小学館
オックスフォード
英語類語辞典

Shogakukan-Oxford
English-Japanese Learner's Thesaurus

監修●田中　実

Shogakukan

小学館 オックスフォード
英語類語辞典
Shogakukan-Oxford
English-Japanese Learner's Thesaurus
© Shogakukan 2011

本辞典は、下記の Oxford Learner's Thesaurus: A dictionary of synonyms を原本とし、日本人にとって有用と思われるものを厳選し、日本語に翻訳したものです。
Oxford Learner's Thesaurus was originally published in English in 2008. This bilingual edition is published by arrangement with Oxford University Press.
Oxford Learner's Thesaurus: A dictionary of synonyms
Chief Editor: Diana Lea
Editors: Jennifer Bradbery, Richard Poole, Helen Warren
ISBN 978 0 19 475201 5
© Oxford University Press 2008

* * * * * *

翻訳・編集協力&DTP　株式会社ジャレックス

校正協力　山崎昭二　岩崎昌子

装丁　岡崎健二

制作　島田浩志
資材　森　雅彦
制作企画　速水健司
販売　前原富士夫　山崎由里佳
宣伝　浦城朋子
編集　井面雄次

まえがき

　この辞典は、2008年に刊行された *Oxford Learner's Thesaurus: A dictionary of synonyms* (Oxford University Press) から、日本人にとって有用と思われる項目を厳選し、編集した日本語版の英語類語辞典です。原書に *Learner's* と銘打たれているだけあって、全体を通して学習者の立場に立った視点が常に貫かれており、日本人にとっても恰好の類語辞典になっていることは論を俟ちません。以下に、この日本語版類語辞典の主な特長を掲げておきます。

① 原書の約65%の内容を厳選収録
② 親見出し約1,300、類語約10,000を誇り、国内では最大・最詳
③ 日本語からも自在に検索できる索引「日本語類語一覧」
④ 日常会話や新聞・雑誌等に現れた生きた用例約26,000を収録
⑤ 類語相互の違いや用法を詳解した約2,600のコラム ノート と注記 ❶
⑥ 類語同士の意味の強弱が矢印で視覚的にわかる123の「類語スケール」
⑦ 文型と結び付きの強い語が一覧できる 文型&コロケーション

　以上7つの特長のほかにも、参照項目や反意語がネットワークさながら相互に確認できるようになっており、類語グループ同士の読み比べに便利です。また、同じ語が別の類語グループでも扱われていれば、意味の違いを探って楽しむこともできます。

　本書は日本語からも引ける最大の類語辞典ですが、例えば、親見出し rise (「上昇する、増す」といった意味) を見てみましょう。類語として grow、increase、climb、go up などが挙げられていますが、各類語がいかに詳述されているかがおわかりになるでしょう。

rise　　（数・水準・量が）上がる，上昇する……
grow　　（大きさ・数・強さが）大きくなる，増す……
increase　（量・水準・数・程度・価値・大きさ・強さが）大きくなる，増す……
climb　　（数字・温度・お金の価値が）上がる，上昇する……
go up　　（水準・価値が）上がる，高くなる

　このように、何が「上昇する、増す」のかが丸括弧内に明示され、さらにコラム（ノート）では rise と grow と increase の使い分けが、次のように簡潔にわかりやすく解説されています。

「rise はこれらの動詞の中で最も頻繁に用いられるが，数や水準について用いられることが一番多い．grow と increase は，大きさや強さについても用いることができる．……」

このような ノート のほかにも注記（ⓘ）が随所にちりばめられており、英語の語彙の習得にうってつけの内容になっています。

　ここで一つ触れておきたいのは、日本人の感覚からすると類語とは思えない、ややずれた感じのする語が類語として扱われている点です。しかし、英語のネイティブスピーカーの感覚からすると、それらはまさに類語なのです。こうした類語に出くわすと、ネイティブスピーカーの思考回路を垣間見ているような気になり、得難い経験になります。

　この辞典は以上のように、日頃から英語を必要とし、望ましい英語や適確な表現に敏感な実務家・ビジネスマンにとってはまさに待望の辞典と言えます。また、英語学習者にとっては、英単語を類語というまとまりで捉えることによって、これまでに習得した語彙を整理し直し、さらなる語彙力アップにつなげることができる辞典と言えるでしょう。

　さらに、26,000もの用例は、どれもが日常会話や実際に新聞・雑誌等に現れた文章で、ネイティブスピーカーの生きた英語の習得には最適なものです。原書に収載するに当たって前後が省かれ、文脈が失われていますが、用例の英語が使われた状況を自ら想像し補いつつ読むことは、単語の意味を追うことにとどまらない読解力を養う一助となるでしょう。

　最後に、この辞典を日常的に大いに活用され、日本人として英語を正しく理解（受信）し、自らの考えを臆することなく表現（発信）する際にお役立ていただければ、監修者としてこれに勝る喜びはありません。

2011年4月
田中　実

目 次

まえがき .... iii - iv

この辞典の使い方（凡例）........................... vi - xvi

日本語類語一覧（日本語索引）.................... (1) - (44)

英語類語辞典 .... 1 - 865

INDEX（英語索引）................................. 866 - 931

この辞典の仕組み

※本文の内容は一部省略しています。

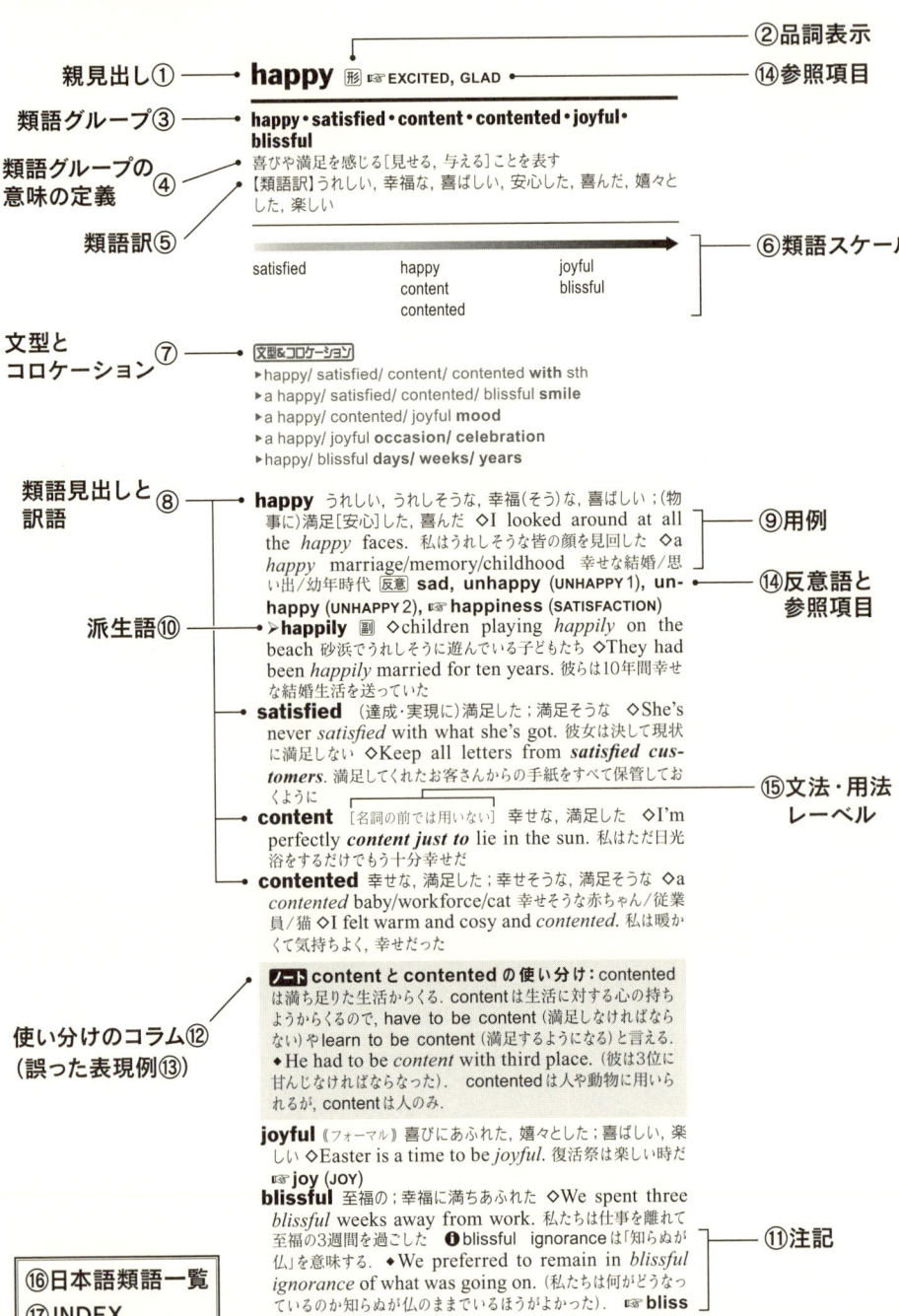

この辞典の使い方

①親見出し

類語グループを代表する見出し語のことです。個々の類語見出し(⑧)と区別するために、「親見出し」と呼びます。約1,300収録しています。

親見出しは品詞ごとに立てられています。同じ綴りで名詞や動詞、あるいは名詞や形容詞など複数の品詞がある場合は、別々に親見出しを立てています。

> **answer** 名
> answer・reply・response・acknowledgement・retort

> **answer** 動
> answer・reply・respond・retort・acknowledge・write back・get back to sb

②品詞表示

品詞は以下のような記号で表示しています。

名	名詞	
動	動詞	
形	形容詞	
副	副詞	
前	前置詞	
限定詞	限定詞	例：last, first
略	略語	
連結動詞	連結動詞	例：become, seem
句動詞	句動詞	例：bring sb up, deal with sb/sth, depend on/upon sth
イディオム	イディオム	例：lose your temper
フレーズ	フレーズ	例：in operation, put a figure on sth
連結形	連結形	例：ex-

③類語グループ

類語グループとは、ある共通する意味によって集められた類語のまとまりのことです。各類語は、使用頻度の高いものから順に並んでいます。したがって、最もよく使われる最初の類語がグループを代表する親見出しになっています。「この辞典の仕組み」にある **happy** の例のように、親見出しと類語グループが一対一の対応をすることが多いのですが、例えば **choice** の

> **choice** 名
> **1** choice・selection・nomination・election・pick
> 二人[二つ]以上の人, 物事, 可能性から選ぶこと
> 【類語訳】選択, 選定, 指名, 選任, 当選

> **2** choice・favourite・preference・selection・pick
> 選ばれる[他よりも好まれる]人や物
> 【類語訳】お気に入り, 好物

ように、一つの親見出しに対して二つ以上の類語グループに分かれているものもあります。その場合は **1**, **2**, **3**……のように番号を付けて区別しています。したがって、親見出し約1,300に対して類語グループは約1,500を数えます。

④ 類語グループの意味の定義
類語グループ(③)に属する類語がどのような意味によって集められているのか、その意味の定義を提示します。

⑤ 類語訳
日本語版で独自に設けた【類語訳】は、類語グループの意味の定義(④)から導き出される日本語の言葉、いわば日本語の類語に相当し、個々の類語見出しで挙げた訳語(⑧)以外のものも採録しています。

【類語訳】は、日本語から引くために設けた**日本語類語一覧**に登録されており、調べたい言葉に近い類語訳を検索することによって、その類語訳のある親見出しにたどり着くことができます。

⑥ 類語スケール
類語グループ内の各類語は、ある共通する意味によって集められていますが、各類語が相対的にどのような意味の強弱の関係にあるかを矢印のスケールで視覚的に表示したのが「類語スケール」です。ネイティブスピーカーではない日本人読者にとっては非常に興味深い情報だと言えます。強さの度合いは右側に行くほど増します。全部で123の「類語スケール」を収録しています。

例えば、親見出し happy 形 では「うれしい, 幸福な, 喜ばしい, ……」といった意味の類語が扱われますが、happy が中程度の強さで、satisfied はやや控えめ、joyful や blissful が最も喜びの度合いが強いことがわかります。joyful に「喜びにあふれた, 嬉々とした；……」、blissful には「至福の；幸福に満ちあふれた」という訳語が与えられていることもうなずけます。

また、このような類語スケールが示されているのは形容詞ばかりとは限りません。動詞や名詞でも、意味の強弱に関わりのある場合には、類語スケールが示されています。

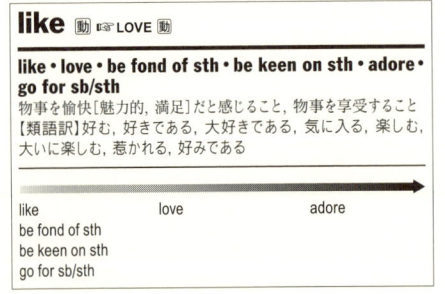

⑦ 文型とコロケーション 文型&コロケーション

共通の意味を持つ類語同士は、文型や構文、あるいは語と語の結び付き（コロケーション）においてもある程度の共通性が見られますが、ここではその特徴的なものが提示されています。スラッシュ（/）は前後の語を入れ替えることができることを表します。

右は親見出し **fast** の例ですが、結び付きの強い前置詞や名詞、副詞などが太字で示されています。また、文型や結び付きに応じて、使える類語が異なることがわかります。

---

fast 形 ☞ QUICK

fast・quick・high-speed・brisk・supersonic・

文型&コロケーション
▶ to be fast/ quick **at** doing sth
▶ a fast/ supersonic **speed**
▶ a fast/ quick/ brisk **movement/ pace/ walk/ run**
▶ quick/ brisk **footsteps**
▶ a fast/ quick **reader/ worker/ learner/ rhythm**
▶ a fast/ a high-speed/ an express **train/ link**
▶ a fast/ a high-speed **computer/ modem**
▶ a fast/ an express **bus/ coach/ lane**
▶ **very/ quite/ fairly** fast/ quick/ brisk

---

⑧ 類語見出しと訳語

それぞれの類語はここで、訳語、用例（⑨）、注記（⑪）などによって詳しく記述されます。類語の意味は説明的な定義ではなく訳語が与えられています。右の親見出し **atmosphere** の各類語のように、「雰囲気」という訳語だけでは微妙な違いが区別できない場合は、「どのような」雰囲気なのかが（ ）で明示されています。さらに、[C] [U] による可算・不可算名詞の区別や、《英》《米》による英用法と米用法の違い、《フォーマル》《インフォーマル》による使用場面の指示など、用法上の違いにも細かく配慮しています。

---

atmosphere 名

atmosphere・climate・mood・tone・spirit・aura・feeling・feel・flavour
特定の場所や状況で受ける全体的な感覚

atmosphere [C, U] (場所・状況の)雰囲気；(二者間[集
mood [単数で] (一団の人々が抱く)気分、ムード；(一団の人々の間の)雰囲気 ◇The *mood* of the meeting was dis
tone [単数で] (文章などの)調子、(その場の)雰囲気 ◇The
aura [C] (人・場所の)独特の雰囲気、オーラ ◇There was
feel [単数で] (場所・状況がかもし出す)印象、雰囲気 ◇It's a
flavour 《英》《米 flavor》[単数で] (他の物事を思い出させる)特質、雰囲気 ◇The children experience a *flavour* of

---

⑨ 用例

◇（❶や ノート の中では◆）は用例を示します。用例には日常会話や新聞・雑誌などに掲載された実際の英文が採用されています。用例中で類語見出しがどのように使われているかわかるよう、該当箇所をイタリック体で示しています。太字のイタリック体は、特徴的な結び付きの連語です。ほとんどの類語で、2つ以上の豊富な用例が与えられていますので、さまざまな使用例が確認できます。用例は26,000余を収録しています。

---

ability [単数で, U] 能力 ◇The system has the *ability* to run more than one program at the same time. そのシステムは同時に複数のプログラムを実行することができる ◇Everyone has the right to good medical care regardless of their *ability* to pay. 支払い能力にかかわらず誰でも医療を受ける権利がある ◇I try to do the job *to the best of my ability* (= as well as I can). 力を尽くしてその仕事をするつもりです 反意 **inability** ❶単数・不可算 の inability は何かをすることができないことを表す。◆the government's *inability* to provide basic services (政府が基本的なサービスを提供できないこと). ◆Some families go without medical treatment because of their *inability* to pay. (支払い能力がないために医療を受けられずにいる家庭がある).

⑩ 派生語

▶は派生語のしるしです。派生語とは、接尾辞などによって別の品詞になったものです。例えば、形容詞 quick の場合は、▶**quickly** 副 が派生語です。派生語の訳語は、元の語から類推できるため省いていますが、ほとんどの派生語には用例が与えられています。

> **quick** (動作・処理について)速い、素早い、機敏な、敏速な、迅速な、即座の ◇He's a very *quick* worker. 彼は仕事がてきぱきしている ◇The kids were *quick* to learn. 子どもたちは物覚えが速かった ◇She was *quick* (= too quick) to point out the mistakes I'd made. 彼女は私が犯したミスをたちまち指摘した ◇Her *quick* hands suddenly stopped moving. 彼女は素早く動かしていた手を突然止めた ◇Try to *be quick*! We're late already. 早くしなさい. もう遅刻だよ 反意 **slow** (SLOW)
> ▶**quickly** 副 ◇She walked away *quickly*. 彼女は足早に歩き去った

⑪ 注記 ❶

❶が目印の注記では、意味や用法に関する説明の補足や、用例、反意語などについてもさまざまな追加情報が提供されています。用例(◆)を挙げながら具体的でわかりやすい説明をしたり、✕印を付けて誤った表現例(⑬)も挙げて、注意を喚起していることもあります。

> **grow** (徐々に)…になる ◇The skies *grew* dark and it began to rain. 空が暗くなってきて雨が降り始めた ◇As time went on he *grew* more and more impatient. 時間が経つにつれ彼はますますいらいらしてきた ◇I'm sure you'll *grow* to like her in time. きっとそのうち彼女のことを好きになるでしょう ❶ *grow* は突然ではなくある期間にわたって生じる変化について言うときに用いる. 徐々に変化することを表すため, しばしば形容詞の比較級と用いられる. ✕She suddenly *grew* angry. ◆She *grew* braver with time. (だんだんと彼女は勇敢になっていった).

⑫ 使い分けのコラム ノート

ノート 欄は、類語同士を比較対照することによって浮かび上がる、ニュアンスの違いや用い方の注意点などについて詳しく解説しているコラムです。注記❶と同様、用例(◆)や誤った表現例(⑬)も収録しています。

> **ノート located, situated, sited** の使い分け：located と situated は両方とも, 常にその場にあり, 人によって置かれたのではない地勢に用いられる. sited はふつう, 工場, 学校, 病院のような人が建てたり特定の位置に置かれた物にのみ用いられる. ◆Goose Island *is located/situated* in the Chicago River. (グース島はシカゴ川の中にある). ✕Goose Island *is sited* in the Chicago River.

⑬ 誤った表現例

注記❶(⑪)や使い分けのコラム **ノート**(⑫)では、間違った表現、いわゆる非文情報を掲載しています。間違いやすい表現にも注意を向けることによって、正しい表現がはっきりする場合も少なくありません。使ってはいけない表現なので、✕印を付けて区別するとともに、あえて日本語訳は省いています。

> **ノート alive と living** の使い分け：alive は名詞の前には用いない. ✕all *alive* things. living は be 動詞の後に用いることができるが, ほかの連結動詞の後にはふつう用いない. ✕She stole just to stay *living*. ✕Doctors fought to keep the baby *living*.

⑭ 参照項目 ☞ と反意語 反意

☞ は参照のしるしです。例えば、☞ INCOME は、親見出し income を参照せよということを表しています。この辞典での約束事ですが、スモールキャピタルの書体(例：INCOME)は、親見出しを表し、そこを参照せよという意味です。

> **revenue** 名 ☞ INCOME
> revenue・income・turnover・proceeds・receipts・takings・take
> 税の徴収[商品の販売, サービスの提供]で得られるお金
> 【類語訳】税収, 収入, 収益, 歳入, 売上高

> **income** 名 ☞ REVENUE
> income・wage・pay・salary・earnings
> 人が仕事をして稼ぐ[受け取る]お金
> 【類語訳】所得, 収入, 賃金, 給料, 俸給, 給与

また, 例えば luck の ☞ **lucky** (TIMELY) の場合は, スモールキャピタルの TIMELY は親見出しを表しているので, 親見出し **timely** の類語見出し **lucky** を参照せよという意味になります。

> **luck** [U] (幸[不])運, つき ◇*The best of luck with your exams.* 試験がうまくいくことを祈ってます ◇*Bad luck, Helen, you played very well.* ついてなかったね, ヘレン, でもすごくよくやったよ ◇*Never mind — better luck next time.* 気にするな一次はうまくいくよ ◇*It was his hard luck that he wasn't chosen.* 彼が選ばれなかったのは運が悪かったね ◇*It's hard luck on him that he wasn't chosen.* 《英》彼が選ばれなかったのは運が悪かったね ◇*Just my luck to arrive after they had left* (= used to show you are not surprised sth bad has happened to you, because you are not often lucky). 彼らがいなくなってから着くなんて, 案の定, ついてない ☞ **lucky** (TIMELY)

> **timely** 形 ☞ PROMISING
> timely・lucky・happy・fortunate
> 物事が適切な時に起こることを表す語
> 【類語訳】時を得た, 適時の, 折よい, 運のよい, 幸運な
>
> **timely** [ふつう名詞の前で] 時を得た, 適時の, 折よい ◇*A nasty incident was prevented by the timely arrival of the police.* 折よく警察が到着して不快な事件は防がれた ◇*This has been a timely reminder to us all.* これは私たち皆にとって折よい合図であった
> **lucky** 運のよい, 幸運な ◇*It was lucky for us that he didn't see us.* 運よく私たちは彼に見られなかった ◇*That was the luckiest escape of my life.* それは私の生活からの願ってもない逃避であった ◇*I didn't know he was*

一方, 反意 は対をなす反対の意味の語, つまり「反意語」を表します。右の evening の 反意 morning の例では, morning が evening の反意語であることが示されています。ここではただ反意語が提示されているだけですが, relaxed の 反意 **nervous** (WORRIED) の例では, nervous が反意語であることが示され, さらに参照項目の場合と同様, 親見出し **worried** の類語見出し **nervous** を参照せよということが表されています。

happy の 反意 sad, unhappy (UNHAPPY 1), unhappy (UNHAPPY 2) では, sad と unhappy が反意語です。sad と unhappy は親見出し **unhappy** の **1** の類語グループで, もう一つの unhappy は親見出し **unhappy** の **2** の類語グループで, それぞれ該当類語見出しがあるので, 参照せよということになります。

> **evening** [U, C] (午後の終わりから就寝時間までの)夜, 晩 ◇*I'll come and see you this evening.* 今晩あなたに会いに行きます ◇*The evening performance begins at 7.30.* 夜の部は7時半に開演です ◇*We spent the long winter evenings inside by the fire.* 私たちは冬の夜長を屋内の炉辺で過ごした 反意 **morning**

> **relaxed** くつろいだ, リラックスした ◇*I had to learn to be more relaxed about things.* 物事に対してもっとリラックスできるようにならなくてはいけなかった ◇*She appeared relaxed and confident before the match.* 彼女は試合前リラックスして自信に満ちているように見えた 反意 **nervous** (WORRIED)

> **happy** うれしい, うれしそうな, 幸福(そう)な, 喜ばしい; (物事に)満足[安心]した, 喜んだ ◇*I looked around at all the happy faces.* 私はうれしそうな皆の顔を見回した ◇*a happy marriage/memory/childhood* 幸せな結婚/思い出/幼年時代 ◇*Those were the happiest days* ... ◇*Happy birthday!* お誕生日おめでとう ◇*If there's anything you're not happy about, come and ask.* もし何か不満なことがあれば, 聞きに来てください ◇*I said I'd go, just to keep him happy.* 私はただ彼を喜ばせておくために「私は行きます」と言った 反意 **sad, unhappy** (UNHAPPY 1), **unhappy** (UNHAPPY 2), ☞ **happiness** (SATISFACTION)

また、land の ☞ land (COUNTRY 2), land (SOIL) では同じ land の類語が別の親見出し **country 2** と **soil** の2か所で扱われていることがわかります。**country 2** の land は「田舎, 田園, 地方, ……」、**soil** の land は「(特定の種類の) 土地」と言う訳語が与えられています。このように同じ類語が別のグループで扱われている場合は、グループ相互の意味の違いに注目してください。

land 名

1 land・estate・real estate・farmland

land [U] (またはフォーマル **lands** [複数形で]) (売買可能な資産として人が所有する)土地, 地所, 所有地 ◇The price of *land* is rising rapidly. 地価が急騰している ◇During the war their *lands* were occupied by the enemy. 戦時中彼らの土地は敵に占領されていた ☞ land (COUNTRY 2), land (SOIL)

⑮ **文法・用法レーベルなど**
  ● 使用地域・文体など
    《英》   イギリス用法、英用法
    《米》   アメリカ用法、米用法
    《フォーマル》   改まった言葉で、日常会話にはなじまない
    《ややフォーマル》   やや改まってはいるが、普通の状況で使うことができる
    《インフォーマル》   くだけた言葉で、友達同士や改まらない場面で使われる
    《ややインフォーマル》   インフォーマルほどではないが、ややくだけた言葉
    《俗語》   非常にくだけた言葉
    《話し言葉》   インフォーマルな表現と重なる場合が多いが、フォーマルな状況で用いられるものもある
    《書き言葉》   文章表現で用いられる言葉
    《文語》   もっぱら文学や創作で用いられる言葉
    《古風》   古風な言葉
    《専門語》   ある専門分野で用いられる言葉
    《ほめて》   好ましい意味合いで用いられる言葉
    《けなして》   不快に感じる言葉
    《おどけて》   おどけた、おかしみのある表現
    《皮肉で》   字義とは反対あるいは異なる意味となる表現
    《比喩的》   比喩的な言葉
    《侮蔑的》   侮蔑的な言葉
    《卑語》   下品でタブーとされる言葉
  ● 専門分野
    《医学》《音楽》《化学》《金融》《経済》《コンピューター》《ジャーナリズム》《宗教》《心理》《スポーツ》《政治》《生物》《ビジネス》《物理》《文法》《法律》
  ● 文法レーベル
    ◆ 名詞
    [C]   可算名詞：単数形と複数形がある。単数のときはふつう a, the, each などの限定詞が付く。複数のときは限定詞が付く場合も付かない場合もある。

[U]　　　　　　不可算名詞：複数形にはならない。限定詞は付く場合も付かない場合もある。
　　　　　　　　＊場合によって可算名詞として、あるいは不可算名詞として用いられるものは、[C,U][U,C] と表示している。
[複数で]　　　常に複数形で用いられる名詞
[単数で]　　　常に単数形で用いられる名詞
[単数＋単数・複数動詞]
[C＋単数・複数動詞]
[U＋単数・複数動詞]

《英》で、グループや組織を表すいわゆる集合名詞の中で、単数形または不可算名詞でありながら動詞が複数形で受ける場合がある名詞です。

> **the competition** [単数＋単数・複数動詞] (ビジネス・スポーツでの)競争相手, ライバル ◇We'll be able to assess *the competition* at the conference. 会議ではライバルを値踏みできるだろう ☞ **compete** (COMPETE)

> **council** (または **Council**) [C＋単数・複数動詞] 勧告・規則づくり・調査・資金提供などを行う)協議会, 審議会 ◇In Britain, the Arts *Council* gives grants to theatres. イギリスでは芸術協議会が劇場に補助金を出している ◇There are

> **logistics** [U＋単数・複数動詞] (複雑な計画を成功させるための実際的な)準備, 用意, 備え, 手配, 手はず, 段取り ◇We have the aid money, but the *logistics* of getting it to those in need are daunting. 我々のところに義援金が寄せられているが、その義援金を必要としている人々のところにどのようにして届けたらよいかその段取りを思うと気が重い

英和辞典ではふつう、《単数・複数扱い》と表示されているものです。《米》では、これらの名詞は単数形であれば動詞も単数形で受けることになっています。＊本書では、このような名詞の用例については原則として、《英》《米》のどちらでも許容されるよう、動詞は単数形を取る形にしています。

[複数扱い]　語形は単数形だが複数として扱われる名詞

> ▶**the old** 图 [複数扱い] ◇*The old* (= old people) feel the cold more than the young. 高齢者は若者より寒さを感じやすい

◆動詞
　[自]　　　自動詞
　[他]　　　他動詞
◆形容詞
　[名詞の前で][ふつう名詞の前で]
　　　　　　名詞の前に置かれて名詞を修飾する形容詞

> **budget** [名詞の前で] 《特に広告で》(基本的サービスだけの提供で)割安の, 安い ◇Save pounds on *budget* flights to the sun. 割安航空便で太陽のもとへ ◇a *budget* airline/

> **live** [ふつう名詞の前で] 生きている ◇We saw a *real live* rattlesnake! 私たちは本物の生きたガラガラヘビを見た

[名詞の前では用いない][名詞の前はまれ]
　　　　　　名詞を修飾するのではなく、動詞の補語として用いられる形容詞

> **all 'right** [名詞の前では用いない] かろうじて十分と言える, まあまあの ◇Your work is *all right*, but you could do better. あなたの仕事はまあまあの出来ですが、本来ならもっとうまくできるでしょう

> **counterproductive** [名詞の前はまれ] 逆効果の ◇Increases in taxation would be *counterproductive*. 増税は逆効果となるだろう ◇It would be *counterproduc-*

●略語、かっこ、記号など
　sb　　　(＝somebody)「人」を表す。
　sth　　 (＝something)「物、物事、事柄」を表す。

your	親見出し、類語見出し、「文型&コロケーション」および句例では、your は「人の」の意味で用いられる。英和辞典などではふつう one's が用いられることが多い。	**lose your temper** 〖イディオム〗 **clear your 'throat** 〖イディオム〗咳払いをする ◇She *cleared her throat*. 'I hope I'm not interrupting,' she said. 彼女は咳払いをして、「邪魔しちゃったかしら」と言った ▶to lose your/its ... appearance/ air/ looks **button** [C] 丸いボタン ◇to do up/undo your *buttons* 《英》ボタンを留める/外す ◇to button/unbutton your *buttons* 《米》ボタンを留める/外す ◇The top *button* of
( )	丸かっこは、補足や注記など幅広く使われますが、特に訳語では「省略可能」の意味で用いられます。 例：推薦(文) →「推薦」と「推薦文」の2つを同時に表しています。	**plug** [C] 《インフォーマル》(新刊本・映画の売り上げを伸ばすために寄せる) 推薦(文) 宣伝 ◇He managed to get in a
[ ]	直前の語句と交換可能を表す。 例：却下[棄却]する →「却下する」と「棄却する」の2つを表しています。	**dismiss** [他]《法律》(証拠不十分で訴訟を)却下[棄却]する
/	/の前後の語句との交換可能を表す。 特に 文型&コロケーション 欄と用例中で(文例でなく)句例の場合に使用されます。 例：to adjust/ modify/ revise your ideas は adjust, modify, revise をそれぞれ入れ替えて to adjust your ideas, to modify your ideas, to revise your ideas のように3つの句が表されています。 　　　to turn blue/red/white の場合は、blue と red と white を入れ替えて使うことができることを表しています。(青く/赤く/白くなる) のように用例訳にも対応しています。	文型&コロケーション ▶to adjust/ modify/ revise your **ideas** ▶to modify/ amend/ revise a **text**/ **constitution** ▶to modify/ amend/ qualify a **statement** ▶to adjust/ modify/ amend/ revise sth **slightly** ▶to modify/ amend/ revise/ qualify sth **heavily** ▶to adjust/ modify/ revise sth **constantly** の政治家だ ❶turn は ◆to *turn* blue/red/white (青く/赤く/白くなる) のように色や、◆to *turn* cold/warm/chilly (寒く/暖かく/肌寒くなる) のように天気や、◆to *turn* nasty/ mean/sour/bad (ひどく/下品に/酸っぱく/悪くなる) のよう
▶	派生語を示す → ⑩	
❶	注記を示す → ⑪	
ノート	使い分けのコラムを示す → ⑫	
×	誤った表現であることを示す → ⑬	
反意	反意語を示す → ⑭	
☞	参照項目を示す → ⑭	

⑯日本語類語一覧

日本語類語一覧は、日本語からも検索して自在に活用できるよう日本語版で独自に設けた日本語の索引です。検索キーワードは類語訳(⑤)で、類語訳を介して親見出しが検索できるようになっています。

アーティスト → あのひと   (1)

日本語類語一覧

この日本語類語一覧は、日本語から検索して利用するために、各類語グループで挙げた【類語訳】を五十音順に配列したものです。スモールキャピタルで示された英語は、その類語訳が収録されている親見出しを示しています。例えば、以下のようになります。

アーティスト ▶ ACTOR → 「アーティスト」が親見出し actor に収録されています。

あ

アーティスト ▶ ACTOR	赤くなる ▶ FLUSH	あさる ▶ ROB	悪化する ▶ WORSEN
相いれない	証 ▶ EVIDENCE, SIGN 1	あざ笑う	厚かましい ▶ RUDE
▶ INCONSISTENT	赤字 ▶ LOSS-MAKING	▶ LAUGH AT SB/STH	厚かましく…する ▶ DARE
相方 ▶ PARTNER 1	明かす ▶ CONVEY	足音 ▶ STEP	厚切り ▶ PIECE
愛好 ▶ TASTE	赤ちゃん ▶ CHILD	アジト ▶ REFUGE	熱くなる ▶ HEAT
愛好家 ▶ FAN	あか抜けた	足止めする	厚さが…の ▶ WIDE 2
愛国心 ▶ RACISM	▶ SOPHISTICATED	▶ HOLD SB/STH UP	圧制者 ▶ DICTATOR
挨拶する ▶ GREET	あからさまな ▶ PLAIN 2	足取り ▶ SIGN 1	圧制的な ▶ REPRESSIVE
愛されていない	上がる ▶ RISE	味見する ▶ TRY 2	あっという間 ▶ MINUTE
▶ UNWANTED	明るい ▶ BRIGHT,	味わう ▶ APPRECIATE,	圧倒的勝利 ▶ VICTORY
愛情 ▶ LOVE 名 1, 2	CHEERFUL, OPTIMISTIC	EAT, FEEL	圧倒的な ▶ COMPLETE
愛情に満ちた ▶ LOVING	明るみに出る ▶ TURN OUT	味を知る ▶ FEEL	集まり ▶ GROUP 1
愛情を抱いた ▶ LOVING	赤ん坊 ▶ CHILD	足を引っかける ▶ FALL 3	集まる ▶ COLLECT,
	空き ▶ JOB	焦り ▶ SPEED	COME 1, MEET 1
	飽き飽き ▶ FAMILY 2	焦る ▶ HURRY	集める ▶ COLLECT, HAVE 4
	親切な ▶ FRIENDLY 1,		
	KIND 形, POLITE		

例えば「親切な」を引くと、
親切な ▶ FRIENDLY 1, KIND 形, POLITE と出ています。スモールキャピタルの英字で親見出しが示されているので、親見出し **friendly 1** を見ると、warm, pleasant, welcoming, ……といった類語が調べられます。

また、【類語訳】にある「気さくな」「感じのよい」「愛想のよい」……などもキーワードになっているので、それらの語を介しても **friendly 1** の類語が検索できます。

---

friendly 形

1 ☞ NICE 2
friendly • warm • pleasant • welcoming • amiable • good-natured • genial • hospitable • approachable
人が他人に対して思いやりを持って心地よく振る舞うことを表す
【類語訳】親切な, 気さくな, 感じのよい, 愛想のよい, 気立てのよい, 温厚な, 穏やかな, 親しみやすい

xvi

⑰ INDEX

一方、**INDEX** は英語索引です。親見出しと全類語が検索できます。つまり、例えば前ページの friendly の例で言うと、親見出し **friendly** とその類語 friendly, warm, pleasant, welcoming, amiable, …… がキーワードになっています。

866　　　　　　　　　　　abandon → adjust

INDEX

このインデックスは、親見出しとすべての類語をアルファベット順に配列したものです。スモールキャピタルで示された英語は親見出しを表し、親見出しの収録ページと、個々の類語が収録されている親見出しがわかります。例えば、以下のようになります。

ABILITY 名 *p.1* → 親見出し ability が1ページに収録されています。
abandon 動 ▶ LEAVE 4, STOP → abandon という類語が親見出し leave 4 と stop の2か所に収録されています。

A

abandon 動
　▶ LEAVE 4, STOP
abandoned 形
　▶ DESERTED
abbey 名
　▶ CHURCH
abbreviated 形
　▶ SHORT 3
abduct 動
　▶ KIDNAP
abhor 動
　▶ HATE
abide by sth

absurd 形
　▶ RIDICULOUS
abuse 動
　▶ OFFEND
abusive 形
　▶ OFFENSIVE
academic 形
　▶ EDUCATIONAL, INTELLECTUAL 1
ACCELERATE 動 *p.2*
accelerate 動
　▶ ACCELERATE
accept 動
　▶ AGREE, GET 2, GREET, AGGRESSIVE 1

warm 形
　▶ DARK 2, FRIENDLY 1, HOT

accredited 形
　▶ OFFICIAL
accrue 動
　▶ COLLECT
accumulate 動
　▶ COLLECT
accurate 形
　▶ EXACT
accusation 名
　▶ CHARGE 2
ACCUSE 動 *p.3*
accuse 動
　▶ ACCUSE
accustomed to sth
　▶ USED TO STH

action 名
　▶ ACTION, CASE, EFFECT, WAR
ACTIVE 形 *p.6*
active 形
　▶ ACTIVE, BUSY 1, ENERGETIC
activity 名
　▶ PROJECT
act on/upon sth
　▶ FOLLOW 3
ACTOR 名 *p.6*
actor 名
　▶ ACTOR
actress 名

例えば warm を引くと、

warm 形 ▶ DARK 2, FRIENDLY 1, HOT とあり、3つの親見出しで warm が扱われていることがわかります。

親見出しは、**FRIENDLY** 形 *p.302* のように収録ページを掲載しています。

FRIEND 名 *p.301*
friend 名
　▶ FRIEND
FRIENDLY 形 *p.302*
friendly 形
　▶ FRIENDLY 1, 2
FRIENDSHIP 名 *p.303*
friendship 名
　▶ FRIENDSHIP

　▶ DETAILED
fully 副
　▶ QUITE 2
fuming 形
　▶ FURIOUS
FUN 名 *p.306*
fun 名
　▶ ENTERTAINMENT, FUN
function 名

日本語類語一覧

この日本語類語一覧は，日本語から検索して利用するために，各類語グループで挙げた【類語訳】を五十音順に配列したものです．スモールキャピタルで示された英語は，その類語訳が収録されている親見出しを示しています．例えば，以下のようになります．

アーティスト ▶ ACTOR → 「アーティスト」が親見出し actor に収録されています．

あ

アーティスト ▶ ACTOR
相いれない ▶ INCONSISTENT
相方 ▶ PARTNER 1
愛好 ▶ TASTE
愛好家 ▶ FAN
愛国心 ▶ RACISM
挨拶する ▶ GREET
愛されていない ▶ UNWANTED
愛情 ▶ LOVE 名 1, 2
愛情に満ちた ▶ LOVING
愛情を抱いた ▶ LOVING
愛情をささげた ▶ LOVING
愛情をささげる ▶ LOVE 動
愛情を示した ▶ LOVING
合図 ▶ SIGNAL
愛すべき ▶ SWEET
愛する ▶ LOVE 動
愛する人 ▶ DARLING
愛蔵する ▶ APPRECIATE
愛想のよい ▶ FRIENDLY 1, SOCIABLE
間柄 ▶ RELATIONSHIP 1
愛着 ▶ LOVE 名 2
アイデア ▶ IDEA 1
空いている ▶ DESERTED, EMPTY, FREE 形 3
アイデンティティー ▶ IDENTITY
哀悼 ▶ SYMPATHY
会いに行く ▶ VISIT 動
あいにく… ▶ SORRY
あいにくの ▶ UNFORTUNATE 2
相反する ▶ INCONSISTENT
相棒 ▶ FRIEND, PARTNER 1
合間 ▶ PAUSE
あいまいな ▶ MISLEADING, UNSURE, VAGUE
会う ▶ MEET 1, 2
あえて…する ▶ DARE
青ざめた ▶ CLEAR 形 3
青写真 ▶ PLAN 2
赤くなる ▶ FLUSH
証 ▶ EVIDENCE, SIGN 1
赤字の ▶ LOSS-MAKING
明かす ▶ CONVEY
赤ちゃん ▶ CHILD
あか抜けた ▶ SOPHISTICATED
あからさまな ▶ PLAIN 2
上がる ▶ RISE
明るい ▶ BRIGHT, CHEERFUL, OPTIMISTIC
明るみに出る ▶ TURN OUT
赤ん坊 ▶ CHILD
空き ▶ JOB
飽き飽きする ▶ ANNOYING
空き時間 ▶ LEISURE
飽き足りない ▶ UNHAPPY 2
商い ▶ TRADE
明らかな ▶ CLEAR 形 1, VISIBLE
明らかにする ▶ FIND 1, INFORMATIVE, REVEAL
明らかになる ▶ TURN OUT
あきらめる ▶ STOP
悪 ▶ EVIL 名
悪行 ▶ CRIME 2, EVIL 名
悪事 ▶ CRIME 2
悪質な ▶ HARMFUL, TERRIBLE 1
悪臭 ▶ ODOUR
握手する ▶ SHAKE 1
悪循環 ▶ MESS 2
悪性の ▶ FATAL
アクセサリー ▶ DECORATION
悪戦苦闘する ▶ TRY 1
悪徳の ▶ CORRUPT
空ける ▶ CLEAR 動, TEAR
開ける ▶ UNDO
あげる ▶ GIVE 1
挙げる ▶ POINT STH OUT
あこがれる ▶ HOPE 動
あざができる ▶ INJURE
あざけり ▶ CONTEMPT
欺く ▶ CHEAT 動
鮮やかな ▶ BRIGHT
あさる ▶ ROB
あざ笑う ▶ LAUGH AT SB/STH
足音 ▶ STEP
アジト ▶ REFUGE
足止めする ▶ HOLD SB/STH UP
足取り ▶ SIGN 1
味見する ▶ TRY 2
味わう ▶ APPRECIATE, EAT, FEEL
味を知る ▶ FEEL
足を引っかける ▶ FALL 3
焦り ▶ SPEED
焦る ▶ HURRY
唖然とさせる ▶ SURPRISE
唖然とした ▶ SILENT
遊び ▶ ENTERTAINMENT, FUN, INTEREST 名 2
遊ぶ ▶ PLAY 動 1
値する ▶ WORTHY
与えない ▶ REFUSE
与える ▶ GIVE 1, PROVIDE
温かい ▶ HOT
温まる, 暖まる ▶ HEAT
温める, 暖める ▶ HEAT
頭 ▶ MIND
頭金 ▶ PAYMENT
頭にくる ▶ LOSE YOUR TEMPER
頭のおかしい ▶ CRAZY, MAD
頭の切れる ▶ INTELLIGENT, SHREWD
頭の柔軟な ▶ TOLERANT
頭の鈍い ▶ STUPID
頭の悪い ▶ STUPID
新しい ▶ NEW 1, 2, RECENT
当たる ▶ HIT 1
暑い ▶ HOT
熱い ▶ HOT
厚い ▶ WIDE 2
厚板 ▶ PIECE
扱いづらい ▶ ANNOYING
扱いにくい ▶ SENSITIVE 2, UNCONTROLLABLE
悪化する ▶ WORSEN
厚かましい ▶ RUDE
厚かましく…する ▶ DARE
厚切り ▶ PIECE
熱くなる ▶ HEAT
厚さが…の ▶ WIDE 2
圧制者 ▶ DICTATOR
圧制的な ▶ REPRESSIVE
あっという間 ▶ MINUTE
圧倒的勝利 ▶ VICTORY
圧倒的な ▶ COMPLETE
集まり ▶ GROUP 1
集まる ▶ COLLECT, COME 1, MEET 1
集める ▶ COLLECT, HAVE 4
あつらえ向きの ▶ IDEAL
あつらえる ▶ CHANGE 動 1
圧力 ▶ PRESSURE 2
圧力団体 ▶ PARTY 1
宛先 ▶ HOME
当て推量 ▶ SPECULATION
宛名を書く ▶ SEND
当てにする ▶ EXPECT, TRUST
当てにできる ▶ RELIABLE 1
当てはまらない ▶ IRRELEVANT
当てはまる ▶ RELEVANT
艶やかさ ▶ STYLE
充てる ▶ DEVOTE
跡 ▶ MARK
後押しする ▶ SUPPORT
後に続く ▶ RELATED
後の ▶ NEXT
アドバイザー ▶ ADVISER
アドバイス ▶ ADVICE
アドバイスする ▶ RECOMMEND 1
アドレス ▶ HOME
後をつける ▶ FOLLOW 1
穴 ▶ HOLE 1, 2
アナウンサー ▶ PRESENTER
あなた ▶ DARLING
アナリスト ▶ ANALYST
あの人 ▶ THING 1

あばく → いせき

日本語類語一覧

暴く ▶ REVEAL
アパルトヘイト ▶ DISCRIMINATION
アバンギャルドな ▶ EXPERIMENTAL
浴びせる ▶ SOAK
危ない ▶ DANGEROUS
あふれ出る ▶ FLOW
あふれる ▶ FLOOD 動
あほう ▶ FOOL
甘やかす ▶ TOLERANT
あまり…ない ▶ INADEQUATE
雨（あられ）▶ FLOOD 名 2
雨が降る ▶ RAIN
危うくする ▶ DAMAGE 動, THREATEN
怪しい ▶ SUSPICIOUS 2
怪しんで ▶ SUSPICIOUS 1
あやふやな ▶ VAGUE
誤った ▶ WRONG 1
誤り ▶ MISTAKE 2
歩み ▶ STEP
歩み寄り ▶ COMPROMISE
洗う ▶ CLEAN 動, WASH
洗える ▶ CLEAN 動
嵐の ▶ ROUGH
粗筋 ▶ SUMMARY
争い ▶ FIGHT 名, WAR
改めさせる ▶ IMPROVE 1
改める ▶ ADJUST, IMPROVE 1
洗った ▶ CLEAN 形
荒っぽい ▶ VIOLENT, WILD
あらゆる点で ▶ QUITE 2
現す ▶ SHOW 2
表れ ▶ SIGN 1
現れる ▶ APPEAR, ARRIVE
ありうる ▶ POSSIBLE 2
ありえない ▶ IMPOSSIBLE
ありか ▶ PLACE
ありそうに思われる ▶ LIKELY
ありそうにもない ▶ UNLIKELY 1
（…で）あり続ける ▶ REMAIN
ありのままの ▶ HONEST, PLAIN 2
ありふれた ▶ GENERAL, NORMAL, USUAL
（場所に）ある ▶ BASE
（…で）ある ▶ REPRESENT 1
歩く ▶ WALK 1, 2

アルコール飲料 ▶ DRINK 名
ある種の ▶ PARTICULAR
ある程度は ▶ PARTLY
荒れ狂う ▶ ROUGH
荒れた ▶ ROUGH
荒れ地 ▶ HILL
淡い ▶ PALE
慌ただしい ▶ BUSY 2, QUICK
泡立てる ▶ STIR
慌てた ▶ RESTLESS
慌てふためいた ▶ HYSTERICAL
慌てふためく ▶ PANIC
慌てる ▶ HURRY
哀れな ▶ SAD
哀れみ ▶ SYMPATHY
哀れむ ▶ SORRY FOR SB
哀れむべき ▶ UNFORTUNATE 2
案 ▶ PLAN 1
アンカー ▶ PRESENTER
暗記する ▶ LEARN
行脚 ▶ TRIP
案件 ▶ FACTOR
暗殺 ▶ MURDER
暗殺する ▶ KILL
暗殺部隊 ▶ TEAM 1
暗示する ▶ SUGGEST
安心 ▶ RELIEF, SILENCE
安心した ▶ HAPPY
安全 ▶ SECURITY
安全な ▶ SAFE
安息の地 ▶ REFUGE
暗たんたる ▶ SERIOUS 2
安定した ▶ FIRM, STEADY
安堵 ▶ RELIEF
案内 ▶ ADVICE, INFORMATION
案内書 ▶ BOOK
案内状 ▶ LEAFLET
案内する ▶ TAKE 2
アンパイア ▶ JUDGE 名
安楽死 ▶ MURDER
安楽な ▶ COMFORTABLE

い

言い争い ▶ ARGUMENT 1, DEBATE
言い争う ▶ ARGUE, DISAGREE
言い表す ▶ SAY 2
いい加減な ▶ RECKLESS
言い方 ▶ LANGUAGE

言い直す ▶ REPEAT
言い張る ▶ CLAIM
言い分 ▶ ARGUMENT 2, VIEW 1
言い間違い ▶ MISTAKE 2
Eメール ▶ LETTER
言い寄り ▶ OFFER 1
言い寄る ▶ FLIRT
言い訳 ▶ REASON
委員 ▶ OFFICIAL 名
委員会 ▶ COMMITTEE
委員長 ▶ LEADER 1
言う ▶ SAY 1, 2
家 ▶ HOME, SHELTER
家柄 ▶ FAMILY 3
意外な ▶ SURPRISING
いかがわしい ▶ SUSPICIOUS 2
医学 ▶ TREATMENT
いかさま師 ▶ CRIMINAL
いかさまをする ▶ CHEAT 動
いかめしい ▶ STERN
怒り ▶ ANGER 名, TEMPER
怒り狂う ▶ LOSE YOUR TEMPER
怒り狂った ▶ FURIOUS
怒り狂わせる ▶ ANGER 動
怒りを買う ▶ ANGER 動
いかれた ▶ MAD
遺憾 ▶ GUILT
移管する ▶ GIVE 1
遺憾な ▶ UNFORTUNATE 2
意気 ▶ DETERMINATION, MOOD
異議 ▶ DEBATE, OPPOSITION
行き当たりばったりの ▶ RANDOM
行き当たる ▶ HAVE 3
生き生きとした ▶ LIVELY
勢い ▶ INCENTIVE
生き方 ▶ LIFE 3
息苦しい ▶ HUMID
意気消沈 ▶ GLOOM
意気消沈させる ▶ NEGATIVE
行き詰まる ▶ FAIL 2, HOLD SB/STH UP
生きて（いる）▶ ALIVE
憤り ▶ ANGER 名, FRUSTRATION
粋な ▶ ELEGANT, FASHIONABLE
生き長らえる ▶ REMAIN, SURVIVE

生き残り ▶ LIFE 1
生き残る ▶ SURVIVE
異議のない ▶ UNDOUBTED
生き延びる ▶ SURVIVE
偉業 ▶ MIRACLE
意気揚々とした ▶ LIVELY
異議を唱える ▶ DISAGREE, DOUBT 動
息をのませる ▶ IMPRESS
息をのむような ▶ AMAZING
行く ▶ GO 1, 2
意気地なし ▶ COWARD
行く手 ▶ WAY 3
いくぶん ▶ PARTLY
畏敬 ▶ ADMIRATION
意見 ▶ CONCLUSION, STATEMENT, VIEW 1
威厳 ▶ DIGNITY
威厳のある ▶ PROUD 1
意見を聞く ▶ TALK
意見を持つ ▶ THINK
意向 ▶ PURPOSE, VIEW 1, WISH
居心地のよい ▶ COMFORTABLE
意固地な ▶ STUBBORN
いさかい ▶ ARGUMENT 1
いざこざ ▶ TROUBLE 1
勇ましい ▶ BRAVE
意志 ▶ DETERMINATION
意思 ▶ WISH
意識 ▶ AWARENESS, UNDERSTANDING
意識的な ▶ DELIBERATE
維持する ▶ CONTINUE 2, MAINTAIN
異質の ▶ FOREIGN, PARTICULAR, STRANGE 2
意志の強い ▶ STUBBORN
意地の悪い ▶ MEAN 形
いじめ ▶ REPRESSION
異臭 ▶ ODOUR
移住者 ▶ REFUGEE
移住する ▶ LEAVE 2
異種の ▶ FOREIGN
衣装 ▶ CLOTHES
異常 ▶ DEFECT
異常な ▶ SURPRISING
意地悪 ▶ EVIL 名
意地悪な ▶ EVIL
意思を疎通する ▶ TALK
威信 ▶ REPUTATION, STATUS
遺跡 ▶ REMAINS

いぜんの → うごかない

日本語類語一覧

以前の ▶ FORMER, PREVIOUS
急いで逃げる ▶ FLEE
忙しい ▶ BUSY 1, 2
急がせる ▶ ACCELERATE
急ぎ ▶ SPEED
急ぐ ▶ HURRY
依存する ▶ NEED 動
依存性の ▶ ADDICTIVE
痛い ▶ PAINFUL 1
偉大な ▶ GREAT 2, POWERFUL
いたずら ▶ JOKE, TRICK
板挟み ▶ MESS 2
痛ましい ▶ PAINFUL 2, SAD
痛み ▶ ILLNESS, PAIN
痛みを与える ▶ INJURE
痛む ▶ HURT 2
痛める ▶ INJURE
傷んだ ▶ ROTTEN
市 ▶ MARKET 2
一群 ▶ SERIES
一個人の ▶ OWN
一時停止する ▶ BREAK 2
一時的な ▶ SHORT 1
一族 ▶ FAMILY 2, 3
一団 ▶ GROUP 1, 2, PARTY 2
市場 ▶ MARKET 2
一番目の ▶ FIRST
一部分は ▶ PARTLY
一瞥 ▶ LOOK 名
一味 ▶ PARTY 2, TEAM 1
一様な ▶ EQUAL
一覧表 ▶ LIST 名, SERIES
一覧表を作る ▶ LIST 動
一流 ▶ STYLE
一流の ▶ EXCELLENT, TOP
一例である ▶ REPRESENT 2
一列 ▶ SERIES
一連 ▶ FLOOD 名 2, SERIES
一家 ▶ FAMILY 1
一回 ▶ STAGE
一見 ▶ LOOK 名
一行 ▶ PARTY 2
一式 ▶ GROUP 1
一瞬の ▶ SHORT 1
一生 ▶ LIFE 2
一生懸命になる ▶ TRY 1
一生残る ▶ PERMANENT
一緒に ▶ PARALLEL
一緒にする ▶ MATCH 2
一斉射撃 ▶ FLOOD 名 2
一隊 ▶ PARTY 2
一体感 ▶ FRIENDSHIP

行ったり来たりする ▶ WALK 1
一致しない ▶ INCONSISTENT
一致する ▶ MATCH 1
一定の ▶ STEADY
いっぱいにする ▶ FILL
いっぱいになる ▶ FILL
いっぱいの ▶ FULL
一般的な ▶ GENERAL, NORMAL, USUAL
一般の ▶ GENERAL
一風変わった ▶ UNUSUAL
一片 ▶ PIECE
一変させる ▶ TURN 2
一変する ▶ CHANGE 動 2
一歩 ▶ STEP
いつもと異なる ▶ UNUSUAL
いつもの ▶ USUAL
いつものように ▶ USUALLY
いつもは ▶ USUALLY
逸話 ▶ STORY
偽りのない ▶ DEEP 1
イデオロギー ▶ VALUES
移転させる ▶ LEAVE 2
移転する ▶ LEAVE 2
遺伝的な ▶ NATURAL
意図 ▶ MEANING, PURPOSE
移動 ▶ MOVEMENT, TRAVEL
移動する ▶ GO 1
異動する ▶ LEAVE 2
糸口 ▶ SUGGESTION
居所 ▶ PLACE
いとしい ▶ DEAR, SWEET
意図する ▶ DESIGN 動 2, INTEND
意図的でない ▶ UNCONSCIOUS
意図的な ▶ DELIBERATE
挑む ▶ TRY 1
いないこと ▶ LACK
田舎 ▶ COUNTRY 2
田舎道 ▶ ROAD
いなくなる ▶ LEAVE 1
居眠りする ▶ SLEEP
居残る ▶ STAY 1
命 ▶ LIFE 1
違反 ▶ CRIME 2
違反者 ▶ CRIMINAL
違反する ▶ BREAK 3
畏怖 ▶ ADMIRATION
衣服 ▶ CLOTHES, THING 2
遺物 ▶ REMAINS

イベント ▶ EVENT 2
違法行為 ▶ CORRUPTION, CRIME 2
違法な ▶ ILLEGAL
今の ▶ RECENT
忌まわしい ▶ DISGUSTING 2, UGLY
意味 ▶ MEANING
意味する ▶ MEAN 動
移民 ▶ REFUGEE
イメージ ▶ IDEA 1, REPUTATION
いやいやながらの ▶ RELUCTANT
嫌がる ▶ HESITATE
医薬品 ▶ DRUG 2
嫌気 ▶ HATRED
卑しい ▶ EVIL 形
いやす ▶ CURE
嫌だと思う ▶ CARE
嫌な ▶ BAD, DISGUSTING 2, PAINFUL 2, TERRIBLE 1
嫌なにおい ▶ ODOUR
嫌みな ▶ IRONIC
異様な ▶ STRANGE 1, UGLY
意欲 ▶ INCENTIVE
意欲を起こさせる ▶ INSPIRE
依頼 ▶ REQUEST, WISH
依頼人 ▶ CUSTOMER
いらいらさせる ▶ ANNOY, ANNOYING, OFFENSIVE, WORRY, WORRYING
いらいらした ▶ IRRITABLE, RESTLESS, TENSE, UNHAPPY 2
いら立たせる ▶ ANGER 動, ANNOY, ANNOYING
いら立ち ▶ FRUSTRATION, TEMPER
いら立った ▶ ANGRY, ANNOYED
入り口 ▶ HALL 2
入り組んだ ▶ COMPLEX
医療 ▶ TREATMENT
いる ▶ STAY 1
衣類 ▶ CLOTHES, THING 2
異例の ▶ SPECIAL, UNUSUAL
入れ替える ▶ REPLACE 2
色目を使う ▶ FLIRT
異論のない ▶ UNDOUBTED
祝う ▶ PLAY 動 1
陰鬱な ▶ CLOUDY, NEGATIVE

陰気 ▶ GLOOM
印刷出力 ▶ COPY 名 1
陰惨な ▶ TERRIBLE 3
因子 ▶ FACTOR
因習 ▶ TRADITION
飲酒する ▶ DRINK 動
印 ▶ LOGO
印象 ▶ APPEARANCE, ATMOSPHERE, EFFECT, REPUTATION, SENSE
印象的な ▶ IMPRESSIVE, MAGNIFICENT
印象を与える ▶ SEEM
飲食物 ▶ FOOD
インスピレーション ▶ INSPIRATION
引退する ▶ LEAVE 3
インタビュー ▶ INTERVIEW 1
インタビューする ▶ QUESTION 動
インフレ ▶ INCREASE 名
陰謀 ▶ CONSPIRACY
陰謀を企てる ▶ PLOT
引用 ▶ REFERENCE
引用句 ▶ REFERENCE
引用する ▶ MENTION, QUOTE

う

ウイルス ▶ DEFECT
ウイルス性疾患 ▶ DISEASE
飢えている ▶ HUNGRY
右往左往した ▶ HYSTERICAL
うかつな ▶ CARELESS
浮き彫りにする ▶ POINT STH OUT
請け合い ▶ PROMISE 名
受け入れ ▶ APPROVAL
受け入れられない ▶ UNACCEPTABLE
受け入れる ▶ AGREE, APPROVE, GREET, LET SB IN, TAKE 4
請け負う ▶ DO
受付 ▶ HALL 2
受け止め方 ▶ AWARENESS
受取通知 ▶ ANSWER 名
受け取る ▶ GET 2, TAKE 4
受けのよい ▶ POPULAR
受ける ▶ TAKE 4
動かす ▶ OPERATE
動かない ▶ STILL

うごき → おいやる

日本語類語一覧

- 動き ▶ MOVEMENT, TREND
- 動く ▶ WORK 動 2
- うさんくさい ▶ SUSPICIOUS 2
- 後ろ盾 ▶ SPONSOR
- 後ろ向きの ▶ NEGATIVE
- 後ろめたく思って ▶ SORRY
- 後ろめたさ ▶ DOUBT 名 2
- 薄い ▶ NARROW, PALE
- うずき ▶ PAIN
- 薄汚い ▶ DIRTY
- 薄切り ▶ PIECE
- うずく ▶ HURT 2
- 薄暗い ▶ CLOUDY
- 渦を巻く ▶ SPIN
- 嘘 ▶ LIE, TRICK
- 嘘つきの ▶ DISHONEST
- 疑い ▶ DOUBT 名 1, 2
- 疑い深い ▶ SUSPICIOUS 1
- 疑いを抱いた ▶ UNSURE
- 疑う ▶ DOUBT 動, SUSPECT
- 疑う余地のない ▶ CLEAR 形 1
- 疑って ▶ SUSPICIOUS 1
- 疑わしい ▶ SUSPICIOUS 2, UNLIKELY 1, 2, UNSURE
- うたた寝する ▶ SLEEP
- 打ち勝つ ▶ WIN
- 内気な ▶ SHY, SOLITARY
- 打ち込む ▶ PUSH 1
- 打ち込んでいる ▶ BUSY 1
- 打ち解けた ▶ FRIENDLY 2
- 打ち負かす ▶ DEFEAT
- 打ち身 ▶ TUMOUR
- 有頂天 ▶ JOY
- 有頂天の ▶ EXCITED
- 内輪の ▶ SECRET
- 打つ ▶ BEAT, HIT 1, 2
- 美しい ▶ BEAUTIFUL 1, 2, WONDERFUL
- 美しくない ▶ UGLY
- 訴え ▶ REQUEST
- うっとりした ▶ INTERESTED
- 移る ▶ CHANGE 動 2
- 腕前 ▶ SKILL 1
- うとうとした ▶ TIRED
- うなる ▶ SHOUT, WHISPER
- うぬぼれ ▶ PRIDE
- うぬぼれた ▶ PROUD 2
- 奪う ▶ ROB, SUPPRESS 1
- うぶな ▶ NAIVE
- うまい ▶ DELICIOUS
- うまくいかない ▶ FAIL 2

- うまくいく ▶ DO WELL, WIN
- うまさ ▶ SKILL 2
- 生まれ育つ ▶ BRING SB UP
- 生まれつきの ▶ NATURAL
- 海 ▶ SEA
- 生み出す ▶ MAKE 1
- 海辺 ▶ COAST
- 生む ▶ PROVIDE
- うめく ▶ WHISPER
- 埋め尽くす ▶ PACK
- 紆余曲折のある ▶ COMPLEX
- 裏表のある ▶ DISHONEST
- 裏切る ▶ CHEAT 動
- 裏づけ ▶ EVIDENCE
- 裏づけのない ▶ IRRATIONAL
- 裏づける ▶ CONFIRM 1, 2, SHOW 1
- 裏通り ▶ ROAD
- 恨み ▶ TENSION
- 裏目に出る ▶ FAIL 2
- 売上高 ▶ REVENUE
- 売り込む ▶ ADVERTISE
- 売り台 ▶ STALL
- 売り出す ▶ INTRODUCE, PRESENT 1, PUBLISH 2
- 売りに出されて ▶ AVAILABLE
- 売り場 ▶ STALL
- 売り払う ▶ SELL 1
- 売る ▶ SELL 1
- うるさい ▶ LOUD
- うれしい ▶ GLAD, HAPPY, NICE 1, WONDERFUL
- うれしがらせる ▶ PLEASE
- うれしさ ▶ JOY, SATISFACTION
- 売れ筋商品 ▶ LEADER 2
- うろ ▶ HOLE 2
- うろたえた ▶ UPSET
- うろたえる ▶ PANIC
- うろつく ▶ STAY 1, WALK 1
- 浮気する ▶ FLIRT
- 噂 ▶ REPUTATION
- 噂話 ▶ DISCUSSION
- 上の空の ▶ CARELESS
- うわべの ▶ APPARENT
- 上向き ▶ INCREASE 名
- 上向く ▶ IMPROVE 2
- 上役 ▶ MANAGER
- 運 ▶ LUCK, RISK 2
- 運営する ▶ GOVERNMENT 2
- 運営者 ▶ MANAGEMENT

- 運営する ▶ ORGANIZE, RUN 2
- 運行する ▶ GO 2
- うんざりさせる ▶ BAD, BORING
- うんざりした ▶ ANGRY
- 運送 ▶ DELIVERY
- 運賃 ▶ RATE
- 運動 ▶ SPORT
- 運動する ▶ CAMPAIGN 動
- 運動をする[させる] ▶ TRAIN 2
- 運のよい ▶ TIMELY
- 運命 ▶ LUCK
- 運輸業 ▶ DELIVERY

え

- 絵 ▶ PICTURE
- エアロビクス ▶ SPORT
- 永遠の ▶ PERMANENT
- 映画スター ▶ ACTOR
- 永久の ▶ PERMANENT
- 影響 ▶ EFFECT, RESULT
- 営業 ▶ TRADE
- 営業している ▶ WORK 動 2
- 影響する ▶ AFFECT
- 営業部員 ▶ STAFF
- 影響力 ▶ EFFECT, INVOLVEMENT
- 影響力のある ▶ POWERFUL
- 影響を与える ▶ INFLUENCE 動
- 栄光 ▶ STATUS
- 衛生的な ▶ CLEAN 形
- 衛星都市[国] ▶ TERRITORY
- 永続的な ▶ CONTINUOUS
- 英知 ▶ KNOWLEDGE
- 鋭敏な ▶ SHREWD
- 栄誉 ▶ STATUS, VALUE
- 栄誉ある ▶ FAMOUS
- 栄養の ▶ HEALTHY
- 栄養分 ▶ FOOD
- 栄養満点の ▶ HEALTHY
- 営利の ▶ SUCCESSFUL 2
- 描く ▶ DRAW, PRESENT 2
- エキスパート ▶ EXPERT
- 液体 ▶ MATERIAL
- 液体を流す ▶ FLOW
- エグゼクティブ ▶ EXECUTIVE
- えこひいき ▶ DISCRIMINATION
- えさ ▶ BRIBE

- エチケット ▶ RESPECT 名
- 謁見 ▶ INTERVIEW 1
- エッセイ ▶ PAPER
- エラー ▶ MISTAKE 1
- 選ばれる ▶ FAVOURITE
- 選ぶ ▶ APPOINT, CHOOSE, DECIDE, PREFER
- 偉ぶった ▶ PROUD 2
- エリート ▶ ELITE
- エリートの ▶ TOP
- 得る ▶ GAIN, GET 1, 2
- 絵を描く ▶ DRAW
- 沿岸 ▶ COAST
- 延期する ▶ DELAY, HOLD SB/STH UP
- 演技する ▶ PLAY 動 2
- 縁起の悪い ▶ UNFORTUNATE 1
- 演芸 ▶ INTEREST 名 2
- 演劇 ▶ DRAMA
- 援護 ▶ SECURITY
- 演者 ▶ ACTOR
- 演習 ▶ TRAINING
- 援助 ▶ AID, HELP 名
- 炎症 ▶ TUMOUR
- 炎症を起こした ▶ PAINFUL 1
- 援助金 ▶ GIFT
- 援助する ▶ HELP 動 1
- 演じる ▶ PLAY 動 2, PRESENT 2, PRETEND
- 演説 ▶ SPEECH
- 演奏 ▶ PERFORMANCE
- 演奏する ▶ PLAY 動 2
- 遠征 ▶ TRIP
- エンターテイナー ▶ ACTOR
- 延滞の ▶ LATE
- 延長した ▶ LONG
- 延長する ▶ EXPAND, MAINTAIN
- 遠慮 ▶ LIMIT 1
- 遠慮する ▶ HESITATE
- 遠慮のない ▶ SOCIABLE
- 縁を切る ▶ REJECT

お

- 追いかける ▶ FOLLOW 1
- おいしい ▶ DELICIOUS
- おいしそうな ▶ DELICIOUS
- 追い出す ▶ EXCLUDE 2
- 追いつく ▶ GET 3
- 追いはぎ ▶ THIEF
- 追いやる ▶ EXPEL, FORCE

おいわいをいう → おもいだす

お祝いを言う ▶ PRAISE 動
応援 ▶ HELP 名
応援する ▶ HELP 動 1
応じられる ▶ FREE 形 3
応じる ▶ ANSWER 動, FOLLOW 3, TAKE 4
往診 ▶ VISIT 名
王朝 ▶ FAMILY 3
応答 ▶ ANSWER 名
横柄な ▶ PROUD 2, RUDE
横暴さ ▶ REPRESSION
応募者 ▶ CANDIDATE
応用 ▶ USE 名
応用する ▶ APPLY
横領 ▶ THEFT
横領する ▶ STEAL
終える ▶ END 動, FINISH
大雨 ▶ FLOOD 名 1
多い ▶ LARGE
覆い隠す ▶ HIDE
大急ぎの ▶ QUICK
大いなる ▶ LARGE
大いに ▶ VERY 副
大いに楽しむ ▶ LIKE
覆う ▶ SPREAD
大きい ▶ LARGE
大きくする ▶ EXPAND
大きくなる ▶ EXPAND
多くの場合 ▶ USUALLY
大げさに言う ▶ EXAGGERATE
大御所 ▶ STAR
大仕事 ▶ PROJECT
大詰め ▶ END 名
オーディション ▶ INTERVIEW 2
大通り ▶ ROAD
オーバーホールする ▶ REPAIR
大広間 ▶ HALL 1
大目に見る ▶ FORGIVE, IGNORE
大物 ▶ AUTHORITIES, EXECUTIVE, STAR
公の ▶ PUBLIC, SOCIAL
おおよその ▶ VAGUE
大喜びさせる ▶ DELIGHT
大喜びの ▶ GLAD
オーラ ▶ ATMOSPHERE
大笑いする ▶ LAUGH, SCREAM
丘 ▶ HILL
おかしい ▶ FUNNY
おかしな ▶ RIDICULOUS, STRANGE 1
(過失などを)犯す ▶ DO

お金 ▶ MONEY 1
起き上がる ▶ STAND 1
おきて ▶ VALUES
お気に入り ▶ CHOICE 2
お気に入りの ▶ FAVOURITE
置く ▶ BASE, PUT
憶測 ▶ SPECULATION
憶測する ▶ SAY 3
臆病な ▶ SHY
臆病者 ▶ COWARD
お悔やみ ▶ SYMPATHY
遅らせる ▶ DELAY, HOLD SB/STH UP
送り届ける ▶ TAKE 1
贈り物 ▶ GIFT
送る ▶ CONVEY, SEND, TAKE 2
遅れた ▶ LATE
怠る ▶ FAIL 1
怒った ▶ ANGRY, ANNOYED
行い ▶ ACTION
行う ▶ DO, HAVE 4
行われる ▶ HAPPEN
怒らせる ▶ ANGER 動, ANNOY, HURT 1
起こり ▶ SOURCE
起こりうる ▶ LIKELY
起こりそうにもない ▶ UNLIKELY 1
怒りっぽい ▶ IRRITABLE, SENSITIVE 3
起こる ▶ FOLLOW 2, HAPPEN
怒る ▶ LOSE YOUR TEMPER, SCOLD
抑えがたい ▶ UNCONTROLLABLE, WILD
抑えきれない ▶ URGENT
抑える ▶ SUPPRESS 2
幼い ▶ YOUNG
おさらいする ▶ PRACTISE
押し入り ▶ THEFT
押し入る ▶ ROB
押し売りする ▶ ADVERTISE
教え ▶ KNOWLEDGE, VALUES
教える ▶ CONVEY, SHOW 1, TEACH, TELL 1, TRAIN 1
おじけづかせる ▶ DISCOURAGE 2
おじけづく ▶ PANIC
押し込み ▶ THEFT

押し込み強盗 ▶ THEFT
押し込む ▶ PACK, PUSH 1, PUT
推し進める ▶ CONTINUE 2
押しつける ▶ PRESS 2, PUSH 1
押しのける ▶ PUSH 2
押しの強い ▶ AGGRESSIVE 2
おしゃべり ▶ DISCUSSION
押しやる ▶ PUSH 1
おしゃれな ▶ ELEGANT, FASHIONABLE
汚職 ▶ CORRUPTION
押し分ける ▶ PUSH 2
押す ▶ PRESS 1, PUSH 1
お世辞 ▶ PRAISE 名
お世辞の ▶ GOOD 6
遅い ▶ SLOW
遅い時間の ▶ LATE
襲う ▶ ATTACK 動 1
遅くなった ▶ LATE
遅まきの ▶ LATE
おぞましい ▶ DISGUSTING 2
お粗末な ▶ POOR 2, UNFORTUNATE 2
おそらく ▶ PROBABLY
恐れ ▶ FEAR, RISK 1
恐れさせる ▶ FRIGHTEN
恐れ知らずの ▶ BOLD
恐れて ▶ AFRAID
恐れを知らない ▶ BRAVE
おそろいの ▶ EQUIVALENT
恐ろしい ▶ EVIL 形, FRIGHTENING, TERRIBLE 1, 3
教わる ▶ LEARN
おたく ▶ FAN
おだての ▶ GOOD 6
おだてる ▶ PERSUADE
穏やかな ▶ CALM, FRIENDLY 1, GENTLE, QUIET 1, 2
陥る ▶ HAVE 3
落ちこぼれの人 ▶ LOSER 2
落ち込ませる ▶ DISCOURAGE 2
落ち込んだ ▶ DEPRESSED
落ち着いた ▶ CALM
落ち着かない ▶ EMBARRASSED, WORRIED, WORRYING
落ち度のある ▶ GUILTY
おちょくる ▶ ANNOY

落ちる ▶ FAIL 3, FALL 2, WORSEN
追っかけ ▶ FAN
夫 ▶ PARTNER 2
お手洗い ▶ TOILET
おでき ▶ TUMOUR
おどおどした ▶ SHY
おどかす ▶ FRIGHTEN
おどけ ▶ JOKE
男 ▶ MAN 1, PARTNER 2
男の子 ▶ CHILD
男の人 ▶ MAN 1
落とし穴 ▶ DISADVANTAGE
陥れる ▶ PLOT
落とす ▶ FAIL 3, REDUCE
おどす ▶ FRIGHTEN
訪れる ▶ VISIT 動
劣った ▶ POOR 2
おとなしい ▶ SENSITIVE 1
大人っぽい ▶ ADULT
大人の ▶ ADULT
おとり ▶ BRIBE
衰える ▶ WORSEN
驚かす ▶ SURPRISE
驚き ▶ FEAR, SHOCK 名
驚くべき ▶ AMAZING, FRIGHTENING, REMARKABLE, SURPRISING, WONDERFUL
音を立てない ▶ QUIET 1
同じ ▶ EQUAL
同じである ▶ MATCH 1
同じような[で] ▶ LIKE 前 形
尾根 ▶ HILL
お願いする ▶ ASK 2
おびえて ▶ AFRAID
おびえる ▶ PANIC
脅かす ▶ THREATEN
オプションの ▶ VOLUNTARY 1
オフレコで ▶ UNOFFICIAL
覚えている ▶ REMEMBER
覚える ▶ FEEL, LEARN
お前 ▶ DARLING
おまる ▶ TOILET
お恵み ▶ AID
思い上がった ▶ PROUD 2
思い上がり ▶ PRIDE
思い浮かべる ▶ IMAGINE
思い描く ▶ IMAGINE
思い起こす ▶ REMEMBER
思い切った ▶ SERIOUS 1
思い込んでいる ▶ THINK
思い出す ▶ REMEMBER

日本語類語一覧

おもいちがい → かきまわす

思い違い ▶ ILLUSION
思いつき ▶ DESIRE, IDEA 1
思いつく ▶ ESTIMATE 動, IMAGINE
思い出 ▶ MEMORY
思い出話 ▶ MEMORY
思いとどまらせる ▶ DISCOURAGE 1
思いもよらない ▶ SURPRISING, UNLIKELY 2
思いやり ▶ ATTENTION, LOVE 名 2, SYMPATHY, TACT
思いやりのある ▶ LOVING, SENSITIVE 1
思いやりのない ▶ CRUEL, INSENSITIVE
思う ▶ FIND 1, IMAGINE, REGARD, SUPPOSE, THINK
思える ▶ SEEM
重々しい ▶ SERIOUS 2
重苦しい ▶ SERIOUS 2
面白い ▶ FUNNY, INTERESTING, POPULAR
面白がった ▶ INTERESTED
面白くない ▶ BORING
面白さ ▶ FUN, INTEREST 名 1
面白み ▶ HUMOUR
表向きの ▶ APPARENT
重荷 ▶ CARGO, RESPONSIBILITY
趣 ▶ INTEREST 名 1
重んじる ▶ APPRECIATE
お役所仕事 ▶ BUREAUCRACY
お役人 ▶ OFFICIAL 名
折り合いのつかない ▶ INCONSISTENT
折にふれて ▶ SOMETIMES
折よい ▶ TIMELY
折る ▶ BREAK 1
折れる ▶ BREAK 1, GIVE WAY
愚かな ▶ CRAZY
愚か者 ▶ FOOL
卸売業者 ▶ DEALER
おろそかにする ▶ IGNORE
終わったばかりの ▶ LAST 2
終わらせる ▶ END 動
終わり ▶ END 名
終わりの ▶ LAST 1
終わる ▶ END 動, STOP
恩恵 ▶ BENEFIT

温厚な ▶ FRIENDLY 1
音信 ▶ COMMUNICATION
温暖な ▶ SUNNY
女 ▶ WOMAN
女友達 ▶ FRIEND
女の子 ▶ CHILD, GIRL
温和な ▶ KIND 形
恩を感じる ▶ GRATEFUL

か

科 ▶ DEPARTMENT
階 ▶ FLOOR
害 ▶ DAMAGE 名
会員 ▶ LECTURER
海運 ▶ DELIVERY
絵画 ▶ PICTURE
海外の ▶ FOREIGN
開花する ▶ DO WELL
快活な ▶ CHEERFUL, LIVELY
海岸 ▶ COAST
概観 ▶ SUMMARY
海岸線 ▶ COAST
会期 ▶ MEETING 1
会議 ▶ MEETING 1
会議場 ▶ HALL 1
懐疑 ▶ SCEPTICISM
懐疑的な ▶ SUSPICIOUS 1
階級 ▶ CATEGORY, CLASS 3
開業 ▶ WORK 名 1
開業している ▶ WORK 動 1
解決 ▶ SOLUTION
解決する ▶ DEAL WITH SB/STH, RESOLVE
外見 ▶ APPEARANCE
解雇 ▶ UNEMPLOYMENT
会合 ▶ MEETING 1
外交員 ▶ SALESMAN
外交術 ▶ TACT
会合する ▶ MEET 1
外向的な ▶ SOCIABLE
開口部 ▶ HOLE 1
外国からの ▶ FOREIGN
外国人居住者 ▶ REFUGEE
外国人嫌い ▶ RACISM
外国との ▶ FOREIGN
外国の ▶ FOREIGN
解雇された ▶ UNEMPLOYED
解雇する ▶ FIRE
介護する ▶ LOOK AFTER SB
買い込む ▶ KEEP 1
開催する ▶ PLAY 動 2

開催地 ▶ PLACE
開催を求める ▶ HAVE 4
解散 ▶ DIVISION 1, UNEMPLOYMENT
概算 ▶ ESTIMATE 名
概算する ▶ ESTIMATE 動
開始 ▶ ARRIVAL, START 名
開始する ▶ BEGIN, INTRODUCE
開示する ▶ REVEAL
会社 ▶ COMPANY
解釈 ▶ DEFINITION
解釈する ▶ EXPLAIN 1
解釈的な ▶ DESCRIPTIVE
会場 ▶ PLACE
外傷 ▶ INJURY
改心させる ▶ PERSUADE
海図 ▶ MAP
害する ▶ DAMAGE 動, RUIN
快晴の ▶ SUNNY
解説 ▶ ASSESSMENT
概説 ▶ REPORT 1
解説者 ▶ ANALYST
解説的な ▶ DESCRIPTIVE
改善 ▶ CHANGE 名 2
改善される ▶ IMPROVE 2
改善する ▶ CORRECT, IMPROVE 1
階層 ▶ AREA 2, CLASS 3
回想録 ▶ MEMORY
海賊 ▶ THIEF
海賊版の ▶ ILLEGAL
解体 ▶ DIVISION 1
買いだめする ▶ KEEP 1
会長 ▶ LEADER 1
買い手 ▶ CUSTOMER
快適な ▶ COMFORTABLE
回転させる ▶ TURN 1
回転する ▶ SPIN
ガイド ▶ ADVISER
解答 ▶ SOLUTION
該当する ▶ INCLUDE
介入する ▶ INTERVENE
解任する ▶ FIRE
概念 ▶ IDEA 1, SENSE, UNDERSTANDING
概念化する ▶ IMAGINE
概念的な ▶ INTELLECTUAL 1
開発 ▶ DEVELOPMENT
開発事業 ▶ PROJECT
開発する ▶ DEVELOP 2
会費 ▶ RATE
回避する ▶ ESCAPE, PREVENT
快復 ▶ TREATMENT

回復する ▶ IMPROVE 2, RECOVER
解放される ▶ FREE 動
解放する ▶ FREE 動, RELEASE
開放的な ▶ TOLERANT
解明する ▶ FIND 3
壊滅させる ▶ DESTROY
外面的な ▶ APPARENT
買い物客 ▶ CUSTOMER
解約する ▶ ABOLISH, CANCEL
潰瘍 ▶ TUMOUR
概要 ▶ SUMMARY
外来の ▶ FOREIGN
回覧する ▶ PUBLISH 1
戒律 ▶ RULE
概略 ▶ SUMMARY
改良される ▶ IMPROVE 2
街路 ▶ ROAD
会話 ▶ DISCUSSION
下院議員 ▶ POLITICIAN
買う ▶ BUY
飼う ▶ KEEP 4
カウンセラー ▶ ADVISER
カウンセリング ▶ ADVICE
カウント ▶ ESTIMATE 名
返す ▶ RETURN 2
変える ▶ CHANGE 動 1, TURN 2
替える ▶ REPLACE 2
帰る ▶ RETURN 1
顔見知り ▶ FRIEND
香り ▶ SMELL
抱える ▶ HAVE 2, HOLD
価格 ▶ PRICE
化学物質 ▶ MATERIAL
輝かしい ▶ SUCCESSFUL 2
輝く ▶ SHINE
かかりっきりの ▶ BUSY 1
(病気に)かかる ▶ SUFFER FROM STH
関わらせる ▶ AFFECT
関わり ▶ INVOLVEMENT
関わる ▶ AFFECT
鍵 ▶ SOLUTION
書き写す ▶ WRITE
書き起こす ▶ WRITE
かき込む ▶ EAT
かき立てる ▶ STIMULATE
書き手 ▶ WRITER
書き留める ▶ WRITE
書き取らせる ▶ QUOTE
かき混ぜる ▶ STIR
書き間違い ▶ MISTAKE 2
かき回す ▶ STIR

かきゅうの → かのうせい

日本語類語一覧

火急の ▶ URGENT
限られた ▶ LIMITED 1, 2
嗅ぎ分ける ▶ FIND 4
鍵をかける ▶ CLOSE 動
格 ▶ CATEGORY
核 ▶ POINT
かく ▶ SCRATCH
書く ▶ WRITE
額 ▶ NUMBER
学位論文 ▶ PAPER
架空の ▶ FICTIONAL, SUPPOSED
角切り ▶ PIECE
格差 ▶ DIFFERENCE, GAP
学識 ▶ KNOWLEDGE
確実な ▶ CERTAIN, FINAL
確実にする ▶ ENSURE
隠し場所 ▶ REFUGE
学者ぶった ▶ INTELLECTUAL 2
学習 ▶ EDUCATION
学術 ▶ KNOWLEDGE
学術的な ▶ EDUCATIONAL, INTELLECTUAL 1
革新 ▶ DEVELOPMENT
確信 ▶ FAITH
核心 ▶ POINT
確信がない ▶ UNSURE
確信させる ▶ CONVINCE
確信して ▶ SURE
革新者 ▶ LEADER 2
確信する ▶ CHECK 2
革新的な ▶ CREATIVE, RADICAL
隠す ▶ HIDE
隠すもの ▶ PRECAUTION
覚醒剤 ▶ DRUG 1
愕然とさせる ▶ SHOCK 動
楽想 ▶ SUBJECT
拡大する ▶ EXPAND, RISE
拡張 ▶ INCREASE 名, PROGRESS
格付けする ▶ RANK
確定する ▶ CONFIRM 3
確定的な ▶ FINAL
格闘 ▶ FIGHT 名
格闘する ▶ FIGHT 動
獲得する ▶ ACHIEVE, GAIN
確認する ▶ CHECK 2, CONFIRM 2, FIND 3
撹拌する ▶ STIR
学部 ▶ DEPARTMENT
格別に ▶ SPECIAL
確保する ▶ ENSURE, GAIN
かくまう ▶ HIDE, PROTECT
革命 ▶ REVOLUTION

革命家 ▶ GUERRILLA
革命的な ▶ RADICAL
学問 ▶ KNOWLEDGE
学問的な ▶ EDUCATIONAL, INTELLECTUAL 1
学問の ▶ EDUCATIONAL
確約する ▶ PROMISE 動
隔離 ▶ DIVISION 1
隔離する ▶ ISOLATE
隠れ家 ▶ REFUGE
賭け ▶ RISK 2
影 ▶ SHAPE
家系 ▶ FAMILY 3
かけがえのない ▶ VALUABLE 1
掛け勘定 ▶ BILL
過激な ▶ RADICAL
欠けた ▶ INADEQUATE
駆け出す ▶ FLEE
影法師 ▶ SHAPE
かけら ▶ BIT, FRAGMENT
駆ける ▶ RUN 1
懸ける ▶ THREATEN
賭ける ▶ THREATEN
火口 ▶ HOLE 2
下降する ▶ FALL 2
過酷な ▶ HARD, STRICT
過去の ▶ PREVIOUS
過去の人 ▶ LOSER 2
飾り ▶ DECORATION
飾り板 ▶ SIGN 2
飾り気のない ▶ PLAIN 1
飾る ▶ DECORATE
家事 ▶ TASK
かじかんだ ▶ FREEZING
賢い ▶ INTELLIGENT, WISE
過失がある ▶ GUILTY
貸付金 ▶ LOAN
カジュアルな ▶ INFORMAL
かじる ▶ BITE
課す ▶ APPLY, CHARGE 動
数 ▶ NUMBER
ガス ▶ OIL
かすかな ▶ DIM, QUIET 2
かすめる ▶ TOUCH
かする ▶ TOUCH
化石燃料 ▶ OIL
稼ぐ ▶ MAKE 2
仮説 ▶ THEORY 2
画像 ▶ PICTURE
仮想された ▶ SUPPOSED
仮想の ▶ FICTIONAL
数える ▶ COUNT
家族 ▶ FAMILY 1
加速する ▶ ACCELERATE
ガソリン ▶ OIL

型 ▶ KIND 名
堅い, 固い ▶ SOLID, TIGHT
硬い ▶ SOLID
課題 ▶ ASSIGNMENT, PROBLEM, PROJECT
ガタガタと鳴る ▶ SHAKE 2
堅気の ▶ RESPECTABLE
堅く締まる[締める] ▶ TIGHTEN
堅苦しい ▶ FORMAL
堅苦しさ ▶ RESPECT 名
形 ▶ SHAPE
片づける ▶ CLEAR 動, TIDY
肩で押す ▶ PUSH 2
過多な ▶ EXCESSIVE
かたまり ▶ GROUP 1
傾く ▶ LEAN
傾ける ▶ LEAN
偏った ▶ BIASED
偏らせる ▶ INFLUENCE 動
偏りのない ▶ OBJECTIVE
語る ▶ DESCRIBE, SAY 2
カタログ ▶ LIST 名
肩を並べる ▶ FOLLOW 4
価値 ▶ PRICE, VALUE
価値がある ▶ WORTHY
価値観 ▶ VALUES
勝ち取る ▶ GAIN, GET 2, WIN
ガチャンとぶつかり合う[合わせる] ▶ BANG 1
勝つ ▶ DEFEAT, WIN
学科 ▶ AREA 2, DEPARTMENT
学会 ▶ ORGANIZATION
がっかりさせる ▶ DISAPPOINT, DISAPPOINTING
がっかりして ▶ UPSET
がっかりな ▶ TERRIBLE 1
活気に満ちた ▶ LIVELY
活気のある ▶ CROWDED
活気のない ▶ QUIET 1
楽曲 ▶ WORK 名 2
かつぐ ▶ CHEAT 動
かっこいい ▶ ELEGANT, GREAT 1
学校教師 ▶ TEACHER
確固たる ▶ FINAL, GOOD 3, UNDOUBTED
喝采 ▶ PRAISE 名
喝采する ▶ SHOUT
活性化させる ▶ STIMULATE

活性の ▶ ACTIVE
買ったばかりの ▶ NEW 2
ガッツのある ▶ BRAVE
活動 ▶ PROJECT
活動中で ▶ ACTIVE
活動的な ▶ ACTIVE, BUSY 1, ENERGETIC
カットする ▶ DELETE
かっとなる ▶ LOSE YOUR TEMPER
活発な ▶ BUSY 2, ENERGETIC, LIVELY, VARIABLE
かっぷくのよい ▶ FAT
活用 ▶ USE 名
活用する ▶ USE 動 1
仮定 ▶ SPECULATION
家庭 ▶ FAMILY 1
家庭教師 ▶ TEACHER
家庭教師をする ▶ TEACH
仮定された ▶ SUPPOSED
仮定上の ▶ SUPPOSED
仮定する ▶ SAY 3
家庭生活 ▶ FAMILY 1
カテゴリー ▶ CATEGORY
合点のいく ▶ INFORMATIVE
角 ▶ CORNER
稼働させる ▶ OPERATE
稼動する ▶ WORK 動 2
可撓(とう)性のある ▶ FLEXIBLE 2
門出 ▶ OPPORTUNITY
過度の ▶ EXCESS, EXCESSIVE
かなえる ▶ ACHIEVE
金切り声の ▶ HIGH 3
金切り声を上げる ▶ SCREAM
悲しい ▶ UNHAPPY 1
悲しさ ▶ GRIEF
悲しみ ▶ GRIEF
悲しみに沈んだ ▶ UNHAPPY 1
悲しむべき ▶ SAD, UNFORTUNATE 2
悲しんで ▶ UPSET
かなり ▶ QUITE 1, VERY 副
かなりの ▶ LARGE
加入する ▶ JOIN
金では買えない ▶ VALUABLE 1
金に困った ▶ POOR 1
金持ちの ▶ RICH
可能性 ▶ POSSIBILITY, POTENTIAL

日本語類語一覧

可能性のある ▶ LIKELY
可能な ▶ POSSIBLE 1
可能にする ▶ HELP 動 2
彼女 ▶ PARTNER 2
かび臭い ▶ ROTTEN
かびた ▶ ROTTEN
下部 ▶ BOTTOM
株 ▶ THING 2
貨幣 ▶ MONEY 2
構え ▶ POSITION
我慢する ▶ PERSIST, STAND 2, SUPPRESS 2
我慢強い ▶ CALM
我慢強さ ▶ PATIENCE
我慢できない ▶ HATE, UNACCEPTABLE
我慢の限界を超える ▶ LOSE YOUR TEMPER
噛み砕く ▶ BITE
過密の ▶ FULL
神業の ▶ IMPRESSIVE
仮眠をとる ▶ SLEEP
噛む ▶ BITE
寡黙な ▶ QUIET 3
貨物 ▶ CARGO
かもる ▶ CHEAT 動
かゆい ▶ HURT 2, PAINFUL 1
通う ▶ VISIT 動
辛い ▶ STRONG 2
からかう ▶ ANNOY, LAUGH AT SB/STH
がらくた ▶ THING 2
枯らす ▶ KILL
体つき ▶ SHAPE
体の引き締まった ▶ THIN
体を鍛える ▶ TRAIN 2
空にする ▶ CLEAR 動
空の ▶ EMPTY
借方 ▶ DEBT
カリキュラム ▶ CLASS 1
カリスマ性 ▶ CHARM
カリスマ的な ▶ NICE 2
駆り立てる ▶ FORCE 動
仮の ▶ SHORT 1
軽い ▶ SLIGHT
軽く触れる ▶ TOUCH
軽はずみな ▶ RECKLESS
がれき ▶ REMAINS
彼氏 ▶ PARTNER 2
枯れた ▶ DEAD
枯れる ▶ DIE
カレンダー ▶ SCHEDULE
かわいい ▶ SWEET
かわいくない ▶ UGLY

かわいそうに思って ▶ UPSET
かわいらしい ▶ BEAUTIFUL 1
変わった ▶ STRANGE 1
変わらない ▶ STEADY
変わり者 ▶ PERSON
変わりやすい ▶ VARIABLE
代わりをする ▶ REPLACE 1
変わる ▶ CHANGE 動 2, TURN 2
代わる ▶ REPLACE 1
勘 ▶ IDEA 2, INSTINCT
…観 ▶ VIEW 1
考え ▶ CONSIDERATION, IDEA 1, VIEW 1
考えうる ▶ POSSIBLE 2
考え方 ▶ ATTITUDE
考え方の古い ▶ TRADITIONAL
考えつく ▶ ESTIMATE 動, IMAGINE
考えている ▶ INTEND
考えられない ▶ IMPOSSIBLE, UNLIKELY 2
考える ▶ IMAGINE, SUPPOSE, THINK
考えを抱く ▶ IMAGINE
感覚 ▶ SENSE, UNDERSTANDING
感化される ▶ HAVE 3
感化する ▶ INFLUENCE 動
喚起する ▶ STIMULATE
観客 ▶ AUDIENCE, CROWD
観客席 ▶ HALL 1
環境 ▶ CONTEXT, ENVIRONMENT, SITUATION
監禁する ▶ JAIL
換金する ▶ SELL 1
関係 ▶ RELATION, RELATIONSHIP 1, 2
歓迎会 ▶ EVENT 2
歓迎されていない ▶ UNWANTED
関係者 ▶ PARTICIPANT
関係する ▶ AFFECT
歓迎する ▶ GREET, LET SB IN
関係のある ▶ RELEVANT
関係ない ▶ IRRELEVANT
関係を断つ ▶ REJECT
間欠的な ▶ OCCASIONAL
簡潔な ▶ SHORT 3

甘言で釣る ▶ PERSUADE
看護 ▶ TREATMENT
慣行 ▶ TRADITION
観光 ▶ TRAVEL, VISIT 名
観光客 ▶ TOURIST
観光産業 ▶ TRAVEL
刊行する ▶ PUBLISH 2
刊行物 ▶ BOOK
勧告 ▶ PROPOSAL
頑固な ▶ STERN, STUBBORN
監査 ▶ INSPECTION
監査委員 ▶ INSPECTOR
贋作 ▶ FAKE
観察者 ▶ ANALYST, WITNESS
観察する ▶ LOOK 動 1
監視 ▶ INSPECTION
感じ ▶ APPEARANCE, ATMOSPHERE, IDEA 2, SENSE
幹事 ▶ OFFICIAL 名
監視員 ▶ GUARD, INSPECTOR
監視機関 ▶ INSPECTOR
監視者 ▶ ANALYST
監視する ▶ REGULATE
感じ取る ▶ FEEL
感じのよい ▶ FRIENDLY 1, NICE 2
感謝(の言葉) ▶ THANKS
患者 ▶ PATIENT
癇癪(かんしゃく) ▶ TEMPER
感謝している ▶ GRATEFUL
感謝の念 ▶ THANKS
観衆 ▶ AUDIENCE, MARKET 1
慣習 ▶ HABIT, TRADITION
慣習的な ▶ CONSERVATIVE, TRADITIONAL
慣習にとらわれない ▶ UNUSUAL
甘受する ▶ STAND 2
感受性 ▶ TACT
感傷 ▶ EMOTION
勘定 ▶ ESTIMATE 名
感情 ▶ DIGNITY, EMOTION
感情移入する ▶ UNDERSTAND 2
勘定書 ▶ BILL
完勝する ▶ DEFEAT
干渉する ▶ INTERVENE
感情的な ▶ INTENSE
鑑賞力 ▶ UNDERSTANDING
寒色の ▶ PALE

感じる ▶ FEEL, THINK
関心 ▶ ATTENTION, INVOLVEMENT
関心がある ▶ CARE
関心事 ▶ ISSUE
感心させる ▶ IMPRESS
感心する ▶ APPRECIATE, RESPECT 動
肝心な ▶ ESSENTIAL
完遂する ▶ ACHIEVE
冠水する ▶ FLOOD 動
関税 ▶ TAX
完成させる ▶ FINISH
間接費 ▶ COSTS
感染症 ▶ DISEASE
感染する ▶ SUFFER FROM STH
完全な ▶ COMPLETE, PERFECT, WHOLE
完全な物 ▶ THING 1
感想 ▶ VIEW 1
乾燥した ▶ SUNNY
簡素な ▶ PLAIN 1
寛大 ▶ PATIENCE
歓待する ▶ GREET
寛大な ▶ KIND 形
甲高い ▶ HIGH 3
感嘆させる ▶ IMPRESS
感嘆する ▶ RESPECT 動
簡単な ▶ EASY 1
勘違い ▶ ILLUSION
勘違いする ▶ MISUNDERSTAND
感知する ▶ NOTICE
感づく ▶ FIND 4
鑑定 ▶ VALUATION
鑑定家 ▶ EXPERT, JUDGE 名
観点 ▶ ATTITUDE, VIEW 1
感動させる ▶ IMPRESS, STIMULATE
感動的な ▶ IMPRESSIVE, MAGNIFICENT
監督 ▶ CONTROL, GOVERNMENT 2
監督機関 ▶ INSPECTOR
監督する ▶ REGULATE, RUN 2
カンニングをする ▶ CHEAT 動
かんぬきをかける ▶ CLOSE 動
観念 ▶ IDEA 1, SENSE, UNDERSTANDING
がんばり ▶ DETERMINATION

がんばる → きてん

頑張る ▶ PERSIST
看板 ▶ SIGN 2
看病する ▶ LOOK AFTER SB
幹部 ▶ AUTHORITIES, EXECUTIVE, MANAGEMENT
感服する ▶ RESPECT 動
幹部職員 ▶ OFFICIAL 名
完璧な ▶ PERFECT
願望 ▶ DESIRE, HOPE 名 2, WISH
緩慢な ▶ SLOW
感銘深い ▶ IMPRESSIVE
感銘を与える ▶ IMPRESS
含有する ▶ INCLUDE
関与 ▶ INVOLVEMENT
寛容 ▶ PATIENCE
寛容な ▶ KIND 形, TOLERANT
関与する ▶ JOIN
官吏 ▶ OFFICIAL 名
管理 ▶ CONTROL, GOVERNMENT 2, RESPONSIBILITY
管理者 ▶ ORGANIZER
管理職 ▶ EXECUTIVE
管理する ▶ DEAL WITH SB/STH, RUN 2
簡略な ▶ PLAIN 1
官僚 ▶ AUTHORITIES, OFFICIAL 名
官僚社会 ▶ AUTHORITIES
完了する ▶ FINISH
官僚制 ▶ AUTHORITIES
慣例 ▶ TRADITION
関連 ▶ RELATION, RELATIONSHIP 1, SIMILARITY
関連した ▶ RELATED, RELEVANT
関連づける ▶ RELATE
関連のない ▶ PARTICULAR
貫禄 ▶ CHARM
貫禄のある ▶ PROUD 1
緩和 ▶ RELIEF
緩和する ▶ EASE

き

キー ▶ BUTTON 1
議員 ▶ OFFICIAL 名
消える ▶ DISAPPEAR
記憶している ▶ REMEMBER

記憶する ▶ LEARN
記憶力 ▶ MEMORY
気後れする ▶ PANIC
キオスク ▶ STALL
気落ちした ▶ DEPRESSED
戯画 ▶ PARODY
機会 ▶ OPPORTUNITY, TIME
気概 ▶ DETERMINATION
議会 ▶ GOVERNMENT 1
奇怪な ▶ STRANGE 1, UGLY
着替える ▶ WEAR
気がかりな ▶ WORRIED, WORRYING
気が狂った ▶ MAD
気が向く ▶ WANT
機関 ▶ ORGANIZATION, SERVICE
期間 ▶ PERIOD
危機 ▶ CRISIS, RISK 1
機器 ▶ TOOL
聞き入れる ▶ HEAR
聞き込み調査 ▶ RESEARCH
切り裂く ▶ TEAR
嬉々とした ▶ HAPPY
棄却する ▶ ABOLISH
企業 ▶ COMPANY
企業家 ▶ EXECUTIVE
起業家 ▶ EXECUTIVE
企業グループ ▶ GROUP 3
企業連合 ▶ GROUP 3
戯曲 ▶ DRAMA
基金 ▶ FUND 名
聞く ▶ FIND 1
聴く ▶ HEAR
危惧 ▶ CONCERN, DOUBT 名 2
器具 ▶ TOOL
気配り ▶ TACT
気配りのない ▶ INSENSITIVE
聴く人 ▶ AUDIENCE
喜劇 ▶ PLAY 名
危険 ▶ DISADVANTAGE, RISK 1
機嫌 ▶ MOOD
起源 ▶ SOURCE, START 名
危険な ▶ DANGEROUS, SERIOUS 1
危険な人 ▶ THREAT
危険な物事 ▶ THREAT
危険にさらされた ▶ VULNERABLE
危険にさらす ▶ THREATEN
危険分子 ▶ THREAT

危険要因[因子] ▶ THREAT
期限を過ぎた ▶ LATE
機嫌を損ねる ▶ OFFEND
機構 ▶ STRUCTURE, SYSTEM
紀行 ▶ TRAVEL
記号 ▶ FIGURE
技巧 ▶ SKILL 2, WAY 2
寄稿者 ▶ REPORTER
聞こえない ▶ QUIET 2
聞こえる ▶ HEAR, SEEM
気骨 ▶ CHARM
記載する ▶ LIST 動, RECORD
気さくな ▶ FRIENDLY 1, 2
きざし ▶ SIGN 1
記事 ▶ ARTICLE, REPORT 2
儀式 ▶ EVENT 2
気質 ▶ ATMOSPHERE, PERSONALITY
議事日程 ▶ SCHEDULE
記者 ▶ REPORTER
記者会見 ▶ INTERVIEW 1
奇襲 ▶ ATTACK 名 1
奇襲する ▶ ATTACK 動 2
記述 ▶ DESCRIPTION
技術 ▶ SKILL 1, 2, WAY 2
記述する ▶ DESCRIBE
記述的な ▶ DESCRIPTIVE
基準 ▶ CRITERION, QUALITY
記章 ▶ LOGO
希少価値の高い ▶ VALUABLE 1
偽証罪 ▶ LIE
希少な ▶ RARE, SCARCE
傷 ▶ INJURY
築く ▶ BUILD, ESTABLISH
傷つきやすい ▶ FRAGILE, SENSITIVE 3, VULNERABLE
傷つける ▶ HURT 1, RUIN
きずな ▶ RELATIONSHIP 1
規制 ▶ GOVERNMENT 2, LIMIT 1
規制された ▶ LIMITED 2
規制する ▶ REGULATE
奇跡 ▶ MIRACLE
奇跡的な ▶ AMAZING
偽善的な ▶ DISHONEST
基礎 ▶ BASICS, BOTTOM
起訴 ▶ CASE, CHARGE 名
競う ▶ COMPETE
寄贈 ▶ GIFT
寄贈者 ▶ SPONSOR
起草する ▶ PREPARE 1

寄贈する ▶ GIVE 3
偽造物 ▶ FAKE
規則 ▶ RULE 名, THEORY 1
貴族 ▶ ELITE
規則的な ▶ STEADY
起訴状 ▶ CHARGE 名
起訴する ▶ ACCUSE
期待 ▶ HOPE 名 1, 2
気体 ▶ MATERIAL
議題 ▶ SUBJECT
期待する ▶ EXPECT, HOPE 動, TRUST
期待外れの ▶ DISAPPOINTING
期待外れの人 ▶ LOSER 2
期待を裏切る ▶ DISAPPOINT
期待をかける ▶ TRUST
鍛える ▶ TRAIN 2
気立てのよい ▶ FRIENDLY 1
汚い ▶ CORRUPT, DISGUSTING 1, OFFENSIVE, UNTIDY
来るべき ▶ NEXT
機知 ▶ HUMOUR
機知に富んだ ▶ FUNNY
基調 ▶ SUBJECT
議長 ▶ LEADER 1
貴重な ▶ DEAR, VALUABLE 1, 2
貴重品 ▶ THING 2
きちょうめんな ▶ EFFICIENT
議長を務める ▶ LEAD
きちんとした ▶ EFFICIENT, NEAT, RESPECTABLE, RIGHT 形 2
きちんとしていない ▶ UNTIDY
きつい ▶ DIFFICULT 1, HARD, STRICT
気づいて ▶ AWARE
気遣い ▶ SYMPATHY
気遣う ▶ CARE
きっかけ ▶ SIGNAL
気づく ▶ FIND 1, KNOW, NOTICE
キックオフ ▶ START 名
キックバック ▶ BRIBE
ぎっしり詰まった ▶ FULL
規定 ▶ LIMIT 1, RULE 名
規定する ▶ EXPLAIN 1, RULE 動 2
機転 ▶ HUMOUR, INTELLIGENCE, TACT

日本語類語一覧

日本語類語一覧

- 起点 ▶ SOURCE
- 軌道 ▶ WAY 3
- 奇特な ▶ KIND 形
- 気取らない ▶ AVERAGE, REALISTIC
- 気に入らない ▶ UNHAPPY 2
- 気に入る ▶ LIKE 動
- 気にする ▶ CARE
- 気に留めない ▶ IGNORE
- 記入する ▶ KEEP 3, RECORD
- 疑念 ▶ DOUBT 名 1, 2, SCEPTICISM
- 記念式典 ▶ BIRTHDAY
- 記念日 ▶ BIRTHDAY
- 機能 ▶ SYSTEM
- 技能 ▶ SKILL 2
- 機能障碍 ▶ DISEASE
- 機能する ▶ WORK 動 2
- 機能的な ▶ USEFUL
- 気の置けない ▶ FRIENDLY 2
- 気の利いた ▶ FUNNY, INTELLIGENT
- 気の利かない ▶ INSENSITIVE
- 気の利く ▶ SENSITIVE 1
- 気の狂った ▶ CRAZY
- 気の小さい ▶ SHY
- 気の毒な ▶ UNFORTUNATE 2
- 気の毒に思う ▶ SORRY FOR SB
- 気の毒に思って ▶ UPSET
- 気のない ▶ INDIFFERENT
- 気乗りしない ▶ INDIFFERENT
- 気迫 ▶ DETERMINATION
- 奇抜な ▶ STRANGE 1
- 気晴らし ▶ ENTERTAINMENT, INTEREST 名 2, PROJECT
- 規範 ▶ TRADITION, VALUES
- 忌避 ▶ HATRED
- 厳しい ▶ SERIOUS 1, STERN, STRICT
- 気品 ▶ RESPECT 名, STYLE
- 機敏な ▶ FAST
- 寄付 ▶ GIFT, INVESTMENT, PAYMENT
- 基部 ▶ BOTTOM
- 寄付金 ▶ INVESTMENT
- 寄付者 ▶ SPONSOR
- 寄付する ▶ GIVE 3
- 気分 ▶ ATMOSPHERE, DIGNITY, MOOD
- 気分のよい ▶ WELL
- 気分の悪い ▶ TERRIBLE 1
- 気分を害した ▶ ANNOYED
- 希望 ▶ HOPE 名 1
- 技法 ▶ SKILL 1, 2, WAY 2
- 希望する ▶ RECOMMEND 1
- 希望のない ▶ NEGATIVE
- 希望の持てる ▶ PROMISING
- 希望を与える ▶ INSPIRE
- 基本 ▶ BASICS
- 基本的な ▶ FUNDAMENTAL
- 基本方針 ▶ SUBJECT
- 気まずい ▶ EMBARRASSED
- 決まり ▶ LAW, PRINCIPLE 2, RULE 名
- 決まり文句 ▶ SLOGAN
- 決まる ▶ DEPEND ON/UPON STH
- 欺瞞 ▶ FRAUD 1
- 機密の ▶ SECRET
- 気味の悪い ▶ FRIGHTENING
- 奇妙な ▶ STRANGE 1, UNUSUAL
- 義務 ▶ PRESSURE 2, RESPONSIBILITY, TASK
- 気難しい ▶ IRRITABLE, STERN
- 義務的な ▶ NECESSARY
- 決める ▶ CHOOSE, DECIDE, DETERMINE
- 気持ち ▶ DIGNITY, EMOTION, SENSE
- 肝っ玉 ▶ COURAGE
- 疑問 ▶ DOUBT 名 1, QUESTION 名
- 疑問の余地のない ▶ UNDOUBTED
- 疑問符 ▶ DOUBT 名 1
- 規約 ▶ LAW
- 逆 ▶ OPPOSITE 名
- ギャグ ▶ JOKE
- 逆上した ▶ HYSTERICAL
- 規約に関する ▶ LEGAL
- 逆の ▶ OPPOSITE 形, WRONG 1
- 脚本 ▶ PLAY 名
- 脚本家 ▶ WRITER
- きゃしゃな ▶ THIN
- キャスター ▶ PRESENTER
- 却下する ▶ ABOLISH, REFUSE
- 客観的な ▶ OBJECTIVE
- 逆境 ▶ TROUBLE 2
- キャッチフレーズ ▶ SLOGAN
- キャットウォーク ▶ CORRIDOR
- ギャップ ▶ GAP
- ギャング ▶ PARTY 2
- キャンセルする ▶ ABOLISH, CANCEL
- キャンペーン ▶ CAMPAIGN 名
- 旧… ▶ PREVIOUS
- 求愛 ▶ RELATIONSHIP 2
- 求愛する ▶ GO OUT
- 救援 ▶ HELP 名
- 休暇 ▶ HOLIDAY 1, 2
- 急カーブ ▶ CORNER
- 休会 ▶ HOLIDAY 1
- ぎゅうぎゅう詰めの ▶ FULL
- 休憩 ▶ PAUSE
- 休憩する ▶ REST
- 急激な ▶ SERIOUS 1
- 急行する ▶ HURRY
- 急行の ▶ FAST
- 求婚者 ▶ PARTNER 2
- 求婚する ▶ GO OUT
- 救済 ▶ AID
- 救済策 ▶ SOLUTION
- 救済する ▶ SAVE 1
- 休止 ▶ END 名, PAUSE
- 旧式の ▶ OLD-FASHIONED
- 休日 ▶ HOLIDAY 1
- 急襲 ▶ ATTACK 名 1
- 急襲する ▶ ATTACK 動 1, 2
- 救出する ▶ FREE 動, SAVE 1
- 救助 ▶ HELP 名
- 窮状 ▶ DISTRESS
- 急上昇する ▶ RISE, SOAR
- 救助する ▶ SAVE 1
- 急進的な ▶ RADICAL
- 急成長する ▶ DO WELL
- 急増 ▶ INCREASE 名
- 急増する ▶ SOAR
- 休息する ▶ REST
- 急速な ▶ QUICK
- 糾弾 ▶ CRITICISM
- 糾弾する ▶ BLAME
- 窮地 ▶ MESS 2, PROBLEM
- 急騰する ▶ SOAR
- 旧弊な ▶ OLD-FASHIONED
- 窮乏 ▶ MESS 2, POVERTY
- 究明する ▶ FIND 3, INVESTIGATE
- 給与 ▶ INCOME
- 休養する ▶ REST
- 旧来の ▶ TRADITIONAL
- 急落する ▶ SLUMP
- 急流 ▶ FLOOD 名 1
- 丘陵 ▶ HILL
- 給料 ▶ INCOME, RATE
- 急を要する ▶ URGENT
- 寄与 ▶ INVOLVEMENT
- …業 ▶ INDUSTRY
- 凶悪な ▶ VIOLENT
- 驚異 ▶ MIRACLE
- 脅威 ▶ RISK 1
- 教育 ▶ EDUCATION
- 教育者 ▶ TEACHER
- 教育する ▶ TEACH, TRAIN 1
- 教育専門家 ▶ TEACHER
- 教育的な ▶ EDUCATIONAL
- 教育の ▶ EDUCATIONAL
- 教育を受けた ▶ INFORMED
- 教育を受ける ▶ TRAIN 1
- 驚異的な ▶ AMAZING
- 脅威となる人 ▶ THREAT
- 脅威となる物事 ▶ THREAT
- 脅威を与える ▶ THREATEN
- 教員 ▶ TEACHER
- 教科 ▶ AREA 2
- 教化 ▶ KNOWLEDGE
- 教会 ▶ CHURCH
- 境界 ▶ EDGE, LIMIT 2
- 協会 ▶ ORGANIZATION, UNION
- 業界 ▶ INDUSTRY
- 業界最大手 ▶ LEADER 2
- 驚愕の ▶ AMAZING
- 教科書 ▶ BOOK
- 共感 ▶ SYMPATHY
- 共感する ▶ UNDERSTAND 2
- 共感的な ▶ SENSITIVE 1
- 教義 ▶ VALUES
- 協議 ▶ DISCUSSION
- 協議会 ▶ COMMITTEE, MEETING 1
- 競技会 ▶ COMPETITION 1
- 行儀がよい ▶ GOOD 7
- 狂喜した ▶ EXCITED, HYSTERICAL
- 協議する ▶ NEGOTIATE
- 供給 ▶ SUPPLY
- 供給源 ▶ FACILITIES
- 供給する ▶ DISTRIBUTE, PROVIDE
- 境遇 ▶ SITUATION
- 教訓 ▶ VALUES
- 恐慌 ▶ RECESSION

強国 ▶ COUNTRY 1
強固な ▶ CONVINCING
強固にする ▶ CONFIRM 3
器用さ ▶ SKILL 2
教材 ▶ FACILITIES
教師 ▶ LECTURER, TEACHER
凝視 ▶ LOOK 名
行事 ▶ EVENT 2
凝視する ▶ STARE
教授 ▶ LECTURER
郷愁にかられた ▶ LONELY
享受する ▶ HAVE 2
供述 ▶ STATEMENT
強靭な ▶ STRONG 1
強制 ▶ PRESSURE 2
強制する ▶ FORCE 動, PRESS 2
強制的な ▶ NECESSARY
行政部 ▶ GOVERNMENT 1
強勢を置く ▶ STRESS
業績の悪い
 ▶ LOSS-MAKING
競争 ▶ CAMPAIGN 名, COMPETITION 2
競争相手 ▶ ENEMY, PARTICIPANT
競争意識 ▶ COMPETITION 2
競争する ▶ COMPETE
競争力 ▶ COMPETITION 2
強大な ▶ POWERFUL
協調 ▶ PLANNING
強調 ▶ PRIORITY
強調する
 ▶ POINT STH OUT, STRESS
協調的な ▶ HELPFUL
共通点 ▶ SIMILARITY
共通の ▶ COMMON
協定 ▶ AGREEMENT, CONTRACT
仰天させる ▶ SURPRISE
協同組合 ▶ GROUP 3
共同経営会社 ▶ GROUP 3
共同経営者 ▶ PARTNER 1
共同事業者 ▶ PARTNER 1
共同事業体 ▶ GROUP 3
共同の ▶ COMMON
競売にかける ▶ SELL 1
競売人 ▶ SALESMAN
強迫観念 ▶ OBSESSION
強迫観念にとりつかれた
 ▶ ADDICTIVE
共犯証言をする ▶ TELL 2
恐怖 ▶ FEAR, SHOCK 名
共謀 ▶ CONSPIRACY

共謀する ▶ PLOT
凶暴な ▶ WILD
興味 ▶ ATTENTION
興味がある ▶ INTERESTED
興味深い ▶ INTERESTING
興味深げな ▶ INTERESTED
興味をそそる
 ▶ INTEREST 動, POPULAR
興味を引く ▶ INTEREST 動
興味を引く特性
 ▶ INTEREST 名 1
共有する ▶ SHARE 動
共有の ▶ COMMON
強要する ▶ DEMAND 動, FORCE 動, PRESS 2
共用する ▶ SHARE 動
教養のある ▶ INFORMED, INTELLECTUAL, SOPHISTICATED
狂乱した ▶ HYSTERICAL
狭量な ▶ LIMITED 1
協力 ▶ HELP 名
協力関係
 ▶ RELATIONSHIP 1
協力者 ▶ PARTICIPANT
協力する ▶ HELP 動 1
協力的な ▶ HELPFUL
強力な ▶ CONVINCING, POWERFUL
強烈な ▶ STRONG 2
虚栄心 ▶ PRIDE
許可 ▶ APPROVAL, PERMISSION
許可証 ▶ CERTIFICATE, LICENCE
許可する ▶ ALLOW
許可を与える ▶ AGREE
虚偽 ▶ LIE
虚偽の ▶ FICTIONAL, WRONG 1
極端な ▶ RADICAL, SERIOUS 1
極度の ▶ SERIOUS 1
局面 ▶ SITUATION, STAGE
虚構 ▶ LIE
虚構の ▶ FICTIONAL
居住者 ▶ RESIDENT, TENANT
居住する ▶ LIVE
巨匠 ▶ STAR
拒絶 ▶ REFUSAL
拒絶する ▶ REFUSE, REJECT
巨大な ▶ HUGE
許諾する ▶ ALLOW
ぎょっとした ▶ AFRAID

拠点 ▶ ORGANIZATION
拠点にする ▶ BASE
拒否 ▶ REFUSAL
拒否権 ▶ REFUSAL
拒否する ▶ REFUSE
許容できない
 ▶ UNACCEPTABLE
距離 ▶ RANGE 2
嫌う ▶ HATE
気楽な ▶ EASY 2, FRIENDLY 2
きらめく ▶ BRIGHT, SHINE
切り替え ▶ CHANGE 名 2
切り換える ▶ SWITCH
切り刻む ▶ CUT 2, DIVIDE 1
切り傷 ▶ INJURY
切り倒す ▶ DEMOLISH
切り立った ▶ HIGH 2
規律 ▶ PRINCIPLE 2
起立する ▶ STAND 1
切り取る ▶ DELETE
切り抜ける ▶ SURVIVE
切り離す ▶ ISOLATE
技量 ▶ SKILL 1
切り分ける ▶ CUT 2, DIVIDE 1
切る ▶ CUT 2
着る ▶ WEAR
ギルド ▶ UNION
儀礼 ▶ RESPECT 名
儀礼的な ▶ POLITE
きれいな ▶ BEAUTIFUL 1, 2
きれいになる ▶ CLEAN 動
切れ端 ▶ PIECE
キレる
 ▶ LOSE YOUR TEMPER
記録する ▶ KEEP 3, RECORD
記録簿 ▶ LIST 名
議論 ▶ DEBATE, DISCUSSION, RESEARCH
議論する ▶ ARGUE, TALK
議論の余地のない
 ▶ MARKED, UNDOUBTED
際立たせる ▶ STRESS
際立った ▶ MAIN, REMARKABLE, SPECIAL
際どい ▶ SENSITIVE 2
きわめて ▶ VERY 副
きわめて重要な
 ▶ ESSENTIAL
金 ▶ NUMBER, PRICE
緊急性 ▶ IMPORTANCE
緊急の ▶ URGENT
銀行業 ▶ FINANCE
筋骨隆々の ▶ STRONG 1

僅差での ▶ CLOSE 形
禁止された
 ▶ FORBIDDEN
禁止する ▶ BAN 動
均質な ▶ EQUAL
近似的な ▶ VAGUE
禁じられた
 ▶ FORBIDDEN
禁止令 ▶ BAN 名
禁ずる ▶ BAN 動
禁制の ▶ FORBIDDEN
金銭の ▶ ECONOMIC
禁断の ▶ FORBIDDEN
緊張 ▶ PRESSURE 1
緊張関係 ▶ TENSION
緊張させる ▶ TIGHTEN
緊張した ▶ TENSE, WORRIED
緊張する ▶ TIGHTEN
均等 ▶ JUSTICE
緊迫 ▶ PRESSURE 1
緊迫した ▶ STRESSFUL
吟味する ▶ EXAMINE, TEST 動 1
禁輸 ▶ BAN 名
金融の ▶ ECONOMIC
筋力 ▶ FORCE 動

く

区域 ▶ AREA 1, COUNTY, PLACE
ぐいぐい飲む ▶ DRINK 動
食いしばる ▶ TIGHTEN
クイズ ▶ COMPETITION 1
食い違い ▶ CONFLICT
食い違う ▶ CONFLICT 動, INCONSISTENT
食い止める ▶ RESIST
空位 ▶ JOB
空間 ▶ HOLE 1, LIMIT 2
空襲 ▶ ATTACK 名 1
空席 ▶ JOB
偶然 ▶ LUCK
偶然の一致 ▶ LUCK
偶然の出来事 ▶ LUCK
偶然発見する ▶ MEET 2
空想 ▶ IMAGINATION
クーデター ▶ REVOLUTION
空洞 ▶ HOLE 2
空腹な ▶ HUNGRY
区画 ▶ COUNTY
釘付けにする
 ▶ INTEREST 動
釘付けになるような
 ▶ INTERESTING

日本語類語一覧

く

- 苦境 ▶ MESS 2
- 具現 ▶ EXAMPLE 2
- 臭い ▶ DISGUSTING 1, ROTTEN
- 腐った ▶ ROTTEN
- 草分け ▶ LEADER 2
- くじく ▶ INJURE
- くしでとかす ▶ BRUSH
- くしゃみをする ▶ COUGH
- 苦渋の ▶ PAINFUL 2
- くず ▶ FRAGMENT, WASTE
- くすくすと笑う ▶ LAUGH
- くすぐる ▶ HURT 2
- 薬 ▶ DRUG 2
- ぐずる ▶ CRY
- 崩れる ▶ FALL 3
- くすんだ ▶ PALE
- 癖 ▶ HABIT
- くそまじめな ▶ FORMAL
- 具体的な ▶ FINAL, PARTICULAR
- くだらない ▶ RIDICULOUS
- 口数の少ない ▶ QUIET 3
- 口きき料 ▶ BRIBE
- 口汚い ▶ OFFENSIVE
- 口げんか ▶ ARGUMENT 1
- 口止め料 ▶ BRIBE
- 口に出す ▶ SAY 1, 2
- 口のうまい ▶ CONVINCING
- 口の重い ▶ QUIET 3
- 口の利けない ▶ SILENT
- 愚痴る ▶ COMPLAIN
- 口を挟む ▶ INTERRUPT
- 苦痛 ▶ DISTRESS, PAIN
- 覆す ▶ DISPROVE
- くっきりした ▶ BRIGHT
- 屈辱を与える ▶ EMBARRASS
- 屈する ▶ GIVE WAY
- 靴紐 ▶ BUTTON 2
- くつろいだ ▶ CALM, COMFORTABLE, FRIENDLY 2
- くつろぐ ▶ REST
- 口説き ▶ OFFER 1
- 口説く ▶ FLIRT
- 苦難 ▶ TROUBLE 2
- 国 ▶ COUNTRY 1
- 国の ▶ NATIONAL, PUBLIC
- くねり ▶ CORNER
- 苦悩 ▶ CONCERN, DISTRESS
- 配る ▶ DISTRIBUTE
- 首にする[なる] ▶ FIRE
- 首を突っ込む ▶ INTERRUPT
- 工夫 ▶ INSPIRATION, TACTIC
- 区分 ▶ CATEGORY
- 区分する ▶ DIVIDE 1
- 区別 ▶ DIFFERENCE
- くぼみ ▶ HOLE 2
- 組 ▶ TEAM 2
- 組合 ▶ UNION
- 組み合わせる ▶ COMBINE, RELATE
- 組み入れる ▶ INCLUDE
- 組み立てる ▶ BUILD
- くむ ▶ PUMP
- 曇りの ▶ CLOUDY
- 苦悶 ▶ DISTRESS
- 苦悶に満ちた ▶ PAINFUL 2
- 苦悶の ▶ UPSET
- 暗い ▶ DARK 1, NEGATIVE
- クライマックス ▶ PEAK
- ぐらぐらする ▶ SHAKE 2
- 暮らし ▶ LIFE 3
- 暮らし方 ▶ LIFE 3
- 暮らし向き ▶ SITUATION
- クラス ▶ CATEGORY
- 暮らす ▶ LIVE
- クラスメート ▶ PARTNER 1
- ぐらつかない ▶ FIRM
- クラッシュする ▶ BREAK 2
- クラブ ▶ TEAM 2, UNION
- グラフィックス ▶ PICTURE
- 繰り返し言う ▶ REPEAT
- 繰り返し書く ▶ REPEAT
- 来る ▶ COME 1, 2
- グループ ▶ GROUP 2, PARTY 1
- ぐるぐる回る ▶ SPIN
- 苦しい ▶ DIFFICULT 2, PAINFUL 1, 2
- 苦みのある ▶ BITTER
- 苦しむ ▶ SUFFER FROM STH
- くるりと回す ▶ TURN 1
- クレーター ▶ HOLE 2
- クレジット ▶ LOAN
- 苦労 ▶ RESPONSIBILITY
- グローバルな ▶ INTERNATIONAL
- 黒字 ▶ PROFIT
- 黒っぽい ▶ DARK 2
- 黒幕 ▶ GENIUS
- 詳しい ▶ USED TO STH
- 企て ▶ ATTEMPT, PROJECT
- 企てる ▶ TRY 1
- 加わる ▶ JOIN
- 軍 ▶ ARMY
- 郡 ▶ COUNTY
- 群衆 ▶ CROWD
- 勲章 ▶ AWARD
- 軍隊 ▶ ARMY
- 軍団 ▶ ARMY
- 軍法会議 ▶ CASE
- 君臨する ▶ RULE 動 1
- 訓練 ▶ EDUCATION, TRAINING
- 訓練する ▶ TRAIN 1
- 訓練生 ▶ RECRUIT
- 訓練を受ける ▶ TRAIN 1
- 訓話 ▶ SPEECH

け

- 敬意 ▶ ADMIRATION, REPUTATION, RESPECT 名, STATUS
- 敬意を示す ▶ POLITE
- 経営 ▶ GOVERNMENT 2
- 経営者 ▶ MANAGEMENT
- 経営陣 ▶ MANAGEMENT
- 経営する ▶ RUN 2
- 敬遠する ▶ HESITATE
- 警戒して ▶ AWARE
- 計画 ▶ PLAN 1, PROJECT, PURPOSE, SCHEDULE
- 計画者 ▶ ORGANIZER
- 計画する ▶ DESIGN 動 2, INTEND, ORGANIZE
- 計画的な ▶ DELIBERATE
- 景観 ▶ COUNTRY 2
- 警官 ▶ POLICEMAN
- 景気後退 ▶ RECESSION
- 経験 ▶ EVENT 1, KNOWLEDGE, LIFE 3
- 経験する ▶ HAVE 3
- 軽減する ▶ EASE
- 経験不足 ▶ IGNORANCE
- 経験豊富な ▶ EXPERIENCED, SOPHISTICATED
- 傾向 ▶ TENDENCY, TREND
- 稽古する ▶ PRACTISE
- 稽古をつける ▶ PRACTISE
- 軽罪 ▶ CRIME 2
- 経済学 ▶ FINANCE
- 経済効果 ▶ FINANCE
- 掲載する ▶ PUBLISH 1
- 経済性 ▶ FINANCE
- 経済的な ▶ CHEAP, SHORT 3
- 経済の ▶ ECONOMIC
- 警察官 ▶ POLICEMAN
- 計算 ▶ ESTIMATE 名
- 計算する ▶ CALCULATE, COUNT
- 刑事 ▶ POLICEMAN
- 形式 ▶ STRUCTURE
- 軽視する ▶ IGNORE
- 掲示板 ▶ SIGN 2
- 軽侮 ▶ TREND
- 芸術作品 ▶ WORK 名 2
- 形状 ▶ SHAPE
- 軽食 ▶ FOOD
- 計数 ▶ FIGURE
- 形成する ▶ APPEAR
- 形跡 ▶ SIGN 1
- 継続する ▶ CONTINUE 1, REMAIN
- 継続的な ▶ CONTINUOUS, FREQUENT
- 軽率な ▶ CARELESS, RECKLESS
- 形態 ▶ DESIGN 名
- 系統 ▶ SERIES, SYSTEM
- 傾倒している ▶ RELIABLE 1
- 系統立てる ▶ ARRANGE
- 系統的な ▶ RATIONAL
- 軽度の ▶ GENTLE
- 芸人 ▶ ACTOR
- 芸能人 ▶ STAR
- 啓発 ▶ KNOWLEDGE
- 経費 ▶ COSTS
- 警備 ▶ SECURITY
- 警備員 ▶ GUARD
- 警備する ▶ PROTECT
- 系譜 ▶ FAMILY 3
- 軽蔑 ▶ CONTEMPT
- 軽蔑する ▶ HATE
- 軽妙洒脱な ▶ FUNNY
- 刑務所に入れる ▶ JAIL
- 啓蒙 ▶ KNOWLEDGE
- 契約 ▶ AGREEMENT, CONTRACT
- 契約する ▶ EMPLOY
- 経理 ▶ FINANCE
- 計略 ▶ FRAUD 2, TRICK
- 経歴 ▶ LIFE 2, WORK 名 1
- 系列 ▶ SERIES
- 痙攣 ▶ SHIVER
- 痙攣する ▶ SHAKE 3
- 経路 ▶ WAY 3
- ゲーム ▶ INTEREST 名 2
- けが ▶ INJURY
- 外科 ▶ TREATMENT
- けがを負わせる ▶ INJURE
- 劇 ▶ DRAMA, PLAY 名
- 激化する ▶ RISE
- 劇作家 ▶ WRITER

激しやすい ▶ INTENSE
激情 ▶ EMOTION, LOVE 名 1
劇場 ▶ HALL 1
激の ▶ CLOSE 形
激痛 ▶ PAIN
劇的な ▶ EXCITING
劇的にする ▶ EXAGGERATE
激怒 ▶ ANGER 名, FRUSTRATION, TEMPER
激怒させる ▶ ANGER 動
激した ▶ ANGRY, ANNOYED, FURIOUS
激突する ▶ CRASH
激励する ▶ INSPIRE
けしからぬ ▶ OUTRAGEOUS
景色 ▶ COUNTRY 2, VIEW 2
景色のよい ▶ BEAUTIFUL 2
下宿人 ▶ TENANT
消す ▶ DELETE, DISAPPEAR, REMOVE, TURN STH OFF
削りくず ▶ FRAGMENT
気高い ▶ WORTHY
気だるい ▶ SLOW
けちる ▶ SAVE 2
決意 ▶ DETERMINATION
欠員 ▶ JOB
結果 ▶ EFFECT, RESULT, VICTORY
結果的な ▶ LAST 1
結果として起こる ▶ FOLLOW 2
結果をもたらす ▶ CAUSE
欠陥 ▶ DEFECT
結局…になる ▶ REPRESENT 1
結合する ▶ COMBINE
傑作 ▶ WORK 名 2
傑出した ▶ EXCELLENT, GREAT 2
欠如 ▶ LACK
決勝 ▶ GAME
決勝の ▶ SUCCESSFUL 1
決心させる ▶ CONFIRM 3
決心する ▶ DECIDE
結束させる ▶ COMBINE
結託する ▶ PLOT
決着をつける ▶ CONFIRM 3
決定 ▶ CONCLUSION
決定される ▶ DEPEND ON/UPON STH

決定する ▶ DECIDE, DETERMINE
決定的な ▶ CERTAIN, ESSENTIAL, FINAL
欠点 ▶ DISADVANTAGE
血統 ▶ FAMILY 3
潔白な ▶ INNOCENT
欠乏 ▶ LACK
結末 ▶ END 名, RESULT
決裂 ▶ FAILURE
決裂する ▶ FAIL 2
結露 ▶ MOISTURE
結論 ▶ CONCLUSION, END 名
結論を下す ▶ CONCLUDE
けなすような ▶ INSULTING
懸念 ▶ CONCERN, DOUBT 名 2, FEAR
気配 ▶ APPEARANCE, SUGGESTION
下品な ▶ OFFENSIVE
下落 ▶ REDUCTION
下落する ▶ FALL 1
ゲリラ ▶ GUERRILLA
険しい ▶ STERN
県 ▶ COUNTY
険悪にする ▶ INFLUENCE 動
険悪になる ▶ INFLUENCE 動
権威 ▶ AUTHORITIES, EXPERT
権威ある ▶ GREAT 2
検印 ▶ LOGO
原因 ▶ FAULT, SOURCE
牽引する ▶ PULL 1
原因の究明 ▶ INVESTIGATION
検閲 ▶ INSPECTION
嫌悪 ▶ HATRED, SHOCK 名
嫌悪感 ▶ FEAR
嫌悪感を催させる ▶ DISGUSTING 2
嫌悪する ▶ HATE
けんか ▶ FIGHT 2
見解 ▶ ASSESSMENT, DEFINITION, STATEMENT, VIEW 1
限界 ▶ LIMIT 2
見学 ▶ VISIT 名
減額する ▶ DISCOUNT
厳格な ▶ STRICT
原価計算 ▶ VALUATION
けんかする ▶ ARGUE
玄関 ▶ HALL 2
嫌疑 ▶ DOUBT 名 2

元気づけられる ▶ PROMISING
元気づける ▶ ENCOURAGE
元気で ▶ SAFE
元気な ▶ ENERGETIC, LIVELY, WELL
元気のよい ▶ CHEERFUL
研究 ▶ REPORT 1, RESEARCH
言及 ▶ REFERENCE
研究家 ▶ ANALYST
研究会 ▶ CLASS 2
研究課題 ▶ ASSIGNMENT
研究する ▶ EXAMINE, INVESTIGATE, LEARN
言及する ▶ MENTION
現金 ▶ MONEY 2
現金化する ▶ CASH, SELL 1
権限 ▶ CONTROL, PERMISSION, RIGHT 名
権限のない ▶ UNOFFICIAL
健康(な状態) ▶ HEALTH
健康な ▶ WELL
健康に ▶ HEALTHY
健康を管理する ▶ LOOK AFTER SB
健康を保つ ▶ TRAIN 2
検査 ▶ INSPECTION, TEST 名 1
健在で ▶ SAFE
現在の ▶ RECENT
検査官 ▶ INSPECTOR
検索 ▶ SEARCH
検索する ▶ LOOK 2
検査する ▶ CHECK 1, LOOK 動 2, TEST 動 1
原産 ▶ SOURCE
検死 ▶ INVESTIGATION
見識 ▶ UNDERSTANDING
見識のある ▶ TOLERANT
現実 ▶ FACT
現実的な ▶ POSSIBLE 1, REALISTIC
堅実な ▶ STEADY
現実の ▶ RELIABLE 2
現実の世界 ▶ FACT
研修生 ▶ RECRUIT
厳粛な ▶ SERIOUS 2
憲章 ▶ LAW
現象 ▶ EVENT 1
減少 ▶ REDUCTION
懸賞金 ▶ AWARD
減少する ▶ FALL 1, WORSEN
原初の ▶ FIRST

減じる ▶ DISCOUNT
検診 ▶ INSPECTION
献身する ▶ DEVOTE
献身的な ▶ LOVING, RELIABLE 1
献身的な愛情 ▶ LOVE 名 2
献身的に愛する ▶ LOVE 動
厳正な ▶ STRICT
建設 ▶ PRODUCTION
建設者 ▶ MAKER
建設する ▶ BUILD
厳然たる ▶ FINAL
健全な ▶ GOOD 3
元素 ▶ MATERIAL
幻想 ▶ ILLUSION
建造者 ▶ MAKER
建造する ▶ BUILD
原則 ▶ BASICS, PRINCIPLE 2
現存 ▶ LIFE 1
現代的でない ▶ OLD-FASHIONED
現代の ▶ RECENT
言質 ▶ PROMISE 名
建築 ▶ PRODUCTION
限定の ▶ LIMITED 2
限度 ▶ LIMIT 1, 2, RANGE 2
見当 ▶ SENSE
検討する ▶ EXAMINE, INVESTIGATE
見当違いの ▶ IRRELEVANT, WRONG 1
原動力 ▶ INFLUENCE 名
現場 ▶ PLACE
現場監督 ▶ MANAGER
見物 ▶ VISIT 名
見物客 ▶ TOURIST
見物する ▶ LOOK 動 1, STAY 2, VISIT 動
見物人 ▶ WITNESS
検分する ▶ CHECK 1
見聞の広い ▶ INFORMED
憲法 ▶ LAW
憲法に関する ▶ LEGAL
厳密な ▶ EXACT
言明 ▶ STATEMENT
賢明な ▶ BEST, WISE
幻滅 ▶ SHOCK 名
倹約する ▶ SAVE 2
原油 ▶ OIL
権利 ▶ RIGHT 名
原理 ▶ BASICS, THEORY 1
権力 ▶ RIGHT 名
権力層 ▶ AUTHORITIES
権利を与える ▶ ALLOW

こ

故…▶DEAD
濃い▶DARK 2, STRONG 2
語彙▶LANGUAGE
恋心▶LOVE 名 1
恋した▶IN LOVE
恋して▶IN LOVE
故意でない▶UNCONSCIOUS
恋仲で▶IN LOVE
故意の▶DELIBERATE
恋人▶DARLING, PARTNER 2
請う▶ASK 2
公安▶PEACE
考案する▶DESIGN 動 1, DEVELOP 2
行為▶ACTION
好意▶LOVE 名 2
合意▶AGREEMENT, APPROVAL
好意的な▶GOOD 6
高位の▶GREAT 2, TOP
好意を抱く▶LOVE 動
工員▶WORKER 1
強引な▶AGGRESSIVE 2
豪雨▶FLOOD 名 1
幸運▶LUCK
幸運な▶TIMELY
光栄▶PLEASURE, STATUS
公営の▶PUBLIC
交易▶TRADE
交易する▶SELL 2
校閲▶CHANGE 名 2
後援▶HELP 名, INVESTMENT
講演▶SPEECH
後援者▶SPONSOR
後援する▶FUND 動
公演する▶PLAY 動 2
後悔▶GUILT
梗概▶SUMMARY
後悔して▶SORRY
公開する▶PRESENT 1, PUBLISH 1, 2
口外する▶TELL 2
合格した▶SUCCESSFUL 1
合格する▶GRADUATE
狡猾な▶DISHONEST
効果的な▶PRODUCTIVE, SUCCESSFUL 1
高価な▶EXPENSIVE, VALUABLE 1
効果のない▶INEFFECTIVE, USELESS

好感▶ADMIRATION
交換▶EXCHANGE
強姦▶ATTACK 名 2
交換する▶REPLACE 2, SWITCH
好機▶OPPORTUNITY
講義▶CLASS 1, SPEECH
抗議▶DEBATE, OPPOSITION
抗議運動▶TROUBLE 1
抗議者▶PROTESTER
好奇心を抱かせる▶INTEREST 動
高貴な▶GREAT 2
後期の▶LAST 1
高級▶STYLE
恒久的な▶PERMANENT
高級な▶FASHIONABLE
高級の▶TOP
工業▶INDUSTRY, PRODUCTION
公共事業▶FACILITIES
興行主▶SPONSOR
公共の▶COMMON, PUBLIC, SOCIAL
講義をする▶TEACH
工具▶TOOL
口径▶HOLE 1
光景▶VIEW 2
合計する▶COUNT
合計の▶WHOLE
工芸品▶THING 1
攻撃▶ATTACK 名 1, 2, CRITICISM
攻撃する▶ATTACK 動 1, 2
攻撃性▶TENSION
攻撃的な▶AGGRESSIVE 1
高潔▶INTEGRITY, MORALITY
高潔な▶GOOD 5, RESPECTABLE, WORTHY
貢献▶INVOLVEMENT
交互▶CHANGE 名 1
広告▶ADVERTISEMENT
広告を出す▶PUBLISH 1
恍惚▶JOY
講座▶CLASS 1
交際▶FRIENDSHIP
交際する▶GO OUT
交錯した▶CONFUSING
考察▶CONSIDERATION
講師▶LECTURER
行使▶USE 名
抗しがたい▶UNCONTROLLABLE
公式会見▶INTERVIEW 1

公式の▶OFFICIAL 形
行使権▶USE 名
行使する▶USE 動 1
口実▶REASON
公衆の▶SOCIAL
公衆便所▶TOILET
口述する▶QUOTE
工場▶COMPANY, FACTORY
向上▶PROGRESS
向上させる▶IMPROVE 1
向上心▶HOPE 名 2
交渉する▶NEGOTIATE
向上する▶DEVELOP 1, IMPROVE 2
高尚な▶GREAT 2
強情な▶STUBBORN
交渉人▶NEGOTIATOR
高尚ぶった▶INTELLECTUAL 2
控除する▶DISCOUNT
行進する▶WALK 1
香辛料の利いた▶STRONG 2
構図▶STRUCTURE
洪水▶FLOOD 名 1
構成▶DESIGN 名, STRUCTURE, SYSTEM
公正▶JUSTICE
合成▶STRUCTURE
公正な▶REASONABLE
合成の▶ARTIFICIAL
功績▶VALUE
公設の▶PUBLIC
交戦▶WAR
好戦的な▶AGGRESSIVE 1
控訴院▶COURT
構想▶STORY
構造▶STRUCTURE
構想する▶IMAGINE
高層の▶HIGH 2
拘束する▶KIDNAP
高速の▶FAST
後退▶REDUCTION
交替▶CHANGE 名 1
交替する▶REPLACE 1, 2
交代する▶SWITCH
広大な▶HUGE, LARGE
交替要員▶REPLACEMENT
強奪する▶ROB, TAKE 3
豪胆な▶BRAVE
高地▶HILL
耕地▶LAND 1
交通▶TRAFFIC
交通渋滞▶TRAFFIC
交通渋滞区間▶TRAFFIC

交通麻痺▶TRAFFIC
好都合である▶MEET 4
校訂▶CHANGE 名 2
工程▶WAY 2
肯定的な▶GOOD 6, OPTIMISTIC
好敵手となる▶COMPARE 2
好適の▶HEALTHY
好転▶INCREASE 名
好転する▶IMPROVE 2
好天の▶SUNNY
高騰▶INCREASE 名
行動▶ACTION
講堂▶HALL 1
強盗▶THEFT
口頭試験▶TEST 名 2
強盗犯▶THIEF
購入者▶CUSTOMER
購入する▶BUY
後任▶REPLACEMENT
後任となる▶REPLACE 1
公認の▶OFFICIAL 形
効能▶FEATURE 名
広範囲にわたる▶LARGE
広範囲の▶GENERAL
広範な▶WIDE 1
後半の▶LAST 1
公表▶STATEMENT
公表する▶DECLARE, PUBLISH 1, SAY 2
高品質▶VALUE
高品質の▶GOOD 1
幸福▶SATISFACTION
幸福な▶HAPPY
好物▶CHOICE 2
興奮▶EXCITEMENT
興奮剤▶DRUG 1
興奮させる▶EXCITING, STIMULATE
興奮した▶EXCITED, RESTLESS
公文書▶DOCUMENT
公平▶JUSTICE
公平な▶FINE
広報▶ADVERTISEMENT
合法の▶LEGAL
候補者▶CANDIDATE, PARTICIPANT
傲慢▶PRIDE
高慢な▶PROUD 2
傲慢な▶PROUD 2, RUDE
巧妙さ▶SKILL 2
高名な▶GREAT 2
公民▶CITIZEN
公務員▶OFFICIAL 名

日本語類語一覧

公務上の ▶ OFFICIAL 形
公務の ▶ PUBLIC
こうむる ▶ HAVE 3
公明正大な
　▶ REASONABLE
項目 ▶ ISSUE
荒野 ▶ HILL
公約 ▶ PROMISE 名,
　RESPONSIBILITY
公約する ▶ PROMISE 動
交友関係 ▶ FRIENDSHIP
高揚感 ▶ EXCITEMENT
高揚した ▶ EXCITED
行楽 ▶ HOLIDAY 2
行楽客 ▶ TOURIST
行楽地 ▶ HOLIDAY 2
合理化する ▶ CUT 1
小売業者 ▶ DEALER
小売りする ▶ SELL 2
合理性 ▶ LOGIC
効率 ▶ EFFICIENCY
効率的な ▶ EFFICIENT
公立の ▶ COMMON,
　PUBLIC
合理的な ▶ RATIONAL
攻略する ▶ INVADE
勾留する ▶ JAIL
拘留する ▶ JAIL
考慮 ▶ CONSIDERATION
綱領 ▶ PLAN 1
考慮する ▶ CONSIDER
高齢の ▶ OLD 2
航路 ▶ WAY 3
口論 ▶ ARGUMENT 1,
　FIGHT 名
講和 ▶ PEACE
護衛 ▶ GUARD
護衛する ▶ PROTECT,
　TAKE 2
コーチを務める ▶ TRAIN 1
氷で覆われた ▶ FREEZING
ゴールイン ▶ END 名
誤解 ▶ ILLUSION,
　MISTAKE 1
誤解する
　▶ MISUNDERSTAND
誤解を招く ▶ MISLEADING
互角の ▶ CLOSE 形
小型の ▶ SMALL
枯渇させる ▶ USE 動 2
小柄の ▶ SHORT 2
顧客 ▶ CUSTOMER,
　MARKET 1
極悪な ▶ EVIL 形
刻印 ▶ LOGO
国営の ▶ PUBLIC

国際試合 ▶ GAME
国際人の
　▶ INTERNATIONAL
国際的な
　▶ INTERNATIONAL
国際の ▶ INTERNATIONAL
告示 ▶ STATEMENT
酷似して ▶ LIKE 前 形
国事の ▶ PUBLIC
告訴 ▶ CHARGE 名
告訴する ▶ ACCUSE
告知 ▶ STATEMENT
国内の ▶ NATIONAL
告白 ▶ STATEMENT
告発 ▶ CHARGE 名
告発する ▶ ACCUSE
黒板 ▶ SIGN 2
酷評する ▶ SCOLD
酷評的な ▶ CRITICAL
極貧 ▶ POVERTY
極貧の ▶ POOR 1
ごく普通の ▶ USUAL
国民 ▶ CITIZEN, PEOPLE
国民的な ▶ CULTURAL
国民投票 ▶ ELECTION
国有の ▶ PUBLIC
国立の ▶ PUBLIC
固形の ▶ SOLID
小声で話す ▶ WHISPER
凍える ▶ COOL
凍えるほど寒い
　▶ FREEZING
心地よい ▶ BEAUTIFUL 2,
　COMFORTABLE,
　SATISFYING, WONDERFUL
個々の ▶ PARTICULAR
心 ▶ MIND
心当たりがある ▶ INTEND
心からの ▶ DEEP 1,
　HONEST
心に訴える ▶ INTEREST 動
心待ちにする ▶ EXPECT,
　HOPE 動
試み ▶ ATTEMPT
試みる ▶ TRY 1
心を動かす ▶ IMPRESS
心を打つ ▶ IMPRESS
心を奪う ▶ DELIGHT
心を奪われた ▶ IN LOVE,
　INTERESTED
心を開いた ▶ TOLERANT
故殺 ▶ MURDER
古参の ▶ EXPERIENCED
腰掛ける ▶ SIT
ごしごし磨く ▶ BRUSH
こじつけの ▶ UNLIKELY 2

固執する ▶ FOLLOW 3,
　PERSIST
ゴシップ ▶ DISCUSSION
腰抜け ▶ COWARD
故障させる ▶ BREAK 2
故障した ▶ SICK 1
故障する ▶ BREAK 2
誤植 ▶ MISTAKE 2
腰を下ろす ▶ SIT
個人 ▶ PERSON
誤信 ▶ ILLUSION
個人教授をする ▶ TEACH
個人的な ▶ OWN, SECRET
個人の ▶ OWN
個人用の ▶ OWN
コスト ▶ COSTS
個性 ▶ IDENTITY,
　PERSONALITY
個性的な ▶ UNIQUE
小銭 ▶ MONEY 2
小競り合い ▶ FIGHT 名,
　WAR
小競り合いをする
　▶ FIGHT 動
固体 ▶ MATERIAL
誇大広告する
　▶ ADVERTISE
固体の ▶ SOLID
古代の ▶ OLD 1
答え ▶ ANSWER 名,
　SOLUTION
答える ▶ ANSWER 動
ごちゃごちゃ ▶ MESS 1
ごちゃ混ぜ ▶ MESS 1
ごちゃ混ぜになった
　▶ UNTIDY
誇張する ▶ EXAGGERATE
こぢんまりした ▶ SMALL
こつ ▶ SKILL 1
国家 ▶ COUNTRY 1
国会 ▶ GOVERNMENT 1
小遣い ▶ FUND 名
国会議員 ▶ POLITICIAN
国家の ▶ CULTURAL
小突く ▶ PUSH 1
こっけいな ▶ FUNNY,
　RIDICULOUS
ごった返した ▶ CROWDED
骨重の ▶ OLD 1
固定された ▶ STILL
固定する ▶ ATTACH
古典派の ▶ TRADITIONAL
事柄 ▶ ISSUE
孤独な ▶ LONELY
異ならせる ▶ DIVIDE 2

異なる ▶ DIFFER,
　DIFFERENT
言葉 ▶ LANGUAGE
子ども ▶ CHILD
子どもじみた ▶ CHILDISH
子どもの ▶ CHILDISH
子どものころ
　▶ CHILDHOOD
子どもらしい ▶ CHILDISH
断る ▶ REFUSE
この前の ▶ LAST 2
好ましい ▶ BETTER,
　NICE 2, POPULAR
好ましくない
　▶ DIFFICULT 2
好まれる ▶ FAVOURITE
好み ▶ TASTE, TENDENCY
好みである ▶ LIKE
好む ▶ LIKE 動, PREFER,
　WANT
小走りする ▶ RUN 1
拒む ▶ REFUSE
湖畔 ▶ COAST
コピー ▶ COPY 名 1
コピーする ▶ COPY 動
こぶ ▶ TUMOUR
鼓舞する ▶ INSPIRE
個別の ▶ PARTICULAR
語法 ▶ LANGUAGE
こぼれる ▶ FLOOD 動
コマーシャル
　▶ ADVERTISEMENT,
　PAUSE
ごまかしの ▶ WRONG 1
ごまかす ▶ HIDE
ごまかす人 ▶ CHEAT 名
困った ▶ SENSITIVE 2
困らせる ▶ HURT 1,
　WORRY
ごみ ▶ WASTE
小道 ▶ PATH
コミュニケーション
　▶ COMMUNICATION
コメディアン ▶ ACTOR
コメディー ▶ PLAY 名
コメンテーター
　▶ ANALYST, PRESENTER
コメント ▶ STATEMENT
コメントする ▶ COMMENT
顧問 ▶ ADVISER
固有の ▶ UNIQUE
雇用 ▶ WORK 名 1
雇用する ▶ EMPLOY
雇用主 ▶ MANAGER
古来の ▶ OLD 1

日本語類語一覧

こらえる ▶ RESIST, SUPPRESS 2
娯楽 ▶ ENTERTAINMENT, FUN, INTEREST 名 2
コラム ▶ ARTICLE
コラムニスト ▶ REPORTER
孤立 ▶ DIVISION 1
孤立させる ▶ ISOLATE
孤立した ▶ LONELY
これまでにない ▶ NEW 1
頃合い ▶ OPPORTUNITY
語呂合わせ ▶ JOKE
転がる ▶ SPIN
殺す ▶ KILL
転ぶ ▶ FALL 2, 3
怖い ▶ FRIGHTENING
怖かった ▶ WORRIED
怖がって ▶ AFRAID
怖がらせる ▶ FRIGHTEN, SHOCK 動
壊す ▶ FALL 2, RUIN
壊れやすい ▶ FRAGILE
壊れる ▶ FALL 2
弧を描く ▶ CURVE
根幹 ▶ NATURE 1
懇願 ▶ REQUEST
根気強さ ▶ DETERMINATION
困窮 ▶ MESS 2
根拠 ▶ EVIDENCE, REASON
根拠のない ▶ IRRATIONAL
コンクール ▶ COMPETITION 1
権化 ▶ EXAMPLE 2
根源 ▶ SOURCE
根源的な ▶ FUNDAMENTAL
混合の ▶ DIVERSE
混雑した ▶ CROWDED, FULL
コンサルタント ▶ ADVISER
根性 ▶ COURAGE
根性のある ▶ BRAVE
混成の ▶ DIVERSE
痕跡 ▶ SIGN 1
根底 ▶ SOURCE
コンテスト ▶ COMPETITION 1
困難 ▶ EFFORT, OBSTACLE, PROBLEM, TROUBLE 2
困難な ▶ DIFFICULT 1, HARD
困難にする ▶ BLOCK 1
今日の ▶ RECENT
コンペ ▶ COMPETITION 1

梱包する ▶ FILL
根本 ▶ NATURE 1, SOURCE
根本的な ▶ FUNDAMENTAL
混乱 ▶ MESS 2
混乱した ▶ CONFUSED

さ

差 ▶ GAP
サービス業 ▶ INDUSTRY
差異 ▶ DIFFERENCE
最愛の ▶ DEAR
罪悪 ▶ EVIL 名
罪悪感 ▶ GUILT
最悪な ▶ TERRIBLE 1
災害 ▶ CRISIS
再開する ▶ CONTINUE 3
才覚 ▶ INTELLIGENCE
才気あふれる ▶ INTELLIGENT
猜疑心 ▶ FEAR
再起動する ▶ CONTINUE 3
最近の ▶ LAST 2, RECENT
財源 ▶ MONEY 1, SUPPLY
再検討する ▶ EXAMINE
最後 ▶ END 名
在庫 ▶ SUPPLY
最高位 ▶ PEAK
最高位の ▶ TOP
最高級の ▶ TOP
最高経営責任者 ▶ LEADER 1
最高限度 ▶ LIMIT 1
最高潮 ▶ PEAK
最高の ▶ EXCELLENT, IDEAL, TOP, WONDERFUL
最後に残った ▶ LAST 1
最後の ▶ LAST 1
さい先のよい ▶ PROMISING
財産 ▶ MONEY 3, THING 2
採算の取れない ▶ LOSS-MAKING
再試合 ▶ GAME
再始動する ▶ CONTINUE 3
在住者 ▶ RESIDENT
最終的な ▶ LAST 1
最終の ▶ FINAL, LAST 1
最重要の ▶ MAIN
最初 ▶ START 名
最上級の ▶ EXCELLENT
最小限にする ▶ REDUCE
最上の ▶ GOOD 1
最初の ▶ FIRST
細心の ▶ DETAILED

最新の ▶ LAST 2, MODERN, NEW 1, RECENT
財政 ▶ FINANCE, MONEY 1
最盛期 ▶ PEAK
財政支援 ▶ INVESTMENT
財政支援する ▶ FUND 動
再生する ▶ TURN STH ON
最前線 ▶ LIMIT 2
最先端の ▶ MODERN
最善の ▶ BEST
最善の方策 ▶ OPTION
最大化する ▶ INCREASE 動
採択する ▶ CHOOSE
財団 ▶ CHARITY
裁定する ▶ COMPENSATION, CONCLUSION
裁定する ▶ RULE 動 2
最適の ▶ BEST, FAVOURITE, IDEAL
災難 ▶ DISASTER, TROUBLE 2
歳入 ▶ REVENUE
罪人 ▶ CRIMINAL
才能 ▶ SKILL 1
才能がある ▶ GOOD 4
さいの目 ▶ PIECE
さいの目に切る ▶ CUT 2
栽培地 ▶ FACTORY
栽培する ▶ KEEP 4
裁判 ▶ CASE
裁判所 ▶ COURT
細部にわたる ▶ DETAILED
細片 ▶ FRAGMENT
債務 ▶ DEBT
財務 ▶ FINANCE
最有力候補 ▶ LEADER 2
採用する ▶ CHOOSE, EMPLOY
在留者 ▶ RESIDENT
材料 ▶ MATERIAL
最良の ▶ GOOD 1
サイン ▶ SIGNAL
サインする ▶ WRITE
さえぎる ▶ BLOCK 2, INTERRUPT
栄える ▶ DO WELL
捜し出す ▶ FIND 4, LOOK 動 2
捜し回る ▶ LOOK 動 2
捜し求める ▶ LOOK 動 2
探す, 捜す ▶ LOOK 動 2
逆らう ▶ OPPOSE
下がる ▶ FALL 1, 2
詐欺 ▶ FRAUD 1, 2
詐欺師 ▶ CHEAT 名

先立つ ▶ PREVIOUS
詐欺的な ▶ CORRUPT, DISHONEST
先の ▶ LAST 2, PREVIOUS
先延ばしにする ▶ DELAY
作業 ▶ PROJECT, TASK
作業員 ▶ WORKER 1
作業場 ▶ FACTORY
昨… ▶ LAST 2
索引 ▶ LIST 名
削減 ▶ REDUCTION
削減する ▶ CUT 1, FIRE, REDUCE, REMOVE
作者 ▶ WRITER
削除する ▶ DELETE
作成する ▶ PREPARE 1
作戦 ▶ PROJECT, TACTIC
策定する ▶ PREPARE 1
作品 ▶ WORK 名 2
作文 ▶ PAPER
策略 ▶ CONSPIRACY, FRAUD 2, PLAN 1, TACTIC, TRICK
探る ▶ INVESTIGATE
酒 ▶ DRINK 名
さげすみ ▶ CONTEMPT
叫ぶ ▶ SCREAM, SHOUT
避けられない ▶ INEVITABLE
避ける ▶ ESCAPE, HESITATE, PREVENT
裂ける ▶ TEAR
些細 ▶ INFORMATION
些細な ▶ MINOR, SLIGHT
支え ▶ HELP 名
支える ▶ HELP 動 1
ささげる ▶ DEVOTE
査察 ▶ INSPECTION
ささやく ▶ WHISPER
指し示す ▶ SUGGEST
指図する ▶ RULE 動 2
差し迫った ▶ URGENT
差し引く ▶ DISCOUNT
詐取する ▶ DEFRAUD
挫折 ▶ FRUSTRATION
させないようにする ▶ PREVENT
…させる ▶ FORCE 動
定める ▶ RULE 動 2
殺意のある ▶ VIOLENT
撮影審査 ▶ INTERVIEW 2
作家 ▶ WRITER
殺害 ▶ MURDER
殺害する ▶ DESTROY, KILL
錯覚 ▶ ILLUSION
殺菌した ▶ CLEAN 形

さつじん → しじして

日本語類語一覧

殺人 ▶ MURDER
殺人未遂 ▶ ATTACK 名 2
雑然とした ▶ UNTIDY
雑談 ▶ DISCUSSION
察知する ▶ KNOW
殺到 ▶ FLOOD 名 2
殺到する ▶ HURRY
さっと向ける ▶ TURN 1
ざっと読む ▶ READ
さっぱりする ▶ WASH
さっぱりとした ▶ NEAT
殺風景な ▶ PLAIN 1
雑用 ▶ TASK
査定 ▶ ASSESSMENT, VALUATION
サディスティックな ▶ CRUEL
作動させる ▶ OPERATE
作動して ▶ ACTIVE
作動しなくなる ▶ BREAK 2
作動する ▶ WORK 動 2
里親となる ▶ BRING SB UP
悟る ▶ KNOW
…さばく ▶ SKILL 2
サバティカル ▶ HOLIDAY 1
差別 ▶ DISCRIMINATION, DIVISION 1
差別的な ▶ BIASED
作法 ▶ PRINCIPLE 2, RESPECT 名, VALUES
サポーター ▶ FAN
さまざまである ▶ DIFFER
さまざまな ▶ DIVERSE, WIDE 1
冷ます ▶ COOL
妨げる ▶ BLOCK 1, PREVENT
寂しい ▶ LONELY, UNHAPPY 1
寒い ▶ COLD 1
冷めた ▶ INDIFFERENT
冷める ▶ COOL
左右される ▶ DEPEND ON/UPON STH
左右する ▶ DETERMINE
座右の銘 ▶ SLOGAN
作用 ▶ EFFECT
作用する ▶ AFFECT, WORK 動 2
さりげない ▶ IRONIC
去る ▶ GO AWAY, LEAVE 1
騒がしい ▶ LOUD
触って調べる ▶ TOUCH
触ってみる ▶ TOUCH
触る ▶ TOUCH

参加 ▶ INVOLVEMENT
残骸 ▶ REMAINS
参加者 ▶ CANDIDATE, PARTICIPANT
参加する ▶ JOIN
残虐行為 ▶ CRIME 2
残虐な ▶ VIOLENT
産業 ▶ INDUSTRY
残酷な ▶ CRUEL, RUTHLESS
惨事 ▶ CRISIS
賛辞 ▶ PRAISE 名
産出 ▶ PRODUCTION
算出する ▶ CALCULATE
斬新な ▶ NEW 1
賛成 ▶ APPROVAL, PRAISE 名
賛成する ▶ AGREE, IN FAVOUR, SUPPORT
賛成で ▶ IN FAVOUR
燦然たる ▶ MAGNIFICENT
残存している ▶ REMAIN
残存する ▶ SURVIVE
山地 ▶ HILL
山頂 ▶ HILL
賛同 ▶ PRAISE 名
賛同の ▶ GOOD 6
賛同を得る ▶ PERSUADE
残忍な ▶ VIOLENT
残念 ▶ FRUSTRATION, GRIEF
残念な ▶ TERRIBLE 1, UNFORTUNATE 2
残念ながら… ▶ SORRY
散発的な ▶ OCCASIONAL
賛美する ▶ PRAISE 動
産物 ▶ RESULT
散歩する ▶ WALK 2
酸味のある ▶ BITTER
散乱 ▶ MESS 1
散乱物 ▶ MESS 1

し

詩 ▶ WORK 名 2
試合 ▶ GAME
試合開始 ▶ START 名
仕上げる ▶ FINISH
幸せ ▶ SATISFACTION
飼育場 ▶ FACTORY
飼育する ▶ KEEP 4
シースルーの ▶ CLEAR 形 3
強いられた ▶ NECESSARY
寺院 ▶ CHURCH
試飲する ▶ TRY 2

シェア ▶ SHARE 名
ジェスチャー ▶ MOVEMENT
支援 ▶ AID, HELP 名, INVESTMENT
支援する ▶ HELP 動 1
塩味の利いた ▶ STRONG 2
自我 ▶ MIND
視界 ▶ SIGHT
司会者 ▶ PRESENTER
司会を務める ▶ PRESENT 4
仕返し ▶ REVENGE
資格 ▶ RIGHT 名
自覚 ▶ AWARENESS
資格を与える ▶ ALLOW
資格を得る ▶ GRADUATE
仕方 ▶ WAY 1
自活する ▶ TAKE CARE OF YOURSELF
しがみつく ▶ HOLD
叱る ▶ SCOLD
しかるべき ▶ RESPECTABLE, RIGHT 形 1, 2
時間 ▶ TIME
志願者 ▶ CANDIDATE
志願の ▶ VOLUNTARY 1
時間のある ▶ FREE 形 3
指揮 ▶ CONTROL, GOVERNMENT 2
士気 ▶ MOOD
時機 ▶ OPPORTUNITY
時期 ▶ PERIOD
式辞 ▶ SPEECH
識字能力 ▶ KNOWLEDGE
時期尚早の ▶ RECKLESS
指揮する ▶ RUN 2
しきたり ▶ TRADITION
敷地 ▶ LAND 2, PLACE
仕切っている ▶ RUN 2
識別できる ▶ VISIBLE
支給 ▶ SHARE 名
支給する ▶ PROVIDE
至急の ▶ URGENT
事業 ▶ PROJECT, TRADE
支局 ▶ DEPARTMENT
死去した ▶ DEAD
資金 ▶ FUND 名, MONEY 1, SUPPLY
試金石 ▶ CRITERION
資金提供 ▶ INVESTMENT
資金を提供する ▶ FUND 動
しぐさ ▶ MOVEMENT
ジグザグ ▶ CORNER

ジグザグになる ▶ CURVE
しくしく泣く ▶ CRY
地口 ▶ JOKE
シグナル ▶ SIGN 1
刺激 ▶ INCENTIVE
刺激剤 ▶ DRUG 1
刺激する ▶ INSPIRE, STIMULATE
刺激的な ▶ EXCITING, INTERESTING
しけた ▶ ROUGH
自決権 ▶ INDEPENDENCE
試験 ▶ INTERVIEW 2, TEST 名 1, 2
資源 ▶ SUPPLY
時限 ▶ CLASS 2, TIME
試験官 ▶ INSPECTOR, JUDGE 名
試験する ▶ TEST 動 1, 2
試験的研究 ▶ TEST 名 1
試験的に使う ▶ TEST 動 1
試験問題 ▶ TEST 名 2
事故 ▶ ACCIDENT
自己 ▶ IDENTITY
思考 ▶ CONSIDERATION
嗜好 ▶ TASTE
志向 ▶ TENDENCY
指向 ▶ TENDENCY
事項 ▶ ISSUE
施行する ▶ APPLY
思考する ▶ CONSIDER
自己管理する ▶ TAKE CARE OF YOURSELF
時刻 ▶ TIME
自国の ▶ NATIONAL
自己主張 ▶ CONFIDENCE
自己主張が強い ▶ AGGRESSIVE 2
自己像 ▶ DIGNITY
自己中心的な ▶ SELFISH
仕事 ▶ JOB, RESPONSIBILITY, TASK, WORK 名 1
自己評価 ▶ DIGNITY
しこり ▶ TUMOUR
示唆 ▶ SUGGESTION
示唆する ▶ SUGGEST
視察 ▶ INSPECTION, VISIT 名
自殺 ▶ MURDER
資産 ▶ THING 2
持参する ▶ TAKE 1
支持 ▶ APPROVAL, ENDORSEMENT
指示 ▶ SIGN 1
支持して ▶ IN FAVOUR

しじする → しばる

日本語類語一覧

支持する ▶ APPROVE, IN FAVOUR, SUPPORT
指示する ▶ ORDER 1, RULE 動 2
資質 ▶ FEATURE 名
事実 ▶ FACT, INFORMATION
事実どおりの ▶ TRUE
事実に基づいた ▶ OBJECTIVE
事実無根の ▶ IRRATIONAL
支社 ▶ DEPARTMENT
自主 ▶ FREEDOM
自主運営 ▶ INDEPENDENCE
支出 ▶ COSTS
思春期 ▶ CHILDHOOD
思春期の ▶ YOUNG
地所 ▶ LAND 1
支障 ▶ OBSTACLE
市場 ▶ MARKET 1, TRADE
事情 ▶ FACTOR, SITUATION
市場占有率 ▶ SHARE 名
市場に出回って ▶ AVAILABLE
支障をきたす ▶ HARMFUL
試食する ▶ TRY 2
辞職する ▶ LEAVE 3
支持を得る ▶ PERSUADE
詩人 ▶ WRITER
自信 ▶ CONFIDENCE
自信があって ▶ SURE
自信がない ▶ UNSURE
自身の ▶ OWN
自信のある ▶ CONFIDENT
自信のない ▶ SHY
静かな ▶ QUIET 1, 2
滴 ▶ DROP
静けさ ▶ PAUSE, SILENCE
システム ▶ SYSTEM
地滑り的勝利 ▶ VICTORY
静まり返った ▶ STILL
沈める ▶ SOAK
姿勢 ▶ ATTITUDE, POSITION, TENDENCY
施政 ▶ GOVERNMENT 2
自制 ▶ LIMIT 1
時世 ▶ PERIOD
自責の念 ▶ GUILT
施設 ▶ FACILITIES
使節団 ▶ COMMITTEE
視線 ▶ LOOK 名
慈善 ▶ AID
慈善家 ▶ SPONSOR
自然界 ▶ NATURE 2
自然環境 ▶ NATURE 2
慈善団体 ▶ CHARITY

事前の ▶ PREVIOUS
…しそうな ▶ LIKELY
氏族 ▶ PEOPLE
持続する ▶ CONTINUE 1, MAINTAIN
持続的な ▶ PERMANENT
自尊心 ▶ DIGNITY, PRIDE
自尊心のある ▶ PROUD 1
…したい ▶ WANT
事態 ▶ SITUATION, STATE
時代 ▶ PERIOD
時代遅れの ▶ OLD-FASHIONED
時代区分 ▶ PERIOD
辞退する ▶ LEAVE 3, REFUSE
時代の風潮 ▶ TREND
従う ▶ FOLLOW 3, 4
下書き ▶ PLAN 2
従わない ▶ OPPOSE
自宅 ▶ HOME
下稽古 ▶ TRAINING
親しくなる ▶ MEET 3
親しみやすい ▶ FRIENDLY 1
したたり ▶ DROP
自堕落な ▶ WILD
師団 ▶ DEPARTMENT
自治 ▶ FREEDOM, INDEPENDENCE
自治都市 ▶ CITY
視聴者 ▶ MARKET 1
質 ▶ QUALITY, VALUE
実演 ▶ PRESENTATION
実家 ▶ HOME
失格者 ▶ LOSER 2
失格の ▶ INCOMPETENT
しっかりした ▶ FIRM, GOOD 3, TIGHT
しっかり締まる[締める] ▶ TIGHTEN
疾患 ▶ DISEASE
実感 ▶ AWARENESS
失業 ▶ UNEMPLOYMENT
実業家 ▶ EXECUTIVE
実況解説 ▶ REPORT 2
失業した ▶ UNEMPLOYED
失業者数 ▶ UNEMPLOYMENT
失業中の ▶ UNEMPLOYED
失業手当を受けて ▶ UNEMPLOYED
実況放送 ▶ REPORT 2
失業率 ▶ UNEMPLOYMENT
湿気 ▶ MOISTURE
湿気の多い ▶ HUMID

しつける ▶ BRING SB UP
実験 ▶ TEST 名 1
実現可能な ▶ POSSIBLE 1
実現させる ▶ ACHIEVE
実験する ▶ TEST 動 1
実現する ▶ HAPPEN
実験的な ▶ EXPERIMENTAL
しつこい ▶ CONTINUOUS
実行 ▶ USE 名
実行する ▶ DO
しつこく繰り返される ▶ FREQUENT
実際 ▶ FACT
実際的な ▶ POSSIBLE 1, REALISTIC
実際の ▶ REAL, VERY 形
実在の ▶ REAL, RELIABLE 2
実施する ▶ APPLY, INTRODUCE
実習 ▶ TEST 名 2
実習生 ▶ RECRUIT
湿潤な ▶ HUMID
実証 ▶ EVIDENCE
実状 ▶ FACT
実情 ▶ SITUATION
実証する ▶ CONFIRM 1
実証できる ▶ RELIABLE 2
叱責する ▶ SCOLD
実戦 ▶ WAR
実践 ▶ USE 名
実践する ▶ APPLY, DO
疾走する ▶ HURRY, RUN 1
質素な ▶ PLAIN 1
失態 ▶ MISTAKE 1
実態をあばく ▶ DISPROVE
実地試験 ▶ TEST 名 1
知って ▶ AWARE
知っている ▶ FEEL, KNOW, LEARN
嫉妬 ▶ JEALOUSY
湿度 ▶ MOISTURE
じっとしている ▶ STAY 1
じっと見る ▶ STARE
しっとりした ▶ WET
実に ▶ QUITE 2, VERY 副
ジッパー ▶ BUTTON 2
ジッパーを外す ▶ UNDO
失敗 ▶ DISASTER, FAILURE
失敗する ▶ FAIL 2
実物の ▶ REAL
しっぺ返し ▶ ANSWER 名
失望 ▶ GLOOM, SHOCK 名

失望させる ▶ DISAPPOINT, DISAPPOINTING, SHOCK 動
質問 ▶ QUESTION 名
質問する ▶ ASK 1, QUESTION 動
実用的な ▶ USEFUL
実用品 ▶ THING 1
実力者 ▶ INFLUENCE 名
実例 ▶ EXAMPLE 1
失礼な ▶ INSULTING, RUDE
指定する ▶ LIST 動
指摘する ▶ POINT STH OUT
私的な ▶ SECRET
…してほしい ▶ WANT
支店 ▶ DEPARTMENT
視点 ▶ ATTITUDE, VIEW 1
時点 ▶ TIME
指導 ▶ ADVICE, EDUCATION, GOVERNMENT 2
始動させる[する] ▶ TURN STH ON
指導者 ▶ LEADER 1
指導する ▶ RUN 2, TRAIN 1, 2
児童の ▶ YOUNG
指導部 ▶ MANAGEMENT
指導力 ▶ GOVERNMENT 2
しない ▶ FAIL 1
品ぞろえ ▶ RANGE 1
品物 ▶ PRODUCT, THING 1
しなやかな ▶ FLEXIBLE 2, SOFT
シナリオライター ▶ WRITER
死に至る ▶ FATAL
辞任する ▶ LEAVE 3
死ぬ ▶ DIE
忍び寄る ▶ FOLLOW 1
忍び笑いをする ▶ LAUGH
支配 ▶ CONTROL
芝居 ▶ PERFORMANCE, PLAY 名
支配する ▶ AFFECT, DETERMINE, INVADE, RULE 動 1
支配体制 ▶ AUTHORITIES
支配的な ▶ POWERFUL
しばしば ▶ OFTEN
自発的な ▶ HELPFUL, SPONTANEOUS, VOLUNTARY 1
自腹 ▶ FUND 名
支払い ▶ PAYMENT
縛る ▶ ATTACH

慈悲 ▶ SYMPATHY
慈悲深い ▶ KIND 形
指標 ▶ SIGN 1
持病 ▶ DISEASE
辞表を提出する
　▶ LEAVE 3
しびれを切らす
　▶ LOSE YOUR TEMPER
支部 ▶ DEPARTMENT
自負 ▶ DIGNITY
至福 ▶ JOY
しぶしぶの ▶ RELUCTANT
渋る ▶ HESITATE
自分 ▶ IDENTITY
自分勝手な ▶ SELFISH
自分自身の ▶ OWN
自分本位の ▶ SELFISH
思弁的な ▶ SUPPOSED
志望者 ▶ CANDIDATE
搾り出す ▶ PUMP
しぼる ▶ PRESS 1
資本 ▶ MONEY 1
閉まる ▶ CLOSE 動
自慢する ▶ BOAST
染み ▶ MARK
染みだらけの ▶ DIRTY
地味な ▶ PLAIN 1
市民 ▶ CITIZEN, RESIDENT
市民としての ▶ SOCIAL
市民の ▶ NATIONAL
事務局 ▶ SERVICE
事務所 ▶ COMPANY, SERVICE
事務的な ▶ REALISTIC
使命 ▶ TASK
指名 ▶ CHOICE 1
指名する ▶ APPOINT
自明の ▶ CLEAR 形 1, OBVIOUS
じめじめした ▶ WET
じめじめする ▶ HUMID
示す ▶ PRESENT 2, SHOW 1, SUGGEST
締め出す ▶ EXCLUDE 2
湿った ▶ WET
湿らす ▶ SOAK
閉める ▶ CLOSE 動
地面 ▶ SOIL
霜の降りた ▶ FREEZING
指紋 ▶ MARK
視野 ▶ SIGHT
邪悪 ▶ EVIL 名
邪悪な ▶ EVIL 形, WRONG 3
ジャーナリスト
　▶ REPORTER

謝意 ▶ THANKS
謝意を示す ▶ GRATEFUL
社員 ▶ WORKER 1
社会的な ▶ SOCIAL
社会の ▶ SOCIAL
社会保障 ▶ AID
借地人 ▶ TENANT
尺度 ▶ CRITERION
灼熱の ▶ HOT
釈放する ▶ RELEASE
釈明する ▶ EXPLAIN 2
借家人 ▶ TENANT
社交辞令の ▶ POLITE
社交的な ▶ SOCIABLE
社主 ▶ EXECUTIVE
写真複写 ▶ COPY 名 1
社説 ▶ ARTICLE
遮断 ▶ PAUSE
社長 ▶ LEADER 1
借金 ▶ DEBT
射程距離 ▶ RANGE 2
車道 ▶ ROAD
しゃぶる ▶ DRINK 動
遮蔽する ▶ PROTECT
遮蔽物 ▶ PRECAUTION
しゃべる ▶ SAY 1
邪魔 ▶ OBSTACLE, PAUSE
邪魔されない ▶ QUIET 1
邪魔者 ▶ OBSTACLE
邪魔をする ▶ INTERRUPT
しゃれ ▶ JOKE
謝礼 ▶ AWARD
シャワーを浴びる
　▶ WASH
ジャンル ▶ KIND 名
首位 ▶ LEADER 2, PEAK
首位の ▶ TOP
州 ▶ COUNTY
自由 ▶ FREEDOM
重圧 ▶ PRESSURE 1
周囲 ▶ EDGE, ENVIRONMENT
自由意志の
　▶ VOLUNTARY 1
収益 ▶ PROFIT, REVENUE
収益を上げる ▶ MAKE 2
集会 ▶ MEETING 1
収穫高 ▶ OUTPUT
習慣 ▶ HABIT, TRADITION
習慣的に ▶ OFTEN
習慣的に行われる
　▶ FREQUENT
習慣の ▶ USED TO STH
住居 ▶ HOME
就業 ▶ WORK 名 1

従業員 ▶ STAFF, WORKER 1
住居侵入 ▶ THEFT
住居侵入者 ▶ THIEF
襲撃 ▶ ATTACK 名 2
襲撃者 ▶ THIEF
終結 ▶ END 名
重罪 ▶ CRIME 2
自由裁判 ▶ FREEDOM
自由裁量の
　▶ VOLUNTARY 1
従事 ▶ INVOLVEMENT
自由時間 ▶ LEISURE
従事する ▶ JOIN
充実感 ▶ SATISFACTION
充実する ▶ DO WELL
収集する ▶ COLLECT
自由主義の ▶ TOLERANT
収縮する ▶ SHRINK
従順な ▶ GOOD 7
住所 ▶ HOME
住所氏名録 ▶ LIST 名
執心 ▶ OBSESSION
修正する ▶ ADJUST, CORRECT
修繕する ▶ REPAIR
十代 ▶ CHILDHOOD
渋滞させる
　▶ HOLD SB/STH UP
渋滞した ▶ FULL
重大性 ▶ IMPORTANCE
重大な ▶ HUGE, IMPORTANT, SERIOUS 1
集団 ▶ GROUP 1, 2, PARTY 2
集団の ▶ WIDE 1
周知の ▶ FAMOUS
集中 ▶ ATTENTION
集中する ▶ FOCUS
集中的な ▶ INTENSE
集中力 ▶ ATTENTION
重点 ▶ POINT, PRIORITY
重点を置く ▶ STRESS
習得する ▶ LEARN
重篤の ▶ SERIOUS 1
重度の ▶ SERIOUS 1
自由な ▶ FREE 形 1, 3
柔軟性のない ▶ STRICT
柔軟な ▶ FLEXIBLE 1, SOFT
自由にする ▶ RELEASE
収入 ▶ INCOME, MONEY 1, REVENUE
住人 ▶ RESIDENT
10年間 ▶ PERIOD
私有の ▶ OWN
収納する ▶ KEEP 1

自由の身の ▶ FREE 形 1
宗派主義 ▶ RACISM
修復する ▶ CORRECT, REPAIR, RESOLVE
十分な ▶ ADEQUATE, FINE
周辺的な ▶ MINOR
自由放任の ▶ TOLERANT
自由奔放な ▶ WILD
住民 ▶ PEOPLE, RESIDENT
周遊旅行 ▶ TRIP
重要視 ▶ PRIORITY
収容する ▶ JAIL
重要性 ▶ IMPORTANCE, VALUE
重要でない
　▶ IRRELEVANT, MINOR
重要な ▶ FAMOUS, FUNDAMENTAL, IMPORTANT, POWERFUL
重要な地位
　▶ IMPORTANCE
従来型の ▶ TRADITIONAL
従来の ▶ TRADITIONAL
修理する ▶ REPAIR
終了 ▶ END 名
終了する ▶ END 動, FINISH
修了する ▶ FINISH
主演させる ▶ FEATURE 動
主演する ▶ FEATURE 動
主義 ▶ ATTITUDE, PRINCIPLE 1, VALUES
授業 ▶ CLASS 1, 2
授業料 ▶ RATE
祝賀会 ▶ EVENT 2
熟視する ▶ LOOK 動 1
縮尺 ▶ RATIO
淑女 ▶ WOMAN
縮小する ▶ CUT 1, SHRINK
宿題 ▶ ASSIGNMENT
熟達 ▶ SKILL 2
熟達した ▶ IMPRESSIVE
熟知した ▶ USED TO STH
祝典 ▶ EVENT 2
熟年の ▶ OLD 2
宿泊客 ▶ TENANT
祝福する ▶ PRAISE 動
宿命 ▶ LUCK
縮約した ▶ SHORT 3
熟慮 ▶ CONSIDERATION
熟練 ▶ SKILL 2
熟練した ▶ EXPERIENCED, GOOD 4, IMPRESSIVE
主権 ▶ INDEPENDENCE
取材 ▶ INTERVIEW 1
主催者 ▶ ORGANIZER, SPONSOR

日本語類語一覧

- 主催する ► HAVE 4, ORGANIZE
- 主宰する ► LEAD
- 趣旨 ► MESSAGE
- 種々雑多な ► DIVERSE
- 手術 ► TREATMENT
- 手術不能の ► FATAL
- 首席 ► PEAK
- 首席の ► TOP
- 主題 ► MESSAGE, SUBJECT
- 受諾する ► AGREE
- 手段 ► TOOL, WAY 2
- 首長 ► LEADER 1, OFFICIAL 名
- 主張 ► VIEW 1
- 主張する ► CLAIM, SAY 2
- 術 ► SKILL 1, 2
- 出演する ► FEATURE 動, PLAY 2
- 出現 ► ARRIVAL
- 術語 ► LANGUAGE
- 熟考 ► CONSIDERATION
- 熟考する ► CONSIDER
- 出資者 ► SPONSOR
- 出場者 ► CANDIDATE, PARTICIPANT
- 出身 ► FAMILY 3
- 出世 ► PROGRESS
- 出生 ► FAMILY 3
- 出席簿 ► LIST 名
- 十中八九 ► PROBABLY
- 出発 ► START 名
- 出発する ► GO 1, LEAVE 1
- 出発点 ► SOURCE
- 出版する ► PUBLISH 2
- 出版物 ► BOOK
- 出費 ► COSTS, PRICE
- 出品する ► PRESENT 1
- 首都 ► CITY
- ジュニア ► CHILD
- ジュニアの ► YOUNG
- 首脳部 ► PEAK
- 首尾一貫しない ► VARIABLE
- 守備隊 ► GUARD
- 首謀者 ► GENIUS
- 趣味 ► INTEREST 名 2
- 寿命 ► LIFE 1, 2
- 呪文 ► SLOGAN
- 腫瘍 ► TUMOUR
- 需要 ► DEMAND 名
- 主要な ► MAIN
- 授与する ► GIVE 1
- 樹立する ► ESTABLISH
- 主流の ► TRADITIONAL
- 受領する ► GET 2
- 主力商品 ► LEADER 2
- 種類 ► KIND 名
- 手腕 ► SKILL 1
- 順位 ► SERIES
- 瞬間 ► MINUTE, TIME
- 循環させる ► FLOW
- 循環する ► FLOW
- 純潔 ► MORALITY
- 巡査 ► POLICEMAN
- 順序 ► SERIES
- 潤色する ► EXAGGERATE
- 順調な ► VALUABLE 2
- 順応性のある ► FLEXIBLE 1
- 順番 ► OPPORTUNITY, SERIES
- 準備 ► PLANNING
- 準備金 ► FUND 名
- 準備をする ► INVESTIGATE, PREPARE 1, 2
- 巡礼者 ► TOURIST
- 巡礼の旅 ► TRIP
- 使用 ► USE 名
- 省 ► DEPARTMENT
- 賞 ► AWARD
- 掌握する ► INVADE
- 上位の ► TOP
- 証印 ► LOGO
- 上院議員 ► POLITICIAN
- 上映する ► PRESENT 1
- 上演 ► PERFORMANCE, PLAY 名
- 上演する ► PLAY 動 2, PRESENT 1
- 紹介 ► MEETING 2
- 傷害 ► INJURY
- 障害 ► OBSTACLE, PROBLEM
- 生涯 ► LIFE 2
- 渉外係 ► NEGOTIATOR
- 紹介する ► PRESENT 4
- 障碍のある ► DISABLED
- 障害物 ► BARRIER
- 昇格 ► PROGRESS
- 召喚する ► ACCUSE
- 試用期間 ► TEST 名 1
- 正気ではない ► MAD
- 小球 ► DROP
- 昇給 ► INCREASE 名
- 商業 ► TRADE
- 状況 ► CONTEXT, SITUATION
- 商業的な ► SUCCESSFUL 2
- 商業の ► ECONOMIC
- 消極的な ► NEGATIVE
- 消去する ► DELETE
- 常軌を逸した ► UNUSUAL
- 賞金 ► AWARD
- 笑劇 ► PLAY 名
- 衝撃 ► SHOCK 名
- 衝撃を与える ► SHAKE 2
- 条件 ► CONDITION, SITUATION
- 証拠 ► CASE, EVIDENCE
- 称号 ► AWARD
- 条項 ► CONDITION
- 商工名鑑 ► LIST 名
- 証拠となる ► CONFIRM 1
- 証拠のある ► FINAL
- 証拠のない ► IRRATIONAL
- 証拠文書 ► CERTIFICATE
- 詳細な ► DETAILED
- 小冊子 ► LEAFLET
- 賞賛, 称賛 ► ADMIRATION, PRAISE 名, STATUS
- 賞賛した ► GOOD 6
- 賞賛すべき ► WORTHY
- 賞賛[称賛]する ► PRAISE 動, RESPECT 動
- 上司 ► MANAGER
- 情事 ► RELATIONSHIP 2
- 正直 ► INTEGRITY
- 正直な ► HONEST, RESPECTABLE
- 生じさせる ► CAUSE
- 消失する ► DISAPPEAR
- 上質の ► GOOD 1
- 乗車券 ► LICENCE
- 招集する ► HAVE 4
- 常習的な ► FREQUENT
- 詳述する ► EXAMINE, EXPLAIN 1, LIST 動
- 証書 ► CERTIFICATE, DOCUMENT
- 少女 ► CHILD
- 症状 ► PATIENT, SIGN 1
- 上昇 ► INCREASE 名
- 上昇させる ► INCREASE 動
- 上昇する ► RISE
- 生じる ► APPEAR, FOLLOW 2, PROVIDE
- 昇進 ► PROGRESS
- 小数 ► FIGURE
- じょうずな ► GOOD 4
- 使用する ► USE 動 1
- 試用する ► TEST 動 1
- 情勢 ► ATMOSPHERE, SITUATION
- 小説 ► BOOK
- 小説家 ► WRITER
- 小説の ► FICTIONAL
- 常設の ► PERMANENT
- 上訴 ► CASE
- 肖像画 ► PICTURE
- 上層部 ► AUTHORITIES
- 状態 ► POSITION, SITUATION, STATE
- 上体を傾ける ► LEAN
- 承諾 ► APPROVAL, PERMISSION
- 承諾する ► IN FAVOUR
- 上達 ► PROGRESS
- 上達する ► IMPROVE 2
- 冗談 ► ENTERTAINMENT, JOKE
- 承知して ► AWARE
- 承知する ► CONCLUDE
- 使用中で ► ACTIVE
- 省庁 ► SERVICE
- 象徴 ► LOGO, SIGN 1
- 象徴する ► REPRESENT 2
- 象徴的な ► TYPICAL
- 象徴となる ► TYPICAL
- 冗長な ► BORING
- 小テスト ► TEST 名 2
- 小テストをする ► TEST 動 2
- 商店街 ► MARKET 2
- 焦点となる ► FEATURE 動
- 焦点を当てる ► FOCUS
- 衝動 ► DESIRE
- 衝動的な ► SPONTANEOUS
- 譲渡する ► GIVE 1
- 衝突 ► CONFLICT 名, FIGHT 名, MEETING 2
- 衝突事故 ► ACCIDENT
- 衝突する ► ARGUE, CONFLICT 動, CRASH, FIGHT 動, HIT 1
- 情にもろい ► SENSITIVE 1
- 商人 ► DEALER
- 証人 ► WITNESS
- 承認 ► APPROVAL
- 承認する ► AGREE, ALLOW, APPROVE
- 情熱的な ► INTENSE
- 少年 ► CHILD, GIRL
- 少年少女の ► YOUNG
- 私用の ► OWN
- 賞杯 ► AWARD
- 商売 ► TRADE
- 商売する ► SELL 2
- 消費者 ► CUSTOMER
- 消費者団体 ► INSPECTOR
- 消費する ► USE 動 2
- 商標 ► LOGO
- 商品 ► PRODUCT

賞品 ▶ AWARD
上品さ ▶ RESPECT 名, STYLE
上品な ▶ ELEGANT, SOPHISTICATED
勝負 ▶ GAME
承服できない ▶ UNACCEPTABLE
丈夫な ▶ WELL
性分 ▶ PERSONALITY
障壁 ▶ OBSTACLE
小片 ▶ BIT, FRAGMENT
譲歩 ▶ COMPROMISE
情報 ▶ INFORMATION, REPORT 2
情報機関 ▶ INFORMATION
情報に基づいた ▶ INFORMED
情報を持っている ▶ INFORMED
譲歩する ▶ GIVE WAY
乗務員 ▶ TEAM 1
証明された ▶ FINAL
証明書 ▶ CERTIFICATE, ENDORSEMENT
証明する ▶ CONFIRM 1, 2, FIND 3, SHOW 1
消滅させる ▶ DESTROY
消耗させる ▶ USE 動 2
条約 ▶ CONTRACT
剰余 ▶ PROFIT
情欲 ▶ LOVE 名 1
将来性 ▶ POTENTIAL
将来の ▶ NEXT
勝利 ▶ VICTORY
上陸する ▶ ARRIVE
勝利した ▶ SUCCESSFUL 1
勝利する ▶ WIN
上流階級 ▶ ELITE
上流社会 ▶ ELITE
蒸留酒 ▶ DRINK 名
少量 ▶ BIT
使用料 ▶ RATE
小旅行 ▶ TRIP
症例 ▶ PATIENT
条例 ▶ RULE 名
奨励する ▶ RECOMMEND 1
小論文 ▶ PAPER
錠を下ろす ▶ CLOSE 動
ショー ▶ PERFORMANCE
ジョーク ▶ JOKE
ショービジネス ▶ DRAMA
除外する ▶ EXCLUDE 1, PREVENT
所感 ▶ VIEW 1
書簡 ▶ LETTER

初期 ▶ START 名
初期の ▶ FIRST
初期費用 ▶ COSTS
除去する ▶ REMOVE
ジョギングする ▶ RUN 1
職 ▶ JOB
職員 ▶ STAFF, WORKER 1, 2
職業 ▶ WORK 名 1
食事 ▶ FOOD
職長 ▶ MANAGER
職人 ▶ MAKER
私欲のない ▶ OBJECTIVE
食品 ▶ FOOD
植民地 ▶ TERRITORY
職務 ▶ JOB, RESPONSIBILITY, TASK
職務上の ▶ OFFICIAL 形
食糧 ▶ FOOD
食料品 ▶ FOOD
処刑する ▶ KILL
所見 ▶ STATEMENT, VIEW 1
助言 ▶ ADVICE
助言者 ▶ ADVISER
助言を求める ▶ ASK 1
徐行の ▶ SLOW
所在地 ▶ HOME
如才ない ▶ INTELLIGENT
女子 ▶ WOMAN
所持金 ▶ FUND 名
所持する ▶ HAVE 1
所持品 ▶ THING 2
序章 ▶ INTRODUCTION
徐々に ▶ SLOW
初心者 ▶ BEGINNER
女性 ▶ WOMAN
助成金 ▶ INVESTMENT
助成金を支給する ▶ FUND 動
書籍 ▶ BOOK
所蔵する ▶ HAVE 1
所蔵品 ▶ THING 2
所帯 ▶ FAMILY 1
除隊 ▶ UNEMPLOYMENT
除隊させる ▶ FIRE
処置 ▶ TREATMENT
助長する ▶ HELP 動 2
ショッキングな ▶ OUTRAGEOUS
ショック ▶ SHOCK 名
ショックを与える ▶ OFFEND, SHOCK 動
職権 ▶ RIGHT 名
職権乱用 ▶ CRIME 1
しょっちゅう ▶ OFTEN
ショッピングする ▶ BUY

ショッピングセンター ▶ MARKET 2
ショッピングモール ▶ MARKET 2
所得 ▶ INCOME
序文 ▶ INTRODUCTION
処分する ▶ REMOVE
処方箋 ▶ DRUG 2
処方薬 ▶ DRUG 2
初歩的な ▶ FUNDAMENTAL
署名する ▶ WRITE
書物 ▶ BOOK
女優 ▶ ACTOR
所有権 ▶ RIGHT 名
所有する ▶ HAVE 1
所有地 ▶ LAND 1
所有物 ▶ THING 2
処理する ▶ DEAL WITH SB/STH, REMOVE
助力 ▶ HELP 名
助力する ▶ HELP 動 1
書類 ▶ DOCUMENT
書類仕事 ▶ BUREAUCRACY
しょんぼりした ▶ DEPRESSED
知らされている ▶ INFORMED
じらす ▶ FLIRT
知らず知らずの ▶ UNCONSCIOUS
知らせ ▶ INFORMATION
知らせる ▶ CONVEY, TELL 1
知らない ▶ IGNORANT, STRANGE 2
シラバス ▶ CLASS 1
調べる ▶ INVESTIGATE, LOOK 動 1, 2
知り合い ▶ FRIEND
知り合いになる ▶ MEET 3
尻込みする ▶ HESITATE
じりじりした ▶ RESTLESS
退く ▶ LEAVE 2
自立 ▶ FREEDOM, INDEPENDENCE
自立した ▶ CONFIDENT
自立する ▶ TAKE CARE OF YOURSELF
資料 ▶ INFORMATION
資力 ▶ MONEY 1
思慮のない ▶ INSENSITIVE
思慮深い ▶ WISE
知る ▶ FIND 1
シルエット ▶ SHAPE

しるし ▶ SIGN 1, SUGGESTION
事例 ▶ EXAMPLE 1
じれったい ▶ RESTLESS
ジレンマ ▶ MESS 2
じろじろ見る ▶ STARE
(…を)し忘れる ▶ FAIL 1
死をもたらす ▶ FATAL
親愛の情 ▶ LOVE 名 2
神意 ▶ LUCK
人員 ▶ STAFF
陣営 ▶ PARTY 1
真価 ▶ VALUE
侵害 ▶ ATTACK 名 1
侵害する ▶ BREAK 3
人格 ▶ PERSONALITY
進化する ▶ TURN 2
震撼させる ▶ SHOCK 動
審議会 ▶ COMMITTEE
辛苦 ▶ TROUBLE 2
神経過敏な ▶ SENSITIVE 3
神経質な ▶ SENSITIVE 3
真剣な ▶ INTENSE, SERIOUS 2
侵攻 ▶ ATTACK 名 1
振興 ▶ PROGRESS
親交 ▶ FRIENDSHIP
信号 ▶ SIGNAL
侵攻する ▶ INVADE
新興の ▶ YOUNG
人工の ▶ ARTIFICIAL
進行方向 ▶ WAY 3
深刻さ ▶ IMPORTANCE
深刻な ▶ SERIOUS 1
審査 ▶ RESEARCH
人材 ▶ STAFF
審査員 ▶ JUDGE 名
審査する ▶ JUDGE 動
診察 ▶ INSPECTION, INTERVIEW 1
診察する ▶ CHECK 1
新参の ▶ NEW 3
信じがたい ▶ INCREDIBLE, UNLIKELY 2
シンジケート ▶ GROUP 3
真実 ▶ FACT
真実の ▶ TRUE
真実味のない ▶ UNLIKELY 2
紳士的な ▶ POLITE
真摯な ▶ DEEP 1
信じない ▶ SUSPECT
信じやすい ▶ NAIVE
人種 ▶ PEOPLE
伸縮性のある ▶ FLEXIBLE 2

じんしゅさべつ → すねること

人種差別 ▶ RACISM
人種の ▶ CULTURAL
心象 ▶ IDEA 1
信条 ▶ PRINCIPLE 1, VALUES
信じられない ▶ AMAZING, INCREDIBLE
信じられる ▶ POSSIBLE 2
信じる ▶ TRUST
信じること ▶ FAITH
新人 ▶ BEGINNER, RECRUIT
心酔 ▶ LOVE 名 1
心酔する ▶ LOVE 動
浸水する ▶ FLOOD 動
人生 ▶ LIFE 2, 3
人生観 ▶ ATTITUDE, VALUES
申請する ▶ ASK 2
親戚 ▶ FAMILY 2
親切な ▶ FRIENDLY 1, KIND 形, POLITE
親善 ▶ FRIENDSHIP
真相 ▶ FACT
人造の ▶ ARTIFICIAL
親族 ▶ FAMILY 2
迅速な ▶ FAST, IMMEDIATE, QUICK
死んだ ▶ DEAD
甚大な ▶ HUGE, TERRIBLE 3
信託機関 ▶ CHARITY
診断する ▶ JUDGE 動
慎重さ ▶ TACT
慎重な ▶ WISE
心痛 ▶ DISTRESS
進歩 ▶ PROGRESS
神殿 ▶ CHURCH
進展する ▶ DEVELOP 1
親展の ▶ SECRET
神童 ▶ GENIUS
振動する ▶ SHAKE 2
陣頭に立つ ▶ LEAD
しんとした ▶ QUIET 1
進入 ▶ ATTACK 名 1
信念 ▶ FAITH, IDEA 1, VIEW 1
真の ▶ REAL
心配 ▶ CONCERN, FEAR, SYMPATHY
心配させる ▶ FRIGHTEN, WORRY
心配して ▶ AFRAID
心配する ▶ CARE
心配な ▶ STRESSFUL, WORRYING

審判員 ▶ JUDGE 名
新品同様の ▶ PERFECT
新品の ▶ NEW 2
人物 ▶ PERSON
新兵 ▶ RECRUIT
進歩 ▶ PROGRESS
信望 ▶ REPUTATION, STATUS
信望がある ▶ GREAT 2
辛抱する ▶ PERSIST, STAND 2
辛抱強さ ▶ PATIENCE
親睦 ▶ FRIENDSHIP
進歩する ▶ DEVELOP 1, IMPROVE 2
進歩的な ▶ RADICAL
シンボル ▶ SIGN 1
新米 ▶ BEGINNER
親密さ ▶ FRIENDSHIP
親身の ▶ SENSITIVE 1
人命 ▶ LIFE 1
審問 ▶ CASE
尋問 ▶ INTERVIEW 1
尋問する ▶ QUESTION 動
深夜 ▶ NIGHT 1
親友 ▶ FRIEND
信用 ▶ FAITH
陣容 ▶ TEAM 2
信用貸し ▶ LOAN
信用詐欺 ▶ CONSPIRACY, FRAUD 2
信用しない ▶ SUSPECT
信用証明書 ▶ CERTIFICATE
信用する ▶ TRUST
信用できる ▶ CERTAIN, POSSIBLE 2
信頼 ▶ FAITH
信頼する ▶ TRUST
信頼できる ▶ CERTAIN, DEEP 1, POSSIBLE 2, RELIABLE 1, 2
辛辣な ▶ SHREWD
人力 ▶ STAFF
心理的な ▶ INTELLECTUAL 1
侵略 ▶ ATTACK 名 1
侵略する ▶ INVADE
親類 ▶ FAMILY 2
人類 ▶ MAN 2
進路 ▶ WAY 3
針路 ▶ WAY 3

す

水域 ▶ SEA

随意の ▶ VOLUNTARY 1
吸いこむ ▶ DRINK 動
水準 ▶ QUALITY
水蒸気 ▶ MOISTURE
推奨する ▶ RECOMMEND 1
推薦 ▶ ENDORSEMENT
推薦状 ▶ ENDORSEMENT
推薦する ▶ RECOMMEND 2
推測 ▶ SPECULATION
推測する ▶ CONCLUDE, ESTIMATE 動, SAY 3
衰退 ▶ REDUCTION
衰退する ▶ WORSEN
推断する ▶ CONCLUDE
スイッチ ▶ BUTTON 1
スイッチを入れる
　▶ TURN STH ON
スイッチを切る
　▶ TURN STH OFF
推定 ▶ SPECULATION
推定する ▶ PREDICT, SAY 3
随筆 ▶ PAPER
水分 ▶ MOISTURE
ずいぶん ▶ QUITE 1, VERY 副
水平 ▶ FLAT
推量 ▶ SPECULATION
推論 ▶ CONCLUSION
推論する ▶ CONCLUDE
推論的な ▶ SUPPOSED
数字 ▶ FIGURE
ずうずうしい ▶ RUDE
ずうずうしく…する
　▶ DARE
趨勢 ▶ TREND
数値 ▶ FIGURE
スーパースター ▶ STAR
崇拝者 ▶ FAN
崇拝する ▶ LOVE 動
数量 ▶ FIGURE, NUMBER
据える ▶ PUT
姿形 ▶ SHAPE
姿を現す ▶ APPEAR
過ぎ去った ▶ PREVIOUS
過ぎ去ったばかりの
　▶ LAST 2
好きである ▶ LIKE 動, LOVE 動
好きであること
　▶ LOVE 名 2
透き通った ▶ CLEAR 形 3
すき間 ▶ HOLE 1
救う ▶ SAVE 1
少ない ▶ INADEQUATE, SCARCE, SMALL

すぐの ▶ IMMEDIATE
スクラップ ▶ WASTE
スクリーンテスト
　▶ INTERVIEW 2
優れた ▶ EXCELLENT, GOOD 1, WORTHY
すくんで ▶ AFRAID
スケジュール ▶ SCHEDULE
スケッチ ▶ PICTURE
すごい ▶ AMAZING, GREAT 1
すごく ▶ QUITE 2, VERY 副
すさまじい
　▶ TERRIBLE 2, 3
すじ ▶ MARK
筋 ▶ LOGIC, STORY
筋の通った ▶ GOOD 3, RATIONAL
筋の通らない
　▶ IRRATIONAL
筋道 ▶ MESSAGE
涼しい ▶ COLD 1
涼しげな ▶ PALE
進む ▶ GO 1, 2, WALK 1
勧める ▶ RECOMMEND 1
薦める ▶ RECOMMEND 2
すすり泣く ▶ CRY
進んだ ▶ TOLERANT
進んでいる
　▶ FASHIONABLE
スター ▶ STAR
スタート ▶ OPPORTUNITY, START 名
スターの座 ▶ FAME
スタイル ▶ FASHION
スタッフ ▶ STAFF
廃れる ▶ DISAPPEAR
スタンス ▶ ATTITUDE
スタント ▶ ACTION
すっかり ▶ VERY 副
すっきりとした ▶ NEAT
すっぱい ▶ BITTER
すてきな ▶ GREAT 1, NICE 2, SWEET, WONDERFUL
ステップ ▶ STAGE
捨てる ▶ REMOVE, STOP
ストーカー行為をする
　▶ FOLLOW 1
ストレス ▶ PRESSURE 1
ストレスの多い
　▶ STRESSFUL
砂煙 ▶ SOIL
砂浜 ▶ COAST
すねた ▶ IRRITABLE
すねること ▶ TEMPER

ずのう → ぜっきょうする

日本語類語一覧

頭脳 ▶ INTELLIGENCE
素早い ▶ FAST, QUICK
素晴らしい ▶ EXCELLENT, GOOD 1, GREAT 1, NICE 2, REMARKABLE, WONDERFUL, WORTHY
図版 ▶ PICTURE
スピーチ ▶ SPEECH
スピードアップする ▶ ACCELERATE
ずぶ濡れにする ▶ SOAK
スペアの ▶ EXCESS
すべての ▶ WHOLE
スポーツ ▶ SPORT
スポンサー ▶ SPONSOR
スポンサーになる ▶ FUND 動
済ます ▶ FINISH
すみか ▶ SHELTER
速やかな ▶ QUICK
住む ▶ LIVE
図面 ▶ PLAN 2
すらりとした ▶ THIN
すり ▶ THIEF
すり傷 ▶ INJURY
すり減る ▶ SCRATCH
すりむく ▶ SCRATCH
スリムな ▶ THIN
スリリングな ▶ EXCITING
スリル ▶ EXCITEMENT
する ▶ DO
ずるそうな ▶ SUSPICIOUS 2
…するようになる ▶ FIND 1
すれる ▶ SCRATCH
スローガン ▶ SLOGAN
座る ▶ SIT
ずんぐりした ▶ SHORT 2
寸劇 ▶ PLAY 名
澄んだ ▶ CLEAR 形 3

せ

せい ▶ FAULT
税 ▶ TAX
制圧する ▶ INVADE
聖域 ▶ SHELTER
精鋭の ▶ TOP
声援する ▶ SHOUT
成果 ▶ RESULT
性格 ▶ PERSONALITY
正確な ▶ EXACT, VERY 形
生活 ▶ LIFE 3
生活保護を受けて ▶ UNEMPLOYED

生活様式 ▶ LIFE 3
成果のない ▶ USELESS
請願する ▶ ASK 2
世紀 ▶ PERIOD
正義 ▶ JUSTICE, MORALITY
生気に満ちた ▶ LIVELY
請求 ▶ REQUEST
請求権 ▶ RIGHT 名
請求書 ▶ BILL
請求する ▶ CHARGE 動
性急な ▶ QUICK, RECKLESS
制御する ▶ OPERATE
税金 ▶ TAX
生計を立てる ▶ WORK 動 1
清潔な ▶ CLEAN 形
政権 ▶ GOVERNMENT 1
制限 ▶ LIMIT 1
制限された ▶ LIMITED 1, 2
性向 ▶ DESIRE, TENDENCY
成功した ▶ SUCCESSFUL 1, 2
成功者 ▶ MIRACLE
成功する ▶ ACHIEVE, DO WELL, SUCCEED, WIN
精巧な ▶ BEAUTIFUL 2, COMPLEX
精査 ▶ RESEARCH
制裁 ▶ BAN 名
制作 ▶ PERFORMANCE
政策 ▶ PLAN 1
製作 ▶ PRODUCTION
製作者 ▶ MAKER
制作する ▶ PLAY 動 2
精査する ▶ CHECK 1
性差別 ▶ RACISM
清算 ▶ PAYMENT
生産 ▶ PRODUCTION
生産者 ▶ MAKER
生産する ▶ MANUFACTURE
生産性 ▶ OUTPUT
生産性のない ▶ INEFFECTIVE
生産高 ▶ OUTPUT
生産的な ▶ PRODUCTIVE
生産物 ▶ PRODUCT
生産量 ▶ OUTPUT
生産力 ▶ OUTPUT
静止 ▶ PAUSE
政治家 ▶ POLITICIAN
正式の ▶ OFFICIAL 形
正式用の ▶ FORMAL
静止した ▶ STEADY, STILL
性質 ▶ ATMOSPHERE, NATURE 1

誠実 ▶ INTEGRITY
誠実な ▶ DEEP 1, RELIABLE 1
静寂 ▶ SILENCE
脆弱な ▶ VULNERABLE
税収 ▶ REVENUE
成熟した ▶ ADULT
清純 ▶ MORALITY
青春時代 ▶ CHILDHOOD
正常な ▶ STEADY
精神 ▶ ATMOSPHERE, MIND
精神的な ▶ INTELLECTUAL 1
成人の ▶ ADULT
整然とした ▶ NEAT
製造 ▶ PRODUCTION
製造機械 ▶ MAKER
製造業 ▶ PRODUCTION
製造業者 ▶ MAKER
製造所 ▶ FACTORY
正装する ▶ WEAR
清掃する ▶ CLEAN 動, TIDY
製造する ▶ MANUFACTURE
生息する ▶ LIVE
勢ぞろい ▶ RANGE 1
生存 ▶ LIFE 1
政体 ▶ GOVERNMENT 1
生態系 ▶ NATURE 2
盛大な ▶ MAGNIFICENT
成長 ▶ PROGRESS
精通 ▶ KNOWLEDGE
精通した ▶ USED TO STH
制定する ▶ RULE 動 2
性的関係 ▶ RELATIONSHIP 2
制度 ▶ PLAN 1, SYSTEM
政党 ▶ PARTY 1
正当化する ▶ EXPLAIN 2
正当性 ▶ MORALITY
正統的な ▶ TRADITIONAL
正当な ▶ GOOD 3, RIGHT 形 2
正当な理由 ▶ LOGIC
生得の ▶ NATURAL
整頓された ▶ NEAT
整頓する ▶ ARRANGE, TIDY
青年 ▶ GIRL
青年期の ▶ YOUNG
青年時代 ▶ CHILDHOOD
制覇する ▶ SUCCEED
正反対 ▶ OPPOSITE 名
整備する ▶ REPAIR
製品 ▶ PRODUCT
政府 ▶ GOVERNMENT 1

征服する ▶ INVADE
生物 ▶ NATURE 2
製法 ▶ WAY 2
精密な ▶ DETAILED, EXACT
声明 ▶ STATEMENT
生命 ▶ LIFE 1
生命のある ▶ ALIVE
制約 ▶ LIMIT 1
誓約 ▶ PROMISE 名
誓約する ▶ PROMISE 動
静養地 ▶ REFUGE
性欲 ▶ LOVE 名 1
生来の ▶ NATURAL
整理 ▶ EFFICIENCY
整理する ▶ ARRANGE, CLASSIFY, TIDY
成立させる ▶ FINISH
勢力 ▶ FORCE 名
精力 ▶ EFFORT
精力的な ▶ ENERGETIC
整列させる ▶ ARRANGE
清廉潔白 ▶ INTEGRITY
清廉な ▶ GOOD 5
世界観 ▶ ATTITUDE
世界主義的な ▶ INTERNATIONAL
世界的規模の ▶ INTERNATIONAL
世界的な ▶ INTERNATIONAL
急かす ▶ HURRY
せき立てる ▶ PRESS 2
石炭 ▶ OIL
責任 ▶ FAULT, RESPONSIBILITY
責任がある ▶ DEAL WITH SB/STH, GUILTY, REGULATE
責任者 ▶ MANAGER
咳払いをする ▶ COUGH
赤貧 ▶ POVERTY
責務 ▶ RESPONSIBILITY
赤面する ▶ FLUSH
石油 ▶ OIL
咳をする ▶ COUGH
セクシーな ▶ BEAUTIFUL 1
世間知らず ▶ IGNORANCE
世間知らずの ▶ NAIVE
…せずにはいられない ▶ URGENT
世帯 ▶ FAMILY 1
世代 ▶ PERIOD
説 ▶ THEORY 2
説教 ▶ SPEECH
絶叫する ▶ SCREAM, SHOUT

せっきょうをする → そうぞうせい

日本語類語一覧

説教をする ▶ SCOLD
積極的な ▶ BUSY 1
接近 ▶ ARRIVAL
接近する ▶ COME 1
接近方法 ▶ ACCESS
設計 ▶ DESIGN 名, DEVELOPMENT
設計図 ▶ DEVELOPMENT, PLAN 2
設計する ▶ DESIGN 動 1
絶好の ▶ WONDERFUL
接触 ▶ COMMUNICATION
雪辱 ▶ REVENGE
接戦の ▶ CLOSE 形
絶大な ▶ COMPLETE
設置する ▶ BUILD
接着する ▶ ATTACH
絶頂 ▶ PEAK
節度 ▶ LIMIT 1
セット ▶ EQUIPMENT
窃盗 ▶ THEFT
説得する ▶ PERSUADE
説得力 ▶ FAITH, LOGIC
説得力のある
　▶ AGGRESSIVE 2, CONVINCING
説得力のない
　▶ UNLIKELY 2
刹那 ▶ TIME
切迫した ▶ URGENT
せっぱ詰まった ▶ BUSY 1
設備 ▶ FACILITIES
切望した ▶ EAGER
説明する ▶ DESCRIBE, EXPLAIN 1, PROPOSE
説明的な ▶ DESCRIPTIVE
絶滅する ▶ DISAPPEAR
絶滅の危機に瀕した
　▶ VULNERABLE
節約する ▶ SAVE 2
摂理 ▶ LUCK
設立する ▶ ESTABLISH
是認 ▶ PRAISE 名
是認する ▶ APPROVE, PRAISE 動
背の低い ▶ SHORT 2
狭まる ▶ SHRINK
狭い ▶ LIMITED 1, NARROW, SMALL
迫る ▶ COME 2, PRESS 2
ゼミ ▶ CLASS 2
攻め落とす ▶ INVADE
責めさいなむ ▶ HURT 1
責める ▶ BLAME, SCOLD
セレブ ▶ STAR

世話をする
　▶ LOOK AFTER SB
背を向ける ▶ LEAVE 4
善 ▶ MORALITY
全員の ▶ WHOLE
先鋭的な ▶ RADICAL
前衛的な
　▶ EXPERIMENTAL
線画 ▶ PICTURE
旋回する ▶ SPIN, TURN 1
選挙 ▶ ELECTION
先駆者 ▶ LEADER 2
先駆者になる
　▶ DEVELOP 2
全景 ▶ VIEW 2
宣言 ▶ STATEMENT
宣言する ▶ DECLARE, RULE 動 2
先見の明 ▶ EXPECTATION, INSPIRATION
善行 ▶ MORALITY
選考会 ▶ INTERVIEW 2
前後関係 ▶ CONTEXT
宣告する ▶ DECLARE
全国的な ▶ NATIONAL
潜在識 ▶ MIND
潜在意識下の
　▶ UNCONSCIOUS
潜在的な ▶ LIKELY
潜在能力 ▶ POTENTIAL
繊細な ▶ FRAGILE, SENSITIVE 1, 3
詮索する ▶ INVESTIGATE
漸次の ▶ SLOW
選手 ▶ PARTICIPANT
選手権 ▶ AWARD
戦術 ▶ TACTIC
選出する ▶ APPOINT
染色する ▶ PAINT
前進する ▶ GO 1
全身全霊の ▶ DEEP 1
先進の ▶ MODERN
先陣を切る ▶ LEAD
センス ▶ UNDERSTANDING
センスの良さ ▶ STYLE
先生 ▶ TEACHER
宣誓 ▶ PROMISE 名
全盛期 ▶ PEAK
全盛期に ▶ LIFE 2
専制君主 ▶ DICTATOR
専制国家 ▶ REPRESSION
宣誓する ▶ PROMISE 動
専制政治 ▶ REPRESSION
専制の ▶ REPRESSIVE
センセーショナルな
　▶ AMAZING

全然 ▶ QUITE 2
戦争 ▶ WAR
全体主義の ▶ REPRESSIVE
全体の ▶ WHOLE
選択 ▶ CHOICE 1, TASTE
選択肢 ▶ OPTION, RANGE 1
選択する ▶ CHOOSE, DECIDE
選択の ▶ VOLUNTARY 1
選択の自由 ▶ OPTION
前兆 ▶ SIGN 1
選定 ▶ CHOICE 1
前提 ▶ SPECULATION, THEORY 2
前提とする ▶ SAY 3
宣伝 ▶ ADVERTISEMENT
宣伝する ▶ ADVERTISE, PUBLISH 1
先天的な ▶ NATURAL
宣伝文 ▶ ADVERTISEMENT
宣伝文句 ▶ SLOGAN
戦闘 ▶ WAR
先導 ▶ INFLUENCE 名
先頭者 ▶ LEADER 2
先導する ▶ LEAD, TAKE 2
先頭に立つ ▶ LEAD
前途有望な ▶ PROMISING
選任 ▶ CHOICE 1
専念した ▶ RELIABLE 1
全部の ▶ WHOLE
前文 ▶ INTRODUCTION
羨望 ▶ JEALOUSY
全滅させる ▶ DESTROY
全面的な ▶ COMPLETE, DETAILED, WIDE 1
全面的に ▶ QUITE 2
専門家 ▶ ANALYST, EXPERT
専門職 ▶ WORK 名 1
専門知識 ▶ SKILL 2
専門用語 ▶ LANGUAGE
占有者 ▶ TENANT
占有する ▶ LIVE
専用の ▶ LIMITED 2, OWN, UNIQUE
戦慄 ▶ SHOCK 名
戦略 ▶ PLAN 1, TACTIC
善良 ▶ MORALITY
占領する ▶ INVADE
善良な ▶ GOOD 5
先例 ▶ INFLUENCE 名
洗練された
　▶ INTELLECTUAL 2, SOPHISTICATED
洗練する ▶ IMPROVE 1

栓を開ける
　▶ TURN STH ON
栓を締める
　▶ TURN STH OFF

そ

層 ▶ CATEGORY, FLOOR
像 ▶ PICTURE
創案 ▶ DEVELOPMENT
創意 ▶ INSPIRATION
相違 ▶ DIFFERENCE
憎悪 ▶ HATRED, TENSION
相応の ▶ EQUIVALENT
憎悪する ▶ HATE
増加 ▶ INCREASE 名
増加させる ▶ INCREASE 動
増加する ▶ RISE
相関関係 ▶ RELATION
送還する ▶ EXPEL
壮観な ▶ MAGNIFICENT
操業 ▶ TRADE
遭遇 ▶ MEETING 2
遭遇する ▶ FIND 2, HAVE 3, MEET 2
総計 ▶ ESTIMATE 名
造詣 ▶ UNDERSTANDING
総計の ▶ WHOLE
相互依存 ▶ RELATION
奏功する ▶ WIN
相互関係 ▶ RELATION
相互に関係する
　▶ MATCH 1
荘厳な ▶ MAGNIFICENT
捜査 ▶ INVESTIGATION
捜索 ▶ SEARCH
捜索する ▶ LOOK 動 2
創作的な ▶ CREATIVE
創作物 ▶ DEVELOPMENT
捜査する ▶ INVESTIGATE
操作する ▶ OPERATE
掃除する ▶ BRUSH, CLEAN 動
贈収賄 ▶ CORRUPTION
装飾する ▶ DECORATE
装飾物 ▶ DECORATION
増進する ▶ IMPROVE 2
創設する ▶ ESTABLISH
創造 ▶ DEVELOPMENT
想像(力) ▶ IMAGINATION
騒々しい ▶ LOUD, WILD
想像上の ▶ FICTIONAL, SUPPOSED
想像する ▶ IMAGINE
創造する ▶ MAKE 1
創造性 ▶ INSPIRATION

創造的な ▶ CREATIVE
想像できる ▶ POSSIBLE 2
想像もつかない
　▶ IMPOSSIBLE
相対的な ▶ RELATIVE
壮大な ▶ MAGNIFICENT
総体の ▶ COMMON
相談 ▶ INTERVIEW 1
相談する ▶ TALK
装置 ▶ EQUIPMENT, SYSTEM, TOOL
早朝 ▶ NIGHT 1
総長 ▶ LEADER 1
想定 ▶ SPECULATION
想定する ▶ ESTIMATE 動, SAY 3, SUPPOSE
贈呈する ▶ GIVE 1
争点 ▶ ISSUE
騒動 ▶ TROUBLE 1
(…に)相当する
　▶ REPRESENT 1
相当に ▶ VERY 副
造反 ▶ REVOLUTION
造反者 ▶ PROTESTER
装備 ▶ EQUIPMENT
装備させる ▶ EQUIP
送付する ▶ PRESENT 3
聡明な ▶ INTELLIGENT
壮麗な ▶ MAGNIFICENT
挿話 ▶ EVENT 1
疎遠 ▶ DIVISION 2
疎遠である ▶ DIVIDE 2
疎外 ▶ DIVISION 2
疎外感を感じた ▶ LONELY
疎開者 ▶ REFUGEE
疎外する ▶ DIVIDE 2
族 ▶ PARTY 2
即座の ▶ FAST, IMMEDIATE, QUICK
促進 ▶ PROGRESS
属性 ▶ FEATURE 名
俗説 ▶ ILLUSION
ぞくぞくさせる
　▶ EXCITING
ぞくぞくするような
　▶ FRIGHTENING
ぞくっとする ▶ SHAKE 3
測定する ▶ FIND 3
速度 ▶ SPEED
速配便の ▶ FAST
続発 ▶ SERIES
続落する ▶ SLUMP
属領 ▶ TERRITORY
そぐわない ▶ WRONG 2
底 ▶ BOTTOM
損なう ▶ DAMAGE 動, RUIN

素材 ▶ INFORMATION
組織 ▶ ORGANIZATION, SYSTEM, TEAM 1
組織者 ▶ ORGANIZER
阻止する ▶ RESIST
素質 ▶ NATURE 1, SKILL 1
訴訟 ▶ CASE
組成 ▶ STRUCTURE
蘇生させる ▶ CURE
注ぐ ▶ DEVOTE
育てる ▶ BRING SB UP
措置 ▶ ACTION
訴追 ▶ CASE
卒業する ▶ GRADUATE
即興の ▶ SPONTANEOUS
卒業論文 ▶ PAPER
そっくりである ▶ MATCH 1
そっくりの ▶ EQUAL
続行する ▶ CONTINUE 2
率直な ▶ HONEST, PLAIN 2
ぞっとさせる ▶ SHOCK 動
ぞっとする ▶ TERRIBLE 3, UGLY
備え ▶ PLANNING, PRECAUTION
備え付ける ▶ EQUIP
備える ▶ HAVE 2, PREPARE 2
その後の ▶ RELATED
そのとおり ▶ FACT
そびえ立つ ▶ HIGH 2
ソプラノの ▶ HIGH 3
素朴な ▶ AVERAGE
染める ▶ PAINT
そわそわした
　▶ RESTLESS, WORRIED
そわそわする ▶ SHAKE 2
損害 ▶ DAMAGE 名
損害を与える
　▶ DAMAGE 動
尊敬 ▶ ADMIRATION, REPUTATION
尊敬する ▶ RESPECT 動
尊敬に値する ▶ WORTHY
尊厳 ▶ DIGNITY
存在 ▶ LIFE 1
存在感 ▶ CHARM
損失 ▶ DEBT
損傷 ▶ DAMAGE 名
存続 ▶ LIFE 1
存続期間 ▶ LIFE 2
存続する ▶ SURVIVE
尊大 ▶ PRIDE
尊大な ▶ PROUD 2
尊重 ▶ RESPECT 名

尊重する ▶ APPRECIATE, RESPECT 動
損をする ▶ LOSS-MAKING

た

隊 ▶ TEAM 1
体位 ▶ POSITION
大意 ▶ MESSAGE
体育 ▶ SPORT
第一の ▶ FIRST, MAIN
第一級の ▶ EXCELLENT, TOP
大家 ▶ EXPERT
大会 ▶ COMPETITION 1, GAME
大海 ▶ SEA
対外的な ▶ FOREIGN
退学させる ▶ FAIL 3
退学になる ▶ FAIL 3
大家の ▶ IMPRESSIVE
大規模な ▶ WIDE 1
退去させる ▶ EXPEL
大金 ▶ MONEY 3
退屈な ▶ BORING
大群衆 ▶ CROWD
体系 ▶ STRUCTURE
体系的な ▶ EFFICIENT
体験 ▶ LIFE 3
体現 ▶ EXAMPLE 2
体験する ▶ HAVE 3
体現する ▶ REPRESENT 2
対抗意識
　▶ COMPETITION 2
対抗者 ▶ PROTESTER
大国 ▶ COUNTRY 1
滞在 ▶ VISIT 名
題材 ▶ SUBJECT
滞在する ▶ STAY 2
対策 ▶ PRECAUTION
第三者的な ▶ OBJECTIVE
大事故 ▶ CRISIS
体質 ▶ HEALTH
大失敗 ▶ DISASTER
大事な ▶ DEAR
大事にする ▶ APPRECIATE
大衆の ▶ SOCIAL
大衆向けの ▶ WIDE 1
退出する ▶ LEAVE 1
対照 ▶ DIFFERENCE
対象 ▶ TARGET
対照する ▶ COMPARE 1
大勝する ▶ DEFEAT
対照的である
　▶ CONFLICT 動
対象とする ▶ FOCUS

対象にする ▶ INCLUDE
大丈夫で ▶ WELL
大丈夫な ▶ SAFE
退職 ▶ UNEMPLOYMENT
退職する ▶ LEAVE 3
対処法 ▶ SOLUTION
退陣する ▶ LEAVE 3
大好きである ▶ LIKE 動
体制 ▶ STRUCTURE, SYSTEM
大成功 ▶ MIRACLE
大切な ▶ DEAR, IMPORTANT
大切な人 ▶ DARLING
大切に思う ▶ LOVE 動
大切に思う気持ち
　▶ LOVE 名 2
対戦する ▶ COMPETE
体操 ▶ SPORT
代替 ▶ EXCHANGE
大々的な ▶ WIDE 1
大打撃を与える
　▶ DESTROY
対談 ▶ DISCUSSION
大胆 ▶ COURAGE
大胆な ▶ BOLD, BRAVE
大胆不敵な ▶ BOLD
体調 ▶ HEALTH
体調のよい ▶ WELL
体調の悪い ▶ SICK 1
たいてい ▶ USUALLY
態度 ▶ APPEARANCE, ATTITUDE, TENDENCY
台頭 ▶ PROGRESS
タイトル ▶ AWARD
台無しにする ▶ RUIN
大人気の ▶ DEAR
退任する ▶ LEAVE 3
滞納金 ▶ DEBT
大破させる ▶ CRASH
対比する ▶ COMPARE 1
代表する ▶ REPRESENT 2
代表団 ▶ COMMITTEE, PARTY 2
代表的な ▶ TYPICAL
タイプ ▶ KIND 名, PERSON
たいへん ▶ VERY 副
待望 ▶ HOPE 名 1
大望 ▶ HOPE 名 2
逮捕する ▶ KIDNAP
怠慢な ▶ CARELESS
代役 ▶ REPLACEMENT
ダイヤル ▶ BUTTON 1
ダイヤルする ▶ CALL 2
大要 ▶ SUMMARY
代用 ▶ EXCHANGE

日本語類語一覧

- 代用する ▶ REPLACE 2
- 代用となる ▶ REPLACE 1
- 代用品 ▶ REPLACEMENT
- 平らげる ▶ EAT
- 平らな ▶ FLAT
- 代理 ▶ REPLACEMENT
- 大陸間の ▶ INTERNATIONAL
- 対立 ▶ CONFLICT 名, DEBATE, DIVISION 2
- 対立候補者 ▶ PARTICIPANT
- 対立した ▶ AGAINST SB/STH
- 対立している ▶ DISAGREE
- 対立する ▶ ARGUE, CONFLICT 動
- 代理店 ▶ SERVICE
- 大量の ▶ WIDE 1
- 体力 ▶ FORCE 名, HEALTH
- 代理をする ▶ REPLACE 1
- 第六感 ▶ INSTINCT
- 対話 ▶ DISCUSSION
- 耐え抜く ▶ SURVIVE
- 耐えられない ▶ HATE, UNACCEPTABLE
- 耐える ▶ PERSIST, STAND 2
- 倒れ込む ▶ FALL 2
- (水準・程度が)高い ▶ HIGH 1
- (高さが)高い ▶ HIGH 2
- (声・音が)高い ▶ HIGH 3
- 高くつく ▶ EXPENSIVE
- 多額の ▶ LARGE
- 高潮 ▶ FLOOD 名 1
- 高波 ▶ FLOOD 名 1
- 高まり ▶ INCREASE 名
- 高まる ▶ INCREASE 動, RISE
- 高める ▶ INCREASE 動
- 多感な ▶ NAIVE
- 抱きかかえる ▶ HUG
- 抱き締める ▶ HOLD, HUG
- 妥協 ▶ COMPROMISE
- 抱く ▶ TAKE 3
- 卓越 ▶ VALUE
- 卓越した ▶ GREAT 2
- 巧みな ▶ GOOD 4
- たくらみ ▶ FRAUD 2
- たくらむ ▶ PLOT
- 蓄え ▶ SUPPLY
- 蓄えておく ▶ SAVE 3
- 蓄える ▶ KEEP 1
- 蛇行する ▶ CURVE
- 多国間の ▶ INTERNATIONAL
- 多国籍の ▶ INTERNATIONAL
- 他言する ▶ TELL 2
- 多才の ▶ FLEXIBLE 1
- ダサい奴 ▶ FOOL
- 多作の ▶ PRODUCTIVE
- 多産の ▶ PRODUCTIVE
- 出し合う ▶ SHARE 動
- 確かな ▶ CERTAIN, RELIABLE 2, UNDOUBTED
- 多湿の ▶ HUMID
- たしなめる ▶ SCOLD
- 出し物 ▶ PERFORMANCE
- 駄じゃれ ▶ JOKE
- 足す ▶ COUNT
- 助け ▶ AID, HELP 名
- 助け出す ▶ SAVE 1
- 助けとなる ▶ HELP 動 2
- 助けになる ▶ HELPFUL, POWERFUL, USEFUL
- 助ける ▶ HELP 動 1
- 携わっている ▶ WORK 動 1
- 尋ねる ▶ ASK 1, INVESTIGATE
- 訪ねる ▶ VISIT 動
- たそがれ ▶ NIGHT 2
- 称える ▶ PRAISE 動
- 闘い ▶ CAMPAIGN 名
- 戦い ▶ WAR
- 闘う ▶ CAMPAIGN 動, COMPETE, FIGHT 動, RESIST
- 戦う ▶ FIGHT 動
- たたきつける ▶ BEAT
- たたく ▶ BEAT, HIT 1, 2, KNOCK
- (道徳的に)正しい ▶ GOOD 5
- 正しい ▶ RIGHT 形 1, 2, TRUE
- 但し書き ▶ CONDITION
- ただの[で] ▶ FREE 形 2
- だだをこねた ▶ IRRITABLE
- 立会人 ▶ INSPECTOR
- 立ち上がる ▶ STAND 1
- 立ち上げる ▶ INTRODUCE
- 立ち直る ▶ RECOVER
- 立ち退く ▶ LEAVE 2
- 立場 ▶ ATTITUDE, SITUATION
- 立ち向かう ▶ OPPOSE
- 立ち寄り ▶ VISIT 名
- 立ち寄る ▶ STAY 2, VISIT 動
- 立つ ▶ STAND 1
- 奪取する ▶ INVADE
- 達人の ▶ IMPRESSIVE
- 達する ▶ ACHIEVE
- 達成可能な ▶ POSSIBLE 1
- 達成感 ▶ SATISFACTION
- 達成する ▶ ACHIEVE
- たっぷりの ▶ LARGE
- 脱落 ▶ MISTAKE 1
- 盾 ▶ PRECAUTION
- 建てる ▶ BUILD
- 立てる ▶ BUILD, PUT
- 妥当な ▶ FINE, GOOD 2, 3, REASONABLE, SLIGHT
- 例えば ▶ SAY 3
- たどり着く ▶ GET 3
- 棚上げする ▶ DELAY
- 多難な ▶ DIFFICULT 2
- 楽しい ▶ FUNNY, HAPPY, NICE 1, SATISFYING, WONDERFUL
- 楽しく過ごす ▶ PLAY 動 1
- 楽しさ ▶ FUN, JOY
- 楽しみ ▶ ENTERTAINMENT, PLEASURE, PROJECT
- 楽しみにする ▶ EXPECT
- 楽しむ ▶ LIKE 動, PLAY 動 1
- 頼み ▶ WISH
- 頼む ▶ ASK 2
- 束 ▶ GROUP 1
- 旅する ▶ GO 2
- たびたび起こる ▶ FREQUENT
- たびたび繰り返される ▶ FREQUENT
- タブー ▶ BAN
- たぶん ▶ PROBABLY
- 食べていく ▶ SURVIVE
- 食べ物 ▶ FOOD
- 食べる ▶ EAT
- 多忙な ▶ BUSY 2
- 打撲傷 ▶ TUMOUR
- だまされやすい ▶ NAIVE
- だまし ▶ TRICK
- 魂 ▶ MIND
- だまし取る ▶ DEFRAUD
- だます ▶ CHEAT 動
- 玉突き事故 ▶ ACCIDENT
- 黙った ▶ SILENT
- たまの ▶ OCCASIONAL, RARE
- 多民族の ▶ INTERNATIONAL
- ため息をつく ▶ WHISPER
- ダメージ ▶ DAMAGE 名
- 貯め込む ▶ COLLECT, KEEP 1
- 試し ▶ ATTEMPT, TEST 名 1
- 試しに使う ▶ TRY 2
- 試す ▶ TEST 動 1, TRY 2
- 貯めておく ▶ SAVE 3
- 駄目にする ▶ RUIN
- ためになる ▶ HELP 動 2, INFORMATIVE, VALUABLE 2
- ためらう ▶ HESITATE
- ためらった ▶ UNSURE
- 貯める ▶ COLLECT
- 多目的の ▶ FLEXIBLE 1
- 保つ ▶ CONTINUE 2, KEEP 2, 3, MAINTAIN, SAVE 1
- 多様性 ▶ RANGE 1
- 多様な ▶ DIVERSE
- 頼りにする ▶ TRUST
- 頼りになる ▶ RELIABLE 1
- 堕落した ▶ CORRUPT
- 墜落する ▶ CRASH
- だらしのない ▶ UNTIDY
- たれ込む ▶ TELL 2
- タレント ▶ STAR
- たわごと ▶ NONSENSE
- 団 ▶ TEAM 1
- 段 ▶ FLOOR
- 弾圧 ▶ REPRESSION
- 弾圧する ▶ SUPPRESS 1
- 弾圧的な ▶ REPRESSIVE
- 単位 ▶ ELEMENT
- 段階 ▶ STAGE
- 弾劾 ▶ CRITICISM
- 弾劾する ▶ ACCUSE
- 嘆願 ▶ REQUEST
- 嘆願する ▶ ASK 2
- 短期滞在 ▶ VISIT 名
- 短気な ▶ IRRITABLE, SENSITIVE 3
- 短期の ▶ SHORT 1
- 探求 ▶ SEARCH
- 探究 ▶ RESEARCH
- 探検 ▶ RESEARCH, TRIP
- 断言する ▶ CLAIM, DECLARE, PROMISE 動, SAY 2
- 断固たる ▶ STERN, STRICT
- 探査 ▶ RESEARCH
- 探索 ▶ SEARCH
- 探索する ▶ LOOK 動 2
- 短時間の ▶ QUICK
- 短縮形の ▶ SHORT 3
- 短縮する ▶ SHRINK
- 単純な ▶ AVERAGE, EASY 1, PLAIN 1
- 誕生 ▶ START 名

たんじょうび → ちょめいじん (27)

誕生日 ▶ BIRTHDAY
暖色の ▶ DARK 2
男性 ▶ MAN 1
弾性のある ▶ FLEXIBLE 2
断然 ▶ QUITE 2
断続的な ▶ OCCASIONAL
断続的に ▶ SOMETIMES
団体 ▶ ORGANIZATION, TEAM 2, UNION
淡々とした ▶ INDIFFERENT, REALISTIC
単純な ▶ BORING
担当している ▶ RUN 2
単独の ▶ PARTICULAR
段取り ▶ PLANNING
段取りをつける ▶ ORGANIZE
断念する ▶ STOP
堪能な ▶ GOOD 4
断片 ▶ BIT, PIECE
短命の ▶ SHORT 1
男優 ▶ ACTOR
弾力のある ▶ FLEXIBLE 2
談話 ▶ SPEECH

ち

治安 ▶ PEACE, SECURITY
治安紊乱(攵) ▶ TROUBLE 1
地位 ▶ CLASS 3, JOB, STATUS
地域 ▶ AREA 1, COUNTY
小さい ▶ SHORT 2, SMALL
小さくする ▶ REDUCE
小さくなる ▶ SHRINK
小さな ▶ SLIGHT
チーム ▶ TEAM 1, 2
チームメート ▶ PARTNER 1
知恵 ▶ INTELLIGENCE, KNOWLEDGE
チェーン ▶ SERIES
チェックリスト ▶ LIST 名
知恵のある ▶ WISE
遅延した ▶ LATE
近い ▶ LIKE 前 形
誓い ▶ PROMISE 名
違い ▶ DIFFERENCE
誓う ▶ PROMISE 動
知覚 ▶ AWARENESS
近づく ▶ COME 1, 2
違った ▶ DIFFERENT
近寄りがたい ▶ STERN
力 ▶ ABILITY, FORCE 名
力持ちの ▶ STRONG 1
地球儀 ▶ MAP

地球上の ▶ INTERNATIONAL
ちぎる ▶ TEAR
ちぎれる ▶ TEAR
知己を得る ▶ MEET 3
地区 ▶ AREA 1, COUNTY
蓄積 ▶ SUPPLY,
蓄積する ▶ COLLECT, KEEP 3
地形 ▶ COUNTRY 2, DESIGN 名
遅刻した ▶ LATE
知識 ▶ KNOWLEDGE, UNDERSTANDING
致死の ▶ FATAL
恥辱 ▶ DISGRACE, GUILT
知人 ▶ FRIEND, PARTNER 1
地図 ▶ MAP
血筋 ▶ FAMILY 3
地図帳 ▶ MAP
地勢 ▶ COUNTRY 2
治世 ▶ GOVERNMENT 1, PERIOD
知性 ▶ INTELLIGENCE
知性のある ▶ INTELLECTUAL 2
地層 ▶ FLOOR
地帯 ▶ AREA 1, COUNTY
縮む ▶ SHRINK
チック ▶ SHIVER
秩序 ▶ EFFICIENCY, PEACE
秩序のある ▶ NEAT
窒息する ▶ COUGH
チップ ▶ GIFT
知的な ▶ INTELLECTUAL 1, 2
地点 ▶ PLACE
血生臭い ▶ VIOLENT
知能 ▶ INTELLIGENCE
知能の高い ▶ INTELLIGENT
ちびちび飲む ▶ DRINK 動
地方 ▶ COUNTRY 2, COUNTY
地方(財産)税 ▶ TAX
緻密な ▶ COMPLEX
血みどろの ▶ VIOLENT
致命的な ▶ FATAL
知名度 ▶ FAME, REPUTATION
血も涙もない ▶ RUTHLESS
チャーターする ▶ ORDER 2
着実な ▶ STEADY
着手する ▶ BEGIN, DO
着色する ▶ PAINT

着席する ▶ SIT
着服 ▶ THEFT
着服する ▶ STEAL
着陸する ▶ ARRIVE
茶番劇 ▶ PLAY 名
チャペル ▶ CHURCH
茶目っ気 ▶ HUMOUR
チャンス ▶ OPPORTUNITY
治癒 ▶ TREATMENT
注意 ▶ ATTENTION
注意事項 ▶ CONDITION
注意を払う ▶ NOTICE
中央政府の ▶ PUBLIC
仲介者 ▶ NEGOTIATOR
忠告する ▶ RECOMMEND 1
仲裁する ▶ INTERVENE
仲裁人 ▶ NEGOTIATOR
中止 ▶ PAUSE
中止する ▶ ABOLISH, STOP
注視する ▶ LOOK 動 1
忠実な ▶ GOOD 7, RELIABLE 1
中止になる ▶ FAIL 2
注釈 ▶ ASSESSMENT
抽出する ▶ PUMP
抽象概念 ▶ IDEA 1
中傷的な ▶ INSULTING, MEAN 形
抽象的な ▶ INTELLECTUAL 1
中心地 ▶ ORGANIZATION
中心的な ▶ MAIN
中断 ▶ END 名, PAUSE
中断させる ▶ INTERRUPT
中断する ▶ STOP
躊躇する ▶ HESITATE
中道 ▶ COMPROMISE
中毒性の ▶ ADDICTIVE
注目 ▶ ATTENTION, FAME
注目すべき ▶ IMPORTANT
注目する ▶ NOTICE
注目に値する ▶ IMPORTANT
注文 ▶ REQUEST
注文する ▶ ORDER 2
中立 ▶ COMPROMISE
中立的な ▶ OBJECTIVE
長 ▶ LEADER 1
弔意 ▶ SYMPATHY
長期間かかる ▶ LONG
長期的な ▶ LONG
調教する ▶ TRAIN 1, 2
兆候 ▶ SIGN 1, SUGGESTION
兆候となる ▶ MEAN 動 1, SUGGEST

調査 ▶ INSPECTION, INVESTIGATION, REPORT 1, RESEARCH, TEST 名 1
調査官 ▶ INSPECTOR
調査結果 ▶ CONCLUSION
調査する ▶ CHECK 1, INVESTIGATE, SURVEY, TEST 動 1
調査報告 ▶ REPORT 1
調子 ▶ ATMOSPHERE, STATE
聴衆 ▶ AUDIENCE
徴収する ▶ CHARGE 動
長寿の ▶ OLD 2
長所 ▶ BENEFIT, VALUE
頂上 ▶ HILL
嘲笑的な ▶ IRONIC
調整 ▶ CHANGE 名 2, PLANNING
調整する ▶ ADJUST
調節する ▶ ADJUST
挑戦 ▶ PROBLEM
挑戦者 ▶ PARTICIPANT
挑戦する ▶ TRY 1
超然とした ▶ INDIFFERENT
調停者 ▶ NEGOTIATOR
調停する ▶ INTERVENE
頂点 ▶ PEAK
ちょうどの ▶ VERY 形
懲罰的な ▶ STRICT
諜報 ▶ INFORMATION
諜報部 ▶ INFORMATION
町民 ▶ RESIDENT
長命の ▶ OLD 2
跳躍する ▶ JUMP
調和させる ▶ MATCH 2
調和する ▶ MATCH 2
(…の)長を務める ▶ LEAD
貯金 ▶ FUND 名
貯金する ▶ SAVE 2, 3
直情的な ▶ SPONTANEOUS
直面する ▶ HAVE 3
著作集 ▶ WORK 名 2
著者 ▶ WRITER
著書 ▶ WORK 名 2
貯蔵 ▶ SUPPLY
貯蔵する ▶ KEEP 1
貯蓄する ▶ SAVE 3
直感 ▶ IDEA 2, INSTINCT
直観 ▶ INSTINCT
ちょっとした ▶ SLIGHT
ちょっとの間 ▶ MINUTE
著名 ▶ FAME
著名人 ▶ STAR

日本語類語一覧

日本語類語一覧

著名な ▶ FAMOUS, GREAT 2
ちらし ▶ LEAFLET
ちらっと見る ▶ SEE
治療 ▶ TREATMENT
治療する ▶ CURE
治療法 ▶ DRUG 2
治療薬 ▶ DRUG 2
知力 ▶ INTELLIGENCE
鎮圧する ▶ SUPPRESS 1
賃借りする ▶ ORDER 2
賃金 ▶ INCOME
沈思(黙考)
　▶ CONSIDERATION
椿事 ▶ LUCK
賃借人 ▶ TENANT
陳述 ▶ STATEMENT
賃貸料 ▶ RATE
沈黙した ▶ QUIET 2
陳列 ▶ EXHIBITION
陳列されて ▶ VISIBLE
陳列する ▶ PRESENT 1
陳列台 ▶ STALL

つ

追憶 ▶ MEMORY
追加料金 ▶ PAYMENT
追求 ▶ SEARCH
追跡 ▶ SEARCH
追跡する ▶ FOLLOW 1
追想 ▶ MEMORY
付いて行く ▶ FOLLOW 1
ついていなくて
　▶ UNFORTUNATE 1
追放する ▶ EXCLUDE 2, EXPEL
費やす ▶ DEVOTE, USE 動 2
通 ▶ EXPERT
通貨 ▶ MONEY 2
通行人 ▶ WITNESS
通行料 ▶ RATE
通じた ▶ USED TO STH
通商 ▶ TRADE
通常の ▶ NORMAL, USUAL
通常は ▶ USUALLY
通信員 ▶ REPORTER
通信文 ▶ LETTER
通則 ▶ PRINCIPLE 2
通知書 ▶ LEAFLET
通知する ▶ TELL 1
通報する ▶ TELL 1
ツール ▶ TOOL
通例の ▶ USUAL
通例は ▶ USUALLY

痛烈な ▶ SHREWD, STERN
通路 ▶ CORRIDOR
使い勝手のよい ▶ USEFUL
使いきる ▶ USE 動 2
使い尽くす ▶ USE 動 2
使い果たす ▶ USE 動 2
使いものにならない
　▶ USELESS
使う ▶ USE 動 1
司る ▶ REGULATE, RUN 2
つかの間の ▶ SHORT 1
捕まえる ▶ TAKE 3
捕まっていない
　▶ FREE 形 1
つかみ合う ▶ FIGHT 動
つかむ ▶ HOLD, TAKE 3
疲れた ▶ TIRED
疲れ果てた ▶ TIRED
付き合う ▶ GO OUT
突き上げる ▶ SHAKE 1
突き刺す ▶ PUSH 1
突き進む ▶ PUSH 1
付き添う ▶ TAKE 2
突き止める ▶ FIND 3, 4
次の ▶ NEXT
継ぎを当てる ▶ REPAIR
着く ▶ ARRIVE, GET 3, GO 1
造り ▶ STRUCTURE
作り話 ▶ ILLUSION, LIE
作る ▶ BUILD, MAKE 1
繕う ▶ REPAIR
つけ ▶ BILL
付け合わせる
　▶ DECORATE
告げ口する ▶ TELL 2
付け値 ▶ OFFER 2
付ける ▶ ATTACH
つける ▶ SOAK
(電気などを)つける
　▶ TURN STH ON
都合のよい ▶ GOOD 2
伝える ▶ CONVEY, SHOW 1, TALK, TELL 1
土 ▶ SOIL
土ぼこり ▶ SOIL
続いて起こる ▶ FOLLOW 2
つつく ▶ PUSH 1
続く ▶ CONTINUE 1
続ける ▶ CONTINUE 2, 3
突っ込む ▶ PUT
包み隠しのない
　▶ HONEST
つて ▶ PARTNER 1
務め ▶ BUSINESS
努める ▶ TRY 1

つながり
　▶ RELATIONSHIP 1
つながる ▶ CAUSE
津波 ▶ FLOOD 名 1
常にある ▶ PERMANENT
粒 ▶ BIT, DROP
つぶやく ▶ WHISPER
つまずく ▶ FALL 3
つまらない ▶ BORING
罪 ▶ CRIME 2, FAULT
積み込む ▶ FILL
積荷 ▶ CARGO
罪のない ▶ INNOCENT
詰め込む ▶ FILL, PACK
冷たい ▶ COLD 1, RUTHLESS
つもり ▶ PURPOSE
(…する)つもりである [言う] ▶ INTEND
(…の)つもりで言う
　▶ MEAN 動 2
つやのない ▶ PALE
露 ▶ MOISTURE
強気 ▶ COURAGE
強まる ▶ INCREASE 動, RISE
強み ▶ BENEFIT
強める ▶ INCREASE 動
つらい ▶ HARD, PAINFUL 2, TERRIBLE 1
つらさ ▶ DISTRESS
釣り合い ▶ RATIO
釣り銭 ▶ MONEY 2
連れ ▶ FRIEND
連れ合い ▶ PARTNER 2
連れて行く ▶ TAKE 1, 2
連れて来る ▶ TAKE 1
(鼻に)つんとくる
　▶ BITTER

て

出会い ▶ MEETING 2
出会う ▶ MEET 2
手当たり次第の
　▶ RANDOM
手当 ▶ SHARE 名
手当て ▶ TREATMENT
手当てをする
　▶ LOOK AFTER SB
提案 ▶ OFFER 1, PROPOSAL
提案する ▶ PROPOSE
ディーゼル油 ▶ OIL
ディーラー ▶ DEALER
定員 ▶ SHARE 名

ティーンエイジャー
　▶ GIRL
ティーンエイジャーの
　▶ YOUNG
低音の ▶ DEEP 2
低下 ▶ REDUCTION
低価格の ▶ CHEAP
低下する ▶ FALL 1, WORSEN
定款 ▶ RULE 名
定義 ▶ DEFINITION
提起する ▶ ASK 1
定義する ▶ EXPLAIN 1
提議する ▶ PROPOSE
定期的な ▶ STEADY
提供 ▶ OFFER 1
提供者 ▶ SPONSOR
提供する ▶ GIVE 3, ORGANIZE, PROVIDE
提携者 ▶ PARTNER 1
提言 ▶ PROPOSAL
抵抗 ▶ OPPOSITION
抵抗した
　▶ AGAINST SB/STH
抵抗する ▶ OPPOSE, RESIST
偵察 ▶ INSPECTION
停止 ▶ END 名, PAUSE
提示 ▶ PROPOSAL
提示額 ▶ OFFER 2
停止して ▶ STILL
停止する ▶ STOP
提示する ▶ PRESENT 1, 3
提出する ▶ PRESENT 3, PROPOSE
提唱する ▶ PROPOSE
ディスカウントする
　▶ DISCOUNT
訂正 ▶ CHANGE 名 2
訂正する ▶ CORRECT
貞操 ▶ MORALITY
停滞させる
　▶ HOLD SB/STH UP
丁重さ ▶ RESPECT 名
丁重な ▶ POLITE, SOPHISTICATED
抵当 ▶ LOAN
丁寧さ ▶ RESPECT 名
丁寧な ▶ POLITE
定理 ▶ THEORY 1
出入許可証 ▶ LICENCE
手入れ ▶ STATE
手入れをする
　▶ LOOK AFTER SB
データ ▶ INFORMATION
テーマ ▶ SUBJECT

てがかり → とうぜんのこととおもう

手がかり ▶ IDEA 2, SOLUTION, SUGGESTION
出かける ▶ LEAVE 1, VISIT 動
手紙 ▶ LETTER
敵 ▶ ENEMY
溺愛する ▶ LOVE 動
敵意 ▶ HATRED, TENSION
敵意のある ▶ AGGRESSIVE 1
適応させる ▶ CHANGE 動 1
適応力のある ▶ FLEXIBLE 1
的確な ▶ SHREWD
適合させる ▶ CHANGE 動 1
出来事 ▶ EVENT 1
適した ▶ GOOD 2
適時の ▶ TIMELY
テキスト ▶ BOOK
適性 ▶ SKILL 1, 2
適正な ▶ REASONABLE
適切な ▶ GOOD 2, RELEVANT, RIGHT 形 1, 2
敵対 ▶ OPPOSITION
敵対感情 ▶ TENSION
敵対行為 ▶ TENSION
敵対者 ▶ PROTESTER
敵対的な ▶ AGGRESSIVE 1
適当な ▶ FINE, RIGHT 形 2, TRUE
適度の ▶ SLIGHT
適法の ▶ LEGAL
摘要 ▶ SUMMARY
適用 ▶ USE 名
適用される ▶ INCLUDE
適用する ▶ APPLY
適用できる ▶ RELEVANT
手際の良さ ▶ STYLE
出口調査 ▶ ELECTION
出くわす ▶ FIND 2, MEET 2
手ごろな ▶ CHEAP, SLIGHT, USEFUL
デザイン ▶ DEVELOPMENT
デザインする ▶ DESIGN 動 1
手順 ▶ WAY 2
手数料 ▶ RATE, SHARE 名
テスト ▶ TEST 名 2
テストする ▶ TEST 動 2
テストマッチ ▶ GAME
でたらめな ▶ RANDOM
でたらめな話 ▶ LIE
手帳 ▶ SCHEDULE

撤回する ▶ BREAK 4, GIVE WAY
哲学 ▶ VALUES
哲学的な ▶ INTELLECTUAL 1
デッキ ▶ FLOOR
デッサン ▶ PICTURE
手伝う ▶ HELP 動 1
でっち上げ ▶ TRICK
徹底的な ▶ FUNDAMENTAL
鉄砲水 ▶ FLOOD 名 1
出て行く ▶ LEAVE 1
出てくる ▶ APPEAR
テナント ▶ TENANT
手に入れたい ▶ POPULAR
手に入れる ▶ GET 1, 2
手に負えない ▶ UNCONTROLLABLE, WILD
手に取る ▶ TAKE 3
手のかかる ▶ DIFFICULT 1
手の込んだ ▶ COMPLEX
手配 ▶ PLANNING
手配する ▶ ORGANIZE
手はず ▶ PLANNING
手はずを整える ▶ ORGANIZE
手引書 ▶ BOOK
でぶの ▶ FAT
手本 ▶ EXAMPLE 2, INFLUENCE 名
手本とすべき ▶ PERFECT
手本とする ▶ FOLLOW 4
手間取らせる ▶ HOLD SB/STH UP
手短な ▶ SHORT 3
出迎える ▶ GREET
デモンストレーション ▶ PRESENTATION
デリケートな ▶ SENSITIVE 2
照る ▶ SHINE
出る ▶ LEAVE 1
テレビ視聴者 ▶ AUDIENCE
テロリスト ▶ GUERRILLA
手渡す ▶ GIVE 2
手を貸す ▶ HELP 動 1
手を切る ▶ REJECT
手を出す ▶ FLIRT
手を引く ▶ REJECT
手を振る ▶ SHAKE 1
店員 ▶ SALESMAN
田園 ▶ COUNTRY 2
展開する ▶ ORGANIZE
転換 ▶ CHANGE 名 1
転換する ▶ SWITCH

伝記作家 ▶ WRITER
転勤させる ▶ LEAVE 2
転勤する ▶ LEAVE 2
典型 ▶ EXAMPLE 2
典型である ▶ REPRESENT 2
典型的な ▶ NORMAL, TYPICAL
点検 ▶ INSPECTION
電源を入れる ▶ TURN STH ON
電源を切る ▶ TURN STH OFF
転向させる ▶ PERSUADE
伝言 ▶ LETTER
天才 ▶ GENIUS
展示 ▶ EXHIBITION, PERFORMANCE
展示会 ▶ EXHIBITION
展示されて ▶ VISIBLE
展示する ▶ PRESENT 1
店主 ▶ DEALER
転職する ▶ LEAVE 2
伝染病 ▶ DISEASE
転送する ▶ SEND
伝統 ▶ TRADITION
転倒する ▶ FALL 3
伝統的な ▶ CONSERVATIVE, TRADITIONAL
添付する ▶ ATTACH
天分 ▶ INTELLIGENCE
展望 ▶ POTENTIAL
天文学的な ▶ HIGH 1
転落する ▶ FALL 2
展覧会 ▶ EXHIBITION
電話が切れる ▶ TURN STH OFF
電話帳 ▶ LIST 名
電話をする ▶ CALL 2

と

問い ▶ QUESTION 名
問い合わせ ▶ QUESTION 名, RESEARCH
問いただす ▶ QUESTION 動
問い詰める ▶ ASK 1, QUESTION 動
トイレ ▶ TOILET
問う ▶ ASK 1, QUESTION 動
答案 ▶ TEST 名 2
同意 ▶ PERMISSION

同意する ▶ AGREE, IN FAVOUR
同一 ▶ SIMILARITY
倒壊させる ▶ DEMOLISH
投函する ▶ SEND
討論 ▶ DEBATE, DISCUSSION
動機 ▶ INCENTIVE, REASON
動議 ▶ PROPOSAL
道心 ▶ INTEGRITY
投棄する ▶ REMOVE
動機付け ▶ INCENTIVE
同義の ▶ EQUAL
等級 ▶ CATEGORY, CLASS 3, QUALITY
投球する ▶ THROW
同級生 ▶ PARTNER 1
当局(者) ▶ AUTHORITIES
道具 ▶ EQUIPMENT, TOOL
凍結した ▶ FREEZING
動向 ▶ TREND
同好会 ▶ UNION
統合する ▶ COMBINE
投獄する ▶ JAIL
動作 ▶ MOVEMENT
当座借越額 ▶ LOAN
洞察 ▶ UNDERSTANDING
洞察力 ▶ EXPECTATION, INSPIRATION, UNDERSTANDING
投資 ▶ INVESTMENT
当時の ▶ FORMER
同時発生 ▶ LUCK
投書 ▶ LETTER
登場 ▶ ARRIVAL
同情 ▶ SYMPATHY
搭乗員 ▶ TEAM 1
同情する ▶ SORRY FOR SB
同情的な ▶ SENSITIVE 1
どうしようもない ▶ POOR 2
どうしようもない人 ▶ LOSER 2
当初の ▶ FIRST
統制 ▶ CONTROL, LIMIT 1
統制する ▶ RUN 2
当選 ▶ CHOICE 1
当選した ▶ SUCCESSFUL 1
…も同然 ▶ ALMOST
(…も)同然である ▶ REPRESENT 1
当然の ▶ OBVIOUS, RIGHT 形 2
当然のこととおもう ▶ TRUST

日本語類語一覧

闘争 ▶ CAMPAIGN 名, WAR
闘争する ▶ COMPETE
逃走する ▶ FLEE
盗賊 ▶ THIEF
統率 ▶ CONTROL
統率者 ▶ LEADER 1
到達する ▶ ACHIEVE
同値 ▶ SIMILARITY
統治 ▶ GOVERNMENT 2
統治する ▶ RULE 動 1
到着 ▶ ARRIVAL
到着する ▶ ARRIVE, GET 3
登頂する ▶ CLIMB
統治領 ▶ TERRITORY
動的な ▶ VARIABLE
同等 ▶ SIMILARITY
同等である ▶ COMPARE 2
堂々とした ▶ PROUD 1
同等の ▶ EQUIVALENT
道徳 ▶ MORALITY, PRINCIPLE 1, VALUES
道徳上の ▶ MORAL
道徳的な ▶ GOOD 5
投入口 ▶ HOLE 1
投入する ▶ DEVOTE
導入する ▶ APPLY, INTRODUCE
当の ▶ VERY 形
党派 ▶ PARTY 1
党派主義 ▶ RACISM
投票 ▶ ELECTION
投票者 ▶ CITIZEN
投票する ▶ SUPPORT
投票を求める ▶ SURVEY
逃亡する ▶ FLEE
透明な ▶ CLEAR 形 3
投薬治療 ▶ DRUG 2
動揺させる ▶ FRIGHTEN, WORRY, WORRYING
動揺した ▶ WORRIED
同様の ▶ PARALLEL
到来 ▶ ARRIVAL
到来する ▶ COME 2
動乱 ▶ REVOLUTION, TROUBLE 1
道理 ▶ LOGIC
同僚 ▶ PARTNER 1
同量 ▶ SIMILARITY
道路 ▶ ROAD
登録する ▶ LET SB IN, RECORD
討論 ▶ DEBATE
討論会 ▶ CLASS 2
当惑させる ▶ CONFUSING
当惑した ▶ CONFUSED

通し稽古をする ▶ PRACTISE
遠回しに言う ▶ MEAN 動 2
通り ▶ ROAD
通り過ぎる ▶ GO 1
通り道 ▶ WAY 3
通る ▶ GO 1
都会風の ▶ SOPHISTICATED
とがめる ▶ BLAME
時 ▶ TIME
時折 ▶ SOMETIMES
時折の ▶ OCCASIONAL
時たまの ▶ OCCASIONAL
ときどき ▶ SOMETIMES
時々の ▶ OCCASIONAL
時には ▶ SOMETIMES
ドキュメント ▶ DOCUMENT
度胸 ▶ COURAGE
度胸のある ▶ BOLD
途切れ ▶ PAUSE
時を得た ▶ TIMELY
説く ▶ CLAIM
得意でない ▶ INCOMPETENT
得意な ▶ FAVOURITE, GOOD 4
特異な ▶ SPECIAL, UNIQUE
独裁国家 ▶ REPRESSION
独裁者 ▶ DICTATOR
独裁政権 ▶ REPRESSION
独裁的な ▶ REPRESSIVE
独自性 ▶ IDENTITY
特質 ▶ FEATURE 名, NATURE 1, SIGN 1
独自の ▶ UNIQUE
読者 ▶ MARKET 1
特集 ▶ ARTICLE
特集する ▶ FEATURE 動
特殊な ▶ PARTICULAR, SPECIAL
特色 ▶ NATURE 1
独身の ▶ SINGLE
特性 ▶ FEATURE 名, PERSONALITY
特徴 ▶ FEATURE 名, SIGN 1
特徴とする ▶ FEATURE 動
特徴づける ▶ FEATURE 動
特定する ▶ FIND 3
特定の ▶ PARTICULAR
独特さ ▶ IDENTITY

独特の ▶ TYPICAL, UNIQUE, UNUSUAL
特筆する ▶ COMMENT
特別の ▶ PARTICULAR, SPECIAL, UNIQUE
特有の ▶ TYPICAL, UNIQUE
独立 ▶ FREEDOM, INDEPENDENCE
独立した ▶ PARTICULAR
とげ ▶ FRAGMENT
都市 ▶ CITY
年老いた ▶ OLD 2
年取った ▶ OLD 2
土壌 ▶ SOIL
閉じる ▶ CLOSE 動
塗装する ▶ PAINT
土台 ▶ BOTTOM
途絶え ▶ PAUSE
途絶える ▶ STOP
土地 ▶ LAND 1, 2
特許 ▶ LICENCE
特許状 ▶ LICENCE
取っ組み合い ▶ FIGHT 名
取っ組み合う ▶ FIGHT 動
突撃する ▶ ATTACK 動 2
特権 ▶ LICENCE, RIGHT 2
突進する ▶ HURRY, RUN 1
突然変異する[させる] ▶ TURN 2
どっちつかずの ▶ UNSURE, VAGUE
取っ手 ▶ BUTTON 1
取っておく ▶ KEEP 2
取って代わる ▶ REPLACE 1
とっぴな ▶ STRANGE 1, UNLIKELY 2
トップ ▶ LEADER 2
とても ▶ VERY 副
届く ▶ ARRIVE
届け出る ▶ PRESENT 3, RECORD, TELL 1
届ける ▶ CONVEY
整える ▶ TIDY
整った ▶ NEAT
留まる ▶ REMAIN, STAY 1
ドナー ▶ SPONSOR
唱える ▶ QUOTE
どなりつける ▶ SCOLD
隣の ▶ NEXT
どなる ▶ SHOUT
とびきりの ▶ EXCELLENT
跳び越える ▶ JUMP
飛び跳ねる ▶ JUMP
飛び火 ▶ RESULT
跳ぶ ▶ JUMP

途方に暮れた ▶ CONFUSED
途方もない ▶ HIGH 1, REMARKABLE
乏しい ▶ INADEQUATE, LIMITED 1, SCARCE
止まった ▶ STILL
泊まる ▶ SLEEP, STAY 2
富 ▶ MONEY 3
留め具 ▶ BUTTON 2
留める ▶ ATTACH
止める ▶ PREVENT, STOP, TURN STH OFF
友達 ▶ FRIEND
伴う ▶ RELATED
共に ▶ PARALLEL
トライアウト ▶ INTERVIEW 2
トライアル ▶ INTERVIEW 2
ドライな ▶ REALISTIC
とらえ方 ▶ ATTITUDE
捕らえる ▶ KIDNAP, TAKE 3
トラブル ▶ PROBLEM, TROUBLE 1, 2
ドラマ ▶ DRAMA, PLAY 名
取扱説明書 ▶ BOOK
取り扱う ▶ DEAL WITH SB/STH, SELL 2
取り合わせ ▶ RANGE 1
取り合わない ▶ IGNORE
取り入れる ▶ INTRODUCE
取り替え ▶ EXCHANGE
取り替える ▶ REPLACE 2
取り掛かる ▶ BEGIN
取り決め ▶ AGREEMENT
取り決めをする ▶ NEGOTIATE
取り組み方 ▶ WAY 1
取り消す ▶ BREAK 4, CANCEL, GIVE WAY
取り壊す ▶ DEMOLISH
取締役会 ▶ COMMITTEE
取り締まる ▶ REGULATE
取り調べ ▶ INTERVIEW 1, INVESTIGATION
取り調べる ▶ INVESTIGATE
取り出す ▶ CLEAR 動
取り散らかった ▶ UNTIDY
取り付ける ▶ ATTACH
取り残す ▶ LEAVE 4
取り除く ▶ CLEAR 動, REMOVE
取り外す ▶ UNDO

とりひき → にゅうもんてきな

取り引き
　▶ COMMUNICATION, TRADE
取り引きする ▶ SELL 2
取引高 ▶ TRADE
取り分 ▶ SHARE 名
取り乱した ▶ HYSTERICAL, UPSET
取りやめる ▶ ABOLISH
努力 ▶ ATTEMPT, EFFORT
努力する ▶ TRY 1
取り寄せる ▶ ORDER 2
取る ▶ GET 1
(盗み)取る ▶ STEAL
取るに足らない ▶ MINOR, SLIGHT, IRRELEVANT
トレーニング ▶ TRAINING
トレーニングをする[させる] ▶ TRAIN 2
トレッキングをする
　▶ WALK 2
トレンド ▶ FASHION
泥 ▶ SOIL
どろどろした ▶ SOFT
トロフィー ▶ AWARD
泥棒 ▶ THIEF
泥棒に入る ▶ ROB
泥まみれの ▶ DIRTY
度を越した ▶ EXCESSIVE
鈍感な ▶ INSENSITIVE
鈍行の ▶ SLOW
どんちゃん騒ぎをする
　▶ PLAY 動 1
とんでもない ▶ BAD, OUTRAGEOUS, TERRIBLE 2
どんよりした ▶ CLOUDY

な

内閣 ▶ GOVERNMENT 1
内腔 ▶ HOLE 2
内向的な ▶ SOLITARY
ないこと ▶ LACK
内緒の ▶ SECRET
内省する ▶ CONSIDER
内服薬 ▶ DRUG 2
内部告発する ▶ TELL 2
内包する ▶ INCLUDE
内密の ▶ SECRET
内容 ▶ MESSAGE
直す ▶ REPAIR
治す ▶ CURE
治る ▶ RECOVER
(時間的に)長い ▶ LONG
流し出す ▶ FLOW, PUMP

流す ▶ FLOW
仲立ち ▶ NEGOTIATOR
長続きさせる ▶ MAINTAIN
長続きする ▶ PERMANENT
仲直りする ▶ RESOLVE
なかなか ▶ QUITE 1
中に入れる ▶ LET SB IN
仲に入る ▶ INTERVENE
長年に及ぶ ▶ OLD 1
仲のよい ▶ FRIENDLY 2
仲のよさ ▶ FRIENDSHIP
長引かせる
　▶ HOLD SB/STH UP, MAINTAIN
仲間 ▶ FRIEND, GROUP 2, PARTNER 1, PARTY 2
仲間意識 ▶ FRIENDSHIP
眺め ▶ VIEW 2
眺める ▶ LOOK 動 1
流れ出る ▶ FLOW, PUMP
流れる ▶ FLOW
仲を裂く ▶ DIVIDE 2
仲を取り持つ
　▶ INTERVENE
泣きじゃくる ▶ CRY
泣きべそをかく ▶ CRY
泣く ▶ CRY
慰め ▶ RELIEF
慰める ▶ ENCOURAGE
なくす ▶ REMOVE
亡くなった ▶ DEAD
亡くなる ▶ DIE
なくなる ▶ DISAPPEAR
殴る ▶ BEAT, HIT 2
投げ上げる ▶ THROW
嘆かわしい
　▶ OUTRAGEOUS, UNFORTUNATE 2
投げ出す ▶ PUT
投げつける ▶ THROW
投げる ▶ THROW
和やかな ▶ FRIENDLY 2, INFORMAL, SOCIABLE
情けない ▶ POOR 2, UNFORTUNATE 2
情け容赦のない ▶ CRUEL, RUTHLESS, STERN
成し遂げる ▶ ACHIEVE
なじみのある
　▶ USED TO STH
なじみのない
　▶ STRANGE 2
名高い ▶ FAMOUS
なだめすかす
　▶ PERSUADE
懐かしい ▶ LOVING

名づける ▶ CALL 1
納得させる ▶ CONVINCE, PERSUADE, PLEASE
納得して ▶ SURE
納得する ▶ AGREE
納得のいかない
　▶ UNLIKELY 2
納得のいく ▶ FINE
生意気な ▶ CONFIDENT, PROUD 2, RUDE
生ごみ ▶ WASTE
なまぬるい ▶ COLD 1
波立つ ▶ ROUGH
並々ならない
　▶ TERRIBLE 3
並みの ▶ AVERAGE, NORMAL
並外れた ▶ REMARKABLE
滑らかな ▶ FLAT
悩ませる ▶ HURT 1, WORRY, WORRYING
悩み ▶ CONCERN
習う ▶ LEARN
倣う ▶ FOLLOW 4
鳴り響く ▶ DEEP 2
成り行き ▶ EVENT 1
成り行き任せの
　▶ RANDOM
なる ▶ BECOME
ナレーションを入れる
　▶ QUOTE
慣れた ▶ USED TO STH
難局 ▶ CRISIS
難色を示す ▶ DISAPPROVE
ナンセンス ▶ NONSENSE
難題 ▶ PROBLEM
難点 ▶ DEFECT, DISADVANTAGE, PROBLEM
何とかいう人[物]
　▶ THING 1
何度も ▶ OFTEN
ナンパする ▶ FLIRT
難破船 ▶ REMAINS
難民 ▶ REFUGEE

に

2位になるチーム
　▶ LOSER 1
2位になる人 ▶ LOSER 1
煮えたぎった ▶ HOT
におい ▶ ODOUR, SMELL
におわせる ▶ SUGGEST
苦い ▶ BITTER

にぎやかな ▶ CROWDED, LIVELY
握り締める ▶ HOLD, TIGHTEN
握る ▶ HOLD
憎しみ ▶ HATRED
肉体労働者 ▶ WORKER 2
憎む ▶ HATE
憎むべき ▶ DISGUSTING 2
憎めない ▶ SWEET
逃げた ▶ FREE 形 1
逃げ場 ▶ REFUGE
逃げ道 ▶ SOLUTION
逃げる ▶ ESCAPE, FLEE
にこにこしている ▶ SMILE
にせの ▶ ARTIFICIAL
偽物 ▶ FAKE
偽物の ▶ FICTIONAL
似た ▶ LIKE 前 形
似たような ▶ PARALLEL
日常の ▶ USUAL
日没 ▶ NIGHT 2
日課 ▶ TASK
荷造りする ▶ FILL
にっこりと笑う ▶ SMILE
似て ▶ LIKE 前 形
似ていない ▶ DIFFERENT
似ている ▶ EQUIVALENT, SEEM
鈍い ▶ PALE, QUIET 2, SLOW
荷物 ▶ THING 2
にやにや笑う ▶ LAUGH, SMILE
入会(許可) ▶ ACCESS
入会金 ▶ RATE
入会させる ▶ LET SB IN
入会する ▶ JOIN
入学させる ▶ LET SB IN
入札 ▶ OFFER 2
乳児期 ▶ CHILDHOOD
入手する ▶ GAIN
入手することができる
　▶ AVAILABLE
入場 ▶ ARRIVAL
入場(許可) ▶ ACCESS
入場券 ▶ LICENCE
入場させる ▶ LET SB IN
入場料 ▶ RATE
ニュース ▶ REPORT 2
ニュースキャスター
　▶ PRESENTER
入念な ▶ COMPLEX, DETAILED
入門書 ▶ BASICS
入門的な ▶ FIRST

日本語類語一覧

日本語類語一覧

入浴させる ▶ WASH
入力する ▶ RECORD
にらみつける ▶ STARE
にらむこと ▶ LOOK 名
二流の ▶ POOR 2
任意の ▶ RANDOM, VOLUNTARY 1
認可 ▶ APPROVAL, PERMISSION
認可された ▶ OFFICIAL 形
認可する ▶ ALLOW
任官する ▶ APPOINT
人気のある ▶ POPULAR
人気のない ▶ UNWANTED
人間 ▶ MAN 2, PERSON
認識 ▶ AWARENESS, SENSE, VIEW 1
認識する ▶ KNOW
認識できる ▶ VISIBLE
人情 ▶ SYMPATHY
忍耐力 ▶ PATIENCE
認知 ▶ ATTENTION
任務 ▶ ASSIGNMENT, JOB, TASK
任命 ▶ JOB
任命する ▶ APPOINT

ぬ

ヌードの ▶ NAKED
脱がせる ▶ TAKE STH OFF
ぬかるみ ▶ SOIL
抜き出す ▶ PUMP
抜き取る ▶ CLEAR 動
脱ぐ ▶ TAKE STH OFF
拭い去る ▶ SUPPRESS 2
抜け ▶ MISTAKE 1
抜け目のない ▶ INTELLIGENT, SHREWD
盗人 ▶ THIEF
盗み ▶ THEFT
盗む ▶ STEAL
濡らす ▶ SOAK
ぬるぬるした ▶ SOFT
濡れた ▶ WET

ね

ネイティブ ▶ RESIDENT
ねえ ▶ DARLING
願い ▶ WISH
願う ▶ HOPE 動, WANT
寝かせる ▶ PUT
ねじる ▶ TURN 1
ねたみ ▶ JEALOUSY
値段 ▶ PRICE

…熱 ▶ OBSESSION
熱意のない ▶ INDIFFERENT
根っからの ▶ NATURAL
熱情 ▶ EMOTION, LOVE 名 1
熱心な ▶ BUSY 1, EAGER, INTENSE, RELIABLE 1, SERIOUS 2
熱する ▶ HEAT
熱中 ▶ INVOLVEMENT, LOVE 名 1, OBSESSION, TASTE
熱中させる ▶ INTEREST 動, INTERESTING
熱中した ▶ INTERESTED
熱中している ▶ BUSY 1
熱中の対象 ▶ TASTE
ネットワーク ▶ SYSTEM
熱望した ▶ EAGER
熱望する ▶ HOPE 動
熱烈な ▶ EAGER, INTENSE
値の張る ▶ EXPENSIVE
ねばねばした ▶ SOFT
眠い ▶ TIRED
眠気を催させる ▶ TIRED
眠そうな ▶ TIRED
眠る ▶ SLEEP
根も葉もない ▶ IRRATIONAL
狙う ▶ DESIGN 動 2
寝る ▶ SLEEP
念願 ▶ HOPE 名 2
捻挫する ▶ INJURE
年少者 ▶ CHILD
年代ものの ▶ OLD 1
粘土 ▶ SOIL
念頭に置く ▶ REMEMBER
年配の ▶ OLD 2
年表 ▶ SERIES
燃料 ▶ OIL

の

脳 ▶ MIND
農産物 ▶ PRODUCT
納税者 ▶ CITIZEN
農地 ▶ LAND 1
ノウハウ ▶ SKILL 2
膿瘍 ▶ TUMOUR
能率的な ▶ EFFICIENT
能率の悪い ▶ INEFFECTIVE
能力 ▶ ABILITY, SKILL 1, 2
ノー ▶ REFUSAL
逃れる ▶ ESCAPE

のけものにする ▶ EXCLUDE 2
残っている ▶ REMAIN
載せる ▶ PUT
のぞく ▶ STARE
除く ▶ EXCLUDE 1, REMOVE
望ましい ▶ BEST, BETTER, POPULAR
望まれていない ▶ UNWANTED
望み ▶ DESIRE, HOPE 名 1, WISH
望みのない ▶ USELESS
望みを託す ▶ TRUST
望む ▶ HOPE 動, WANT
ノックする ▶ KNOCK
のどかな ▶ QUIET 1
ののしりの ▶ OFFENSIVE
ののしる ▶ OFFEND
伸ばす ▶ EXPAND, PUSH 1
野放しの ▶ FREE 形 1
伸び ▶ INCREASE 名
のびのびした ▶ SPONTANEOUS
延び延びになった ▶ LATE
伸びる ▶ EXPAND, RISE
ノブ ▶ BUTTON 1
述べる ▶ COMMENT, DESCRIBE, SAY 2
のぼせ上がった ▶ IN LOVE
上る, 登る ▶ CLIMB
飲み込む ▶ EAT
ノミネートする ▶ RECOMMEND 2
飲み干す ▶ DRINK 動, EAT
飲む ▶ DRINK 動, EAT
乗り切る ▶ SURVIVE
乗組員 ▶ TEAM 1
載る ▶ FEATURE 動
のろい ▶ SLOW
のんびりした ▶ EASY 2
のんびりする ▶ REST

は

場合によって ▶ SOMETIMES
把握する ▶ UNDERSTAND 1
バージョン ▶ KIND 名
バースデー ▶ BIRTHDAY
パーティー ▶ EVENT 2
ハードコピー ▶ COPY 名 1
パートナー ▶ PARTNER 1, 2
ハードル ▶ BARRIER

這い上がる ▶ CLIMB
徘徊する ▶ WALK 1
廃棄する ▶ REMOVE
廃棄物 ▶ WASTE
売却する ▶ SELL 1
廃墟 ▶ REMAINS
ハイキングをする ▶ WALK 2
背景 ▶ CONTEXT, ENVIRONMENT
廃止する ▶ ABOLISH
敗者 ▶ LOSER 1
排出する ▶ PUMP
賠償 ▶ COMPENSATION
排除する ▶ EXCLUDE 1, PREVENT, REMOVE
廃水 ▶ WASTE
排斥する ▶ EXCLUDE 2
配送 ▶ DELIVERY
配属 ▶ JOB
配達 ▶ DELIVERY
配達する ▶ TAKE 1
配置 ▶ DESIGN 名, POSITION
配置する ▶ ARRANGE, PUT
売店 ▶ STALL
配当 ▶ PROFIT, SHARE 名
売買 ▶ TRADE
売買する ▶ SELL 2
配布資料 ▶ LEAFLET
廃物 ▶ WASTE
俳優 ▶ ACTOR
俳優業 ▶ DRAMA
ハイライト ▶ PEAK
ハイリスクな ▶ DANGEROUS
配慮 ▶ ATTENTION
入る ▶ ENTER
配列 ▶ SERIES
ばか ▶ FOOL
破壊する ▶ DEMOLISH, DESTROY, KILL
破壊的な ▶ HARMFUL, WILD
ばかげた ▶ CRAZY, RIDICULOUS
ばかな ▶ STUPID
はかない ▶ SHORT 1
ばかにする ▶ LAUGH AT SB/STH
ばかばかしい ▶ RIDICULOUS
秤にかける ▶ COMPARE 1
バカンス ▶ HOLIDAY 2
吐き気を催させる ▶ DISGUSTING 1

吐き気を催して ▶ SICK 2
破棄する ▶ ABOLISH
歯切れの悪い ▶ SILENT
掃く ▶ BRUSH
迫害 ▶ REPRESSION
迫害する ▶ SUPPRESS 1
博学な ▶ INTELLECTUAL 2
博識の ▶ INFORMED
爆笑させる ▶ LAUGH
薄情な ▶ RUTHLESS
漠然とした ▶ VAGUE
莫大な ▶ HIGH 1, HUGE, LARGE
剥奪する ▶ SUPPRESS 1
白熱した ▶ INTENSE
爆発させる
  ▶ TURN STH ON
薄片 ▶ FRAGMENT
薄暮 ▶ NIGHT 2
暴露する ▶ REVEAL
激しい ▶ ROUGH, TERRIBLE 3
激しくする[なる]
  ▶ INCREASE 動
励ます ▶ ENCOURAGE
励みになる ▶ PROMISING
派遣団 ▶ PARTY 2
破産した ▶ BANKRUPT
端 ▶ EDGE
恥 ▶ DISGRACE
はしがき ▶ INTRODUCTION
バシッと鳴らす ▶ BANG 1
恥じて ▶ SORRY
始まり ▶ SOURCE, START 名
始まる ▶ BEGIN, START 動
初め ▶ START 名
始める ▶ BEGIN, START 動
はしゃいだ ▶ LIVELY
場所 ▶ LAND 2, PLACE
走り書きする ▶ WRITE
走り去る ▶ FLEE
走る ▶ GO 2, HURRY, RUN 1
恥をかかせる
  ▶ EMBARRASS
恥ずかしい
  ▶ EMBARRASSED
恥ずかしがりの ▶ SHY
恥ずかしさ ▶ GUILT
外す ▶ FREE 動, UNDO
(眼鏡などを)外す
  ▶ TAKE STH OFF
パステル調の ▶ PALE
バスの ▶ DEEP 2
恥ずべき ▶ OUTRAGEOUS
弾み ▶ INCENTIVE

斜向かいに置く ▶ LEAN
旗 ▶ LOGO
裸にする[なる]
  ▶ TAKE STH OFF
裸の ▶ NAKED
果たす ▶ ACHIEVE, DO
ばたつく ▶ SHAKE 1
働いている ▶ WORK 動
働かせる ▶ USE 動
働きかけ ▶ OFFER 1
働く ▶ WORK 動 2
破綻 ▶ FAILURE
破綻する ▶ FAIL 2
バタンと閉まる[閉める]
  ▶ BANG 1
バタン[ピシャリ]と閉める ▶ CLOSE 動
罰当たりの ▶ EVIL 形
発育 ▶ PROGRESS
発覚する ▶ TURN OUT
発揮 ▶ EXPRESSION
発議する ▶ PROPOSE
はっきりした ▶ MARKED, PLAIN 2
はっきりしない
  ▶ QUIET 2, SILENT, UNCLEAR, VAGUE
はっきり見える ▶ VISIBLE
罰金 ▶ RATE
罰金を科す ▶ CHARGE 動
発掘する ▶ FIND 2
バックパッカー ▶ TOURIST
バックル ▶ BUTTON 2
抜群の ▶ REMARKABLE,
発言 ▶ STATEMENT
発見する ▶ FIND 2, 3, 4, NOTICE
発行する ▶ PROVIDE, PUBLISH 2
伐採する ▶ DEMOLISH
発症 ▶ START 名
発祥 ▶ SOURCE
発生させる ▶ MAKE 1
発生する ▶ HAPPEN
発送 ▶ DELIVERY
発送する ▶ SEND
発達 ▶ PROGRESS
発達する ▶ DEVELOP 1
はったり ▶ TRICK
発注する ▶ ORDER 2
発展 ▶ PROGRESS
発展させる ▶ DEVELOP 2
発展する ▶ DEVELOP 1, DO WELL, RISE
発売中で ▶ AVAILABLE

発表 ▶ PRESENTATION, STATEMENT
発表する ▶ INTRODUCE, PRESENT 1, PUBLISH 1, REVEAL
発奮させる
  ▶ INTERESTING
抜本的な ▶ SERIOUS 1
発明 ▶ DEVELOPMENT
発明する ▶ DESIGN 動 1
発明の才 ▶ INSPIRATION
はつらつとした ▶ LIVELY
果てしない ▶ PERMANENT
パトロン ▶ SPONSOR
花形 ▶ STAR
放された ▶ FREE 形 1
話 ▶ SPEECH, STORY
話し合い ▶ DISCUSSION
話し合う ▶ TALK
話の腰を折る
  ▶ INTERRUPT
話をする ▶ TALK
話す ▶ DESCRIBE, SAY 1, 2, TALK
放す ▶ FREE 動
放たれる ▶ FREE 動
放つ ▶ RELEASE
鼻にかける ▶ BOAST, PROUD 2
華やかな ▶ FASHIONABLE
離れる ▶ LEAVE 1
はにかんだ ▶ SHY
歯に衣着せぬ ▶ HONEST, PLAIN 2
パニックになる ▶ PANIC
はね ▶ DROP
跳ね上がる ▶ SOAR
はねつける ▶ REFUSE
パノラマ ▶ VIEW 2
幅が…の ▶ WIDE 2
はばかる ▶ HESITATE
羽ばたく ▶ SHAKE 1
派閥 ▶ PARTY 1
派閥主義 ▶ RACISM
幅の広い ▶ WIDE 2
幅広い ▶ WIDE 2
幅広さ ▶ RANGE 1
阻む ▶ BLOCK 1, 2
羽振りのよい ▶ RICH
破片 ▶ FRAGMENT, REMAINS
浜辺 ▶ COAST
場面 ▶ CONTEXT
波紋 ▶ RESULT
破門する ▶ EXCLUDE 2
早足で歩く ▶ RUN 1

早足の ▶ FAST
速い ▶ FAST
速さ ▶ SPEED
早まった ▶ RECKLESS
早める ▶ ACCELERATE
速める ▶ ACCELERATE
はやり ▶ FASHION
はやり言葉 ▶ SLOGAN
はやりの ▶ FASHIONABLE
払い戻し金
  ▶ COMPENSATION
ばら色の ▶ PROMISING
ばらす ▶ KILL, REVEAL
腹立たしい ▶ ANNOYING, DISGUSTING 2, OFFENSIVE
腹立ち ▶ TEMPER
ばらばらになる ▶ DIVIDE 1
ばらばらの ▶ PARTICULAR
ぱらぱらめくる ▶ READ
腹を立てた ▶ ANGRY
腹を立てる
  ▶ LOSE YOUR TEMPER
バランス ▶ RATIO
波瀾に富んだ ▶ BUSY 2
張り合う ▶ ARGUE
貼り紙 ▶ SIGN 2
バリケード ▶ BARRIER
貼り付く ▶ ATTACH
張り詰めた ▶ STRESSFUL, TENSE
パルチザン ▶ GUERRILLA
腫れ ▶ TUMOUR
晴れ上がった ▶ SUNNY
晴れた ▶ SUNNY
腫れ物 ▶ TUMOUR
晴れやかな ▶ CHEERFUL
パロディー ▶ PARODY
歯を食いしばる
  ▶ TIGHTEN
版 ▶ KIND 名
班 ▶ TEAM 1
晩 ▶ NIGHT 2
範囲 ▶ AREA 2, LIMIT 1, 2, PLACE, RANGE 1, 2
反意語 ▶ OPPOSITE 名
繁栄 ▶ MONEY 3, PROGRESS
繁栄した ▶ RICH, SUCCESSFUL 2
反感 ▶ HATRED, TENSION
反感を持つ ▶ HATE
反感を持った
  ▶ AGAINST SB/STH
反逆 ▶ REVOLUTION
反逆者 ▶ GUERRILLA

反逆する ▶ OPPOSE
半狂乱の ▶ HYSTERICAL
番組表 ▶ SCHEDULE
番狂わせ ▶ VICTORY
判型 ▶ DESIGN 名
判決 ▶ CONCLUSION
番号 ▶ FIGURE
反抗する ▶ OPPOSE
犯罪 ▶ CRIME 2
犯罪行為 ▶ CRIME 1
犯罪者 ▶ CRIMINAL
犯罪の ▶ ILLEGAL
ハンサムな ▶ BEAUTIFUL 1
反証する ▶ DISPROVE
反する ▶ CONFLICT 動
反省会 ▶ INVESTIGATION
反対 ▶ OPPOSITE 名, OPPOSITION
反対語 ▶ OPPOSITE 名
反対者 ▶ ENEMY, PROTESTER
反対する
　▶ AGAINST SB/STH, COMPLAIN, DISAGREE, DISAPPROVE, OPPOSE
反体制派 ▶ PROTESTER
反対の ▶ OPPOSITE 形, WRONG 1
反対票 ▶ REFUSAL
判断 ▶ VIEW 1
判断する ▶ CONCLUDE, JUDGE 動, THINK
範疇 ▶ CATEGORY
パンチをくらわす ▶ HIT 2
判定 ▶ CONCLUSION
ハンディキャップ
　▶ OBSTACLE
斑点 ▶ MARK
半透明の ▶ CLEAR 形 3
パンと鳴る ▶ BANG 1
ハンドル ▶ BUTTON 1
犯人 ▶ CRIMINAL
晩年の ▶ LAST 1
反応 ▶ ANSWER 名
万能の ▶ FLEXIBLE 1
販売員 ▶ SALESMAN, STAFF
販売している ▶ SELL 2
反駁する ▶ DENY, DISPROVE
反発 ▶ REVOLUTION
反発する ▶ OPPOSE
パンフレット ▶ LEAFLET
半分は ▶ PARTLY
判明する ▶ TURN OUT
反乱 ▶ REVOLUTION

氾濫 ▶ FLOOD 名 1
反乱者 ▶ GUERRILLA
氾濫する ▶ FLOOD 動
伴侶 ▶ FRIEND, PARTNER 2
反論する ▶ DISAGREE, DISPROVE
番をする
　▶ LOOK AFTER SB

ひ

比 ▶ RATIO
悲哀 ▶ GRIEF
ひいき ▶ TASTE
ピーク ▶ PEAK
非営利の ▶ LOSS-MAKING
冷えた ▶ COLD 1
冷える ▶ COOL
被害 ▶ DAMAGE 名
被害妄想の ▶ AFRAID
控え ▶ HELP 名
控え選手 ▶ REPLACEMENT
控えめな ▶ QUIET 3, SHY, SLIGHT
日帰り旅行 ▶ TRIP
控える ▶ HESITATE
比較して ▶ RELATIVE
比較する ▶ COMPARE 1
比較的な ▶ RELATIVE
日陰の ▶ DARK 1
干からびた ▶ ROTTEN
光る ▶ SHINE
惹かれる ▶ LIKE 動
悲観的な ▶ NEGATIVE
引き合いに出す
　▶ MENTION
引き上げる ▶ INCREASE 動
率いる ▶ LEAD
引き受ける
　▶ DEAL WITH SB/STH, DO, TAKE 4
引き起こす ▶ CAUSE
引き返す ▶ RETURN 1
引きこもりがちな
　▶ SOLITARY
引き裂く ▶ TEAR
引き下げ ▶ REDUCTION
引きずる ▶ PULL 1
引き継ぐ ▶ CONTINUE 3
ひきつけ ▶ SHIVER
引きつける ▶ NICE 2
引きつる ▶ SHIVER
引き止めておく ▶ JAIL
引き止める
　▶ HOLD SB/STH UP
引き抜く ▶ STEAL

引き離す ▶ ISOLATE, UNDO
引き紐 ▶ BUTTON 2
卑怯な ▶ CORRUPT
引き寄せる ▶ PULL 1, 2
引き渡す ▶ EXPEL, GIVE 2
引く ▶ PRESS 1, PULL 2
(音が)低い ▶ DEEP 2
ぴくっと動く ▶ SHAKE 3
ピクニック ▶ TRIP
びくびくさせる
　▶ WORRYING
びくびくした ▶ WORRIED
日暮れ ▶ NIGHT 2
悲劇 ▶ PLAY 名
悲劇的な ▶ SAD
秘訣 ▶ SOLUTION
ひけらかす ▶ BOAST
引けを取らない
　▶ COMPARE 2
非現実的な ▶ HIGH 1
非公開の ▶ SECRET
非行グループ ▶ PARTY 2
非公式の ▶ INFORMAL, UNOFFICIAL
尾行する ▶ FOLLOW 1
非公認の ▶ UNOFFICIAL
非行の ▶ ILLEGAL
非業の死をとげる ▶ DIE
非合法化する ▶ BAN 動
非合法の ▶ ILLEGAL
微細の ▶ SMALL
悲惨な ▶ NEGATIVE, PAINFUL 2, SAD, TERRIBLE 1
非識字の ▶ IGNORANT
非社交的な ▶ SOLITARY
批准する ▶ APPROVE
非常事態 ▶ CRISIS
非情な ▶ RUTHLESS, STERN
非常に ▶ VERY 副
微小の ▶ SMALL
びしょ濡れの ▶ WET
ヒステリー ▶ FEAR
ヒステリックな
　▶ HYSTERICAL
秘蔵 ▶ SUPPLY
秘蔵する ▶ KEEP 1
ひそひそ話す ▶ WHISPER
浸す ▶ SOAK
悲嘆 ▶ GRIEF
悲嘆に暮れた
　▶ UNHAPPY 1
備蓄 ▶ SUPPLY
備蓄する ▶ KEEP 1

悲痛 ▶ GRIEF
悲痛な ▶ SAD
ひっかく ▶ SCRATCH
引っ掛け ▶ TRICK
ひっくり返る ▶ FALL 2
びっくり仰天して
　▶ AFRAID
びっくりさせる
　▶ AMAZING, FRIGHTEN, SHOCK 動, SURPRISE
びっくりした ▶ AFRAID
日付 ▶ TIME
引っ越す ▶ LEAVE 2
引っ込み思案な
　▶ QUIET 3, SHY
必死の ▶ SERIOUS 1
筆者 ▶ WRITER
必需品 ▶ NEED 名
必須の ▶ ESSENTIAL, INEVITABLE, NECESSARY
必然性 ▶ NEED 名
必然的な ▶ INEVITABLE
ひったくる ▶ TAKE 3
ぴったりの ▶ IDEAL
ひっつかむ ▶ TAKE 3
匹敵する ▶ COMPARE 2, EQUIVALENT
引っ張る ▶ PULL 1, 2
必要 ▶ NEED 名
必要条件 ▶ CONDITION
必要書類 ▶ CERTIFICATE, DOCUMENT
必要性 ▶ NEED 名
必要とする ▶ CONTINUE 1, NEED 動
必要な ▶ INEVITABLE, NECESSARY
否定 ▶ REFUSAL
否定する ▶ DENY
否定的な ▶ HARMFUL
美点 ▶ BENEFIT, VALUE
人 ▶ PERSON
ひどい ▶ BAD, PAINFUL 2, POOR 2, REMARKABLE, TERRIBLE 1, 2, 3
一息 ▶ PAUSE
人影 ▶ SHAPE
一かたまり ▶ PIECE
一切れ ▶ PIECE
美徳 ▶ MORALITY
人込み ▶ CROWD
等しい ▶ EQUAL, EQUIVALENT
等しくない ▶ DIFFERENT
人好きのする ▶ NICE 2
一そろい ▶ GROUP 1

ひとづきあいのよい → ふくつの

人付き合いのよい ▶ SOCIABLE
一続き ▶ SERIES
人手 ▶ STAFF
一またぎ ▶ STEP
一目 ▶ LOOK 名
一人ぼっちの ▶ LONELY
独りよがり ▶ PRIDE
独り笑いをする ▶ LAUGH
避難 ▶ SHELTER
非難 ▶ CRITICISM
避難所 ▶ REFUGE
避難する ▶ FLEE
非難する ▶ ACCUSE, BLAME, DISAPPROVE, SCOLD
避難民 ▶ REFUGEE
皮肉 ▶ JOKE
皮肉な ▶ IRONIC
皮肉を含んだ ▶ IRONIC
否認する ▶ DENY
ひねる ▶ TURN 1
非の打ち所のない ▶ PERFECT
批判 ▶ CRITICISM
批判する ▶ BLAME
批判的な ▶ CRITICAL
ひびが入る ▶ BREAK 1
響き渡る ▶ DEEP 2
批評家 ▶ ANALYST, REPORTER
批評文 ▶ ASSESSMENT
びびる ▶ PANIC
ひびを入れる ▶ BREAK 1
疲弊させる ▶ USE 動 2
非凡さ ▶ VALUE
非凡な ▶ REMARKABLE
暇 ▶ LEISURE
暇な ▶ FREE 形 3
肥満の ▶ FAT
秘密にする ▶ HIDE
秘密の ▶ SECRET
秘密を漏らす ▶ TELL 2
美味な ▶ DELICIOUS
微妙な ▶ SENSITIVE 2
非民主的な ▶ REPRESSIVE
悲鳴を上げる ▶ SCREAM, SHOUT
秘めた ▶ SECRET
ひもじい ▶ HUNGRY
冷やす ▶ COOL
費用 ▶ COSTS, PRICE, RATE
表 ▶ LIST 名
秒 ▶ MINUTE

評価 ▶ ASSESSMENT, VALUATION, VIEW 1
評価価格 ▶ VALUATION
評価する ▶ JUDGE 動, TEST 動 2
病気 ▶ DISEASE, ILLNESS
評議員 ▶ OFFICIAL 名
病気にかかっている ▶ SICK 1
票決 ▶ ELECTION
評決 ▶ CONCLUSION
表現 ▶ EXPRESSION
表現する ▶ PRESENT 2, SAY 2
標語 ▶ SLOGAN
標示 ▶ ASSESSMENT
標識 ▶ SIGN 2
描写 ▶ DESCRIPTION
病弱な ▶ SICK 1
描写する ▶ PRESENT 2
描写的な ▶ DESCRIPTIVE
表出 ▶ EXPRESSION
標準 ▶ QUALITY
標準的な ▶ NORMAL
標準の ▶ USUAL
表象 ▶ DESCRIPTION
病状 ▶ PATIENT
評する ▶ REGARD
表題 ▶ CATEGORY
氷点下の ▶ FREEZING
平等 ▶ JUSTICE
病人 ▶ PATIENT
評判 ▶ REPUTATION
表明する ▶ DECLARE, PRESENT 3, SAY 2
表面的な ▶ APPARENT
評論 ▶ PAPER
評論家 ▶ ANALYST, EXPERT, REPORTER
病気がちの ▶ SICK 1
肥沃な ▶ PRODUCTIVE
ビラ ▶ LEAFLET
開き ▶ DIFFERENCE
開く ▶ HAVE 4, SPREAD
ひらめき ▶ INSPIRATION
比率 ▶ RATIO
(舌に)ぴりっとくる ▶ BITTER
ぴりぴりした ▶ HYSTERICAL, SENSITIVE 3, TENSE
ひりひりする ▶ PAINFUL 1
微量の ▶ SMALL
比類ない ▶ REMARKABLE
翻す ▶ BREAK 4
昼寝する ▶ SLEEP

ひるませる ▶ DISCOURAGE 2
ひるむ ▶ HESITATE
比例した ▶ RELATIVE
卑劣な ▶ EVIL 形
広い ▶ LARGE, WIDE 1
拾い読みする ▶ READ
披露 ▶ EXPRESSION
疲労困憊の ▶ TIRED
広がり ▶ LAND 2
広がる ▶ EXPAND, SPREAD
広げる ▶ EXPAND, SPREAD
広まった ▶ GENERAL
非論理的な ▶ IRRATIONAL
秘話 ▶ STORY
卑猥な ▶ OFFENSIVE
ピン ▶ BUTTON 2
品格 ▶ STYLE
敏感さ ▶ TACT
敏感な ▶ SENSITIVE 1, 3
貧窮 ▶ POVERTY
貧困 ▶ POVERTY
貧困の ▶ POOR 1
敏速な ▶ FAST
ぴんたする ▶ HIT 2
ぴんと張った ▶ TIGHT
頻繁な ▶ FREQUENT
頻繁に ▶ OFTEN
品評会 ▶ EXHIBITION
貧乏 ▶ POVERTY
貧乏な ▶ POOR 1
品目 ▶ THING 1

ふ

歩合 ▶ SHARE 名
無愛想な ▶ SOLITARY
ファイル ▶ DOCUMENT
ファイルする ▶ CLASSIFY
ファックス ▶ LETTER
ファッション ▶ FASHION
不安 ▶ CONCERN, FEAR, TROUBLE 1
ファン ▶ EXPERT, FAN
不安な ▶ STRESSFUL, WORRIED
不案内の ▶ NEW 3
不安にさせる ▶ FRIGHTEN
フィアンセ ▶ PARTNER 2
フィナーレ ▶ END 名
フィニッシュ ▶ END 名
部員 ▶ STAFF
風景 ▶ COUNTRY 2, VIEW 2
封鎖する ▶ BLOCK 2
風刺 ▶ PARODY
風刺的な ▶ IRONIC

風刺漫画 ▶ PICTURE
風習 ▶ TRADITION
ブース ▶ STALL
風潮 ▶ ATMOSPHERE, TREND
…ふうに ▶ LIKE 前 形
風味のよい ▶ DELICIOUS
ブーム ▶ FASHION
不運 ▶ TROUBLE 2
不運な[で] ▶ UNFORTUNATE 1
不運な事故 ▶ TROUBLE 2
フェアプレー ▶ JUSTICE
増える ▶ COLLECT, RISE
不穏 ▶ TROUBLE 1
不快感 ▶ FRUSTRATION, PAIN
不快な ▶ BAD, DISGUSTING 1, OFFENSIVE
不快にさせる ▶ OFFEND
不可解な ▶ CONFUSING, STRANGE 1
賦課金 ▶ PAYMENT
不確実な ▶ SENSITIVE 2
不可欠な ▶ INEVITABLE
不可欠の ▶ ESSENTIAL
不可能な ▶ IMPOSSIBLE
不可能にする ▶ PREVENT
不可避の ▶ INEVITABLE
深みのある ▶ DARK 2
不寛容 ▶ DISCRIMINATION
不機嫌 ▶ FRUSTRATION, TEMPER
不機嫌な ▶ IRRITABLE, UNHAPPY 2
不規則な ▶ VARIABLE
不吉な ▶ UNFORTUNATE 1
不気味な ▶ FRIGHTENING, STRANGE 1
不況 ▶ RECESSION
部局 ▶ SERVICE
不均衡 ▶ DIFFERENCE
不具合 ▶ DEFECT, PROBLEM
複合企業体 ▶ GROUP 3
複雑な ▶ COMPLEX
複写する ▶ COPY 動
復讐 ▶ REVENGE
服従する ▶ GIVE WAY
復唱する ▶ QUOTE
複製 ▶ COPY 名 2
複製画 ▶ PICTURE
複製する ▶ COPY 動
服装 ▶ CLOTHES
不屈の ▶ STUBBORN

日本語類語一覧

日本語類語一覧

副本 ▶ COPY 名 2
含む ▶ INCLUDE
含める ▶ INCLUDE
ふくよかな ▶ FAT
服を着る ▶ WEAR
服を脱ぐ ▶ TAKE STH OFF
不景気 ▶ RECESSION
不経済な ▶ LOSS-MAKING
不敬な ▶ RUDE
不潔な ▶ DIRTY
不健康 ▶ ILLNESS
不健康な ▶ SICK 1
不幸 ▶ TROUBLE 2
不合格 ▶ REFUSAL
不合格にする[なる]
　▶ FAIL 3
不幸な ▶ UNFORTUNATE 1
不公平 ▶ INEQUALITY
不公平な ▶ WRONG 3
不合理な ▶ IRRATIONAL,
　RIDICULOUS
布告 ▶ STATEMENT
房 ▶ GROUP 1
負債 ▶ DEBT
不在 ▶ LACK
不採用 ▶ REFUSAL
ふさぎ込ませる
　▶ DISCOURAGE 2
ふさぎ込んだ
　▶ DEPRESSED,
　UNHAPPY 1
ふさぐ ▶ BLOCK 2
ふざけ ▶ JOKE
無作法な ▶ OFFENSIVE,
　RUDE
ふさわしい ▶ GOOD 2,
　RESPECTABLE,
　RIGHT 形 1, WORTHY
不幸せな ▶ UNHAPPY 1
不思議な ▶ STRANGE 1
ぶしつけな ▶ CONFIDENT,
　HONEST, RUDE
無事な ▶ SAFE
不死の ▶ PERMANENT
不治の ▶ FATAL
不自由 ▶ POVERTY
不自由な ▶ DISABLED
不十分な
　▶ DISAPPOINTING,
　INADEQUATE
負傷させる ▶ INJURE
不正直な ▶ DISHONEST
不条理な ▶ WRONG 3
侮辱する ▶ OFFEND
侮辱的な ▶ INSULTING,
　OFFENSIVE

不信 ▶ SCEPTICISM
婦人 ▶ WOMAN
不信感 ▶ DOUBT 名 2
不信仰 ▶ SCEPTICISM
不親切な ▶ MEAN 形
不審な ▶ SUSPICIOUS 2
付随する ▶ RELATED
不正 ▶ CORRUPTION
不正確な ▶ WRONG 1
不成功 ▶ FAILURE
不正行為 ▶ CRIME 1,
　FRAUD 1
不誠実な ▶ DISHONEST
不正な ▶ CORRUPT,
　WRONG 3
不正な金もうけ
　▶ FRAUD 2
不正をする ▶ CHEAT 動
防ぐ ▶ PREVENT, PROTECT
不相応の ▶ EXCESSIVE
武装する[させる]
　▶ EQUIP
不足 ▶ LACK
部族 ▶ PEOPLE
足した ▶ SCARCE
不足な ▶ INADEQUATE
不測の ▶ SURPRISING
不測の事態 ▶ EVENT 1
付属品 ▶ DECORATION
不ぞろいの ▶ VARIABLE
部隊 ▶ ARMY,
　DEPARTMENT
舞台 ▶ CONTEXT
舞台芸術 ▶ DRAMA
不確かさ ▶ DOUBT 名 1
不確かな ▶ UNCLEAR,
　UNLIKELY 1
負担 ▶ PRESSURE 1,
　RESPONSIBILITY,
　SHARE 名
負担が大きい
　▶ DIFFICULT 1
普段着の ▶ INFORMAL
負担金 ▶ PAYMENT
普段の ▶ USUAL
普段は ▶ USUALLY
縁 ▶ EDGE
縁飾りをする ▶ DECORATE
ぶち壊し ▶ RUIN
縁取る ▶ DECORATE
不注意な ▶ CARELESS
不調 ▶ DEFECT
部長 ▶ LEADER 1
不調和 ▶ DIVISION 2
普通でない ▶ UNUSUAL

普通の ▶ AVERAGE,
　GENERAL, NORMAL,
　USUAL
普通は ▶ USUALLY
ぶつかる ▶ BANG 2,
　FIGHT 動, HIT 1, SHAKE 2
ぶっきらぼうな ▶ HONEST
ぶつける ▶ BANG 2, BEAT
不都合 ▶ DISADVANTAGE
不都合な ▶ DIFFICULT 2,
　WRONG 2
復刻品 ▶ COPY 名 2
物質 ▶ MATERIAL
物体 ▶ THING 1
ぶっつけ本番の
　▶ SPONTANEOUS
物品 ▶ THING 1, 2
ぶつぶつ言う ▶ WHISPER
物々交換 ▶ EXCHANGE
物々交換する
　▶ REPLACE 2
不釣合いな ▶ EXCESSIVE,
　WRONG 3
不定期の ▶ VARIABLE
不定の ▶ VARIABLE
不適格者 ▶ LOSER 2
不適格な ▶ INCOMPETENT,
　WRONG 2
不適切な ▶ WRONG 2
不適当な ▶ WRONG 2
(声が)太い ▶ DEEP 2
不動産 ▶ LAND 1
舞踏場 ▶ HALL 1
不道徳な ▶ WRONG 3
不当な ▶ CORRUPT,
　HIGH 1, ILLEGAL,
　WRONG 3
太った ▶ FAT
船荷 ▶ CARGO
不慣れな ▶ NEW 3
無難な ▶ FINE
不買運動 ▶ BAN 名
腐敗した ▶ CORRUPT,
　ROTTEN
不備 ▶ DEFECT
不必要な ▶ EXCESS
不評 ▶ DISGRACE
不平等 ▶ INEQUALITY
不平等な ▶ WRONG 3
部品 ▶ ELEMENT
不品行 ▶ EVIL 名
不品行な ▶ WRONG 3
不憫な ▶ SAD
不服な ▶ UNHAPPY 2
部分 ▶ ELEMENT, PLACE
部分的には ▶ PARTLY

不平を言う ▶ COMPLAIN
侮蔑 ▶ CONTEMPT
侮蔑的な ▶ INSULTING
不便 ▶ DISADVANTAGE
不変の ▶ STEADY
不偏不党の ▶ OBJECTIVE
不法侵入 ▶ THEFT
不法な ▶ ILLEGAL
不本意ながらの
　▶ RELUCTANT
不満 ▶ CRITICISM,
　FRUSTRATION
不満足な
　▶ DISAPPOINTING
不満で ▶ UNHAPPY 2
不満な ▶ ANGRY,
　UNHAPPY 2
不満を言う ▶ COMPLAIN
不満を示す ▶ DISAPPROVE
不明確な ▶ UNCLEAR
不明の ▶ STRANGE 2
不名誉 ▶ DISGRACE
不明瞭 ▶ DOUBT 名 1
不明瞭な ▶ UNCLEAR
不滅の ▶ PERMANENT
不面目 ▶ DISGRACE
部門 ▶ DEPARTMENT,
　SERVICE
増やす ▶ COLLECT
富裕 ▶ MONEY 3
富裕な ▶ RICH
不愉快な ▶ MEAN 形
冬らしい ▶ FREEZING
不用になった ▶ DESERTED
プライド ▶ DIGNITY, PRIDE
プラグを抜く
　▶ TURN STH OFF
ブラシをかける ▶ BRUSH
ふらつかない ▶ FIRM
ぶらつく ▶ STAY 1, WALK 1
ぶらぶらする ▶ REST
フランチャイズ
　▶ LICENCE
不利 ▶ DISADVANTAGE
不利益な ▶ HARMFUL
不利な ▶ DIFFICULT 2
振り向かせる ▶ TURN 1
振り向く ▶ TURN 1
不良な ▶ POOR 2
武力 ▶ FORCE 名
振り分ける ▶ SHARE 動
振りをする ▶ PRETEND
不倫 ▶ RELATIONSHIP 2
プリントアウト
　▶ COPY 名 1
(人を)振る ▶ LEAVE 4

振る ▶ SHAKE 1
古い ▶ OLD 1
部類 ▶ CATEGORY
奮い立たせる ▶ INSPIRE
震え ▶ SHIVER
震えない ▶ FIRM
震える ▶ SHAKE 3
古株の ▶ EXPERIENCED
古臭い ▶ FORMAL, OLD-FASHIONED
無礼講の ▶ SOCIABLE
無礼な ▶ INSULTING, MEAN 形, RUDE
プレーオフ ▶ GAME
プレート ▶ SIGN 2
ブレーン ▶ GENIUS
プレゼンテーション ▶ PRESENTATION
プレゼント ▶ GIFT
プレッシャー ▶ PRESSURE 1
触れる ▶ MENTION, TOUCH
プログラム ▶ PLAN 1, SCHEDULE
プロジェクト ▶ PROJECT
ブロック ▶ PIECE
風呂に入れる ▶ WASH
プロフィール ▶ DESCRIPTION
プロフェッショナルな ▶ GOOD 4
プロモーション ▶ ADVERTISEMENT
不和 ▶ DIVISION 2, OBSTACLE
ふわふわした ▶ SOFT
分 ▶ MINUTE
雰囲気 ▶ ATMOSPHERE
憤慨 ▶ FRUSTRATION, TEMPER
憤慨させる ▶ ANGER 動, SHOCK 動
憤慨した ▶ FURIOUS
分割 ▶ DIVISION 1
分割する ▶ DIVIDE 1, SHARE 動
文化の ▶ CULTURAL
墳丘 ▶ HILL
分散する ▶ DIVIDE 1
噴出 ▶ FLOOD 名 2
噴出させる ▶ FLOW
噴出する ▶ FLOW
粉飾する ▶ EXAGGERATE
文書ファイル ▶ DOCUMENT
分数 ▶ FIGURE

分析 ▶ RESEARCH
分析する ▶ EXAMINE
扮装 ▶ PARODY
紛争 ▶ WAR
分隊 ▶ ARMY, DEPARTMENT, TEAM 1
分担金 ▶ PAYMENT
分担分 ▶ SHARE 名
文通 ▶ COMMUNICATION
奮闘 ▶ ATTEMPT
奮闘する ▶ OPPOSE, TRY 1
ぶん殴る ▶ HIT 2
分派 ▶ DEPARTMENT
分配する ▶ DISTRIBUTE, SHARE 動
文筆家 ▶ WRITER
分別のある ▶ ADULT, REALISTIC, REASONABLE, WISE
文脈 ▶ CONTEXT
分野 ▶ AREA 2
分離 ▶ DIVISION 1
分離する ▶ ISOLATE
分量 ▶ NUMBER
分類する ▶ CLASSIFY
分裂 ▶ DIVISION 2
分裂する ▶ DIVIDE 1, 2

へ

平安 ▶ SILENCE
平易な ▶ AVERAGE, CLEAR 形 2, PLAIN 1
平穏 ▶ PEACE, SILENCE
平穏な ▶ QUIET 1
平滑な ▶ FLAT
平均的な ▶ NORMAL
並行した ▶ PARALLEL
併合する ▶ INVADE
平常は ▶ USUALLY
平静 ▶ SILENCE
平坦な ▶ FLAT
並置する ▶ COMPARE 1
平凡な ▶ AVERAGE, CONSERVATIVE, NORMAL, USUAL
平和 ▶ PEACE
へそくり ▶ FUND 名
下手くそな ▶ POOR 2
隔たり ▶ GAP
下手な ▶ POOR 2
別居した ▶ SINGLE
別個の ▶ PARTICULAR
別々の ▶ PARTICULAR
ベテランの ▶ EXPERIENCED

ぺてん ▶ FRAUD 2
ペテン師 ▶ CRIMINAL
へとへとになった ▶ TIRED
へま ▶ MISTAKE 1
減らす ▶ CUT 1, REDUCE
ベルクロ ▶ BUTTON 2
便 ▶ FACILITIES
変化 ▶ CHANGE 名 1, DIFFERENCE
弁解 ▶ REASON
変化する ▶ BECOME, CHANGE 動 2
返還 ▶ COMPENSATION
返還する ▶ RETURN 2
変換する ▶ SWITCH
便所 ▶ TOILET
返却する ▶ RETURN 2
勉強 ▶ EDUCATION
勉強する ▶ LEARN
偏狭な ▶ BIASED, LIMITED 1
ペンキを塗る ▶ PAINT
返金 ▶ COMPENSATION
変形させる ▶ TURN 2
偏見 ▶ DISCRIMINATION, RACISM, TENDENCY
偏見のある ▶ BIASED
偏見のない ▶ OBJECTIVE
偏見を抱かせる ▶ INFLUENCE 動
弁護 ▶ ARGUMENT 2, SECURITY
偏向 ▶ DISCRIMINATION
変更 ▶ CHANGE 名 2
変更する ▶ SWITCH
弁護士 ▶ LAWYER
弁護士業 ▶ LAWYER
弁護する ▶ EXPLAIN 2
弁護団 ▶ LAWYER
返済 ▶ PAYMENT
返事 ▶ ANSWER 名
編集長 ▶ REPORTER
便所 ▶ TOILET
弁償 ▶ COMPENSATION
返事をする ▶ ANSWER 動
編成 ▶ SYSTEM
返送する ▶ RETURN 2
返答 ▶ ANSWER 名
変動 ▶ CHANGE 名 1
返答する ▶ ANSWER 動
変動する ▶ CHANGE 動 2
変な ▶ STRANGE 1
変な奴 ▶ FOOL
返品する ▶ RETURN 2
弁明 ▶ ARGUMENT 2
弁明する ▶ EXPLAIN 2

変容させる ▶ TURN 2
便利な ▶ USEFUL

ほ

ボイコット ▶ BAN 名
法 ▶ RULE 名
某… ▶ SECRET
方位 ▶ WAY 3
防衛 ▶ PRECAUTION, SECURITY
防衛する ▶ PROTECT
貿易 ▶ TRADE
貿易商 ▶ DEALER
崩壊 ▶ FAILURE
崩壊する ▶ FAIL 2
妨害する ▶ BLOCK 1, 2
法外な ▶ EXCESSIVE, HIGH 1
方角 ▶ WAY 3
包括する ▶ INCLUDE
包括的な ▶ DETAILED
包含する ▶ INCLUDE
法規 ▶ LAW
蜂起 ▶ REVOLUTION
放棄する ▶ STOP
俸給 ▶ INCOME
防御 ▶ PRECAUTION, SECURITY
防御する ▶ PROTECT
暴君 ▶ DICTATOR
冒険 ▶ RISK 2
暴言を吐く ▶ OFFEND
防護 ▶ SECURITY
方向 ▶ WAY 3
芳香 ▶ SMELL
暴行 ▶ ATTACK 名 2
暴行する ▶ ATTACK 動 1
方向づける ▶ DETERMINE
方向転換 ▶ CORNER
報告 ▶ REPORT 2
報告する ▶ TELL 1
報告を求める ▶ QUESTION 動
防塞 ▶ BARRIER
方策 ▶ ACTION, HABIT, PLAN 1, TACTIC
防止 ▶ LIMIT 1
方式 ▶ WAY 2
防止する ▶ BAN 動
報酬 ▶ AWARD, RATE
宝飾品 ▶ DECORATION
方針 ▶ ATTITUDE, HABIT, PLAN 1
呆然とした ▶ CONFUSED
包装する ▶ FILL

ぼうそうする → まちがいなく

暴走する ▶ RUN 1
包装を解く ▶ UNDO
法則 ▶ THEORY 1
膨大な ▶ HIGH 1, HUGE
法治 ▶ PEACE
放置する ▶ LEAVE 4
膨張する ▶ EXPAND
傍聴人 ▶ INSPECTOR
法廷 ▶ COURT
法定の ▶ LEGAL
法的手続き ▶ CASE
法的な ▶ LEGAL
法的に有効な ▶ LEGAL
法典 ▶ LAW
暴徒 ▶ CROWD
報道 ▶ REPORT 2
冒頭 ▶ START 名
暴動 ▶ REVOLUTION
暴騰した ▶ HIGH 1
報道する ▶ DESCRIBE
冒頭の ▶ FIRST
ほうび ▶ AWARD
暴風雨の ▶ ROUGH
報復 ▶ REVENGE
方法 ▶ TACTIC, WAY 1, 2
亡命 ▶ SHELTER
亡命者 ▶ REFUGEE
方面 ▶ WAY 3
訪問 ▶ VISIT 名
訪問客 ▶ TOURIST
訪問する ▶ VISIT 動
抱擁する ▶ HUG
暴落する ▶ SLUMP
放り込む ▶ PUT
法律 ▶ LAW, RULE 名
法律違反の ▶ ILLEGAL
法律で定められた
 ▶ LEGAL
法律で認められた
 ▶ LEGAL
法律に関する ▶ LEGAL
放り投げる ▶ THROW
暴力 ▶ FORCE 名,
 PRESSURE 2
暴力団 ▶ PARTY 2
暴力的な ▶ VIOLENT
暴力による ▶ VIOLENT
法令 ▶ RULE 名
ポーズ ▶ POSITION
ホームシックにかかった
 ▶ LONELY
ホール ▶ HALL 1
他ならぬ ▶ VERY 形
保管記録 ▶ DOCUMENT
保管する ▶ CLASSIFY,
 KEEP 1

ボクシングをする
 ▶ FIGHT 動
ほくそえむ ▶ LAUGH
保険料 ▶ PAYMENT
保護 ▶ SECURITY, SHELTER
保護区 ▶ REFUGE
保護施設 ▶ REFUGE
保護する ▶ PROTECT
誇り ▶ SATISFACTION
誇り高い ▶ PROUD 1
ほこりだらけの ▶ DIRTY
誇りとする ▶ BOAST
ほこりを拭き取る
 ▶ BRUSH
誇る ▶ HAVE 2
ほしがる ▶ WANT
保持している ▶ KEEP 3
保持する ▶ KEEP 2, 3
補充する ▶ FILL
保守的な
 ▶ CONSERVATIVE,
 OLD-FASHIONED
補助 ▶ HELP 名
歩哨 ▶ GUARD
補償 ▶ COMPENSATION
保証 ▶ PROMISE 名
保証する ▶ CONFIRM 2,
 ENSURE, PROMISE 動
保障する ▶ PROMISE 動
保証人 ▶ SPONSOR
保証人になる ▶ FUND 動
補助器具 ▶ TOOL
補助金 ▶ GIFT,
 INVESTMENT
細い ▶ NARROW, THIN
細くなる ▶ SHRINK
ぼそぼそ言う ▶ WHISPER
保存する ▶ KEEP 1, 3,
 PROTECT
ボタン ▶ BUTTON 1, 2
ボタンを外す ▶ UNDO
勃興 ▶ PROGRESS
欲する ▶ WANT
ほっそりした ▶ THIN
ぼったくる ▶ DEFRAUD
発端 ▶ SOURCE
ぽっちゃりした ▶ FAT
没頭 ▶ INVOLVEMENT,
 OBSESSION
没頭させる
 ▶ INTEREST 動,
 INTERESTING
没頭した ▶ INTERESTED
ほっとした ▶ GLAD
ホットな ▶ POPULAR
ボディガード ▶ GUARD

ほてる ▶ FLUSH
歩道 ▶ PATH
ほどく ▶ FREE 動,
 SPREAD, UNDO
ほどける ▶ SPREAD
施し ▶ AID, GIFT
ほとばしり ▶ FLOOD 名 2
ほどほどの ▶ ADEQUATE
程よい ▶ SLIGHT
ほとんど ▶ ALMOST
ほとんど同じで
 ▶ LIKE 前形
ほとんど…ない ▶ RARELY
ほとんどの場合
 ▶ USUALLY
骨折り ▶ EFFORT
骨の折れる ▶ DIFFICULT 1,
 HARD
ほのかな ▶ PALE
ほの暗い ▶ DIM, PALE
ほのめかし ▶ REFERENCE
ほのめかす ▶ MEAN 動 2,
 MENTION, SUGGEST
歩幅 ▶ STEP
ほぼ ▶ ALMOST
ほほ笑む ▶ SMILE
ほめる ▶ PRAISE 動
保有し続ける ▶ KEEP 2
保有する ▶ HAVE 1
ボランティアで働く
 ▶ VOLUNTARY 2
ボランティアの
 ▶ VOLUNTARY 2
掘り出す ▶ FIND 2
ほれ込んだ ▶ IN LOVE
ぼろぼろの ▶ ROTTEN
ホワイエ ▶ HALL 2
歩を進める ▶ WALK 1
本 ▶ BOOK
本気の ▶ DEEP 1,
 SERIOUS 2
本質 ▶ NATURE 1, SOURCE
本質的な ▶ FUNDAMENTAL
本性 ▶ NATURE 1,
 PERSONALITY
本当に ▶ QUITE 2, VERY 副
本当の ▶ REAL, TRUE
ポンと鳴る[鳴らす]
 ▶ BANG 1
本能 ▶ INSTINCT, THEORY 1
本能的な ▶ NATURAL
本分 ▶ RESPONSIBILITY
本物の ▶ REAL
本文 ▶ POINT
ぼんやりした ▶ CARELESS

ぼんやりとした ▶ DIM,
 PALE, VAGUE
本来の ▶ FIRST
奔流 ▶ FLOOD 名 1

ま

間 ▶ PAUSE
マーケティングする
 ▶ ADVERTISE
真新しい ▶ NEW 1, 2
まあまあ ▶ QUITE 1
まあまあの ▶ FINE
埋蔵量 ▶ SUPPLY
マイナスの ▶ HARMFUL
マイナス面
 ▶ DISADVANTAGE
前置き ▶ INTRODUCTION
前口上 ▶ INTRODUCTION
前の ▶ PREVIOUS
前払い金 ▶ LOAN
前向きな ▶ OPTIMISTIC
満足のゆく ▶ SATISFYING
曲がり角 ▶ CORNER
曲がりくねる ▶ CURVE
曲がる ▶ CURVE
巻き込む ▶ AFFECT
紛らわしい ▶ CONFUSING,
 MISLEADING
紛れもない ▶ MARKED,
 UNDOUBTED
まぐれ ▶ MIRACLE
負け犬 ▶ LOSER 2
負け嫌いの
 ▶ AGGRESSIVE 2
負けたチーム ▶ LOSER 1
負けた人 ▶ LOSER 1
曲げられる ▶ FLEXIBLE 2
負ける ▶ GIVE WAY
曲げる ▶ CURVE
まごつかせる
 ▶ WORRYING
まことしやかな
 ▶ POSSIBLE 2
まさにその ▶ VERY 形
勝る ▶ WIN
まじめくさった
 ▶ SERIOUS 2
まじめな ▶ SERIOUS 2
まずい ▶ WRONG 2
貧しい ▶ POOR 1
まず…ない ▶ RARELY
まずまずの ▶ ADEQUATE
町 ▶ CITY
間違い ▶ MISTAKE 1
間違いなく ▶ QUITE 2

まちがいのない → みをまかせる

間違いのない ▶ RIGHT 形 1
間違った ▶ WRONG 1
間近の ▶ NEXT
待ち望む ▶ HOPE 動
真っ赤になる ▶ FLUSH
末期患者 ▶ PATIENT
末期疾患を患った ▶ FATAL
末期の ▶ FATAL
真っ暗な ▶ DARK 1
末梢的な ▶ MINOR
まったく ▶ QUITE 2, VERY 副
まったくの ▶ COMPLETE, VERY 形, WHOLE
的外れの ▶ IRRELEVANT
まとめ役 ▶ ORGANIZER
まとめる ▶ FINISH
まともな ▶ RESPECTABLE, RIGHT 形 2
間取り ▶ DESIGN 名
マナー ▶ RESPECT 名
学ぶ ▶ LEARN
マニア ▶ EXPERT
間に合う ▶ GET 3
マニフェスト ▶ PLAN 1
マニュアル ▶ BOOK
免れえない ▶ INEVITABLE
免れる ▶ ESCAPE
間抜け ▶ FOOL
招かれていない ▶ UNWANTED
招き入れる ▶ LET SB IN
まねる ▶ FOLLOW 4
まばらな ▶ INADEQUATE, OCCASIONAL
魔法 ▶ INTEREST 名 1
(…の)ままでいる ▶ REMAIN
守る ▶ FOLLOW 3, PROTECT
麻薬 ▶ DRUG 1
迷った ▶ UNSURE
真夜中 ▶ NIGHT 1
魔力 ▶ INTEREST 名 1
まる… ▶ WHOLE
まるごとの ▶ WHOLE
丸っこい ▶ FAT
まれな ▶ RARE
まれに ▶ RARELY
回す ▶ GIVE 2
回る ▶ SPIN
満員の ▶ FULL
満席の ▶ FULL
満足(感) ▶ SATISFACTION

満足させる ▶ MEET 4, PLEASE
満足のいく ▶ FINE
万引き ▶ THEFT
万引きする ▶ STEAL
万引き犯 ▶ THIEF
満腹の ▶ FULL
満面の笑みを浮かべる ▶ SMILE

み

見合った ▶ RELATIVE
見誤る ▶ MISUNDERSTAND
見出す ▶ SEE
実入りのよい ▶ SUCCESSFUL 2
身内 ▶ FAMILY 2
見えなくなる ▶ DISAPPEAR
見える ▶ SEEM
見えること ▶ LOOK 名
見落とし ▶ MISTAKE 1
未解決の ▶ UNCLEAR
未回答の ▶ UNCLEAR
見返り ▶ AWARD
見返り金 ▶ BRIBE
見限られた ▶ DESERTED
見かけ上の ▶ APPARENT
見かける ▶ FIND 2
見方 ▶ ATTITUDE, VIEW 1
味方する ▶ EXPLAIN 2, SUPPORT
見きわめる ▶ SEE
見くびり ▶ CONTEMPT
見くびるような ▶ INSULTING
見苦しい ▶ UGLY
未決定の ▶ UNCLEAR, UNSURE
見事な ▶ MAGNIFICENT, WONDERFUL, WORTHY
見込み ▶ EXPECTATION, HOPE 名 1, POSSIBILITY, POTENTIAL
見込みのある ▶ LIKELY, PROMISING
見込む ▶ HOPE 動
未婚の ▶ SINGLE
短い ▶ SHORT 1, 2
短くする ▶ CUT 1, SHRINK
惨めさ ▶ DISTRESS, GRIEF
惨めな ▶ TERRIBLE 1, UNFORTUNATE 2, UNHAPPY 1
未熟さ ▶ IGNORANCE

未熟な ▶ NAIVE
ミス ▶ MISTAKE 1
水煙 ▶ MOISTURE
水しぶき ▶ MOISTURE
見捨てられた ▶ DESERTED
見捨てる ▶ LEAVE 4
水浸しにする ▶ SOAK
水ぶくれ ▶ TUMOUR
ミスプリント ▶ MISTAKE 2
店 ▶ COMPANY
未成熟の ▶ CHILDISH
未成年者 ▶ CHILD, GIRL
見せかけ ▶ IMAGINATION
見せかけの ▶ MISLEADING, WRONG 1
見せかける ▶ PRETEND
店のおごりで ▶ FREE 形 2
見せる ▶ PRESENT 1, 2, SHOW 2
溝 ▶ GAP
見出し ▶ CATEGORY
満たす ▶ FILL, MEET 4
見た目のよい ▶ BEAUTIFUL 2
道 ▶ PATH, ROAD, WAY 3
道順 ▶ WAY 3
道筋 ▶ WAY 3
未知の ▶ STRANGE 2
満ちる ▶ FILL
見つけ出す ▶ FIND 4
見つける ▶ FIND 2, 3, SEE
密告する ▶ TELL 2
密通 ▶ RELATIONSHIP 2
みっともない ▶ OUTRAGEOUS
密売 ▶ TRADE
密売する ▶ SELL 2
見つめること ▶ LOOK 名
見積もり ▶ ESTIMATE 名, VALUATION
見積もる ▶ ESTIMATE 動
密漁者 ▶ THIEF
見て見ぬ振りをする ▶ IGNORE
見通し ▶ IDEA 1, POTENTIAL
見通しの暗い ▶ NEGATIVE
認める ▶ ADMIT, IN FAVOUR, SEE
見取り図 ▶ PLAN 2
見直す ▶ ADJUST, EXAMINE
見なす ▶ REGARD
源 ▶ SOURCE
見習い ▶ RECRUIT

見習う ▶ FOLLOW 4
身なりのよい ▶ ELEGANT
見に行く ▶ LOOK 動 1
醜い ▶ UGLY
ミニチュアの ▶ SMALL
身につける ▶ GET 1, LEARN
身に着ける ▶ WEAR
見抜く ▶ SEE
峰 ▶ HILL
未納金 ▶ DEBT
身の毛もよだつ ▶ TERRIBLE 3
実りの多い ▶ PRODUCTIVE
未発達の ▶ CHILDISH
見放す ▶ LEAVE 4
見張り人 ▶ GUARD
身振り ▶ MOVEMENT, SIGNAL
身震い ▶ SHIVER
身震いする ▶ SHAKE 3
身分 ▶ STATUS
身分証明書 ▶ CERTIFICATE
見本 ▶ FAKE
見本市 ▶ EXHIBITION
見舞いに行く ▶ VISIT 動
見守る ▶ LOOK 動 1, REGULATE
耳にする ▶ NOTICE
耳を貸す ▶ HEAR
耳を澄ます ▶ HEAR
耳をつんざくような ▶ HIGH 3, LOUD
未明 ▶ NIGHT 1
脈絡 ▶ MESSAGE
未来の ▶ NEXT
魅了する ▶ DELIGHT, INTEREST 動
魅力 ▶ CHARM, INTEREST 名 1, LOVE 名 1
魅力的な ▶ BEAUTIFUL 1, 2, NICE 1, POPULAR
魅力のない ▶ UGLY
見る ▶ LOOK 動 1, SEE
見ること ▶ LOOK 名
見る人 ▶ AUDIENCE
魅惑 ▶ INTEREST 名 1, LOVE 名 1
魅惑する ▶ DELIGHT
魅惑的な ▶ INTERESTING
見分けのつく ▶ VISIBLE
見分ける ▶ SEE
身を引く ▶ LEAVE 3
身を任せる ▶ GIVE WAY

みんかんの → もうしたてる

日本語類語一覧

民間の ▶ CULTURAL
民族 ▶ PEOPLE
民族意識 ▶ RACISM
民族主義 ▶ RACISM
民俗の ▶ CULTURAL
民族の ▶ CULTURAL

む

無意識下の ▶ UNCONSCIOUS
無一文の ▶ BANKRUPT, POOR 1
向いていない ▶ INCOMPETENT
無意味な ▶ USELESS
ムード ▶ ATMOSPHERE
無益な ▶ USELESS
無縁の ▶ STRANGE 2
向かう ▶ GO 1
迎え入れる ▶ LET SB IN
迎える ▶ GREET
無学の ▶ IGNORANT
昔かたぎの ▶ OLD-FASHIONED
昔の ▶ FORMER, PREVIOUS
昔ふうの ▶ OLD-FASHIONED
むかつく ▶ TERRIBLE 1
むかむかさせる ▶ DISGUSTING 1
無関心な ▶ INDIFFERENT
無傷の ▶ SAFE
むき出しの ▶ NAKED, PLAIN 1
無記名投票 ▶ ELECTION
無給で働く ▶ VOLUNTARY 2
無給の ▶ VOLUNTARY 2
無教養な ▶ IGNORANT
無許可の ▶ UNOFFICIAL
向きを変える ▶ LEAN, TURN 1
無菌の ▶ CLEAN 形
無口な ▶ QUIET 3, SOLITARY
無垢な ▶ NAIVE
むくれること ▶ TEMPER
向けられる ▶ FOCUS
向ける ▶ FOCUS
無効にする ▶ CANCEL
向こう見ずな ▶ RECKLESS
無言の ▶ SILENT
無罪の ▶ INNOCENT
無作為の ▶ RANDOM
蒸し暑い ▶ HUMID

蒸し暑さ ▶ MOISTURE
無視する ▶ IGNORE
無実の ▶ INNOCENT
無地の ▶ PLAIN 1
無慈悲な ▶ RUTHLESS, STERN, STRICT
無邪気さ ▶ IGNORANCE
矛盾 ▶ CONFLICT 名
矛盾する ▶ CONFLICT 動, INCONSISTENT
無情な ▶ RUTHLESS
無償の ▶ VOLUNTARY 2
無色の ▶ CLEAR 形 3
無神経な ▶ INSENSITIVE, RUTHLESS
無人の ▶ DESERTED
難しい ▶ DIFFICULT 1, SENSITIVE 2
結び付ける ▶ ATTACH, RELATE
結びの ▶ LAST 1
むずむずする ▶ PAINFUL 1
無政府状態 ▶ TROUBLE 1
無責任な ▶ RECKLESS
むせる ▶ COUGH
夢想 ▶ IMAGINATION
無駄な ▶ USELESS
無知 ▶ IGNORANCE
無秩序な ▶ UNTIDY
無知な ▶ IGNORANT
夢中 ▶ LOVE 名 1, TASTE
夢中にさせる ▶ DELIGHT
むっつりした ▶ IRRITABLE
むっとさせる ▶ ANNOY
むっとする ▶ LOSE YOUR TEMPER
むっとすること ▶ TEMPER
無頓着な ▶ INDIFFERENT
胸くそ悪い ▶ DISGUSTING 1
胸騒ぎ ▶ IDEA 2
無認可の ▶ UNOFFICIAL
無念 ▶ FRUSTRATION
無能な ▶ INCOMPETENT, INEFFECTIVE
無分別な ▶ RECKLESS
無法な ▶ WILD
無謀な ▶ RECKLESS
無防備な ▶ VULNERABLE
謀反 ▶ REVOLUTION
無味乾燥な ▶ BORING
無免許の ▶ UNOFFICIAL
無用の ▶ USELESS
村 ▶ CITY
無理強い ▶ PRESSURE 2
無理な ▶ IMPOSSIBLE

無理もない ▶ OBVIOUS
無料の ▶ FREE 形 2
無力な ▶ INCOMPETENT, INEFFECTIVE, VULNERABLE
群れ ▶ GROUP 1

め

明快な ▶ CLEAR 形 2
明快にする ▶ EXPLAIN 1
明確な ▶ CLEAR 形 2, EXACT, PARTICULAR, PLAIN 2
明確に述べる ▶ LIST 動
明記する ▶ LIST 動
明言する ▶ DECLARE
明細な ▶ EXACT
名士 ▶ STAR
明示する ▶ EXPLAIN 1, LIST 動, SHOW 1
明示的な ▶ CLEAR 形 2
命じる ▶ ORDER 1, RULE 動 2
名人の ▶ IMPRESSIVE
名声 ▶ FAME, REPUTATION, STATUS, VALUE
瞑想 ▶ CONSIDERATION
瞑想にふける ▶ CONSIDER
命題 ▶ THEORY 2
明白な ▶ CLEAR 形 1, MARKED, OBVIOUS
銘板 ▶ SIGN 2
明敏な ▶ SHREWD
名簿 ▶ LIST 名
命名する ▶ CALL 1
盟友 ▶ PARTNER 1
名誉 ▶ INTEGRITY, PLEASURE, REPUTATION, STATUS
名誉ある ▶ GREAT 2
名誉職の ▶ VOLUNTARY 2
名誉な ▶ FAMOUS
名誉を傷つけるような ▶ INSULTING
命令する ▶ ORDER 1, RULE 動 2
メーカー ▶ MAKER
メール ▶ LETTER
目が離せない ▶ INTERESTING
目利き ▶ EXPERT, JUDGE 名
恵まれている ▶ HAVE 2
巡り合う ▶ FIND 2

巡り合わせ ▶ LUCK, RISK 2
目指す ▶ INTEND
目障りな ▶ UGLY
珍しい ▶ RARE, UNUSUAL
目線 ▶ LOOK 名
めそめそ泣く ▶ CRY
目立たない ▶ AVERAGE
目立つ ▶ MARKED, VISIBLE
メダル ▶ AWARD
めちゃくちゃにする ▶ RUIN
メッセージ ▶ LETTER, MESSAGE
めったにない ▶ RARE
めったに…ない ▶ RARELY
目にする ▶ NOTICE
目に見える ▶ VISIBLE
目の肥えた ▶ SHREWD
メモ ▶ LETTER
目安 ▶ CRITERION
目を奪う ▶ IMPRESS
目をつぶる ▶ IGNORE
目を通す ▶ READ
目を引く ▶ MARKED
目を向ける ▶ LOOK 動 1
免許 ▶ LICENCE
免許証 ▶ LICENCE
免職 ▶ UNEMPLOYMENT
免職する ▶ FIRE
面接 ▶ INTERVIEW 2
面接する ▶ QUESTION 動
メンター ▶ ADVISER
面談 ▶ INTERVIEW 1
面談する ▶ QUESTION 動
面倒を見る ▶ DEAL WITH SB/STH, LOOK AFTER SB
メンバー ▶ TEAM 2
面目 ▶ REPUTATION
面目をつぶす ▶ EMBARRASS

も

儲からない ▶ LOSS-MAKING
儲かる ▶ SUCCESSFUL 2
儲け ▶ PROFIT
儲ける ▶ MAKE 2
申し入れ ▶ OFFER 1
申し込む ▶ ASK 2
申し立て ▶ ARGUMENT 2
申し立て事実 ▶ CASE
申し立てる ▶ CLAIM, PRESENT 3

日本語類語一覧

もうしで → ゆうずうのきかない

申し出 ▶ OFFER 1, PROPOSAL
申し分のない ▶ EXCELLENT, FINE, PERFECT
妄想 ▶ ILLUSION
猛烈な ▶ INTENSE, ROUGH
模擬店 ▶ STALL
目撃者 ▶ WITNESS
目撃する ▶ FIND 2, NOTICE
黙諾 ▶ APPROVAL
目的 ▶ MEANING, PURPOSE, TARGET
目的とする ▶ DESIGN 動 2
黙認 ▶ APPROVAL
黙認する ▶ AGREE
目標 ▶ PURPOSE, TARGET
目標 ▶ FOCUS
目録 ▶ LIST 名
もくろむ ▶ INTEND
模型 ▶ COPY 名 2, FAKE
模写 ▶ COPY 名 2
模写する ▶ COPY 動
もじり ▶ PARODY
模造する ▶ COPY 動
模造の ▶ ARTIFICIAL
模造品 ▶ COPY 名 2, FAKE
モダニズムの ▶ EXPERIMENTAL
モダンな ▶ EXPERIMENTAL, RECENT
持ち味 ▶ FEATURE 名
持ち合わせる ▶ HAVE 1
持ち衣装 ▶ CLOTHES
モチーフ ▶ SUBJECT
用いる ▶ USE 動 1
持ちこたえる ▶ REMAIN
持ち去る ▶ STEAL
持ち続ける ▶ KEEP 2
持ち物 ▶ THING 2
持ち寄る ▶ SHARE 動
持つ ▶ HOLD
もったいぶった ▶ PROUD 2
持って行く ▶ TAKE 1
持っている ▶ HAVE 1, 2, KEEP 3
持って来る ▶ TAKE 1
モットー ▶ SLOGAN
もっともな ▶ GOOD 3, OBVIOUS, REASONABLE
もっともらしい ▶ POSSIBLE 2
もてあそぶ ▶ FLIRT
もてなす ▶ GREET

もどかしい ▶ RESTLESS
もどかしさ ▶ FRUSTRATION
戻す ▶ RETURN 2
元の ▶ FORMER, PREVIOUS
求められていない ▶ UNWANTED
求める ▶ ASK 2, DEMAND 動
もともとの ▶ FIRST
戻る ▶ CONTINUE 3, RETURN 1
物 ▶ MATERIAL, THING 1, 2
物語 ▶ STORY
物悲しさ ▶ GRIEF
物腰 ▶ APPEARANCE
ものすごい ▶ REMARKABLE, TERRIBLE 2, 3
物まね ▶ PARODY
物わかりのよい ▶ SENSITIVE 1
模範 ▶ EXAMPLE 2, INFLUENCE 名
模範とする ▶ FOLLOW 4
模倣作品 ▶ FAKE
模倣する ▶ FOLLOW 4
模倣品 ▶ COPY 名 2
もめごと ▶ PROBLEM, TROUBLE 1, 2
催し ▶ EVENT 2
催し物 ▶ INTEREST 名 2
催す ▶ HAVE 4
もらう ▶ GET 1
モラル ▶ PRINCIPLE 1
漏れる ▶ TURN OUT
もろい ▶ FRAGILE
文句を言う ▶ COMPLAIN
文言 ▶ LANGUAGE
紋章 ▶ LOGO
問題 ▶ EVENT 1, ISSUE, OBSTACLE, PROBLEM, QUESTION 名
問題点 ▶ DISADVANTAGE, FACTOR, POINT

や

やあ ▶ DARLING
やかましい ▶ LOUD
夜間 ▶ NIGHT 1
焼きもち ▶ JEALOUSY
役員 ▶ OFFICIAL 名
約束 ▶ AGREEMENT, MEETING 2, PROMISE 名, RESPONSIBILITY

約束する ▶ PROMISE 動
役立たずの ▶ INCOMPETENT
役立たずの人 ▶ LOSER 2
役立つ ▶ HELP 動 2, VALUABLE 2
役に立たない ▶ INEFFECTIVE, USELESS
役に立つ ▶ HELP 動 1, HELPFUL, MEET 4, USEFUL
薬物 ▶ DRUG 1
薬物療法 ▶ DRUG 2
役割 ▶ INVOLVEMENT
やさしい ▶ EASY 1
優しい ▶ KIND 形, LOVING, POLITE
優しさ ▶ LOVE 名 2
野次馬 ▶ CROWD
社(やしろ) ▶ CHURCH
野心 ▶ HOPE 名 2
野心的な ▶ AGGRESSIVE 2
安い ▶ CHEAP
休み ▶ HOLIDAY 1
休む ▶ REST
安物の ▶ POOR 2
安らぎ ▶ RELIEF
やすりくず ▶ FRAGMENT
野生動物 ▶ NATURE 2
やせこけた ▶ THIN
やせた ▶ THIN
屋台 ▶ STALL
家賃 ▶ RATE
奴 ▶ MAN 1
厄介な ▶ DIFFICULT 2, HARD, SENSITIVE 2, WORRYING
厄介な状況 ▶ TROUBLE 2
やって来る ▶ ARRIVE, COME 1, 2
宿 ▶ SHELTER
雇う ▶ EMPLOY
破る ▶ BREAK 3, 4, TEAR
破れる ▶ TEAR
野望 ▶ HOPE 名 2
山 ▶ HILL
やましい ▶ SORRY
山場 ▶ PEAK
やめさせようとする ▶ DISCOURAGE 1
やめさせる ▶ PREVENT
やめる ▶ ABOLISH, PREVENT, STOP
辞める ▶ LEAVE 2
ややこしい ▶ COMPLEX

揶揄する ▶ LAUGH AT SB/STH
やりがい ▶ SATISFACTION
やりがいのある ▶ DIFFICULT 1, SATISFYING, VALUABLE 2
やり方 ▶ HABIT, WAY 1
やりすぎの ▶ EXCESSIVE
やり取り ▶ DISCUSSION
やる気 ▶ INCENTIVE
柔らかい ▶ DIM, SOFT
和らぐ ▶ EASE
和らげる ▶ EASE

ゆ

唯一の ▶ UNIQUE
優位 ▶ BENEFIT
有意義な ▶ PRODUCTIVE
優位な ▶ POWERFUL
憂鬱 ▶ GLOOM
憂鬱な ▶ DEPRESSED, NEGATIVE, UNHAPPY 1
憂鬱にさせる ▶ DISCOURAGE 2
有益 ▶ BENEFIT
有益な ▶ INFORMATIVE, USEFUL, VALUABLE 2
優越感 ▶ PRIDE
誘拐する ▶ KIDNAP
有害な ▶ DANGEROUS, HARMFUL
優雅さ ▶ STYLE
優雅な ▶ ELEGANT, FASHIONABLE
勇敢 ▶ COURAGE
勇敢な ▶ BRAVE
勇気 ▶ COURAGE
遊戯 ▶ INTEREST 名 2
勇気づける ▶ ENCOURAGE
夕暮れ ▶ NIGHT 2
有権者 ▶ CITIZEN
有効で ▶ ACTIVE
友好的な ▶ FRIENDLY 2
有効な ▶ SUCCESSFUL 1, USEFUL
有罪 ▶ FAULT
有罪の ▶ GUILTY
融資 ▶ LOAN
優秀さ ▶ STYLE, VALUE
優秀な ▶ INTELLIGENT
湧出 ▶ FLOOD 名 2
友情 ▶ FRIENDSHIP
優勝する ▶ WIN
友人 ▶ FRIEND
融通の利かない ▶ STRICT

ゆうずうのきく → よろこばせる

日本語類語一覧

融通の利く ▶ FLEXIBLE 1
優勢である ▶ WIN
優勢な ▶ POWERFUL
優勢になる ▶ DEFEAT
優先 ▶ PRIORITY, TASTE
優先順位をつける
　▶ STRESS
郵送する ▶ SEND
優待の ▶ FREE 形 2
有能な ▶ GOOD 4
郵便物 ▶ LETTER
裕福 ▶ MONEY 3
裕福な ▶ RICH
有望 ▶ POTENTIAL
有望性 ▶ POTENTIAL
有名 ▶ FAME
有名人 ▶ FAME, STAR
有名な ▶ FAMOUS,
　IMPORTANT
有名になる ▶ SUCCEED
ユーモア ▶ HUMOUR
有用な ▶ USEFUL,
　VALUABLE 2
有利 ▶ BENEFIT
有利な ▶ VALUABLE 2
有力者 ▶ AUTHORITIES,
　INFLUENCE 名
有力な ▶ POWERFUL
憂慮すべき ▶ SERIOUS 1
誘惑 ▶ DESIRE
愉快な ▶ FUNNY
雪で覆われた ▶ FREEZING
輸出する ▶ SELL 2
ゆすぐ ▶ CLEAN 動
ゆすり ▶ CORRUPTION
譲り合い ▶ COMPROMISE
輸送する ▶ TAKE 1
輸送料 ▶ DELIVERY
豊かな ▶ PRODUCTIVE
ゆったりした ▶ EASY 2,
　SLOW
輸入する ▶ SELL 2
夢 ▶ HOPE 名 2
ゆゆしい ▶ SERIOUS 1
由来 ▶ SOURCE
ゆらめく ▶ SHINE
揺るぎない
　▶ CONVINCING, FINAL,
　STEADY, STUBBORN,
　UNDOUBTED
許されていない
　▶ FORBIDDEN
許しがたい
　▶ OUTRAGEOUS
許す ▶ ALLOW, FORGIVE
ゆるやかな ▶ SLOW

揺れない ▶ FIRM
揺れる ▶ SHAKE 2

よ

夜明け ▶ START 名
(品質が)よい ▶ GOOD 1
(評価が)よい ▶ GOOD 6
用意 ▶ PLANNING
用意する ▶ PROVIDE
容易な ▶ EASY 1
容易にする ▶ HELP 動 2
用意をする
　▶ PREPARE 1, 2
要因 ▶ FACTOR
容疑 ▶ DOUBT 名 2
容疑が晴れて ▶ INNOCENT
陽気な ▶ CHEERFUL,
　LIVELY, OPTIMISTIC
要求 ▶ REQUEST, WISH
要求する ▶ ASK 2,
　DEMAND 動
要求物 ▶ NEED 名
容疑をかける ▶ SUSPECT
用具 ▶ EQUIPMENT,
　THING 2, TOOL
要件 ▶ CONDITION
用語 ▶ LANGUAGE
擁護 ▶ SECURITY
擁護する ▶ EXPLAIN 2,
　SUPPORT
要旨 ▶ MESSAGE
幼児 ▶ CHILD
用事 ▶ TASK
幼児期 ▶ CHILDHOOD
養子にする
　▶ BRING SB UP
容赦できない
　▶ OUTRAGEOUS
容赦のない ▶ STERN
養殖する ▶ KEEP 4
用心深さ ▶ TACT
用心棒 ▶ GUARD
様子 ▶ APPEARANCE
要請 ▶ REQUEST, WISH
養成する ▶ TRAIN 1
要素 ▶ ELEMENT, FACTOR
様相 ▶ APPEARANCE
容体 ▶ HEALTH
容態 ▶ PATIENT
用地 ▶ LAND 2, PLACE
幼稚な ▶ CHILDISH
要点 ▶ FACTOR,
　FEATURE 名, MESSAGE,
　POINT
容認 ▶ PATIENCE

容認する ▶ ADMIT
容認できない
　▶ UNACCEPTABLE
容認できる ▶ FINE
幼年期 ▶ CHILDHOOD
用品 ▶ EQUIPMENT,
　THING 2
用法 ▶ LANGUAGE
容貌 ▶ APPEARANCE
要望 ▶ REQUEST, WISH
要約 ▶ SUMMARY
要領 ▶ SKILL 1
要を得た ▶ RELEVANT
余暇 ▶ LEISURE
予感 ▶ IDEA 2
予期する ▶ EXPECT
予期せぬ ▶ SURPRISING
余儀なく…させる
　▶ FORCE 動
余興 ▶ FUN, INTEREST 名 2
預金 ▶ FUND 名
預金口座 ▶ FUND 名
預金する ▶ SAVE 3
抑圧的な ▶ REPRESSIVE
よくある ▶ GENERAL
抑止 ▶ LIMIT 1
よく知った ▶ USED TO STH
欲情 ▶ LOVE 名 1
よく知らない ▶ NEW 3
よく知られた ▶ FAMOUS
抑制 ▶ LIMIT 1
抑制する ▶ SUPPRESS 2
よくなる ▶ IMPROVE 2,
　RECOVER
よく似た ▶ LIKE 前 形
抑留する ▶ JAIL
予言 ▶ EXPECTATION
予言する ▶ PREDICT
予行演習 ▶ TRAINING
横顔 ▶ SHAPE
予告編 ▶ ADVERTISEMENT
横取りする ▶ STEAL
汚れ ▶ MARK
汚れた ▶ DIRTY
良さ ▶ BENEFIT
予算 ▶ FUND 名
予算の ▶ ECONOMIC
予算を組む ▶ SAVE 2
よしとする ▶ GOOD 6
よじ登る ▶ CLIMB
余剰人員とする ▶ FIRE
余剰の ▶ EXCESS
予選 ▶ INTERVIEW 2
予想 ▶ EXPECTATION,
　IDEA 1

予想される ▶ LIKELY,
　PREDICTABLE
予想する ▶ EXPECT,
　IMAGINE, PREDICT
予想どおりの
　▶ PREDICTABLE
装う ▶ PRETEND
予測 ▶ EXPECTATION
予測可能な
　▶ PREDICTABLE
予測する ▶ PREDICT
よそよそしい ▶ COLD 2,
　FORMAL
よそよそしさ ▶ DIVISION 2
予知する ▶ PREDICT
予知できる
　▶ PREDICTABLE
欲求 ▶ DESIRE
欲求不満 ▶ FRUSTRATION
欲求不満を抱いた
　▶ UNHAPPY 2
酔って ▶ SICK 2
予定 ▶ PURPOSE,
　SCHEDULE
予定する ▶ INTEND
予定表 ▶ SCHEDULE
予定を立てる ▶ ORGANIZE
世慣れた
　▶ SOPHISTICATED
予備 ▶ HELP 名, SUPPLY
呼びかけ ▶ REQUEST
予備金 ▶ FUND 名
予備的な ▶ FIRST
予備の ▶ EXCESS
呼ぶ ▶ CALL 1
夜更け ▶ NIGHT 1
余分な ▶ EXCESS
予報 ▶ EXPECTATION
予防 ▶ PRECAUTION
予報する ▶ PREDICT
読み上げる ▶ READ
読み書きのできない
　▶ IGNORANT
読み取る ▶ CONCLUDE
読む ▶ READ
予約 ▶ MEETING 2,
　REQUEST
予約する ▶ ORDER 2
より優れた ▶ BETTER
より勝った ▶ BETTER
よりよい ▶ BETTER
夜 ▶ NIGHT 1, 2
喜ばしい ▶ HAPPY,
　SATISFYING
喜ばせる ▶ PLEASE

喜び ▶ FUN, JOY, PLEASURE
喜んだ ▶ GLAD, HAPPY
世論調査 ▶ INVESTIGATION
世論調査をする ▶ SURVEY
弱い ▶ DIM, VULNERABLE
弱まる ▶ WORSEN
弱虫 ▶ COWARD
世をすねた ▶ SUSPICIOUS 1

ら

礼賛 ▶ PRAISE 名
ライセンス ▶ LICENCE
ライター ▶ REPORTER
ライバル ▶ ENEMY
来訪 ▶ VISIT 名
烙印を押す ▶ CALL 1
落書きする ▶ WRITE
落後者 ▶ LOSER 1
楽勝する ▶ DEFEAT
落選者 ▶ LOSER 1
落第させる ▶ FAIL 3
落第する ▶ FAIL 3
落胆 ▶ GLOOM, GRIEF, SHOCK 1
落胆させる ▶ DISCOURAGE 2, HURT 1
落胆しきった ▶ UPSET
楽天的な ▶ OPTIMISTIC
楽な ▶ EASY 2
ラジオ聴取者 ▶ AUDIENCE
拉致する ▶ KIDNAP
落下する ▶ FALL 2
楽観的な ▶ OPTIMISTIC
欄 ▶ ARTICLE
ランク付けする ▶ RANK
乱雑 ▶ MESS 1
乱雑な ▶ UNTIDY
乱闘騒ぎ ▶ FIGHT 名
乱暴な ▶ VIOLENT, WILD

り

リーフレット ▶ LEAFLET
利益 ▶ INCREASE 名, PROFIT
利益になる ▶ VALUABLE 2
利益の上がらない ▶ LOSS-MAKING
利益を得る ▶ MAKE 2
理解 ▶ DEFINITION, KNOWLEDGE, UNDERSTANDING
利害 ▶ INVOLVEMENT
理解している ▶ UNDERSTAND 2
理解しやすい ▶ CLEAR 形 2
理解する ▶ THINK, UNDERSTAND 1
理解力 ▶ UNDERSTANDING
力説する ▶ STRESS
力量 ▶ SKILL 1
リクエスト ▶ WISH
陸軍 ▶ ARMY
理屈 ▶ LOGIC
履行する ▶ DO
利口な ▶ INTELLIGENT
利己心 ▶ PRIDE
利己的な ▶ SELFISH
離婚した ▶ SINGLE
利子 ▶ PROFIT
理事 ▶ OFFICIAL 名, ORGANIZER
理事会 ▶ COMMITTEE
履修科目 ▶ CLASS 1
利潤 ▶ PROFIT
リスキーな ▶ DANGEROUS
リスク ▶ RISK 1
リスト ▶ LIST 名
理性を失った ▶ IRRATIONAL
理性を欠いた ▶ UNACCEPTABLE
理想 ▶ EXAMPLE 2, HOPE 名 2, PRINCIPLE 1
理想的な ▶ IDEAL, PERFECT
理想の ▶ IDEAL
利息 ▶ PROFIT
立案者 ▶ ORGANIZER
立証する ▶ CONFIRM 1, SHOW 1
立証できる ▶ RELIABLE 2
立派な ▶ LARGE, RESPECTABLE, WORTHY
立腹 ▶ FRUSTRATION
立法者 ▶ POLITICIAN
立法する ▶ RULE 動 2
利点 ▶ BENEFIT
理にかなった ▶ BEST, OBVIOUS, RATIONAL, REASONABLE
理念 ▶ PRINCIPLE 2
リハーサル ▶ TRAINING
リハーサルする ▶ PRACTISE
リハビリさせる ▶ CURE
離反 ▶ DIVISION 2
リベート ▶ BRIBE
略装の ▶ INFORMAL
略奪 ▶ THEFT
略奪者 ▶ THIEF
略奪する ▶ ROB
理由 ▶ ARGUMENT 2, REASON
留意 ▶ ATTENTION
留意して ▶ AWARE
流儀 ▶ WAY 1
流血の ▶ VIOLENT
流行 ▶ FASHION
流行遅れの ▶ OLD-FASHIONED
流行の ▶ FASHIONABLE
粒子 ▶ BIT
流出する ▶ PUMP
隆盛 ▶ PROGRESS
流体 ▶ MATERIAL
留置する ▶ JAIL
流通 ▶ DELIVERY
流通させる ▶ DISTRIBUTE
流動的な ▶ VARIABLE
利用 ▶ USE 名
量 ▶ NUMBER
領域 ▶ AREA 2, PLACE
了解 ▶ AWARENESS
領海 ▶ SEA
両替 ▶ EXCHANGE
両替する ▶ CASH, REPLACE 2
利用価値の高い ▶ VALUABLE 2
料金 ▶ RATE
良識的な ▶ BEST
了承 ▶ APPROVAL
良心の呵責 ▶ DOUBT 名 2
利用する ▶ USE 動 1
利用する権利[機会] ▶ ACCESS
領地 ▶ TERRITORY
領土 ▶ TERRITORY
領分 ▶ BUSINESS
療法 ▶ TREATMENT
料理 ▶ FOOD
両立しない ▶ INCONSISTENT
旅行 ▶ HOLIDAY 2, TRAVEL, TRIP
旅行者 ▶ TOURIST
理論 ▶ THEORY 1
理論上の ▶ SUPPOSED
理論的な ▶ INTELLECTUAL 1
輪郭 ▶ SHAPE
臨機応変の才 ▶ TACT
臨時の ▶ SHORT 1, SPECIAL
倫理 ▶ PRINCIPLE 1, VALUES
倫理上の ▶ MORAL

る

類縁 ▶ SIMILARITY
類似 ▶ SIMILARITY
類似の ▶ EQUIVALENT
ルーツ ▶ FAMILY 3, SOURCE
ルート ▶ WAY 3
ルール ▶ RULE 名
ルックス ▶ APPEARANCE

れ

例 ▶ EXAMPLE 1
レイアウト ▶ DESIGN 名
レイアウトする ▶ ARRANGE
例外的な ▶ SPECIAL
礼儀 ▶ RESPECT 名
礼儀正しい ▶ POLITE, SOPHISTICATED
冷酷な ▶ COLD 2, CRUEL, RUTHLESS, STERN
例証 ▶ EXAMPLE 1
令状 ▶ LICENCE
冷笑的な ▶ IRONIC, SUSPICIOUS 1
冷静な ▶ REALISTIC
冷製の ▶ COLD 1
冷淡な ▶ COLD 2, RUTHLESS
冷凍保存する ▶ COOL
レイプ ▶ ATTACK 名 2
黎明 ▶ START 名
歴史的に有名な ▶ FAMOUS
歴史の浅い ▶ YOUNG
レジャー ▶ LEISURE
レセプション ▶ EVENT 2
列 ▶ FLOOR
劣化する ▶ WORSEN
列挙する ▶ LIST 動
裂傷 ▶ INJURY
レッスン ▶ CLASS 2
劣勢 ▶ LACK
劣等な ▶ POOR 2
裂片 ▶ FRAGMENT
レバー ▶ BUTTON 1
レビュー ▶ ASSESSMENT
レフェリー ▶ JUDGE 名

レベル ▶ CATEGORY, QUALITY
レポート ▶ REPORT 2
恋愛 ▶ LOVE 名 1, RELATIONSHIP 2
恋愛関係 ▶ RELATIONSHIP 2
連合 ▶ UNION
連合する ▶ COMBINE
連鎖 ▶ SERIES
練習 ▶ SPORT, TRAINING
練習時間 ▶ TRAINING
練習する ▶ PRACTISE
練習問題 ▶ ASSIGNMENT
練習をする[させる] ▶ TRAIN 2
連想する ▶ RELATE
連続 ▶ FLOOD 名 2, SERIES
連続的な ▶ CONTINUOUS
連帯感 ▶ FRIENDSHIP
レンタルする ▶ ORDER 2
連発 ▶ FLOOD 名 2
連邦政府の ▶ PUBLIC
連盟 ▶ UNION
連絡 ▶ COMMUNICATION, LETTER
連絡する ▶ TALK
連絡通路 ▶ CORRIDOR
連絡票 ▶ LETTER

ろ

漏洩する ▶ REVEAL
廊下 ▶ CORRIDOR
朗唱する ▶ QUOTE
労働組合 ▶ UNION
労働者 ▶ WORKER 1, 2
労働人口 ▶ STAFF
狼狽 ▶ FEAR
老齢の ▶ OLD 2
朗々とした ▶ DEEP 2
ローン ▶ LOAN
ロゴ ▶ LOGO
路地 ▶ ROAD
路線 ▶ WAY 3
露店 ▶ STALL
ロビー ▶ HALL 2
ロビー活動する ▶ CAMPAIGN 動
ロマンス ▶ RELATIONSHIP 2
論外の ▶ IMPOSSIBLE
論拠 ▶ ARGUMENT 2
論考 ▶ RESEARCH
論旨 ▶ POINT
論述 ▶ ASSESSMENT
論証 ▶ EVIDENCE
論説 ▶ ARTICLE
論争 ▶ ARGUMENT 1, DEBATE
論題 ▶ SUBJECT
論点 ▶ FACTOR, ISSUE
論評 ▶ STATEMENT
論評記事 ▶ ASSESSMENT
論文 ▶ PAPER
論理 ▶ LOGIC
論理的な ▶ RATIONAL

わ

賄賂 ▶ BRIBE
若い ▶ YOUNG
若い女性 ▶ GIRL
若かりし頃に ▶ LIFE 2
若さ ▶ CHILDHOOD
わかっている ▶ KNOW, UNDERSTAND 2
わかってくる ▶ TURN OUT
わがままな ▶ SELFISH, STUBBORN
若者 ▶ CHILD, GIRL
わかりきった ▶ CLEAR 形 1
わかりづらい ▶ UNCLEAR
わかりやすい ▶ AVERAGE, EASY 1
わかる ▶ FIND 1, LEARN, NOTICE, TURN OUT, UNDERSTAND 1
分かれた ▶ PARTICULAR
分かれる ▶ DIVIDE 1
別れる ▶ LEAVE 1, 4
枠組み ▶ STRUCTURE
わくわくさせる ▶ EXCITING
わけ ▶ REASON
分け与える ▶ SHARE 動
わけのわからない ▶ CONFUSING
分け前 ▶ DIVISION 1, SHARE 名

わざ ▶ SKILL 1
災い ▶ DISASTER
災いする ▶ FAIL 2
わずかな ▶ INADEQUATE
わずかの ▶ SLIGHT, SMALL
患う ▶ SUFFER FROM STH
忘れっぽい ▶ CARELESS
話題 ▶ SUBJECT
渡す ▶ GIVE 1, 2
罠 ▶ DISADVANTAGE, TRICK
わびしい ▶ LONELY
和平 ▶ PEACE
わめく ▶ SCREAM, SHOUT
笑う ▶ LAUGH, LAUGH AT SB/STH
笑える ▶ RIDICULOUS
割当分 ▶ SHARE 名
割り当てる ▶ SHARE 動
割り込む ▶ INTERRUPT
割引 ▶ REDUCTION
割引して売る ▶ DISCOUNT
割り振る ▶ SHARE 動
割増金 ▶ PAYMENT
割安の ▶ CHEAP
割る ▶ BREAK 1
悪い ▶ BAD, EVIL 形, HARMFUL, POOR 2, WRONG 3
悪がき ▶ CHILD
悪くする ▶ INFLUENCE 動
割れる ▶ BREAK 1, TEAR
ワンマン ▶ DICTATOR
腕力 ▶ FORCE 名

A a

ability 名

ability・capability・capacity・power
何かをすることができること、または何かをするために必要とされる資質
【類語訳】能力、力

文型&コロケーション
▶ a capability/ capacity **for** sth
▶ the ability/ capability/ capacity/ power **to do** sth
▶ **beyond/ within** your ability/ capability/ capacity/ power
▶ (a/ an) **great/ remarkable/ extraordinary/ amazing** ability/ capability/ capacity/ powers
▶ **natural/ physical/ intellectual/ mental/ limited** ability/ capability/ capacity/ powers
▶ to **have/ develop/ acquire/ lack/ lose** the ability/ capability/ capacity/ power
▶ to **demonstrate/ show** your ability/ capability/ capacity/ power
▶ to **restrict** sb's ability/ capability/ capacity/ power

ability [単数で, U] 能力 ◇The system has the *ability* to run more than one program at the same time. そのシステムは同時に複数のプログラムを実行することができる ◇Everyone has the right to good medical care regardless of their *ability* to pay. 支払い能力にかかわらず誰でもよい医療を受ける権利がある ◇I try to do the job *to the best of my ability* (= as well as I can). 力を尽くしてその仕事をするつもりです [反意] **inability** ❶ 単数・不可算の inability は何かをすることができないことを表す. ◆ the government's *inability* to provide basic services (政府が基本的なサービスを提供できないこと). ◆ Some families go without medical treatment because of their *inability* to pay. (支払い能力がないために医療を受けられないご家庭がある).
➤ **able** 形 ◇You must be *able* to speak French for this job. この仕事をするにはフランス語が話せなくてはいけない ◇A viral illness left her barely *able* to walk. ウイルス性の疾患で彼女は歩くのがやっとという状態になった [反意] **unable to do sth** ❶ not able も用いられる. ◆ He lay there, *unable to* move. (彼は動くことができず, そこに横になった). ◆ Unfortunately they weren't *able to* come. (残念なことに彼らは来ることができなかった).

capability [U, C] 能力, 素質 ◇Animals in the zoo have lost the *capability of* catching food for themselves. 動物園の動物たちは自ら餌を取る能力を失っている ◇Age affects the range of a person's *capabilities*. 年齢は人の能力の範囲に影響を及ぼす ❶ capability は企業・国が何かを作り出す能力がどのくらいあるかというときによく用いられる. ◆ a company/country's manufacturing/production/processing/defence/weapons/nuclear *capability* (企業[国]の製造力/生産力/加工処理能力/防衛力/兵器力/核能力).
➤ **capable** 形 ◇You are *capable* of better work than this. あなたにはこれ以上によい仕事をする能力が ◇I'm perfectly *capable* of doing it myself, thank you. 私は自分でちゃんとやることができますから

capacity [C, ふつう単数で]《ややフォーマル》(知的)能力 ◇She has an enormous *capacity* for hard work. 彼女には激務をものともしない力がある ◇A habit becomes an addiction when it reduces your *capacity* to enjoy life. 習慣もとらわれすぎるとただの中毒になる ❶ capacity は社会生活面での能力, 教育面での能力, 仕事面での能力に関することをいうときによく用いられる. ◆ a *capacity* for hard work/humour/enjoying life/learning languages/love/reflective thinking (激務に耐える能力/ユーモアを解する力/人生を楽しむ力/言葉を学ぶ力/愛する力/内省的思考力).

power [U](または **powers**[複数形で]) 能力；体力, 知力 ◇He had lost the *power* of speech. 彼は話す能力を失ってしまっていた ◇The drug may affect your *powers* of concentration. その薬は集中力に影響を及ぼすことがある ◇At 26, he is *at the height of his powers* and ranked fourth in the world. 彼は26歳で全盛期にあり, ランクは世界第4位だ ❶ 不可算の power は, 特に (not) within sb's power (…の能力の範囲内で(ない)), beyond sb's power (…の能力を超えて), do everything within your power (…ができるだけのことはする) のような句で用いられる. ◆ It is *not within my power* (= I am unable) to help you. (あなたを助けることは私にはできない). ◆ I will *do everything in my power* to help you. (あなたを助けるためにあらゆる手を尽くします).

abolish 動 ☞ CUT 1, REMOVE

abolish・cancel・scrap・dismiss・do away with sth・axe・call sth off
計画を変更する, これ以上起こらないようにする
【類語訳】廃止する, 取りやめる, キャンセルする, 解約する, 破棄する, 却下する, 棄却する, やめる, 中止する

文型&コロケーション
▶ to abolish/ cancel/ scrap/ axe a **service**
▶ to abolish/ scrap a **system/ plan/ scheme/ tax**
▶ to cancel/ call off a/ an **game/ match/ engagement**
▶ to scrap/ axe **jobs**
▶ to abolish/ scrap sth **completely**
▶ to cancel/ scrap sth **altogether**

abolish [他, しばしば受身で]《法律・制度・慣習などを正式に》廃止する ◇Slavery was *abolished* in the US in 1865. 奴隷制度はアメリカでは1865年に廃止された ◇Over the past six years we have *abolished* a whole range of direct taxes. 過去6年にわたってあらゆる直接税を廃止してきた
➤ **abolition** 名 [U] the *abolition* of slavery/apartheid/the death penalty 奴隷制度/アパルトヘイト/死刑の廃止

cancel (-II-, 米 -I-)[他, しばしば受身で]《予定されていたことを》取りやめる, キャンセルする ◇All flights have been *cancelled* because of bad weather. 悪天候のためすべ

ての航空便が欠航になった ◇Don't forget to *cancel* the newspaper (= arrange for it not to be delivered) before going away. 留守にする前に新聞を止めてもらうのを忘れないように ☞ **postpone** (DELAY)
▶**cancellation** (米でまた **cancelation**) [名] [U, C] We need at least 24 hours' notice of *cancellation*. 少なくとも24時間前の解約予告が必要だ ◇*Cancellations* must be made in writing. 解約は書面にて行われなくてはならない

scrap (-pp-) [他, しばしば受身で]《ややインフォーマル, 特にジャーナリズム》(現実的でない)[役に立たない]計画などを)取りやめる ◇The government has been forced to *scrap* plans for a proposed tax reform. 政府は税制改革案の破棄を強いられた

dismiss [他]《法律》(証拠不十分で訴訟を)却下[棄却]する ◇Judges have to state their reasons for *dismissing* a case. 裁判官は訴訟を却下する理由を述べなくてはならない ◇'Case *dismissed*!' 却下

do a'way with sth [句動]《ややインフォーマル, 特に話し言葉, しばしばほめて》(そうしたほうがよいと思って)廃止する ◇He thinks it's time we *did away with* the monarchy. 彼は君主制は廃止していい時だと思っている

axe (英)(米 **ax**) [他, しばしば受身で]《ややインフォーマル, ジャーナリズム》(サービス・システムを)やめる, (経費を大幅に)削減する ◇Other less profitable services are to be *axed* later this year. 他の収益性の低いサービスは今年後半に打ち切りになる ◇The series was *axed* after only six episodes. そのシリーズはたった6話で打ち切りになった

call sth 'off [句動](大勢の人が関わっている計画を)取りやめる, 中止する ◇Union leaders last night called *off* strike action planned for today. 昨夜労働組合の幹部たちは今日予定されていたストを中止した ◇They have called *off* their engagement (= decided not to get married). 彼らは婚約を破棄した

accelerate [動]

accelerate・speed (sth) up・speed・hasten・quicken
もっと早く行かせたり, 進めたりすること
【類語訳】加速する, 速める, スピードアップする, 急がせる, 早める

▶to accelerate/ speed up/ speed/ hasten/ quicken the **pace/ progress** (of sth)
▶to accelerate/ speed up/ speed/ hasten the **development** (of sth)
▶to accelerate/ speed/ hasten the **death** of sb/ sth
▶to **greatly** accelerate/ speed up/ speed/ hasten sth

accelerate [自, 他] (乗り物・人が)加速する ◇The car *accelerated* to overtake me. その車は私を追い越そうと加速した ◇Inflation continues to *accelerate*. インフレは加速し続けている ◇Exposure to the sun can *accelerate* the ageing process. 日光を浴びると老化が早まるかもしれない 反意 **retard** (HOLD SB/STH UP), **decelerate** ❶ decelerate は accelerate よりフォーマルで, 主に文書で用いられる. ◆Economic growth *decelerated* sharply in January. (《フォーマル, 書き言葉》経済成長は1月に急激に減速した)
▶**acceleration** [名] [U, 単数형で] ◇a car with good *ac-*
celeration 加速のいい車 ◇an *acceleration* in the rate of growth 成長率の加速

,speed 'up, ,speed sth 'up [句動]《ややインフォーマル》速度を速める, スピードアップする ◇The train soon *speeded up*. 電車はまもなく速度を上げた ◇Can you try and *speed* things *up* a bit? もう少しペースを上げてもらえませんか ◇They have *speeded up* production of the new car. 新車の生産のスピードを速めた 反意 **slow down** ❶反意語は slow down. ◆*Slow down!* I can't keep up with you. (ゆっくりやって. ついていけない)

speed [他]《書き言葉》急がせる, (回復・開発などを)早める ◇The drugs will *speed* her recovery. そうした薬は彼女の回復を早めるだろう ◇More is needed to *speed* the development of a safe and effective vaccine. 安全で効能のあるワクチンの開発を急ぐためにはもっと多くのものが必要である ☞ **speedy** (QUICK)

ノート speed sth up と speed の使い分け: speed は speed sth up よりフォーマルで, 物事を急がせる[速める]ときに用いるが, 乗り物を加速する場合には用いない. ×The train soon *speeded*. この意味では speed up も speed も過去・過去分詞は speeded を用い, 不規則変化の sped は用いない.

hasten [他]《書き言葉》急がせる, (死・破壊・物事の終わりなどを)早める ◇The treatment she received may, in fact, have *hastened* her death. 彼女の受けた治療は, 実際には彼女の死を早めたのかもしれない ◇News of the scandal certainly *hastened* his departure from office. そのスキャンダルのニュースは確実に彼の辞任を早めた 反意 **delay** (DELAY)

quicken [自, 他]《書き言葉》速くなる, 急がせる ◇She felt her heartbeat *quicken* as he approached. 彼が近づくにつれて彼女は鼓動が早くなるのを感じた ◇He *quickened* his pace to catch up with them. 彼らに追いつこうと彼は足取りを速めた ❶ quicken は heartbeat (鼓動), pulse (拍), breathing (呼吸), pace (足取り) といった体の働きや動きに関連してよく用いられる. 反意 **slacken** ❶反意語は slacken. ◆She *slackened* her pace a little (= walked more slowly). (彼女は少しペースを落とした).

access [名]

access・entry・admission・entrance
ある場所に入る方法や, ある場所に入ったり, グループに加わったりする権利や機会を表す
【類語訳】接近方法, 利用する権利[機会], 入場(許可), 入会(許可)

▶access/ entry/ admission/ entrance **to** sth
▶access/ entry **for** sb
▶**free** access/ entry/ admission/ entrance
▶**unlimited** access/ entry
▶to **refuse/ deny** (sb) access/ entry/ admission/ entrance
▶to **gain** access/ entry/ admission/ entrance
▶an entry/ admission/ entrance **charge/ fee**

access [U] 接近方法, 利用する権利[機会] ◇Double doors *give access to* the terrace. 両開きのドアからテラスに行けます ◇There is easy *access* by road. 車で楽に着けます ◇There is *wheelchair access* to most of the facilities. 施設のほとんどは車椅子で入れます ◇Students

must **have access** to good resources. 学生たちは優れた資料を利用する機会を持たなければなりません ◇You need a password to **get access** to the computer system. コンピューターシステムにアクセスするにはパスワードが必要です ◇Journalists were denied *access* to the President. ジャーナリストたちは大統領との面会の機会を絶たれた
▶ **access** [他] ◇The loft can be *accessed* by a ladder.《フォーマル》はしごを使えば屋根裏部屋に行けます

entry [U] 入場(の権利/機会), 入会, 参加 ◇A sign said: No *Entry*. 標識には「立入禁止」と書かれてあった ◇*Entry* to the museum is free. その博物館への入場は無料です ◇How did the thieves gain *entry* into the building? 泥棒たちはどうやってそのビルに忍び込んだのだろうか ◇That was before the American *entry* into the war. それはアメリカがあの戦争に加わる前のことだった ☞ **enter** (ENTER)

admission [U, C] 入場(許可)の権利), 加入(許可(の権利)) ◇*Last admission* 30 minutes before closing time. 最終入場は閉館[閉園]30分前です ◇Hospital *admissions* for asthma attacks have doubled. 喘息発作による入院数は倍増した ◇*Admission* is by ticket only. チケットがなければ入場できません ◇The country has applied for *admission* to the European Union. その国はEUへの加盟を申請した ☞ **admit** (LET SB IN)

entrance [U] 入場(の権利), 加入(の権利) ◇They were refused *entrance* to the club. 彼らはそのクラブへの入店を断られた ◇The police were unable to gain *entrance* to the house. 警察官はその家に立ち入ることができなかった ◇What are the *entrance* requirements for this course? これを受講するのに必要な要件は何ですか

accident 名

accident・crash・collision・wreck・mishap・pile-up
(特に乗り物などによる)予期しない出来事を表す
【類語訳】事故, 衝突事故, 玉突き事故

文型&コロケーション
▶ **in** an accident/ a crash/ a collision/ a wreck/ a pile-up
▶ a **serious** accident/ crash/ collision/ wreck/ mishap
▶ a **major** accident/ crash/ collision/ wreck/ pile-up
▶ a **minor** accident/ collision
▶ a **slight**/ **little** accident/ mishap
▶ a **car**/ **train** accident/ crash/ wreck
▶ a **plane** crash/ wreck
▶ a **head-on** crash/ collision
▶ to **have** an accident/ a collision/ a mishap
▶ to **cause** an accident/ a crash/ a collision/ a wreck/ a pile-up
▶ an accident/ a crash/ a collision/ a wreck/ a mishap/ a pile-up **happens**/ **occurs**

accident [C] (乗り物などの)事故 ◇a road/traffic *accident* 交通事故 ◇a climbing/riding *accident* 登山/落馬事故 ◇It's Dad. He's had an *accident* at work. 親父なんだ. 仕事中に事故に遭ったのね ◇I didn't mean to break it ― it was an *accident*. わざと壊したのではありません. 事故だったのです ◇It is the first fatal *accident* (= in which sb is killed) to have occurred at the factory. それは工場で起きた最初の死亡事故だ
▶ **accidental** [形] ◇a verdict of *accidental* death 事故死という評決 反意 **deliberate** (DELIBERATE)
▶ **accidentally** [副] ◇As I turned around, I *acciden-*

tally hit him in the face. 振り向いたら誤って彼の顔を殴ってしまった 反意 **deliberately** (DELIBERATE)

crash [C] (乗客のけが・死亡を伴う乗り物の)衝突事故 ◇A girl was killed in a *crash* involving a stolen car. 盗難車による衝突事故で女の子が亡くなった ☞ **crash** (CRASH)

collision [C] (人・乗り物の)衝突 ◇Stewart was injured in a *collision* with another player. スチュアートは他のプレーヤーとぶつかってけがをした ◇His car was *in collision with* a motorbike. 彼の車はバイクと衝突した ☞ **collide** (CRASH)

wreck [C] (米)衝突[墜落]事故 ◇The *wreck* occurred at milepost 534, just west of Greenup, Kentucky. その事故はケンタッキー州グリーナップのまさに西, 里程標534の地点で起きた ☞ **wreck** (CRASH)

mishap [C, U] (ややフォーマル) ちょっとした事故[災難] ◇I'm afraid your son had a slight *mishap* in the playground. 申し上げにくいのですが, あなたの息子さんが運動場でちょっとした事故に遭われました ◇I managed to get home without further *mishap*. それ以上のトラブルはなくなんとか家へ帰った

'pile-up [C] (ややインフォーマル, 特にジャーナリズム) 玉突き事故 ◇Three people died in a multiple *pile-up* in freezing fog. 着氷性の霧で何重もの玉突き事故があり3人が亡くなった

accuse 動

accuse・charge・prosecute・indict・impeach・cite
悪事や犯罪を働いた人を法廷に立たせること
【類語訳】非難する, 告訴する, 告発する, 起訴する, 弾劾(愆)する, 召喚する

文型&コロケーション
▶ to prosecute/ indict/ impeach/ cite sb **for** sth
▶ to charge/ indict sb **with** sth
▶ to be prosecuted/ indicted/ impeached/ cited **on** charg**es**/ **on a charge** of sth

accuse [他] (悪・不正行為のかどで)責める, 非難する; 告訴[告発]する ◇She *accused* him *of* lying. 彼女は彼がうそをついたと非難した ◇The government was *accused* of incompetence. 政府は無能さを非難された ◇They **stand** *accused* of crimes against humanity.《フォーマル》彼らは非人道的犯罪で告発[告訴]されている ☞ **accusation** (CHARGE 名)

charge [他, ふつう受け身で] 告訴[告発]する ◇He was *charged* with murder. 彼は殺人罪で告発された ◇Several people were arrested but nobody was *charged*. 数人が逮捕されたが誰も告発されなかった ❶ フォーマルな用法では charge に「不正行為のかどで公に非難する」という意味がある. ◆ Opposition MPs *charged* the minister with neglecting her duty. (野党の下院議員が大臣を職務怠慢で非難した). ☞ **charge** (CHARGE 名)

prosecute [他, 自] 起訴する ◇The company was *prosecuted* for breaching the Health and Safety Act. その企業は衛生安全法違反で起訴された ◇The police decided not to *prosecute*. 警察は起訴しないことを決定した ☞ **prosecution** (CASE)

indict [他, ふつう受け身で]《法律》(米国の大陪審が)起訴する ◇The senator was *indicted* for murder. その上院議員は殺人罪で起訴された ◇They were *indicted* on a

↪accuse　　　　　　　　　　　　　　　　　　achieve

number of corruption charges. 彼らは数々の汚職疑惑で起訴された ☞ **indictment** (CHARGE 名)

ノート **charge**と**indict**の使い分け：イギリスでは起訴する(charge)かどうかは公訴局が決定する。アメリカでは検察官が起訴するときにchargeを用い、大陪審によるときはindictを用いる。

impeach [他]（米国の公務員を）弾劾する ◇The President was *impeached* by Congress for lying. 大統領は虚偽の罪で議会により弾劾された ☞ **impeachment** (CHARGE 名)

cite [他, ふつう受身で]《法律》召喚する；告発する ◇He was *cited* for contempt of court. 彼は法廷侮辱罪で召喚された ◇She was *cited* in the divorce proceedings. 彼女は離婚手続きで召喚された

achieve [動]

achieve・manage・succeed・reach・accomplish・effect・arrive at sth・pull sth off・attain・get there・fulfil
物事がうまくいくことを表す
【類語訳】成し遂げる、到達する、実現させる、成功する、達成する、完遂する、達する、獲得する、かなえる、果たす

文型&コロケーション

▶ to achieve/ succeed in/ reach/ accomplish/ attain/ fulfil a/ an **goal/ objective**
▶ to achieve/ reach/ attain/ fulfil a **target**
▶ to achieve/ succeed in/ accomplish/ attain/ fulfil a/ an **aim**
▶ to achieve/ accomplish/ attain a/ an **purpose/ end**
▶ to achieve/ succeed in/ accomplish/ fulfil a **task**
▶ to achieve/ accomplish/ fulfil an **ambition**
▶ to achieve/ attain/ fulfil an **ideal**
▶ to achieve/ reach/ arrive at a/ an **agreement/ result**
▶ to achieve/ accomplish/ effect a **change/ transformation**
▶ to reach/ pull off/ attain a **deal**
▶ to achieve/ reach/ attain a **balance**
▶ to achieve/ manage/ accomplish/ pull off a **feat**
▶ to achieve/ pull off a **coup/ victory**
▶ to **actually** achieve/ manage/ succeed in/ reach/ accomplish/ arrive at/ pull off/ attain/ fulfil sth
▶ to **finally** achieve/ manage/ succeed in/ reach/ accomplish/ arrive at/ attain/ fulfil sth

achieve [他]（長い時間努力して目標[地位, 基準]に）到達する；成し遂げる ◇He had finally *achieved* success. 彼はついに成功を収めた ◇I haven't *achieved* very much today. 今日はまだそれほど目標をこなせていません ◇All you've *achieved* is to upset my parents. あなたがやったことと言えば私の両親を動揺させただけだ ☞ **achieve** (SUCCEED)
　▶ **achievement** [名] [U] ◇Even a small success gives you *a sense of achievement* (= a feeling of pride). 小さな成功でも達成感がある

manage [他, 自]（困難なことを）どうにか成し遂げる ◇In spite of his disappointment, he *managed* a weak smile. 失望していたにもかかわらず彼は少々弱々しい笑顔を見せた ◇I don't know exactly how we'll *manage it*, but we will, somehow. どうやって成し遂げられる

かははっきりわからないが、なんとかやれるだろう ◇We *managed to* get to the airport in time. なんとか間に合って空港に着いた ◇How did you *manage* to persuade him? どうやって彼をうまく説得したの ◇We couldn't have *managed* without you. あなたがいなければ私たちはうまくいかなかっただろう ◇'Need any help?' 'No, thanks. I can *manage*.' 「お手伝いしましょうか」「いいえ結構です, 自分でなんとかできます」

succeed [他]（努力し続けて）成し遂げる[手に入れる]；成功する ◇He *succeeded in* getting a place at art school. 彼は美術学校に籍を得ることができた ◇I tried to discuss it with her but *only succeeded* in making her angry (= I failed and did the opposite of what I intended). 彼女とそのことについて話し合おうとしたが, 怒らせてしまっただけだった ◇Our plan *succeeded*. 私たちの計画は成功した 反意 **fail** (FAIL 2), ☞ **succeed** (SUCCEED), **successful** (SUCCESSFUL 1)
　▶ **success** [U] ◇I didn't have much *success in* finding a job. 私は就職活動があまりうまくいかなかった ◇commercial/economic/electoral *success* 商業での/経済での/選挙での成功 反意 **failure** (FAILURE)

reach [他]（議論・熟考の末に決定[合意, 結論]などに）達する, （目的に）達する ◇The jury took two days to *reach* a verdict. 陪審は2日間かけて評決に至った ◇Greater efforts are needed to *reach* the goal of universal education. 普遍的教育という目標に達するためにはさらなる努力が必要だ

accomplish [他]《ややフォーマル》成し遂げる, 完遂する ◇The first part of the plan has been safely *accomplished*. 計画の第一段階は無事に遂行された ◇That's it. *Mission accomplished* (= we have done what we aimed to do). 以上だ. 任務完了 ❶ *accomplish*はtask, mission, plan, jobなどを成し遂げたというときに用いられる.

effect [他]《フォーマル》実現させる, もたらす ◇These drugs can sometimes *effect* miraculous cures. これらの薬は時に奇跡的な効き目をもたらすことがある

ar'rive at sth [句動詞]（議論・熟考の末に決定[結論]に）達する ◇We need to make sure we have all the facts before *arriving at* a decision. 決定を出す前にすべての事実がそろっているかを確認する必要がある ❶ *arrive at* sthはreachよりわずかにインフォーマルな表現である. しかし, achieve a goalの意味では用いることはできない. ◆to *reach* a goal/a target/an objective（目標/目的に達する）. ✕to *arrive at* a goal/a target/an objective.

,pull sth 'off [句動詞]《インフォーマル, 話し言葉》（困難な事を）成し遂げる ◇We *pulled off* the deal. 取り引きを成功させた ◇I never thought you'd *pull* it *off*. 君がうまくやってのけるとは思ってもみなかった

attain [他]《フォーマル》（苦労して）獲得する ◇Most of our students *attained* five 'A' grades in their exams. うちのほとんどの学生は試験でAを5つ取った ❶ *attain*はobjectives（目標）や status（地位）といった語以外にも, 次のような語と共にふつう用いられる. ◆*attain* (a) degree/standard/level/proficiency/mastery（学位を得る/水準を達成する/技能を獲得する/技能を獲得する）
　▶ **attainment** [名] [U] ◇schools with high levels of academic *attainment* 高水準の学力を付けさせる学校

'get there [伝用]《インフォーマル, 話し言葉》目的を達成する, 仕事を完遂する ◇I'm sure you'll *get there* in the end. あなたは最後にはきっと目的を達成するでしょう ◇It's not perfect but we're *getting there* (= making progress). 完璧ではないが順調にいっている

ノート pull sth off と get there の使い分け：get there は目的を達成するまでの長く懸命な努力に，pull sth off は目的の達成に重点が置かれる．

fulfil 《英》（米 **fulfill**）(-ll-) [他]（望み・期待を）かなえる［果たす］ ◇*Fulfil* your dreams with a new career. 新しい仕事で夢をかなえなさい ◇Turkey is a market that has never quite *fulfilled* its potential. トルコはまだまだ可能性のある市場だ

action [名]

action・measure・step・act・move・gesture・deed・stunt・doing
人がすることを表す
【類語訳】行動，行為，措置，行い，方策，スタント

文型&コロケーション
▸ an action/ a measure/ a step/ an act/ a move/ a gesture/ a deed/ a stunt **by** sb
▸ a step/ move/ gesture **towards** sth
▸ a **heroic/ brave/ daring** action/ step/ act/ move/ gesture/ deed
▸ a **kind/ charitable/ generous** action/ act/ gesture/ deed
▸ a/ an **evil/ terrible** act/ deed
▸ to **take** actions/ measures/ steps
▸ to **do** an action/ an act/ a deed/ a stunt
▸ to **perform** an action/ an act/ a deed/ a stunt
▸ to **make** a step/ move/ gesture

action [C, U] 行動, 行為 ◇Her quick *action* saved the child's life. 彼女のすばやい行動が子どもの命を救った ◇Each of us must take responsibility for our own *actions*. 私たちは各自自分の行動に責任を持たなければならない ◇Only the priest can perform these *actions*. 聖職者だけがこういった行為をすることができる ◇We shall take whatever *actions* are necessary. 必要とあらばいかなる行動も取る ◇Firefighters **took** *action* immediately to stop the blaze from spreading. 消防士はただちに延焼を食い止める行動を取った ◇What is the best *course of action* in the circumstances? この状況下でどういった行動方針がベストだろうか ◇She began to explain her *plan of action* to the group. 彼女はそのグループに自分の行動計画を説明し始めた

measure [C]（目標達成のための）対策, 措置 ◇Special *measures* are being taken to protect the local water supplies. 地域の給水を保全するために特別な措置が取られつつある ◇Tougher *measures against* racism are needed. 人種差別に対するより厳しい措置が必要だ ◇This is just a temporary *measure*, while the emergency exists. これは緊急時のほんの一時的な措置にすぎません ◇The government introduced emergency *measures* to stave off an economic crisis. 政府は経済危機を回避するための緊急措置を導入した

step [C]（目標達成のための）手段, 一歩 ◇This was a first *step* towards a united Europe. これはヨーロッパ統一への第一歩だった ◇We are taking *steps* to prevent pollution. 我々は汚染防止の対策を講じているところです ◇This won't solve the problem but it's *a step in the right direction*. これで問題が解決するわけではありませんが，正しい方向に向けての一歩です ◇The new drug is a major *step forward* in the treatment of the disease. その新

薬はその病気の治療にとっての大いなる前進です

act [C] 行為, 行い ◇an *act* of kindness/generosity/love/aggression/desperation 親切な／寛容な／愛の／敵対的な／自暴自棄的な行為 ◇You have committed a serious criminal *act*. あなたは重大な犯罪を犯した ◇The very *act* of writing out your plan clarifies what you need to do. 自分の計画を書き出す行為そのものによりあなたがやらなければならないことがはっきりする ◇He was *caught in the act* of stealing (= caught stealing). 彼は窃盗の現行犯で捕まった

ノート action と act の使い分け：この2つの語は同じ意味を持っているが使い方が違う．act はふつう of を伴い, 形容詞と共に用いる. action はふつう of とは用いないが his, her など と用いられることが多い． ◆a heroic *act* of bravery（勇敢な英雄的行為）．×a heroic *action* of bravery． ◆his heroic *actions/acts* during the war（戦争中の彼の英雄的行為）．action は take と共に用いるが act は take とは用いられない．×We shall take whatever *acts* are necessary.

move [C]《特にジャーナリズム》（目標達成のための）行動, 方策, 措置 ◇This latest *move* by the government has aroused fierce opposition. 政府によるこの最新の措置に猛烈な反対が起こった ◇The management has made no *move* to settle the strike. 経営側はスト収拾に何の措置も講じなかった ◇If he wants to see me, he should *make the first move*. もし彼が私に会いたいのなら彼が最初に行動を起こすべきだ ◇Getting a job in marketing was a good *career move*. マーケティングの仕事が得られたのはキャリア対策としてはよかった

gesture [C]（感情・意思を表示する）行為 ◇It was a *nice gesture* (= it was kind) to invite his wife too. 彼の奥さんも招待するとは気がきいていたね ◇Words and *empty gestures* are not enough — we demand action! 言葉やうわべだけの態度ではだめだ―我々は行動を求めます ◇We do not accept responsibility but we will refund the money as a *gesture of goodwill/a goodwill gesture*. 我々は責任を認めるものではありませんが, 善意のしるしとして返金はいたします

deed [C]《フォーマル or 文語》（善意・悪意の）行為, 行動 ◇It's a stirring tale of heroic *deeds*. それは英雄的行為の感動的な話です ◇These were evil *deeds* perpetrated by wicked people. これらは悪人たちが行った悪質な行為だ ◇I took Sarah's children to school so I've done *my good deed for the day*.（ややインフォーマル, 特に話し言葉）一日一善として私はサラの子どもたちを学校に連れて行った

stunt [C]（人を楽しませるための危険で困難な）行為, （映画などの）スタント ◇He did all his own *stunts* in the movie. その映画では彼は自分ですべてスタントをこなした ◇a *stunt* pilot/rider/team スタントパイロット／ライダー／チーム ◇a *stunt*man/*stunt*woman スタントマン／スタントウーマン ❶ *stunt* は時に人目を引くための非難されるような行為についても用いる． ◆They jumped off London Bridge as a publicity *stunt*.（彼らは世間の注目を集めようとしてロンドンブリッジから飛び降りた）.

doing [C, ふつう複数で, U] 行い ◇I've been hearing a lot about your *doings* recently. 最近あなたがなさっていることをよく耳にします

active 形

active・in operation・in force・in action・up and running・operational

人や物事がその典型的な活動や仕事に従事していることを表す
【類語訳】活動的な、活性の、活動中で、使用中で、有効で、作動して

active 活動的な；(化学的に)活性の ◇These animals are *active* only at night. これらの動物は夜行性だ ◇Numbers of sexually *active* teenagers have continued to rise. 活発な性行動に走るティーンエイジャーの数が増え続けている ◇The virus is still *active* in the blood. そのウイルスは血液中で活性をまだ保っている ◇What is the *active* ingredient in aspirin? アスピリンの活性成分は何ですか 反意 **inactive** ❶ inactive は人・物事が「活動していない、使われていない、機能していない、効果のない」ことを表す ◆Some animals are *inactive* during the daytime. (日中は活動しない動物もいる)。◆an *inactive* drug/disease (効果の現れない薬／不活性な疾患).

in ope'ration フレーズ 《ややフォーマル》 (システムが)活動中[使用中]で、有効で ◇The system needs to be *in operation* for six months before it can be assessed. そのシステムは査定前に6か月間動かしておく必要がある ◇Temporary traffic controls are *in operation* on New Road. ニューロードで一時的な交通規制が敷かれている ❶システムが comes into operation と言うとき、「動き始める、効果が出始める」という意味である。◆The new rules *come into operation* from next week. (来週から新しい規則が施行される)。put sth into operation は、物事を「使い始める、始動させる」という意味である。◆It's time to *put* our plan *into operation*. (我々の計画を実施する時が来た)。☞ operate (ORGANIZE), operate (WORK 動 2)

in 'force フレーズ (法律・規則などが)施行されて、効力があって ◇The new regulations are now *in force*. 新しい規則が今や有効になっている ❶come/enter into force は「(法律・規則などが)施行される」という意味である。◆When do the new regulations *come into force*? (その新しい規則はいつ施行されるのですか)。bring sth into force は「…を施行する」の意味である。◆They are hoping to *bring* the new legislation *into force* by the end of the year. (年内に新しい規則を実施できればと思っている)。

in 'action フレーズ (人・物がその典型的な)活動をして ◇I've yet to see all the players *in action*. すべての選手がプレーしているところをまだ見たことがない

,up and 'running フレーズ (コンピュータシステムなどが)作動して、使用中で ◇By that time the new system should be *up and running*. その時までには新システムを作動させなくてはならない ❶up and running は何かが始動するとき、あるいは開発期間を経て使用されるようになるときに用いられる。☞ **run** (WORK 動 2)

operational [名詞の前にまれ] 《ややフォーマル》 使用[実用]可能な；使用[稼動]中の ◇The new airport should be fully *operational* by the end of the year. 新しい空港は今年中に完全に使用できるようになるだろう ❶operational は fully operational というフレーズでよく用いられる。☞ **operate** (WORK 動 2)

actor 名

actor・actress・performer・artist・comedian・entertainer・movie/film star・artiste

観客を楽しませる仕事をする人
【類語訳】男優、女優、俳優、演者、アーティスト、コメディアン、エンターテイナー、映画スター、芸人

文型&コロケーション
▶ a **young** actor/ actress/ performer/ artist/ comedian/ entertainer/ artiste
▶ a **famous** actor/ actress/ performer/ artist/ comedian/ entertainer/ movie star
▶ a/ an **talented/ aspiring** actor/ actress/ performer/ artist/ comedian/ entertainer

actor [C] (舞台・テレビ・映画などでの)男優、俳優 ◇She is one of the country's leading *actors*. 彼女はその国のトップ俳優の一人だ

actress [C] 女優 ◇In 1940 he married *actress* Jane Wyman. 1940年に彼は女優のジェーン・ワイマンと結婚した

ノート **actor** と **actress** の使い分け：actor は男性にも女性にも用いられる。女性に actor を用いる場合、プロとして演技力のあることを強調する。actress は俳優が女性であることを強調する場合に用いられる。

performer [C] (ショー・コンサートなどでの)演者、演奏者 ◇By the age of 15, Allan had become an experienced circus *performer*. 15歳の頃にはアランは熟練したサーカスの演技者になっていた

artist [C] (ミュージシャン・俳優などの)アーティスト ◇After the band broke up, Joe relaunched his career as a solo *artist*. バンド解散後、ジョーはソロアーティストとして再出発した ◇A mime *artist's* movements must be clear to the audience. パントマイム演者の動きは観客にはっきりとわかるようにしなくてはならない

comedian [C] コメディアン ◇Peter was in his thirties when he decided to be a **stand-up comedian**. ピーターは30歳台でソロのお笑い芸人になろうと決めた ❶stand-up comedy は「一人でやるお笑い芸」。

entertainer [C] (歌手・漫才師・ダンサーなど)エンターテイナー、芸人 ◇Covent Garden is famous for its street *entertainers*. コベントガーデンは大道芸人で有名だ ☞ **entertain** (ENTERTAIN)

'movie star (特に米) (英ふつう **'film star**) [C] 映画スター ◇I always wanted to be a *movie star*, even when I was a child. ぼくは子どもの時でもいつも映画スターになりたいと思っていた

artiste [C] (特に英、時に皮肉で) (歌手・ダンサー・俳優などの)優れたエンターテイナー ◇He was a true *artiste*: sensitive, dramatic and tragic. 彼は本物のエンターテイナーだった。感性が鋭く、劇的かつ悲劇的で

addictive 形

addictive・obsessive・compulsive・obsessional consuming

やめたり抑制したりすることが困難、不可能であることを表す
【類語訳】中毒性の、依存性の、強迫観念にとりつかれた

adequate, adjust

文型&コロケーション
- obsessive/ compulsive/ obsessional **about** sth
- the addictive/ obsessive/ compulsive **nature** of sth
- addictive/ obsessive/ compulsive/ obsessional **behaviour**
- an obsessive/ a compulsive/ a consuming **need/ desire**
- almost obsessive/ compulsive/ obsessional

addictive (薬物・活動が)中毒性の, 依存性の ◇Tobacco is highly *addictive*. タバコは常習性が高い ◇The game is very *addictive*. そのゲームはやみつきになる ◇Some people have an *addictive* personality (= they easily get addicted to things). 物事にはまりやすい人がいる ☞**addict** (FAN)

obsessive (けなして) 執拗に；強迫観念にとりつかれた ◇An *obsessive* fan was making the singer's life a misery. ある執拗なファンがその歌手の生活を悲惨にしていた ◇He's becoming more and more *obsessive* about punctuality. 彼は時間を守るという強迫観念がますます強くなっている ◇The play is about *obsessive* jealousy. その芝居は異常なまでの嫉妬についてである
- ▶**obsessively** 副 ◇She was *obsessively* tidy. 彼女は異常なまでにきれい好きだった

compulsive (行為などが)やめられない, 抑制できない ◇His family had been unaware of his *compulsive* gambling. 彼の家族は彼がギャンブルをしないではいられないことに気づいていなかった
- ▶**compulsively** 副 ◇He was *compulsively* generous. 彼は気前よくしないではいられなかった

obsessional (《フォーマル or 医学》) 強迫観念にとりつかれた ◇She is *obsessional* about cleanliness. 彼女は過度のきれい好きだ ◇They were receiving medical treatment for *obsessional* symptoms. 彼らは強迫症状で治療を受けていた

ノート obsessive と obsessional の使い分け：これらは2つとも人・行為について用いられるが, obsessional はより医学的な文脈で用いられる.

consuming ［名詞の前で］(感情・興味が)激しい, 焼き尽くすような ◇They both had a *consuming interest* in cricket. 彼らは二人ともクリケットにのめり込んでいた ◇Theatre was his *consuming passion*. 演劇に彼の熱情は注ぎ込まれていた

adequate 形 ☞FINE, GOOD 2

adequate・not bad・reasonable・all right・acceptable
物事が非常によいわけではなく, そこそこであることを表す
【類語訳】十分な, まずまずの, ほどほどの

文型&コロケーション
- to be adequate/ not bad/ reasonable/ all right/ acceptable **for** sb/ sth
- an adequate/ a reasonable/ an acceptable **level/ degree/ standard** of sth
- adequate/ reasonable/ acceptable **provision** for sb/ sth
- just (about) adequate/ all right/ acceptable
- barely/ scarcely adequate/ acceptable

adequate (ある用途のために質・量において)十分な, まずまずの ◇They'll need an *adequate* supply of hot water. 十分なお湯の供給が必要だ ◇The room was small but *adequate*. その部屋は狭いが十分だ ◇The space available is not *adequate* for our needs. 使えるスペースは我々が必要としている十分な広さではない ◇The training given should be *adequate to* meet the future needs of the industry. 提供される訓練はその産業が将来必要とするものに十分見合うものであるべきだ 反意 **inadequate** (INADEQUATE)
- ▶**adequately** 副 ◇Are you *adequately* insured? 十分な保険を掛けていますか

not 'bad (《インフォーマル, 話し言葉》) まあまあの; 思ったよりよい ◇'How are you?' '*Not too bad*.' 「元気ですか」「まあまあです」 ◇That wasn't *bad* for a first attempt. 最初の試みにしては悪くなかった

reasonable まずまずの, ほどほどの ◇Most people here have a *reasonable* standard of living. ここにいる人の大部分はまずまずの生活水準だ ◇The hotel was *reasonable*, I suppose. そのホテルはまずまずだったと思う ☞**reasonably** (QUITE 1)

all 'right ［名詞の前では用いない］ かろうじて十分と言える, まあまあの ◇Your work is *all right*, but you could do better. あなたの仕事はまあまあの出来ですが, 本来ならもっとうまくできるでしょう

acceptable 一応満足できる, 可もなく不可もない ◇The food was *acceptable*, but no more. 食べ物は可もなく不可もなかったが, しょせんそんなところだった

adjust 動 ☞CHANGE 動 1

adjust・modify・amend・revise・qualify
状況に合わせて物事を多少変えることを表す
【類語訳】調整する, 調節する, 修正する, 改める, 見直す

文型&コロケーション
- to adjust/ modify/ revise your **ideas**
- to modify/ amend/ revise a **text/ constitution**
- to modify/ amend/ qualify a **statement**
- to adjust/ modify/ amend/ revise sth **slightly**
- to modify/ amend/ revise/ qualify sth **heavily**
- to adjust/ modify/ revise sth **constantly**

adjust ［他］ (新しい状況・条件に合うように)調整[調節]する ◇This button is for *adjusting* the volume. このボタンは音量を調節するためのものです ◇*Adjust* your language *to* the age of your audience. 観客の年齢に応じて言葉を使い分けなさい ◇The brakes need to be *adjusted*. ブレーキを調整しなくてはならない ☞**adjustment** (CHANGE 名 2), **adjustable** (FLEXIBLE 1)

modify ［他］ (《ややフォーマル》) (ある目的に適合するように)修正する ◇Patients are taught how to *modify* their diet. 患者たちは食生活をどのように変えればよいかを教えられる ◇We found it cheaper to *modify* existing equipment rather than buy new. 今ある装置に手を加えるほうが新しい物を買うより安くつくことがわかった ☞**adapt** (CHANGE 動 1), **modification** (CHANGE 名 2)

ノート adjust と modify の使い分け：adjust は装置などの設定を変えるときに用いられる. ◆to *adjust* the setting/ dial/ volume/ speed/ angle/ level/ tension/ clock/ sails/ straps (設定/ダイヤル/音量/速度/角度/水準/電圧/時計/帆/(肩)ひもを調節する). 状況の変化に応じた継続的なものであることが多い. ◆to *adjust* sth continual-

↪adjust

ly/constantly/accordingly （継続的に/絶えず/状況に応じて調節する）．modify は新たな機能を果たさせるため，またその状況に応じた新装置により永続的な変更を加えるときに用いる．またその時の状況に応じて adjust [modify] your behavior, adjust [modify] your language のようにいずれの語も使える．

amend ［他］《ややフォーマル》（法律・文書・声明などを）修正する，改める ◇He asked to see the *amended* version. 彼は修正案を見せるように言った ◇The law has been *amended* to read as follows:... その法は以下のような文言に修正された ☞ **amendment** (CHANGE 名 2)

revise ［他］（新たな情報を得るなどして意見・計画を）変える，見直す ◇I can see I will have to *revise* my opinions of his abilities now. 今の彼の能力について私の考えを変えざるをえないことはわかっている ◇The government may need to *revise* its policy in the light of this report. この報告を踏まえて政府は方針を見直す必要があるかもしれない ❶ revise your plans/arrangements と共に revise your opinion/ideas/decision と言うことができる．公的機関であれば revise the constitution/a policy/a law/guidelines と言うこともある．ビジネスの場では revise a draft/an estimate/figures/a proposal と言うこともある．☞ **revision** (CHANGE 名 2)

qualify ［他］《ややフォーマル》（意味を弱めたりするために）前言に付け加える ◇I want to *qualify* what I said earlier — I didn't mean he couldn't do the job, only that he would need supervision. 前言を取り消したいと思います．彼が仕事ができないと言ったつもりなどなく，彼には監督が必要だと言っただけです ☞ **qualification** (CONDITION)

admiration 名

admiration • respect • awe • recognition • esteem • appreciation
人の功績，物事の質の良さなどに感銘を受けて抱く好印象を表す
【類語訳】賞賛，尊敬，敬意，畏敬，畏怖，好感

respect	admiration	awe
recognition		
esteem		
appreciation		

⬛ 文型&コロケーション

▶ admiration/ respect/ recognition **for** sb
▶ to do sth **in** admiration/ awe/ recognition/ appreciation
▶ **great** admiration/ respect/ awe/ esteem/ appreciation
▶ **deep/ genuine** admiration/ respect/ appreciation
▶ **mutual** admiration/ respect/ esteem/ appreciation
▶ **grudging** admiration/ respect/ recognition
▶ to **have** a lot of, no, etc. admiration/ respect/ appreciation (for sb/ sth)
▶ to **show** your admiration/ respect/ appreciation (for sb/ sth)
▶ to **win/ gain/ deserve** admiration/ respect/ recognition
▶ to **earn** respect/ recognition/ esteem
▶ to **inspire** admiration/ respect/ awe

admiration ［U］賞賛 ◇I have great *admiration* for her as a writer. 作家としての彼女に感服しています ◇We watched in *admiration* as the gymnasts practised their routines. 体操選手たちの規定演技に賞賛の目で見

入った ☞ **admire** (RESPECT 動), **admiring** (GOOD 6)

respect ［U, 単数で］尊敬，敬意 ◇I have the greatest *respect* for your brother. あなたのお兄さんをとても尊敬しています ◇A two-minute silence was held as a *mark of respect*. 敬意のしるしとして2分間の黙祷があった ☞ **respect** (RESPECT 動)

📝 **admiration** と **respect** の使い分け：admiration はその人のことが好きでそのようになりたいことを表す． ◆ He was full of *admiration* for the way she never lost her patience. （彼は彼女が決してしびれを切らさないことにいたく感心した）．respect はその人のことがあまり好きではない場合でも用いることができる． ◆ She had a lot of *respect* for him as an actor, but didn't like the way he treated other members of the cast. （彼女は彼を役者として非常に尊敬していたが，他の出演者に対する彼の態度は気に入らなかった）．admiration は賞賛の気持ちだけを表すが，respect は尊敬の気持ちを抱いているゆえに人に丁寧な態度を取ることをも表す． ◆ I have nothing but *admiration/respect* for the winning team. （勝利チームには賞賛/尊敬の念しかない）． ◆ He always treated me with *respect*. （彼はいつも私に敬意を持って接してくれた）．× He always treated me with *admiration*.

awe ［U］畏敬，畏怖 ◇They gazed in *awe* at the beauty of the scene. その景色の美しさを畏敬の念を持って見つめた ◇While Diana was *in awe of* (= she admired and was slightly afraid of) her grandfather, she adored her grandmother. ダイアナは祖父には畏怖の念を抱いていた一方，祖母へは敬愛の念を抱いていた ☞ **be/stand in awe of sb** (RESPECT 動)

recognition ［U］（作品・行為に対する）評価 ◇She gained only minimal *recognition* for her work. 彼女は自分の作品に対してごくわずかな評価しか得なかった ◇He received the award *in recognition of* his success over the past year. 彼はこの1年の功績が評価され受賞した

esteem ［U］《フォーマル》（人に対する）尊敬，賞賛の念 ◇She is *held in high esteem* by her colleagues. 彼女は同僚から高い評価を得ている ☞ **esteem** (RESPECT 動), **self-esteem** (DIGNITY)

appreciation ［U］（人・物事の良さを理解した上での）正しい評価，鑑賞（力） ◇She shows little *appreciation* of good music. 彼女はいい音楽を鑑賞する耳を持たない ◇The crowd murmured in *appreciation*. 観衆は賞賛のつぶやきを漏らした ☞ **appreciate** (APPRECIATE)

admit 動

admit • acknowledge • recognize • concede • confess • grant
事実であると受け入れることを表す
【類語訳】認める，容認する

⬛ 文型&コロケーション

▶ to admit/ confess **to** sth
▶ to admit/ concede/ confess sth **to** sb
▶ to admit/ acknowledge/ recognize/ concede/ confess/ grant **that**...
▶ **It is/ was (generally)** admitted/ acknowledged/ recognized/ conceded/ granted **that**...
▶ to admit/ acknowledge/ recognize **the truth**
▶ to admit/ confess your **mistakes/ ignorance**
▶ you **must** admit/ acknowledge/ recognize/ concede/ con-

fess/ grant sth
▶ to admit/ acknowledge/ concede/ confess/ grant sth **freely/ readily**
▶ to admit/ acknowledge/ concede/ confess sth **grudgingly/ privately/ reluctantly**

admit (**-tt-**) [自, 他] (不本意ながら事実であると)認める
◇She *admits* to being strict with her children. 彼女は子どもたちに対して厳しいと認めている ◇It was a stupid thing to do, I *admit*. 確かにばかなことをした ◇*Admit* it! You were terrified! 認めなさい。君は怖がっていたね ◇Why don't you just *admit defeat* (= recognize that you cannot do sth and let sb else try)? 手に余ると認めたらいいじゃないか ◇You must *admit* that it all sounds very strange. あなたはすべてが変だと認めざるをえない ◇The appointment is now generally *admitted* to have been a mistake. その任命は間違いだったと今や広く認められている ❶ このようなパターンでは受身形でのみ用いられる。

acknowledge [他]《ややフォーマル》(物事が真実であると)認める ◇She refuses to *acknowledge* the need for reform. 彼女は改善の必要性を認めようとはしない ◇He did not *acknowledge* that he had done anything wrong. 彼は悪いことをしたとは認めなかった ◇It is generally *acknowledged* to be true. それは事実だと一般に認められている

recognize (英でまた **-ise**) [他] (物事の存在・真実性を)認める ◇They *recognized* the need to take the problem seriously. 彼らはその問題を真剣に取り上げる必要があると認めた ◇Drugs were not *recognized as* a problem then. 当時ドラッグは問題視されていなかった ◇Nobody *recognized* how urgent the situation was. その状況がどれほど緊迫したものであるか誰も認識していなかった
▶**recognition** [名] [単数で, U] ◇a growing *recognition* that older people have potential too 高齢者も潜在能力を持っているという高まりつつある認識 ◇There is general *recognition* of the urgent need for reform. 緊急に改善の必要があるという一般的な認識がある

concede [他]《ややフォーマル》(不本意ながら物事が事実である[理にかなっている]と)認める ◇He was forced to *concede* (that) there might be difficulties. 困難なことがあるかもしれないと彼は認めざるをえなかった ◇He reluctantly *conceded the point* to me. 彼はしぶしぶその点で私に譲歩した

ノート **admit** と **concede** の使い分け：admit は自ら間違いである事実を認める場合。concede は事実・意見が筋が通っていると不本意ながら認める場合。

confess [他, 自]《ややフォーマル》(恥ずかしい[みっともない]と感じることを)認める ◇She was reluctant to *confess* her ignorance. 彼女は自分の無知を認めたがらなかった ◇I must *confess* to knowing nothing about computers. 私はコンピューターについては何も知らないと言わざるをえません

grant [他] (主張などが正しいと)認める ◇She's a smart woman, I *grant* you, but she's no genius. 彼女が頭のいい女性であることは認める、しかし決して天才ではない ◇*Granted*, he is a beginner, but he should know the basic rules. 確かに彼は初心者だ、しかし初歩的なルールは知っておくべきだ ❶ grantはふつうI/I'll grant you (that)...や、文頭でGranted...という表現で用いられる。grantを用いるときはよく文の後半にbutを付ける。

adult

adult [形]

adult・mature・grown・grown-up
精神的・肉体的に十分に成長していることを表す
【類語訳】成人の, 成熟した, 分別のある, 大人っぽい, 大人の

文型&コロケーション
▶ to be mature/ grown-up **about** sth
▶ an adult/ a mature/ a grown **man/ woman**
▶ a mature/ grown-up **child/ boy/ girl**
▶ **fully** mature/ grown

adult 成人の, 成熟した；大人の ◇*adult* monkeys 大人の猿 ◇the *adult* population 成人人口 ◇preparing young people for *adult* life 大人としての生活に向けての若者の備え ◇When my parents split up, it was all very *adult* and open. 両親の離婚に際してはすべてがいかにも大人らしくオープンだった 反意 **juvenile** (YOUNG), **childish** (CHILDISH)
▶**adult** [名] [C] ◇Children must be accompanied by an *adult*. 子どもには大人の付き添いが必要です ◇The fish return to the river as *adults* in order to breed. その魚は成長すると産卵のために川へ戻る ◇Why can't you two act like civilized *adults*? 君たち二人とも分別のある大人らしくしたらどうだ 反意 **child, minor**

mature (子ども・若者が)分別のある, 大人っぽい；(人・樹木・鳥・動物が)十分に成長[生長]した, 成熟した ◇Jane is very *mature* for her age. ジェーンは年の割にとても大人っぽい ◇He shows a *mature* and sensible attitude. 彼の態度は大人びていて分別がある ◇a *mature* oak/eagle/elephant 成長したオークの木/鷲(ワシ)/象 反意 **immature** (CHILDISH), ☞ **mature** (OLD 2), **sensible** (WISE)
▶**maturity** [名] [U] ◇He has *maturity* beyond his years. 彼は年よりも大人びている 反意 **immaturity**

ノート **adult** と **mature** の使い分け：adult は肉体的な発達を, mature は精神的な発達を言うことが多い。◆an *adult* male (成人男性). ◆*adult* education (= for adults, not children) (成人教育) ◆a *mature* conversation/attitude (= sensible, not childish) (大人の会話/態度). それほど頻繁ではないがadultが精神的な発達を表し, matureも肉体的な発達を表すのに用いられることもある。◆She dealt with it in a very *adult* way (= in a sensible way, as an adult should). (彼女は非常に大人らしいやり方でそれを処理した). ◆a *mature* fish (= fully grown) (成魚).

grown [名詞の前で] (精神的・肉体的に)大人の ◇It's pathetic that *grown* men have to resort to violence like this. 大人がこのように暴力に訴えなくてはならないとは情けないことだ ◇The little girl she remembered was now a *grown* woman. 彼女が覚えていた小さな少女は今や大人の女性だった

grown-'up (精神的・肉体的に)大人の, 大人らしい ◇What do you want to be when you're *grown-up*? 大人になったら何になりたいの ◇She has a *grown-up* son. 彼女には成人した息子がいる
▶**'grown-up** [名] [C] ◇If you're good you can eat with the *grown-ups*. お行儀よくしていれば大人と一緒に食事ができますよ 反意 **child** (CHILD) ❶ grown-upは子どもがよく用いたり, 子どもに向かって言うときに用いられる。◆Wow, look at you! You look so *grown-up*! (うわー, すごい。と

ても大人っぽく見えるよ). ◆Ask a *grown-up* to help you cut this shape out. (この形に切るように大人に手伝ってもらいなさい).

advertise 動

advertise・market・promote・push・merchandise・hype・plug
人々に商品やサービスなどを買わせたり使わせたりするよう、または新しい考えを受け入れるよう働きかけること
【類語訳】宣伝する、マーケティングする、売り込む、押し売りする、誇大広告する

文型&コロケーション
- to advertise/ market/ promote/ push/ merchandise/ hype/ plug sth **as** sth
- to advertise/ market/ promote/ merchandise sth **through** sth
- to advertise/ market sth **to** sb
- to advertise/ market/ promote/ push/ merchandise/ hype/ plug a **product**
- to advertise/ market/ promote/ hype/ plug a/ an **book/ film/ movie/ CD/ album**
- to advertise/ market/ promote a **service**
- to market/ promote/ push an **idea**
- to advertise/ market/ promote/ hype sth **heavily**

advertise [自,他] 広告する、宣伝する ◇If you want to attract more customers, try *advertising* in the local paper. もっと多くの顧客を引き付けたいなら、地元の新聞に広告を打ちなさい ◇The cruise was *advertised* as the 'journey of a lifetime'. その船旅の宣伝文句は「生涯の旅」だった ☞ **advertise** (PUBLISH 1)
　▷**advertising** 名 [U] ◇She's hoping to make a career in *advertising*. 彼女は広告業界で働きたいと思っている
market [他] 売り出す、マーケティングする ◇It is *marketed* as a low-alcohol wine. それは低アルコールワインとして売り出されている ◇School meals need to be *marketed* to children in the same way as other food. 他の食品と同様に学校給食も子どもたちに対するマーケティングを怠ってはならない
　▷**marketing** 名 [U] ◇He works in *sales and marketing*. 彼は営業とマーケティングの仕事をしている
promote [他] (商品・サービスの販売を)促進する、広める ◇The band has gone on tour to *promote* their new album. そのバンドは新発売のアルバムのプロモーションのためにツアーに出た ◇The area is being *promoted* as a tourist destination. その地域は観光地振興の対象となっている
push [他] 《ややインフォーマル》(新商品・新しい考えを)押し売りする、強いる ◇She didn't want to *push* the point any further at that moment. その時には彼女はそれ以上その点を主張したくなかった ◇Sales promotion is designed to *push* certain products. 販売促進は特定の商品を売り込むことを目的としている
merchandise [他] 《ビジネスで》(人気映画・有名人・イベントに関連した商品を)宣伝して売り込む ◇She works with companies that want to make or *merchandise* products related to the company's films. 彼女は自社の映画に関連した商品の製造・販売をしてくれる会社と仕事をしている
hype [他] 《インフォーマル、けなして》大げさに宣伝する、誇大広告する ◇This week his much *hyped* new movie opens in London. 大々的に宣伝した彼の新作映画が今週ロンドンで公開される
plug (**-gg-**) [他] 《インフォーマル》(番組で)売り込む、宣伝する ◇She came on the show to *plug* her latest album. 彼女は最新アルバムを売り込むためにその番組に出た

advertisement 名

advertisement・publicity・ad・commercial・promotion・advert・trailer・blurb・plug
商品、仕事、サービスのことを知らせるためのビラ、写真、映画など
【類語訳】広告、宣伝、広報、コマーシャル、プロモーション、予告編、宣伝文

文型&コロケーション
- an advertisement/ publicity/ an ad/ a commercial/ a promotion/ an advert/ a trailer/ a blurb/ a plug **for** sth
- (a) **TV/ television/ radio/ cinema** advertisement/ ad/ commercial/ promotion/ advert
- to **run/ show** an advertisement/ an ad/ a commercial/ an advert/ a trailer
- to **put/ place/ take out** an advertisement/ ad/ advert
- the advertisement/ ad/ commercial/ advert/ blurb **says/ states/ claims...**
- the advertisement/ ad/ commercial/ advert/ trailer **appears/ shows sth/ features sb/ sth**

advertisement [C, U] 広告、宣伝 ◇Put an *advertisement* in the local paper to sell your car. 車を売るには地元の新聞に広告を打ちなさい ◇Dirty streets and homelessness are no *advertisement* for a prosperous society. 汚れた街角やホームレスは裕福な社会の宣伝にはならない ◇We are employing an assistant to help with the *advertisement* of the group's activities. そのグループの活動の宣伝に役立つようなアシスタントを雇おうとしているところです
publicity [U] 宣伝[広報]業務；宣伝内容 ◇She works in *publicity*. 彼女は広報の仕事をしている ◇There has been a lot of advance *publicity* for her new film. 彼女の新作映画は盛んに前宣伝をしていた ◇*publicity* material 宣伝材料 ◇a *publicity* campaign 宣伝活動 ◇The band dressed up as the Beatles as a *publicity stunt*. そのバンドは宣伝用パフォーマンスとしてビートルズに扮した
ad [C] 《インフォーマル》広告 ◇We put an *ad* in the local paper. 我々は地元の新聞に広告を出した ◇They've produced an *ad* for a new chocolate bar. 彼らは新製品のチョコレートバーの広告を制作した
commercial [C] コマーシャル、広告放送 ◇The company has made *commercials* for leading sportswear manufacturers. その会社は一流スポーツウエアメーカーのコマーシャルを作った ◇a *commercial* break (= a time during or between shows when advertisements are broadcast) (番組の途中に入る)コマーシャルの時間
promotion [C, U] (宣伝・販売促進といった)プロモーション ◇We are doing a special *promotion* of Chilean wines. チリワインの特別プロモーションを行っている ◇Her job is mainly concerned with sales and *promotion*. 彼女の仕事は主に販売促進です
advert [C] 《英、インフォーマル》広告、宣伝 ◇I never watch the *adverts* on TV. 私はテレビでは広告は決して見ません
trailer [C] 《特に英》(映画・テレビ番組の)予告編 ◇The

advice, adviser, affect

review said that if you've seen the *trailer*, you needn't bother watching this film. 批評によれば予告編を見たのならば、この映画をわざわざ見ることはなさそうだった

blurb [C] （製作者側による本・映画などの）宣伝文 ◇The *blurb* says that this is Tarantino's greatest movie. 宣伝文句によればこの映画はタランティーノの最高傑作だそうだ ❶ blurb はふつう本の表紙、DVD のケースなどに書かれている。

plug [C] （インフォーマル）（新刊本・映画の売り上げを伸ばすために寄せる）推薦（文），宣伝 ◇He managed to get in a *plug* for his new book. 彼は自分の新刊本の宣伝となるコメントをなんとか取り付けた

advice 名

advice・counselling・tip・guidance
ある状況で人がすべきことについての意見や提案
【類語訳】アドバイス，助言，カウンセリング，案内，指導

文型&コロケーション
▸ advice/ counselling/ tips/ guidance **on** sth
▸ advice/ counselling/ tips **for** sb/ sth
▸ advice/ guidance **about** sth
▸ **helpful/ practical/ useful/ valuable/ general** advice/ tips/ guidance
▸ **professional** advice/ counselling/ tips/ guidance
▸ **spiritual** advice/ counselling/ guidance
▸ **to give** sb advice/ counselling/ a tip/ guidance
▸ **to offer/ provide/ seek** advice/ counselling/ guidance

advice [U] アドバイス，助言 ◇Can you give me some *advice* on where to buy good maps? いい地図を買うにはどこへ行けばよいか教えてください ◇We were advised to seek *legal advice*. 我々は法的なアドバイスを求めるように忠告された ◇Let me give you a *piece of advice*. 君に一つ忠告しておこう ◇*Take my advice* — don't get married. 私の忠告を聞いて。結婚してはだめですよ ◇I chose it *on his advice*. 彼のアドバイスに従って私はそれを選んだ ◇Permission was given *against the advice* of the planning officers. 企画官たちの助言に反して許可が下りた ❶ advice はふつう，経験豊富な人や権力のある人が与える。もし年上の人や経験豊かな人に take my advice と言ったとしたら不快感を与えることになる。 ☞**advise** (RECOMMEND 1), **recommendation** (ENDORSEMENT)

counselling 《英》《米 **counseling**》 [U] （個人的・精神的な問題について専門的な助言を行う）カウンセリング ◇Many of the victims of the tragedy still need *counselling*. その惨事の犠牲者の多くがいまだにカウンセリングを必要としている

tip [C] 《ややインフォーマル》（ちょっとした実践的な）助言；（賭け事についての）内密の情報，専門的助言 ◇There are lots of useful *tips* on how to save money. お金を貯めるのに役立つヒントがたくさんある ◇He said he'd been given a *hot tip* for that afternoon's race. 彼はその日の午後のレースの有力情報を手に入れたと言った

guidance [U] （やり方・問題対処に関する年長者・経験者からの）指導，案内 ◇Activities take place *under the guidance of* an experienced tutor. 活動は経験のある教員の指導のもとに行われる ◇The handbook gives helpful *guidance* on writing articles. そのハンドブックは記事を書くのに役立つ内容が書かれている

adviser 名

adviser・consultant・counsellor・mentor・guide
個人的に，または仕事として助言する人のことを表す
【類語訳】助言者，アドバイザー，顧問，コンサルタント，カウンセラー，メンター，ガイド

文型&コロケーション
▸ an adviser/ a consultant/ a mentor **to** sb
▸ an adviser/ a consultant **on** sth
▸ a **political** adviser/ consultant/ mentor
▸ a **spiritual** adviser/ counsellor/ mentor/ guide
▸ **to act as** an adviser/ a consultant/ a mentor/ a guide

adviser (または頻度は低いが **advisor**) [C] 助言者，アドバイザー ◇He works as an *adviser* on environmental issues. 彼は環境問題のアドバイザーとして働いている ◇As your legal *adviser*, it is my duty to warn you against it. 顧問弁護士として，そうしないようあなたに警告することが私の義務です

consultant [C] 顧問，コンサルタント ◇The professor also acted as a *consultant* to the Department of Education. その教授は教育省の顧問もやっていた ◇*Management consultants* were brought in to sort out the mess. 混乱した事態を収拾するために経営コンサルタントが招かれた

ノート **adviser** と **consultant** の使い分け：adviser は企業，政府，政治家などに永続的に雇われたり，特定の問題やプロジェクトに関して助言を求められて招かれる一個人である。consultant は企業や政治家などに特定の分野での助言をする人で，adviser のように個人や企業などに永続的に雇われることはふつうないが，コンサルタント会社に勤めていることは多い。

counsellor 《特に英》《米でふつう **counselor**》 [C] （個人的な問題に助言する訓練を積んだ）カウンセラー ◇The centre is staffed by specially trained *counsellors*. そのセンターは特別に訓練されたカウンセラーを置いている ◇Have you thought of talking to a *marriage guidance counsellor*? 《英》結婚カウンセラーに相談しようと思ったことがありますか ◇a *marriage counselor* 《米》結婚カウンセラー

mentor [C] （一定期間にわたって人に助言を与える経験豊富な）メンター ◇The agent was a friend and *mentor* to many young artists. その代理人は多くの若いアーティストにとって友達でありメンターであった ☞**guru** (EXPERT), **mentoring** (EDUCATION)

guide [C] （生き方・振る舞い方を）助言する人，案内人，ガイド ◇His sister had been his *guide*, counsellor and friend. 彼の姉は彼にとってガイドで，カウンセラーで，友達でもあった

affect 動 ☞INFLUENCE 動

affect・involve・concern・influence・work・impact・take (a) hold・leave a mark・act・colour
人や物事に影響をもたらすことを表す
【類語訳】影響する，関わらせる，巻き込む，関係する，関わる，支配する，作用する

↪affect / afraid

文型&コロケーション
- to impact/ act/ leave a mark **on** sth
- to be involved/ concerned **in** sth
- to affect/ influence **what** happens
- to affect/ influence **how/ why/ when/ where** sth happens
- to affect/ influence/ colour sb's **judgement/ attitude**
- to **directly/ indirectly** affect/ involve/ concern/ influence/ impact on/ act on sb/ sth
- to **adversely/ inevitably** affect/ influence/ impact on sth

affect [他, しばしば受身で] (人・物事に)影響する ◇How will these changes *affect* us? この変化が我々にどう影響するだろうか ◇Your opinions will not *affect* my decision. あなたの意見は私の決断に影響を与えないだろう ◇The south of the country was worst *affected* by the drought. その国の南部が干ばつで一番ひどい影響を受けた ◇The type of audience will *affect* what you say and how you say it. 聴衆次第であなたは発言内容や話し方を変えざるをえないだろう ☞ **effect** (EFFECT), **bias** (INFLUENCE 動)

involve [他] (状況・事件・活動に)関わらせる, 巻き込む ◇There was a serious incident *involving* a group of youths. 若者のグループを巻き込んだ重大な事件があった ◇How many vehicles were *involved* in the crash? その衝突事故に何台の車が巻き込まれたのだろう

concern [他, しばしば受身で]《ややフォーマル》(問題・状況・事件が人に)関係する, かかわる ◇Don't interfere in what doesn't *concern* you. 君に関係のないことは口出ししないでくれ ◇The meetings were often embarrassing for *all concerned*. 会議はしばしば関係者一同に気まずいものになった ◇The individuals *concerned* will have some explaining to do. 関係する個々人が説明をしなくてはならない

> **ノート** **involve** と **concern** の使い分け: involve は人の出来事への関与の程度を問題にする場合。×an incident *concerning* a group of youths. ×the vehicles *concerned* in the crash. concern は人の関心や責任への関わりの程度を問題にする場合。

influence [他] (ある状況やその展開に)影響を及ぼす ◇A number of social factors *influence* life expectancy. 多くの社会的要因が寿命に影響を及ぼす ◇The local climate is *influenced* by the Gulf Stream. メキシコ湾流が地域の気候に影響を及ぼしている ◇At college she met the two people who most *influenced* her artistic career. 彼女は大学でその芸術面でのキャリアに非常に影響を与えた二人の人に出会った ☞ **influence** (INFLUENCE 動), **influence** (EFFECT)

work [自]《副詞や前置詞と共に》(人・状況に特定の)影響を与える ◇Your age can *work against* you in this job. この仕事はあなたの年齢が不利になるかもしれない ◇Speaking Italian should *work in his favour*. イタリア語を話せることが彼に有利に働くだろう

impact [自, 他]《特にジャーナリズム or ビジネス》(物事に(悪い))影響を与える ◇The border dispute could *impact* on the work of aid agencies. 国境紛争は救援機関の活動に影響を与えるかもしれない ◇The company's performance was *impacted* by the high value of the pound. その企業の業績はポンド高の影響を受けた ☞ **impact** (EFFECT)

take (a) 'hold [イディオム] (物事に強い)影響を及ぼし始める, (人・物事を)支配する ◇Panic *took hold of* him and he couldn't move. パニックが彼を襲い, 彼は動けなかった ◇It was in the sixties that the cult of the teenager first *took hold*. 初めてティーンエイジャーがもてはやされたのは60年代のことだった

leave your/its/a 'mark [イディオム] (人・物事に(悪い))影響を長く残す ◇Such a traumatic experience is bound to *leave its mark*. そういったトラウマ的な体験は当然後々まで影響を残すだろう

act [自] (薬物や化学的[物理的]な力が物事に)作用する, 影響を及ぼす ◇Alcohol *acts* quickly on the brain. アルコールはすぐに脳に影響を及ぼす ◇It took a few minutes for the drug to *act*. その薬は数分で作用した ☞ **action** (EFFECT)

colour 《英》(米では **color**)[他] (意見・態度に(よくない))影響を与える ◇The experience moulded and *coloured* her whole life. その経験が彼女の全人生を形作り影響を与えた ◇Don't let your judgement be *coloured* by personal feelings. あなたの判断が個人的な感情に左右されないようにしなさい

---

afraid [形] ☞ WORRIED

afraid・frightened・scared・terrified・alarmed・fearful・paranoid・intimidated・startled・petrified

恐ろしいと感じることや, その表れを表す
【類語訳】恐れて, 怖がって, 心配して, おびえて, 被害妄想の, ぎょっとした, びっくりした, びっくり仰天して, すくんで

→

startled	afraid	terrified	petrified
alarmed	frightened		
intimidated	scared		
	fearful		
	paranoid		

文型&コロケーション
- frightened/ scared/ fearful/ paranoid **about** sth
- afraid/ frightened/ scared/ terrified/ fearful/ petrified **of** sb/ sth
- terrified/ alarmed/ intimidated/ startled **by** sb/ sth
- afraid/ frightened **for** sb
- afraid/ frightened/ scared/ terrified/ fearful/ petrified **that**...
- afraid/ frightened/ scared **to do** sth
- **Don't be** afraid/ frightened/ scared/ alarmed/ intimidated.
- **There's no need to be** afraid/ frightened/ scared/ alarmed/ paranoid/ intimidated.
- to **feel** afraid/ frightened/ scared/ terrified/ alarmed/ paranoid/ petrified
- to **look** afraid/ frightened/ scared/ terrified/ alarmed/ startled/ petrified
- to **sound** afraid/ frightened/ scared/ terrified/ alarmed
- to **get** frightened/ scared/ paranoid
- frightened/ scared/ terrified **out of your wits**
- frightened/ scared **to death**

afraid [名詞の前には用いない] 恐れて, 怖がって;(悪いことが起こるのではないかと)心配して ◇There's nothing to be *afraid* of. 何も恐れることはないよ ◇Aren't you *afraid* (that) you'll fall? 落ちるのが怖くないのですか ◇Don't be *afraid* to ask if you don't understand. わからないことがあったら遠慮なく質問しなさい [反意] **unafraid** ❶ unafraid は

ややフォーマルで書き言葉にのみ用いられる. not afraidを用いるほうが一般的. ◆I'm *not afraid* of you! (私は君を恐れてはいないぞ.) ◆He felt calm and *unafraid*. (《ややフォーマル, 書き言葉》彼は落ち着いていて恐れていなかった.)

frightened 恐れた, 怖がって, (悪いことが起こるのではないかと)心配して ◇a *frightened* child おびえた子ども ◇She was *frightened* that the glass would break. 彼女はガラスが割れるのではないかと怖がった ◇I'm *frightened* for him (= for example, that he will be hurt). 私は彼のことを心配している (例えば, けがするのではないかと) ☞ **frighten** (FRIGHTEN), **frightening** (FRIGHTENING), **fright** (FEAR)

scared 《ややインフォーマル》 恐れて, 怖がって ; (悪いことが起こるのではないかと)心配して ◇The thieves got *scared* and ran away. 泥棒どもは怖くなり逃げ出した ◇a very *scared* face/expression 非常におびえた顔/表情 ☞ **scare** (FRIGHTEN), **scary** (FRIGHTENING)

ノート afraid, frightened, scared の使い分け :
scaredはインフォーマルな語で, 話し言葉で用いられ, 小さな恐怖を表すことが多い. afraidは名詞の前では用いない. ×an *afraid* child. afraidは前置詞ofのみを取り, aboutは用いない. afraid/frightened/scared of sb/sth/doing sthは afraid/frightened/scared to do sthというとき, 身の危険にさらされている, あるいは苦しい目に遭っていることを表す. frightened/scared about sth/doing sthは身の安全より何か嫌なことが起こる恐れを表している. ◆*frightened* about the exam tomorrow (明日の試験を恐れて). ×*frightened* of the exam tomorrow.

terrified (非常に)怖がって, おびえて ◇I was *terrified* (that) she wouldn't come. 彼女が来ないのではないかと不安だった ◇She looked at him with wide, *terrified* eyes. 彼女は大きく見開いたおびえた目で彼を見た ☞ **terror** (FEAR), **terrify** (FRIGHTEN), **terrifying** (FRIGHTENING)

alarmed 《名詞の前では用いない》(危険・不快な出来事が起こるのではと[心配して]) 恐れて ◇She was *alarmed* at the prospect of travelling alone. 彼女は一人旅に不安を感じた ☞ **alarm** (FEAR), **alarm** (FRIGHTEN)

fearful 《フォーマル》おびえて, 心配して ◇*Fearful* of an attack, the government declared a state of emergency. 攻撃を恐れて政府は非常事態を宣言した ◇Parents are ever *fearful* for their children. 親は常に子どものことを心配している 《反意》**fearless** (BRAVE), ☞ **fear** (FEAR)
▸ **fearfully** 《副》◇We watched *fearfully*. 我々は恐る恐る見た

paranoid 《ややインフォーマル》被害妄想の ◇She's getting really *paranoid* about what other people say about her. 彼女は自分に対する他人のうわさに非常に被害妄想的になっている ◇You're just being *paranoid*. あなたは被害妄想になっているだけです ☞ **paranoia** (FEAR)

intimidated 《名詞の前では用いない》(特定の状況で自信が持てなくて)おびえて ◇We try to make sure children don't feel *intimidated* on their first day at school. 最初の登校日に子どもたちが必ず不安にならないようにしようと注意しています ☞ **intimidate** (THREATEN 1)

startled ぎょっとした, びっくりした ◇She looked at him with *startled* eyes. 彼女はぎょっとした目で彼を見た ◇He seemed *startled* to see me. 彼は私を見てびっくりしたように見えた ☞ **startle** (SURPRISE)

petrified びっくり仰天して, (恐怖で)何もできなくなって, すくんで ◇I'm *petrified* of snakes. 私, 蛇にはすくんでしまうの ◇They were *petrified with* fear. 彼らは恐怖ですくんだ

against sb/sth, aggressive

be **against sb/sth**

against・hostile・opposed・resistant・antagonistic
人がある事に賛成できず, それをやめさせたり, 妨げたりしたいと思うことを表す
【類語訳】反対する, 反感を持った, 抵抗した, 対立した

文型&コロケーション
▸ hostile/ opposed/ resistant/ antagonistic **to** sb/ sth
▸ hostile/ antagonistic **towards** sb/ sth
▸ against/ hostile to/ opposed to/ resistant to **the idea of** sth
▸ **strongly** against/ hostile/ opposed to sth
▸ **openly/ bitterly/ fiercely** hostile/ opposed/ antagonistic

be against sb/sth 《フレーズ》 [名詞の前では用いない] (人・物事に)反対する, 同意しない ◇I'm strongly *against* animal testing. 私は動物実験に猛反対 ◇Are you *for or against* the death penalty? あなたは死刑に賛成ですか, 反対ですか ◇If you are not with us, you *are against* us. 我々の側につかないのならあなたは我々に反対していることになる 《反意》**for**

hostile 《形》(人・物事に)反感を持った, 強く反対の ◇Many of the employees were *hostile* to the idea of change. 従業員の多くは変更する考えに反感を持っていた ◇The proposals have provoked a *hostile* response from opposition parties. その提案は野党からの強い反発を招いた ☞ **hostility** (OPPOSITION)

opposed 《形》[名詞の前はまれ] (物事に強く)反対の ◇They are totally *opposed* to abortion. 彼らは中絶に全面的に反対している 《反意》**in favour of sth** (IN FAVOUR), ☞ **opposition** (OPPOSITION)

resistant 《形》 (自分に影響が及ばないように)抵抗した ◇Elderly people are not always *resistant* to change. 年配者は必ずしも変化に抵抗しているわけではない ☞ **resistance** (OPPOSITION)

antagonistic 《形》《フォーマル》(ある階級の人々や考え方を)対立した ◇Marx saw these issues in terms of *antagonistic* class relationships. マルクスはこれらの問題を対立する階級関係の観点から見ていた

aggressive 《形》

1 aggressive・hostile・militant・warlike
攻めたり争うことが好きであることを表す
【類語訳】攻撃的な, 敵対的な, 敵意のある, 好戦的な

文型&コロケーション
▸ aggressive/ hostile **towards** sb/ sth
▸ an aggressive/ a hostile/ a militant/ a warlike **attitude**
▸ an aggressive/ a hostile/ a militant **person**
▸ a hostile/ warlike **nation**
▸ aggressive/ hostile **behaviour/ feelings**
▸ **very** aggressive/ hostile/ militant/ warlike

aggressive 攻撃的な ◇He warned that his dog could be *aggressive* towards strangers. 自分の犬が知らない人に攻撃的になることもあると彼は警告した ◇It is important at all times to discourage *aggressive* behaviour in young children. 小さな子どもたちの攻撃的な振る舞いをやめさせるのは常に大事なことだ ☞ **aggression**

↪**aggressive** (TENSION)
▸**aggressively** 副 ◇'What do you want?' she demanded *aggressively*. 「何か用」と彼女はけんか腰に尋ねた
hostile 敵対的な, 敵意のある ◇The speaker got a very *hostile* reception from the audience. 話し手は聴衆に強い敵意を持って迎えられた ◇She was openly *hostile* towards her parents. 彼女は両親に対して敵意をむき出しにしていた 反意 **friendly** (FRIENDLY 2), ☞ **hostility** (TENSION)
militant 《ややフォーマル》(社会的・政治的改革のため武力[圧力]を用いて)攻撃的な ◇*Militant* groups have been blamed for a series of attacks in the region. 武闘派グループのその地域の一連の攻撃が非難されてきた
warlike 《ややフォーマル》好戦的な ◇It is *the most warlike* nation on earth, and perhaps in all of history. それは世界で最も好戦的な国だ, おそらく歴史上でも 反意 **peace-loving** ❶ peace-loving people は議論や戦いを避けて平和に暮らす人を指す. ◆*peace-loving* citizens (平和を愛する市民).

---

2 aggressive・ambitious・competitive・assertive・pushy・forceful
成功したことや自分の意見を表すのに懸命になっている人が, 決然と自信を持って振る舞っていることを表す
【類語訳】押しの強い, 強引な, 野心的な, 負けず嫌いな, 自己主張が強い, 説得力のある

[文型&コロケーション]
▸aggressive/ ambitious/ competitive/ assertive **in** sth
▸aggressive/ assertive/ forceful **in doing** sth
▸an aggressive/ a competitive/ an assertive/ a forceful **approach/ attitude/ manner**
▸an aggressive/ a competitive/ a pushy/ a forceful **style**
▸aggressive/ competitive/ assertive **behaviour**
▸an aggressive/ an ambitious/ a competitive/ an assertive/ a forceful **person**
▸ambitious/ pushy/ forceful **parents**

aggressive 《時にけなして》(成功やほしいものを手に入れるために)押しの強い, 強引な ◇I was put off by his *aggressive* sales pitch. 彼の強引な売り込みにうんざりした ◇We need to be more *aggressive* in our strategy. 我々はもっと強気な戦略を展開する必要がある
▸**aggressively** 副 ◇The products were *aggressively* promoted. その商品は強引に宣伝された
ambitious (成功・富・権力に対して)野心的な ◇She's a great student — dedicated, hardworking and *ambitious*. 彼女はすばらしい学生だ—ひたむきで, 勤勉で, 野心的だ ◇They became fiercely *ambitious* for the boy. 彼らはその少年の将来に露骨な野望を抱くようになった 反意 **unambitious** ❶ unambitious people は成功したり, 金持ちになったり, 権力を持ったりすることに興味を持たない人を指す.
competitive 負けず嫌いの ◇He has a strong *competitive* streak. 彼にはとても負けず嫌いなところがある
assertive 《しばしばほめて》(注目を集めるよう)自信を持ってはっきりと意見[願望]を述べる, 自己主張が強い ◇Learn to be *assertive* and stand up for your rights. 自分の意見を述べ, 自己の権利を守れるようになりなさい ◇There was a new *assertive* foreign policy in the White House. 米国政府には新たな強い主張の外交政策があった ☞ **assertiveness** (CONFIDENCE), **confident** (CONFIDENT)
▸**assertively** 副 ◇You are taught to handle tricky situations *assertively*. あなたは扱いにくい状況を独断的に処理することを教えられるよ
pushy 《インフォーマル, けなして》(無礼なほど)押しの強い ◇What's the best way to get rid of a *pushy* salesman? 押しの強いセールスマンを追い返す一番いい方法は何だろうか
forceful (意見が明瞭できっぱりとしており)説得力のある ◇His mother was a *forceful* character and had a big influence on him. 彼の母親は説得力があり, 彼に多大な影響を与えた
▸**forcefully** 副 ◇He argued his case *forcefully*. 彼は自分の件を余すところなく論じた

> [ノート] **aggressive, assertive, pushy, forceful** の使い分け: これらの語はほしいものを手に入れようとしたり, 自分の意見を述べるときの行為や態度を表す. **aggressive** と **pushy** はふつう非難を込めて, 押しが強く無礼に感じさせる人に用いられる. **assertive** と **forceful** は肯定的な語で, 強く自信にあふれていて, その様が礼儀正しく適切であることを指す.

---

agree 動

agree・accept・approve・go along with sb/sth・consent・take sth on board・acquiesce
人が望むことをしたり, 物事が起こるのに任せることを表す
【類語訳】賛成する, 同意する, 納得する, 受諾する, 受け入れる, 承認する, 許可を与える, 黙認する

[文型&コロケーション]
▸to agree/ consent/ acquiesce **to** sth
▸to agree/ consent **to do** sth
▸to agree to/ accept/ approve/ go along with/ consent to a **plan/ scheme/ proposal**
▸to agree to/ accept/ approve/ go along with/ acquiesce in a **decision**
▸to agree to/ accept/ approve/ consent to a **change**
▸to agree to/ accept/ approve/ take on board a **suggestion**
▸to agree to/ accept/ approve a **request**
▸to **meekly** accept/ go along with sth/ acquiesce

agree [自, 他] 賛成する, 同意する ◇I asked for a pay rise and she *agreed*. 私は賃上げを要求し, 彼女は同意した ◇Do you think he'll *agree* to their proposal? 彼が彼らの案に賛成すると思いますか ◇She *agreed (that)* we could finish early. 我々が早く終えてもいいと彼女は同意した ◇He *agreed* to let me go early. 彼は私を早く行かせることに同意した ◇Next year's budget has been *agreed*. 来年度の予算がまとまった 反意 **refuse** (REFUSE), ☞ **agreement** (APPROVAL)
accept [他] 受諾する, 受け入れる ◇They *accepted* the court's decision. 彼らは裁判所の決定を受け入れた ◇He *accepted* all the changes we proposed. 彼は我々が提案した変更をすべて受け入れた ◇She won't *accept* advice from anyone. 彼女は誰の忠告にも耳を貸そうとしない ☞ **acceptance** (APPROVAL)
approve [他] (案・要求などを正式に)承認する ◇The committee unanimously *approved* the plan. 委員会は全会一致でその案を承認した ◇His appointment has not been formally *approved* yet. 彼の役職はまだ正式には承認されていない 反意 **reject** (REFUSE), ☞ **approval** (APPROVAL)

go a'long with sb/sth 句動詞 《ややインフォーマル》(他人が決めたこと・提案に)賛成する ◇She just *goes along with* everything he suggests. 彼女は彼が提案するすべてにただ賛成するだけです ◇I don't *go along with* her views on abortion. 私は中絶に関する彼女の意見には賛成しない

consent [自]《ややフォーマル》同意する, 許可を与える ◇When she told them what she intended they readily *consented*. 彼女が自分の意図を彼らに話したら, 彼らはあっさりと同意した ◇He reluctantly *consented* to his daughter's marriage. 彼は娘の結婚をしぶしぶ承諾した
☞ **consent** (PERMISSION)

take sth on 'board 行句《ややインフォーマル》(考え・提案を理解して)受け入れる ◇I told him what I thought, but he didn't *take* my advice *on board*. 私は彼に自分の考えを話したが彼は私のアドバイスを受け入れてくれなかった

acquiesce [自]《フォーマル》黙認する, 不本意ながら同意する ◇Senior government figures must have *acquiesced in* the cover-up. 政府高官たちの隠蔽工作を黙認したに違いない ◇She explained her plan and reluctantly he *acquiesced*. 彼女は自分の計画を説明し, 彼は不本意ながら同意した ☞ **acquiescence** (APPROVAL)

agreement 名 ☞ CONTRACT

agreement・deal・settlement・arrangement・pact・bargain・understanding
複数の人の間でなされる意見の一致や請け合い
【類語訳】合意, 協定, 契約, 取り決め, 約束

文型&コロケーション

▸ an agreement/ a deal/ a settlement/ an arrangement/ a pact/ a bargain/ an understanding **with** sb
▸ an agreement/ a deal/ an arrangement/ a pact/ a bargain/ an understanding **between** sb and sb
▸ an agreement/ a deal/ a settlement/ an arrangement/ a pact/ an understanding **on** sth
▸ an agreement/ a deal/ a settlement/ an arrangement/ an understanding **over** sth
▸ **under** an agreement/ a deal/ an arrangement/ a pact
▸ an agreement/ an arrangement/ a pact/ an understanding **that**...
▸ an agreement/ an arrangement/ a pact **to do sth**
▸ an **informal** agreement/ arrangement/ understanding
▸ a **political** agreement/ deal/ settlement/ arrangement/ pact/ bargain
▸ a **financial** agreement/ deal/ settlement/ arrangement/ bargain
▸ to **have** an agreement/ an arrangement/ a pact/ an understanding
▸ to **enter into** an agreement/ an arrangement/ a pact
▸ to **negotiate** an agreement/ a deal/ a settlement/ an arrangement/ a pact
▸ to **reach** an agreement/ a deal/ a settlement/ an arrangement/ an understanding
▸ to **make/ sign** an agreement/ a deal/ a pact
▸ to **conclude** an agreement/ a deal/ a settlement/ a pact

agreement [C] 合意; 協定, 契約, 取り決め ◇An *agreement* was finally reached between management and employees. 労使間でようやく合意に達した ◇We are working towards a formal cease-fire *agreement*. 我々は正式な停戦協定に取り組んでいる ◇The *agreement* will be legally binding. その協定は法的拘束力を持つだろう ◇They had made a verbal *agreement* to sell. 彼らは口頭で販売契約を結んであった ◇They had an *agreement* never to talk about work at home. 彼らは家では仕事の話をいっさいしないという約束をした

deal [C] (ビジネスでの)合意, 取り決め ◇The unions were ready to *do a deal* over pay. 組合はいつでも賃金交渉の用意ができていた ◇The company expects to *close the deal* (= finish making it) in the first quarter of next year. その会社は来年の第1四半期に契約を結ぶつもりにしている ◇The *deal fell through* (= no agreement was reached). その契約は成立しなかった ◇I got a *good deal* on the car (= a good price). 私はその車を安く買った ◇*It's a deal!* (= I agree to your terms).《話し言葉》じゃあそうしよう ◇*This is the deal* (= this is what we have agreed and are going to do). これで決まりだ
☞ **do a deal** (NEGOTIATE)

settlement [C] (二者間の正式な)合意;(金銭・財産の)付与 ◇There have been efforts to broker a peace *settlement* with the militia groups. 武装集団との和平協定を仲介する努力がなされてきた ◇Lawyers are seeking an *out-of-court settlement*. 弁護士たちは示談を模索している ◇The house was put on the market as part of a *divorce settlement*. 離婚の財産分与の一部としてその家が売りに出された ☞ **settle** (RESOLVE)

arrangement [C, U] (こまごまとした)取り決め ◇The company has a special *arrangement* with the bank. その会社は銀行と特別な取り決めを結んでいる ◇We can come to an *arrangement* over the price. 我々は価格について折り合える ◇Viewing of the property is only possible *by arrangement* with the owner. 所有者との申し合わせがある場合のみ, その物件を見ることができる ◇You can cash cheques here *by prior arrangement* with the bank. 銀行との事前の取り決めによりここで小切手を現金化することができます ☞ **arrange** (ORGANIZE)

pact [C] (人・グループ・国同士における相互扶助の正式な)協定 ◇He helped to negotiate a non-aggression *pact* between the two countries. 彼は2国間の不可侵条約の交渉を手助けした ◇The two parties agreed on an electoral *pact*. 両党は選挙協力に合意した ◇She died with her lover in a *suicide pact* (= an agreement by two or more people to kill themselves at the same time). 彼女は恋人と合意の心中で亡くなった

bargain [C] (二者以上の間でなされる)約束, 協定 ◇Finally the two sides *struck a bargain*. ついに両者は協定を結んだ ◇I've done what I promised and I expect you to keep your side of the *bargain*. 私は約束を守ったのだからあなたのほうも当然そうしてくれますよね ☞ **bargain** (NEGOTIATE)

ノート **pact** と **bargain** の使い分け: お互いの目的が同じで, その達成に協力することを合意するときは pact を用いる. 目的は異なっているが, お互い自分たちがやりたいことをすることに合意するときは bargain を用いる. ×a non-aggression/suicide *bargain*. ×I expect you to keep your side of the *pact*.

understanding [C, ふつう単数で] (二者以上での非公式な)了解, 合意 ◇We finally came to an *understanding* about what hours we would work. 我々は何時

↳agreement

間働くかということについてようやく了解にたどり着いた ◇I thought you gave me the book *on the understanding* that I could keep it. 私はあなたがその本を私にくれたものとばかり理解していました

aid 名

aid・help・welfare・relief・charity・social security・handout
貧しい人、病人、その他困っている人への手助け、金品
【類語訳】援助、助け、支援、救済、慈善、社会保障、施し、お恵み

文型&コロケーション
▸aid/ help/ welfare/ relief/ charity/ social security/ handouts **for** sb
▸to be **on** welfare/ social security
▸**emergency** aid/ help/ relief
▸**government/ state** aid/ help/ welfare/ relief/ handouts
▸**direct/ immediate/ financial/ medical** aid/ help/ relief
▸to **get/ receive** aid/ help/ welfare/ relief/ charity/ social security/ handouts
▸to **accept** aid/ help/ charity
▸to **give (sb)** aid/ help/ relief/ charity/ handouts
▸to **provide/ send/ promise** aid/ help/ relief
▸to **ask for** aid/ help/ welfare/ relief/ charity
▸to **rely/ depend on** help/ welfare/ charity/ social security/ handouts
▸to **live on** welfare/ charity/ social security

aid [U] （厳しい状況下にある国への）援助 ◇An extra £10 million in foreign *aid* has been promised. 1000万ポンドの追加対外援助が約束されている ◇Much of the funding has come from international *aid agencies* (= organizations that provide help). 財源の大半は国際救援組織から来ている
help [U] （問題解決のための）助け、援助 ◇I decided to seek legal *help*. 私は法的援助を求めることにした ◇The organization offers practical *help* in dealing with paperwork. その組織では事務処理を実際に支援しています ☞ **help** (HELP 動 2)
welfare [U] （人々・動物のための）福祉的援助 ◇The state is still the main provider of *welfare*. 今でも国家が主導的に福祉を提供している ◇Animal *welfare* groups want this practice banned altogether. 動物保護団体はこの慣行が完全に禁止されることを願っている ❶（米）では welfare は政府が貧しい人、失業者、病人などに定期的に支給するお金のことも指す。《英》ではこのことを social security と言う。
◆They would rather work than live on *welfare*. （彼らは生活保護で暮らすより働きたいと思っている）☞ **on welfare** (UNEMPLOYED)
relief [U] （戦争・災害などに遭った人々の）救済（物資） ◇We raised £5,000 for famine *relief*. 飢餓救済のために我々は5000ポンド寄付を集めた ☞ **relieve** (EASE)

ノート **aid** と **relief** の使い分け：aid は財政難にある国へ送られる援助金を指す場合に用いられ、長期にわたる場合もしばしばである。relief はふつう緊急事態に対する早急な対応として、戦争や災害に遭った人々へ送られる援助金、医薬品、食料などを指すことが多い。

charity [U] 慈善 ◇Most of the runners in the London Marathon are *raising money for charity*. たいていのロンドンマラソンのランナーはチャリティー募金をしてい

aid, alive

る ◇He refused to live on *charity* (= to live on money which other people give you because you are poor). 彼は施しを受けたくなかった
,social se'curity [U] 《英》 社会保障、生活保護費［給付金］ ◇He's been living on *social security* for the past two months. 彼はこの2か月間生活保護で暮らしている
handout [C] 《時にけなして》 施し(物)、お恵み ◇I don't want to be dependent on *handouts*. 私は施し物に頼りたくない ☞ **handout** (GIFT), **hand sth out** (DISTRIBUTE)

alive 形

alive・living・live・animate
命があることを表す
【類語訳】生きて(いる), 生命のある

文型&コロケーション
▸a living/ live **animal/ plant/ bird**
▸a living/ live **organism/ creature**
▸**still** alive/ living

alive ［名詞の前では用いない］ 生きて ◇We don't know whether he's *alive* or dead. 彼が生きているのか死んだのか我々にはわからない ◇She had to steal food just to *stay alive*. 彼女はただ生きて行くために食べ物を盗まなくてはならなかった ◇Doctors fought to *keep* the baby *alive*. 医者は赤ちゃんの命を守るために奮闘した ◇I was glad to hear you're *alive and well*. あなたが健在だと聞いてうれしかった ◇He was buried *alive* in the earthquake. 彼は地震で生き埋めになった 反意 **dead** (DEAD)
living 《ややフォーマル》 生きて(いる) ◇She taught us to show respect for all *living* things. 彼女は生きとし生けるものに敬意を払うよう私たちに教えた ◇Many people say he is the finest *living* pianist. 多くの人が彼は存命中の最高のピアニストだと言う 反意 **dead** (DEAD)

ノート **alive** と **living** の使い分け：alive は名詞の前には用いない。×all *alive* things。live は動詞の後に用いることができるが、ほかの連結動詞の後にはふつう用いない。×She stole just to stay *living*. ×Doctors fought to keep the baby *living*.

live ［ふつう名詞の前で］ 生きている ◇We saw a *real live* rattlesnake! 私たちは本物の生きたガラガラヘビを見た ◇the number of *live births* (= babies born alive) 正常出産の数 反意 **dead** (DEAD)

ノート **living** と **live** の使い分け：living はふつう人や動物などに広く用いられる。◆The elephant is the biggest *living* land animal = elephants in general, not one particular elephant). （象は陸上の動物で最も大きな生き物だ）。×The elephant is the biggest *live* land animal. ◆ the finest *living* pianist (= out of all pianists alive today) （存命中の最高のピアニストだ）。×the finest *live* pianist. live はふつう瞬時に反応する人や動物に用いられる。◆I need to talk to a *live* person (= not a recorded message). （私は生身の人間と話す必要がある）。×I need to talk to a *living* person. ◆Customs officials seized 400 *live* snakes packed in crates. （税関職員は木箱に入った400匹の生きた蛇を押収した）。×Customs officials seized 400 *living* snakes.

animate 《フォーマル》 生きている、生命のある ◇Children

quickly learn to distinguish between *animate* and inanimate motion. 子どもたちはすぐに生命のあるものとないものの動きの違いがわかるようになる 反意 **inanimate** ❶ inanimate は人, 動物, 植物のような生命のあるものではないものに用いられる。◆ A rock is an *inanimate* object. (岩は生命のない物体だ)

allow [動]

allow・let・grant・permit・entitle・authorize・license・qualify・OK・sanction・empower・clear

人が…してもよい, または物を受け取ってもよい, あるいは事が行われてもよいと決定したり発言したりすることを表す
【類語訳】許可する, 許す, 権利を与える, 認可する, 許諾する, 資格を与える, 承認する

文型&コロケーション
▶ to allow/ permit/ entitle/ authorize/ license/ empower/ clear sb to do sth
▶ to let sb do sth
▶ to allow/ let/ permit **yourself** sth/ (to) do sth
▶ to allow/ be entitled to/ authorize/ sanction **payment**
▶ to be **legally** allowed/ permitted/ entitled/ authorized/ sanctioned/ empowered
▶ to be **officially** allowed/ permitted/ entitled/ authorized/ sanctioned
▶ to be (**not**) **normally** allowed/ granted/ permitted/ entitled
▶ to **automatically** grant sth/ entitle sb to sth/ qualify sb for sth

allow [他] 許可する ◇His parents won't *allow* him to stay out late. 彼の両親は彼に夜遊びを許そうとしません ◇He **is not** *allowed* **to** stay out late. 彼は夜遊びすることを許されていない ◇Smoking is not *allowed* in here. ここでは喫煙は禁止されています ◇No dogs *allowed* (= you cannot bring them in). 犬お断り ◇The prisoners are *allowed* out of their cells for two hours a day. 囚人たちは一日に2時間独房から出ることを許されている ◇You're *allowed* half an hour to complete the test. そのテストの制限時間は30分です ◇I sometimes *allow* myself the luxury of a cigar. 私は時々葉巻を吸う贅沢を自分に許している ◇He *allowed* his mind to wander. 彼はとりとめのない思いをめぐらせた 反意 **forbid** (BAN [動])

let [他] (やめさせようとせずに人に)…させておく, (事が起こるに)まかせておく ◇They never *let* the children play outside. 彼らは決して子どもたちを外で遊ばせない ◇I wanted to drive but she wouldn't *let* me. 私は運転したかったが彼女がどうしてもさせてくれなかった ◇Don't *let* it upset you. 怒らないでね ◇*Let* me help you with your luggage. お荷物を運びましょう ❶この意味のletは受身文では用いられない。✕The children are never *let* play outside. しかしながら, letには「人が出入りできるようにドアを開ける」の意味もあり, この意味では能動文でも受身文でも構わない。◆ I'll give you a key so you can *let* yourself *in*. (中に入れるようにあなたに鍵を渡すね) ◆ The cat wants to be *let out*. (猫が外へ出してもらいたがっている) let sb out (人にドアを開けてやる)とallow sb out (人に外出の許可を与える)の違いに注意。

grant [他, しばしば受身で](ややフォーマル)(公式・法的な)許可を与える ◇Planning permission for the development was *granted* last week. 先週, その開発計画の許可が下りた ◇The government *granted* an amnesty to all political prisoners. 政府はすべての政治犯に大赦を与えた ◇She was *granted* a divorce. 彼女の離婚が承認された ◇Her *wish* was *granted*. 彼女の願いは聞き入れられた ☞ **award** (GIVE 1)

permit (-tt-)[他](フォーマル)(人に…する)許可を与える; (事が発生するのを)許す ◇The banks were not *permitted* to invest overseas. それらの銀行は海外への投資を許可されなかった ◇The rules of the club do not *permit* it. クラブの規則ではそれは許されない ◇Radios are not *permitted* in the library. 図書館内でのラジオは禁止 ◇*Permit* me to make a suggestion. 私に提案をさせてください 反意 **ban, forbid, prohibit** (BAN [動]), ☞ **permission** (PERMISSION), **permit** (LICENCE)

entitle [他, しばしば受身で](…する)権利を与える ◇Passengers will be *entitled to* a full refund of the cost of the ticket. 乗客にはチケット代の全額払い戻しを求める権利がある ◇Of course, he's *entitled* to his opinion but I think he's wrong. もちろん彼には意見を言う権利はあるが, 彼は間違っていると思う ☞ **entitlement** (RIGHT [名])

authorize (英でまた **-ise**) [他] (事を)正式に認可する; (人に…する)権限を正式に与える ◇I can *authorize* payments up to £5,000. 5千ポンドまで報酬を認めることができる ◇I have *authorized* him to act for me while I am away. 私の留守中に彼に私の代行をさせている 反意 **prohibit** (BAN [動]), ☞ **authorization** (PERMISSION), **authorization** (LICENCE)

license (英でまた, 頻度は低いが **licence**) [他] (人に…する)正式な許可を与える, (事を)正式に認可する ◇The drug is not *licensed* for long-term use. その薬は長期服用を認可されていない ◇The hotel is *licensed* to sell alcohol. そのホテルはお酒の販売を許可されている ◇The company plans to *license* the technology to others. その会社はその技術の使用を他社に許諾する予定だ ☞ **licence** (LICENCE)

qualify [自, 他] (…する)資格がある; (人に)資格を与える ◇You have to be over 60 to *qualify*. 60歳以上にならないと資格はない ◇She didn't *qualify for* a full pension. 彼女には満額の年金を受給する資格がなかった ◇Membership of the scheme *qualifies* you for the discount. その組織の会員になれば割引サービスが受けられる

OK (または **okay**) [他] (インフォーマル)(事を)正式に承認する ◇The chairman *OK'd* the request. 議長はその要求を承認した ◇The property has to be valued before a mortgage loan is *OK'd*. 担保付きローンが承認される前に資産価値を査定する必要がある

sanction [他] (フォーマル)(事を)認可する ◇The military refused to *sanction* a transfer of power to a civilian government. その軍は文民政権への政権移譲を容認しようとはしなかった

empower [他, しばしば受身で](フォーマル)(人に…する)権力[権限]を与える ◇The courts were *empowered* to impose the death sentence for certain crimes. それらの裁判所は特定の犯罪に対して死刑を課す権限があった

clear [他] (事の正式な)認可を得る[与える]; (人・船などに)出入りの許可を与える, (特別任務や特別文書の閲覧を)正式に認める ◇I'll have to *clear it with* the manager before I can refund your money. あなたに代金を払い戻す前に部長から許可をもらわないといけない ◇The plane had been *cleared* for take-off. その飛行機は離陸の許可を得ていた ◇She hasn't been *cleared* by security. 彼女は警備係に足止めされている ☞ **clearance** (PERMISSION)

almost 副

almost・nearly・virtually・more or less・not quite・practically・about・pretty much/well
度合いは大きいが100パーセントではないことを表す
【類語訳】ほとんど, ほぼ, …も同然

文型&コロケーション
- ▶almost/ nearly/ virtually/ more or less/ not quite/ practically/ pretty much **all/ every**
- ▶almost/ virtually/ more or less/ practically/ pretty much **any/ anything**
- ▶almost/ nearly/ virtually/ more or less/ practically **always**
- ▶almost/ nearly/ virtually/ more or less/ not quite/ practically **empty**
- ▶almost/ virtually/ more or less/ practically **impossible**
- ▶almost/ nearly/ virtually/ more or less/ not quite/ practically **finished**

almost ほとんど ◇I like *almost* all of them. 私はそれらほとんど全部が好きだ ◇It's a mistake they *almost* always make. それは彼らがたいがいいつもやる間違いだ ◇The story is *almost certainly* false. その話はほぼ間違いなく嘘だ ◇Dinner's *almost* ready. もうすぐ夕飯ができるよ ◇Their house is *almost* opposite ours. 彼らの家は我が家のほぼ向かいにある ◇He slipped and *almost* fell. 彼は滑って転びそうになった

nearly ほとんど ◇I've worked here for *nearly* two years. 私はここで既に2年間働いている ◇The bottle's *nearly* empty. 瓶はほとんど空だ ◇It's *nearly* time to leave. そろそろ帰る時間です ◇He's *nearly* as tall as you are. 彼はあなたとほぼ同じくらいの背の高さです ◇She *very nearly* died. (特に英)彼女は危うく死ぬところだった

ノート almostとnearlyの使い分け：多くの場合どちらの語も使用可能. ◆I've got *almost/nearly* every CD they've made. (彼らのCDはほとんどどれも持っている). ◆She *almost/nearly* missed her train. (彼女はもう少しで電車に乗り遅れるところだった). この二語を否定文で用いることもできるが, only justを用いて肯定文を作るのがより一般的. ◆We *only just* got there in time. (私たちはぎりぎりそこに間に合った). ◆ *nearly* は数字と共に用いられるほうが一般的. ◆There were *nearly* 200 people at the meeting. (会議にはほぼ200人の出席者がいた). any, anybody, anythingなどの語の前にalmostを用いることはできるが, nearlyは用いることはできない. ◆They'll eat *almost* anything. (彼らは何でも食べるでしょう). ×They'll eat *nearly* anything. また, no, nobody, neverの前にalmostを使用することはできるが, any, anybody, everと共にhardlyやscarcelyを使うほうがより一般的. ◆She's *hardly* ever in. (彼女はほとんどいつもいない). almostは, ある物が他の物に似ていることを言うときにも用いられる. ◆The boat looked *almost* like a toy. (そのボートはほとんどおもちゃみたいに見えた). 《英》ではveryやsoを*nearly*の前に置くことができる. ◆He was very *nearly* caught. (《英》彼はもう少しで捕まるところだった.)

virtually ほぼ, …も同然 ◇He *virtually* admitted he was guilty. 彼は容疑を認めたも同然だった ◇This year's results are *virtually* the same as last year's. 今年の結果は昨年とほぼ同じだ ◇The red squirrel has become *virtually* extinct in most of the country. 国の大部分で

地域でアカリスはほぼ絶滅している

,more or 'less フレーズ ほとんど ◇The story is *more or less* true. その話はおおむね本当だ ◇His estimate has turned out to be *more or less* correct. 彼の推定はほぼ正しかった ◇The two houses were *more or less* identical. その2つの家はほとんど同じだった ◇I've *more or less* finished the book. 私はその本をほぼ読み終えた ❶ more or less は virtually ほど近接性の度合いは大きくなく, 完全さの度合いは重要ではない.

not quite (完全ではないが)ほとんど ◇The theatre was *not quite* full. 劇場は満席とまではいかなかった ◇That's *not quite* the same thing, is it? それってまったく同じことだというわけではないよね ◇The room was full of old furniture that *didn't quite* match. その部屋は完璧にマッチしているとまでは言えない古い家具でいっぱいだった ◇He didn't feel *quite* ready for marriage. 彼は結婚に今一つ気乗りがしなかった ❶ not quite はこのグループの他の語句ほど肯定的な表現ではない. しばしばほぼ完全な, または満足のゆくことよりも, わずかに不完全さや不満があることを強調する.

practically 《特に話し言葉》 ほぼ, …も同然 ◇She *practically* accused me of starting the fire! 彼女は火を点けたかどで私を告発したも同然だった ◇With that crack in it, the vase is worth *practically* nothing. そのひびのせいで, 花瓶はほとんど何の価値もない ◇There's *practically* no difference between the two options. その二つの選択肢にはほとんど何の違いもない

ノート virtually と practically の使い分け：多くの場合どちらの語も使用可能. ◆This drug was *virtually/practically* unknown in Britain. (この薬はイギリスではほとんど知られていなかった). 両語とも否定文で用いることが可能だが, hardly や scarcely を any, anything, ever などと一緒に用いることも可能. ◆There's *virtually/practically* no money left. (ほとんどお金は残っていない). ◆There's *hardly any* money left. (ほとんどお金は残っていない). practically は virtually よりもややくだけた表現で, 特に口語で用いられる.

about 《特に話し言葉》 ほとんど; ほぼ ◇I'm *just about* ready. もうすぐ準備できます ◇This is *about* the best we can hope for. これが期待しうるほぼ最善に近いものだ

pretty 'much/'well 《話し言葉》 ほぼ, ほとんど ◇One sheep looks *pretty much* like another to me. 私には羊の区別がほとんどつかない ◇He goes out *pretty well* every night. 彼はほとんど毎晩出かけている ◇The first stage is *pretty much* finished. 第一ステージはほぼ終わった

amazing 形 ☞ REMARKABLE, SURPRISING

amazing・astonishing・awesome・staggering・breathtaking・miraculous・stunning・sensational
しばしば通常よりも素晴らしくて非常に驚嘆させられることを表す
【類語訳】驚くべき, びっくりさせる, 驚異的な, 信じられない, すごい, 息をのむような, 奇跡的な, 驚愕の, センセーショナルな

文型&コロケーション
- ▶to be amazing/ astonishing/ staggering/ miraculous **that...**
- ▶to be amazing/ astonishing/ staggering **how...**
- ▶an amazing/ an astonishing/ an awesome/ a staggering **achievement**

- an amazing/ astonishing/ awesome **feat**
- an amazing/ an astonishing/ a miraculous/ a stunning/ an astounding **success**
- an amazing/ an astonishing/ a stunning **victory/ result**
- amazing/ astonishing/ breathtaking/ stunning **news**
- an amazing/ an astonishing/ an awesome/ a breathtaking/ a stunning **sight**
- astonishing/ awesome/ breathtaking/ stunning **beauty**
- **quite** amazing/ astonishing/ awesome/ staggering/ breathtaking/ miraculous/ stunning/ sensational
- **truly** amazing/ astonishing/ awesome/ staggering/ breathtaking/ sensational
- **absolutely** amazing/ astonishing/ staggering/ breathtaking/ stunning
- **pretty** amazing/ awesome/ sensational

amazing（喜び・賞賛を感じさせるほど）驚くべき ◇I made an *amazing* discovery today. 今日はびっくりするような発見をした ◇The virus spread at *amazing* speed. そのウイルスは驚異的なスピードで広まった ◇It's *amazing* what you can do if you have to. 切羽詰まった状況に置かれたときの人の可能性には驚かされる ◇It's *amazing* the difference a few polite words make. 少し丁寧な言葉を使うと驚くほど違いが出る ◇The *amazing* thing is, he really believes he'll get away with it. 驚くべきことに彼は逃げ切れると本当に信じている ☞ **amaze** (SURPRISE)
▶ **amazingly** 副 ◇*Amazingly*, they won. 驚いたことに彼らは勝利した ◇The meal was *amazingly* cheap. その食事は驚くほど安かった

astonishing（信じられないほど）驚くべき ◇The painting was sold at auction for an *astonishing* $30 million. その絵はオークションで何と3千万ドルで売られた ◇Then he had an *astonishing* piece of luck. その後彼は信じられないほどの幸運をつかんだ ◇During this period London grew at an *astonishing* rate. この時期にロンドンは驚異的な速さで発展した ☞ **astonish** (SURPRISE)
▶ **astonishingly** 副 ◇He took the news *astonishingly* well. 彼はそのニュースを思いもよらぬほど歓迎した

awesome（畏怖の念を起こさせるほど）すごい ◇It is a region of *awesome* gorges and spectacular peaks. そこは圧倒されるような峡谷や壮観な峰々がある地域です ◇After the war the country faced the *awesome* task of reconstruction. 戦後その国は復興というとんでもない課題に取り組んだ

staggering（ややインフォーマル）驚異的な、（信じがたいほど）すごい ◇The attention to detail is *staggering*. 細部への気配りには信じがたいものがある ◇The paintings on the wall were evidence of a *staggering* lack of talent. 壁に掛かった絵画は驚くほどの才能のなさを物語っていた ☞ **stagger** (SURPRISE)
▶ **staggeringly** 形 ◇The painting sold for a *staggeringly* high figure. その絵は信じられないほど高額で売れた

breathtaking 息を呑むような; 驚くべき ◇The scene was *breathtaking* in its beauty. その景色は息を呑むほど美しかった ◇He spoke with *breathtaking* arrogance. 彼の語り口は唖然とするほど横柄だった ☞ **spectacular** (MAGNIFICENT), **take sb's breath away** (IMPRESS)
▶ **breathtakingly** 副 ◇*breathtakingly* beautiful 息を呑むほど美しい

miraculous 奇跡的な、驚くべき ◇The child had a *miraculous* escape when the firework exploded in her hand. 花火が手の中で爆発したにもかかわらずその女の子は奇跡的に怪我を免れた ◇Doctors feared she would die but she's made a *miraculous* recovery. 医者たちは彼女は死ぬのではないかと思ったが彼女は奇跡的に快復した ☞ **miracle** (MIRACLE)
▶ **miraculously** 副 ◇*Miraculously*, no one was hurt. 奇跡的に誰も負傷しなかった

stunning（ややインフォーマル）驚くべき、驚愕の ◇The election result was a *stunning* blow for the party. 選挙結果はその党に大きな衝撃をもたらした ◇The team is celebrating a *stunning* victory. チームは見事な大勝利を祝っているところだ ☞ **stun** (SURPRISE)

sensational 驚くべき、センセーショナルな ◇Police have uncovered *sensational* new evidence. 警察はあっと言わせるような新証拠を公表した ◇It was the most *sensational* 24 hours of the jockey's career. それはその騎手の経歴の中で最も世間を騒がせた24時間だった
▶ **sensationally** 副 ◇The trial ended *sensationally*. その裁判はセンセーショナルな結末を迎えた

analyst 名

analyst・critic・observer・commentator・watcher

テレビ、ラジオ、新聞で意見を言うために、出来事や状況を観察して分析する人

【類語訳】アナリスト、評論家、批評家、観察者、監視者、コメンテーター、解説者、研究家、専門家

- an analyst/ a critic/ a commentator **for** sb/ sth
- an **astute/ independent** analyst/ critic/ observer/ commentator
- a **keen** analyst/ critic/ observer
- a **social** analyst/ critic/ commentator/ observer
- a/ an **media/ industry** analyst/ critic/ commentator/ observer/ watcher
- a **political/ military** analyst/ observer/ commentator
- to **surprise** analysts/ critics/ commentators/ observers/ watchers
- to **strike** critics/ observers/ watchers

analyst [C]（経済・政治などの分野での）アナリスト ◇City *analysts* forecast pre-tax profits of £40 billion this year. 今年シティの経済アナリストは400億ポンドの税引き前利益を予想している

critic [C]（書籍・映画・音楽などの分野での）評論家、批評家 ◇He's a restaurant *critic* for 'The Times'. 彼は『タイムズ』誌のレストラン評論家である ◇The *critics* loved the movie. 評論家たちはその映画にほれ込んだ

observer [C] 観察者、監視者、評者 ◇*Observers* noted an absence of the violence which had been a feature of previous elections. 立会人たちは前回の選挙の特徴だった暴力行為がないことに注目した

commentator [C]（テレビ・ラジオなどでの）コメンテーター、解説者 ◇She's a political *commentator* for the BBC. 彼女はBBCの政治コメンテーターである ◇He is best known as a *commentator on* culture and the arts. 彼は文化と芸術に関する解説者として最もよく知られている

watcher [C]《しばしば複合語で》（ややインフォーマル、特にジャーナリズム）専門家 ◇There are now several books on the princess by various royal *watchers*. さまざまな王室ウォッチャーによる王女に関する本が今では何冊もある

↪**analyst**

A **ノート** analysts, critics, commentators はふつう会社や組織に雇われている、もしくは勤務している人を指す. observers, watchers はふつう定職には就かず、本や記事を書いたり、アドバイスをしたりして収入を得る情報通の人を言う. ×She's a political *observer/watcher* for the BBC. commentator はテレビ、ラジオ、新聞で一般人に対してあるテーマの解説を行ったり意見を述べたりする職業の人. analyst は他の専門職に就いている人に対してあるテーマの解説を行ったり、意見を述べたり、アドバイスをしたりする職業の人.

anger 名

anger・rage・fury・outrage・indignation
(激しい)立腹を表す
【類語訳】怒り, 激怒, 憤り

anger	outrage	rage
indignation		fury

文型&コロケーション

▶ to do sth **in** anger/ rage/ fury/ outrage/ indignation
▶ **public/ widespread** anger/ indignation
▶ to **provoke** anger/ fury/ outrage/ indignation
▶ to **arouse** sb's anger/ fury/ indignation
▶ to **be filled/ shake/ tremble/ seethe with** anger/ rage/ fury/ outrage/ indignation
▶ to **express** anger/ rage/ fury/ outrage/ indignation
▶ to **vent** your anger/ rage/ fury
▶ to **fly into** a rage/ fury

anger [U] (不当でよくないと思う事への) 怒り ◇Jan slammed the door in *anger*. ジャンは怒ってドアをバタンと閉めた ◇I am acutely aware of the growing *anger* and frustration of young unemployed people. 若い失業者たちの怒りと欲求不満が高まりつつあるのを痛切に感じている

rage [U, 単数で] (抑えがたい)激しい怒り, 激怒 ◇She was speechless with *rage*. 彼女は激怒のあまり口が利けなかった ◇She stormed out of the room in a *rage*. 彼女は怒り狂って部屋から飛び出した ☞ **rage** (TEMPER), **enraged** (FURIOUS)

fury [U, 単数で]《書き言葉》激怒, 激昂 ◇Her face was white with *fury*. 彼女の顔は激しい怒りで青ざめていた ◇In a cold *fury* my uncle hurled his son from the room. 冷静を装ってはいるが激昂しておじは息子を部屋から放り出した ☞ **furious** (FURIOUS)

ノート rage と fury の使い分け: 両語とも暴力的な振る舞いをもたらす可能性があるが、ふつう fury のほうが rage よりコントロールされた感情を言う. rage は hot または cold, red または white と共に用いられることがある. ◆His face was red/ white with *rage*.(彼の顔は怒りで真っ赤/真っ青だった). fury は cold, white のみ.

outrage [U] 激怒, 憤り ◇The judge's remarks caused public *outrage*. その裁判官の発言は一般市民の強い怒りを買った ◇She was filled with an overwhelming sense of moral *outrage*. 彼女はどうしようもない義憤に満ち溢れていた ☞ **outraged** (FURIOUS), **outrageous** (OUTRAGEOUS)

indignation [U] (不当・理不尽だと思う事への)怒り, 憤り ◇Some benefits apply only to men, much *to the indignation of* working women. 働く女性が大変憤ることなのだが、手当の中には男性にしか適用されないものがある ◇She was full of *righteous indignation* (= the belief that you are right to be angry even though other people do not agree). 彼女は自分としては義憤に満ちていた

ノート outrage と indignation の使い分け: 両語とも怒りだけでなく驚きの感情を含んでいるが、outrage のほうが強い感情を表す. しばしば indignation は本人が不当な扱いを受けていると感じていることを含意し、outrage は個人が持つ感情というよりは世間一般が持つ怒りを表す.

anger 動 ☞ ANNOY

anger・infuriate・antagonize・drive sb mad/crazy・outrage・enrage・rankle・rile・incense・piss sb off
人に(激しく)腹を立てさせることを表す
【類語訳】怒らせる, 激怒させる, 怒り狂わせる, 憤慨させる, 怒りを買う, いら立たせる

rankle	anger	drive sb mad	infuriate
rile	antagonize	outrage	enrage
	piss sb off		incense

文型&コロケーション

▶ **What really** angers/ infuriates/ enrages/ riles/ incenses **me is...**
▶ **What pisses us off/ drives us mad/ crazy is...**
▶ **It** infuriated/ enraged/ riled/ incensed **him that...**

anger [他] 怒らせる ◇The question clearly *angered* him. その質問は明らかに彼を怒らせた ◇They stayed silent but were *angered* by the decision. 彼らは黙っていたがその決定に怒っていた ❶ インフォーマルな表現または話し言葉において make sb angry と言うことも一般的である. ◆It really *makes* me *angry* the way they keep changing the rules.(《話し言葉》彼らのルールを変え続けるやり方には本当に腹が立つ).

infuriate [他] 激怒させる ◇Her silence *infuriated* him even more. 彼女が黙り込むと彼はさらにいっそう激怒した ☞ **infuriating** (ANNOYING)

antagonize (英でまた **-ise**) [他] 怒らせる事をする ◇Not wishing to *antagonize* her further, he said no more. それ以上彼女を怒らせたくないと思い, 彼はもう何も言わなかった ☞ **antagonism** (TENSION)

drive sb mad/crazy 行他《インフォーマル》怒り狂わせる ◇That noise is *driving* me *mad*! あの騒音は頭にくる ◇He *drove* me *crazy* with his constant questions. 彼のたび重なる質問に私は腹が立った

outrage [他] (大きなショックを与えて)憤慨させる ◇The killings have *outraged* the entire community. それらの殺人は地域全体に憤りをもたらした ☞ **outraged** (FURIOUS), **outrageous** (OUTRAGEOUS)

enrage [他]《ややフォーマル, 書き言葉》激怒させる ◇The newspaper article *enraged* him. その新聞記事に彼は激怒した ☞ **enraged** (FURIOUS)

rankle [自] (発言・出来事が長期間の)怒りを買う ◇Her comments still *rankled*. 彼女のコメントはいまだに反感を買っていた ◇His decision to sell the land *rankled*

angry, annoy

with her. 土地を売却するという彼の決定が彼女を後々まで腹立たしい思いにさせた
rile [他] いら立たせる, 怒らせる ◇Nothing ever seemed to *rile* him. 今まで彼が怒ることなどないように思われた ◇She regretted at once that she had let herself become *riled*. 彼女はいら立たせたことをすぐに後悔した
incense [他] (道徳的理由で)激怒させる ◇The decision *incensed* the entire workforce. その決定に全従業員が激怒した ☞ **incensed** (FURIOUS)

> **ノート** **infuriate, enrage, incense の使い分け**：ふつう infuriate は他人の理不尽な振る舞いをどのように感じたかを強調し, enrage は怒っている人の振る舞いが理不尽であることを含意する. incense はしばしば怒って当然だと思うときに用いられる.

,piss sb 'off [句動詞]《卑語, 俗語》怒らせる, いら立たせる ◇Her attitude really *pisses* me *off*. 彼女の態度は本当に頭にくる

angry [形] ☞ ANNOYED, FURIOUS

angry・mad・indignant・cross・irate・pissed off
人が怒りを感じていることや, それを表に出していることを表す
【類語訳】怒った, 腹を立てた, いら立った, 激怒した, うんざりした, 不満な

cross	angry	irate
	mad	
	indignant	
	pissed off	

文型&コロケーション
- ▶ angry/ mad/ indignant/ cross/ pissed off **about/ at** sth
- ▶ angry/ indignant **over** sth
- ▶ angry/ cross/ pissed off **with** sb **for** sth
- ▶ to be angry/ mad/ indignant/ cross/ pissed off **that**...
- ▶ to **get** angry/ mad/ cross/ pissed off
- ▶ to **make sb** angry/ mad/ cross

angry 怒った, 腹を立てた ◇Please don't be *angry* with me. どうか私を怒らないでください ◇I was very *angry* with myself for making such a stupid mistake. 私はこんな馬鹿げた間違いをして自分自身にすごく腹が立った ◇Thousands of *angry* demonstrators filled the square. 何千もの怒ったデモ参加者で広場はいっぱいになった ◇an *angry* voice/letter/response 怒りの声/手紙/反応
> **angrily** [副] ◇Some senators reacted *angrily* to the President's remarks. 上院議員の中には大統領の発言に怒りの反応を示す者もいた ◇He swore *angrily*. 彼は腹立たしげに毒づいた

mad [名詞の前では用いない]《特に米, インフォーマル》怒った ◇He got *mad* and walked out. 彼は怒って出て行った ◇She's *mad at me* for being late. 彼女は遅刻した私に腹を立てている ◇That noise is *driving me mad*. あの騒音は頭にくる ❶《米》では mad はインフォーマルな場面で angry の代わりによく使う.《英》で用いられる場合は特に go mad の句で「非常に怒った」の意味を持つ. ◆ Dad'll *go mad* when he sees what you've done. (お前がしたことを見たらお父さんは怒り狂うよ) . go mad には「気が狂う」または「非常に興奮する」の意味もある. ☞ **mad** (MAD), **maddening** (ANNOYING)

indignant (他人の不当な扱いに)怒った ◇an *indignant* look/letter 怒りの表情/手紙 ◇She was very *indignant* at the way she had been treated. 彼女は自分の扱われ方にとても腹を立てた
> **indignantly** [副] ◇'I'm certainly not asking him!' she retorted *indignantly*. 「はっきり言って彼に尋ねているのではありません」と彼女は腹立たしげに切り返した

cross《特に英, ややインフォーマル》(かなり)怒った, いら立った ◇If you don't do as you're told I shall get very *cross*. 言われたとおりにやらないと怒るぞ ❶ cross はしばしば子どもによってまたは子どもに対して用いられる.
> **crossly** [副] ◇'Well, what did you expect?' she said *crossly*. 「ところで何を期待していたの」と彼女は腹立たしげに言った

> **ノート** **angry と cross の使い分け**：cross man は性格上いつも不機嫌な人. angry man はいつも怒っている人, または特定の場合に怒っている人.

irate 激怒した ◇*irate* customers/callers 激怒した客/激怒して電話を掛けてきた人 ◇an *irate* letter/phone call 怒りの手紙/電話 ❶ irate はふつう前置詞を伴わない. ✕ She was *irate* with me/about it.

,pissed 'off《米でまた **pissed**》《卑語, 俗語》(あまりにも長い間続く状況に対して)怒った, うんざりした ◇I'm *pissed off* with the way they've treated me. 私に対する彼らの扱い方に腹が立っている ◇a very *pissed off* taxi driver かなり頭にきているタクシー運転手

annoy [動] ☞ ANGER

annoy・frustrate・irritate・get on sb's nerves・wind sb up・bug・displease・exasperate
人を(少し)腹立たしい思いにさせることを表す
【類語訳】怒らせる, むっとさせる, いら立たせる, いらいらさせる, からかう, おちょくる

displease	annoy	exasperate
bug	frustrate	
	irritate	
	get on sb's nerves	
	wind sb up	

文型&コロケーション
- ▶ It annoys me/ irritates me/ gets on my nerves/ bugs me **that/ when**...
- ▶ What annoys me/ frustrates me/ irritates me/ gets on my nerves/ bugs me **is the way/ the fact that**...
- ▶ to **really** annoy sb/ irritate sb/ get on sb's nerves/ wind sb up/ bug sb

annoy [他] (少し)怒らせる, むっとさせる ◇His constant joking was beginning to *annoy* her. 彼がひっきりなしに冗談ばかり言うので彼女はいらつき始めていた ◇It really *annoys* me when people don't say thank you. 人がありがとうを言わないと本当に腹が立つ ◇*It annoys me to* see him getting ahead of me. 彼が自分より出世しているのを見るとむかつく ☞ **annoyance** (FRUSTRATION)

frustrate [他] (したいことができないで少し)怒らせる, いら立たせる ◇What *frustrates* him is that there's too little money to spend on the project. 彼がいら立たしい思いをしているのはその事業の投資額があまりにも少ないことだ

↪annoy

annoyed, annoying

☞ frustration (FRUSTRATION), frustrated (UNHAPPY 2)

irritate [他]（しきりに行われたり発生したりするので少し）怒らせる, いらいらさせる ◇The way she puts on that accent really *irritates* me. 彼女のあの訛りのあるしゃべり方には本当にいらいらさせられる ◇She was *irritated* by his continued refusal to believe her. 彼がずっと自分の言うことを信じようとしないので彼女はいら立っていた ☞ **irritable** (IRRITABLE), **irritation** (FRUSTRATION)

get on sb's 'nerves [行動]《インフォーマル》（少し）怒らせる, いら立たせる ◇That music is *getting on my nerves*. あの音楽は神経に障る ◇It didn't take long before we started *getting on each other's nerves*. 私たちがお互いの神経を逆なでし始めるのに時間はかからなかった

,**wind sb 'up** [句動]《英, インフォーマル》（少し）怒るような事をわざと言う[する], からかう, おちょくる ◇Calm down! Can't you see he's only *winding you up*? 落ち着いて. 彼はただあなたをからかっているだけなんだから ◇That can't be true! You're *winding me up*! そんなはずはないよ. からかっているんでしょ

bug (-gg-) [他]《インフォーマル》（少し）いら立たせる, 悩ませる ◇What's the matter? Is there something *bugging* you? どうしたの. 何か悩み事でもあるの

displease [他]《フォーマル》機嫌を損なわせる, （少し）怒らせる, 不快にする ◇The tone of the letter *displeased* her. 彼女はその手紙の調子が気に入らなかった 反意 **please** (PLEASE), ☞ **displeasure** (FRUSTRATION)

exasperate [他] 激怒させる ◇Her moods *exasperated* him. 彼女の不機嫌さに彼は激怒した ◇She was clearly *exasperated* by all my questions. 私のすべての質問に彼女は明らかに激怒していた ☞ **exasperation** (FRUSTRATION)

annoyed [形] ☞ ANGRY

annoyed・irritated・exasperated・put out
人が物事について（少し）腹立っていることを表す
【類語訳】怒った, いら立った, 激怒した, 気分を害した

【文型&コロケーション】
▶ annoyed/ irritated/ put out **at** sth
▶ irritated/ exasperated **by** sb/ sth
▶ annoyed/ put out **about** sth
▶ annoyed/ irritated/ exasperated **with** sb
▶ annoyed/ irritated/ put out **that**...
▶ annoyed/ irritated/ put out **to find/ see**...
▶ to **feel** annoyed/ irritated/ exasperated/ put out
▶ **a bit/ slightly/ quite/ rather** annoyed/ irritated/ put out

annoyed （少し）怒った, いら立った ◇I was *annoyed* **with myself** for giving in so easily. あんなにも簡単に降参してしまい私は自分自身に腹が立っていた ◇I bet she was *annoyed* at having to write it out again. 彼女はもう一度清書しなければならなくて怒ったに違いない ◇He tried to ignore the *annoyed* looks from the other customers. 彼は他の客たちのいらついた表情を見て見ぬ振りをしようとした ☞ **annoyance** (FRUSTRATION)

irritated （少し）怒った, いら立った ◇She was getting more and more *irritated* by his comments. 彼女は彼の意見を聞いてますますいらいらしてきた ☞ **irritable** (IRRITABLE), **irritation** (FRUSTRATION)

【ノート】 annoyed と irritated の使い分け : 多くの場合には両語とも使用可能だが, 特に話し言葉では annoyed が頻繁に用いられる. ふつう irritated は他人の言動に対して用いられるが, annoyed は自分自身や自分がしなければならない事に対しても用いられる.

exasperated （状況を改善する事ができずに）激怒した ◇She was becoming *exasperated* with all the questions they were asking. 彼女は彼らが尋ねてくるすべての質問に腹が立ってきた ◇'Why not?' he asked in an *exasperated* voice. 「どうして」と彼は怒った口調で聞いた ☞ **exasperation** (FRUSTRATION)

,**put 'out** [名詞の前では用いない]《ややインフォーマル, 特に話し言葉》（人の言動に少し）怒った, 気分を害した ◇She looked really *put out* when I said I didn't agree. 私が賛成しないと言うと彼女は本当に気分を害したようだった

annoying [形]

annoying・irritating・frustrating・tiresome・infuriating・maddening・galling・trying・pesky
人や物事が怒りを感じさせたり, 腹立たしくさせたりすることを表す
【類語訳】いらいらさせる, 腹立たしい, いら立たせる, 飽き飽きする, 扱いづらい

【文型&コロケーション】
▶ annoying/ irritating/ frustrating/ tiresome/ infuriating/ galling/ trying **for** sb
▶ **an** annoying/ **an** irritating/ **a** tiresome/ **an** infuriating/ **a** pesky **man**
▶ **an** annoying/ **an** irritating/ **a** tiresome/ **an** infuriating/ **a** maddening **habit**
▶ to **find** sb/ sth annoying/ irritating/ frustrating/ tiresome/ infuriating/ galling
▶ **very** annoying/ irritating/ frustrating/ tiresome/ galling/ trying
▶ **absolutely** infuriating/ maddening

annoying 腹立たしい, いらいらさせる ◇I find her very *annoying*. 彼女はかなりいらつかせる女だと思う ◇The *annoying* thing was that I only had myself to blame. むかつくことにまったくの自業自得だった ☞ **annoyance** (FRUSTRATION)

▶ **annoyingly** [副] *Annoyingly*, I'd left my wallet at home. 腹立たしいことに私は財布を家に忘れてしまった

irritating （少し）腹立たしい, いらいらさせる ◇The way she stares at me is extremely *irritating*. 彼女の私をじっと見る目にひどくいらいらさせられる ◇His most *irritating* habit was eating with his mouth open. 彼の最も腹立たしい癖はくちゃくちゃ音を立てて食べることだった ☞ **irritable** (IRRITABLE), **irritation** (FRUSTRATION)

▶ **irritatingly** [副] He was *irritatingly* quiet all day. 彼は腹立たしいほど一日中口をきかなかった

【ノート】 annoying と irritating の使い分け : ふつうどちらの語も使用できるが, annoying のほうが特に話し言葉では頻繁に用いられる. irritating はふつう人や人の癖について用いられるが, annoying は腹立たしい事や状況にも用いられる.

frustrating （したいことができないので少し）腹立たしい, いら立たせる ◇It's *frustrating* to have to wait so long. そんなに長く待たないといけないなんていらいらするね ◇The *frustrating* thing is, they probably won't even be in

when we get there. いらつくことに私たちが着いても彼らは恐らく居さえしないだろう ❶ frustrating は事実や状況について用い、人や人の癖には用いない。×a frustrating man/habit. ☞ **frustrated** (UNHAPPY 2), **frustration** (FRUSTRATION)
▸**frustratingly** 副 ◇Progress was frustratingly slow. 進捗状況はいらいらするほど遅かった
tiresome 《特に書き言葉》 いらいらさせる, 飽き飽きする ◇The children were being very tiresome. 子どもたちはすっかり飽き飽きしてきた ◇Buying a house can be a tiresome business. 家を買うことにはうんざりすることが付き物だ
infuriating ひどく腹立たしい ◇an infuriating child/delay ひどく腹立たしい子ども/遅れ ◇It is infuriating trying to talk to someone who just looks out of the window. ただ窓の外を見ているだけの人に話しかけようとするのは腹立たしい ☞ **infuriate** (ANGER 動)
▸**infuriatingly** 副 ◇He just smiled infuriatingly. 彼は憎たらしげにほほ笑んだだけだった ◇Infuriatingly, the shop had just closed. むかつくことにその店は閉店したばかりだった
maddening ひどく腹立たしい, 頭にくる ◇He found her behaviour maddening. 彼女の振る舞いを彼は実に腹立たしく思った ☞ **mad** (ANGRY)
▸**maddeningly** 副 ◇Progress is maddeningly slow. 進捗状況は頭にくるほど遅い
galling 《不公平・不当で》腹立たしい ◇It was galling to have to do it all over again. もう一度やり直ししなければならなくて腹が立った
trying (少し)腹立たしい, つらい ◇She can be very trying. 彼女にはとても癇(かん)に障るところがある ◇These are trying times for all of us. 私たち全員にとってつらい時だ
pesky [名詞の前で]《特に米, インフォーマル》うるさい, 厄介な, 嫌な ◇those pesky insects/kids あのうっとうしい虫/子ども ◇I can't go out tonight — I've got that pesky interview tomorrow. 今夜は外出できないよ—明日, あの嫌な面接があるんだ

answer 名

answer・reply・response・acknowledgement・retort
質問や状況に反応するために言ったり, 書いたり, したりすることを表す
【類語訳】答え, 返答, 返事, 反応, 受取通知, しっぺ返し

〖文型&コロケーション〗
▸an answer/ a reply/ a response/ a retort **to** sb/ sth
▸an answer/ reply/ a response/ an acknowledgement **from** sb
▸**in** answer/ reply/ response **to** sb/ sth
▸a/ an **quick/ immediate/ appropriate/ suitable** answer/ reply/ response/ retort
▸a **written** answer/ reply/ response/ acknowledgement
▸a/ an **sharp/ angry/ curt** reply/ response/ retort
▸a **formal** reply/ response/ acknowledgement
▸to **get/ receive** an answer/ a reply/ a response/ an acknowledgement
▸to **give/ write/ elicit/ produce/ wait for** an answer/ a reply/ a response
▸to **send** an answer/ a reply/ an acknowledgement

▸to **make no** answer/ reply/ response

answer [C] 答え, 返答, 返事 ◇Have you had an answer to your letter? 手紙への返事はあったの ◇As if in answer to our prayers, she offered to lend us the money. まるで我々の願いに応えるかのように彼女はお金を貸すと申し出てくれた ◇I rang the bell, but there was no answer. ベルを鳴らしたがなんの返事もなかった ◇I expect a **straight answer** to a straight question. 率直な質問に対しては率直な答えを期待しています
reply [C, U]《特に書き言葉》返事, 答え, 返答 ◇We had over 110 replies to our advertisement. 広告を出したところ110件を上回る返事があった ◇I haven't received a reply from him yet. 彼からはまだ返事一つない ◇What did they say **in reply**? 彼らはなんと返答してきましたか ◇I asked her what her name was but she made no reply. 彼女に名前を尋ねたが返事はなかった
response [C, U]《ややフォーマル》反応, 返答, 応答 ◇95% of customers can expect a response to their enquiries within 10 days. 顧客の95パーセントが問い合わせに対して10日以内に返事がもらえると思う ◇I knocked on the door but there was no response. ドアを叩いてはみたが反応はなかった

〖ノート〗 answer, response, reply の使い分け：reply は answer よりもいくぶんフォーマルで, 特に書き言葉で用いられる. また reply は会話における返事や宣伝, 招待状への書面による返事に関してよく用いられる. response は reply よりもフォーマルでビジネス関係でよく用いられる.

acknowledgement (または **acknowledgment**) [C] 《ややフォーマル》受け取り通知 ◇I didn't receive an acknowledgement of my application. 願書を送ったのに受領通知がなかった
retort [C]《ややフォーマル, 書き言葉》しっぺ返し, (当意即妙の)言い返す ◇He opened his mouth to **make a** caustic retort. 彼は口を開いて辛辣に言い返した ◇She bit back (= stopped herself from making) a sharp retort. 彼女は痛烈な反論を控えた

answer 動

answer・reply・respond・retort・acknowledge・write back・get back to sb
質問や状況に対する反応として, 言ったり, 書いたり, 行動したりする
【類語訳】答える, 応じる, 返事をする, 返答する

〖文型&コロケーション〗
▸to reply/ respond/ get back/ write back **to** sb/ sth
▸to answer/ reply/ respond/ retort/ acknowledge sth/ get back to sb **with** sth
▸to answer/ reply/ respond/ retort/ write back **that**...
▸to answer/ reply to/ respond to/ acknowledge a/ an **question/ letter/ email**
▸to answer/ reply/ respond to **mail/ correspondence**
▸to answer/ reply/ respond to an **ad/ advert/ advertisement/ accusation**
▸to answer/ reply/ acknowledge a **claim**
▸to answer/ reply to/ acknowledge a/ an **query/ enquiry/ charge**
▸to answer/ reply/ respond/ acknowledge sth **quickly**
▸to answer/ reply/ respond **directly/ promptly/ personal-**

▶to answer/ reply/ respond/ retort **coldly/ curtly/ sharply/ stiffly/ angrily/ bitterly/ indignantly/ sarcastically/ bluntly**
▶to answer/ reply/ respond **honestly/ politely/ truthfully/ vaguely/ cautiously/ calmly/ quietly/ slowly**

answer [自, 他] 答える、応じる ◇I repeated the question, but she didn't *answer*. 私は質問を繰り返したが彼女は答えなかった ◇You haven't *answered* my question. あなたは私の質問に答えていません ◇Come on, *answer* me! Where were you? ほら早く答えてよ。どこにいたの ◇Could somebody ***answer the phone*** (= pick up the phone when it rings)? 誰か電話に出てくれませんか ◇They never bother to ***answer the door*** (= open the door when sb knocks/rings). 彼らはわざわざ玄関先まで応対に出ることなんてしない ◇My *prayers have been answered* (= I have got what I wanted). 私の願いはかなえられた ◇'I'd prefer to walk,' she *answered*. 「私は歩くほうがいいわ」と彼女は答えた

reply [自, 他]《特に書き言葉》返事をする、応じる ◇He never *replied* to any of my letters. 私が書いたどの手紙にも彼は決して返事をくれなかった ◇She only *replied* with a smile. 彼女は笑顔を返しただけだった ◇The senator *replied* that he was not in a position to comment. その上院議員は自分はコメントする立場にないと返答した

respond [自, 他]《ややフォーマル、特にビジネスで》返事をする、応じる ◇I asked him his name, but he didn't *respond*. 私は彼に名前を尋ねたが彼は答えなかった ◇More than fifty people *responded* to the advertisement. 50人以上の人がその広告に反応した ◇'I'm not sure,' she *responded*. 「よくわかりませんね」と彼女は答えた

ノート answer, reply, respond の使い分け: answer は answer sb/sth または単に answer だけでも用いることができるが、answer to sb/sth は不可。reply と respond は reply/respond to sb/sth または単に reply/respond だけでも用いることができるが、reply/respond sb/sth は不可。reply は answer よりもやや formal で、特に書き言葉で用いられる。respond は reply よりもフォーマルで、特にビジネスの文脈でも用いられる。これら3語は多くの場合代用できるが、目的語が the phone/the door/sb's prayers の場合、answer しか用いることができない。×*reply/respond to* the phone/the door/sb's prayers. answer/respond to a call とは言えるが、×*reply to* a call は不可。

retort [他]《ややフォーマル、書き言葉》（怒って[おどけて]）言い返す ◇'Don't be ridiculous!' Pat *retorted* angrily. 「ばかげたことを言うな」とパットは怒って言い返した

acknowledge [他]《ややフォーマル》（物を送ってくれた人に）受け取ったことを伝える；（質問・意見を聞いて）理解したことを示す ◇All applications will be *acknowledged*. すべての応募に対して受領を通知いたします ◇Please *acknowledge* receipt of this letter. この手紙を受け取ったら知らせてください

,**write 'back** [句動]（手紙の）返事を書く ◇I'm afraid I never *wrote back* to him. 残念ですが彼にはいっさい返事を書いていません ◇She *wrote back* saying that she couldn't come. 彼女は行けそうにないと返事を書いた

,**get 'back to sb** [句動]《インフォーマル》（返事のため）後で再度連絡する ◇I'll find out and *get back to you*. 調べてからまた後で連絡するよ

apparent 形

apparent・outward・purported・seeming・superficial・ostensible

実際はどうかわからないが、本物または真実のように見えること
【類語訳】見かけ上の、うわべの、外面的な、表面的な、表向きの

文型&コロケーション
▶apparent/ outward **calm**
▶an apparent/ a purported **attack**
▶an apparent/ a seeming **contradiction/ failure/ inability/ indifference/ reluctance**
▶an apparent/ a superficial **similarity**
▶an outward/ a superficial **appearance**
▶the apparent/ ostensible **purpose/ reason**

apparent [ふつう名詞の前で] 見かけ上の、うわべの ◇My parents were concerned at my *apparent* lack of enthusiasm for school. 私の両親は私が学校に行く気がなさそうに見えることを心配していた ◇Their affluence is more *apparent* than real (= they are not as rich as they seem to be). 彼らは見掛けほど実際は裕福ではない ☞ **apparent** (CLEAR 形 1), **appear** (SEEM)
➤**apparently** 副 ◇I thought she had retired, but *apparently* (= in fact) she hasn't. 彼女は退職していたと思っていたが、どうやらそうではなかった ◇He paused, *apparently* lost in thought. 彼は考え込むようなそぶりで立ち止まった

outward [名詞の前で] 外面的な、うわべの ◇Mark showed no *outward* signs of distress. マークは悩んでいるそぶりも見せなかった ◇*To all outward appearances* (= as far as it was possible to judge from the outside) they were perfectly happy. はたから見る限り、彼らはまったく幸せそうだった ◇*outward* と結び付くのは form, appearance, display, expression, indication, sign など、特に形や様子を表すさまざまな語が挙げられる。反意 **inward**
❶ inward は「心の内にあって他人には見せない」ことを表す。
♦ Her calm expression hid her *inward* panic. (彼女の冷静な表情からは内心パニック状態にあることはわからない).
➤**outwardly** 副 ◇Though badly frightened, she remained *outwardly* composed. ひどくおびえていたが、彼女は外見上は平静を保っていた ◇*Outwardly*, the couple seemed perfectly happy. 外見上、その夫婦はまったく幸せそうだった 反意 **inwardly**

purported [名詞の前で]《フォーマル》…だとされている ◇He was seen at the scene of the *purported* crime. 犯罪が行われたとされる現場で彼は目撃された
➤**purportedly** 副 ◇a letter *purportedly* written by Mozart モーツァルトによって書かれたとされる手紙

seeming [名詞の前で]《フォーマル》見かけ上の、うわべの ◇We discussed the *seeming* contradiction of his arguments. 私たちは彼の主張が矛盾しているように思われる点について話し合った ☞ **seem** (SEEM)
➤**seemingly** 副 ◇a *seemingly* endless journey 終わりのないように思われる旅 ◇a *seemingly* impossible task 一見不可能な任務 ◇*Seemingly*, he borrowed the money from the bank. どうやら彼は銀行からお金を借りたようだ

superficial 見かけ上の、表面的な ◇*Superficial* similarities can be deceptive. 見かけの類似性は当てにならな

appear, appearance

いかもしれない ◇When you first meet her, she gives a *superficial* impression of warmth and friendliness. 彼女と初めて会うと、表面上は優しくて好意的な印象を受ける ❶この意味における superficial の典型的な結び付きとしては、impression や appearance、また likeness, resemblance, similarity といった類似性を表す語が挙げられる。

ostensible [名詞の前で][フォーマル] 見せかけの、表向きの ◇The *ostensible* reason for his absence was illness. 彼が欠席した表向きの理由は病気だった ❶ostensible は人の行いの理由や目的について言うときに用いられる。

▶ **ostensibly** 副 ◇Troops were sent in, *ostensibly* to protect the civilian population. 一般市民を守るという名目で軍隊が送り込まれた

appear 動

appear・emerge・show・loom・pop・manifest itself・form・come out
ある場所で見られるようになることを表す
【類語訳】現れる、出てくる、姿を現す、生じる、形成する

文型&コロケーション
▶ to appear/ emerge from sth
▶ to loom/ pop into view/ up
▶ to appear/ emerge/ loom/ pop out of sth
▶ to suddenly appear/ emerge/ show/ loom/ pop/ come out
▶ to gradually appear/ emerge/ manifest itself/ form
▶ to eventually appear/ emerge/ show
▶ to finally appear/ emerge/ loom

appear [自]《ふつう副詞や前置詞と共に》現れる ◇She suddenly *appeared* in the doorway. 彼女は突然戸口に現れた ◇If a rash *appears*, call a doctor immediately. 発疹が現れたら、医者をすぐに呼んでください ◇Posters for the gig *appeared* all over town. 街の至る所にそのライブのポスターが貼ってあった ◇New shoots are just *appearing* at the base of the plant. その植物の根元から新芽がちょうど出てきている ◇Her dead mother *appeared to* her in a dream. 彼女の死んだ母親が夢の中で彼女の前に現れた
[反意] disappear (DISAPPEAR)

emerge [自]《ふつう副詞や前置詞と共に》(暗い[閉じられた、隠された]場所から)出てくる、現れる ◇The swimmer *emerged* from the lake. 泳いでいた人が湖から現れた ◇They suddenly *emerged* into brilliant sunshine. 彼らは突然明るい日なたに出た ◇The crabs *emerge* at low tide to look for food. 蟹は餌を探して干潮時に出てくる

show [自, 他] 見えるようになる[する] ◇The cloth was folded so that the stain didn't *show*. 染みが見えないようにその布は畳まれていた ◇His hands were clenched, the whites of the knuckles *showing*. 彼は拳を握り締め、指の関節部分が白くなっていた ◇She had a warm woollen hat on that left only her eyes and nose *showing*. 彼女は暖かいウールの帽子をかぶり、目と鼻だけしか出ていなかった ◇A white carpet will *show* every mark. 白のカーペットならどんな汚れも目立ちます ◇Come out and *show* yourselves (= let us see you)! 出てきて姿を見せなさい

loom [自]《ふつう副詞や前置詞と共に》《書き言葉》(脅かすように)ぼんやりと大きな姿を現す ◇Something huge and black *loomed* out of the mist. 巨大で黒い何かが霧の中からぼうっと現れた ◇The city walls *loomed* up ahead of them. その街の城壁が彼らの前にぬっと現れた

pop (-pp-) [自]《副詞や前置詞と共に》突然現れる ◇The window opened and a head *popped* out. 窓が開いて頭がひょいっと現れた ◇When you send a fax, a dialog box *pops* up on the screen. ファックスを送信する際に画面上にダイアログボックスが現れます ◇An idea suddenly *popped* into his head. ある考えが突然彼の頭に浮かんだ

manifest itself [他]《フォーマル》見える[目立つ]ようになる ◇Heatstroke sometimes *manifests itself* as red spots on the skin. 熱射病になると時に皮膚に赤い斑点が現れることがある ◇A new trend seems to have *manifested* itself. 新しい流行が現れたようだ

form [自]《ややフォーマル》(自然物が)形となって現れる ◇Flowers appeared, but fruits failed to *form*. 花は咲いたが実はならなかった ◇Storm clouds are *forming* on the horizon. 暗雲が地平線上に出てきている

come 'out 句動詞 (太陽・月・星が)見えるようになる、現れる、出る ◇The rain stopped and the sun *came out*. 雨がやんで太陽が顔を出した

appearance 名

appearance・look・manner・air・looks
人や物事の見え方、振る舞い方、ありさまを表す
【類語訳】外見、様相、様子、態度、物腰、感じ、印象、気品、容貌、ルックス

文型&コロケーション
▶ (a) striking/ distinctive appearance/ look/ looks
▶ sb's general appearance/ manner/ air
▶ a confident appearance/ manner/ air
▶ to have a ... appearance/ look/ manner/ air
▶ to lose your/ its ... appearance/ air/ looks
▶ to improve sb/ sth's appearance/ look/ looks
▶ to like sb/ sth's appearance/ look/ manner/ looks
▶ to give sb the appearance/ look/ air of sth

appearance [C] 外見、様相 ◇The dog was similar in general *appearance* to a spaniel. その犬は全体的に見た目がスパニエル犬に似ていた ◇She had never been greatly concerned about her *appearance*. 彼女は自分の外見を大して気にしたことはなかった ◇*To all appearances* (= as far as people could tell) he was dead. どう見ても彼は死んでいた ◇He *gave every appearance of* (= seemed very much to be) enjoying himself. 彼はとても楽しんでいるようだった ◇When she lost all her money, she was determined to *keep up appearances* (= hide the true situation and pretend that everything was going well). お金をすべて失ったとき彼女は努めて平静を装った ☞ **appear** (SEEM)

look [C, ふつう単数で] 様子、外見 ◇It's going to rain today, *by the look of it* (= judging by appearances). この様子では今日は雨が降るだろう ◇I *don't like the look of* that guy (= I don't trust him, judging by his appearance). あいつは見た目からしてうさんくさい ◇*Looks* can be deceptive. 物事は見掛けによらぬものだ ☞ **look** (SEEM)

ノート **appearance** と **look** の使い分け：appearance はしばしば人や物事の外見が実際とどれほど対照的であるかについて言うときに用いられる。outward や external と結び付き、keep up appearances の句でも用いられる。appearance はまた「容姿」について言うときにも用いられる。◆She

↳**appearance**

was always very particular about her *appearance*. (彼女はいつもとてもおしゃれに気を遣っていた). **look** は話し言葉でよく用いられ、特に **by the look of it/him/her/...** や **(not) like the look of sb** の句で用いられる。

manner [単数で] 態度, 物腰 ◇She has a friendly, relaxed *manner*. 彼女は気さくでのんびりした人だ ◇His *manner* was polite but cool. 彼の態度は丁寧だが冷淡だ

air [単数で] 雰囲気, 態度 ◇The room had an *air* of luxury. その部屋には高級な雰囲気があった ◇There was an *air* of complete confidence about her. 彼女には絶対的な自信が漂っていた ☞ **aura** (ATMOSPHERE)

looks [複数で] (魅力的な) 外見, 容貌, ルックス ◇She has her father's good *looks*. 彼女には父親譲りの美貌が備わっている ◇He lost his *looks* (= became less attractive) in later life. 後年彼の容貌は衰えた ☞ **good-looking** (BEAUTIFUL 1)

apply 動 ☞ USE 動 1

apply・impose・enforce・put sth into effect・put sth into practice

法律, 知識, 技術などを働かせることを表す
【類語訳】適用する, 応用する, 導入する, 課す, 施行する, 実施する, 実践する

▸ to apply/ impose/ enforce/ put into effect/ put into practice **measures**
▸ to apply/ impose/ enforce/ put into practice a **law**
▸ to apply/ impose/ enforce a **rule/ regulation/ restriction/ penalty/ punishment/ regime/ sanction/ standard**
▸ to apply/ impose/ enforce **guidelines/ discipline**
▸ to enforce/ put into effect/ put into practice **recommendations**
▸ to apply/ impose/ put into practice a **principle**
▸ to apply/ impose/ put into effect/ put into practice **ideas**

apply [他] 《ややフォーマル》(法律・罰則などを) 適用する, (知識・技術などを) 応用する ◇Political pressure has been *applied to* the colony's government in an attempt to win the contract. 契約を獲得するために植民地政府に対しては政治的圧力が掛けられてきた ◇The new technology was *applied* to farming. 新しい科学技術が農業に応用された ◇Now is the time to *apply* the insights you have gained from your studies. 今こそ研究で得た洞察力を使う時だ ☞ **application** (USE 名)

impose [他] 《ややフォーマル》(税・罰則などを) 課す ◇A new tax was *imposed on* fuel. 新税が燃料に課せられた ◇A prison sentence of 25 years is *imposed* on each of the defendants. 懲役25年の刑がそれぞれの被告に課された ◇The time limits are *imposed* on us by factors outside our control. 私たちの力が及ばぬ要因によって制限時間が課せられている

enforce [他] 《ややフォーマル》施行する, 実施する ◇The legislation will be difficult to *enforce*. その法律を施行するのは難しいだろう ◇United Nations troops *enforced* a ceasefire in the area. 国連軍はその地域で停戦を実施した

,put sth into ef'fect フレーズ (規則・勧告などを) 実施する ◇The recommendations will soon be *put into effect*. 勧告がまもなく実施される予定だ

,put sth into 'practice フレーズ (考え・知識を) 実行する ◇She's determined to *put* her new ideas *into practice*. 彼女は新たな考えを実行に移そうとしている ☞ **practice** (USE 名)

appoint 動 ☞ EMPLOY

appoint・elect・name・nominate・designate・co-opt・commission・vote sb in・vote sb into/onto sth

公式または正式に人を重要な仕事や責任のある地位に就ける
【類語訳】選ぶ, 任命する, 指名する, 選出する, 任官する

▸ to appoint sb/ name sb/ nominate sb/ designate sb/ commission sb/ vote sb in **as** sth
▸ to appoint/ elect/ name/ nominate sb **to** sth
▸ to appoint/ elect/ name/ nominate/ designate/ co-opt sb **to do sth**
▸ to **officially/ formally** appoint/ name/ nominate/ designate sb

appoint [他] 任命する, 指名する ◇They have *appointed* a new principal at my son's school. 息子の学校では新しい校長が任命された ◇She has recently been *appointed* to the committee. 彼女は委員会のメンバーに最近任命された ◇They *appointed* him (as) captain of the national team. 彼が国の代表チームのキャプテンに指名された ◇A lawyer was *appointed* to represent the child. 弁護士がその子どもの代理人に指名された 反意 **dismiss** (FIRE)

▸ **appointment** 名 [C, U] ◇Following her recent *appointment* to the post... 最近彼女がそのポストへ任命されたのに続き… the *appointment* of a new captain for the England team イングランド・チームの新キャプテンの指名 ☞ **appointment** (JOB)

elect [他] 投票によって選ぶ, 選出する ◇an *elected* assembly/leader/representative 選出議会/選ばれた指導者/選ばれた代表者 ◇the newly *elected* government 新たに選挙で選ばれた政府 ◇She became the first black woman to be *elected* to the Senate. 彼女は黒人女性初の上院議員に選ばれた ◇What changes will he make if he gets *elected*? もし彼が当選したらどんな改革を行うのだろうか ❶ **elect** は政治の文脈で最も頻繁に用いられ, 正式な書面投票によって政府, 指導者, 代表者を選ぶことを言う。 ☞ **election** (CHOICE 1), **election** (ELECTION)

▸ **electoral** 形 ◇*electoral* systems/reforms 選挙制度/改革

name [他] 指名する, 任命する ◇I had no hesitation in *naming* him (as) captain. 私は彼をキャプテンに指名することに何のためらいもなかった ◇Mr Shah has been *named* to run the new research unit. シャー氏が新しい調査団を指揮する立場に指名された

nominate [他] 《ややフォーマル》任命する, 指名する ◇I have been *nominated* to the committee. 私は委員会のメンバーに任命された ◇She was *nominated* to speak on our behalf. 彼女が私たちを代表してスピーチをするよう指名された ☞ **nomination** (CHOICE 1)

designate [他] 《フォーマル》任命する, 指名する ◇The director is allowed to *designate* his/her successor. 取締役は自分の後継者を指名することができる

appreciate, approval

ノート name, nominate, designate の使い分け: name が最もよく用いられ、特に書き言葉では多い。しばしばビジネスの文脈において、新たな社員や委員などを任命するのに用いられる。nominate は一定期間継続する仕事や地位ではなく、特定の任務について言うときに用いられる。×She was *named* to speak on our behalf. designate は name のフォーマルな表現である。

,co-'opt [他] メンバーの一員にする ◇She was *co-opted* onto the board. 彼女は委員会のメンバーに選出された
commission [他, ふつう受身で] 軍の将校に選ぶ, 任官する ◇He has just been *commissioned* (as a) pilot officer. 彼は空軍少尉に任命されたばかりだ
,vote sb 'in, ,vote sb 'into/'onto sth 句動詞 投票によって人を…に選出する ◇He was *voted* in as treasurer. 彼は財務官に選出された ◇She was *voted* onto the board of governors. 彼女は理事会のメンバーに選出された 反意 **vote sb out, vote sb out of/off sth**, ☞ **vote** (ELECTION)

appreciate 動

appreciate・value・admire・treasure・cherish・prize
人や物事が重要[特別]であると考える
【類語訳】味わう、尊重する、重んじる、感心する、愛蔵する、大事にする

文型&コロケーション
▸ to value/ prize sb/ sth **as/ for** sth
▸ to value/ treasure/ prize sb's **friendship**
▸ to treasure/ cherish a **memory**
▸ to **really** appreciate/ value/ treasure/ cherish sb/ sth
▸ to value/ prize sth **highly**

appreciate [他]《進行形なし》評価する, 良さがわかる ◇You can't really *appreciate* foreign literature in translation. 翻訳では外国文学を本当には味わうことができない ◇His talents are not *fully appreciated* in that company. その会社では彼の才能は十分には評価されていない ◇Her family doesn't *appreciate* her. 家族は彼女の良さをわかっていない ☞ **appreciation** (ADMIRATION), **appreciative** (GOOD 6)
value [他]《進行形なし》評価する, 尊重する, 重んじる ◇I really *value* him as a friend. 私は彼を友人として本当に大切に思っている ◇They don't seem to *value* honesty very highly. 彼らは誠実であることをあまり重視していないようだ ☞ **value** (VALUE), **valuable** (VALUABLE 2)

ノート appreciate と value の使い分け: value は人や物事を大切にすることを指す。例えば your friends, your health, your freedom, sb's opinion などを目的語にとる。appreciate は人や物事の価値を認めることを言うが, それらは個人的には大切でないこともある。また, 認められるべき良さが認められていないことを表す否定文の中でよく用いられる。

admire [他] ほれぼれと眺める, 見とれる ◇He stood back to *admire* his handiwork. 彼は後ろに下がって彼の手製品をほれぼれと眺めた ◇Let's just sit and *admire* the view. ちょっと座って景色をめでよう ◇I've just been *admiring* your new car. 君の新車に見とれていたところだよ
treasure [他]《進行形なし》大事にする, 愛蔵する ◇I shall always *treasure* the memory of our time together. 一緒に過ごした思い出をいつまでも心にとどめておきます

☞ **treasured** (DEAR)
cherish [他]《進行形なし》《フォーマル》(人・物事を)大事にする;(思い出・喜びを)長い間心にとどめる ◇Children need to be *cherished*. 子どもたちは大事にされる必要がある ◇*Cherish* the memory of those days in Paris. パリにいたあの頃の思い出を心にとどめておこう ☞ **cherished** (DEAR)
prize [他, ふつう受身で] (物事を高く)評価する, 珍重する ◇an era when honesty was *prized* above all other virtues 他のあらゆる美徳以上に誠実さが重んじられていた時代 ◇Oil of cedarwood is highly *prized* for its use in medicine and perfumery. シーダーから取れる油は薬や香料への用途に珍重されている ☞ **prized** (DEAR)

approval 名 ☞ PERMISSION

approval・acceptance・agreement・favour・assent・blessing・thumbs up・acquiescence
ある事が好ましいと思われるので, それが行われることを許すこと
【類語訳】許可, 認可, 承認, 承諾, 受け入れ, 了承, 合意, 支持, 賛成, 黙認, 黙許

acquiescence	acceptance	approval	blessing
	agreement	favour	thumbs up
	assent		

文型&コロケーション
▸ approval/ acceptance/ agreement/ assent/ thumbs up **for** sth
▸ **with** the approval/ agreement/ assent/ blessing/ acquiescence **of** sb
▸ **full** approval/ acceptance/ agreement/ blessing
▸ **widespread/ total/ tacit/ prior** approval/ acceptance/ agreement
▸ (the) **official** approval/ acceptance/ blessing
▸ to **give** your approval/ your agreement/ your assent/ your blessing/ the thumbs up **to** sth
▸ to **get** sb's approval/ sb's acceptance/ sb's agreement/ sbs' assent/ sb's blessing/ the thumbs up
▸ to **secure** approval/ acceptance/ agreement/ assent/ acquiescence
▸ to **receive** approval/ acceptance/ sb's assent/ sb's blessing
▸ to **gain** approval/ acceptance/ agreement/ assent
▸ to **nod** approval/ agreement/ your assent

approval [U] (計画・要求などに対する)公式の許可, 認可, 承認 ◇The treaty still required *approval* by the Senate. その協定はいぜんとして上院の承認を必要としていた ◇The plan will be submitted for *approval* next month. 来月その計画は承認を求めて提出される予定だ ◇The offer is *subject to approval* by the shareholders (= they need to agree to it). その提案は株主の承認が必要である ◇The project needs the bank's *seal of approval* (= official approval). この計画には銀行のお墨付きが必要である ☞ **approve** (AGREE)
acceptance [U] (集団の構成員[一般の人々]による)承認, 承諾, 受け入れ ◇A new theory emerged that quickly gained wide *acceptance*. ある新しい理論が生まれ急速に広く受け入れられた ◇The Assembly voted against *acceptance* of constitutional reform. 下院は憲法改正に

ついて投票で承認しないことに決めた 反意 **refusal, rejection** (REFUSAL), ☞ **accept** (AGREE)
agreement [U] （個人・団体の要求に対する）承認, 了承, 合意 ◇No images may be reproduced without the artist's *agreement*. アーティストの承認なしではいかなる画像もコピーできない ◇The museum secured the *agreement* of the owners *to* the loan of the statue. 博物館は彫像の貸し出しに対する所有者の了承を得た ❶ *agreement* は *approval* よりも公式的な意味合いは弱く, ふつう個人的なことに用いられる. 反意 **refusal** (REFUSAL), ☞ **agree** (AGREE)
favour （英）（米 *favor*）[U] （集団・個人による）支持, 賛成 ◇The suggestion to close the road has *found favour with* (= been supported by) local people. 道路を閉鎖する提案は地元住民から支持された ◇The show has *lost favour* with viewers recently. その番組は最近視聴者の支持を失っている ◇It seems Tim is *back in favour* with the boss (= the boss likes him again). ティムはまた上司に気に入られているようだ
assent [U] 《フォーマル》承認, 同意 ◇There was a general murmur of *assent*. みんなが口々に同意の声を漏らした ◇She gave her *assent* to publication. 彼女は刊行に同意した 反意 **dissent** (DEBATE)
blessing [単数で] （よいことなのでうまくいってほしいという思いからの）承認, 賛成 ◇This arrangement received the full *blessing* of the committee. この取り決めは委員会の全面的な承認を得た
thumbs 'up 《口語》《ややインフォーマル》（結果・計画に対する）賛成, 支持 ◇The programme is getting a big *thumbs up* from our target audience. その番組はターゲットとする視聴者層から絶大な支持を受けつつある ◇The government is likely to give the *thumbs up* to the merger. 政府はその合併を支持する見込みである ❶ thumbs up はほぼ常に get または give と共に用いられる. 反意 **thumbs down** ❶ give sth the thumbs down は, ある事への不満足や不賛成を表す. ◆The proposals were *given the thumbs down*. （その提案は支持されなかった）.
acquiescence [U] 《フォーマル》（望み・意見の）黙諾, 黙認 ◇The best one can hope for is grudging *acquiescence* from the majority in the party. 党内の過半数がしぶしぶでも認めてくれることがベストです ☞ **acquiesce** (AGREE)

approve 動

approve・confirm・recognize・uphold・ratify・sustain・validate・certify
公式に受け入れて認める
【類語訳】是認する, 承認する, 受け入れる, 支持する, 批准する

文型&コロケーション
▶ to approve/ confirm/ recognize/ uphold/ ratify/ validate/ certify sth **as** sth
▶ to approve/ recognize/ validate a **course**
▶ to approve/ uphold/ ratify a **treaty**
▶ to confirm/ uphold/ ratify a/ an **decision/ agreement**
▶ to be approved/ confirmed/ recognized/ upheld/ sustained by the **court**
▶ to **officially** approve/ confirm/ recognize/ ratify sth

approve [他, しばしば受身で] 承認する, 是認する ◇The course is *approved* by the Department for Education. その課程は教育省によって承認されている ◇The auditors *approved* the company's accounts. 会計監査官は会社の収支計算書を是認した

confirm [他] （地位・合意を）より確かな[正式な]ものにする, 承認する ◇After a six-month probationary period, her position was *confirmed*. 6か月の試用期間の後, 彼女は正式に採用された ◇He was *confirmed* as captain for the rest of the season. 彼はシーズンの残りの間にキャプテンの座をより確かなものにした
▶ **confirmation** 名 [U, C] ◇You will receive written *confirmation* of our decision in the next few days. 数日後には我々の決定に関する確認の書面をお届けします

recognize [英でまた -**ise**] [他, しばしば受身で] （人・事を）正式に受け入れる[承認する] ◇The qualifications are internationally *recognized*. その資格は国際的に認められている ◇The UK has refused to *recognize* the new regime. イギリスは新政権の承認を拒否した

uphold [他] （法廷が前の決定を）支持する, （要求を）是認する ◇The conviction was *upheld* by the Court of Appeal. その有罪判決は控訴院でも支持された ◇The Press Council refused to *uphold* the complaint. 新聞評議会はその申し立てを承認しなかった

ratify [他] （投票・署名によって）正式に合意を有効なものとする, 批准する ◇The treaty was *ratified* by all the member states. その条約は全加盟国によって批准された
▶ **ratification** 名 [U] ◇The agreement is subject to *ratification* by the Senate. その合意は議会により批准されるものとする

sustain [他] 《法律》（法廷において異論・反論が）正当であると認める ◇The court *sustained* his claim that the contract was illegal. 法廷は契約は違法であるという彼の主張を認めた ◇Objection *sustained*! (= said by a judge when a lawyer makes an objection in court) 異議を認めます

validate [他] 《フォーマル》（事が有益で受け入れられる水準にあることを）正式に認める ◇Check that their courses have been *validated* by a reputable organization. それらの課程が信頼できる組織によって認可されているか確認してください

certify [他, ふつう受身で] 《ややフォーマル》（特定の職業の）免許状を与える ◇I was *certified* as a teacher in 1989. 私は教員免許を1989年に取得した

area 名

1 area・region・part・zone・neighbourhood・district・belt・climate・quarter
土地や都市の一部
【類語訳】地域, 地帯, 区域, 地区

文型&コロケーション
▶ (a/ an) **eastern/ northern/ southern/ western** area/ region/ parts/ zone/ district/ quarter
▶ the **central** area/ region/ part/ zone/ district
▶ the **whole/ entire** area/ region/ zone/ neighbourhood/ district
▶ the **surrounding** area/ region/ neighbourhood/ district
▶ a **remote** area/ region/ part
▶ a **border/ coastal/ geographical** area/ region/ zone/ district
▶ an **industrial** area/ region/ zone/ district/ belt/ quarter
▶ a **residential** area/ zone/ neighbourhood/ district/ quar-

▶(a) **rural** area/ region/ parts/ zone/ district
▶an **urban** area/ region/ zone/ neighbourhood/ district
▶a **military** area/ region/ zone/ district

area [C] 地域, 地帯 ◇mountainous/desert *areas* 山岳/砂漠地帯 ◇She knows the local *area* very well. 彼女は地元地域をとてもよく知っている ◇The farm and surrounding *area* was flooded. その農場と周辺地域が洪水に遭った ◇There is heavy traffic in the downtown *area* tonight. 今夜は市街地で交通渋滞が起きています ◇Wreckage from the plane was scattered over a **wide** *area*. 飛行機の残骸が広範囲にわたって散乱していた ◇John is the London *area* manager. ジョンはロンドン地区のエリアマネージャーだ

region [C] (広い)地域 ◇This is one of the most densely populated *regions* of North America. ここは北アメリカの中で最も人口密度の高い地域の一つだ ◇Soil erosion is particularly serious in dry tropical *regions*. 土壌浸食は乾燥した熱帯地域で特に深刻である ☞ **region** (COUNTY)

ノート **area** と **region** の使い分け：**area** のほうが **region** よりも意味の幅が広い。**region** は特に地理的特徴や経済的[政治的]な重要度の観点から国[大陸]のかなり広大な地域を指す。**area** は国[大陸]，都市[町]，建物[部屋]またはさらに小さな場所の一部を指すこともある。☞ **area** (PLACE)

part [C] 《ふつう of を伴って》(世界・国・町などの)一地域[区域] ◇Apples grow in many *parts* of the world. りんごは世界各地で生育する ◇The northern *part* of the country is richer than the south. その国の北部は南部よりも裕福である ◇Which *part* of London do you come from? ロンドンのどの地域出身ですか

zone [C] (特徴・用途のある)地域, 区域；(地球表面を緯度で5分割したうちの一つである)帯 ◇Medical teams are on standby to fly out to the *war zone*. 医療チームが戦闘地域へ飛び立つため待機している ◇Aid workers were advised to leave the *danger zone*. 援助活動の関係者たちは危険地帯を離れるよう忠告された ◇This species is found widely distributed throughout the northern *temperate zone*. この種は北部温帯地域全体に広く分布している ❶*time zone* は世界を24分割したうちの一つで, それぞれ東隣の時間帯よりも時刻が1時間早い。☞ **zone** (COUNTY)

neighbourhood 《英》《米 **neighborhood**》[C] (町の)一地域；地域住民 ◇We grew up in the same *neighbourhood*. 私たちは同じ地域で育った ◇He shouted so loudly that the whole *neighbourhood* could hear him. 彼は近所全体に聞こえるほど大きな声で叫んだ

district [C] (特徴のある国[町]の)一地域 ◇The financial *district* of London is usually referred to as 'the City'. ロンドンの金融街はふつう「シティ」と呼ばれる ◇The house was like all the others in this exclusive residential *district*. その家はこの高級住宅地にある他の家々と似たり寄ったりだった ☞ **district** (COUNTY)

belt [C] (形容詞と共に) (特徴のある, または特定の人々が住む)地帯 ◇Towns in the country's industrial *belt* were particularly affected by the recession. 国内の産業地帯にある街が不景気の影響を受けていた ◇the US *corn belt* アメリカのとうもろこし地帯 ◇We live in the *commuter belt*. 《英》私たちはベッドタウン地域に住んでいる ◇Buffalo is an American *rust belt* city (= in an

area that used to have a lot of heavy industry) that was home to several steel mills. バッファローはアメリカのかつての重工業地帯の都市で、そこにはいくつかの製鋼所があった

climate [C] (特定の気候を持つ)地域 ◇They wanted to move to a warmer *climate*. 彼らはより温暖な地域へ移り住みたがっていた

quarter [C, ふつう単数で] (町の)一地域, 一部；地区 ◇The historic *quarter* of the city is full of grand buildings. その都市の歴史的地区には壮大な建造物がたくさんある

2 area・sector・field・domain・subject・discipline・sphere・specialty・realm・branch・specialism
活動, 学問, 興味の区分
【類語訳】範囲, 領域, 分野, 学科, 教科, 階層

文型&コロケーション

▶**within/ outside** the area/ sector/ field/ domain/ discipline/ sphere/ realm of sth
▶**beyond** the domain/ sphere/ realm of sth
▶the **public/ private/ domestic** sector/ domain/ sphere/ realm
▶the **cultural** sector/ field/ domain/ sphere/ realm
▶the **social** sector/ field/ sphere/ realm
▶the **economic/ military** sector/ field/ sphere
▶(the) **financial** area/ sector/ sphere
▶the **political** field/ domain/ sphere/ realm
▶(the) **scientific** field/ subjects/ disciplines/ sphere
▶to **open up** a (new) area/ field/ realm of sth
▶to **work in** the area/ sector/ field/ domain of sth
▶to **fall within/ move into** the area/ sector/ domain/ realm of sth

area [C] (仕事・学問・政治などの)範囲, 領域, 分野 ◇The report covers several *areas* of social policy. その報告書は社会政策のいくつかの分野を扱っている ◇Don't ask me about finance — that's Mark's *area*. 財務のことは私に聞かないでくれ—それはマークの担当分野だ ◇The big growth *area* of recent years has been in health clubs. 近年大きく成長した分野はスポーツクラブ業界だ

sector [C] (経済・産業などの)一部門 ◇Public *sector* institutions have much to learn from private *sector* companies. 政府系機関は民間企業から学ぶべきことがたくさんある ◇the manufacturing/service *sector* 製造/サービス部門

field [C] (仕事・研究の)分野 ◇He was equally famous in the *fields* of politics and of science. 彼は政治と科学の分野で同じくらい有名だった ◇All of them are experts in their *chosen field*. 彼らは皆それぞれの道の達人だ ◇This discovery has opened up a whole new *field* of research. この発見でまったく新しい研究分野が切り開かれた ◇How big was the bomb if it did all that damage?' 'I don't know. It's not my *field* (= that is not one of the subjects I know about).' 「あれほどの被害をもたらしたとすると, その爆弾の大きさはどのくらいでしたか」「わかりません。専門外なので」

domain [C] (活動・学問の担当の)分野 ◇Physics used to be very much a male *domain*. 物理学は以前はまさに男性の領域だった ◇Sensitive information should not be released into the public *domain*. 機密情報は一般に公開されるべきではない

subject [C] (学校・大学での)学問の分野[科目] ◇My fa-

↳area

vourite *subject* is biology. 私の好きな教科は生物です ◇The core *subjects* are English, maths and science. 主要科目は英語と数学と科学だ ☞ **subject** (SUBJECT)
discipline [C]《フォーマル》(学問)分野；(大学で学ぶ)学科 ◇Scholars from various *disciplines* have been working on these problems. さまざまな分野の学者がこれらの問題に取り組んでいる
sphere [C]《活動・影響・興味の及ぶ》分野, 範囲；(特定の)社会的階層 ◇Debate should be confined to the *sphere* of economics rather than politics. 議論は政治ではなく経済の分野にとどめたほうがよい ◇This area was formerly within the **sphere of influence** of the US. 以前までこの地域はアメリカの勢力圏内だった ◇He and I moved in totally different social *spheres*. 彼と私はまったく異なる社会的階層に移った
specialty [C]《特に米》(仕事・研究の)分野, 専門, 専攻；得意なもの ◇He is a lawyer with a *specialty* in international tax. 彼は国際税法が専門の弁護士だ ◇Telling jokes is my *specialty*! 冗談を言うのは得意だぜ
realm [C]《活動・興味・学問の及ぶ》分野, 領域 ◇Questions of consciousness lie outside the *realm* of physics. 意識に関する問題は物理学の範囲外である ◇At the end of the speech he seemed to be moving **into the realms of** fantasy. スピーチの最後では空想の領域に入り始めているように思われた ❶ realm はしばしば「分野」内か「分野」外かが問題になるときに用いられ, 事が主語の場合, within/outside/beyond the realms of sth の形で, 人が主語の場合, enter/move into the realms of sth の形で用いられる.
branch [C] (教科の)分野, 部門 ◇The aim is to bring together researchers from different *branches* of geography. 目的は地理学のさまざまな分野の研究者を集めることだ
specialism [C, U] (研究・業務の)専門分野 ◇He's doing a business degree with a *specialism* in computing. 彼はコンピュータ処理についての経営学学位を取得中だ ◇Dr Crane's *specialism* is tropical diseases. クレーン博士の専門は熱帯病です

argue 動

argue • quarrel • bicker • fight • clash • squabble • row • fall out
同意できないために熱くなって話し合いをすることを表す
【類語訳】議論する, 言い争う, けんかする, 張り合う, 衝突する, 対立する

[文型&コロケーション]

▶ to argue/ quarrel/ bicker/ fight/ clash/ squabble/ row/ fall out **with** sb
▶ to argue/ quarrel/ bicker/ fight/ clash/ squabble/ row/ fall out **over** sth
▶ to argue/ quarrel/ bicker/ fight/ squabble/ row/ fall out **about** sth

argue [自] 議論する, 言い争う ◇You two are always *arguing*. 君たち二人はいつも言い争ってばかりじゃないか ◇We're always *arguing* with each other about money. ぼくたちは互いにお金のことでいつももめてばかりだ ◇I don't want to *argue* with you — just do it! 君と議論する気はないね —— いいからやれよ
quarrel (-ll-, 米 -l-) [自] (個人的に)けんかする, 口論する, 言い争う ◇My sister and I used to *quarrel* all

argue, argument

the time. 妹とぼくは始終けんかしていたものだ ◇She *quarrelled* with her brother over their father's will. 彼女は父親の遺言の件で弟と口論した
bicker [自] (些細なことで)言い争う ◇The children are always *bickering* about something or other. その子どもたちはいつも何かのことで言い争ってばかりいる ◇I'm fed up with their constant *bickering*. 彼らの相も変わらぬ言い争いにはうんざりだ
fight [自]《米》(よく知っている相手と)口論する, 張り合う ◇It's a trivial matter and not worth *fighting* about. それはつまらないことで, 口論にも値しない ◇I remember lying in bed listening to my parents *fighting*. ベッドで横になって両親の言い争いを聞いていた覚えがある
clash [自]《特にジャーナリズム》(意見などが)衝突する, 対立する ◇The leaders **clashed** with party members **on** the issue. 指導者たちはその問題で党員たちと対立した ◇The Prime Minister and his old rival *clashed* over European policy. 首相と昔からの政敵はヨーロッパの政策を巡って衝突を見た
squabble [自] 口論する, 言い合う ◇My sisters were *squabbling* over what to watch on TV. 妹たちはテレビで何を見るかで言い合っていた ◇Will you two stop *squabbling*! 君たち二人, 口論するのをやめてくれないか

> [ノート] **bicker**と**squabble**の使い分け：squabbleはふつう騒々しい些細な言い争いで, とりわけ家族, 親しい友達, 子ども同士のものを指す. bickerは, 傍目からは大人げないと思われるもので, 恋人同士の言い争いを指すことが多い.

row [自]《英, インフォーマル》(騒々しく)言い争う, 口論する ◇Mike and Sue are always *rowing*. マイクとスーはいつも言い争ってばかりいる ◇She *rowed* with her parents about her new boyfriend. 彼女は新しいボーイフレンドのことで両親と口論した
ˌfall ˈout 句動詞 (友人や家族の一員と)けんかして仲が悪くなる ◇He had *fallen out* with his family. 彼は家族の者と不仲になっていた

argument 名

1 ☞ DEBATE

argument • row • fight • quarrel • squabble • tiff • shouting match
意見が合わず, 怒って言い合う状況
【類語訳】口論, 論争, 口げんか, 言い争い, いさかい

[文型&コロケーション]

▶ an argument/ a row/ a fight/ a quarrel/ a squabble/ a tiff/ a shouting match **with** sb
▶ an argument/ a row/ a fight/ a quarrel/ a squabble/ a tiff/ a shouting match **between** two people
▶ an argument/ a row/ a fight/ a quarrel/ a squabble **about/ over** sth
▶ a **bitter/ fierce/ violent** argument/ row/ quarrel
▶ a **big** argument/ row/ fight
▶ to **become/ get involved in** an argument/ a row/ a fight/ a quarrel
▶ to **have** an argument/ a row/ a fight/ a tiff
▶ to **get into/ start** an argument/ a fight
▶ to **pick** a fight/ a quarrel
▶ to **win/ lose** an argument/ a fight
▶ an argument/ a row/ a fight/ a quarrel **breaks out**

argument [C, U] 口論, 論争 ◇She got into an *argument* with the teacher. 彼女は先生と口論になった ◇After some heated *argument* a decision was finally made. 激論の末, ついにある決定が下された

row [C] (《英, インフォーマル》)(個人的な問題に関する)騒々しい口論 ◇She left him after a *blazing row*. 激しい口論の末, 彼女は彼を残して去った ◇He'd had a *row* with his son. 彼は息子と口論してしまった ❶報道において, rowは人々や団体の間の公の不和についても用いられる.

fight [C] (《特に米》)(家族・友達・恋人・知り合い同士の)口げんか, 言い争い ◇Did you two have a *fight*? 君たち二人はけんかでもしたの ◇We had a *fight* over money. 私たちはお金のことでけんかになった

quarrel [C] (《特に書き言葉》)(個人的な問題に関する)口げんか, いさかい ◇I don't want to pick a *quarrel* with her. 彼女と言い争いたくはない ❶不可算のquarrelは「不平やけんかの原因」の意味もある. ♦We have no *quarrel* with his methods. (私たちは彼のやり方に関して何ら不満がない).

ノート **argument, row, fight, quarrel の使い分け**：row, fight, quarrelはふつう知り合い同士による個人的な問題に関するものを指す. ♦We had an *argument* with the waiter about the bill. (私たちは勘定のことでウェイターと口論になった). ✗We had a *row/fight/quarrel* with the waiter about the bill. rowは(《英》)でしか実際には用いられず, fightはたいてい(《米》)で用いられる. quarrelはふつうrowやfightほど激しくないが, 長い間続く「仲たがい」を指すこともある. argumentは「激しい口論」の意味でも, 「(意見や立場を守るための真剣な)討論」の意味でも用いられる.

squabble [C] (《ややインフォーマル》)(些細な事に関する)騒々しい口論 ◇There were endless *squabbles* over who should sit where. 誰がどこに座るのかでつまらないけんかがとめどなく続いていた

tiff [C] (《インフォーマル》)(親密な友達・恋人同士の)ちょっとしたけんか ◇She was upset because she'd had a *tiff* with her boyfriend. 彼女は彼氏とちょっとしたけんかをしてむしゃくしゃしていた ◇It's just a lovers' *tiff*. 単なる痴話げんかだよ

'shouting match [C] どなり合いのけんか ◇The meeting had turned into a *shouting match* between the tenants and the landlord. 会議は借地人と地主とのどなり合いのけんかになっていた

2 ☞REASON
argument・case・defence・plea
事が真実[正しい]と説明するために用いる一連の根拠
【類語訳】理由, 論拠, 言い分, 弁護, 弁明, 申し立て

文型&コロケーション
▶an argument/ a case/ a defence **for/ against** sth
▶a **strong/ robust/ legal** argument/ case/ defence
▶to **put forward/ strengthen/ weaken** an argument/ a case/ a defence
▶to **support** an argument/ a case

argument [C] (事が真実[正しい]と説明するために用いる一連の)理由, 論拠 ◇There are strong *arguments* for and against childhood vaccinations. 小児期予防接種に関しては強い賛否両論がある ◇His *argument* was that public spending must be reduced. 彼は公共支出を削減しなければならないと論じた ◇He was able to see both sides of the *argument*. 彼はその論拠を双方の立場から見ることができた ☞ **argue** (CLAIM)

case [C, ふつう単数で] (裁判・討論において一方の支えを支える一連の)事実, 論拠; 言い分 ◇Our lawyer didn't think we had a *case* (= had enough good arguments to win in court). 弁護士は私たちに十分な言い分があるとは思っていなかった ◇The report *makes out* a strong *case* (= gives good arguments) for spending more money on hospitals. その報告書は病院により多くの資金を費やすべき論拠となる ◇the *case* for the defence/prosecution 被告/検察を利する証拠 ◇the *case* for/against private education 私学支持[不支持]の論拠

defence (《英》) (《米》)**defense**) [C] (裁判での)弁護, 弁明 ◇Her *defence* was that she was somewhere completely different at the time of the crime. 彼女の答弁は犯行時には自分はまったく別の所にいたというものだった ◇He wanted to conduct his own *defence*. 彼は自分自身で弁護を行いたいと望んだ

▷**defend** [動] (他, 自) ◇He has announced that he will *defend* himself in the case. 彼はその裁判での弁護を彼自身が行うと発表した ◇Who's *defending*? 誰が弁護しているのですか

plea [C] (《of を伴って》)(《法律》)(法廷への)申し立て ◇He was charged with murder, but got off on a *plea* of insanity. 彼は殺人の容疑が掛けられていたが, 精神異常であると主張して刑を免れた

▷**plead** [動] (他) ◇They hired a top lawyer to *plead* their case. 彼らは自分たちの言い分を述べる一流の弁護士を雇った

army 名

army・force・unit・contingent・legion
組織された軍人の集団
【類語訳】陸軍, 軍, 軍隊, 部隊, 分隊, 軍団

文型&コロケーション
▶(a/ the) **British/ French, etc.** army/ forces/ unit
▶(a/ an) **enemy/ rebel** army/ forces/ units
▶(a) **military** forces/ unit/ contingent
▶to **deploy** an army/ a force/ a unit/ a contingent
▶to **command/ be in command of** an army/ a force/ a unit/ a contingent
▶an army/ a force/ a legion **invades** a place
▶an army/ a force/ a unit/ a legion **advances/ retreats**
▶an army/ a force/ a unit/ a contingent/ a legion **withdraws/ is withdrawn**

army [C+単数・複数動詞] 陸軍 ◇The two opposing *armies* faced each other across the battlefield. 敵対する二つの陸軍が戦場を挟んで互いに向き合った ❶数+単数・複数動詞]は国軍の中の地上で戦う部門. ♦Her husband is *in the army*. (彼女の夫は陸軍に所属している). ♦After leaving school, Mike *went into the army*. (退学してマイクは陸軍に入った). ♦He's an *army* officer. (彼は陸軍将校だ).

force [C+単数・複数動詞] 軍隊 ◇A peace-keeping *force* was deployed to the area. 平和維持軍がその地域に配置された ◇The country now has its own army, air *force* and navy. その国は今や自国の陸軍, 空軍, 海軍を持っている ◇A UN-led *task force* of 28,000 troops was sent to the area. 国連主導による2万8千人から成る機動部隊がその地域に派遣された ❶複数形の forces は陸軍

が所有する武器と兵士, すなわち「軍隊, 軍勢」のこと. ◆The government is negotiating cuts to nuclear *forces*. (政府は核戦力の削減を協議している) ◆the armed forces (または《英》で単にthe forces)は陸・海・空軍全体を指す.

unit [C] (陸軍の)部隊 ◆The army is collaborating with guerrilla *units* in the border region. 国境地帯では陸軍がゲリラ部隊に協力している ◆Medical *units* were operating in the disaster area. 医療部隊が被災地で活動していた ☞ **unit** (DEPARTMENT), **detachment** (TEAM 1)

contingent [C＋単数・複数動詞] (派遣)部隊 ◆The French *contingent* in the UN peacekeeping force withdrew. 国連平和維持軍のフランス派遣部隊が撤退した

legion [C, 単数+単数・複数動詞] (古代ローマ軍の)軍団, レギオン; 軍隊, 部隊 ◆A Roman *Legion* consisted of 6,000 men. ローマ軍の一軍団は6千人から成っていた

arrange 動

arrange • manage • organize • set sth out • lay sth out • sort sth out • align • line sb/sth up
整える[能率よく使う]ため特定の順序に物を置くことを表す
【類語訳】配置する, 整頓する, 整理する, 系統立てる, レイアウトする, 整列させる

── 文型&コロケーション ──
▸ to arrange/ manage/ organize/ set out/ lay out/ align/ line up sth **in** a particular way
▸ to arrange/ manage/ organize/ set out/ lay out/ sort out (your) **things**
▸ to arrange/ manage/ organize/ set out/ sort out your **thoughts/ ideas**
▸ to arrange/ manage/ organize/ set out **information/ data**
▸ to arrange/ manage/ organize/ sort out your **affairs**
▸ to organize/ set out/ lay out your **work**
▸ to arrange/ manage/ organize/ set out/ lay out/ align sth **carefully**
▸ to arrange/ organize/ set out/ lay out sth **neatly**
▸ to arrange/ manage/ organize/ set out/ lay out sth **well/ systematically**

arrange [他] 配置する; 整頓する, 見栄えよく整える ◆The books are *arranged* alphabetically by author. 本は著者名のアルファベット順に並べられている ◆I must *arrange* my financial affairs and make a will. 私は財務関係を整理して遺書を書かねばならない ◆She *arranged* the flowers in a vase. 彼女は花瓶に花を生けた ☞ **arrangement** (DESIGN 名)

manage [他] (金・時間・情報などを)有効的に活用[整理]する, 管理する ◆Don't tell me how to *manage* my affairs. 自分のことは自分でやるから口を出すな ◆It's a computer program that helps you to *manage* data efficiently. コンピュータープログラムこそがデータ管理を効率的にする

organize (英でまた *-ise*) [他] (特定の順序・構成に)整理する, 系統立てる ◆Modern computers can *organize* large amounts of data very quickly. 現代のコンピューターのおかげで大量のデータを非常にすばやく整理することができる ◆You should try and *organize* your time better. 時間のやりくりを改善したほうがいいよ

,set sth 'out 句動詞 (家具などを)配置する, (意見・情報などを)整理する ◆We'll need to *set out* some chairs for the meeting. 会議用にいすをいくつか並べる必要がある ◆Her work is always very well *set out*. 彼女の仕事はいつもとても良く整理されている

,lay sth 'out 句動詞 [しばしば受身で] (計画に従って)配置する, レイアウトする ◆The gardens were *laid out* with lawns, flower beds and fountains. 庭には芝生, 花壇, 噴水が配置されていた ◆This is a very well *laid out* magazine. この雑誌はとてもよくレイアウトされている ☞ **lay-out** (DESIGN 名)

> ノート set sth out と lay sth out の使い分け： set outは個々の物の配置のされ方について言うことが多く, lay outは家, 庭, 店などの配置計画について言うことが多い. 紙面について言うときは, set outはふつう意見や情報の順番を, lay outはページの実際の見た目について用いられる.

,sort sth 'out 句動詞 《インフォーマル》(物の山・中身を)整理する; (考えを)整理する ◆Have you *sorted out* all those things on the floor in the hall? 玄関の床に置いてある物を整理したのか ◆The closet needs *sorting out*. クローゼットを整理する必要がある ◆She wanted to be alone to *sort out* her muddled thoughts. 彼女は混乱した考えを整理するため一人になりたかった

align [他, 自] 《ややフォーマル》 配列する[させる]; 一直線に並ぶ[並べる] ◆Make sure the shelf is *aligned with* the top of the window. 必ず棚が窓の上部と一直線になるようにしてください ◆The top and bottom line of each column on the page should *align*. ページの各段の天地がそろっていたほうがいい

,line sb/sth 'up 句動詞 (人・物を)一列に整列させる ◆The suspects were *lined up* against the wall. 容疑者たちを壁に向かって一列に並ばされた ◆He *lined* the bottles *up* along the shelf. 彼は棚に沿って瓶を一列に並べた

arrival 名

arrival • appearance • coming • advent • approach • entrance
場所に到着する行為や物事の新たな始まりを表す
【類語訳】到来, 出現, 到着, 登場, 開始, 接近, 入場

── 文型&コロケーション ──
▸ sb's/ sth's arrival/ appearance **at/ in** sth
▸ a **sudden** arrival/ appearance/ entrance
▸ sb/ sth's **imminent** arrival/ appearance/ approach
▸ a **dramatic** arrival/ appearance/ entrance
▸ to **signal** sb/ sth's arrival/ coming/ advent/ approach/ entrance
▸ to **announce** sb/ sth's arrival/ coming/ advent/ approach
▸ to **await** sb/ sth's arrival/ appearance/ coming/ approach
▸ the arrival/ coming/ advent/ approach of **spring**
▸ the arrival/ coming/ advent of **television/ the railways**

arrival [C, ふつう単数で, U] 到着; (新技術の)到来, 出現 ◆Her *arrival* was a complete surprise. 彼女が来たことにすっかり驚いた ◆A rainstorm greeted our *arrival*. 雨嵐が我々の到着を迎えた ◆We apologize for the late *arrival* of the Paris train. パリ発[行き]の電車が遅れて到着しましたことをお詫びいたします ◆There are 30 *arrivals and departures* at the ferry terminal daily. そのフェリーターミナルでは一日30便フェリーが発着する ◆Tea will be served *on arrival* at the hotel. ホテルに到着するとティーが出されます ◆the *arrival* of pay TV 有料放送テレ

ビの出現 反意 **departure**
appearance [C, ふつう単数で]（人・物の予期せぬ）到着，出現，出席；（物の）登場 ◇They were startled by the young man's sudden *appearance*. 彼らはその若い男の突然の登場に驚いた ◇I suppose I'd better **put in an appearance** at the party (= go there for a short time). パーティーに顔を出したほうがよさそうだ ◇Gas lighting made its first *appearance* in 1802. ガス照明は1802年に初めて登場した 反意 **disappearance (DISAPPEAR)**
coming [C, ふつう単数で] 到着，（新しい物事の）開始 ◇Her *coming* meant that the department could complete the project on time. 彼女が来たことでその課は時間どおりに計画を完了できた ◇From her window she could watch the *comings and goings* of visitors. 窓から彼女は訪問者の出入りを見ることができた ◇Many jobs were lost with **the coming of** modern technology. 現代の科学技術の到来で多くの仕事がなくなった 反意 **going,** ☞ **come (COME 2)**
advent [単数で]《フォーマル，書き言葉》（重要な人物・時代・発明の）到来 ◇The fighting continued until the *advent* of winter. 戦闘は冬の到来まで続けられた ◇Before the *advent* of the railways, communications were slow and difficult. 鉄道が登場するまで連絡のやり取りはスピードが遅く，また困難なものだった
approach [単数で]（距離的・時間的な）接近 ◇She hadn't heard his *approach*. 彼女には彼の接近が聞こえていなかった ◇They felt apprehensive about the *approach* of war. 戦争が間近に迫っていると危惧していた ☞ **approach (COME 1)**
entrance [C, ふつう単数で]（人目に触れるように）入ること，入場 ◇A fanfare signalled the *entrance* of the king. ファンファーレが王様の入場を知らせた ◇After so many years in show business he knew how to **make an entrance**. 芸能界に長年いたので彼は舞台への登場のしかたを心得ていた ◇The hero **makes his entrance** (= comes onto the stage) in scene two. 主人公は第二幕で登場する 反意 **exit,** ☞ **enter (ENTER)**

arrive

arrive 動 ☞ GET 3

arrive・come・get here/there・turn up・get in・come in・land・show up・appear・roll in・show
場所に至ることを表す
【類語713】到着する，着く，届く，現れる，やって来る，上陸する，着陸する

文型&コロケーション
▶ to arrive/ turn up/ land/ show up/ appear **at/ in/ on** a place
▶ to arrive/ come **for** sb
▶ to arrive/ come/ turn up/ land/ show up/ appear **here/ there**
▶ to **have just** arrived/ come/ got here/ turned up/ got in/ come in/ landed/ appeared
▶ to **be the first/ last to** arrive/ come/ get here/ turn up/ get in/ come in/ land/ show up/ roll up/ appear
▶ to arrive/ come/ get here/ turn up/ get in/ come in/ appear **late**
▶ to arrive/ come/ get here/ turn up/ get in/ come in **early**
▶ to arrive/ get here/ turn up/ get in/ come in/ land **on time**
▶ to arrive/ come/ turn up/ show up/ appear **soon**

▶ to arrive/ get here/ land **safely**
▶ to **finally** arrive/ come/ get here/ turn up/ get in/ come in/ show up/ appear/ show
▶ to **eventually** arrive/ come/ get here/ get in/ come in/ show up/ appear/ roll in

arrive [自]（人が旅の目的地などに）到着する；（物が）届く ◇What time did they *arrive*? 彼らは何時に到着したの ◇We were the first to *arrive*. 私たちが一番に到着した ◇She'll *arrive* in New York at around noon. 彼女はニューヨークに正午到着する予定だ ◇We didn't *arrive back* at the hotel till very late. 私たちはかなり遅くまでホテルに戻らなかった ◇Ambulances quickly *arrived at the scene*. 救急車がすぐに現場に駆けつけた ◇A package *arrived* for you this morning. 今朝荷物が一つあなたに届きました ◇Your application should *arrive* by 29 June. 申込書は6月29日必着です 反意 **leave, depart (LEAVE 1)**
come [自]（場所に）到着する；（…のため）到着する ◇They continued until they *came to* a river. 彼らは歩き続けて川にたどり着いた ◇Your breakfast is *coming* soon! 朝食がもうすぐできますよ ◇Have any letters *come* for me? 手紙が私に届いていない ◇Help *came* at last. ついに助けが来た ◇I've *come for* my book. 本を取りに来ました ◇I've *come to* get my book. 本を取りに来ました ◇I've *come about* my book. 本を取りに来ました ◇He *came* looking for me. 彼は私を探しに来た
'get here/there フレーズ《ややインフォーマル，特に話し言葉》ここ［そこ］へ到着する ◇Email me when you *get there*. そこに着いたら私にメールして ◇Why did it take you so long to *get here*? ここに着くのにどうしてそんなに時間がかかったの ◇By the time I *got there*, I was very cold and hungry. そこへ到着する頃には私はとても寒くて空腹だった
,turn 'up 句動詞《ややインフォーマル，特に話し言葉》（予期せず）現れる，やって来る ◇She was surprised when they *turned up* on her doorstep. 彼らが玄関前の階段に現れると彼女は驚いた ◇After two days the child *turned up safe and well*. 2日後その子どもは無事健康な状態で見つかった ◇She hadn't *turned up* for work that morning. その日の朝，彼女は職場に姿を現さなかった
,get 'in, ,get 'into sth 句動詞《ややインフォーマル，特に話し言葉》（家・職場・旅の終着地に）到着する ◇What time did you *get in* (= arrive home) last night? 昨日の夜は何時に戻ったの ◇I *got in* (= at work) late that morning. その日の朝は遅刻した ◇I'll ask him as soon as he *gets in*. 彼が戻ったらすぐに聞いてみる ◇His train *gets into* Glasgow at 12.22. 彼が乗っている列車はグラスゴーに12時22分に到着します
,come 'in 句動詞（旅の終着点に）到着する；（ニュースが）入ってくる ◇A few minutes later our train *came in*. 数分後，私たちの乗る電車が到着した ◇*Come in* (= enter) and make yourself at home. 中へ入ってくつろいでよ ◇News is *coming in* of a serious accident. 重大事故のニュースが入ってきている
land [自]《ふつう副詞や前置詞と共に》（飛行機・船に）到着［上陸，着陸］する；（厄介な物が）届く ◇Troops *landed* on the island. 軍隊がその島に上陸した ◇We were due to *land* at Gatwick. 私たちはガトウィック空港に到着する予定だ ◇Who were the first men to *land* on the moon? 初めて月に着陸した人たちは誰ですか ◇Why do complaints always *land on my desk* (= why do I always have to deal with them)? どうしてこう不平不満ばか

↳**arrive**

,show 'up 句動 《インフォーマル》（予定どおり）到着する ◇When she *failed to show up* by eight we got worried. 8時になっても彼女が姿を見せなかったので私たちは心配した

appear 自 《ふつう副詞や前置詞と共に》姿を現す ◇By ten o'clock Lee still hadn't *appeared*. 10時になってもリーは来ていなかった ◇A man *appeared* at the door and asked to see her. 一人の男が戸口に姿を現し彼女との面会を求めた ◇The file *appeared* on my desk yesterday. 昨日私の机の上にファイルが置かれていた

,roll 'in 句動 《インフォーマル》（時間を気にせず）到着する ◇Steve eventually *rolled in* around lunchtime. スティーブはようやく昼頃姿を現した

show 自 《しばしば否定文で》《インフォーマル》（待っている場所に）現れる ◇I waited till ten o'clock but she didn't *show*. 私は10時まで待っていたが彼女は来なかった ◇What if nobody *shows*? 誰も来なかったらどうする

article 名 ☞PAPER

article・editorial・piece・column・feature
新聞や雑誌の中の読み物
【類語訳】記事, 社説, 論説, コラム, 欄, 特集

文型&コロケーション
▸ an article/ an editorial/ a piece/ a column/ a feature **in/ on/ about** sth
▸ a **recent** article/ editorial/ piece/ column/ feature
▸ a **newspaper** article/ editorial/ column/ feature
▸ a **magazine** article/ piece/ column/ feature
▸ to **write/ read/ run/ publish** an article/ an editorial/ a piece/ a column/ a feature

article [C] （新聞・雑誌の特定のテーマに関する）記事 ◇Have you seen that *article* about skyscrapers? 超高層ビルに関するあの記事を見ましたか

editorial [C] （新聞の）社説, 論説 ◇In a scathing *editorial*, the paper called on the director to resign. 社説の中で, その新聞は容赦なく理事の辞任を求めた ❶《米》では *editorial* はラジオ[テレビ]局やその経営者などの意見である「声明」を指すこともある.

piece [C] （新聞・雑誌の）記事,（テレビ・ラジオの）ニュース ◇Did you see her *piece* about the Internet in the paper today? 今日の新聞の中でインターネットに関する彼女の記事を見ましたか ☞ **piece** (WORK 名 2)

column [C] コラム, 欄 ◇He writes a *gossip column* (= a column about social events and famous people) for the local paper. 彼は地元紙にゴシップ記事を書いている ◇The website runs an online advice *column* for teenagers. そのウェブサイトには十代の若者向けの人生相談欄がオンラインで掲載されている ☞ **columnist** (REPORTER)

feature [C] （新聞・雑誌の）特集記事,（テレビ・ラジオの）特集 ◇In today's programme we have a special *feature* on education. 今日は番組の中で教育に関する特集を組んでいます

artificial 形

artificial・synthetic・false・man-made・fake・imitation
物が本物でない, 自然に生産されたものでないことを表す
【類語訳】人工の, 合成の, 人造の, 模造の, にせの

文型&コロケーション
▸ artificial/ synthetic/ man-made **fabrics/ fibres/ materials/ products**
▸ artificial/ synthetic/ fake/ imitation **fur/ leather**
▸ artificial/ synthetic/ false/ fake/ imitation **diamonds/ pearls**

artificial （自然のものをまねた）人工の; 本物でない ◇The patient was kept alive by the *artificial* heart for nearly two months. 2か月近くの間, その患者は人工心臓によって生かされていた ◇All food served in the restaurant is completely free from any *artificial* colours and flavours. そのレストランで出されるすべての食べ物には人工着色料と香味料はいっさい含まれておりません ◇I don't like having to do detailed work in *artificial* light. 人工光照明で細かい仕事をさせられるのは好きではない 反意 **natural** ❶ *natural* things は「自然の」もので, 人間によって作られたものではない. ◆ *the natural world* (= of trees, rivers, animals and birds) (自然界). ◆ a country's *natural resources* (= its coal, oil, forests, etc.) (国の天然資源). ◆ My hair soon grew back to its *natural* colour (= after being dyed). (私の髪はすぐに元の地毛の色に戻った).
➤ **artificially** 副 ◇*artificially* created lakes 人造湖

synthetic （化学物質による）合成の ◇*synthetic* drugs/dyes 合成薬品/染料 ◇shoes with *synthetic* soles 底が合成物質でできている靴 反意 **natural**
➤ **synthetically** 副 ◇*synthetically* produced drugs 合成薬品

false 天然ではない; 人工の ◇*false* teeth/eyelashes 入れ歯/付けまつげ ◇a *false* beard and moustache 付けあごひげと口ひげ

,man-'made 人造の; 天然ではない ◇*man-made* fibres such as nylon and polyester ナイロンやポリエステルなどの人造繊維 ◇Europe's largest *man-made* lake ヨーロッパ最大の人造湖 反意 **natural**

fake 模造の; 本物ではない, にせの ◇a *fake* fur jacket 模造の毛皮のジャケット ◇We sprayed *fake* snow over the trees to make it look like winter. 私たちは冬らしく見えるように木の上ににせ物の雪をスプレーでかけた 反意 **genuine** (REAL), ☞ **fake** (FAKE)

imitation [名詞の前で] 模造の; 本物ではない ◇She would never wear *imitation* pearls. 彼女は模造真珠を着けるようなことは絶対にしない ◇He threatened them with an *imitation* gun. 彼はにせ物の銃で彼らを脅した 反意 **genuine** (REAL), ☞ **imitation** (FAKE)

ask 動

1 ask・enquire・demand・pose・consult
情報を得るために口頭[文面]で聞く
【類語訳】尋ねる, 質問する, 問う, 問い詰める, 提起する, 助言を求める

文型&コロケーション
▸ to ask/ enquire **about/ after** sb/ sth
▸ to ask/ enquire/ demand sth **of** sb
▸ to ask/ enquire/ demand **what/ who/ how...**, etc.
▸ to ask/ enquire **politely**

▶to ask/ enquire/ demand **angrily**
▶to ask/ demand **fiercely/ aggressively**

ask [他, 自] 質問する, 尋ねる ◇'Where are you going?' she *asked*.「どこへ行くの」と彼女は聞いた ◇The interviewer *asked* me about my future plans. 面接官は私に将来の計画について質問した ◇Did you *ask* the price? 値段を聞きましたか ◇She *asked* the students their names. 彼女は生徒たちに名前を尋ねた ◇I often get *asked* that! よくそのことを聞かれるよ ◇She *asked* where I lived. 彼女は私がどこに住んでいるか尋ねた ◇I was *asked* if/whether I could drive. 私は運転できるかどうか聞かれた ◇Can I *ask a question*? 質問してもよろしいでしょうか ◇How old are you, *if you don't mind me/ my asking*? おいくつですか. 差し支えなければお聞かせください ◇He *asked* about her family. 彼は彼女の家族について質問した ❶ask to sbのようには言えない. ×I *asked* to my friend what had happened.

enquire (または特に米で **inquire**) [自, 他]《ややフォーマル》質問する, 尋ねる, 問う ◇I called the station to *enquire* about train times. 私は電車の発車時刻について聞くために駅に電話を掛けた ◇She *enquired* after my father. 彼女は私の父の健康状態を尋ねた ◇She *enquired as to* your whereabouts. 彼女が君の居所に関して問い合わせてきました ◇Might I *enquire* why you never mentioned this before? なぜこのことについて以前話さなかったのかお聞かせいただけますか ◇He *enquired* her name. 彼は彼女の名前を尋ねた ☞ **enquiry** (QUESTION 名)

demand [他] 問い詰める ◇'And where have you been?' he *demanded* angrily. 「それで, 君はどこにいたの」と彼は怒って尋ねた ◇'What's your name?' she *demanded* of the girl. 「名前は」と彼女は少女に尋ねた

pose [他]《question と共に》《フォーマル》質問を投げかける[提起する] ◇The new play *poses* some challenging *questions*. その新しい劇は挑戦的な問いをいくつか投げかけている

consult [他] 助言[情報]を求める ◇If the pain continues, *consult* your doctor. もし痛みが続くようなら, 医者に診てもらってください ☞ **consultation** (INTERVIEW 1)

2 ☞ DEMAND 動
ask・seek・call for sth・request・apply・invite・appeal・claim・petition
人に…してほしいと言う
【類語訳】求める, 頼む, お願いする, 申し込む, 申請する, 請う, 要求する, 請願する, 嘆願する

文型&コロケーション
▶to ask/ call/ apply/ appeal/ petition **for** sth
▶to ask for/ seek/ call for/ request/ invite/ appeal for/ claim sth **from** sb
▶to ask/ request sth **of** sb
▶to ask/ call for/ request/ invite/ appeal for/ petition sb **to do** sth
▶to ask/ apply **to do** sth
▶to ask/ request **that**…
▶to **formally** ask for/ seek/ call for/ request/ apply for/ invite sb to do/ claim/ petition for sth
▶to **repeatedly** ask for/ call for/ request/ apply for/ appeal for sth
▶to **explicitly** ask for/ call for/ request/ invite sth

ask [自, 他] 求める, 頼む ◇If you want anything, just *ask*. ほしい物があれば, まあ試しに言ってください ◇I went up to the bar and *asked* for a beer. 私はバーに行ってビールを頼んだ ◇He *asked* me for a job yesterday. 昨日彼は私に仕事がないか尋ねた ◇Why don't you *ask* David's advice? デービッドに助言を求めてみたら ◇Can I *ask* a favour of you? 君にお願いしてもいい ◇I *asked* to see the manager. 私は責任者との面会を求めた ◇All the students were *asked* to complete a form. 生徒全員が用紙に記入するよう求められた ◇I'll *ask* if it's all right to park here. ここに駐車させてもらえないか頼んでくるよ

seek [他]《フォーマル》求める ◇I think it's time we *sought* legal advice. そろそろ法律相談を受けたいのですが ◇She managed to calm him down and *seek* help from a neighbour. 彼女は何とか彼を落ち着かせて近所の人に助けを求めた ☞ **seek** (LOOK 動 2), **seek** (TRY 1)

'call for sth 句動詞《特にジャーナリズム》《公然と》求める ◇The group *called for* the immediate release of the hostages. その集団は人質の即時解放を求めた ◇The opposition is *calling for* the prime minister to resign. 野党は首相の辞任を求めている ☞ **call** (REQUEST)

request [他]《フォーマル》《丁寧・正式に》求める, 頼む, …するようお願いする ◇She *requested* permission to film at the White House. 彼女はホワイトハウスでの撮影許可を求めた ◇You are politely *requested* not to smoke in this restaurant. このレストランでは喫煙を控えていただいております ☞ **request** (REQUEST), **request** (WISH)

apply [自]《文面で就職・大学入学などに》正式に申し込む, 申請する ◇to *apply* for a job/ passport/ grant 仕事/パスポート/助成金を申請する ◇I decided to *apply* to Manchester University. マンチェスター大学に出願することに決めた ◇You can *apply* by letter or on-line. 申し込みは書面またはオンラインで可能です ◇He's *applied* to join the army. 彼は陸軍への入隊を志願している ☞ **applicant** (CANDIDATE), **application** (REQUEST)

invite [他]《フォーマル》《正式に》求める, 請う ◇Successful candidates will be *invited* for interview next week. 合格者には来週面接に来ていただく予定です ◇He *invited* questions from the audience. 彼は聴衆に質問を勧めた

appeal [自]《真剣・緊急に》求める ◇Nationalist leaders have *appealed* for calm. 国民党の指導者たちは事態の沈静化を訴えた ◇Organizers *appealed to* the crowd not to panic. 主催者側は観客にパニックを起こさないよう求めた ◇I am *appealing* on behalf of the famine victims (= asking for money). 私は飢餓の犠牲者を代表して募金の協力を呼びかけているところです ☞ **appeal** (REQUEST)

claim [他, 自]《当然の権利として政府・企業に金銭を》要求する ◇He's not entitled to *claim* unemployment benefit. 彼には失業手当給付金を請求する資格がない ◇She *claimed* damages from the company for the injury she had suffered. 彼女は自分が負った傷害に対して会社に損害賠償を求めた ◇You can *claim on your insurance* for that coat you left on the train. 電車に置き忘れたそのコートに対しては保険請求ができるよ ☞ **claim** (REQUEST)

petition [自, 他] 請願する, 嘆願する; (法廷で正式に)申し立てる ◇Local residents have successfully *petitioned against* the proposals. 地元住民はその計画に反対してうまく請願した ◇The group intends to *petition* the governor for reform of the law. その団体は知事に対し法改正を求める嘆願書を提出するつもりだ ◇His wife *petitioned for divorce* in 1997. 彼の妻は1997年に離婚を申し立てた ☞ **petition** (REQUEST)

assessment 名

assessment・evaluation・review・appraisal・commentary・critique・criticism・estimation
書き物に関する意見や判断
【類語訳】評価, 査定, 論評記事, レビュー, 解説, 注釈, 論述, 標示, 批評文, 見解

文型&コロケーション

- **in** an assessment/ an evaluation/ a review/ an appraisal/ a commentary/ a critique/ sb's estimation
- a **detailed/ general** assessment/ evaluation/ appraisal/ commentary/ critique
- a **critical** assessment/ evaluation/ review/ appraisal/ commentary
- a/ an **thorough/ subjective/ effective** assessment/ evaluation/ appraisal/ critique
- a/ an **objective/ careful** assessment/ evaluation/ appraisal/ criticism
- a **searching** assessment/ appraisal/ critique/ criticism
- a **written** assessment/ appraisal/ commentary/ critique
- to **give** an assessment/ a review/ an appraisal/ a critique
- to **write** an assessment/ a review/ a commentary/ a critique
- to **carry out/ make** an assessment/ evaluation/ appraisal

assessment [C, U] 《ややフォーマル》 評価, 査定, 見解 ◇What is your *assessment* of the situation? その状況に対する君の判断はどうですか ◇We need to make a detailed *assessment* of the risks involved. 関わってくるリスクに関する詳細な査定が必要だ ◇written and oral exams and other forms of *assessment* 筆記試験および口頭試験などの評価形態 ◇We are developing new methods of *risk assessment* for chemicals. 私たちは化学薬品に対する危険性評価のための新たな方法を開発している ❶ assessment はふつう学生の成績や能力, ある状況に関わる問題[危険性, 必要性]に対して用いられる. ☞ TEST 名 2, ☞ **assess** (JUDGE 動), **assess** (TEST 動 2)

evaluation [C, U] 《ややフォーマル》(量・価値・質についての)評価 ◇We've still got to carry out an *evaluation* of the results. 私たちはまだそれらの結果の評価を行わなければならない ◇The new programme is still under *evaluation*. 新計画はまだ評価を受けている段階だ

review [C, U] (本・劇・映画などに関する新聞・雑誌の)論評記事, レビュー ◇The book received **mixed reviews** (= some people liked it, some did not). その本の評価には賛否両論あった ◇The new musical opened to **glowing reviews**. 新しいミュージカルは上演が始まると賞賛に満ちた論評を受けた ◇He submitted his latest novel for *review*. 彼は書評してもらうため新作の小説を提出した ❶《米》では, review には労働者が経営者に対して仕事の成果を報告する面談による「評定」や, その制度の意味もある. ◆ I have my **performance review** tomorrow. 《米》明日私の勤務評定がある. ◆ A formal performance *review* system was introduced five years ago. (正式な勤務評定の制度は5年前に導入された). 《英》ではこれは appraisal と呼ばれる. ☞ **reviewer** (REPORTER)
▷**review** 動 他 ◇The play was *reviewed* in the national newspapers. 其の劇は全国紙で論評された

appraisal [C, U] 《ややフォーマル》評価, 値踏み ◇She read many detailed critical *appraisals* of his work. 彼女は彼の作品に対して詳しく書かれた批判的な評価をたくさん読んでいた ◇She made a quick *appraisal* of the other guests. 彼女は他の招待客を素早く値踏みした ❶《英》では appraisal はふつう労働者の「勤務評定」を意味する(上記). ◆ I've got my *appraisal* tomorrow. 《特に英》明日私の勤務評定がある. ◆ A formal system of **performance appraisal** was introduced five years ago. (正式の勤務評定の制度は5年前に導入された). 《米》ではふつう review と呼ばれるが appraisal も用いられる.
▷**appraise** [T] ◇She stepped back to *appraise* her workmanship. 《フォーマル》彼女は一歩離れて出来栄えを確かめた

commentary [C, U] (本・劇などに関する)解説, 注釈 ; (質のよしあしについての)論評, 標示 ◇He wrote a *commentary on* Paul's letters to the Romans. 彼はローマ人(宛)に宛てたパウロの手紙に関する解説を書いた ◇The film is part love story and part *social commentary*. その映画はある部分は恋愛物語で, またある部分は社会批評だ ❶人が主語で本・劇・映画に関する「解説」を「書く」場合は write a commentary on a book/play/film. 本・劇・映画が主語で社会[政治]的な問題に関する「批評」の場合は be a commentary on social/political issues.

critique [C] (思想・芸術などに関する)批評文 ◇She wrote a feminist *critique* of Freud's theories. 彼女はフロイト理論に関するフェミニスト側からの批評を書いた
▷**critique** 動 他 ◇Her job involves *critiquing* designs by fashion students. ファッション専攻の学生のデザインを批評することも彼女の仕事だ

criticism [U] (本・音楽などに関する)批評 ◇She has written several works of **literary criticism**. 彼女は文芸批評の作品をいくつか書いている ◇art *criticism* 芸術批評
▷**criticize** 《英でまた-ise》 動 他 ◇We were taught how to *criticize* poems. 《英》私たちは詩の批評の仕方を教わった

estimation [単数で] 《ややフォーマル》(個人の)判断, 意見, 評価, 見解 ◇Who is the best candidate *in your estimation*? あなたの評価では誰が一番の候補者ですか ◇Since he left his wife, he's certainly **gone down in my estimation** (= I have less respect for him). 彼が奥さんと別れて以来, 私の彼に対する評価は確実に下がっている ◇She **went up in my estimation** (= I have more respect for her) when I discovered how much charity work she does. 彼女がどれだけ慈善活動を行っているかを知って, 私の中で彼女の株は上がった

assignment 名 ☞ PAPER, TASK

assignment・project・homework・exercise
なすべき仕事, 特に勉強の一環としてやるべき事柄
【類語訳】任務, 課題, 研究課題, 宿題, 練習問題

文型&コロケーション

- a project/ homework/ an exercise **on** sth
- a/ an **easy/ difficult** assignment/ exercise
- (a) **geography/ history/ biology, etc.** project/ homework
- to **do** an assignment/ a project/ your homework/ an exercise
- to **have** an assignment/ some homework **to do**
- to **get on with** an assignment/ a project/ your homework
- to **finish** an assignment/ a project/ your homework

▶ to **give sb/ set (sb)** an assignment/ their homework/ some exercises

assignment [C] (仕事・勉強の一環として割り当てられた)任務, 課題 ◇You will be expected to complete three written *assignments*. あなたは3つの課題を書き上げることを求められるだろう ◇I'd set myself a tough *assignment*. 私は自らきつい課題に取り組んでいた ◇She's **on assignment** in Greece at the moment. 今彼女はギリシャに派遣されている

project [C] (学生の一定期間にわたる)研究課題 ◇My class is doing a *project* on medieval towns. 私のクラスでは中世都市に関する研究課題に取り組んでいます ◇The final term will be devoted to *project work*. 最終学期は研究課題の作業に専念することになるだろう

homework [U] 宿題 ◇I still haven't done my geography *homework*. 私はまだ地理の宿題をやっていません ◇How much *homework* do you get? 宿題はどれくらいの量ですか ◇I have to write up the notes **for** *homework*. 宿題で講義ノートをまとめなければならない

exercise [C] 練習問題 ◇grammar *exercises* 文法の練習問題 ◇Do one *exercise* for homework. 宿題として練習問題を一つやりなさい

atmosphere 名

atmosphere・climate・mood・tone・spirit・aura・feeling・feel・flavour
特定の場所や状況で受ける全体的な感覚
【類語訳】雰囲気, 感じ, 風潮, 情勢, 気分, ムード, 調子, 性質, 気質, 精神, オーラ, 印象

[文型&コロケーション]

▶ the **general** atmosphere/ climate/ mood/ tone/ spirit/ feeling/ feel/ flavour
▶ an **international** atmosphere/ climate/ feel/ flavour
▶ (a) **hostile** atmosphere/ climate/ tone
▶ a **festive** atmosphere/ mood/ spirit/ feel
▶ a **welcoming** atmosphere/ aura/ feel
▶ the **political** atmosphere/ climate/ mood/ tone/ flavour
▶ to **create** an atmosphere/ a climate/ a mood/ a spirit/ an aura/ a feeling/ a feel
▶ to **reflect** the atmosphere/ climate/ mood/ tone/ spirit/ feeling (of sth)
▶ to **capture** the atmosphere/ mood/ tone/ spirit/ feeling/ flavour of sth
▶ to **evoke** an atmosphere/ a mood/ a spirit/ a feeling
▶ to **take on** an atmosphere/ a tone/ an aura/ a feel/ a flavour
▶ to **convey** an atmosphere/ a mood/ a spirit/ a feeling/ a flavour

atmosphere [C, U] (場所・状況の)雰囲気;(二者間[集団の中]にある)感じ ◇The hotel offers a friendly *atmosphere* and personal service. そのホテルは親しみやすい雰囲気と個人に合わせたサービスを提供している ◇The children grew up in an *atmosphere* of violence and insecurity. 子どもたちは暴力と危険を感じながら育った ◇The old house is full of *atmosphere* (= it is very interesting). その古い家はとても趣がある ◇There was an *atmosphere* of mutual respect between them. 彼らはお互いを尊敬し合っている感じがした

climate [C] (ある時代の)風潮;(場所の)情勢 ◇The new policies have created a *climate* of fear. 新しい政策は恐怖の風潮を生み出した ◇There's been a change in the *climate of opinion* (= what people generally are thinking about a particular issue). 世論に変化が起きている ◇He admitted that the economic *climate* has rarely been worse. 彼は経済情勢が極めて悪化していることを認めた ❶ *climate* の後には fear, suspicion, distrust, despair, hostility など否定的な語をしばしば伴う.

mood [単数で] (一団の人々が抱く)気分, ムード;(一団の人々の間の)雰囲気 ◇The *mood* of the meeting was distinctly pessimistic. 会議のムードは明らかに悲観的だった ◇We need a leader who can gauge the **popular** *mood*. 私たちは市民感情が推し量れる指導者を必要としている ◇The movie captures the *mood* of the interwar years perfectly. その映画は両大戦間の時代の人々の雰囲気を完璧にとらえている

> **ノート** atmosphere と mood の使い分け : atmosphere は特に場所について用い, 一定期間同じ状態を保つ可能性があるもの. mood はある時の人々の「気分」について用い, 時と共に移ろいやすいものである. ×The hotel offers a friendly *mood*. ×The children grew up in a *mood* of violence. ×a leader who can gauge the popular *atmosphere*.

tone [単数で] (文章などの)調子, (その場の)雰囲気 ◇The overall *tone* of the book is gently nostalgic. その本には全般的になつかしさがゆったりと漂っている ◇The article was moderate **in tone** and presented both sides of the case. 記事の調子は穏やかで意見の両面を伝えていた ◇She **set the tone for** the meeting with a firm statement of company policy. 彼女は社の方針をはっきりと述べて会議の雰囲気を作った ◇Trust you to **lower the tone** of the conversation! 君は相変わらず会話の品を落としてくれるね

spirit [単数で] 特質, 精神 ◇The exhibition captures the *spirit* of the Swinging Sixties. その展覧会は活気に満ちた60年代の精神を見事にとらえている ◇His poetry summed up **the spirit of the age**. 彼の詩はその時代の精神を凝縮していた ❶ spirit は特に特定の時代の人々の感情・態度・振る舞いについて言うときに用いられる. ◆ the *spirit* of the 70s/the age/the times/the Enlightenment (70年代/その時代/啓蒙運動の精神).

aura [C] (人・場所の)独特の雰囲気, オーラ ◇There was a faint *aura* of mystery about him. 彼にはかすかに謎めいた雰囲気があった ◇The mountains have a magical *aura*. その山々には不思議なオーラがある ☞ **air** (APPEARANCE)

feeling [単数で] (場所・状況が人に与える)雰囲気, 感じ ◇They have managed to recreate the *feeling* of the original theatre. 元の劇場が持っていた雰囲気が何とか再現された ◇There was a general *feeling* of change in the air. 雰囲気の変化をみんなが感じていた ☞ **feel** (SEEM)

feel [単数で] (場所・状況がかもし出す)印象, 雰囲気 ◇It's a big city but it has the *feel* of a small town. 大都市だが小さな町のような感じがする ◇There is an international *feel to* the restaurant. そのレストランには国際的な雰囲気がある

flavour (《英》(米 **flavor**)) [単数で] (他の物事を思い出させる)特質, 雰囲気 ◇The children experience a *flavour* of medieval life. 子どもたちは中世の生活の雰囲気を味わっている ◇The music festival has taken on a distinctly

↪atmosphere   attach, attack

German *flavour*. その音楽祭は明らかにドイツ的な雰囲気を帯びていた

A attach 動

attach・tie・fix・put・stick・secure・strap・glue・tape・fasten
何かを使ってある物を他の物の中や上に、あるいは一緒にくっ付けることを表す
【類語訳】付ける、添付する、結び付ける、縛る、固定する、貼り付く、留める、接着する、取り付ける

文型&コロケーション

▶ to attach/ tie/ fix/ stick/ secure/ strap/ glue/ tape/ fasten sth **to** sth
▶ to tie/ fix/ put/ stick/ strap/ glue/ tape/ fasten sth **on** sth
▶ to tie/ fix/ stick/ fasten sth **into** sth
▶ to tie/ fix/ stick/ strap/ glue/ tape/ fasten sth **together**
▶ to tie/ fix/ stick/ strap/ glue sth **down**
▶ to tie/ fix/ fasten sth **back**
▶ to tie/ glue/ tape sth **up**
▶ to attach/ tie/ fix/ stick/ secure sth **firmly**
▶ to attach/ tie/ fix/ tape/ fasten sth **securely**

attach [他]（ある物を他の物に）付ける、添付する ◇He *attached* the rope securely to a tree. 彼はロープを木にしっかりと結び付けた ◇I *attach* a copy of the contract for your records. 契約書のコピーを記録用に添付します ◇I am *attaching* the image as a PDF file (= sending it with an email). 画像をpdfファイルとして添付します ❶ *attach* はビジネスレターを書くときによく用いられる。 反意 **detach** (UNDO)
tie [他]《ふつう副詞や前置詞と共に》（ひも・ロープなどで）結び付ける、縛る ◇Her hands had been *tied* together. 彼女は両手を縛られていた ◇The label was *tied* on with string. ラベルはひもで付けられていた ◇She *tied* back her hair with a ribbon. 彼女はリボンで髪を後ろ縛りにした
反意 **untie** (UNDO)
fix [他]《特に英》（動かないように）固定する ◇Start by *fixing* a post in the ground. 柱を地中に固定することから始めよう ◇He *fixed* the shelf to the wall. 彼は壁に棚を取り付けた
put [他]《副詞や前置詞と共に》（ある物を他の物に）付ける、固定する ◇We're not allowed to *put* posters on the walls. 壁にポスターを貼ることは許されていません ◇We had to *put* new locks on all the doors. すべてのドアに新しい錠を取り付けなければならなかった
stick [他, 自]《ふつう副詞や前置詞と共に》（粘着性物質で）付ける；貼り付く ◇I forgot to *stick* a stamp on the envelope. 封筒に切手を貼るのを忘れた ◇Her wet hair was *sticking* to her head. 濡れた髪が彼女の頭に貼り付いていた ◇This glue's useless — the pieces just won't *stick*. この接着剤は使えない—部品がまったく付かないもの
▷ **sticky** 形 ◇*sticky* tape 粘着テープ
secure [他]《ふつう副詞や前置詞と共に》（ある物を他の物に）しっかりと付ける ◇She *secured* the rope to the back of the car with a firm knot. 彼女は車の後ろにロープを固く結んでしっかりと付けた ◇Wrap a bandage around the arm and *secure* it with tape or a pin. 包帯を腕に巻いてテープやピンで留めましょう
strap (-**pp**-) [他]《ふつう副詞や前置詞と共に》（人・物が場所から離れないように）ひもで留める ◇He *strapped* the knife to his leg. 彼はナイフを足に結わえ付けた ◇Make sure your passengers are *strapped* in (= wearing their seat belts). 同乗者がシートベルトをしているか確認しましょう
glue [他]《ふつう副詞や前置詞と共に》接着剤で貼り付ける、接着する ◇She *glued* the label onto the box. 彼女は箱にラベルを貼った ◇*Glue* the pieces of wood together. いくつかの木片を接着してください ◇Make sure the edges are *glued* down. 両端がぴったりと接着されているか確認してください
tape [他]《ふつう副詞や前置詞と共に》 粘着テープで留める；粘着テープで取り付ける ◇Put it in a box and *tape* it up securely. 箱の中に入れてテープでしっかりと留めましょう ◇Someone had *taped* a message onto the door. 誰かがドアに伝言をテープで貼っていた
fasten [他]《ふつう副詞や前置詞と共に》（何かで）特定の位置に固定する、他の物に取り付ける ◇She opened the window and *fastened* back the shutters. 彼女は窓を開けてから雨戸を元に戻した ◇He *fastened* the papers together with a paper clip. 彼はクリップで書類を留めた

attack 名

1 attack・strike・invasion・raid・assault・offensive・aggression・incursion
敵に対する軍事行動を表す
【類語訳】攻撃、急襲、空襲、侵攻、奇襲、侵略、侵害、進入

文型&コロケーション

▶ an attack/ a strike/ a raid/ an assault/ an offensive/ aggression **against** sb/ sth
▶ an attack/ a strike/ an assault/ an offensive/ an incursion **on** sb/ sth
▶ **in** an attack/ a strike/ an invasion/ a raid/ an assault/ an offensive/ an incursion
▶ (a) **military** attack/ strike/ invasion/ raid/ assault/ offensive/ aggression/ incursion
▶ a **full-scale** attack/ invasion/ assault/ offensive
▶ a **successful** attack/ strike/ invasion/ raid/ assault/ offensive
▶ an **all-out** attack/ assault/ offensive
▶ an **air** attack/ strike/ raid/ assault/ offensive
▶ to **plan/ launch** an attack/ a strike/ an invasion/ a raid/ an assault/ an offensive
▶ to **mount** an attack/ an assault/ an offensive
▶ to **make** an attack/ a raid/ an assault/ an incursion
▶ to **resist** (an) attack/ an invasion/ an assault/ (an) aggression

attack [C, U]（戦争での）攻撃 ◇He ordered his men to mount an *attack* on the city. 彼は部下に対してその都市に攻撃を仕掛けるよう命令した ◇The patrol came under *attack* from all sides. パトロール隊が四方八方から攻撃を受けた
strike [C]（軍事的な）急襲、空襲 ◇The effects of the air *strikes* had been devastating. 空襲の効果は壊滅的なものだった ◇They launched a **pre-emptive strike** (= before the enemy could attack). 彼らは先制攻撃を仕掛けた
invasion [C, U]（軍の武力による他国への）侵入、侵攻 ◇She left Czechoslovakia after the Russian *invasion* in 1968. 1968年のロシアによる侵攻の後、彼女はチェコスロヴァキアを後にした ◇The *invasion* force comprised

attack

3,000-5,000 heavily armed troops. 侵攻軍は3〜5千人の重武装した部隊から成っていた ☞ **invade** (INVADE)

raid [C] (兵隊・戦艦・戦闘機による)急襲, 奇襲 ◇Hundreds of civilians were killed in the air *raids*. 何百人もの市民がその突然の空襲で命を落とした

assault [C] (場所を制圧するための)攻撃 ◇An *assault* on the capital was launched in the early hours of the morning. 首都に対する攻撃は早朝に行われた

offensive [C] (時に長期にわたる)計画的な軍事攻撃 ◇The final *offensive* was launched in the spring. 最終攻撃は春に行われた

aggression [U] (他国への)攻撃, 侵害 ◇Each country agreed to halt all *acts of aggression* against the other's territory. 各国は他国の領土に対するあらゆる侵略行為の停止に合意した

incursion [C] 《フォーマル》(突然の・一時的な越境による敵の支配地への)進入 ◇Border patrols were increased to deter further *incursions* by foreign forces. 外国軍のさらなる進入を防ぐため国境警備隊が増員された

2 attack・rape・assault・attempt
人を殺傷するために暴力を用いる行為
【類語訳】攻撃, 襲撃, 強姦, レイプ, 暴行, 殺人未遂

【文型&コロケーション】
▶ an attack/ a rape/ an assault **by** sb
▶ an attack/ assault **on/ against** sb
▶ a/ an **violent/ brutal/ savage/ vicious/ alleged** attack/ rape/ assault
▶ a/ an **serious/ unprovoked/ racial/ sexual/ physical** attack/ assault
▶ an **attempted** rape/ assault
▶ to **carry out** an attack/ assault

attack [C] (人を殺傷するために暴力を用いる)攻撃, 襲撃 ◇Police have reported a series of racist *attacks*. 警察は人種差別主義者による一連の襲撃を報告した ◇A child is recovering in hospital after a serious *attack* by a stray dog. 野良犬のひどい襲撃に遭ったが、子どもは病院で快復しつつある

rape [U, C] 強姦, レイプ ◇He was charged with *rape*. 彼は強姦の罪で告発された ◇There has been an increase in the number of reported *rapes*. 強姦の届け出件数が増加している

assault [U, C] 《ややフォーマル》暴行 ◇Both men were charged with *assault*. 男は二人とも暴行の罪で告発された ◇A significant number of *indecent assaults* on women go unreported. 女性に対する強制わいせつ行為かなりの件数が届け出られないままである

attempt [C] 殺人の試み, 殺人未遂 ◇Someone has *made an attempt on* the President's *life*. 大統領を殺害しようとした者がいる

attack 動

1 attack・assault・beat sb up・mug・strike
人を殺傷したり、人から金品を奪うために暴力を用いることを表す
【類語訳】攻撃する, 襲う, 暴行する, 急襲する

【文型&コロケーション】
▶ to attack/ assault/ beat up sb **with** sth
▶ to **get** beaten up/ mugged
▶ to **violently** attack sb/ assault sb/ beat sb up

attack [他, 自] 攻撃する, 襲う ◇The man *attacked* him with a knife. 男は彼をナイフで襲った ◇Most dogs will not *attack* unless provoked. たいていの犬は怒らせなければ襲ってこない

assault [他] 《ややフォーマル》(犯罪行為として)暴行する ◇He has been charged with *assaulting* a police officer. 彼は警察官への暴行の罪で告発されている ◇He admitted *indecently assaulting* the child. 彼は子どもに対する強制わいせつ行為を認めた

,beat sb 'up 句動詞 (殴る蹴るの)暴行を加える ◇He was badly *beaten up* by a gang of thugs. 彼は暴漢たちから手ひどい暴行を受けた

mug (**-gg-**) [他, しばしば受身で] (公衆の場で金を)強奪する ◇She was *mugged* in the street in broad daylight. 彼女は真っ昼間に路上で強盗の被害に遭った

▶ **mugging** 名 [U, C] *Mugging* is on the increase in the area, especially after dark. その地域では特に暗くなってからの強盗の被害が増えている ◇Murders, kidnaps and *muggings* are reported daily in the newspapers. 新聞では殺人, 誘拐, 強盗が毎日報道されている

strike [自] 攻撃する, 急襲する ◇Police fear that the killer may *strike* again. 警察は殺人犯の再犯を心配している ◇The lion crouched ready to *strike*. ライオンは身をかがめて攻撃態勢に入った

2 ☞ INVADE
attack・strike・storm・charge・raid
戦争において敵を襲うことを表す
【類語訳】攻撃する, 急襲する, 突撃する, 奇襲する

【文型&コロケーション】
▶ to strike/ charge **at** sb/ sth
▶ to attack/ strike/ charge **the enemy**
▶ to attack/ strike **a target**
▶ to attack/ storm a/ an **house/ building/ embassy**
▶ **soldiers/ troops/ police** attack/ storm/ charge/ raid sth
▶ **aircraft** attack/ strike/ raid sth

attack [他, 自] 攻撃する ◇At dawn the army *attacked* the town. 夜明けに軍はその街を攻撃した ◇The guerrillas usually *attack* at night. ゲリラはふつう夜に攻撃を仕掛ける

strike [自, 他] 攻撃する, 急襲する ◇The guerrillas *struck* with deadly force. ゲリラが殺傷能力の高い武器で急襲を仕掛けた ◇Warplanes *struck* several targets in the city. 戦闘機がその都市のいくつかの標的を急襲した

storm [他, 自] (占拠するため襲う)急襲する ◇Police *stormed* the building and captured the gunman. 警察は建物を急襲して武装犯を捕まえた ◇Soldiers *stormed* into the city at dawn. 兵士たちは夜明けに都市を急襲した

charge [自, 他] 突進して襲う, 突撃する ◇We *charged* at the enemy. 私たちは敵に突撃した ◇The bull put its head down and *charged*. 雄牛は頭を下げて突進した ◇He ordered his troops to *charge* the enemy lines. 彼は自分の隊に敵陣へ突撃するよう命令した

raid [他] 不意に襲撃する, 奇襲[急襲]する ◇Villages along the border are regularly *raided*. 国境沿いの村々は何度も不意の襲撃を受けている ◇a *raiding* party (= a group of soldiers, etc. that attack a place) 奇襲部隊

attempt 名

attempt・effort・try・go・shot・stab
何か、とりわけ困難なことをしてみようとする行為を表す
【類語訳】試み、企て、努力、奮闘、試し

文型&コロケーション
- an attempt/ a try/ a go/ a shot/ a stab **at** sth
- an attempt/ effort **to do** sth
- **in** an attempt/ effort to do sth
- a **first/ last/ good** attempt/ effort/ try/ go/ shot/ stab
- a **serious** attempt/ effort/ try/ go/ shot
- a/ an **valiant/ brave/ feeble/ unsuccessful** attempt/ effort/ stab
- to **have** a try/ go/ shot/ stab
- to **make** an attempt/ an effort/ a stab
- to **give** sth a try/ go/ shot
- to **take** a shot/ stab at sth
- to **be worth** a try/ go/ shot/ stab

attempt [C, U] (失敗することも多い)試み、企て ◇Two factories were closed in an *attempt* to cut costs. 二つの工場が経費削減を試みて閉鎖された ◇The couple made several *attempts* at a compromise. その二人は何度か和解を試みた ◇They **made no attempt to** escape. 彼らは逃げようとはしなかった ◇I passed my driving test **at the first attempt**. 一発で運転免許試験に合格した ◇The previous *attempt* on the world record was abandoned last year due to bad weather. 世界記録樹立への前回の試みは昨年は悪天候により断念された
☞ **attempt** (TRY 1)

effort [C] 努力、奮闘 ◇I'll make a special *effort* to finish on time this week. 今週は予定どおりに終わるように特別に努力するつもりです ◇I didn't really feel like going out, but I'm glad I **made the effort**. あまり外出したくなかったけれど、頑張ってよかったと思う ◇The local clubs are **making every effort** to interest more young people. 地元のクラブはあらゆる努力を払ってもっと若者たちの気を引こうとしている ◇Despite **our best efforts**, we didn't manage to win the game. 最善の努力はしたがどうにも試合には勝てなかった

> ノート **attempt**と**effort**の使い分け：多くの場合、どちらを使っても構わない。◆They met once more in an *attempt/effort* to find a solution. (彼らは解決策を見いだそうとしてもう一度会った)。**attempt**はしばしば、何かをしようとする、何かを達成しようといった行動を強調する。◆ a coup/ assassination/suicide *attempt* (クーデター/暗殺/自殺の企て)。✗a coup/assassination/suicide *effort*。**effort**は、何かをしようとして投じる作業や労力を特に強調する。◆ a great/enormous/strenuous *effort* (大変な/途方もない/懸命の努力)。✗a great/enormous/strenuous *attempt*。

try [C, ふつう単数で] ((ややインフォーマル)) (うまくいかない可能性を念頭においた)試み、努力 ◇I don't think I'll be any good at tennis, but I'll give it a *try*. テニスは少しもうまくならないと思うけどやってみようは思う ◇I doubt they'll be able to help, but it's **worth a try** (= worth asking them). 彼らが手を貸してくれるとは思えないけれど、頼んでみて損はない ◇Never mind — it was a good *try*. 気にしなくていい—よく試みた ◇The US negotiators decided to **make** another **try at** reaching a settlement. ((米)) 米国の交渉人は合意を目指してもう一度やってみることにした
☞ **try** (TRY 1)

go [C] ((英、ややインフォーマル)) (うまくいかない可能性を念頭においた)試み、努力 ◇You should have a *go* at answering all the questions. すべての質問に答えてみるべきだね ◇It took three *goes* to get it right. 三回やってみてようやくうまくいった

shot [C, ふつう単数で] ((インフォーマル)) (達成するための)試み、企て ◇The team are looking good for a *shot* at the title. そのチームは選手獲得に向けてうまくいっているようだ ◇Just **give it your best shot** (= try as hard as you can) and you'll be fine. やれるだけのことがやれれば大丈夫だよ

stab [C, ふつう単数で] ((インフォーマル)) (経験・技量の伴わない)試み ◇I've always enjoyed acting, but I'd like to have a *stab* at directing one day. いつも演じるのを楽しんできたけど、いつか監督をやってみたいなあ

attention 名

attention・interest・notice・concentration・regard
重要なことだと思うので注意深く聴いたり、見たり、考えたりする行為
【類語訳】注意、留意、注目、関心、興味、認知、集中力、集中、配慮、思いやり

文型&コロケーション
- **close/ media/ personal/ special** attention/ interest
- **deep/ growing/ great/ intense** interest/ concentration
- **full/ total/ undivided** attention/ concentration
- **careful/ public** attention/ notice
- to **catch/ get/ grab/ lose** sb's attention/ interest
- to **lose** interest/ concentration
- to **hold/ focus** sb's attention/ interest/ concentration
- to **attract/ bring** sth **to/ come to/ escape** sb's attention/ notice
- to **turn** your attention/ interest/ concentration **to** sth
- to **pay (no)** attention/ regard **to** sth

attention [U] 注意、留意、注目 ◇He wanted to **call/ draw attention to** the problem. 彼はその問題への注目を促したかった ◇Now, please sit up and **pay attention** (= listen carefully) to what I am going to say. それでは、きちんと座って私の言うことを注意して聴いてください ◇Don't **pay** any *attention* to what they say (= don't think that it is important or be upset by it). 彼らの言うことに耳を貸すな ◇She tried to attract the waiter's *attention*. 彼女はウェイターの注意を引こうとした ◇Films with the big stars always attract great *attention*. 例の大スターが出演する映画はいつも大きな注目を集める ◇Small children have a very **short attention span** (= become easily bored). 小さな子どもは集中力の持続が非常に短い ◇Can I have your *attention* please? ((フォーマル、話し言葉)) ご注目いただけますか ◇The child was used to being the **centre of attention**. その子どもは注目の的になることに慣れていた

interest [単数で, U] 関心、興味 ◇I told him about it but he showed no *interest*. 彼にそれについて話したが、まったく興味を示さなかった ◇Several people expressed an *interest* in learning the game. 何人かがその遊びを覚えることに興味を示した ◇Does she **take an interest in**

your research? 彼女はあなたの研究に興味を持っていますか ◇*As a matter of interest* (= I would like to know) what time did the party finish? お聞きしたいのですがパーティーは何時に終わりましたか ◇*Just out of interest,* (= I would like to know but it is not important) how much did it cost? 興味本位で知りたいだけなんですが, 費用はどれくらい掛かりましたか

notice [U] 注目, 注意 ◇*Don't take any notice of* what you read in the papers. 新聞に書かれていることなんて気にすることはない ◇*Take no notice of* what he says. 彼の言うことなんて気にするな ◇It was Susan who brought the problem to my *notice* (= told me about it). 《フォーマル》私にその問題を知らせたのはスーザンだった ◇It will not have escaped your *notice* that there have been some changes in the company. 《フォーマル》会社内のいくつかの変化に気づいたはずです ☞ **notice** (NOTICE)

concentration [U] 集中; 集中力 ◇Tiredness affects your powers of *concentration*. 疲労は集中力に影響を及ぼす ◇The noise had disturbed his *concentration*. 騒音で彼の集中力はかき乱されていた ◇He stressed the need for greater *concentration* on environmental issues. 彼は環境問題にもっと集中する必要性を強調した
▷ **concentrate** 動 [自, 他] ◇I can't *concentrate* with all that noise going on. あんな騒音がしていたら集中できない ◇I decided to *concentrate* all my efforts on finding somewhere to live. 住む場所を見つけることに全力を注ぐことに決めた

regard [U] 《フォーマル》注意, 配慮, 思いやり ◇They show scant *regard for* other people's property. 彼らは他人の所有物に対する配慮が足りない ◇He was driving *without regard to* speed limits. 彼は制限速度などお構いなしに運転していた ◇Social services should *pay proper regard to* the needs of inner-city areas. 社会事業はスラム化した都心部が必要としていることにきちんと目を向けるべきだ

attitude 名 ☞ VIEW 1

attitude・view・perspective・point of view・stance・position・outlook・level・line・angle・side・stand
人や物事に関する特定の思いや感じ方
【類語訳】態度, 姿勢, とらえ方, 考え方, 観点, 見方, スタンス, 立場, 人生観, 世界観, 見方, 主義, 方針

【文型&コロケーション】
▶sb's view/ a perspective/ a stance/ a position/ an outlook/ a line/ an angle/ a stand **on** sth
▶a stance/ stand **against** sb/ sth
▶**from** the perspective/ point of view/ position/ angle of sb/ sth
▶**different/ various** attitudes/ views/ perspectives/ points of view/ stances/ positions/ outlooks/ levels/ angles/ sides
▶an **alternative** view/ perspective/ point of view/ position/ angle
▶a **personal** attitude/ view/ perspective/ point of view/ stance/ position/ level/ angle/ stand
▶the **general** attitude/ view/ perspective/ point of view/ position/ outlook
▶a **popular** attitude/ view/ perspective
▶a **positive/ negative** attitude/ view/ perspective/ point of view/ stance/ outlook/ angle
▶a **sympathetic** attitude/ view/ point of view/ angle
▶a **critical** attitude/ view/ perspective/ point of view/ stance
▶a **practical** attitude/ view/ perspective/ point of view/ outlook
▶to **take** an attitude/ a view/ a perspective/ a point of view/ a stance/ a position/ a line/ a side/ a stand
▶to **adopt** an attitude/ a view/ a perspective/ a point of view/ a stance/ a position/ an outlook/ a line
▶to **have** an attitude/ a view/ a perspective/ a point of view/ an outlook/ a line/ an angle
▶to **change** an attitude/ your view/ your perspective/ your point of view/ your stance/ your position/ your outlook/ sides
▶to **challenge** an attitude/ a view/ a perspective

attitude [C] 態度, 考え方, 姿勢 ◇Her *attitude to* her parents has always been somewhat negative. 彼女の両親に対する態度はいつもやや否定的である ◇What is your *attitude towards* the job as a whole? 仕事に対するあなたの考え方は総じてどんなものですか ◇I tend to take the *attitude* that it's best to leave well alone. 私は現状のままでよしとする態度を取りがちだ ◇If you want to pass your exams you'd better change your *attitude*. 試験に合格したいならば考え方を変えたほうがいい

view [C, ふつう単数で] 物事のとらえ方 [考え方] ◇He has a pretty optimistic *view* of life. 彼はかなり楽観的な人生観を持っている ◇The traditional *view* was that marriage was for life. 結婚は死ぬまで続くものというのが伝統的な考え方だった

perspective [C, ふつう単数で] (問題に対する) 見方, 観点; (物事に関する) 考え方 ◇Try to approach the problem from a different *perspective*. 異なる観点から問題に取り組んでみよう ◇We need to take a global *perspective* on the environment. 私たちは環境に対してグローバルな視点に立つ必要がある

,point of 'view [C] 観点, 見方 ◇These statistics are important from an economic *point of view*. 経済的な観点からしてこれらの統計は重要である ◇The book is written from a child's *point of view*. その本は子どもの視点で書かれている

stance [C] (公の) 見解, 立場, スタンス ◇What's the newspaper's *stance* on the war? 戦争に対するその新聞のスタンスはどんなものですか ◇He's known for his anti-immigration *stance*. 彼は移民排斥の立場で知られている

position [C] (自分たちの行動に影響を与える特定の問題に対する) 態度, 立場 ◇Our party's *position* on education is very clear. 教育に関するわが党の見解はとても明確だ ◇The official *position* was that of refusing to talk to terrorists. 当局の姿勢はテロリストとの対話を拒否するものだった

【ノート】**stance** と **position** の使い分け: stance は有名人・新聞が時事的な問題に対する「見解」を述べるときに用いられ, position よりも一時的 [個人的] な「見解」を指す. position は長期にわたる [公的な] もので, 特定の問題に対する発言よりは実際に取る「態度」を指す.

outlook [C] (人生・世界に関する) 見解, 態度 ◇He has a very practical *outlook* on life. 彼は非常に実際的な人生観を持っている ◇Most western societies are liberal *in outlook*. たいていの西洋社会では考え方は自由である

↪attitude

audience, authorities

level [C] 特定の見方[とらえ方], レベル ◇On a more personal *level*, I would like to thank Jean for all the help she has given me. より個人的には、ジーンのあらゆる助力に感謝したい ◇Fables can be understood on various *levels*. 寓話はさまざまな観点からとらえることができる

line [C, ふつう単数で] (政府・政党・政治家などによる公式の)態度、主義、方針 ◇The government took a *hard line* on the strike. 政府はストライキに対し強硬路線を取った ◇The MP supported the *official line* on education. その下院議員は教育に関する政府の方針を支持した ◇He was expelled from the party for refusing to *toe the party line* (= follow the party's official opinions and policies). 彼は党の方針に従うことを拒否したかどで党から追放された

angle [C] (状況・問題・テーマに関する)考え方 ◇We're looking for a new *angle* for our next advertising campaign. 次の広告キャンペーンの新たな切り口を探しています ◇The article concentrates on the human *angle* (= the part that concerns people's emotions) of the story. 記事はその話の人情的な部分にスポットを当てている

side [C] (議論・契約における)一方の意見 [姿勢、立場] ◇You need to listen to both *sides* of the argument. その議論の双方の意見に耳を傾ける必要がある ◇The other *side* maintains that the project will not be affordable. もう一方の意見ではその計画には費用面で無理があると主張し続けている ◇Will you keep your *side* of the bargain? 契約に関するそちらの約束を守ってくれますか

stand [C, ふつう単数で] (あることに反対する公式の)態度、立場 ◇We need to take a tough *stand* on tax avoidance. 税金逃れに関しては毅然たる態度を取る必要がある

audience 名 ☞WITNESS

audience・viewer・spectator・listener
公演やショー、スポーツを見たり聞いたりする人々を表す
【類語訳】聴衆、観衆、観客、テレビ視聴者、見る人、ラジオ聴取者、聴く人

▸ before/ in front of an audience/ spectators
▸ a television/ TV/ cinema audience/ viewer
▸ to attract the audience/ viewers/ spectators/ listeners
▸ to draw an audience/ spectators
▸ to pull in an audience/ viewers
▸ to entertain/ be a hit with/ shock the audience/ viewers/ listeners
▸ an audience/ a viewer/ a spectator sees/ watches sb/ sth
▸ an audience/ a listener hears/ listens to sb/ sth
▸ an audience/ a spectator cheers/ applauds/ boos

audience [C+単数・複数動詞] 聴衆、観衆、観客、視聴者 ◇The debate was televised in front of a *live audience*. ディベートは生の観客の前でテレビ放映された ◇An *audience* of millions watched the wedding on TV. 何百万もの視聴者がテレビでその結婚式に見入った ☞ **audience** (MARKET 1)

viewer [C] テレビ視聴者、見る人 ◇The show attracted millions of *viewers*. そのショーは何百万人もの視聴者を(テレビに)釘づけにした ◇Some of her art is intended to shock the *viewer*. 彼女の芸術の一部は見る者に衝撃を与えるよう意図されている

spectator [C] (特にスポーツの)観客、観衆 ◇The new football stadium will hold 75,000 *spectators*. 新設のフットボールスタジアムの収容人数は7万5千人になる予定だ ◇I think soccer is the best *spectator sport* (= a sport that many people watch or that is interesting to watch) there is. 思うにサッカーは見て楽しむスポーツとして最高だ

listener [C] ラジオ聴取者、聴く人 ◇Regular *listeners* will know this is the Year of Czech Music. いつも聴いている人たちは今年がチェコ音楽年であることを知っているだろう

the authorities 名

the authorities・bureaucracy・the establishment・the system・the top brass・officialdom
組織や国などにおいて決定権を持つ人や、その仕組みを指し、一般の人の手には及ばないため不公平だと思わせる
【類語訳】当局(者)、官僚制、官僚社会、官僚、有力者、権力層、権威、支配体制、上層部、幹部、大物

▸ within the bureaucracy/ establishment/ system
▸ the military authorities/ bureaucracy/ establishment/ top brass
▸ the medical/ political authorities/ / bureaucracy/ establishment
▸ the local/ federal/ government/ state authorities/ bureaucracy
▸ to rebel against/ fight the establishment/ system

the authorities [複数で] (国・地域の)当局(者) ◇The *health authorities* are investigating the problem. 保健当局がその問題を調査している ◇Someone *reported him to the* immigration *authorities*. 誰かが彼のことを入国管理局に通報した

bureaucracy [U, C] 官僚制;官僚社会 ◇Many people believed that the state *bureaucracy* was corrupt. その国の官僚社会は腐敗していると多くの人が思った ◇We are living in a modern *bureaucracy*. 私たちは近代的な官僚制社会で暮らしている ☞ **bureaucracy** (BUREAUCRACY), bureaucrat (OFFICIAL 名)

the establishment (または **the Establishment**) [単数＋単数・複数動詞] (しばしばけなして) 特権階級、権力[支配者]層 ◇As a young designer she soon became known for kicking *against the Establishment*. 権威に歯向かう若いデザイナーとして彼女はすぐに有名になった ◇His ideas have not been widely accepted within *the* academic *establishment*. 彼の思想は学会の権威たちに広くは受け入れられていない

the system (国・組織の)支配体制 ◇You should know you can't *beat the system* (= you must accept the way things are done). 支配体制を打ち破ることなどできないと知るべしだ ◇Graham knew how to *work the system* (= make it work to his own advantage). グレアムは体制の動かし方がわかっていた

the ,top 'brass 《英》《米 **the brass**》[単数＋単数・複数動詞] 《インフォーマル》(組織・活動の場などの)上層部、幹部、大物たち ◇There will be a meeting of *the* sport's *top brass* in Paris this week. 今週パリでスポーツ界の大物たちの会合が開かれる予定だ

officialdom [U] 《けなして》(規則に固執する)官僚、役

人，(大きな組織の)幹部 ◇The report is critical of attempts by *officialdom* to deal with the problem of homelessness. その報道はホームレスの問題を扱う官僚の試みに対して批判的である

available 形

available・for sale・on the market・on sale
物を買う[手にする，見つける]ことができる
【類語訳】入手することができる，売りに出されて，発売中で，市場に出回って

▸ available/ on sale **from** sb/ sth
▸ to **go** on the market/ on sale
▸ **now/ still** available/ for sale/ on the market/ on sale

available (ややフォーマル) 入手する[買う，見つける]ことができる ◇This was the only room *available*. ここが唯一空いている部屋だった ◇When will the information be made *available*? 情報はいつ入るようになりますか ◇We have used all *available* resources. 私たちは利用可能な資源をすべて使ってしまった
▸ **availability** 名 [U] the *availability* of cheap flights 格安便が利用可能であること ◇This offer is *subject to availability*. これは在庫[空き]があればご提供できます

for 'sale フレーズ (所有者から)売りに出されて ◇I'm sorry, it's not *for sale*. 申し訳ありません。それは売り物ではございません ◇They've *put their house up for sale*. 彼らは家を売りに出している ◇There has been an increase in the number of stolen vehicles being *offered for sale*. 売りに出される盗難車数が増加している

on the 'market フレーズ 売りに出されて，市場に出回って ◇There are hundreds of different brands *on the market*. 何百もの異なるブランドが市場に出回っている ◇Don't put your house *on the market* until spring. 春までは家を売りに出さないように ◇The house came *on the market* last year. 昨年その家は売りに出された

on 'sale フレーズ (店で)発売中で ◇Tickets are *on sale* from the booking office. 切符は切符売り場で発売しています ◇The new model goes *on sale* next month. 新型が来月発売されます

average 形

average・simple・ordinary・plain・unremarkable
物事や人が特別でないことを表す
【類語訳】並みの，平凡な，素朴な，単純な，普通の，平易な，わかりやすい，気取らない，目立たない

▸ an average/ ordinary **sort of** person/ thing
▸ an average/ a simple/ an ordinary/ an unremarkable **person**
▸ average/ ordinary **players**
▸ simple/ plain **ignorance/ common sense**
▸ **pretty** average/ ordinary/ unremarkable
▸ **very** average/ simple/ ordinary

average (しばしばけなして) 並みの ◇He was quite an *average* sort of student, nothing out of the ordinary.

---

available, average, award　43

彼はまったく平凡な生徒で，これといって変わったところなどなかった ◇The quality has been pretty *average*. それは質的にはごく普通だった ☞ **average** (NORMAL)

simple [ふつう名詞の前で] (しばしばほめて) (人が)気取らない，純真な；(物事・形が)単純な ◇They were *simple* country people. 彼らは純朴な田舎の人々だった ◇In some cases his argument is based on *simple* ignorance. 彼の論点は単なる無知からきているところもある ❶ simple は人や良質なものについて言うときはほめる意味になり，質のよくないものを表すときはけなす感じになる。

ordinary (けなして) 平凡な，並みの，ありきたりの ◇The meal was very *ordinary*. 食事はごく平凡だった ◇I lead a very *ordinary* life. 私はごく平凡な生活を送っている ❶ この意味では ordinary は very を伴うことが多く，否定的な印象が強調される。 反意 **extraordinary** (REMARKABLE), ☞ **ordinary** (NORMAL)

plain [名詞の前で] (しばしばほめて) (質が)普通の；(人が)気取らない ◇It doesn't require special skills, just *plain* common sense. それには特別な技術は必要なく，ただ普通の常識があればよい ◇He prided himself on being a *plain*, honest man with no nonsense about him. 彼は気取らない誠実な男で，ばかなまねはしないと自負していた ☞ **plain** (PLAIN 2)

ノート **simple と plain の使い分け**：両語とも人や性質について用いることができるが，simple は人について，plain は性質について用いることがより多い。人について用いるとき simple は他人に気取らず，素朴であるといったよい印象があるときに用いられるのに対して，plain はその人自身が気取ったりしてはいないことを表すときに用いられる。

unremarkable 目立たない ◇It was a pleasant but *unremarkable* town. そこは居心地はよいがどうということのない街だった 反意 **remarkable** (REMARKABLE)

award 名

award・prize・reward・title・medal・trophy・honour・cup・championship
勝利したり達成したりして与えられる物や地位を表す
【類語訳】賞，賞金，賞品，ほうび，報奨，見返り，懸賞金，謝礼，タイトル，選手権，メダル，勲章，トロフィー，称号，賞杯

▸ an award/ a prize/ a reward/ a medal/ a trophy/ a cup **for** sth
▸ a **major** award/ prize/ title/ trophy/ honour/ championship
▸ a **coveted/ prestigious** award/ prize/ title/ trophy
▸ a/ an **special** award/ prize/ reward/ honour
▸ a/ an **top/ academic** award/ prize/ honour
▸ the **supreme** award/ prize/ title
▸ a **European/ world** title/ trophy/ cup/ championship
▸ a **championship** title/ medal/ trophy
▸ to **win** an award/ a prize/ a reward/ a title/ a medal/ a trophy/ an honour/ a cup/ the championship
▸ to **take** an award/ a prize/ a reward/ the title/ a medal/ the trophy/ the championship
▸ to **earn** an award/ a prize/ a reward/ a title/ a medal
▸ to **receive** an award/ a prize/ a reward/ a medal/ a trophy/ an honour
▸ to **accept** an award/ a prize/ a reward/ a title/ an honour
▸ to **lose** a title/ medal/ the cup/ the championship
▸ to **defend/ retain** a title/ a trophy/ the championship

▶ an award/ a prize/ a title/ a medal/ a trophy/ an honour/ a cup/ the championship **goes to** sb

award [C] (成果・業績に対して与えられる)賞 ◇He was nominated for the best actor *award*. 彼は最優秀男優賞にノミネートされた ◇Stephen's quick thinking has earned him a bravery *award*. 機転の良さからスティーブンはその勇気を讃える賞を手にした ◇The association is presenting its annual *awards* this week. 今週協会は毎年恒例の賞を発表する予定だ ◇Helen received her prize at an *awards ceremony* in New York. ヘレンはニューヨークでの授賞式で賞品を受け取った ☞ **award** (GIVE 1)

prize [C] (競技・レースの勝利者[すぐれた仕事をした人]に与えられる)賞;価値のあるもの ◇She was awarded the Nobel *Prize* for Literature. 彼女はノーベル文学賞を受賞した ◇He took *first prize* in the woodwind section. 彼は木管楽器部門で一位を獲得した ◇I won £500 in *prize money*. 賞金で500ポンドを獲得した ◇Win a car in our grand *prize draw*! 大抽選会で車を手に入れよう ◇World peace is the greatest *prize* of all. 世界平和はあらゆるものの中で最大に価値あるものだ

reward [C, U] (よい事・努力をして与えられる)ほうび, 報酬, 見返り;(犯罪者の逮捕[遺失物の発見])に対する懸賞[謝礼]金 ◇You deserve a *reward* for being so helpful. とても役に立ってくれたからこうびをあげよう ◇The company is now *reaping the rewards* of their investments. 会社は今資本を投下した見返りを得ている ◇Winning the match was *just reward* for the effort the team made. 試合に勝利することはチームが努力した当然の見返りだった ◇The look on her face when I told her was *reward enough*. 彼女に告げたときの彼女の表情で十分報われた ◇A $100 *reward* has been *offered* for the return of the necklace. そのネックレスが持ち主の手元に戻れば100ドルの謝礼金が支払われることになっている ◇The company has *put up* a *reward* of £25,000 for information. 会社は情報提供に対し2万5千ポンドの懸賞金を賭けている 反意 **punishment, penalty**

▶**reward** [動] [他,しばしば受身で] ◇She was *rewarded* for her efforts with a cash bonus. 彼女の努力は現金によるボーナスという形で報われた ◇Our patience was finally *rewarded*. 私たちの忍耐がついに報われた

title [C] (スポーツの)タイトル, 選手権 ◇She has three world *titles*. 彼女は3つの世界タイトルを持っている ◇She'll be defending her *title* at this week's French Open. 彼女は今週のフレンチ・オープンでタイトル防衛に臨むことになっている

medal [C] (競技の勝者への)メダル, (戦争などの功労者への)勲章 ◇He received a *medal* for his service in the war. 彼は戦争中の軍務に対して勲章を授かった ◇Anyone who does that job *deserves a medal*! その仕事を果たした者は誰でも勲章に値する ◇She won the *gold medal* at the World Championships. 彼女は世界選手権で金メダルを獲得した

trophy [C] (競技の勝者への)トロフィー ◇He picked up a *trophy* for best news editor. 彼は最優秀ニュース編集者のトロフィーを獲得した ◇The team paraded their League Championship *trophy*. チームはリーグ優勝のトロフィーをパレードで披露した

honour 《英》(米では **honor**) [C] (業績に対する)賞, 称号 ◇It was the British who scooped the *honours* at last night's Oscars. 昨晩アカデミー賞をさらったのはイギリス人たちだった ◇He was buried *with full military honours* (= with a special military service as a sign of respect). 彼は正式な軍葬で埋葬された

cup [C] (競技で与えられる)賞杯, カップ ◇She has won several *cups* for skating. 彼女はスケートでカップをいくつも獲得している

championship [C] 優勝者の地位, チャンピオンの座, 選手権 ◇They've held the *championship* for the past two years. 彼らは過去2年間チャンピオンの座を守っている

aware [形]

aware・conscious・mindful・alert to sth
わかっていたり、認識していたりすることを表す
【類語訳】知って, 気づいて, 承知して, 留意して, 警戒して

▶ aware/ conscious/ mindful **of** sth
▶ aware/ conscious/ mindful **that**...
▶ **very** aware/ conscious/ mindful/ alert
▶ **keenly** aware/ conscious/ alert

aware [名詞の前では用いない] 気づいて;承知して ◇He was *well aware* of the problem. 彼はその問題を十分承知していた ◇Were you *aware* that something was wrong? 何かおかしいと気づいていましたか ◇*As far as I'm aware* no one has done anything about it. 私の知っている限り, そのことに関しては誰も何もやっていません ◇Helen slipped out without him being *aware* of it. ヘレンは彼に気づかれないようにそっと抜け出した 反意 **unaware**

conscious [名詞の前では用いない]《ややフォーマル》(責任・不安などを感じつつ)気づいて ◇He was painfully *conscious* of his mother's embarrassment. 彼には母親の恥ずかしさが痛いほどわかった ◇I was vaguely *conscious* that I was being watched. 私は何となく見られているように感じた

mindful [名詞の前では用いない]《フォーマル》心に留めて, 留意して ◇*Mindful* of his advice, I decided to return to my hotel. 彼の助言を念頭に置いて私はホテルに戻ることに決めた

alert to sth [名詞の前では用いない] (問題・危険に)気づいて, 警戒して ◇Soldiers must be *alert* to danger but not constantly frightened. 兵士は危険を警戒していなくてはならないが, びくついてばかりはいられない

awareness [名]

awareness・knowledge・consciousness・realization・perception
知っていたり, 気づいていたり, 認識したりしていること, またはその能力を表す
【類語訳】認識, 了解, 自覚, 意識, 実感, 知覚, 受け止め方

▶ an awareness/ the knowledge/ a consciousness/ the realization/ a perception **of** sth
▶ an awareness/ the knowledge/ a consciousness/ the realization/ a perception **that**...
▶ **a sudden** awareness/ realization/ perception
▶ **a/ the growing/ increasing/ greater** awareness/ knowledge/ consciousness/ realization/ perception
▶ **full** awareness/ knowledge/ consciousness/ realization

awareness

- a **heightened** awareness/ consciousness/ perception
- (a/ the) **public** awareness/ knowledge/ consciousness/ perception
- to **raise** awareness/ consciousness
- to **develop/ increase** sb's awareness/ knowledge/ perception
- to **heighten** sb's awareness/ perception
- a **lack** of awareness/ knowledge/ consciousness/ perception

awareness [U, 単数で] 知って[認識して]いること ◇There is growing *awareness* of the link between diet and health. 食事と健康との関連性の認識が高まっている ◇I seemed to have a heightened *awareness* of my surroundings. 周囲の状況を認識する力が高まったように思えた ◇It's the start of Breast Cancer *Awareness* week. 乳がんへの意識を高める週間の始まりだ

knowledge [U] (事実・状況を)知っていること, 了解 ◇She sent the letter ***without my knowledge***. 私の知らない間に彼女は手紙を送った ◇The documentary was made ***with*** the singer's full ***knowledge*** and permission. ドキュメンタリーはその歌手に十分な了解と許可を得て制作された ◇They could relax, ***safe/secure in the knowledge*** that the money would be available. 彼らは金が入るだろうとわかって安心し, 緊張が緩むかもしれない ◇He ***denied all knowledge*** of the affair. 彼はその件に関してまったく知らないと主張した ◇Their relationship is ***common/public knowledge*** (= everyone knows about it). 彼らの関係は周知の事実だ 反意 **ignorance** (IGNORANCE), ☞ **know** (KNOW)

consciousness [U, 単数で] 自覚, 意識;ものの考え方 ◇We need to raise people's *consciousness* of environmental issues. 人々の環境問題に対する意識を高める必要がある ◇The memory remained deep in his *consciousness*. その思い出は彼の意識の奥深くに残ったままだ

realization (英でまた **-isation**) [U, 単数で] 気づくこと, 実感 ◇The *realization* of what she had done suddenly hit her. 自分がしてしまったことに彼女は突然気づいた ◇the gradual *realization* that they were losing the war 戦争に負けそうだという徐々に迫りくる彼らの実感 ☞ **realize** (KNOW 1)

perception [U, 単数で] 《フォーマル or 専門語》(五感による)知覚;(物事を理解したうえでの)受け止め方 ◇Everyone's *perception* of reality is slightly different. 人は皆現実に対する受け止め方がやや異なる ◇There's a general *perception* that standards of health care are falling. 保健水準が下がっているというのが一般的な見方だ ☞ **perceive** (NOTICE)

B b

bad 形 ☞ TERRIBLE 1

bad・nasty・unpleasant・grim・lousy・wretched・ghastly

問題をたくさんはらみ、人を動揺させたり、不快にさせたり、気を滅入らせたりすることを表す
【類語訳】悪い、うんざりさせる、嫌な、ひどい、不快な、とんでもない

bad	nasty	wretched
unpleasant	grim	ghastly
	lousy	

文型&コロケーション

▶ a bad/ a nasty/ an unpleasant/ a grim/ a ghastly **situation**
▶ a bad/ a nasty/ an unpleasant/ a grim/ a ghastly **experience/ feeling**
▶ bad/ nasty/ unpleasant/ grim/ lousy/ wretched/ ghastly **weather**
▶ a bad/ a nasty/ an unpleasant/ a grim **mood**
▶ a bad/ a nasty/ an unpleasant **taste/ smell**
▶ bad/ grim/ ghastly **news**
▶ a bad/ a grim/ a lousy/ a wretched **day/ night/ time**
▶ a nasty/ an unpleasant/ a grim/ a wretched/ a ghastly **thought**
▶ the nasty/ unpleasant/ grim **truth/ reality/ facts**
▶ to find sth unpleasant/ grim
▶ **very** bad/ nasty/ unpleasant/ grim/ wretched
▶ **really** bad/ nasty/ unpleasant/ grim/ lousy/ wretched/ ghastly
▶ **pretty** bad/ nasty/ unpleasant/ grim/ lousy/ ghastly
▶ **rather** bad/ nasty/ unpleasant/ grim/ ghastly
▶ **particularly** bad/ nasty/ unpleasant/ grim/ ghastly

bad 望ましくない、悪い ◇I'm having a really *bad* day. まったくついてない日 ◇It was the *worst* experience of her life. それは彼女の人生で最悪の経験だった ◇Smoking gives you *bad* breath. タバコを吸うと息が臭くなる ◇Things are *bad* enough without our own guns shelling us. 味方からの砲撃がなくても状況は特にひどい 反意 **good** (NICE 1)
nasty 非常に悪い[深刻な]; 動揺させる、うんざりさせる、嫌な ◇He had a *nasty* accident. 彼はひどい事故に遭った ◇The news gave me a *nasty* shock. そのニュースを聞いて私はひどく衝撃を受けた ◇He had a *nasty* moment when he thought he'd lost his passport. 彼はパスポートをなくしたと思い一瞬どきっとした ◇This coffee tastes *nasty*. このコーヒーはひどい味がする ◇Don't buy that coat — it looks *cheap and nasty*. あのコートを買ってはいけないよ。安かろう悪かろうだよ 反意 **nice** (NICE 1)
unpleasant 《ややフォーマル》楽しくない、快適でない、不快 ◇There was an *unpleasant* atmosphere in the room. 部屋に気まずい空気が漂っていた ◇The minerals in the water made it *unpleasant* to drink. ミネラルを含んでいるせいでその水はのど越しが悪かった ◇He may make life *unpleasant* for the rest of us. 彼はこのあとずっと私たちの生活を不愉快なものにするかもしれない ❶ふつう unpleasant は nasty よりも控えめな表現であり、「深刻な」の意味には用いられない。×He had an *unpleasant* accident. しかしながら、やや丁寧でフォーマルな表現だが、非常に不快なことを表すときに、その不快さをはっきり言いたくない場合には用いられることもある。◆Things started to get *unpleasant* when the neighbours called in the police.（近所の人が警察を呼んだときにはひどい事態になり始めていた）反意 **pleasant** (NICE 1)
grim 不愉快な、嫌な ◇The accident serves as a *grim* reminder of what drinking and driving can do. その事故は飲酒運転が行きつくところを嫌というほど思い出させてくれる ◇The outlook is pretty *grim*. 見通しはかなり厳しい ◇Things are looking *grim* for workers in the building industry. 建設業界で働く人々には事態は悪化しているように見える ❶ grim は特にたった今起こったことや将来起こりそうなことについて用いられる。news, reminder, discovery, reality, picture, legacy, fate, future, prospect, forecast, outlook, warning などと結びつく。
lousy 《インフォーマル》非常に悪い[がっかりさせる], ひどい ◇What *lousy* weather! なんてひどい天気だ ◇I've had a *lousy* day. さんざんな一日だった ❶ lousy は特にがっかりさせられた事・人について言うときに用いられる。day, food, husband, lover, summer, weather などと結びつく。
wretched 《書き言葉》極度に悪い、非常に不快な、とんでもない ◇She had a *wretched* time of it at school. 彼女は学校でさんざんな目に遭った ◇The animals are kept in the most *wretched* conditions. 動物たちは最悪の状態で飼育されている ❶ wretched は特に人や動物が苦しみ、気の毒であるような極端な状況について言うときに用いられる。
ghastly 《インフォーマル》極度に悪い、非常に不快な ◇The weather was *ghastly*. 天気は最悪だった ◇It's all been a *ghastly* mistake. それはまったくとんでもない間違いだった ❶ ghastly は特に人に心理的影響を与えるような最悪の状況について言うときに用いられる。

ban 名

ban・sanction・boycott・embargo・prohibition・moratorium・veto・taboo

行いをやめさせる規則[命令、風習、活動]を表す
【類語訳】禁止令、制裁、ボイコット、不買運動、禁輸、タブー

文型&コロケーション

▶ a ban/ sanctions/ a boycott/ an embargo/ a prohibition/ a veto/ a moratorium/ a taboo **on** sb/ sth
▶ a ban/ sanctions/ a boycott/ an embargo/ a prohibition/ a veto/ a taboo **against** sb/ sth
▶ a **total** ban/ boycott/ embargo/ prohibition/ moratorium
▶ (an) **international** ban/ sanctions/ boycott/ embargo/ moratorium
▶ (a) **trade** ban/ sanctions/ boycott/ embargo
▶ (an) **economic** sanctions/ boycott/ embargo

ban, bang

▶ to **impose** a ban/ sanctions/ a boycott/ an embargo/ a prohibition/ a moratorium/ a veto
▶ to **call for/ introduce** a ban/ sanctions/ a boycott/ a prohibition/ a moratorium
▶ to **enforce/ tighten/ ease** a ban/ sanctions/ an embargo
▶ to **comply with** a ban/ sanctions/ a prohibition
▶ to **break** a ban/ sanctions/ an embargo/ a taboo
▶ to **lift** a ban/ sanctions/ a boycott/ an embargo/ a prohibition/ a veto
▶ a ban/ sanctions/ an embargo **come/ comes into force**

ban [C] 公式の禁止，禁止令 ◇There is to be a total *ban* on smoking in the office. オフィス内は全面禁煙にすべきです ◇The students took to the streets, defying a *ban* on political gatherings. 学生たちは政治的集会の禁止に公然と反抗して街頭デモをした ◇The sprinter received a lengthy *ban for* failing a drugs test. その短距離走者はドーピングに引っかかり，長期の出場停止処分を受けた ◇He faces a possible life *ban from* international football. 彼はサッカーの国際試合への永久出場停止処分を受ける可能性がある

sanction [C, ふつう複数で] (国際法の立場から特定の国との貿易・接触を制限する)公式命令, 制裁 ◇Trade *sanctions* were imposed against any country that refused to sign the agreement. その条約への署名を拒否した国すべてに対し貿易制裁が課せられた

boycott [C] ボイコット, 不買運動 ◇Opposition groups declared a *boycott* of the elections. 反対派は選挙のボイコットを表明した ◇The group is calling for a *consumer boycott* of the company's products. そのグループはその会社の製品の不買運動を訴えている

embargo [C] (特定品目の)禁輸 ◇There is a strict *embargo* on oil imports. 石油の輸入が厳しく禁止されている ◇We knew the *arms embargo* was being broken. 武器禁輸が守られていないことがわかった

prohibition [U, C] 禁止, 禁止令 ◇The RSPB has called for the *prohibition* of all imports of wild birds. RSPB(王立鳥類保護協会)はあらゆる野鳥の輸入禁止を求めている

moratorium (複 **moratoriums, moratoria**) [C] (正式合意による活動の)一時停止 ◇The convention called for a two-year *moratorium* on commercial whaling. その協定では商業捕鯨に対して二年間の活動停止が求められた

veto (複 **-oes**) [C] 拒否権 ◇For months there was a *veto* on employing new staff. 何か月もの間, 新規従業員の採用に同意が得られないでいた ☞ **veto** (REFUSAL), **veto** (REFUSE)

taboo [C] タブー ◇Death is one of the great *taboos* in our culture. 我々の文化において死は主なタブーの一つだ ◇There is still a *taboo* on the subject in our family. うちではそのことはまだタブーだ ☞ **taboo** (FORBIDDEN)

ban 動 ☞ EXCLUDE 2

ban・prohibit・bar・forbid・outlaw
公式に[法によって]やめさせる
【類語訳】禁止する, 禁ずる, 防止する, 非合法化する

【文型&コロケーション】
▶ to ban/ prohibit/ bar sb **from** sth
▶ to ban/ prohibit/ bar/ forbid sb **from doing** sth
▶ to ban/ prohibit/ forbid/ outlaw the **practice/ use/ sale** of sth
▶ to ban/ prohibit the **import/ export** of sth
▶ to be **effectively** banned/ prohibited/ barred/ forbidden/ outlawed
▶ to be **officially** banned/ prohibited
▶ to be **strictly** prohibited/ forbidden

ban (-nn-) [他] (公式に)禁止する；締め出す ◇There are plans to *ban* smoking in public places. 公の場所での喫煙を禁止する計画がある ◇He claimed that the government had tried to *ban* the book. 政府がかつてこの本を発禁にしようとしたと彼は訴えた ◇He was *banned* from the meeting. 彼は会合への出席を禁じられた ◇The sprinter has been *banned for life* after failing a drugs test. ドーピングに引っかかりその短距離走者は生涯にわたり出場禁止になった 反意 **permit** (ALLOW), ☞ **banned** (FORBIDDEN)

prohibit [他, しばしば受身で] (《フォーマル》(法によって)禁止する ◇The convention strictly *prohibits* the dumping of waste at sea. 国際協定によって海への廃棄物投棄は厳しく禁じられている ◇The import of these products is *prohibited by law*. これらの製品の輸入は法律によって禁じられている 反意 **permit, authorize** (ALLOW), ☞ **prohibited** (FORBIDDEN)

bar (-rr-) [他] 《ややフォーマル》(規則・法律が)禁止する, 防止する ◇The curfew has effectively *barred* migrant workers from their jobs. 夜間外出禁止令によって移民労働者の不法労働は効果的に阻止された ◇Certain activities are still *barred to* women. いくつかの活動がいまだに女性たちに禁止されている

forbid [他] 《ややフォーマル》禁ずる, 命令する ◇You are all *forbidden to* leave. 皆さんは出ないようにしてください ◇Her father *forbade* the marriage. 彼女の父親はその結婚を禁じた ◇Smoking is strictly *forbidden*. 喫煙は厳しく禁じられています 反意 **allow, permit** (ALLOW), ☞ **forbidden** (FORBIDDEN)

outlaw [他] 非合法化する ◇There are plans to *outlaw* the carrying of knives. ナイフの所持を禁止する計画がある ◇He was found to be a member of the *outlawed* rebel movement. 彼は非合法の反乱組織の一員であるとわかった

bang 動

1 bang・crash・pop・crack・explode・clash
突然短い音を立てる動きを表す
【類語訳】バタンと閉まる[閉める], ポンと鳴る[鳴らす], バンと鳴る, バシッと鳴らす, ガチャンとぶつかり合う[合わせる]

【文型&コロケーション】
▶ a door bangs/ crashes
▶ thunder crashes/ cracks/ explodes
▶ cymbals crash/ clash
▶ to bang/ crash/ pop/ crack/ explode **loudly**

bang [他, 自] (ドア・窓が[を])バタンと閉まる[閉める] ◇Don't *bang* the door when you go out! 出るときにドアをバタンと閉めないでね ◇A window was *banging* somewhere (= opening and closing noisily). どこかの窓が(開閉を繰り返して)ガタガタと音を立てていた ◇The door *banged* shut behind her. 彼女の後ろでドアがバタンと閉まった ☞ **bang** (HIT 1)

↪**bang**

crash [自] (波・雷が)すさまじい音を立てる ◇The waves *crashed* deafeningly. 波が耳をつんざくような音を立てて砕けた ◇Thunder *crashed* overhead. 雷が頭上でとどろいた

pop (-pp-) [自, 他] ポンと鳴る；ポンと鳴らす ◇Flashbulbs were *popping* all around them. 彼らの周りであちこちフラッシュがパシャパシャたかれた ◇He *popped* the cork on the champagne bottle. 彼はシャンパンの瓶のコルクをポンと抜いた

crack [自, 他, 受身なし] バンと鋭い音が鳴る；バシッと鳴らす ◇A shot *cracked* across the ridge. 尾根の向こう側で銃声が鳴った ◇He *cracked* his whip and galloped away. 彼は馬にむちをバシッとくれて走り去った

explode [自] とどろく ◇Thunder *exploded* overhead. 頭上で雷の音がとどろいた

clash [自, 他] ガチャンとぶつかり合う；ガチャンとぶつかり合わせる ◇The long blades *clashed* together. 長い剣がガチャッとぶつかり合った ◇She *clashed* the cymbals. 彼女はシンバルを打ち鳴らした

---

2 bang・knock・hit・crack・bump
体の一部が偶然にあたる
【類語訳】ぶつける, ぶつかる

【文型&コロケーション】
▸ to bang/ knock/ hit/ crack/ bump your **head**/ **knee**, etc. **on**/ **against** sth
▸ to bang/ knock/ hit/ crack/ bump your **head**/ **forehead**
▸ to bang/ knock/ hit/ bump your **arm**/ **knee**/ **elbow**

bang [他] ぶつける ◇He *banged* his head as he tried to stand up. 立ち上がろうとして彼は頭をぶつけた ◇She tripped and *banged* her knee on the desk. 彼女はつまづいて膝を机に打ちつけた ☞ **bang** (HIT 1)

knock [他, 自] ぶつける ◇The door's very low — mind you don't *knock* your head! ドアがとても低いので, 頭をぶつけないように注意して ◇Her hand *knocked* against the glass. 彼女の手がガラスにぶつかった ☞ **knock** (HIT 1)

hit [他] ぶつける ◇He fell, *hitting* his head on the hard stone floor. 彼は転んで頭を硬い石の床にぶつけた ☞ **hit** (HIT 1, 2)

crack [他] (頭を)ぶつける ◇He stood up suddenly, *cracking* his head on the low ceiling. 彼は突然立ち上がって, 頭を低い天井にぶつけた

bump [他] ぶつける ◇Toddlers are always falling over and *bumping* their heads. よちよち歩きの子どもたちはいつも転んで頭をぶつけてばかりいる ☞ **bump** (HIT 1)

> **ノート** これらの語は非常によく似た使われ方をする。knockとhitは一般的に, 強く[弱く]ぶつけて痛むとき, bangはとりわけ体の一部がぶつかって痛みを伴うときに最も頻繁に使われる。crackは特に頭をぶつけたとき。bumpは特に前置詞なしで用いられ, bangも同様。hitとcrackは必ず前置詞句を伴う。×Toddlers are always falling over and *hitting*/ *cracking* their heads.

---

bankrupt [形] ☞ POOR 1

bankrupt・bust・insolvent・broke
個人[会社]がつぶれたことを表す
【類語訳】破産した, 無一文の

【文型&コロケーション】
▸ to **go** bankrupt/ bust/ broke
▸ to **declare sb** bankrupt/ insolvent
▸ **virtually** bankrupt/ bust/ insolvent

bankrupt 破産した ◇The firm went *bankrupt* in 2003 and all its assets were sold off. その会社は2003年に破産し, 全資産は売却された
▸ **bankrupt** [動] [他] ◇The company was almost *bankrupted* by legal costs. その会社は訴訟費用によって破産寸前に追い込まれた
▸ **bankruptcy** [名] [U, C] ◇The company filed for *bankruptcy* (= asked to be officially bankrupt) in 2006. その会社は2006年に破産申請した ◇There could be further *bankruptcies* among small farmers. 小規模農家のあいだで更なる破産が続く可能性がある

bust [名詞の前のみ] 《インフォーマル》 破産した ◇We lost our money when the travel company went *bust*. その旅行会社が破産して我々はお金を失った

insolvent 《金融》破産した ◇The company has been declared *insolvent*. その会社は破産宣告された [反意] **solvent** ❶人や会社が solvent ならば, 借金を返済する資金がある, ということ. ◆The company managed to remain *solvent* during the recession. (その会社はどうにか不況下に生き残ることができた)
▸ **insolvency** [名] [U, C] ◇The company is close to *insolvency*. その会社は破産寸前だ

broke [名詞の前では用いない] 《ややインフォーマル》 無一文の ◇I'm always *broke* by the end of the month. 月末までにはいつも無一文になっている

---

barrier [名]

barrier・barricade・obstacle・roadblock・obstruction・hurdle
道路や入り口などを塞いで人々の通過を妨げる物
【類語訳】バリケード, 障害物, 防塞, ハードル

【文型&コロケーション】
▸ **behind** a barrier/ barricade
▸ **over** a barricade/ hurdle
▸ **at**/ **through** a barrier/ roadblock
▸ a **physical** barrier/ obstacle/ obstruction
▸ a **police** barrier/ barricade/ roadblock
▸ to **erect**/ **set up** a barrier/ barricade/ roadblock
▸ sth **forms** a barrier/ a barricade/ an obstacle
▸ to **clear** a barricade/ an obstacle/ an obstruction/ a hurdle
▸ to **hit** a barrier/ an obstacle/ an obstruction/ a hurdle
▸ to **remove** a barricade/ a roadblock/ an obstruction

barrier [C] (道路・入り口に建てる)柵 ◇The crowd had to stand behind *barriers*. 群衆は柵の後ろに立たされた ◇Show your ticket at the *barrier*. ゲートでチケットを見せてください ◇*Crash barriers* were erected along the roads to be used for the race. レース用にガードレールが道路沿いに建てられた ☞ **bar** (BLOCK 2)

barricade [C] バリケード(特に抗議の一環として通り抜けできないように道路などに一列に並べて設置される物) ◇The police **stormed** the **barricades** the demonstrators had put up. デモ参加者が張ったバリケードに警察が突入した ◇The protesters formed a human *barricade*. 抗議者

base, basics

らは人間バリケードを作った ☞ **barricade** (BLOCK 2)

obstacle [C] (行く手を阻む)障害物;(障害物競技で馬が飛び越える)柵 ◇The area was full of streams and bogs and other natural *obstacles*. その地域には川や沼をはじめとする天然の障害物がたくさんあった ◇This huge open ditch forms the biggest *obstacle* on the course. この巨大な開渠がコース上で最大の障害物となっている

roadblock [C] (検問用に警察・軍隊によって道路に設置される)防塞 ◇They were stopped at an army *roadblock* leaving the city. 街を出るとき彼らは軍の路上防塞で車を止められた

obstruction [C]《書き言葉》(道路・入り口などをふさぐ)障害物 ◇The train driver receives a warning if there's an *obstruction* on the line ahead. 行く手の線路上に障害物がある場合、列車の運転士は警報を受信する ☞ **obstruct** (BLOCK 2)

hurdle [C] (人・馬がレースで連続して飛び越える)ハードル ◇She cleared the first *hurdle* (= jumped over it without hitting it) in the lead. その雌馬は先頭で一つ目のハードルをクリアした ☞ **hurdle** (JUMP)

base 動

base・locate・be situated・site
特定の場所に建設または設置する
【類語訳】拠点にする、(特定の場所に)置く、ある

文型&コロケーション
▶to be based/ located/ situated/ sited **in/ at/ close to** sth
▶to be based/ located/ situated/ sited **between** A and B
▶**conveniently** based/ located/ situated/ sited
▶**strategically** located/ situated/ sited
▶**centrally** located/ situated

base, be based [他、しばしば受身形](特定の都市・地域を商売などの)本拠地とする;(仕事・旅行などで地方の特定の場所を)拠点にする ◇She works for a company *based* in Chicago. 彼女は本社がシカゴにある会社で働いている ◇a Chicago-*based* company シカゴが本拠地の会社 ◇We're going to *base* ourselves in Tokyo and make trips from there. 私たちは東京を拠点にしてそこから旅行する予定です

▶**base** 名 [C] ◇The town is an ideal *base* for touring the area. その地域を旅行するのにその街は理想的な拠点となる

locate, be located [他、しばしば受身形]《副詞や前置詞と共に》《ややフォーマル、特に書き言葉》(特定の場所に)置く[建設する];(特定の場所に)ある[建てられている] ◇They *located* their headquarters in Paris. 彼らは本部をパリに置いた ◇The offices are conveniently *located* just a few minutes from the main station. オフィスは主要駅からたった数分のところにあって便利だ ❶特に《米》では自動詞の *locate* は特定の場所に会社が移転するという意味でも用いられる。◆There are tax breaks for businesses that *locate* in rural areas. (地方に移転する企業に対して税の控除がある) ☞ **location** (PLACE), **relocate** (LEAVE 2)

be situated [他]《副詞や前置詞と共に》《フォーマル》(特定の場所・位置に)ある[置かれている] ◇My bedroom *was situated* on the top floor of the house. 私の寝室は家の最上階にあった

site, be sited [他、しばしば受身形]《ややフォーマル》《副詞や前置詞と共に》(特定の場所・位置に)建てる ◇There was a meeting to discuss the *siting* of the new school. 新しい学校の立地について話し合う会合が開かれた ◇The castle is magnificently *sited* high up on a cliff. その城は崖の上高くに壮麗なたたずまいを見せている ☞ **site** (PLACE)

ノート **located, situated, sited** の使い分け：*located* と *situated* は両方とも、常にその場所にあり、人によって置かれたのではない地勢に用いられる。*sited* はふつう、工場、学校、病院のような人が建てたり特定の位置に置かれた物にのみ用いられる。◆Goose Island *is located/situated* in the Chicago River.(グース島はシカゴ川の中にある)。×Goose Island *is sited* in the Chicago River.

basics 名

basics・fundamentals・introduction・essentials・practicalities
特定の状況に置かれた人々が必要とする最も重要な事柄、事実、知識を表す
【類語訳】基礎、基本、原則、原理、入門書

文型&コロケーション
▶**the/ a basic** fundamentals/ introduction/ essentials
▶to **teach/ grasp** the basics/ fundamentals/ essentials
▶to **learn/ master** the basics/ fundamentals
▶to **understand/ know/ cover/ concentrate on** the basics/ essentials

basics [複数で] 基礎、基本 ◇I need to learn the *basics* of computer programming. コンピュータ・プログラミングの基礎を勉強する必要がある ◇Managers should *get back to basics* and examine the kind of products people really want. 経営者は基本に立ち戻って、人々が本当に必要とする製品とはどんなものかを検討すべきだ ☞ **basic** (FUNDAMENTAL)

fundamentals [複数で]《ややフォーマル、特に書き言葉》(ある分野の知識の中で最も重要な)規則、原則、原理；基礎 ◇He wrote 'The *Fundamentals* of Modern Physics'. 彼は『現代物理学の基礎』を書いた ◇She taught me the *fundamentals* of the job. 彼女は仕事のイロハを私に教えてくれた ☞ **fundamental** (FUNDAMENTAL)

introduction [C] 入門書 ◇An *Introduction* to Astronomy『天文学入門』 ◇It's a useful *introduction* to an extremely complex subject. それは極めて複雑なテーマにとって役立つ入門書だ ☞ **introductory** (FIRST)

essentials [複数で] (ある分野の知識の中で最も重要な)事実、原則、基礎 ◇We will concentrate on the *essentials* of English grammar. 英文法の基礎に重点を置くことにしましょう ☞ **essential** (FUNDAMENTAL)

ノート **basics, fundamentals, essentials** の使い分け：多くの場合これらの語のうちどの語を使用しても構わないが、*basics* はふつう最も実用的なもの、必要な方法や技術に関して用いられる。◆the *basics* of dinghy sailing/ good nutrition/how to set it up and operate it (小型ヨットの航法/十分な栄養/組み立てと操作方法の基本)。*essentials* はやや理論的なもの、理論および実際の方法に関してしばしば用いられる。◆the *essentials* of arithmetic/design/how we communicate using language (算数/デザイン/言語によるコミュニケーションの基礎)。*fundamentals* は最も理論的なもの。システム、知識、信仰のもととなる考え方や原理に関して用いられる。◆the *fun-*

damentals of Christian belief/microbiology/the western concept of law (キリスト教信仰/微生物学/西洋の法観念の根本原則).

practicalities [複数で] (概念・理論ではなく)実際 ◇It sounds like a good idea; let's look at the *practicalities* and work out the costs. それはいい考えですね。現実的にみてコストを計算してみましょう ❶ふつう動詞には consider, look at, discuss などが用いられる。☞ **practical** (REALISTIC)

beat 動 ☞ HIT 2

beat・batter・pound・lash・hammer・dash・pummel
強く人や物を何度もぶつ
【類語訳】たたく, 殴る, 打つ, たたきつける, ぶつける

〔文型&コロケーション〕
▶ to beat/ batter/ pound/ lash/ hammer/ pummel sb/ sth **with** sth
▶ to beat/ batter/ pound/ lash/ hammer/ pummel **at** sb/ sth
▶ to beat/ batter/ pound/ lash/ hammer/ dash sb/ sth **against** sth
▶ to beat/ batter/ pound/ hammer **on** sth
▶ to beat/ batter/ hammer sth **down**
▶ to beat/ batter/ pound/ lash/ hammer/ dash sb **to death**
▶ to beat/ batter sb **about/ around the head**
▶ the **rain/ wind/ sea** beats/ batters/ pounds/ lashes/ dashes (at) sth
▶ **waves** beat/ batter/ pound/ lash/ dash (at) sth
▶ **storms** beat/ batter/ pound/ lash (at) sth

beat [自, 他] (人・物を強く何度も)たたく ◇Someone was *beating* at the door. 誰かがドアをたたいていた ◇Hailstones *beat* against the window. 雹が窓に打ちつけた ◇Someone was *beating* a drum. 誰かが太鼓をたたいていた ◇A young man was found *beaten* to death at his home last night. 昨晩自宅で若い男性が殴り殺されているのが発見された

batter [自, 他] (大きなダメージを与えるように人・物を)何度もたたく[殴る] ◇She *battered* at the door with her fists. 彼女はドアをこぶしで何度もたたいた ◇Severe winds have been *battering* the north coast. 激しい風がずっと北岸に吹きつけている ◇The police had to *batter* the door down. 警察はドアを打ち壊さねばならなかった

pound [自, 他] (人・物を音を立てて)何度もたたく ◇The machines *pounded* away day and night. その機械は四六時中ドンドンと音を立てていた ◇She *pounded* him with her fists. 彼女はこぶしで彼を何度も殴った

lash [自, 他] (人・物を力一杯)たたく ◇The rain *lashed* at the window. 雨が窓に打ちつけた ◇Great waves *lashed* the shore. 大波が岸に打ちつけた ❶ *lash* の主語にはしばしば rain, wind, hail, sea, waves などが用いられる。

hammer [自, 他] (人・物を音を立てて荒々しく何度も)たたく ◇I was so scared my heart was *hammering* (= beating very fast) in my chest.《比喩的》とても怖くて心臓がどきどきしていた ◇He *hammered* the door with his fists. 彼はこぶしでドアを何度もたたいた

〔ノート〕 **pound** と **hammer** の使い分け: これら 2 語には意味の違いは大きくないが, pound はときにより規則的な行為を表す。×The machines *hammered* away day and night. hammer はより荒々しく, しばしば比喩的に用いられる。

dash [他, 自]《副詞や前置詞と共に》(かたいものに)たたきつける; ぶつける ◇The boat was *dashed* repeatedly against the rocks. ボートは何度も岩にたたきつけられた ◇The waves were *dashing* against the harbour wall. 波が港の岸壁にたたきつけていた

pummel (-II-, 米 -I-) [他, 自] (人・物をこぶしで)何度も殴る (**pommel** とも綴る) ◇Her fists *pummelled* at his chest. 彼女はこぶしで彼の胸をたたいた ◇He *pummelled* the pillow with his fists. 彼はこぶしを枕に繰り返し打ちつけた

beautiful 形

1 beautiful・pretty・handsome・attractive・lovely・cute・good-looking・gorgeous・stunning・striking
見た目のよい人々を表す
【類語訳】美しい, かわいらしい, ハンサムな, 魅力的な, きれいな, セクシーな

pretty	beautiful	gorgeous
handsome	lovely	stunning
attractive		
cute		
good-looking		
striking		

〔文型&コロケーション〕
▶ a beautiful/ a pretty/ a handsome/ an attractive/ a lovely/ a cute/ a good-looking/ a gorgeous/ a stunning/ a striking **girl/ woman**
▶ a beautiful/ a pretty/ a handsome/ an attractive/ a lovely/ a cute/ a good-looking/ a gorgeous **boy**
▶ a beautiful/ a handsome/ an attractive/ a cute/ a good-looking/ a gorgeous **man**
▶ a beautiful/ a pretty/ a handsome/ an attractive/ a lovely/ a cute/ a good-looking **child**
▶ a beautiful/ a pretty/ a handsome/ an attractive/ a lovely/ a cute/ a good-looking/ a striking **face**
▶ a beautiful/ a handsome/ an attractive/ a lovely/ a cute/ a gorgeous **body**
▶ **really/ quite** beautiful/ pretty/ handsome/ attractive/ lovely/ cute/ good-looking/ gorgeous/ stunning/ striking
▶ **very/ rather** beautiful/ pretty/ handsome/ attractive/ lovely/ cute/ good-looking/ gorgeous/ striking
▶ **strikingly** beautiful/ pretty/ handsome/ attractive/ lovely/ good-looking
▶ **almost** beautiful/ pretty/ handsome/ attractive/ good-looking

beautiful (女性・少女が)美しい ◇What a *beautiful* baby! なんてかわいらしい赤ちゃんでしょう ◇She looked stunningly *beautiful* that night. その晩彼女は驚くほど美しく見えた ◇She had a classically *beautiful* face. 彼女は古典的な美しい顔立ちであった 〔反意〕 **ugly** (UGLY)
▶ **beauty** 名 [U] ◇She was a woman of great *beauty*. 彼女はすばらしく美しい女性だった

pretty (少女・女性が)かわいらしい ◇She's got a very *pretty* face. 彼女はとてもかわいらしい顔をしている ◇A *pretty* little girl was standing in the doorway. かわ

beautiful

いい小さな女の子が戸口に立っていた ◇You look so *pretty* in that dress! あの服を着るとすごくかわいく見えるよ ❶ *pretty* は少女について言うとき最もよく用いられる。大人の女性に用いる場合、ふつう少女のように小柄で華奢であることを含意する。 反意 **plain** (UGLY)

handsome （男性が）ハンサムな；（女性が）大柄で美しい ◇He was aptly described as '*tall, dark, and handsome*'. 彼をうまく描写すると「背が高く、色が黒くて、かっこよかった」 彼女は背の高い美しい女性だった ◇The bride and groom made a *handsome* couple. その花嫁と花婿はすばらしいカップルだった

attractive （性的に）魅力的な ◇She's a very *attractive* woman. 彼女はとても魅力的な女性だ ◇I like John as a person, but I don't **find him attractive** physically. ジョンのことは人間的には好きだけど、肉体的魅力は感じないわ 反意 **unattractive** (UGLY)

lovely 《特に英》 きれいな；とても魅力的な ◇You've got *lovely* eyes. あなたは目がすてきですね ◇She looked particularly *lovely* that night. あの晩彼女は特に美しく見えた ❶人を lovely と表現する場合、ふつうその人に対し強い愛情を持っていることを示す。

cute 《特に米，インフォーマル》 性的に魅力的な、セクシーな ◇Check out those *cute* guys over there! あそこにいい男たちがいるから見て

good-looking （性的に）魅力的な ◇She arrived with a very *good-looking* man. 彼女はすごくハンサムな男と一緒に到着した ☞**looks** (APPEARANCE)

ノート **attractive** と **good-looking** の使い分け：attractive と人を表現するとしばしば外見だけでなく人柄も感じのよい人を意味するが、good-looking は人の外見しか表さない。

gorgeous 《インフォーマル》（性的に）とても魅力的な ◇He's got *gorgeous* eyes. 彼はすごくすてきな目をしている ◇You look *gorgeous*! すごくすてきだよ

stunning 《インフォーマル》 すごく美しい、魅力的な ◇You look absolutely *stunning*! すごくすてきだよ

striking （並外れて）魅力的な ◇He was a young man with dark hair and *striking* good looks. 彼は濃い色の髪の驚くほどハンサムな若者だった ☞**striking** (MARKED)

2 ☞ MAGNIFICENT
beautiful・lovely・attractive・pretty・charming・scenic・exquisite・picturesque
物や場所の見た目の良さを表す
【類語訳】心地よい、美しい、きれいな、見た目のよい、魅力的な、景色のよい、精巧な

attractive	charming	beautiful
pretty		lovely
scenic		exquisite
picturesque		

文型&コロケーション

▶ a beautiful/ a lovely/ an attractive/ a pretty/ a charming/ a picturesque **place/ town/ village**

▶ a beautiful/ a lovely/ an attractive/ a charming/ a scenic/ an exquisite/ a picturesque **setting/ view**

▶ a beautiful/ lovely/ pretty/ scenic/ picturesque **spot**

▶ beautiful/ lovely/ attractive/ picturesque **countryside/**

scenery/ surroundings

▶ a beautiful/ a lovely/ an attractive/ a pretty/ an exquisite **design**

▶ a beautiful/ a lovely/ an attractive/ a pretty/ a charming/ an exquisite **voice**

▶ a beautiful/ a lovely/ an attractive/ a charming **smile**

▶ very beautiful/ lovely/ attractive/ pretty/ charming/ scenic/ picturesque

▶ quite beautiful/ lovely/ attractive/ pretty/ charming/ exquisite

▶ rather beautiful/ lovely/ attractive/ pretty/ charming

▶ absolutely beautiful/ lovely/ charming/ exquisite

beautiful （目・感覚・心を楽しませてくれて）美しい、きれいな ◇'They're just *beautiful*,' breathed Jo, when she saw the earrings. そのイヤリングを見て、「ほんとにきれい」とジョーはため息まじりに言った ◇We sat and listened to the *beautiful* music. 私たちは座って美しい音楽を聴いた ◇What a *beautiful* thing to say! なんて美しい言葉が口を衝くのだろう 反意 **ugly** (UGLY)

▶ **beautifully** 副 ◇She sings *beautifully*. 彼女は歌がうまい ◇a *beautifully* decorated house 美しい装飾がされた家

▶ **beauty** 名 [U] The woods were designated an area of outstanding natural *beauty*. その森は屈指の景勝地と称された

lovely 《特に英》 きれいな；（感覚的に）心地よい ◇We travelled through some *lovely* countryside. 私たちはすてきな田園の中を通り抜けた ◇It was a *lovely* evening — calm and still. 気持ちのいい夕方だった —一穏やかで ◇He has a *lovely* voice. 彼はいい声をしている

ノート **beautiful** と **lovely** の使い分け：lovely は beautiful よりもややインフォーマルで、書き言葉よりも話し言葉で用いられる。lovely な物には常に目だけでなく心に訴える温かい性質があり、単に物理的な外見を表すだけではない。beautiful な物にもしばしばこの性質があるが、心というより目と知性に訴えると言える。 ◆The designs were pure, austere and coldly *beautiful*. （そのデザインには素朴で飾り気がなく冷たい感じの美しさがあった） ✕The designs were pure, austere and coldly *lovely*.

attractive （見て）心地よい、見た目のよい ◇This is a big house with an *attractive* garden. ここはきれいな庭付きの大きな家だ ◇Antique furniture is used to make an *attractive* contrast with a modern setting. アンティークの家具が現代的な設備と好対照をなすように用いられています ❶ *attractive* はしばしば話し手・書き手の個人的感情を押し出したくないときに用いられる。 反意 **unattractive** (UGLY)

▶ **attractively** 副 ◇The room is arranged very *attractively*. その部屋は家具がとても魅力的に配置されている

pretty （魅力的で）心地よい ◇That's a *pretty* flower — what's it called? あの可愛い花、なんていう花かな ◇Lydia — what a *pretty* name! リディア。なんて可愛らしい名前なの ❶ *pretty* はしばしば女性・少女にとって魅力的に思えるような物について用いられる。否定的におどけた表現として用いられることもある。 ◆You should have seen him in his swimming trunks — **not a pretty sight**! （彼のトランクスの水着姿を見せたかった。あまりいい眺めじゃないけどね）

charming 《特に書き言葉》 （やや古風だが）とても感じがよい（魅力的な） ◇The cottage is tiny, but *charming*. このコテージは小さいけどいいね ◇What a *charming* name. なんていい名前なんだろう ❶ *charming* はしばしば場所を表

↪beautiful　　　　　　　　　　　　become

現するのに用いられるが、田舎を表現するのには用いられない。
☞ **charm** (INTEREST 名 1)
scenic ［ふつう名詞の前で］景色のよい ◇Loch Lomond is an area of *scenic* beauty. ローモンド湖は景勝地だ ◇We took the ***scenic route*** (=using country roads, not the motorway) back to the hotel. 私たちはホテルに戻るのに景色のよい田園の道を通った

exquisite （ややフォーマル）たいへん美しい、精巧な ◇Look at the *exquisite* craftsmanship in this vase. この花瓶の精巧な職人技を見てください ❶*exquisite* は壮大な美しさではなく細かく繊細な美しさを指す。

picturesque （場所が）古風で美しい ◇This *picturesque* setting is perfect for a relaxing holiday. この絵のようにきれいな環境はのんびりできる休日にはもってこいだ

become　連結動詞

become・get・go・grow・come・turn
…になり始める、ある状態から別の状態に変わる
【類語訳】なる、変化する

▶文型&コロケーション
▶ to get/ grow/ come **to know/ like** sb/ sth
▶ to become/ get/ grow/ turn **cold/ warm/ chilly**
▶ to become/ get/ grow **fat/ old**
▶ to become/ get/ grow **angry/ hungry/ tired**
▶ to become/ get **annoyed/ confused/ involved/ worried**
▶ to become/ get/ grow **used/ accustomed to sth**
▶ to become/ get **engaged/ pregnant**
▶ to become/ go/ turn **red/ white/ blue, etc.**
▶ to become/ go **blind/ crazy/ mad**
▶ to become/ come **loose**
▶ to go/ turn **bad/ sour**

become …になる ◇She was *becoming* confused. 彼女は混乱してきた ◇It was *becoming* more and more difficult to live on his salary. 彼の給料では生活がますます困難になってきた ◇She *became* queen in 1952. 彼女は1952年に女王になった ◇The bill will *become* law next year. その法案は来年には法律になるだろう

get （特定の状態に）なる，（ある点に）達する ◇You'll soon *get* used to the climate here. すぐにここの天候に慣れますよ ◇We ought to go; it's *getting* late. もう行かないと、遅くなってきたから ◇to *get dressed/undressed* (= to put your clothes on/take your clothes off) 服を着る/脱ぐ ◇They plan to *get married* in the summer. 彼らは夏に結婚する予定だ ◇She's upstairs *getting ready*. 彼女は二階で準備をしている ◇Don't *get* your dress dirty! 服を汚さないでね ◇She soon *got* the children ready for school. すぐに彼女は子どもたちに学校に行く準備をさせた ◇You'll like her once you *get to know* her. いったん知り合いになれば彼女のことを好きになるよ ◇She's *getting* to be an old lady now. 彼女はもう老いた女性になってきている

╱ート **become** と **get** の使い分け：両方とも人の状態の変化を指し、◆to *become/get* tired/cold/angry/scared/ pregnant/thin/old/better（疲れる/寒くなる/怒る/怖くなる/妊娠する/やせる/年を取る/よくなる）のように用いることができる。一般的に become のほうがフォーマルで、get は話し言葉でより頻繁に用いられる。しかしながら、どちらか一方しか使用できない場合がいくつかある。 ◆I *became/got*

hungry/upset. (動詞+形容詞. 腹が減った/気が立った). ◆She *became* Queen/a teacher/a member of the club. (動詞+名詞. 彼女は女王/教師/クラブのメンバーになった). ×She *got* Queen, etc. ◆Don't *get* your dress dirty! (動詞+名詞+形容詞. ドレスを汚さないで). ×Don't *become* your dress dirty! ◆It took me a long time to *get* to know her properly. (動詞+to 不定詞. 彼女のことをちゃんと理解するのに時間がかかった). ×to *become* to know her.
意図的な行動の結果生じる変化については get を用いる。 ◆to *get* dressed/married/divorced/killed/ mugged/fired（服を着る/結婚する/離婚する/殺される/襲われる/解雇される）など。 ×to *become* dressed/married, etc. また、get ではなく、become としか用いることができない形容詞もいくつかある。能力に関する able/unable/proficient/skilled など、知識に関する aware, certain, convinced など、有用性に関する available, common, extinct, useful など、明瞭さに関する clear, obvious, evident, apparent などがそうである。

go （好ましくない状態）になる ◇Her hair is *going* grey. 彼女の髪は白くなってきている ◇This milk has *gone* sour. このミルクは酸っぱくなってしまった ◇The children *went* wild with excitement. 子どもたちは興奮して大騒ぎした ◇She *went* to sleep. 彼女は眠りについた ◇That colour has *gone* out of fashion. その色はもはやらなくなった ❶しばしば go red/white/grey など色の変化や、特に go mad/ bad/bald/crazy/wrong/bankrupt など好ましくない変化について言うときに用いられる。

grow （徐々に）…になる ◇The skies *grew* dark and it began to rain. 空が暗くなってきて雨が降り始めた ◇As time went on he *grew* more and more impatient. 時間が経つにつれ彼はますますいらいらしてきた ◇I'm sure you'll *grow* to like her in time. きっとそのうち彼女のことを好きになるでしょう ❶*grow* は突然ではなくある期間にわたって生じる変化について言うときに用いる。徐々に変化することを表すため、しばしば形容詞の比較級と用いられる。×She suddenly *grew* angry. ◆She *grew* braver with time. （だんだんと彼女は勇敢になっていった）

come …になる；…するようになる ◇The buttons had *come* undone. ボタンがはずれてしまっていた ◇Everything will *come right* in the end. 最後には万事うまくくだろう ◇I've *come* to expect this kind of behaviour from him. 私は彼がこうした振る舞いをしてくれるものと思うようになった

╱ート **grow** と **come** の使い分け：この意味においては両語とも形容詞(come loose/grow calm) または to 不定詞(came/grew to realize, understand, believe, etc.)を伴う。

turn （特定の状態に）変化する[変化させる] ◇The leaves were *turning* brown. 葉が茶色になり始めていた ◇He *turned nasty* when we refused to give him the money. 私たちがお金を渡すのを拒むと彼は態度を荒らげた ◇She *turned* a deathly shade of white when she heard the news. その知らせを聞くと彼女はぞっとするほど青ざめた ◇He's a lawyer *turned* politician (= he used to be a lawyer but is now a politician). 彼は元弁護士の政治家だ ❶*turn* は ◆to *turn* blue/red/white（青く/赤く/白くなる）のように色や、◆to *turn* cold/warm/chilly（寒く/暖かく/肌寒くなる）のように天気や、◆to *turn* nasty/ mean/sour/bad（ひどく/下品な/酸っぱく/悪くなる）のよう

に好ましくない変化について用いられる。

begin 動 ☞ ESTABLISH, INTRODUCE, START 動

begin・start・open・embark on/upon sth・take sth up・set about sth・go about sth・commence
物事の初めの部分を行う、初めて…する、初めて物事を起こす[存在させる]
【類語訳】始める、始まる、着手する、開始する、取り掛かる

文型&コロケーション
▶ to begin/ start/ take up/ set about/ go about/ commence **doing sth**
▶ to begin/ start **to do sth**
▶ to begin/ start sth **by doing/ with** sth
▶ to begin/ start/ open/ embark on a/ an **campaign/ enquiry**
▶ to begin/ start/ open a **discussion/ conversation**
▶ to begin/ start/ embark on a **war/ scheme**
▶ to begin a/ start a/ commence **battle**
▶ to begin/ start/ take up/ commence **work**
▶ to begin/ start/ open a **story/ letter/ sentence**
▶ to begin/ start/ open a **day/ year/ meeting**
▶ to begin/ start/ open/ embark on/ take up/ commence a **career/ life**
▶ to begin/ start/ embark on a **journey/ search/ relationship**
▶ to begin/ start/ take up a/ your **employment/ duties/ hobby**
▶ to begin/ start/ commence **production**
▶ to **immediately** begin/ start/ embark on/ set about/ commence/ launch into sth
▶ to have **just** begun/ started/ opened/ embarked on/ taken up/ launched into sth

begin [自, 他] 始める、始まる ◇She *began* by thanking us all for coming. 彼女は私たち皆に対して来場のお礼から言い始めた ◇We *began* work on the project in May. 5月にそのプロジェクトの仕事に着手した ◇I *began* (= started reading) this novel last month and I still haven't finished it. 先月この小説を読み始めてまだ読み終えていない ◇She *began* to cry. 彼女は泣き始めた ◇I was *beginning* to think you'd never come. 君はもう来ないと考え始めていたところだ ◇Everyone *began* talking at once. 皆が一斉にしゃべり始めた 反意 **end** (END 動), ☞ **beginning** (START 名), **begin** (START 動)

start [他, 自] 始める；開始させる ◇I *start* work at nine. 私は9時に仕事を始めます ◇The kids *start* school next week. 子どもたちは来週から学校です ◇We need to *start* (= begin using) a new jar of coffee. 新しいコーヒージャーを使い始めなくてはならない ◇It *started* to rain. 雨が降り始めた ◇Mistakes were *starting* to creep in. 知らず知らず間違いが始めていた ◇She *started* laughing. 彼女は笑い始めた ◇Let's *start* by reviewing what we did last week. 先週やったことの再検討から始めよう ◇It's time you *started on* your homework. 宿題を始める時ですよ ◇Who *started* the fire? 誰が火をつけたのか ◇Do you *start* the day with a good breakfast? 十分な朝食で一日をスタートさせていますか 反意 **finish, stop** (END 動), **finish** (FINISH), **stop** (STOP), ☞ **start** (START 名), **start** (START 動)

ノート **begin** と **start** の使い分け：意味の違いはあまりないが、**start** は話し言葉やビジネスの文脈で、**begin** は書き言葉で頻繁に用いられる。**start** には「物事を発生させる」や「機械を動かし始める」の意味もあるが、**begin** にはない。×Who *began* the fire? ×I can't *begin* the car.

open [他] (活動・イベント・物語・期間を)開始させる ◇Who is going to *open* the conference? 誰がその会議の開会を宣言するのですか ◇The police have *opened* an investigation into the death. 警察は死因の調査を始めた ◇They will *open* the new season with a performance of 'Carmen'. 『カルメン』の公演で新たなシーズンが開幕する ◇I *opened* the story with Viola because I wanted the reader to 'meet' everybody through her eyes. 私は物語をヴァイオラから始めた、なぜなら彼女の目を通して読者に皆に「会って」もらいたかったからだ 反意 **close** (END 動), ☞ **open** (START 動), **opening** (START 名), **opening** (FIRST)

em'bark on/upon sth 句動詞 《ややフォーマル》(新しい事・困難な事を)始める ◇She is about to *embark on* a diplomatic career. もうすぐ彼女は外交官職に乗り出すことになっている ◇Remember these basic rules before *embarking upon* major home improvements. 大規模な家のリフォームに着手する前にこれらの基本的なルールを覚えておきなさい

'take sth 'up 句動詞 [受身なし] (仕事・趣味などを)始める ◇He *takes up* his duties next week. 彼は来週から任務を開始する ◇She has *taken up* (= started to learn to play) the oboe. 彼女はオーボエを始めた 反意 **give sth up** (STOP)

'set about sth 句動詞 [受身なし] …し始める ◇She *set about* the business of cleaning the house. 彼女は家を清掃するビジネスを始めた ◇We need to *set about* finding a solution. 私たちは解決策を捜し始める必要がある

'go about sth 句動詞 [受身なし] 《しばしば否定文およびhowの疑問文で》(特定の方法で)…に取り掛かる ◇You're not *going about* the job in the right way. そのやり方はそもそも始めから違っている ◇How should I *go about* finding a job? どうやって仕事を見つければいいんだろう

commence [他] 《フォーマル》開始する ◇The company *commenced* operations in April. その会社は4月に業務を開始した ☞ **commence** (START 動)

beginner 名 ☞ RECRUIT

beginner・novice・rookie
ある事を始めたばかりでほとんど知識や経験のない人
【類語訳】初心者、新米、新人

文型&コロケーション
▶ a beginner/ novice **in** sth
▶ a/ an **absolute/ complete** beginner/ novice

beginner [C] (学び始めたばかりの)初心者 ◇She's in the *beginners'* class. 彼女は初級クラスにいます ◇Italian for *beginners* 初心者向けのイタリア語

novice [C] (仕事・活動を始めたばかりの)初心者 ◇I'm a complete *novice at* diving. ダイビングはまったくの初心者です ◇Some ski resorts are ideal for *novices*. スキー場のなかには初心者に最適なところもある

rookie [C] 《特に米, インフォーマル》新米、新人 ◇The transition from *rookie* to fighter pilot starts with selection day. 新米から戦闘機パイロットになるにはまず選抜を受ける ❶rookieはしばしば兵士・警官・スポーツ選手について言うときに用いられる. ◆Derek Jeter was voted American League *Rookie* of the Year in 1996. (1996年デレク・ジーターはアメリカンリーグの新人王に選ばれた). ◆a *rookie* quarterback (ルーキーのクォーターバック).

benefit 名

benefit・advantage・strength・merit・good・virtue・asset・plus・good point
物事の有益な効果や性質
【類語訳】有益, 恩恵, 利点, 優位, 有利, 長所, 強み, 美点, 良さ

文型&コロケーション

- some/ any/ no benefit/ advantage/ virtue **in** sth
- a benefit/ an advantage/ an asset **for** sb/ sth
- to be to **sb's** benefit/ advantage
- to do sth **for sb's** benefit/ good
- to be **with/ without the** benefit/ advantage **of** sth
- to **be of** great/ major/ real, etc. benefit/ advantage/ merit
- **considerable/ great/ real** benefits/ advantages/ strengths/ merits/ good/ virtues/ assets
- **maximum/ additional** benefit/ advantage
- **relative** benefits/ advantages/ strengths/ merits/ virtues
- to **have** the benefit/ advantage/ merit/ virtue
- to **see** the benefit/ advantage/ merit/ good/ virtue

benefit [U, C] (物事の有益な)効果 ◇She had the *benefit* of a good education. 彼女はよい教育の恩恵を受けた ◇The new regulations will be of *benefit* to everyone. 新しい規則は皆に利点があるだろう ◇For maximum *benefit*, take the tablets before meals. 薬が最もよく効くように, この錠剤は食前にお飲みください ◇It was good to see her finally *reaping the benefits* (= getting the results) of all her hard work. 彼女の努力のすべてがやっと報われてよかった ☞ **beneficial** (VALUABLE 2)

advantage [C, U] (人 [他の物事] よりも)有利, 優位 ◇Having a degree is a huge *advantage* when it comes to getting a job. 仕事を得る段になると学位を持っているととても有利だ ◇You will be *at an advantage* (= have an advantage) if you have thought about the interview questions in advance. 事前に面接で質問されるようなことについて考えておくと有利になる ◇Is there any *advantage* in getting there early? そこに早く着くと何かいいことがありますか ◇A small car has the added *advantage* of being cheaper to run. 小さな車は燃費がいいというさらなる利点があります ◇Each of these systems has its *advantages and disadvantages*. これらのシステムにはそれぞれメリットとデメリットがある 反意 **disadvantage** (DISADVANTAGE)

strength [C] (人・物事が有利になる)長所, 強み ◇The ability to keep calm is one of her many *strengths*. 平常心を保つ能力は彼女の数ある強みのひとつだ ◇Consider all the *strengths and weaknesses* of the argument. その論のあらゆる長所と短所をよく考えなさい 反意 **weakness**

merit [C, ふつう複数で] (人・物事が持つ)利点, 長所 ◇We will consider each case *on its (own) merits* (= without considering any other issues, feelings, etc.). 他のことがらや感情などを考慮せずにそれぞれのメリットをよく考えるようにしま

す ◇They weighed up the relative *merits* of the four candidates. 彼らは候補者4人の長所を比較検討した

good [U] (人・物事にとって)役立つこと, 利益 ◇Cuts have been made for *the good of* the company. 会社の利益のために賃金が引き下げられた ◇I'm telling you this *for your own good*. 君のためを思ってそう言っているんだ ◇*What's the good of* earning all that money if you've no time to enjoy it? 使う時間がないならそんなにお金を稼いで何の意味があるだろう ◇*What good would it do* to tell her about it after all this time? 今さら彼女にそれについて話して何の意味がある

virtue [C, U] 《ややフォーマル》(物事の)美点, 良さ ◇The plan has the *virtue* of simplicity. その計画は簡単なところがいい ◇They could see no *virtue* in discussing it further. 彼らはそれについてさらに話し合うことに何の利点も見出せなかった

ノート **benefit, advantage, merit, virtue の使い分け**: benefitは行動することによってもたらされるもの. advantage, merit, virtueは人・物・計画・行為が本来持っているもの. advantageは人・物が他より優れていること. merit, virtueは他と比べるわけではないが, relative advantages/merits/ virtues of sb/sthのように言える. meritsはふつう複数形で, 人・物事の総合的に見た良さを指すときに用いられる. virtueは単数形・複数形・不可算でも用いることができ, 魅力的な[有益な]良さを指すときに用いられる.

asset [C] (成功への助けとなる)価値ある[有益な]人[物] ◇She'll be a great *asset to* any company she works for. 彼女ならどこでも入った会社で貴重な人材になるだろう ◇I'm not sure if his forcefulness is an *asset* or a liability. 彼の強引さが吉と出るか凶と出るかは定かではありません 反意 **liability** ❶liabilityは多くの問題を引き起こす人・物事を指す. ◆Since his injury, Jones has become more of a *liability* than an asset to the team. (怪我をして以来ジョーンズはチームにとって貴重な財産というよりはお荷物になっていた).

plus [C] 《ややインフォーマル》有利さ, 利点 ◇Being able to speak French is *a definite plus* when you're travelling in North Africa. 北アフリカを旅行するときフランス語を話せたら間違いなく有利だ ◇You should carefully consider *the pluses and minuses* (= good and bad points) of going to live in the country. 田舎暮らしをすることの長所と短所をよく考えないといけないよ 反意 **minus**

good point [C] (人・物事の)好ましい特徴, よい点 ◇One of the *good points* about the system is that it treats everyone equally. その制度のよい点のひとつは皆を平等に扱うところだ ◇His one *good point* is that he knows how to fix cars. 彼の強みのひとつは車の修理法を知っていることだ ❶good pointはadvantage, merit, virtueと似ているが, 本来の良さというよりは後から得られた良さを指す.

best 形 ☞ FAVOURITE, IDEAL

best・wise・desirable・sensible・advisable
特定の状況においてベストであることを表す
【類語訳】最適の, 最善の, 賢明な, 望ましい, 良識的な, 理にかなった

文型&コロケーション

- to be best/ wise/ desirable/ sensible/ advisable **to do sth**
- the best/ a wise/ a sensible **choice/ thing to do/ use of sth**

▶the best/ a wise/ a sensible **course (of action)/ investment**
▶it is/ it might be best/ wise/ desirable/ sensible/ advisable (to do sth)

best 最適の、最善の ◇What's the *best* way to cook steak? ステーキを焼く一番いい方法は何ですか ◇The *best* thing to do would be to apologize. 謝罪するのが一番だろう ◇He's the *best* man for the job. 彼こそその仕事にうってつけの男だ ◇I'm not in the *best* position to advise you. 私は君にアドバイスをする最適の立場にはない ◇It's *best* if you go now. 今出かけるのが最善だよ [反意] **worst** ❶worstは最も不適切な事、人、行動を表す。◆Going back now is just about the *worst* thing you could do. (今戻るのはまさに最悪の選択だ)。

wise (適切な判断に基づいているので)賢明な ◇Locking your car doors is always a *wise* precaution. 車のドアにロックをかけるのはいつだって賢い安全対策です ◇The *wisest* course of action is just to say nothing. ただ何も言わないのが最も賢明なやり方だ ◇It was very *wise* of you to leave when you did. あの時君が帰ったのはとても賢明だった [反意] **unwise** (RECKLESS)
▶**wisely** 副 ◇He *wisely* decided to tell the truth. 彼は賢明にも真実を話すことを決心した

desirable (フォーマル)望ましい ◇It is *desirable that* interest rates be reduced. 金利の引き下げが望ましい ◇It is no longer *desirable for* adult children to live with their parents. もはや、成人した子どもが親と同居するのは望ましいとは言えない ◇An end to the hostilities remains a highly *desirable* objective. 戦闘行為の終結が強く望まれる目標であることに変わりはない [反意] **undesirable** (UNWANTED)

sensible (特に書き言葉)(的確判断力・理性に基づき)良識的な、賢明な ◇That wasn't a very *sensible* thing to do! それをやったのはあまり賢明ではなかったね ◇The *sensible* thing would be to take a taxi home. タクシーで家に帰るのが賢明だろう ◇I think it's a very *sensible* idea. それはとても賢明な考えだと思うよ ◇Choose a *sensible* diet and stick to it. 理にかなった食事を選んでそれを続けましょう [反意] **stupid** (CRAZY)
▶**sensibly** 副 ◇Try to drive carefully, courteously and *sensibly*. 慎重に、思いやりと良識をもって運転してください

advisable [名詞の前にはまれ] (ややフォーマル)(目的を達成する のに)よい ◇Early booking is *advisable*. お早めにご予約されることをお勧めします ◇It is *advisable* to practise each exercise individually at first. まずそれぞれの運動を別々に行うことをお勧めします [反意] **inadvisable** ❶inadvisableは賢明でなく勧められない行動に用いられる。◆It is *inadvisable* to bring children on this trip. (今回の旅行には子どもたちを連れて行かないことをお勧めします)。

better 形 ☞ GOOD 1

better・superior・preferable
ある物[人]が別の物[人]よりいいことを表す
【類語訳】よりよい、より優れた、より勝った、好ましい、望ましい

文型&コロケーション
▶superior/ preferable **to** sb/ sth
▶better than/ superior to/ preferable to **the rest**
▶far/ greatly/ vastly/ infinitely better/ superior/ prefera-ble
▶slightly better/ superior

better 《good の比較級》(水準・質などが)よりよい、より優れた ◇The weather should get *better* towards the end of the week. 天気は週末に向けて好転するはずだ ◇Her new movie is *much better* than her last one. 彼女の新作映画は前作よりもずっとよい ◇Your work is *getting better all the time*. 君の作品は常によくなってきている ◇Her work is getting *better and better*. 彼女の作品はますますよくなっている ◇There's *nothing better than* a long soak in a hot bath. 熱い風呂に長くつかる以上のものはない ◇If you only exercise once a week, that's *better than nothing* (= better than no exercise at all). 1週間に1回だけの運動なら何もやらないよりましと言ったところだ [反意] **worse** ❶worseであるものは水準や品質が劣る。◆The weather *got worse* during the day. (天気は昼間のうちにいっそう悪くなった)。◆The interview was *much worse than* he had expected. (そのインタビューは彼が考えていた以上にはるかにひどかった)。

superior (ややフォーマル)より優れた、より勝った ◇This model is far *superior* to its competitors. このモデルのほうが競争相手よりもはるかに優れている ◇Her *superior* intellect makes her the ideal candidate for the position. より優れた知性によって彼女はその地位にふさわしい候補者になっている ◇This computer is technically *superior* to the others, but it's not as user-friendly. このコンピューターは技術的にはほかより優れているが、使い勝手はそれほどよくない ◇They won the battle because of their *superior* numbers. 数的優位から彼らは戦いに勝利した [反意] **inferior** (POOR 2)

preferable 好ましい、望ましい ◇Anything was *preferable* to the tense atmosphere at home. 家での張り詰めた空気に比べたら何であってもましだった ◇It would be *preferable* to employ two people rather than one. 一人よりも二人雇うのが望ましいだろう
▶**preferably** 副 ◇We're looking for a new house, *preferably* near the school. 私たちは新しい家を探しているところです、できることなら学校の近くで

biased 形

biased・prejudiced・partisan・discriminatory・intolerant・one-sided・unbalanced
不公平が生じるくらい、不当に人や物事を毛嫌いしたりひいきしたりすることを表す
【類語訳】偏った、偏見のある、差別的な、偏狭な

文型&コロケーション
▶biased/ prejudiced/ discriminatory **against** sb/ sth
▶biased/ prejudiced **in favour of** sb/ sth
▶a partisan/ a prejudiced/ a discriminatory/ an intolerant **attitude**
▶a biased/ a prejudiced/ a partisan/ a one-sided/ an unbalanced **view**
▶a biased/ prejudiced/ partisan **opinion**
▶a biased/ partisan/ one-sided **account**
▶biased/ partisan/ one-sided **coverage**
▶somewhat/ rather biased/ prejudiced/ partisan/ one-sided/ unbalanced

biased 《けなして》(特定の人・集団・考えに)偏った ◇They

↪biased

admit that they're ***biased towards*** the Republican Party. 彼らは共和党をひいきしていると認めている ◇The article was heavily *biased* against the current regime. その記事は現政権をひどく毛嫌いしていた ◇There is little doubt that most media coverage is *biased*. マスコミの報道の大半が偏見に満ちていることはまず間違いない ◇She gave a somewhat *biased* account of the proceedings. 事態の推移に関して彼女はやや偏った説明をした 反意 **unbiased** (OBJECTIVE)，☞ **bias** (DISCRIMINATION)，**bias** (INFLUENCE 動)

prejudiced《けなして》(人種・宗教・性別・年齢などを理由に)(理不尽に)毛嫌いする，ひいきする，偏見を持つ ◇Few people will admit to being racially *prejudiced*. 甘んじて人種的偏見を受け入れる人はほとんどいないだろう ◇They are strongly *prejudiced* against older candidates. 彼らは年配の候補者たちに強い反感を抱いている ☞ **prejudice** (DISCRIMINATION)，**prejudice** (INFLUENCE 動)

partisan《ふつうけなして》(特定の人・集団・考えに)偏った ◇Most newspapers are politically *partisan*. 新聞の大半は政治的に偏っている ◇The speakers were encouraged by a large *partisan* crowd. 演説者たちは熱狂的に支持する大群衆に勇気づけられた 反意 **non-partisan** (OBJECTIVE)

discriminatory《フォーマル，けなして》差別的な ◇Women's groups claim that the laws are *discriminatory*. 女性の権利グループがそれらの法律が差別的であると訴えている ◇Companies were urged to tackle sexually and racially *discriminatory* recruitment practices. 企業は新規採用の際の性差別，人種差別の実態に取り組むことを迫られている ☞ **discrimination** (DISCRIMINATION)

intolerant《ややフォーマル，けなして》(自分とは異なる意見・振る舞いに対して)偏狭な ◇He was deeply ***intolerant*** *of* all opposition. 彼はあらゆる反対意見に対してまったく聞く耳をもたなかった 反意 **tolerant** (TOLERANT)，☞ **intolerance** (DISCRIMINATION)

,one-'sided《けなして》(議論・意見・説明などが)偏った ◇The debate was very *one-sided*, and lacking in any serious thinking. その討論はとても偏っていていかなる真剣な考えにも欠けていた

unbalanced [ふつう名詞の前で]《ふつうけなして》(物事の一面だけを過大[過小]評価して)偏った，アンバランスな ◇The media often presents a somewhat *unbalanced* picture of scientific progress. マスコミはしばしば科学的進歩についてやや偏った描き方をする 反意 **balanced ❶** *a balanced view/ treatment* は「あらゆる側面を適切に評価して，公平に見たり扱ったりすること」を意味する． ◆The programme presented *a balanced view* of the two sides of the conflict. 《ほめて》その番組は争っている双方を偏りなく扱った

bill 名

bill・account・invoice・check・tab
購入[利用]した商品やサービスに対して，いくら支払う義務があるかを記録したもの
【類語訳】請求書，掛け勘定，つけ，勘定書

文型&コロケーション
▶the bill/ invoice/ check/ tab **for** sth
▶to **pay/ settle** a bill/ an account/ an invoice/ a check
▶to **pick up** the bill/ check/ tab

▶to **put** sth **on** the bill/ (sb's) account/ the tab
▶to **send/ submit** a bill/ an invoice to a customer
▶to **ask for/ get** the bill/ check

bill [C]（商品・サービスの）請求書；金額，費用 ◇*the telephone/ electricity/ gas **bill*** 電話／電気／ガス料金請求書 ◇We ***ran up*** a massive hotel ***bill***. 私たちはホテルの膨大な請求書の合計を計算した ◇Is the company going to *foot the bill* (= pay) for the repairs? その会社は修理費用を払ってくれるの ◇I'll be sending you the *bill* (= I will expect you to pay) for the dry-cleaning! クリーニングの請求書を送っておくよ ◇The waiter brought the *bill* to their table.《特に英》ウェイターが彼らのテーブルに勘定書を持って行った[きた] ☞ **bill** (CHARGE 動)

account [C]（商品・サービスの）掛け勘定，つけ ◇Put it on my *account* please. それはつけておいてください ◇We have *accounts* with most of our suppliers. 当社は大半の仕入先とつけで取り引きしている ◇She bought the furniture she wanted ***on account*** (= she would pay for it later). 彼女は欲しかった家具をつけで買った

invoice [C]《ややフォーマル》（商品・仕事の）請求書 ◇The timber merchants sent an *invoice* for £250. 木材業者は250ポンドの請求書を送付した ☞ **invoice** (CHARGE 動)

ノート **bill** と **invoice** の使い分け：bill はレストラン，バー，ホテル，ガス会社，電気会社からの請求書，または人からの損害賠償の請求時に受け取るもの．invoice は供給された商品，行われた仕事に対するもので，顧客と供給会社の間で了解されている．また，invoice はふつう商品が届けられた後，仕事が完了した後に送付される．

check [C]《米》（レストランの）勘定書 ◇Can I have the *check*, please? お勘定をお願いします ❶《英》ではふつうcheck の代わりに bill が用いられる．

tab [C]《ややインフォーマル》（レストラン・バーの）後日支払う勘定書；物の値段，費用 ◇*a bar **tab*** バーの未払い勘定書 ◇Can I put it on my *tab*? それ，つけておいてくれる ◇He walked out of the restaurant and left me to pick up the *tab* (= pay) for the whole meal. 彼はレストランから出てしまい，食事の勘定を全部私に支払わせた

birthday 名

birthday・anniversary・commemoration・jubilee
1年前または何年か前に起こった出来事を記念する時
【類語訳】誕生日，バースデー，記念日，記念式典

文型&コロケーション
▶a **first/ second/ fiftieth** birthday/ anniversary
▶a **silver/ golden/ diamond** anniversary/ jubilee
▶**it is** sb/ sth's birthday/ anniversary/ jubilee
▶to **have** a birthday/ anniversary
▶to **celebrate/ mark** a birthday/ an anniversary/ a jubilee
▶to **forget/ remember** sb's birthday/ anniversary
▶a birthday/ an anniversary **party/ present/ card**
▶**Happy** Birthday/ Anniversary!

birthday [C] 誕生日 ◇My *birthday* is in August. 私の誕生日は8月です ◇It's Sam's *birthday* tomorrow. He'll be seven. 明日はサムの誕生日です．7歳になります ◇Would you like a piece of ***birthday cake***? バースデーケーキを一切れいかが

anniversary [C] 記念日 ◇Today is the *anniversary*

of his wife's death. 今日は彼の奥さんの命日だ ◇It's our **wedding anniversary** tomorrow. 明日は私たちの結婚記念日だ ◇She's organizing the theatre's 25th *anniversary* celebrations (= it is 25 years since it began). 彼女はその劇場の25周年の式典の準備をしている

commemoration [U, C]《ややフォーマル》記念式典；記念行為[物] ◇a *commemoration* service/service of *commemoration* in the cathedral 大聖堂での記念礼拝 ◇a statue **in commemoration of** the founder of the nation/of the soldiers' sacrifice 国の創設者／戦没者を記念する像

jubilee [C] (25, 50または60周年を記念する特別な)記念日[記念式] ◇Queen Victoria had been on the throne for 60 years and her diamond *jubilee* was being celebrated. ヴィクトリア女王が戴冠60周年を迎え、60周年式典が祝われていた ◇The school's silver *jubilee* will be marked in style. その学校の25周年記念式典は盛大に行われる予定だ

ノート **anniversary**と**jubilee**の使い分け：silver wedding anniversary/wedding anniversary/jubileeは25周年、goldenの場合は50周年、diamondの場合は60周年を記念する。(英)ではsilver/golden/diamond weddingと言い、(米)ではsilver/golden/diamond anniversaryと言うほうが一般的。

bit 名 ☞ FRAGMENT, PIECE

bit・piece・scrap・grain・particle・morsel・speck
量が少ないことを表す
【類語訳】少量、小片、かけら、断片、粒、粒子

文型&コロケーション
▶a bit/ piece/ scrap/ grain/ particle/ morsel/ speck **of** sth
▶a **small/ tiny** bit/ piece/ scrap/ grain/ particle/ morsel/ speck
▶a **little** bit/ piece/ scrap/ speck
▶a **large** bit/ piece/ particle
▶**odd** bits/ pieces/ scraps
▶a grain/ particle/ speck **of** dust
▶a bit/ piece/ scrap **of information/ news**
▶a bit/ piece/ scrap **of paper**
▶to **smash** sth **to** bits/ pieces
▶to **pick up** the bits/ pieces of sth

bit [C]《特に英、ややインフォーマル》少量、小片 ◇Do you want a *bit* of pizza? ピザを少し食べませんか ◇Can you save me a *bit*? 私に少しとっておいてくれますか ◇You've got *bits* of grass in your hair. 髪に少し草がついていますよ ◇A big *bit* of plaster just fell down from the ceiling. 大きな漆喰のかけらが天井から落ちてきたばかりだ ◇I've got a *bit* of shopping to do. 少し買いたい物があります ◇With a *bit* of luck, we'll be there by 12. うまくすれば12時までにはそこに着くだろう

piece [C] 一片、破片；一例、一定量 ◇There were tiny *pieces* of glass all over the road. 道路一面に細かいガラス片が散乱していた ◇The vase lay **in *pieces*** on the floor. 花瓶が床の上で粉々になっていた ◇It was an interesting *piece* of research. それは面白い調査だった ❶a *piece* ofは advice, bread, chewing gum, equipment, furniture, information, luck, luggage, news, paper, researchなどいろいろな不可算名詞と共に用いられる。☞ PIECE

scrap [C] (紙・布の)小片, (情報の)断片 ◇She scribbled his phone number on a *scrap* of paper. 彼女は紙切れに彼の電話番号を走り書きした ◇We need to check every *scrap* of information that might give us a clue as to what happened. 何が起こったかに関する手がかりになるかもしれない情報の断片を一つ一つチェックする必要がある

grain [C] (特定の物質の硬い)小片[粒] ◇She sprinkled a few more **grains of rice** into the pan. 彼女はさらにもう少し米粒を平鍋の中へ振り入れた ◇I got a *grain* of sand caught in my eye. 砂粒が目に入った ❶*grain*は以下の連語で用いられる。◆a *grain* of rice/wheat/salt/sugar/sand (米／小麦／塩／砂糖／砂の粒)。

particle [C] 微細な粒子 ◇He watched the *particles* of dust floating in the light. 彼は光のなかに浮かぶ埃の粒子を見ていた ◇There was **not a particle of evidence** (= no evidence at all) to prove his case. 彼の言い分を立証する証拠はまったくなかった

morsel [C]《ややフォーマル》(食べ物の)少量, 小片 ◇They put out some **tasty *morsels*** for the hedgehogs. 彼らはハリネズミのためにごちそうを少し取り出した

speck [C] (埃の)小さな粒子 ◇There wasn't a *speck* of dirt anywhere. どこにも塵一つ落ちていなかった ◇He brushed a few *specks* of dust from his sleeve. 彼は袖についた埃を少し払い落とした

bite 動

bite・chew・munch・nibble・gnaw・crunch
食べ物を食べるための歯の使い方を表す
【類語訳】噛む、かじる、噛み砕く

文型&コロケーション
▶to bite/ chew/ munch/ gnaw/ crunch **through** sth
▶to bite/ chew/ munch/ nibble/ gnaw **at** sth
▶to bite/ chew/ munch/ nibble/ crunch **on** sth
▶to chew/ munch/ nibble/ gnaw **away at** sth
▶to bite/ munch/ nibble/ crunch an **apple**
▶to chew on/ gnaw/ crunch a **bone**
▶to bite/ chew your **lip/ nails**
▶to chew/ munch/ nibble/ gnaw/ crunch **your way through** sth

bite [自, 他] 噛む ◇She *bit into* a ripe juicy pear. 彼女は熟したジューシーな梨にかぶりついた ◇Does your dog *bite*? あなたの犬は噛みますか ◇She was *bitten* by the dog. 彼女は犬に噛まれた ◇He *bit off* a large chunk of bread. 彼はパンをがぶりとかじった ◇Stop *biting* your nails. 爪を噛むのはやめなさい
▶**bite** 名 [C] ◇She took a huge *bite* out of the chocolate bar. 彼女はチョコレートバーを大きく一かじりした ◇The dog gave me a playful *bite*. 犬が私をじゃれて噛んだ

chew [他, 自] 噛み砕く；噛み続ける ◇*Chew* your food *up* well before you swallow it. 食べ物はよく噛んでから飲み込みなさい ◇He is always *chewing* gum. 彼はいつもガムを噛んでばかりいる ◇After the operation you may find it difficult to *chew* and swallow. 術後は噛んで飲み込むのが難しいかもしれません ◇The dog was *chewing* on a bone. 犬が骨を噛んでいた ◇Rosa *chewed* on her lip and stared at the floor. ローザは唇を噛んで床を見つめた ❶食べるために口の中で噛むことはchew sthまたはchew sth upと言い、食べるためではなく例えば唇などをずっと噛んでいることはchew on sthと言う。

munch [自, 他]（歯切れのよい音をさせて）食べ続ける ◇She *munched* on an apple. 彼女はリンゴをシャキシャキと食べた ◇He sat in a chair *munching* his toast. 彼は椅子に座ってトーストをムシャムシャ食べていた ◇I *munched* my way through a huge bowl of cereal. 私は大盛りのシリアルをひたすら食べ続けた

nibble [他, 自]（食べ物を）少しずつ噛む ◇We sat drinking wine and *nibbling* olives. 私たちは座ってワインを飲みオリーブをかじっていた ◇She took some cake from the tray and *nibbled* at it. 彼女はトレーからケーキを取り出して少しずつ口に入れた

gnaw [他, 自]（徐々になくなるまで続けて）かじる ◇The dog was *gnawing* a bone. 犬が骨をかじっていた ◇Rats had *gnawed* through the cable. ネズミがケーブルをかじって穴を開けてしまった

crunch [他, 自] 音を立てて噛み砕く ◇She *crunched* her apple noisily. 彼女はリンゴをムシャムシャ音を立てて食べた ◇He was *crunching* on a piece of toast. 彼はトーストを一枚ムシャムシャ食べていた

bitter 〔形〕

bitter・pungent・sour・acrid・sharp・acid
味やにおいが強くて，不快であることを表す
【類語訳】苦い，苦みのある，（舌に）ぴりっとくる，（鼻に）つんとくる，ぴりっとする，すっぱい，酸味のある

〔文型&コロケーション〕
- a bitter/ a pungent/ an acrid/ a sharp/ an acid **taste/ flavour**
- a bitter/ a pungent/ a sour/ an acrid/ a sharp/ an acid **smell/ odour**
- a bitter/ a pungent/ an acrid/ a sharp **scent**
- a bitter/ a sour/ a sharp/ an acid **fruit**
- a pungent/ sharp **cheese**
- pungent/ acrid **smoke**
- to **taste** bitter/ sour/ sharp
- to **smell** bitter/ sharp

bitter 苦い，苦みのある ◇*bitter* coffee/chocolate 苦みのあるコーヒー/チョコレート ◇The drink tasted *bitter*. その飲み物は苦みがあった ◇This plant is ignored by livestock because of the *bitter* taste. この植物は苦いので家畜から敬遠されている

pungent（舌に）ぴりっとくる，（鼻に）つんとくる ◇the *pungent* smell of burning rubber 鼻につんとくる焼けているゴムの臭い ◇The air was *pungent* with the smell of spices. 辺りはスパイスのつんとくる臭いが漂っていた

sour すっぱい ◇Too much pulp produces a *sour* wine. 果肉が多すぎるとすっぱいワインができる 〔反意〕**sweet** ❶ sweetな食べ物には砂糖か砂糖の味が含まれている ◆I need a cup of hot *sweet* tea.（温かくて甘い紅茶を1杯ほしい）◆This wine is too *sweet* for me.（このワインは私には甘口すぎる）☞ **sour (ROTTEN)**

acrid（舌に）ぴりっとする，（鼻に）つんとくる ◇The fog was yellow and *acrid* and bit at the back of the throat. 煙は黄色く，鼻につんとくて，のどの奥がひりひりした

sharp（味・においが）ぴりっとする ◇The cheese has a distinctively *sharp* taste. そのチーズは独特のぴりっとした味がする

acid すっぱい，酸味のある ◇It's a very juicy fruit with a slightly *acid* flavour. それはすっぱい風味のあ

る，とても果汁たっぷりの果物だ

> 〔ノート〕**bitter, pungent, sour, acrid, sharp, acid の使い分け**: bitter, sour, sharp, acid はどれも味について，pungent と acrid はにおいについて多く用いられる。bitter はふつう不快なものだが，コーヒーやチョコレートの苦みを好む人もいる。この味を表すのに使える他の語はない。× *pungent/sour/acrid/sharp/acid* coffee/chocolate. sour と acid は両語ともレモンやまだ熟していないフルーツの味をイメージさせる。sour はふつう否定的な語だが，acid は否定的にもなりうるし，ただ単にすっぱいことを表すこともある。sharp または pungent な味は，不快というより強烈で，チーズについて述べるときに特に用いられる。× *bitter/sour/acrid/acid* cheese. pungent なにおいはふつう不快ではないが，濃厚でスパイシーな料理の pungent なにおいを好む人もいる。acrid なにおいは常に不快で，食べ物のにおいを表すのに acrid を使うことはない。

blame 〔動〕☞ SCOLD

blame・criticize・condemn・attack・denounce・censure
好ましくないことをしたとして人・事を支持しない
【類語訳】非難する，批判する，責める，糾弾する，とがめる

〔文型&コロケーション〕
- to blame/ criticize/ condemn/ attack/ denounce/ censure sb/ sth **for** sth
- to blame/ criticize/ condemn/ attack/ denounce/ censure the **government/ president**
- to criticize/ condemn/ attack/ denounce/ censure a **decision**
- to criticize/ condemn/ attack/ denounce sb/ sth **strongly**
- to blame/ criticize/ condemn/ attack/ denounce/ censure sb/ sth **publicly**
- to blame/ criticize/ attack sb/ sth **unfairly**
- to be **widely** blamed/ criticized/ condemned/ attacked/ denounced
- to be **roundly** criticized/ condemned/ attacked

blame [他] 非難する，責める ◇She *blamed* the government for failing to respond to the crisis. 危機への対応がまずかったとして彼女は政府を非難した ◇A dropped cigarette is being *blamed* for the fire. タバコの投げ捨てがその火事の原因と見られている ◇Police are *blaming* the accident **on** dangerous driving. 警察はその事故の原因は危険な運転にあると見ている ◇If you lose your job you'll **only have yourself to blame** (= it will be your fault). 職を失っても自業自得だからね ◇'I just slammed down the phone when he said that.' '*I don't blame you!* (= I think that was reasonable and the right thing to do)'〔話し言葉〕「彼がそう言うと私はただ電話をガチャンと切ったよ」「無理もないよ」◇Call her if you like but *don't blame me* (= because I have advised you not to do it) if she's angry. 彼女に電話したければすればいい。でも彼女が怒っても私は知らないよ
☞ **blame (FAULT), to blame (GUILTY)**

criticize（英でも **-ise**）[他, 自] 非難する，批判する ◇The decision was *criticized* by environmental groups. その決定は環境保護団体から非難された ◇The government has been *criticized* for not taking the problem seriously. 政府はその問題を深刻に捉えなかったと非難されて

block

いる ◇All you ever do is *criticize*! 君のやる事といえば批判ばかりだ 反意 praise (PRAISE 動), ☞ critical (CRITICAL), criticism (CRITICISM)
▶**critic** [名] [C] ◇She is one of the ruling party's most outspoken *critics*. 彼女は与党に対して非常に遠慮のない批判をする批評家の一人だ ◇She is looking for a chance to prove her *critics* wrong. 彼女は自分を批判する人間が間違っていることを証明するチャンスをうかがっている
condemn [他]《ややフォーマル》(道徳的理由で)強く責める，糾弾する ◇The government issued a statement *condemning* the killings. 政府は殺害を強く非難する声明を発表した 反意 condone (FORGIVE), ☞ condemnation (CRITICISM)
attack [他]《ややインフォーマル》(尊敬されなくなるようにするため)強く非難する ◇The studio audience repeatedly *attacked* the minister for her stance. スタジオの観覧者はその大臣の姿勢を何度も激しく非難した ◇He *attacked* the idea that the company's practices were bad for the environment. 彼はその会社の業務が環境によくないという考え方に対して激しく攻撃を加えた ☞ attack (CRITICISM)
denounce [他]《ややフォーマル》(公式に)激しく非難する ◇The project was *denounced* as a scandalous waste of public money. そのプロジェクトは公的資金の恥ずべき浪費だとして激しく非難された ❶単に嫌いだからという理由で，間違っていると思うときに denounce を用いる。☞ **denunciation** (CRITICISM)
censure [他]《フォーマル》(公式に)激しく非難する，とがめる ◇He was *censured* by the council for leaking information to the press. 彼は報道機関への情報漏洩のかどで議会から激しく非難された ☞ **censure** (CRITICISM)

block 動

1 ☞ HOLD SB/STH UP
block・interfere with sth・handicap・inhibit・
hamper・hinder・obstruct・hold sb/sth back
事が発生［発展，進歩］するのを止める
【類語訳】妨害する，妨げる，困難にする，阻む

文型&コロケーション

▶to hamper sb/ hinder sb/ hold sb back **from (doing)** sth
▶to block/ interfere with/ inhibit/ hamper/ hinder/ obstruct/ hold back **progress**
▶to block/ interfere with/ handicap/ inhibit/ hamper/ hinder/ hold back **growth**
▶to block/ interfere with/ inhibit/ hamper/ hinder/ obstruct **development**
▶to block/ interfere with/ inhibit/ hinder/ obstruct a **process**
▶to interfere with/ inhibit/ hamper/ hinder/ obstruct sb's **work**
▶to block/ interfere with/ inhibit/ hamper/ hinder sb's **ability** (to do sth)
▶to inhibit/ hamper/ hinder/ hold back the **recovery** of sb/ sth
▶to block/ hamper/ hinder/ obstruct an **investigation**
▶to block/ hamper/ hinder sb's **efforts**
▶to **seriously** interfere with/ handicap/ inhibit/ hamper/ hinder sb/ sth
▶to **deliberately** block/ hinder/ obstruct sth
▶to **greatly/ significantly/ severely** handicap/ hamper/ hinder

block [他]（公式の規則・手順を用いて）妨害する ◇The proposed merger has been *blocked* by the government. 合併案は政府によって差し止められている ◇The new rules would effectively *block* protesters' attempts to assert their rights. 新規則は抗議者たちが権利を主張しようとするのを阻止するのに効果的だろう

inter'fere with sth 句動詞 （計画どおりの事の達成・進行を）妨げる ◇She never allows her personal feelings to *interfere with* her work. 彼女は仕事に私情を差し挟むことは決してしない ◇Poor language skills can seriously *interfere with* communication. 語学のスキルが乏しいとコミュニケーションに深刻な支障をきたすことがある
▶**interference** [名] [U] ◇We will not allow any *interference with* the normal democratic processes. 私たちは正常な民主的プロセスに対するいかなる妨害も許さない

ノート **block** と **interfere with sth** の使い分け：ふつう人が plans または efforts などを故意に妨げるのが block で，物事が意図せず妨害されるときに interfere with を用いる。

handicap (-pp-) [他，ふつう受身で]（事を成し遂げるのに）不利な状況になる ◇British exports have been *handicapped* by the strong pound. イギリスの輸出はポンド高のため不利な状況が続いている ◇The team was *handicapped* by the loss of their key striker early in the game. 試合開始後まもなく重要なストライカーを失い，そのチームは不利な状況に立たされた ☞ **handicap** (OBSTACLE)

inhibit [他]《フォーマル》(迅速な[通常どおりの]発生・発展を)妨げる ◇A lack of oxygen may *inhibit* brain development in the unborn child. 酸素不足が胎児の脳の発達を妨げる可能性がある ◇Alcohol significantly *inhibits* the action of the drug. アルコールは薬の作用を著しく抑制する

hamper [他]（達成を）困難にする，阻止する ◇High winds *hampered* the rescue attempt. 強風で救助活動が難航した ◇Our efforts were severely *hampered* by a lack of money. 我々の努力に資金不足が大きく立ちはだかった 反意 help (HELP 動 2)

hinder [他]（進行を遅らせて達成を）妨げる ◇These killings have seriously *hindered* progress towards peace. これらの殺害によって和平への前進が著しく阻まれた ◇Some teachers felt *hindered* by a lack of resources. 教材不足でうまくいかないと感じる教師もいた 反意 help (HELP 動 2), ☞ **hindrance** (OBSTACLE)

ノート **handicap, hamper, hinder** の使い分け：人，計画，プロセスが handicapped である場合，お金・設備の不足，不利な規則・規制で，物事の進行・達成は困難である。人が hindered または hampered である場合，不利な状況のため，物事を進めることは同じく困難である。また，例えば悪天候や非協力者など積極的に進行を妨げる外的要因があるかもしれない。

obstruct [他]《ややフォーマル》(故意に進捗を)妨害する ◇They were charged with *obstructing* the police in the course of their duty. 彼らは警察の公務執行妨害で告発された ◇He accused terrorists of attempting to *obstruct* the peace process. 彼は和平プロセスの妨害を企てたとしてテロリストたちを非難した

hold sb/sth back 句動詞 （人・事を）妨害する，遅らせる ◇Do you think that mixed ability classes *hold back* better students? 能力別ではないクラスは成績のよい生徒の足を引っ張ると思いますか ◇They are determined that nothing should *hold back* the negotiations. 彼らは何があってもその交渉が妨げられてはならないのだと意を決している 反義 **encourage**

2 block・be/get in sb's/the way・obstruct・barricade・cut sth off・block sth off・seal・bar
前方に立ったり、行く手に物を置いたりして人がどこかへ行けなくする
【類語訳】妨害する、さえぎる、ふさぐ、封鎖する、阻む

文型&コロケーション
▶ to block/ obstruct/ bar an **entrance**
▶ to block/ obstruct/ bar sb's **path/ way**
▶ to block/ cut off/ bar sb's **retreat**
▶ to block/ barricade/ block off a **road**
▶ to block/ bar sb's **progress/ exit**
▶ to block/ cut off sb's **escape**
▶ to block/ obstruct sb's **view**
▶ to **deliberately** block/ obstruct sb/ sth

block [他]（人の前方[行く手]に立って）妨害する、さえぎる ◇She had her back to the door, *blocking* his exit. 彼女はドアを背にして立ち彼の退路をふさいだ ◇An ugly new building *blocked* the view from the window. 新しく建った見苦しい建物のせいで窓からの景色が見られなくなった
be/get in sb's/the way 句動 （人が動く[…する]のを前方[行く手]に立って）妨害する ◇You'll have to move — you're *in my way*. どいてください。邪魔なんです ◇Do you want me to move my bike — is it *getting in your way*? 邪魔でしたら私の自転車をどかしましょうか 反義 **get out of sb's/the way**
obstruct [他]《フォーマル》（人・物が通る道路・入り口を）ふさぐ ◇You can't park here, you're *obstructing* my driveway. ここに駐車はできません。うちの車用通路をふさいでいますよ ◇First check that the accident victim doesn't have an *obstructed* airway. 事故の被害者の気道がふさがっていないかまず確認してください
barricade [他]（道路・戸口を）バリケードでふさぐ ◇They *barricaded* all the doors and windows. 彼らはすべてのドアと窓をバリケードでふさいだ ◇He had *barricaded himself* inside his room. 彼はバリケードを築いて部屋に立てこもった ☞ **barricade** (BARRIER)
,cut sth 'off 句動詞 （前方[行く手]に立って人がどこかへ）行けないようにする ◇They *cut off* the enemy's retreat. 彼らは敵の退路を断った ◇The only other escape route was *cut off* by the rising tide. 他の唯一の避難ルートは満ち潮で閉ざされていた

ノート **block, cut sth off, be/get in sb's/the way** の使い分け：**block** は一か所に静止して意図的に人の行く手を遮ること。**cut off** は意図的に人の逃げ道や経路に移動して行く手を阻むこと。**get in sb's way** は意図せずたまたま邪魔すること。

,block sth 'off 句動詞 （道路[通路]の端に柵などを配置して）封鎖する ◇The main roads out of the city have been *blocked off*. その街から外へ伸びている幹線道路は封鎖されている
seal [他]（警察・軍が国境などを）封鎖する ◇Troops have *sealed the border* between the countries. 軍隊がそれらの国の国境を封鎖した
bar (-rr-) [他]（道路・路上に立って[あって]）ふさぐ ◇Two police officers were *barring* her exit. ふたりの警官が彼女が出て行くのを阻んでいた ◇We found our way *barred* by rocks. 私たちの行く手を岩が阻んでいた ☞ **barrier** (BARRIER)

boast 動

boast・show off・pride yourself on sth・brag・gloat・congratulate yourself
過度にうぬぼれる、誇りに感じる
【類語訳】自慢する、ひけらかす、誇りとする、鼻にかける

文型&コロケーション
▶ to boast/ show off/ brag/ gloat **about** sth
▶ to show off/ brag/ crow **to** sb
▶ to boast/ brag **of** sth
▶ to boast/ brag/ congratulate yourself **that** ...

boast [自]《ふつうけなして》（能力・業績・所有物について）自慢する ◇I don't want to *boast*, but I can actually speak six languages. 自慢じゃないけど実際に6か国語を話すことができるんだ ◇She is always *boasting* about how wonderful her children are. 彼女はいつも自分の子どもたちがいかに素晴らしいか自慢している ◇He openly *boasted* of his skill as a burglar. 彼は悪びれもせず強盗としての技術を自慢した ☞ **boastful** (PROUD 2)
▶**boast** [名][C] ◇It was her *proud boast* that she had never missed a day's work because of illness. 病気で仕事を一日も休んだことがないのが彼女の大の自慢だった
,show 'off 句動詞 《ややインフォーマル, けなして》（能力・所有物について）ひけらかす ◇He's just *showing off* because that girl he likes is here. 好きなあの子がここにいるから彼はいいところを見せようとしているだけだ ◇They drive around in their new cars, *showing off* to their friends. 彼らは新車を乗り回して、友達に見せびらかしている
▶**'show-off** [名][C] ◇She's always been a real *show-off*. 彼女はいつだってほんとに目立ちたがり屋なんだ
'pride yourself on sth 句動詞 （能力・性質を）誇りとする ◇The school *prides itself on* its academic record. その学校は優秀な学業成績を誇っている ☞ **pride** (SATISFACTION), **proud** (GLAD)
brag (-gg-) [自]《けなして》（行為・所有物について人をいらつかせるほど）自慢する、鼻にかける ◇I'm not *bragging* but I think I did very well in the interview. 鼻にかけるわけじゃないけど面接はとてもうまくいったと思うよ
gloat [自]《けなして》（自分の成功・好運[他人の失敗・不運]を）ほくそ笑む、にんまりする ◇She was still *gloating over* her rival's disappointment. 彼女はいまだにライバルの落胆をほくそ笑んでいた
congratulate yourself [他]（達成感を感じるほど）誇りに思う ◇You can *congratulate yourself on* having done an excellent job. いい仕事をしたのだから誇りに思っていいんだよ

bold 形 ☞ BRAVE

bold・adventurous・daring
人・事が危険を恐れないことを表す
【類語訳】度胸のある、大胆な、恐れ知らずの、大胆不敵な

文型&コロケーション
▶ a bold/ an adventurous **design/ spirit**
▶ a bold/ a daring **plan/ move**

▶adventurous/ daring **exploits**

bold (人・行為が)勇敢で度胸のある, 大胆な；恐れ知らずの ◇It was a *bold* move on their part to open a branch of the business in France. フランスに支店を開くとは彼らは思い切った行動に出たね ◇The wine made him *bold* enough to approach her and introduce himself. ワインのせいで彼は彼女に近寄って自己紹介をするほど大胆になった ◇The slaughter of his family turned him into a *bold* and fearless warrior. 家族が殺害されて彼は恐れ知らずの戦士になった 反意 timid (**SHY**)
▶**boldly** 副 ◇He stepped forward *boldly* to speak. 彼はスピーチするため堂々と歩み出た

adventurous (人が)冒険好きな, 大胆な；(事が)目新しい, 刺激的な, 危険な ◇For the more *adventurous* tourists, there are trips into the mountains with a local guide. 冒険をしてみたい観光客のために地元ガイドと行く山岳旅行があります ◇Many teachers would like to be more *adventurous* and creative. 多くの教師たちはもっと失敗を恐れず, 独創的になりたいと思っている ◇The menu contained traditional favourites as well as more *adventurous* dishes. メニューには伝統的な人気料理のみならず野心的な創作料理もある 反意 **unadventurous** ❶ unadventurousな人は危険を冒したがらず, 新しい刺激的なことに挑戦したがらない.

daring (人が)勇敢で恐れ知らずの, 大胆不敵な；(事が)危険を伴う ◇'Should you be drinking so much?' she asked, **greatly daring**. 「そんなにお酒を飲んでいいんですか」と大胆にも彼女は聞いた ◇There are plenty of activities at the resort for the less *daring*. 少し怖がりの人にもその行楽地には遊べる物がたくさんある ◇She wore a *daring* strapless dress in black silk. 彼女は肩紐のない黒のシルクのドレスを着ていた ☞ **daring** (**COURAGE**), **dare** (**DARE**)
▶**daringly** 副 ◇This house would have looked *daringly* modern when it was built. できた時にはこの家はずいぶんとモダンに見えただろう

book 名

book • publication • novel • guide • title • manual • textbook • text • volume
表紙の内側で印刷された頁が綴じられた物
【類語訳】本, 出版物, 刊行物, 小説, 案内書, 手引書, 取扱説明書, マニュアル, 教科書, テキスト, 書籍, 書物

文型&コロケーション
▶a book/ publication/ novel/ guide/ manual/ textbook/ text/ volume **about** sb/ sth
▶a book/ publication/ guide/ title/ manual/ textbook/ text/ volume **on** sb/ sth
▶a book/ publication/ novel/ title/ text/ volume **by** sb
▶a **reference** book/ publication/ guide/ title/ manual
▶a **best-selling** book/ novel/ guide/ title/ textbook
▶a **paperback** book/ publication/ novel/ title/ volume
▶a **children's** book/ novel/ guide/ title
▶to **read** a book/ publication/ novel/ guide/ manual/ textbook/ text/ volume
▶to **publish** a book/ a novel/ a guide/ titles/ manuals/ textbooks/ a volume
▶to **write** a book/ publication/ novel/ guide/ manual/ textbook/ text/ volume

book [C] 本；(紙・電子媒体で出版される)著作物 ◇His desk was covered with piles of *books*. 彼の机は本の山で覆われていた ◇The *book* has received some terrible reviews. その本はいくつかの書評でこき下ろされた ◇a library/hardback *book* 図書館の/ハードカバーの本

publication [C] 《ややフォーマル》(本・雑誌・新聞・文書などの)出版物[刊行物] ◇Her work has appeared in a wide variety of mainstream *publications*. 彼女の作品はいろいろの主だった出版物に掲載されている

novel [C] (架空の人物・出来事を扱う)小説 ◇detective/ historical/romantic *novels* 探偵/歴史/恋愛小説 ◇His first *novel* was published in 1934. 彼の最初の小説は1934年に出版された ☞ **novelist** (**WRITER**)

guide [C] 案内書, 手引書 ◇a *Guide* to Family Health 家庭の健康の手引書 ◇Let's have a look at the TV *guide* and see what's on. テレビ案内を見て, 何が放送されているか見てみよう ❶ guide, guidebookは「旅行ガイドブック」の意味もある. ◆He has written a number of travel *guides*. (彼はたくさんの旅行ガイドブックを執筆している). ◆a *guidebook* to Peru (ペルー旅行のガイドブック).

title [C] (人・会社によって出版[販売]される)刊行物 ◇The company publishes twenty new *titles* a year. その会社は年に20冊の新刊を発行している

manual [C] 手引書, (機械などの)取扱説明書, マニュアル ◇Why do you never read the instruction *manual*? どうして取扱説明書を読まないの

textbook (《米でまた **text**) [C] (学校・大学で使用する)教科書 ◇a school/medical/history *textbook* 学校の/医学の/歴史の教科書 ◇I would not recommend it as a classroom *textbook*. 授業で使う教科書としてはお勧めしません

text [C] (研究の対象としての)書物[戯曲, 文章], テキスト ◇It is one of the most difficult literary *texts* of all time. それは史上最も難しい文学テキストの一つである ◇'Macbeth' is a *set text* for the exam. 『マクベス』がその試験の指定教材だ ❶《米》ではtextが教科書を意味することもある. ◆Students are requested not to buy *texts* prior to the first class. (学生は最初の授業が始まる前に教科書を買わないように言われている).

volume [C] 《フォーマル》本, 書籍, 書物 ◇She published her first book, a slim *volume* of poetry, at the age of sixteen. 彼女は16歳のとき自身初の本である薄い詩の冊子を出版した ❶ volumeはフォーマルな文脈で本の大きさ・巻数を言うのに用いられることもある. ◆a slim/thick *volume* (薄い/厚い本. ◆a library of over 50,000 *volumes* (5万冊以上の蔵書を持つ図書館). 以下のような(特にフォーマルではない)一般的な文脈では用いられない. ✗His desk was covered with piles of *volumes*. ✗The *volume* has received some terrible reviews.

boring 形

boring • dull • tedious • repetitive • monotonous • uninteresting • dry
テーマ, 活動, 人や場所が刺激的でないことを表す
【類語訳】面白くない, つまらない, 退屈な, 冗長な, うんざりさせる, 単調な, 無味乾燥な

文型&コロケーション
▶to be boring/ dull/ tedious/ uninteresting **for** sb
▶boring/ dull/ tedious/ dry **subjects/ books**
▶boring/ dull/ tedious/ repetitive/ monotonous **jobs/ work**

↳boring

- ▶boring/ dull/ tedious **games/ lectures/ details**
- ▶a boring/ dull/ tedious **evening**
- ▶a boring/ a dull/ an uninteresting **place**
- ▶a boring/ dull **man/ woman/ person**
- ▶**rather** boring/ dull/ tedious/ repetitive/ monotonous/ uninteresting/ dry
- ▶**very** boring/ dull/ tedious/ repetitive/ uninteresting/ dry
- ▶**pretty** boring/ dull/ tedious/ uninteresting

boring (けなして) 面白くない, つまらない；退屈な ◇He's such a *boring* man! 彼はすごく退屈な男だ ◇Try not to make the diet *boring*. 食生活をつまらないものにしないでください ◇That film was ***dead boring***.《英, インフォーマル, 話し言葉》あの映画はまったくつまらなかった 反意 **interesting** (INTERESTING)
▶**boredom** 名 [U] ◇Television helps to relieve the *boredom* of the long winter evenings. テレビは長い冬の晩の退屈しのぎに役に立つ

dull (けなして) 面白くない, 刺激的でない, つまらない ◇Life in a small town could be ***deadly dull***. 小さな町の生活はすごくつまらないかもしれない ◇The work gets a bit *dull* at times. その仕事は時々少し退屈だ ◇There's ***never a dull moment*** when John's around. ジョンがいれば退屈することはない 反意 **interesting** (INTERESTING)

tedious (けなして) 長くてあきあきする, 冗長な, うんざりさせる ◇The journey soon became *tedious*. その旅にはすぐにあきた ◇It was *tedious*, repetitive work. それはうんざりする反復作業だった ◇We had to listen to all the *tedious* details of his operation. 彼の仕事のつまらない詳細を全部聞かされるはめになった
▶**tedium** 名 [U] ◇She longed for something to relieve the *tedium* of everyday life.《書き言葉》彼女は退屈な日常生活から救ってくれる何かをしきりに求めた

repetitive (しばしばけなして)（繰り返しが多くて）退屈な ◇Machines can now perform many *repetitive* tasks in the home. 今や機械が多くの家庭内の退屈な作業を行ってくれる

monotonous (けなして) 単調な ◇a *monotonous* voice/diet/routine 単調な声/食事/日課 ◇New secretaries came and went with *monotonous regularity*. 新しい秘書がやって来ては去るという単調な繰り返しだった
▶**monotonously** 副 ◇As the clock ticked *monotonously* on the wall Mr Simons slowly and methodically cut up and ate his food. 壁に掛かった時計が単調に時を刻むのに合わせて, サイモンズ氏はゆっくりと几帳面に食べ物を刻んで食べた
▶**monotony** 名 [U] ◇She watches television to relieve the *monotony* of everyday life. 彼女は日々の生活の単調さを紛らわすためテレビを見ている

uninteresting (けなして) 面白くない ◇The food was dull and *uninteresting*. 料理はつまらない味でどうということはなかった 反意 **interesting** (INTERESTING), ☞ **uninterested** (INDIFFERENT)

dry (けなして) 無味乾燥な ◇Government reports tend to make *dry* reading. 政府の報告書は無味乾燥な読み物になりがちだ

bottom 名

bottom・base・foundation・foot
物の一番低い部分

【類語訳】底, 下部, 基部, 土台, 基礎

文型&コロケーション
- ▶**at/ near/ towards** the bottom/ base/ foot of sth
- ▶**on** the bottom/ base of sth
- ▶(a) **firm/ solid/ strong** base/ foundations
- ▶to **have** a bottom/ a base/ foundations

bottom [C, ふつう単数で] 底, 下部 ◇Footnotes are given at the *bottom* of each page. 各ページの下に脚注がある ◇The wind blew through gaps at the top and *bottom* of the door. ドアの上と下にある隙間から風が吹き込んだ ◇I waited for them at the *bottom* of the hill. 私は丘の麓で彼らを待った ◇The book I want is right at the *bottom* of the pile. 私が欲しい本はちょうど一番下にあります 反意 **top** (TOP)

base [C, ふつう単数で] 基部, 土台 ◇The lamp has a heavy *base*. そのスタンドは基部が重い ◇He felt a sharp pain at the *base* of his spine. 彼は背骨の基底部に刺すような痛みを感じた ◇Four bronze lions stand at the *base* of the column. その柱の土台のところに4体のライオンの銅像が立っている

foundation [C, ふつう複数で] (建物の)土台, 基礎 ◇The builders are now beginning to **lay the foundations** of the new school. 建設業者は現在新しい学校の基礎を築く工事に取り掛かり始めている ◇The explosion shook the *foundations* of the houses nearby. その爆発で近隣の家の土台部分が揺れた

foot [単数で] 最下部 ◇At the *foot* of the stairs she turned to face him. 階段の下で彼女は振り返って彼に向き合った

ノート **bottom** と **foot** の使い分け：foot は tree, hill, mountain, steps, stairs, page などの「最下部」によく用いられる. bottom はもっと広く用いられる. foot はふつう文語的な文脈で用いられる.

brave 形 ☞ BOLD

brave・courageous・heroic・gallant・fearless・gutsy
人が困難や危険なことをいとわないことを表す
【類語訳】勇敢な, 大胆な, 恐れを知らない, 勇ましい, 豪胆な, ガッツのある, 根性のある

文型&コロケーション
- ▶a brave/ courageous/ heroic/ gallant **attempt/ effort/ action/ resistance/ struggle**
- ▶a brave/ courageous **decision**
- ▶brave/ heroic **deeds**
- ▶a brave/ courageous/ gallant/ fearless **soldier**
- ▶a brave/ fearless **warrior**

brave (人が)勇敢な；(行動が)恐れを知らない, 大胆な ◇Be *brave*! 勇気を持って ◇I wasn't *brave* enough to tell her what I thought of her. 彼女のことをどう思っているか私には彼女に伝える勇気がなかった ◇She died after a *brave* fight against cancer. 彼女はガンとの勇気ある闘いの末に亡くなった ◇I had to **put on a brave face** and try to show him that I wasn't worried. 私は何食わぬ顔をして, 彼に心配していないふりをするしかなかった 反意 **cowardly** (COWARD), ☞ **bravery** (COURAGE)

break

▶**bravely** 副 ◇Though they fought *bravely*, they were no match for the trained mercenaries. 彼らは勇敢に戦ったが、訓練を受けた傭兵の敵ではなかった
courageous (正しいと信じる事をするので)勇ましい、勇気ある ◇I think he made a very *courageous* decision to resign. 彼は辞任というとても勇気ある決断を下したと私は思う ◇I hope people will be *courageous* enough to speak out against this injustice. 人々はこのような不正に対して断固反対する勇気を持つようになってほしい ☞ **courage** (COURAGE)
heroic (並外れていて称賛されるほど)勇敢な ◇She is a *heroic* figure we can all look up to. 彼女は私たち皆が尊敬できる勇敢な人物だ ◇Rescuers made *heroic* efforts to save the crew. 救助隊員は乗組員を救出するために多大な努力を傾けた ☞ **heroism** (COURAGE)
▶**heroically** 副
gallant (古風 or 文語) (戦争・窮地において)勇ましい ◇Our *gallant* soldiers have had to endure many hardships in the field. 我が国の勇敢なる兵士たちは戦場で数多くの困難に耐えなければならなかった ◇She made a *gallant* attempt to hide her tears. 彼女は気丈にも涙を隠そうとした
▶**gallantly** 副
fearless 〈書き言葉〉 (称賛に値するほど)恐れ知らずの、豪胆な ◇He was known as a powerful king and a *fearless* warrior. 彼は勢力絶大な王及び恐れ知らずの戦士として知られていた ◇She was *fearless* and full of energy. 彼女は怖いもの知らずでエネルギッシュだった [反意] **fearful** (AFRAID)
gutsy (インフォーマル) ガッツ[根性]のある ◇Her *gutsy* performance in the game impressed everyone, even her teammates. 試合での彼女のガッツ溢れるプレーは皆、いやチームメイトにさえ感銘を与えた ☞ **guts** (COURAGE)

break 動

1 break・crack・fracture・snap
物に力を加えて2つ以上の部分に損傷させる
【類語訳】割る、割れる、折る、折れる、ひびが入る、ひびを入れる

▢文型&コロケーション▢
▸ to break/ crack/ fracture **a bone/ rib**
▸ to break/ fracture **your hip/ jaw/ wrist**
▸ to crack/ fracture **your skull**
▸ to break/ crack a/ an **cup/ egg/ mirror**
▸ a **branch/ cable/ rope** breaks/ snaps
▸ a **broken/ cracked/ fractured pipe**

break [自, 他] (力を加えて2つ以上の断片に)割る[割れる], 折る[折れる] ◇She dropped the plate and it *broke into pieces*. 彼女は皿を落とし、皿は粉々に割れた ◇She fell off a ladder and *broke* her arm. 彼女ははしごから落ちて腕の骨を折った ◇I didn't mean to *break* the window. 窓を割るつもりはなかった ◇He *broke* the chocolate *in two* and gave me half. 彼はチョコレートを2つに割って半分を私にくれた ◇How did this dish *get broken*? どうしてこのお皿は割れたの
▶**breakage** 名 [U, C] ◇The last time we moved house there were very few *breakages*. この前引っ越したときにはほとんど破損物はなかった ◇Wrap it up carefully to protect against *breakage*. 慎重に包んで壊れないようにしてください

crack [自, 他] (硬い物が[に])ひびが入る[ひびを入れる] ◇The ice *cracked* as I stepped on it. 氷を踏んだらひびが入った ◇The leather/mud/paint/plaster had *cracked*. 革/泥/絵の具/漆喰にひびが入っていた ◇He has *cracked* a bone in his arm. 彼の腕の骨にひびが入った ◇Her lips were dry and *cracked*. 彼女の唇は乾燥していてひび割れていた ❶前置詞と一緒に用いられると、「割る」という意味を持つこともある。◆She *cracked* an egg into the pan. (彼女はフライパンに卵を割って入れた)。

fracture [自, 他] 《ややフォーマル》割れる[割る], ひびが入る[ひびを入れる] ◇Cast iron is not only heavy, but likely to *fracture*. 鋳鉄は重いだけでなく割れやすい ◇A gas escape from a *fractured* pipe was the likely cause of the explosion. ひびの入ったパイプからのガス漏れが爆発の原因だと考えられた ◇He fell and *fractured* his skull. 彼は倒れて頭蓋骨を骨折した
▶**fracture** 名 [C, U] ◇She sustained two *fractures to* her leg. 彼女は脚を2か所[2度]骨折した ◇Ground movements could cause *fracture* of the pipe. 地盤の移動がパイプの破損の原因になることもある

┌─ ノート **break, crack, fracture の使い分け**：どの語も骨や関節に用いることは可能だが、**crack** だけは関節に用いることができない。✕He *cracked* his hip/jaw/wrist. break だけが腕と脚の骨について用いることが可能。✕She *cracked/fractured* her arm/leg. fracture はふつう頭蓋骨について用いる。頭蓋骨には break は用いないが crack を用いることは可能。✕He fell and *broke* his skull. ─┘

snap (-pp-) [自, 他] (突然鋭い音を立てて)割れる[割る], 折れる[折る], 切れる[切る] ◇Suddenly the rope *snapped*. 突然ロープがプツンと切れた ◇The wind had *snapped* the tree in two. その風で木が真っ二つにバキッと折れた

2 break・fail・break down・go wrong・crash・go down
欠陥が原因で機械が動かなくなる
【類語訳】故障する, 故障させる, 作動しなくなる, クラッシュする, 一時停止する

▢文型&コロケーション▢
▸ a **video/ watch** breaks/ goes wrong
▸ a **washing machine** breaks down/ goes wrong
▸ an **engine** fails/ breaks down
▸ a **computer** goes wrong/ crashes
▸ a **system** fails/ crashes/ goes down

break [自, 他] (装置・小型機器が[を])故障する[故障させる] ◇My watch has *broken*. 腕時計が故障した ◇I think I've *broken* the video. ビデオを壊しちゃったみたい
fail [自] (システム全体、機械[システム、体]の一部が)動かなくなる、故障する ◇The air-conditioning system *failed* on the hottest day of the year. その年の一番暑い日に空調設備が故障した ◇The brakes on my bike *failed* halfway down the hill. 丘を半分下ったところで自転車のブレーキが故障した
▶**failure** 名 [U, C] ◇patients suffering from heart/kidney *failure* 心/腎不全を患う患者 ◇A *power failure* plunged everything into darkness. 停電で何もかも真っ暗になった

break 'down 句動詞 (機械・乗り物が欠陥が原因で)動かなくなる ◇The washing machine has *broken down*

again. 洗濯機がまた動かなくなった ◇We (= our car) broke down on the motorway. 高速道路で車が故障した
▶**breakdown** [名] ◇a breakdown on the motorway 高速道路での車の故障

,**go 'wrong** [フレーズ] 正常に動かなくなる ◇My watch keeps going wrong. 私の腕時計は狂っている ◇The new television set will contain fewer components to go wrong. 新型のテレビに含まれる部品には故障するものが少なくなる予定だ ❶ go wrongは機器、装置、機械の部品、乗り物の部品を主語にすることができるが、乗り物全体を主語にすることはできない。×The car has gone wrong again. go wrongの場合、breakやbreak downとは違い、完全に動かなくなるとは限らない。

crash [自, 他] (コンピューター(システム)が[を])突然クラッシュする[クラッシュさせる] ◇Files can be lost if the system suddenly crashes. システムが突然クラッシュするとファイルが失われる可能性がある
▶**crash** [名] [C] ◇A systems crash in the morning and a bomb scare in the afternoon provided enough excitement. 午前中にシステムがクラッシュし、午後には爆破事件があり大騒ぎだった

,**go 'down** [句動詞] [自] (コンピューターシステムが)一時停止する ◇The system is going down in ten minutes. システムが10分間停止します

[ノート] **crashとgo downの使い分け**：crashは個々のコンピューターまたはシステム全体が、突然予期せず動かなくなること。go downはシステムの使用を意図的に止めるような場合に用いる。

---

3 break・breach・infringe・violate
法律や協約、主義に反することを表す
【類語訳】違反する、破る、侵害する

[文型&コロケーション]
▶to break/ breach/ infringe a **regulation**
▶to break/ breach/ violate a **rule/ law/ treaty**
▶to break/ infringe/ violate a **code**
▶to break/ violate a **ceasefire/ truce**
▶to breach/ infringe/ violate **copyright**
▶to breach/ infringe/ violate **Article** 12 of the treaty

break [他] (法律・規則・協約に)違反する ◇to break an agreement/a contract 協約/契約に違反する ◇Would you be willing to break the law to achieve your goal? 目的を達成するためには法律を破ることもいとわないのですか ◇They insist that they have not broken any rules. いかなる規則にも反していないと彼らは主張している ◇He was breaking the speed limit (= driving faster than the law allows). 彼はスピード違反をしていた [反意] **obey** (FOLLOW 3)

breach [他] 《協約・法律》に従わない ◇The government is accused of breaching the terms of the treaty. 政府はその条約の条項に違反したとして非難されている [反意] **comply** (FOLLOW 3)
▶**breach** [名] [C, U] ◇a breach of contract/copyright/ warranty 契約不履行/著作権侵害/保証違反 ◇This action is **in breach of** Article 119 of the Constitution. この行為は憲法第119条に違反している

[ノート] **breakとbreachの使い分け**：breachのほうがフォーマル。特定の規則の違反にはbreachを、法律全般の違反にはbreakを用いる。◆areas where EU limits were breached (EUの制限が守られていなかった地域)。×They are breaching the law and could be in serious trouble. break lawsは主語は人だが、breach rulesは人も行為も主語にすることができる。

infringe [他, 自] 《フォーマル》(行為・計画が法律を)破る；(人の法的権利を)侵害する ◇The material can be copied without infringing copyright. その資料はコピーしても著作権侵害とならない ◇They said that compulsory identity cards would infringe civil liberties. 身分証明書の強制は市民の自由を侵害するだろうというのが彼らの立場である ◇She refused to answer questions that infringed on her private affairs. 彼女はプライバシーを侵害する質問には答えたくないと言った
▶**infringement** [名] [U, C] ◇copyright infringement 著作権侵害 ◇an infringement of his personal liberty 彼の個人的自由の侵害

violate [他] 《フォーマル》(法律・主義・協約に)従わない[守らない]；(プライバシーを)侵害する ◇The directive violates fundamental human rights. その指示は基本的人権を侵害している ◇She accused press photographers of violating her privacy. 彼女は報道カメラマンたちをプライバシーを侵害したとして告発[非難]した [反意] **respect** (FOLLOW 3)
▶**violation** [名] [C, U] ◇gross violations of human rights はなはだしい人権侵害 ◇They were in open violation of the treaty. 彼らはその協約に公然と違反していた

[ノート] **infringeとviolateの使い分け**：violateはしばしば単なる違法行為ではなく道徳的に間違った行為を表す。infringeは人の個人的権利に関して用いられるが、人権全般に関して用いられるviolateほど意味は強くない。

---

4 break・withdraw・do a U-turn・retract・recant・take sth back・backtrack・go back on sth
以前の発言や意見、約束を変える
【類語訳】破る、撤回する、取り消す、翻す

[文型&コロケーション]
▶to break/ withdraw/ go back on a **promise**
▶to break/ go back on **your word/ an agreement**
▶to withdraw/ retract a/ an **claim/ allegation/ confession**

break [他] (約束・協約を)破る[守らない] ◇I've never broken my word; why should I do it now? 私は約束を破ったことはこれまで一度もない。今回だってそんなことをするわけないでしょう ◇She has already broken three appointments (= not gone to them). 彼女は既に会う約束を3件すっぽかしている [反意] **keep**

withdraw [他] 《フォーマル》(以前の発言を)撤回する ◇The newspaper withdrew the allegations the next day. 翌日の新聞はそうした主張を撤回した

,**do a 'U-turn** 《インフォーマル、特にジャーナリズム》(みっともなくも方針・言動を)完全に変える ◇The Prime Minister may be forced to do another humiliating U-turn on Europe. 屈辱的にも首相はもう一度ヨーロッパについての方針の180度転換を強いられるだろう ❶ do a U-turnは政治・ビジネスに関する文脈で最も頻繁に見受けられる。不面目なことに用いられるので、ふつうhave toやbe forced toといった動詞を伴う。

retract [他] 《フォーマル》(以前の発言は正しくないと)取り消

bribe, bright, bring sb up

◇He made a false confession which he later *retracted*. 彼は虚偽の供述をしたが後に取り消した

ノート withdraw と retract の使い分け: 多くの場合どちらの語も使用可能。◆ to *withdraw/retract* a claim/an allegation/a confession (主張/申し立て/自白を撤回する[取り消す])。しかし、retract は強制的に発言させられたことの撤回によく用いられる。withdraw は立証できなかった訴えや告発を取り下げざるをえないときに用いられることが多い。

recant [他, 自] 《フォーマル》(信条・意見を)正式に撤回する ◇In 1633 he was forced to *recant* his assertion that the earth orbited the sun. 1633年彼は地球が太陽の周りを回っているという主張を撤回することを強いられた

,take sth 'back [句動詞] 《ややインフォーマル, 特に話し言葉》(発言を)取り消す ◇OK, I *take* it all *back*! わかった, 全部取り消すよ ❶ take sth back は Would you like to take that back? (その発言を取り消しますか), Can I take that back? (その発言を取り消せますか), I take it (all) back. (その発言を[すべて]取り消します)などの口語表現で頻繁に用いられる。

backtrack [自] 《特にビジネス or 政治》(圧力で)発言[約束]を翻す ◇The trade unions have had to *backtrack on* their main demand. 労働組合は最も重要な要求を翻さねばならなくなった

,go 'back on sth [句動詞] 《ややインフォーマル》(約束を)破る;(気が)変わる ◇They have no intention of *going back on* any of their commitments. 彼らはいずれの公約も破るつもりはまったくない

bribe [名] ☞ INCENTIVE

bribe・bait・pay-off・kickback
人がある事をするように仕向けるために用いられるもの
【類語訳】賄賂, えさ, おとり, 見返り金, 口止め料, キックバック, リベート, 口きき料

文型&コロケーション
▶bait/ a pay-off/ a kickback **for** sb
▶a £1,000/ $500, etc. bribe/ pay-off
▶to **offer** (sb) a bribe/ a pay-off
▶to **offer sth as** a bribe/ bait
▶to **pay** sb a bribe/ kickback
▶to **take** bribes/ the bait/ kickbacks

bribe [C] 賄賂 ◇She had been offered a $50,000 *bribe* to drop the charges. 彼女は告訴を取り下げるよう5万ドルの賄賂の申し出を受けていた ◇It was alleged that he had taken *bribes* while in office. 彼は在職中に賄賂を受けていたという容疑がかけられた ◇The tax cut was described as a pre-election *bribe*. 減税は選挙前の賄賂だと書き立てられた ▶**bribery** (CORRUPTION)
▶**bribe** [動][他] ◇They *bribed* the guards with cigarettes. 彼らはタバコで看守を買収した ◇She was *bribed into* handing over secret information. 彼女は賄賂をもらって機密情報を渡した

bait [U, C] えさ, おとり ◇The police used him as *bait* to trap the killers. 殺人犯を捕らえるため警察は彼をおとりとして使った ◇She covered her face and began to sob, but he wouldn't *rise to the bait* (= react as she wanted him to). 彼女は顔を覆って泣きじゃくり始めたが彼はまったく引っかからなかった

'pay-off [C] 《インフォーマル, ふつうくけて》見返り金, 口止め料 ◇The government are investigating *pay-offs* to high-ranking officials. 政府は高級官僚への贈賄を調査している ◇The Chief Executive left a year early with a £1.5 million *pay-off*. その最高経営責任者は150万ポンドの退職金を受け取って1年早く退職した
▶**,pay sb 'off** [句動詞] ◇All the witnesses had been *paid off*. 目撃者全員に口止め料が支払われていた

kickback [C] 《特に米, やや인フォーマル》(商取引がらみで政治家・役人に支払われる) キックバック, リベート, 口きき料 ◇They were accused of paying *kickbacks* to politicians to obtain public contracts. 彼らは公的機関から契約を得ようと政治家へリベートを贈った容疑で告発された

bright [形]

bright・brilliant・vivid・vibrant・bold
物が輝いていること, 色が鮮やかで目立つことを表す
【類語訳】明るい, きらめく, 鮮やかな, くっきりした

文型&コロケーション
▶bright/ brilliant/ vivid/ vibrant/ bold **colours**
▶bright/ brilliant **light/ sunlight/ sunshine/ eyes**

bright 光に満ちた, 明るい;強く輝いている;(色が)鮮やかで目立つ ◇a *bright* room 明るい部屋 ◇a *bright* morning (= with the sun shining) 明るい晴れた朝 ◇Her eyes were *bright* with tears. 彼女の目には涙が光っていた ◇a *bright* yellow dress 鮮やかな黄色のドレス ◇a *bright* tie 明るい色のネクタイ **反意 dim, faint** (DIM), **grey, dull** (CLOUDY)
▶**brightly** [副] ◇a *brightly* lit room 明るい部屋

brilliant 非常に明るい, きらめく ◇*brilliant* blue eyes きらきらと輝く青い目 ◇The sky was a *brilliant* blue. 空は青く澄みわたっていた
▶**brilliantly** [副] ◇It was *brilliantly* sunny. その日は快晴だった

vivid 《ほめて》(色が)鮮やかな ◇His eyes were a *vivid* green. 彼の目は鮮やかな緑色をしていた

vibrant 《ほめて》(色が)鮮やかな ◇The room was decorated in *vibrant* blues and greens. 部屋は鮮やかな青と緑に塗り上げられていた

ノート vivid と vibrant の使い分け: vivid は一つの色がいかに鮮やかであるかを強調し, vibrant はより生き生きとした刺激的な単色または複数の色の組み合わせを含意する。

bold (色が)くっきりとした, はっきりしていて目立つ ◇a *bold* black and yellow sign 黒と黄色のよく目立つ標識 ◇The furniture was painted in *bold*, primary colours. 家具は目立つ原色で塗られていた
▶**boldly** [副] ◇*boldly* patterned/coloured くっきりとした模様の

ノート bright と bold の使い分け: bold は周りの物との対比でその色がいかに目立つかを強調し, 明るい色と共に用いられる bright よりも使用できる色の範囲が広い。

bring sb up [句動詞]

bring sb up・adopt・raise・rear・foster・be born and bred
子どもの成長や世話に関わることを表す
【類語訳】育てる, しつける, 養子にする, 里親となる, 生まれ育つ

↪bring sb up　　　　　　　　　　**brush, build**

文型&コロケーション
- to be brought up/ raised/ reared/ born and bred **in** a place
- to be brought up/ raised/ reared/ born and bred **as** sth
- to be brought up/ raised/ reared/ born and bred (as) a **Catholic/ Protestant/ Muslim/ Jew,** etc.
- to bring up/ adopt/ raise/ foster a **child**
- to bring up/ adopt/ raise/ rear a **daughter/ son/ family**
- to bring up/ adopt/ raise/ foster a **baby**
- to raise/ rear **young/ animals/ sheep/ chickens/ poultry**

,bring sb 'up [句動詞] [しばしば受身で] (子どもを)世話する[しつける]，育てる ◇She *brought up* five children. 彼女は5人の子どもを育てた ◇He was *brought up* by his aunt. 彼はおばに育てられた ◇What a well *brought up* child! なんてよくしつけられた子なの ◇They were *brought up* (= taught as children) to respect authority. 彼らは権威に敬意を示すよう育てられた

adopt [自，他] 養子にする ◇He led a campaign to encourage childless couples to *adopt*. 彼は子どものいない夫婦の養子の受け入れを勧めるキャンペーンを指揮した ◇She was forced to have her baby *adopted*. 彼女は自分の赤ちゃんを養子に出さねばならなかった
▶**adoption** [名] [U, C] ◇She put the baby up for *adoption*. 彼女は赤ちゃんを養子に出した

raise [他，しばしば受身で] (特に米) (人間・動物の子どもを)世話する，育てる ◇They were both *raised* in the South. 彼らは二人とも南部育ちだった ◇These kids have been *raised* on a diet of hamburgers. この子たちはハンバーガーを食べて育った ◇I was **born and raised** a city boy. 私は生まれも育ちも都会っ子だった ☞ **raise** (KEEP 4)

ノート bring sb up と **raise** の使い分け：(英)において子どもを育てることについて用いられるとき，**raise** のほうが **bring sb up** よりもややフォーマルである。

rear [他, しばしば受身で] (ややフォーマル) (動物・人間の子どもを)世話する，育てる ◇She *reared* a family of five on her own. 彼女は一家5人を独りで養った ◇Lions usually manage to *rear* about half the number of cubs born to them. ライオンはふつう生まれてきた子のおよそ半分を育て上げる ☞ **rear** (KEEP 4)

ノート raise と **rear** の使い分け：**raise** は人間の子について，**rear** は動物の子についてより頻繁に用いられる。

foster [他，自] (特に英) 里親となる ◇They have *fostered* over 60 children during the past ten years. 彼らは最近10年間で60人以上の子どもの里親となってきた ◇We couldn't adopt a child, so we decided to *foster*. 私たちは養子を取ることはできなかったので里親になることに決めた
▶**foster** [形] [名詞の前で] ◇a *foster* mother/father/family/child/home 育ての母/育ての父/里親の家族/里子/里親の家庭 ◇*foster* parents 里親 ◇*foster* care 里親制度

be ,born and 'bred [句動] (特定の環境のもとで教育を受けて)生まれ育つ ◇He *was born and bred* in Boston. 彼はボストンで生まれ育った ◇I'm a Londoner, *born and bred*. 私は生粋のロンドンっ子です

brush [動] ☞ CLEAN [動]

brush・scrub・sweep・dust・comb・groom
ブラシや布，くしなどを使ってきれいにすることを表す

【類語訳】ブラシをかける，ごしごし磨く，掃く，掃除する，ほこりを拭き取る，くしでとかす

文型&コロケーション
- to brush/ sweep/ dust sth **off/ from** sth
- to brush/ sweep sth **away**
- to brush/ comb your **hair**
- to scrub/ sweep the **floor**
- to scrub/ dust the **table/ surfaces**
- to brush/ scrub/ sweep sth **clean**

brush [他] ブラシをかける，ブラシ[手]で払いのける ◇to *brush* your hair/teeth/shoes 髪をブラッシングする/歯を磨く/靴を磨く ◇The non-slip surface is easy to *brush* clean. 滑らない表面はブラシできれいにしやすい ◇He *brushed* the dirt off his jacket. 彼はブラシをかけて上着のほこりを払った ◇She *brushed* the fly away. 彼女はハエを払いのけた
▶**brush** [名] [単数で] ◇to give your hair/teeth a good *brush* 髪をきれいにブラッシングする/歯をきれいに磨く

scrub (**-bb-**) [他, 自] (石鹸などを使って)ごしごし磨く ◇She *scrubbed* the counters down with bleach. 彼女は漂白剤でカウンターを磨き上げた ◇The woman *scrubbed at* her face with a tissue. その女性はティシューで顔をごしごし拭いた
▶**scrub** [名] [単数で] ◇I've given the floor a good *scrub*. 床をごしごしときれいに磨いた

sweep [他] (ほうき・手で)掃く，掃除する ◇to *sweep* the floor/street/stairs 床を掃く/通りを掃除する/階段を掃く ◇She *swept* the crumbs into the wastebasket. 彼女はパンくずを掃き集めてくずかごに入れた ◇He *swept* the leaves *up* into a pile. 彼は葉っぱを掃き上げた

dust [自, 他] (布などに)(ほこりを)拭き取る，払う ◇I broke the vase while I was *dusting*. ほこりを拭き取っているうちに花瓶を割ってしまった ◇Could you *dust* the sitting room? 居間のほこりを拭き払っていただけませんか ◇She *dusted* some ash from her sleeve. 彼女は袖から灰を払い落とした

comb [他] くしでとかす ◇Don't forget to *comb* your hair. くしで髪をとかすのを忘れないように
▶**comb** [名] [単数で] ◇Your hair needs a good *comb*. あなたの髪はくしできれいにとかす必要がある

groom [他] (動物に)毛づくろいする ◇to *groom* a horse/dog/cat 馬/犬/猫に毛づくろいする
▶**grooming** [名] [U] ◇*Grooming* is a vital part of caring for your dog. 毛づくろいは犬の世話に欠かせません

build [動]

build・construct・assemble・erect・set sth up・put sth up
部品を組み立てて物を形成する
【類語訳】作る，建てる，建設する，建造する，組み立てる，築く，立てる，設置する

文型&コロケーション
- to build/ construct sth **from/ out of/ of** sth
- to build/ construct/ assemble a **machine/ engine**
- to build/ construct/ erect/ set up/ put up a **barrier**
- to build/ construct/ erect/ put up a **house/ shelter/ wall/ fence**
- to build/ construct/ erect/ put up some **shelves**

bureaucracy, business

▶to **build**/ **construct**/ **erect** a **bridge**
▶to **build**/ **construct** a **road**/ **railway**/ **railroad**/ **tunnel**/ **nest**
▶to **erect**/ **put up** a **tent**/ **statue**/ **monument**

build [他, 自] （部品を組み立てて）作る, （建物を）建てる ◇Robins *build* nests almost anywhere. コマドリはどんどこにでも巣を作る ◇a house *built* of stone 石造りの家 ◇apartment blocks *built in* brick and concrete 煉瓦とコンクリートで建てられたアパート ◇They had a house *built* for them. 彼らは自分たちの家を建てた ◇David *built* us a shed in the backyard. デービッドが裏庭に小屋を建ててくれた ◇They're going to *build* on the site of the old power station. もと発電所のあった場所に建物の建設が予定されている [反意] **demolish** (DEMOLISH), ☞ **building** (PRODUCTION)

construct [他, しばしば受身で]《ややフォーマル》（道路・建物・機械などを）建設[建造]する ◇When was the bridge *constructed*? いつその橋は架けられたのですか ◇They *constructed* a shelter out of fallen branches. 彼らは落ちていた枝で避難小屋を建てた [反意] **demolish** (DEMOLISH), ☞ **construction** (PRODUCTION), **construction** (STRUCTURE)

assemble [他]《ややフォーマル》（家具・機械などの部品を）組み立てる ◇The shelves are easy to *assemble*. その棚は組み立てが簡単です ◇The company *assembles* vehicles for Renault and Toyota. その会社はルノーとトヨタの車を組み立てている ☞ **assembly** (PRODUCTION)

erect [他]《フォーマル》（建物を）建てる, 建立する ;（物を）築く, 立てる ◇The church was *erected* in 1582. その教会は1582年に建てられた ◇Police had to *erect* barriers to keep crowds back. 警察は群衆を押しとどめるため防御柵を築かなければならなかった

set sth 'up [句動詞]（建物を）建てる, （物を）設置する ◇The police *set up* roadblocks on routes out of the city. 警察はその街から出る道路にバリケードを築いた ◇We decided to *set up camp* for the night. その晩私たちはテントを張ることに決めた

put sth 'up [句動詞]（建物を）建てる, （物を）設置する ◇They're *putting up* new hotels to boost tourism in the area. その地域の観光振興のため新しくホテルが建てられる予定だ ◇Do you know how to *put* this tent *up*? このテントの張り方を知っていますか

[ノート] **set sth up** と **put sth up** の使い分け : set sth up は常設の建築には用いられない. ×They're *setting up* new hotels. 目的語が camp と tent の場合はそれぞれ set up camp, put up a tent と決められているが, 他の仮設構造物に関しては両方とも使用可能. ◆ to *set up/put up* a fence/barrier/shelter（フェンス／障壁／避難所を設置する）.

bureaucracy [名]

bureaucracy • paperwork • red tape • rules and regulations
複雑で時間の無駄に思えるような役所の規則またはやり方
【類語訳】お役所仕事, 書類仕事

[文型&コロケーション]
▶**unnecessary**/ **too much**/ **endless** bureaucracy/ paperwork/ red tape
▶**government** bureaucracy/ red tape/ rules and regulations

▶to **involve** bureaucracy/ paperwork/ red tape
▶to **reduce**/ **cut** bureaucracy/ paperwork/ red tape
▶to **deal with** bureaucracy/ paperwork

bureaucracy [U]《しばしばけなして》お役所仕事 ◇She is initiating a project to eliminate unnecessary *bureaucracy*. 彼女は不必要なお役所仕事を根絶するプロジェクトを開始する予定だ ❶ **paperwork** ☞ **bureaucracy** (AUTHORITIES), **bureaucrat** (OFFICIAL [名])

paperwork [U] 書類仕事 ◇She spent the day catching up on the vast mound of *paperwork* that had built up. たまっていた膨大な量の書類仕事に取り組んで挽回するのに彼女は一日を費やした ❶ paperwork は bureaucracy, red tape のように常に非難を表すとは限らない. たとえやりたくなかったり, 他のことに時間を使いたいとしても, やらなければならないと理解している「書類仕事」のことを言う. また,「必要書類」を指すこともある. ☞ **paperwork** (DOCUMENT)

,red 'tape [U]《けなして, ジャーナリズム》お役所風[流] ◇Plans may take longer and involve more *red tape* than you expect. 計画が思ったよりも長期間に及んだりお役所流になったりするかもしれない

,rules and regu'lations [フレーズ] お役所的な規則[やり方] ◇They seem to be more concerned with enforcing petty *rules and regulations* than really improving employee safety. 彼らは従業員の安全を実際に改善することよりも, つまらぬお役所的な規則を守らせることに関心があるように思える

business [名]

business • concern • preserve • affair
特定の人, 集団, 団体に関連する事柄を表す
【類語訳】務め, 領分

[文型&コロケーション]
▶(a) **private**/ **personal** business/ concern/ affair
▶sth is sb's **own** business/ concern/ affair
▶to be **none** of sb's business/ concern
▶sth is **no** business/ concern **of** sb

business [単数で]（特定の人・団体がやるべき）本分, 務め ◇It is the *business* of the police to protect the community. 地域社会を守ることは警察の務めだ ◇My private life is none of your *business* (= you do not have a right to know about it). 私の私生活はあなたには関係のないことです ◇It's no *business* of yours who I invite to the party. 私が誰をパーティーに招待するかはあなたには関係のないことです ◇I shall **make it my business** to find out who is responsible. 私が必ず誰に責任があるかを突き止めましょう

concern [C, ふつう単数で]《フォーマル》関心事, 務め ◇This matter is their *concern*. この事は彼らに任せておけばよい ◇How much money I make is none of your *concern*. 私がいくら稼いでいるかなんてあなたには関係のないことです

[ノート] **business** と **concern** の使い分け : これらの語には意味の違いはないが, concern のほうがフォーマルでよく書き言葉で用いられる. 両語とも sth is sb's business/concern の句で用いられるが, sth is the business of sth の句では代わりに concern を用いることはできない. ×It is the *concern* of the police to protect the community. **make it your business to do sth**「…する権利[知る権利]があり、そうする」の意味だが、concernはこのようには用いられない。×I shall make it my *concern* to find out who is responsible.

preserve ［単数で］（特定の人・集団にふさわしいと考えられている）領分 ◇Higher education is no longer the *preserve* of the wealthy. 高等教育はもはや富裕層だけのためにあるものではない ◇I began my career in the days when nursing was a female *preserve*. 私は看護が女性のための仕事であった時代にこの仕事を始めた

affair ［単数で］《ややフォーマル》個人的問題［事情］ ◇How I spend my money is my *affair*. 私の金をどのように使うかは私の問題だ ◇The details of your relationship should be a private *affair*. あなたのこまごまとした人間関係は個人的問題のはずだ ❶ affairはThat's my business/concern/affair.のように business, concernと同じように用いることができるが、以下の形で用いることはできない。×none of sb's *affair*. ×no *affair* of sb. しかしながら、sth is [should be] a private/personal affairと言うのは非常に一般的である。

busy ［形］

1 busy・active・engaged・involved・occupied・hard-pressed・at work
人がすべきことがたくさんあることを表す
【類語訳】忙しい、活動的な、熱心な、積極的な、熱中している、打ち込んでいる、かかりっきりの、せっぱ詰まった

文型&コロケーション
▸ **busy/ involved/ occupied with** sth
▸ **active/ engaged/ involved/ occupied in** sth
▸ **engaged/ at work on** sth
▸ to keep sb **busy/ active/ involved/ occupied**
▸ **very/ particularly/ quite busy/ active/ involved**
▸ **currently busy/ active/ engaged/ involved/ occupied/ at work**
▸ **constantly busy/ engaged/ involved/ occupied/ at work**
▸ **actively engaged/ involved in** sth

busy 忙しい、多忙な、手がふさがっている ◇Are you *busy* tonight? 今夜は忙しいですか ◇I'm afraid the doctor is *busy* at the moment. Can he call you back? 申し訳ありませんが、今先生は手が離せません。折り返しお電話させましょうか ◇The principal is a very *busy* woman. 校長は非常に多忙な女性です ◇She was always too *busy* to listen. 彼女はいつも忙しくて人の話を聞いていられなかった ◇James is *busy* practising for the school concert. ジェームズは学校のコンサートの練習に忙殺されている
▸ **busily** ［副］ ◇He was *busily* engaged in repairing his bike. 彼はせっせと自転車の修理に没頭していた

active 《ややフォーマル》活動的な、熱心な；積極的な ◇They were both politically *active*. 彼らはふたりとも政治活動に熱心だった ◇She takes an *active* part in school life. 彼女は学校生活に積極的に参加している ◇The parents were *active* in campaigning against cuts to the education budget. 親たちは教育予算の削減に対する反対運動に積極的に関わっていた ◇They took *active* steps to prevent the spread of the disease. 彼らはその病気の蔓延を防ぐため積極的な方策を講じた ［反意］ **inactive, pas-**

sive. ❶ この意味におけるactiveの反意語はinactiveまたはpassive. ◆The area has a large, but politically *inactive* population. (その地域は人口は多いが、政治には無関心である). ◆He played a *passive* role in the relationship. (彼はその関係において消極的な役割しか果たさなかった). ☞ **active (ENERGETIC)**
▸ **actively** ［副］ ◇She was *actively* looking for a job. 彼女は精力的に就職活動をしていた

engaged ［名詞の前では用いない］《フォーマル》忙しい、没頭している ◇They were *engaged* in conversation. 彼らは話に夢中だった ◇He is now *engaged* on his second novel. 彼は今二作目の小説にかかりっきりだ ◇I can't come to dinner on Tuesday — I'm *otherwise engaged* (= I have already arranged to do sth else). 火曜日は食事には行けない — 他の用でふさがっているので ☞ **engagement (MEETING 2)**

involved ［名詞の前まれ］（人・物事に）熱心な、打ち込んでいる ◇She was deeply *involved* with the local hospital. 彼女は地元の病院と深く関わっていた ◇I was so *involved* in my book I didn't hear you knock. 本に夢中で君のノックが聞こえなかったよ ◇He's a very *involved* father (= he spends a lot of time with his children). 彼はとても子煩悩な父だ ☞ **involvement (INVOLVEMENT)**

occupied ［名詞の前では用いない］《ややフォーマル》（人・物事に）専念した、忙しい ◇He's fully *occupied* looking after three small children. 彼は3人の小さい子どもの面倒をみるのに手一杯だ ◇Only half her time is *occupied* with politics. 彼女は片手間で政治に関わっている ◇The most important thing is to keep yourself *occupied*. 最も重要なことは取り組むべきことがあることだ

ノート **involvedとoccupiedの使い分け**: involvedはふつう人が個人的・感情的な結びつきから「打ち込んでいる」ことを含意する。occupiedは単に人にすべきことがたくさんあることを示唆する。

hard-'pressed (仕事・時間に)せっぱ詰まった，(お金に)困窮した ◇*Hard-pressed* junior doctors want shorter working hours. 忙しい[かせぎの少ない]若手の医者たちは勤務時間の短縮を望んでいる

at 'work ［名詞の前では用いない］…することに忙しい［従事している］ ◇He is still *at work* on the painting. 彼はまだせっせと絵を書いている ◇Danger — men *at work*. 危険 — 工事中

2 busy・hectic・full・eventful・lively
仕事や活動がたくさん詰まった期間を表す
【類語訳】多忙な、忙しい、慌ただしい、波瀾に富んだ、活発な

文型&コロケーション
▸ a **busy/ a hectic/ a full/ an eventful day/ weekend/ week**
▸ a **busy/ a hectic/ full/ lively programme**
▸ a **busy/ a hectic/ full schedule/ timetable**
▸ a **busy/ a hectic/ a full/ an eventful life**
▸ **very busy/ hectic/ full/ eventful/ lively**

busy 多忙な、忙しい ◇Have you had a *busy* day? 今日は忙しかったの ◇This is one of the *busiest* times of the year for the department. 今はこの売り場にとって一年で最も忙しい時期の一つです ［反意］ **quiet (QUIET 1)**

hectic 慌ただしい、忙しすぎる ◇I don't want to lead such a *hectic* life any more. こんな慌ただしい生活を送るのはもうこりごりだ ◇We were involved in the *hectic*

last-minute preparations. 私たちは準備の最後の追い込みにおおわらわだった
full 《しばしばほめて》忙しい；たくさんの活動を伴う ◇He'd had a very *full* life. 彼は非常に忙しい[充実した]生活を送っていた ◇Her life was too *full* to find time for hobbies. 彼女の生活はやることがいっぱいで趣味の時間を作ることができなかった

ノート busy, hectic, full の使い分け：busy が最も一般的な語。full は人の生活がよい意味で忙しいことを表す。hectic は過度に忙しいことを表す。

eventful 波瀾に富んだ ◇It had been a long and *eventful* journey. 長くそして波瀾に富んだ旅だった 反意 **uneventful**
lively 《特に英》(忙しくて)活動的な、活発な ◇They do a *lively* trade in souvenirs and gifts. 彼らは土産物や贈り物の貿易を活発に行っている ❶この意味では、lively は主に trading, business, bidding, the market などに用いられる。

button 名

1 button・switch・control・wheel・key・handle・lever・knob・dial
機械や乗り物、装置の一部で押したり回したり動かしたりして作動を開始させるもの
【類語訳】ボタン、スイッチ、ハンドル、キー、レバー、ノブ、ダイヤル

文型&コロケーション
▶ a button/ switch/ key/ handle/ lever/ knob/ dial **on** sth
▶ the **on/ off/ on-off** button/ switch
▶ a **control** button/ switch/ key/ level/ knob
▶ a **door** handle/ knob
▶ a **volume control** button/ switch/ knob/ dial
▶ to **be at/ take** the controls/ wheel
▶ to **press** a button/ switch/ key/ lever
▶ to **push** a button/ switch/ handle/ lever
▶ to **pull** a switch/ handle/ lever
▶ to **turn** a wheel/ handle/ knob/ dial
▶ to **hit** a button/ switch/ key
▶ to **adjust** the controls/ lever/ knob/ dial
▶ a button/ switch/ handle/ lever/ knob/ dial **controls** sth
▶ a/ the button/ switch/ controls/ wheel/ handle/ lever **operates** sth
▶ a/ the button/ switch/ controls/ lever/ knob/ dial **adjusts** sth

button [C] ボタン ◇the play/stop/rewind *button* 再生/停止/巻き戻しボタン ◇Adam pressed a *button* and waited for the doors to open. アダムはボタンを押してドアが開くのを待った ◇Choose 'printer' from the menu and click with the right *mouse button*. メニューから「プリンター」を選択してマウスの右のボタンをクリックしてください ◇The windows slide down **at the touch of a button**. その窓はボタンに触れるとスライドして降りてくる
switch [C] スイッチ ◇a light *switch* 電気のスイッチ ◇That was in the days before electricity was available **at the flick of a switch**. それはスイッチをカチッと入れると電気が利用できる以前の時代のことだった ◇Which *switch* do I press to turn it off? オフにするにはどのスイッチを押すの ◇to throw a *switch* (= to move a large switch) スイッチを入れる ☞ **switch sth off** (TURN STH

OFF), **switch sth on** (TURN STH ON)
control [C, ふつう複数で] (機械・乗り物を操作するために用いる)スイッチ/ハンドル類 ◇the *controls* of an aircraft 飛行機の操縦装置 ◇the *control* panel 制御盤 ◇the volume *control* of a CD player CDプレーヤーの音量調節つまみ ◇The co-pilot was at the *controls* when the plane landed. 飛行機が着陸したときの副操縦士は操縦席にいた ☞ **control** (OPERATE)
wheel [C, ふつう単数で] ハンドル ◇He drummed his fingers on the **steering wheel** and waited. 彼は指でハンドルをトントンたたきながら待っていた ◇This is the first time I've sat **behind the wheel** since the accident. 事故以来運転席に座るのは今日が初めてです ◇A car swept past with Laura at the *wheel*. 通り過ぎた車はローラが運転していた ◇Do you want to take the *wheel* (= drive/steer) now? 今運転したいの
key [C] (コンピューター・タイプライターなどの)キー ◇Press the return *key* to enter the information. リターン・キーを押して情報を入力してください ◇His hands flew over the piano *keys* and beautiful sounds filled the theatre. 彼の手がピアノの鍵盤の上を舞うと美しい音色で劇場が満たされた
▶**key** 動 [他] ◇*Key* (in) your password. あなたのパスワードを入力してください
handle [C] 取っ手、ハンドル ◇She turned the *handle* and opened the door. 彼女は取っ手を回してドアを開けた ◇He tried the *handle* but the window was locked. 彼は取っ手を回してみたが、窓には鍵がかけられていた
lever [C] レバー、握り ◇Pull the *lever* towards you to adjust the speed. スピードを調節するにはレバーを自分の方に引いてください
knob [C] (オン・オフに用いるラジオなどの)丸型のスイッチ；(ドア・引き出しの)丸型の取っ手、ノブ ◇the volume control *knob* 音量の操作つまみ ◇I've tried twiddling the *knobs*, but nothing seems to happen. つまみを回してみたけど何も起こらないみたい ◇She turned the heavy brass door *knob*. 彼女は重い真鍮製のドアノブを回した
dial [C] ダイヤル ◇You can tune into our station at 1460 on the radio *dial*. ラジオのつまみを1460にすると当局に合わせることができます ◇Set the *dial* for the number of copies requested. コピーしたい枚数に合わせてダイヤルを調節してください

2 button・pin・buckle・zip・zipper・fastener・clasp・catch・Velcro™・lace/shoelace・drawstring
衣服などを留めたり締めたりするのに用いられる物
【類語訳】ボタン、ピン、バックル、ジッパー、留め具、締め具、ベルクロ、靴紐、引き紐

文型&コロケーション
▶ to **do up/ undo** a/ your button/ buckle/ zip/ zipper/ clasp/ catch/ laces/ shoelaces
▶ to **fasten/ unfasten** a/ your button/ buckle/ zip/ zipper/ clasp
▶ a/ your button/ buckle/ zip/ zipper/ clasp/ catch/ laces/ shoelaces **is/ are/ comes/ come undone**
▶ a zip/ zipper/ fastener/ fastening/ clasp/ catch **is/ gets stuck**

button [C] 丸いボタン ◇to do up/undo your *buttons* 《英》ボタンを留める/外す ◇to button/unbutton your *buttons* 《米》ボタンを留める/外す ◇The top *button* of

↪**button**

his shirt was undone. 彼はシャツの一番上のボタンを外していた ◇My coat has lost a *button*. コートのボタンが一つなくなっている ◇I need to sew this *button* back on. このボタンを縫い付け直さないといけない ☞ **unbutton** (UNDO)

pin [C] ピン ◇Use *pins* to keep the patch in place while you sew it on. 縫い付けている間、継ぎ当てが動かないようにピンを使いましょう ◇The map had a lot of little *pins* stuck into it. その地図には小さなピンがたくさん刺さっていた ◇Fasten the baby's nappy with ***a safety pin*** (= a pin with a point bent back towards the head, that is covered when closed so that it cannot hurt you). 赤ちゃんのおしめを安全ピンで留めましょう
▸ **pin** [動] [他] ◇She *pinned* the badge onto her jacket. 彼女はそのバッジを上着にピンで留めた ◇*Pin* all the pieces of material together. すべての生地をピンで留めましょう

buckle [C] バックル ◇He adjusted his belt *buckle*. 彼はベルトのバックルを調節した
▸ **buckle** [動] [他, 自] ◇She *buckled* her belt. 彼女はベルトのバックルを締めた ◇These shoes *buckle* at the side. この靴は脇のバックルで留めるタイプです 反意 **unbuckle**

zip [英] [C] ジッパー ◇My *zip*'s stuck. ジッパーが引っかかってしまった ◇a bag with a *zip* ジッパー付きのバッグ ☞ **unzip** (UNDO)

zipper 《特に米》[C] ジッパー ◇My *zipper*'s stuck. ジッパーが引っかかってしまった

fastener (または **fastening**) [C] 留め具、締め具 ◇*buttons*, *zippers* and other *fasteners* ボタンやジッパーを始めとする留め具 ◇She fumbled with the unfamiliar *fastening* of the seatbelt. 彼女は馴染みのないシートベルトの締め方にまごついた ☞ **unfasten** (UNDO)

clasp [C] (バッグ・ベルト・宝飾品などの) 留め具 ◇the *clasp* of a necklace/handbag ネックレス／ハンドバッグの留め金 ◇He tried to undo the *clasp* on the briefcase, but it was stuck. ブリーフケースの留め金を外そうとしたが、固くて開かなかった

catch [C] (ドア・窓・箱を締める) 留め金 ◇a *catch* on the door ドアの掛け金 ◇safety *catches* for the windows 窓の安全ロック ◇I can't open the *catch* on this bracelet. このブレスレットの留め金をはずせない

Velcro™ [U] (マジックテープの一種である) ベルクロ ◇He did up the *Velcro* straps on his shoes. 彼は靴のベルクロを締めた

lace (または **shoelace**) [C, ふつう複数で] 靴紐 ◇to tie/untie your *laces*/*shoelaces* 靴紐を締める／ほどく ◇a pair of *shoelaces* 一組の靴紐 ◇My *shoelaces* came undone and I nearly tripped. 靴紐がほどけて私は転びそうになった
▸ **lace 'up**, **lace sth 'up** [句動] ◇a dress that *laces up* at the side 脇を紐で締めるタイプのドレス ◇He was sitting on the bed *lacing up* his shoes. 彼はベッドに座って靴紐を締めていた

drawstring [C] (袋・衣服の開口部を締める) 引き紐 ◇They fasten with a *drawstring*. それらは引き紐で締めます ◇a *drawstring* waist 引き紐で締めるウエスト部分

buy [動]

buy • get • purchase • acquire • shop • take • pick sth up • snap sth up
お金を支払って物を手に入れる
【類語訳】買う、購入する、ショッピングする

buy

文型&コロケーション

▸ to buy sth/ get sth/ purchase sth/ acquire sth/ shop/ pick sth up/ snap sth up **for £10, $2 million**, etc.
▸ to buy sth/ get sth/ go shopping **for sb**
▸ to buy/ get/ purchase/ acquire sth **from sb**/ a particular shop
▸ to buy/ get/ purchase/ acquire/ pick up/ snap up **shares**
▸ to buy/ get/ purchase/ acquire/ snap up (a) **property**/ **company**/ **house**
▸ to buy/ get/ purchase/ acquire/ take **goods**/ **a lease**
▸ to buy/ get/ purchase/ acquire **land**/ **premises**/ **a site**/ **tickets**
▸ to buy/ get/ purchase/ take a **newspaper**/ **magazine**
▸ to get/ pick up/ snap up a **bargain**
▸ to buy sth/ purchase sth/ acquire sth/ pick sth up **cheaply**

buy [他, 自] 買う;(お金が) 足りる ◇I *bought* this from a friend for £10. 私は友人から10ポンドでこれを買った ◇He *bought* me a new coat. 彼は私に新品のコートを買ってくれた ◇If you're thinking of getting a new car, now is a good time to *buy*. 新車の購入をお考えなら、今が買い時ですよ ◇Five pounds doesn't *buy* much nowadays. 最近は5ポンドでは大した買い物はできない ◇He gave his children the best education that money can *buy*. 彼はお金が許す範囲で最高の教育を子どもたちに受けさせた ☞ **buyer** (CUSTOMER)

get [他, 受身なし]《ややインフォーマル、特に話し言葉》手に入れる、買う;(新聞・雑誌などを) 定期的に購入する ◇Did you *get* a present for your mother? お母さんにプレゼントを買ったかい ◇Did you *get* your mother a present? お母さんにプレゼントを買ったかい ◇You can *get* the basic model for $100. ベーシックモデルを100ドルで購入できます ◇Which newspaper do you *get*? どこの新聞を購読してますか ❶ get はお金を払ったかどうかに関係なく「手に入れる」という広い意味も持っている。以下の文を比べてみよう。◆'Where did you *get* that skirt?' 'I bought it.' (あのスカートどうやって手に入れたの」「買ったの」). ◆'Where did you *buy*/*get* that skirt?' 'Top Shop.' (「どこのスカートを買ったの」「トップショップで」). get は特に話し言葉で大して高価でない物を「購入する」の意味で頻繁に用いられるが、お金を払ったかどうかを明確にする必要がある場合は buy を用いる。☞ **get** (GET 1)

purchase [他]《フォーマル》購入する ◇The equipment can be *purchased* from your local supplier. その装置は地元の販売元から購入することができる ◇Please ensure that you *purchase* your ticket in advance. 必ずチケットは前もってご購入ください ☞ **purchaser** (CUSTOMER)

acquire [他]《フォーマル、特にビジネス》(購入して物を) 手に入れる ◇The company has just *acquired* new premises. その会社は新しい土地建物を購入したばかりだ ◇How did the gallery come to *acquire* so many Picassos? どうやってその画廊はピカソの絵をそんなにたくさん購入できるようになったの

ノート **purchase** と **acquire** の使い分け: acquire は company, firm, franchise, land, lease, premises, site, stake, subsidiary などビジネスに関連する語と一緒に用いられる。purchase は単に buy のフォーマルな代用語で、いろいろな名詞と共に用いられる。acquire には人からもらって「手に入れる」という意味もあるので、お金を払ったかどうかを明確にする必要がある場合は、buy や purchase を用いる。☞ **acquire** (GET 1)

shop (-pp-) [自] (物を店で)買う, ショッピングする ◇We tend to go into Edinburgh to ***shop for*** clothes. 私たちは服を買いにエディンバラに行くことが多い ◇He likes to *shop* at the local market. 彼は地元の市場で買い物をするのが好きだ ❶ go shopping は店に行って買う物を探すことに費やすことを指す. ◆There should be plenty of time to *go shopping* before we leave New York. (ニューヨークを出発する前にショッピングする時間がたくさんあるはずだ). ☞ **shopper** (CUSTOMER)

take [他] (選んで物を)買う ◇I'll *take* the grey jacket. グレーのジャケットをください ❶この意味では take は特に I'll take... の言い回しで, 選んで買うことが明白な場合にのみ用いられる. 例えば She took the grey jacket. という文では took が「盗む」の意味に誤解される可能性がある. take は「新聞や雑誌を定期購読する」の意味で用いる場合, get のフォーマルな表現として用いられることもある. ◆We *take* the 'Express'. (《フォーマル》私たちは『エクスプレス』を購読しています).

,pick sth 'up 句動詞 《インフォーマル》(安く[偶然に]物を)買う ◇We managed to *pick up* a few bargains at the auction. 私たちはうまい具合にオークションで掘り出し物をいくつか買うことができた

,snap sth 'up 句動詞 (-pp-)《インフォーマル》(安い[ほしかった]から)即座に購入[入手]する ◇All the best bargains were *snapped up* within hours. 最特価品は全部数時間ですぐに売り切れた

C c

calculate [動] ☞ COUNT, ESTIMATE [動]

calculate・work sth out・compute・quantify・figure sth out・figure・put a figure on sth
数字を用いて総計を出す
【類語訳】計算する、算出する

文型&コロケーション

- to calculate/ compute/ figure sth **at** 400, $1,000, 25%, etc.
- to calculate/ work out/ compute/ quantify/ figure out/ figure/ put a figure on **how much/ how many ...**
- to calculate/ work out/ figure out/ figure **that ...**
- to calculate/ work out/ compute/ quantify/ figure out/ figure/ put a figure on the **cost/ number/ amount** (of sth)
- to calculate/ work out/ compute **a total**
- to calculate sth/ work sth out/ quantify sth/ figure sth out **exactly**

calculate [他, 自]《ややフォーマル》計算する、算出する ◇Use the formula to *calculate* the volume of the container. 公式を用いて容器の容量を計算しなさい ◇The sum involved was *calculated* at $82 million. 関連したものの総額は8200万ドルと算出された ◇*It has been calculated that* at least 47,000 jobs were lost last year. 昨年は少なくとも47000の雇用が失われた計算になる ☞ **calculate** (ESTIMATE [動]), **calculation** (ESTIMATE [名])

work sth 'out [句動]《ややインフォーマル、特に話し言葉》(物事を)計算する[算出する] ◇I just need a minute to *work out* the answer. 答を出すのにほんの少し時間がいります ◇I can't *work* this *out* — have you got a calculator? この計算ができない—計算機を持ってますか ◇You'll need to *work out* how much time the assignment will take. この課題にどれくらいの時間がかかるか算出する必要があるだろう

compute [他]《フォーマル》計算する、算出する ◇The losses were *computed* at £5 million. 損失は500万ポンドと算出された

> ノート **calculate, work sth out, compute** の使い分け: 書き言葉では **calculate** が最もよく用いられる。話し言葉では **work sth out** がよく用いられ、特に小さな数字をふつうの人が計算するときに用いられる。**compute** はフォーマルな書き言葉で、特に機械による計算を表す。

quantify [他]《ややフォーマル》量[数]で表す ◇The risks to health are impossible to *quantify*. 健康へのリスクを数値で表すことはできない

figure sth 'out [句動]《インフォーマル》(量・費用を)計算する、算出する ◇Have you *figured out* how much the trip will cost? 旅行の費用がいくらかかるか計算しましたか

figure [他]《米》(量・費用を)計算する ◇We *figured* the attendence at 150,000. 我々は出席者は15万人と計算した ☞ **figure** (ESTIMATE [動])

> ノート **figure sth out** と **figure** の使い分け: **figure** は《米》のみで用いられる。**figure sth out** は《英》でも《米》でも用いられるが、総計を表すのに **at** と共には用いない。 ×We *figured out* the attendence at 150,000.

put a figure on sth [フレーズ]《ふつう疑問文と否定的な文で》(物事の)正確な値段[数]を言う ◇It's impossible to *put a figure on* the number of homeless people in the country. この国のホームレスの正確な数を出すのは不可能だ

call [動]

1 call・name・term・entitle・label・designate・dub・brand・nickname・address・christen
人や物事に名前や名称をつける
【類語訳】名づける、命名する、呼ぶ、烙印を押す

文型&コロケーション

- to label/ designate/ brand/ address sb/ sth **as** sth
- to call/ address sb **by** their full name, their first name, etc.
- to call/ name/ dub/ nickname/ christen sb **Mary, Ali etc.**
- to call/ dub/ nickname sb **captain, the wizard, etc.**
- **officially** called/ named/ termed/ entitled/ labelled/ designated/ dubbed/ christened
- **aptly** called/ named/ termed/ entitled/ nicknamed
- **commonly** called/ termed/ labelled

call [他] 名づける;(名前で)呼ぶ ◇They decided to *call* the baby Mark. 彼らはその赤ちゃんをマークと名づけることに決めた ◇His name's Hiroshi but everyone *calls* him Hiro. 彼の名前はヒロシだがみんな彼のことをヒロと呼ぶ ◇What do they *call* that new fabric? あの新しい生地はなんという名前ですか ◇They *called* their first daughter after her grandmother. 彼らは長女を祖母の名前にちなんで命名した ◇We *call* each other by our first names here. ここでは我々はお互いファーストネームで呼び合っている

name [他] 名づける、命名する ◇They *named* their son John. 彼らは息子をジョンと名づけた ◇He was *named after* his father (= given his father's first name). 彼は父親の名前をとって命名された ◇The planet Mars is *named for* the Roman god of war. 《特に米》Mars(火星)はローマ神話の戦争の神の名をとってつけられている ❶新しい名前をつけることを **rename** という。 ◆ Leningrad was *renamed* St Petersburg. (レニングラードはサンクトペテルブルグに改称された). ◆ to *rename* a file (= on a computer) (ファイルに新しい名前をつける[をリネームする]).

term [他, ふつう受身で]《フォーマル》(科学的・専門的な文脈で)特定の名前・語で)呼ぶ ◇At his age, he can hardly be *termed* a young man. 彼の年齢では、とても若者とは呼べない ◇REM sleep is *termed* 'active' sleep. レム睡眠は「賦活」睡眠といわれる

entitle [他, ふつう受身で] (本・芝居・映画・絵画などに)題をつける ◇The company launched a huge marketing campaign *entitled* 'Buy Blue'. その会社はBuy Blueと題した大々的な販売活動を始めた ◇He read a poem *entitled* 'Salt'. 彼はSaltという題の詩を読んだ

label (-ll-, 米 -l-) [他, しばしば受身で]《時にけなして》(不当で よくない)レッテルをはる ◇He was *labelled* (as) a traitor by his former colleagues. 彼は元同僚から裏切り者のレッテルをはられていた ◇It is unfair to *label* a small baby as naughty. 小さな赤ん坊を行儀が悪いと決めつけるのは正しくない

designate [他, ふつう受身で] (ややフォーマル) 指定する；称する ◇This area has been *designated* (as) a National Park. この地域は「国立公園」とされている ◇*designated* seats for the elderly お年寄りのための指定席

dub (-bb-) [他, しばしば受身で] (メディアでユーモラスな[批判をこめた]) 通称をつける ◇The media *dubbed* anorexia 'the slimming disease'. メディアは拒食症を「ダイエット病」と呼んだ

brand [他]《時にけなして》(不当に人に)烙印を押す ◇They were *branded* as liars and cheats. 彼らは嘘つきで詐欺師だという烙印を押された ◇The newspapers *branded* her a hypocrite. 新聞は彼女に偽善者という烙印を押した

nickname [他, しばしば受身で] あだな[ニックネーム]をつける, 愛称で呼ぶ ◇She was *nicknamed* 'The Ice Queen'. 彼女は「氷の女王」というあだ名をつけられた ❶ニックネームは本当の名前, 個性, 外見, 特性, やったこと, できることなどに結びつくものからつけられる. ◆Michael Jackson, *nicknamed* 'Jacko' [マイケル・ジャクソン, ニックネームはジャコ]. ◆He was *nicknamed* 'Stretch' because he was so tall. (彼は非常に背が高かったので「ストレッチ」というあだ名が付いた.)

address [他] [敬称[特定の名前]で]呼びかける ◇The judge should be *addressed* as 'Your Honour'. 裁判官には「Your Honour」と呼ぶべきだ ◇How should I *address* her? 彼女を何とお呼びすればいいですか ◇Please *address* my client by his full name, Mr Babic. バビックさん, 私のクライアントをフルネームで呼んでください

christen [他, しばしば受身で] (赤ん坊に)洗礼を施して命名する, 洗礼名をつける；(人・物事に)命名する ◇The child was *christened* Mary. その子どもはメアリという洗礼名を授けられた ◇Did you have your children *christened*? あなたは子どもたちに洗礼名を付けてもらいましたか ◇They *christened* the boat 'Oceania'. 彼らはその船を「オセアニア」と命名した

▶**christening** 名 [C] ◇my nephew's *christening* (= the ceremony in which a baby is christened) 私の甥の命名式

---

2 call・ring・phone・dial・telephone・reach・call sb up
電話をかける
【類語訳】電話をする, ダイヤルする

文型&コロケーション

▶to call sb/ ring sb/ phone sb/ telephone sb/ call sb up **about** sth
▶to call/ ring/ phone/ telephone **from** somewhere
▶to call/ ring/ phone/ telephone **to do** sth
▶to call/ ring/ phone/ dial/ telephone **a number/ a hotline/ the switchboard/ reception**
▶to call/ ring/ phone/ dial/ telephone **New York/ India, etc.**
▶to call/ ring/ phone/ telephone the **doctor/ fire brigade/ police/ hospital**
▶to call/ ring/ phone/ telephone **home**
▶to call/ ring/ phone/ dial/ telephone **direct**
▶to call/ ring/ phone (sb) **up/ back**

---

call [他, 自] 電話をかける；電話で呼び出す ◇My brother *called* me from Germany last night. 兄が昨夜ドイツから電話をかけてきた ◇I *called* the office to tell them I'd be late. 私は遅くなるとオフィスに電話を入れた ◇Has anyone *called* the police? 誰か警察を呼びましたか ◇I'll *call* you a taxi. タクシーを呼んであげましょう ◇I'll *call* back later. 後でかけ直そう

▶**call** 名 [C] to get/have/receive a *call* from sb 人から電話をもらう ◇to give sb/to make a *call* 人に電話する ◇Were there any *calls* for me while I was out? 私が出かけている間に電話がありましたか ◇I'll *take* (= answer) *the call* upstairs. 私が2階で電話をとります

ring [他, 自]《英, ややインフォーマル, 特に話し言葉》電話をかける ◇I'll *ring* you later. 後で電話します ◇When is the best time to *ring* New York? ニューヨークに電話するのはいつが一番いいですか ◇David *rang* up while you were out. あなたが出かけているときにデイヴィッドから電話してきた ◇He said he was *ringing* from London. 彼はロンドンから電話をかけていると言った ◇Could you *ring* for a cab? タクシーを呼んでいただけませんか ◇She *rang* to say she'd be late. 彼女は電話して遅れると伝えた

phone [自, 他]《英, ややインフォーマル, 特に話し言葉》電話をする ◇Could you *phone* back later? あとで折り返し電話をいただけませんか ◇I'm *phoning* about your ad in the paper. 私は新聞広告のことでお電話しています ◇For reservations, *phone* 0207 281 3964. ご予約は0207 281 3964へお電話ください

▶**phone** 名 [C, U] ◇The *phone* rang and Pat answered it. 電話が鳴ってパットが出た ◇They like to do business *by phone/over the phone*. 彼らは好んで電話でビジネスをする ◇He's been *on the phone* (= using the phone) to Kate for more than an hour. 彼はケイトと1時間以上も電話している

ノート call, ring, phone の使い分け：これら3つの語のうち《米》で用いられるのはcallのみ. ringとphoneは《英》の話し言葉で最もよく用いられるが, 緊急の呼び出しには《英》でもふつうはcallが好まれる. call the police/fire brigade (警察/消防隊を呼ぶ)はring/phone the police/fire brigadeより頻繁に用いられる. 人, 場所, 施設などに電話をするときはcall/ring/phoneを用い, タクシー (cab, taxi), 救急車 (ambulance)を呼ぶときはcallを用いる. ×I'll *ring/phone* you a cab.

dial (-ll-, 米 -l-) [他, 自] ダイヤルする；電話をかける ◇He *dialled* the number and waited. 彼は電話番号をダイヤルして待った ◇*Dial* 0033 for France. フランスへの電話は0033をダイヤルしてください ◇She picked up the receiver, paused a moment, and then *dialled*. 彼女は受話器を取り, 少し間をおいてから番号をダイヤルした

telephone [自, 他]《特に英, フォーマル》 電話をかける ◇Please write or *telephone* for details. 詳細を手紙や電話で知らせてください ◇You can *telephone* your order 24 hours a day. 注文は24時間電話で受け付けています ◇I was about to *telephone* the police. 警察に電話するところだった

▶**telephone** 名 [C, U] ◇The *telephone* rang and Pat answered it. 電話が鳴ってパットが出た ◇You're wanted (= sb wants to speak to you) *on the telephone*. あなたにお電話ですよ

reach [他] (電話で)連絡をとる ◇Do you know where I can *reach* him? 彼はどこでつかまりますか ◇You can *reach* me at this number. この番号にかければ私につなが

ります
,call sb' up 句動詞 《特に米, ややインフォーマル》(人に)電話をかける ◇I *called* him *up* and asked him how he was doing. 私は彼に電話をして, どうしているか尋ねた

calm 形

calm・patient・cool・relaxed・controlled・easy-going・placid・laid-back・unperturbed・unfazed・composed
人が感情を抑え, 興奮したり不安になったり怒ったりしないことを表す
【類語訳】落ち着いた, 我慢強い, 穏やかな, くつろいだ

文型&コロケーション
▸ calm/ patient/ cool/ easy-going/ laid-back **about** sth
▸ unperturbed/ unfazed **by** sth
▸ a calm/ a cool/ a relaxed/ a controlled/ an easy-going/ a laid-back **manner**
▸ a calm/ cool/ relaxed/ controlled/ placid **voice**
▸ a calm/ a cool/ a relaxed/ a controlled/ an easy-going **way**
▸ a calm/ cool/ placid **exterior**
▸ a relaxed/ an easy-going/ a laid-back **atmosphere**

calm 落ち着いた, 平静な ◇Strangely, she felt quite *calm* about it. 不思議にも彼女はそのことに対してとても落ち着いていた ◇It is important to keep *calm* in an emergency. 緊急時に平静でいることは大事なことです ◇She handled the situation with *calm* assurance. 彼女はその状況に落ち着きはらって対処した 反意 **agitated** (RESTLESS), **excitable** (MOODY)
➤**calmly** 副 ◇'I'll call the doctor,' he said *calmly*. 「私が医者を呼ぼう」と彼は落ち着いた調子で言った
patient 辛抱強い, 我慢強い ◇You'll just have to be *patient* and wait till I'm finished. 私が終わるまでじっと我慢して待っていなさい ◇She's very *patient with* the children. 彼女はその子どもたちにとても寛容だ 反意 **impatient** (RESTLESS), ☞ **patience** (PATIENCE)
➤**patiently** 副 ◇to listen/sit/wait *patiently* 辛抱強く [じっと]聞く/座る/待つ
cool 落ち着いた, 冷静な ◇Keep *cool*. We'll sort this out. 落ち着いて。これを解決しよう ◇She tried to remain *cool, calm and collected*. 彼女は冷静で落ち着いていようとした ◇He has a *cool head* (= he stays calm in an emergency). 彼は冷静な人だ
relaxed くつろいだ, リラックスした ◇I had to learn to be more *relaxed* about things. 物事に対してもっとリラックスできるようにならなくてはいけなかった ◇She appeared *relaxed* and confident before the match. 彼女は試合前リラックスして自信に満ちているように見えた 反意 **nervous** (WORRIED)

ノート **calm, cool, relaxed** の使い分け: relaxed は物事に対して本当に心配や不安がないことを示す。cool は人の振る舞いに対して冷静に行動することを表す。calm は感情と行為の両面について用いられる。

controlled 感情を抑えた ◇He spoke in a *controlled*, even voice. 彼は感情を抑えた落ち着いた口調で話した
,easy-'going のんびりした, おおらかな, のんきな ◇His friends described him as an *easy-going* person. 彼の友達は彼をのんきな人だと言った ❶ easy-going は人の性

格や普段の振る舞いを表すときに用いられる。反意 **uptight** (TENSE), ✔ **tolerant** (TOLERANT)
placid (人・動物が)おとなしい, 穏やかな ◇The cattle are *placid*, so easy to work with. 牛はおとなしいので扱いやすい ◇My second child was a *placid* baby. 2番目の子は赤ん坊の時はおとなしかった 反意 **high-spirited** ❶馬のような動物は high-spirited (気性が荒い)と形容されることがある
➤**placidly** 副 ◇'Of course,' said Helen *placidly*. 「もちろんよ」とヘレンは穏やかな調子で言った
,laid-'back 《ややインフォーマル》くつろいだ; 心配事のなさそうな, のんきな ◇Steve was very *laid-back* about it all. スティーヴはそのことについてまったく気にしていなかった ◇He loved the *laid-back* Caribbean lifestyle. 彼はのんびりしたカリブ海風のライフスタイルが好きだった
unperturbed [名詞の前はまれ] (びっくりするような[嫌な]ことにも)平然とした, 動じない ◇She seemed *unperturbed* by the news. 彼女はそのニュースに動じてはいないようだった
unfazed [名詞の前はまれ] 《ややインフォーマル》(予期せぬことが起きても)動じない ◇The President seems *unfazed* by the ongoing crises around the world. 世界中で起きている危機に大統領は動じる様子はない
composed [名詞の前はまれ] 落ち着いた, 沈着な ◇She sat with a book on her lap, apparently quite *composed*. 彼女は膝の上に本をのせて, 見たところとても落ち着いて座っていた 反意 **flustered** (RESTLESS)

campaign 名

campaign・battle・struggle・drive・war・fight・crusade
何かを達成したり防いだりするための努力を表す
【類語訳】キャンペーン, 競争, 闘争, 闘い

文型&コロケーション
▸ a campaign/ battle/ struggle/ drive/ fight/ crusade **for** sth
▸ a campaign/ battle/ struggle/ drive/ war/ fight/ crusade **against** sth
▸ a battle/ struggle/ war/ fight **between** people
▸ a **big/ major** campaign/ battle/ struggle/ drive
▸ a **successful** campaign/ battle/ struggle/ drive/ fight
▸ a/ an **national/ international** campaign/ battle/ struggle/ drive/ crusade
▸ a **personal/ one-man/ one-woman** campaign/ battle/ struggle/ war/ crusade
▸ a **bitter** campaign/ battle/ struggle/ fight
▸ a **brave/ desperate** battle/ struggle/ fight
▸ a **political** campaign/ battle/ struggle
▸ to **launch/ embark on** a campaign/ battle/ drive/ crusade
▸ to **lead/ continue** the campaign/ battle/ struggle/ drive/ war/ fight/ crusade
▸ to **win/ lose** the battle/ struggle/ war/ fight
▸ to **give up** the battle/ struggle/ fight
▸ The campaign/ battle/ war/ fight **is on**.

campaign [C] (社会的・商業的・政治的目的達成のための)一連の活動[運動], キャンペーン ◇She led the *campaign* for parliamentary reform. 彼女は議会改革運動の先頭に立った ◇We're launching an anti-smoking *campaign* in the New Year. 我々は新年に禁煙運動を始めるつもりだ ◇The advertising *campaign* was responsible for the massive rise in sales. 宣伝活動のおかげで販売総額で大幅な上昇が見られた

battle [C] （権力・支配権を勝ち取るための）競争, 闘争, 闘い ◇She finally won the legal *battle* for compensation. 彼女はついに賠償を求める法廷論争に勝った ◇Looking after a two-year-old needn't be a constant *battle of wills* (= when each side is very determined to win). 2歳の子の世話のことでいつも意地を張り合うことはない ◇He had been conducting a personal *battle of wits* (= when each side uses their ability to think quickly to try and win) with the sales manager since his first day at work. 彼は働き始めた日からずっと営業部長と個人的な知恵比べを展開している

struggle [C] （権力・支配権を勝ち取るための）競争, 闘争, 闘い ◇He was a major player in the *struggle* for independence. 彼は独立を求める闘争で主要な役割を果たした ◇It is an epic tale of the *struggle* between good and evil. それは善と悪の闘いの壮大な物語だ ◇She will not give up her children without a *struggle*. 彼女は臆せずに子どもたちのことをあきらめはしないだろう ☞ **struggle** (RESIST)

ノート battle と struggle の使い分け：さまざまな場面でどちらの語も用いることができるが, struggle は常に生, 死, 自由といった必要不可欠な事柄に対して用いられる. battle は必要不可欠な事柄ではなく単に望ましいもの, 勝利の喜びといったものを求めて用いられる. ◆ the *battle/struggle* between good and evil/man and nature （善と悪／人間と自然の闘争） × a legal *struggle* for compensation. × a *struggle* of wills/wits.

drive [C] （何かを達成するための）組織的運動 ◇He played a crucial role in the *drive* for greater efficiency. いっそうの効率化への動きの中で彼は決定的な役割を果たした ◇She is leading the recruitment *drive*. 彼女は会員募集活動の先頭に立っている

ノート campaign と drive の使い分け：campaign はふつうある事を他人にさせることを目的とする. drive は当事者自身があることをするように仕向ける動きを表す. ◆ From today, we're going on an *economy drive* (= we must spend less). (今日から我々は節約志向でやっていこう). × an economy *campaign*. campaignのほうが driveよりも大規模であり, フォーマルかつ組織立ったものを指す.

war [U, 単数で] （悪に対する）闘い, 撲滅運動 ◇The government *has declared war on* drug dealers. 政府は麻薬の売人への戦いを宣言した ◇We seem to be winning the *war* against crime. 犯罪撲滅の戦いが功を奏しているようだ

fight [単数で] （悪［善］への）闘争；（スポーツでの）闘志 ◇Workers won their *fight* to stop compulsory redundancies. 労働者は強制解雇をやめさせることに成功した ◇The team *put up a good fight* (= they played well) but were finally beaten. そのチームは善戦したが結局敗れてしまった

crusade [C] （善への）運動, （悪に対する）撲滅運動 ◇We must continue the *crusade* against crime. 我々は犯罪撲滅運動を続けなくてはならない ◇Her moral *crusade* began in 1963. 彼女の道徳運動は1963年に始まった ◇He led a *crusade* to give terminally ill people the right to die. 彼は末期患者に死ぬ権利を与える運動の先頭に立った

ノート war, fight, crusade の使い分け：war は麻薬や犯罪など誰もが悪いと思うことをやめさせること. fight は自分自身が正しいと思うことを達成することに用いる. crusade はしばしば自分と同じ善悪の考えを共有するよう人を説得する場合に用いられる.

campaign 動

campaign・fight・lobby・work・agitate
人への要求, 説得, 影響を通じて, あることを達成できるよう多大の努力をする
【類語訳】運動する, 闘う, ロビー活動する

文型&コロケーション
▸ to campaign/ fight/ lobby/ work/ agitate **for** sth
▸ to campaign/ lobby/ agitate **against** sth
▸ to campaign/ fight/ lobby **on behalf of** sb
▸ to campaign/ fight/ lobby/ work/ agitate **to do** sth
▸ to campaign/ fight/ lobby **for changes**
▸ to campaign/ fight/ agitate for **reform**
▸ a **group** campaigns/ fights/ lobbies/ works
▸ to campaign/ fight/ lobby/ work **hard**
▸ to campaign/ lobby/ work **actively/ vigorously**
▸ to **successfully** campaign/ fight/ lobby for sth

campaign [自] （政治的・社会的目的達成のための）運動を起こす［進める］ ◇We have *campaigned* against whaling for the last 15 years. 我々はこの15年間捕鯨反対運動をしてきた ◇The group *campaigns on* environmental issues. そのグループは環境問題について活動している ◇They are *campaigning* to save the area from building development. 彼らはその地域を建築のための開発から守る運動をしている

fight [自, 他] （何かを得る［達成する］ために）闘う ◇He's still *fighting* for compensation after the accident. 彼はいまだに事故後の補償を求めて争っている ◇Campaigners *fought* to save the hospital from closure. 運動家たちはその病院を閉鎖させないように闘った ◇She gradually *fought her way* to the top of the company. 彼女は一歩一歩会社のトップへと困難を押して登りつめた

ノート campaign と fight の使い分け：campaign にはしばしば演説をする, 新聞に広告を出す, 政府のメンバーに手紙を書くなどの活動が伴う. その目的の多くは政治的, 社会的な変化が必要であることや, ある慣行をやめるべきだということを人にわからせようとすることである. fight も政治的, 社会的な変化のために奮闘することを意味するが, この語は何かする権利を得るなど, 自分自身で正義を勝ち取ることに用いる. そして fight では達成に向けての決意が強調される.

lobby [自, 他] （法改正などへの支持・反対を）政治家・政府に働きかける, ロビー活動をする ◇Teachers have *lobbied* hard against education cuts. 教師たちは教育費の削減に反対する激しいロビー活動を展開した ◇Farmers will *lobby* Congress for higher subsidies. 農業従事者は助成金を上げるよう議会に働きかけるだろう ☞ **lobby** (PARTY 1)

work [自] （他人と共に）働いて［努力して］成し遂げる ◇She dedicated her life to *working* for peace. 彼女は平和のために働くことに人生をささげた ◇The police and public need to *work* together to combat crime. 警察と一般の人々は犯罪と闘うために協力する必要がある

agitate [自] 《ややフォーマル》（法改正・社会情勢の変化などを

求めて)強く主張する, 運動する ◇Some militant groups have been *agitating* for autonomy for the region. ずっとその地方の自治権を強く主張している過激派組織もある ☞**agitation** (TROUBLE 1)

cancel 動

cancel・lift・revoke・repeal・invalidate・annul
正式に法律や協定を廃止する, 文書や方針が有効でなくなったことを公的に言う
【類語訳】キャンセルする, 取り消す, 解約する, 無効にする

文型&コロケーション
- to cancel/ revoke an **agreement**
- to cancel/ revoke/ invalidate a **will**
- to cancel/ invalidate a **contract**
- to lift/ revoke/ repeal a **ban**
- to revoke/ repeal/ annul a **law**
- to revoke/ invalidate the **constitution**
- to revoke/ invalidate a **licence/ permit**
- to invalidate/ annul a **marriage**

cancel (-ll-, 米 -l-) [他, 自] (取り決め・注文などを)キャンセルする, 取り消す, 解約する, 無効にする ◇to *cancel* a policy/subscription 方針を取り消す/定期購読を解約する ◇Is it too late to *cancel* my order? 注文を取り消すにはもう遅いですか ◇The US has agreed to *cancel* debts (= say that they no longer need to be paid) totalling $10 million. アメリカは総額1千万ドルもの債務を帳消しにすることに合意した ◇No charge will be made if you *cancel* within 10 days. 10日以内にキャンセルすれば支払いは発生しない
➤**cancellation** 名 [U, C] ◇the *cancellation* of a contract 契約の解除 ◇*Cancellations* must be made in writing. 解約は文書でしなくてはならない

lift [他] (制限などを)解く, 解除する ◇to *lift* a ban/curfew/blockade 禁止令/外出禁止令/封鎖を解く ◇Martial law has now been *lifted*. 戒厳令はもう解かれている

revoke [他] 《フォーマル》(文書・決定・協定などを法的に)無効にする ◇Your licence may be *revoked* at any time. 免許はいつ無効になるとも限らない

repeal [他] 《ややフォーマル》(法律を)無効にする ◇The committee does not have the power to *repeal* the ban. 委員会にはその禁止令を無効にする権限がない

invalidate [他] 《ややフォーマル》無効にする ◇Misuse of the mattress will *invalidate* the guarantee. 誤ってマットレスを使用した場合保証は無効になります ❶ふつうあることの発生や人の行為の結果によって物がinvalidateされるのであり, 人が意図してinvalidateするのではない. 反意 **validate** ❶ *validate* は法的に有効にすることを表す. ◆An official stamp was used to *validate* the voting papers. (投票用紙を有効にするために公印が押された).

annul (-ll-) [他] 《フォーマル》(結婚・法律・選挙結果などを)無効にする ◇Their marriage was *annulled* after just six months. たった6か月で彼らの結婚は無効になった

candidate 名 ☞PARTICIPANT

candidate・nominee・applicant・entrant
仕事や地位に志願している人
【類語訳】候補者, 志願者, 志望者, 応募者, 出場者, 参加者

文型&コロケーション
- a candidate/ a nominee/ an applicant/ an entrant **for** sth
- a candidate/ an entrant **in** sth
- a nominee/ an applicant/ an entrant **to** sth
- the **successful** candidate/ applicant
- a **potential/ prospective** candidate/ applicant/ entrant
- a/ an **good/ ideal/ suitable** candidate/ applicant
- a **Democratic/ Republican/ presidential** candidate/ nominee
- to **attract** candidates/ applicants/ entrants
- to **interview/ choose/ select/ shortlist/ reject** a candidate/ an applicant
- to **appoint** a candidate/ a nominee/ an applicant

candidate [C] 候補者, 志願者, 志望者 ◇The committee will select the best *candidate* for the job. 委員会はその仕事に最適な候補者を選ぶだろう ◇Prospective *parliamentary candidates* met party leaders last week. 議員候補者と目される人たちが先週党の幹部と会った ◇The party intends to *field a candidate* in the next general election. その党は次の総選挙で候補者を立てる予定だ ◇He *stood as a candidate* in the local elections. 《英》彼は地方選挙で立候補した ❶《英》ではcandidateは試験の受験者のことも指す. ◆*Candidates* are allowed to use dictionaries in this examination. 《英》この試験では辞書の使用が認められている).

nominee [C] (仕事・賞・選挙などの正式な)候補者 ◇And here are the *nominees* for Best Director. そしてこちらが監督賞の候補者の方々です ◇The President will present his *nominee* for Supreme Court Justice to Congress for approval. (これから)大統領が議会の承認を求めるために最高裁判事指名候補を紹介します ◇He was chosen as the party's presidential *nominee*. 彼は党の大統領候補に選ばれた ☞**nominate** (RECOMMEND 2)

ノート **candidate** と **nominee** の使い分け: 政治的な選挙, 特にアメリカの大統領選挙では党の代表として数人が任命され (nominated), このような人を nominee という. 政党はこの任命された人の中から他の政党の対立候補として選挙戦を戦うために candidate を (多くは投票によって) 選ぶ. 他にも仕事や賞などの候補者を表すときに自薦他薦にかかわらず一般的に candidate が用いられる. nominee は常に他の人によって候補に挙げられる人である.

applicant [C] (仕事・大学などの)志願者, 応募者 ◇There were over 500 *applicants* for the job. その仕事に500人を超える応募者があった ◇What can be done about the falling number of *applicants* to medical schools? 医学部の志願者数の減少にどう対処すればよいでしょうか ◇The factory was accused of turning away *job applicants* who belong to a union. その工場は組合に所属している求職者の採用を断ったかどで告訴された ☞**apply** (ASK 2)

entrant [C] (レース・コンテストなどの)出場者[動物], 参加者 ◇You will automatically be registered as an *entrant* in the Prize Draw. あなたは福引きの参加者として自動的に登録されます ◇The *winning entrant* received tickets to the theatre. 当選者は劇場のチケットをもらった ❶《英》ではentrantは試験の受験者のことも指す. ◆The average score for all A-level *entrants* was 5.4. (Aレベル試験全受験者の平均点は5.4だった).

care 動

care・mind・be bothered
重要だと思えるので、強い感情を持つことを表す
【類語訳】気遣う、心配する、関心がある、気にする、嫌だと思う

文型&コロケーション
- to care/ mind/ be bothered **about** sth
- to care/ mind/ be bothered **that** ...
- to **not** care/ mind/ be bothered **what people think**
- to **not seem to** care/ mind/ be bothered
- to care/ mind **very much**
- to **not** care/ mind **very much/ at all**
- to **not really** care mind
- to **not** be **really/ at all** bothered

care [自]《進行形なし》気遣う、心配する、関心がある ◇She *cares* passionately about environmental issues. 彼女は環境問題に大いに関心がある ◇*I don't care* (= I will not be upset) if I never see him again! 彼に二度と会えなくても構わないわ ◇He threatened to leave me, *as if I cared*! 彼は私と別れるぞと脅したけど、知ったことじゃないわ ◇He genuinely *cares* about his customers. 彼は心から顧客を大事にしている

mind [他、自、受身なし]《特に疑問文で or 否定語と共に；進行形では用いない》《特に話し言葉》気にする、嫌だと思う ◇I don't *mind* the cold — it's the rain I don't like. ぼくは寒さなんかへっちゃらだよ―嫌なのは雨なんだよ ◇Did she *mind* (about) not getting the job? 彼女はその職に就けないことを気にしていました ◇I wouldn't have *minded* so much if you hadn't lied about it. 君がそのことについて嘘をついていなかったらぼくもそれほど気にも留めなかったんだけど ❶ *mind* は、何かをする許可を求めるときに、または人に何かをしてほしいと丁寧にお願いするときに用いられる ◇Do you *mind* if I open a window? (窓を開けてもいいですか)。 ◆ How old are you, if you don't *mind* me asking? (お聞きして差し支えなければ、何歳ですか)。 ◆ Would you *mind* explaining that again? (それをもう一度説明していただけますか)。 ❶ *not mind* は、気にしない、または何かを気遣っていることを表す。 ◆No, I don't *mind* a bit. (いいや、ちっとも気にならないね)。 ◆'Would you prefer tea or coffee?' 'I *don't mind* — either's fine.' (紅茶とコーヒーではどちらがお好きですか」「どちらでも構いません」)。 ◆*Don't mind* her — she didn't mean what she said. (彼女のことは気にするな―本気に何にも言ったんだから)。 ◆*Don't mind* me (= don't let me disturb you) — I'll just sit here quietly. (私のことは気にしないで―ここに静かに座っていようと思っているだけですから)。

> **ノート** care と mind の使い分け: mind は丁寧な質問や返事で用いられる。どれがいいかと人に聞かれて「どれでも結構です」と答えるとき、I don't mind. は丁寧だが、I don't care. はとても失礼である。

be bothered フレーズ 《特に否定語と共に》《特に英、インフォーマル、話し言葉》気にする ◇Where shall we have lunch?' 'Anywhere, I'm not *bothered*.' 「どこで昼食にしましょうか」「別にどこでもいいですよ」 ◇I'm not all that *bothered* about the delay. 遅刻の件はそれほど気にしていません

careless 形

careless・negligent・forgetful・absent-minded
十分な注意や思慮なく行動するので、人が忘れたり間違いを犯すことを表す
【類語訳】不注意な、うかつな、軽率な、怠慢な、忘れっぽい、上の空の、ぼんやりした

文型&コロケーション
- **very** careless/ negligent/ forgetful
- **extremely** careless/ negligent
- **a bit** careless/ forgetful

careless 不注意な、うかつな、軽率な ◇It was *careless of me* to leave the door open. 私はうっかりドアを開けたままにしていた ◇Don't be so *careless about* spelling. もう少し綴りに気をつけなさい ◇He's very *careless with* money. 彼はお金にひどく無頓着だ
> **carelessly** ◇Someone had *carelessly* left a window open. 誰かがうっかり窓を開けっぱなしにしていた
> **carelessness** 名 [U] ◇a moment of *carelessness* うっかりしている時 反意 care

negligent 《フォーマル or 法律、特に書き言葉》怠慢な、不注意な ◇The school had been *negligent in* not informing the child's parents about the incident. 学校側は生徒の親にその事件を報告していなかったという点では怠慢であった
> **negligence** 名 [U] ◇The accident was caused by *negligence* on the part of the driver. その事故は運転手側の過失が原因で起きた
> **negligently** 副 ◇The defendant drove *negligently* and hit a lamp post. 被告は不注意な運転をして街灯にぶつかった

forgetful 忘れっぽい ◇She has become very *forgetful* in recent years. ここ数年のうちに彼女はとても忘れっぽくなった

absent-'minded (他のことを考えていて)忘れっぽい、上の空の、ぼんやりした ◇Grandpa's becoming quite *absent-minded*. おじいちゃんはかなり忘れっぽくなってきた ❶ 非常に賢くても現実的でない人は absent-minded と形容される。 ◆an *absent-minded* professor/scientist (学者ばか/科学者ばか)。
> **absent-mindedly** 副 ◇She *absent-mindedly* twisted a strand of hair around her fingers. 彼女は何気なく指に髪の毛の細い束を巻きつけていた

cargo 名

cargo・goods・load・freight・burden
道路、鉄道、船、飛行機などで輸送されるもの
【類語訳】積荷、貨物、船荷、重荷

文型&コロケーション
- a cargo/ load **of** sth
- (a) **heavy** cargo/ goods/ load/ freight/ burden
- (a) **bulk** cargo/ goods/ freight
- to **carry** a cargo/ goods/ a load/ freight/ a burden
- to **handle** cargo/ goods/ freight
- to **transport/ deliver** goods/ freight
- a goods/ freight **train**
- goods/ freight **traffic**

cargo (複 -oes, 米でまた -os) [C, U] (船・飛行機で輸送される)荷, 積荷, 貨物 ◇The tanker began to spill its *cargo* of oil. そのタンカーから積荷の原油が漏れ始めた ◇a *cargo* ship/jet 貨物船/貨物機

goods (複数で)《英》(道路・鉄道で輸送される)貨物 ◇The road was closed both to passengers and *goods*. 人にも貨物にもその道路は閉鎖されていた ◇You need a special licence to drive a ***heavy goods vehicle***. 重量物運搬車を運転するには特別な免許が必要だ ❶ heavy goods vehicle (重量物運搬車)はHGVと略される。◆Do you have an *HGV* licence? (HGVの免許を持っていますか)

load [C] (大量に車・人・動物で運ばれる)荷, 積荷 ◇They struggled down the hill with their *loads* of firewood. 彼らは苦労して受け持ち分の薪材を山からおろした ◇A truck had ***shed its load*** (= accidentally dropped its load) on the way to the depot. トラックが1台倉庫への輸送中に誤って積荷を落とした

freight [U]《ややフォーマル or ビジネス》(道路・鉄道・船・飛行機で輸送される)貨物 ◇The trains were designed specifically to haul (= carry) *freight*. その列車は貨物運搬用に作られていた ◇A *freight* train pulled into the station. 貨物列車が駅に入ってきた

burden [C]《フォーマル》(運ぶのが困難な)重荷 ◇She shifted her *burden* from one arm to the other. 彼女は重い荷を一方の腕からもう片方の腕に持ち替えた ◇The donkey was the traditional ***beast of burden*** (= animal used for carrying things). ロバは昔から荷役用の動物だった

case 名

case・trial・hearing・appeal・action・suit・lawsuit・proceeding・prosecution・litigation・court martial
正式な法廷論争を表す語
【類語訳】訴訟, 証拠, 申し立て事実, 裁判, 審問, 上訴, 法的手続き, 起訴, 訴訟, 軍法会議

[文型&コロケーション]
▸ (a) **legal** case/ hearing/ appeal/ action/ proceedings
▸ (a) **criminal** case/ hearing/ appeal/ action/ proceedings/ prosecution/ litigation
▸ (a) **civil** case/ hearing/ appeal/ action/ suit/ lawsuit/ proceedings/ litigation
▸ a **murder/ rape/ fraud** case/ trial
▸ (a) **libel** case/ trial/ hearing/ action/ suit/ proceedings
▸ to **bring** a case/ an action/ a suit/ a lawsuit/ proceedings/ a prosecution (**against** sb/ sth)
▸ to **take** action/ proceedings (**against** sb/ sth)
▸ to **file** an appeal/ a suit/ a lawsuit
▸ to **face** trial/ a hearing/ an action/ a suit/ a lawsuit/ proceedings/ prosecution/ litigation/ court martial
▸ to **hear** a case/ an appeal
▸ to **win/ lose** a case/ an appeal/ an action/ a suit/ a lawsuit

case [C] (裁判所で判決が下される)訴訟;(告発[弁護]用の)証拠, 申し立て事実 ◇The *case* will be heard next week. その訴訟は来週審理される ◇The new evidence weakened the *case for* the defence. 新たな証拠で弁護側の主張は弱められた ◇Our lawyer didn't think we ***had a case*** (= had good enough arguments to win in court). 弁護士は我々が裁判に勝てる十分な論拠を持っているとは思っていなかった

trial [U, C] (裁判官および陪審員による)裁判 ◇He's ***on trial*** for murder. 彼は殺人罪で裁判にかけられている ◇She will ***stand trial*** for fraud. 彼女は詐欺罪で裁判を受けるだろう ◇The men were arrested but not ***brought to trial***. 男たちは逮捕されたが裁判にはかけられなかった ◇The case never ***came to trial***. その事件は裁判にかけられることはなかった ◇He did not receive a fair *trial*. 彼は公正な裁判を受けられなかった

hearing [C] 聴聞会, 審問, 審理 ◇a court/disciplinary *hearing* 法廷審問/懲戒審問 ◇At a preliminary *hearing* the judge announced that the trial would begin on March 21. 裁判官は予審で裁判は3月21日に開始すると告げた ◇She was granted a divorce in a five-minute *hearing*. 彼女は5分間の審問で離婚が認められた

appeal [C, U] 控訴, 上訴, 上告 ◇to lodge an *appeal*《英》上訴する ◇to file an *appeal*《米》上訴する ◇an *appeal* court/judge《英》上訴裁判所/上訴裁判所判事 ◇an *appeals* court/judge《米》上訴裁判所/上訴裁判所判事 ◇He lost his *appeal against* the 3-match ban. 彼は3試合出場停止撤回の要請を退けられた

action [C, U]《ややフォーマル》法的手続き, 訴訟 ◇A libel *action* is being brought against the magazine that published the article. その記事を掲載した雑誌に対して名誉毀損訴訟が起こされている ◇He is considering taking legal *action* against the hospital. 彼はその病院に対して法的手段をとろうと考えている

suit [C]《ややフォーマル》不服の申し立て, 訴訟 ◇His former business associate filed a *suit* against him claiming £5 million damages. 彼の以前の仕事仲間が500万ポンドの損害をうけたとして彼に対して訴訟を起こした ◇Their arguments grew worse and worse and ended with a divorce *suit*. 彼らの言い争いはますます悪化し, 最後は離婚訴訟になった

lawsuit [C]《ややフォーマル》訴訟 ◇The opening of the factory was delayed because of a *lawsuit* brought by an environmental group. 環境保護団体による訴訟のため工場の開業が延期された

proceeding [C, ふつう複数で]《ややフォーマル》訴訟手続き ◇The company has started legal *proceedings* against its competitor. その会社はライバル社に対して法的手続きを始めた

prosecution [U, C] (犯罪行為についての)起訴, 訴追 ◇*Prosecution* for a first minor offence rarely leads to imprisonment. 軽犯罪の起訴では初犯であれば禁固刑になることはまれだ ◇He threatened to bring a private *prosecution* against the doctor. 彼はその医師に対して私人訴追を行うと脅した ☞ **prosecute** (ACCUSE)

litigation [U]《ややフォーマル》告訴, 訴訟 ◇The company has been in *litigation* with its auditors for a full year. その会社は丸一年監査役と係争中だ

court 'martial (複 **courts martial**) [C, U] 軍法会議(の審理) ◇He was convicted at a *court martial*. 彼は軍法会議で有罪判決を受けた ◇All the soldiers now face *court martial*. すべての兵士たちが今軍法会議にかけられている

cash 動

cash・exchange・cash sth in・change・clear
お金を同価値の別の通貨に変える

category, cause

【類語訳】現金化する，両替する

【文型&コロケーション】
- to cash/ change traveller's cheques
- to cash/ clear a cheque
- to exchange/ change your currency/ pounds/ dollars for/ into pounds/ dollars/ the local currency

cash [他]（小切手を）現金化する ◇The company *cashed* my cheque but then failed to send the goods I'd ordered. その会社は私の小切手を現金に換えたが私の注文した商品を送ってこなかった ☞ **cash** (MONEY 2)

exchange [他]（お金を）両替する ◇You can *exchange* your currency for dollars in the hotel. ホテルでお手持ちの通貨をドルに両替できます

cash sth 'in [句動]（満期日前に保険証券などを）現金に替える ◇It's not a good idea to *cash in* your bonds before the five years are up. 5年の満期前に公債を現金にするのは勧められない

change [他]《特に話し言葉》（お金を）両替する ◇Where can I *change* my traveller's cheques? トラベラーズチェックはどこで現金に替えられますか ◇Can you *change* a £20 note? 20ポンド札をくずせますか ☞ **change** (MONEY 2)

clear [自, 他]（小切手が）交換清算[現金化]される；（銀行が）交換清算[現金化]する ◇Cheques usually take three working days to *clear*. 小切手はふつう清算されるのに3営業日かかる

category 名 ☞ KIND 名

category・class・heading・league・bracket・classification
ある特徴を共有する人やものの集まり
【類語訳】範疇，カテゴリー，等級，階級，クラス，表題，見出し，レベル，格，部類，区分，層

【文型&コロケーション】
- to be **under** a category/ heading/ classification
- to be **in/ within** a category/ class/ league/ bracket/ classification
- the **same** category/ class/ heading/ league/ bracket/ classification
- a **different** category/ class/ heading/ league/ classification
- a/ the **main/ broad/ general/ separate** category/ class/ heading/ classification
- a **subject** category/ heading/ classification
- to **fall/ come under** a category/ heading
- to **fall into** a category/ bracket
- to **belong to** a category/ class/ league
- to **divide sb/ sth into** categories/ classes/ headings
- to **group sb/ sth under** categories/ headings
- to **put sb/ sth in/ into** a category/ bracket

category [C] 範疇，カテゴリー ◇We have created a special *category* for part-time workers. 我々はパート従業員に特別部門を作った ◇Patients fell into two broad *categories*. 患者は二つのカテゴリーに大別できた ◇There are two main *categories* of homicide according to the law. 法律的には殺人には2つの大きな区分がある ☞ **categorize** (CLASSIFY)

class [C] 等級，階級，部類，クラス ◇It was pretty cheap for this *class* of hotel. このクラスのホテルにしてはかなり安かった ◇There are several distinct *classes* of drugs. いくつかの異なった等級の薬物がある ◇Dickens was *in a different class from* (= much better than) most of his contemporaries. ディケンズは同時代のたいていの人よりはるかに優れていた ◇As a jazz singer she's *in a class of her own* (= there is no one as good as her). ジャズシンガーとして彼女は比類なき存在だ ☞ **class** (CLASSIFY)

heading [C] 総合的なカテゴリー[分類]；表題，見出し ◇Sex education often came under the general *heading* of 'Biology' or 'Health'. 性教育はしばしば「生物学」や「保健」の枠の中で扱われた ◇We can examine these issues under four *headings*. 我々はこういった問題を4つに分類して検討することができます

league [C]《ややインフォーマル》（品質・能力の）レベル，格，部類 ◇As a painter, he is *in a league of his own* (= there is no one as good as him). 画家として彼は比類なき存在だ ◇They're *in a different league* from us. 彼らは我々とは格が違う ◇When it comes to cooking, I'm *not in her league*. 料理のことになるととうてい彼女には及ばない ◇A house like that is *out of our league* (= too expensive for us). あのような家はとうてい私たちの手の届くものではない

bracket [C]《ややフォーマル，特に書き言葉》（価格・収入・行政状態・年齢などによる）区分，層 ◇This model remains firmly in the upper price *bracket*. このモデルが高価格帯のものであることは揺るぎない ◇Most respondents were in the 45-60 age *bracket*. ほとんどの回答者は45歳から60歳の年齢層だった ❶ この意味のbracketと結びつくのはprice, income, earnings, tax, ageなどである. ☞ **bracket** (CLASSIFY)

classification [C]《共有する特徴にしたがった》部類，級 ◇The material was put into the highest security *classification*. その物質は最高度のセキュリティ区分に入れられた ◇The *classification* 'science' covers a great many different subjects. 「科学」という部類には非常に多くの異なる主題が含まれる ☞ **classify** (CLASSIFY)

cause 動 ☞ STIMULATE

cause・result in sth・lead (sth) to sth・produce・bring sth about・give rise to sth・create・make・induce
物事を発生させる
【類語訳】引き起こす，結果をもたらす，つながる，生じさせる

【文型&コロケーション】
- to cause/ result in/ lead to/ produce/ bring about/ give rise to a/ an **change/ shift/ increase**
- to cause/ result in/ lead to/ produce/ bring about a **reduction** in sth
- to cause/ result in/ lead to/ produce/ give rise to/ create **problems/ difficulties**
- to cause/ result in/ lead to/ produce **damage/ friction**
- to cause/ result in/ lead to/ bring about the **collapse/ destruction/ demise** of sth
- to cause/ lead to/ produce/ give rise to/ create **speculation/ uncertainty**
- to cause/ lead to/ give rise to/ create **discontent/ dissatisfaction/ resentment**
- to result in/ lead to/ produce **improvements/ success**

↪cause

▶to **inevitably** cause/ result in/ lead to/ produce/ bring about/ give rise to/ create sth

cause [他] (悪い[不快な]ことを)引き起こす ◇Do they know what *caused* the fire? 何が原因で火事になったのかはわかっているのですか ◇Are you *causing* trouble again? 君はまた厄介ごとを起こしてるの ◇Doctors say her condition is *causing* some concern. 医者によれば彼女の体調にはちょっと心配なところがあるとのことだ ◇The project is still *causing* him a lot of problems. その企画のせいで彼にはいまだに多くの問題が起こっている ◇The poor harvest *caused* prices to rise sharply. 不作で急激な物価の上昇が引き起こされた ☞ **cause** (SOURCE)

re'sult in sth [句動詞] (損失・増加などの)結果をもたらす ◇Closure of the plant could *result in* the loss of thousands of jobs. その工場が閉鎖されれば何千人もの失業者を出すことになりかねない ◇In 1965 their work *resulted in* a Nobel Prize. 彼らの業績は1965年のノーベル賞受賞をもたらした ◇These policies *resulted in* many elderly and disabled people suffering hardship. これらの政策は多くの高齢者や障害者を苦しませる結果となった ☞ **result** (RESULT), **resulting**, **resultant** (RELATED)

lead to sth, lead sth to sth [句動詞] …の理由となる, …につながる; 物事に…の結果をもたらす ◇The scandal ultimately *led to* his resignation. そのスキャンダルは最終的に彼の辞任につながった ◇A reward was offered for information *leading to* an arrest. 逮捕につながる情報に対して報奨金が支払われた ◇These policies could *lead* the country *to* environmental catastrophe. これらの政策によってその国の環境が大きく損なわれる恐れがある ❶ lead to sth はしばしば何かを説明するときや理解するときの過程の一端として用いられる.

produce [他] (特定の結果・反応を)もたらす ◇A phone call to the manager *produced* the result she wanted. マネージャーにかけた電話は彼女が望む結果をもたらした ◇The prime minister's speech *produced* an angry response from opposition parties. 首相の演説は野党から怒りの反応を招いた ◇The drug *produces* a feeling of great happiness and excitement. その薬物は至福感と興奮をもたらす

,bring sth a'bout [句動詞] (徐々に変化をもたらすことを)引き起こす ◇What *brought about* the change in his attitude? 何が彼の態度を変えさせたのだろう ◇It was this scandal that finally *brought about* her downfall. 最終的に彼女を失脚させたのはこのスキャンダルだった

give 'rise to sth [句動] 《フォーマル》(物事を)引き起こす, 生じさせる ◇The novel's success *gave rise to* a number of sequels. その小説の成功はいくつかの続編を生んだ ◇The ocean *gave rise to* the first life on Earth. 海は地球上で最初の生物を生じさせた

create [他] (感情・印象などを)引き起こす, 生み出す ◇The company is trying to *create* a young energetic image. その企業は若いエネルギッシュなイメージを作り出そうとしている ◇The announcement only succeeded in *creating* confusion. その発表はただ混乱を引き起こしただけだった

make [他] (目に見える結果を)もたらす ◇The rock *made* a dent in the roof of the car. 岩で車の屋根にへこみができた ◇The holes in the cloth were *made* by moths. 虫が食って服に穴があいた

induce [他] 《フォーマル》(害に)引き起こす, 誘発する ◇A glass of warm milk at bedtime may help to *induce* sleep. 寝る前の1杯の温かいミルクには眠りを催させる効果が期待できることがある ◇Doctors will begin bringing him out of a drug-*induced* coma on Sunday. 医者は日曜日に薬物による昏睡状態から彼を目覚めさせる予定だ ❶ induce は薬, 病気, けがなどが身体へ及ぼす影響について言うときによく用いられる. ◆Hearing loss is often *induced* by exposure to loud noise. (難聴は大音響にさらされて引き起こされることが多い).

certain [形]

certain・bound・sure・definite・destined・guaranteed・assured
必ず起きること, 間違いなく真実であることを表す
[類語訳] 確実な, 確かな, 信用できる, 信頼できる, 決定的な

[文型&コロケーション]
▶certain/ sure/ assured **of** sth
▶certain/ bound/ sure/ destined/ guaranteed **to do** sth
▶certain/ definite **that**...
▶I couldn't say for certain/ sure/ definite.
▶to **seem** certain/ bound to.../ sure/ definite/ destined/ guaranteed/ assured
▶to **look** certain/ sure/ definite/ destined/ guaranteed/ assured
▶**by no means** certain/ sure/ definite/ guaranteed/ assured
▶fairly/ quite/ absolutely certain/ sure/ definite

certain 確実な, 確かな ◇It's *certain* that they will agree. 彼らが賛成するのは確かだ ◇She looks *certain* to win an Oscar. 彼女がオスカーを受賞するのは確実と見える ◇If you want to be *certain* of getting into the concert, buy your ticket now. そのコンサートに確実に行きたいのなら, 今すぐにチケットを買いなさい ◇The climbers face *certain* death if the rescue attempt is unsuccessful. もし救出活動が失敗すれば登山者たちは絶体絶命となる [反意] **uncertain**

▷**certainly** [副] ◇This will *certainly* make them think again. このことできっと彼らは考え直すだろう ◇She was *certainly* attractive but you couldn't call her beautiful. 彼女は確かに魅力的だったが美しいとは言えなかった

bound [名詞の前では用いない] (…する[になる]ことが)確実な, 確かな ◇There are *bound* to be changes when the new system is introduced. 新しいシステムが導入されたら必ず変化が起こる ◇You've done so much work — you're *bound* to pass the exam. 一生懸命やったのだから, きっと試験に通るでしょう ◇It was *bound* to happen sooner or later (= we should have expected it). 遅かれ早かれそれは当然起こるべきことだった ❶ bound は bound to do, bound to be の形でのみ用いられる.

sure 確実な, 確かな; 信用[信頼]できる ◇She's *sure* to be picked for the team. 彼女は必ずそのチームに選ばれるだろう ◇There's only one *sure* way of knowing. 確実に知る方法が一つだけある ◇It's a *sure sign* of economic recovery. それは景気回復の確かな兆しだ ◇He's a *sure bet* for the presidential nomination (= he is certain to get it). 《ややインフォーマル》彼は大統領候補指名の大本命だ

definite 《特に話し言葉》確実な; 変わることのない ◇Is it *definite* that he's leaving? 彼がやめるのは確かなの

◇I've heard rumours, but nothing *definite*. うわさを聞いたことがあるが確実なものは何もない ◇Can you give me *a definite answer* by tomorrow? 明日までにはっきりした返事をくださいますか ◇Have they made you a *definite* offer of a job? あなたは就職を確約してもらいましたか
▸ **definitely** 副 ◇I *definitely* remember sending the letter. 私は手紙を送ったことをはっきり覚えている ◇'Do you plan to have children?' 'Definitely not!'「子どもを作る予定はありますか」「まったくありません」◇The date of the move has not been *definitely* decided yet (= it may change). 引っ越しの日にちはまだはっきりと決めていません ◇Please say *definitely* whether you will be coming or not. 来るのか来ないのかはっきり言ってください

destined 《フォーマル》(…することを)運命づけられた ◇He was *destined for* a military career, like his father before him. 父親と同様に彼は将来軍人の道を歩む運命にあった ◇We seem *destined* never to meet. 我々は二度と会うことのない運命であるように思われる ☞ **destiny** (LUCK)

guaranteed (特定の結果になることが)確かな ◇If we try to keep it a secret, she's *guaranteed* to find out. 我々がそれを秘密にしようとしても彼女にばれるのは間違いない ◇That kind of behaviour is *guaranteed* to make him angry. そんな行動をすれば間違いなく彼を怒らせる

assured 《書き言葉》(起こること[手に入れること]が)確実な ◇Victory seemed *assured*. 勝利は確かなものと思われた ◇The French team are now *assured* of a place in the final. フランスチームが決勝戦まで行くのは今や確実だ

certificate 名 ☞ LICENCE

certificate・documentation・papers・ID・credentials
証明するための公式な文書
【類語訳】証明書, 証書, 必要書類, 証拠文書, 身分証明書, 許可証, 信用証明書

文型&コロケーション

▸ **on** a certificate/ the documentation
▸ **in** the documentation/ papers
▸ (an) **official/ necessary** certificate/ documentation/ papers
▸ to **have** (a) certificate/ documentation/ papers/ ID/ credentials
▸ to **get/ obtain** (a) certificate/ documentation/ papers/ credentials
▸ to **issue/ give** (sb) (a) certificate/ documentation/ papers
▸ to **see/ check** sb's certificate/ documentation/ papers/ ID/ credentials
▸ to **examine** sb's documentation/ papers/ ID/ credentials
▸ to **show/ present** your certificate/ documentation/ papers/ ID/ credentials

certificate [C] 証明書, 証書 ◇This *certificate* is an important document. Keep it in a safe place. この証書は重要な書類です。安全な場所に保管してください ◇a birth/marriage/death *certificate* 出生/結婚/死亡証明書 ◇She showed her *certificate* of insurance. 彼女は保険証書を見せた

documentation [U] 必要書類, 証拠文書 ◇I couldn't enter the country because I didn't have all the necessary *documentation*. 私は必要な書類がそろっていなかったため入国できなかった ◇We send comprehensive travel *documentation*, including tickets, hotel vouchers and a detailed itinerary. チケット, ホテルの宿泊券, 詳細な日程を含めた旅行の関係書類一式を送ります ◇If the technical *documentation* is inadequate, your system is not a quality product. もし技術文書が不十分であれば, 御社のシステムは高品質の製品とはいえない ☞ **document** (DOCUMENT)

papers [複数で] (公)文書, 身分証明書 ◇We had to show our *papers* at the border. 国境では身分証明書を見せる必要があった ◇Do you have your identification *papers* with you? 身分証明書類をお持ちですか ◇He hasn't received his divorce *papers* yet. 彼はまだ離婚届を受け取っていません ☞ **papers** (DOCUMENT)

ノート **documentation** と **papers** の使い分け：どちらの語も特に各国を旅行する際に必要な, 身分を証明する文書の意味で用いられる。しかし travel *documentation* はふつうチケットを意味する。*documentation* はまた機械やコンピューターシステムなどの製品の技術情報が詳しく書かれたものも意味する。*papers* は認可を与えたりする法的文書でもある。

ID [U, C] 《ややインフォーマル》身分証明書(identity または identification の略) ◇Do you have any *ID*? 何か身分証明書をお持ちですか ◇You must carry *ID* at all times. 身分証明書は常に携帯していなくてはならない ◇The police checked *IDs* at the gate. 警察が入り口で身分証明書を確認した ◇You will need some form of *photo ID*. 何らかの形の写真つきの身分証明書が必要でしょう

credentials [複数で] 信用[人物]証明書, 信任状 ◇The ambassador presented his diplomatic *credentials*. 大使は信任状を提示した ◇Check the *credentials* of any unknown caller. 知らない人が訪ねてきたら人物証明書を確認しなさい

change 名

1 change・shift・variation・swing・fluctuation・variability・alternation
(頻繁に)変わること
【類語訳】変化, 転換, 変動, 交互, 交替

文型&コロケーション

▸ a change/ a shift/ a variation/ a swing/ a fluctuation/ variability/ an alternation **in** sth
▸ a shift/ a variation/ a fluctuation/ an alternation **between** A and B
▸ a shift/ swing **towards** sth
▸ (a) **considerable** change/ shift/ variation/ fluctuation/ variability
▸ a **big/ dramatic/ massive** change/ shift/ variation/ swing
▸ (a) **small** change/ shift/ variation/ swing/ fluctuations
▸ (a) **rapid** change/ shift/ fluctuation/ alternation
▸ (a) **random** change/ variation/ fluctuation/ alternation
▸ (a) **seasonal** change/ variation/ fluctuation
▸ to **cause** a change/ a shift/ a variation/ a swing/ fluctuations/ variability
▸ to **produce** a change/ a shift/ a variation/ a swing/ fluctuations
▸ to **show** a change/ a shift/ a variation/ a swing/ a fluctuation/ an alternation/ variability
▸ a change/ a shift/ a variation/ a swing/ fluctuation **occurs**

change [C, U] 変化 ◇We're hoping for a *change* in the weather. 天気が変わってくれることを願っている ◇There was **no change** in the patient's condition overnight. 一晩中患者の容態にはなんら変化はなかった ◇She is someone who hates *change*. 彼女は変化を嫌う人だ ◇How far does war bring about social *change*? 戦争はどこまで社会的変化をもたらすだろうか ❶単数形で用いる change は状況、場所、経験などがいつもと違い、面白く[楽しく]なりそうなことを意味する。◆Let's stay in tonight *for a change*. (今夜は気分を変えて家にいることにしよう。) ◆It *makes a change* to read some good news for once. (たまにいいニュースを目にすると楽しくなる)。

shift [C] (特にジャーナリズム) (位置・方向の)変化、転換 ◇These results mark a dramatic *shift* in public opinion. これらの結果は世論の劇的な変化を印するものだ ◇There was a gradual *shift* in the population *away from* the countryside to the towns. 田舎を離れ都会へと人々が次第に移動する流れが見られた ◇I detected a subtle *shift* towards our point of view. 私は我々の見解への微妙な変化を見て取った ◇These climate *shifts* occurred over less than a decade. こういった気候の変化は十年足らずの間に起こった

variation [C, U] (量・質・レベルの頻繁な)変化、変動 ◇The dial records very slight *variations* in pressure. その目盛り盤は気圧のごくわずかな変化をも表示します ◇Currency exchange rates are always subject to *variation*. 為替レートは常に変動する ◇We need to take seasonal *variation* into account (= depending on the time of year). 我々は季節による変動を考慮する必要がある ☞ **variation** (DIFFERENCE)

swing [C] (考え・状況の)変動(量)、転換 ◇He is liable to abrupt *mood swings* (= for example from being very happy to being very sad). 彼は突然気分が変わることがある ◇Voting showed a 10% *swing* to Labour. 投票で10パーセントが労働党へ動いたことが示された ◇There are indications of a *swing* towards nuclear power. 原子力への支持傾向が現れている ❶ swing は mood swings や swings of mood のような気分の変化と同様に、特に政治的、社会的、文化的変化について言うときにも用いられる。

fluctuation [C, U] 《ややフォーマル》(大きさ・量・レベル・質の大幅な)変動 ◇The situation led to wild *fluctuations* in interest rates. その状況が金利の大幅な変動をもたらした ◇Recent ice-cap surveys reveal climatic *fluctuation*. 最近の山頂を覆う雪の調査で気候変動が明らかになっている

variability [U] 《書き言葉》変わりやすさ、変動性 ◇The changes were attributed to natural climatic *variability*. その変化は自然の気候変動性に起因しているとされた ◇There is always a degree of *variability* in the exchange rate. 為替レートには常にある程度の変動がある ☞ **variable** (VARIABLE)

alternation [U, C] 《ややフォーマル》(状況・感情・行動・考えの)交互、交替 ◇the *alternation* of day and night 昼と夜が交互に来ること ◇Such rapid *alternations* of mood are a feature of her writing. そのように雰囲気がころころ変わるのは彼女の文章の特徴だ ❶ alternations はある状況から別な状況へも移り変わり、また最初の状況へ戻ることをも指す。

2 change・amendment・transition・adjustment・conversion・modification・switch・alteration・revision・adaptation
違いを生じさせる行為、違いを生じさせた結果

【類語訳】変更、改善、訂正、調整、切り替え、校閲、校訂

文型&コロケーション

▶a change/ an amendment/ a transition/ an adjustment/ a conversion/ a modification/ a switch/ an alteration/ a revision/ an adaptation **to** sth
▶a change/ an adjustment/ a modification/ a switch/ an alteration **in** sth
▶(a) **major** change/ amendment/ transition/ adjustment/ modification/ alteration/ revision/ adaptation
▶(an) **important** change/ amendment/ transition/ adjustment/ modification/ switch/ alteration/ revision
▶(a) **radical** change/ adjustment/ alteration/ revision/ adaptation
▶(a) **slight** change/ amendment/ adjustment/ modification/ alteration/ revision
▶(a) **constant** change/ adjustment/ modification/ alteration/ revision/ adaptation
▶to **propose/ suggest** a change/ an amendment/ a modification/ an alteration/ a revision/ an adaptation
▶to **make** a change/ an amendment/ the transition/ an adjustment/ a modification/ a switch/ an alteration/ a revision/ an adaptation
▶to **carry out/ undertake** a conversion/ modification/ an alteration/ revision
▶to **need/ require** amendment/ adjustment/ modification/ alteration/ revision
▶to **undergo** a transition/ modification/ alteration/ revision

change [C, U] 変更 ◇I made a couple of minor *changes* to the opening paragraph. 私は冒頭のパラグラフに2,3か所小さな手直しをした ◇He made a rapid gear *change* as he approached the bend. 彼はカーブに近づくとすばやくギアチェンジをした ◇He called for a *change* of mood in Scottish politics. 彼はスコットランドの政治に雰囲気の変化を求めた ◇Train times are subject to *change* without notice. 発車時刻は予告なしに変わることがある ☞ **change over** (SWITCH)

amendment [C, U] 《ややフォーマル》(法・文書の)修正、改正 ◇A major *amendment* was introduced into the legislation. 法律に大がかりな修正が施された ◇Parliament passed the bill without further *amendment*. 更なる修正を加えることなく議会は法案を可決した ☞ **amend** (ADJUST)

transition [U, C] 《ややフォーマル》推移、移行 ◇The company was slow to make the *transition* from paper to computer. その会社は紙からコンピューターへの移行が遅かった ◇He will remain head of state during the *period of transition* to democracy. 彼は民主政治への移行期間国家元首に留まるだろう ◇This class is useful for students who are *in transition* (= in the process of changing) from one training programme to another. このクラスはあるトレーニングプログラムから次のプログラムへの移行段階にある学生にとって役立つ ◇We need to ensure a smooth *transition between* the old system and the new one. 古いシステムから新しいシステムへの円滑な移行を確実にする必要がある

▶**transitional** 形 ◇a *transitional* period 過渡期 ◇*transitional* government 暫定政府

adjustment [C, U] 《ややフォーマル》調整；(行動[思考]様式の適応[合] ◇I've made a few *adjustments* to the design. 私はデザインを2,3か所手直しした ◇Some *ad-*

justment of the lens may be necessary. いくらかレンズの調整が必要かもしれない ◊She went through a period of emotional *adjustment* after her marriage broke up. 彼女は結婚生活が破綻してから情緒不適応期を経験した ❶ *adjustment* はふつう文書などではなく物事に小さな変化を加えることをいう。☞ **adjust** (ADJUST)

conversion [U, C] (形式・用法・システムの)変換, 転換 ◊Their main business is the *conversion* of farm buildings *into* family homes. 彼らの主なビジネスは農家の建物を家庭用住宅に変えることだ ◊*Conversion* to gas central heating will save you a lot of money. ガスのセントラルヒーティングに変えれば大幅な節約になります ◊The firm specializes in house *conversions* (= turning large houses into several smaller flats or apartments). その会社は大きな一戸建て住宅から小さなアパートへの改築を専門としている ☞ **convert** (TURN 2), **conversion** (SWITCH)

modification [U, C] (ややフォーマル) 修正, 改善 ◊Considerable *modification* of the existing system is needed. 現行の体制のかなりの修正が必要とされている ◊It might be necessary to make a few slight *modifications* to the design. そのデザインはちょっとした手直しがいくつか必要かもしれない ☞ **modify** (ADJUST)

switch [C] (ややインフォーマル, 特にジャーナリズム) (急(完全))な転換, 切り替え ◊She made the *switch* from full-time to part-time work when her first child was born. 彼女は最初の子供が生まれたときフルタイムの仕事からパートタイムに変えた ◊He has vehemently opposed the policy *switch*. 彼は政策転換に激しく反対した ☞ **switch** (SWITCH)

alteration [C, U] 変更, 改変, 改造 ◊They are making some major *alterations* to the house. 彼らは大掛かりな家の改築をしている ◊The dress will not need much *alteration*. その服はそれほど手直しをしなくていいだろう

ノート adjustment, modification, alteration の使い分け: adjustment はデザインや装置などに加えられるわずかな変更のことをいう。modification はより幅広い種類の変更をいうときに用いるが, システムや乗り物などに対するより大掛かりな変更について表すときにも用いられる。alteration は建物, 特に家の改築などについて用いる。

revision [U, C] (ややフォーマル) 修正, 改訂; 修正(改訂)したもの ◊The system is in need of *revision*. そのシステムは修正が必要だ ◊He made some minor *revisions* to the report before printing it out. 彼はプリントアウトする前にそのレポートを少し手直しした ❶ *revision* はふつう間違っているものを正したり, 最新の状態にするというときに用いられる。☞ **revise** (ADJUST)

adaptation [U] (ややフォーマル) 適応, 適合 ◊We've been studying the *adaptation* of species to hot conditions. 我々は高温条件への種の適応を研究している

change 動

1 ☞ ADJUST
change・alter・adapt・shift・tailor・vary
人や物事に変化を加えること
【類訳語】変える, 適応させる, 適合させる, あつらえる

文型&コロケーション
▶ to change/ alter/ adapt/ tailor sth **for** sb/ sth
▶ to change/ alter/ adapt a **plan/ story**
▶ to change/ alter/ shift/ vary the **emphasis**
▶ to change/ alter/ shift the **balance/ perspective**
▶ to change/ alter/ adapt your **behaviour**
▶ to change/ alter/ adapt/ vary your **routine**
▶ to change/ alter/ shift your/ sb's **attitude/ opinion**
▶ to change/ alter/ adapt/ tailor sth **accordingly**
▶ to change/ adapt/ tailor sth **specially/ carefully**

change [他] 変える ◊Information technology has *changed* the way people work. 情報技術は人々の働き方を変えた ◊This incident *changed* the whole course of events. この出来事は事の成り行き全体を変えた ◊What made you *change your mind* (= change your opinion)? どうして気が変わったのですか ◊The fruit *changes colour* as it ripens. 果実は熟すにつれて色が変わる ◊Don't keep *changing the subject*. 話をころころ変えないでください

alter [他] 変える ◊This development will *alter* the character of the town. この開発は町の性格を変えるだろう ◊Nothing can *alter* the fact that we are to blame. 我々に責任があるという事実はどうあろうと変わらない

ノート change と alter の使い分け: どちらの語でも使えることがある。◆Fame hasn't really *changed/altered* him. (有名になっても彼はあまり変わらなかった). change がしばしば完全に変わったことを表すのに対し, alter はわずかな変化を表すことがある。◆This law needs to be *altered* (= changed slightly in order to improve it). (この法律は多少改変が必要だ). ◆This law needs to be *changed* (= changed completely or got rid of). (この法律は改変が必要だ). alter は「変わらない」という否定の意味でよく用いられる。◆It doesn't *alter* the way I feel. (そのことで私の気持ちは変わらない). また物事の特定の側面を変えることについていう。◆They can *alter* the programme until success is achieved. (そのプログラムはうまくいくまで手直しして構わない). change も上記のようなすべての場合に用いることができるが, その使用範囲は alter よりはるかに広く, change your mind, change your name, change colour, change tack, change the subject といった特定のコロケーションでも見られる。

adapt [他] (新たな用途・状況に合うように)改造する, 適応(適合)させる ◊Most of these tools have been specially *adapted* for use by disabled people. これらの道具は障害者用に改造されている ◊These styles can be *adapted* to suit individual tastes. これらのスタイルは個々の好みに合うように変えることができる ☞ **modify** (ADJUST), **adaptable** (FLEXIBLE 1)

shift [他] (考え方などを)変える ◊They are trying to *shift* public attitudes about the nature of old age. 彼らは老齢というものの性質について国民の考え方を変えようとしている ◊We need to *shift* the focus of this debate. 我々はこの議論の焦点を変えなければならない ❶ shift とよく結びつくのは attitudes, opinions, balance, emphasis, focus, perspective などである。

tailor [他] (物事を特定の目的・人のために)合わせる ◊Special programmes of study are *tailored to* the needs of specific groups. 特定のグループの要望に合わせて特別研究プログラムが作られている ◊Most travel agents are prepared to *tailor* travel arrangements to meet individual requirements. ほとんどの旅行代理店は個々の要望に合わせた旅行日程を用意している

vary [他] (少し)変化を加える ◊The job enables me to

↪change　　　　　　　　　　　　　　charge

vary the hours I work. その仕事のおかげで私は働く時間に変化をつけられる　◇The aerobics instructor *varies* the routine each week. エアロビクスのインストラクターは毎週振りを変えます　❶*vary*はいつも規則的にやっていることに少し変化を加えるようなときに用いられる。

2 change・vary・shift・fluctuate・swing・alter・alternate
変化が加わることを表す
【類語訳】変わる, 変化する, 移る, 変動する, 一変する

▷文型&コロケーション
▶to change/ shift/ swing **from** sth **to** sth
▶to vary/ fluctuate/ swing/ alternate **between** A **and** B
▶to change/ vary/ fluctuate **according to** sth
▶to change/ vary/ fluctuate/ swing **wildly**
▶to change/ vary/ shift/ fluctuate/ swing/ alter **dramatically/ sharply**
▶to change/ vary/ shift/ fluctuate/ alter **significantly**
▶to change/ vary/ shift/ fluctuate **constantly/ continually**
▶to change/ shift/ fluctuate/ swing **rapidly**
▶to change/ shift/ swing **suddenly**
▶to change/ vary/ alter **little/ slightly/ somewhat**
▶to **hardly/ never** change/ vary/ alter

change [自] 変わる, 変化する　◇Rick hasn't *changed*. He looks exactly the same as he did at school. リックは変わっていない。見た目は彼は学生のころのままだ　◇We examined *changing* attitudes towards education. 我々は教育に対する姿勢の変化を調べた　◇The language is *changing* all the time. 言葉は絶え間なく変化している　◇Leeds *changed* from a small market town into a busy city. リーズは小さな市場の町からにぎやかな都市に変わった　◇Her life *changed* completely when she won the lottery. 宝くじが当たってから彼女の人生はすっかり変わった

vary [自]（頻繁に[状況によって]）変わる　◇The menu *varies with* the season. 季節によりメニューは変わります　◇Prices *vary* according to the type of room you require. ご要望の部屋のタイプによって値段が変わります　◇Class numbers *vary* between 25 and 30. クラスあたりの生徒数は25から30の間だ　◇Pulse rates *vary* slightly from person to person. 脈拍数は人によって微妙に異なる　◇'What time do you start work?' '*It varies.*' 「何時から仕事を始めますか」「日によって違う」

shift [自]《特にジャーナリズム》（状況・考えが）変わる, 移る　◇The balance of power *shifted away* from workers *towards* employers. 力の均衡が労働者から雇用者へと傾いた　◇Public attitudes towards marriage have *shifted* over the past 50 years. この50年で結婚に対する世間の考え方が変わった

fluctuate [自]《ややフォーマル or 書き言葉》（大きさ・量・レベル・質が極端に よく）変わる, 変動する　◇During the crisis, oil prices *fluctuated* between \$30 and \$50 a barrel. その危機の間, 石油の値段は1バレル当たり30ドルから50ドルの間で変動した　◇Temperatures can *fluctuate by* as much as 10 degrees. 気温は10度程度上下することがあるかもしれない　◇My weight *fluctuated* wildly depending on how much I ate. 私の体重は食べる量によって激しく変動した

swing [自]《特にジャーナリズム》（意見・気分・状況が極端に）変わる　◇The state has *swung* from Republican to Democrat. その州は共和党から民主党支持に大転換した　◇His emotions *swung* between fear and curiosity. 彼の気持ちは恐怖と好奇心の間で揺れた　◇The game could *swing* either way (= either side could win it). その試合はどっちにも転びそうだろう

alter [自] 変わる　◇Property prices did not significantly *alter* during 2007. 不動産価格は2007年中は大きな変化はなかった　◇He had not *altered* greatly in the last ten years. この10年間で彼は大して変わっていなかった

▷ノート **change** と **alter** の使い分け：どちらの語でも使えることがある。◆Rick hasn't *changed/altered* much. (リックはそんなに変わっていなかった). しかし **change** は alterよりずっと頻繁に, 幅広く用いられ, しばしば大切なものがすっかり変わることを示唆する。◆Her life *changed* completely when she won the lottery. (宝くじが当たってから彼女の人生はすっかり変わった). ×Her life *altered* completely. また変化の過程にある事柄についてもいう。◆*changing* attitudes to education (教育に対する姿勢の変化). ×*altering* attitudes to education. alterはわずかに変わるか, まったく変わらないような場合に用いられる。◆The party's policies have hardly *altered*, but public opinion has. (政党の政策はほとんど変わらなかったが世論は変わった).

alternate [自]《**between**を伴って》変動する　◇Her mood *alternated* between happiness and despair. 彼女の気分は幸福と絶望の間で揺れ動いた

charge 名

charge・accusation・indictment・impeachment・recrimination
人が悪いことをした[罪を犯した]と訴えること
【類語訳】告訴, 告発, 起訴状, 起訴

▷文型&コロケーション
▶a charge/ an accusation/ an indictment/ recriminations **against** sb
▶a charge/ an accusation **of** sth
▶a charge/ an accusation **that**...
▶a **formal/ serious** charge/ accusation/ indictment
▶**bitter** accusations/ recriminations
▶to **face** a charge/ an accusation/ an indictment/ impeachment
▶to **make/ deny** a charge/ an accusation
▶to **issue/ bring/ drop** a charge/ an indictment

charge [C]（警察による）告訴 ;（人の悪事の）告発　◇The investigation resulted in criminal *charges* against three police officers. 捜査により3人の警官を刑事告発する結果となった　◇After being questioned by the police, she was released *without charge*. 警察に事情聴取された後彼女は告訴されることなく釈放された　◇She rejected the *charge* that the story was untrue. その話は偽りだという告発を彼女は否認した　☞ **charge** (ACCUSE)

accusation [C, U]（人の悪事・犯罪の）告発, 非難　◇No one believed her wild *accusations* against her husband. 夫に対する彼女のとんでもない告発を誰も信じなかった　◇There was a hint of *accusation* in her voice. 彼女の口調はかすかに非難めいていた　☞ **accuse** (ACCUSE)

indictment [C, U]《特に米》起訴状 ; 起訴　◇There is sufficient evidence against him to support an *in-*

dictment for murder. 彼を殺人罪で起訴するための十分な証拠がある ◇This led to his *indictment* on allegations of conspiracy. このことが陰謀の疑惑に関する彼の起訴につながった ☞ **indict** (ACCUSE)

impeachment [C, U]《米》重要な公人に対する)弾劾 ◇If Congress should rule that the President's actions were unconstitutional, it would be a big step towards his *impeachment*. 大統領の行為が憲法に違反していると議会が裁定を下せば弾劾への大きな一歩となるだろう ☞ **impeach** (ACCUSE)

recrimination [C, ふつう複数で, U] 非難のし返し ◇There were bitter *recriminations* within the party about who was to blame for the disastrous election results. 悲惨な選挙結果の責任を誰が取るかということで党内で激しい非難の応酬があった ◇We spent the rest of the evening in mutual *recrimination*. その夜はそれ以降お互いを非難しあっていた

charge 動

charge・fine・ask・levy・bill・invoice
商品、サービスの代金や税の支払いを人に要求することを表す
【類語訳】請求する, 罰金を科す, 徴収する, 課す

文型&コロケーション
▶ to charge (sb)/ levy sth **on** sth
▶ to charge (sb)/ fine sb/ ask sth/ bill sb/ invoice sb **for** sth
▶ to be charged/ levied **at** one per cent/ 17%
▶ to charge/ bill sth **to sb's account**
▶ to charge/ ask a high/ low **price/ fee/ commission/ rent**

charge [他, 自]（商品・サービスの代金・税の支払いを）請求する ◇What did the builders *charge* for the repairs? 建築業者は修理作業にいくら請求しましたか ◇Calls are *charged* at 36p per minute. 1分間に36ペンスの通話料がかかります ◇Your broker will *charge* you a 6% commission on the transaction. 仲介業者は6パーセントの取引手数料を取るでしょう ☞ **charge** (RATE)

fine [他, しばしば受身で]（人に）罰金を科す ◇She was *fined* for speeding. 彼女はスピード違反で罰金を科せられた ◇The company was *fined* £20,000 for breaching safety regulations. その企業は安全規則に違反して2万ポンドの罰金を科せられた ☞ **fine** (RATE)

ask [他]《ふつう進行形で》（代金を）請求する ◇He's *asking* £2,000 for the car. 彼はその車に2000ポンド請求している

levy [他]《フォーマル or 法律》（罰金・税金を）徴収する[課す] ◇It was a local tax *levied* by the council on the occupiers of land and buildings. それは地方議会が土地や建物の占有者に課す地方税だった ◇A $30 million fine was *levied against* the company. その企業に3000万ドルの罰金が課せられた

bill [他]《ややフォーマル》（商品・サービスに対しての）請求書を送る ◇You will be *billed* monthly for the service. 毎月そのサービスの請求書が送られてきます ◇The cost will be *billed* to your account. その費用はあなたの口座に請求されます ☞ **bill** (BILL)

invoice [他]《ややフォーマル》（商品・仕事に対しての）送り状［インボイス］を送る ◇You will be *invoiced* for these items at the end of the month. 月末にこれらの商品の送り状が届きます ☞ **invoice** (BILL)

ノート **bill** と **invoice** の使い分け: ふつう毎月または3か月に1度、電話・ガス・電気などを供給する会社が顧客に請求書を送るとき bill を用いる。商品などを供給した会社や仕事をした人が顧客や雇用者に請求書を送るときはふつう invoice を用いるが、この意味では bill も用いることができる。動詞の bill と invoice はややフォーマルで、send sb a bill/an invoice はそれほどフォーマルではない。

charity 名

charity・cause・foundation・trust
困っている人を助ける団体を表す
【類語訳】慈善団体, 財団, 信託機関

文型&コロケーション
▶ a charity/ foundation/ trust **for** sth
▶ a **local** charity/ cause/ foundation/ trust
▶ a **deserving/ worthwhile/ worthy** charity/ cause
▶ a **charitable** foundation/ trust
▶ a/ an **national/ private/ independent/ family/ educational/ medical/ conservation/ housing** charity/ foundation/ trust
▶ to **help/ support** a charity/ cause/ foundation/ trust
▶ to **give/ donate to** a charity/ cause/ foundation
▶ to **set up** a charity/ foundation/ trust
▶ to **establish/ create** a foundation/ trust

charity [C] 慈善団体 ◇Many *charities* sent money to help the victims of the famine. 多くの慈善団体が飢えに苦しむ人々を助けるために義援金を送った ◇The concert will raise money for local *charities*. そのコンサートは地元の慈善団体のための募金集めとなる
▷ **charitable** 形 ◇a *charitable* institution/foundation/trust 慈善施設/団体/信託 ◇a *charitable* donation/gift 慈善寄付

cause [C] 主義, 大義, 運動 ◇Animal welfare campaigners raised £70,000 for their *cause* last year. 動物保護活動家たちは去年自分たちの運動のために7万ポンドの資金を集めた ◇Oh well, it's all for a *good cause* (= an organization that does good work, such as a charity). ああ、すべては慈善活動のためなんだ ◇He dedicated his life to fighting for the Republican *cause*. 彼は共和主義のための闘いに生涯を捧げた

foundation [C] 財団 ◇The money will go to the San Francisco AIDS *Foundation*. その金はサンフランシスコ・エイズ財団に入る ◇Many of the hospitals were originally established by religious *foundations*. 病院の多くはもともとは宗教団体により設立された ☞ **organization** (ORGANIZATION)

trust [C]《法律》（資金・財産の寄付や貸与を受けて, そこから発生する利益で慈善事業を援助する）信託機関 ◇She's hoping a charitable *trust* will soon pay for her operation. 彼女は慈善トラストが活動資金をすぐに払ってくれることを願っている

ノート **foundation** と **trust** の使い分け: trust は「trustee と呼ばれる二人以上の個人が慈善目的で資金、土地、その他の財産を管理する団体」と法律で定義されており, foundation は法的な構成よりむしろその目的で定義されており, 信託機関のこともあれば, ある種の会社組織のこともある。

charm 名

charm・personality・character・charisma・presence

人を魅力的に[面白く、印象的に]する特性
【類語訳】魅力、気骨、カリスマ性、貫禄、存在感

▸文型&コロケーション
- **great** charm/ character/ charisma/ presence
- **natural** charm/ charisma
- **personal** charm/ charisma/ presence
- to **lack** charm/ personality/ character/ charisma
- to **have** charm/ charisma/ presence

charm [U]《しばしばほめて》魅力 ◇He was a man of great *charm*. 彼はとても魅力的な男性だった ◇He oozes *charm*, but I wouldn't trust him. 彼は魅力にあふれているが、どうも信用できない ☞ **charm (DELIGHT), charming (NICE 2)**

personality [U]《ほめて》人柄(からくる魅力) ◇We need someone with lots of *personality* to head the project. 我々はプロジェクトを率いる魅力あふれる人を必要としている

character [U]《ほめて》(困難・危険な状況に対応できる)気骨 ◇He showed great *character* returning to the sport after his accident. 彼は事故の後スポーツ界に復帰するという大いなる気骨を見せた ◇Everyone admires her **strength of character** and determination. 誰もが彼女の気概と決断力に敬服している

charisma [U]《ほめて》(人々が引きつけられる[感動させられる、影響を受ける])カリスマ性 ◇The President has great personal *charisma*. その大統領は絶大なカリスマ性を持っている ☞ **charismatic (NICE 2)**

presence [U, 単数で]《ほめて》(容姿・話し方・所作からくる)貫禄、存在感 ◇She has a strong voice but absolutely no **stage presence**. 彼女は力強い声の持ち主だが舞台上ではまったく存在感がない ◇He had a commanding *presence* in meetings. 彼は会議では堂々たる存在だった

cheap 形

cheap・competitive・budget・affordable・reasonable・inexpensive・economical・half-price

製品やサービスが安い値段であったり、思っていたより費用がかからないことを表す
【類語訳】安い、低価格の、割安の、手ごろな、経済的な

competitive	cheap	half-price
affordable	budget	
reasonable	economical	
inexpensive		

▸文型&コロケーション
- cheap/ competitive/ budget/ affordable/ reasonable/ economical **prices/ rates/ fares**
- cheap/ competitive/ budget/ affordable/ inexpensive/ economical **products/ services**
- cheap/ competitive/ affordable/ inexpensive **goods**
- **very/ quite** cheap/ competitive/ affordable/ reasonable/ inexpensive/ economical
- **highly** competitive/ economical
- **relatively** cheap/ competitive/ affordable/ inexpensive

cheap (思っていたよりも)費用がかからない、安い、安価な ◇A good education is not *cheap*. いい教育は安くはない ◇A quality pair of Italian shoes **doesn't come** *cheap*. 質のよいイタリア製の靴は安くはない ◇They've got brand new CD players **going** *cheap*. 彼らは新品のCDプレーヤーを安く手に入れた ◇Her school managed to get a couple of computers **on the** *cheap*. 彼女の学校はコンピューター数台をなんとか安く買い入れた ◇The town is full of immigrant workers, used as a source of ***cheap labour*** (= workers who are paid very little, especially unfairly). その町は安い賃金で働く移民の労働者であふれている ◇We found a ***cheap and cheerful*** *cafe* (= one that is simple and charges low prices but is pleasant).《英》安くてごきげんなカフェを見つけた ❶ *cheap* は値段が低くて質が悪いという意味にも用いられる。◆It was just a bottle of *cheap* perfume. (それは安っぽい香水だった). ◆a ***cheap and nasty*** bottle of wine (《英》安くて質の悪い[安かろう悪かろうの]ワイン). 反意 **expensive (EXPENSIVE)**, ☞ **cheap (POOR 2)**

▸**cheaply** 副 ◇I'm sure I could buy this more *cheaply* somewhere else. どこか別なところではきっとこれをもっと安く買える ◇You can live very *cheaply* in Greece. ギリシアではとても安く生活できる

competitive 《特にビジネス》(価格・商品・サービスが)競争力のある ◇We aim to provide a first-rate *competitive* service. 我々はどこにも絶対負けないサービスの提供を目指しております ◇We need to work harder to remain *competitive* **with** other companies. 我々は他社との競争力を維持するためによりいっそうがんばらなくてはならない ◇They had gained a ***competitive advantage*** over rival companies. 彼らはライバル社に競争力で優位に立っていた
反意 **uncompetitive** ❶ *uncompetitive* goods [services] は商品やサービスが他社より安くない[劣っている]ために対等な競争ができないことを意味する。◆an *uncompetitive* industry (競争力のない産業). ◆ *uncompetitive* prices (競争力のない価格).

▸**competitively** 副 ◇*competitively* priced goods 価格競争力のある商品

budget [名詞の前で]《特に広告で》(基本的サービスだけの提供で)割安の、安い ◇Save pounds on *budget* flights to the sun. 割安航空便で太陽のもとへ ◆a *budget* airline/ hotel 安い航空会社/ホテル

affordable (ほとんどの人が買えるほど)安い、手ごろな ◇We offer the best at *affordable* prices. 私たちは手ごろな価格で最高のものを提供します ◇There is less and less *affordable* housing in this town. この街では手の届く価格の家が少なくなっている

reasonable (価格が)高くない、ほどほどの、手ごろな ◇We sell good quality food at *reasonable* prices. 私たちは高品質の食品を手ごろな値段で売っています 反意 **unreasonable (HIGH 1)**

▸**reasonably** 副 ◇The apartments are *reasonably* priced. そのアパートは手ごろな値段だ

inexpensive 《ややフォーマル》安い ◇Can you recommend an *inexpensive* hotel? 割安なホテルを紹介してくださいますか ❶ *inexpensive* はしばしば値段のわりに十分な価値があることを意味する。*cheap* は品質が悪いことも示唆するため、*cheap* の代わりに *inexpensive* が用いられる。反意 **expensive (EXPENSIVE)**

economical 経済的な ◇These cars are very *economical* to run (= they do not use too much fuel). これらの車はとても燃費がよい ◇It would be more *economical* to buy the bigger size. 大きいサイズを買ったほうがより経済的だ。 反意 **uneconomical** ❶ *uneconomical* なものは費用・時間・材料などがかかりすぎて、利益になりそうもない。 ◆ It soon proved to be *uneconomical* to stay open 24 hours a day. (24時間営業は不経済だということがすぐにわかった。)

➤ **economically** 副 ◇I'll do the job as *economically* as possible. 私はできるだけ経済的に仕事をするつもりです

half-'price 半額の ◇We waited in line and managed to get two *half-price* tickets. 私たちは列に並び、なんとか半額のチケットを2枚手に入れた 反意 **full-price**

➤ **'half-'price** 副 ◇Children aged under four go *half-price*. 4歳未満の子どもは半額です

➤ **'half price** [U] ◇We have many items at *half price* or less. 半額以下の商品がたくさんあります

cheat 名

cheat · cheater · con man · hustler · swindler

人をだましたり、ごまかしたりする人

【類語訳】ごまかす人、詐欺師

cheat [C]《けなして》（ゲームで）ごまかす人 ◇You little *cheat*! ずるいやつだな ◇The government has announced a plan to crack down on tax *cheats*.《インフォーマル、ジャーナリズム》政府は脱税に対して断固たる措置をとると発表した ❶《米》では、*cheat* は主に書き言葉で用いられ、話し言葉では *cheater* が用いられる。

cheater [C]《米、けなして》ごまかす人 ◇You *cheater* — I saw you looking at my cards! ずるいね — 君が私のカードを見ているのを知っていたよ

'con man [C]《インフォーマル》（人をだまして金を取る）詐欺師 ◇The screenplay focuses on the friendship between a dim-witted stud and a petty *con man*. その映画のシナリオは間抜けな男と小物詐欺師の友情を中心としている

hustler [C]《インフォーマル、特に米》（強引[不正]に物を売って金をかせぐ）路上売り；（ギャンブルで）金を巻き上げる人 ◇a street *hustler* selling fake designer T-shirts 偽物のデザイナーTシャツの路上売人 ◇Johnny was a small-time pool room *hustler*. ジョニーは場末のいかさま球突き師だった

swindler [C]《書き言葉、けなして、特にジャーナリズム》（人をだまして金を取る）詐欺師 ◇A *swindler* who tricked banks out of £2.2 million was jailed for four years yesterday. 銀行から220万ポンドをだましとった詐欺師が昨日4年間の禁固刑を受けた

cheat 動 ☞ DEFRAUD

cheat · fool · deceive · betray · take sb in · trick · con · dupe

望むものを得るために人に真実でないことを信じ込ませる

【類語訳】だます、不正をする、いかさまをする、カンニングをする、かつぐ、欺く、裏切る、かもる

文型&コロケーション

▸ to cheat/ trick/ con/ dupe sb **out of** sth
▸ to cheat/ fool/ deceive/ trick/ con/ dupe sb **into doing** sth
▸ to cheat/ fool/ deceive/ trick/ con/ dupe sb into **believing** sth
▸ to cheat/ trick/ con **your way** into sth
▸ to fool/ deceive **yourself**
▸ to **feel** cheated/ deceived/ betrayed/ tricked
▸ to **easily** cheat/ fool/ deceive/ take in/ trick/ con/ dupe sb
▸ to **completely** cheat/ fool/ deceive/ take in/ trick sb

cheat [他]《けなして》（金品などを得るために人を）だます, 不正[いかさま, カンニング]をする ◇She is accused of attempting to *cheat* the taxman. 彼女は税務署員をだまそうとした容疑で告発されている ◇He *cheated* his way into the job. 彼は不正をしてその仕事にありついた ❶ *cheat* には特に試合・競争・試験において有利に立つために「不正をする」という意味もある。 ◆ He *cheats at* cards. (彼はトランプでいかさまをする。) ◆ You're not allowed to look at the answers — that's *cheating*. (解答を見てはいけません — カンニングになりますよ。) ◆ Anyone caught *cheating* will automatically be disqualified from the examination. (カンニングが見つかった者は自動的に受験資格を失うことになります。)

fool [他]《時にけなして》（人をあざ笑う[望むものを得る]ために人を）だます, かつぐ ◇Ha! *Fooled* you! You really thought I was going to jump, didn't you? はは、だまされたね。ぼくが跳ぶと本当に思ったんだろう ◇You can't/ don't *fool* me! だまされないよ ◇She certainly *had me fooled* — I really believed her! 彼女は確かに私をだましたんだ — 本当に彼女を信じてたのに

deceive [他]《けなして》（望むものを得るために人を）だます, 欺く ◇Her husband had been *deceiving* her for years. 何年もの間、夫は彼女を欺いてきた ◇She *deceived* him into handing over all his savings. 彼女は彼から貯金を全額だまし取った ☞ **deception** (FRAUD 1)

betray [他]《けなして》（だまして[不実を働いて]人を）裏切る ◇She felt *betrayed* when she found out the truth about him. 彼について真実を知ってしまったとき、彼女は裏切られたと感じた ◇She *betrayed his trust* over and over again. 彼女は何度も彼の信頼を裏切った ◇I have never known him to *betray a confidence* (= tell other people sth that should be kept secret). 彼が秘密を漏らすなど経験したことがない ☞ **betray** (TELL 2)

,take sb 'in [動詞]《しばしば受身で》《けなして》（望むものを得るために人を）だます ◇I was completely *taken in* by her story. 私は彼女の話にすっかりだまされた ◇Don't be *taken in* by his charm — he's ruthless. 彼の魅力にだまされてはいけない — 彼は残酷な男だよ

trick [他]《時にけなして》（望むものを得るために巧みに人を）だます ◇I realized that I'd been *tricked* and then I felt so stupid. 私はだまされていたことに気づいて、ひどくばかを見た気分だった ◇He managed to *trick* his way past the security guards. 彼はうまくごまかして警備をすり抜けた ☞ **trick** (TRICK)

con (-nn-) [他]《ややインフォーマル》（金品を得る[あるとをさせる]ために人を）だます ◇I was *conned* into buying a useless car. 私はだまされて使い物にならない車を買わされた ◇They had been *conned* out of £100,000. 彼らは10万ポンドをだまし取られていた ☞ **con** (FRAUD 2)

dupe [他、しばしば受身で]《けなして》（物を得るためにばかを見させる形で人を）だます ◇They soon realized they had been *duped*. 彼らはかもられたことにすぐに気づいた ◇He was *duped* into giving them his credit card. 彼はだま

されて彼らに自分のクレジットカードを渡してしまった

check 動

1 check・look at sth・examine・inspect・audit・visit・go over sth・look sth over・check over sth・view・check through sth
すべてが正確[良い状態,許容範囲内]であることを確認するために人や物を入念に見る
【類語訳】検査する,調査する,診察する,検分する,精査する

文型&コロケーション

▶ to check/ examine/ inspect/ check over/ check through (sth) **for** sth
▶ to check/ look at/ examine/ inspect sth **to see if/ whether…**
▶ to check/ look at/ examine/ inspect/ go over/ look over/ check over/ check through sth **carefully**
▶ to check/ examine/ inspect/ go over sth **thoroughly**
▶ to check/ look at/ examine/ inspect sth **closely**
▶ to check/ examine/ inspect/ visit sth **regularly/ daily**

check [他] (入念に)調べる, 検査する ◇*Check* your work before handing it in. 提出する前に書類を点検しなさい ◇*Check* the container for cracks or leaks. 容器にひびや漏れ口がないか調べなさい ☞ **check** (INSPECTION)
'look at sth 句動詞 (入念に)調べる, 検査する;読む ◇Your ankle's swollen — I think a doctor ought to *look at* it. 足首が腫れているよ—医者に診てもらうべきだと思う ◇I haven't had time to *look at* (= read) the papers yet. これまでのところ書類にじっくり目を通す時間がなかった ☞ **look** (LOOK 名)
examine [他] 検査[調査, 診察]する ◇The goods were *examined* for damage on arrival. 到着時に商品は傷がないか検査された ◇The doctor *examined* her but could find nothing wrong. 医者は彼女を診察したが悪いところは何も見つからなかった ☞ **examination** (INSPECTION), **examiner** (INSPECTOR)
inspect [他] (入念に)調べる;(学校・工場などを)視察する ◇The teacher walked around the classroom *inspecting* the children's work. 教師は教室の中を歩きながら子どもたちの作業を見て回った ◇The Tourist Board *inspects* all recommended hotels at least once a year. 観光局は少なくとも年に1度すべての推奨ホテルを視察している ☞ **inspection** (INSPECTION), **inspector** (INSPECTOR)

ノート **check, examine, inspect** の使い分け:これらの語は実際に起こりうる問題を探す場合に使用することが可能。checkだけは間違いを探すことについて用いられる。✗*Examine/Inspect* your work before handing it in. examineのみ問題の原因を探す場合に用いられる。✗The doctor *checked/inspected* her but could find nothing wrong. また, examineは専門家の「調査」によく用いられる。◆The surveyor *examined* the walls for signs of damp. (検査官は湿気の兆候がないか壁を調査した)。inspectは公務員が行う「視察」によく用いられる。◆Public health officials were called in to *inspect* the restaurant. (公衆衛生局員がレストランの視察に呼ばれた)

audit [他] 《ビジネスで》(企業の財務会計を)検査[監査]する ◇The National *Audit* office is responsible for auditing the accounts of a wide range of bodies. 国家監査局が広範囲にわたる団体の会計監査を担当している ☞ **audit**

(INSPECTION)
visit [他] (調査・勧告などのため)視察する ◇Government inspectors are *visiting* all schools in the area next month. 来月政府の検査官たちがその地域のすべての学校を視察する予定だ
,go 'over sth 句動詞 (間違い・傷・危険がないか物事を)入念に調べる ◇*Go over* your work for spelling mistakes before you hand it in. 提出する前に綴りの間違いがないか書いたものを確認しなさい ◇The Health and Safety Officer *went over* the whole school, checking every fire door. 健康安全委員会の職員が学校全体を調査し, すべての防火扉を点検した
,look sb/sth 'over 句動詞 (人・物を入念に)調べる ◇We *looked over* the house again before we decided to rent it. 借りることを決める前に私たちはもう一度その家を見た ◇The sergeant *looked* him *over* and told him to polish his shoes. 軍曹は彼の身だしなみをチェックして靴を磨くように言った
,check 'over sb/sth 句動詞 (人・物を入念に)調べる ◇We *checked over* the house, looking for damp or rot. 私たちは湿気のあるところや腐っているところがないか探しながら家をチェックした ◇The doctor *checked* him *over* and said he was fit and healthy. 医者は彼を検診して, 元気で健康だと言った
view [他] 《ややフォーマル》(買う[借る]かどうかを決めるため家などを)見学する, 検分する ◇The property can only be *viewed* by appointment. その不動産物件は予約が必要です
,check 'through sth 句動詞 (物をくまなく)調べる, 精査する ◇We *checked through* the photographs to make sure there were none missing. 私たちは写真をくまなくチェックして一枚もなくなっていないか確認した

2 check・make sure・verify・assure yourself
物事が真実であるかどうかを調べる
【類語訳】確認する, 確信する

文型&コロケーション

▶ to check/ verify sth **with** sb
▶ to check/ make sure/ verify/ assure yourself **that…**
▶ to check/ verify **what/ whether…**
▶ to check/ verify the **accuracy/ authenticity/ results** (of sth)
▶ to go and check/ make sure
▶ to **always** check/ make sure/ verify sth

check [自, 他] 確認する ◇Go and *check* that I've locked the windows. 私が窓の鍵を掛けたか行って見てきて ◇'Is Mary in the office?' 'Just a moment. I'll go and *check*.'「メアリーはオフィスにいますか」「少し待ってください。私が行って見てきます」 ◇You'd better *check* with Jane what time she's expecting us. 何時に私たちが来るものと思っているのかジェーンに確かめたほうがいい
make 'sure フレーズ 確認する ◇She looked around to *make sure* that she was alone. 彼女は辺りを見回して周りに人がいないか確認した ◇I think the door's locked, but I'll just go and *make sure*. ドアに鍵を掛けたと思うがちょっと行って確かめてくる
verify [他, 自] 《フォーマル》確認する ◇We have no way of *verifying* his story. 彼の話の真偽を確かめる方法はない ◇Please *verify* that your password was entered correctly. パスワードを正確に入力したかご確認ください ☞ **ver-**

ifiable (RELIABLE 2)
assure yourself《フォーマル》確認する；確信する ◇He *assured himself of* her safety. 彼は彼女の無事を確認した ◇She *assured herself* that the letter was still in the drawer. 手紙はまだ引き出しの中にあると彼女は思った

cheerful 形

cheerful・bright・cheery・jolly・in a good mood
幸せな気分が振る舞いに表れていることを表す
【類語訳】陽気な, 元気のよい, 快活な, 明るい, 晴れやかな

文型&コロケーション
▶ a cheerful/ bright/ cheery/ jolly **face**
▶ a cheerful/ cheery/ jolly **person/ manner**
▶ **in** a cheerful/ cheery/ jolly/ good **mood**
▶ **bright and** cheerful/ cheery/ jolly

cheerful（振る舞い・表情から見て）陽気な, 快活な ◇She tried to sound *cheerful* and unconcerned. 彼女は陽気で何も気にしていないように見せようとした ◇You're not *your usual cheerful self* today. 今日はいつもの元気がないね ◇She wrote him a chatty, *cheerful* letter. 彼女は彼におしゃべり口調の心弾む手紙を書いた 反意 **gloomy** (DEPRESSED), **miserable** (UNHAPPY 1)
▶ **cheerfully** 副 ◇He waved *cheerfully* at them and hurried on. 彼は彼らに元気よく手を振ると急いで行ってしまった ◇She *cheerfully* admitted that she had no experience at all (= she wasn't afraid to admit it). 彼女は自分にまったく経験がないことを屈託なく認めた
bright（人・表情が）明るい, 晴れやかな, はつらつとした ◇He felt *bright* and cheerful and full of energy. 彼は明るい快活な気分で気力がみなぎってくる感じがした ◇His face was *bright with* excitement. 彼の顔は興奮で輝いていた
▶ **brightly** 副 ◇'Hi!' she called *brightly*. 「こんにちは」と彼女は明るく呼びかけた

ノート **cheerful** と **bright** の使い分け：人を修飾する場合, both **bright and** cheerful の句か, 動詞の**be**または**feel**の後で用いられる. ◆ I was not feeling very *bright* that morning. (その日の朝はあまり気分がすぐれなかった). a cheerful boy/girl は「快活な男の子/女の子」を意味するが, a bright boy/girl は「快活な」ではなく「利発な男の子/女の子」を指す. ☞ **bright** (INTELLIGENT)

cheery《インフォーマル, 特に話し言葉》（人・態度が）陽気な, 元気のよい ◇He left with a *cheery* 'See you again soon.' 彼は陽気に「近いうちにまた会いましょう」と言って立ち去った
jolly《ややインフォーマル》（人・態度が）陽気な元気のよい ◇The manager was fat and *jolly*. その支配人は太っていて陽気な人だった ◇He had a round, *jolly* face. 彼は丸顔で陽気な表情をしていた
in a ˌgood ˈmood 行れ（よい事があって人が）気分[機嫌]のよい ◇He was not *in a good mood* with her. 彼は彼女に対して不機嫌だった ◇This announcement put the fans *in a good mood*. このアナウンスを聞いてファンはいい気分になった

child 名 ☞ GIRL

child・boy・girl・baby・kid・infant・youngster・toddler・minor・brat・junior
まだ大人になっていない若者を表す
【類語訳】子ども, 少年, 男の子, 少女, 女の子, 赤ん坊, 赤ちゃん, 幼児, 若者, 未成年者, 悪がき, 年少者, ジュニア

文型&コロケーション
▶ a **young** child/ boy/ girl/ baby/ kid/ infant
▶ a **little** child/ boy/ girl/ baby/ kid/ brat
▶ a **small/ good/ naughty** child/ boy/ girl/ baby/ kid
▶ a **healthy/ normal** child/ boy/ girl/ baby/ kid/ infant
▶ a **bright/ local** child/ boy/ girl/ kid/ youngster
▶ a **difficult** child/ boy/ baby/ toddler
▶ a **spoilt/ spoiled** child/ kid/ brat
▶ to **look after/ take care of** a child/ baby/ kid
▶ a child/ boy/ girl/ baby/ kid/ infant/ youngster/ toddler **learns** sth
▶ a child/ boy/ girl/ baby/ kid/ youngster/ toddler/ junior **plays**
▶ a child/ boy/ girl/ baby/ kid/ youngster **grows (up)**

child（複 **children**）[C] 子ども ◇a *child* of three/ a three-year-old child 3歳の子ども ◇men, women and *children* 男たち, 女たち, そして子どもたち ◇I lived in London as a *child*. 子どものころにロンドンに住んでいた ◇The group campaigns for the rights of the unborn *child*. このグループは胎児の権利を求めて運動しています ◇She was a *child star* but never made it as an adult. 彼女は子役スターだったが大人になってパッとしなかった 反意 **adult, grown-up** (ADULT)
boy [C] 少年, 男の子 ◇The older *boys* at school used to tease him. 上級生の男の子たちは彼をよくいじめていた ◇Be a good *boy* and get me my coat. いい子だからぼくのコートを取ってきて 反意 **girl**
girl [C] 少女, 女の子 ◇She's a bright little *girl*. 頭のいい愛らしい子だ 反意 **boy**, ☞ **girl** (GIRL)
baby [C] 赤ん坊, 赤ちゃん ◇The *baby*'s crying! 赤ちゃんが泣いている ◇He just broke down and cried like a *baby*. 彼はちょっと取り乱して赤ん坊のように泣いた ◇The illness is common in *newborn babies* and is easily treated. それは新生児にはよくある病気で, 治療は簡単です
kid [C]《インフォーマル, 特に話し言葉》子ども ◇He's only a *kid*. You can't expect him to understand what's going on. 彼はほんの子どもだよ. 何が起きているか彼に理解しろと言うのがだいたい無理な話だよ ◇A bunch of *kids* were hanging around outside. 多くの子どもたちが外でたむろしていた

ノート **child** と **kid** の使い分け：《米》のインフォーマルな話し言葉では, **child** より **kid** が頻繁に使われる. **kid** はまた child より年上の子どもにも構わない. **a kid of 15** (15歳の子ども) と言えるが, child はふつう12歳くらいまでしか使われない. 12歳より上の子どもには, **kids, teenagers, young people, girls, youths, lads** を使う.

infant [C]《フォーマル or 専門語》幼児, 赤ん坊 ◇We studied newborn *infants* up to two months old. 私たちは生後2か月以下の新生児を調査した ◇The country has an appallingly high *infant mortality rate*. この国の乳児死亡率は驚くほど高い ❶ イギリスとオーストラリアの教育制度では, infant は4歳から7歳までの学童も指す. ◆The majority of *infant* teachers are women. (幼児担当の先生の多くは女性だ). ◆ I've known her since we were in the *infants* (= at infant school). (彼女とは幼稚学校のころからの知り合いだ).

youngster [C]《インフォーマル》子ども, 若者 ◇The camp is for *youngsters* aged 8 to 14. そのキャンプは8歳から14歳までの子どもが対象だ

toddler [C] よちよち歩きの幼児 ◇She was left at home with a *toddler* and a four-month-old baby to care for. 彼女は世話のかかるよちよち歩きの幼児と4か月の赤ん坊と一緒に家に残された

minor [C]《法律》未成年者 ◇It is an offence to serve alcohol to *minors*. 未成年者にアルコールを出すのは違法行為だ ◇He was jailed for having sex with a *minor*. 彼は未成年者とセックスをして拘留された 反意 **adult** (ADULT)

brat [C]《インフォーマル, けなして》悪がき ◇He's a spoilt little *brat*! 彼は甘やかされた幼い悪がきだ

junior [C]《英》(スポーツで)年少者, ジュニア；(7～11歳の)学童 ◇At 16, he's still eligible to play for the *juniors*. 彼は16歳で, まだジュニア資格でプレーできる ◇Sam is going to be a *junior* next year. サムは来年から小学生だ ◇a *junior* school 小学校

childhood 名

childhood・youth・adolescence・teens・infancy・puberty
人の子ども[若者]である期間
【類語訳】幼年期, 子どものころ, 青春時代, 青年時代, 若さ, 思春期, 十代, 幼児期, 乳幼期

infancy	childhood	youth
		adolescence
		teens
		puberty

文型&コロケーション
▶ in (sb's) childhood/ youth/ adolescence/ teens/ infancy
▶ during (sb's) childhood/ youth/ adolescence/ teens/ infancy/ puberty
▶ from (sb's) childhood/ youth/ infancy
▶ since/ throughout (sb's) childhood/ youth/ adolescence/ teens/ infancy
▶ (sb's) early childhood/ youth/ adolescence/ teens/ infancy
▶ (sb's) late childhood/ adolescence/ teens
▶ a/ an happy/ unhappy childhood/ youth
▶ to reach adolescence/ your teens/ puberty
▶ to spend your childhood/ youth/ adolescence/ teens...

childhood [U, C] 幼年時代, 幼年期, 子どものころ ◇From her earliest *childhood* she'd had a love of dancing. ごく幼い頃から彼女はダンスが好きだった ◇She had a very happy *childhood*. 彼女はとても幸せな幼年期を過ごした ◇*childhood* memories/experiences 幼年時代の思い出/経験

youth [U, 単数で] (思春期から成人までの)若い[青春, 青年]時代；若さ ◇He had been a talented musician in his *youth*. 若い頃彼は才能のあるミュージシャンだった ◇His lack of qualification was taken as a sign of *a misspent youth* (= having wasted his time when he was young). 彼が資格のなかったのは青春時代を無為に過ごした証だと考えられた ◇She brings to the job a rare combination of *youth* and experience. 彼女は珍しいことに若さと経験を兼ね備えて仕事をしている ❶ *youth* には

「若い人」の意味もある。☞ **youth** (GIRL)

adolescence [U]《ややフォーマル》(子どもから大人になる)思春[青春, 青年]期 ◇*Adolescence* brings about major changes in a young person's body. 思春期に若者の体に大きな変化が生じる ◇She developed the problem in early *adolescence*. その問題は彼女の思春期初期に起こった ❶ *adolescence* はしばしば大人になりつつある若者が問題を抱えているような場合に用いられる。☞ **adolescent** (GIRL)

teens [複数で] (13歳から19歳までの)十代 ◇She began writing poetry in her *teens*. 彼女は十代の頃に詩を書き始めた ◇An eyewitness described a boy in his mid to late *teens* wearing a dark jacket. 目撃者は少年は十代半ばから後半で黒っぽい上着を着ていたとその特徴を述べた ❶ *teens* は常に my, his, her など代名詞所有格の後に用いられる。× I met him in *teens*. ☞ **teen** (GIRL)

infancy [U] 幼児期, 乳児期 ◇Tragically, she died in *infancy*. 悲しいことに彼女は乳児期に亡くなった ◇The vaccination is given in early *infancy*. そのワクチンは幼児期の初期に接種される ❶ *infancy* はしばしば病気や命の危険のある乳幼児について用いられる。 ◆ to survive *infancy* (乳児期を生き延びる)。 ◆ deaths during *infancy* (乳児期の死亡)。

puberty [U] (性器の発達・身体の変化が起こる)思春期 ◇He reached *puberty* at the age of fourteen. 彼は14歳で思春期を迎えた ◇The body undergoes many changes during *puberty*. 思春期に多くの変化が体に起こる ❶ *puberty* は子ども時代に関する個人的な事柄を言う場合よりは医学的・科学的な文脈でよく用いられる。

childish 形

childish・immature・youthful・boyish・childlike・girlish
人や動物が成長しきっていないことや, 若さの特徴を備えていることを表す
【類語訳】子どもの, 子どもらしい, 子どもじみた, 幼稚な, 未成熟の, 未発達の

文型&コロケーション
▶ childish/ immature/ childlike behaviour
▶ youthful/ boyish charm/ energy/ enthusiasm/ (good) looks
▶ a youthful/ boyish/ girlish figure
▶ very childish/ immature/ youthful
▶ almost childish/ childlike/ girlish

childish 子どもの, 子どもらしい, 子どもじみた ◇At the front of the book I found her name, written in *childish* handwriting. 私は本の表に彼女の名前が子どもらしい手書きの字で書かれているのを見つけた ❶ *childish* は愚かな振る舞いをする大人・年長児をけなして用いられることもある。 ◆ Don't be so *childish*! (《けなして》そんな子どもじみたことしないの)。反意 **adult** (ADULT)
▶ **childishly** 副 ◇to behave *childishly* 子どもらしく振舞う

immature 《けなして》幼稚な, 未成熟[発達]の, 子どもじみた ◇Oh, don't be so *immature*. もう, そんな子どもみたいなことしないの ◇Although she was older than her husband, she was emotionally quite *immature*. 彼女は夫より年上だったが, 感情的にかなり幼稚だった ❶ *immature* はまだ十分成長していない動植物にも用いられる。 ◆ The im-

choice, choose

mature birds have shorter tails and brown, speckled plumage. (未成熟の鳥は尾が短く, 羽毛は茶色で斑紋がある). 反意 **mature** (ADULT)
▶**immaturity** 名 [U] ◇I'm fed up with his selfishness and *immaturity*. 彼のわがままと幼稚さにはうんざりしている 反意 **maturity**
youthful 若者らしい ◇She brought a tremendous *youthful* enthusiasm to the job. 彼女が仕事に注ぐ若者らしい熱心さはすごかった
boyish 《ふつうほめて》(見た目・振る舞いが魅力的で)少年のような ◇She had a slim, almost *boyish* figure. 彼女はすらっとしていてほとんど男の子のような体つきをしていた ◇Jane fell for his *boyish* charm. ジェーンは彼の少年っぽい魅力に夢中になった
childlike 《ふつうほめて》(無邪気で)子どもらしい ◇She responded with *childlike* simplicity. 彼女は子どもらしいあどけなさで返事をした ☞ **innocent** (NAIVE)
girlish (見た目・振る舞いに関して)少女のような ◇His face was delicate, almost *girlish*. 彼の顔は優美でほとんど女の子のようだった ◇She gave a *girlish* giggle. 彼女は少女のようにくすくす笑った

choice 名

1 choice・selection・nomination・election・pick
二人[二つ]以上の人, 物事, 可能性から選ぶこと
【類語訳】選択, 選定, 指名, 選任, 当選

文型&コロケーション
▶sb's selection/ nomination/ election **as** sth
▶sb's selection/ nomination **for** sth
▶a/ an **careful/ initial/ final** choice/ selection
▶to **make** a choice/ selection/ nomination
▶to **have** a choice/ your pick
▶to **take** your choice/ pick
▶to **get first** choice/ pick
▶to **secure** selection/ the nomination/ election
▶to **win** selection/ the nomination

choice [C]（二つ以上の可能性から）選ぶこと, 選択 ◇Many women are forced to make a *choice* between family and career. 多くの女性は家庭か仕事のどちらかを選ばざるを得ない ◇We aim to help students make more informed career *choices*. 私たちの目的は学生がより多くの情報を得て仕事を選択できるよう助けることです ◇We are faced with a difficult *choice*. 私たちは難しい選択に直面している ☞ **choice** (OPTION)
selection [U] 《ややフォーマル》(グループの中から手順に従って)人・物事を)選ぶこと, 選択, 選定 ◇The final team *selection* will be made tomorrow. チームの最終選考は明日行われる予定だ ◇The game is based on the *random selection* of numbers. そのゲームは数字の無作為抽出に基づいて行われる ◇What are their *selection* criteria? その選考基準は何ですか
nomination [U, C] (選挙・職業・賞の候補者の)指名(をされること), 推薦 ◇Membership of the club is by *nomination* only. クラブの会員には指名を受けた場合に限り, なることができる ◇They opposed her *nomination to* the post of Deputy Director. 彼らは彼女が副理事の候補となることに反対した ◇How many Oscar *nominations* has she had in her career? 今までのキャリアで彼女は何回オスカー候補になりましたか ☞ **nominate** (APPOINT), **nominate**

(RECOMMEND 2)
election [U] (選挙で)選ばれたこと, 選任, 当選 ◇We welcome his *election* as president. 私たちは彼が大統領に選ばれたことを歓迎します ☞ **elect** (APPOINT)
pick [単数で]《ややインフォーマル》(人・物事を)選ぶこと, 選択 ◇Red or green? *Take your pick* (= choose). 赤か緑か, 好きに選んで ◇The winner *gets first pick* of the prizes. 勝者が賞品の中から一番最初に選びます ◇She had her *pick of* the young single men at the party. 彼女は若い独身男性たちを好きに選んでパーティーに呼んだ ❶ **pick** はほとんど常に上記の用例中に示された句で用いられる.

2 choice・favourite・preference・selection・pick
選ばれる[他よりも好まれる]人や物
【類語訳】お気に入り, 好物

文型&コロケーション
▶sb's choice/ favourite/ pick **for** sth
▶sb's choice/ favourite/ selection/ pick **as** sth
▶an **obvious** choice/ favourite/ selection
▶a/ an **excellent/ good/ popular/ fine** choice/ selection

choice [C] (一人[一つ]の)選ばれた人[物] ◇She's the obvious *choice* for the job. その仕事にはどうみても彼女がうってつけだ ◇This colour wasn't my *first choice*. この色は私の第一希望ではなかった ◇I don't like his *choice* of friends (= the people he chooses as his friends). 私は彼が友人に選ぶ人たちが好きではない ☞ **choice** (OPTION), **of choice** (FAVOURITE)
favourite [英] (米 **favorite**) [C] お気に入り ◇This song is a particular *favourite of* mine. この歌は特に私のお気に入りだ ◇These *cakes* are great *favourites with* the children. 子どもたちはこのケーキが大好きだ ◇The show has become a *firm favourite* with young people. その番組は若者から根強い人気を得るようになった ☞ **favourite** (FAVOURITE)
preference [C] 好物 ◇They are undertaking a study of consumer *preferences*. 彼らは消費者の嗜好の研究に着手している ◇Tastes and *preferences* vary from individual to individual. 趣味嗜好は人それぞれ異なる ☞ **preference** (TASTE), **prefer** (PREFER), **preferred** (FAVOURITE)

ノート **favourite** と **preference** の使い分け：favourite は最も好きで, よく持たれたり[されたり, 聴かれたり など]する物. preference は選ぶことができる場合に持たれたり[された り]する物.

selection [C] (多数の中からいくつか)選ばれた人[物] ◇A *selection* of readers' comments are published below. 読者のご意見から選んだものを以下に掲載します ◇The orchestra played *selections* from Hollywood musicals. オーケストラはハリウッド・ミュージカルから選んだ曲を演奏した
pick [単数で]《特に米, ややインフォーマル》(一人[一つ])の選ばれた人[物] ◇She was his *pick* for best actress. 彼女は彼に最優秀女優に選ばれた

choose 動

choose・select・pick・decide・opt・go for sth・single sb/sth out・adopt
選択可能なものの中から望ましい人や物を決める

↪choose

【類語訳】選ぶ, 決める, 選択する, 採用する, 採択する

文型&コロケーション
▶ to choose/ select/ pick/ single out **A from** B
▶ to choose/ select/ pick/ decide **between** A **and**/ **or** B
▶ to choose/ select/ pick/ opt for/ go for/ single out/ adopt sb/ sth **as** sb/ sth
▶ to choose/ select/ pick/ single out sb/ sth **for** sb/ sth
▶ to choose/ select/ pick/ opt for/ go for/ single out/ adopt sb/ sth **to do sth**
▶ to choose/ decide/ opt **to do sth**
▶ to pick/ single sb/ sth **out**
▶ to choose/ select/ pick sb/ sth **carefully**/ **at random**
▶ **randomly** chosen/ selected/ picked
▶ **well** chosen/ selected

choose [自, 他] (選択可能なものの中から人・物事を)選ぶ, 決める ◇You *choose* — I can't decide. あなたが選んで—私は決められない ◇There are plenty of restaurants to *choose* from. たくさんのレストランから選ぶことができる ◇She had to *choose* between giving up her job or hiring a nanny. 彼女は仕事を辞めるか子守を雇うかのどちらかを選択せねばならなかった ◇You have to take any job you can get — you can't *pick and choose*. もらえる仕事は何でも引き受けなくてはならない—選り好みはできないよ ◇He *chose* banking as a career. 彼は仕事として銀行業を選んだ ◇You'll have to *choose* whether to buy it or not. それを買うか買わないか決めなくてはならないだろう ◇We *chose* Paul Stubbs to be chairperson. 私たちはポール・スタッブズを議長に選んだ ☞ **choice** (OPTION), **choice** (RANGE 1)

select [他, しばしば受身で] 《ややフォーマル》 (グループの中から手順に従って人・物事を)選ぶ, 選択する ◇He hasn't been *selected* for the team. 彼はチームの選手に選ばれたことがない ◇All our hotels have been carefully *selected* for the excellent value they provide. 私どものホテルが優れた価値を提供するということで厳選されました ◇a randomly *selected* sample of 23 schools 例として無作為に選ばれた23校 ◇*selected* poems of T.S. Eliot T.S.エリオットの詩選集 ◇*Select* 'New Mail' from the 'Send' menu. 「送信」メニューから「新しいメール」を選択してください ☞ **selection** (RANGE 1)

pick [他] 《ややインフォーマル》 (グループの中から人・物事を)選ぶ ◇*Pick* a number from one to twenty. 1〜20の数字から一つ選びなさい ◇Names were *picked* at random out of a hat. 名前が思いつくままに無作為に選ばれた ◇He was *picked* out as the best player. 彼は最優秀選手に選ばれた

ノート **choose, select, pick の使い分け**: choose はこれらの語の中で最も一般的で, 唯一目的語なしで用いることができる. ×You *select*/*pick* — I can't decide. select は randomly/at random を伴わない限り「慎重に選ぶ」ことを意味する. pick は よりインフォーマルな語で, 特にあまり重要でない選択に用いられ, しばしばほど慎重な選択ではない. ×*Select* a number from one to twenty.

decide [自] (二つ以上の選択可能なものの中から)選ぶ, どれかに決める ◇It was difficult to *decide* between the two candidates. その二人の候補のうちどちらに決めるかは難しかった ◇We're still trying to *decide on* a venue. 私たちは開催地を検討中だ ◇You *choose* — I can't *decide*. あなたが選んで—私は決められない ☞ **de-**cide (DECIDE)

opt [自] (採るべき道を)選ぶ, 選択する ◇After graduating she *opted for* a career in music. 卒業後彼女は音楽関連の仕事を選んだ ◇After a lot of thought, I *opted against* buying a motorbike. よくよく考えて私はバイクを買わないことに決めた ◇Many workers *opted* to leave their jobs rather than take a pay cut. 多くの従業員が賃金カットを受け入れるのではなく仕事を辞めることを選んだ ◇Employees may *opt out of* the company's pension plan. 従業員は会社の年金制度への不参加を選択してもよい ☞ **option** (OPTION)

'go for sth 句動詞 《ややインフォーマル》 (物事を)選ぶ ◇I think I'll *go for* the fruit salad. フルーツサラダにしようかな

,single sb/sth 'out 句動詞 (グループの中から人・物事を)選び出す ◇She was *singled out* for criticism. 彼女が槍玉に挙げられた ◇He was *singled out* as the outstanding performer of the games. 彼はその大会の優秀選手に選出された

adopt [他] (新しい名前・国などを)採用する, 自分のものとする ◇The royal family *adopted* the name of Windsor early in the last century. 前世紀初頭, 英国王室はウィンザーという名称を採用した

church 名

church・temple・mosque・shrine・cathedral・chapel・synagogue・abbey・sanctuary・place of worship
宗教的建造物を表す
【類語訳】教会, 神殿, 寺院, 社(やしろ), チャペル

文型&コロケーション
▶ to go to church/ temple/ chapel/ synagogue

church [C, U] (キリスト教の)教会(堂); (教会での)礼拝 ◇The procession moved into the *church*. 行列は教会の中に入って行った ◇a *church* tower 教会の塔 ◇*church* services 礼拝 ◇How often do you go to *church*? どのくらい教会へ行きますか ◇They're *at church* (= attending a church service). 彼らは礼拝中だ ◇They're *in church*. 《米》彼らは礼拝中だ ◇*Church* is at 9 o'clock. 礼拝は9時からです

temple [C] (キリスト教以外の)神殿, 寺院, 礼拝堂 ◇a Buddhist/Hindu/Sikh *temple* 仏教/ヒンドゥー教/シーク教寺院 ◇the *Temple* of Diana at Ephesus エフェソスにあるアルテミス神殿 ◇to go to *temple* (= to a service in a synagogue, where Jews worship) 《米》(ユダヤ教のシナゴーグへ)礼拝に行く

mosque [C] (イスラム教の礼拝堂である)モスク ◇We were woken by the call to prayer from a nearby *mosque*. 私たちは近くのモスクから礼拝の時刻を知らせる呼びかけで目が覚めた

shrine [C] (聖人・聖なる出来事と関連のある)聖堂, 聖地, 社(やしろ) ◇a *shrine to* the Virgin Mary 聖母マリアを祀る聖堂 ◇to visit the *shrine of* Mecca メッカを訪れる

cathedral [C] (司教管区内の中心的な教会である)大聖堂 ◇St Paul's *Cathedral* セントポール大聖堂 ◇a *cathedral* city 《英》大聖堂のある都市

chapel [C] (学校・刑務所・大邸宅内にあるキリスト教の)チャペル[礼拝堂[室]]; (教会・大聖堂の)分会堂, 支聖堂; (共同墓地・火葬場内で葬儀を執り行う)礼拝堂 ◇the school/

college *chapel* 学校/大学のチャペル ◊Evening prayer will be held in the Lady *Chapel*. 晩祷式はレディー・チャペルで行われます ◊a tiny *chapel* in the mountains 山の中にある小さな礼拝堂 ◊a *chapel* of rest 霊安室 ❶（英）では chapel [C, U]は非国教会などいくつかのキリスト教宗派の教会を指すこともある． ◆a Methodist/Mormon *chapel*（メソジスト派/モルモン教の教会）． ◆She always went to *chapel* on Sundays.（彼女はいつも毎週日曜日に礼拝に通った）．

synagogue [C]（ユダヤ教の礼拝堂である）シナゴーグ ◊They went to *synagogue* every Saturday. 彼らは毎週土曜日にシナゴーグに通った

abbey [C]（修道士[女]が生活する）大修道院 ◊Westminster *Abbey* ウェストミンスター寺院 ◊a ruined *abbey* 廃墟と化した修道院

sanctuary [C] 神聖な建物，（建物内の一番）神聖な場所 ◊Women were excluded from entering the *sanctuary* where the priest stood at the altar. 司祭が祭壇に立つ神聖な場所に女性は立ち入ることがまったく許されていなかった

ˌplace of ˈworship（複 **places of worship**）[C]《ややフォーマル》（教会・神殿・寺院・モスク・シナゴーグのような）礼拝所 ◊The statistics show the number of people who regularly attend a *place of worship*. その統計データは定期的に礼拝所へ通う人の数を示している ❶ place of worship は国・都市・地域に住む人々に関する公式の情報収集を行うような文脈で用いられる

citizen 名

citizen・voter・taxpayer・native・national・subject
特定の国に属し法的権利を有する人を表す
【類語訳】国民，市民，公民，投票者，有権者，納税者

▶a citizen/ native/ national of a country
▶a British citizen/ voter/ taxpayer/ national/ subject
▶a US/ Australian, etc. citizen/ voter/ taxpayer/ national
▶an ordinary/ average citizen/ voter/ taxpayer
▶a foreign/ fellow citizen/ national

citizen [C]（特定の国の市民権を持つ）国民，市民，公民 ◊She's Italian by birth, but is now an Australian *citizen*. 彼女は生まれはイタリアだが，現在はオーストラリア国民です ☞ **citizen** (RESIDENT)
▷**citizenship** 名 [U] ◊You can apply for *citizenship* after five years' residency. 5年以上居住すれば，市民権を申請することが可能です

voter [C] 投票者，有権者 ◊Only 60% of eligible *voters* actually used their vote. たった60%の有権者しか実際に投票権を行使しなかった

taxpayer [C]（所得税の）納税者 ◊The changes make an average *taxpayer* £2.50 a week better off. この改革により平均的な納税者の暮らし向きが週2.5ポンドよくなる ◊Hundreds of thousands of pounds of *taxpayers' money* have been spent on the project. 何十万ポンドという納税者の金がその事業に費やされている ❶ taxpayer は政府の支出について述べる場合，しばしば国民全体を指す． ◆What is **the cost to the taxpayer** of hosting the Olympics?（オリンピックの開催で国民に与える負担額はいくらになるのか）． ◆Should politicians be able to travel first class **at the taxpayer's expense**?（政治家は国民の金でファーストクラスで旅行してよいのだろうか） ◆It was estimated to have cost **the US taxpayer** $35 billion.（それはアメリカ国民に350億ドルの負担をさせる見積もりになった）．

native [C]（特定の国・地域）生まれの人 ◊She was not a *native* of the island, but had lived there for many years. 彼女はその島で生まれた人間ではなかったが，長年そこで生活していた ☞ **native** (RESIDENT), **native** (CULTURAL)

national [C]《ややフォーマル》（特定の国の）国民，市民 ◊The government has advised British *nationals* to leave the area. 政府はイギリス国民にその地域を離れるよう勧告している ❶ nationals は特定の国籍を有する人で特に外国で暮らしていたり，働いていたりする人について用いられる．
▷**nationality** 名 [U, C] ◊She has *dual nationality* (= is a citizen of two countries). 彼女は二重国籍を持っている ◊The college attracts students of all *nationalities*. その大学はあらゆる国籍の学生を集めている

subject [C]《ややフォーマル》（君主国の）国民，臣民 ◊British *subjects* and Commonwealth citizens do not need visas. イギリス国民およびイギリス連邦市民はビザが不要である ◊The prince had to tax his *subjects* heavily to raise money for the war. 戦争資金を調達するため王子は臣民に対し重税を課さなければならなかった

city 名

city・town・village・borough・municipality・metropolis・conurbation
人々が生活や仕事をする通りや建物がある場所
【類語訳】都市，町，村，自治都市，首都

▶in a city/ town/ village/ borough/ municipality/ metropolis/ conurbation
▶a small city/ town/ village/ borough/ municipality
▶a major city/ town/ metropolis/ conurbation
▶a big city/ town/ village/ metropolis
▶a large city/ town/ village/ conurbation
▶a great city/ metropolis
▶a provincial city/ town
▶the local borough/ municipality
▶the city/ town/ village/ borough council

city [C] 都市，大きな町 ◊The *city* of Boston is one of America's most historic cities. ボストン市はアメリカで最も歴史的な都市の一つである ◊Ely is a *cathedral city* in East Cambridgeshire. イーリーはイーストケンブリッジシャーにある大聖堂の町である

town [C] 町（villageより大きくcityより小さい） ◊The nearest *town* is ten miles away. 最寄の町は10マイル離れている ◊Sackville is a small *university town* in eastern Canada. サックビルはカナダ東部にある小さな学園都市である ❶（米）では不可算のtownが，人が生活し仕事をする特定の町を意味することもある． ◆I'll be **in town** next week if you want to go out for a drink.（君が飲みに行きたいなら，私は来週町に行くよ）． ◆He married a girl from **out of town**.（彼はよそから来た女の子と結婚した）． ◆They live in a rough part of *town*.（彼らは町の荒廃した地域に住んでいる）． ◆This restaurant serves the best steaks in *town*.（このレストランは町一番のステーキを出す）． 単数の **the town** は「田舎での生活に対し一般的な「都会[町]」での生活」という概念を指すこともある． ◆Do you prefer *the town*

↳city

to the country? (田舎での生活より町での生活のほうが好きですか)

ノート **city**と**town**の使い分け：cityはふつうtownより大きいが、常にそうとは限らない。公式的にはcityはイギリスでは王・女王によって、アメリカでは州政府によって認可される。時が経てばtownやcityの規模も変わるので、最近ではcityの中にはtownより小さいものも見受けられる。《米》ではあまりvillageという語は用いられず、townがその代わりに用いられることがある。

village [C] 村, (小さな)町 ◇Appledore is a fishing *village* on the north coast of Devon. アップルドアはデボンの北岸にある漁村である ◇Most basic items are available from the *village* shop. 《特に英》たいていの必需品は村の店で入手可能だ ◇Her books are about *village* life. 彼女の本は村の生活に関するものだ ❶《米》ではvillageはtownより古びた感じのする小地域を指す.

borough [C] 自治都市[町村, 区] ◇She served as a local councillor in the London *Borough* of Westminster. 彼女はロンドン自治区ウェストミンスターの地元議員として働いた

municipality [C] 《フォーマル》(市・町村・区などの)地方自治体(当局) ◇The *municipality* provides services such as electricity, water and rubbish collection. 地方自治体が電気・水道・ごみ収集といったサービスを提供している
➤**municipal** 形 《ふつう名詞の前で》◇*municipal* elections 地方議会議員選挙

metropolis [C] (地方の)主要[大]都市, (国の)首都 ◇Barcelona has all the amenities you would expect to find in a great *metropolis*. バルセロナには大都市に見られるありとあらゆる施設がそろっている
➤**metropolitan** 形 [名詞の前で] ◇the New York *metropolitan* area ニューヨーク都市圏

conurbation [C] 《フォーマル》コナベーション, 連接[集合]都市 ◇The region has several medium-sized towns and cities, but no major *conurbations*. その地域にはいくつかの中規模の町や都市はあるが、主要な連接都市はない

claim 動

claim・argue・insist・allege・contend・maintain・assert・protest・affirm
事が事実であると述べる
【類語訳】主張する, 説く, 言い張る, 申し立てる, 断言する

文型&コロケーション
▶to claim/ argue/ insist/ allege/ contend/ maintain/ assert/ protest/ affirm **that**...
▶It is claimed/ argued/ alleged/ contended/ maintained/ asserted/ affirmed **that**...
▶to insist on/ maintain/ assert/ protest **your innocence**
▶to argue/ insist/ protest/ assert sth **strongly**

claim [他] (十分な証拠のないままに)主張する ◇He *claims* (that) he was not given a fair hearing. 彼は発言の機会が公平に与えられなかったと主張している ◇I don't *claim* to be an expert. 私は自分が専門家だと言うつもりはない ◇Scientists are *claiming* a major breakthrough in the fight against cancer. 科学者たちはがんとの戦いにおける大きな前進だと主張している ◇It was *claimed* that some doctors were working 80 hours a week. 医者の中には1週間に80時間働いている者もいるとの主張がなされた
argue [自, 他] (説得するために理由を述べて)主張する, 説く, (賛成・反対の)論を唱える ◇They *argued* for the right to strike. 彼らはストライキの権利を主張した ◇He was too tired to *argue the point* (= discuss the matter). 彼はとても疲れていてその件について議論することができなかった ◇She *argued* that they needed more time to finish the project. 彼女はその事業を完成するにはもっと時間が必要だと主張した ☞**argument** (ARGUMENT 2)
insist [自, 他] (信じてくれないときに断固として繰り返し)主張する, 言い張る ◇He *insisted on* his innocence. 彼は自分の無実を強く主張した ◇He *insisted* (that) he was innocent. 彼は無実であると強く主張した
➤**insistence** 名 [U] ◇No one was convinced by her *insistence* that she was not to blame. 自分に責任はないとする彼女の主張に誰も納得しなかった
allege [他, しばしば受身で] 《フォーマル》(法的な争いのもとで)主張する, 申し立てる ◇It is *alleged* that he mistreated the prisoners. 申し立てによれば彼は囚人に虐待を加えたとのことだ ◇He is *alleged* to have mistreated the prisoners. 彼は囚人に虐待を加えたと申し立てられている ◇This procedure should be followed in cases where dishonesty has been *alleged*. 不正が申し立てられている場合にはこの手順にしたがって事が進められます ☞**alleged** (SUPPOSED)
contend [他] 《フォーマル》(議論で)主張する ◇I would *contend* that the prime minister's thinking is flawed on this point. 首相の考えはこの点で間違っていると私は主張するものだ
maintain [他] 《ややフォーマル》(同意[信用]してくれなくても)主張し続ける ◇The men *maintained* (that) they were out of the country when the crime was committed. 男たちは犯行が行われたとき自分たちは国外にいたと主張し続けた ◇She has always *maintained* her innocence. 彼女は一貫して自分の無実を主張し続けている
assert [他] 《フォーマル》(はっきり・断固として)主張する, 断言する ◇She continued to *assert* her innocence. 彼女は自分の無実を断固として主張し続けた ◇She continued to *assert* that she was innocent. 彼女は自分が無実であることを断固として主張し続けた
protest [他] (告発されている[信じてくれない]ときに断固として)主張する, 抗議する ◇She has always *protested* her innocence. 彼女は常に自分の無実を主張している ◇He *protested* that the journey was too far by car. 彼はその旅(程)は車では遠すぎると言い張った ◇'That's not what you said earlier!' Jane *protested*. 「前に言ったことと違うじゃない」とジェーンは抗議した
affirm [他] 《フォーマル》(断固として[公然と])主張する, 断言する, 支持を表明する ◇I can *affirm* that no one will lose their job. 誰も職を失うことはないと断言できます ◇Both sides *affirmed* their commitment to the ceasefire. 双方とも停戦を確約した

ノート **assert**と**affirm**の使い分け：assertは人からの信用と支持を求めるときに「主張」し、affirmは人を安心させるために「断言」する.

class 名

1 class・course・programme・curriculum・syllabus
教育[養成]を目的として教えられる[学ばれる]一連の教科や技能
【類語訳】授業, 講義, 履修科目, 講座, カリキュラム, シラバス

class

文型&コロケーション

- a/ the course/ programme/ curriculum/ syllabus **for** sb/ sth
- **in** a/ the class/ course/ programme/ curriculum/ syllabus
- **on** a/ the course/ programme/ curriculum/ syllabus
- a **narrow/ wide/ broad** curriculum/ syllabus
- a **core** programme/ curriculum/ syllabus
- a **day/ evening** class/ course/ programme
- a/ an **English/ history/ mathematics, etc.** class/ course/ programme/ curriculum/ syllabus
- to **design/ plan** a class/ course/ programme/ curriculum/ syllabus
- to **follow/ teach/ offer** a/ the course/ programme/ curriculum/ syllabus
- to **run/ take/ do/ enrol on/ sign up for** a class/ course/ programme
- to **complete** a class/ course/ programme/ syllabus
- a/ the **class/ course/ programme/ curriculum/ syllabus covers** sth

class [C] (または **classes** [複数で]) (特定の教科・技能に関する)授業, 講義 ◇I'm taking a management *class* this semester. 今学期は経営の授業を取るつもりだ ◇The college runs specialist language *classes*. その大学では学習者の専門分野別の語学講座が開かれている ◇Are you still doing your French evening *class*?《英》まだフランス語の夜間授業を取っていますか ◇I'm taking *night classes* in art appreciation.《米》私は美術鑑賞の夜間講義を受講している

course [C]《英 or フォーマル, 米》(特定の教科に関する)授業 [講義], 講座 ◇She's taking a *course in* Art and Design. 彼女は「アートとデザイン」の講義を取っている ◇I've signed up for an evening *course on* media techniques. 私は「メディア・テクニック」の夜間の講義を履修登録した ◇Over 50 students have enrolled *on the course*.《英》50名以上の学生がその講義に登録している ❶《米》ではこの意味でのcourseはフォーマルあるいは公式な言い回しでしか用いられない。◆ Registration for *courses* begins tomorrow. (科目の履修登録は明日から始まる). 日常会話ではclassを用いる。◆ What *classes* did you register for? (どの科目を登録したの).《英》ではcourseはフォーマルな書き言葉にも日常の話し言葉にも用いられる。《英》ではcourseは試験や資格取得のための大学の「課程」を意味することもある。この意味では《米》ではcourseの代わりにprogramが用いられる。◆ It's a four-year *course*. (それは4年課程です). ◆ She had taught on a range of undergraduate *courses*. (彼女は学部課程のさまざまな講座で教鞭をとった).

programme《英》(または特に米で **program**) [C] (大学の)教育課程 ◇Take a look at our new history and language *programs*. 当校の新しい歴史と語学の教育課程を見てください ◇We especially encourage those from minorities to apply for our *degree programs*. 特に少数民族の受験生に当大学の学位課程に志願することを勧めています ◇We urge as many people as possible to enrol on our management training *programme*. 当校はできるだけ多くの人々への管理者養成講座への登録を促しております ❶《米》ではprogramは大学での「課程」を表す一般的な語であり、この場合はdegree program (教育[学位]課程)の短縮形である。degree programは数多くのclasses (講義)・courses (講座)から成る。program は《英》ではundergraduate programmes (学部課程)を指す言葉として一般的になりつつある。

curriculum (複 **curricula, curriculums**) [C, ふつう単数で] (学校・大学の)カリキュラム, 履修課程 ◇The school *curriculum* should be as broad as possible. 学校のカリキュラムはできるだけ幅広いものであるべきだ ◇These subjects are not part of the core *curriculum* (= consisting of the most basic and important subjects). これらの科目はカリキュラムの中心をなすものではない ◇They all have to study French because it's *on the curriculum*.《英》カリキュラムに含まれているので必ず全員フランス語を学ばなければならない ◇Nutrition education is now *in the curriculum*.《米》現在では栄養教育がカリキュラムに含まれています

> ノート **on** と **in** の使い分け:《英》では学生が course (講座) や programme (課程) を on (受講している)、または科目が curriculum (カリキュラム) や syllabus (シラバス) に on (含まれている) と用いるのがふつう。《米》では学生が program (課程) に in (登録している)、科目が curriculum (カリキュラム) や syllabus (シラバス) に in (含まれている) と用いられる。

syllabus [C, ふつう単数で]《英》(学校・大学の)シラバス, 講義概要 ◇A group of experienced teachers were asked to design a new English *syllabus*. 経験豊かな教師のグループが新しい英語のシラバスを作成するよう求められた ◇The courses do not follow any particular exam *syllabus*. それらの科目はシラバスで特に試験のことは触れていない ❶《米》ではsyllabusは履修科目の「講義概要」を指し、学生に学期中の講義内容を知らせるためにそのコピーが授業の初日に配られることがある。

2 class・session・lesson・seminar・workshop・tutorial・period

学習に費やされるある一定の時間を表す
【類語訳】授業, レッスン, ゼミ, 研究会, 討論会, 時限

文型&コロケーション

- a class/ session/ lesson/ seminar/ workshop/ tutorial **on** sth
- **in/ during** a class/ session/ lesson/ seminar/ workshop/ tutorial/ period
- **at** a class/ session/ lesson/ seminar/ workshop/ tutorial
- to **go to/ attend** a class/ session/ lesson/ seminar/ workshop/ tutorial
- to **miss** a class/ session/ lesson/ seminar/ workshop/ tutorial/ period
- to **have** a class/ lesson/ seminar/ workshop/ tutorial
- to **give/ conduct** a class/ session/ lesson/ seminar/ workshop/ tutorial
- to **teach** a class/ session/ lesson/ seminar
- to **hold/ run** a class/ session/ lesson/ seminar/ workshop
- a class/ session/ lesson/ seminar/ workshop/ tutorial **takes place**

class [C, U] 授業(時間) ◇I have an English *class* at 11. 英語の授業が11時からあります ◇Please see me after *class*. 授業の後で私のところに来てください ◇She works hard *in class* (= during lessons). 彼女は授業に熱心に参加している

session [C] 授業時間, 課業 ◇a photo/recording/ training *session* 撮影/レコーディング/トレーニングの時間 ◇Your presentation will be part of the morning *session*. あなたの発表は午前の部で行われる予定です ◇The programme is made up of 12 two-hour *sessions*. そ

の課程は12回の2時間授業から成っています

lesson [C] 授業[稽古]時間, レッスン ◇New students get *lessons in* how to use the library. 新入生は図書館の利用法に関する講習を受けている ◇piano/driving *lessons* ピアノのレッスン/自動車運転の教習 ◇I've decided to *take* golf *lessons*. 私はゴルフのレッスンを受けることに決めた ◇She made a living giving private *lessons* in English. 彼女は英語の個人レッスンをして生計を立てた ◇What did we do last *lesson*?《特に英》前回の授業では何をしましたか

|ノート| **class**と**lesson**の使い分け：classは常にグループで一緒に学ぶもの. lessonはグループあるいは個人で学ぶもの.

seminar [C] (大学での)ゼミ；(養成・議論を目的とした)セミナー, 研究[討論]会 ◇Teaching is by lectures and *seminars*. 授業は講義形式とゼミ形式で行われます ◇a *seminar* room/group ゼミの教室/グループ ◇The company organizes management *seminars*. その会社はマネージメント研究会を開いている

workshop [C] (特定のテーマに関する)研究[討論, 講習]会 ◇a drama/poetry *workshop* 劇[詩]の研究会 ◇There are two management development *workshops* per year. 管理職養成の勉強会が年に2回行われている

tutorial [C] (大学での)個別指導授業 ◇Students have to write an essay for each weekly *tutorial*. 学生たちは毎週1回の個別指導授業で小論を一つ書かねばならない ☞ **tutor** (TEACHER)

period [C] (学校・大学の)授業時間, 時限, こま ◇We've got French next *period*. 次の時間はフランス語だ ◇I have two *free/study periods* (= for private study) on Tuesday afternoons. 毎週火曜日の午後は自由[自習]時間が2こまある

---

3 class・level・position・rank・status・rating・standing・ranking・grade
地位や権限の程度に基づく社会や組織内での位置づけ, 人や物事の良し悪しや重要性の尺度
【類語訳】階級, 階層, 地位, 等級

|文型&コロケーション|
▶ sb's **class**/ **level**/ **position**/ **rank**/ **status**/ **standing**/ **ranking** **in**/ **within** sth
▶ a/ the **high**/ **higher** level/ position/ rank/ status/ rating/ standing/ ranking/ grade
▶ a/ the **low**/ **lower** class/ level/ position/ rank/ status/ rating/ standing/ ranking/ grade
▶ the **top** level/ rank/ rating/ ranking/ grade
▶ the **upper** class/ level/ rank
▶ the **middle** class/ level/ rank/ ranking/ grade
▶ a/ the **senior** level/ position/ rank/ grade
▶ sb's **social** class/ position/ rank/ status/ standing/ ranking
▶ a/ sb's **professional** class/ status/ standing
▶ to **improve** your position/ status/ standing/ ranking
▶ to **have** a ... rank/ rating/ status/ standing
▶ to **give (sb/ sth)** a status/ rating/ ranking
▶ to **achieve** a rank/ status/ rating
▶ sb's **class**/ position/ rank/ status/ standing **in society**
▶ a/ the **class**/ level/ ranks **of society**

class 《C+単数・複数動詞, U》(社会的・経済的な)階級, 階層；階級[身分]制度 ◇His ideas had an appeal among the wealthy, professional *classes*. 彼の思想は富裕層, 知的職業階級の間で受けた ◇Do you consider yourself to be middle *class*? あなたは自分が中流階級であると思いますか ◇A lot of British comedy is based on *class* differences. イギリスの喜劇の多くは階級格差に基づいたものだ ◇The old *class system* is not appropriate in a modern age. 古い階級制度は現代にはふさわしくない ☞ **the upper class** (ELITE)

level [C] (社会・組織内における)地位, 職位 ◇He promised reforms at all *levels* of government. 彼は政府のあらゆる階層における改革を約束した ◇She reached a very high *level* at a very young age. 彼女はとても若くして非常に高い地位まで昇りつめた ◇The decision is being made at top *level*. その決定は首脳部で下されることになっている

position [C, U] (人[組織内で]の)地位, 立場 ◇We need to improve the *position* of women and girls in these societies. 私たちはこれらの社会での女性と少女の地位を向上させる必要がある ◇The company has a dominant *position* in the world market. その会社は世界市場において支配的な地位を占めている ◇Wealth and *position* are not important to her. 富や地位は彼女にとって重要なことではない

rank [C, U] (組織・社会での重要な)地位, 職位；(軍隊・警察における)階級, 等級 ◇She *rose through the ranks* to become managing director (= she started in a low position). 彼女は出世の階段を上り取締役となった ◇She was not used to mixing with people of high social *rank*. 彼女は社会的地位の高い人々との交流に慣れていなかった ◇He was promoted to the *rank* of major. 彼は少佐の階級に昇進した ◇I gave them only my name, *rank* and serial number. 私は彼らに名前と階級と認識番号のみを伝えた

status [U, C, ふつう単数で] (社会的・職業的)地位, 身分 ◇The only jobs on offer were of low *status* and badly paid. 募集のある仕事には地位・給料ともに低いものしかなかった ◇How do people perceive the *status* of the full-time mother? 世間では専業主婦の身分はどのように考えられていますか

rating [C] (良し悪し・重要性・人気などに関する)格付け, 等級 ◇It was a very good *rating* for an amateur performance. その評価は素人の演奏に対するものとしては非常に高いものだった ◇The poll gave an *approval rating* of 39% for the president. 世論調査の結果, 大統領に対する支持率は39%だった ☞ **rate** (RANK), **rate** (JUDGE)

standing [U] (グループ・組織内における)地位, 評判 ◇The prime minister needs to improve his *standing with* the public. 首相は国民からの評判を向上させる必要がある ◇Their *standing* as a profession has declined in recent years. 彼らの職業の評判は近年下がっている

ranking [C] (スポーツにおける)ランキング, 番付 ◇She has retained her No. 1 *world ranking*. 彼女は世界ランキング1位を保持している ◇The product has consistently been given a high *ranking* by consumer groups. その製品は消費者グループの評価ランキングで常に上位を占めてきた ☞ **rank** (RANK)

grade [C] (組織内での報酬と関わる)地位, 職位, 階級, 等級 ◇She's still only on a secretarial *grade*. 彼女の身分はまだ一介の秘書でしかない ◇The higher *grades* within the organization usually get bigger pay rises. 組織内での職位が上級であればあるほど, ふつう昇給も大きい

classify 動

classify・file・sort・categorize・class・group・bracket
人や物事を類似のものに仕分ける
【類語訳】分類する，保管する，ファイルする，整理する

文型&コロケーション
- to classify/ sort/ categorize/ group sb/ sth **according to** sth
- to classify/ file/ categorize/ class/ group/ bracket sb/ sth **as** sth
- to classify/ file/ sort/ categorize/ class/ group sb/ sth **under** sth
- to classify/ categorize/ class/ group/ bracket sb/ sth **with** sth
- to classify/ sort/ categorize/ group sb/ sth **into** sth
- to classify/ sort/ categorize/ group sb/ sth **by** sth
- to classify/ file/ class sth **alongside** sth
- to classify/ file/ class/ group/ bracket sb/ sth **together**

classify [他] (共通の特徴に従って) 分類する ◇The books in the library are *classified* according to subject. 図書館の本はテーマ別に分類されている ◇Soils can be *classified* under two main headings. 土壌は大きく2つの項に分けられる ◇The study recorded and *classified* accidents over a period of a year. その調査では1年間に起きた事故を記録し分類した ◇Eleven accidents were *classified* as major. 11件の事故が大事故と分類された ☞ **classification** (CATEGORY)

file [他] (特定の場所・順序に) 保管する, ファイルする; (書類を) ファイルに綴じる ◇The forms should be *filed* alphabetically. 用紙はアルファベット順にファイルするのが決まりだ ◇Wynne-Jones should be *filed* under 'W'. ウィン＝ジョーンズは「W」の項目にファイルされます ◇The report was *filed away* in the archives. 報告書は整理の上書庫に保管された ☞ **file** (DOCUMENT)

sort [他] (種類別に) 分類 [整理, 分別] する ◇The mail is *sorted* automatically. 郵便物は自動的に分別されます ◇The documents were *sorted* by age and type. 書類は年代と種類別に分類された ◇Waste is *sorted* for recycling. ごみは再利用の目的で分別されます ☞ **sort** (KIND)

categorize (英でまた -**se**) [他] 分類する ◇Her latest work cannot be *categorized* as either a novel or an autobiography. 彼女の最新作は小説にも自伝にも分類することができない ◇Some types of investment risk are difficult to *categorize*. 投資リスクの種類には分類し難いものもある ☞ **category** (CATEGORY)

class [他, しばしば受身で] 分類する, (特定の種類であると) 判断する ◇Prisoners *classed* as illiterate were given a basic education. 読み書きができないと判断された囚人には基礎教育が施された ◇I wouldn't have *classed* you as a Shakespeare fan. 私ならあなたをシェイクスピアのファンだとは見分けはしなかっただろう ☞ **class** (CATEGORY)

group [他] (共通の特徴に従って) 分類する, ひとまとまりにして考える ◇Topics for the second year can be *grouped* under three headings. 2年次で学ぶテーマは三つの種類にまとめることができる

bracket [他, しばしば受身で] (類似 [関連] 性によって) 一くくりにする, 同類とみなす ◇The two writers are often *bracketed* together by critics. その二人の作家は評論家からしばしば一くくりにして扱われる ☞ **bracket** (CATEGORY)

clean 動 ☞ BRUSH

clean・wash・rinse・cleanse・hose・shampoo・dry-clean・bathe
水や石鹸を使って物から汚れを取り除く
【類語訳】掃除する, 清掃する, きれいになる, 洗う, 洗える, ゆすぐ

文型&コロケーション
- to clean/ wash/ rinse/ cleanse/ bathe sth **in/ with** sth
- to clean/ wash/ rinse sth **from** sth
- to clean/ wash/ rinse sth **out**
- to clean/ wash/ hose sth **down**
- to clean/ wash/ cleanse/ bathe a **wound**
- to clean/ wash/ rinse the **glasses**
- to clean/ wash/ hose (down) the **car**
- to clean/ wash the **windows/ floor**
- to wash/ rinse/ shampoo your **hair**
- to **have** sth cleaned/ washed/ shampooed/ dry-cleaned

clean [他, 自] (水・化学薬品などで) きれいにする, 掃除 [清掃] する; きれいになる ◇The villa is *cleaned* twice a week. 週に2度の屋敷は清掃される ◇This product *cleans* baths very effectively. この製品でお風呂は非常にきれいになる ◇Have you *cleaned* your teeth? 歯は磨いたの ◇This coat is filthy. I'll have it *cleaned* (= dry-cleaned). このコートはひどく汚い。クリーニングに出そう ◇I must *clean* the fish tank out. 魚の水槽をきれいに掃除しないと ◇I spent all day cooking and *cleaning*. 一日中，料理やら掃除やらをしていた ◇This oven *cleans* easily (= is easy to clean). このオーブンは掃除が楽だ ☞ **clean (sth) up** (TIDY)

wash [他, 自] (水・石鹸で) 洗う, 洗濯する; (衣類・織物が色落ちせず [傷めず] に) 洗濯できる, 洗える ◇He quickly *washed* his hands and face. 彼は急いで手と顔を洗った ◇*Wash* the fruit thoroughly before eating. 食べる前に果物はよく洗いましょう ◇These jeans need *washing*. このジーンズは洗濯する必要がある ◇She *washed* the blood from his face. 彼女は彼の顔から血を洗い落としてやった ◇The beach had been *washed* clean by the tide. 浜は潮に洗われてきれいになっていた ◇*Wash* down the walls before painting them. 塗装する前に壁をきれいに洗います ◇This sweater *washes* well. このセーターはしっかり洗濯できる ☞ **wash, wash up** (WASH)

rinse [他] ゆすぐ, 水 [すすぎ] で洗う; (石鹸を) 洗い [すすぎ] 落とす ◇*Rinse* the dishes in warm water. 温水で皿をゆすいでください ◇*Rinse* the cup out before use. 使用前にカップをよくゆすいでください ◇Make sure you *rinse* all the soap out. 必ず石鹸を完全に洗い落としてください ◇I wanted to *rinse* the taste out of my mouth. 口をゆすいでその後味を洗い落としたかった ☞ **rinse** (BATH)

cleanse [他] (肌・傷を) 洗浄 [浄化] する ◇a lotion to *cleanse* the face/skin 顔/肌を洗浄するローション ◇This is a treatment to *cleanse* the body **of** toxins. これは体を浄化して毒素を取り除く治療法だ

hose [他] ホースで水をかける ◇I'll just *hose* down the car. ホースで車の水洗いだけするよ ◇Firemen *hosed* the burning car. 消防士は燃えている車にホースで水をかけた

shampoo [他] (髪・カーペット・家具を) シャンプー [液体洗剤] で洗う ◇She showered and *shampooed* her hair. 彼女はシャワーで髪をシャンプーした ◇If you can afford it, have the carpet *shampooed* professionally. お金の余

↪clean　　　　　　　　　　　　　　　clean, clear

裕があれば、カーペットを業者にクリーニングしてもらいなさい
,dry-'clean [他, しばしば受身で] ドライクリーニングする ◇I took the coat in to be *dry-cleaned*. 私はコートをクリーニングに出した
bathe [他] (傷・体の一部を)水で洗う ◇*Bathe* the wound and apply a clean dressing. 傷を水で洗って清潔な包帯を巻きなさい

clean 形

clean・pure・sterile・hygienic・spotless
物が汚れていないことを表す
【類語訳】清潔な、洗った、無菌の、殺菌した、衛生的な

▸ 文型&コロケーション
▸ clean/ pure/ sterile **(drinking) water**
▸ clean/ pure **air**
▸ clean/ sterile/ hygienic **conditions**
▸ (a) clean/ sterile **equipment/ dressing/ needle**
▸ **to keep sth** clean/ pure/ sterile/ spotless
▸ **very** clean/ pure/ hygienic
▸ **completely** clean/ sterile

clean 清潔な;きれいな;汚染されていない ◇Are your hands *clean*? 手はきれい ◇He wiped his plate *clean* with a piece of bread. 彼は一切れのパンで皿をきれいにふいた ◇It is your responsibility to keep the room ***clean and tidy***. 《英》部屋を清潔に整理整頓しておくのはあなたの責任です ◇Keep your room ***neat and clean***. 《米》部屋をきちんときれいにしておくように ◇I can't find a *clean* shirt (= one that I haven't worn since it was washed). 洗濯したシャツが見つからない ◇Cats are very *clean* animals. ネコはとてもきれい好きな動物だ ◇Thousands were left without food or *clean* drinking water. 何千もの人々が食料もきれいな飲み水もないままにされた 反意 **dirty (DIRTY)**
pure (空気・水が)きれいな、澄んだ ◇Much of the population still does not have access to *pure* drinking water. 今もなお住民の多くがきれいな飲み水を手にできない状態にある ◇The mountain air was sweet and *pure*. 山の空気はおいしくて澄んでいた
sterile 無菌の、殺菌[滅菌]した ◇All the equipment used is new and *sterile*. 使用器具はすべて未使用で無菌です
hygienic 衛生的な ◇Food must be prepared in *hygienic* conditions. 食べ物は衛生的な状態で用意されなければならない ◇The kitchen didn't look very *hygienic*. 台所はあまり衛生的には見えなかった 反意 **unhygienic**
▸ **hygienically** 副 ◇Medical supplies are disposed of *hygienically*. 医療用品は衛生的に廃棄されている
spotless 染み[汚れ, ちり]一つない ◇She keeps the house absolutely *spotless*. 彼女は家中まったくちり一つないようにしている ◇He wore a smart jacket and a *spotless* white shirt. 彼はきちんとしたジャケットと染み一つない白のシャツを着ていた
▸ **spotlessly** 副 ◇The room was poorly furnished but *spotlessly* clean. 家具は貧相だったが、その部屋にはちり一つ落ちていなかった

clear 動

clear・empty・drain・unload・unpack

ある場所から物をのける、ある物の中から物を出す
【類語訳】片づける、取り除く、空にする、空ける、抜き取る、取り出す

▸ 文型&コロケーション
▸ to clear/ empty/ drain sth **of** sth
▸ to empty/ drain/ unload the **contents** of sth
▸ to empty/ unpack a **suitcase/ bag**
▸ to unload/ unpack **a car/ the shopping**
▸ to empty/ drain **water** from sth
▸ to empty/ drain your **glass**

clear [他] (不要な物を)片づける、取り除く ◇*Clear* those papers off the desk. 机の上の書類を全部片づけなさい ◇It's your turn to ***clear the table*** (= take away the dirty plates and other things after a meal). 君が食卓を片づける番だよ ◇She *cleared* a space on the sofa for him to sit down. 彼女は彼が座れるようにソファの上を片づけた ◇It was several hours before the road was *cleared* after the accident. 事故後の道路の片づけに数時間かかった ◇It's time your toys were ***cleared away***. おもちゃを片づける時間ですよ ❶ clear away は目的語なしで用いることも可能。◆ He *cleared away* and made coffee. (彼はテーブルの上を片づけてからコーヒーを淹れた).
empty [他] (容器を)空にする ;(中身を)出す、空ける ◇I *emptied out* my pockets but could not find my keys. 私はポケットの中を空にしたが鍵は見つからなかった ◇She *emptied* the water out of the vase. 彼女は花瓶の水を空けた ◇He *emptied* the ashtrays, washed the glasses and went to bed. 彼は灰皿を空け、グラスを洗ってから寝た ◇The room had been *emptied* of all furniture. 部屋から家具がすべて撤去されていた ◇She *emptied* the contents of her bag onto the table. 彼女はバッグの中身をテーブルの上に出した 反意 **fill (FILL)**, ☞ **empty (EMPTY)**
drain [他] (液体を)抜く、水気を切る ◇*Drain* and rinse the pasta. パスタのゆで湯を切って水洗いをして ◇The marshes have been *drained*. 沼地は水抜きされている ◇You will need to turn off the water and *drain* the tank. 水道を止めて、タンクの水を抜く必要があるだろう
unload [他, 自] (乗り物・船から)荷を降ろす ;(弾丸・フィルムを)銃器[カメラ]から抜き取る ◇Everyone helped to *unload* the luggage from the car. 全員で協力して車から荷物を降ろした ◇This isn't a suitable place to *unload* the van. ここはバンの荷降ろしに適した場所ではない ◇The truck driver was waiting to *unload*. トラックの運転手は荷降ろしを待っていた ◇Each time a gun is laid down it must first be broken and *unloaded*. 小銃を横にして置く場合は、毎回まず二つに折って弾丸を抜き取らなければならない 反意 **load (FILL)**
unpack [他, 自] (スーツケース・バッグなどの中身を)取り出す、荷[包み]を解く ◇I *unpacked* my bags as soon as I arrived. 到着後すぐに私はバッグの中身を取り出した ◇She *unpacked* all the clothes she needed and left the rest in the case. 彼女は必要な衣類をすべて取り出し、残りをケースの中に残しておいた ◇She went to her room to *unpack*. 彼女は荷を解きに自分の部屋に行った 反意 **pack (FILL)**

clear

clear 形 ☞ VISIBLE

1 ☞ MARKED
clear・obvious・apparent・evident・plain・self-evident
事実[性質, 状況]を把握しやすくて疑いのないことを表す
【類語訳】明らかな、明白な、疑う余地のない、自明の、わかりきった

文型&コロケーション
▸ clear/ obvious/ apparent/ evident/ plain/ self-evident **to** sb/ sth
▸ clear/ obvious/ apparent/ evident/ plain/ self-evident **from/ in** sb/ sth
▸ clear/ obvious/ apparent/ evident/ self-evident **what.../ that...**
▸ clear/ obvious/ apparent/ evident/ plain **who/ how/ where/ why...**
▸ to **seem** clear/ obvious/ apparent/ evident/ plain/ self-evident
▸ to **become/ make sth** clear/ obvious/ apparent/ evident/ plain
▸ **very/ quite/ perfectly** clear/ obvious/ apparent/ evident/ plain
▸ **all too** clear/ obvious/ apparent/ evident/ plain
▸ **fairly** clear/ obvious/ evident/ plain/ self-evident
▸ **far from** clear/ obvious/ evident/ self-evident
▸ **by no means** clear/ obvious/ self-evident

clear 明らかな、明白な、疑う余地のない ◇It was quite *clear* to me that she was lying. 彼女が嘘をついていることは私にははっきりしていた ◇It is not *clear* what they want us to do. 彼らが私たちに何をさせたいのかよくわからない ◇It is *clear* from the graph that sales have dropped sharply. グラフから明らかなとおり、売り上げが急激に落ち込んでいる ◇This is a *clear* case of fraud. これは紛れもない詐欺事件だ ◇She won the election by a *clear majority*. 彼女は明白に過半数を得て選挙に勝利した
反義 **unclear** (UNCLEAR)
▸ **clearly** 副 ◇*Clearly*, this will cost a lot more than we realized. 明らかにこれは思った以上にコストがかかるだろう

obvious 明らかな、明白な ◇It's *obvious* from what she said that something is wrong. 彼女の発言からおかしいことは明らかだ ◇I know you don't like her but try not to make it so *obvious*. 君は彼女を好きじゃないってことはわかるが、そんなにあからさまにしないように ◇He put his book down with *obvious* annoyance. 彼は見るからにいらいらして本を下に置いた ◇*For obvious reasons*, I'd prefer not to give my name. おわかりいただけると思いますが私は名前を言いたくありません
▸ **obviously** 副 ◇He was *obviously* drunk. 彼は見るからに酔っていた ◇I didn't realize it was a formal occasion.' '*Obviously*!' (= I can see by the way you are dressed) 「ここがフォーマルな場だとは気づかなかった」「(服装を見る限り)そうだろうね」

apparent [名詞の前はまれ] 《ややフォーマル》 明らかな、明白な ◇His devotion to her was increasingly *apparent*. 彼の彼女に対する一途な思いはだんだん明らかになった ◇It soon became *apparent* to everyone that he couldn't sing. 彼が歌えないことはすぐに皆にわかった ◇Then, *for no apparent reason*, the train suddenly stopped. その時、理由は定かではないが、電車が突然止まった

evident 《ややフォーマル》明らかな、明白な ◇The growing interest in history is clearly *evident* in the number of people visiting museums. 博物館を訪れる人々の数から歴史に対する関心の高まりがはっきりわかる ◇The orchestra played with *evident* enjoyment. オーケストラは見るからに楽しそうに演奏した
▸ **evidently** 副 ◇She walked slowly down the road, *evidently* in pain. 明らかに痛そうに彼女は道をゆっくり歩いておりた ◇'I'm afraid I couldn't finish the work last night.' '*Evidently* not.' 「あいにく昨晩は仕事を終わらせることができなくて」「見ればわかるよ」

plain 明らかな、明白な ◇He *made it* very *plain* that he wanted us to leave. 彼は私たちに立ち去ってほしいとはっきり意思表示した ◇She made her annoyance *plain*. 彼女はいら立ちを表に出した ◇The facts were *plain to see*. そうした事実は一目瞭然だった
▸ **plainly** 副 ◇She had no right to interfere in what was *plainly* a family matter. 家庭の事情だとはっきりしていることに口を挟む権利は彼女にはなかった ◇*Plainly* something was wrong. 明らかに何かがおかしかった

|ノート| これらの語はほとんど同じ意味で用いられるが、言語使用域や用法にわずかな違いがある。make sth clear/plain は意図的な行為。make sth obvious はふつう意図せず行うことを指す。◆I hope I *make* myself *clear/plain*. (私は自分の気持ちをわかってもらいたい)。✗I hope I *make* myself *obvious*. ◆Try not to *make* your dislike so *obvious*. (そんなにあからさまに嫌がるのはよしなさい)。✗Try not to *make* it so *clear/plain*. clear majority, for obvious reasons, for no apparent reason, plain to seeという表現では、他の語とは置き換えはできない。apparentとevidentは両語ともややフォーマルだが、obviousとの言い換えは常に可能。obviousとevidentは感情を表す名詞の前に用いられることもあり、その感情が目に見えることを意味する。◆Jane took the letter and read it out with *obvious/evident* reluctance. (ジェーンは手紙を取り上げ、見るからに嫌そうに読み上げた)。apparent reluctance (一見嫌そうな様子)のapparentは「見せかけの」の意味。☞ **apparent** (APPARENT)

self-'evident 自明の、わかりきった ◇The dangers of such action are *self-evident*. そのような行為がもたらす危険はわかりきっている ◇a *self-evident* truth 自明の真理

2 clear・explicit・plain・express・accessible・unambiguous・intelligible・comprehensible・lucid
話や文章がわかりやすくて混乱を招かないことを表す
【類語訳】明確な、明快な、理解しやすい、明示的な、平易な

文型&コロケーション
▸ clear/ explicit/ unambiguous **about** sth
▸ clear/ plain/ accessible/ intelligible/ comprehensible **to** sb
▸ clear/ explicit/ express **instructions/ directions**
▸ a clear/ an accessible/ a lucid **style**
▸ clear/ plain/ intelligible/ comprehensible **language/ English**
▸ to **make** sth clear/ explicit/ plain/ accessible/ intelligible/ comprehensible (to sb)
▸ to **make yourself** clear/ explicit/ plain
▸ to **make it** clear/ explicit/ plain **that...**
▸ **quite** clear/ explicit/ plain/ accessible/ unambiguous/ intelligible/ comprehensible
▸ **perfectly** clear/ plain/ intelligible/ comprehensible

↳**clear**

clear 明確な, 明快な, 理解しやすい, はっきりとした ◇She gave me *clear* and precise directions. 彼女は私に明確で的確な指示をくれた ◇Your meaning needs to be *crystal clear*. あなたの意図を極めて明確にする必要がある ◇You'll do as you're told. Is that *clear*? 君は言われたとおりにしなさい。わかった ◇This behaviour must stop! Do I make myself *clear*? (= used when you are angrily telling sb what they should do). こんなことはやめなさい。わかったか 反意 **unclear** (UNCLEAR), **confusing** (CONFUSING)
▶**clearly** 副 ◇She explained everything very *clearly*. 彼女はすべてを非常に明確に説明した

explicit (ややフォーマル) 明確に[はっきりと]述べられた, 明示的な; あからさまな ◇The author is quite *explicit* about her political bias. 作者は彼女の政治的偏向に関して実に明確に述べている ◇The reasons for the decisions should be made *explicit*. 決定の理由を明示すべきだ ◇She made some very *explicit* references to her personal life. 彼女は私の私生活についていくつか非常にはっきりと言及した ❶ explicit はあからさまで詳細な性描写の本・映画・言葉遣い・絵画についても用いられる。◆sexually *explicit* films/material/language (性描写があからさまな映画/題材/言葉遣い)。explicit language は sexuallyと明記されていなくても常に「卑猥な言葉遣い」を意味する。「明快でわかりやすい言葉遣い」を言いたい場合は clear, plain, unambiguous を用いる。
▶**explicitly** 副 ◇He made this point much more *explicitly* in his next speech. 彼は次のスピーチでこの点についてさらにはっきりと述べた

plain 明確な, 明快な, 理解しやすい, はっきりとした, 平易な ◇He made it *plain* that we should leave. 彼は私たちはもう立ち去るべきだとはっきりさせた ◇Her intentions were *plain* enough. 彼女の意図は見え見えだった ◇Teachers should encourage students to write in *plain* English. 教師は生徒に平易な英語で書くよう促すべきだ ☞ **plain** (PLAIN 2)
▶**plainly** 副 ◇The agreement *plainly* states that all damage must be paid for. 契約書にはあらゆる損害が賠償の対象となると明確に書かれている

express (フォーマル) (希望・目的が)明確に[はっきりと]述べられた ◇It was his *express wish* that you should have his gold watch after he died. 自分が死んだら金時計をあなたに託すことを彼は言葉にして望んでいた ◇I came here with the *express purpose* of speaking with the manager. 支配人と話をするという明確な目的を持って私はここに来た
▶**expressly** 副 ◇She was *expressly* forbidden to touch my papers. 私の書類には触れてはいけないと彼女ははっきり言われていた

accessible (特に書き言葉) (たいていの人にとって)理解しやすい ◇Her poetry is always very *accessible*. 彼女の詩はいつもとてもわかりやすい ◇The programme tries to make science more *accessible* to young people. その番組は若い人たちにとって科学をもっととっつきやすいものにしようと試みている

unambiguous (一つの解釈しかないため)曖昧でない, 明確な ◇The message was clear and *unambiguous*: get out of town. メッセージは明確ではっきりとしていた。町から出て行け, と 反意 **ambiguous** (MISLEADING)
▶**unambiguously** 副 ◇The essential information should be displayed clearly and *unambiguously*. 極めて重要な情報は明確かつ曖昧さを残さずに開示されるべきだ

intelligible (ややフォーマル) 理解可能な ◇The child's speech was barely *intelligible*. その子の話はかろうじて理解可能なものだった 反意 **unintelligible** (CONFUSING)
▶**intelligibly** 副 ◇You need to be able to write clearly and *intelligibly*. 君ははっきりとわかりやすく書けるようにならないといけない

comprehensible (ややフォーマル) 理解可能な ◇The novel is easily *comprehensible* to the average reader. その小説はふつうの読者なら簡単に理解できる 反意 **incomprehensible** (CONFUSING)

ノート **intelligible** と **comprehensible** の使い分け: これらの語は非常によく似ているので, たいていの場合はどちらも使用できる。intelligible は人の話・言葉遣いについて, comprehensible は思想・行動・方法について用いられる傾向がいくぶん強い。

lucid (特に書き言葉) (書き方が)明快な, 理解しやすい ◇She writes in a very *lucid* style. 彼女は非常に明快な文体で書く ◇It was a *lucid* account of the main facts of the case. それは事件の重要な事実をわかりやすく伝える説明だった

3 clear • transparent • translucent • colourless • see-through
物が透けて見えることを表す
【類語訳】透明な, 透き通った, 澄んだ, 半透明の, 無色の, 青ざめた, シースルーの

文型&コロケーション
▸ clear/ transparent/ translucent **glass**
▸ clear/ transparent/ see-through **plastic**
▸ clear/ transparent/ colourless **varnish**
▸ a clear/ colourless **liquid**
▸ clear/ translucent **skin**
▸ almost *transparent/ translucent/ colourless*

clear 透明な, 透き通った, 澄んだ ◇Items must be carried in a *clear* plastic bag. 商品は必ず透明なビニール袋に入れてお持ちください ◇The water was so *clear* we could see the bottom of the lake. 水が澄んでいたので湖の底を見ることができた ◇The water comes out of the spring *crystal clear* (= completely clear) and totally pure. その水は文字通り澄みきっていてこの上なく清らかな泉から湧き出ている 反意 **cloudy** ❶ cloudy は液体が塵などの小さな粒子をたくさん含んでいて「濁った」の意味。◆The water looked *cloudy* and not fit to drink. (その水は濁っていて飲むのに適していないように見えた)

transparent 透明な ◇The insect's wings are almost *transparent*. その虫の翅(はね)はほとんど透明だ ◇I've covered the photographs with *transparent* plastic sheets. 私は写真を透明なプラスチックのシートで包んだ 反意 **opaque** ❶ opaque はガラス・液体が「不透明で・光を通さないこと」を表す。◆If you add water to the glass the liquid will go milky and *opaque*. (そのグラスに水を加えると液体は白濁し不透明になります)。

ノート **clear** と **transparent** の使い分け: clear はほとんどの場合, 水を表すのに用いられる。水以外の物を表す場合は, ふつう名詞の前に用いられる。◆*clear* blue water (青く澄んだ水)。◆The water was blue and *clear*. (水は青く澄んでいた)。◆a *clear* plastic bag (透明なビニール袋)。✕The plastic bag was *clear*. transparent はふつう液体(ニスは除く)ではなく, 固体について用いられる。

translucent《書き言葉》(透明ではないが光を通す)半透明の ◇The sky was a pale *translucent* blue. 空は薄曇りで青白い色をしていた ◇His skin was *translucent* with age. 彼の肌は年齢でくすんでいた

colourless〈英〉(〈米〉**colorless**) 無色の, 青ざめた ◇Water is a *colourless* compound of hydrogen and oxygen. 水は水素と酸素の無色の化合物である ◇Her illness had left her face deathly white and her lips *colourless*. 病気のせいで彼女の顔はぞっとするほど白く, 唇も青ざめていた

'see-through《ふつう名詞の前で》(衣類・織物が)シースルーの, 非常に薄くて透けて見える ◇She was wearing a *see-through* blouse. 彼女はシースルーのブラウスを着ていた

climb 動

climb・go up (sth)・scramble・clamber・mount・ascend・scale

最上部に向かって移動する
【類語訳】登る, 這い上がる, 上る, よじ登る, 登頂する

〉文型&コロケーション

▶ to climb/ go/ scramble/ clamber **up** sth
▶ to climb/ scramble/ clamber **over** sth
▶ to cilmb/ go up/ mount/ ascend a **hill**
▶ to climb/ go up/ ascend/ scale a **mountain**
▶ to climb/ ascend/ scale a **peak**
▶ to climb/ go up/ scramble up/ clamber up/ ascend/ scale a **ladder**
▶ to climb/ go up/ mount/ ascend the **stairs/ steps**
▶ to climb/ scramble over/ clamber over/ scale a **wall**
▶ to climb/ clamber over/ scale a **fence**

climb [他, 自] (苦労して)登る, 這い上がる ◇I loved *climbing* trees when I was a kid. 子どもの頃私は木登りが好きだった ◇The car slowly *climbed* the hill. 車はゆっくりと丘を上った ◇As they *climbed* higher, the air became cooler. 高く登れば登るほど, 空気は冷たくなった ◇I *climbed* through the window. 私はよじ登って窓から侵入した ◇Can you *climb* down? 降りられますか ❶ go *climbing* は趣味・スポーツとしての「山[岩]登りに行く」こと. ◆He goes *climbing* most weekends. (彼は週末はたいてい登山に行く).
➤**climb**[名][C] ◇It's an hour's *climb* to the summit. 頂上まで登るのに1時間かかります

,**go 'up sth**, ,**go 'up** 句動詞 (…に)上る, 登る ◇She went up the stairs to bed. 彼女は寝ようと思って階段を上った ◇It gets colder as you *go up* (by 0.5℃ with each 100 m rise). 上に行くほど寒くなる(100m毎に0.5℃ずつ) 反意 **go down (sth), come down (sth)** (FALL 2)

ノート **climb と go up** の使い分け:climbはふつうgo upよりも労力を必要とする行為を指す. climb/go up a hill/mountainと言うことができるが, climbは費やされる労力により大きな重点を置く. そのため, climb a wall/fence/tree(壁/柵/木によじ登る)とは言えないが, 次のようには言えない. ×go up a wall/fence/tree. 階段を上るのに疲労を感じたり, 階段が急なときはclimb the stairsと言えるが, その他の場合は単にgo up the stairsと言う.

scramble[自]《副詞や前置詞と共に》(手を使い苦労しながらすばやく)よじ登る[移動する] ◇She managed to *scramble* over the wall. 彼女は何とか壁をよじ登った ◇He *scrambled to his feet* as we came in. 私たちが中に入ると彼はあたふたと立ち上がった
➤**scramble**[名]《単数で》◇It was a stiff two-hour walk, followed by a difficult *scramble* over slimy rock faces. 2時間に及ぶ難儀な歩行の後, ぬるぬるした岩場の難しい登攀が続いた

clamber[自]《副詞や前置詞と共に》(手を使い苦労しながら)よじ登る, 移動する ◇The children *clambered* up the steep bank. 子どもたちは急な土手をよじ登った

ノート **scramble と clamber** の使い分け:scramble はスピードに, clamberは伴う困難・労力に重点を置く.

mount[他]《フォーマル》上る, 登る ◇She slowly *mounted* the steps. 彼女はゆっくりと階段を上った ◇He *mounted* the platform and addressed the crowd. 彼は演壇に上って群衆に呼びかけた

ascend[自, 他]《フォーマル》上る, 登る ◇The air became colder as we *ascended*. 登るにつれ空気は冷たくなった ◇Her heart was thumping as she *ascended* the stairs. 階段を上るにつれて彼女の心臓はどきどきした 反意 **descend** (FALL 2)
➤**ascent**[名][C, ふつう単数で] the first *ascent* of Mount Everest エベレスト山への初登攀

scale[他]《書き言葉》(非常に高く険しい物に)登頂する ◇He somehow managed to *scale* the sheer outside wall of the tower. 彼はどうにかこうにか塔の険しい外壁を上りきった

close 動

close・shut・lock・slam・draw・bolt

物の開口部を覆ったり, 開かないようにする
【類語訳】閉じる, 閉める, 閉まる, 錠を下ろす, 鍵をかける, バタン[ピシャリ]と閉める, かんぬきをかける

〉文型&コロケーション

▶ to close/ shut/ lock/ slam/ bolt a **door/ gate**
▶ to close/ shut/ lock a **window/ drawer/ case/ suitcase**
▶ to close/ shut/ slam a **shutter**
▶ to close/ shut/ bolt a **hatch**
▶ to close/ shut a/ an/ your **box/ lid/ eyes/ mouth/ flap/ valve/ book/ umbrella**
▶ to close/ draw the **curtains/ blinds**
▶ a **door/ gate** closes/ shuts/ slams
▶ sb's **eyes** close/ shut
▶ to **hear** sth close/ shut/ slam
▶ to close/ shut/ lock/ slam/ bolt sth **behind** you
▶ to close/ shut/ lock/ bolt sth **firmly**
▶ to close/ shut sth **tightly**
▶ to **half/ partly** close/ shut/ draw sth

close [他, 自] 閉じる, 閉める;閉まる ◇She *closed* the gate behind her. 彼女は入ってから門を閉めた ◇She *closed* her eyes and fell asleep immediately. 彼女は目を閉じるとすぐに眠り込んだ ◇The doors open and *close* automatically. それらは自動ドアです. 反意 **open** ❶反意語は open. ◆She *opened* her bag and took out her passport. (彼女はバッグを開けて, パスポートを取り出した). ◆The door *opened* and Alan walked in. (ドアが開いてアランは歩いて中に入った).

shut [他, 自] 閉める, 閉じる ◇I can't *shut* my suitcase — it's too full. スーツケースが閉められない — 中

↪**close**

に詰めすぎろ ◇I *shut* my eyes against the bright light. まぶしい光で目を閉じた ◇He *shut* his book and looked up. 彼は本を閉じて、見上げた ◇The window won't *shut*. 窓がどうしても閉まらない 反意 **open**

ノート **close**と**shut**の使い分け：closeとshutはどちらも同じような名詞と共に用いることができるが、箱やスーツケースなどの容器にはshutのほうがよく用いられる。またshutが、それが突然の行為であったり、closeよりも音がうるさいことを暗示する。一方closeは、よりゆっくりとそっと閉める[閉まる]ことを暗示する。 ◆*Close* your eyes and go to sleep. 目を閉じて、寝なさい) ◆She quietly *closed* the window and crept out of the room. 彼女は物音立てずに窓を閉めて、部屋からこっそり抜け出した)

lock [他, 自] 錠を下ろす、鍵をかける；鍵がかかる ◇The gates are *locked* at 6 o'clock. 門は6時に閉まる ◇This suitcase doesn't *lock*. このスーツケースは鍵がかからない ◇She *locked* her passport and money in the safe. 彼女はパスポートとお金を金庫に入れて鍵をかけた ❶名詞の lock はドア、窓、蓋などを閉めた状態にする装置で、開けるのにふつう鍵を必要とする。 反意 **unlock** ❶unlockとは鍵を使ってドア、窓、蓋などを開けることを言う。

slam (-mm-) [自, 他] バタン[ピシャリ]と閉める ◇I heard the door *slam* behind him. 彼が中に入ってドアをバタンと閉めるのが聞こえた ◇He stormed out of the house, *slamming* the door as he left. 彼はドアをバタンと閉めると、慌てて家から飛び出して行った ☞ **slam** (CRASH)
▶**slam** 名 [C, ふつう単数で] ◇The front door closed with a *slam*. 玄関のドアはバタンと閉まった ◇She gave the door a good hard *slam*. 彼女はそのドアをかなりきつくバタンと閉めた

draw [他] (カーテンなどを)引っ張る ◇*Draw* the curtains — it's dark outside. カーテンを閉めて―外が暗いから ◇She *drew* back the curtains and let the sunlight in. 彼女はカーテンを開けて、日の光を入れた

bolt [他, 自] かんぬきをかける、かんぬきがかかる ◇Don't forget to *bolt* the door. ドアにかんぬきをかけるのを忘れないで ◇The gate *bolts* on the inside. その門は内からかんぬきがかかる ❶名詞の bolt は、ドアや窓を閉めるために、内側を滑る長くて小幅の金属片を指す。

close 形

close・even・near・narrow・level・marginal・hard-fought・neck and neck
二人の選手や二つのチームの互角のレース[試合]、ある事がもう少しで起こりそうな状況
【類語訳】接戦の、互角の、僅差での、激戦の

close	even
near	level
narrow	neck and neck
marginal	
hard-fought	

文型&コロケーション
▶level/ neck and neck with sb
▶a close/ an even/ a hard-fought **contest**
▶a close/ hard-fought **battle/ finish**
▶a narrow/ hard-fought **win/ victory**
▶a narrow/ marginal **lead**
▶a close/ narrow **vote**
▶**desperately** close/ hard-fought

close (レース・試合が)接戦の、拮抗[伯仲]した；(危険・不快な状況が)もう少しで起こりそうな ◇It's a desperately *close* race — I can't quite see who is ahead. まったくきわどいレースだ―誰が先にいるのかよくわからない ◇The California election looks *too close to call* (= it is impossible to predict the result) as voters go to the polls. 有権者が投票を行うにつれ、カリフォルニアの選挙は予測がつかない接戦の様相となっている ◇The invasion never happened but it was *a close run thing* (= it almost did). 侵入は決してなかったが、すんでのところまでいった ◇Phew! That was *close* — the motorbike nearly hit us. ふー。危ないところだった―バイクがぶつかってきそうだった

even (量が)均等な；(二人の選手・二つのチームが)互角の ◇The scores were *even* at 2-2. スコアは2対2の同点だった ◇The political goal was a more *even* distribution of wealth. 政治の目標は富をより均等に分配することだった ◇The two players were pretty *even*. 二人の選手はほぼ互角だった ◇This seems to be a more *even* contest. この試合はより互角の戦いに思える 反意 **uneven** ❶uneven contestは一方のグループ[チーム、選手]が他方よりも断然勝っている試合を表す。

near [名詞の前で]《比較・最上級なし》もう少しで起こりそうな ◇The election proved to be a *near disaster* for the party. その党はもう少しで選挙に惨敗を喫するところだった ◇We won in the end but it was a *near thing*. 私たちは最終的には勝ったが、辛勝だった ◇The climbers had already had one *near miss* (= almost had an accident) on the summit. 登山者たちはすでに一度頂上であわやという目に遭っていた

narrow [ふつう名詞の前で] かろうじて[ぎりぎり]の、僅差での ◇He blamed the goalkeeper for the *narrow defeat* against Ireland. 彼はアイルランドに惜敗したことでゴールキーパーを責めた ◇She lost the race by the *narrowest* of margins. そのレースで彼女はあり得ないほどの僅差で負けた ◇She was elected by a *narrow majority*. 彼女はぎりぎりの過半数で選出された ◇He had a *narrow escape* (= nearly had a bad accident) when his car skidded on the ice. 車が氷の上でスリップしたが彼はかろうじて事故を免れた

level [名詞の前では用いない]《特に英》(スポーツで)同点で並んだ ◇A good second round brought him *level with* the tournament leader. 2日目でスコアを伸ばして彼は首位に並んだ ◇The clubs are *level on* points. それらのクラブは勝ち点で並んでいる ◇The score was *level* at 5 points each. スコアは5対5の同点だった ◇France took an early lead but Wales soon *drew level* (= scored the same number of points). フランスが先にリードしたがウェールズがすぐに追いついた

marginal [ふつう名詞の前で]《特に英》(政治で)僅差で勝った[負けた] ◇Their campaign targeted *marginal constituencies*. 彼らの選挙運動は勝てるかどうかが微妙な選挙区をターゲットにしていた ◇They risk losing key *marginal seats* at the next election. 彼らは僅差で得た重要な議席を次の選挙で失うおそれがある 反意 **safe** ❶《英》の政治では safe seat は特定の党が多くの支持を得ていて、選挙に負けそうにない選挙区での議席を指す。

,**hard-'fought** (試合・競技が)激戦の ◇It was a lively and *hard-fought* match. その試合は活気に満ちた激し

clothes, cloudy

闘いだった ◇It was a *hard-fought* game. その試合は激戦だった

ˌneck and ˈneck 〖形式〗（レース・競技で）互角［接戦］の ◇The cyclists were *neck and neck* as they approached the final lap. 最終ラップに近づくとサイクリストたちは接戦を繰り広げた ◇He was running *neck and neck with* his Democrat rival. 彼は民主党の対立候補との接戦を繰り広げていた

clothes 〖名〗

clothes・clothing・garment・dress・costume・apparel・wear・wardrobe・gear
身に着けるもの
【類語訳】衣服，衣類，服装，衣装，持ち衣装

〖文型&コロケーション〗
▶ **casual** clothes/ clothing/ dress/ apparel/ wear/ gear
▶ **evening/ formal** clothes/ dress/ wear
▶ (sb's) **summer/ winter** clothes/ clothing/ apparel/ wear/ wardrobe
▶ **designer/ sports** clothes/ clothing/ apparel/ wear/ gear
▶ **children's/ men's/ women's** clothes/ clothing/ garments/ apparel/ wear
▶ (sb's) **new** clothes/ garments/ wardrobe/ gear
▶ (sb's) **old** clothes/ garments/ gear
▶ **warm** clothes/ clothing/ garments
▶ to **have/ buy** ... clothes/ apparel/ wardrobe/ gear
▶ to **have on/ be in** ...clothes/ garments/ dress/ gear
▶ to **wear** ... clothes/ garments/ dress/ costume/ gear
▶ to **be dressed in** ... clothes/ garments/ costume/ gear

clothes 〖複数で〗衣服 ◇I bought some new *clothes* for the trip. 私は旅行用に新しい服を何着か買った ◇I quickly threw on some *clothes* and ran downstairs. 私は急いで服を引っかけて階段を駆け下りた ◇Bring a *change of clothes* with you. 着替えを持ってきてください ❶ change/put on/remove/take off your clothes（衣服を着替える/着る/脱ぐ）という表現が使えない場合、この類義語グループの他の語と置き換えて言うことはできない。また，get changed/dressed/undressedと言うほうがはるかに一般的である．

clothing 〖U〗《やや形式》（特定の種類の）衣類 ◇Please make sure you bring warm *clothing*. 必ず防寒着を持ってください ◇What was the last item of *clothing* you bought? 最近どんな服を買いましたか

〖ノート〗**clothesとclothingの使い分け**：clothingはclothesよりもフォーマルで「特定の種類の衣類」を意味する。両語ともドレスやシャツの1着について言う場合はa piece/an item/an article of clothingという形が用いられる．

garment 〖C〗《フォーマル》（1着の）衣類 ◇He was wearing a strange shapeless *garment*. 彼は奇妙な形のくずれた服を着ていた ❶ garmentはフォーマルまたは文語的な文脈でのみ用いられ、日常の場面ではa piece of clothingが用いられる．

dress 〖U〗（特定のスタイル・機会で着る）服装 ◇All the guests were in evening *dress*. 来賓は皆イブニングドレスに身を包んでいた ◇He has no *dress sense* (= no idea of how to dress well). 彼のセンスが悪い ◇The company has a strict *dress code* — all male employees are expected to wear suits. その会社は服装規

定が厳しい—男性社員は全員スーツの着用を求められる

costume 〖C, U〗（特定の地方・時代の）衣装 ◇Some of the singers wore the Welsh *national costume*. 歌手の中にはウェールズの民族衣装を着ている者もいた ◇The film is a *costume drama* based on a 19th-century novel. その映画は19世紀の小説に基づいた時代劇だ

apparel 〖U〗《米》（店で売られている）衣類 ◇The store sells women's and children's *apparel*. その店は婦人服と子ども服を売っている

wear 〖U〗《ふつう複合語で》（特定の目的［機会］用の店で販売されている）衣類，ウェア ◇We headed straight for the children's *wear* department. 私たちは子ども服売り場へ直行した ◇They manufacture designer sports*wear*. その会社はデザイナーブランドのスポーツウェアを製造している

wardrobe 〖C, ふつう単数で〗《ややフォーマル》持ち衣装 ◇We have everything you need for your summer *wardrobe*. 当店では御用向きのあらゆる夏着を取り揃えております

gear 〖U〗《インフォーマル》衣服 ◇Her friends were all wearing the latest *gear* (= fashionable clothes). 彼女の友達はみんな流行の服を着ていた ☞ **gear** (EQUIPMENT)

cloudy 〖形〗

cloudy・misty・grey・foggy・hazy・overcast・dull・murky
空に雲がたくさんある天候を表す語
【類語訳】曇りの，どんよりした，薄暗い，陰鬱な

〖文型&コロケーション〗
▶ cloudy/ grey/ foggy/ dull **weather**
▶ misty/ foggy/ overcast **conditions**
▶ a cloudy/ misty/ grey/ overcast/ dull **day**
▶ a cloudy/ misty/ foggy/ murky **night**
▶ a dull/ grey/ misty **morning**
▶ a dull/ grey **afternoon**
▶ (a) cloudy/ grey/ dull/ overcast **sky/ skies**
▶ misty/ grey/ hazy/ dull/ murky **light**

cloudy 曇りの ◇It was a dark, *cloudy* night. 雲の多い暗い夜だった 〖反意〗**clear, sunny** (SUNNY)

misty もやのたちこめた ◇It was a beautiful *misty* morning. もやのかかった美しい朝だった 〖反意〗**clear** (SUNNY)

grey 《特に英》《米でふつうgray》《ふつうけなして》どんよりした；雲に覆われた ◇I hate when *grey* days. 近頃のどんよりした天気が嫌いだ 〖反意〗**bright** (BRIGHT)

foggy 霧のかかった ◇He was driving much too fast for the *foggy* conditions. 彼は霧のかかった状況にそぐわないものすごいスピードで運転していた 〖反意〗**clear** (SUNNY)

hazy かすみ［もや］のかかった ◇There will be a dry start to the day with some *hazy sunshine* in the east. 東部では初めのうちは幾分かすみがかった日差しのある乾燥した天気になるでしょう ◇The mountains were *hazy* in the distance. 遠方に山々がぼんやりと見えた

〖ノート〗**misty, foggy, hazyの使い分け**：mistyとfoggyは寒い日に，hazyはふつう暑い日に見られる天候．foggyはmistyよりも霧が深い．

overcast どんよりした；雲に覆われた ◇The sky was *overcast* and we needed to use artificial light. 空が雲に覆われていて、私たちは人工光を使用する必要があった

dull 〖時にけなして，特に書き言葉〗どんよりした；雲に覆われた

↱cloudy　　　　　　　　　　　　　　　　coast, cold

◇The town seemed deserted in the *dull* afternoon light. どんよりとした午後の光をうけて町はさびれた感じがした　反意 **bright** (BRIGHT)

> **ノート cloudy, grey, overcast, dull の使い分け：** grey, overcast, dull は空全体が雲に覆われていて青空が見えないことを表す。cloudy は雲は多いが一部青空は見える。grey と dull はしばしば話し手がその天候を不満に思っていることを暗示する。overcast は青空の見えない空を表す中立的な語。dull は使われる頻度が他の語よりも低く、文語的・描写的な文章で用いられる。

murky 《しばしばなしで》（霧・煙で大気・空・日光が）薄暗い, 陰鬱な；見通しの悪い ◇The light was *murky* and it was difficult to see ahead. 日の光は薄暗く前が見えにくかった

coast 名 ☞SEA

coast・beach・seaside・coastline・waterfront・shoreline・sand・lakeside・seaboard・seashore
海、川、湖のそば［近く］にある陸地を表す
【類語訳】海岸, 沿岸, 海辺, 浜辺, 海岸線, 砂浜, 湖畔

文型&コロケーション
▸**along** the coast/ beach/ coastline/ waterfront/ shoreline/ sand/ seaboard/ seashore
▸**on** the coast/ beach/ coastline/ waterfront/ shoreline/ sands/ lakeside/ seaboard/ seashore
▸**at** the coast/ beach/ seaside/ waterfront/ seashore
▸**by** the coast/ seaside/ waterfront/ seashore/ lakeside
▸**a long/ beautiful/ rocky** coast/ beach/ coastline/ shoreline
▸**a/ an spectacular/ unspoilt** coast/ beach/ coastline
▸**a rugged** coast/ coastline/ shoreline
▸**the north/ northern/ south/ southern, etc.** coast/ coastline/ seaboard
▸**to go to** the coast/ beach/ seaside/ seashore
▸**to follow** the coast/ coastline/ shoreline
▸the coast/ beach/ coastline/ sand **stretches** for miles

coast [C, ふつう単数で, U] 海岸, 沿岸, 海辺 ◇We live in a town on the south *coast* of England. 私たちはイングランドの南岸にある町に住んでいる ◇Have you visited any of the islands off the west *coast* of Ireland? アイルランドの西岸沖にある島のどこかに行ったことはありますか ◇We walked along the *coast* for five miles. 私たちは海岸沿いを5マイル散歩した ◇The *coast* road is closed due to bad weather. 海岸沿いの道路は悪天候のため通行止めです ❶ coast は不可算の場合と a sea coast という《英》表現を除いて、ほとんど常に the coast という形で用いられる。 ◆That's a pretty stretch of *coast*. (きれいに伸びた海岸だ).　◆The next scene is famously set on '*a sea coast* in Bohemia'. ((英))次の場面はかの有名な「ボヘミアの海岸」です：シェイクスピアの *The Winter's Tale* の一場面。Bohemia には海はないがシェイクスピアはそのことを知らないかのような場面を設定した。

beach [C]（海・湖の, 砂・小石に覆われた）浜辺 ◇We could see tourists sunbathing on the *beach*. 浜辺で日光浴をする観光客が見えた ◇There are miles of beautiful sandy *beaches*. きれいな砂浜が何マイルも続いている

seaside [単数で]《特に英》（休日などに）海辺 ◇The children would love a day at the *seaside*. 子どもたちは海辺で1日過ごせるなら大喜びだろう［過ごす1日を好んだものだ］ ❶ seaside は名詞の前に用いる場合を除いて、常に the seaside という形で用いられる。 ◆a *seaside* resort/ hotel/ villa（海辺のリゾート/ホテル/別荘）。《米》では定冠詞なしで名詞の前でのみ用いられる。

coastline [C, ふつう単数で, U] 海岸線 ◇The highway gives stunning views of California's rugged *coastline*. ハイウェーからはカリフォルニアのぎざぎざした海岸線の素晴らしい景色が見られる ◇Here are long stretches of unspoilt *coastline*. ここには手つかずの海岸線が長く伸びている

waterfront 《しばしば the waterfront》[C, ふつう単数で]（町・地域の）水辺［臨海, 湖岸, 河岸］地区 ◇We stayed in a beautiful apartment on the *waterfront*. 私たちは臨海地区にある美しいアパートの一室に滞在した

shoreline 《しばしば the shoreline》[C] 海岸［湖岸］線 ◇We walked along the rocky *shoreline*. 私たちは岩の多い海岸線を歩いた

> **ノート coastline と shoreline の使い分け：** coastline は湖岸ではなく常に海岸線を指し、ふつう shoreline よりも距離の長い地域について用いられる。 ◆the British/ Mediterranean/ Saudi/ Turkish *coastline* (イギリス/地中海/サウジアラビア/トルコの海岸線). ◆the Dublin *shoreline* (ダブリンの海岸線). the shoreline は the seashore と同じように「海辺」を指すこともある。 ◆She ran along the *shoreline*. (彼女は海辺に沿って走った).

sand [U, C, ふつう複数で] 砂浜 ◇We went for a walk along the *sand*. 私たちは砂浜に散歩に出かけた ◇With its miles of golden *sands*, this resort is heaven on earth. このリゾートは黄金の砂浜が何マイルも続く地上の楽園だ

lakeside [単数で]《ふつう the lakeside》湖畔 ◇We went for a walk by the *lakeside*. 私たちは湖畔を散歩しに出かけた

seaboard [C, ふつう単数で]（国の）沿岸, 海岸 ◇The whales have been sighted along the north-eastern *seaboard*, from Maine to New Jersey. 鯨はメイン州からニュージャージー州までの北東部沿岸で目撃されている ❶ seaboard はほとんどの場合 eastern/ western/ Atlantic seaboard (東海岸/西海岸/大西洋岸)の句で用いられる。他国についても可能だが特にアメリカ合衆国で用いられる。

seashore 《ふつう the seashore》[C, ふつう単数で]（砂・岩のある）海岸, 海辺 ◇He liked to look for shells on the *seashore*. 彼は海辺で貝殻を探すのが好きだった

> **ノート beach と seashore の使い分け：** beach はふつう休日などに人々が日光浴をしたり、遊んだりする海の砂浜を指す。seashore は波・貝殻・岩場などと関連して用いられ、人々が散歩を楽しむ海辺を指す傾向がある。

cold 形

1 cold・cool・chilly・chill・lukewarm・tepid・crisp
温度が低いことを表す
【類語訳】冷たい, 寒い, 冷製の, 冷えた, 涼しい, なまぬるい

lukewarm	cool	chilly	cold
tepid		chill	
		crisp	

cold

【文型&コロケーション】
- ▸ a cold/ cool/ chilly/ chill/ crisp **day/ morning**
- ▸ a cold/ cool/ chilly **night/ afternoon/ evening**
- ▸ cold/ cool/ chilly/ chill/ crisp **air**
- ▸ a cold/ cool/ chilly/ chill **wind**
- ▸ cold/ cool/ chilly **weather**
- ▸ cold/ cool/ lukewarm/ tepid **water**
- ▸ cold/ cool/ lukewarm/ tepid **shower**
- ▸ a cold/ lukewarm/ tepid **bath**
- ▸ a cold/ cool **temperature**
- ▸ cold/ lukewarm/ tepid **tea/ coffee/ food**
- ▸ a cold/ cool **climate/ drink**
- ▸ to feel cold/ cool/ chilly/ chill
- ▸ to get cold/ cool/ chilly
- ▸ It's cold/ chilly **outside**.

cold (普段より)冷たい, 寒い；(食べ物・飲み物が)冷たい, 冷製の；(調理後に)冷えた, 冷めた ◇I'm *cold*. Turn the heating up. 寒いよ. 暖房を上げて ◇It's freezing *cold*! 凍えるほど寒い ◇The stream was icy *cold*. 川は氷のように冷たかった ◇A *cold* wind blew. 冷たい風が吹いた ◇It was the *coldest* winter on record. 記録上最も寒い冬だった ◇Every room has hot and *cold* water. すべての部屋に給水・給湯設備がある ◇It's *cold* chicken for lunch. 昼食はコールド・チキンです 【反意】**hot, warm** (HOT), **mild** (SUNNY)

▸**cold** 名 [U] ◇He shivered with *cold*. 彼は寒さで身震いした ◇Don't stand outside **in the cold**. 寒い外に立たないで ◇She doesn't seem to **feel the cold**. 彼女は寒くないようだ

▸**coldness** 名 [U] ◇the icy *coldness* of the water 氷のように冷たい水

cool (ふつうほめて) (心地よく)冷たい, 涼しい ◇a long *cool* drink 背の高いグラスに入れた冷たい飲み物 ◇Store medicines in a *cool* dry place. 薬は涼しい乾燥した場所に保管してください ◇A *cool* breeze played in the trees. 涼しい風が木々の間を吹いていった ◇*Cooler* weather is forecast for the weekend. 予報では週末は涼しくなるそうだ ◇The water was blissfully *cool*. 水はすばらしく冷たかった ◇Let's sit in the shade and keep *cool*. 日陰に座って涼みましょう 【反意】**warm** (HOT), 【参照】**cool** (COOL)

chilly (ややインフォーマル) (不快に)寒い ◇Bring a coat. It might turn *chilly* later. コートを持ってくるように. 後で寒くなるかもしれないから ◇She was beginning to feel *chilly*. 彼女は寒くなり始めていた ◇The room was uncomfortably *chilly*. 部屋は冷え冷えとしていた

chill (ややフォーマル) (天候・風・空気が不快に)寒い ◇the *chill* grey dawn 寒くてどんよりした夜明け ◇Their breath steamed in the *chill* air. 彼らの息は冷気の中で白くなった ◇It was a *chill* day in February. それは2月の寒い日だった

▸**chill** 名 [単数で] ◇There's a *chill* in the air this morning. 今朝の空気は冷たい

【ノート】**chilly** と **chill** の使い分け：chilly は chill よりもインフォーマル. 人を主語にして feel, chilly とは言うが, ふつう feel chill とは言わない. 次のような表現はふつう. ◆It's quite *chilly* outside. (外はかなり寒い). ◆A *chill* wind was blowing. (冷たい風が吹いていた).

lukewarm (比較級なし) (しばしばけなして) (時に不快に)なまぬるい, なま温かい ◇The food was barely *lukewarm*. 食べ物はわずかになま温かかった ◇Add half a cup of *lukewarm* water to the mixture. 混ぜ合わせたものにぬるま湯を半カップ加えてください

tepid (比較級なし) (しばしばけなして) (時に不快に)なまぬるい, なま温かい ◇The tea was weak and *tepid*. お茶は薄くてなまぬるかった ◇She stood under the *tepid* shower. 彼女はなまぬるいシャワーを浴びた

【ノート】**lukewarm** と **tepid** の使い分け：意味・用法に実質的な違いはない.

crisp (ほめて) (空気・天候がひんやりしていて)すがすがしい, さわやかな ◇It was a *crisp* winter morning. すがすがしい冬の朝だった ◇The air was *crisp* and clear and the sky was blue. 空気はすがすがしく澄んでいて, 空は青かった

2 cold・impersonal・unfriendly・cool・aloof・frosty・remote・distant

人や場所が冷ややかな[温か味のない]ことを表す
【類語訳】冷淡な, 冷酷な, よそよそしい

impersonal	cold	frosty
cool	unfriendly	
	aloof	
	remote	
	distant	

【文型&コロケーション】
- ▸ unfriendly/ cool **towards** sb
- ▸ a cold/ an unfriendly/ a cool/ a frosty **look**
- ▸ a cold/ an impersonal/ an unfriendly/ a cool/ an aloof/ a frosty **manner**
- ▸ a cold/ an unfriendly/ a cool **voice**
- ▸ a cold/ cool/ frosty **stare**
- ▸ a cold/ an unfriendly/ a cool **glance**
- ▸ a cool/ frosty **reception**
- ▸ an impersonal/ an unfriendly/ a cool **attitude**

cold (けなして) 冷淡な, 冷酷な；冷ややかな, よそよそしい ◇Her manner was **cold and distant**. 彼女の態度は冷ややかでよそよそしかった ◇He was portrayed as a *cold*, calculating terrorist. 彼は冷酷で抜け目のないテロリストとして描かれた ◇He was staring at her with **cold eyes**. 彼は冷めた目つきで彼女を見つめていた 【反意】**warm** (FRIENDLY 1)

▸**coldly** 副 to stare/smile/reply *coldly* 冷ややかに見つめる/ほほ笑む/返事をする

▸**coldness** 名 [U] ◇She was hurt by the *coldness* in his voice. 彼女は彼の声の冷淡さに傷ついた

impersonal (ふつうけなして) 人間味[温か味]のない；そっけない ◇Business letters do not always need to be *impersonal* and formal. ビジネスレターが常に人間味のない, 堅苦しいものである必要はない ◇The hotel room looked bare and *impersonal*. そのホテルの部屋はがらんとしていて温か味がないように見えた ◇You should write your report in an *impersonal* manner. 感情を交えずに報告書を書くべきだ 【反意】**personal** ❶ personal は集団[一般]の人々に対してではなく, 特定の個人に向けられたサービス・行為に用いられる. ◆We offer a ***personal service*** to all our customers. (私どもはすべてのお客様に対しそれぞれの方に合わせたサービスをご提供します).

unfriendly 友好的でない, 不親切な ◇The report said that the Church can appear ***unfriendly to*** outsid-

↳**cold**

collect, combine

ers. 報告によれば(国) 教会は部外者に対して友好的でないように見えることもあるとのことだった ◇The atmosphere in the room was distinctly *unfriendly*. 部屋の雰囲気は明らかに友好的ではなかった 反意 **friendly (FRIENDLY 1)**

cool (友好的でなく)冷たい, (熱意・関心がなく)冷めた ◇She was decidedly *cool about* the proposal. 彼女はその提案にはまったく冷淡だった ◇He has been *cool* towards me ever since we had the argument. 喧嘩して以来, 彼は私に冷たくなった 反意 **warm (FRIENDLY 1)**
▸**coolly** 副 ◇He received my suggestion *coolly*. 彼は冷ややかに私の提案を受け入れた

aloof [名詞の前はまれ]《書き言葉》(人と)打ち解けない ◇She had always *kept herself aloof from* her colleagues. 彼女は常に同僚とは打ち解けようとしていなかった

frosty (不満を示して)冷ややかな ◇He received a *frosty* reception from the US media. 彼はアメリカのメディアから冷ややかな反応を受けた
▸**frostily** 副 ◇'No thank you,' she said *frostily*.「結構です」と彼女は冷ややかに言った

remote [名詞の前はまれ] よそよそしい; 打ち解けない ◇He somehow remains a *remote* figure. どうも彼は相変わらずよそよそしい
▸**remoteness** 名 [U] ◇His *remoteness* made her feel unloved. 彼のそっけなさから彼女は愛されていないと感じた

distant よそよそしい; 打ち解けない ◇He seemed *distant* and distracted. 彼はそっけなくて上の空のように思えた
☞ **distance** (DIVISION 2)

collect 動

collect・gather・accumulate・rack up sth・run sth up・amass・accrue
ある期間に何かを入手したり, 量を増やしたりすることを表す
【類語訳】集める, 収集する, 集まる, 増える, 蓄積する, 貯め込む, 貯める, 蓄積する

【文型&コロケーション】
▸to collect/ gather/ accumulate/ amass **data/ evidence/ information**
▸to accumulate/ rack up/ run up/ amass/ accrue **debts**
▸to accumulate/ rack up/ run up/ accrue **losses**
▸to accumulate/ rack up **profit**
▸to accumulate/ amass a **fortune**
▸to accumulate/ accrue **interest**
▸**debts** accumulate/ accrue
▸**dirt/ dust/ debris** collects/ accumulates
▸to **gradually/ slowly/ steadily** collect/ gather/ accumulate (sth)

collect [他, 自] 集める, 収集する; 集まる ◇We've been *collecting* data from various sources. 私たちはさまざまな情報源からデータを集めてきている ◇Samples were *collected* from over 200 patients. サンプルは200人以上の患者から集められた ◇We seem to have *collected* an enormous number of boxes (= without intending to). 膨大な数の箱を集めてしまったようだ ◇Dirt had *collected* in the corners of the room. 部屋の隅々にほこりがたまってしまった ❶私たちはときどき趣味で特定の種類のものを collect する。▸to *collect* stamps/postcards/fossils（切手/はがき/化石を収集する）

gather [他] 集める ◇I waited while he *gathered up* his papers. 彼が書類をかき集める間, 私は待っていた ◇She *gathered* her things *together* and got to her feet. 彼女は自分の持ち物をまとめて, 立ち上がった ◇Detectives have spent months *gathering* evidence. 探偵たちは何か月もかけて証拠を集めた

ノート **collect** と **gather** の使い分け：データ, 情報, 証拠を集める場合にはどちらの語も用いることができる。物を集める場合, すぐ近くに散らばっている物を集めるのであれば gather を用いて, things, belongings, papers のような語と共に用いることができる。collect は, 物理的に離れたさまざまな人たちやいろいろな場所から何かのサンプルを集めるような場合に用いられる。

accumulate [他, 自]《ややフォーマル》集める, 増やす; 溜まる, 増える ◇I seem to have *accumulated* a lot of books. 本をたくさん集めてしまったようだ ◇By investing wisely she *accumulated* a fortune. 賢く投資して彼女は富を築いた ◇Debts began to *accumulate*. 債務が累積し始めた ◇Dust and dirt soon *accumulate* if a house is not cleaned regularly. 家は定期的に掃除しないとちりやほこりがすぐにたまる
▸**accumulation** 名 [U, C] ◇the *accumulation* of wealth 富の蓄積 ◇an *accumulation* of toxic chemicals 有毒化学物質の蓄積

ノート **collect** と **accumulate** の使い分け：ほこりや泥などの物質がある場所で時間と共に少しずつたまっていく場合, collect も accumulate も用いることができる。ある少量のほこりや泥が除去するのが困難な場所にたまったときには collect を用いる。◆Food debris *collects* in holes in the teeth.（食べかすは歯間にたまる）。accumulate は, より多量の物が非常に長い時間を経て堆積していく場合に用いられる。◆The sediment *accumulates* over millions of years.（堆積物は何百万年もの時を経て堆積する）

,**rack 'up sth** 句動詞《ややインフォーマル, ビジネス or ジャーナリズム》(利益・損失・得点などを)蓄積する, 貯め込む ◇The company *racked up* $200 million in losses in two years. その会社は2年間で2億ドルの損失を重ねた ◇In ten years of boxing he *racked up* a record 176 wins. 彼は10年のボクサー生活で176勝挙げた

,**run sth 'up** 句動詞《ややインフォーマル》(料金・損失を)かさませる ◇She had *run up* a huge phone bill during the course of the relationship. 彼女は恋愛中の電話代がとんでもなくかさんだ ❶ run sth up はほとんど常に bill, debt, loss と共に用いられる。

amass [他]《特に書き言葉》(お金・借金・情報などを大量に)貯める, 蓄積する ◇He *amassed* a fortune from silver mining. 彼は銀の採掘で一財産を築いた ◇They *amassed* enough evidence to convict her. 彼らは彼女を有罪にするために十分な証拠をそろえた

accrue [他]《フォーマル》(利子などを)増やす, 増加させる ◇The money was placed in a special account to *accrue* interest. 利子が付くようにそのお金は特別な口座に移された ◇The firm had *accrued* debts of over $6m. その会社の負債は600万ドル以上にふくらんでいた

combine 動

combine・integrate・merge・consolidate・unify・unite・fuse
合わせて一つの物事[グループ]になる, 二つの物事[グループ]を合わせて一つにする

come

【類語訳】結合する, 組み合わせる, 統合する, 結束させる, 連合する

文型&コロケーション
- to combine/ integrate/ merge/ consolidate/ unify/ unite/ fuse (sth) **with** sth
- to combine/ integrate/ merge/ consolidate/ fuse (sth) **into** sth
- to combine/ integrate/ merge/ fuse (sth) **together**
- to combine/ merge/ unite/ fuse **to form** sth
- to combine/ integrate/ consolidate/ unify **knowledge**
- to combine/ integrate/ consolidate **resources/ skills**
- to combine/ integrate/ fuse **elements**
- to unify/ unite a/ an **country/ area**
- to **successfully** combine/ integrate/ merge/ consolidate/ unite/ fuse sth
- to **fully** integrate/ consolidate/ unify sth

combine [自, 他] 結合する, 結びつく；(二つ以上の物事・グループ・特徴・性質を)組み[混ぜ]合わせる；(二つの物事を)兼ねる, 両立させる ◇Hydrogen *combines* with oxygen to form water. 水素は酸素と結合して水になる ◇Several factors had *combined* to ruin our plans. いくつかの要因が重なって我々の計画が潰れた ◇*Combine* all the ingredients in a bowl. すべての材料をボウルの中で混ぜ合わせましょう ◇The German team scored a **combined total** of 652 points. ドイツチームは通算652得点を挙げた ◇The hotel *combines* comfort with convenience. そのホテルは利便性と快適性を兼ね備えている ◇The other room was a kitchen and dining room *combined*. もう一つの部屋はダイニング・キッチンだった ◇The trip will *combine business with pleasure*. その旅行は仕事と遊びを兼ねることになるだろう

integrate [他, 自] 《ややフォーマル》(二つ以上の物事を)統合する, 統合[調和]させる；(他の物事と)融合[調和]する ◇The department has successfully *integrated* new ideas into the traditional course structure. その学部は新しい考え方をうまく従来の課程構成に組み入れた ◇These programs will *integrate* with your existing software. これらのプログラムはあなたが今お使いのソフトウェアと一緒に動かせます 反意 segregate (ISOLATE)
➤ **integration** [名] [U] ◇The aim is to promote closer economic *integration*. 目的は経済統合をいっそう促進することにある

merge [自, 他] (二つ以上のグループが)合併する；(性質が)融合する, 同化する；(グループ・性質を)合併[融合]させる ◇The banks are set to *merge* next year. 来年その銀行は合併することが決まっている ◇His department will *merge* with mine. 彼の課は私の課と合併することになるだろう ◇Fact and fiction *merge* together in his latest thriller. 彼の最新作の推理小説には事実とフィクションが融合している ◇The company was formed by *merging* three smaller firms. その会社は比較的小さな規模の3社が合併して作られた ❶*merge* は特にビジネスや政治の文脈で用いられ, 団体や組織の統合を指す.
➤ **merger** [名] [C] ◇a *merger* between the two banks 二つの銀行の合併

consolidate [他, 自] 《ビジネス or 専門語》(いくつかのものを)一つにまとめる；一つになる, 合併[合同]する ◇All the debts have been *consolidated*. すべての借金が一つにまとめられた ◇The two companies *consolidated* for greater efficiency. 二つの企業がさらなる効率を求めて合同した
➤ **consolidation** [名] [U] ◇the *consolidation* of Japan's banking industry 日本の銀行業界の合併

unify [他] (国・地域・システムの一部を)統一する；(国・地域・組織の人々を)結束[団結]させる ◇What we need is a *unified* transport system. 私たちに必要なのは統合された輸送システムだ ◇The new leader hopes to *unify* the party. 新しい党首は党を結束させたいと思っている
➤ **unification** [名] [U] ◇the *unification* of Germany in the 19th century 19世紀におけるドイツの統一

unite [他, 自] (国などを)統一[統合]する；(人々を)結束[団結]させる；(異質なものを)合体[結合]する[させる]；(国などが)統一[結合]される, 連合[結合]する ◇His aim was to *unite* Italy. 彼の目的はイタリアを統一することだった ◇A special bond *unites* our two countries. 特別な絆で我々2か国は結ばれている ◇She *unites* keen business skills with a charming personality. 彼女は鋭い経営手腕と魅力的な性格を併せ持つ人物だ ◇The two countries *united* in 1887. その二つの国は1887年に統合した 反意 divide (ISOLATE)

ノート **unify** と **unite** の使い分け：両語とも集団[地域]内に個々の部分が一つにまとまる場合に用いられる. ◆to *unify/unite* the country/the party/Europe (国を統一する/党内部を結束させる/ヨーロッパを統合する). **unite** は単に個々の部分が一つにまとまるにすぎない場合にも用いられる. ◆to *unite* two political parties/the two Germanies/the people (二つの政党/二つのドイツを統合する/人々を団結させる). ✕to *unify* two political parties/the two Germanies/the people. **unify** はシステムの部分を一つにまとめる場合に用いられる. ◆to *unify* the tax/transport system (税制/輸送システムを統一する). ✕to *unite* the tax/transport system.

fuse [自, 他] 《フォーマル or 専門語》(物質・グループ・考え・性質を新しい形に)結合[融合]する ◇As they heal, the bones will *fuse* together. 回復するにつれて骨は結合するでしょう ◇Our different ideas *fused* into a plan. 私たちの異なる考え方が溶け合って一つの計画になった ◇Atoms of hydrogen are *fused* to make helium. 水素の原子が結合してヘリウムになる
➤ **fusion** [名] [U, 単数で] ◇the *fusion* of copper and zinc to produce brass 真鍮を作るための銅と亜鉛の結合 ◇The movie displayed a perfect *fusion* of image and sound. その映画は映像と音響との完璧な融合を見せた

come [動]

1 come・approach・draw・come along・near・close in・converge
人や場所に向かって移動する
【類語訳】来る, 近づく, やって来る, 接近する, 集まる

文型&コロケーション
- to come/ draw **in/ into** sth
- to come/ draw **up/ up to sb/ sth**
- to close in/ converge **on** sb/ sth
- to come/ draw **close/ near/ closer/ nearer**
- to **slowly** come/ approach/ draw/ close in on sb

come [自] 《ふつう副詞や前置詞と共に》来る ◇He *came* into the room and shut the door. 彼は部屋に入るとドアを閉めた ◇She *came* to work wearing a very smart suit.

彼女はとても洗練されたスーツを着て職場に来た ◇*Come here!* ここへおいで ◇*Come and* see us soon! また会いに来てね ◇*Come* see us soon!《米》また会いに来てね ◇*Here comes* Jo (= Jo is coming)! ジョーが来たよ ◇He's *come* all the way from Tokyo. 彼ははるばる東京からやって来た ◇Why don't you *come* with us? 私たちと一緒に行きませんか ◇It looks as if there's a storm *coming*. まるで嵐が近づいているみたいだ ◇The kids *came running* into the room. 子どもたちが部屋の中へ駆け込んで来た ❶ *come* はふつうある人が向かっている人物・場所の視点[立場]から用いられる. 反意 go (GO1), ☞ **coming** (ARRIVAL)

approach [自, 他]《ややフォーマル》近づく ◇We could hear the train *approaching*. 電車が近づいてくるのが聞こえた ◇Police said the suspect should not be *approached*. 警察は容疑者に近づいてはいけないと述べた ◇She *approached* the crossroads cautiously. 彼女は慎重に交差点に近づいた ☞ **approach** (ARRIVAL)

draw [自]《書き言葉》《副詞や前置詞と共に》近づく ◇The train *drew* into the station. 電車は駅に近づいた ◇Their car *drew alongside* ours. 彼らの車が私たちの車に迫ってきて横並びになった ◇She waved to me as I *drew* up (= arrived in a car and stopped). 私が車で到着すると彼女は私に手を振った ◇As he *drew* near, I could see that he was limping. 彼が近づいてくると足を引きずっていることに私は気づいた

come a'long 句動詞 やって[近づいて]来る ◇We'll get the next bus that *comes along*. 次にやって来るバスに乗る予定だ ◇I'd hate someone to *come along* and see me like this. 誰かがやって来てこんなありさまの私を見ると思うだけでいやだ

near [自, 他]《フォーマル》近づく ◇As the bus *neared* we could see someone waving. バスが近づくと, 誰かが手を振っているのが見えた ◇We were obviously *nearing* the airport. 私たちは明らかに空港に近づいていた

,close 'in 句動詞 (襲撃・捕獲するために)接近する ◇They knew the police were *closing in*. 彼らは警察が迫っていることを知っていた ◇It was a shark *closing in for the kill*. とどめを刺しに来たのはサメだった ◇Rebel troops were *closing in* on the city. 反乱軍が町に迫っていた

converge [自]《ふつう副詞や前置詞, 特にonと共に》(人・乗り物が)集まる, 集結する ◇Thousands of supporters *converged* on Washington for the rally. その大会のために何千ものサポーターがワシントンに集結した

2 come・arrive・approach・near・draw near
待ち続けていた時間や出来事の生起を表す
【類語訳】来る, やって来る, 到来する, 近づく, 迫る

文型&コロケーション
▶ **spring/ summer/ autumn/ fall/ winter** comes/ arrives/ approaches/ draws near
▶ **the day/ time** comes/ arrives/ approaches/ draws near
▶ to come/ arrive **early/ late**
▶ to finally **come**/ arrive

come [自] 来る ◇When the moment actually *came*, I began to feel a little nervous. その瞬間が実際にやって来ると, 私は少し神経質になり始めた ◇Business improved as Christmas *came* nearer. クリスマスが近づくにつれて景気はよくなった ◇The deadline *came and went*, but there was no reply from them. 締め切りは過ぎたが彼らからはなんの音沙汰もなかった

arrive [自]《書き言葉》(待っていた時が)やって来る, 到来する ◇The day of the wedding finally *arrived*. 結婚式の日がついにやって来た ◇The age of industrialization had *arrived*. 産業化の時代が到来していた

approach [自, 他] (時間が)近づく, 迫る ◇The deadline was *fast approaching*. 締め切りはどんどん近づいていた ◇He was *approaching* a turning point in his life. 彼は人生の転機を迎えつつあった

near [自, 他]《ややフォーマル》(時間が)近づく, 迫る ◇It was *nearing* midnight. 真夜中になろうとしていた ◇The project is *nearing* completion. その企画は完成に近づきつつある ◇Many of the teachers were *nearing* retirement. 教師の多くが退職間近だった

draw near [自]《ややフォーマル》(時間が)近づく, 迫る ◇The time for her departure was *drawing near*. 彼女の出発の時間は迫っていた

comfortable 形

comfortable・cosy・snug・homely・comfy・homey
屋内や物が気持ちよい[暖かさを感じる]状態を表す
【類語訳】快適な, 心地よい, くつろいだ, 安楽な, 居心地のよい, 着心地のよい

文型&コロケーション
▶ a comfortable/ cosy/ homely/ homey **atmosphere**
▶ a comfortable/ cosy/ snug/ homely **room**
▶ a comfortable/ cosy/ snug **house**
▶ a comfortable/ cosy/ snug/ comfy **bed**
▶ a comfortable/ cosy/ comfy **armchair**
▶ a comfortable/ cosy/ snug/ homely/ homey **little place**
▶ to feel comfortable/ cosy/ snug/ homely/ comfy/ homey
▶ very/ quite comfortable/ cosy/ snug/ homely/ comfy/ homey
▶ **nice and** comfortable/ cosy/ snug/ homely/ comfy
▶ **warm and** comfortable/ cosy/ homely/ comfy/ homey
▶ comfortable/ cosy/ snug **and warm**

comfortable 《ほめて》(衣類・家具・場所が)快適な, 着[座り, 居]心地のよい; (人が)気持ちよく感じる, くつろいだ; (暖かく痛みがなくて)安楽な ◇It is advisable to wear loose, *comfortable* clothing. ゆったりとした着心地のよい服を着ることをお勧めします ◇Let me slip into something more *comfortable*. (= change into more comfortable clothing). もっとくつろげる服に着替えさせてください ◇It's an elegant, *comfortable* house with good views from the windows. それは窓からの景色が素晴らしい, 上品で快適な家です ◇She shifted into a more *comfortable* position on the chair. 彼女は椅子の上でもっと楽な姿勢をとった ◇Please *make yourself comfortable* while I get some coffee. コーヒーを持って来ますので, どうぞおくつろぎください ◇The patient is *comfortable* (= not in pain) after his operation. 術後その患者は苦痛が取れて楽にしている 反意 **uncomfortable** ❶衣類・家具などがuncomfortableの場合, 肉体的に快適でないことを指す. ◆I couldn't sleep because the bed was so *uncomfortable*. (ベッドの寝心地があまりにも悪くて私は眠れなかった). 人がuncomfortableな場合, 肉体的にくつろげない[暖かくない]などを表す. ◆She still finds it *uncomfortable* to stand without support. (彼女はまだ支えなしで立つことに苦痛を感じる).

➤ **comfortably** 副 ◇All the rooms were *comfortably* furnished. すべての部屋には快適な家具が備え付けられていた ◇If you're all sitting *comfortably*, then I'll begin. 皆さん全員が楽に座られているようなら、始めたいと思います

cosy《英》《米**cozy**》(ほめて)(こぢんまりとして[囲いがあって])心地よい ◇We stopped in a *cosy* little cafe for a cup of tea. 私たちは一服しに居心地のよいこぢんまりとした喫茶店に立ち寄った ◇I felt warm and *cosy* sitting by the fire. 炉辺に座っていると私は暖かくて気持ちよかった

➤ **cosily** 副《英》《米**cozily**》◇We were sitting *cosily* by the fire. 私たちは気持ちよく炉辺に座っていた

➤ **cosiness**《英》《米では**coziness**》名 [U] ◇I wished I was back in the *cosiness* and warmth of the kitchen. 私は快適で暖かいキッチンに戻りたかった

snug(ほめて)(寒くなくて)心地よい ◇I spent the afternoon *snug* and warm in bed. 私はベッドの中でぬくぬくと午後を過ごした ◇It had rained during the night but our tents were *snug* and dry. 一晩中雨が降っていたが私たちのテントは乾燥していて暖かかった

➤ **snugly** 副 ◇I left the children tucked up *snugly* in bed. 私は子どもたちに布団をかけてやって暖かくしておいた

[ノート] **cosyとsnugの使い分け**：両語とも場所・人について用いられるが、snugは人について、cosyは場所について用いるほうがやや一般的。

homely《英,ほめて》(場所が自分の家に居るように)居心地のよい ◇The hotel has a lovely *homely* feel to it. そのホテルはとても居心地がよい

comfy《インフォーマル,ほめて》快適な ◇These slippers aren't as *comfy* as my old ones. この上靴は前のほど履き心地がよくない ◇Put some pillows behind you so you're nice and *comfy*. 枕を背にあてれば楽ですよ

homey(または**homy**)《特に米,インフォーマル,ほめて》(場所が自分の家に居るように)居心地のよい ◇The lamp in the window made the room feel *homey* and welcoming. 窓に灯がともりその部屋には温かく人を迎え入れる雰囲気があった

comment 動

comment・note・remark・observe
事実や意見を口述[記述]する
【類語訳】述べる、コメントする、特筆する

[文型&コロケーション]
▶ to comment/ remark **on** sth
▶ to comment/ remark/ observe **to** sb
▶ to comment/ note/ remark/ observe **that**...
▶ to comment on/ note/ remark/ observe **how**...
▶ to comment/ note/ remark/ observe **drily/ wryly**
▶ to comment/ remark/ observe **coolly/ acidly/ casually**

comment [自,他] 意見[事実]を述べる、コメントする ◇He refused to *comment* until after the trial. 彼は裁判が終わるまでコメントを断った ◇We were just *commenting* on how well you look. 君が元気そうだねって話していたところだよ ◇'Not his best performance,' she *commented* to the woman sitting next to her. 「彼は最高の出来栄えではないですね」と彼女は隣に座っている女性に言った ☞ **comment** (STATEMENT)

note [他]《ややフォーマル》(重要な[興味深い]ので)とりたて述べる、特筆する ◇It is worth *noting* that the most successful companies had the lowest prices. 最も成功している会社が最低価格であったことは特筆に値する ❶ **note** はしばしば重要な[興味深い]事実に対して人の注目を引くために用いられる。◆Visitors should *note* that the tower is not open to the public. (観光客の皆さんはそのタワーが一般に公開されていないことにご留意ください)。◆There are two other points to *note* from this graph. (このグラフから注目すべき点がもう二つある)。

remark [自,他](状況について気づいた事を)述べる ◇The judges *remarked* on the high standard of entries for the competition. 審査員たちは競技会の参加者のレベルの高さについて述べた ◇Critics *remarked* that the play was not original. 評論家たちはその劇がオリジナルではないと指摘した ☞ **remark** (STATEMENT)

observe [他]《進行形はまれ》《フォーマル》(状況について気づいた事を)述べる ◇She *observed* that it was getting late. 彼女は時間が押してきていると述べた ☞ **observation** (STATEMENT)

[ノート] **comment, remark, observe の使い分け**：comment on は物事について述べること。remark on と observe は物事について気づいた点を述べること。ほとんどの場合、これらの語に大きな違いはないが、refuse to comment と言えるのに対して、refuse to remark または refuse to observe とは言えない。×He refused to *remark/observe* until after the trial.

committee 名

committee・council・commission・board・jury・panel・delegation・body・task force・mission
特定の事柄に関する決定を下す[勧告を行う、問題を処理する]などの機能を持つ人の集団
【類語訳】委員会、協議会、審議会、取締役会、理事会、代表団、使節団

[文型&コロケーション]
▶ a committee/ commission/ panel/ task force **on** sth
▶ a committee/ council/ commission/ board/ delegation/ body **for** sth
▶ to be **on** a committee/ council/ commission/ board/ jury/ panel/ body
▶ a **special** committee/ commission/ task force/ mission
▶ a/ an **joint/ independent** committee/ council/ commission/ board/ delegation/ body/ task force/ mission
▶ a **government/ parliamentary** committee/ commission/ board/ delegation/ body
▶ a **congressional** committee/ commission/ delegation/ body
▶ an **official** committee/ commission/ delegation/ body
▶ a **governing** committee/ council/ commission/ board/ body
▶ a/ an **executive/ management** committee/ council/ board/ body
▶ a/ an **advisory/ consultative** committee/ council/ board/ panel/ body
▶ a **research** committee/ council/ commission/ board/ body
▶ to **choose/ select** a committee/ jury/ panel
▶ to **head** a committee/ council/ commission/ board/ delegation/ task force/ mission

↪**committee**

- ▶to **chair** a committee/ council/ commission/ board/ panel/ body
- ▶to **lead** a commission/ delegation/ task force/ mission
- ▶to **serve on/ sit on** a committee/ council/ commission/ board/ jury/ panel/ body
- ▶to **send** a delegation/ task force/ mission

committee [C＋単数・複数動詞] (選ばれた人たちからなる) 委員会 ◇They have set up a *committee* on the safety of medicines. 医薬品の安全性に関する委員会が設立された ◇She's on the management *committee*. 彼女は経営委員会の一員である

council (または **Council**) [C＋単数・複数動詞] (勧告・規則づくり・調査・資金提供などを行う) 協議会, 審議会 ◇In Britain, the Arts *Council* gives grants to theatres. イギリスでは芸術協議会が劇場に補助金を出している ◇There are plans to establish a funding *council* for higher education. 高等教育のための資金配分協議会を設立する計画がある

commission [C＋単数・複数動詞] (政府の公的)委員会 ◇Sweden's Environment *Commission* has ruled against the dam project. スウェーデンの環境委員会がそのダム計画を覆す裁決を下した ◇The *commission* is expected to report its findings next month. 来月委員会は結果を報告するように求められている

ノート committee, council, commission の使い分け: これらの語はすべて類似した機能を持つ人々の団体を指す。団体名に用いる場合, どの語を用いるかは団体の自由である。committee は最も一般的な語であり, 政府・企業の一部, または労働組合・政党・大学などの「委員会」を指す。組織内でお決まりの決定を下し, 高いレベルの「委員会」にも地方レベルの「委員会」にも用いられる。council は独立した専門家から成る「審議会」である場合が多い。例えば, the Medical Research Council (医学研究審議会) など。その役割は芸術・スポーツ・学術研究などの振興である。commission はふつう大物の政治家や専門家から成る「委員会」で, 政府や政治団体が設立する。貿易・農業など特定の分野を扱ったり, 重大事故・社会問題など特定の問題を調査したりする。◆the Atomic Energy *Commission* (原子力委員会). ◆the United Nations High *Commissioner* for Refugees (UNHCR) (国連難民高等弁務官(UNHCR)).

board [C＋単数・複数動詞] 取締役[理事]会 ◇The project will have to go to the *board* for consideration. その計画は検討してもらうために取締役会に回さねばならないだろう ◇There have been discussions about the issue *at board level*. 理事会レベルでその問題に関して議論が行われている ◇She has a seat on the *board of directors*. 彼女は取締役会の一員である

jury [C＋単数・複数動詞] 陪審;(競技会の)審査員団 ◇Everyone should have the right to *trial by jury*. すべての人が陪審裁判を受ける権利をもつべきだ ◇The *jury* was *sworn in*. 陪審が宣誓就任した ◇The *jury* has retired to consider its verdict. 陪審は評決を検討するために退席した ◇It was the second time he had been called up for *jury service* (= to be a member of a jury). 《英》彼が陪審に召集されたのはそれが2度目だった ◇*jury* duty 《米》陪審義務 ◇He was on the *jury* for this year's Booker Prize. 彼は今年のブッカー賞の審査員だった

panel [C＋単数・複数動詞] (専門家の)委員会, (テレビ・ラジオの)パネリスト団 ◇The designs will be judged by a *panel of experts*. デザインは専門家委員会によって審査される予定だ ◇A distinguished *panel* of speakers considered the role of global corporations. 有名な論客パネリストたちがグローバル企業の役割を考えた ◇The decision of the judging *panel* is final. 審査委員会によって最終決定が行われます

delegation [C＋単数・複数動詞] (組織・国の)代表団 ◇The prime minister met with an all-party *delegation from* the city council. 首相は超党派の市議会の代表団と会談した ◇The Canadian *delegation* walked out of the talks in protest. カナダの代表団は抗議して協議の場を退席した

body [C＋単数・複数動詞] (公的な目的を持つ)団体, 組織 ◇The government is consulting trade unions and other professional *bodies*. 政府は労働組合を始めとする他の職業団体の意見を聞いている ❶ *body* は共に働く人々の集団を表す一般的な語で, 特に管理・決定などを行う公的団体を指す。例えば, sport's governing body (スポーツ運営組織) としばしば言うが, 団体の実際の名称は, the Football Association (FA) (イングランドサッカー協会) などに見られる association や the International Association of Athletics Federations (IAAF) (国際陸上競技連盟) などに見られる federation, the International Olympic Committee (IOC) (国際オリンピック委員会) などに見られる committee などであったりする。

'task force [C] (特定の問題に対処するための政府の)特別委員会, タスクフォース ◇She is expected to lead a *task force* on health care reform. 彼女には医療保険改革委員会を指揮することが求められている

mission [C＋単数・複数動詞] (重要な公的業務を行う)使節団;使節団の任務地 ◇She led a recent trade *mission* to China. 最近彼女は中国への貿易使節団の団長を務めた ◇He will be part of a four-member UN *fact-finding mission* to the disputed region. 彼は4人から成る国連の紛争地域への視察調査団のメンバーになる予定だ

common 形

common・public・joint・collective・popular・communal・cooperative
物事に多数の人が加わったり, 関わったりしている状態
【類語訳】共通の, 共有の, 公共の, 公立の, 共同の, 総体の

文型&コロケーション

- ▶common/ public/ joint/ collective/ communal **property**
- ▶common/ public/ communal **land**
- ▶common/ joint/ collective/ communal **ownership/ responsibility**
- ▶a common/ joint/ collective/ communal/ cooperative **enterprise**
- ▶a joint/ collective/ communal/ cooperative **effort**
- ▶joint/ collective/ communal/ cooperative **action**
- ▶a joint/ collective/ communal **decision**
- ▶common/ collective/ popular **opinion**

common [ふつう名詞の前で] 共通の, 共有の ◇They share a *common interest* in photography. 彼らは共に写真に興味がある ◇This decision was taken for *the common good* (= the advantage of everyone). この決定は共通の利益のために下された ◇It is, *by common consent*, Scotland's prettiest coast (= everyone agrees that it is). それは万人が認めるスコットランドで最も美しい海岸だ ◇Some basic features are *common to* all human languages. いくつかの基本的な特徴が人間のあらゆる言語に共通している

public [名詞の前で] 公共の, 公立の ◇There is a desperate need to improve *public transport* in the city. 《英》その都市の公共交通機関の改善が切実に求められている。 ◇*public transportation*《米》公共輸送[交通]機関 ◇The information is available in any *public library*. その情報はどの公立図書館でも入手可能である ◇He was charged with destroying *public* property. 彼は公共財産損壊で告発された **反意** **private** (**OWN**)

joint [名詞の前で] 共同の, 共有の ◇They were *joint owners* of the house. 彼らはその家の共同所有者だった ◇We opened a *joint account* when we got married. 結婚したとき私たちは共同口座を開設した ◇They divorced two years ago, but he has *joint custody* of the children (= he shares care of the children with his ex-wife). 彼らは2年前に離婚したが, 彼には子どもたちへの共同親権がある ◇They finished in *joint* first place. 彼らは共に首位タイでゴールした **反意** **separate** (**PARTICULAR**)

▶**jointly** 副 ◇The event was organized *jointly* by students and staff. そのイベントは学生と職員が共同で開催した

collective [ふつう名詞の前で] 集団全体の; 社会全体の; 総体の ◇MPs heaved a *collective sigh of relief* when the news was announced last night. 昨晩そのニュースが発表されると下院全体が安堵のため息を漏らした ◇The austerities of wartime Europe were still fresh in the *collective memory* (= memories shared by the whole of society). 戦時中のヨーロッパの耐乏生活はいまだに社会全体の記憶の中に鮮明に残っていた ◇The *collective* name for mast, boom and sails on a boat is the 'rig'. 船の帆柱と下桁, 帆を総称して「艤装」と言う **反意** **individual** (**PARTICULAR**)

▶**collectively** 副 ◇We have had a successful year, both *collectively* and individually. 集団全体としても個々人としても, 私たちは満足のゆく一年を送った

popular [名詞の前で] (考え・信条・意見が) 共有の ◇By *popular demand*, the tour has been extended by two weeks. たくさんの要望があり, コンサートツアーは2週間延長された ◇Contrary to *popular belief*, women cause fewer road accidents than men. 世間の常識に反して女性は男性ほど交通事故を起こさない

▶**popularly** 副 ◇a *popularly* held belief 世間一般の常識

communal (同居者の) 共有の, 共同使用の ◇As a student I tried *communal* living for a few years. 学生の頃, 私は数年間共同生活をしてみた ◇He led me down the corridor to the *communal* kitchen. 彼は廊下を通って共同キッチンへ私を案内した **反意** **individual** (**OWN**), **separate** (**PARTICULAR**)

▶**communally** 副 ◇The property was owned *communally*. その不動産は共同で所有されていた

cooperative (英でまた **co-operative**) [ふつう名詞の前で] 共同[協同]の, 力を合わせて行う ◇*Cooperative* activity is essential to effective community work. 共同作業は効果的な社会事業に欠くことができない ◇This is a *cooperative* venture with the University of Copenhagen. これはコペンハーゲン大学との共同事業だ

communication 名

communication・contact・dealings・correspondence
人と連絡を取る活動
【類語訳】コミュニケーション, 連絡, 音信, 接触, 取り引き, 文通

文型&コロケーション

▶communication/ contact/ dealings/ correspondence **with** sb
▶communication/ contact/ dealings/ correspondence **between** people
▶**regular** communication/ contact/ dealings/ correspondence
▶**business** communication/ dealings/ correspondence
▶to **be in** communication/ contact/ correspondence (with sb)
▶to **have** contact/ dealings with sb

communication [U] コミュニケーション ◇Speech is the fastest method of *communication* between people. 口頭での話が人間のコミュニケーションの中で最も短時間ですむ方法だ ◇All *channels of communication* need to be kept open. あらゆるコミュニケーションの道を閉ざさないでおく必要がある ◇Doctors do not always have good *communication skills*. 医者が必ずしもコミュニケーション能力が高いとは限らない ◇non-verbal *communication* such as gestures or facial expressions 身ぶりや顔の表情といった非言語的コミュニケーション ☞ **communication** (**LETTER**), **communicate** (**CONVEY**), **communicate** (**TALK**)

contact [U] (人との定期的な) 連絡, 音信, 接触 ◇Have you *kept in contact* with any of your friends from college (= do you still see them or speak or write to them)? 大学からの友達の誰かと連絡を取り合っていますか ◇She's *lost contact with* (= no longer sees or writes to) her son. 彼女は息子と音信不通になっている ◇I finally *made contact with* (= succeeded in speaking to or meeting) her in Paris. 私はついにパリにいる彼女と連絡が取れた ◇In her job she often *comes into contact with* (= meets) lawyers. 彼女は仕事でよく弁護士と接する ◇The organization *put me in contact with* other people in a similar position (= gave me their addresses or phone numbers). その団体は似たような境遇にいる人たちと私が連絡が取れるようにしてくれた ◇He carefully avoided *eye contact* (= looking directly at sb else's eyes). 彼は慎重に視線を合わせないようにした

▶**contact** 動 [他] I've been trying to *contact* you all day. 一日中あなたに連絡を取ろうとしていた

dealings [複数で]《ややフォーマル》(仕事上の) 取り引き; 取引関係 ◇Have you had any previous *dealings* with this company? 以前この会社と取り引きしたことはありますか ◇I knew nothing of his business *dealings*. 私は彼の仕事の取引関係は何も知らなかった ☞ **deal with sb** (**NEGOTIATE**)

correspondence [U, C]《フォーマル》文通, 書面による通信 ◇I refused to *enter into* any *correspondence* (= to exchange letters) with him about it. 私はそのことに関して彼とはいかなる手紙のやり取りも始めたくないと言った ◇We kept up a *correspondence* for many years. 私たちは長年文通を続けた ☞ **correspondence** (**LETTER**)

▶**correspond** 動 [自] ◇I have *corresponded* with

him in the past. 私はこれまで彼と文通してきた

company 名 ☞ GROUP 3

company・firm・business・operation・corporation・enterprise・practice・house
商品やサービスを生産したり、販売したりしてお金をかせぐ組織
【類語訳】会社, 事務所, 店, 工場, 企業

文型&コロケーション

▶ a **multinational** company/ firm/ business/ operation/ corporation/ enterprise
▶ a **state-owned** company/ firm/ business/ corporation/ enterprise
▶ a **private** company/ firm/ business/ operation/ corporation/ enterprise/ practice/ ... house
▶ a **family** company/ firm/ business/ operation/ enterprise/ practice/ ... house
▶ a **commercial** company/ firm/ business/ operation/ corporation/ enterprise/ ... house
▶ a **business** company/ firm/ operation/ corporation/ enterprise
▶ to **manage/ run/ have/ own** a company/ a firm/ a business/ an operation/ a corporation/ an enterprise/ a ... house
▶ to **buy/ acquire/ take over** a company/ firm/ business/ an operation/ an enterprise
▶ to **set up** a company/ firm/ business/ an operation/ a corporation/ an enterprise/ a practice/ a ... house
▶ to **found** a company/ firm/ business/ practice/ ... house
▶ to **work for/ join/ leave/ resign from** a company/ firm/ business/ corporation/ practice/ ... house
▶ a company/ a firm/ a business/ a corporation/ an enterprise/ a ... house **fails**

company [C+単数・複数動詞] 会社 ◇During the 1980s it was one of the largest computer *companies* in the world. 1980年代の間その会社は世界最大のコンピューター会社の一つだった ◇Mike gets a *company* car with his new job. マイクには新しい任務と共に社用車が与えられる
firm [C] 会社, 事務所 ◇He got a job with a London engineering *firm*. 彼はロンドンの工業技術系の会社に就職した ◇the city's oldest and most prestigious law *firm* その都市で最も古くて名の通った法律事務所 ◇I'm working for a *firm of* accountants. 私は会計事務所で働いています

> **ノート company と firm の使い分け**: firm はしばしば専門的な助言・サービスを提供する小規模な組織について用いられる。◆a/an engineering/law/consulting/insurance/security *firm*（工業技術系の会社／法律事務所／コンサルティング会社／保険会社／警備会社）. ◆a *firm* of accountants/consultants/lawyers/solicitors（会計事務所／コンサルタント会社／弁護士事務所／事務弁護士事務所）. firm はまたしばしば家族経営の会社についても用いられる。◆a/the family *firm*（同族会社）. ◆his father's *firm*（彼の父親が経営する会社）. 長年営業している会社についても用いられる。◆a/an old/long-established/old-fashioned/reputable/renowned *firm*（歴史の長い／昔ながらの／名のある／有名な会社）. company はより幅広い種類の会社を指し、商品・サービスを生産・販売し利益を上げる組織であればいかなる会社にも用いることができる。

business [C]（商業的組織としての）会社, 店, 工場 ◇I've decided to start my own *business*. 私は自分で事業を起こすことに決めた ◇They've got a small catering *business*. 彼らは小さな仕出し屋を営んでいる ◇This legislation will hurt small *businesses*. この法律で小さな事業所は痛手を受けるだろう ❶ business は種類・規模を問わず商業的組織を表す一般的な語。◆Almost all *businesses* will be closed on Christmas Day (= shops, factories, offices, etc.).（ほとんどすべての事業がクリスマスの日は休業するだろう）. また特に従業員のいない個人・家族経営の会社を含む小規模な組織についても用いられる（company と firm には必ず従業員がいる）. business はしばしば start up, set up などの動詞を伴い、事業を開始する場合に用いられる。a big business とも言えるが、big business の形で「一グループとしての大企業群」を意味する不可算名詞として用いられることのほうがはるかに多い。☞ **business** (INDUSTRY), **business** (TRADE)
operation [C]（多くの部門を持つ）会社, 企業；大会社[企業]の一部門 ◇It's a huge multinational *operation*. それは巨大な多国籍企業だ ◇Network Computing Inc. plans to open a UK *operation* in Britain next year. 来年株式会社ネットワーク・コンピューティングはイギリスに支社を開業する予定だ
corporation（略 **Corp.**）[C] 大会社, 大企業 ◇They provide banking facilities to multinational *corporations*. 彼らは銀行業務を多国籍企業に提供している ❶ corporation はしばしば非常に巨大なアメリカ系企業について用いられる。
enterprise [C]（ビジネス, ジャーナリズム）会社, 企業 ◇They plan to privatize over 100 state-owned *enterprises*. 当局は100社以上の国有企業を民営化する計画である ❶ enterprise はしばしば政府の文書や商業ジャーナリズムにおいて用いられる。
practice [C]（法律・医療関係の）開業[営業]場所, 事務所 ◇She runs a successful law *practice*. 彼女の法律事務所の経営はうまくいっている ☞ **practice** (WORK 名 1)
house [C]（複合語で）（特定の種類の）会社 ◇The publishing *house* made its name by encouraging first-time writers. その出版社は初めて本を書く作家を奨励することで有名になった ❶ house は a/an fashion/publishing/software/investment/auction *house*（ファッション／出版／ソフトウェア／投資／競売会社）などのように複合語として用いられる。

compare 動

1 compare・contrast・juxtapose・balance sth against sth・match sth against sth
人や物事がどれほど似て[違って]いるか吟味する
【類語訳】比較する, 対照する, 対比する, 並置する, 秤にかける

文型&コロケーション

▶ to compare/ contrast/ juxtapose A **and/ with** B
▶ to compare/ contrast sth **favourably/ unfavourably** with sth

compare [他]（相似・相違を見るために人・物事を）比較する ◇It is interesting to *compare* their situation and ours. 彼らと私たちの状況を比較すると興味深い ◇We *compared* the two reports carefully. 私たちは二つの報告書を慎重に比較した ◇My own problems seem insignificant *compared* with other people's. 他の人と比べれ

ば私自身の問題なんてちっぽけなもののように思える ◇Standards in health care have improved enormously *compared to* 40 years ago. 40年前と比べれば健康保険の水準は格段に良くなった ❶この用法では*to*ではなく*with*のみを用いることを好む人もいるが, *with*も*to*も実際にとても頻繁に用いられる. compare sth to sth は常に「二人・二つの物事をなぞらえる[たとえる]」という意味で用いられる. ◆The critics *compared* his work *to* that of Hemingway. (評論家たちは彼の作品をヘミングウェイの作品になぞらえた).

contrast [他]《ややフォーマル》(相違を示すために二つの物事を)対照[対比]する ◇It is interesting to *contrast* the British legal system with the American one. イギリスとアメリカの法制度を対比すると興味深い ◇The poem *contrasts* youth and age. その詩は若さと老いを対比している ◇*Compare and contrast* the two main characters in the play. 劇中の二人の主要人物を比較対照しなさい
☞ **contrast** (DIFFERENCE), **contrast** (OPPOSITE) 图

juxtapose [他, ふつう受身で]《フォーマル》(相違・新しい関係を示すために人・物事を)並置[並列]する ◇In the exhibition, abstract paintings are *juxtaposed* with shocking photographs. その展覧会では抽象画が衝撃的な写真と並置されている ❶*juxtapose*はしばしば *crudely, sharply, starkly, dramatically* などの副詞や *to good/great/maximum effect* のような句と共に用いられる.

balance sth against sth 句動《ややフォーマル》(二つの対照的な物事の重要性を)比較検討する, 秤[天秤]にかける ◇The cost of obtaining legal advice needs to be *balanced against* its benefits. 法的助言を得る費用とその恩恵を秤にかける必要がある

'match sth against sth 句動 (相似を調べるために二つの物事を)照合する ◇New information is *matched against* existing data in the computer. コンピューター上で新しい情報が既存のデータと照合されている ❶*match* sth *against* sthはしばしばコンピューター上または記憶の中にある大量の情報の蓄積, すなわちデータベースを持つ語群のような二つの物事を比較する場合に用いられる.

2 compare・match・rival・equal・be on a par with sb/sth
人や物事と同じくらいによい
【類語訳】匹敵する, 引けを取らない, 好敵手となる, 同等である

文型&コロケーション
▸to match/ rival/ equal sth in/ for sth
▸to compare with/ match/ rival/ be on a par with sth in terms of sth
▸to compare with/ match/ equal sb's achievements
▸to match/ rival/ equal the performance of sth
▸to match/ equal a feat/ record
▸to be matched/ rivalled/ equalled only by sth

compare [自] (良さの点で)匹敵[比肩]する ; (よい意味でも悪い意味でも)引けを取らない ◇Few trees can *compare with* our native rowan for ease of cultivation. 栽培のしやすさは我が国国産のナナカマドに匹敵する樹木がないほどない ◇How do these results *compare with* last year's (= are they better or worse)? これらの結果は昨年のものと比べてどうですか ◇This Roman gold doesn't *compare to* (is not as good as) a recent find by a local farmer, which is worth millions. このローマ時代の金は地元の農民によって最近発見された何百万の価値があるものには引けを取る ◇This government's record *com-* *pares favourably with* (= is better than) that of our predecessors. 現政府の実績は前政府の残したそれと比べて引けを取らない ◇The profit of £23 million *compares* (= contrasts) with a £32 million loss in the previous financial year. 2千3百万ポンドの利益は前年度の3千2百万ポンドの損失とは好対照だ ☞ **comparable** (EQUIVALENT)

match [他] (良さ・面白さ・成功の点で)匹敵[比肩]する ◇The teams are *evenly matched* (= of a similar standard). それらのチームは力量が互角だった ◇The two firms are quite *closely matched* in terms of size and profitability 規模と収益性の観点から見てその二つの会社はほぼ互角だ ◇The firm was unable to *match* the salaries offered by their rivals. その会社は給料をライバル会社のそれに比肩させることができなかった

rival (-ll-, 米 -l-) [他] (良さ・印象深さの点で)好敵手となる ◇You will find scenery to *rival* anything you can see in the Alps. アルプスの景色に匹敵するものが見られるだろう ◇Golf cannot *rival* football for excitement. 興奮を求めるならゴルフはサッカーに及ばない

equal (-ll-, 米 -l-) [他] (良さの点で)匹敵する ; (他の人と)同等のことを成し遂げる ◇Half-year profits *equalled* the best expectations. 半期の利益が予想最高値を達成した ◇With his last jump he *equalled* the world record. 彼は最後のジャンプで世界記録に並んだ

be on a par with sb/sth 句動《ややインフォーマル》(良さ・悪さ・重要性などの点で)同等である ◇Profits should *be on a par with* last year. 利益はきっと昨年並だろう ◇It's quite impressive, but it's not *on a par with* the stadiums we have back home. その競技場はなかなか立派なものだが, 私たちの国にあるスタジアムには及ばない

compensation 图

compensation・refund・rebate・award・restitution・reimbursement
人, 金銭, 所有物の損害を償うお金などを表す
【類語訳】補償, 賠償, 払い戻し金, 返金, 裁定, 弁償, 返還

文型&コロケーション
▸compensation/ a refund/ a rebate/ an award/ restitution/ reimbursement from sb to sb
▸compensation/ a refund/ a rebate/ an award/ restitution/ reimbursement for sth
▸a refund/ rebate on sth
▸to pay/ receive, etc. money as/ in compensation/ restitution
▸(a) full compensation/ refund/ rebate/ restitution/ reimbursement/ reparation/ redress
▸to receive compensation/ a refund/ a rebate/ an award/ restitution/ reimbursement
▸to get compensation/ a refund/ a rebate/ an award/ restitution
▸to pay compensation/ a refund/ a rebate/ restitution/ reimbursement
▸to make compensation/ a refund/ an award/ restitution/ reimbursement
▸to offer (sb) compensation/ a refund/ a rebate/ restitution/ reimbursement
▸to be entitled to compensation/ a refund/ a rebate/ restitution/ reimbursement
▸to seek compensation/ a refund/ restitution/ reimbursement

↪**compensation**

▶ to **claim** compensation/ a refund/ a rebate/ restitution/ reimbursement
▶ to **demand** compensation/ a refund/ restitution/ reimbursement

compensation [U, C]（傷害・損害に対する）補償[賠償]（金）◇The employer has a duty to pay full *compensation* for injuries received at work. 雇用主には就業中に被る傷害に対して完全に補償する義務がある ◇She received a cash sum by way of *compensation*. 彼女は賠償として現金を受け取った

refund（過払いによる）払い戻し金，（店からの）返金 ◇If there is a delay of 12 hours or more, you will receive a full *refund* of the price of your trip. もし12時間以上の遅延があれば，旅行代金を全額返金いたします

rebate（過払いによる）払い戻し金 ◇You may be entitled to a *rebate* on your car insurance. あなたは自動車保険の払い戻し金を受け取る資格があるかもしれない

ノート **refund** と **rebate** の使い分け：**refund** のほうが **rebate** よりも一般的。**rebate** は過払いに対してのみ用いられ，特に税金の「払い戻し金」を指す。**refund** は商品などに返品したり，購入した商品・サービスが当然期待する質・水準を満たさない場合に受け取る「返金」を指すこともある。

award [C, U]（裁判で勝訴側に支払われる）賠償金；（損害賠償などの）裁定 ◇an *award* of £600,000 libel damages 60万ポンドの賠償の裁定がなされた名誉棄損 ◇The court must specify the different elements in its *award*of compensation. 裁判所はその賠償金裁定の内訳を明確にしなければならない ☞ **award** (GIVE 1)

restitution [U]《フォーマル or 法律》（遺失・盗難に対する持ち主への）弁償，返還；（傷害・損害に対する）賠償 ◇The family's lawyer is demanding the *restitution* of all family property seized under the previous regime. その家族の顧問弁護士は前政権下で没収された全家産の返還を要求している ◇The company has a legal duty to make *restitution* to passengers for any inconvenience caused. その会社には発生したいかなる不便に対しても乗客への賠償を行う法的義務がある

reimbursement [U]《ややフォーマル》（本人の責任でない支払い[遺失]に対する）償還，払い戻し ◇You will receive *reimbursement* for any additional costs incurred while on company business. 会社の業務でかかったいかなる追加費用に対しても払い戻しを受けられるだろう

compete 動

compete・fight・battle・take sb on・struggle・contest・vie・pit sb/sth against sb/sth

競争，競技，選挙などで他の人に勝とうとすることを表す
【類語訳】競う，競争する，闘争する，闘う，対戦する

文型&コロケーション

▶ to compete/ fight/ battle/ struggle/ vie **for** sth
▶ to compete/ battle/ struggle/ vie **with** sb
▶ to compete/ battle/ vie **to do** sth
▶ to compete for/ battle for/ contest/ vie for a (first/ second/ etc.) **place**
▶ to compete/ fight/ struggle/ vie **for power**
▶ to fight/ battle/ struggle/ vie **for control**
▶ to compete/ fight/ vie **for a share of** sth
▶ to compete/ fight/ battle/ struggle **hard**

▶ to **successfully** compete for/ fight (for)/ contest sth

compete [自] 競う，張り合う ◇Small bookshops can't *compete* with the large stores. 小規模の書店はそうした大規模店と張り合うことはできない ◇Several projects are *competing against* each other for scarce resources. いくつかの事業が乏しい資源を奪い合っている ◇Travel firms are *competing* fiercely on price. 旅行会社は激しい価格競争をしている ◇Colleges will have to *compete* to attract the best students. 大学は最も優秀な学生たちを引きつけるための競争を強いられるだろう ☞ **competitor, the competition** (ENEMY)

fight [自, 他]（競技などで）激しく争う ◇She's *fighting* for a place in the national team. 彼女は国の代表チームの座を争っている ◇Collins *fought back* to level the match at 2 sets all. コリンズが反撃に転じ，試合を2セット・オールのイーブンにした ◇There are twelve parties *fighting* the election.《特に英》選挙を戦う党は12ある

battle [自]《特にジャーナリズム》（競技・論争などで）競争[闘争]する，（難事と）闘う ◇Unions are *battling* with the company **over** the job losses. 労組が雇用削減に関して会社と争っている ◇The players have *battled* hard. 選手たちは懸命に戦ってきた ◇The two sides will **battle it out** in the final next week. 来週の決勝戦で両者は死闘を演じることになるだろう ❶ *battle* には「不快[危険]な事に立ち向かう」の意味もある。◆ She's still *battling* with a knee injury.（彼女はまだ膝の故障と闘っている）．この意味では《米》では目的語を伴うこともある。◆ He *battled* cancer for four years.（彼は4年間ガンと闘った）．☞ **fight** (OPPOSE)

,take sb 'on [句動詞]《受身なし》（競争相手と）対戦[対決]する ◇He'll *take on* the former Olympic champion in the 5,000 metres. 彼は前オリンピック・チャンピオンと5千メートルで対戦することになっている ◇Why don't you *take him on at* chess? 彼とチェスで勝負したらどうだい

struggle [自]（物事を得るために）争う ◇The two men *struggled* for control of the party. 二人の男が党の覇権を争った ◇The firms are *struggling* for market share. それらの会社は市場占有率を争っている

contest [他]（競技・選挙で）競う，争う ◇Three candidates *contested* the leadership. 三人の候補者が指導者の地位を争った ◇It turned out to be another *hotly contested* tournament. またも激戦の大会となった

vie [自]《ややフォーマル》（物事を得るために）激しく争う ◇The boys would *vie* with each other to impress her. 男の子たちは競い合って彼女の気を引こうとしていた ◇They are all *vying* for a place in the team. 彼らは皆チームのメンバーの座を争っている

'pit sb/sth against sb/sth [句動詞] (-tt-)（競技などで人・力・知力・決断力を）競わせる ◇The issue of water supply *pitted* farmers *against* environmentalists. 水の供給問題で農家と環境保護論者が争った ◇They *pit their wits against* each other in the weekly sports quiz. 週に一度のスポーツクイズで彼らは互いに知力を競わせている

competition 名

1 competition・contest・quiz

賞を獲得する[誰が一番であるかを決める]ために人々が競い合う行事
【類語訳】競技会，大会，コンペ，コンテスト，コンクール，クイズ

competition

文型&コロケーション
- a competition/ contest **between** sb
- a competition/ contest **for** sth
- **in** a competition/ contest/ quiz
- a/ an **international/ national/ sporting** competition/ contest
- to **enter/ take part in/ win/ have/ hold** a competition/ contest/ quiz

competition [C] 競技会, 大会, コンペ ◇I won a car in a *competition*. 私は競技会で車を獲得した ◇We're going to have a *competition* to see who can swim the furthest. 誰が最も長距離を泳げるかを競う競技会を開催します ◇The *competition* is open to all readers of the magazine. そのコンペは雑誌の読者なら誰でも参加できます
☞ **competitor** (PARTICIPANT)

contest [C] 競技会, コンテスト, コンクール ◇They won the doubles *contest against* the Williams sisters. 彼らはウィリアムズ姉妹に勝ってダブルス競技を制した ◇Jackson has injured his knee and is now out of the *contest*. ジャクソンは膝を負傷したので、コンテストからは外れている ◇She's the favourite for this year's Eurovision Song *Contest*. 彼女は今年のユーロヴィジョン・ソング・コンテストの優勝候補だ ◇a beauty/talent *contest* 美人/芸能コンテスト ❶be no contest は一方が強すぎて楽勝することが確実なため「試合にならない」ことを意味する.

ノート competition と contest の使い分け：両語ともスポーツ・ゲームで人々が競い合う行事, または演奏[演技]・芸術・著述など才能・知識を披露する行事を指す. competition のほうがいくぶん一般的な語で, チーム・団体・個人による競い合いについて用いることができる. contest は賞を獲得するために少数の個人が競い合うことを指すことが多い.《英》では competition は多数の人が郵便・電話で参加する行事を指すこともある. それには例えば, 無作為に名前が選び出された人が一等を得るような, 才能・技術によってではなく運によって勝者が決まる行事も含まれる. ♦ *Competition*: to win an Oxford Mini car, customers must guess how many copies of the Oxford Minidictionary will fit into the car. (抽選会：オックスフォード小辞典が何冊積み込めるかを当てれば, オックスフォード・ミニ・カーがもらえます).《米》では contest がこのような意味で用いられることもある. ♦ To enter the *contest*, simply send an email to this address... (抽選会への応募は, このアドレスにEメールを送信するだけです). ☞ **contestant** (PARTICIPANT)

quiz (複 **quizzes**) [C] クイズ(大会) ◇I'm useless at *general knowledge quizzes*. 私は常識クイズはだめだ ◇He's the host of a popular *TV quiz show*. 彼はテレビの人気クイズ番組の司会者だ ◇The club has weekly *quiz nights*. そのクラブは週に一度クイズ・ナイトを開催している

2 competition・race・contest・rivalry・competitiveness
人や組織が何かを争うべく互いに競い合う状況を表す
【類語訳】競争, 競争意識, 対抗意識, 競争力

文型&コロケーション
- competition/ a race/ a contest/ rivalry **for** sth
- competition/ a race/ a contest/ rivalry **between** people
- **in** competition/ a race/ a contest/ rivalry **with** sb/ sth
- competition/ a race **to do** sth
- (a) **fierce** competition/ contest/ rivalry/ competitiveness
- (an) **open** competition/ race/ contest
- **international** competition/ rivalry/ competitiveness
- to **enter/ win/ lose** the race/ contest

competition [U] (人・組織同士の)競争 ◇There is now intense *competition* between schools to attract students. 今学校の間では生徒募集の激しい競争が行われている ◇We are in *competition* with four other companies. 当社は他の4つの会社と競い合っている ◇We face strong *competition from* other countries. 我が国は他国との激しい競争に直面している ◇They won the order *against* fierce international *competition*. 彼らは熾烈な国際競争を制して注文を取り付けた ◇The company is having to lay off workers in the face of *stiff competition*. その会社は厳しい競争に直面し, 従業員を解雇せざるをえなくなっている ☞ **competitor** (PARTICIPANT)

race [単数で]《特にジャーナリズム》(人・団体・組織同士の)競争 ◇Polls give him the edge over his Democratic rival in the *race* for the presidency. 世論調査の結果, 彼は大統領の座を争う戦いで民主党対立候補より優位に立っている ◇Two right-wing candidates *lead the* presidential *race*. 右派の候補者2名が大統領選挙戦をリードしている ◇The rival TV companies are in a *race* to bring out the first film drama of her life. 競合するテレビ会社が彼女の人生の初のドラマ化をめぐってしのぎを削っている ◇*The race is on* (= has begun) to find a cure for this disease. この病気の治療法を見つける競争が始まっている

contest [C]《特にジャーナリズム》(候補者・企業同士の)競争 ◇During the election *contest* newspapers are not allowed to publish opinion polls. 選挙戦の間, 新聞は世論調査を報道することを許されていない ◇The other bidders for the contract complained that it had not been a fair *contest*. その契約に入札した他の業者たちから, それが公正な競争ではなかったという不満の声が上がった

ノート race と contest の使い分け：両語とも政治選挙について用いられ, ほとんどの場合どちらの語を使用しても構わない. しかしながら, contest はふつう選挙それ自体を指し, 時には選挙日直前の2〜3週間の選挙戦を指すこともある. race は特にアメリカの大統領選の場合など, 数か月に及ぶこともある選挙運動の全期間を含む. 人を主語にして wins/loses a race/ contest や leads/is ahead in the race for sth と言うが, leads/is ahead in the contest for sth とはふつう言わない. race はまた, まだ誰も達成していない物事を成し遂げようとする競争についても用いられる.

rivalry [C, U] (二人の人・二つのチーム[団体, 会社]同士の)競争 ◇Bitter ethnic *rivalries* within the region have grown. 地域内での激しい民族間競争が起こっている ◇There is a certain amount of *friendly rivalry* between the teams. それらのチームの間には多少のよい意味での対抗意識がある ◇Her parents had been very aware of the problems of *sibling rivalry* (= between brothers and sisters) before the younger child was born. 彼女の両親は下の子が生まれる前から兄弟間の競争意識の問題をよく心得ていた

ノート competition と rivalry の使い分け：この意味では competition はビジネスの文脈で最も頻繁に用いられる. rivalry は政治・スポーツ・個人的な人間関係に用いられることが多い.

competitiveness [単数で, U] (人・物事同士の)競争[対

抗]意識；競争力 ◇Jenny brings a fierce *competitiveness* to the team. ジェニーは激しい競争意識をチーム内に持ち込んでいる ◇The move is an attempt to improve the *competitiveness* of British industry. その措置にはイギリス産業の競争力を増進する狙いがある

➤ **competitive** 形 ◇It's a fiercely *competitive* market. それは競争の激しい市場である

complain 動

complain・protest・object・grumble・moan・whine・carp

人や物事に関して困っている[不満である]と述べる
【類語訳】不平を言う，不満を言う，文句を言う，反対する，愚痴る

文型&コロケーション

▶ to complain/ protest/ grumble/ moan/ whine/ carp **about** sth
▶ to grumble/ moan/ carp **on** about sth
▶ to complain/ protest/ grumble/ moan **at** sth
▶ to complain/ protest/ grumble/ moan/ whine **at** sb
▶ to complain/ protest/ object/ grumble/ moan/ whine **to** sb
▶ to complain/ protest/ object/ grumble/ moan/ whine **that...**
▶ to complain/ protest/ grumble **loudly**

complain [自, 他] 不平[不満, 文句]を言う ◇She never *complains*, but she's obviously exhausted. 彼女は決して泣き言を言わないが明らかに疲れている ◇I'm going to *complain* to the manager about this. 私はこの件に関して支配人に文句を言うつもりだ ◇'It's not fair,' she *complained*. 「不公平だわ」と彼女は文句を言った ◇The defendant *complained of* intimidation during the investigation. 《ややフォーマル》被告は取調べ中の脅しに関して不服を申し立てた

protest [自, 他] (発言・行動によって公然と)抗議する；異議を申し立てる ◇Students took to the streets to *protest against* the decision. 学生たちが街頭に繰り出してその決定に抗議した ◇It's no use *protesting*, I won't change my mind. 反対しても無駄だ。私は考えを変えるつもりはない ◇She *protested* that she could not receive a fair trial. 公正な裁判を受けられなかったと彼女は異議を申し立てた ❶《米》では protest は目的語として名詞を取ることもできる．
・ They fully intend to *protest* the decision. 《米》彼らは完全にその決定に抗議するつもりだ）．☞ **protest** (OPPOSITION), **protester** (PROTESTER)

object [自, 他] (発言によって)反対する, 抗議する；反対理由を挙げる ◇If nobody *objects*, we'll postpone the meeting till next week. 異論がなければ会議を来週まで延期しよう ◇I really *object* to being charged for parking. 私は駐車料金を請求されることに断固反対する ◇He *objected* that the police had arrested him without sufficient evidence. 彼は証拠不十分にもかかわらず警察に逮捕されたと抗議した ☞ **objection** (OPPOSITION)

grumble [自, 他]《ややインフォーマル, けなして》(不機嫌に)文句[愚痴]を言う ◇She's always *grumbling* to me about how badly she's treated at work. 彼女はいかに自分が職場でひどい扱いを受けているかについて私にぼやいてばかりいる

moan [自, 他]《ややインフォーマル, けなして》(うるさく)文句[愚痴]を言う, 愚痴る ◇They're always *moaning and groaning* about how much they have to do. 彼らは自分たちがいかに忙しいかについて愚痴ってばかりいる ◇What are you *moaning on* about now? 《英》今度は何が気に入らないの ☞ **moan** (WHISPER)

whine [自, 他]《ややインフォーマル, けなして》(泣き声で)文句[愚痴]を言う, ぐずる ◇Stop *whining*! ぴーぴー泣かないの ◇'I want to go home,' *whined* Toby. 「おうちに帰りたい」とトビーはぐずった ❶whine はしばしば幼い子どもが文句を言って困らせることについて用いられる．

carp [自]《ややインフォーマル, けなして》(他の人への)文句[難癖]を繰り返す ◇I've had enough of him constantly *carping* and criticizing. 絶え間ない彼の難癖や批判にはもううんざりだ ◇Lord, how you *carp* on, Lucy! ああ, ルーシー, どれだけ文句を言うんだ ❶carp は文句が繰り返されることを強調する **on** を伴ってよく用いられる．

complete 形

complete・total・real・absolute・outright・utter・perfect・positive・downright

物事の度合いがいかにすごいかを強調して表す
【類語訳】まったくの, 完全な, 全面的な, 絶大な, 圧倒的な

文型&コロケーション

▶ a complete/ a total/ a real/ an absolute/ an utter **disaster**
▶ a complete/ a total/ a real/ an absolute **mess**
▶ a complete/ a total/ a real **idiot**
▶ a complete/ a total/ an absolute/ an utter **fool**
▶ complete/ total/ absolute/ utter **rubbish/ nonsense/ darkness**
▶ complete/ total/ absolute/ utter/ perfect **silence**
▶ a complete/ total/ perfect **stranger**
▶ a complete/ a real/ an absolute **beginner**
▶ a complete/ a total/ an absolute/ an outright **ban**

complete [ふつう名詞の前で] まったくの, 完全なる ◇We were in *complete* agreement. 私たちは完全に意見が一致していた ◇It came as a *complete* surprise. それにはまったく驚いた ◇The whole thing has been a *complete* waste of time. すべて完全に時間の無駄だった ☞ **completely** (QUITE 2)

total [名詞の前で] まったくの, 完全なる, 全面的な ◇The room was in *total* darkness. その部屋は真っ暗だった ◇I always expect *total* honesty from my employees. 私は常に従業員に完全な誠実さを求めている ◇Six years of *total war* had left no citizen untouched. 6年にわたる全面戦争で無傷の市民は誰一人いなかった ☞ **total** (WHOLE), **totally** (QUITE 2)

> ノート **complete と total の使い分け**：ほとんどすべての場合において両語とも使用可能． ◆ *complete/total* agreement/honesty/darkness （完全なる意見の一致／誠実さ／暗闇）． ◆ a *complete/total* surprise/idiot/waste of time/lack of understanding （まったくの驚き／ばか／時間の無駄／理解力の欠如）． total war は決まった表現なので complete との置き換えは不可． ✕Six years of *complete* war... total は名詞の前でのみ用いられ, complete は頻度は低くややフォーマルだが連結動詞の後でも用いることが可能．
> ◆ Her misery was made *complete* when she was separated from her children. 《ややフォーマル》子どもと離れ離れになって彼女は本当に悲しかった）． ✕Her misery was made *total*...

real [名詞の前で]《ややインフォーマル、特に話し言葉》まったく[本当]の ◇He looks like a *real* idiot. 彼は本当にばかみたいだ ◇This accident could have produced a *real* tragedy. この事故は大惨事をもたらしかねなかった ◇Her next play was a *real* contrast. 彼女の次の芝居はまったく対照的なものだった ❶ *real* はややインフォーマルな言い回しに用いられ、物事の好ましくない[異なる]度合いを強調する。☞ **really** (VERY 副)

absolute [ふつう名詞の前で]《特に話し言葉》まったくの、完全なる、絶大な ◇He must earn an *absolute* fortune. 彼は大もうけするにちがいない ◇'You're wrong,' she said with *absolute* certainty. 「あなたが間違っているわ」と彼女は絶対的な確信を持って言った ❶ *absolute* は特に話し言葉で用いられ、物事がいかに好ましくない[大きい]かを強調する。少しフォーマルな書き言葉では、感情・性質を表すのにも用いられる。ふつう名詞の前で用いられるが、文語的な文脈では連結動詞の後で用いられることもある。◆Around them the darkness was *absolute*, the silence oppressive. (《文語》辺りは真っ暗闇で、静寂が重苦しかった). ☞ **absolutely** (QUITE 2)

outright [名詞の前で] まったくの、完全なる、全面[圧倒]的な ◇She was the *outright* winner. 彼女は完全なる勝者だった ◇No one party is expected to gain an *outright* majority. 圧倒的過半数を獲得すると目される政党は一つとない ◇They may introduce tougher restrictions or even an *outright* ban. より厳しい制限あるいは全面的な禁止までもが打ち出されるかもしれない ❶ この意味における *outright* は win, victory, winner, majority, ban, rejection, refusal, lie と結びつく。
▷**outright** ◇Neither candidate won *outright*. どちらの候補者も圧勝ではなかった

utter [名詞の前で] まったくの、完全なる ◇That's *complete and utter* nonsense! それはまったくばかな話だ ◇To my *utter* amazement she agreed. まったく驚いたことに彼女は同意した ❶ *utter* は特に驚き・嫌悪・絶望・混乱・信念・平穏など感情・性質を表すのにも用いられる。surprise, disgust, despair, failure, confusion, chaos, conviction, delight, silence, stillness といった語と結びつく。☞ **utterly** (QUITE 2)

perfect [名詞の前で] まったくの、完全なる ◇I don't know her — she's a *perfect* stranger. 彼女のことは知らない—赤の他人だ ◇I have a *perfect right* to ask you — and you have the right not to answer. 私にはあなたに質問する完全な権利がある—そしてあなたには答えなくてもいい権利がある ❶ この意味における perfect は stranger, gentleman, right, accuracy, freedom, harmony, happiness と結びつく。☞ **perfectly** (QUITE 2)

positive [名詞の前で]《ややインフォーマル》まったくの、完全なる ◇He has a *positive* genius for upsetting people. 彼は人を怒らせるまったくの天才だ ◇It was a *positive* miracle that we survived. 私たちが生き残れたのはまったくの奇跡だった

downright [名詞の前で]《ややインフォーマル、ふつうけなして》(否定的[不愉快]な事を強調して)まったくの ◇It's a *downright* disgrace that they still haven't paid you. 彼らがあなたへまだ支払いをしていないなんてもってのほかだ
▷**downright** 副 ◇It's not just stupid — it's *downright* dangerous. ただの愚かどころか—まったくもって危険だ

complex 形

complex・complicated・elaborate・intricate・tortuous・involved・convoluted・tangled

complex 117

物事に多くの要素や細部があって理解するのが難しいことを表す
【類語訳】複雑な、入り組んだ、ややこしい、精巧な、緻密な、手の込んだ、入念な、紆余曲折のある

―――――――――――――――

文型&コロケーション

▶a complex/ a complicated/ an elaborate/ an intricate **system**
▶a complex/ a complicated/ an elaborate/ an intricate/ a convoluted **story/ plot**
▶a complex/ a complicated/ an elaborate/ an intricate **design/ structure/ network**
▶a complex/ a complicated/ an intricate/ a tangled **web/ relationship**
▶complex/ complicated/ elaborate **machinery**
▶a complex/ complicated/ tortuous **process**
▶extremely complex/ complicated/ elaborate/ intricate/ involved
▶highly complex/ complicated/ elaborate/ intricate

complex 複雑な、入り組んだ、ややこしい ◇This is a highly *complex* matter. これは極めて複雑な問題だ ◇The mechanism involves a *complex* arrangement of rods and cogs. その機械装置には連接棒と歯車の複雑な組み合わせが含まれている ◇She managed to put over a fairly *complex* argument in a brilliantly simple way. 彼女は相当に入り組んだ論旨を見事なわかりやすさで説明しきってみせた 反意 **simple** (EASY 1)

complicated 複雑な、入り組んだ、ややこしい ◇The instructions look very *complicated*. その使用説明書はとてもややこしそうに見える ◇This is where the story gets *complicated*. ここで話が複雑になる ◇It's all very *complicated* — but I'll try and explain. すべてとてもややこしいです—しかし説明してみましょう 反意 **uncomplicated, straightforward** (EASY 1), ☞ **complication** (PROBLEM)

―――――――――――――――

ノート **complex** と **complicated** の使い分け：多くの場合、両語とも使用可能。◆a *complex/complicated* problem (複雑な問題). ◆ *complex/complicated* instructions (ややこしい指示). complicated のほうが会話において用いられることが若干多い。◆I'll send you map of how to get here. It's a bit too *complicated* to describe. (ここまでの地図を送るよ。少し複雑すぎて説明しづらいから). complex のほうが書き言葉で用いられることがいくぶん多く、重大[学問的、科学的、専門的]な問題について用いられる。◆a *complex* mathematical equation/ formula (複雑な数学の方程式/公式). また、両語とも物事それ自体がそもそも理解しがたいことを指すが、complicated はしばしば、何らかの出来事、変化、問題などによっていっそう複雑になったり、こんがらがったり、理解[扱い]が難しくなってしまったことを言う場合に使われる。

―――――――――――――――

elaborate [ふつう名詞の前で] 精巧な、緻密な、手の込んだ、入念な ◇The ceiling was tiled in an *elaborate* pattern. 天井には凝った模様にタイルが張られていた ◇She had prepared a very *elaborate* meal. 彼女はとても手の込んだ食事を用意していた ◇This *elaborate* deception fooled his family for ages. この巧みな嘘に彼の家族はずいぶん長いことだまされていた 反意 **simple** (EASY 1)

intricate 精巧な、緻密な ◇The building has *intricate* geometric designs on several of the walls. その建物のいくつかの壁には緻密な幾何学模様が施されていた ◇It is difficult to describe the *intricate* network of loyal-

ties and relationships. 忠誠心と人間関係との込み入った絡み合いを言葉にするのは難しい
▸**intricately** 副 ◇*intricately* carved/decorated/patterned 精巧に彫られた/緻密に装飾された/複雑な模様の
tortuous [ふつう名詞の前で]《書き言葉、しばしばけなして》紆余曲折のある；回りくどく複雑な ◇the long, *tortuous* process of negotiating peace in the region 長く、紆余曲折のあるその地域の和平交渉のプロセス
involved 入り組んだ、込み入った ◇Avoid long, *involved* debates which could be just delaying tactics. 戦略を遅らせるだけの長たらしくややこしい議論は避けなさい 反意 **straightforward** (EASY 1)
convoluted 《書き言葉、しばしばけなして》(必要以上に)複雑で分らない ◇The book has a rather *convoluted* plot. その本のプロットはやや複雑すぎる
tangled 複雑でわかりにくい、入り組んだ、ややこしい ◇The series involves the *tangled* relationships of two London families. そのシリーズではロンドンに住む二つの家族の複雑に絡み合った関係が描かれている ◇He spent the next few days wrestling with very *tangled* emotions. それから数日間、彼はよじれによじれた感情と闘った ❶元々はまったく単純で複雑でないものでも、重なり合って複雑で理解困難な状況を引き起こす変化や問題ゆえに、時間と共に*tangled*となることがしばしばある。

compromise 名

compromise・concession・trade-off・middle ground・sop・give and take
合意や問題解決のために二者間の要望が均衡すること、相反する二つの事物が均衡すること
【類語訳】妥協、譲歩、歩み寄り、中立、中道、譲り合い

文型&コロケーション
▸a compromise/ a trade-off/ middle ground/ give and take **between** sb/ sth and sb/ sth
▸a compromise/ concession **on/ over** sth
▸a concession/ a sop **to** sb
▸**as** a compromise/ concession/ trade-off/ sop
▸a **necessary** compromise/ concession/ trade-off
▸a/ an **possible/ obvious** compromise/ concession/ trade-off
▸to **make** a compromise/ a concession/ a trade-off
▸to **look for/ seek/ offer/ reject** a compromise/ concession

compromise [C, U] 妥協、譲歩、歩み寄り；妥協[折衷]案 ◇They came to a *compromise* over the exact amount to be paid. 彼らは正確な支払額に関して妥協に達した ◇In any relationship, you have to make *compromises*. どんな交渉においても妥協せねばならない ◇This model represents the best *compromise* between price and quality. このモデルは価格と品質とが最高の形で折り合っている ◇*Compromise* is an inevitable part of life. 妥協は人生において避けては通れないものだ
▸**compromise** 動 [自, 他] ◇Neither side is prepared to *compromise*. どちらの側も妥協する用意はない ◇We are not prepared to *compromise on* safety standards. 私たちは安全基準に関して妥協する用意はない ◇I refuse to *compromise* my principles. 私は自分の信条を曲げることを拒否する

concession [C, U] (争いの終了・難しさの緩和などの)譲歩 ◇The management will be forced to make *concessions* to the union. 経営者側は労働組合に譲歩することを強いられるだろう ◇The pressure group has **won** a number of *concessions* on environmental policy. その圧力団体は環境政策に関して多くの譲歩を引き出している ◇Military support was offered in return for the *concession of* territory. 領土に関する譲歩の見返りとして軍事支援が提供された
'trade-off [C] (相反する二つの事物の)釣り合いを保つこと、兼ね合いを考量すること ◇There is a *trade-off* between the benefits of the drug and the risk of side effects. その薬物については有用性と副作用の危険性との兼ね合いが問題である
'middle ground [U] (反対派の合意を得る)妥協[折衷]案；中立、中道 ◇Negotiations have failed to establish any *middle ground*. 交渉ではいかなる妥協案も成立しなかった ◇The ballet now **occupies the middle ground between** classical ballet and modern dance. 現在のバレエはクラシックバレエとモダンダンスの中道を行っている
sop [C, ふつう単数で]《特に書き言葉》(ささやかな)ご機嫌取り ◇The move was seen as another *sop* to the moderates in the party. その措置は党内の穏健派に対するもう一つのご機嫌取りのようなものと見なされた
,give and 'take [U] 譲り合い、歩み寄り、持ちつ持たれつ ◇We must accept a certain amount of *give and take*. 私たちはある程度譲り合わなければならない

concern 名

concern・worry・anxiety・apprehension・unease・angst・agitation
気をもんでいる状態やその原因を表す
【類語訳】懸念、心配、悩み、不安、危惧、苦悩

unease　　　anxiety　　　concern
　　　　　　apprehension　worry
　　　　　　angst
　　　　　　agitation

文型&コロケーション
▸concern/ worry/ anxiety/ apprehension/ unease/ angst **over/ about** sth
▸concern/ worry/ anxiety/ apprehension/ unease **that**...
▸**great/ considerable/ growing** concern/ worry/ anxiety/ apprehension/ unease/ agitation
▸**deep** concern/ anxiety/ unease
▸to **express** concern/ your worries/ anxiety/ apprehension/ unease
▸to **voice** your concern/ unease
▸to **share** your concerns/ worries
▸to **cause** concern/ anxiety/ apprehension/ unease

concern [U, C]《ややフォーマル》(多くの人々による)懸念；懸念事項 ◇She hasn't been seen for four days and there is *concern* for her safety. 彼女は4日間消息不明で安否が懸念されている ◇The report expressed *concern* over continuing high unemployment. その報告では高い失業率が継続していることへの懸念が示された ☞ **concern (WORRY), concerned (WORRIED)**
worry [U, C] 心配、悩み；心配事、悩みの種 ◇He claims

conclude, conclusion 119

the illness was caused by stress and *worry*. 彼はその病気がストレスと悩みによって引き起こされたと主張していた ◇He was *sick with worry*. 彼は気苦労がたたって体調を崩していた ☞*financial/family worries* 家計/家族に関する心配事 ☞**worried** (WORRIED)
anxiety [U, C] 不安, 心配；不安の種, 心配事 ◇Some hospital patients experience high levels of *anxiety*. 入院患者の中には高度に不安を持つ人がいる ◇She felt a nagging *anxiety* that could not be relieved. 彼女は癒すことのできないしつこい不安につきまとわれた ☞**anxious** (WORRIED)

> ノート **concern, worry, anxiety** の使い分け：worry は concern や anxiety よりもインフォーマルな語であるが、インフォーマルな言い回しでは、これらの名詞よりも **be worried** という表現を用いるほうが一般的。worry と anxiety は特に個人が抱くものを指し、concern はしばしば大勢の人が抱くものを指す。

apprehension [U, C]《ややフォーマル》（好ましくない事が起こるかもしれないという）不安, 心配, 危惧 ◇There is growing *apprehension* that fighting will begin again. 戦闘が再び開始されるかもしれないという不安が高まっている ◇She felt some *apprehension* at seeing him again. 彼女は彼にまた会うのではないかと案じた ☞**apprehensive** (WORRIED)
unease [U, 単数で]（軽度の）不安, 気がかり ◇He was unable to hide his *unease* at the way the situation was developing. 事態の進展ぶりに彼は不安を隠せなかった ☞**uneasy** (WORRIED)
angst [U]（状況・人生に対する）不安, 心配, 苦悩 ◇songs full of teenage *angst* 十代の苦悩に満ちた歌
agitation [U]（振る舞いに表れる）心配, 不安, の動揺 ◇Dot arrived in a state of great *agitation*. ドットはあわてふためいた様子で到着した ◇He started to pace up and down the room in *agitation*. 彼は心配で部屋を行ったり来たりし始めた ☞**agitated** (RESTLESS)

conclude 動

conclude・understand・figure・infer・deduce・gather・reason・read sth into sth
証拠や情報に従って判断を下したり、信じたりする
【類語訳】結論を下す, 承知する, 判断する, 推測する, 推断する, 推論する, 読み取る

文型&コロケーション

▶ to conclude/ understand/ figure/ infer/ deduce/ gather/ reason **from** sth
▶ to conclude/ understand/ figure/ infer/ deduce/ gather sth **about** sth
▶ to conclude/ understand/ figure/ infer/ deduce/ gather/ reason **that**...
▶ to figure/ deduce **what/ how/ who/ why**...
▶ It is concluded/ understood/ inferred/ deduced/ reasoned **that**...
▶ It can be concluded/ inferred/ deduced **that**...

conclude [他]《進行形なし》（情報に基づいて）結論を下す ◇What do you *conclude* from that? そこからどのような結論を下しますか ◇The report *concluded* that the cheapest option was to close the laboratory. その報告の結論としては最も安上がりな選択肢が研究所を閉鎖することだった

understand [他]《進行形なし》《ややフォーマル》（述べられたとおりに）承知する ◇Am I to *understand* that you refuse? 拒否ととってよろしいでしょうか ◇The prime minister is *understood* to have been extremely angry about the report. 首相はその報告に激怒していることだ ☞**understanding** (DEFINITION)
figure [他]《進行形なし》《ややインフォーマル》（起こる[真実である]と）判断する ◇I *figured* (that) if I took the night train, I could be in Scotland by morning. 夜行列車に乗れば朝までにはスコットランドに着けると思いました ◇There was only one thing to do, he *figured*. すべきことはたった一つしかないと彼は思った
infer (-rr-) [他]《進行形はまれ》（証拠・推論を用いて）推断[推測]する ◇Much of the meaning can be *inferred* from the context. その文脈からは意味するところの多くが推測できる ◇It is reasonable to *infer* that the government knew all about this. 政府がこれに関してすべてを知っていたと推測することは理にかなっている
deduce [他]《進行形なし》（証拠・推論を用いて）推定[推測]する ◇We can *deduce* a lot from what people spend their money on. 人々のお金の使い道から多くのことが推測できる

> ノート **infer** と **deduce** の使い分け：多くの場合両語とも使用可能だが、若干の違いがある。infer は手元にある証拠から考えておそらく真実であるとするが、deduce は事実から考えて論理的に真実であるとする。

gather [他]《進行形なし》《ややインフォーマル, 特に話し言葉》（述べられたとおりに）承知する ◇I *gather* you wanted to see me. 私に用件があったそうですね ◇'There's been a delay.' 'So I *gather*.'「遅れているね」「そう思うよ」◇As far as I can *gather*, he got involved in a fight. 私の知る限りでは彼は喧嘩に巻き込まれたらしい ◇From what they could *gather*, there had been some kind of problem back at the base. 得られた情報によると、何らかの問題が根底にあったようだ

> ノート **understand** と **gather** の使い分け：両語とも話し言葉でよく用いられるが、understand のほうが gather よりフォーマルである。gather は understand よりも重大なことを示唆することがある。understand はふつう質問せずに述べられたとおりに理解すること。gather は述べられたとおりに理解することもの、伝え聞いて知ったりすることもある。gather はしばしば can や could と共に用いられる。×As far as I can *understand*... ×From what they could *understand*...

reason [他, 自]（事実[論理的思考]によって）推論する ◇They *reasoned*, correctly, that the enemy would not attempt an attack at night. 敵は夜は攻撃を仕掛けてこないだろうと彼らは推論した, 正しい推論だった ☞**reason** (REASON), **reasoned** (RATIONAL)
,**read sth 'into sth** 句動詞（過大に特定の意味に）読み取る ◇Yes, he's going over to talk to her, but don't *read too much into it*. はい、彼は彼女に話しに行っていますが、深読みはしないでください

conclusion 名 ☞SPECULATION

conclusion・finding・judgment・ruling・verdict・inference・deduction
状況に関するすべての事実を検討した後で判断を下して確信すること

↪conclusion

condition

【類語訳】結論, 調査結果, 判決, 決定, 裁定, 評決, 判定, 意見, 推論, 結論

文型&コロケーション
- a conclusion/ findings/ a judgment/ a ruling/ an inference/ a deduction **about** sth
- a judgment/ ruling/ verdict **against/ in favour of/ on** sb/ sth
- the conclusion/ finding/ judgment/ ruling/ verdict/ inference/ deduction **that**...
- a/ the **general** conclusion/ finding/ verdict/ inference/ deduction
- a/ the **correct/ wrong** conclusion/ verdict/ inference
- a **logical/ reasonable/ valid** conclusion/ inference/ deduction
- the **final** conclusion/ judgment/ ruling/ verdict
- **reach** a conclusion/ judgment/ verdict
- **make** a judgment/ a finding/ a ruling/ an inference/ a deduction/ a decree
- to **give** judgment/ a ruling/ a verdict
- to **challenge** sb's findings/ a ruling/ a verdict
- to **base** your conclusion/ findings/ judgment/ ruling/ verdict **on** sth

conclusion [C] 結論 ◇We can safely draw some *conclusions* from our discussion. 私たちは間違いなく議論からいくつかの結論を引き出すことができる ◇I've *come to the conclusion* that he's not the right person for the job. 私は彼がその仕事に適任の人材ではないという結論に至った ◇Don't *jump to conclusions* (= do not decide that sth is true without knowing the facts). 結論を急ぎすぎないように

finding [C, ふつう複数で] 調査結果 ◇These *findings* suggest that there is no direct link between unemployment and crime. これらの調査結果は失業と犯罪との間に直接的なつながりはないことを示している ◆The *findings* are based on interviews with more than 2,000 people. その調査結果は2千人以上の人へのインタビューに基づいている ❶フォーマルな[法律上の]言い回しではfindingには法廷における「(裁判官・陪審による)判決・評決」の意味もある. ◆The facts of this case do not justify a *finding* of negligence. (この事件の事実からは過失の判決が正当であるとは認められない). ☞ find (FIND 1)

judgment (または **judgement**) [C, U] (裁判所・裁判官による)判決 ◇They are hoping for a *judgment* in their favour from the European Court of Justice. 彼らは欧州裁判所で自分たちに有利な判決が出ることを望んでいる ◇The court has yet to *pass judgment* (= to say what its decision is) in this case. 裁判所はこの事件に関してまだ判決を下していない ❶たいていの意味において, この単語の通常の綴りは《英》ではjudgement,《米》ではjudgmentであるが, 法律の文脈では《英》《米》共にjudgmentのほうが好まれる.

ruling [C] (権力者・裁判官による公式の)決定, 裁定 ◇The court will make its *ruling* on the case next week. 来週裁判所がその事件に関する裁定を下す予定だ ☞ rule (RULE 動 2)

verdict [C] (陪審による)評決；(検査・検討後の)判定, 意見 ◇The jury *returned a verdict* (= gave a verdict) of not guilty. 陪審は無罪の評決を下した ◇The coroner *recorded a verdict* of accidental death. 検死官は事故死と判定した ◇The panel will give their *verdict* on the latest video releases. パネリストたちが新発売のビデオに関して意見を述べることになっている

ノート finding, judgment, ruling, verdict の使い分け：これらの語はすべて裁判所で下される決定について用いることができる. finding は最もフォーマルな語で, 裁判所が行う犯罪・違法行為の種類を決定する際には, ふつう a finding of negligence/murder/unfair dismissal (過失/殺人/不当解雇の判決[評決]) などの句で用いられる. finding はまた法律上の意味以外で research findings (調査結果) の形で頻繁に用いられる. judgment と ruling は他よりも一般的な語で, 特に裁判所の判決を求める告訴に対して下される決定について用いられる. judgment は裁判官・陪審を問わず, 決定が裁判所によって下されることを強調し, ruling は決定が陪審員団ではなく, 権限を有する個人, しばしば裁判官(常にではない)によって下されることを強調する. ◆The *judgment* of the jury cannot be overturned. (陪審の評決は覆すことができない). ✗the *ruling* of the jury. verdict は刑事事件において犯罪の容疑者が有罪か無罪かに関する陪審による評決を指し, 検死での検死官による判定についても用いられる.

inference [C, U] (既知の事柄から導かれる)推論, 結論；推論すること ◇What *inferences* can we draw from this data? このデータからどんな結論を導き出すことができますか ◇If he is guilty then, *by inference*, so is his partner (= it is logical to think so, from the same evidence). もしそれで彼が有罪ならば, 推論の結果として彼の仲間もそうなる

deduction [U, C] (手持ちの情報からの)推論 ◇He arrived at the solution by a simple process of *deduction*. 彼は単純な推論の過程を経てその解決策に至った ◇If my *deductions* are correct, I can tell you who the murderer is. もし私の推論が正しければ, 殺人犯が誰だか言える

ノート inference と deduction の使い分け：inference は deduction よりもやや確実性に欠け, 既知の事柄から考えておそらく真実であるはずだとすること. deduction は事実に誤りがなければ論理的に真実であるはずだとすること. inference はふつう deduction よりも複雑な推論を指す. ✗He arrived at the solution by a simple process of *inference*.

condition 名

condition • requirement • terms • provision • qualification • prerequisite • proviso • the small print
何かが発生する[合意に達する]前に起こって[了解されて]いなければならない事柄
【類語訳】条件, 必要条件, 要件, 条項, 但し書き, 注意事項

文型&コロケーション
- a condition/ requirement/ terms/ a provision/ a prerequisite **for** sth
- **under** the conditions/ terms/ provisions **of** sth
- **with** the qualification/ proviso **that**...
- an **important** condition/ requirement/ provision/ qualification/ prerequisite/ proviso
- **strict** conditions/ requirements/ terms/ provisions
- the **basic** condition/ requirements/ terms/ provision/ prerequisite
- a/ an **absolute/ essential/ necessary** condition/ requirement/ prerequisite
- **special** conditions/ requirements/ terms/ provisions

- ▶a **legal** requirement/ provision/ prerequisite
- ▶to **lay down** conditions/ requirements/ terms/ provisions
- ▶to **add** a provision/ proviso/ qualification
- ▶to **contain** a requirement/ terms/ provisions/ qualifications/ a proviso
- ▶to **accept/ observe/ comply with** the conditions/ requirements/ terms/ provisions
- ▶to **satisfy/ fulfil** the conditions/ requirements/ terms

condition [C]（契約・合意のための）条件；（物事が発生するための）条件 ◇They agreed to lend us the car *on condition that* (= only if) we returned it before the weekend. 週末前に返却するという条件で彼らは私たちに車を貸すことに同意した ◇They will give us the money *on one condition* — that we pay it back within six months. 6か月以内に返済するという条件一つで彼らは私たちにお金を貸してくれるだろう ◇They agreed *under the condition that* the matter be dealt with promptly.《米》問題に迅速に対応するという条件で彼らは合意した ◇Congress can impose strict *conditions* on the bank. 議会はこの銀行に厳しい条件を課す可能性もある ◇They have agreed to a ceasefire provided their *conditions* are met. 条件が満たされれば彼らは停戦に合意するとしている ◇Stable political leadership is a necessary *condition* for economic growth. 安定した政治的指導力が経済成長にとって必須の条件である

requirement [C]（ややフォーマル，特に書き言葉）（可能にする［許可を受ける］ための）必要条件，要件，資格 ◇What is the minimum entrance *requirement* for this programme? このプログラムに参加するための最低必要条件は何ですか ◇Be sure to check passport and visa *requirements* with your travel agent. 必ずパスポートとビザの要件を旅行代理店に確認してください ☞ **require** (DEMAND 動)

terms [複数形で]（契約・合意のための）条件，条項 ◇Under the *terms* of the agreement, their funding of the project will continue until 2012. 合意の条項によると，プロジェクトへの彼らの資金提供は2012年まで継続される予定だ ◇You should check your *terms and conditions* of employment. あなたは自分の雇用条件を確認すべきだ ☞ **terms** (RATE 2)

provision [C]（ややフォーマル，特に書き言葉）（法的文書の）条件，条項，規定 ◇The Act contains detailed *provisions* for appeal against the court's decision. その法令には裁判所の決定に対する上訴請求の詳細な規定が含まれている

qualification [C, U]（効果・適用を制限するための）条件，制限 ◇I accept his theories, but not without certain *qualifications*. 私は彼の理論を認めるが，条件がない訳ではない ◇The plan was approved *without qualification*. その計画は無条件で承認された ☞ **qualify** (ADJUST)

prerequisite [C，ふつう単数で]《フォーマル》（物事が発生する［行われる］ための）必要［前提］条件 ◇Flexibility of approach is an important *prerequisite to* successful learning. 柔軟なアプローチは効果的な学習にとって重要な必要条件である

proviso (複 -os) [C]《ややフォーマル》（合意のための）条件，但し書き ◇He agreed to their visit with the *proviso* that they should stay no longer than one week. 1週間以上滞在しないという条件で彼は彼らの訪問を了承した

the ˌsmall ˈprint《英》(《米》**the ˌfine ˈprint**) [U]（契約書・法的文書に小さい字で印刷された）注意事項，細字部分 ◇Make sure you *read the small print* before signing. ご署名の前に必ず注意事項をお読みください

confidence 名

confidence・self-confidence・assertiveness・aplomb・assurance
自分自身［自分の能力］を信じること
【類語訳】自信，自己主張

|文型&コロケーション|
- ▶**with** confidence/ self-confidence/ aplomb/ assurance
- ▶**great** confidence/ self-confidence/ aplomb/ assurance
- ▶**growing** confidence/ self-confidence/ assurance
- ▶**total** aplomb/ assurance
- ▶**quiet/ calm/ easy** confidence/ assurance
- ▶sb's **usual** confidence/ aplomb
- ▶to **have/ show** confidence/ self-confidence/ assurance
- ▶to **lose/ be lacking in/ lack** confidence/ self-confidence
- ▶an **air of** confidence/ self-confidence/ assurance

confidence [U]（うまくやれるという）自信 ◇He answered the questions with *confidence*. 彼は自信を持って質問に答えた ◇She has very little *confidence in* her own abilities. 彼女は自分の能力にほとんどなんの自信もない ◇He *gained confidence* when he went to college. 大学に進学すると彼は自信がついた ◇Winning the competition really *boosted* her *confidence*. 試合に勝つことで彼女の自信はいっそう大きなものになった

ˌself-ˈconfidence [U]（自分自身・能力に対する）自信 ◇He constantly tried to undermine her *self-confidence*. 彼はしきりに彼女の自信をぐらつかせようとした ◇A few months living away from home have given him renewed *self-confidence*. 数か月間故郷を離れて生活することで彼は自信を取り戻した

|ノート| **confidence** と **self-confidence** の使い分け：
多くの場合両語とも使用可能。◆to **have/exude/lack/gain/give sb** *confidence/self-confidence*（自信を持っている/にあふれる/を欠く/を得る/を人に与える）。◆to **boost/dent/shake/undermine sb's** *confidence/self-confidence*（人の自信を高める/弱める/揺るがす/傷つける）。しかしながら，confidenceは自分自身の能力全般または特定の物事を行う能力を信じることであるのに対し，self-confidenceは自分自身の能力全般を信じることのみを指すので，**have self-confidence in sth**という表現は不可。◆She had no *confidence* in her ability to persuade anyone.（彼女には誰をも説得する自信がなかった）．✕She had no *self-confidence* in her ability to persuade anyone.

assertiveness [U]《ややフォーマル》（意見・要望をはっきりさせる）自己主張 ◇an *assertiveness* training programme for women managers 女性管理職のための自己主張養成プログラム ❶assertivenessは特に仕事の文脈で用いられる。☞ **assertive** (AGGRESSIVE 2)

aplomb [U]《ややフォーマル，ほめて》（難事を うまく処理するための）落ち着き，自信 ◇He delivered the speech with his usual *aplomb*. 彼は普段どおりの落ち着いた様子でスピーチを行った

assurance [U]（能力・力に対する）自信 ◇There was an air of easy *assurance* and calm about him. 彼には余裕と落ち着いた雰囲気があった

⏎confidence / **confident, confirm**

> **ノート** confidence と assurance の使い分け：confidence または self-confidence は自らが抱く自信、assurance は自信を示す態度・振る舞いを指す。

confident 形

confident・independent・brash・self-confident
人がうまくやれると信じていることを表す
【類語訳】自信のある、自立した、生意気な、ぶしつけな

▶ 文型&コロケーション
▶ **very** confident/ independent/ self-confident

confident (うまくやれる)自信のある；(言動が)自信に満ちた ◇She was in a relaxed, *confident* mood. 彼女はリラックスして自信に満ちた気分だった ◇They gave a very *confident* performance of the piece. 彼らはその曲をとても自信に満ちた様子で演奏した 反意 **insecure** (SHY)、**nervous** (WORRIED)、☞ **assertive** (AGGRESSIVE 2)
independent 自立した、自立心のある ◇Going away to college has made me much more *independent*. 大学に通うため親元を離れることで私はさらに一段と自立した ◇Students should aim to become more *independent* of their teachers. 生徒は教師からもっと自立することを目指すべきだ ☞ **independence** (FREEDOM)
brash (けなして) 生意気な、ぶしつけな ◇Beneath his *brash* exterior, he's still a little boy inside. 外面的な生意気さの裏側では、彼は内面的にまだ幼い少年だ
,self-'confident (自分・能力に)自信のある ◇a *self-confident* child 自分に自信のある子ども

> **ノート** confident と self-confident の使い分け：confident は人・言動の両方に、self-confident は人のみに用いられる。× a *self-confident* performance.

confirm 動

1 confirm・support・bear witness・substantiate・validate・evidence・corroborate・authenticate・testify to sth
物事が真実であることを証明する証拠を提供する
【類語訳】立証する、裏づける、証拠となる、実証する、証明する

▶ 文型&コロケーション
▶ to confirm/ validate/ authenticate sth **as** sth
▶ to bear witness/ testify **to** sth
▶ to confirm/ support/ substantiate/ corroborate **what**...
▶ to confirm/ support/ substantiate/ validate/ corroborate/ authenticate a **claim**
▶ to confirm/ support/ substantiate/ validate/ corroborate a **theory**
▶ to confirm/ support/ substantiate/ validate an **argument**
▶ to confirm/ support/ substantiate/ corroborate a **story**
▶ to confirm/ support/ substantiate a **point**
▶ to confirm/ support/ corroborate a **statement**

confirm [他] (推測・理論を)立証する ◇His guilty expression *confirmed* my suspicions. 彼のやましそうな表情を見て怪しいと思った私の疑念が立証された ◇The results *confirm* the findings of our earlier research. その結果は私たちが以前行った調査で得たことを立証している 反意 **disprove, refute** (DISPROVE)
support [他] (主張・理論を)裏づける ◇The witness's story was not *supported* by the evidence. 目撃者の話は証拠による裏づけがなかった ☞ **support** (EVIDENCE)
bear 'witness 行いが (ややフォーマル、書き言葉) (感情・性質・状況の存在・真実性の)証拠となる ◇The crowd of mourners at his funeral *bore witness* to the great affection in which he was held. 彼の葬儀に集った大勢の参列者こそが彼が大きな愛情に包まれていたことの証だった
substantiate [他] (ややフォーマル) (主張・理論を)立証[実証]する ◇They made accusations which could not be *substantiated*. 彼らは立証不可能な告発を行った
validate [他] (フォーマル) (主張・理論を)立証[実証]する ◇The research findings do not *validate* the claims made by the manufacturer. その調査でわかったことでは製造業者の主張は立証されない

> **ノート** substantiate と validate の使い分け：substantiate は主張の裏づけとなる substance (証拠)に重点が置かれ、validate は主張の validity (真実性・正当性)に重点が置かれる。validate は特に theory, argument, claim (特に claim が物事に対する権利の保有に関する主張である場合)のような理屈・論理に関する語と共に用いられる。substantiate もこのように用いられるが、story, claim (claim が事実に関する主張である場合)のような事実に関する語と共に用いられる。

evidence [他、ふつう受身で] (フォーマル) (一般的な事実・傾向の)証拠となる ◇The legal profession is still a largely male world, *as evidenced by* the small number of women judges. 女性裁判官の数の少なさから明らかなように、法曹界は依然としておおむね男性社会である ☞ **evidence** (EVIDENCE)
corroborate [他、しばしば受身で] (フォーマル) (被疑者の主張・理論に)裏づけを与える ◇Complaints will be investigated only if there is some *corroborating* evidence. ある程度裏づけのある証拠がある場合に限り、抗告は審理される
authenticate [他] (ややフォーマル) (書類などを本物[本当、真実]であると)証明する ◇Experts have *authenticated* the writing as that of Byron himself. 専門家がその筆跡をバイロン自身のものであると証明した
'testify to sth 句動詞 (フォーマル) (物事の強力な)証拠となる ◇The film *testifies to* the courage of ordinary people during the war. その映画は戦時中の庶民の勇敢さの証となるものである

2 confirm・verify・back sb/sth up・certify・bear sb/sth out・testify・vouch for sb/sth
証拠があるので物事が真実であると思うと述べる
【類語訳】確認する、裏づける、証明する、保証する

▶ 文型&コロケーション
▶ to confirm/ verify/ certify sth **as** sth
▶ to confirm/ verify/ certify/ bear out/ testify **that**...
▶ **It was** confirmed/ verified/ certified **that**...
▶ to confirm/ verify/ certify/ bear out **what**...
▶ to confirm/ verify **whether**...
▶ to confirm/ verify/ back up/ bear out a **claim/ statement/ theory/ story/ point**
▶ to **officially** confirm/ certify sth

confirm [他] (真実[正確]であると)確認する、本当だ[間違いない]と言う ◇The doctor *confirmed* my suspicions and prescribed an antibiotic. 医者は私の疑ったとおりだと言って抗生物質を処方した ◇Rumours of job losses were later *confirmed*. 人員削減の噂は後に本当だとわかった ◇Please write to *confirm* your reservation (= say that it is definite). ご記入いただき、予約をご確認ください ◇Has everyone *confirmed* that they're coming? みんな絶対来るって言ってましたか ◇Can you *confirm* what happened? 何が起こったのか確認できますか 反義 **deny** (DENY)

▶**confirmation** 名 [U, C] ◇I'm still waiting for *confirmation* of the test results. 私はまだ検査結果の確定を待っている

verify [他]《フォーマル》(真実[正確]であると)確認する, 本当だ[間違いない]と言う ◇Her version of events was *verified* by neighbours. 事件についての彼女の説明は正しいと近所の人たちも保証した

ノート **confirm** と **verify** の使い分け: verify は意味において confirm と似ている。◆Several witnesses *confirmed/verified* his story. (何人かの目撃者が彼の話は間違いないと述べた). しかしながら, verify は一般的によりフォーマル・専門的な文脈で用いられる。◆Data that would aptly *verify* or refute this are not available. (この真否を適切に確かめるはずのデータが利用できない).

,**back sb/sth 'up** 句動詞《ややインフォーマル》(人の発言を)真実だと言う;(言動によって意見・主張・論を)裏づける ◇I'll *back* you *up* if they don't believe you. 彼らが君を信じなくても私は君の言っていることが本当だと証言するよ ◇The writer doesn't *back up* his opinions with examples. その記者は自分の意見を実例で裏づけていない

certify [自, 他]《フォーマル》(書面で公式に)証明する, 認定する ◇This (= this document) is to *certify* that... この書類は…であることを証明する ◇He was *certified* dead on arrival. 彼は病院到着時に死亡と認定された ◇The accounts were *certified* as correct by the finance department. その計算書に誤りがないことが経理部によって認定された

,**bear sb/sth 'out** 句動詞《特に英, ややフォーマル》(人の正当性[物事の真実性]を)証明する, 裏づける ◇The other witnesses will *bear* me *out*. 他の目撃者たちも私が正しいと言うだろう ◇The other witnesses will *bear out* what I say. 他の目撃者たちも私の言っていることを証明するだろう

testify [自]《ややフォーマル》(証拠に基づき真実であると)証言[証明]する ◇Too many young people are unable to write or spell well, as employers will *testify*. 雇用者なら口を揃えるところだが, あまりにも多くの若者がまともに字が書けない

'**vouch for sb/sth** 句動詞《ややフォーマル》(人[物事の真実性・信頼性]を)保証する, 請け合う ◇Are you willing to *vouch for* him? 進んで彼に太鼓判を押せますか ◇I was in bed with the flu. My wife can *vouch for* that. インフルエンザで寝込んでいました。私の妻がそれを証明できます

3 confirm・settle・decide・clinch
物事に対する感情や信念をさらにいっそう強くする, 物事に関して最終決定を下す
【類語訳】強固にする, 確定する, 決心させる, 決着をつける

文型&コロケーション
▶to confirm/ settle/ clinch an **argument**
▶to **finally** confirm/ settle/ decide/ clinch sth

conflict 123

▶That **settles**/ **clinches** **it**.

confirm [他]（感情・信念を）強固にする ◇The walk in the mountains *confirmed* his fear of heights. 山歩きをして彼の高所恐怖症がますます強まった ◇Both teams played badly, which *confirms* the impression left by earlier games. 両チームとも不甲斐ないプレーだったので, 前の試合で残った印象がさらに強まる

settle [他, しばしば受身で]（最終的に）確定する ◇Good, that's *settled*, then. よし, ではそれで決まりだ ◇Bob will be there? That *settles* it. I'm not coming.《話し言葉》ボブが来るのかい. それで決まりだ. 私は行かない

decide [他]（人に）決心[決意]させる ◇They offered me free accommodation for a year, and that *decided* me. 彼らが1年間無料で泊めてくれるというので, 私は決心がついた ◇That *decided it for* me: I wasn't carrying my bike back up those stairs. それで決めたんだ, あの階段を上って自転車を元の位置に戻しはしないとね

clinch [他]《ややインフォーマル》(物事に)答えを出す;(不確定の物事に)決着をつける ◇'I'll pay your air fare.' 'Okay, *that clinches it* — I'll come with you.'「君の航空運賃をぼくが払うよ」「わかった, じゃあ決まりだ―君と一緒に行くよ」

conflict 名

conflict・contradiction・clash・collision・opposition
二つの物事が互いに大きく異なっていて容易には相容れない状況を表す
【類語訳】対立, 衝突, 矛盾, 食い違い

文型&コロケーション
▶in conflict/ contradiction/ opposition
▶a conflict/ clash/ collision **with** sb/ sth
▶in contradiction/ opposition **to** sb/ sth
▶conflict/ a contradiction/ a clash/ a collision/ an opposition **between** sb/ sth
▶(a/ an) **fundamental/ apparent** conflict/ contradiction/ opposition
▶in **direct** conflict/ contradiction/ opposition
▶to **see/ create** a conflict/ contradiction
▶to **avoid** a conflict/ clash/ collision
▶to **resolve** a conflict/ contradiction/ clash

conflict [C, U]（思想・意見・感情・欲望の）対立, 衝突 ◇The story tells of a classic *conflict* between love and duty. その物語は義理と人情の典型的な対立を描いている ◇There is often a *conflict of interests* between farmers and conservationists. 農家と環境保護論者との間でしばしば利害の衝突が起こる ◇Many of these ideas appear to be in *conflict* with each other. これらの思想の多くは互いに相容れないようだ

contradiction [C, U]（事実・供述の）矛盾, 食い違い ◇A healthy suntan is a *contradiction in terms*. 「健康的な日焼け」は言葉の矛盾である ◇His public speeches are in direct *contradiction* to his personal lifestyle. 彼の演説は自身の実生活と真っ向から矛盾している ☞ **contradictory** (INCONSISTENT)

clash [C]（相容れない物事の）衝突, 対立 ◇Simply put, the conflict comes down to a *clash* of cultures. 簡潔に言えば, その紛争はつまるところ文化の衝突なのだ ◇Personality *clashes* led to the break-up of the band. 個性が衝突し合ってそのバンドは解散することになった

collision [C, U]《書き言葉》(人・相反する思想[意見]の)衝突, 軋轢；(異なる事柄の)接触 ◇The problem comes from a *collision* between two opposing points of view. その問題は相反する二つの考え方の衝突から生じている ◇In his work we see the *collision* of two different traditions. 彼の作品の中で二つの異なる伝統がぶつかり合っているのが見られる

ノート clash と collision の使い分け：collision は二つの異なる事柄の接触を指し, clash は接触がもたらす敵対的な結果を指す。collisionがもたらす結果は時に好ましい[興味深い]ものである。◆ Australian food is an exciting *collision* of native, Asian and European cuisines. (オーストラリア料理は先住民とアジア, ヨーロッパの料理が刺激的に出会ったものだ)

opposition [U, C]《フォーマル》対立；正反対のもの ◇Many fairy stories are based on the *opposition* between good and evil. おとぎ話の多くが善と悪の対立に基づいている ◇His poetry is full of *oppositions* and contrasts. 彼の詩は対立と対照にあふれている

conflict 動

conflict・contrast・contradict・be at odds・clash・go against sth
思想や感情, 個性が大きく異なる
【類語訳】対立する, 衝突する, 食い違う, 対照的である, 矛盾する, 反する

文型&コロケーション
▸ to conflict/ contrast/ be at odds/ clash **with** sth
▸ to be at odds/ clash **over** sth
▸ **stories/ versions** conflict/ contradict each other/ are at odds
▸ **conflicting**/ **contrasting** opinions/ personalities/ emotions

conflict [自] (思想・信念・個性が)対立[衝突]する, (話・説明が)食い違う ◇These results *conflict* with earlier findings. これらの結果は前回の結果と食い違う ◇Reports *conflicted* on how much of the aid was reaching the famine victims. 飢饉に苦しむ人々へどれだけの援助が届けられているかに関する報告が食い違った ◇He was torn between *conflicting* loyalties to family and work. 彼は家族に尽くすべきか仕事に励むべきかの葛藤に苦しんでいた

contrast [自] (二つの物事が)対照的である ◇Her actions *contrasted* sharply with her promises. 彼女の行動は約束とまったく違っていた ◇Her actions and her promises *contrasted* sharply. 彼女の行動と約束はまったく違っていた ☞ **contrast** (DIFFERENCE), **contrast** (OPPOSITE 名), **contrasting** (DIFFERENT)

contradict [他] (供述・証言・証拠が)矛盾する, 食い違う ◇The two stories *contradict* each other. 二つの話は互いに矛盾している ◇This version of events was *contradicted* by eyewitness reports. 事件に関するこの説明は目撃者の報告と食い違った ☞ **contradictory** (INCONSISTENT)

be at 'odds 行動《同一であるべきものが》食い違う ◇Her story was *at odds* with the police report. 彼

女の話は警察の調書と食い違った ☞ **at odds** (INCONSISTENT)

clash [自]《ややインフォーマル, 特にジャーナリズム》(思想・信念・個性が)衝突する ◇He *clashed* with his father over politics. 彼は政治のことで父親と衝突した ◇His views and his father's *clashed*. 彼の意見と父親の意見が衝突した

ノート conflict と clash の使い分け：conflict のほうが使用範囲が広く, しばしば互いに大きく異なる説明・信念・感情について用いられる。clash はまったく異なる意見を持つ人々による険悪な衝突について用いられることが多い。clashの主語には人・意見が用いられるが, conflictに人は不可。×He *conflicted* with his father over politics.

go a'gainst sth 句動詞 (思想・信念に)反する, 当てはまらない ◇Paying for hospital treatment *goes against* her principles. 病院治療に金を払うことは彼女の主義に反する ◇His thinking *goes against* all logic. 彼の思考はいかなる論理にもなじまない

confused 形

confused・puzzled・at a loss・bewildered・dazed・bemused・perplexed・muddled・disoriented・disorientated
何が起きているのかわからないと思う気持ちを表す
【類語訳】混乱した, 途方に暮れた, 当惑した, 呆然とした

文型&コロケーション
▸ to be confused/ puzzled/ perplexed/ muddled **about** sth
▸ to be confused/ bewildered/ bemused/ perplexed **at** sth
▸ to be confused/ puzzled/ at a loss/ perplexed **as to how.../ why...**
▸ a confused/ puzzled/ bewildered/ dazed/ bemused/ perplexed **expression/ look**
▸ puzzled/ bewildered/ dazed **eyes**
▸ **slightly** confused/ puzzled/ at a loss/ bewildered/ dazed/ bemused/ perplexed/ muddled
▸ **rather** confused/ puzzled/ at a loss/ bewildered/ bemused
▸ **a little** confused/ puzzled/ bewildered/ dazed/ bemused
▸ **totally** confused/ bewildered/ bemused/ disoriented/ disorientated
▸ **completely** confused/ at a loss/ bewildered/ disoriented/ disorientated

confused (理解できず・思考が乱れて)混乱した ◇People are *confused* about all the different labels on food these days. この頃のさまざまな種類の食品ラベルに混乱させられる ◇I'm *confused* — say all that again. 頭が混乱してる—もう一度言って ◇She was beginning to get rather *confused*. 彼女はいくぶん混乱し始めていた ◇He was depressed and in a *confused* state of mind. 彼は落胆していて混乱した精神状態にあった ☞ **confusion** (DOUBT 名 1)

puzzled (理解できず・理由がわからず)困惑した ◇He looked *puzzled* so I repeated the question. 彼は困惑しているようだったので私は質問を繰り返した ◇She had a *puzzled* expression on her face. 彼女は困惑の表情を見せた

at a 'loss 行動 (何を言って[すれば]よいかわからず)途方に暮れて ◇I'm *at a loss* to explain what happened.

私は起こったことをどう説明したらよいのかわからない ◇Ruth was completely *at a loss*. ルースはすっかり途方に暮れた ◇His comments left me *at a loss for words*. 彼の意見に私は言葉を失った
bewildered 《ややフォーマル》(何が起きているか[何をすればよいか]わからない)当惑した, 途方に暮れた ◇She was totally *bewildered* by the whole affair. 彼女は事の次第にすっかり当惑した
dazed (ショックで・頭をぶつけて)ぼうっとした, 呆然とした ◇Survivors waited for the rescue boats, *dazed* and frightened. 生存者たちは呆然としたりおびえたりしながら救難ボートを待った
bemused (何が起きているかわからず)呆然とした, 困惑した ◇Her bizarre performance left the audience looking *bemused*. 彼女の異様な演技に観客は呆然とするほかないような様子だった
perplexed 《ややフォーマル》(心配気味に)混乱した, 当惑した ◇We are all *perplexed* as to how this happened. 私たちは皆どうしてこうなったか当惑している
muddled 《特に英》(どれがどれだかわからず)混乱した ◇There were so many names that she became hopelessly *muddled*. たくさん名前がありすぎて彼女はどうしようもないほど混乱した ◇This is the result of *muddled thinking*. 思考が混乱した結果がこうだ
disoriented 《主に米》(周りで何が起きているかわからず)混乱した, 見当識を失った ◇The patient appeared *disoriented*. その患者は見当識を失っているようだった
disorientated 《英, ややフォーマル》(周りで何が起きているかわからず)混乱した, 見当識を失った ◇She felt shocked and totally *disorientated*. 彼女はショックを受けてすっかり混乱した ❶《英》ではどちらの語も用いられるが, disorientated のほうが disoriented よりも頻繁に用いられる.《米》では disoriented のみ用いられる.

confusing 形

confusing・incomprehensible・puzzling・bewildering・inexplicable・unintelligible・baffling
理解しづらいことを表す
【類語訳】紛らわしい, 交錯した, わけのわからない, 当惑させる, 不可解な

[文型&コロケーション]
▸confusing/ incomprehensible/ puzzling/ bewildering/ inexplicable/ baffling **to** sb
▸confusing/ puzzling/ bewildering/ baffling **for** sb
▸confusing/ incomprehensible/ puzzling/ bewildering/ inexplicable/ baffling **that** ...
▸a confusing/ bewildering **experience/ variety**
▸incomprehensible/ unintelligible **language**
▸a puzzling/ baffling **problem**
▸**for sb** incomprehensible/ inexplicable **reason**
▸**totally** confusing/ incomprehensible/ bewildering/ inexplicable/ unintelligible
▸**quite** confusing/ incomprehensible/ puzzling/ bewildering/ baffling
▸**rather/ somewhat** confusing/ puzzling/ bewildering/ baffling

confusing (情報などが)紛らわしい, 混乱させる, 錯綜[交錯]した ◇The news bulletins were *confusing*, giving different versions of what was happening. 起こっていることに関してくるくる変わる報道を行っていてニュース速報は錯綜していた ◇It was all very *confusing*. すべてがとても紛らわしかった ◇The signposts are *confusing* for people who don't know the area. その標識はその地域を知らない人々の混乱を招くものだ ◇She experienced a *confusing* mixture of emotions. 彼女は感情がさまざまに交錯し合うのを実感した 反意 clear (CLEAR 形 2), ☞ confusion (DOUBT 名 1)
▸**confusingly** 副 ◇The biology lectures were in a big hall, *confusingly* called the Physics Theatre. 生物学の講義は紛らわしくも物理教室と呼ばれる大きなホールで行われた
incomprehensible 理解不能の ◇Their dialect is *incomprehensible* to most speakers of Standard English. 彼らの方言は標準英語を話す大半の人にとって理解不能だ ◇From a child's point of view, adult behaviour is often just as *incomprehensible*. 子どもの目には大人の行動はしばしば単に理解不能なものとしてしか映らない 反意 comprehensible (CLEAR 形 2)
puzzling (言葉・行動が)理解[説明]しづらい, わけのわからない ◇I had noticed something *puzzling*. 私は何かわけのわからない物に気づいていた ◇Marlowe was a *puzzling* character. マーローはわけのわからない人物だった ❶ *puzzling* は問題・特徴などに関する problem, question, aspect, feature などの語と結びつく
bewildering (選択肢が多すぎて・理解しづらくて)当惑[困惑]させる ◇Voters have a *bewildering* array of 116 parties to choose from. 投票者は116もある政党の中からとまどいつつ選ばねばならない ◇The complexity of these 'simplest' forms of life is *bewildering*. 「最も単純な」形を持つこれらの生物の複雑さには困惑させられる ❶ *bewildering* は数・範囲・速度などに関する array, choice, variety, rapidity, complexity などの語と結びつく
inexplicable (出来事・行動・感情が)説明のつかない, 不可解な ◇He was shocked at the sudden, *inexplicable* sense of loss he felt. 彼は突然説明のつかない喪失感に襲われた ◇For some *inexplicable* reason her mind went completely blank. どういうわけだか彼女は頭の中がまっ白になった
▸**inexplicably** 副 ◇The switch had *inexplicably* turned itself on. スイッチがどういうわけかひとりでに入っていた
unintelligible (音・話・文書が)理解不能の ◇She murmured something *unintelligible*. 彼女は何かわけのわからないことをつぶやいた ◇Dolphin sounds are *unintelligible* to humans. イルカの出す音は人間には理解できない 反意 intelligible (CLEAR 形 2)
baffling (事実・出来事が)不可解な ◇He is still the chief suspect in this *baffling* case. 彼は依然としてこの不可解な事件の第一容疑者だ

conservative 形 ☞ TRADITIONAL

conservative・conventional・traditionalist・conformist
行動が人並みで, 退屈であることを表す
【類語訳】保守的な, 伝統的な, 慣習的な, 平凡な

[文型&コロケーション]
▸conservative/ conventional/ traditionalist **thinkers/ views/ values**
▸conventional/ conformist **behaviour**

▶very/ highly conservative/ conventional

conservative（社会変化に対して，流儀[価値観]）が)保守的[伝統的]な ◇They were *conservative* in their political outlook. 彼らは政治的見解において保守的だった ◇Popular taste in art remained *conservative*. 芸術に対する一般の人の好みは保守的なままだった 反意 **radical, progressive** (RADICAL)
　▶**conservatively** 副 ◇He was *conservatively* dressed in a dark suit. 彼は地味な黒っぽいスーツを着ていた
conventional《しばしばけなして》因襲[慣習]的な，平凡[月並み，陳腐]な ◇The imagery in the poem is somewhat *conventional*. その詩の比喩的描写はやや陳腐だ ◇They rejected what they saw as the hypocrisy of *conventional* society. 因習的な社会の偽善であると見えるものを彼らは拒絶した 反意 **unconventional** (UNUSUAL)
　▶**conventionally** 副 ◇She was not a *conventionally* beautiful girl. 彼女はいわゆる美少女というタイプではなかった
traditionalist《ややフォーマル》伝統主義(者)の ◇The proposals appeal to *traditionalist* teachers. その提案は伝統を尊ぶ教師たちに訴えるところがある
conformist《しばしばけなして》遵奉[順応]主義の；人と違うのが嫌な，右にならえな ◇Don't forget how *conformist* and resistant to change many people are. 多くの人がどれほど変化に対して消極的で抵抗するかを忘れるな

consider 動

consider・think・look at sth・wonder・reflect・ponder・contemplate・take・deliberate・mull sth over・meditate
理解や意思決定，問題解決などのために頭を働かせる
【類語訳】熟考する，思考する，考慮する，瞑想にふける，内省する

文型&コロケーション
▶to think/ reflect/ ponder/ deliberate/ meditate **on** sth
▶to think/ ponder/ deliberate/ mull/ meditate **over** sth
▶to think/ wonder/ ponder/ contemplate **about** sth
▶to consider/ think/ look at/ wonder/ reflect/ ponder/ contemplate/ deliberate **how/ what/ whether...**
▶to consider/ think/ reflect **that...**
▶to consider/ think/ look at sth/ reflect/ ponder **carefully/ briefly**
▶to consider/ think/ look at sth/ reflect/ contemplate **seriously**
▶to think/ look at sth/ reflect/ ponder/ deliberate **long and hard**

consider [他，自]《意思決定のために》熟考[検討]する ◇She *considered* her options. 彼女は選択肢をよく考えた ◇Let us *consider* the facts. その事実をよく考えてみよう ◇It was a carefully *considered* decision. それは慎重に考えた上での決断だった ◇We're *considering* buying a new car. 私たちは新車の購入を検討している ◇He was *considering* what to do next. 彼は次に何をすべきかを考えていた ◇I'd like some time to *consider*. 少し考える時間がほしい ☞ **consider** (REGARD)
think [自] 考える，思考する ◇Are animals able to *think*? 動物は考えることができるか ◇Let me *think* (= Give me time before I answer). 考えさせてください ◇I can't tell you now — I'll have to *think about it*. 今

はわからない —考えてみよう ◇She had *thought* very deeply about this problem. 彼女はこの問題についてとても深く考えていた ◇All he ever *thinks* about is money. 彼が考えていることといえばお金のことだけだ ◆I'm sorry, I wasn't *thinking* (= said when you have upset or offended sb accidentally). すみません，あさはかでした ◇He was trying to *think* what to do. 彼は何をすべきか考えようとしていた ❶ **think** は頭の中に考え・言葉・イメージが浮かんでいるとき，特に進行時制でも用いられる. ◆You're very quiet. What are you *thinking*? (とても静かだね. 何を考えているの) ◆I was just *thinking* what a long way it is. (遠いなぁって思ってただけだよ) ◆'I must be crazy,' she *thought*. (「私の頭どうかしてるみたい」と彼女は思った)
'look at sth 句動詞 熟考[検討，考察]する ◇The implications of the new law will need to be *looked at*. この新法が導入されるとどうなるかをよく考える必要があるだろう ◇I suggest the government *looks* long and hard *at* this new report. 私は政府がこの新しい報告をじっくり真剣に検討することを提案する ◇In this chapter we will be *looking at* three different theories. この章では三つの異なる理論を考察します ☞ **look at sth** (REGARD)
wonder [自，他] 思いをめぐらす ◇I *wonder* who she is. 彼女は誰だろう ◇'Why do you want to know?' 'No particular reason. I was just *wondering*.'「なぜ知りたいの」「特に理由はないよ. どうなのかなと思っただけで」 ◇We were *wondering* about next April for the wedding. 私たちは結婚式を挙げるのに来年の4月はどうかと考えていた
reflect [自，他]《ややフォーマル》《意思決定・理解のために》熟考[思案]する ◇Before I decide, I need time to *reflect*. 結論を下す前に，私には考える時間が必要です ◇She was left to *reflect* on the implications of her decision. 彼女は自分の決定が及ぼす影響について考えさせられた ◇I paused to *reflect* how I would answer that question. 私は間を置いてその質問にどう答えようか考えた ❶ **reflect** は目的語に名詞句をとることはできないので，代わりに **on, upon, that, how** を用いなければならない. ✕She *reflected* the implications.
ponder [自，他]《特に書き言葉》《理解のために》熟考する ◇She *pondered* over his words. 彼女は彼の言葉をよく考えた ◇The senator *pondered* the question for a moment. 上院議員はその質問についてしばし考えた
contemplate [他，自]《可能性の一つとして》考慮する；《時間をかけて》熟考する ◇He's only 55, but he's already *contemplating* retirement (= thinking about whether he should retire). 彼はまだ55歳だが，すでに退職のことを考えている ◇The thought of war is too awful to *contemplate* (= to think about and accept as a possibility). 戦争が起きるなど恐ろしくて考えられない ◇She lay in bed, *contemplating*. 彼女はベッドに横になって考えていた
take [他]《特に指定で用いて》《一例として》考慮する ◇Lots of couples have problems in the first year of marriage. *Take* Ann and Paul. たくさんの夫婦が結婚1年目に問題を抱えるものだ. アンとポールのことを考えてみなよ
deliberate [自]《ややフォーマル》《慎重に》熟考[検討]する，協議する ◇The jury *deliberated* for five days before finding him guilty. 彼を有罪と評決する前に陪審は5日間協議した ❶ **deliberate** は主に法廷における陪審などが決定を下すために検討[議論]し合う場合に用いられる.
,mull sth 'over 句動詞 《計画・提案などを》熟考[検討]する ◇I need some time to *mull* it *over* before making a decision. 決定を下す前に私にはそれについて検討する時間

consideration, conspiracy

がある程度必要だ
meditate [自]（宗教的理由で・気持ちを落ち着かせるために）瞑想[黙想]にふける, 内省[内観]する ◆She *meditates* for half an hour every evening to help herself relax after work. 彼女は仕事後の緊張を和らげるために毎晩30分間の瞑想にふける ❶*meditate* は「…することを考える・頭の中で計画を練る」ことを意味するのに目的語と共に用いられることがある. この意味ではよりフォーマルであり, 主に書き言葉で用いられる. ◆They were *meditating* revenge.（彼らは復讐をもくろんでいた）.

consideration 名

consideration・thought・look・deliberation・reflection・meditation・contemplation
何かをじっくりと考える行為を表す
【類語訳】考慮, 考察, 考え, 思考, 熟考, 熟慮, 沈思（黙考）, 瞑想

〔文型&コロケーション〕
▸**after** (some, etc.) consideration/ thought/ deliberation/ reflection/ contemplation
▸**on** consideration/ reflection
▸to be **for** (sb's) consideration/ deliberation/ contemplation
▸(a) **serious** consideration/ thought/ look/ deliberation/ reflection/ contemplation
▸(a) **careful** consideration/ thought/ look/ deliberation/ reflection
▸**quiet** consideration/ thought/ deliberation/ reflection/ meditation/ contemplation
▸**deep** consideration/ thought/ reflection/ meditation/ contemplation
▸to **give** sth some consideration/ some thought/ a look
▸to be **deep/ lost in** thought/ meditation/ contemplation
▸a **moment's** consideration/ thought/ reflection

consideration [U, C, ふつう単数で]《ややフォーマル》（決定を下すための）考慮, 考察 ◆Careful *consideration* should be given to matters of health and safety. 健康と安全に関して熟慮すべきです ◆Don't forget to take the cost of insurance *into consideration*. 保険料を考慮することを忘れないように ◆The plan is currently *under consideration* (= being considered). その計画は目下考慮中です ◆There needs to be a *consideration* of the legal issues involved. 関連する法律問題を考慮する必要があります

thought [U] 考え, 思考（力）, 考慮, 熟考 ◆A good teacher always encourages independent *thought*. よい教師は独自に考えることをいつも促してくれる ◆She was lost in *thought* (=thinking very hard about sth and not paying attention to anything else). 彼女は思案に暮れていた ◆I've been giving the matter careful *thought*. その件を熟考し続けている ◆Not enough *thought* has gone into this assignment. この任務については十分な検討がなされていない

look [C, ふつう単数で] 考察 ◆We'll be *taking* a close *look at* the proposals. 私たちはこれらの提案を詳細に検討することになります ◆We need to take a *long hard look* at all the facts. 私たちはそれらすべての事実を時間をかけて厳密に考察する必要がある

deliberation [U, C, ふつう複数で]《フォーマル》（決定を下すための）熟考（の過程）, 熟慮, 審議 ◆After much *delibera-*

ation, we have decided to award the title to Springfield College. 熟慮を重ねて私たちはスプリングフィールド大学にその称号を与えることにした ◆The jury's *deliberations* lasted over five days. 陪審員団は5日間にわたって審議した

reflection [U]《ややフォーマル》（時に長時間にわたる）熟考, 熟慮, 沈思（黙考） ◆She decided, on *reflection*, not to take the job. よくよく考えて彼女はその仕事に就かないことにした ◆A period of calm *reflection* is now needed. 今は冷静になって考えてみる期間が必要だ

meditation [U]《ややフォーマル》瞑想, 沈思（黙考） ◆He was deep in *meditation* and didn't see me come. 彼は深い瞑想に入っていて, 私が来るのが見えなかった ◆More and more people *practise meditation* on a regular basis. 定期的に瞑想した人たちがますます増えている

contemplation [U]《ややフォーマル》沈思（黙考）, 瞑想 ◆He sat by the window, deep in *contemplation*. 彼は深く沈思黙考しながら窓のそばに座った ◆The monks dedicate themselves to a life of prayer and *contemplation*. 修道士たちは明けても暮れても祈りと瞑想にふけっている

conspiracy 名

conspiracy・scheme・plot・intrigue・collusion・sting
違法や有害な事を行ったり, 人をだましたりするひそかな計画
【類語訳】共謀, 陰謀, 策略, 信用詐欺

〔文型&コロケーション〕
▸a conspiracy/ a plot/ intrigue **against** sb
▸a conspiracy/ collusion **between** people/ groups
▸a conspiracy/ scheme/ plot **to do** sth
▸(an) **alleged** conspiracy/ scheme/ plot/ intrigue/ collusion
▸(a) **political/ international** conspiracy/ plot/ intrigue
▸to **be involved in** a conspiracy/ a scheme/ a plot/ intrigue/ collusion/ a sting
▸to **engage in** a conspiracy/ a scheme/ a plot/ intrigue
▸to **uncover** a conspiracy/ scheme/ plot

conspiracy [C, U] 共謀, 陰謀 ◆He claimed there had been a *conspiracy* to overthrow the government. 彼は政府を転覆させる陰謀があったと主張した ◆They were charged with *conspiracy* to murder. 彼らは殺人の共謀容疑で告発された ◆A lot of people subscribe to the *conspiracy theory* (= believe that a conspiracy is responsible for a particular event). 多くの人がその陰謀説を信じている ☞**conspire** (PLOT)

scheme [C]（金・利益を得ようとする）陰謀, たくらみ ◆Police uncovered a *scheme* to steal paintings worth more than $250,000. 警察は25万ドル以上の価値のある絵画を盗む陰謀を暴いた ☞**scheme** (PLOT), **ploy** (TACTIC)

plot [C] 共謀, 陰謀 ◆The military had foiled an assassination *plot* against the president. 軍が大統領の暗殺計画を阻止していた ☞**plot** (PLOT)

〔ノート〕**conspiracy**と**plot**の使い分け : 両語とも人を権力の座から退かせる計画について用いられるが, **plot**のほうが殺人・暴力を伴う傾向が強い.（an assassination plot（暗殺計画）とは言うが, ✗an assassination *conspiracy*とは言わない）. **conspiracy**は権力の座にある人々が物事を隠蔽しておこうとする計画についても用いられる.

intrigue [U, C]《特に書き言葉》陰謀, 策略, 悪だくみ；秘められた関係 ◇The young heroine steps into a web of *intrigue* in the academic world. 若いヒロインが陰謀渦巻く学界に足を踏み入れる ◇Sexual *intrigues* were almost part of the culture of high politics. 不義密通が政界上層部の文化のほぼ一部になっていた

collusion [U]《フォーマル》結託, 共謀, 通謀 ◇The police were operating *in collusion with* the drug dealers. 警察が麻薬の売人と結託して動いていた ☞ **colllude** (PLOT)

sting [C]《特に米》(警察による)おとり捜査；(犯罪者による)信用詐欺 ◇The FBI conducted a *sting* operation to catch heroin dealers in Detroit. デトロイトでヘロインの売人を捕まえるためにFBIはおとり捜査を行った

contempt 名

contempt・scorn・disdain・mockery・ridicule・disrespect・derision
人や物事が尊敬に値しないと思うこと, 人や物事を笑いものにする言葉
【類語訳】軽蔑, 侮蔑, さげすみ, 見くびり, あざけり

【文型&コロケーション】
▶ contempt/ scorn/ disdain/ disrespect **for** sb/ sth
▶ scorn/ mockery/ derision **from** sb
▶ **with** contempt/ scorn/ disdain/ mockery/ ridicule/ disrespect/ derision
▶ **in** scorn/ disdain/ mockery/ derision
▶ **gentle** mockery/ ridicule/ derision
▶ to **risk/ invite** (sb's) contempt/ scorn/ ridicule/ derision
▶ to **show** contempt/ scorn/ disdain/ disrespect
▶ to **treat sb/ sth with** contempt/ disdain/ ridicule/ disrespect
▶ to **feel** contempt/ scorn/ disdain
▶ an **object of** scorn/ ridicule/ derision

contempt [U, 単数で]（嫌悪的な）軽蔑, 侮蔑, さげすみ ◇She looked at him with barely disguised *contempt*. 彼女はかろうじて軽蔑の念を隠して彼を見つめた ◇I shall treat that remark with the *contempt* it deserves. 私は当然その見解を軽蔑します ◇Politicians seem to be generally *held in contempt* by the police. 政治家は一般的に警察から軽蔑されているようだ ◇His treatment of his children is *beneath contempt* (= so unacceptable that it is not even worth feeling contempt for). 子どもに対する彼の仕打ちは軽蔑にも値しない ◇They had shown a *contempt* for the values she thought important. 彼女が大切だと思う価値観を彼らは軽蔑していた 反意 respect (RESPECT 名)

scorn [U]（話し方に表れる）軽蔑, 侮蔑, さげすみ ◇Opposition politicians *poured scorn* on the proposals. 野党の政治家はその案をあざ笑った ◇She was unable to hide the *scorn* in her voice. 彼女はさげすむような口調を隠すことができなかった

disdain [U, 単数で]《ややフォーマル》軽蔑, 侮蔑, さげすみ, 見くびり ◇She turned her head away in *disdain*. 彼女は軽蔑して顔をそむけた ◇Imitation jewellery is regarded with *disdain*. まがい物の宝飾品は蔑視の対象となっている

▷ **disdain** 動 [他] ◇She *disdained* his offer of help. 彼女は彼の援助の申し出に見向きもしなかった

mockery [U] 冷笑, あざけり ◇They left themselves open to *mockery* from the left-wing press. 彼らは自らを左翼メディアの冷笑にさらすこととなった ◇There was a *hint of mockery* in his voice. 彼の口調にはいくぶん人をばかにする感じがあった ☞ **mock** (LAUGH AT SB/STH)

ridicule [U] あざけり ◇She might find herself exposed to *public ridicule*. 彼女は公然と皆の笑いものにされるかもしれない ◇She soon became an object of *ridicule*. 彼女はまもなくもの笑いの種となった ☞ **ridicule** (LAUGH AT SB/STH), **ridiculous** (RIDICULOUS)

disrespect [U, 単数で]《ややフォーマル》尊敬[敬意]を欠くこと, 軽蔑, 軽視 ◇They have shown a total *disrespect* for the law. 彼らはその法律を完全に愚弄する姿勢を示している ◇I mean no *disrespect to* the team, but their performance was poor. 私はそのチームをこけにするつもりはないが, 彼らのプレーはお粗末だった 反意 respect (RESPECT 名), ☞ **disrespectful** (RUDE)

derision [U]《ややフォーマル》あざけり ◇He snorted in *derision*. 彼は鼻で笑った ◇The statement was met with *hoots of derision*. その発言は嘲笑の嵐に遭った

【ノート】contempt, scorn, disdain はあざ笑うことではなく, 人・物事に対して敬意を示さないことに重点が置かれる. contempt は強い嫌悪の念を表し, disdain と scorn には大して良くないという理由での拒絶が伴う. disdain には自分自身への優越感が示され, scorn はしばしば言葉で示されるものを指す. mockery, ridicule, mockery は他の人にも笑いを促そうとするものである. derision はよりフォーマルな語で, 物事が取るに足らないものとしてあざけりを受けることに重点が置かれる.

context 名

context・background・backdrop・setting・milieu
物事が存在および発生する状況を表す
【類語訳】背景, 場面, 状況, 文脈, 前後関係, 舞台, 環境

【文型&コロケーション】
▶ **in** (a) context/ a setting/ a milieu
▶ **against** a background/ backdrop
▶ **cultural/ historical/ economic/ political** context/ background/ setting/ milieu
▶ to **provide** (sb with) a context/ background/ backdrop/ setting
▶ to **describe** the context/ background/ setting

context [C, U] (存在・発生・位置を理解するための)背景, 場面, 状況, 文脈, 前後関係 ◇This speech needs to be set *in the context of* Britain in the 1960s. この演説は1960年代のイギリスという場面に置いて考える必要がある ◇His decision can only be understood *in context*. 彼の決定はその背景があって初めて理解できる ◇Such databases are being used in a wide range of *contexts*. このようなデータベースはさまざまな状況で用いられている

▷ **contextualize**《英でまた **-ise**》動 [他] ◇As important as the photograph is a caption to *contextualize* the image.《フォーマル》写真と同じくらい重要なものが, その画像の状況を説明するキャプションだ

background [C, ふつう単数で, U] (出来事の発生原因となる)背景(情報) ◇The book explains the complex historical *background* to the war. その本にはその戦争

を引き起こした複雑な歴史的背景が説明されている ◇The elections are taking place against a *background* of violence. その選挙は暴力を背景に行われている ◇Encyclopedias are a good source of ***background information***. 百科事典は背景知識の宝庫だ ◇Can you give me more *background* on the company's financial position? その会社の財政状態の背景をもう少し教えていただけますか

backdrop [C]《書き言葉》(出来事が発生した)背景 ◇It was against this *backdrop* of racial tension that the civil war began. この民族間の緊張を背景にして内戦は勃発した

▏ノート▕ **background** と **backdrop** の使い分け：**background** のほうがはるかに使用範囲が広い。**backdrop** は特により文語的な文章で、against a backdrop of sth の句で用いられる。×*backdrop* information. ×Can you give me more *backdrop*?

setting [C]《劇・小説・映画の》場面, 舞台；《物事の》背景, 状況 ◇It is the first story she has written with a contemporary *setting*. それは彼女が初めて書いた現代を舞台にした物語である ◇The writer fails to place the events in their wider political *setting*. その作家は諸々の出来事をより幅広い政治状況の中に位置づけることができていない

▶ **set** [動] [他, ふつう受身で] ◇The movie is *set* in Los Angeles in the year 2019. その映画は2019年のロサンゼルスを舞台にしている

milieu《複 **milieux, milieus**》[C, ふつう単数で]《フランス語から, フォーマル》(生活・職場の社会的)環境 ◇The findings of the report refer to a particular social and cultural *milieu*. その報告書が伝える発見は特定の社会的及び文化的な環境についてのものだ ☞ **environment** (ENVIRONMENT)

continue [動]

1 continue・take・last・go on・carry on・keep on・drag on
一定期間にわたりそれまでどおり起こり続ける
【類語訳】続く, 継続する, 持続する, 必要とする

▕文型&コロケーション▏
▶ to continue/ last/ go on/ carry on/ keep on/ drag on **for** hours/ a week/ two years, etc.
▶ to continue/ last/ go on/ carry on/ keep on/ drag on **until** morning/ next year, etc.
▶ to continue/ last **into** the night/ next week, etc.
▶ to take/ last **a few minutes/ an hour/ all day/ years**, etc.

continue [自]《ややフォーマル, 特に書き言葉》(間断なく)続く, 継続[持続]する ◇The exhibition *continues* until 25 July. その展覧会は7月25日まで開催されている ◇The rain will *continue* into the evening. 雨は夜まで続くでしょう ◇The rain *continued to* fall all afternoon. 雨は午後いっぱい降り続けた ◇The rain *continued* falling all afternoon. 雨は午後いっぱい降り続けた 反意 **suspend**

take [他, 自]《特定の時間を》必要とする ◇The journey to the airport *takes* about half an hour. 空港までの移動は30分くらいかかる ◇*It takes* about half an hour to get to the airport. 空港まで行くには30分くらいかかる ◇It *took* her three hours to repair her bike. 彼女が自転車

を修理するのに3時間かかった ◇It'll ***take time*** (= take a long time) for her to recover from the illness. 彼女がその病気から回復するには時間がかかるだろう ◇I need a shower — I ***won't take long***. シャワーを浴びなきゃ―時間はかけないよ

last [他, 自]《進行形なし》(特定期間)続く, 継続[持続]する ◇Each game *lasts* (for) about an hour. 各試合は1時間くらい続きます ◇The trial is expected to *last* until the end of the week. 裁判は週末まで続く見込みだ ◇The celebrations *lasted* well into the next week. 祝典は軽く翌週に食い込む時点まで続いた ◇How long does the play *last*? 劇の時間はどれくらいですか

go on [句動詞]《特に話し言葉》(変化があってもいいのに変わらず)続く ◇This cannot be allowed to *go on*. これを続けさせるわけにはいかない ◇How much longer will this hot weather *go on* for? この暑い日はいつまで続きますか ◇We ***can't go on like this*** — we seem to be always arguing. こんなこと続けてはいられない―いつも言い争ってばかりいるようにに思われる

carry on [句動詞]《特に英, 特に話し言葉》動き[進み]続ける ◇*Carry on* until you get to the junction, then turn left. このまま交差点まで行って, それから左に曲がってください

keep on [句動詞]《特に話し言葉》(間断なく)続く, 継続[持続]する ◇The rain *kept on* all day. 雨は一日中降り続いた ◇*Keep on* until you get to the church. 教会に行き当たるまでずっと行って ❶ keep on は断固として[迷惑なほど]長い間継続することを暗示することがある.

drag on [句動詞] (-gg-)《けなして》(状況が変わらず)延々と続く ◇The dispute has *dragged on* for months. その議論はもう何か月も続いている

2 continue・keep・go on with sth/go on doing sth・proceed・pursue・carry (sth) on・keep sth up/keep up with sth・press ahead/on・stick with sb/sth
一定期間にわたり間断なく何かする
【類語訳】続ける, 続行する, 推し進める, 保つ, 維持する

▕文型&コロケーション▏
▶ to continue/ keep on/ go on/ proceed/ carry on/ keep up/ press ahead/ stick **with** sth
▶ to continue/ keep/ go on/ pursue/ carry on/ press ahead with **doing** sth
▶ to continue/ go on/ proceed/ pursue/ carry on/ keep up/ press ahead (with) the/ your **work**
▶ to continue/ go on with/ pursue/ carry on/ keep up a **conversation**
▶ to continue/ proceed/ pursue/ carry on/ press ahead (with) **plans**
▶ to continue/ proceed/ pursue/ press ahead (with) **reforms**
▶ to continue/ pursue/ carry on/ keep up/ press ahead/ stick (with) a **policy**
▶ to proceed/ pursue/ press ahead (with) **legislation**
▶ to continue/ proceed/ pursue/ carry on (with) an **investigation**
▶ to continue/ pursue/ carry on/ keep up a **relationship/ tradition**
▶ to continue/ keep/ go on/ carry on **fighting/ working/ talking/ improving sth/ believing/ building sth**
▶ to continue/ go on/ carry on **regardless**

continue [他, 自]《ややフォーマル》続ける, …し続ける ◇She

wanted to *continue* working after the baby was born. 彼女は赤ちゃんが生まれた後も働き続けたかった ◇He *continued to* ignore everything I was saying. 彼は私の言うことすべてを無視し続けた ◇The board of enquiry is *continuing* its investigations. 調査委員会が調査を続行している ◇Are you going to *continue* with the project? その計画を継続するつもりですか

keep [他,自]《特に話し言葉》続ける;(繰り返し)…し続ける ◇*Keep* smiling! 笑顔を絶やさないで ◇I wish you wouldn't *keep* on interrupting me! 私の邪魔ばかりするのはやめてほしい ◇I want to *keep on* with part-time work for as long as possible. 私はパートの仕事をできるだけ長く続けたい ❶話し言葉ではkeep doing sthのほうが、ややフォーマルな響きのあるcontinue doing sthよりもはるかに頻繁に用いられる。この意味ではkeepは常に、動名詞(-ing形)、on+動名詞(-ing形)、on with sthを伴う。

,go 'on with sth, go on doing sth [句動詞] (物事を)続ける、…し続ける ◇She shrugged and went on with her writing. 彼女は肩をすくめると、また書き物を続けた ◇Neil nodded and *went on* eating. ニールはうなずいて食べ続けた

proceed [自]《ややフォーマル》(開始された事を[が])続行する[される] ◇We're not sure whether we still want to *proceed* with the sale. 私たちは自分たちがまだ販売を続けたいのかよくわからない ◇Work is *proceeding* slowly. 作業はゆっくりと進められている ❶ proceed withの目的語には work, plans, reforms, a transaction, an investigationなどが挙げられ、proceedの主語にはconversation, meeting, sale, transaction, trialなどが挙げられる。

pursue [他]《フォーマル》(議論・調査・仕事などを)続行する、推し進める ◇We have no option but to *pursue* legal action. 私たちには法的措置を推し進める他に選択肢はない ◇We have decided not to *pursue* the matter. 私たちはその件は打ち切ることに決めた ❶ pursueとよく結びつく語として enquiry, investigation, lawsuit, line, matter, policy, quest, strategyが挙げられる。

,carry 'on, ,carry sth 'on [句動詞]《特に話し言葉》続ける ◇*Carry on* with your work while I'm away. 私が外出している間、その仕事を続けていなさい ◇After he left I just tried to *carry on* as normal (= do the things I usually do). 彼が出て行った後も私はただ普段どおりにしようとした ◇He *carried on* peeling the potatoes. 彼はポテトの皮をむき続けた

,keep sth 'up, ,keep 'up with sth [句動詞] (高水準の)保つ、続ける;(定期的に)支払い[行為]を続ける ◇The enemy *kept up* the bombardment day and night. 敵は昼も夜も爆撃の手をゆるめなかった ◇Well done! *Keep up the good work/Keep it up.* いいぞ、その調子 ◇If you do not *keep up with* the payments you could lose your home. 支払いが滞るようなら、家を失うことになりかねません

,press a'head/'on [句動詞] (活動・移動を断固として)続ける ◇The company is *pressing ahead* with its plans for a new warehouse. その会社は新倉庫の建設計画を敢行するつもりだ ◇'Shall we stay here for the night?' 'No, let's *press on*.'「夜はここにとどまるかい」「いや、先に行こう」

'stick with sb/sth [句動詞] [受身なし]《インフォーマル》続行[固持、維持]する;…し続ける ◇They decided to *stick with* their original plan. 彼らは当初の計画を推し進めることに決定した ◇Even if you find it hard at first, *stick with it* — it will get easier with practice. 初めは難し

いと思っても、やり続けるように—やっていれば簡単にできるようになります ❶stick with sb/sthはしばしば既知の事柄から変更しない[離れない]ことについて用いられる。◆to *stick with* the old system/the original plan/what you know/what you already have/the status quo (古い体制/当初の計画/知っていること/既に持っているもの/(現)体制を固持[維持]する)。

3 continue・go on・resume・return to sth・renew・reopen・restart・take sth up
しばらく中断した後に再び始める
【類語訳】続ける, 再開する, 戻る, 再起動する, 再始動する, 引き継ぐ

[文型&コロケーション]
▶to continue/ go on **with** sth
▶to continue/ go on/ resume **doing** sth
▶to continue/ resume/ return to/ renew/ reopen/ restart **talks**
▶to continue/ resume/ return to/ reopen a **discussion**
▶to continue/ resume/ return to/ take up a **conversation**
▶to return to/ reopen/ take up a/ an **case/ issue**
▶to continue/ renew/ take up the **campaign**
▶to continue/ resume/ return to/ renew/ take up the **attack**
▶to continue/ resume/ restart **production**
▶to continue/ resume/ return to your **duties**
▶**work** continues/ goes on/ restarts

continue [自,他]《特に書き言葉》続ける, 再開する, 話を続ける ◇The story *continues* in our next issue. 物語の続きは次号です ◇The story will be *continued* in our next issue. 物語の続きは次号です ◇Please *continue* with the work you were doing before. 前にやっていた作業を続けてください ◇Please *continue* — I didn't mean to interrupt. 続けてください—邪魔をするつもりじゃなかったので ◇'In fact,' he *continued*, 'I'd like to congratulate you.'「実のところ」と言って、彼は「君にお祝いを言いたいんだ」と続けた ❶ continueの略語の表記はcont.で、しばしばページの下部に表示される。◆ *cont.* p.161 (161ページへ続く)。ページの上部には◆*cont.* from p.159 (159ページからの続き)。と表示される。

▷**continuation** [名] [C] ◇The new book is a *continuation* of her autobiography. その新刊書は彼女の自伝の続編だ

,go 'on [句動詞]《ややインフォーマル, 特に話し言葉》続ける, 再開する, 話を続ける ◇That's enough for now — let's *go on* with it tomorrow. 今回はこれでおしまい—明日またこの続きをしよう ◇She hesitated for a moment and then *went on*. 彼女は一瞬ためらったが、そのまま続けた ◇'You know,' he *went on*, 'I think my brother could help you.'「ねぇ」と言って、彼は「ぼくの弟が役に立てると思うよ」と続けた

resume [他,自]《フォーマル》再開する;(元の席・場所に)戻る ◇She *resumed* her career after an interval of six years. 6年ぶりに彼女は仕事に復帰した ◇There is no sign of the peace talks *resuming*. 和平交渉が再開されるきざしはない ◇He *resumed* his seat opposite her. 彼は彼女の向かいの席に戻った

▷**resumption** [名] [単数で, U] ◇We are hoping for an early *resumption* of the peace talks. 私たちは和平交渉の早期再開を望んでいる

return to sth [句動詞]《ややフォーマル, 特に書き言葉》(前の

議題・活動に)戻る ◇He *returns to* this topic later in the report. 報告書の後半で彼はこの論題に立ち戻っています ◇She looked up briefly, then *returned to* her sewing. 彼女はしばらく顔を上げたが、縫い物に戻った ◇The doctor may allow her to *return to* work next week. 医者は来週にも彼女が仕事に復帰するのを許可するかもしれない

▶**a return to sth** 图 [単数で] ◇his *return to* public life 彼の公職への復帰

renew [他]《特にジャーナリズム》再開する ◇The army *renewed* its assault on the capital. 軍は首都に対する攻撃を再開した ◇We have to *renew* our efforts to attract young players. 我々は若い選手を引きつけるために改めて努力せねばならない ◇The annual dinner is a chance to *renew* acquaintance with old friends. 毎年恒例の夕食会は旧交を温める機会になっている ❶ renew はしばしば人・国・政府が相手との関係を壊そうとする場合にも築こうとする場合にも用いられる. ◆to *renew* efforts/a bid/calls/demands/threats/an assault/an attack (改めて努力する/値をつけ直す/電話をかけ直す/再度要求する/再度脅迫する/再度強要する/攻撃を再開する). ◆to *renew* a friendship/an acquaintance (旧交を温める).

▶**renewal** 图 [C, U] ◇a *renewal* of interest in traditional teaching methods 伝統的な教授法への新たな関心

reopen [他, 自]《特に書き言葉》再開する ◇The police have decided to *reopen* the file on the missing girl. 警察は行方不明の少女の捜索を再開する決定を下した ◇The trial *reopened* on 6 March. その裁判は3月6日に再開された ❶ reopen の典型的な目的語として debate, discussion, issue, controversy, argument, case, file, negotiations, talks が挙げられる.

restart [自, 他] (活動・進行を[が])再開する;(機械・心臓を[が])再起動[始動]する ◇The umpire tried to *restart* the game after 35 minutes. 審判は35分後に試合を再開しようとした ◇The doctors struggled to *restart* his heart. 医師たちは彼の心臓を再び動かそうと懸命に努めた ◇The engine did not *restart* and the plane dived to the ground. エンジンが再始動せず、その飛行機は地面に激突した

,take sth 'up 句動詞 《特に話し言葉》(他人がやり残した[しばらく話に出なかった]事)を続ける、引き継ぐ ◇She *took up* the story where Tim had left off. 彼女はティムが途中でやめた話の続きをした ◇I'd like to *take up* the point you raised earlier. あなたが先に提起した問題を引き継ぎたいのですが ❶ この意味での take sth up は主に人が前に述べた問題に戻ること、一時中断後に再び話を続けることを指す.

continuous 形

continuous・relentless・continual・persistent・round-the-clock・unbroken・uninterrupted・incessant・non-stop

間断なしに長く続くことを表す
[類語例]継続的な、連続的な、永続的な、しつこい

文型&コロケーション

▶the continuous/ relentless/ uninterrupted/ incessant **flow** of sth
▶continuous/ continual/ relentless **struggle**
▶continuous/ continual/ persistent **change/ conflict**
▶continuous/ relentless/ persistent **pressure**
▶continuous/ relentless/ persistent/ incessant **rain**
▶continuous/ continual/ incessant **noise**
▶perpetual/ unbroken/ uninterrupted **peace**
▶a continuous/ an unbroken/ an uninterrupted **succession/ series/ sequence/ period**
▶almost continuous/ continual/ unbroken/ uninterrupted/ incessant/ non-stop

continuous 絶え間ない、継続[連続]的な ◇It was a week of almost *continuous* sunshine. その週はほとんど晴れの天気が続いた ◇Do the exercise in one *continuous* flowing motion. この運動は動きを止めずに流れるように1回の動作で行ってください ◇You need to have been in *continuous* employment for at least two years. 最低2年間は勤続してきたことが条件です ◇Awards are based on *continuous* assessment of course work as well as a final examination. 奨学金は最終試験だけでなく学習活動の恒常的評価に基づいて決められる [反義] **intermittent** (OCCASIONAL)

▶**continuously** 副 ◇The radio station now transmits *continuously*. 現在そのラジオ放送局は切れ目なく放送を流しています

relentless 絶え間ない、たゆまない、衰えない ◇The wind was *relentless*. 風が容赦なく吹いていた ◇His *relentless* energy made him come alive in every role he played. 衰えを知らぬエネルギーは、演じるすべての役に生気を吹き込んだ ◇The *relentless pursuit of* increased profit at any cost is questionable. 絶え間なくこぎる利益の追求には疑問の余地がある

▶**relentlessly** 副 ◇The sun beat down *relentlessly*. 太陽が容赦なく照りつけた

continual [名詞の前で] 絶え間ない、継続[連続]的な ◇They live in *continual* fear. 彼らは絶え間ない恐怖の中で生活している ◇The body is in a *continual* state of chemical activity. 体の中では化学物質の活動が絶え間ない状態にある ◇He was in a *continual* process of rewriting his material. 彼は休むことなく資料を書き直しているところだった

▶**continually** 副 ◇All living organisms are *continually* in competition with other species. あらゆる生命体は他の種との絶え間ない競争のただ中にある

ノート **continual** と **continuous** の使い分け：多くの場合両者とも使用可能。◆a *continuous/continual* process/movement/struggle (絶え間ない進行/動き/努力)。◆*continuous/continual* change/conflict/noise (絶え間ない変化/争い/騒音). しかしながら、continuous のほうがより頻繁に用いられ、使用範囲も広い. continual は特に長い期間継続する精神や肉体の状態について用いられ、state, fear, pain, delight, threat, reminder などと結びつく. また、両語とも「何度も繰り返された」の意味もある. ☞ **FREQUENT**

persistent 継続[持続, 永続]的な、しつこい ◇*Persistent* heavy rain held up work on the bridge for more than a week. 大雨がなかなかやまず橋の工事が1週間以上も中断された ◇*Persistent* pressure from the water authority forced the company to comply with the rules. 水道局から執拗な圧力を受けて、その会社は規則に従わざるを得なくなった

▶**persistently** 副 ◇*persistently* high interest rates なかなか下がらない高い利率

,round-the-'clock (または **a,round-the-'clock**) [名詞の前で] 昼夜兼行で、四六時中の ◇His family kept a *round-the-clock* vigil at his bedside. 家族は彼の枕元

↳**continuous**　　　　　　　　　　**contract, control**

で昼夜を徹して看病を行った　◇*Round-the-clock* police surveillance was necessary. 昼夜を徹しての警察による張り込みが必要だった
▶*around/round the 'clock* 〔仔ル〕　◇Emergency teams were working *round the clock* to make the homes secure. 緊急救助隊が昼夜を徹して各家庭の安全確保にあたっていた

unbroken 妨害されない；絶え間ない，継続[連続]的な　◇It was the first *unbroken* night of sleep I had had for months. 何か月ぶりかで熟睡することができた夜だった　◇She retired from the company after 45 years of *unbroken* service. 彼女は45年勤続した後その会社を退職した

uninterrupted 中断されない；絶え間ない，継続[連続]的な　◇We had two weeks of *uninterrupted* warm sunshine. 暖かく晴れた天気が2週間通して続いた　◇You need to find a place where you can do *uninterrupted* work. 君は邪魔されずに作業できる場所を見つける必要がある

incessant 《ややフォーマル，けなして》絶え間なく続く，ひっきりなしの　◇She raised her voice above the *incessant* beat of the music. 彼女は絶え間なく続く音楽のビートに負けない声を張り上げた
▶**incessantly** 副　◇The dogs barked *incessantly*. 犬たちがひっきりなしに吠えた

,non-'stop 《ややインフォーマル》(活動が)休憩[中断]なしの　◇It will be a real fun day out for everyone. Seven hours of *non-stop* entertainment. 皆さんにとって戸外で過ごす本当に楽しい一日になるでしょう。7時間ぶっ通しのお楽しみです
▶**non-'stop** 副　◇They talked *non-stop* about the play. 彼らはその劇について絶え間なく話し続けた

contract 名 ☞AGREEMENT

contract・treaty・accord・convention
人々や組織，国家同士の正式な合意を表す
【類語訳】契約，条約，協定

〔文型&コロケーション〕
▶a contract/ a treaty/ an accord/ a convention **between** sb and sb
▶a contract/ a treaty/ an accord **with** sb
▶a treaty/ an accord/ a convention **on** sth
▶a contract/ a treaty/ an accord **to do** sth
▶**under** (a) contract/ a treaty/ an accord/ a convention
▶a **draft** contract/ treaty/ accord/ convention
▶an **international** contract/ treaty/ accord/ convention
▶to **sign** a contract/ a treaty/ an accord/ a convention
▶to **comply with** a contract/ a treaty/ an accord/ a convention
▶to **approve** a contract/ a treaty/ an accord/ a convention
▶to **ratify** a treaty/ an accord/ a convention
▶to **accept/ draw up/ negotiate/ conclude/ violate** a contract/ a treaty/ an accord

contract [C] (個人・会社・組織同士の書面による)契約　◇These clauses form part of the *contract* between buyer and seller. これらの条項は買い手と売り手との契約の一部を成している　◇They won a *contract for* the delivery of five fighter planes. 彼らは戦闘機5機納品の契約を獲得した　◇I was *on* a three-year fixed-term *contract* that expired last week. 私は期限が先週で切れた3年間の期限付き契約を結んでいた　◇She is *under contract to* (= has a contract to work for) a major US computer firm. 彼女はアメリカの一流のコンピューター会社で働く契約をしている　◇All employees have a written *contract of employment*. 全従業員は書面による雇用契約を結んでいる　◇The offer has been accepted, *subject to contract* (= the agreement is not legally binding before contracts are signed). 契約が成立するまで効力はないが申し込みとしては受けつけられた　◇They were sued for *breach of contract* (= not keeping to a contract). 彼らは契約違反で訴えられた ☞**contract** (EMPLOY)

treaty [C] (二つ以上の国家間の)条約，協定　◇The government concluded a *peace treaty* with the rebels. 政府は反乱軍と平和条約を締結した　◇The new law may be in breach of the *Treaty* of Rome. その新法はローマ条約に抵触している可能性がある

accord [C] (二つの組織・国家間の)協定，条約　◇The countries drew up *accords* on economic and technical cooperation. それらの国は経済協力と技術協力に関する協定書を作成した

convention [C] (国家間[代表者同士]の)協定，条約　◇This is forbidden under the European *Convention* on Human Rights. これはヨーロッパ人権条約のもとで禁止されている　◇Over 60 countries have yet to ratify the climate *convention*. 60か国以上の国々が気候に関する協定をまだ批准していない

┃ノート┃ **treaty, accord, convention** の使い分け：treaty と accord は両語とも例えば紛争後の和平再建や貿易・軍事・経済協力などに関する国家間の正式な合意を指す。両語ともしばしば調印場所の地名が付される特定の条約[協定]名の中で用いられる。◆the *Treaty* of Rome (ローマ条約)．◆the Algiers *Accord* (アルジェ協定)．accord は政府・労働組合など組織間の正式な合意にも用いられる。convention は多国間(3か国以上)の国際的な合意を指し，ふつう例えば武器の売り渡し・難民の待遇・汚染管理など特定の活動に関する規約を含むものを言う。convention はふつう多国間にまたがる問題の調整を行うもので，その条約[協定]に調印することで各国はそれに含まれる規約・基準の適用に合意する。

control 名

control・power・rule・authority・jurisdiction・discipline・command・hold・grasp・force
人や物事を抑える力を表す
【類語訳】支配，権限，管理，監督，統制，指揮，統率

〔文型&コロケーション〕
▶control/ power/ rule/ authority/ jurisdiction/ command/ a hold **over** sb/ sth
▶a hold/ grasp **on** sb/ sth
▶to be **in** control/ power/ authority/ command/ force
▶to be **under** sb's control/ rule/ authority/ jurisdiction/ command
▶to be **beyond/ outside** the control/ power/ authority/ jurisdiction **of** sb
▶the power/ authority/ jurisdiction **to do** sth
▶**absolute/ complete** control/ power/ authority/ command
▶**direct** control/ rule/ authority/ command
▶to **have** control/ power/ authority/ jurisdiction/ command/ a hold over sb/ force
▶to **exercise** control/ power/ authority/ jurisdiction

convey

- ▶to **take** control/ power/ command
- ▶to **assume** control/ power/ authority/ command
- ▶to **give** sb control/ power/ authority/ jurisdiction/ command/ a hold over sb
- ▶to **delegate** power/ authority/ command (to sb)
- ▶to **lose** control/ power/ authority/ command/ your hold on sth
- ▶to **relinquish** control/ power/ command/ your hold on sth

control [U] （国家[地域, 組織, 生活]運営に関わる）支配(力), 権限；（人・物事を自分の思い通りにする）支配, 管理, 監督, 統制, 制御, 抑制 ◇The party is expecting to *gain control of* the council in the next election. その党が次回の選挙で議会の支配権を得る見込みだ ◇The aim is to give people more *control* over their own lives. 目的は人々の自らの生活に対する権限を強化することである ◇The city is *under enemy control*. その都市は敵の支配下にある ◇The teacher had no *control* over the children. その教師は子どもたちを監督する能力がなかった ◇She struggled to *keep control of* her voice. 彼女は口調を抑えようと懸命に努めた ◇She lost *control* of her car on the ice. 彼女は凍った路面の上で車を制御できなくなった ◇Owing to *circumstances beyond our control* the flight to Rome has been cancelled. やむを得ない事情により, ローマ行きの便は欠航となった

power [U] （人・物事に対する）支配(力), 権限；（国家・地域に対する）政治的支配 ◇He has the *power* to make life very difficult for us. 彼には私たちの生活を非常に困難なものにする権力がある ◇The Emperor had absolute *power* over all his subjects. 皇帝は全臣民に対して絶対的な力を持っていた ◇She was determined to go through with her plan, now that she *had him in her power* (= was able to do what she liked with him). 彼を支配下に置いたので, 彼女は計画を遂行する決心をした ◇The party *came to power* at the last election. その党が先の選挙で政権を取った ◇He *seized power* in a military coup. 彼は軍事クーデターで政権を握った ◇It was the beginning of a *power struggle* between rival factions within the party. それが党内で対立する派閥間の勢力争いの始まりだった ◇The war brought about a shift in the *balance of power*. その戦争は勢力の均衡に変化をもたらした

rule [U] （特定の人物[集団, 政治体制]による国家・地域の）支配[統治] ◇There was a gradual process of returning the country to civilian *rule*. その国は徐々に民政への移行が進みつつあるところであった ◇The country remained under direct *rule* by the occupying powers. その国は依然として占領する強国による直接支配下にあった ❶ rule はしばしば他の国家[集団]による統治や, 自由がほとんど許されていない（または自由が保障されていない）政治体制による統治を指す. ◆ colonial/British/Ottoman *rule*（植民地主義／英国／オスマントルコによる統治）. ◆ Communist/military *rule*（共産主義／軍事政権）. ◆ a return to civilian/democratic/majority *rule*（文民統治／民主制／多数決原理への回帰）. ☞ **rule** (RULE 動 1)

authority [U] （命令を与える）権限, 権力 ◇She now has *authority* over the people who used to be her bosses. 今や彼女にはかつて自分の上司だった人々に対する指揮権限がある ◇Nothing will be done because no one in *authority* (= who has the power to do sth) takes the matter seriously. 権限を持つ者が誰もその問題を深刻に捉えないので何も行われないだろう

jurisdiction [U, C] 《フォーマル》（法的決定を行う公的機関の）権限, 管轄 ◇These matters do not *fall within* our *jurisdiction*. これらの問題は我々の権限の範囲内にない ◇The agreement doesn't come under the *jurisdiction* of the EU courts. その協定は欧州裁判所の管轄下に入らない

discipline [U] 規律；規律正しさ ◇The school has a reputation for high standards of *discipline*. その学校は規律の水準が高いという評判だ ◇Strict *discipline* is imposed on army recruits. 厳しい規律が陸軍の新兵に課せられている ◇She keeps good *discipline* in class. 彼女はクラスの規律をよく保っている

command [U] （軍隊・警察に対する）指揮[統率](権) ◇He has 1,200 men under his *command*. 彼は1200人の部下を指揮下に納めている ◇Who's in *command* here? この指揮は誰が執っているのか ◇The police arrived and took *command* of the situation. 警察が到着してその場の指揮を執った ☞ **command** (ORDER 1), **command** (RUN 2)

hold [単数で] （人・状況に対する）支配[影響][力[権]] ◇What she knew about his past gave her a *hold* over him. 彼女は彼の過去について知っていたことで, 彼ににらみがきいた ◇Enemy forces have consolidated their *hold* on the northern province. 敵軍は北部州への支配を強化した

grasp [単数で]《ややインフォーマル》（維持するのが難しい）支配(力), 掌握 ◇The company continues to maintain its *grasp* on the business computer market. その会社は業務用コンピューター市場の支配を維持し続けている ◇Don't let the situation escape from your *grasp*. 事態をしっかりと掌握しておくように

|ノート| **hold** と **grasp** の使い分け：この意味では hold のほうが grasp よりも強意的. hold が取る動詞には have, strengthen, consolidate があり, grasp が取る動詞には maintain や slip, escape from（主語は物事）がある.

force [U] （法律・規則が持つ）効力, 拘束力 ◇These guidelines do not have *the force of law*. これらの指針には法的拘束力はない ◇The court ruled that these standards have *force* in British law. これらの規範が英国の法律において効力を持つと裁判所は判決を下した

convey 動 ☞ TELL 1

convey・send・communicate・relay・repeat・impart・get sth across・pass sth on・break

人に物事に関する情報や考え, 感情を知らせたり理解させたりする

【類語訳】伝える, 送る, 届ける, 知らせる, 教える, 明かす

文型&コロケーション

- ▶to convey/ send/ communicate/ relay/ repeat/ impart/ get across/ pass on/ break sth **to** sb
- ▶to convey/ communicate/ relay/ repeat/ break it to sb **that**...
- ▶to convey/ communicate/ relay/ repeat to sb **what**...
- ▶to convey/ send/ communicate/ relay/ repeat/ impart/ get across/ pass on a **message**
- ▶to convey/ communicate/ get across your **ideas**
- ▶to convey/ pass on/ break **the news**
- ▶to convey sth/ communicate sth/ get sth across **clearly/ effectively**

↳ convey

convey [他]《ややフォーマル》(情報・考え・感情を)伝達する, 伝える ◇He tried desperately to *convey* how urgent the situation was. 彼は事態がいかに緊急を要することか必死に伝えようとした ◇Colours like red *convey* a sense of energy and strength. 赤のような色は活力や力強さの意味を表す ◇Please *convey* my apologies to your wife. 《フォーマル, 話し言葉》奥様に私からの謝罪の気持ちをお伝えください

send [他]《メッセージの形で)送る, 届ける, 伝える ◇My parents ***send their love***. 私の両親はよろしくって言っています ◇What sort of message is the irresponsible behaviour of these celebrities *sending* to young people? これらの芸能人の無責任な言動は若者にどんなメッセージを伝えているのか ◇She ***sent word*** that she could not come. 《フォーマル or 文語》彼女は行くことができないという旨の言葉を伝えた

communicate [他, 自]《ややフォーマル》(情報・考え・感情を)伝達する, 知らせる ◇He was eager to *communicate* his ideas to the group. 彼は熱心に自分の考えをそのグループに伝えようとした ◇Her nervousness was *communicating* itself to the children. 彼女のいら立ちが子どもたちに伝わっていた ◇Candidates must be able to *communicate* effectively. 立候補者は効果的に考えを伝えることができなくてはならない ☞ **communication** (COMMUNICATION), **communication** (LETTER)

[ノート] **convey** と **communicate** の使い分け: convey は情報・考え・感情を個人・集団・一般の人々に伝えること, communicate は情報・考えを集団・一般の人々に伝えることで, ふつうは個人に伝えない. ×Please *communicate* my apologies to your wife. convey は必ず目的語を伴い, その目的語は主語とは異なる. ×Her nervousness was *conveying* itself to the children. ×Candidates must be able to *convey* effectively.

relay [他]《ややフォーマル》(自分が受けた情報を)中継する, 伝える ◇He *relayed* the message to his boss. 彼はその伝言を上司に伝えた ◇Instructions were *relayed* to her by phone. 指示が電話で彼女に伝えられた

repeat [他](自分が聞いた[言われた]事を)他言する ◇I don't want you to *repeat* a word of this to anyone. これに関しては一言も誰にも他言しないでもらいたい ◇The rumour has been widely *repeated* in the press. そのうわさは報道機関に広まっていた ◇Why did you go and *repeat* what I said to Ian? なぜ私が言ったことをイアンのところへ行って伝えたのか ☞ **repeat** (REPEAT)

impart [他]《フォーマル》(情報・知識を)知らせる, 教える ◇Her aim was not merely to *impart* knowledge, but rather to help students learn for themselves. 彼女の目的は単に知識を教えることではなく, 生徒が自学自習できるようにすることであった

get sth a'cross [句動詞]《ややインフォーマル》(物事を)うまく伝える ◇He's not very good at *getting* his ideas *across*. 彼は自分の考えを人に伝えることがあまり得意ではない

pass sth 'on [句動詞]《ややインフォーマル》(自分が受けた情報を)中継する ◇I *passed* your message *on* to my mother. あなたの伝言を母に伝えました ❶ pass on の目的語には情報以外の物事も用いられる.

break [他, 自](悪い知らせをうまく)明かす, 知らせる;(知らせが)明らかになる ◇I don't know how to ***break it to*** him. 彼にそのことをどのように打ち明けたらよいかわからない ◇Just *break* the news to her gently. まあ試しに彼女にそっと知らせてごらん ◇There was a public outcry when the scandal *broke*. スキャンダルが明らかになると国民から激しい非難が起きた

convince [動] ☞ PERSUADE

convince・satisfy・persuade
物事が真実であると人に信じさせる
【類義訳】納得させる, 確信させる

[文型&コロケーション]
▶ to convince/ satisfy/ persuade sb **of** sth
▶ to convince/ satisfy/ persuade sb **that**...
▶ to convince/ satisfy/ persuade **yourself**

convince [他]《進行形なし》納得[確信]させる ◇He was like a politician who wants to *convince* you of his sincerity. 彼は自分の誠実さを説きたがる政治家のようだった ◇I had *convinced* myself (that) I was right. 私は自分が正しかったと確信していた ◇The events in Paris *convinced* him that Europe was on the brink of revolution. パリの諸々の事件で彼はヨーロッパに今にも革命が起きようとしていると確信した ◇I wasn't *convinced* by her arguments. 私は彼女の言い分に納得がいかなかった ☞ **convince sb to do sth** (PERSUADE), **convinced** (SURE)

satisfy [他]《進行形なし》《ややフォーマル》納得[確信]させる ◇Her explanation didn't *satisfy* the teacher. 彼女の説明ではその教師は納得しなかった ◇First people need to be *satisfied* of the need for a new system. まず新しい制度の必要性を人々にわからせる必要がある ☞ **satisfied** (SURE)

persuade [他](言葉で)納得[確信]させる ◇No one was *persuaded* by his argument. 彼の主張には誰も納得しなかった ◇It has been difficult to *persuade* people that we have no political objectives. 私たちに政治的な目的などないことを人々にわかってもらうのはなかなか困難だ

convincing [形]

convincing・compelling・persuasive・strong・forceful・cogent
主張や意見, 証拠が真実であると確信させるほどきっぱりと明瞭に提示されることを表す
【類義訳】説得力のある, 口のうまい, 強固な, 強力な, 揺るぎない

persuasive	convincing	compelling
strong		
forceful		
cogent		

[文型&コロケーション]
▶ a convincing/ compelling/ persuasive/ strong/ forceful/ cogent **argument**
▶ convincing/ compelling/ persuasive/ strong/ cogent **evidence**
▶ a convincing/ compelling/ persuasive/ strong/ cogent **reason/ case**
▶ a convincing/ compelling/ cogent **explanation**
▶ **very** convincing/ compelling/ persuasive/ strong/ forceful/ cogent
▶ **extremely** convincing/ compelling/ persuasive/ strong

convincing (主張・理由・証拠が)説得力のある ◇This explanation is not entirely *convincing*. この説明には必ずしも強い説得力があるわけではない ◇She sounded very *convincing* to me (= I believed what she said). 彼女の言うことは私にはなるほどもっともだと聞こえた 反意 **unconvincing** (UNLIKELY 2)
▶**convincingly** 副 ◇Her case was *convincingly* argued. 彼女の事件の弁護には説得力があった
compelling [ふつう名詞の前で]《特に書き言葉》(主張・理由・証拠が非常に)説得力のある、なるほどと思わせる ◇The new studies provide *compelling* evidence in support of these concepts. それらの新たな研究はこれらの概念を裏づけるきわめて有力な証拠を提示している

ノート **convinging** と **compelling** の使い分け：compelling のほうが convincing よりもいくぶん強意的。seem/sound/look convincing は思われているほどには説得力がないことをわずかに示唆することもある。compelling はふつう名詞の前に用いられ、真実であることに疑問の余地が残されていないことを表す。

persuasive (主張・理由などが)説得力のある、(人が)口のうまい ◇Advertising relies heavily on the *persuasive* power of imagery. 広告はイメージが持つ説得力に依存するところが大きい ◇He can be very *persuasive*. 彼はとても口がうまい
▶**persuasively** 副 ◇They argue *persuasively* in favour of a total ban on handguns. 彼らは拳銃の全面禁止を支持する説得力のある主張をしている
strong (主張・理由などが)強固[強力]な、揺るぎない ◇You have a *strong* case for getting your job back. 君には仕事を取り戻すための強力な言い分がある ◇There is *strong* evidence of a link between exercise and a healthy heart. 運動と健康な心臓との関連を示す揺るぎない証拠がある 反意 **weak** (UNLIKELY 2)
forceful (意見・主張が)強力な、力強い ◇The minister launched a *forceful* defence of the policy. 大臣はその政策の強力なてこ入れに乗り出した
cogent 《フォーマル》(主張・理由・証拠が)説得力のある ◇His criticisms still seem *cogent* today as they did twenty years ago. 彼の批評には今日もまだ20年前と変わらぬ説得力があるようだ

cool 動

cool・chill・cool (sb/sth) down・freeze・refrigerate
温かくない状態になる[する]
【類語訳】冷える、冷める、冷やす、冷ます、凍える、冷凍保存する

文型&コロケーション
▶chilled/ frozen food
▶to leave sth to/ allow sth to/ let sth cool/ cool down
▶to keep sth frozen/ refrigerated

cool [自, 他] (物が)冷える、冷める；冷やす、冷ます ◇Glass contracts as it *cools*. ガラスは冷えると収縮する ◇The cylinder is *cooled* by a jet of water. シリンダーは水の噴射によって冷やされる ☞ **cool** (COLD 1)
chill [他, 自] (人を)寒がらせる；(食べ物・飲み物を)よく冷やす、(食べ物・飲み物を)よく冷える ◇They were *chilled* by the icy wind. 彼らは氷のように冷たい風で凍えた ◇This wine is best *served chilled*. このワインはよく冷やして出すのが一番よい ◇Let the pudding *chill* for an hour until set. プディングが固まるまで1時間よく冷やしましょう
,cool 'down, ,cool sb/sth 'down 句動詞 《ややインフォーマル》(人・物が)冷える、冷める；(人・物を)冷やす、冷ます ◇Let the charger *cool down* before using it again. もう一度使用する前に充電器を冷ましておきましょう ◇Drink plenty of cold water to *cool* yourself *down*. 体を冷ますために冷たい水をたくさん飲みなさい ◇Blow on it to *cool* it *down* or you'll burn your mouth. 息を吹きかけて冷まさないと、口を火傷します ❶ *cool off* ともいえるが、目的語なしでは *cool down* ほどは一般的ではない。◆We *cooled off* with a swim in the lake. (私たちは湖で一泳ぎして涼をとった)

ノート **cool** と **cool (sb/sth) down** の使い分け：cool down のほうが cool よりもややインフォーマルで、話し言葉で用いられることが多い。また、cool down は cool よりも myself, yourself, himself などと共に用いられることが多い。※How about a swim to *cool* ourselves *down*? (涼むために一泳ぎするのはどう)。専門的な言い回しに用いる場合、または工程[機構]について言う場合はcoolを用いる。✕The cylinder is *cooled down* by a jet of water.

freeze [自, 他] (人が)凍える、凍死する；(食べ物を)冷凍保存する；(食べ物が)冷凍保存できる ◇Every time she opens the window we all *freeze*. 彼女が窓を開けるたびに私たちは皆凍える ◇Two men *froze to death* on the mountain. 2人の男性が山で凍死した ◇These meals are ideal for home *freezing*. これらの料理は家庭での冷凍保存に最適だ ◇Some fruits *freeze* better than others. 果物の中には他のものよりも冷凍保存に向いているものがある 反意 **melt, thaw, defrost**, ☞ **freezing, frozen** (FREEZING)
refrigerate [他, しばしば受身で]《フォーマル》(食べ物を)冷蔵[冷凍]保存する ◇Once opened, this product should be kept *refrigerated*. 開封後はこの製品は冷蔵してください

copy 名

1 copy・transcript・printout・photocopy・hard copy
原本や原画を手書き[印刷]で写した複写物
【類語訳】コピー、印刷出力、プリントアウト、写真複写、ハードコピー

文型&コロケーション
▶to **make** a copy/ transcript/ photocopy
▶to **send** a copy/ printout/ transcript/ photocopy/ hard copy
▶to **attach/ enclose** a copy/ printout/ photocopy/ hard copy
▶to **keep** a copy/ printout/ transcript/ photocopy

copy [C] (印刷・コピー機による)コピー ◇I will send you a *copy* of the report. その報告書のコピーをお送りします ◇Could I have ten *copies* of this page, please? このページを10部コピーしてもらえますか
transcript [C] (話されたことの手書き・印刷による)写し ◇They are going to publish a *transcript* of the interview. そのインタビューを文字に書き起こした記事が掲載される予定だ ☞ **transcribe** (WRITE)
printout [C, U] (コンピューターからの)印刷出力、プリントアウト(した印刷物) ◇a *printout* of text downloaded

↪**copy**

from the Internet インターネットからダウンロードした文章のプリントアウト ◇There were a few pages of computer *printout* on her desk. 彼女の机の上にコンピューターからのプリントアウトが数枚あった

photocopy [C] (写真複写[コピー]機による)写真複写, コピー ◇Make as many *photocopies* as you need. 必要なだけコピーしてください

ノート copyとphotocopyの使い分け：copyはあらゆる種類の複製印刷に用いられる。photocopyはphotocopier(写真複写機)で複写されるもの。しかし、特にどんなコピーのことを言っているかが既に明らかな場合、photocopyはしばしばcopyとよばれる。

hard 'copy [U] 《コンピューター》(コンピューターからの情報が紙に印刷出力された)ハードコピー ◇Most of our material is online, but this course is still only available in *hard copy*. 資料の大半はオンラインですが、この講座のものはまだハードコピーしかありません

ノート hard copyとprintoutの使い分け：hard copyは電子データとは対照的に印刷されたデータを指す。printoutはプリンターで印刷された紙その物を指す。

2 copy・model・replica・reproduction・facsimile・duplicate・reconstruction・mock-up
他の物を模して作られた物
【類語訳】模写, 複製, 模倣品, 模造品, 模型, 復刻品, 副本

文型&コロケーション
▶in replica/ facsimile/ duplicate
▶a/ an **good/ accurate** copy/ model/ reproduction/ facsimile/ reconstruction
▶an **exact** copy/ replica/ reproduction/ facsimile/ duplicate/ reconstruction
▶a **faithful** copy/ model/ reproduction
▶a **crude** copy/ model
▶a **full-scale/ life-size** model/ replica/ reconstruction
▶a **working** model/ replica/ reconstruction
▶to **make** a copy/ a model/ a replica/ a reproduction/ a facsimile/ a duplicate/ a reconstruction
▶to **keep** a copy/ duplicate

copy [C] (芸術作品・書類・ディスクの)模写, 複製, 模倣[模造]品 ◇The thieves replaced the original painting with a *copy*. その泥棒たちは原画を複製とすり替えた ◇It must be certified as a true *copy* of the original document. それは本当に書類の正本を複製した物であると証明されなければならない ◇You should make a *copy* of the disk as a back-up. バックアップとしてディスクを複製したほうがいい

model [C] (原物より小型の)模型 ◇They have a working *model* (= one in which the parts move) of a water mill. 彼らは水車小屋の動く模型を持っている ◇I used to build *model* aeroplanes. 私は飛行機の模型をよく組み立てたものだ ◇The architect had produced a **scale model** of the proposed shopping complex (= one in which all the parts are the correct size in relation to each other). 建築家は提案されているショッピングセンターの縮尺模型を作った

replica [C] (本物を精巧[正確]に複製した)レプリカ ◇There is even a scaled-down *replica* of the Eiffel Tower there. そこにはエッフェル塔の縮尺レプリカがある

◇The weapon used in the raid was a *replica*. 襲撃に用いられた武器はレプリカだった ◇*replica* guns レプリカ銃

reproduction [C] (芸術作品・家具の)複製[復刻]品 ◇They have a catalogue with colour *reproductions* of the paintings for sale. その店には販売しているカラー複製絵画のカタログがある ◇*reproduction* furniture (= furniture made as a copy of an earlier style) 復刻モデルの家具 ❶reproductionは人をあざむくために作られるものではなく、ふつう合法的に公認された複製物を指す。☞FAKE

facsimile [C] (書籍・書類の)複製, 復刻 ◇A *facsimile* of the document is available in the British Library. その文書の複製は英国図書館で利用できる ◇a *facsimile* edition 復刻版 ❶facsimileは特に古書・古文書の写真複製について言う。

duplicate [C] (正本に対する)複製, 副本 ◇Is this a *duplicate* or the original? これは副本ですか, それとも正本ですか ◇The contract is prepared in *duplicate* (= two copies are made), so that both parties can keep a copy. 契約書は正副2部用意されているので、両者とも1部ずつ保管することができます ❶duplicateはふつう書類・ディスク・鍵について用いられる。

reconstruction [C] (もはや存在しない物の)復元[再現]物 ◇The doorway is a 19th century *reconstruction* of Norman work. その戸口はノルマン様式を19世紀に復元したものだ

'mock-up [C] (試験・展示用に作られた)実物大模型, 実物見本 ◇He was looking at a *mock-up* of the following day's front page. 彼は翌日の第1面の校正刷りを見ていた ❶mock-upはしばしば実物の設計者自身による「見本」について用いられる。

copy [動]

copy・reproduce・photocopy・duplicate
他の物を正確に模して作る
【類語訳】コピーする, 複写する, 複製する, 模造する, 模写する

文型&コロケーション
▶to copy/ reproduce sth **from** sth
▶to copy/ reproduce/ photocopy/ duplicate a **letter/ document**
▶to copy/ photocopy/ duplicate a **form**
▶to copy/ reproduce a **painting**
▶to copy/ duplicate a **disk/ CD**
▶to copy/ reproduce/ duplicate sth **exactly**
▶to copy/ reproduce sth **accurately/ faithfully**
▶to **merely/ simply** copy/ reproduce sth

copy [他] コピー[模写, 複製, 模造, 模写]する; (コピー機で)コピーする ◇They *copied* the designs from those on Greek vases. 彼らはギリシアの花瓶に施された模様を複製した ◇Data can be *copied* from the computer onto a memory stick. データはコンピューターからメモリースティックにコピーすることができる ◇Finally, the notes can be *copied* and distributed to the audience. 最後に(お伝えしておきますが)メモはコピーされ聴衆に配られることもございます

reproduce [他] (ややフォーマル)(画像・文章・情報を)コピー[複写, 複製, 模造, 模写]する ◇All illustrations are *reproduced* by kind permission of the Mercury Gallery. すべての図版はマーキュリー・ギャラリーの寛大な許可

いただいて複製されている ◇The results are *reproduced* in Table 2. 結果は表2に転載されている ❶*reproduce*は特に書籍の中の文章や画像や、絵画・写真・その他の芸術作品を複製することについて用いられる。

photocopy [他,自] (写真複写[コピー]機で書類を)写真複写する, コピーする ◇The *photocopied* letter had been sent to all the houses in the street. コピーされた手紙がその通りにあるすべての家に届けられていた ◇I seem to have spent most of the day *photocopying*. 私は1日の大半をコピーに費やしたみたいだ ❶ *photocopying* (コピー機によるコピー)を指していることが明らかな場合は、しばしば単に copy と言う。◆Can you get these *copied/photocopied* for me by 5 o'clock? (5時までにこれらをコピーしてもらえますか)

duplicate [他, しばしば受身で] 複製[副本]を作る ◇Please keep the *duplicated* form and send us the original. 副本用紙を保管して正本用紙を当方にお送りください ❶ *duplicate* は主として書類・手紙・用紙の副本をコピー機で1枚以上作ることについて用いられるが、コンピューターのディスク・CD の複製を作ることについても言う。
▶**duplicate** [形] ◇a *duplicate* invoice 納品書の副本

corner [名]

corner・turn・bend・zigzag・hairpin bend・twist
道路・河川の方向が変わる湾曲部を表す
【類語訳】角, 曲がり角, 急カーブ, 方向転換, ジグザグ, くねり

文型&コロケーション
▶ **around/ round/ at/ on** a corner/ bend/ hairpin bend
▶ a **left-hand/ right-hand** corner/ turn/ bend
▶ a **left/ right** corner/ turn
▶ a **sharp** corner/ turn/ bend/ twist
▶ a **tight** corner/ turn/ bend
▶ a **blind/ dangerous** corner/ bend
▶ to **negotiate** a corner/ turn/ bend/ hairpin bend
▶ to **round/ take** a corner/ bend/ hairpin bend
▶ to **come around/ round** a corner/ bend/ hairpin bend

corner [C] (2本の道路が合流する交差点の)角;(道路の)曲がり角, 急カーブ ◇There was a large group of youths standing on the street *corner*. 通りの角にたくさんの若者たちが立っていた ◇Turn right at the *corner* of Avalon Road and Radnor Street. アバロン街とラドナー通りの交差点の角を右に曲がってください ◇The wind hit him as he *turned the corner*. その角を曲がると風が彼に吹きつけた

turn [C] (乗り物の)方向転換;(道路の)カーブ, 曲がり角 ◇*Make a* right *turn* into West street. 右折してウェスト・ストリートに入ってください ◇The narrow lane was full of *twists and turns*. その狭い路地は曲がりくねっていた ☞ **turn** (CURVE)

bend [C] (道路・河川の)曲がり, カーブ, 曲がり角 ◇The two vehicles collided on a sharp *bend* in the road. 2台の車が道路の急カーブで衝突した ◇You took that *bend* very fast! あのカーブをすごく速く曲がったね ☞ **bend** (CURVE)

zigzag [C] ジグザグ ◇The path descended the hill in a series of *zigzags*. 道はジグザグの連続でその丘を下っていた ☞ **zigzag** (CURVE)

hairpin 'bend (英) (米 ,**hairpin 'curve** , **hairpin 'turn**) (または **hairpin** 英, 米) [C] (道路・山道の)ヘアピンカーブ ◇The road winds uphill in a series of *hairpin bends*. その道路は上に向かって曲がりくねり、ヘアピンカーブが続いている

twist [C] (道路・河川の)困難[危険]なほどの急カーブ, 曲がり, くねり ◇The car followed the *twists and turns* of the mountain road. 車は曲がりくねった山道をたどった ☞ **twist** (CURVE)

correct [動]

correct・fix・put sth right・set sb/sth straight・remedy・rectify・redress・cure
正確な、あるいは誤りや問題のないものにする
【類語訳】訂正する, 修正する, 改善する, 修復する

文型&コロケーション
▶ to correct/ fix/ put right/ remedy/ rectify/ redress/ cure **what...**
▶ to correct/ fix/ put right/ remedy/ rectify/ redress/ cure a **problem**
▶ to correct/ fix/ put right/ remedy/ rectify/ redress a **situation**
▶ to correct/ fix/ put right/ remedy/ rectify/ redress a/ an **mistake/ error/ fault**
▶ to correct/ remedy/ cure a **defect/ deficiency**
▶ to put right/ rectify/ redress a **wrong**
▶ to **easily** correct sth/ fix sth/ put sth right/ remedy sth/ rectify sth/ cure sth

correct [他] (誤りを)訂正する[修正, 矯正]する ◇Read through your work and *correct* any mistakes that you find. 提出物を読み通して、見つけた間違いをすべて訂正しなさい ◇Minor problems with eyesight can now be *corrected* in a few seconds. 視力のささいな問題ならほんの数秒で矯正できますよ ◇They issued a statement *correcting* what they had said earlier. 彼らは前回の発言を訂正する声明を発表した
▶**correction** [名] [C, U] ◇I've made a few small *corrections to* your report. あなたのレポートに数か所小さな訂正を加えました ◇There are some programming errors that need *correction*. いくつか修正が必要なプログラミングの誤りがある

fix [他] 《ややインフォーマル》 (問題・誤りを)解決[修正]する, (状況を)改善する ◇The company had a bad image that needed *fixing*. その会社には払拭が必要な悪いイメージがつきまとっていた ◇Don't imagine that the law can *fix* everything. 法律ですべてがよくなると思ってはならない ☞ **fix** (SOLUTION)

put sth 'right フレーズ 《特に英, ややインフォーマル》 (問題・誤りを)解決[修正]する, (状況を)改善する ◇If you find a mistake, let your bank know and they will *put it right*. 誤りを見つけたら、銀行に知らせましょう。そうすれば修正してもらえます ◇It's not too late to *put things right*. 今からでも事態の修復はまだ間に合う

ノート **fix** と **put sth right** の使い分け: 両語ともややインフォーマルな表現。**fix** はしばしばビジネスの文脈で用いられる。**put sth right** は特に《米》よりも《英》の話し言葉で用いられることが多い。

set sb/sth 'straight 行/他 《インフォーマル》 (誤った考え[印象]・人の誤りを)正す ◇I just want to *set the record straight* — everything I did was perfectly legal. 私はただ誤解を正したいだけ — 私がしたことはすべてまったく合法的だった ◇Let me just *set* you *straight* on one or two points. 一つか二つの点についてあなたの誤りを少し訂正させてください ❶《英》ではこの表現はほとんど常に set sb straight と set the record straight の句で用いられる.《米》では set the story straight や set things straight の句も用いられる.

remedy [他]《ややフォーマル》(問題・状況を)改善[修復, 矯正]する ◇I tried my best to *remedy* the situation. 私は状況を改善するために最善を尽くした ◇The 1997 law was intended to *remedy* the deficiencies in the previous law. 1997年の法律は以前の法律の欠陥を補正する目的で作られた ☞ **remedy** (SOLUTION)

rectify [他]《フォーマル》(誤りを)訂正[修正]する ◇There were some errors in the report, but these were easy to *rectify*. 報告書の中には誤りがいくつかあったが, これらは簡単に訂正できるものだった ◇It's not too late to *rectify* matters. 今からでも事態の修復はまだ間に合う

redress [他]《フォーマル》(不正・誤りを)正す, 矯正[是正]する ◇Attempts were made to *redress* some of the injustices of the previous regime. 前政権が犯した いくつかの不正を正す試みがなされた ◇For years poorer children have had to put up with a lower quality education, and now is the time to *redress the balance* (= make the situation more fair). 何年もの間貧しい子どもたちは質の低い教育で我慢せざるをえませんでしたが, 今こそその不均衡を是正する時です

cure [他] (問題を)解決[矯正]する ◇Charities alone can't *cure* basic social injustices. 慈善事業だけでは根本的な社会的不公正を解決できない ◇I finally managed to *cure* the rattling noise in my car. 私はやっとのことで車のガラガラ鳴る音を直した
▶**cure** 名 [C] ◇a *cure* for poverty 貧困の救済策

corridor 名 ☞ HALL 2

corridor・hall・hallway・aisle・passage・passageway・walkway・catwalk
場所から場所に歩いていくことのできる壁に囲まれた細長い場所
【類語訳】廊下, 通路, 連絡通路, キャットウォーク

《文型&コロケーション》
▶ **in** the corridor/ hall/ hallway/ aisle/ passage/ passageway/ walkway
▶ **along/ down** the corridor/ hall/ hallway/ aisle/ passage/ passageway/ walkway/ catwalk
▶ **through** the corridor/ hall/ hallway/ passage/ passageway
▶ a **narrow** corridor/ hall/ hallway/ aisle/ passage/ passageway/ walkway/ catwalk
▶ a **long** corridor/ hall/ hallway/ aisle/ passage/ passageway/ walkway
▶ an **underground** passage/ passageway/ walkway
▶ to **stand** in the corridor/ hall/ hallway/ aisle
▶ at/ to the **end of** the corridor/ hall/ hallway/ aisle/ passage/ passageway/ walkway/ catwalk

corridor [C]《特に英》(病院・学校・オフィスビルなどの)廊下, 通路 ◇Go along the *corridor*, turn left, and you'll see his office in front of you. 廊下を進んで左に曲がると目の前が彼の事務所です ❶列車では corridor は客車の中にある客室から別の客室に歩くために利用する壁に囲まれた細長い通路を指す.

hall [C] (部屋・場所同士をつなぐ)廊下, 通路 ◇Her office is just down the *hall*. 彼女のオフィスはその廊下をほんの少し行ったところにある ☞ **hall** (HALL 2)

hallway [C]《特に米》(部屋・建物同士をつなぐ)廊下, 通路 ◇As I walked along the *hallway*, I passed several open doors. 廊下を歩いている間に, 私はいくつか開けっ放しのドアの前を通り過ぎた ☞ **hallway** (HALL 2)

> 「ノート」**corridor, hallway, hall の使い分け**:これらの語は意味が非常によく似ている. corridor はふつう長くてまっすぐなものを指し, 通常は大型の公共建物について言うときに用いられる. hall と hallway は公共建物と大型の私邸の両方について建物同士をつなぐ連絡通路を指すことがある. corridor は主に《英》で用いられ, これらの語の中では《英》で最も頻繁に用いられる. hall は《英》《米》の両方で用いられるが, これらの語の中では《米》で最も頻繁に用いられる. hallway は特に《米》で用いられる.

aisle [C] (教会・劇場・列車などの中央に伸びる座席列間の)通路;(スーパーマーケットの商品棚の間の)通路 ◇She looked radiant as she walked down the *aisle* on her father's arm (= when getting married in a church). 父親と腕を組んで教会の通路を歩いているとき彼女は晴れやかな表情をしていた ◇She managed to get an *aisle* seat (= in a plane). 彼女は何とか通路側の席を取ることができた ◇Coffee and tea are in the next *aisle*. コーヒーと紅茶は隣の通路にあります

passage [C] (部屋・場所同士をつなぐ)廊下, 通路 ◇It is said that the two houses were connected by a secret underground *passage*. その2棟の家屋は秘密の地下通路で結ばれていたそうだ ◇A dark, narrow *passage* led to the main hall. 暗く, 狭い廊下が本堂に通じていた ❶ passage はふつう corridor や hallway よりも狭くしばしば長く暗いものを指す. ☞ **alley** (ROAD)

passageway [C]《特に米》(部屋・場所同士をつなぐ)廊下, 通路 ◇They followed him through a narrow *passageway* into the old town. 彼らは旧市街に通じる狭い通路を彼の後について行った

walkway [C] (屋外の高い位置にある)連絡通路 ◇A covered *walkway* joins the two buildings. 屋根のある連絡通路がその二つの建物を結んでいる

catwalk [C] (橋のわき・劇場の舞台などの上部にある狭い通路である)キャットウォーク ◇The lights were mounted on a *catwalk* above the stage. 照明が舞台上部にあるキャットウォークに取り付けられていた ❶特に《英》では catwalk はファッションショーでモデルが歩く細長い舞台を指すこともある.《米》ではふつうこの意味を表す単語は runway. ◆He presented his latest collection at a *catwalk* show during Paris fashion week. (パリコレの間, 彼は最新のコレクションをキャットウォーク・ショーで発表した).

corrupt 形

corrupt・fraudulent・unscrupulous・dirty・rotten・crooked・unprincipled・amoral
利益を得るために正しくない, あるいは違法な行為を進んですることを表す
【類語訳】不正な, 腐敗した, 堕落した, 詐欺的な, 不当な, 卑怯な, 汚い, 悪徳の

《文型&コロケーション》
▶ corrupt/ fraudulent/ unscrupulous/ unprincipled/ amoral **behaviour**
▶ corrupt/ fraudulent/ unscrupulous/ dirty **dealings**

▶ corrupt/ fraudulent/ unscrupulous **practices**
▶ a corrupt/ rotten/ crooked **system**
▶ a corrupt/ an unscrupulous/ a crooked **businessman/ lawyer/ politician**
▶ thoroughly/ totally corrupt/ unscrupulous/ amoral

corrupt （けなして）（金・利益を見返りに）不正を働く；(行為が)不正な, 腐敗[堕落]した ◊It was seen as the only way to overthrow a *corrupt* regime. それは腐敗した政権を打倒する唯一の方法だと考えられた

fraudulent （フォーマル）詐欺的な, 詐欺による, 不正[不当]な ◊Steps are being taken to crack down on *fraudulent* advertising. 詐欺的な広告を厳しく取り締まるための措置が講じられている ◊The number of *fraudulent* insurance claims has risen. 不正な保険金請求の件数が増えている ❶ fraudulentは人よりも物事・行為について用いられることが多い。このグループの非難を表す他の語よりも中立的で説明に適した語。典型的に結びつく語としてclaim, statement, use, tradingが挙げられる。☞ **fraud** (FRAUD 1)
▷ **fraudulently** 副 ◊She was charged with *fraudulently* obtaining a bank loan. 彼女は銀行からの融資を不正に得たとして告発された

unscrupulous （ややフォーマル, けなして）（金・利益を見返りに）不正を働く；(行為が)不正な, 腐敗[堕落]した ◊The new law will give *unscrupulous* landlords an easy way of getting rid of people. 新しい法律によって悪徳家主は店子を容易に追い出すことが可能になるだろう 反意 **scrupulous** (GOOD 5), ☞ **scruple** (DOUBT 名 2)

ノート **corrupt**と**unscrupulous**の使い分け：corruptはしばしば当局・体制[組織]およびそこに勤務する人々について用いられる。典型的に結びつくのはregime, system, officialなど。unscrupulousは一般的に結びつく語は特に自営業を営む人およびその仕事に関連した、dealer, employer, landlord, lender, operator, people, politician, dealings, practicesが挙げられる。

dirty （ふつう名詞の前で）《インフォーマル, けなして》卑怯な, 汚い ◊You *dirty* liar! この汚い嘘つき野郎め ◊She's a *dirty* player. 彼女は卑怯な手を使う選手だ ◊He always gets someone else to **do the dirty work** for him (= tasks which are unpleasant because they involve being dishonest or unkind to people). 彼はいつも自分のために誰か他の人の手を汚させる ❶ この意味でのdirtyはplay, player, work, jobなどと結びつく。
▷ **dirty** 副 ◊We would have won if the other team hadn't *played dirty* (= cheated). 相手チームが汚いプレーをしなかったら我々が勝利していただろう

rotten ［名詞の前はまれ］《インフォーマル, けなして》(体制・組織が)腐敗した ◊The organization is *rotten to the core*. その組織は芯まで腐敗している

crooked （ややインフォーマル, 特にジャーナリズム, けなして）(事業を行う人が)不正を働く, 悪徳の ◊The president has vowed to jail *crooked* executives. 大統領が不正を働く高官たちを投獄すると宣言した

unprincipled （ややフォーマル, 特に書き言葉, けなして）節操のない；道徳[道義]をわきまえない ◊She saw him as an *unprincipled* opportunist. 彼女は彼を無節操な日和見主義者とみなした 反意 **principled** (GOOD 5), ☞ **principle** (PRINCIPLE 1)

amoral （ややフォーマル, 特に書き言葉, 時にけなして）道徳[道義]心のなさを示す ◊She had led them to believe that she shared their *amoral* values. 彼女は彼らのような道徳心

を欠いた価値観を自分も持っていると彼らに信じ込ませていた 反意 **moral** (GOOD 5), ☞ **morals** (PRINCIPLE 1)

ノート **unprincipled**と**amoral**の使い分け：unprincipledは主に人を修飾する。 ◆an *unprincipled* charlatan/creature/opportunist/scoundrel (節操のないいかさま師/やつ/日和見主義者/ならず者). amoralは人の態度・行為を修飾することが多い。典型的に結びつく語としてbehaviour, society, attitude, valuesが挙げられる。

corruption 名

corruption • bribery • extortion • blackmail
権力のある人々が行う正しくない, あるいは法に反する行為
【類型訳】不正, 違法行為, 汚職, 贈収賄, ゆすり

文型&コロケーション
▶ alleged corruption/ bribery/ extortion
▶ attempted bribery/ extortion/ blackmail
▶ political corruption/ bribery/ blackmail
▶ to **be involved in** corruption/ bribery/ extortion
▶ to **resort to** bribery/ blackmail
▶ to **accuse sb of/ charge sb with** corruption/ bribery/ extortion
▶ a corruption/ bribery **scandal**
▶ **allegations of** corruption/ bribery

corruption [U]（権力のある人々の）不正[違法]行為, 汚職 ◊There were allegations of *bribery and corruption*. 贈収賄や汚職に関する陳述が行われた ◊The new district attorney has promised to fight police *corruption*. 新任の地方検事が警察の汚職と闘うことを約束した

bribery [U]（不正な）贈収賄 ◊She was arrested on *bribery* charges. 彼女は贈収賄の容疑で逮捕された ☞ **bribe** (BRIBE)

ノート **corruption**と**bribery**の使い分け：corruptionはbriberyよりも幅広い活動をカバーする。briberyはcorruptionの一形態である。

extortion [U, C]《ややフォーマル》（暴力をちらつかせての）ゆすり ◊He was arrested and charged with *extortion*. 彼は逮捕されゆすりの罪で告発された
▷ **extort** 動 ［他］ ◊The gang *extorted* money from over 30 local businesses. その暴力団は30社以上の地元企業から金をゆすり取った

blackmail [U]（秘密をばらすと言っての）ゆすり, 恐喝；(脅し・罪の意識を感じさせての)強要 ◊He was convicted of *blackmail* at Bristol Crown Court last month. 先月彼はブリストル刑事裁判所で恐喝の罪で有罪判決を受けた ◊We can't let them practise this emotional *blackmail* on us. 私たちは彼らに感情的な脅しをかけられるわけにはいかない
▷ **blackmail** 動 ［他］ ◊She *blackmailed* him for years by threatening to tell the newspapers about their affair. 彼女は自分たちの不倫関係を新聞社に暴露すると脅迫して, 何年間も彼を恐喝した

costs 名

costs • spending • expenditure • expenses • overheads • outlay
政府や組織, 人が使う金

↪costs

【類語訳】費用, 経費, コスト, 支出, 出費, 間接費, 初期費用

文型&コロケーション
- ▶spending/ expenditure/ outlay **on** sth
- ▶**total** costs/ spending/ expenditure/ expenses/ overheads/ outlay
- ▶**considerable/ low** costs/ spending/ expenditure/ expenses/ overheads/ outlay
- ▶**high** costs/ spending/ expenditure/ expenses/ overheads
- ▶**capital** costs/ spending/ expenditure/ expenses/ outlay
- ▶**government/ public/ education/ health/ defence/ military/ household** costs/ spending/ expenditure/ expenses
- ▶to **increase/ reduce** costs/ spending/ expenditure/ expenses/ overheads/ the outlay
- ▶to **control/ cover** costs/ spending/ expenditure/ expenses/ overheads
- ▶to **cut** costs/ spending/ expenditure/ expenses/ overheads
- ▶to **meet** costs/ expenditure/ expenses/ overheads
- ▶to **incur** costs/ expenditure/ expenses

costs [複数形で]《企業の》費用, 諸経費, コスト ◇*labour/operating/production/running/transport costs* 人件/運営/生産/維持/輸送費 ◇These factories use cheap labour to keep *costs* down. これらの工場は安価な労働力を使ってコストを下げている ◇The money they're making is barely enough to cover their *costs*. 彼らが稼いでいる金では諸経費をまかなうのがやっとだ

spending [U]《政府・組織の》支出, 出費 ◇This government wants to keep a tight rein on public *spending*. 現政府は公共支出を引き締めたいと思っている ◇More *spending* on health was promised. 医療費を増やすことが約束された

expenditure [U, C]《ややフォーマル》《政府/組織・人の》支出, 出費 ◇There are plans to increase *expenditure* on education. 教育費を増やす計画がある ◇The budget provided for a total *expenditure* of £27 billion. 予算は総額270億ポンドの支出に備えるものだった

expenses [複数形で]《人・組織の》出費, 支出 ;《会社に代わって一時的に立て替える》経費 ◇*living/medical/legal expenses* 生活/医療/訴訟費用 ◇Can I give you something towards *expenses*? いくらか経費を渡しておこうか ◇You can claim back your travel *expenses*. 旅費は清算して返金されます ◇Just put the cost of the train fare *on your expense account*. 電車賃の費用はまあ必要経費に入れておいてください ◇The company sent her on a two-day *all-expenses-paid* course in London. 会社は彼女をロンドンで行われる2日間の費用全額会社負担の研修に送り出した ☞ expense (PRICE)

overheads [複数形で]《特に英》 **overhead** [U]《特に米》《企業・組織の家賃・光熱費・賃金などのような》間接費, 諸経費 ◇High *overheads* mean small profit margins. 間接費が高いと利益率が下がる

outlay [C, U]《新しい事業・計画のための》《後の金銭・時間を節約する》ための費用, 支出 ◇The business quickly repaid the initial *outlay* on advertising. その事業は広告にかかった初期費用をすぐに取り返した

cough 動

cough・sneeze・choke・clear your throat

物が肺へ通じる気道をふさいでいるときや, 空気がのどや鼻から勢いよく出るときにする行為を表す

【類語訳】咳をする, 咳払いをする, くしゃみをする, むせる, 窒息する

文型&コロケーション
- ▶to **make** sb cough/ sneeze/ choke
- ▶to cough/ clear your throat **loudly/ nervously**

cough [自] 咳をする, 咳払いをする ◇I couldn't stop *coughing*. 咳が止まらなかった ◇She *coughed* nervously and looked at me. 彼女は神経質に咳払いをして私を見た
▶**cough** [名] [C] ◇She gave a little *cough* to attract my attention. 彼女は私の注意を引くために小さく咳払いをした

sneeze [自] くしゃみをする ◇I've been *sneezing* all morning. 私は午前中ずっとくしゃみばかりしている
▶**sneeze** [名] [C] ◇He gave a violent *sneeze*. 彼は大きなくしゃみをした

choke [自, 他] のどを詰まらせる, むせる, 窒息する ; むせさせる, 窒息させる ◇He was *choking on* a piece of toast. 彼はトーストの一切れでのどを詰まらせていた ◇She almost *choked to death* in the thick fumes. 彼女は濃度の高いガスを吸い込んで窒息死するところだった ◇The device contains small parts which could easily *choke* a child. その装置には子どもがのどを詰まらせやすい小さな部品が含まれています

clear your 'throat [行れ] 咳払いをする ◇She *cleared her throat*. 'I hope I'm not interrupting,' she said. 彼女は咳払いをして, 「邪魔しちゃったかしら」と言った

count 動 ☞ CALCULATE, ESTIMATE 動

count・add・tally・tot sth up・total
総数[量]を計算する
【類語訳】数える, 計算する, 合計する, 足す

文型&コロケーション
- ▶to count/ add/ tally/ tot/ total **up how much/ many...**
- ▶to count/ add/ tally/ tot up **the number of sth**
- ▶to add up/ tot up **the amount/ the cost of sth**
- ▶to count/ add up/ tally/ tot up/ total sb's **points/ score**

count [他, 自]《人・物の総数を》数える, 計算する [合計]する ◇The diet is based on *counting* calories. その規定食はカロリー計算に基づいている ◇She began to *count up* how many guests they had to invite. 彼女は招待すべき客が何人か数え始めた ◇There are 12 weeks to go, *counting* from today. 今日から数えてあと12週ある ☞ count (ESTIMATE 名)

add [他]《数・量を》足す, 合計する ◇*Add* 9 *to* the total. 合計に9を足してください ◇If you *add* all these amounts *together* you get a huge figure. これら全部の量を合計するとものすごい数量になるよ 反意 take, subtract (DISCOUNT)
▶**addition** [名] [U] ◇children learning *addition* and subtraction 足し算と引き算を習っている子どもたち 反意 **subtraction** (DISCOUNT)

ノート count と add の使い分け: add は最低でも二つの数・量を足す(add sth to sth else)こと, count は1つの総数

country 141

を計算する(count sth)こと。add numbers/amountsはいえるが、count amountsとはいえない。◆to *add up/count the number of people* (人の数を合計する)。◆to *add up the amount of rainfall* (降水量を合計する)。×to *count the amount of rainfall*. これは可算名詞だけが数えられ、不可算名詞は数えられないからである。countは人・物も数えることができる。◆add は不可。◆to *count tickets/people/votes* (券/人/票を数える)。×to *add up people/tickets/votes*.

tally [他]《ややインフォーマル、特にビジネス》《物の総数を》計算[合計]する ◇When we *tallied* up the cost of moving, we decided against it. 私たちは移動の費用を計算して、そうしないことに決めた ❶tallyはしばしばビジネスで売上高・費用を始めとする経済上の結果について言うときに用いる。☞ **tally** (ESTIMATE [名])

,tot sth 'up [句動]《-tt-》《英、インフォーマル》《いくつかの数・いくらかの量を》足す、合計する ◇Let's *tot up* everybody's points and see who's won. 全員の点を計算して誰が勝ったか見ようよ ◇The trip isn't really that cheap when you *tot* everything *up*. 旅行は全部を合計すると実際にはそれほど安くない

total (-ll-、米 -l-)[他、ふつう受身で]《人[物]の数・得点を》合計する ◇Each student's points were *totalled* and entered in a list. 各生徒の点数は合計されて表に記入された ☞ **total** (WHOLE)

country [名]

1 country・nation・state・land・superpower・power
独自の政府と法律を持つ地域を表す
【類語訳】国、国家、大国、強国

文型&コロケーション
▶a **foreign** country/ nation/ state/ land/ power
▶a/ an **great/ major/ leading/ industrial/ colonial** country/ nation/ state/ power
▶a/ an **independent/ free/ powerful/ Third World/ Communist/ democratic** country/ nation/ state
▶an **allied/ enemy** country/ nation/ power
▶a **sovereign** nation/ state/ power
▶to **rule** a country/ nation/ state/ land
▶to **govern** a country/ nation/ state
▶to **lead** a country/ nation
▶to **serve** your country/ nation

country [C] 国、国家 ◇They are holding special events *all over the country*. 全国的に特別行事が開催されている ◇This is just one of 30 sites *around the country*. ここは国中に30か所ある遺跡の一つにすぎない ◇It's good to meet people from *different parts of the country*. 国内のさまざまな地域の人々と会うことはよいことだ ◇'It's a free *country*!' he shouted. 'I can do what I like.'「ここは自由の国だ」と彼は叫んだ。「好きなことができるんだ」 ◇Sugar is only produced in tropical *countries*. 砂糖は熱帯諸国でのみ生産されている ◇She represented her *country* at the Olympics. 彼女はオリンピックで国を代表した

nation [C]《言語・文化・歴史を共有する人々の集合体としての》国、国家 ◇This is an important moment in our *nation*'s history. これは我が国の歴史において重大な節目

だ ◇They are a *nation of* food lovers. 彼らは食べ物が大好きな国民だ ◇Leaders of the G8 leading industrial *nations* backed the plan. G8の各主要工業国の指導者はその計画を支持した ☞ **national** (NATIONAL), **national** (CULTURAL)

state (または **State**)[C]《政治共同体としての》国、国家 ◇It has not yet been recognized as an independent sovereign *state*. そこは独立主権国家としてまだ認められていない ◇The action was opposed by several UN member *states*. その行動はいくつかの国連加盟国の反対を受けた ◇Many Third World countries are *one-party states* of one type or another. 第三世界諸国の多くはどのような形にせよ一党支配国家である ◇After the collapse of the Soviet Union, many new *nation states* were created. ソビエト連邦の崩壊後、新しい民族国家が多く誕生した ☞ **state** (PUBLIC)

ノート country, nation, state の使い分け：政治的単位・政府としての国を指す場合はcountry, nation, stateのいずれの語を使用してもよい。◆relations between the two *countries/nations/states* (その2国間の関係)。◆a newly independent *country/nation/state* (新しく独立した国)。countryとnationは国民が居住する地域・経済・文化などを指すこともできる。◆a rich/ wealthy *country/nation* (富裕国)。◆an oil-producing *country/nation* (産油国)。countryは地理的地域としての国を指すことのできる唯一の語。◆a hot/cold/tropical *country* (暑い/寒い/熱帯の国)。

land [C]《文語》《感情や想像を込めて言う》国 ◇She longed to return to her native *land*. 彼女は生まれ故郷に戻りたくて仕方なかった ◇America was seen as the *land* of freedom and opportunity. アメリカは自由とチャンスの国だと考えられていた

superpower [C]《巨大な軍事力・経済力を持つ》(超)大国 ◇The United States was left as the only *global superpower*. 合衆国は世界で唯一の超大国として残った ◇Japan's status as an economic *superpower* 経済大国としての日本の地位

power [C]《大きな軍事力を持つ》強国 ◇Major European *powers*, such as France and Germany, are against the plan. フランスやドイツといった主要ヨーロッパの列強はその計画に反対している ◇He transformed a backward country into a *world power*. 彼は発展途上国を世界の強国に変貌させた

2 country・landscape・countryside・terrain・land・scenery・topography
町や都市から離れていて畑や森林、農場がある地域を表す
【類語訳】田舎、田園、地方、風景、景観、地形、地勢、景色

文型&コロケーション
▶the **surrounding** country/ landscape/ countryside/ terrain/ land/ scenery
▶**mountain/ mountainous/ wild/ rugged** country/ landscape/ countryside/ terrain/ scenery
▶**beautiful/ glorious/ stunning/ dramatic/ magnificent/ spectacular** country/ landscape/ countryside/ scenery
▶**open** country/ landscape/ countryside/ terrain/ land
▶**rolling** country/ landscape/ countryside
▶to **protect** the landscape/ countryside/ land

country [U]《しばしばthe country》《特徴のある自然を有する》

↳country county, courage

田舎, 田園, 地方 ◇She lives in the *country*. 彼女は田舎に住んでいる ◇We came to an area of wooded *country*. 私たちは森の多い田舎の地域に出た ◇a little *country* town 小さな田舎町 ◇I don't really enjoy *country* life. 私は田舎の生活を満喫してはいない ◇There have often been disagreements between town and *country*. 都会と地方との間で意見の不一致が度々起こっている

landscape [C, ふつう単数で] (田園)風景, 景観 ◇This pattern of woods and fields is typical of the English *landscape*. この森と野原が織りなす模様は典型的なイングランドの風景だ ◇The mountains dominate the *landscape*. 山脈が風景を見下ろすかのようにそびえ立っている ◇The power station is a ***blot on the landscape*** (= completely spoils the landscape). 発電所が景観を損なっている

countryside [U] (野原・森林・農園のある)田舎, 田園, 地方 ◇a little village in the French *countryside* フランスの田舎にある小さな村 ◇You can walk through miles and miles of unspoilt *countryside*. 手つかずの自然が残る田園地帯を何マイルも何マイルも歩くことができる ❶ *countryside* はふつう田舎の美しさ・平穏さについて言うときに用いられる。☞ **nature** (NATURE 2)

terrain [U, C] 《書き言葉》 地形, 地勢 ◇Make sure you have equipment that is suitable for the *terrain*. 必ず地形に適した用具類を持参してください ◇There were several miles of ***difficult terrain*** to be covered. 踏破するには険しい地形が数マイル続いていた ❶ *terrain* は地域の地形の特徴(例えば起伏に富むとか平坦であるなど)を述べる場合に用いられる。

land [U] 《ふつう the *land*》 田舎, 田園, 地方;(都会の生活に対する)田舎の生活 ◇Many younger people are leaving the *land* to find work in the cities. 多くの若者が都会で就職するために田舎を離れている ◇Almost a third of the population ***live off the land*** (= grow or produce their own food). 人口の約3分の1が自給自足の生活を送っている ◇Her family had ***farmed the land*** for generations. 彼女の家は代々田畑を耕作していた ☞ **land** (LAND 1)

scenery [U] (自然の美しい)風景, 景色 ◇Alpine *scenery* アルプスの風景 ◇We stopped on the mountain pass to admire the *scenery*. 私たちは景色を眺めるために山道で足を止めた ◇They went abroad for ***a change of scenery*** (= to see and experience new surroundings). 《特に米》 彼らは環境の変化を求めて海外へ行った ❶《英》では a change of scene と言うほうが一般的。☞ **scene** (VIEW 2), **nature** (NATURE 2)

topography [U] 《専門語》 地勢, 地形;地形学 ◇a map showing the *topography* of the island その島の地勢を示す地図

county 名

county・state・district・province・region・zone
国の一部分を形成する、正式な境界を持つ地域
【類語訳】州、県、郡、区域、地区、地区画、地方、地帯、区域

文型&コロケーション
▶ in a county/ state/ district/ province/ region/ zone
▶ a **border/ coastal** county/ state/ district/ province/ region/ zone
▶ the **northern, southern, etc.** counties/ states/ districts/ provinces/ region/ zone

county [C] (イギリスの)州, (アイルランドの)県, (アメリカの)郡 ◇The US state of California is divided into 58 *counties*. アメリカ合衆国のカリフォルニア州は58の郡に分けられている ◇Originally, *county* boundaries often followed the course of a river. もともと郡の境界線は多くの場合川筋に沿っていた

state (または **State**) [C] (アメリカ・オーストラリアなどの)州 ◇The hurricane swept across the southern *states* of the US. そのハリケーンはアメリカの南部諸州を通り抜けた

district [C] (国・町・州内における行政上の)区域, 地区, 区画 ◇Delivery is free within the London postal *district*. 配送はロンドンの郵便区域内は無料です ◇The *district* council granted planning permission for ten new houses. 地区議会は10棟の新築家屋に対し建築許可を与えた ☞ **district** (AREA 1)

province [C] (カナダ・南アフリカなどの)州, 省 ◇Canada is divided into ten *provinces* and two territories. カナダは10の州と2つの準州に分けられている
▷ **provincial** 形 ◇the *provincial* assembly 州議会

ノート county, state, province の使い分け: これらの語の使われ方は一様でなく、国の慣習や構成によってさまざまな区域が表される。イギリスとアイルランドは複数の county から成るが、アイルランドでは county は4つの大きな province (地方)を構成する。イギリスには province はない。アメリカは複数の state から成り、これらほとんどすべての state は複数の county から成る。カナダは複数の province から成るが、いくつかの province はさらに複数の county に分けられる。state と province はふつう county よりも大きな区域を指す。

region [C] (独自の慣習や行政府を持つ)地方 ◇Bilbao is the largest city in the Basque *region* in northern Spain. ビルバオはスペイン北部のバスク地方の中で最大の都市だ ☞ **region** (AREA 1)
▷ **regional** 形 ◇the *regional* council 地方議会

zone [C] (地域をさらに分割した)地区, 区間, 地帯, 地域, 区域 ◇The ticket may be used on any bus in *zone* 2. その切符はゾーン2のすべてのバスで使えます ◇All countries in *zones* 1 and 2 have free incoming calls. ゾーン1とゾーン2の中のすべての地域で電話の受信は無料です ☞ **zone** (AREA 1)

courage 名

courage・bravery・nerve・guts・heroism・valour・audacity・daring
危険や困難に立ち向かって行おうとする気持ち
【類語訳】勇気, 勇敢, 度胸, 強気, 肝っ玉, 根性, 大胆

文型&コロケーション
▶ **great** courage/ bravery/ nerve/ heroism/ valour/ audacity/ daring
▶ **true** courage/ bravery/ heroism
▶ to **have** the courage/ bravery/ nerve/ guts/ audacity
▶ to **show** courage/ bravery
▶ doing sth **takes** courage/ bravery/ nerve/ guts
▶ an **act of** courage/ bravery/ heroism/ valour

courage [U] (危険・苦痛・反対に対する)勇気, 勇敢さ, 度胸 ◇She displayed remarkable ***courage in the face of*** danger. 彼女は危険に直面してすばらしい勇気を見せた ◇I haven't yet ***plucked up the courage*** to ask her. 私はまだ勇気を出して彼女に尋ねることができないでいる ◇Unfortunately, they lack the ***moral courage*** to speak out against what is happening. 残念なことに彼らは起きていることに対して敢然と反対する道徳的勇気に欠けている ◇You need to have ***the courage of your convictions*** (= be brave enough to do what you believe to be right). 信念を貫く勇気を持ちなさい 反意 **cowardice** (COWARD), ☞ **courageous** (BRAVE)

bravery [U] (危険・苦痛・困難に対する)勇気, 勇敢さ ◇My great grandfather received the medal as an award for outstanding *bravery* in World War I. 私の曽祖父は第1次世界大戦での卓越した勇敢さを称える賞としてメダルを授与された ☞ **brave** (BRAVE)

ノート **courage** と **bravery** の使い分け：**courage** は体罰・拷問を受ける恐れがあるほか、経歴・名声が脅かされる可能性があり、道徳的理由から反対者に立ち向かう場合に頻繁に用いられる。**bravery** は肉体的な危険・苦痛に進んで立ち向かう場合に用いられることが多い。×They lack the moral *bravery* to speak out. ×He received the medal as an award for *courage*.

nerve [U] (困難・危険に対する)勇気, 度胸, 強気 ◇It took a lot of *nerve* to take the company to court. その会社に対して訴訟を起こすにはかなりの勇気を要した ◇I was going to have a go at parachuting but ***lost my nerve*** at the last minute. 私はスカイダイビングに挑戦しようと思ったが、いざという段になって気後れした ◇She ***kept her nerve*** to win the final set 6-4. 彼女は弱気になることなく最終セットを6-4で獲った

guts [複数で]《インフォーマル》(困難・嫌な事に対する)度胸, 肝っ玉, 気合, 根性 ◇He doesn't have the *guts* to walk away from a well-paid job. 彼は高報酬の仕事から足を洗う度胸はない ☞ **gutsy** (BRAVE)

heroism [U] (他の人から称賛を受ける)勇敢さ ◇He showed great *heroism* in going back into the burning building. 彼は偉大な勇気を見せ、燃え盛る建物の中に再び飛び込んだ ☞ **heroic** (BRAVE)

valour《英》《米 **valor**》[U]《文語》(戦争で兵士が見せる)武勇, 勇猛 ◇The purpose of the award is to recognize acts of *valour* by members of the armed services. その賞の目的は軍務に服する兵士たちの勇猛果敢な行為を称えることである

audacity [U] 大胆さ, 無鉄砲 ◇The sheer *audacity* of the plan amazed everyone. その計画のまったくの大胆さに皆驚いた

daring [U] (危険に対する)勇敢[豪胆]さ ◇He was saved by the skill and *daring* of the mountain rescue team. 彼は山岳救助隊の技術と豪胆さで救われた ☞ **daring** (BOLD), **dare** (DARE)

court 名

court・tribunal・courtroom・court of law・court of appeal・courthouse・law court
裁判や訴訟が行われて判決が下される場所を表す
【類語訳】裁判所, 法廷, 控訴院

文型&コロケーション

▶in a court/ tribunal/ courtroom/ court of law/ courthouse/ law court
▶before a court/ tribunal/ court of law/ court of appeal
▶at a court/ tribunal/ law court
▶a local court/ tribunal/ courthouse/ law court
▶to take sb to/ come before/ set up/ apply to a court/ tribunal/ court of appeal
▶to go to/ refer sth to/ appear before/ attend/ tell/ preside over a court/ tribunal
▶a court/ tribunal/ court of appeal hears/ dismisses/ upholds sth
▶a court/ tribunal orders/ rules sth

court [C, U] 裁判所, 法廷 ◇She will appear in *court* tomorrow. 明日彼女は出廷することになっている ◇They took their landlord to *court* for breaking the contract. 彼らは契約違反で家主を告訴した ◇The case took five years to ***come to court***. その事件は裁判が行われるまでに5年かかった ◇There wasn't enough evidence to ***bring*** the case ***to court***. その事件を裁判に持ち込む十分な証拠がなかった ◇The case was ***settled out of court*** (= a decision was reached without a trial). その事件は示談の成立で決着した ◇He won the ***court case*** and was awarded damages. 彼は勝訴して損害賠償を受けた ❶ 単数形の court は法廷に参加する人々、特に裁判官や陪審など判決[評決]を下す人々を指す。♦ The case is now before *the court*. (その事件は今審理中だ). ♦ Please tell *the court* what happened. (何が起きたかこの法廷の中でお話しください).

tribunal [単数+単数・複数動詞] (特定の問題・争いを扱う)裁判所, 法廷 ◇A war crimes *tribunal* was set up to prosecute those charged with atrocities. 戦犯法廷が設置され残虐行為の容疑者が起訴された ◇The fee for the player will be decided ***by tribunal***. その選手の年俸は裁判所によって決定が下される予定 ◇He lost his appeal against the decision at an ***industrial tribunal*** (= a court that can decide on disputes between employees and employers).《英》労働裁判所の決定を不服とする彼の上訴は敗訴した

courtroom [C] (裁判・訴訟が実際に行われる)法廷 ◇The judge came back into the packed *courtroom*. 裁判官が満員の法廷に戻ってきた ◇She could face a bitter ***courtroom battle***. 彼女は法廷内での激しいやり取りを目の当たりにすることになるかもしれない

,**court of 'law**〔複 **courts of law**〕[C]《フォーマル》司法裁判所, 法廷 ◇There was nothing that could be proved in a *court of law*. 法廷で立証しうるものなど何もなかった

,**court of ap'peal**（または **appeal court**）〔複 **courts of appeal**, **appeal courts**〕[C] 控訴裁判所,（イギリスの）控訴院 ◇There is a right of appeal to the *court of appeal*. 控訴裁判所に控訴する権利がある ❶《英》では Court of Appeal (控訴院) は House of Lords (上院) から独立した最高司法機関で下級裁判所での判決を変更することができる。《米》の最高司法機関は Supreme Court (最高裁判所) である。この下位に一審判決を変更することのできる Court of Appeal が多数ある。

courthouse《米》裁判所の庁舎 ◇The prison is opposite the *courthouse*. 刑務所が裁判所の向かいにある

'**law court** [C]《英》裁判所, 法廷; 裁判所の庁舎 ◇He has a job as an interpreter in the *law courts*. 彼は裁判所の通訳官として働いている

ノート **court, courtroom, court of law, courthouse, law court** の使い分け：**court** がこれらの語の中で最も一般的で、裁判が行われる部屋または建物や、訴訟の開廷・審理・判決の過程について用いられる。♦ to go/take sb/bring a case to *court* (人を告訴する/事件を裁判

持ち込む). court of lawはcourtのフォーマルな表現で、裁判の過程ではなく特に場所または建物についていうときに用いられる. courtroomは実際に裁判が行われる部屋を指し、特に大勢の人が部屋の中に押し寄せたり、部屋の中で互いに向き合っていることを示す場合に用いられる. law court(英)は法廷がある建物を指すことが多く、(米)ではcourthouseがlaw courtの代わりに用いられる.

coward 名

coward・wimp・sissy・nervous wreck・chicken・wuss

勇気や強さ、自信のない人を表す
【類語訳】臆病者, 腰抜け, 意気地なし, 弱虫

文型&コロケーション
▶ You're such a/ Don't be a coward/ wimp/ sissy/ chicken/ wuss!
▶ You coward/ wimp/ sissy/ chicken/ wuss!

coward [C] (けなして)臆病者, 腰抜け ◇I'm a real *coward* when it comes to going to the dentist. 歯医者に行くとなると私は本当に臆病者だ
  ➤ **cowardice** [U] ◇The lieutenant had displayed *cowardice* in the face of the enemy. 敵を前にして中尉は臆病さを見せていた 反意 **courage** (COURAGE)
  ➤ **cowardly** 形 ◇a weak, *cowardly* man 弱くて臆病な男 ◇your *cowardly* refusal to tell the truth あなたが真実を語ることの臆病にも拒否すること 反意 **brave** (BRAVE)
wimp [C] (インフォーマル, けなして) 意気地なし, 弱虫 ◇He won't go on his own — he's a complete *wimp*! 彼は自力でやっていく気がない―本当に意気地なしだよ
sissy (英でまた **cissy**) [C] (インフォーマル, けなして)(男の子の)意気地なし, 弱虫 ◇The other boys kept calling him a *sissy*. 他の男の子たちは彼のことを弱虫と呼び続けた
nervous 'wreck [C] (インフォーマル) ノイローゼの[神経のまいった]人 ◇The interview reduced him to a *nervous wreck*. その面談で彼は神経がまいってしまった
chicken [C] (インフォーマル, けなして)意気地なし, 弱虫 ◇He called me a *chicken* because I wouldn't swim in the river. どうしても川で泳ごうとしなかったので、彼は私のことを弱虫と呼んだ
  ➤ **chicken** 形 [名詞の前では用いない] ◇They were too *chicken* to follow us. 彼らは臆病で私たちの後をついても来られない程だった
wuss [C] (話し言葉, けなして) 意気地なし, 弱虫 ◇Don't be such a *wuss*! She won't hurt you! そんな弱虫でどうする. 彼女がお前を傷つけたりするわけでもあるまいし

crash 動

crash・slam・collide・smash・plough into sth・bang into sth・wreck・write sth off・total

物や乗り物同士が激しくぶつかる
【類語訳】衝突する, 激突する, 墜落する, 大破させる

文型&コロケーション
▶ to crash/ slam/ smash/ plough/ bang **into** sth
▶ to crash/ slam/ smash **sth into** sth
▶ two vehicles crash/ collide
▶ two vehicles crash/ slam/ smash/ bang **into each other**
▶ to crash/ smash/ wreck/ write off/ total a **car/ truck/ vehicle**
▶ to crash/ collide **head-on**

crash [自, 他] (ややインフォーマル) 衝突[激突, 墜落]する; 衝突[激突, 墜落]させる ◇I was terrified that the plane would *crash*. 私は飛行機が墜落するのではないかと怖かった ◇Look out! We're (= our car is) going to *crash*! 危ない, 車がぶつかるぞ ◇He *crashed* the car into a tree. 彼は車を木に激突させた ☞ **crash** (ACCIDENT)
slam (**-mm-**) [自, 他] (intoやagainstと共に) 激突させる ◇The car skidded and *slammed* into a tree. 車は横滑りして木に激突した ◇The force of the explosion *slammed* me against the wall. 爆発の力で私は壁にたたきつけられた
collide [自] (ややフォーマル) 衝突する; 衝突する ◇The car and the van *collided* head-on in thick fog. 濃い霧の中で車とバンが正面衝突した ◇As he fell, his head *collided with* the table. 彼は転んで頭をテーブルにぶつけた ☞ **collision** (ACCIDENT)
smash [自, 他] (ややインフォーマル) 激突する; 激突させる ◇A bullet *smashed* into the wall behind them. 一発の弾丸が彼らの後ろの壁に撃ち込まれた ◇Ramraiders *smashed* a stolen car through the shop window. 強盗が盗難車を店のウインドーに突っ込ませた

ノート **crash, slam, smash** の使い分け: crash は特に乗り物について用いられ、前置詞なしで用いることが可能.
◆ We're going to *crash*, aren't we? (ぶつかるんじゃないの). この意味ではslamとsmashは必ず前置詞を伴う.
✕ We're going to *slam/smash*, aren't we? この二つの語は乗り物だけではなくさまざまな物について用いられる. crashも前置詞を伴う場合は物について用いることもできる.
◆ He *crashed* down the telephone receiver. (彼は電話の受話器をガチャンと置いた).

'plough into sth 句動詞 (英)(米 **plow into sth**) (スピードの出しすぎ[前方不注意]で) 激突する ◇A truck *ploughed into* the back of the bus. トラックがバスの後部に追突した
'bang into sth 句動詞 (ややインフォーマル)(誤って)激突する ◇I *banged into* a chair and hurt my leg. 私は椅子にぶつかって脚を怪我した
wreck [他] (乗り物を)大破させる ◇The road was littered with *wrecked* cars. 道路は大破した車の破片が散乱していた ☞ **wreck** (ACCIDENT), **wreck** (REMAINS1)
write sth 'off 句動詞 (英, ややインフォーマル)(乗り物を)大破させる ◇He's *written off* two cars this year. 今年彼は2台の車を大破させた
  ➤ **'write-off** 名 [C] ◇She survived the crash with minor injuries, but the car was a *write-off*. 彼女はその衝突事故で軽傷を負っただけで生き残ったが、車は大破した
total [他] (**-ll-**, 米 **-l-**) (特に米, インフォーマル, 話し言葉)(乗り物を)大破させる ◇She never forgave him for *totaling* her car. 彼女は自分の車を大破させたことで彼を決して許さなかった

ノート **wreck, write sth off, total** の使い分け: write sth offとtotalは事故によって乗り物を大破させること. wreckは事故による(特におもしろ半分)によっても乗り物を大破させること. ◆ youths who steal and *wreck* fast cars (スピードの出る車を盗んでは大破させる若者).

crazy, creative

crazy 形 ☞ RECKLESS

crazy・stupid・silly・foolish・dumb・mad・insane・idiotic
良識や分別のない人を表す
【類語訳】頭のおかしい、気の狂った、ばかげた、愚かな

stupid	crazy	insane
silly	mad	
foolish	idiotic	
dumb		

文型&コロケーション
- crazy/ stupid/ silly/ foolish/ dumb/ mad/ insane/ idiotic **to do sth**
- crazy/ stupid/ silly/ foolish/ dumb/ mad/ insane/ idiotic **of sb to do sth**
- a crazy/ a stupid/ a silly/ a foolish/ a dumb/ a mad/ an insane/ an idiotic **idea**
- a crazy/ a stupid/ a silly/ a foolish/ a dumb/ a mad/ an insane/ an idiotic **thing to do**
- a crazy/ a stupid/ a silly/ a foolish/ a dumb/ an idiotic **question**
- a stupid/ a silly/ a foolish/ a dumb/ an idiotic **mistake**
- to **seem/ look/ sound** crazy/ stupid/ silly/ foolish/ dumb/ insane/ idiotic
- to **act** crazy/ stupid/ dumb
- to **feel** stupid/ silly/ foolish/ dumb
- **Are you** crazy/ stupid/ dumb/ mad/ insane?
- **Sb must be** crazy/ stupid/ mad/ insane!
- **really/ plain/ a bit/ a little/ quite** crazy/ stupid/ silly/ foolish/ dumb/ mad/ insane
- **completely/ totally** crazy/ stupid/ dumb/ mad/ insane
- **pretty/ rather** crazy/ stupid/ silly/ foolish/ dumb/ mad

crazy《特に米、インフォーマル、ふつうなしで》頭のおかしい、ばかげた、むちゃくちゃな ◇Are you *crazy*? We could get killed doing that. 気は確かか。そんなことしたら殺されるぞ ◇She must be *crazy* to lend him money. 彼に金を貸すなんて彼女は気が狂っているにちがいない ◇I know it sounds *crazy*, but it just might work. むちゃに聞こえるのはわかっているが、本当にうまくいくかもしれないんだ ◇What a *crazy* idea! 何てばかげた考えだ ❶この意味では crazy は行動よりも人について用いられることが多い。

stupid《しばしばなしで》愚かな、ばかな ◇I've made a *stupid* mistake. 愚かな間違いをしてしまった ◇I was *stupid* enough to believe him. 彼を信じた私がばかだった ◇It was *stupid* of you to get involved. かかわり合いになるなんて君はばかだったね ❶人に stupid であると言うのは侮蔑的とみなされる。反意 **sensible** (BEST), **sensible** (WISE)
▷**stupidity** 名 [U, C, ふつう複数形で] ◇I couldn't believe my own *stupidity*. 私は自分の愚かさが信じられなかった ◇the errors and *stupidities* of youth 若気の至り
▷**stupidly** 副 ◇I *stupidly* agreed to lend him the money. 私は愚かにも彼に金を貸すことに同意してしまった
silly《ややインフォーマル、特に話し言葉、ふつうなしで》ばかな、ばかげた ◇No, actually that's a *silly* idea. いや、実際そればかげた考えだ ◇I can walk home.' 'Don't be *silly* — it's much too far!'「家まで歩いて帰れるよ」「ばかな

と言わないで―遠すぎるよ」◇You *silly* boy! ばかな子ねえ ◇How *silly* of me to expect them to help! 彼らの助けを期待するなんて私は本当にばかだった
foolish《ややフォーマル、特に書き言葉》愚かな ◇She's just a vain, *foolish* woman. 彼女はただ見栄っ張りで愚かな女だ ◇How could she have been so *foolish* as to fall in love with him? 彼に恋してしまうなんて彼女はどうしてそこまで愚かになれたのだろう ◇It was a very *foolish* thing to do. それはとても愚かな行為だった 反意 **wise** (WISE), ☞ **unwise** (RECKLESS), **fool** (FOOL)
dumb《特に米、インフォーマル、ふつうなしで》ばかな、ばかげた ◇That was a pretty *dumb* thing to do. それはとてもばかげた行為だった ◇That's the *dumbest* idea I ever heard. それは私が今まで聞いた中で一番ばかげた考えだ

ノート **crazy, stupid, silly, foolish, dumb** の使い分け：crazy はふつう人を修飾し、行為を修飾するのはふつう意図的な行為(危険を伴ったりなんらかの形で人を傷つける可能性があるもの)を指す。◆That was a *crazy* thing to do! Are you trying to get us killed? (あれはむちゃな行為だったよ。私たちを殺す気かい). stupid, silly, foolish, dumb は人・行為を修飾する。これらは意図的な行為または何気なしに行われる不注意な行為を指すこともある。◆a *stupid/silly/foolish/dumb* mistake（愚かな/ばかげた間違い）. × a *crazy* mistake. stupid はしばしば侮蔑的とみなされる。dumb はやや侮蔑の度合いが弱く、親しみを込めて友人に対して用いられることもある。silly はややかな表現で、特に子どもに対して用いられるが、大人に対して用いる場合はやはり侮蔑的とみなされることもある。foolish はややフォーマルな語で、特に書き言葉で用いられる。

mad《特に英、インフォーマル、時にけなして》頭のおかしい、気の狂った；まったくばかげた、分別がまるでない ◇You must be *mad* to risk it. 危険を冒すなんて、君、どうかしてるよ ◇'I'm going to buy some new clothes.' 'Well, don't *go mad* (= spend more than is sensible).'「新しい服を買ってくるよ」「いいけど、あまり度を越さないように」❶《米》ではふつう mad の代わりに crazy が用いられる。この意味では mad は行為よりも人について用いられることが多い。
▷**madness** 名 [U] ◇In a *moment of madness* she had agreed to go out with him. 一瞬分別を失って彼女は彼とデートに行くことに同意してしまった
insane《インフォーマル、ふつうなしで》正気でない、狂気の沙汰 ◇I must have been *insane* to agree to the idea. そんな考えに賛成するなんて私はどうかしていたに違いない ◇It was an *insane* risk to take. そんな危険を冒すなんて正気の沙汰ではなかった
▷**insanity** 名 [U] ◇It would be sheer *insanity* to attempt the trip in such bad weather. こんな悪天候の中で出かけようとするのはまったく正気の沙汰ではない
idiotic《けなして》ばかな、ばかげた ◇What an *idiotic* question. 何てばかげた質問だ ◇Don't be so *idiotic*! そんなばかな真似するな ❶ idiotic はしばしば怒っている人が用いる。☞ **idiot** (FOOL)

creative 形

creative・artistic・innovative・original・imaginative・ingenious・inventive
新しくて面白い物事を生み出す技術や想像力があることを表す
【類語訳】創造的な、独創的な、創作的な、革新的な

↳**creative**

文型&コロケーション
▶ a creative/ an artistic/ an innovative/ an original/ an imaginative/ an ingenious/ an inventive **mind**
▶ creative/ artistic **ability/ achievement/ skill/ talent**
▶ a creative/ an innovative/ an original/ an imaginative/ an ingenious/ an inventive **idea/ design/ solution**
▶ creative/ innovative/ original/ imaginative **thinking**
▶ a creative/ an innovative/ an original **thinker**
▶ **highly** creative/ innovative/ original/ imaginative/ ingenious/ inventive

creative 創造[独創, 創作]的な；創造[独創, 創作]力のある ◇classes on *creative writing* (= writing stories, plays and poems) 文芸の授業 ◇the company's *creative* team その会社の創作チーム ◇She's very *creative* — she writes poetry and paints. 彼女はとても創造的だ — 詩を書いたり絵を描いたりしている ☞ **create** (MAKE 1), **creation** (DEVELOPMENT), **creativity** (INSPIRATION)

artistic 芸術に秀でた, 芸術のわかる, 芸術を愛好する；芸術的な ◇He comes from a very *artistic* family. 彼はたいへんな芸術一家の出だ ◇The decor inside the house was very *artistic*. その家の中の装飾はとても芸術的だった

innovative 《ほめて》革新的な ◇their *innovative* use of existing technology 彼らの既存の技術の革新的な利用法 ☞ **innovation** (DEVELOPMENT), **innovator** (LEADER 2)

original 《ふつうほめて》独創的な ◇The film is challenging and highly *original*. その映画は挑戦的かつ極めて独創的だ ◇This work is the product of a highly *original* mind. この作品は極めて独創的な精神の賜物だ ☞ **originality** (INSPIRATION), **novel** (NEW 1)

imaginative 《ふつうほめて》想像力[創意工夫]に富む ◇an *imaginative* child 想像力豊かな子ども ◇recipes that make *imaginative* use of seasonal vegetables 季節の野菜を想像力豊かに使用したレシピ 反意 unimaginative ☞ **imagination** (IMAGINATION), **imagination** (INSPIRATION)
▷ **imaginatively** 副 ◇The stables have been *imaginatively* converted into offices. その馬小屋は豊かな発想で事務所に改装された

ingenious 独創的な, 創意工夫に富む；発明の才に富む ◇an *ingenious* device/invention/experiment 工夫のこらされた装置/発明/実験 ◇She's very *ingenious* when it comes to finding excuses. 口実を見つけることに関しては彼女は大変発想豊かだ ☞ **ingenuity** (INSPIRATION)
▷ **ingeniously** 副 ◇*ingeniously* designed 独創的なデザインの

inventive 《しばしばほめて》独創的な, 創意工夫に富む；発明の才に富む ◇She is one of the most *inventive* of modern writers. 彼女は現代の作家の中で最も独創的な一人だ ◇This is a courageous and *inventive* piece of film-making. これは勇気あるそして創意工夫に富む映画作品だ ☞ **invent** (DESIGN 動 1), **invention** (DEVELOPMENT), **inventiveness** (INSPIRATION)

| ノート innovative, original, imaginative, ingenious, inventive の使い分け: innovative はしばしば実用面やビジネス分野で新しいアイデアを実践する場合に用いられる。original, imaginative, inventive はしばしば芸術分野で用いられる。original/imaginative ideas 《独創的な考え》は実用性のあるなしに関わらず面白いもの。ingenious は創 |

crime

に富んでいて実用的なもの(実用性がなければ ingenious とは言わない)だが, innovative や original ほど独創的ではないことがある。

crime 名

1 crime・wrongdoing・misconduct・delinquency・vice
法律や規則を破る行為を表す
【類語訳】犯罪行為, 違法行為, 不正行為, 職権乱用

文型&コロケーション
▶ **serious** crime/ wrongdoing/ misconduct/ delinquency
▶ **sexual** crime/ misconduct/ vice
▶ **male/ female** crime/ delinquency/ vice
▶ **juvenile** crime/ delinquency
▶ **cause/ tackle/ control/ prevent** crime/ delinquency
▶ to **be driven/ turn** to crime/ vice
▶ to **deny** wrongdoing/ misconduct

crime [U] 犯罪(行為) ◇This month's figures show an increase in *violent crime*. 今月の統計数字は暴力犯罪の増加を示している ◇More needs to be done to help the *victims of crime*. 犯罪被害者を援助するためにもっと多くのことがなされる必要がある ◇These youngsters are often involved in *petty crime* such as shoplifting and casual theft. こうした若者は万引きや出来心の窃盗などの軽犯罪にしばしばかかわっている ◇There is a strong link between drugs and *organized crime*. 麻薬と組織犯罪は強く結びついている ◇The *crime rate* is rising. 犯罪率が上昇している ◇She writes *crime* novels (= stories about crime). 彼女は犯罪小説を書いている ☞ **criminal** (ILLEGAL)

wrongdoing [U, C] 《フォーマル》違法[不正]行為 ◇The company denies any *wrongdoing*. その会社はいかなる違法行為をも否定している ❶ wrongdoing はしばしば不正行為に関して身の潔白を主張したり, または潔白が証明されるような場合に用いられる。

misconduct [U] 《フォーマル》(知的職業人による)違法[不正]行為, 職権乱用 ◇The doctor was accused of *gross misconduct* (= very serious misconduct). その医者は目に余る違法行為で起訴された

delinquency [U, C] 《ややフォーマル》(若者による)犯罪行為, 非行 ◇There has been an increase in *juvenile delinquency*. 青少年犯罪が増加している ◇The boys drift into minor *delinquencies* while hanging around the streets. その少年たちは街をうろつくうちに, 知らず知らず非行に手を染めている ☞ **delinquent** (ILLEGAL)

vice [U] (売春・麻薬がらみの)犯罪行為 ◇At the door were two plain-clothes detectives from the *vice* squad. ドアのところに風紀犯罪特捜班の私服刑事が二人いた

2 crime・offence・sin・felony・misdemeanour・atrocity・wrong・outrage
違法な, あるいは不正な, 容認できない行為を表す
【類語訳】犯罪, 違反, 罪, 重罪, 軽罪, 残虐行為, 悪事, 悪行

文型&コロケーション
▶ a **crime/ an offence/ a sin/ an atrocity/ an outrage against** sb/ sth

- ▶a **serious** crime/ offence/ felony/ misdemeanour/ wrong
- ▶a **terrible** crime/ sin/ wrong
- ▶a **capital** crime/ offence/ felony
- ▶a **minor/ petty** crime/ offence/ misdemeanour
- ▶a **sexual** crime/ offence/ sin/ misdemeanour
- ▶a **terrorist** crime/ offence/ atrocity/ outrage
- ▶to **commit** a crime/ an offence/ a sin/ a felony/ a misdemeanour/ an atrocity/ an outrage
- ▶to **forgive** a crime/ an offence/ a sin/ a misdemeanour/ a wrong/ an outrage

crime [C]（刑罰が科される）犯罪 ◇The massacre was a *crime* against humanity. その虐殺は非人道的犯罪だった ◇Many *crimes* are never reported to the police. 警察に届け出がなされない犯罪がたくさんある ◇No weapon was found at *the scene of the crime*. 犯罪現場では凶器は見つからなかった

offence《英》(《米》**offense**) [C]（ややフォーマル）(刑罰が科される)犯罪, 違反 ◇It is a criminal *offence* to inflict cruelty on any wild animal. いかなる野生動物に対する残虐行為も刑事犯罪である ◇He was given a warning since it was a *first offence* (= the first time that he had been found guilty of a crime). 初犯だったので彼は警告を受けるにとどまった ◇The rebels could face charges of treason, a capital *offence* (= one for which sb may be punished by death). 反逆者は反逆罪, つまり死刑にも問われかねない罪を負う可能性がある

▷ **offend** 動〔自〕◇He started *offending* at the age of 16.《フォーマル》彼は16歳で犯罪に手を染めた

ノート crime と offence の使い分け：crime は日常会話ではofferceよりも頻繁に用いられ, 殺人や強盗などより重大な違法行為について用いられる。offence はスピード違反などの違法行為について用いられることが多い。◆a driving/motoring *offence*（《英》交通違反）, ◆a traffic *offense*（《米》交通違反）, 銃の所持に対しては ◆a firearms *offence*（《英》銃刀法違反）, 麻薬の使用に対しては ◆a drugs *offence*（《英》薬物取締法違反）, ◆a drug *offence*（《米》薬物取締法違反）。しかしながら, 法律の文脈では offence はあらゆる違法行為を表す専門用語として好まれる。

sin [C]（神・戒律・道徳律に対する）罪 ◇Confess your *sins* to God and he will forgive you. 神にあなたの罪を告白すれば, 神はお許しになるでしょう

▷ **sin** 動〔自〕◇Forgive me, Lord, for I have *sinned*. 主よ, 罪を犯した私をお許しください

felony [C, U]《米 or 古風, 法律》(殺人・強姦などの) 重罪 ◇He was indicted on three *felony* charges of lying to the grand jury. 彼は大陪審に3度嘘をついた重罪の容疑で起訴された

misdemeanour《英》(《米》**misdemeanor**) [C]（特に米, 法律）(felonyよりも軽い)罪, 軽罪 ◇He pleaded guilty to the *misdemeanor* of domestic violence. 彼は家庭内暴力の罪を認めた ❶《英》《米》のフォーマルな表現ではmisdemeanourにはそれほど重大ではない「悪事」の意味もある。◆He thought about his own youthful *misdemeanours*.（彼は若い頃の悪事について思いめぐらした）.

atrocity [C, ふつう複数で, U]《ややフォーマル》(戦時中の)残虐行為 ◇They have accepted responsibility for the *atrocities* committed during the war. 彼らは戦争中に行った残虐行為に対する責任を認めた

wrong [C]《フォーマル》悪事, 悪行, 不正〔違法〕行為 ◇It is time to forgive past *wrongs* if progress is to be made. もし改善が見られるようなら, 過去の悪事は許されてもいい頃だ ◇It's the job of the newspapers to expose the *wrongs* suffered by such people. このような人々がこうむる違法行為を暴くのは新聞の仕事だ ❶wrongは被害者に重点を置き, ◆to suffer a *wrong*（害を受ける）のように用いる。しばしば悪い行いを正そうとする場合に使う。◆to redress/right/forgive a *wrong*（不正を正す/許す）

outrage [C]（ショック・怒りを招く）非道な行為 ◇No one has yet claimed responsibility for this latest bomb *outrage*. 最近起こったこの非道な爆破行為の犯行声明はまだ出されていない

ノート atrocity と outrage の使い分け：outrage はほとんどの場合, テロ行為について用いられ, atrocity は戦時中の行為とテロ行為の両方に用いられる。

criminal 名

criminal・offender・culprit・sinner・felon・crook・delinquent
悪事, 不正, 違法行為を働く人を表す
【類語例】犯罪者, 罪人, 犯人, 違反者, いかさま師, ペテン師

文型&コロケーション
- ▶a **convicted/ habitual** criminal/ offender/ felon
- ▶to **catch** a criminal/ an offender/ the culprit/ a crook
- ▶to **identify/ apprehend** a criminal/ an offender/ a culprit
- ▶to **convict/ sentence** a criminal/ an offender
- ▶to **punish** criminals/ offenders/ the culprit/ sinners/ felons

criminal [C] 犯罪者, 罪人, 犯人 ◇Society does not know how to deal with *hardened criminals* (= people who regularly commit crimes and are not sorry for what they do). 世間は常習犯の処遇に困っている ◇I was treated just like a common *criminal*. 私はまるでふつうの犯人と何ら変わらぬ扱いを受けた ◇Sending these youngsters to prison simply trains them to become professional *criminals*.《英》これらの少年を刑務所に送ることは単に彼らを筋金入りの犯罪者に仕立て上げるだけだ ◇career *criminals*《米》常習犯

offender [C]（ややフォーマル）違反者, 犯罪者；(悪事の)元凶 ◇He spent some time in a young *offender* institution. 彼はしばらく少年院に入っていた ◇*First offenders* (= people who had never committed a crime before this one) were treated more leniently. 初犯者はより寛大な扱いを受けた ◇He favours tougher punishments for *repeat offenders* (= people who commit the same crime more than once). 彼は再犯者に対してより重い刑罰を科することに賛成している ◇Child protection groups are calling for a national register of *sex offenders* (= people found guilty of illegal sexual acts). 児童保護団体は全国の性犯罪者登録名簿を要求している ◇When it comes to pollution, the chemical industry is a major *offender*. 汚染について言えば, 化学工業こそ主たる元凶だ

ノート criminal と offender の使い分け：criminal は犯罪を犯した人だけでなく, 犯罪を犯す傾向のある人についても言う。offender は少なくとも一度法律に違反した人のみを指す。例えば, スピード違反をした運転手は offender であるが, criminal とは呼ばない。offender は法律違反者を扱う仕事に従事する人々が好んで使う。

criminal

culprit [C] 違反者, 犯罪者；(問題の)元凶 ◇The police quickly identified the real *culprits*. 警察はすぐに真犯人を特定した ◇The main *culprit* in the current crisis seems to be modern farming techniques. 現在の危機を招いた主たる元凶は先進農業技術であるようだ

> ノート **offender** と **culprit** の使い分け：culprit は特定の物事の原因となる人・人々・物事について用いられるため, ほとんど常に定冠詞 the の後に置かれる. culprit を修飾する最も一般的な形容詞には biggest, main, major, prime, real, worst が挙げられる. offender もこのような用いられ方をするが, culprit よりもいくぶんフォーマルである.

sinner [C]《フォーマル》(神の掟を破る)罪人 ◇God forgives all *sinners* who repent. 神は罪を悔い改めるすべての罪人をお許しになる

felon [C]《特に米, 法律》(殺人・強姦などの)重罪犯人 ◇The law requires convicted *felons* entering the state to register their address with the police. 有罪が確定した重罪犯は入国する場合に住所を警察に届け出ることが法律により義務づけられている

crook [C]《インフォーマル》いかさま[ペテン]師 ◇That salesman is a real *crook*. あの営業マンはまさにペテン師だ ◇The film portrays a world of *small-time crooks*, petty crime and drinking clubs. その映画は三流いかさま師, けちな犯罪, 飲酒業界のあれこれの世界を描いている

delinquent [C]《ややフォーマル》(若い)非行者 ◇What can be done to help these *juvenile deliquents* turn away from crime? これらの非行青少年に犯罪から足を洗わせるために何ができるだろうか

crisis 《名》

---

crisis・emergency・disaster・tragedy・catastrophe・calamity

困難な状況を作り出す[多くの人の命が犠牲になる, 多大な損害を引き起こす]予期せぬ事態や出来事を表す
【類語訳】危機, 難局, 非常事態, 災害, 惨事, 大事故

---

crisis	calamity	disaster
emergency		tragedy
		catastrophe

文型&コロケーション

▶ a crisis/ disaster/ tragedy/ catastrophe/ calamity **for** sb
▶ **in** a crisis/ an emergency
▶ a **major** crisis/ emergency/ disaster/ tragedy/ catastrophe/ calamity
▶ a **great** crisis/ disaster/ tragedy/ catastrophe/ calamity
▶ a/ an **awful/ dreadful/ terrible** disaster/ tragedy/ catastrophe/ calamity
▶ a **potential** crisis/ disaster/ tragedy/ catastrophe
▶ a **national** crisis/ emergency/ disaster/ tragedy/ catastrophe/ calamity
▶ an **environmental** crisis/ emergency/ disaster/ tragedy/ catastrophe
▶ a/ an **ecological/ personal** crisis/ disaster/ tragedy/ catastrophe
▶ a/ an **economic/ financial** crisis/ disaster/ catastrophe
▶ a **nuclear** disaster/ catastrophe
▶ to **cause** a crisis/ an accident/ a disaster/ a tragedy/ a catastrophe

▶ to **bring** disaster/ tragedy/ catastrophe/ calamity
▶ to **deal with/ cope with** a crisis/ an emergency/ a disaster
▶ to **avert** a crisis/ a disaster/ tragedy/ catastrophe/ calamity
▶ a disaster/ tragedy/ catastrophe/ calamity **happens/ occurs**
▶ disaster/ tragedy/ catastrophe **strikes**

crisis (複 **crises**) [C, U] 危機, 難局 ◇It is hoped that his resignation will end the latest political *crisis* in the country. 彼の辞任によって最近のその国の政治的危機が終息することが期待されている ◇The Communist Party was facing an *identity crisis*. 共産党は自らの存在意義を見出せなくなっていた ◇The party was suffering a *crisis of confidence* among its supporters (= they did not trust it any longer). その政党は支持者からの信頼の失墜の危機に苦しんでいた ◇The business is still *in crisis* but it has survived the worst of the recession. その企業は依然として危機に瀕しているが, 不況のどん底は切り抜けた ◇In *times of crisis* I know which friends I can turn to. いざという時にはどの友達に頼ればよいかわかっている

emergency [C, U] 緊急[非常]事態, 危機的状態 ◇This door should only be used in an *emergency*. このドアは緊急時にのみ使用してください ◇I always have some extra cash with me *for emergencies*. 私はいつも緊急事態に備えていくらか余分に現金を持つようにしている ◇The government has declared a *state of emergency* following the earthquake. その地震の直後に政府は非常事態を宣言した ◇There is an *emergency* exit (= to be used in an emergency) on each side of the aeroplane. 飛行機の両側に非常口がある

disaster [C, U] (多くの死者・損害をもたらす)災害, 惨事, 大事故 ◇Thousands died in the *disaster*. その災害で何千もの人々が亡くなった ◇They were involved in the 2001 ferry *disaster*. 2001年のフェリー事故に彼らは巻き込まれた ◇They will not insure you against a natural *disaster* (= one that is caused by nature). 保険会社は天災に対しては補償しないだろう ◇Although there was always the possibility of flooding, the Nile seldom brought *disaster* to Egypt. 洪水が起こる可能性は常にあったが, ナイル川はめったにエジプトに災害をもたらさなかった ☞ **disaster** (DISASTER)

tragedy [C, U] (死者をもたらす)悲惨な出来事, 惨事, 悲劇 ◇*It's a tragedy that* she died so young. 彼女がそれほど若くして亡くなったことは悲劇だ ◇*Tragedy* struck the family when their three-year-old son was hit by a car and killed. その家族を悲劇が襲った, 彼らの3歳になる息子が車にひかれて死んだのだ ◇The whole affair *ended in tragedy*. すべては悲劇に終わった ☞ **tragic** (SAD)

catastrophe [C] 大災害, 大惨事 ◇Early warnings of rising water levels prevented another major *catastrophe*. 水位の上昇を早期に警告することでさらなる大惨事はまぬがれた ☞ **catastrophe** (DISASTER)

> ノート **disaster** と **catastrophe** の使い分け：両語とも nuclear, environmental, ecological, economic などの語と共に用いられるが, disaster は多くの死者を出した有名な出来事について言うときに用いられる傾向がある. ◆ the Chernobyl/ Lockerbie/ Challenger *disaster* (チェルノブイリ原発事故/ロッカービー航空機爆破事件/チャレンジャー号爆発事故).

calamity [C, U] (国・組織・個人に降りかかる政治的・財政的な)災難, 惨状 ◇Sudan suffered a series of *calami-*

criterion, critical 149

ties during the 1980s. スーダンは1980年代に一連の災害に見舞われた ◇His financial help saved the magazine from total *calamity*. 彼からの財政援助のお陰で雑誌をどん底状態から救った ❶ *calamity*は, disaster や catastrophe よりも重大さの度合いは小さく, ふつうは死者を伴わない出来事に用いられる.

criterion 名

criterion・standard・test・measure・benchmark・guide・guideline・gauge・yardstick・norm
人や物事の評価[判断]に用いられる質の程度[水準]を表す
【類語訳】基準, 試金石, 尺度, 目安

▶ 文型&コロケーション
- a criterion/ measure/ benchmark/ yardstick/ norm **for** sth
- **by** any criteria/ standard/ measure/ yardstick
- **against** the criteria/ standard/ benchmark/ yardstick/ norm
- a **useful** criterion/ test/ measure/ benchmark/ guide/ gauge/ guideline/ yardstick
- (an) **objective** criterion/ standards/ test/ measure/ guide
- (a) **general** standards/ measure/ guide/ guideline
- (a) **reliable** test/ measure/ guide/ gauge/ guidelines
- to **serve as** a criterion/ measure/ guide/ gauge/ guideline/ yardstick
- to **provide** a criterion/ standard/ measure/ benchmark/ guide/ yardstick
- to **set/ establish** criteria/ a standard/ the benchmark/ norms

criterion [C, ふつう複数で] (評価・判断の)基準 ◇The *sole criterion* is the market price of the land. 唯一の判断基準は土地の市場価格だ ◇What are the *criteria* used in evaluating student performance? 学生の成績を評価するのに用いられる基準は何ですか ◇The listing in the guide is proof that the restaurant *meets* certain *criteria*. ガイドブックの一覧表を見れば, そのレストランがある程度の基準を満たしていることは明らかだ

standard [C, ふつう複数で] (特定の人・状況が定める)基準, 水準, 標準 ◇No matter how hard I tried I could never *reach their standards*. どんなに頑張っても, 私は彼らの水準に達することができなかった ◇You'd better *lower your standards* if you want to find somewhere cheap to live. どこか安く住める所を見つけたいなら, 君の水準を下げたほうがいいよ ◇I don't know if it's *up to your standards*. あなたの基準を満たしているかどうかはわかりません ◇It was a simple meal, by Eddie's *standards*. エディーの基準によれば, それは質素な食事だった ◇The equipment was slow and heavy *by modern standards*. 現代の水準からすれば, その装置はスピードが遅くて重たかった

test [C] (人・物事の力量・価値を問う)試練, 試金石 ◇The local elections will be a good *test* of the government's popularity. 地方選挙は政府の人気を問うよい試金石となるだろう ◇The game against Dundee will be a real *test of character* for us. ダンディーとの試合で私たちの人間としての真価が問われるだろう ◇The latest pay dispute has really *put* her management skills *to the test*. 最近の賃金闘争で彼女の経営手腕の真価が問われた

measure [C] (判断・評価の)尺度, 物差し ; (物事の大きさ・力を示す)度合い ◇Exam results are only one *meas-ure of* a school's success. 試験結果は個々の学校の教育成果を測る一つの物差しでしかない ◇Is this test a good *measure* of reading comprehension? このテストで読解力は適切に測れますか ◇Her hand trembled slightly, a *measure* of her anxiety. 彼女の手は少し震えていたが, それは彼女がどれくらい不安なのかを表すものだった

benchmark [C] (比較対照の)基準, ベンチマーク ◇The German recycling system is seen as a *benchmark* for schemes throughout Europe. ドイツのリサイクル制度はヨーロッパ中の要項作りの基準とされている ◇The central bank has cut its *benchmark* interest rate four times. 中央銀行は基準となる利率を4回引き下げた

guide [C, ふつう単数で] (判断・意見の材料となる)目安 ◇As a general *guide*, large dogs need more exercise than small ones. 一般的な目安として, 大型犬は小型犬よりも多く運動をする必要がある ◇These figures should be taken as a *rough guide*. これらの数字はおおよその目安と考えるべきだ

guideline [C] (判断・意見の材料となる)指標, 指針 ◇These prices are a *guideline* only. これらの価格は指標にすぎない ◇It may help to have a few *guidelines* to follow. それに倣えば事足りるような指針がいくつかあれば役立つかもしれない

🔖 **guide と guideline の使い分け**: これら二つの語の意味の違いはほとんどない. guide はしばしば正確さがあまり問題とならない状況で用いられる. guideline はしばしばビジネスの文脈で用いられ, まったく正確であることは不可能でも, できるだけ正確であることが重要とされる状況で用いられる. guide はふつう複数形では用いられない. ✗It may help to have a few *guides* to follow.

gauge [米でまた **gage**] [C, ふつう単数で] 《書き言葉, 特にビジネス》(評価・判断の)基準, 目安 ◇The company was regarded as a *gauge* of Britain's industrial well-being. その会社はイギリス産業の繁栄度を測る基準とみなされていた ☞ **gauge** (ESTIMATE 動), **gauge** (JUDGE 動)

yardstick [C] (比較対照の)基準, 物差し ◇Exam results are not the only *yardstick* of a school's performance. 試験結果は学校の教育成果を測る唯一の物差しではない ◇Rates of progress are difficult to compare without a common *yardstick*. 進行速度は共通の基準がないと比較するのは困難だ

🔖 **benchmark と yardstick の使い分け**: benchmark はふつう特定の物事を評価するために利用[推奨]される基準. yardstick は利用可能ないくつか考え得る基準の中の一つを指すことが多い.

norm [C] (果たすべき義務としての[合意の上での])基準, 水準, 標準 ◇The level of background radioactivity is well below international *norms*. バックグラウンド放射能のレベルは国際基準をはるかに下回っている

critical 形

critical・disapproving・judgemental・damning
好ましくないと思う人や物事に対する反応を表す
【類語訳】批判的な, 酷評的な

▶ 文型&コロケーション
- critical/ disapproving **of** sb/ sth
- a critical/ disapproving **glance/ look/ voice**
- a critical/ disapproving/ judgemental **tone/ attitude**

↪**critical**   **criticism**

▶ critical/ disapproving/ judgemental/ damning **comments**
▶ a critical/ judgemental **person**
▶ to **cast** a critical/ disapproving **eye** at sb/ sth
▶ **very** critical/ disapproving/ judgemental
▶ **mildly** critical/ disapproving

critical 批判的な ◇They issued a *critical* report on the government's handling of the crisis. 彼らは政府の危機への対応に関して批判的な報道を行った ◇Tom's parents were highly *critical* of the school. トムの両親は学校に対してとても批判的だった 反意 **uncritical** ❶ uncritical にはふつう非難が込められている。 ◆ Her *uncritical* acceptance of everything I said began to irritate me. (彼女は私の言うことをすべて無批判に受け入れるので私はいら立ち始めた). ☞ **criticize** (BLAME)
▷ **critically** 副 ◇He spoke *critically* of the government. 彼は批判的に政府のことを話した

disapproving 非難[不満, 不賛成]を表す ◇She gave him a *disapproving* glance. 彼女は彼を非難するような目で見た ◇She sounded *disapproving* as we discussed my plans. 私の計画について話し合ったのだが、彼女は賛成ではないようだった 反意 **approving** (GOOD ❻), ☞ **disapprove** (DISAPPROVE)
▷ **disapprovingly** 副 ◇He shook his head *disapprovingly*. 彼は首を横に振って反対した

judgemental 《英》(または特に米で **judgmental**)(けなして)性急に決めつける ◇Stop being so *judgemental*! そうやってすぐに決めつけるのはやめて ☞ **judge** (JUDGE 動)

damning 酷評的な; 有罪を証明する ◇a *damning* criticism/evidence 辛辣な批判/有罪を示す証拠 ◇a *damning* conclusion/report 極めて批判的な結論/報道 ◇Her report is expected to deliver a *damning* indictment of education standards. 彼女は報告書の中で、教育水準に対して極めて批判的な攻撃を加えるはずだ 反意 **glowing** (GOOD ❻)

criticism 名

criticism・attack・disapproval・condemnation・
denunciation・censure・assault・rap・quibble・flak
人や物事に対して否定的な意見を述べる行為を表す
【類語訳】批判, 非難, 攻撃, 不満, 糾弾, 弾劾

文型&コロケーション

▶ criticism/ disapproval/ condemnation/ a denunciation/ censure **of** sb/ sth
▶ an attack/ assault **on** sb/ sth
▶ criticism/ an attack/ condemnation/ flak **from** sb/ sth
▶ (a) **strong** criticism/ attack/ disapproval/ condemnation
▶ a **fierce/ severe** criticism/ attack/ denunciation/ censure
▶ (a) **public** criticism/ attack/ disapproval/ condemnation/ denunciation/ censure
▶ to **launch** a criticism/ an attack/ an assault
▶ to **make** a criticism/ an attack/ a denunciation/ an assault
▶ to **express** criticism/ disapproval/ condemnation
▶ to **bring/ draw** criticism/ condemnation from sb/ sth
▶ to **come under** criticism/ attack/ censure/ assault
▶ to **take** criticism/ flak

criticism [U, C] 批判, 非難 ◇The plan has ***attracted criticism*** from consumer groups. その計画に消費者団体から非難が集まった ◇People in public life must always be ***open to criticism*** (= willing to accept being criticized). 公職にある者は常に批判を受け止めねばならない ◇Ben is very sensitive, he just can't take *criticism*. ベンはとても傷つきやすいし、非難にも少しも耐えられない ◇I didn't mean it as a *criticism*. 私は非難するつもりでそう言ったのではない ◇My only *criticism* of the house is that it is on a busy main road. その家の唯一の難点は交通量の多い幹線道路に面していることだ ☞ **criticize** (BLAME)

attack [C, U] 《特にジャーナリズム》(口頭・文面による)攻撃, 非難 ◇She launched a scathing *attack* on the government's policies. 彼女は政府の方針に対して痛烈な非難を浴びせた ◇The school has come under *attack* for failing to encourage bright students. その学校は優秀な生徒に奨学金を与えないとして攻撃の的となっている ☞ **attack** (BLAME)

disapproval [U] (考え・行動に対する)非難, 不満, 不賛成 ◇He shook his head *in disapproval*. 彼は首を横に振って反対した ◇She looked at my clothes *with disapproval*. 彼女は「何それ」というような目で私の装いを一瞥した 反意 **approval** (PRAISE 名), ☞ **disapprove** (DISAPPROVE)

condemnation [U, C] 《ややフォーマル》(道徳的理由による)糾弾, 非難 ◇There was widespread *condemnation* of the invasion. その侵略に対して非難が巻き起こった ◇The report will be seen by many as a strong *condemnation* of the prison system. 多くの人はその報告を刑務所制度に対する激しい糾弾であるとみなすだろう ☞ **condemn** (BLAME)

denunciation [C, U] 《フォーマル》(公然の)弾劾, 非難 ◇The bishop made an angry *denunciation* of the government's policies. 主教は政府の方針を怒りを込めて非難した ◇All parties joined in bitter *denunciation* of the terrorists. 全政党が一丸となってテロリストを激しく非難した ☞ **denounce** (BLAME)

censure [U] 《フォーマル》(裁判所・議会など公的機関による)激しい非難 ◇Her dishonest behaviour came under severe *censure*. 彼女の不正行為は激しい非難の的となった ☞ **censure** (BLAME)

assault [C] (口頭・文面による)激しい攻撃, 非難 ◇The paper's *assault* on the president was totally unjustified. 大統領に対するその新聞の攻撃はまったく不当なものだった

ノート **attack** と **assault** の使い分け：attack は assault 以上に「非難」を表す語として用いられる。assault は激しい「非難」を表し、本気かつ故意に人の評判を傷つけたり、政策にダメージを与えようとすることを暗示する。

rap [C] 《米, インフォーマル》(不当な)非難 ◇He denounced the criticisms as 'just one bum *rap* after another'. 彼はその批判に対し「不当な非難を連発している」であると非難した ◇Wolves ***get a bad rap***, says a woman who owns three. オオカミには悪評がつきもの、と3頭のオオカミの飼い主である女性は言う

quibble [C] (取るに足らない)難癖, けち, 難点 ◇The only *quibble* about this book is the lack of colour illustrations. この本の唯一の難点はカラーのイラストがないことだ

flak [U] 《インフォーマル》(複数の方面からの)激しい攻撃, 非難 ◇He's taken a lot of *flak* for his left-wing views. 彼はその左翼的な物の見方で多方面から激しい非難を浴びている ◇She ***came in for a lot of flak*** from the press. 彼女は報道機関からここぞとばかりに集中砲火を浴びた

crowd 名

crowd・mob・horde・throng・drove・crush・rabble
一緒にいる多くの人々を表す
【類語訳】群衆, 人込み, 観客, 暴徒, 野次馬, 大群衆

文型&コロケーション
- a crowd/ hordes/ a throng/ droves/ a crush **of** people
- a crowd/ mob/ horde/ rabble **of** youths
- a crowd/ throng **of** journalists/ photographers
- people do sth **in** hordes/ droves
- a/ an **angry/ unruly/ hostile** crowd/ mob
- a **disorderly** crowd/ rabble
- to **push/ fight/ force your way through** the crowd/ mob/ hordes/ throng/ crush
- to **break up/ disperse** a crowd/ mob
- to **join** the crowd/ throng
- a crowd/ mob/ throng **gathers**

crowd [C＋単数・複数動詞] （公共の場所にいる）群衆, 人込み, 観客 ◇A small *crowd* had gathered outside the church. 教会の外には小さな人だかりができていた ◇*Crowds* of people poured into the street. 人々の群れが通りに押し寄せた ◇I want to get there early to avoid the *crowds*. 人込みを避けるために私はそこには早く着きたい ◇The game attracted a **capacity** *crowd* of 80,000. その試合に引き寄せられて8万人もの満員の観客がやって来た ◇Nearly 300 marshals will be involved in *crowd* **control**. ほぼ300名の係員が群衆の整理に駆り出されるだろう ◇A whole *crowd* of us (= a lot of us) are going to the ball. 私たちの多くが舞踏会に行くことになっている

mob [C＋単数・複数動詞] 《しばしばけなして》 暴徒, 野次馬 ◇An angry *mob* of demonstrators came charging around the corner. デモ中の怒った暴徒たちが角を回って突進して来た ◇*mob* **rule** (= a situation in which a mob has control, rather than people in authority) 暴徒支配 ◇a **lynch** *mob* (= a group of people who capture and kill sb illegally because they consider them guilty of a crime) リンチをする暴徒

horde [C] 《時にけなして》 大群衆 ◇There are always *hordes* of tourists here in the summer. ここは夏になるといつも観光客でごった返している ◇Football fans turned up in *hordes*. サッカーファンが大挙して押し寄せた

throng [C] 《書き言葉》 （人の）群れ, 群衆 ◇We pushed our way through the *throng*. 私たちは群衆をかき分けて進んだ ◇He was met by a *throng* of journalists and photographers. 彼は群がったジャーナリストとカメラマンに迎えられた

ノート **crowd** と **throng** の使い分け: crowd はthrong より頻繁に使われる一般的な語である。throng は, 大勢の人がせわしなく, あるいは興奮気味に群がっている様子を描写する文章で特によく使われる。throng は, 参加したい, あるいは何が行われているのか知りたがっている人たちを引きつけるものである。crowd を避けたい (avoid/get away from the crowd) と思うかもしれないが, throng を避けるとは限らない。スポーツ競技に集まる群衆は crowd であって, throng とは言わない。

drove [C, ふつう複数で] （行動を共にする人・動物の）群 ◇People are leaving the countryside **in** *droves* to look for work in the cities. 人々は都会に仕事を求めて集団で田舎から離れている

crush [C, ふつう単数で] 《時にけなして》 （ひしめき合っている） 群衆 ◇There's always a big *crush* in the bar during the interval. バーでは幕間の休憩中にはいつも押すな押すなの賑わいだ

rabble [単数・複数扱い] 《けなして》 騒然とした群衆, 暴徒 ◇As he arrived he was met by a *rabble* of noisy youths. 彼が着くと多くのうるさい若者たちに迎えられた

crowded 形 ☞FULL

crowded・busy・lively・bustling・vibrant
多くの人がいることを表す
【類語訳】混雑した, ごった返した, にぎやかな, 活気のある

文型&コロケーション
- crowded/ busy/ bustling **with** people
- a crowded/ busy/ lively/ bustling/ vibrant **city**
- crowded/ busy/ lively/ bustling **streets**
- a crowded/ busy/ lively/ bustling **place/ town/ resort/ port/ harbour/ market/ bar**
- a crowded/ busy/ lively **pub**
- crowded/ busy/ bustling **shops**

crowded 《時にけなして》 混雑した, ごった返した ◇We made our way through the *crowded* streets. 私たちは混雑した通りを人の間を縫って進んだ ◇In the spring the place is *crowded* with skiers. 春になるとその場所はスキー客でごった返す ◇London was very *crowded*. ロンドンはとても混雑していた

busy 人［交通量］の多い, にぎやかな ◇We have to cross a *busy* main road to get to school. 学校へ行くには交通量の多い幹線道路を渡らなければならない ◇Victoria is one of London's *busiest* stations. ビクトリア駅はロンドンの中でも最も列車発着の多い駅の一つだ

lively 《ほめて》 活気のある, にぎやかな ◇'Les vignes' is a *lively* bar just off the main street. 「レ・ビーニュ」は表通りから少し離れたところにあるにぎやかなバーだ ◇Younger people may prefer a *livelier* resort such as Malia. 若者はマリアのような人でにぎわうリゾート地を好むかもしれない

bustling 《書き言葉, ほめて》 にぎやかな, 活気のある ◇Naples is a *bustling* city located in a beautiful natural setting. ナポリは美しい自然の中に位置するにぎやかな都市だ

vibrant 《書き言葉, ほめて》 活気にあふれる ◇Thailand is at its most *vibrant* during the New Year celebrations. タイは正月の祝賀期間が最も活気に満ちている ❶ vibrant はしばしば観光案内に用いられ, さまざまな人種が行き交い, 商業活動が盛んな都市に用いられる。また夜間にも明るい照明や刺激的な雰囲気で彩られ, さまざまな活動が行われていることを示す。

cruel 形 ☞RUTHLESS

cruel・brutal・savage・vicious・sadistic・barbaric・inhuman・inhumane
意図的に苦痛や苦悩をもたらす人を表す
【類語訳】残酷な, 冷酷な, 情け容赦のない, サディスティックな, 思いやりのない

文型&コロケーション
- cruel/ brutal/ savage/ vicious/ sadistic/ barbaric/ inhu-

↪**cruel**   **cry**

man/ inhumane **treatment**
- cruel/ brutal/ savage/ vicious/ sadistic/ barbaric/ inhuman **acts**
- cruel/ brutal/ sadistic **torture**
- a cruel/ an inhuman/ inhumane **punishment**
- a cruel/ brutal/ vicious **man**
- cruel/ savage/ sadistic/ inhuman **eyes**
- brutal/ vicious/ barbaric **crimes**
- brutal/ savage/ sadistic **violence**
- a brutal/ savage/ vicious/ barbaric **murder**
- a brutal/ savage/ vicious **attack/ assault**
- a brutal/ savage **killing/ beating**
- a brutal/ vicious/ sadistic **killer/ murderer**

cruel 残酷な，冷酷な；残酷[冷酷]さを示す ◇He was known to be a *cruel* dictator. 彼は無慈悲な独裁者として知られていた ◇I can't stand people who are *cruel to* animals. 私は動物を虐待する人のことが我慢ならない ◇Her eyes were *cruel* and hard. 彼女は冷酷で厳しそうな目をしていた 反意 **kind** (KIND 形), **humane** (SENSITIVE 1)
➤ **cruelly** 副 ◇The dog had been *cruelly* treated. その犬は虐待を受けていた

brutal 残忍な，情け容赦のない ◇We did not want to hear the details of the *brutal* attack. 私たちは情け容赦のない襲撃の詳細を聴きたくなかった ◇He had escaped from a *brutal* and repressive *regime*. 彼は残忍かつ弾圧的な政権から逃れてきた ☞ **brutal** (RUTHLESS)
➤ **brutally** 副 ◇He had been *brutally* assaulted. 彼は残忍な襲撃に遭っていた

ノート **cruel**と**brutal**の使い分け：brutalはふつう殺人・攻撃，またはこれらの行為を行う人・政権について用いられる．cruelも肉体的な攻撃について用いられるが，精神的な苦痛・苦悩をもたらす行為についても用いられる．cruelはしばしば人が暴力行為を楽しむ印象を与え，その人の表情を浮かべさせる語と共に用いられることもある．◆a *cruel* mouth/grin/look（冷酷そうな口／笑み／目つき）．cruelは「冷酷な」を意味することもあるが，単に「思いやりのない」を意味することも意味の強弱に幅があるが，brutalの意味は常に強い．☞ **unkind** (MEAN 形)

savage 《特にジャーナリズム》凶暴な；甚大な被害をもたらす ◇She had been badly hurt in what police described as 'a *savage* attack'. 彼女は警察の言うところの「凶暴な襲撃」に遭い重傷を負った

vicious 凶暴な，凶悪な ◇He was set upon by *vicious* thugs. 彼は凶悪な暴漢に襲われた ◇She has a *vicious temper*. 彼女には凶暴な気質がある ❶ viciousは時に attackと共に，口頭・文面による攻撃についてもしばしば用いられる．

sadistic （性的快感について）加虐的な，サディスティックな ◇He took *sadistic* pleasure in taunting the boy. 彼は少年をからかうことにサディスティックな快感を覚えた

barbaric 野蛮な，残忍な ◇It was described as a particularly *barbaric* act. それは特に野蛮な行為だと述べられていた ◇The way these animals are killed is *barbaric*. これらの動物の殺害手口は残忍である

inhuman 《ややフォーマル》非人間的な，無慈悲な ◇We regard their treatment of the prisoners as *inhuman*. 私たちは彼らの捕虜への処遇を非人間的とみなします ◇The photos showed *inhuman* and degrading conditions. それらの写真は非人間的で退廃した状況を写していた
➤ **inhumanity** 名 [U] ◇man's *inhumanity* to man 人

間の人間に対する非人間性 反意 **humanity** (SYMPATHY)
inhumane 《ややフォーマル》（処遇・処罰について）思いやりのない ◇They protested about the *inhumane* treatment of the prisoners. 彼らは捕虜に対する思いやりのない処遇に抗議した 反意 **humane** (SENSITIVE 1)

cry 動

cry • **sob** • **be in tears** • **weep** • **whimper** • **snivel** • **whine**

悲しくて[傷ついて]（声を出して）涙を流す
【類語訳】泣く，すすり泣く，泣きじゃくる，泣きべそをかく，しくしく泣く，めそめそ泣く，ぐずる

文型&コロケーション
- to cry/ be in tears/ whimper/ snivel/ whine **about** sth
- to cry/ sob/ weep/ whimper **with** an emotion
- to cry/ sob/ weep/ whimper **softly/ quietly**
- to cry/ sob/ weep **a little/ silently/ bitterly/ loudly/ uncontrollably/ hysterically**

cry [自] （悲しくて・傷ついて）泣く ◇It's all right. Don't *cry*. 大丈夫だよ．泣かないで ◇There's nothing to *cry* about. 泣くようなことじゃないでしょう ◇The baby was *crying for* (= because it wanted) its mother. 赤ちゃんが母親を求めて泣いていた ◇I found him *crying his eyes out* (= crying very much). 私は彼が大泣きしているのを見た ◇That night she *cried herself to sleep*. その夜，彼女は泣き疲れて寝入った
➤ **cry** 名 [単数で] ◇I felt a lot better after a good long *cry*. 私はさんざん泣いたら気分がすごくよくなった

sob (-bb-) [自, 他] すすり泣く，泣きじゃくる；すすり泣きながら言う ◇I heard a child *sobbing* loudly. 子どもが大きな声で泣きじゃくっているのが聞こえた ◇'I hate him,' she *sobbed*. 「彼なんか大っ嫌い」と彼女はすすり泣きながら言った ◇She flung herself at his chest and *sobbed her heart out*. 彼女は彼の胸に飛び込んで胸も張り裂けんばかりに泣きじゃくった
➤ **sob** 名 [C] ◇Her body was racked (= shaken) with *sobs*. 彼女の体はすすり泣きに震えた

be in 'tears フレーズ 泣いている ◇As she left the room I could see that she *was in tears*. 彼女が部屋を出るとき，私は彼女が泣いているのがわかった

ノート **cry**と**be in tears**の使い分け：be in tearsはcryよりもややフォーマルで，しばしば大人が泣くのに用いられる．cryは子どもが泣く[子どもに泣くのをやめるように言う]場合に用いることが多い．

weep [自, 他] 《フォーマル or 文語》（悲しくて）泣く ◇She started to *weep* uncontrollably. 彼女はこらえきれずに泣き始めた ◇He *wept for joy*. 彼はうれし泣きした ◇I could have *wept* thinking about what I'd missed. 失ったもののことを考えると泣けてきそうだった ◇She *wept* bitter tears of disappointment. 彼女は失意の苦い涙に暮れた

whimper [自, 他] しくしく泣く，泣きべそをかく；しくしく泣きながら言う ◇The child was lost and began to *whimper*. 子どもは道に迷ってべそをかき始めた ◇'Don't leave me alone,' he *whimpered*. 「独りにしないで」と彼はしくしく泣きながら言った
➤ **whimper** 名 [C] ◇The puppy gave a little *whimper* of fear. 子犬は恐怖で弱弱しくくんくんと鳴いた

snivel (-ll-, 米で-l-) [自] （けなして）めそめそ泣く，めそめそ泣

きごとを言う ◇Stop *snivelling*! I can't stand it. めそめそするな。もうたくさんだ ◇What a *snivelling* little brat! 何てよく泣くがきだ

whine [自] (苦痛で[悲しくて])哀れっぽく泣く[鳴く]、ぐずる ◇The dog *whined* and scratched at the door. 犬が哀れっぽく鳴いてドアを引っかいた

cultural [形]

cultural・national・ethnic・native・racial・tribal・indigenous・folk
特定の国や文化、人々の集団と関連があることを表す
【類語訳】文化の、国家の、国民的な、民族の、人種の、民俗の、民間の

文型&コロケーション

▸ native/ indigenous **to** somewhere
▸ a cultural/ a national/ an ethnic/ a racial/ a tribal/ an indigenous **group**
▸ a cultural/ an ethnic/ a native/ a tribal/ an indigenous **community**
▸ native/ tribal/ indigenous **population/ peoples/ leaders**
▸ cultural/ national/ tribal/ indigenous/ folk **traditions**
▸ a national/ an ethnic/ a native/ a tribal/ an indigenous **language**
▸ national/ ethnic/ native/ tribal/ folk **dress/ costume**
▸ ethnic/ native/ indigenous/ folk **art/ music**
▸ sb's cultural/ national/ ethnic/ racial **identity/ origin**
▸ a cultural/ national/ racial **stereotype**
▸ cultural/ ethnic/ racial/ tribal **divisions**
▸ cultural/ ethnic/ racial **differences/ factors/ background/ diversity/ minorities**
▸ native/ indigenous **species/ plants**

cultural [ふつう名詞の前で] 文化の、文化的な ◇Teachers need to be aware of *cultural* differences. 教師は文化の違いを心がけておく必要がある ◇The custom is deeply rooted in the religious and *cultural* heritage of the region. その風習はその地域に受け継がれる宗教と文化に深く根づいている
▸**culturally** [副] ◇a *culturally* diverse society 文化の多様な社会

national [ふつう名詞の前で] (特定の)国家の、国家的な、ある国に特有の；全国的な、国民的な ◇During your visit, you should take the opportunity to sample the *national* dish. 滞在中に機会をとらえてその国の料理を試してみるといいよ ◇This is not just a sporting event; for many it is a matter of *national* pride. これは単なるスポーツイベントではありません。多くの人にとって国の威信をかけた大会なのです ☞ **nation** (COUNTRY 1)

ethnic [ふつう名詞の前で] (共通の伝統文化を持つ)民族[人種、部族]の[に属する]；民族[人種、部族]間に起こる；(西洋文化と異なる)民族特有の、エスニックな ◇This region of Bulgaria has a large *ethnic* Turkish population. ブルガリアのこの地域にはトルコ系住民が多く住んでいる ◇The conference strongly condemned the practice of *ethnic cleansing* (= mass killing of one ethnic group by another). 会議では民族浄化の実践に対し激しい非難が浴びせられた ◇The country is divided along *ethnic* lines. その国は民族ごとに分割されている ◇There was a stall selling *ethnic* jewellery from Afghanistan. アフガニスタンの民族宝飾品を売る露店があった ❶ eth-

nic は *ethnic group/origin/minority* などの句で、人の生い立ち・出生・帰属集団を修飾する一般的な語として近年用いられるようになった。*race* や *tribe* などの語よりも一般的で侮蔑的でないと考えられている。人々の人種的な生い立ちに限らず、宗教・習俗・文化を修飾することもできる。☞ **ethnic group** (PEOPLE)
▸**ethnically** [副] ◇an *ethnically* divided region 民族ごとに分割された地域

native [名詞の前で] (ある場所に)生まれ育った、生粋の ◇It's a long time since he visited his *native* Poland. 彼が故国ポーランドを訪れてからもう久しい ◇Her *native* language is German. 彼女の母語はドイツ語だ ◇His work is barely known in his *native country* of Sweden. 彼の作品は生まれ故郷のスウェーデンではわずかに知られているだけ ◇Are you a *native* Berliner (= a person who has always lived in Berlin)? あなたは生粋のベルリンっ子ですか ❶ native には「先住[土着]民の」の意味もある。◆The *native* peoples depend on the forest for their livelihoods. (先住民は生活を森に頼っている)。この語の使用を侮蔑的と考えて *indigenous* という語を好む人もいるが、Native American (先住アメリカ人) という語句は今もなお先住アメリカ人自身によって好んで用いられている。人種を表す多くの語についても同じだが、最も無難な用語は時代と共にしばしば変わる。❶ native はまたある場所に自生する動植物を修飾することもある。この意味では名詞の前、または native to +「場所」の句で用いられる。◆ Introduced species are often a threat to *native* plants. (外来種はしばしば自生植物にとっての脅威となる)。◆There are about 17 hedgehog species *native* to Europe, Asia and Africa. (ヨーロッパ、アジア、そしてアフリカ原産のハリネズミは約17種存在する)。反意 **foreign, alien** (FOREIGN), ☞ **native** (CITIZEN), **native** (RESIDENT)

racial [ふつう名詞の前で] 人種[民族]間に起こる[ある]；人種[民族]の ◇The killings came at the end of a week of *racial* violence. その殺害事件は1週間に及ぶ人種間の暴力ざたの果てに起こった ◇He struggled to overcome *racial prejudice*. 彼は人種差別と懸命に闘った ☞ **race** (PEOPLE)
▸**racially** [副] ◇The attacks were not *racially* motivated. その襲撃は人種を動機としたものではなかった ◇*racially* mixed schools 人種の混ざった学校

tribal [ふつう名詞の前で] 部族の；部族間に起こる[ある] ◇In rural areas, family and *tribal loyalties* remain important. 地方では、家族と部族に対する忠誠は依然として重要である ◇The area had been ravaged by *tribal warfare*. その地域は部族間闘争によって破壊されていた ☞ **tribe** (PEOPLE)

indigenous 《フォーマル》(人・文化が)土着[現地]の；(動植物が)固有[原産、自生]の ◇Antarctica has no *indigenous* population. 南極大陸には土着民はいない ◇The reserve supports a wide range of *indigenous* species. その保護区はさまざまな固有種を支えている ◇The kangaroo is *indigenous* to Australia. カンガルーはオーストラリア原産である

folk [名詞の前で] (芸術・文化が)民俗の；民間(伝承)の ◇Scottish *folk dancing* スコットランドの民俗舞踊 ◇a Russian *folk song* ロシア民謡 ◇Garlic is widely used in Chinese *folk medicine*. ニンニクは中国の民間療法で広く用いられている

cure 動

cure・heal・resuscitate・rehabilitate・make sb better
人を健康な状態に戻す
【類語訳】治す, 治療する, いやす, 蘇生させる, リハビリさせる

文型&コロケーション

▶to cure sb/ heal sb/ rehabilitate sb/ make sb better **by** doing sth
▶to cure/ heal sb **of** sth

cure [他]（人・動物・病気を）治す, 治療する ◇She was *miraculously cured*. 彼女は奇跡的に回復した ◇They will try to *cure* her of her alcoholism. 彼らは彼女のアルコール依存症を治療しようとするだろう ◇It is better to prevent rather than *cure* diseases. 病気を治療することよりも予防することのほうが大事だ ☞ **cure** (DRUG 2), **cure** (TREATMENT)

heal [他]（薬を用いずに人を）治す, 治療する；（人を）いやす ◇He told stories of Jesus *healing the sick*. 彼は病人を治すイエスの話をした ◇The children were *healed* by a local witch doctor. 子どもたちは地元の呪術医に病気を治してもらった ◇I felt *healed* by his love. 私は彼の愛でいやされた ❶ heal はしばしば信仰・呪術による治療について用いられる。☞ **healing** (TREATMENT)

resuscitate [他]（危篤状態の人を）蘇生させる ◇He had a heart attack and all attempts to *resuscitate* him failed. 彼は心臓発作を起こしたが, 蘇生させるあらゆる試みは失敗に終わった
▸**resuscitation** [名] [U] ◇mouth-to-mouth *resuscitation* (= breathing air into the mouth of an unconscious person to make them start breathing again) マウス・ツー・マウスの人工呼吸法

rehabilitate [他]《ややフォーマル or 書き言葉》（病人・囚人を）社会復帰できるようにする, リハビリさせる ◇He was sent to a unit for *rehabilitating* drug addicts. 彼は薬物中毒者にリハビリテーションを施す病棟に移された ❶ rehabilitate は比喩的な意味で用いられることが多い。◇He played a major role in *rehabilitating* Magritte as an artist (= causing people to again think highly of Magritte as an artist). (彼はマグリットの画家としての名誉回復において大きな役割を果たした.)
▸**rehabilitation** [名] [U] ◇a drug *rehabilitation* centre 薬物中毒リハビリテーション・センター

,make sb 'better [フレーズ]《ややインフォーマル, 特に話し言葉》（人を）治す ◇Here, take this medicine, it'll *make you better*. さあ, この薬を飲めばよくなりますよ

curve 動

curve・turn・wind・snake・bend・twist・arc・zigzag
形や動きがまっすぐでないことを表す
【類語訳】曲がる, 曲げる, 曲がりくねる, 蛇行する, 弧を描く, ジグザグになる

文型&コロケーション

▶to curve/ snake/ wind/ bend/ twist **around/ round** sth
▶to curve/ snake/ wind/ twist/ arc/ zigzag **through/ across** sth
▶to curve/ turn/ snake/ wind/ arc **away** (from sth)
▶to curve/ turn/ wind/ arc **toward/ towards** sth
▶to curve/ turn/ bend **(to the) left/ right/ north/ south**, etc.
▶the **road/ path** curves/ turns/ snakes/ winds/ bends/ twists/ zigzags
▶the **river** curves/ turns/ snakes/ winds/ bends
▶to curve/ turn/ wind/ bend/ twist **sharply/ slightly**

curve [自, 他]《ふつう副詞や前置詞と共に》曲る[曲げる]；（形が）曲線状になる ◇The ball *curved* through the air. ボールが空中で曲がった ◇The road *curved* around the bay. 道が湾に沿って曲がっていた ◇His lips *curved* in a smile. 彼の口元が笑顔でほころびた ◇A smile *curved* his lips. 笑顔で彼の口元がほころびた

turn [自]《ふつう副詞や前置詞と共に》（道路・河川が）曲がる ◇The road *turns* to the left after the church. 道路は教会を過ぎると左に曲がっている ☞ **turn** (CORNER)

wind [自, 他]《副詞や前置詞と共に》（道路・小道・河川が）曲がりくねる ◇The path *wound* down to the beach. 道は曲がりくねって砂浜に通じていた ◇The river *winds* its way between two meadows. 川は2か所の牧草地の間を曲がりくねって流れている ◇The walk follows a *winding* path through the forest. その道は森の中の曲がりくねった道に続いている

snake [他, 自]《書き言葉》《ふつう副詞や前置詞と共に》蛇行する, 蛇行して進む ◇The procession *snaked* its way through narrow streets. 行進は狭い通りを蛇行して進んだ ◇The road *snaked* away into the distance. 道路は蛇行して遠くまで続いていた

bend [自]（形が）曲線状になる, 角をなして曲がる；（物を曲線状に［角をつけて］）曲げる ◇The road *bent* sharply to the right. 道路は右へ急カーブしていた ◇Glass and water both *bend* light. ガラスと水は両方とも光を屈折させる ☞ **bend** (CORNER)

twist [自]（道路・河川が危険なほど）曲がりくねる ◇The road *twists and turns* along the coast. 道路は海岸沿いを曲がりくねっている ◇From the cellar a *twisting* staircase leads down to the dungeon. 地下食料室から曲がりくねった階段が地下牢に通じている ☞ **twist** (CORNER)

arc [自]《ふつう副詞や前置詞と共に》《専門語》（空中に）弧を描く ◇For a few seconds a perfect rainbow *arced* across the city. 数秒間完璧な虹がその町の上に弧を描いた

zigzag (-gg-) [自]《ふつう副詞や前置詞と共に》ジグザグになる［進む］ ◇The narrow path *zigzags* up the cliff. 細い道がジグザグに崖を上っている ☞ **zigzag** (CORNER)

customer 名

customer・client・consumer・buyer・purchaser・shopper・patron・punter・regular・end-user
店や企業から商品やサービスを購入する人あるいは団体を表す
【類語訳】顧客, 依頼人, 消費者, 買い手, 購入者, 買い物客

文型&コロケーション

▶to **have/ deal with/ get/ lose** a customer/ client/ buyer
▶to **attract** customers/ clients/ consumers/ buyers/ shoppers/ punters
▶to **encourage** customers/ clients/ consumers/ buyers/ shoppers
▶to **entice/ persuade** customers/ clients/ consumers/ buyers
▶to **tempt** customers/ buyers/ shoppers

▶customers/ clients/ consumers/ buyers/ purchasers/ shoppers **buy/ spend** sth

customer [C] （個人・団体としての）顧客, 銀行の利用客 ◇He comes in twice a week and is one of our best *customers*. 彼は週に2度来てくれる, この店のお得意さんの一人です ◇Schools are among the biggest *customers* for this service. このサービスの最大の顧客に学校が含まれている ◇I'd like to speak to someone in the *customer* service department, please. 顧客サービス部のどなたかと話したいのですが

client [C] （専門職業人・法人の）依頼人 ◇She's a well-known lawyer with many famous *clients*. 彼女は著名な依頼人を多く抱える有名弁護士だ ◇It is our job to act on behalf of the *client*. クライアントの代理として行動するのが我々の仕事だ ☞ **clientele** (MARKET 1)

consumer [C] （商品・サービスの）消費者 ◇Health-conscious *consumers* want more information about the food they buy. 健康に関心の高い消費者は購入する食品についてより詳しい情報を求めている ◇The big stores are, of course, responding to *consumer* demand. 当然ながら大型店は消費者の需要に応えている ◇We live in a *consumer society* (= one in which buying and selling is considered to be very important) 私たちは消費社会に暮らしている ❶ *consumer* はふつう特定の消費者ではなく, 一般の消費者について用いられる。consumer はしばしば demand, boycott, boom, confidence, spending などの名詞の前で形容詞的に用いられる。

buyer [C] （高額物件の）買い手, 購入者 ◇Have you found a *buyer* for your house? 君の家の買い手は見つかったかい ❶ *buyer* はほとんどの場合, 家・車の購入者または商品を大量購入する会社について用いられる。☞ **buy** (BUY)

purchaser [C] （フォーマル, 特に書き言葉）（高額物件の）買い手, 購入者 ◇The *purchaser* reserves the right to change his or her mind. 買い手は購入を考え直すことのできる権利を留保する ❶ *purchaser* はほとんどの場合, フォーマルな書き言葉で用いられ, 家・車の購入者またはビジネスにおける企業・株式の買収者を指す。☞ **purchase** (BUY)

shopper [C] （店の）買い物客 ◇Crowds of *shoppers* had to be evacuated from the store after the bomb threat. 爆破予告の後で大勢の買い物客が店から避難させられるはめになった ◇Competition between stores can result in big savings for *shoppers*. 店舗間の競争で買い物客は大いにお得な買い物ができることになるかもしれない ❶ *shopper* はほとんどの場合, hundreds/thousands/crowds of など多数に関連する語句, または Christmas/Saturday-morning など多くの人が店で買い物をする時期に関連する語句の後で複数形で用いられる。☞ **shop** (BUY)

patron [C] 《フォーマル》（特定の店・レストラン・劇場などの）顧客 ◇*Patrons* are requested not to smoke. お客様にはおたばこをご遠慮ください

punter [C] 《英, インフォーマル》（特定の製品・サービスの）客 ◇It's important to keep the *punters* happy. 客を満足させておくことが重要だ ◇Your average *punter* won't notice the difference. お店に来るふつうの客はその違いには気づきませんよ

regular [C] （特定の店・バー・レストランなどの）常連 ◇He's one of our *regulars*. 彼は私どもの常連の一人だ

,end-'user [C] （コンピュータ関連製品の）最終[一般]使用者, エンドユーザー ◇Programs are tailored to meet the needs of *end-users*. プログラムはエンドユーザーのニーズに合わせて作られている

cut 動

1 ☞ ABOLISH, REDUCE, SAVE 2
cut • slash • cut sth back • cut sth down • scale sth back • rationalize • downsize • scale sth down
金額や事業などを少なく[小さく]する
【類語инфо】減らす, 削減する, 縮小する, 短くする, 合理化する

文型&コロケーション

▶to cut sth/ cut sth back/ cut sth down/ downsize sth/ scale sth down **from** $50,000 **to** $40,000
▶to cut sth/ cut sth back/ cut sth down/ scale sth down **by** $5,000/ 30%
▶to cut/ slash/ cut down **on** sth
▶to cut/ slash/ cut back on/ cut down on/ scale back/ rationalize **spending/ production**
▶to cut/ slash/ cut back on **jobs**
▶to cut/ slash/ downsize **the workforce**
▶to cut/ slash/ rationalize **the cost** of sth
▶to cut sth/ slash sth/ cut sth back/ cut sth down/ scale sth down **drastically**
▶to cut sth/ cut sth back/ cut sth down **considerably**

cut [他]（金額を）減らす, 削減する；（規模を）縮小する, 短くする ◇The President has promised to *cut* taxes significantly. 大統領は大幅な減税を行うことを約束した ◇Could you *cut* your essay from 5,000 to 3,000 words? エッセイの語数を5000語から3000語に減らしていただけませんか ☞ **cut** (REDUCTION)

slash [他, しばしば受身で]《ややインフォーマル, ジャーナリズム》（大幅に）削減する ◇The workforce has been *slashed* by half. 従業員数は半分に削減された ◇A slump in the retail trade has forced the company to *slash* prices. 小売の不振により, その会社は価格を大幅に引き下げざるを得なくなった

,cut sth 'back, ,cut 'back on sth 句動詞 （金額・事業を）削減[縮小]する ◇If we don't sell more we'll have to *cut back* production. もっと多く売り上げないと生産を縮小しなければならなくなるだろう ◇The local authority is trying to *cut back* significantly *on* spending this year. 地方自治体は今年度の支出を大幅に削減しようとしている ☞ **cutback** (REDUCTION)

,cut sth 'down, ,cut 'down on sth 句動詞 （規模・数量を）削減[縮小]する ◇The doctor told him to *cut down* on his drinking. 医者は彼に酒の量を減らすように言った ◇I won't have a cigarette, thanks — I'm trying to *cut down* (= smoke fewer). 一服はやめておくよ, ありがとう一本数を減らそうとしているんだ

,scale sth 'back 句動詞 《特に米 or ビジネス》（金額・事業を）削減[縮小]する ◇The IMF has *scaled back* its growth forecasts for the next decade. 国際通貨基金は今後10年間の成長予測を下方修正した

rationalize 《英でまた **-ise**》[他, 自]《英, ビジネス》（企業・組織を）合理化する ◇Twenty workers lost their jobs when the department was *rationalized*. その部門が合理化される際, 20人の従業員が職を失った

▶**rationalization** 《英でまた **-isation**》图 [U, C] ◇a need for *rationalization* of the industry 事業の合理化の必要性

downsize [自, 他]《ビジネスで》（企業・組織を）削減[縮小]する ◇The worsening situation forced the company to *downsize* from 39 employees to 7. 状況の悪化に伴い、その会社は従業員を39人から7人に削減せざるを得なかった ◇The larger companies are all planning to *downsize* their US operations. 大企業はこぞってアメリカでの業務の縮小を計画している ❶ downsize は否定的な響きのある fire, dismiss, lay sb off, make sb redundant などのより露骨な表現を好まない人によってしばしば用いられる。

ˌscale sth ˈdown 句動詞 (規模・数量・範囲を)削減[縮小]する ◇We are thinking of *scaling down* our training programmes next year. 当社は来年度の研修プログラムの縮小を検討しています ◇He was using *scaled-down* versions of his father's tools. 彼は父親の道具の小型版を使用している

ノート cut, cut sth back, cut sth down, scale sth back, scale sth down の使い分け：cut がこれらの語の中で最も一般的。cut sth back と scale sth back は両方とも特に金額・事業について用いられる。cut sth down と scale sth down も一般的であるが、金額・事業以外の物事について用いられることが多い。

2 cut・chop・slice・carve・dice
ナイフのように鋭利な物を使って、物をより小さな部分にする
【類語訳】切る、切り刻む、(薄く)切る、切り分ける、さいの目に切る

文型&コロケーション
▶to cut/ chop/ slice/ carve sth **into** sth
▶to cut/ chop/ slice sth **off** sth
▶to cut/ slice sth **in half/ two**
▶to cut/ chop/ slice sth **up**
▶to cut/ chop/ slice/ carve/ dice **meat**
▶to cut/ slice **bread/ cake**
▶to chop/ slice an **onion**
▶to cut/ chop/ slice/ dice sth **finely**
▶to cut/ slice sth **thinly**

cut [他] 切る ◇He *cut* four slices from the loaf. 彼はパンのかたまりを4切れに切った ◇He *cut* the loaf into thick slices. 彼はパンのかたまりを厚切りにした ◇Shall I *cut* you a piece of cake? ケーキを一切れ切ってあげましょうか ◇Don't *cut* the string; untie the knot. ひもを切っては駄目、結び目をほどいて ◇The climbers *cut* steps in the ice. 登山家たちは足の置き場として氷に刻み目を入れた

chop (-pp-) [他] 小さく切る、切り刻む ◇He was *chopping* logs for firewood. 彼は薪用に丸太を切っていた ◇Roughly *chop* the herbs. ハーブを荒く刻みなさい

slice [他, 自] (薄く)切る ◇*Slice* the cucumber thinly. きゅうりを薄切りにしなさい ◇a *sliced* loaf 薄切りのパン ◇a loaf of *sliced* bread ひとかたまりの薄切りのパン ◇He accidentally *sliced through* his finger. 彼は誤って指を切った ☞ **slice (PIECE)**

carve [他, 自] (調理した肉を)切り分ける ◇She taught me how to *carve* a leg of lamb. 彼女は私に子羊の脚の切り分け方を教えてくれた ◇Lunch is ready. Who's going to *carve*? ランチはできています、誰か切り分けてくれない

dice [他] さいの目に切る ◇*diced* carrots/lamb さいの目に切ったにんじん/ラム肉

D d

damage 名

damage・harm・detriment
事故や犯罪、病気などの不運な出来事が人や物事にもたらす悪影響
【類語訳】損害、損傷、ダメージ、被害、害

文型&コロケーション
- damage/ harm/ detriment **to** sth
- damage/ harm **from** sth
- **great/ serious/ severe/ lasting/ long-term/ environmental** damage/ harm/ detriment
- **real/ irreparable/ permanent/ physical/ bodily/ personal/ emotional/ psychological** damage/ harm
- to **cause/ do/ inflict/ suffer/ escape/ prevent** damage/ harm
- damage/ harm **results from** sth

damage [U] (事故・犯罪・病気などによる)損害、損傷、ダメージ ◇The earthquake caused *damage* to property estimated at $60 million. その地震で推定6千万ドルの物的損害がもたらされた ◇We assessed the storm *damage*. 私たちはその嵐による被害を査定した ◇He was hit by a car and suffered severe **brain damage**. 彼は車にはねられて重篤な脳障碍(⁉)を負った ◇I insist on paying for the *damage*. 私は損害に対する賠償を求めている ◇I'm going — I've done enough *damage* here already. もう行くよ—ここにはすでに十分なダメージを与えてしまった
☞ **damaging** (HARMFUL)

harm [U] (人・物事に対する)損害[被害]、害 ◇The accident could have been worse; luckily **no harm was done**. その事故はもっとひどいことになっていてもおかしくなかったが、好運にも被害がまったくなかった ◇The treatment they gave him did him **more harm than good**. 彼に施された治療は効果があるというよりむしろ害になった ◇Hard work **never did anyone any harm**. 一所懸命やってったかを見ただけなんてことは決してない ◇He may look fierce, but he **means no harm**. 彼は恐そうに見えるかもしれないが、悪意はないよ ◇Don't worry, we'll see that the children **come to no harm**. 心配しないでください、子どもたちに危害が及ばないよう見ておきますから ◇I prefer the children to play in the garden where they're **out of harm's way**. 私は子どもたちを安全な庭で遊ばせたい
☞ **harmful** (HARMFUL)

ノート damage と harm の使い分け: damage は嵐・洪水・火事などによる建物などへの「被害」を指す。◆ storm/ flood/ fire/ smoke/ bomb/ structural *damage* (嵐/洪水/火/煙/爆弾/構造上の被害). damage はまた体内器官の「損傷」についても用いる。◆ liver/ kidney/ lung/ brain *damage* (肝臓/腎臓/肺/脳の損傷). damage も harm も精神的苦痛について用いることができる。◆ emotional/ psychological/ social *damage/harm* (心的/精神的/社会的ダメージ). harm は上記の用例に見られる決まった句で、被害の原因や被害の発生の有無に関して用いられる。

detriment [U, C, ふつう単数で]《フォーマル》被害[損害](の原因) ◇Wood accounts for 90% of energy production in some countries, with consequent environmental *detriment*. 木材がエネルギー生産の90%を占める国々もあり、その結果環境被害がもたらされる ◇He was engrossed in the job **to the detriment of** his health. 彼は仕事にのめり込んで健康を害した ◇The tax cannot be introduced **without detriment to** people's living standards. 人々の生活水準を損なうことなくその税を導入することはできない ☞ **detrimental** (HARMFUL)

damage 動

damage・hurt・harm・impair・compromise
人や物事に悪影響を及ぼす
【類語訳】損害を与える、害する、損なう、危うくする

文型&コロケーション
- to damage/ hurt/ harm/ impair/ compromise sb's **chances**
- to damage/ hurt/ harm/ compromise sb's **reputation**
- to damage/ hurt/ harm sb's **interests/ image**
- to damage/ harm/ impair/ compromise sb's **health**
- to **seriously** damage/ hurt/ harm/ impair/ compromise sb/ sth
- to **greatly** damage/ hurt/ harm/ impair sb/ sth
- to **severely/ badly** damage/ hurt/ impair sb/ sth

damage [他] (物事に)損害を与える；(人の生命・健康・幸福・成功の可能性などを)損なう ◇Several vehicles were *damaged* in the crash. その衝突事故で何台かの車が損傷した ◇Smoking seriously *damages* your health. 喫煙は健康を著しく害する ◇The allegations are likely to *damage* his political career. その申し立ては彼の政治生命を損なう可能性がある ◇He works with emotionally *damaged* children. 彼は心に傷を負った子どもたちのために働いている ☞ **damaging** (HARMFUL)

hurt [他] 《ややインフォーマル》(物事・人の生命[健康、幸福、成功の可能性など]に)悪影響を与える ◇Many people on low incomes will be *hurt* by the government's plans. 多くの低所得者が政府の計画によって痛手を被るだろう ◇Hard work never *hurt* anyone. 勤勉が災いをもたらしたことはない ◇High interest rates are *hurting* the local economy. 高金利は地域経済に打撃を与えている

harm [他] (人・物事に)悪影響を与える、害する、損なう ◇Pollution can *harm* marine life. 汚染が海洋生物に被害をもたらす可能性がある ◇These revelations will *harm* her chances of winning the election. これらが暴露されると彼女が選挙に勝つ可能性は損なわれるだろう ☞ **harmful** (HARMFUL)

ノート damage, hurt, harm の使い分け: hurt は特に否定的な文で用いられるときは、damage や harm よりフォーマルな感じは弱い。◆ It won't *hurt* him to have to wait a bit. (彼は少しくらい待ってもいいじゃないか). ◆ These prices won't *hurt* your wallet. (この値段

↳damage

なら財布は痛くない). ×It won't *damage/harm* him to have to wait a bit. ×These prices won't *damage/harm* your wallet. harmはしばしばbirds, animals, wildlife, environmentなどの自然界の物が人間の活動によってどのように影響されているかを述べるときにも用いられる。また、harmはある行為がunborn child/baby, foetus (胎児)にいかに悪影響を与えるかを述べるときにも用いられる。

impair [他]《ややフォーマル》(人の健康・能力・可能性を)害する[損なう] ◇There are a number of factors which can directly *impair* memory. 記憶力を直接損なう可能性のある数多くの要因がある ◇Even one drink can *impair* driving performance. たった一杯飲むだけでも運転能力は損なわれる 反意 **improve** (IMPROVE 1)
▶**impaired** [形]《複合語で》◇the problems faced by people who are *visually/hearing impaired* 視覚/聴覚障碍のある人々が直面している問題

compromise [他] (浅はかな行為をして人・事・身を)危うくする ◇She has already *compromised herself* by accepting his invitation. 彼の招待に応じることで彼女はすでに自らを危険にさらしている ◇Defeat at this stage would *compromise* their chances of reaching the finals of the competition. この段階で敗れれば彼らが決勝まで残る可能性は危うくなるだろう

dangerous [形]

---

dangerous・hazardous・risky・unsafe・high-risk・treacherous

人や物事にとって危ういものとなることを表す
【類語訳】危険な, 危ない, 有害な, リスキーな, ハイリスクな

文型&コロケーション
▶ dangerous/ hazardous/ risky/ unsafe **for** sb (to do sth)
▶ dangerous/ hazardous **to** sb/ sth
▶ dangerous/ hazardous/ risky/ unsafe **to do sth**
▶ a dangerous/ a hazardous/ a risky **business/ situation**
▶ a dangerous/ a hazardous/ high-risk **occupation/ operation**
▶ **very** dangerous/ hazardous/ risky/ unsafe/ treacherous
▶ **highly** dangerous/ hazardous/ risky

dangerous (人・物事にとって)危険な, 危ない ◇Flu can be a *dangerous* illness for some people, including the very young. 幼児を含む一定の人々にとってインフルエンザが危険な病気となることもある ◇He received a conviction for *dangerous driving*. 彼は危険運転の罪で有罪判決を受けた ◇It would be *dangerous* for you to stay here. 君がここに留まるのは危険だろう ◇The prisoners who escaped are violent and *dangerous*. 脱獄囚たちは暴力的で危険だ ◇We'd be *on dangerous ground* if we asked about race or religion (= it might make people angry). 人種や宗教に関する質問をすれば人々の感情を害することもある 反意 **safe, harmless**, ☞ **danger** (RISK 1), **danger** (THREAT)
▶**dangerously** [副] ◇She was standing *dangerously* close to the fire. 彼女は火に危険なほど近づいて立っていた ◇His father is *dangerously* ill (= so ill that he might die). 彼の父親は危篤である

hazardous 《ややフォーマル》(人の健康・安全に)危険を伴う, 危険な, 有害な ◇Britain produces almost five million tonnes of *hazardous* waste each year. イギリスは毎年5百万トン近くの有害廃棄物を出している ◇They endured a *hazardous* journey through thickening fog. 次第に濃くなる霧の中を進む危険な道程に彼らは耐えた ◇They attached a list of products that are potentially *hazardous* to health. 健康を害する可能性のある生産物のリストが添付された ☞ **hazard** (THREAT)

risky (ビジネスにおいて)リスキーな, 危険な ◇Predicting the weather is a *risky* business for farmers. 天気がどうなるかを予測することは農家にとってリスクを伴う問題だ ◇Even a very good company can be a *risky* investment if it is overvalued. 過大評価されていると優良企業でさえもリスキーな投資先になりうる ◇It's far too *risky* to generalize from one set of results. 限られた結果から一般論を導き出すのはあまりにも危険だ ☞ **risk** (RISK 1, 2)

unsafe (場所・行為・活動的で)安全でない, 危険な ◇The roof was *declared unsafe*. その屋根は危険であると判定された ◇It was considered *unsafe* to release the prisoners. 囚人たちを釈放することは危険だと考えられた ◇*Unsafe sex* (= for example, sex without a condom) carries a high risk of spreading HIV. 安全でない性行為でHIVが蔓延する危険性が高くなる 反意 **safe**

,high-'risk 《ふつう名詞の前で》(損失・損害・傷害・死亡の)危険性が高い, ハイリスクな; (人が)特定の病気にかかりやすい ◇It's a *high-risk* venture that will require a lot of capital. それは多大な資本が必要なハイリスクな事業だ ◇Ideally the technique should be limited to *high-risk* patients. 理想を言えば, その処置は高リスクの患者に限定されるべきだ ❶ high-riskは特にビジネスや医学の文脈で用いられる。結びつく語には investment, strategy, venture, projectや patients, subjects, children, category, group などが挙げられる。 反意 **low-risk** ❶ low-riskな活動とは「危険が少なく, 損失, 損害の危険性が低い活動」を指す。また, low-riskな患者とは「特定の病気にはまずかからない患者」のことを言う。

treacherous (安全そうに見えて)危険な ◇The ice on the roads made driving conditions *treacherous*. 道路上に氷があり油断のならない走行条件だった ❶ treacherousは特に悪天候の文脈で用いられる。

dare [動]

---

dare・risk・go so/as far as to...・venture・hazard・stick your neck out・pluck up (the) courage・presume・chance

失敗するかもしれないことを勇気を持って試みる
【類語訳】あえて…する, 厚かましく…する, ずうずうしく…する

文型&コロケーション
▶ to dare/ go so far as/ venture/ pluck up courage/ presume **to do sth**
▶ to risk/ chance **doing sth**
▶ to venture/ hazard an **opinion**
▶ to risk/ chance a **look** (at sth)
▶ to risk/ chance **it**

dare [自]《進行形はまれ》あえて…する; 厚かましく[ずうずうしくも]…する ◇She said it as loudly as she *dared*. 彼女は精一杯大きな声でそう言った ◇He didn't *dare* (to) say what he thought. 彼は自分の考えを言う勇気がなかった ◇*Dare* to be different! あえて人と違うことをせよ ◇They *daren't* ask for any more money. 《英》それ以上の金を要求する勇気は彼らになかった ◇'I'll tell her about it.' '***Don't you dare!***' 《話し言葉》「彼女にそのこ

とについて話すよ」「やめとけよ」 ◇*How dare you* talk to me like that! よくも私にそんなような口の利き方ができるね ☞ **daring** (BOLD), **daring** (COURAGE)

risk [他] あえて…する, …する恐れがある ◇There was no choice. If they stayed there, they *risked* death. 仕方がなかった. そこに留まるなら彼らには死の危険性があった ◇They knew they *risked* being arrested. 彼らは捕まるリスクを承知していた ◇He *risked* a glance at her furious face. 彼は思い切って彼女の怒った顔をちらっと見た ◇It was a difficult decision but we decided to *risk* it. 難しい決断だったが私たちは賭けに出た ☞ **risk** (RISK 1, 2)

go so/as 'far as to... [フレーズ]《極端な[人が驚くような]ところまで》行う ◇In June 2006 he *went so far as to* offer his resignation. 2006年6月, 彼は辞任するとまで言い出した ◇I wouldn't *go as far as to* say that he's a liar (= but I think he may be slightly dishonest). 私は彼が嘘つきであるとまでは言うつもりはない

venture [他]《フォーマル》(人を怒らせるかもしれないが)思い切って言う[する] ◇She hardly dared to *venture* an opinion. 彼女は思い切って意見を言うようとしたがほとんど不発に終わった ◇I *ventured* to suggest that she might have made a mistake. 私は彼女がミスを犯したかもしれないことをほのめかしてみた

hazard [他, 自] (間違っているかもしれない提案・推測を)あえて行う ◇Would you like to *hazard a guess*? 山勘で当ててみますか ◇'Is it Tom you're going with?' she *hazarded*. 「付き合ってるのはトムなの」と彼女は当てずっぽうで聞いてみた

stick your 'neck out [慣用]《インフォーマル》(間違っているかもしれないことを)あえて言う[行う] ◇I'll *stick my neck out* and say that Bill is the best candidate for the job. あえて言いますが, ビルがその仕事に最も適任です

pluck up (the) 'courage [慣用]《ふつうほめて》(恐れながらも)勇気をふるって…する ◇I finally *plucked up the courage* to ask her for a date. 私はついに勇気を奮い起こして彼女をデートに誘った

presume [自]《フォーマル, ふつう否定して》おこがましくも…する ◇I wouldn't *presume* to tell you how to run your own business. あなたに事業のやり方を教えるなんておこがましいことをするとは思いません

chance [他]《インフォーマル》(失敗するかもしれないことを)あえて行う ◇'Take an umbrella.' 'No, I'll *chance* it (= take the risk that it may rain).' 「傘を持って行きなさい」「いや, 降らないほうに賭けるよ」 ◇She was *chancing her luck* driving without a licence.《特に英》彼女は一か八か無免許で運転をしていた

dark [形]

1 dark・black・shady・shadowy・unlit
光がほとんど[まったく]ないことを表す
【類語訳】暗い, 真っ暗な, 日陰の

▶ 文型&コロケーション
- a dark/ shady/ shadowy **place/ corner**
- a dark/ shadowy/ unlit **room**
- a dark/ unlit **road**
- a dark/ black **night**
- black/ shadowy **darkness**
- to go dark/ black
- pitch dark/ black
- cool and dark/ shady

dark (特に夜なので)光がまったく[ほとんど]ない, 暗い ◇What time does it *get dark* in summer? 夏は何時に暗くなりますか ◇It was *dark* outside and I couldn't see much. 外は暗くてあまりよく見えなかった ◇He stumbled along through the *dark* forest. 彼は暗い森の中をつまずきながら歩いた 反意 **light**

black 光のない; 真っ暗な ◇Through the *black* night came the sound of thunder. 雷鳴が闇夜に轟いた ◇It's pitch *black* (= very dark) outside. 外は真っ暗だ ◇My head banged on a rock and everything went *black*. 私は岩に頭をぶつけて目の前が真っ暗になった

shady (木々・建物などによって)日陰になった ◇We went to find somewhere cool and *shady* to have a drink. 私たちは一杯やるために涼しい日陰の場所を探しに行った ◇This is a nice *shady* spot for a picnic. ここはピクニックにうってつけの日陰だ 反意 **sunny** (SUNNY)

shadowy [ふつう名詞の前で] 暗い, 影の多い ◇Someone was hiding in the *shadowy* doorway. 誰かが暗い戸口に隠れていた ◇The lights went out, plunging the room into a *shadowy* darkness. 電気が消えて何も見えない暗闇に変わった

unlit (光がなくて[消灯していて])暗い ◇The room was *unlit* and they could hardly see the man in the gloom. 部屋の中は光がなく, 彼らには暗がりにいる男がほとんど見えなかった ◇Avoid walking through parks or down quiet, *unlit* roads. 公園内や人通りの少ない明かりのない道を通るのは避けましょう 反意 **lighted**

2 dark・rich・deep・warm・mellow
好ましい濃い色を表す
【類語訳】黒っぽい, 濃い, 深みのある, 暖色の

▶ 文型&コロケーション
- a dark/ rich/ deep/ warm **colour/ tone/ shade**
- (a) dark/ rich/ deep/ warm **red/ orange**
- (a) dark/ rich/ deep **blue/ green/ purple**
- very dark/ deep

dark (色が)濃い, 黒っぽい ◇*Darker* colours are more practical and don't show stains. 暗い色のほうがより実用的で汚れが見えない ◇Mahogany is a *dark*-coloured wood. マホガニーは黒っぽい木材だ ◇He was dressed in a *dark* suit and a plain white shirt. 彼は黒っぽいスーツと無地の白いシャツを着ていた ◇The *dark* clouds in the sky meant that a storm was coming. 空にある暗雲は嵐が近づいていることを意味していた 反意 **pale, light** (PALE)

rich [ふつう名詞の前で] (色が鮮やかで)濃い ◇The colour of the flower is a *rich* deep red. その花の色は濃い赤色だ ◇the *rich* tones of autumn 秋の深みのある色合い

deep [ふつう名詞の前で] (色が)暖かみのある, 暖色の ◇He had a pale face with *deep* blue eyes. 彼は色白の顔で, 深みのある青い目をしていた ◇The colour is *deeper* when the grapes are dried. 葡萄は乾くと色が濃くなる 反意 **pale** (PALE)

warm [ふつう名詞の前で] (色が)暖かみのある, 暖色の ◇The house is decorated in *warm* shades of red and orange. その家は赤とオレンジ色の暖かい色調のペンキで塗られている 反意 **cool** (PALE)

mellow (色が)やわらかで落ち着いた ◇The floor was of *mellow* golden stone. 床はやわらかで落ち着いた黄金色の石でできていた

darling 名

darling • honey • love • baby • sweetheart • dear • sweetie • loved one • babe • beloved
大好き[大切]な人に対する呼びかけ[呼称]
【類語訳】ねえ、あなた、愛する人、大切な人、やあ、恋人、お前

文型&コロケーション
▶thank you, hello, yes, etc. darling/ honey/ love/ baby/ sweetheart/ dear/ sweetie/ babe
▶my darling/ love/ baby/ sweetheart/ dear/ beloved

darling [C]《特に英、インフォーマル、話し言葉》(愛する人へ呼びかけて)ねえ、あなた、お前 ◇What's the matter, *darling*? ねえ、どうしたの ◇I love you too, my *darling*. 私も愛してるわ、あなた ☞ **darling** (DEAR)

honey [C]《特に米、インフォーマル、話し言葉》(愛する人へ呼びかけて)ねえ、あなた、お前 ◇Have you seen my keys, *honey*? ねえ、鍵を見なかったかい

love [C] 愛する人；(愛する人へ呼びかけて)あなた、お前 ◇Take care, my *love*. じゃあまたね ◇He was **the love of my life** (= the person I loved most). 彼は最愛の人だった

baby [C]《特に米、インフォーマル、話し言葉》(恋愛感情を伴う愛する人へ呼びかけて)ねえ、あなた、君 ◇Come on *baby*, let's dance! ねえ、おいでよ。踊ろう ❶baby は男性から見知らぬ女性に対して用いられた場合は侮蔑的なこともある。

sweetheart [単数で]《インフォーマル、話し言葉》(愛する人へ呼びかけて)ねえ、君、お前 ◇Do you want a drink, *sweetheart*? ねえ、一杯どう ❶sweetheart は特に男性から女性へ、女性から子どもへ用いられる。

dear [C]《やや古風、インフォーマル、話し言葉》(愛する人へ呼びかけて)ねえ、あなた、君 ◇Come here, my *dear*. ねえ、こっちへおいで ❶dear は特に年配の人が用いる。☞ **dear** (DEAR)

sweetie [単数で]《インフォーマル、話し言葉》(愛する人へ呼びかけて)ねえ、あなた、君 ◇Oh, *sweetie*. Don't cry. ねえ、泣かないで ◇If you ask me, *sweetie*, you're making a big mistake. 私に言わせれば、ねえ、君は大きな間違いを犯してるよ ❶(英)ではsweetieはふつう女性が子どもに対して用いるが、(米)では女の友達同士でも用いられる。

'loved one [C]《ややインフォーマル、特に書き言葉》(特に家族を指して)大切な人 ◇He longed to be at home with his *loved ones*. 彼は愛する家族のいる家に戻りたいと願った ❶loved one はこのグループの語で唯一呼びかけには用いることができない。×Are you all right, *loved one*?

babe [C]《インフォーマル、話し言葉》(親友・愛する人へ呼びかけて)やあ、かわいこちゃん ◇Hi, *babe*, how are you doing? やあ、元気かい ❶babe は特に若者に用いられる。男性から見知らぬ女性に対して用いられた場合は侮蔑的なこともある。babesも用いられるが、使用頻度は低い。

beloved [C]《古語 or 文語》愛する人、恋人 ◇It was a gift from her *beloved*. それは彼女の恋人からの贈り物だった ☞ **beloved** (DEAR)

dead 形

dead • late • deceased • lifeless • at peace
人、動物、植物がもはや生きていない
【類語訳】死んだ、枯れた、亡くなった、故…、死去した

文型&コロケーション
▶to lie dead/ lifeless/ at peace
▶a dead/ late/ deceased wife/ husband/ mother/ father/ brother/ sister/ relative
▶a/ sb's dead/ lifeless body
▶almost/ nearly/ apparently/ seemingly dead/ lifeless

dead 死んだ、枯れた ◇a *dead* person/animal/tree 死人/死んだ動物/枯れ木 ◇*dead* leaves/wood/skin 枯れ葉/枯れ木/壊死した皮膚 ◇My mother's *dead*; she died in 1997. 母は死んでいます。1997年に亡くなりました ◇He was shot *dead* by a gunman outside his home. 彼は家の外で銃を持った犯人に射殺された ◇He **dropped dead** (= died suddenly) last week.《インフォーマル》彼は先週急死した 反意 **alive, living, live** (ALIVE), ☞ **die** (DIE)
▶**the dead** 名 [複数扱い] ◇*The dead* and wounded in that one attack amounted to 6,000. あの一回の攻撃における死傷者は6千人に上った
▶**death** 名 [C, U] ◇a sudden/violent/peaceful *death* 突然死/変死/安らかな死 ◇the anniversary of his wife's *death* 彼の奥さんの命日 ◇Two children were burnt **to death** in the fire (= they died as a result of the fire). 二人の子どもが火事で焼け死んだ ◇Police are still trying to establish the cause of *death*. 警察はいまだに死因を特定しようとしている 反意 **life** (LIFE 1)

late [名詞の前で]《ややフォーマル》亡くなった、故… ◇She spoke of her *late* husband with passion. 彼女は亡くなった夫のことを熱心に話した ◇The event was organized in memory of the *late* Christopher Reeve. そのイベントは故クリストファー・リーヴ氏を追悼して催された ❶この意味のlateはふつう sb's late husband/wife/father/mother などや、the late John Smith/Mary Brown などの句で、ごく最近亡くなった人について言うときに用いられる。

deceased《法律 or フォーマル》死んだ、死去した、亡くなった ◇She took over her *deceased* parents' business. 彼女は亡くなった両親の商売を引き継いだ
▶**the deceased** 名 [C] ◇The funeral was attended by only the male relations of *the deceased*. 葬式には亡くなった人の男性の親戚のみが出席した ❶the deceased は特に最近亡くなった人について用いられる。

lifeless《フォーマル》死んだ、死んでいるように見える ◇He knelt beside her *lifeless* body. 彼は彼女の遺体のそばでひざまずいた ❶lifelessはふつう体または体の一部について言うときに用いられる。◆his/her *lifeless* body/form/eyes/hand 彼・彼女の遺体/生気のない目/活気のない姿/冷たくなった手)

at 'peace 供述 死んだ、安らかな ◇Her illness would develop, and soon she would be *at peace*. 病気が進行しやがて彼女は亡くなるだろう

dealer 名

dealer • trader • supplier • seller • merchant • retailer • vendor • distributor • wholesaler • shopkeeper
物を売買する仕事を持つ人[会社]
【類語訳】商人、ディーラー、貿易商、小売業者、卸売業者、店主

文型&コロケーション
▶to buy/ sell sth through a dealer/ distributor/ wholesaler
▶a small dealer/ trader/ supplier/ merchant/ retailer/ vendor/ distributor/ wholesaler/ shopkeeper

deal with sb/sth

▶ a **large** dealer/ trader/ supplier/ merchant/ retailer/ vendor/ distributor/ wholesaler
▶ a **local** dealer/ trader/ supplier/ merchant/ retailer/ vendor/ distributor/ wholesaler/ shopkeeper
▶ an **international** dealer/ trader/ supplier/ merchant/ distributor/ wholesaler
▶ a **foreign** dealer/ trader/ supplier/ seller/ merchant/ vendor
▶ a **street** trader/ seller/ vendor
▶ an **independent** dealer/ trader/ supplier/ retailer/ vendor/ distributor/ wholesaler
▶ a **licensed** dealer/ trader/ seller/ retailer/ vendor/ distributor
▶ a **leading** dealer/ supplier/ merchant/ retailer/ distributor/ wholesaler
▶ a/ an **food/ clothing/ electrical** supplier/ retailer/ distributor/ wholesaler
▶ a dealer/ trader/ supplier/ seller/ merchant/ vendor/ distributor/ wholesaler/ shopkeeper **sells** sth
▶ a dealer/ trader/ merchant/ retailer/ distributor/ wholesaler **buys** sth

dealer [C] 商人, 売買業者, ディーラー ◇She set up in business as an antiques *dealer*. 彼女は骨董商の事業を始めた ◇He's a ***dealer in*** second-hand cars. 彼は中古車のディーラーだ ❶dealerは絵画, 骨董品, 車, 武器の売買をする人によく用いられる. your dealerは物を最近購入した人に助言をする文脈でしばしば用いられる. ♦ Contact *your dealer* for more information. (詳細は取扱業者へお問い合わせください). ♦ Return the unit to *your dealer* for repair. (修理は取扱業者へ商品ごと返送ください). この場合のdealerは商品を販売するあらゆる企業[店]を指す. ❶(英)ではdealerは証券取引市場で通貨や株式などを売買する人を指すことが多い. ◇She's a *dealer* in the financial futures market. (英)彼女は金融先物取引市場のディーラーだ. (米)ではふつうtraderと言う. ☞ **dealing** (TRADE)

trader [C] 商人 ◇Many of the small local *traders* have been forced to close. 《特に英》地元の小規模な販売業者の多くが廃業を迫られている ◇Being a ***sole trader*** (= a person who runs a business on their own) is a risky venture. 《特に英》個人事業主になるのはリスクの高い企てだ ◇Numerous risks are taken every day by currency *traders*. 《特に米》為替トレーダーは毎日数多くのリスクを冒している ❶《英》ではtraderはさまざまな文脈で用いられる. small/local/independent traderは町で店を自営する人. market/street traderは通り・市場で食べ物・日用品を売買する人.《米》でcurrency/bond/commodity traderは証券取引市場で通貨・株式などを売買する人を指す.《英》ではdealerを用いる. ☞ **trade, trading** (TRADE)

supplier [C] 製品製造[供給]業者, 納入業者 ◇They are a leading *supplier* of computers in the UK. その会社はイギリスにおけるコンピューターの大手メーカーだ ◇You will need to be able to deal with both customers and *suppliers*. 顧客と製造業者の両方に対応できるようにならなければならない

seller [C] 販売人, 売り手 ◇The law is intended to protect both the buyer and the *seller*. その法律は買い手と売り手の双方を保護することを目的としている ◇She stopped to buy a bunch of violets from a flower *seller* in the market square. 市場で花売りから一束のスミレを買うために彼女は立ち止まった

merchant [C] （大掛かりな売買をする）商人, 貿易商 ◇Venice was once a city of rich *merchants*. ヴェニスはかつて裕福な商人の町だった ◇He was the eldest son of a wealthy wine *merchant*. 彼は裕福なワイン商人の長男だ

retailer [C] 《特に書き言葉》（一般の消費者に物を売る）小売業者 ◇They are one of the country's largest food *retailers*. その店は国内最大の食料品小売業者の一つだ

vendor [C] （街頭で食料・新聞などを売る）商人, 露天商人 ◇Jewellery, leather and clothes are offered by street *vendors* at every corner. あちこちで露天商人が宝石や革製品, 衣服を売っている ❶法律用語ではvendorは家などの不動産を販売する人を指す. ♦ The cost to the *vendor* of selling land by auction is normally higher than by private treaty. （オークションで土地の売り主に支払う金額はふつう当事者売買より高い).《米》ではvendorはsupplierと同じ意味で用いられることもある. ♦ Get a list of *vendors* who deliver frozen food. （冷凍食品を配達する供給業者の一覧を入手してください).

distributor [C] （店に物を供給する）卸売業者, 配給業者 ◇They are Japan's largest software *distributor*. その会社は日本最大のソフトウェアの卸売業者だ

📝 **supplier** と **distributor** の使い分け：supplier は distributor よりも使用範囲が広い. supplier は商品を企業や店に販売する業者, 商品を製造する会社つまりメーカー, メーカーに原料を販売する会社を指す. distributor はメーカーが製造した商品を購入し小売店に販売する業者. また, supplier とも distributor ともいえる会社もある. 自社の商品を売るメーカーは自らを商品を売る distributor と見なすこともあるし, メーカーから購入する企業はそのメーカーを原料や装置を供給する supplier と見なすこともある.

wholesaler [C] （大量の物を仕入れて転売して利益を出す）卸売業者, 問屋 ◇The majority of stock is bought through *wholesalers*, before being repackaged for retailing to the public. 一般消費者への小売用に包装される直す前に, 仕入れ品の多くは卸売業者を通して購入される

shopkeeper [C] （小さな）店を営む人, （小売）店主 ◇the village *shopkeeper* 村で店を営む人

deal with sb/sth 句動詞

deal with sb/sth・handle・take care of sth・look after sth・contend with sb/sth・see to sth
仕事に関わる問題を取り仕切る
【類語訳】解決する, 取り扱う, 管理する, 責任がある, 処理する, 面倒を見る, 引き受ける

[文型&コロケーション]

▶ to deal with/ handle sth **with** ease, assurance, etc.
▶ to deal with/ handle/ take care of/ look after/ see to **the matter**
▶ to deal with/ handle/ take care of/ look after/ contend with **a problem**
▶ to deal with/ handle/ take care of/ look after the **correspondence/ paperwork/ customers**
▶ to **have sth to** deal with/ contend with/ attend to
▶ to deal with/ handle/ look after sb/ sth **properly**
▶ to deal with/ handle/ take care of sth **easily**

'**deal with sb/sth** 句動詞 対処する, 処理する ◇There are various possible ways of *dealing with* this problem. この問題を処理するにはさまざまな方法が可能だ

↳ **deal with sb/sth**　　**dear, debate**

◇My job is to *deal with* enquiries from the public. 私の仕事は一般の人からの問い合わせに対応することです ◇She smiled the same smile she used when *dealing with* difficult customers. 彼女は厄介な客を相手にするときの笑顔と同じ笑顔を見せた ◇He's good at *dealing with* pressure. 彼はプレッシャーを上手に処理する

handle [他] 扱う, 処理する ◇We can *handle* up to 500 calls an hour at our new offices. 新しいオフィスでは1時間に500本までの電話に対処することができる ◇She's very good at *handling* patients. 彼女は患者を扱うのがとても上手だ ◇We all have to learn to *handle* stress. 私たちは皆ストレスの対処法を身につける必要がある ◇The matter has been *handled* very badly. その問題への対応は非常にまずかった ◇'Any problems?' '*Nothing I can't handle.*' 《インフォーマル》「何か問題でも」「私の手に負えない問題なんてないよ」
▶**handling** [名] [U] ◇I was impressed by his *handling* of the situation. 私は彼の状況への対処の仕方に感動した ◇This horse needs firm *handling*. この馬はしっかりとした手綱さばきが必要だ

ノート **deal with** と **handle** の使い分け：handle はしばしば感情を抑えて, 問題に対応することができる (capable of handling, can handle) ことを表す. deal with はふつうてきぱきしたやり方 (ways, methods, means) で問題を処理することを表す.

take care of sth [フレーズ] 責任を持って引き受ける, 処理する ◇Don't worry about the travel arrangements. They're all being *taken care of*. 旅行の手配については心配しないで. すべてやっていますから ◇Celia *takes care of* the marketing side of things. セリアはマーケティング的な側面を担当している

,look 'after sth [句動詞] 《特に英, ややフォーマル》責任を持つ, 担当する ◇I'm *looking after* his affairs while he's in hospital. 彼の入院中は私が彼の案件の担当をしています ◇She also *looks after* quality control. 彼女は品質管理も担当しています ❶look after は特に人の経済面の面倒を見たり, 特定業務を担当する場合に用いられる.

con'tend with sb/sth [句動詞] （問題[困難な状況]に）対処する ◇Nurses often have to *contend with* violent or drunken patients. 看護師は暴力的な患者や酔っ払った患者をしばしば相手にしなければならない ◇He had troubles enough of his own to *contend with*. 彼は対処しなければならない自分自身の問題をたくさん抱えていた ❶contend with は人が自分の置かれた状況に対処しなければならないので, have to contend with sth や have sth to contend with の形で用いられる. 自らすすんで contend with することはない. ✗ Don't worry — I'll *contend with* it.

'see to sth [句動詞] 《話し言葉》 取り計らう, 引き受ける ◇Will you *see to* the arrangements for the next meeting? 次回の会議の準備をやってもらえますか ◇Don't worry — *I'll see to it*. 心配しなくていい—私が責任を持つから ◇We'll have to get that door *seen to* (= repaired). 《英》あのドアを見てもらわないといけない

dear [形]

dear・beloved・precious・prized・cherished・darling・treasured・much loved
物事や人が人にとってとても大切なことを表す
【類語訳】いとしい, 大切な, 最愛の, 大人気の, 貴重な, 大事な

文型&コロケーション
▶beloved/ prized/ cherished/ treasured/ much loved **by** sb
▶dear/ precious **to** sb
▶a/ sb's dear/ beloved/ cherished/ darling/ much loved **friend**
▶a/ sb's dear/ beloved/ darling/ much loved **daughter/ son**
▶a prized/ cherished/ treasured/ much loved **possession**
▶a precious/ cherished/ treasured **memory**
▶dear/ darling **Henry/ Sarah**, etc.
▶**very** dear/ precious
▶**much** beloved/ prized/ cherished/ treasured/ loved

dear 《書き言葉 or やや古風》 いとしい, 大切な ◇He's one of my *dearest* friends. 彼は私の親友の一人です ◇They lost everything that was *dear* to them. 彼らは大切なものをすべて失った ❶dear は話し言葉で用いられるとやや古くさく, 書き言葉で用いられるとやや文語的な響きがある. 日常語として用いるなら one of my closest/best friends や, everything that is important/special to me のほうが普通. ☞ **dear** (DARLING)

beloved 《フォーマル》 最愛の；大人気の ◇in memory of our dearly *beloved* son, John 我々の親愛なる最愛の息子ジョンを追悼して ◇They were glad to be back in their *beloved* Ireland. 彼らは愛するアイルランドに戻ることができて喜んだ ◇the deep purple flowers so *beloved* by artists 画家たちに大変愛された濃い紫色の花々 ☞ **beloved** (DARLING)

precious いとしい, 大切な, 貴重な ◇My family is the most *precious* thing I have in my life. 人生の中で家族が一番大切だ ◇They managed to salvage a few *precious* possessions from the fire. 彼らはどうにかこうにか火災からいくつかの貴重品を運び出すことができた

prized [名詞の前で] 貴重な, 大切な, 大事な ◇I lost some of my most *prized* possessions in the fire. 私は火事でかけがえのない大事な物をいくつか失った ❶prized は人ではなく物についてのみ用いられる. ✗ my *prized* daughter. ☞ **prize** (APPRECIATE)

cherished 大切な ◇her most *cherished* possession 彼女の最も大切な持ち物 ☞ **cherish** (APPRECIATE)

darling [名詞の前で] 《インフォーマル》 最愛の；いとしい ◇my *darling* daughter 私の最愛の娘 ◇'*Darling* Henry,' the letter began. 「いとしいヘンリー」でその手紙は始まっていた ❶darling は物ではなく人についてのみ用いられる. ✗ *darling* possessions/memories. ☞ **darling** (DARLING)

treasured 貴重な, 大切な ◇This ring is my most *treasured* possession. この指輪は私の一番大切な物です ❶treasured は人ではなく物についてのみ用いられる. ✗ my *treasured* daughter. ☞ **treasure** (APPRECIATE)

much loved とても大切な ◇the boys' *much loved* grandfather, James 少年が大好きなお祖父さんジェームズ ◇She is *much loved* in this town. 彼女はこの町で皆にとても好かれている

debate [名] ☞ ARGUMENT 1

debate・conflict・dispute・controversy・disagreement・difference・war・dissent・contention
人[団体, 国]同士の話し合い
【類語訳】討論, 討議, 議論, 対立, 論争, 異議, 言い争い

文型&コロケーション
▶a debate/ conflict/ a dispute/ controversy/ disagreement/

differences/ a war/ contention **about/ over/ between** sb/ sth
- to be **in** debate/ conflict/ dispute **with** sb/ sth
- (a) **serious** debate/ conflict/ dispute/ controversy/ disagreement/ differences/ dissent/ contention
- (a) **growing** debate/ conflict/ controversy/ differences/ dissent
- (an) **unresolved** debate/ conflict/ dispute/ differences
- a **bitter** debate/ conflict/ dispute/ controversy/ disagreement/ war
- (an) **internal** debate/ conflict/ dispute/ controversy/ disagreement/ differences/ dissent
- **open** debate/ conflict/ disagreement/ dissent
- (a) **political** debate/ conflict/ dispute/ controversy/ disagreement/ differences/ war/ dissent/ contention
- to **cause** debate/ conflict/ a dispute/ controversy/ dissent
- to **lead to/ avoid** debate/ conflict/ controversy/ a war
- to **resolve** a debate/ a conflict/ a dispute/ a controversy/ a disagreement/ sb's differences
- a **debate**/ conflict/ dispute/ controversy/ disagreement/ difference **arises**
- a conflict/ dispute/ controversy/ war **breaks out**
- a debate/ conflict/ dispute/ controversy **continues**

debate [C, U]《ふつうほめて》《異なる意見を出し合う有益で必要な》討論, 討議, 議論 ◇This accident has sparked off an intense *debate*. この事故は激しい議論を引き起こした ◇the current *debate* about tax 税に関する現在行われている討論 ◇There has been much *debate* on the issue of childcare. 保育の問題に関する討論が盛んに行われている ◇Whether he deserved what happened to him is *open to debate/a matter for debate* (= cannot be certain or decided yet). 彼に起こったことが本人にふさわしかったかどうかについては議論の余地がある

conflict [C, U]《やや堅く, ふつうよくない》《人・団体・国同士の》対立[抗争] ◇The violence was the result of political and ethnic *conflicts*. その暴力行為は政治的・民族的対立の結果であった ◇John often *comes into conflict* with his boss. ジョンはよく社長と衝突する

dispute [C, U]《二者の人・団体・国同士の》議論[不和]; 論争 ◇His job is to settle pay *disputes*. 彼の仕事は賃金紛争を解決することだ ◇The cause of the accident was still *in dispute* (= being argued about). 事故原因はまだ係争中だった ◇The matter was settled *beyond dispute* by the court judgment (= it could no longer be argued about). その問題は判決により議論の余地なく解決された ◇His theories are *open to dispute* (= can be disagreed with). 彼の理論は議論の余地がある ☞ **dispute** (DISAGREE)

ノート conflict と dispute の使い分け: conflict は一般に dispute よりも深刻な内容のものを指す. dispute は所有権・収入などに関する問題について用いられ, conflict はしばしば長期に及び, 権力・宗教などのより幅広い問題について用いられる.

controversy [U, C]《やや堅い》《公の》論争, 議論 ◇The President resigned amid continuing *controversy*. 論争が続く最中, 大統領が辞任した ◇A fierce *controversy* has broken out over the issue. その問題をめぐって激しい論争が巻き起こった

disagreement [U, C]《意見の》不一致[衝突] ◇*Disagreement* arose about exactly how to plan the show. ショーの具体的な構想に関して意見の衝突が起こった ◇They have had several *disagreements* with their neighbours. 彼らは何度か近所の人たちとの間で意見の衝突があった 反意 **agreement**, ☞ **disagree** (DISAGREE)

difference [C]《ややフォーマル》《意見の》不一致 ◇We *have our differences*, but she's still my sister. 私たちの意見は違うが彼女が私の妹であることに変わりはない ◇There was a *difference of opinion* over who had won. 誰が勝ったかについて意見の相違があった ☞ **differ** (DISAGREE) ❶ difference は怒りや言い争いは避けようとするけれども意見が合わない場合に用いられる. 実際に言い争いがあったのになかったように見せかけたいときに difference を用いて, There was an argument/a fight... のソフトな表現として There was a difference of opinion... が使える.

war [C, U]《複合語で》《団体・企業・国家間の》闘争[競争] ◇The US threatened a trade *war* with Europe after the breakdown of the talks. 協議が決裂した後, アメリカはヨーロッパとの貿易戦争の恐れを匂わせた ◇The country seemed at times to be close to class *war*. 時折その国は階級闘争寸前であるように思えた

dissent [U]《フォーマル》《公式見解に対する》異議[抗議] ◇The authorities continue their suppression of political *dissent*. 当局は政治的な反対意見の弾圧を続けている 反意 **assent** (APPROVAL)

contention [U]《フォーマル》《怒りを伴う》論争, 言い争い ◇One area of *contention* is the availability of nursery places. 論争の一つの争点は保育所の利用の可能性である ❶ a bone/point of contention は議論や意見の衝突における争点[論点]を意味する. ◆ Privatization of the health service remains a point of *contention*. (健康保険の民営化は依然として争点のまま解決されていない).

debt 名

debt・loss・liability・arrears・debit
金を借りている[失う]こと, 借りている[失った]金額
【類語訳】負債, 借金, 損失, 債務, 滞納金, 未納金, 借方

文型&コロケーション
- **in** debt/ arrears/ debit
- **heavy/ massive** debts/ losses
- **mortgage/ tax/ outstanding** debts/ liabilities/ arrears
- to **fall/ get into** debt/ arrears
- to **have** debts/ liabilities
- to **run up** debts/ losses
- to **pay off** debts/ arrears

debt [C, U] 負債; 借金 ◇She had run up credit card *debts* of thousands of dollars. 彼女はクレジットカードの負債が何千ドルもたまっていた ◇He died *heavily in debt*. 彼は膨大な借金を抱えて亡くなった ◇It's hard to *stay out of debt* when you are a student. 学生のときは借金をせずにいるのは困難だ

loss [C]《企業・組織の》損失(額) ◇The company has announced net *losses* of $1.5 million. 会社は150万ドルの純損失を公表した ◇We *made a loss on* (= lost money on) the deal. 我々はその取引で損失を出した ◇We are now operating *at a loss*. 今私たちは赤字で操業している 反意 **profit** (PROFIT), ☞ **gain** (INCREASE 名), **loss-making** (LOSS-MAKING)

liability [C, ふつう複数で]《金融》(人・会社の)負債金額, 債務 ◇The company is reported to have *liabilities* of

↪**debt**

decide, declare

nearly $90,000. その会社は9万ドルに近い負債を抱えていると報じられている ◇Our financial advisers will concentrate on minimizing your tax *liabilities* and maximizing your income. 当社のフィナンシャル・アドバイザーは貴社の税負担を最小にして収益を最大にすることに専念いたします 反意 **asset** (THING 2)

arrears [複数形]《(フォーマル or 金融)》滞納金, 未納金 ◇Unions are demanding the settlement of pay *arrears*. 組合は給料の未払金の解決を要求している ❶be in arrears または get/fall into arrears は「金の支払いが遅れている」ことを表す. ◆Our tenants have fallen into *arrears* with their rent. (私たちの借家人は家賃を滞納している). また, be paid in arrears は人・金を主語にして給料などが「後払いで支払われる」ことを意味する. ◆You will be paid monthly in *arrears*. (給与は毎月後払いで支払われます).

debit [C] 《金融》借方 ; (口座からの)引出金額 ◇This expenditure should all be shown on the *debit* side of the account. この支払いはすべて借方欄に示されるはずだ ◇If the *debits* exceed the credits you're in trouble. もし支払い額が入金額を超過すると困ったことになるよ 反意 **credit** ❶ credit は「銀行口座に振り込まれる金額」, または「振り込み記録」を意味する. ☞ **credit** (LOAN), **debit** (DISCOUNT)

decide 動

decide・choose・determine・make up your mind・elect・resolve
どうすべきかについてよく考え, 実行可能な事柄を選択する
【類語訳】決める, 決定する, 選ぶ, 選択する, 決心する

文型&コロケーション

▶ to decide/ determine/ resolve **on** sth
▶ to decide/ choose/ determine/ make up your mind/ elect/ resolve **to do** sth
▶ to decide/ determine/ resolve **that**...
▶ to decide/ choose/ make up your mind **whether/ what/ how**...
▶ to **be free to** decide/ choose/ determine
▶ to **be difficult to** decide/ make your mind up
▶ to **eventually/ consciously** decide/ choose/ resolve
▶ to **finally** decide/ make up your mind/ resolve

decide [自, 他] 決める, 決定する ◇It's up to you to *decide*. あなた次第で決まります ◇They *decided against* taking legal action. 彼らは法的措置を取らないことに決めた ◇We've *decided* not to go away after all. 結局私たちは出かけないことに決めた ◇I can't *decide* what to do. 何をすべきか決められない ◇I can't tell you what to do — you'll have to *decide for yourself*. どうしたらいいかは言えない—君が自分で決めないと ◇*It was decided (that)* the school should purchase new software. 学校では新しいソフトウェアを購入することが決定された ◇We might be hiring new people but nothing has been *decided* yet. 新しく人を雇うかもしれないが, まだ何も決まっていない ☞ **decide** (CHOOSE), **undecided** (UNSURE)
▷ **decision** 名 [C, U] ◇to *make a decision* (= to decide) 決定を下す ◇to *take a decision* 《英》決定を下す ◇We need a *decision on* this by next week. 私たちは来週までにこれに関しての判断が必要だ ◇We finally *reached a decision* (= decided after some difficulty). 私たちはついに決定に至った ◇a big (= important) *decision* 重大な決断 ◇The moment of *decision* had arrived. 決断の時が来ていた

choose [自] 選ぶ, 選択する ◇Employees can retire at 60 *if they choose*. 従業員たちはもしそうしたいならば, 60歳で退職することができる ◇Many people *choose* not to marry. 多くの人が結婚しないことを選んでいる ☞ **choice** (OPTION)

determine [他, 自]《(フォーマル)》(正式に)決定する[取り決める] ; …することを固く決心する ◇A date for the meeting has yet to be *determined*. 会議の日取りはまだ決まっていない ◇As she walked home, she *determined* to speak to her boss the next day. 家へ歩いて帰りながら, 彼女は翌日上司に話そうと固く決心した ◇The government *determined* on a change of policy. 政府は政策の変更を決定した

make up your 'mind (または **make up your 'mind up**) (よく考えた末に)固い決心をする ◇I couldn't *make up my mind about* the new job. 私は新しい仕事について考えを固めることができなかった ◇He had clearly *made up his mind* to leave. 彼ははっきりと辞める決心をしていた ◇You'll never persuade him to stay — *his mind's made up*. 決して彼に留まるよう説得できない—彼の気持ちは固まっているから

elect [他]《(ふつう elect to do sth の形で)》《(フォーマル)》(指示・強制によらずに)…することを選ぶ ◇Increasing numbers of people *elect* to work from home nowadays. 近頃自宅で仕事することを選ぶ人の数が増えている

resolve [自]《(ややフォーマル, 書き言葉)》…することを固く決心する ; (会議などで投票により)決定に至る ◇We had *resolved* on making an early start. 早く始めることに決めていた ◇She *resolved* that she would never see him again. 彼女は彼に二度と会わないと固く決心した ◇The Supreme Council *resolved* to resume control over the press. 最高評議会は報道に対する規制の再開を決定した
▷ **resolution** 名 [C] ◇She *made a resolution* to visit her relatives more often. 彼女はもっと頻繁に親戚に会いに行くことに決めた ◇The UN Security Council unanimously adopted a *resolution* calling for a halt to hostilities. 国連安全保障理事会は満場一致で戦闘の停止を求める決議を採択した

declare 動 ☞ SAY 2

declare・state・indicate・announce・proclaim・pronounce
公の場で毅然と明確に述べる
【類語訳】宣言する, 明言する, 断言する, 表明する, 公表する, 宣告する

文型&コロケーション

▶ to declare/ state/ indicate/ announce/ proclaim/ pronounce sth **to sb**
▶ to declare/ state/ indicate/ announce/ proclaim/ pronounce **that**...
▶ **It** was declared/ stated/ indicated/ announced/ proclaimed **that**...
▶ to declare/ state/ proclaim/ pronounce sb/ sth **to be** sth
▶ to declare/ state/ indicate/ announce/ proclaim your **intention to do** sth
▶ to declare/ state/ indicate/ announce your **support**
▶ to declare/ state/ announce/ proclaim/ pronounce sth **formally/ officially**

▶to declare/ state/ announce/ proclaim sth **publicly/ proudly/ boldly**
▶to declare/ state/ announce/ pronounce sth **confidently/ firmly**

declare [他]《ややフォーマル》宣言する；明言[断言]する
◇Germany *declared war* on France on 1 August 1914. 1914年8月1日ドイツはフランスに対して宣戦布告した ◇The president *declared* a state of emergency. 大統領は緊急事態を宣言した ◇The court *declared* that strike action was illegal. 裁判所はそのストライキ行動は違法であると宣した ◇The painting was *declared* to be a forgery. その絵画は偽造であると断言された ◇The area has been *declared* a national park. その地域は正式に国立公園とされている ◇I *declare* this bridge open. この橋の開通を宣言します ☞ **declaration** (STATEMENT)

state [他]《ややフォーマル》明言する，表明する ◇The facts are clearly *stated* in the report. それらの事実は報告書に明記されている ◇There is no need to *state the obvious* (= to say sth that everyone already knows). わかりきったことを言う必要はない ◇*State* clearly how many tickets you require. 必要なチケットの枚数をはっきりと指定してください ☞ **statement** (STATEMENT)

indicate [他]《ややフォーマル，特に話し言葉 or ジャーナリズム》（やや間接的に）述べる，示す ◇As I've already *indicated* to you, what we do next depends on a number of factors. 既に君に言ったとおり，次にすべきことは多くの要因によって変わってくるよ ◇During our meeting, he *indicated* his willingness to cooperate. 会合の席で，彼は協力する意思をほのめかした ☞ **indication** (SIGN 1), **indicate** (SHOW 1), **indicate** (SUGGEST)

announce [他]（決定・計画など）を公表する；（拡声器を通して）アナウンスする；（大声で[厳粛に]）言う ◇They haven't formally *announced* their engagement yet. 彼らはまだ正式には婚約を発表していない ◇Has our flight been *announced* yet? 私たちの乗る便はもうアナウンスされましたか ◇'I've given up smoking,' she *announced*.「タバコはやめました」と彼女は宣言した ☞ **announcement** (STATEMENT)

[ノート] **declare** と **announce** の使い分け：**declare** は「判断を下す」場合に，**announce** は「事実を提供する」場合によく用いられる。×The painting was *announced* to be a forgery. ×They haven't formally *declared* their engagement yet.

proclaim [他]《ややフォーマル》公言する，宣言する ◇The charter *proclaimed* that all states would have their own government. 憲章にはすべての州が独自の自治政府を持つことがうたわれていた ◇He *proclaimed* himself emperor. 彼は自らが皇帝であることを宣言した ❶*proclaim* はしばしば全員に影響を及ぼすようなことを権力者が発言する場合に用いられる。*proclaim* される状況はふつう好ましいものとして提示される。

pronounce [他]《フォーマル》宣告する，申し渡す ◇The judge will *pronounce sentence* today. 裁判官は今日判決を言い渡す予定だ ◇I now *pronounce* you man and wife (= in a marriage ceremony). 今ここにあなた方を夫婦と宣言します ◇She was *pronounced* dead on arrival at the hospital. 病院に着くと同時に彼女は死亡と告された

decorate [動]

decorate • adorn • garnish • illustrate • edge • hang • festoon • deck • ornament • trim
飾りを付けて物をより見栄えよくする
[類語訳] 飾る，装飾する，付け合わせる，縁取る，縁飾りをする

[文型&コロケーション]
▶to decorate/ adorn/ garnish/ illustrate/ edge/ hang/ festoon/ deck/ ornament/ trim sth **with** sth
▶to decorate/ festoon/ deck sth **in** sth
▶**richly** decorated/ adorned/ ornamented

decorate [他]（見栄えよくするために）飾る，装飾する ◇They *decorated* the room with flowers and balloons. 彼らは部屋を花や風船で飾りつけた ◇The cake was *decorated* to look like a car. そのケーキは車に見えるように飾りつけられていた ◇Photographs of actors *decorated* the walls of the restaurant. 何枚もの俳優の写真がレストランの壁を飾っていた

adorn [他，しばしば受身で]《フォーマル》（見栄えよくするために）飾る，装飾する ◇The walls were *adorned* with paintings. 壁は絵で飾られていた

garnish [他]（料理に）付け合わせる ◇*Garnish* the chicken with almonds. チキンにアーモンドを添えましょう ◇soup *garnished* with croutons クルトンで付け合わせたスープ

illustrate [他，ふつう受身で]（絵・写真・図などを）用いる，添える，入れる ◇a beautifully *illustrated* book きれいに挿絵が入った本 ◇His lecture was *illustrated* with slides taken during the expedition. 彼の講義には調査旅行の間に撮られたスライド写真が彩りを添えた

edge [他，ふつう受身で] 縁に飾りを付ける，縁取る ◇The handkerchief was *edged* with lace. そのハンカチはレースで縁取りされていた

hang [他，ふつう受身で]《with と共に》（壁に絵画などを）掛ける ◇The room was *hung* with tapestries. その部屋はタペストリーが壁に飾られていた

festoon [他，ふつう受身で]《文語》（お祝いの一環として）花[電飾，色紙]で飾る ◇The streets were *festooned* with banners and lights. 通りは旗や電飾で飾られていた

deck [他，ふつう受身で]（カラフルなもので）飾る ◇The Conservative candidate and his supporters were *decked* in blue rosettes. 保守党の立候補者とその支持者たちは青のバラ飾りを付けていた ◇The room was *decked out* in flowers and balloons. 部屋は花や風船で飾られていた ❶ふつう **deck** は **decked (out) in/with** sth の形でのみ用いられる。能動態は文語あるいは詩的文脈でのみ用いられる。 ◆*Deck* the halls with boughs of holly!（ホールをヒイラギの大枝で飾りましょう；クリスマスの歌の句）

ornament [他，ふつう受身で]《フォーマル》（物に）装飾を加える ◇The room was richly *ornamented* with carving. その部屋は彫刻で豪華に飾り立てられていた

trim (-mm-) [他，ふつう受身で]（衣類の縁に）飾りを付ける，縁飾りをする ◇She wore gloves *trimmed* with fur. 彼女は毛皮の縁取りがされた手袋をしていた

▶**trimming** [名] [U, C, ふつう複数で] a white blouse with navy-blue *trimming* ネイビーブルーの縁取りがされた白のブラウス

decoration 名

decoration • accessory • ornament • frills • finery • garnish

飾るために物に添えられる物
【類語訳】装飾物, 付属品, アクセサリー, 飾り, 宝飾品

文型&コロケーション
- without decoration/ frills
- little/ no decoration/ ornament
- few/ no accessories/ frills
- personal decoration/ ornament/ finery

decoration [C, U] 装飾; 装飾様式 ◇We admired the elaborate *decorations* on the carved wooden door. 私たちは彫刻を施した木製のドアの手の込んだ装飾に見とれた ◇They chose a Chinese theme in the interior *decoration*. 彼らは中国風のインテリア装飾を選んだ

accessory [C, ふつう複数で] 付属品, (ベルト・バッグなどを含む)アクセサリー ◇We stock a large range of bicycle *accessories*. 当店は自転車の付属品を幅広く取りそろえております ◇Why not invest in some *fashion accessories* to dress up your wardrobe? 持ち衣装をおしゃれに見せるファッションアクセサリーをいくつか奮発してみたらどう

ornament [U] (フォーマル) 装飾 ◇The clock is simply for *ornament* — it doesn't work any more. その時計は単なる飾りだよ—もう動かないんだ

frills [複数で] 《否定文で》(なくてもかまわない)飾り ◇It was a simple meal, with no *frills*. それは飾り気のない質素な食事だった

finery [U] 《書き言葉》(特別なとき用の)華やかで豪華な衣服 [宝飾品] ◇The mayor was dressed in all his *finery*. 市長は豪華な装いに身を包んでいた

garnish [C, U] (料理の)付け合わせ ◇Add a *garnish* of tomato. トマトの付け合わせを加えましょう ◇Keep some olives to one side for *garnish*. 付け合わせ用にオリーブをいくつか片側に置いておきましょう

deep 形

1 deep • sincere • real • genuine • heartfelt • from the heart • wholehearted

感情や信じる気持ちの強さを表す
【類語訳】心からの, 真摯な, 本気の, 偽りのない, 誠実な, 信頼できる, 全身全霊の

文型&コロケーション
- sincere/ genuine **about** sth
- deep/ sincere/ real/ genuine/ heartfelt **sympathy/ concern**
- deep/ sincere/ real/ genuine **affection/ respect/ regret**
- a deep/ real/ genuine **sense of** sth
- sincere/ heartfelt **thanks/ apologies**
- a sincere/ genuine **attempt** (to do sth)
- a sincere/ genuine **person**
- very deep/ real/ sincere/ genuine
- really/ completely sincere/ genuine

deep 心からの, 真摯な ◇He expressed *deep* concern over the government's handling of the incident. 彼は政府のその事件への対応に強い関心を示した ◇I felt a *deep* sense of loss when I heard of her death. 彼女の死を知らされたとき私は深い喪失感を覚えた
▶ **deeply** 副 ◇They were *deeply* disturbed by the accident. 彼らはその事故でひどく動揺していた

sincere 心からの, 真摯な ◇Please accept our *sincere* apologies. 心よりお詫び申し上げます ◇I would like to express my *sincere* gratitude for your care and concern during this past week. この1週間お心遣いをいただき深く感謝いたします 反意 **insincere**
▶ **sincerely** 副 ◇I *sincerely* believe that this is the right decision. これは正しい決断であると心から信じています

real (感情・態度が)本気の ◇I had no *real* interest in politics. 私は政治に真剣に興味を持ってはいなかった ◇She was making a *real* effort to be nice to her. 彼女は一生懸命彼女にやさしくしていた

genuine (人・感情・意図が)偽りのない, 誠実な; 信頼できる ◇She always showed *genuine* concern for others. 彼女はいつも他人に偽りのない心遣いを示した ◇He came across as a very *genuine* person. 彼はとても誠実な人だという印象を与えた 反意 **forced**
▶ **genuinely** 副 ◇He seemed *genuinely* sorry for what had happened. 彼は起こったことを本当に気の毒に思っているようだった

ノート **sincere** と **genuine** の使い分け: 多くの場合両語とも使用可能。しかしながら, sincere は自分自身の感情や意図について用いられ, genuine は人の感情や意図に関する判断を表すのに用いられる傾向が強い。 ♦ She insisted that they were making a *sincere* attempt to resolve the problem. (彼女は彼らがその問題の解決を本気で試みようとしていると主張した)。 ♦ He made a *genuine* attempt to improve conditions. (彼は状況を改善しようと本気で試みた)。 ×Please accept our *genuine* apologies.

heartfelt [ふつう名詞の前で] 心からの ◇She made a *heartfelt* plea for her son to give himself up. 彼女は息子に降服するよう心から呼びかけた ◇Christina breathed a *heartfelt* sigh of relief. クリスティーナは心から安堵のため息をついた

from the (bottom of your) 'heart 〔行句〕 心からの, 心の底からの ◇I beg you, *from the bottom of my heart*, to spare his life. 心からのお願いです。彼の命を助けてやってください ◇It was clearly an offer that came *from the heart*. それは明らかに心からの申し出だった

wholehearted (ほめて) 真心のこもった, 全身全霊の ◇The plan was given *wholehearted* support. その計画は全面的な支持を受けた
▶ **wholeheartedly** 副 ◇I *wholeheartedly* agree with you. 心からあなたに賛成します

2 deep • low • rich • bass • sonorous • full • resounding

声や音が高くなく[静かで]よく響くことを表す
【類語訳】(声が)太い, 低音の, (音が)低い, 朗々とした, バスの, 響き渡る, 鳴り響く

文型&コロケーション
- a deep/ low/ rich/ bass/ sonorous/ full **voice**
- a deep/ low/ rich/ bass/ full/ resounding **sound**
- a deep/ low **groan/ roar/ rumble**
- a deep/ resounding **thud/ thump/ thwack**

defeat

deep (声が)男性のような, 太い; (音が)低音階の, 低い ◇I heard his *deep* warm voice filling the room. 彼の低く暖かい声が部屋中に響き渡るのが聞こえた ◇We heard a *deep* roar in the distance. 遠くで低いうなり声が聞こえた 反意 **high** (HIGH 3)

low (音が)低音の, 低い; (声が)静かで低い, 男性のような ◇The cello is *lower* than the violin. チェロはバイオリンよりも低音だ ◇They were speaking in *low* voices. 彼らは小声で話していた 反意 **high** (HIGH 3)

ノート **deep** と **low** の使い分け: low は静かな声・音を表すが、高くか低いかを表すことができない。音階について言うときのみ low は大きな音でも静かな音でも用いることができる。deep は大きな声・音にも、静かな声・音にも用いることができる。音階については deep は非常に低いことを表す。

rich 《ほめて》(歌声・音が)太くてよく響く, 朗々とした ◇Her *rich* contralto voice filled the concert hall. 彼女のよく響くコントラルトの声がコンサートホールに鳴り響いた ❶ *rich* は話す声ではなく、ふつう歌声に用いられる

bass 《音楽》(声・楽器・音楽が)低音の, バスの ◇He was musically talented, with a fine *bass* voice. 彼は音楽的才能があり美しい低音の声を持っていた ◇a *bass* drum ベース・ドラム ❶ bass は low や deep より以上に, 歌声に関する専門的な語 反意 **treble** (HIGH 3)

sonorous 《フォーマル, ほめて》(声・音が)よく響く ◇Her clear, *sonorous* voice is perfect for opera. 彼女の澄んでいてよく響く声はオペラにうってつけだ
▶ **sonorously** 副

full 《ほめて》(音が)豊かな, よく響く ◇He draws a unique *full* sound from the instrument. 彼はその楽器で独特な豊かな響きの音を奏でる

resounding 《名詞の前で》《書き言葉》(音が)響き渡る, 鳴り響く ◇The boulder hit the ground with a *resounding* thud. 巨石がドシーンと音を鳴り響かせて地面に落ちた

defeat 動 ☞ WIN

defeat・beat・overcome・vanquish・get the better of sb・rout・trounce・best・prevail・thrash
スポーツ[コンテスト, 争い]で人に勝つ
【類語訳】勝つ, 打ち負かす, 優勢になる, 完勝する, 大勝する, 楽勝する

get the better of sb	defeat	vanquish
best	beat	rout
prevail	overcome	trounce
		thrash

文型&コロケーション
▶ to defeat/ beat/ rout/ trounce/ thrash sb **by** 10 points/ 4 goals, etc.
▶ to defeat/ beat/ overcome/ vanquish/ get the better of/ rout/ trounce/ thrash an **opponent**
▶ to defeat/ beat/ overcome/ vanquish/ trounce a **rival**
▶ to defeat/ beat/ vanquish a **foe**
▶ to **finally** defeat/ beat/ overcome/ get the better of/ rout sb
▶ to **totally** defeat/ overwhelm/ thrash sb
▶ to **easily** defeat/ beat/ overcome sb

defeat [他]《特に書き言葉》(戦争・競争・スポーツ・投票で)勝つ, 打ち負かす ◇The English were *heavily defeated* here by the Scots in 1314. 1314年イングランドはここでスコットランドに惨敗した ◇He *defeated* the champion in three sets. 彼は3セットでチャンピオンを打ち破った ◇The government was *defeated* by 200 votes to 83. 政権与党は200票対83票で敗北した
▶ **defeat** 名 [C, U] ◇The battle ended in humiliating *defeat*. 戦闘は屈辱的敗北に終わった ◇He was gracious *in defeat*, acknowledging his opponent's greater skill. 相手の技術のほうがすごいことを認め、彼は敗北しても潔かった ◇The Prime Minister *conceded defeat* and resigned. 首相は敗北を認めて辞任した ◇They finally had to *admit defeat* (= stop trying to be successful). 彼らはついに負けを認めざるを得なかった 反意 **victory** (VICTORY), ☞ **defeat** (VICTORY)

beat [他]《特に話し言葉》(スポーツ・ゲーム・選挙・戦争で)勝つ, 打ち負かす ◇He *beat* me *at* chess. 彼はチェスで私を打ち負かした ◇He was *beaten* into second place by the American. 彼はアメリカの選手に負けて準優勝に終わった ◇She *beat* him *hands down* (= easily). 彼女は彼に楽勝した ◇Their recent wins have proved that they're still *the ones to beat* (= the most difficult team to beat). 彼らの最近の勝利は彼らがいまだに最強であることを証明している

ノート **defeat** と **beat** の使い分け: defeat は特定の競争, 戦いにおいて一人[一団体]の相手に勝利する場合によく用いられる。◆He *defeated* the incumbent president. (彼は現職大統領を打ち負かした). beat はゲーム, 競争, レースにおいて一人[一団体]の相手または複数の相手に勝利する場合に用いられる。◆She won the 100 metres, *beating* a number of top Europeans. (たくさんのヨーロッパのトップ選手を打ち破り、彼女は100メートル走で優勝した). beat は日常的な話し言葉で、defeat は書き言葉で使われることが多い。

overcome [他]《書き言葉》(難敵に)打ち勝つ ◇She *overcame* strong opposition to take the title. 彼女は強敵に打ち勝ってタイトルを獲得した ◇In the final, Sweden easily *overcame* France. 決勝戦でスウェーデンがフランスに快勝した

vanquish [他]《文語》(戦争・競争で)完全に打ち負かす ◇Government forces *vanquished* the rebels. 政府軍が反乱軍を制圧した

get the better of sb [自]《闘い・議論・競争で》打ち負かす, 優勢になる ◇No one can *get the better of* her in an argument. 議論で彼女の右に出る者はいない

rout [他]《書き言葉》(戦い・競争で)完全に打ち負かす ◇The Royalist forces were *routed*. 王党派の軍は完敗した
▶ **rout** 名 [単数で] ◇The offensive into rebel-held territory had ended in a *rout*. 反政府支配下の領地への攻撃は大敗に終わっていた

trounce [他]《書き言葉》(スポーツで)完勝[大勝]する ◇Brazil *trounced* Italy 5-1 in the final. 決勝戦でブラジルはイタリアに5対1で大勝した

best [他, ふつう受け身で]《フォーマル》打ち負かす, 優勢になる ◇A great colonial power was nearly *bested* by a few farmers. 強大な植民地政権が数名の農場主に危うく打ち負かされそうになった

prevail [自]《フォーマル》(長い戦いの末)打ち勝つ ◇Ultimately, Rome *prevailed over* her neighbours. 最終的にローマ帝国は近隣諸国を征服した ◇In a one-sided fi-

↪**defeat**

nal, Spain *prevailed against* title-holder Croatia 40-34. 一方的な展開の決勝戦で、スペインは前回優勝国のクロアチアを40対34で打ち破った ☞ **prevail** (WIN)

thrash [他]《特に英, インフォーマル》(スポーツ・ゲームで)楽勝[快勝]する ◇They were *thrashed* 5-0 in the League. 彼らはリーグの試合で5対0で完敗した

defect [名]

defect・fault・flaw・virus・bug・glitch・imperfection
物や事の(作られ方)に不備があり、完璧で[適切に機能し]ないこと
【類語訳】欠陥, 異常, 不具合, 不備, ウイルス, 不調, 難点

[文型&コロケーション]
▶ a defect/ a fault/ a flaw/ a virus/ a bug/ a glitch/ an imperfection **in** sth
▶ a **small/ minor** defect/ fault/ flaw/ bug/ glitch/ imperfection
▶ a **major/ serious** defect/ fault/ flaw
▶ a **temporary** fault/ flaw/ glitch
▶ a **technical/ mechanical** defect/ fault/ flaw/ glitch
▶ a **structural/ design** defect/ fault/ flaw
▶ a **computer/ software** fault/ virus/ bug/ glitch
▶ to **have** a defect/ a fault/ a flaw/ a virus/ a bug/ a glitch/ an imperfection
▶ to **detect** a defect/ fault/ flaw/ virus
▶ to **look for/ discover** a defect/ fault/ flaw/ bug
▶ to **identify/ correct** a defect/ fault/ flaw

defect [C] (機械・システム・体の)欠陥, 異常 ◇The manufacturer is responsible for any *defects* that may cause damage. 製造者は被害を引き起こす可能性のあるいかなる欠陥に対しても責任がある ◇Vulnerable people are going short of money because of *defects* in the payment system. 賃金体系の欠陥により、その影響を受けやすい人が資金不足になりつつある ◇The drug is widely known to cause **birth** *defects*. その薬は先天性異常を引き起こすことで広く知られている

fault [C] (機械・システムなどの)欠陥, 不具合 ◇The book's virtues far outweigh its *faults*. その本の長所はその欠点よりはるかに勝る ◇There seemed to be some *fault* **with** the cooling system. 冷却装置に何らかの不具合がありそうだった ◇The healthcare system, *for all its faults*, is far better than ever before. 欠陥はあるけれども医療制度は以前よりはるかによくなっている ◇The fire was caused by an electrical *fault*. 火事の原因は電気系統の不良だった ◇If a *fault* develops in the equipment, you can call us 24 hours a day. 機器の不具合が発生したときには、24時間いつでもお電話ください

[ノート] **defect** と **fault** の使い分け：多くの場合両語とも使用可能。◆ a technical/mechanical/structural/design *defect*/*fault* (技術/機械/構造/設計の欠陥)。 *fault* は常に人が作った物に潜む欠陥について用い、ずっと続くものか一時的なもの、最初から後から発生したものかは問われない。**defect** は体の一部について用いられる場合、これは必ず先天的なものを言う。◆ birth/congenital/genetic *defects* (先天的/遺伝的異常など)。◆ birth/congenital/genetic *faults*. **defect** はどんな種類の欠陥も最初から[先天的に]あるもので、後から発生したものではない。修理は可能だが、「欠陥」は進行するものでもなく一時的なものでもない。

でもない。× If a *defect* develops in the equipment... × We're hoping this is just a temporary *defect*.

flaw [C] 欠陥, 不備 ◇There are some very basic *flaws* in his argument. 彼の論法には非常に基本的な不備がいくつかある ◇Engineers have detected serious design *flaws*. 技術者は重大な設計上の欠陥を発見した
▷ **flawed** [形] ◇a *flawed* argument 不備のある論

virus [C] (コンピューターの)ウイルス ◇Most *viruses* can only **spread** if you open an email attachment. たいていのウイルスはEメールの添付ファイルを開いた場合にのみ感染する ◇My computer has **caught** some kind of *virus*, and it won't let me log on to the Internet. 私のコンピューターは何らかのウイルスに感染していてインターネットにログオンできない ◇*anti-virus* software (= software that finds and destroys viruses in a computer system) ウイルス駆除ソフト

bug [C] 《ややインフォーマル》(コンピューターのプログラム・システムの)欠陥, バグ ◇The latest software is full of *bugs*. その最新ソフトは欠陥だらけだ ◇My computer's really slow at the moment — it must be some kind of *bug*. 今私のコンピューターは動作が遅い──何らかのバグに違いない

glitch [C] 《インフォーマル》(一時的な小さな)不具合, 不調 ◇It was only a temporary *glitch* but it could have put people's lives in danger. それは単なる一時的な不具合だったが人の命を危険にさらす可能性はあった

imperfection [C, U] (外見上の小さな)欠点, 難点, 不完全さ ◇The only slight *imperfection* in the painting is a scratch in the corner. その絵の唯一のささいな欠点は角に引っかき傷があることだ ◇Nature is full of *imperfection*. 自然は不完全さに満ちている ☞ **blemish** (MARK)
▷ **imperfect** [形] ◇All our sale items are slightly *imperfect*. 当店の特売品はすべて小さな難があります

definition [名]

definition・interpretation・understanding・reading
事が理解[説明]される特定の方法
【類語訳】定義, 解釈, 理解, 見解

[文型&コロケーション]
▶ (a) **careful** definition/ interpretation/ understanding/ reading
▶ a **clear/ precise/ narrow/ broad/ wide/ conventional** definition/ interpretation/ understanding
▶ a **literal** interpretation/ understanding/ reading
▶ **different** definitions/ interpretations/ understandings/ readings
▶ to **give/ provide/ offer** a definition/ an interpretation

definition [C, U] (辞書の語・句[特定の人・集団にとっての観念])の定義 ◇The dictionary provides clear, simple *definitions*. その辞書は明確で簡潔な定義を載せている ◇The term 'partner' requires careful *definition*. 「partner」という語は定義付けに注意が必要だ ◇Neighbours *by definition* live close by (= this is what being a neighbour means). 「隣人」はその定義上当然だが近くに住んでいる ◇What's your *definition* of happiness? あなたの幸せの定義は何ですか ☞ **define** (EXPLAIN 1), **define** (LIST [動])

interpretation [C, U] 《ややフォーマル》解釈, 説明, 理解 ◇Her evidence suggests a different *interpretation*

of the events leading to his death. 彼女の証言は彼が死亡した事件に異なる解釈をもたらしている ◇Dreams are **open to interpretation** (= they can be explained in different ways). 夢はいろいろな解釈が可能だ
▶**interpret** 動 [他] ◇I didn't know whether to *interpret* her silence as acceptance or refusal. 彼女の沈黙を承諾、拒絶のいずれと解釈すればよいかわからなかった ◇The data can be *interpreted* in many different ways. そのデータはさまざまに解釈されうる ☞ **interpret** (EXPLAIN 1), **interpretative** (DESCRIPTIVE)
understanding [U, C] 理解 ◇My *understanding* of the situation is... 私は…であるとその状況を理解している ◇Students will gain an active *understanding* of the workings of Parliament. 生徒たちは国会の仕組みを進んで理解することになるだろう ☞ **understand** (CONCLUDE)
reading [C] 《ややフォーマル、特に書き言葉》解釈、見解 ◇Those conclusions are based on a literal *reading* of the text. それらの結論はテキストを文字どおり読んだ解釈に基づいている ◇My own *reading* of events is less optimistic. 私自身の事柄の展開に対する見解はやや悲観的です
▶**read** 動 [他] ◇How do you *read* the present situation? 今の状況をどう解釈しますか

ノート interpretation, understanding, reading の使い分け：場合によってどの語も使用可能．◆a different *interpretation/understanding/reading* of the situation/history（状況/歴史の異なる解釈/理解/読み方）．しかしながら、interpretation は特に生じたことの意味合いに関する「解釈」に用いられる．◆*interpretation* of data/information/results/findings/events/the law/sb's theory/dreams （データ/情報/結果/発見/事件/法/理論/夢の解釈）．understanding は特に物事の働き方や関わり方に関する「解釈」に用いられる．◆an *understanding* of a process/a relationship/sb's role/the workings of sth/the principles of sth/a problem/an issue（プロセス/関連/役割/働き/原理/問題/論点などの解釈）．reading は特に文章に関する「解釈」に用いられる．◆my *reading* of the text/poem/novel/story（テキスト/詩/小説/話の解釈）．

defraud 動 ☞ CHEAT 動

defraud・rip sb off・swindle・fleece・bilk・screw・short-change
人から不正[違法]に金品などを得る
【類語訳】だまし取る、詐取する、ぼったくる

文型&コロケーション
▶to defraud/ swindle/ fleece/ bilk/ screw sb **out of** sth
▶to defraud/ rip off/ fleece/ bilk/ short-change **customers**
▶to defraud/ swindle/ bilk **investors**
▶to defraud/ rip off/ bilk a **company**
▶to defraud/ swindle/ bilk the **government**
▶to rip off/ fleece **tourists**

defraud [他, 自]《ややフォーマル、けなして》だまし取る、詐取する ◇They were accused of *defrauding* the company *of* $14,000. 彼らは会社から1万4千ドルをだまし取った容疑で告訴された ◇All three men were charged with conspiracy to *defraud*.《法律》三人とも詐欺を共謀した容疑をかけられていた ☞ **fraud** (FRAUD 1), **fraud** (FRAUD 2)

,**rip sb 'off** 句動詞 (-pp-) [しばしば受身で]《インフォーマル、けなして》ぼったくる ◇Tourists complain of being *ripped off* by local cab drivers. 観光客たちは地元のタクシー運転手がぼったくるとこぼしている
▶'**rip-off** 名 [C, ふつう単数で] ◇$70 for a T-shirt! What a *rip-off*! Tシャツ1枚で70ドル。何てぼったくりだ
swindle [他]《けなして》だまし取る、詐取する ◇They *swindled* him out of thousands of dollars. 彼らは彼から何千ドルもだまし取った
▶**swindle** 名 [C, ふつう単数で] ◇We think she was mixed up in an insurance *swindle*. 私たちは彼女が保険金詐欺に関わっていたと思っています

ノート defraud と swindle の使い分け：目的語なしで用いられる場合、defraud は swindle よりもフォーマル．swindle は必ず目的語を伴う．

fleece [他]《インフォーマル、けなして》ぼったくる ◇Some local shops have been *fleecing* tourists. 地元の店には以前から観光客からぼったくっている店もある
bilk [他]《特に米、インフォーマル、けなして》だまし取る ◇He was a con man who *bilked* investors out of millions of dollars. 彼は投資家たちから何百万ドルもだまし取った詐欺師だった
screw [他]《俗語、けなして》ぼったくる ◇We've been *screwed*. ぼったくられたよ ◇How much did they *screw you for* (= how much did you have to pay)? 彼らにいくらぼったくられたか
,**short-'change** [他, しばしば受身で]《けなして》釣銭をごまかす ◇I think I've been *short-changed* at the bar. バーで釣銭をごまかされたみたいだ

delay 動

delay・postpone・adjourn・wait・put sth off・defer・suspend・shelve・reschedule
…する[…が起こる]ことを延ばす
【類語訳】遅らせる、延期する、先延ばしにする、棚上げする

文型&コロケーション
▶to delay sth/ postpone sth/ adjourn sth/ wait/ put sth off/ defer sth/ suspend sth/ shelve sth **for** a few days/ the time being, etc.
▶to wait/ reschedule sth **for** later in the year, etc.
▶to delay sth/ postpone sth/ adjourn sth/ wait/ put sth off/ defer sth **until** sth
▶to postpone/ defer sth **to** sth
▶to delay/ postpone/ put off/ defer **doing sth**
▶to delay/ postpone/ adjourn/ reschedule a **meeting**
▶to delay/ postpone/ adjourn a **case/ trial**
▶to delay/ postpone/ put off your **departure/ return**
▶to delay/ postpone/ put off/ reschedule a **visit**
▶to delay/ postpone a **flight**
▶to suspend **visits/ flights**
▶to delay/ postpone/ put off/ defer a **decision**
▶to delay/ postpone/ suspend **plans**
▶to delay/ postpone/ adjourn/ put off/ defer/ suspend/ shelve sth **indefinitely**

delay [他]《ややフォーマル》(…する[…が起こる]ことを)遅らせる ◇The judge will *delay* his verdict until he receives medical reports on the offender. 犯罪者に関する医療報告書が届くまで裁判官は判決の言い渡しを遅らせるだ

↪delay   delete

ろう ◇He *delayed* telling her the news, waiting for the right moment. 彼は時機が来るまで彼女にその知らせを伝えるのを待った ◇These drugs can significantly *delay* the onset of the disease. これらの薬は病気の発症を大きく遅らせることができる ◇She's suffering a *delayed reaction* (= a reaction that did not happen immediately.) 彼女は遅延型反応に苦しんでいる 反意 **hasten** (ACCELERATE), ☞ **delay** (HOLD SB/STH UP)

postpone [他, しばしば受身で] 《ややフォーマル》(催し物・行動を)延期する ◇The game has already been *postponed* three times. 試合はすでに3度延期になっている ◇They have agreed to *postpone* repayment of the loan to a future unspecified date. 彼らは貸付金の返済を将来の不特定日までに延期することに合意した ☞ **cancel** (ABOLISH)

▶**postponement** [名][U, C] ◇Riots led to the *postponement* of local elections. それらの暴動で地方選挙が延期された

adjourn [自, 他, しばしば受身で] 《フォーマル》(会議・公式手続を)一定期間休止する, (法廷を)休廷にする ◇The court *adjourned* for lunch. 法廷は昼食で休廷になった ◇The trial has been *adjourned* until next week. 裁判は来週まで休廷になりました

▶**adjournment** [名][C, U] ◇The judge granted us a short *adjournment*. 裁判官は我々に短時間の休廷を認めた

wait [自] 《ややインフォーマル》(緊急ではないので)後回しにする ◇I've got some calls to make but they *can wait* until tomorrow. 何件か電話をかけないといけないんだが, 明日に回すこともできる ◇I'm afraid this *can't wait*. It's very important. あいにく, これは待ったなしです. 非常に重要です ❶ **wait** は目的語ではなく主語が後回しになる点に注意。×I can *wait* those calls.

put sth 'off [句動詞]《ややインフォーマル》(催し物を)延期する;(…することを)後回し[先延ばし]にする ◇We've had to *put off* our wedding until September. 私たちは9月まで結婚式を延期しなければならなくなっていた ◇He keeps *putting off* going to the dentist. 彼は歯医者に行くのをずっと先延ばしにしている

defer (-rr-) [他]《フォーマル》(決定・行動を)遅らせる, 延期する ◇The department *deferred* the decision for six months. 課ではその決定を6か月間延期した ◇She had applied for *deferred* admission to college. 彼女は大学への入学期限の延期を求めていた

suspend [他]《ややフォーマル》(正式に)遅らせる;システムの作動を一時停止する ◇The jury was asked to *suspend* judgement. 陪審は審判を延期するよう求められた ◇Aid flights have been *suspended* for a week after fighting near the city's airport. その都市の空港付近で戦闘があってから救援便の発着は1週間停止になっている ❶ **suspend** には開始を遅らせるという意味も, すでに開始された事を中止するという意味もある. 目的語には plans, work, aid, flights, visit, payments などが挙げられる.

▶**suspension** [名][U, 単数で] ◇These events led to the *suspension* of talks. これらの出来事は話し合いの延期をもたらした

shelve [他]《ややフォーマル》(一時的[恒久的]に計画などを)中止[棚上げ]する ◇The government has *shelved* the idea until at least next year. 政府は少なくとも来年までその考えを棚上げにした ◇Plans to expand the company have been quietly *shelved*. 会社を拡大する計画は知らない間に棚上げされた

reschedule [他, しばしば受身で]《ややフォーマル》日程を変更する, 延期する ◇The meeting has been *rescheduled* for next week. 会議は来週に日程が変更された

ノート **postpone** と **reschedule** の使い分け: **postpone** はしばしば失望感を与え, 否定的なことを連想させる. しばしば have to, be forced to, be obliged to などと共に用いられる. **reschedule** はむしろ肯定的な感じで, しばしば for + 日付・時間を伴う. ♦The event has been *rescheduled* for 5 June/Sunday/the spring. (その催し物は6月5日/日曜日/春に延期された).

delete [動]

delete • erase • cut • cross sth out • wipe • strike sth out • rub sth out • cross sb/sth off
書かれた情報を取り除く
【類語訳】削除する, 消す, 消去する, カットする, 切り取る

文型&コロケーション
▶to delete/ erase/ cut/ wipe sth **from** sth
▶to delete/ erase/ cross out/ strike out/ rub out a **word**
▶to delete/ cut/ cross out a **sentence**
▶to delete/ cut/ cross out/ strike out a **paragraph**
▶to delete sth from/ cross sb/ sth off a **list**
▶to delete/ erase/ wipe a **file** (on a computer)
▶to delete/ erase/ wipe sth **accidentally**
▶to erase/ wipe sth **completely**

delete [他]《ややフォーマル or コンピューター》削除する ◇Your name has been *deleted* from the list. 君の名前がリストから削除されている ◇This command *deletes* files from the directory. このコマンドはファイルをディレクトリから削除します ◇I *deleted* your last email by mistake — could you send it again? 私はあなたからの最新のEメールを間違って消してしまいました — もう一度送ってもらえますか

▶**deletion** [名][C, U] ◇He made several *deletions* to the manuscript. 彼は原稿からいくつか文言を削除した

erase [他] (記憶から)取り除く;(記号・文字などを)消す;(テープ[コンピューター]から)記録・情報を)消去する ◇She tried to *erase* the memory of that evening. 彼女はあの晩の記憶を拭い去ろうとした ◇All doubts were suddenly *erased* from his mind. すべての疑念が突然彼の心から消えた ◇All the phone numbers had been *erased*. 電話番号がすべて消されていた ◇Parts of the recording have been *erased*. 記録の一部が消去されている

cut [他, 自] (文章・録音・映像の一部を)削除する;(コンピューター上で文の一部を)カットする[切り取る] ◇This scene was *cut* from the final version of the movie. この場面はその映画の最終版からカットされた ◇You can *cut* this whole paragraph without losing any of the impact. このパラグラフ全体はインパクトをいっさい失わずに省くことができるよ ◇You can *cut and paste* between different programs. 異なるプログラム間でカットアンドペーストすることができます

▶**cut** [名][C] ◇The director objected to the *cuts* ordered by the film censor. 監督は映画検閲官が命令した削除部分に異議を唱えた

cross sth 'out [句動詞] (誤っているため語などに)線を引いて消す ◇She *crossed out* 'Miss' and wrote 'Ms'. 彼女は「Miss」に線を引いて消して「Ms」と書いた ◇He's *crossing* the days *out* on the calendar until the start of the World Cup. ワールドカップの開幕まで彼はカレンダーの日付に線を引いて消している

wipe [他]（コンピューター・テープ・ビデオの情報[音, 画像]を）消去する ◇You must have *wiped off* that show I recorded. 私が録画したあの番組を君が消したに違いない ◇Somebody had *wiped* all the tapes. 誰かがすべてのテープを消去していた

,strike sth 'out 句動詞 （線を引いて）削除する ◇The editor *struck out* the whole paragraph. 編集者はそのパラグラフ全体を削除した

,rub sth 'out 句動詞 (-bb-)《英》（鉛筆・チョークなどによる記号・文字を）消す ◇She reached up and *rubbed out* the words on the board. 彼女は手を伸ばして黒板の文字を消した ◇Use a pencil so you can *rub* it *out* if you make a mistake. 間違ったときに消せるよう鉛筆を使いましょう ❶《米》では erase を用いる。

,cross sb/sth 'off, ,cross sb/sth 'off sth 句動詞（名前・項目に）線を引いて消す ◇We can *cross* his name *off* the list — he's not coming. 彼の名前をリストから削除しよう―彼は来ないよ

deliberate 形

deliberate・intended・conscious・intentional・wilful・calculated・premeditated・purposeful
行為が意図的になされる[事前に計画される, 達成をもくろまれる]ことを表す
【類語訳】故意の, 意図的な, 意識的な, 計画的な

文型&コロケーション
▶a deliberate/ a conscious/ an intentional/ a wilful/ a calculated/ a premeditated/ a purposeful **act**
▶a deliberate/ an intended/ a conscious/ an intentional/ a calculated/ a purposeful **action**
▶deliberate/ conscious/ wilful **neglect**
▶deliberate/ intentional/ wilful **cruelty**
▶deliberate/ conscious/ calculated **attempts/ manipulation**

deliberate 故意の, 意図的な ◇The speech was a *deliberate* attempt to embarrass the government. その演説は政府を苦境に陥らせようという意図を込めたものだった ◇The emphasis on Europe was quite *deliberate*. ヨーロッパを強調したのはまったく意図的なものだった 反意 **accidental** (ACCIDENT)
➤**deliberately** 副 ◇She was accused of *deliberately* misleading Parliament. 彼女は意図的に国会を欺いたとして告訴された ◇Her tone was *deliberately* insulting. 彼女の口調はわざと侮蔑的だった 反意 **accidentally** (ACCIDENT)

intended [名詞の前で] 意図された ◇The bullet missed its *intended* target. 弾は狙われた標的から外れた ◇The *intended* victims were selected because they seemed vulnerable. 弱々しそうな者が攻撃対象者に選ばれた 反意 **unintended** (UNCONSCIOUS), ☞ **intend** (INTEND)

conscious (行為・感情の）意識的な ◇She made a *conscious* decision to spend more time with her family. 彼女は家族との時間をもっと増やそうと意識的に決めた ◇I made a *conscious* effort to get there on time. 私は時間どおりに到着しようと意識的に努力した 反意 **unconscious, subconscious** (UNCONSCIOUS)

➤**consciously** 副 ◇I never really *consciously* set out to be a war photographer. 私は決して意図的に戦場カメラマンになろうとしたのではない ◇Whether *consciously* or unconsciously, you made a choice. 意識的にせよ無意識的にせよ, 君は選択したんだ 反意 **unconsciously** (UNCONSCIOUS)

intentional 《ややフォーマル》意図的な, 故意の ◇I'm sorry I left you off the list — it wasn't *intentional*. あなたをリストから落としてしまい申し訳ありません―故意ではなかったのです ◇She felt she was a victim of *intentional* discrimination. 彼女は意図的な差別による被害者だと感じた 反意 **unintentional** (UNCONSCIOUS)
➤**intentionally** 副 ◇He'd never *intentionally* hurt anyone. 彼は故意に誰かを傷つけることは決してなかった ◇*Intentionally* or not, police procedures may be biased. 意図的にせよそうでないにせよ, 警察のやり方は偏向している可能性がある 反意 **unintentionally** (UNCONSCIOUS)

ノート **deliberate** と **intentional** の使い分け：実質的な意味の違いはないが, **intentional** のほうが低頻度かつフォーマルで, 結びつく語の種類も少ない。

wilful 《特に英》《米でふつう **willful**》《ふつう名詞の前で》《フォーマル, けなして or 法律》（悪行・悪事が）故意の ◇He was charged with *wilful* damage to property. 彼は故意による器物損壊の容疑をかけられた
➤**wilfully** 副 ◇They were charged with *wilfully* neglecting their children. 彼らは故意に子どもたちを放置した罪に問われていた

calculated [ふつう名詞の前で] 計画的な ◇It was either a ridiculous mistake or a *calculated* insult. それは愚かな過ちか計画的な侮辱だった ◇He took a *calculated risk* (= a risk that you decide is worth taking even though you know it might have bad results). 彼はリスクを承知で賭けに出た ❶ *calculated* はしばしば人に危害を及ぼす意図的な行為について用いられる。

premeditated 《しばしばけなして》（犯行・悪行が）前もって計画された ◇The killing had not been *premeditated*. その殺害は前もって計画されたものではなかった ◇This was a callous, *premeditated* attack on a defenceless young man. これは無防備な若い男性に対する冷酷で計画的な襲撃だった **unpremeditated** ❶ *unpremeditated* な crimes（犯行）とは前もって計画された犯行ではないことを意味する。

purposeful 目的のある, 断固とした ◇She looked *purposeful* and determined. 彼女は目的を持ち, 決然としているように見えた ◇He approached each task in the same *purposeful* manner. 彼は同じように目的意識を持ってそれぞれの仕事に取り組んだ
➤**purposefully** 副 ◇Edward strode *purposefully* towards the door. エドワードは決然とドアのほうへ歩いて行った

delicious 形

delicious・tasty・appetizing・mouth-watering・yummy
食べ物や飲み物が味がよいことを表す
【類語訳】おいしい, 風味のよい, 美味な, おいしそうな, うまい

tasty yummy delicious
appetizing mouth-watering

↪delicious

delight, delivery

文型&コロケーション
- delicious/ tasty/ appetizing **food**
- a delicious/ tasty **meal**
- a delicious/ an appetizing **smell**
- a delicious/ tasty **lunch**
- delicious/ tasty/ mouth-watering **dishes**
- to **look** delicious/ tasty/ appetizing/ mouth-watering
- **really** delicious/ tasty/ yummy
- **not very** tasty/ appetizing

delicious おいしい、風味のよい ◇Who cooked this? It's absolutely *delicious*. 誰がこれを料理したの。ものすごくおいしい ◇What's that? It smells *delicious*. あれは何。おいしそうなにおいだね ◇Lentils cooked with garlic make a *delicious* accompaniment to sausages or red meat. ヒラマメをニンニクで調理したものは、ソーセージや赤身肉のおいしい付け合わせになる

▸**deliciously** 副 ◇*deliciously* creamy soup クリーミーでおいしいスープ

tasty おいしい、美味な ◇The food is wholesome, *tasty* and well-presented. その食べ物はヘルシーで、おいしくて見た目もよい ◇There is a range of *tasty* snacks available at the bar. そのバーではおいしい軽食がいろいろ食べられる

appetizing (英でまた -sing) (食べ物が)食欲をそそる、おいしそうな ◇The *appetizing* aroma of sizzling bacon was coming from the kitchen. ジュージュー音を立てるベーコンの食欲をそそる香りが台所からしてきた ◇The meals he cooked were always nourishing but never particularly *appetizing*. 彼の作る料理はいつも栄養満点だったが特に食欲をそそるものではなかった ❶ *appetizing* は否定文以外ではふつう be 動詞と共に用いられない。◇The food wasn't very *appetizing*. (その食べ物はあまりおいしそうではなかった。)×The food was very *appetizing*. 反意 un-appetizing

'**mouth-watering** [ふつう名詞の前で] よだれの出そうな、おいしそうな ◇They looked through the window at the *mouth-watering* display of cakes. 彼らはウインドー越しにおいしそうなケーキが並べられているのを見た

yummy (インフォーマル、話し言葉) おいしい、うまい ◇These biscuits are *yummy*. このビスケットはおいしい ◇Chocolate cake? *Yummy*! チョコレートケーキなの。おいしいね ❶ yummy は特に子どもによって、または子どもに対して用いられる。反意 **yucky** ❶ yucky はまずい食べ物を表すインフォーマルな表現で特に子どもが用いる。

delight 動 ☞INTEREST 動, PLEASE

delight • charm • captivate • entrance • enthral • enchant • bewitch
人を大いに喜ばせる、人に強く欲させる
【類語訳】大喜びさせる、魅了する、心を奪う、夢中にさせる、魅惑する

→
delight	captivate
charm	entrance
	enthral
	enchant
	bewitch

文型&コロケーション
▸ to be delighted/ charmed/ captivated/ enthralled/ enchanted/ bewitched **by** sb/ sth

delight [他, 自] (人を)大喜びさせる ◇This news will *delight* his fans all over the world. この知らせに世界中の彼のファンは大喜びするだろう ◇She had a limitless capacity to astonish and *delight*. 《書き言葉》彼女は驚異と歓喜をもたらす限界なき能力の持ち主だった ☞ **delight** (JOY), **delight** (PLEASURE)

charm [他, 自] (自分の思いどおりのことをしてもらうために人を)魅了する、虜にする ◇He *charmed* his mother into letting him have his own way. 彼は母親に取り入って自分の思うとおりにさせてもらった ◇Her words had lost their power to *charm*. 彼女の言葉からは人を魅了する力が失われていた ☞ **charm** (CHARM), **charming** (NICE 2)

captivate [他, しばしば受身で] 《特に書き言葉》(おもしろさ・魅力で人の)心を奪う ◇The children were *captivated* by her stories. 子どもたちは彼女の話に心を奪われた ◇Men were *captivated* by her charm. 男たちは彼女の美しさの虜になった

entrance [他, ふつう受身で] 《書き言葉》(楽しさ・あこがれで人を)夢中にさせる ◇He listened to her, *entranced*. 彼は夢中になって彼女に聞き入った ◇I was *entranced* by the bird's beauty. 私はその鳥の美しさにうっとりしていた

enthral (英) (米 **enthrall**) (-ll-) [他, しばしば受身で] 《特に書き言葉》(おもしろさ・魅力で人の)心を奪う ◇This book will *enthral* readers of all ages. この本はあらゆる年齢の読者の心を奪うだろう ◇The child watched, *enthralled* by the bright moving images. その子は鮮やかな動画に夢中になって見入っていた

> ノート **captivate, entrance, enthral** の使い分け：
> captivated は人の容姿・魅力・言動に心奪われた状態。entranced は人のほか、音楽・芸術・美しさなど五感に訴える物事に心奪われた状態。enthralled は目にしている物・想像力に訴える物語などに心奪われた状態。

enchant [他, 自] 《特に書き言葉》(人を)魅了する ◇The happy family scene had *enchanted* him. 幸せな家族のシーンを彼はとても気に入っていた

bewitch [他, しばしば受身で, 自] 《書き言葉》(人をすっかり)魅惑する ◇He was completely *bewitched* by her beauty. 彼はすっかり彼女の美しさの虜になった

delivery 名

delivery • distribution • freight • transport • transit • shipment • shipping • haulage • handling
ある場所から別の場所へ商品を運ぶ[送る]行為[商売]
【類語訳】配達、配送、流通、運送、運輸業、海運、発送、輸送料

文型&コロケーション
▸ **for** delivery/ distribution/ freight/ transport/ shipment/ shipping/ haulage
▸ delivery/ distribution/ freight/ transport/ transit/ shipping/ haulage/ handling **costs**
▸ a/ the delivery/ freight/ handling **charge**
▸ a delivery/ distribution/ freight/ transport/ shipping/ haulage **company/ business**
▸ the freight/ transport/ transit/ shipping/ haulage **industry**

delivery [U, C] (商品・手紙の)配達, 配送 ◇We offer free *delivery* on orders over $200. 200ドル以上の注文で送料は無料になります ◇Allow 28 days for *delivery*. 配達まで28日間を見込んでください ◇Please pay for goods *on delivery* (= when they are delivered). 商品の到着時にお支払いください ◇When will you be able to *take delivery of* the car? 《フォーマル》いつなら車の受け取りが可能ですか ◇At the moment there are two *deliveries* a day (= of mail). 現在, 1日に2回配達が行われています ◇She had *made a delivery* to the address earlier that day. 彼女はその日もっと早い時間帯にその住所に配達を行っていた ☞ **deliver** (TAKE 1)

distribution [U] 《ビジネスで》配給；流通 ◇They have systems in place for sales, *distribution* and marketing. 彼らのところでは販売, 流通, マーケティングのシステムが整っている ◇He worked in the milk *distribution* business. 彼は牛乳の配達の仕事をしていた ☞ **distribute** (DISTRIBUTE)

freight [U] (車・飛行機・鉄道による)運送(システム) ◇We tend to use air *freight* for lighter goods. 軽量の品物は空輸を利用する傾向にある ☞ **freight** (CARGO)

transport 《特に英》(または特に米で **transportation**) [U] (車・鉄道による)輸送, 運送業 ◇We need stricter controls on the *transport* of nuclear waste. 核廃棄物の輸送に関するより厳しい規制が必要だ ◇*Transportation* costs have virtually crippled our business. 事実上, 輸送費が我々の商売の足かせになっています ☞ **transport** (TAKE 1)

transit [U] 輸送 ◇The total cost includes *transit*. 総費用には輸送料が含まれている ◇Your insurance should cover *transit* by air, sea or rail. あなたの保険は飛行機, 船, 鉄道の輸送に適用されるはずです ◇We will pay for any goods lost or damaged *in transit*. 輸送中に遺失または損傷した商品すべてに対して賠償します

shipment [U] (国外への)出荷, (海路・陸路・空路での)発送 ◇The goods are ready for *shipment*. 商品は出荷の準備ができています ◇The illegal *shipment* of weapons continues to be a multimillion dollar industry. 武器の違法な出荷は依然として数百万ドル規模の産業だ ☞ **ship** (TAKE 1)

shipping [U] (船による人・荷物の)輸送, 海運 ◇She arranged for the *shipping* of her furniture to England. 彼女は家具をイングランドへ船便で送る手配をした ◇She married a *shipping magnate* (= sb who has made a lot of money from shipping) in 1997. 彼女は1997年に海運王と結婚した ❶《米》では shipping は, 消費者に販売される商品の「発送」という意味で shipment の代わりに用いられることもある. ◆ We offer free *shipping* on orders over $50.《米》50ドル以上のご注文で送料は無料になります ☞ **ship** (TAKE 1)

haulage [U]《英》(道路・鉄道による)輸送業, 運送業 ◇There have been protests from the road *haulage* industry. 道路輸送業界から抗議があった ◇How much will *haulage* be (= how much will it cost)? 送料はいくらになりますか

handling [U]《フォーマル》(梱包を含む)配送, 発送手数料 ◇There is a $5 *handling* charge for each order. 注文ごとに5ドルの発送手数料がかかります ◇You pay only $29.95 plus *shipping and handling*.《米》送料および手数料29.95ドルのお支払いのみです ❶《英》では postage and packing と言う.

demand

demand・market・a run on sth・(no) call for sth
商品やサービスを求めている人々の数
【類語訳】需要

▸ demand/ a market/ (no) call **for** sth
▸ (a) **big/ buoyant/ huge/ growing/ steady/ changing/ current/ potential/ total/ falling** demand/ market
▸ (the) **consumer/ domestic/ local/ export/ foreign/ worldwide** demand/ market
▸ to **create** demand/ a market
▸ to **stimulate/ boost/ increase** demand/ the market

demand [U, 単数で]《特にビジネス》需要 ◇We are struggling to *meet the demand* for the product. 我々はその製品の需要を満たそうと努力している ◇*Demand* is exceeding supply. 需要が供給を上回っている ◇There's an increased *demand* for organic produce these days. 最近では無農薬野菜の需要が高まっている

market [単数で]《ビジネスで》需要 ◇The second-hand car *market* is declining. 中古車の需要は下がりつつある ◇There's not much of a *market* for black and white televisions nowadays. 最近白黒テレビの需要はあまりない ☞ **market** (MARKET 1)

> ノート **demand** と **market** の使い分け：基本的には同じ意味であるが, demand のほうがより一般的で, market のほうがより専門的なビジネス用語である. これらの語は文法と結びつく語のパターンが異なる. market は the housing/labour market や product markets という形を取るが, demand は demand for housing/labour/a product という形を取る. 以下は結びつきのパターン. create demand/a market (需要を生む). meet [satisfy]/increase demand (需要を満たす/高める). supply/expand the market (需要にこたえる/を拡大する). influence/forecast demand (需要に影響を与える/を予測する). find/identify a market (需要を開拓/把握する). a fall/a decline/an increase/growth in demand (需要の低迷/増加). a slump/recovery in market (需要の低迷/回復). 商品の生産が需要に追いつかない状況では market ではなく demand を用いる. ✕We're struggling to meet the *market*. ✕The *market* exceeds supply.

a run on sth フレーズ《ビジネスで》(突然の)需要 ◇There's been *a run on* the dollar. ドルに対して買いが殺到している ◇When the new currency measures were announced there was *a run on the bank* (= a lot of people suddenly took their money out of the bank). 新しい通貨対策が発表されるとその銀行で取り付け騒ぎが起こった ❶ run はしばしば金融に関する文脈で見られるが, 天気の変化などが起こると突然の需要が生まれて, 店・企業には例えば, experience a run on sun cream/petrol/red roses (日焼け止めクリーム/ガソリン/赤いバラに対して買いが殺到する)

(no) call for sth フレーズ [単数で]《ややインフォーマル》(商品・サービスに対する)需要(がないこと) ◇There isn't a lot of *call for* small specialist shops nowadays. 最近, 小さな専門店の需要は大きくない

demand 動 ☞ASK 2

demand・require・expect・insist・press (sb) for sth・ask・stipulate・clamour・hold out for sth・exact

人が…をする[持つ]べきだと主張する
【類語訳】要求する、求める、強要する

文型&コロケーション
▶ to demand/ require/ expect/ ask/ exact sth **from** sb
▶ to demand/ require/ expect/ ask sth **of** sb
▶ to ask/ press/ push/ clamour/ hold out **for** sth
▶ to demand/ require/ expect/ insist/ ask/ stipulate **that**…
▶ to require/ expect/ ask **sb to do sth**
▶ to demand/ require/ expect/ insist on **high standards**
▶ to demand/ require/ expect/ insist **a lot/ too much/ a great deal**
▶ to **be too much to** expect/ ask

demand [他] 強く要求する ◇She *demanded* an immediate explanation. 彼女は即座に説明を求めた ◇The group *demands* a high level of loyalty from its members. その集団は会員に非常に強い忠誠心を要求している ◇The UN has *demanded* that all troops be withdrawn. 国連はすべての軍隊を撤退させることを要求した ◇They *demanded to* see the ambassador. 彼らは大使との面会を求めた ☞ **demand** (REQUEST)

require [他、しばしば受身で]《進行形はまれ》《ややフォーマル》(法律・規則・基準によって)…をする[持つ]よう求める ◇The wearing of seat belts is *required* by law. シートベルトの着用は法律によって義務付けられている ◇Several students failed to reach the *required* standard. 何人かの学生は必要な水準に達することができなかった ◇'Hamlet' is *required reading* (= must be read) for the class. 『ハムレット』はその授業での指定必読図書だ ☞ **requirement** (CONDITION)

expect [他] (義務・責任があるので)…をする[を持つ, である]ことを求める ◇Are you clear about what is *expected* of you? あなたは何が求められているかわかっていますか ◇Don't *expect* too much from him. 彼に多くを求めすぎるな ◇They *expected* all their children to be high achievers. 彼らは子どもたち全員が成績優秀者になることを求めた ◇I *expect* to be paid promptly for the work. 仕事に対して遅滞なく給与が支払われることを求める
▷ **expectation** 名 [C, ふつう複数で] ◇Some parents have unrealistic *expectations* of their children. 親の中には子どもたちに非現実的な期待をかける者もいる ◇Unfortunately the new software has failed to *meet expectations*. 残念ながら、その新しいソフトは期待はずれだった

insist [自, 他] 強く求める ◇I didn't want to go but he *insisted*. 私は行きたくなかったが、彼がどうしても言うものでしたから ◇We *insist on* the highest standards at all times. 私たちは常に最高水準を求めている ◇Stay and have lunch. I *insist*! 《話し言葉》お昼を食べて行ってください。是非 ◇'Please come with us.' 'All right, *if you insist*.' 「私たちと一緒に来てください」「わかりました。どうしてもとおっしゃるなら」 ◇The company *insisted* that the money be paid immediately. その会社は金を即座に支払うよう強く求めた ❶句動詞のinsist on/uponには「要求がすべてであると言って、それ以外は受け入れない」の意味がある。

◆We *insisted on* a refund of the full amount. (私たちは全額払い戻しを譲らなかった).
▷ **insistence** 名 [U] ◇their *insistence on* strict standards of behaviour 彼らが厳格な行動規範を求めること ◇*At her insistence*, the matter was dropped. 彼女の強い求めに応じて、その問題は打ち切られた

'press for sth, 'press sb for sth 句動詞 強く求め続ける、しつこく求める ◇They are *pressing for* a change in the law. 彼らは法律の改正を求め続けている ◇The bank is *pressing* us *for* repayment of the loan. 銀行がローンの返済をしつこく催促してきている ☞ **press** (PRESS 2)

ask [他] 求める ◇I know I'm *asking* a great deal. 多くを求めていることは承知 ◇You're *asking* too much of him. 君は彼に多くを求めすぎ ◇It's *asking* a lot to expect them to win again. 彼らにもう一度勝つことを期待するのは荷が重い

ノート **demand, expect, ask** の使い分け：命令に近いdemandやexpectほどaskの意味は強くない。

stipulate [他]《フォーマル》(条件として)明記する, 要求する ◇A delivery date is *stipulated* in the contract. 納品日は契約書に明記されている ◇The job advertisement *stipulates* that the applicant must have teaching experience. 求人広告には応募者は教育経験を有することが明記されている

clamour《英》《米 clamor》[自]《ややフォーマル, 書き言葉》声高に要求する, 騒ぎ立てる ◇People began to *clamour* for his resignation. 人々は彼の辞任を求めて騒ぎ始めた ◇Everyone was *clamouring* to know how much they would get. 皆いくらもらうことになるのか知りたいと声高に要求していた

hold 'out for sth 句動詞 《受身なし》(合意が遅れるくらい)求めて譲らない ◇They are *holding out for* a 10% raise. 彼らは あくまでも10％の昇給を求めている

exact [他]《フォーマル》強要する ◇She was determined to *exact* a promise from him. 彼女は彼から強制的に約束を取り付けようと決心していた

demolish 動

demolish・tear sth down・knock sth down・raze・cut sth down・fell・level・flatten・bulldoze

建物[樹木]を壊す
【類語訳】取り壊す、破壊する、切り倒す、伐採する、倒壊させる

文型&コロケーション
▶ to demolish/ tear down/ knock down/ level/ flatten a **building/ house**
▶ to demolish/ tear down/ knock down a **factory/ wall**
▶ to raze/ level/ flatten/ bulldoze an **area**
▶ to raze/ level/ flatten a **village/ town/ city**
▶ to raze/ cut down/ fell/ bulldoze a **forest**
▶ to cut down/ fell/ bulldoze **trees**

demolish [他]《ややフォーマル》(建物を)取り壊す ◇The old slums are being *demolished* to make way for a new housing project. 古いスラム街は新しい住宅計画を進めるため取り壊されている ❶demolishは老朽化・不要化・土地の転用のため意図的に建物を取り壊すことを意味する。特に《米》でのインフォーマルな用法では、建物・乗り物などが事故・災害などで破壊されることにも用いられる。 ◆Tornadoes de-

molished trailers and blew roofs off houses. (《特に米、インフォーマル》トルネードがトレーラーを破壊し、家々の屋根を吹き飛ばした). 反意 **build, construct**

▶**demolition** 名 [U, C] ◇The whole row of houses is scheduled for *demolition*. その家並み全体が取り壊される予定だ 反意 **construction, building (PRODUCTION)**

,**tear sth 'down** 句動 (時にけなして)（建物・壁・柵を）取り壊す；（絵・カーテンなどを）引きはがす [むしりとる] ◇They're *tearing down* these old houses to build a new office block. これらの古い家々は取り壊されて、新しいオフィスビルが建てられる予定だ ◇Demonstrators *tore down* posters of the president. デモ参加者は大統領のポスターを引きはがした

,**knock sth 'down** 句動 (建物・壁・柵を)取り壊す；(ドアを)打ち破る ◇You could *knock* this wall *down* and make one large room. この壁を取り壊せば一つの大きな部屋になりますよ ◇They didn't need to *knock* the door *down*! 彼らはドアを打ち破る必要はなかった

ノート **demolish, tear sth down, knock sth down** の使い分け：**tear sth down** は乱暴な様子や、話し手がその行為に対して否定的な感情を抱いていることを示唆する。**demolish** と **knock sth down** は肯定的でも否定的でもなく中立的な語である。

raze [他、ふつう受身で] (建物・町・森林などを) 跡形もなく破壊する ◇The village was *razed to the ground*. 村は跡形もなく破壊された ❶**raze** は徹底的な破壊を意味し、広大な土地に関してよく用いられる。ふつう意図的に、戦争行為として地域を焼き払うことを表す。

,**cut sth 'down** 句動 (木を) 切り倒す ◇Some care must be taken before deciding to *cut down* large trees. 巨木を切り倒す決定をする前には何らかの保護措置を施さなければならない

fell [他]（ややフォーマル）(木を) 伐採する ◇Trees were *felled* and floated downstream. 木は伐採され、下流へ流送される ◇illegally *felled* timber 違法に伐採された材木

ノート **cut sth down** と **fell** の使い分け：**fell** はよりフォーマルな語で商業的な文脈で用いられ、大量の木々や森林全体を対象にする。

level (-ll-, 米 -l-) [他] (建物・町・木々を) 完全に倒壊させる、なぎ倒す ◇Bulldozers are now waiting to *level* their home. 今ブルドーザーが彼らの家を取り壊すために待機している ◇The blast *levelled* several buildings in the area. 突風がその地域のいくつかの建物をなぎ倒した

flatten [他] (建物・町・木・庭などを) 完全に倒壊させる ◇The hurricane *flattened* thousands of homes. ハリケーンによって何千棟という家が倒壊した ◇Most of the factory was *flattened* by the explosion. その工場の大半が爆発によって跡形もなくなった

ノート **level** と **flatten** の使い分け：**level** は土地を再利用するため意図的に取り壊す、あるいはテロリストが爆弾によって爆破することを表す。**flatten** は事故、自然災害、爆発による破壊を表す。

bulldoze [他]（時にけなして）(ブルドーザーで建物・木々などを)破壊する ◇The trees are being *bulldozed* to make way for a new superstore. スーパーマーケットを新設するためブルドーザーでなぎ倒されている ❶**bulldoze** は乱暴な様子や、話し手がその行為に対して否定的な感情を抱いていることを示唆する。**knock sth down** や **cut sth down** のほうがより中立的である。

deny 動

deny・contradict・repudiate・refute・disclaim
報告・主張が真実ではないと述べる
【類語訳】否認する、否定する、反駁する

文型&コロケーション

▶ to deny/ contradict/ repudiate/ refute a **report/ suggestion**
▶ to deny/ repudiate/ refute a **claim**
▶ to deny/ repudiate an **accusation/ allegation**
▶ to deny/ disclaim **knowledge/ responsibility**
▶ to flatly deny/ contradict sth
▶ to strongly/ publicly deny/ repudiate/ refute sth

deny [他] 否認する、否定する ◇He *denied* accusations of corruption and mismanagement. 彼は汚職と不正行為の容疑を否認した ◇There's no *denying* the fact that quicker action could have saved them. 迅速に行動していれば彼らを救出できたことは否定できない事実だ ◇He *denies* attempting to murder his wife. 彼は妻の殺害を企てたことを否認している ◇She *denied that* there had been any cover-up. 彼女は隠ぺい工作が行われていたことを否定した ◇It can't be *denied* that we need to devote more resources to this problem. この問題にもっと多くの資金を注入する必要があることは否定できない ◇She *denied* all knowledge of the incident. 彼女はその事件への関知をいっさい否認した 反意 **confirm (CONFIRM 2)**

contradict [他] 反対する、反駁する ◇All evening her husband *contradicted* everything she said. 一晩中夫は彼女の言うことすべてに反駁した ◇You've just *contradicted yourself* (= said the opposite of what you said before).あなたが言ったことは矛盾している

repudiate [他]《フォーマル》(正式・公式に) 否定する ◇A spokeswoman *repudiated* the article, calling it unbalanced and inaccurate. 女性スポークスマンはその記事を偏っていて不正確なものであると公に否定した

refute [他]《特にジャーナリズム》否定する ◇She strongly *refutes* any suggestion that she behaved unprofessionally. 彼女はプロらしからぬ振る舞いをしたといういかなる指摘も彼女は強く否定している ❶**refute** は現在では、しばしば **deny** の同意語として用いられる。この用法を嫌う人もいるが、今や標準英語として広く受け入れられており、特にジャーナリズムで用いられる。☞ **refute (DISPROVE)**

disclaim [他]《フォーマル》(公式に) 否定する ◇The rebels *disclaimed* all responsibility for the explosion. 反乱勢力はその爆発への関与を全面的に否定した

department 名

department・division・branch・unit・arm・wing
組織の一部
【類語訳】部門、学部、学科、省、師団、支社、支店、支局、支部、科、部隊、分派、分隊

文型&コロケーション

▶ an **administrative** department/ division/ branch/ arm
▶ a **research** department/ division/ unit/ arm
▶ the **finance/ marketing** department/ division/ arm
▶ a **political** department/ unit/ arm/ wing
▶ a **military** unit/ arm/ wing

↳department

▶a **regional** department/ division/ branch/ unit

department [C]（企業・店・大学・政府・病院などの）部門, 学部, 学科, 省 ◇I work in the sales *department*. 私は営業部で働いています ◇The children's *department* sells a wide range of good quality clothes. 子ども服売り場には高品質の衣類が幅広く揃っている ◇Several professors from the history *department* will also speak at the event. 史学科の教授数人もその行事でスピーチする予定だ ◇The *Department* of Trade and Industry refused to comment on the allegations. 貿易産業省はそれらの申し立てに関するコメントを拒否した

division [C]（軍隊・企業などの）部門, 師団 ◇The commander of the fourth infantry *division* defied orders. 第4歩兵師団の司令官が命令に逆らった ◇The company's sales *division* is going to be restructured. その会社の営業部ではリストラが行われるようだ

branch [C]（大企業・組織の）支社, 支店, 支局, 支部 ◇The bank has *branches* all over the country. その銀行は国中至る所に支店を持っている ◇Our New York *branch* is dealing with the matter. 我が社のニューヨーク支店がその件に対応しています ❶政府などの組織のdepartmentの中にはbranchという語が名前に含まれているものもある. ◆Scotland Yard's anti-terrorist *branch* swung into action. (ロンドン警視庁の)テロ対策部が乗り出した

unit [C]（病院の）科,（軍隊の）部隊 ◇She was taken to the *intensive care unit*. 彼女は集中治療室に運ばれた ◇The hospital's *maternity unit* is to be closed. その病院の産婦人科は閉鎖される予定だ ◇*Enemy units* have infiltrated the territory. 敵の部隊が領土に侵入した ☞ unit (ARMY)

arm [C, ふつう単数で]《特に複合語として》(組織の)部門 ◇The report was published by the research *arm* of the Department of Transport. その報告は運輸省の調査部門から発表された ◇The bank plans to sell part of its US finance *arm*. その銀行はアメリカでの金融部門の一部を売却する計画だ

wing [C]（政治組織・軍隊の）党派, 側面部隊 ◇The radical *wing* of the party was dissatisfied with the policies. 党内の急進派はその方針に満足していなかった

depend on/upon sth 句動詞

depend on/upon sth • rest on sth • hinge on/upon sth • hang on sth
事によって影響される
【類語訳】左右される, 決定される, 決まる

文型&コロケーション
▶It depends (on)/ rests on/ hinges on **what/ how/ who/ where/ whether...**
▶a **case** depends on/ rests on/ hinges on sth
▶to **entirely/ solely/ largely/ mainly/ partly/ ultimately** depend on/ rest on sth
▶It all depends on/ hinges on sth.

de'pend on/upon sth 句動詞《進行形なし》…によって左右[決定]される ◇Does the quality of teaching *depend on* class size? 授業の質はクラスの規模によって違いますか ◇It would *depend on* the circumstances. 状況次第だろう ◇We might need more food, *depending on* how many people turn up. 何人来るかによって

depend on/upon sth, depressed

もっと多くの食べ物が必要かもしれない ❶インフォーマルな表現では what, how, whether などの語の前では depend on よりも depend を用いることがかなり一般的である. ◆It *depends what* you mean by 'hostile'. (それは「hostile」をどういう意味で使っているかによる). フォーマルな書き言葉では depend は常に on か upon を伴わなければならない. ◆It *depends on how* you define the term 'hostile'. (それは「hostile」をどう定義するかによります). upon はこのようなフォーマルで頻度は低い. 話し言葉で, 他のことも考慮せねばならず確証がもてないとき, that depends や it (all) depends と言える. ◆'Is he coming?' '*That depends*. He may not have the time.'（《話し言葉》「彼は来るの?」「状況次第だね. 時間が取れないかもしれないんだ」）. ◆I don't know if we can help — *it all depends*. (手伝えるかどうかわかりません — 状況次第です).

'rest on sth 句動詞《特に書き言葉》（決定・議論・未来が）…に基づいている, …によって決まる ◇The whole argument *rests on* a false assumption. 議論全体が間違った仮定に基づいている ◇The case *rests on* who owned the knife. その事件は誰がナイフを所持していたかが鍵だ ◇Europe's political future *rests on* its economic strength. ヨーロッパの政治的未来は経済力次第である ❶rest on は特に決定[判断]の理由や事実に基づいているかどうかを述べるときに用いられる. ◆The argument/case/decision/evidence/theory *rests on* sth. (議論/事件/決定/証言/理論は…に基づいている). また, 名声, 将来, 望み (fame, future, hopes) についても rest on sth で言うことができる.

'hinge on/upon sth 句動詞《特に書き言葉, 特にジャーナリズム》（行為・結果が）…によって決まる ◇Everything *hinges on* the outcome of these talks. すべてがこの話し合いの結果次第だ ◇His success *hinged on* how well he did at the interview. 彼の成功はいかにうまく面接をこなすかどうかにかかっていた ❶hinge on/uponはしばしば話し合い[選挙, 討論, 裁判, 試合]の結果について述べるときに用いられる.

'hang on sth 句動詞《ややインフォーマル》…によって決まる ◇A lot *hangs on* this decision. 多くのことがこの決定にかかっている ❶hang on はふつう三人称・現在形で用いられる. 典型的な主語として everything, it all, a lot, sb's reputation などが挙げられる.

depressed 形 ☞ UNHAPPY 1

depressed • gloomy • demoralized • glum • despondent • dejected • down
人が悲しくて希望を失っていることを表す
【類語訳】気落ちした, 落ち込んだ, ふさぎこんだ, しょんぼりした, 憂鬱な

文型&コロケーション
▶depressed/ gloomy/ glum/ despondent **about** sth
▶a depressed/ gloomy/ glum **silence/ mood**
▶to **feel** depressed/ gloomy/ demoralized/ despondent/ dejected/ down
▶to **look** depressed/ gloomy/ glum
▶to **get** depressed/ gloomy/ demoralized
▶**increasingly** depressed/ gloomy/ despondent

depressed 気落ちした, 憂鬱な ◇She felt very *depressed* about the future. 彼女は将来についてとても憂鬱な気分になった ◇He was really *depressed at* the thought of going into the office. 彼は職場に行くことを考えると本当に憂鬱だった ◇You mustn't let yourself get *depressed*. 落ち込まないでよ ☞ **depress** (**DIS-COURAGE** 2), **depressing** (**NEGATIVE**), **depression** (**GLOOM**)

gloomy (表情・態度に表れる形で)希望を失った, 落ち込んだ, 憂鬱な ◇Don't look so *gloomy*. Things aren't that bad. そんな暗い顔をするなよ. 状況はそれほど悪くないんだから ◇He mopes around all the time with that *gloomy* expression on his face. 彼は暗い表情を顔に浮かべてずっと塞ぎ込んでいる [反意] **cheerful** (**CHEERFUL**), ☞ **gloom** (**GLOOM**)

▷ **gloomily** 副 ◇He stared *gloomily* at the phone. 彼は浮かない顔で電話を見つめていた

demoralized (英でまた **-sed**) (失敗したり, 進展がないことで)自信[希望]を失った, やる気を失くした ◇The workers here seem very *demoralized*. ここの従業員たちはとてもやる気を失っているように見える ◇What can we do to revitalize a *demoralized* sales force? 意気消沈した営業陣を蘇生させるにはどうしたらよいのだろうか ❶ *demoralized* は特にチーム・軍隊・従業員などの集団が持つ感情が一定期間にわたって悪化して, morale (士気)が下がっているときに用いられる. ☞ **morale** (**MOOD**)

glum (表情・態度に表れる形で)ふさぎこんだ, しょんぼりした ◇The couple looked distinctly *glum*. 夫婦は明らかにしょんぼりしていた ◇Her tone was flat and *glum*. 彼女の口調は抑揚がなくて元気がなかった

▷ **glumly** 副 ◇We sat *glumly* looking out to sea. 私たちはしょんぼり座って海を眺めていた

despondent (ややフォーマル, 特に書き言葉) 気落ちした, 落ち込んだ ◇She was becoming increasingly *despondent* about the way things were going. 彼女は事態の推移にますます気落ちしていった ☞ **despondency** (**GLOOM**)

dejected (ややフォーマル, 特に書き言葉) がっかりした, しょげた ◇She looked so *dejected* when she lost the game. 彼女は試合に負けてがっくりしているようだった

down [名詞の前では用いない] (ややインフォーマル) 憂鬱な, 元気のない ◇I feel a bit *down* today. 今日は少し憂鬱です ◇Don't let the weather *get you down*. 天気が悪くても元気を出していきましょう

describe 動 ☞ PRESENT 2

describe・report・tell・unfold・recount・relate・weave・chronicle・cover・narrate
人や物事がどんなものであるかを述べる, 出来事の説明をする
【類意訳】述べる, 記述する, 報道する, 語る, 話す, 説明する

【文型&コロケーション】
▶ to describe/ report/ tell/ recount/ relate **what/ how**...
▶ to report/ recount/ relate **that**...
▶ to describe/ report/ recount/ relate/ chronicle/ cover/ narrate **events/ a series of events**
▶ to describe/ report/ recount/ relate your **adventures**
▶ to tell/ unfold/ recount/ relate/ weave/ cover/ narrate a **story**
▶ to tell/ unfold/ recount/ relate/ weave/ narrate a **tale**
▶ to report/ recount **details**
▶ to describe/ report sth **accurately/ clearly**
▶ to describe/ tell/ recount sth **vividly**

describe [他] 述べる, 記述する, 説明する ◇Can you *describe* him *to* me? 彼がどんな人か私に教えてもらえますか ◇The current political situation in Vietnam is *described* in chapter 8. 現在のベトナムの政治情勢は第8章で記述されています ◇*Describe* how you did it. どんなふうにしたか説明しなさい ◇Several people *described* seeing strange lights in the sky. 何人かの人たちが空に奇妙な光を見たと述べた ☞ **describe** (**REGARD**)

report [他, 自] (新聞・テレビなどで)報じる, 報道する ◇The stabbing was *reported* in the local press. その刺傷事件は地元の報道機関で報じられた ◇*It was reported that* several people had been arrested. 数人が逮捕されたと報じられた ◇She *reports on* royal stories for the BBC. 彼女はBBCで王室の話題を報道している ☞ **report** (**REPORT** 2), **reporter** (**REPORTER**)

tell [他] 語る, 話す, 言い表す ◇They *told* stories and jokes while sitting around the camp fire. 彼らはキャンプファイヤーの周りに座って話をしたり冗談を言ったりした ◇Are you *telling* the truth? あなたは真実を述べていますか ◇She is always *telling* lies. 彼女は嘘ばかりついている ◇Did anyone *tell* you what happened? 何が起こったか誰かあなたに話しましたか ◇*I can't tell you* how happy I am. どれくらい幸せかは言い表せない ☞ **tell** (**TELL** 1)

unfold (自, 他) 《文語》 徐々に明かされる[明らかにする] ◇The audience watched the story *unfold* before their eyes. 観客は目の前で徐々に明かされる事のてんまつを見つめた ◇Dramatic events were about to *unfold*. 劇的な出来事が明かされようとしていた ◇She *unfolded* her tale to us. 彼女は私たちに話を打ち明けた

recount [他]《フォーマル》(自分に起こった出来事を)説明する ◇She was asked to *recount* the details of the incident to the court. 彼女は裁判官に事件の詳細を説明するよう求められた

relate [他]《フォーマル》物語る, 話す ◇She *relates* her childhood experiences in the first chapters. 彼女は幼年期の経験を第1章で語っている ◇He *related* the whole conversation to the police. 彼は警察に会話のやり取りをすべて話した

ノート tell, recount, relate の使い分け: recount と relate は tell よりもフォーマル. 経験した出来事に関するインフォーマルで面白いような話をするときは, recount のほうが relate よりも使用頻度が高い. ◆Brian and I *recounted* the awful story. (ブライアンと私は恐ろしい話をした). relate はよりフォーマルで中立的な説明をするのによく用いられる. ◆An audio-visual presentation *relates* the story of the Battle of Hastings. (視聴覚素材を使った展示ではヘースティングズの戦いの話が説明されている).

weave [他]《文語》(事実・出来事・詳細をまとめて話を)作り上げる ◇The author *weaves* the narrative around the detailed eyewitness accounts. その著者は目撃者の詳細な話をまとめて物語を作り上げている

chronicle [他]《フォーマル》年代順に記す ◇Her achievements are *chronicled* in a new biography. 彼女の業績は新刊の伝記に年代順に記されている ☞ **chronicle** (**STORY** 2)

cover [他] (テレビなどで)報じる ◇She's *covering* the party's annual conference. 彼女はその党の年次大会を報じている ◇The BBC will *cover* all the major games of the tournament. BBCはトーナメントの主要な試合をすべて放送する予定です

narrate [他]《フォーマル》物語る ◇She entertained them by *narrating* her adventures in Africa. 彼女はアフリカでの冒険の話をして彼らを楽しませました ◇The story is

↪describe

description, descriptive

narrated in flashback. その話は過去の回想の形で語られている ☞ **narrative** (STORY)

description 名 ☞ REPORT 2

description・picture・representation・profile・portrayal・portrait・depiction・evocation
人や物事を文章[絵, 写真, 映画, 画面]で描くこと[描いたもの]
【類語訳】記述, 描写, 表象, プロフィール

▸ **文型&コロケーション**
- a/ an description/ picture/ representation/ profile/ portrayal/ portrait/ depiction/ evocation **of** sb/ sth
- an **accurate** description/ picture/ representation/ profile/ portrayal/ portrait/ depiction/ evocation
- a **true/ realistic** description/ picture/ representation/ portrayal/ depiction
- a **detailed** description/ picture/ representation/ profile/ depiction/ evocation
- a **vivid** description/ picture/ representation/ portrayal/ depiction/ evocation
- to **give** a description/ picture/ representation
- to **draw/ paint** a picture/ a portrait
- to **build up** a picture/ profile

description [C, U] 記述, 描写 ◇Police have issued a *description* of the gunman. 警察は狙撃犯の人相を発表した ◇'Scared stiff' is an apt *description* of how I felt at that moment. 「ゾッとした」というのがその時私がどう感じたかを表す適切な表現だ ◇There was no mention of any cleaning in my **job description**. 私の職務経歴書では清掃作業のことにはまったく触れていなかった ◇I experienced a personal pain that goes **beyond description** (= is too great to express in words). 筆舌に尽くしがたい個人的な苦痛を経験した

picture [C, ふつう単数で] (生き生きとした)描写 ◇The writer paints a gloomy *picture* of the economy. その作家は経済情勢の悲観的な状況を描いている ◇From newspaper reports a *picture* emerges of a country barely under control. 新聞の報道から, 辛うじて統制されているに過ぎない国の様子が浮かび上がってくる ☞ **picture** (IMAGINE)

representation [C, U] 《やや形式》描写;表象 ◇The snake swallowing its tail is a *representation* of infinity. 尻尾を呑み込んでいる蛇は無限性を表したものである ◇the negative *representation* of single mothers in the media メディアにおけるシングルマザーの否定的な報じられ方 ☞ **represent** (PRESENT 2), **represent** (REPRESENT 2)

profile [C] (有益な情報をもたらす)プロフィール, 横顔 ◇We first build up a detailed *profile* of our customers and their requirements. 私たちはまず顧客と彼らの要望に関する詳細なプロフィールを作成する ◇His psychological *profile* is revealing. 彼の心理的な特性が明らかにされつつある

portrayal [U, C] 《やや形式》(絵・本・映画などでの)描写(の行為・方法) ◇The article examines the *portrayal* of gay men in the media. その記事はメディアにおける男性同性愛者の描かれ方を調査している ◇He is best known for his chilling *portrayal* of Hannibal Lecter. 彼はハンニバル・レクター役の身の毛もよだつ演技で最も有名である ☞ **portray** (PRESENT 2)

portrait [C] (本・映画などでの詳細な)描写 ◇Her first film was a stunning *portrait* of life in the sugar plantations of her native Martinique. 彼女が手がけた初の映画は彼女が生まれたマルティニーク島の砂糖農園での生活を見事に描写した作品だった

▸ **ノート** **portrayal**と**portrait**の使い分け:**portrayal**は言葉・画像で表されるものを指し, **portrait**は描写, 劇, 映画そのものを指す。☞ **portrait** (PICTURE)

depiction [C, U] 《フォーマル》描写画;(新聞・映画などでの)描写 ◇The latest addition to the gallery is a *depiction* of Amsterdam. その美術館の最新の所蔵品はアムステルダムの描画だ ◇They object to the movie's *depiction* of black people. 彼らはその映画における黒人の描かれ方に反発している ☞ **depict** (PRESENT 2)

▸ **ノート** **representation, portrayal, depiction**の使い分け:**representation**が最も一般的。書き言葉による描写・絵画・芸術作品に用いることは可能だが, 映画や動いたり変化したりするものにはふつう用いられない。**representation**はまた人・集団・場所・物事についても用いられる。**portrayal**は描写・演じぶりを指し, 必ずしも絵を指すわけではない。ふつう**portrayal**は人・集団について用いられ, しばしば俳優が演じる実在[架空]の登場人物を指す。**depiction**はしばしば芸術作品である絵画, 特に風景画を表すフォーマルな表現。**depiction**はまた人・集団の描写・演出上の表現にも用いられる。

evocation [C, U] 《書き言葉》(感情・思い出・像を呼び起こす)描写 ◇The film is a brilliant *evocation* of childhood in the 1940s. その映画は1940年代の幼年期を鮮やかに思い起こさせる作品だ ◇The artist's work has been praised for its richness of *evocation*. その芸術家の作品は回想を引き出す力の豊かさで賞賛されている

descriptive 形

descriptive・explanatory・interpretative・illustrative
物事を他の物事で描写[説明]する
【類語訳】記述的な, 描写的な, 説明的な, 解説的な, 解釈的な

▸ **文型&コロケーション**
- **for** descriptive/ explanatory/ interpretative/ illustrative **purposes**
- descriptive/ explanatory/ interpretative **notes**
- a descriptive/ explanatory/ interpretative **statement/ passage**
- descriptive/ explanatory/ illustrative **material**

descriptive 記述的な, 描写的な ◇She read out some of the *descriptive* passages in the novel. 彼女は小説の中の描写的な文章をいくつか読み上げた ◇The term I used was meant to be purely *descriptive* (= not judging). 私が用いた言葉は純粋に事実を述べたものであった

explanatory [ふつう名詞の前で] 《やや形式》説明[解説]的な ◇There are *explanatory* notes at the back of the book. 本の巻末には解説が付けられている ❶ self-explanatoryは「自明の」「説明を要しない」という意味。◆I think the title is *self-explanatory*. (そのタイトルは説明不要だと思う)。☞ **explain** (EXPLAIN 1)

interpretative (または特に米で **interpretive**) [ふつう名詞の前で] 《フォーマル》解釈的な ◇The *interpretative* problems arise from concepts that may be understood

deserted, design

in different ways by different people. 解釈上の問題は人によって理解の仕方が異なる概念から生じる ☞ **interpret** (EXPLAIN 1), **interpretation** (DEFINITION)

illustrative 《フォーマル》説明に役立つ ◇Be sure to include plenty of *illustrative* examples. 必ず役立つ実例をたくさん入れるようにしなさい ☞ **illustrate** (EXPLAIN 1), **illustration** (EXAMPLE 1)

> ノート **explanatory** と **illustrative** の使い分け：explanatory notes とは直接的に言葉で説明するものを、illustrative materials とは実例を挙げて示すものを言う。

deserted 形

deserted・abandoned・disused・unoccupied・uninhabited
もはや人のいなくなった場所や置き去りにされた人や物を表す
【類語訳】見捨てられた、見限られた、不用になった、空いている、無人の

> 文型&コロケーション
> ▸ a deserted/ an abandoned/ an unoccupied/ an uninhabited **area**
> ▸ a deserted/ an abandoned/ a disused/ an unoccupied **building**
> ▸ a deserted/ an abandoned/ an unoccupied **house**
> ▸ a deserted/ an abandoned/ a disused **warehouse**
> ▸ an abandoned/ a disused **mine/ railway/ railroad**
> ▸ a deserted/ an abandoned **village**
> ▸ a deserted/ an uninhabited **island**
> ▸ **largely/ completely/ totally** deserted/ abandoned/ uninhabited

deserted （場所が）人のいない；（場所・人・物が）見捨てられた ◇The office was completely *deserted*. そのオフィスは完全に引き払われた後だった ◇A large proportion of the remaining community was made up of widows and *deserted* wives. 残された地域社会の相当部分が未亡人や夫に見捨てられた妻から成っていた

abandoned （人・場所・物が）見捨てられた ◇The charity's work involves finding foster homes for *abandoned* children. その慈善事業には捨て子の養育家庭を探す活動も含まれている ◇Police found several guns in an *abandoned* car. 警察は乗り捨てられた車から数丁の銃を発見した

disused ［ふつう名詞の前で］不用になった、もはや使用されていない ◇The party was held in a *disused* warehouse. そのパーティーはもう使われていない倉庫で開かれた ❶「これまで使われたことのない」「その時使われていない」を意味するunused と disused とを混同しないよう注意が必要。

unoccupied 住む[使う]人のいない、空いている ◇The building appeared to be *unoccupied*. その建物は空家のように見えた ◇Children must sit on a parent's lap unless an *unoccupied* seat is available. 空いている席がなければ子どもたちは親の膝に座らなければならない 反意 **occupied** ❶建物・部屋・席などが occupied ならば、人に使用されていることを意味する。◆Only half the rooms are *occupied* at the moment. ただ今、半分の部屋しか使われていません。☞ **vacant** (EMPTY)

uninhabited 人の住んでいない、無人の ◇They landed on an *uninhabited* island off the Newfoundland coast. 彼らはニューファンドランド海岸沖にある無人島に上陸した ◇The area is largely *uninhabited*. その地域の大部分には人は住んでいない ❶ **desert island** は「熱帯の無人島」を意味する一般的な語句である。

design 名

design・format・layout・configuration・arrangement・geography
構成要素の配置のされ方
【類語訳】設計、構成、形態、判型、レイアウト、間取り、配置、地形

> 文型&コロケーション
> ▸ a design/ format/ layout/ configuration **for** sth
> ▸ **in** a/ the (...) design/ format/ layout/ configuration/ arrangement/ geography **of** sth
> ▸ **in** design/ format/ layout
> ▸ a/ the **basic/ simple** design/ format/ layout/ arrangement
> ▸ a **complex** design/ format/ layout/ arrangement
> ▸ a **new** design/ format/ layout/ configuration/ arrangement
> ▸ the **original** design/ format/ layout
> ▸ a **similar/ different** design/ format/ layout/ arrangement
> ▸ the **same** design/ format/ layout/ arrangement
> ▸ the **standard** design/ format/ layout/ configuration/ arrangement
> ▸ a **traditional** design/ format/ layout/ arrangement
> ▸ to **use** a design/ format/ layout/ configuration
> ▸ to **follow** a design/ format/ layout
> ▸ to **change** the format/ layout/ configuration

design [U, C]（建物・本・機械などの）設計、造り ◇The machine's unique *design* prevents it from overheating. その機械の独特の設計はオーバーヒートを防ぐ ◇The equipment is quite complex in *design*. その装置はかなり設計が複雑だ ◇Our house was built to a traditional *design*. 我が家は伝統的な造りで建てられた ◇There was a basic *design fault* in the new computer. 新型のコンピューターには基本的な設計ミスがあった ◇What new *design features* does the TV have? そのテレビにはどんな新しい設計上の特徴がありますか ☞ **design** (DEVELOPMENT)

format [C]（行事・活動の）構成、形態；（本・雑誌の）判型 ◇The *format* of the new quiz show has proved very popular. 新しいクイズ番組の形態は非常に人気をよんでる ◇We will follow the same *format* as last year. 昨年と同じ形式に従う予定だ ◇Books are available in a larger *format*. より大きな判型の本が売られている

layout [C, ふつう単数で, U]（ページ・庭・建物などの）レイアウト、配置 ◇You'll soon get used to the *layout* of the building. 建物の間取りにすぐに慣れますよ ◇Editing and *layout* is now usually done on computer. 現在、編集とレイアウトはふつうコンピューター上で行われる ☞ **lay sth out** (ARRANGE)

configuration [C]《フォーマル or 専門語》（要素の）配置 ◇The design is based on four *configurations* of squares. そのデザインは正方形の4つの配置に基づいている ◇The stars seemed to appear in a different *configuration*. 星の配置が変わって見えるように思えた

arrangement [C, U] 配列、配置（すること） ◇Has the seating *arrangement* been worked out yet? 座席の配置はもう決まりましたか ◇She's taking a class in flower *arrangement*. 彼女は生け花の授業を受けている ☞ **arrange** (ARRANGE)

geography [単数で] (場所の)地形, 地勢, 配置 ◇She knew the *geography* of the building well. 彼女は建物の間取りをよく知っていた ◇The island's *geography* is very simple. その島の地形はいたってシンプルだ

design 動

1 design・invent・engineer
どのように見せる[機能させる]か決定して物を新しく生み出す
【類語訳】デザインする, 設計する, 発明する, 考案する

文型&コロケーション
▶ to design/ invent/ engineer a **new kind of motor**
▶ to design/ invent a **new product**
▶ to design/ engineer a **new car/ bridge**

design [他] (図を描いたり, 模型を作ったりして)デザイン[設計]する ◇to *design* a dress/an office ドレス/オフィスを設計する ◇a badly *designed* kitchen 設計のまずい台所 ◇He *designed* and built his own house. 彼は自分で家を設計して建てた ◇They asked me to *design* a poster for the campaign. 私はそのキャンペーンのポスターのデザインを頼まれた ☞ **design** (DEVELOPMENT 名)

invent [他] 発明[考案]する ◇I wish television had never been *invented*! テレビなんて発明されなければよかったのに ◇Louis Braille *invented* an alphabet to help blind people. ルイ・ブライユは目の不自由な人を助けるための文字体系を考案した ☞ **invention** (DEVELOPMENT), **inventive** (CREATIVE)

engineer [他, ふつう受身で] (乗り物・機械・構造物を)設計して造る ◇The car is beautifully *engineered* and a pleasure to drive. その車は素晴らしい設計で, 運転する喜びがある ◇the men who *engineered* the tunnel トンネルを設計し建設した男たち

> **ノート** design, invent, engineer の使い分け: invent はまったく新しい[それまで存在しなかった]物事に関して用いられる. ◆Who *invented* the motor car? (誰が自動車を発明したの). ✕Who *designed/engineered* the motor car? design, engineer は既存の物事の新バージョンに関して用いることが可能. ◆They've *designed/engineered* a new car. (彼らは新型車を設計した). invent はその車が本当に斬新なものでない限りこのような文脈では用いられない. ◆They've *invented/designed/engineered* a revolutionary new car. (彼らは革命的な新型車を考案/設計した). ◆They've *invented/designed/engineered* a whole new type of car. (彼らはまったく新しいタイプの車を考案/設計した)

2 design・be aimed at sth・be intended for/as/to be sth・mean
特定の目的や役割に合うように作る
【類語訳】計画する, 意図する, 目的とする, 狙う

文型&コロケーション
▶ to be designed/ intended/ meant **for/ as** sth
▶ to be designed/ intended/ meant **to be/ do** sth
▶ to be **clearly** designed for/ aimed at/ intended for/ meant to be sth
▶ to be **specifically/ primarily/ mainly/ principally/ largely** designed for/ aimed at/ intended for sth

design [他, ふつう受身で] 《進行形なし》(特定の目的に合うように)計画する, 意図する ◇The method is specifically *designed* for use with small groups. その方法は特に少人数のグループで用いられるよう考えられている ◇These classes are primarily *designed* as an introduction to the subject. これらの授業は主にその教科への入門講座として位置づけられている ◇The programme is *designed* to help people who have been out of work for a long time. そのプログラムは長期間失業している人を援助するためのものだ

be aimed at sth フレーズ 目的としている, 狙う ◇These measures *are aimed at* preventing violent crime. これらの対策には暴力犯罪を防止する狙いがある

be intended for/as/to be sth フレーズ (特定の目的・人々用に)計画[設計]されている ◇The book *is intended for* children. その本は子ども向けだ ◇The notes *are intended as* an introduction to the classes. その注意書きはそれらの授業への導入として作成されている ◇The programme *was intended to* encourage more local involvement in education. そのプログラムは教育への地域社会の参加を促進する狙いがあった

mean [他, ふつう受身で] 《進行形なし》計画[意図, 期待]する ◇The house was clearly *meant* to be a family home. その家は明らかに家族向けに作られていた ◇His father *meant* him to be an engineer. 《特に英》父親は彼にエンジニアになってもらいたかった ◇I was *never meant for* the army (= did not have the qualities needed to become a soldier). 私は決して軍人に向いてはいなかった ◇Philip and Kim were *meant for each other* (= are very suitable as partners). フィリップとキムはお似合いのパートナーだった

desire 名 ☞ HOPE 名 2

desire・need・wish・temptation・urge・impulse・inclination・whim・want・compulsion
所有[行動]することへの強い思い
【類語訳】欲求, 願望, 望み, 誘惑, 衝動, 性向, 思いつき

文型&コロケーション
▶ a desire/ a need/ a wish/ an urge/ an inclination **for** sth
▶ the desire/ need/ wish/ temptation/ urge/ impulse/ inclination/ compulsion **to do** sth
▶ a **strong** desire/ need/ wish/ temptation/ urge/ impulse/ inclination
▶ an **overwhelming** desire/ need/ temptation/ urge/ impulse
▶ an **irresistible** desire/ temptation/ urge/ impulse
▶ a **natural** desire/ wish/ temptation/ urge/ impulse/ inclination
▶ a **sudden** desire/ need/ urge/ impulse/ inclination/ whim
▶ **sexual** desires/ needs/ urges/ impulses/ inclinations
▶ to **have** a desire/ a need/ a wish/ a temptation/ an urge/ an impulse/ an inclination/ wants/ a compulsion
▶ to **feel** a desire/ a need/ a temptation/ an urge/ an impulse/ an inclination/ a compulsion
▶ to **express/ make known** a desire/ need/ wish
▶ to **satisfy** a desire/ a need/ an urge/ impulse/ sb's whims/ sb's wants
▶ to **pander to** sb's wishes/ whims/ wants
▶ to **resist/ fight** a desire/ a temptation/ an urge/ an impulse

desire [C, U]《ややフォーマル, 特に書き言葉》欲求, 欲 ◇Most children have an insatiable *desire* for knowledge. たいていの子どもたちは飽くなき知識欲を持っている ◇She felt an overwhelming *desire* to return home. 彼女は家に帰りたくてたまらなかった ◇He now had enough money to satisfy all his *desires*. 彼は今やあらゆる欲求を満たすだけの金を持っていた ◇I have no *desire* (= I do not want) to discuss the matter further.《フォーマル》これ以上そのことについて話し合いたくない ☞ **desire** (WANT)

need [C, U] 強い欲求, 必要性 ◇She felt the *need* to talk to someone. 彼女は誰かに話しかけていなくてはいられなかった ◇I'm *in need of* some fresh air. 新鮮な空気に当たりたい ◇It can be difficult to express our *needs* and *desires*. 私たちの欲求を言い表すのは難しいこともある ☞ **need** (NEED 名), **need** (NEED 動)

ノート **desire** と **need** の使い分け：need はふつう desire よりも強い欲求を意味し, ただ単にしたい事ではなく, しなければならないと感じる事について用いられる。しかしながら, 否定文では, 必要がない事を意味する。◆ She *had no* more *need of* me (= did not want me any more).（彼女は私をこれ以上必要としていなかった）

wish [C]《特に書き言葉》願望, 望み ◇I can understand her *wish* for secrecy. 彼女が内密にしておきたいのは理解できる ◇He *had no wish* to start a fight. 彼には喧嘩を始めたい気持ちなどなかった ◇His *dearest wish* (= what he wants most of all) is to see his grandchildren again. 彼の一番の望みは孫たちにもう一度会うことだ ◇It was her *dying wish* that I should have it. 私にそれを託すことが彼女の最期の望みだった ☞ **wish** (WANT), **wish** (WISH)

ノート **desire** と **wish** の使い分け：単独で用いられる場合, desire は wish よりもやや強い欲求を表すだけだが, desire はしばしば deep, great, urgent, burning, insatiable, overwhelming などの形容詞と共に用いられ, 非常に強い欲求を表す。wish はこれらの形容詞とあまり結び付かない。

temptation [C, U]（よくないことを承知の上での）欲求, 誘惑 ◇The *temptation* of easy profits was too much for them. 楽して儲けるという誘惑に彼らは勝てなかった ◇Don't give in to *temptation*. 誘惑に負けるな ◇I couldn't resist the *temptation* to open the letter. 私はその手紙を開けたいという思いを我慢できなかった

urge [C]（抑えがたい）衝動 ◇I had a sudden *urge* to hit him. 私は突然彼を殴りたい衝動に駆られた ◇Freud claimed that this behaviour was caused by the repression of sexual *urges*. フロイトはこの行動は性的衝動の抑圧によって引き起こされると主張した ☞ **urgent** (URGENT)

ノート **need** と **urge** の使い分け：両語ともしばしば精神ではなく肉体から生じると思われる感情を表す。◆ a/an biological/instinctive/primitive *need/urge*（生物学的な/本能的な/根源的な欲求）◆ sexual *needs/urges*（性的欲求）。しかしながら, needs はふつう多くの人が共有しているので理解しやすい感情を指す。urge はやや理解されがたく, 実際に言動に移すことを我慢しようとする感情を指す。◆ She felt a violent *urge* to laugh, but suppressed it, with difficulty.（彼女は笑いたいという激しい欲求に駆られたが, やっとの思いで我慢した）

impulse [C, ふつう単数で, U]（後先を考えない）衝動 ◇He had a sudden *impulse* to stand up and sing. 彼は立ち上がって歌いたいという衝動に突然駆られた ◇Her first *impulse* was to run away. 彼女はまず逃げたいと思った ◇The door was open and *on an impulse* she went inside. ドアが開いていたので, つい中に入った ◇He tends to act *on impulse*. 彼は衝動的に行動しがちだ ☞ **impulsive** (SPONTANEOUS)

inclination [U, C]《ややフォーマル》…したい気持ち, 性向 ◇He did not show the *slightest inclination* to leave. 彼は帰りたいというそぶりは少しも見せなかった ◇He was a loner by nature and *by inclination*. 彼は生まれつき人と交わらない性格の男だった ◇You must follow your own *inclinations* when choosing a career. 仕事を選ぶ際は, 自分がやりたいことに従いなさい ❶ inclination は大して強い感情ではないかもしれないが, それに勝る理由がなければ, 人は自分の inclination に従って行動するものである。inclination がないということは, まったくその気がないことを意味する。

whim [C]（しばしばけなして）気まぐれ, 思いつき ◇He was forced to pander to *her every whim*. 彼は彼女の気ぐれすべてに付き合わされた ◇We bought the house *on a whim*. 私たちはふと思いついてこの家を買った ◇She hires and fires people *at whim* (= as and when she wants to, without good reason). 彼女は気まぐれに人を雇ったり解雇したりする

want [C, ふつう複数で] 望み ◇She spent her life pandering to the *wants* of her children. 彼女は子供たちの望みに迎合しながらの生活を送った ❶ この意味では wants はふつう my/your/his/her/our/their/the customers' wants または the wants of sb など所有を表す句で用いられる。☞ **want** (NEED 名), **want** (WANT)

compulsion [C, U]《ややフォーマル, 書き言葉》（よくない[ばかげた, 危険な] 抑えがたい）衝動；衝動強迫 ◇He felt a great *compulsion* to drive too fast. 彼は猛スピードで運転したいという強い衝動に駆られた ◇Obsessions and *compulsions* often develop in people who live stressful lives. 強迫観念や衝動強迫はストレスの多い生活を送る人にしばしば現れる ☞ **compelling** (URGENT)

destroy 動

destroy・wipe sb/sth out・devastate・ravage・decimate・annihilate・exterminate・zap

存在できないように人や物事を傷つける[除去する, 殺害する]
【類語訳】破壊する, 壊滅させる, 消滅させる, 殺害する, 全滅させる, 大打撃を与える

文型&コロケーション

▶ to destroy/ wipe out/ devastate/ ravage/ decimate a village/ town/ city
▶ a bomb/ blast destroys/ devastates buildings
▶ to destroy/ wipe out/ decimate/ annihilate/ exterminate/ zap the enemy
▶ to destroy/ wipe out profits/ savings
▶ a/ an earthquake/ flood/ fire destroys/ devastates/ ravages sth

destroy [他]（物事を）破壊する；（人などを）殺害する, 滅ぼす ◇The building was completely *destroyed* by fire. 建物は火事で全壊した ◇They've *destroyed* all the evidence. 彼らはすべての証拠を破棄した ◇Heat gradually *destroys* vitamin C. 熱は徐々にビタミンCを破壊する ◇Failure was slowly *destroying* him (= making him less confident and happy).《比喩的》失敗により彼はゆっくりと破滅の道をたどっていった

↪**destroy**

➤**destruction** 名 [U] ◇a tidal wave bringing *death and destruction* in its wake 死と破壊をもたらす高波 ◇*weapons of mass destruction* 大量破壊兵器

wipe sb/sth 'out 句動詞 (人・物事を)全滅[壊滅, 消滅]させる ◇Whole villages were *wiped out* by the earthquake. 地震で村々がまるごと全滅した ◇a campaign to *wipe out* malaria マラリア撲滅運動 ◇Their life savings were *wiped out*. 彼らの老後の蓄えは消え去った

devastate [他] (場所・地域・建物を)壊滅させる ◇The bomb *devastated* much of the old part of the city. 爆弾でその都市の旧市街地の大半が壊滅した

➤**devastation** 名 [U] ◇The bomb caused widespread *devastation*. 爆弾で広範囲の地域が壊滅した

ノート destroy と devastate の使い分け: devastate は destroy よりも意味は強いが, 場所と建物以外のものには用いられない. devastate は人について用いる場合は意味が変わってくる.

ravage [他, ふつう受身で]《ややフォーマル》(場所・商売に)大打撃[被害]を与える ◇The countryside has been *ravaged* by pollution. その田園地帯は汚染で大被害を被った ◇the flood-/quake-/tornado-/war-*ravaged* country 洪水/地震/トルネード/戦禍に見舞われた国 ◇a recession that has *ravaged* the textile industry 繊維産業に大打撃を与えた不況

➤**ravages** 名 [複数形] ◇*the ravages of* inflation/poverty/war インフレーション/貧困/戦争の大打撃 ◇Her looks had not survived *the ravages of time*. 彼女の容貌は寄る年波には勝てなかった

decimate [他, ふつう受身で](特定地域内の動植物・人間を)多量に滅ぼす;(産業・サービスを)大幅に衰退させる ◇The rabbit population was *decimated* by the disease. その病気で多くのウサギが死んだ ◇Rural transport provision has been *decimated*. 地方の輸送事業はかなり衰退している

➤**decimation** 名 [U] ◇the *decimation* of the rainforests 熱帯雨林の破壊

annihilate [他] (人を)絶滅[全滅]させる ◇The human race has enough weapons to *annihilate* itself. 人類は自らを絶滅させるのに十分な兵器を所有している

➤**annihilation** 名 [U] ◇the *annihilation* of the whole human race 全人類の絶滅

exterminate [他] (故意に人・動物を)全滅させる ◇They use poison to *exterminate* moles. モグラの駆除に毒薬が用いられる

ノート decimate と exterminate の使い分け: decimate はふつう災難, 特に病気の結果, 人・動植物の多く(すべてではない)が死ぬことを言う. exterminate は人が意図的に動物・人のすべてを殺すことを言う.

zap (-pp-) [他]《インフォーマル》(暴力で突然人・物事を[に])殺す[破壊する, 衝撃を与える] ◇The monster *got zapped* by a flying saucer (= in a computer game). モンスターは空飛ぶ円盤にやっつけられた ◇He jumped like a man who'd been *zapped with* 1,000 volts. 彼は1000ボルトで感電した人のように跳ねた

detailed 形

detailed・comprehensive・careful・thorough・close・rigorous・minute・in-depth・exhaustive・full-scale

detailed

細部や全体に大きな注意を払って検討[研究, 検査]する行為を表す
【類語訳】詳細な, 細部にわたる, 包括的な, 入念な, 細心の, 精密な, 全面的な

文型&コロケーション

▸ a detailed/ a comprehensive/ a careful/ a thorough/ a close/ a rigorous/ a minute/ an in-depth/ an exhaustive **analysis**

▸ a detailed/ a comprehensive/ a careful/ a thorough/ a close/ a rigorous/ an in-depth/ an exhaustive/ a full-scale **study/ investigation**

▸ a detailed/ a comprehensive/ a careful/ a thorough/ a close/ a rigorous/ a minute/ an exhaustive **examination** of sth

▸ a detailed/ a comprehensive/ a careful/ a thorough/ a close/ an in-depth **look** at sth

▸ a detailed/ a careful/ a thorough/ a rigorous/ an exhaustive/ a full-scale **search**

▸ detailed/ comprehensive/ careful/ thorough/ rigorous/ in-depth/ exhaustive **research**

▸ detailed/ comprehensive/ thorough/ rigorous/ exhaustive **tests**

▸ a detailed/ a comprehensive/ a thorough/ an in-depth/ an exhaustive **survey**

▸ detailed/ comprehensive/ thorough/ in-depth/ exhaustive **coverage**

▸ detailed/ comprehensive/ careful/ minute **instructions**

▸ a detailed/ a comprehensive/ a thorough/ an in-depth/ an exhaustive **discussion**

▸ detailed/ comprehensive/ thorough/ in-depth/ exhaustive **knowledge**

▸ detailed/ careful/ thorough/ close **consideration**

▸ detailed/ careful/ close/ rigorous/ minute **attention**

detailed 詳細な; 細部にわたる ◇She was able to give a *detailed* description of her attacker. 彼女は自分を襲った犯人のことを詳しく述べることができた ◇He gave *detailed* instructions on what to do in an emergency. 彼は緊急時に何をすべきかについて細かい指示を与えた

comprehensive 包括[総合]的な, 広範囲にわたる ◇a *comprehensive* list of addresses 広範囲にわたる住所録 ◇You are advised to take out *comprehensive* insurance (= covering all risks). 総合的に損害をカバーする保険に入ることをお勧めします

➤**comprehensively** 副 ◇The matter has been *comprehensively* discussed. その問題は包括的に議論されている

careful 入念な, 慎重な ◇This is a very *careful* piece of work. これはとても入念に作られた作品だ ◇After *careful* consideration we have decided to offer you the job. よく考えた後, 私たちはあなたを採用することに決めました 反意 **careless**

➤**carefully** 副 ◇Read the contract *carefully* before signing it. 契約書をよく読んでからサインしてください ◇He chose his words *carefully*. 彼は言葉を慎重に選んだ

thorough 徹底的な ◇You will need a *thorough* understanding of the subject. そのテーマをとことん理解している必要があるでしょう ◇The police carried out a *thorough* investigation. 警察は徹底的な捜査を行った ❶ thorough は特に人の知識・理解・仕事のやり方について用いられる.

➤**thoroughly** 副 ◇Wash the fruit *thoroughly* before use. お使いになる前に果物をよく洗ってください ◇The work had not been done very *thoroughly*. その仕事はあまり徹底的に行われていなかった

close [名詞の前で] (見たり、考えたりすることが)入念な、綿密な ◇Take a *close* look at this photograph. この写真をよく見てください ◇**On closer examination** the painting proved to be a fake. さらによく調べてみると、その絵は偽物であることがわかった

➤**closely** 副 ◇I sat and watched everyone very *closely*. 私は座って全員を入念に観察した

rigorous (研究・調査・問題への取り組みに関して)厳密な ◇Few people have gone into the topic in such *rigorous* detail. そのテーマをこれほど綿密に追求した人はほとんどいない ◇The second team adopted a much more *rigorous* approach to the problem. 2番目のチームはその問題により厳密な手法で取り組んだ

➤**rigorously** 副 ◇Each product is *rigorously* tested before being put on sale. それぞれの製品は販売前に厳密な検査を受けています

➤**rigour** 《英》《米では rigor》 名 ◇academic/intellectual/scientific *rigour* 学問的/知的/科学的な厳密さ

minute 細心の、精密な ◇A *minute* inspection of the vase revealed tiny cracks in the glaze. 花瓶を細かに検査したところ、つやのある表面に小さなひびが見つかった ◇She remembered everything **in minute detail/in the minutest detail(s)**. 彼女は事細かにすべてを覚えていた

➤**minutely** 副 ◇The agreement has been examined *minutely*. その契約は事細かに検討された

,in-'depth [ふつう名詞の前で] (問題について)掘り下げた、突っ込んだ ◇We will be providing *in-depth* coverage of the election as the results come in. 結果が入ってくる中で選挙を深く掘り下げた内容の報道をお届けする予定です ◇Tonight's programme is an *in-depth* look at the long-term effects of unemployment. 今夜の番組では失業が及ぼす長期的影響を掘り下げてみます

exhaustive (議論・研究・検査が)徹底的な、完全な ◇*Exhaustive* research has been carried out into the effects of the drug. その薬の効用に対する徹底的な調査が実行されている ◇The information in this leaflet is not intended to be *exhaustive*, but it does tell you the basic facts. このパンフレットは情報をすべて網羅する意図で作られておりませんが、基本的な事実はわかります

➤**exhaustively** 副 ◇Every product is *exhaustively* tested before being sold. すべての製品は販売前に徹底的な検査を受けています

full-scale [名詞の前で] (組織的な活動が)総力を挙げた、全面的な ◇Rebel troops launched a *full-scale* attack on the city. 反乱軍がその都市に対して総攻撃を仕掛けた ◇The police made a *full-scale* search of the area. 警察はその地域を全面的に捜索した

ノート このグループの語にはまた、ある意味への焦点の当て方という点で次のような違いが見られる。すなわち、detailed, close, minute, in-depth などは、細部への理解や詳細な情報の提示といった「深さ」に焦点を当てたもの、comprehensive, exhaustive, full-scale などは、あらゆる観点から一つの主題に関してすべてを包括するという「幅」に焦点を当てたもの。thorough, rigorous はこの「深さ」と「幅」の両方に焦点を当てたものである。

determination 名

determination・persistence・resolve・spirit・purpose・tenacity・perseverance
困難[不快]なことを継続する助けとなる個人的資質
【類語訳】決意、根気強さ、気概、気迫、意気、意志、がんばり

文型&コロケーション
▶determination/ resolve **to do** sth
▶**great** determination/ persistence/ resolve/ spirit/ purpose/ tenacity/ perseverance
▶**sheer/ dogged** determination/ persistence/ perseverance
▶**to show** (your) determination/ persistence/ resolve/ spirit/ tenacity
▶**to have** determination/ persistence/ spirit/ purpose/ tenacity/ perseverance

determination [U] 《しばしばほめて》(困難でも試み続けようとする)決意 ◇The key to his success was his dogged *determination* to see things through. 彼の成功の鍵は物事を見極めようとする不退転の決意だった ◇She fought the illness with courage and *determination*. 彼女は勇気と決意を持って病気と闘った

persistence [U] (困難にめげない)根気強さ、粘り強さ、しぶとさ ◇His *persistence* was finally rewarded when the insurance company agreed to pay for the damage. 彼の粘りはついに報われ、保険会社は損害賠償に同意した ◇It was her sheer *persistence* that wore them down in the end. 彼女の不屈の粘り強さに彼らはついに根負けした ☞ **persist** (PERSIST)

resolve [U] 《フォーマル、しばしばほめて》(強固な)決意 ◇The difficulties in her way merely strengthened her *resolve*. 前途にある困難も彼女の決意を強固なものにするだけだった ◇He did not weaken in his *resolve*. 彼は決意を曲げなかった

spirit [U] 《ほめて》(勇気・決意・エネルギーの合わさった)気概、気迫、意気 ◇Show a little **fighting spirit**. 少しは闘志を見せなさい ◇Although the team lost, they played with tremendous *spirit*. チームは負けたが、彼らは非常に素晴らしい気迫でプレーした ◇They took away his freedom and **broke his spirit**. 彼の自由は奪われ気力はくじかれた ☞ **spirited** (LIVELY)

purpose [U] 《ややフォーマル》(計画を立て完遂する)決意、意志 ◇He has enormous confidence and **strength of purpose**. 彼には大きな自信と意志の力がある

tenacity [U] 《ややフォーマル、書き言葉》(試み続けようとする)決意、粘り強さ ◇They competed with skill and *tenacity*. 彼らは巧みにまた粘り強く競い合った

ノート **determination と tenacity の使い分け**：determination は tenacity よりも意味の幅が広い。determination はしばしば困難・危険・苦悩に直面した状況において発揮され、よく courage and determination の句で用いられる。tenacity の場合、勇気は不要で、それほど重要[深刻]ではない状況において発揮され、成功するための粘り強さを表す。

perseverance [U] 《ややフォーマル、ほめて》(失敗・困難にめげず目的を達成しようとする)粘り強さ、がんばり ◇They showed great *perseverance* in the face of difficulty. 彼らは困難に直面しながらも素晴らしいがんばりを見せた
☞ **persevere** (PERSIST)

persistence と perseverance の使い分け： perseverance はふつう病気・不況・不運など人の力が及ばない状況がもたらす困難に直面した状況で発揮される。persistence は他人が助けてくれなかったり，妨害したりして困難をもたらす場合に発揮される。

determine 動

determine・shape・govern・dictate・form・decide・rule
人や物事の発展の仕方や事の生じ方に影響を与える
【類語訳】決定する，決める，左右する，方向づける，支配する

shape	govern	determine
form	rule	dictate
		decide

【文型&コロケーション】
▶ to determine/ shape/ govern/ dictate/ decide **how**...
▶ to determine/ govern/ dictate/ decide **what/ when/ why**...
▶ to determine/ dictate **that** ...
▶ to determine/ shape/ dictate/ decide the **outcome/ result** (of sth)
▶ to determine/ shape/ dictate the **course/ direction/ future** (of sth)
▶ to determine/ shape/ form the **character** of sb/ sth
▶ to determine/ shape/ govern **behaviour**
▶ a **factor** determines/ shapes/ governs/ decides sth
▶ a **force** determines/ shapes/ governs sth
▶ to be **largely** determined/ governed/ dictated by sth

determine [他，しばしば受身で]《フォーマル》(事の生じ方・タイプを)決定する，決める，左右する ◇Female employment was *determined* by economic and social factors. 経済的・社会的要因によって女性の雇用は左右された ◇The physical capabilities of a plant *determine* where it can and cannot live. 植物の生物的能力によってどこに生息できるかできないかが決まる ◇Upbringing plays an important part in *determining* a person's character. しつけは人の性格を決定する上で重要な役割を果たす

shape [他] (人・物事の発展の仕方を)決定づける，方向づける ◇Historical events helped to *shape* the town. 歴史上の出来事がこの町の今を形成する一助となった ◇She had a leading role in *shaping* party policy. 彼女は党の政策の方向づけに主要な役割を果たした ◇Religion had long been losing its power to *shape* and control behaviour. 宗教は行動を方向づけ，制御する力を長い間かけて失っていった

govern [他，しばしば受身で]《ややフォーマル》(事の生じ方・人の振る舞い方を)決定[左右]する ◇Prices are very much *governed* by market demand. 価格は市場の需要によって大きく左右される ◇We need changes in the *law governing* school attendance. 就学を規定する法律を改正する必要がある ◇All his decisions had been entirely *governed* by self-interest. 彼は私利私欲によってすべての決定を下していた

dictate [他，自] (特定の状況が)決定する ◇It's generally your job that *dictates* where you live now. 現在住んでいる場所を選ばせているのは一般的に言って仕事である ◇Circumstances *dictated* that I had to wait nearly two years. いろいろな事情で私は2年近く待たされることになった ◇This is clearly the best choice, unless financial considerations *dictate otherwise*. 財政的に考慮しても事情が変わらなければ，これは明らかに最善の選択 ◇She had to remain indoors for 30 days before the wedding, as **custom dictates**. しきたりで結婚式まで彼女は30日間屋内にいなければならなかった

form [他] (人の性格・考え方を)決定する ◇Positive and negative experiences *form* a child's character. 好ましい経験とそうでない経験が子どもの性格を決定する ◇No other work of fiction has had such an influence in *forming* public attitudes. 他のいかなる小説も大衆の考え方を方向づける上でこれほどの影響力はなかった

shape と form の使い分け： 両語とも shape/form sb's character/ideas/attitude/opinions など，人の性格・考え方への影響を言うときに用いられる。form は不可だが，shape はまた人の行動・事の成り行きに及ぼす影響について言うときにも用いられる。×Historical events helped to *form* the town. ×the power of religion to *form* behaviour.

decide [他，自] (結果を)決定する ◇A mixture of skill and good luck *decided* the outcome of the game. 技術と好運とが相まってその試合の結果がもたらされた ◇In the end, price was the *deciding* factor. 最終的に，価格が決め手となった

rule [他，しばしば受身で]《しばしばなしで》(生活・選択などを)左右する，支配する ◇The pursuit of money *ruled his life*. 金銭の追求が彼の人生を支配していた ◇We live in a society where we are *ruled* by the clock. 私たちは時計に支配された社会に暮らしている

develop 動

1 ☞ IMPROVE 2
develop・move・evolve・progress・gain ground・advance・shape up・come on/along・mature
徐々により大きく[よく，強く]なったり，より進歩したりする
【類語訳】発達する，発展する，進展する，向上する，進歩する

【文型&コロケーション】
▶ to develop/ move/ evolve/ progress/ mature **from** sth
▶ to develop/ move/ evolve/ progress **to** sth
▶ to develop/ evolve/ mature **into** sth
▶ to develop/ move/ evolve/ progress/ advance **towards** sth
▶ to develop/ move/ evolve/ progress/ advance **beyond** sth
▶ an **idea** develops/ evolves/ gains ground
▶ a **style/ theory** develops/ evolves
▶ a **war/ campaign** develops/ progresses
▶ to develop/ move/ evolve/ progress/ gain ground/ advance/ mature **rapidly/ slowly**
▶ to develop/ move/ evolve/ progress/ gain ground/ advance **steadily**
▶ to develop/ move/ evolve/ progress/ advance **further**
▶ to be developing/ progressing/ shaping up/ coming on **well**

develop [自] 発達する，発展する ◇The child is *developing* normally. その子は正常に発育している ◇The place has rapidly *developed* from a small fishing community into a thriving tourist resort. その場所は

development

小さな漁村から、景気のよい観光リゾート地へと急速に発展した ◇Their relationship has *developed* over a number of years. 彼らの関係は長年にわたって育まれてきた ☞ **development** (PROGRESS)

move [自]《副詞や前置詞と共に》《ややインフォーマル》進展する ◇Time is *moving on*. 時間はどんどん過ぎている ◇Share prices *moved ahead* today. 今日、株価が上がった ◇Things are not *moving* as fast as we hoped. 事態は私たちが望んだほど早くは進展していない ❶ *move* は ふつう on, ahead, up など方向を示す副詞や fast, slowly, quickly, rapidly, steadily など速度を示す副詞を伴う。

evolve [自]《ややフォーマル》(単純な形から複雑な形へ)徐々に発展する ◇The idea *evolved* from a drawing I discovered in the attic. そのアイデアは私が屋根裏部屋で見つけたスケッチから生まれた ◇The company *evolved* into a major chemical manufacturer. その会社は化学薬品製造の大会社へと発展した ☞ **evolve** (TURN 2)

➤ **evolution** [名] [U] In politics Britain has preferred *evolution* to revolution (= gradual development to sudden violent change). 政治においてイギリスは革命よりも漸進的変化を好んできた

progress [自] (一定期間にわたって)向上[発展]する; 進歩する ◇The course allows students to *progress* at their own speed. その課程では学生は自分自身のペースで進んでいくことができる ◇Work on the new road is *progressing* slowly. 新しい道路の工事はゆっくりと進行している ❶ この意味での progress は一定期間学ぶ学生や仕事・計画について用いられる。☞ **progress, progression** (PROGRESS)

gain 'ground [慣れ] 有力[優勢]になる ◇Sterling continues to *gain ground* against the dollar. スターリングがドルに対して強い傾向が続いている ◇These ideas slowly *gained ground* over the next ten years. これらの考え方はその後10年にわたってゆっくり浸透していった ❶ gain ground はほとんどの場合 system, party, movement, sb's views [ideas] について用いられる。

advance [自] (知識・科学技術が)発展[向上]する ◇Our knowledge of the disease has *advanced* considerably in recent years. その病気についての我々の知識は近年かなり向上している ◇As medical science *advances*, treatments are becoming more and more expensive. 医学の進歩に伴い、治療がますます高額になっている
☞ **advance, advancement** (PROGRESS)

,shape 'up [句動] (しばしば進行形で)《ややインフォーマル、特にジャーナリズム》(順調に)進展する ◇Our plans are *shaping up* nicely (= showing signs that they will be successful). 私たちの計画はうまくいっている ◇It's *shaping up* to be an exciting climax to the championships. 優勝を決めるエキサイティングなクライマックスになりそうな展開だ

,come 'on/along [句動] 《ふつう進行形で》《話し言葉》(望みどおりに)進展する ◇'How's the project going?' 'Oh, it's *coming on*.' 「プロジェクトはどう」「ええ、うまくいっていますよ」 ◇It was spring, and the garden was *coming along* nicely. 春になり庭はとてもいい感じになってきた

mature [自]《ややフォーマル》成熟[熟達]する ◇She has *matured* into one of the country's finest actresses. 彼女はその国で最も素晴らしい女優の一人に成長した

2 ☞ MAKE 1
develop・pioneer・evolve
新しいアイデア[製品]を考え出す、開発する

【類語訳】考案する、開発する、先駆者になる、発展させる

▸ to develop/ pioneer/ evolve a/ an **idea/ technique/ method/ strategy/ system/ way/ style/ design/ policy/ plan**
▸ to develop/ pioneer a/ an **concept/ model/ approach/ scheme/ project/ service/ technology**
▸ to develop/ evolve a **theory/ framework/ programme**
▸ a/ an **scientist/ team/ group/ institute/ company/ authority** develops/ pioneers sth

develop [他] (新しいアイデア・製品を)考案[開発]する ◇The company *develops* and markets new software. その会社は新しいソフトウェアを開発・販売している ◇A new type of painkilling drug has recently been *developed*. 新しいタイプの鎮痛剤が最近開発された ☞ **developer** (DESIGNER)

pioneer [他、しばしば受身で] (特に書き言葉) 開拓する、(新技術などを)開発する ◇This is a new technique, *pioneered* by surgeons in a London hospital. これはロンドン病院の外科医が開発した新しい技術です ❶ pioneer は科学的な文脈でしばしば用いられる。典型的な目的語には treatment, new approach, technique などが挙げられる。しばしば受身で、治療法や技術がどこで初めて開発されたかについて言うときに用いられる。☞ **pioneer** (LEADER 2)

evolve [他] 《ややフォーマル、書き言葉、特にビジネス》(単純な形から複雑な形へ)徐々に発展させる、進化させる ◇Each school must *evolve* its own way of working. それぞれの学校は独自の運営法を編み出さなければならない ❶ evolve の場合、組織(に属する人)が主語となり、目的語に method, system, policy, style, technique などをとる場合が多い。

development 名

development・design・creation・innovation・invention
新しい物事の開発および開発された物事
【類語訳】開発、設計、デザイン、設計図、創造、創作物、革新、発明、創案

▸ sb's **new/ latest** design/ creation/ innovation/ invention
▸ a **brilliant** design/ innovation/ invention
▸ a/ an **ingenious/ wonderful** design/ invention
▸ **product** development/ design/ innovation
▸ the development/ design **process**

development [U, C] 開発;開発された製品 ◇the *development* of vaccines against tropical diseases 熱帯病ワクチンの開発 ◇A more powerful version of this engine is currently *in development* (= being developed). このエンジンのより強力なバージョンは現在開発中です ◇*developments* in aviation technology 航空技術の開発

design [U, C] (図・模型を使った)設計、デザイン;設計図 ◇the *design* and development of new products 新製品の設計と開発 ◇a course in *art and design* 美術とデザインの課程 ◇*designs for* aircraft 飛行機の設計図 ◇I made this one *to my very own design*. 私は自分が設計したとおりにこれを作った ☞ **design** (DESIGN 名), **design** (DESIGN 動 1)

devote, dictator

creation [U, C] 創造；(芸術的・独創的な)創作物 ◇Job *creation* needs to be the top priority. 雇用創出が最優先であるべきだ ◇The committee recommended the *creation* of a new government agency to be responsible for the environment. 委員会は環境問題を担当する新しい政府系機関の創設を勧告した ◇a literary *creation* 文学作品 ☞ **create** (MAKE 1), **creative** (CREATIVE)

innovation [U, C] 革新；新しいアイデア[手法] ◇an age of technological *innovation* 技術革新の時代 ◇recent *innovations* in steel-making technology 製鋼技術の最近の先端技法 ☞ **innovative** (CREATIVE), **innovator** (LEADER 2)

▸**innovate** [自] ◇We must constantly adapt and *innovate* to ensure success in a growing market. 拡大する市場において成功を収めるため絶えず順応し革新せねばならない

invention [C, U] 発明品；発明, 考案 ◇Fax machines were a wonderful *invention* at the time. ファックス機は当時驚くべき発明品だった ◇Such changes have not been seen since the *invention* of the printing press. 印刷機の発明以来このような変化は見られていない ☞ **invent** (DESIGN [動] 1), **inventive** (CREATIVE)

devote [動]

devote・dedicate・commit・give sth over to sth
多大な時間や努力を重要だと思う特定の活動や目的に向ける
【類語訳】注ぐ, 献身する, ささげる, 費やす, 投入する, 充てる

〔文型&コロケーション〕
▸to devote sth/ dedicate sth/ commit sth/ give sth over **to** sb/ sth
▸to devote/ dedicate **yourself** to sb/ sth
▸to devote/ dedicate/ commit/ give over your **life/ time** to sb/ sth
▸to devote/ dedicate/ commit (your) **resources/ funds** to sb/ sth
▸to devote/ dedicate/ give over (a) **space/ page/ chapter/ section**
▸to devote/ dedicate your **effort/ energy**
▸to devote/ give over your **attention/ thoughts**
▸to **entirely/ mainly** devote/ dedicate sth/ yourself to sb/ sth
▸to **exclusively/ solely/ specifically** devote sth/ yourself/ dedicate sth/ yourself/ give sth over to sb/ sth

devote [他]《ややフォーマル》注ぐ, ささげる ◇I could only *devote* two hours a day to work on the project. 私はそのプロジェクトの取り組みに1日に2時間しか割けないだろう ◇He *devoted* all his attention to his mother. 彼は献身的に母親の世話をした ◇Most companies *devote* resources to quality control and product testing. たいていの会社は資金を品質管理と製品検査に充てている ☞ **devotee** (FAN)

▸**devotion** [名] [U, 単数で] ◇Her *devotion* to the job left her with very little free time. 《ほめて》仕事に打ち込んでいたので彼女にはほとんど自由な時間がなかった ◇The judge praised the firefighters for their courage and *devotion* to duty. 裁判官は消防員たちの勇気と義務への献身を賞賛した ☞ **devotion** (LOVE [名] 2)

dedicate [他]《ややフォーマル, ふつうほめて》ささげる, 専心する ◇She *dedicates* herself to her work. 彼女は仕事に専心する人だ ◇He *dedicated* his life to helping the poor. 彼は貧者を援助することに一生をささげた ☞ **dedicated** (RELIABLE 1)

▸**dedication** [名] [U] ◇I really admire Gina for her *dedication* to her family. 《ほめて》ジーナの家族への献身は本当にすごいと思う ◇The job requires total *dedication*. その仕事には完全な献身が求められる

〔ノート〕**devote** と **dedicate** の使い分け：意味の違いはほとんどない。dedicate はふつうほめ言葉として用いられ, devote はほめ言葉としても中立的にも用いられるが, devotion と dedication という名詞は両方ともほめ言葉として用いられる。devote は thoughts, attention などと共に用いることもでき, 目的語に取る語の種類がやや多い。×He *dedicated* all his attention to his mother. dedicate とは oneself や one's life がよく結びつく。

commit (-tt-) [他]《ややフォーマル》(お金・時間を)費やす[投入する] ◇The council has *committed* large amounts of money to housing projects. 議会は巨額の資金を住宅事業に投入してきた ☞ **committed** (RELIABLE 1)

▸**commitment** [名] [U] ◇He was best known for his lifelong *commitment* to the socialist cause. 《ほめて》彼は生涯にわたって社会主義の理念に力を注いだことで最もよく知られていた ◇I was saddened to see their *lack of commitment*. 私は彼らの責任の欠如を見て悲しかった

give sth 'over to sth [句動詞] [ふつう受身で] (特定の目的に)充てる, ささげる ◇This gallery is *given over to* British art. このギャラリーは英国美術品のみを扱っています

dictator [名]

dictator・tyrant・despot・autocrat
国を独裁的に支配する人, 人を完全に支配する力があるかのごとく思っている人
【類語訳】独裁者, 専制君主, 暴君, 圧制者, ワンマン

〔文型&コロケーション〕
▸a/ an **cruel/ brutal/ evil/ ruthless** dictator/ tyrant/ despot
▸a **benevolent** dictator/ despot
▸a dictator/ tyrant/ despot **rules** a country

dictator [C]《けなして》(軍事力で権力の座についた)独裁者, 専制君主；独裁的に振る舞う人 ◇The country suffered at the hands of a series of *military dictators*. その国は代々続く軍事独裁者の手に苦しめられた ◇He was seen by many as a benevolent *dictator* (= one who tries to use his power in a good way). 彼は多くの人から慈悲深い独裁者と思われていた ◇Her father was a *dictator* and the whole family was afraid of him. 彼女の父親は独裁的で家族全員が彼を恐れていた ☞ **dictatorship** (REPRESSION), **dictatorial** (REPRESSIVE)

tyrant [C]《けなして》暴君, 圧制者 ◇The country was ruled by a succession of *tyrants*. その国は次々と暴君によって支配された ◇Many of the naval officers were no more than *petty tyrants*. 海軍将校の多くがただの狭量な圧制者に過ぎなかった ☞ **tyranny** (REPRESSION), **tyrannical** (REPRESSIVE)

despot [C]《けなして, ややフォーマル》暴君, 専制君主 ◇It is the story of a military coup which brings a brutal *despot* to power. それは残忍な暴君に権力を与える軍事クーデターの話だ ◇He was seen by many as *an en-*

die, differ, difference

lightened despot (= one who tries to use his power in a good way). 彼は多くの人から物わかりのいい専制君主と思われていた
autocrat [C]《しばしばなして、ややフォーマル、書き言葉》専制君主；専制的に振る舞う人、ワンマン ◇He governed as an *autocrat*. 彼は専制君主として統治を行った ◇The article painted her as an *autocrat*, angry with her husband and out of touch with her family. 夫に逆上し、家族のことなどおかまいなしの彼女をその記事でワンマンな人間として描いた ☞ **autocratic** (REPRESSIVE)

ノート **dictator, tyrant, despot, autocrat** の使い分け：tyrant は必ず残忍であり、一国の支配者にも、複数の人に対して権力をふるう経営者や教師にも用いる。dictator や despot は絶対的な権力を持ち、ふつう残忍であるが、benevolent dictator/despot や enlightened despot のように権力をよい形で用いようとする支配者を指すこともある。一国の支配者について用いられる場合、autocrat は必ずしもけなして用いられる語ではなく、単に絶対的な権力を持つ支配者を事実に基づいて表す語でもある。しかしながら、autocrat はけなして用いられることのほうが多く、家庭や組織において権力を持つ地位にいて、家族や部下に常に有無を言わさず服従を求める人を指す。

die 動

die・perish・pass away
生きることをやめる
【類語訳】死ぬ、枯れる、非業の死をとげる、亡くなる

文型&コロケーション
▸ to die/ perish **of / from** sth
▸ to die/ perish **in** an accident, a fire, etc.
▸ to die/ pass away **peacefully**

die [自, 他] 死ぬ、枯れる ◇Her father *died* of cancer. 彼女の父親はがんで死んだ ◇He *died* for his beliefs. 彼は信念のために命を投げうった ◇That plant's *died*. あの植物は枯れている ◇She *died* young. 彼女は若くして死んだ ◇He *died* a poor man. 彼は貧困の中死んだ ◇I'll never forget it **to my dying day** (= when I die). 私は死ぬまでそれを決して忘れないだろう ◇She *died* a natural death. 彼女は天寿をまっとうした ☞ **dead** (DEAD)
perish [自]《フォーマル or 文語》(天寿をまっとうせずに)死ぬ、非業の死をとげる ◇A family of four *perished* in the fire. 家族4人がその火事で死んだ ◇Thousands *perished* at the hands of the invading forces. 侵略軍の手により何千もの人が殺された ❶ perish はふつう戦争や事故の結果を述べる文章で用いられる。
‚pass a'way 《句動詞》死ぬ、亡くなる ◇His mother *passed away* last year. 彼の母親は昨年亡くなった ❶ pass away は die の婉曲表現。

differ 動

differ・range・vary・diverge
他の人や物事と違う
【類語訳】異なる、さまざまである

文型&コロケーション
▸ to differ/ range/ vary/ diverge **in** size, shape, etc.
▸ to differ/ diverge **from** sth
▸ to range/ vary **from** sth **to** sth
▸ to differ/ range/ vary **between** things/ A and B
▸ to differ/ vary **according to** sth
▸ to differ/ range/ vary/ diverge **widely**
▸ to differ/ range/ vary **enormously**
▸ to differ/ vary/ diverge **considerably/ markedly/ significantly**

differ [自]《ややフォーマル》(他の人・物事と)異なる；(二つの物事が)異なる ◇French *differs* from English in this respect. フランス語はこの点で英語と異なる ◇French and English *differ* in this respect. フランス語と英語はこの点で異なる ◇They hold *differing* views. 彼らは異なる意見を持っている ◇Ideas on childcare may *differ* considerably between the parents. 養育に対する考え方は両親によってかなり異なることもある
range [自]《副詞や前置詞と共に》(範囲が)…に及ぶ〔わたる〕 ◇The disease *ranges* widely in severity. その病気の深刻さは多方面にわたる ◇Estimates of the damage *range* between $1 million and $5 million. 損害の見積もりは100万ドルから500万ドルと幅広い ◇The opinions they expressed *ranged* right *across* the political spectrum. 彼らが表明した意見はまさに政治勢力全体に及ぶものだった ◇She has had a number of different jobs, *ranging* from chef to swimming instructor. 彼女はシェフから水泳のインストラクターまで幅広く、多種多様な仕事をしてきた ◇The conversation *ranged* widely (= covered a lot of different topics). 会話は多岐にわたった ☞ **range** (RANGE 1)
vary [自]《同種のものの質・大きさなどが》さまざまである ◇The students' work *varies* considerably in quality. 生徒の作品は質の点でかなり幅がある ◇The quality of the students' work *varies* considerably. 生徒の作品の質はかなり幅がある ◇New techniques were introduced with *varying degrees of* success. 新技術が導入されたが成功の度合いはさまざまだった ☞ **varied** (DIVERSE), **variable** (VARIABLE), **variety** (RANGE 1)
diverge [自]《フォーマル》(意見が)異なる ◇Opinions *diverge* greatly on this issue. この問題に関しては意見が大きく食い違っている

difference 名

difference・contrast・distinction・variation・imbalance・variance・disparity・divergence
人や物事が互いに似ていないこと
【類語訳】相違、違い、差異、変化、対照、区別、不均衡、格差、開き

文型&コロケーション
▸ a difference/ a contrast/ a distinction/ a variation/ an imbalance/ a variance/ a disparity/ a divergence **between** A and B
▸ a difference/ a contrast/ a variation/ an imbalance/ a variance/ a disparity/ a divergence **in** sth
▸ a **huge** difference/ contrast/ variation/ imbalance/ disparity
▸ a **considerable** difference/ contrast/ variation/ imbalance/ variance/ disparity/ divergence
▸ a **major/ fundamental** difference/ contrast/ distinction/ variation/ imbalance
▸ a **clear** difference/ contrast/ distinction/ variation/ disparity

▶ a **slight** difference/ variation/ variance/ divergence
▶ a **regional/ gender** difference/ variation/ imbalance
▶ to **show** a difference/ a contrast/ a distinction/ a variation/ an imbalance/ a variance/ a disparity/ a divergence
▶ to **see/ be aware of/ look at** a difference/ a contrast/ distinction/ variation
▶ to **highlight** a difference/ contrast/ distinction/ variation/ disparity
▶ to **explain** a difference/ a distinction/ a variation/ an imbalance/ a variance/ a disparity/ a divergence
▶ to **cause** a difference/ a variation/ an imbalance/ a divergence
▶ to **make** a difference/ contrast/ distinction

difference [C, U] 相違, 違い, 差異；変更, 変化 ◇There are no significant *differences* between the education systems of the two countries. その二つの国の教育制度に大きな違いはない ◇She noticed a marked *difference* in the children on her second visit. 彼女は2度目の訪問で子どもたちの著しい変化に気がついた ◇***What a difference***! You look great with your hair like that. すごく変わるね。髪をそんなふうにしてると素敵だよ ◇I can never ***tell the difference*** (= distinguish) between the twins. 私はその双子の区別がつかない 反意 **similarity** (SIMILARITY).

contrast [C, U] (二人以上の人・二つ以上の物事の)顕著な相違, コントラスト；対照 ◇There is an obvious *contrast* between the cultures of East and West. 東と西の文化には明らかな違いがある ◇A wool jacket with silk trousers provides an interesting *contrast* in texture. ウールの上着にシルクのズボンを合わせると面白い生地のコントラストができる ◇The company lost $7 million this quarter ***in contrast to*** a profit of $6.2 million a year earlier. 1年前の620万ドルの利益とは対照的に, 今四半期, その会社は7百万ドルの損失を出した ◇The poverty of her childhood ***stands in*** total ***contrast to*** her life in Hollywood. 彼女の子ども時代の貧困生活とハリウッドでの今の生活とはまったく対照的だ ◇When you look at their new system, ours seems very old-fashioned ***by contrast***. 彼らの新しいシステムを見ると, 私たちのは対照的に時代遅れのように思える ☞ **contrast** (COMPARE 1), **contrast** (CONFLICT 動).

distinction [C] 《やや堅い》(似た[関連のある]人・物事の)顕著な相違, 区別 ◇Philosophers did not make a *distinction* between arts and science. 哲学者たちは芸術と科学を区別しなかった ◇She tends to ***blur the distinctions*** between family and friends. 彼女は家族と友達との区別を明確にしない傾向がある ❶この意味では**make/draw a distinction between A and B**の句で用いられる。最初は似ているように思える物事を慎重に検討して区別することを指す。 ◆We need to ***draw a distinction*** between democratic socialism and social democracy. (民主社会主義と社会民主主義とは区別する必要がある).

variation [C, U] 相違, 差 ◇There may be striking *variations* within a species. 一つの種において著しい変異が起こる可能性もある ◇regional *variations* in voting patterns 投票パターンの地域差 ◇There is considerable *variation* in tastes across the country. 地方によって味覚がかなり違う ◇There is little ***variation by*** sex or social class in these attitudes. これらの考え方については性別や社会階級による差はほとんどない ❶ **variation** はふつう異なる場所・地域・文化における同種の人・物事の明らかな相違について言うときに用いられる。 ◆local/regional/geographical/environmental/climatic/cultural/ethnic *variation* (地域的/地理的/環境的/気候的/文化的/民族的相違). ☞ **variation** (CHANGE 名1).

imbalance [C, U] 《やや堅い or 専門語》不均衡, アンバランス ◇a global *imbalance* of/in power 世界の国力の不均衡 ◇Attempts are being made to redress (= put right) the *imbalance* between our import and export figures. 輸出入高の不均衡を調整する試みがなされている ◇Postnatal depression is usually due to hormonal *imbalance*. 産後のうつ病はふつうホルモンバランスの不均衡が原因で起こる 反意 **balance** ❶**balance**は「均衡」が取れている状況を意味する。◆Try to keep a *balance* between work and relaxation. (仕事と休息のバランスを保つようにしましょう). ◆This newspaper maintains a good *balance* in its presentation of different opinions. (この新聞は異なる意見の掲載のバランスをうまくとっている).

variance [U, C] 《フォーマル》変動, 差異 ◇There is considerable *variance* in pay across the company. 会社の中で給与はかなりの差がある ◇a note with subtle *variances* of pitch 高さが微妙に変わる音

disparity [U, C] 《フォーマル》格差 ◇The wide *disparity* between rich and poor was highlighted. 貧富の大きな格差が目立った ◇There are growing regional *disparities* in economic prosperity. 経済的繁栄の地域格差が広がりつつある

divergence [C, U] 《フォーマル》差異, 開き ◇There is a wide *divergence* of opinion within the group. 大きな意見の相違がグループ内にある

ノート **variance** と **divergence** の使い分け：**variance** は特に専門的な文脈, 例えば数字の分析で用いられる。 **divergence** は特に集団の **opinions** や **views** について言うときに用いられる。×considerable *divergence* in pay. ×a wide *variance* of opinion.

different 形 ☞ DIVERSE

different・unlike・contrasting・disparate・dissimilar・unequal
人[物事]が他の人[物事]と同じではない
【類語訳】似ていない, 異なる, 違った, 等しくない

文型&コロケーション
▶ different/ dissimilar **from** sth
▶ different/ contrasting/ disparate **views/ ways**
▶ to **look** different/ unlike sth/ dissimilar
▶ **very** different/ unlike/ disparate/ dissimilar/ unequal
▶ **quite/ totally** different/ unlike/ disparate/ dissimilar
▶ **not altogether/ not entirely** different/ unlike/ dissimilar

different 異なる, 違った ◇The room looks *different* without the furniture. その部屋は家具がないと違って見える ◇People often give very *different* accounts of the same event. 人は同じ出来事に関してしばしばまったく異なる説明をするものだ ◇American English is significantly *different* from British English. アメリカ英語はイギリス英語と大きく異なる ◇He saw he was no ***different than*** anybody else. 《米》彼は自分が他の人たちと全然違わないことがわかった ◇It's very ***different to*** what I'm used to. 《英, 話し言葉》それは私が慣れ親しんだ物とはまった

difficult

く違う ❶書き言葉では different to sb/sth は正しくないと考えられており、代わりに different from sb/sth を用いる。 反意 the same (EQUAL), similar (LIKE) 前形
▷**differently** 副 ◇Boys and girls behave *differently*. 男の子と女の子では振る舞いが違う ◇The male bird has a *differently* shaped head. オスの鳥は違う形の頭をしている

unlike 前 [名詞の前では用いない] 似ていない、異なる ◇Music is quite *unlike* any other art form. 音楽は他のどんな芸術形態ともかなり異なる ◇The sound was *not unlike* that of birds singing.《書き言葉》その音は鳥の鳴き声とよく似ていた ◇They are both teachers. Otherwise they are quite *unlike*. 彼らは二人とも教師。他の点ではまったく似ていないが ❶unlike は比較の場合 quite, most, so, very などの副詞と共に用いられたり、not の後で用いられる。 not unlike は「よく似ている」ことを意味する。 反意 **like** (LIKE 前形)

contrasting 形 [ふつう名詞の前で] (スタイル・色・態度が) 非常に異なる、対照的な ◇Choose bright, *contrasting* colours for a child's room. 子ども部屋には明るい対照的な色を選びましょう ◇The book explores *contrasting* views of the poet's early work. その本はその詩人の初期の作品に対する様々な対照的な見方を探究している ☞ **contrast** (CONFLICT 動), **contrast** (OPPOSITE 名)

disparate《フォーマル》(二つ以上の物が) 本質的に異なる ◇It's an ambitious book that tries to cover such *disparate* forms as Anglo-Saxon poetry and the modern novel. それは古英語の詩と現代小説というような本質的に異なるジャンルを合わせて論じようとする意欲的な本だ ◇The machine can keep the *disparate* parts of the system coordinated. その機械はシステムのまったく異なる部分同士の調和を保つことができる

dissimilar [しばしば否定文で] 《フォーマル》 同じでない、似ていない ◇These wines are *not dissimilar* (= are similar). これらのワインは似ている ◇They had spent their childhoods in highly *dissimilar* circumstances. 彼らはまったく異なる環境で幼年期を過ごしていた 反意 **similar** (LIKE 前形)

unequal (大きさ・量・価値などが) 等しくない、異なる ◇The sleeves are *unequal* in length. 袖の長さが違う ◇The rooms upstairs are of *unequal* size. 2階の部屋は大きさが異なる 反意 **equal** (EQUAL)

difficult 形

1 difficult・hard・challenging・demanding・taxing・testing

事が容易ではなく、行うのに多大な努力と技術が求められること
【類語訳】難しい、困難な、やりがいのある、骨の折れる、負担が大きい、きつい

文型&コロケーション

▸ difficult/ hard/ challenging/ demanding/ taxing **for** sb
▸ difficult/ hard **to do sth**
▸ difficult/ hard **to believe/ see/ tell/ say**
▸ a difficult/ hard/ challenging/ demanding/ taxing/ testing **time/ week/ year**
▸ a difficult/ hard/ challenging/ demanding/ taxing **work**
▸ a difficult/ hard/ challenging/ demanding/ taxing **job**
▸ a difficult/ hard/ challenging/ demanding **task/ target**
▸ a difficult/ hard/ challenging/ taxing/ testing **question**
▸ very/ quite difficult/ hard/ challenging/ demanding/ tax-

ing/ testing
▸ **physically** difficult/ hard/ challenging/ demanding/ taxing
▸ **emotionally** difficult/ hard/ challenging/ demanding/ taxing
▸ **technically** difficult/ hard/ challenging/ demanding
▸ **mentally/ intellectually** challenging/ demanding/ taxing

difficult 難しい、困難な ◇It's really *difficult* to read your writing. あなたの筆跡は本当に読みづらい ◇It can be *difficult* for young people to find jobs around here. 若者がこの辺りで仕事を見つけるのは難しいかもしれない ◇We didn't realize how *difficult* it was going to be. 私たちはそれがどれほど困難になろうとしているのかわからなかった ◇Senior lawyers handle the most *difficult* cases. 上級の弁護士が最も厄介な事件を扱う 反意 **easy, simple** (EASY 1), ☞ **difficulty** (PROBLEM)

hard 難しい、困難な ◇I always found languages quite *hard* at school. 学校ではいつも語学がすごく難しいと思っていた ◇It was one of the *hardest* things I ever did. それは私が今まで経験した中で最も困難なことの一つだった ◇It must be *hard* for her, bringing up four children on her own. 4人の子どもを彼女独りだけで育てるのは困難に違いない ◇It's *hard* to believe she's only nine years old. 彼女がたった9歳だなんて信じがたい ◇'When will the job be finished?' 'It's *hard* to say.'「その仕事はいつ終わるの」「わからない」 ◇I find his attitude quite *hard to take* (= difficult to accept). 彼の態度はまったく受け入れがたいものだ 反意 **easy** (EASY 1)

> ノート **difficult** と **hard** の使い分け： hard は difficult よりもややインフォーマルで、hard to believe/say/find/take/come by などの形で特に用いられるが、difficult もこれらの形で用いられることがある。

challenging (ほめて) やりがいのある、難しい ◇I have had a *challenging* and rewarding career as a teacher. 私は教師というやりがいと実りのある仕事をしてきた ◇We have changed the programme to make it more academically *challenging*. 私たちは講義内容をもっと学問的にやりがいのあるものに変更した ☞ **challenge** (PROBLEM)

demanding 要求の厳しい、骨の折れる、手のかかる ◇It is a technically *demanding* piece of music to play. それは技術的に演奏の難しい楽曲だ ◇This event is considered one of the most *demanding* in the sporting calendar. このスポーツの大会は日程の中で最も厳しいものの一つと思われる 反意 **undemanding** (EASY 1)

taxing [しばしば否定文で] 負担が大きい、きつい ◇This shouldn't be too *taxing* for you. これはあなたにとってそれほどきつくないはずだ ◇There was nothing intellectually *taxing* about the exercise. その練習問題には頭を悩ますことは何もなかった

testing 試練の、きわめて難しい ◇This has been a *testing* time for us all. これは私たち全員にとって試練の時だ

> ノート **demanding, taxing, testing** の使い分け： demanding が最も意味の強い語で、仕事や経験について言う。しばしば more, most, physically, mentally, emotionally などの副詞と共に用いられる。 taxing は特に否定的な文で用いられ、精神的努力を要する [要しない] 問題や仕事について言うときに用いられる。 testing は仕事ではなく経験について言い、特に time, week, year と共に用いられる。

2 difficult・tough・bad・hard・adverse・rough・unfavourable・disadvantageous

↳**difficult**

問題が多いことや多くの問題を引き起こすことを表す
【類語訳】多難な、厄介な、不都合な、苦しい、好ましくない、不利な

文型&コロケーション

▸ difficult/ tough/ bad/ hard/ unfavourable/ disadvantageous **for** sb
▸ tough/ hard/ rough **on** sb
▸ unfavourable/ disadvantageous **to** sb
▸ a difficult/ a bad/ a hard/ an adverse/ an unfavourable/ a disadvantageous **position**
▸ a difficult/ a tough/ a bad/ a hard/ a rough/ an unfavourable **situation**
▸ difficult/ tough/ bad/ adverse/ rough/ unfavourable **conditions**
▸ difficult/ tough/ adverse/ unfavourable **circumstances**
▸ a difficult/ tough/ bad/ hard/ rough **time/ day/ week/ year**
▸ a difficult/ tough/ hard/ rough **life/ childhood**
▸ a bad/ an adverse/ an unfavourable/ a disadvantageous **effect**

difficult 問題の多い、多難な ◇The next few months were quite *difficult*. 次の数か月はかなり多難だった ◇My boss is making life very *difficult* for me. 上司が私をひどく困らせている ◇What's the most *difficult* personal situation you've ever been in? 今まで経験した個人的な場面の中で最も苦しかったのはどんなこと ◇There was a great deal of *difficult* terrain to be covered. 踏破の難所がずいぶんあった ☞ **difficulty** (PROBLEM)

tough (個人的な)問題の多い ◇She's been having a *tough* time of it. 彼女には大変な時期が続いている ◇This will be the *toughest* test of his leadership yet. これは彼のリーダーシップに対する今までで最も厳しい試練となるだろう ◇It's *tough* out there in the real world. 現実の世の中は厳しいものだ ❶ **tough** は **difficult** ほど一般的な語ではない。物理的な状態ではなく個人的な問題について用いられる。
✗ *tough* terrain/weather conditions.

bad 問題の多い；厄介な ◇Things were *bad* enough without her interfering. 彼女のじゃまがなくても事態は十分に悪いものだった ◇The situation couldn't get any *worse*. 状況はそれ以上悪くなりようがなかった ◇It was the *worst* time of my life. それは人生の中で最悪の時だった ◇I think it was probably a *bad* time to ask him. 彼に頼むタイミングがおそらく悪かったんだと思う ◇He realized it had been a *bad* decision. 彼はそれがまずい決断であったことに気がついた

hard (状況が悪くて・お金がなくて)問題の多い ◇My grandmother had a *hard* life. 祖母は苦しい生活を送っていた ◇Times were *hard* at the end of the war. 終戦時は厳しい時期だった ◇Conditions were extremely *hard* in the camps. 収容所の状況は過酷なものだった ☞ **hardship** (TROUBLE 2)

adverse [ふつう名詞の前で]《ややフォーマル》不都合な；悪影響をもたらす ◇Lack of money will have an *adverse* effect on the research programme. 資金不足で研究プログラムに悪影響が出るだろう ◇*Adverse* weather conditions meant the rescue had to be abandoned. 悪天候は救援を断念せざるを得ないことを意味していた ◇They have attracted strong *adverse* criticism. 彼らは強く非難された

▸ **adversely** 副 ◇This move could *adversely* affect the UK's position in the market. この措置はイギリスの市場での立場に悪影響を及ぼしかねなかった

rough (問題が多くて)つらい、苦しい ◇He's had a really *rough* time recently. 彼は最近本当につらい日々を送っている ◇Life was *rough* on the streets. 路上での生活はきつかった ◇They set sail in *rough* conditions. 悪天候の中、彼らは出港した ❶ **life**, **times** は個人的問題や暴力がらみで **rough** でありうるし、**conditions** は物理的に困難で **rough** な

unfavourable 《英》《米 **unfavorable**》《フォーマル》(状態・状況が)好ましくない、不都合な ◇The conditions were *unfavourable* for increased crop production. 穀物生産量の増加に対して状況は好ましいものではなかった ◇The country's geographical position is *highly unfavourable*. その国の地理的位置は極めてよくない 反意 **favourable** (VALUABLE 2)

disadvantageous 《フォーマル》不利な；都合の悪い ◇The deal would not be *disadvantageous* to your company. その取り引きは御社にとって不利にはならないでしょう ◇Growing conditions here are *disadvantageous*. ここの生育条件はよくない 反意 **advantageous** (VALUABLE 2), ☞ **disadvantage** (DISADVANTAGE)

dignity 名

dignity • ego • pride • self-esteem • feelings • self-respect • self-image • sensibilities

自分への意識や自分自身の重要性[価値]を表す
【類語訳】威厳、尊厳、自尊心、自負、プライド、自己評価、気分、感情、気持ち、自己像

文型&コロケーション

▸ **injured** dignity/ pride/ self-esteem/ feelings
▸ **wounded** ego/ pride/ self-esteem/ feelings
▸ **personal** dignity/ pride/ self-esteem/ feelings
▸ **professional** dignity/ pride/ self-respect
▸ to **damage** sb's dignity/ ego/ pride/ self-esteem/ self-respect
▸ to **hurt** sb's pride/ feelings
▸ to **bolster** sb's ego/ pride/ self-esteem/ self-image
▸ to **boost** sb's ego/ self-esteem/ self-respect/ self-image
▸ to **restore** sb's dignity/ pride/ self-esteem/ self-respect
▸ to **lose/ keep** sb's dignity/ pride/ self-respect
▸ a **loss of** dignity/ pride/ self-esteem
▸ a **lack of** dignity/ ego/ self-esteem

dignity [U] 威厳、尊厳 ◇It's difficult to preserve your *dignity* when you have no job and no home. 仕事と家を失えば尊厳を保つのは難しい ◇He needed a way to retreat with his *dignity* intact. 彼には尊厳が傷つかないように引き下がる道が必要だった ☞ **dignified** (PROUD 1)

ego (複 **-os**) [C, U] 《時にけなして》自尊心、自負 ◇He has the *biggest ego* of anyone I've ever met. 彼は私が今まで会った誰よりも強い自尊心を持っている ◇Winning the prize really boosted her *ego* (= made her feel more confident). 賞を獲得して彼女の自尊心は大いに高まった ◇It was a huge blow to his *ego* to find out he was so unpopular. 自分が非常に不人気であることがわかり彼の自尊心は大きく傷つけられた ☞ **egoism** (PRIDE)

pride [U] プライド ◇She refused their help *out of pride*. 彼女は誇り高きがゆえに彼らの援助を断った ◇*Pride* would not allow him to accept the money. プライドが

彼に金を受け取ることを許さないだろう ◇It's time to *swallow your pride* (= hide your feelings of pride) and ask for help. 君はプライドを捨てて助けを求めてもいい頃だ ☞ **proud** (PROUD 1)

,self-e'steem [U] (自分の性質・能力への)自尊心, 自負, 自己評価 ◇Some children suffer from *low self-esteem* and expect to do badly. 子どもたちの中には自己評価が低くできなくて当たり前と思ってしまう者もいる ◇You need to build your *self-esteem*. 君は自尊心を確立する必要がある ☞ **esteem** (ADMIRATION)

feelings [複数形で] 気分, 感情, 気持ち ◇I didn't mean to hurt your *feelings*. あなたの感情を害するつもりはなかった ◇I kept off the subject of divorce so as to *spare her feelings*. 彼女のことを考えて離婚の話題は避けた

,self-re'spect [U] 自尊心 ◇Despite poverty and appalling conditions, these people still manage to keep their dignity and *self-respect*. 貧困と劣悪極まる状況にあっても, この人たちは尊厳と自尊心をどうにか持ち続けている ☞ **self-respecting** (PROUD 1)

,self-'image [C, ふつう単数で, U] (外見・能力についての)自己像 [評価] ◇It's very easy to get a *negative self-image* and lose confidence. 否定的な自己評価をして自信を失うのはとても簡単なことだ

sensibilities [複数形で] 《ややフォーマル, 書き言葉》 (傷つきやすい, 影響され)やすい)感情 ◇The article offended her religious *sensibilities*. その記事は彼女の信仰心を傷つけた

dim 形

dim・faint・weak・soft・thin
あまり強くない光を表す
【類語訳】ほの暗い, ぼんやりとした, かすかな, 弱い, 柔らかい

文型&コロケーション
▸ dim/ faint/ weak/ soft/ thin **light**
▸ a dim/ faint/ soft **glow**
▸ a dim/ soft **lamp**
▸ dim/ soft **lighting**
▸ faint/ thin **moonlight**
▸ a dim/ faint **outline**

dim (光が)ほの暗い; (光がなくて物が)よく見えない, かすかに見える ◇It was hard to see in the *dim* glow of the streetlights. それは街灯の薄明かりの下では見づらかった ◇The light is too *dim* to read by. 光が暗くて読めない ◇I could see a *dim* shape in the doorway. 戸口にぼんやりと人影が見えた 反意 **bright** (BRIGHT)
▸ **dimly** 副 ◇a *dimly* lit room ほの暗い照明の部屋
▸ **dimness** 名 [U] ◇It took a while for his eyes to adjust to the *dimness*. 彼の目が薄暗さに慣れるまでしばらくかかった

faint (光・物が)かすかな ◇There was a *faint* glimmer of light from her window. 彼女の部屋の窓からかすかな光がちらちらもれていた ◇We saw the *faint* outline of the mountain through the mist. 霧の中, 山のかすかな輪郭が見えた 反意 **bright** (BRIGHT)
▸ **faintly** 副 ◇A streetlight glowed *faintly* through the frosted glass. 曇りガラスの街灯がかすかに光を放っていた

weak (光が)弱い ◇The *weak* winter sunlight spread across the lake. 冬の弱い日差しが湖に広がった 反意 **strong** (STRONG 2)

▸ **weakly** 副 ◇The sun was shining *weakly*. 太陽が弱々しく輝いていた

ノート **dim, faint, weak の使い分け**: dim は空・部屋・場所の光が明るくなく, はっきりと物が見えづらいときに用いられる. faint はしばしば glimmer や glow などの光が見えづらい状態を表す. weak は特に明るくなく暖かさを感じない太陽光に用いられ, 物ははっきりと見えるが光自体は物に反射して輝かせるほど強くない.

soft [ふつう名詞の前で] (光が)柔らかい, ぎらぎらしない ◇The kitchen was filled with the *soft* cosy glow of candlelight. 台所はろうそくの柔らかく心地よい光に満ちていた 反意 **dazzling, harsh**
▸ **softly** 副 ◇The room was *softly* lit by a lamp. 部屋はランプで優しく照らされていた

thin [ふつう名詞の前で] 《文語》(光が)弱い ◇the *thin* grey light of dawn 夜明けの淡い灰色の光

dirty 形

dirty・dusty・filthy・muddy・soiled・grubby・stained・messy・unwashed・grimy
人や物が清潔でない
【類語訳】不潔な, 汚れた, ほこりだらけの, 泥まみれの, 薄汚い, 染みだらけの

文型&コロケーション
▸ dirty/ dusty/ filthy/ muddy/ soiled/ grubby/ stained/ unwashed **clothes**
▸ dirty/ dusty/ filthy/ grubby/ unwashed/ grimy **hands**
▸ dirty/ dusty/ filthy/ grubby/ grimy **windows**
▸ a dirty/ dusty/ filthy **room**
▸ a dirty/ filthy/ messy **job**
▸ to **look** dirty/ dusty/ grubby/ messy/ grimy
▸ to **get** dirty/ dusty/ filthy/ muddy/ stained/ messy
▸ **rather** dirty/ dusty/ muddy/ grubby/ messy/ grimy
▸ **a bit** dirty/ dusty/ muddy/ grubby/ messy
▸ **slightly** dirty/ dusty/ grubby/ soiled/ stained
▸ **really** dirty/ dusty/ filthy/ messy/ grimy
▸ **very/ extremely** dirty/ dusty/ muddy/ messy

dirty 不潔な; (ほこり・土・泥・油などで)汚れた ◇If your hands are *dirty*, go and wash them. 手が汚れているなら, 洗いに行きなさい ◇My thumb had left a *dirty* mark on the paper. 紙に親指の汚い跡が付いた ◇Try not to get too *dirty*! あまり汚れないようにしなさい ◇The soot had made everything *dirty*. すすで何もかもが汚れていた ◇I always get given the *dirty* jobs (= jobs that make you become dirty). 私はいつも汚れる仕事ばかりさせられる 反意 **clean** (CLEAN 形)

dusty ほこりだらけの; ほこりをかぶった ◇The room was dark and *dusty*. 部屋は暗くほこりだらけだった ◇We tramped for miles down the *dusty* road. 私たちは土ぼこりの上がる道を何マイルも重い足取りで歩いた ◇There were shelves full of faded *dusty* books. 色あせてほこりをかぶった本が詰まった棚があった

filthy ひどく汚い, 汚らしい ◇Why are the streets so *filthy* in this part of the city? この町のこのあたりってなぜこんなに汚いの ◇It's absolutely *filthy* in here. ここはめっぽう汚い ◇There were two beggars dressed in *filthy* rags. 汚いぼろを着た乞食が二人いた

muddy 泥まみれの ◇Don't you come in here with

↪dirty

those *muddy* boots on! その泥まみれのブーツを履いたままここに入らないで ◇We drove along the *muddy* track. 私たちはぬかるんだ道を車で通った ◇Look, you've made the floor all *muddy*. こら、床中泥まみれにしやがって ☞ **mud** (SOIL)

soiled《ややフォーマル》(体の老廃物で)汚れた ◇She changed the *soiled* bedding. 彼女は汚れた寝具類を取り替えた

grubby《ややインフォーマル》(洗っていなくて)薄汚れた、薄汚い ◇My hands are a bit *grubby*. 手が少し汚れている ◇He hoped she wouldn't notice his *grubby* shirt cuffs. 彼は彼女に汚れたシャツの袖口に気づかれたくなかった

stained《しばしば複合語で》染みだらけの; 染みの付いた ◇The sheets were old and *stained*. シーツは古くて染みだらけだった ◇The shirt was heavily *stained* with blood. シャツには大量の血痕が付いていた ◇She was wearing a pair of paint-*stained* jeans. 彼女はペンキの染みの付いたジーンズをはいていた ☞ **stain** (MARK)

messy《ややインフォーマル》(液体・粘性のある物で)汚れた[汚れる] ◇The children got really *messy* painting and gluing. 子どもたちは絵の具や糊を使ううちにすごく汚れた ◇Painting can be a *messy* job. ペンキ塗りは下手をすると汚れる仕事だ ❶ *messy* house/room/desk (取り散らかした家/部屋/机)はしばしば「汚い」「取り散らかした」を意味する。 ☞ **messy** (UNTIDY), **mess** (MESS 1)

unwashed《特に書き言葉》洗っていない ◇The sink was full of *unwashed* dishes. シンクは洗っていない食器でいっぱいだった ◇Their clothes were dirty and their hair *unwashed*. 彼らの服は汚れていて髪は洗われていなかった

grimy(ほこり・土・泥・油などで)汚れた ◇Her hands were *grimy* from changing the car wheel. 彼女の手は車のタイヤ交換で汚れていた

disabled 形

disabled・handicapped・lame
体を申し分なく[円滑に]使うことができない
【類語訳】障碍(がい)のある、不自由な

文型&コロケーション

▶a disabled/ handicapped **person/ child**
▶to **be born** disabled/ handicapped
▶to **leave sb** disabled/ handicapped/ lame
▶**badly/ profoundly/ seriously/ severely/ permanently/ mentally/ physically** disabled/ handicapped

disabled(体調・病気・けがで身体的・知的)障碍(がい)のある ◇My son is *disabled* and needs extra support at school. 息子には障碍があって学校では特別な援助が必要だ ◇The museum has special facilities for *disabled* people. その博物館には障碍者用の特別な設備がある ◇Does the theatre have *disabled* access? その劇場は障碍者は利用できますか 反意 **able-bodied** ❶ able-bodied は disabled とは反対に、「身体的に健全である」ことを表す。 ● Military service is compulsory for every *able-bodied* male between 18 and 27. (18歳から27歳までの身体的に健全なすべての男子に兵役が義務付けられている).
▶**the disabled** 名[複数扱い] ◇She spends a lot of her free time caring for *the disabled*. 彼女は自由な時間の多くを障碍者の介護に充てている ❶ the disabled より disabled people や people with disabilities という表現がしばしば好まれる。

disabled, disadvantage

handicapped《古風、時に侮蔑的》障碍(がい)のある ◇The accident left him physically *handicapped*. 事故で彼は身体障碍者になった

ノート disabled と handicapped の使い分け:「永続的に身体的・知的障碍のある」という意味の handicapped は今ではやや古風で侮蔑的に受け取られることもあるので避けるべき。 be mentally disabled/handicapped と言う代わりに have a learning disability (学習障碍がある)を用いる。

lame(けがのため人・動物が)足の不自由な ◇The accident left her slightly *lame*. 事故で彼女はやや足が不自由になった ◇His horse had **gone lame**. 彼の馬は足を悪くしていた ❶ 人について用いるとき、lame はふつう長期的な障碍(がい)を指す。一時的な足[脚]のけがならば、limp や walk with a limp を用いる。しかし、馬に go lame を用いる場合は、単に一時的なけがを指すことがある。

disadvantage 名

disadvantage・drawback・pitfall・snag・downside・catch
物事に伴う問題[困難]や物事の否定的な側面を表す
【類語訳】不利、不都合、不便、問題点、欠点、難点、危険、落とし穴、マイナス面、罠

文型&コロケーション

▶a/ the disadvantage/ drawback/ snag/ downside/ catch **to** sth
▶a/ the disadvantage/ drawback/ pitfall/ snag/ downside **for** sb
▶a disadvantage/ pitfall/ snag **in** sth
▶the disadvantages/ drawbacks/ pitfalls **associated with** sth
▶The disadvantage/ drawback/ snag/ downside/ catch **is that**...
▶a **possible** disadvantage/ drawback/ pitfall/ snag/ downside
▶the **only** disadvantage/ drawback/ pitfall/ snag/ catch
▶a/ an **major/ obvious/ potential** disadvantage/ drawback/ pitfall/ snag
▶a/ the **big/ main/ minor/ slight** disadvantage/ drawback/ snag
▶to **have** a disadvantage/ drawback/ snag/ downside
▶to **overcome** a disadvantage/ drawback/ pitfall/ snag

disadvantage [C, U]《成功・進展をはばむ》不利、不都合、不便、問題点、欠点 ◇There are *disadvantages* to the plan. その計画には問題点がある ◇The fact that he didn't speak a foreign language **put him at a** distinct *disadvantage*. 外国語を話せないということで彼は明らかに不利な立場に立たされた ◇I hope my lack of experience won't **be to my disadvantage**. 経験不足が仇(あだ)とならないことを望む ◇The advantages of the plan far **outweigh the disadvantages**. その計画の利点はその欠点を補って余りある ◇Many children in the class suffered severe social and economic *disadvantage*. そのクラスの多くの子どもたちは社会的・経済的にひどく恵まれない立場にあった 反意 **advantage** (BENEFIT), ☞ **disadvantageous** (DIFFICULT 2)
▶**disadvantage** 動[他] ◇Some pension plans may *disadvantage* women. 年金制度の中には女性に不利に働く可能性のあるものもある

drawback [C]（物事の魅力を損なう）障害, 問題, 難点, 欠点 ◇The main *drawback* to it is the cost. その一番のネックは費用だ ◇This strategy has its *drawbacks*. この戦略には欠点がある

pitfall [C]（潜在的な）危険, 落とし穴 ◇We need to be alert to potential *pitfalls*. 陰に潜む落とし穴に注意する必要がある ◇Buying property holds many *pitfalls* for the unwary. 騙されやすい人にとっては不動産の購入には多くの落とし穴が潜んでいる

snag [C]《ややインフォーマル》（小さな[隠れた, 思わぬ]）問題, 難点 ◇The only *snag* with the course is that it's quite short. その講座[コース]の唯一の難点は非常に短いことだ ◇There is just one *small snag* — where is the money coming from? 小さな問題がほんの一つだけある—どこから資金が出るかだ ◇We've *hit* a technical *snag*: the printer isn't compatible with my PC. 私たちは思わぬ技術上の問題にぶつかった. それはそのプリンターが私のパソコンと対応していないことだ

downside [単数形]《一般的には好ましくない事の》マイナス面, 難点 ◇The *downside* of all this success is that I don't get to spend much time with my family. この成功のマイナス面は家族との時間を取れなくなることだ ◇On the *downside*, such improvements in efficiency often mean job losses. 否定的側面としては, このような効率の改善はしばしば雇用の喪失を生む [反意] **upside** ❶ upside は「（全般的には好ましくない事の）良い面」を指す. ◆The *upside* is that I do get to spend more time with my family.（良い面は家族との時間を多く取れるようになることだ）

catch [C, ふつう単数で]《ややインフォーマル》隠れた問題, 罠, 落とし穴 ◇It sounds too good. There must be a *catch*. うますぎる話だ. きっと罠があるに違いない ◇All that money for two hours' work — *what's the catch*? 2時間の仕事でそんなにも多くの金がもらえるなんて—どんな落とし穴があるのか

▸ **catch sb 'out** 句動詞 ◇Many investors were *caught out* by the fall in share prices. 株価の暴落で多くの投資家が落とし穴に陥った

disagree 動

disagree・differ・dispute・be at odds・take issue with sb・not see eye to eye with sb
人が異なる意見を持つ
【類語訳】反対する, 言い争う, 異議を唱える, 対立している, 反論する

文型&コロケーション

▸ to disagree/ differ/ dispute/ be at odds/ take issue/ not see eye to eye **with** sb/ sth
▸ to disagree/ differ/ be at odds/ take issue/ not see eye to eye **on** sth
▸ to disagree/ differ/ be at odds/ take issue **over** sth
▸ to disagree/ differ/ take issue **about** sth
▸ to disagree/ differ **as to** sth
▸ to **agree to** disagree/ differ

disagree [自] 意見が異なる[合わない] ◇Even friends *disagree* sometimes. 友達でさえも時には意見が分かれる ◇He *disagreed* with his parents on most things. 彼は両親とたいてい意見が合わなかった ◇Some people *disagree* with this argument. この主張に反対する人もいる ◇No, I *disagree*. I don't think it would be the right thing to do. いいえ. 私は反対です. それが正しいことであるとは思いません ◇She *disagreed that* building more roads was the only way to handle traffic congestion. 彼女はさらなる道路建設が交通渋滞を緩和する唯一の方法だとすることに異議を唱えた [反意] **agree**, ☞ **disagreement** (DEBATE)

differ [自]《ややフォーマル》意見が異なる ◇I have to *differ* with you on that. その件についてはあなたと意見を異にしなければならない ◇Medical opinion *differs* as to how to treat the disease. 病気の治療法に関して医師たちの意見が異なる ◇I think you're wrong. Let's just agree to *differ*. あなたは間違っていると思う. 意見が違うという点だけは一致しておきましょう ☞ **difference** (DEBATE)

ノート **disagree** と **differ** の使い分け：disagree は理由を述べ, 自分が正しいことを相手に説得しようとする場合. differ はよりフォーマルな語で, 意見が異なる理由ではなく事実を述べるときに用いられる. disagree の主語は人のみだが, differ は人も意見も主語となる. ×Medical opinion *disagrees* as to how to treat the disease.

dispute [他, 自]（所有権に関して）言い争う, 異議を唱える ◇The ownership of this land has been *disputed* for centuries. 何世紀もの間, この土地の所有権をめぐり論争が続けられている ◇The United Nations recognizes the area as a *disputed territory*. 国際連合はその地域を係争中の領土と認定している ◇The issue remains *hotly disputed*. その問題はいまだに激しく論争されている ☞ **dispute** (DEBATE)

be at 'odds 行札 対立している ◇He's always *at odds* with his father over politics. 彼は政治のことで父親と対立ばかりしている

take 'issue with sb 行札《フォーマル》（人に）反論する ◇I must *take issue with* you on that point. その点ではあなたに反対せねばなりません

not see eye to 'eye with sb 行札（人と）意見が合わない ◇The two of them have *never seen eye to eye* on politics. 彼ら二人は政治のことで意見が合った試しがない

disappear 動

disappear・vanish・fade・die out・dissolve・clear・melt
ある場所に存在しなくなる
【類語訳】見えなくなる, なくなる, 消える, 絶滅する, 廃れる, 消失する, 消す

文型&コロケーション

▸ to disappear/ vanish/ fade/ dissolve/ melt **into** sth
▸ to fade/ melt **away**
▸ **anger/ hope** disappears/ vanishes/ fades/ melts
▸ a **smile** disappears/ vanishes/ fades
▸ **cloud/ smoke/ mist** disappears/ clears
▸ a **species** disappears/ vanishes/ dies out
▸ a **tradition/ custom** disappears/ dies out
▸ disappear/ vanish/ fade/ die out/ dissolve/ clear **completely**
▸ disappear/ fade/ die out/ dissolve/ clear **gradually**
▸ to disappear/ vanish/ fade **from view/ sight**
▸ to disappear/ vanish/ melt **into thin air**

disappear [自] 見えなくなる；存在しなくなる；なくなる，見つからなくなる ◇The plane *disappeared* behind a cloud. 飛行機は雲に隠れて見えなくなった ◇The problem won't just *disappear*. その問題はまずなくならないだろう ◇Our countryside is *disappearing* at an alarming rate. 我が国の田園風景は驚くべき速さで消滅しつつある ◇The child *disappeared from* his home some time after four. その子は4時を回ったくらいの時刻に家からいなくなった 反意 appear (APPEAR)
▶**disappearance** [名] [U, C] ◇Police are investigating the *disappearance* of a young woman. 警察は若い女性の失踪について捜査している 反意 **appearance** (ARRIVAL)

vanish [自] （突然，説明のしようもなく）消える；存在しなくなる，なくなる ◇The magician *vanished* in a puff of smoke. 一筋の煙だけ残してマジシャンはパッと消えた ◇My glasses seem to have *vanished*. 私の眼鏡がなくなったみたいだ ◇The boys *vanished* without trace during a snowstorm. 吹雪の中で少年たちは足取りも残さぬまま消えた ◇All hopes of a peaceful settlement had now *vanished*. もはや平和的解決の望みがすべて絶たれていた

fade [自] 次第に消える ◇Her smile *faded*. 彼女の笑みは薄れていった ◇The laughter *faded away*. 笑い声が小さくなっていった ◇His voice *faded to* a whisper (= gradually became quieter). だんだん彼は声を潜めていった ◇All other issues *fade into insignificance* compared with the struggle for survival. 生存競争の現実に直面すると他の問題は取るに足らなくなっていく

,die 'out [句動] （動植物の種が）絶滅する；（慣習・伝統が）廃れる ◇The report estimates that up to 40,000 species will have *died out* by the end of the century. その報告書の見積もりでは最高で4万もの種が世紀末までに絶滅しているだろうとのことだ ◇Most of these traditions *died out* during the 19th century. これらの伝統の内の大半が19世紀に廃れてしまった

dissolve [自, 他] 《やや フォーマル or 文語》 消える, 消失する ；（物を）消す ◇When the ambulance had gone, the crowd *dissolved*. 救急車が行ってしまうと, 野次馬たちはいなくなった ◇His calm response *dissolved* her confusion. 彼の冷静な反応で彼女の混乱は落ち着いた

clear [自] （空・天気・煙・霧が）晴れる ◇The sky *cleared* after the storm. 嵐の後, 空は晴れた ◇The rain is *clearing* slowly. 雨がだんだんとやんできた ◇As the smoke *cleared*, two fighter planes came into view. 煙が晴れると2機の戦闘機が姿を現した 反意 cloud

melt [自] 《ふつう副詞か前置詞と共に》 （人・感情が）次第に消える ◇At the first sign of trouble, his supporters *melted away*. トラブルの兆候が見え始めただけで, 彼の支持者たちは徐々に消えていった ◇All her anger and hurt *melted away in* his embrace. 彼の胸の中で彼女の怒りと心の傷は徐々に消えていった

disappoint [動]

disappoint・let sb down・fail・leave sb in the lurch
人の望み[期待]どおりに援助[支持, 行動]しない
【類語訳】失望させる, 期待を裏切る, がっかりさせる

disappoint	let sb down fail	leave sb in the lurch

文型&コロケーション
▶to disappoint/ let down/ fail your **fans/ children/ family/ colleagues/ friends**
▶to be **sorry to** disappoint sb/ let sb down/ leave sb in the lurch
▶sb **won't** disappoint sb/ let sb down/ fail sb/ leave sb in the lurch

disappoint [他, 自] （人を）失望させる, （人の期待を）裏切る ◇Her decision to cancel the concert is bound to *disappoint* her fans. 彼女のコンサート中止の決定でファンは間違いなくがっかりするだろう ◇I hate to *disappoint* you, but I'm just not interested. あなたをがっかりさせて悪いが, 全く興味がないんだ ◇The movie had *disappointed* her (= it wasn't as good as she had expected). その映画は彼女の期待にそむく内容だった ◇His latest novel does not *disappoint*. 彼の最新の小説は期待を裏切らない

,let sb 'down [句動] （けなして） （援助・支持に関して人の）期待を裏切る ◇I'm afraid she *let* us *down* badly. 残念ながら彼女は私たちの期待をひどく裏切った ◇This machine won't *let* you *down*. この機械はあなたの期待を裏切りませんよ ◇He trudged home feeling lonely and *let down*. 彼は孤独と失望を胸にとぼとぼと家路についた

fail [他] 《ややフォーマル》 （人の期待を）裏切る ◇When he lost his job, he felt he had *failed* his family. 仕事を失って彼は家族を裏切ってしまったと感じた ◇She tried to be brave, but her courage *failed* her. 勇気を持とうとしたが彼女にはできなかった ◇***Words fail me*** (= I cannot express how I feel). 《比喩的》何と言えばよいかわからない ❶fail は family, children, friends, colleagues など自分を頼りにしてくれる人を目的語に取ったり, me を目的語にして courage, nerve, heart を主語に用いたりする.

leave sb in the 'lurch [句動] 《インフォーマル, けなして》 （困っている人を）助けられない, 見捨てる ◇I'm sorry to *leave* you *in the lurch* but I can't do the presentation with you this afternoon. 力になれず申し訳ありませんが, 午後にあなたとプレゼンを行うことはできません ◇She felt she had been *left in the lurch* by all her colleagues. 彼女は同僚達皆に見捨てられたと感じた ◇leave sb in the lurch は letting sb down の意味を強めた表現と言える. 人を失望させるだけではなく, 人を苦境に追いやることを意味する.

disappointing [形]

disappointing・unsatisfactory・wanting・discouraging
望んだり, 期待していたほどよくないことを表す
【類語訳】期待外れの, 失望させる, 不満足な, 不十分な, がっかりさせる

文型&コロケーション
▶disappointing/ unsatisfactory/ discouraging **that**...
▶a disappointing/ an unsatisfactory/ a discouraging **result/ experience**
▶a disappointing/ an unsatisfactory **outcome/ performance**
▶to **find sth** disappointing/ unsatisfactory/ wanting/ discouraging

disappointing 期待外れの ◇They gave a very *dis-*

appointing performance. 彼らの演奏はとても期待外れだった ◇The outcome of the court case was *disappointing* for the family involved. 裁判の結果は当事者家族の期待を裏切るものであった

unsatisfactory《ややフォーマル》不満足な ◇The results were considered to be thoroughly *unsatisfactory*. 結果はまったく不満足なものであると考えられた ◇He reflected on the *unsatisfactory* nature of his relationship with the school principal. 彼は校長との不本意な関係について思案した 反意 **satisfactory** (FINE), ☞ **INADEQUATE**

wanting［名詞の前では用いない］《フォーマル》不十分な ◇This explanation is *wanting* in many respects. この説明は多くの点で不十分である ◇The new system was tried and found *wanting*. 新しいシステムが試され基準を満たしていないことがわかった

discouraging がっかりさせる ◇The response to our appeal has been rather *discouraging*. 私たちの訴えに対する反応はやや不満の残るものであった 反意 **encouraging** (PROMISING), ☞ **discourage** (DISCOURAGE 2)

disapprove 動

disapprove・deplore・frown on/upon sth
人や物事を妥当［適切, 容認可能］でないと思う
【類語訳】反対する, 不満を示す, 非難する, 難色を示す

frown on/upon sth   disapprove   deplore

文型&コロケーション
▸ to disapprove of/ deplore/ frown on a/ an **practice**/ **action**
▸ to disapprove of/ deplore/ frown on **the use of** sth
▸ to disapprove of/ deplore **the way** sb does sth
▸ to **strongly** disapprove of/ deplore sth

disapprove［自］反対する ◇She wants to be an actor but her parents *disapprove*. 彼女は女優になりたいが両親は反対している ◇He strongly *disapproved of* the changes that had been made. 彼は行われた変更に強い不満を示した 反意 **approve** (IN FAVOUR), ☞ **disapproval** (CRITICISM), **disapproving** (CRITICAL)

deplore［他］《ややフォーマル》(公然と)非難する ◇Like everyone else, I *deplore* and condemn this killing. 他の皆さんと同様, 私はこの殺人行為を遺憾とし厳しく非難するものです ◇He *deplored the fact that* these criminals were treated by many as heroes. 彼はこれらの犯罪者たちが多くの人から英雄のように扱われている事実を槍玉にあげた ☞ **deplorable** (OUTRAGEOUS)

'frown on/upon sth 句動詞《ややフォーマル》(事に)難色を示す ◇In her family, any expression of feeling was *frowned upon*. 彼女の家では少しでも感情を表に出すのはよしとされなかった ◇According to the Home Office, this practice is *frowned upon*, but it is not illegal. 内務省によれば, この慣習は望ましくはないが違法ではないとのことだ

disaster 名

disaster・failure・catastrophe・fiasco・debacle・flop・washout
まったくうまくいかないこと, 問題［失望］を招くこと
【類語訳】災難, 失敗, 災い, 大失敗

文型&コロケーション
▸ a disaster/ failure/ catastrophe **for** sb
▸ a fiasco/ debacle **over** sth
▸ a **total** disaster/ failure/ catastrophe/ fiasco/ flop/ washout
▸ a **complete** disaster/ failure/ catastrophe/ fiasco/ flop
▸ a **financial** disaster/ failure/ fiasco/ debacle
▸ an **economic** disaster/ failure/ catastrophe
▸ to **prove** a disaster/ failure/ fiasco/ flop

disaster [C, U] 災難；大失敗 ◇Losing your job doesn't have to be such a *disaster*. たかが失職したくらいのことでそんなにじたばたするもんじゃない ◇*Disaster struck* when the wheel came off. 車輪が外れたのが惨事の幕あけだった ◇Letting her organize the party is a *recipe for disaster* (= sth that is likely to go badly wrong). 彼女にパーティーを準備させるのは災いの元だ ◇The play's first night was a total *disaster*. その劇の初日は完全な大失敗だった ☞ **disaster** (CRISIS)

failure [C] 失敗 ◇The whole thing was a complete *failure*. すべてが完全な失敗だった ◇A team learns from experience, both successes and *failures*. チームは成功も失敗も経験から学ぶものである ◇The venture proved to be a costly *failure*. その事業の失敗は高くついた 反意 **success**, ☞ **failure** (FAILURE)

catastrophe [C] 大失敗 ◇The attempt to expand the business was a *catastrophe* for the firm. 事業の拡大を企てたのがその会社にとって大失敗だった ◇We've had a few *catastrophes* with the food for the party. パーティー用の料理の件でとんでもないことが既にいくつか起きているんだ ☞ **catastrophe** (CRISIS)

fiasco [C]《ややインフォーマル》(計画・段取りのまずさで起こる決まりの悪い)大失敗 ◇What a *fiasco*! 大失敗だ ◇After the *fiasco* over the brochures, I decided to take charge of the marketing. パンフレットで大失敗があった後, 私はマーケティングを引き受けることにした

debacle [C]《ややインフォーマル》(意見の決裂による決まりの悪い)大失敗 ◇He should take responsibility for the *debacle* and resign. 彼は失敗の責任を取り辞任すべきだ

flop [C]《インフォーマル》(映画・パーティー・製品などの)失敗(作) ◇The film has been labelled the year's biggest box-office *flop*. その映画は興行面でこの年最大の失敗作と呼ばれている ◇The share sale has been a *flop* with investors. その株は投資家たちに不人気だ 反意 **hit**

washout [C, ふつう単数で]《インフォーマル》(雨による)大失敗 ◇They feared that the wedding was going to be a *washout* after torrential rain. 彼らは集中豪雨の後で結婚式が台無しになることを懸念した

discount 動

discount・deduct・take・subtract・knock sth off (sth)・take sth out of sth・take sth off sth・debit・dock
ある数［量］を別の数［量］から引く
【類語訳】割引して売る, ディスカウントする, 差し引く, 控除する, 減らす, 減額する

↪discourse / discourage

文型&コロケーション
- to deduct/ take/ subtract/ debit/ dock sth **from** sth
- to discount/ deduct/ take/ subtract/ knock sth off/ debit an **amount** (from sth)
- to take/ subtract one **number** from another
- to discount/ knock sth off/ take sth off **prices**
- to deduct/ knock off/ take off/ dock **points/ marks**
- to deduct sth from/ take sth out of/ dock sb's **pay/ wages**

discount [他, ふつう受身で]《特にビジネス》(物を)割引して売る, ディスカウントする ◇We're offering *discounted* prices throughout March. 3月中は割引価格でのご提供です ◇You can find *discounted* flights on the Internet. インターネットで割引[格安]航空便を見つけることができる ◇Most of our stock has been *discounted* by up to 40%. 在庫品の大部分が最大40%割引になっています ❶ *discount* の目的語には prices, rates, fees, fares, tickets, books, subscriptions などが挙げられる.
▷**discount** [名] [C, U] ◇The store manager gave us a 10% *discount* on the drum set. 店長がドラム一式を10%引きにしてくれた ◇They were selling everything *at a discount*. そこでは全品割引価格で売られていた ◇Do you give any *discount*? いくらか割引してくれませんか

deduct [他, しばしば受身で]《ややフォーマル》(金額・ポイントを)差し引く, 控除する ◇The cost of your uniform will be *deducted* from your wages. 制服代は給料から引かれます ◇Ten points will be *deducted* for a wrong answer. 答えを間違えると10点引かれます ❶お金の面では deduct はほとんどの場合, 給与などから引かれる税金について用いられる. ◇Tax is *deducted* at source (= before you actually receive the payment). (税金は源泉で徴収される). 他に deduct は主に競技や格付けシステムにおいて前もって与えられていたポイント・星数が引かれることについて用いられる.
▷**deduction** [名] [C, U] ◇*deductions* from your pay for tax and pension contributions 給与からの税と年金負担の控除

take [他]《進行形なし》(別の数字から)数字を引く ◇*Take* 5 from 12 and you're left with 7. 12から5を引くと7が残ります ◇28 *take away* 5 is 23.《インフォーマル, 話し言葉》28 −5=23だ [反意] **add** (COUNT)

subtract [他]《ややフォーマル》(別の数字から)数字を引く, 減らす ◇6 *subtracted* from 9 is 3 (9 − 6 = 3). 9−6=3だ ◇If you *subtract* 6 from 9, you get 3. 9から6を引くと3になります [反意] **add** (COUNT)
▷**subtraction** [名] [U] ◇children learning addition and *subtraction* 足し算と引き算を習う子どもたち [反意] **addition** (COUNT)

,knock sth 'off, ,knock sth 'off sth [句動詞]《ややインフォーマル》(金額・ポイントなどを)差し引く ◇They *knocked off* $60 because of a scratch. 引っかき傷があったので60ドル値引きしてくれた ◇The news *knocked* 13% *off* the company's shares. そのニュースでその会社の株が13%下がった

,take sth 'out of sth [句動詞](支払いから金額を)差し引く ◇The fine will be *taken out of* your wages. 罰金は給料から引かれます ❶ take sth out of の二つ目の sth にはふつう wages や pay が用いられる.

,take sth 'off sth [句動詞](金額・ポイントなどを)差し引く ◇The manager *took* $10 *off* the bill. 店長が勘定から10ドルを割引いてくれた ◇That experience *took* ten years *off* my life (= made me feel ten years older).《ややインフォーマル》あの経験で私は10歳年取った ◇That

discourage

new hairstyle *takes* years *off* you (= makes you look several years younger)! その新しい髪型で君は何歳か若返って見えるよ

debit [他]《ややフォーマル, 金融》(銀行が口座からお金を)引き落とす, (口座の)借方に記入する ◇The money will be *debited* from your account each month. その金額はお客様の口座から毎月引き落とされます ◇The bank will *debit* your account *with* any withdrawals made using your payment card. カードを使用すると銀行がお客様の口座からその金額を引き落とします [反意] **credit** ❶ *credit* は口座の貸方に金額を記入することを意味する. ◆Your account has been *credited with* $50,000. (お客様の口座の貸方に5万ドルが記入されています). ◆$50,000 has been *credited to* your account. (5万ドルがお客様の口座の貸方に記入されています). ☞ **debit** (DEBT)

dock [他](罰金として給与から)差し引く, 給与を減額する ◇If you're late, your wages will be *docked*. 遅刻すると給与が減額されます ◇They've *docked* 15% off my pay for this week. 今週分として給料から15%が差し引かれた ❶ dock の主語には雇用者, 目的語には給与から差し引かれる pay, wages, money などが用いられる.

discourage [動]

1 discourage・dissuade・talk sb out of sth・warn sb off (sth)
…しないよう人を説得する
【類語訳】やめさせようとする, 思いとどまらせる

文型&コロケーション
- to discourage/ dissuade sb **from doing sth**
- to talk sb out of/ warn sb off **doing sth**
- to **try to** discourage/ dissuade/ talk sb out of/ warn sb off sth
- to **manage to** dissuade sb/ talk sb out of sth

discourage [他] (妨害・反対して)人が…するのをやめさせようとする ◇They are launching a new campaign to *discourage* smoking among teenagers. 10代の若者の喫煙をやめさせる新たな運動が開始されようとしている ◇I leave a light on when I'm out to *discourage* burglars. 泥棒がその気にならないように外出するとき私は電気を点けたまま出る ◇His parents tried to *discourage* him from being an actor. 両親は彼が俳優になるのを思いとどまらせようとした [反意] **encourage**
▷**discouragement** [名] [U, C] ◇the government's *discouragement* of political protest 政府が政治的抗議行動をやめさせること

dissuade [他]《ややフォーマル, 特に書き言葉》…しないよう人を説得する, 思いとどまらせる ◇I tried to *dissuade* him from resigning. 私は彼に辞職を思いとどまらせようとした ◇They were going to set off in the fog but were *dissuaded*. 彼らは霧の中を出発しようとしたが忠告を受けて思いとどまった [反意] **persuade** (PERSUADE)

,talk sb 'out of sth [句動詞]《ややインフォーマル》…しない人を説得する ◇I tried to *talk* him *out of* giving up his job. 私は彼に仕事を辞めないよう説得しようとした [反意] **talk sb into sth** (PERSUADE)

ノート dissuade と talk sb out of sth の使い分け: dissuade は主に書き言葉・フォーマルな話し言葉で用いられる. talk sb out of sth は特に会話などインフォーマルな文脈

discrimination

で用いられる. persuade sb not to do sth はあらゆる文脈で非常に一般的に用いられる. ◆I tried to **persuade him not to** resign/give up his job. (私は彼に仕事を辞めないよう説得しようとした).

,warn sb 'off, **,warn sb 'off sth** 〖句動詞〗《ややインフォーマル》人に…しない[…をやめる]よう忠告する ◇We were *warned off* buying the house. 私たちはその家を買わないよう忠告された ◇She wanted to ask him about it but the look in his eyes *warned* her *off*. 彼女はそれについて彼に聞きたかったが, 彼の目つきを見てやめた

2 discourage・demoralize・depress・daunt・crush・get sb down・oppress

人の自信[熱意, 幸せ]を失わせる
【類語訳】憂鬱にさせる, 落胆させる, ひるませる, おじけづかせる, 落ち込ませる, ふさぎ込ませる

〖文型&コロケーション〗

▶a thought depresses/ daunts/ oppresses sb

discourage [他, しばしば受身で] (人を)落胆させる, がっかりさせる ◇Don't be *discouraged* by the first failure ― try again! 一度くらいの失敗でくじけるな―もう一度やってみろ ◇The weather *discouraged* most people *from* attending. 天気のせいで, たいていの人は出席する気をなくした ◇High interest rates will *discourage* investment. 金利が高いと投資は冷え込む 〖反意〗 **encourage** (ENCOURAGE), ☞ **discouraging** (DISAPPOINTING)
▷**discouragement** [名] [U, C] ◇an atmosphere of *discouragement* and despair 落胆と絶望の雰囲気 ◇Despite all these *discouragements*, she refused to give up. こんなふうに落胆だらけだったにもかかわらず彼女は頑としてあきらめなかった 〖反意〗 **encouragement** (ENCOURAGE)

demoralize (英でまた **-ise**) [他, しばしば受身で] (人の士気を)くじく, (人を)意気消沈させる ◇Constant criticism is enough to *demoralize* anybody. ひっきりなしに非難されたら誰だって意気消沈する ◇Many members were *demoralized* by the leadership's failure to implement reforms. 指導部が改革を実行できず多くのメンバーの士気が下がった ☞ **morale** (MOOD)
▷**demoralizing** (英でまた **-ising**) [形] ◇the *demoralizing* effects of unemployment 失業による士気の低下

depress [他] (人を)憂鬱にさせる, 落胆させる ◇Wet weather always *depresses* me. 雨が降るといつも私は憂鬱になる ◇It *depresses* me to see so many young girls smoking. こんなにも多くの若い女の子がタバコを吸うのを見ると私は気がめいる ☞ **depressed** (DEPRESSED), **depressing** (NEGATIVE), **depression** (GLOOM)

daunt [他, しばしば受身で] (人を)ひるませる, おじけづかせる ◇She was a brave woman but she felt *daunted* by the task ahead. 彼女は勇敢な女性だったが, これから取組まなければならない仕事にはひるむ思いがあった ☞ **daunting** (FRIGHTENING)

crush [他]《特に書き言葉》(人の自信・幸せを)打ち砕く, 打ちひしぐ ◇She felt completely *crushed* by the teacher's criticism. 先生の批評に彼女は完全に打ちひしがれた ◇Their new self-confidence could not be *crushed*. 彼らの新たな自信は打ち砕かれることはないだろう
▷**crushing** [形] ◇a *crushing defeat* in the election 選挙での惨憺たる敗北

,get sb 'down 〖句動詞〗《ややインフォーマル, 特に話し言葉》(人を)憂鬱に[悲しく]させる, 落ち込ませる ◇Don't let it *get* you *down* too much. あまり落ち込まないでくださいね ◇The lack of sleep is *getting* me *down*. 睡眠不足でもうばてそう 〖反意〗 **cheer sb up** (ENCOURAGE)

oppress [他]《ややフォーマル, 書き言葉》(悲しみ・不安で人を)憂鬱にする, ふさぎ込ませる ◇The gloomy atmosphere in the office *oppressed* her. 職場の重苦しい雰囲気に彼女は憂鬱になった

discrimination 〖名〗☞ RACISM

discrimination・prejudice・bias・apartheid・affirmative action・intolerance・favouritism

人種, 性別, 宗教などを理由とした社会における特定の人々に対する不公平な扱い
【類語訳】差別, 偏見, 偏向, アパルトヘイト, 不寛容, えこひいき

〖文型&コロケーション〗

▶discrimination/ prejudice/ bias/ intolerance/ favouritism **towards/ toward** sb/ sth
▶discrimination/ prejudice/ bias **in favour of/ against** sb/ sth
▶**sexual** discrimination/ prejudice/ bias/ apartheid
▶**racial/ religious** discrimination/ prejudice/ bias/ intolerance
▶**race/ class/ age/ political** discrimination/ prejudice/ bias
▶**blatant/ clear** discrimination/ prejudice/ bias
▶to **have** a prejudice/ bias
▶to **show** discrimination/ prejudice/ a bias/ intolerance/ favouritism
▶to **fight** discrimination/ prejudice/ apartheid
▶to **reduce/ eliminate** discrimination/ prejudice/ bias

discrimination [U]《けなして》(人種・性別・宗教を理由とした)差別 ◇This is blatant *discrimination* against people with disabilities. これは障碍(ﾏﾏ)を持つ人たちに対するあからさまな差別だ ◇Our policy forbids *discrimination on the grounds of* a person's race, sex or sexuality. 私たちの方針では人種・性別・性的志向を理由とした差別は禁止です ◇Some colleges feel there is a real need for *positive discrimination* in favour of applicants from poorer backgrounds (= more favourable treatment for that group).《英, ほめて》貧困家庭からの志願者を好遇する積極的差別が実際に必要だと感じている大学もある ❶《米》ではふつう affirmative action (下記参照)と言う. 逆のケースを指す reverse discrimination は《英》《米》の両方で用いられる. ◆The court heard arguments that programs to reserve some public works contracts for minorities cause *reverse discrimination*.《けなして》少数民族のための公共事業契約を確保する計画が逆差別を引き起こすという申し立てが法廷で行われた). ☞ **segregation** (DIVISION 1), **discriminatory** (BIASED)
▷**discriminate** [動] [自] ◇practices that *discriminate against* women 女性を差別する慣習 ◇It is illegal to *discriminate on grounds of* race, sex or religion. 人種・性別・宗教を理由として差別することは違法である

prejudice [U, C]《けなして》(人種・性別・宗教などを理由とする)偏見 ◇*Prejudice* towards new immigrants meant that many were unable to find work. 新しい移民に対する偏見が多くの人が仕事を見つけることができなくな

ることにつながった ◇He was just talking out of ***blind prejudice***. 彼はひどい偏見で話をしていただけだった ◇I'm afraid all the debate did was confirm my own *prejudices*. 残念ながら討論は偏見を再確認するものでしかなかった ❶prejudice には特定の人・集団に対する「ひいき」を意味することもあるが、「偏見」という否定的な意味のほうが一般的。
♦ I must admit to a *prejudice* in favour of British universities. (イギリスの大学をひいきしてしまうのを認めざるを得ない)。☞ **prejudiced** (BIASED)

bias [U, C, ふつう単数で] (けなして) (公平な判断を欠いた)偏見, 偏愛, 偏向 ◇There is plenty of evidence of gender *bias* in the classroom. 教室には性差による偏見の証拠がたくさんある ◇Employers must consider all candidates without *bias*. 雇用者は偏見をもたずにすべての志願者を検討しなければならない ◇There is a systematic *bias* in favour of employers in this country. この国には雇用者に対して有利に働く構造的偏向がある ☞ **biased** (BIASED)

apartheid [U] (南アフリカの)アパルトヘイト, 人種隔離政策 ◇*Under apartheid*, white people were not allowed to marry non-white people. アパルトヘイトの下では白人は非白人と結婚することを許されていなかった ◇He was jailed for advocating the violent overthrow of the *apartheid system*. 彼はアパルトヘイト制度の武力による打倒を唱えたかどで投獄された ❶南アフリカにはアパルトヘイト制度はもはや存在しないが、apartheid という語は人の集団が優勢なグループよりも不当な扱いを受ける状況について用いられることもある。♦ It was a system of educational *apartheid* in which children were divided, at the age of eleven, into 'achievers' and 'non-achievers'. ((けなして))それは子どもたちが11歳で「優秀者」と「非優秀者」に分けられる教育的アパルトヘイト制度だった)。☞ **segregation** (DIVISION 1)

af,firmative 'action [U] ((ふつうほめて)) ((米))の)アファーマティブアクション, マイノリティー優遇措置 ◇The City Council implemented the *affirmative action* hiring plan in response to critics' charges that the police department did not reflect the city's racial makeup. 警察が市の人種構成を反映していないという批判者の追及に応えて, 市議会はマイノリティーを優遇する雇用計画を実施した

intolerance [U] ((ややフォーマル, けなして)) (自分と異なる考え・行動様式への)不寛容 ◇Refugees are people whose lives have been shattered by *intolerance*, persecution, torture and fear of death. 難民とは不寛容, 迫害, 拷問, そして死の恐怖によって生活を打ち砕かれてきた人々のことである 反意 **tolerance** (PATIENCE), ☞ **intolerant** (BIASED)

favouritism ((英)) ((米 **favoritism**)) [U] ((けなして)) (権力者による)偏愛, えこひいき ◇She tries not to show any *favouritism* towards her own children. 彼女は自分の子どもたちを決してひいきしないようにしている

discussion 名

discussion・conversation・dialogue・talk・debate・consultation・chat・gossip・chatter・exchange
人々が話し合う機会を表す
【類語訳】議論, 討議, 会話, 対話, 対談, 話し合い, 協議, 雑談, 噂話, ゴシップ, おしゃべり, やり取り

文型&コロケーション

▸a discussion/ a conversation/ a dialogue/ a talk/ a debate/ a consultation/ a chat/ a gossip/ chatter/ an exchange **about** sth
▸a discussion/ conversation/ dialogue/ debate/ consultation **on** sth
▸a discussion/ a conversation/ a dialogue/ a talk/ a debate/ a consultation/ a chat/ a gossip/ an exchange **with** sb
▸a discussion/ a conversation/ a dialogue/ a debate/ a consultation/ an exchange **between** two people/ groups
▸**in (close)** discussion/ conversation/ dialogue/ debate/ consultation **with** sb
▸to **have** a discussion/ a conversation/ a dialogue/ a talk/ a debate/ a consultation/ a chat/ a gossip/ an exchange
▸to **hold** a discussion/ conversation/ debate/ consultation
▸to **be involved in/ join in/ participate in/ take part in/ engage in** (a) discussion/ conversation/ dialogue/ debate
▸to **get into** (a) discussion/ conversation with sb
▸to **conclude/ end/ continue** a discussion/ conversation/ debate
▸to **break off** a discussion/ conversation

discussion [C, U] (重要なことについての詳細な)議論, 討議 ◇*Discussions* are still taking place between the two leaders. 二人の指導者の間で討議はまだ行われている ◇We will choose a different topic for *discussion* each week. 毎週異なる議題を選びます ◇After considerable *discussion*, they decided to accept our offer. かなり議論した後, 彼らは私たちの申し出を受け入れる決定を下した ◇The plans have been ***under discussion*** (= being talked about) for a year now. 計画はもう1年もの間討議中である ◇We can use the draft document as ***a basis for discussion***. その草案文書を基にして協議することができる ☞ **discuss** (TALK)

conversation [C, U] (私的な・くだけた)会話 ◇a telephone *conversation* 電話での会話 ◇He struggled to keep the *conversation* going. 彼は一生懸命会話をつなごうとした ◇The *conversation* turned to gardening. 会話はガーデニングの話に変わった ◇The main ***topic of conversation*** was the likely outcome of the election. 話題の中心は選挙結果がどうなるかということであった ◇Don was ***deep in conversation*** with the girl on his right. ドンは右隣の女の子との会話に夢中だった ◇I tried to ***make polite conversation*** (= to speak in order to appear polite). 私は礼儀正しく話をしようとした ◇I ***got into conversation*** with a man on the bus. ((英))私はバスの中で男の人と話し始めた ◇I ***got into a conversation with*** a man on the bus. ((米))私はバスの中で男の人と話し始めた

dialogue ((米でまた **dialog**)) [U, C] (本・劇・映画の)対話, 会話部分 ; (問題解決に向けての二者間の)対談 ◇The novel has long descriptions and not much *dialogue*. その小説は描写部が長くて, 会話部はあまり多くない ◇Learners are asked to listen to three short *dialogues*. 学習者は三つの短い対話を聞き取るよう求められる ◇The President told waiting reporters there had been a constructive *dialogue*. 大統領は待ち構える記者に対し建設的な対談が行われたと述べた

talk [C] (当事者にとっての問題や重要案件についての)話し合い ◇I had a long *talk* with my boss about my career prospects. 私は自分の昇進の見通しについて上司と長いこと話し合った ◇She looked worried so we had a *talk*. 彼女が不安そうに見えたので私たちは話し合った ☞ **talk** (TALK)

debate [C, U] (決定が投票に付される公的集会・国会での)

disease

討論 ◇a *debate* on prison reform 刑務所改革に関する討論 ◇The prime minister opened the *debate* (= was the first to speak). 首相が議論の口火を切った ◇After a long *debate*, Congress approved the proposal. 長時間の討議の結果、国会はその法案を承認した ◇The motion **under** *debate* (= being discussed) was put to a vote. 審議中の動議は投票にかけられた ☞ **debate** (TALK)

consultation [C, U] (決定を下す前の)協議 ◇There have been extensive *consultations* between the two countries. 2国間で広範囲にわたる協議が行われている ◇The decision was taken after close *consultation* with local residents. 地元住民との綿密な協議の末、決定が下された ◇A *consultation* period will be required. 協議期間が必要だろう ☞ **consult** (TALK)

chat [U, C] 雑談, (くつろいだ)おしゃべり ◇I just called in for a *chat* about the kids.《特に英》子どものことで雑談をしに来ただけだ ◇That's enough *chat* from me — on with the music! 私の話はここまで—音楽を続けましょう ❶特に《英》で chat の可算名詞としての用法が見受けられる

gossip [C, ふつう単数で] (他人についての)噂話, ゴシップ ◇We had a good *gossip* about the boss. 私たちは上司の噂話を楽しんだ

chatter [U] (くだらない)おしゃべり ◇Jane's constant *chatter* was beginning to annoy him. ジェーンの絶え間ないおしゃべりに彼はいらいらし始めていた

exchange [C] (短い・激しい)やり取り ◇There was only time for a brief *exchange*. 短いやり取りの時間しかなかった ◇There was a **heated** *exchange* between the parents and the school managers. 保護者と学校関係者の激しいやり取りがあった ☞ **exchange** (REPLACE 2)

disease 名 ☞ ILLNESS

disease・illness・disorder・infection・condition・ailment・bug・complaint・virus・sickness
健康がよくない状態を表す
【類語訳】病気, 機能障害(:), 疾患, 感染症, 伝染病, 持病, ウイルス性疾患

文型&コロケーション

▶a **serious/ chronic** disease/ illness/ disorder/ infection/ condition/ ailment
▶a **minor** disease/ illness/ disorder/ infection/ ailment
▶a **common/ rare** disease/ illness/ disorder/ infection/ condition/ ailment/ virus
▶an **infectious** disease/ illness/ condition/ virus
▶a **childhood** disease/ illness/ disorder/ infection/ ailment
▶to **have/ suffer from** a disease/ an illness/ a disorder/ an infection/ a condition/ an ailment/ a bug/ a complaint/ a virus/ sickness
▶to **cause** a disease/ an illness/ a disorder/ an infection/ a condition/ an ailment/ sickness
▶to **catch/ contract/ get/ pick up** a disease/ an illness/ an infection/ a bug/ a virus
▶to **diagnose/ treat** a disease/ an illness/ an infection/ a condition/ an ailment/ a virus
▶to **cure** a disease/ an illness/ a disorder/ an infection/ a condition/ an ailment
▶to **recover from** a disease/ an illness/ a disorder/ an infection/ a bug/ a virus/ a sickness
▶to **die from/ of** a disease/ an illness/ a disorder/ an infection/ a condition/ a bug/ a virus

▶a disease/ an illness/ an infection/ a virus/ a sickness **spreads**

disease [C, U] (感染による人間・動植物の)病気 ◇He suffers from a rare blood *disease*. 彼は珍しい血液の病気にかかっている ◇The problem was finally diagnosed as heart *disease*. その症状は最終的に心臓病であると診断された ◇Measures have been taken to prevent the spread of *disease*. 病気の蔓延を防ぐ対策が取られている

illness [C] 病気(の期間) ◇Have you suffered from any serious *illnesses* in the past six months? 最近6か月の間に何か重篤な病気にかかりましたか ◇He died after a long *illness*. 彼は長い間病気を患い亡くなった ☞ **ill** (SICK 1)

ノート **disease** と **illness** の使い分け: disease は特に臓器に影響を及ぼす比較的重度の病気について言うときに用いられる。illness は重度・軽度を問わず、精神に影響を及ぼす病気に用いられる。◆ heart/kidney/liver *disease* (心臓／腎臓／肝臓病). × heart/kidney/liver *illness*. ◆ mental *illness* (精神疾患). × mental *disease*. disease は病気の期間について用いることはできない。× He died after a long *disease*. illness は「病気にかかっている状態」を意味することもある。☞ ILLNESS

disorder [C, U] (ややフォーマル) (身体の)機能障害, 疾患 ◇This is a rare *disorder* of the liver. これは珍しい肝機能障害だ ◇Most people with acute mental *disorder* can be treated at home. 急性の精神障害を患う人の大半は自宅療養が可能だ ❶ disorder はふつう感染症ではない。次例のように、精神面での不調に用いられる。◆ a/an psychiatric/personality/mental/depressive/eating *disorder* (精神／人格／知能／抑鬱／摂食障害). 体の不調について言う場合、ほとんどの場合、blood, bowel, kidney や serious, severe, rare などと共に用いられる

infection [C] 感染症, 伝染病 ◇He's been off work with a throat *infection*. 彼はのどの感染症で仕事を休んでいる ◇Sneezing is the most common way of spreading an *infection*. くしゃみによって感染症が蔓延するのが最も一般的だ

condition [C] (ややフォーマル) (治癒不可能な)持病 ◇Does your child have any kind of medical *condition* that we should know about? お子さんには私たちが知っておくべき持病が何かありますか ◇He suffers from a serious heart *condition*. 彼は重い心臓病を患っている

ailment [C] (ややフォーマル) (軽度の)病気 ◇Below is a list of common childhood *ailments*. 以下が子どもがかかる軽い病気の一覧です

bug [C] (インフォーマル) (軽度の)感染症 ◇There's a stomach *bug* going round (= people are catching it from each other). 胃腸炎が流行っている

complaint [C] (ややフォーマル) (軽度で特定の部位に影響する)病気 ◇He suffers from a skin *complaint* called 'rosacea'. 彼は「酒さ」という皮膚の病気を患っている

virus [C] (インフォーマル) ウイルス性疾患 ◇There's a *virus* going around the office. 職場でウイルス性疾患が流行っている ❶ この意味では *virus* よりフォーマルな表現は viral infection と言う

sickness [U, C, ふつう単数で] (複合語で) (特定の)病気 ◇Do you need any travel *sickness* tablets? 何か酔い止めの錠剤が必要ですか ❶ sickness と共に複合語を作る語に altitude, morning, mountain, radiation, travel などが挙げられる

disgrace 名

disgrace・disrepute・shame・dishonour・discredit
他人からの尊敬や賛同を失うこと
【類語訳】不名誉, 不面目, 不評, 恥辱, 恥

▸文型&コロケーション
- ▶ in disgrace/ disrepute
- ▶ to **bring** disgrace/ shame/ dishonour/ discredit **on** sb/ sth
- ▶ to **fall into** disgrace/ disrepute
- ▶ **There is no** disgrace/ shame/ dishonour **in** sth.

disgrace [U] 不名誉, 不面目 ◇Her behaviour has brought *disgrace* on her family. 彼女の振る舞いは家族の面目をつぶした ◇The swimmer was *sent home* from the Olympics *in disgrace*. その水泳選手は不名誉にもオリンピックから本国に送り返された ◇Sam was in *disgrace* with his parents. サムは両親にのけ者にされていた ☞ **disgraceful** (OUTRAGEOUS)
▸**disgrace** 動 [他] ◇I *disgraced myself* by drinking far too much. 私は大幅に飲み過ぎて面目を失った ◇He had *disgraced* the family name. 彼は家名を傷つけた過去があった

disrepute [U] 《ややフォーマル, 特に書き言葉》不評 ◇The players' behaviour on the field is likely to *bring* the game *into disrepute*. その選手のフィールドでの振る舞いは試合の評判を落とすことになるだろう ❶ bring ～ into disrepute の～には, 特にサッカーなどの試合の価値を落とす不正や乱闘などの好ましくない行為によって試合の価値を落とすことを言う. theory, system, law などが in disrepute や fall into disrepute の主語になり, それらがもはや有効でなくなったことを意味する.

shame [U] 不名誉, 恥 ◇There is no *shame* in wanting to be successful. 成功を望むことは恥ずべきことではない ◇She felt that her failure would bring *shame* on her family.《フォーマル》失敗したら家族の面目がつぶれてしまうと彼女は思った ☞ **shame** (EMBARRASS), **shameful** (OUTRAGEOUS)

dishonour 《英》(《米 **dishonor**) [U] 《フォーマル》不名誉, 恥辱 ◇Her actions have brought shame and *dishonour* on the profession. 彼女の行動はその職業の名誉を失墜させた ◇There is no *dishonour* in such a defeat. そのような敗北には不名誉なことは何もない 反意 **honour** (INTEGRITY), **honour** (REPUTATION)
▸**dishonour** 《英》(《米 **dishonor**) [他] ◇You have *dishonoured* the name of the school. 君が学校の名を汚したのだ

discredit [U] 《フォーマル》(集団・組織にとっての公然となった)不名誉, *to its discredit*, Britain, *to its discredit*, did not speak out against these atrocities. イギリスは不名誉にもこれらの残虐行為を非難しなかった ◇My brother's behaviour did great *discredit to* the family. 弟の振る舞いは家族に大きな不名誉をもたらした

┌─ノート disgrace, shame, dishonour, discredit の使い分け: 時としてどの語を使用しても構わない. ◆Her behaviour has brought *disgrace/shame/dishonour/discredit* on her family. (彼女の振る舞いの面目をつぶした). disgrace はこれらの語の中で最も頻繁に用いられ, 結びつく語の種類も一番多い. ×The swimmer was sent home in *shame/dishonour/discredit*.

×Sam was in *shame/dishonour/discredit* with his parents. disgrace は一般の人や身近な人からの尊敬を失うこと. shame, dishonour, discredit はすべて一般の人からの尊敬を失うことを指す. shame と dishonour は特に bring shame/dishonour on sb/sth や There is no shame/dishonour in (doing) sth の句で用いられる. 実質的な意味の違いはないが, dishonour のほうがよりフォーマルである. discredit は構成員[代表者]の振る舞いによって特に家族・集団・組織・国家に対する尊敬が失われることについて用いられる. 特に to sb/sth's discredit や do discredit to sb/sth の句で用いられる.

disgusting 形

1 ☞ TERRIBLE 1
disgusting・foul・revolting・repulsive・offensive・gross・nauseating
ひどく不快で気分を悪くさせる臭い, 味, 癖などを表す
【類語訳】むかむかさせる, 汚い, 臭い, 不快, 胸くそ悪い, 吐き気を催させる

▸文型&コロケーション
- ▶ disgusting/ repulsive/ offensive **to** sb
- ▶ a disgusting/ a foul/ a revolting/ an offensive/ a gross/ a nauseating **smell**
- ▶ a disgusting/ foul/ gross/ nauseating **taste**
- ▶ a disgusting/ revolting/ gross/ nauseating **habit**
- ▶ disgusting/ offensive/ gross **behaviour**
- ▶ a disgusting/ revolting/ repulsive **man/ woman/ person**
- ▶ to **find sb/ sth** disgusting/ revolting/ repulsive/ offensive/ nauseating
- ▶ to **smell/ taste** disgusting/ foul/ gross
- ▶ **really** disgusting/ foul/ revolting/ offensive/ gross/ nauseating
- ▶ **quite** disgusting/ revolting/ offensive/ gross
- ▶ **absolutely** disgusting/ foul/ revolting

disgusting 《特に話し言葉》気持ちが悪い, むかむかさせる, とてもひどい ◇The kitchen was in a *disgusting* state. 台所はとてもひどい状態だった ◇What a *disgusting* smell! 何てひどい臭いだ ◇The sink was full of a *disgusting* black slime. シンクは気持ちの悪い黒いドロドロしたもので一杯だった ◇This tastes absolutely *disgusting*. この味は本当に気持ちが悪い ◇Picking your nose is a *disgusting* habit. 鼻をほじる癖は最低だよ ☞ **disgust** (SHOCK 動)
▸**disgust** 名 [U] ◇She wrinkled her nose *in disgust* at the smell of urine. おしっこの臭いを嫌がって彼女は鼻にしわを寄せた
▸**disgustingly** 副 ◇The kitchen was *disgustingly* dirty. 台所はひどく汚れていた

foul 汚い, 嫌な味の, 臭い ◇This tastes *foul*! 嫌な味がする ◇The air in the cell was *foul*. 独房の空気は臭かった ◇She could smell his *foul* breath. 彼女は彼の息の臭さを感じた ◇*Foul* drinking water was blamed for the epidemic. 汚い飲み水が伝染病の原因とされた

revolting ひどく不快な, むかむかさせる ◇The stew looked *revolting*. そのシチューは見るからに吐き気を催すほどだった ◇He's an absolutely *revolting* man. 彼は本当にむかつく男だよ
▸**revoltingly** 副 ◇a *revoltingly* sentimental story

dishonest

むかむかするほどセンチメンタルな物語

ノート disgusting と revolting の使い分け：両語とも嫌な臭い[味]のする物，不快な癖(を持つ人)を表すのに用いられる．実質的な意味の違いはないが，特に話し言葉においては disgusting のほうがより頻繁に用いられる．

repulsive (ややフォーマル)[腹が立つ[気分が悪くなる]ほど]ひどく不快 ◇What a *repulsive* person! なんて不快なやつなんだろう ◇He found her habits quite *repulsive*. 彼は彼女の癖をかなり不快に思った．❶ repulsive はふつう，身体的・道徳的理由から不快だと思う人・行動・癖を修飾する． ☞ **repel** (SHOCK ❶)

offensive (フォーマル)(臭いが)ひどい ◇The problem is how to eliminate *offensive* smells from the processing plant. 問題は加工処理プラントからどうやって悪臭を除去するかです

gross (インフォーマル，話し言葉)(臭い・味・癖が)ひどく不快な，胸くそ悪い ◇'He ate it with mustard.' 'Oh, *gross*!'「彼はそれにマスタードを塗って食べたんだ」「ええっ，気持ち悪いね」

nauseating 吐き気を催させる ◇He woke to the *nauseating* smell of burning flesh. へどが出るような肉が燃える臭いで彼は目を覚ました ☞ **nauseous** (SICK 2)

---

2 disgusting・distasteful・sickening・hateful・repugnant・abominable

容認できないぞっとするようなことを表す
【類語訳】腹立たしい，嫌な，嫌悪感を催させる，おぞましい，憎むべき，忌わしい

disgusting	sickening	hateful
distasteful		repugnant
		abominable

文型&コロケーション
▸ disgusting/ distasteful/ hateful/ repugnant/ abominable **to** sb
▸ disgusting/ distasteful/ sickening/ hateful/ repugnant/ abominable **that...**
▸ a disgusting/ an abominable **practice**
▸ a sickening/ an abominable **crime**
▸ to **find** sth disgusting/ distasteful/ repugnant
▸ **absolutely/ quite** disgusting/ sickening/ hateful/ repugnant

disgusting (ややインフォーマル，特に話し言葉)(道徳的理由から)腹立たしい，嫌な ◇I think it's *disgusting* that they're closing the hospital. 腹が立つことに病院が閉鎖されると思う ◇That's a *disgusting* thing to say. それは口に出すのも腹立たしいことだ ❶ disgusting はふつう話し言葉で道徳的によくないと思うことを表すのに用いられるが，それ他のいくつかの語が表すほどのひどい悪行ではない． ×a cruel and *disgusting* regime which tortures its opponents. ☞ **disgust** (SHOCK ❶)
▸ **disgust** 名 [U] ◇Much **to my disgust** they refused to help. 彼らが協力しようとしないことには大いにむかついた ◇He walked away **in** *disgust*. 彼はむかっとして歩き去った

distasteful (ややフォーマル)(死・性・犯罪を扱って)嫌悪[不快]感を催させる ◇Parts of this story may be *distasteful*, even shocking. この物語の一部は嫌悪感や，場合によっては衝撃をももたらすかもしれない ◇Some viewers might find the pictures *distasteful*. その絵を見る人の中には嫌悪感を抱く人もいるかもしれない
▸ **distaste** 名 [U, 単数で] ◇He looked around the filthy room in *distaste*. 彼は汚い部屋を嫌悪の思いで見回した ◇She felt a *distaste for* anything to do with bodily functions. 彼女は身体の機能に関する事には何でも嫌悪感を抱いた

sickening (肉体的損傷に関して)おぞましい ◇She was the victim of a *sickening* attack. 彼女はおぞましい襲撃事件の被害者だった ◇His head hit the ground with a *sickening* thud. 彼の頭は地面にゴツンと嫌な音を立ててぶつかった ❶ sickening はしばしば人・物がけが[ひどく損傷]したことを思わせる音を表すのに用いられる．

hateful (ややフォーマル)憎むべき，いまいましい ◇I tried to ignore her *hateful* words. 私は彼女のいまいましい言葉を無視しようとした ◇The idea of fighting their own people was *hateful* to them. 自国民と戦うのは考えるだにおぞましいことだった

repugnant (フォーマル)(信念・道徳に反していて)到底受け入れられない ◇We found his suggestion quite *repugnant*. 私たちは彼の提案をまったく意外だと思った ◇The idea of eating meat was *repugnant* to her. 肉を食べるという考えは彼女にとってはありえないことだった

ノート hateful と repugnant の使い分け：hateful はふつう大半の人が受け入れられないと思う考えを表す．repugnant は特定の人にとっては受け入れられない考えを表すこともできる． ◆We found his suggestion quite *repugnant*. (私たちは彼の提案をまったく論外だと思った). ✗We found his suggestion quite *hateful*.

abominable (ややフォーマル) 忌わしい ◇The judge described the attack as an *abominable* crime. 裁判官はその襲撃を忌わしい犯罪であると述べた ❶ abominable はときどき，肉体的には残酷ではないが思いやりに欠ける行為を表すときに，大げさにややインフォーマルな言い回しとして用いられる． ◆I think you are utterly selfish and your behaviour has been *abominable*. (あなたはまったく自己中心的で，あなたの振る舞いたるや最悪だったと思う).

---

dishonest 形

dishonest・devious・hypocritical・deceitful・underhand・lying・two-faced

人が誠実でなく他人をだまそうとすることを表す
【類語訳】不誠実な，不正直な，詐欺的な，狡猾な，偽善的な，嘘つきの，裏表のある

文型&コロケーション
▸ to be dishonest/ devious/ hypocritical **of** sb to do sth
▸ a dishonest/ a devious/ a hypocritical/ a deceitful/ an underhand **manner/ way**
▸ dishonest/ devious/ deceitful/ underhand **tactics/ means**
▸ a dishonest/ a devious/ underhand **method**
▸ dishonest/ underhand **dealings**
▸ a lying/ two-faced **hypocrite**
▸ to do **something/ nothing** dishonest/ underhand

dishonest (ややフォーマル) 不誠実な，不正直な；不正の，詐欺的な ◇Beware of *dishonest* traders in the tourist areas. 観光地の悪徳商人には気をつけてください ◇I don't like him, and it would be *dishonest* of me to pretend otherwise. 私は彼が嫌いだし，そうでない振りをす

るのも欺瞞的な気がする 反意 **honest** (HONEST), ☞ **dis-honesty** (FRAUD 1)
➤**dishonestly** 副 ◇He was accused of *dishonestly* obtaining property. 彼は不正に財産を得た容疑で起訴された

devious (物を得るために)狡猾な、ずるい ◇He's as *devious* as a politician needs to be. 彼には政治家に必要な狡猾さがある ◇They got rich by *devious* means. 彼らはずるいやり方で金持ちになった ❶ *devious* は人のほか、minds, plans, schemes, ways, means, methods, tactics などを修飾する.

hypocritical (ややフォーマル) 偽善的な ◇It would be *hypocritical* of me to have a church wedding when I don't believe in God. 神なんて信じていない私が教会で結婚式を挙げるのは偽善的だろう
➤**hypocrisy** 名 [U, C] ◇It's *hypocrisy* for them to pretend they were shocked at the news. 《ややフォーマル》彼らがそのニュースに衝撃を受けた振りをするのは偽善的だ ◇She refused to conform to the usual practices and *hypocrisies* of high society. 彼女は上流社会の慣習や偽善的実態に順応したくはないと言った
➤**hypocrite** 名 [C] ◇Charles was a liar and a *hypocrite* who married her for her money. チャールズは彼女と金目当てで結婚した嘘つきかつ偽善者だった

deceitful (ややフォーマル) 詐欺的な ◇The government was accused of being hypocritical and *deceitful*. 政府は偽善的かつ詐欺的であるとして非難された ☞ **deceit** (FRAUD 1)

> ノート **dishonest** と **deceitful** の使い分け: dishonest は dishonest workmen (悪徳建築業者) と同様、ビジネスにおいてごまかしが行われる dishonest dealings/practices/conduct (不正取引/業務/処理) といった表現で用いられる. deceitful は特に嘘をつく人を指すのに用いられる.

underhand (ややフォーマル) (行為が)こそこそした、陰険な ◇I would never have expected her to behave in such an *underhand* way. 彼女がそんなにこそこそと行動するとは思ってもみなかった ◇I promise you there's nothing *underhand* about this agreement. 誓ってこの合意には何もやましいことはありません ❶ *underhand* は望むものを手に入れるための ways, methods, means, tactics について言うときに用いられる.

lying (インフォーマル、特に話し言葉) 嘘つきの ◇You *lying* little toad! 嘘つき

two-'faced (インフォーマル) 裏表のある、二枚舌の ◇He accused her of being a *two-faced* liar. 彼は彼女を二枚舌の嘘つきだと言って非難した

disprove 動

disprove • refute • discredit • rebut • confound • debunk • invalidate • explode • demolish
物事が間違っていることを表す
【類語訳】反証する、反論する、反駁する、実態をあばく、覆す

文型&コロケーション
▸ to disprove/ refute/ discredit/ debunk/ invalidate/ explode/ demolish a **theory**
▸ to disprove/ refute/ debunk/ invalidate/ explode/ demolish a **myth**
▸ to disprove/ refute/ discredit/ rebut/ confound/ demolish an **argument**
▸ to disprove/ refute/ discredit/ rebut/ invalidate/ explode/ demolish **claims**
▸ to disprove/ refute/ confound/ invalidate a **thesis**
▸ to disprove/ refute/ rebut an **allegation**
▸ **evidence** disproves/ refutes/ discredits/ rebuts sth
▸ to **successfully** refute/ confound/ debunk/ demolish sth
▸ to be **easily** disproved/ refuted/ discredited/ rebutted/ demolished

disprove [他] (説・主張などの)誤りを立証する、反証する ◇It is difficult to confirm or *disprove* the existence of such a group. そのようなグループの存在を立証または反証することは難しい ◇It cannot be *disproved that* a meeting took place. 会議が行われたことを否定することはできない 反意 **prove** (SHOW 1), **confirm** (CONFIRM 1)

refute [他] 《フォーマル》(論・説・主張などの)誤りを証明する、反論[反証]する ◇She tried to think how to *refute* the argument on moral grounds. 彼女は道徳的根拠に基づいてその主張に反論する方法を考えようとした ◇This study cannot provide data to confirm or *refute* this hypothesis. この研究ではこの仮説を立証あるいは反証するデータを提供することはできない 反意 **confirm** (CONFIRM 1), ☞ **refute** (DENY)

discredit [他] 信用できないものにする ◇These theories are now largely *discredited* among linguists. これらの学説は今や言語学者の間ではおおかた信用できないものとされている ◇This new evidence *discredits* earlier findings. この新証拠によって以前の調査結果の信頼性は失われている

rebut (-tt-) [他] 《フォーマル》(主張・告発の)誤りを示す、反論[反証]する、反駁する ◇An attempt was made to publicly *rebut* rumours of a divorce. 離婚の噂に公の場で反論する試みがなされた ◇The defendants were unable to *rebut* the charges of negligence. 被告側は過失の告発に対し反論することができなかった

> ノート **disprove, refute, rebut** の使い分け: 場合によってどの語でも使うことが可能. ◆ to *disprove/refute/rebut* a claim/an allegation/an argument (主張/論などに反証する). *disprove* は他の2語よりも頻繁に用いられ、ややインフォーマルな語. 特に科学的・歴史的事実に関する事を言うときに用いられる. *refute* は主張や告発についてより頻繁に用いられ、*rebut* は特に法的文脈で用いられる. *rebut* はある主張に対して反証を挙げずにただ否定することを指すこともできる. *refute* は元来反証を挙げてある主張の誤りを立証するという意味だが、現代の用法では「否定する」という意味でもしばしば用いられる. ☞ **refute** (DENY)

confound [他] 《フォーマル》(予想に反する事をして人・物事の)誤りを示す ◇She *confounded* her critics and proved she could do the job. 彼女は自分に批判的な人たちの裏をかいて、自分がその仕事をできることを証明した ◇The rise in share prices *confounded* expectations. 予想に反して株価は上昇した

debunk [他] 《ややインフォーマル》(長い間考え[信じ]られてきたことの)誤りを示す; 実態をあばく ◇Let's start by *debunking* a few myths. まず、いくつかの神話の誤りを指摘しましょう ◇She attempts to *debunk* unrealistic expectations about marriage. 彼女は結婚に関する非現実的な期待を打ち砕こうとしている

invalidate [他] (間違いを含んでいることを示して考え・話・論などの)誤りを証明する ◇This new piece of evidence *invalidates* his version of events. この新しい証拠で事

件に関する彼の説明は説得力を失う ◇Flawed research methods may *invalidate* the study's conclusions. 欠陥のある調査方法ではその研究結果が無に帰する可能性がある ❶ *invalidate* は人の反証によってではなく、証拠・状況証拠にもとづいて考え・話などを無効にすることを言う。 ×She tried to think how to *invalidate* the argument on moral grounds.

explode ［他］（一般的に考え［信じ］られていることを）覆す
◇At last, a women's magazine to *explode* the myth that thin equals beautiful. 細い＝美しいという神話を覆す女性誌がついに誕生

demolish ［他］《やや インフォーマル》（考え・理論などを）完全に覆す ◇A recent book has *demolished* this theory. 最近出た本でこの理論は完全に覆された

distress ［名］

distress・pain・suffering・anguish・torture・agony・hurt・misery
出来事や人の言動により傷つけられたときに抱く非常につらい気持ち
【類語訳】苦悩, 心痛, つらさ, 苦痛, 苦悶, 窮状, 惨めさ

distress	anguish	torture
pain	misery	agony
suffering		
hurt		

文型＆コロケーション

▸ distress/ pain/ anguish/ hurt/ misery **at** sth
▸ **in** distress/ pain/ anguish/ agony/ misery
▸ **great** distress/ pain/ suffering/ anguish/ agony/ hurt/ misery
▸ **real** distress/ pain/ suffering/ anguish/ torture/ agony/ hurt/ misery
▸ **sheer/ absolute** torture/ agony/ misery
▸ **physical/ emotional** distress/ pain/ suffering/ anguish/ torture/ agony/ hurt
▸ **mental** distress/ pain/ suffering/ anguish/ torture/ agony
▸ **personal** distress/ pain/ suffering/ anguish/ agony/ hurt/ misery
▸ to **endure** the distress/ pain/ suffering/ torture/ agony/ misery
▸ to **bear** the pain/ suffering/ anguish/ torture/ misery
▸ to **go through** pain/ suffering/ agony/ hurt/ misery
▸ to **suffer** distress/ pain/ anguish/ torture/ agony/ hurt/ misery
▸ to **inflict** pain/ suffering/ anguish/ torture/ agony/ hurt/ misery
▸ to **cause (sb)** distress/ pain/ suffering/ anguish/ agony/ hurt/ misery
▸ to **spare** sb the distress/ pain/ suffering/ anguish/ agony/ misery
▸ to **ease** sb's distress/ pain/ suffering/ anguish/ agony/ misery

distress ［U］苦悩, 心痛 ◇He was obviously in *distress* after the attack. 非難を浴びて彼は明らかに悩んでいた ◇The newspaper article caused the actor considerable *distress*. 新聞記事にその俳優はとても心を痛めた

☞ **distress** (HURT 1), **distressed** (UPSET), **distressing** (PAINFUL 2)

pain ［U］苦悩, 心痛 ◇The *pain* of separation remained intense. 離別のつらさがまだ強く残っていた ◇She had never meant to cause him any *pain*. 彼女には彼を苦しめるつもりは決してなかった ❶ *pain* には「肉体的苦痛」の意味もある。 ☞ **pain** (PAIN) 反意 **pleasure** (FUN), **pleasure** (PLEASURE), ☞ **pain** (HURT 1), **painful** (PAINFUL 2)

suffering ［U］苦悩, 心痛 ◇The taunts of her schoolmates caused her intense mental *suffering*. 学校の友達からからかわれ、彼女は激しい精神的苦痛を味わった ◇This war has caused widespread human *suffering*. この戦争は広範囲の人々に苦悩をもたらした ❶ *suffering* には「肉体的苦痛」の意味もある。 ☞ **suffering** (PAIN)

ノート *distress, pain, suffering* の使い分け：これらの語はすべて「非常につらい気持ち」を表す。*distress* には「心配」の意味もある。◆I was in such *distress*, wondering what had happened to them. (彼らに何が起こったのかとても心配だった). ×I was in such *pain/suffering*, wondering what had happened to them. *pain* と *suffering* は両語とも肉体的苦痛の意味もあり、時に肉体的・精神的苦痛を同時に表すこともある。◆It was a life full of *pain* and *suffering*. (それは苦痛と苦悩に満ちた人生だった). *pain* は特により個人的な苦痛で、愛する者の死や人の心ない言動によって引き起こされる。*suffering* は特に多くの人にとっての苦痛で、戦争・自然災害などによって大規模に引き起こされる。

anguish ［U］《やや インフォーマル》（精神的）苦痛, 苦悶 ◇Tears of *anguish* filled her eyes. 苦悩の涙が彼女の目に溢れた ◇He groaned in *anguish*. 彼は苦悶のうなり声を上げた
☞ **anguished** (UPSET)

torture ［U］《インフォーマル》（精神的な）非常な苦痛（の種）◇Falling in love with a man she could never have was exquisite *torture*. 自分のものには決してできない定めの男との恋は彼女には絶大な苦しみだった ◇The interview was sheer *torture* from start to finish. その面接は開始から終了までまったくの苦痛だった ❶このグループでは *torture* だけが前置詞 *in* の後に用いることができない。×He cried out in *torture*.

agony ［U, C］（精神的な）非常な苦痛（の種）, 苦悶 ◇It was *agony* not knowing where the children were. 子どもたちがどこにいるのかわからないことは苦痛の極みだった ◇She waited in an *agony* of suspense. 彼女は不安にさいなまれながら待っていた ◇The worst *agonies* of the war were now beginning. 戦争の最悪の苦しみが今始まりつつあった ❶ *agony* には「肉体的苦痛」の意味もある。 ☞ **agony** (PAIN)

hurt ［U, 単数で］《やや インフォーマル》（人の心ない［不当な］仕打ちによる精神的）苦痛, 苦悩 ◇There was *hurt* and real anger in her voice. 彼女の声には苦痛と心底からの怒りが表れていた ◇It was a *hurt* that would take a long time to heal. その心の痛手は癒えるのに時間のかかるものだった ☞ **hurt** (HURT 1), **hurt** (UPSET), **hurtful** (MEAN 形)

misery ［U, C］（長く続く精神的な）苦悩, 惨めさ ◇Fame brought her nothing but *misery*. 名声は彼女に苦悩以外の何ものももたらさなかった ◇The bad news had plunged him into abject *misery*. 悪い知らせで彼は絶望に追い込まれていた ◇My old boss used to **make my life a misery**. 《英》あの例の上司が私によく辛く当たったものだった

↳distress

distribute, diverse

❶《米》では make my life miserable と言う．☞ **miserable (NEGATIVE), miserable (UNHAPPY 1)**

ノート anguish, torture, agony, misery の使い分け：これらの語の主な違いは、苦痛の程度とフォーマル・インフォーマルのレベル．agony は最も大きな苦痛．torture は極度の苦痛を指すが、インフォーマルな言葉で大げさな表現として用いられ、苦痛をもたらす状況が実際は大して深刻ではないこともある．anguish はややフォーマルな語で、agony や torture よりも苦痛の程度は少し小さい．misery は比較的小さな苦痛を指すがより長い間継続することがある．

distribute 動

distribute・hand sth out・give sth out・dispense・dole sth out・pass sth out・dish sth out・deal
物を多くの人に与える
【類語訳】分配する，流通させる，配る，供給する

文型&コロケーション
▶ to distribute/ hand out/ give out/ dispense/ dish out **food**
▶ to distribute/ hand out/ give out/ dispense/ dole out **money**
▶ to distribute/ hand out/ dispense **cash**
▶ to distribute/ hand out/ give out/ pass out **copies**
▶ to distribute/ hand out/ give out/ pass out/ dole out/ dish out **leaflets**
▶ to distribute/ hand out/ give out/ dish out **awards/ prizes**
▶ to hand out/ give out/ dole out/ dish out **punishments**

distribute [他]《ややフォーマル》（大きな集団内の各人に）分配する；（店・企業に商品を）流通させる ◇The organization *distributed* food and blankets to the earthquake victims. その団体が食料と毛布を地震被災者たちに配給した ◇The newspaper is *distributed* free. その新聞は無料で配られている ◇The money was *distributed* *among* schools in the area. そのお金は地域の学校に分配された ◇'Plastika' *distributes* our products in the UK. イギリスでは「プラスティカ」が当社の製品を配給しています
▷ **distribution** [名] [U] ◆the *distribution* of food and medicine to the flood victims 洪水被災者への食料と医薬品の配給 ☞ **distribution (DELIVERY)**

ˌhand sth ˈout 句動詞 （集団内の各人に）配る ◇Could you *hand* these books *out*, please? これらの本を配ってもらえますか ◇She *handed out* medals and certificates to the winners. 彼女はメダルと証書を受賞者たちに手渡した ☞ **handout (AID), handout (GIFT), handout (LEAFLET)**

ˌgive sth ˈout 句動詞《特に話し言葉》（集団内の各人に）配る ◇The teacher *gave out* the exam papers. 教師は問題用紙を配った

ノート hand sth out と give sth out の使い分け：実質的な意味の違いはない．give sth out は書き言葉よりも話し言葉で頻繁に用いられ、hand sth out は書き言葉でも話し言葉でも同じくらいに用いられる．

dispense [他]《ややフォーマル》（機械が食べ物・飲み物・お金を）供給する ◇The machine *dispenses* a range of drinks and snacks. その機械からはさまざまな飲み物や軽食が出てくる

ˌdole sth ˈout 句動詞《インフォーマル》（集団内の各人に食べ物・お金を）配る ◇Dad began to *dole out* the porridge from the saucepan. お父さんがおかゆを鍋から取り分け始めた

ˌpass sth ˈout 句動詞 《特に米》（集団内の各人に）配る ◇Information sheets were *passed out* before the talk. 情報シートが協議の前に配られた

ˌdish sth ˈout 句動詞《インフォーマル》（多くの人に大量に）配る ◇Students *dished out* leaflets to passers-by. 学生たちが通行人にチラシを一斉配布した ◇She's always *dishing out* advice, even when you don't want it. 彼女は君の迷惑お構いなしに助言を押しつけてくる

deal [自, 他]（カードゲームでプレーヤーにカードを）配る ◇Whose turn is it to *deal*? 誰が親になる番かい ◇Start by *dealing out* ten cards to each player. それぞれのプレーヤーにカードを10枚配って開始してください ◇He *dealt* me two aces. 彼は私にエースを2枚配った

diverse 形 ☞ **DIFFERENT, WIDE 1**

diverse・varied・mixed・assorted・miscellaneous・heterogeneous・eclectic・motley
物事が非常に異なり、いろいろな種類のあることを表す
【類語訳】さまざまな，多様な，混成の，混合の，種々雑多な

文型&コロケーション
▶ a diverse/ a varied/ a mixed/ an assorted/ a miscellaneous/ a heterogeneous/ a motley **group**
▶ a diverse/ varied/ mixed/ miscellaneous/ heterogeneous/ motley **collection**
▶ a diverse/ varied/ mixed/ heterogeneous/ motley **array**
▶ a diverse/ varied/ mixed/ motley **assortment**
▶ diverse/ assorted/ miscellaneous **items**
▶ **very** diverse/ varied/ mixed/ heterogeneous/ eclectic
▶ **rather** diverse/ mixed/ heterogeneous
▶ **racially/ ethnically/ culturally/ socially** diverse/ varied/ mixed

diverse 《ややフォーマル》 異なった，さまざまな；多様な ◇People from *diverse* cultures were invited to the event. さまざまな文化を持つ人々がその行事に招待された ◇My interests are very *diverse*. 私の興味はとても多岐にわたる ◇The US is a vast and *diverse* country. アメリカは広大で多様性に富む国だ ☞ **diversity (RANGE 1)**

varied 《しばしばほめて》さまざまな；多様な ◇The opportunities the job offers are *many and varied*. その仕事がもたらす機会は多種多様である ◇They stock a wide and *varied* selection of cheeses. その店はチーズの品揃えが豊富だ ☞ **vary (DIFFER), variety (RANGE 1)**

mixed [名詞の前で] 混成の，混合の ◇She was born to parents of *mixed race*. 彼女は人種の異なる両親の子として生まれた ◇a *mixed marriage* (= between two people of different races or religions) 異人種[宗教]間の結婚 ◇Do you have experience of teaching *mixed-ability* classes? 能力混成方式のクラスを教えた経験はありますか ❶この意味での mixed はここにあげた決まった連語で用いられる．

assorted [名詞の前で]《ややフォーマル》さまざまな種類の ◇The meat is served with salad or *assorted* vegetables. 肉はサラダや野菜の盛り合わせと共に出されます ◇The sweater comes in *assorted* colours. そのセーターはさまざまな色が売られている ◇a box of *assorted* chocolates 一箱のチョコの詰め合わせ ❶ assorted は特にレストラン・店・メーカーによる商品・サービスの説明に用いられる．☞ **assortment (RANGE 1)**

miscellaneous ［ふつう名詞の前で］《ややフォーマル》種々雑多な ◇The museum houses a *miscellaneous* collection of iron age artefacts. その博物館には種々雑多な鉄器時代の工芸品のコレクションが所蔵されている ◇She gave me some money to cover any *miscellaneous* expenses. 彼女は種々雑多な出費を埋め合わせるお金を私にくれた

heterogeneous ［《フォーマル》］異なる人［物］から成る, 雑多な ◇She cited the *heterogeneous* population of the United States to support her argument. 彼女は持論を補強するためアメリカの住民がさまざまな人々から成っていることを引き合いに出した 反意 **homogeneous** (EQUAL 形)

eclectic 《フォーマル》 取捨選択された, 織り交ぜられた ◇She has very *eclectic* tastes in literature. 彼女の文学の趣味はとても幅広い ◇His house is an *eclectic* mixture of the antique and the modern. 彼の家は古いものと新しいものを織り交ぜて建ててある

motley ［名詞の前で］《特に書き言葉, しばしばけなして》種々雑多な ◇The room was filled with a *motley* collection of furniture and paintings. その部屋は種々雑多な家具や絵画のコレクションでいっぱいだった ◇The audience was a *motley crew* of students and tourists. 見物人は学生や観光客など種々雑多な群衆の寄せ集めだった ❶ motleyはふつうbunch, collection, crew, groupなどの語と結びついて, しばしば人・物のまとまりがなく乱雑で, 奇妙［滑稽］な様子であることを表す.

divide 動

1 divide・break (sth) up・split・cut sth up・subdivide・split (sb) up・separate (sth) out
全体を二つ以上にする
【類語訳】分かれる, 分裂する, 分割する, ばらばらになる, 切り分ける, 切り刻む, 分散する, 区分する

[文型&コロケーション]
▶ to divide/ break/ split/ cut sth **up**
▶ to divide (sth)/ break sth up/ split sth/ subdivide sth **into parts**
▶ to divide (sth)/ break sth up/ split sth **into sections**
▶ to divide (sth)/ split sth/ cut sth up **into pieces**
▶ to divide (sb)/ split sb/ subdivide sth/ split (sb) up **into groups**
▶ to divide/ split (sth) **in two/ in half**

divide ［自, 他］分かれる, 分裂する, 分割する; 分ける ◇The cells began to *divide* rapidly. 細胞が急速に分裂し始めた ◇We reached the point where the river *divides* in two. 私たちは川が二手に分かれるポイントに到着した ◇This report is *divided* broadly into two parts. この報告書は大きく二つの部分に分かれている ◇A sentence can be *divided* up into meaningful segments. 一つの文はいくつかの有意味な部分に分解できる

,break 'up, ,break sth 'up 句動詞 分かれる［分ける］, ばらばらになる［する］ ◇The grey clouds had begun to *break up*. 灰色の雲がちぎれて分かれ始めていた ◇Much has changed since the Soviet Union *broke up*. ソ連が崩壊してずいぶんと変わった ◇*Break up* the chocolate and place it in a bowl. チョコレートを小さく割ってボウルに入れましょう ◇The ship was *broken up* for scrap metal. 船はスクラップ目的で解体された ◇Sentences can be *broken up* into clauses. 文は節に分けることができる

split ［自, 他］分かれる, 分ける ◇The results *split* neatly into two groups. その結果はきれいに二つのグループに分かれた ◇Slate *splits* easily into thin sheets. スレートは簡単に薄い板状に切り分けることができる ◇Which scientist first *split the atom*? どの科学者が初めて原子を分裂させたか ◇She *split* the class into groups of four. 彼女はクラスを4人ずつのグループに分けた ◇The day was *split* up into six one-hour sessions. その日は6つの1時間単位のセッションに分割された

ノート divide, break up, split の使い分け: divide は break up や split よりもややフォーマル. break up はしばしばある程度の力を加えて, 人・状況が物事を強制的に分割することを表す. 分割された部分はもはや全体の一部とは見なされない. ◆ The empire was *broken up* into different parts (= it was no longer an empire). (帝国はさまざまな国々に分裂した). ◆ The empire was *divided*/*split* into different parts (= it was still an empire but contained separate areas). (帝国はさまざまな地域に分割された). divide, split は物を主語に自動詞として用いられるので, Cells divide naturally. という言い方が自然だが, 原子は大きな力をかけてのみ分裂させられるので Atoms can be split. のように split を他動詞として用いる.

,cut sth 'up 句動詞 （ナイフ・はさみで）細かく切る, 切り分ける, 切り刻む ◇He *cut up* the meat on his plate. 彼は肉を皿の上で切り分けた ◇I *cut* the paper *up* into small segments. 私は紙を細かく切り分けた

subdivide ［他, しばしば受身で］《ややフォーマル》再分割する ◇Each of the chapters is *subdivided* into several double-page spreads. 各章はさらにいくつかの見開きページに分けられている

,split 'up, ,split sb 'up 句動詞 （小グループに）分ける ◇Let's *split up* now and meet again at lunchtime. ではここで小グループに分かれて, 昼食時にまた会いましょう ◇We were *split up* into groups to discuss the question. 私たちは問題を話し合うためグループに分けられた ◇You two are talking too much. I'm going to have to *split* you *up*. あなたたち二人は私語が多過ぎます. 分けないといけませんね

,separate 'out, ,separate sth 'out 句動詞 分散する, 分別する ◇Particles will *separate out* as the smoke disperses. 煙が消散するにつれ, 粒子は分散するだろう ◇More and more households are *separating out* recyclable waste. リサイクル可能なゴミを分別する家庭がますます増えている ◇We need to *separate out* fact *from* speculation. 推測から事実を選り分ける必要がある ❶ separate out は各部分それ自体が完全体と考えられることを強調する. ◆ The particles *separate out* (= they move away from each other). (粒子は分散するだろう). ◆ The particles will *divide* (= each particle will become two or more separate parts). (粒子は分裂するだろう).

2 divide・split・alienate・separate・be/become estranged・come between sb and sb
人の意見を対立させる, 人を感情的に引き離す
【類語訳】分裂する, 疎外する, 異ならせる, 疎遠である, 仲を裂く

[文型&コロケーション]
▶ to be divided/ split **over** sth
▶ to be alienated/ estranged **from** sb
▶ to be **increasingly** divided/ split/ alienated/ separated/ estranged

↪**divide**

▶ to be **deeply** divided/ split
▶ to be **totally** alienated/ separated
▶ to be **completely** separated/ estranged

divide [他] (問題で)意見を対立させる ◇The issue has bitterly *divided* the community. その問題に関して地域社会の意見が激しく対立した ◇The government is *divided* on the question of tax cuts. 政府内で減税の問題に関して意見が分かれている

split [自, 他] (意見の違いで)分裂する；(問題で)分裂させる ◇The committee *split* over government subsidies. 委員会は政府の補助金に関して意見が分かれた ◇The debate has *split* the country ***down the middle***. 論争はその国を真っ二つにした

ノート divide と split の使い分け：divide は一時的な意見の不一致を, split は恒久的な意見の不一致を暗示する. この意味での divide はふつう目的語を伴う.

alienate [他] (ややフォーマル) (人を)疎外する ◇Very talented children may feel *alienated* from the others in their class. 非常に有能な子たちはクラスの他の子たちから疎外されていると感じるかもしれない ◇It is important that the new policies do not *alienate* our core supporters. 新しい政策が我々の主な支持者を疎外しないということが大切だ

separate [他] (他と)異ならせる ◇Politics is the only thing that *separates* us (= that we disagree about). 私たちの意見が分かれるのは政治に関してだけだ ◇Her lack of religious faith *separated* her from the rest of her family. 信仰心のなさが彼女と家族とを分け隔てた ◇Only four points *separate* the top three teams. トップの3チームとの差はたった4ポイントだ

be/become estranged [自] (ややフォーマル) (家族と)疎遠である[になり] ◇He *became estranged* from his family after the argument. その口論があって以来, 彼は家族と疎遠になった

come be'tween sb and sb 句動詞 (受身なし) (二人の)関係を壊す, 仲を裂く ◇I'd hate anything to *come between* us. 私たちの仲を裂こうとするものは何でも憎むだろう ◇Must she always *come between* us? 彼女はいつも私たちの仲をぶち壊すではおれないの ❶ come between sb and sb の主語には人・問題・感情・口論・状況などほとんど何でも用いられる.

division 名

1 division・separation・isolation・segregation・quarantine・split・partition・dissolution
物事や人を分ける行為, 分けた結果
【類語訳】分割, 分離, 孤立, 差別, 分け前, 解散, 解体

文型&コロケーション
▶ division/ separation/ isolation/ segregation **from** sb/ sth
▶ (a) division/ separation/ segregation/ split **between** sth and sth else
▶ (a) division/ segregation/ segregation/ split **into** parts
▶ (a) division/ isolation/ segregation **within** sth
▶ **strict** division/ separation/ isolation/ segregation/ quarantine
▶ (a) **clear** division/ separation/ split
▶ **complete** separation/ isolation/ segregation

division [U, 単数で] 分割(する行為[した結果]) ◇The organism begins as a single cell and grows by cell *division*. 生物は単細胞として始まり, 細胞分裂によって成長する ◇We need to ensure a fair *division* of time and resources. 時間と資金を適切に分割することを保証する必要がある ◇In many traditional societies, the *division* of labour between the sexes is strict. 多くの伝統的社会において, 性差による労働の分割は厳密である ☞ **divide** (SHARE 動)

separation [U, 単数で] 分離(している状態) ◇Many years passed before the state's eventual *separation* from the federation. 最終的にその州が連邦から分離するまで何年もが経過した ◇He argued for the need for a clear *separation* between Church and State. 彼は教会と国家の明確な分離の必要性を訴えた

isolation [U] (完全な)分離, 孤立 ◇The country has been threatened with complete *isolation* from the international community unless the atrocities stop. もし残虐行為をやめなければその国は国際社会から完全に孤立する危機にさらされている ◇He lives in *splendid isolation* (= far from, or in a superior position to, everyone else). 彼は孤高の生活を送っている ☞ **isolate** (ISOLATE)

ノート separation と isolation の使い分け：separation のほうが一般的. isolation は国家や政治について用いられ, diplomatic, geographical, political, international などと結びつく. この種の isolation はふつう好ましくないものと見なされるが, separation (例えば between Church and State (教会と国家の分離)や between the executive and the judiciary in government (政府内における行政と司法の分離)) はしばしば好ましいものと考えられる. isolation は感染症の蔓延を防止する文脈でも用いられる. ♦ an *isolation* hospital/ward (隔離病院/病棟)

segregation [U] (人種・宗教・性別に基づく)分離(政策), 差別 ◇The social structure was based on the policy of *racial segregation*. その社会構造は人種分離政策に基づいていた ◇*Segregation by* sex and age is relatively common in these societies. 性別と年齢による差別はこれらの社会においては比較的一般的だ ❶ segregation はフォーマルな言い回しで人や物事を大きくグループ分けする行為を意味することもある. ♦ the *segregation* of smokers and non-smokers in restaurants (レストランにおける喫煙者と非喫煙者の分離). ☞ **segregate** (ISOLATE), discrimination, apartheid (DISCRIMINATION)

quarantine [U] (病気の蔓延防止のための動物・人の)隔離 ◇The dog was kept *in quarantine* for six months. その犬は6か月間隔離されていた ◇*Quarantine* regulations have been introduced. 隔離に関する法規が導入された ☞ **quarantine** (ISOLATE)

split [単数で] (ややインフォーマル) 分け前 ◇He demanded a 50-50 *split* in the profits. 彼は儲けの半分を要求した ☞ **split** (SHARE 動)

partition [U] (国の)分割 ◇The effects of the *partition* of Germany can still be seen today. ドイツの分裂の影響は今日もまだ見受けられる

dissolution [U] (ややフォーマル) (組織・協会などの)解散, 解体 ◇The company was set up following the *dissolution* of the Soviet Union. ソビエト連邦の解体を受けてその会社は設立された

2 division・split・rift・alienation・schism・distance・disunity・estrangement

人々の間の意見の不一致や違い
【類語訳】対立, 不和, 疎外, 分裂, よそよそしさ, 不調和, 疎遠, 離反

【文型&コロケーション】
▶ division/ a split/ a rift/ a schism/ distance/ disunity/ estrangement **between** people or groups
▶ division/ disunity **among** people or groups
▶ division/ a split/ a rift/ a schism/ disunity **within** a group
▶ a split/ rift **with** sb
▶ a split/ alienation/ distance/ estrangement **from** sb
▶ (a/ an) **deep/ serious/ internal/ ideological** division/ split/ rift
▶ (a) **growing** division/ split/ rift/ alienation/ distance/ estrangement
▶ (a) **political** division/ split/ rift/ alienation/ disunity
▶ to **cause/ lead to** divisions/ a split/ a rift/ alienation/ a schism
▶ to **create** divisions/ a rift/ a distance
▶ to **heal** divisions/ a split/ a rift

division [C, U] (社会・組織内における意見の)対立 ◇We need to work together to heal the *divisions* within society. 私たちは社会にある対立をなくすため協力する必要がある ◇The party was weakened by *division* between various factions. さまざまな派閥間の対立が原因でその政党は弱体化した

split [C]《ややインフォーマル》(恒久的な)対立, 不和 ◇A damaging *split* within the party leadership has occurred. 由々しき対立が党執行部内で生じた ◇He found it difficult to cope in the years following his bitter *split* with his wife. 彼はにがい離婚を経て数年で妻とよりを戻すのは無理だと思った

rift [C] (恒久的とは限らない)対立, 不和 ◇The *rift* within the party deepens. 党内の溝は深まっている ◇Efforts to heal the *rift* between the two countries have failed. 2国間の対立を解消する努力は失敗に終わった

ノート **split と rift の使い分け**：rift はしばしば split につながるような深刻な意見の対立を表すが, それが解消される可能性は split 以上に大きい.

alienation [U] 疎外 ◇The new policy resulted in the *alienation* of many voters. 新しい政策は多くの投票者を遠ざける結果となった ◇Many immigrants suffer from a feeling of *alienation*. 多くの移民が疎外感に苦しんでいる

schism [C, U]《フォーマル》(宗教組織内での)分裂 ◇The disagreement eventually led to a *schism* within the Church. その意見の不一致はついに教会内に分裂をもたらした ◇By 1914 the party was dangerously close to *schism*. 1914年までにその政党は危うく分裂しそうだった

distance [U, C] よそよそしさ ◇He worried about the increasing *distance* between his children and himself. 彼は子どもたちとの間の広がりつつある隔たりのことを心配した ◇The coldness and *distance* in her voice took me by surprise. 彼女の声の冷たさとよそよそしさに私は驚いた ☞ **distant** (COLD 2)

disunity [U]《フォーマル》(人々の)不調和, 分裂 ◇*Disunity* among opposition groups will prevent real change from happening. 野党がまとまらなくては真の改革が行われることはないだろう 反義 **unity**

estrangement [U, C]《フォーマル》疎遠, 離反 ◇A period of *estrangement* from his wife had left him feeling isolated and alone. 妻と別居しているあいだ, 彼は孤独と寂寞を感じていた ◇The misunderstanding had caused a seven-year *estrangement* between them. 誤解が原因で彼らは7年もの間疎遠になっていた ☞ **estranged** (SINGLE)

do 動

do・carry sth out・conduct・undertake・perform・implement・commit・practise・go through sth
活動したり, 作業したりすることを表す
【類語訳】する, 実行する, 果たす, 行う, 引き受ける, 請け負う, 着手する, 履行する, (過失などを)犯す, 実践する

【文型&コロケーション】
▶ to do/ carry out/ conduct/ undertake/ perform the **work**
▶ to do/ carry out/ conduct/ undertake/ perform a/ an **activity/ analysis/ investigation/ review/ assessment/ evaluation**
▶ to do/ carry out/ conduct/ undertake **business**
▶ to do/ carry out/ conduct/ perform/ go through a **test**
▶ to do/ carry out/ undertake/ perform a **task/ job**
▶ to do/ carry out/ perform/ go through a **manoeuvre**
▶ to do/ carry out/ perform/ practise **surgery**
▶ to do/ carry out/ implement a **plan/ policy/ strategy**
▶ to do/ carry out/ conduct/ undertake/ perform/ implement sth **effectively/ efficiently/ properly/ successfully**
▶ to do/ conduct/ perform/ implement sth **well/ poorly**

do [他] する ◇I *do* aerobics once a week. 週に一度エアロビクスをやります ◇I'm *doing* some research on the subject. そのテーマで研究をしています ◇I have a number of things to *do* today. 今日済まさなければならないことがたくさんある ◇**What do you do** (= what is your job)? お仕事は何ですか ◇What did she *do for a living*? 彼女は何をして生計を支えたのですか ❶ do は, 名指しではっきり言えない行為や知らない行為についてしばしば用いられる. ◆What are you *doing* this evening? (今晩は何をするつもりなの). ◆There's *nothing to do* (= no means of passing the time in an enjoyable way) in this place. (この場所では何もすることがない). ◆The company ought to *do something* about the poor service. (その会社はお粗末なサービスに関して何らかの手を打たなければならない). ◆There's *nothing we can do* about it (= we can't change the situation). (その件で私たちは打つ手がない). ◆*What can I do for you* (= how can I help)? (どのようなご用件でしょうか). ❶ do は, 買い物や掃除のような活動や作業を表す名詞と共によく用いられる. ◆I like listening to the radio when I'm *doing* the ironing. (《英》アイロンがけをしているときにラジオを聞くのが好きです). ◆She *did* a lot of acting when she was at college. (彼女は大学時代によく芝居に出た). ◆You could help me by *doing* (= washing) the dishes. (皿洗いだったらあなたは手伝えるわね). ◆I like the way you've *done* your hair. (あなたのヘアスタイルが気に入っている).

carry sth 'out 句動《ややフォーマル》実行する, 果たす ◇We *carry out* routine maintenance of the equipment. 私たちは日常的に設備を保守しています ◇The company has just *carried out* a major cost-cutting exercise. その会社はまさに大幅な経費削減に踏み切った ◇The pilot has to *carry out* a series of complex manoeuvres. パイロットは一連の複雑な操作を実行しなければならない ◇The massacre was *carried out* by enemy troops. 大虐殺は敵の軍隊によって実行された ❶ *carry sth out* は仕事, 作業, 犯罪について用いられるが, 犯罪の場合には入念に練られた[指示された]犯罪であることが多い.

conduct [他]《フォーマル》(特定のことを)行う ◇We *conducted* the experiment under controlled circumstances. 私たちは管理された状況下でその実験を行った ◇The negotiations have been *conducted* in a positive manner. その交渉は前向きに行われてきている ◇The interrogation was *conducted* by senior police officers. その取り調べは巡査長によって行われた ❶ *conduct* は, enquiry, inquest, interview, interrogation, investigation, survey, study といった語と共によく用いる.

undertake [他]《フォーマル》引き受ける, 請け負う, 着手する ◇The directors of the company refused to *undertake* such a risky venture. その会社の重役たちはそのようなリスクの高い事業を請け負おうとしなかった ◇A group of enthusiasts has *undertaken* the reconstruction of a steam locomotive. 熱狂的なファンのグループが1台の蒸気機関車の復元に着手した ❶ *undertake* は, ふつう人・集団が責任を負う重要な仕事について用いられる.
☞ **undertaking** (PROJECT)

perform [他]《ややフォーマル, 特に書き言葉》(仕事・義務などを)行う, 果たす ◇A computer can *perform* many tasks at once. コンピューターは一度に多くのタスクをこなすことができる ◇She *performs* an important role in our organization. 彼女は我々の組織では重要な役割を果たしている ◇He *performed miracles* to get everything ready in time. 彼はすべてを時間に間に合わせるという奇跡を起こした

ノート carry sth out と perform の使い分け: *carry sth out* は作業の量に重点が置かれる. 特にその作業が一定時間[期間]に及んだり, 計画に基づいて行われたりする場合にそうである. *perform* はしばしば作業の技量に重点が置かれる. ✗*carry out* miracles/an important role. ✗*perform* inquiries/a cost-cutting exercise. carry sth out は attack, abuse, assault, assassination, killing などの否定的な行為についても用いることができるが, perform はできない.

implement [他]《ややフォーマル》(公式に決められたことを)実行する, 履行する ◇We have not yet begun to *implement* the changes. 我々はまだそれらの変更を実行に移し始めていない ◇We are *implementing* a new system of stock control. 私たちは在庫管理の新システムを始動しているところだ

commit (-tt-) [他]《過失などを》犯す ◇What leads someone to *commit* murder? 何が人を殺人に駆り立てるのだろうか ◇We heard of some of the appalling crimes *committed against* innocent children. 私たちは罪もない子どもたちに対する忌まわしい犯罪のいくつかを聞き及んだ ❶ *commit* は crime, offence, atrocity, outrage, sin, その他 murder, assault, robbery, adultery, blasphemy といったさまざまな種類の罪を表す語と結びつくことが多い. commit suicide は「自殺する」を意味する.

practise [英]《米 **practice**》[他]《ややフォーマル》(ふだんの行いとして)行う, 実践する ◇A lot of couples now *practise* safe sex. カップルの多くは今では(コンドームなどを使った)安全なセックスをする ◇Do you still *practise* your religion? あなたはいまだに自分の宗教を信仰しているのですか ◇Train yourself to *practise* self-restraint. 自

制できるように訓練しなさい ☞ **practice** (USE [名])

go through sth [句動詞] (一連のことを)する, (手続きなどを)踏む ◇Certain formalities have to be *gone through* before you can emigrate. 移住する前には一定の手続きを踏む必要がある ◇We *go through* the same old routine every morning. 私たちは毎朝, 昔から変わらぬ同じ日課をこなしている

document [名]

document・file・papers・archive・deed・paperwork・dossier

情報や記録が記されている書類
【類語訳】公文書, ドキュメント, 文書ファイル, ファイル, 書類, 保管記録, 証書, 必要書類

文型&コロケーション

▶ a document/ a file/ the paperwork/ a dossier **on** sb/ sth
▶ **in** a document/ a file/ the archives/ the paperwork/ a dossier
▶ the **relevant** document/ file/ papers/ paperwork
▶ the **necessary** documents/ papers/ paperwork
▶ (an) **important** document/ papers/ archive
▶ **confidential** documents/ files/ papers
▶ (a) **personal**/ **secret** documents/ file/ papers/ archive/ dossier
▶ (a/ an) **official**/ **government**/ **state** document/ file/ paper/ archive
▶ to **prepare** a document/ a file/ the paperwork/ a dossier
▶ to **draw up** a document/ papers/ the paperwork
▶ to **release** a document/ a file/ papers
▶ to **keep** a document/ a file/ papers/ an archive/ the deeds/ the paperwork/ a dossier
▶ to **leak** a document/ a file/ papers
▶ to **read (through)** a document/ a file/ the papers/ the paperwork/ a dossier
▶ to **study** a document/ papers/ a dossier

document [C] (公式の)書類, 公文書; (コンピューターの)ドキュメント, 文書ファイル ◇Keep all your travel *documents* in a safe place. 渡航文書はすべて安全な場所に保管しましょう ◇This is an important legal *document*. これは重要な法律文書だ ◇They have produced a new *policy document*. 彼らは新しい保険関係書類を作った ◇The committee presented a *discussion document* (= to be discussed) at yesterday's meeting. 昨日の会議で委員会は討議資料を提出した ◇Save the *document* before closing. 閉じる前にドキュメントを保存してください
☞ **documentation** (CERTIFICATE)

file [C] (特定の人・問題などについてまとめた)ファイル; (コンピューターの)ファイル ◇The police were accused of keeping secret *files* on political activists. 警察は政治活動家に関するファイルを隠し持っていたことで非難された ◇Please add this document to your *files*. この書類をファイルに加えてください ◇Exactly what information is kept in these *files*? 正確に言ってどんな情報がこれらのファイルに保管されているのですか ◇Your application will be *kept on file*. あなたの願書はファイルに保管されます ◇Every *file* on the same disk must have a different name. 同じディスク上のすべてのファイルには異なる名前を付けなければならない ☞ **file** (CLASSIFY)

papers [複数形で] 書類 ◇His desk was covered with

books and *papers*. 彼の机は本や書類で覆われていた ◊I was sorting through his *papers* when I came upon a letter from my mother. 彼の書類を選り分けていたら私の母からの手紙が偶然出てきた ❶ *papers* は免許や身分証などの公式文書を意味することもある。☞ **papers** (CERTIFICATE)

archive [C]（または **archives** [複数形]）（政府・一家・組織などの）古[保管]文書, 保管資料 ◊These papers are an important part of the national *archive*. これらの書類は国の保管文書の重要な一部です ◊The data is now held in the company *archives*. そのデータは今、会社の書庫に保管されている ◊The recording is preserved in the BBC's *sound archive*. その音声はBBCの録音資料室に保管されている ◊It is one of the most important *film archives* in the world. それは世界で最も重要な映像資料の一つである

deed [C]（しばしば英では複数形）（家・建物・土地の）証書 ◊The *deeds to* the property are with my lawyer. 財産証書は私の弁護士が持っている ◊Who currently keeps the *title deed* (= a deed showing who owns sth)? 権利証書は現在誰が保管していますか

paperwork [U]（必要）書類 ◊We can get the necessary *paperwork* signed tomorrow. 明日私たちは必要書類に署名をすることができる ☞ **paperwork** (BUREAUCRACY)

dossier [C]《フォーマル》（人・事件・テーマに関する）調書 ◊They kept *dossiers* on all trade union members. 彼らは組合員全員に関する調書を保管していた ◊The group *compiled a dossier* of patients' complaints. その団体が患者の苦情に関する調書をまとめた

doubt 名

1 doubt・question・uncertainty・confusion・a question mark over sth・indecision
人や物事に関して確信が持てない感じ
【類語訳】疑い, 疑念, 不確かさ, 不明瞭, 疑問符

文型&コロケーション

▸ doubt/ uncertainty/ confusion/ a question mark/ indecision **over** sth
▸ doubt/ uncertainty/ confusion/ indecision **about/ as to** sth
▸ **in** doubt/ question/ uncertainty
▸ **beyond/ without** doubt/ question
▸ **considerable** doubt/ uncertainty/ confusion
▸ **serious** doubt/ confusion
▸ **slight** uncertainty/ confusion
▸ to **come into/ be open to** doubt/ question
▸ to **express** doubt/ uncertainty
▸ to **clear up/ dispel** doubt/ uncertainty/ confusion

doubt [U] 疑い, 疑念 ◊*There is some doubt* about the best way to do it. それを行う最善の方法に関していくらか疑問がある ◊*There is no doubt* at all that we did the right thing. 私たちは正しいことをしたということに疑いの余地はまったくない ◊New evidence has *cast doubt on* the guilt of the man jailed for the crime. 新証拠はその罪で服役している男の有罪に疑いを投げかけた ◊The success of the system is not in *doubt*. そのシステムの成功は確実である ◊*If in doubt*, wear black. 迷ったら、黒っぽい服を着ましょう ◊He's made some great movies. There's *no doubt about it*. 彼はいくつか素晴らしい映画を制作した。それは間違いない ◊The prosecution was able to establish *beyond reasonable doubt* that the woman had been lying.《法律》検察はその女性が嘘をついていたことは合理的に考えて疑いがないと証明した ☞ **doubtful** (UNLIKELY 1), **doubtful** (UNSURE)

question [U] 疑問 ◊Her honesty is beyond *question*. 彼女の正直さに疑問の余地はない ◊His suitability for the job is open to *question*. その仕事に彼が向いているかに関しては疑問が残る ◊Her version of events was accepted without *question*. 事件に関する彼女の説明は疑われることなく受け入れられた ◊The incident *brought into question* the safety of travellers in the region. その事件でその地域の観光客の安全性に疑問が生じた

uncertainty [U]《ややフォーマル》不確かさ ◊There is considerable *uncertainty* about the company's future. その会社の将来性に関してはかなり不透明だ ◊He had an air of *uncertainty* about him. 彼には自信のない雰囲気があった 反義 **certainty** (FAITH), ☞ **uncertain** (UNSURE)

ノート **doubt** と **uncertainty** の使い分け: doubt はしばしば人や物事に対して積極的に疑いをかけることを言う。
◆ Religious *doubt* is an integral element of faith.（宗教的疑念は信仰に不可欠な要素である）. uncertainty はそれほど積極的ではなく、物事に関して消極的にしか確信が持てないことを意味する。✗ Religious *uncertainty* is an integral element of faith.

confusion [U, C] 不明瞭, 不確入 ◊There is some *confusion* about what the correct procedure should be. 正しい手順がどうあるべきかよくわからない ◊There was a *confusion* as to what to do next. 次に何をすべきかはっきりしなかった ☞ **confused** (CONFUSED), **confusing** (CONFUSING)

a 'question mark over sth 行礼《ややインフォーマル》（特に将来への）疑問符 ◊There's still *a big question mark* hanging over his future with the team. そのチームとの関係で彼の今後がどうなるかについては依然として大きな疑問符が付いている

indecision [U] 優柔不断, 躊躇 ◊After a moment's *indecision*, he said yes. 一瞬迷って彼は承諾した ◊She went through a period of terrible uncertainty and *indecision*. しばらくの間彼女はまったく確信がもてず何も決められない状態が続いた
▸ **indecisive** 形 ◊a weak and *indecisive* man 弱気で優柔不断な男

2 doubt・suspicion・uncertainty・misgiving・second thoughts・qualm・scruple・compunction
正しいことをしていないかもしれないという思い
【類語訳】疑念, 疑い, 不信感, 嫌疑, 容疑, 懸念, 危惧, 後ろめたさ, 良心の呵責

文型&コロケーション

▸ doubts/ suspicions/ uncertainties/ misgivings/ second thoughts/ qualms/ scruples/ compunction **about** sth
▸ **without** a doubt/ misgivings/ a qualm/ scruples/ compunction
▸ **considerable/ great/ grave/ deep/ serious** doubts/ suspicion/ misgivings
▸ to **have** doubts/ suspicions/ misgivings/ second thoughts/ qualms/ scruples

▶ to **have no** doubts/ suspicions/ misgivings/ qualms/ scruples/ compunction
▶ to **feel (no)** doubt/ qualms/ compunction
▶ to **express** doubts/ suspicions/ misgivings
▶ to **raise/ arouse/ voice** doubts/ suspicions

doubt [C] 疑念, 疑い ◇His failure to appear raises serious *doubts as to* his reliability. 姿を見せないとなると彼の信頼性に関して大きな疑念が生じることになる ◇*Doubts* have arisen *over* the viability of the schedule. スケジュールの実行可能性に関して疑問が生じている ◇They say they'll be here on time but I *have my doubts* about that. 彼らは時間どおりにここに来ると言っているが, それは疑わしいと思う ◇I had been aware of a *nagging doubt* growing in my mind. 私は心の中にある払い切れない疑念が広がってくるのに気づいていた ☞ **doubt (SUSPECT)**
suspicion [U, C] 不信感, 嫌疑, 容疑 ◇He was arrested *on suspicion of* murder. 彼は殺人の容疑で逮捕された ◇They drove away slowly to avoid arousing *suspicion*. 彼らは疑惑をかき立てさせないように車でゆっくりと立ち去った ◇I have a *sneaking suspicion* that she's not telling the truth. 私は彼女が真実を語っていないのではないかとひそかに疑っている ◇She was reluctant to voice her *suspicions*. 彼女は疑いの念を口に出す気にはなれなかった ☞ **suspicion (SCEPTICISM), suspect (SUPPOSE), suspicious (SUSPICIOUS 1, 2)**
uncertainty [C] 不安定；不安をいだかせる状況 ◇All of us are a bit afraid of life's *uncertainties* and unexpected problems. 私たちは皆人生の不確実さや予期せぬ問題に少々不安を抱いている ◇She tried to get on with her life amidst the *uncertainties* of war. 戦争という不安な状況のただ中で彼女はなんとか生活していこうとした 反義 **certainty, uncertain (UNCLEAR)**
misgiving [C, ふつう複数で, U] 《ややフォーマル》《起こるかもしれないこと[正しい行いかどうか]に関する》懸念, 危惧 ◇I had grave *misgivings* about making the trip. 旅に出ることに大きな懸念があった ◇I read the letter with a sense of *misgiving*. 懸念を抱きながら私はその手紙を読んだ
second thoughts [フレーズ] 再考 ◇You're not having *second thoughts* about it, are you? それについて考え直す気はないんですね ◇I'll wait here. No, *on second thoughts*, I'll come with you. 《英》ここで待つよ。いや, やっぱり, 君と行くよ ◇*On second thought*, I'll come with you. 《米》やっぱり, 君と行くよ ❶ *second thoughts* は have second thoughts と on second thoughts 《《米》では on second thought》の二つのイディオムで用いられる。
qualm [C, ふつう複数で]《正しい行いかどうかに関する》気のとがめ, 後ろめたさ ◇He had been working very hard so he had no *qualms* about taking a few days off. 彼は非常にがんばって働いていたので, 休日を数日取ることにまったく気がとがめることはなかった
scruple [C, ふつう複数で, U]《道徳的に間違っているのではないかという》ためらい ◇I overcame my moral *scruples*. 私は道徳的なためらいを振り切った ◇He had no *scruples* about spying on her. 彼は彼女の素行を調査することに何のやましさも感じなかった ◇She is totally without *scruple*. 彼女はまったく良心のとがめを感じていない ☞ **scrupulous (GOOD 5), unscrupulous (CORRUPT)**
compunction [U] 《フォーマル》良心の呵責 ◇She felt no *compunction* about leaving her job. 彼女は仕事を辞めることに何の良心の呵責も感じなかった ❶《米》では compunction は可算名詞で使われることもある。 ◆She has no *compunctions* about rejecting the plan. 《《米》彼女は計画を却下することに何の良心の呵責も感じない）.

doubt 動

doubt・question・challenge・dispute・contest・query
人や物事に関して疑いの念を抱く[示す]
【類語訳】疑う, 異議を唱える

文型&コロケーション

▶ to **doubt/ question/ challenge/ dispute/ query whether**...
▶ to **doubt/ dispute that**...
▶ to **doubt/ question/ challenge/ dispute/ contest** the **validity** of sth
▶ to **doubt/ question/ challenge** the **wisdom** of sb/ sth
▶ to **doubt/ question/ challenge** a **story**
▶ to **doubt/ question** sb's **integrity/ motives**
▶ to **question/ challenge/ dispute/ contest/ query** a **decision**
▶ to **seriously doubt/ question/ challenge/ dispute/ contest** sth

doubt [他] 疑いを抱く, 疑う；疑問に思う ◇There seems no reason to *doubt* her story. 彼女の話を疑う理由はないように思われる ◇'Do you think England will win?' —'I *doubt* it.'「イングランドが勝つと思うかい」—「思わないね」 ◇I never *doubted* (that) she would come. 私は彼女が必ず来ると思っていた ◇I *doubt if* the new one will be any better. 新しいものが少しでも良いものになるかどうか疑わしい ☞ **doubtful (UNLIKELY 1), doubtful (UNSURE), undoubted (UNDOUBTED)**
question [他] 疑う ◇I just accepted what he told me. I never thought to *question* it. 彼が私に言ったことをうのみにしました。それに疑いをさしはさむなど思ってもみませんでした ◇No one has ever *questioned* her judgement. これまで誰も彼女の判断に疑問を抱いたことはなかった ◇He *questioned* whether the accident was solely the truck driver's fault. 彼はその事故がトラック運転手の過失だけによるものかどうか疑いを抱いた ☞ **unquestioned (UNDOUBTED)**
challenge [他] 《真実[合法]かどうかに》疑いを示す；《(物事に)異議を唱える ◇The story was completely untrue and was successfully *challenged* in court. その話はまったくの嘘で, 法廷において徹底的に追及された ◇This discovery *challenges* traditional beliefs. この発見で伝統的に信じられてきたことに疑問が持たれている ◇She does not like anyone *challenging* her authority. 彼女は自分の権威にたて突く人間が嫌いだ ☞ **unchallenged (UNDOUBTED)**
dispute [他] 《真実性・正当性に関して》異議を唱える, 疑念を示す ◇These figures have been *disputed*. これらの数字は疑問視されている ◇The players *disputed* the referee's decision. 選手たちは審判の決定に異議を唱えた ◇No one is *disputing* that there is a problem. 誰も問題があることに異議はない ☞ **undisputed (UNDOUBTED)**
contest [他] 《決定・発言などに正式に》異議を唱える ◇Her son *contested* the will, stating that she was not of sound mind when she signed it. 彼女の息子は母親が遺書にサインをしたとき健全な精神状態になかったとして, 遺書の無効を申し立てた ◇The divorce was not *contested*.

do well, drama

離婚について異議の申し立てはなかった ☞ **uncontested** (UNDOUBTED)

query [他]（物事が正しいかどうか）疑念を示す ◇We *queried* the bill as it seemed far too high. あまりにも高いように思われたので私たちは請求書がおかしいのではと疑う問い合わせをした

> **ノート** questionとqueryの使い分け：意味はとても近いが、questionのほうがより頻繁に用いられる。queryはしばしば請求書・報告書・請求金額などの明細に関して疑問を示すのに用いられる。questionは物事の存在自体を疑うことを含み、より強い疑念を示す。◆I question the existence of life on other planets. (私は他の惑星の生命体の存在に疑問を抱いている)。×I query the existence of life on other planets.

do well [動]

do well・flourish・thrive・prosper・boom・blossom・bloom・be going places

成功していることや、成長や発展が速いことを表す

【類語訳】うまくいく、栄える、発展する、成功する、急成長する、開花する、充実する

文型&コロケーション

▶ to flourish/ thrive/ prosper **on/ under** sth
▶ to do well/ prosper/ blossom **as** sth
▶ to blossom/ bloom **into** sth
▶ a **business** does well/ flourishes/ thrives/ prospers/ is booming/ blossoms
▶ an **industry** does well/ flourishes/ thrives/ prospers
▶ **tourism/ trade/ a market** flourishes/ thrives/ prospers/ is booming
▶ the **economy** does well/ flourishes/ thrives/ prospers/ is booming
▶ a **plant/ town** does well/ flourishes/ thrives
▶ to **really** flourish/ thrive/ blossom
▶ to do **really** well/ be **really** going places

do 'well [自]《特に話し言葉》うまくいく、順調である ◇Jack is *doing* very *well* at school. ジャックは学校での成績がとてもよい ◇Her last play had *done well*. 彼女の最後の芝居は当たっていた ◇The company is *doing well* now after a difficult start. 初めは苦戦したが今やこの会社はうまくいっている ◇This shrub will *do well* even in a small city garden. 都会の小さな庭でもこの低木は立派に成長するだろう ❶ do well は人・場所・商売・植物について用いられる。

flourish [自]《特に書き言葉》急速に発展する、栄える；すこやかに[よく]成長する ◇His international career has *flourished* under captain James Murray. 彼はジェームズ・マーレイ主将の下、国際舞台で華々しい活躍を見せている ◇The arts began to *flourish* at that time. その当時、芸術が栄え始めた ◇There was a *flourishing* black market. 栄えている闇市があった ◇The plants *flourish* in a damp climate. その植物は湿度の高い気候でよく育つ ❶ flourish は人・職業・関係・場所・伝統・商売・植物について言うときに用いられる。特に歴史的な文脈で芸術・文化について用いられる。

thrive [自]急速に発展する、栄える；すごく[よく]成長する ◇He's clearly *thriving* in his new job. 彼は新しい仕事で確かに活躍している ◇New businesses *thrive* in this area. 新しいビジネスがこの地域で栄えている ◇These animals rarely *thrive* in captivity. これらの動物は飼

育がほとんど困難だ ◇She seems to *thrive on* stress (= enjoy it). 彼女はストレスを楽しんでいるように思える ❶ thrive は人・商売・場所・動植物について用いられる。特に人・動植物がよく成長する状況について用いられる。 ☞ **thriving** (SUCCESSFUL 2)

prosper [自]《特に書き言葉》（人・商売・経済が）発展する、繁栄する；（財政的に）成功する ◇The economy *prospered* under his administration. 彼の政権下で経済は発展した ◇The railway *prospered* from the new mining traffic. 新たな鉱山物資輸送の必要から鉄道が栄えた ☞ **prosperity** (MONEY 3), **prosperous** (RICH)

boom [自]《特に進行形で》（ややインフォーマル、特にジャーナリズム）（商売・経済が）急成長する；より大きくなる、より活発になる ◇The club scene was *booming*. クラブシーンが大盛況だった ◇Business is *booming*! 大繁盛だ ◇Tourist numbers have *boomed* in recent years. 近年観光客の数が急増した
▶ **boom** [名] [C] ◇a *boom* in car sales 自動車販売の急増 ◇a property/housing *boom* 不動産/住宅ブーム ◇a *boom* year for exports 輸出好況の年 反義 **slump** (RECESSION)

blossom [動] [自]（人が）より充実する；（関係・仕事・才能が）発展する、開花する ◇She has visibly *blossomed* over the last few months. 彼女はここ数か月で目に見えてよくなった ◇The friendship *blossomed* into love. 友情が愛情へと発展した

bloom [自]（人が）健康になる[である]、充実する ◇She was *blooming* with good health. 彼女は健康的で生き生きとしていた

be 'going places [行自]《ややインフォーマル》（人が）成功[出世]しつつある ◇He's a young architect who's really *going places*. 彼は実に前途有望な若手の建築家だ

drama [名]

drama・theatre・stage・acting・show business・the performing arts・showbiz

芝居を演じる行為およびその職業

【類語訳】劇、戯曲、ドラマ、演劇、俳優業、ショービジネス、舞台芸術

文型&コロケーション

▶ **improvisational/ serious** drama/ theatre/ acting
▶ **classical/ Elizabethan/ modern** drama/ theatre
▶ to **study** drama/ theatre/ acting
▶ a drama/ theatre/ stage/ acting/ performing arts **school**
▶ a drama/ theatre/ acting/ performing arts **student**
▶ a drama/ theatre **critic**

drama [U]（文学の一形式としての）劇、戯曲、ドラマ ◇Television *drama* is a powerful cultural medium. テレビドラマは強い影響力のある文化的メディアだ ☞ **drama** (PLAY [名])
▶ **dramatic** [形]《ふつう名詞の前で》◇Students will study various plays and *dramatic* texts. 学生はさまざまな演劇や脚本を研究することになっています

theatre [英]《米 **theater**》[U]（娯楽の一形式としての）演劇 ◇I like music, *theatre* and cinema. 《英》私は音楽や演劇、映画が好きです ◇The play challenges current ideas about what makes good *theatre* (= what makes good entertainment when performed). その劇はこんにちよい演劇の条件とされている考え方に疑問を投げかけている

↪**drama**

>**theatrical** 形 [名詞の前で] ◇a *theatrical* career 演劇の経歴
stage《しばしば the stage》[単数で] (職業・娯楽の一形式としての)演劇 ◇His parents didn't want him to *go on the stage* (= to be an actor). 両親は彼に役者になってほしくなかった ◇She was a popular star of *stage and screen* (= theatre and cinema). 彼女は舞台と映画の人気スターだった ☞ **stage** (PLAY 動 2)
acting [U] (劇・映画などの)俳優業 ◇She started her *acting* career while still at school. 彼女はまだ学生のときに女優業をスタートさせた ☞ **act** (PLAY 動 2)
'show business [U] (劇・映画・テレビなどの)芸能界, ショービジネス ◇The whole family is in *show business*. 家族全員ショービジネスに携わっている
the per,forming 'arts [C, 複数で] (ややフォーマル) (音楽・舞踊・劇などの)舞台[公演]芸術, パフォーミングアーツ ◇The book examines recent trends in *the performing arts*. その本は舞台芸術における最近の流行について調査している
showbiz [U] (インフォーマル) (劇・映画・テレビなどの)芸能産業, ショービジネス ◇The club is a favourite haunt of *showbiz* stars and celebrities. そのクラブは芸能界のスターや有名人御用達の場所だ ◇That's *showbiz*! それがショービジネスさ

draw 動

draw・paint・sketch・colour
人や物を描写する
【類語訳】描く, 絵を描く, 図を描く

文型&コロケーション
▶to draw/ paint/ sketch/ colour a **picture**
▶to draw/ paint/ sketch a **landscape/ portrait**
▶to draw/ sketch a **diagram/ graph**

draw [他, 自] (鉛筆・ペン・チョークで)絵[図]を描く ◇She *drew* a house (= a picture of a house). 彼女は家の絵を描いた ◇He *drew* a circle in the sand with a stick. 彼は棒で砂に丸を描いた ◇You *draw* beautifully. 君は絵を上手に描くね
>**drawing** 名 [U] ◇I'm not very good at *drawing*. 私は絵を描くのがあまり上手くない ◇technical *drawing* 製図 ☞ **drawing** (PICTURE)
paint [他, 自] (絵の具で)絵[図]を描く ◇A friend *painted* the children for me (= a picture of the children). 友人が子どもたちの絵を私のために描いてくれた ◇She *paints* in oils. 彼女は油絵を描く ◇My mother *paints* quite well. 母はとても上手に絵を描く ☞ **paint** (PAINT 動), **painter** (ARTIST)
>**painting** 名 [U] ◇Her hobbies include music and *painting*. 彼女の趣味には音楽と絵画が含まれる ☞ **painting** (PICTURE)
sketch [他, 自] (ペン・鉛筆で)スケッチを描く ◇He quickly *sketched* the view from the window. 彼は窓からの景色を素早くスケッチした ◇He enjoyed *sketching*, writing poetry and playing music. 彼はスケッチしたり, 詩を書いたり, 音楽を演奏するのが好きだった ☞ **sketch** (PICTURE)
colour (英) (米では color) [自, 他] (カラーペン・色鉛筆などで)色をつける ◇The children love drawing and *colouring*. 子どもたちは絵を描いて色を塗るのが大好きだ ◇I'll

draw a tree and you can *colour it in* (= put colour inside the lines). 私が木を描くから, それに色を塗ってください ◇a *colouring* book (= with pictures that you can colour in) 塗り絵の本 ☞ **colour** (PAINT)

drink 名

drink・alcohol・liquor・spirit・booze
アルコールを含む飲み物
【類語訳】酒, アルコール飲料, 蒸留酒

文型&コロケーション
▶**alcoholic** drinks/ liquor
▶**strong** drink/ liquor
▶to **drink** alcohol/ liquor/ spirits/ booze
▶to **consume** alcohol/ liquor
▶to **turn to/ keep off/ stay off** (the) drink/ alcohol/ booze
▶a drink/ an alcohol/ a booze **problem**

drink [C, U] 酒; アルコール飲料 ◇Let's *go for a drink*. 一杯飲みに行きましょう ◇He *downed* his *drink*. 彼は酒をぐっと飲み干した ◇I need a *stiff drink* (= a strong drink). 強い酒がほしい ◇She bought another *round of drinks*. 彼女は酒のおかわりを注文した ◇The *drinks are on me* (= I'll pay for them) 飲み代は私がおごります ◇Jim's got a *drink* problem. (英) ジムはアルコール依存症だ ◇a *drinking* problem (米) アルコール依存症
alcohol [U] (ビール・ワイン・ウィスキーなどの)アルコール類 ◇He never *touches alcohol*. 彼は一滴もアルコールは飲まない ◇The level of *alcohol* in his blood was over the legal limit. 彼の血液中のアルコールの濃度は法定限度を超えていた
liquor [U] (特に米) 強いアルコール飲料, 蒸留酒 ◇They were standing outside the *liquor store*. 彼らは酒屋の外で立っていた ◇She drinks beer and wine but no *hard liquor*. 彼女はビールとワインは飲むが強い酒は飲まない ❶ (英)の専門語としては liquor はアルコール飲料全般を指す. ◆The sale of *liquor* to persons under 18 is prohibited. (18歳未満の未成年者への酒の販売は禁止されている)
spirit [C, ふつう複数で] (特に英) 強いアルコール飲料, 蒸留酒 ◇I don't drink whisky or brandy or any other *spirits*. 私はウィスキーやブランデーなどの強い酒は飲まない ◇A standard *measure of spirits* is 25ml. 蒸留酒の標準的な量は25mlだ
booze [U] (インフォーマル) アルコール飲料, 酒 ◇The party was great but we had run out of *booze* by midnight. パーティーは素晴らしかったが, 夜の12時までに酒がなくなってしまった

drink 動

drink・sip・suck・drain・booze・swig
液体を口から摂取する
【類語訳】飲む, 飲酒する, ちびちび飲む, 吸いこむ, しゃぶる, 飲み干す, ぐいぐい飲む

文型&コロケーション
▶to sip/ suck/ swig **at** sth
▶to drink/ sip/ swig **from** a bottle/ glass of sth
▶to drink/ suck sth **up**
▶to drink/ sip/ drain your **drink/ pint**

drop, drug

▶ to drink/ sip/ swig **beer/ wine**
▶ to drink/ sip **tea/ coffee/ water**

drink [他,自] (液体を)飲む;(定期的に)酒を飲む, 飲酒する ◇What would you like to *drink*? 飲み物は何がよろしいですか ◇I don't *drink* coffee. 私はコーヒーは飲まない ◇He was *drinking* straight from the bottle. 彼は瓶から直に飲んでいた ◇He doesn't *drink* (= doesn't drink alcohol). 彼はお酒を飲みません ◇Don't *drink and drive* (= drive a car after drinking alcohol). 飲酒運転はやめましょう ◇She's been *drinking heavily* since she lost her job. 彼女は仕事を失ってから酒に溺れている ◇I *drank* far too much last night. 昨晩は飲みすぎた

sip (-pp-) [他,自] ちびちび飲む ◇He slowly *sipped* his wine. 彼はゆっくりとワインをちびちび飲んだ ◇She sat there, *sipping at* her tea. 《英》彼女はそこに座って紅茶を少しずつ飲んでいた

suck [他,自]《液体・空気を》吸い込む;(物を)しゃぶる ◇She was noisily *sucking* up milk through a straw. 彼女はストローでミルクを音を立てて吸っていた ◇He *sucked* a mint. 彼はミントキャンディーをなめた ◇He *sucked on* a mint. 彼はミントキャンディーをなめた

drain [他] (コップ・グラスなどを)空にする, 飲み干す ◇In one gulp, he *drained* the glass. 彼はグラスを一息で空けた ◇She quickly *drained* the last of her drink. 彼女は素早く最後の残りを飲み干した

booze [自] (ふつう進行形で)《インフォーマル》(大量に)アルコールを飲む, 大酒を飲む ◇He's out *boozing* with his mates. 彼は仲間と飲みに出かけている

swig (-gg-) [他]《インフォーマル》(アルコール・飲み物を)ぐいぐい飲む ◇They sat around *swigging* beer from bottles. 彼らは車座になって瓶のままビールをぐいぐい飲んでいた

drop [名]

drop・bead・splash・globule・blob・drip
少量の液体
【類語訳】滴, 粒, はね, 小球, したたり

[文型&コロケーション]
▶ a drop/ bead/ splash of **blood**
▶ a drop/ bead of **moisture/ perspiration/ sweat**
▶ a drop/ splash of **water**
▶ a splash/ blob of **paint**

drop [C] (液体の)滴 ◇A few *drops of rain* fell. 雨がぽつぽつ落ちてきた ◇Mix a few *drops* of milk into the cake mixture. ケーキの生地に牛乳を数滴混ぜてください ◇He drained the last few *drops* from his glass. 彼はグラスから最後の数滴を飲み干した

bead [C] (*of*を伴って) (汗などの)粒, 滴 ◇There were *beads* of sweat on his forehead. 彼の額に汗の粒が現れていた

splash [C] (液体の)はね;はねの跡 ◇There were dark *splashes* of mud on her skirt. 彼女のスカートに黒い泥のはねた跡が残っていた

globule [C] (液体・溶けた固体の)粒, 小球, 滴 ◇The milk's small *fat globules* make it easy to digest. 小さな乳脂肪球のおかげで牛乳は消化されやすくなる

blob [C]《インフォーマル》(粘性のある液体の)少量, 滴 ◇A *blob* of ketchup was rolling down his chin. ケチャップが一滴彼のあごに垂れていた

drip (物から落ちる液体の)滴, したたり ◇We put a bucket under the hole in the roof to catch the *drips*. 私たちは落ちてくる水滴を受けるために屋根の穴の下にバケツを置いている

ノート **splash**と**drip**の使い分け：splashはdripよりも大きく, 偶然に1回以上物にかかる[落ちる]液体。dripsは穴や割れ目から規則的[継続的]に落ちる液体。splashは何に液体がかかるかを強調し, dripはどこから液体が落ちるかを強調する。

drug [名]

1 drug・dope・narcotic・stimulant
人が摂取すると精神に何らかの影響を及ぼす, 特に違法な物質
【類語訳】薬物, 麻薬, 覚醒剤, 興奮剤, 刺激剤

[文型&コロケーション]
▶ to **use** drugs/ dope/ narcotics/ stimulants
▶ to **take** drugs/ narcotics/ stimulants
▶ to **abuse** drugs/ narcotics
▶ to **deal** drugs/ dope
▶ a drug/ dope **test**
▶ a drug/ dope/ narcotics **dealer**
▶ drug/ narcotics **trafficking/ traffickers**
▶ the drug/ narcotics **trade**

drug [C] 麻薬, 薬物 ◇He does not smoke or take *drugs*. 彼はたばこも麻薬もやらない ◇I found out Tim was *on drugs* (= regularly used drugs). ティムが麻薬をやっていることがわかった ◇I don't *do drugs* (= use them).《インフォーマル》私は麻薬をやらない ◇*hard drugs* (= very harmful drugs, such as heroin) ハードドラッグ(ヘロインなどの中毒性の強い麻薬) ◇*soft drugs* (= drugs that are not considered so harmful) ソフトドラッグ(マリファナなどの中毒性の弱い麻薬) ◇*drug* and alcohol abuse 麻薬とアルコールの乱用 ◇a *drug* addict/dealer 麻薬常用者/密売人 ◇*Drugs* have been seized with a street value of 2 million dollars. 末端価格にして2百万ドルの麻薬が押収された

dope [U]《インフォーマル》(大麻・《米》ヘロインなどの)麻薬;(スポーツ選手・競走馬に影響を与える)薬物 ◇He has admitted *smoking dope* as a teenager. 彼は十代の頃に麻薬を吸引したことを認めた ◇The athlete had failed a *dope* test (= a medical test showed that he had taken such drugs). そのアスリートは薬物検査に引っかかったことがあった

narcotic [C]《ややフォーマル》(ヘロイン・コカインなどの中毒性の強い)麻薬 ◇*Narcotics* trafficking represents 30 to 50 per cent of organized crime's take. 麻薬取引は組織犯罪の利益の30〜50%を占めている ◇a *narcotics* agent (= a police officer investigating the illegal trade in drugs) 麻薬捜査官 ❶narcoticは特に麻薬の違法取引や警察の捜査について言うときに用いられる。

stimulant [C] 覚醒剤, 興奮[刺激]剤 ◇Coffee and tea are mild *stimulants*. コーヒーと紅茶は軽い興奮剤だ

2 drug・medicine・prescription・medication・cure・remedy・placebo・antidote
病気の治療に用いるもの
【類語訳】医薬品, 薬, 内服薬, 処方箋, 処方薬, 投薬治療, 薬物療法, 治療薬, 治療法

↳drug

drug

文型&コロケーション

- a drug/ medicine/ a prescription/ medication/ a cure/ a remedy/ an antidote **for** sth
- (an) **effective** drug/ medicine/ medication/ cure/ remedy
- a **herbal** medicine/ cure/ remedy
- to **take** your medicine/ your medication/ a remedy/ a placebo/ the antidote
- to **prescribe** drugs/ medicine/ medication/ a cure/ a remedy
- to **find** a cure/ a remedy/ an antidote

drug [C] (病気・症状を治す)医薬品, 薬 ◇The doctor put me on a course of pain-killing *drugs*. 医者は私に鎮痛剤1クールを出した ◇***Drug companies*** are always developing new products. 製薬会社は常に新製品を開発している ❶合法の医薬品に関しては take drugs とは言わない. ✕Are you *taking* any *drugs* for your headaches? ◆Are you taking anything for your headaches? (頭痛に何か薬を飲んでいますか)

medicine [U, C] (液体の)内服薬 ◇She gave me a dose of cough *medicine*. 彼女は私に一回分の咳止めの薬をくれた ◇Food and *medicines* are being airlifted to the flood-hit area. 食料と医薬品が洪水被災地に空輸されている ☞ **medicine** (TREATMENT)

prescription [C] 処方箋；処方薬 ◇The doctor gave me a *prescription* for antibiotics. 医者は私に抗生物質の処方箋を出した ◇Antibiotics are only available **on** *prescription*. 抗生物質は処方箋がないと入手できません ◇The pharmacist will make up your *prescription*. 薬剤師が処方薬を調合します

▶**prescribe** [動] [他] ◇The doctor may be able to *prescribe* something for that cough. 医者はその咳に何らかの薬を処方できるだろう

medication [U, C] 《ややフォーマル》医薬品；投薬治療, 薬物療法 ◇Are you currently taking any *medication*? 現在, 何か薬を服用していますか ◇My grandmother has been **on** *medication* for years. 祖母は何年も投薬治療をしている ◇Many flu *medications* are available without a prescription. 多くのインフルエンザ薬が処方箋なしで入手できる

> **ノート** drug, medicine, medication の使い分け: drug は物質の成分を強調し, 特にそれらを製造する化学工業について話す時に用いられる. medicine と medication は化学物質の用途を強調する. medicine は特に病気全般に対する治療薬. medication は特に特定の病気・患者に対する治療薬. medication のほうがしばしばより重い病気に対する治療薬について用いられる.

cure [C] 治療薬, 治療法 ◇Although there is no *cure* for this illness, it can be treated to reduce the pain. この病気に対する治療法はないが, 痛みを軽減する治療は可能だ ◇The only real *cure* is rest. 唯一本当に効くのは休息だ ☞ **cure** (CURE), **cure** (TREATMENT)

remedy [C] (軽度の病気に対する)治療薬[法], 療法 ◇I prefer to use herbal *remedies* when I have a cold. 私は風邪を引いたら漢方薬を好んで用いる ◇The best **home** *remedy* for a sore throat is honey and lemon. のどの痛みに一番効く家庭薬は蜂蜜レモンだ

placebo (複 **-os**) [C] 偽薬, プラセボ, プラシーボ(薬が必要だと思い込んでしまっている患者に与えられる[新薬をテストするときに用いられる]薬効のない薬) ◇Half of the people taking part in the experiment were given a *placebo*. 実験に参加した人の半数にプラセボが投与された

antidote [C] 解毒剤 ◇There is no known *antidote* to the poison produced by this fish. この魚が作り出す毒に対する解毒剤はわかっていない

E e

eager 形

eager・enthusiastic・keen・anxious・hungry・avid・mad・zealous・impatient
何かがしたい, 何かが起きてほしいと強く願うこと
【類語訳】熱望した, 切望した, 熱心な, 熱烈な

文型&コロケーション

▶eager/ keen/ anxious/ hungry/ avid/ mad/ impatient **for** sth
▶enthusiastic/ mad **about** sth
▶keen/ mad **on** sth
▶eager/ enthusiastic/ keen/ anxious/ impatient **to do sth**
▶eager/ keen/ anxious **that...**
▶an enthusiastic/ a keen **supporter/ admirer**
▶an enthusiastic/ a keen/ an avid **collector/ fan**
▶a keen/ an avid **reader/ interest**
▶**very** eager/ enthusiastic/ keen/ anxious/ impatient
▶**extremely** enthusiastic/ keen/ anxious/ zealous/ impatient

eager 熱望した, 熱心な ◇*Eager* crowds waited outside the stadium. 熱心な観客がスタジアムの外で待っていた ◇She is *eager* for (= wants very much to get) her parents' approval. 彼女は両親の賛同をしきりに求めている ◇Everyone in the class seemed *eager* to learn. クラス全員が勉強熱心なようだった ◇They're *eager to please* (= they want to be helpful). 彼らは役に立ちたい気持ちでいる 反意 **reluctant** (RELUCTANT)
➤**eagerly** 副 ◇the band's *eagerly* awaited new CD そのバンドの待望の新作CD
➤**eagerness** 名 [U, 単数で] ◇I couldn't hide my *eagerness* to get back home. 故郷に帰りたい気持ちを隠しきれなかった

enthusiastic 熱烈な, 熱狂的な ◇I love playing to such an *enthusiastic* audience. そういった熱狂的な聴衆の前で演奏するのが大好きだ ◇They gave her an *enthusiastic* welcome. 彼らは彼女を熱烈に歓迎した ◇You don't sound very *enthusiastic* about the idea. その考えにあまり乗り気でないようですね 反意 **lukewarm** (INDIFFERENT), ☞ **enthusiast** (FAN)
➤**enthusiastically** 副 ◇They responded *enthusiastically* to the plan. 彼らはその計画に熱烈な(支持の)反応を示した
➤**enthusiasm** 名 [U, 単数で] ◇I can't say I share your *enthusiasm* for the idea. その考えに対してあなたのように熱心にはなれない

ノート **eager**と**enthusiastic**の使い分け：enthusiasticはeagerよりも惜しみない気持ちを表す。人が求めるものについて言うときはしばしばeagerを用いる。◆The low prices still pull in crowds of *eager* buyers. (低価格は今でも熱心な買い手を大勢引きつける)。他人や他人の考え, 成果について言うときはしばしばenthusiasticを用いる。◆an *enthusiastic* welcome/reception/response (熱烈な歓

迎/出迎え/反応). ◆*enthusiastic* support/applause/praise (熱烈な支持/拍手/賞賛).

keen [名詞の前にまれ]《特に英, ややインフォーマル》切望した, 熱心な ◇John was very *keen* to help. ジョンはとても手伝いたがった ◇We are *keen* that Britain should get involved too. 我々は英国も参加することを切望している ◇I wasn't too *keen* on going to the party. あまりパーティーに出かける気がしなかった ❶ *keen*は名詞の前に置いて, ある活動や思想に非常に熱心な人を表す場合にも用いられる。◆He's a *keen* sportsman and enjoys football, fishing and rugby. (彼は熱心なスポーツマンでサッカー, 釣り, ラグビーを楽しむ). ◆She takes a *keen* interest in politics. (彼女は政治に強い関心を抱いている). 活動や思想に熱心な人としてはa keen collector/fisherman/footballer/gardener/golfer/photographer/sailor/sportsman/swimmer/travellerなど。思想に熱心な人については, keen interest in sth や keen supporter of sthのような形で用いられる。keen interestという句を除いて, keenは《米》ではあまり用いられない。代わりに, eager to help や avid sportsman/collector/photographerなどと言うほうがふつうである。☞ **be keen on sth** (LIKE 動)

anxious [名詞の前にまれ] 切望した ◇He was *anxious* to finish school and get a job. 彼は学校を出て仕事に就くことを切望していた ◇I'm *anxious* for her to do as little as possible. 彼女にはできるだけ何もしないでほしい ◇She was *anxious* that he should meet her father. 彼女は彼が自分の父親に会うことを切に望んでいた ❶ *anxious*の意味には, 物事が通常の状態に戻ることを人が「望む」場合にしばしば用いられる。◆He seemed *anxious* to return to more familiar ground. (彼はもっと慣れていることにしきりに戻りたがっているようだった). ◆She was *anxious* to put the past behind her/set the record straight/get the whole thing over with. (彼女は過去を捨てること/誤解を正すこと/すべてにけりをつけることを強く望んでいた).
➤**anxiety** 名 [U] ◇A couple of photographers fell over themselves in their *anxiety* to get a shot of her. 2人の写真家が何とかして彼女の写真を撮ろうとやっきになっていた

hungry 渇望した, 熱望した ◇Both parties are *hungry* for power. 両党とも政権を渇望している ◇We like to use small agencies that are *hungry* for our business. 我々の事業を熱望してくれている小さな代理店を使いたい ❶ *hungry* for にはふつう change/company/excitement/information/knowledge/news/power/success/victoryなどが続く。

avid [ふつう名詞の前で]（趣味などに）熱心な ◇I have always been an *avid* reader. 私は以前からずっと読書に熱心だ ❶ *avid* for sthは, 物事を手に入れたいと強く願っていることを意味する。◆She was *avid* for more information. (彼女はもっと多くの情報がどうしてもほしかった).《英》では, avidはややフォーマルな語で, フォーマルな状況以外ではkeenを用いるほうがふつう。《米》ではavidは日常語。
➤**avidly** 副 ◇She reads *avidly*. 彼女は熱心な読書家だ

mad [名詞の前にまれ]《インフォーマル》（人・物事に）夢中の ◇She's *mad* on tennis. 彼女はテニスに夢中だ ◇He's always been *mad* about kids. 彼は以前からずっと子どもが大好きだ ◇*football-mad* boys サッカー狂の少年 ◇She's completely power-*mad*. 彼女は完全に権力亡者だ

zealous [《ややフォーマル, 書き言葉》(強い道徳的・宗教的な信条から)熱心な ◇He was a *zealous* reformer, utterly devoted to rooting out corruption. 彼は汚職の一掃に徹底的に取組んだ熱心な改革家だった

▶**zeal** 图 [U, 単数で] ◇her missionary/reforming/religious/political *zeal* 彼女の布教/改革/宗教/政治に対する熱意

impatient [名詞の前はまれ] 切望した ◇She was clearly *impatient* to leave. 彼女が帰りたくてたまらないのは明らかだった ◇We are *impatient* for change. 我々は変化を待ち望んでいる ❶ しばしば impatient for success/change や, impatient to leave/get away/escape/go home/get on の形で用いる.

▶**impatience** 图 [U] ◇She was bursting with *impatience* to tell me the news. 彼女はその知らせを私に伝えたくてうずうずしていた

ease 動

ease • relieve • alleviate • soften • allay • cushion • soothe • lighten
物事が不快[深刻]でなくなる, 物事を不快[深刻]でなくする
【類語訳】和らげる, 緩和する, 軽減する, 和らぐ

[文型&コロケーション]
▶to ease/ relieve/ alleviate/ soothe the **pain**
▶to ease/ relieve/ alleviate/ allay/ soothe sb's **fear/ anxiety**
▶to ease/ relieve/ alleviate sb's **problems/ suffering**
▶to ease/ relieve/ alleviate/ soften/ allay/ soothe/ lighten a **feeling**
▶to ease/ relieve/ alleviate **pressure/ stress/ poverty**
▶to ease/ relieve/ alleviate/ lighten the **burden**
▶to ease/ relieve/ lighten the **load**
▶to ease/ alleviate/ soften/ cushion the **impact** of sth
▶to **do little/ nothing to** ease/ relieve/ alleviate/ soften/ allay/ soothe/ lighten sth

ease [他, 自] (物事のつらさ・深刻さ・激しさを[が])軽減する, 和らげる[和らぐ] ◇The plan should *ease* traffic congestion in the town. その計画によって町の交通渋滞は緩和するはずだ ◇It would *ease my mind* (= make me less worried) to know that she was happy. 彼女が幸せだとわかれば安心できます ◇The pain gradually *eased* a little. 痛みは徐々に少し和らいだ ◇The snow was *easing up* and people were leaving their houses. 雪が小降りになってきたので, 人々は家から出てきていた

relieve [他] (不快な感情・苦痛などを)軽減する, 緩和する, 和らげる ◇Take painkillers and hot drinks to *relieve* the symptoms. 症状を緩和するために痛み止めと温かい飲み物を飲みなさい ◇Don't resort to alcohol to *relieve* stress. ストレス解消にアルコールに頼るな ◇Being able to tell the truth at last seemed to *relieve* her. ようやく真実を話せるようになって, 彼女は安心したようだった ◇Aid workers called for further effort from governments to *relieve* the famine. 救援部隊は飢饉を緩和するよう, 各国政府に更なる努力を求めた ☞ **relief** (RELIEF), **relief** (AID)

alleviate [他] 《ややフォーマル》(感情・問題を)緩和する, 軽減する ◇Her words did little to *alleviate* his fears. 彼女が言葉をかけたが彼の恐怖はほとんど薄れなかった ◇A number of measures were taken to *alleviate* the problem. 問題軽減にいくつかの対策が講じられた [反意] **aggravate**

soften [他] (何かの力・不快な物の影響を)軽減する, 和らげる ◇Airbags are designed to *soften* the impact of a car crash. エアバッグは車の衝突時の衝撃を和らげるように設計されている ◇The government may try to *soften the blow* (= make things seem less unpleasant and easier to accept) with a cut in interest rates. 政府は利率の引き下げによってダメージを軽減しようとするかもしれない

allay [他] 《フォーマル》(不快な感情を)和らげる, 鎮める ◇The government is keen to *allay* the public's fears. 政府は国民の不安を鎮めたいと思っている ◇The inquiry has done little to *allay* suspicion. 調査ではほとんど疑惑は晴れなかった

cushion [他] (何かの害・不快な物の影響を)和らげる ◇The south of the country has been *cushioned from* the worst effects of the recession. 国の南部は不況の最悪の影響からは守られている ◇He broke the news of my brother's death to me, making no effort to *cushion the blow* (= make the news less shocking). 彼はショックを少しも和らげようともせずに, 兄の訃報を私に伝えた

[ノート] **soften**と**cushion**の使い分け: 多くの場合, どちらの語も使える. しかしcushionは受身で用いると, 軽減・緩和されるものより状況から恩恵を受ける人や物事に焦点が置かれる. ◆Homeowners will be *cushioned* from any tax rises. (住宅所有者はあらゆる増税から守られるだろう). ◆All grief is *softened* with time. (すべての悲しみは時と共に薄れる).

soothe [他] (不快な感情・苦痛を)軽減する ◇Only when Maisie came to hold him and *soothe* his fears did he feel safe. メイジーがやってきて彼を抱きしめ不安を和らげてくれるまでは, 彼は安心できなかった ◇Take a warm bath to *soothe* tense, tired muscles. 暖かいお風呂に入って, 筋肉のこりや疲れをほぐしてください

[ノート] **relieve**と**soothe**の使い分け: 苦痛やつらい感情にはどちらも使えるが, 痛みのある体の部分にはsootheしか使えない. ×Take a warm bath to *relieve* tense, tired muscles. 痛みや感情の原因にrelieveは使えるが, sootheは使えない. ×Don't resort to alcohol to *soothe* stress.

lighten [他] (仕事・借金・心配などを)減らす, 軽減する ◇This equipment is designed to *lighten* the load of domestic work. この装置は家事の負担を軽くする意図で作られている ◇The measures will *lighten* the tax burden on small businesses. その措置は中小企業への税負担を軽減するだろう ❶この意味のlightenは, ほぼ常にloadかburdenを後ろに伴う.

easy 形

1 easy • simple • straightforward • effortless • uncomplicated • undemanding • painless • cushy • plain sailing
物事が難しくないし, 大した骨折りや問題もなく実行[入手, 理解]できることを表す
【類語訳】簡単な, 容易な, やさしい, わかりやすい, 単純な

easy

文型&コロケーション

- to be easy/ simple/ straightforward/ plain sailing **for** sb
- to be easy/ simple/ straightforward/ painless/ plain sailing **to do sth**
- an easy/ a simple/ a straightforward/ an undemanding/ a cushy **job**
- an easy/ a simple/ a straightforward/ an undemanding **task**
- an easy/ a simple/ a straightforward/ a painless **method**
- an easy/ a simple/ a straightforward **matter/ decision/ test/ question**
- There's no easy/ simple/ straightforward **answer**.
- **relatively** easy/ simple/ straightforward/ uncomplicated/ undemanding/ painless
- **apparently** easy/ simple/ straightforward/ effortless

easy 簡単な, 容易な, 楽な ◇It was a really *easy* exam. 実に簡単な試験だった ◇This encyclopedia is designed for quick and *easy* reference. この百科事典は手早く簡単に引けるように作られている ◇Their house isn't the *easiest* place to get to. 彼らの家はたやすくたどり着ける所ではない ◇It can't be *easy* for her, on her own with the children. 彼女が子どもを抱えて自活していくのは容易ではない得ない ◇Several schools are *within easy reach* (= not far away). いくつかの学校がすぐ近くにある 反意 **difficult, hard** (DIFFICULT 1)
▷**ease** 图 [U] ◇He passed the exam with *ease*. 彼は試験に楽々受かった ◇The computer is popular for its good design and *ease of use*. そのコンピューターはデザインのよさと使いやすさで人気がある 反意 **difficulty**
▷**easily** 副 ◇The museum is *easily* accessible by car. 博物館へは車で簡単に行ける ◇Learning languages doesn't come *easily* to him. 語学は彼にはたやすいことではない

simple 簡単な, 単純な, わかりやすい ◇I used a very *simple* method to obtain the answer. 答えを出すのに非常に簡単な方法を用いた ◇This machine is *simple* to use. この機械は使いやすい ◇Give the necessary information but *keep it simple*. 必要な情報を与えなさい, ただし, 簡潔に ◇We lost because we played badly. It's *as simple as that*. 《特に話し言葉》ひどいプレーをしたので負けたんだ. ただそれだけのことさ 反意 **complex, elaborate** (COMPLEX), **difficult** (DIFFICULT 1)
▷**simplicity** 图 [U] ◇the relative *simplicity* of the new PC 新作PCの比較的の簡素な作り ◇*For the sake of simplicity*, let's divide the discussion into two parts. わかりやすくするために議論を二つに分けましょう
▷**simply** 副 ◇Anyway, *to put it simply*, we still owe them £2,000. とにかく, 簡単に言えば, 彼らにまだ2千ポンド借りがあるんだ

ノート easy と simple の使い分け：easy は「難しくない」ことを意味する. easy test/task は能力や理解力があるので問題なくできるものである. その人の能力次第で easy ともそうでないとも感じる. simple は「複雑でない」ことを意味する. simple test/task はごくわずかの非常に基本的な行為しか要しないもので, 人の能力はあまり関係がない. easily は「何の困難もなく」を意味する. ◆I can *easily* finish it tonight. (今夜わけなくそれを済ませられます). simply は「理解するのに困難なことなく」を意味する. ◆The book explains grammar *simply* and clearly. (その本は文法を単純明快に説明している).

straightforward 簡単な, わかりやすい ◇It's a relatively *straightforward* process. それは比較的わかりやすい手順である ◇It's quite *straightforward* to get here from your house. お宅からここへ来られるのは実に簡単です 反意 **complicated, involved** (COMPLEX)

ノート simple と straightforward の使い分け：両語の意味・用法はよく似ていて, どちらも question, answer, case, matter, method, procedure, exercise などの語と結びつく.

effortless 努力を(ほとんど)要しない, たやすい ◇She dances with *effortless* grace. 彼女は苦もなく優雅に踊る ◇He made playing the guitar look *effortless*. 彼にかかるとギターの演奏をたやすく見えた
▷**effortlessly** 副 ◇Your presentation must move *effortlessly* from one point to the next. プレゼンテーションは1つの論点から次の論点へスムーズに移行しなければならない

uncomplicated [U] 《ややフォーマル》複雑でない, 単純な ◇It's an *uncomplicated* computer interface that is truly easy to use. 実に使いやすい単純なコンピューター・インターフェイスだ ◇It came as a relief to hold a light, *uncomplicated* conversation with an ordinary guy. 普通のやつと気軽で難しくない会話をするとほっとした ❶ uncomplicated は生活・人間関係・感情について用いられる. umcomplicated な関係や感情を持つ人にも用いることができる. ◆He was an easygoing, *uncomplicated* young man. (彼はのんきで単純な若者だった). 医学的な文脈で「合併症を伴わない」の意味でも用いる. ◆an *uncomplicated* pregnancy/birth (合併症を伴わない妊娠/出産) 反意 **complicated** (COMPLEX)

undemanding 《書き言葉》さほど労力[思慮]を必要としない, きつくない ◇I wanted an *undemanding* job which would leave me free to pursue my hobbies. 気ままに趣味を追求できるような, きつくない仕事がよかった 反意 **demanding** (DIFFICULT 1)

painless 《書き言葉》困難[不快]でない, 楽な ◇The interview turned out to be relatively *painless*. 面接は実際には比較的楽なものだった

cushy 《インフォーマル, しばしばけなして》非常に簡単で楽な；(ほとんど)労力を要しない ◇His father found him a *cushy* job in the office. 父親は仕事場で彼に楽な仕事をあてがった

plain 'sailing 形容 簡単で手間のかからない ◇If you get the measurements right, the rest of the job should be *plain sailing*. 寸法をきちんと測れば, 残りの仕事は簡単に済むはずだ

2 ☞ **SLOW**
easy • leisurely • languid • unhurried • at leisure • lazy
人[活動]が心地よく, くつろいだ状態である[行われる]ことを表す【類語訳】楽な, 気楽な, ゆったりした, のんびりした

文型&コロケーション

- an easy/ a leisurely/ a languid/ an unhurried **manner**
- a leisurely/ an unhurried/ a lazy **way**
- an easy/ a leisurely/ a lazy **day/ morning/ afternoon/ time**
- an easy/ a leisurely/ an unhurried **pace**
- an easy/ a leisurely **trip/ stroll/ ride/ drive**

easy 気楽な, 心配のない ◇I'll agree to anything for an *easy life*. 楽な生活のためなら何にでも同意します ◇His *easy* charm soon won her over. 彼女はすぐに彼のおっとりした魅力に引き付けられた ◇I don't feel *easy* about letting the kids go out alone. 子どもたちだけで出かけさせるのは不安だ ❶ *easy* は人・行動・生活様式を表すのに用いることができる。☞ **uneasy** (WORRIED)

leisurely [ふつう名詞の前で] ゆったりした; ゆっくりした, のんびりした ◇We went for a *leisurely* stroll after dinner. 私たちは夕食後のんびりと散歩した ◇They set off at a *leisurely* pace. 彼らはゆったりした足取りで出発した ❶ *leisurely* は急がない移動について最も頻繁に用いられる。◆ a *leisurely* trip/stroll/ride/pace/drive (ゆったりした旅/散歩/車での移動/歩調/ドライブ). 急がずにくつろいだ食事についても用いる。◆ a *leisurely* breakfast/lunch/dinner (ゆったりした朝食/昼食/夕食).

languid [書き言葉] (身のこなし・話し方などが)ゆったりした ◇She gave a *languid* wave of the hand. 彼女はゆっくり手を振った ◇'Ah, my dear,' said the *languid* voice. 「ああ、私のいとしい人よ」とけだるそうな声がした ❶ 暑すぎて活発になれなくなると、しばしば人の動きが languid となる。

unhurried [書き言葉] ゆったりした; ゆっくりした ◇His conversation was relaxed and *unhurried*. 彼の会話はくつろぎ、ゆったりしたものだった ◇It's a quiet resort where life is taken at an easy, *unhurried* pace. そこは、穏やかでゆったりとしたペースで生活が送れるリゾート地だ 反意 **hurried** (QUICK)

at 'leisure ゆっくりと、のんびりと; 暇で ◇Spend the afternoon *at leisure* in the city. 町でゆっくり午後を過ごしてください ◇Let's have lunch so we can talk *at leisure*. 一緒にお昼にしましょう、のんびり話せるでしょう ◇I suggest you take the forms away and read them *at your leisure*. 用紙をお持ちになって、手の空いたときにお読みになってはいかがですか ❶ at leisure は特に、物事の好き嫌いや善し悪しの決定に関わる動詞と共に、誰にもせかされずにゆっくりと行う場合に用いられる。◆ to discuss sth/talk/study sth/examine sth/look round/browse/try sth on *at leisure* (のんびりと話し合う/話す/調べる/検討する/見回る/見て回る/試着する). (英)では、旅行パンフレットの中で、自由行動の時間について言うときにしばしば at leisure が用いられる。

lazy (あまり精力・活動を伴わないで)ゆっくりした、のんびりした ◇We spent a *lazy* day on the beach. 浜辺で一日のんびりと過ごした ◇She smiled a *lazy* smile. 彼女はゆっくりと笑みを浮かべた

eat 動

eat・have・swallow・consume・finish・ingest・devour・taste・wolf・stuff・tuck in/tuck into sth
飲食物を口から胃に入れる
【類語訳】食べる、飲む、飲み込む、平らげる、飲み干す、味わう、かき込む

▷ 文型&コロケーション

▶ to eat/ finish sth **up**

▶ to eat/ swallow/ consume/ devour/ wolf down/ stuff yourself with/ tuck into your **food**

▶ to eat/ have/ finish/ devour/ tuck into a **meal**

▶ to eat/ have/ finish/ wolf/ tuck into your **lunch/ dinner**

▶ to eat/ have/ consume/ taste some **meat/ fruit**

eat [自, 他] 食べる ◇I was too nervous to *eat*. 緊張しすぎて食べられなかった ◇She doesn't *eat* sensibly (= doesn't eat food that is good for her). 彼女はまともな食事をとっていない ◇***Eat up!*** (= Eat all your food.) 残さずに食べなさい ◇I don't *eat* meat. 肉は食べません ◇Would you like something to *eat*? 何か食べませんか ◇I couldn't *eat* another thing (= I have had enough food). それ以上何も食べられなかった

have [他] 食べる、飲む ◇Have you *had* breakfast yet? もう朝食はお済みですか ◇I just *had* a sandwich for lunch. 昼食にサンドイッチを食べただけです ◇I'll *have* the salmon (= in a restaurant). (レストランで)サーモンにします

swallow [他, 自] (飲食物・薬を)飲み込む ◇Always chew food well before *swallowing* it. 食べ物を飲み込む前に必ずよく噛みなさい ◇The pills should be *swallowed whole* (= in one piece). 錠剤はかまずに飲み込まなければいけません ◇I had a sore throat and it hurt to *swallow*. のどがひりひりして飲み込むと痛かった

consume [他] 《フォーマル》食べる、飲む ◇Red meat should be *consumed* in moderation. 赤身の肉はほどほどに食べるほうがよい ◇Before he died he had *consumed* a large quantity of alcohol. 彼は死ぬ前に大量の酒を飲んでいた ☞ **consume** (USE 動 2)

▶ **consumption** [名] [U] The meat was declared unfit for ***human consumption***. その肉は食用に適さないと発表された ◇She was advised to reduce her alcohol *consumption*. 彼女はアルコール摂取量を減らすようアドバイスされた

finish [他] 平らげる、飲み干す、食べ[飲み]終える ◇He ***finished off*** his drink with one large gulp. 彼は飲み物をごくんと一気に飲み干した ◇We might as well *finish* up the cake — there isn't much left. ケーキは全部食べてしまおうか——大して残っていないし ◇We'll go out after you've *finished* your dinner. 君が夕食を終えたら出かけよう

ingest [他] 《専門語》摂取する ◇Food is the major source of *ingested* bacteria. 主に食品から細菌は摂取される

devour [他] 《フォーマル》(空腹なために)がつがつ食べる、むさぼり食う ◇He *devoured* half of his burger in one bite. 彼はハンバーガーの半分を一口でむさぼった

taste [他] (ふだん飲み食いしない物を)食べる、飲む、味わう ◇I've never *tasted* anything like it. そんなもの、食べたことないよ ◇I haven't *tasted* meat since I started the journey. 旅に出てから肉を食べていません

wolf [他] (ややインフォーマル) (一度に口いっぱいに押し込んで)かき込む、がつがつ食べる ◇He *wolfed down* his breakfast and left the house in a hurry. 彼は朝食をかき込むと急いで家を出た

stuff [他] (インフォーマル) たくさん食べる[食べさせる]、食べすぎる ◇He sat at the table ***stuffing himself***. 彼はテーブルに着いて腹いっぱい食べた ◇We ***stuffed our faces*** at the party. 私たちはパーティーでたらふく食べた ◇Don't *stuff* the kids with chocolate before their dinner. 夕食前に子どもにチョコレートをたくさん食べさせてはいけません

,tuck 'in, ,tuck 'into sth 句動詞 《英, 特に話し言葉》(夢中になってすばやく)たくさん食べる、がつがつ食べる ◇Come on everyone, *tuck in*! さあ皆さん、どんどん食べて ◇He was *tucking into* a huge plateful of pasta. 彼は超大盛りのパスタをがつがつ食べていた

economic 形

economic・financial・commercial・monetary・budgetary
(特に企業や国家による)金銭の使用に関連した活動[状況]を表す
【類語訳】経済の, 金融の, 商業の, 金銭の, 予算の

▸文型&コロケーション

▸economic/ financial/ commercial/ monetary/ budgetary **policy/ arrangements/ systems/ problems**
▸economic/ financial/ commercial/ monetary **gain/ loss/ value**
▸economic/ financial/ commercial/ monetary **affairs/ consequences**
▸economic/ financial/ commercial/ budgetary **data/ decisions**
▸the economic/ financial/ commercial/ budgetary **climate**
▸economic/ financial/ commercial **advantage/ interest**
▸economic/ financial/ commercial **markets/ centres**
▸the economic/ financial/ commercial **side/ status** of sth
▸economic/ financial/ monetary/ budgetary **control/ restrictions**
▸an economic/ a financial/ a monetary/ a budgetary **crisis**
▸economic/ financial/ budgetary **planning**

economic [名詞の前で] 経済の ◇This book deals with the social, *economic* and political issues of the period. この本はその時代の社会・経済・政治問題を扱っている ◇*Economic growth* was fastest in Japan. 経済成長は日本が一番急速だった ◇She's a lecturer in *economic* history. 彼女は経済史の講師だ ☞**economics** (FINANCE)
▸**economically** 副 ◇The factory is no longer *economically* viable. その工場はもはや採算が取れない
financial [ふつう名詞の前で] 金銭の, 金融の, 財政の ◇He is an independent *financial* adviser. 彼は独立した財務アドバイザーである ◇She had got into *financial* difficulties. 彼女は財政難に陥っていた ◇banks and other *financial* institutions 銀行などの金融機関 ◇The firm made a loss in the first quarter of the current *financial year*. 《英》その会社は今会計年度の第1四半期に赤字を出した ❶《米》では fiscal year が用いられる。☞**finance** (FINANCE)
▸**financially** 副 ◇She is still *financially* dependent on her parents. 彼女はまだ経済的に両親に頼っている
commercial [ふつう名詞の前で] 商業の ◇They have offices in the *commercial* heart of the city. 彼らは市の商業中心地にオフィスを設けている ◇She is developing the *commercial* side of the organization. 彼女はその組織の商業面を展開させている ☞**commerce** (TRADE)
▸**commercially** 副 ◇The product is not yet *commercially* available. その製品はまだ市販されていない
monetary [名詞の前で] 《フォーマル or 金融》金銭の, 通貨の ◇The sculptures were of little *monetary* value. その彫刻はほとんど金銭的な価値がなかった ◇closer European political, *monetary* and economic union ヨーロッパの政治・通貨・経済のより緊密な統合
budgetary [名詞の前で] 《金融》予算の ◇The new accounting procedures will improve *budgetary* control. 新しい会計処理によって予算管理は改善されるだろう ☞**budget** (FUND 名)

edge 名

edge・end・side・perimeter・limit・fringe・periphery・margin
物事の中心から最も離れた部分
【類語訳】端, 縁, 周囲, 境界

▸文型&コロケーション

▸**at** the edge/ end/ side/ perimeter/ limits/ fringe/ periphery/ margins
▸**on** the edge/ end/ side/ perimeter/ fringe/ periphery/ margins
▸**beyond** the edge/ end/ perimeter/ limits/ fringe/ margins
▸**along/ around** the edge/ sides/ perimeter/ fringe/ periphery/ margins
▸the **outer** edge/ end/ perimeter/ limit/ fringe/ periphery/ margins of sth
▸the **inner** edge/ end/ perimeter of sth
▸the **northern/ eastern/ southern/ western** edge/ end/ side/ limit/ fringe/ periphery/ margins of sth
▸the **very** edge/ end/ limit/ fringe of sth
▸to **reach** the edge/ end/ perimeter/ limit/ fringe/ periphery
▸to **remain on/ stand on** the edge/ end/ fringe

edge [C] 端, 縁 ◇He stood on the *edge* of the cliff. 彼は崖の縁に立っていた ◇They live right on the *edge* of town. 彼らは町のまさに端に暮らしている ◇I sat down at the water's *edge*. 水辺に腰を下ろした ◇Stand the coin on its *edge* and spin it. コインを立てて回転させてごらん ◇She tore the page out roughly, leaving a ragged *edge* in the book. 彼女がページを乱暴に破り取ると, 綴じ合わせのところでぎざぎざになった 反意 **the middle**
end [C] 端, 突き当たり ◇Turn right at the *end* of the road. 道の突き当たりを右に曲がりなさい ◇His wife sitting at the far *end* of the table. テーブルの向こうの端に座っているあの人が彼の奥さんです ◇Go to the *end* of the line! 列の最後尾に並んでください ◇You've got something on the *end* of your nose. 鼻の頭に何かついているよ ◇Tie the *ends* of the string together. ひもの両端を結んでください ◇These two products are from opposite *ends* of the price range. この二つの製品は価格帯の両端にあるものだ ◇We walked along the whole promenade *from end to end*. 私たちは遊歩道の全長を端から端まで歩いた ◇They arranged the tables *end to end*. 彼らはテーブルの端と端をくっつけて並べた ◇Stand the box *on end*. 箱を立てて置きなさい ◇They live in the *end* house. 彼らは端の家に住んでいる 反意 **the middle**
side [C] 端 ◇She sat on the *side* of the bed. 彼女はベッドの端に座った ◇A van was parked at the *side* of the road. バンが道路の端に停めてあった ◇the south *side* of the lake 湖の南端 反意 **the middle**

[ノート] **edge, end, side** の使い分け: 物や場所の **edge** はその周辺部分. 物や場所の二つの **end** は, 互いに最も離れた反対位置にある部分. **side** は反対位置にある端部分だが, 最も離れているわけではない.

perimeter [C] 《ややフォーマル》(囲まれた場所の)周辺, 囲, 境界 ◇Guards patrol the *perimeter* of the estate. 守衛が地所の周囲を巡回します ◇There is a 15-foot *perimeter* fence. 高さ15フィートの境界フェンスがある
limit [C] (地域・場所の)境界, 果て ◇We were reaching

↳edge

the *limits* of civilization. 我々は文明社会の果てに達しようとしていた ◇The houses lie outside the *city limits* (= the official boundary of the city). その家々は市の境界の外側にある

fringe [C] (端に沿って細く延びる木・建物などの)連なり ◇West of the river there was a *fringe* of woodland along its bank. 川の西側は土手沿いに森林が延びていた ◇Along the coast, an industrial *fringe* had already developed. 海岸沿いにはすでに細長い工業地帯が発達していた ❶(英)では, fringeは地域や群れ[集まり]のはずれを表すこともある. ◆The factories are located on the northern *fringes* of the city. (工場群は市の北端に位置している)

periphery [C, ふつう単数で] 《フォーマル》(地域の)周辺；(活動・政治(社会))集団の)非主流部, 外縁 ◇There is a lot of industrial development on the *periphery* of the town. 町の外縁部でかなり産業開発が進んでいる ◇It is a minor party on the *periphery* of American politics. それは米国の政界における非主流の小政党だ ☞ **peripheral** (MINOR)

margin [C] 《フォーマル》(地域(特に水域)の)端；(活動・政治(社会))集団の)非主流部 ◇The island is on the eastern *margin* of the Indian Ocean. その島はインド洋の東端にある ◇These are desperate people, often homeless, living on the *margins* of society. この人たちは社会の片隅で生活する絶望故に必死になっている人たちで, 家もないことが多い

education 名

education・training・study・teaching・learning・instruction・tuition・schooling・mentoring・coaching・tutoring
学ぶ過程や教わる過程を表す
【類語訳】教育, 訓練, 指導, 学習, 勉強

〖文型&コロケーション〗

▶education/ training/ teaching/ instruction/ tuition/ schooling/ coaching/ tutoring **in** sth
▶education/ training/ study/ teaching/ tuition/ coaching **for** sth
▶education/ teaching/ learning/ instruction **about** sth
▶(a) **good** education/ training/ teaching/ instruction/ schooling/ mentoring
▶**formal** education/ training/ study/ teaching/ learning/ instruction/ tuition/ schooling/ coaching
▶(a) **basic** education/ training/ teaching/ instruction/ tuition/ schooling/ coaching
▶**compulsory** education/ training/ study/ schooling
▶**private** education/ teaching/ study/ tuition/ schooling/ coaching/ tutoring
▶**public/ state** education/ schooling
▶**individual/ one-to-one** education/ training/ teaching/ learning/ instruction/ tuition/ mentoring/ coaching/ tutoring
▶**college/ university** education/ teaching/ study/ tuition
▶to **have** an education/ training/ instruction/ tuition/ schooling/ coaching/ tutoring
▶to **get/ receive** an education/ training/ instruction/ tuition/ coaching/ tutoring
▶to **provide** an education/ training/ instruction/ tuition/ schooling/ mentoring/ coaching/ tutoring

▶to **give sb** an education/ training/ instruction/ tuition/ coaching/ tutoring
▶to **continue/ complete/ finish** your education/ training/ studies/ schooling

education [U, 単数で]（(学校・大学における)教育 ◇He had little formal *education* (= education in school, college, etc.). 彼は正規の教育をほとんど受けなかった ◇It is only through *education* that prejudice can be overcome. 教育を通じてしか偏見を克服することはできない ◇Will she go on to **higher education** (= university or college)? 彼女は高等教育[大学]に進むつもりですか ◇*Sex education* in schools needs to be improved. 学校での性教育は向上させる必要がある ◇In those days it was very difficult for poorer people to get a university *education*.《英》当時, 貧困者が大学教育を受けることは非常に難しかった ◇a college *education*《米》大学教育 ☞ **educate** (TEACH), **educate** (TRAIN 1), **educator** (TEACHER)

training [U] 訓練, (実地)教育 ◇Few candidates had any *training* in management. 経営の訓練を受けたことのある志願者はほとんどいなかった ◇No one is allowed to operate the machinery without proper *training*. 適切な訓練を受けずにその機械を操作することは誰にも許されていない ◇*Vocational training* should not be seen as less important than an academic education. 職業訓練を進学教育より軽視してはいけない ◇She's an accountant *by training*. 彼女は会計士の教育を受けている ☞ **train** (TRAIN 1)

study [U] 学習, 研究 ◇Physiology is the *study* of how living things work. 生理学は生物の仕組みについての研究である ◇There's a quiet room set aside for private *study*. 自習用の静かな部屋が取ってあります ◇It's important to develop good *study* skills. 優れた学習技能を身につけることが重要である ◇Students in the same field of *study* may have very different skill levels. 同じ研究分野の学生でも技能水準には大きなばらつきがあることもある ❶複数形でフォーマルな*studies*は, 大学などにおける特定の人の研究活動を表す. ◆Many undertake further *studies* after passing their exams. (試験に合格したあと多くの者がさらなる研究に着手する) ☞ **study** (LEARN)

teaching [U] 教職, 教育, 授業 ◇What made you go into *teaching*? なぜ教師になったのですか ◇The system should reward good classroom *teaching*. クラスでの優れた授業に対しては, 制度として報酬を与えるべきだ ◇She retired at the end of a 40-year *teaching* career. 彼女は40年の教師生活を終えて退職した ☞ **teach** (TEACH), **teacher** (TEACHER)

learning [U] 学ぶこと, 学習 ◇Effective teaching inevitably leads to effective *learning*. 効果的な教育は必然的に効果的な学習をもたらす ◇They run special classes for students with *learning difficulties*. 学習障害を持つ学生のための特別クラスが開設されている ◇You may get extra help if your child has a *learning disability*. お子さんに学習障害があれば, 特別な支援を受けられます ◇They're new to the job and will be on a steep *learning curve* (= will have to learn a lot in a short time). 彼らはこの仕事が初めてなので, 急ピッチで学習しなければならないだろう ☞ **learn** (LEARN)

instruction [U]《フォーマル》教えること, 教育 ◇She had no formal *instruction* in music. 彼女は正式な音楽教育を受けていなかった ◇Religious *instruction* is banned in all state schools in the country. 国内のすべての公立学校では宗教教育は禁止されている ◇The medium of *instruction* in these classes is English. これらのクラスでは授業で使う言葉は英語である ☞ **instruct** (TRAIN 1)

tuition [U]《ややフォーマル》(個人・小グループに)教えること, 教授, 指導 ◇The price includes two weeks' horse riding plus expert *tuition*. 価格には2週間の乗馬とプロによる指導が含まれます ◇One-to-one *tuition* can be arranged in certain languages. 言語によってはマンツーマン指導をご用意できます

schooling [U]《フォーマル》学校教育 ◇He received very little formal *schooling*. 彼は正規の学校教育をほとんど受けなかった

mentoring [U] 個人指導(経験豊かな人が経験の少ない若手の仕事の習得に個人的に助力する) ◇The company provides *mentoring* programmes as well as specialized training for its new employees. その会社は新入社員のために, 専門研修だけでなく個人指導プログラムも行っている ☞ **mentor** (ADVISER)

coaching [U]《英》(特定の科目の学生への)個人指導 ◇Extra *coaching* is available for students who might need a little more help. もう少し助けが必要かと思われる学生は特別個人指導が受けられる ❶《米》では, スポーツ・演技などの活動中の特別指導についてだけ用いるのがふつう. ☞ **coach** (TRAIN 1)

tutoring《特に米》個人指導 ◇Volunteer *tutoring* programs help children who are having trouble reading. ボランティアによる個人指導プログラムは, 読むことに困難をかかえている子どもたちの助けになっている ☞ **tutor** (TEACH), **tutor** (TEACHER)

educational 形

educational・academic・scholarly・informational・instructional・pedagogic・didactic
教育や教育[情報]を与えることに関連していることを表す
【類語訳】教育の, 教育的な, 学術的な, 学問の, 学問的な

文型&コロケーション
▶an **educational**/ an **academic**/ an **informational**/ an **instructional**/ a **pedagogic programme**
▶**educational**/ **academic**/ **scholarly**/ **informational**/ **instructional**/ **pedagogic value**/ **use**
▶**educational**/ **academic**/ **scholarly**/ **pedagogic practice**/ **methods**
▶an **educational**/ an **academic**/ a **scholarly career**
▶**educational**/ **academic**/ **scholarly standards**/ **excellence**
▶**educational**/ **academic**/ **informational**/ **pedagogic needs**
▶an **academic**/ a **scholarly**/ an **instructional**/ a **pedagogic**/ a **didactic work**

educational 教育の, 教育に役立つ, 教育的な ◇The two women were from similar social and *educational* backgrounds. その二人の女性は育った社会や受けた教育が似ていた ◇Many of the kids here have special *educational* needs (= they need extra help that is not given to all children). ここの子どもたちの多くが特別な教育を必要としている ◇Sometimes television can be highly *educational*. 時として, テレビは教育にとても役立つことがある
▷**educationally** 副 ◇Children living in inner-city areas may be *educationally* disadvantaged. 都心部に住んでいる子どもたちは教育上の不利益を被っているのかもしれない

academic《ふつう名詞の前で》学術[学究]的な, 学業の, 学問の ◇*academic* research 学術研究 ◇He retired from *academic life* and went into politics. 彼は学究生活を退いて政界に進出した ◇The *academic year* usually starts in September. 学年度は通例9月から始まる
▷**academically** 副 ◇She was always regarded as *academically* gifted. 彼女は常に勉強がよくできると思われていた

scholarly《しばしばほめて》学術的な, 学問的な ◇The issue has given rise to much *scholarly* debate. その問題は多くの学問的な論争を引き起こした ◇They have produced a detailed and *scholarly* study of the composer's works. 彼らはその作曲家の作品の詳細な学術的研究を行った ☞ **scholarship** (KNOWLEDGE)

informational《ふつう名詞の前で》《ややフォーマル, 書き言葉》情報提供的な ◇The materials do not have much real *informational* content. 資料には本当に情報らしい情報はあまりない

instructional《ふつう名詞の前で》《ややフォーマル, 書き言葉》教えるための, 教育的な ◇The activities are intended to be both interesting and *instructional*. その活動は面白くかつためになるように意図されたものである

pedagogic(または **pedagogical**)《フォーマル, 書き言葉》教授法[教育方法]の ◇Most teachers have excellent *pedagogic* skills. ほとんどの教師は優れた教育技術を備えている

didactic《フォーマル, 書き言葉》教訓的な ◇This form of *didactic* literature was popular in Victorian times. こういった形式の教訓的な文学はヴィクトリア朝時代に人気があった

effect 名 ☞ RESULT

effect・impact・influence・power・force・impression・action
人や物事によって引き起こされる変化
【類語訳】影響, 影響力, 結果, 印象, 作用

文型&コロケーション
▶an **effect**/ **impact**/ **influence**/ **impression on**/ **upon** sb/ sth
▶**under** the **effect**/ **impact**/ **influence of** sth/ sb
▶(a) **considerable**/ **tremendous**/ **great effect**/ **impact**/ **influence**/ **power**/ **force**/ **impression**
▶a **profound**/ **significant**/ **strong**/ **big**/ **positive**/ **lasting effect**/ **impact**/ **influence**/ **impression**
▶a/ an **cultural**/ **economic**/ **political**/ **social effect**/ **impact**/ **influence**
▶to **have** an **effect**/ **impact**/ **influence**
▶to **make** an **impact**/ **impression**
▶to **feel** the **effect**/ **impact of** sth

effect [C, U] 影響, 結果 ◇Despite her ordeal, she seems to have suffered no *ill effects*. つらい体験をしたにもかかわらず, 彼女は悪影響を実感しなかったようだ ◇Her criticisms *had the effect of* discouraging him completely. 彼女の批評は彼をすっかり落胆させる結果となった ◇It's not always easy to distinguish between *cause and effect*. 原因と結果を区別するのは必ずしも容易ではない ◇The management changes had *little or no effect* on output. 経営陣の交代は生産高にほとんど何の影響も与

↳**effect**

なかった ☞ **affect** (AFFECT)

impact [C, ふつう単数で, U] (人・物事に与える)強い影響 ◇Her speech made a profound *impact* on everyone. 彼女のスピーチはみんなに多大な影響を与えた ◇The programme examined the environmental *impact* of power generation. その事業では発電の環境への影響が調査された ◇We are trying to **minimize the impact** of price rises on customers. 値上げが消費者に与える影響を最小限にとどめようとしているところです ☞ **impact** (AFFECT)

influence [U, C] (人の考え方・行動様式[物事の作用・展開]に与える)影響 ◇Children around the age of eight are especially vulnerable to the *influence* of television. 8歳くらいの子どもはテレビの影響を特に受けやすい ◇The artists **exerted** a strong *influence* on a younger generation. その芸術家たちは若い世代に強い影響を及ぼした ◇They said she was a **bad** *influence* on the other children. 彼女はほかの子どもたちに悪い影響を与えると彼らは言った ☞ **influence** (AFFECT)

power [U] (特定の物事・集団による)影響力 ◇He talked about the enormous *power* of the mass media. 彼はマスメディアの強大な影響力について語った ◇The government promised greater opportunities for **parent** *power*. 政府はもっと親の影響力を発揮できる機会を約束した

force [U] (人の主張・個性が及ぼす)迫力 ◇She spoke **with** *force* and deliberation. 彼女は力強くかつ慎重に話した ◇He felt the full *force* of her criticism. 彼は彼女の批評にすっかり圧倒された ◇He controlled himself by **sheer** *force* **of will**. 彼はもっぱら意志の力で自制した

impression [C, ふつう単数で] (将来の考え方・行動に与える)影響, 印象 ◇The stillness and silence leave a deep *impression* on visitors. その静寂と沈黙は訪れる者に深い印象を残す ◇You'll have to play better than that if you really want to **make an** *impression* (= to make people admire and remember you). 本当に強い印象を残したいなら、もっといいプレーをしなければならないだろう ◇My words **made no** *impression* on her. 私の言葉は彼女にまったく響かなかった ☞ **impress** (IMPRESS), **impressive** (IMPRESSIVE)

action [U] 《of を伴って》(物質・薬品が他の物質・薬品に与える)影響, 作用 ◇Vitamin D can be made in the body by the *action* of sunlight on the skin. 日光の皮膚に対する作用によってビタミンDは体内で生成される ☞ **act** (AFFECT)

efficiency 名

efficiency・order・coherence・organization・structure・method
よくまとまっていて、うまく機能する性質
【類語訳】効率, 整理, 秩序

文型&コロケーション
- *efficiency/ coherence/ method* **in** sth
- **great** *efficiency/ coherence*
- **to bring/ give** *order/ coherence/ structure* **to** sth
- **to have** *order/ coherence/ organization/ structure*
- **to impose** *order/ coherence/ structure* **on** sth
- **to achieve** *efficiency/ coherence*
- **to create** *order/ coherence*
- **to lack** *order/ coherence/ organization/ structure*
- **a lack of** *order/ coherence/ organization/ structure*

efficiency, efficient

efficiency [U] 効率, 能率 ◇The new computer system will cut costs and increase *efficiency*. 新しいコンピューターシステムはコストを削減し効率を上げるだろう ◇New standards of *energy efficiency* (= not wasting energy) are being introduced. エネルギー効率の新基準が導入されているところです 反意 **inefficiency** (INEFFECTIVE)

order [U] 整理, 秩序 ◇Get your ideas into some sort of *order* before you begin to write. 書き始める前に考えを何らかの形に整理しなさい ◇She always liked creating *order* out of chaos. 彼女はいつも混沌の中から秩序を生み出すのが好きだった ◇The house had been kept **in good** *order*. 家は以前は整理整頓されていた ◇I felt it was time to **put** my life **in** *order*. 私は生活を整え直すべき時だと感じた 反意 **disorder** (MESS 1), **chaos**, ☞ **ordered, orderly** (NEAT)

coherence [U] 《フォーマル》首尾一貫性, 統一 ◇Some of the points you make are good, but the essay as a whole lacks *coherence*. あなたの主張のいくつかはよいが, 論文全体としては首尾一貫性に欠ける ◇The party tried to find some kind of ideological *coherence*. その政党は何らかの類のイデオロギーの統一性を見出そうとした ☞ **coherent** (RATIONAL)

organization 《英でまた **-isation**》 [U] 秩序 ◇She's highly intelligent but her work lacks *organization*. 彼女はとても聡明だが, 彼女の仕事は秩序立っていない ◇As a manager he's obsessed with *organization*. 彼は経営者として、きちんとしていないと気がすまない

> **ノート** *order* と *organization* の使い分け: *order* は生み出される「秩序」. *organization* はすでに存在する「秩序」.
> × Get your ideas into some sort of *organization*.
> × creating *organization* out of chaos.

structure [U, C] 構成, 秩序 ◇In terms of *structure* the novel has several flaws. その小説は構成の点でいくつか欠点がある ◇Children need *structure* in their lives. 子どもたちには生活における秩序が必要だ ☞ **structure** (STRUCTURE)

method [U] 計画性, 筋道 ◇We have to apply some *method* to this investigation. この調査には計画性をもたせなければならない ❶ *method* は仕事[問題解決]の仕方について用いられる

efficient 形

efficient・systematic・orderly・tidy・businesslike・methodical・organized・neat
物事をうまく[完全に, 体系的に]行える[行う]ことを表す
【類語訳】効率的な, 能率的な, 体系的な, きちょうめんな, きちんとした

文型&コロケーション
- *efficient/ systematic/ businesslike/ methodical/ organized* **in** sth
- **in a** *systematic/ an orderly/ a businesslike/ a methodical/ an organized* **fashion**
- **an** *efficient/ a systematic/ an orderly/ a businesslike/ a methodical/ an organized* **approach/ way**
- **relatively** *efficient/ systematic/ orderly/ organized*
- **fairly** *efficient/ systematic/ orderly/ tidy*
- **quite** *efficient/ businesslike/ methodical*
- **extremely** *efficient/ organized/ neat*
- **highly** *efficient/ systematic/ organized*

efficient 効率的な, 能率的な ◇It's an incredibly *efficient* system. それは信じられないほど効率的なシステムだ ◇The more *efficient* firms have lower costs. 効率性の高い会社の方がコストは抑えられる ◇More *efficient* use of energy resources is vital. エネルギー資源のより効率的な利用が不可欠である ◇Our bodies become less *efficient* at burning off calories. 我々の体はカロリーを消費する際に効率が落ちる ◇She was helpful, quietly *efficient* and tactful. 彼女は役に立ち, 目立たないが有能で気がきいた ◇Which software is the most *efficient* at processing the data? そのデータの処理には, どのソフトウェアが最も効率的ですか 反意 **inefficient (INEFFECTIVE)**
▶**efficiently** 副 ◇They began to work harder and more *efficiently*. 彼らはより一生懸命に, より効率的に働き出した 反意 **inefficiently (INEFFECTIVE)**

systematic 体系的な, 組織的な ◇No *systematic* analysis has ever been carried out in this area. この領域では系統立った分析が一度も行われていない ◇This was a *systematic* attempt to infiltrate a democratic organization. これは民主的な組織に潜入しようとする組織的な企てだった 反意 **unsystematic (RANDOM), system (WAY 1)**
▶**systematically** 副 ◇The topic has never been *systematically* studied. このテーマは体系的な研究がまったくなされていない

orderly 秩序ある, 整然とした, 規律正しい ◇She had led a calm and *orderly* life. 彼女は平穏で規律正しい生活を送っていた ◇Public policy changes can be made in an *orderly* and rational manner. 公共政策の変更は整然と合理的になしえる ◇It was a civilized and *orderly* society. それは文明化された秩序ある社会だった 反意 **disorderly (WILD)**

tidy (特に英) 整理整頓した, きれい好きな, きちょうめんな ◇I'm not a very *tidy* person. 私はあまりきれい好きではない ◇Even young children can be taught *tidy* habits. 幼い子どもたちにでも整理整頓の習慣は教えられる ◇He is obsessively *tidy*. 彼は異常なくらいきれい好きだ 反意 **untidy (RANDOM)**, ☞ **tidy (NEAT)**

businesslike 能率的な, 事務的な ◇Wearing the suit made him feel more *businesslike*. 彼はスーツを着ると仕事をてきぱき片づける気分になった ◇She adopted a brisk, *businesslike* tone. 彼女はそっけなく事務的な口調で話すことにした

methodical きちょうめんな, 整然とした, 順序だった ◇He was slow, *methodical* and reliable. 彼はおっとりしていてきちょうめんで信頼できた ◇Police carried out a *methodical* search of the premises. 警察は敷地内を順序だてて捜索した
▶**methodically** 副 ◇The investigation was proceeding slowly but *methodically*. 調査はゆっくりとだが, 整然と進行していた

organized (英ではまた **-sed**) (生活・仕事に関して人が)きちんとした ◇The chairman is one of the most *organized* people I know. 私の知るかぎり, 議長はもっともきちんとした人の一人だ ◇Isn't it time you started to get *organized*? もうそろそろちゃんとしてもいいんじゃないの 反意 **disorganized (RANDOM)**

neat (人が)きれい好きな, きちょうめんな, (身なりが)きちんとした ◇She was a very efficient, *neat* woman. 彼女はとても有能できちょうめんな女性だった ◇The children are always *neat and tidy*. その子たちはいつもきちんとした身なりをしている ◇By nature he was *clean and neat*. 生まれつき彼は清潔できれい好きだった ❶(米)では, 物事や場所にも用いることができる. ◆Each resident is expected to keep their room *neat*. ((米)住人はみな部屋をきれいにしておくことを求められている). ☞ **neat (NEAT)**

effort 名

effort • hard work • struggle • endeavour • energy • exertion

多大なエネルギーのいる事をするのに必要な体力や気力
【類語訳】努力, 骨折り, 困難, 精力

文型&コロケーション
▶(a) **great** effort/ struggle/ endeavour/ exertion
▶(a) **physical** effort/ struggle/ exertion
▶(a) **mental** effort/ struggle/ exertion
▶(a) **creative** effort/ endeavour/ energies
▶to **need** effort/ hard work/ your energies/ exertion
▶to **take/ demand** effort/ hard work
▶to **put** effort/ hard work/ your energies **into** sth
▶to **expend** effort/ your energies

effort [U, C] 努力 ◇It's a long climb to the top, but well worth the *effort*. 山頂まで登るのは長いが, 苦労する価値は十分ある ◇A lot of *effort has gone into* making this event a success. このイベントを成功させるために多大な労力が費やされた ◇Getting up this morning was quite an *effort* (= it was difficult). 今朝は起きるのにかなり苦労した

,hard 'work [U] 努力, 骨折り ◇She earned her grades through sheer *hard work*. 彼女は猛勉強してその成績を取った ◇They put in a lot of *hard work* to achieve this result. 彼らは一生懸命に力を注いでこの成果を上げた ◇It's *hard work* trying to get him to do anything for himself. 彼に何であれ自分のことは自分でやらせようとするとかなり骨が折れます

struggle [単数형] 苦闘, 努力 ◇It was a real *struggle to* be ready on time. 時間どおりに準備するのは実に大変だった ◇They face an *uphill struggle* to get to the finals of the competition. 彼らは競技会の決勝戦に進むための苦しい闘いに直面している ☞ **struggle (TRY 1)**

endeavour 《英》《米 **endeavor**》 [U]《フォーマル》(新しい)[困難な]ことをするための)努力 ◇There have been great advances in the field of scientific *endeavour*. 科学的目標への努力において大いなる向上が見られた ☞ **endeavour (TRY 1)**

energy [U] (または **energies** [複数で]) 活(動)力, 精力 ◇She put all her *energy* into her work. 彼女は仕事に全精力を注いだ ◇Provide a means of channelling your child's creative *energies*. お子さんの創造力が伸びるように手立てを講じてあげなさい ❶ energy, energies はふつう所有代名詞 his, her, my, your, our, their のあとで用いられる. concentrate, devote, direct, focus, channel などの動詞と結びつく.

exertion [U] (または **exertions** [複数で])《ややフォーマル》尽力, 努力 ◇She was hot and breathless from the *exertion* of cycling uphill. 彼女は上り坂を苦労して自転車で登ったので, 体がほてり息が切れていた ◇He needed to relax after the *exertions* of a busy day at work. 職場で一日忙しく働いた後, 彼はリラックスする必要があった

↪**effort**

ノート effort と exertion の使い分け：exertion はふつう，活動するのに精力を費やすことおよびその結果について用いる．♦ His voice was breathless from *exertion*. (きつい作業をして彼の声は息切れしていた)．effort は何かを達成するために人々がする仕事について用いる傾向がある．♦ A lot of *effort* has gone into achieving this result. (この成果をあげるのにかなりの労力が費やされた)．

election 名

election・vote・poll・referendum・ballot・exit poll・straw poll・show of hands
代表を選んだり，投票で何かを決定したりする行事
【類語訳】選挙，投票，票決，国民投票，無記名投票，出口調査

文型&コロケーション

▸ an election/ a vote/ a poll/ a referendum/ a ballot **on** sth
▸ a **democratic/ free** election/ vote/ poll/ ballot
▸ a **secret** election/ vote/ ballot
▸ a **national/ local** election/ poll/ referendum/ ballot
▸ a **state** election/ poll/ referendum
▸ to **conduct** an election/ a vote/ a poll/ a referendum/ a ballot/ an exit poll
▸ to **have** an election/ a vote/ a poll/ a referendum/ a ballot/ a show of hands
▸ to **hold** an election/ a vote/ a poll/ a referendum/ a ballot
▸ to **call/ lose/ win** an election/ a vote/ a referendum/ a ballot
▸ an election/ a vote/ a poll/ a referendum/ a ballot **takes place**
▸ the **outcome/ result of** an election/ a vote/ a poll/ a referendum/ a ballot

election [C, U] 選挙 ◇Who did you vote for in the last *election*? この前の選挙で誰に投票しましたか ◇The first *election* results will be coming in very soon. 最初の選挙結果はまもなく出ます ◇Labour won a landslide victory in the 1945 *general election* (= a national election for a new government). 《英》労働党は1945年の総選挙で地滑り的勝利を収めた ◇He first **stood for election** when he was 21. 《英》彼は21歳のとき初めて選挙に立候補した ◇She's yet to say whether she will be **running for election**. 彼女はまだ選挙に出馬するかどうか明言していない ☞ **elect** (APPOINT)
vote [C] 投票，票決 ◇They **took a vote** on who should be their new leader. 彼らは誰が新しいリーダーになるべきかを票決した ◇I think it's time to **put this** issue **to the vote**. この問題を投票にかけるべき時だと思います ◇The *vote* was unanimous (= everyone voted the same way). 票決は満場一致だった ◇Let me propose a *vote of thanks* (= a vote to formally thank sb). 《英》感謝決議を提案します ☞ **vote sb in** (APPOINT)
poll [C] (または **the polls** [複数形])《特にジャーナリズム》投票 ◇The final result of the *poll* will be known tomorrow. 投票の最終結果は明日判明します ◇They suffered a resounding defeat **at the polls**. 彼らは投票で大敗を喫した ◇The **polls close** (= voting ends) at 10 pm. 投票は午後10時で終了します ◇Thursday is traditionally the day when Britain **goes to the polls** (= votes in an election). 木曜日が英国では昔からの投票日だ
referendum [C] 国民投票 ◇The president called a *referendum* on the new divorce laws. 大統領は新しい離婚法に関する国民投票の実施を決定した ◇The issue will be decided **by referendum**. その問題は国民投票で決定されるだろう
ballot [U, C] 無記名投票，投票 ◇The leader will be chosen by secret *ballot*. リーダーは無記名投票で選ばれるでしょう ◇The union cannot call a strike unless it holds a *ballot* amongst its members. 組合は組合員の間で投票を実施しなければ，ストライキを行うことはできない ❶ *ballot* はふつう一般大衆が投票する場合よりも組織内での投票に用いられる．☞ **ballot** (SURVEY)
'exit poll [C] 出口調査 ◇*Exit polls* show that the Republicans are slightly ahead. 出口調査によれば共和党がわずかに優勢である
,straw 'poll [C] (非公式の)世論調査 ◇I took a quick *straw poll* among my colleagues to see how many agreed. どれだけの人が賛成したか見てみようと同僚に速やかに意見調査をした
show of 'hands (賛否を問う)挙手 ◇OK, let's have a *show of hands*. Who's in favour of the proposal? それでは，挙手で採決しましょう．案に賛成の人は

elegant 形 ☞ FASHIONABLE

elegant・smart・stylish・graceful・classic・well dressed
人や物の魅力的でかっこいい様子を表す
【類語訳】おしゃれな，かっこいい，粋な，身なりのよい，優雅な，上品な

文型&コロケーション

▸ an elegant/ a smart/ a stylish/ a graceful/ a well-dressed **woman**
▸ an elegant/ a smart/ a well-dressed **man**
▸ smart/ stylish/ well-dressed **people**
▸ an elegant/ a smart/ a stylish/ a classic **suit/ dress**
▸ an elegant/ a stylish/ a classic **cut/ design**
▸ an elegant/ a smart/ a classic **style**
▸ an elegant/ a smart/ a stylish **restaurant**
▸ an elegant/ a graceful **movement**
▸ elegant/ graceful/ classic **lines**

elegant 《ほめて》(人・服・場所・物が)上品な，おしゃれな ◇She was tall, slim and *elegant*. 彼女は背が高く，ほっそりとしていて品がよかった ◇She was looking for something cool and *elegant* to wear. 彼女はかっこよくておしゃれな服を探していた ◇Guests can dine and relax in comfortable *elegant* surroundings. お客様は快適な素晴らしい環境で食事を取り，くつろぐことができます ☞ **elegance** (STYLE)
▸ **elegantly** 副 *elegantly* dressed women 品のいい服を身に着けた女性たち
smart 《特に英，ほめて》(身なりが)きちんとしている；(衣服などが)おしゃれな ◇You look very *smart* in that suit. そのスーツを着るととてもきちんとして見えますよ ◇They wear *smart* blue uniforms. 彼らはおしゃれな青い制服を着ている 反意 scruffy
▸ **smartly** 副 *smartly* dressed おしゃれをした
stylish 《ほめて》流行の，おしゃれな，粋な，かっこいい ◇His pale grey suit was *stylish*. 彼の淡い灰色のスーツはいきだった ◇It was a *stylish* performance by both artists. どちらのアーティストもかっこいい演奏だった ☞ **style**

element, elite

(STYLE), **style** (FASHION)
▶**stylishly** 副 ◇*stylishly* cut hair おしゃれな髪型
graceful 優雅な, 優美な ◇He gave a *graceful* bow to the audience. 彼は観衆に向かって優雅にお辞儀した ◇The flowers have *graceful*, arching stems. その花の茎は優美に弧を描いている ☞ **grace** (STYLE)
▶**gracefully** 副 ◇He bowed *gracefully*. 彼は優雅にお辞儀した
classic《特に書き言葉》オーソドックスな, 正統派の ◇She was wearing a *classic* little black dress. 彼女はオーソドックスなリトルブラックドレスを着ていた ◇The shop specializes in *classic* English style. その店は正統派のイングランドスタイルを専門的に扱っている ☞ **class** (STYLE)
▶**classically** 副 ◇*classically* beautiful オーソドックスな美しさを備えた
,well 'dressed《特に書き言葉》身なりのよい, おしゃれな
◇It's what today's *well-dressed* man is wearing. それは近頃のおしゃれな男性が身につけている物です ◇She was always *well dressed*. 彼女はいつも身なりがよかった

element 名

element・component・module・unit・part・piece・ingredient・section
より大きなものの一部分だが, それとは別個にとらえることのできるもの
【類語訳】要素, 単位, 部品, 部分

文型&コロケーション

▶an element/ a component/ an ingredient **in** sth
▶an **individual** element/ component/ module/ unit/ part/ piece/ ingredient
▶a **basic** element/ component/ module/ unit/ part/ ingredient
▶a **core** element/ component/ module/ unit
▶a/ an **major/ important/ fundamental** element/ component/ unit/ ingredient
▶a/ an **necessary/ essential** element/ component/ part/ ingredient
▶the **main/ principal** element/ component/ ingredient
▶**component/ constituent** elements/ modules/ parts

element [C]（必須の[典型的な]）要素 ◇Cost was a key *element* in our decision. 経費は我々の決定において重要な要素だった ◇The story has all the *elements* of a soap opera. その物語はメロドラマの要素をすべて備えている
component [C]《ややフォーマル》（全体を構成する一つの）要素, 部品 ◇Car *components* are manufactured in the other factory. 自動車部品はもう一つの工場で製造されている ◇Trust is a vital *component* in any relationship. 信頼はどんな関係においても不可欠な要素である
▶**component** 形 [名詞の前で] ◇This concept can be broken down into its *component* parts. この概念は構成要素に分けることができる
module [C]（英国の大学における）（学習）単位；（機械・構造物の）モジュール, ユニット ◇The course consists of ten core *modules* and five optional modules. その課程は10の必修単位と5つの選択単位からなります ◇Each student takes five *modules*. 学生はそれぞれ5つの単位をとります ◇Ships are now built in *modules* rather than built in a whole from the base up. 現在, 船は基部から上へと全体を組み立てるのではなく, ユニットごとに建造される
❶コンピュータの分野では, *module* は特定の機能を持ったコンピューターシステム[プログラム]の一部をさす. ◆New *soft-ware modules* include a virtual memory tool.（新しいソフトウェア・モジュールは仮想記憶ツールを含んでいる）. *module* は母船から独立して機能できる宇宙船の一部でもある. ◆Photographs were taken from a lunar *module*.（写真は月着陸船から撮られた）.
unit [C]（構成）単位 ◇The cell is the *unit* of which all living organisms are composed. 細胞はすべての生物を構成する単位である ◇The basic *unit* of society is the family. 社会の基本単位は家族である
part [C]（機械・構造物の）一部分, 部品, 部分 ◇Where can I get *spare parts* for my motorbike? どこでオートバイの予備部品を入手できますか ◇Although it is no longer a working watermill, several of the *working parts* remain. それは水車場としてはもはや稼動していないが, 作動部品のいくつかは残っている
piece [C]（何かを作りあげている）一部分 ◇He took the clock *to pieces*. 彼は時計をばらばらに分解した ◇He broke the clock *down into pieces*.《米》彼は時計をばらばらに分解した ◇The bridge was taken down *piece by piece*. 橋は徐々に解体された ◇She's been doing a 500-*piece* jigsaw. 彼女は500ピースのジグソーパズルをずっとしている ◇There had to be some missing *piece* of the story. その話には欠けた部分があるに違いなかった
ingredient [C]（料理などの）材料, 成分；（成功に必要な）要素 ◇Coconut is a basic *ingredient* in many curries. ココナッツは多くのカレーの基本的な材料だ ◇Our skin cream contains only **natural** *ingredients*. 私どものスキンクリームは天然成分しか使っておりません ◇The only **active** *ingredient* in this medicine is aspirin. この薬の有効成分はアスピリンだけだ ◇Determination is one of the essential *ingredients* **for** success. 決断力は成功に欠かせない要素の一つである ◇It has **all the ingredients** of a good mystery story. それは優れたミステリー小説の要素をすべて備えている ◇The **magic/secret ingredient** is love. 秘訣は愛だよ
section [C]（組み立て式の構造物の）一部, 部品 ◇The shed comes in *sections* that you assemble yourself. 物置は自分で組み立てる部品の形で販売されている

elite 名

elite・society・the nobility・the aristocracy・the gentry・the upper class
社会の上流階級の集団や多大な権力, 富, 影響力を持つ集団
【類語訳】エリート, 上流社会, 上流階級, 貴族

文型&コロケーション

▶**among** the elite/ nobility/ aristocracy/ gentry/ upper class
▶the **local** elite/ nobility/ aristocracy/ gentry
▶the **British/ French, etc.** elite/ nobility/ aristocracy/ gentry/ upper class
▶the **landed/ landowning/ minor/ lesser** nobility/ aristocracy/ gentry
▶to **belong to** an elite/ the nobility/ the aristocracy/ the gentry/ the upper classes

elite [C＋単数・複数動詞] エリート ◇In these countries, only the *elite* can afford an education for their children. これらの国では, エリートにしか子どもの教育費を出す経済的な余裕がない ◇He came from the country's *intellectual elite*. 彼はその国の知的エリートの出身だった ☞ **elite** (TOP)

↳elite

embarrass, embarrassed

society [U] 上流社会 ◇She was a poor Irish girl who married into New York *society*. 彼女はもとはと言えばニューヨークの上流社会に結婚して紛れ込んだアイルランド人の貧しい少女だった ◇She moved in **high society** and had many literary friends. 彼女は上流社会に入り, 文学界の友人がたくさんいた ◇The revelations have outraged *polite society*. 驚くべき新事実に上流社会の人々は激怒した ◇He was a popular photographer for *society weddings*. 彼は上流社会の結婚式で人気の写真家だった

the nobility [単数+単数・複数動詞] 貴族(階級) ◇She had some influential supporters, including members of *the nobility*. 彼女には貴族を含む有力な支持者たちがいた

the aristocracy [C+単数・複数動詞] 貴族(階級) ◇He claimed to be a member of *the* minor *aristocracy* (= with a lower title). 彼は自分が下級貴族だと主張した

the gentry [複数扱い] (昔の)上流階級の人々 ◇The influence of the Church and *the* landed *gentry* (= those owning a lot of land) at that time cannot be overemphasized. 当時の教会と地主貴族の影響力はいくら強調しても十分ほど強大だ

ノート **nobility, aristocracy, gentry** の使い分け: the nobility や the aristocracy は一部の国で, 特に過去において, 王族を除いた最上級階級出身の人々を指す。公爵(Duke, Duchess), 伯爵(Count, Earl)のような特別な称号を持つ。ふつう裕福な有力者で, しばしば土地を所有する。the gentry は昔は, the nobility のすぐ下の上流階級の人々を指し, ふつう裕福で土地を所有したが, 必ずしも特別な称号を持たず, 全国レベルではなく地方レベルの有力者であった。

the ˌupper ˈclass [単数+単数・複数動詞]《(特に米)》(または **the ˌupper ˈclasses** [複数で]) 上流階級 ◇They produced luxury furniture for *the* middle and *upper classes*. 彼らは中・上流階級向けの高級家具を製造していた ❶the upper class は時には the aristocracy だけを言うのに用いられる。しかし多くの場合, もっと広い意味を持ち, the gentry や, 時には他の上流階級との社交ができるだけの財産, 教育, 教養を有する実業界や専門職の人々を含むこともある。
♦ Wealthy industrialists joined *the upper class* by virtue of their newly acquired spending power. (裕福な実業家たちは, 新たに獲得した購買力のおかげで上流階級に加わった). ☞**class** (CLASS 3)

embarrass 動

embarrass・humiliate・shame・mortify
人に気まずく恥ずかしい思いをさせる
【類語訳】恥をかかせる, 屈辱を与える, 面目をつぶす

embarrass	humiliate shame	mortify

文型&コロケーション

▶ to embarrass/ humiliate sb **in front of** sb
▶ to be embarrassed/ mortified **at** sth
▶ to embarrass/ humiliate/ shame sb **by doing** sth
▶ to be embarrassed/ humiliated/ mortified **to do** sth
▶ to embarrass/ humiliate/ shame **yourself**
▶ to **publicly/ deeply/ utterly** embarrass/ humiliate/ shame sb

embarrass [他] 照れくさい[気まずい, 恥ずかしい]思いをさせる; 当惑[困惑]させる ◇Her questions about my private life *embarrassed* me. 私生活についての彼女の質問に私は照れくさくなった ◇*It embarrassed her to* meet strange men in the corridor at night. 夜の廊下で知らない男性に会うと彼女は恥ずかしくなった ◇The speech was deliberately designed to *embarrass* the prime minister. 演説は首相を当惑させるように仕組まれたものだった

➤**embarrassing** 形 ◇an *embarrassing* mistake/ question/situation 恥ずかしいミス/照れくさくなるような質問/厄介な状況 ◇It was so *embarrassing* having to sing in public. 人前で歌わなければならなくてひどく恥ずかしかった

➤**embarrassment** 名 [U, C] ◇Much **to her embarrassment** she realized that everybody in the room had heard her. 部屋のみんなが自分の話を聞いていることに気づいて彼女はとても恥ずかしかった ◇His resignation will be a severe *embarrassment* to the party. 彼が辞任したら党はひどく困惑するだろう

humiliate [他] 屈辱を与える, 恥をかかせる ◇I didn't want to *humiliate* her in front of her colleagues. 同僚の前で彼女に恥をかかせたくなかった ◇The party was *humiliated* in the recent elections. 最近の選挙でその党は屈辱を味わった

➤**humiliating** 形 ◇a *humiliating* defeat 屈辱的な敗北

➤**humiliation** 名 [U, C] ◇She suffered the *humiliation* of being criticized in public. 彼女は人前で批判される屈辱を受けた

shame [他]《書き言葉 or フォーマル》恥ずかしい思いをさせる; 面目をつぶす ◇His generosity *shamed* them all. 彼の気前のよさに彼らはみな面目をつぶされた ◇She *shamed* her father ***into*** promising to help (= persuaded him to do it by making him feel ashamed to not do it). 彼女は父親の義侠心をくすぐって援助を約束させた ◇The companies that pollute our rivers should be ***named and shamed***. 我々の川を汚染する企業は名指しで非難するべきだ ☞**shame** (GUILT), **shame** (DISGRACE)

mortify [他, ふつう受身で] 非常に恥ずかしい[ばつの悪い]思いをさせる, 屈辱を与える ◇She was *mortified* to realize he had heard every word she said. 自分が口にした言葉を彼が全部聞いていたことを知って, 彼女はひどく恥ずかしい思いをした ❶mortify は話し言葉で大げさに用いられることがあり, 実際は「非常に恥ずかしい思いをする」でなく「ちょっと恥ずかしい思いをする」の意味で用いられることがある。♦ I was *mortified* when I realized I had forgotten our lunch date. (ランチデートの約束を忘れていたのに気づいてばつが悪かったわ).

➤**mortification** 名 [U] ◇Imagine my *mortification* when I found out. 気づいたときの恥ずかしい思いといったら

➤**mortifying** 形 ◇How *mortifying* to have to apologize to him! 彼に謝らなければならないとは何たる屈辱

embarrassed 形

embarrassed・uncomfortable・awkward・self-conscious・sheepish
人が不安な[恥ずかしい, 落ち着かない]思いをしたり, 人にそういう思いをさせたりすること
【類語訳】恥ずかしい, 落ち着かない, 気まずい

文型&コロケーション

- embarrassed/ uncomfortable/ awkward/ self-conscious/ sheepish **about** sth
- an embarrassed/ uncomfortable/ awkward **silence**
- an embarrassed/ a self-conscious/ a sheepish **smile**
- to **feel/ look** embarrassed/ uncomfortable/ awkward/ self-conscious/ sheepish
- **a little/ a bit** embarrassed/ uncomfortable/ self-conscious/ sheepish
- **slightly/ somewhat/ acutely/ highly** embarrassed/ uncomfortable/ self-conscious

embarrassed 恥ずかしい, 落ち着かない, 気まずい ◇She's *embarrassed* about her height. 彼女は自分の身長のことを恥ずかしく思っている ◇He felt *embarrassed at* being the centre of attention. 彼は注目の的になって照れくさかった ◇Some women are too *embarrassed to* consult their doctor about the problem. 女性の中には, 恥ずかしくてとても医者にその問題を相談できない人もいる ◇Her remark was followed by an *embarrassed* silence. 彼女が発言すると気まずい沈黙が訪れた

uncomfortable 落ち着かない, 不愉快な, 気まずい ◇He looked distinctly *uncomfortable* when the subject was mentioned. その話題が出ると, 彼は見るからに落ち着かない様子になった ◇It was an *uncomfortable* situation for everyone. それは誰にとっても不愉快な状況だった 反意 **comfortable** ❶ある状況でcomfortableである場合は, 自信に満ち, 心配や不安はない. ◆I never feel very *comfortable* in her presence. (彼女の前ではあまり落ち着かない).

▷**uncomfortably** 副 ◇I became *uncomfortably* aware that no one else was laughing. 他に誰も笑っていないのに気づいて気恥ずかしかった ◇Her comment was *uncomfortably* close to the truth. 彼女のコメントは不愉快だが真実に近かった

awkward 落ち着かない, 気まずい ◇She is *awkward* with people she doesn't know. 彼女は知らない人と一緒だと落ち着かない ◇There was an *awkward moment* when they asked about his wife. 彼の妻のことが尋ねられると気まずい間があった

▷**awkwardly** 副 ◇'I'm sorry,' he said *awkwardly*. 「ごめん」と彼はきまり悪そうに言った

ノート **embarrassed, uncomfortable, awkward** の使い分け: embarrassedは, 自分がみんなに見られて[笑われて]いると思うときや, 自分のあまりに個人的なことをみんなが知っていると思うときの気持ちを表すのに用いる. uncomfortableは, 触れたくないが避け方のわからない話題があって, どう振る舞ったらいいかよくわからない状況で用いられることが多い. awkwardは特定の場合の感情だけでなく, その人の性格や日ごろの態度を表すのにもよく用いる. しかし多くの場合, どの語を用いてもよい. ◆He felt *embarrassed/uncomfortable/awkward* about being the centre of attention. (彼は注目の的になることに不安を覚えた). ◆an *embarrassed/uncomfortable/awkward* silence (気まずい沈黙).

‚self-'conscious 人目を気にする, 自意識過剰の ◇He's always been *self-conscious* about being so short. 彼は背が低いことをずっと気にしている ◇She was a shy, *self-conscious* girl. 彼女ははにかみ屋で自意識過剰な女の子だった 反意 **unselfconscious** ❶unselfconsciousであれば, 自分のことを人が気にしたり意識したりしない.

▷**‚self-'consciously** 副 ◇She was *self-consciously* aware of his stare. 彼女は彼の視線を自分に向けられたものと強く意識した

sheepish (ばかげた[間違った]ことをして)きまり悪そうな, 恥ずかしい ◇He came into the room looking distinctly *sheepish*. 彼は見るからにきまり悪そうに部屋へ入ってきた ◇Mary gave a *sheepish grin*. メアリーは照れ笑いを浮かべた

emotion 名

emotion・feeling・passion・fervour・heat・sentiment
愛, 恐怖, 怒りなど, 人が強く感じるもの
【類語訳】感情, 気持ち, 激情, 熱情, 感傷

emotion	heat	passion
feeling		fervour
sentiment		

文型&コロケーション

- **with** emotion/ feeling/ passion/ fervour/ heat
- **intense/ considerable/ profound/ strong/ violent** emotion/ feelings/ passion
- **great** emotion/ passion/ fervour
- **human** emotion/ feelings/ passion
- **personal** emotion/ feeling/ sentiment
- to **arouse** emotion/ feelings/ passion
- to **stir up** emotion/ feelings/ fervour
- to **be full of** emotion/ passion/ fervour
- emotions/ feelings/ passions **are running high**

emotion [U, C] (愛・恐怖・怒りなどの)感情 ◇She spoke with deep *emotion*. 彼女は強い感情を込めて話した ◇She showed no *emotion* at the verdict. 彼女は評決には何の感情も見せなかった ◇He lost control of his *emotions*. 彼は感情を抑えきれなかった ☞ **emotional** (INTENSE)

feeling [C, U] (理性に対する)感情, 気持ち ◇He hates talking about his *feelings*. 彼は自分の気持ちについて語るのをいやがる ◇The debate aroused strong *feelings* on both sides. 論争によって双方の気持ちが高ぶった ◇She still harboured *feelings* of resentment. 彼女は依然として憤りの気持ちを抱いていた ◇She spoke with *feeling* about the plight of the homeless. 彼女はホームレスの窮状について感情をあらわにして語った ☞ **feel** (FEEL), **feeling** (SENSE)

passion [C, U] (愛・憎しみ・怒り・熱意などの)激しい感情, 激情, 情熱 ◇He's a man of violent *passions*. 彼は激情家だ ◇She argued her case with considerable *passion*. 彼女はかなり激しく自分の言い分を主張した ◇She killed her husband's lover in a *crime of passion*. 彼女は激情に駆られて夫の愛人を殺害する罪を犯した ☞ **passionate** (INTENSE)

fervour 《英》(《米》**fervor**) [U] (書き言葉)(強く信じていることへの)熱情, 熱烈さ ◇She kissed him with unusual *fervour*. 彼女は彼に非常に熱烈なキスをした ◇They were fired by religious *fervour*. 彼らは宗教的熱情で燃え立っていた ☞ **fervent** (INTENSE)

heat [U] 強い感情, 興奮, 怒り ◇'No, I won't,' he said with *heat* in his voice. 「いいえ, しません」と彼は興奮し

た声で言った ◇The chairman tried to take the *heat out of the situation* (= to make people calmer). 議長はその場の興奮を冷まそうとした ◇*In the heat of the moment* she forgot what she wanted to say (= because she was so angry or excited). かっとなって[興奮のあまり]彼女は言いたいことを忘れてしまった ☞ **heated** (INTENSE)

sentiment [U] 《ややフォーマル、時にけなして》感情、感傷、私情、情 ◇There is no room for *sentiment* in business. ビジネスには私情の入る余地はない ◇There was no fatherly affection, no display of *sentiment*. 父親らしい愛情もなければ、情を表に出すこともなかった

▶**sentimental** ◇She kept the letters for *sentimental* reasons. 彼女は感傷的な理由で手紙をとっておいた ◇The ring wasn't worth much but it had great *sentimental value*. その指輪はあまり金銭的価値はなかったが、心情的にはとても大切なものだった ◇a slushy, *sentimental* love story 《けなして》たわいのない感傷的なラブストーリー ◇He's not the sort of man who gets *sentimental about* old friendships. 彼は旧友のことで感傷的になるような男ではない

employ 動 ☞ APPOINT

employ・hire・recruit・sign・contract・engage・retain・take sb on
人に報酬のある仕事を与える
【類語訳】雇う、雇用する、採用する、契約する

┌─ 文型&コロケーション ─┐
▶to employ/ hire/ recruit/ sign/ engage/ retain/ take on sb **as** sth
▶to employ/ hire/ recruit/ sign/ contract/ engage/ retain/ take on sb **to do** sth
▶to hire/ recruit/ sign sb **from** a place/ company/ group
▶to employ/ hire/ recruit/ contract/ take on **workers/ staff**
▶to employ/ hire/ recruit a **manager**
▶to employ/ hire/ engage/ retain a **lawyer**
▶to sign/ contract a **player**
▶to engage/ retain sb's **services**

employ [他] 雇う、雇用する ◇How many people does the company *employ*? その会社は何人雇用しますか ◇A number of people have been *employed* to deal with the backlog of work. 残務処理をするのに数名が雇われている ☞ **be employed** (WORK 動 1), **employer** (MANAGER), **employment** (WORK 名 1)

hire [他, 自]《特に米》雇う、採用する ◇She was *hired* three years ago. 彼女は3年前に雇われた ◇He does the *hiring and firing* in our company. 彼はわが社で採用と解雇を担当している ◇We're not *hiring* right now. わが社は現在採用をしていません ❶《英》《米》共に, *hire* には「特定の仕事のために短期間雇用する」の意味もある。◆They *hired* a firm of consultants to design the new system. (彼らは新システムを設計するためにコンサルタント事務所を臨時に雇った) 反意 **fire** (FIRE)

recruit [他, 自]《ややフォーマル》(会社・組織・軍隊に)採用する ◇The police are trying to *recruit* more officers from ethnic minorities. 警察は少数民族からもっと警官を採用しようとしている ◇They *recruited* several new members to the club. 彼らは何人かのメンバーをクラブに採用した ◇He is responsible for *recruiting* at all levels. 彼はあらゆるレベルの採用を担当している ☞ **recruit** (RECRUIT)

sign [他, 自] (ミュージシャン・スポーツ選手に)雇用契約を結ばせる；(会社・チームと)雇用契約を結ぶ, 契約する ◇The team has just *signed* a new goalkeeper. チームは新しいゴールキーパーと契約したばかりだ ◇He *signed* for United yesterday. 《英》彼は昨日ユナイテッドと契約を交わした ◇He *signed* with the San Francisco 49ers. 《米》彼はサンフランシスコ・フォーティナイナーズと契約を結んだ ◇The band *signed* with Virgin Records. そのバンドはヴァージン・レコードと契約を結んだ

contract [他, ふつう受身で] 《ややフォーマル》(一定期間正式に)契約する, 契約を結ぶ ◇The player is *contracted to* play until August. その選手は8月までプレーする契約をしている ◇Several computer engineers have been *contracted* to the finance department. コンピューター・エンジニア数人が財務部と契約を結んでいる ❶ *contract* はこの意味では、うしろに *to* を伴う。《米》では、時に *with* を伴う。◆He can't work for them because he is *contracted* with another company. (彼は他社と契約しているので, 彼らの所で働くことはできない). ☞ **contract** (CONTRACT)

engage [他] 《フォーマル、特に英》(特定の仕事のために)雇う ◇He is currently *engaged* as a consultant. 彼は現在相談役として雇われている ◇We will have to *engage* the services of a translator. 翻訳業務に携る人を雇わなければならないだろう

retain [他] 《法律》(弁護士などの専門職の人に定期的に[前もって]金を支払って)雇っておく ◇You will need to *retain* the services of a lawyer. 弁護士業務に携る人を雇っておく必要があるでしょう ◇You will be paid a *retaining* fee. 依頼料が支払われます ❶弁護士などは企業だけでなく一般個人によっても *retain* される。また *retain* されていても他の会社や個人の仕事をすることもできる。

,take sb 'on 句動詞 (人に)仕事を与える；(人を)雇う, 採用する ◇We're not *taking on* any new staff at present. 目下のところ新しい職員を雇うつもりはありません 反意 **lay sb off** (FIRE)

empty 形

empty・vacant・bare・free
中に誰もいない[何もない]こと
【類語訳】空の、空いている

┌─ 文型&コロケーション ─┐
▶empty/ bare/ free **of** sth
▶an empty/ a vacant/ a bare **room**
▶an empty/ a vacant/ a free **seat**
▶an empty/ a vacant **house**
▶an empty/ a bare **cupboard**

empty 誰もいない、空の ◇an *empty* box/glass 空き箱/空のグラス ◇an *empty* house/room/bus 空き家/空室/乗客のいないバス ◇The theatre was half *empty*. 劇場は半分が空席だった ◇*empty* hands (= not holding anything) 空いている手 ◇an *empty* plate (= with no food on it) 空の皿 ◇The house had been *standing empty* (= without people living in it) for some time. その家はだいぶ前から空き家だった ◇It's not good to drink alcohol *on an empty stomach* (= without having eaten sth). すきっ腹での飲酒は体によくない ◇The room was *empty* of furniture. 《フォーマル》部屋には家具がなかった

encourage, end

反意 **full** (FULL), ☞ **empty** (CLEAR 動)
vacant 《ややフォーマル》（席・ホテルの部屋・家・土地が）空いている，使われていない ◇There are very few *vacant* properties available in the area. その地域では空き物件はほとんど手に入らない ◇The seat next to him was *vacant*. 彼の隣の席は空いていた ◇a *vacant* lot (= a piece of land in a city that is not being used) 《特に米》空き地 ◇There is a room *vacant*, as it happens. ちょうど空き部屋が一つあります ☞ **unoccupied** (DESERTED)
bare （部屋・食器棚にふつうあるものが）ない，空の ◇At many stores *bare* shelves greeted shoppers. 多くの店では，空の棚が買い物客を迎えた ◇The room was *bare* of furniture. 部屋には家具がなかった
free （必要なものが）空いている，すぐに使える ◇Is this seat *free*? この席は空いていますか ◇The device allows you to talk on the phone with both hands *free*. その装置を使えば，両手があいたままで電話で話せます

encourage 動

encourage・cheer sb up・cheer・uplift・lift/raise sb's spirits
人に勇気[希望，自信]を与える
【類語訳】励ます，勇気づける，元気づける，慰める

文型&コロケーション
▶to be **greatly** encouraged/ cheered

encourage [他] 励ます，勇気づける ◇My parents have always *encouraged me in* my choice of career. 職業を選ぶ際，両親はずっと私を励ましてくれた ◇We were greatly *encouraged* by the positive response of the public. 私たちは大衆の好意的な反応に大いに勇気づけられた ◇'Good girl, you're doing fine,' he *encouraged* her. 彼は「いい子だ，立派だよ」と彼女を励ました 反意 **discourage** (DISCOURAGE 2)
▶**encouragement** [名] [U] ◇He needs all the support and *encouragement* he can get. 彼には得られる限りすべての支えと励ましが必要だ 反意 **discouragement** (DISCOURAGE 2)
,cheer sb 'up [句動詞] （人を）元気づける，励ます ◇I asked her out to lunch to *cheer* her *up*. 元気づけようと彼女をランチに誘った ◇Give John a call — he needs *cheering up*. ジョンに電話しなさい―彼には励ましが必要よ 反意 **get sb down** (DISCOURAGE 2)
cheer [他，ふつう受身で] 励ます，安心させる ◇She was *cheered* by the news from home. 彼女は家からの知らせに励まされた

ノート **encourage と cheer の使い分け**: encourage の主語は人や出来事，cheer の主語は物や出来事。cheer することによって安心感を与え，encourage することによって自信を与える。

uplift [他，ふつう受身で] 《フォーマル》 幸せな気分にする，希望を与える ◇Although it is an emotional play you leave the theatre feeling strangely *uplifted*. 感傷的な芝居だが，劇場を出るときは妙に幸せな気分になる
lift/raise sb's 'spirits [句動] （人を）元気にする，勇気づける ◇The sunny weather *raised* my *spirits* a little. 好天のおかげで少し元気になった

end 名

end・close・conclusion・finish・ending・termination・finale・cessation
一定の時間や出来事，活動，物語の末尾の部分を表す
【類語訳】終わり，最後，結論，ゴールイン，フィニッシュ，大詰め，終結，終了，フィナーレ，停止，休止，中断

文型&コロケーション
▶a/ an (...) end/ finish/ ending/ finale **to** sth
▶**at** the end/ close/ conclusion/ finish/ finale
▶an **abrupt** end/ conclusion/ finish/ ending/ termination
▶a **dramatic** end/ conclusion/ finish/ ending/ finale
▶a **fitting** end/ conclusion/ finish
▶to **have** a/ an (...) end/ conclusion/ ending/ finale
▶to **provide** a/ an (...) conclusion/ finish/ ending/ finale
▶to **bring sth to** an end/ a close/ a conclusion
▶to **come/ draw to** an end/ a close
▶to **reach** the end/ finish

end [C] 終わり，最後 ◇I hope to finish this by the *end* of the week. 今週末までにはこれを終えたいと思っています ◇They finally get named at the *end* of the book. 彼らは本の結末でついに身元を突き止められる ◇There'll be a chance to ask questions at the *end*. 最後に質問する機会があるでしょう ◇We had to hear about the whole journey *from beginning to end*. 私たちは旅行の一部始終を最初から最後まで聞かなければならなかった ◇It's the *end* of an era. それは一つの時代の終わりだ ◇It was the *end* of all his dreams. それは彼のあらゆる夢の最後だった ◇The war was finally *at an end*. その戦争はついに終決した ◇Let's *put an end to* (= stop) these rumours once and for all. このような噂話はこれっきりにしよう 反意 **beginning** (START 名)
close [単数形で]《フォーマル，特にビジネス》終わり，最後 ◇Can we bring this meeting to a *close*? この会議を終わりにできますかね ◇By the *close* of London trading, Wall Street was up 9.78 points. ロンドン株式市場取り引きの引け際にはダウは9.78ポイント上がっていた ❶ *close* は，ビジネスやクリケット，野球といったスポーツ関係でしばしば用いられる。
◆At the *close of play*, the scores were almost level. (試合の終盤ではスコアはほとんど互角だった).
conclusion [C, ふつう単数形で]《ややフォーマル》結論，結末 ◇The *conclusion* of the book was disappointing. その本の結末にはがっかりだった ◇If we took this argument to its *logical conclusion*... もし私たちがこの議論から論理的帰結を導くとしたら… ◇*In conclusion*, (= finally) I would like to thank... 最後に私は…に感謝したい
finish [C, ふつう単数形で] 終わり，ゴールイン，フィニッシュ ◇It was a *close finish*, as they had predicted. それは彼らの予想どおりきわどいゴールインだった ◇He led the race *from start to finish*. 彼は最初から最後までそのレースを引っ張った ◇I want to see the job right through to the *finish*. その仕事をきちっと最後まで見守っていたい ❶ finish は主に，スポーツ大会（特にレース），時間が重視される活動などについて用いられる。反意 **start** (START 名)
ending [C] （物語・映画などの）大詰め，結末，終わり，終結 ◇His stories usually have a *happy ending*. 彼の物語はどれもいつもハッピーエンドで終わる ◇Today is the anniversary of the *ending* of the Pacific War. 今日は太平

↪end

end, endorsement

洋戦争の終戦記念日だ ◇It was the perfect *ending* to the perfect day. 申し分のない日で締めも言うことなしだった 反意 **opening**, **beginning** (START 名)

termination [U]《フォーマル、特にビジネス》終了、終結、最後 ◇Failure to comply with these conditions will result in *termination* of the contract. これらの条件にうまく応じないと契約は解除されるだろう

finale [C] (ショー・楽曲などの)大詰め、フィナーレ ◇the rousing *finale* of Beethoven's Ninth Symphony ベートーヴェンの交響曲第9番の躍動するフィナーレ ◇The festival ended with a **grand finale** of fireworks and music. そのお祭りは花火と音楽で盛大に幕を閉じた ❶ *finale* は、形容詞の後に用いられ、話題にしていることについて「…な最後」といった意味合いで用いられる。◆It was a fitting *finale* to the day's events. (それはその日の出来事にふさわしいフィナーレだった。)

cessation (単数で)《フォーマル、特にジャーナリズム》停止、休止、中断 ◇Mexico called for an immediate *cessation* of hostilities. メキシコは戦闘行為の即時停止を要求した

end 動 ☞ FINISH

end・finish・stop・terminate・conclude・close・wind (sth) up
終わる[終わらせる]こと
【類語訳】終わる、終わらせる、終える、終了する

文型&コロケーション
▶to end/ finish/ conclude **by/ with** sth
▶to end/ finish/ conclude/ close/ wind up a **meeting**
▶to end/ finish/ conclude/ wind up a **speech**
▶a **play/ show/ film** ends/ finishes/ concludes
▶a **concert** ends/ finishes
▶a **story/ letter/ note** ends/ concludes
▶to **almost/ nearly/ effectively** end/ finish/ stop/ terminate/ conclude
▶to **virtually/ all but/ never** end/ finish/ stop/ terminate/ conclude
▶to end/ finish/ stop/ terminate/ conclude **at last/ eventually/ finally**
▶to end/ stop/ terminate **suddenly/ abruptly/ automatically**

end [自、他] 終わる；終わらせる、終える ◇The road *ends* here. ここで道は行き止まりだ ◇How does the story *end*? その物語はどのような結末ですか ◇The speaker *ended* by suggesting some topics for discussion. 講演者は最後に討議すべきテーマをいくつか提案した ◇They decided to *end* their relationship. 彼らは関係を解消することにした ◇They *ended* the play with a song. 彼らは歌で芝居を終えた 反意 **begin** (BEGIN), **begin** (START 動)

finish [自、他] 終わる；(うまく)終わらせる ◇The play *finished* at 10.30. 芝居は10時半に終演した ◇The symphony *finishes* with a flourish. その交響曲はファンファーレで終わる ◇A cup of coffee *finished* the meal perfectly. コーヒーが出て食事は申し分なく終わった ◇They *finished off* the show with one of their most famous songs. 彼らは最も有名な持ち歌の一つで公演の幕を下ろした 反意 **start** (BEGIN)

stop (-pp-) [自、他] 終わる；終える、止める ◇When is this fighting going to *stop*? この戦いはいつ終わるのだろうか ◇The bus service *stops* at midnight. バスの運行は夜12時に終わります ◇Has it *stopped* raining yet? 雨はもうやみましたか ◇Doctors couldn't *stop* the bleeding. 医者は出血を止められなかった ◇The referee was forced to *stop* the game because of snow. 審判は降雪で試合を中止せざるをえなかった 反意 **start** (BEGIN)

terminate [自、他]《フォーマル》(協定・契約が)終了する、切れる；(協定・契約・妊娠を)終わらせる、打ち切る ◇Your contract of employment *terminates* in December. あなたの雇用契約は12月に切れます ◇to *terminate* a pregnancy (= to have an abortion) 中絶する

conclude [自、他]《フォーマル》終了する[させる] ◇Let me make just a few *concluding remarks*. 結びの言葉を少しだけ述べさせてください ◇The commission *concluded* its investigation last month. 委員会は先月調査を終えた

ノート **end, stop, finish, conclude の使い分け**：end は時間的に終わるものだけでなく空間的に終わるものにも用いることができる。◆The road *ends* here. (ここで道路は行き止まり)。end, finish, conclude は、特に終わると再開しないと思われるものについて用いられる。◆The war *ended* in 1945, after almost six years of fighting. (6年近い戦闘の末、1945年に戦争は終わった)。◆The concert should *finish* by 10 o'clock. (コンサートは10時までには終わるだろう)。◆She *concluded* her speech with a quotation from Shakespeare. (彼女はシェークスピアからの引用で演説を終えた)。finish と conclude は、特に終結したことを示す。finish はいつ終わるかについて、conclude はどう終わるかについて言うことが多い。stop は、再び始まる(可能性がある)こと、決して「完了」しえないことについて用いる。◆The rain *stopped* just long enough for us to have a quick walk in the park. (私たちがちょっと公園を散歩する間だけ雨がやんだ)。

close [他、自] (会議・調査などを)終わらせる、終える；(会議・売り出しなどが)終わる、終了する ◇Mr Hunt then *closed* the debate for the government. ハント氏はそこで政府擁護のための議論を終えた ◇A police spokesman said that the case was now *closed*. 警察のスポークスマンは事件はもう終結したと述べた ◇The offer *closes* at the end of the week. 売り出しは週末に終了します ❶事件・調査・問題が close されれば、それ以上の調査・議論は行われない。しかし、必ずしも、調査・議論中の事件・問題が解決したことを意味しない。単に解決する努力をやめる場合もある。反意 **open** (BEGIN), **open** (START 動)

,wind 'up, ,wind sth 'up 句動詞 (演説・会議などを)終わりにする ◇The speaker was just *winding up* when the door was flung open. 演説者が話を終えようというときにドアが勢いよく開いた ◇If we all agree, let's *wind up* the discussion. 全員が賛成なら議論を終了しましょう 反意 **kick off** (START 動)

endorsement 名

endorsement・recommendation・reference・testimonial
人や物事を支えること、人がある仕事に向くだろうと発言すること
【類語訳】支持、推薦、推薦状、証明書

文型&コロケーション
▶an endorsement/ a recommendation/ a reference/ a testimonial **from** sb
▶an endorsement/ a reference **for** sb/ sth
▶a **glowing** endorsement/ recommendation/ reference

testimonial
- a **written** reference/ testimonial
- a **personal** endorsement/ recommendation
- to **give/ get/ receive** an endorsement/ recommendation
- a **letter of** endorsement/ recommendation/ reference

endorsement [C, U] 支持, 是認；(有名人・有力者による製品の)推薦, 推奨 ◇The election victory is a clear *endorsement* of their policies. 選挙の勝利は彼らの政策への明らかな支持である ◇We are happy to give the product our full *endorsement*. 喜んでその製品を全面的に推薦しましょう ☞ **endorse** (RECOMMEND 2)

recommendation [U, C] 推薦, 推薦状 ◇We chose the hotel *on their recommendation*. 彼らの薦めでそのホテルを選びました ◇It's best to find a builder through personal *recommendation*. 個人の推薦で建築業者を見つけるのが一番だ ◇The new housekeeper *came on* the highest *recommendation*. 新しい家政婦は最大級の推薦を受けてやってきた ◇The company gave her a glowing *recommendation*. 会社は彼女にとても好意的な推薦状を書いてやった ☞ **recommend** (RECOMMEND 2), **advice** (ADVICE)

reference [C] (新しい雇用主に向けての)(人物)証明書, 推薦状 ◇You should supply a *reference* from your current employer. 現在の雇用主からの推薦状を用意した方がいい ◇We will *take up references* after the interview.《英》面接のあとで, 推薦状を見ます

> **ノート** **recommendation** と **reference** の使い分け：
> reference は, ある人が新しい仕事などに適していることを述べる手紙を指す一般的な語。書き手は元の雇用主, かつての教師のような社会的信用のある人で, その人物をよく知る人である。recommendation は, ふつう元の雇用主からのもので, 手紙または改まった陳述の形をとる。《米》では, 学生が recommendation letter を書いてもらうこともある。 ◆ a *recommendation letter* for an internship/a scholarship/college (実務研修/奨学金/大学入学のための推薦状)

testimonial [C] (能力・資質・性格・品質についての)証明(書), 推薦文 ◇Other *testimonials* to his character proved hard to come by. ほかに彼の性格を証明するものを手に入れるのは難しいことがわかった ◇The catalogue is full of *testimonials* from satisfied customers. カタログには満足した顧客からの推薦の辞がいっぱい載っている

enemy 名

enemy・competitor・rival・opponent・the opposition・the competition・foe・adversary
人や物と戦う[争う, 競い合う]人, グループ, 国家
【類語訳】敵, 競争相手, ライバル, 反意語

文型&コロケーション

- a competitor/ rival **for** sth
- **against** an enemy/ a competitor/ a rival/ an opponent/ the opposition/ the competition/ a foe/ an adversary
- the **main** enemy/ competitor/ rival/ opponent/ opposition/ competition/ adversary
- a **formidable/ worthy** enemy/ competitor/ rival/ opponent/ foe/ adversary
- an **old** enemy/ rival/ opponent/ foe/ adversary
- a **dangerous** enemy/ rival/ opponent/ foe/ adversary
- **bitter** enemies/ rivals/ opponents/ foes
- to **have** an enemy/ a competitor/ a rival/ an opponent/ a foe
- to **face** an enemy/ an opponent/ the opposition/ the competition/ a foe
- to **fight** an enemy/ an opponent/ the opposition/ a foe
- to **defeat** an enemy/ a rival/ the opposition/ a foe/ an adversary

enemy [C] 敵 ◇After just one day, she had already *made an enemy of* her manager. たった一日で, 彼女はすでに主任の反感を買っていた ◇They used to be friends but now they are *sworn enemies*. 彼らはかつては友人だったが, 今や不倶戴天の敵同士だ ◇Birds are the natural *enemies* of many insect pests. 鳥は多くの害虫の天敵である ❶ the enemy [単数+単数・複数動詞]は戦争の敵国, あるいはその軍隊。 ◆*The enemy* was forced to retreat. (敵軍は撤退を余儀なくされた)。 この意味で, enemy はしばしば, 他の名詞の前でも用いられる。(敵軍, 敵機)。 ◆ to go *behind enemy lines* (敵陣に入る)。 反意 **ally** (PARTNER 1), **friend** ❶自分と同じ利害関係・意見を持ち, 援助・支持してくれるような人が friend (味方)である。 ◆You're among *friends* here — you can speak freely. (ここにいるのはみな味方ですから―遠慮なく話してください)。

competitor [C] (ビジネスにおける)競争相手 ◇The company has no serious *competitors*. その会社には手ごわい競争相手はいない ☞ **compete** (COMPETE)

rival [C] (同じものを求め合う[同じ地域で競い合う])競争相手, ライバル ◇They were *rivals in* love. 彼らは恋敵だった ◇Grand it may be, but this cathedral is no *rival to* the great cathedral of Amiens. 確かにこの大聖堂は壮麗だが, 巨大なアミアンの大聖堂にはまったくかなわない ◇The Japanese are our biggest economic *rivals*. 日本人は我々にとって経済上の最大のライバルである
▶ **rival** 形 [名詞のみ] ◇a *rival* bid/claim/offer 競合する入札/要求/オファー ◇He was shot by a member of a *rival* gang. 彼は敵対するギャングの一員に撃たれた

opponent [C] 反対者；(政治・ビジネス・スポーツでの)敵 ◇As a man he was greatly respected, even by his political *opponents*. 人として, その敵愾にさえ大いに尊敬されていた ◇He drew his sword and turned to face his *opponent*. 彼は剣を抜き, 振り返って敵に相対した ☞ **oppose** (OPPOSE)

the opposition [単数+単数・複数動詞] (ビジネス・競技会・試合などでの)競争相手, ライバル ◇He's gone to work for *the opposition*. 彼はライバル会社に移籍してしまった

the competition [単数+単数・複数動詞] (ビジネス・スポーツでの)競争相手, ライバル ◇We'll be able to assess *the competition* at the conference. 会議ではライバルを値踏みできるだろう ☞ **compete** (COMPETE)

foe [C] 《古風, フォーマル》敵 ◇He knew that Burton could be an implacable *foe*. 彼はバートンが不倶戴天の敵となり得ることはわかっていた ◇She was unsure yet whether he was *friend or foe*. 彼女は彼が敵か味方かまだよくわからなかった 反意 **friend**

adversary [C] 《フォーマル》 (議論・戦闘での)敵, 反対者 ◇The two of them were old *adversaries*. 彼らのうち二人は昔からの敵同士だった

energetic 形 ☞ LIVELY

energetic・vigorous・active・dynamic・mobile

↳**energetic**

人や行為がエネルギーにあふれること
【類語訳】精力的な, 活発な, 元気な, 活動的な

文型&コロケーション
▸ an energetic/ an active/ a dynamic **person/ man/ woman**
▸ an energetic/ active **member** of sth
▸ a vigorous/ an active **supporter/ opponent** of sb/ sth
▸ an energetic/ a vigorous/ an active/ a dynamic **campaign**
▸ a vigorous/ an active **interest** in sth
▸ energetic/ vigorous **exercise**

energetic 精力的な, エネルギッシュな, 活発な ◇He knew I was *energetic* and would get things done. 彼は私が精力的に物事をやり遂げるだろうとわかっていた ◇The heart responds well to *energetic* exercise. 心臓は活発な運動によく反応する ◇For the more *energetic* (= people who prefer physical activities) we offer windsurfing and diving. もっとエネルギッシュな方には, ウインドサーフィンとダイビングをご用意しております
▸**energetically** ◇He strode out *energetically* towards the gate. 彼は門の方へ元気いっぱいに大またで出て行った

vigorous 精力的な, 活発な ◇They conducted a *vigorous* campaign against tax fraud. 彼らは精力的に脱税撲滅運動を展開した ◇Take *vigorous* exercise for several hours a week. 《英》週に数時間は活発な運動をしなさい 《反意》gentle (GENTLE)
▸**vigorously** ◇She shook her head *vigorously*. 彼女は勢いよく首を振った ◇The accusation was *vigorously* denied. その告発は断固として否定された

ノート energetic と vigorous の使い分け: どちらの語も使える場合がある. ◆ *energetic/vigorous* exercise (活発な運動). energetic は体力や身体活動についてよく用いられる. vigorous はしばしばビジネスや政治活動によく用いられる. vigorous man/woman は実にたくましくて健康な人のことであるが, vigorous が人に用いられる場合, 多くはビジネスや政治に従事する人たちに用いられる. ◆ a *vigorous* opponent/supporter/campaigner (精力的な対抗者/支持者/運動家).

active 元気な, 活発な, 活動的な ◇Although he's nearly 80, he is still very *active*. 彼はもう少しで80歳だが, いまだにとても元気だ ◇Before our modern age, people had a more physical and *active* lifestyle. 今より以前は, 人々はもっと体を使う活動的な生活をしていた ❶ active は特にいつも忙しくしている年配の人を表すのに用いられる. life や lifestyle と共に用いるのも一般的である. 何かに多くの時間と手間をかけている人を表すこともできる. ☞ **active** (BUSY 1)

dynamic 《ほめて》活動的な, 精力的な ◇She has a *dynamic* personality. 彼女は活動的な性格です ◇He was a *dynamic* young advertising executive. 彼は精力的な若い宣伝担当重役だった

mobile [名詞の前はまれ]（人が）動き回れる ◇The kitchen is specially designed for the elderly or people who are less *mobile*. そのキッチンは高齢者やあまり動けない人のために特別に設計されたものだ ◇You really need to be *mobile* (= have a car) if you live in the country. 田舎に住んでいると, 本当に車が必要になる
▸**mobility** [名] [U] ◇An electric wheelchair has given her greater *mobility*. 電動車椅子のおかげで彼女は移動しやすくなった

ensure, enter

ensure [動]

ensure・make sure・guarantee・assure・see to it that...
何かが起きるのを確かなものにする
【類語訳】確実にする, 確保する, 保証する

文型&コロケーション
▸ to ensure/ make sure/ guarantee/ see to it **that**...
▸ to ensure/ guarantee/ assure the **success/ survival/ quality** of sth
▸ to **absolutely** ensure/ guarantee/ assure sth
▸ to make **absolutely** sure
▸ to **virtually** ensure/ guarantee/ assure sth

ensure (または特に米で **insure**) [他, 自]《ややフォーマル》確実にする; 確かめる ◇The book *ensured* his success. その本で彼の成功が確実になった ◇Please *ensure* that all lights are switched off. 必ず明かりを全部消すようにしてください

make 'sure [フレーズ] 確実にする, 確かめる ◇*Make sure* (that) no one else finds out about this. 他の誰にも絶対にこのことを知られないようにしなさい ◇They scored another goal and *made sure of* victory. 彼らはもう1点取って勝利を確実なものにした

guarantee [他] 確実にする, 確保する ◇Tonight's victory *guarantees* the team's place in the final. 今夜の勝利でチームの決勝進出が確実になる ◇These days getting a degree doesn't *guarantee* you a job. 近頃では学位を取っても仕事は確保されない

assure [他] 確実にする ◇Victory would *assure* a place in the finals. 勝利によって決勝進出が確実になるだろう ◇This achievement has *assured* her a place in the history books. 彼女はこの業績で確実に歴史に名を残すことになった

ノート ensure, guarantee, assure の使い分け: ensure はしばしば, 命令や指図で用いられる. ✕Please *guarantee/assure* that all lights are switched off. assure と guarantee は何かに対する不安や疑念が取り除かれることを示す. guarantee はしばしば, 不安や疑念が取り除かれることを示す否定文で用いられるが, assure はそうでない. ✕Getting a degree doesn't *assure* you a job.

'see to it that... [フレーズ] 確実にする ◇Can you *see to it that* the fax goes this afternoon? 今日の午後に確実にファックスが送信できるようにしてもらえますか

enter [動]

enter・go in/go into sth・come in/come into sth・set foot in/on sth
場所の中の方に移動する
【類語訳】入る

文型&コロケーション
▸ to enter/ go in/ come in **by/ through** sth
▸ to enter/ go into/ come into/ set foot in a **room/ building/ country/ town**

enter [自, 他]《受身はまれ》《フォーマル》入る ◇I knocked and a bored voice said, '*Enter*'. ノックすると, 「お入り」

entertainment, environment

と退屈しきった声がした ◇*Enter* Hamlet and three of the players (= used in the text of a play to say who should go onto the stage). ハムレットと3人の役者が登場 ◇He was refused permission to *enter* the country. 彼は入国許可を得られなかった ◇Where did the bullet *enter* the body? 弾は体のどこに貫通したのですか 反意 **exit, leave** (LEAVE 1), ☞ **entrance** (ARRIVAL), **entry** (ACCESS)

,go 'in, ,go 'into sth 句動詞 （建物・部屋に）入る ◇It's getting cold. Let's *go in*. 寒くなってきた。中に入ろう ◇They *went into* the kitchen. 彼らは台所へ入った ◇Don't *go in* there — it could be dangerous. そこに入っちゃダメだ—危険かもしれない ◇Troops *went in* (= to a city or region) to restore order. 秩序を回復するために軍隊が突入した

,come 'in, ,come 'into sth 句動詞 （建物・部屋に）入る ◇Tell her to *come in*. 彼女に入るように言って ◇I knocked at the door and he shouted, 'Come in!' ドアをノックすると、彼は「どうぞ」と大声をあげた ◇Two more customers *came into* the shop. さらに二人の客が店に入ってきた ☞ **come** (GO 2)

ノート **go in** と **come in** の使い分け：go in は移動している人の視点で用いる。come in は人の移動先にすでにいる人の視点で用いる。

set 'foot in/on sth 句動 入る, 行く ◇I vowed never to *set foot in* the place again. そこへは二度と行かないと誓った ◇He was the first person to *set foot on* the moon. 彼は月面に初めて足を踏み入れた人だった

entertainment 名

entertainment・fun・recreation・relaxation・play・pleasure・amusement
仕事をしていない時に人を楽しませる物事や活動
【類語訳】楽しみ，娯楽，冗談，気晴らし，遊び

文型&コロケーション
▶ to do sth **for** entertainment/ fun/ recreation/ relaxation/ pleasure/ amusement
▶ to do sth **for sb's** entertainment/ amusement
▶ **pure** entertainment/ fun/ pleasure
▶ to **provide** entertainment/ fun/ recreation/ relaxation/ amusement
▶ a **form of** entertainment/ recreation/ relaxation/ amusement

entertainment [U] (映画・テレビ・音楽などの)楽しみ，娯楽 ◇There are three bars, with *live entertainment* seven nights a week. バーが3つあり、毎晩ライブが楽しめる ◇There was no TV or radio so we had to make our own *entertainment* (for example by playing games). テレビもラジオもなかったので，自分たちで楽しみをつくらなければならなかった ◇The stories will be judged purely on their *entertainment value*. ストーリーは純粋に娯楽性のみによって審査される
fun [U]《ややインフォーマル》楽しみ，冗談，おふざけ ◇She's very lively and *full of fun*. 彼女はとても快活ですごくおもしろい ◇It wasn't serious — it was all done *in fun*. 本気じゃなかったんだよ—みんな冗談でやってたんだ ◇Teaching isn't all *fun and games*, you know. 教えるというのは楽しいばかりではないんだ，わかるよね ❶ fun はしばしば

定型句で危ない[ばかばかしい]と思われかねない行為を擁護しようとする際に用いられる。◆The lottery provides *harmless fun* for millions. (宝くじはたくさんの人に罪のない楽しみを与える)。◆We didn't mean to hurt him. It was just *a bit of fun*. (《英》彼を傷つけるつもりはなかった。ちょっとふざけただけだったんだ)。☞ **have fun** (PLAY 動 1)
recreation [U]《ややフォーマル》気晴らし，娯楽 ◇She cycles for *recreation*. 彼女は気晴らしに自転車に乗る ◇His only form of *recreation* is playing cards. 彼の唯一の気晴らしの方法はトランプ遊びです
▷ **recreational** 形 ◇*recreational* activities/facilities 娯楽活動/施設
relaxation [U]《ややフォーマル》息抜き，気晴らし ◇I go hillwalking for *relaxation*. 息抜きに山歩きに行きます ◇a chance for *relaxation from* work 仕事の息抜きをする機会 ◇It's a good idea to learn some *relaxation* techniques. リラックスの方法を身につけるのはいいことだ ☞ **relax** (REST)

ノート **recreation** と **relaxation** の使い分け：どちらの単語も広範囲の身体的・精神的活動に用いることができるが、**relaxation** は特に **recreation** より穏やかな活動に用いる。◆I play the flute in a wind band for *recreation*. (気晴らしに吹奏楽団でフルートを演奏します)。◆I listen to music for *relaxation*. (気晴らしに音楽を聴きます)。**relaxation** は楽しみばかりでなく技能にも適用されるが、**recreation** はそうではない。× *recreation* techniques.

play [U] (子どもの)遊び ◇the happy sounds of children *at play* 遊んでいる子どもたちの楽しそうな声 ◇the importance of learning through *play* 遊びを通じて学ぶことの重要性 ☞ **play** (PLAY 動 1)
pleasure [U] (仕事に対する)遊び ◇Are you in Paris *on business or pleasure*? パリへはお仕事ですか、遊びですか ◇I never *mix business with pleasure*. 仕事と遊びは決して混同しません 反意 **business** (TASK)
amusement [U]《ややフォーマル》娯楽，気晴らし ◇What do you do for *amusement* around here? このあたりは娯楽と言えば何ですか ◇I write purely *for my own amusement*. I don't expect to make money out of it. ただ自分の気晴らしで物を書いています。それで金儲けできるとは思っていません

environment 名

environment・setting・surroundings・background・backdrop
人や物が存在[位置]する場所
【類語訳】環境，周囲，背景

文型&コロケーション
▶ **in** an environment/ a setting/ surroundings
▶ **against** a/ the background/ backdrop (of sth)
▶ (a/ an) **attractive/ perfect** environment/ setting/ surroundings/ background/ backdrop
▶ (a/ an) **pleasant/ idyllic** environment/ setting/ surroundings
▶ (a) **beautiful** setting/ surroundings/ backdrop
▶ a **dramatic** setting/ background/ backdrop
▶ (a) **peaceful** environment/ setting/ surroundings
▶ (a/ an) **new/ unfamiliar** environment/ setting/ surroundings
▶ sb/ sth's **immediate** environment/ surroundings

- (a) **rural** environment/ setting/ surroundings/ backdrop
- the/ sb's/ sth's **natural** environment/ setting/ surroundings/ backdrop
- to **provide/ create** an environment/ a setting/ surroundings/ a background/ a backdrop
- to **adapt to/ blend in with** your/ the environment/ surroundings

environment [C] (何らかの影響を与える)環境 ◇For many, school seemed to be a hostile *environment*. 多くの者にとって、学校は敵意にあふれた環境に思えた ◇An unhappy *home environment* can affect children's behaviour. 不幸な家庭環境は子どもの行動に影響を与える可能性がある ◇We aim to provide a pleasant *working environment*. 私たちは心地よい職場環境を提供することを目指しています ☞ milieu (CONTEXT)

setting [C] (特定の)環境 ◇It was the perfect *setting* for a wonderful celebration. 素晴らしい祝典には申し分のない環境だった ◇People behave differently in different social *settings*. 人は異なる社会環境では異なる行動をとる

surroundings [複数で] 周囲(の状況)、環境 ◇His paintings try to capture the beauty of the *surroundings*. 彼の絵画は周囲の美しさをとらえようとしている ◇She was not aware of her *surroundings* for a while. 彼女はしばらくの間、周囲の状況に気づかなかった

background [C, ふつう単数で] (場所・写真などでの中心的な物・人の後ろ[周り]にある)背景 ◇The mountains in the *background* were capped with snow. 背景の山々は雪をかぶっていた ◇The areas of water stand out against the dark *background*. 水域は暗い背景を背にくっきり見える ☞ 反意 **the foreground**

backdrop [C, ふつう単数で] (書き言葉) (事件の[場所の中心的な物の後ろにある])背景 ◇The events took place against the dramatic *backdrop* of the Atlas mountains. 事件は壮大なアトラス山脈を背景に発生した ◇White walls provide the perfect *backdrop* for wooden furniture. 白壁が木製の家具の見事な背景となっている

equal 形

equal・the same・identical・uniform・synonymous・homogeneous・indistinguishable・tantamount to sth・interchangeable
物事の大きさ[量、価値]が同一であることを表す
【類語訳】同じ、等しい、そっくりの、一様な、同義の、均質な

〖文型&コロケーション〗
- equal/ identical/ tantamount **to** sth
- identical/ synonymous/ interchangeable **with** sth
- to **become** equal/ synonymous/ homogeneous/ indistinguishable/ interchangeable
- **exactly** equal/ the same/ identical/ synonymous
- **almost** equal/ the same/ identical/ uniform/ synonymous/ indistinguishable/ interchangeable
- **apparently** the same/ identical/ uniform/ homogeneous
- **roughly** equal/ the same/ synonymous

equal (大きさ・量・価値などが)同じ、等しい ◇There is an *equal* number of boys and girls in the class. クラスは男女同数である ◇Take two pieces of wood of *equal* length. 同じ長さの材木を2本選んでください ◇Cut it into four *equal* parts. それを4等分に切ってください ◇One unit of alcohol is *equal* to half a pint of beer. アルコール1単位量はビール半パイント分に相当する ◇The two books are more or less *equal in* length. その2冊の本はほぼ同じ長さだ 反意 **unequal (DIFFERENT)**

▶ **equally** 副 ◇The money was divided *equally* among her four children. お金は彼女の4人の子どもたちの間で等分された ◇They share the housework *equally*. 彼らは家事を平等にしている

the same (触れられている物事と)同じ ◇I bought *the same* car as yours (= another car of that type). 君のと同じ車を買ったよ ◇She was wearing *the same* dress that I had on. 彼女は私が着ていたのと同じドレスを着ていた ◇*The same* thing happened to me last week. 私にも先週同じことがありました 反意 **different (DIFFERENT)**

identical (細部に至るまで)まったく同じの、そっくりの ◇I came to a row of *identical* houses. そっくりの家が一列に立ち並ぶ場所にやってきた ◇The two pictures are similar, although not *identical*. 2枚の絵はまったく同じではないが似ている ◇The number on the card should be *identical* with the one on the cheque book. カードの数字は小切手帳の数字と一致していなければならない

▶ **identically** 副 ◇The children were dressed *identically*. 子どもたちはまったく同じ服装をしていた

uniform (すべての部分が)同じ、一様な、一律の ◇The walls were a *uniform* grey. 壁は一様に灰色だった ◇Growth has not been *uniform* across the country. 成長は全国一律に進んでいない ☞ **uniformity (SIMILARITY)**

▶ **uniformly** 副 ◇The principles were applied *uniformly* across all the departments. 原則は全部門に一律に適用された ◇The quality is *uniformly* high. 質は一様に高い

synonymous (ややフォーマル)(単語・表現が(ほぼ)同じ意味の、同義の ◇Few words are truly *synonymous*. 全く同義の単語は少ない ◇Wealth is not necessarily *synonymous* with happiness. 富は必ずしも幸福と同義ではない

homogeneous (フォーマル)均質な、一様な ◇Old people are not a *homogeneous* group, as some people seem to think. そう考える人もいるようだが、高齢者は均質な集団ではない ◇We no longer live in a culturally *homogeneous* society. 私たちはもはや文化的に均質な社会に暮らしてはいない 反意 **heterogeneous (DIVERSE)**

indistinguishable (ややフォーマル)(二つの物が)区別がつかない ◇The male of the species is almost *indistinguishable from* the female. その種の雄は、雌とほとんど区別がつかない ◇The two parties' policies are almost *indistinguishable*. その二つの政党の政策にはほとんど差がない 反意 **distinguishable**

'tantamount to sth フレーズ (書き言葉)(悪い結果になる点で)…に等しい ◇If he resigned it would be *tantamount to* admitting that he was guilty. 彼が辞任するなら、自分が有罪だと認めるに等しいだろう ❶ tantamountは通例 crime, declaration of war, cruelty, killing, stealing, treachery, treasonといった名詞と結びつく

interchangeable (ややフォーマル)交換可能な、互換性のある ◇The two words are virtually *interchangeable* (= have almost the same meaning). その2語は実質的に交換可能である ◇The V8 engines are all *interchangeable* with each other. V8エンジンはすべて互換性がある

▶ **interchangeably** 副 ◇These terms are used *interchangeably*. これらの用語は互いに入れ替えて用いられる

equip, equipment

equip 動

equip・arm・stock・outfit・fit sb/sth out・provision・kit sb/sth out

目的[活動]に必要な物を人[物,自分自身]に与えることを表す
【類語訳】装備させる、武装する[させる]、備え付ける

文型&コロケーション

- to equip sb/ sth/ arm sb/ stock sth/ fit sb/ sth out/ provision/ kit sb out **with** sth
- to equip/ arm **yourself**
- to equip/ outfit/ fit out/ provision a **ship**
- to equip/ arm **soldiers**
- to equip/ provision an **army**
- to be **well** equipped/ armed/ stocked/ provisioned
- to be **fully/ properly/ poorly** equipped/ armed/ stocked

equip (-pp-) [他]《ややフォーマル》(特定の目的・活動に必要な物を)備え付ける、装備[携帯]させる ◇She got a bank loan to rent and *equip* a small workshop. 小さな作業場を賃借して装置を取りつけるために彼女は銀行ローンを借りた ◇He *equipped* himself with a street plan. 彼は市街地図を携行した ◇We travelled in a specially *equipped* medical jeep. 我々は特別装備の医療用ジープで移動した ◇The centre is well *equipped for* canoeing and mountaineering. そのセンターはカヌーと登山のための装備が充実している

arm [他, 自] (戦闘・戦争のため)武装させる[する] ◇The crowd *armed* themselves with sticks and stones. 群衆は棒や石で武装した ◇The country was *arming* against the enemy. その国は敵国に対して武装を進めていた

stock [他, しばしば受身で] (食料・書籍・植物・魚などを)(仕)入れる、蓄える、在庫として置く ◇The pond was well *stocked* with fish. 池には魚がたくさんいた ◇The college has a well-*stocked* library. 大学には蔵書の充実した図書館がある ❶(well) stocked は通例、garden/pond/shop/library/fridge などに用いられる。☞**stock** (SUPPLY)

outfit (-tt-) [他, しばしば受身で] (特に米)(特別の目的のために人・物に)装備[衣類]を与える ◇The ship was *outfitted* with a 12-bed hospital. 船は10床の病室を備えていた ◇They had enough swords and suits of armour to *outfit* an army. 彼らには一つの軍隊を武装させるのに十分な剣と甲冑があった ❶outfit はしばしば、船・兵士・スポーツ選手に装備を与える場合に用いられる。

,fit sb/sth 'out (-tt-) [他, しばしば受身で]《英》(人・物に必要な物を)備え付ける ◇It was their job to *fit out* ships before long voyages. 長い航海の前に艤装するのが彼らの仕事だった ◇The room has been *fitted out* with a stove and a sink. 部屋にはレンジと流しが備え付けられている ❶fit out はふつう部屋・家・乗り物に用いられる。

provision [他, しばしば受身で]《フォーマル》(ある期間持ちこたえるのに十分な)食糧を供給する ◇The main business of the port is to *provision* passing ocean liners. その港の主要な務めは、そこを通る遠洋定期船に食糧を供給することである ❶provision はふつう、船への食糧供給について用いられるが、都市・軍隊など人の集団への食糧供給についても用いることができる。

,kit sb/sth 'out 句動詞 (-tt-) 《ふつう受身で》《英、ややインフォーマル》(特定の活動用の)服[服装]を与える ◇They were all *kitted out in* brand new ski outfits. 彼らはみな新品のスキーウエアを身につけていた ◇The London stu-dio is lavishly *kitted out* with six cameras. ロンドンのスタジオはぜいたくにも6台のカメラを備えている ❶kit sb/sth out with＋装備、kit sb out in＋服装、の形で用いられる。

equipment 名 ☞ THING 2

equipment・material・gear・kit・apparatus・hardware・tackle

特定の目的や活動に必要な物
【類語訳】装備、装置、用品、用具、道具、セット

文型&コロケーション

- **basic** equipment/ materials/ kit/ apparatus/ hardware
- **state-of-the-art/ up-to-date/ the latest** equipment/ gear/ kit/ hardware
- **electronic/ electrical** equipment/ gear/ apparatus/ hardware
- **laboratory** equipment/ apparatus/ hardware
- to **have** the right equipment/ materials/ gear/ kit/ apparatus/ hardware
- to **use** the equipment/ materials/ gear/ kit/ apparatus/ hardware
- a **piece of** equipment/ apparatus

equipment [U] 装備、装置、用品 ◇We loaded the camping *equipment* into the car. 私たちはキャンプ用品を車に積み込んだ ◇The plane uses state-of-the-art navigation *equipment*. その飛行機は最新式の航法装置を用いている

material [C, ふつう複数で, U] 用品、道具 ◇You have to buy your own art *materials*. 自分の美術用具は自分で買わなければならない ◇Many household cleaning *materials* are highly toxic. 多くの家庭用洗剤は毒性が強い ◇We usually produce our own teaching *material*. 本校ではふだん教材は独自に作っています

> **ノート** equipment と material の使い分け：equipment はふつう固形物で、特に大きな物. material は小さい固形物だけでなく、液体や粉末、書物、情報の入ったテープの場合もある.

gear [U] 用具、道具 ◇Skiing *gear* can be expensive. スキー用具は高くつくことがある ☞**gear** (CLOTHES)

kit [C, U] 道具[備品]一式、セット ◇a first-aid *kit* 応急処置セット[救急箱] ◇a tool *kit* 工具セット ◇a wine-making *kit* ワイン醸造道具一式 ◇They left most of their *kit* at the camp. 彼らはキャンプ地に用具のほとんどを置いてきた ❶《英》では、kit は特定の活動で着用する「衣類」を指す場合もある。

apparatus [U] 装置、機器 ◇The firefighters had to use breathing *apparatus*. 消防士たちは呼吸装置を使わなければならなかった ◇Science departments say they are lacking basic *apparatus*. 科学部門では基本的な機器が不足していると言っている ❶apparatus は特に科学、医学、技術のものである。

hardware [U] (家庭・庭用の道具・備品である)金物 ◇a *hardware* store 金物店 ❶hardware はこの意味ではふつう、こうした備品を売買する店に関して用いられる。また、兵器などの軍事装備・車両も指す。◆The cargo consisted entirely of military *hardware* — rifles, machine guns, hand grenades and rockets. 《専門語》貨物はライフル、機関銃、手榴弾、ロケット弾といった兵器類ばかりだった。

tackle [U] (釣り)道具 ◇You can hire bait and *fishing tackle* from the outdoor centre. アウトドア用品店で餌と釣り道具を賃借できます

equivalent 形 ☞ RELATIVE

equivalent・comparable・corresponding・matching・analogous
物事が価値[数量, 意味, 重要性など]の点で同じであること
【類語訳】等しい, 同等の, 類似の, 匹敵する, 相応の, おそろしの, 似ている

文型&コロケーション
▶ equivalent/ comparable/ corresponding/ analogous **to** sth
▶ comparable/ analogous **with** sth
▶ equivalent/ comparable **in** size, amount, etc.
▶ an equivalent/ a comparable/ a corresponding **increase**
▶ an equivalent/ a comparable **size/ amount/ proportion**
▶ **broadly/ roughly/ directly** equivalent/ comparable/ analogous
▶ **exactly** equivalent/ comparable/ matching/ analogous
▶ **closely** equivalent/ comparable/ analogous

equivalent 〈ややフォーマル〉 (価値・数量・意味・重要性等)等しい, 同等の ◇Eight kilometres is roughly *equivalent* to five miles. 8キロメートルは5マイルにほぼ等しい ◇You'll need 250 grams or an *equivalent* amount in ounces. 250グラム, またはオンスで同等の量が必要となります ◇The new regulation was seen as *equivalent* to censorship. 新たな規制は検閲に等しいと見なされた ☞ **equivalence** (SIMILARITY)

comparable 〈ややフォーマル〉 対比[比較]できる, 類似の, 匹敵する ◇A *comparable* house in the south of the city would cost twice as much. 市の南部では類似の住宅は価格が2倍するだろう ◇Inflation is now at a rate *comparable* with that in other European countries. 現在のインフレ率は, 他のヨーロッパ諸国のものに匹敵する ◇The situation in the US is not directly *comparable* to that in the UK. 米国の状況は, 英国の状況と直接比較できるものではない ❶ comparable は《米》ではそれほどフォーマルな語ではない ☞ **compare** (COMPARE 2)

corresponding 〈ややフォーマル〉対応した, 相応の ◇A change in the money supply brings a *corresponding* change in expenditure. 通貨供給量の変化は支出において相応の変化をもたらす ◇Profits have risen by 15 per cent compared with the *corresponding* period last year. 利益は昨年同期に比べて15%増加した ◇Give each picture a number *corresponding* to its position on the page. 写真それぞれに, ページ上の位置に対応した番号をつけなさい ☞ **correspond** (MATCH 1), **correspondence** (SIMILARITY)
➤ **correspondingly** 副 ◇a period of high demand and *correspondingly* high prices 高い需要とそれに相応した高い価格の時期

matching [名詞の前で] (衣類・生地・物体の色[模様, 型]が同じで)おそろいの, 釣り合った ◇We got a pine table with four *matching* chairs for only £240. マツ材のテーブルとおそろいの椅子4脚をたった240ポンドで手に入れた ☞ **match** (MATCH 2)

analogous 〈フォーマル〉 (ある点で)対比可能な, 似ている ◇Sleep has often been thought of as being in some way *analogous* to death. 眠りはしばしば, ある意味で死に似ていると考えられてきた

ノート **comparable** と **analogous** の使い分け : comparable は同じ種類の物が比較可能ということから, 類似点や相違点を見るために比較している. analogous はふつう, 種類の違うものがある点で類似していることから, どの点で似ているかを示すために比較している.

escape 動

escape・get away・elude・evade・lose
追跡の手や脅威となる危険な状況から離れることを表す
【類語訳】逃れる, 逃げる, 回避する, 避ける, 免れる

文型&コロケーション
▶ to escape/ get away **from** sb/ sth
▶ to escape/ evade **being** captured, hit, killed, etc.
▶ to escape/ get away from/ elude/ evade/ lose your **pursuers**
▶ to escape/ elude/ evade **capture/ detection/ the police**
▶ to escape/ evade **arrest**
▶ to **manage to** escape sb/ get away from sb/ elude sb/ evade sb

escape (自, 他, 受身なし) (嫌な[危険な]状況・出来事から)逃れる, 逃げる, 免れる;(まったく[思っていたほど]害を被らずに)済む ◇She managed to *escape* from the burning car. 彼女は燃えている車からやっとのことで脱出した ◇As a child he would often *escape* into a dream world of his own. (比喩的)子どもの頃, 彼はしばしば自分の夢の世界へ逃げ込んだものだった ◇There was no *escaping* the fact that he was overweight. 彼が太りすぎだということとは逃れようもない事実だった ◇The police will not *escape* criticism in this affair. この事件では警察は非難を免れないだろう ◇She managed to *escape* the fate of the other rebels. 彼女はどうにか他の反逆者と同じ目に遭わずに済んだ ◇The pilot *escaped* death by seconds. パイロットは数秒の差で命拾いした ◇He *narrowly escaped* being killed. 彼はかろうじて殺されずに済んだ ◇She only just *escaped* with her life. 彼女はやっとのことで命からがら逃げた ◇Both drivers *escaped unhurt*. どちらの運転手も無傷で済んだ ❶捕まること・罰せられることを「免れる」のを escape で表せる. ◆ to *escape* detection/capture/ arrest/justice/prosecution/conviction/punishment/ prison (発覚/捕縛/逮捕/法の裁き/起訴/有罪/刑罰/投獄を免れる). *escape* prison は「投獄を免れる」を意味し, 投獄されてから「脱獄する」は escape from prison なので注意. 殺害・負傷を免れることも escape で表せる. ◆ to *escape* death/assassination/the massacre/drowning/injury/ being hit/the fighting (死/暗殺/大量虐殺/溺死/けが/殴打/殴り合いを免れる). 何かの責任を免れることを escape で表せる. ◆ to *escape* blame/censure/criticism/sb's wrath (責任/非難/批判/人の憤りを免れる). また, fate (運命)や destiny (宿命), bankruptcy (破産)や recession (不況)といった重大問題を免れることにも用いられる. 特に only just (やっとのことで), narrowly (かろうじて)と共に用いられたり, lucky to escapeの形で用いられたりする.
➤ **escape** 名 [C, U] ◇I had a *narrow escape* (= I was lucky to have escaped). 間一髪で助かった ◇There was no hope of *escape* from her disastrous marriage. 彼女が悲惨な結婚生活から逃れられる見込みはなかった ◇As soon as he turned his back, she would *make her*

escape. 彼が背中を向けるとすぐに, 彼女は逃げ出そうとした
▸**get a'way** 自動詞 (人・場所・状況から)逃れる, 逃げる ◇He felt that he had to *get away* from home, away from his parents and their efforts to rule his life. 家, 両親, そして両親が彼の人生を支配しようとすることから逃れなければならないと彼は感じた ◇You'd better *get away* — the soldiers are coming. 逃げた方がいい—兵隊たちがやってくる
▸**getaway** 名 [C, ふつう単数で] ◇We'll have to *make a quick getaway*. すぐに逃げなければならないだろう ◇a *get-away* car 逃走車

elude [他] 《ややフォーマル》回避する, うまく逃れる ◇The two men managed to *elude* the police for six weeks. 6週間の間, 二人の男は何とか警察の手を逃れた ◇How did the killer *elude* detection for so long? 殺人犯はどうやってそんなに長い間発覚を免れたのですか

evade [他] 《ややフォーマル》回避する, 逃れる ◇For two weeks they *evaded* the press. 彼らは2週間報道陣から逃れた ◇He managed to *evade* capture. 彼は何とか逮捕を免れた

📝 **elude** と **evade** の使い分け：多くの場合どちらの語も用いることができる。◆ to *elude/evade* detection/capture/the police/your pursuers (発覚/逮捕/警察/追っ手を逃れる). elude は, 捕まるのを避けるのに必要な巧みさ・賢さを強調する. evade は単に捕まらない事実を強調する.

lose [他] (追っ手から[を])逃れる[まく] ◇We managed to *lose* our pursuers in the darkness. 暗闇の中, 何とか追っ手をまいた

essential 形 ☞ IMPORTANT, NECESSARY

essential・vital・crucial・critical・decisive・indispensable・imperative・pivotal・of the essence
特定の状況や活動が左右されるほど, 非常に大切[絶対に必要]であることを表す
【類語訳】きわめて重要な, 不可欠の, 必須の, 肝心の, 決定的な

文型&コロケーション
▸essential/ vital/ crucial/ critical/ decisive/ indispensable/ imperative/ of the essence **for** sth
▸essential/ vital/ crucial/ critical/ indispensable/ pivotal **to** sth
▸to be essential/ vital/ crucial/ critical/ imperative **that**...
▸to be essential/ vital/ crucial/ critical/ imperative **to do** sth
▸an essential/ a vital/ a crucial/ a critical/ a decisive/ an indispensable/ a pivotal **part/ factor**
▸an essential/ a vital/ a crucial/ a critical/ an indispensable **ingredient/ tool**
▸an essential/ a vital/ a crucial/ a critical **component**
▸essential/ vital/ crucial **services**
▸the crucial/ critical/ decisive/ pivotal **moment**
▸to **play** an essential/ a vital/ a crucial/ a critical/ a decisive/ a pivotal **part/ role** in sth
▸of crucial/ critical/ decisive **importance**
▸**absolutely** essential/ vital/ crucial/ critical/ decisive/ indispensable/ imperative/ pivotal
▸**quite** essential/ vital/ crucial/ critical/ decisive/ indispensable

essential 絶対に必要な, 不可欠な, 必須の ◇Experience is *essential* for this job. この仕事には経験が不可欠だ ◇Money is not *essential* to happiness. お金は幸せに絶対に必要というわけではない ◇It is *essential* that you have some experience. あなたにいくらか経験があることが必須である ◇It is *essential* to keep the two groups separate. 二つのグループを別々にしておくことが不可欠です ◇The museum is closed while *essential* repairs are being carried out. 重要な修復作業が行われる間, 博物館は休館します 反意 **inessential** ❶ *inessential* は「必要でない」こと. ◆ *inessential* luxuries (不必要なぜいたく品).
☞ **essential** (NEED 名)

vital 不可欠な, 必須の, きわめて重要な ◇Bean sprouts contain many of the vitamins that are *vital* for health. 豆もやしは健康に不可欠なビタミンの多くを含む ◇Good financial accounts are *vital* to the success of any enterprise. 健全な財政状態はどんな企業の成功にも必須である ◇It is *vital* that you keep accurate records when you are self-employed. 自営の場合, 正確な記録をつけておくことがきわめて重要である ◇The police play a *vital* role in our society. 警察は私たちの社会で不可欠な役割を果たしている
▸**vitally** 副 ◇Education is *vitally important* for the country's future. 教育は国の将来にきわめて重要である

📝 **essential** と **vital** の使い分け：2語の間に実質的な意味の違いはなく, 用いる名詞や構文も同じである. しかし, ニュアンスにわずかな違いがある. essential は威厳を持って事実や意見を述べる場合に用いられる. vital は, ある物事に不安がある場合, あるいは事実や意見が本当に[正しい, 重要だ]と人に説得する必要がある場合にしばしば用いられる. vital は否定文ではあまり用いられない. ◆ It was *vital* to show that he was not afraid. (彼が恐れていないことを示すことが肝要だった). ✗ Money is not *vital* to happiness.

crucial (特定の状況・活動が左右されるので)きわめて重要な, 肝心な ◇Winning this contract is absolutely *crucial* to our long term success. この契約を獲得することは我々の長期的な成功にきわめて重要である ◇It is *crucial* that we get this right. このことを正しく理解することが非常に重要です ◇He wasn't there at the *crucial* moment (= when he was needed most). 肝心なときに彼はそこにいなかった
▸**crucially** 副 ◇These things are all *crucially* important. これらのことはみなきわめて重要である

critical きわめて重要な, 決定的な ◇Price and availability are the *critical* factors that will determine product success. 価格と入手のしやすさは製品の成功を左右する決定的な要因である ◇If the temperature drops those *critical* two degrees, the engine will stop functioning. 温度がその境目となる2度下がると, エンジンは動かなくなる
▸**critically** 副 ◇The next few days will be *critically* important to the President's election chances. これからの数日間は大統領選挙での勝利にとってきわめて重要になるでしょう

📝 **crucial** と **critical** の使い分け：2語の間に実質的な意味の違いはなく, 用いる名詞や構文も同じである. しかし, 文脈にわずかな違いがある. critical は主にビジネスや科学の専門的な事柄に用いられるのに対して, crucial は不安などの感情を引き起こす事柄について用いられる.

essential — establish, estimate

decisive (最終結果に影響する上で)最も重要な、決定的な、決め手になる ◇Gettysburg was the *decisive* battle of the Civil War. ゲティスバーグは南北戦争の勝敗を決する戦いだった ◇Signing the treaty was a *decisive* step (= an important action that will change a situation) towards a cleaner environment. その条約の調印はよりクリーンな環境に向けての決定的な一歩だった ❶*decisive* は単に「非常に重要な」を意味するだけではない。×Reducing levels of carbon dioxide in the atmosphere is of *decisive* importance. ある人や物事が過去や将来の特定の状況の結果に最も重要な影響を与えると判断されるときに用いられる。◆Morrison scored the *decisive* goal in the 75th minute of the game. (モリソンは試合開始75分に決定的な得点を挙げた)

➤**decisively** 副 ◇The governing party is expected to win *decisively* in the elections. 与党は選挙で決定的な勝利を収めると見られている

indispensable 不可欠な;(非常に重要で)なくてはならない ◇Cars have become an *indispensable* part of our lives. 車は私たちの生活に不可欠なものとなった ◇She made herself virtually *indispensable* to the department. 彼女は事実上その部門になくてはならない存在になった 反意 **dispensable** ❶*dispensable* なものは、なくて済むものであり取り除くことができる。◆They looked on music and art lessons as *dispensable*. (彼らは音楽と美術の授業をなくてもいいとみなしていた)

imperative [名詞の前まれ]《フォーマル》絶対に必要な、緊急の ◇It is absolutely *imperative* that we finish by next week. 来週までに終えることが絶対に必要だ

pivotal 《ややフォーマル, 特に書き言葉》きわめて重要な ◇The Foreign Secretary has played a *pivotal* role in European affairs. 外務大臣はヨーロッパ情勢においてきわめて重要な役割を果たしてきた ◇Accountancy, law and economics are *pivotal* to a successful career in any financial services area. 会計, 法律, 経済学は金融サービス分野での仕事を成功させるにはきわめて重要です ❶*pivotal* は特定の状況で人・物事が果たす「非常に重要な」役割を表すのに用いられる。単に「非常に重要な」項目・行動を表すのには用いない。×*pivotal* services/supplies/repairs. ×It is *pivotal* that we get this right.

of the 'essence フレーズ 《ややインフォーマル》不可欠な、きわめて重要な ◇In this situation **time is of the essence** (= we must do things as quickly as possible). この状況では、時間はきわめて重要です ◇Speed is *of the essence* when transporting casualties to hospital. 負傷者を病院へ搬送する際、スピードがきわめて重要だ

establish 動 ☞ BEGIN

establish・set sth up・form・found
組織[体制]を始める[つくり出す]
【類語訳】創設する、築く、設立する、樹立する

文型&コロケーション
▸ to establish/ set up/ form/ found a/ an **group/ society/ club/ party/ company/ institute/ movement/ colony/ republic**
▸ to establish/ set up/ form a/ an **relationship/ partnership/ alliance/ government/ committee/ team/ network/ database**
▸ to establish/ set up/ found a **business/ firm/ programme**
▸ to establish/ set up a/ an **fund/ initiative/ project/ scheme/ procedure/ monopoly/ regime/ monarchy**
▸ to establish/ found a/ an **dynasty/ empire/ church**

establish [他]《ややフォーマル, 特に書き言葉》(長期にわたって存続することを意識して)創設する;(正式な関係を)築く ◇The new treaty *establishes* a free trade zone. 新条約は自由貿易圏を創設する ◇Let's *establish* some ground rules. いくつか基本原則を打ち立てましょう ◇The school has *established* a successful relationship with the local community. 学校は地域社会と良好な関係を築いている

,set sth 'up 句動詞 (組織・体制などを)始める[創設する] ◇I'm planning to *set up* my own business. 自分で商売を始めるつもりです ◇A fund will be *set up* for the dead men's families. 故人の遺族のために基金が創設されるだろう ◇The company has *set up* its European headquarters in the UK. その会社はイギリスにヨーロッパ本部を設立した ❶*set sth up* は商売を始めたり、金融の仕組みを整えたりする場合にしばしば用いられる。◆to *set up* a business/a company/a firm/a fund/ a project/a scheme/a venture/an initiative/a monopoly/a headquarters/a base (商売/会社/企業/基金/プロジェクト/計画/事業/構想/独占事業/本部/基地を始める[設立する]).

form [他, 自] 組織する, 結成する;形をとる ◇They hope to *form* the new government. 彼らは新政府樹立を望んでいる ◇We are a newly-*formed* political party. 我々は新しく結成された政党である ◇The band *formed* in 2005. そのバンドは2005年に結成された ❶*form* はしばしば政治関係にしばしば用いられる。◆to *form* a government/an administration/a cabinet/a coalition/a committee/a council/an assembly/a party/a league/an alliance/a trade union/a syndicate (政府/政権/内閣/連立/委員会/協議会/集会/政党/連盟/同盟/労働組合/シンジケートを樹立[設立]する). バンドを組むことについて用いる最も一般的な動詞でもある。

found [他]《特に書き言葉》(資金を提供して)始める[創設する] ◇He *founded* the company 20 years ago. 彼は20年前にその会社を設立した ◇Her family *founded* the college in 1895. 彼女の一族が1895年にその大学を設立した ◇The town was *founded* by English settlers in 1790. その町は1790年にイギリスの移住者によって作られた ❶*found* は institute, society, company, firm, town, city, church, monastery, convent などを目的語に取る。

estimate 名

estimate・count・calculation・tally・reckoning
数量や合計の割り出しの仕方
【類語訳】概算、見積もり、勘定、総計、カウント、計算

文型&コロケーション
▸ a/ an **accurate/ precise** estimate/ count/ calculation
▸ a **rough/ quick/ approximate** estimate/ count/ calculation
▸ to **make** an estimate/ a calculation
▸ to **do** a count/ calculation
▸ to **keep** a count/ tally **of** sth
▸ **By** my/ his, etc. estimate/ calculations/ reckoning...

estimate [C] 概算, 見積もり ◇I can give you a rough *estimate* of the amount of wood you will need. 必

要な量の木材を大ざっぱに見積もることはできます ◇a **ball-park** *estimate* (= an approximate estimate) 概算見積もり ◇These are the official government *estimates* of traffic growth over the next decade. これらがこの先10年の交通量の増加についての正式な政府見積もりです ◇At least 5,000 people were killed, and that's a **conservative** *estimate* (= the real figure will be higher). 少なくとも5千人が殺されたが, これは控え目な見積もりだ

count [C, ふつう単数で] (総数を確認するために) 数えること, 勘定; (確かめた) 総数, 総計; (1から順番に数字を言う) カウント ◇If the election result is close, there will be a second *count*. 選挙結果が僅差なら, 数え直すことになるでしょう ◇**At the last** *count* she had 43 cats! [英] 最近数えたところによると, 彼女は43匹の猫を飼っていた ◇**At last** *count* she had 43 cats! [米] 最近数えたところによると, 彼女は43匹の猫を飼っていた ◇The body *count* (= the total number of people who have died) stands at 24. 死者の数は24人に達する ◇I've **lost** *count* of the (= forgotten how many) times I've heard that joke. その冗談を何度聞いたかわからない ◇On the *count* of three, take one step forward. 3つ数えたら, 一歩前に出てください ☞ **count** (COUNT)

calculation [C, U] 計算 (すること) ◇She made a rough *calculation* in her head. 彼女は暗算で概算した ◇By my *calculations*, we made a profit of £20,000 last year. 私の計算では, 昨年2万ポンドの利益が出た ◇Our guess was confirmed by *calculation*. 我々の推量は計算によって確かめられた ☞ **calculate** (CALCULATE)

[ノート] **count** と **calculation** の使い分け: count は数を合計することを指す. calculation は, 数字の掛け算や割り算などの数学上の働きを指すことが多い.

tally [C] (加え続ける) 数 [量] の記録 ◇Keep a *tally* of how much you spend while you're away. 外出中いくら使うか記録をつけなさい ◇She scored four more points, taking her *tally* to 15. 彼女はさらに4点を獲得して合計15点となった ☞ **tally** (COUNT)

reckoning [U, C] (あまり正確でない形での) 計算 ◇By my *reckoning* you still owe me £5. 私の計算ではまだ5ポンド君に貸しだ

estimate [動] ☞ CALCULATE, COUNT

estimate・guess・judge・reckon・calculate・gauge・figure・extrapolate

経費 [大きさ, 価値など] についておよその見当をつける
【類語訳】見積もる, 概算する, 想定する, 思いつく, 考えつく, 推測する

[文型&コロケーション]

▸ to estimate/ guess/ judge/ reckon/ calculate/ gauge/ extrapolate sth **from** sth

▸ to estimate/ reckon/ calculate sth **at** sth

▸ to estimate/ guess/ judge/ reckon/ calculate/ figure/ extrapolate **that...**

▸ to estimate/ guess/ judge/ figure/ calculate/ gauge **how much/ how many/ how far, etc.**

▸ to estimate/ guess/ judge/ reckon/ calculate/ gauge/ figure sth **to be sth**

▸ to estimate/ guess/ judge/ calculate/ gauge the **amount/ value/ size/ distance**

▸ to estimate/ guess/ calculate sb/ sth's **age**

▸ to estimate/ judge/ gauge the **depth**

estimate [他, しばしば受身で]《ややフォーマル》見積もる, 概算する ◇Police *estimated* the size of the crowd at 50,000. 警察は群集の規模を5万人と見積もった ◇*Estimate* the time it will take to complete each section. 各セクションの完了にかかる時間を見積もりなさい ◇The satellite will cost an *estimated* $500m. 衛星は概算で5億ドルかかるでしょう ◇It is *estimated* that the project will last about four years. プロジェクトはほぼ4年続くと見られている ☞ **estimate** (VALUATION)

guess [他] 推測する, 思いつく, 言い当てる ◇She *guessed* the answer straight away. 彼女はすぐに答えを言い当てた ◇I *guessed*, rightly, that the keys would be under the doormat. 鍵はドアマットの下にあるだろうと正しく言い当てた ◇**You'll never** *guess* where they've gone. 彼らがどこへ行ってしまったか絶対に思いつかないでしょう ☞ **guess** (SPECULATION)

judge [他] 見積もる, 判断する ◇Young children are unable to *judge* the speed of traffic. 幼い子どもたちは通行する車の速さの見当がつかない ◇I *judged* him to be about 50. 彼は50歳くらいだと私は見た

[ノート] **estimate** と **judge** の使い分け: estimate は正確に把握するためには計算しなければならない経費 (cost) などに用いる. judge は正確に把握するためには測定しなければならない距離 (distance), 深さ (depth), 速度 (speed) などに用いることが多い. estimate は正確には計算できない将来の経費や時間の長さを, 手元の情報から慎重に見積もる場合によく用いられる. judge は距離や速度を過去の経験に照らして見当をつける場合によく用いられる.

reckon [他, しばしば受身で] (おおよその数量・時間を) 見積もる, 推測する ◇The age of the earth is *reckoned* to be about 4,600 million years. 地球の年齢は約46億年と推定される ◇They *reckon* that their profits were down by 30%. 利益は30%減少したと推定される ◇The trip was *reckoned* to take over two days. 旅は2日以上かかると思われた ❶ reckon の結果得られる数量や時間は, estimate の結果より大ざっぱである可能性がある.

calculate [他] (手元の情報をよく用いて) 推測する [意見をまとめる], 算定する ◇It's impossible to *calculate* the extent of his influence on her. 彼が彼女に与える影響度を推測するのは不可能だ ◇Environmentalists *calculate* that hundreds of plant species may be affected. 環境問題の専門家たちは何百もの植物種が影響を受けるかもしれないと推測している ☞ **calculate** (CALCULATE)

gauge (米でまた **gage**) [他]《ややフォーマル》推測する, 測る ◇We were able to *gauge* the strength of the wind from the movement of the trees. 木々の動きから風の強さを推定することができた ☞ **gauge** (CRITERION)

figure [他]《特に米, ややインフォーマル》(数量・経費・年齢を) 見積もる ◇If we can *figure* roughly how much it will cost, we can decide what to do. いくらかかるかざっと計算できるなら, やるべきことを決められます ❶《米》では, 物事を正確に計算するのにも用いることができる. ☞ **figure** (CALCULATE)

extrapolate [自, 他]《フォーマル》(既存の事実から未知の事柄を) 推定する ◇The figures were obtained by *extrapolating* from past trends. その数値は過去の傾向から推量することで得られた ◇These results cannot be *extrapolated to* other patient groups. これらの結果から他の患者群について推測することはできない

➤ **extrapolation** 图 [U, C] ◇Their age can be determined by *extrapolation* from their growth rate. それらの年齢は成長率からの推測で確定することができる

event 图

1 event・affair・incident・experience・phenomenon・episode・business・development・occurrence・proceedings・eventuality
発生する事柄
【類語訳】出来事、経験、現象、挿話、問題、成り行き、不測の事態

文型&コロケーション
- ▶ the **whole** event/ affair/ incident/ experience/ phenomenon/ episode/ business/ proceedings
- ▶ (a) **strange** event/ affair/ incident/ experience/ phenomenon/ development/ occurrence
- ▶ (a) **terrible** event/ affair/ incident/ experience/ business
- ▶ (a) **dramatic** event/ incident/ experience/ episode/ development
- ▶ an **enjoyable** event/ affair/ experience
- ▶ (an) **everyday** event/ affair/ incident/ experience/ occurrence
- ▶ an **isolated** event/ incident/ experience/ phenomenon/ episode/ occurrence
- ▶ a **rare/ common** event/ experience/ phenomenon/ occurrence
- ▶ to **witness** an event/ an incident/ a phenomenon/ an episode
- ▶ an event/ an incident/ an experience/ a phenomenon/ an episode **occurs**
- ▶ an event/ an incident/ an experience/ a phenomenon/ an episode/ proceedings **takes place/ take place**

event [C] (重要な)出来事 ◇The election was the main *event* of 2005. その選挙は2005年の主要な出来事だった ◇In the light of later *events* the decision was proved to be right. のちの出来事を踏まえると、その決定の正しいことが証明された ◇The decisions we take now may influence the *course of events* (= the way things happen) in the future. 私たちが今下す決定はこれからの事の成り行きに影響を与えるかもしれない ◇Everyone was frightened by the strange *sequence of events*. 一連の不思議な出来事には誰もがおびえた

affair [C, ふつう単数で] (個々に語られる[表現される])出来事 ◇I ended up disillusioned and bitter about the whole *affair*. 出来事全体に幻滅し苦い思いをする結果となった ◇The debate was a pretty disappointing *affair*. 論戦はかなり期待外れのものだった ◇She wanted the celebration to be a simple family *affair*. 彼女はお祝いを家庭内のあっさりしたものにしてほしかった ❶ *affair* の複数形は、世間の関心がある[政治的な重要性のある]出来事を指す
- ◆ world/international/business *affairs* (世界情勢/国際問題/ビジネス業務). ◆ He's an expert on *foreign affairs*. (彼は外交問題の専門家である). ◆ He believed in a strict separation of the *affairs of state* and those of the church. (彼は厳密な政教分離の正当性を信じていた). ◆ The talk ranged over a variety of topics, from sport to *current affairs* (= events of political or social importance that are happening now). (話はスポーツから時事問題まで多岐のテーマに及んだ).

incident [C, U] 《ややフォーマル》(非日常的[不愉快]な)出来事；(犯罪・事故・攻撃などの深刻[暴力的]な)事件 ◇His bad behaviour was just an isolated *incident*. 彼の不品行はその場限りの出来事にすぎなかった ◇There was a shooting *incident* near here last night. 昨夜この近くで発砲事件があった ◇The demonstration passed off *without incident*. デモは何事もなく終了した

experience [C] (何らかの形で人に影響を及ぼす)経験、体験 ◇It was her first *experience* of living alone. 彼女にとって初めての一人暮らしの経験だった ◇Living in Africa was very different from home and *quite an experience* (= unusual for us). アフリカでの生活は故郷とは全く違い本当に凄い経験であった ◇I had a bad *experience* with fireworks once. 花火については少々一つ嫌な経験をした ◇He seems to have had some sort of religious *experience*. 彼はある種の宗教体験をしたようだ ☞ **experience** (KNOWLEDGE), **experience** (LIFE 3), **experience** (HAVE 3)

phenomenon (複 **phenomena**) [C] (十分理解できない自然[社会]の)現象、事象 ◇natural/cultural/social *phenomena* 自然/文化的/社会現象 ◇This kind of crime is a *phenomenon* of the modern age. この種の犯罪は現代の不思議な出来事の一つである

episode [C] (何らかの意味で重要な[興味深い])出来事、逸話、挿話、エピソード ◇I'd like to try and forget the whole *episode*. その出来事は全部忘れてしまいたい ◇It turned out to be one of the funniest *episodes* in the novel. それはその小説で最もこっけいな挿話の一つだとわかった

business 《ふつう形容詞と共に》[単数で] 《ややインフォーマル、特に話し言葉》問題、出来事、状況 ◇I found the whole *business* very depressing. 状況全体はとても気の滅入るようなものだとわかった ◇That plane crash was a terrible *business*. その飛行機事故は悲惨な出来事だった ◇The *business* of the missing tickets hasn't been sorted out. チケットをなくした件は解決していない

development [C] 新しい状況[段階]、進展 ◇the latest *developments* in the war 戦争の最新情勢 ◇Are there any further *developments* in the investigation? 捜査にさらなる進展はありますか

occurrence [C] 《フォーマル》事件、出来事、出現 ◇Vandalism has become a regular *occurrence* in recent times. 破壊活動は最近では日常茶飯事となっている ◇The program counts the number of *occurrences* of any word or group of words, within the text. そのプログラムはテキスト内の単語や単語の集まりの出現数を計算するものです ☞ **occur** (HAPPEN)

proceedings [複数で] 行動、一連の活動、成り行き ◇The Mayor will *open the proceedings* at the City Hall tomorrow. 市長は明日から市役所で一連の活動を始めるでしょう ◇We watched the *proceedings* from the balcony. 私たちはバルコニーから成り行きを見守った

eventuality [C] 《フォーマル》(不愉快な)起こりうる事柄、不測の事態 ◇We were prepared for every *eventuality*. 我々はあらゆる不測の事態に備えていた ◇This strategy will allow us to cope with all *eventualities* which may arise. この戦略に従えば、起こりうるすべての事態に対処できるだろう

2 event・celebration・occasion・function・reception・reunion・festivities・get-together
人目につく[社交的な]場面に人が招かれること

evidence

【類語訳】行事, 催し, イベント, 祝典, 祝賀会, 儀式, 歓迎会, レセプション, パーティー

文型&コロケーション

- (a) **special** event/ celebration/ occasion/ reception/ reunion/ festivities
- (a) **family** event/ celebration/ occasion/ reunion/ festivities/ get-together
- a **social** event/ occasion/ function
- a **school** event/ function/ reunion
- (a) **wedding** celebrations/ reception
- **Christmas** celebrations/ festivities
- an **annual** event/ celebration/ reunion/ get-together
- an event/ celebrations/ a function/ a reception/ a reunion/ festivities **is/ are held**
- an event/ celebrations/ a reception/ a reunion/ festivities **takes place/ take place**

event [C] 行事, 催し, イベント ◇Details of meetings and social *events* are sent out to all club members. 会合と社交行事の詳細はクラブのメンバー全員に送られています ◇The hospital is planning a major fund-raising *event* for June. 病院は6月に向けて資金集めの大イベントを計画している

celebration [C, ふつう複数で] 祝典, 祝賀会 ◇They are already preparing for his 80th birthday *celebrations* in October. 彼らはすでに10月の彼の80歳の誕生祝賀会に向けて準備をしています ◇The *celebrations* continued with a cabaret dinner. お祝いはキャバレーディナーの場に引き継がれた ☞ **celebrate, celebration** (PLAY ⓓ 1)
▶ **celebrate** ⓓ [自, 他] ◇Jake's passed his exams. We're going out to *celebrate*. ジェイクが試験に合格した。お祝いに出かけよう ◇How do people *celebrate* New Year in your country? あなたの国では新年をどうお祝いしますか

occasion [C] (特別な)行事, 儀式, 祝典 ◇Turn every meal into a special *occasion*. 毎回の食事を特別な事としなさい ◇Their wedding turned out to be quite an *occasion*. 彼らの結婚式はすごいお祝いになった ◇They marked the *occasion* (= celebrated it) with an open-air concert. 彼らは慶事を野外コンサートで記念した ◇He was presented with the watch **on the occasion of** his retirement. 彼は引退の節目に際して腕時計を贈られた

function [C] 《ややフォーマル》(社会的な)行事, (公式の)式典 ◇The hall provided a venue for weddings and other *functions*. そのホールは結婚式やその他の目的に会場を提供していた ◇He and his wife were guests of honour at a *function* held by the society last weekend. 彼と彼の妻は先週末, その協会が開いた式典の来賓であった

reception [C] 歓迎会, 祝賀会, レセプション ◇They held a *reception* for 100 guests at the golf club. ゴルフクラブで100人の客を迎えて歓迎会が行われた ◇The hall is a popular venue for wedding *receptions*. そのホールはよく結婚披露宴の会場に使われる

reunion [C] 再会の集い ◇The seventh annual *reunion* will take place in March. 7回目を数える毎年恒例の同窓会[クラス会]が3月に行われます ◇a school *reunion* 同窓会

festivities [複数で] 《ややフォーマル》祝祭行事 ◇Bonfires and fireworks will form part of the *festivities*. 大かがり火や花火が祝祭行事の一部となります

'get-together [C] 《インフォーマル》(非公式の)会合；パーティー ◇I'm going back for the usual family *get-together* at Thanksgiving. 慣例となっている感謝祭の家族パーティーのため帰るつもりです ☞ **get together** (MEET 1)

evidence 名

evidence・proof・support・testimony・demonstration
物事が真実だと信じさせる事実[痕跡, 物体]
【類語訳】証拠, 根拠, 裏づけ, 証, 実証, 論証

文型&コロケーション

- evidence/ support **for** sth
- evidence/ proof/ testimony/ a demonstration **that**...
- (a) **clear/ convincing** evidence/ proof/ support/ testimony/ demonstration
- (a) **conclusive** evidence/ proof/ support/ demonstration
- (an) **ample/ adequate** evidence/ proof/ testimony/ demonstration
- **sufficient/ good/ direct** evidence/ proof/ testimony
- to **provide/ give** evidence/ proof/ support/ testimony/ a demonstration
- to **find** evidence/ proof/ support

evidence [U] 証拠, 根拠 ◇Have you any *evidence* to support this allegation? この主張を裏づける証拠はありますか ◇There is **not a shred of evidence** that the meeting actually took place. 会合が実際に行われた形跡はかけらもない ◇A **body of evidence** emerged suggesting that smoking tobacco caused serious diseases. 喫煙が重大な病気を引き起こすと示唆する証拠が山ほど明らかになった ◇**On the evidence of** their recent games, it is unlikely the Spanish team will win the cup. 最近の試合を根拠にすると, スペインチームが優勝杯を勝ち取る見込みはない ◇I was asked to **give evidence** (= to say what I knew, describe what I had seen, etc.) at the trial. 私は公判での証言を依頼された ◇The jury **heard evidence** from 38 witnesses. 陪審団は38人の証人から証言を聴取した ☞ **evidence** (CONFIRM 1)

proof [U, C] 証拠 ◇There is no *proof* that the knife belonged to her. そのナイフが彼女の物だったという証拠はない ◇Can you provide any **proof of identity**? 身元を証明するものを何か提示してもらえますか ◇Keep the receipt as **proof of purchase**. 購入した証拠として領収書をとっておきなさい ◇These results are a further *proof* of his outstanding ability. これらの結果は彼の並外れた能力のさらなる証明である ☞ **prove** (SHOW 1)

ノート evidence と proof の使い分け：evidence は物事が真実だと信じさせるもの, proof は物事が真実だと誰も反論できない形で示すもの.

support [U] (理論・考えを支える)証拠, 裏づけ ◇The statistics offer further *support* for our theory. その統計は我々の理論をさらに裏づける ☞ **support** (CONFIRM 1)

testimony [U, 単数で] 《フォーマル》(別の物の存在・真実を示す)証拠, 証 ◇The pyramids are an eloquent *testimony to* the ancient Egyptians' engineering skills. ピラミッドは古代エジプト人の工学技術を雄弁に語る証拠である ◇This increase in imports *bears testimony to* the successes of industry. この輸入増加は産業の成功の証である

demonstration [C, U] 証明（すること）, 実証, 論証
◇This is a clear *demonstration* of how something that seems simple can turn out to be very complicated. これは単純に見えるものが実は極めて複雑でありうるその有様をはっきりと証明する一例である ☞**demonstrate** (SHOW 1)

evil 名

evil・sin・wrong・wickedness・immorality・vice
道徳的不品行や悪いことを引き起こす力を表す
【類語訳】悪, 邪悪, 悪行, 罪悪, 意地悪, 不品行

▸ 文型&コロケーション
▸ to **do** evil/ wrong
▸ to **turn (away) from** evil/ sin/ wickedness
▸ a **life of** evil/ sin/ wickedness/ vice

evil [U] 悪, 邪悪；悪行 ◇The film is about the eternal struggle between good and *evil*. その映画は善悪の永遠の争いを取り上げている ◇He believed he could rid the world of the forces of *evil*. 彼は世の中から悪の力を一掃できると信じていた ◇Humans have the capacity to do more *evil* than any other species on earth. 人間は地球上の他のどの種類より邪悪なことをする力を持っている 反意 **good** (MORALITY)

sin [U]《ややフォーマル》(宗教[道徳]上の)罪悪 ◇Believers are called on to turn away from *sin* and embrace a life of prayer. 信者たちは罪悪から目をそむけ, 祈祷生活に取り組むよう求められている

wrong [U] 悪, 悪行 ◇Children must be taught the difference between right and *wrong*. 子どもには善悪の違いを教えなければならない ◇Her son can do no *wrong* in her eyes. 彼女の目から見れば, 息子は悪事を働くことなどできない ◇I see no *wrong* in taking a little time off. 少しの時間休むのは何も悪いことだとは思わない ❶この意味では, do/see no wrongや right and wrongの句で用いるのがほとんどである. 反意 **right** (MORALITY), ☞ **wrong** (WRONG 3)

wickedness [U] 意地悪 ◇They started to beat me for no reason except sheer *wickedness*. 全くの意地悪以外の何の理由もなく彼らは私を殴りはじめた

immorality [U, C]《ややフォーマル》不品行, (性的)ふしだら ◇For him, the besetting sins of the age were greed and sexual *immorality*. 彼は当時, ややもすると強欲と性的ふしだらの罪に陥った 反意 **morality** (MORALITY), ☞ **immoral** (WRONG 3)

vice [U]《特にジャーナリズム》悪行, 悪徳 ◇The film ended most satisfactorily: *vice* punished and virtue rewarded. その映画は非常に満足のいく結末だった；勧善懲悪だった ❶ジャーナリズムやインフォーマルな文脈では, viceはふつうセックス・麻薬の使用・飲酒・ギャンブルなどの意を指す. 反意 **virtue** (MORALITY)

evil 形

evil・wicked・bad・dark・satanic・base・demonic・sinful
残酷[不道徳]な人間[行動]を表す
【類語訳】極悪な, 邪悪な, 意地悪な, 悪い, 恐ろしい, 卑しい, 卑劣な, 罰当たりの

▸ 文型&コロケーション
▸ an evil/ a wicked/ a bad/ a sinful **man/ woman/ person/ life/ act/ thought**
▸ an evil/ a wicked/ a bad **character**
▸ an evil/ a wicked/ a base/ a sinful **creature**
▸ an evil/ a wicked **demon**
▸ a wicked/ bad **child**
▸ an evil/ a wicked/ a bad/ a dark/ a sinful **deed**
▸ an evil/ a wicked **crime**
▸ an evil/ a bad/ a satanic **influence**
▸ an evil/ a bad **omen**
▸ evil/ dark/ demonic **forces/ powers**

evil 極悪な；邪悪な；悪魔の ◇He gave an *evil* laugh. 彼は悪意のある笑い方をした ◇In his speech he described the *evil* effects of racism. 演説で彼は人種差別のもたらす害悪について語った ◇It was an ancient charm to ward off *evil spirits*. それは悪霊を払うための古代のお守りだった 反意 **good** (GOOD 5)

wicked 極悪な；意地悪な, 邪悪な ◇She despised herself for being selfish, even *wicked*. 彼女は自分勝手で意地悪でさえある自分が嫌だった ◇That was a *wicked* thing to do! そんなことしちゃ駄目でしょ ◇The *wicked* witch casts a spell on the princess. 邪悪な魔女がお姫様に魔法をかけるのです 反意 **good** (GOOD 5)

▸ ノート **evilとwickedの使い分け**：どちらも非常に悪い人や行動を表す激しい言葉. 十分注意して用いなければならない. evilはwickedよりも強烈である. wickednessとは, 邪悪であることの喜びが引き起こす悪行のこと. 基本的には人間の特性である. evilは人に悪行をさせる外部の力で, しばしば悪魔と関連付けられる. wickedな人間は, 邪悪であることや他人の感情を傷つけることを楽しむ. evilな人間は, 人を肉体的に傷つけることを楽しみ, 人の感情を顧みることすらしない. 特に童話では, 子ども(child), 魔女(witch), 継母(stepmother)がwickedである. 特に大人向けの物語や大衆向けの報道では, 霊(spirit), 怪物(monster), 殺人犯(killer), 黒幕(mastermind)がevilである.

bad 悪い, 不正の, 不道徳な ◇The hero gets to shoot all the *bad* guys. 主人公が悪人すべてを撃ち殺す役回りなんだ ◇He said I must have done something *bad* to deserve it. 私が何かその報いを受けるような悪いことをしたに違いないと彼は言った 反意 **good** (GOOD 5)

dark 邪悪な, 恐ろしい ◇There was a *darker* side to his nature. 彼の人間性にはより邪悪な一面があった ◇There are *dark* forces at work here. ここには邪悪な力が働いている

satanic (または **Satanic**) 悪魔崇拝の ◇There was no evidence of *satanic* rituals. 悪魔崇拝の儀式の証拠はなかった

base《フォーマル》卑しい, 卑劣な ◇He acted from *base* motives. 彼は卑しい動機で行動した

demonic 悪霊の, 悪霊のような ◇This was a society in which *demonic* possession was greatly feared. ここは悪霊がとりつくことがひどく恐れられている社会だった

sinful《フォーマル》道徳的に間違った；罰当たりの ◇He tried to keep his *sinful* thoughts to himself. 彼は罰当たりな考えを隠そうとした

exact 形

exact・precise・accurate・specific
物事の詳細すべてを正しく伝えることを表す

exaggerate

【類語訳】正確な, 明確な, 精密な, 厳密な, 明細な

文型&コロケーション
▶ precise/ accurate/ specific **about** sb/ sth
▶ exact/ precise/ accurate/ specific **instructions/ details**
▶ exact/ precise/ accurate **measurements**
▶ an exact/ a precise/ an accurate **answer/ description**
▶ a precise/ an accurate **account**
▶ an exact/ an accurate **picture/ copy**
▶ the exact/ precise **time**
▶ quite exact/ precise/ accurate/ specific

exact [ふつう名詞の前で] 正確な ◇She gave an *exact* description of the attacker. 彼女は攻撃してきた者について正確に説明した ◇What were his *exact* words? 彼は正確には何と言ったのですか ◇She's in her mid-thirties — 36, to be *exact*. 彼女は30代半ば―正確には36歳です 反意 approximate, rough (VAGUE), ☞ **exact** (VERY) 形
▶ **exactly** 副 ◇Do *exactly* as I tell you. 言われたとおりにやりなさい ◇It happened almost *exactly* a year ago. それはほぼちょうど一年前に起きた

precise 正確な；精密な ◇Please give *precise* details about your previous experience. あなたの過去の体験について詳細を正確に教えてください ◇She was reasonably *precise* about the time of the incident. 彼女は事件の発生時刻に関してかなり正確だった ◇It measures 3.4 metres, to be *precise*. 正確には, それは3.4メートルです 反意 imprecise (VAGUE), ☞ **precise** (VERY) 形
▶ **precisely** 副 ◇That's *precisely* what I meant. 私が言ったのはまさにそういうことです
▶ **precision** 名 [U] ◇Her writing is imaginative but lacks *precision*. 彼女の著述は想像力に富んでいるが正確さに欠ける

accurate 正確な ◇*Accurate* records must be kept at all times. 常に正確な記録が取られなければならない ◇The test results are *accurate* in 99% of cases. 実験結果は99%のケースで間違いない ◇The novel wasn't intended to be historically *accurate*. その小説は史実に忠実であろうとする意図はなかった 反意 **inaccurate** (WRONG 1), ☞ RELIABLE 2
▶ **accuracy** 名 [U] ◇They questioned the *accuracy* of the information in the file. 彼らはファイルの情報の正確さについて疑問を持った
▶ **accurately** 副 ◇The report *accurately* reflects the current state of the industry. 報告書はその産業の現状を正確に反映している

ノート **exact, precise, accurate の使い分け**：accurateはしばしば, exact, preciseと同じように名詞の前で用いることができる. ◆ *exact/precise/accurate* records（正確な記録）．連結動詞のあとに用いるとき, 特に否定文において少し強調のしかたが違う. 描写がnot very exact/preciseの場合は, 詳細に欠けることだが, not very accurateなら, 詳細は詳細でも誤りがあることになる. preciseには, はっきりしていて確信があり, 正しいというニュアンスがあり, be precise about sthという句で人を表すのに用いることができる. exactはふつうこの形で用いない. ×She was reasonably *exact* about the time of the incident. reasonably accurate about sthという場合, 物事についてかなり正しいという, ほど確信があるわけではない.

specific 明確な ◇I gave you *specific* instructions. 君にははっきり指示したよ ◇'I'd like your help tomorrow.'

'Can you *be more specific* (= tell me exactly what you want)?' 「明日君の手を借りたいんだ」「もっとはっきりと言ってくれ」 ❶ specificはしばしばpreciseと同じように用いられる. 誰かにさらにpreciseであるよう求めたり, 誰かがpreciseではなかったと不満を漏らしたり, (例えば, 相手が自分の指示を無視したりしたときなど)自分はpreciseだったと主張する場合によく用いられる.

exaggerate 動

exaggerate • overstate • dramatize • embellish • inflate

実際以上に関心を引かせたり, 重要に見せかけたりする
【類語訳】誇張する, 大げさに言う, 劇的にする, 潤色する, 粉飾する

文型&コロケーション
▶ to exaggerate/ overstate/ inflate the **importance/ significance** of sth
▶ to exaggerate/ overstate the **extent** of sth
▶ to exaggerate/ dramatize/ embellish a **story**
▶ to **greatly/ grossly/ vastly/ wildly/ somewhat** exaggerate/ overstate/ inflate sth

exaggerate [自, 他] 誇張する ◇The hotel was really filthy and I'm not *exaggerating*. 大げさじゃなくて, ホテルはほんとに汚かった ◇Demand for satellite television has been greatly *exaggerated*. 衛星テレビの需要量はかなり誇張されてきた
▶ **exaggerated** 形 ◇He made some wildly *exaggerated* claims about what they had achieved. 彼は彼らが成し遂げたことをひどく大げさに主張した
▶ **exaggeration** 名 [C, ふつう単数で, U] ◇That's a slight *exaggeration*! それって, ちょっと大げさじゃない ◇He told his story simply and without *exaggeration*. 彼は話を飾り気もなく誇張もせずに述べた

overstate [他]《ややフォーマル》大げさに言う ◇He tends to *overstate the case* when talking politics. 彼は政治を語るとき, 実情を大げさに言うきらいがある ◇The seriousness of the crime *cannot be overstated*. その犯罪の重大さはどれだけ誇張してもしすぎるということはない ❶ 一般的に は, importance, significance, seriousness, the caseと結びつく. 反意 **understate**
▶ **overstatement** 名 [C, U] ◇It is not an *overstatement* to say a crisis is imminent. 危機が差し迫っているというのは大げさな表現ではない ◇He was well known for his fondness for *overstatement*. 彼は大げさな表現を好むことでよく知られていた

dramatize [英でまた **-ise**] [他, 自]《ややフォーマル》劇的に見せる ◇Don't worry too much about what she said — she tends to *dramatize* things. 彼女の言ったことを気にしすぎないでね―物事を脚色しがちな人だから

embellish [他]《ややフォーマル》潤色する, 粉飾する ◇His account of his travels was *embellished* with details of famous people he met. 彼の旅の話は, 出会った有名人についてのあれこれで尾ひれがついていた

inflate [他]《特にジャーナリズム》誇張する ◇The media have grossly *inflated* the significance of this meeting. メディアはこの会議の重要性を露骨に誇張してきた ❶ この意味では一般的に, importance, significance, valueと結びつく.
▶ **inflated** 形 ◇She has an *inflated* sense of her own importance. 彼女は自らの重要性を過大に見ている

examine 動

examine・analyse・review・study・discuss・go into sth・take stock・survey
綿密に考える[調べる, 説明する]
【類語訳】研究する, 吟味する, 分析する, (再)検討する, 見直す, 詳述する

文型&コロケーション

▶ to examine/ analyse/ review/ study/ discuss/ go into/ take stock of/ survey **what/ how/ whether...**
▶ to examine/ analyse/ review/ study/ discuss/ take stock of/ survey the **situation**
▶ to examine/ analyse/ review/ study/ discuss the **possibility** of sth
▶ to examine/ analyse/ review/ study/ discuss a/ an **proposal/ idea**
▶ to examine/ analyse/ review/ study/ discuss the **evidence/ sb's work**
▶ to examine/ analyse/ review/ study/ discuss/ go into sth **in depth/ in detail**
▶ to examine/ analyse/ review/ study/ discuss sth **in the light of** sth
▶ to examine/ analyse/ review/ study/ discuss/ survey sth **carefully/ critically/ systematically/ briefly**

examine [他] 調べる, 検討する, 吟味する ◇These ideas will be *examined* in more detail in Chapter 10. これらの考え方については第10章でもっと詳しく考察します ◇It is necessary to *examine* how the proposals can be carried out. 提案をいかにして実現できるか吟味する必要がある ☞ **examination** (RESEARCH)

analyse 《英》 **analyze**) [他] 分析する ◇The job involves gathering and *analysing* data. データを収集・分析するのもその仕事の一つだ ◇He tried to *analyse* his feelings. 彼はその男の気持ちを分析しようとした ◇We need to *analyse* what went wrong. 我々は何がうまくいかなかったのか分析する必要がある ☞ **analysis** (RESEARCH)

review [他] 再検討する, 見直す ◇Staff performance is *reviewed* annually. 職員の業績は毎年見直される ◇The decision may need to be *reviewed* in the light of new evidence. 新しい証拠を考慮して, 判決を見直す必要があるかもしれない ◇Safety procedures are being urgently *reviewed* after a chemical leak at the factory. 工場の化学薬品漏出後, 安全手順が至急再検討されているところだ

▶ **review** [名] [U, C] ◇The case is *subject to* judicial *review*. この訴訟は司法審査の対象だ ◇The terms of the contract are *under review*. 契約条件は検討されている最中だ ◇a pay/salary *review* 賃金/給与査定 ☞ **review** (REPORT 1)

study [他] 調べる, 研究する ◇We will *study* the report carefully before making a decision. 我々は決定を下す前に報告書を慎重に検討するつもりです ◇The group will *study* how the region coped with the loss of thousands of jobs. その地域が何千人もの失業にどう対処したかをグループで調査することになっている ☞ **study** (RESEARCH), **study** (REPORT 1)

ノート **examine** と **study** の使い分け: examine は, 例えば執筆などを通じて, 物事を理解したり他人の理解を手助けしたりするために「調べる」. study は, 物事を自分で理解するために「調べる」.

discuss [他] 詳細に述べる ◇This topic will be *discussed* at greater length in the next chapter. このテーマは次章でもっと詳細に論じます ☞ **discussion** (RESEARCH)

go 'into sth 句動詞 《ややインフォーマル, 特に話し言葉》 (実際上の理由で問題[質問]を)入念に調べる ◇We need to *go into* the question of costs. 経費の問題を詳しく調べる必要がある

take 'stock 仔仗 (次に何をすべきかを)慎重に考える, 検討する ◇It was time to stand back and *take stock of* his career. 距離を置いて彼の経歴についてよく検討してみるときだった

survey [他] 精査する, 概説[概観]する ◇This chapter briefly *surveys* the current state of European politics. この章はヨーロッパ政治の現状について簡潔に概観している ☞ **survey** (REPORT 1)

example 名

1 example・case・instance・specimen・illustration
特定のグループ[セット]に典型的で, 時としてある主張の裏付けとして用いられる物や状況
【類語訳】例, 事例, 実例, 例証

文型&コロケーション

▶ **in a particular** case/ instance
▶ **for example**/ instance
▶ a **typical** example/ case/ instance/ specimen/ illustration
▶ a **classic** example/ case/ instance/ illustration
▶ a **famous/ well-known** example/ case/ instance
▶ a **prime** example/ case/ specimen
▶ a/ an **good/ fine/ excellent/ perfect** example/ specimen/ illustration
▶ to **give sb/ provide** an example/ an instance/ a specimen/ an illustration
▶ to **cite/ take/ highlight** an example/ a case/ an instance
▶ an example/ a case/ an illustration **shows** sth

example [C] 例；典型 ◇Can you give me an *example* of what you mean? おっしゃっることの例を挙げていただけますか ◇It is important to cite *examples* to support your argument. あなたの主張を裏付ける例を挙げることが大切です ◇It is a classic *example* of how not to design a new town. それはどのようにして計画に基づいて新しい町を作るのをやめるべきかを象徴する典型的な例である

case [C] 場合, 事例 ◇In some *cases* people have had to wait several weeks for an appointment. 場合によっては, 予約を数週間待ちだった ◇Many professions feel they deserve higher pay, and nurses are a *case in point*. 多くの専門職の人はもっと高給に値すると感じており, 看護師はそのいい例だ ◇In this *case*, we are prepared to be lenient. この場合, 我々は大目に見てもいいと思っている

instance [C] 《ややフォーマル》 例, 実例, 場合 ◇The report highlights a number of *instances* of injustice. その報道は数多くの不正の実例にスポットを当てている ◇What would you do, for *instance*, if you found an employee stealing. 例えば従業員の盗みを目撃したら, どうしますか

specimen (動植物の)実例, 見本 ◇The aquarium has

some interesting *specimens* of unusual tropical fish. その水族館には珍しい熱帯魚の興味深い見本が何匹かいる ◇Redwood trees can live for a long time; one *specimen* is 4,000 years old. セコイアは長年生きることができる。樹齢4千年という実例が1本ある

illustration [C, U] 《ややフォーマル, 特に書き言葉》 例, 実例, 例証 ◇The statistics are a clear *illustration* of the point I am trying to make. その統計は私の主張の明確な例証である ◇Let me, *by way of illustration*, quote from one of her poems. 実例として, 彼女の詩を一つ引用しましょう ☞ **illustrate** (EXPLAIN 1), **illustrate** (SHOW 1), **illustrative** (DESCRIPTIVE)

ノート example と illustration の使い分け : illustration はしばしば物事が真実であることを示すために用いられ, example は物事の説明の手助けとするために用いられる。

2 example・model・ideal・role model・embodiment・epitome・inspiration・archetype
物事のよい例と考えられる人[物]
【類語訳】手本, 模範, 理想, 具現, 体現, 典型, 権化

文型&コロケーション
▶an example/ a model/ the embodiment/ the epitome/ the archetype **of** sth
▶an example/ inspiration **to** sb

example [C] 《ほめて》手本, 模範 ◇Her courage is an *example* to us all. 彼女の勇気は私たちみんなの手本です ◇She is a *shining example* of what people with disabilities can achieve. 彼女は障害(%)を持つ人が何を成し遂げられるかという輝かしい模範です ◇He is a captain who *leads by example*. 彼は範を示して指揮をとる司令官である ☞ **example** (INFLUENCE 名), **exemplify** (REPRESENT 2)

model [C] 《ほめて》模範, 手本 ◇Her essay was a *model* of clarity. 彼女のエッセーは明快さの好例だった ◇He's a *model* student. 彼は模範生だ ❶ a model of sb/sth の句や, 形容詞のように他の名詞の前で用いるのがふつう。◆ a *model* farm (= one that has been specially designed to work well) (モデル農場)

ideal [C, ふつう単数で] 理想 ◇It's my *ideal* of what a family home should be. それは私にとってあるべき家族の理想の姿です ❶ my, his, her などの所有代名詞と共に用いることが多い。

'**role model** [C] 模範人物 ◇We need positive *role models* for young men to aspire to. 若者が憧れるよい模範人物が必要だ

embodiment [C, ふつう単数で]《フォーマル》具現, 体現, 権化 ◇He is the *embodiment* of the young successful businessman. 彼は成功を収めた若き実業家を絵に描いたような存在だ ❶ embodiment は良い場合にも悪い場合にも用いることができる。☞ **embody** (REPRESENT 2)

epitome [単数形で]《フォーマル, 特に書き言葉》典型, 権化 ◇Her clothes are the *epitome* of good taste. 彼女の服はセンスの良さの典型だ ❶ epitome はほぼ常に, the epitome of sb/sth の句で用いる。人の外見・振る舞い方について用いることが多い。よい場合に用いられることが多いが, そうでない場合もあり, 例えば the epitome of evil の句もよく見られる。☞ **epitomize** (REPRESENT 2)

inspiration [C, ふつう単数で]《向上心から》刺激[鼓舞]する人[物] ◇Her charity work is an *inspiration* to us all. 彼女の慈善事業は我々みんなを鼓舞するものである ☞ **inspire** (INSPIRE)

archetype [単数で]《ややフォーマル, 書き言葉》典型 ◇She is the *archetype* of an American movie star. 彼女はアメリカの映画スターの典型だ ❶ archetype は通例, kindness, style のような質を表す単語と共には用いない。特定の階級[職業, 種類]の人や物に対して抱くイメージにどれだけマッチしているかを言うために, 具象名詞と共に用いることが多い。

excellent [形] ☞ GOOD 1, GREAT 1, WONDERFUL

excellent・outstanding・perfect・superb・classic・first-rate
非常に優れていることを表す
【類語訳】優れた, 素晴らしい, 傑出した, 申し分のない, とびきりの, 最高の, 最上級の, 一流の, 第一級の

文型&コロケーション
▶an excellent/ an outstanding/ a perfect/ a superb/ a first-rate **performance/ job**
▶an excellent/ an outstanding/ a perfect/ a superb/ a first-rate **service**
▶an excellent/ an outstanding/ a superb **achievement**
▶**really** excellent/ outstanding/ perfect/ superb/ first-rate
▶**absolutely** excellent/ outstanding/ perfect/ superb/ classic
▶**quite** excellent/ outstanding/ perfect/ superb

excellent 非常に優れた, 素晴らしい ◇The rooms are *excellent* value at $20 a night. 部屋は一晩20ドルにしては素晴らしい ◇The meals here are generally *excellent* (= usually excellent). ここの食事はだいたいとてもおいしい ◇She made one factual error in her otherwise *excellent* article. 彼女の記事は一つ事実誤認があったが, それ以外は素晴らしかった ◇He speaks *excellent* English. 彼は見事な英語を話す ❶ excellent は特に, サービスや人が働いて作った物の水準について用いる。反意 **mediocre**, ☞ **excellence** (VALUE)

outstanding 非常に優れた, 素晴らしい, 傑出した ◇She's one of their most *outstanding* young players. 彼女は彼らのチームの最も素晴らしい若手選手の一人だ ◇The valley has been designated an Area of *Outstanding* Natural Beauty. その渓谷は特別自然美観地域に指定されている ❶ outstanding は特に, 人がどれだけうまくやるか[得意か]を言うために用いる。
▸**outstandingly** [副] ◇The team has been *outstandingly* successful. チームは抜きん出て素晴らしい実績を収めてきた ◇He performed well but not *outstandingly*. 彼はよくやったが, 傑出しているというほどではなかった

perfect 非常に優れた, 申し分ない ◇The weather was *perfect*. 天気は申し分なかった ◇Conditions were *perfect* for walking. 散歩するには言うことのない状況だった ❶ perfect は特に, 状態, あるいは物事がいかに目的に適しているかについて用いる。

superb 《インフォーマル, 特に話し言葉》非常に優れた, とびきりの, 素晴らしい ◇The car's in *superb* condition. 車はとびきりいい状態にある ◇It was a *superb* goal, scored just seconds before half-time. それは前半終了直前に打ち込まれた素晴らしいゴールだった
▸**superbly** [副] ◇a *superbly* illustrated book 素敵な挿絵の入った本

classic [ふつう名詞の前で] 最高の(名に値する) ◇This *clas-*

sic novel was first published in 1938. この傑作小説は1938年に最初に出版された ▶**classic** [名] [C] ◇The second goal was an absolute *classic*. 2本目のゴールは本当に最高だった
first-rate 非常に優れた、最上級の、一流の、第一級の ◇They did a *first-rate* job. 彼らは最高の仕事をした ◇We aim to provide a *first-rate* service. 私どもは最上級のサービスを提供することを目指しています 反意 **second-rate** (POOR 2)

excess [形]

excess・spare・surplus・superfluous・leftover
求める[必要]以上の量[数]を表す
【類語訳】余分な、過度の、予備の、スペアの、余剰の、不要な

文型&コロケーション
▸ an excess/ a surplus **amount**
▸ excess/ surplus **demand/ supply**
▸ excess/ spare/ surplus **cash/ capacity/ energy**
▸ excess/ surplus/ leftover **food**

excess [名詞の前で] 余分な、過度の ◇*Excess* food is stored as fat. 余分な栄養分は脂肪として蓄えられる ◇Driving with *excess* alcohol in the blood is a serious offence. 過度の血中アルコール濃度での運転は重罪にあたる
▶**excess** [名] [U, 単数で] ◇The drug can be harmful if taken in *excess*. その薬物は過度に摂取すれば害となり得る ◇He started drinking *to excess* after losing his job. 彼は失業後暴飲し始めた ◇The increase will not be *in excess of* (= more than) two per cent. 増加は2%を上回らないだろう ◇Are you suffering from an *excess* of stress in your life? 生活中で過剰なストレスにお悩みですか
spare [ふつう名詞の前で] 予備の、スペアの ◇We've got a *spare* bedroom, if you'd like to stay. お泊りになりたければ、空いている寝室があります ◇I'm afraid I haven't got any *spare* cash. あいにく、余分な現金を持ち合わせていないんだ ◇Take some *spare* clothes in case you get wet. 濡れるといけないから、予備の服を持って行きなさい
surplus 余分な、余剰の ◇*Surplus* grain is being sold for export. 余剰穀物は輸出用に売られている ◇These items are *surplus to requirements* (= not needed). これらの品は必要以上に多い
▶**surplus** [名] [C, U] ◇Agricultural *surpluses* lead to the disposal of thousands of tonnes of food every year. 《ややフォーマル》余剰農産物は毎年何千トンもの食糧廃棄につながっている ◇After meeting domestic needs any *surplus* will be exported. 国内需要を満たした後、どの余剰物も輸出されます 反意 **deficit, shortage** (LACK)

ノート **excess, spare, surplus** の使い分け：spare が最もインフォーマルで、話し言葉や日常的な文脈で用いられる。surplus は余分な商品や金銭についてビジネス絡みで用いられる。◆*surplus* stock/material/products/capital/funds/income/profits（余剰在庫/物資/生産物/資本/資金/収入/収益）. excess は悪いものの余剰量に対してよく用いられる。◆*excess* body fat/carbon dioxide/baggage（余分な体脂肪/二酸化炭素/荷物）.

superfluous [名詞の前はまれ]《ややフォーマル》不要な、余計の ◇She gave him a look that made words *superfluous*. 彼女は言葉はいらないくらいの視線を彼に送った

leftover [名詞の前で] 食べ[飲み、使い]残しの ◇Use any *leftover* meat to make a curry. 食べ残しの肉を使ってカレーを作りなさい ❶特に食べ物について用いるが、他の物資についても用いることができる。◆*leftover* vegetables/porridge（食べ残しの野菜/おかゆ）. ◆*leftover* paper/paint/wool（余った紙/ペンキ/羊毛）.

excessive [形] ☞ HIGH 1

excessive・undue・over the top・disproportionate・inordinate・a bit much
必要[妥当、適切]の域を超えていると思われる人の行動[物事の]数量を表す
【類語訳】過度の、過多な、やりすぎの、度を越した、不釣合いな、不相応の、法外な

文型&コロケーション
▸ an excessive/ an undue/ a disproportionate/ an inordinate **amount** of sth
▸ an excessive/ a disproportionate/ an inordinate **number** of sth
▸ an excessive/ an undue/ a disproportionate/ an inordinate **burden**
▸ an excessive/ an undue/ a disproportionate **influence**
▸ excessive/ undue/ inordinate **delays/ emphasis**
▸ to **seem** excessive/ over the top/ disproportionate/ a bit much
▸ a bit/ a little/ slightly/ rather excessive/ over the top
▸ **grossly** excessive/ disproportionate
▸ **totally** over the top/ disproportionate

excessive 過度の、過多な ◇The amounts she borrowed were not *excessive*. 彼女の借りた額は過度ではなかった ◇*Excessive* drinking can lead to stomach disorders. 過度の飲酒は胃の調子を壊すことがある ◇He claimed that the police had used *excessive* force. 警察が度を越えた実力行使をしたと彼は主張した
▶**excessively** [副] ◇*excessively* high prices 法外な高値
undue [名詞の前で]《ややフォーマル》過度の ◇They are taking *undue* advantage of the situation. 彼らは状況を不当に利用している ◇We did not want to put any *undue* pressure on them. 彼らに必要以上のプレッシャーをかけたくなかった

ノート **excessive** と **undue** の使い分け：excessive は、excessive use/growth/heat/drinking のように、少ない場合には問題のない、過度の事実について用いることが多い。undue は、undue delay/hardship/alarm のように、見解の分かれる問題について、不当だと感じる時に用いることが多い。undue はしばしば、without/no undue pressure などのように否定の句で用いられ、通例不可算名詞を後に従える。

over the 'top [任意]《特に英、インフォーマル》やりすぎの、度を越した ◇His performance in the movie is completely *over the top*. その映画における彼の演技はまったくのやりすぎだ ◇OK, you've already thanked me, there's no need to *go over the top*! わかった、もう礼は言ってもらったから、それ以上はいらないよ

disproportionate 《ややフォーマル》（サイズ・数・量・度合いが）大き[多]すぎる、不釣合い[不相応]な ◇The area contains a *disproportionate* number of young unemployed people. その地域には無職の若者が多すぎる

◇The punishment was grossly **disproportionate to the crime**. その罰は犯罪に対してひどく不相応だった [反対]**proportionate** (RELATIVE)
▶**disproportionately** [副] ◇The lower-paid spend a *disproportionately* large amount of their earnings on food. 低賃金の人にかぎって食べ物に稼ぎをかけすぎる

inordinate [（フォーマル）]過度の, 法外な ◇They spent an *inordinate* amount of time and money on the production. 彼らは生産に時間と金を使いすぎた ◇The strike has led to *inordinate* delays. ストライキで極端な遅れが出た
▶**inordinately** [副] ◇*inordinately* high prices 法外な高値

a bit 'much《インフォーマル, けなして》（人の迷惑な行動が）あんまりな, ひど過ぎる ◇I think it's *a bit much* calling me at three in the morning, don't you? 朝の3時に電話してくるなんてあんまりだと思わない ◇The noise from next door is getting *a bit much*. 隣家からの騒音はだんだんひどくなっている

exchange 名

exchange・replacement・substitution・swap・barter・reversal
人に物を与えて[人のために何かをして]見返りをもらう行為
【類語訳】交換, 両替, 取り替え, 代用, 代替, 物々交換

〔文型&コロケーション〕
▶an exchange/ a swap/ a reversal **between** A and B
▶a **direct** exchange/ replacement/ substitution
▶a **straight** exchange/ swap
▶a **complete/ total** replacement/ reversal
▶to **result in** an exchange/ the replacement/ the substitution of sth

exchange [C, U] 交換；(通貨の)両替 ◇There was a brief *exchange* of glances. ちらっと視線を交わした ◇Woollen cloth and timber were sent to Egypt **in exchange for** linen. 毛織物と材木がリネンと交換にエジプトに送られた ◇I'll type your report if you'll babysit **in exchange**. 引き換えにベビーシッターをしてくれるなら, あなたの報告書をタイプしてあげるわ ◇I get you out of the country and you keep your mouth shut. Is that a **fair exchange**? 国外に出してやるから, 何もしゃべるな. 公平な取り引きだろう ◇We have currency *exchange* facilities. 両替サービスを行っています ◇Where can I find the best **exchange rate/rate of exchange**? どこが為替レートが最もいいですか ☞ **exchange** (REPLACE 2)

replacement [U]（新しい[よい]物との）交換, 取り替え ◇Complete *replacement* of the roof tiles would be very expensive. 屋根瓦を全部取り替えるととても費用がかかるでしょう ◇The original furnishings are now in need of *replacement*. 元々の調度品はもう取り替える必要があります ☞ **replace** (REPLACE 2), **replacement** (REPLACEMENT)

substitution [U, C]《ややフォーマル》代用, 交代 ◇the *substitution* of low-fat spreads for butter バターの代わりの低脂肪スプレッドの使用 ◇Two *substitutions* were made during the game (= two players were taken off and two others sent on in their place). 試合中交代が2件あった ☞ **substitute** (REPLACEMENT), **substitute** (REPLACE 1, 2)

swap（または **swop**）[C, ふつう単数で]《特に英, ややインフォーマル, 話し言葉 or ジャーナリズム》交換 ◇Let's **do a swap**. You work Friday night and I'll do Saturday. 取り替えよう. 君が金曜の夜働いて, ぼくが土曜に働く ◇Why not arrange a **job swap** with someone in another city or state? 他の市や州にいる人との職場交換を手配してはどうですか ❶ swap は語が短く, exchange のややインフォーマルな語としてジャーナリストがよく用いる. だが, exchange ほど多様な形では用いられない. do/make a swap (交換する)や, job/spy swap (仕事/スパイの交換)といった言い方で用いられる. ☞ **swap** (REPLACE 2), **swap** (SWITCH)

barter [U] 物々交換 ◇The islanders use a system of *barter* instead of money. 島民はお金の代わりに物々交換方式を用います ☞ **barter** (REPLACE 2)

reversal [C, U]（立場・役目の）交換 ◇It's a complete **role reversal/reversal of roles** (= for example when a husband cares for the house and children while the wife works). それは完全な役割交代である ❶ この意味では, ほとんど常に role reversal か reversal of roles の句で用いられる. ☞ **reverse** (REPLACE 2)

excited 形 ☞ HAPPY

excited・ecstatic・elated・euphoric・rapturous・exhilarated
人が喜び, 熱狂しているさまを表す
【類語訳】興奮した, 有頂天の, 狂喜した, 高揚した

〔文型&コロケーション〕
▶excited/ ecstatic/ elated/ euphoric **at** sth
▶excited/ ecstatic/ elated **about** sth
▶excited/ elated/ exhilarated **by** sth
▶ecstatic/ elated/ exhilarated **with** sth
▶ecstatic/ rapturous **applause/ praise**
▶an ecstatic/ a rapturous **welcome**
▶to **feel** excited/ elated/ euphoric/ exhilarated

excited 興奮した ◇The kids seem pretty *excited* about the trip. 子どもたちは旅行にかなり興奮しているようだ ◇He was really *excited* to be asked to play for Wales. 彼はウェールズの代表選手に起用され, 本当にわくわくしていた ◇The buzz of *excited* chatter was quite deafening. 興奮した話し声のざわめきがたまらなく耳障りだった
▶**excitedly** [副] ◇She waved *excitedly* as the car approached. 彼女は車が近づくにつれ興奮して手を振った

ecstatic 有頂天の, 狂喜した ◇Sally was *ecstatic* about her new job. サリーは新しい仕事に有頂天だった ◇He gave an *ecstatic* sigh of happiness. 彼は実に幸福そうな吐息を漏らした ❶ 時として, 宗教・セックス・死と結びつく. ◆an *ecstatic* vision of God（恍惚状態の中で見た神の幻）◆their brief but *ecstatic* honeymoon（短いがめくるめくような彼らの新婚旅行）◆a strange kind of *ecstatic* death by drowning（一風変わった恍惚状態の溺死）. ☞ **ecstasy** (JOY)
▶**ecstatically** [副] ◇He sighed *ecstatically*. 彼は喜悦の吐息をついた ◇For a time, we were *ecstatically* happy. 私たちは一時, 有頂天となった

elated（素晴らしいことのおかげで）高揚した ◇I was *elated* by the prospect of the new job ahead. 私はこれからの新しい仕事への期待でわくわくした ◇I was *elated* with the thrill of success. 成功の興奮で高揚していた

↪excited

excitement, exciting

euphoric (短い間だけ)非常に高揚した ◇My *euphoric* mood could not last. 私の高揚感は続かなかった ❶ euphoric は皮肉の効果を狙って否定文でしばしば用いられる。◆His parents were less than *euphoric* at the news of his engagement. (両親は彼の婚約の知らせを聞いても喜ぶどころではなかった)．☞**euphoria** (JOY)

rapturous (ふつう名詞の前で)熱狂的な，狂喜する ◇He was greeted with *rapturous* applause. 彼は熱狂的な拍手で迎えられた

exhilarated (運動の後)高揚した ◇She felt *exhilarated* with the speed and the rush of air. 彼女はスピードと吹きつけてくる強風に高揚感を覚えた

excitement 名

excitement・thrill・buzz・charge・exhilaration・high・kick
刺激的なことを(期待)しているときに感じる気持ち
【類語訳】興奮，スリル，高揚感

文型&コロケーション
▶(a) **real** excitement/ thrill/ buzz/ charge/ high/ kick
▶a **big** thrill/ high/ kick
▶to **give sb** a thrill/ buzz/ high/ kick
▶to **get** a thrill/ buzz/ charge/ kick **out of** sth

excitement [U, C] 興奮；興奮させるもの ◇The news caused great *excitement* among her friends. その知らせに彼女の友人たちは非常に興奮した ◇In her *excitement* she dropped her glass. 彼女は興奮してグラスを落とした ◇A shiver of *excitement* ran through her. 彼女は興奮で身震いした ◇The new job was not without its *excitements*. 新しい仕事には刺激がないわけでもなかった

thrill [C] わくわくする感じ，スリル；スリルを与えてくれる体験 ◇It gave me a big *thrill* to meet my favourite author in person. 大好きな作家に生で会ってすごくどきどきした ◇They were just in search of *cheap thrills* (= excitement that has no real value). 彼らはただお手軽なスリルを探していただけだった

buzz [単数で]《インフォーマル》快感，興奮，達成感 ◇Flying gives me a real *buzz*. 空を飛ぶのは実に興奮する ◇There was a *buzz* of excitement all around the room. 興奮が部屋中に渦巻いていた ◇You can sense the creative *buzz* in the city. その町では創造する喜びが肌身に感じられる

charge [単数で]《ややインフォーマル》快感[興奮，達成感](をもたらす力) ◇I get a real *charge* out of working hard and seeing good results. 私は懸命に取り組んだ好結果を目にすると心からやってよかったと思う ◇a film in which every scene carries an emotional *charge* どの場面も気持ちを高ぶらせる映画

exhilaration [U] (運動から得る)強い高揚感 ◇the *exhilaration* of galloping over miles of open country 広々とした土地を何マイルも馬で疾駆することの高揚感

high [C]《インフォーマル》(楽しいことをして[成功して])強い高揚感 ◇He was *on a real high* after winning the competition. 彼は競技に勝ってとても心躍っていた ◇the *highs and lows* of her acting career 彼女の俳優人生の浮き沈み ❶ある種の薬物を飲んで得られる強い高揚感も指す。◆The *high* lasted all night. (ハイな気分は一晩中続いた)．

kick [C]《インフォーマル》(少し危険なことをして得る)強い高揚感 ◇I get a *kick* out of driving fast cars. 高速

で車を運転するのはわくわくする ◇He gets his *kicks* from skiing. 彼はスキーをすることに非常なスリルを感じる ◇What do you do *for kicks*? スリルを得るために何をしますか

exciting 形

exciting・dramatic・heady・thrilling・exhilarating・stirring
出来事[体験，感情]が刺激をもたらすことを表す
【類語訳】刺激的な，興奮させる，劇的な，わくわくさせる，スリリングな，ぞくぞくさせる

```
exciting            thrilling           exhilarating
dramatic
heady
stirring
```

文型&コロケーション
▶exciting/ dramatic/ heady/ thrilling/ exhilarating/ stirring **stuff**
▶an exciting/ a dramatic/ a heady/ a thrilling/ an exhilarating **experience/ moment**
▶an exciting/ a dramatic/ a heady **atmosphere**
▶an exciting/ a dramatic/ a thrilling/ an exhilarating/ a stirring **performance**
▶an exciting/ a dramatic/ a thrilling/ a stirring **finish/ finale/ victory/ win**
▶an exciting/ a dramatic/ a stirring **tale**

exciting 刺激的な，興奮させる ◇They waited and waited for something *exciting* to happen. 彼らは何か心踊ることが起きるのを待っていた ◇This is one of the most *exciting* developments in biology in recent years. これは近年の生物学における最も興奮をもたらす進展の一つである ◇I still find the job *exciting*. いまだに仕事を刺激的だと感じる 反意 **unexciting**

dramatic (出来事・光景が)刺激[印象]的な，劇的な ◇They watched *dramatic* pictures of the police raid on TV. 彼らは警察の手入れの劇的な映像をテレビで見た ◇The village is set against the *dramatic* backcloth of Mont Blanc. その村はモンブランの印象的な眺めが背景となっている
➢**dramatically** 副 ◇The mountains rose *dramatically* behind them. 山々はその背後に印象的にそびえ立っていた

heady [ふつう名詞の前で] 刺激的な；気分を浮き立たせる ◇the *heady* scent of hot spices 香辛料の刺激的な香り ◇a *heady* mixture of desire and fear 欲望と恐怖の混じった高揚感 ◇Profits grew last year by a *heady* 35%. 昨年の利益は35%とめざましく伸びた

thrilling わくわくさせる，スリリングな ◇Don't miss next week's *thrilling* episode! 次週の胸躍るエピソードをお見逃しなく ◇The game had a *thrilling* finale, with three goals scored in the last five minutes. 最後の5分間に3点入って，試合はスリリングな結末を迎えた

exhilarating わくわくさせる，うきうきさせる ◇My first parachute jump was an *exhilarating* experience. 私のパラシュートジャンピング初体験は爽快なものだった

ノート exciting, thrilling, exhilarating の使い分け：
これらの単語の中で，exhilarating が最も激しく，exciting は

最も弱い. exciting は最も一般的で, 興奮を与えてくれるあらゆる活動, 体験, 感情, 出来事について用いることができる. thrilling は, 特に結末がはっきりしていない競争や話について用いられる. exhilarating は, 特にスピードや危険を伴う身体的活動について用いる.

stirring [ふつう名詞の前で] 強い感情[興奮]をかきたてる ◇a *stirring* performance of Beethoven's Fifth Symphony ベートーベンの第5交響曲の感動的な演奏 ◇*stirring* memories of past victories 過去の勝利の胸を熱くする思い出

exclude 動

1 exclude・eliminate・rule sb/sth out
物事を意図的に含めないことを表す
【類語訳】除外する, 除く, 排除する

文型&コロケーション
▶ to exclude/ eliminate/ rule out sth **as** sth
▶ to exclude/ eliminate sth **from** sth
▶ to be excluded/ eliminated/ ruled out **by** sb/ sth
▶ to exclude/ eliminate/ rule out a/ an **possibility/ explanation**
▶ to eliminate/ rule out sb **as a suspect**
▶ to exclude/ rule out **the idea of** sth
▶ to **completely/ entirely/ totally/ effectively** exclude/ eliminate/ rule out sth

exclude [他] 除外する, 除く ◇The cost of borrowing has been *excluded* from the inflation figures. 借入れコストはインフレの数値から除外されてきた ◇Try to *exclude* sugar and fat from your diet. 食事から糖分と脂肪を除くように心がけなさい ◇Buses run every hour, Sundays *excluded*. 日曜日を除き, バスは毎時走っています ◇We should not *exclude* the possibility of negotiation. 交渉の可能性を除外すべきではない ◇The police have *excluded* theft as a motive for the murder. 警察は殺害動機として窃盗を除外した 反意 **include** (INCLUDE)
▸ **excluding** 前 ◇Lunch costs £10 per person, *excluding* drinks. ランチは飲み物を別として, 一人10ポンドします 反意 **including** (INCLUDE)
▸ **exclusion** 名 [U, C] ◇Memories of the past filled her mind **to the exclusion of** all else. 他のものは何もなく, 過去の思い出で彼女は頭が一杯だった 反意 **inclusion** (INCLUDE)

eliminate [他] 《やゝフォーマル》排除する, 除く ◇The police have *eliminated* two suspects from their investigation. 警察は捜査から二人の容疑者を除外した ◇Malaria was *eliminated* as a cause of death. マラリアは死因から除かれた ◇We can only be certain once we have *eliminated* every other possible explanation. いったん他のあらゆる可能な説明を排除すれば, 確信だけが残る
▸ **elimination** 名 [U] ◇You can crack the code by *a process of elimination*. 消去法で暗号を解くことができます

,rule sb/sth 'out 句動詞 (人・物事を)除外する, 排除する ◇The proposed solution was *ruled out* as too expensive. 提案された解決策は費用がかかりすぎるとして除外された ◇We aren't *ruling* anything *out* at this stage. この段階では何も排除するつもりはない ◇He has not explicitly *ruled out* increasing taxes. 彼は増税することをはっきりとは排除しなかった

2 ☞ BAN 動, EXPEL
exclude・expel・keep sb/sth out・drop・shut sb/sth out・ostracize・blacklist・excommunicate
人や物を参加させない[場所に入らせない]こと, 人を場所から去らせることを表す
【類語訳】締め出す, 追放する, 追い出す, 排斥する, のけものにする, 破門する

文型&コロケーション
▶ to exclude/ expel/ drop/ excommunicate sb **from** sth
▶ to exclude/ expel/ drop/ ostracize/ blacklist/ excommunicate sb **for** sth
▶ to exclude/ expel a **pupil/ student/ child**
▶ to **feel** excluded/ ostracized

exclude [他, しばしば受身で] 締め出す ◇Women are still *excluded* from some golf clubs. 女性はいまだにいくつかのゴルフクラブから締め出されている ◇Large multinationals can make bids which effectively *exclude* local firms. 大規模な多国籍企業は地元企業を効率的に締め出す付け値での入札ができる ◇Many local people feel *excluded* from decisions that affect their own community. 地元民の多くは自分たちの地域社会に影響する決定から締め出されていると感じている ❶《英》では, exclude は不品行で学生を停学にすることを意味することもある. ◆Concern is growing over the number of children *excluded* from school. 《英》停学になる児童数に対する懸念が高まっている). 《米》では expel を用いる. 反意 **admit** (LET SB IN), **involve** (INCLUDE)
▸ **exclusion** 名 [U, C] ◇the causes of social *exclusion* 《やゝフォーマル》社会的疎外の原因 ◇Two *exclusions* from one school in the same week is unusual. 《英》一校から同じ週に二名が停学となるのは異常である

expel (-ll-) [他] (規則違反・悪行を理由に学校・組織から)追放する, 追い出す ◇She was *expelled* from school at 15. 彼女は15歳で退学となった ◇A number of Olympic athletes were *expelled* for drug-taking. 多くのオリンピック選手が薬物使用で除名された ◇They were forcibly *expelled* from their farm by the occupying authorities. 彼らは占領当局者によって農場から強制退去させられた
▸ **expulsion** 名 [U, C] ◇The principal threatened the three girls with *expulsion*. 校長は除籍にするぞと言って3人の少女を脅した

,keep sb/sth 'out 句動詞 (人・物を場所に)入らせない ◇*Keep* that dog *out* of my study! その犬を私の書斎に入れるな ◇They took security precautions to *keep* intruders *out*. 彼らは侵入者を入らせないために安全措置を講じた ◇The house has extra insulation to *keep out* the cold. その家は寒気を遮断するために断熱材を増量してある 反意 **let sb in** (LET SB IN)

drop (-pp-) [他] (人をチーム・グループから)いさせない ◇She's been *dropped* from the team because of injury. 彼女はけがを理由にチームのメンバーから外されている

,shut sb/sth 'out 句動詞 (人・物を場所に)入らせない, 締め出す ◇Mum, Ben keeps *shutting* me *out* of the bedroom! ママ, ベンが寝室に入れてくれないの ◇They make sunglasses which *shut out* 99% of the sun's harmful rays. 彼らは太陽の有害光線を99%遮るサングラスを作っている ◇He carefully locked the door behind him, *shutting out* the world. 彼は部屋に入ると背後のドアに慎重に鍵をかけて、世間を遮断した

|ノート| **exclude, keep sb/sth out, shut sb/sth out**の使い分け：exclude はややフォーマルで、ふつう規則や方針により人を建物やイベント会場などに入らせない場合に用いる。keep sb/sth out と shut sb/sth out はややインフォーマルで、ふつう人が場所に入るのを物理的に阻止する場合に用いられる。shut sb/sth out はドアなどの物的障壁を強調する。

ostracize (英でまた **-ise**) [他]《フォーマル》(グループ・社会などから)排斥する、のけものにする ◇He was *ostracized* by his colleagues for refusing to support the strike. 彼はストライキを支援するのを拒んだことを理由に同僚からのけ者にされた ◇The regime risks being *ostracized* by the international community. その政権は国際社会から排斥される危険を冒している

blacklist [他] (組織・政府が人・物の名前を)ブラックリストに載せる ◇She was *blacklisted* by all the major Hollywood studios because of her political views. 彼女はその政治的見解のせいで、ハリウッドのすべての大手スタジオのブラックリストに載っていた ◇At present, anything except specifically *blacklisted* substances can be dumped at sea. 現在、明確にブラックリストに載っている物質以外は何でも海に投棄できる ❶人・製品・国家のリストがブラックリストと呼ばれる。◇a *blacklist* of countries where illegal copying of software is thought to be widespread (ソフトの違法コピーが蔓延していると考えられる国家のブラックリスト)。

excommunicate [他] (ローマカトリック教会が人を)破門する ◇The Vatican upheld its decision to *excommunicate* seven women who were ordained as priests last year. ローマ教皇庁は、昨年司祭に任命されたとする7人の女性を破門する決定を支持した
▶ **excommunication** [名] [U, C] ◇They were threatened with *excommunication*. 彼らは破門するぞと脅された

executive [名]

executive・businessman/businesswoman/business person・entrepreneur・industrialist・magnate・tycoon
会社経営者[組織管理者]としての要職にある人
【類語訳】エグゼクティブ、管理職、幹部、実業家、起業家、社主、企業家、大物

|文型&コロケーション|
▶ a **local** executive/ businessman/ businesswoman/ entrepreneur/ industrialist/ magnate
▶ a **leading** executive/ businessman/ businesswoman/ entrepreneur/ industrialist/ magnate
▶ a **successful/ wealthy** businessman/ businesswoman/ entrepreneur/ industrialist
▶ an **ambitious** executive/ businessman/ businesswoman/ entrepreneur
▶ a **business** executive/ entrepreneur/ magnate/ tycoon
▶ a **media/ property** executive/ entrepreneur/ magnate/ tycoon
▶ a/ an **newspaper/ publishing/ oil** executive/ magnate/ tycoon

executive [C] エグゼクティブ、管理職、幹部 ◇He's a senior *executive* in a computer firm. 彼はコンピューター会社の上級幹部である ☞ **executive** (MANAGEMENT)

businessman, businesswoman, business person [C] (責任ある地位の)実業家 ◇For many years he was a successful *businessman*, running his own small business. 長年の間、彼はビジネスで成功を収めており、自分で小さな会社を経営していた ◇She's a brilliant and highly successful *businesswoman*. 彼女は大成功を収めた優秀な女性実業家だ ◇a hotel that caters to *business people* 実業家を対象にしたホテル ❶ businessman, businesswoman はしばしば、従業員のためというより自分自身のために働く人を表すのに用いる。またビジネスや金融関係に長けた人を表すのにも用いる。◆I should have got a better price for the car, and I'm not much of a *businessman*. (車にもっと高値を付けるべきだった、商売が下手でね)。business person はしばしば複数形(business people)で、男女の実業家をまとめて言う場合に用いられる。個人について言う場合は、businessman や businesswoman を用いるのがふつう。× She's a highly successful *business person*.

entrepreneur [C] 起業家、アントレプレナー ◇A creative *entrepreneur*, he was continually dreaming up new projects. 創造的な起業家だった彼は、次々と新しい事業を思い描き続けていた

industrialist [C] (大工場・大事業会社を所有[経営]する)社主、企業家 ◇He was the son of a wealthy *industrialist*. 彼は裕福な企業家の息子だった

magnate [C] 大事業家 ◇The company was owned by shipping *magnate* Fred Olsen. その会社は海運王フレッド・オルセンの所有だった

tycoon [C]《時にけなして》大物、巨頭 ◇Tapie, business *tycoon* and football club owner, was appointed Minister for Cities. 実業界の大物でサッカークラブのオーナーであるタピエは、都市担当大臣に任命された

|ノート| **magnate** と **tycoon** の使い分け：magnate はよい意味合いで用いられる傾向にあるが、tycoon は時として、ある点で人々の尊敬を失いがちな不誠実な種類の人間を示唆する。◆the disgraced/fallen/discredited media *tycoon* (面目を失った/堕落した/評判を落としたメディア王)。

exhibition [名]

exhibition・show・display・exhibit・fair・trade show/trade fair
コレクションが一般に公開されること
【類語訳】展示、展示会、展覧会、陳列、品評会、見本市

|文型&コロケーション|
▶ to be **on** exhibition/ show/ display/ exhibit
▶ a **big** exhibition/ show/ display/ exhibit/ fair
▶ a **major** exhibition/ show/ display/ exhibit
▶ an **international** exhibition/ show/ exhibit/ trade show/ trade fair
▶ a **public** exhibition/ show/ display/ exhibit
▶ a **permanent/ temporary** exhibition/ display/ exhibit
▶ an **annual** show/ fair/ trade show/ trade fair
▶ a **travelling/ touring** exhibition/ show/ display/ exhibit
▶ to **see** an exhibition/ a show/ a display/ an exhibit
▶ to **attend/ go to/ visit** an exhibition/ a show/ an exhibit/ a fair/ a trade show/ a trade fair
▶ to **have/ hold/ host** an exhibition/ a show/ an exhibit/ a

expand

fair/ a trade show/ a trade fair
▶ to **mount/ present/ put on** an exhibition/ a display/ an exhibit
▶ The exhibition/ show/ exhibit/ fair/ trade show/ trade fair **opens/ closes/ ends** on a particular date.

exhibition [C]《特に英》(美術品などのコレクションの)展示(品), 展覧会 ◇They are putting on an *exhibition* of old photographs. 古い写真の展示会が催されている ◇The Mappa Mundi is now on permanent *exhibition* at Hereford Cathedral. マッパ・ムンディは現在, ヘレフォード大聖堂で常設展に出されている ❶《米》で可算名詞のexhibitionを意味する語はふつうexhibitである.

show [C, U]《物のコレクションが寄せ集められる)展示(会), 展覧会 ◇They hold an agricultural *show* once a year. 彼らは年に一度農芸展示会を開く ◇The first couple of days at the Paris fashion *shows* are always a thrill. パリのファッションショーの最初の数日間はいつもわくわくする ◇The latest technology will be on *show* at the trade fair. 最新技術が見本市で展示されることになっている
☞ **show** (PRESENT 1)

ノート **exhibition** と **show** の使い分け: show は通例一時的なもの. exhibition は多くは一時的だが, 常設もありうる. 一時的な場合, 数か月続いたり, 他の都市や国の美術館へ何度か移設されることもある. exhibition は通例, 美術品や特別な文化的[科学的]興味を引く品目を含む. show はより一般的な語で, 幅広い層の人々に訴えるイベントを示唆する.

display [C]（人々を楽しませる[商品を宣伝するための])公共の場での)展示, 陳列 ◇The window *display* changes once a month. ショーウィンドウの商品展示は月に一度変わります ◇The medals can be seen in a *display* cabinet on the first floor. メダルは1階の陳列棚で見ることができます ☞ **show** (PRESENT 1)

exhibit [C]《米》展覧会, 展示会 ◇a Matisse *exhibit* at the National Gallery ナショナル・ギャラリーでのマチス展

fair [C]《米》(広場・公園での家畜・農産物の)品評会 ◇We all went south for the state *fair*. 私たちはみな州の品評会のため南に向かった ❶《英》ではan agricultural showと言う.《英》でも, an art/a craft *fair* では芸術家が自分たちの作品を展示・販売するイベントである. **a jobs/careers fair** は, 仕事を探している人たちが雇ってくれる可能性のある会社についての情報を入手できるイベントである.

trade show, trade fair [C]（多くの会社が製品を展示・販売する)(産業)見本市 ◇Opening on June 11, the *trade show* will feature a wide range of goods. 産業見本市は6月11日に始まり, 幅広い製品が出展されます

expand 動

expand・widen・extend・enlarge・broaden・lengthen・stretch
物がより大きくなる, 物をより大きくする
【類語訳】膨張する, 拡大する, 広がる, 広げる, 延長する, 大きくする, 大きくなる, 伸ばす, 伸びる

文型&コロケーション
▶ to **expand/ widen/ extend/ enlarge/ lengthen/ stretch** to a particular amount
▶ to **expand/ widen/ extend/ lengthen** by a particular amount
▶ to **expand/ widen/ extend/ enlarge/ broaden** sth's **scope**/ range
▶ to **expand/ widen/ extend/ broaden** your **knowledge**
▶ to **widen/ broaden/ extend** your **experience**
▶ to **expand/ extend/ enlarge** your **vocabulary**
▶ sth is **considerably/ slightly** expanded/ widened/ extended/ enlarged/ broadened
▶ sth is **greatly** expanded/ widened/ extended/ enlarged

expand [自, 他]（大きさ・数・重要性が[を])膨張する, 拡大する, 広がる, 広げる ◇Metals *expand* when they are heated. 金属は熱せられると膨張する ◇Student numbers are *expanding* rapidly. 学生数が急激に増加している ◇The waist *expands* to fit all sizes. 胴囲はすべてのサイズに合うように伸びます ◇The new system *expanded* the role of family doctors. 新システムはかかりつけの医者の役割を広げた ◇There are no plans to *expand* the local airport. 地元の空港を拡張する計画はない 反意 **contract** (SHRINK), ☞ **grow** (RISE)

▶ **expansion** 名 [U, C] ◇The *expansion* of higher education will continue. 高等教育の拡充は継続するだろう ◇The book is an *expansion* of a series of lectures given last year. その本は昨年行われた一連の講義を発展させたものである

widen [自, 他]（物が[を])広くなる[広くする]; (物の程度・範囲が[を])大きくなる[大きくする] ◇Her eyes *widened* in surprise. 彼女の目は驚いて広がった ◇Here the stream *widens* into a river. ここで小川は広がって川となります ◇They may have to *widen* the road to cope with the increase in traffic. 交通量の増加に対処するため道路を広げなければならないかもしれない ◇The legislation will be *widened* to include all firearms. その法律は範囲が広げられてすべての火器を含むことになるだろう 反意 **narrow** (SHRINK)

extend [他]（物を)拡大する, 延長する; (考え・影響力・業・活動)を広める ◇You can add value to your house by *extending* or renovating it. 拡張や改修によってあなたの家の価値を高めることができます ◇There are plans to *extend* the road network in the north of the country. 国の北部に道路網を拡張する計画がある ◇The school is *extending* the range of subjects taught. その学校は教える学科の範囲を広げている ◇The company plans to *extend* its operations into Europe. その会社にはヨーロッパへの事業拡大計画がある

▶ **extension** 名 [C, U] ◇the gradual *extension* of the powers of central government 中央政府の力の段階的な拡大 ◇a planned *extension* to the hospital《特に英》計画されている病院の増築

enlarge [他, 自]（物を)大きくする, 拡大する; (物が)大きくなる ◇There are plans to *enlarge* the recreation area. レクリエーション区域を拡大する計画がある ◇Reading will *enlarge* your vocabulary. 読書は語彙を増やします ◇The little blisters *enlarge* and eventually burst to form ulcers. 小さな疱疹は大きくなって, 最終的には破れて潰瘍を形成する ❶ enlarge は特に受動態でも用いて「写真[書類]を拡大コピーする」を意味する. ◆ We're going to have this picture *enlarged*. (この写真を引き伸ばしてもらうつもりです)

ノート **extend** と **enlarge** の使い分け: extend はふつう, enlarge より大規模に行われる. house などの建物は extend され, picture や部屋[場所, 建物]内の area は enlarge される.

broaden [自, 他] 広くなる, 広がる; 広める, 広げる ◇Her smile *broadened*. 彼女の顔に笑みが広がった ◇The party needs to *broaden* its appeal to voters. その政党は有権者たちへのアピールを広げる必要がある [反意] **narrow** (SHRINK)

lengthen [自, 他] 長くなる, 伸びる; 長くする, 伸ばす ◇The afternoon shadows *lengthened*. 午後の影が伸びた ◇I need to *lengthen* this skirt. このスカートの丈を伸ばさなきゃ ◇He *lengthened his stride* to catch up with them. 彼は彼らに追いつくために歩幅を広くした [反意] **shorten** (SHRINK)

stretch [自, 他] 引っぱって伸びる; 引き伸ばす ◇This sweater has *stretched*. このセーターは伸びてしまった ◇Stop *stretching* your sleeves like that! そんなふうに袖を引っぱるのはやめなさい ❶ stretchする生地は引っぱると大きく[長く]なるが, はなすと元の形に戻る. ◆The jeans *stretch* to provide a perfect fit. (そのジーンズは伸び縮みしてぴったりフィットします).

expect [動] ☞ HOPE [動]

expect・think・anticipate・await・look forward to sth・look for sth・look ahead・watch for sb/sth・bargain for/on sth
物事の発生を信じる[待つ]
【類語訳】予期する, 予想する, 心待ちにする, 当てにする, 期待する, 楽しみにする

文型&コロケーション
▶ to expect/ think/ anticipate **that**...
▶ **It is** expected/ thought/ anticipated that...
▶ to anticipate/ look forward to/ bargain on **doing sth**
▶ to expect/ anticipate/ await/ look forward to/ look for **results**
▶ to expect/ anticipate/ await/ look forward to a **reply**
▶ to expect/ anticipate/ await/ look forward to the **arrival** of sb/ sth
▶ to await/ look for/ watch for **signs** of sth
▶ to expect/ anticipate/ watch for **trouble**
▶ to **eagerly** anticipate/ await/ look forward to/ look for/ watch for sth
▶ to **confidently** expect/ anticipate/ await/ look forward to sth
▶ to **anxiously** expect/ await/ watch for sth

expect [他] 予期する, 予想する; (予定されている人・物の到着を)心待ちにする, 当てにする ◇You can't *expect to* learn a foreign language in a few months. 数か月で外国語を覚えられると思っちゃいけない ◇I looked back, *half expecting* to see someone following me. 誰かがついていると半ば予想しながら振り返った ◇It is *expected* that the report will suggest some major reforms. 報告書がいくつかの大改革を提唱するものと予想されている ◇Don't *expect* sympathy from me! 私に同情するな ◇Are you *expecting* visitors? お客が来るんですか ◇I'm *expecting* an important call. 大切な電話を待っているんです ☞ **to be expected** (PREDICTABLE)

think [他] 予期する, 予想する ◇I never *thought* (that) I'd see her again. 彼女に再会するとはまったく思っていなかった ◇The job took longer than we *thought*. 仕事は私たちが思っていたより時間がかかった ◇You'd *think* she'd have been grateful for my help (= but she wasn't). 彼女が私の手助けにずっと感謝してきたとあなたは思うでしょうが ◇Who would have *thought* (= I didn't expect) to find you here? 誰がここであなたに出くわすと思っただろうか ❶ think は予想が間違いであるとわかるときにのみ, expectを意味するのに用いる. ×It is *thought* that the report will suggest some major reforms. 通例(thatが省略されていても) that節がつづき, 名詞句を目的語にとることはできない. ×Don't *think* sympathy from me.

anticipate [他] 《ややフォーマル》予期する; 楽しみに待つ ◇We don't *anticipate* any major problems. 重大な問題が起こることなど予期していない ◇They *anticipate* moving to bigger premises by the end of the year. 彼らは年末までにもっと大きな屋敷に引っ越すのを楽しみにしている ◇We *anticipate* that sales will rise next year. 来年は売り上げが伸びるだろうと期待します ◆The band today announced details of their *widely anticipated* third album. バンドは本日, 広く期待を集めていた3枚目のアルバムの詳細を公表しました

ノート expect と anticipate の使い分け: expect は, 日常会話を含め, フォーマル・インフォーマル, いずれのスピーチやライティングにも用いられる. anticipate は特にビジネスや公式声明のような, わずかにフォーマルな話し言葉・書き言葉の中で用いられる.

await [他] 《フォーマル》待ち受ける, 待ち構える ◇He is in custody *awaiting* trial. 彼は拘留されて裁判を待ち受けている ◇Her latest novel is eagerly *awaited*. 彼女の最新小説が熱望されている

ˌlook¹ forward to sth [句動詞] 《しばしば進行形で》心待ちにする, 楽しみに待つ ◇We're really *looking forward to* seeing you again. 再会するのを本当に心待ちにしています ◇Customers can *look forward to* a 5% cut in their bills. お客様は請求金額の5%の割引が期待できます ◇It will give her *something to look forward to*. そこから彼女は後になってのお楽しみが期待できるでしょう ❶ 進行形 I'm looking forward to... はしばしば, 楽しみに待っている物事について用いられる. 現在形 I/We look forward to... はしばしば, フォーマルあるいは商用通信の結びに儀礼上の常套句として用いられる. ◆I *look forward to* hearing from you (= please reply). (お返事を心待ちにしております). ◆We *look forward to* working with you again in the future. (またいつか仕事でご一緒するのを楽しみにしています). 手紙の結びにexpectは用いてはならない. ×I *expect* your reply. [反意] **dread** (FEAR)

ˈlook for sth [句動詞] 《ややフォーマル》(物事を)期待する; (物事が起きるのを)予期する ◇We are a peaceful people and we are not *looking for* revenge. 私たちは平和を愛する民族であり, 復讐を望んではいません ◇We shall be *looking for* an improvement in your work this term. 今学期, あなたの学習面での向上を期待しています

ˌlook aˈhead [句動詞] 将来のことを考える, 先を見越す ◇They have to learn to *look ahead to* the possible consequences of their actions. 彼らは自分たちの行動が引き起こすであろう結果について考えられるようにならなければならない ◇*Looking ahead*, nuclear power may have the best growth prospects. 将来を見越せば, 原子力は最も成長の見込みがあるかもしれない

ˈwatch for sb/sth [句動詞] (人・物を)待ち構える, 待ち受ける ◇*Watch for* the early signs of stress. ストレスの初期兆候に注意しなさい ◇The cat was on the wall *watching for* birds. 猫は塀の上で鳥を待ち構えていた

'**bargain for/on sth** 句動詞 《ふつう否定文で》《ややインフォーマル》(物事が起きるのを)予期する ◇He obviously hadn't *bargained on* finding you there already. 彼がそこで早くもあなたに出会うと予期していなかったのは明らかだった ◇When he agreed to answer a few questions, he *got more than he bargained for*. いくつかの質問に応じることにしたらそれどころではない事態に至った

expectation 名

expectation・forecast・prediction・projection・anticipation・prophecy・foresight
未来に生じることに関する言明[信念]や、そうした言明を行える能力
【類語訳】見込み、予想、予測、予報、予言、先見の明、洞察力

▫文型&コロケーション▫
- expectations/ a forecast/ a prediction/ a projection/ a prophecy **about** sth
- expectations/ a forecast/ predictions/ projections **for** sth
- **contrary to/ against** expectation/ predictions
- **in** expectation/ anticipation **of** sth
- (a/ an) **current/ optimistic** expectations/ forecast/ prediction/ projection
- an expectation/ a forecast/ a prediction/ projections/ anticipation/ a prophecy **that**…
- **future** expectations/ predictions/ projections
- an **official** forecast/ prediction/ projection
- an **accurate** forecast/ prediction/ prophecy
- to **make** a forecast/ prediction/ projection/ prophecy
- to **revise** expectations/ a forecast/ predictions / projections
- sth **is based on** an expectation/ a forecast/ a projection
- an expectation/ a forecast/ a prediction/ a projection **is based on** sth

expectation [C, U] (どうやらそうなりそうな)見込み、予想 ◇We are confident in our *expectation* of a full recovery. 我々は全面回復の見込みに自信がある ◇The *expectation* is that property prices will rise. 不動産価格は上昇するだろうという予想だ ◇*Against all expectations*, she was enjoying herself. すべての予想に反して、彼女は楽しく過ごしていた ◇I applied for the job more in hope than *expectation*. 見込みは薄くても願いを込めてその仕事に応募した ☞ **expectation** (HOPE 名 2)

forecast [C] (現在手に入る情報に基づいた)予報、予想 ◇It is too early to make firm *forecasts* about demand. 需要に関する確固たる予想を出すには早すぎる ◇The *sales forecasts* are encouraging. 販売予測は良好である ◇The *weather forecast* wasn't too bad. 天気予報はさほど悪くなかった ☞ **forecast** (PREDICT)

prediction [C, U] (将来起きると思うことについての)予言(をすること) ◇Not many people agree with the government's *prediction* that the economy will improve. 経済は改善するだろうという政府予測に同意しない人が多い ◇Our *prediction* turned out to be correct. 我々の予言は正しかった ◇Skilled readers make use of context and *prediction*. 読書に熟達した人たちは文脈と予測を活用する ☞ **predict** (PREDICT)

projection [C] (現在起こっていることに基づいた)見込み、予測 ◇Sales have exceeded our *projections*. 売り上げは我々の見積もりを上回った ◇*On* current *projec-*

tions, there will be more than ten million people aged 65 and over in 2010. 現在の推定では、2010年には65歳以上の人は1千万人を超える ◇Calculations are based on a *projection* of existing trends. 計算は現在の動向からの予測に基づいている ☞ **project** (PREDICT)

anticipation [U] 予想、先見 ◇People are buying extra groceries in *anticipation* of heavy snowstorms. 人々は猛吹雪を見越して余分の食糧雑貨を購入している ☞ **anticipate** (EXPECT)

prophecy [C, U]《魔力・宗教的な力による》予言；予言能力 ◇Macbeth believed the witches' *prophecy* about his future. マクベスは自分の将来に関する魔女の予言を信じた ◇Low expectations can become a *self-fulfilling prophecy*. 期待値の低い見込みを立てると自らそのレベルに甘んじてしまいかねない ◇She was believed to have the gift of *prophecy*.《フォーマル》彼女には予言の力があると信じられていた ☞ **prophesy** (PREDICT)

foresight [U]《ほめて》先見の明、洞察力 ◇She had *had the foresight to* prepare herself financially in case of an accident. 事故に備えて財政的な準備をする先見の明が彼女には備わっていた ◇The government's policies show a remarkable *lack of foresight*. 政府の方針は著しく将来への洞察に欠けている 反意 **hindsight** ❶ hindsightとは「後知恵」のことで、先にわかっていれば違ったことをしていただろうという意味を持つ。◆*With hindsight* it is easy to say that they should not have released him. (後から考えて、彼らは彼を解放すべきではなかったというのは簡単だ). ◆What looks obvious in *hindsight* was not at all obvious at the time. (後から考えれば明らかに見えることでも、そのときはまったく明らかではなかった). ☞ **foresee** (PREDICT)

expel 動 ☞ EXCLUDE 2

expel・deport・exile・banish・extradite・repatriate・displace
人を無理やり他国に行かせる
【類語訳】退去させる、追放する、引き渡す、送還する、追いやる

▫文型&コロケーション▫
- to expel/ deport/ exile/ banish/ extradite/ repatriate sb **to/ from** a country
- to expel/ deport/ repatriate/ displace **refugees**
- to expel/ deport/ repatriate **immigrants**
- to **forcibly** expel/ deport/ repatriate sb

expel (-ll-) [他] 国外に退去させる ◇Foreign journalists are being *expelled*. 外国人ジャーナリストが国外に退去させられている
▸ **expulsion** 名 [U, C] ◇These events led to the *expulsion* of senior diplomats from the country. これらの事件のせいで上級外交官は国外退去となった

deport [他]《違法行為・不法滞在を理由に》国外に退去させる ◇He was convicted of drug offences and *deported*. 彼は麻薬犯罪で有罪となり強制国外退去となった
▸ **deportation** 名 [U, C] ◇Several of the asylum seekers now face *deportation*. 数人の亡命希望者が現在、国外退去に直面している

exile [他、ふつう受身で]《政治的理由で・刑罰として》国外に追放する ◇*Exiled* opposition leaders have made an appeal to the international community. 国外追放された野党の指導者たちは国際社会に理解を求めている
▸ **exile** 名 [U] ◇to be/live *in exile* 追放されている／亡命

生活を送る ◇to go/be forced/be sent ***into exile*** 亡命する/強制追放される/追放の身となる ◇a place of *exile* 流刑地 ◇He returned after 40 years of *exile*. 彼は40年の亡命生活の末帰国した ☞ **exile (REFUGEE)**

banish [他, ふつう受身で] (処罰として)去るよう命じる, 追放する ◇He was *banished* to Australia, where he died five years later. 彼はオーストラリアへの追放を宣告され, 5年後その地で死亡した ◇The servants were *banished* from the upstairs rooms. 使用人たちは2階の部屋を出て行くよう命じられた ❶ banish は過去の出来事について用いることが多い. 現在の場面や法律関係の場面ではあまり用いない.
▸ **banishment** [名][U] ◇Lady Montague dies of grief at Romeo's *banishment*. モンタギュー夫人はロミオの追放への悲しみから亡くなります

extradite [他] (犯罪者を犯罪を犯した国へ)引き渡す ◇The courts have refused to *extradite* the suspects from Spain. 裁判所はスペイン出身の容疑者たちを引き渡すのを拒んだ
▸ **extradition** [名][U] ◇The *extradition* of terrorist suspects will cause controversy. テロの容疑者の引き渡しは物議をかもすだろう ◇an *extradition* treaty 犯罪人引き渡し条約 ◇to start *extradition* proceedings 身柄引き渡しの手続きを始める

repatriate [他] 本国へ送還する[連れ戻す] ◇The refugees were forcibly *repatriated*. 難民たちは本国へ強制送還された ◇Tourists who are injured or fall sick are *repatriated*. 傷病を抱えた旅行者は本国に送還されます
▸ **repatriation** [名][U, C] ◇Several refugees took part in the voluntary *repatriation* programme. 数人の難民たちが自主帰還計画に基づいて帰国した

displace [他, しばしば受身で]《ややフォーマル》(自宅から)追いやる[強制退去させる] ◇An estimated 50,000 people have been *displaced* from their homes by the conflict. 推定5万人が紛争によって自宅を追われている
▸ **displacement** [名][U] ◇the largest *displacement* of civilian population since World War Two《フォーマル》第2次世界大戦後最大の一般市民の強制退去

expensive 形 ☞ HIGH 1

expensive・costly・overpriced・pricey
多額の金がかかることを表す
【類語訳】高価な, 値の張る, 高くつく

文型&コロケーション
▸ expensive/ costly/ pricey for sb/ sth
▸ expensive/ costly to do sth
▸ very/ too/ fairly/ quite/ pretty expensive/ costly/ pricey

expensive 多額の金のかかる; 高価な, 値段の高い ◇Art books are enormously *expensive* to produce. 美術書の製作費は巨額である ◇Making the wrong decision could prove to be *expensive*. 誤った決定を下すことは高くつくとわかるだろう ◇That dress was an *expensive* mistake. そのドレスは高くつき過ぎだった ◇an *expensive* restaurant 高いレストラン [反義] **cheap, inexpensive (CHEAP)**, ☞ **expense (PRICE)**
▸ **expensively** 副 ◇*expensively* dressed/furnished 高価なドレスを着た/高価な家具の付いた

costly 《ややフォーマル》(予想以上に)多額の金がかかる, 高くつく ◇You want to avoid *costly* legal proceedings if you can. できれば費用のかかる法的手続きを避けたいのでしょう

overpriced 高すぎる ; (値打ち以上に)金のかかる ◇ridiculously *overpriced* designer clothes ばかばかしいほど高価なデザイナーブランドの服 ◇The commission is set to investigate claims that CDs are *overpriced*. CDの値段が高すぎるという声を調査するために委員会が設置されている

pricey《インフォーマル》高価な ◇Houses in the village are now too *pricey* for local people to afford. その村の住宅は今やあまりに高くて地元住民には買うことができない

experienced 形

experienced・veteran・seasoned・practised・long-serving
人が特定の活動について経験が十分であることを表す
【類語訳】熟練した, 経験豊富な, ベテランの, 古参の, 古株の

文型&コロケーション
▸ to be experienced/ practised in sth
▸ an experienced/ a veteran/ a seasoned campaigner
▸ an experienced/ a veteran actor/ diplomat/ politician/ soldier
▸ an experienced/ a seasoned observer
▸ an experienced/ a practised eye/ hand
▸ well seasoned/ practised

experienced 熟練した, 経験豊富な ◇She's a very *experienced* teacher. 彼女は非常に経験豊かな教師である ◇He's very *experienced* in looking after animals. 彼は動物の世話に非常に熟練している ☞ **experience (KNOWLEDGE), experienced (SOPHISTICATED)**

veteran [名詞の前で]《特にジャーナリズム》経験豊かな, ベテランの ◇The speech was given by the *veteran* British actor and producer, Sir Richard Attenborough. スピーチの主は, 英国のベテラン俳優でプロデューサーのリチャード・アッテンボロー卿だった ❶ veteran は特に, 俳優・スポーツ選手・兵士・政治家について用いる. ふつう, かなり高齢でその分野で実績豊富な人に用いる.

seasoned [ふつう名詞の前で]《特に書き言葉》経験豊富な ◇Mitchell is a *seasoned* campaigner for peace. ミッチェルは経験豊富な平和運動家である ❶ seasoned は一般的に, traveller, campaigner, performer, observer と結びつく.

practised《英》《米 practiced》《特に書き言葉》(定期的に行っているので)長けている, 経験を積んだ ◇It takes a *practised* eye to spot the difference. 違いを見極めるには熟練の目を必要とする ◇He has good ideas but he isn't *practised* in the art of marketing. 彼はいいアイデアを持っているが, 販売の手腕には長けていない ❶ *practised* は人の身体能力について用いることが多い. (a) *practised* eye/hand/skill (熟練の目/手腕/技術). 時として, practised ease (経験からくるゆとり)を持って物事を行うと言うこともある. ☞ **practise (PRACTISE)**

long-serving [名詞の前で] (仕事・地位について)古参の, 古株の ◇Several *long-serving* employees are due to retire this year. 古株の従業員の何人かは, 今年退職予定である ❶ long-serving は一般に, employees, a member of staff/a committee/the Cabinet, a councillor, minister, senator, representative について用いる.

experimental, expert

experimental 形 ☞ MODERN

experimental • modern • modernist • futuristic • avant-garde • postmodernist

旧来のものとは異なるよう意図され、意外で衝撃的な場合もあり、新しくて珍しい考え、様式、方法に基づいていることを表す
【類語訳】実験的な、モダンな、モダニズムの、前衛的な、アバンギャルドな

文型&コロケーション
- an experimental/ a modern/ a modernist **approach**
- experimental/ modern/ modernist/ avant-garde/ post-modernist **art/ writing/ works**
- experimental/ modern/ modernist/ postmodernist **fiction/ novels**
- experimental/ modern/ avant-garde **music/ theatre**
- a modern/ a modernist/ a futuristic/ an avant-garde **style**
- a modern/ modernist/ futuristic **building**

experimental 実験的な、試験的な ◇The equipment is still at the *experimental* stage. その装置はまだ実験段階にある ◇Doctors stress that this kind of treatment is still *experimental*. 医師たちはこの種の治療はまだ実験的な段階にあると強調する
> **experimentally** 副 ◇The new drug is being used *experimentally* on some patients. 新しい薬は数人の患者に実験的に用いられている

modern (必ずしも受け入れられるとは限らない)新式の、モダンな ◇She has very *modern* ideas about educating her children. 彼女は自分の子どもの教育についてとても新しい考えを持っている 反意 **old-fashioned** (OLD-FASHIONED), **traditional** (TRADITIONAL), ☞ **modern** (MODERN)

modernist [名詞の前で] モダニズムの、現代[近代]主義の
❶ モダニズムとは、20世紀半ばに普及した芸術、建築、文学における様式や運動であり、そこでは旧来の考え、方法、材料よりも現代的なものが用いられた。 ◆The museum devotes a large gallery to *modernist* art. (その美術館はモダニズムの芸術に広い展示室を充てている)

futuristic (建築・デザインが)未来を先取りしたような、超近代的な ◇The cover of the novel shows a *futuristic* city on the moon. その小説の表紙には月面上の未来都市が描かれている

avant-garde (美術・音楽・文学が驚愕(がく)的)[衝撃的]な ほど)前衛的な、アバンギャルドな ◇The theatre shows a lot of *avant-garde* work. その劇場は前衛的な作品を多く上演する

postmodernist [名詞の前で] ポスト・モダニズムの ❶ ポスト・モダニズムとは、20世紀後半の芸術、建築、文学における様式や運動であり、例えば、旧来の様式と現代的な様式の特徴を取り混ぜることによって、現代的な分野に反発する。 ◆an analysis of *postmodernist* cultural forms (ポスト・モダニズムの文化様式についての分析)

expert 名

expert • specialist • authority • guru • pundit • buff • connoisseur • aficionado

特定のテーマについて知識が豊富な人
【類語訳】専門家、エキスパート、権威、大家、評論家、通、ファン、マニア、目利き、鑑定家

文型&コロケーション
- an expert/ a specialist/ an authority **in/ on** sth
- an expert/ a specialist/ an authority **in the field** (of sth)
- a **great** expert/ authority/ connoisseur
- a **leading** expert/ specialist/ authority/ pundit
- a **recognized** expert/ specialist/ authority
- an **independent/ outside** expert/ specialist/ authority
- a **financial/ technical** expert/ specialist/ guru
- a **media** expert/ specialist/ guru/ pundit
- a **computer** expert/ specialist/ guru/ buff
- a **wine/ food** expert/ guru/ buff/ connoisseur
- a **film/ cinema/ movie** pundit/ buff/ connoisseur

expert [C] (特別な知識を持った[技術を備えた、訓練を積んだ])専門家、エキスパート ◇She's a leading *expert* in child psychology. 彼女は児童心理学における卓越した専門家である ◇He's an *expert* at getting his own way. 彼はわが道を行く達人だ ◇I'm no *expert*, but I think you should get that cut seen to. 私は専門家でないが、その切り傷は治療してもらうべきだと思う ☞ **expert** (IMPRESSIVE), **expertise** (SKILL 2)

specialist [C] (仕事・研究の特定領域における)専門家; (特定の医学分野を熟知した)専門医 ◇He's a noted *specialist* in his field. 彼はその分野で有名な専門家である ◇I was sent to see a *specialist* at the local hospital. 専門医に診てもらうために地元の病院に送られた ◇a cancer/ ear/eye/heart *specialist* がん/耳/目/心臓の専門医
> **specialist** 形 ◇You need some *specialist* advice. あなたには専門家のアドバイスが必要です
> **specialize** (英ではまた **-ise**) [自] [動] ◇He *specialized* in criminal law. 彼は刑法を専門とした ◇Many students prefer not to *specialize* too soon. 多くの学生はあまり早く専門を定めることを好まない

authority [C] (ある問題について特別な知識を持った)権威、大家 ◇She is an *authority* on early musical instruments. 彼女は古楽器の権威である ☞ **authoritative** (RELIABLE 2)

> ノート **expert** と **authority** の使い分け：expert はふつう、何かに熟練し、人に役立つアドバイスやトレーニングを与えられる人を指す。 authority は、学術的なテーマを熟知した人を指すが、そのテーマは非常に興味深いかもしれないが、他の人にとっては知りたりアドバイスを受けたりすることが必要[有用]なものでないこともある。

guru 《インフォーマル、特にジャーナリズム》(ビジネス・政治・ファッションの分野での)専門家、大家 ◇Most management *gurus* base their appeal on one big theme. ほとんどの経営の大家は一つの大きなテーマに自分の有用性の基礎を置いている ❶ guru は一般的には、business, management, leadership, investment, marketing, fashion, design, style などと結びつく。 ☞ **mentor** (ADVISER)

pundit [C] (テレビで公に語る)評論家 ◇Football *pundit* Ron Atkinson has resigned from his TV job. サッカー評論家のロン・アトキンソンはテレビの仕事から退いた ◇Political *pundits* agree that the government has scored a major victory. 政治評論家たちは政府が大勝利を収めたとの意見で一致している

buff [C] (複合語で) (特定のテーマ・活動への関心・知識を持つ)通、ファン、マニア ◇Opera *buffs* should enjoy the summer season this year. オペラファンは今年のサマーシーズンを楽しむべきである ☞ **enthusiast** (FAN)

connoisseur [C] (食べ物・音楽などの質の判断に長けた)

↳ expert / explain

目利き, 鑑定家 ◇She's a respected *connoisseur* and collector of modern sculpture. 彼女は評判の高い現代彫刻の鑑定家であり収集家である

aficionado [C] (特定のテーマ・活動への関心・知識を持つ) 通, ファン, マニア ◇He's an *aficionado* of the history of the game. 彼はゲームの歴史の愛好家である ◇Jazz *aficionados* gathered at the Hollywood Bowl last night for a tribute concert. ジャズファンは昨晩, トリビュート・コンサートのためにハリウッド・ボウルに集まった

ノート buff と aficionado の使い分け: buff は常に, 他の名詞の後に付いて複合語として用いられる. opera, wine, film, movie, cinema, theatre, computer, cricket と最も頻繁に結びつく. aficionado は, 複合語の形あるいは an aficionado of の形で用いられるが, 結びつく名詞はより多岐にわたる.

explain 動

1 explain・illustrate・define・clarify・ shed/cast/throw light on sth・spell sth out・ interpret・expound
理解できるように物事を人に語る
【類語訳】説明する, 明示する, 定義する, 明快にする, 解釈する, 詳述する

文型&コロケーション
▶ to explain/ clarify/ spell sth out/ expound sth **to** sb
▶ to explain/ spell out **that**...
▶ to explain/ illustrate/ clarify/ shed light on/ spell out **how/ what.../ why...**
▶ to explain/ clarify/ shed light on a/ an **situation/ issue**
▶ to explain/ illustrate/ clarify/ expound an **idea**
▶ to explain/ illustrate/ clarify a **point**
▶ to explain/ illustrate/ define/ clarify the **position/ role/ nature/ meaning** of sth
▶ to explain/ illustrate/ expound a **theory**
▶ to **clearly** explain/ illustrate/ define/ spell out/ expound sth

explain [他, 自] 説明する ◇First, let me *explain* the rules of the game. まずゲームのルールを説明します ◇I tried to *explain* the problem to the technician. 問題を専門技術者に説明しようとした ◇She *explained* to them what to do in the event of an emergency. 彼女は緊急の場合に何をすべきかを彼らに説明した ◇'It was like this,' she *explained*. 「こんなふうでした」と彼女は説明した ◇There's no need to *explain*. We understand. 説明の必要はない. 我々は理解している ❶explain me/him/her などとは言えない. ◆Can you *explain* the situation to me? (私に状況を説明してくれますか). ✗Can you *explain* me the situation? ☞ **explanatory** (DESCRIPTIVE)
▶ **explanation** [C] ◇For a full *explanation* of how the machine works, turn to page 5. 機械の仕組みについての詳細な説明は5ページを開いてください

illustrate [他] (例・絵・図表などを用いて)説明する, 明示する ◇To *illustrate* my point, let me tell you a little story. 要点を説明するために, ちょっとしたお話をさせてください ◇Last year's sales figures are *illustrated* in Figure 2. 昨年の売上高は図表2に明示してあります ☞ **illustrate** (SHOW 1), **illustration** (EXAMPLE 1), **illustrative** (DESCRIPTIVE)

define [他] 説明する, 定義する, 規定する ◇The term 'mental illness' is difficult to *define*. 「精神疾患」という用語は定義するのが難しい ◇Life imprisonment is *defined as* 60 years under state law. 終身刑は州法で60年と規定されている ☞ **definition** (DEFINITION)

clarify [他]《ややフォーマル》明快[明らか]にする ◇Let me *clarify* my position on this matter. この問題における私の立場をはっきりさせておきましょう ◇There are one or two issues that need to be *clarified*. 明らかにしなければならない問題が一つ二つあります ◇I hope I managed to *clarify* things a little. 何とか事を少しは明らかにできたと思います
▶ **clarification** [名] [U, C] ◇I am seeking *clarification* of the regulations. 私はその規定の説明を求めているところです

shed/cast/throw 'light on sth [句動] (物事を)解明する ◇Recent research has *thrown* some new *light on* the causes of the disease. 最近の研究で病因が新たに解明されてきている ◇The report *cast* no *light on* (= does not explain) why some children are still failing to achieve at school. 報告書はなぜいまだに学校で成果を上げられずにいる子どもたちがいるのか, まったく明らかにしていない ❶人や人が言ったり書いたりするもの, 新発見は, shed/cast/throw light on の主語になることができる.

,spell sth 'out [句動詞] (物事を)明快[詳細]に説明する ◇You know what I mean — I'm sure I don't need to *spell* it *out*. 私の言うことがわかるだろう—詳しく説明する必要はないね

interpret [他] (文章・芸術品などの意味を)説明する, 解釈する ◇The students were asked to *interpret* the poem. 学生たちはその詩の解釈を求められた ☞ **interpretation** (DEFINITION), **interpretative** (DESCRIPTIVE)

expound [他, 自]《フォーマル》詳細に説明する, 詳述する ◇She *expounded* her theory further in the course of her talk. 彼女は講演の中で自分の理論についてさらに詳述した ◇He was there to *expound on* the government's latest policy initiative. 彼は政府の最新の政策構想について説明するためにそこにいた

2 explain・justify・account for sth・defend・ stand up for sb/sth・stick up for sb/sth
批判や攻撃を受けている人[物事]を支える[説明する]こと
【類語訳】釈明する, 弁明する, 正当化する, 弁護する, 擁護する, 味方する

文型&コロケーション
▶ to explain/ justify/ account for/ defend sth **to** sb
▶ to explain/ justify/ account for **what/ why/ how...**
▶ to explain/ justify/ defend/ stand up for/ stick up for **yourself**
▶ to explain/ justify/ account for/ defend a **decision**
▶ to explain/ justify/ account for/ defend your/ sb's **behaviour**
▶ to defend/ stand up for/ stick up for sb's **rights**

explain [自, 他] 理由を説明する, 釈明する ◇She tried to *explain* but he wouldn't listen. 彼女は釈明しようとしたが, 彼は聞こうとしなかった ◇Ed *explained that* his car had broken down. エドは車が故障したと釈明した ◇The government now has to *explain* its decision to the public. 政府は今, 国民にその決定の理由を明らかにしなければならない ◇Well, that doesn't *explain* why you

expression

didn't call me. だけど、それじゃ私に電話をくれなかった説明になっていない ◇Oh well then, that *explains it* (I understand now why sth happened).《話し言葉》ああ、なるほど。それでわかったよ ☞ **explanation** (REASON)

justify [他] 正しい[妥当だ]と示す；説明[弁明]する，正当化する ◇How can they *justify* paying such huge salaries? どうやってそんな多額の給与を支払っていることを彼らは正当化できるんですか ◇Her success had *justified* the faith her teachers had put in her. 彼女の成功で、先生たちが彼女に託した信頼が正しかったことが証明された ◇You don't need to *justify* yourself to me. 私に対して弁明する必要はない ☞ **justification** (REASON)

ac'count for sth [句動詞]《ややフォーマル》(物事の)原因である；(物事の理由を)説明する ◇The poor weather may have *accounted for* the small crowd. 悪天候が少ない人出の原因かもしれなかった ◇How do you *account for* the show's success? 番組のヒットをどう説明しますか

defend [他] 弁護する ◇Politicians are skilled at *defending* themselves *against* their critics. 政治家は自分を批判する者に対して弁明することに熟達しているものだ ◇How can you *defend* such behaviour? そんな行動をどう申し開きできると言うの ☞ **defence** (SECURITY)

,stand 'up for sb/sth [句動詞] [受身なし] (批判されてきた人・物事を)強く擁護する[弁護する]，味方する ◇Always *stand up for* your friends. つねに友達の支えとなりなさい ◇You must *stand up for* your rights. 自分の権利を自分で守らなければなりません ◇She had learnt to *stand up for* herself. 彼女は自立する力を習得していた

,stick 'up for sb/sth [句動詞] [受身なし]《ややインフォーマル》(批判されてきた人・物事を)擁護[弁護]する ◇*Stick up for* what you believe. 自分の信じることを貫きなさい ◇She taught her children to *stick up for* themselves at school. 彼女は子どもたちに学校では自分のことは自分で守るよう教えた ❶ 他に擁護する者がいないときに人や自分を擁護して用いる。

expression [名]

expression・display・show・demonstration・exhibition
感情や本質を示したり，意見や考えを表したりすること
【類語訳】表現，表出，発揮，披露

文型&コロケーション

▸an expression/ a display/ a show/ a demonstration of **support/ affection**
▸an expression/ a display/ a show of **concern/ emotion**
▸an expression/ a display of **sympathy**
▸an expression/ a show of **gratitude**

▸a display/ show/ demonstration of **strength**
▸a display/ show of **unity/ force**
▸a display/ demonstration of **skill**
▸a **public** expression/ display/ show/ demonstration of sth
▸an **open** expression/ display of sth
▸an **impressive** display/ show/ demonstration of sth
▸a **great** display/ show of sth

expression [C, U]《ややフォーマル》(言葉・行動による)表現 ◇The riots are the most serious *expression* of anti-government feeling yet. 暴動は依然として、反政府感情の最も深刻な表現である ◇*Freedom of expression* (= freedom to say what you think) is a basic human right. 表現の自由は基本的人権である ◇Only in his dreams does he *give expression to* his fears.《フォーマル》彼は夢の中でのみ自分の恐怖を表現する ◇The poet's anger *finds expression in* (= is shown in) the last verse of the poem. 詩人の怒りは詩の最後の一行[節，連]に表れている ☞ **express** (SAY 2)

display [C] 発揮，表出 ◇My family has never gone in for open *displays* of affection. 私の家族は愛情をおおっぴらに見せることを好ましく思ったことはありません ◇an ostentatious *display* of wealth これ見よがしに富をひけらかすこと ◇a magnificent *display* of goalkeeping 見事なゴールキーパーぶり

show [C] 発揮，表出 ◇He was completely unmoved by her little *show* of temper. 彼女がちょっとかんしゃくを起こしても、彼はまったく動じなかった ◇She made a great *show* of wanting to leave, but I knew she didn't mean it. 彼女は帰りたがっているそぶりを懸命に見せようとしたが、本気でないのはわかっていた ☞ **show** (SHOW 2)

demonstration [C]《ややフォーマル》発揮，表出 ◇She was given to quite embarrassing public *demonstrations* of emotion. 感情が公然と表出されて彼女は実に当惑した ◇The performance was a remarkable *demonstration* of his abilities. その演技は彼の能力を見事に表すものだった

ノート display, show, demonstration の使い分け：
display と show は不誠実に、誇張して、わざとらしく、本心ではない表出の仕方を指すことがある。◆a *display/show* of temper（腹を立ててみせること）. demonstration はふつうもっと誠実な表出の仕方を指す。

exhibition [C]《特に英、ややフォーマル》(技能・ある種の行為の)発揮，披露 ◇We were treated to an *exhibition* of the footballer's speed and skill. 我々はそのサッカー選手が発揮するスピードと技術に酔いしれた ◇It was an appalling *exhibition* of bad manners. それは驚くばかりの無作法ぶりだった

F f

facilities 名

facilities・service・utility・resource・amenity
人々が使用するためにある場所に備えられているもの
【類語訳】設備, 施設, 公共事業, 便, 教材, 供給源

[文型&コロケーション]
▶ **public/ basic/ local** facilities/ services/ utilities/ resources/ amenities
▶ **essential/ limited/ adequate** facilities/ services/ resources
▶ **recreational/ leisure** facilities/ services/ resources/ amenities
▶ the facilities/ services/ resources/ amenities **available**
▶ to **provide/ lack** facilities/ services/ resources/ amenities
▶ to **have access to** facilities/ services/ resources

facilities [複数で]（特定の目的で備えられた）設備, 施設 ◇Each apartment has basic *cooking facilities* and a small bathroom. アパートの各部屋には基本的な調理設備と小さなバスルームがあります ◇All rooms have private *facilities* (= a private bathroom). すべての部屋に専用のバス・トイレが付いています ◇The hotel has special *facilities* for welcoming disabled people. そのホテルには障害者を迎え入れるための特別な設備がある

service [C]（政府・民間企業による）公共[公益]事業,（公共輸送機関の）便, 運行 ◇A free bus *service* to and from the venue is available. 会場を往復する無料バスの便が利用できます ◇The *postal service* here is rather unreliable. ここの郵便業務は大して当てになりません ◇The government aims to improve public *services*, especially education. 政府は公共事業, 特に教育の改善を目指している ◇Essential *services* (= the supply of water, gas and electricity) will be maintained. 生活に不可欠の公益事業は維持されるでしょう ◇A massive operation was launched by the **emergency services** (= the police, fire and ambulance services). 警察・消防・救急の緊急救援隊によって大規模な作戦が開始された ❶《米》では, ふつう **first responders**（緊急救援隊）と総称される.

utility [C]《特に米》（水道・ガス・電気などの）公共[公益]事業 ◇Public *utilities* such as water, gas and electricity come under the control of the government. 水道・ガス・電気などの公益事業は政府の管理下で行われている ◇Legislation will be introduced to regulate the ***privatized utilities***. 民営化された公共事業を規制する法律が導入されるだろう

resource [C]（教師・学生用の）教材,（知識・情報などの）供給源 ◇The database could be used as a teaching *resource* in colleges. そのデータベースは大学の教材として利用することができるだろう ◇Time is your most valuable *resource*, especially in exams. 特に試験において時間は最も貴重な頼みの綱となる

amenity [C, ふつう複数で]《ややフォーマル》（快適に[住みやすく]するための）設備, 施設 ◇Many of the houses lacked even basic *amenities* (= for example baths, showers or hot water). 多くの家には最低限の設備さえなかった ◇The area now has a far higher standard of *amenity*.《特に英》現在その地域にははるかに高水準の施設がある

fact 名

fact・the truth・reality・so・the real world・real life
虚構ではないと思われる状況
【類語訳】事実, 現実, 実際, 真実, 真相, 実状, そのとおり, 現実の世界

[文型&コロケーション]
▶ **in** fact/ reality/ the real world/ real life
▶ the fact/ truth (of the matter) **is that...**
▶ to **face/ accept/ ignore** the fact/ the truth/ reality
▶ to be **based on** fact/ the truth

fact [単数で, U]（存在する）事実, 真実, 実際；(虚構ではない)事実 ◇I could no longer ignore the *fact* that he was deeply unhappy. 私は彼が不幸のどん底にいるという現実をもはや無視することができなかった ◇***Despite the fact that*** she was wearing a seat belt, she was thrown sharply forward. 実際にシートベルトをしていたにもかかわらず, 彼女は激しく前方へ投げ出された ◇***The fact remains*** that we are still two teachers short. まだ教師が二人足りないという事実に変わりはない ◇I thought the work would be difficult. In *actual fact*, it's very easy. その仕事は難しいだろうと思ったが, 実際はとても簡単です ◇The story is based on *fact*. この物語は事実に基づいている ◇It's important to distinguish *fact* from fiction. 事実と虚構を区別することが大切である [反意] **fiction** (LIE), **factual** (RELIABLE 2), **the case** (SITUATION)

the truth [単数で]（虚構・憶測ではない）真実, 真相, 事実 ◇Do you think she's ***telling the truth***? 彼女は真実を語っていると思いますか ◇We are determined to get at (= discover) *the truth*. 私たちは真相を突き止めることを固く決意しています ◇I don't think you are telling me ***the whole truth*** about what happened. あなたが起きたことをありのままに語っているとは私には思えない ◇*The sad truth* is that, at 72, he is past his prime. 悲しいことに彼は72歳で人生の盛りを過ぎている [⇒] **true** (TRUE)

reality [U]（願望に対する）現実, 実状, 実際 ◇You're out of touch with *reality*. あなたは現実を知らない ◇Outwardly she seemed confident but in *reality* she felt extremely nervous. 外見上は彼女は自信に満ちているようだったが, 実際は極度に緊張していた [反意] **fantasy** (IMAGINATION)

so 副《特に話し言葉》（前言を受けて）そのとおり, そう ◇I hear that you're a writer — ***is that so*** (= is that true)? あなたは作家だそうですね—そうなんですか ◇He thinks I dislike him but that just ***isn't so***. 彼は私に嫌われていると思っているけど, まったくそうではない ◇I might be away next week. ***If so***, I won't be able to see you. ひょっとすると来週は留守にするかもしれない. そうだとし

factor, factory, fail

たら君と会えないね ❷副詞のsoは物事の真否を確かめる場合や, 物事が事実ではないと否定する場合に, is that so? または that isn't soの句で用いられる. また, 物事の真否が定かではなく, 他の物事がそれに左右される場合に, if soの句で用いられる.

the ,real 'world 〔慣用〕 (空論・仮定ではない)現実の世界 ◇Politicians seem to be out of touch with *the real world*. 政治家たちは現実の世界からかけ離れているように思える ❶*the real world* という表現は時に, 実生活の苦しみなどは守られている学校や職場などの特定の施設の外の世界を指すことがある. ◆The purpose of school is to prepare students to go out into *the real world*. (学校の目的は生徒に実社会に出て行く準備をさせることである)

,real 'life 〔慣用〕 (物語・映画などの架空の世界ではない)現実の世界 ◇In the movies guns kill people instantly, but it's not like that in *real life*. 映画では銃は人を殺すが, 現実の世界ではそういうことにはならない

factor 名

factor・point・consideration
ある状況において重要な[影響力を持つ]物事
【類語訳】要因, 要素, 因子, 要点, 論点, 問題点, 案件, 事情

〔文型&コロケーション〕
▶ a factor/ consideration **in** sth
▶ a/ an/ the **additional/ main/ major/ important/ key/ vital/ chief/ crucial/ essential/ prime** factor/ point/ consideration
▶ **political/ practical** factors/ points/ considerations
▶ **economic/ environmental** factors/ considerations
▶ factors/ points/ considerations **to be taken into account**

factor [C] (複数の中の一つの)要因, 要素, 因子 ◇The closure of the mine was the single most important *factor* in the town's decline. 鉱山の閉鎖がその町を衰退させた唯一にして最大の要因だった ◇Money proved to be the *deciding factor*. お金が決め手であることがはっきりした ◇Studies have established that smoking is a *risk factor* for cancer. 喫煙はがんの危険因子であることが研究で立証されている

point [C] (主張・論における)要点, 論点, 問題点 ◇She made several interesting *points* in the article. 彼女はその記事の中で興味深い問題点をいくつか挙げた ◇How long it will last is a *moot point* (= sth which is uncertain or not agreed). それがどのくらい長く続くかが争点となっている ❶sb's pointは単なる「要点」ではなく, 人の「主張・論」を指すことがある. ☞ point (VIEW 1)

consideration [C] (計画・決定に際して考慮すべき)案件, 事情, 問題 ◇Financial *considerations* will obviously play a big part. 財政上の問題が大きなウェイトを占めるであろうことは明らかだ ☞ concern (ISSUE)

factory 名

factory・plant・mill・works・yard・workshop・foundry
物が製造される建物や場所
【類語訳】工場, 製造所, 作業場, 栽培場, 飼育場

〔文型&コロケーション〕
▶ a **car/ chemical/ munitions** factory/ plant
▶ an **engineering** plant/ works
▶ to **manage/ run** a factory/ plant/ mill/ works/ yard/ workshop/ foundry
▶ to **work in/ at** a factory/ plant/ mill/ yard/ workshop/ foundry
▶ a factory/ plant/ mill/ works/ workshop/ foundry **makes/ manufactures/ produces** sth
▶ factory/ mill/ foundry **owners/ managers/ workers**

factory [C] (商品が製造される)工場, 製造所 ◇a chocolate/cigarette/clothing/soap *factory* チョコレート/タバコ/衣料品/せっけん工場 ◇The *factory* closed down ten years ago. その工場は10年前に閉鎖された

plant [C] (電力などを作る)工場, 製造所 ◇a nuclear power *plant* 原子力発電所 ◇a/an assembly/manufacturing/production *plant* 組立/製造/生産工場 ◇a sewage (treatment) *plant* (= a place where chemicals are used to clean sewage) 下水処理場

mill [C] (しばしば複合語で)(材料・原料を生産する)工場, 製造所 ◇a cotton/paper/textile/woollen *mill* 紡績/製紙/織物/毛織物工場

works [C＋単数・複数動詞]《しばしば複合語で》(物を製造する)工場, 製造所 ◇a steel*works* 製鋼所 ◇Raw materials were carried to the *works* by barge. 原料は平底荷船で製造所に運ばれた

yard [C] 《ふつう複合語で》(建造・飼育・栽培が行われる)作業場, 栽培[飼育]場 ◇a ship*yard* 造船所 ◇a construction *yard* 建設作業場 ◇a vine*yard* (= for growing grapes to make wine) ぶどう園

workshop [C] (製造・修理が行われる)工場, 作業場 ◇a car repair *workshop* 自動車修理工場 ◇The craftsmen worked in a freezing cold *workshop*. 職工たちは凍てつくほど寒い作業場で働いた

foundry [C] (金属・ガラスの加工が行われる)工場, 鋳造所 ◇an iron *foundry* 鋳鉄工場

fail 動

1 fail・forget・neglect・omit
すべきことを行わない
【類語訳】しない, 怠る, し忘れる

〔文型&コロケーション〕
▶ to fail/ forget/ neglect/ omit **to do** sth
▶ to **completely/ totally/ almost/ never/ conveniently** fail/ forget to do sth

fail [他, 自]《ややフォーマル》…しない, 怠る ◇He *failed* to keep the appointment. 彼は会う約束を守らなかった ◇She never *fails* to email every week. 彼女は毎週欠かさずeメールを送る ◇I *fail to see* (= I don't understand) why you won't even give it a try. なぜあなたがそれを試そうともしないのかわからない ◇He felt he would be *failing* in his duty if he did not report it. 彼はそれを報告しないと義務を怠ることになると思った
▷ **failure** 名 [U, C] ◇*Failure* to comply with the regulations will result in prosecution. 規則に従わないと起訴されます ◇His confession followed repeated *failures* to appear in court. 何度も出廷を拒否した後で彼は自白した

forget [自, 他](すべき事を)し忘れる ◇'Why weren't you at the meeting?' 'Sorry — I *forgot*.'「どうして会議に出

なかったの」「ごめん, 忘れてた」◇Take care, and don't *forget* to write. 元気でね, 忘れずに手紙書いてよ ◇*Aren't you forgetting something?* (= I think you have forgotten to do sth). 《話し言葉》何かやり忘れてないか [反意] **remember** (REMEMBER)

neglect [自]《フォーマル》(すべきことを)しない, し忘れる ◇You *neglected* to mention the name of your previous employer. あなたは以前勤めていた会社の名前を言いませんでしたよ

omit (-tt-) [自]《特に英, フォーマル》…しない, 怠る ◇She *omitted* to mention that they were staying the night. 彼女は彼らが泊まるつもりであることを言わなかった

> [ノート] **neglect** と **omit** の使い分け: neglect は人が単に必要な行動をし忘れた[わざわざしなかった]のだと話し手や書き手が考えていることを示唆する。omit は…しなかった[言わなかった]ことが意図的であることを示唆する。omit はほとんどの場合, ask, disclose, inform, mention, say, tell など, 話すことに関連する動詞と共に用いられる。

---

2 fail・go wrong・collapse・break down・get/go nowhere・backfire・founder・fall through・come to nothing

一定期間何かをしようと試みて, 成功しないことを表す
【類語訳】失敗する, うまくいかない, 災いする, 崩壊する, 決裂する, 破綻する, 行き詰まる, 裏目に出る, 中止になる

[文型&コロケーション]
- a **plan** fails/ goes wrong/ backfires/ founders/ falls through/ comes to nothing
- a **relationship/ marriage** fails/ goes wrong/ collapses/ breaks down
- **talks** fail/ collapse/ break down/ founder/ fall through
- a **project** fails/ collapses/ founders/ falls through
- a **deal** goes wrong/ collapses/ falls through
- to fail/ backfire **badly**
- to **completely** fail/ break down
- to go **badly/ completely** wrong

fail [自, 他](人・物事が)失敗する, 成功しない, 達成できない ◇They had tried and they had *failed*. 彼らは挑戦したが失敗した ◇I *failed in* my attempt to persuade her. 私は彼女を説得しようとして失敗した ◇I tried to cheer her up, but *failed miserably*. 私は彼女を元気づけようとしたが, 無残にも失敗した ◇She *failed to* get into art college. 彼女は芸大[美大]への入学に失敗した [反意] **succeed** (ACHIEVE), **succeed** (SUCCEED), ☞ **failure** (LOSER2)

go' wrong [仔イル]《ややインフォーマル》(物事が)うまくいかない, 狂う, 問題が起きる, 災いする;(人が)失敗する[過ち, 間違い]を犯す ◇The relationship started to *go wrong* when they moved abroad. 海外に移住して彼らの関係は狂い始めた ◇What would you do if something *went wrong*? 何か問題が起きたらどうするつもりですか ◇He was badly injured when the joke *went horribly wrong*. 冗談が思わぬ方向に飛び火して彼は手ひどい目に遭った ◇Where did we *go wrong* with those kids (= what mistakes did we make for them to behave so badly)? 私たちはどこであの子どもたちのしつけを間違えたのだろう ◇If you do what she tells you, you *won't go far wrong*. 彼女が言うようにすれば, それほど道を誤ることはないだろう

collapse [自](物事・人の集団が)崩壊[瓦解]する, 決裂[破綻]する ◇Talks between management and unions

have *collapsed*. 経営陣と組合の話し合いは決裂した ◇All opposition to the plan has *collapsed*. その計画に対する反対はことごとく押しつぶされた ◇The home side *collapsed* spectacularly in the second half. 後半, 地元チームは目を覆うほど総崩れになった

break 'down [句動詞](話し合い・関係が)決裂[破綻]する ◇The agreement *broke down* almost immediately. その協定はほぼ即座に決裂した ◇Communication between the two sides has *broken down*. 二者間の連絡は途絶えている ◇They were divorced on the grounds that their marriage had *broken down irretrievably*. 結婚生活が取り返しのつかないほどに破綻したことを理由に彼らは離婚した

get/go 'nowhere, get sb 'nowhere [仔イル]《ややインフォーマル》(人が)成果[進展]を得られない, 行き詰まる, うまくいかない;(人に)無駄骨を折らせる, 行き詰まらせる ◇We discussed it all morning but *got nowhere*. 我々は午前中ずっとそれについて話し合ったが, 何の進展も得られなかった ◇Do you ever get the feeling your job is *going nowhere*? 仕事がうまくいっていないと思うことはありますか ◇Talking to him will *get* you *nowhere*. 彼と話しても無駄だよ [反意] **get somewhere** ❶ be getting somewhere は行っていることが「はかどって[うまくいって]いる」ことを意味する。◆ At last I feel we're *getting somewhere*. (ようやく私たちは何とかなっている気がする).

backfire [自](計画が)逆効果になる, 裏目に出る ◇Unfortunately the plan *backfired*. 不運にも計画は裏目に出た ◇The surprise I had planned *backfired on* me. 私が計画していた不意打ちが裏目に出て自分に返ってきた

founder [自]《ややフォーマル, 書き言葉》(計画・試みが)頓挫[失敗]する ◇The peace talks *foundered on* a basic lack of trust. 和平交渉は基本的な信頼感が欠如していたために頓挫した ◇The project *foundered* after problems with the funding. その計画は財政上の問題が生じて, 頓挫した

fall 'through [句動詞](計画が)中止[駄目]になる, 失敗[不成立]に終わる ◇The deal *fell through* when the author received a more attractive offer. 作家はより魅力的な申し出を受けて, その契約は不成立に終わった

come to 'nothing, not 'come to anything [仔イル]《ややインフォーマル》(計画・試みが)失敗[徒労]に終わる, 水の泡となる ◇How sad that all his hard work should *come to nothing*. 彼の努力がすべて徒労に終わるとはなんと悲しいことか ◆Her plans didn't *come to anything*. 彼女の計画は水の泡となった

---

3 fail・flunk

テスト[試験]に合格しない, テスト[試験]で人を合格させない
【類語訳】落ちる, 不合格になる, 落第する, 退学になる, 落とす, 不合格にする, 落第させる, 退学させる

[文型&コロケーション]
- to fail/ flunk a/ an **exam/ examination/ test/ course**

fail [自, 他](人・物がテスト・試験・科目に)落ちる, 不合格になる, 落第する;(テスト・試験・科目で人・物を)落とす, 不合格にする, 落第させる ◇Once a student has *failed on* a few tasks, they lose motivation. 生徒が数回の課題でいったん落第点を取るとやる気をなくす ◇What will you do if you *fail*? 不合格になったらどうするの ◇He *failed* his driving test. 彼は運転免許の試験に落ちた ◇She was disqualified after *failing* a drugs test. 彼女は薬物検

査にひっかかり失格になった ◇My car *failed* its MOT. 私の車は車検を通らなかった ◇The examiners *failed* over half the candidates. 試験官は志願者の半分以上を不合格にした 反意 **pass** (GRADUATE)

flunk [自, 他]《特に米, インフォーマル》(人がテスト・試験・科目に)落ちる, 落第点[赤点]を取る, 退学になる；(テスト・試験・科目で人を)落とす, 落第点[赤点]を付ける, 退学させる ◇I *flunked* math in second grade. 私は2年生のとき数学で落第した ◇She's *flunked* 13 of the 18 students. 彼女は18人中13人の学生に落第点を付けた ◇He *flunked out of* college after four semesters (= had to leave because his grades were not good enough). 彼は成績不振のため4学期目で大学を退学になった 反意 **pass** (GRADUATE)

failure 名

failure・collapse・breakdown
物事がうまくいかない状況を表す
【類語訳】失敗, 不成功, 崩壊, 決裂, 破綻

文型&コロケーション
▶a failure/ collapse/ breakdown **in** sth
▶a/ an **complete/ total/ general/ apparent** failure/ collapse/ breakdown
▶(an) **economic** failure/ collapse/ breakdown
▶to **contribute to/ lead to/ result in/ cause/ avoid** the failure/ collapse/ breakdown (of sth)
▶to **end in** failure/ the breakdown (of sth)

failure [U] (行動・達成における)失敗, 不成功 ◇The success or *failure* of the plan depends on you. 計画の成功も不成功もあなたにかかっている ◇All my efforts ended in *failure*. 私の努力はすべて徒労に終わった ◇There is a high *failure* rate with this treatment. この治療法は失敗する確率が高い 反意 **success** (ACHIEVE), ☞ **failure** (DISASTER)

collapse [C, ふつう単数で, U] (制度・商取引・試みの)崩壊, 瓦解, 決裂, 破綻, 失敗 ◇The war has led to the *collapse* of agriculture in the area. 戦争はその地域の農業を崩壊させた ◇He charted the villagers' *collapse into* poverty. 彼は村民の貧困化を図で示した ◇The peace talks were **on the verge of** *collapse*. 和平交渉は決裂寸前だった

breakdown [C, U] (関係・話し合い・制度の)破綻, 決裂, 崩壊 ◇A growing proportion of children are affected by family *breakdown*. 家庭崩壊の影響を受ける子どもの比率が上昇している ◇The *breakdown* of negotiations was not expected. 交渉の決裂は予想外だった ◇There seems to be a complete *breakdown* in law and order. 法と秩序は完全に崩壊しているように思える

faith 名

faith・belief・trust・confidence・certainty・conviction
人や物事の能力[良さ]に対する確信を表す語
【類語訳】信じること, 信念, 信頼, 信用, 確信, 説得力

文型&コロケーション
▶faith/ belief/ trust/ confidence **in** sb/ sth
▶**great/ absolute** faith/ belief/ trust/ confidence/ certainty/ conviction
▶**public** faith/ belief/ trust/ confidence
▶to **have/ show** faith/ trust/ confidence
▶to **lack** faith/ belief/ confidence/ conviction
▶to **lose** faith/ sb's trust/ confidence
▶to **undermine** faith/ belief/ trust/ confidence/ certainty
▶to **shake** sb's faith/ belief/ confidence/ conviction
▶to **destroy** sb's faith/ belief/ trust/ confidence
▶to **put/ place** your faith/ trust **in** sb/ sth
▶**a lack of** faith/ belief/ trust/ confidence/ certainty/ conviction

faith [U, 単数で] (人の能力・良さを[への])信じること, 信念；(約束への)信頼, 信用 ◇I have great *faith* in you — I know you'll do well. 君をとても信頼してる—君ならいい結果を出すのは間違いない ◇Her friend's kindness restored her *faith* in human nature. 友達の優しさに触れ, 彼女は人間を信頼する心を取り戻した ❶人や物事に対する blind *faith* (盲信) とは, 理性を欠いていると思えるほど疑うことのない信念を表す. **faithful** (RELIABLE 1)

belief [U] (人・物事の存在・真実性を)信じること；(人・物事の良さ・正当性への)信念 ◇I admire his passionate *belief* in what he is doing. 取り組んでいることに対する彼の熱い思い入れを私は素晴らしいと思う ◇*Belief* in God is more than a matter of logic. 神の存在を信じることは論理の問題を超えている ☞ **believe in sth** (IN FAVOUR), **believe in sb** (TRUST)
▷**believe** [動] [他, 自]《進行形なし》◇I don't *believe* you! あなたの言うことなんか信じない ◇People used to *believe that* the earth was flat. 昔の人は地球が平らであると信じていたものだ ◇The god appears only to those who *believe*. 神は信じる者の前にのみ姿を現す 反意 **disbelieve** (SUSPECT)

trust [U] (善良さ・誠実さ・正直さからの)信頼, 信用 ◇It has taken years to *earn their trust*. 彼らの信頼を得るのに何年もかかった ◇She will not *betray your trust* (= do sth that you have asked her not to do). 彼女はあなたの信頼を裏切らないだろう ◇Many people feel it is a *breach of trust* to give out information about their loved one. 最愛の人に関する情報を公表するのは背信行為であると多くの人は感じる ☞ **trust** (TRUST), **trusted** (RELIABLE 1), **trusting** (NAIVE)

confidence [U] (人・物事の能力・良さへの)信頼, 信用 ◇A fall in unemployment will help to restore *consumer confidence*. 失業率の低下は消費者の信頼を回復するのに役立つだろう ◇She has *every confidence* in her students' abilities. 彼女は自分の生徒たちの能力を全面的に信頼している ☞ **confident** (SURE), **have confidence in sb/sth** (TRUST)

ノート faith と confidence の使い分け: faith は特に人間関係の文脈で用いられ, confidence は特にビジネスの文脈で用いられる.

certainty [U] (物事の真実性・正当性への)確信 ◇There is no *certainty* that the president's removal will end the civil war. 大統領の解任で内戦が終わるとは確信できない ◇I can't say with any *certainty* where I'll be next week. 私が来週どこにいるか確かなところはまるで言えない 反意 **uncertainty** (DOUBT 名 1), ☞ **certain** (SURE)

conviction [U] (物事に対する)確信, 信念, 説得力 ◇'Not true!' she said with *conviction*. 「真実ではありません」と彼女は自信を持って言った ◇The leader's speech in de-

↪faith　　　　　　　　　　　　fake, fall

fence of the policy didn't *carry* much *conviction*.
政策を擁護するリーダーの演説はあまり説得力がなかった

fake 名 ☞COPY 名 2

fake・imitation・forgery・dummy
本物ではないが,本物そっくりに作られた物
【類語訳】偽物,模造品,贋作,模倣作品,偽造物,模型,見本

▸**文型&コロケーション**
▸ a **good** fake/ imitation/ forgery
▸ a **cheap** fake/ imitation
▸ a **poor/ crude** imitation/ forgery

fake [C]（芸術作品・硬貨・宝石などの)偽物,模造[偽造]品,贋作 ◇All the paintings proved to be *fakes*. すべての絵画は贋作だとわかった ◇She had long ago sold the diamonds and replaced them with *fakes*. 彼女はずっと前にダイヤモンドを売っていて,それらを偽物と擦り替えてあった ☞ **fake** (ARTIFICIAL)

imitation [C]（高価・有名な製品・素材・作品の)偽物,模造[偽造]品,模倣作品 ◇Many tourists cannot tell the difference between authentic Indian craftwork and imported *imitations*. 多くの観光客にはアメリカ先住民の本物の工芸品と輸入された模造品との違いがわからない ◇The remake is a *pale imitation* of the original 1966 film (= it is not nearly as good). そのリメーク版は1966年のオリジナル映画には及びもつかない模倣作品である ❶ *imitation* はしばしば本物には劣る複製であることを示唆する. ◆ a poor/cheap/pale/second-rate *imitation*（お粗末な/安っぽい/見劣りの/二流の模造品). 製造の元となる原料［材料]について言う場合には形容詞のように用いられることもある. ◆ *imitation* fur/gold/leather/marble/silk/pearls (人造の毛皮/金/皮革/大理石/絹/真珠). また,武器の複製にも用いられる. ◆ an *imitation* sword/firearm/gun/bomb (偽物の刀/小火器/拳銃/爆弾) ☞ **imitation** (ARTIFICIAL)

forgery [C] (人をあざむくための書類・紙幣・絵画などの)偽造物,贋作 ◇Experts are dismissing claims that the painting is a *forgery*. 専門家たちはその絵画が贋作であるという主張を退けている ◇If the signature on the deed is a *forgery*, the whole legal position changes. 証書の署名が偽造であれば,法的見解は一変する

▸**forge** 動 [他] ◇She was getting good at *forging* her mother's signature. 彼女は母親のサインを偽造するのがだんだんうまくなっていた

ノート fake と forgery の使い分け:forgery は人をあざむくために主として書く[描く,印刷する,絵の具で描く]ことのできる物について用いられる. fake は製品や作品だけでなく,(宝石などの)自然物の人工複製品を指すこともある. fake は人をあざむくためのものである場合もあればそうでない場合もある.

dummy [C] (本物に見えるが複製にすぎない)模型,見本,ダミー ◇The bottles of whisky on display are all *dummies*. 陳列されているウィスキーの瓶はすべて見本です ❶ dummy は本物そっくりに作られるので,しばしば運転[操縦・射撃]など危険を伴う技能訓練や映画・演劇のために使用される.

fall 動

1 ☞ SLUMP
fall・decline・drop・diminish・decrease・sink・come down
物事の量,水準,数が減る
【類語訳】低下する,減少する,下がる,下落する

▸**文型&コロケーション**
▸ to fall/ decline/ drop/ diminish/ decrease/ sink/ come down **by** 100, 25%, a half, etc.
▸ to fall/ decline/ drop/ decrease/ sink/ come down **from** 15,000 **to** 1,000
▸ to decline/ diminish/ decrease/ come down **in** number, level, size, etc.
▸ to decline/ diminish/ decrease **with** age, time, experience, etc.
▸ **numbers** fall/ decline/ drop/ diminish/ decrease/ come down
▸ **levels** fall/ decline/ drop/ decrease
▸ **prices/ rates** fall/ decline/ drop/ decrease/ sink/ come down
▸ **profits/ sales** fall/ decline/ drop/ decrease/ sink
▸ the **temperature** falls/ drops
▸ sb's **voice** falls/ drops/ sinks
▸ to fall/ decline/ drop/ diminish/ decrease/ sink **sharply/ rapidly**
▸ to fall/ decline/ drop/ decrease **dramatically/ suddenly**
▸ to fall/ decline/ drop/ diminish/ decrease **slightly/ slowly/ gradually/ steadily**

fall [自,他] (水準・数・強さが)低下[減少]する ◇Their profits have *fallen* by 30 per cent. 彼らの利益は30%減少した ◇The temperature *fell* sharply in the night. 気温は夜になると急激に低下した ◇*Falling* birth rates could have an impact on future economic growth. 出生率の低下は将来の経済成長に影響を及ぼす可能性があるだろう ◇Her voice *fell* to a whisper. 《書き言葉》彼女の声は小さくなってささやき声になった ◇Share prices *fell* 30p. 株価は30ポイント下落した 反意 **rise** (RISE), ☞ **fall** (REDUCTION)

decline [自]《ややフォーマル,特に書き言葉》(水準・数・大きさ・強さ・重要性が)低下[減少]する ◇The number of tourists visiting the resort *declined* by 10% last year. リゾート地を訪れる観光客の数は昨年10%減少した ◇Manufacturing industry has slowly *declined* in importance. 製造業の重要性は徐々に低下している 反意 **increase** (RISE), ☞ **decline** (REDUCTION)

drop (-pp-) [自]《進行形なし》(水準・数・強さが)低下[減少]する ◇The Dutch team have *dropped* to fifth place. オランダチームは5位に順位を下げた ◇At last the wind *dropped*. ようやく風がやんだ 反意 **rise, climb** (RISE), ☞ **drop** (REDUCTION)

ノート fall, decline, drop の使い分け:多くの場合どの語も使用可能. ◆ Sales have *fallen/declined/dropped* by 20%.(売り上げが20%減少した). どの語もすべて数,水準,率,価格,利益,売り上げについて用いることができる. 特定の場所や産業における経済力の低下については decline を用いる. ◆ The area/city/industry/market/sector has *declined* (in importance).(その地域/都市/市場/部門の重要性は低下している). decline は支持,興味,健康,

fall

ついても用いられる. 人の声には fall や drop が用いられることがある. 気温には fall や drop を用いる. 風には drop のみ用いることができる. fall と decline は一定期間にわたって低下[減少]することを表し, 進行形で用いられるが, drop は進行形では用いることができない. ◆ Sales have been *falling/declining*. (売り上げは減少し続けてきている). ◆ *falling/declining* sales (売り上げの落ち込み). ×Sales have been *dropping*. ×*dropping* sales.

diminish [自]《ややフォーマル, 特に書き言葉》(数・量・強さが)低下[減少]する ◇The world's resources are rapidly *diminishing*. 世界の資源は急激に減少している ◇His influence has *diminished* with time. 彼の影響力は時と共に低下してきている ◇Our efforts were producing *diminishing* returns (= we achieved less although we spent more time or money). 我々の努力に反して収益は減少しつつあった ❶ diminish は物事の数や量に用いることはできるが, 数字, 率, 水準, 利益, 売り上げには用いることはできない. [反意] **enhance** (IMPROVE 1)

decrease [自]《ややフォーマル》(数・水準などが)低下[減少]する ◇The number of new students *decreased* from 210 to 160 this year. 新入生の数は今年210名から160名に減少した ◇The number of quarrels among children *decreases* with age (= the older they are, the fewer quarrels they have). 子どもたちのけんかの数は年齢と共に減る [反意] **increase** (RISE), ☞ **decrease** (REDUCTION)

sink [自]《特にビジネス》(価値・強さが)低下する ◇The pound has *sunk* to its lowest recorded level against the dollar. ポンドはドルに対して記録に残る最低水準にまで低下している ◇His voice *sank* almost to a whisper. 彼の声はほとんどささやき声になった [反意] **rise** (RISE)

,come 'down [動詞]《価格が》下がる, 下落する ◇The price of gas is *coming down*. ガスの価格が下落している ◆ Gas is *coming down* in price. ガスの価格が下落している [反意] **go up** (RISE)

---

2 fall・go down (sth)・come down (sth)・descend・drop・sink・crash・tumble・topple・plunge
突然[誤って]下方へ動く
【類語訳】落ちる, 落下する, 転落する, 下がる, 転ぶ, 下降する, 倒れ込む, 壊れる, 壊す, ひっくり返る

文型&コロケーション
▶to fall/ go/ come/ drop/ sink/ crash/ tumble **down**
▶to go down/ come down/ descend the **stairs/ steps**
▶to go down/ come down/ descend a **ladder**
▶to fall/ plunge **to your death**

fall [自]《ふつう副詞や前置詞と共に》(突然・誤って)落ちる, 落下する, 転落[墜落]する ◇Several of the books had *fallen* onto the floor. 本が何冊か床に落ちていた ◇One of the kids *fell* into the river. 子どもたちの一人が川に転落した ◇September had come and the leaves were starting to *fall*. 9月になって葉が落ち始めていた ◇He *fell* 23 metres onto the rocks below. 彼は下の岩場で23メートル落下した
▶**fall** [名] [C] ◇She was killed in a *fall* from a horse. 彼女は落馬して亡くなった

,go 'down sth, ,go 'down [句動詞] 下がる, 下りる;(地面に)落ちる, 下る ◇I've been *going* up and *down* the stairs all day. 私は一日中階段を上ったり下りたりしていた ◇The sun *went down* below the horizon. 太陽

地平線に沈んだ ◇She tripped and *went down* with a bump. 彼女はつまずいてドテッと転んだ [反意] **go up (sth)** (CLIMB)

,come 'down sth, ,come 'down [句動詞] 下がる, 下りる;(地面に)崩れ落ちる ◇She *came down* the steps two at a time. 彼女は一段飛ばしで階段を下りた ◇The ceiling *came down* with a terrific crash. すさまじい音を立てて天井が崩れ落ちた [反意] **go up (sth)** (CLIMB)

ノート go down と come down の使い分け: go はふつうどこかへ移動している人の視点から用いられる. come はふつう来る人や物が向かっている先の人や場所の視点から用いられる.

descend [自, 他]《フォーマル》下降[降下]する ◇The plane began to *descend*. 飛行機が降下し始めた ◇She *descended* the stairs slowly. 彼女はゆっくりと階段を下りた [反意] **ascend** (CLIMB)
▶**descent** [名] [C, ふつう単数形で] ◇The plane began its *descent* to Heathrow. 飛行機はヒースロー空港に向かって降下を始めた

drop (-pp-) [自] (誤って)落ちる, 落下する, 転落[墜落]する;(立っていられずに)倒れ[座り]込む ◇The climber slipped and *dropped* to his death. その登山者は滑落死した ◇He staggered in and *dropped* into a chair. 彼はよろめきながら入ってくると, 崩れるように椅子に座り込んだ

sink [自]《ふつう副詞や前置詞と共に》(人が)倒れ[座り]込む;(物がゆっくりと)下降[沈下]する ◇She *sank back* into her seat. 彼女は自分の席に座り込んだ ◇The old man had *sunk to his knees*. 老人は膝を突いて座り込んでしまっていた ◇The foundations of the building are starting to *sink*. 建物の土台が沈み始めている

crash [自]《ふつう副詞や前置詞と共に》(物にぶつかって)音を立てる, 壊れる, 壊す ◇A brick *crashed* through the window. れんがが窓を突き破った ◇With a sweep of his hand he sent the glasses *crashing* to the floor. 彼は手でグラスをさっと払って床に落として割った ◇The door *crashed* open. ドアがバタンと開いた

tumble [自] (突然劇的に)崩れ落ちる ◇The scaffolding came *tumbling* down. 足場が崩れ落ちてきた
▶**tumble** [名] [C, ふつう単数形で] ◇The jockey took a nasty *tumble* at the third fence. その騎手は3つ目の障害でひどい転落をした

topple [自]《副詞や前置詞と共に》(不安定になって)崩れ落ちる, ひっくり返る ◇The pile of books *toppled over*. 本の山が崩れ落ちた

plunge [自]《副詞や前置詞と共に》(前方・下方へ)突っ込む, 落下する ◇She lost her balance and *plunged* 100 feet to her death. 彼女はバランスを失って100フィート落下して死亡した

---

3 fall・fall over・stumble・trip・fall down
立っている状態から突然倒れる
【類語訳】転ぶ, 転倒する, つまずく, 足を引っかける, 崩れる

文型&コロケーション
▶to stumble/ trip **over** sth

fall 《ふつう副詞や前置詞と共に》[自]《特に書き言葉》転ぶ, 転倒する ◇She slipped and *fell* on the ice. 彼女は氷の上で滑って転倒した

,fall 'over [句動詞]《特に話し言葉》転倒する ◇I *fell over* and cut my knee. 私は転んで膝を切った

stumble [自] (物に足が当たって)つまずく ◇The child *stumbled* and fell. その子どもはつまずいて転んだ ◇I *stumbled* over a rock. 私は岩につまずいた
trip (-pp-) [自] (ふつう副詞や前置詞と共に) (物に足を取られて)つまずく, 足を引っかける ◇Someone will *trip* over that cable. 誰かがそのケーブルに足を引っかけるよ ◇Be careful you don't *trip up* on the step. 階段でつまずかないように気をつけなさい
fall 'down 句動詞 転ぶ, 崩れる ◇The house looked as if it was about to *fall down*. その家は今にも崩れそうに見えた

ノート **fall, fall over, fall down の使い分け**: この意味では fall と fall over は人についてのみ用いる。fall down は人や建物について用いられ, 立って[建って]いる状態から転ぶ[崩れる]ことを指す。fall は書き言葉で用いられることが多い。《英》では fall over は話し言葉で用いられることが多い。《米》では fall down は話し言葉で用いられることが多い。

fame 名

fame・publicity・prominence・celebrity・stardom
その活動[存在]によって世間によく知られている状態を表す語
【類語訳】名声, 有名, 注目, 知名度, 著名, 有名人, スターの座

文型&コロケーション
▶ fame/ prominence/ celebrity **as** sth
▶ **international** fame/ publicity/ prominence/ celebrity/ stardom
▶ to **achieve/ shoot to** fame/ prominence/ stardom

fame [U] 名声, 有名 ◇She *found fame* on the stage. 彼女は舞台で名を成した ◇Tennis brought him *fame and fortune*, but it didn't bring happiness. テニスは彼に富と名声をもたらしたが, 幸せを運んではくれなかった ◇He disappeared in 1934, *at the height of his fame*. 彼はその名声の絶頂期の1934年に失踪した ◇The town's only *claim to fame* is that it is the birthplace of Einstein. その町が自慢できるのはアインシュタイン生誕の地であることだけだ 反意 **obscurity ①** obscurity はよく知られていない[忘れられている]状態を指す。◆The actress was only 17 when she was plucked from *obscurity* and made a star. (無名から一躍スターになったとき, その女優はまだ17歳だった。☞ **famous, famed** (FAMOUS))
publicity [U] (新聞・テレビなどでの)注目, 知名度 ◇Taking part in the event will be good *publicity* for our school. その大会に出場すれば我が校の知名度は上がるだろう ◇There has been a great deal of *publicity* surrounding his disappearance. 彼の失踪をめぐって大きな注目が集まっている
prominence [U, 単数で]《書き言葉》重要, 著名, 注目 ◇She *came to prominence* as an artist in the 1960s. 彼女は1960年代に芸術家として有名になった ◇The issue was given great *prominence* in the press. その問題は報道で大きな注目を浴びた ☞ **prominent** (FAMOUS)
celebrity [U] (メディアにおける)有名[著名]人 ◇Does she find her new *celebrity* intruding on her private life? 有名になると私生活が侵害されることを彼女は受け止めていますか ◇He briefly achieved *celebrity* as a radical politician. 彼は急進的な政治家として一時的に有名になった ☞ **celebrity** (STAR), **celebrated** (FAMOUS)

ノート **fame** と **celebrity** の使い分け: fame は多くの人に知られている状態を表す一般的な語。人, 集団, 行事, 場所について用いられ, 短期間[長期間]持続するものを指す。celebrity はふつう個人について用いられ, 特に頻繁にメディアに登場する俳優, 歌手, スポーツ選手など, 特定の期間よく知られている人を指す。

stardom [U] (俳優・歌手・音楽家としての)スターの座 ◇The group is being *tipped for stardom* (= people say they will be very famous). そのグループはスターの座につくと予想されている ◇He achieved almost instant *stardom*. 彼はほとんどアッという間にスターになった ☞ **star** (STAR)

family 名

1 family・household・home・house
同じ建物で一緒に暮らす人々
【類語訳】家族, 家庭, 一家, 世帯, 所帯, 家庭生活

文型&コロケーション
▶ a **low-income/ poor/ high-income/ wealthy/ rich** family/ household/ home
▶ a **middle-class/ working-class** family/ household/ home
▶ a **one-parent/ single-parent** family/ household/ home
▶ a **large/ big/ small** family/ household
▶ a **friendly/ happy** family/ home/ house
▶ an/ the **average** family/ household/ home
▶ to **come from** a ...family/ home
▶ to **be one of the** family/ household
▶ family/ household **income**
▶ sb's family/ home **life/ background/ situation**
▶ a/ the **member/ head** of the family/ household

family [C+単数・複数動詞] (親と子どもから成る)家族, 家庭, 一家 ◇a *family* of four 4人家族 ◇*families* with young children 幼い子どものいる家族 ◇the other members of my *family* 私の家族で私以外の者 ◇All my *family* enjoy skiing. 家族は皆スキーが好きです ◇Almost every *family* in the country owns a television. 国中のほぼ全家庭にテレビがある ◇He's a friend of the *family* (= he is known and liked by the parents and the children). 彼は家族全員の友達である ◇Not everybody lives in the conventional *nuclear family* (= a family that consists of father, mother and children). すべての人が一般的な核家族として生活しているわけではない ◇a *family* business/car 家業/自家用車
household [C] (経済単位としての)家庭, 世帯, 所帯 ◇Most *households* now own at least one car. 今ではほとんどの家庭が車を少なくとも1台所有している ◇House prices are rising, driven by the big increase in the number of *single-person households*. 単身者世帯数の大幅な増加によって住宅価格は上昇している ◇The average *household* pays 27p a day in water rates. 平均的な家庭は1日に27ペンスを水道代として支払う ◇*household* bills/chores/goods 世帯ごとの請求書/家事/家財道具

ノート **family** と **household** の使い分け: family の構成員は互いに関係があるが, household の構成員は, 例えば家の部屋の賃借人や住み込みで働く人であることもありうる。family は関係する個人を強調し, どんな人であるか, どんな

family

活動が好きか，人間関係の善し悪しなどについて用いられる．household はしばしばニュース報道やビジネス文書で用いられるが，社会での地位や収入・支出などが話題のときは特に最小単位としての一団のことである．

home [C] 家庭(生活[環境]) ◇They wanted to give the boy a secure and loving *home*. 彼らはその少年に安心と愛情のある家庭環境を与えたかった ◇She comes from a *broken home* (= a family in which the parents are divorced or separated). 彼女は崩壊した家庭の出だ ◇She had never had a stable *home* life. 彼女は安定した家庭生活を送ったことがなかった

house [単数f] 家族全員 ◇Be quiet or you'll wake the whole *house*! 静かにしなさい．家中皆起きちゃうでしょ

2 family・relative・relation・kin・connections
互いに関係のある人や人々の集団
【類語訳】親族，身内，一族，親戚，親類

▸ **文型&コロケーション**
- a relative/ relation **of mine, yours, his,** etc.
- (a) **close/ near/ distant** relative/ relation/ kin
- the/ sb's **immediate** family/ relatives/ relations
- (a) **female/ male** relative/ relation/ kin
- a **living/ surviving** relative/ relation
- to **have** family/ relatives/ relations (in Australia, abroad, in the car trade, etc.)
- to **stay with/ visit** family/ relatives/ relations
- **friends and** family/ relatives/ relations

family 《C＋単数・複数動詞, U》親族，身内，一族 ◇All our *family* came to Grandad's eightieth birthday party. 一族全員がおじいちゃんの80歳の誕生パーティーに来た ◇The support of *family* and friends is vital. 親類縁者と友達の応援が不可欠です ◇I always think of you as one of the *family*. 私はあなたのことをいつも身内の一人だと考えている ◇She's *family* (= she is related to us). 《インフォーマル》彼女は親族だ ◇She grew up surrounded by a large *extended family* (= a family group that includes not only parents and children but also uncles, aunts, grandparents, etc.). 彼女は親戚を含めた大家族に囲まれて育った

relative [C] 親戚，親類；近縁種 ◇I have close *relatives*. 私には親しい親戚がいる ◇She's looking after an elderly *relative*. 彼女は年配の親戚の面倒を見ている ◇The ibex is a distant *relative* of the mountain goat. アイベックスはロッキーヤギの遠い仲間である

▸ **related** [形] ◇We're distantly *related*. 私たちは遠縁にあたる親戚だ ◇The llama is *related* to the camel. ラマはラクダの近縁種である

relation [C] 親戚, 親類 ◇She's a distant *relation* of mine. 彼女は私の遠い親戚です ◇He's called Brady too, but we're *no relation* (= not related). 彼もブレーディーという名前だが，親戚関係ではありません ◇Is he any *relation* to you? 彼はあなたと親戚関係にありますか

▸ **ノート** relative と relation の使い分け：時に両語とも使用可能．◆She's a distant *relative/relation* of mine. (彼女は私の遠い親戚です). relative はしばしば正確な関係がはっきりしない[重要でない]場合に用いられる．◆On his death, the house will pass to the nearest surviving *relative* (= whichever relative that happens to be).

(彼が亡くなったときには，家屋は最も近親の存命者に譲渡されることになっています).
relation は特に関係の度合いについて述べる[質問する]場合に用いられる．◆We're no *relation*. (私たちは親戚関係にありません). ◆What *relation* is Rita to you? (リタはあなたとどんな親戚関係にありますか). poor relation は文字どおりの意味にも比喩的な意味にも用いられる．◆Our branch of the family was always regarded as the *poor relations*. (一族の分家である我が家は常に身分の低い親戚と見なされていた). ◆He believes that interior design is the *poor relation* of (= inferior to) architecture. (《比喩的》内装デザインは建築より劣っていると彼は信じている).

kin [複数扱い] 《古風，フォーマル》親族，親戚 ◇Marriage between close *kin* is prohibited. 親族間の結婚は禁止されている ◇I'm her *next of kin* (= her closest living relative). 私は彼女の最近親者です ❶ kin はほとんどの場合，next of kin の表現で用いられる．

connections [複数で]（遠縁の）親戚，親類 ◇She is British but also has German *connections*. 彼女はイギリス人だがドイツ人の親戚もいる ◇He has a whole network of family *connections* in Italy. 彼の一族の親戚関係は全員イタリアにいる

3 family・origin・dynasty・lineage・blood・descent・ancestry・birth・pedigree・roots・parentage
先祖を含めた互いに関係のあるすべての人々
【類語訳】家系，一族，家柄，出生，出身，血統，王朝，血筋，系譜，ルーツ

▸ **文型&コロケーション**
- **by** origin/ descent/ birth
- to **be of** noble, Scottish, etc. origin/ lineage/ blood/ descent/ ancestry/ birth/ pedigree/ parentage
- **ethnic/ racial/ social/ cultural** origin/ descent/ ancestry/ pedigree/ roots
- **African, Scottish, Italian, etc.** family/ origin/ lineage/ blood/ descent/ ancestry/ roots/ parentage
- (of) **humble/ lowly** family/ origins/ birth/ roots
- (of) **noble** family/ origins/ lineage/ blood/ descent/ ancestry/ birth
- (of) **unknown** origin/ descent/ parentage
- **middle-class/ working-class/ peasant** family/ origins/ roots
- to **trace** your family/ origin/ lineage/ ancestry/ pedigree/ roots

family [C＋単数・複数動詞]（先祖を含めた）家系，一族 ◇Some *families* have farmed in this area for hundreds of years. 何百年もの間この地域で農業を営んできた一族がいくつかある ◇This painting has *been in our family* for generations. この絵画は我が一族が先祖代々所有してきた ◇How far back can you trace your *family tree* (= a diagram that shows the relationship between members of a family over a long period of time)? あなたはどのくらいまで家系をさかのぼることができますか ◇Heart disease *runs in the family*. その家族には心臓病の体質がある

origin [C, U] （または **origins** [複数で]）（社会的背景としての）家柄，出身，出身，血統 ◇children of various ethnic *origins* さまざまな種族出身の子どもたち ◇people of German *origin* ドイツ人の血を引く人々 ◇a person's country of *origin* (= where they were born) 人の出生国 ◇She has risen from humble *origins* to immense wealth. 彼女は卑しい家柄から出世して巨額の富を築いた ☞**origin** (SOURCE)

dynasty [C] (国家君主の)一族；(歴代の)王朝 ◇the Nehru-Gandhi *dynasty* ネール=ガンジー一族 ◇a Ming *dynasty* vase 明王朝期の花瓶 ◇Eventually the *dynasty* was overthrown, and the country became a Republic. ついに王朝は打倒されて、その国は共和国になった

▶**dynastic** 形 〔ふつう名詞の前で〕*dynastic* history 王朝史

lineage [U, C] 《フォーマル》(歴代の高貴な)血統, 血筋, 家系 ◇a French nobleman of ancient *lineage* 古い血統のフランス貴族 ☞**line** (SERIES)

blood [U] 《やや フォーマル》血統, 血筋, 家柄, 家系 ◇She is of noble *blood*. 彼女は高貴な家柄の出だ ◇There is some Polish *blood* on his father's side. 父方がポーランド系である

descent [U] 《やや フォーマル》家柄, 家系, 出身, 血統 ◇people of West Indian *descent* 西インド諸島の出身者たち ◇He traces his **line of descent** from the Stuart kings. 彼はスチュアート王家の血筋を引いている

ancestry [C, ふつう単数で, U] 《やや フォーマル》家柄, 家系, 血統 ◇His eyes owed their startling blueness to his Irish *ancestry*. 息を飲むほどの彼の目の青さはアイルランド系の家系に由来していた ◇He was able to trace his *ancestry* back over 1,000 years. 彼は家系を1000年以上さかのぼることができた

▶**ancestor** 名 [C] ◇His *ancestors* had come to America from Ireland. 彼の祖先はアイルランドから米国にやって来ていた ◇a reptile that was the common *ancestor* of lizards and turtles とかげと亀の共通の祖先であった爬虫類 反意 **descendant**

〔ノート〕**blood, descent, ancestry の使い分け**：これらの語はすべて人の家系を表すややフォーマルな表現. trace your descent from sb は過去を始点に現在に向けて近づくことを指す. trace your ancestry back to sb は現在を始点に過去にさかのぼることを意味する. blood は特に家系の社会的地位のある[異なる場所の異なる種類の家系の子孫であること]を強調する. ◆of noble *blood*（高貴な血筋の）. ◆of mixed Chinese and Portuguese *blood*（中国人とポルトガル人の混血の）. ◆some Polish *blood* on his father's side（父方がポーランド系の血筋）.

birth [U] (現状と異なる[高い社会的地位にある])家柄, 家系, 出自, 血統 ◇Anne was French by *birth* but lived most of her life in Italy. アンは生まれはフランスだが, 人生の大半をイタリアで過ごした ◇a woman of noble *birth* 高貴な生まれの女性

pedigree [C, U] (すごい)家柄, (物の)系譜 ◇She was proud of her long *pedigree*. 彼女は歴史ある家柄を誇りに思っていた ◇The product has a *pedigree* going back to the last century. その製品の系譜は前世紀にまでさかのぼる

roots [複数で] (自分・先祖の)心の故郷 (略式), ルーツ ◇I'm proud of my African *roots*. 私はアフリカにルーツがあることを誇りに思います ◇After 20 years in America, I still feel my *roots* are in Ireland. 渡米して20年, 等の心の故郷はアイルランドだといまだに感じます ☞**root** (SOURCE)

parentage [U] (両親の)家柄, 家系, 血統 ◇a young American of German *parentage* ドイツ人の血統を引く若いアメリカ人 ◇Nothing is known about her *parentage* and background. 彼女の家系や素性については何もわかっていない

famous 形

famous・historic・well known・prominent・public・legendary・renowned・famed・glorious・celebrated

人, 場所, 物事が多くの人に知られていて, しばしば好まれたり[たたえられたり]することを表す

【類語訳】有名な, 歴史的に有名な, よく知られた, 重要な, 著名な, 周知の, 名高い, 栄誉ある, 名誉

文型&コロケーション

▶ famous/ well known/ prominent/ renowned/ famed/ celebrated **as** sb
▶ famous/ well known/ legendary/ renowned/ famed/ celebrated **for** sth
▶ a famous/ historic/ well-known/ prominent/ legendary/ glorious/ celebrated **name**
▶ a famous/ historic/ well-known/ prominent/ public/ legendary/ renowned **figure**
▶ a famous/ well-known/ prominent/ renowned/ celebrated **writer/ author/ actor/ architect/ artist/ collection**
▶ a famous/ well-known/ prominent **politician/ personality**
▶ a famous/ well-known/ renowned **brand**
▶ **very** famous/ well known/ prominent/ celebrated
▶ **justly** famous/ renowned/ famed/ celebrated
▶ **internationally** famous/ renowned/ celebrated

famous 有名な ◇He became a world-*famous* conductor. 彼は世界的に有名な指揮者になった ◇Loch Ness is probably the most *famous* lake in Scotland. ネス湖は恐らくスコットランドで最も有名な湖だろう ◇One day, I'll be **rich and famous**. いつの日か私は金持ちになって有名になるんだ ◇So this is the *famous* dress! (= the one we have heard a lot about but have not seen) じゃあ, これがその有名なドレスなんだね ☞**fame** (FAME)

▶**famously** 副 ◇the words he *famously* uttered on his deathbed 彼が死の間際に発した有名な言葉

historic 歴史的に有名な[重要な]な；(将来的に)歴史に残る, 歴史的な ◇a *historic* building/monument 歴史的に有名な建造物/記念碑 ◇The area is of special *historic* interest. その地域は歴史的に特別興味深い ◇The party has won a *historic* victory at the polls. その政党は選挙で歴史的勝利を収めた ☞**ancient** (OLD 1)

,well 'known よく知られた, 有名な ◇She's married to a *well-known* actor, whose name I've forgotten. 彼女は, 名前は忘れたが, 有名な俳優と結婚している ◇His books are not *well known*. 彼の著書はあまり知られていない ❶ well known は名詞の前に用いる場合, 必ず **well-known** とハイフンを入れる.

prominent 《やや フォーマル, 特に書き言葉》重要な, 有名な, 著名な ◇A number of *prominent* politicians made public statements supporting the change. 数多くの著名な政治家たちがその改革を支持する公式声明を出した ◇He played a *prominent* part in the campaign. 彼はキャンペーンで重要な役割を果たした ◇She was *prominent* in the fashion industry. 彼女はファッション業界で有名だった ❶ prominent はしばしば政界[ビジネス界]の人々

について用いられる。☞ **prominence** (FAME), GREAT 2, TOP
public 公に知られた、有名な、周知の ◇She entered *public life* (= started a job in which she became known to the public) at the age of 23. 彼女は23歳のとき知名度の上がる職に就いた ◇Details of the government report have not yet been made *public*. 政府の報告書の詳細はまだ公表されていない 反意 **private** (SECRET), ☞ **public figure** (STAR)
legendary 《伝説に残るほど》有名な ◇We once received a visit from the *legendary* Orson Welles. 私たちはかつて伝説的に名高いオーソン・ウェルズの訪問を受けた ◇Her patience and tact are *legendary*. 彼女の忍耐と機転は今なお語り種になっている ❶ *legendary* はしばしば依然として話題に上り賞賛される故人[年配者]について用いられる。☞ **legend** (STAR)
renowned 《特に書き言葉》有名な、名高い、誉れ高い ◇We asked for advice from the *renowned* legal expert, Sam Pincher. 私たちは有名な法律専門家のサム・ピンチャーに助言を求めた ◇It is *renowned* as one of the region's best restaurants. そこはその地域で最高のレストランの一つとして名高い ◇She is *renowned* for her patience. 彼女は忍耐強さで誉れ高い ❶ *renowned* は、人の場合は、仕事ぶりが優秀である[特殊技能や能力を持っている]ために尊敬されていること、場所や作品の場合は、非常に高水準のサービスを提供することで評判が高いという意味である。
famed 《書き言葉》《人・場所がその質の高さで》有名な ◇As a player she was *famed* for her grace and artistry, as well as her success. 彼女は演奏者として、その成功だけでなく、優美さや芸術性においても名を馳せていた ◇The movie was filmed in the *famed* Blue Ridge Mountains, possibly the last forested wilderness in the United States. おそらくアメリカに唯一残された原生林であろう有名なブルーリッジ山脈でその映画は撮影された ☞ **fame** (FAME)
glorious [ふつう名詞の前で]《フォーマル》栄誉ある、名誉な、輝かしい ◇We congratulate you on this *glorious* victory. この栄誉ある勝利をお祝いします ◇This is a *glorious* chapter in our country's history. これは我が国の歴史における輝かしい一章です ❶ *glorious* は特に歴史[政治]文学で用いられる。☞ **glory** (STATUS)
celebrated [ふつう名詞の前で]《書き言葉》《質の高さで》有名な ◇He is one of France's most *celebrated* painters. 彼はフランスで最も有名な画家の一人である ◇'The Kiss' is one of Rodin's most *celebrated* works. 「接吻」はロダンの最も有名な作品の一つである ❶ *celebrated* はしばしば芸術およびその作品において成功を収めている人について用いられる。◆ a *celebrated* artist/painter/sculptor/poet/novelist/actor/actress/painting/work/poem/novel《著名な芸術家／画家／彫刻家／詩人／小説家／俳優／女優／絵画／作品／詩／小説》☞ **celebrity** (FAME)

fan 名

fan・enthusiast・supporter・lover・admirer・fanatic・devotee・groupie・follower・addict・freak
特定の物事[活動、人]がとても好きな人
【類語訳】ファン、愛好家、サポーター、崇拝者、おたく、追っかけ

文型&コロケーション
▸ a great fan/ enthusiast/ lover/ admirer
▸ a true fan/ enthusiast/ admirer
▸ a keen fan/ enthusiast/ supporter/ admirer/ follower
▸ a real fan/ enthusiast/ fanatic/ freak
▸ a big fan/ supporter/ admirer
▸ a music/ art/ jazz fan/ enthusiast/ lover/ fanatic/ devotee
▸ a sports/ football/ boxing/ cricket, etc. fan/ enthusiast/ fanatic/ devotee
▸ a fitness/ health enthusiast/ fanatic/ freak

fan [C] 《人・チーム・趣味・鑑賞などの》ファン、愛好家 ◇Movie *fans* will be familiar with his work already. 映画ファンはすでに彼の作品になじんでいることでしょう ◇Crowds of football *fans* filled the streets. サッカーファンの群衆が通りを埋めた ◇He's always been a big *fan* of Pavarotti. 彼は昔からずっとパヴァロッティの大ファンだ ◇She received bags of *fan mail* (= letters from her fans). 彼女はファンレターをどっさり受け取った ◇He's a big Yankees *fan*. 《米》彼はヤンキースの大ファンだ
enthusiast [C] 《趣味に対する》ファン ◇Railway *enthusiasts* were given the chance to ride on the old steam train during the weekend. 鉄道ファンは週末に古い蒸気機関車に乗る機会を得た ◇She was a lifelong *enthusiast* of dancing, running and waterskiing. 彼女は生涯にわたってダンス、ランニング、水上スキーに熱中した ☞ **enthusiastic** (EAGER)

ノート **fan** と **enthusiast** の使い分け：どちらの語も活動や対象について用いることができるが、*enthusiast* は人についてはいえることができない。 ◆jazz/fishing/DIY *fans/enthusiasts*《ジャズファン／釣り好き／日曜大工好き》◆*fans* of the pop star Madonna《ポップスターのマドンナのファン》. ×*enthusiasts* of the pop star Madonna. *enthusiast* は *fan* よりも物事により積極的に取り組むことを表す。*enthusiast* は人が物事に自由な時間を多くかけるという事実を強調し、*fan* は物事の楽しみを強調する。☞ **buff** (EXPERT)

supporter [C] 《英》《サッカーチームなど特定のスポーツチームの》サポーター ◇They are both keen Arsenal *supporters*. 彼らはどちらもアーセナルの熱烈なサポーターだ ❶ *support* はスポーツチームの試合を観戦する[その成長を熱烈に応援する]などを意味する。《米》では *supporter* の代わりに *fan* などを用いる。
lover [C] 愛好家《しばしば複合語で》 ◇He was a devoted animal *lover*, and had a large number of pets at home. 彼は熱心な動物愛好家で、たくさんのペットを家で飼っていた ◇She was a great *lover* of the arts, and of Greek architecture in particular. 彼女は芸術、特にギリシャ建築をとても愛していた ◇an art-*lover*/a nature-*lover*《美術／自然愛好家》☞ **love** (LIKE 動)
admirer [C] 《ややフォーマル》《有名な人・物事の》崇拝者 ◇He is a great *admirer* of Picasso's early paintings. 彼はピカソの初期の絵画を非常に崇拝している ☞ **admire** (RESPECT)
fanatic [C] 《ややインフォーマル、時にけなして》《狂信的な》おたく、…狂 ◇He's a non-smoking, non-drinking, fitness *fanatic*. 彼は禁煙、禁酒、健康にご熱心だ ▸ *fanatical* interest in football サッカーに対する熱狂的な関心 ◇She's *fanatical* about healthy eating. 彼女は健康的な食事に異常なまでに熱心だ
devotee [C] 《熱狂的な》ファン、愛好家 ◇He's been a golf *devotee* for 23 years. 彼は23年間ゴルフ一筋の愛好家だ ◇a *devotee* of science fiction SFにのめり込むファン ❶ *devotee* は人が物事に時間と労力を惜しまず注ぎ込む事

↳fan **fashion, fashionable**

実を強調する. ☞**devote** (DEVOTE)
groupie [C]《ややインフォーマル, 時にけなして》(ポップ・ミュージシャンに付きまとう) 追っかけ[親衛隊]の女の子 ◇The *groupies* were waiting around at the exit, hoping for a glimpse of the band. 追っかけの女の子たちはそのバンドを一目見ようと出口付近で待っていた
follower [C]（特定の活動[最新情報]に注目する）ファン, 追っかけ ◇He is a keen *follower* of both football and cricket. 彼はサッカーとクリケットの熱心なファンだ ◇a *follower* of fashion 最新ファッションを追いかける人 ☞**follow** (FOLLOW 4)
addict [C]《しばしばけなして》(物事に没頭する) 中毒者, おたく ◇I used to be a video game *addict* ─ I literally spent all my free time playing games. かつて私はテレビゲームおたくだった─文字どおり空いている時間を全部使ってゲームをしていた ☞**addictive** (ADDICTIVE)
freak《ふつう複合語で》[C]《インフォーマル, しばしばけなして》(特定のテーマに異常に関心を持つ)おたく, …狂 ◇He's a real fitness *freak* ─ he goes to the gym every single day. 彼はほんと健康おたくだ─一日も欠かさずジムへ行く

fashion 名 ☞ STYLE

fashion・style・vogue・fad・trend・look・craze
特定の物事がある限られた期間に非常に人気のあることを表す
【類語訳】流行, はやり, ファッション, スタイル, ブーム, トレンド

【文型&コロケーション】
▶ a fashion/ vogue/ fad/ trend/ craze **for** sth
▶ a fashion/ style/ trend **in** sth
▶ a fashion/ trend/ craze **among** people
▶ **in** fashion/ style/ vogue/ trend
▶ a **new** fashion/ style/ vogue/ fad/ trend/ look/ craze
▶ the **latest** fashion/ style/ fad/ trend/ look/ craze
▶ the **current** fashion/ style/ vogue/ fad/ trend
▶ a **passing** fashion/ fad/ craze
▶ to **come (back) into/ (be) go out of** fashion/ vogue
▶ to **set** a fashion/ style/ trend
▶ to **create** a style/ vogue/ trend/ look
▶ to **follow** fashion/ a style/ a trend

fashion [U, C] (服装・髪型・行為・活動などの) 流行, はやり, ファッション；ファッション業 ◇Long skirts have come into *fashion* again. ロングスカートが再び流行している ◇The stores are full of the spring *fashions*. 店は春物のファッションであふれている ◇*Fashions* in art and literature come and go. 美術と文学の流行は移り変わる ◇a *fashion* designer/magazine/show ファッションデザイナー/雑誌/ショー ◇the *fashion* industry ファッション産業 ◇the world of *fashion* ファッション業界
style [C, U] (服装・髪型の)型, スタイル；流行 ◇We stock a wide variety of *styles* and sizes. 当店はさまざまな型とサイズの品を置いております ◇Why not have your hair cut in a shorter *style*? もっと短い髪型にしたらどう ◇hot tips for *style*-conscious teenagers 流行に敏感なティーンエージャーにとっての最新情報 ◇Short skirts are back in *style*. 短いスカートがまたはやっている ☞**stylish** (ELEGANT)
vogue [C, U, ふつう単数で]《ややフォーマル, 書き言葉》(物事の) 流行, はやり, ブーム ◇the *vogue* for child-centred education 子ども主体の教育ブーム ◇Black is in *vogue* again this winter. この冬はまた黒がはやっている
fad [C]《けなして》一時的流行[熱中] ◇It's just a *fad*. It

won't last. それは一時的な流行にすぎない. 長続きはしないだろう ◇*Fads* for vitamin supplements have been overtaken by a vogue for minerals and trace elements. ビタミン補助食品の一時的な流行はミネラルと微量元素の流行に取って代わられた
trend [C] (ある方向に移り変わる全体的な) 流行, はやり, トレンド ◇You seem to have set (= started) a new *trend*. あなたが新しい流行を生み出したようです ◇fashion *trends* in sunglasses サングラスのファッション・トレンド ◇Their new knitwear is very **on trend** (= in the latest fashion).《英, ややインフォーマル》彼らの新しいニットウエアは最新のトレンドです ☞**trend** (TREND)
look [単数で] (見た目による特定の)型, 装い, 格好 ◇The punk *look* is in again. パンクルックが再来している ◇She said she was aiming for a more sophisticated *look*. もっと洗練された格好を目指していると彼女は言った
craze [C] (一時的な) 熱狂的流行；熱狂的 ◇I don't understand this *craze* for collecting labels. 私はこのラベル収集熱が理解できない ◇Pet pigs are the latest *craze*. ペットの豚が最近ものすごくはやっている

fashionable 形 ☞ ELEGANT

fashionable・glamorous・trendy・classy・smart・hip
物事が特定の時期に多くの人々によって称賛される[欲される]こと
【類語訳】流行の, はやりの, おしゃれな, 華やかな, 優雅な, 高級な, 粋な, 進んでいる

【文型&コロケーション】
▶ fashionable/ glamorous/ trendy/ classy/ smart **people**
▶ fashionable/ glamorous/ smart **women**
▶ fashionable/ smart **men**
▶ fashionable/ glamorous/ trendy/ smart **clothes**
▶ a fashionable/ trendy/ classy/ smart **hotel/ restaurant**
▶ a fashionable/ trendy/ smart **audience/ shop**
▶ **very** fashionable/ glamorous/ trendy/ classy
▶ **quite** fashionable/ glamorous/ trendy/ classy/ smart
▶ **rather** fashionable/ glamorous/ classy/ smart

fashionable 流行の, はやりの；おしゃれな, 上流の ◇Everything Italian suddenly became *fashionable*. イタリアのものすべてが突然おしゃれということになった ◇The play is a satire on ***fashionable society*** (= the upper classes) in Victorian times. その劇はビクトリア朝時代の上流社会に対する諷刺である ◇Such thinking is ***fashionable among*** right-wing politicians at the moment. 現在そういった考えが右派の政治家たちの間ではやっている ◇It's a very *fashionable* part of London. そこはロンドンのとりわけおしゃれな区域です 反意 **unfashionable**
❶ unfashionable は物事, 場所, 人々が特定の時期に人気がない[流行していない]ことを表す. ◆an *unfashionable* part of the city (都市の流行遅れの区域). ◆ *unfasionable* ideas/attitudes (古くさい考え/態度).
▶**fashionably** 副 ◇*fashionably* dressed おしゃれな装をした
glamorous (ふつうと違って物事・人々が) 華やかな, 優雅な ◇*glamorous* movie stars 華やかな映画スターたち ◇*glamorous* lifestyle 優雅な生活 ☞ **glamour** (INTEREST 名 1), **glamour** (STYLE)
▶**glamorously** 副 ◇*glamorously* dressed 華やかな装いの

trendy《インフォーマル、時にけなして》(デザイン・考えにおいて) 最新流行の、今はやりの、流行に飛びつく、おしゃれな ◇She wasn't a *trendy* sort of person. 彼女は流行に飛びつくタイプの人間ではなかった ◇People are buying them just to be *trendy*. 人々はただ最新流行だからというだけでそれらを買っている

classy《インフォーマル、ほめて》上等の;高級な、粋な ◇United play some *classy* football. ユナイテッドはかなり洗練されたサッカーをする ◇The car was a *classy* German make. その車はドイツ製の高級車だった ☞ **class** (STYLE)

smart《特に英》優雅な、高級な、粋な、おしゃれな ◇The restaurant has a *smart* new décor. そのレストランには優雅で現代的な内装が施されている ◇The reception would be very grand and *smart*. 歓迎会はとても盛大でおしゃれなものになるだろう

hip《インフォーマル、ほめて》(服装・音楽において)流行に敏感な、おしゃれな、進んでいる ◇He said it was the *hip* place to hang out. そこは彼がよく行くおしゃれな場所だと彼は言った ◇It's hard to be *hip* and forty. 流行に敏感な40歳でいることは難しい

fast 形 ☞ QUICK

fast・quick・high-speed・brisk・supersonic・express
物や人が速さを伴って動いたり、事を行ったりすることを表す
【類語訳】速い、高速の、素早い、敏速な、迅速な、機敏な、即座の、早足の、急行の、速配便の

fast	high-speed	supersonic
quick	express	
brisk		

文型&コロケーション
▶ to be fast/ quick at doing sth
▶ a fast/ supersonic **speed**
▶ a fast/ quick/ brisk **movement/ pace/ walk/ run**
▶ quick/ brisk **footsteps**
▶ a fast/ quick **reader/ worker/ learner/ rhythm**
▶ a fast/ a high-speed/ an express **train/ link**
▶ a fast/ a high-speed **computer/ modem**
▶ a fast/ an express **bus/ coach/ lane**
▶ very/ quite/ fairly **fast/ quick/ brisk**

fast (動作・処理について)速い、高速の、素早い、敏速な;高速を生み出す、高速向きの ◇She loves driving *fast* cars. 彼女は速い車を運転するのが大好きだ ◇Are you a *fast* reader with the ability to retain the key points? あなたは要点を押さえて速読できますか ◇These are complex programs needing very large and *fast* computers. これらは非常に大型で高速のコンピューターを必要とする複雑なプログラムである ◇It's a very *fast* road and people do not realize what speed they are doing. その道路はすごい速さで走ることができるので、人はどのくらいスピードを出しているのか気づかない 反意 **slow** (SLOW)
▶ **fast** 副 ◇Don't drive so *fast*! そんなに飛ばさないように ◇I can't go any *faster*. これ以上スピードを出せないよ

quick (動作・処理について)速い、素早い、機敏な、敏速な、迅速な、即座の ◇He's a very *quick* worker. 彼はすばしこくてきぱきしている ◇The kids were *quick to* learn. 子どもたちは物覚えが速かった ◇She was *quick* (= too quick) to point out the mistakes I'd made. 彼女は私が犯したミスをたちまち指摘した ◇Her *quick* hands suddenly stopped moving. 彼女は素早く動かしていた手を突然止めた ◇Try to **be quick**! We're late already. 早くしなさい。もう遅刻だよ 反意 **slow** (SLOW)
▶ **quickly** 副 ◇She walked away *quickly*. 彼女は足早に歩き去った

ノート **fast** と **quick** の使い分け: fast は特に乗り物の移動について用いられる一般的な語。×a *quick* car/road. ×Don't drive so *quickly*! 人が素早く事を行えることを表す場合は両語とも使用可能。• a *fast/quick* reader/ worker/runner/thinker/learner/brain (速読する人/仕事の速い人/俊足の人/理解の速い人/物覚えの速い人/頭の回転の速い人)。ただし、fast は be 動詞の後では用いられない。× The kids were *fast* to learn. ×Try to be *fast*! We're late already. ☞ QUICK

high-'speed [ふつう名詞の前で](移動・処理・発生について)高速(度)の ◇We are talking about a network of modern highways, *high-speed* trains, airports and air routes. 私たちは現代の幹線道路、高速列車、空港、航空路の交通網について話しているところです ◇There should be a large market for cheap *high-speed* modems. 安価な高速モデムの市場は大きいはずだ ◇A police officer was injured during a *high-speed* chase across two counties. 一人の警官が二つの郡にまたがって高速度で追跡中に負傷した

brisk (徒歩について)早足の ◇We went for a *brisk* walk before lunch. 私たちは昼食前に早足でウォーキングに出かけた ◇They set off at a *brisk* pace. 彼らは早足で出発した
▶ **briskly** ◇He walked *briskly* down the street. 彼は足早に通りを歩いて行った

supersonic 超音速の ◇Until then, no aircraft was capable of *supersonic* flight. それまで超音速飛行が可能な飛行機はなかった

express [名詞の前で](移動について)高速の、急行の;(運送・処理について)急行便の、速配便の ◇An *express* coach runs once an hour from the airport. 高速バスが1時間に1本空港から出ている ◇We provide *express* delivery services seven days a week. 当社は週に7日速配サービスを提供しております ❶ express は運送などのサービスについて用いられる

fat 形

fat・overweight・plump・obese・chubby・stout
体にぜい肉が付きすぎていて体重が重すぎることを表す
【類語訳】太った、肥満の、でぶの、ふくよかな、丸っこい、ぽっちゃりした、かっぷくのよい

ノート 人は自分の体格・体重についてよく話をするが、一般的に人の大きな体格・体重について本人に向かって話をすることは失礼であると考えられている。

| plump | stout | fat | obese |
| chubby | | overweight | |

文型&コロケーション
▶ a fat/ an overweight/ a plump/ an obese/ a chubby/ stout **man/ woman**
▶ a fat/ an overweight/ a plump/ an obese/ a chubby **child**

▶a fat/ an overweight/ a plump/ a chubby **baby**
▶a fat/ plump/ chubby **boy/ girl**
▶a fat/ plump/ chubby/ stout **body/ face**
▶fat/ plump/ chubby **arms/ cheeks/ fingers/ legs/ hands**

fat (人・体の部位が)太った, 肥満の, でぶの ◇A big *fat* man walked into the room. 太った大男が部屋に入って行った ◇You'll get *fat* if you eat so much chocolate. チョコレートを食べすぎると太っちゃうよ ◇I was ashamed of my *fat* flabby legs. 私は太ってるんだ脚が恥ずかしかった ❶fatは最も一般的で直接的な語だが, 人がfatである(太っている)ことを本人に向かって言うのは失礼である. 書き言葉よりも話し言葉で用いられることが多い. 反意 **thin** (THIN)
▶**fatness** 名 [U] ◇*Fatness* tends to run in families. 肥満は遺伝する傾向がある

overweight (人が)肥満の; 標準体重を超えた ◇She was only a few pounds *overweight*. 彼女は標準体重を数ポンド超えただけだった ◇A number of medical conditions are due to being *overweight*. 疾患は肥満によるものが多い ❶overweightはfatほど侮蔑的ではないが, やはり人がoverweightである(肥満である)ことを本人に向かって言うのは失礼である. 反意 **underweight** (THIN)

plump (人・体の部位が)ふっくら[ぽっちゃり]した, ふくよかな, 丸っこい; 太り気味の ◇Our new teacher was a short, *plump* woman. 私たちの学校の新任教師は背が低くてぽっちゃりした女の人だった ◇His *plump* face was pink with embarrassment. 彼の丸っこい顔は恥ずかしさで赤くなっていた ❶plumpは人が魅力的に少し太っていることを指す. 反意 **slim** (THIN)

obese 《ややフォーマル or 医学》(人が病的に)肥満体の, 太りすぎの ◇*Obese* patients are given dietary advice. 肥満患者たちは食餌療法の指導を受ける ❶obeseは太りすぎで不健康な人について医者が用いる語. 「太りすぎの」の意味で一般的にも用いられる.
▶**obesity** 名 [U] ◇*Obesity* can increase the risk of heart disease. 肥満により心臓病の危険性が高まることがある

chubby 《しばしばほめて》(人・体の部位が)ふっくら[ぽっちゃり]した ◇Aah, look at his *chubby* little hands! まぁ, 彼のふっくらした小さな手を見てよ ◇She was eleven years old and pretty in a *chubby* sort of way. 彼女は11歳で, ちょっとぽっちゃりしてかわいかった ❶chubbyは主に赤ちゃんや子どもについて用いられる. 反意 **skinny** (THIN)

stout 《特に英, ややフォーマル》(男性・女性が)かっぷく[肉づき]のよい ◇He was a *stout* man with a red face. 彼は赤ら顔のかっぷくのよい男だった
▶**stoutly** 副 ◇He was tall and *stoutly* built. 彼は背が高くてかっぷくがよかった

fatal 形

fatal・deadly・lethal・malignant・terminal・incurable・inoperable
死を引き起こす(可能性のある)ことを表す
【類語訳】死をもたらす, 死に至る, 致死の, 悪性の, 末期の, 不治の, 末期疾患を患った, 手術不能の

文型&コロケーション
▶fatal/ deadly/ lethal **to** sb/ sth
▶fatal/ lethal **for** sb/ sth
▶a fatal/ a deadly/ a lethal/ a malignant/ a terminal/ an incurable **disease**
▶a fatal/ a terminal/ an incurable **illness/ condition**
▶a deadly/ lethal **cocktail/ poison/ venom/ weapon**
▶**potentially** fatal/ deadly/ lethal/ malignant

fatal 死をもたらす, 死に至る, 致命的な ◇They were involved in a *fatal* accident. 彼らは死亡事故に巻き込まれた ◇He suffered *fatal* injuries when he was struck by a car. 彼は車にひかれて致命傷を負った ❶fatalは事故, 傷害, 病気, 人への攻撃について用いられる. 毒物や武器には用いられない.
▶**fatally** 副 ◇*fatally* injured/wounded 致命傷を負った

deadly 死をもたらす(可能性のある), 死に至る, 致死の, 命に関わる ◇The cobra is one of the world's *deadliest* snakes. コブラは世界で最も強い毒を持つヘビの1種である ◇The terrorists have chosen to play a *deadly* game with the civilian population. テロリストたちは一般市民と命を賭けたゲームをすることを選んだ ❶deadlyは毒物, 有毒動物, 武器, 攻撃について用いられる. 事故や傷害には用いられない. 連語としてdisease, virusと一緒に用いられるが, illnessとは結びつかない.

lethal 死をもたらす(可能性のある), 致死の ◇She had been given a *lethal* dose of poison. 彼女は致死量の毒薬を飲まされていた ◇He has been sentenced to death by *lethal* injection. 彼は薬物注射による死刑を宣告された ❶lethalは dose, cocktail, mixture, injection, weaponと共に用いられるのが最も一般的である. 事故, 傷害, 攻撃には用いられない.

malignant 《医学》(疾患・腫瘍が)悪性の ◇The tests found some *malignant* cells. 検査で悪性細胞がいくつか見つかった ❶malignantはほとんどの場合, disease, tumourと共に用いられる. tumourは本来は成長するはずのない体内[体表]で成長する細胞の塊のこと. malignantと共によく用いられる他の語に, carcinoma, melanomaなど, この種の細胞を表すより専門的な医学用語が挙げられる.

terminal 《ややフォーマル》(病気・疾患・患者が)末期の, 不治の, 死に至る; (人が)末期疾患[不治の病]を患った ◇He has *terminal* lung cancer. 彼は末期の肺がんを患っている ◇Many *terminal* patients would prefer to end their days at home. 多くの末期患者たちは自宅で死を迎えることを望むものである
▶**terminally** 副 ◇*terminally* ill patients 末期患者たち

incurable (病気・疾患が)不治の ◇He's suffering from an *incurable* disease. 彼は不治の病に苦しんでいる 反意 **curable** は病気や疾患が治療可能であることを表す. ◆Most skin cancers are *curable* if treated early. (たいていの皮膚がんは早期治療すれば治る).
▶**incurably** 副 ◇*incurably* ill 不治の病の

ノート terminal と incurable の使い分け: 両語とも連語としてdisease, condition, illnessと一緒に用いられる. terminalのほうがフォーマルで, 専門的な医学の文脈で用いられる. incurableは日常会話で用いられる傾向が強い. terminalはがんについて言うときに好まれる用語である.

inoperable (疾患・腫瘍が)手術不能の ◇He was diagnosed with an *inoperable* brain tumour. 彼は手術不能な脳腫瘍があると診断された 反意 **operable** ❶operableは疾患や腫瘍が手術可能であることを表す.

fault 名

fault・responsibility・blame・guilt

favourite

起きてしまった過ち・過失を背負うことを表す
【類語訳】責任, 原因, せい, 罪, 有罪

文型&コロケーション
- the responsibility/ blame/ guilt **for** sth
- (not) **without** fault/ responsibility/ blame/ guilt
- to **admit** your fault/ responsibility/ your guilt
- to **bear** the responsibility/ blame/ guilt for sth
- to **accept/ share/ absolve sb from/ shift** the responsibility/ blame/ guilt
- to **take/ shoulder/ carry/ lay/ place/ put/ attribute** the responsibility/ blame
- to **deny** responsibility/ your guilt
- the fault/ responsibility/ blame/ guilt **lies with sb**
- the fault/ responsibility/ blame **rests with sb**

fault [U]《特に話し言葉》(過ち・過失に対する)責任, 原因, せい ◇Why should I say sorry when it's not *my fault*? 私のせいじゃないのにどうして謝らないといけないの ◇It's nobody's *fault*. 誰のせいでもない ◇It was his *fault that we were late*. 私たちが遅刻したのは彼のせいだった ◇It's *your own fault* for being careless. 不注意だったのは自業自得だよ ◇Many people live in poverty *through no fault of their own*. 多くの人たちが自分たちが悪いわけではないのに, 貧しい暮らしをしている ◇I think the owners are *at fault* (= responsible) for not warning us. 私たちに警告をしなかった責任はオーナーにあると私は思う ☞ **at fault** (GUILTY).

responsibility [U]《ややフォーマル》(過ち・過失に対する)責任 ◇The bank refuses to accept *responsibility* for the mistake. 銀行はその手違いに対する責任を負うことを拒否している ◇Nobody has *claimed responsibility* for the bombing. その爆破事件の犯行声明はまだ出されていない ◇We must all bear some *responsibility* for what happened. 起きたことに対する何らかの責任が私たち全員にある ☞ **responsible** (GUILTY).

ノート fault と responsibility の使い分け:どちらの語も意味は基本的に同じだが, 使用パターンと連語が異なる。fault はふつう my/your/his/her/our/their/sb's (own) fault や sb is at fault の句で用いられる。×It was his *responsibility* that we were late. ×I think the owners are at *responsibility*. responsibility の典型的な連語として, accept/share/admit/claim/deny responsibility (責任を負う/分担する/認める/主張する/否定する)が挙げられる。×The bank refuses to accept *fault* for the mistake. ◆The bank refuses to accept that it is at *fault* for the mistake.(銀行はその手違いが自分たちの責任であることを認めていない)。◆He refused to accept that the mistake was his *fault*.(彼はその間違いが自分のせいであることを認めなかった)。

blame [U](過ち・過失に対する)責任;(事実に反して)責任を人になすりつけること, 人のせいにすること ◇She *put the blame* on me. 彼女は私に責任をなすりつけた ◇The government will have to *take the blame* for the riots. 政府は暴動の責任を取らなければならないだろう ◇Why do I always *get the blame* for everything that goes wrong? うまくいかないことすべてがどうしていつも私のせいになるの ❶ 実際に事を行った張本人でなくても, 人が **gets/takes/accepts/bears/shoulders the blame for sth**(事に対する責任を負う/取る/認める/負う/引き受ける)ことがよくある。また, 事実に反していても, 人がその事を行ったのだと主張する

ることで, **lay/pin/place/put the blame on sb for sth**(他の人に事の責任をなすりつける)人もいる。反意 **credit** (PRAISE 名), ☞ **blame** (BLAME), **to blame** (GUILTY), **blameless** (INNOCENT).

guilt [U]《ややフォーマル, 特に書き言葉》(違法行為に対しての)罪, 有罪;(過ち・過失に対する)責任, 罪 ◇His *guilt was proved* beyond all doubt by the prosecution. 彼の有罪は検察当局によって疑いの余地なく立証された ◇Do you think this statement amounts to an admission of *guilt*? この供述は罪を認めることになると思いますか ❶ 典型的な結びつきとして, 自分の guilt (罪)には admit (認める)が, 他人の guilt (罪)には establish, prove (立証[証明]する)が挙げられる。 反意 **innocence** (INNOCENT), ☞ **guilty** (GUILTY).

favourite 《英》《米 favorite》 形 ☞ BEST, IDEAL

favourite・preferred・favoured・of choice・pet・best-loved

人や物, 場所が同種の他のものよりも望まれることを表す
【類語訳】お気に入りの, 最適の, 選ばれる, 好まれる, 得意の

文型&コロケーション
- sb's **least** favourite/ preferred/ favoured sth
- sb's favourite/ preferred/ favoured **food/ activity/ method/ way/ type**
- sb's **method of choice**
- sb's favourite/ preferred **choice**
- sb's favourite/ pet **subject/ topic**
- sb's preferred/ favoured **option/ approach/ strategy/ version/ location/ candidate/ school**

favourite《英》《米 **favorite**》(同種の他のものより)お気に入りの, 特に好きな ◇It's one of my *favourite* movies. それは私のお気に入りの一つです ◇Who is your *favourite* writer? あなたの特に好きな作家は誰ですか ☞ **favourite** (CHOICE 2), **favour** (PREFER).

preferred [名詞の前で]《特にビジネス》(たいていの人に)最も好まれる, 最適の ◇The company has not yet identified a *preferred* candidate for the job. 会社はその職に最適の候補者をまだ特定していない ◇Watching TV was high on the children's list of *preferred* activities. テレビを観ることは子どもたちの最も好きな活動リストの上位にあった ☞ **prefer** (PREFER), **preference** (CHOICE 2), **preference** (TASTE).

favoured《英》《米 **favored**》《ややフォーマル, 特に書き言葉》(たいていの人に)最も好まれる, 最適の ◇David Prince is widely viewed as the *favoured* candidate to replace Mr Wallace. デイヴィッド・プリンスはウォーレス氏に代わる最有力候補と広く見なされている ☞ **favour** (PREFER).

ノート preferred と favoured の使い分け:これらの語に意味による違いはほとんどない。話し言葉では preferred のほうが favoured よりもずっと一般的である。

of 'choice [行法][名詞の後で](特定の人の集団に[特定の目的のために])選ばれる, 好まれる, 最適の ◇It's the software *of choice* for business use. それはビジネスの使用に最適のソフトです ◇Cheap handguns are the weapon *of choice* for young criminals. 安価な拳銃は若い犯罪者が好んで使う武器である ☞ **choice** (CHOICE 2).

pet [名詞の前で] お気に入りの, 特に好きな[興味のある], 得意の ◇One of the council's *pet* projects is to re-

→favourite

duce traffic speeds in residential areas. 議会が特に関心を持つ計画の一つは住宅地における走行速度を下げることである ❶《英》では特に嫌いな物事をpet hateと言い,《米》ではpet peeveと言う. ◆According to our survey, your number one *pet peeve* is junk email.（調査によると嫌なものの1位は迷惑メールです）.

,best-'loved 最も(多くの人に)愛される ◇It remains one of the best-known and *best-loved* movies of all time. それはいまだに史上最も有名で最も愛される映画の一つだ ❶best-lovedはしばしば映画,書籍,音楽など,またそれらを生み出す人(作家,俳優,音楽家など)について用いられる. また,一般に人気のある人や物事について用いられることもある. ◆This play has become the *best-loved* of all his works.（この劇は彼の全作品の中で最も愛される作品になった）. しばしば特定の国で最も愛される場合にも用いられる. ◆one of Britain's *best-loved* comedians（英国で最も愛されているコメディアンの一人）. さらに,特定の時期に最も愛される場合にも用いられる. ◆one of the *best-loved* authors of the last century（前世紀で最も愛された作家の一人）.

fear 名

fear・terror・panic・alarm・fright・hysteria・dread・paranoia・phobia

怖がるときに抱く悪感情

【類語訳】恐怖, 恐れ, 心配, 不安, 懸念, 狼狽, 驚き, ヒステリー, 嫌悪感, 猜疑心

alarm	fear	panic	terror
	fright	paranoia	hysteria
		dread	
		phobia	

文型&コロケーション

▶ a fear/ terror/ dread **of** sth
▶ panic/ alarm/ paranoia/ a phobia **about** sth
▶ **in** fear/ terror/ panic/ alarm/ fright/ dread
▶ fear/ terror/ panic/ alarm/ dread **that**...
▶ **absolute/ pure/ sheer** terror/ panic/ hysteria/ dread
▶ to be **filled with** fear/ terror/ panic/ alarm/ dread
▶ to **have** a fear/ panic/ fright/ dread/ phobia
▶ a **feeling of** fear/ terror/ panic/ alarm/ hysteria/ dread/ paranoia

fear [U, C]（危険・災いなどに対する）恐怖, 恐れ, 心配, 不安, 懸念 ◇(a) *fear* of the dark/spiders/flying 闇／蜘蛛／空を飛ぶことに対する恐怖 ◇Her eyes showed no *fear*. 彼女の目に恐怖心は表れなかった ◇The child was shaking with *fear*. その子どもは恐怖で震えていた ◇We lived in constant *fear* of losing our jobs. 私たちは絶えず失業の不安を抱えて生活していた ◇He spoke of his ***fears for*** the future. 彼は将来に対する不安を口にした ◇The doctor's report confirmed our worst *fears*. その医者の報告内容は私たちの最悪の懸念を裏づけた 反意 **hope** (HOPE 名 2), ☞ **fearful** (AFRAID)

▶**fear** 動 [他] to *fear* death/danger/persecution《書き言葉》死／危険／迫害を恐れる ◇Hundreds of people are *feared* dead. 何百人もの人々が死亡したのではと懸念されている ◇We *feared for* their safety. 私たちは彼らの安否を気遣った ◇Don't worry, you have ***nothing to***

fear

fear from us. 心配するな, 私たちを怖がることはない ❶動詞fearの用法はたくさんあるが, be afraid/frightened/scared of sb/sth/doing sthという表現を用いるほうがより一般的で自然である. ☞ **AFRAID**

terror [U, 単数で]（極度の）恐怖 ◇Her eyes were wild with *terror*. 彼女の目は恐怖で狂気じみていた ◇People fled from the explosion in *terror*. 人々は怖くて爆発から逃げ出した ◇Some women have a *terror* of losing control in the birth process. 女性の中には出産のときに感情の抑えがきかなくなることを恐れている人もいる ☞ **terrified** (AFRAID)

panic [U, C, ふつう単数で]（抑制できない突然の）恐怖, 狼狽,（恐怖による）驚き ◇I had a sudden moment of *panic*. 私は一瞬びくっとした ◇There's no point getting into a *panic* about the exams. 試験のことでびくびくしてもしょうがない ☞ **panic** (PANIC), **panicky, panic-stricken** (HYSTERICAL)

alarm [U]（危険に対する突然の[継続的な]）恐怖, 心配, 不安,（恐怖による）驚き ◇'What have you done?' Ellie cried in *alarm*. 「何をしでかしたの」とエリーはびっくりして叫んだ ◇The doctor said there was ***no cause for alarm***. 医者は心配することはないと言った ☞ **alarm** (FRIGHTEN), **alarmed** (AFRAID)

fright [U, C]（突然の）恐怖,（恐怖による）驚き ◇She cried out in *fright*. 彼女はびっくりして大声を上げた ◇He suffered from *stage fright* (= nervous feelings felt by performers before they appear in front of an audience). 彼はあがり症に悩んでいた ❶frightは怖い体験[出来事]を指すこともある. ☞ **frighten** (FRIGHTEN), **frightened** (AFRAID)

ノート **fear**と**fright**の使い分け:frightはたった今起こったばかりの[今起こっている]物事に対する反応を指す. 常に怖い物事や将来起こるかもしれない物事についてはfrightではなくfearを用いる. ✕I have a *fright* of spiders. ✕his *fright* of what might happen.

hysteria [U] ヒステリー,（感情の高ぶりによる極度の）興奮[恐怖, 激昂]状態 ◇A note of *hysteria* crept into her voice. ヒステリーの兆候が彼女の声に表れてきた ◇Fear infected people with mass *hysteria*. 恐怖で人々は集団ヒステリーに陥った ☞ **hysterical** (HYSTERICAL)

dread [U, C, ふつう単数で]《ややインフォーマル》（将来に対する）心配, 不安, 恐怖；心配[不安, 恐怖]の種 ◇The prospect of growing old alone fills me with *dread*. 独りで老いていくのかと思うと私は不安な気持ちでいっぱいです ◇She has an irrational *dread* of hospitals. 彼女は異常に病院を怖がる

▶**dread** 動 [他] ◇This was the moment he had been *dreading*. これこそ彼が恐れていた瞬間だった ◇She *dreads* her husband finding out. 彼女は夫が知ることになるのを恐れている ◇***I dread to think*** what would happen if there really was a fire. 火事が実際に起こったらどんなことになるか考えただけでぞっとする 反意 **look forward to sth** (EXPECT)

paranoia [U]《インフォーマル》（他人に対する根拠のない）恐怖心, 猜疑心 ◇his *paranoia* that people might find out 人が見つけ出すのではないかという彼の恐怖心 ☞ **paranoid** (AFRAID)

phobia [C]《ややフォーマル》（病的な）恐怖[嫌悪]感, 恐怖症, 毛嫌い ◇He has a *phobia* about flying 彼は飛行機恐怖症だ ◇One of the symptoms of the disease is water *phobia*. この病気の症状の一つは水恐怖症です ❶pho-

bia は特定の恐怖症の名称を表すために複合語でも用いられる。
- arachno*phobia* (= fear of spiders) (蜘蛛恐怖症).
- claustro*phobia* (= fear of enclosed spaces) (閉所恐怖症). ◆ xeno*phobia* (= fear or hatred of people from other countries) (外人嫌い).

feature 名

feature・characteristic・quality・property・attribute・trait・point
人や物事が他との違いを典型的に示すもの
【類語訳】要点, 特質, 特徴, 特性, 持ち味, 資質, 効能, 属性

文型&コロケーション

▸ a/ an **essential/ desirable/ individual** feature/ characteristic/ quality/ property/ attribute/ trait
▸ a **distinctive** feature/ characteristic/ quality/ attribute/ trait
▸ a/ an **important/ natural/ special/ useful** feature/ characteristic/ quality/ property/ attribute
▸ a **unique** feature/ characteristic/ quality/ property
▸ a **common** feature/ characteristic/ property/ attribute/ trait
▸ a **positive/ negative** feature/ characteristic/ quality/ attribute/ trait
▸ a **human/ physical** feature/ characteristic/ quality/ attribute/ trait
▸ a **psychological/ mental** characteristic/ quality/ attribute/ trait
▸ a **biological** feature/ characteristic/ property/ trait
▸ to **possess/ display/ share** a feature/ a characteristic/ a quality/ a property/ an attribute/ a trait/ ...points
▸ to **show** a feature/ a characteristic/ a quality/ an attribute/ a trait/ ...points
▸ to **exhibit** a feature/ a characteristic/ a quality/ a property/ a trait

feature [C] (場所・物事の重要な [興味深い, 特有の]) 点, 要点, 特質, 特徴 ◇An interesting *feature* of the city is the old market. その都市の面白さの一つは古い市場にある ◇Teamwork is a key *feature* of the training programme. 共同作業がこの研修プログラムの主な特徴だ ◇The one *redeeming feature* of the plan was its low cost to the council. 議会にとってその計画の唯一の救いは低コストという点であった ◇The design has many new built-in *safety features*. その設計には新しい安全機能が多く内蔵されている *feature* は人の注意を引くものであることが多く, ふつう望ましいものを指す.

characteristic [C] (人の性格・外見・行動の) 特性, 特徴, 持ち味 ; (場所・物事の) 特質, 特徴, 特性, 特色 ◇The need to communicate is a key *characteristic* of human society. 意思疎通の必要性は人間社会の一つの重要な特徴です ◇His melodies have distinguishing *characteristics* which make them instantly identifiable. 彼の旋律にはすぐに識別できる際立った特徴がある ◇Personal *characteristics*, such as age, sex and marital status are taken into account. 年齢, 性別, 配偶者の有無などの個人の特性が考慮されます ❶ *characteristic* はふつう人や物事の他との違いをはっきりと示すものを指す.

quality [C, U] (人の能力・行動の優れた) 特性, 資質, 特長 ; (物事の違いを示す物の) 特質, 特徴, 特長 ◇*personal qualities* such as honesty and generosity 正直さや寛大さといった個人的特性 ◇It's hard to find

people with the right *qualities* for the job. その仕事にぴったりの適性を持つ人を見つけるのは困難です ◇He showed great energy and *leadership qualities*. 彼は卓越した行動力と指導力を発揮した ◇The ancient city of Assisi has a wonderful magical *quality*. アッシジの古代都市は素晴らしく魅惑的な特質を備えている

property [C, ふつう複数で] (フォーマル or 専門語) (物理的形状 [作用] に関する物質・成分の) 特性, 効能 ◇Compare the physical and chemical *properties* of the two substances. この二つの物質が持つ物理的・化学的特性を比較しなさい ◇The plant is thought to have medicinal *properties*. その植物には薬効があると考えられている

attribute [C] (ややフォーマル) (人・物事の優れていると思われる) 特質, 特性, 属性 ◇Patience is an essential *attribute* for a teacher. 忍耐は教師に不可欠な特性である ◇The most basic *attribute* of all animals is consciousness. すべての動物が持つ最も基本的な属性は意識である

trait [C] (特定の行動を伴う人の) 特性, 特質 ◇*personality/character traits* 人格/性格の特性 ◇Awareness of class is a typically British *trait*. 階級に対する意識はイギリス人を象徴する国民性である

point [C, ふつう複数で] (人・物事の) 特性, 特質, (善し悪しなどの) 点 ◇Tact is not one of her *strong points*. 機転がきくことは彼女の長所の一つには挙げられない ◇Living in Scotland *has its good points* but the weather is not one of them. スコットランドに住むことにはいい点もあるが, 天候はその一つではない ◇One of the hotel's *plus points* is that it is very central. そのホテルの好ましい点の一つはまさに中心部にあることです ❶ *point* はしばしば物事の長所と短所を考えるときに用いられる.

feature 動

feature・star・figure・appear
物事が重要な部分を占める, 人や物事を重要な部分として含む
【類語訳】特徴とする, 主演させる, 特集する, 特徴となる, 主演する, 焦点となる, 出演する, 載る

文型&コロケーション

▸ to feature/ star/ figure/ appear **in** sth
▸ to feature/ star/ figure/ appear **as** sb/ sth
▸ a **film/ movie** features/ stars sb
▸ to feature/ star/ appear in a **film/ movie**
▸ to feature/ figure/ appear **prominently** in sth

feature [他, 自] (特定の人・物事を) 特徴とする, 主演させる, 特集する ; (物事の) 特徴となる ◇The film *features* Anne Hathaway as Jane Austen. その映画はアン・ハサウェイがジェーン・オースティン役で主演している ◇The latest model *features* alloy wheels and an electronic alarm. 最新モデルは合金ホイールと電子アラームを特徴としている ◇Many of the hotels *featured* in the brochure offer special deals for weekend breaks. パンフレットで特集されたホテルの多くが週末に向けた特別サービスを提供しています ◇Olive oil and garlic *feature* prominently in his recipes. オリーブ油とにんにくは彼の調理法の顕著な特徴です

star (-rr-) [自, 他, 受身なし] (映画・劇・番組の) 主演する ; (映画・劇・番組が特定の人を) 主演させる ◇She *starred* opposite Johnny Depp in 'Pirates of the Caribbean'. 彼女は『パイレーツ・オブ・カリビアン』でジョニー・デップの相手役として主演した ◇No one has yet been chosen for the

starring role (= the main part). まだ主役は決まっていない ◊The movie *stars* Aishwarya Rai. その映画にはアイシュワリヤ・ラーイが主演している

figure [自]《ふつう副詞や前置詞と共に》(過程・状況に)重要な位置を占める, 焦点[中心]となる ◊The question of the peace settlement is likely to *figure* prominently in the talks. 和平調停の問題がその会議の際立った焦点となりそうだ ◊It did not *figure* high on her list of priorities. それは彼女にとって優先順位は高くなかった ◊Do I still *figure* in your plans? あなたの計画の中で私がまだ中心になっているのですか

appear [自]《ふつう副詞や前置詞と共に》(映画・劇・番組に)出演する; (紙面・誌面に)載る ◊He has *appeared* in over 60 movies. 彼は60本以上の映画に出演している ◊She regularly *appears* on TV. 彼女はテレビにレギュラー出演している ◊Your name will *appear* at the front of the book. あなたの名前が本の巻頭に載るでしょう

feel [動]

feel・know・sense・experience・taste
特定の感情[身体的感覚]を抱いたり, 自覚したりする
【類語訳】感じる, 覚える, 味わう, 感じ取る, 知っている, 味を知る

▶ to feel/ know/ experience/ taste **joy**
▶ to feel/ know/ experience **pain/ satisfaction/ shame**
▶ to feel/ sense/ experience a **need**
▶ to feel/ experience a/ an **sense/ sensation/ emotion/ urge/ pang/ surge/ rush/ stab**
▶ to know/ experience **poverty/ hardship/ difficulties**
▶ to experience/ taste **success/ life**
▶ to have never felt/ known/ experienced/ tasted sth
▶ to **actually** feel/ know/ sense/ experience sth
▶ to feel/ experience sth **suddenly/ sometimes/ often**
▶ to know/ experience sth **directly/ first-hand**

feel [自, 他] (特定の感覚・感情を)感じる, 覚える, 味わう; (物の触感・身体的影響を)感じる; (第六感で直感的に物事を)感じる, 感じ取る ◊The heat made him *feel* faint. 彼は熱で目まいがした ◊She sounded more confident than she *felt*. 彼女は自分が感じている以上に自信に満ちているように思われた ◊How are you *feeling* today? 今日の気分はどうだい ◊I know exactly how you *feel* (= I feel sympathy for you). 君の気持ちはよくわかるよ ◊He *felt* no remorse at all. 彼はまったく自責の念を感じなかった ◊I could *feel* the warm sun on my back. 私は背中に暖かい日差しを感じることができた ◊She could not *feel* her legs. 彼女は両脚の感覚がなかった ◊He *felt* a hand on his shoulder. 彼は肩に手が触れるのを感じた ◊Can you *feel* the tension in this room? この部屋の緊張感を感じることができますか ❶feel は外界にある物事を感じることについて言う場合は, ふつう進行形では用いられない. ◆I was *feeling* guilty. (私は後ろめたさを感じていた) ×I was *feeling* the sun on my back. ×Are you *feeling* the tension in this room? ☞ **feeling** (EMOTION), **feeling** (SENSE)

know [他]《進行形なし》(個人的経験として感情・状況を)知っている, 感じる ◊She thought she would never *know* the joy of seeing a child grow up in her care. 彼女は自分が世話をする子どもの成長を見る喜びを決して知ることはないだろうと思っていた ◊She may be successful now,

but she has *known* what it is like to be poor. 彼女は今成功しているかもしれないが, 貧乏がどういうものかを知っている

sense [他]《進行形なし》(第六感で直感的に外界の物事を)感じる, 感じ取る ◊*Sensing* danger, they started to run. 彼らは危険を感じて走り出した ◊I *sensed* a note of tension in his voice. 私は彼の声に緊張した響きを感じ取った ◊Lisa *sensed that* he did not believe her. リサは彼が自分を信じていないと感じた ☞ **sense** (SENSE)

|ノート| **feel** と **sense** の使い分け: feel はふつう自分の感覚や感情について用いられるが, sense は他人の感覚や感情について用いられる. ◆He *felt* a terrible pain in his chest. (彼は胸に激痛を感じた). ×He *sensed* a terrible pain in his chest. ◆She *sensed* the terrible pain he was *feeling* (= she was aware of it). (彼女は彼が感じている激痛に気づいた). ◆I *feel* your pain (= I know how you are suffering and it makes me suffer too). (あなたの苦しみはよくわかります).

experience [他]《ややフォーマル》(特定の感情・身体的感覚を)感じる, 覚える, 味わう ◊I have never *experienced* such pain before. 私はこんな痛みをこれまで感じたことがなかった ◊I *experienced* a moment of panic as I boarded the plane. 私は飛行機に乗るときに恐怖の瞬間を味わった

taste [他]《特に書き言葉》(もっと経験したい物事の)味を知る ◊He had *tasted* freedom only to lose it again. 彼は自由の味を知ったが, 結局また失う羽目になった ❶典型的な目的語に victory, success, freedom が挙げられる.

fictional [形]

fictional・virtual・non-existent・fictitious・imaginary・pretend
本物ではなくて物語や人の心にのみ存在することを表す
【類語訳】架空の, 虚構の, 小説の, 仮想の, 偽物の, 虚偽の, 想像上の

▶ a fictional/ a fictitious/ an imaginary **story/ character**
▶ a fictional/ a virtual/ an imaginary **world**
▶ **purely/ wholly** fictional/ fictitious/ imaginary
▶ **totally** non-existent/ fictitious

fictional (物語について)架空の, 虚構の, 実在しない; 小説の, 小説的な ◊a *fictional* account of life on a desert island 無人島生活の架空の物語 ◊the *fictional* world of J.K. Rowling J・K・ローリングの虚構の世界 ◊*fictional* techniques 小説の手法 ❶fiction は実在しない人や出来事を描いた文学の一形式. 反意 **real-life** (RELIABLE 2)

virtual [名詞の前で] バーチャルな, 仮想の(コンピューター・ソフトを利用したかも存在するように見えるものについて用いる) ◊The technology has enabled development of an online *virtual* library. その技術によってオンラインの仮想図書館の開発が可能になった ◊Immersion in a *virtual* world of monsters and aliens helped alleviate pain in children with severe burns. 怪物や宇宙人のいる仮想世界に没頭させて, 重度のやけどを負った子どもの痛みが緩和された

,non-e'xistent 存在[実在]しない; 本物でない, 偽物の ◊They would waste their time worrying about *non-existent* dangers. 彼らは存在しない脅威に神経を使う

時間を浪費するだろう ◇Hospital beds were scarce and medicines were practically *non-existent*. 病院のベッドは不足しており、医薬品はないに等しかった ❶non-existentはしばしば人や物が（存在しないのに）存在すると言い張るときに用いる．◆She was claiming welfare for two *non-existent* children. (彼女は実在しない二人の子どものための生活保護を請求していた).

fictitious [（物語について）架空の，虚構の，実在しない；（詐欺について）虚偽の，架空の ◇All the places and characters in my novel are *fictitious* (= they do not exist in real life). 私の小説に登場する場所や登場人物はすべて実在しない ◇The account he gives of his childhood is *fictitious*. 子ども時代についての彼の話は虚偽である 反意 **factual** (RELIABLE 2)

ノート **fictional** と **fictitious** の使い分け：両語とも物語のために創作された登場人物，場所，出来事について用いられる．fictional は小説を執筆する過程を表すこともあるが，fictitious は不可．×*fictitious* techniques. fictitious は特に人をあざむくために物事をでっち上げて，真実であるかのように装う場合に用いられるが，fictional は不可．◆Police said the name John Haydon was *fictitious*, but the address given was genuine. (ジョン・ヘイドンは偽名だが，提示された住所は本当であると警察は述べた). ×The name John Haydon was *fictional*.

imaginary [想像[空想]上の，実在しない ◇I had an *imaginary* friend when I was a child. 子どものとき私には想像上の友達がいた ◇Children experience a lot of *imaginary* fears at this age. この歳になると子どもは空想上の恐怖をたくさん経験する ◇The equator is an *imaginary* line around the middle of the earth. 赤道は地球の真ん中を一周する実在しない線である 反意 **real** (REAL)

pretend [ふつう名詞の前で]《インフォーマル》偽物の，おもちゃの；想像[空想]上の，実在しない（主に幼児語）◇The children gave out their *pretend* cakes on little plastic plates. 子どもたちは小さなプラスチックの皿に載せたおもちゃのケーキを配った 反意 **real** (REAL)

fight 名

fight・clash・brawl・struggle・scuffle・tussle
人々が身体的な力を用いて互いに打ち負かそうとする状況を表す
【類語訳】けんか，格闘，小競り合い，衝突，乱闘騒ぎ，争い，取っ組み合い，口論

文型&コロケーション
▶ a fight/ clash/ brawl/ struggle/ scuffle/ tussle **with** sb
▶ a fight/ clash/ brawl/ struggle/ scuffle/ tussle **between people**
▶ a fight/ clash/ brawl/ struggle/ scuffle/ tussle **over** sth
▶ **in** a fight/ clash/ brawl/ struggle/ scuffle/ tussle
▶ a **violent** fight/ clash/ struggle
▶ to **be in/ get into/ be involved in** a fight/ clash/ brawl/ scuffle/ tussle
▶ to **have** a fight/ brawl/ scuffle
▶ to **break up** a fight/ brawl
▶ a fight/ clash/ brawl/ scuffle **breaks out**

fight [C] （二人以上の人による身体的な）けんか，格闘 ◇He got into a *fight* with a man in the bar. 彼はバーにいた男とけんかになった ◇A *fight* broke out between rival groups of fans. ライバルのファン同士の間でけんかが起こった ◇They got tickets to watch the world title *fight* (= fighting as a sport). 彼らは世界タイトル戦の観戦チケットを手に入れた

clash [C] 《ジャーナリズム》（二つの集団による短時間の）小競り合い，衝突 ◇Eight people were wounded in a *clash* with border guards. 国境警備隊との小競り合いで8人が負傷した

brawl [C] （集団による公共の場での）けんか[乱闘]騒ぎ ◇a street/pub/tavern/nightclub/bar-room *brawl* 路上/パブ/居酒屋/ナイトクラブ/バーでの乱闘騒ぎ

struggle [C] （二人の人［二つの集団］による）争い，取っ組み合い（一方が逃げよう［相手から何かを奪おう］とする状況で用いられる）◇There were no signs of a *struggle* at the murder scene. 殺人現場に争った形跡はなかった

scuffle [C] （あまり暴力的ではない短時間の）小競り合い，取っ組み合い ◇He was involved in a *scuffle* with a photographer. 彼はカメラマンとの小競り合いに巻き込まれた

tussle [C] （何かを得ようとする短時間の）争い，小競り合い，口論 ◇He was injured during a *tussle for* the ball. 彼はボールを奪い合ってけがをした

fight 動

fight・struggle・wrestle・clash・brawl・grapple・box・scuffle
二人以上の人々が互いに身体的な力を使い合うことを表す
【類語訳】戦う，格闘する，闘う，取っ組み合う，ぶつかる，衝突する，つかみ合う，ボクシングをする，小競り合いをする

文型&コロケーション
▶ to fight/ struggle/ wrestle/ clash/ brawl/ grapple/ scuffle **with** sb
▶ to fight/ struggle/ box **against** sb
▶ to fight/ struggle **fiercely/ furiously**
▶ to struggle/ clash **violently**

fight [自, 他] 戦う，格闘する；ボクシングをする ◇My little brothers are always *fighting*. 弟たちはいつもけんかばかりしている ◇She *fought* her attacker, eventually forcing him to flee. 彼女は襲ってきた男と戦い，ついには撃退した ◇Doctors fear he may never *fight* again following his injury in last night's match. 昨夜の試合での負傷の結果彼が二度と戦うわけにはいかないかもしれないと医者たちは心配している

struggle [自] 戦う，（逃げようとして）闘う ◇Ben and Jack *struggled* together on the grass. ベンとジャックは芝生の上で取っ組み合った ◇I *struggled* and screamed for help. 私はもがきながら助けを求めて悲鳴を上げた ◇How did she manage to *struggle* free? 彼女はどうあがいて自由になれたのだろう

wrestle [自, 他] 取っ組み合う，レスリングをする ◇As a boy he had boxed and *wrestled*. 彼は少年の頃ボクシングとレスリングをやっていた ◇Armed guards *wrestled* with the intruder. 武装衛兵が侵入者と取っ組み合った ◇Shoppers *wrestled* the raider to the ground. 買い物客たちは侵入者と取っ組み合って地面に組み伏せた

clash [自] 《特にジャーナリズム》ぶつかる，衝突する ◇The two teams *clash* in tomorrow's final. その2チームは明日の決勝戦でぶつかり合う ◇Demonstrators *clashed* with police. デモ参加者は警官隊と激しく衝突した

brawl [自] （公の場で）派手にけんかをする ◇They were arrested for *brawling* in the street. 彼らは通りで派手

↪**fight**

けんかをして逮捕された

grapple [自, 他] つかみ合う ◇Passers-by *grappled* with the man after the attack. 通行人たちは攻撃されてその男ともみ合った ◇They managed to *grapple* him to the ground. 彼らはつかみ合ってなんとか彼を地面に組み伏せた

box [自, 他] ボクシングをする ◇He *boxed* for Ireland in the Olympics. 彼はアイルランド代表としてオリンピックでボクシングに出場した ◇The newcomer *boxed* the champion for the full twelve rounds. その新人はチャンピオン相手に最終12ラウンドまで打ち合った

scuffle [自] 小競り合いをする ◇She *scuffled* with photographers as she left her hotel. 彼女はホテルから出るとカメラマンたちと小競り合いになった

figure 名 ☞ INFORMATION

figure・number・statistics・fraction・stats
特定の数や量を表す語[記号]
【類語訳】数字, 数量, 数値, 計数, 記号, 番号, 分数, 小数

【文型&コロケーション】
▶ a high/ low/ round figure/ number
▶ exact figures/ numbers/ statistics
▶ approximate figures/ numbers/ statistics
▶ accurate/ reliable/ alarming figures/ statistics
▶ to add/ multiply/ subtract/ divide figures/ numbers/ fractions
▶ to publish figures/ statistics

figure [C] （公式の）数字, 数量, 数値, 計数統計 ◇Viewing *figures* for the series have dropped dramatically. そのシリーズものの視聴率は劇的に低下している ◇*Figures* for April show a slight improvement on previous months. 4月の数字は過去の月よりもわずかに改善が見られる ◇By 2004, this *figure* had risen to 14 million. 2004年までにこの数値は1400万まで上昇した

number [C] 数字, 記号, 番号 ◇Think of a *number* and multiply it by two 数字一つを思い浮かべてそれに2を掛けてください ◇The houses on this side of the road are all *even numbers* (= 2, 4, 6, etc.). 道路のこちら側の家々はみな偶数番地です ◇Pick out all the *odd numbers* (= 1, 3, 5, etc.). 奇数をすべて選びなさい ◇'So you owe me 28 dollars?' 'Make it 30, that's a good round *number*.' 「じゃあ28ドルの貸しでいいね」「30ドルにしてよ, そのほうが切りのいい数字だから」

statistics [複数で] 《ややフォーマル》統計 ◇According to official *statistics* the disease kills 10,000 people a year. 公式統計によると, その病気で年間1万人が死亡している **❶** a statistic は数字で示される一つの情報を指す. ◆An important *statistic* is that 94 per cent of crime relates to property. (重要な統計値は犯罪の94%が財産に関連しているということだ.) ◆I felt I was no longer being treated as a person but as a *statistic*. (私はもはや人でなく統計上の一つの数値として扱われている気がした.)

▶ **statistical** 形 ◇*statistical* analysis/methods/data 統計分析/方法/データ
▶ **statistically** 副 ◇The difference between the two samples was not *statistically* significant. この二つのサンプルの違いは統計上大ではなかった

[ノート] **figures** と **statistics** の使い分け: 多くの場合, 両語とも使用可能. ◆ official/government/crime/un-

employment *figures/statistics* （公式/政府/犯罪/失業統計）. statistics は科学や計算のより高い水準を示す（例えば, 単に数字を合計するのではなく, パーセンテージや時系列の変化を算定する）ことができる. statistics は figures よりも一般的に用いられることもある. ◆ *Statistics* show that far more people are able to ride a bicycle than can drive a car. （統計によると, 車を運転できる人より自転車に乗れる人のほうがはるかに多い）. figures を用いる場合は, ふつうどの種の数値かを明確にする必要がある. ◆ Government/Inflation *figures* show that... (政府/インフレ計数によると…). ×*Figures* show that...

fraction [C] 分数 ◇How do you express 25% as a *fraction*? 25%は分数でどう表すか

stats [複数で] 《インフォーマル》統計 ◇The match *stats* show that there were 16 instances of players being offside. 試合の統計によると, 延べ16選手がオフサイドを犯していた **❶** stats はしばしばスポーツの試合の結果[分析]について用いられる.

fill 動

fill・pack・load・fill (sth) up・refill・replenish・top sb/sth up・restock
一定量の物を容器にぎりぎりまで入れる
【類語訳】いっぱいにする, 満たす, いっぱいになる, 満ちる, 詰め込む, 荷造りする, 梱包する, 包装する, 積み込む, 補充する

【文型&コロケーション】
▶ to fill/ pack/ load/ fill up/ refill/ replenish/ top up/ restock sth **with** sth
▶ to fill/ pack/ load sth **in/ into** sth
▶ to fill/ fill up/ refill/ replenish/ top up sb's **glass**

fill [他, 自] いっぱいにする, 満たす; いっぱいになる, 満ちる ◇She *filled* the kettle from the tap. 彼女は蛇口をひねってやかんをいっぱいにした ◇Smoke *filled* the room. 煙が部屋に充満した ◇The school is **filled to capacity** (= completely full). その学校は定員いっぱいだ ◇The room was *filling* quickly (= with people). 部屋はすぐに人で満杯になろうとしていた ◇Her eyes suddenly *filled* with tears. 《比喩的》彼女の目に突然涙があふれた [反意] **empty** (CLEAR 動)

pack [自, 他] （旅行に備えてかばんに）詰め込む, 荷造りする; （貯蔵[輸送, 販売]用に容器に）梱包する[包装]する ◇I haven't *packed* yet. 私はまだ荷造りしていない ◇He *packed* a bag with a few things and was off. 彼はかばんに物をいくつか詰め込んだと思ったらもういなくなっていた ◇He *packed* a few things into a bag. 彼は物をいくつかかばんに詰めた ◇He found a part-time job *packing* eggs. 彼は卵を梱包するアルバイトの仕事を見つけた [反意] **unpack** (CLEAR 動)

load [他, 自] （大量に）積み[詰め]込む ◇We *loaded* the car in ten minutes. 私たちは10分で車に荷物を積み込んだ ◇Can you help me *load* the dishwasher? 食器洗い機に入れるのを手伝ってくれますか ◇Men were *loading* up a truck with timber. 男たちがトラックに材木を積んでいた ◇Sacks were being *loaded* onto the truck. 麻袋がトラックに積み込まれていた ◇We finished *loading* and set off. 私たちは荷積みを終えて出発した [反意] **unload** (CLEAR 動)

,fill 'up, ,fill sth 'up 句動詞 一杯になる; （物を）一杯にす

る ◇The ditches had *filled up* with mud and debris. 排水溝は泥とくずで一杯になっていた ◇First we need to *fill up* the tank with water. まずタンクを水で一杯にする必要がある ◇We can't be out of petrol! I *filled up* (= put petrol in the car) yesterday. ガソリンが切れるはずはないよ．私が昨日満タンにしたんだから

refill [他] 再び一杯にする[満たす]，補充[補給]する ◇She *refilled* the kettle with fresh water. 彼女はやかんに新鮮な水を補充した

▶**refill** [名] [C] ◇Would you like a *refill* (= another drink of the same type)? お代わりはいかがですか

replenish [他]《フォーマル》（使用された物と取り替えて）再び一杯にする[満たす]，補充[補給]する ◇Sailors used the islands to *replenish* their food and water supplies. 船員たちは島々に寄って食糧や水を補給した

ノート **refill** と **replenish** の使い分け：ふつう **refill** は容器を目的語に取るが，**replenish** は供給物を目的語に取る．両語とも飲用グラスを目的語に取るが，**replenish** のほうがフォーマルである．

top sb/sth 'up 句動詞 (-pp-)《特に英，ややインフォーマル》（容器に入っている液体に）注ぎ足す ◇I want to *top up* the oil in the car before we set off. 私は出発前に車にオイルを注ぎ足しておきたい ◇Can I *top* you *up* (= give you some more to drink)?《インフォーマル》飲み物を注ぎ足しましょうか

▶**'top-up** [名] [C] ◇Can I give anybody a *top-up* (= some more to drink)?《英，ややインフォーマル》誰かにお注ぎしましょうか

restock [他，自]（使用された[販売された，持ち去られた]物を取り替えて）再び一杯にする[満たす]，補充[補給]する ◇Environmentalists are planning to *restock* the river with fish. 環境保護論者たちは川に魚を放流することを計画している

final [形]

final・firm・concrete・proven・definitive・hard・absolute・positive・categorical

情報や決定が確定されていて，変更できないことを表す
【類語訳】最終の，決定的な，確固たる，揺るぎない，確定的な，確実な，具体的な，証明された，厳然たる，証拠のある

文型&コロケーション
▶ firm/ concrete/ definitive/ hard/ absolute/ positive **evidence**
▶ final/ firm/ concrete/ definitive/ absolute/ positive **proof**
▶ a final/ firm/ definitive **decision/ conclusion/ diagnosis/ agreement/ answer**
▶ a final/ firm **offer**
▶ concrete/ proven/ hard **facts**
▶ a final/ definitive **judgement/ ruling**

final （議論・変更の余地がなくて）最終の，最終[決定]的な ◇The judge's decision is *final*. 裁判官の決定が最終的なものです ◇Who has the *final* say around here? この辺りで最終的な決定権を持っているのは誰ですか ◇I'll give you $500 for it, and that's my *final* offer! それに500ドル出しましょう，それがぎりぎりの線です ◇I'm not coming, *and that's final*! (= I will not change my mind)《話し言葉》私の言い分，それが（最終的な）答えよ

▶**finally** [副] ◇The matter was not *finally* settled un-

til much later. その問題はずっと後まで最終的な解決を見なかった

firm （変わりそうになく）確固[断固]たる，揺るぎない，確定的な ◇At the age of 87 he is still a *firm* believer in socialism. 87歳で彼はなお社会主義を固く信じている ◇No *firm* date has yet been set for the launch. 確実な打ち上げの日程はまだ決まっていない ◇She is a *firm favourite* with the children. 彼女は子どもたちに根強い人気がある ◇They remained *firm friends*. 彼らはいつまでも固い友情で結ばれていた

▶**firmly** [副] ◇It is now *firmly* established as one of the leading brands in the country. 現在それはその国の主要ブランドの一つとして確固たる地位を確立している

concrete （意見・推測ではなく）現実に即した，具体的な ◇By the end of the meeting some fairly *concrete* proposals had been put forward. 会議終了までにかなり具体的な案がいくつか出された ◇'It's only a suspicion,' she said, 'nothing *concrete*.'「それは疑いにすぎず，具体的なことは何もない」と彼女は言った [反意] **abstract** (INTELLECTUAL 1)

proven [名詞の前で]《ややフォーマル》（試験・検査で）証明[立証]された ◇The award will be presented to a student of *proven* ability. その賞は能力が証明された学生に与えられる ◇The candidate should have a *proven* track record of handling large projects. 志願者は大きなプロジェクトを担当した実績を示さなければならない [反意] **unproven** ❶ unproven は証明[試験，検査]されていない事を表す．◆*unproven* theories（立証されていない理論）
☞ **prove** (SHOW 1)

definitive 《ややフォーマル》（変更・追加の余地[必要性]がなくて）最終[決定]的な ◇The *definitive* version of the text is ready to be published. そのテキストの決定版は出版の準備ができている

▶**definitively** [副] ◇The question has never been *definitively* resolved. その問題は最終的な解決に至っていない

hard [名詞の前で]（証明可能な情報に基づいていて）厳然[確固]たる，確実な，証拠[裏づけ]のある ◇Is there any *hard* evidence either way? どちらにしても何か確かな証拠はありますか ◇The newspaper story is based on *hard* facts. その新聞記事は厳然たる事実に基づいている

absolute （他に依存することがなくて）厳然[確固]たる，確実な，絶対的な ◇There was no *absolute* proof. 動かぬ証拠は何もなかった ◇He taught us that the laws of physics were *absolute*. 物理の法則は絶対的であることを彼は私たちに教えた ◇The divorce became *absolute* last week. 先週離婚が確実となった

positive （証拠・情報があって）決定的な，明確な ◇We have no *positive* evidence that she was involved. 彼女が関与していたという決定的な証拠はない

▶**positively** [副] ◇Her attacker has now been *positively* identified by police. 彼女を襲った犯人は現在警察によって明確に特定されている

categorical [ふつう名詞の前で]《フォーマル》（発言などが）断固たる，明確な ◇The government has yet to make a *categorical* statement on the issue. 政府はその問題についてまだ明確な声明を出していない

▶**categorically** [副] ◇He *categorically* rejected our offer. 彼は断固として我々の申し出を拒否した

finance [名]

finance・economics・banking

↳finance

政府や会社, 銀行による多額の金の管理[やりくり]の方法を表す
【類語訳】財政, 財務, 経理, 経済学, 経済性, 経済効果, 銀行業

finance [U] (政府・会社の)財政, 財務, 財務管理, 経理 ◇the Minister of *Finance* 財務大臣 ◇Please send all invoices to the *finance* department. 経理部にすべての請求明細書をお送りください ◇The bank offers advice and guidance on personal *finance*. その銀行は個人に向けた財務管理に関する助言と指導を行っている ◇He's a big wheel in the world of **high finance** (= finance involving large companies or countries). 彼は財界の大物である ☞ **finance** (MONEY 1), **financial** (ECONOMIC)

economics [U, 複数で] 経済学；経済的側面[意味], 経済性[効果] ◇He studied politics and *economics* at Yale. 彼はイェール大学で政治学と経済学を学んだ ◇Keynesian/Marxist *economics* ケインズ/マルクス経済学 ◇The *economics* of the project are very encouraging. その事業の経済効果は非常に有望である ☞ **economic** (ECONOMIC)

ノート **finance** と **economics** の使い分け：finance は金銭を管理する実務を指す. economics はいかに金銭が機能するかに関する理論を指す.

banking [U] 銀行業(務) ◇She's thinking about a career in *banking*. 彼女は銀行業務の職を検討している

F find 動

1 find・find out (sth)・hear・discover・learn
物事に気づく, 人や物事に関する情報を得る
【類語訳】知る, わかる, 気づく, 思う, 明らかにする, 聞く, …するようになる

文型&コロケーション
▶ to find out/ hear/ learn **about** sth
▶ to hear/ learn **of** sth
▶ to find/ find out/ hear/ discover/ learn **that**...
▶ It was **found**/ **discovered that**...
▶ to find/ hear/ discover/ learn **how/ what/ why**...
▶ to find/ discover **sb/ sth to be/ have, etc. sth**
▶ to find/ find out/ discover/ learn the **facts/ truth/ secret/ identity**
▶ to **be surprised/ saddened/ shocked/ delighted/ pleased/ interested to** find/ hear/ discover/ learn sth
▶ to **quickly/ eventually** find/ discover/ learn sth

find [他] (試して[検査して, 経験して]真実であると)知る, わかる, 思う ◇I *find* (that) it pays to be honest. 私は正直は報われると思う ◇The report *found* that 30% of the firms studied had failed within a year. その報告書によると, 調査した企業の30%が1年以内に倒産していたことがわかった ◇We *found* the beds very comfortable. 私たちはそのベッドがとても快適だとわかった ◇Her blood was *found* to contain poison. 彼女の血液に毒が含まれていることがわかった ☞ **finding** (CONCLUSION)

ˌfind ˈout, ˌfind ˈout sth 句動詞 (質問[読書, 調査, 話]によって情報を[が, に])知る, わかる, 明らかにする ◇She'd been seeing the boy for a while, but didn't want her parents to *find out*. 彼女はしばらくその少年と会っていたが, 自分の両親には知られたくなかった ◇Did your sister ever *find out* about it? お姉さんにそのことを知られましたか ◇I haven't *found* anything *out* about

him yet. 私は彼についてまだ何もわかっていない ◇Can you *find out* what time the meeting starts? 会議が何時に始まるかわかりますか ◇We *found out* later that we had been at the same school. 後になって私たちは同じ学校にいたことがわかった ◇She was determined to *find out* the truth. 彼女は真相を明らかにしようと決めていた

hear 《進行形はまれ》[自, 他] 《特に話し言葉》(人に関する情報を人づてに)聞く ◇Haven't you *heard*? She's resigned. まだ聞いてなかったのかい. 彼女, 辞めたんだって ◇'He's being promoted.' '*So I've heard*.'「彼, 昇進するんだって」「私もそう聞いてる」 ◇I was sorry to *hear* about your accident. 事故のこと聞きました, お気の毒でしたね ◇We had *heard* nothing for weeks. 私たちは何週間もの間何も聞かされていなかった ◇I was delighted to *hear* your good news. あなたの朗報を聞いて私は嬉しかった

discover [他] 《進行形はまれ》(驚異[衝撃]的な情報を)知る, わかる, 気づく ◇It was a shock to *discover* that he couldn't read. 彼が読むことができないと知ってショックだった ◇We never did *discover* why she gave up her job. 私たちは彼女がなぜ仕事を辞めたのかまったくわからなかった ◇He was later *discovered* to be seriously ill. 後になって彼が重病であることがわかった ◇It was later *discovered* that the diaries were a fraud. その日記が偽物であると後でわかった
▷ **discovery** [C, U] ◇He was shocked by the *discovery* that she had been unfaithful. 彼女が不倫をしていたと知って彼はショックを受けた

learn [自, 他] 《進行形はまれ》《ややフォーマル》(人から聞いて[読んで])知る, わかる, (態度を徐々に改めて)…するようになる, …することを学ぶ ◇I *learned* of her arrival from a close friend. 私は彼女の到着を親友から聞いて知った ◇We were very surprised to *learn* that she had got married again. 私たちは彼女が再婚していたと知ってとても驚いた ◇I'm sure she'll *learn* from her mistakes. 彼女は自らの過ちから学ぶだろうと私は確信している ◇I soon *learned* not to ask too many questions. 私はすぐにあまり質問をしすぎないようになった

2 find・discover・come across sb/sth・catch・turn sth up・unearth・come upon sb/sth・stumble on/upon/across sb/sth
人や物の存在[位置]に偶然に気づく
【類語訳】見つける, 発見する, 見かける, 出くわす, 目撃する, 掘り出す, 発掘する, 巡り合う, 遭遇する

文型&コロケーション
▶ to find/ discover/ come across/ catch sb **doing sth**
▶ to find/ discover/ unearth the **remains** (of sth)
▶ to find/ discover a **fault/ wreck**
▶ to find/ discover/ stumble upon a **body**
▶ to **happen to** find/ discover/ come across sth
▶ to find/ discover/ stumble upon sth **by accident**

find [他] (思いがけなく・偶然に)見つける, 発見する ◇Look what I've *found*! 私が見つけた物を見てごらん ◇We've *found* a great new restaurant near the office. 私たちはオフィスの近くにすてきな新しいレストランを見つけた ◇A whale was *found* washed up on the shore. 1頭のクジラが海岸に打ち上げられているのが見つかった ◇I didn't expect to come home and *find* him gone. 彼がいなくなっていることに帰宅して気づくとは思わなかった
▷ **find** [名] [C] ◇This is an important archaeological

find

find. これは考古学上重要な発見だ

discover [他] (初めて)発見する;(隠されていた人・物を思いがけず)見つける ◇Cook is credited with *discovering* Hawaii. クックはハワイを発見したと信じられている ◇Police *discovered* a large stash of drugs while searching the house. 警察は隠されていた大量の麻薬を家宅捜索中に発見した ◇He was *discovered* hiding in the shed. 彼は納屋に隠れているところを見つかった ◇She was *discovered* dead at her home in Leeds. 彼女はリーズの自宅で死体となって発見された

▶ **discovery** [名] [C, U] ◇All these were chance *discoveries* made by scientists engaged in other investigations. これらはすべて他の調査に携わっていた科学者たちによって偶然発見されたものだった ◇The *discovery* of a child's body in the river has shocked the community. 川で子どもの死体が見つかったことは地域社会に衝撃を与えた

,come a'cross sb/sth [句動] (受身なし) (偶然に人・物を)見かける, 出くわす, 見つける ◇I *came across* children sleeping under bridges. 私は橋の下で寝ている子どもたちに出くわした ◇She *came across* some old photographs in a drawer. 彼女は引き出しの中から古い写真を数枚見つけた ☞ **encounter** (MEET 2)

catch [他] (悪い事をしているところを)見つける, 目撃する ◇I *caught* her smoking in the bathroom. 私は彼女がバスルームでタバコを吸っているところを見つけた ◇He was *caught with* bomb-making equipment in his home. 彼は自宅に爆弾製造器具を所有しているところが発見された ◇Mark walked in and *caught them at it* (= in the act of doing sth wrong). マークは中に入り, 悪事を働いている彼らを目撃した ◇You've *caught* me at a bad time (= at a time when I am busy). 都合の悪い時に来ちゃったね

,turn sth 'up [句動] (長期間の捜索の末に物を)見つける, 発見する ◇Our efforts to trace him *turned up* nothing. 我々は懸命に彼の後をつけたが何も発見できなかった ◇If I *turn* anything *up*, I'll let you know 何か見つけたら君に教えるよ ❶ turn sth up は何が見つかるか前もって正確にわからない場合の, 全般的な捜索行動の一環を指すことが多い.

unearth [他] (地面を掘って)掘り出す, 発掘する;(偶然/捜索の末)長期間隠されていた物を見つける, 発見する ◇Police have *unearthed* a human skeleton. 警察は人間のがい骨を掘り出した ◇I *unearthed* my old diaries when we moved house. 私は引っ越しの際に自分の古い日記を見つけた ◇The newspaper has *unearthed* some disturbing facts. 憂慮すべき事実を新聞がいくつか暴き出した

,come upon sb/sth [句動] [受身なし] (ややフォーマル) (偶然に人・物を)見かける, 出くわす, 見つける ◇Jamie *came upon* her unawares. ジェイミーは思いがけなく彼女と出くわした ◇He was on vacation in Italy when he *came upon* the engravings in a local market. 彼は休暇でイタリアにいたとき地元の市場でその彫版を見つけた

'stumble on/upon/across sb/sth [句動] (偶然に驚くべき[重大な]結果をもたらす人・物に)巡り合う, 遭遇する, 見つける, 発見する ◇He was killed after he *stumbled* on a cocaine factory. 彼はコカイン製造工場を偶然見つけて殺害された

---

3 find・establish・identify・determine・ascertain・discover

入念な捜索[調査, 考察]によって気づく

【類語訳】見つける, 発見する, 特定する, 解明する, 証明する, 測定する, 突き止める, 確認する

[文型&コロケーション]

▶ to establish/ identify/ determine/ ascertain **what/ how/ when/ where/ why/ whether...**
▶ to establish/ ascertain **that...**
▶ It was established/ ascertained **that...**
▶ to find/ establish/ identify/ determine/ ascertain/ discover the **cause**
▶ to find/ establish/ identify/ determine/ discover the **correlation**
▶ to find/ establish/ identify/ discover a **connection**
▶ to find/ identify/ discover a **solution**
▶ to find/ discover the **answer**
▶ to find/ discover a **cure**
▶ to establish/ ascertain the **facts**

find [他] (人・物事を)見つける, 発見する ◇Scientists are still trying to *find* a cure for cancer. 科学者は今ながんの治療法を発見しようとしている ◇I'm having trouble *finding* anything new to say on this subject. 私はこのテーマについて発言すべき何か新しい内容を見つけるのに苦労している ◇Have they *found* anyone to replace her? 誰か彼女の代わりになる人が見つかりましたか ◇Can you *find* me a hotel? 私のためにホテルを見つけてもらえますか

establish [他] 《ややフォーマル》 (状況に関する事実を)特定[解明, 究明]する, 証明[立証]する ◇Police are still trying to *establish* the cause of death. 警察はまだ死因を特定しようとしている ◇They have *established* that his injuries were caused by a fall. 彼のけがは転落によるものであると立証された ◇We need to *establish* where she was at the time of the shooting. 狙撃が行われたときに彼女がどこにいたかを解明する必要がある

identify [他] 《ややフォーマル》 (問題の関連性[原因, 解決策]を)特定[解明, 究明]する ◇Scientists have *identified* a link between diet and cancer. 科学者は食べ物とがんとの一つの関連性を解明した ◇As yet they have not *identified* a buyer for the company. 今のところまだ会社の買い手を特定していない ◇They are trying to *identify* what is wrong with the present system. 彼らは現システムの不具合の原因を究明しようとしている ❶ identify はふつう, まず最初に考えうる関連性[原因]などを考察してから, それを立証[反証]する証拠を探すことを指す.

determine [他] 《フォーマル》 (物事に関する事実を)特定する;(物事を正確に)測定する ◇An enquiry was set up to *determine* the cause of the accident. 事故原因を究明するために調査が始まった ◇Computer models help to *determine* whether a particular area is likely to flood. コンピューター・モデルによって特定の地域が氾濫する可能性を測定できる

ascertain [他] 《フォーマル》 (状況に関する事実を)突き止める, 確認する ◇It should be *ascertained* that the plans comply with the law. 計画が順法であることを確認しなければならない

[ノート] **establish** と **ascertain** の使い分け: ascertain は establish よりもさらにフォーマルな語である. establish はふつう公式[科学的]調査の文脈で用いられる. ascertain は人の個人的な意図や感情を見いだそうとする場合に用いられる. ◆ Could you *ascertain* whether she will be coming to the meeting? (彼女は会議に出席するつも

りがあるのかどうか確かめていただけますか). ×Could you *establish* whether she will be coming to the meeting.

discover [他] (特定の物事・場所の存在を初めて)発見する ◇Scientists around the world are working to *discover* a cure for AIDS. 世界中の科学者がエイズの治療法の発見に取り組んでいる
  ▶**discovery** 图 [C, U] ◇Researchers have *made* some important new *discoveries*. 研究者たちはいくつか新たに重要な発見をした ◇the *discovery* of antibiotics in the 20th century 20世紀における抗生物質の発見

4 find・locate・trace・track sb/sth down・search sb/sth out・sniff sb/sth out
人や物がどこにいる[ある]かを発見したり, 捜したりした末にそれを取り戻す
【類語訳】見つけ出す, 捜し出す, 発見する, 突き止める, 嗅ぎ分ける, 感づく

〘文型&コロケーション〙
▶to find sth/ locate sth/ track sth down/ search sth out **for sb/ sth**
▶to find/ trace/ track down the **killer/ location**
▶to locate/ trace/ track down/ sniff out sb's **whereabouts**
▶to find/ locate/ trace/ track down the **missing** ...
▶to **finally/ eventually** find/ locate/ trace/ track down sb/ sth

find [他] (遺失した[行方不明の]人・物を)見つけ[捜し]出す, 発見する ◇I can't *find* my keys. 鍵が見つからない ◇Can you *find* my bag for me? 私のかばんを捜してくれますか ◇The child was eventually *found* safe and well. 結局その子は無事で元気な状態で発見された ◇He went through the drawers but *found* nothing. 彼は引き出しをくまなく調べたが何も見つからなかった ◇I wanted to talk to him but he was *nowhere to be found*. 私は彼と話したかったが, 彼はどこにも見当たらなかった

locate [他] (ややフォーマル) (人・物の正確な位置を)突き止める ◇The mechanic *located* the fault immediately. 整備士はすぐに欠陥を突き止めた ◇Rescue planes are trying to *locate* the missing sailors. 救難機は行方不明の船員たちの位置を突き止めようとしている ☞ **location** (PLACE)

trace [他] (失踪した人や遺失した物を)突き止める, 見つけ[捜し]出す(人・物が以前いた[あった]場所の痕跡から捜し出して突き止める場合に用いられる) ◇We finally *traced* him *to* an address in Chicago. 私たちはついにシカゴのとある住所に彼がいることを突き止めた ◇We have not been able to *trace* the original letter. その手紙の原物を見つけ出すことはできていない ☞ **trace** (SIGN 1)

,track sb/sth 'down 句動詞 (時間をかけて人・物を)突き止める, 見つけ[捜し]出す ◇The police have so far failed to *track down* the attacker. 警察はこれまでのところ襲撃者の特定に失敗している ◇I finally *tracked* the reference *down* in a book of quotations. 私は引用集の本の中にようやく引用箇所を見つけ出した

,search sb/sth 'out 句動詞 (見つかるまで人・物を)捜し出す ◇Fighter pilots *searched out* and attacked enemy aircraft. 戦闘機のパイロットは敵機を捜し出して攻撃した

,sniff sb/sth 'out 句動詞 (ややインフォーマル) (嗅覚を使って人・物を)嗅ぎ分ける[つける]; (見る[尋ねる]ことで)人・物事に感づく ◇The dogs are trained to *sniff out* drugs. その犬たちは麻薬を嗅ぎ分けるように訓練されている ◇Journalists are good at *sniffing out* a scandal. ジャーナリストはスキャンダルを嗅ぎつけるのが得意だ

fine 形 ☞ ADEQUATE, GOOD 2

fine・all right・fair・OK・acceptable・satisfactory・reasonable・in order・right
物事を受け入れるのに問題ないことを表す
【類語訳】申し分のない, 十分な, まあまあの, 適当な, 公平な, 無難な, 容認できる, 満足のいく, 納得のいく, 妥当な

〘文型&コロケーション〙
▶to be fine/ all right/ fair/ OK/ acceptable/ satisfactory/ reasonable/ in order **to do sth**
▶to be fine/ all right/ fair/ OK/ acceptable/ satisfactory/ reasonable/ in order **that**...
▶a fair/ an acceptable/ a satisfactory/ a reasonable **solution**
▶a fair/ an acceptable/ a reasonable **wage/ price**
▶a fair/ reasonable **question**
▶That's fine/ all right/ OK **by me**.
▶**perfectly** fine/ all right/ fair/ OK/ acceptable/ satisfactory/ reasonable/ in order
▶**(not) entirely** fair/ acceptable/ satisfactory/ reasonable

fine (しばしば感嘆詞として) (話し言葉) (行動・提案・決定・状況が)申し分のない, 構わない, 十分な, 満足な ◇'I'll leave this here, OK?' '*Fine*.' 「ここにこれを置いて行くけど, いいかい」「構わないよ」 ◇Bob wants to know if he can come too. 'That's *fine* by me.' 「ボブが自分も行っていいかどうか知りたがってるんだけど」「私はいいよ」 ◇Your speech was *absolutely fine*. 君のスピーチはまったく申し分なかったよ ◇'Can I get you another drink?' 'No thanks. *I'm fine*.' 「もう1杯飲み物いかが?」「ありがとう, 結構です」

all 'right (名詞の前では用いない) (インフォーマル, 特に話し言葉) 申し分のない, まあまあの, うまくいく ; 了承[了解]した, 構わない ◇Is the coffee *all right*? このコーヒーはまあまあかな ◇Is it *all right* for me to leave early? 早めにおいとましますが構いませんか ◇Is it *all right* if I leave early? 早めにおいとましても構いませんか ◇'I'm afraid I have to go now.' 'That's *all right*.' 「悪いけど, もう行かなくちゃいけないんだ」「了解だよ」
  ▶**all right** 副 ◇Are you getting along *all right* in your new job? 新しい仕事はうまくこなせていますか

fair (特定の状況において) 申し分のない, まあまあの, 適当な, 適正な, 公平な, 公正な ◇Scoring twenty points was a *fair* achievement. 20点の得点はまあまあの成績だった ◇It wasn't really *fair* to ask him to do all the work. 彼にすべての仕事を頼むのは本当のところ公平ではなかった ◇It seems only *fair* that they should give us something in return. 何らかの返礼があっても罰は当たらないように思える ◇*It's fair to say that* they're very pleased with the offer. 彼らがその申し出に大変満足していると言っても過言ではない ◇*To be fair*, she behaved better than we expected. 公正を期するために言えば, 彼女は私たちの予想以上に立派な振る舞いを見せた ☞ **fair** (REASONABLE)

OK (または **okay**) [名詞の前にまれ] (インフォーマル, 話し言葉) 了承[了解]した, 構わない ; 申し分のない, うまくいく ◇Is it *OK* if I leave now? もう帰っても構わないかな ◇Is it *OK* for me to come too? 私も行っていいかな ◇She

looks *OK* to me. 彼女はぼくにはまあまあに見えるよ ◇We had an *okay* time on the trip — not great. 旅はまあまあだったよ—最高とは言えないけどね
▶**OK** 副 ◇I think I did *OK* in the exam. 試験の出来はまあまあだったと思うよ

ノート all right と OK の使い分け：OK は話し言葉でしか用いられない. all right は インフォーマル だが，書き言葉で用いられることがある.

acceptable 受け入れられる，無難な，どうにか間に合う，許容［容認］できる ◇We want a solution that is *acceptable* to all parties. すべての当事者に受け入れられる解決策が必要だ ◇To get on this course, a pass in English at grade B is *acceptable*. この科目を履修するには、英語で合格点がBであれば大丈夫です ◇Air pollution in the city has reached four times the *acceptable* level. その都市の大気汚染は許容レベルの4倍に達している 反意 **unacceptable** (UNACCEPTABLE)

satisfactory (特定の目的にとって)申し分のない，満足［納得］のいく ◇Their work is *satisfactory* but not outstanding. 彼らの仕事は満足いくものだが突出しているわけではない ◇You haven't yet given us a *satisfactory* explanation. あなたからまだ納得のいく説明をしてもらっていません 反意 **unsatisfactory** (DISAPPOINTING)
▶**satisfactorily** 副 ◇Our complaint was dealt with *satisfactorily*. 私たちの苦情は納得のいく形で処理された

reasonable (特定の状況において)納得のいく，まずまずの，適当な，妥当な，手ごろな ◇The furniture is in *reasonable* condition. その家具はまずまずの状態である ◇You must submit your claim within a *reasonable* time. 妥当な期間内に請求の申し出をしなければならない ◇If the price is *reasonable*, we'll buy it. 価格が手ごろなら買いますよ ☞ **reasonable** (REASONABLE)
▶**reasonably** 副 ◇The instructions are *reasonably* straightforward. その指示はかなり直接的である

ノート fair と reasonable の使い分け：多くの場合，両語とも使用可能だが，fair は話し言葉で用いられ，reasonable はふつう用いられない．また，fair は time (時間)と共に用いられることはない．×You must submit your claim within a *fair* time.

in 'order 形[句] (フォーマル) 正常な状態で，順調で ◇Is *everything in order*, sir? 万事順調ですか ◇We need to check that all your papers are *in order*. あなたの書類がすべて万全かを確認する必要があります

right [名詞の前では用いない] (特に否定的な文で) 正常な状態で，うまくいって ◇That sausage doesn't smell *right*. そのソーセージは変な臭いがする ◇Things aren't *right* between her parents. 彼女の両親はうまくいっていない ◇If only I could have helped *put* matters *right*. 事態を収拾する手助けができてさえいたらなぁ 反意 **wrong**
▶**right** 副 ◇Nothing's going *right* for me today. 今日は何をやってもうまくいかない

finish 動 ☞ END 動

finish • be done • complete • finalize • wrap sth up • follow (sth) through • round sth off • round sth out
物事をすべてやり遂げたり、完璧にしたりする
【類語訳】終える、済ます、終了する、完了する、修了する、まとめる、成立させる、完成させる

文型&コロケーション
▶to finish sth/ be done/ follow through/ round sth off/ round sth out **with** sth
▶to finish sth/ complete sth/ follow through/ round sth off/ round sth out **by** doing sth
▶to finish/ complete/ finalize the **preparations/ arrangements**
▶to finish/ complete/ wrap up/ round off/ round out a/ an **discussion/ evening/ meal**
▶to finish/ complete/ wrap up the **championship/ game/ series**
▶to finish/ complete/ round off/ round out the **day/ season**
▶to finish/ complete/ round off/ round out a/ an **tour/ interview/ campaign**
▶to complete/ finalize/ wrap up a **deal**
▶to **finally** finish sth/ be done/ complete sth/ round sth off/ round sth out

finish [他, 自]《特に話し言葉》(完成させて)終える、済ます、終了[修了]する ◇Haven't you *finished* your homework yet? 宿題はまだ終わってないのかい ◇I'll just *finish* the chapter, then I'll come. その章だけ読み終えて、それから行きます ◇She *finished* law school last year. 彼女は去年ロースクールを修了した ◇Be quiet! He hasn't *finished* speaking. 静かにしなさい。彼は話し終えてないのよ ◇She *put the finishing touches* to her painting (= did the things that made it complete). 彼女は自分の絵に最後の仕上げを施した ◇I thought you'd never *finish*! 君は絶対終えないと思ったよ 反意 **start** (BEGIN)

be 'done [フレーズ]《特に米，特に話し言葉》終えている ◇Aren't you *done* with your homework yet? まだ宿題を終えていないのかい ◇No, I'll *be done* in a minute. いいや、すぐに終わるよ ◇Be quiet — he's not *done* yet. 静かに—彼はまだ終えてないんだよ ◇I thought you'd never *get done*.《ややインフォーマル》君は絶対終えられないと思ったよ

complete [他, しばしば受身で]《ややフォーマル，特に書き言葉》(完成させて)終える、終了[修了]する ◇She's just *completed* a master's degree in Law. 彼女は法学の修士号を受けたばかりだ ◇The project should be *completed* within a year. その事業は1年以内に完了させなくてはいけない ❶この意味では complete はしばしば仕事・研究について用いられる．▶to *complete* a project/an assignment/ a thesis/a deal/an apprenticeship (事業/任務/学位論文/取り引き/年季奉公を終了[完了、修了]する)．また、complete には「完全[完璧]にする、全部そろえる、完成させる」の意味もある．◆I only need one more card to *complete* the set. (あと1枚カードがあれば一組が全部そろう)。この意味の連語として set, collection, scene, picture, series, sequence, transformation が挙げられる．
▶**completion** 名 [U] ◇The project is *due for completion* in the spring. その事業は春に完了する予定である ◇The road is *nearing completion* (= it is nearly finished). その道路は完成間近だ

ノート finish, be done, complete の使い分け：finish は話し言葉で、complete は書き言葉で用いられることが多い．finish は doing sth を目的語に取ることができるが、complete は doing sth は不可であることに注意．×He hasn't *completed* speaking.《米》の話し言葉では、finish も用いられるが、be done のほうが頻繁に用いられる．

finalize《英 -ise》[他]《特にビジネス》(計画・契約の最後の部分を)完了[完結]する、仕上げる、まとめる、決着をつける、成

↪finish

立させる ◇We need to *finalize* our plans. 私たちは計画を確定する必要がある ◇They met to *finalize* the terms of the treaty. 彼らはその条約の条項を決定するために集まった ❶*finalize* はしばしば商取引の契約, 取り決め, 計画について用いられる. ビジネスで用いられることもあり, 販売に関する合意を完結することを指す. ◆to *finalize* a deal/transaction/sale (取り引き/売買/売り渡しを成立させる).

,**wrap sth 'up** 句動詞 (-pp-) (インフォーマル, 特にビジネスや スポーツ) (満足のいく形で契約・会議・スポーツ競技会などを) 締めくくる, まとめる, 仕上げる, 切り上げる ◇That just about *wraps* it *up* for today. それでもってまあ今日のところは終わりかな ◇He is the one driver who could have beaten the Brazilian and *wrapped up* the world championship. 彼こそがそのブラジル人を破って世界選手権を締めくくったドライバーだ

,**follow 'through, ,follow sth 'through** 句動詞 《ややインフォーマル, 特に話し言葉》(開始した事を) 最後までやり通す ◇The key to success is having the motivation to *follow through* with your ideas. 成功の鍵は考えを最後まで貫くモチベーションを持つことにある ◇The project only has any value if you *follow* it *through*. その計画はやり遂げて初めてそれなりの価値が出てくる

,**round sth 'off** 句動詞 《英》 (好ましい[ふさわしい]形で活動・物事を) 締めくくる, 仕上げる, 完了[完結]する, 完成させる ◇She *rounded off* the tour with a concert at Carnegie Hall. 彼女はカーネギーホールでコンサートツアーを締めくくった ❶ round offの言い回しとしては, round off a day/an evening/a campaign with sports/dancing/a party (一日/夜会/選挙運動をスポーツ/ダンス/パーティーで締めくくる). mealを目的語に取って, round off a meal with coffee/cheese (食事をコーヒー/チーズで締めくくる). 主語がスポーツチームなら, round off the season with a win (シーズンを勝利で締めくくる) が挙げられる.

,**round sth 'out** 句動詞 《米》(好ましい形で活動・物事を) 締めくくる, 仕上げる, 完了[完結]する, 完成させる ◇The book is *rounded out* with a new cover and introduction. その本は新しい表紙と序文で仕上げられている ❶round out は人や物事のリスト[グループ] を表す語 (例えばcast) を目的語に取ることもある. ◆Julia Roberts and Gwyneth Paltrow *round out* the cast. (ジュリア・ロバーツとグウィネス・パルトロウが出演者の取りを飾ります).

fire 動

fire・lay sb off・dismiss・sack・axe・make sb redundant・let sb go・discharge・give sb/get the sack
人を正式に仕事から外す
【類語訳】解雇する, 首にする, 解任する, 免職する, 削減する, 余剰人員とする, 除隊させる, 首になる

文型&コロケーション
▸ to fire sb/ lay sb off/ dismiss sb/ sack sb/ make sb redundant/ discharge/ get the sack **from** a job
▸ to fire sb/ dismiss sb/ sack sb/ give sb the sack **for** sth
▸ to fire/ lay off/ dismiss/ sack/ axe **staff/ workers/ employees**
▸ to make **staff/ workers/ employees** redundant
▸ to let **staff/ employees** go
▸ to make **jobs/ posts/ positions** redundant
▸ to axe **jobs/ posts/ positions**
▸ to **get** fired/ laid off/ dismissed/ sacked/ made redundant

fire

▸ to be **unfairly/ summarily** fired/ dismissed/ sacked
▸ to be **wrongfully** fired/ dismissed

fire [他, しばしば受身で] 《米, ややインフォーマル; 英》(正式に) 解雇する, 首にする ◇We had to *fire* him for dishonesty. 我々は不正を理由に彼を解雇しなければならなかった ◇She got *fired* from her first job. 彼女は最初の仕事を首になった ◇He was responsible for *hiring and firing* employees. 彼は従業員の雇用と解雇を担当していた 反意 **hire** (EMPLOY)

lay sb 'off 句動詞 [しばしば受身で] (十分な仕事がないために人を) 一時解雇する ◇200 workers at the factory have been *laid off*. その工場で働く200人の従業員が解雇されている 反意 **take sb on** (EMPLOY), ☞ **lay-off** (UNEMPLOYMENT)

dismiss [他, ふつう受身で] 《ややフォーマル》 (正式に) 解雇[解任, 免職]する ◇She claims she was unfairly *dismissed* from her position. 彼女は地位を不当に解任されたと主張している ❶*dismiss* は法律の文脈で好まれる用語で, 特にunfairly/wrongfully dismissedの句で用いられる. 反意 **appoint** (APPOINT), ☞ **dismissal** (UNEMPLOYMENT)

sack [他, しばしば受身で] 《特に英, インフォーマル》(不正行為を理由に) 首にする ◇She was *sacked* for refusing to work on Sundays. 彼女は日曜出勤を拒否して首になった ☞ **sacking** (UNEMPLOYMENT)

axe 《英》 (《米》**ax**) [他, ふつう受身で] 《ジャーナリズム》 解雇[削減]する ◇300 jobs are to be *axed* at a local chemical works. 地元の化学工場で300の職が削減されることになっている ◇Jones has been *axed* from the team. ジョーンズはそのチームから解雇された ❶*axe* は多くの人々が同時に余剰人員となる場合に, 特にジャーナリズムで用いられる. 人よりも削減される職について用いられるほうが一般的である.

,**make sb re'dundant** フレーズ [ふつう受身で] 《英》(仕事の空きがないために人を) 解雇する, 余剰人員とする ◇She was *made redundant* from her job. 彼女は仕事を解雇された ◇A further five senior posts are to be *made redundant*. さらに5つの上級職が余剰となる予定だ ❶正式には目的語はjob(s) (仕事)やpost(s) (職) であるが, 実際には, 解雇される人を目的語に取るほうが一般的である. ☞ **redundant** (UNEMPLOYED), **redundancy** (UNEMPLOYMENT)

,**let sb 'go** 句動 (人を) 解雇する ◇They're having to *let* 100 employees *go* because of falling profits. 減益のために100人の従業員を解雇しなければならなくなるだろう ❶let sb go は fire, sack, make sb redundantの婉曲的な表現として用いられる.

discharge [他, ふつう受身で] 《ややフォーマル》(軍の職・地位から正式に) 除隊させる, 解雇[解任, 免職]する ◇He was *discharged* from the army following his injury. 彼はけがをして軍を除隊となった ◇She was *discharged* from the police force for bad conduct. 彼女は不品行がために警察を免職となった ☞ **discharge** (UNEMPLOYMENT)

,**give sb the 'sack, ,get the 'sack** フレーズ 《特に英, インフォーマル》(不正行為を理由に人を[が]) 首にする; 首になる ◇I've never had to *give* anyone *the sack*. 私は誰も首にする必要がなかった ◇He *got the sack* from his last job. 彼は前の仕事を首になった

ノート sackとgive sb the sack の使い分け: sackは give sb the sack よりも唐突[劇的]な響きを与えることがあり, ジャーナリズムで用いられることが多い. give sb the sack は日常の話し言葉で用いられることが多い.

firm, first

firm 形

firm・secure・steady・stable
物が場所に強く固定されていて動きそうにないことを表す
【類語訳】安定した、しっかりした、ぐらつかない、揺れない、震えない、ふらつかない

[文型&コロケーション]
▸ a firm/ secure/ steady/ stable **foundation**
▸ a firm/ secure/ stable **base**

firm (重い[頑丈な]物の上に固定されて)安定[しっかり]した ◇Stand the fish tank on a *firm* base. 安定した土台の上に水槽は置きましょう ◇No building can stand without *firm* foundations, and neither can a marriage. しっかりした土台なしに建物は建たないし、結婚もまた同様である ☞ **firm** (SOLID), **firm** (TIGHT)
▸ **firmly** 副 ◇Make sure the cover is *firmly* fixed in place. カバーが定位置にしっかりと固定されているか確かめましょう
secure (強く[正しく]固定されて)安定[しっかり]した、ぐらつかない、びくともしない ◇The aerial doesn't look very *secure* to me. そのアンテナはあまり安定しているようには私には見えない ◇It was difficult to maintain a *secure* foothold on the ice. 氷の上にしっかりした足場を保つのは難しかった
steady (支えられていて・バランスが取れていて)安定[しっかり]した;揺れ[震え]ない、ぐらつか[ふらつか]ない ◇He held the boat *steady* as she got in. 彼女が乗り込むとき、彼はボートをしっかりと押さえていた。◇Such fine work requires a good eye and a *steady hand*. そのような細かい作業には良い視力と震えない手が必要とされる ◇She's not very *steady on her feet* these days. このごろ彼女は足元があまりおぼつかない 反意 **unsteady** ❶ unsteady は自分の体を完全に制御できずに倒れそうになったり、体の部分が震えたり勝手に動いたりすることを表す。◆She is still a little *unsteady on her feet* after the operation. (手術後、彼女はまだ少し足元がふらついている). ◆With *unsteady* hands he opened the door and peered out. (彼は震える手でドアを開け、外をうかがった). ☞ **steady** (STEADY)
stable (倒れそうになく)安定[しっかり]した、ぐらつか[ふらつか]ない ◇This ladder doesn't seem very *stable*. このはしごはあまり安定性がないようだ 反意 **unstable**, ☞ **stable** (STEADY)

first 限定詞 形

first・initial・original・preliminary・opening・earliest・primary・introductory・preparatory
発生や存在が初めてであることを表す
【類語訳】最初の、第一の、一番目の、初期の、当初の、原初の、本来の、もともとの、予備的な、冒頭の、入門的な

[文型&コロケーション]
▸ preliminary/ preparatory **to** sth
▸ the first/ initial/ preliminary/ opening/ earliest/ primary/ introductory/ preparatory **stage**
▸ first/ initial/ original/ preliminary/ opening/ introductory **remarks**
▸ a first/ an initial/ an original/ a preliminary **estimate/ draft/ version**
▸ the first/ initial/ preliminary/ introductory/ preparatory **meeting**
▸ a first/ an initial/ a preliminary **step/ appointment/ visit**
▸ the first/ opening/ introductory **chapter/ paragraph**
▸ the initial/ the original/ a preliminary/ a preparatory **study**
▸ the initial/ original/ preliminary **findings**

first 限定詞 (同類のうちで)最初の、最も早い;第一の、一番目の ◇his *first* wife 彼の最初の妻 ◇King Richard *I* (= said as 'King Richard the *First*') 国王リチャード1世 ◇It was the *first* time they had ever met. それが彼らが出会った最初の時だった ◇She resolved to do it at the *first* opportunity. 彼女は最初の機会にそうする決心をした ◇*First* impressions can be misleading. 第一印象が誤解につながることもある ◇You can have *first choice* of all the rooms. 一番先にすべての部屋からお選びできます ◇We're having chicken for the *first course*. 最初の一品にチキンをいただきます 反意 **last** (LAST 1, 2)
▸ **first!** 副 ◇*First* I had to decide what to wear. 私はまず何を着るかを決めなければならなかった ◇Who came *first* in the race (= who won)? そのレースでは誰が1着だったの
▸ **at first** フレーズ ◇*At first* I thought she was joking but then I realized he meant it. 初めは彼女が冗談を言っているのだと思ったが、次に彼がそのつもりで言ったのだと悟った ◇I didn't like the job much *at first*. 私は最初はその仕事があまり好きではなかった
initial [名詞の前で] (発生について)初期の、当初の、;(同類のうちで)最初の、最も早い、第一の、一番目の ◇My *initial* reaction was to decline the offer. 私は当初その申し出を断った ◇It is the *initial* preparation that takes the time. それだけの時間がかかるのは初期の準備の部分だ ◇There is an *initial* payment of £60 followed by ten instalments of £25. 60ポンドの頭金に25ポンドの10回払いです ❶ initial は特にあまり長く続かない反応[感情]について用いられる。◆By 1960 the *initial* optimism had evaporated. (1960年までには当初の楽観論は消滅していた). ◆sb's *initial* response/impression/instinct/shock/surprise/enthusiasm/euphoria/excitement/scepticism/reluctance (人の当初の反応/印象/直観/衝撃/驚き/熱中/幸福感/興奮/疑念/嫌気). 過程の段階について、◆ the *initial* stage/phase/step/planning/preparation (第一段階/第一期/第一歩/第一案/最初の準備). お金の支払い[使用]について、◆the *initial* investment/ payment/outlay (初期投資/頭金/当初の支出) 反意 **final** (LAST 1)
▸ **initially** 副 ◇My contract is *initially* for three years. 私の契約は当初は3年間である ◇*Initially*, the system worked well. そのシステムは始めのうちはうまく機能した
original [名詞の前で] (変化する前の)原初の、最初の、本来の、元来の、もともとの、そもそもの ◇The room still has many of its *original* features. その部屋は依然として本来の特徴をたくさん備えている ◇I think you should go back to your *original* plan. あなたは元の案に立ち返るべきだと私は思います
▸ **originally** 副 ◇The school was *originally* very small. その学校はもともとはとても小さかった ◇He comes *originally* from Peru. 彼は元をただればペルー出身だ
preliminary (重要な行動[出来事]に[の])先立つ、予備[準備]的な、序の、前置きの ◇After a few *preliminary* remarks he announced the winners. 少し前置きを述べた後、彼は優勝者を発表した ◇This is just a pilot study

preliminary to a full-scale study. これは本格的な研究に先立つ予備的研究にすぎない

opening [名詞の前で]（発言・著述・楽曲などの）冒頭の, 序の, 前置きの, 開始の ◇She was humming the *opening* bars of a song she had heard on the radio. 彼女はラジオで聞いたことのある歌の前奏を鼻歌で歌っていた ◇United scored in the *opening* minutes of the game. ユナイテッドは試合開始後数分で得点した [反意] **closing** (LAST 1), ☞ **opening** (START 名), **open** (BEGIN)

earliest （出来事・期間が）初期の, 初頭の, 最古の, 最も早い ◇The *earliest* description of this species dates from 1816. この種に関する最古の記述は1816年にさかのぼる ◇The *earliest* possible date I can make is the third. 私が都合のつく最も早い日は3日です

primary [ふつう名詞の前で]《フォーマル or 専門語》（発達・発生が）初期の, 最初の, 第一の ; （出来事・期間が）初期の, 初頭の, 最古の, 最も早い ◇The disease is still in its *primary* stage. その病気はまだ初期段階だ ◇It is not self-evident what the *primary* causes of this phenomenon are. この現象の第一要因が何であるかは自明ではない ☞ **primary** (MAIN)

introductory （後に続くものの）序の, 前置きの, 入門的な ◇The booklist at the end of the chapter contains some *introductory* reading on the subject. 章末にある本の一覧にはこのテーマに関する何冊かの入門書が含まれている ◇I took an *introductory* class in psychology during my first year at college. 私は大学1年のとき心理学の入門クラスを取った ☞ **introduction** (BASICS), **introduction** (INTRODUCTION)

preparatory [名詞の前で]《特に英, フォーマル》準備の[予備]的な ◇After a few *preparatory* drawings, she completed the portrait in one session. 数回下描きをした後, 彼女は1回の授業で肖像画を完成させた ◇Security checks had been carried out *preparatory* to (= to prepare for) the President's visit. 大統領の訪問に備えてセキュリティーチェックが行われていた ☞ **preparation** (PLANNING), **prepare** (PREPARE 1, 2)

flat [形]

flat・smooth・level・horizontal
物の表面が湾曲していない, 傾斜していない, でこぼこになっていないことを表す
【類語訳】平らな, 平坦な, 滑らかな, 平滑な, 水平な

[文型&コロケーション]
▸ a flat/ smooth/ level/ horizontal **surface**
▸ a flat/ smooth/ level **road/ floor**
▸ a flat/ smooth **rock/ stone**
▸ flat/ level **ground/ land**
▸ **completely** flat/ smooth/ level/ horizontal

flat 平らな, 平坦な ◇The town consisted mainly of low buildings with *flat* roofs. その町には主に平屋根の低い建物が多い ◇People used to think the earth was *flat*. 以前, 地球は平らだと思われていた ◇The road stretched ahead across the *flat* landscape. その道は平坦な地形を横切るように前方に伸びていた ◇I need a *flat* surface to write on. 書き物をするので平らな面がいる

smooth [しばしばほめて] 滑らかな, 平滑な ◇The water was as *smooth* as glass. 水面は（波一つなく）とても穏やかだった ◇Use a paint that gives a *smooth*, silky finish. 滑らかで絹のような仕上がりを見せる塗料を使いなさい ◇Over the years, the stone steps had worn *smooth*. 長い年月を経てその石段は磨り減って滑らかになってしまった [反意] **rough**

level 水平な, 平らな, 平坦な ◇Pitch the tent on *level* ground. 平らな地面にテントを張りなさい ◇Add a *level* tablespoon of flour (= enough to fill the spoon but not so much that there is a round heap on the spoon). 大さじすりきり1杯の小麦粉を足しなさい

[ノート] flat と level の使い分け: level は ground や floor と共に最もよく用いられ, 特に平らであり, あるいは望ましいものとしてよく用いられる. flat は, 湾曲していない表面を言うときに用いられる. ◆ a *flat* screen/base/bottom/sheet/stomach/surface （フラットスクリーン／平台／平底／フラットシーツ／出っ張っていない腹／平面）. （例外は, 傾斜のない a *flat* roof （平ら[陸]屋根））. flat はまた丘のない風景にも用いられる. ◆ a *flat* field/landscape/plateau/plain/region/beach （起伏のない野原／平坦な風景／平らな台地／平原／平面領域／平坦な砂浜）. flat landscape は, しばしば変化がなく退屈だと思われる. level ground は, 上に建物を建てることができるとか, 歩きやすいとかの理由で, 好ましいものとされる.

horizontal 水平な ◇Draw a grid of *horizontal* and vertical *lines*. 横線と縦線から成る格子を描きなさい [反意] **vertical**

flee [動]

flee・run away・run off・take off・make off・bolt・run for it
人や物を避けるために非常に素早くある場所から離れる
【類語訳】逃げる, 避難する, 逃走する, 逃亡する, 走り去る, 急いで逃げる, 駆け出す

[文型&コロケーション]
▸ to flee/ run away/ bolt **from** sb/ sth
▸ to flee/ run away/ run off/ bolt **to** sth
▸ to run/ take/ make/ bolt **off**
▸ to flee/ run away/ run off/ take off/ make off/ bolt **down/ into** sth
▸ to run away/ run off/ take off/ make off **with** sb/ sth
▸ to **turn and** flee/ run away/ run off

flee [自, 他]《特に書き言葉》（危険な状況から素早く）逃げる, 避難する, 逃走[逃亡]する ◇Refugees *fled* from the city. 難民たちはその都市から避難した ◇People *fled in terror* as the bomb exploded. 爆弾が爆発して人々は恐れをなして逃げた ◇Hundreds of people were forced to *flee their homes*. 何百人もの人々が家を捨てて避難せざるをえなかった ◇They *fled the country* in 1987. 彼らは1987年に国外へ逃亡した ◇The man looked at me in horror, and then turned and *fled*. その男はおびえたように私を見ると, きびすを返して逃げ出した

,run a'way [句動詞]《特に話し言葉》（危険・困難を避けるため素早く[突然]）逃げる, 逃げ出す, 走り[逃げ]去る ◇'Don't *run away*', the stranger said, 'We're here to help.' 「逃げるな. 私たちは助けに来たんだ」とその見知らぬ人は言った ◇I tried to *run away from home* several times when I was a kid. 私は子供の頃, 何度か家出しようとした

,run 'off [句動詞]《特に英》（人・場所から素早く）走り[逃げ]去る ◇The dog *ran off* across the park, barking loudly. その犬はやかましく吠えながら公園を横切って走り去った ◇She *ran off* when I tried to talk to her. 私が話しかけようとすると彼女は走り去った

ノート **run away**と**run off**の使い分け：《英》では、run offはまさに今自分がいる場所にいる人[直面している危険]から逃げることを指す．run awayもこのように用いられることもあるが、人生におけるより一般的な困難[問題]から逃れるために突然旅に出かけることを意味することもある．◆*Why don't we run away to Paris?* (パリに逃亡したらどうかって). ×*Why don't we run off to Paris?* run awayは、ふつう驚いて逃げること．run offは、恐怖で[単に逃げたいから]逃げることを指す．《米》では、run awayはこのどちらの意味でも用いられる．

,**take 'off** 句動詞 《インフォーマル》(場所から急いで)走り[逃げ]去る ◇When he saw me coming he *took off* in the opposite direction. 彼は私が近づいて来るのを見ると、反対方向に走り去った

,**make 'off** 句動詞 (犯罪[過ち]を犯して場所から急いで)走り[逃げ]去る ◇The robbers *made off* before the police arrived. 強盗は警察が到着する前に逃げ去った ❶**make off with** sthは「物を盗んで急いで持ち去る」ことを意味する．◆The raiders *made off with* £20,000 worth of jewellery. (襲撃犯は2万ポンド相当の宝石類を持ち去った).

bolt (馬などが驚いて突然)駆け[逃げ]出す；(人が逃亡のために)走り[逃げ]去る ◇The plane swooped down low and the horses *bolted*. 飛行機が低く舞い降りてきたので、馬たちは駆け出した ◇For a moment I thought about *bolting*, but there was no escape. 私は一瞬逃げることを考えたが、逃げ道がなかった

'**run for it** 成句 (人・物から)急いで逃げる(しばしば命令形で用いられる) ◇'*Run for it!*' Billy yelled. 「急いで逃げろ」とビリーは叫んだ

flexible 形

1 flexible・versatile・adjustable・convertible・adaptable・multi-purpose・all-purpose
人や物事が変化して新しい条件[状況]に適応できることを表す
【類語訳】順応性のある、柔軟な、融通の利く、多才の、万能の、適応力のある、多目的の

文型&コロケーション
▸convertible/ adaptable **to** sth
▸a flexible/ a versatile/ an adaptable **system**
▸a flexible/ versatile **workforce/ approach**
▸a versatile/ multi-purpose **machine**
▸**highly/ very/ wonderfully/ fairly/ quite** flexible/ versatile/ adaptable
▸**easily/ readily** adjustable/ convertible/ adaptable

flexible 《ほめて》(新しい条件[状況]に)順応性のある、柔軟な、融通の利く ◇What is needed is a more *flexible* design. 必要なのはより柔軟なデザインである ◇We can offer you *flexible* working hours. フレックスタイム制を勧めます ◇Can you be *flexible* about when you take your leave? 休暇をいつ取るか、融通がききますか 反意 **inflexible**
▸**flexibility** 名 [U] ◇Computers offer a much greater degree of *flexibility* in the way work is organized. コンピューターによって作業の進め方にはるかに大きな柔軟性が生まれる
▸**flexibly** 副 ◇Managers must respond *flexibly* to

new developments in business practice. 経営者たちはビジネス手法の新たな進展に対して柔軟に対応しなければならない

versatile 《ほめて》(人が)多才の、多芸な；(物が)多用途の、万能の ◇He's a *versatile* actor who has played a wide variety of parts. 彼は幅広い役どころを演じてきた多芸多才な俳優である ◇Eggs are easy to cook and are an extremely *versatile* food. 卵は調理しやすく、極めて用途の広い食品である

adjustable (位置・形・大きさが)調整[調節]自在の[可能な] ◇The golf buggy comes equipped with fully *adjustable* seat belts. そのゴルフカートは完全に調節自在のシートベルトが備え付けられるようになります ◇The height of the bicycle seat is *adjustable*. 自転車のサドルの高さは調節可能である ☞ **adjust** (ADJUST)

convertible (形・用途が)変換[転換、切り換え、兌換、転用]可能な ◇a *convertible* sofa (= one that can be used as a bed) ソファーベッド ◇The bonds are *convertible into* ordinary shares. その社債は普通株に転換できる ❶ convertibleはほとんどの場合、ソファーあるいは金融関係の語と共に用いられる．◆*convertible* bonds/currencies/debt/shares/stocks/securities (転換社債/兌換通貨/転換社債/転換株式/転換株/転換証券) ☞ **convert** (TURN 2)

adaptable 《ほめて》(新しい状況に)順応性[適応力]のある ◇Older workers can be as *adaptable* and quick to learn as anyone else. 年配の労働者でも他の労働者と同じくらい適応力があり、物覚えの早い人もいる ◇Successful businesses are highly *adaptable* to economic change. 成功している企業は経済的変化に対して順応性が高い ☞ **adapt** (CHANGE 動 1)

ノート **flexible** と **adaptable** の使い分け：flexible は労働状況が頻繁に変わる場合(例えば、顧客の要望、金融上の規制など)の人や制度の順応性[柔軟性]について用いられる．adaptable は長期間にわたって条件が変わる場合(例えば、気候の大きな変動、特定の食糧の不足、経済の破綻など)の人や動物の順応性[適応力]について用いられることが多い．

,**multi-'purpose** [名詞の前で] 多目的の ◇Just one *multi-purpose* cleaner should be enough for the whole house. 多目的クリーナー1台で家全体には十分なはずだ ◇The concert hall is actually a *multi-purpose* building that doubles as a theatre, exhibition hall and community centre. そのコンサートホールは実は劇場、展示場、公民館を兼ねる多目的ビルである

,**all-'purpose** [名詞の前で] 万能の、汎用の、多用途の ◇Cheddar is an *all-purpose* cheese for cooking and eating. チェダーチーズは万能チーズで調理用にも食用にもなる ◇Each child had one pair of *all-purpose* shoes. 子どもたちはそれぞれ万能靴を1足持っていた

ノート **multi-purpose** と **all-purpose** の使い分け：multi-purpose は all-purpose よりも肯定的な語であり、物がいかに有用で用途が広いかを強調するときに用いられる．all-purpose は単に何にでも用いられているだけのごくふつうの物であることが多く、用途にわざわざ異なる物を作る[手に入れる]余裕がないときに用いられる．all-purpose は《米》で用いられることが多い．

2 flexible・springy・elastic・supple
物が容易に折れることを表す
【類語訳】曲げられる、しなやかな、可撓(とう)性のある、弾力のあ

↪flexible

る, 弾性のある, 伸縮性のある

文型&コロケーション
▶flexible/ elastic materials
▶very flexible/ springy/ elastic/ supple

flexible (素材が)曲げられる, しなやかな, 可撓性のある ◇You'll need 2 metres of *flexible* plastic tubing. 曲げられるプラスチックチューブが2m必要となるだろう 反意 **rigid** (SOLID)

springy (すぐに元の形に戻る)弾力[弾性]のある ◇We walked across the *springy* grass. 私たちはふわふわした芝生を歩いて横切った ❶ springyは主に hair, grass, moss, heatherなどと共に用いられる.

elastic (素材が)伸縮性[弾力, 弾性]のある ◇An *elastic* material is usually placed around the upper arm. 弾性材はふつう上腕の周りに取り付けられる

supple (柔らかくて)曲げやすい, しなやかな ◇Moisturizing cream helps to keep your skin soft and *supple*. 保湿クリームは肌を柔らかくしなやかに保ってくれます ❶ suppleはほとんどの場合, 肌, 指, 背骨, 動作など, 体に関連する語と共に用いられる.

flirt 動

flirt • chat sb up • tease • come on to sb • make a pass at sb
特定の方法で話しかける[振る舞う]ことで人を性的に魅了しようとする
【類語訳】もてあそぶ, 手を出す, ナンパする, 浮気する, 口説く, 言い寄る, じらす, 色目を使う

flirt [自] もてあそぶ, 手を出す, ナンパする, 浮気する ◇He *flirts* outrageously *with* his female clients. とんでもないことに彼は女性依頼人たちを口説いている
▶**flirt** 名 [C, ふつう単数で] ◇She's a real *flirt*. 彼女は本当に浮気者だ
▶**flirtatious** 形 ◇a *flirtatious* young woman 浮気な若い女性 ◇a *flirtatious* giggle 誘いかけるような忍び笑い

,chat sb 'up 句動詞 (-tt-) 《英, インフォーマル》(人に[を])なれなれしく話しかける, ナンパする, 口説く, 言い寄る ◇She went straight over and tried to *chat* him *up*. 彼女はすっと彼に近寄り, なれなれしく話しかけようとした
▶**'chat-up** 名 [C, U] ◇Is that your best *chat-up* line? それがあなたの最高の口説き文句なの

ノート flirtとchat sb upの使い分け: chat sb upは人が実際に話す言葉について言うだけだが, flirtは人の行動についても言う. chat sb upはふつう交際を求めるものであるが, flirtは必ずしもそうではない.

tease [自, 他]《けなして》じらす, 思わせぶりな態度を見せる ◇She *teased* the men with an expression that was both innocent and knowing. 彼女は清純とも狡猾とも取れる表情で男たちをじらした
▶**tease** 名 [C, ふつう単数で] ◇She's a wicked little *tease*. 彼女はたちの悪い思わせぶりな小娘だ

,come 'on to sb 句動詞《インフォーマル》(人に[を])色目を使う, 誘いかける, 口説く, 言い寄る ◇When he started *coming on to* me, I assumed he wasn't married. 彼が私を口説き始めたときは, 彼は結婚していないと思った
▶**'come-on** 名 [C, ふつう単数で] ◇She tried to ignore his *come-ons*.《インフォーマル》彼女は彼の誘いかけを無視し

flirt, flood

ようとした
make a 'pass at sb 行為《インフォーマル》(人を[に])口説く, 言い寄る ◇Are you *making a pass at* me? 私を口説こうとしてるの

flood 名

1 flood • torrent • flash flood • tidal wave • deluge • tsunami
速く[普段は水のない場所に]流れる非常に大量の水
【類語訳】洪水, 氾濫, 急流, 奔流, 鉄砲水, 高潮, 大雨, 豪雨, 津波

文型&コロケーション
▶a great flood/ torrent
▶to cause a flood/ flash flood/ tidal wave/ tsunami
▶floods/ flash floods/ a tidal wave/ a tsunami hit/ hits sth
▶a flood/ tidal wave/ tsunami destroys sth
▶a torrent/ deluge of rain

flood [C, U] 洪水, 氾濫 ◇The heavy rain has caused *floods* in many parts of the country. 大雨は全国各地に洪水をもたらした ◇The building was evacuated as *flood* water filled the basement. 洪水で地階が浸水したので, 人々はその建物から避難させられた ◇The river is *in flood* (= has more water in it than normal and has caused a flood).《特に英》川が氾濫している ☞ **flood** (SOAK)

torrent [C] 急流, 奔流 ◇After the winter rains, the stream becomes a raging *torrent*. 冬の雨で, その川は荒れ狂う奔流となる ◇The rain was coming down in *torrents*. 雨は滝のように降っていた
▶**torrential** 形 ◇*torrential* rain 土砂降りの雨

'flash flood [C] (大雨が引き起こす)鉄砲水 ◇More than 80 people were feared dead last night after *flash floods*, the worst in 34 years. 昨夜の鉄砲水で80人以上の人が死亡したと見られ, これは34年間で最悪の事態だった

,tidal 'wave [C] (地震・火山の噴火が引き起こす)高潮 ◇According to one account, the explosion caused a *tidal wave* 65 feet high. ある報告によれば, その爆発によって高さ65フィートの高波が起きた

deluge [C, ふつう単数で]《特に書き言葉》(突然の)大雨, 豪雨 ◇The earlier *deluge* had given way to more normal rain. 初期の豪雨はより普通の雨に変わった

tsunami [C] (地震・火山の噴火などが引き起こす)津波 ◇The *tsunami* caused immeasurable damage. 津波は計り知れない損害をもたらした

ノート tidal waveとtsunamiの使い分け: 地震によって引き起こされる非常に巨大な波(津波)を表す正確な科学用語はtsunamiまたはseismic sea waveである. tidal wave (高潮)は, 専門的には潮の干満をもたらす月と太陽の引力によって引き起こされるものであるが, 一般的な言い回しでは, tidal waveはふつう「津波」を意味する.

2 flood • stream • barrage • shower • battery • torrent • hail • outpouring • volley
大量の物事[多くの人々]が同時に発生[到来]すること
【類語訳】殺到, ほとばしり, 連続, 連発, 雨(あられ), 一連, 噴出, 湧出, 一斉射撃

文型&コロケーション

- a flood/ stream/ torrent of **words**
- a flood/ stream of **calls**
- a flood/ barrage of **complaints**
- a stream/ barrage/ torrent of **abuse**
- a barrage/ torrent/ hail of **criticism**
- a barrage/ battery/ volley of **questions**
- floods/ a torrent of **tears**
- a torrent/ an outpouring of **emotion**
- a shower/ hail/ volley of **arrows/ bullets/ stones**
- a hail/ volley of **shots/ fire**
- a **constant/ continuous** stream/ barrage of sth
- to **unleash** a flood/ barrage/ torrent/ volley of sth

flood [C]《ふつう of を伴って》(人・物の)殺到、ほとばしり ◇They took on temporary workers in anticipation of a *flood* of calls. 彼らは電話が殺到することを見越して臨時職員を採用した ◇Authorities are struggling to cope with the *flood* of refugees. 当局は殺到する難民に懸命に対処しようとしている ◇The child was in *floods* of tears (= crying a lot). その子どもは大泣きしていた

stream [C]《of を伴って》(物事の)連続 ◇She had to deal with a constant *stream* of enquiries. 彼女は絶え間なく続く質問に対処しなければならなかった ◇He let loose a *stream* of insults and obscenities. 彼は侮辱と卑猥な雑言をひとしきり吐き続けた ◇The agency provided me with a steady *stream* of work. 代理店は私に仕事を絶えず提供してくれた ❶ stream は人や乗り物の絶え間ない流れを指すこともある。☞ **stream** (FLOW)

barrage [単数で]《《ふつう of を伴って》》(攻撃的に矢継ぎ早に発せられる質問・批評などの)連発 ◇She had not been prepared to face this *barrage* of questions. 彼女はこんな矢継ぎ早の質問に向かう心構えができていなかった

shower [単数で]《ふつう of を伴って》《書き言葉》(落下物の)雨(あられ) ◇A log in the fire broke and fell, sending out a *shower* of sparks. 火だるまになった丸太がものすごい数の火の粉を散らしながら崩れ落ちた

battery [C, ふつう単数で]《of を伴って》(同類の物事の)一続き、一連 ◇A whole *battery* of measures was tried in an attempt to get them to give up cigarettes. 彼らにタバコをやめさせようとして一連の方法がすべて試された ❶ この意味での battery の連語に questions, tests, measures が挙げられる。

torrent [C]《《ふつう of を伴って》》(突発的で激しい言葉・感情の)ほとばしり、奔出 ◇A *torrent* of words poured out as thoughts raced around in his head. 考えが彼の頭の中を駆け巡る中、とめどなく言葉が溢れ出した ◇She was subjected to a *torrent* of abuse. 彼女は罵詈雑言の嵐にさらされた

hail [単数で]《of を伴って》《書き言葉》(弾丸・石・矢の)雨(あられ);(批判の)連発 ◇A passer-by was caught in the *hail* of bullets. 通行人の一人が弾丸の雨に巻き込まれた ◇The attempt to bring in new legislation was met by a *hail* of criticism. 新法導入の企ては批判の嵐にさらされた

outpouring [C]《書き言葉》(突発的で激しい感情の)ほとばしり、噴出;(短期間の物事の)湧出 ◇Her death prompted huge *outpourings* of grief. 彼女の死で抑えられていた深い悲しみが一気に噴出した ◇His early career was characterized by a remarkable *outpouring* of new ideas. 彼が仕事に就いた初期の頃は驚くほど新しいアイデアが湧き起こったものだ

volley [C, ふつう単数で] (弾丸[石, 矢]の)一斉射撃, 雨(あられ);(矢継ぎ早に発せられる質問[批評, 侮辱]の)連発 ◇A *volley* of shots rang out. 一斉射撃の音が鳴り響いた ◇Police fired a *volley* over the heads of the crowd. 警察は群衆の頭上に一斉射撃を浴びせた ◇She faced a *volley* of angry questions from her mother. 彼女は母親から怒りの質問を連発された

ノート hail と volley の使い分け: a hail of bullets/arrows/stones/shots/fire はふつう、それらが降りかかる人の視点から用いられ、人を主語にして be caught/be killed/die in a hail of bullets と言える。a volley はふつう、発射[投石]を行う人の視点から用いられる。

flood 〔動〕

flood・overflow・spill over (sth)・burst its banks
川や容器が一杯になりすぎて両側からあふれ出ることを表す
【類語訳】浸水する、冠水する、氾濫する、あふれる、こぼれる

文型&コロケーション

- a **river** floods/ overflows/ bursts its banks
- a river overflows/ bursts **its** banks
- **tears** overflow/ spill over

flood [自] 浸水[冠水]する, 水浸しになる;(川が)氾濫する ◇The cellar *floods* whenever it rains heavily. 大雨になるといつも地下室は浸水する ◇When the Ganges *floods*, it causes considerable damage. ガンジス川が氾濫すると甚大な被害を引き起こす ☞ **flood** (SOAK)

overflow [自, 他] (容器・川が)あふれる、こぼれる、氾濫する ◇The bath is *overflowing*! 風呂があふれているよ ◇My heart *overflowed* with love. 《比喩的》彼女の心は愛に満ちあふれていた ◇If it keeps raining the river could *overflow* its banks. 雨が降り続けると、川が堤防を越えてあふれ出ることもありうるだろう

,spill 'over, ,spill 'over sth [句動] (容器の両側[縁, 表面]から)あふれる、こぼれる ◇The bag was so full of presents that it was *spilling over*. 袋はプレゼントがこぼれ落ちそうだった ◇The tears *spilled over* and trickled down her cheeks. 涙があふれ、彼女の頬をしたたり落ちた ◇A few drops of wine *spilled over* the edge of her glass. 彼女のグラスの端からワインが数滴こぼれ落ちた ◇She lay with her hair *spilling over* the pillow. 彼女は枕からはみ出て髪が横たわっていた

,burst its 'banks 〔他〕(川が)堤防を決壊させる ◇Many sheep were swept to their deaths when the river *burst its banks* after rising eight feet overnight. 一晩で8フィート増水し、川の堤防が決壊したとき、たくさんの羊が押し流されて死んだ

floor 〔名〕

floor・storey・level・deck・tier
建物や場所, 船, バスの異なる平面[階層]
【類語訳】階, 地層, デッキ, 列, 段, 層

文型&コロケーション

- on the **top,** etc. floor/ storey/ level/ deck/ tier
- the **upper/ lower** floors/ storeys/ levels/ decks/ tiers
- the **top** floor/ storey/ level/ deck/ tier
- the **main** floor/ deck

floor [C] (建物の)階 ◇Her office is on the second floor. 彼女のオフィスは3階[2階]にある ◇the Irish guy who lives two floors above 2階上に住んでいるアイルランド人男性 ◇Their house is on three floors (= it has three floors). 彼らの家は3階分ある ❶《英》では、建物の1階を ground floor, その一つ上の階を first floor, 一つ下の階を basement, またそれが公共の建物であれば lower ground floor と言う。《米》では、1階はふつう first floor, その一つ上の階を second floor, 一つ下の階を basement と言う。公共の建物の地階は ground floor と言うこともある。

storey 《特に英》《米でふつう **story**》[C] (建物の)階 ◇a single-storey/two-storey/three-storey building 1階[2階, 3階]建ての建物

> **ノート** floor と storey の使い分け: floor は特に建物のどの階に人がいるか[行くか]といった場合に用いられる。◆His office is on the fifth floor. (彼の職場は5階にある). storey は特に建物が何階建てかといった場合に用いられる。◆a five-storey house (5階建ての家). ◆The office building is five storeys high. (そのオフィスビルは5階建ての高さがある).

level [C] (建物の)階; 地層 ◇The library is all on one level. 図書館は全体が一つの階にあります ◇Archaeologists found pottery in the lowest level of the site. 考古学者たちは遺跡の最も下の堆積層で陶器を見つけた ◇a multi-level parking lot 多くの階から成る駐車場 ❶建物や遺跡の level は必ずしも他の level の上にあるとは限らない。level はしばしば、建物や遺跡の異なる領域が異なる高さにある場合に用いられる。場所の上位や下位について用いられることもある。大型の多層階の駐車場(ビル)の場合を除いて、数字で数えられる建物の階にはあまり用いられない。×His office is on the fifth level. ◆Remember that we parked on level 5. (5階に駐車したこと覚えておいてね).

deck [C] (船・バスの)階, デッキ ◇My cabin is on deck C. 私の船室はCデッキにあります ◇We sat on the top deck of the bus. 私たちはバスの2階に座った

tier [C] (上下に配置された[ひな段状になった])列, 段, 階, 層 ◇a wedding cake with three tiers 3段のウェディングケーキ ◇The seating is arranged in tiers. 座席は階段状に配列されている

flow 動

flow・run・pour・stream・circulate・spew・pump・cascade・spurt・gush
液体や気体がある場所から別の場所に大量に移動する
【類語訳】流れる, 液体を流す, 流す, 循環する, 循環させる, 噴出する, 噴出させる, あふれ出る, 流れ出る, 流し出す

文型&コロケーション

▶ to flow/ pour/ stream/ spew/ pump/ cascade/ spurt/ gush **out**
▶ to flow/ run/ pour/ stream/ spew/ pump/ spurt/ gush **out of** sth
▶ to flow/ run/ pour/ stream/ spew/ pump/ cascade/ spurt/ gush **from** sth
▶ to flow/ run/ pour/ stream/ cascade/ spurt/ gush **into** sth
▶ to flow/ run/ pour/ stream/ cascade/ pump/ cascade/ spurt/ gush **through** sth
▶ to flow/ run/ pour/ stream/ cascade/ gush **down** (sth)
▶ to flow/ circulate/ pump (sth) **around/ round** sth
▶ to be flowing/ running/ streaming/ gushing **with** sth

▶ water flows/ runs/ pours/ streams/ circulates/ cascades/ spurts/ gushes
▶ blood flows/ runs/ pours/ streams/ circulates/ pumps/ cascades/ spurts/ gushes
▶ tears flow/ run/ pour/ stream/ gush
▶ adrenalin flows/ pours/ pumps
▶ a waterfall pours/ cascades/ gushes
▶ light flows/ pours/ streams/ cascades
▶ smoke pours/ streams/ spews
▶ to flow/ run/ circulate **freely/ slowly**

flow [自]《ふつう副詞や前置詞と共に》(液体・気体・電気が)流れる, 流れ込む ◇It's here that the river flows down into the ocean. その川が海に流れ込むのはここです ◇This can prevent air from flowing freely to the lungs. これで空気が自由に肺に入るのを防げる ◇The current flowing in a circuit is measured by connecting an ammeter. 回路に流れる電流は電流計につなぐことで測定される

run [自](液体が)流れる; 液体を流す ◇The tears ran down her cheeks. 涙が彼女の頬を流れ落ちた ◇Who left the tap running? 蛇口の水を流しっ放しにしたのは誰? ◇Your nose is running. 鼻水が出ているよ ◇The smoke makes my eyes run. 煙で目から涙が出る ❶sth is running with は, 主語の物が液体であふれていることを表す。◆His face was running with sweat. (彼は顔に大汗をかいていた).

pour [自]《副詞や前置詞と共に》(液体・煙・光が)噴き[あふれ]出る ◇Blood was pouring from the wound. 傷から血が噴き出ていた ◇Thick black smoke was pouring out of the roof. 濃い黒煙が屋根からもくもくと出ていた ◇The kitchen door opened and light poured into the hallway. 台所のドアが開いて光が廊下に差し込んだ

stream [自, 他]《目的語がない場合は副詞や前置詞を用いて》(液体・気体・煙・光が)流れる;(液体・気体・煙を勢いよく)流す ◇Sunlight streamed through the windows. 日射しが窓から差し込んだ ◇Her head was streaming with blood. 彼女の頭に血が流れていた ◇The exhaust streamed black smoke. その排気管は黒煙を吐いた

circulate [自, 他](液体・気体が場所[システム])で)循環する;(液体・気体を場所[システム]で)循環させる ◇The condition prevents blood from circulating freely. その症状で血液が自由に流れない ◇Cooled air is circulated throughout the building. 冷却された空気がビル中を循環している

spew [自, 他]《副詞や前置詞と共に》(煙・炎が)噴き出する;(煙・炎を)噴出させる ◇Flames spewed from the aircraft's engine. 飛行機のエンジンが火を噴いた ◇Massive chimneys were spewing out smoke and flames. 巨大な煙突が煙と炎を吐いていた

pump [自]《副詞や前置詞と共に》(液体がポンプで押し出されるかのように)噴き出る, あふれ出る ◇Blood was pumping out of the wound on his shoulder. 肩の傷から血が噴き出ていた

cascade [自]《書き言葉》(液体が大量に)流れ落ちる ◇Water cascaded down the mountainside. 水は山の斜面を滝のように流れ落ちた

spurt [自, 他]《目的語がない場合は副詞や前置詞を用いて》(液体・気体・炎が)噴き[流れ]出る;(液体・気体・炎を)噴き[流し]出す ◇Blood was spurting from her nose. 彼女の鼻から血が噴き出ていた ◇The volcano spurted clouds of steam and ash high into the air. 火山が空高く水蒸気と灰をもうもうと噴き出した

▶**spurt** [C] ◇*a spurt* of blood 血液の噴出
gush [自, 他]《目的語がない場合は副詞や前置詞を用いて》(液体が)噴く[流れ]出る；(容器・乗り物が液体を)噴き[流し]出す ◇Water *gushed* out of the pipe. パイプから水がほとばしった ◇The tanker was *gushing* oil. タンカーから油が流れ出ていた

flush [動]

flush・blush・glow・colour・burn
恥ずかしさなどの感情で顔が紅潮する
【類語訳】赤くなる、赤面する、ほてる、真っ赤になる

colour	flush	burn
	blush	
	glow	

文型&コロケーション

▶ to flush/ blush/ glow/ colour/ burn **with** sth
▶ sb's **cheeks** flush/ glow/ colour/ burn
▶ sb's **face** flushes/ glows/ colours/ burns
▶ to flush/ blush **scarlet**

flush [自] (恥ずかしくて[興奮して, 怒って, 暑くて])赤くなる ◇He *flushed* with anger at her reply. 彼女の返事に怒って彼の顔は赤くなった ◇She felt her cheeks *flush* red and she looked away in embarrassment. 彼女は頬が赤くなるのを感じ、きまり悪そうに顔を背けた ◇A patient with a fever may be very hot and *flushed*. 発熱している患者は体がとても熱く顔が赤い場合がある
▶**flush** [C, ふつう単数で] ◇There was an unhealthy *flush* across his thin face. 彼のやせこけた顔は健康とは言えないほど赤かった
blush [自] (恥ずかしくて)赤面する ◇She felt herself *blushing* scarlet at the thought. その考えに彼女は顔が真っ赤になるのを感じた ◇I *blush to think* (= feel embarrassed or ashamed to think) of how I behaved the last time we met. この前にお会いしたときの自分の振る舞いを考えると赤面します
▶**blush** [C] ◇She felt a warm *blush* rise to her cheeks. 彼女は頬が熱くて赤くなるのを感じた

ノート blushとflushの使い分け：blushは人が恥ずかしさを覚える場合にのみ用いられる。flushは他の状況でも用いられる。また、blushの主語は人でなければならない。×Her cheeks/face *blushed*.

glow [自] (運動後に[興奮して, 恥ずかしくて])ほてる、赤面する ◇glowはしばしば物事に対する肯定的な反応を表す。 ◆She *glowed* with pleasure at the compliment. 彼女はほめ言葉にうれしくなって顔を赤らめた
▶**glow** [単数で] ◇The fresh air had brought a healthy *glow* to her cheeks. 新鮮な空気が彼女の頬に健康的な赤みが差していた
colour《英》(米では**color**) [自] (進行形がまれ) (恥ずかしくて[怒って])赤面する ◇Everyone in the room stared at Gerry, and he *coloured* slightly. 部屋にいる者みんなが見つめたのでゲリーは少し赤面した ◇He grinned at Mary, who *coloured up* instantly. 彼がメアリーににこっと笑いかけると、彼女はすぐに赤面した
▶**colour**《英》(米では**color**) [U] ◇*Colour* flooded her face when she thought of what had happened. 起きたことを考えると、彼女は顔中真っ赤になった ◇His face was drained of *colour* (= he looked pale and ill). 彼の顔からは赤みが引いていた
burn [自] (きまり悪くて[恥ずかしくて])真っ赤になる、ほてる ◇Her cheeks *burned* with embarrassment. きまり悪くて彼女の両頬は真っ赤になった

focus [動]

focus・target・direct・be aimed at sb・turn・address・orient・pitch
特定の人や集団に注意を払う[メッセージを送る]
【類語訳】焦点を当てる、集中する、対象とする、目標とする、向ける、向けられる

文型&コロケーション

▶ to focus/ target/ turn sth **on** sb/ sth
▶ to target/ direct sth/ be aimed at/ pitch sth **at** sb/ sth
▶ to target/ direct/ orient sth **towards** sb/ sth
▶ to turn/ address/ orient sth **to** sb/ sth
▶ **efforts/ resources/ campaigns** are focused on/ targeted at/ directed at sb/ sth
▶ **attention** is focused on/ directed at/ turned to sb/ sth
▶ **research** is focused on/ directed at/ oriented towards sth
▶ sth is focused on/ targeted at a/ directed at/ an **group/ area**
▶ **primarily** focused on/ targeted at/ directed at/ aimed at/ addressed to/ oriented towards/ pitched at sb/ sth
▶ **particularly** focused on/ targeted at/ directed at/ aimed at/ oriented towards/ pitched at sb/ sth
▶ **specifically** focused on/ targeted at/ directed at/ aimed at/ addressed to/ oriented towards sb/ sth
▶ **principally** targeted at/ directed at/ addressed to/ oriented towards sb/ sth
▶ **directly** focused on/ targeted at/ aimed at/ addressed to/ pitched at sb/ sth
▶ **mainly/ clearly** focused on/ targeted at/ directed at/ aimed at sb/ sth

focus [自, 他] (注意・努力・時間などに関して特定の人・物事・状況に)焦点を当てる、集中する ◇The discussion *focused* on three main issues. 話し合いは3つの主要問題に焦点を当てた ◇Schools should not *focus* exclusively on exam results. 学校は試験の結果にばかり焦点を当ててはいけない ◇I was finding it hard to *focus* my mind properly. 私はまともに精神集中することは難しいと気づきかけていた ◇The visit helped to *focus* world attention *on* the plight of the refugees. その訪問は難民の窮状に世界の注目を集める助けとなった ◇Much recent concern has been *focused upon* sea level rises. 最近海面上昇に多くの関心が寄せられている ◇Where do you really wish to *focus* your time and energy? 時間とエネルギーを本当にどこに集中したいと思っているのか
target [他, しばしば受身で] (製品・サービスに関して特定の人の集団に)対象[目標]とする ◇The booklet is *targeted* at people approaching retirement. その小冊子は退職間近の人々を対象としている ◇We *target* our services towards specific groups of people. 私たちのサービスは特定の集団の人々に向けられている ◇This hospital is *targeted for* additional funding. このホテルは追加融資を目標にしている

direct [他]《前置詞と共に》(言動を特定の人・集団・状況・問題に)向ける ◇Was that remark *directed* at me? その言葉は私に向けられていたの ◇Most of his anger was *directed against* himself. 彼の怒りの矛先はほとんど自分自身に対してであった ◇There are three main issues we need to *direct* our attention to. 我々が注意を向けなければならない主要問題は3つある

be aimed at sb [フレーズ] (製品・サービス・発言が特定の人・集団に)向けられる ◇The book *is aimed at* very young children. その本は幼い子ども向けのものである ◇My criticism *wasn't aimed at* you. 私の批判はあなたに向けられたものではなかった

turn [他](特定の人・テーマ・状況に注意の)向きを変える ◇She looked at him, then *turned* her attention *back to* me. 彼女は彼を見てから再び私に注意を向けた ◇Don't *turn* your anger on the children. 怒りを子どもたちに向けてはいけません ◇His thoughts *turned* to his dead wife. 彼の思いは死んだ妻に向かった

address [他]《フォーマル》(特定の人に向かって)話す, 書く ◇I was surprised when he *addressed* me in English. 彼に英語で話しかけられて驚いた ◇Any questions should be *addressed* to your teacher. どんな質問でも先生に向けるべきです ◇The book is *addressed* to the general reader. その本は一般読者に向けて書かれている

orient [英でまた **orientate**] [他, ふつう受身で] (特定のテーマ・人・状況に対する関心・注意・努力を人・物事に)向けさせる; (特定の目的に人・物事を)適合させる ◇Our students are *oriented* towards science subjects. 本校の生徒は理科系の教科に対する志向が強い ◇We run a *commercially oriented* operation. 我々は営利志向の業務を行っている

pitch [他, しばしば受身で]《ややインフォーマル, 特にビジネス》(製品・サービスを特定の人の集団に)向ける ◇The new software is being *pitched* at banks. その新しいソフトウェアは銀行向けに売り出されている最中だ ◇Orange juice is being *pitched as* an athlete's drink. オレンジジュースは運動選手の飲料として売られている

follow [動]

1 follow・chase・hunt・pursue・stalk・tail・trail・track
特定の理由から人や動物の後を追う
【類語訳】付いて行く, 後をつける, 追いかける, 追跡する, 忍び寄る, ストーカー行為をする, 尾行する

〖文型&コロケーション〗
▸ to follow/ chase/ pursue sb/ sth **into** sth
▸ to follow/ chase/ pursue/ stalk/ tail/ trail/ track a **person**
▸ to follow/ chase/ hunt/ pursue/ stalk/ trail/ track an **animal**
▸ to chase/ hunt/ pursue/ stalk (its) **prey**
▸ to chase/ hunt/ pursue a **criminal**
▸ the **police** follow/ chase/ hunt/ pursue/ tail sb
▸ to follow/ pursue sb/ sth **closely**

follow [他, 自] (人・物の後を)付いて行く[来る], つける ◇*Follow* me, please. I'll show you the way. どうぞ私に付いて来てください. 道を教えましょう ◇I think we're being *followed*. 私たちはつけられていると思います ◇She walked in and we all *followed*. 彼女が中に入って行き, 私たちもみな後を付いて行った [反語] **lead** (TAKE 2)

chase [他, 自] (捕まえるために人・物を)追いかける, 追跡する ◇My dog likes *chasing* rabbits. うちの犬は兎を追いかけるのが好きです ◇The boys were *chasing each other* around the yard. 少年たちは庭の周りを追いかけっこしていた ◇They *chased after* the burglar but didn't catch him. 彼らは泥棒を追いかけたが, 捕まえられなかった
▸ **chase** [C] ◇a high-speed car *chase* 猛スピードでのカーチェイス ◇We lost him in the narrow streets and had to *give up the chase*. 私たちは細い通りで彼を見失い, 追跡をあきらめなければならなかった

hunt [自, 他] (食べるために[スポーツとして, 金もうけのために]野生の動物・鳥を)狩る ◇Lions sometimes *hunt* alone. ライオンは時として単独で狩りをする ◇The animals are *hunted for* their fur. その動物たちは毛皮を得るために狩られる ◇It is now illegal to *hunt* otters. 今やカワウソ狩りは違法である ◇They *hunt* (= chase and kill foxes as a sport, riding horses and using dogs) when they stay with friends in Ireland.《英》アイルランドでは友人同士泊まり込むときは狐狩りをします
▸ **hunt** [C]《しばしば複合語で》: a tiger/seal *hunt* 虎/アザラシ狩り
▸ **hunting** [名] [U] ◇traditional country pursuits like *hunting*, shooting and fishing 狩猟, 射撃, 釣りといった田舎の伝統的な楽しみ

pursue [フォーマル or 書き言葉] (捕まえたくて人・物を)追跡する ◇She drove away, *hotly pursued* by the photographers. 彼女はカメラマンに追い回され, 車で走り去った ◇Police *pursued* the car at high speed. 警察は猛スピードでその車を追跡した
▸ **pursuit** [名] [U] ◇We drove away with two police cars *in pursuit* (= following). 私たちは2台のパトカーに追跡されながら車で逃走した

stalk [他, 自] (殺す[捕まえる, 傷つける]ために動物・人に)忍び寄る;(長期にわたり違法に人を)つけ回す, ストーカー行為をする ◇The lion was *stalking* a zebra. ライオンが縞馬に忍び寄っていた ◇He *stalked* his victim as she walked home, and then attacked her. 彼は帰宅途中の彼女に狙いをつけて忍び寄り, それから彼女を襲った ◇He was arrested and accused of *stalking* the actor over a period of three years. 彼は, その俳優に対する3年にわたるストーカー行為で逮捕, 起訴された
▸ **stalking** [名] [U] ◇the deer *stalking* season 鹿の獲物を追いかける季節 ◇An undercover detective said '*Stalking* has become a problem that we must take seriously.' 潜入捜査官は「ストーカー行為は深刻に取り上げるべき問題となっている」と述べた

tail [他] (行き先[行為]を見るために人を)尾行する ◇A private detective had been *tailing* them for several weeks. 私立探偵が彼らを数週間尾行し続けていた

trail [他] (その場にいた痕跡を探して人・物の)跡をたどる, 追跡する ◇The police *trailed* Dale for years. 警察は何年もデールを追跡した ◇Sharks were *trailing* the ship. 鮫たちはその船の後を追っていた

track [他, 自] (残された痕跡[しるし, 情報]を追って人・物の)跡をたどる ◇The men earned their living *tracking* and shooting bears. 男たちは熊の足跡をたどって狩りをして生計を立てた

2 follow・result・arise・stem from sth・ensue
時間[順序]的に他の人や物事の後に続く
【類語訳】続いて起こる, 起こる, 生じる, 結果として起こる

〖文型&コロケーション〗
▸ to follow/ result/ arise/ stem/ ensue **from** sth

▶to follow/ result/ arise **out of** sth
▶sth follows/ results/ arises/ stems **from the fact that**...

follow [他, 自]《進行形なし》(時間[順序]的に他の人・物の)後に続く；(他の物事の結果として)続いて起こる ◇The first two classes are *followed* by a break of ten minutes. 最初の二つの授業の後10分間の休憩があります ◇A period of unrest *followed* the president's resignation. 大統領辞任後しばらく不安な状態が続いた ◇A detailed news report will *follow* shortly. すぐに詳細な報道があるでしょう ◇There *followed* a short silence. 短い沈黙が続いた ◇Our opening hours are **as follows**... 私どもの営業時間は次のとおりです… ◇A new proposal *followed on* from the discussions. 話し合いの後で新たな提案があった
result [自]《進行形なし》(最初に起きた物事の結果として)起きる ◇job losses *resulting* from changes in production 生産量の変化に起因する雇用喪失 ◇When water levels rise, flooding *results*. 水位が上がると洪水が起こる ☞ **resulting, resultant (RELATED)**
arise [自]《進行形なし》《ややフォーマル》(問題・質問・困難が特定の状況の結果として)起こる, 生じる ◇The current debate *arose* out of the concerns of parents. 目下の議論は両親の心配から生じた ◇Are there any **matters** *arising* from the minutes of the last meeting? この前の会議の議事録に起因する問題が何かありますか
stem from sth [句動]《-mm-》《進行形なし》(問題・困難が物事の結果として)起こる ◇Most people's insecurities *stem from* something that happened in their childhood. 人々の不安はたいてい子どもの頃に起きたことに起因する
ensue [自]《進行形なし》《ややフォーマル, 書き言葉》(けんか・混乱状態が他の出来事に)続いて[結果として]起こる ◇The riot police swooped in and chaos *ensued*. 機動隊が襲ってきて, 結果として混乱が起きた ☞ **ensuing (RELATED)**

3 follow・comply・obey・act on/upon sth・adhere to sth・abide by sth・observe・carry sth out・respect
忠告[指示, 規則]を受け入れて言われた[教えられた]とおりにする
【類語訳】従う, 応じる, 固執する, 守る

【文型&コロケーション】
▶to follow/ comply with/ obey/ adhere to/ abide by/ observe/ respect the **conventions/ rules/ regulations/ law**
▶to follow/ comply with/ obey/ abide by/ respect sb's **will/ wishes**
▶to follow/ comply with/ adhere to/ abide by/ carry out a **policy**
▶to follow/ obey/ act on/ carry out **instructions/ orders**
▶to follow/ act on/ carry out a **recommendation**
▶to comply with/ carry out/ respect an **obligation**
▶to follow/ obey/ adhere to/ observe/ carry out sth **faithfully**
▶to comply with/ adhere to/ observe/ carry out/ respect sth **fully**
▶to follow/ comply with/ adhere to/ abide by/ observe sth **strictly**

follow [他] (忠告・指示)に従う ◇I didn't really *follow* the recipe. すべてレシピどおりにはやらなかった ◇He has trouble *following* simple instructions. 彼は簡単な指示でもそのとおりにできない ❶*follow* はしばしば recipe, timetable, syllabus などの書面による指示に従うだけでなく, orders, commands に従うことを表す
comply [自]《ややフォーマル》(規則・法律)に従う ◇They refused to *comply with* the UN resolution. 彼らは国連決議に従うことを拒否した ◇What sanctions can they take against us if we fail to *comply*? 我々が従わなければ彼らは我々にどんな制裁を課すのだろうか ❶*comply* はふつう法律や外交情勢に関連する文脈で用いられる. 反意 **breach (BREAK 3)**
➤**compliance** [名][U] ◇to ensure full *compliance* with the law 法律の完全遵守を確実にする
obey [他, 自] (言われた[期待された]とおり)に従う, 応じる ◇He consistently refuses to *obey* rules. 彼は規則に従うことを一貫して拒んでいる ◇He had always *obeyed* his parents without question. 彼は両親にいつも言われるままに従ってきた ◇'Sit down!' Meekly, she *obeyed*. 「お座りなさい」彼女は素直に従った ❶*obey* は目的語に人 (例えば両親) や物事 (例えば規則) を取ることがある. *obey* はしばしば人々の間の力関係を強調する. 反意 **disobey (OPPOSE), break (BREAK 3),** ☞ **obedient (GOOD 7)**
'act on/upon sth [句動] (忠告・情報・感情)に従って行動する ◇*Acting on* information from a member of the public, the police raided the club. 警察は一般人からの情報を受けてそのクラブに踏み込んだ ◇Why didn't you *act on* her suggestion? なぜ彼女の忠告に従わなかったの ◇*Acting on* impulse, he picked up the phone and dialled her number. 彼は, 衝動の赴くままに受話器を取り, 彼女の電話番号をダイヤルした
ad'here to sth [句動]《フォーマル》(法律・規則・指示)に従う；(特定の信条[決まった方法])に固執する ◇For ten months he *adhered to* a strict no-fat low-salt diet. 彼は10か月間, 厳格な無脂肪・低塩ダイエットの指示に従った ◇She *adheres to* teaching methods she learned over 30 years ago. 彼女は自分が30年以上前に学んだ教授法に固執している
➤**adherence** [名][U] ◇strict *adherence* to the rules 規則の厳守
a'bide by sth [句動]《フォーマル》(法律・契約・決定)に従う ◇You'll have to *abide by* the rules of the club. あなたはクラブの規則に従わなければならないだろう ◇We will *abide by* their decision. 我々は彼らの決定に従います
observe [他]《フォーマル》(法律・契約・慣習)に従う ◇Will the rebels *observe* the ceasefire? 反乱軍は停戦に従うだろうか ◇We *observed* a two-minute silence for the victims of the bombing. 爆撃の犠牲者のために2分間の黙祷を捧げた
,carry sth 'out [句動] (頼まれていること)に応じる ◇He made it clear that they must *carry out* orders immediately. 彼は彼らが即座に命令に応じなければならないと表明した
respect [他] (法律・原則)を守る ◇The new leader has promised to *respect* the constitution. 新しい指導者は憲法を守ることを約束した ◇*respect* は, 規則を破っても罰せられることはないが, 原則として破らないことを期待される人についてしばしば用いられる. 反意 **violate (BREAK 3),** ☞ **respect (RESPECT [名])**

4 follow・imitate・emulate・follow suit・mimic・copy・follow in sb's footsteps・model yourself/sth on sb/sth

→follow

他人と同じ方法で振る舞う[事を行う]
【類語訳】従う、まねる、模倣する、模範とする、見習う、肩を並べる、手本とする、倣う

【文型&コロケーション】
- to follow/ imitate/ emulate/ copy a **style**
- to imitate/ mimic/ copy sb/ sth's **movements**
- to imitate/ mimic sb/ sth's **appearance**
- to follow/ mimic/ copy sb/ sth **exactly**
- to follow/ copy sb/ sth **faithfully/ slavishly**
- to imitate/ mimic sb/ sth **accurately**
- to mimic/ model sth/ yourself on sb/ sth **closely**

follow [他, 自] (人・物事を指針[指導者, 手本]として)従う; (他人を)まねる ◇They *followed* the teachings of Buddha. 彼らは仏陀の教えに従った ◇He always *followed* the latest fashions (= dressed in fashionable clothes). 彼はいつも最新ファッションを追っていた ◇I don't want you to ***follow my example*** and rush into marriage. 君には私のまねをして急いで結婚などしないでほしい ◇The movie *follows* the book faithfully. 映画は忠実にその本に倣っている ◇It wasn't in his nature to *follow* blindly. やみくもに従うのは彼の性に合わなかった ☞ **follower** (FAN)

imitate [他] 《ややフォーマル》 (他人を)模倣する, 模範とする ◇Her style of painting has been *imitated* by other artists. 彼女の絵画のスタイルは他の画家に模倣されてきた ◇Teachers provide a model for children to *imitate*. 教師は子どもたちの模範となる手本を提供する ◇No computer can *imitate* the complex functions of the human brain. 人間の脳の複雑な機能を模倣できるコンピューターなどありえない ❶ *imitate* の典型的な連語に crime, movements, sound, model, style, behaviour が挙げられる

▷**imitation** [名] [U] ◇A child learns to talk by *imitation*. 子どもは真似ることから話すことを覚える ◇Many corporate methods have been adopted by American managers ***in imitation of*** Japanese practice. 日本の慣例に倣って多くの企業手法がアメリカ人経営者によって導入されてきた

emulate [他] 《フォーマル》 (尊敬の念から他人の行いを)見習う, 肩を並べる ◇She hopes to *emulate* her sister's sporting achievements. 彼女はスポーツの実績で姉と肩を並べることを望んでいる

follow 'suit [句動] 《特にビジネス or ジャーナリズム》 (他人が行ったばかりの方法で)後に続く ◇The Bank of England has announced a 0.5% rise in interest rates, and other banks are expected to *follow suit*. イングランド銀行が0.5%の利上げを発表したが、他行も追随すると思われる

mimic (-ck-) [他] 《ややフォーマル or 専門用語》 (他人を)まねる, 擬態する ◇The robot was programmed to *mimic* a series of human movements. そのロボットは人間の一連の動きをまねるようにプログラムされた ◇Scientists have created a vaccine that *mimics* the virus. 科学者たちはそのウイルスに擬態するワクチンを作り出した

▷**mimicry** [名] [U] ◇Parrots specialize in vocal *mimicry*. オウムは声をまねることを得意とする

copy [他] (他人を)模倣する, 模範とする ◇She *copies* everything her sister does. 彼女は姉のすることすべてを模倣している ◇Their tactics have been *copied* by other terrorist organizations. 彼らの戦術は他のテロ組織にも模

food

された ❶ *copy* は一般的に, work, style, behaviour, ideas, actions, movements と結びつく

follow in sb's 'footsteps [句動] (同じ仕事[生活様式]を選んで家族と)同じ道を歩む ◇She works in television, *following in* her father's *footsteps*. 彼女は父親と同じ道を歩んでテレビの仕事に就いている

'model yourself/sth on sb/sth [句動詞] (-ll-, 米 -l-) 《書き言葉》 (好きな[尊敬する]人や物事の行動[スタイル]を)手本とする, ;(他の物事に)倣う ◇As a politician, he *modelled himself on* Churchill. 彼は政治家としてチャーチルを手本とした ◇The country's parliament is *modelled on* the British system. その国の議会は英国方式を模範としている

food [名]

food · meal · diet · foodstuff · refreshment · fare · nourishment

人々が食べる物
【類語訳】食べ物, 食糧, 食品, 料理, 食事, 食料品, 飲食物, 軽食, 栄養分

【文型&コロケーション】
- (a) **delicious** food/ meal/ fare
- (a) **staple** food/ diet/ foodstuff/ fare
- (a) **simple/ traditional/ vegetarian** food/ meal/ diet/ fare
- (a/ an) **English/ Chinese, etc.** food/ meal/ diet/ fare
- (an) **adequate** food/ meal/ diet/ nourishment
- (a) **healthy/ nourishing** food/ meal/ diet
- to **provide** food/ a meal/ a ... diet/ refreshment/ nourishment
- to **serve** food/ a meal/ ... fare
- to **eat** food/ a meal/ a... diet/ ...fare
- to **obtain** food/ a meal/ nourishment

food [U, C] (人・動物の)食べ物, 食糧; (特定の種類の)食品, 料理 ◇He obviously enjoys good *food*. 彼がおいしい物を食べているのは明らかだ ◇Gina had prepared *food and drink* for the work party. ジーナは作業班のために飲食物を用意してあげていた ◇Do you like Italian *food*? イタリア料理は好きですか ◇Could you buy a can of *dog food*? ドッグフードを一缶買っていただけますか ◇This street is full of *fast food* restaurants. この通りにはファストフード・レストランがあふれている ◇You shouldn't eat so much *junk food*. そんなにたくさんジャンクフードを食べてはいけない ◇The store specializes in *frozen foods*. その店は冷凍食品が専門である

meal [C] (人が席に着いて食べる)食事 ◇Enjoy your *meal*. 食事をお楽しみください ◇They gave us a three-course *meal*. 彼らは3品から成る食事を出してくれた

diet [C, U] (常食としている)食べ物, 食品 ◇It is important to have a healthy, balanced *diet*. 健康的でバランスの取れた物を食べることが大切です ◇I loved the Japanese *diet* of rice, vegetables and fish. 米、野菜、魚から成る日本食が大好きだった ◇For general advice on *diet*, see pages 26-27. 食品についての一般的なアドバイスについては、26-27ページを参照してください

foodstuff [C, ふつう複数で] 《フォーマル or 専門用語》 食糧, 食料品 ◇Rationing of basic *foodstuffs* was introduced. 基本的な食糧の配給制が導入された

refreshment [U] 《フォーマル》 飲食物, 軽食 ◇In York we had a short stop for *refreshment*. 私たちはヨークで

軽食を取るために少し休憩した
fare [U]《書き言葉，特にジャーナリズムで出される》料理 ◇The restaurant serves good traditional *fare*. そのレストランはおいしい伝統料理を出しています ❶ *fare* は日常会話で用いられる場合，古めかしく聞こえる．しかし，特にその食べ物が **simple, plain, traditional, staple, English, Scottish, local** である場合には，ジャーナリズムや広告において，レストランで提供される食べ物について今なお頻繁に用いられる．

nourishment [U]《フォーマル or 専門語》《生命[成長，健康]の維持に必要な食べ物の》栄養分 ◇Can plants obtain adequate *nourishment* from such poor soil? 植物はそんなやせた土地から十分な栄養を摂ることができるのですか ◇You need natural, fresh food with lots of *nourishment*. 栄養分の多い新鮮な自然食品が必要です

fool 名

fool・idiot・jerk・moron・bimbo・prat・dork
どうかしていると思われる人を表す
【類語訳】ばか，あほう，間抜け，愚か者，変な奴，ダサい奴

ノート これらの語はすべて，特に人に向かって直接 fool, idiot, jerk などと言う場合，侮蔑的となりうる．jerk, moron, bimbo は最も侮蔑的である．その他の語は時として，友人同士で親しみを込めて用いられることもある．

文型&コロケーション
▶ **like a/ an** fool/ idiot/ jerk/ bimbo/ prat
▶ **What a/ an** fool/ idiot/ jerk/ moron/ prat/ dork!
▶ **You** fool/ idiot/ jerk/ moron/ prat/ dork!
▶ a **complete** fool/ idiot/ jerk/ moron/ prat/ dork
▶ an **absolute** fool/ idiot/ moron/ prat/ dork
▶ a/ an **stupid/ utter** fool/ idiot/ jerk/ prat
▶ to **feel/ look like** a fool/ an idiot/ a jerk/ a moron/ a prat/ a dork
▶ to **act like** a fool/ an idiot/ a jerk/ a moron/ a prat
▶ to **call sb** sb a fool/ an idiot/ a jerk
▶ to **make** a fool/ an idiot/ a prat/ a dork **of yourself**

fool [C]《けなして，時に侮蔑的》《知性[的確な判断]に欠ける》ばか，あほう，間抜け，愚か者 ◇Don't be such a *fool*! そんなばかなはよせ ◇I felt like such a *fool* when I realized my mistake. 自分の間違いに気づいたときとんだばかだったと思えた ◇He told me he was an actor and I *was fool enough to* believe him. 彼は俳優だと名乗り，私は愚かにも彼を信じた ☞ **foolish** (CRAZY), **foolish** (RIDICULOUS)

idiot [C]《ややインフォーマル，けなして，時に侮蔑的》《非常に[気に障る]》ばか，あほう，間抜け ◇I just stood there like an *idiot* with my mouth open. 私は口を開けたままばかみたいにただそこに突っ立っていた ◇Not that switch, you *idiot*! そのスイッチじゃないだろ，ばか ◇What stupid *idiot* left their shoes on the stairs? 階段に靴を置き忘れるなんてどんな大ばか者なのだ ☞ **idiotic** (CRAZY)

jerk [C]《特に米，インフォーマル，けなして，侮蔑的》《男性・少年の》ばか，あほう，間抜け ◇He was acting like a complete *jerk*. 彼は完全なばかを演じていた ◇He silently swore at himself for being such a *jerk*. 彼は心の中で何てばかな奴なんだと自分を罵った

moron [C]《ややインフォーマル，けなして，侮蔑的》《尊敬に値しない》ばか，あほう，間抜け ◇Shut up, you *moron*! 黙れ，間

抜け野郎 ◇The people responsible for this are mindless *morons*. これに関与している連中は思慮のない能なしだ

bimbo 《複 **-os**》[C]《インフォーマル，けなして，侮蔑的》《若い女性で性的に魅力的だが，あまり知的でない》ばか，あほう，間抜け ◇He's going out with an empty-headed *bimbo* half his age. 彼は頭が空っぽで，自分の半分の年齢の娘と付き合っている

prat [C]《英，インフォーマル，けなして，時に侮蔑的》《非常に[厄介な]》ばか，あほう，間抜け ◇You look a right *prat* in that outfit. あんな服装じゃあ本当のばかに見えるよ ◇He got drunk and made a complete *prat* of himself. 彼は酔っ払ってまったくばかなまねをした

dork [C]《特に米，インフォーマル，けなして，時に侮蔑的》《妙な振る舞い[時代遅れの服装]による》変なダサい奴 ◇He's such a *dork*! あいつは何てダサいんだ ◇Oh no, what a *dork* I am! まったく，俺は何てイケてねえーんだ

forbidden 形

forbidden・banned・prohibited・taboo
物事が認可されていないことを表す
【類語訳】許されていない，禁じられた，禁止された，禁制の，禁断の

文型&コロケーション
▶ forbidden/ banned/ prohibited/ taboo **areas**
▶ forbidden/ banned/ prohibited **books**
▶ banned/ prohibited **substances/ weapons**
▶ forbidden/ prohibited **foods/ places**
▶ a forbidden/ taboo **subject**
▶ **officially/ specifically** forbidden/ banned/ prohibited
▶ **strictly** forbidden/ taboo
▶ forbidden/ banned/ prohibited **by law**

forbidden 許されていない，禁じられた ◇Smoking is strictly *forbidden* in the museum. 美術館では喫煙は厳禁だ ◇Entry to the room was *forbidden to* the children. その部屋への入室は子どもには許されていなかった ◇It is not *forbidden* to dream of a better world. よりよい世界を夢見ることは禁じられていない ☞ **forbid** (BAN 動)

banned 《公式に》禁止された；《罰として》禁止された ◇He belongs to one of the *banned* opposition parties. 彼は禁止された野党の一つに所属している ◇Traces of a *banned* pesticide were found in chocolate. チョコレート中に禁止農薬の痕跡が見つかった ◇The group included several athletes *banned* for using illegal substances. そのグループには違法薬物の使用で出場禁止となったスポーツ選手が数名含まれていた ☞ **ban** (BAN 動)

prohibited 《フォーマル》禁止された；《罰として》禁止された ◇The police searched the vehicle for stolen or *prohibited* articles. 警察は車を捜索して盗品や禁制品を探した ◇He was the leader of a *prohibited* right-wing organization. 彼は禁止された右翼団体の指導者だった ☞ **prohibit** (BAN 動)

taboo 《行動[発言，使用]が宗教・社会習慣によって》禁止された，禁制の，禁断の ◇The subject is still *taboo* in many families. その話題はいまだに多くの家庭でタブーとなっている ◇The guide includes a list of swear words and *taboo* words. 手引書には罵り言葉と忌み言葉のリストが載っている ☞ **taboo** (BAN 名)

force 名

force・strength・power・might
肉体上の強さ(の行使)を表す語
【類語訳】腕力, 体力, 暴力, 武力, 筋力, 勢力, 力

文型&コロケーション
▸ **physical** force/ strength/ power
▸ **brute** force/ strength
▸ to **use** force/ your strength/ your power/ your might

force [U] (暴力行為で用いられる)腕力, 体力 ; (物事の獲得[達成]のために用いられる)暴力, 武力 ◇We had to resort to *force* to get the door open. ドアを開けるために腕力に頼らなければならなかった ◇The police were accused of using excessive *force*. 警察は過剰な武力行使で告訴[非難]された ◇The rioters were taken away *by force*. 暴徒たちは力ずくで排除された ◇We achieve much more by persuasion than by brute *force*. (けなして)暴力より説得によるほうがずっと多くのことが達成される ☞ **force** (PUSH 1)

strength [U] 筋力 ; (肉体仕事[活動]に必要な)体力 ◇His superior physical *strength* won him the title. 彼はその並外れた体力でタイトルを勝ち取った ◇It may take a few weeks for you to build up your *strength* again. あなたが再び体力を取り戻すためには2,3週間かかるでしょう ◇She didn't have the *strength* to walk any further. 彼女はそれ以上歩く体力はなかった ☞ **strong** (STRONG 1), **strong** (WELL)

power [U] (活動に用いられる)体力 ; (人が持っている)体力 ◇He hit the ball with as much *power* as he could. 彼は持てる力でボールを打った ◇the sheer physical *power* of the man その男の真の体力 ☞ **powerful** (STRONG 1)

might 《フォーマル or 文語》(強大な)体力, 勢力, 力 ◇America's military *might* アメリカの軍事力 ◇He pushed against the rock *with all his might*. 彼は力一杯岩を押した

force 動

force・make・oblige・compel・drive・impel
したくない物事をしなければならない状況に人を置く
【類語訳】強制する, 強要する, 余儀なく…させる, …させる, 追いやる, 駆り立てる

文型&コロケーション
▸ to drive/ impel sb **to** sth
▸ to force sb/ be made/ be obliged/ compel sb/ drive sb/ impel sb **to do** sth
▸ to **feel** obliged/ compelled/ impelled to do sth

force [他, しばしば受身で] (人にしたくない事を)強制[強要]する, 余儀なく…させる ◇Ill health *forced him into* early retirement. 彼は健康が優れず早期引退に追い込まれた ◇I was *forced* to take a taxi because the last bus had left. 最終バスが出てしまったのでタクシーに乗らざるをえなかった ◇She *forced herself* to be polite to them. 彼女は無理して彼らに礼儀正しく接した ◇Public pressure managed to *force* a change in the government's position. 大衆の圧力によって, 政府は方針転換せざるをえない事態に追い込まれた ◇He didn't *force* me ― I wanted to go. 彼が強制したんじゃない―私が行きたかったんだ ☞ **force** (PRESSURE 2)

make [他] (意ız にかかわらず人に)…させる ◇They *made* me repeat the whole story. 彼らは私に話のすべてを繰り返させた ◇His snoring was so bad, she *made* him sleep on the sofa downstairs. 彼のいびきがとてもひどかったので, 彼女は彼を階下のソファで眠らせた ◇We were *made* to work very hard. 私たちは猛烈に働かされた

ノート force と make の使い分け: make のほうが少しインフォーマルで, 特に会話で用いられる. ふつう, 特に決然として命じる[言いつける]とき他人に何かをやらせることを表す. ◆Mum *makes* us eat lots of vegetables. (母親は私たちに野菜をたくさん食べさせます). force はしばしば人からの強い説得[脅し]を示唆したり, 何をすべきかについて選択の余地がない状況を表す. ◆The hijackers *forced* the passengers to lie on the ground. (ハイジャック犯たちは乗客たちを地面に伏せさせた). ◆The plane was *forced* to make an emergency landing because of bad weather. (飛行機は悪天候で緊急着陸を余儀なくされた). 受動態では, 両語とも後に to 不定詞を伴う. ◆to be *forced*/*made* **to do sth** (…せざるをえない, …させられる). しかし, 能動態におけるこの二つの動詞の用法の違いに注意すること. ◆to *force* sb *to do sth* (人に…するよう強制する). ◆to *make* sb *do sth* (人に…させる).

oblige [他, ふつう受身で] (to 不定詞を伴って)《ややフォーマル》(法律・義務などによって人に)…するよう強制する[義務づける] ◇Parents are *obliged by law* to send their children to school. 両親は子どもを学校へ送って行くよう法律で義務づけられている ◇Suppliers aren't *legally obliged to* provide a warranty. 供給業者は法律上の保証を義務づけられていない ❶ oblige は特に公式な文書で用いられ, 法律によって[責任として]人が物事を実行することを求められることを表す. ◆The landlord is *obliged* to give tenants 24 hours' notice of a visit. (大家は, 借家人に対し24時間前に訪問通知をするよう義務づけられている). 道徳上の[社会的な]義務を表すこともあるが, この文脈ではフォーマルである. ◆We felt *obliged* to sit with them. (彼らと一緒に座らなければ悪いと感じた). ☞ **obligation** (RESPONSIBILITY)

compel (-ll-) [他] 《フォーマル》(権力を行使して人に)…するよう強制する ; (物事を)強制[強要]する ◇The law can *compel* fathers to make regular payments for their children. 子どもに定期的な支払いをするよう法律で父親に強制できる ◇Last year ill health *compelled* his retirement. 昨年, 健康が優れず彼はやむなく引退した ☞ **compulsion** (PRESSURE 2)

drive [他] (極限まで人を)追いやる, 余儀なく…させる ◇The urge to survive *drove them on*. 生き延びたいという衝動が彼らを駆り立てた ◇It's the story of a teenager *driven to despair* by the hypocrisy of the adult world. それは大人の世界の偽善によって絶望に追いやられるティーンエイジャーの物語です

impel (-ll-) [他, しばしば受身で] 《フォーマル》(抑えがたい感情[考え]によって人を)駆り立てる, …せずにはいられなくする ◇He felt *impelled* to investigate further. 彼はもっと調査しなければならないと感じた ◇There are various reasons that *impel* me to that conclusion. 私をその結論に至らせるさまざまな理由がある

foreign 形

foreign・overseas・external・alien

物事が他の国々に関連することを表す
【類語訳】外国の, 外国との, 対外的な, 海外の, 外国からの, 異質の, 異種の, 外来の

文型&コロケーション
- a foreign/ an overseas/ an alien **country**
- foreign/ an overseas/ alien **territory**
- foreign/ overseas/ external **trade/ markets/ debt/ policy**
- a foreign/ an overseas **bank/ firm/ holiday/ tour/ trip**
- foreign/ overseas **demand/ visitors/ buyers/ investors**
- foreign/ external **affairs/ interference/ relations**
- a foreign/ an alien **culture/ language/ species/ system**

foreign 外国(から)の; 外国との, 対外的な ◇What *foreign* languages do you speak? どんな外国語を話せますか ◇Tourism is the country's biggest *foreign* currency earner. 観光はその国で最大の外貨の稼ぎであ る ◇You could tell she was *foreign* by the way she dressed. 彼女のことは服装から外国人だとわかるだろう ◇She was working as a *foreign* correspondent (= one who reports on foreign countries in the media). 彼女は外国特派員として働いていた [反意] **native** (CULTURAL), **domestic, home** (NATIONAL)

overseas [名詞の前で]《特にビジネス》海外の[に関する];(人が)外国からの, 外国で生活している ◇The *overseas* aid budget has been cut. 海外援助予算は削減された ◇The hotel is popular with *overseas* visitors to London. そのホテルはロンドンを訪れる外国人に人気がある [反意] **domestic, home** (NATIONAL)

▷ **overseas** 副 ◇He was working *overseas* for an oil company. 彼は石油会社で海外勤務していた

external [名詞の前で]《ビジネス or 政治》外国の[に関する], 対外的な ◇*External* trade increased last year. 昨年, 対外貿易が増加した ◇The country was promised military aid in the case of *external* threat. その国は対外的脅威が発生した場合の軍事援助を約束された [反意] **internal** (NATIONAL)

▷ **externally** 副 ◇*Externally* borrowed funds were used to stimulate economic growth. 外国からの借り入れ資金が経済成長を促進するのに使われた

alien 《しばしばけなして》(別の国[社会]に由来し)異質の, 異種の, 外来の;外国(から)の ◇His last years were spent alone and insecure in an *alien* land. 彼はその晩年を異国の地で独り心もとなく過ごした ◇Native woodland was destroyed and *alien* conifers were planted. 原生林地帯は破壊され, 外来種の針葉樹が植えられた [反意] **native** (CULTURAL)

> ノート **foreign** はこれらの語の中で最も頻繁に用いられ, 使用範囲も最も広範にわたる. **visitors, investors, buyers** など人々の集団を表す語に外国に暮らす本国人が含まれる場合, **overseas** が好まれる. ♦ In this constituency only 65 *overseas* voters registered in time to vote. (この選挙区では, わずか65人の海外有権者しか投票時に登録できなかった). **foreign voters** は本国ではない国に住む「外国人の有権者」を意味する. **overseas, external** はいずれも, 特にビジネスや政治の文脈で用いられる. これらは事実を表すだけで, **foreign** に時折含まれる「違い」「違和感」といったニュアンスはない. **alien** はより文語的な語で, 違いや違和感の意味合いを強く持ち, 否定的に[けなして]用いられることが多い. また, 外来の植物や動物についても用いられる.

forgive 動

forgive・pardon・condone・excuse
人の間違い[不品行]を受け入れる, 間違いを犯した[行儀の悪い行いをした]人に腹を立てるのをやめる
【類語訳】許す, 大目に見る

文型&コロケーション
- to forgive/ pardon/ condone/ excuse sb **for** sth
- to forgive/ condone/ excuse sb's **behaviour**
- Forgive/ Pardon/ Excuse **my ignorance**.

forgive [他]《特に話し言葉》(傷つけ[困らせ, 動揺させ]ようとした人を)許す;(自分を)許す ◇I'll never *forgive* her for what she did. 私は彼女のしたことを絶対に許さない ◇I can't *forgive* that type of behaviour. そういった類の振る舞いは許せません ◇She'd *forgive* him anything. 彼女なら彼のことは何でも許すだろう ◇I'd never ***forgive myself*** if she heard the truth from someone else. 彼女が真実を他人から聞いたりしたら, 私は自分を許せないでしょう ◇I know what he did was wrong but don't you think it's time to ***forgive and forget*** (= stop being angry with him about it and behave as if it had not happened). 彼のしたことが間違っているのはわかるが, 水に流してやる時じゃないか ❶ フォーマルな話し言葉では, 自分の言動が無礼[愚か]だと思える場合に, forgive を用いて丁寧に弁解することができる. ♦ *Forgive* my ignorance, but what exactly does the company do? (知らなかったのは申し訳ないが, それはいったい何の会社なの. ♦ *Forgive* me, but I don't see that any of this concerns me. (悪いけど, 私がこのどれにも関係があるとは思えないんだ).

pardon [他]《ややフォーマル, 話し言葉》(言動の無礼さ[愚かさ]を)許す(丁寧な謝罪に用いられる) ◇*Pardon* my ignorance, but what is a 'duplex'? ごめん, 知らないんだけど, 「duplex」って何 ◇The place was, ***if you'll pardon the expression***, a dump. あそこは, 言葉は悪いけど, ごみだめだったよ ◇*Pardon* me for interrupting you. お話中すみません

condone [他]《しばしば否定文で》《ややフォーマル》(道徳的に間違った振る舞いを)許す, 大目に見る ◇Terrorism can never be *condoned*. テロを決して許すことはできない ◇The college cannot *condone* any behaviour that involves illicit drugs. 大学は違法薬物に関わるどんな行為も大目に見ることができない ▽ **condone** は目的語に人を取ることができないことに注意. 目的語に取ることができるのは行動だけである. [反意] **condemn** (BLAME)

excuse [他]《特に米, 特に話し言葉》(無礼[小さな間違い]などを)許す(謝罪に用いられる) ◇Please *excuse* the mess. 散らかっていて申し訳ない ◇I hope you'll *excuse* me for being so late. こんなに遅れてほんとうにごめんね ◇You'll have to *excuse* my father — he's not always that rude. 父を許してやって—いつもあんなに無作法というわけじゃないの ☞ **excuse** (REASON)

formal 形

formal・staid・stuffy・stiff
非常にまじめに振る舞い, しばしば退屈な[古風な, 愛想がない, 張り詰めた]人のことを表す
【類語訳】堅苦しい, 正式用の, くそまじめな, 古臭い, よそよそしい

↪formal

former, fragile, fragment

文型&コロケーション
- formal/ stuffy **about** sth
- a formal/ stiff **manner**
- rather formal/ staid/ stuffy/ stiff
- a staid/ stuffy/ stiff **old** sb

formal 堅苦しい；正式用の ◇She has a very *formal* manner, which can seem unfriendly. 彼女は非常に態度が堅苦しく、無愛想に見えたりもする ◇He insisted on *formal* dress for dinner. 彼はディナーに正装して行くと言い張った ◇He kept the tone of the letter *formal* and businesslike. 彼の手紙の語調は堅苦しく事務的だった 反意 **informal**, **casual** (INFORMAL), ☞ **formality** (RESPECT 名)
➢ **formally** 副 ◇'How do you do?' she said *formally*. 「はじめまして」と彼女は改まって言った

staid (けなして) くそまじめな；古臭い ◇The museum is trying to get rid of its *staid* image. その美術館は古臭いイメージを取り除こうと努めている

stuffy (ややインフォーマル、けなして) くそまじめな、堅苦しい、古臭い ◇He reminded her of a *stuffy* old headmaster she had once had. 彼は彼女に昔の堅苦しい老校長を思い出させた

stiff (ふつうけなして) よそよそしい、堅苦しい ◇The speech he made to welcome them was *stiff* and formal. 彼らに対する彼の歓迎のスピーチはよそよそしく堅苦しかった 反意 **relaxed** (INFORMAL)

former 形

former • old • then • ex-
人や物事が過去に特定の身分[地位]にあったことを表す
【類語訳】元の、以前の、昔の、当時の

文型&コロケーション
- sb's former/ old/ then/ ex-**partner/ boyfriend/ girlfriend**
- sb's former/ then/ ex-**husband/ wife**
- sb's former/ old/ then **boss**
- a former/ an old/ an ex-**lover/ colleague/ member**
- a former/ an old **friend/ ally/ enemy**
- the former/ then/ ex-**president/ ambassador**
- a former/ an old/ an ex-**student**
- a former/ an ex-**communist/ king/ patient/ smoker**
- a former/ an old/ an ex-**colony**

former [名詞の前で] 《ややフォーマル》 元の ◇She's the *former* world champion. 彼女は元世界チャンピオンだ 反意 **current** (RECENT), **future** (NEXT)

old [名詞の前で] 以前の、昔の ◇We had more room in our *old* house. 私たちの以前の家にはもっと空間があった ◇I met up with some *old* school friends. 私は昔の学校の友達数人と約束して出会った 反意 **new** ❶ new は以前に会ったことない人[経験したことない物事]を指す。◆He's made a lot of *new* friends. (彼には新しい友達がたくさんできた)。◆When do you start your *new* job? (新しい仕事はいつ始めるの)。◆This is a *new* experience for me. (これは私にとって初体験です)。◆Our system is probably *new to* you. (我々のシステムはあなたはおそらく初めてでしょう)。

then [名詞の前で] 当時の ◇That decision was taken more than ten years ago by the *then* president. その決定は10年以上前に当時の大統領によってなされた 反意 **current** (RECENT)

ex- 連結形 元の ◇My *ex*-wife and I are not on speaking terms. 先妻とは口も利かない間柄だ 反意 **current** (RECENT), **future** (NEXT)

ノート **former** と **ex-** の使い分け：former は ex- よりも幅広い連語を持つ。×sb's *ex*-boss/friend/ally/enemy. ex- は former よりもインフォーマルで話し言葉で好まれる。

fragile 形

fragile • delicate • brittle
物が容易に壊れることを表す
【類語訳】壊れやすい、傷つきやすい、もろい、繊細な

文型&コロケーション
- fragile/ delicate/ brittle **bones/ glass**
- fragile/ delicate **china**
- a fragile/ delicate **thread**
- the fragile/ delicate **ecology**

fragile 壊れ[傷つき]やすい、もろい ◇Be careful not to drop it, it's very *fragile*. 落とさないように気を付けて、とても壊れやすいから ◇*fragile* habitats threatened by pollution 公害の脅威にさらされる脆弱な生息環境

delicate 繊細な、壊れ[傷つき]やすい、もろい ◇The eye is one of the most *delicate* organs of the body 眼は体の中で最も傷つきやすい器官の一つである ◇the *delicate* ecological balance of the rainforest (熱帯)雨林の崩れやすい生態学的バランス

ノート **fragile** と **delicate** の使い分け：ウールや絹などの delicate (繊細な) 生地には特別な手入れが必要です。◆cool wash for *delicate* fabrics (繊細な生地のための熱を加えない洗濯). fragile (もろい) 生地はふつう非常に古くなっているために、さらなる注意が必要である。◆What sort of cleaning method will avoid damaging these *fragile* old fabrics? (どんな洗濯方法なら、これらのもろい古生地を傷めずに済みますか).

brittle (触感・表面は硬いが) 壊れ[傷つき]やすい、もろい ◇Bones become more *brittle* with age. 骨は年齢と共にもろくなる ◇She had thin, *brittle*, permed hair. 彼女は細くて傷みやすいパーマのかかった髪をしていた ❶ brittle は bones, nails, hair, glass などの硬い素材について用いられる。折れやすい骨について、年齢や病気によるものには brittle, fragile を、小さく軽いものには delicate, fragile を用いる。

fragment 名 ☞ BIT, PIECE

fragment • flake • shard • splinter • chip • sliver • crumb • shred • shavings • filings
壊れた[より大きな物から切り取られた]物の小片を表す
【類語訳】破片、薄片、裂片、とげ、かけら、くず、小片、細片、削りくず、やすりくず

文型&コロケーション
- in fragments/ flakes/ shards/ slivers/ shreds
- (a) small fragments/ flakes/ shards/ splinters/ chip/ sliver
- (a) tiny fragments/ flakes/ shard/ sliver/ shreds
- (a) thin flakes/ splinters/ sliver/ shreds
- flying fragments/ shards
- glass/ metal fragments/ shards/ splinters
- wood chips/ shavings

▶a fragment/ shard/ splinter/ sliver of **glass**
▶a fragment/ shard of **pottery**

fragment [C]（ガラス・石・金属・陶器の）破片 ◇Police found *fragments* of glass near the scene. 警察は現場近くでガラスの破片を見つけた ◇The shattered vase lay in *fragments* on the floor. 砕けた花瓶の破片が床に散らばっていた

flake [C]（物質・材料の）薄片 ◇Large *flakes* of paint were peeling off the walls. ペンキの大きな薄片が壁から剥がれていた ◇As they neared home the first *flakes* of snow fell. 彼らが家に近づくと最初の雪片が落ちた

shard (または**sherd**) [C]《ややフォーマル, 書き言葉》(ガラス・金属・プラスチック・陶器の鋭い)破片 ◇The brickwork exploded in dust and flying *shards* of clay. 煉瓦造りの建物が爆発して土ぼこりや粘土の破片が舞い散った

splinter [C]（人の肉に刺さった木・ガラス・金属・骨・氷の細く鋭い）裂片, 破片, とげ ◇I've got a *splinter* in my finger (= a small piece of wood). 指にとげが刺さった ◇A small *splinter* of metal had lodged in his thumb. 小さな金属片が親指に刺さっていた ❶特に断りのない限り, splinterは木の裂片(とげ)を指す. 他の物質の破片の場合, a splinter of または a glass/metal splinter などの形で用いられる.

chip [C]（ガラス・陶磁器・木・歯の）かけら, くず ◇She had a slight *chip* off her front tooth. 彼女は前歯がほんの少し欠けていた ◇The gutted raw fish are smoked slowly over wood *chips*. はらわたを取り除いた生の魚が木くずの上でゆっくりいぶされるのだ ❶chipは欠け落ちた元の場所を表すために用いられることが多い. ◆This mug has a *chip* in it. (このマグは縁が欠けている)

sliver [C]（ガラス・氷・木・食べ物の）小片, 細片 ◇*Slivers* of glass crackled and crunched beneath her feet. ガラス片が彼女の足の下でバリバリ音を立てて割れた ◇Top each canapé with a *sliver* of cheese. カナッペにチーズのかけらを載せなさい

ノート **fragment** と **sliver** の使い分け: fragment はふつう粉々に砕けた物の一片. sliver も一片ではあるが, ある物から欠けた一片で, 元の物は部分を欠いただけでそのまま残っていることもある.

crumb [C]（パン・ケーキなどの食べ物の）かけら, くず ◇She stood up and brushed the *crumbs* from her sweater. 彼女は立ち上がって, セーターに付いた食べかすをブラシで払い落とした

shred [C, ふつう複数で]（生地・紙の）細片 ◇His jacket had been *torn to shreds* by the barbed wire. 彼のジャケットは有刺鉄線でぼろぼろに裂けていた ☞ **shred** (TEAR)

shavings [複数形で]（鋭利な道具を使って木片から切り離された）削りくず ◇His study smelled of dust, ink and pencil *shavings*. 彼の書斎はほこり, インク, 鉛筆の削りかすのにおいがした

filings [複数形で]（金属片にやすりをかけるときに出る）やすりくず ◇copper/iron *filings* 銅/鉄のやすりくず

fraud 名

1 fraud・deception・dishonesty・deceit
人をだます行為
【類語訳】詐欺, 欺瞞, 不正行為

文型&コロケーション
▶to **be guilty of/ accuse sb of** fraud/ deception/ dishonesty/ deceit
▶to **practise/ obtain sth by** fraud/ deception/ deceit
▶to **use/ admit/ confess to/ deny** fraud/ deception

fraud [U]《金品を得るために人をだます犯罪行為としての》詐欺 ◇She was charged with credit card *fraud*. 彼女はクレジットカード詐欺で起訴された ☞ **defraud** (DEFRAUD), **fraudulent** (CORRUPT)

deception [U]《ややフォーマル or 法律》(人に真実でないことを故意に信じ込ませる)欺瞞, 詐欺 ◇It's a drama full of lies and *deception*. それは嘘と欺瞞だらけのドラマだ ☞ **deceive** (CHEAT 動)

dishonesty [U]《ややフォーマル》（嘘をつく［盗む, だます］などの）不正行為 ◇Five civil servants were dismissed for *dishonesty* and misconduct. 5人の公務員が不正行為と職権濫用で解雇された 反義 **honesty** (INTEGRITY), ☞ **dishonest** (DISHONEST)

deceit [U]《ややフォーマル, 特に書き言葉》(人に真実でないことを故意に信じ込ませる)欺瞞, 詐欺 ◇He did not want to get drawn into this web of *deceit*. 彼はこんな詐欺の陰謀に巻き込まれたくなかった ☞ **deceitful** (DISHONEST)

ノート **deception** と **deceit** の使い分け: deception はしばしば法的文脈で用いられる. ◆She admitted two charges of *deception*. (彼女は2件の詐欺容疑を認めた). ×She admitted two charges of *deceit*. deception も小説や文学作品で用いられることがあるが, deceit ほど頻繁ではない. いずれも実際には人に嘘をつかずに真実でないことを信じ込ませる行為について用いられる.

2 fraud・game・scam・racket・con
不正な計画
【類語訳】詐欺, 策略, 計略, たくらみ, 信用詐欺, ぺてん, 不正な金もうけ

文型&コロケーション
▶a **$1 million** fraud/ scam/ racket
▶a/ an **insurance/ financial** fraud/ scam
▶to **operate/ run/ be involved in** a fraud/ scam/ racket
▶to **control** a fraud/ racket

fraud [C] 詐欺 ◇He helped prevent a $100 million *fraud*. 彼は1億ドルの詐欺を防ぐ手助けをした ☞ **defraud** (DEFRAUD)

game [C]《インフォーマル》策略, 計略 ◇So that's his *little game* (= now I know what he has been planning). なるほど, それは彼のちょっとした策略だな

scam [C]《インフォーマル》信用詐欺, ぺてん ◇She got involved in an insurance *scam*. 彼女は保険金詐欺に巻き込まれた

racket [C]《インフォーマル》(組織的な)不正な金もうけ ◇They believe that he was the victim of a protection *racket*. 彼はゆすりの犠牲者だと思われている

ノート **scam** と **racket** の使い分け: racket はふつう薬物売買や人を恐喝して金を巻き上げるといった, 不正行為のための金のやり取りを指す. ◆an extortion/protection *racket*（ゆすり/みかじめ料）. scam はふつう何らかの方法で組織的にだまして金を手に入れる行為を指す. ◆a gambling/insurance/credit card/VAT *scam*（ギャンブル/保険金/クレジットカード/付加価値税詐欺）.

con [単数で]《インフォーマル》信用詐欺, ぺてん ◇The so-called bargain was just a *con*! その取り引きというやつはぺてんにすぎなかった ◇It was all one big *con trick*. 《英》それはすべて一つの大きな信用詐欺だった ◇a *con game* 《米》信用詐欺 ◇He's a real *con artist* (= a person who regularly cheats others). 彼は本物のぺてん師だ ❶con は《英》の confidence trick または《米》の confidence game という語句の短縮形。☞ **con** (CHEAT 動)

free 動

free・let (sb/sth) go・cut・release・disengage・disentangle
人や物を捕らえることをやめる, 人や物を捕らわれている場所[位置]から移動させる
【類語訳】解放する, 救出する, 外す, 放す, 放たれる, 解放される, ほどく

▶ 文型&コロケーション
▶ to free/ cut/ release/ disengage/ disentangle sb/ sth from sth
▶ to free/ release/ disengage/ disentangle yourself from sth
▶ to free/ release a passenger
▶ to free/ let go of/ release/ disengage/ disentangle your/ sb's arm/ hand
▶ to let go of/ release a strap

free [他]《捕らわれている[留められている]人・物を》解放[救出]する, 外す ◇Three people were *freed* from the wreckage. 瓦礫から3名が救出された ◇He managed to *free* his arms from their bonds. 彼は何とか手かせから両腕を外した ◇A good kick finally *freed* the door. うまく蹴ってついにドアを開けた ◇Counselling may help you to *free* yourself from the past. 《比喩的》過去からあなた自身を解放するのにカウンセリングが役立つかもしれません ☞ **free** (RELEASE)
,let 'go, ,let sb/sth 'go [フレーズ]《しばしば命令で》《特に話し言葉》《自由に落ちる[動く]ことができるように人・物を》放す ◇Don't *let go of* the rope. ロープから手を放すな ◇*Let go*! You're hurting me! 放して. 痛いわ ◇*Let me go*! 私を放して ☞ **let sb go** (RELEASE)
cut [他]《拘束しているロープ・物体などを切断して人を》解放[救出]する ◇The injured driver had to be *cut* from the wreckage. 負傷した運転手を大破した車を切断して助け出さなければならなかった ◇Two survivors were *cut free* after being trapped for twenty minutes. 20分間閉じ込められた後, 2名の生存者が解放された
release [他]《ややフォーマル》《捕らわれている人・物を》解放[救出]する;《自由に動く[飛ぶ, 落ちる]ことができるように物を》放つ ◇Firefighters took two hours to *release* the driver from the wreckage. 消防士たちは残骸から運転手を救い出すのに2時間かかった ◇He refused to *release* her arm. 彼は彼女の腕を放すことを拒んだ ◇10,000 balloons were *released* at the ceremony. その儀式では1万個の風船が放たれた ◇Death *released* him from his suffering. 《比喩的》彼は死んで苦しみから解き放たれた ☞ **release** (RELEASE)
disengage [他, 自]《フォーマル》《人・物を》放す, 解放する;《人・物が》放たれる, 解放される ◇She gently *disengaged* herself from her sleeping son. 彼女は眠っている息子からそっと体を離した ◇We saw the booster rockets *disengage* and fall into the sea. 我々は打ち上げロケットが

離脱して海中に落ちるのを見た ◇They wished to *disengage* themselves from these policies. 《比喩的》彼らはこれらの方針から自由になりたかった ❶disengage は音を立てたり盛んに活動することなく, しばしば状況から gently (そっと) 自らを解放する場合に用いられる.
disentangle [他]《巻[絡]みついた物から人・物を》ほどく ◇He tried to *disentangle* his fingers from her hair. 彼は彼女の髪から指をほどこうとした

free 形

1 free・loose・at large
人や動物が管理されずに動き回ることができることを表す
【類語訳】自由の身の, 放された, 自由な, 野放しの, 逃げた, 捕まっていない

▶ 文型&コロケーション
▶ to set sb/ sth free/ loose
▶ to break/ get/ run free/ loose
▶ to remain free/ loose/ at large

free 《人が囚人[奴隷]ではなく》自由の身の;《動物がつながれていなくて[檻・かごの中にいなくて]》放された ◇He walked out of jail *a free man*. 彼は刑務所から自由の身になって出ていた ◇The protesters set the animals *free*. その抗議者たちは動物たちを解き放った ◇He subdues one of the wild horses and then allows it to *go free*. 彼は野生馬のうち1頭を服従させ, その後自由にしてやる ☞ **free** (RELEASE)
▶ **freedom** 名 [U] ◇He finally won his *freedom* after twenty years in jail. ついに彼は20年の刑務所暮らしのあと自由を勝ち取った
loose [名詞の前はまれ]《管理されずに》自由な, 野放しの;《つながれていなくて[閉じ込められていなくて]》放された, 逃げた ◇The sheep had got out and were *loose* on the road. 羊たちは逃げ出した後, 道路で野放し状態だった ◇The horse had broken *loose* (= escaped) from its tether. その馬はつなぎ縄から抜け出してしまった ◇During the night, somebody had cut the boat *loose* from its moorings. 夜の間に誰かがボートを係留ロープから切り離してしまった ☞ **let sb/sth loose** (RELEASE)
at 'large [形詞]《危険な人・動物が》捕まっていない, 野放しで; 逃亡中で, 自由で ◇Her killer is still *at large*. 彼女を殺害した人間はまだ捕まっていない

2 free・free of charge・complimentary・for nothing・on the house
物事が支払いなしでもらえる[手に入る]ことを表す
【類語訳】無料の, ただの, 優待の, ただで, 店のおごりで

▶ 文型&コロケーション
▶ a free/ complimentary ticket/ sample/ copy/ subscription
▶ to get sth free/ free of charge/ for nothing

free 無料の, ただの ◇Admission is *free*. 入場は無料だ ◇We're offering a fabulous *free gift* with each copy you buy. 1冊お買い上げごとにすてきな景品を差し上げます ◇There's a new website that offers *free* legal advice to homeowners. 住宅所有者に無料で法的アドバイスをする新しいウェブサイトがある ◇You can't expect people to work *for free* (= without payment). 人がただで

働いてくれると思ってはいけない
free of 'charge フレーズ (ビジネスにおいて)無料の ◇Delivery is *free of charge*. 配達は無料です
complimentary 《ややフォーマル》(ビジネスにおいて)無料の, 優待の ◇The hotel offers a *complimentary* breakfast and evening cocktails. そのホテルでは無料の朝食と夜のカクテルを提供している
for 'nothing 行れ《インフォーマル》ただで ◇We could have got in *for nothing* — nobody was collecting tickets. 入ろうと思えばただで入れただろう―誰もチケットをもぎっていなかったから ◇Don't expect somebody to give you a big salary *for nothing*! じっとしていりゃ誰かが高い給料をくれるだろうなんて期待するな
on the 'house 《ややインフォーマル》(バー・レストランにおいて飲食物が)店のおごり ◇Have a drink *on the house*. 店のおごりで1杯どうぞ

---

3 free・available・spare
人が特に予定[約束]がない, 人が忙しくない
【類語訳】空いている, 時間のある, 暇な, 応じられる, 自由な

文型&コロケーション
▶free/ available **for** sth
▶free/ available **to do** sth
▶free/ available **spare time**
▶a free/ spare **afternoon/ morning/ weekend/ moment**

free (人・時間が)空いている, 時間がある, 暇な; 応じられる ◇If Sarah is *free* for lunch I'll take her out. サラがランチの時間に空いているなら, ぼくが連れ出そう ◇Keep Friday night *free* for my party. 金曜の夜はぼくのパーティーのために空けておいてよ ☞ **free time** (LEISURE)
available 《ややフォーマル》(人が会見・話に)応じられる ◇The director was not *available* for comment. 監督はコメントに応じられない事情があった
spare (時間が)暇な, 自由な ◇I haven't had a *spare* moment this morning. 今朝は暇な時間がまるでなかった ☞ **spare time** (LEISURE)

freedom 名

freedom・independence・autonomy・liberty・leeway
他人の支配を受けず[助けを必要とせず]に物事[決定]を行う権利や能力
【類語訳】自由, 独立, 自立, 自主, 自治, 自由裁量

文型&コロケーション
▶freedom/ liberty/ leeway **to do sth**
▶**greater** freedom/ independence/ autonomy/ liberty/ leeway
▶**complete/ individual/ personal** freedom/ independence/ autonomy/ liberty
▶to **have** freedom/ independence/ autonomy/ liberty/ leeway
▶to **enjoy/ lose** freedom/ independence/ autonomy/ liberty
▶to **encourage/ promote** freedom/ independence/ autonomy
▶to **undermine** sb's freedom/ independence/ autonomy

freedom [U, C] (好きに言動を行える)自由 ◇Branch managers have considerable *freedom in* running their offices. 支店長には職場を切り盛りする上でのかなりの自由裁量がある ◇This case is about protecting our *freedom of speech*. この裁判は言論の自由を守ることに関するものである ◇The new syllabus allows students greater *freedom of choice*. 新しい要綱は学生により大きな選択の自由を与えている ◇The constitution contains guarantees of democratic *rights and freedoms*. 憲法には民主的な権利と自由の保障が含まれる ❶この意味ではfreedomはしばしばthe freedom of sthという言い回しで用いられる. ◆*freedom of* speech/thought/expression/worship/choice/action/movement (言論/思想/表現/信仰/選択/行動/運動の自由). freedom of information (情報の自由)とは国民や団体に関する機密情報を政府が知る権利を指す. freedom of association (結社の自由)は共通の目的のために集団を組織する権利を指す. press/academic freedom (報道/学問の自由)や freedom of the press (報道の自由)は真実である限り何でも著述, 出版できる権利を指す.
▶**free** 形 ◇I have no ambitions other than to have a happy life and be *free*. 楽しく暮らして束縛されないこと以外には何も望まない ◇Students have a *free choice* of classes in their final year. 学生たちは最終学年ではクラスを自由に選択できる ◇You are *free to* come and go as you please. 好きなように自由に行き来していいよ ◇A true democracy complete with *free speech* and a free press was called for. 言論と出版の自由を備えた真の民主主義が求められた

independence [U] 独立, 自立, 自主 ◇Some people have questioned the *independence* of the inspectors. 検査官の独立性に疑義を唱える人も出ている ◇Her work gave her a degree of financial *independence*. 彼女は仕事に就いてある程度経済的に自立した ◇The car became a symbol of *independence*. 車は自立の象徴となった 反意 **dependence** ❶dependenceは生き残る[成功する]ために人や物事の助け[支援]が必要な状態を指す. ◆his *dependence on* his parents (彼の両親への依存). ◆financial/economic *dependence* (財政的/経済的依存). ☞ independence (INDEPENDENCE)
▶**independent** 形 ◇It was important to me to be financially *independent*. 経済的に自立することが私には重要だった ☞ **independent** (CONFIDENT)

autonomy [U] 《フォーマル》自主(性), 自治(権), 独立 ◇Schools have gained greater *autonomy from* government control. 学校は政府統制下で今まで以上に大きな自治を獲得した ◇One of the aims of modern nursing is to encourage patient *autonomy*. 現代看護の目的の一つは患者に自主性を促すことである ❶autonomyはindependenceのフォーマルな表現. 特に公的な支配を受けない組織やさまざまな階級の人々について用いられる. 個人にはあまり用いられない. ✗She doesn't want to lose her hard-won *autonomy*. ☞ **autonomy** (INDEPENDENCE)
▶**autonomous** 形 ◇Teachers help children to become *autonomous* learners. 教師は子どもが自主的に学べるように手助けします

liberty [U] (政府・当局からの規制を受けない)自由 ◇The system allows us complete *liberty* to do the task as we like. 私たちはそのシステムによって好きなように仕事をする完全な自由を得る ◇The concept of individual *liberty* is enshrined in the constitution. 個人の自由の概念は憲法に正式に記されている

leeway [U] (物事を変える[好きなように行う])自由裁量(の余地) ◇How much *leeway* should parents give their children? 親は子どもに自由裁量の余地をどれくらい与えるべきか

freezing 形

freezing・icy・snowy・wintry・frozen・bitter・frosty
人や物が極度に冷たいことを表す
【類語訳】凍えるほど寒い、氷点下の、氷で覆われた、雪で覆われた、冬らしい、かじかんだ、凍結した、霜の降りた

文型&コロケーション
- freezing/ icy/ snowy/ wintry/ bitter/ frosty **weather**
- freezing/ icy/ snowy/ wintry/ frozen/ frosty **conditions**
- a freezing/ an icy/ a wintry/ a bitter **wind**
- freezing/ icy/ wintry/ frosty **air**
- a freezing/ an icy/ a snowy/ a wintry/ a frosty **day/ night/ morning**
- freezing/ icy/ bitter **cold**
- a freezing/ an icy/ a bitter **winter**
- freezing/ icy **water**
- an icy/ a snowy/ a wintry/ a frozen **landscape**
- I'm freezing/ frozen.
- It's freezing/ bitter **outside**.

freezing 凍えるほど寒い；氷点下の、着氷性の ◇It's absolutely *freezing* outside. 外はまったく凍えるほど寒い ◇I'm *freezing*! Close the window! 凍えそうだ。窓を閉めてくれ ◇Expect icy roads and *freezing* fog tonight. 今夜は道路の凍結と着氷性の霧があるものと思ってください 反意 **boiling** (HOT), ☞ **freeze** (COOL)
▶ **freezing** 副 ◇It was a *freezing* cold morning. 今朝は凍えるほど寒かった

icy 《特に書き言葉》(天気・大気・景色が)氷のように寒い[冷たい]；氷で覆われた ◇An *icy* blast (= of wind) hit them. 身を切るように冷たい突風が彼らを襲った ◇the *icy* wastes of the Russian Steppes ロシアの大草原の氷で覆われた荒野 ◇The car skidded on the *icy* road. 車は凍結した道路の上で滑った
▶ **icy** 副 ◇The water was *icy* cold. 水は氷のように冷たかった

snowy 雪で覆われた、雪の積もった；雪の多い、雪の降る ◇*snowy* fields/peaks 雪原/雪に覆われた峰々 ◇a *snowy* weekend 雪が降る週末 ◇The weather in January is often cold and *snowy*. 1月の天気はしばしば寒く雪が多い

wintry (天気・大気・景色が)冬の、冬らしい、冬に特有な ◇The weather will turn *wintry* over the next few days. 今後数日間は冬らしい天気になるでしょう ◇There will still be one or two *wintry* showers (= with snow or sleet) around. 冬特有のみぞれや雪が一、二度あるでしょう ◇She gazed out at the *wintry* landscape (= with frost and snow). 彼女はその冬景色を見つめた

ノート **icy** と **wintry** の使い分け：**icy** は単に「極度に寒い[冷たい]」ことを意味し、特に文学作品において、風について用いられる。**wintry** は寒さ[冷たさ]だけでなく雪や霜を想起させ、文学作品だけでなくテレビ・ラジオの天気予報の解説でもよく用いられる。

frozen (人・体の部位が)かじかんだ、凍るほど冷たい；(川・湖・景色が)凍結[氷結]した ◇My hands are *frozen*. 両手がかじかんでいる ◇The surface of the lake is permanently *frozen*. その湖面は常に凍結している ◇You look *frozen stiff*. 君は寒さでコチコチのようだね ☞ **freeze** (COOL)

bitter 《けなして》(天気が)肌を刺す[身を切る]ように寒い ◇They had no protection against the *bitter* cold. 彼らには身を切るような寒さから身を守る物はなかった ◇It's really *bitter* out today. 今日は外は本当に肌を刺すように寒い

frosty (天気が)霜の降りるほど寒い；霜で覆われた、霜の降りた ◇It was a bright, *frosty* day. 霜の降りるほど寒く晴れた日だった ◇I looked out over the *frosty* fields. 私は霜に覆われた野原を見渡した
▶ **frost** 名 [U, C] ◇It will be a clear night with some ground *frost*. 地面に霜が降りる快晴の夜となるでしょう ◇a sharp/hard/severe *frost* 霜の降りる厳しい寒さ

frequent 形

frequent・constant・regular・persistent・perpetual・continual・continuous・habitual
物事がしょっちゅう起こる[行われる]ことを表す
【類語訳】頻繁な、たびたび起こる、習慣的に行われる、しつこく繰り返される、たびたび繰り返される、継続的な、常習的な

frequent	persistent	constant
regular		perpetual
habitual		continual
		continuous

文型&コロケーション
- frequent/ constant/ regular/ persistent/ continual/ continuous/ habitual **use**
- frequent/ constant/ regular/ continual/ continuous **attacks**
- frequent/ constant/ regular/ continual/ continuous **changes**
- a frequent/ constant/ persistent/ perpetual/ continual/ continuous **problem**
- frequent/ constant/ perpetual **interruptions**
- a frequent/ constant/ regular **visitor**
- a frequent/ constant/ perpetual/ continual/ continuous **source** of sth
- frequent/ constant/ regular/ persistent **reports/ complaints**

frequent 頻繁な、たびたび起こる[行う] ◇There is a *frequent* bus service into town. 町へのバスの便は頻繁にある ◇Power failures are *frequent* occurrences in the city. その町では停電が頻発している ◇His calls became less *frequent*. 彼からの電話はあまり頻繁でなくなった ◇The case was reviewed *at frequent intervals*. その事件はたびたび再審理された ◇He was a *frequent* guest at the palace. 彼は宮殿にたびたび招かれる賓客だった 反意 **infrequent** (RARE), **occasional** (OCCASIONAL), ☞ **frequently** (OFTEN)

constant [ふつう名詞の前で] 四六時中[ひっきりなしに]起こる[行う] ◇He is very ill and needs *constant* attention. 彼は非常に具合が悪く、付きっきりの看病が必要だ ◇Her *constant* chatter was beginning to annoy him. 彼女のひっきりなしのおしゃべりは彼を悩ませ始めていた ◇Her daughter is a *constant* source of worry to her. 娘は彼女にとって常に悩みの種だ
▶ **constantly** 副 ◇How can I finish if I am *constantly* interrupted? しょっちゅう話の腰を折られたら、どうやって話し終えたらいいの

friend

regular 習慣的に[たびたび]行われる[起こる, 行う] ◇In the 1950s he made *regular* appearances on Broadway. 1950年代に彼はブロードウェーの舞台にたびたび出ていた ◇Eat a healthy diet and take *regular* exercise. 健康的な食事をして運動する習慣を身に付けましょう ◇He became a *regular* visitor to Hamilton Road. 彼はハミルトン通りをたびたび訪れるようになった 反意 **irregular** (VARIABLE), **occasional** (OCCASIONAL), ☞ **regular** (STEADY)

▶**regularly** 副 ◇She *regularly* wins prizes for her designs. 彼女はそのデザインで何度も賞を受けている

ノート **frequent** と **regular** の使い分け：frequent のほうがこの意味では一般的であるが, regular は人々が積極的に物事に取り組む場合に用いられることが多い. ×Take *frequent* exercise. regular はまた「決まった間隔で起こる」ことを指し,「頻繁に起こる」ことを指す場合とあいまいになることがある. 例えば, a regular bus service は「頻繁なバス便」も「毎日[毎時]同じ時間にくるバス」も意味する.

persistent (迷惑なほど)しつこく[何度も]繰り返される, 継続的な ◇The most common symptom is a *persistent* cough. 最も一般的な症状はしつこい咳である ◇He resigned over *persistent* rumours of his part in the scandal. 彼はそのスキャンダルに関わっているとの執拗な噂で辞任した

▶**persistently** 副 ◇a prison for juveniles who *persistently* reoffend 何度も再犯を犯す年少者のための刑務所

perpetual [ふつう名詞の前で]《特に書き言葉》(迷惑なほど)ひっきりなしに繰り返される, 継続的な ◇The *perpetual* interruptions made conversation difficult. ひっきりなしに邪魔が入って会話が難しかった ◇Lack of time is a *perpetual* problem for nurses on the ward. 時間不足が病棟における看護師にとっての永久の課題である

continual [名詞の前で] (迷惑なほど)たびたび繰り返される, 継続的な ◇There were *continual* arguments because he felt he was being treated unfairly. 彼は自分が不当な待遇を受けていると感じていたので, たびたび議論を呼び起こした ◇He seemed to need *continual* reassurance. 彼には継続的に元気づけてやる必要がありそうだった

▶**continually** 副 ◇People were *continually* tripping over the cable. 人々は相も変わらずそのケーブルにつまずいていた

continuous (迷惑なほど)たびたび繰り返される, 継続的な ◇The soldiers suffered *continuous* attacks for four days. 兵士たちは4日間絶え間なく攻撃を受けた ◇The company said the reasons for closure were poor margins and *continuous* losses. 閉店の理由は利益(率)の縮小と継続的な損失にあると会社は述べた

ノート **persistent, perpetual, continual, continuous** の使い分け：場合によって, どの語も使用可能. ・a *persistent/perpetual/continual/continuous* problem (継続的な問題). persistent は健康[社会]問題に関する事実に基づく著述や報告で用いられることが多い. perpetual は人を悩ます個人的な癖[問題]に関する私的な著述や創作で用いられることが多い. continual と continuous は一般的な意味ではあまり区別なく用いられ, しばしば話し言葉では類似の文脈で好まれる. これらの単語すべてに「間断なく長い間続く」という意味もあり, continuous はこの意味で用いられることが多く,「何度も繰り返される」の意味で用いるべきではないとする人もいる. ☞ CONTINUOUS

habitual (行動が迷惑なほど)習慣[常習]的な ◇The mechanic had been dismissed for *habitual* lateness. その機械工は遅刻の常習で解雇されてしまった ☞ **habit** (HABIT), **habitually** (OFTEN)

friend 名 ☞ PARTNER 1

friend・companion・mate・buddy・pal・acquaintance・the girls・confidant・the boys・crony

よく知っていて一緒に楽しく時を過ごす人

【類語訳】友達, 友人, 仲間, 連れ, 相棒, 伴侶, 知人, 知り合い, 顔見知り, 女友達, 親友

文型&コロケーション
- a friend/ mate/ buddy/ pal **of mine/ yours/ his/ hers/ ours/ theirs/ my mother's/ Diana's**, etc.
- an **old** friend/ mate/ buddy/ pal/ acquaintance
- a/ sb's **close** friend/ companion/ pal/ acquaintance
- a/ sb's **good** friend/ companion/ mate/ buddy/ pal
- a/ sb's **loyal** friend/ companion/ mate/ pal
- sb's **best** friend/ mate/ buddy/ pal
- a **real/ true** friend/ mate/ pal
- a **drinking** companion/ buddy/ pal
- to **become** friends/ mates/ buddies/ pals
- to **have** friends/ mates/ buddies/ pals/ acquaintances
- a **night out with** the girls/ boys
- sb's **friend and** companion/ confidant

friend [C] (家族以外の)友達, 友人 ◇This is my *friend* Tom. こちらは友達のトムです ◇Is he a *friend* of yours? 彼はあなたの友達ですか ◇She's an old *friend* (= I have known her a long time). 彼女とは長年の付き合いです ◇He's one of my best *friends*. 彼は親友の一人です ◇I heard about it through *a friend of a friend*. 友人の友人を介してそのことを聞きました ◇She has a wide *circle of friends*. 彼女には友人が多い ◇He finds it difficult to *make friends*. 彼は友達を作るのは難しいと実感している ◇a childhood/family/lifelong *friend* 幼なじみ/家族ぐるみの友人/生涯の友 ☞ **friendship** (FRIENDSHIP)

companion [C] (気の合う)仲間, 友；(旅(多くの時間)を共にする)連れ, 相棒, 伴侶 ◇His younger brother is not much of a *companion* for him. 彼の弟は彼とはあまり気が合わない ◇He was an entertaining travelling *companion*. 彼は愉快な旅の連れだった ◇Jeff was my *companion* on the journey. ジェフは私にとってその旅の相棒だった ☞ **companionship** (FRIENDSHIP)

mate [C]《英, インフォーマル》友達, 友人 ◇They've been best *mates* ever since they were at school together. 彼らは学校で一緒になって以来ずっと親友だ ◇I was with a *mate*. 私は友達と一緒だった

buddy [C]《米, インフォーマル》友達, 友人 ◇I'd like you to meet an old college *buddy* of mine. ぼくの大学時代の旧友に会ってほしいんだ ◇Howard and Mick were drinking *buddies* (= they went out drinking together). ハワードとミックは飲み友達だった

pal [C]《インフォーマル, 古風》友達, 友人 ◇We've been *pals* for years. 私たちは長年の友人です ◇Thanks — you're a real *pal*. ありがとう — 君はぼくの本当の友達だ

ノート **mate, buddy, pal** の使い分け：mate は《英》でインフォーマルに用いられ, buddy は《米》でインフォーマルに用いられる. これらは両語とも男性による他の男性へのインフォー

マルな親しみを込めた呼びかけとしても用いられる。◆Sorry *mate*, you'll have to wait. (やあごめんね、待たせることになるけど). ◆'Where to, *buddy*?' the driver asked. (「どこへ行きましょうか、お客さん」と運転手は尋ねた). palは《英》《米》の両方で用いられるが、呼びかけとして用いられる以外は現在では古風である。しかし、呼びかけとして用いられても、好意的ではない。◆If I were you, *pal*, I'd stay away from her! (俺があんただったら、よう兄ちゃん、彼女相手は出さないね).

acquaintance [C] （親密な友人ではなく）知人、知り合い、顔見知り ◇Claire has a wide circle of *friends and acquaintances*. クレアには多くの友人や知人がいる ◇I don't know him socially, he's just a business *acquaintance*. 彼のことは付き合い程度にしか知らない、仕事上の知人ってだけさ ◇I bumped into an old *acquaintance* on the train. 私は列車で昔の知り合いにばったり出会った ☞**acquaintance** (FRIENDSHIP), make sb's acquaintance (MEET 3)

the girls [複数で]（女性にとっての）女友達 ◇I'm having a night out with *the girls*. 夜、女友達と出かけるの

confidant [C] （私事[秘め事]について話せる信頼のおける）親友、腹心の友 ◇He was a trusted *confidant* of the President. 彼は大統領が信頼する腹心の友だった ❶ confidantは男性にも女性にも用いられる。女性の場合はconfidanteと綴ることもある。両語とも用法、発音共に同じ。

the boys [複数で]《インフォーマル》(よく一緒に出かける)男友達の仲間 ◇Are you free tomorrow? How about a night out with *the boys*? 明日空いてるかい。夜、男連中で出かけるのはどう

crony [C、ふつう複数で]《しばしばけなして》(多くの時間を一緒に過ごす)仲間 ◇He was playing cards with his *cronies*. 彼は仲間たちとトランプをしていた ❶ cronyは自分の友人ではなく他人の友人をけなして[おもしろおかしく]言うときに用いられる。

friendly 形

1 ☞ NICE 2
friendly・warm・pleasant・welcoming・amiable・good-natured・genial・hospitable・approachable
人が他人に対して思いやりを持って心地よく振る舞うことを表す
【類語訳】親切な、気さくな、感じのよい、愛想のよい、気立てのよい、温厚な、穏やかな、親しみやすい

▸文型&コロケーション
▸ friendly/ pleasant/ welcoming/ hospitable **to** sb
▸ a friendly/ a warm/ a pleasant/ an amiable/ a good-natured/ a genial/ a hospitable/ an approachable **person**
▸ a welcoming/ genial/ hospitable **host/ hostess**
▸ a friendly/ a warm/ a pleasant/ a welcoming/ an amiable/ a genial/ a hospitable **manner**
▸ a friendly/ warm/ pleasant/ welcoming/ good-natured/ genial **smile**
▸ a friendly/ a pleasant/ an amiable/ a genial **tone**
▸ a friendly/ an amiable/ a genial **mood**

friendly （好意を持って）親切な；気さくな ◇Everyone was exceptionally *friendly towards* me. 誰もが私に対してことのほか親切にした ◇John gave me a *friendly* smile. ジョンは私に気さくにほほ笑んだ 反意 **unfriendly** (COLD 2)

warm （愛情[熱意]を持って）温かい、心からの、熱烈な ◇Please send her my *warmest* congratulations. 彼女に私の心からの祝福を伝えてください ◇His comments were greeted with *warm* applause. 彼の発言は温かい拍手をもって迎えられた 反意 **cold, cool** (COLD 2)
▸**warmly** 副 ◇He kissed her *warmly* on both cheeks. 彼は彼女の両頬に愛情を込めてキスした
▸**warmth** 名 [U] ◇Her *warmth* and kindness made her universally liked. 彼女はその温かさと親切さから万人に好かれた

pleasant 《ややフォーマル》(気さくで礼儀正しくて)感じ[愛想]のよい ◇He seemed a very *pleasant* young man. 彼はとても感じのよい若者に見えた ◇Please try to be *pleasant* to our guests. お客様には愛想よく努めてね 反意 **unpleasant** (MEAN 形)
▸**pleasantly** 副 ◇'Can I help you?' he asked *pleasantly*. 「どうされましたか」と彼は愛想よく尋ねた

welcoming （客を）歓迎して；（訪問者に）温かい、気さくな ◇He found the locals extremely *welcoming*. 彼は地元民がとても歓迎していることに気づいた 反意 **unwelcoming** ❶ unwelcomingは訪れる[到着する]人に対して人が好意的でないことを表す。◆The locals were distinctly *unwelcoming*. （地元民が歓迎していないのは明らかだった）. ☞ **welcome** (GREET)

amiable 《ややフォーマル、書き言葉》(気さくで人なつっこくて)感じ[愛想]のよい ◇Her parents seemed very *amiable*. 彼女の両親はとても感じよく見えた ◇He uses an *amiable* tone of voice to soothe stressed clients. 彼はストレスがたまっている依頼人を落ち着かせるために愛想よく語りかける

good-'natured （人の扱いに際して）気立てのよい、温厚、穏やかな ◇Anthony is so *good-natured* — he finds it difficult to hate anyone. アンソニーはとても温厚だ―彼は誰をも憎めないと思っている ◇The discussion was *good-natured* and positive. 話し合いはスムーズで前向きだった

genial 《書き言葉》(気さくで朗らかで)感じ[愛想]のよい、にこやかな ◇Graham was a *genial* and modest host. グレアムはにこやかで控え目な主人だった

hospitable 《ややフォーマル》(客を)歓迎して；(訪問者に)温かい、気さくな ◇The local people are very *hospitable* to strangers. 地元の人々はとても温かく見知らぬ人を受け入れる ❶ hospitableはwelcomingほど頻繁に用いられず、よりフォーマルな語。

approachable (気さくで話しかけやすくて)近づき[親しみ]やすい；理解しやすい ◇Despite being a big star, she's very *approachable*. 彼女は大スターにもかかわらず、とても親しみやすい ◇It's quite an *approachable* piece of music. 実に親しみやすい曲だ 反意 **unapproachable** ❶ unapproachableは人がよそよそしくて話しかけにくいことを表す。◆Librarians have a reputation for being difficult and *unapproachable*. (司書たちは気難しく近寄りがたいという定評がある).

2 friendly・cordial・amicable・easy
感じがよく礼儀正しくて、攻撃的でない[口論の少ない]関係[雰囲気]を表す
【類語訳】仲のよい、和やかな、友好的な、気さくな、気の置けない、気楽な、くつろいだ、打ち解けた

▸文型&コロケーション
▸ a friendly/ a cordial/ an amicable/ an easy **relationship**
▸ friendly/ cordial/ amicable/ easy **relations**

friendship

- a friendly/ a cordial/ an amicable **meeting**
- a friendly/ cordial **atmosphere**
- to be **on** friendly/ cordial/ amicable/ easy **terms** (with sb)

friendly 仲のよい、和やかな、親しみを込めた;(国家間の関係が)友好的な、親善の ◇The boss had a *friendly* chat with me about the problem after work. 上司は仕事の後、その問題について私と親しげに話してくれた ◇We soon became *friendly* with the couple next door. 私たちはすぐに隣のカップルと仲よくなった ◇We were not on the *friendliest* of terms (= we were not friendly at all). 私たちは実に仲が悪かった ◇The government has maintained *friendly* relations with the Japanese. 政府は日本人との友好関係を維持してきた 反意 **hostile** (AGGRESSIVE 1)

cordial 《フォーマル》(関係・会議・雰囲気が)和気あいあいの、誠心誠意の ◇The talks took place in a *cordial* atmosphere. 会談は和気あいあいの雰囲気で行われた

amicable (関係・合意に至る形が)友好[平和]的な ◇The government and the union managed to reach an *amicable* settlement of the dispute. 政府と(労働)組合は何とか友好的に論争の解決を見た ◇It was an *amicable* divorce. それは協議離婚だった

easy 〖名詞の前で〗(人の態度・関係が)気さくな、気の置けない、気楽な;くつろいだ、打ち解けた ◇He had a very *easy* manner. 彼の態度はとても気さくだった ◇Their success at the game did not make for an *easy* relationship off court. 試合が終わっても彼らにはコートを離れて打ち解けた関係は生まれなかった

friendship 名

friendship・intimacy・acquaintance・companionship・camaraderie・fellowship・closeness・togetherness・comradeship
人との近親感[親しい状態]を表す
【類語訳】交友関係、交際、友情、親交、親善、親睦、親密さ、仲間意識、連帯感、仲のよさ、一体感

acquaintance	friendship companionship camaraderie fellowship togetherness comradeship	intimacy closeness

〖文型&コロケーション〗
- friendship/ intimacy/ acquaintance/ companionship/ camaraderie/ fellowship/ closeness/ comradeship **with** sb
- the friendship/ intimacy/ companionship/ camaraderie/ fellowship/ closeness/ comradeship **between** A and B
- **close** friendship/ intimacy/ companionship/ camaraderie/ fellowship
- **great** friendship/ intimacy/ camaraderie/ fellowship
- **real** friendship/ intimacy/ togetherness/ comradeship
- **true** friendship/ intimacy/ camaraderie/ fellowship
- to **make** a friendship/ sb's acquaintance
- to **develop** a friendship/ an intimacy/ a camaraderie/ a closeness
- to **offer** friendship/ companionship/ fellowship/ closeness
- friendship/ intimacy/ camaraderie/ closeness/ comrade-

ship **develops**
- a **feeling of** friendship/ intimacy/ companionship/ camaraderie/ togetherness/ comradeship

friendship [C, U] 交友関係、交際;友情、親交、親善、親睦、親しい状態 ◇Theirs was a lifelong *friendship*. 彼らの友情は生涯にわたるものだった ◇He had already **struck up** (= begun) *a friendship* with Jo. 彼はすでにジョーと親しくなり始めていた ◇Your *friendship* is very important to me. 君の友情は私にはとても大切だ ◇a conference to promote international *friendship* 国際親善推進会議 ☞ **friend** (FRIEND)

intimacy [U, 単数で] 親交、親密さ ◇The old *intimacy* between them had gone for ever. 彼らの間にあった親密さは永遠になくなってしまった ◇I sensed a close *intimacy* between them. 彼らの間にはかなりの親密さがあるのを感じた

▸ **intimate** 形 ◇*intimate* friends 親友 ◇We're not *on intimate terms with* our neighbours. 私たちは近所の人たちと親しい間柄ではない

〖ノート〗**friendship** と **intimacy** の使い分け: friendship が圧倒的に頻繁に用いられる一般的な語。intimacy はより強い意味を持ち、例えば恋人同士[夫婦など]、非常に親しい友人同士の関係[恋愛で結ばれた人々の関係]について用いられる。

acquaintance [U, C] 《フォーマル》知り合いであること、面識;(少しばかりの)交際、付き合い ◇I'm delighted to **make your acquaintance**, Mrs Baker. お知り合いになれて光栄です、ベイカー夫人 ◇No one else *of my acquaintance* was as rich and successful. 私の知人でそれほど裕福で成功した人はほかにいなかった ◇He hoped their *acquaintance* would develop further. 彼は自分たちの交際がさらに発展することを望んでいた ☞ **acquaintance** (FRIEND), **make sb's acquaintance** (MEET 3)

companionship [U] 《ややフォーマル》親交、親睦、交友 ◇They meet at the club for *companionship* and advice. 彼らは親交とアドバイスを求めてクラブで会うのです ◇She has only her cat for *companionship*. 彼女が親しく付き合えるのは飼い猫だけだ ☞ **companion** (FRIEND)

camaraderie [U] 《特に書き言葉》(一緒に働く[多くの時間を過ごす]人々の間の)仲間[同志]意識、友情 ◇the wartime spirit of *camaraderie* 戦時中の仲間意識

fellowship [U] 《ややフォーマル》(一緒に物事を行う[興味を共有する]人々の間の)仲間意識、連帯感 ◇The sessions offer students counselling and *fellowship*. その集まりは学生たちに助言と連帯感を提供します

closeness [U] 親密さ、仲のよさ ◇She couldn't help feeling jealous of the *closeness* between him and Dylan. 彼とディランの親密さに彼女は嫉妬を覚えずにはいられなかった

▸ **close** 形 ◇Jo is a very *close* friend. ジョーはとても親しい友達です ◇She and her father are very *close*. 彼女と父親は非常に仲がいい

togetherness [U] (家族[友人]など好きな人と一緒にいるときに抱く)一体[連帯]感 ◇By the end of the week, there was a tremendous feeling of *togetherness* in the group. 週末までにグループの中に強い連帯感が生まれた

comradeship [U] (一緒に働く[戦争を戦う]人々の間の)仲間[同志]意識、友情 ◇After a few weeks together, there was a real sense of *comradeship* between them. 数週間一緒にいた後、彼らの間には真の仲間意識が芽生えた

frighten, frightening

frighten 動

frighten・scare・alarm・terrify・traumatize・spook
人をおびえさせる
【類語訳】怖がらせる、おどかす、びっくりさせる、心配させる、動揺させる、不安にさせる、恐れさせる、おどす

alarm	frighten	terrify
	scare	traumatize
	spook	

文型&コロケーション
- to frighten/ scare sb/ sth **away/ off**
- to frighten/ scare/ terrify sb **into** doing sth
- It frightens/ scares/ alarms/ terrifies me **that**...
- It frightens/ scares/ alarms/ terrifies me **to** think, see, etc.

frighten [他] (不意に人を)怖がらせる、おどかす、びっくりさせる ◇Stop it! You're *frightening* me! やめて、びっくりするじゃない ◇Oh sorry. I didn't mean to *frighten* you. ああ、ごめん。おどかすつもりはなかったんだ ◇He brought out a gun and *frightened* them off. 彼は銃を持ち出し、彼らをおどかして追い払った ☞ **frightened** (AFRAID), **fright** (FEAR)

scare [他] 《ややインフォーマル》(不意に人を)怖がらせる、おどかす、びっくりさせる ◇It *scared* me to think I was alone in the building. 建物の中で一人きりだと思うと怖くなった ◇They managed to *scare* the bears away. 彼らはうまい具合に熊をおどかして追い払った ◇The very thought of flying *scares him silly/stiff*. 《インフォーマル》空を飛ぶと思っただけで彼は怖くなって気が遠くなる [動けなくなる] ☞ **scared** (AFRAID)

ノート frighten と scare の使い分け: scare は frighten よりも少しインフォーマルなので、書き言葉よりも話し言葉で用いられることが多いが、両語とも自動詞としても用いられる。
- He doesn't *frighten/scare* easily. (彼は簡単には怖がらない). しかし、次のように言うほうが自然である。
- Nothing *frightens/scares* him. (彼に怖いものはない) または、
- He doesn't get *frightened/scared* easily. (彼は簡単には怖がらない).

alarm [他] 《進行形はまれ》(人を)心配 [動揺] させる、不安にさせる、おどかす ◇It *alarms* me that nobody takes this problem seriously. 誰もこの問題を真剣に受け止めてくれず心配になる ◇The captain knew there was a problem but didn't want to *alarm* the passengers. 機長は問題があるのを知っていたが、乗客を動揺させたくなかった ❶ alarm は将来において不快 [危険] なことが起こるかもしれないという感情を人が抱くときに用いられる。その感情はしばしば実際の恐怖ではなく不安である。 ☞ **alarm** (FEAR), **alarmed** (AFRAID), **startle** (SURPRISE)

terrify [他] (人を極度に)恐れさせる、ぎょっとさせる ◇Flying *terrified* her. 彼女は空を飛んで肝をつぶした ◇He *terrified* employees at the bank into handing over cash. 彼は銀行員をおどして現金を渡させた ☞ **terrified** (AFRAID)

traumatize (英でまた **-ise**) [他、ふつう受身で] (正常に考えられ [動け] なくなるほど人に) 精神的ショックを与える、心を傷つける ◇We were *traumatized* by what we saw. 私たちは目にしたものに精神的ショックを受けた ◇He was *traumatized* for life. 彼は死ぬまでずっと心に傷を負っていた ☞ **traumatic** (PAINFUL 2)

spook [他] 《インフォーマル》(不意に人・動物を)怖がらせる、おどかす、びっくりさせる ◇We were *spooked* by the strange noises and lights. 私たちは不思議な音や光にびっくりした

frightening 形 ☞ WORRYING

frightening・terrifying・scary・alarming・daunting・chilling・eerie・intimidating・spooky・creepy・hair-raising
人や物事、出来事などが人をおどかすことを表す
【類語訳】怖い、恐ろしい、驚くべき、不気味な、気味の悪い、ぞくぞくするような

alarming	frightening	terrifying
daunting	scary	chilling
intimidating	eerie	hair-raising
	spooky	
	creepy	

文型&コロケーション
- frightening/ terrifying/ scary/ alarming/ daunting/ intimidating **for** sb
- It's frightening/ terrifying/ scary/ daunting **to think**...
- a frightening/ a terrifying/ a scary/ an alarming/ a daunting/ a chilling **experience/ thought/ prospect**
- a frightening/ a terrifying/ a scary/ an eerie/ an intimidating/ a spooky/ a creepy **place**
- a scary/ an intimidating/ a creepy **woman**
- an eerie/ an intimidating/ a spooky/ a creepy **atmosphere**
- an eerie/ a spooky/ a creepy **feeling**
- to **find sth** frightening/ terrifying/ scary/ daunting/ chilling/ intimidating/ creepy
- **rather/ pretty** frightening/ terrifying/ scary/ alarming/ daunting/ chilling/ eerie/ intimidating/ spooky
- **very** frightening/ scary/ alarming/ daunting/ intimidating/ spooky
- **a bit** frightening/ scary/ daunting/ spooky/ creepy

frightening 怖い、びっくりさせるような ◇It's *frightening* to think it could happen again. またそれが起こるかもしれないと思うと怖い ◇The noise was *frightening*. その音にびっくりした ❶ frightening は《米》ではややフォーマルな語。☞ **frightened** (AFRAID)

terrifying (極度に)恐ろしい、ぎょっ[ぞっ]とさせるような ◇The sudden silence was *terrifying*. 突然の沈黙にぞっとした ☞ **terrified** (AFRAID)

scary 《インフォーマル》怖い、びっくりさせるような ◇a *scary* movie 恐怖映画 ◇This is the *scariest* thing I've ever done in my life. これは今まで人生でやった中で一番怖いことです ◇a *scary*-looking guy こわもての男 ☞ **scared** (AFRAID)

alarming 憂慮すべき、驚くべき ◇an *alarming* increase in the number of cases of skin cancer 皮膚がんの症例数の憂慮すべき増加 ◇The rainforest is disappearing *at an alarming rate*. (熟語) 雨林は驚くべき割合で姿を消している ❶ alarming は《米》ではややフォーマルな語。 [反意] **reassuring**

▶**alarmingly** 副 ◇Prices have risen *alarmingly*. 物価は驚くほど上昇している

ノート **frightening, scary, alarming** の使い分け：
alarmingはふつう将来における不快な事、特に快適な[好ましい]状態を損なわせる事が起こる状況に対する警告の際に用いられる。frighteningとscaryは人や状況の現在[将来]における恐怖を指す。これは単に快適さを失うことだけでなく、個人の安全に関する恐怖を指すこともある。

daunting （緊張して[自信がなく]）大変な, 気の滅入るような ◇Starting a new school can be very *daunting*. 学校を新設するにはとても大変なこともあるだろう ◇She has the *daunting* task of cooking for 20 people every day. 彼女は毎日20人分の料理を作るという気の滅入るような仕事をしている ☞ **daunt (DISCOURAGE 2)**

chilling （暴力的[残忍]で）恐ろしい, 身の毛のよだつような ◇a *chilling* tale of murder and revenge 身の毛のよだつような殺人と復讐の話 ◇The film evokes *chilling* reminders of the war. その映画はあのおぞましい戦争を思い出させる

eerie 不気味な, 薄気味の悪い ◇an *eerie* green light 不気味な緑色の光 ◇He had an *eerie* feeling that he was not alone. 彼は自分だけではないという不気味な感覚に包まれていた

▶**eerily** 副 ◇It was *eerily* quiet. 薄気味悪いほど静かだった

intimidating （ややフォーマル）（自信を失わせるほど）威圧[脅迫]的な ◇He had a very *intimidating* manner. 彼の態度は非常に脅迫的だった ◇The atmosphere was less *intimidating* than I had imagined. 雰囲気は想像していたほど威圧的ではなかった

ノート **daunting** と **intimidating** の使い分け：dauntingはやっている[やろうとしている]事に用いられる。◆a *daunting* experience （大変な経験）。◆a *daunting* thought/prospect/task/challenge（気の滅入るような考え/見通し/仕事/挑戦）。intimidatingは人や場所に用いられる。

spooky 《インフォーマル》気味の悪い ◇a *spooky* old house 気味の悪い古い家 ◇I was just thinking about her when she phoned, which was a bit *spooky*. ちょうど彼女のことを考えていたときに彼女から電話があったので、ちょっと気味が悪かった

creepy 《インフォーマル》気味の悪い ◇It's kind of *creepy* down in the cellar! 地下室にいるとなんだか気味が悪い！ ◇What a *creepy* coincidence. 何ともぞっとする偶然だ ◇a *creepy* little man with a nervous tic 神経質なチックのある気味の悪い小柄な男

ノート **eerie, spooky, creepy** の使い分け：これらの語は特に、何か奇妙で[不自然な]事が起ころうとしている[迫っている]と感じていることを表している。spookyとcreepyはともに科学的に説明できない出来事について用いるが、creepyは場所、出来事、状況だけでなく人にも用いることができ、気味の悪さや不快さを暗示する。eerieは他の二語ほどインフォーマルではない。

'hair-raising （恐怖・興奮で）身の毛のよだつような, 鳥肌の立つ[ぞくぞく]するような ◇a *hair-raising* adventure/journey ぞくぞくするような冒険/旅

frustration 名

frustration・irritation・annoyance・exasperation・displeasure・chagrin・pique
少し怒っている感情
【類語訳】欲求不満, 挫折, いら立ち, もどかしさ, 立腹, 不快感, 激怒, 憤慨, 不満, 不機嫌, 無念, 残念, 憤り

文型&コロケーション

▶ frustration/ irritation/ annoyance/ exasperation/ displeasure **at** sth
▶ irritation/ annoyance/ exasperation/ displeasure **with** sb/ sth
▶ to do sth **in** frustration/ irritation/ annoyance/ exasperation
▶ to do sth **with** irritation/ annoyance/ exasperation/ displeasure/ chagrin
▶ **to my/ his/ her, etc.** irritation/ annoyance/ chagrin
▶ **great/ considerable** frustration/ irritation/ annoyance/ displeasure
▶ **intense** frustration/ irritation/ annoyance
▶ **deep** frustration/ displeasure
▶ **to hide** your frustration/ irritation/ annoyance/ exasperation/ displeasure/ chagrin
▶ **to show** your frustration/ irritation/ annoyance/ displeasure
▶ **to cause** frustration/ irritation/ annoyance/ displeasure

frustration [U, C, ふつう複数で] 欲求不満, 挫折, いら立ち, もどかしさ；欲求不満[挫折, いら立ち, もどかしさ]の種 ◇Dave thumped the table in *frustration*. デイヴはいらいらしてテーブルを強く叩いた ◇She couldn't stand the *frustration* of not being able to help. 彼女は手助けできないもどかしさを抑えられなかった ◇Every job has its difficulties and *frustrations*. どんな仕事にも困難と挫折は付き物だ ◇Inevitably she took out her *frustrations* on the children. 必然的に彼女は子どもたちに八つ当たりした ☞ **frustrate (ANNOY), frustrated (UNHAPPY 2), frustrating (ANNOYING)**

irritation [U, C] いら立ち, 立腹, 不快感；いら立ち[立腹, 不快感]の種 ◇He noted, with some *irritation*, that the letter had not been sent. 彼はいくぶん腹を立てながら、その手紙が出されていないと言った ◇He could hear the *irritation* in her voice. 彼は彼女の声にいら立ちを聞き取ることができた ◇the minor *irritation* of having to wait 待たなければならないというちょっとしたいら立ち ☞ **irritable (IRRITABLE), irritate (ANNOY), irritated (ANNOYED), irritating (ANNOYING)**

annoyance [U, C] いら立ち, 立腹, 不快感；いら立ち[立腹, 不快感]の種 ◇He could not conceal his *annoyance* at being interrupted. 彼は邪魔されていら立ちを隠すことができなかった ◇Much to our *annoyance*, they decided not to come after all. 私たちはとても不快に思ったのだが、彼らは結局来ないと決めた ◇petty *annoyances* and irritations ささいな不快感といら立ち ☞ **annoy (ANNOY), annoyed (ANNOYED), annoying (ANNOYING)**

ノート **irritation** と **annoyance** の使い分け：この2語の用法にはほとんど違いはない。

exasperation [U] （状況を変えられないときに抱く）激怒, 憤慨 ◇He shook his head in *exasperation*. 彼は憤慨し

↳**frustration**　　　　　　　　　　　　　　　　　**full, fun**

て首を横に振った ◇a groan/look/sigh of *exasperation* 憤慨の唸り声/表情/ため息 ☞ **exasperate** (ANNOY), **exasperated** (ANNOYED)

displeasure [U]《フォーマル》不満, 不快感, 不機嫌 ◇She made no attempt to hide her *displeasure* at the prospect. 彼女はその見通しに対する不快感を隠そうともしなかった ◇The incident has heightened public *displeasure* with the authorities. その事件は当局に対する国民の不満を増大させた 反意 **pleasure** (FUN), ☞ **displease** (ANNOY)

chagrin [U]《フォーマル》無念, 残念 ◇To her *chagrin*, neither of her sons became doctors. 残念なことに, 彼女の息子は二人とも医者にはならなかった

pique [U]《フォーマル》(自尊心を傷つけられて抱く)立腹, 憤り ◇When he realized nobody was listening to him, he left in a *fit of pique*. 誰も自分の話を聞いていないと気づいて, 彼は急にむかっときて立ち去った ◇She'd lied about it *out of pique*. 彼女は腹立ち紛れにそのことで嘘をついてしまった

full 形 ☞ CROWDED

---

full · packed · crammed · overcrowded · congested · stuffed

人や物をたくさん含んだ状態を表す
【類語訳】いっぱいの, ぎっしり詰まった, 満員の, 満席の, ぎゅうぎゅう詰めの, 過密の, 渋滞した, 混雑した, 満腹の

文型&コロケーション
▶ full/ packed/ crammed/ overcrowded/ congested **with** sb/sth
▶ packed/ crammed **full** of sb/ sth
▶ overcrowded/ congested **cities/ roads**

---

full (物で)いっぱいの, ぎっしり詰まった, 満ちた ; (感情・特徴などで)いっぱいの ◇a *full* bottle of wine ボトル丸ごと1本のワイン ◇She could only nod, because her mouth was *full*. 口の中がいっぱいで, 彼女はうなずくことしかできなかった ◇There were cardboard boxes *stuffed full of* clothes. 衣類がぎっしり詰まった段ボール箱があった ◇The sky was *full of* brightly coloured fireworks. 空は色鮮やかな花火でいっぱいだった ◇She was *full of* admiration for the care she had received. 彼女はしてもらった看護に感心しきりだった ❶《英》では full up も隙間のないことを表すが, 大量の物事には用いられない. ◇Sorry, the hotel is *full up* tonight. (申し訳ありません. 今夜ホテルは満室です). ×Life is *full up* of coincidences.　full《英》では full up)は人が十分に食べたときにも用いられる. ◆ The kids still weren't *full*, so I gave them an ice cream each. (子どもたちはまだ満腹ではなかったので, 私はそれぞれにアイスクリームを与えた). ◆You shouldn't swim *on a full stomach*. (満腹で泳いではいけません). ◆No more for me, thanks — I'm *full up*.《英》私はもう結構です, ありがとうございます—満腹です) 反意 **empty** (EMPTY)

packed (部屋・建物が)満員の, 満席の, ;(特定の物事で)いっぱいの ◇The restaurant was *packed*. レストランは満席だった ◇The show played to *packed houses* (= large audiences). ショーは大入り満員で上演された ◇The book is *packed* with information. その本には情報がぎっしり詰まっている ◇The train was absolutely *jam-packed*.《インフォーマル》列車はまったくすし詰め状態だった ☞ **pack** (PACK)

crammed [名詞の前では用いない]《with sb/sth や full of sb/sth を伴って》(人・物で)ぎゅうぎゅう詰めの, ぎっしり詰まった ◇The room was *crammed full* of people. 部屋は人でぎゅうぎゅう詰めだった ◇All the shelves were *crammed* with books. すべての棚は本がぎっしり詰まっていた ◇The article was *crammed* full of ideas. その記事にはアイデアがいっぱい詰まっていた ☞ **cram** (PACK)

ノート **packed** と **crammed** の使い分け : crammed は packed よりもたくさん人や物が入っている場所や物を表し, そのためしばしば, (人でいっぱいなら)不快であったり, (物でいっぱいなら)散らかっていたりする. 出し物が人気で全席が埋まっている劇場[映画館]などには crammed ではなく, packed が用いられる. ◆The theatre was *packed* every night. (その劇場は毎晩満席だった). ×The theatre was *crammed* every night.

overcrowded (けなして)(場所が人・物で)超満員の, 過密の ◇Drugs and violence are rife in our filthy, *overcrowded* prisons. 麻薬と暴力が我が国の不潔で超満員の刑務所にはびこっている ◇Too many poor people are living in *overcrowded* conditions. あまりにも多くの貧困者たちが過密状態で生活している

congested (ふつうけなして)(交通量が多すぎて)渋滞[混雑]した ◇Traffic engineers believe that the new road could free up *congested* city streets. 交通工学者たちは新しい道路により市街地の渋滞を解消できるだろうと信じている ◇Many of Europe's airports are heavily *congested*. ヨーロッパの空港の多くはひどく混雑している ☞ **congestion** (TRAFFIC)

stuffed [名詞の前では用いない]《インフォーマル》満腹の ◇I couldn't eat another thing. I'm absolutely *stuffed*. もう何も食べられません. すっかり満腹です

fun 名

---

fun · pleasure · good time · enjoyment · great time · blast

楽しむ思い[行為, 時間]
【類語訳】楽しさ, 面白さ, 余興, 娯楽, 遊び, 喜び

文型&コロケーション
▶ to do sth **for** fun/ pleasure/ enjoyment
▶ to do sth **with** pleasure/ enjoyment
▶ **great** fun/ pleasure/ enjoyment
▶ a **really** good/ great time
▶ to **have** fun/ a good time/ a great time/ a blast
▶ to **get**/ **derive** pleasure/ enjoyment **from** sth
▶ to **bring** (sb) pleasure/ enjoyment
▶ to **spoil** the fun/ sb's pleasure/ sb's enjoyment

---

fun [U]《ややインフォーマル, 特に話し言葉》楽しさ, 面白さ ; 余興, 娯楽, 遊び ◇We had a lot of *fun* at Sarah's party. サラのパーティーはすごく楽しかった ◇Sailing is *good fun*.《特に英》ヨットは実に楽しい ◇I decided to learn Spanish just for *fun*. 遊び半分にスペイン語を習うことにした ◇I didn't do all that work just *for the fun of it*. あんなにたくさんの仕事をただの遊び心でやったわけではない ◇It's not much *fun* going to a party on your own. 一人でパーティーに出かけても大して面白くないね ◇*Have fun* (= Enjoy yourself!)《話し言葉》楽しんで来てね ☞ **have fun** (PLAY 動 1)

pleasure [U]《ややフォーマル》楽しさ, 喜び ◇Reading for

pleasure and reading for study are not the same. 楽しむための読書と勉強のための読書は同じではない ◇He takes no *pleasure in* his work. 彼は仕事に喜びを覚えない ◇**It gives me great pleasure** to introduce our guest speaker. 《フォーマル, 話し言葉》ゲストスピーカーをご紹介するのは大変光栄です ◇We request the *pleasure* of your company at the marriage of our daughter Lisa. 《フォーマル, 書き言葉》娘のリサの結婚式にはぜひご同席くださればと思います [反意] **displeasure** (FRUSTRATION), **pain** (DISTRESS)

good 'time [C]《ややインフォーマル》楽しい時間 ◇Did you have a *good time* in Spain? スペインでは楽しかったですか ◇Mike and I shared some really *good times*. マイクと私は実に楽しい時を共にしました

enjoyment [U]《ややフォーマル》楽しさ, 喜び ◇I get a lot of *enjoyment* from gardening. ガーデニングを大いに楽しんでいる ☞ **enjoy yourself** (PLAY 動 1)

> [ノート] **pleasure** と **enjoyment** の使い分け：enjoyment はふつう, 自分で行った行為によって感じる楽しさ・喜び, pleasure は自分で行った事柄あるいはその時起こった出来事による楽しさ・喜びである. ◇He beamed with *pleasure* at seeing her. (彼は彼女に会う喜びで輝いていた). ×He beamed with *enjoyment* at seeing her.

great 'time [C]《ややインフォーマル》素晴らしい時間 ◇We had a really *great time* together. 私たちは実に素晴らしい時間を共に過ごした

blast [単数で]《米, インフォーマル, 話し言葉》(とても)楽しいひととき ◇The party was a *blast*. パーティーはとても楽しかった ◇We had a *blast* at the party. 私たちはパーティーを大いに楽しんだ

fund 名

fund・budget・account・savings・reserve・pocket・purse・stash

貯めている[特定の目的に使うことのできる]お金
【類語訳】資金, 基金, 預金, 予算, 預金口座, 貯金, 準備金, 予備金, 所持金, 小遣い, 自腹, へそくり

[文型&コロケーション]

▶ to pay sth **from/ out of** a fund/ a budget/ an account/ your savings/ your reserves/ your own pocket/ the purse
▶ to have sth **in** a fund/ a budget/ an account
▶ (a) **small** fund/ budget/ reserves/ stash
▶ (a) **large** fund/ budget/ reserves
▶ sb's **private** fund/ budget/ account/ savings/ purse
▶ sb's **family** fund/ budget/ savings/ purse
▶ sb's **personal** budget/ account/ savings/ stash
▶ a/ the **public** fund/ budget/ purse
▶ to **have** a fund/ a budget/ an account/ savings/ a stash
▶ to **dip into** a fund/ a budget/ your savings/ your reserves/ your pocket/ your purse
▶ to **build up** a fund/ savings/ reserves
▶ to **spend** a fund/ a budget/ your savings/ your reserves
▶ to **manage** a fund/ a budget/ an account/ your savings/ your reserves

fund [C] 資金, 基金, 預金 ◇She made a donation to the local cancer relief *fund*. 彼女は地元のがん救済基金に寄付した ◇He's been paying into the firm's pension *fund* for thirty years. 彼は30年間会社の年金基金にずっと払い込みを続けてきている ☞ **funds** (MONEY 1)

budget [C, U] 予算 ◇The government is planning to double the education *budget*. 政府は教育予算を倍増する計画だ ◇It's one of those big-*budget* Hollywood movies. それは巨額予算を投じたハリウッド映画の一つです ◇We decorated the house **on a tight budget** (= without much money to spend). 窮屈な予算で家の装飾に手を入れた ◇Every year the school has a struggle to **balance its budget** (= not spend more than it has). 毎年学校は予算の帳尻を合わせるのに苦労している ◇The work was finished on time and **within budget** (= did not cost more money than was planned). 仕事はスケジュールどおり予算内で仕上がった ◇The company must not go **over budget** (= spend too much money). 会社は予算をオーバーしてはいけない ☞ **budget** (SAVE 2), **budgetary** (ECONOMIC)

account [C] 預金口座 ◇I don't have a **bank account**. 私は銀行口座を持っていません ◇to open/close an *account* 口座を開く[閉じる] ◇I paid the cheque into my current *account*. 《英》小切手を当座預金口座に振り込んだ ◇She deposited the check in her *account*. 《米》彼女は自分の口座に小切手を入金した

savings [複数で] 預金, 貯金 ◇Your *savings* will grow if you invest them wisely. 賢く投資すれば預金は増えるよ ◇He put all his *savings* into buying a boat. 彼は貯金をすべてボートの購入に投じた ☞ **save** (SAVE 2), **save** (SAVE 3)

reserve [C, ふつう複数で]《金融》準備金, 予備金 ◇The company has substantial *reserves* of capital to fall back on if necessary. その会社には必要なら頼ることのできるかなりの資本準備金がある

pocket [C]《ややインフォーマル》所持金, 小遣い, 自腹, 懐 ◇We have a range of gifts to suit every *pocket*. 私どもはどんな懐具合にも応じられる贈り物を取りそろえております ◇He had no intention of paying for the meal **out of his own pocket**. 彼は自腹を切ってまで食事代を支払うつもりはなかった ◇That one mistake left him thousands of pounds **out of pocket** (= having lost thousands of pounds). 《特に英》その一つのミスで彼は何千ポンドもの所持金を失った ☞ **pocket** (MAKE 2)

purse [単数で]《ややインフォーマル》資金 ◇Should spending on the arts be met out of the public *purse* (= from government money)? 芸術への支出は国庫から賄うべきですか

> [ノート] **pocket** と **purse** の使い分け：pocket は purse よりもインフォーマルで, 個人のお金について用いられることが多い. purse は公的なお金について用いられることが多い.

stash [C, ふつう単数で]《インフォーマル》へそくり ◇Luckily the thieves never found my small *stash* of ten pound notes. 幸運にも10ポンド紙幣のわずかなへそくりは泥棒に見つからなかった ☞ **stash** (KEEP 1)

fund 動

fund・support・finance・sponsor・guarantee・subsidize・underwrite・endow・bankroll

役割[成功]を手助けするために人や物事にお金を提供する
【類語訳】資金を提供する, 財政支援する, スポンサーになる, 後援する, 保証人になる, 助成金を支給する

↪fund　　　　　　　　　　**fundamental**

文型&コロケーション

▶ to fund/ support/ finance/ sponsor/ subsidize/ underwrite/ bankroll a **project/ programme**
▶ to fund/ support/ finance/ sponsor/ underwrite/ bankroll a **campaign**
▶ to fund/ support/ finance/ sponsor/ subsidize **research**
▶ sth is **fully/ properly** funded/ financed/ guaranteed/ underwritten
▶ sth is **generously** funded/ supported/ sponsored/ endowed
▶ sth is **poorly** funded/ supported/ financed/ endowed
▶ sth is **privately** funded/ financed/ sponsored/ endowed
▶ sth is **publicly** funded/ financed/ sponsored/ subsidized

fund [他]（長期にわたって公的な物事に）資金を提供する ◇There is an annual dance festival *funded* by the Arts Council. 芸術協議会が資金を提供する毎年恒例のダンスフェスティバルがあります ◇She used the stolen money to *fund* her extravagant lifestyle. 彼女は盗んだ金をぜいたくな生活スタイルを維持するのに使った ☞ **funding** (INVESTMENT), **funds** (MONEY 1)

support [他]（成功の手助けのため物事に）財政支援［援助］する ◇Several major companies are *supporting* the project. 大企業数社がその事業に財政支援している ▷**support** [名] [U] ◇Local businesses have provided financial *support*. 地元企業が財政援助している

finance [他]（物事に）資金［資本］を調達［供給］する ◇The building project will be *financed* by the government and by public donations. その建設事業は政府や一般からの寄付によって資金調達する予定だ ◇He took a job to *finance* his stay in Germany. 彼は仕事をしてドイツの滞在資金を賄った ☞ **finance** (MONEY 1)

ノート fund と finance の使い分け：これら二つの語は非常によく似ているが、fund は finance よりも継続する［毎年繰り返される］計画［事業］に用いられることが多い．

sponsor [他]（会社などの）スポンサー［広告主］になる；（訓練［教育］費用を支払って人を）後援する ◇Many sports events on TV used to be *sponsored* by the tobacco industry. テレビのスポーツイベントの多くは、以前はタバコ産業がスポンサーを務めていた ◇She found a company to *sponsor* her through college. 彼女は大学卒業まで後援してくれる会社を見つけた ☞ **sponsor** (SPONSOR), **sponsorship** (INVESTMENT)

guarantee [他]《金融》保証人になる ◇His father agreed to *guarantee* the bank loan. 彼の父は銀行ローンの保証人となることを了承した

subsidize 〈英では〉-ise [他]（個人［団体］が必要とする）助成［補助、奨励］金を支給する ◇The housing projects are *subsidized* by the government. 〈米〉その住宅事業は政府から助成を受けている ◇She's not prepared to *subsidize* his gambling any longer. 彼女はもはや彼に金を貢いでギャンブルを許すつもりはない ☞ **subsidy** (INVESTMENT)

underwrite [他]《金融》（事業・行動の）費用負担を引き受ける ◇The British government ended up *underwriting* the entire project. 英国政府が結局は事業全体の費用を負担する結果となった ◇The record company may *underwrite* the costs of a band's first tour. レコード会社があるバンドの初ツアーの費用負担を引き受けるかもしれない

endow [他]（特定の目的のために学校［大学］などの施設に）基金を寄付する ◇In her will, she *endowed* a schol-arship in the physics department. 彼女は遺言で物理学科の奨学基金に寄付した ☞ **endowment** (INVESTMENT)

bankroll [他]《特に米、ややインフォーマル》（人・物事に）財源［資金］を供給する ◇They claimed his campaign had been *bankrolled* with drug money. 彼の選挙運動は麻薬絡みの金が資金源だったと彼らは主張した

fundamental [形]

fundamental・underlying・radical・basic・essential・elementary・ultimate・rudimentary
問題や考えなどが最も大切で欠かせないものであることを表す
【類語訳】重要な、基本的な、根本的な、徹底的な、本質的な、初歩的な、根源的な

文型&コロケーション

▶ fundamental/ basic **to** sth
▶ a fundamental/ an underlying/ a radical/ a basic/ an essential **difference/ distinction**
▶ a fundamental/ an underlying/ a radical/ a basic **change/ improvement**
▶ a fundamental/ radical/ basic **approach**
▶ a fundamental/ an underlying/ a basic/ an essential/ an elementary **rule/ principle**
▶ a fundamental/ an underlying/ a basic/ an essential/ the ultimate **truth**
▶ a fundamental/ an underlying/ a basic/ an essential/ the ultimate **cause/ reason**
▶ a fundamental/ an underlying/ a basic/ an essential **assumption/ aim/ problem/ cause/ reason/ need/ weakness**
▶ a fundamental/ a basic/ an elementary/ a rudimentary **skill/ understanding/ knowledge/ level**
▶ a fundamental/ a basic/ an elementary **error/ mistake**

fundamental 《ややフォーマル、特に書き言葉》重要な、基本的な；根本［抜本］的な；基本［基礎、土台］となる ◇There is a *fundamental* difference between the two points of view. その二つの視点には基本的な違いがある ◇A *fundamental* change in the organization of health services was required. 医療業務機関は根本的な変化が必要とされていた ◇Hard work is *fundamental* to success. 勤勉が成功への基本だ ☞ **fundamentals** (BASICS)
▷ **fundamentally** [副] ◇The two approaches are *fundamentally* different. その二つのアプローチは根本的に違っている ◇By the 1960s the situation had changed *fundamentally*. 1960年代までに状況は根本から変わっていた

underlying [名詞の前で]《ややフォーマル、特に書き言葉》基本となる、根底にある ◇The *underlying* assumption is that the amount of money available is limited. 使える金額が限られているというのが基本となる前提である ◇Unemployment may be an *underlying* cause of the rising crime rate. 失業は犯罪率の上昇の根底にある原因かもしれない ❶典型的な連語には cause, assumption, reason, motive, trend, theme, problem, reality, aim が挙げられる．

radical [ふつう名詞の前で]《ややフォーマル、特に書き言葉》（変化・違いが）根本［抜本］的な；徹底的な、完全な ◇There have been demands for *radical* reform of the law. その法律の抜本的改革を求める声がずっとある ◇This document marks a *radical* departure from earlier recommendations. 初期の勧告から完全に逸脱していることが

この公文書から明らかだ ☞ **radical** (RADICAL)
▶**radically** 副 ◇The new methods are *radically* different from the old. 新しい手法は古いものと根本的に異なる ◇Attitudes have changed *radically*. 態度が根本から変わった

ノート **fundamental** と **radical** の使い分け：fundamental は物事の基礎となる制度[原理]の構造全体に関わる変化[相違]に用いられる。radical は広範囲に影響を及ぼす重要な変化に用いられる。

basic 基本的な ◇They haven't even given us the most *basic* information we need. 彼らは私たちが必要としている最も基本的な情報さえ与えてくれなかった ◇During the first term, we will concentrate on the *basic* principles of law. 一学期間は法律の基本原理に注意を傾けよう ◇Drums are *basic* to African music. 太鼓はアフリカ音楽の基本である ❶ *basic* は名詞の前で用いられ、「すべての人にとって必要かつ重要な」を意味することもある。
◆Aren't food and shelter *basic* human rights? (食住は基本的人権ではないのか) ◆The report sets out the cost of *basic* foods in several European countries. (報告書はヨーロッパの数か国における基本的な食糧の価格を体系的に説明している). ☞ **basics** (BASICS)
▶**basically** 副 ◇Yes, that's *basically* correct. ええ、それは基本的に合っています ◇There have been some problems but *basically* it's a good system. いくつか問題はあったものの、それは基本的にはよいシステムである

essential [名詞の前で] 本質的な ◇The *essential* difference between Sara and me is our attitude to money. サラと私の本質的な違いはお金に対する姿勢だ ◇The *essential* character of the town has been destroyed by the new road. 町本来の特徴が新しい道路によって破壊されてしまっている ☞ **essence** (NATURE 1), **essentials** (BASICS)
▶**essentially** 副 ◇There are three *essentially different* ways of tackling the problem. その問題に取り組む上で3つの本質的に異なる方法がある ◇The pattern is *essentially the same* in all cases. そのパターンはすべての場合、本質的に同じである

ノート **basic** と **essential** の使い分け：basic は物事を行う[理解する]ために重要であることに焦点を当て、実用的な観点から物事を見ている。essential は物事の本質そのもの、および物事と異なっていて[似ている]要素を考察して、哲学的な観点から物事を見ている。

elementary 《ややフォーマル》初歩的な、基本の ◇How could you make such an *elementary* mistake? どうしてそんな初歩的なミスをするのかなあ ◇It's an *elementary* law of economics: the scarcer the commodity, the higher the price. 商品が少なくなれば価格が上昇する、それは経済学の基本原理だ ❶ *elementary* はふつう教科を学ぶ上での水準[段階]を表す。
◆I'm taking classes in *elementary* Italian. (初級イタリア語のクラスを取っています)

ultimate [名詞の前で] 根源的な、根本的な ◇the *ultimate* truths of philosophy and science 哲学と科学の根源[根本]の真理 ◇We could not trace the *ultimate* source of the rumours. 噂の根源を突き止めることはできなかった
▶**ultimately** 副 ◇All life depends *ultimately* on oxygen. すべての生命は究極的に酸素に依存している

rudimentary 《フォーマル》初歩の、基礎の ◇His understanding of the language is very *rudimentary*. 彼の

その言語の理解度はほんの初歩の段階です ◇They were given only *rudimentary* training in the job. 彼らはその仕事の基礎訓練しか受けていなかった ❶ *rudimentary* はほとんどの場合、knowledge, understanding, skill, training を修飾する。

funny 形

funny・amusing・entertaining・witty・humorous・comic・hilarious・light-hearted

人や物事が笑わせて[ほほ笑ませて]くれることを表す
【類語訳】面白い、おかしい、こっけいな、楽しい、愉快な、気の利いた、軽妙洒脱な、機知に富んだ

humorous	funny	hilarious
light-hearted	amusing	
	entertaining	
	witty	
	comic	

文型&コロケーション

▶ a funny/ an amusing/ an entertaining/ a witty/ a humorous/ a comic/ a light-hearted **story**
▶ a funny/ an amusing/ a witty/ a humorous/ a light-hearted **speech**
▶ a funny/ an entertaining/ a witty/ a humorous/ a comic **writer**
▶ a funny/ an entertaining/ a witty/ a humorous **speaker**
▶ a funny/ an amusing/ a witty **guy/ man/ woman**
▶ a funny/ an amusing/ a humorous/ a hilarious **incident**
▶ a funny/ an amusing/ a hilarious **joke**
▶ to **find sth** funny/ amusing/ entertaining/ witty/ humorous/ hilarious

funny 面白い、おかしい、こっけいな ◇That's the *funniest* thing I've ever heard. そんなこっけいなことは今まで聞いたことないよ ◇It's not *funny*! Someone could have been hurt. 面白くなんかないよ。誰かが傷ついたかもしれないじゃないか ◇I was really embarrassed, but then I *saw the funny side of it*. ほんとにばつが悪かったが、そのあとそのこのこっけいな側面が見えてきた ◇'What's so *funny*?' she demanded. 「何がそんなに面白いの」と彼女が聞いてきた
amusing 面白い、楽しい、おかしい、愉快な ◇This can be a very *amusing* game to play. これはやってみるととっても面白いゲームなのかもしれない ◇He writes very *amusing* letters. 彼は非常に愉快な手紙を書く
▶**amuse** 動 [他] ◇My funny drawings *amused* the kids. 私の面白い絵が子どもたちを楽しませた ◇This will *amuse* you. これには笑うでしょう
▶**amusement** 名 [U] ◇She could not hide her *amusement* at the way he was dancing. 彼女は彼が踊っている様がおかしくて笑いを隠しきれなかった ◇Much *to their amusement* I couldn't get the door open. 彼らに大いに受けたのは、私がそのドアを開けられなかったことだ
entertaining 《ややフォーマル》面白い、楽しい、愉快な ◇It was a very *entertaining* evening. とっても楽しい夜だった ◇She found him a charming and *entertaining* companion. 彼女は彼を魅力的で愉快な仲間だと思った
witty 気の利いた、軽妙洒脱な；機知に富んだ、しゃれのうまい ◇Somebody made a *witty* remark about needing a forklift truck. フォークリフト車がいるね、と気の利い

た感想を述べる人がいた ◇He was much in demand as a *witty* public speaker. 彼は機知に富んだ演説家として引っ張りだこだった ☞ wit (HUMOUR)

humorous 面白い, おかしい, こっけいな；ひょうきんな, おどけな ◇It's a *humorous* look at the world of fashion. それはファッション界に対するユーモア溢れる見方だね ◇She had not intended to be *humorous*. 彼女にはおどけるつもりはなかった ☞ humour (HUMOUR)

comic 面白い, おかしい, こっけいな, 笑える ◇Many of the scenes in the book are richly *comic*. その本の多くの場面はおかしさ満載です ◇She can always be relied on to provide *comic relief* (= sth to make you relax and laugh) at a boring party. 退屈なパーティーで笑いを誘って緊張をほぐすなら彼女はいつも頼りになる ❶ *comic* には「喜劇に関する」の意味もある。この意味では, 名詞の前でしか用いられない。◆a *comic* opera (喜歌劇) ◆a very fine *comic* actor (とても素晴らしい喜劇俳優). ☞ comedy (HUMOUR)

> **ノート funny, amusing, humorous, comic の使い分け**: amusing はこれらの語の中で最も一般的な語。それに楽しめるだけでなく人を笑わせるという意味合いがあって, 出来事, 活動, 機会について用いられる。◆an *amusing* party/game/evening（楽しいパーティー／ゲーム／夕べ）×a *funny/humorous/comic* party/game/evening. humorous は funny や comic ほど強い意味を持たず, 実際に人を大声で笑わせることよりも, ある状況でユーモアがわかること表す。comic は特に意図的でわざとらしい面白い著作や劇などに用いられる。comic writer（喜劇作家）を除いて, 人には用いられない。funny は人, 冗談, 物語, 出来事など, 人を笑わせるものなら何でも用いることができる。

hilarious とても面白い ◇Lynn found the whole situation absolutely *hilarious*. リンはその状況全体を滑稽の極みと思った ◇Do you know Pete? He's *hilarious*. ピートを知ってるの。彼って, とても面白いわね

light-'hearted 陽気な, 気楽な ◇She gave a *light-hearted* speech that was just right for the occasion. 彼女はその場にうってつけの陽気なスピーチを披露した 反意 **serious** (SERIOUS 2)

furious 形 ☞ ANGRY

furious • outraged • enraged • incensed • fuming • seething
非常に怒っていることを表す
【類語訳】激怒した, 憤慨した, 怒り狂った

文型&コロケーション
▶ furious/ outraged/ incensed/ fuming/ seething **about/ at/ over** sth
▶ furious/ outraged/ incensed **that**...
▶ a furious/ an outraged **expression**
▶ **absolutely** furious/ outraged/ incensed/ fuming

furious ひどく腹を立てた, 激怒した ◇I was *furious* at the way we'd been treated. 私は自分たちが受けた待遇にひどく腹が立った ◇She was *furious with* me when she found out. 彼女は悪事を看破して私に激怒した ◇He was *furious with himself* for letting things get so out of control. 彼はそんなにも収拾のつかない事態にしてしまったことで激しい自責の念に駆られていた ☞ **fury** (ANGER 名)
▶ **furiously** 副 ◇*furiously* angry ひどく腹を立てている ◇He banged the door *furiously*. 彼は激怒してドアをバタンと閉めた

outraged （不当な［道徳的に間違っている］物事に）激怒した, 憤慨した ◇I was *outraged* when I heard of the decision. その決定を聞いたとき私は激怒した ◇a group of *outraged* customers/residents/passengers 憤慨した顧客／住民／乗客の一団 ◇She wrote an *outraged* letter to the newspaper. 彼女は新聞に怒りの投書を送った ☞ **outrage** (ANGER 名), **outrage** (ANGER 動), **outrageous** (OUTRAGEOUS)

enraged 《書き言葉》（自制心を失う［暴力的になる］ほど）激怒した, 怒り狂った ◇She was *enraged* at his stupidity. 彼女は彼の愚かさに激怒していた ◇an *enraged* mob 怒り狂った暴徒 ☞ **rage** (ANGER 名), **enrage** (ANGER 動)

incensed （不当な扱い［評価］を受けたと思って）激怒した, 憤慨した ◇Workers were *incensed* by the decision to lengthen working hours. 労働者たちは労働時間を延ばす決定に激怒した ☞ **incense** (ANGER 動)

> **ノート outraged と incensed の使い分け**: 多くの場合, 両語とも使用可能だが, outraged は物事が道徳的に間違っているという強い感情を表し, incensed は個人的にひどい扱いを受けたという強い感情を表す。

fuming ［名詞の前では用いない］（怒りを表す効果的な方法がなく）ひどくいら立つ ◇She sat in the car, silently *fuming* at the traffic jam. 彼女は車の中に座り, 交通渋滞に無言でいら立っていた

seething ［名詞の前では用いない］（内心では）はらわたの煮えくり返った ◇Inwardly *seething*, she did as she was told. 内心はらわたが煮えくり返りながらも, 彼女は言われた通りにした

G g

gain 動 ☞GET 1

gain・win・secure・earn・land・procure・net
技量や優れた資質, 努力によって物事を手に入れる
【類語訳】獲得する, 勝ち取る, 得る, 確保する, 入手する

文型&コロケーション
- to gain/ win/ secure/ earn/ procure sth **by** (doing) sth
- to gain/ win/ secure/ earn/ procure sth **for** sb
- to gain/ win/ secure/ earn **support/ approval**
- to gain/ win/ earn **respect/ admiration**
- to gain/ earn a **reputation**
- to gain/ earn **notoriety**
- to win/ secure/ land a **contract**
- to gain/ secure **access/ entry**
- to gain/ win/ secure/ earn/ land **yourself** sth

gain [他]《ややフォーマル》(必要な[ほしい]物事を)手に入れる, 獲得する, 得る ◇The country *gained* its independence ten years ago. その国は10年前に独立を果たした ◇The party *gained* over 50% of the vote. その党は投票総数の過半数を獲得した ◇Her unusual talent *gained* her worldwide recognition. 彼女の非凡な才能は世界的な評価を得た ❶ gain は特に, 自由(access, entry, independence), 人からの評価(recognition, reputation), 知識(insight, experience, knowledge, understanding)を手に入れることについて用いられる.

win [他](努力・能力・資質によってほしい物事を)手に入れる, 得る ◇She *won* the admiration of many people in her battle against cancer. 彼女は自らの癌との闘いで多くの人々の称賛を得た ◇He *won* a scholarship to study at Stanford. 彼はスタンフォード大学で学ぶための奨学金を得た ❶ win はこの意味では特に, お金(scholarship (奨学金))や仕事(contract (契約))をもらう合意のほかに, 人々の admiration (称賛), support (支援), respect (尊敬)を得る場合に用いられる.

secure [他]《フォーマル》(努力・能力によってほしい物事を)手に入れる, 獲得する, 確保する ◇He's just *secured* a $5 million contract. 彼は500万ドルの契約をちょうど獲得したところだ ◇She *secured* 2,000 votes. 彼女は2000票を確保した ◇He *secured* himself a place at law school. 彼はロースクールに入学できた ❶ secure はしばしば, 法律・金融などのビジネス関連の場面で用いられる.

earn [他](よい行い・資質によって自らにふさわしい物事を)手に入れる, 得る ◇He *earned* a reputation as an expert on tax law. 彼は税法の専門家としての評価を得た ◇Her outstanding ability *earned* her a place on the team. 彼女は傑出した能力でチームの一員となれた

land [他](賞などを首尾よく)手に入れる, 物にする ◇He's just *landed* a starring role in Spielberg's next movie. 彼はスピルバーグの次回作の主役を物にしたところだ ◇She's just *landed* herself a company directorship. 彼女は晴れて企業の取締役に就任したばかりである

procure [他]《フォーマル》(苦労して物事を)手に入れる, 入手する ◇She managed to *procure* a ticket for the concert. 彼女はどうにかそのコンサートのチケットを入手した ◇They *procured* us a copy of the report. 彼らは報告書の写しを調達してくれた

net (**-tt-**) [他]《書き言葉, 特にジャーナリズム》(巧みに人[物]を)捕らえる, 獲得する ◇A swoop by customs officers *netted* a large quantity of drugs. 税関職員による手入れで大量の薬物が押収された ❶ net は business (商取引), contract (契約), customer (顧客)などを獲得するのにも用いることができる.

game 名

game・match・final・test・tie・fixture・play-off・fight・round・replay・bout
人[チーム]同士が競うスポーツイベントを表す
【類語訳】試合, 勝負, 決勝, 国際試合, テストマッチ, 大会, プレーオフ, 再試合

文型&コロケーション
- a game/ match/ final/ test/ tie/ fixture/ play-off/ fight/ replay/ bout **against/ between/ with** sb
- an **exciting** game/ match/ final/ tie/ fight
- a **tough** game/ match/ tie/ fixture/ fight/ bout
- a **big** game/ match
- a **home** game/ match/ test/ tie/ fixture
- an **away** game/ match/ tie/ fixture
- a/ an **international/ friendly** game/ match/ fixture
- a **football** game/ match/ final/ fixture
- a **tennis** game/ match/ final
- a **rugby** game/ match/ test
- a **cricket** match/ test
- to **win/ lose** a game/ match/ final/ test/ tie/ play-off/ fight/ replay/ bout
- to **play** a game/ a match/ in a final/ a test/ a tie/ a fixture/ a round
- to **go to/ see/ watch** a game/ match/ final/ test/ tie/ play-off/ fight/ replay

game [C] 試合, 勝負 ◇a *game* of chess チェスの試合 ◇Will he be available for Saturday's *game* against the Bears? 彼は土曜日のベアーズとの試合に出場できる[を見に行ける]だろうか

match [C]《特に英》試合 ◇They're playing an important *match* against Chelsea on Saturday. 彼らは土曜日にチェルシーとの大切な試合に臨みます ◇I'll probably watch the *match* on TV. 私はたぶんテレビでその試合を見ますよ

ノート **game** と **match** の使い分け: game は match より使用範囲が広く, チームスポーツや個人が互いに競う活動について用いられる. ◆a *game* of football/chess/cards (サッカーの試合/チェスの試合/トランプの勝負). しかし, テニスのような個人競技にはあまり用いられない. テニスでは, game は match (試合)の一部を指す.《英》では, match は個人競技やチームスポーツ以外の活動には用いられない. ×a chess/cards *match*.《米》では, match は個人競技に用

↪**game**

いられるが, **game** はチームスポーツに用いるほうが好まれる.
- a football *match* (《英》サッカーの試合). ◆ a football *game* (《英》サッカー [《米》アメリカンフットボール]の試合). a game of football や a football game/match とは言えるが, 次のようには言えない. ×a *match* of football. また a chess *game* a game of chess ほど頻繁に用いられない. 《英》では, a card game はトランプの勝負でなく, ブリッジやポーカーといったトランプのゲームの種類を指すが, 《米》ではどちらも指す.

final [C] 決勝(戦) ◇She reached the *final* of the 100m hurdles. 彼女は100メートルハードルの決勝にたどり着いた ◇The players *met in* last year's *final*. その選手たちは昨年の決勝で対戦した ◇The country will stage next year's World Cup *finals* (= the last few games in the competition). その国で来年のワールドカップ本戦が開催されます

test [C] (または **Test**) (または '**test match**) [C] 《英》(クリケット・ラグビーの一連の)国際試合, テストマッチ ◇They played well in the first *test* against South Africa. 彼らは初の南アフリカ相手との国際試合で善戦した

tie [C] 《英》(サッカーの)試合 ◇It was the first leg of the Cup *tie* between Leeds and Roma. それはカップ戦におけるリーズ対ローマの第1戦だった

fixture [C] 《英》(日程の決まった)大会, 試合 ◇There are plans to make the race an ***annual fixture***. そのレースを毎年恒例の大会にする計画がある ◇It will be difficult to fit the match into an already crowded ***fixture list*** (= list of planned matches to be played). その試合をすでに立て込んでいる開催リストに組み入れるのは難しいだろう

'**play-off** 《英》(《米》**playoff**) [C] プレーオフ (同点・同順位の2チーム [2選手]の勝者を決定する(一連の)試合) ◇Britain now face a *play-off* for the bronze medal against South Korea. イギリスは, 今度は韓国と銅メダルを争ってプレーオフを戦う ❶ アメリカの多くのスポーツでは, the playoffs はレギュラーシーズン終了後に上位チームが優勝を争ってプレーオフを戦うシーズンの一部である. ◆ It looks like the Red Sox and the Yankees will meet in *the playoffs* again this year. (今年もまた, レッドソックスとヤンキースがプレーオフで対戦することになりそうだ).

fight [C] (ボクシング・レスリングなどの)試合 ◇He is unbeaten in 34 *fights*. 彼は34戦無敗である ◇He has lined up a world title *fight* against Lewis. 彼はルイス相手の世界タイトルマッチを組んだ

round [C] (ゴルフの)ラウンド; (馬術の障害飛越競技などの)コース1周 ◇We played a *round* of golf. 私たちはゴルフを一ラウンドプレーした ◇It was the first horse to jump a clear *round*. それが減点なしでコース1周をクリアした最初の馬だった

replay [C] 《英》再試合 (前の試合で勝者が決まらなかったために行われる) ◇They scored a late goal to force a *replay*. 彼らは終了間際にゴールを決めて再試合に持ち込んだ

bout [C] (ボクシング・レスリングなどの)試合 ◇It was hailed as one of the best heavyweight *bouts* of recent times. その一戦は近年最高レベルのヘビー級の試合と評価された

gap 名

gap • margin • gulf
人や集団間に見られる考え方や生き方, 競争力の違いを表す

【類語訳】差, 格差, 隔たり, ギャップ, 溝

margin　　　　　gap　　　　　　　　gulf

文型&コロケーション
▶ the gap/ margin/ gulf **between** A and B
▶ to **bridge** the gap/ gulf between A and B
▶ a gap/ gulf **separates** A and B

gap [C] (考え方・生き方・感じ方の)差, 格差, ギャップ; (二つの考え・行動・理想と現実の)差, 隔たり ◇The *gap* between rich and poor gets wider every year. 貧富の差は年々広がっている ◇the *gap* between theory and practice 理論と実践の隔たり ◇a movie that is sure to bridge the ***generation gap*** (= the difference in attitude or behaviour between younger and older people that causes a lack of understanding) 必ずや世代間のギャップを埋めるであろう映画

margin [C, ふつう単数で] (時間・得票・得点の)差 ◇He won by a ***narrow margin***. 彼は僅差で勝利した ◇She beat the other runners ***by a margin of*** ten seconds. 彼女は他の走者たちを10秒差で破った

gulf [C, ふつう単数で] (考え方・生き方・感じ方の)大きな隔たり, 深い溝 ◇There appeared to be a growing *gulf* between the prosperous south and the declining towns of the north. 繁栄する南部と衰退する北部の町の差がますます広がっているようだった ◇It felt as if a *gulf* had opened up between his life and mine. 彼の生活と私の生活との間に深い溝が生じてしまったような感じだった

general 形 ☞ WIDE 1

general • common • widespread • universal • prevalent • commonplace • ubiquitous • rife
物事がしばしば [ほぼ必ず] 見られる [行われる, 考えられる, 感じられる] ことを表す
【類語訳】一般的な, 一般の, 広範囲の, 広まった, よくある, ありふれた, 普通の

文型&コロケーション
▶ the **disease** is common/ widespread/ prevalent/ rife
▶ **violence** is common/ widespread/ commonplace/ rife
▶ **in** general/ common/ widespread/ universal **use**
▶ the general/ common/ widespread/ universal/ prevalent **view**
▶ a general/ common/ widespread/ universal/ prevalent **problem**
▶ a general/ common/ widespread/ universal **feeling**
▶ general/ widespread/ universal **acclaim**

general 一般的な, (世間)一般の, 広範囲の ◇The *general* opinion is that a new bridge is needed. 新しい橋が必要だという意見が一般的である ◇As a foreigner and a teacher, I was the object of *general* interest. 外国人および教師として, 私は世間一般の興味の的だった ◇The unions threatened a further ***general strike*** (= one that affects all workers in an industry or country). 労働組合はさらにゼネストを続けると脅しをかけた ◇The bad weather has been fairly *general* (= has affected most areas). 悪天候はかなり広範囲にわたっている ☞ **general** (USUAL)

▸**generally** 副 ◇The software will be *generally* available from January. そのソフトは1月から一般販売されます

common よくある；ありふれた，普通の ◇Jones and Davies are *common* Welsh names. ジョーンズとデービスはウェールズではありふれた名前である ◇The fungus is a *common sight* in woodlands at this time of year. そのキノコはこの時期に森林地帯でよく[普通に]見られる ◇It's a *common enough* situation, I know. それって，非常によくある状況ですよね 反意 **rare, uncommon (RARE)**, ☞ **commonly (USUALLY)**

widespread 広範囲にわたる，広まった ◇The storm caused *widespread* damage. その嵐は広範囲にわたる被害をもたらした ◇The decision met with *widespread* approval. その決定は広く受け入れられた ◇The use of steroids was *widespread* in many sports. ステロイドの使用は多くのスポーツに広まっていた

universal 世界共通の，全世界の，万人の，すべての人の(ための)，一般的な ◇A representative assembly is a near *universal* feature of modern democracies. 代議院は現代の世界の民主主義国家にほぼ共通する特徴である ◇Agreement on this issue is almost *universal*. この問題に関してはほとんどの人の意見が一致している ◇The party wanted to introduce a *universal* health care system. その党は国民皆保険制度の導入を望んでいた

▸**universally** 副 ◇The document is now *universally* acknowledged as a forgery. その文書は現在では偽造品だという認識が一般的だ

prevalent (フォーマル) (特定の時・場所に)非常によく見られる，一般的な ◇Temporary working is most *prevalent* among people in service occupations. 臨時の仕事はサービス業に携わる人たちの間でごく一般的である ◇Our diet contributes to the high levels of heart disease *prevalent* in this country. 我が国で心臓病になる確率が高いのは私たちの食事にも一因がある

commonplace (ごく)普通の，ありふれた ◇It is *commonplace* for soldiers to get very little sleep. ほとんど睡眠がとれないのは兵士にとってごく普通のことである ◇Violent incidents of this kind have become *commonplace*. この種の暴力事件がありふれたものになってしまった

ubiquitous [ふつう名詞の前で] (フォーマル or おどけて) (同時に)至る所に[何か所にも]あるような，どこにでもある ◇The *ubiquitous* portraits of the president usually showed him in military uniform. どこにでもある大統領の肖像画は，たいていはその軍服姿を見せていた

rife [名詞の前では用いない] (悪い物事が)広まった，蔓延した ◇Rumours have been *rife* in media circles all summer. 夏の間ずっとメディア界では噂が飛び交っていた ◇Speculation is *rife* that the company is about to be sold. その会社は売却間近だという憶測が広まっている

genius 名

genius・prodigy・mastermind・brain
知能または，音楽[美術，科学など]の技量が非常に高い人
【類語訳】天才，神童，首謀者，黒幕，ブレーン

文型&コロケーション
▸the genius/ mastermind/ brains **behind** sth
▸a **great** genius/ brain
▸a **true** genius/ prodigy
▸an **evil** genius/ mastermind

▸a **child** genius/ prodigy
▸a **musical** genius/ prodigy/ mastermind
▸a **scientific** genius/ brain

genius [C] 天才 ◇He was undoubtedly the greatest comic *genius* of his age. 彼は明らかに当時最高の喜劇の天才だった ◇She's a *genius at* getting things organized. 彼女は物を整理する天才だ ◇You don't have to be a *genius* to see that this plan is not going to work. この計画がうまくいかないことぐらい誰でもわかるよ ❶*genius* は人がとてもよい考えを思いついたり，物事を見事に行ったりしたときに，くだけた表現で用いられることもある．◆You're an absolute *genius*! (君ってほんとに天才だね)

prodigy [C] 天才(少年[少女])，神童 ◇The 12-year-old *prodigy* will play America's reigning chess champion next week. その12歳の天才少年は来週，アメリカのチェスの現チャンピオンと対戦する

mastermind [C] (違法で込み入った計画[活動]を立案・指揮する)首謀者，黒幕 ◇There's a criminal *mastermind* behind all this. このすべての裏には犯罪の黒幕がいる

brain [C, ふつう複数形で] 非常に知能の高い人，ブレーン ◇We have the best scientific *brains* in the country working on this. 我々にはこれに取り組んでいる国内で最も優秀な科学ブレーンがいる ◇the brains (単数扱い) は，特定の集団で最も知能の高い人や物事の立案や計画に責任を持つ人を指す．◆She's always been *the brains* of the family. (彼女はいつも家族の知恵袋だった)．◆The band's drummer is *the brains* behind their latest venture. (そのバンドのドラマーは彼らの最近の冒険的試みの仕掛人だ)．

gentle 形

gentle・light・mild
物事が強く[極端で]なく，あまり人を傷つけないことを表す
【類語訳】穏やかな，軽度の

文型&コロケーション
▸a gentle/ light **breeze/ wind/ rain**
▸gentle/ light **work/ exercise**
▸a light/ mild **punishment**

gentle 強くない；(疲れ[傷つけ]させないほど)穏やかな ◇the *gentle* swell of the sea 海の穏やかなうねり ◇Cook over a *gentle* heat. 弱火で調理してください ◇We went for a *gentle* stroll. 軽い散歩に出かけた ◇This soap is very *gentle* on the hands. この石けんは手にとてもやさしい 反意 **vigorous (ENERGETIC)**

light 強くない；(疲れさせ[ひどい目に遭わせ]ないほど)軽度の，厳しくない ◇The forecast is for *light* showers. 天気予報では軽いにわか雨です ◇*light* traffic 少ない交通量 ◇After his accident he was moved to *lighter* work. 彼は事故の後，より負担の軽い仕事に異動となった ◇He was convicted of assaulting a police officer but he got off with a *light sentence*. 彼は警官暴行で有罪判決を受けたが，軽い刑で済んだ 反意 **heavy** ❶heavyな状態[活動，処罰]は通常より程度の重い[悪い]ものを指す．◆*heavy* traffic (交通渋滞)．◆*heavy* frost/rain/snow (ひどい霜/豪雨/大雪)．◆*heavy* drinking/fighting (深酒/激しい戦闘)．◆The penalty for speeding can be a *heavy fine*. (スピード違反の処罰は重い罰金のこともある)．

mild 強くない，穏やかな；(傷つけ[ひどい目に遭わせ]ないほ

↪gentle

ど)軽度の, 厳しくない ◇a *mild* form of the disease 病気の軽症例 ◇It's safe to take a *mild* sedative. 弱い鎮静剤を服用するのが安全だ ◇It was a very *mild* criticism but he took it very badly. 非常に穏やかな批評だったが, 彼はそれをとても悪く受け取った 反意 **severe** (SERIOUS 1)

ノート gentle, light, mild の使い分け：gentle は特に, 天候・気温・仕事・運動を表すのに用いる. light は特に, 天候・仕事・運動・処罰を表すのに用いる. mild は特に, 病気・薬物・批評・処罰を表すのに用い, 天候を表すのにも用いることができる.
☞ **mild** (SUNNY)

get 動

1 ☞ GAIN
get・obtain・acquire・take・pick sth up・take sth out・get hold of sth
何かして必ず物事を手にする
【類語訳】得る, 手に入れる, 身につける, 取る, もらう

文型&コロケーション
▶ to get/ obtain/ acquire/ take/ pick up sth **from** sb/ sth
▶ to get/ obtain/ acquire/ pick up/ get hold of a **ticket**
▶ to get/ obtain/ take out a **loan/ mortgage/ patent**
▶ to get/ obtain/ take out **insurance/ cover**
▶ to get/ obtain/ take **water/ oil/ minerals** (from sth)
▶ to get/ obtain/ acquire/ take/ get hold of **information**
▶ to get/ obtain/ take a/ an **extract/ example/ sample**
▶ to get/ obtain/ acquire a **licence/ permit**
▶ to get/ obtain **permission/ approval/ advice**
▶ to get/ acquire a **reputation/ taste** for sth

get [他, 受身なし]《進行形まれ》《ややインフォーマル, 特に話し言葉》得る, 手に入れる ◇Did you manage to *get* tickets for the concert? 何とかコンサートのチケット, 手に入った ◇Try to *get* some sleep. 少し眠るようにしなさい ◇He has just *got* a new job. 彼は新しい仕事に就いたばかりだ ◇Did you *get* a present for your mother? お母さんにプレゼント, 買った ◇Did you *get* your mother a present? お母さんにプレゼント, 買った ☞ **get** (BUY)
obtain [他]《ややフォーマル, 特に書き言葉》(努力して)得る, 手に入れる ◇I finally manged to *obtain* a copy of the report. やっとのことでその報告書を1部入手した ◇Further details can be *obtained* by writing to the above address. さらに詳しくは上記の住所にお便りください ☞ **extract** (PUMP)
acquire [他]《ややフォーマル》(努力・能力・行動によって)得る, 身につける ; (与えられて)手に入れる ◇She has *acquired* a good knowledge of English. 彼女は十分英語力を身につけている ◇He has *acquired* a reputation for dishonesty. 彼は不誠実だと評されている ◇I have recently *acquired* a taste for olives. 私は最近オリーブが好きになった ◇How did the gallery come to *acquire* so many Picassos? その画廊はどうやってそんなに多くのピカソ作品を手に入れることになったのですか ❶ *acquire* はしばしば, 人があり様子や振る舞い方を見せ始める時や物事が変わり始める時について用いられる. ◆ to *acquire* a/an reputation/bad name/criminal record/tan/look/appearance (評判を得る/悪評を得る/前科がつく/日焼けする/様子をおびる/体裁を身につける). ◆ to *acquire* a love of/ taste for sth (物事を好きになる/食物の味を覚える). 人が新しい技能を習得するときにも用いられる. ☞ **acquire** (BUY),

get

acquire (LEARN)
take [他] (特定の源から)得る, 取る ◇The scientists are *taking* water samples from the river. 科学者たちはその川から試料の水を採取している ◇Part of her article is *taken* straight (= copied) out of my book. 彼女の記事の一部は私の本からのそのままの引用である ◇The machine *takes* its name from its inventor. その機械の名前は発明者から取られている ❶ *take* はこの意味では, 科学者や技師が特定の源から, サンプル, 標本, 水, 細胞, 鉱物などを手に入れるときにしばしば用いられる. より大きな文書から, 情報, 記事, 抜粋, 例を得るときにも用いられる.
,pick sth 'up 句動詞《ややインフォーマル》(物事を)手に入れる, もらう ◇I *picked up* a few leaflets when I was out today. 私は今日外出時に数枚のチラシをもらった ◇I *picked up* £30 in tips today. 今日は30ポンド, チップをもらった ◇I seem to have *picked up* a terrible cold from somewhere. どこかでひどい風邪をうつされてしまったようだ ❶ *pick sth up* はしばしば, どこかに出かけているときに物事を得ることを表す. また, お金を稼いだり, 勝ち取ったりすること, 傷病を負うことについても用いられる. ☞ **SUFFER FROM STH**
,take sth 'out 句動詞 (公式文書を)手に入れる, (サービスを)受ける ◇We had to *take out* a loan to pay for the car. 自動車代金を払うためにローンを組まなければならなかった ◇How much does it cost to *take out* an ad in a newspaper? 新聞に広告を出すのにいくらかかりますか ❶ 一般的に, 保険[年金]をかける, 購読の申し込みをする, ローンを組む, 担保をつけて借り入れをする, 広告を出すのに *take out* を用いる.
get 'hold of sth フレーズ (ほしい[必要な]ものを)見つける ◇It's almost impossible to *get hold of* tickets for the final. 決勝戦のチケットを手に入れるのはほとんど不可能です ◇How did the press *get hold of* the story? 記者たちはどうやってその話をつかんだのだろう

2 **get・receive・accept・derive sth from sth・reap・collect**
与えられるか, 送られるかによって入手する
【類語訳】得る, 手に入れる, 受け取る, 受領する, 勝ち取る

文型&コロケーション
▶ to get/ receive/ accept/ derive/ reap/ collect sth **from** sb/ sth
▶ to get/ receive/ accept/ collect a/ an **medal/ award/ prize**
▶ to get/ receive/ accept/ collect (your) **winnings/ compensation**
▶ to get/ receive/ accept **treatment/ payment/ help**
▶ to get/ receive/ accept a/ an **call/ message/ complaint/ invitation/ request/ answer**
▶ to get/ receive/ derive/ reap (a/ the) **benefit**
▶ to get/ receive/ reap the **dividends/ profits/ rewards**
▶ to get/ receive a/ an **reply/ letter/ impression/ shock/ prison sentence**
▶ to get/ derive **amusement/ enjoyment/ pleasure/ satisfaction/ comfort** from sth

get [他, 受身なし]《ややインフォーマル, 特に話し言葉》得る, 手に入れる, 受け取る ◇I *got* a letter from Dave this morning. デイヴからは手紙を受け取った ◇He *gets* (= earns) about $40,000 a year. 彼は年に4万ドル稼ぎます ◇This room *gets* very little sunshine. この部屋は日当たりはとんどありません ◇I *get* the impression that he is bored with his job. 彼は仕事にうんざりしているような印象を受ける ◇I *got* a shock when I saw the bill. 請求書を見てショックを受けた ◇She *got* great satisfaction from seeing his embarrassment. 彼女は彼の当惑ぶりを見て大いに気をよくした

receive [他]《ややフォーマル、特に書き言葉》受け取る、受領する ◇I've just *received* this letter from an old friend. 旧友からちょうどこの手紙を受け取ったところだ ◇Please let me know as soon as you *receive* payment. 支払いを受けたらすぐに知らせてください ◇He *received* an award for bravery from the police service. 彼は勇敢さに対して警察から賞を受けた

ノート **get**と**receive**の使い分け：両語の主な違いは使用領域。receiveはややフォーマルで、特に書き言葉で使われるのに対して、getは話し言葉で普通に使われる語である。shockやimpressionのような突然の感情はgetまたはreceiveすることができる。一方enjoyment, pleasure, satisfactionなどの、ある一定の時間にわたって経験する感情はふつうgetすることはできるがreceiveすることはできない。

accept [他]《ややフォーマル》受け取る、受け入れる ◇My article has been *accepted* for publication. 私の記事は採用され掲載された ◇This machine only *accepts* coins. この機械は硬貨しか使えません ◇Will you *accept* a cheque? 小切手でも構いませんか

de'rive sth from sth 句動詞《フォーマル》(行為からよい感情[結果]を)得る、引き出す ◇He *derived* great pleasure *from* painting. 彼は絵を描くのが何より楽しみだった ❶概して人は何かからamusement, benefit, comfort, enjoyment, fulfilment, inspiration, pleasure, satisfactionなどをderiveする。

reap [他]《特に書き言葉》(行為の結果として)受ける、手に入れる ◇They are now *reaping the fruits* of all their hard work. 彼らは今、懸命にやった仕事の成果を手に入れつつある ❶概して人は仕事からdividends, fruits, profits, rewardsをreapする。自分が行った何か悪いことの結果をきにもreap the consequencesと言うことができる。

collect [他] 勝ち取る、(代償として)手に入れる ◇We were invited to London to *collect* our prize. 授賞のためにロンドンに招待された ◇She *collected* £25,000 in compensation. 彼女は代償として2万5千ポンド受け取った

3 get・reach・make・make it・hit・catch up
移動の末に特定の場所に到る
【類語訳】着く、到着する、たどり着く、間に合う、追いつく

文型&コロケーション
▶to get/ make it **to** a place
▶to get/ reach/ make it **here/ home/ there**
▶to get **to**/ reach/ make it **to** your **destination**
▶to get **to**/ reach/ make/ make it **to the summit**
▶to get **to**/ reach/ make it **to**/ hit the **border**

get [自]《副詞や前置詞と共に》《特に話し言葉》着く、到着する ◇We're aiming to *get* to the party at about nine. 私たちは9時ごろパーティーに着くことを目指しています ◇I *got back* an hour ago. 一時間前に戻った ◇They *got in* very late last night. 彼らは昨晩とても遅く帰宅した ◇We only *got as far as* the next town. 隣町までしかたどり着かなかった ☞ **get** (GO 1)

reach [他]《特に書き言葉》(目的地に)着く、着する；人の目に留まる[耳に入る] ◇It took them three hours to *reach* the opposite shore. 彼らは対岸にたどり着くのに3時間かかった ◇The beach can only be *reached* by boat. そのビーチにはボートでしか行けません ◇I hope this letter *reaches* you. この手紙があなたに届きますように ◇The rumours eventually *reached* the President. 噂はとうとう大統領の耳に届いた

ノート **get**と**reach**の使い分け：これらの単語の主たる違いは使用域である。reachは特に書き言葉で、getは話し言葉でふつうに用いられる。getは目的語をとらないが、常に副詞または副詞句をとる。意味する場所を聞き手が理解できると思われる場合には、there, in, backのように具体的ではないものをとることも多い。reachは常に目的語をとり、ふつう到着する場所についてより具体的である。

make [他、受身なし]《ややインフォーマル》(首尾よく特定のイベント・場所・位置に)たどり着く ◇I'm sorry I didn't *make* the party last night. ゆうべはパーティーに行けなくて残念でした ◇He'll never *make* (= get a place in) the team. 彼はチームには入れないだろう ◇The story *made* (= appeared on) the front pages of the national newspapers. その記事は全国紙の第1面を飾った

'make it フレーズ《ややインフォーマル》(首尾よくイベント・場所に)たどり着く、時間どおりに間に合う ◇I don't think I'll be able to *make it* to the meeting. 会議には出席できないと思います ◇Even if we take a taxi I don't think we'll *make it in time*. タクシーに乗っても時間には合わないと思うよ ◇The flight leaves in twenty minutes — we'll never *make it*. その便は20分後に出てしまう一絶対に間に合わない

hit [他]《インフォーマル》(場所に)到着する、(道に)出る ◇Traffic was heavy when they *hit* the main road. 幹線道路に入ると渋滞していた ◇The president *hits town* (= is visiting the town) tomorrow. 大統領が明日街に来られます

,catch 'up《英でまた,catch sb 'up》(先を行っている人に)追いつく ◇We stopped for a few minutes to let the others *catch up*. 私たちは数分立ち止まって他の人たちが追いつくのを待った ◇On lap 45 Hunt's car was *catching up* fast. 45周目でハントの車は急速に追い上げていた ◇You go on ahead. I'll *catch up with* you. 先に行ってください。追いつきますから ◇She hurried to *catch* him *up*.《英》彼女は彼に追いつこうと急いだ

gift [名]

gift・present・donation・contribution・tip・gratuity・handout
特別な機会[手助けするため、礼を述べるためなど]に人に与える物
【類語訳】贈り物、プレゼント、寄付、寄贈、チップ、補助金、援助金、施し

文型&コロケーション
▶a gift/ present/ donation/ contribution/ tip/ gratuity/ handout **for/ from** sb
▶a gift/ present/ donation/ contribution **to** sb/ sth
▶£50,000, $10, etc. **in** gifts/ donations/ contributions/ tips/ handouts
▶a **small** gift/ present/ donation/ contribution/ tip/ gratuity
▶a **large/ generous** gift/ present/ donation/ contribution/ tip
▶a/ an **birthday/ wedding/ anniversary/ Christmas** gift/ present

▶a **cash** gift/ donation/ handout
▶a **free** gift/ handout
▶to **get** a gift/ present/ donation/ contribution/ tip/ handout
▶to **receive** a gift/ present/ donation/ contribution/ gratuity
▶to **send** (sb) a gift/ present/ donation/ contribution
▶to **leave** (sb) a gift/ present/ donation/ tip/ gratuity
▶to **give** (sb) a gift/ present/ donation/ tip
▶to **make** a donation/ contribution

gift [C]（ややフォーマル，特に書き言葉）（金品の）贈り物 ◇There's a free *gift* for every reader. 読者全員に景品があります ◇The gift of love is the greatest *gift* a person can give or receive. 愛という贈り物は，人が与えたり受けたりできる最も素晴らしい贈り物である ◇The party was originally funded by a *gift* of £50,000 from a top motor manufacturer. その党は元々，大手自動車メーカーからの5万ポンドの贈与という資金提供を受けていた ◇All such posts are *in the gift of* the managing director (= only given by the managing director).《英》そういったすべてのポストは最高経営責任者だけが与えることができる ☞ **give** (GIVE 3)

present [C]（特別な機会[礼として]の）贈り物，プレゼント ◇What can I get him for a birthday *present*? 彼の誕生日プレゼントに何がいいかしら

|ノート| **gift**と**present**の使い分け：gift は，present よりも頻繁に，特にビジネス関連で用いられる。商店はクリスマス用の gift (Christmas gift ideas) について宣伝し，買い物客たちは家族や友人のために買ったクリスマスの present (Christmas presents) について語るものである。present はふつう，個人から個人へ与えられるもの。gift は，会社が与えることもあり (a corporate gift)，組織に向けて与えられることもある。present はふつう品物であるが，gift はお金や，愛／命という贈り物 (the gift of love/life) のこともある。×funded by a *present* of £50,000. ×She gave me the *present* of love. だが特に《米》では，gift は必ずしもフォーマルなものではなく，時として個人的な文脈で present の代わりに用いられることもある。◆The watch was a *gift/present* from my mother.（その時計は母からの贈り物だった）

donation [C]（人・慈善団体などへの）寄付（行為）◇I made a £200 *donation* to charity. 200ポンドを慈善目的で寄付した ◇The work of the charity is funded by voluntary *donations*. その慈善事業は自発的な寄付によって資金を得ている ◇Organ *donation* (= allowing doctors to use organs from your body after your death in order to save a sick person's life) has not kept pace with the demand for transplants. 臓器提供は移植の需要に対応できていない ☞ **donate** (GIVE 3)

contribution [C, U]（費用のまかなel[資金調達]用の）寄付金，寄贈品；寄付行為 ◇He has made several valuable *contributions towards* the upkeep of the cathedral. 彼は大聖堂保存のために何度か高額の寄付をしてきた ◇*Contributions* of cakes and other items for the cake sale can be left in the school office. ケーキセールのために寄付されたケーキやその他の品物は，学校の事務所に置いていくことができます ◇We rely entirely on voluntary *contribution*. 私たちは有志の寄付にすっかり頼っています ☞ **contribute** (GIVE 3)

|ノート| **donation**と**contribution**の使い分け：contribution は他人がすでに与えたものに付け加えられて全体の一部となる金や物を強調する。contribution はしばしば，期待さ

れたり求められたりするものだが，donation は自発的な贈り物としてとらえられる。

tip [C]（レストランなどでの）チップ ◇Are we supposed to leave a *tip*? チップを置かなくちゃならないの ◇He gave the waiter a generous *tip*. 彼はそのウェイターにチップを弾んだ
▶**tip** 動 [他, 自] ◇Did you remember to *tip* the waiter? 忘れずにウェイターにチップをやりましたか ◇Americans were always welcome because they tended to *tip* heavily. アメリカ人はチップを弾むことが多かったので，いつも歓迎された

gratuity [C]《フォーマル》（レストランなどでの）チップ ◇Our employees may not accept *gratuities*. うちの従業員はチップの受け取りを禁じている

handout [C]（しばしば悪口）（政府からの）補助金，援助金，施し ◇The company is currently thriving thanks to a £70,000 government *handout*. その会社は，7万ポンドの政府補助金のおかげで，現在成長を続けている ❶ handout は貧困者たちにも与えられることがある。☞ **handout** (AID), **hand sth out** (DISTRIBUTE)

girl 名 ☞ CHILD

▶**girl・youth・lad・teenager・teen・adolescent・juvenile**
まだ大人でない若い人々を表す
【類語訳】若い女性，女の子，若者，少年，青年，ティーンエイジャー，未成年者

|文型&コロケーション|
▶a **young** girl/ lad/ teenager/ adolescent
▶an **older** girl/ youth/ teenager
▶a **local** girl/ youth/ lad/ teenager
▶an **awkward** teenager/ teen/ adolescent
▶youth/ juvenile **crime/ unemployment**

girl [C]《時に侮辱的》若い女性，女の子 ◇Alex is not interested in *girls* yet. アレックスはまだ女の子に興味がない ◇One of the *girls* at work told me about it. 職場の女の子の一人がそのことを教えてくれた ◇He married the *girl* next door. 彼は隣の娘と結婚した ❶ girl はしばしば，インフォーマルまたはうちとけた話で若い女性に言及するのに用いる。だが，よりフォーマルまたは専門的な仕事の話の中で girl と呼ばれると，侮辱的で敬意を欠くと感じる若い女性もいる。反意 **guy** (MAN 1), **girl** (CHILD)

youth [C]《しばしば悪口》（品行の悪い[違法行為をする]）若者 ◇The fight was started by a gang of *youths*. その喧嘩は若者の一団が始めた ❶ youth や the youth（複数扱い）は，若者を集合的に表す句で用いられる。◆The Royal Family is facing an uncertain future, according to *the nation's youth*.（国の若者たちによれば，王室は不確かな将来に直面している）◆Many people think *the youth of today* are not taught proper standards of behaviour.（今日の若者は適切な行動基準を教えられていないと，多くの人たちが考えている）◆*youth* politics/culture（若者の政治活動／若者文化）◆an increase in *youth* unemployment（若年失業者の増加）。つまり，(the) youth は，単独ではなく，常により長い句の一部として用いられる。×*The youth* are not taught proper standards of behaviour. ☞ **youth** (CHILDHOOD)

lad [C]《特に英，インフォーマル》少年，青年 ◇He's a nice *lad*. 彼はいいやつだ ◇Things have changed since I was a *lad*. 少年の頃からすると、状況は変わってしまった

teenager [C] (13〜19歳の)ティーンエイジャー ◇a magazine aimed at *teenagers* ティーンエイジャー向けの雑誌 ◇Many *teenagers* are embarrassed by their parents. ティーンエイジャーの多くは両親にきまり悪い思いをさせられる ☞ **teenage** (YOUNG)

ノート **youth, lad, teenager の使い分け**：teenager は性別を問わないが、13から19歳の年齢でなければならない。youth は、それよりは厳密ではなく、20代初めまでの人を表すことができる。lad もあまり厳密ではないが、19歳以上の人にはふつう用いない。若者を指す場合、lad も teenager より否定的で、結びつく語も(常にというわけではないが)否定的なことが多い。◆ angry/drunken/masked *youths* (怒れる/酔った/覆面をした若者) lad に結びつく語も ◆ a handsome/decent/fine/good/great/lovely/nice/smashing/bright/sensible *lad* (ハンサムな/きちんとした/優れた/善良な/立派な/きれいな感じのよい/素晴らしい/聡明な/分別のある若者)。特に新聞やよりフォーマルな英語において、一般的な若者について語る場合には、youth は teenager よりふつうに用いられる。◆ unemployed/modern/educated *youth* (失業した/現代の/教養のある若者) ◆ *youth* crime/employment (若者の犯罪/失業率)

teen [C] 《インフォーマル、特に米》ティーンエイジャー ◇Two plain-looking *teens* were sitting on the couch watching TV. 見かけの地味なティーンエイジャーが二人ソファに座ってテレビを見ていた ☞ **teen** (YOUNG), **teens** (CHILDHOOD)

adolescent [C] 《ややフォーマル》(子どもから大人に成長しつつある)若者 ◇*adolescents* between the ages of 13 and 18, and the problems they face 13〜18歳の年齢の若者と、彼らが直面している問題 ◇Stop acting like an *adolescent*! 若造みたいなことをするのはやめろ ☞ **adolescence** (CHILDHOOD), **adolescent** (YOUNG)

juvenile [C] 《フォーマル or 法律》(違法行為をする[で罪に問われる])未成年者 ◇Most of the suspects were *juveniles* under the age of 17. 容疑者たちの大半は17歳以下の未成年者だった ☞ **juvenile** (YOUNG)

give 動

1 give・award・present・confer・transfer・accord・bestow・lavish sth on/upon sb/sth
人に何かを持たせる
【類義訳】渡す、あげる、与える、授与する、贈呈する、移管する、譲渡する

文型&コロケーション
▶ to give/ award/ present/ transfer/ accord sth **to** sb
▶ to confer/ bestow/ lavish sth **on** sb
▶ to give/ award/ accord sb **sth**
▶ to give/ present/ bestow **gifts**
▶ to lavish **gifts** on/ upon sb/ sth
▶ to give/ present/ bestow an **award**
▶ to give/ award/ present a **prize**
▶ to give/ confer/ accord/ bestow (a/ an) **honour/ title/ status**
▶ to confer/ bestow a **favour**
▶ to give/ accord/ bestow an **accolade**

give [他, 自] (プレゼントとして)渡す、あげる、与える ◇What are you *giving* your father for his birthday? お父さんの誕生日には何をあげるの ◇Did you *give* the waiter a tip? ウェイターにチップをあげましたか ◇We don't usually *give* presents to people at work. ふつうは職場の人たちにプレゼントをあげたりしません ◇They say it's better to *give* than to receive. もらうよりあげる方がいいと言われている

award [他] (報酬・賞を正式に)授与する、与える ◇He was *awarded* damages of £50,000. 彼に5万ポンドの損害賠償金が支払われた ◇The judges *awarded* equal points to both finalists. 審判は決勝進出者両者に同じ得点を与えた ❶ award は一般的に、points, prize, trophy, compensation, damages と結びつく。 ☞ **award** (AWARD), **award** (COMPENSATION), **grant** (ALLOW)

present [他] (式典で正式に)贈呈する、授与する、与える ◇The local MP will start the race and *present* the prizes. その地元選出の下院議員がレースをスタートさせ、賞を贈呈する予定だ ◇The sword was *presented* by the family to the museum. その刀は家族によって博物館に寄贈された ◇On his retirement, colleagues *presented him with* a set of golf clubs. 彼の引退に際して、仲間たちは彼にゴルフクラブ一式をプレゼントした ❶ present sth, present sb with sth, present sth to sb の形で用いられる。

confer [-rr-] [他] 《フォーマル》(賞・学位・称号・権利を)授与する、与える ◇An honorary degree was *conferred* on him by Oxford University in 2005. 2005年にオックスフォード大学から名誉学位が彼に授与された

transfer (-rr-) [他] (正式に)移管する、譲渡する ◇He *transferred* the property to his son. 彼は資産を息子に譲渡した

accord [他] 《フォーマル》(権威・地位・待遇を)授ける、与える ◇Our society *accords* the family great importance. 私たちの社会ではその一族に重きを置いている ◇There were complaints about the special treatment *accorded* to some minority groups. いくつかの少数派集団に与えられた特別待遇に対して苦情が出ていた ❶ accord はしばしば職業や宗教など特定のグループに地位や承認を与える場合に用いられる。

bestow [他] 《フォーマル》(敬意を示すために)授与する、与える ◇It was a title *bestowed* upon him by the king. それは彼に王から授けられた称号だった ❶ bestow は、人々に rights, respect, honours, titles を与えることを言う場合に最も頻繁に用いられるが、敬意を示すために与えられる特別な贈り物についても用いることができる。

lavish sth on/upon sb/sth 句動詞 《書き言葉》(人・物事に)惜しみなく[ふんだんに]与える ◇She *lavishes* most of her attention *on* her youngest son. 彼女はほとんど末の息子ばかりをかまっている ❶ lavish sth on/upon sb/sth は一般的に、gifts, praise, attention と結びつく。

2 give・hand・hand sb/sth over・pass
人の(両)手に物を持たせる、容易に手の届く場所に物を置く
【類義訳】渡す、手渡す、引き渡す、回す

文型&コロケーション
▶ to give/ hand/ hand sb/ sth over/ pass sth **to** sb
▶ to **just** give/ hand/ hand over/ pass sth
▶ to give/ hand/ hand over/ pass sth **immediately/ promptly**

give [他] (手に)渡す ◇They were all *given* a box to carry. 彼らみんなに運搬用の箱が渡された ◇She *gave*

her ticket to the woman at the check-in desk. 彼女はチェックイン・デスクの女性に自分のチケットを渡した
hand [他] (手に) 渡す, 手渡す ◇She *handed* the letter to me. 彼女は私に手紙を手渡した ◇She *handed* me the letter. 彼女は私に手紙を手渡した
,hand sb/sth 'over 句動詞 (公式 [正式] に) 人・物を) 引き渡す ◇He *handed over* a cheque for $20,000. 彼は2万ドルの小切手を渡した ◇I knew I should have *handed* you *over* to the police! 君を警察に引き渡すべきだったのはわかっていた
pass [他] 手渡す, (手の届くところに) 回す ◇*Pass* the salt, please. 塩を回してください ◇Could you *pass* me that book? その本を取ってくださいますか ❶ *pass* はしばしば、人が自分の手が届かない物を取って渡してくれるよう別の人に頼むときに、話し言葉で用いられる。

ノート give, hand, pass の使い分け: hand は、話し言葉より (特に、文語的な語で) 用いられることが多い。give は、書き言葉・話し言葉どちらでも頻繁に用いられるが、話し言葉で特によく用いられる。pass は、話し言葉での要望で用いることが多いが、書き言葉・文語でも用いる。

3 give・contribute・donate・chip in (sth)
援助のためにお金や品物を与える
【類語訳】寄付する, 寄贈する, 提供する

文型&コロケーション
▶ to give/ contribute/ donate (sth) **to** sth
▶ to give/ contribute/ donate chip in **£10/ $100,000**, etc.
▶ to give/ contribute/ donate **cash/ a sum**
▶ to give/ chip in with a **donation**
▶ to give/ donate **blood**
▶ to give/ contribute/ donate **generously**

give [他, 自] (慈善団体に金・食糧・衣料を) 寄付する, 寄贈する; 献血する ◇We need your help — please *give* generously. みなさんのご協力を必要としています—気前よくご寄付をお願いします ◇They both *gave* regularly to charity. 彼らは二人ともしばしば慈善事業に寄付した ◇I *gave* a small donation. 私は少しだけ寄付した ☞ **gift** (GIFT)
contribute [他, 自] 《ややフォーマル》 (援助のためにお金・品物を) 寄付する, 寄贈する ◇The writer personally *contributed* £5,000 to the earthquake fund. その作家は地震基金に5千ポンドを個人的に寄付した ◇Would you like to *contribute* to our collection? 私どものコレクションに寄贈していただけますか ◇Do you wish to *contribute*? 寄付をなさることを御希望ですか ☞ **contribution** (GIFT), **contributor** (SPONSOR)
donate [他] 《ややフォーマル》(慈善団体にお金・品物を) 寄付する, 寄贈する; (血液・臓器を) 提供する ◇I would like to thank our sponsors, The Woodworks, for *donating* the prizes for this competition. このコンペの賞品を提供してくださった, 我々のスポンサーであるウッドワークス社に感謝いたします ◇All *donated* blood is tested for HIV and other infections. 献血された血液は全部, HIVなどの感染症の検査を受けている ☞ **donation** (GIFT), **donor** (SPONSOR)

ノート **contribute** と **donate** の使い分け: contribute は、数多くの人がお金、食べ物、衣類などを慈善事業や基金に与えることを表す。donate は、物を与えた主 (で) である個人や

会社を強調する。contribute が個人について用いられる場合、ふつう大きな寄付をした人物を指す。
chip in, chip in sth 句動詞 (-pp-) 《インフォーマル》 (共同購入できるように金を) 出し合う ◇If everyone *chips in* we'll be able to buy her a really nice present. みんなでお金を出し合えば、彼女にとって素晴らしいプレゼントを買ってあげられるわ ◇We each *chipped in (with)* £5. 私たちはそれぞれ5ポンドを出し合った

give way 動

give way・give in・submit・bow to sth・back down・relent・yield
人や物事からの圧力 [要求] に抵抗するのをやめる
【類語訳】譲歩する, 身を任せる, 屈する, 服従する, 撤回する, 取り消す, 折れる, 負ける

文型&コロケーション
▶ to give way/ give in/ submit/ bow/ yield **to** sb/ sth
▶ to give way/ give in/ back down/ relent **on** sth
▶ to give way/ give in/ submit/ bow/ yield to sb's **demands**
▶ to give way/ give in/ submit/ bow/ yield to **pressure**
▶ to give in/ submit to **authority**
▶ to give in/ yield to **temptation**
▶ to **be forced to** give way/ give in/ submit/ bow to sth/ back down/ yield
▶ to **refuse to** give in/ submit/ bow to sth/ back down/ yield

give 'way 仔仂 《特に英》 (気は進まないが) 譲歩する; (感情に) 身を任せる ◇He refused to *give way* on any of the points. 彼はどの点についても譲歩したくなかった ◇In the end she always *gave way* to him because she could not bear his moods. 彼女は彼の不機嫌に耐えられず、結局いつも彼に譲歩した ◇She never *gave way* to anger. 彼女は怒りに身を任せることは決してなかった
,give 'in 句動詞 譲歩する, 屈する ◇The authorities have shown no signs of *giving in* to the kidnappers' demands. 当局には誘拐犯の要求に屈服する気配がまったくなかった ◇He reluctantly *gave in* to the pressure. 彼はしぶしぶ圧力に屈した ◇In the end, they were forced to *give in*. 結局彼らは譲歩せざるを得なかった 反意 **resist** (RESIST)

ノート **give way** と **give in** の使い分け: 多くの場合、どちらも用いることができる。give way は、人の要求や圧力に対してよりも人に対して譲歩する場合に give in より用いられることが多い。give way は感情に身を任せることにも用いることができるが、give in はできない。×She never *gave in* to anger.

submit (-tt-) [自, 他] 《ややフォーマル》 (権威・支配・強い力に) 服従する ◇She refused to *submit* to threats. 彼女は脅しには屈服しようとはしなかった ◇He *submitted himself* to a search by the guards. 彼は警備員による所持品検査を受け入れた 反意 **resist** (RESIST)
'bow to sth 句動詞 (他の人が望むので) いやいや同意する ◇He felt he had to *bow to* her wishes. 彼女の意向に従わざるを得ないと思った ◇She *bowed to the inevitable* (= accepted a situation in which she had no choice) and resigned. 彼女はやむを得ず事態を受け入れて辞任した
,back 'down 句動詞 (他の人が強く反対する要望・意見を

glad, gloom

撤回する, 取り消す ◇She refused to *back down* on a point of principle. 彼女は主義主張を撤回しようとはしなかった ◇We cannot *back down from* the decision, which we believe is right and just. 正しく公正だと信じているその決定を撤回することは出来ない

relent [自]《ややフォーマル》(拒んだ末に結局)同意する, 折れる ◇'Well, just for a little while then,' she said, finally *relenting*. 「じゃあ, ほんのちょっとだけよ」と彼女はついに折れて言った

yield [自]《ややフォーマル, 書き言葉》(圧力に)屈する；(自らの欲求に)負ける ◇After a long siege, the town was forced to *yield*. 長い包囲攻撃の後, 町は降伏を余儀なくされた ◇I *yielded* to temptation and had a chocolate bar. 誘惑に勝てずチョコレートバーを食べた

glad [形] ☞GRATEFUL

glad・happy・pleased・delighted・proud・relieved・thrilled・overjoyed
人々が起きた事[これから起こる事]に幸せを感じることを表す
【類義訳】うれしい, 喜んだ, ほっとした, 大喜びの

relieved	glad happy pleased proud	delighted	thrilled overjoyed

文型&コロケーション

▸ glad/ happy/ pleased/ delighted/ relieved/ thrilled/ overjoyed **about** sth
▸ pleased/ delighted/ relieved/ thrilled/ overjoyed **at** sth
▸ pleased/ delighted/ thrilled/ overjoyed **with/ by** sth
▸ glad/ happy/ pleased/ delighted/ relieved/ thrilled/ overjoyed **for** sb
▸ glad/ happy/ pleased/ delighted/ proud/ relieved/ thrilled/ overjoyed **that**...
▸ glad/ happy/ pleased/ delighted/ relieved/ thrilled/ overjoyed **to see/ hear/ find/ know**...
▸ glad/ happy/ pleased/ delighted/ proud **to say (that**...**)**
▸ a happy/ delighted **smile/ laugh**
▸ **very** glad/ happy/ pleased/ proud/ relieved
▸ **absolutely** delighted/ thrilled

glad [名詞の前はまれ] うれしい, 喜んだ ◇'He doesn't need the pills any more.' 'I'm *glad about* that.' 「彼にはもうその錠剤は必要ないよ」「それを聞いて嬉しいよ」 ◇He was *glad* he'd come. 彼は来られたことを喜んだ ◇She's absolutely fine, I'm *glad* to say. 嬉しいことに, 彼女はすっかり元気だよ ◇She was *glad* when the meeting was over. 会議が終わって彼女はほっとした 反意 sorry (UPSET)

happy 喜んだ, うれしい ◇We are *happy* to announce the engagement of our daughter. 娘の婚約をご報告できることをうれしく思います ◇'We're getting married!' 'I'm so *happy for* you both!' 「私たち結婚します」「お二人とも本当におめでとう」 反意 sorry (UPSET)

pleased [名詞の前では用いない] 喜んだ, うれしい ◇She was very *pleased* with her exam results. 彼女は試験の結果にとても満足していた ◇I was *pleased* to hear you've been promoted. 昇進されたと聞いてうれしかったです ◇*Pleased to meet you* (= said when you are introduced to sb).《特に英, フォーマル, 話し言葉》お会いできてうれしいです 反意 **displeased** (UNHAPPY 2), ☞ **please** (PLEASE)

ノート **glad, happy, pleased** の使い分け: **pleased** は, 人や物事について判断してよいと認めたことを暗示する. 反対の **displeased** は, 判断の結果よくなかったことを表す. **pleased** は, 特に自分に好都合なことが起きたことも意味する. その反対の意味を持つのは **disappointed** である. **glad** は, 自分や他人のために物事に感謝する場合に用いられることが多い. その反対の **sorry** には, 同情は含まれるが, 判断は含まれない. **happy** は, **glad, pleased, satisfied** の意味にもなる.
☞ HAPPY

delighted 大喜びの；うれしそうな ◇I'm *delighted* by your news. 君の知らせにとても喜んでいる ❶ *delighted* はしばしば, 招待に応じる場合に用いられる. ◆'Can you stay for dinner?' 'I'd be *delighted* (to).'「夕食までいられる?」「喜んで」

▸ **delightedly** [副] ◇She laughed *delightedly*. 彼女はうれしそうに笑った

proud (所有物・行為・関わり事について)喜ばしく[誇らしく]思う ◇*proud* parents 誇らしげな両親 ◇the *proud owner* of a new car 新車を自慢する所有者 ◇He was *proud of* himself for not giving up. 彼はあきらめない自分のことを誇りに思っていた ◇Your achievements are *something to be proud of*. 君の功績は誇るべきものだ ◇I feel very *proud* to be a part of the team. チームの一員であることを非常に誇りに思います ☞ **pride** (SATISFACTION), **pride yourself on sth** (BOAST)

▸ **proudly** [副] ◇She *proudly* displayed her prize. 彼女は誇らしげに賞品を見せた

relieved (不快な物事が終わって[起こらなくて])ほっとした(様子の) ◇You'll be *relieved* to know your jobs are safe. 自分の仕事が大丈夫だとわかるとほっとするでしょう ◇I'm just *relieved* that nobody was hurt. 誰も傷ついていなくて本当にほっとしています ◇They exchanged *relieved* glances. 彼らは安堵して顔を見合わせた ☞ **relief** (RELIEF), **thankful** (GRATEFUL)

thrilled [名詞の前では用いない]《ややインフォーマル》興奮して大喜びの ◇I was *thrilled* to be invited. 招かれて大喜びした

overjoyed [名詞の前では用いない] 大喜びの ◇She was *overjoyed* at the birth of her daughter. 彼女は娘の誕生に大喜びした

ノート **delighted, thrilled, overjoyed** の使い分け: **overjoyed, thrilled** は **delighted** より強い感情を表すことがある. **delighted** は **absolutely, more than, only too** を伴ってより強い意味を表せる. ◆I was *more than delighted* at the great success he had achieved. (彼が収めた大成功がとてもうれしかった). **overjoyed** と **thrilled** は, **not exactly, less than** を伴って否定的・反語的な意味を表すことができる. ◆She was *not exactly overjoyed* at the prospect of looking after her niece. (彼女は姪の面倒を見ることになるのが必ずしもうれしいわけではなかった). ◆He's *less than thrilled* at the prospect of working for his old rival. (彼はかつてのライバルのもとで働くことになる事態に, わくわくしているというわけでは決してない).

gloom [名] ☞GRIEF

gloom・depression・the blues・despondency
悲しくて希望が持てない感情を表す

↳**gloom**

【類語訳】憂鬱, 陰気, 意気消沈, 落胆, 失望

文型&コロケーション
▶ gloom/ despondency **about** sth
▶ **deep/ deepening** gloom/ depression/ despondency
▶ **to fill sb with/ sink into/ plunge into** gloom/ depression
▶ the gloom/ depression **deepens/ lifts**
▶ **a feeling of** gloom/ depression/ despondency
▶ **a fit of** gloom/ depression/ the blues

gloom [U, 単数で] (一団の人々の間の)憂鬱, 陰気 ◇There is general *gloom* about the farming industry. 農業界には憂鬱な気分が広がっている ◇The *gloom* deepened as the election results came in. 選挙結果が入ってくるにつれ雰囲気がさらに暗くなった ◇An air of *gloom and despondency* settled over the household. 陰鬱と失望の空気が一家をおおった ☞**gloomy** (DEPRESSED), **gloomy** (NEGATIVE)

depression [U] (困難に対しての)意気消沈, 憂鬱 ◇These results should not be a cause for *depression*. これらの結果が憂鬱の種となってはならない ◇Her mood swung from *the depths of depression* to coping well. 彼女は憂鬱のどん底から抜け出してうまくそれに対処できるようになった ☞**depress** (DISCOURAGE 2), **depressed** (DEPRESSED), **depressing** (NEGATIVE)

the blues [複数で] (ややインフォーマル) 憂鬱, 気のふさぎ ◇Everyone has had the feeling of *the* Monday morning *blues*. 誰もが月曜の朝の憂鬱な気分を味わっていた ◇I'm planning a break in the sun as a way to *beat the blues*. 憂鬱な気分を追い払う方法として日差しの中で休息を取ることにしています

despondency [U] (ややフォーマル) (やっていることがうまく行かないことへの)落胆, 失望 ◇Their earlier enthusiasm has been replaced by a mood of *despondency*. 彼らのかつての熱意はすっかり失意へと変貌を遂げていた ☞**despondent** (DEPRESSED)

go 動

1 go・get・head・pass・move・travel・make your way・make for sth・advance・proceed・run
ある場所から別の場所へ移る
【類語訳】行く, 着く, 向かう, 進む, 出発する, 通る, 通り過ぎる, 移動する, 前進する

文型&コロケーション
▶ to go/ get/ pass/ move/ travel/ make your way/ advance/ proceed/ run **from... to...**
▶ to go/ get/ head/ move/ travel/ make your way/ advance/ proceed **to** sb/ sth
▶ to go/ head/ move/ travel/ make your way/ advance/ proceed/ run **towards** sb/ sth
▶ to head/ make **for** sb/ sth
▶ to go/ get somewhere/ make your way **by** bus/ train/ car, etc.
▶ to go/ get/ head/ make your way/ make for **home**

go [自] (副詞や前置詞と共に) 行く ◇She *went* into her room and shut the door behind her. 彼女は部屋に入って背後のドアを閉めた ◇She's *gone* to see her sister. 彼女は妹[姉]に会いに行った ◇Could you *go and* get me a towel? タオルを取りに行っていただけますか ◇*Go* get me

a towel. (米) タオルを取ってきて ◇Slow down — you're *going* too fast. スピードを落として一番すぎるよ ◇The car *went* skidding off the road. 車は横滑りして道路を外れて行った ❶been は人がある場所に行って戻っていた場合に過去分詞で用いられるが, gone はそうではない. ◆She's *gone* to town (= and is there now or on her way there). 彼女は町へ出かけた；現在は町にいるか, 向かっている途中 ◆I've just *been* to town (= I went to town and have now returned). (町に行ってきたところだ). ❶go はふつう, どこかへ移動している人の視点で用いられる. 反意 **come** (COME 1)
☞**go** (LEAVE 1)

get [自, 他] (副詞や前置詞と共に) (時に苦労して)行く, 着く, 行かせる ◇How can we *get* to the other side of town? どうしたら町の反対側へ行けますか ◇I don't know how he managed to *get* down from the roof. 彼がどうやって屋根から下りられたのかわからない ◇She *got* back into bed. 彼女はベッドに戻った ◇Where have they *got* to (= where are they)? 彼らはどこにいるの ◇We'd better call a taxi and *get* you home. タクシーを呼んでそれで君に帰宅してもらった方がいいね ☞**get** (GET 3)

head [自] (副詞や前置詞と共に) (ややインフォーマル) 向かう, 進む, 出発する ◇Where are we *heading*? どこに向かってるの ◇She *headed* for the door. 彼女はドアの方に進んだ ◇The boat was *heading* out to sea. 船は沖へ向かっていた

pass [自] (ややフォーマル) (副詞や前置詞と共に) (沿って[経由して])通る, 行く, (特定の地点を)通り過ぎる ◇The procession *passed* slowly along the street. 行列は通り沿いをゆっくり進んだ ◇Bomber planes were *passing* overhead all night. 爆撃機が一晩じゅう頭上を飛んでいた

move [自] (副詞や前置詞と共に) (特定の方向へ短距離を)移動する, 行く ◇Phil *moved* towards the window. フィルは窓の方に移動した ◇We *moved* a little nearer. 私たちはさらに少し近づいた ◇The traffic *moved* slowly along the highway. 幹線道路の車の流れはゆっくりだった

travel (-ll-, 米 -l-) [自] (特定の速度で[方向へ, 距離を])行く, 移動する ◇The truck was *travelling* at 90 mph when it veered off the road. 道路からそれたとき, トラックは時速90マイル出ていた ◇Messages *travel* from the nerve endings to the brain. メッセージは神経終末から脳に伝わる ◇News *travels fast* these days. 近頃ではニュースはすぐに伝わる

make your 'way フレーズ (副詞や前置詞と共に) (ゆっくりと[苦労して])行く, 向かう ◇Will you be able to *make your own way* to the airport (= get there without help or a ride)? 空港へ一人で行けますか ◇She turned and *made her way* home. 彼女はくるりと背を向けて家路についた

'make for sth 句動詞 (急いで[行く[去る]必要を感じて])向かう ◇People were *making for* the exits. 人々は出口に向かって急いでいた ◇He advised us to get out of the city and *make for* the coast. 彼は私たちに町を出て海岸にでも向かってはと助言した

advance [自] (ややフォーマル) (威嚇するために)進む, 前進する ◇Troops were given the order to *advance*. 部隊は前進命令を受けた ◇They had *advanced* 20 miles by nightfall. 彼らは日暮れまでに20マイル前進していた ◇The mob *advanced on* us, shouting angrily. 暴徒は怒号を発しながら私たちに迫ってきた 反意 **retreat**
▶ **advance** 名 [C] ◇Their *advance on* the city seemed unstoppable. 彼らの町への進攻は制止できないように思われた

go away

proceed [自]《副詞や前置詞と共に》《フォーマル》(特定の方向に)[旅を続けるために])進む ◇The marchers *proceeded* slowly along the street. デモの参加者たちは通り沿いをゆっくりと前進した ◇Passengers for Frankfurt should *proceed* to Gate 14. フランクフルトへ向かう乗客の皆さんは14番ゲートにお進みください

run [自]《副詞や前置詞と共に》(すばやく滑らかに)進む ◇The car *ran* off the road into a ditch. 車は道路を外れて排水溝に落ちた ◇A shiver *ran* down my spine. 背筋がぞくっとした ◇The sledge *ran* smoothly over the snow. そりは雪の上をすいすいと滑った ◇The old tramlines are still there but no trams *run* on them now. 古い路面電車の軌道はまだ残っているが、現在その軌道を走る電車はない

2 go・fly・travel・come・do・drive・ride・run・cover
異なる場所間の長い距離を移動する
【類語訳】行く、旅する、進む、走る、運行する

[文型&コロケーション]
▶ to go/ fly/ travel/ come/ drive/ ride/ run **from/ to** sth
▶ to go/ fly/ travel/ come/ drive/ ride **with** sb
▶ to go/ fly/ travel/ come/ do/ drive/ ride/ cover **50 miles/ 1,000 km**
▶ to go/ travel/ come **by air/ sea/ boat/ ship/ train/ car**
▶ to go/ fly/ travel/ come/ do sth/ cover sth **on foot**
▶ to go/ fly/ travel/ come/ drive **east/ north/ south/ west**
▶ to go/ travel/ come/ drive **overland**
▶ to travel/ come/ drive **a long distance**

go [自] (特定の距離を)行く、旅する ◇I usually *go* to work by bus. ふだんバスで通勤しています ◇She's *gone* to Brazil on vacation. 彼女は休暇でブラジルに行っています ◇I have to *go* to Rome on business. 私はローマへ出張しなければならない ◆Here's a list of things to remember before you *go*. これは出かける前に覚えておくべき事柄のリストです ◇We had *gone* many miles without seeing another car. 我々は他の車に出会うことなく何マイルも進んだ ❶ *been* は人がある場所に行って戻っている場合に過去分詞で用いられるが、*gone* はそうではない。◆She has *gone* to China (= she is now in China or is on her way there). (彼女は中国に行ってしまった；現在中国にいるか、向かう途中). ◆She's *been* to China (= she went to China and has now returned). (彼女は中国に行ったことがある；中国に行っていたが、今は戻っている). ☞ *go* (LEAVE 1)

fly [自, 他] 飛行機で行く ◇When are you *flying* to Bangkok? バンコクへはいつ発つ予定ですか ◇It was the first time I'd ever *flown*. 飛行機に乗るのは初めてだった ◇She always *flies* business class. 彼女はいつもビジネスクラスで旅をする ◇Who was the first person to *fly* the Atlantic (= travel over it in an aircraft)? 初めて大西洋を飛行機で横断したのは誰ですか

travel (-ll-, 米 -l-) [自, 他] (長い距離を)行く、旅する ◇I spent a year *travelling* around Africa. 一年をかけてアフリカをあちこち旅して回った ◇Here are some tips on how to keep healthy while you're *travelling*. ここに旅行中健康を保つのに役立つヒントがいくつかあります ◇He *went travelling* (= spent time visiting different places) for six months. 彼は半年間の旅行に出た ◇We *travelled the length and breadth of* (= all over) the country. 私たちはその国の津々浦々を旅して回った ◇Children under five *travel free*. 5歳未満の子どもは運賃無料です ☞ *travel* (TRAVEL)

come [自, 他] (特定の距離を[特定の種類の乗り物で])行く、旅する ◇People *came* from all over the world to settle here. 世界中から人々がやってきてここに住みついた ◇How far have you *come*? どのくらいの距離をやって来たのですか ◇He *came* to England by ship. 彼は船でイングランドにやって来た ☞ **come in** (ENTER)

[ノート] *go* と *come* の使い分け：*go* は、旅が始まる場所にいる人の視点で語るときに用いられる。*come* は、旅が終了する場所にいる人の視点で語るときに用いられる。◆We're *going* to Australia to visit our daughter. (私たちはオーストラリアに娘を訪ねる予定です) ◆I hope you can *come* to Australia to visit us. (オーストラリアまで私たちに会いに来てくれるといいな).

do [他] (特定の距離を特定の速度で)進む、行く；旅を完了する ◇How many miles did you *do* yesterday? 昨日は何マイル進みましたか ◇My car *does* 40 miles to the gallon (= uses one gallon of petrol to travel 40 miles). 私の車は1ガロンで40マイル走ります ◇The car was *doing* 90 miles an hour. その車は時速90マイルで走っていた ◇We *did* the round trip (= went there and back) in under three hours. 私たちは3時間以内で往復した

drive [自, 他] 車で行く ◇Shall we *drive* or go by train? 車で行こうか、それとも列車にするかい ◇We must have *driven* over 600 kilometres today. 今日は600キロ以上車で走ったに違いない ◇We *drove* the rest of the way in silence. 残りの道のりは黙って車を走らせた

ride [自, 他] (ふつう副詞や前置詞と共に)《特に米》(乗客として)乗り物で行く；(乗り物に)乗る ◇The men loaded my stuff onto the pick-up and I *rode* with them in the cab. 男たちは私の荷物を小型トラックに積み込み、私は彼らと一緒にタクシーに乗って行った ◇You could *ride* right along the coast by tram. 路面電車に乗ってまさに海岸沿いを行くことができるだろう ◇He *rides* the subway every day. 《米》彼は毎日地下鉄に乗る

run [自] (バス・列車などが特定の路線を)走る、運行する ◇The buses *run* every thirty minutes. バスは30分ごとに出ています ◇He claimed that 95 per cent of trains *run on time*. 列車の95%が時間通り走っていると彼は主張した ◇The train was *running late* (= was not going to arrive on time). 列車は遅れていた ❶ *run* はふつう、どのくらいの頻度で、あるいは何時に[バス[列車など]があるかについて述べるときに用いられる。

cover [他] (ある距離を)行く ◇We must have *covered* over 20 miles. 20マイル以上の距離を移動したに違いない ◇I *covered a lot of ground* rapidly and soon caught up with them. 長い距離を急ぎ、まもなく彼らに追いついた

go away [句動詞]

go away・get out of here・get away・go off・decamp・be/go on your way・clear out
ある場所から離れる
【類語訳】去る

[ノート] *go away* と *leave* の使い分け：親見出し *leave* の項の語は人や物事から離れる行為や時間を強調する。本項 *go away* の各類語は自身やほかの人のためにどこか別の場所へ行く必要性やその望みを強調する。☞ **LEAVE 1**

go away

文型&コロケーション
- ▶ to go away/ get away/ decamp **from** sb/ sth
- ▶ to go off/ decamp **to** sth
- ▶ to go off/ decamp/ clear out **with** sth
- ▶ to go away/ get out of here/ get away **now/ soon**

,go a'way 句動詞 《特に命令で》(人・場所から)去る ◇Just *go away* and leave me alone! ちょっと行って一人にしてちょうだい ◇*Go away* and think about it. 帰ってそのことについて考えてみなさい ◇I told her to *go away*. 去るように彼女に告げた ◇It's been over seven years since he *went away*. 彼が去って7年以上経つ 反意 **come back** (RETURN 1)

get 'out of here フレーズ 《特に命令で》《特に米, インフォーマル》(人・場所から)去る ◇I'm bored — let's *get out of here*. 退屈だ——ここを出ようよ ◇Hey you two, you'd better *get out of here* before the teacher catches you! おいそこの二人、先生に捕まる前にここからずらかった方がいいぜ ❶《米》の非常にインフォーマルな話し言葉では、I'm/We're leaving の意味で I'm/We're outta here! と言うことができる。去る理由は、いつもというわけではないが、怒っていたり退屈だったりすることが多い。◆I wasn't going to listen to her yell at me anymore so I just said, 'Bye — *I'm outta here*.'《米, 俗語》それ以上彼女が私にわめくのを聞くつもりはなかったので「じゃあねーさいなら」とだけ言った。

,get a'way 句動詞 《首尾よく場所から》去る ◇I won't be able to *get away* from the office before seven. 7時前に退社することはできないだろう

,go 'off 句動詞 (何かをするために人・場所から)去る ◇'Where did David go?' 'He *went off* to find his dad.' 「デイヴィッドはどこに行ったの?」「お父さんを探しに行ったよ」 ◇She *went off* to college last year and I haven't seen her since. 昨年彼女は大学に行ってしまい、以来姿を見ていない ◇Matt *went off* in search of a flashlight. マットは懐中電灯を探しに行った

decamp 自 《特に英, 書き言葉》(突然[ひそかに]場所から)去る ◇The first person to take up the job *decamped* after a few days. その仕事の最初の引き受け手が数日後姿をくらました ◇The firm's production unit has *decamped* to California. その会社の製造部は引き払ってカリフォルニアに移った

be/go on your 'way イディオム 《特に英》(人・場所から)去る ◇It's time we *were on our way* (= we should leave). 出かける時間だ ◇He *went on his way* and I never saw him again. 彼は立ち去り、その姿を二度と見かけることはなかった

,clear 'out 句動詞 《特に英, インフォーマル》(所持品をすべて携えて場所から)すばやく去る ◇He *cleared out* with the money and left her with the kids. 彼は彼女の元に子どもたちを残したまま、金を持って立ち去った ◇You'd better *clear out* of here before they find you. やつらに見つかる前にここをたたんじまったほうがいいよ ❶《米》では、*clear out* は個人ではなく一団の人々が場所を去る際にのみ用いられる。◆Homeless people in the camp have been given 72 hours to pack up and *clear out*. (仮設施設にいる)ホームレスの人たちには、荷物をまとめて退去するのに72時間が与えられた

good

物事の質の良さを表す
【類語訳】(品質が)よい, 高品質の, 上質の, 素晴らしい, 最上の, 最良の, 優れた

文型&コロケーション
- ▶ (of) good/ fine/ sterling/ prime/ superior **quality**
- ▶ a good/ fine/ quality/ high quality/ sterling/ superior **performance/ service**
- ▶ a good/ fine/ quality/ high quality/ superior **product**

good 質の高い, よい, まあまあの ◇I think that make of car's pretty *good*. その型の車はかなり高品質だと思い ◇The old piano was in *good* condition. その古いピアノの状態はよかった ◇Your work is not just not *good* enough. あなたの仕事はちょっといただけない ◇This is as *good* a place as any to spend the night. ここは夜を過ごすにはどこにも引けを取らない格好の場所だ ❶*good* は特に, 日用品, ありふれた場所, ふだんする仕事に用いられる。 反意 **bad** (POOR 2)

fine 《ふつう名詞の前で》質の高い, よい ◇It's a particularly *fine* example of Saxon architecture. それは特に素晴らしいサクソン建築の実例である ◇They enjoy good food and *fine wines*. 彼らはおいしい食事と上質のワインを楽しむ ◇people who enjoy the *finer things* in life (= for example, art, good food etc.) 人生で良質な物事を楽しむ人々 ◇It was his *finest hour* (= most successful period) as manager of the England team. それが彼のイングランドチームの監督としての最良のときだった ❶*fine* は特に, 芸術・文化・食事について用いられる。 反意 **poor** (POOR 2)

quality 《名詞の前で》《ややインフォーマル》質の高い, よい ◇We specialize in *quality* furniture. 私どもは高品質家具を専門に扱っております ◇We offer a *quality* service to all customers. 私どもはすべてのお客様に質の高いサービスをご提供します ❶*quality* は特に, 広告や販売で用いられる。☞ **quality** (VALUE)

high quality 《名詞の前で》 質のよい, 高品質の, 上質の ◇We always use the *highest quality* ingredients. 私どもは常に最も質の高い食材を使用しております ◇*High quality* TV shows are getting rarer all the time. 質の高いテレビ番組はつねに減り続けている

ノート *quality* と *high quality* の使い分け: これらの単語は意味は同じだが, *quality* は *high quality* よりくだけており, 物事を宣伝[販売]しようとする人たちだけが用いる。

sterling 《ふつう名詞の前で》《特に英, フォーマル》非常に良質な, 素晴らしい ◇He's done some *sterling work*. 彼は素晴らしい仕事をものにした ◇Thanks to all your *sterling efforts*, we've raised over £12,000. あなたの素晴らしいお骨折りのおかげで, 1万2千ポンド以上を調達できた ◇She has some *sterling qualities*. 彼女は優れた資質をいくつか備えている

prime 《名詞の前で》最上の, 最良の ◇Use only *prime cuts* (= pieces) of beef. 牛肉の最上の部分だけを使ってください ◇a *prime location* in the centre of town 町の中心の一等地

superior 《ふつう名詞の前で》非常に良質な；(他の類似した物事より)優れた ◇The hotel offers *superior* accommodation and leisure facilities. そのホテルは上質の宿泊設備とレジャー施設を提供しています ❶*superior* は特に, 広告で用いられる。 反意 **inferior** (POOR 2)

good 形

1 ☞ BETTER, EXCELLENT, GREAT 1, WONDERFUL
good • fine • quality • high quality • sterling • prime • superior

good

2 ☞ ADEQUATE, FINE
good・appropriate・suitable・right・convenient・fitting・apt・cut out for/to be sth・fit

人や物事が特定の目的や状況で十分に機能することを表す
【類語訳】適した, 都合のよい, 適切な, 妥当な, ふさわしい

【文型&コロケーション】
- good/ appropriate/ suitable/ right/ convenient/ fitting/ apt/ cut out/ fit **for** sb/ sth
- good/ appropriate/ suitable **as** sb/ sth
- good/ appropriate/ suitable/ right/ convenient/ fitting/ apt/ fit **that**...
- good/ appropriate/ suitable/ right/ convenient/ fitting/ fit **to do sth**
- a good/ an appropriate/ a suitable/ the right/ a convenient **time** to do sth/ **place** for sth
- a good/ an appropriate/ a suitable/ the right/ a fitting **thing** to do/ say
- a good/ an appropriate/ a suitable/ the right **person** for sth

good (特定の目的・人に)適した, 都合のよい ◇Now is a *good* time to buy a house. 今や家の買いどきだ ◇Do you think she would be *good* for the job? 彼女はその仕事に向くと思いますか ◇Can we change the time of the meeting? Monday is no *good* for me. 会議の時間を変えられますか. 月曜は都合が悪いんですよ 【反意】 **bad** (WRONG 2)

appropriate (特定の状況・人に)適切な, 妥当な, ふさわしい ◇Jeans are not *appropriate* for a formal interview. ジーンズは公式会見にふさわしくない ◇Would it be *appropriate* to take him a small gift? 彼にちょっとした贈り物を持っていってもいいかしら ◇We must make sure that *appropriate* action is taken. 必ず適切な行動がとられるようにしなければならない 【反意】 **inappropriate** (WRONG 2)
▸**appropriately** 副 ◇Make sure you dress *appropriately* for the meeting. 服装は必ず会議にふさわしいものにするように

suitable (英 or フォーマル, 米) (特定の目的・状況・人に)適切な, 妥当な, ふさわしい ◇The exercise-with-answer-key format makes the book *suitable* for self-study. 解答書付きの練習問題形式なので, その本は独学に適している ◇I don't think he's a *suitable* partner for her. 彼が彼女にぴったりのパートナーだとは思わない ◇Do you think he's *suitable* as a babysitter for such young kids? 彼があんな幼い子どものベビーシッターに適任だと思う ❶《米》では, *suitable* はフォーマルな言葉遣いとしてのみ用いられる.《米》の日常的な話し言葉や書き言葉では *appropriate* や *right* を用いる. 【反意】 **unsuitable** (WRONG 2)
▸**suitably** 副 ◇*suitably* qualified candidates 相応の資格を持った候補者たち

right (特定の目的・状況・物事に)適切な ◇He's definitely the *right* man for the job. 彼はその仕事にうってつけの人物です ◇I don't think she was *right* for you (= for you to have a relationship with). 彼女はあなたの相手には向いていないと思う ◇Next time we'll get it *right*. 次回はきちんとやろう ◇You're not holding it *the right way up*. 正しい方を上にして持っていないよ ◇Are you sure that sweater's on *the right way round*?《英》そのセーターの前後ろ本当に合ってる, 大丈夫 ◇Are you sure that sweater's on *the right way (around)*?《米》そのセーターの前後ろ本当に合ってる, 大丈夫 【反意】 **wrong** (WRONG 2)

【ノート】 **good, appropriate, suitable, right** の使い分け: 人や物事がいかに appropriate, あるいは suitable であるかは, 判断の問題であり, 何が他人に受け入れられるかにかかっている. 人や物事がいかに good かは, 自分が何を好むかとか, 何が都合が良いかということにより左右される. 人や物事がいかに right かはより実際的な問題である. ◆Do you think she would be a/an *good/appropriate/suitable* person to ask? (彼女は頼むのに適切な人物だと思いますか). ✗a *right* person to ask. ✗She's definitely the *good/appropriate/suitable* person to ask. ◆She's definitely the *right* person to ask. (彼女は頼むのにまさにうってつけの人物だ). good, suitable, right はすべて, 物事が特定の目的に適切な場合にも用いられるが, appropriate は人・状況にしか用いない.

convenient (時間・取決めが)都合のよい, 何の問題もない ◇I can't see them now. It's not *convenient*. 今は彼らに会えないな. 都合が悪いんだ ◇We'll arrange a *mutually convenient* meeting place. お互いに会うのに都合のいい場所を設定しましょう 【反意】 **inconvenient** (WRONG 2)

fitting 《フォーマル》(機会に)ふさわしい, 適切な ◇The award was a *fitting tribute* to her years of devoted work. その賞は彼女の長年の仕事への讃えるのにふさわしかった ◇It was a *fitting end* to a glamorous career. それは華やかな経歴にふさわしい結末だった

apt (特定の状況に)適している ◇That question seemed quite *apt* in the circumstances. その質問はそういう状況下では実に当を得ていると思えた ◇'Love at first sight' is an *apt* description of how I felt when I first saw her. 「一目ぼれ」は私が彼女に初めて会ったときの気持ちを適切に表したものだ
▸**aptly** 副 ◇the *aptly* named Grand Hotel 文字どおりの名前のグランドホテル

cut 'out for sth, cut 'out to be sth 《ややインフォーマル》(特定の仕事・活動に)向いている, 適任の ◇He's not *cut out for* teaching. 彼は教職に向いていない ◇He's not *cut out to be* a teacher. 彼は教師に向いていない

fit 適している; 適任の ◇The food was not *fit* for human consumption. その食物は人が食べるのには適さなかった ◇It was a meal *fit for a king* (= of very good quality). それは申し分のない食事だった 《英》He's *in no fit state* to see anyone.《英》彼は誰にも会えない状態だ ❶《米》ではこの場合, fit は必要ない. ◆He's in no state to see anyone. 《米》彼は誰にも会えない状態だ 【反意】 **unfit** (WRONG 2)

3 ☞ RATIONAL
good・solid・sound・valid・legitimate・well founded

物事に適切で論理的な根拠とちゃんとした存在理由が備わっていることを表す
【類語訳】もっともな, 正当な, しっかりした, 確固たる, 妥当な, 健全な, 筋の通った

【文型&コロケーション】
- a good/ solid/ sound/ valid/ legitimate **reason/ basis**
- good/ solid/ sound/ valid **evidence**
- good/ solid/ sound **advice**
- a good/ sound/ valid/ legitimate **argument**
- a good/ sound **conclusion**

▶to have good/ sound **judgement**
▶a good/ valid/ legitimate **question/ point/ excuse**
▶perfectly good/ sound/ valid/ legitimate

good もっともな, 正当な ◇They won't be able to find the way without a map.' '***Good point***.' 「地図がなければ彼らは道を見つけられないだろう」「まったくその通り」 ◇You'll have to think of a ***better*** excuse than that! それよりはましなもっといい言い訳を考えなくちゃね ◇That's a really ***good idea***. それは実に妙案だね ◇Students are not allowed to miss classes ***without good reason***. 学生たちは正当な理由なくして授業を休むことは許されていない ◇I ***have good reason*** to be suspicious. 疑うに十分な理由があるんです ❶goodは特に, 人の考え, 発言, 質問, 理由について用いられる. 反意 **bad** (WRONG 2)

solid (分別があり論理的で)しっかりした; 確固たる ◇Her advice is always ***solid*** and practical. 彼女のアドバイスはいつもしっかりとした実際的なものである ◇There's ***solid*** evidence to show he wasn't there when the crime took place. その犯罪が起きたときに彼がそこにいなかったことを示す確固たる証拠があります ◇Their friendship provided a ***solid*** foundation for their future together. 彼らの友情は二人が一緒に暮らす将来への յとっての基礎を築いた 反意 **flimsy** ❶ flimsy excuse (見えすいた口実), flimsy evidence (お粗末な証拠)を人は信じることはできない. ◆He keeps calling on the ***flimsiest*** of pretexts. (彼はこの上なく見えすいた口実で電話をかけ続けている).
▶**solidly** 副 ◇Their argument was ***solidly*** based on fact. 彼らの議論はしっかりと事実に基づいていた

sound (当てにできるほど[よい結果をもたらす点で])妥当な, しっかりした, 健全な ◇He's a person of very ***sound*** judgement. 彼は非常に真っ当な判断ができる人だ ◇The proposal makes ***sound*** commercial sense. その提案は商業的には妥当だ ◇Their policies are *environmentally **sound***. 彼らの政策は環境保護の観点からは健全だ 反意 **unsound** ❶ unsoundな方法には, ミスが含まれ, よい結果をもたらせるかどうか当てにできない. unsoundな考えや実践は, 特に道徳的[政治的]な理由から受け入れられない. ◆The use of disposable products is considered ecologically ***unsound***. (使い捨て製品の利用は, 環境保護の視点から不健全だと考えられる).

valid (決定・主張が)根拠のしっかりした, 妥当な ◇The point you make is perfectly ***valid***. あなたの指摘はまったく妥当である ◇Accepting ***valid*** criticism is an important part of the learning process. 正当な根拠のある批判を受け入れることは, 学びの過程の大切な一部である 反意 **invalid** ❶ invalidな点[批判, 議論など]は, 事実に基づいているわけではないので正しくない.
▶**validity** 名 [U] ◇Of course we recognize the ***validity*** of that argument. もちろん我々はその主張の正当性を認めています

legitimate (ややフォーマル) (公正で受け入れられる根拠に基づいているので)筋の通った, 正当な ◇All ***legitimate*** grievances should be raised with your line manager. 筋の通った不平[不満]は直属の上司に訴えるべきだ ◇The court ruled that celebrities' children were not a ***legitimate target*** for press intrusion. 有名人の子どもたちを当たり前のように過剰報道の対象としてよいわけではないとの裁判所の裁定が下った

,**well founded** (ややフォーマル) (原因・支持に)十分な根拠[証拠]がある ◇His fears proved to be ***well founded***. 彼の恐怖は十分な根拠に基づいていたと判明した

4 ☞ IMPRESSIVE
good・skilled・great・able・competent・talented・capable・gifted・skilful・proficient・accomplished・professional
人が物事を見事にこなすことを表す
【類語訳】有能な, 熟練した, 得意な, じょうずな, 才能がある, 巧みな, 堪能な, プロフェッショナルな

文型&コロケーション

▶good/ skilled/ great/ competent/ gifted/ skilful/ proficient/ accomplished **at** sth
▶good/ skilled/ great/ competent/ gifted **with** sb/ sth
▶skilled/ competent/ gifted/ proficient/ professional **in** sth
▶a good/ a skilled/ a great/ an able/ a competent/ a talented/ a capable/ a gifted/ a skilful **teacher**
▶a good/ a skilled/ a great/ a talented/ a capable/ a skilful/ an accomplished **performer**
▶a good/ a skilled/ a great/ a competent/ a talented/ a gifted/ a skilful/ an accomplished **player**
▶a good/ a great/ a competent/ a talented/ a gifted/ an accomplished **actor/ musician/ singer/ artist/ painter/ writer**
▶a good/ great/ competent/ capable **manager**
▶sb's competent/ skilful/ professional **handling** of sth
▶**very** good/ skilled/ able/ competent/ talented/ capable/ gifted/ skilful/ proficient/ accomplished/ professional
▶**extremely** good/ skilled/ able/ competent/ talented/ capable/ gifted/ skilful/ accomplished/ professional
▶**highly** skilled/ able/ competent/ capable/ gifted/ proficient/ accomplished/ professional
▶**perfectly** able/ competent/ capable
▶**naturally** good at sth/ talented/ gifted
▶**technically** skilled/ able/ competent/ proficient/ accomplished

good 有能な, うまい ◇She's a really ***good*** actor. 彼女は本当に実力のある女優だ ◇I'm not really a very ***good*** cook. 私はそれほど料理が上手くありません ◇Are you any ***good*** at languages? 語学はいくらかお得意ですか ◇Nick has always been ***good*** at finding cheap deals. ニックはいつも安上がりな取引条件を見つけてくるのが得意だ ◇Jo's very ***good*** with her ***hands*** (= able to make things, etc.). ジョーは手先が非常に器用だ 反意 **bad, poor** (INCOMPETENT)

skilled (人が)熟練た; (仕事が)熟練を要する ◇We need more ***skilled*** engineers. より多くの熟練度の高いエンジニアを必要としています ◇***Skilled*** workers can expect to earn pretty high wages after a few years. 熟練労働者は, 2, 3年後にはかなり高い賃金を稼ぐことが望まきす ◇There's a shortage of ***skilled*** labour (= workers who are able to do jobs that need particular skills). 熟練労働者が不足している ◇Furniture-making is very ***skilled*** work. 家具作りは非常に熟練を要する仕事である 反意 **unskilled** ❶ unskilledな人々は, 特別な技術を持っていない. unskilledな仕事には特別な技能を必要としない. ◆***unskilled*** manual workers (熟練していない肉体労働者たち). ☞ **skill** (SKILL 1, 2)

great (インフォーマル, 特に話し言葉)非常に得意な[じょうずな] ◇She's ***great*** at chess. 彼女はチェスの名手だ ◇You're a ***great*** cook — this is delicious! 君はすばらしい料理人だね — これはおいしいよ ◇He's ***great*** with the kids. 彼はそ

good

の子どもたちの扱いが非常にうまい 反意 **rotten** (INCOMPETENT)

able (ややフォーマル)（知性[学力]のいる仕事・活動に関して）有能な ◇He was a very *able* man in business matters. 彼はビジネスにかけては非常に有能な人物だった ◇We aim to help the less *able* in society to lead an independent life. 私たちは社会でより能力的に劣る人たちが自立した生活を送るのを支援することを目指しています ☞ **ability** (SKILL 1)
▶ **ably** 副 ◇We were *ably* assisted by a team of volunteers. 私たちはボランティアグループによってうまく支えられていた

competent （うまく[必要な水準まで]物事を行えるほど）有能な, 能力のある ◇Make sure the builders are *competent to* carry out the work. 建築業者たちにその仕事を遂行する力量があるかどうか確かめなさい ❶ *competent* は, 人が物事をうまく行えることも, まずまず行えることも意味することができる. ◆He's very *competent* in all his work. (彼は仕事すべてについて非常に有能である). ◆Ron was a *competent* player — more than that, he was good! (ロンは選手としてはまあまあだった — それ以上に, 彼は善良だった). 反意 **incompetent** (INCOMPETENT), ☞ **competence** (SKILL 2)
▶ **competently** 副 ◇You must be able to perform *competently* and efficiently the following task:... 以下の仕事は十分な能力で効率的に行うことが求められる:...

talented （美術・音楽・文学・演劇・スポーツに）天賦の才がある, 才能がある ◇We're looking for *talented* young designers to join our team. 私たちのチームに参加してくれる才能のある若いデザイナーを探しています ◇The kids at this school are all exceptionally *talented* in some way. この学校の子どもたちはみな, 何かしら並外れた才能がある ☞ **talent** (SKILL 1)

capable （物事を何とかうまく成し遂げる）能力がある ◇She's an extremely *capable* teacher. 彼女はとても有能な教師である ◇I'll leave things **in** your *capable* **hands** (= leave you to deal with sth because I know you will deal with it well). あなたの優れた能力に託します

gifted 天賦の才[知性]にあふれている, 天分に恵まれた ◇She goes to a school for *gifted* children. 彼女は英才児向けの学校に通っている ◇He's an extremely *gifted* young player. 彼は非常に才能に恵まれた若い選手だ ◇She's especially *gifted* at art. 彼女は特に美術に天分がある ☞ **gift** (SKILL 2)

|ノート| **talented** と **gifted** の使い分け: **talented** な人たちはふつう, 音楽やスポーツといった特定の物事を得意とする. **gifted** な人たちは, 特定の物事を得意とするか, 単に非常に知的であることもある. *academically* **gifted** とは言えるが, ×*academically* *talented* とは言えない. 物事について天分に恵まれていれば多くの経験を必要としないことから, **gifted** は子どもや若者について用いられることが多い.

skilful (英) (米 **skillful**)（人が）得意な;（行動が）巧みな ◇As Foreign Secretary he proved to be a *skilful* diplomat. 彼は外務大臣として, 腕のある外交官であることを証明した ◇Everyone admired her *skilful* handling of the affair. その一件での彼女の巧みな手腕を誰もが高く評価した ☞ **skill** (SKILL 1, 2)

proficient (ややフォーマル) 〔訓練[実践]のおかげで〕じょうずな, 堪能な ◇She's *proficient* in several languages. 彼女は数か国語に堪能である ◇With practice, you should become *proficient* within six months. 練

習すれば半年以内に上達するはずです ☞ **proficiency** (SKILL 2)

accomplished (ややフォーマル) （訓練[経験]を通じて）熟達した; 多くの技能を身につけた ◇He was an *accomplished* linguist, fluent in French and German. 彼は語学に堪能で, フランス語とドイツ語を流暢に操った ◇She was an elegant and *accomplished* woman. 彼女は上品でたしなみのある女性だった

professional くろうとの, プロフェッショナルな ◇He dealt with the problem in a highly *professional* way. 彼はきわめてプロフェッショナルなやりかたでその問題に対処した ❶ この意味では, *professional* はしばしば, very, highly と共に用いられることが多い. 仕事の名称と共には用いない. *professional* teacher/actor/singer などは, 「仕事として教える/演じる/歌う人」である. 反意 **amateurish** ❶ 物事に対する *amateurish* な試みは, うまく[巧みに]行われない. ◆Detectives described the burglary as 'crude and *amateurish*'. （刑事たちはその押し込み強盗を「粗雑で素人くさい」と評した）.

---

5 good・ethical・moral・principled・virtuous・scrupulous
人およびその振る舞いや行動, 考え方が道にはずれていないこと
【類語訳】（道徳的に）正しい, 善良な, 道徳的な, 高潔な, 清廉な

|文型&コロケーション|
▶ a good/ moral/ principled/ virtuous/ scrupulous **person**
▶ a good/ principled/ virtuous/ scrupulous **man/ woman**
▶ a good/ moral/ virtuous **life**
▶ good/ ethical/ moral **behaviour/ practices/ principles**
▶ an ethical/ a moral/ a principled **stand/ stance/ position**
▶ **very** good/ ethical/ moral/ virtuous/ scrupulous
▶ **highly** moral/ principled

good （道徳的に）正しい, 善良な;（道徳的に）正しく振る舞う ◇Giving her that money was a *good* thing to do. その金を彼女にやるのは正解だった ◇He prayed that God would make him a *better* person. 彼は神が自分をより善き人間にしてくださるよう祈った 反意 **bad, evil, wicked** (EVIL 形), ☞ **good** (KIND 形), **good, goodness** (MORALITY)

ethical 道徳[倫理]にかなった, 道徳的な ◇Is it *ethical* to promote cigarettes through advertising? 広告を通じてタバコの販売促進をするのは倫理にかなっていますか ◇There needs to be a greater emphasis on *ethical* investment (= investing money in businesses that are considered to be morally acceptable). 倫理的投資をより重視する必要がある ❶ *ethical* は人を表すのには用いないが, 人の振る舞いを表すことはできる. 行動やビジネス活動について用いることが多い. 反意 **unethical** (WRONG 3), ☞ **ethical** (MORAL), **ethics** (PRINCIPLE 1)
▶ **ethically** 副 ◇Most people find the commercial exploitation of children *ethically* unacceptable. たいていの人たちは, 子どもたちを商業的に搾取することは倫理的に受け入れられないと思っている

moral 道義をわきまえた, 道徳的な ◇He led a very *moral* life. 彼は非常に道徳的な生活を送った ◇We try to teach our students to be conscientious, *moral* young people. 私どもは学生たちに実直で道義をわきまえた若者であるよう努力をしています 反意 **immoral** (WRONG 3), ☞ **amoral** (CORRUPT), **moral** (MORAL), **morals, morality** (PRINCIPLE 1)

▶**morally** 副 ◇They try to live a life that is *morally* pure. 彼らは道徳的に清らかな生活を送ろうとしている
principled (善悪に関して)強い信念を持っている；強い信念に基づいた ◇The new biography presents her as a deeply *principled* woman. 新しい伝記は彼女を強い信念を持った女性として描いている ◇We need to take a *principled* stand against the government's actions. 政府の措置に対して我々は信念を持って反対の態度をとる必要がある 反意 **unprincipled** (CORRUPT)
virtuous 《ややフォーマル》高潔な ◇Unmarried women were expected to live modest, *virtuous* lives. 未婚女性は質素で高潔な生活を送るのが当然と思われていた ☞ **virtue** (MORALITY)
scrupulous 清廉な ◇She has a reputation for *scrupulous* honesty. 彼女は清廉潔白であるとの評判だ ◇He is *scrupulous in* all his business dealings. 彼はあらゆる商取引に関して誠実である 反意 **unscrupulous** (CORRUPT), ☞ **scruple** (DOUBT 名2)
▶**scrupulously** 副 ◇All court proceedings need to be *scrupulously* fair to each side. すべての公判手続きは双方に対して徹底して公平である必要がある

---

6 good・positive・favourable・glowing・admiring・complimentary・appreciative・flattering・approving
人が人や物事に対して賛意を示すことを表す
【類語訳】(評価などが)よい、肯定的な、好意的な、賞賛した、お世辞の、おだての、よしとする、賛同の

文型&コロケーション
▶ positive/ complimentary **about** sb/ sth
▶ favourable/ complimentary **to** sb/ sth
▶ admiring/ appreciative/ approving **of** sb/ sth
▶ a good/ a positive/ a favourable/ a complimentary/ an appreciative/ a flattering/ an approving **comment**
▶ a good/ a positive/ a complimentary/ an appreciative/ a flattering/ an approving **remark**
▶ a good/ positive/ favourable **response**
▶ a good/ positive/ favourable/ glowing **report**
▶ a good/ positive/ favourable **opinion/ impression/ reaction/ response**
▶ to **show** sb/ sth in a good/ positive/ favourable **light**
▶ **very** good/ positive/ favourable/ complimentary/ appreciative/ flattering/ approving
▶ **highly** positive/ favourable/ complimentary

good (評価などが)よい ◇The school has an extremely *good* reputation. その学校は非常に評判がよい ◇Initial reactions to the proposal have been *good* so far. その提案に対する当初の反応はこれまでのところよい ◇Her school report was much *better* this year. 彼女の通信簿は今年はずっとよかった
positive (人・物事に対して)肯定的な ◇Most of his remarks were *positive*, but there were a few criticisms. 彼の発言のほとんどは肯定的だったが、批判も多少あった ◇You should try to be a bit more *positive* about your students. 君は自分の学生たちのよい面をもっと見てやるとすべきです 反意 **negative** (NEGATIVE)
▶**positively** 副 ◇She was portrayed very *positively* in the movie. 彼女はその映画の中でとても肯定的に描かれていた
favourable (英) (米 **favorable**) 《ややフォーマル》(人・物事に対して)好意的な ◇The performance drew a lot of *favourable* comments from reviewers. その上演は批評家たちから多くの好評を得た ◇The report was very *favourable* to the existing government. その報告書は現政権に対して非常に好意的だった 反意 **unfavourable** ❶ *unfavourable* な発言や態度は、人や物事に対する不同意を示す。◆The documentary presents him in a very *unfavourable* light. (そのドキュメンタリーは彼のことを非常に悪く描き出している)
▶**favourably** 副 ◇He speaks very *favourably* of your work. 彼はあなたの仕事に対して非常に好意的な発言をしています

ノート **good** と **favourable** の使い分け：**favourable** は、**good** よりフォーマルな言い方。この意味で **good** を用いることができない構文や語の結びつきがいくつかある。**favourable comment** は賛同を示す評言だが、**good comment** は賢明な評言をさす。物事が **favourable to sb** である場合は賛同を示すが、**good to sb** はその人たちに親切であることを示す。

glowing [ふつう名詞の前で] 熱烈に称賛した ◇He described her performance *in glowing terms*. 彼は彼女の演技をべた褒めした 反意 **damning** (CRITICAL)
admiring 称賛した、うっとりした ◇She was used to receiving *admiring* glances from men. 彼女は男性たちから称賛のまなざしを向けられることに慣れっこになっていた ❶ この単語は一般的に、glance, look, gaze, smile, audience/crowd と結びつく。
▶**admiringly** 副 ◇'That's very clever,' he said *admiringly*.「そいつは実に賢明だ」と彼は感心して言った ☞ **admire** (RESPECT 動), **admiration** (ADMIRATION)
complimentary 称賛した ◇She was extremely *complimentary* about his work. 彼女は彼の作品を褒めちぎった ☞ **compliment** (PRAISE 動)
appreciative (人・物事に対して)称賛した、喜んで[楽しんで]いる ◇The audience was highly *appreciative*. 観客は非常に楽しんでいた ◇She watched them with an *appreciative* smile. 彼女は嬉しそうにほほ笑んで彼らを見た ☞ **appreciate** (APPRECIATE)
flattering お世辞の、おだての ◇He made several *flattering* remarks. 彼はお世辞をいくつか並べた
approving よしとする、賛同の ◇He gave me an *approving* nod. 彼は賛同して私にうなづいてくれた 反意 **disapproving** (CRITICAL)
▶**approvingly** 副 ◇'Your work's very good,' she said *approvingly*.「あなたの作品は非常に素晴らしい」と彼女は褒めた

---

7 good・obedient・dutiful・well behaved
人[子ども]が品行のよいことを表す
【類語訳】行儀がよい、従順な、忠実な

文型&コロケーション
▶ a good/ an obedient/ a dutiful/ a well-behaved **child**
▶ a good/ an obedient/ a dutiful **daughter/ son/ wife/ servant**
▶ a good/ an obedient/ a well-behaved **boy/ girl**
▶ a good/ an obedient **dog**

good (子どもが)行儀がよい ◇You can stay up late if you're *good*. 行儀よくしてるなら、遅くまで起きててもいいわよ ◇Get dressed now, there's a *good* boy. さあ着替えて、いい子から ◇'That's a *good* dog,' I said, patting its head. 「いい子だね」と犬の頭をなでながら言ってやった ❶この意味のgoodはふつう、子どもや犬に用いられるが、特に妻・使用人を表すのにも用いることができる。誠実な妻・使用人を表すのにも用いることができる。good husbandも誠実で妻の面倒を見るが、言いなりになるとは限らない。 反意 **bad, naughty**

obedient (人・動物が)従順な ◇He was always *obedient to* his father's wishes. 彼はいつも父親の望みに従順だった ◇Did he really expect her to trot right after him, like an *obedient* dog? 彼は本当に彼女が、忠犬のように自分のすぐ後を小走りでついてくるなんて思っていたのですか 反意 **disobedient,** ☞ **obey (FOLLOW 3)**

▶**obedience** [名] [U] ◇blind/unquestioning *obedience* 盲目的に従うこと／絶対的服従 ◇He has acted in *obedience* to the law. 彼は法律に則って行動してきた 反意 **disobedience**

▶**obediently** [副] ◇He ate up his dinner *obediently*, like a child. 彼は子どものように素直に夕食を平らげた

dutiful (ややフォーマル、書き言葉)(息子・娘・妻が)忠実な; (行動が)忠実さを示す ◇It's about time she helped out like a *dutiful* daughter. そろそろ孝行娘のように彼女が手伝う時だ ◇He paid a *dutiful* visit to his grandmother. 彼は律儀に祖母を訪ねた

,well be'haved (子どもが)行儀がよい ◇All her children were cheerful and *well behaved*. 彼女の子どもたちはみんな朗らかで行儀がよかった ◇On the whole, the crowd was pretty *well behaved*. 全体的に見ると、群衆はかなり行儀がよかった

go out 句動詞

go out・see・date・be together・court・woo
人と恋愛関係にある
【類語訳】付き合う、交際する、求愛する、求婚する

go 'out 句動詞 《特に進行形で》(若者が)付き合う、恋愛[性的]関係にある ◇Tom has been *going out with* Lucy for six weeks. トムはルーシーと6週間付き合っている ◇How long have Tom and Lucy been *going out*? トムとルーシーは付き合ってどのくらいになりますか

see [他]《特に進行形で》 付き合う、恋愛[性的]関係にある ◇Are you *seeing* anyone at the moment? 今付き合ってる人いるの

date [他, 自]《特に進行形で》《特に米》 付き合う、恋愛[性的]関係にある ◇She's been *dating* Ron for several months. 彼女はロンと数か月交際してる ◇How long have you two been *dating*? 君たち二人はどのくらい付き合ってるの ☞ **date (MEETING 2), date (PARTNER 2)**

> ノート **go out, see, date** の使い分け: これらの表現はすべて、how long, for three months などといった時間表現と共に、一般的に進行形で用いられる。これはより真剣「永続的」なものになることもあるがそれが必ずしも一時的な関係であることを示唆している。date は《英》ではあまり用いられず、《米》でも古臭く聞こえ始めているところである。go outもdateもパートナーと一緒にどこかに出かけたり何かをすることに重点を置いているが、see はそうではない。

be together フレーズ 《ややインフォーマル、特に話し言葉》(一定期間)付き合う、恋愛[性的]関係にある ◇We've been *together* seven years — that's practically married, isn't it? 私たちは7年一緒に過ごしている—それって、実質的な結婚だよね

court [自, 他]《古風》(結婚を前提に)交際する、付き合う ◇At that time they had been *courting* for several months. 当時彼らの交際はすでに数か月に及んでいた ◇He *courted* Jane for two years before she finally agreed to marry him. 彼はジェーンが結局は結婚に同意してくれるまで2年間交際した ❶court は現在、すっかり時代遅れの言葉であるが、昔の人について言うときには今なお用いられる。年配の人たちが、自分たちの婚前の関係について用いることがある。 ♦Your grandfather and I were still *courting* at the time (= we spent time together as a couple, but were not married yet). (おじいさんと私はその頃まだ交際中だったのよ). ☞ **courtship (RELATIONSHIP 2)**

woo [他]《古風 or 文語》(男性が)求愛する、求婚する ◇He *wooed* her with flowers, poetry and compliments. 彼は花と詩と褒め言葉で彼女に求愛した

government 名

1 government・administration・regime・cabinet・reign・parliament・the executive
国家を統治する一団の人々、その人たちが統治する期間
【類語訳】政府, 政権, 政体, 内閣, 治世, 国会, 議会, 行政部

> 文型&コロケーション

▶ **under** a government/ an administration/ a regime/ sb's reign
▶ the **former/ previous/ current** government/ administration/ regime
▶ the **central/ local/ national** government/ administration
▶ a **left-wing/ right-wing/ communist/ fascist** government/ administration/ regime
▶ a/ an **authoritarian/ totalitarian/ repressive/ military/ revolutionary** government/ regime
▶ to **elect** a government/ an administration
▶ to **form** a government/ an administration/ a cabinet
▶ to **bring down/ overthrow** a government/ an administration/ a regime
▶ a government/ an administration/ a regime **comes to power**
▶ a government/ an administration **takes office/ is in office**

government [C+単数・複数動詞] (しばしば **the government**) [単数で] 政府 ◇The *government* has been considering further tax cuts. 政府はさらなる減税を考えている ◇She has resigned from the *government*. 彼女は政府の職を辞任した ◇The interests of the state should not be confused with the interests of ***the government of the day*** (= the people in government at a particular time). 国益を時の政府の利益と混同してはならない ☞ **govern (RULE 動 1)**

administration [C+単数・複数動詞] 政府；政権期間 ◇The current *administration* will remain in office until elections in November. 現政府は11月の選挙まで政権を維持することになる ◇He was Secretary of Education in Bush's first *administration* (= first period as president). 彼は一期目のブッシュ政権で教育長官だった

> ノート **government** と **administration** の使い分け: administrationは特に、大統領が率いる政府、とりわけ米国政府について用いられる。ふつう特定の大統領の政府や、その政府が持続する期間をさす。 ♦during/under the Rea-

↳ **government**

gan/Clinton/Bush *Administration* (レーガン/クリントン/ブッシュ政権中[下]). ×*during/under the Reagan/ Clinton/Bush government.* ふつう大統領や政権が変わっても不変である政府の機関や措置について言及するのには用いない. ◆ *Approximately 2.7 million people are employed by the federal government.* (およそ270万人の人々が連邦政府に雇用されている). ×*employed by the federal administration.* 大統領より権力に制限のある首相が政府を率いる諸国, 特に英国ではふつう *government* が好まれる. ◆ *the Thatcher/Major/Blair/Brown government* (サッチャー/メージャー/ブレア/ブラウン内閣[政権]). ◆ *government employees* (政府職員). 首相の名前の後に *administration* という単語を用いることは時として, 大統領のごとく振る舞おうとする首相に対する非難を示す.

regime [C] (公正な形で選ばれたものではない)政権, 政体
◇*She was imprisoned because of her opposition to the regime.* 彼女は政権に反対して投獄された ◇*They are investigating human rights abuses under the previous military regime.* 彼らは以前の軍事政権下での人権侵害を調査している ☞ **leadership (MANAGEMENT)**

cabinet (または **Cabinet**) [C+単数・複数動詞] 内閣 ◇*Several cabinet ministers have been implicated in the scandal.* 数人の閣僚がスキャンダルにかかわっている ◇*The issue was discussed at yesterday's cabinet meeting.* その問題は昨日の閣議で話し合われた ◇*She lost her position as Health Minister in a recent cabinet reshuffle* (= change). 彼女は最近の内閣改造で厚生相の職を失った ◇*He is a member of the Shadow Cabinet* (= senior politicians of the party not in government). 彼は影の内閣の一員である

reign [C] (王・女王・皇帝などが)支配している期間, 治世 ◇*The house was built during the reign of Henry VIII.* その家はヘンリー8世の治世に建てられた ◇*By the end of his reign, the vast empire was in decline.* 彼の治世の終わりには, 広大な帝国は衰退の道をたどっていた ☞ **reign (RULE 動) 1)**

parliament [C, U] 国会, 議会(の会期) ◇*We are now into the second half of the parliament.* 私たちは現在議会会期の後半に入っている ◇*The prime minister unexpectedly dissolved parliament* (= formally ended its activities) and called a general election. 首相は突然議会を解散し, 総選挙を行った ◇*The legislation is expected to be introduced early in the next session of parliament.* その法案は次の議会の会期の早いうちに提出される見込みだ

the executive (法律の施行に責任のある政府の)行政部
◇*The constitution calls for a separation of the powers of the executive, the legislature and the judiciary.* 憲法は, 行政府・立法府・司法部の権力分立を求めている

2 government・management・leadership・ regulation・administration・supervision・direction
会社や組織, 国家をまとめる行為を表す
【類語訳】統治, 施政, 運営, 経営, 指導力, 規制, 管理, 監督, 指揮, 指導

文型&コロケーション

▶ leadership/ supervision/ direction **from** sb
▶ regulation/ supervision **by** sb
▶ **under** the management/ leadership/ administration/ supervision/ direction **of** sb
▶ (to be/ work, etc.) **in** government/ management/ administration
▶ **good** government/ management/ leadership/ administration
▶ **firm/ strong** government/ management/ leadership/ direction
▶ **effective** government/ management/ leadership/ regulation/ administration/ supervision/ direction
▶ **weak** government/ management/ leadership
▶ **poor** management/ leadership/ regulation/ administration/ supervision
▶ **day-to-day** government/ management/ administration/ supervision
▶ **general** management/ regulation/ administration/ supervision
▶ **government** regulation/ administration/ supervision/ direction
▶ to **be responsible for** the management/ regulation/ administration/ supervision **of** sth
▶ to **take over** the management/ leadership/ administration

government [U] 統治(方法), 施政 ◇*The Nationalists had been in government for most of the 1980s.* 国家主義者たちが1980年代の大半に政権の座にあった ◇*Democratic government has now replaced military rule.* 今や民主政治が軍政に取って代わった ☞ **govern (RULE 動) 1)**

management [U] (会社などの組織の)運営(方法), 経営 ◇*She studied hotel management in Munich.* 彼女はミュンヘンでホテル経営を学んだ ◇*The report blames bad management.* その報告書は経営のまずさが問題であると指摘している ◇*The company's top-down management style made decision-making slow.* その会社のトップダウンの経営スタイルが意思決定を遅くしていた ☞ **management (MANAGEMENT), manage (RUN 2), manager (MANAGER)**

leadership [U] 指導者としての活動[立場]; 指導者に必要な能力[資質], 指導力 ◇*The party thrived under her leadership.* その党は彼女の指導の下で勢力を伸ばした ◇*In the crisis he showed real leadership.* 危機に瀕して彼は真の指導力を発揮した ☞ **lead (LEAD), leader (LEADER 1)**

regulation 規制 ◇*There are calls for tighter regulation of the industry.* その産業をより厳しく規制する必要がある ◇*Theatre, cinema and broadcasting are all subject to regulation by local authorities.* 演劇・映画・放送はすべて, 地方自治体の規制を受ける ☞ **regulation (RULE 名), regulate (REGULATE)**

administration [U] (会社などの組織の)管理, 運営 ◇*A large part of his job involves routine administration.* 彼の仕事の相当部分は日常的な管理にかかわることだ ◇*Administration costs are passed on to the customer.* 管理費は顧客に転嫁される ☞ **administer (RUN 2), administrator (ORGANIZER)** ❶ administration は, (製品を製造[販売]するような)会社の実務ではなく, 会社の組織・運営に必要な活動すべてを指すが, 特に, 書類に記入する, 手紙・電子メールを書く, 申請するなど, 必要な文書業務に用いられることが多い.

supervision [U] (すべてが正しく[安全に]行われるようにする)監督, 管理 ◇*New employees are trained to work without direct supervision.* 新しい従業員たちは直接監督されることなく仕事ができるように訓練されている ◇*There was inadequate supervision of children in the* swimming pool. 水泳プールにおける子どもの監視が不十分だった ☞**supervise** (REGULATE), **supervisor** (MANAGER)

direction [U]《ややフォーマル》(人・物事の)指揮, 指導, 管理 ◇All the work was produced by the students under the *direction* of John Williams. その作品は全面的にジョン・ウィリアムズの指揮の下, 学生によって製作された ◇The teacher provided *clear direction*, but allowed children some autonomy. その教師は明確な指示を与える一方で, 子どもたちにはある程度の自主性を与えた ☞**direct** (RUN 2), **director** (MANAGER)

graduate [動]

graduate・pass・qualify・get through (sth)・sail through (sth)
首尾よく教科課程を修了する, 試験[テスト]に合格する
【類語訳】卒業する, 合格する, 資格を得る

【文型&コロケーション】
▶ to graduate/ qualify **as** sth
▶ to graduate/ pass **with** sth
▶ to pass/ get through/ sail through a/ an **course/ exam/ test**
▶ **students** graduate/ pass/ qualify/ sail through

graduate [自] (大学を)卒業する, (大学卒業で)学位を受ける；(米国の高校などを)卒業する ◇Only thirty students *graduated* in Chinese last year. 昨年, 中国語を専攻して卒業した学生はたった30人だった ◇She taught in France after *graduating*. 彼女は卒業後フランスで教鞭をとった ◇Martha *graduated from* high school two years ago. マーサは2年前高校を卒業した ❶《米》では from は省略できる. ● Martha *graduated* high school two years ago. 《米》マーサは2年前高校を卒業した).
▷**graduate** [名] [C] ◇a science *graduate* 科学系の卒業生 ◇high school *graduates* 高校の卒業生たち

pass [自, 他] (試験・テストに)合格する, 通る ◇I'm not really expecting to *pass* first time. 一回目で合格するとはあまり思っていません ◇I *passed* my driving test. 運転試験に合格した 〔反意〕 **fail, flunk** (FAIL 3)
▶ **pass** [名] [C] ◇She *got a pass* in French. 《特に英》彼女はフランス語で合格点をとった ◇12 *passes* and 3 fails 12の可と3の不可

qualify [自] 《特に英》(仕事に必要な)資格を得る ◇How long does it take to *qualify*? 資格を取得するのにどのくらい(の期間)かかりますか ◇She *qualified* as a doctor last year. 彼女は昨年医師の資格を得た
▷**qualification** [名] [U, C, ふつう複数形] ◇Nurses in training should be given a guarantee of employment following *qualification*. 訓練中の看護師は資格取得後の雇用が保証されるべきだ ◇He left school with no formal *qualifications*. 《英》彼は正式な資格を何も取得せずに卒業[退学]した

,get 'through sth, ,get 'through [句動詞]《英, ややインフォーマル》(困難な)試験[テスト]に合格する, 通る ◇I *got through* the final exam by avoiding questions that required factual knowledge. 事実に基づく知識を必要とする設問は避けて最終試験に合格した

,sail' through sth, ,sail 'through [句動詞]《ややインフォーマル》楽に試験[テスト]に合格する, やすやすと学習過程を終了する ◇She's very bright and *sailed through*

college. 彼女は非常に聡明で, 楽に大学に合格した

grateful [形] ☞GLAD

grateful・thankful・glad・indebted・appreciative
人が親切な[頼んだ]ことをしてもらいありがたく思うことを表す
【類語訳】感謝している, 恩を感じる, 謝意を示す

【文型&コロケーション】
▶ grateful/ thankful **for** sth
▶ grateful/ indebted **to** sb
▶ grateful/ thankful **that**...
▶ grateful/ thankful **to be/ have,** etc....
▶ a grateful/ an appreciative **smile**
▶ to **feel** grateful/ thankful/ glad/ indebted
▶ **deeply** grateful/ thankful/ indebted/ appreciative
▶ **very** grateful/ thankful/ glad/ appreciative

grateful 感謝している, 謝意を示す ◇I am extremely *grateful* to all the teachers for their help. すべての先生の助力にとても感謝しています ◇Kate gave him a *grateful* look. ケイトは彼に感謝のまなざしを向けた ❶ grateful は, 特に手紙やフォーマルな状況で, 頼み事をするときに用いられることが多い. ◆I would be grateful if you could send the completed form back as soon as possible. (《フォーマル》できるだけ早く記入済みの書類を返送していただければ幸いです). ☞**gratitude** (THANKS)
▷**gratefully** [副] ◇All donations will be *gratefully* received. 寄付はすべてありがたくお受けします

thankful [名詞の前はまれ] (よくないことが起きなくて)うれしい, 感謝している ◇I was *thankful* to see they'd all arrived safely. 彼らがみな無事に到着したのを見てうれしかった ◇He wasn't badly hurt — that's something to be *thankful* for. 彼はひどくは傷ついていなかった — それは喜ばしいことだ ☞**thanks** (THANKS), **relieved** (GLAD)
▷**thankfully** [副] ◇There was a fire in the building, but *thankfully* no one was hurt. その建物で火事があったが, 誰も負傷しなかったのはよかった

glad (of や if を伴って) (物事に)感謝している ◇She was very *glad of* her warm coat in the biting wind. 身を刺すような風の中にあって, 彼女は暖かいコートにとてもありがたみを感じた ◇I'd be *glad if* you could help me. あなたが助けてくれたらうれしいんだけど

indebted [名詞の前はまれ]《フォーマル》(人の助けに)恩を感じる, 感謝している ◇I am deeply *indebted* to my family for all their help. 家族には支援してもらった大きな恩がある

appreciative《ややフォーマル》(人の親切に)感謝を覚える, 謝意を示す ◇The company was very *appreciative of* my efforts. 会社は私の尽力に深く感謝してくれていた ❶一般的に appreciative of には sb's **work/efforts/support/loyalty** などが続く. ☞**appreciation** (THANKS)

great [形]

1 ☞EXCELLENT, GOOD 1
great・cool・fantastic・fabulous・terrific・brilliant・tremendous・awesome・wicked
人や物事が好ましい[楽しい]ことを表す
【類語訳】素晴らしい, すてきな, かっこいい, すごい

↳great

文型&コロケーション

▶ a great/ a cool/ a fantastic/ a fabulous/ a terrific/ a brilliant/ an awesome/ a wicked **place**
▶ to **have** a great/ a cool/ a fantastic/ a fabulous/ a terrific/ a brilliant/ a tremendous/ an awesome **time**
▶ a great/ cool/ fantastic/ fabulous/ terrific/ brilliant **guy/ girl**
▶ a great/ a fantastic/ a terrific/ a brilliant/ a tremendous/ an awesome **achievement**
▶ a great/ cool/ fantastic/ fabulous/ terrific/ brilliant **goal**
▶ to **look/ sound** great/ cool/ fantastic/ fabulous/ terrific/ brilliant/ awesome
▶ **really** great/ cool/ fantastic/ fabulous/ terrific/ brilliant/ tremendous/ awesome/ wicked
▶ **absolutely** great/ cool/ fantastic/ fabulous/ terrific/ brilliant/ awesome
▶ **That's** great/ cool/ fantastic/ fabulous/ terrific/ brilliant/ tremendous/ awesome/ wicked.

great 《インフォーマル》素晴らしい；とてもうれしい ◇That was a *great* goal! あれは見事なゴールだった ◇It's *great* to see you again. またお会いできてとてもうれしい ◇We had a *great* time in Madrid. 私たちはマドリッドで素晴らしい時間を過ごした ◇'I'll pick you up at seven.' 'That'd be *great*, thanks.'「7時に車で迎えに行きますよ」「それは助かる, ありがとう」◇Oh, *great*! They left without us!《皮肉に》まあ, うれしいね. 置いてけぼりとは ◇You've been a *great* help, I must say (= no help at all). 《皮肉に》本当に, 大いに助かりましたよ 反意 **awful** (TERRIBLE 3)

cool 《インフォーマル, 話し言葉》すてきな, かっこいい ◇His new car's pretty *cool*. 彼の新車, すごくかっこいい ◇What's his new girlfriend like?' 'She's *cool*.'「彼の新しい恋人って, どんな人」「彼女, いかしてるわよ」❶人や物事を認めたり, 提言に同意することを示すために, Cool!, That's cool!と言う. ◆'We're meeting Jake later.' 'Cool!'「後でジェイクに会うことになってる」「いいね」. 反意 **uncool** ❶ *uncool* の物事は流行を追う若者に受け入れられないと考えられる. ◆My mum is so *uncool* it's funny. (うちのママは本当に野暮ったいの, 笑っちゃうわ).

fantastic 《インフォーマル》非常に素晴らしい ◇We found a *fantastic* beach about a mile away. 1マイルほど離れたところにとっても素晴らしいビーチを見つけたよ ◇You look *fantastic*! 素敵だね ◇'How was your trip?' '*Fantastic*!'「旅はどうだった」「素晴らしかったよ」◇'You've got the job?' '*Fantastic*!'「仕事が見つかったの」「すごいでしょ」

fabulous 《インフォーマル》非常に素晴らしい ◇Jane's a *fabulous* cook. ジェーンの料理はとても素晴らしい ◇Enter our *fabulous* free draw now! さあ, すてきな無料のくじ引きに参加してください ❶ *fabulous* はこのグループのどの単語よりも少し古臭い.

terrific 《インフォーマル》非常に素晴らしい, すごい ◇She's doing a *terrific* job. 彼女はすごい仕事をしている ◇'How do you feel today?' '*Terrific*!'「今日の気分は」「最高だよ」◇To win one of our *terrific* prizes, answer these three questions. 素晴らしい賞の一つを獲得するために, この3問にお答えください

brilliant 《英, インフォーマル, 話し言葉》非常に素晴らしい ◇'How was the show?' '*Brilliant*!'「ショーはどうだった」「素晴らしかったよ」◇Thanks. You've been *brilliant* (= very kind or helpful). ありがとう. ほんとにどうも助かりました

tremendous 《インフォーマル》非常に素晴らしい ◇It was a *tremendous* experience. 素晴らしい経験でした ◇The support they gave us was *tremendous*. 彼らの私たちへの支援は非常に素晴らしかった

awesome 《特に米, インフォーマル, 話し言葉》非常に素晴らしい[印象的な, 楽しい] ◇The show was just *awesome*. お芝居はほんとすごく楽しかった ◇Hey, come look at this! It's *awesome*! おい, ちょっと来てこれ見ろよ. すげえぞ

wicked 《俗語》素晴らしい, すごい ◇'What do you think of her?' 'She's *wicked*!'「彼女のことどう思う」「彼女は素晴らしいよ」◇'OK, we can all go to the beach now.' '*Wicked*!'「よし, じゃあみんなでビーチに行こう」「最高」◇Jo just bought a *wicked* new computer game. ジョーは新しいすごいコンピューターゲームを買ったばかりだ ❶ *wicked* は特に若者が用いる.

2 great・prestigious・distinguished・eminent・exalted

人や物事に非常に素晴らしい能力[資質]があり, それゆえに多くの人に高く評価されていることを表す
【類語訳】偉大な, 信望がある, 権威ある, 名誉ある, 卓越した, 傑出した, 高名な, 著名な, 高位の, 高貴な, 高尚な

文型&コロケーション

▶ a great/ a distinguished/ an eminent **scientist/ painter/ poet/ writer/ architect/ historian/ philosopher/ scholar/ professor**
▶ a great/ prestigious/ distinguished **collection**
▶ a great/ prestigious **university/ award**
▶ a great/ distinguished **achievement/ career/ tradition**
▶ a prestigious/ a distinguished/ an exalted **position**
▶ **very** prestigious/ distinguished/ eminent
▶ **highly** prestigious/ distinguished

great 偉大な, たいした ◇He has been described as the world's *greatest* violinist. 彼は世界最高のヴァイオリニストと言われている ◇Sherlock Holmes, the *great* detective 偉大な私立探偵であるシャーロック・ホームズ ◇*Great* art has the power to change lives. 偉大な芸術には人生を変える力がある ☞ **great** (STAR)

prestigious [ふつう名詞の前で] 信望がある, 権威[名誉]ある ◇The Gold Cup is one of the most *prestigious* events in the racing calendar. ゴールドカップは, レース日程の中で最も権威あるイベントの一つである ◇It's the city's most *prestigious* and exclusive hotel. そこはその都市で最も格式がある高級なホテルです ☞ **prestige** (STATUS)

distinguished 《特に書き言葉》(特定の職業で)卓越した, 傑出した, 著名な ◇His eldest brother was the *distinguished* mathematician and geologist John Playfair. 彼の長兄は, あの著名な数学者で地質学者のジョン・プレイフェアだった ◇He has had a long and *distinguished* career in medicine. 彼は医学において長きにわたって顕著なキャリアを積み上げてきた ◇Wales has a long and *distinguished* tradition of choral singing. ウェールズには聖歌合唱の長く輝かしい伝統がある 反意 **undistinguished**

eminent [ふつう名詞の前で] 《特に書き言葉》(特定の職業で)高名な, 著名な ◇The house was designed by the *eminent* architect, Robert Adam. その家は著名な建築家ロバート・アダムの設計だった

ノート distinguished と eminent の使い分け: どちらも, 職業の観点から人を表すのに用いることができる. ◆a *distinguished*/an *eminent* scientist/artist/painter/

poet/writer/architect/historian/philosopher/scholar/professor （著名[高名]な科学者／芸術家／画家／詩人／作家／建築家／歴史家／哲学者／学者／教授）．distinguished は，人の career, achievement, record, position，あるいは組織やグループの record, tradition にも用いることができるが，eminent ではない．×a long and eminent career in medicine/tradition of choral singing. ☞ **prominent** (FAMOUS)

exalted 《フォーマル or おどけて，書き言葉》高位の，高貴な，高尚な，非常に重要な ◇She was the only woman to rise to such an *exalted* position. 彼女はそのような高い地位にまで登りつめた唯一の女性だった ◇You're moving in very *exalted* circles! あなたはとても高尚な人たちと交際しているんだね

greet 動

greet・accept・welcome・entertain・meet・receive
人が到着したときなどに温かく迎え入れて言葉を交わす
【類語訳】挨拶する，出迎える，受け入れる，迎える，もてなす，歓迎する，歓待する

▸文型&コロケーション

▸ to greet/ welcome/ meet/ receive sb **with** a smile, etc.
▸ to accept/ receive sb **as** sth
▸ to accept/ receive sb **into** sth
▸ to greet/ welcome/ entertain/ meet/ receive a **guest/ visitor**
▸ to **be there to** greet/ welcome/ entertain/ meet/ receive sb
▸ to greet/ accept/ welcome sb **formally**
▸ to greet/ welcome/ receive sb **enthusiastically/ warmly/ with open arms**

greet [他]（到着した人に）挨拶する，出迎える ◇He *greeted* all the guests warmly as they arrived. お客さんが到着すると，彼は全員を暖かく出迎えた ◇She *greeted* us with a smile. 彼女は私たちに笑顔で挨拶した ◇The winning team was *greeted* by cheering crowds. 凱旋チームは歓呼する群衆に出迎えられた

accept [他]（進行形はまれ）（グループの一員として）受け入れる，迎える ◇She had never been *accepted* into what was essentially a man's world. 彼女は本質的に男の世界とされるところに受け入れられたことなど決してなかった 反意 **reject** (REJECT), ☞ **accept** (LET SB IN)

welcome [他, 自]（到着した人に）親しげに挨拶する，出迎える ◇They were at the door to *welcome* us. 彼らは戸口で私たちを出迎えてくれた ◇It is a pleasure to *welcome you to* our home. あなたを我が家にお迎えできて光栄です ☞ **welcome** (LET SB IN), **welcoming** (FRIENDLY 1)

ノート greet と welcome の使い分け：greet は，いつもはそうではないがふつうは親しげに，人に挨拶するときに用いる．人に greet するのは，街頭でのこともあれば，訪問を受けた時のこともある．welcome は訪問を受けた時や，久しぶりに戻ってきた人に対して用いる．そして，一緒にいられてうれしいことを示し，相手にもそう感じてもらえるよう特別な努力をする．

entertain [自, 他]（自宅に客として人を招いて飲食で）もてなす ◇The job involves a lot of *entertaining*. その仕事には多くのおもてなしが含まれる ◇Barbecues are a favourite way of *entertaining* friends. バーベキューは皆が

greet, grief

友人のもてなし方の一つです

meet [他] 出迎える ◇Will you *meet* me at the airport? 空港に迎えに来てくれますか ◇The hotel bus *meets* all incoming flights. そのホテルはすべての到着便に出迎えのバスを出す

receive [他，しばしば受身で]《フォーマル》（正式に客を）歓迎[歓待]する ◇He was *received* as an honoured guest at the White House. 彼はホワイトハウスで賓客として歓迎された ☞ **receive** (LET SB IN)

grief 名 ☞ GLOOM

grief・sadness・regret・unhappiness・sorrow・melancholy・heartache・heartbreak
悲しい感情を表す
【類語訳】悲嘆，悲しみ，悲しさ，残念，落胆，惨めさ，悲哀，悲痛，物悲しさ

▸文型&コロケーション

▸ grief/ sadness/ regret/ unhappiness/ sorrow/ melancholy/ heartache/ heartbreak **at/ about/ over** sth
▸ grief/ sadness/ regret/ sorrow **for** sth
▸ **to** your grief/ regret/ sorrow
▸ **with** sadness/ regret/ sorrow
▸ **deep/ great/ real/ personal/ private** grief/ sadness/ regret/ unhappiness/ sorrow/ melancholy/ heartache/ heartbreak
▸ to be **filled with/ full of/ overcome with** grief/ sadness/ regret/ unhappiness/ sorrow/ melancholy/ heartache/ heartbreak
▸ to **feel/ experience** grief/ sadness/ regret/ unhappiness/ sorrow/ melancholy/ heartache/ heartbreak
▸ to **bring/ cause** (sb) grief/ sadness/ regret/ unhappiness/ sorrow/ heartache/ heartbreak
▸ to **cope with/ deal with** grief/ sadness/ regret/ unhappiness/ sorrow/ heartache/ heartbreak
▸ to **express/ show/ hide** your grief/ sadness/ regret/ unhappiness/ sorrow

grief [U, C]（人が死んだ際の）深い悲しみ，悲嘆 ◇She was *stricken with grief* when her husband died. 夫が死んだとき，彼女は悲嘆に暮れた ◇Children can feel real *grief* at the loss of a pet. ペットを亡くすと子どもたちは本当に悲しい気持ちを味わうことがある ◇They were able to share their common joys and *griefs*. 彼らは共通の喜びや悲しみを分かち合うことができた 反意 **joy** (JOY), **joy** (PLEASURE)

sadness [U, 単数で]《ややフォーマル》（他人[楽しい時が終わること]への）悲しみ，悲しさ ◇His memories of that time were tinged with *sadness*. 当時の彼の記憶は悲しみに満ちていた ◇I felt a deep *sadness* for them all. 私はみんなに対して深い悲しみを感じた ❶ *sadness* は *grief* よりも一般的な語だが，あまり頻繁には用いられず，ふつうはむしろフォーマル．形容詞の *sad* を用いる方がフォーマルさは弱まり，一般的である．◆ I felt very *sad* when I heard that she had died. （彼女が亡くなったと聞いてとても悲しかった）反意 **happiness** (SATISFACTION), ☞ **sad** (SAD), **sad** (UNHAPPY 1)

regret [U, C]（起こったこと[行ったこと，行わなかったこと]への）残念，悲しみ，落胆 ◇He gave up teaching in 2007, *much to the regret of* his students. 彼は2007年教職を捨て，学生たちは非常に残念がった ◇What is your

↪grief

greatest *regret* (= the thing that you are most sorry about doing or not doing)? あなたの最も残念に思っていることは何ですか ◊I **have no regrets** about leaving Newcastle (= I do not feel sorry about it). ニューキャッスルを去ることは少しもつらくない ❶自分が行った悪いことについて遺憾に思うときにもregretを用いることができる. 反意 **sat-isfaction** (SATISFACTION), ☞ **regret** (GUILT)
▶**regret** [動][他] ◊If you don't do it now, you'll only *regret* it. 今それをしないと、悔やむことになるだけだ ◊He bitterly *regretted* ever having mentioned it. 彼はかつてそのことに言及したことをひどく後悔した

unhappiness [U] (人生が困難[不愉快]であることによる)惨めさ, 悲哀 ◊A marriage break-up can cause a lot of *unhappiness*. 結婚生活の破綻でひどく惨めな気分になるかもしれない 反意 **happiness** (SATISFACTION), ☞ **unhappy** (UNHAPPY 1)

sorrow [U,C] 《ややフォーマル》(悪いことが起きたことによる)大きな悲しみ, 悲痛；悲しい出来事[状況] ◊He found to his *sorrow* that his childhood home was no longer there. 悲しいことに, 彼は子どもの頃の自分の家がもはやないことを知った ◊His death was a great *sorrow to* everyone who knew him. 彼を知る人みんなにとって, その死は大きな悲しみだった ◊It was an opportunity to share the *joys and sorrows* of the past few months. それは過去数か月の喜びや悲しみを分かち合う機会になった 反意 **joy** (PLEASURE)

melancholy [U] 《文語》(長く持続する説明のつかない)物悲しさ ◊A mood of *melancholy* descended on us that evening. その夜, 物悲しい気分が私たちを襲った ☞ **melancholy** (UNHAPPY 1)

heartache [U,C] 《ややインフォーマル》心痛, 悲痛 ◊The relationship caused her a great deal of *heartache*. その関係は彼女に多大な心痛をもたらした ◊I remember the *heartaches* of being a parent. 親なるがゆえの心痛を思い出します

heartbreak [U, C] 《ややインフォーマル》(悪いことに見舞われたことによる)大きな悲しみ, 悲嘆, 悲痛 ◊They suffered the *heartbreak* of losing a child through cancer. 彼らはガンで子どもを亡くす悲嘆を身をもって体験した ☞ **heartbreaking** (SAD), **heartbroken** (UNHAPPY 1)

group [名]

1 group・set・cluster・collection・bunch・clump
数多くの物[人]が同じ場所に一緒にある[いる]ことを表す
【類語訳】集団, 集まり, 一式, 一そろい, かたまり, 房, 群れ, 一団, 束

文型&コロケーション
▶a group/ set/ cluster/ collection/ bunch/ clump **of** sth
▶**in** a group/ set/ cluster/ bunch/ clump
▶**as** a group/ set
▶a **large/ small/ little** group/ set/ cluster/ collection/ bunch/ clump
▶a **big** group/ set/ bunch/ clump
▶to **form** a group/ set/ cluster/ clump
▶to **divide** sth **into** groups/ sets/ clusters

group [C＋単数・複数動詞] (同じ場所にある[いる])物・人の)集団, 集まり ◊On the hillside was a little *group* of houses. 丘の中腹に小さな集落があった ◊A *group* of us are going to the theatre this evening. 今晩私たち

group

のグループは観劇に出かけます ◊Students were sitting around in *groups* on the grass. 学生たちは芝生の上に三々五々座っていた ◊Classes will involve both individual and *group* activities. 授業には個人活動もグループ活動もあります

set [C] (同類のものの)一式, 一そろい ◊a *set* of six matching chairs 6脚のそろいの椅子一式 ◊She had a complete *set* of the author's novels. 彼女はその作家の全小説を一式そろえていた ◊You can borrow my keys — I have a spare *set*. 私の鍵を貸すよ—スペアが一そろいあるから

cluster [C] (近接して育つ[現れる]同種の物の)かたまり, 房；(一緒にいる人・動物・物の)群れ, 一団, 集まり ◊The plants have *clusters* of white flowers in early June. その植物は6月初めに白い花の房をつけます ◊The telescope is focused on a dense *cluster* of stars at the edge of the galaxy. 望遠鏡は銀河の端にある密集した星団に焦点をあわせています ◊A woman had emerged from the *cluster* of buildings. ビル群の中から一人の女性が姿を現していた

collection [C] (異なる種類の物[人]の)集まり ◊There was a *collection* of books and shoes on the floor. 床の上には本と靴が山となっていた ◊They appeared to be a *motley collection* (= a rather strange group of people) of college students. 彼らは大学生の雑多な集団に見えた

bunch [C] 房, 束 ◊a *bunch* of keys 鍵束 ◊a *bunch* of flowers/grapes/bananas 花束/ブドウ一房/一本のバナナ ❶この意味ではbunchはkeys, grapes, bananas, または異なる種類のflowers, herbsについて用いる.

clump [C] (木々・植物・人々などの)小集団；(草・髪などの)房, 束 ◊They planted trees in *clumps* around the park. 彼らは公園の周りに少しずつまとめて植樹した ◊He tore out a *clump* of her hair. 彼は彼女の髪を一房かきむしった

2 ☞ PARTY 2, TEAM 1
group・circle・bunch・crowd・gang・set・clique
物事を共有し, しばしば一緒に時間を過ごす何人かの人々を表す
【類語訳】グループ, 集団, 仲間, 一団

文型&コロケーション
▶a group/ circle/ bunch/ crowd/ gang/ clique **of** sth
▶a group/ circle/ bunch/ crowd/ gang/ set of **friends**
▶**in** a group/ circle/ set/ clique
▶a **small** group/ circle/ clique
▶a **mixed/ motley** group/ circle/ bunch/ clique
▶a **social** group/ circle/ set/ clique
▶to **belong to** a group/ set/ clique
▶to **join** a group/ circle/ set
▶**part of** a group/ circle/ crowd/ gang/ clique
▶a **member of** a group/ circle/ clique

group [C＋単数・複数動詞] (興味[問題, 体験]を共有する[時間を共に過ごす]人々の)グループ, 集団 ◊She worked with *groups* of college students who had literacy problems. 彼女は読み書きに問題を抱えた大学生のグループを対象とする活動をしていた ◊The college has a small but active women's *group*. その大学には小さいが活発な女性の集まりがある ◊People in the younger *age groups* tended to vote less. 年齢の低いグループに属する若者は投票に行かない傾向にあった ◊Members of some *ethnic groups* say that the law is discriminatory. いくつかの

group

民族グループのメンバーたちはその法律は差別的だと言っている ◇**Minority groups** are entitled to equal protection under the law. 少数派だって法律のもとで平等の保護を受ける権利がある

circle [C] (（同じ興味[仕事]を持つ）[社交的な交流のある]）仲間, 集団, グループ ◇He has a ***wide circle*** of friends 彼は幅広い交友関係がある ◇Talk of religion was forbidden in the ***family circle***. 身内の間では, 宗教の話は禁じられていた ◇He maintained influence in the ***inner circle*** of the president's political advisers. 彼は大統領の政治顧問の中枢グループ内において影響力を維持していた ◇Her ideas have caused controversy in scientific ***circles*** in recent years. 彼女の考えは近年科学界において物議をかもしてきた ◇My brother and I ***move in*** completely different ***circles*** (= we have very different friends). 兄と私はまったく異なる仲間と付き合っている

bunch [単数で]《インフォーマル》（友人関係にある[同じ興味[仕事]を持つ]）一団, 仲間 ◇The people that I work with are a great ***bunch***. 一緒に働いている人たちは最高の仲間だ ◇He's been hanging out with a ***bunch*** of yobs and hooligans. 彼は不良ならずもの連中とずっとつるんでいる

crowd [C+単数·複数動詞]《インフォーマル》（友人関係にある[同じ興味[仕事]を持つ]）一団, 仲間 ◇Do you ever see any of the ***old crowd*** (= people who used to be friends) from college? 大学時代の旧友の誰かと会っていますか ◇Bob introduced him to some of ***the usual crowd*** (= people who often meet each other). ボブは彼をふだん付き合っている仲間の何人かに紹介した ◇He got in with the ***wrong crowd*** (= people you disapprove of). 彼は悪い連中と付き合った

ノート **bunch** と **crowd** の使い分け：多くの場合, どちらの語も用いることができる. ◆They are a great ***bunch/crowd*** of people to work with. (彼らは一緒に働くには最高の仲間だ) ◆They were a bit of a motley ***bunch/crowd*** (= a strange mix of types of people). (彼らは少しばかり雑多な集まりだった) しかし, crowdのほうがより大きな人々の集団で, わずかだが結びつきの弱いことを示唆することもある. one/some of the usual crowdとは言えるが, ×one/some of the usual bunch とは言えない. bunch はひとまとまりのものとして見られる傾向がより強い.

gang [C+単数·複数動詞]《インフォーマル》（よく会う友達の）一団, 仲間 ◇There was a ***whole gang*** of us who went out together at weekends. 私たちは週末になると連れ立って出かける仲間たちがいた ◇Her friends made me feel welcome and treated me like ***one of the gang***. 彼女の友人は私を温かく迎え, 仲間の一人のように扱ってくれた

set [C+単数·複数動詞]《時にけなして》（同じ興味を持つ[社交的な時間を共にする]）一団, 仲間 ◇It's a favourite meeting place for Berlin's ***smart set*** (= rich, fashionable people). そこはベルリンの社交界の名士たちにとってお気に入りの会合の場だ ◇Several members of Dublin's literary ***set*** turned up for her funeral. ダブリンの文士仲間のメンバー数人が彼女の葬儀に出席した ❶setは金持ちや教養人の集まりのことが多いが, これはしばしば社会階級についての概念と結びつき, そのグループは特徴的で一般人とは別だし, けなす意味が含まれることもある.

clique [C+単数·複数動詞]（しばしばけなして）（同じ興味[社交的な時間を共にする]排他的な）小集団 ◇The club is dominated by a small ***clique*** of intellectuals. そのクラブは知識人の小派閥に牛耳られている

3 ☞ COMPANY
group • partnership • conglomerate • consortium • outfit • syndicate • cooperative

ビジネスで連携する数多くの人々[会社]を表す
【類語訳】企業グループ, 共同経営会社, 複合企業体, 共同事業体, シンジケート, 企業連合, 協同組合

文型&コロケーション
▶ a **large** group/ partnership/ conglomerate/ consortium/ outfit/ syndicate
▶ an **international** group/ partnership/ conglomerate/ consortium/ syndicate
▶ a **multinational** group/ conglomerate/ consortium
▶ a **small** group/ partnership/ outfit/ syndicate/ cooperative
▶ a **local** partnership/ consortium/ outfit/ cooperative
▶ a **business/ financial** group/ partnership/ conglomerate/ consortium
▶ a **media** group/ partnership/ conglomerate/ consortium/ outfit
▶ to **form** a group/ a partnership/ a conglomerate/ a consortium/ an outfit/ a syndicate/ a cooperative
▶ to **set up** a partnership/ a consortium/ an outfit/ a syndicate/ a cooperative
▶ to **join** a group/ a partnership/ a consortium/ an outfit/ a syndicate/ a cooperative
▶ to **run** a group/ a conglomerate/ a consortium/ an outfit/ a syndicate/ a cooperative

group [C+単数·複数動詞]《ビジネスで》（同一人物[組織]が所有する）企業グループ ◇This acquisition will make them the largest newspaper ***group*** in the world. この買収で彼らは世界最大の新聞関連の企業グループとなるだろう ◇Our ***group*** sales director attended the conference in Munich this year. 私たちの企業グループの営業部長は今年, ミュンヘンでの会議に出席した

partnership [C] （利益を分かち合う二人以上が所有する）共同経営会社 ◇a junior member of the ***partnership*** 下位の共同経営者 ☞ **partner** (PARTNER 1)

conglomerate [C]《ビジネスで》（異なる事業を結合させた）複合企業体, コングロマリット ◇He turned the business into a huge media ***conglomerate***. 彼はその会社を巨大な複合的メディア企業体に変えた

ノート **group** と **conglomerate** の使い分け：conglomerateには非常に大きな規模の印象が伴う. 一般的な結びつきは, ビジネスにおける産業領域に関連した語である. ◆a/an chemical/industrial/engineering/mining ***conglomerate*** (化学/産業/工学/鉱業コングロマリット). 他に, financial, media, publishingだけでなく, 規模や広がりに関連した語とも一般的に結びつく. ◆a/an huge/vast/international/multinational ***conglomerate*** (巨大/巨大/国際的/多国籍コングロマリット). groupにはより幅広い意味があり, 連携している会社の集まりならどんなものでも表すことができる.

consortium （複 **consortia, consortiums**）[C]《ビジネスで》（特定事業で連携している人々[国家, 会社]の）コンソーシアム, 共同事業体 ◇He led the Anglo-French ***consortium*** that built the Channel Tunnel. 彼は英仏海峡トンネルを建設した英仏の共同事業体を率いていた ❶consortiumはふつう, 特定の目的を持って暫定的に組まれたものを指す. ☞ UNION

outfit [C+単数・複数動詞]《インフォーマル》(組織[会社、チーム]として連携する人々の)一団、一群 ◇A London-based market research *outfit* has been appointed for the job. ロンドンに拠点を置いた市場調査組織にその仕事は指名された ◇This was the fourth album by the top rock *outfit*. これはこの一流のロックグループによる4枚目のアルバムだった ❶ *outfit* は、特に独立した小さな、スポーツチーム、ロックバンド、企業組織に最も頻繁に用いられる。

syndicate [C] (特定の目的を達成するために連携・協力する人々[会社]の)シンジケート、企業連合 ◇It is the home of the largest *crime syndicate* in Japan. そこは日本最大の犯罪組織の本拠地である ❶ *syndicate* は犯罪組織について最も頻繁に用いられる。◆a drug(s)/crime *syndicate* (麻薬シンジケート/犯罪組織)、また金(钱)を勝ちとろうとする人々の一団 ◆a lottery *syndicate* (宝くじシンジケート)や、連携する金融会社の一群 ◆a/an banking/insurance/investment *syndicate* (銀行/保険/投資シンジケート)に用いられることもある。☞ UNION

cooperative (英ではまた **co-operative**) [C] (関係者によって所有・運営・利益分配される)協同組合 ◇The 'Daily Worker' was run as a *cooperative*. 「デイリー・ワーカー」は協同組合として運営された ❶ *cooperative* の形をとる会社はしばしば、地元や地域社会に拠点を置き、食品の製造販売に関わる。◆a/an local/community/farming/agricultural/food/dairy *cooperative* (地元の/地域/農業/農芸/食品/酪農協同組合)。

guard 名

guard・bodyguard・sentry・garrison・minder・bouncer・lookout

人や物事を守ることを仕事とする人を表す
【類語訳】警備員、護衛、ボディガード、歩哨、守備隊、用心棒、見張り人、監視員

文型&コロケーション
▸ a/ an **armed**/ **uniformed** guard/ bodyguard
▸ to **stand** guard/ sentry
▸ to **post** a guard/ sentry/ lookout
▸ guard/ sentry/ garrison **duty**

guard [C] (兵士・警官のように場所[人々]を守る)警備員、護衛 ◇The *border guard* checked our papers before waving us through. 国境警備兵は通過するよう合図する前に私たちの書類をチェックした ◇She saw the *security guards* wrestle him to the ground. 彼女は警備員たちが彼を地面に組み伏せるのを見た ❶ *guard* [C+単数・複数動詞]は「警備員の集団」を意味することもできる。◆The President always travels with an armed *guard* (= a group of armed guards). (大統領はいつも武装警備隊を伴って移動する)。◆A group of tourists was watching *the changing of the guard* outside the palace (= when one group of guards replaces another). (観光客の一団は宮殿の外の衛兵たちの交代を見ていた)。☞ **guard** (PROTECT)

bodyguard [C+単数・複数動詞] (他人に攻撃される危険のある人を守る)ボディガード、護衛(の一群) ◇A personal *bodyguard* was assigned to her and is with her day and night. 専属のボディガードが彼女につけられ、昼夜はりついている

sentry [C] (入り口に立って警護する)歩哨 ◇People approaching the gate were challenged by the *sentry*. ゲートに近づく人たちが歩哨に呼び止められ身分を尋ねられた

garrison [C+単数・複数動詞] (防衛[統制]のために町[基地]で生活する)守備隊、駐屯兵団 ◇The Romans maintained a *garrison* of 5,000 soldiers in the city. ローマ人はその都市に5千人からなる守備隊を保持した ❶ **fort** (とりで、要塞)は、攻撃に対して地域を防衛するために建てられた建物(の一群)である。

minder [C]《特に英、ややインフォーマル》(有名人を危険[世間の注目]から守る)ボディガード ◇Her *minders* hurried her past the journalists and into a waiting car. ボディガードたちが彼女をせき立てて報道陣をやり過ごさせ、待機の車に押し込んだ

bouncer [C] (クラブ[バー]の入り口に立つ)用心棒 ◇The *bouncers* threw him out when he became aggressive. 彼がけんか腰になったとき、用心棒たちは彼をたたき出した

lookout [C] 見張り人、監視員 ◇One of the men stood at the door to act as a *lookout*. 男たちの一人は戸口に立って見張り番を務めた

guerrilla (または guerilla) 名

guerrilla・rebel・terrorist・insurgent・revolutionary・partisan・bomber・paramilitary

政府などの権威に対して暴力を用いる人を表す
【類語訳】ゲリラ、反逆者、テロリスト、反乱者、革命家、パルチザン

文型&コロケーション
▸ **armed** guerrillas/ rebels/ terrorists/ insurgents/ revolutionaries
▸ to **support** the guerrillas/ rebels/ terrorists/ insurgents/ partisans/ paramilitaries
▸ to **join** the guerrillas/ rebels/ insurgents/ partisans
▸ to **lead** the guerrillas/ rebels/ rebels
▸ guerrillas/ rebels/ terrorists/ insurgents/ partisans/ bombers **attack**/ **kill** sb/ sth
▸ a guerrilla/ a rebel/ a terrorist/ an insurgent/ a revolutionary/ a paramilitary **group**
▸ guerrilla/ rebel/ terrorist/ insurgent/ revolutionary/ paramilitary **activity**
▸ a guerrilla/ a rebel/ a terrorist/ an insurgent/ a paramilitary **attack**

guerrilla (または **guerilla**) [C] (政府に対し武器を使って戦う非正規軍武装組織の)ゲリラ兵 ◇Seven soldiers and two *guerrillas* were killed after an attack on a border post. 国境の軍駐屯地への攻撃後、7人の兵士と2人のゲリラ兵が死亡した ◇The peace talks have put an end to the 17-year *guerrilla* war. 和平交渉は17年にわたるゲリラ戦に終止符を打った

rebel [C] (母国政府と戦う)反逆者 ◇A group of armed *rebels* seized control of the national radio headquarters. 武装した反逆者たちの一団は国営ラジオ局本社を占拠した ◇*Rebel* forces clashed with government troops. 反乱軍は政府軍と激しく衝突した ☞ **rebellion** (REVOLUTION)

terrorist [C]《(けなして)》(政治的意図で暴力行為に訴える)テロリスト ◇International *terrorists* are threatening to blow up the plane. 国際テロリストたちは飛行機を爆破すると脅しをかけている ◇Three suspected *terrorists* have been arrested. テロリストと疑われる者3名が逮捕された

guilt, guilty 335

▶**terrorism** [名] [U] ◇an act of *terrorism* テロ行為
insurgent [C, ふつう複数で] 《フォーマル》(母国の政府[軍隊]と戦う)反乱者 ◇Government forces continue to face deadly attacks by armed *insurgents*. 政府軍、武装反乱兵の決死的攻撃になお対峙中 ☞ **insurgency** (REVOLUTION)

[ノート] **rebel** と **insurgent** の使い分け: 政府[当局]に対する戦いの初期段階では insurgent を用いる。insurgent よりフォーマルでなくよく用いられる rebel は、紛争の初期段階にも後期にも用いることができる。

revolutionary [C] (政治的な)革命家、革命支持者 ◇The *revolutionaries* tried to encourage soldiers to mutiny or desert. 革命家たちは兵士たちに反乱や脱走をそそのかした 関連 **revolution** (REVOLUTION), **revolutionary** (RADICAL)
partisan [C] (国家を掌握している敵軍とひそかに戦う武装集団の一員の)パルチザン ◇By the end of 1944 German forces had driven the Italian *partisans* out of the region. 1944年の終わりまでには、ドイツ軍はその地域からイタリアのパルチザンを追い出してしまっていた ❶ partisan はふつう、現在よりもむしろ歴史上の戦争や紛争、特に第二次世界大戦に関わる人について用いる。
bomber [C] 爆弾犯人 ◇The suicide *bomber* blew himself up in a crowded restaurant, killing twelve people. 自爆犯は混雑したレストランで自爆し12人を殺害した
paramilitary [C, ふつう複数で] (反政府を掲げる)準軍事的組織[構成員] ◇The army has blamed *paramilitaries* for heavy civilian casualties in the area. 軍隊はその地域の多数の民間犠牲者について準軍事的組織を非難した

guilt [名]

guilt・shame・regret・remorse・repentance
行った[行わなかった]ことを残念に[愚かに、悲しいと]思う気持ち
【類語訳】罪悪感、恥ずかしさ、恥辱、遺憾、後悔、自責の念

[文型&コロケーション]
▶ guilt/ shame/ regret/ remorse **at** sth
▶ guilt/ regret/ remorse **over** sth
▶ guilt/ regret **about** sth
▶ regret/ remorse/ repentance **for** sth
▶ to do sth **without** guilt/ shame/ regret/ remorse/ repentance
▶ **deep** shame/ regret/ remorse
▶ **genuine** regret/ remorse/ repentance
▶ to **feel** (no) guilt/ shame/ regret/ remorse
▶ to **have** no shame/ regret/ remorse
▶ to **show** regret/ remorse/ repentance
▶ a **pang/ stab** of guilt/ regret/ remorse

guilt [U] 罪悪感 ◇She had feelings of *guilt* about leaving her children and going to work. 彼女は子どもたちを置いて仕事に出かけることに罪悪感があった ◇Many survivors were left with a sense of *guilt*. 多くの生存者たちに罪悪感が残った ☞ **guilty** (SORRY)
shame [U] (間違った[愚かな]ことをしたゆえに抱く)恥ずかしさ、恥辱 ◇His face burned with *shame*. 彼は恥ずかしくて顔から火が出る思いだった ◇She hung her head in *shame*. 彼女は恥ずかしくてうなだれた ◇I would die of *shame* if she ever found out. 万一彼女に知られたら恥ずかしくて死んでしまうだろう ▶**To my shame** (= I feel

shame that) I refused to listen to her side of the story. 恥ずかしいことだが、私は彼女の側の話を聞こうとしなかった ❶ フォーマルな言葉では、shame は自分がしたことを恥ずかしいと感じられるかどうかという意味でも用いるが、疑問文・否定文においてのみである。◆ Have you no *shame*? (恥だと思わないの). 反意 **pride** (SATISFACTION), ☞ **shame** (EMBARRASS), **ashamed** (SORRY)

[ノート] **guilt** と **shame** の使い分け: 間違っていると自分が思っていることをしたときに guilt を感じる。他人がそれを知っているか否かは問題ではない。一方、自分が間違った[愚かな]ことをしてしまったことを他人に知られ、彼らからの尊敬を失ったと思うときに shame を感じる。◆ He could not live with the *guilt* of knowing it was all his fault. (それはすべて自分のせいだと認識して罪悪感を抱きながら生きることは彼にはできなかった). ◆ He could not live with the *shame* of other people knowing the truth. (他人が真実を知っているという恥ずかしさを感じながら生きることは彼にはできなかった).

regret [U, C] (自分が行った[行わなかった]ことへの)遺憾(の念)、後悔 ◇The police offered no expression of *regret* at his wrongful arrest. 警察は彼の不法逮捕に対して何ら遺憾の意を表明しなかった ❶ 行った[行わなかった]ことや逸した機会について悲しんだり失望したりするときに、regret を用いることができる。☞ **regret** (GRIEF)
remorse [U] (ややフォーマル、特に書き言葉) (自分の行った間違った[悪い]ことへの)深い後悔、自責の念 ◇I felt guilty and full of *remorse*. 私は罪悪感を覚え、自責の念で一杯だった ◇He was filled with *remorse* for not believing her. 彼は彼女を信じなかった後悔の念で一杯だった ❶ 罪を犯して show no remorse (後悔が見られない)であれば、法廷でより重い罰を受ける可能性が高くなる。
repentance [U] 《フォーマル、特に宗教》(間違った行いに対する)悔い改め ◇He shows no sign of *repentance*. 彼は改悛のそぶりも見せない ◇Sins are wiped out by sincere *repentance*. 心から悔い改めることで罪はすすがれる
▶**repent** [動] [自, 他] ◇She had *repented of* what she had done. 彼女は自分がしたことを悔やんでいた ◇He came to *repent* his hasty decision. 彼は性急な判断を悔やむことになった

guilty [形]

guilty・responsible・to blame・at fault・in the wrong
人が正しくない[違法な]ことを行ったことを表す
【類語訳】有罪の、責任がある、落ち度のある、過失がある

[文型&コロケーション]
▶ responsible/ to blame/ at fault **for** sth
▶ to **feel** guilty/ responsible/ to blame
▶ to **consider/ hold sb** guilty/ responsible/ to blame/ at fault
▶ **clearly** guilty/ responsible/ to blame/ at fault
▶ **entirely/ partly/ partially** responsible/ to blame/ at fault

guilty 有罪の; 罪を犯した ◇The jury found the defendant *not guilty*. 陪審は被告を無罪とした ◇My lawyer urged me to *plead guilty* (= say in court that I was guilty of a crime). 弁護士に罪を認めるよう勧められた ◇Under the UK judiciary system, everyone is *innocent until proved guilty*. 英国の司法制度

では, 有罪が立証されるまでは誰もが無実である ◇Who was the ***guilty party*** (= the person who was mainly responsible) in the affair? その事件の犯人は誰だったか ◇We've all been ***guilty of*** selfishness at some time in our lives. 私たちはみな, 人生のあるときに身勝手なことをしでかしてきたのだ 反意 **innocent, not guilty** (INNOCENT), ☞ **guilt** (FAULT)

responsible [名詞の前では用いない] (間違った事[まずい状況を招いたこと]への) 責めを負うべき, 責任がある ◇Who's *responsible* for all this mess? このひどいありさまは誰の責任なの ◇Everything will be done to bring those *responsible* to justice. 責めを負うべき者たちを裁判にかけるためにあらゆる手が打たれることになろう ◇Smoking is *responsible* for over 90% of deaths from lung cancer. 肺がんによる死亡の9割以上は喫煙が原因である ☞ **responsibility** (FAULT)

to 'blame フレーズ (まずい状況についての)責めを負うべき, 責任がある ◇For once, the government was not *to blame*. 今回に限って, 政府に非はなかった ◇If anyone's *to blame*, it's me. 誰かが責めを負うとすれば, それは私です ◇Modern intensive farming methods are largely *to blame* for this loss of habitat. 主として現代の集約農法が, この生息環境の喪失の責めを負うべきである ❶ to blame は特に, 否定的な発言や質問において, 多くの人々や事柄の間で責任をいかにして分かち合うかを決定するときに用いられる. ☞ **blame** (FAULT), **blame** (BLAME)

,at 'fault フレーズ (まずい状況についての)責めを負うべき; 落ち度のある, 過失がある ◇I think it's the law that's *at fault*. おかしいのは法律だと思う ◇The manager was *at fault in* refusing to listen to her initial concerns. 彼女の当初の懸念に耳を貸そうとしなかったことが経営者の過ちだった ☞ **fault** (FAULT)

in the 'wrong フレーズ (事故・ミスについての)責めを負うべき; 間違って, 誤って ◇The motorcyclist was clearly *in the wrong*. オートバイに乗っていたその人に非があるのは明らかだった ◇You're just trying to ***put me in the wrong*** (= prove that I am to blame), aren't you? 私のせいにしようとしているだけなんだろ ◇Why do you keep on arguing when you must know you are *in the wrong*? 自分が間違っていると悟るべきときに, どうして文句を言い続けるんだ ❶ responsibility, blame, fault は分担可能なものであり, 人や物事を主語にして, partly responsible/to blame/at fault (責任の一端がある)と言うことができる. ×partly *in the wrong*. in the wrong は一方の人が間違っていて他方が正しいという状況で用いられる. 反意 **in the right**

H h

habit 名

habit・practice・policy・ways・ritual・rule
しばしば行う事柄、日ごろの行い
【類語訳】癖、習慣、慣習、方針、方策、やり方

▶文型&コロケーション
- to **be** sb's habit/ practice/ policy **to do** sth
- **as is** sb's habit/ practice
- the/ sb's **usual** habit/ practice/ policy/ ritual
- sb's **personal** habits/ practice/ ritual
- **bad** habits/ practices/ policy/ ways
- to **make** a habit/ practice **of** doing sth
- to **make it** a habit/ practice/ policy/ rule **to do** sth
- to **become** a habit/ practice/ ritual
- to **have** a habit/ policy/ ritual/ rule
- to **follow** a policy/ ritual/ rule
- to **change** a/ your habit/ practice/ policy/ ways

habit [C, U] (なかなかやめられない)癖; (個人的な)習慣 ◇You need to change your eating *habits* (= what and how you eat). あなたは食習慣を変える必要があります ◇It's all right to borrow money occasionally, but don't ***let it become a habit***. 時々お金を借りるのは問題ないが、それを習慣にしてはいけない ◇I'm not ***in the habit of*** letting strangers into my apartment. 私には見知らぬ人を自分のアパートの部屋に招き入れる習慣はない ◇I ***got into the habit of*** going there every night for dinner. 私は毎晩夕食を食べにそこへ行くようになった ◇I do it ***out of habit***. 私は習慣でそうしている ◇When it comes to clothes, men are ***creatures of habit*** (= have fixed and regular ways of doing things). 服のことになると、男はいつも決まった服を着るものだ ☞ **habitual** (FREQUENT), **habitual** (USUAL)

practice [C] (ややフォーマル) (もっともな理由のある)習慣、(社会的な)慣習 ◇I like the German *practice* of giving workers a say in how their company is run. 会社の運営に関して従業員に発言権を与えるドイツ人流のやり方が私は好きだ ◇Established *practices* can be difficult to modify. 定着した習慣を変えるのは難しいかもしれない

policy [C, U] (《フォーマル》) (個人的な)方針、方策;(いつものやり方 ◇It is my *policy* not to say anything to the press. 記者には何も答えないのが私のやり方だ ◇As the old saying goes, honesty is the best *policy*. 古いことわざにあるように、正直は最良の策さ

ways [複数で] (個人的な)習慣、癖、(いつもの)やり方 ◇It's unlikely that your boss will change his *ways*. あなたの上司がやり方を変えることはなさそうだ ◇They seem to have seen ***the error of their ways***. 彼らは自分たちのやり方の間違いに気づいたようだ ◇You're going to have to ***mend my ways*** (= stop behaving badly). 君は心を入れ替えなければならないだろう ◇She had become ***set in her ways*** (= did not want to or was not able to change her habits and opinions). 彼女は自分のやり方に凝り固まっていた

ritual [C] 儀式的習慣[行為] ◇She had been following this daily *ritual* for several months. 数か月の間彼女はこの毎日行われる儀式的習慣に従っていた ◇It was all part of the *ritual* of returning home. それはいつもと何ら変わらないただ帰宅するという行為にすぎなかった ❶ritual はしばしば特定の時間に[状況で]行われるちょっとした一連の行為を指す。それらの行為が行われるのは、同じ形や状況で長期にわたって行われてきたり、人がそれらを続けたいと思ったりするからにすぎない。

rule [C, ふつう単数で] (個人的に決めた)習慣、主義 ◇I make it a *rule* never to mix business with pleasure. 私は仕事と遊びを決して混同しないようにしている ◇He occasionally allowed himself to break his own *rule*. 彼は時々自分で決めた習慣を自ら破ることを許した ☞ **rule** (PRINCIPLE 2), **as a rule** (USUALLY)

hall 名

1 hall・theatre・auditorium・chamber・ballroom・amphitheatre
多くの人を収容することができ、公共の[社交的な]行事に利用される広間
【類語訳】ホール、講堂、大広間、劇場、観客席、会議場、舞踏場

▶文型&コロケーション
- a **500-seat** hall/ theatre/ auditorium/ chamber/ amphitheatre
- a **crowded/ packed** hall/ theatre/ auditorium
- a **huge** hall/ auditorium
- an **open-air** theatre/ auditorium/ amphitheatre
- a **conference** hall/ chamber

hall [C] (集会・食事・コンサートなど用の)ホール、会堂、講堂、食堂、大広間 ◇It's important for a *concert hall* to have good acoustics. コンサートホールには優れた音響効果があることが重要だ ◇There are three *dining halls* on campus. キャンパスには大食堂が3か所ある ◇They will be performing at The Royal Albert *Hall*. 彼らはロイヤル・アルバートホールで演奏することになっている ❶(英)では hall には全校集会や催し物に利用される学校の「講堂」の意味もあるが、これは(米)では auditorium と呼ばれる。

theatre (《英》)(《米》**theater**) [C] 劇場 ◇She left the *theatre* a few minutes after the curtain fell. 彼女は幕が下りたあと数分で劇場を出た ◇How often do you ***go to the theatre***? どのくらいの頻度で劇を観に行きますか

auditorium (複 **auditoriums, auditoria**) [C] (劇場・コンサート会場の)観客[聴衆]席;(集会・コンサートなど用の)会館、会場、講堂、公会堂、大広間 ◇He stood at the back of the packed *auditorium*. 彼は満員の観客席の後方に立っていた ◇The new building will include an exhibition hall, *auditorium*, bookshop and restaurant. その新しい建物の中には展示場、公会堂、書店、レストランが入る予定だ ❶(米)では auditorium には全校集会や催し物に利用される学校の「講堂」の意味もあるが、これは(英)では school hall と呼ばれる。

chamber [C] (公共施設内の)会議場[室] ◇The members left the council *chamber*. 評議員たちは会議場を後にした ◇He had to answer some tricky questions from the floor of the *debating chamber*. 彼は議事堂の議員席から発せられるいくつかの巧妙な質問に答えねばならなかった

ballroom [C] 舞踏場 ◇He entered the palatial *ballroom* and took in his surroundings. 彼は宮殿の舞踏場に入ると中にある物にじっくりと見入った

amphitheatre [英] (米 **amphitheater**) [C] (古代ギリシャ・古代ローマの)円形劇場[闘技場]; (階段式座席のある円形[半円形]の)会場[講堂, 劇場] ◇The Roman *amphitheatre* stands just outside the fortress walls. 古代ローマの円形闘技場は要塞の城壁のすぐ外に立っている ◇Here in a vast *amphitheatre* you can dance the night away. こんなに広々とした円形劇場の中なら一晩中踊り明かすこともできるのだ

2 ☞ CORRIDOR
hall・lobby・reception・foyer・hallway・entry・entryway
建物に入るときに通り抜ける部屋[空間]
【類語訳】玄関, ロビー, 受付, ホワイエ, 入り口

<文型&コロケーション>
▶in the hall/ the lobby/ reception/ the foyer/ the hallway/ the entry/ the entryway
▶at reception/ the entry/ the entryway
▶an entrance hall/ lobby/ foyer
▶the main lobby/ foyer/ entry/ entryway
▶(a) hotel lobby/ reception/ foyer

hall [C] (住宅・アパート・建物の)玄関(の広間) ◇She ran into the *hall* and up the stairs. 彼女は玄関に駆け込んで階段を駆け上がった ☞ **hall** (CORRIDOR)
lobby [C] (応接[待合]に利用される公共施設の)ロビー ◇Long-distance calls can only be made from the *lobby* of the hotel. 長距離電話の使用はホテルのロビーからのみ可能です
reception [U] (特に英) (病院・ホテル・オフィスビルなどの)受付 ◇We arranged to meet in *reception* at 6.30. 私たちは6時30分に受付で会う約束をした ◇You can leave a message with *reception*. 受付に伝言を残すことができます ❶この意味ではreceptionは主に《英》で用いられる, reception deskという語句は《英》《米》の両方で用いる。◆For more information, please contact the *reception desk*. 《英,米》詳細については受付までお問い合わせください。
foyer [C] (ややフォーマル) (応接・待合に利用される劇場・ホテルの)ホワイエ, ロビー, (住宅・アパートの)玄関(の広間) ◇I'll meet you in the *foyer* at 7 o'clock. 7時にロビーで会いましょう ❶《米》ではfoyerには個人宅やアパートの「玄関(の広間)」の意味もある。◆An elegant *foyer* leads directly to the living room. (豪華な玄関が直接居間に通じている)
hallway [C] (特に英) (建物の)玄関(の広間); (入り口の)廊下, 通路 ◇He walked down the tiled *hallway* and into the kitchen. 彼はタイル張りの廊下を通って台所に入った ☞ **hallway** (CORRIDOR)

> **ノート** hallとhallwayの使い分け: これらの語に意味による違いはほとんどない。hallのほうが頻繁に用いられ, 横幅の広いものを指す。hallwayは特に細長いhall (玄関)を指す。

entry [C] 《米》 (建物の)入り口, 玄関(の広間); (入り口の)廊下, 通路 ◇You can leave your umbrella in the *entry*. 入り口に傘を置くことができます
entryway [C] 《米》 (建物の玄関に通じる内側[外側]の)通路 ◇The glass-enclosed *entryway* gives access to the lobby. ガラス張りの通路はロビーに通じている

happen [動]

happen・occur・take place・arise・come up・come about・turn out・materialize・crop up
事態が生じたり, 状況が存在し始めたりする
【類語訳】起こる, 発生する, 行われる, 実現する

<文型&コロケーション>
▶a change happens/ occurs/ takes place/ arises/ comes about
▶a situation happens/ occurs/ arises/ comes about
▶an event/ accident happens/ occurs/ takes place
▶a problem occurs/ arises/ comes up/ crops up
▶to be likely to happen/ occur/ take place/ arise/ come up/ come about/ materialize/ crop up
▶to happen/ occur/ take place/ arise/ come up in the future

happen [自] (出来事・事態が偶然に)起こる; (事の結果として)起こる ◇Let's see what *happens* next week. 来週どういうことになっているか見てみよう ◇**What happens if** nobody comes to the party? もし誰もパーティーに来なければ, どうなるのですか ◇I don't know how this *happened*. どうしてこうなったのかわかりません ◇Is this really *happening* or is it a dream? これは現実に起こっているのか, それとも夢なのか ◇I'll be there *whatever happens*. どんなことがあろうと私はそこへ行くつもりだ ◇She pressed the button but nothing *happened*. 彼女はボタンを押したが何も起こらなかった
occur (-rr-) [自] 《フォーマル》(犯罪・事故など予期せぬ出来事が)起こる, 発生する ◇When exactly did the incident *occur*? 正確にはいつその事件は発生したのですか ◇Something unexpected *occurred*. 不測の事態が起こった ☞ **occurrence** (EVENT 1)
take 'place [行わ] (行事が準備[計画]されて)行われる; (出来事・事態が偶然に)起こる ◇The film festival *takes place* in October. 映画祭は10月に行われる ◇When did this conversation *take place*? この会話はいつあったのですか
arise [自] 《フォーマル》(問題・論争・困難が)発生する ◇We keep them informed of any changes as they *arise*. 私たちは変化が起きたらどんなことでも彼らに逐次連絡している ◇Children should be disciplined *when the need arises* (= when it is necessary.) 必要なときには子どもたちをしつけることも大切だ ◇A storm *arose* during the night. 夜間に嵐が発生した
,come 'up [句動詞] (問題・機会が突然)起こる; (行事・時期が)近づいてくる ◇I'm afraid something urgent has *come up*. あいにく急用ができてしまいました ◇We'll let you know if any vacancies *come up*. 空きができましたらお知らせします ◇Her birthday is *coming up* soon. 彼女の誕生日がもうすぐ来る
,come a'bout [句動詞] (事の結果として)起こる ◇How did this dramatic transformation *come about*? どうしてこの劇的な変化は起こったのですか ◇How has it

come about that such a small group has been able to achieve such influence? どのようにしてこのような少人数のグループがこれほどの支配力をもてるようになったのですか ❶ **come about** は特に賛成できないような事がどのようにして起こったのか説明[質問]するために用いられる.

ˌturn ˈout 句動詞 《副詞や形容詞と共に, howの疑問文で》（特定の形で）起こる；（特定の形に）進展する, 終わる ◇*Despite our worries everything turned out* well. 私たちの心配をよそに, 万事うまくいった ◇*You never know how your children will turn out!* お前の子供たちがどうなるかわかったもんじゃないぞ ◇*If the day turns out* wet, we may have to change our plans. もし当日雨になれば, 計画を変更しなければならないかもしれない

materialize（英でまた -**ise**）[自]《ふつう否定文で》（予測[計画]どおりに）実現する, 実行される ◇*The promotion he had been promised failed to materialize.* 彼の約束されていた昇進は実現しなかった ◇*The hoped-for boom never materialized.* 期待された好況はまったく起こらなかった

ˌcrop ˈup 句動詞（-**pp**-）《ややインフォーマル》（時々・予期せず）現れる, 起こる ◇*It's the kind of problem that crops up* from time to time. その種の問題は時々起こる ◇*I'll be late — something's cropped up* at the office. 遅くなるよ — 会社でちょっとあってね

happy ☞ EXCITED, GLAD

happy・satisfied・content・contented・joyful・blissful
喜びや満足を感じる[見せる, 与える]ことを表す
【類語訳】うれしい, 幸福な, 喜ばしい, 安心した, 喜んだ, 嬉々とした, 楽しい

satisfied	happy content contented	joyful blissful

▷ 文型&コロケーション
▸ happy/ satisfied/ content/ contented **with** sth
▸ a happy/ satisfied/ contented/ blissful **smile**
▸ a happy/ contented/ joyful **mood**
▸ a happy/ joyful **occasion/ celebration**
▸ happy/ blissful **days/ weeks/ years**
▸ to **feel** happy/ satisfied/ content/ joyful
▸ **very/ perfectly/ quite** happy/ satisfied/ content/ contented

happy うれしい, うれしそうな, 幸福(そう)な, 喜ばしい；（物事に）満足[安心]した, 喜んだ ◇*I looked around at all the happy faces.* 私はうれしそうな皆の顔を見回した ◇*a happy marriage/memory/childhood* 幸せな結婚/思い出/幼年時代 ◇*Those were the happiest days of my life.* その頃が私の人生の中で一番幸せな時だった ◇*The story has a happy ending.* その物語はハッピーエンドで終わる ◇*Happy birthday!* お誕生日おめでとう ◇*If there's anything you're not happy about*, come and ask. もし何か不満があれば, 聞きに来てください ◇*I said I'd go, just to keep him happy.* 私はただ彼を喜ばせておくために「私は行きます」と言った 反意 **sad, unhappy** (UNHAPPY 1), **unhappy** (UNHAPPY 2), ☞ **happiness** (SATISFACTION)

▷ **happily** 副 ◇*children playing happily on the beach* 砂浜でうれしそうに遊んでいる子どもたち ◇*They had been happily married for ten years.* 彼らは10年間幸せな結婚生活を送っていた

satisfied （達成・実現に）満足した；満足そうな ◇*She's never satisfied with what she's got.* 彼女は決して現状に満足しない ◇*Keep all letters from satisfied customers.* 満足してくれたお客さんからの手紙をすべて保管しておくように ◇*Sarah watched, a satisfied expression on her face.* サラは彼女の満足そうな顔の表情をじっと見ていた 反意 **dissatisfied** (UNHAPPY 2), ☞ **satisfaction** (SATISFACTION), **satisfy** (PLEASE)

content 《名詞の前では用いない》幸せな, 満足した ◇*I'm perfectly content just to* lie in the sun. 私はただ日光浴をするだけでもう十分幸せです ◇*Not content with* stealing my boyfriend (= not thinking that this was enough) she has turned all my friends against me. 私の彼氏を奪うだけでは物足りなくて, 彼女は私の友達全員を私の敵に回すよう仕向けた ☞ **contentment** (SATISFACTION)

contented 幸せな, 満足した；幸せそうな, 満足そうな ◇*a contented baby/workforce/cat* 幸せそうな赤ちゃん/従業員/猫 ◇*I felt warm and cosy and contented.* 私は暖かくて気持ちよく, 幸せだった ◇*He gave a long contented sigh.* 彼は満足そうに長いため息を漏らした 反意 **discontented** (UNHAPPY 2), ☞ **contentment** (SATISFACTION)

▷ **contentedly** 副 ◇*She smiled contentedly.* 彼女は満足げに笑った

▷ ノート **content** と **contented** の使い分け：**contented** は満ち足りた生活からくる. **content** は生活に対する心の持ちようなので, **have to be content**（満足しなければならない）や **learn to be content**（満足するようになる）と言える.
◆ *He had to be content with third place.* (彼は3位に甘んじなければならなかった). ◆ *I really should try to be like her, she is so content.* (私は本当に彼女を見習うべきだ, だって彼女はとても幸せなんだもの). **contented** は人や動物に用いられるが, **content** は人のみ.

joyful 《フォーマル》喜びにあふれた, 嬉々とした；喜ばしい, 楽しい ◇*Easter is a time to be joyful.* 復活祭は楽しい時だ ☞ **joy** (JOY)

blissful 至福の；幸福に満ちあふれた ◇*We spent three blissful weeks away from work.* 私たちは仕事を離れて至福の3週間を過ごした ❶ *blissful ignorance* は「知らぬが仏」を意味する. ◆ *We preferred to remain in blissful ignorance of what was going on.* (私たちは何がどうなっているのか知らぬが仏のままでいるほうがよかった). ☞ **bliss** (JOY)

▷ **blissfully** 副 ◇*blissfully* happy この上なく幸せな ◇*blissfully* ignorant/unaware 知らぬが仏の状態で

▷ ノート **joyful** と **blissful** の使い分け：**joyful** のほうがより活発な感情を指し, **blissful** のほうがより平穏な心を指す.

hard 形

hard・strenuous・arduous・gruelling・punishing
多くの労力[努力]が要ることを表す
【類語訳】骨の折れる, 困難な, つらい, きつい, 厄介な, 過酷な

▷ 文型&コロケーション
▸ hard/ strenuous/ arduous/ gruelling **work**

↪hard

- a hard/ a strenuous/ an arduous **climb**
- a hard/ an arduous/ a gruelling **journey**
- a hard/ gruelling/ punishing **schedule**
- a hard/ gruelling **day**

hard （ある期間にわたり）労力［努力］が要る, 骨の折れる, 困難な, つらい ◇It's *hard* work shovelling snow. 雪かきは重労働だ ◇I've had a long *hard* day. 長くつらい一日だった

▶**hard** 副 ◇They work *hard* at school. 彼らは学校で勉強に励んでいる ◇I trained as *hard* as I could. 私はできる限りの猛練習をした ◇You must **try harder**. 君はもっと頑張らなくてはならない ◇She **tried her hardest** not to show her disappointment. 彼女はがっかりした様子を見せないように精一杯努力した

strenuous 労力［努力］が要る, 骨の折れる, きつい; 必死の, 熱心な, 激しい ◇Avoid tasks which require *strenuous* physical activity. 激しい肉体的作業を必要とする仕事は避けなさい ◇The ship went down although *strenuous* efforts were made to save it. 救助するために必死の努力がなされたが, その船は沈没した

▶**strenuously** 副 ◇He still works out *strenuously* every morning. 彼はいまだに毎朝熱心にトレーニングしている ◇The government *strenuously* denies the allegations. 政府はそれらの根拠のない主張を必死に否定している

arduous （ある期間にわたり）労力［努力］が要る, 骨の折れる, 厄介な ◇She was now faced with an *arduous* trek across the mountains. 彼女は今度は山脈を越える険しい行程に直面していた ◇an *arduous* task/process 厄介な仕事/方法

ノート strenuous と arduous の使い分け： strenuous のほうが arduous よりも多大な努力を要することがあるが, 時間は比較的かからないこともある. ◆ The exercise need not take long, but it should be fairly *strenuous*. (その運動は時間をかける必要はないが, かなりきついだろう).

gruelling 《特に英》《米でふつう **grueling**》（ある期間にわたり）労力［努力］が要る, 過酷な, へとへとに疲れさせる ◇a *gruelling* work schedule 厳しい仕事のスケジュール ◇a sporting event that represents a *gruelling* test of endurance 過酷な我慢比べの象徴であるスポーツ大会

punishing （予定の活動［作業］が）労力［努力］を要する, 骨の折れる, 過酷な, へとへとに疲れさせる ◇a *punishing* exercise regime 過酷な運動療法 ◇The president has a *punishing* schedule for the next six months. 大統領は今後6か月間にわたってスケジュールがぎっしり詰まっている

ノート punishing と gruelling の使い分け： punishing は予定の活動［作業］にしか用いられず, 結びつくのも schedule, programme, regime だけである.

harmful 形

harmful・destructive・negative・damaging・bad・
ill・detrimental・pernicious
害をもたらす可能性のあることを表す
【類語訳】有害な, 破壊的な, 否定的な, マイナスの, 悪い, 不利益の, 支障をきたす, 悪質な

文型＆コロケーション
- harmful/ destructive/ damaging/ detrimental **to** sb/ sth
- harmful/ damaging/ bad **for** sb
- a harmful/ destructive/ negative/ damaging/ bad/ detrimental/ pernicious **effect**
- ill **effects**
- a harmful/ destructive/ negative/ damaging/ bad/ pernicious **influence**
- harmful/ destructive/ negative/ damaging/ detrimental/ pernicious **consequences**
- harmful/ negative/ damaging/ bad **publicity**
- **very**/ **extremely** harmful/ destructive/ negative/ damaging/ bad/ detrimental
- **potentially** harmful/ destructive/ damaging/ detrimental
- **positively** harmful/ damaging/ detrimental
- **highly** destructive/ damaging/ detrimental
- **environmentally**/ **socially** harmful/ destructive/ damaging/ detrimental

harmful 《ややフォーマル》（健康・環境に対して）有害な ◇The *harmful* effects of alcohol are well established. アルコールの有害性は十分に立証されている ◇Keep food chilled to prevent the spread of *harmful* bacteria. 有害細菌の増殖を防ぐために食品は冷蔵保存しましょう ◇pesticides that are *harmful* to the environment 環境に有害な農薬 [反意] **harmless**, ☞ **harm** (DAMAGE 名), **harm** (DAMAGE 動)

destructive 《ややフォーマル》 有害な, 破壊的な ◇The war demonstrated the *destructive* power of modern weapons. その戦争で近代兵器の破壊力が実証された ◇People have to learn how to handle *destructive* emotions like anger. 怒りのような人の気持ちを荒立てる感情への対処の仕方を身に付けなければならない

negative （関係・商売・経済・健康・幸福に）有害な, 否定的な, マイナスの ◇The crisis had a *negative* effect on trade. その危機は商売に悪影響を及ぼした ◇The whole experience was definitely more positive than *negative*. その経験が総じてマイナスよりプラスに働いたことは間違いない ❶ negative は特に effect, impact, influence, consequences, side effects を修飾する. [反意] **positive** (VALUABLE 2), ☞ **negative** (NEGATIVE)

damaging （健康・環境・幸福・評判に）有害な, 損害［悪影響］を与える ◇A strike would hit public services and be politically *damaging* for the government. ストライキになれば公共サービスへの打撃となり政府側には政治的損害を与えることになろう ◇Lead is potentially *damaging* to children's health. 鉛は子どもの健康に有害である可能性がある ☞ **damage** (DAMAGE 名), **damage** (DAMAGE 動)

ノート harmful と damaging の使い分け： harmful は環境・健康に害を及ぼす場合. damaging は環境・健康についても用いられるが, 社会［経済］的幸福・評判に害を及ぼす場合に用いられることが多い.

bad 《ややインフォーマル, 特に話し言葉》（健康・商売・性質・評判に）有害な, 悪い ◇Sugary drinks are *bad* for your teeth. 甘い飲み物は歯に悪い ◇Weather like this is *bad* for business. このような天候は商売によくない ◇That girl's a *bad* influence on Tom. あの娘はトムに悪影響を与えている ◇Sunbeds have received a lot of *bad* publicity in recent years. Are they safe? 近年日焼け器具は悪い評判だらけですが安全なものなのでしょうか ❶ この意味では bad は bad **for** sb/sth の句や influence, publicity, effect と結びついて用いられる. [反意] **good** (VALUABLE 2)

ill ［名詞の前で］《ややフォーマル》（健康・快適さ・評判に）有害

な，好ましくない ◇He resigned because of *ill* health. 彼は体調不良のため辞任した ◇She suffered no *ill* effects from the experience. 彼はその経験による悪影響を受けなかった ◇I *bear you no ill will* (= do not wish any harm to come to you), but I am simply not in a position to help you. 《フォーマル》悪意はないんだけど，ただ君を助ける立場にないだけなんだ ❶この意味では ill は特に health, effects, treatment, will, repute と結びつく．

detrimental 《フォーマル》（環境・健康・幸福に）有害な，不利益な；（試みに）障害[支障]をきたす ◇Emissions from the factory are widely suspected of having a *detrimental* effect on health. 工場からの排気ガスは健康に悪影響を及ぼすと各方面から懸念されている ◇The policy will be *detrimental* to the peace process. その政策は和平プロセスに支障をきたすだろう ❶*detrimental* はほとんど常に detrimental effect/effects や detrimental to sb/sth の句で用いられる．反意 **beneficial** (VALUABLE 2), ☞ **detriment** (DAMAGE 名)

pernicious 《フォーマル》（社会・道徳にじわじわと）有害な，害悪となる，悪質な ◇They discussed the *pernicious* influence of TV violence on children. 彼らはテレビの暴力シーンが子どもたちに与える悪影響を議論した ◇Ageism is just as offensive and *pernicious* as sexism. 年齢差別は性差別とまったく同様に侮辱的で悪質なものだ

hate 動

hate・dislike・can't stand・despise・can't bear・loathe・detest・abhor
人・物事に対して嫌悪感を強く抱く
【類語訳】憎む，嫌う，反感を持つ，我慢できない，耐えられない，軽蔑する，憎悪する，嫌悪する

dislike	hate	can't bear	loathe
despise	can't stand		detest
			abhor

〔文型&コロケーション〕
▶ to hate/ dislike/ despise/ loathe/ detest sb/ sth **for** sth
▶ to hate/ dislike/ despise/ loathe/ detest sth **about** sb/ sth
▶ I hate/ dislike/ can't stand/ can't bear/ loathe/ detest **do**-**ing** sth
▶ I hate/ can't bear **to do** sth
▶ I hate/ dislike/ can't stand/ can't bear **it when**…
▶ to hate/ despise/ loathe **yourself**
▶ they hate/ dislike/ can't stand/ despise/ loathe/ detest **each other**
▶ I **really** hate/ dislike/ can't stand/ despise/ can't bear/ detest sb/ sth
▶ I **absolutely** hate/ dislike/ can't stand/ loathe/ detest/ abhor sb/ sth

hate [他, 自]《進行形なし》憎む，(ひどく)嫌う ◇He *hates* violence in any form. 彼はいかなる形の暴力も嫌う ◇I've always *hated* cabbage. 私はずっとキャベツが嫌いだ ◇Sometimes I really *hate* her. 時々私は本当に彼女を憎むことがある ◇I *hated* myself for feeling jealous. 私は焼きもちを焼いた自分を憎んだ ◇She *hates* making mistakes. 彼女は間違えることをひどく嫌う ◇I would *hate* him to think he wasn't welcome here. 彼が私はここに歓迎されていないとは思ってもらいたくない ◇I *hate*

to think what would have happened if you hadn't been there. あなたがそこにいなかったらどうなっていただろうなんてことは考えたくもない ◇She *hated* it in France (= did not like the life there). 彼女はフランスでの生活をひどく嫌がった ◇When children are taught to *hate*, the whole future of society is in danger. 子どもたちが憎むことを教わると，社会の先行き全体は危険にさらされる ❶*hate* は通例は非常に強い意味の動詞だが，話し言葉やインフォーマルな言い回しでもふつうに用いられ，人や，例えば嫌いな食べ物の種類など重要性の薄い事柄にも用いられる．反意 **love** (LOVE 動), love (LIKE 動)

dislike [他]《進行形なし》《ややフォーマル》嫌う，反感を持つ ◇Why do you *dislike* him so much? どうして彼がそんなに嫌いなの ◇Not only would she rather not go swimming, she *actively dislikes* it. どちらかと言えば泳ぎに行きたくないというのではなく，彼女はまったくその気になれないんだ ◇The new regime is *universally disliked*. その新政権は全世界から反感を持たれている ◇*Much as she disliked* asking for help, she knew she had to. 彼女は人に助けを求めるのが嫌いだったが，そうしなければならないことはわかっていた ❶*dislike* はややフォーマルな語．特に話し言葉では don't like と言うほうがフォーマルでなく一般的. ◆I *don't like* it when you phone me so late at night. (こんなに夜遅く電話されるのは嫌なんですが). 反意 **like** (LIKE 動), **like** (LOVE 動)

stand [他, 受身なし]《進行形なし，否定文・疑問文で》《ややインフォーマル，特に話し言葉》我慢する，耐える ◇I can't *stand* his brother. 私は彼の弟のことが我慢できない ◇She can't *stand* the sight of blood. 彼女は血を見るとたえられない ◇I can't *stand* it when you do that. 私は君がそうすることに我慢ならない ◇How could she have *stood* such treatment for so long? そんなにも長い間，彼女はどうしてうした待遇に耐えられたのだろうか

despise [他]《進行形なし》嫌う，軽蔑する ◇She *despised* gossip in any form. 彼女はいかなる形のうわさ話も嫌った ◇He *despised* himself for being so cowardly. 彼はそんなにも臆病な自分を軽蔑した

bear [他]《進行形なし，否定文・疑問文で》 我慢する，耐える ◇How can you *bear* to eat that stuff? どうしてあんな物を我慢して食べられるの ◇I just can't *bear* it any more! もうこれ以上我慢できない ◇The pain was almost more than he could *bear*. その苦痛に彼は耐えられなくなりそうだった ◇She *couldn't bear the thought of* losing him. 彼女は彼を失うことを考えるとたまらなくなった

〔ノート〕**can't stand** と **can't bear** の使い分け：ほとんどの場合両方とも使用可能だが，**can't stand** のほうが **can't stand** よりもいくぶん強意的でフォーマルな表現．**bear** は肯定文でも用いられ，「嫌な物事に耐える」という意味を持つ．◆She *bore* it all with her usual patience. (いつもどおり忍耐強く彼女はそのすべてに耐えた). ✗She *stood* it all with her usual patience. ☞ STAND 2

loathe [他]《進行形なし》ひどく[忌み]嫌う，大嫌いである ◇They *loathe* each other. 彼らはひどく嫌い合っている ◇Many of the people fear and *loathe* the new government. 国民の多くが新政府を恐れ，忌み嫌っている ◇He *loathed* hypocrisy. 彼は偽善を忌み嫌った ❶*loathe* は *hate* よりもさらに強意的な動詞であるが，比較的インフォーマルで，それほど重要でない物事について「大嫌いである」の意味で用いられることもある. ◇Whether you *love* or *loathe* their music, you can't deny their talent. (彼らの音楽が大好きでも大嫌いでも，彼らの才能を否定することはで

きないよ). 反意 **love, adore** (LOVE 動), **adore** (LIKE 動)

detest [他]《進行形なし》《ややフォーマル》ひどく憎む[嫌う]
◇They absolutely *detest* each other. 彼らはまったく互いに憎み合っている ◇I *detest* being treated like a child. 私は子ども扱いされるのが本当に嫌だ 反意 **love** (LOVE 動)

abhor 《進行形なし》《フォーマル》(道徳的理由で)憎む[嫌悪]する ◇Most decent people *abhor* corruption in government. 大半のまともな国民は政府内の腐敗を憎悪している

hatred 名

hatred・dislike・hate・aversion・loathing
人や物事を嫌う強い気持ち
【類語訳】憎しみ、憎悪、嫌悪、反感、敵意、忌避、嫌気

| dislike | hatred | loathing |
| aversion | hate | |

文型&コロケーション
▶ hatred/ dislike/ hate/ loathing **for/ of** sb/ sth
▶ **deep** hatred/ dislike/ aversion/ loathing
▶ **absolute** hatred/ hate/ loathing
▶ to **be filled with** hatred/ hate/ loathing
▶ to **develop** a hatred/ an aversion/ a loathing
▶ **fear and** hatred/ hate/ loathing

hatred [U, C] (人・物事への)憎しみ、憎悪、激しい嫌悪 ◇She felt nothing but *hatred* for her attacker. 彼女は襲撃者に対して憎しみ以外の何も覚えなかった ◇He was accused of stirring up *racial hatred*. 彼は人種の憎悪を扇動したかどで告発された ◇The debate simply revived old *hatreds*. その討議は過去の憎しみが再燃しただけだった

dislike [U, C] (人・物事への)嫌気、反感;嫌いなもの ◇He did not try to hide his *dislike* of his boss. 彼は上司に対する反感を隠そうとしなかった ◇She **took an instant dislike to** the house and the neighbourhood. 彼女はその家と地域が急に嫌いになった ◇I've told you all my **likes and dislikes**. 私の好き嫌いを全部あなたに話したでしょ 反意 **liking** (LOVE 名 2), **likes** ❶ likesは好きなものを指すが、この語は実際にはsb's likes and dislikesの句でしか用いられない

hate [U] (人への)憎しみ、敵意 ◇His eyes were flashing with *hate* and anger. 彼の目は憎しみと怒りで燃え上がっていた ◇He had received racist *hate mail*. 彼に人種差別主義者から嫌がらせの手紙が届いていた 反意 **love** (LOVE 名 2)

ノート **hatred** と **hate** の使い分け：hatredのほうがいくぶんフォーマルで、特に書き言葉で用いられることが多い。抽象的な概念を指すことが多いが、特定の人や物事に対する非常に強い嫌悪感を表すこともある ◆ Her deep *hatred* of her sister was obvious. (彼女が妹に対して深い憎しみを抱いていることは明らかだった) ◆ a cat's *hatred* of water (猫の水嫌い) 一般的にはhateを用いることが多い ◆ a look of pure *hate* (純然たる憎しみの表情) ◆ people filled with *hate* (憎しみに満ちた人々)、hateはインフォーマルで話し言葉の文脈で用いられることが多い。また、a hate campaign (嫌がらせ)やa hate figure (憎むべき人物)の句のように他の名詞の前で用いられることもある。

aversion [C, U] (人・物事への)強い嫌悪、忌避、大の苦手 ◇He had an *aversion to* getting up early. 彼は早起きが大の苦手だった ◇She has a deep-rooted *aversion* to dogs, almost amounting to a phobia. 彼女は根っからの犬嫌いで、ほとんど恐怖症に等しい

loathing [単数形、U]《フォーマル》(人・物事への)憎悪、激しい嫌悪、嫌気、愛想尽かし ◇Many soldiers returned with a deep *loathing* of war. 多くの兵士が戦争を心から憎しみながら帰還した ◇She looked at her attacker with fear and *loathing*. 彼女は恐怖と憎悪に満ちた目で襲撃者を見た

have 動

1 have・have got・own・hold・possess
自分のものであることを表す
【類語訳】所有する、持っている、持ち合わせる、所持する、保有する、所蔵する

文型&コロケーション
▶ to have/ have got/ own/ possess a **car/ house**
▶ to have/ have got/ own a **company**
▶ to have/ have got/ hold a **driving licence/ passport**
▶ to have/ have got **money**
▶ to own/ hold sth **legally/ jointly**

have [他, 受身なし]《進行形なし》所有する、持っている;持ち合わせる、所持する ◇He *had* a new car and a boat. 彼は新車とボートを所有していた ◇I don't *have* that much money on me. そんな多額の持ち合わせはないよ ◇She *has* a BA in English. 彼女は英語の学士号を持っている ▶ **the haves** 名 [複数で] ◇the division between **the haves and the have-nots** (= between the people who have enough money and possessions and those who don't) 持てる者と持たざる者との格差

have got [他, 受身なし]《特に英》《進行形なし》所有する、持っている;持ち合わせる、所持する ◇He's *got* a new job. 彼は新しい仕事に就いている ◇We *haven't got* much time, I'm afraid. あいにく私たちには時間があまりありません ◇*Have* you *got* a belt I could borrow? 私が借りられるようなベルトを持ってる？

ノート **have** と **have got** の使い分け：これらの2語に意味の違いはないが、have got は《米》ではあまり用いられない。《英》では一般的で、特に話し言葉とインフォーマルな書き言葉において、特に現在時制で用いられる。過去時制では have got (had got, hadn't got) よりも have (had, didn't have) のほうが頻繁に用いられる。◆ He *had* a house by the sea. (彼は海辺に家を所有していた) × He *had got* a house by the sea. ◆ Did you *have* this toy when you were a child? (子どもの頃にこのおもちゃを持っていたかい). ◆ We *didn't have* enough bedrooms. (私たちの家には十分な数の寝室がなかった). ◆ I *hadn't got* a car at the time. (《didn't have》より使用頻度が少ない) 当時私は車を持っていなかった).

own [他]《進行形なし》(購入により法的に)所有する ◇Do you *own* your house or do you rent it? お住まいは持ち家ですか、それとも借家ですか ◇I don't *own* anything of any value. 私は少しでも価値のある物はいっさい持っていない ◇Most of the apartments are privately *owned*. そのアパートの部屋の大半は個人により所有されています ◇an American-*owned* company アメリカ系企業 ◇Don't tell me what to do — you don't *own* me! あれこれ指図しないで —私はあなたの所有物じゃないわ

hold [他]《進行形なし》《ややフォーマル》(金・株・公文書などを)所有[保有]する ◇Employees *hold* 30% of the shares. 従業員が株の30%を保有している ◇The company has *held* the advertising contract since 2005. 2005年からその会社は広告契約を結んでいる ◇Applicants must *hold* a full driving licence. 応募者は制限条件なしの運転免許を有する者に限る ❶hold の目的語には opinion, views, job, position, office, record, title も挙げられる。 ◆He *holds* strange *views* on education. 彼は教育に関して変わった考えを持っている。 ◆How long has he *held office*? (彼が着任してからどのくらい経ちますか[彼はもうどのくらい在職していますか]). ◆She *held the title* of world champion for three years. 彼女は3年間世界チャンピオンのタイトルを保持した)。

possess [他]《進行形なし》《フォーマル》(特別[高価]な物を)所有[所持, 所蔵]する ◇He was charged with *possessing* a shotgun without a licence. 彼は無免許で散弾銃を所持した罪で起訴された ◇I'm afraid this is the only suitcase I *possess*. あいにく私はこれしかスーツケースを持っていない ◇The gallery *possesses* a number of the artist's early works. その美術館はその画家の初期の作品をいくつも所蔵している ☞ **possession** (THING 2)

2 have・have got・enjoy・possess・boast・be endowed with sth・be blessed with sb/sth
特性や特徴を見せる
【類語訳】備える, 持っている, 抱える, 享受する, 誇る, 恵まれている

文型&コロケーション

▸ to have/ have got/ possess/ be blessed with **charm/ talent/ charisma**
▸ to have/ have got/ possess/ be endowed with **intelligence**
▸ to have/ have got/ possess **beauty**
▸ to have/ have got/ enjoy/ possess/ be endowed with/ be blessed with an/ the **ability to do sth**
▸ to have/ have got/ possess/ be endowed with/ be blessed with a **talent** (for sth)
▸ to have/ have got/ be blessed with a **child**

have [他, 受身なし]《進行形なし》《特性・特徴を》備える, 持っている;(人間関係として)抱える ◇The ham *had* a smoky flavour. そのハムは薫製の風味がした ◇The car *has* four-wheel drive. その車は四輪駆動だ ◇They *have* a lot of courage. 彼らは勇気に満ちている ◇Do you *have* a client named Peters? ピーターズという名の依頼人を抱えていますか

have got [他, 受身なし]《特に英》《進行形なし》(特性・特徴を)備える, 持っている;(人間関係として)抱える ◇He's *got* a front tooth missing. 彼は前歯が一本欠けている ◇*Has* the house *got* a garden? その家には庭がありますか ◇I've *got* three children and two cats! 私には3人の子どもと2匹の猫がいるんだ

> **ノート** have と have got の使い分け: これらの2語に意味の違いはないが, have got は《米》ではあまり用いられない。《英》では一般的で, 特に話し言葉やインフォーマルな書き言葉において, 特に現在時制で使う。過去時制では have (had got, hadn't got) よりも have (had, didn't have) のほうが頻繁に用いられる。× He *had got* a special talent. ◆You *had* blond hair as a child. (あなたは

の頃はブロンドの髪だったね)。◆The hotel *didn't have* a swimming pool. (そのホテルにプールはなかった)。◆I *hadn't got* a clue what they were talking about. (《didn't have より使用頻度が少ない》私は彼らが何について話しているのか見当がつかなかった)。

enjoy [他]《進行形なし》《フォーマル》(他の人にはない利益などを)享受する ◇People in this country *enjoy* a high standard of living. この国の国民は高い生活水準を享受している ◇He has always *enjoyed* good health. 彼は昔からずっと健康に恵まれている

possess [他]《進行形なし》《フォーマル》(人が特性・特徴を)備える ◇I'm afraid he doesn't *possess* a sense of humour. 残念ながら彼はユーモアのセンスを持ち合わせていない ◇He credited her with a maturity she did not *possess*. 彼は彼女が成熟しているものと買い被っていた

boast [他]《進行形や受身では用いない》《特に書き言葉》(誇りとして)持っている; 誇る ◇The hotel *boasts* two swimming pools and a golf course. そのホテルは二つのプールと一つのゴルフコースを誇っている ◇Rhodes *boasts* 300 days of sunshine a year. ロードス島は年間300日の好天を誇る ◇This is a region which proudly *boasts* its own distinct culture. ここは独自の特異な文化を誇る地域である ❶boast はホテルや都市などの観光客向けの案内などで宣伝文句として用いられる。

be en'dowed with sth [フレーズ]《ややフォーマル》(生来の能力・特性に)恵まれている, 備えている ◇She *was endowed with* intelligence and wit. 彼女は知性と機知に恵まれていた ◇The stones are believed to *be endowed with* magical powers. その石には不思議な力が宿ると信じられている

be 'blessed with sb/sth [フレーズ]《ややフォーマル》(幸福・喜びなどに)恵まれている ◇She's *blessed with* excellent health. 彼女は素晴らしい健康に恵まれている ◇We're *blessed with* five lovely grandchildren. 私たちは5人のかわいい孫に恵まれている ❶この表現は神などの大いなる力によって, 幸運にも授けられているという気もちを示す。

3 have・suffer・experience・receive・feel・undergo・go through sth・take・encounter・run into sth・meet
特定の状況[出来事]に影響を受けたり, 出くわしたりする
【類語訳】経験する, こうむる, 体験する, 感化される, 遭遇する, 行き当たる, 陥る, 直面する

文型&コロケーション

▸ to have/ experience/ encounter/ run into/ meet **problems**
▸ to have/ experience/ encounter/ run into **difficulties/ trouble**
▸ to experience/ encounter/ run into/ meet **resistance**
▸ to receive/ encounter/ run into/ meet **opposition**
▸ to have/ suffer/ experience/ receive/ encounter a **setback**
▸ to have/ suffer/ experience/ receive/ feel a/ the **shock**
▸ to suffer/ experience/ undergo/ go through an **ordeal**
▸ to have/ experience/ receive/ undergo **treatment**
▸ to have/ suffer/ experience/ receive/ encounter sth **directly**

have [他] 経験する, (困難などを)覚える ◇I went to a few parties and *had* a good time. 私はいくつかパーティーに出て, 楽しい時間を過ごした ◇I was *having* difficulty in

→have

have

staying awake. 私は今にも睡魔に身を委ねようとしていた ◇She'll *have* an accident one day. 彼女はいつか事故に遭うよ ❶*have* の典型的な目的語には problems, difficulties, shock, fright, accident, good [bad] time が挙げられる.

suffer [他]《ややフォーマル》(不快な出来事を)経験する, (けが・敗北・損失などを)負う, こうむる ◇He *suffered* a massive heart attack. 彼は重篤な心臓発作を起こした ◇The party *suffered* a humiliating defeat in the general election. その政党は総選挙で屈辱的敗北を喫した ◇The company *suffered* huge losses in the last financial year. 前会計年度にその会社は巨額の損失を出す憂き目に遭った

experience [他]《ややフォーマル》経験[体験]する ◇The country *experienced* a foreign currency shortage for several months. 数か月の間その国は外貨不足に陥った ◇He had not directly *experienced* the fighting in the city. 彼は市街戦を直接経験したわけではなかった ☞ **experience** (EVENT 1), **experience** (LIFE 3)

receive [他]《ややフォーマル》(けが・扱いを)負う, 受ける ◇Several of the passengers *received* severe injuries. 乗客のうち数人が重傷を負った ◇Emergency cases will *receive* professional attention immediately. 救急患者は即座に専門家による処置を受けることになります ◇We *received* a warm welcome from our hosts. 私たちは主催者から温かい歓迎を受けた

ノート **suffer** と **receive** の使い分け：両語とも injury (けが)を目的語に取るが, receive はそのけがに対してそれほどの感情を伴わないが, suffer は人がこうむる悪影響や苦痛により重点が置かれる.

feel [他] (体調の変化を)覚える, (出来事に強く)影響を受ける, 感化される ◇He *feels* the cold a lot. 彼はひどく寒気がしている ◇She *felt* her mother's death very deeply. 彼女は母親の死を心の奥底で受けとめた ◇The effects of the recession are being *felt* everywhere. 不況の影響が至る所に感じられる ◇We all *felt* the force of his arguments. 私たちは皆彼の主張の説得力を肌身に感じた

undergo [他]《ややフォーマル, 特に書き言葉》(変化・不快な事を)経験する, 受ける, こうむる ◇Some children *undergo* a complete transformation when they become teenagers. 子どもの中には10代になるとすっかり変貌する子もいる ◇My mother *underwent* major surgery last year. 昨年私の母は大手術を受けた ◇The drug is currently *undergoing* trials in America. その薬は現在アメリカで治験を受けている ❶*undergo* の典型的な目的語には tests, trials や, operations, examinations などの医療処置, changes, transformation, metamorphosis が挙げられる.

go through sth [句動]《ややインフォーマル》(不快な経験[困難な時期]を)経験する, 味わう, こうむる ◇She's *going through* a bad patch recently. 近頃彼女は不運な目に遭っている ◇He's amazingly cheerful considering all he's had to *go through*. 彼はつらい試練を経てきた割には驚くほど陽気だ ◇I *went through* hell in my first year at the school. 私はその学校の1年生のときに地獄のような苦しみを味わった ❶*go through sth*の後に phase, patch, period, stage など困難な時期について言うときに用いられる. また, 極めて不快な状況については hell, agony, ordeal などの語と共に用いられることもある.

take [他]《進行形はまれ》(打撲・けがなどを)負う, 受ける, こうむる ◇She's *taken* a nasty fall and has her leg in plaster. 彼女は激しく転倒して脚にギプスをはめている ◇The

team *took* a terrible beating. そのチームは惨敗を喫した ◇The school *took* the full force of the explosion. その学校は爆発の影響をもろに受けた

encounter [他]《フォーマル, 特に書き言葉》(思いがけなく不快[困難]な事に)遭遇する, 行き当たる ◇We *encountered* a number of difficulties in the first week. 最初の1週間私たちは数々の困難に行き当たった ◇I had never *encountered* such resistance before. 私はそのような抵抗に遭うことはこれまで一度しなかった

'run into sth [句動]《ややインフォーマル》(困難に)ぶち当たる, 陥る ◇Be careful not to *run into* debt. 借金地獄に陥らないように注意しなさい ◇We were worried that she may have *run into* trouble. 彼女が困難な目に遭っているかもしれないと私たちは心配した ❶debt, bad weather以外に, *run into* の典型的な目的語には problems, difficulties, trouble が挙げられる.

meet [他] (不快な事に)遭遇[直面]する ◇Others have *met* similar problems. 他の人たちも同じような問題に直面している ◇How she *met her death* will probably never be known. 彼女がどのような最期を遂げたかはおそらく決してわからないだろう ❶*meet*の典型的な目的語には problems, resistance, death, fate が挙げられる.

---

4 have・hold・host・call・give・convene・throw
特別な目的のために人が集まるように手配する
【類語訳】開く, 催す, 行う, 主催する, 招集する, 開催を求める, 集める

文型&コロケーション

▶ to have/ hold/ host/ call/ give/ convene a **conference**
▶ to have/ hold/ call/ convene a **meeting**
▶ to have/ hold/ host/ give/ throw a **party**
▶ to have/ hold/ host/ give a **dinner**
▶ to have/ hold/ call an **election**
▶ to have/ hold/ host a **competition/ contest**
▶ to have/ hold a **conversation/ debate/ discussion**

have [他] 開く, 催す ◇Let's *have* a party to celebrate. お祝いの会を開こう ◇We *had* a very interesting discussion about climate change. 私たちは気候変動について大変興味深い討論会を催した

hold [他, しばしば受身で]《ややフォーマル》開く, 催す, 行う ◇The next conference will be *held* in Ohio. 次の会議はオハイオで開かれることになっている ◇It's impossible to *hold* a conversation with all this noise. こんなにうるさくては話会するのは無理だ

host [他] 主催する ◇The President *hosted* a banquet in her honour. 大統領が彼女に敬意を表して宴会を催した ◇Germany *hosted* the World Cup finals. ドイツがワールドカップ本大会の開催国だった
▶ **host** [名] [C] ◇Ian, our *host*, introduced us to the other guests. ホスト役のイアンが私たちを他の招待客に紹介してくれた ◇The college is *playing host to* a group of visiting Russian scientists. その大学がロシアからの訪問科学者たち一行の世話役校となっている

call [他] 招集する, 開催を求める ◇The principal *called* a staff meeting to discuss the changes. それらの変更内容を検討するために校長は職員会議を招集した ◇The drivers were going to *call* a strike. 運転手たちはスト入りを宣言しようとしていた

give [他] (人を招いて)開く, 催す, 公演する ◇The Chancellor will be *giving* a press conference later today.

首相はきょう後ほど記者会見を開くことになるだろう ◇She gave a reading from her latest novel. 彼女は最新の小説を朗読した

convene [他]《フォーマル》(公式な会議のために)招集する、集める ◇A Board of Enquiry was *convened* immediately after the accident. 事故の直後に調査委員会が招集された

throw [他]《ややインフォーマル》(パーティーを)開く、催す ◇They *threw a party for* him on his birthday. 彼らは彼に誕生パーティーを開いてあげた ◇He always *throws* a big bash on Oscar night.《インフォーマル》彼はオスカー賞の夜にはいつも盛大なパーティーを開く ❶この意味では throw は常に party か bash と結び付く.

health [名]

health・condition・fitness・well-being・shape・constitution
人の健やかな[健やかでない]身体の状態を表す
【類語訳】健康(な状態)、体調、容体、体力、体質

▶文型&コロケーション◀
▶ sb's **general/ physical** health/ condition/ fitness/ well-being
▶ sb's **personal** health/ fitness/ well-being
▶ **full** health/ fitness
▶ sb's health/ condition/ fitness **deteriorates/ improves**
▶ to **maintain/ regain** your health/ fitness
▶ to **be in good** health/ shape

health [U] (心身の)健康；健康な状態 ◇Exhaust fumes are *bad for your health*. 排ガスは健康に悪い ◇Smoking can seriously *damage your health*. 喫煙によって健康が著しく損なわれることがある ◇She was forced to resign because of *ill health*. 彼女は体調不良のため辞任を余儀なくされた ◇He has been *in poor health* for some time now. 彼はかなり前から健康を害している ◇She has always enjoyed *the best of health*. 昔からずっと彼女はとても健康に恵まれている ◇Her *mental health* began to deteriorate. 彼女の心の健康は悪化し始めた ◇He was nursed back to *health* by his wife. 彼は妻に看病してもらった結果健康を回復した ☞**healthy** (WELL)

condition [U, 単数で]《ややフォーマル》(病後・けが後の)体調、容体；妊娠状態 ◇You are *in no condition* (= too ill or injured) to go anywhere. あなたはどこかへ行ける体調ではない ◇The cyclist was in a *critical condition* in hospital last night. 昨夜彼の自転車競技の選手は病院で危篤状態だった ◇Her *condition is* said to be *stable*. 彼女の容体は安定しているとのことだ ◇She shouldn't be drinking so much *in her condition* (= because she is pregnant). 妊娠しているのだから彼女はそんなにお酒を飲んでいてはいけない

fitness [U] (身体の)健康な状態、体力 ◇She has a good level of physical *fitness*. 彼女の体力は十分だ ◇a *fitness* instructor フィットネス・インストラクター ☞ **fit** (WELL)

'well-being [U] 健康で幸福なこと ◇Being with my family gives me a wonderful *sense of well-being*. 家族と一緒にいることが私にとって最高の幸せだ

shape (in や into と共に)《ややインフォーマル》体調 ◇He's in good *shape* for a man of his age. 彼は年齢の割に元気だ ◇I need to *get myself into shape* for the race on Saturday. 私は土曜日のレースのためにシェイプアップする必

要がある ◇She always manages to *stay in shape*. 彼女は何とかいつも体調を保っている

constitution [U] (丈夫な)体質 ◇I have a *strong constitution* and my stomach can handle anything. 体質的に丈夫なので、私の胃は何でもこなせる

healthy [形]

healthy・nutritional・good・nutritious・nourishing
食べ物が体によいことを表す
【類語訳】健康によい、栄養の、栄養満点の、好適の

▶文型&コロケーション◀
▶ a healthy/ nutritional/ good/ nutritious/ nourishing **meal/ diet**
▶ healthy/ good/ nutritious/ nourishing **food**

healthy [ふつう名詞の前で] 健康によい、健康的な ◇More public awareness of *healthy eating* has made us think more about our diet. 健康的な食事に対する人々の認識の深まりが食物に関する意識をさらに高めている ◇Many people today are adopting a *healthy lifestyle*. 今日多くの人々が健康によいライフスタイルを身につけている [反意] **unhealthy**
▶ **healthily** [副] ◇Try to eat *healthily*. 健康的な食事を心がけましょう

nutritional 栄養の[に関する] ◇Parents may be unaware of the *nutritional value* of certain foods. 親たちはある種の食べ物の栄養価に気づいていないかもしれない ◇Check the *nutritional* information on the side of the packet before you eat it. 食べる前にパックの側面に表示してある栄養価の情報を確認しましょう
▶ **nutritionally** [副] ◇a *nutritionally* balanced menu 栄養的にバランスの取れたメニュー

good 《食べ物が》よい ◇Too much sun isn't *good* for you. 日光に当たり過ぎることは健康によくない ◇He doesn't seem to have a very *good* diet. 彼はあまり健康によい食事を取っていないようだ ◇Citrus fruits are a *good* source of vitamin C. かんきつ類の果物はビタミンCの宝庫だ [反意] **bad**

nutritious (食べ物が)栄養価の高い ◇Lentil soup is *highly nutritious* and easy to prepare. ヒラマメのスープは栄養価が高く調理が簡単だ

nourishing (食べ物が)栄養満点の；(何かを育てるのに)好適の ◇Vegetarian food can be both *nourishing* and cheap. 菜食系の料理は栄養満点で安上がりでもある ◇The environment was *nourishing to* the young girl's developing personality. その環境は幼い少女の個性を伸ばすのにうってつけだった

hear [動]

hear・listen・pay attention・heed・catch・tune in
声や音、人の言葉の意味に気づいていることを表す
【類語訳】聞こえる、聴く、耳を澄ます、耳を貸す、聞き入れる

▶文型&コロケーション◀
▶ to listen/ pay attention/ tune in **to** sb/ sth
▶ to hear/ listen to/ tune in to/ catch a **radio programme**
▶ to hear/ listen to **music**
▶ to hear/ listen to/ pay attention to a **conversation**
▶ to hear/ listen to/ pay attention to/ heed/ catch sb's

↳hear　　　　　　　　　　　　　　　　heat

words/ what sb says
▶to hear/ listen to/ heed **advice/ a warning**
▶an **audience** hears/ listens to/ tunes in to sb/ sth

hear ［自, 他］《進行形なし》聞こえる；(注意して)聴く ◇I can't *hear* very well. あまりよく聞こえません ◇I couldn't *hear* anything. 何も聞こえなかった ◇He could *hear* a dog barking. 彼は犬が吠えているのが聞こえた ◇Did you *hear* him go out? 彼が出かける音が聞こえた ◇Didn't you *hear* what I said? 私の言ったことが聞こえなかった ◇Did you *hear* that play on the radio last night? 昨日の夜ラジオのあのドラマ聴いた ◇Don't decide until you've *heard* both sides of the argument. 双方の意見を聞くまでは結論を下さないでください

listen ［自］(注意して)聴く、耳を澄ます[傾ける]；(人の言うことを)聞く、耳を貸す、聞き入れる、従う ◇'What were you doing?' 'Just *listening* to the radio.' 「何をしていたの」「ラジオを聴いていただけだよ」◇*Listen*! What's that noise? 聴いて。あの音は何 ◇Sorry, I wasn't really *listening*. すみません、ちゃんと聞いてませんでした ◇He had been *listening* at the door. 彼は戸口で聞き耳を立てていた ◇Can you **listen out for** the doorbell? 玄関の呼び鈴の音を聞き漏らさないようにしてくれる ◇None of this would have happened if you'd *listened* to me. 私の言うことに耳を貸していればこんなことにはならなかったろう ◇Why won't you **listen to reason**? どうして理性に従おうとしないんだ ◇*Listen*, there's something I have to tell you. 《話し言葉》ねぇ聞いて、話したいことがあるんだ ◇OK everyone, *listen* **up**! 《特に米》では皆さん、よく聞いてください ❶ listen sb/sth (前置詞 to なし) は不可. I'm fond of *listening* to classical music. (私はクラシック音楽を聴くのが好きだ). ✗I'm fond of *listening* classical music.

［ノート］**hear と listen の使い分け**：hear はふつう注意を払っているかどうかにかかわらず、物音や話し声などが耳に入ること。listen は意図的に音や声を聴こうとすることを意味する. ◆She *heard* them talking to each other (= she became aware of their conversation). (彼女には彼らが互いに話し合っているのが聞こえた). ◆She *listened to* them talking to each other (= she was trying to hear what they were saying). (彼女は彼らが互いに話し合っているのを聴いた). hear もときどき listen と同じ意味を持つことがある. ◆Don't decide until you've *heard*/*listened to* both sides of the argument. (双方の意見を聞くまでは結論を下さないでください). しかしながら、hear は進行形では用いられないし、その行為は一つの完結したものである. hear a radio programme/broadcast/lecture/debate (ラジオ番組/放送/講義/討論を聴く)とは言えるが、hear music/the radio (音楽/ラジオが聞こえる)と言うと、意図的に聴いているのではなく、それらが偶然に聞こえることを意味する. ◆I could *hear* music playing/the radio blaring out in the next room. (私は隣の部屋で音楽が流れている/ラジオががんがん鳴っているのが聞こえた). ✗He enjoys *hearing* music. ✗'What were you doing?' 'Just *hearing* the radio.'

,pay at'tention ［フレーズ］(人の言うこと・物音を注意して)聴く、耳を澄ます[傾ける、貸す] ◇Can you all **pay attention** please? 皆さん聴いてもらえますか ◇Don't **pay** any **attention** to what they say (= don't think that it is important). 彼らの言うことに耳を貸すな ［反意］ **ignore** (IGNORE)

heed ［他］《フォーマル》(警告・忠告などを)心に留める、聞き入

れる、従う ◇They failed to *heed* the lessons of history. 彼らは歴史の教訓を心に留めなかった ◇Calls for more legislation to protect tenants were not *heeded*. 賃借人を守るためのさらなる法律制定を求める声は聞き入れられなかった

catch ［他］はっきりと聞き取る、よく理解する ◇Sorry, I didn't quite *catch* what you said. すみませんが、おっしゃったことがよくわかりませんでした ◇Did you *catch* that show on the radio? ラジオのあの番組ははっきりと聞き取れた ❶ catch は特に否定文で用いられ、聞き取れなかった[理解できなかった]ことを表す.

,tune 'in ［句動詞］(テレビ[ラジオ]番組に)チャンネル[ダイヤル]を合わせる ◇More than five million listeners *tuned in* to his afternoon radio show. 5百万人以上のリスナーが彼の午後のラジオ番組にチャンネルを合わせた もう少しインフォーマルな言い回しでは、tune in to sb/sth は「人の考え・気持ちを感じ取る」を意味することがある. ◆She can understand what babies need by listening to their cries and *tuning in* to their body language. (《ややインフォーマル》彼女は泣き声を聞いたり身振りを察したりして、赤ちゃんが何を求めているかを理解することができる).

heat ［動］

heat・warm・warm (sth) up・heat (sth) up・reheat
人や物が温まる[暖まる、熱くなる]、人や物を温める[暖める、熱する]
【類語訳】熱する、暖める、温める、暖まる、温まる、熱くなる

[文型&コロケーション]
▶to heat/ warm sth **through**
▶to heat/ warm up/ heat up/ reheat **soup**
▶to heat/ warm/ warm up a **room/ house**
▶to heat/ warm/ reheat sth **gently**
▶to heat sth/ warm sth/ warm sth up/ heat sth up/ reheat sth **in the oven/ microwave**

heat ［他］(物を)熱する、温[暖]める ◇*Heat* the oil and add the onions. 油を熱してタマネギを加えましょう ◇The system produced enough energy to *heat* several thousand homes. その装置は数千軒の家庭を暖めるのに十分なエネルギーを産み出した ◇Metals expand when *heated*. 金属は熱せられると膨張する ◇Check the lasagne is *heated* through (= that all parts of it are hot) before serving. お出しする前にラザニアに火が通っているかをチェックして ☞ **heated** (HOT)

warm ［他, 自］(人・物を)温[暖]める；(人・物が)温[暖]まる ◇Come in and *warm yourself* by the fire. 中へ入って暖炉のそばで体を温めてください ◇The alcohol *warmed* and relaxed him. アルコールで彼は温まってリラックスした ◇As the climate *warms* the ice caps will melt. 気候が温暖になると氷冠は解けるだろう ☞ **warm** (HOT)

,warm sth 'up, ,warm 'up ［句動詞］《ややインフォーマル、特に話し言葉》(人・物を)温[暖]める；(人・物が)温[暖]まる ◇I'll *warm up* some milk. ミルクを温めるね ◇Come in and get *warmed up*. 中へ入って温まってください ◇When spring comes the weather begins to *warm up*. 春になると天候は暖かくなり始める

［ノート］**warm と warm (sth) up の使い分け**：warm (sth) up は warm よりもいくぶんインフォーマルで、話し言葉で用いられることが多い. warm は文語またはフォーマルな書き言葉で用いられることが多い.

,heat sth 'up, ,heat 'up 句動詞 (物を)熱する, 温[暖]める; (物が)熱くなる, 温[暖]まる ◇I'll just *heat up* some soup. スープを少し温めるね ◇The oven takes a while to *heat up*. オーブンは温まるのにしばらく時間がかかる

ノート **heat**と**heat (sth) up**の使い分け: heat (sth) upはheatよりもいくぶんインフォーマルで, 話し言葉で用いられることが多い. heatはふつう目的語なしでは用いられない.
◆The oven is *heating up*. (オーブンが温まってきている). ×The oven is *heating*. 専門用語で用いる場合や装置[工程](例えば建物の暖房装置など)について言う場合はheatを用いる. ×The system produced enough energy to *heat up* several thousand homes.

reheat [他] (調理済みの冷めた食べ物を)温め直す, 再加熱する ◇*Reheat* the sauce carefully without boiling it. 沸騰させないように注意してソースを温め直しましょう

help 名

help・assistance・support・aid・service・cooperation・backup
人を助ける行為
【類語訳】助け, 援助, 協力, 救助, 救援, 支援, 助力, 支え, 応援, 補助, 後援, 予備, 控え

文型&コロケーション
▶ help/ assistance/ support/ cooperation **in** doing sth
▶ **without** help/ assistance/ support/ aid/ sb's services/ cooperation/ backup
▶ **with** the help/ assistance/ support/ aid/ services/ cooperation **of** sb/ sth
▶ **valuable** help/ assistance/ support/ services
▶ **mutual** help/ assistance/ support/ aid/ cooperation
▶ **to get** help/ assistance/ support/ aid/ sb's services/ cooperation/ backup
▶ **to have** help/ assistance/ support/ sb's services/ cooperation/ backup
▶ **to call for** help/ assistance/ support/ aid/ backup
▶ **to offer** help/ assistance/ support/ your services/ cooperation
▶ **to need** help/ assistance/ support/ sb's services/ sb's cooperation
▶ **to come to sb's** help/ assistance/ support/ aid
▶ **to enlist** sb's help/ assistance/ support/ aid

help [U] 助け, 援助, 協力, 救助, 救援; 助けになること, 役に立つこと ◇None of this would have been possible without her *help*. 今回のことはすべて彼女の協力なしではありえなかっただろう ◇The passengers were screaming for *help*. 乗客たちは救助を求めて叫んでいた ◇Quick, run and get *help*! 早く, 急いで助けを呼ぶんだ ◇The place was difficult to find and the map *wasn't much help*. その場所は見つけにくくて, 地図は大して役に立たなかった ⇨ **helpful** (VALUABLE 2)

assistance [U] 《フォーマル》援助, 支援, 助力, 救助, 救援; 助けになること, 役に立つこと ◇technical/economic/military *assistance* 技術的/経済的/軍事的支援 ◇financial *assistance* for people on low incomes 低所得者に対する財政援助 ◇The other passengers went to her *assistance*. 他の乗客たちは彼女の救助に向かった ◇Good afternoon Sir, *can I be of any assistance*? いらっしゃいませ, 何かお役に立つことはありますか

support [U] (不幸[困難]な状況にある人への)支え, 励まし, 応援, 支援 ◇We'll need to give her lots of *support* when she comes out of hospital. 彼女が退院したら私たちがいろいろと支えてあげる必要があるだろう ◇He needed constant emotional *support*. 彼には心の支えが常時必要だった ◇Friends came to the lecture to give me *moral support* (= encouragement). 友達が私を勇気づけるために講演会に集まってくれた

▷**supportive** 形 ◇My sister was very *supportive* when my baby was ill. 私の赤ちゃんが病気のときに, 姉はとてもよく支えてくれた ◇a *supportive* family 応援してくれる家族

aid [U] 《フォーマル》(仕事の遂行に必要な)助力, 援助, 補助; (困難[危険]な状況にある人への)救助, 救援 ◇The job would be impossible without the *aid* of a computer. その仕事はコンピューターの助けなしでは不可能だろう ◇Two other swimmers came to his *aid*. 他に二人の人が泳いで彼を助けに来た

service [C, ふつう複数で] 《ややフォーマル》(専門的な)助力, 援助 ◇I think you are going to need the *services* of a good lawyer. 君には腕の立つ弁護士の助けが必要になると思うよ ◇I offered my *services* as a babysitter for the evening. 私はベビーシッターとしてその晩は役に立てると申し出た

cooperation (英でまた **co-operation**) [U] 《ややフォーマル》協力, 援助 ◇We would be grateful for your *cooperation* in leaving as quietly as possible. 極力お静かにご退出いただくようご協力のほどよろしくお願いいたします

backup [U, C] (非常時に備えての)後援, 応援, 予備, 控え ◇The police called for *backup* from the army. 警察は陸軍の応援を要請した ◇We can use him as a *backup* if one of the team can't play. 我々はチームの一員が出場できない場合の控えとして彼を使うことがある ◇The hospital has a *backup* power supply. 病院には予備電源の備えがある

help 動

1 help・assist・support・cooperate・help (sb) out・aid・aid and abet・lend (sb) a hand・be of service
人のために…する[必要なものを与える]ことで人が…するのを容易[可能]にする
【類語訳】手伝う, 助ける, 援助する, 協力する, 役に立つ, 助力する, 支える, 応援する, 支援する, 手を貸す

文型&コロケーション
▶ to help/ assist/ help out/ lend a hand **with** sth
▶ to help/ assist/ support/ cooperate/ aid (sb) **in** sth
▶ to help/ assist/ cooperate/ aid (sb) **in doing** sth
▶ to help/ assist/ aid (sb) **to do** sth
▶ to be **greatly/ considerably** helped/ assisted/ aided
▶ to **actively** help/ assist/ support/ cooperate with sb/ sth
▶ to be **ably** assisted/ supported by sb

help [自, 他] 手伝う, 助ける, 援助[協力]する, 助けになる, 役に立つ ◇*Help*, I'm stuck. 助けて, 行き詰まっちゃった[体が抜けない] ◇I was only trying to *help*. 私はただ手伝おうとしていただけだ ◇He always *helps* with the housework. 彼はいつも家事を手伝ってくれる ◇I need contacts that could *help* in finding a job. 私には就職に役立つコネが必要だ ◇We must all try and *help* each other. 私

たちは皆で協力し合おうとせねばならない ◇Jo will *help* us with some of the organization. ジョーは私たちのために準備・手配に一役買ってくれるだろう ◇She *helped* (to) organize the party. 彼女はパーティーの準備を手伝ってくれた
assist [他, 自]《ややフォーマル, 特に書き言葉》援助[支援, 助力]する, 助手[補佐]を務める ◇We'll do all we can to *assist* you. 私たちはあなたを援助するためにできることは何でもします ◇The play was directed by Mike Johnson, *assisted* by Sharon Gale. その劇はマイク・ジョンソンが監督で, シャロン・ゲールが助監督を務めた ◇Anyone willing to *assist* can contact this number. ご支援いただける方はどなたでもこの番号にご連絡ください
support [他]（不幸[困難]な状況にある人を）支える, 励ます, 応援[支援]する ◇She *supported* her husband through many difficult times. 彼女は多くの困難な時期にわたって夫を支え続けた ◇The organization *supports* people with AIDS. その団体はエイズ患者を支援している
cooperate（英でまた **co-operate**）[自]（目的達成のために）協力[協同, 提携]する；（求めに応じて）援助する ◇The two groups agreed to *cooperate with* each other. その二つの団体は提携することに合意した ◇They had *co-operated* closely in the planning of the project. 彼らはそのプロジェクトの計画において緊密に協力し合っていた ◇Their captors told them they would be killed unless they *cooperated*. 彼らを捕らえた者たちは協力しなければ殺すと彼らに告げた
help 'out, help sb 'out 句動［困難[多忙]な状況にある人を］手伝う, 助ける, 援助する ◇He's always willing to *help out*. 彼はいつも手伝いすることをいとわない ◇When I bought the house, my sister *helped* me *out* with a loan. 家を買うときに姉がローンの援助をしてくれた
aid [他]《ややフォーマル, 書き言葉》助力[援助, 補助]する ◇Each group is *aided* by a tutor or consultant. 各団体は助言者または顧問の助けを借りている ◇They were accused of *aiding* him in his escape. 彼らは彼の逃亡をほう助した罪に問われた
,aid and a'bet 行動 (-tt-)《法律 or おどけて》（違法[不正]行為を）ほう助する；手助けする ◇He stands accused of *aiding and abetting* the bombing. 彼は爆破をほう助した罪に問われている ◇His black mood receded, *aided and abetted* by two glasses of wine. 2杯のワインのおかげで彼の暗い気分は薄らいだ
lend (sb) a 'hand 行動《ややインフォーマル》（実際に）手を貸す ◇I went over to see if I could *lend a hand*. 私は手を貸そうかどうか見に出かけた ◇I'll be there to *lend* him *a hand* with anything if required. 私は必要な場合は何であれ彼に手を貸すためにそこへ行くつもりだ ◇She's always ready to *lend a helping hand*. 彼女はいつでも救いの手を差し伸べる構えです
be of 'service 行動《フォーマル, 話し言葉》助けになる, 役に立つ ◇Can I *be of service to* anyone? 私は誰かの役に立てるかな［お待ちの方どうぞ］ ◇Glad to *be of service*. お役に立てて光栄です

2 help・facilitate・benefit・assist・aid・clear the way・ease・open the way
事が発生する［事を改善する］のを容易にする
【類義訳】役立つ, 助けとなる, 可能にする, 容易にする, ためになる, 助長する

文型&コロケーション
▶ to help/ assist/ aid in (doing) sth

▶ to clear the way/ open the way for sth
▶ to help/ clear the way for/ open the way for sb **to do sth**
▶ to help/ facilitate/ assist/ aid/ ease a **process**
▶ to help/ facilitate/ assist/ aid/ ease the **development** of sth
▶ to facilitate/ assist/ ease the **flow/ transition/ transfer/ passage/ introduction** of sth
▶ to help/ facilitate/ ease **matters**
▶ to clear/ ease/ open the **way** (for sth)
▶ to **undoubtedly** help/ facilitate/ benefit/ assist/ aid sth
▶ to **greatly/ certainly** help/ facilitate/ benefit/ assist/ aid sth
▶ to **considerably** help/ benefit/ assist sth

help [自, 他]（状況を）改善［救済］する；（事を[に]）容易にする, 役立つ, 助長[促進]する ◇The money raised *helped towards* the cost of organizing the event. 集められた資金はイベントの企画費に充てられた ◇Iron *helps in* the formation of red blood cells. 鉄は赤血球の形成に役立つ ◇This should *help (to)* reduce the pain. これは痛みを軽減する助けとなるはずだ ◇The exhibition *helped* her establish herself as an artist. その展覧会は彼女が画家としての地位を確立するのに役立った ◇It certainly *helped* being able to talk about it. それについて話すことができたのは確かによかったです 反意 **hinder, hamper** (BLOCK 1), ☞ **help** (AID), **helpful** (VALUABLE 2)
facilitate [他]《フォーマル》（行動・進行を）可能[容易]にする, 助長[促進]する ◇The new trade agreement should *facilitate* more rapid economic growth. この新たな貿易協定でより急速な経済成長が可能になるはずだ ◇Structured teaching *facilitates* learning. 組織だった指導で学習が容易になる
benefit (**-t-, -tt-**) [他]（特定の人の集団[生活]に）利益を与える, ためになる ◇We should spend the money on something that will *benefit* everyone. 私たちは万人のためになることにこのお金を使うべきだ ◇The new tax laws will clearly *benefit* those on low wages. この新しい税法で間違いなく低所得者に利益がもたらされるだろう 反意
disadvantage ❶ disadvantage は人・集団に「不利益をもたらす」ことを意味する. ◆ In the past women have been *disadvantaged* by the narrow range of occupations open to them. （昔は女性には限られた職業にしか門戸が開かれておらず不利だった）. ☞ **beneficial** (VALUABLE 2)
assist [自, 他]《ややフォーマル, 特に書き言葉》（事を[に]）容易にする, 役立つ, 助長[促進]する ◇Two approaches might *assist* in tackling the problem. その問題への取り組みに役立つかもしれない方法が二つある ◇These activities will *assist* the decision-making process. これらの活動は政策決定の進行を促すだろう
aid [他, 自]《フォーマル》（事を[に]）容易にする, 役立つ, 助長[促進]する ◇New drugs are now available to *aid* recovery. 回復を助ける新薬がもう入手できます ◇*Aided* by fire and strong winds, the fire quickly spread. 火が強風にあおられ, 火事は急速に広がった ◇Computers can be used to *aid* in management decision-making. コンピューターは経営の意思決定に役立てられることがある

ノート **facilitate, assist, aid** の使い分け：場合によってどの語も使用可能. ◆ to *facilitate/assist/aid* a process/transition （進行/変化を促す）. ◆ to *facilitate/assist/aid* the development of sth （事の発展を助長[促進]する）. **facilitate** と **assist** は **aid** よりも多種多様な語（passage, flow, transition, transfer, introduction, removal など進行[変化]を表す多くの名詞を含む)と結び付く. assist はしばしばinを伴う. ◆ *assist* in the development of sth (事の発展を助長[促進]する). aidもinと共に用いられることがあるが, facilitateは不可. ×*facilitate* in the development of sth. facilitateはほとんど常に「有用な事の進行を容易にする」ことについて用いられる. aidは「有用でない事の進行」についても用いられる. ×*Facilitated/assisted* by fire and strong winds, the fire quickly spread.

clear the way [句動] (障害を取り除いて)円滑に運ばせる ◇The ruling could *clear the way* for extradition proceedings. その裁定のおかげで身柄引渡手続きが円滑に行われた[行われる可能性がある]

ease [他] (障害を取り除いて[改めて])容易にする ◇Ramps have been built to *ease* access for the disabled. 傾斜路が身体障害者の利用を容易にするために設置された

open the way [句動] (不可能だった事を[に])可能にする, 道を開く ◇The agreement could *open the way* for the country to pay off its debts. その協約によって国が借金を返済することが可能になった

helpful [形]

helpful・cooperative・willing・obliging・accommodating・neighbourly
人が友好的で他の人を助けることをいとわない
【類語訳】助けになる, 役に立つ, 協力的な, 自発的な, 協調的な

[文型&コロケーション]
▸ helpful/ obliging/ accommodating **to** sb
▸ to **find sb** helpful/ cooperative/ willing
▸ **friendly and** helpful/ cooperative/ obliging/ accommodating

helpful 助け[ため, 頼り]になる, 役に立つ ◇I called the police but they weren't very *helpful*. 私は警察を呼んだが, 彼らはあまり頼りにならなかった ◇The staff couldn't have been more *helpful*. スタッフの助けはこの上なく有益だった ◇She's one of the most *helpful* people I know. 彼女は私が知っている中で最も頼りになるうちの一人だ [反意] **unhelpful**
▸ **helpfully** [副] ◇She *helpfully* suggested that I try the local library. 彼女は地元の図書館にあたってみることを私に勧めてくれて, それが役立った

cooperative (英でまた **co-operative**) 協力的な ◇Employees will generally be more *cooperative* if their views are taken seriously. 自分たちの意見を真剣に考えてもらえば, ふつう従業員はもっと協力的になるだろう [反意] **uncooperative**

willing [ふつう名詞の前で] 進んで[喜んで]行う, 自発的な;熱心[熱烈]な ◇*willing* helpers/volunteers 自発的な協力者/熱心なボランティア ◇*willing* support/consent 熱心な支援/熱烈な同意 ◇She's very *willing*. 彼女はとても自発的だ [反意] **unwilling** (RELUCTANT)
▸ **willingly** [副] ◇People would *willingly* pay more for better services. 人々はよりよいサービスに対してなら喜んでもっとお金を支払うだろう

obliging 《フォーマル》 進んで[喜んで]人のためになる, とても親切[協力]な ◇They were very *obliging* and offered to wait for us. 彼らはとても親切で私たちを待とうと申

し出てくれた
▸ **obligingly** [副] ◇'I'll go for you,' she said, *obligingly*. 「あなたのために[代わりに]行くわ」と彼女は親切にも言ってくれた

accommodating 《ややフォーマル》 協調的な, 融通のきく ◇They are very *accommodating* to people with special needs. 彼らは特別な支援を必要とする人々の面倒見がとてもよい

neighbourly (米 **neighborly**) 人付き合いのよい, 親切な ◇It was a *neighbourly* gesture of theirs. それは彼らからの好意の意志表示だった

hesitate [動]

hesitate・shy away from sth・shrink from sth・hold back・think twice・baulk・recoil
困難である[面白くない]かもしれないと迷って何かをすることをやめる
【類語訳】ためらう, 躊躇する, 避ける, 嫌がる, 敬遠する, ひるむ, 尻込みする, 控える, はばかる, 遠慮する, 渋る

[文型&コロケーション]
▸ to shy away/ shrink/ hold back/ recoil **from** sth
▸ to baulk/ recoil **at** sth
▸ to shy away from/ shrink from/ think twice about/ baulk at **doing** sth
▸ to shy away from/ shrink from/ recoil from a/ an **idea/ thought/ prospect**
▸ to shy away from/ shrink from the **truth**
▸ to **make sb** hesitate/ hold back/ think twice/ baulk/ recoil
▸ to hesitate/ hold back **(for) a moment**
▸ to hesitate/ hold back/ recoil **a little**

hesitate [自] 《ややフォーマル》 (自信がなく)ためらう, 躊躇する, 遠慮する ◇Please do not *hesitate* to contact me if you have any queries. 何かご質問がございましたら, 遠慮なさらず私にご連絡ください
▸ **hesitation** [名] [U] ◇She agreed *without* the slightest *hesitation*. 彼女はまったく躊躇することなく同意した ◇I *have no hesitation* in recommending her for the job. 私は彼女をその仕事に推薦することに何のためらいもない

,**shy a'way from sth** [句動詞] (心配[不安]で・恥ずかしがって)避ける, 嫌がる, 敬遠する ◇Hugh never *shied away from* his responsibilities. ヒューは決して責任逃れをしなかった ◇The newspapers have *shied away from* investigating the story. 新聞各社はそのうわさの真相究明を避けてきた ❶ shy away from sth で from の目的語となる典型的なものに question, subject, idea, prospect, commitment, truth, publicity, scandal が挙げられる.

'**shrink from sth** [句動詞] 《書き言葉》 (困難[嫌]な事を[に])避ける, ひるむ, 尻込みする ◇We made it clear to them that we would not *shrink from* confrontation. 私たちは対決も辞さないことを彼らにはっきりと伝えた ◇They did not *shrink from* doing what was right. 彼らはひるまずに正しいことを行った

,**hold 'back** [句動詞] (言動について)控える, はばかる, 遠慮する ◇He wanted to tell her about it, but *held back* for fear of upsetting her again. 彼はそのことについて彼女に話したかったが, また彼女の気分を害するのではと恐れて話を控えた ◇She *held back* from saying what she really thought about it. 彼女は自分のことについて本

↪hesitate　　　　　　　　　　　　　　　　　　　　　　　hide, high

当はどう思っているか伝えるのを遠慮した

ノート **hesitate**と**hold back**の使い分け：**hesitate**はどうすべきか自信が持てず、間違っているのではないかと迷う場合。**hold back**は本当にしたいことが実際には最善[他の人が求めていること]ではないと思う場合に用いられる。

think 'twice 行礼 （決定する前に）考え直す、もう一度よく考える ◇You should *think twice about* employing someone you've never met. 一度も会ったことがない人を雇い入れるなんてもう一度よく考えたほうがいい

baulk 《英》《米でふつう**balk**》 [自] 《ややフォーマル》（困難[危険, 高価]なため）ためらう、尻込みする、渋る ◇Many parents may *baulk at* the idea of paying $100 for a pair of shoes. 多くの親は1足の靴に100ドル出すなんてと渋るかもしれない ❶baulkは値段や新たな考えなどを聞かされて突然やめることを暗示し、shy away from sthやshrink from sthと比べてより強い抵抗感を示す。

recoil [自]《書き言葉》（考え・状況に）嫌悪[恐怖]感を示す、ひるむ、尻込みする ◇She *recoiled* from the idea of betraying her own brother. 彼女は自分の兄を裏切ることになるという思いにひるんだ

ノート **shrink from sth**と**recoil**の使い分け：**recoil**は衝撃・恐怖への反応を示し、**shrink from sth**は…したくないという強い感情を示すが、感情自体は**recoil**ほど強くない。

hide 動

hide・conceal・cover・disguise・mask・bury・camouflage
人や物を見えない[見つからない]場所に置く[保管する]、真実や感情を秘密にしておく
【類語訳】隠す、かくまう、秘密にする、覆い隠す、ごまかす

文型&コロケーション
▶ to hide/ conceal/ disguise/ mask/ camouflage sth **behind** sth
▶ to hide/ conceal/ bury sth **under** sth
▶ to hide/ conceal sth **from** sb
▶ to hide/ conceal/ disguise/ mask the **the truth/ the fact that...**
▶ to hide/ conceal/ disguise/ mask/ bury your **feelings**
▶ to hide/ conceal/ cover/ disguise/ mask your **disappointment/ surprise**
▶ to hide/ conceal/ disguise your **emotion/ shock**
▶ to hide/ conceal/ cover your **embarrassment**
▶ to hide/ conceal/ mask your **anger**
▶ to **completely/ partly** hide/ conceal/ cover/ disguise/ mask/ bury sth
▶ to **carefully** hide/ conceal/ cover/ disguise/ camouflage sth
▶ to **cleverly** hide/ conceal/ disguise sth
▶ to **barely/ scarcely** hide/ conceal/ cover/ disguise sth

hide [他]（人・物を）隠す、かくまう；(感情を)隠す、秘密にする ◇He *hid* the letter in a drawer. 彼は手紙を引き出しの中に隠した ◇I keep my private papers *hidden*. 私は自分の私的文書を隠してある ◇They *hid* me from the police in their attic. 彼らは警察から私を屋根裏にかくまってくれた ◇She struggled to *hide* her disappointment. 彼女は失望感を必死に隠そうとした ◇They claim that they **have nothing to hide** (= there was nothing wrong or illegal about what they did). 彼らは隠し立てすることは何もないと主張している ◇His brusque manner *hides* a shy and sensitive nature. 彼の無愛想な振る舞いが内気で繊細な性格を隠している

conceal [他]《フォーマル》（人・物を）隠す、かくまう；(事を)隠す、秘密にする ◇The paintings were *concealed* beneath a thick layer of plaster. 絵画は壁土の厚い層の裏に隠されていた ◇For a long time his death was *concealed* from her. 長い間彼の死は彼女に知らされていなかった ◇She sat down to *conceal* the fact that she was trembling. 彼女は震えていることを隠そうとして腰を下ろした ❶感情について言う場合、concealはしばしば否定的な文で用いられる。◆He could not *conceal* his joy/disappointment. (彼は喜び/失望感を隠すことができなかった)。◆She could barely/scarcely/hardly *conceal* her delight.

cover [他]（物を）覆い隠す；(感情を)隠す、ごまかす ◇She *covered* her face with her hands. 彼女は両手で顔を覆い隠した ◇He laughed to *cover* (= hide) his embarrassment. 彼は笑ってきまり悪さをごまかした

disguise [他]（物事の本質を）偽る、隠す、ごまかす ◇He tried to *disguise* his accent. 彼はなまりを隠そうとした ◇She made no attempt to *disguise* her surprise. 彼女は驚きを隠そうとしなかった ◇It was a ***thinly disguised*** attack on the President. それはお粗末にも名指しを避けた委員長批判だった

mask [他]（感情・臭い・事実などを）隠す、ごまかす ◇She *masked* her anger with a smile. 彼女は怒りを笑顔でごまかした ◇Spices were used to *mask* the unpleasant taste of the meat. 肉の臭みを隠すのに香辛料が用いられた

bury [他]（物を地面に）埋めて隠す、埋蔵する；(感情・間違いなどを)隠す ◇We used to dig for hours, looking for *buried* treasure. 私たちは何時間も地面を掘って、埋蔵された宝を探したものだ ◇She had learnt to *bury* her feelings. 彼女は感情を隠すことができるようになっていた

camouflage [他]（人・物に）迷彩を施す ◇The soldiers *camouflaged* themselves with leaves and twigs. 兵士たちは葉っぱと小枝で自分たちに迷彩を施した

high 形

1 ☞ EXCESSIVE, EXPENSIVE

high・inflated・steep・prohibitive・unreasonable・exorbitant・astronomical・extortionate
標準以上の水準[値段, 価格]を表す
【類語訳】(水準・程度が)高い、暴騰した、法外な、不当な、非現実的な、途方もない、天文学的な、莫大な、膨大な

high	unreasonable	prohibitive
inflated		exorbitant
steep		astronomical
		extortionate

文型&コロケーション
▶ high/ inflated/ steep/ prohibitive/ unreasonable/ exorbitant/ astronomical/ extortionate **prices**
▶ high/ steep/ prohibitive/ exorbitant/ astronomical/ extortionate **costs**
▶ high/ exorbitant/ astronomical/ extortionate **rates**
▶ high/ exorbitant/ extortionate **charges/ taxes/ fees/ rents**
▶ a high/ an unreasonable/ an astronomical **level**
▶ a high/ an inflated/ an astronomical **figure**

high

high (水準・程度が)高い ◇They charge very *high* prices for a pretty average service. いたってふつうのサービスに対してとても高い料金が請求される ◇a *high* level of pollution 高レベルの環境汚染 ◇a *high* standard of craftsmanship 高水準の職人技 ◇A *high* degree of accuracy is needed. 高度の正確性が求められる ◇Demand is *high* at this time of the year. 1年のうちでこの時期は需要が高い ◇The cost in terms of human life was *high*. 人命の観点から考えてその代償は大きかった ◇We had *high* **hopes** for the business (= we believed it would be successful). 私たちはその事業に強く期待していた 反意 **low** (POOR 2)

inflated (量・水準が)異常に高い、騰貴[暴騰]した ◇company directors with *inflated* salaries 異常に高い給料を得ている会社役員 ◇Consumers are paying *inflated* prices for food. 消費者は食品に暴騰価格を支払っている

steep (インフォーマル)(値段・要求が)法外な、むちゃな ◇£2 for a cup of coffee seems a little *steep* to me. コーヒー1杯に2ポンドは私には少し高すぎるように思える

prohibitive (値段・価格が)法外な、高すぎて手が出せない ◇a *prohibitive* tax on imported cars 輸入車に対する法外な税 ◇The price of property in the city is *prohibitive*. その都市の不動産の価格は高すぎて手が出せない

▶**prohibitively** 副 ◇Car insurance can be *prohibitively* expensive for young drivers. 自動車保険は若い運転者にとって手が出せないほど高いことがある

unreasonable (しばしば否定文で)(値段・水準が)不当な、法外な、非現実的な ◇The fees they charge are not *unreasonable*. 彼らの請求額は法外ではない 反意 **reasonable** (CHEAP)

▶**unreasonably** 副 ◇The bank was found to be charging *unreasonably* high prices for its services. その銀行はサービスに対して不当に高い料金を請求していることが発覚した

exorbitant 《やや形式,けなして》(値段が)法外な、途方もない ◇The lawyer charged us an *exorbitant* fee for two days' work. その弁護士は2日間の仕事に対して私たちに途方もない報酬を請求した

astronomical 《インフォーマル》(値段・量が)天文学的な、莫大(膨大)な、めちゃくちゃ高い ◇the *astronomical* costs of land for building 莫大な建設用地費用 ◇The figures are *astronomical*. その数字は天文学的だ

▶**astronomically** 副 ◇Interest rates are *astronomically* high. 金利が天文学的に高い

extortionate 《ややインフォーマル,けなして》(値段)が法外な、べらぼうに高い ◇They are offering loans at *extortionate* rates of interest. 彼らはべらぼうに高い利息で金を貸し付けている

〔ノート〕 **exorbitant** と **extortionate** の使い分け：exorbitant のほうが extortionate よりも頻繁に用いられ、フォーマルな語だが、両者に実質的な意味の違いはない。

2 high・tall・towering・high-rise・lofty
下から上までの距離が長い；地面[水面]から離れた位置にある【類語訳】(高さが)高い、そびえ立った、高層の

〔文型&コロケーション〕
▶a high/ tall/ towering/ lofty **mountain / cliff**
▶a high/ tall/ high-rise/ lofty **tower/ building**
▶high/ tall/ towering **walls**
▶high/ tall **trees/ grass**
▶a high/ tall/ lofty **peak**
▶a high/ lofty **ceiling**
▶towering/ lofty **heights**

high (高さが)高い；(地面・海水面から)高い位置にある ◇What's the *highest* mountain in the US? アメリカで一番高い山はどれですか ◇Her shoes were black, with *high heels*. 彼女の靴は高いヒール付きの黒だった ◇He has a round face with a *high* forehead. 彼は額の広い丸顔をしている ◇They were flying at *high altitude*. 彼らは高高度を飛行していた ◇I can't reach the top shelf — it's too *high*. 一番上の棚に手が届かない—高すぎるよ ❶*high* は物の下から上までの高さについて言う[聞く]ときにも用いられる。◆How *high* is Everest? (エベレスト山はどのくらい高いですか)。◆It's only a low wall — about a metre *high*. (それはただの低い壁さ—1メートルくらいの高さだよ)。◆The grass was *waist-high*. (その草は腰くらいの高さがあった)。反意 **low** ❶上の例のlowには同義語がない。◆a *low* wall/ building/ table (低い壁/建物/テーブル)。◆a *low* range of hills (低い丘陵地)。◆flying at *low* altitude (低高度飛行)。◆The sun was *low* in the sky. (太陽は空の低いところにあった)。

tall (平均の身長・丈よりも)高い；(高さが)高い ◇What's the *tallest* building in the world? 世界で最も高い建物は何ですか ◇Pollutants are dispersed through *tall chimneys*. 汚染物質が高い煙突からまき散らされている ◇a *tall glass* of iced tea 細長いグラスに入ったアイスティー

〔ノート〕 **high** と **tall** の使い分け：多くの場合、両語とも「下から上までの高さが高い」の意味で用いられるが、ふつう以下のような連語で用いられる。◆a *high* mountain/cliff/peak/ wall (高い山/崖/頂/壁)。◆(a) *tall* building/tower/ tree/grass (高い建物/塔/木/草)。*tall* は地面から高い位置にある物についてではなく、物の下から上までの高さについてのみ用いられる。◆The room has *tall windows* (= the windows stretch from the bottom of the wall to the top). (その部屋には丈の高い窓が付いている)。The room has *high windows* (= they are at the top of the wall, near the ceiling). (その部屋には高い所に窓がある)。

towering [名詞の前で] 非常に高い、そびえ立った、切り立った ◇The coastline consists of wild, *towering* cliffs. その海岸線は荒れ果てて切り立った崖から成っている ◇The building erupted in a *towering inferno* (= a very tall fire). 建物から火柱が高々と噴き上がった

high-rise [名詞の前で] (建物が)高層の ◇These *high-rise apartment blocks* were built in the 1960s. この高層団地群は1960年代に建てられた

lofty 《ふつう名詞の前で》《フォーマル or 文語》非常に高い、そびえ立つ ◇From the *lofty* heights of his apartment you could see right across New York. とても高い所にある彼の部屋からはニューヨークが一望できた

3 high・shrill・high-pitched・sharp・treble・piercing
声や音の音域が最上部(近く)にあり、太くも低くもないことを表す【類語訳】(声・音が)高い、甲高い、金切り声の、ソプラノの、耳をつんざくような

〔文型&コロケーション〕
▶a high/ shrill/ high-pitched/ sharp/ treble/ piercing **voice**
▶a high/ shrill/ high-pitched/ sharp/ piercing **sound**

▶a high/ shrill/ sharp **note**
▶a shrill/ high-pitched/ sharp/ piercing **scream/ whistle**
▶a shrill/ high-pitched/ piercing **shriek**
▶a high/ high-pitched **laugh**
▶in shrill/ sharp/ piercing **tones**

high 《声・音が》高い, 甲高い ◇She has a *high* voice. 彼女は甲高い声をしている ◇That note is definitely too *high* for me. その音程は私には間違いなく高すぎる 反意 **low, deep** (DEEP 2)

shrill 《けなして》《声・音が》甲高い, 切切りの ◇The PE teacher's *shrill* voice rang out across the school fields. 体育教師の金切り声が校庭に響き渡った ◇A *shrill* scream rent the air. 甲高い悲鳴が空気を切り裂いた
▷**shrilly** 副 ◇She laughed *shrilly*. 彼女は甲高く笑った

high-'pitched 《時にけなして》《音が》甲高い, 高い調子の ◇She had a *high-pitched* giggle which irritated me intensely. 彼女は甲高くキャッキャッと笑って私をひどくいら立たせた 反意 **low-pitched** ❶high-pitchedの反意語はlow-pitchedだが, この語はあまり頻繁に用いられず, 単にlowを用いるほうが一般的である. lowにはhigh-pitchedに伴うような不快さはない.

ノート high と high-pitched の使い分け: この意味の highはいくつかの音を表す名詞とはしか結び付かない. ◆a *high* voice/note/key 《高い声/音/調子》. これら以外の音を表す名詞と用いられる. ◆a *high-pitched* noise/scream/whistle/tone 《甲高い雑音/悲鳴/笛の音/口調》. 両語ともsoundと共に用いられることがある. ◆a *high/high-pitched* sound 《高い/甲高い音》. high-pitchedは時にやや不快な音を示すこともある.

sharp [ふつう名詞の前で] 《声・音が》鋭い, 甲高い, 金切り声の ◇She read out the list in *sharp*, clipped tones. 彼女は鋭く歯切れのよい口調で一覧表を読み上げた ◇There was a *sharp* knock on the door. ドアを鋭く叩く音が聞こえた 反意 **soft** (QUIET 2) ❶音楽用語ではsharpは正しいピッチの音よりも高い音を表す. 反意語はflat. この意味のsharpは副詞でも用いる. ◇That note was slightly *sharp*. (その音はいくぶんシャープだった). ◆You played that note *sharp*. (君はその音をシャープで演奏したね).
▷**sharply** 副 ◇He rapped *sharply* on the window. 彼は窓を鋭く叩いた

treble [名詞の前で]《音楽》《声・音程が》甲高い, 最高音域の, ソプラノの ◇He sang in a high, clear *treble* voice. 彼は甲高くはっきりとした最高音部の声で歌った 反意 **bass** (DEEP 2)

ノート high と treble の使い分け: treble は high よりも専門的な語で, 声楽に用いられる.

piercing [ふつう名詞の前で]《けなして》《声・音が》甲高い, 耳をつんざくような ◇She gave a *piercing* scream. 彼女は絹を裂くような悲鳴を上げた ◇She has such a *piercing* voice. 彼女はとても甲高い声をしている

ノート shrill と piercing の使い分け: piercing は大きな声・音を指し, shrill よりもさらに高く耳ざわりであることを表す.

hill 名

hill • mountain • moor • summit • ridge • peak • mound • moorland • fell • highlands • foothills

周囲の土地よりも高くなった地域
【類語訳】山, 丘, 丘陵, 荒野, 荒れ地, 頂上, 山頂, 尾根, 峰, 墳丘, 高地, 山地

mound	hill	mountain
	moor	summit
	moorland	ridge
	fell	peak
	foothills	highlands

文型&コロケーション

▶**on** a hill/ a mountain/ the moors/ the summit/ a ridge/ a peak/ a mound/ the fells
▶**in** the hills/ mountains/ fells/ highlands/ foothills
▶a **steep** hill/ mountain/ ridge/ mound
▶a **grassy** hill/ mound
▶**open** hills/ moors/ moorland/ fells
▶to **climb** a hill/ mountain/ ridge/ peak/ fell

hill [C] 《低い》山, 丘, 丘陵 ;《道路の》坂 ◇a region of gently rolling *hills* 緩やかな起伏のある丘陵地帯 ◇a *hill* farm/town/fort 丘の上の農場/町/砦 ◇I love walking in the *hills* (= in the area where there are hills). 私は山歩きが好きだ ◇Always take care when driving down steep *hills*. 急な坂道を下りるときは常に運転に気をつけてください 反意 **valley**
▷**hilly** 形 ◇a *hilly* area/region 丘陵地帯

mountain [C]《高い》山, 山岳 ◇a chain/range of *mountains* 連山/山脈 ◇We stopped to enjoy the *mountain* scenery. 私たちは立ち止まって山の景色を楽しんだ ◇*mountain* roads/streams/villages 山道/山岳渓流/山村 ◇a *mountain rescue team* 山岳救助隊
▷**mountainous** 形 ◇*mountainous* regions 山岳地帯

moor [C, ふつう複数で, U]《特に英》《高地の》荒野, 荒れ地 ◇the North York *Moors* ノース・ヨーク・ムーアズ ◇We went for a walk on the *moors*. 私たちは荒野を散歩に出かけた ◇*moor* and rough grassland 荒野と未開の草原

summit [C]《山の》頂上, 山頂,《物の》てっぺん ◇We reached the *summit* at noon. 私たちは正午に頂上へ到着した

ridge [C]《丘・山の》尾根 ◇walking along the *ridge* 尾根歩き ◇the north-east *ridge* of Mount Everest エベレスト山の北東側の尾根

peak [C]《山の》峰 ;《峰のある》山 ◇a mountain *peak* 山の峰 ◇snow-capped/jagged *peaks* 雪を頂く/ぎざぎざの連峰 ◇The climbers made camp halfway up the *peak*. 登山者たちは山の中腹でキャンプをした

ノート summit と peak の使い分け: 1つの mountain (山) には1つ以上の peak (峰) がある. 山にただ1つある the highest peak (最高峰) が summit (頂上) である. 1つの山全体をpeakと呼ぶこともある. ただその頂上は summit とも呼ばれる.

mound [C]《土[石]を積んで築いた》塚, 墳丘 ;《小さな》丘 ◇a Bronze age burial *mound* 青銅器時代の墳丘 ◇The castle was built on top of a natural grassy *mound*. その城は草で覆われた天然の小さな丘の上に建てられていた

moorland [U, C, ふつう複数で]《特に英》《高地の》荒野[荒れ]地帯 ◇walking across open *moorland* 広々とした荒野地帯を横切って歩くこと

fell [C]《北イングランドの》丘, 丘陵地帯 ◇The long green

line of the *fells* rose before me. 緑の丘の長い稜線が私の前に現れた

highlands [複数で]（丘・山の多い）高地, 山地 ◇Peru's Andean *highlands* ペルーのアンデス山地 ❶ the Highlands はふつう「スコットランド高地」を指す。 反意 **lowland**

foothills [複数で]（高山・山脈のふもとの）丘陵地帯 ◇the *foothills* of the Himalayas ヒマラヤ山脈のふもとの丘陵地帯

hit 動

1 hit・knock・bang・strike・bump・bash
大きな力が物に加わる
【類語訳】ぶつかる, 衝突する, 当たる, 打つ, たたく

▸ 文型&コロケーション
▸ to hit/ knock/ bang/ bump/ bash against sb/ sth
▸ to knock/ bang/ bump/ bash into sb/ sth
▸ to hit/ strike the ground/ floor/ wall

hit [他, 自]（損傷を伴って物に）ぶつかる, 衝突する, 当たる；（バットなどで）打つ, 打ち飛ばす ◇The boy was *hit* by a speeding car. 男の子は猛スピードで走る車にひかれた ◇The grenade will explode as soon as it *hits* the ground. 手投げ弾は地面にぶつかると同時に爆発するだろう ◇The boat *hit* against an object under the surface of the water. ボートが水面下の物体に当たった ◇She *hit* the ball too hard and it went out of the court. 彼女はボールの打ち方が強すぎたため, ボールはコートの外に飛んで行った 反意 **miss** ❶ miss は人・物に「当て[当たり]そこなう」の意味。 ◆The bullet *missed* her by about six inches. （弾は彼女からおよそ6インチそれた）. ◆She threw a plate at him and *narrowly missed* hitting him. （彼女は彼に向かって皿を投げたが, わずかのところで当てそこなった）. ☞ **hit** (BANG 2)
▸ **hit** 名 [C] ◇The bomber scored a *direct hit* on the bridge. 爆撃機はその橋直撃の戦果を上げた ◇We finished the first round with a score of two *hits* and six misses. 私たちは2発命中・6発外れの得点で第一ラウンドを終えた

knock [他]（物を）打ち動かす[壊す]；（人・物を）打って…の状態にする ◇Someone had *knocked* a hole in the wall. 誰かが壁に穴をぶちあけていた ◇The two rooms had been *knocked* into one. 二つの部屋は壁を打ち抜いて一つになっていた ◇They had to *knock* the door *down* to get into the apartment. 彼らはアパートの部屋に入るためにドアを打ち破らねばならなかった ◇I accidentally *knocked over* his drink. 私は誤って彼の飲み物をひっくり返してしまった ◇The blow *knocked* him senseless (= he became unconscious). その一撃で彼は意識を失った ☞ **knock** (KNOCK), **knock** (BANG 2)
▸ **knock** 名 [C] ◇*Knocks* and scratches will lower the value of antique furniture. 打ち傷や擦り傷があるとアンティーク家具の価値は下がるだろう

bang [他, 自]（大きな音を立てて物を）たたく ◇The baby was *banging* the table with his spoon. 赤ちゃんがスプーンでテーブルをトントンたたいていた ◇She *banged* on the door angrily. 彼女は怒ってドアをドンドンたたいた ◇A branch *banged* against the window. 枝がバタバタ窓をたたいた ☞ **bang** (BANG 1, 2)

strike [他]《フォーマル》（激しく人・物に）ぶつかる, 衝突する ◇The ship *struck* a rock. その船は岩礁に衝突した

◇The stone *struck* him on the forehead. その石が彼の額に当たった ◇The old tree had been *struck by lightning*. 昔の古木には雷が落ちていた

bump [自, 他]（誤って人・物に）ぶつかる, 衝突する ◇In the darkness I *bumped* into a chair. 暗闇の中で私は椅子にぶつかった ◇The car *bumped* against the kerb. その車は縁石にぶつかった ◇Their boat came up alongside, *bumping* the side of ours. 彼らのボートが平行に近づいてきて, 私たちのボートの側面にぶつかった ☞ **bump** (BANG 2)
▸ **bump** 名 [C] ◇He fell to the ground *with a bump*. 彼はドシンと地面に落ちた

bash [自, 他]《インフォーマル》（非常に激しく物に）ぶつかる, 衝突する ◇I braked too late, *bashing* into the car in front. 私はブレーキをかけるのが遅すぎて, 前の車に突っ込んだ ◇He stood up, *bashing* his head on the low ceiling. 彼は立ち上がって頭を低い天井にぶつけた

2 ☞ BEAT
hit・punch・slap・strike・smack・spank・thump・whack・swat・sock
手[手に持った物]で人や物に非常に力強く触れる
【類語訳】たたく, 殴る, 打つ, パンチをくらわす, びんたする, ぶん殴る

▸ 文型&コロケーション
▸ to hit/ strike/ whack/ swat sb/ sth with sth
▸ to hit/ strike/ thump/ whack sb over the head
▸ to hit/ punch/ strike/ thump sb in the stomach/ chest
▸ to hit/ punch sb on the nose
▸ to hit/ punch/ slap/ smack/ spank/ thump/ whack/ sock sb hard
▸ to hit/ punch/ strike sb repeatedly

hit [他]（手・物で人・物を）たたく, 殴る, 打つ ◇I felt like *hitting* him. 私は彼を殴りたい気分だった ◇She *hit* him hard in the stomach. 彼女は彼のお腹を強くたたいた ◇He *hit* the nail squarely on the head with the hammer. 彼は金づちで釘の頭をまっすぐ打った ☞ **hit** (BANG 2)
▸ **hit** 名 [C] ◇Give it a good *hit*. 一発ぶちかましてやれ

punch [他]（拳で人・物を力一杯）殴る, パンチをくらわす ◇They repeatedly kicked and *punched* the man as he lay on the ground. 彼らは地面に横たわっている男性に殴る蹴るを繰り返した ◇He was *punching the air* in triumph. 彼は勝利して拳を突き上げていた
▸ **punch** 名 [C] ◇a *punch* in the face 顔へのパンチ ◇Hill *threw a punch* at the police officer. ヒルは警官を殴りつけた

slap (-pp-) [他]（平手で人・物を）たたく, びんたする ◇I'll *slap* you if you do that again. それをもう一度やったらびんただよ ◇She *slapped* him hard across the face. 彼女は彼の顔を強く横さまにひっぱたいた ◇'Congratulations!' he said, *slapping* me on the back. 「おめでとう」と彼は言って, 私の背中をたたいた
▸ **slap** 名 [C] ◇She gave him a *slap* across the face. 彼女は彼の顔をびんたした

strike [他]《フォーマル》（手・物で人・物を）たたく, 殴る, 打つ ◇She *struck* him hard across the face. 彼女は彼の顔を強く横さまにたたいた ◇Did she ever *strike* you? 今まで君をたたいたことがあるのか ◇He *struck* the table with his fist. 彼は拳でテーブルをたたいた ◇Who *struck the first blow* (= started the fight)? 誰が先に手を出したの

↪hit

smack [他]《特に英》(罰として平手で子どもを)たたく, たたいてしかる ◇I think it's wrong to *smack* children. 私は子どもをたたくのはよくないと思う
➤**smack** [名] [C] ◇You'll get a *smack* on your backside if you're not careful. 気をつけないとお尻をたたかれるよ

spank [他] (罰として子どもの)お尻をたたく ◇She says she's never *spanked* her children. 彼女は子どもたちのお尻をたたいたことは一度もないと言っている ❶《米》では spank は smack の代わりとして一般的に用いられる。spank は《英》でも用いられるが、使用頻度は少ない。

thump [他] (手で人・物を)強烈にたたく, 殴る, 打つ ◇She *thumped* the table angrily. 彼女は怒ってテーブルをたたいた ◇She couldn't get her breath and had to be *thumped* on the back. 彼女は息ができなくなり, 背中をたたいてもらわねばならなかった
➤**thump** [名] [C] ◇She gave him a *thump* on the back.《英, インフォーマル》彼女は彼の背中をたたいた

whack [他]《インフォーマル, 特に話し言葉》(手で人・物を)強烈にたたく, 殴る, 打つ ◇She *whacked* him around the head. 彼女は彼の頭のあたりを強烈にたたいた ◇He *whacked* the ball back over the net. 彼はネットの上を越えてボールを激しく打ち返した
➤**whack** [名] [C] ◇He gave the ball a good *whack*. 彼はボールをしっかり強打した

swat (-tt-) [他] (手で・物で虫を)たたく ◇She *swatted* the fly with a rolled-up newspaper. 彼女は丸めた新聞紙でハエをたたいた ◇He *swatted away* the mosquitoes that were buzzing around his head. 彼は顔の周りをブンブン飛び回る蚊をたたいて追い払った

sock [他]《インフォーマル, 特に話し言葉》(拳で人を)強烈に殴る ◇She got mad and *socked* him in the mouth. 彼女は怒って彼の口元をぶん殴った ◇I had to stop myself from *socking him one*. 私は彼を一発ぶん殴るのをやめざるをえなかった
➤**sock** [名] [C, ふつう単数で] ◇He gave Mike a *sock* on the jaw. 彼はマイクのあごに一発くらわせた

hold

hold・hold on・cling・clutch・grip・grasp・clasp・handle・hang on
人や物を手や腕で持つことを表す
【類語訳】持つ, 握る, 抱える, しがみつく, つかむ, 握り締める, 抱き締める

文型&コロケーション
▶ to hold/ clutch/ grip/ clasp sth **in your hand/ hands/ arms**
▶ to hold/ clutch/ clasp sb/ sth **in your arms**
▶ to hold/ hold on to/ cling to/ clutch/ grip/ grasp/ clasp/ hang on to sb/ sth **by/ with** sth
▶ to hold/ clutch/ grip/ grasp/ clasp/ hang **on to** sth
▶ to hold/ cling/ hang **on**
▶ to hold/ clutch/ clasp sth **to** you
▶ to hold/ hold on to/ cling on to/ clutch/ grip/ grasp/ clasp sb's **hand**
▶ to hold/ hold on to/ cling to/ clutch/ grip/ grasp/ clasp hang on to sb/ sth **tightly**
▶ to hold/ hold on to/ clutch/ grip/ clasp/ grasp sb/ sth **firmly**
▶ to hold/ hold on to/ cling to/ clutch/ grip/ clasp/ hang on to sb/ sth **tight**

hold [他] 持つ, 握る, 抱える ◇She was *holding* a large box. 彼女は大きな箱を抱えていた ◇The captain *held* the trophy in the air. キャプテンはトロフィーをかざした ◇I *held* the baby gently in my arms. その赤ん坊をそっと腕に抱いた ◇The girl *held* her father's hand tightly. その女の子はお父さんの手をしっかり握った ◇They walked along the street, *holding hands*. 彼らは手をつないで通りを歩いた ◇He *held* her by the shoulders. 彼は彼女の肩を抱いた ◇The lovers *held* each other close. 恋人たちは互いに抱き合っていた
➤**hold** [名] [単数で, U] ◇His *hold on* her arm tightened. 彼は彼女の腕をさらにしっかりとつかんだ ◇She tried to *keep hold of* the child's hand. 彼女は子どもの手を放さないようにした

hold 'on, hold 'onto sb/sth [句動詞] 《受身なし》(人・物に)つかまる, つかむ ◇*Hold on* and don't let go until I say so. 私が言うまでつかまって放しちゃ駄目よ ◇It's very windy — you'd better *hold on to* your hat. とても風が強い一帽子をつかんでいなさい ◇He *held onto* the back of the chair to stop himself from falling. 彼は自分が倒れないように椅子の背につかまっていた

cling [自] しがみつく ◇Survivors *clung to* pieces of floating debris. 生存者たちは浮遊している破片にしがみついた ◇Leaves still *clung* to the branches. 木の葉はまだ枝にしがみついていた ◇*Cling* on tight! しっかりしがみついて ◇They *clung together*, shivering with cold. 彼らは寒さで震えながらも互いにしがみついていた

clutch [他, 自] ぐいとつかむ, 握り締める ◇She stood there, the flowers still *clutched* in her hand. 花を手に握り締めたまま彼女はそこに立っていた ◇He gasped, and *clutched* his stomach. 彼はあえいで腹を押さえた ◇He felt himself slipping and *clutched at* a branch. 彼は自分が滑り落ちると感じ, 1本の枝をぐいとつかんだ

grip (-pp-) [他, 自] しっかりつかむ ◇'Please don't go,' he said, *gripping* her arm. 彼女の腕をしっかりつかみながら彼は「行かないでほしい」と言った ◇*Grip* the rope as tightly as you can. できるだけしっかりロープにつかまりなさい ◇She *gripped* on to the railing with both hands. 彼女は手すりにしっかりつかまった
➤**grip** [名] [C, ふつう単数で] ◇Keep a tight *grip on* the rope. ロープをしっかりつかまえていなさい ◇The climber slipped and lost his *grip*. その登山者は滑って手を放した

grasp [他] しっかり握る ◇He *grasped* my hand and shook it warmly. 彼はぼくの手をしっかり握って, 熱烈に握手した ◇Kay *grasped* him by the wrist. ケイは彼の手首をぎゅっとつかんだ ◇He *grasped* the pan by its handle. 彼は浅鍋の取っ手をぐっとつかんだ ❶graspの目的語にはしばしば hand や wrist がくる。
➤**grasp** [名] [C, ふつう単数で] ◇I grabbed him, but he slipped from my *grasp*. 私は彼をつかまえたが, するりと逃げられた

clasp [他]《書き言葉》強く握る, 抱き締める ◇He leaned forward, his hands *clasped* tightly together. 彼は両手を握り締めて身を乗り出した ◇They *clasped* hands (= held each other's hands). 彼らは手と手を握りしめた ◇She *clasped* the children in her arms. 彼女は子どもたちを腕に抱き締めた ◇He *clasped* her to him. 彼は彼女を抱き締めた ❶claspの目的語にはしばしば自分の hands や他人の (の hand) がくる。
➤**clasp** [名] [単数で] ◇He took her hand in his firm *clasp*. 彼は彼女の手を強く握った

handle [他] 手を触れる, 手で扱う ◇Our cat hates being

handled. うちの猫は手で触られるのが嫌だ ◇The label on the box said: 'Fragile. Handle with care.' 箱に貼ってあるラベルには「壊れ物。取扱い注意」と書かれていた

,hang 'on 句動詞 [受身なし] (体を支えるため) しがみつく ◇Hang on tight. We're off! しっかりつかまって。スタートしたぞ ◇I hung on to him for support. 倒れないように彼にしがみついた

hold sb/sth up 句動詞 ☞BLOCK 1

hold sb/sth up・delay・keep・stall・be/get bogged down・retard・set sb/sth back・stunt・detain
人や物事の進行 [動き, 発展] のスピードを緩める
【類語訳】遅らせる, 停滞させる, 渋滞させる, 足止めする, 引き止める, 手間取らせる, 延期する, 長引かせる, 行き詰まる

【文型&コロケーション】
▸ to be held up/ delayed/ stalled/ set back **by/ for hours/ days/ months, etc.**
▸ to hold up/ delay/ retard/ stunt the **development/ growth** of sth
▸ to delay/ bog down/ stall/ retard a **process**
▸ to hold up/ delay/ retard the **progress** of sth
▸ to hold up/ delay (a) **flight/ traffic/ work**
▸ to **seriously** hold up/ delay/ retard sth
▸ to be **unavoidably** delayed/ detained

,hold sb/sth 'up 句動詞 (動き・進行を) 遅らせる, 妨げる, 停滞 [渋滞] させる, 引き止める ◇The launch was held up for several hours by environmental protesters. 環境保護活動家によって開始が数時間遅らされた ◇An accident is holding up traffic. 事故で交通渋滞が起きている ◇I'm holding everybody up — you go ahead without me. 私が皆を引き止めておく—君は私抜きで先に行くんだ

▸ **'hold-up** 名 [C] ◇We should finish by tonight, barring hold-ups. 私たちは順調なら今晩までに終わりそう ◇What's the hold-up (= what is causing it)? 何が原因で遅れているの

delay [他, しばしば受身に] (人を) 遅らせる, 手間取らせる；(事を予定よりも) 遅らせる, 延期する ◇Thousands of commuters were delayed for over an hour. 何千人もの通勤客が1時間以上遅れた ◇What could have delayed him? どうして彼は遅れてしまうことになったの ◇These arguments will inevitably delay the start of construction. この議論をしていたら建設の開始が延期されるのは必至だ ◇The government is accused of using delaying tactics (= deliberately doing sth to delay a process, decision, etc). 政府は牛歩戦術を用いていると非難されている ☞ **delay** (DELAY)

▸ **delay** 名 [C] ◇Commuters will face long delays on the roads today. 本日車で通勤する人は長い渋滞に遭うでしょう ◇We apologize for the delay in answering your letter. 手紙の返事が遅くなり申し訳ございません

keep [他] 《特に話し言葉》 (移動中の人を) 遅らせる, 引き止める ◇You're an hour late — what kept you? 1時間の遅刻だよ—どうして遅れたの ◇I won't keep you long. I've just got a couple of quick questions. 長くはお引き止めしません。すぐに終わる質問がほんのいくつかあるだけです ◇I must go now. I've kept you from your dinner too long. もう行かないと。君の夕飯が遅くなってしまったね

stall [他, 自] (事を) 延期する, 引き延ばす, 長引かせる；(進行

を) 遅らせる, 妨げる ◇They could stall the process further by asking for a judicial review. 彼らは司法審査を求めることで訴訟手続きをさらに引き延ばすことができるだろう ◇There have been several attempts to revive the stalled peace plan. 遅れていた和平計画を再開する試みがいくつかなされている ◇Discussions have once again stalled. 議論がまた長引いている

be/get bogged down フレーズ 〔困難な [取るに足らない] 問題で〕 動きが取れなくなる, 行き詰まる, はまり込む ◇We mustn't **get bogged down in** details. 私たちは細かいことに行き詰まってはいられない ◇Try to avoid becoming **bogged down with** routine reporting procedures. 所定の報告処理だけで手一杯にならないようにしましょう

retard [他] 《フォーマル》 (発展・進行を) 遅らせる ◇The progression of the disease can be retarded by early surgery. その病気の進行は早期に手術することで遅らせることができる ◇The lack of a rail link retarded the town's development. 鉄道が通っていないことでその町の発展は遅れた 〔反意〕 **accelerate** (ACCELERATE)

,set sb/sth 'back (進行を特定期間) 遅らせる ◇The bad weather set back the building schedule by several weeks. 悪天候により数週間建設の日取りが遅れた ◇Her recovery was going well, but this latest infection has really set her back. 彼女は順調に回復に向かっていたが、最近かかったこの感染症によって非常に回復が遅れている

stunt [他] (成長・発展を) 妨げる ◇The constant winds had stunted the growth of plants and bushes. やむとのない風に草木の生長が妨げられていた ◇His illness had not stunted his creativity. 病気も彼の創造力を衰えさせてはいなかった

detain 《フォーマル》 (話・仕事などで人を) 遅らせる, 引き止める, 手間取らせる ◇I'm sorry — he'll be late; he's been detained at a meeting. すみません—彼は遅れます。会議が長引いておりまして

hole 名

1 hole・space・gap・opening・slot・aperture
物にあいた [の間にある], 通り抜けることのできる [欠落している] 広がり
【類語訳】穴, 空間, すき間, 開口部, 投入口, 口径

【文型&コロケーション】
▸ a hole/ space/ gap/ opening/ slot/ aperture **in** sth
▸ a space/ gap **between** A and B
▸ a **small/ narrow** hole/ space/ gap/ opening/ slot/ aperture
▸ a **large/ wide** hole/ space/ gap/ opening/ aperture
▸ to **leave** a hole/ a space/ a gap/ an opening
▸ to **make** a hole/ an opening/ a slot

hole [C] (貫通した) 穴 ◇to drill/bore/punch/kick a hole in sth 物にドリルで/錐で/パンチで/蹴って穴をあける ◇There were holes in the knees of his jeans. 彼のジーンズには膝のところに穴があいていた ◇The children climbed through a hole in the fence. 子どもたちがフェンスの穴を潜って通り抜けた ◇a bullet hole 弾痕

space [C] (物の間 [中間] にある) 空間, 場所, 面積 ◇a space two metres by three metres 2m×3mの面積 ◇a parking space 駐車場 ◇I'll clear a space for your books. あなたの本を置く場所をつくりましょう ◇Put it in

↪hole

holiday

the *space* between the table and the wall. テーブルと壁の間のスペースにそれを置きましょう
gap [C] (物の間[中間]にある)すき間 ◇a *gap* in a hedge/ fence/wall 生垣/フェンス/壁のすき間 ◇Leave a *gap* between your car and the next. あなたの車と隣の車との間にすき間を残しておいてください
opening [C] (物が通り抜ける)開口部, 穴, 空間 ◇The hall is lit by an *opening* in the roof. その広間は屋根の開口部から光が入ってくる ◇the dark *opening* of the tunnel トンネルの真っ暗な入り口 ◇The adult parasites have a simple mouth *opening*. その寄生虫の成虫には単純な口の機能をもつ穴がある
slot [C] (細長い)投入[差込]口 ◇He slid a coin into the *slot* of the jukebox. 彼はジュークボックスの硬貨入れにコインを滑らせた ◇a *slot* machine スロット・マシーン
aperture [C] 《フォーマル or 専門語》(小さな)開口部, 穴, 空間 ; (カメラのレンズなどの)口径, 絞り, 窓 ◇The bell ropes passed through *apertures* in the ceiling. 鐘のひもが天井にある小さな穴に通されていた ◇Open up the lens *aperture* to maximize the brightness of the shot. レンズの絞りを開けて撮影の明るさを最大にしましょう

2 hole・pit・hollow・crater・cavity
地面[物の内部]にある空っぽの空間
【類語訳】穴, くぼみ, 空洞, うろ, 火口, クレーター, 内腔

〖文型&コロケーション〗
▸ a hole/ pit/ hollow/ crater/ cavity in sth
▸ a deep/ shallow hole/ pit/ hollow/ crater
▸ a huge hole/ pit/ crater
▸ to dig a hole/ pit
▸ a bomb blows a hole/ crater in sth

hole [C] (固体内部の・物の表面にあいた)穴, くぼみ, 空洞 ◇He managed to dig out a small snow *hole*. 彼は何とか小さな雪の穴を掘った ◇Water had collected in *holes* in the road. 道路に水たまりができていた ◇an operation for a *hole* in her heart 彼女の心臓の空洞に対する手術
pit [C] (地面の大きくて深い)穴 ◇The body had been dumped in a *pit*. 死体は穴には遺棄されていた

〖ノート〗**hole と pit の使い分け : pit** は常に「地面の大きな穴」を指す。hole は物や大きさを問わずの「穴・くぼみ」を意味する。hole は不可欠だが, pit はしばしば比喩的な用いられる。 ♦ The human mind is a dark, bottomless *pit*. (《比喩的》人間の精神は底なしの暗い穴である) . ✗The human mind is a dark, bottomless *hole*.

hollow [C] (地面の)くぼみ, くぼ地 ; (物の内部の)空洞, うろ ◇The village lay secluded in a *hollow* of the hills (= a small valley). その村は丘のくぼ地にあり孤立していた ◇She noticed the slight *hollows* under his cheekbones. 彼女は彼のほおが少しこけているのに気づいた ◇The squirrel disappeared into a *hollow* at the base of the tree. リスは木の根元にあるうろの中に消えた
▸**hollow** 形 ◇a *hollow* ball/centre/tube/tree へこんだボール/くぼんだ中心/中空のチューブ/中が空洞の木 ◇*hollow* eyes/cheeks くぼんだ目/こけた目
crater [C] (火山の)火口 ; (爆弾の破裂[爆発]によって地面にできた)穴, 弾孔, クレーター ◇volcanic peaks which tower above deep *craters* 深い火口の上にそびえる火山の峰 ◇The bomb blew a *crater* 80 metres across. その爆弾で直径80mの弾孔ができた

cavity 《フォーマル or 専門語》(固体内部・体内の)空洞, 内腔 ; (虫歯の)穴 ◇the abdominal/nasal *cavity* 腹腔/鼻腔 ◇Most dentists fill *cavities* right away. たいていの歯医者はすぐに虫歯の穴に詰め物をする

holiday 名

1 holiday・vacation・break・leave・time off・day off・recess・sabbatical
仕事や学校, 大学の休業[校]期間
【類語訳】休日, 休み, 休暇, 休会, サバティカル

〖文型&コロケーション〗
▸ **during** the holidays/ the vacation/ the break/ the recess/ a sabbatical
▸ to be **on** holiday/ vacation/ leave
▸ (the) **summer/ Christmas** holiday/ vacation/ recess
▸ **annual** holiday/ vacation/ leave
▸ **paid/ unpaid** holiday/ vacation/ leave/ time off/ sabbatical
▸ **three weeks'/ two days'/ a month's**, etc. holiday/ vacation/ leave/ recess/ sabbatical
▸ to **take** leave/ time off/ a day off/ a sabbatical
▸ to **spend** your holiday/ vacation/ leave/ time off/ day off/ sabbatical doing sth

holiday [U] (または **holidays** [複数で])《英》(仕事・学校・大学の)休業[校]期間, 休日, 休み, 休暇 ◇My assistant is on *holiday* this week. 今週私の助手は休みを取っている ◇You are entitled to four weeks' annual *holiday*. あなたには4週間の年次休暇を取る権利がある ◇Your *holiday entitlement* is 25 days a year. あなたの休暇日数は年に25日です ◇My sister's coming to stay in the *holidays*. 私の妹が今度の休暇に来ることになっている ❶《英》《米》の両方で, holiday には「宗教的な[国の]祝祭日」の意味もあり, 大半の人は仕事[学校]を休む. ◆The president's birthday was declared a national *holiday*. (大統領の誕生日は国の祝日とされた). ◆Today is a *holiday* in Scotland. (今日はスコットランドでは祝日です).《米》では the *holidays* はクリスマス, ハヌカー, 正月を含む12月下旬〜1月上旬の期間を意味する.
vacation [U, C] 《米》(仕事・学校・大学の)休業[校]期間, 休日, 休み, 休暇 ◇Their son is home on *vacation*. 彼らの息子は休みで家にいる ◇The schools were closed for summer *vacation*. 学校は夏休みの間閉じられていた ◇*Vacation* time and other benefits were cut. 休暇や他の手当が削減された ❶《英》では vacation は大学, 裁判所が閉まる期間を指す. ◆the Christmas *vacation* (クリスマス休暇). ◆the long (= university summer) *vacation* (大学の夏休み).《米》では国会や委員会と同様, 裁判所にも **recess** (休廷期間)(以下参照)がある.
break [U, C] 《インフォーマル》(学校・大学の)休校期間, 休日, 休み, 休暇 ◇A lot of students go to Florida for Spring *Break*. 《米》春休み期間の多くの学生がフロリダへ行く ◇Have you got any plans for the Easter *break*? 《英》イースター休暇に何か予定はあるか ❶この意味では break は《米》では不可算名詞だが,《英》では可算名詞である.
leave [U] (特別な理由による)休暇 ◇Sylvia's on *maternity leave* (= after having a baby). シルビアは産休中だ ◇Fathers are allowed a week's *paternity leave* (= after the birth of a baby). 父親たちには1週間の育児休暇が与えられる ◇There are new provisions for *pa-*

home

rental leave (= for parents of young children). 育児休暇のための新たな規定がある ◇He was on *sick leave* following a heart attack. 彼は心臓発作の後、病気休暇を取っていた ◇She was given *compassionate leave* to attend the funeral. 葬儀に参列するため彼女には忌引休暇が与えられた ◇He applied for *study leave* (= from teaching at a university) to write the book. 彼は本を執筆するため研究休暇を申請した

,time 'off [U] (仕事・学校の)休み ◇Why not come with me if you can get the *time off*? 休みが取れたら私と一緒に行きませんか ◇Can you get some *time off work*? 少し仕事を休めますか ◇The children were given *time off school* to watch the ceremony. 子どもたちは式典を見学するため学校を休むことを許された

,day 'off [C] (仕事・学校の1日の)休み ◇She's had only two *days off* in the past year. この一年間彼女は休みが2日しかなかった ◇I've got the *day off* from school. 今日私は学校を休んだ ◇Sunday is my only *day off*. 日曜日が私の唯一の休日だ

recess [C, U] (議会・委員会の)休会(期間) ◇Tomorrow MPs break for the Christmas *recess*. 明日はクリスマス休会のため下院議員は休みだ ◇The peace talks resumed after a month-long *recess*. 和平交渉は1か月間の休会後に再開した ◇The report was published while Congress was *in recess*. その報道は国会の休会期間中に行われた

sabbatical [C, U] (大学教師の研究・執筆・旅行のための)サバティカル、休暇 ◇He's been given a year's *sabbatical*. 彼は1年間のサバティカルを与えられている ◇She's on *sabbatical* until January. 彼女は1月までサバティカル中だよ

2 ☞ TRIP
holiday・vacation・break・getaway
自宅を離れて行楽[旅行]に費やす期間
【類語訳】休暇、旅行、行楽、バカンス、行楽地

〖文型&コロケーション〗
▶ a **great/ relaxing** holiday/ vacation/ break/ getaway
▶ a **dream/ family** holiday/ vacation
▶ a **summer/ winter** holiday/ vacation/ break/ getaway
▶ a holiday/ vacation **abroad**
▶ a holiday/ vacation **destination/ home/ resort/ spot**
▶ to **go/ be on** holiday/ vacation
▶ to **take** a holiday/ vacation
▶ to **cancel** a holiday/ vacation/ break
▶ a **week's/ three-day, etc.** holiday/ vacation/ break

holiday [C] 《英》(自宅を離れての)休暇、旅行、行楽 ◇The neighbours are away on *holiday*. 近所の人たちは旅行に出かけている ◇He's never had a *holiday* abroad. 彼は海外で休暇を過ごしたことがない ◇We're going on a *skiing holiday* in Austria. 私たちはオーストリアにスキー旅行に行ってきます ◇*Package holidays* (= in which your flight, accommodation, etc. are all organized for you and included in the price) are generally becoming less popular. パック旅行は一般的に人気が下落になっている ◇Let's have a look at your *holiday* photos. 君の休暇の写真を見ようよ

vacation [C] 《米》(自宅を離れての)休暇、バカンス、旅行、行楽 ◇The senator is on *vacation* in Maine. その議員はメーンで休暇中だ ◇How was your *vacation*? 休暇はどうだった ◇They usually go on a *ski vacation* this time of year. 彼らは1年のこの時期にたいていスキー旅行に行く ◇The area is a popular *vacation* choice for families. その地域は家族連れに選ばれる人気の行楽地だ

break [C] (短い)休暇、旅行 ◇The prize is a three-night *break* in Paris. 賞品はパリ3泊の旅行です ◇Choose from our range of city *breaks*. いろいろな都市滞在型休暇の中からお選びください ◇It's a great city for a *weekend break*. そこは週末旅行にうってつけの都市だ

getaway [C] 《ふつう単数で》(ややインフォーマル) (短い)休暇、旅行；行楽地 ◇a romantic weekend *getaway* in New York 恋人と行くニューヨークへの週末旅行 ◇the popular island *getaway* of Penang 人気の行楽地であるペナン島

▶ **,get a'way** 句動詞 We're hoping to *get away* (= go away on holiday) for a few days at Easter. 私たちはイースターに数日旅行に行きたいと思っている

home 名

home・address・place・dwelling・residence・abode
人が住んでいる場所
【類語訳】家、自宅、実家、住所、所在地、住居、宛先、アドレス

〖文型&コロケーション〗
▶ **at** (a) home/ an address/ sb's place/ a residence
▶ **in** a home/ sb's place/ a dwelling/ a residence
▶ a **comfortable** home/ place/ dwelling/ residence
▶ a **private** home/ address/ dwelling/ residence
▶ a **family** home/ dwelling/ residence
▶ a **permanent** home/ address/ dwelling/ residence/ abode
▶ a **temporary** home/ address/ dwelling/ residence/ abode
▶ **no fixed** address/ abode
▶ to **have** a home/ an address/ a place of your own

home [C, U] (家族と共に住む)家、自宅、実家 ◇We're not far from my *home* now. 今私たちは私の家から遠くないところにいます ◇Old people prefer to stay in their own *homes*. 高齢の人は自宅にいるほうが好きだ ◇She leaves *home* at 7 every day. 彼女は毎日7時に家を出る ◇She *left home* (= left her parents) and began an independent life at sixteen. 彼女は親元を離れて、16歳で自立し始めた ◇Nowadays a lot of people *work from home*. この頃多くの人が在宅勤務をしている

▶ **home** 副 Come on, it's time to *go home*. さあ、家に帰る時間ですよ ◇What time did you *get home* last night? 昨日の夜は何時に家に着いたの

address [C] (自宅・職場の)住所、所在地、住居、(手紙・メールなどの)宛先、アドレス ◇What's your *name and address*? お名前とご住所をお願いします ◇Is that your *home address*? それはあなたのご自宅の住所ですか ◇Half the names in his *address book* (= that you write addresses and phone numbers in) are crossed out. 彼のアドレス帳の中にある名前の半分が削除されている ◇an email *address* eメール・アドレス ◇a web *address* ウェブ・アドレス ◇Please note my *change of address*. 私あての住所の変更に注意してください ◇Police found him at an *address* (= a house or flat) in West London. 警察は西ロンドンにある住居で彼を発見した ☞ **address** (SEND)

place [C] 〖単数で〗《インフォーマル》(戸建・アパート・マンションを含む)住居、住宅；(人の)家、自宅 ◇What about dinner at *my place*? 私の家で夕食はいかが ◇I'm fed up with living with my parents, so I'm looking for *a place of* *my own*. 両親との同居にうんざりしていて、自分の家を探しているところだ ◇I thought I'd better clean the *place* up. 私は家の掃除をしたほうがいいと思った

dwelling [C]《フォーマル or 文語》(戸建・アパート・マンションなどを含む)住居, 住宅 ◇The development will consist of 66 *dwellings* and a number of offices. その造成地は66の住宅といくつかのオフィスから成る予定だ

residence [C]《フォーマル》(大きな)邸宅；(人の住む)住居, 住宅, 住所 ◇This desirable family *residence* is situated in the heart of the town (= in an advertisement). この素敵な家族向けの邸宅は町の中心部に位置しています ◇10 Downing Street is the British Prime Minister's official *residence*. ダウニング街10番地とは英国首相官邸のことです ☞*residence* [U]は特定の地域での居住を指す。 ☞ **reside** (LIVE)

abode [C, ふつう単数で]《フォーマル or おどけて》(人の住む)住居, 住宅, 住所 ◇His sole residence is in a hostel for people of *no fixed abode* (= with no permanent home). 彼の唯一の住み家は住所不定の人用の宿泊所だ ◇Welcome to my humble *abode*. 狭苦しい我が家へようこそ ❶ **right of abode**（居住権）は正式に特定の国で生活することが許された権利を指す。 ◆The island's citizens' will not be given the *right of abode* in Britain. (その島の住民にはイギリスでの居住権は与えられないだろう)。

honest 形 ☞ PLAIN 2

honest・frank・direct・open・outspoken・straight・blunt・sincere・truthful・candid・straightforward・forthright

人が感情や意見、事実を隠そうとせずにはっきり言うことを表す
【類語訳】率直な, ありのままの, 包み隠しのない, 歯に衣着せぬ, ぶっきらぼうな, ぶしつけな, 心からの, 正直な

【文型&コロケーション】

▶ honest/ frank/ direct/ open/ outspoken/ straight/ sincere/ truthful/ candid/ straightforward/ forthright **about** sth
▶ honest/ frank/ direct/ open/ straight/ blunt/ truthful/ candid/ straightforward **with** sb
▶ honest/ frank/ outspoken/ sincere/ candid/ forthright **in** your views/ criticism, etc.
▶ an honest/ an outspoken/ a forthright **opinion/ view**
▶ an honest/ a direct/ a straight/ a blunt/ a truthful **answer**
▶ an honest/ a direct/ an open/ a sincere/ a truthful **person**
▶ a frank/ direct/ blunt/ forthright **manner**
▶ **quite/ very** honest/ frank/ direct/ open/ outspoken/ blunt/ sincere/ truthful/ candid/ straightforward/ forthright
▶ **extremely** honest/ frank/ direct/ open/ outspoken
▶ **completely** honest/ frank/ open/ straight/ sincere/ truthful
▶ **absolutely** honest/ frank/ open/ truthful
▶ **perfectly** honest/ frank/ / sincere/ candid
▶ **To be/ Let's be** honest/ frank/ blunt...

honest《しばしばほめて》正直な, 率直な, ありのままの, 偽りのない ◇Give me your *honest* opinion. 君の率直な意見を聞かせてくれ ◇Are you being completely *honest* about your feelings? 自分の感情を偽っているということはまったくありませんか ◇Thank you for being so *honest* with me. 本当に正直に話してくれてありがとう ◇To be *honest*, it was one of the worst books I've ever read. 《話し言葉》正直に言えば、それは私が今まで読んだ中で最低の本の一つだ ◇Let's be *honest*, she's only interested in Mike because of his money. 正直なところ, 彼女はマイクのお金にしか興味がないんだ 反意 **dishonest** (DISHONEST)

▶**honestly** 副 ◇I didn't tell anyone, *honestly*! 本当に誰にも言わなかったよ ◇I *honestly* can't remember a thing about last night. 私は本当に昨晩のことを何一つ覚えていない

▶**honesty** 名 [U] ◇She answered all my questions with her usual *honesty*. 彼女は私の質問のすべてにいつもどおり正直に答えてくれた ◇The book isn't, *in all honesty*, as good as I expected. 正直なところ、その本は期待していたほどよくない

frank《しばしばほめて》率直な, ありのままの, 包み隠しのない；(他人の反感を買うほど)あけっぴろげな ◇a full and *frank* discussion 十分かつ率直な議論 ◇a *frank* admission of guilt ありのままの罪の告白 ◇He was very *frank* about his relationship with the actress. 彼は非常にあけっぴろげにその女優との関係について話した

▶**frankly** 副 ◇He spoke *frankly* about the ordeal. 彼はつらい体験について包み隠さず話した ◇Quite *frankly*, I'm not surprised you failed. はっきり言って, 君が失敗したことに驚いてはいないよ

▶**frankness** 名 [U] ◇They outlined their aims with disarming *frankness*. 彼らは構えず率直に自分たちの目的の概要を語った

direct（誰もとはけることができないほど）率直な, 単刀直入の, 端的な ◇I need a *direct* answer to a *direct* question. 端的な質問に対しては端的に答える必要がある ❶ *direct* は *indirect*（回りくどい）とは反対に好意的に受け止められるが、時に人がぶしつけであることを「婉曲的に」言うときにも用いられる。 ◆She has a very *direct* way of speaking (= she does not bother to be polite to people when speaking to them). (彼女はとてもあからさまなもの言いをする). 反意 **indirect** ❶回答や話し方が *indirect* であるとは「遠回しである」ということ。

▶**directness** 名 [U] ◇'What's that?' she asked with her usual *directness*. 「それってどういうこと」と彼女らしく単刀直入に聞いた ◇He presents his case with refreshing clarity and *directness*. 彼は胸がすくほど明快かつ端的に論点を提示する

open《ほめて》(人が)隠し立てをしない, 包み隠しのない ◇She was always *open* with her parents. 彼女はいつも両親に隠し事をしなかった ◇He was quite *open* about his reasons for leaving. 彼は辞任の理由をまったく包み隠さず話した

▶**openly** 副 ◇The men in prison would never cry *openly* (= so that other people could see). 獄中の男たちは決しておおっぴらに泣くようなことはしないものだ

outspoken（人を驚かせる[怒らせる]ことをいとわないほど）率直な, 歯に衣着せない, 遠慮のない ◇He was known as an *outspoken* opponent of the leadership. 彼は首脳部に対する歯に衣着せぬ敵対者として知られていた ◇She was *outspoken* in her criticism of the plan. 彼女はその計画を率直に批判した

▶**outspokenly** 副 ◇*outspokenly* critical 歯に衣着せず批判的な

straight《ふつうほめて》率直な, 正直な, 単刀直入の, 端的な ◇I don't think you're being *straight* with me. 君が正直に話してくれているとは思えない ◇It's time for some *straight talking*. そろそろ率直な話し合いが必要な時です

blunt 無遠慮な, あからさまな, ぶっきらぼうな, そっけない ◇She has a reputation for *blunt* speaking. 彼女は話し

hope

方がぶっきらぼうという評判だ ◇To be *blunt*, your work is appalling. 遠慮なく言えば、あなたの作品にはあきれ果てていう

▶**bluntly** 副 ◇*To put it bluntly*, I want a divorce. あからさまに言うと、私は離婚したいんです ◇'Is she dead?' he asked *bluntly*. 「彼女は死んだのですか」と彼は何のためらいもなく聞いた

sincere 《ほめて》偽りのない、裏表のない、心からの ◇He seemed *sincere* enough when he said he wanted to help. 力になりたいと言ったとき彼は心からそう言っているように思えた ◇She is never completely *sincere* in what she says about people. 彼女は人について話す際に、すべて心のままを語ることは決してない 反意 **insincere**

▶**sincerely** 副 ◇I *sincerely* believe that this is the right decision. これは正しい決断であると心から思っています

truthful 《ほめて》正直な；ありのままの ◇Are you being completely *truthful* with me? 全部私に正直に話してくれているのか ◇She was unable to give a *truthful* answer. 彼女はありのままを答えることができなかった

▶**truthfully** 副 ◇He answered all their questions *truthfully*. 彼は彼らの質問にすべて正直に答えた

candid 《ややフォーマル、しばしばほめて》率直な、包み隠しのない ◇The ex-minister gave a *candid* interview about his reasons for resigning. 元大臣は辞任理由について取材に包み隠さず答えた

▶**candidly** 副 ◇She *candidly* admitted her mistakes. 彼女は自分のミスを率直に認めた

▶**candour** 《英》《米では**candor**》名 ◇'I don't trust her,' he said, in a rare moment of *candour*. 「私は彼女を信頼していない」と彼は珍しく率直に言った

straightforward 《ほめて》率直な、正直な；隠し立てをしない ◇She's nice: very *straightforward* and easy to get on with. 彼女は素敵な人だ。とても正直で誰とでもすぐに仲良くなる ❶ *straightforward* は広く好まれる人の性格を表す。intelligent, honest, fair などの肯定的な語と並べて用いられる。

forthright (思っていることを)ずばりと言う；率直な、歯に衣着せない ◇a woman of *forthright* views 意見をずばりと言う女性 ◇He spoke in a *forthright* manner but without anger. 彼は率直に、だが怒ることなく話した

ノート honest, frank, candid は下で示す話し方と同様に話の内容についても用いられる。◆a/an *honest/frank/candid* admission of guilt (正直な[ありのままの]罪の告白)。これらの語はすべて一般的には肯定的な語であるが、frank は他人の反感を買うほど度の過ぎた率直さを表す可能性もある。direct, outspoken, blunt, forthright はすべて思っていることを口にする場合の話し方を指す。forthright が最も肯定的な意味を持ち、他人がどう思おうと恐れずに話すことを示す。outspoken は人に衝撃を与えることをいとわず正しいと思うことを話すこと、blunt と direct はしばしば正直であることを優先させて礼儀をわきまえずに話すこと、open と straightforward は最も肯定的で人の性格を表す。◆He's a very *open*/*straightforward* person. (彼はとても正直な人です)

hope 名

1 hope・optimism・expectancy・wishful thinking
好ましい事が起こるだろうという思い
【類語訳】希望、望み、期待、見込み、待望

文型&コロケーション
▶hope/ optimism **for** sth
▶hope/ optimism **that**...
▶**great/ considerable/ false/ renewed** hope/ optimism
▶to **express/ share** your hope/ optimism
▶hope/ optimism **grows/ rises**

hope [U, C] 希望、望み、期待、見込み ◇There is now *hope of* a cure. 今は快復の見込みがある ◇They have *given up hope* of finding any more survivors. 彼らはこれ以上の生存者を発見する望みを放棄した ◇There is still a *glimmer of hope*. まだかすかな望みがある ◇She *has high hopes* of winning (= is very confident about it). 彼女は勝てる見込みが極めて大きいと思っている ◇Don't *raise your hopes* too high, or you may be disappointed. 高望みしすぎると、がっかりするかもしれないよ ❶ hope はふつう事が一般的にうまくいくことへの思いだけではなく、特別の事が起こることへの思いに用いられる。 反意 **despair, hopelessness,** ☞ **hopeful** (OPTIMISTIC), **hopeful** (PROMISING)

optimism [U] 《ややフォーマル》楽観；楽観主義、楽観する傾向 ◇He returned with renewed *optimism* about the future. 彼は将来を改めて楽観視する気持ちになって戻ってきた ◇Some people talked of a mood of cautious *optimism*. 慎重かつ楽観的なムードを話題にする人もいた ❶ optimism はビジネス[政治]の文脈で、経営者[政治家]が自分たちの会社[政策]がうまくいくだろうといった確信を表す場合によく用いられる。 反意 **pessimism** (NEGATIVE), ☞ **optimistic** (OPTIMISTIC)

expectancy [U] 《ややフォーマル、特に書き言葉》《好ましい[わくわくするような]ことへの》期待、待望 ◇There was an *air of expectancy* among the waiting crowd. 待ち受ける大勢の人々の間に期待感が漂った ❶ expectancy はしばしばテレビ[ラジオ]で、わくわくさせる出来事が起こるのを大勢の人が待ち望んでいる様子を表すのに用いられる。 ☞ **expectant** (OPTIMISTIC)

wishful 'thinking [U] (実現しそうもない)甘い考え、希望的観測、幻想 ◇I've got a feeling that Alex likes me, but that might just be *wishful thinking*. アレックスは私のことが好きなんだと思っているけど、それは単なる希望的観測にすぎないかもしれない

2 ☞ DESIRE
hope・dream・aspiration・ambition・fantasy・expectation
何かを持ちたい[したい]という思い
【類語訳】願望、期待、夢、理想、向上心、野心、野望、念願、大望

文型&コロケーション
▶hopes/ aspirations/ expectations **for** sth
▶aspirations/ an ambition **to do** sth
▶**high** hopes/ aspirations/ ambitions/ expectations
▶(a) **personal** hope/ dream/ aspiration/ ambition/ fantasy/ expectations
▶**political** hopes/ aspirations/ ambitions
▶to **have** hopes/ a dream/ aspirations/ an ambition/ a fantasy/ expectations
▶to **cherish/ harbour/ nurture** a hope/ a dream/ an ambition/ a fantasy
▶to **fulfil** your hopes/ dreams/ aspirations/ ambitions/ fantasies/ expectations

▶ to **achieve** your dreams/ aspirations/ ambitions
▶ to **abandon/ give up** a hope/ a dream/ an ambition
▶ to **shatter** a hope/ dream/ fantasy

hope [C] 願望, 期待 ◇She told me all her *hopes*, dreams and fears. 彼女は私に自分の願望, 夢, 不安をすべて語ってくれた ◇They **have high hopes** for their children. 彼らは子どもたちにすごく期待している 反意 **fear** (FEAR)

dream [C] (達成困難な)夢, 理想 ◇Her lifelong *dream* was to be a famous writer. 彼女の生涯の夢は有名な作家になることだった ◇If I win it will be a ***dream come true***. もし私が勝てば, それで夢が実現することになる ◇What would be your *dream* job? あなたの夢の[理想とする]仕事って何だろう ◇I've finally found the man *of my dreams*. 私はついに理想の男性を見つけた

▷ **dream** 動 [自, 他] ◇It was the kind of trip most people only *dream* about. それはたいていの人にとっては夢でしかないような旅だった ◇I *never dreamed* I'd actually get the job! 私が実際にその仕事を手に入れるなんて夢にも思わなかった

aspiration [C, ふつう複数で] 《ややフォーマル》(偉業を達成したい[生活・地位を向上させたい]という)願望, 向上心 ◇He had never had any *aspirations* to enter politics. 彼には政界に入りたいという願望はまったくなかった ◇What changes are needed to meet women's *aspirations* for employment? 女性たちの雇用に抱く願望を満たすためにどのような変革が必要ですか

ambition [C] 野心, 野望, 念願, 大望 ◇She never achieved her *ambition* of becoming a famous writer. 彼女の有名な作家になりたいという野望は実現することはなかった ◇His burning *ambition* was to study medicine. 彼の強い志望は医学の道に進むことだった

ノート **aspiration** と **ambition** の使い分け: aspiration はふつう ambition よりも一般的な願望について用いられる. これらの語はすべて人生において達成したい物事, 特に物質的財産や社会的・職業的成功について用いられる. これらの語はまた, しばしば and と共に句で用いられる. ◆your hopes/ needs/dreams/interests/fears and *aspirations* (期待/要望/夢/興味/不安と願望). ambitionはしばしば職業上の成功に関連して用いられる. aspirationは have aspirations (願望を抱く)という形でよく用いられるのに対して, ambitionは achieve/fulfil/realize/satisfy one's ambitions (念願[野望]を叶える/実現する)といった形で用いられる.

fantasy [C] (実現しそうもない)空想, 夢想, 幻想 ◇He spoke of his childhood *fantasies about* becoming a famous football player. 彼は有名なサッカー選手になるという子ども時代の夢を語った ☞ **fantasy** (IMAGINATION)

▷ **fantasize** 《英でまた -ise》動 [自] ◇Many people *fantasize* about winning the lottery. 多くの人が宝くじを当てる夢想を抱く

expectation [C, ふつう複数で, U] 《ややフォーマル》(好ましい事に対する)期待, 予想 ◇The results exceeded our *expectations*. 結果は私たちの予想を上回った ◇The event did not live up to *expectations*. その催し物は期待に沿うものではなかった ◇There was an air of *expectation* and great curiosity. 期待感と強い好奇心が漂っていた ❶典型的な言い回しに exceed/surpass/meet/fulfill expectations (期待を上回る/に沿う)が挙げられる. ☞ **expectation** (EXPECTATION)

hope

hope 動 ☞ EXPECT

hope • wait • wish • aspire • set your sights on sth • set your heart on sth

事が起こってほしいと強く思う
【類語訳】望む, 願う, 期待する, 見込む, 待ち望む, 心待ちにする, 熱望する, あこがれる

文型&コロケーション
▶ to hope/ wait/ wish **for** sth
▶ to hope/ wish **that**...
▶ to hope/ wait/ aspire **to do** sth
▶ to **still** hope for/ wait for/ wish for/ aspire to sth
▶ to **really/ secretly/ always/ never** hope for/ wish for/ aspire to sth
▶ to **just/ only** hope/ wish

hope [自, 他] 望む, 願う, 期待する, 見込む ◇We're *hoping* for good weather on Sunday. 私たちは日曜日がいい天気になることを望んでいる ◇All we can do now is wait and *hope*. 今は期待しつつ待つほかない ◇'Do you think it will rain?' '*I hope not*.' 「雨が降ると思う」「降らないことを願うよ」 ◇'Will you be back before dark?' '*I hope so*, yes.' 「暗くなる前に戻ってくる」「そうしたいね, うん」 ◇*Let's hope* we can find a parking space. 駐車スペースがあるといいんだけど ◇*It is hoped that* over £10,000 will be raised. 1万ポンド以上のお金が集まると期待されている ◇She is *hoping* to win the gold medal. 彼女は金メダルを獲得したいと思っている

wait [自, 他] (長い間)待ち望む, 心待ちにする ◇The team had *waited* for success for eighteen years. そのチームは18年もの間成功することを待ち望んでいた ◇This is just the opportunity I've been *waiting* for. これこそが私が待ち望んでいた好機だ ◇He's *waiting* for me to make a mistake. 彼は私が失敗を犯すのを心待ちにしている ◇I *waited my chance* and slipped out when no one was looking. 私は機会をうかがって, 誰も見ていないときに抜け出した

wish [自] (幸運[不思議な力]でしか達成できない事を)切望する, 祈る ◇If you *wish* really hard, maybe you'll get what you want. 懸命に祈れば, もしかすると願いが叶うかもしれないよ ◇It's no use *wishing* for the impossible. 不可能なことを望んでも仕方ない ◇He has everything he could possibly *wish* for. 彼は願わずともすべてを持っている ☞ **wish** (WISH), **wish** (WANT)

aspire [自] 《ややフォーマル》(達成したい[なりたい]と)熱望する, あこがれる ◇She *aspired to* a scientific career. 彼女は科学分野の職業にあこがれた ◇He *aspired* to be their next leader. 彼は彼らの次期指導者になることを熱望した

set your sights on sth [行れ] 《特にジャーナリズム》(物事を)目標に定める, 目指す ◇I had *set my sights on* a career in journalism. 私はジャーナリズムの仕事を目指していた ❶ set your sights on sthはふつうスポーツ[ビジネス]で達成したいと思う事について用いられる.

set your 'heart on sth, have your heart 'set on sth [行れ] (物事を)心に決める ◇They've *set their heart on* a house in the country. 彼らは田舎に家を持つと心に決めている

hot, hug

hot [形] ☞ HUMID

hot・warm・heated・burning・feverish・red-hot・boiling
場所、人、物が寒く[冷たく]ないことを表す
【類語訳】熱い、暑い、温かい、灼熱の、煮えたぎった

warm	hot	burning
heated	feverish	red-hot
		boiling

【文型&コロケーション】
- hot/ warm **weather/ sunshine/ water**
- a hot/ warm **climate/ sun**
- a hot/ burning/ feverish **forehead**
- hot/ burning **cheeks**
- hot/ burning/ red-hot **coals**
- to **feel/ look** hot/ warm/ feverish
- to **keep sth** hot/ warm/ heated
- **nice and** hot/ warm

hot (温度が)暑[熱]い、温かい；(人が)暑[熱]く感じる；(人に)暑[熱]く感じさせる ◇It's *hot* today, isn't it? 今日は暑くないかい ◇It was the *hottest* July on record. 記録上それが最も暑い7月だった ◇Be careful — the plates are *hot*. 気をつけてください—お皿が熱いので ◇I'll feel better after a *hot* bath. 熱い風呂に入れば気分がよくなるだろう ◇The canteen provides *hot* meals as well as salads and snacks. その食堂はサラダや軽食だけでなく温かい食事も出している ◇Eat it while it's *hot*. 温かいうちに食べなさい ◇Is anyone too *hot*? 誰か暑すぎる人はいますか ◇Her cheeks grew *hot* with embarrassment. 彼女のほおは恥ずかしさで熱くなった ◇It had been a long *hot* journey. それは長く暑い旅であった 反意 **cold** (COLD 1)

warm (温度が心地よく)暖[温]かい；(衣類・建物が)暖[温]かい ◇It's nice and *warm* in here. この中は気持ちよくて暖かいですね ◇Are you *warm* enough? 十分暖かいですか ◇They stood on the corner, stamping their feet to keep *warm*. 彼らは町かどに立って、足踏みして体を温めていた ◇The leaves swayed slowly in the soft, *warm* breeze. 葉っぱがやさしく暖かい風の中でゆっくり揺れていた ◇Wash the blouse in *warm* soapy water. そのブラウスを温かい石けん水で洗ってください ◇Make sure you pack some *warm* clothes. 必ず暖かい衣類を何枚か荷物に入れてください 反意 **cold, cool** (COLD 1), ☞ **warm** (HEAT)

heated (部屋・建物・場所が)暖房の効いた、暖[温]められた ◇The hotel has a *heated* swimming pool, spa and sauna. そのホテルには温水プール、温泉、サウナがある **unheated** ❶ unheatedは部屋・建物などが暖房のない[効いていない]ことを表す。◆ an *unheated* bathroom (暖房のない風呂場). ☞ **heat** (HEAT)

burning 灼熱の、煮えたぎった；(病気・感情が)燃える[焼ける] ◇They felt the *burning* heat of the sun on their backs. 彼らは背中に灼熱の太陽を感じた ◇The skin of his forehead was *burning*. 彼の額の肌は燃えるように熱かった ◇She was *burning hot* with embarrassment and guilt. 彼女は恥ずかしさと罪の意識で燃えるように熱くなっていた ☞ **burn** (HURT 2)

feverish 発熱している；発熱による ◇She was aching and *feverish*. 彼女には痛みと発熱の症状があった ◇He fell into a troubled, *feverish* sleep. 彼は不安定な発熱による眠りに陥った ☞ **delirious** (HYSTERICAL)
▶ **feverishly** [副] ◇Her mind raced *feverishly*. 彼女は内心焦って体が熱くなった

,red-'hot (金属・物が)真っ赤に焼けた ◇*Red-hot* coals glowed in the fire. 石炭が炎の中で赤々と燃えさかった

boiling (《ややインフォーマル》) うだるように暑い、煮えたぎった ◇You must be *boiling* in that sweater! そんなセーターを着ていては暑苦しいどころじゃないだろう 反意 **freezing** (FREEZING)
▶ **boiling** [副] ◇It's *boiling hot* in here! 《インフォーマル》ここはうだるような暑さだね

hug [動]

hug・embrace・cuddle・cradle・snuggle
愛情を表現するために人を両腕で囲む
【類語訳】抱き締める、抱擁する、抱きかかえる

【文型&コロケーション】
- to hug/ embrace/ cuddle/ cradle a/ your **child/ son/ daughter**
- to hug/ cuddle/ cradle a **baby/ doll**
- to hug/ embrace/ cuddle your **wife/ husband**
- to hug/ cuddle your **girlfriend/ boyfriend**
- to hug/ cuddle a **teddy**
- to hug/ embrace **each other**
- to hug/ embrace/ cradle sb **gently**
- to hug/ embrace sb **tightly/ warmly**

hug (-gg-) [他, 自] (愛情[友情]表現で人を)抱き締める、抱擁する ◇They *hugged* each other. 彼らは互いに抱き締め合った ◇She *hugged* him tightly. 彼女は彼をきつく抱き締めた ◇He *hugged* Anna *to* him. 彼はアンナを抱き寄せた ◇They put their arms around each other and *hugged*. 彼らは両腕を互いに回して抱き締め合った
▶ **hug** [名] [C] ◇She gave her mother a big *hug*. 彼女は母親を包み込むように抱き締めた ◇He stopped to receive *hugs* and *kisses* from the fans. 彼は立ち止まってファンから抱擁やキスを受けた

embrace [自, 他]《フォーマル》(愛情[友情]表現で人を)抱擁する ◇They *embraced* and wept and promised to keep in touch. 彼らは抱擁して泣き、連絡を取り合うことを約束した ◇She *embraced* her son warmly. 彼女は息子を温かく抱擁した
▶ **embrace** [名] [C, U] ◇There were tears and *embraces* as they said goodbye. 彼らは別れの言葉を交わす中涙を流し抱擁し合った ◇She tried to escape from his *embrace*. 彼女は彼の抱擁から逃れようとした

cuddle [自, 他] (愛情表現で人・物を)抱き締める、抱擁する ◇A couple of teenagers were kissing and *cuddling* on the doorstep. 十代のカップルが戸口の階段でキスして抱き合っていた ◇The little boy *cuddled* the teddy bear close. 小さな男の子はクマのぬいぐるみをしっかりと抱き締めた ☞ **cuddly** (SWEET)
▶ **cuddle** [名] [C, 単数形] ◇She gave him a *cuddle*. 彼女は彼を抱き締めた

cradle [他] (赤ちゃんを抱くように)人・物を)抱きかかえる ◇The old man *cradled* the tiny baby in his arms. そのおじいさんは小さな赤ちゃんを両腕で抱きかかえた

snuggle [自, 他]《副詞や前置詞と共に》(心地よく[ぬくぬくと])人・物に)すり寄る、寄り添う、(体の部位などを)すり寄せ

↪hug

◇The child *snuggled up to* her mother. その子は母親にすり寄った ◇He *snuggled down* under the bedclothes. 彼は布団の下にもぐり込んだ ◇She *snuggled* closer. 彼女はもっと近くに寄り添った ◇He *snuggled* his head onto her shoulder. 彼は彼女の肩に顔をすり寄せた

huge 形 ☞LARGE

huge・massive・vast・enormous・giant・tremendous・gigantic・immense・monumental・colossal
極めて大きなことを表す
【類語訳】巨大な, 膨大な, 莫大な, 広大な, 重大な, 甚大な

文型&コロケーション

▶a huge/ a massive/ a vast/ an enormous/ a tremendous/ a colossal **amount of** sth
▶a huge/ a massive/ a vast/ an enormous/ a tremendous **number of** things
▶the huge/ massive/ vast/ enormous/ tremendous/ colossal **cost**
▶a huge/ a massive/ a vast/ an enormous **crowd/ area**
▶a huge/ a massive/ an enormous/ a tremendous/ a monumental **task**
▶a huge/ a massive/ a vast/ a giant/ a tremendous/ a gigantic **step**
▶a huge/ a massive/ an enormous/ a tremendous/ a colossal **explosion**
▶huge/ massive/ enormous/ tremendous/ immense **pressure**
▶a huge/ a massive/ an enormous/ a tremendous **problem/ success**
▶huge/ vast/ enormous/ tremendous/ immense/ colossal **power**
▶massive/ enormous/ tremendous/ immense **strength**
▶to be of huge/ massive/ enormous/ gigantic/ monumental **proportions**
▶to be of/ have huge/ enormous/ tremendous/ immense/ monumental **significance/ importance**
▶on a huge/ massive/ vast/ enormous/ monumental/ colossal **scale**
▶**absolutely** huge/ massive/ enormous/ tremendous
▶**really** huge/ massive/ enormous/ tremendous/ gigantic

huge (大きさ・量・程度が)非常に大きい, 巨大[膨大, 莫大]な ◇A *huge* crowd had gathered in the square. 大勢の人が広場に集まっていた ◇He gazed up at her with *huge* brown eyes. 彼は大きな茶色の目で彼女を見つめた ◇The company ran up *huge* debts. その会社の負債は巨額に及んだ ◇The party was a *huge* success. パーティーは大成功だった 反意 **tiny** (SMALL)

massive 非常に大きい, 巨大[重大, 甚大]な ◇The explosion made a *massive* hole in the ground. その爆発で地面に巨大な穴ができた ◇The Chancellor is to announce a *massive* increase in spending. 首相は支出の大幅な増加を発表する予定だ ◇He suffered a *massive* heart attack. 彼は重篤な心臓発作に見舞われた ❶ *massive* はふつうフォーマルでもインフォーマルでもないが, 《英》の話し言葉では特に物の物理的な大きさについて言うときにインフォーマルな響きを持つことが多々ある. ◆They've got a *massive great* house. (《英, インフォーマル, 話し言葉》)家はものすごく大きい).

vast (面積・量・数・大きさが)非常に広い[大きい], 広大[巨大, 膨大, 莫大]な ◇To the south lay a *vast* area of wilderness. 南方には広大な荒野が広がっていた ◇At dusk bats appear in *vast* numbers. 夕方になると膨大な数のコウモリが現れる ◇His business empire was *vast*. 彼の企業帝国は巨大だった ◇In the *vast* majority of cases this should not be a problem. 圧倒的に多くの場合こんなことは問題にならないはずだ
▶**vastness** 名 [U] ◇the *vastness* of space (《書き言葉》)空間の大きな広がり

enormous (大きさ・量・程度が)非常に大きい, 巨大[膨大, 莫大]な ◇They've bought an *enormous* house in the country. 彼らは田舎に大豪邸を購入した ◇The council has spent an *enormous* amount of money on this project. 議会はこのプロジェクトに莫大な金額を費やしている ◇The implications of such a proposal are *enormous*. このような提案の意味するところはとてつもなく大きい 反意 **tiny** (SMALL)

ノート **huge** と **enormous** の使い分け: これらの語に意味による実質的な違いはなく, たいていの場合両語とも使用可能だが, **huge** は物理的な大きさ, 特に物の一片[部分]について用いられることが若干多い. ◆a *huge* chunk/pile/boulder/slab/mound/expanse (非常に大きな塊/山積み/岩/厚板/盛り土/空間). **enormous** は感情・重要性・可能性などの程度について用いられることが若干多い. ◆*enormous* fun/pleasure/importance/significance/flexibility/scope (非常に大きな楽しみ/喜び/重要性/意義/適応性/視野).

giant [名詞の前で] 非常に大きい, 巨大な; (大きな寸法[重要性]を表して)大…, オオ… ◇The market is controlled by *giant* corporations which function as monopolies. 市場は独占企業として機能する巨大企業によって支配されている ◇*Giant* clams may grow to be a metre long. オオジャコガイは全長1mにまで成長することがある

tremendous (印象[称賛, 共感]を表して)ものすごく[とてつもなく]大きい ◇The noise of bombs, guns and engines was *tremendous*. 爆弾や銃器, エンジンの爆音がすさまじかった ◇A *tremendous* amount of work has gone into the project. 多大な労力がそのプロジェクトにつぎ込まれている ◇He has been under *tremendous* pressure recently. 最近彼はとてつもない重圧を受けている

gigantic (ややインフォーマル) (物理的に)非常に大きい, 巨大な ◇At the top of the steps stood eight *gigantic* marble columns. 階段をのぼり切ったそこに巨大な大理石の柱が8本立っていた ◇The problem can assume *gigantic* proportions if left untreated. 放置すればその問題は大きくなる可能性がある

immense (程度が)ものすごく[とてつもなく]大きい, 膨大[莫大]な ◇To my *immense* relief, he didn't notice my mistake. すっかり安堵の胸を撫で下ろしたのだが, 彼は私の間違いに気づかなかった ◇The benefits are *immense*. その利点は測り知れない ❶ *immense* は特に感情や性質, とりわけ肯定的なものについて用いられる. ◆*immense* satisfaction/relief/pleasure/respect (非常に大きな満足/安心/喜び/尊敬の念). ◆*immense* prestige/popularity/charm/importance/significance/value (非常に大きな名声/人気/魅力/重要性/意義/価値).
▶**immensity** 名 [U] ◇We were overwhelmed by the sheer *immensity* of the task. 私たちはただただその任務の重大さに圧倒された

monumental [名詞の前で] (ややフォーマル) ものすごく[とて

humid, humour, hungry

つもなく]大きい, 重大[甚大]な ◇This book is a work of *monumental* significance. この本は大変意義のある作品だ ◇She had made one *monumental* error of judgement. 彼女は一つとてつもない判断ミスを犯していた ❶ *monumental* は特に非常に愚かで深刻な結果をもたらす行為について用いられる。◆ an act of *monumental* folly (とてつもなく愚かな行為). ◆ *monumental* incompetence (まったくの無能). ◆ a *monumental* error/disaster/cock-up (とてつもない大失敗/大災害/大混乱).

colossal 非常に大きい, 巨大[膨大, 莫大]な ◇Outside stands a *colossal* statue of Queen Victoria. 外にビクトリア女王の巨大な彫像が立っている ◇They have spent a *colossal* amount of money on construction. 建設に巨額の資金が費やされている

humid 形 ☞ HOT

humid・sultry・stuffy・steamy・stifling・airless
暑くて, 空気がさわやかでないことを表す
【類語訳】湿気の多い, 湿潤な, じめじめする, 蒸し暑い, 多湿の, 息苦しい

文型&コロケーション
▶ a humid/ sultry/ stuffy/ steamy/ stifling **atmosphere**
▶ humid/ sultry/ steamy/ stifling **heat**
▶ humid/ sultry/ stuffy **air**
▶ a stuffy/ an airless **room**
▶ humid **weather**/ the **weather** is sultry
▶ hot and humid/ sultry/ stuffy/ steamy
▶ It's stuffy/ stifling **in here**!

humid (空気・気候が)湿気の多い, 湿潤な, じめじめする ◇These ferns will grow best in a *humid* atmosphere. これらのシダはじめじめした環境で最もよく育つのです ◇The island is hot and *humid* in the summer. 夏になるとその島は高温多湿になる ☞ **humidity** (MOISTURE)

sultry (天候・空気が)むし暑い, うだるような暑さの ◇We went out into the still, *sultry* heat of the afternoon. 私たちは空気のよどんだ午後のむし暑さの中に出て行った

stuffy (部屋・建物が)風通しの悪い, むっとする, むし暑い ◇It gets really *stuffy* in here in summer. 夏この中は本当にむっとするんだ

steamy (水蒸気[湯気]の立ちこめた; むし風呂のような, 多湿の ◇It was cold in London compared with the *steamy* heat of Tokyo. むし風呂のように暑い東京に比べるとロンドンは肌寒かった

stifling (暑くて・風通しが悪くて)息苦しい, むっとする ◇It's *stifling* in here — can we open a window?'「この中は息苦しいね—窓を開けられるかい」

airless (書き言葉)空気のよどんだ, 風通しの悪い, むっとする ◇The night was hot and *airless*. その夜はむし暑かった

humour (英) (米 humor) 名

humour・wit・banter・comedy・funny side
話や文のおかしみ, 話や文におかしみを与える要素
【類語訳】面白み, ユーモア, 茶目っ気, 機知, 機転

文型&コロケーション
▶ gentle/ wry humour/ wit/ comedy
▶ caustic/ sardonic humour/ wit

▶ dry/ deadpan/ black humour/ comedy
▶ to see/ appreciate the humour/ comedy/ funny side of sth

humour (英) (米 **humor**) [U] 面白み, ユーモア, 茶目っ気; ユーモアを解する力 ◇She ignored his feeble attempt at *humour*. 彼はかすかにおどけて見せようとしたが, 彼女は無視した ◇She has her very own brand of *humour*. 彼女には独特の茶目っ気がある ◇He has a good *sense of humour*. 彼はユーモアのセンスがいい ☞ **humorous** (FUNNY)

wit [U, 単数で] (話・文に見られる)機知, 機転 ◇a woman of *wit* and intelligence 機知と知性を備えた女性 ◇a book full of the *wit and wisdom* of his 30 years in politics 彼の政界での30年を描いた機知と英知に富んだ本 ◇He was blessed with great charm and a quick *wit*. 彼は大きな魅力と機転の速さに恵まれていた ☞ **witty** (FUNNY)

banter [U] (うちとけた)冗談の言い合い ◇She engages in friendly *banter* with her customers. 彼女は得意先の人たちと親しげに冗談を言い合う

comedy [U] (面白みを与える)喜劇的要素 ◇He didn't appreciate the *comedy* of the situation. 彼は事態のこっけいさがピンとこなかった ☞ **comic** (FUNNY)

'**funny side** [単数で] (ややインフォーマル, 話し言葉) (状況の)喜劇的側面 ◇Try and see the *funny side* of it. その笑える側面を見分けてごらん

hungry 形

hungry・starving・ravenous
人や動物が食べ物を食べたがっている[食べる必要がある]こと
【類語訳】空腹な, 飢えている, ひもじい

hungry → starving → ravenous

文型&コロケーション
▶ hungry/ starving **for** sth
▶ hungry/ starving **children/ people**
▶ **absolutely** starving/ ravenous

hungry 空腹な; 飢えた, ひもじい; 何か食べたくなるような ◇I'm really *hungry*. 腹ぺこだ ◇Is anyone getting *hungry*? お腹が減ってきている人はいますか ◇All this talk of food is making me *hungry*. こんなに食べ物の話ばかりしてたら何か食べたくなってきたよ ◇There were eight *hungry mouths* to feed at home. 家で腹を空かせて待っている家族が8人いた ◇Thousands are *going hungry* because of the failure of this year's harvest. 今年の凶作で何千もの人々が飢えることになるだろう ◇All this gardening is *hungry* work. この庭仕事をずっとしてるとおなかが減るね

▶ **the hungry** 名 [複数扱い] ◇Shipments of flour were sent to *feed the hungry*. 飢えに苦しむ人々への食料として小麦粉が数度にわたって送られた

▶ **hungrily** 副 ◇They gazed *hungrily* at the display of food. 彼らは陳列されている食べ物をひもじそうに見つめた

starving 飢餓に苦しむ, 餓死しそうな ◇These pictures of *starving* children are very upsetting. これらの飢餓に苦しむ子どもたちの写真にはとても胸が痛くなる ❶インフォーマルな話し言葉では starving は単に「とても腹の減った」を意味

することがある. ◆When's dinner? I'm *starving*! (夕飯はいつ. 腹ぺこだよ.)
▶**the starving** 名 [複数扱い] ◇Food was flown in to help *the starving*. 飢餓に苦しむ人々を救済するため食糧が空輸された

ravenous (人が)とても腹の減った；(動物が)腹を空かせてどう猛な；(空腹・飢えが)とてつもない ◇What's for lunch? I'm absolutely *ravenous*. 昼食は何. ほんと腹ぺこだよ ◇Go back in your imagination to the days when huge, *ravenous beasts* ruled the planet. 巨大でどう猛な獣が地球を支配していた時代にさかのぼって想像してみなさい ◇He has a *ravenous* appetite. 彼の食欲はとてつもない ❶人について言う場合, ravenousはたいていの場合, インフォーマルな話し言葉で連結副詞の後でのみ用いられる. 動物[人]の空腹状況について言う場合は, フォーマルな書き言葉で名詞の前で用いられる.

hurry 動

hurry・rush・dash・fly・run・hasten・get a move on
時間がないのですばやく行ったり, したりする
【類語訳】急ぐ, 慌てる, 急行する, 殺到する, 焦る, 急かす, 突進する, 疾走する, 走る

文型&コロケーション
▶ to hurry/ rush/ run/ hasten **to do sth**
▶ to hurry/ fly/ run **along**
▶ to rush/ dash **off**
▶ to hurry/ rush a **meal**

hurry [自, 他] 急ぐ, 早くする；急がせる, 早くさせる；(特定の方向に)急いで[早く]行く ◇You'll have to *hurry* if you want to catch the train. その電車に乗りたいなら急がないといけないよ ◇I wish the bus would *hurry up* and come. バスが早く来ないかな ◇*Hurry* up! We're going to be late. 急げ, 遅れるぞ ◇The kids *hurried* to open their presents. 子どもたちは急いでプレゼントを開けた ◇A good meal should never be *hurried*. おいしい食事は急いで食べるべきではない ◇I don't want to *hurry* you but we close in twenty minutes. お客様を急がせたくはございませんが, 当店はあと20分で閉店です ◇He picked up his bags and *hurried* across the courtyard. 彼はかばんを手に取ると中庭を急いで突っ切った ❶話し言葉ではhurryは特に人に何かを急いでさせる場合に, to 不定詞の代わりandを伴い別の動詞と共に用いられることがある. ◆*Hurry* and open your present — I want to see what it is. (早くプレゼントを開けてみな—何なのか見たいんだよ). ☞ **hurried** (QUICK)

▶**hurry** 名 [単数形で] ◇Take your time — there's no *hurry*. 時間をかけてかまわないよ—急ぐことないからね ◇What's the *hurry*? The train doesn't leave for an hour. 何を急いでいるの. 電車は1時間は発車しないよ ◇Sorry, I haven't got time to do it now — I'm *in a hurry*. すみません, 今はそれをする時間がありません—急いでるんです ◇Why are you in such a *hurry* to sell? どうしてそんなに急いで売るの

rush [自, 他] (度を超して)急ぐ, 慌てる；性急に[軽率に]…する, (人を)急がす, 焦らせる ◇We've got plenty of time; there's no need to *rush*. 時間はたっぷりある. だから慌てる必要はないよ ◇I've been *rushing around* all day, trying to get everything done. 私は全部終わらせようとして一日中走り回っていた ◇People *rushed* to buy shares in the company. 人々はその会社の株を買いにどっとつめかけた ◇We don't want to *rush into* having a baby. 私たちは急いで子どもを作りたくない ◇Don't *rush* me. I need time to think about it. せきたてないで. 私には考える時間が必要なの ◇I'm not going to *be rushed into* anything. 私は何事にも追い立てられて動くつもりはないよ

▶**rush** 名 [単数で] ◇Shoppers made a *rush for* the exits. 買い物客が出口に殺到した ◇I can't stop — I'm *in a rush*. 止まらない—急いでるんだ ◇What's the *rush*? 何を慌てているの ◇I'll let you have the book back tomorrow.' '*There's no rush.*' 「明日には君にその本を返すよ」「急がなくていいよ」

dash [自] 《ふつう副詞や前置詞と共に》(急いで)駆けて行く, 急行[突進, 疾走]する ◇She *dashed* off to keep an appointment. 彼女は約束を守るために急いで出て行った ◇I must *dash* (= leave quickly), I'm late. 《インフォーマル》すぐに行かなきゃ, 遅れちゃう

▶**dash** 名 [単数で] ◇When the doors opened, there was a *mad dash* for seats. ドアが開くと, 人々は気が狂ったように急いで席を取りに走った ◇We waited for the police to leave, then *made a dash for it* (= left quickly in order to escape). 私たちは警察が出て行くのを待ってから, 一目散に逃げ出した

fly [自] 《ふつう副詞や前置詞と共に》(急いで)飛んで行く, ぱっと動く, さっと通り過ぎる ◇The train was *flying* along. 電車が横をさっと通り過ぎて行った ◇She gasped and her hand *flew* to her mouth. 彼女ははっと息をのんで慌てて口に手をやった ◇It's late — I must *fly* (= leave quickly). 《インフォーマル》遅くなった—すぐに行かないと

ノート **dashとflyの使い分け**：dashは必ず人について用いる. ×The train was *dashing* along. flyは物について用いることが多い. 両語ともI must dash/fly(すぐに行かなきゃ)の句でインフォーマルな場面で用いられることがある.

run [自] 《副詞や前置詞と共に》(急いで)走る ◇I've spent the whole day *running* around after the kids. 私は子どもたちの後を追いかけて一日中走り回っていた

hasten [他] 《ややフォーマル, 特に書き言葉》急いで[慌てて]言う[…する] ◇She saw his frown and *hastened* to explain. 彼女は彼のしかめっ面を見て, 慌てて弁明した ◇He has been described as a 'charmless bore' — not by me, *I hasten to add*. 彼は魅力のない退屈な男と言われている——一言言っておくけど, 私が言ったんじゃないよ ❶文語でhastenには「急いで行う」以外に「急いで行く」の意味もある. ◆We *hastened* back to Rome. 《文語》私たちはローマに急いで戻った. ☞ **haste** (SPEED)

get a 'move on [行他] 《インフォーマル, 話し言葉》急ぐ ◇*Get a move on*! We'll miss the bus. 急ごう. バスに乗り遅れるぞ ◇We'd better *get a move on* if we don't want to be late. 遅れたくないなら急いだほうがいい

hurt 動

1 hurt・upset・wound・distress・break sb's heart・sadden・sting・pain
人を悲しませたり, 腹立たせたりすることを表す
【類語訳】傷つける, 落胆させる, 困らせる, 悩ませる, 怒らせる, 責めさいなむ

文型&コロケーション
▶ It hurt/ upset/ distressed/ saddened/ pained **me to** see/ think/ know...

▶It breaks my heart to see/ think/ know...
▶It hurt/ upset/ distressed/ saddened/ pained me that...
▶to hurt/ wound sb's feelings
▶to upset/ distress yourself
▶to not want/ not mean to hurt/ upset/ wound/ distress sb
▶to really hurt sb/ upset sb/ wound sb/ distress sb/ break sb's heart/ sting sb/ pain sb
▶to hurt/ upset/ wound/ distress/ sting/ pain sb deeply

hurt [他, 自] (人の気持ちを)傷つける, 悲しませる, 落胆させる ◇I didn't want to *hurt* his feelings. 私は彼の気持ちを傷つけたくなかった ◇It *hurt* me to think that he would lie to me. 彼が私にうそをつくだろうと思うと悲しくなった ◇What really *hurt* was that he never answered my letter. 何よりつらかったかと言えば, 彼が私の手紙に1度も返事をよこさなかったことだ ☞ **hurt** (DISTRESS), **hurt** (UPSET), **hurtful** (MEAN 形)

upset [他] (人・自分を)悲しませる, 困らせる, 悩ませる, 腹立たせる ◇This decision is likely to *upset* a lot of people. この決定で多くの人が困るだろう ◇Try not to let him *upset* you. 彼のことで悩まないようにしてください ◇Don't *upset* yourself about it. そのことで腹を立てないでください ◇It *upset* him that nobody had bothered to tell him about it. 誰も彼にそのことをわざわざ教えようとはしなかったことが彼には気に入らなかった ☞ **upset** (UPSET), **upsetting** (PAINFUL 2)

[ノート] **hurt**と**upset**の使い分け: **hurt**は, 好意を感じている人[信じていた考え]が悲しい思いをさせることを言う. **upset**も同じように用いることがあるが, feelingsを目的語に取らないし, 目的語なしで用いることもない. ×*upset* his feelings. ×What really *upset* was... **hurt**は不可だが, **upset**は人を怒らせたり叫ばせたりするほど困らせたり怒らせたりする行為や人について用いることもある. **upset**される状況に人がある程度自らもっていく場合もあるので, **upset** yourselfや, let sb upset youとは言える. ただし ×Don't *hurt* yourself about it. ×Try not to let him *hurt* you. とは言わない.

wound [他, しばしば受身で]《文章》(人の気持ちを)傷つける, 悲しませる ◇She felt deeply *wounded* by his cruel remarks. 彼女は彼のひどい言葉に深く傷ついた
　▶**wounded** [形] She didn't know how to soothe his *wounded* pride. 彼女は彼の傷ついたプライドをどう癒せばよいかわからなかった

distress [他]《ややフォーマル》(人を)非常に悲しませる[困らせる], 思い悩ませる ◇It was clear that the letter had deeply *distressed* her. その手紙に彼女が深く心を痛めていたことは明らかだった ◇Don't *distress* yourself. 思い悩まないでね ❶ distressはupsetよりも強意的かつフォーマルな語で, annoy (腹立たせる)の意味は持たない. ☞ **distress** (DISTRESS), **distressed** (UPSET), **distressing** (PAINFUL 2)

break sb's 'heart [taボ] (立ち直れないほど)心を引き裂く, 胸を張り裂けさせる ◇She broke his heart when she called off the engagement. 彼女は婚約を破棄して彼の心を引き裂いた ◇It *breaks my heart* to see you like this. このような形で君と会うとは胸が張り裂けそうだ

sadden [他, しばしば受身で][進行形なし]《フォーマル》(人を)悲しませる ◇We were deeply *saddened* by the news of her death. 私たちは彼女の死の知らせに深く悲しんだ ◇It *saddened* her that people could be so cruel. 人がそれほど残酷になれることに彼女は胸を痛めた

sting [他][進行形なし]《書き言葉》(人を)怒らせる, 責めさい

なむ, 苦しめる, 駆り立てる ◇He was *stung* by their criticism. 彼は彼らの批判に苦しい思いをした ◇Their cruel remarks *stung her into* action. 彼らのひどい言葉は彼女を行動に駆り立てた

pain [他]《進行形なし》《フォーマル》(人を)悲しませる, 心を痛めさせる, 苦しめる ◇She was deeply *pained* by the accusation. 彼女はその非難にひどく心を痛めた ◇It *pains* me to see you like this. このような形で君と会うとはとてもつらい ☞ **pain** (DISTRESS), **painful** (PAINFUL 2)
　▶**pained** [形] She looked at him with a *pained* expression. 彼女は悲痛な表情で彼を見た

2 hurt・ache・burn・sting・tingle・itch・tickle・throb

体の部位が不快に感じることを表す
【類語訳】痛む, うずく, かゆい, くすぐる

tingle	hurt	burn
itch	ache	throb
tickle	sting	

[文型&コロケーション]
▶your eyes hurt/ ache/ burn/ sting/ itch
▶your skin hurts/ burns/ stings/ tingles/ itches
▶your flesh hurts/ burns/ stings/ tingles
▶your head hurts/ aches/ throbs
▶your stomach/ tummy hurts/ aches
▶to really hurt/ ache/ burn/ sting/ tingle/ itch/ tickle/ throb
▶to hurt/ ache/ sting/ tingle/ itch/ tickle/ throb slightly/ a bit
▶to hurt/ ache/ sting/ itch badly/ a lot
▶It hurts/ stings/ tingles/ itches/ tickles.

hurt [自] (体の部位が)痛む; (動作が)痛みを伴う ◇My feet *hurt*. 私は足が痛かった ◇Ouch! That *hurt*! あいたっ. それ, 痛いよ ◇It *hurts* when I bend my knee. ひざを曲げると痛い ☞ **hurt** (INJURE)

ache [自] (絶えず鈍く)痛む, うずく ◇I'm *aching* all over. 私は体中が痛い ◇Her eyes *ached* from lack of sleep. 彼女は睡眠不足で目が痛かった ☞ **ache** (PAIN)

burn [自] (体の部位が)燃えるように熱い, ひりひり痛む ◇Your forehead's *burning*. Have you got a fever? おでこがものすごく熱いよ. 熱があるんじゃない ◇Her cheeks *burned* with embarrassment. 彼女のほおは恥ずかしさで燃えるように熱かった ☞ **burning** (HOT)

sting [自, 他] (体の部位に)刺す[しみる]ような痛みを与える, つん[ちくっ]と痛ませる; (体の部位が)刺す[しみる]ように痛む, つん[ちくっ]と痛む ◇I put some antiseptic on the cut and it *stung* for a moment. 切り傷に消毒液を塗ると一瞬刺すような痛みが走った ◇My eyes were *stinging* from the smoke. 私の目は煙でしみていた ◇Tears *stung* her eyes. 彼女は涙が目にしみた

tingle [自] (体の部位が)ちくちく[ひりひり]痛む ◇The cold air made her face *tingle*. 冷たい空気に彼女の顔はひりひりした ◇You may get a *tingling* sensation in your fingers. 指にちくちくする感じがあるかもしれない

itch [自] (皮膚が)かゆい; (皮膚に)かゆさを感じさせる ◇I *itch* all over. 私は全身がかゆい ◇Does the rash *itch*? その発疹はかゆいのか ◇This sweater really *itches*. このセーターは本当にかゆい
　▶**itch** [名] [C] ◇to get/have an *itch* かゆくなる

tickle [他, 自] (体の敏感な部位を)くすぐる, ちくちく[むずむず]させる；(体の敏感な部位が)くすぐったく感じる, ちくちく[むずむず]する ◇His beard was *tickling* her cheek. 彼のあごひげが彼女のほおにちくちく当たっていた ◇My throat *tickles*. のどがひりひりする

throb (-bb-) [自] (体の部位が)ずきずき痛む ◇His head *throbbed* painfully. 彼の頭はずきずきとひどく痛んだ

hysterical 形 ☞ RESTLESS

hysterical・frantic・worked up・delirious・panicky・panic-stricken・beside yourself・overwrought・incoherent

非常に心配して[おびえて, 興奮して, 気分が悪くて]自分を抑制できない[明晰な思考ができない]
【類語訳】ヒステリックな, 半狂乱の, 狂乱した, 取り乱した, 逆上した, 狂喜した, 慌てふためいた, 右往左往した, ぴりぴりした

worked up overwrought	panicky	hysterical frantic panic-stricken beside yourself delirious incoherent

文型&コロケーション

▶ hysterical/ frantic/ delirious/ beside yourself/ incoherent **with** anger, rage, joy, etc.
▶ hysterical/ frantic/ worked up/ panicky **about** sth
▶ **to become** hysterical/ frantic/ worked up/ delirious/ incoherent
▶ **to get** hysterical/ frantic/ worked up
▶ **almost** hysterical/ frantic/ delirious/ beside yourself/ incoherent

hysterical ヒステリックな, 理性を失った, 感情的になった ◇Calm down, you're getting *hysterical*. 落ち着いて, ヒステリックになってるよ ◇Her screams broke into *hysterical* laughter. 彼女の悲鳴は突然ヒステリックな笑い声になった ☞ **hysteria** (FEAR)
▸ **hysterically** 副 ◇to laugh/cry/scream/sob *hysterically* ヒステリックに笑う/泣く/叫ぶ/泣きじゃくる

frantic (極度の恐怖・不安で)半狂乱の, 狂乱した, 狂気じみた ◇I've been almost *frantic* with worry for the last half-hour. この30分間私は不安でほとんど半狂乱だった ◇Let's go back. Your parents must be getting *frantic* by now. 帰ろう. 今ごろ君の両親は半狂乱になっているに違いない ◇The children are *driving me frantic* (= making me very annoyed). 子どもたちのせいで私は気が狂いそうだ

,worked 'up [名詞の前では用いない] (《インフォーマル, 話し言葉》非常に興奮した, 取り乱した, 逆上した ◇There's no point in getting *all worked up* about it. そんなことですっかり逆上しても仕方ないよ ◇He was silly to *get himself* so *worked up*. そんなに取り乱すなんて彼は愚かだった

delirious (発熱で)うなされた, うわごとを言う；(喜びで)狂喜した ◇He became *delirious* and couldn't recognize people. 彼はうなされるようになって誰が誰だかわからなくなった ◇The crowds were *delirious* with joy. 群衆は狂喜した ☞ **feverish** (HOT)

panicky 《インフォーマル》(心配で)慌てふためいた, じっとしていられない；あたふたした様子の ◇He was feeling a bit *panicky* about the presentation. 彼はプレゼンテーションのことで少しそわそわしていた ◇I got a *panicky* phone call from Emma yesterday. 昨日私はエマからあたふたした様子の電話を受けた ☞ **panic** (FEAR), **panic** (PANIC)

'panic-stricken パニックに陥った, 右往左往した, 恐怖で凍りついた ◇He sounded *panic-stricken* on the phone. 彼は電話口でパニックに陥っているように聞こえた ◇Jack caught a glimpse of her *panic-stricken* face. ジャックは彼女の恐怖で凍りついた顔をちらっと見た

ノート **panicky** と **panic-stricken** の使い分け：pan-ic-stricken のほうが強意的でより深刻な感情を指す. a bit/ slightly/very panicky とは言えるが panic-stricken にはこのような修飾語句は付かない. panic-stricken は身体に影響を与える感情を表し, panicky は内に秘められた感情を表すことが多い. ◆I was feeling quite *panicky*. (私は内心すっかり慌てふためいていた). ◆I was so *panic-stricken* that I could hardly speak. (私はパニックに陥ってほとんど話すことができなかった).

be'side yourself 行動 (不安[恐怖, 怒り, 興奮など]で)我を忘れて, 取り乱して ◇Bella drew her breath in sharply, almost *beside herself* with rage. ベラは怒りでほとんど我を忘れて, 激しく息を吸い込んだ

overwrought 《ややフォーマル》(不安・いら立ちで)ぴりぴりした；極度に緊張した ◇She was still a little *overwrought*. 彼女はまだ少しぴりぴりしていた

incoherent (感情的になって)言葉がまとまらない, 取り乱した, 錯乱した ◇She broke off, *incoherent* with anger. 彼女は怒りで取り乱して急に話をやめた 反意 **coherent**

I i

idea 名

1 idea・thought・concept・notion・image・prospect・abstraction・picture

考えている[頭に浮かんだ]こと

【類語訳】考え, 思いつき, アイデア, 観念, 概念, 信念, イメージ, 見通し, 予想, 抽象概念, 心象

文型&コロケーション

- an idea/ a thought/ a concept/ a notion **about** sth
- the idea/ thought/ concept/ notion **that...**
- an **interesting** idea/ thought/ concept/ notion/ picture
- an **exciting** idea/ thought/ concept/ prospect/ picture
- a **clear** idea/ thought/ concept/ notion/ image/ picture
- a/ an **new/ original** idea/ thought/ concept/ notion
- a **basic** idea/ concept/ notion/ image/ picture
- an **abstract** idea/ concept/ notion/ image
- to **have** an idea/ a thought/ a concept/ a notion/ an image/ a picture
- to **give sb** an idea/ a thought/ a notion
- to **conjure up** an idea/ an image/ a picture
- to **understand/ grasp** an idea/ a concept/ a notion/ an abstraction
- to **discuss/ consider/ explore** an idea/ a concept/ a notion
- an idea/ a thought/ a notion **strikes** sb
- an idea/ a thought/ an image/ a picture **forms**

idea [C] 考え, 思いつき, アイデア ◇That's a brilliant *idea*! それは素晴らしい考えだ ◇The party was Jane's *idea*. そのパーティーはジェーンの発案だった ◇The *idea* never crossed my mind. その考えが頭をよぎったことはない ◇It seemed like a good *idea* at the time. その時はいい考えのように思えた ◇I like the *idea* of living in a boat. 船上での生活という考えはいいと思います ◇He already had an *idea for* his next novel. 彼にはすでに次の小説の構想があった ◇Her family wanted her to go to college, but she **had other ideas**. 家族は彼女に大学に行ってほしかったが, 彼女には別の考えがあった ◇The latest *big idea* is to get more women into the construction industry. 最近抱いている大きな考えはもっと多くの女性を建設業に送り込むということだ

thought [C] 考え, 思いつき ◇I don't like the *thought* of you walking home alone. あなたが一人で歩いて帰宅するという考えはよいとは思えません ◇I've just had a *thought*. ちょうど考えが浮かんだところだ ◇What a horrible *thought*! 何てひどい考えなんだ ◇All kinds of *thoughts* raced through her mind. さまざまな考えが彼女の頭の中を駆けめぐった ◇I'd be interested to hear your *thoughts* on the matter. その問題についてのあなたの考えを聞くのは興味深いと思う ◇She tried to put the *thought* out of her mind. 彼女はその考えを頭から追い払おうとした

concept [C]《ややフォーマル》(抽象的な事柄に関する)観念, 概念, 考え ◇We discussed *concepts* such as 'democracy' and 'equality'. 我々は「民主主義」「平等」といった概念について論じた ◇The *concept* of infinity is almost impossible for us to comprehend. 無限という概念は, 私たちにはほとんど理解不能である ☞ **conceptual** (INTELLECTUAL 1)

notion [C]《ややフォーマル》概念, 観念, 考え, 信念 ◇Our political system is based on *notions* of justice and equality. 我々の政治体制は正義と平等の概念に基づいている ◇I had only the vaguest *notion* of what he was like. 彼がどんな人かごくぼんやりとしか知らなかった ❶ notion はふつう, 想像上のものや抽象的な[実際的な]ものについて用いられる. 人や事物について clear notion と言えるが, ×a vivid/imaginative notion とは言えない. ☞ **notional** (SUPPOSED)

image [C] (頭に絵として浮かぶ)イメージ ◇I always had an *image* of her standing by that window gazing out. 窓のそばに立って外を眺めている彼女の姿をいつも心に思い浮かべていた ◇Do human beings think in words or in *images*? 人間は言葉とイメージのどちらで考えるのですか

prospect [単数で] (将来の)考え, 見通し, 予想 ◇Travelling alone around the world is a daunting *prospect*. 世界中を一人旅するのは容易ではなさそうだ ◇The *prospect* of becoming a father filled him with alarm. 父親になるという思いが彼を不安で一杯にした

abstraction [C, U]《フォーマル》(実在の人物[事物, 状況]に基づかない)抽象概念 ◇Ideological *abstractions* are never going to attract many voters. イデオロギーに関する抽象概念は決して多くの有権者たちを引きつけないだろう ◇The increasing *abstraction* of modern art has tended to make it increasingly difficult to interpret. 現代美術の抽象性が高まることで, ますますその解釈が難しくなる傾向にある ☞ **abstract** (INTELLECTUAL 1)

picture [C, ふつう単数で] (頭に絵として浮かぶ)心象, イメージ ◇She had formed a *picture* of what the place would look like and was very disappointed. 彼女はその場所がどんなふうか心に描いてみて, とてもがっかりした

ノート image と picture の使い分け：多くの場合, どちらも用いることができる. だが image は, ある瞬間のある人[物]について心に描く像を表すことが多い. picture はしばしば, 複数の異なる細かなことや短期間に起こる出来事を含めた全体像をより完全に思い浮かべることを表す.

2 idea・instinct・feeling・hunch・inkling・suspicion・intuition・premonition・foreboding

証拠はないが, 物事が真実である[物事が起きつつある]と思う感覚を表す

【類語訳】感じ, 予感, 直感, 勘, 手がかり, 胸騒ぎ

文型&コロケーション

- an idea/ an instinct/ a feeling/ a hunch/ an inkling/ a suspicion/ an intuition/ a premonition/ a foreboding **about** sth
- an idea/ an instinct/ a feeling/ a hunch/ an inkling/ a suspicion/ an intuition/ a premonition/ a foreboding **that...**
- sb's **first** idea/ instinct/ inkling/ suspicion

- a **vague** idea/ feeling/ inkling/ suspicion
- a **gut** instinct/ feeling/ intuition
- to **have** an idea/ an instinct/ a feeling/ a hunch/ an inkling/ a suspicion/ an intuition/ a premonition/ a foreboding
- to **get** the idea/ the feeling/ a hunch/ a premonition
- to **give sb** the idea/ the feeling/ an inkling
- to **follow/ go with** your instinct/ hunch/ intuition
- to **confirm** sb's instinct/ feeling/ hunch/ suspicion/ intuition

idea [単数で] (確信があるわけではないが人・物事について抱く)感じ, 予感 ◇I had an *idea* of where it might be. それがありそうな場所が浮かんだ ◇What gave you the *idea* that he'd be here? あなたはどうして彼がここにいると思ったの ◇I have a pretty *good idea* who might have said that. 誰がそう言ったのか大方察しはついている ◇He hadn't had *the slightest idea* about what had been going on. 彼には何が起きつつあるのかさっぱり見当がつかなかった

instinct [C] (事実[根拠]に基づかない)直感 ◇Her *instincts* about him had been right. 彼に関する彼女の直感は正しかった ◇Marshall's *gut instinct* (= basic instinct) was to turn and run. マーシャルの本能的な直感はくるりと向きを変えて走るというものだった ☞ **instinctive** (NATURAL)

feeling [単数で] (不快な物事を真実であると思う)感じ ◇I had a nasty *feeling* that she was lying to me. 彼女は私に嘘をついているという嫌な感じがした ◇He suddenly had the *feeling* of being followed. 彼は突然, 尾行されている気がした

ノート **instinct** と **feeling** の使い分け: この意味では feeling はふつう, ある特定の不快な物事が真実であるという感覚を指し, instinct はより一般的で, 特定の人[状況]について抱くあらゆる感覚を指し, 肯定的な感覚にも否定的な感覚にも用いられる. ◆Her *instincts* had been right — he was someone who could be trusted. (彼女の勘は正しかった—彼は信頼に値する人だった). ✕Her *feelings* about him had been right.

hunch [C] 《ややインフォーマル》勘 ◇My *hunch* is that the burglars are still in the area. 私の勘では強盗団はまだこの辺りにいる ◇I didn't know for certain — I was just going on a *hunch*. 確証はなかった—私はただ勘で動いていた ❶ hunch は特に, 犯罪や謎の解決策について語るときに用いられる.

inkling [C, ふつう単数で] (起こりつつある[起こそうとしている]事についての)わずかな知識, 手がかり ◇He didn't have the slightest *inkling* of what was going on. どうなっているのか彼にはさっぱりつかめなかった

suspicion [C] (不快な事が真実なのではないかという漠然とした)感じ ◇I had a horrible *suspicion* that we'd come to the wrong station. 私たちは間違った駅に来てしまったのではないかと嫌な気分になった ☞ **suspect** (SUPPOSE)

intuition [C] (理由の説明はできない)直感 ◇I had an *intuition* that something awful was about to happen. 何か恐ろしいことが起きつつあるという直感が働いた ☞ **intuitive** (NATURAL)

premonition [C] 《ややフォーマル, 特に書き言葉》(不快な事が起きつつあるという)予感 ◇a *premonition* of disaster 災害の予感 ◇He had a *premonition* that he would never see her again. 彼は彼女には二度と会わないだろうという予感がした

foreboding [U, C] 《ややフォーマル, 特に書き言葉》(不快[危険]な事が起きつつあるという)予感, 胸騒ぎ ◇The letter filled him with *foreboding*. その手紙に彼は強い胸騒ぎがした ◇He knew from her face that his *forebodings* had been justified. 彼は彼女の表情から彼の予感は正しかったのだと知った

ノート **premonition** と **foreboding** の使い分け: premonition はふつう, 特定の不快な事が起きつつあるという感覚を指す. foreboding は, 正確にどんなものかわからないが, 悪い事が起きつつあるという一般的な感覚を指す.

ideal [形] ☞ BEST, FAVOURITE

ideal・perfect・optimum・just right・tailor-made
特定の人や目的に最もかなっていることを表す
【類語訳】理想の, 理想的な, あつらえ向きの, 最高の, 最適の, ぴったりの

文型&コロケーション
- ideal/ perfect/ just right/ tailor-made **for** sb/ sth
- an ideal/ a perfect **opportunity/ solution/ candidate**
- **absolutely** ideal/ perfect

ideal 理想の, 理想的な, あつらえ向きの ◇This beach is *ideal* for children. このビーチは子どもたちにはぴったりだ ◇His apartment would be an *ideal* place to stay. 彼のアパートは滞在するのに絶好の場所でしょう ◇As a solution to the problem it was far from *ideal*. それはその問題の解決策としては程遠かった

ideally [副] ◇They're *ideally* suited to each other. それらは互いにうまく適合している[彼らはお似合いのカップルだ] ◇*Ideally*, I'd like to live in New York, but that's not possible at the moment. 理想を言えば, ニューヨークに住みたいが, 当面は無理だ

perfect 理想の, 理想的な, あつらえ向きの ◇It was a *perfect* day for a picnic. ピクニックには言うことなしの日だった ◇The location of the cottage makes it *perfect* for touring. コテージの場所は小旅行には申し分のないものだ ◇'Will 2.30 be OK for you?' '*Perfect*, thanks.' 「2時半でいいかい」「ばっちりだよ, ありがとう」

ノート **ideal** と **perfect** の使い分け: 意味は同じだが, 結びつきに多少違いがある. ideal day for sth と言えば, 何かに非常に都合のいい日を指す. perfect day for sth と言えば, 何かにとても天気のいい日を指す. perfect には, ideal より少しインフォーマルな感じもある.

optimum [名詞の前で] (可能な限り)最高の, 最適な ◇We aim for *optimum* efficiency in all our operations. 我々はどの事業でも最高の効率を目指します

the optimum [名] [単数で] ◇For efficient fuel consumption a speed of 60 mph is about *the optimum*. 効率的な燃料消費には時速60マイルがほぼ最適です

just 'right [フレーズ] 《話し言葉》(人・物事に)ぴったりの, ちょうどよい, 最適の ◇That coat should be *just right* for Jenny. そのコートはジェニーにぴったりでしょう ◇She adjusted the seasoning until it was *just right*. 彼女はちょうどよくなるまで味付けを調節した

,tailor-'made (特定の人・物事に)最適の, ぴったりの ◇We can offer you a *tailor-made* financial package to suit your needs. あなたのニーズにぴったり合う金融パッケージをご用意できます

identity 名

identity・self・individuality・uniqueness
他とは異なる性質や特徴、他とは異なっていること
【類語訳】個性、独自性、独特さ、アイデンティティー、自己、自分

文型&コロケーション
▶ **human** identity/ individuality/ uniqueness
▶ to **lack** identity/ individuality/ uniqueness
▶ to **express/ lose** your identity/ individuality/ uniqueness
▶ to **retain/ maintain** your identity/ individuality
▶ a **sense of** identity/ self/ individuality/ uniqueness
▶ an **expression of** identity/ the self/ individuality

identity [C, U] 個性、独自性、アイデンティティー ◇a sense of national/cultural/personal/group *identity* 国民性／文化的アイデンティティー／個人のアイデンティティー／集団の独自性の意識 ◇The organization has no clear *corporate identity*. その企業には明確なコーポレートアイデンティティーがない ◇The company forged its own *identity* by producing specialist vehicles. その会社は特殊車両の製造によって独自性を築いた

self [U] (または **the self** [単数で]) 《フォーマル》自己、自分 ◇Many people living in institutions have lost their sense of *self*. 施設で暮らしている多くの人々が自分で自分のことがわからなくなっている ◇the inner *self* (= a person's emotional and spiritual character) 内なる自己 ◇Such problems stem from deep insecurity and a lack of confidence in *the self*. そうした問題は強い不安と自分に対する自信のなさから生じる ☞ **self** (PERSONALITY), **ego** (MIND)

individuality [U] 個性 ◇She expresses her *individuality* through her clothes. 彼女は服装によって個性を表現する ◇The plot is credible but the characters lack *individuality*. 筋は現実味があるが、登場人物が個性に欠けている ☞ **individual** (UNIQUE), **originality** (INSPIRATION)

uniqueness [U] 独自性、独特さ ◇The author stresses the *uniqueness* of the individual. その作家は個人の独自性を強調する ☞ **unique** (UNIQUE)

ignorance 名

ignorance・innocence・inexperience・naivety・incomprehension
物事を知らない[理解していない]状態
【類語訳】無知、無邪気さ、経験不足、未熟さ、世間知らず

文型&コロケーション
▶ ignorance/ innocence/ naivety **about** sth
▶ **in** your ignorance/ innocence/ inexperience/ naivety
▶ **through** ignorance/ inexperience
▶ **complete/ total** ignorance/ innocence/ incomprehension
▶ **youthful** ignorance/ innocence/ inexperience/ naivety
▶ to **betray/ show** (your) ignorance/ inexperience
▶ to **take advantage of** sb's ignorance/ innocence/ inexperience/ naivety

ignorance [U, 単数で] 《時にけなして》知らないこと、無知 ◇There is widespread *ignorance* about the disease. その病気については広く知られていない ◇I remained in blissful *ignorance* of what was going on. のんきなことだが私は何が起こっているのか知らないままだった ◇Children often behave badly *out of ignorance*. 子どもはしばしば無知ゆえに行儀の悪いことをする 反語 **knowledge** (KNOWLEDGE), **knowledge** (AWARENESS)

innocence [U, 単数で] 《ほめて》(世間知らずの)純真さ、無邪気さ ◇The story is about a child's *loss of innocence*. それは子どもの純真さの喪失についての物語である ◇There was a touching *innocence* about the child's request. その子の願いはいじらしいほど無邪気なものだった ☞ **innocent** (NAIVE)

inexperience [U] 経験[知識]不足、未熟さ ◇I'm afraid that in this instance the player's *inexperience* showed. 残念ながら今回はその選手の未熟さが露呈してしまったのではないか 反語 **experience** (KNOWLEDGE), ☞ **inexperienced** (NAIVE)

naivety (または **naïvety**) [U, 単数で] 《しばしばけなして》(人生経験・知識・分別に欠けた)単純さ、世間知らず ◇They laughed at the *naivety* of his suggestion. 彼らは彼の提案の単純さをあざ笑った ◇She showed a certain *naivety* in going to the press about the matter. 彼女はその問題に関してマスコミに出た際に世間知らずなところを見せてしまった ☞ **naive** (NAIVE)

incomprehension [U] 理解しないこと、無理解 ◇His attempts to warn them were met with *incomprehension* and sometimes ridicule. 彼は彼らに警告しようとしたが、理解されず、時として嘲笑された

ignorant 形

ignorant・illiterate・untrained・uneducated・uninformed・clueless
人が知識がないことや教育[教養]がないことを表す
【類語訳】知らない、無知な、読み書きのできない、非識字の、無教養な、無学の

文型&コロケーション
▶ ignorant/ uninformed/ clueless **about** sth
▶ ignorant/ illiterate/ untrained/ uneducated/ uninformed/ clueless **people**
▶ an ignorant/ uninformed **comment**
▶ **completely** ignorant/ illiterate/ untrained/ uneducated/ uninformed/ clueless
▶ **totally** ignorant/ illiterate/ uneducated/ uninformed/ clueless
▶ **largely** ignorant/ illiterate/ untrained/ uneducated/ uninformed

ignorant 《けなして》知らない、無知な ◇At that time I was young and *ignorant*, with little experience of the world. 当時の私は若くて無知で人生経験がほとんどなかった ◇You should never make your students feel *ignorant*. 自分が無知だと生徒が思うようにしてはいけない ◇Too many politicians are *ignorant* about the issues involved. 関連のある問題について知らない政治家が多すぎる ❶多くの場合、人に対して ignorant と言うのは失礼である。反語 **knowledgeable** (INFORMED)

illiterate (人が)読み書きのできない、非識字の；(文章・手紙が)無学さを示す、無教養な ◇A large percentage of the rural population was *illiterate*. 農村人口の大部分が読み書きできなかった ◇Many of the application forms we received were virtually *illiterate*. 我々が

❶ illiterate は名詞・副詞の後に置いて「(ある分野について)よく知らない、疎い」という意味でも用いることができる。◆Even if you're *computer illiterate* you should be able to follow these simple instructions. (たとえコンピューターに疎くても、これらの簡単な指示に従うことはできるはずだ)。 反意 **literate** ❶ literate は「読み書きができる」の意味。

untrained (仕事・技術上の)訓練をされていない ◆It's unreasonable to expect *untrained* workers to achieve spectacular results. 訓練を受けていない労働者に目覚しい成果を上げろと言っても無理な話だ ◆The troops were *untrained in* guerrilla warfare. その軍隊はゲリラ戦の訓練を積んでいなかった 反意 **trained**, ☞ **train** (TRAIN 1)

uneducated (正式な)教育を受けていない、無学な ◆We're trying to work with a largely *uneducated* workforce. 我々は大部分が教育を受けていない労働者と共に働こうと努力しているところです 反意 **educated** (INFORMED)

uninformed 知らない、無知の、無知さを示す ◆The public is largely *uninformed* about this disease. 大衆のほとんどがこの病気について知らされていない ◆*Uninformed* criticism certainly will not help us solve the problem. 無知な批判が我々の問題解決に役立たないのは間違いないだろう 反意 **informed** (INFORMED)

clueless (インフォーマル、けなして) わからない、お手上げの ◆He's completely *clueless* about computers. 彼はコンピューターについてはまったくお手上げだ 反意 **clued-up**, **clued-in** ❶《英》clued-up/《米》clued-in は「よく知っている、よくわかっている」の意味。

ignore 動

ignore・disregard・overlook・turn a blind eye・take no notice・neglect・gloss over sth
物事にきちんと[まったく]注意を払わないこと
【類語訳】無視する、取り合わない、軽視する、大目に見る、見て見ぬ振りをする、目をつぶる、気に留めない、おろそかにする

文型&コロケーション

▶ to ignore/ disregard/ overlook/ turn a blind eye to/ neglect/ gloss over **the fact that...**
▶ to ignore/ disregard/ overlook/ neglect **the importance/ need/ possibility** of sth
▶ to ignore/ disregard sb's **advice/ rules/ wishes**
▶ to ignore/ overlook sb/ sth's **faults/ shortcomings**
▶ to **often** ignore/ disregard/ overlook/ neglect/ gloss over sb/ sth
▶ to **completely/ entirely/ totally/ largely/ generally/ frequently/ deliberately** ignore/ disregard/ overlook/ neglect sth
▶ to **conveniently** ignore/ overlook/ turn a blind eye to/ gloss over sb/ sth
▶ to **consistently** ignore/ overlook/ neglect sth

ignore [他] (注意を払わずに)無視する、取り合わない；(人を見ていない[人がいるのにいない]振りをして)無視する ◆He *ignored* all the 'No Smoking' signs and lit up a cigarette. 彼は「禁煙」の標示をすべて無視してタバコに火をつけた ◆I made a suggestion but they chose to *ignore* it. 私がした提案を彼らは取り合わないことにした ◆We cannot afford to *ignore* their advice. 我々は彼らの忠告を無視するわけにはいかない ◆She *ignored* him and carried on with her work. 彼女は彼を無視して仕事を続けた 反意 **pay attention to sth** (HEAR)

disregard [他]《フォーマル》(考慮せずに)無視する；(取るに足らないものとして)軽視する ◆The board completely *disregarded* my recommendations. 委員会は私の勧告を完全に無視した ◆Safety rules were *disregarded*. 安全規則は軽視された
▷ **disregard** [名] [U] ◆She shows a total *disregard* for other people's feelings. 彼女は他人の感情をまったく無視する

overlook [他]《ややフォーマル》(誤り・間違ったことを)見逃す、大目に見る ◆We could not afford to *overlook* such a serious offence. 我々はそうした重罪を見逃すわけにはいかなかった ◆He's so friendly people are prepared to *overlook* his faults. 彼はとても優しいので、人々は彼の欠点を大目に見てもいいと思っている

turn a blind 'eye 慣用 (起こりつつある悪いことに)見て見ぬ振りをする、目をつぶる ◆The authorities were either unaware of the problem or *turned a blind eye to* it. 当局はその問題に気づいていないか、目をつぶっているかのどちらかだった

ˌtake no ˈnotice フレーズ (いない[存在しない]かのように)気に留めない、取り合わない、無視する ◆*Take no notice of* what he says. 彼の言うことなんかに取り合うな ◆*Don't take any notice of* what you read in the papers. 新聞で読んだことは気に留めるな ◆*Take no notice* and they'll just go away. 無視するんだ、そうすれば彼らは立ち去るだけさ

neglect [他]《ややフォーマル》軽視する、おろそかにする ◆Dance has been *neglected* by television. 舞踊はテレビでは軽んじられてきた ◆She has *neglected* her studies. 彼女は勉強をおろそかにしてきた ☞ **neglect** (LEAVE 4)

ˌgloss ˈover sth 句動詞 (不快[厄介]な事を)はぐらかす、取り繕う ◆There is a strong temptation to *gloss over* potential problems. 潜在的な問題には触れずにおこうという強い誘惑がある ◆He *glossed over* any splits in the party. 彼は党内の分裂を取り繕った

illegal 形 ☞ WRONG 3

illegal・criminal・unlawful・unconstitutional・illicit・punishable・illegitimate・delinquent・pirate
人々や物事、活動が法律によって認められないことを表す
【類語訳】不法な、違法な、法律違反の、犯罪の、非合法の、不当な、非行の、海賊版の

文型&コロケーション

▶ an illegal/ a criminal/ an unlawful/ an unconstitutional/ an illicit/ a delinquent **act**
▶ illegal/ criminal/ unlawful/ illicit/ delinquent **activity/ conduct**
▶ illegal/ criminal/ unlawful/ illicit **possession** of drugs/ weapons
▶ an illegal/ illicit **substance/ drug**
▶ a criminal/ a punishable **offence**
▶ criminal/ unlawful **violence**

illegal 不法な、違法な、法律違反の ◆Most of these jobs are done by *illegal* immigrants. これらの仕事のほとんどは不法滞在者が行っている ◆It's *illegal* to drive through a red light. 車で赤信号を突っ切るのは法律違反です ❶ illegal は名詞の前でも連結動詞の後でも用いることができる。

illness, illusion

よく結びつく語に dumping, gambling, possession, practices, trade, transactions, exports, payments がある。illegal は活動を表すのに用いるのが最もふつうだが、特に illegal drugs/substances/organizations/immigrants の句で、物や人を表すのにも用いることができる。[反意] **legal** (LEGAL)
▶ **illegally** 副 ◇an *illegally* parked car 違法駐車車両 ◇He entered the country *illegally*. 彼は不法入国した

criminal [ふつう名詞の前で][ややフォーマル or 法律] 犯罪の、犯罪に関する ◇It should be a *criminal* offence to inflict cruelty on any wild animal. どんな野生動物に対しても残虐行為を加えることは犯罪とすべきである ◇He had three *criminal* convictions and a history of violence. 彼には刑事事件の有罪判決が3回と暴行の前歴が1回あった ❶ *criminal* は法律関係の、主に行為について用いられる。criminal とよく結びつく語句に activity, acts, assault, behaviour, charges, conviction, damage, gang, negligence, offence, sexual conduct, violence, wrongdoing がある。☞ **crime** (CRIME 1)
▶ **criminally** 副 ◇The owners were very negligent but they were not *criminally* negligent (= their negligence was not a crime). 所有者たちには大きな過失があったが、罪になるほどの過失ではなかった

unlawful [フォーマル or 法律] 不法の、非合法の ◇The jury returned a verdict of *unlawful* killing. 陪審員は殺人の評決を下した ❶ *unlawful* は法律関係の、特に状況が異なれば許されるような行為について用いられる。よく結びつく語に acts, conduct, killing, means, possession, sex, violence, wounding がある。[反意] **lawful** (LEGAL)

unconstitutional [国家・組織の]憲法[憲章]違反の、違憲の ◇The judges declared the decision *unconstitutional*. 判事たちはその決定を憲法違反と宣告した ❶ constitution は国家・組織による制度、法律および基本原則を指す。[反意] **constitutional** (LEGAL)

illicit 非合法の、違法の ◇They do not support any behaviour that involves *illicit* drugs. 彼らは非合法ドラッグに関係するいかなる行動も支援しない ❶ *illicit* はふつう、薬物や薬物関連の活動について用いられる。また *illicit* **sex** とも言えるが、illegal *sex* が法律で認められないのに対して、illicit *sex* は合法だが、社会の通常の規範で認められないものを指す。

punishable [犯罪が]罰すべき、処罰に値する ◇This is a crime *punishable* by/with imprisonment. これは投獄による処罰に値する犯罪だ ◇Giving false information to the police is a *punishable* offence. 警察に虚偽の情報を与えることは処罰に相当する罪である

illegitimate [フォーマル][規則・法律上]不当な、非合法な、違法な ◇He has been accused of *illegitimate* use of company property. 彼は会社の資産の不当な使用で告発されている [反意] **legitimate** (LEGAL)

delinquent [ややフォーマル][若者の]非行の ◇She spent a year in an institution for *delinquent* teenagers. 彼女は非行少年の施設で1年を過ごした ☞ **delinquency** (CRIME 1)

pirate [名詞の前で][本・CD・DVDなどのコピーが]海賊版の;[ラジオ局が]海賊放送の ◇a *pirate* CD/video/DVD/cassette/edition/copy/recording 海賊版のCD/海賊版のビデオ/海賊版のDVD/海賊版のカセット/海賊版のコピー/海賊版の録音物 ◇a *pirate* radio station 海賊ラジオ放送局

illness 名 ☞ DISEASE

illness・sickness・ill health・trouble

肉体的[精神的]に健全でない状態を表す
【類語訳】病気、不健康、痛み

[文型&コロケーション]
▶ **due to/ owing to/ through** illness/ sickness/ ill health
▶ **chronic** illness/ sickness/ ill health
▶ **to suffer from** illness/ sickness/ ill health/ heart, etc. trouble

illness [U] (肉体的・精神的な)病気、不健康 ◇She suffered from mental *illness* throughout her life. 彼女は生涯を通じて精神病を患っていた ◇I missed a lot of school through *illness* last year. 去年は病気で学校をたくさん休んだ ☞ **ill** (SICK 1)

sickness [U] [ややフォーマル] 病気;不健康 ◇I recommend you get insurance against *sickness* and unemployment. 病気と失業に備えた保険に入ることをお勧めします ☞ **sick** (SICK 1)

[ノート] **illness** と **sickness** の使い分け: sickness は特に仕事と保険に関する文脈で用いられる。illness のほうが使用範囲は広く、より一般的な文脈で用いられる。

,ill 'health [U] [ややフォーマル] (肉体的な)不健康、(多くの)健康問題 ◇She was forced to resign because of *ill health*. 彼女は健康問題のために辞職せざるをえなかった ❶ ill health はしばしば長期におよぶもの。

trouble [U] (体の特定の部位の)病気、痛み ◇He suffers from heart *trouble*. 彼は心臓病を患っている ◇I've been having *trouble* with my knee. ずっと膝に痛みを抱えています

illusion 名

illusion・myth・misunderstanding・delusion・misconception・fallacy・misinterpretation・false impression・the wrong idea

人や物事についての間違った[事実に反する]考えを表す
【類語訳】幻想、錯覚、勘違い、思い違い、俗説、作り話、誤解、妄想、誤信

[文型&コロケーション]
▶ **an** illusion/ a myth/ a misunderstanding/ a delusion/ a misconception/ a fallacy/ the wrong idea **about** sb/ sth
▶ **the** illusion/ myth/ misunderstanding/ delusion/ misconception/ fallacy/ false impression **that**...
▶ **under** an illusion/ a delusion/ a false impression
▶ **a dangerous** illusion/ myth/ delusion/ misconception/ fallacy
▶ **a common** myth/ misunderstanding/ delusion/ misconception/ fallacy
▶ **a popular** myth/ misconception/ fallacy
▶ **(a) widespread** misunderstanding/ misconception/ fallacy
▶ **to have** an illusion/ a delusion/ the wrong idea
▶ **to be based on** a myth/ a misunderstanding/ a misconception/ fallacy/ misinterpretation
▶ **to give rise to** a myth/ (a) misunderstanding/ a misconception
▶ **to give sb** a false impression/ the wrong idea
▶ **to correct** a misunderstanding/ misconception/ false impression

illusion [C, U] (人・物事が本当はよくないのによいと思い込

む)幻想, 錯覚, 勘違い, 思い違い ◇I **have no illusions** about her feelings for me (= I know that she does not love me). 私への彼女の感情について勘違いなどしていない ◇He's under the *illusion* that (= wrongly thinks) he will get the job. 彼は仕事が得られるという幻想を抱いている ◇They wanted to create the *illusion* of being a close, happy family. 彼らは親密で幸せな家族であるという錯覚を生み出したかった ◇He could no longer tell the difference between *illusion* and reality. もはや彼には幻想と現実の区別がつかなくなった

▶**illusory** 形 ◇Our new situation gave us an *illusory* sense of freedom. 《フォーマル》私たちは新たな状況下で自由になったという錯覚を抱かされた ◇Any power he may seem to have is purely *illusory*. 彼にはあるかとも思える力はまったくの錯覚だ

myth [C, U] (多くの人が信じているが存在しない[間違っている])俗説, 作り話, 神話 ◇It is time to dispel the *myth* of the classless society (= to show that it does not exist). 無階級社会という作り話を払拭すべき時だ ◇It's a *myth* that cats only swish their tails when they are angry. 猫だけが怒ったときに尾を振り回すというのは俗説です ◇**Contrary to popular myth**, women are not worse drivers than men. 俗説とは反対に, 女性は男性より車の運転が下手ということはない

misunderstanding [C, U] (問題を招くような)誤解 ◇The meeting is a final chance to clear up any *misunderstandings*. その会合はあらゆる誤解を解く最後の機会である ◇There must be some *misunderstanding* — I thought I ordered the smaller model. きっと何かの誤解に違いない. 小さな方の型を注文したと思っていた 反意 **understanding** (UNDERSTANDING), ☞ **misunderstand** (MISUNDERSTAND)

delusion [C, U] (自分自身[自分の状況]についての)妄想, 錯覚; 妄想すること ◇Don't go getting *delusions of grandeur* (= a belief that you are more important than you really are). 自分について誇大妄想を抱くな ◇My mother had a tremendous capacity for *delusion*. 母はものすごい妄想家だった ❶*delusion*は精神病によって引き起こされることもある. ◆Many people with this condition suffer from *delusions*. (この疾患を抱えた多くの人は妄想に苦しむ)

misconception [C, U] 《ややフォーマル》(間違った情報に基づいた)誤った考え, 誤解 ◇It's a widespread *misconception* that only women get breast cancer. 女性だけが乳がんになると広く誤解されている ◇Their views are based on *misconception* and prejudice. 彼らの見解は誤解と偏見に基づいている

fallacy [C, U] 《ややフォーマル》(多くの人が信じる)誤った考え, 誤信; (考え方の)誤り ◇It's a *fallacy* to say that the camera never lies. カメラは嘘をつかないというのは誤信である ◇He detected the *fallacy* of her argument. 彼は彼女の主張に誤りを見つけた

misinterpretation [U, C] 《ややフォーマル》(不十分な[誤った]理解による)誤った考え[解釈], 誤解 ◇What he said could easily be **open to misinterpretation**. 彼の言ったことは誤解を招きやすいだろう ◇Their conclusions were a result of a *misinterpretation* of the data. 彼らの結論は, データの誤った解釈から生まれたものだった ☞ **misinterpret** (MISUNDERSTAND)

,false im'pression [C] (情報が少なすぎることによる)誤った印象 ◇Their main headline gave a completely *false impression*. その大見出しはまったく誤った印象を与えた ☞ **false** (WRONG 1)

the ,wrong i'dea フレーズ 《ややインフォーマル》(人・物事が実際より悪いという)誤った考え, 誤解 ◇Be careful about meeting him alone — you don't want people to *get the wrong idea* (= the idea that you are having a relationship with him). 彼と二人きりで会うときは気をつけてね. 人に誤解されたくないでしょう ❶*the wrong idea*はほぼ決って, 動詞get, have, giveと共に用いられる. ☞ **wrong** (WRONG 1)

imagination 名

imagination・vision・fantasy・make-believe
心の中にイメージを描く行為, 描かれるイメージ
【類語訳】想像(力), 空想, 夢想, 見せかけ

文型&コロケーション
▶(a) **romantic** imagination/ vision/ fantasy
▶(a) **private/ personal** vision/ fantasy
▶a **world of** fantasy/ make-believe

imagination [U, C] 想像(力) ◇He's got no *imagination*. 彼には想像力が欠けている ◇It doesn't take much *imagination* to guess what happened next. 次に何が起こったか推測するのに大した想像力はいらない ◇She has a **vivid imagination**. 彼女にはたくましい想像力がある ◇I won't tell you his reaction — I'll leave that to your *imagination*. 彼が見せた反応をあなたには教えません―ご想像におまかせします ◇Nobody hates you — it's all **in your imagination**. あなたは誰にも嫌われていません―すべてあなたの思い過ごしですよ ◇Is it my *imagination* or have you lost a lot of weight? 私の気のせいかな, だいぶ減量したのでは ☞ **imaginative** (CREATIVE)

vision [C] 心に描く像[考え], ビジョン ◇He had a *vision* of a world in which there would be no wars. 彼は戦争のない世界を思い描いていた ◇I **had visions** of us getting hopelessly lost. 私たちが途方にくれている様が頭に浮かんだ

fantasy [U] 《時にはなして》空想, 夢想 ◇This is a work of *fantasy*. これは空想から生まれた作品だ ◇She was no longer able to distinguish between *fantasy* and reality. 彼女はもはや空想と現実の区別がつかなかった ◇Stop living in a *fantasy world*. 空想の世界に生きるのをやめなさい 反意 **reality** (FACT), ☞ **fantasy** (HOPE 名 2)

ノート **imagination** と **fantasy** の使い分け: imaginationはふつうfantasyよりよい意味合いの語である. vivid imaginationを持っていることはしばしばよいことだと考えられる. それがあれば人々は自分自身を楽しませることができたり, 他の人の立場になって想像することで, その人たちによりいっそう同情することができたりする. fantasyはふつう想像した物事を現実世界と対照させるときに用い, しばしば否定的で, 人が現実を直視したがらないことを示唆する.

'**make-believe** [U] 《時にはなして》見せかけ, 作りごと ◇They live in a world of *make-believe*. 彼らは作りごとの世界に住んでいる ◇'Let's play *make-believe*,' said Sam. ごっこ遊びをしようとサムが言った

imagine 動

imagine・think・see・envisage・envision・picture・visualize・conceptualize・pretend

人や物事がどのようなものであるかを頭の中に浮かばせることを意味する
【類語訳】想像する, 思う, 思いつく, 考えつく, 考える, 予想する, 思い描く, 構想する, 思い浮かべる, 考えを抱く, 概念化する

文型&コロケーション
▶ to imagine/ see/ envisage/ envision/ picture/ visualize/ conceptualize sb/ sth **as** sth
▶ to imagine/ think/ see/ envisage/ envision/ picture/ visualize (sb) **doing** sth
▶ to imagine/ think/ see/ envisage/ envision/ picture/ visualize **who/ what/ how...**
▶ to imagine/ think/ envisage/ envision/ pretend **that...**
▶ **Just** imagine/ think/ pretend.

imagine [他, 自] (人・物事がどのようなものであるかについて) 想像する, 思う ◇The house was just as she had *imagined* it. その家はまさに彼女が想像していたとおりだった ◇I can't *imagine* life without the children now. 今では子どものいない生活など想像できない ◇Close your eyes and *imagine* (that) you are in a forest. 目を閉じて, ご自分が森の中にいると想像してください ◇I can just *imagine* him saying that! 彼がそう言うのをありありと想像できるよ ◇I had *imagined* her to be older than him. 彼女は私より年上だと思っていた ◇'He was furious.' 'I can *imagine*!' 《話し言葉》「彼はかんかんに怒ってたよ」「そうだろうね」

think [他, 受身なし] (《起こる [起きた] かもしれない物事を》) 想像する, 思いつく, 考えつく ◇We couldn't *think* where you'd gone. 君がどこへ行ってしまったのか思いもつかなかった ◇Just *think* how nice it would be to see them again. 彼らに再会するのがどんなに素敵かちょっと想像してごらんよ ◇Try to ***think yourself into*** the role. 自分がその役割をしたらどうかを考えるようにしなさい ◇***Just think*** — this time tomorrow we'll be lying on a beach. 考えてみなよ. 明日の今頃はビーチで横になってるんだよ

see [他] 《進行形なし》(将来の可能性として) 考える;(人・物事を…であると) 想像する ◇I can't *see* her changing her mind. 彼女の気が変わるなんて考えられない ◇His colleagues *see* him as a future director. 同僚たちは彼が将来部長になるだろうと考えている

envisage [他] 《特に英, ややフォーマル》(将来起こることを) 想像する, 予想する, 見込む ◇What level of profit do you *envisage*? どの程度の利益を予想しますか ◇*It is envisaged that* the talks will take place in the spring. 会談は春に行われると見込まれている ❶この意味では,《米》ではふつう envision を用いる.

envision [他] 《ややフォーマル》(努力を傾けるつもりの状況がどうなるかを) 想像する, 思い描く, 構想する ◇They *envision* an equal society, free from poverty and disease. 彼らは貧困や病気のない平等な社会を思い描いている ❶envision は特にビジネスや政治の文脈で用いられる.《米》では envisage の代わりとしても用いられる. ◆What level of profit do you *envision*? (どの程度の利益を予想しますか)

picture [他] (人・物事を) 思い描く, 思い浮かべる ◇I can still *picture* the house I grew up in. 自分が育った家が今でも思い浮かびます ☞ **picture** (DESCRIPTION)

visualize (英でまた **-ise**) [他]《ややフォーマル》(人・物事を) 思い描く, 思い浮かべる ◇Try to *visualize* yourself walking into the interview calmly and confidently. 自分が落ち着いて自信を持って面接に臨む姿を思い浮かべるようにしなさい

▷**visualization** (英でまた **-isation**) [名] [U, C] ◇*Visualization* can be a useful technique in building confidence. 心に思い描くことは自信をつけるのに役立つ方法になりうる

ノート **imagine, picture, visualize** の使い分け: imagine はこれらの中で最も一般的な語で, 人, 場所, 物, 経験がどう見えるか[感じられるか] について了解に抱く思いに用いられる. picture と visualize は, 特に物事を (一連の) イメージで想像する場合に用いられる. この2語は, 意味は非常に近いが, visualize はややフォーマルで, ある目的のために物事を意図的に想像しようとする場合に用いられることが多い.

conceptualize (英でまた **-ise**) [他, 自]《フォーマル》(正確に想像するのが難しい物事について) 考えを抱く, 概念化する ◇How can we *conceptualize* the way the international economy works? 世界経済が機能する方法をどのように概念化できるだろうか ◇The ability to *conceptualize* is one of the most likely indicators of who will be a successful manager. 概念化の能力は, 経営者として成功する人物像を示す最も適切な指標の一つである

pretend [他, 自] (子どもがゲームの一部として物事を真実であると) 想像する, ふりをする ◇Let's *pretend* (that) we're astronauts. 宇宙飛行士ごっこをしよう ◇They didn't have any real money so they had to *pretend*. 彼らは本物のお金を持っていなかったので, そのふりをしなければならなかった

immediate [形]

immediate・instant・prompt・instantaneous
物事が遅れることなく起こる[行われる]ことを表す
【類語訳】即座の, すぐの, 迅速な

prompt　　　immediate　　　instantaneous
　　　　　　　instant

文型&コロケーション
▶ an immediate/ an instant/ a prompt/ an instantaneous **reaction/ response/ return**
▶ immediate/ instant/ prompt **action/ attention/ payment/ relief**
▶ an immediate/ instant **appeal/ answer/ solution/ result/ effect/ impact/ improvement**
▶ an immediate/ a prompt **start/ step**
▶ **almost** immediate/ instant/ instantaneous

immediate 即座の, すぐの ◇Carrie's *immediate* reaction to the news was to laugh in relief. その知らせに接してすぐのキャリーの反応は, 安堵の笑いだった ◇Local police took *immediate* action when they received the bomb alert. 地元警察は爆弾警告を受けると直ちに措置を講じた ◇The cream brings *immediate* relief to dry and rough skin. そのクリームは荒れた乾燥肌に即効性があります 反意 **delayed** ❶delayed な反応は, 原因となる出来事から時間がたってから起こる. ◆She's suffering a *delayed* reaction to the shock. (彼女はそのショックに対する遅延反応に苦しんでいる).

▷**immediately** [副] ◇She answered almost *immediately*. 彼女はほぼ即座に答えた ◇The point of my question may not be *immediately* apparent. 私の質問の主旨はすぐにははっきりわからないかもしれない

instant [ふつう名詞の前で] 即座の, すぐの ◇She took an

↪**immediate**

instant dislike to me, the first time we met. 私たちが初めて会ったとき、私は彼女にすぐ嫌われた ◇This account gives you *instant* access to your money. この口座なら、すぐにご自分のお金を自由に出し入れできます ◇The show was an *instant* success in New York. そのショーはニューヨークでたちまちヒットした
▸**instantly** 副 ◇Her voice is *instantly* recognizable. 彼女の声はすぐにわかる ◇The driver of the car was killed *instantly*. その車のドライバーは即死した
prompt 迅速な, 即座の, すぐの ◇*Prompt* action was required as the fire spread. 火事が広がる中で迅速な措置が必要とされた ◇*Prompt* payment of the invoice would be appreciated. 請求書のお支払いを速やかにしていただければありがたく存じます
▸**promptly** 副 ◇She read the letter and *promptly* burst into tears. 《特に書き言葉》彼女は手紙を読むとすぐさま泣き出した
instantaneous 即座の ◇Her *instantaneous* response was to blame her parents. 彼女の即座の反応は両親への非難だった ◇With certain poisons, death is almost *instantaneous*. ある種の毒物では, ほぼ即死に至る

【ノート】**immediate, instant, prompt, instantaneous の使い分け**: prompt は物事を人が行う速さを, instantaneous は物事が起こる速さを表す。immediate と instant はそのどちらも表すことができるが, instant は物事を人が行う速さより物事が起こる速さを表すのに用いることが多い。prompt な行動 (action) は, immediate, instant, instantaneous な行動や反応 (reaction) ほど速くない。very/fairly prompt action とは言えるが, ×very/fairly *immediate/instant/instantaneous* action とは言えない。反応については, almost immediate/instant/instantaneous reaction とは言えるが, ×almost *prompt* reaction とは言えない。

importance 名

importance • **significance** • **urgency** • **seriousness** • **consequence** • **substance** • **gravity**
人や物事に影響を与えるほど大切な特質
【類語訳】重要性, 重要な地位, 緊急性, 重大性, 深刻さ

▶ 文型&コロケーション
▸to be **of** importance/ significance **to** sb
▸**great** importance/ significance/ urgency/ seriousness/ consequence
▸the **utmost** importance/ significance/ urgency/ seriousness/ gravity
▸**real** importance/ significance/ urgency/ consequence
▸**new/ added** importance/ significance/ urgency/ substance
▸to **have/ gain** importance/ significance/ substance
▸to **give sth** importance/ significance/ urgency/ substance
▸to **assume/ take on** importance/ significance/ an urgency
▸to **appreciate/ realize/ recognize/ understand** the importance/ significance/ urgency/ seriousness/ gravity of sth
▸to **reflect/ show/ underline** the importance/ significance/ urgency/ seriousness of sth
▸to **assess/ exaggerate/ underestimate** the importance/ significance/ seriousness of sth
▸a **matter of** importance/ significance/ urgency/ substance

importance [U] 重要性 ◇She stressed the *importance* of careful preparation. 彼女は周到な準備の重要性を強調した ◇They **attach** great **importance to** the project. 彼らはそのプロジェクトを非常に重要視している ◇State your reasons in **order of importance**. 重要性が高い順に理由を述べなさい ◇He was very aware of his own *importance* (= of his status). 彼は自分が重要な立場にいることをよく知っていた
significance [U, C] 《ややフォーマル, 特に書き言葉》(将来起こることに影響を与えるような) 重要性 ◇This is a decision of major political *significance*. これは政治的にても重要な決定である ◇The new drug has great *significance* **for** the treatment of the disease. 新薬はその病気の治療に多大な重要性を持つものである 反意 insignificance (MINOR)
urgency [U, 単数で] 《ややフォーマル》緊急性, 切迫 ◇This is a matter of some *urgency*. これはいささか急を要する問題だ ◇There was a note of *urgency* in his voice. 彼の声には切迫した響きがあった ◇The attack added a new *urgency* to the peace talks. その攻撃で和平会談に新たな緊急性が生じた ☞ **urgent** (URGENT)
seriousness [U, 単数で] (心配の種があることから生じる) 重大性, 深刻さ ◇He had not understood the *seriousness* of the matter. 彼は事の重大性を理解していなかった ◇The problem was not treated with the *seriousness* it deserved. その問題はそれ相応に真剣に扱われなかった ☞ **serious** (SERIOUS 1)
consequence [U] 《フォーマル》重要性 ◇Don't worry. It's *of no consequence*. 心配するな。まったく取るに足りないことだ ◇His work made him a person of some *consequence* in the art world. 彼は自らの作品によって美術界でいささか重要な人物となった ❶ (あまり) 重要でない物事は, of some/little/no consequence や without consequence で表すことができる。重要なことが起きなければ, Nothing of any consequence happens. と言うことができる。重要な人 [物事] は sb/sth of consequence で表すことができる。
substance [U] 《しばしば否定文で》《フォーマル, 特に書き言葉》(情報・証拠・成果などの) 重要性, 中身, 内容 ◇Nothing of any *substance* was achieved in the meeting. 会議では何も実質的なことは成し遂げられなかった ◇Their accusations were without *substance*. 彼らの非難には中身がなかった ❶ 報告 (report) や噂 (rumour) は, 重要な情報を含んでいたり, それを裏づける証拠がある場合, have substance と言う。そうでない場合は, lack substance と言う。議論の重要な論点は, ... of substance や matter of substance と表せる。
gravity [U] 《フォーマル》重大性, 深刻さ ◇I don't think you realize the *gravity* of the situation. あなたは状況の深刻さを認識していないと思う ◇Punishment varies according to the *gravity* of the offence. 犯罪の重大さによって刑罰は変わる ☞ **grave** (SERIOUS 1)

important 形 ☞ ESSENTIAL

important • **significant** • **big** • **great** • **notable** • **momentous**
物事が大きな影響を与えたり, 際立っていたり, とても価値があったりすることを表す
【類語訳】重要な, 重大な, 大切な, 注目に値する, 注目すべき, 有名な

▶ 文型&コロケーション
▸to be important/ significant **for/ to** sb/ sth

- ▶to be important/ signficant/ notable **that**...
- ▶important/ significant/ big/ great/ notable/ momentous **events/ changes/ developments**
- ▶an important/ a significant/ a big/ a great/ a notable **difference/ feature/ achievement/ success**
- ▶an important/ a big/ a momentous **decision**
- ▶especially/ particularly important/ significant/ notable/ momentous
- ▶really/ quite/ equally important/ significant/ momentous
- ▶very/ highly/ increasingly/ extremely/ enormously/ hugely/ immensely important/ significant

important （大きな影響力［価値］があり）重要な、大切な ◇I have an *important* announcement to make. 重大発表があります ◇Listening is an *important* part of the job. 耳を傾けることはその仕事の重要な一部である ◇*It is important to* follow the manufacturer's instructions. メーカーの指示に従うことが重要です ◇It's very *important* to me that you should be there. あなたがそこにいることが私にはとても大切なのです ◇*The important thing* is to keep trying. 大切なのは挑戦し続けるということです 反意 **unimportant** (MINOR)
▶**importantly** 副 ◇Most *importantly*, can he be trusted? 一番重要なことだけど、彼は信頼できるのか
significant （影響力がある［出した］のぞ）著しい、相当な、重要な ◇There are no *significant* differences between the two groups of students. その二つの学生グループの間には大した違いはない ◇The results of the experiment are not *statistically significant*. その実験の結果は統計的に有意ではない ◇These views are held by a *significant* proportion of the population. こうした見解をかなりの割合の住民が抱いている 反意 **insignificant** (MINOR)
▶**significantly** 副 ◇The two sets of figures are not *significantly* different from each other. その2組の数字には互いに大した違いはない ◇Profits have increased *significantly* over the past few years. ここ数年で利益は著しく増加した

ノート **important** と **significant** の使い分け：**important** のほうがより一般的。**significant** である物事は、特定の文脈で［特定の観点から見て］重要である。**significant** は、物事の重要度が何らかの方法で評価されたことを人が示したい場合によく用いる。数字は *statistically significant* と言えるが、× *statistically important* とは言えない。**significant** は「度合いが大きい」ことも意味するが、**important** はそうではない。 × *an important proportion of the population*.

big ［名詞の前で］（ややインフォーマル、特にジャーナリズムまたはビジネス）重要な、重大な ◇It's a *big* decision to have to make. それは下さなければならない重大な決断だ ◇You are making a *big mistake*. 君は大きな間違いを犯している ◇She took the stage for her *big moment*. 彼女は晴れ舞台のステージに上がった

great ［名詞の前で］重要な、大きな ◇The wedding was a *great* occasion. 結婚式は盛大な催しになった ◇*The great thing* is to get it done quickly. 重要なのはそれを素早く仕上げるということです ◇One *great* advantage of this metal is that it doesn't rust. この金属の大きな利点はさびないことである

notable 《ややフォーマル》（珍しい［重要な、興味深い］ので）注目に値する、注目すべき、有名な ◇The town is *notable* for its ancient harbour. その町は大昔からの港ということで

有名だ ◇It is *notable* that only 15% of senior managers are women. 上級管理者のうち女性がわずかに15%であることは注目すべきです ◇*With a few notable exceptions*, everyone gave something. いくつかの注目すべき例外はあるが、誰もが何がしかの寄付をした
▶**notably** 副 ◇The house had many drawbacks, most *notably* its price. その家には多くの欠点があったが、とりわけその価格がそうだった
momentous 《ややフォーマル》（出来事・行事のもたらすかもしれない結果が）重大な、重要な ◇At the same time, *momentous* events were taking place in Russia. 同時に、ロシアでは重大事件が起こっていた

impossible 形

impossible・out of the question・unthinkable・inconceivable・unattainable
物事が起こる［行われる、真実である］可能性がないことを表す
【類語訳】ありえない、不可能な、無理な、論外の、想像もつかない、考えられない

文型&コロケーション
- ▶to be impossible/ unthinkable/ inconceivable **to** sb
- ▶to be impossible/ out of the question/ unthinkable/ inconceivable **for** sb **to do sth**
- ▶to be impossible/ unthinkable/ inconceivable **that**...
- ▶an impossible/ unattainable **goal/ ideal**
- ▶to **find sth** impossible/ unthinkable/ inconceivable
- ▶quite impossible/ out of the question/ unthinkable/ inconceivable
- ▶almost impossible/ unthinkable/ inconceivable

impossible ありえない、不可能な、無理な ◇That's *impossible*! そんなことあるもんか ◇It's *impossible* for me to be there before eight. 8時前にそこに行くなんて私には無理です ◇I find it *impossible* to lie to her. 彼女に嘘をつくことなんてできないと思う ◇I realized it was an *impossible* dream. それはかなわぬ夢だと悟った 反意 **possible** (POSSIBLE 1, 2), **possible** (LIKELY)
▶**the impossible** 名 ［単数で］◇He decided to *attempt the impossible* and set up an airline from scratch in three months. 彼は不可能なことに挑戦する決意をして、3か月でゼロから航空会社を立ち上げた
▶**impossibly** 副 ◇an *impossibly* difficult problem (= impossible to solve) ありえないほど難しい問題
out of the 'question 行社 （話し合う価値のないほど）不可能な、論外の ◇Another trip abroad this year is *out of the question*. 今年また外国旅行をするなんて論外だ
unthinkable 《特に書き言葉》（とても衝撃的なので）想像もつかない、考えられない、思いもよらない ◇It was *unthinkable* that she could be dead. 彼女が死んでいるようなどとは思いもよらなかった
▶**the unthinkable** 名 ［単数で］◇The time has come to *think the unthinkable* (= consider possibilities that used to be unacceptable). 不測の事態［これまでは考えられなかったこと］を考慮すべき時期がやって来た
inconceivable 《ややフォーマル、特に書き言葉》想像もつかない、考えられない、信じられない ◇It is *inconceivable* that the minister was not aware of the problem. 大臣がその問題に気づいていなかったとは信じられない 反意 **conceivable** (POSSIBLE 2)

↳impossible   impress, impressive

▶**the inconceivable** 名 [単数で] ◇Then *the inconceivable* happened — I lost my job. そして考えられないことが起こった。私が失業したのだ
unattainable (ややフォーマル、書き言葉) 達成[実現、到達]不可能な ◇Setting *unattainable* goals will only lead to frustration. 達成不可能な目標を立てれば挫折するだけだ

impress 動

impress・move・touch・dazzle・take sb's breath away・affect
人に賞賛や同情、悲しみなどを感じさせること
【類語訳】感心させる、感動させる、感銘を与える、心を動かす、心を打つ、目を奪う、嘆嘆させる、息をのませる

| impress | move | dazzle |
| touch | affect | take sb's breath away |

文型&コロケーション
▶ impress/ move/ dazzle sb **with** sth
▶ it impresses/ moves/ touches sb **to see/ hear** sth
▶ impress/ move/ touch/ affect sb **deeply**
▶ to be **profoundly** impressed/ moved/ affected by sth

impress [他、しばしば受身で、自] (人・物事が)感心させる、感動させる、感銘を与える ◇We interviewed a number of candidates, but none of them *impressed* us. 何人かの志願者を面接したが、これはと思うような者は誰もいなかった ◇I was enormously *impressed* by their professionalism. 彼らのプロ意識に大いに感動した ◇She was *suitably impressed* (= as impressed as she had hoped) with the painting. 彼女はその絵に期待したとおりの感銘を受けた ◇It *impressed* me that she remembered my name. 彼女が私の名前を覚えていることに心打たれた ◇The Grand Canyon never fails to *impress*. グランドキャニオンはいつも感動を与えてくれる ☞ **impression** (EFFECT), **unimpressed** (INDIFFERENT)
move [他] (同情・悲しみの強い感情を抱かせて)心を動かす、感動させる ◇The woman's story had really *moved* her. その女性の話に彼女は本当に感動した ◇We were deeply *moved* by her plight. 私たちは彼女の窮状に強く心を動かされた ◇Grown men were ***moved to tears*** at the horrific scenes. 大の男たちがその恐ろしい光景に目頭を熱くした ☞ **unmoved** (RUTHLESS).
touch [他] (感謝・同情の念を抱かせて)心を打つ、感動させる ◇I had been *touched* by his kindness to my aunts. 私のおばたちに対する彼の優しさに心を打たれたことがあった ◇What he said really *touched* my heart. 彼の言葉には本当に感動した
dazzle [他、しばしば受身で] (美しさ・技量・知識・魅力を強く印象づけて)目[心]を奪う、感嘆[驚嘆]させる ◇He was *dazzled* by the warmth of her smile. 彼は彼女の笑顔の温かさに心を奪われた ◇He *dazzled* the chess world as he took the title at his first attempt. 初挑戦でタイトルを取ったので、彼はチェス界を驚嘆させた
take sb's 'breath away [行idiom] (光景・行動・演奏がその美しさ[技量]で)(人の)息をのませる、(人を)大いに驚嘆[感動]させる ◇My first view of the island from the air *took my breath away*. 空から初めて見た島の光景に私は息をのんだ ◇The spectacular two-hour performance *took their breath away*. 2時間にわたる見事な演奏に彼ら

は大いに感動した ☞ **breathtaking** (AMAZING)
affect [他、しばしば受身で] (ややフォーマル) (自分自身・他人に対して)深い悲しみ[哀れみ]を抱かせる、感動させる ◇Mrs Davis and her husband were profoundly *affected* by their experiences. デービス夫妻は彼らの体験に深く感動した ◇They were deeply *affected* by the news of her death. 彼女の訃報に彼らは深い悲しみを抱いた

ノート **move, touch, affect** の使い分け: 「感動する」場合、他人の身に起こったこと、特に悲しいことに **be moved** を、他人がしたこと、特にちょっとした親切な行為に **be touched** を使うことができる。自分[他人]の身に起こったことには **be affected** を用いて、受けた影響を強調する。

impressive 形 ☞ GOOD 4

impressive・expert・spectacular・consummate・masterly・virtuoso
人や物事が多くの技量を見せつけること
【類語訳】印象的、感動的な、感銘深い、熟練した、熟達した、達人の、名人の、大家の、神業の

文型&コロケーション
▶ an impressive/ an expert/ a spectacular/ a masterly/ a virtuoso **performance/ display**
▶ impressive/ expert/ consummate/ masterly/ virtuoso **skill**
▶ an impressive/ a spectacular **achievement**
▶ **quite** impressive/ expert/ spectacular
▶ **really/ truly** impressive/ spectacular

impressive (業績が)印象的な、感動的な、感銘深い、見事な ◇It is one of the most *impressive* novels published in recent years. それは近年出版された小説の中で最も感銘深いものの一つである ◇The team are 12 points ahead after an *impressive* victory last night. そのチームは昨晩の見事な勝利で12ポイント先行している ◇She was very *impressive* in the interview. 彼女は面接で非常に印象的だった 反意 **unimpressive** ❶ unimpressive はどのような点からも大したことのない業績を表すのに用いられる。◆ His academic record was *unimpressive*. (彼の学業成績(表)はぱっとしなかった。 ☞ **impressive** (MAGNIFICENT), **impression** (EFFECT)
▶**impressively** 副 ◇Although very old, the maps are *impressively* accurate. その地図は非常に古いが、見事なまでに正確である
expert 熟練[精通]した、専門家[達人]の ◇It's a good idea to seek *expert* advice. 専門家の助言を求めるのはいい考えだ ◇They're all *expert* in this field. 彼らは皆この分野に精通している ◇She's *expert at* making cheap but stylish clothes. 彼女は安価だけどおしゃれな服を作る達人だ ☞ **expert** (EXPERT), **expertise** (SKILL 2)
▶**expertly** 副 ◇He tied up the boat and *expertly* folded down the sails. 彼はボートをつないで、あざやかな手つきで帆を折りたたんだ
spectacular (業績・技量が)実に見事な、華々しい、目覚ましい ◇Rooney scored a *spectacular* goal. ルーニーが実に見事なゴールを決めた ◇They were absolutely delighted with the show's *spectacular* success. 彼らはショーの華々しい成功にすっかり気をよくしていた 反意 **unspectacular** ❶ unspectacular は業績・技量が刺激的でない[大したことのない]ことを表す。◆ He had a steady but *unspectacular* career. (彼は堅実だがぱっとしない経歴の

持ち主だった). ☞ **spectacular** (MAGNIFICENT), **spectacle** (PERFORMANCE)

▸**spectacularly** 副 ◇It had been a *spectacularly* successful season. それは華々しい成功に彩られたシーズンだった

consummate [ふつう名詞の前で]《フォーマル》(人が)熟達[熟練]した; (技量・質が)神業の, 最高の, 実に見事な ◇a *consummate* performer/actor/politician 熟練した役者/俳優/政治家 ◇He weaved his way past the England defenders with *consummate* ease. 彼はいとも簡単にイングランドのディフェンダーをすり抜けた

masterly 名人[大家]の, 見事な ◇Her handling of the situation was *masterly*. 彼女のその事態への対応は見事だった ◇As a performer he shows a *masterly* sense of timing. 彼は役者として大家にふさわしいタイミングのセンスを示す

virtuoso [名詞の前で](演技・演奏において)名人[大家]の ◇a *virtuoso* pianist/player 名ピアニスト/演奏者 ◇They gave a *virtuoso* display of Spanish dancing. 彼らはスペイン舞踊の大家にふさわしい技を見せた

improve 動

1 improve・enhance・reform・refine・enrich
物事をよりよくする
【類語訳】改善する, 向上させる, 改める, 改めさせる, 洗練する

文型&コロケーション
▸to **improve**/ **enhance**/ **refine**/ **enrich** your **understanding**
▸to **improve**/ **enhance**/ **refine** your **knowledge**
▸to **improve**/ **enhance**/ **enrich** your **life**
▸to **further** improve/ enhance/ refine/ enrich sth
▸to **greatly** improve/ enhance/ enrich sth
▸to **slightly** improve/ enhance/ refine sth

improve [他] (人・物事を以前より)改善[改良, 増進]する, 向上[上達, 進歩]させる ◇You can significantly *improve* your chances of getting a job by compiling a good CV. よい履歴書を作成することで就職の機会を大いに増やすことができます ◇We now offer a much *improved* service to our customers. 我々はただ今, お客様に大幅に改善されたサービスを提供しております ◇I need to *improve* my French. 私はフランス語を上達させる必要がある 反意 **impair** (DAMAGE) 動
▸**improvement** 名 [U, C] ◇There is still **room for** *improvement* in your work. あなたの仕事ぶりにはまだ改善の余地がある ◇This is a great *improvement* **on** your previous work. これはあなたのこれまでの仕事に比べて大いに改善された点です ◇*improvements* **to** the bus service バスの運行に関する改善点

enhance [他, しばしば受身で]《ややフォーマル》(人・物事の質[地位, 価値]を)高める, 向上させる ◇The images can be *enhanced* using digital technology. デジタル技術を用いることで画質を高めることができる ◇Most people seek to *enhance* their status at work in whatever ways they can. 大半の人は可能な限りあらゆる方法を使ってその職場の地位向上を図るものだ 反意 **diminish** (FALL) 1

reform [他, 自](制度[組織, 法律]などを)改革[改善, 改正]する; (振る舞い)を改める, (人)が改心する; (人に振る舞い)を改めさせる, (人)を改心させる ◇There are proposals to *reform* the welfare system. 福祉制度の改革案がある ◇He has promised to *reform*. 彼は改心すると約束した ◇She thought she could *reform* him. 彼女は彼を改心させると思った ◇a *reformed* character/alcoholic 改心した人/アルコール依存症から立ち直った人
▸**reform** 名 [U, C] ◇a government committed to *reform* 改革を約束した政府 ◇*reforms* in education 教育改革

refine [他, しばしば受身で](わずかな変更を加えて物事を)改良[洗練]する, 磨きをかける ◇Our methods have been gradually *refined* over the years. 我々の手法は長年にわたって徐々に改良されてきた ◇They would constantly *refine* their designs until they were almost perfect. 彼らはほぼ完璧になるまで絶えず設計に磨きをかけるつもりだった

enrich [他]《書き言葉》(何かを加えて物事の質を)豊かにする, 高める ◇Reading good literature can *enrich* all our lives. 良質の文学作品を読むことで人生全体を豊かにすることができる ◇Most breakfast cereals are *enriched* **with** vitamins. ほとんどの朝食用シリアルにはビタミンが添加され栄養価が高められている

2 ☞ DEVELOP 1
improve・get better・pick up・look up
以前よりよい方に向く
【類語訳】改善される, 改良される, 向上する, 上達する, 進歩する, 増進する, 回復する, よくなる, 上向く, 好転する

文型&コロケーション
▸to **start**/ **begin**/ **continue to** improve/ get better/ pick up/ look up
▸to **fail to** improve/ get better
▸to **improve**/ **get better**/ **pick up** slowly/ gradually/ slightly/ dramatically

improve [自] 改善[改良]される, 向上[上達, 進歩, 増進, 回復]する ◇His quality of life has *improved* dramatically since the operation. 彼の生活の質は手術以来劇的に改善された ◇The doctor says she should continue to *improve* (= after an illness). 彼女はこれからさらに回復していくはずだと医者は言っている 反意 **worsen, deteriorate** (WORSEN)
▸**improvement** 名 [U, C] ◇Sales figures continue to show signs of *improvement*. 売上高は改善の兆しを見せ続けている ◇an *improvement* in Anglo-German relations イギリス・ドイツの関係改善

get 'better フレーズ《しばしば進行形で》《ややインフォーマル》よくなる ◇*Things got better* after my husband found a job. 夫が仕事を見つけてから事態はよくなった ◇It's not an ideal situation, but *things can only get better*. 理想的な状況ではないが, 事態はよくなる方向しか考えられない ◇Our sales seem to be *getting better and better*. 当社の売上高はどんどんよくなっているようだ ◇Computers are *getting better all the time*. コンピューターは常に改良されている 反意 **get worse** (WORSEN), ☞ **get better** (RECOVER)

,pick 'up 句動詞 (ビジネス・経済が)よくなる, 強まる, 上向いていく ◇Exports are gradually *picking up*. 輸出が徐々に上向いてきている ◇Trade usually *picks up* in the spring. 商売はふつう春になると上向く ◇Sales have *picked up* 14% this year. 売上高は今年14%上昇した

,look 'up 句動詞《ふつう進行形や不定詞で》《ややインフォーマル》(ビジネス・状況が不調から)好転[回復]する, 上向く ◇It had been a bad year, but *things were looking up* at last. 悪い年だったが, ようやく事態は好転しつつあった

inadequate 形

inadequate・insufficient・lacking・meagre・scant・sparse・paltry・deficient
数量[水準]が人の必要[欲求]に満たないことを表す
【類語訳】不十分な, 不足な, わずかな, 乏しい, あまり…ない, まばらな, 少ない, 欠けた

文型&コロケーション

▶ lacking/ deficient **in** sth
▶ inadequate/ insufficient **for** sth
▶ inadequate/ insufficient **to do** sth
▶ an inadequate/ an insufficient/ a meagre/ a paltry **amount/ level/ number**
▶ an inadequate/ an insufficient/ a meagre/ scant **supply**
▶ inadequate/ insufficient/ meagre/ scant/ sparse **resources/ information**
▶ an inadequate/ a meagre/ a paltry **sum**
▶ inadequate/ insufficient/ scant **evidence/ knowledge**
▶ **rather** inadequate/ lacking/ meagre/ scant/ sparse/ paltry
▶ **very** inadequate/ meagre/ scant/ sparse/ deficient
▶ **totally/ seriously/ sadly** inadequate/ lacking/ deficient
▶ **quite/ wholly** inadequate/ insufficient/ lacking
▶ **woefully** inadequate/ insufficient/ lacking/ deficient

inadequate 不十分な, 不足な; 不適当な ◇They are blaming their failure on *inadequate* preparation. 彼らは自分たちの失敗の原因は準備不足にあるとしている ◇The system is *inadequate* for the tasks it has to perform. そのシステムでは実行すべきタスクに不適当である ◇The food supplies are *inadequate* to meet the needs of the hungry. その食糧供給では飢えている人々の必要を満たすには不十分である 反意 **adequate** (ADEQUATE), 反意 **inadequate** (INCOMPETENT), **unsatisfactory** (DISAPPOINTING)
▷ **inadequately** 副 ◇to be *inadequately* prepared/ insured/ funded 準備/保険/資金供給が不十分である

insufficient 《ややフォーマル》(特定の目的に対して大きさ[強さ, 重要性]が)不十分な, 不足な ◇I'm afraid we have *insufficient* evidence. 残念ながら, 私たちが持っている証拠では不十分だ ◇His salary is *insufficient* to meet his needs. 彼の給料では彼の必要を満たし切れない ◇There are fears that the existing flood barrier may prove to be *insufficient*. 既存の防潮壁では不十分と判明する恐れがある 反意 **sufficient** ❶反意語は sufficient である.
◆ Make sure you allow *sufficient* time to get there. (そこまで行くのに十分な時間をとっておくことを忘れないで).
◆ One dose should be *sufficient*. (一回分の服用で十分のはずです).
▷ **insufficiently** 副 ◇ *insufficiently* researched 調査不足の

> ノート **inadequate** と **insufficient** の使い分け: insufficient は物事の量[強さ]を強調する. ◆ There are *insufficient* funds in your account. (あなたの口座には十分な資金がない). ◆ to pay *insufficient* attention to sth (物事に十分注意を払わない). inadequate はしばしば量だけでなく質も強調する. ◆ an *inadequate* understanding of how language works (言語がいかに機能するかについての不適切な理解). ◆ low pay and *inadequate* training (低賃金と行き届かぬ研修).

lacking [名詞の前では用いない] (物事に)欠けて, 不足して ◇She's not usually *lacking* in confidence. 彼女はふだん自信がないわけではない ◇The book is completely *lacking* in originality. その本はまったく独創性に欠けている ☞ lack (LACK)

meagre 《英》(米 *meager*) (量・質が)わずかな, 乏しい ◇They had to exist on a *meagre* diet of bread and water. 彼らはパンと水だけの粗食で生きなければならなかった ◇She supplements her *meagre* income by cleaning offices at night. 彼女は夜間のオフィス清掃でわずかな収入を補っている

scant [名詞の前で] 《ややフォーマル》 あまり[ほとんど]…ない ◇I *paid scant attention* to what she was saying. 私は彼女が言っていることにあまり注意を払わなかった ◇The firefighters went back into the house with *scant regard for* their own safety. 消防士たちは自分たちの安全をほとんど顧みずその家の中に戻って行った

sparse (広域において少量[少数]しか存在せず)まばらな, 少ない, 乏しい ◇One characteristic of the islands is their *sparse* population. その諸島の一つの特色は人口の少なさである ◇Vegetation becomes *sparse* higher up the mountains. 植物は山の比較的高いところではまばらになる
▷ **sparsely** 副 ◇a *sparsely* populated area 過疎地 ◇a *sparsely* furnished room 家具の乏しい部屋

paltry [ふつう名詞の前で] (量・数が取るに足らない[役に立たない]ほど)わずかな ◇This account offers a *paltry* 1% return on your investment. この口座は投資に対してわずか1%の利益しかもたらさない ◇They worked long hours for *paltry* wages. 彼らはわずかな賃金で長時間働いた

deficient (不可欠な物事が)不十分な, 不足な, 欠けた, 欠陥のある ◇Your diet is *deficient* in iron. あなたの食事には鉄分が不足している ◇An educational system which fails to teach basic arithmetic is seriously *deficient*. 算数の基礎を教えない教育制度には著しい欠陥がある ☞ **deficiency** (LACK)

incentive 名 ☞ BRIBE

incentive・motivation・stimulus・impetus・inspiration・inducement
人に何かする[もっと早く進める]ことを促すもの, 人が何かする理由となるもの
【類語訳】動機, やる気, 動機付け, 意欲, 刺激, 勢い, 弾み

文型&コロケーション

▶ the incentive/ motivation/ stimulus/ impetus/ inspiration **for** sth
▶ the incentive/ stimulus/ impetus/ inducement **to** sth
▶ the motivation/ impetus/ inspiration **behind** sth
▶ the incentive/ stimulus/ impetus/ inducement **to do** sth
▶ a **strong** incentive/ motivation/ impetus/ inducement
▶ a **powerful** incentive/ stimulus/ impetus/ inducement
▶ the **main** incentive/ motivation/ stimulus/ impetus/ inspiration
▶ a **new** incentive/ motivation/ stimulus/ impetus
▶ an **extra** incentive/ motivation/ stimulus/ impetus/ inducement
▶ the **necessary** motivation/ stimulus/ impetus/ inducement
▶ **sufficient** incentive/ motivation/ inducement
▶ to **provide/ give** (sb/ sth) the incentive/ motivation/ stim-

ulus/ impetus/ inspiration/ inducement
▶to **offer** an incentive/ an inducement

incentive [C, U] (見返りに何かを手に入れるための)動機, やる気, 起爆剤 ◇There are no *incentives* for people to save fuel. 人々が燃料を節約する動機付けとなるものは何もない ◇The government has created **tax** *incentives* to encourage investment. 政府は投資を奨励する税制上の起爆剤を創出した ◇There is little *incentive* for firms to increase the skills of their workers. 会社には労働者の技術を向上させる気などほとんどない 反意 **disincentive** ❶disincentive は特に行っても多くを得られないので、何もする気がしないことを表す. ◆A sudden fall in profits provided a further *disincentive* to investors. (収益の急落で投資家の意欲はさらにそがれた)

motivation [C, U] (人の特定の行動[振る舞い]の)動機; (成功したいと思う)動機付け, 意欲 ◇What is the *motivation* behind this sudden change? この豹変の裏にある動機は何ですか ◇I soon understood his *motivation in* inviting me. 私は招待してくれた彼の動機がすぐにわかった ◇He's intelligent enough but he *lacks motivation*. 彼は十分に知的だが、意欲に欠けている ☞ **motivate** (INSPIRE), **motive** (REASON)
▶**motivational** 形 ◇an important *motivational* factor 《フォーマル》重要な動機的要因

stimulus (複 **stimuli**) [C, ふつう単数形で] (ややフォーマル) (人・物事に開始[発展]を促す)刺激(策) ◇Books provide children with ideas and a *stimulus* for play. 本は子どもたちに考え方や、遊びに誘う刺激を提供する ◇He stressed the value of public investment as a *stimulus* to growth. 彼は成長を促す刺激策として公共投資の価値を強調した ☞ **stimulate** (INSPIRE)

impetus [U, 単数で] (過程・活動に発展を促す)勢い, 弾み ◇The debate seems to have lost much of its initial *impetus*. その討論は当初の勢いをかなり失ってしまったようだ ◇Each new rumour added a **fresh** *impetus* to the smear campaign. 新しい噂の一つ一つが中傷合戦に新たな弾みをつけた

ノート **stimulus** と **impetus** の使い分け：stimulus が物事を始める際の「刺激」となるものについて用いられることが多いのに対し, impetus は物事の発展過程における「勢い, 弾み」について用いられる. gain/maintain/lose impetus や, added/new/further/fresh impetus と言うことができる. stimulus はよりフォーマルな語で, 学問[ビジネス]の文脈で用いられることが多い. impetus はジャーナリズム[放送]で, 動向や発展を議論する際に用いられることが多い.

inspiration [C, ふつう単数で] (人が物事を生み出す[行う]ことを)鼓舞[激励, 刺激]する人[物事] ◇He says my sister was the *inspiration* for his heroine. 彼は私の妹が彼の作品のヒロインを生むヒントとなった人物だと言っている ◇Clark was the *inspiration* behind Saturday's victory. クラークが土曜日の勝利を陰で支えた立役者だった ☞ **inspire** (INSPIRE)

inducement [C, U] (人にふだん行わない物事を行う)意欲を起こさせる物事[金] ◇The higher payments were offered as an *inducement*. やる気を起こさせる代償としてより高い給与が支払われた ◇There is little *inducement* for them to work harder. 彼らにもっと熱心に働く意欲を起こさせるものがない

---

include

include 動

include • contain • cover • incorporate • encompass • involve • build sth in(to sth) • embrace • take sth in

人や物事を一員[一部]として持つ, 人や物事を一員[一部]とする 【類語訳】含む, 含める, 含有する, 包含する, 内包する, 対象にする, 適用される, 該当する, 組み入れる, 包括する

文型&コロケーション

▶to include/ contain/ incorporate/ involve sth **in** sth
▶to incorporate/ build sth **into** sth
▶to be included/ covered/ incorporated/ encompassed **as** sth
▶to contain/ cover/ incorporate/ encompass/ involve/ embrace particular **aspects** of sth
▶to include/ contain/ cover/ incorporate/ encompass particular **material**
▶to include/ contain/ incorporate particular **features**
▶to cover/ encompass/ embrace particular **subjects/ issues**
▶to contain/ cover/ incorporate/ encompass/ involve/ embrace a (wide) **range** of things
▶to include/ contain/ cover/ incorporate/ involve/ embrace the **whole** of sth
▶to **directly** cover/ encompass/ involve sth
▶to cover/ incorporate/ encompass/ involve sb/ sth **fully**

include [他] 《進行形まれ》(一員[一部]として)含む；(一員[一部]に)含める ◇The tour *included* a visit to the Science Museum. そのツアーには科学博物館の見物が含まれていた ◇Does the price *include* tax? 価格は税込みですか ◇Your duties will *include* typing letters and answering the phone. あなた方の職務には手紙のタイピングと電話応対が含まれます ◇You should *include* some examples in your essay. 小論文には実例をいくつか入れるほうがいい ◇We all went, *me included*. 私を含め, 私たちは皆出かけた ◇Representatives from the country were *included* as observers at the conference. その国の代表者たちは大会のオブザーバーとして(参加者に)含まれていた ❶include が「含む」の意味の場合, 進行形では用いられない. ×Is the price *including* tax? 反意 **exclude** (EXCLUDE 1)
▶**including** 前 《略 **incl.**》 ◇It's £7.50, *including* tax. それは税込みで7.5ポンドです 反意 *excluding* (EXCLUDE 1)
▶**inclusion** 名 [U, C] ◇His *inclusion* in the team is in doubt. 彼のチーム入りは未決定である ◇There were some surprising *inclusions* in the list. 名簿には驚くような名前がいくつか含まれていた 反意 **exclusion** (EXCLUDE 1)

contain [他] 《進行形なし》(内部に[一部として])含む, 含有[包含, 内包]する ◇This drink doesn't *contain* any alcohol. この飲料にはアルコールがまったく含まれていません ◇The bottle *contains* (= can hold) two litres. その瓶には2リットル入ります ◇He handed over a brown envelope *containing* a hundred dollar bills. 彼は100ドル札が入った茶封筒を手渡した ◇Her statement *contained* one or two inaccuracies. 彼女の陳述には一つ二つ誤りがあった

cover [他] (物事を)含む；(物事を)取り扱う, 対象にする；(物事に)適用される, 該当する ◇The survey *covers* all aspects of the business. その調査はそのビジネスのあらゆ

→include ... income

...側面を対象としている ◇The lectures ***covered*** a lot of ***ground*** (= a lot of material or subjects). その講義では多くの分野が取り扱われた ◇He manages the sales team *covering* the northern part of the country (= selling to people in that area). 彼は国の北部を担当する販売チームを統括している ◇Do the rules *cover* (= do they apply to) a case like this? その規則はこのような場合に適用されますか ❶cover が「(物事を)含む」の意味の場合、進行形では用いられない。×The survey is *covering* all aspects of the business.
➤**coverage** [名] [U] ◇magazines with extensive *coverage* of diet and health topics 食事と健康の話題を幅広く網羅した雑誌

incorporate [他]《ややフォーマル》(物事の一部を構成するように)組み[取り]入れる[込む] ◇Many of your suggestions have been *incorporated* into the plan. あなたの提案の多くがその計画に取り入れられている ◇The new car design *incorporates* all the latest safety features. その新車のデザインには最新の安全機能がすべて組み込まれている

encompass [他]《進行形なし》《フォーマル》(数多くの[広範な]物事を)包括[網羅]する ◇The job *encompasses* a wide range of responsibilities. その仕事には多様な責任がः含まれる ◇The group *encompasses* all ages. そのグループにはあらゆる年齢層の人が網羅されている

involve [他]《進行形なし》(人を物事に)参加[従事]させる ◇We want to *involve* as many people as possible in the celebrations. 私たちは祝典にできるだけ多くの人々に参加してほしい ◇Parents should *involve themselves* in their children's education. 両親は自分の子どもの教育に携わるべきです [反意] exclude (EXCLUDE 2), ☞ **involvement** (INVOLVEMENT)

ˌbuild sth 'in, ˌbuild sth 'into sth [句動詞] 〔しばしば受身で〕(物事を構造[計画, システム]の恒久的な部分に)組み[作り]付ける ◇We're having new closets *built in*. 私たちは新しいクローゼットを作り付けているところです ◇The pipes were *built into* the concrete. パイプがコンクリートの中に埋め込まれた ◇A certain amount of flexibility needs to be *built into* the system. ある程度の柔軟性をシステムに組み込む必要がある
➤**ˌbuilt-'in** [形] [名詞の前で] ◇*built-in* wardrobes/closets/cupboards/units 作り付けの衣装だんす/クローゼット/食器棚/設備

embrace [他, 受身なし]《進行形なし》《フォーマル》(物事を)含む, 取り扱う ;(異なる物事を)併せ持つ ◇The talks *embraced* a wide range of issues. 協議では幅広い問題が取り扱われた ◇The word 'mankind' *embraces* men, women and children. mankindという単語には, 男, 女, 子どもが含まれる

ˌtake sth 'in [句動詞] [受身なし]《進行形なし》(観光地を)旅程に入れる ◇The tour *takes in* six European capitals. そのツアーの旅程にはヨーロッパの6つの首都が入っている

income [名] ☞ REVENUE

income・wage・pay・salary・earnings
人が仕事をして稼ぐ[受け取る]お金
【類語訳】所得, 収入, 賃金, 給料, 俸給, 給与

〔文型&コロケーション〕
▶(a) **high**/ **low**/ **basic** income/ wage/ wages/ pay/ salary/ earnings
▶(a) **good** income/ wage/ wages/ pay/ salary/ earnings
▶(an) **inadequate** income/ wage/ wages/ pay/ salary
▶(a/ an) **meagre**/ **average** income/ wage/ wages/ pay/ salary/ earnings
▶to **receive** an income/ a wage/ wages/ a salary/ earnings
▶to **get** an income/ a wage/ wages/ a salary
▶to **earn** an income/ a wage/ wages/ your pay/ a salary
▶to **pay**/ **give sb** an income/ a wage/ wages/ a salary
▶to **have**/ **live off** an income/ a wage/ wages/ a salary/ earnings
▶to **be on** an income/ a wage/ wages/ a salary

income [C, U] (人が仕事[投資, ビジネス]で得る)所得, 収入 ◇Organic food is simply not affordable for people on low *incomes*. 自然食品は低所得の人々には絶対に手が届かない ◇They have a weekly ***disposable income*** (= the money that is left to spend after tax) of £200. 彼らには週200ポンドの可処分所得がある ◇She is definitely in the higher *income* bracket. 彼女は明らかに高所得者層に入っている ❶incomeは会社[国家]がビジネス[投資]で得る収益[歳入]も指す. ☞ **income** (REVENUE), **money** (MONEY 1)

wage [C] (または **wages** [複数で])(毎週支払われる)賃金, 給料 ◇There are extra benefits for people on low *wages*. 低賃金者のために特別給付金がある ◇He gets a weekly *wage* of £300. 彼は週に300ポンドの賃金を得ている ◇She earns £120 a week, which is nothing like a ***living wage*** (= a wage that is high enough for sb to buy the things they need in order to live). 彼女の週給は生活賃金に遠く及ばない120ポンドだ ◇a ***minimum wage*** (= the lowest wage that an employer is allowed to pay by law) 最低賃金

pay [U] (仕事で得る)俸給, 給与, 給料 ◇Her job is hard work, but the *pay* is good. 彼女の仕事は重労働だが, 給料はよい ◇The job offers good rates of *pay* and excellent conditions. その仕事は賃金率の良さと優れた条件を提供する ◇a 3% *pay* rise《英》3%の昇給 ◇a 3% *pay* raise《米》3%の昇給

salary [C] (毎月[月2回]支払われる)俸給, 給与, 給料 ◇He gets a basic *salary* plus commission. 彼は基本給に加えて歩合を得ている ◇What *salary* band will I be on after two years in the company? 入社2年後には私はどの給与体系に置かれますか

〔ノート〕**wage, pay, salary** の使い分け: pay はこれら3つの語の中で最も一般的な語. 工場[店]などで働く従業員は, 週ごとに **wage** を得る. オフィスで働く従業員[教師, 医師などの専門職の人]は, 毎月《英》または月2回《米》支払われる **salary** を受け取るが, ふつう年俸で表される.
◆She's on a(n annual) *salary* of over $80,000. (彼女の年俸は8万ドル超である).

earnings [複数で] (仕事で得る)収入 ◇There has been a definite rise in average *earnings* for factory workers. 工場労働者の平均収入ははっきりと上昇してきている ◇She received compensation for loss of *earnings* caused by the accident. 彼女は事故によって失った収入に対する補償金を受け取った ☞ **earnings** (PROFIT), **earn** (MAKE 2)

〔ノート〕**income** と **earnings** の使い分け: 人の earnings は仕事で得る収入を指す. これには銀行の預金口座の利息な

ど、何もせずに得る不労所得は含まれない。incomeは一般的に当てにできる定期的な収入とみなされる。earnignsは人が何とかして得る収入のすべてを指し、月[年]ごとに変化する可能性もある。

incompetent 形

incompetent・bad・rotten・poor・inept・useless・inadequate
人が当然行われるべき仕事をする技術[能力]を持たないこと
【類語訳】無能な、不適格な、得意でない、向いていない、役立たずの、無力な、失格の

文型&コロケーション
▸ bad/ rotten/ poor/ inept/ useless **at sth**
▸ an incompetent/ a bad/ a rotten/ a poor/ a useless **teacher/ driver**
▸ a bad/ a rotten/ a useless/ an inadequate **mother/ father/ parent**
▸ **hopelessly** incompetent/ inept/ inadequate
▸ **completely/ totally** incompetent/ useless/ inadequate
▸ **very** bad/ poor/ inept/ inadequate

incompetent《ややフォーマル》(仕事をする技術[能力]が)なく)無能な、不適格な ◇She worked for years under an *incompetent* manager. 彼女は無能な部長の下で何年も働いた ◇They criticized his *incompetent* handling of the affair. 彼らはその件の処理に際しての彼の無能ぶりを批判した 反意 **competent** (GOOD 4), ☞ **incompetent** (LOSER 2)
▸**incompetence** 名 [U] ◇government/police *incompetence* 政府/警察の無能ぶり
bad《特に話し言葉》得意でない、長けていない、向いていない、下手な ◇I would be a really *bad* teacher — I've no patience. 私は本当に教えることに向いていないと思う—忍耐力がないもん ◇He's a *bad* loser (= he complains when he loses a game). 彼は負け惜しみを言う ◇She is so *bad* at keeping secrets. 彼女は秘密を守るのがとても苦手だ 反意 **good** (GOOD 4)
▸**badly** 副 ◇He plays really *badly*. 彼のプレーは本当に下手だ
rotten [ふつう名詞の前で]《インフォーマル》とても下手[苦手]な ◇She's a *rotten* singer. 彼女は歌がからっきし駄目だ ◇I've always been *rotten* at maths. 私はずっと前から数学がとても苦手だ 反意 **great** (GOOD 4)
poor《ややフォーマル》得意でない、長けていない、向いていない、下手な、苦手で ◇Such a *poor* swimmer would not survive in that water for long. そんなに泳ぐのが下手ならそんな水の中に長い間いれば助からないだろう ◇She's a good teacher but a *poor* manager. 彼女は教えるのはうまいが、経営は下手だ 反意 **good** (GOOD 4)

ノート **bad** と **poor** の使い分け: poorはbadよりもフォーマルで、書き言葉で用いられ、badは話し言葉で用いられることが多い。

inept《ややフォーマル》(技術・判断力がなく)向いていない、下手な、的外れの、間の抜けた ◇She was left feeling *inept* and inadequate. 彼女は自分には適性も能力も欠けているとの思いが残った ◇He made some particularly *inept* remarks. 彼は特に間の抜けた発言をした ❶ineptはふつう人の社交術の欠如について用いられる。

▸**ineptitude** 名 [U] ◇the *ineptitude* of the police in handling the situation 警察の状況処理のまずさ
useless《インフォーマル》非常に下手[苦手]な;役立たずの ◇I'm *useless* at French. 私のフランス語は使いものになりません ◇Don't ask her to help. She's *useless*. 彼女に助けを求めるな。役に立たない

ノート **rotten** と **useless** の使い分け: rottenはbusinessman, cook, driver, husband, wifeなどの名詞の前で用いられることが最も多い。usefulはuseless at sthという句で用いられることが多い。◆ *useless* at football/your job/remembering names (サッカー/仕事/名前を覚えるのが苦手な) 物事をうまく行えない人は、一般にusefulと表すことができるが、rottenは不可。×Don't ask her to help. She's *rotten*.

inadequate 無力な、失格の ◇I felt totally *inadequate* as a parent. 私は親としてまったく失格だと思った ❶この意味では、inadequateはふつうto feel inadequateという句で用いられる。名詞の前に置かれる場合は、ふつう母親・父親・親を修飾する。☞ **inadequate** (INADEQUATE)

inconsistent 形

inconsistent・incompatible・contradictory・at odds・mutually exclusive・irreconcilable
種類が異なり混ぜ[組み]合わせることができないことを表す
【類語訳】一致しない、相反する、食い違う、矛盾する、両立しない、相入れない、折り合いのつかない

文型&コロケーション
▸ inconsistent/ incompatible/ at odds/ irreconcilable **with sth**
▸ **totally** inconsistent/ incompatible/ contradictory/ at odds/ irreconcilable
▸ **somewhat** inconsistent/ incompatible/ contradictory/ at odds
▸ **apparently** inconsistent/ incompatible/ contradictory/ irreconcilable
▸ **clearly** inconsistent/ incompatible/ at odds
▸ **mutually** inconsistent/ incompatible/ contradictory/ exclusive

inconsistent [名詞の前はまれ]《ややフォーマル》(陳述などが)一致しない、相反する、食い違う、矛盾する ◇The report is *inconsistent* with the financial statements. その報告書は財務表と一致しない ◇The witnesses' statements were *inconsistent*. 目撃者たちの供述は食い違っていた ❶inconsistent withは「行為」が「基準[考え]」と一致しないことに用いられることもある。◆ Her behaviour was clearly *inconsistent* with her beliefs. (彼女の振る舞いが信条に反しているのは明らかだった)。反意 **consistent** ❶consistentは陳述などが互いに一致していることを表す。◆The results are entirely *consistent* with our earlier research. (その結果は私たちが以前行った調査と完全に一致している).
▸**inconsistency** 名 [U, C] ◇There is some *inconsistency* between the witnesses' evidence and their earlier statements. 目撃者たちの証言と前回の彼らの供述との間にはいくらか矛盾がある ◇I noticed a few *inconsistencies* in her argument. 私は彼女の主張の中のいくつかの矛盾に気づいた
incompatible《ややフォーマル、特に書き言葉》(行為・考えが)両立しない、矛盾する; (種類が異なり)適合しない、互換性

↪**inconsistent**

のない ◇The hours of the job are *incompatible* with family life. 仕事の時間と家庭生活とが両立しない ◇New computer software is often *incompatible* with older computers. 新しいコンピューター・ソフトは古いコンピューターと互換性がないことが多い ◇Those two blood groups are *incompatible*. それら二つの血液型は適合しない 反意 **compatible** ❶compatibleは行為・考え・物事が一緒に存在[使用]することができることを表す. ◆*compatible* software (互換性のあるソフトウェア). ◆Are measures to protect the environment *compatible with* economic growth? (環境保護対策は経済成長と両立しますか).

contradictory《ややフォーマル, 特に書き言葉》(事実・意見が)矛盾する, 相反する ◇We are faced with two apparently *contradictory* statements. 私たちは明らかに矛盾する二つの供述に直面している ◇The advice I received was often *contradictory*. 私が受けたアドバイスは自己矛盾することが多かった ☞ **contradict** (CONFLICT 動), **contradiction** (CONFLICT 名)

at 'odds《行わ》(同じであるべきなのに)一致しないで, 食い違って ◇These findings are *at odds* with what is going on in the rest of the country. これらの調査結果はこの国の他の地域で起こっていることと一致しない ☞ **be at odds** (CONFLICT 動)

,**mutually ex'clusive**《フレーズ》《しばしば否定的な文で》《ややフォーマル, 特に書き言葉》(共に存在し[真実たり])得ない, 相反する ◇The two options are not *mutually exclusive* (= you can have them both). その二つの選択肢は両立しうる ❶not mutually exclusiveは異なる[一緒に存在することができない]と考えられがちで, 実は同じだ[まったく一緒に存在することができる]というような場合に用いられる. 典型的な連語には, approaches, alternatives, options, assumptions, categories, possibilities が挙げられる.

irreconcilable《フォーマル》(意見が異なり)和解しがたい, 折り合いのつかない;(考え・意見が)両立しない, 相いれない ◇The break-up was due to '*irreconcilable differences*'. 解散は「和解しがたい意見の相違」によるものだった ◇This view is *irreconcilable* with common sense. この考えは常識と相いれない

increase 名

increase • growth • inflation • rise • gain • surge • hike • spiral • raise • upturn
物事の量や数, 水準が増える[高くなる]状況を表す
【類語訳】増加, 高まり, 拡張, 伸び, 上昇, インフレ, 利益, 急増, 高騰, 昇給, 上向き, 好転

文型&コロケーション

▶an increase/ growth/ inflation/ a rise/ a gain/ a surge/ a hike/ a spiral/ an upturn **in** sth
▶an increase/ growth/ inflation/ a rise/ a gain/ a surge/ a hike **of** 20%
▶(a) **significant/ sharp** increase/ growth/ inflation/ rise/ gain/ surge/ hike/ upturn
▶(a) **large/ considerable/ huge/ massive** increase/ growth/ inflation/ rise/ gain/ surge/ hike
▶(a) **sudden** increase/ growth/ inflation/ rise/ gain/ surge/ hike/ upturn
▶(a) **moderate** increase/ growth/ inflation/ rise/ hike
▶(a) **slow/ gradual/ steady** increase/ growth/ inflation/ rise/ spiral
▶(a) **tax/ price/ wage** increase/ growth/ inflation/ rise/

hike/ raise
▶to **see** an increase/ growth/ inflation/ a rise/ a gain/ a surge/ a hike/ an upturn
▶to **lead to/ mean/ report** an increase/ growth/ inflation/ a rise/ a gain/ a surge/ a hike
▶to **cause/ represent** an increase/ growth/ inflation/ a rise/ a gain/ a surge
▶to **show** an increase/ growth/ inflation/ a rise/ a gain/ a surge

increase [C, U] (量・数・水準の)増加, 高まり ◇There has been a steady *increase* in demand for the service. そのサービスに対する需要は着実に高まっている ◇This year saw an *increase* of nearly 20% in the number of visitors. 今年は来客数がほぼ2割増加した ◇The figures show a significant *increase on* last year's turnover. これらの数字は総取引残高が昨年よりも著しく増加したことを示している ◇Homelessness is *on the increase* (= increasing). ホームレスが増加している 反意 **cut, decrease, reduction** (REDUCTION), ☞ **increase** (RISE)

growth [U, 単数で] (大きさ・量・程度の)増加, 拡張, 高まり, 伸び ◇The report links population *growth* with rural poverty. その報告書は人口の増加と地方の貧困を関連付けている ◇The *growth* in average earnings has remained constant. 平均収入の増加は一定のままである ◇Recent years have seen a huge *growth* of interest in alternative medicine. 近年, 代替医療に対する関心が非常に高まっている ☞ **grow** (RISE)

inflation [U] (物価の)上昇, インフレ(ーション);物価上昇[インフレ]率 ◇The bank is introducing new measures to curb *inflation*. 銀行は新たなインフレ抑制措置を導入しようとしている ◇Wage increases must be *in line with inflation*. 賃上げはインフレに見合ったものでなければならない ◇*Inflation* is currently *running at* 3%. インフレ率は現在3%の水準で

rise [C] (数・量・水準の)増加, 上昇, 高まり ◇The industry is feeling the effects of recent price *rises*. その産業では最近の価格上昇の影響を感じている ◇There has been a sharp *rise* in the number of people out of work. 失業者数が急増している 反意 **fall, decline, drop** (REDUCTION), ☞ **rise** (RISE)

ノート **increase, growth, rise** の使い分け: 多くの場合, これらのどの語も使用可能. ◆a rapid *increase/growth/rise* in the number of private cars (自家用車数の急増). growthはしばしば不可算で, 特に大きさについて用いられる. population growthは population increase/riseよりもずっと一般的な表現. また, 肯定的な物事について用いられるほうが多い. ◆the *growth* in earnings/employment/demand (収益/雇用/需要の増加). increaseとriseはより否定的な物事について用いられることが多い. ◆an alarming *increase/rise* in violent crime (凶悪犯罪の驚くべき急増). increaseはriseよりも一般的で, ひとりでに増加する[意図的に増加させられる]場合に用いられる. riseは意図的な増加よりも, 偶然に増加する場合に用いられる. price risesは販売者ではなく, 購入者の視点から見た言い方. 企業が announce price increases (値上げを告知する)のに対し, 顧客は feel the effects of price increases/rises (値上がりの影響を感じる)ことになる.

gain [C, U] (重量・富の)増加, 利益 ◇a £3,000 *gain* from our investment 私たちの3千ポンドの投資利益 ◇Regular exercise is the best way of preventing weight *gain*.

increase

規則的な運動は体重増加を防ぐ最良の方法である 反意 **loss**
❶ **loss** [U, C]はもはや(同じだけ)持っていない状態[持っていない状態に至る過程]を指す. ◆weight *loss* (減量). ◆*loss* of blood (失血). ◆The closure of the factory will lead to a number of job *losses*. (その工場の閉鎖は多くの雇用の喪失をもたらすだろう). ☞ **loss** (DEBT)

surge [C] (数量の)急増, 高まり;大量 ◆Economists have reported a *surge* in consumer spending. 経済学者たちは消費者支出の急増を報告している ◆After an initial *surge* of interest, there has been little call for our services. 当初は関心がどっと寄せられたが, その後我々のサービスに対する需要はほとんどなくなった ☞ **surge** (SOAR)

hike [C] 《インフォーマル, 特にジャーナリズム》(価格・税金の抜き打ち的な)引き上げ, 高騰 ◆Higher crude oil prices mean price *hikes* for consumers too. 原油価格の上昇は消費者価格の高騰も意味する ◆Borrowers will be hit hard by the latest *hike* in interest rates. 債務者は最近の金利引き上げによって大きな打撃を受けるだろう

spiral [U] (有害な)連鎖的上昇, 悪循環 ◆How can we halt the destructive *spiral* of violence in the inner cities? どうしたら都市部における破壊的な暴力の連鎖を止めることができるだろうか ◆The country is caught in a vicious *spiral* of rising wages and prices. その国は賃金と価格の上昇という悪循環にはまっている ❶ *spiral* は物事の有害な連鎖的低下についても用いられる. ◆The book gives a harrowing account of a *downward spiral* of drink, drugs and despair. (その本は酒, 麻薬, 絶望の悪循環の悲惨さを描いている).

raise [C] 《米》昇給 ◆If I asked my boss for a *raise* he'd fire me. 上司に昇給を求めたりしたら, 解雇されちゃうよ ❶《英》では rise を用いる.

upturn [C, ふつう単数で] (取引高・景気の)上向き, 好転, 上昇 ◆The restaurant trade is on the *upturn*. レストラン業は好転に向かっている ◆an *upturn* in the economy 景気の上昇 反意 **downturn** (REDUCTION)

increase 動

increase • raise • boost • intensify • maximize • heighten • inflate • step sth up • turn sth up
量や数, 水準を増すことを表す
【類語訳】増加させる, 上昇させる, 高める, 引き上げる, 強める, 激しくする, 強まる, 激しくなる, 最大化する, 高まる

【文型&コロケーション】
▸ to increase/ raise/ boost/ inflate/ step up sth **by** 15%, 250, £100, a third, etc.
▸ to increase/ raise/ boost/ inflate/ step up sth **from** 150, $500, etc
▸ to increase/ raise/ boost/ inflate/ step up sth **to** 150, $500, etc
▸ to increase/ raise/ boost/ maximize/ inflate **prices**
▸ to increase/ raise/ boost/ maximize your **income**
▸ to increase/ raise/ boost/ heighten **awareness/ interest**
▸ to increase/ raise/ boost/ maximize **support**
▸ to increase/ raise/ boost **confidence**
▸ to increase/ raise/ intensify/ step up the **pressure**
▸ to increase/ intensify/ maximize/ heighten/ step up **security**
▸ to increase/ raise/ boost/ intensify/ heighten/ inflate sth **greatly/ further**

increase [他] (量・数・水準・程度・価値を)増加[上昇]させる, 高める ◆We need to *increase* productivity. 我々は生産性を高める必要がある ◆They've *increased* the price by 50%. 価格が50%引き上げられた ◆Last month the reward was *increased* from £20,000 to £40,000. 先月, 報酬が2万ポンドから4万ポンドに引き上げられた 反意 **decrease, reduce** (REDUCE), ☞ **increase** (RISE)
▸*increased* 形 《名詞の前で》◆*increased* demand/ pressure/spending 増加した需要/圧力/支出

raise [他] (量・水準を)増加[上昇]させる ◆The government has promised not to *raise* taxes. 政府は増税しないことを約束している ◆They *raised* their offer to $500. 彼らは付け値を500ドルに引き上げた ◆How can we *raise* standards in schools? どうしたら学校の水準を引き上げることができますか ◆Don't tell her about the job until you know for sure — we don't want to *raise her hopes* (= make her hope too much). 確実なことがわかるまで彼女にその仕事のことを言うな―彼女に過剰な期待を抱かせたくないんだ ◆I've never heard him even *raise his voice* (= speak louder because he was angry). 彼が(怒って)声を張り上げるのさえ一度も聞いたことがない 反意 **lower** (REDUCE)

ノート **increase** と **raise** の使い分け:多くの場合, 両語とも使用可能. increase は数・価格・数字について用いられることがいくぶん多い. raise は感情・性質などを表す抽象名詞に用いられることが多い. to raise interest/awareness (関心/認識を高める). また, raise は raise sb's hopes や raise your voice などの慣用語句でも用いられる.

boost [他] 《しばしばほめて, 特にジャーナリズム》(増加[改善, 成功]させて)引き上げる, 伸ばす, 高める ◆The new service helped to *boost* pre-tax profits by 10%. 新サービスは税引き前利益を10%伸ばすのに役立った ◆A last-minute rush by Christmas shoppers *boosted* sales. クリスマス用品の買い物客がぎりぎりになって殺到して売上げが伸びた ◆Getting that job did a lot to *boost his ego* (= make him feel more confident). その仕事に就くことで彼の自尊心はかなり高まった ❶ boost は常に肯定的な増加に用いる. ◆to *boost* productivity/sales/spending (生産性/売り上げ/支出を伸ばす). ◆to *boost* sb's morale/ career/confidence (人の士気/経歴/自信を高める). ✕ *boost* taxes/pressure/tension.

intensify [他, 自] (行動・感情を)強める, 激しくする;(行動・感情が)強まる, 激しくなる ◆The opposition leader has *intensified* his attacks on the government. 野党の党首が政府に対する攻撃を強めている ◆The reforms served only to *intensify* the misery of the poorer peasants. 改革は結局のところ, 貧困層の農民の窮状を悪化させるだけだった ◆Violence *intensified* during the night. 暴力行為は夜中に激しくなった

maximize 《英でまた **-ise**》[他] 《ややフォーマル, 特にビジネスで》(物事を)最大にする;(物事を)最大限に活用する, 最大化する ◆They drew up a six-point plan to *maximize* safety and efficiency in the use of the equipment. 彼らはその装置の使用にあたり, 安全性と効率を最大限にするため6点からなる案を作成した ◆*Maximize* the window to full screen. 《コンピューター》ウィンドウを画面いっぱいに最大化しましょう ◆The purpose of the restructuring is to *maximize* opportunities in the global market. このリストラの目的は世界市場に存在する機会を最大限に活用することである 反意 **minimize** (REDUCE)

heighten [他, 自] (影響・感情を)強める, 高める;(影響・

感情が)強まる, 高まる ◇Fears of further racial conflict were *heightened* by news of the riots. さらなる人種紛争の恐れが, その暴動のニュースで強まった ◇Tension *heightened* after the recent bomb attack. 最近行われた爆発の後で, 緊張が高まった

【ノート】 **intensify** と **heighten** の使い分け: 両語とも他動詞・自動詞として用いるが, heighten は他動詞として, 特に感情・態度について用いられる. intensify は行動についても用いられる. ◆ a *heightened* sense of loneliness/well-being (孤独感/幸福感の高まり) ◆ to *intensify* the campaign/battle (運動/戦闘を激化させる)

inflate [他]《しばしばみなして, 特にジャーナリズム》(価格を)吊り上げる ◇The principal effect of the demand for new houses was to *inflate* prices. 新築住宅に対する需要がもたらす主な影響は, 価格の吊り上げであった ◇The profit margin had been artificially *inflated*. 利ざやは人為的に吊り上げられていた ❶ inflate は自動詞としても用いるが, 頻度は低い. ◆ House prices are no longer *inflating* at the same rate as last year. (住宅価格はもはや昨年と同じ率では高騰していない).

step sth 'up [句動] (-pp-) (活動の水準を)強化する ◇He has *stepped up* his training to prepare for the race. 彼はレースに備えてトレーニングを強化している ◇Security has been *stepped up* in response to the recent terrorist threat. 最近のテロの脅威に対応して警備が強化されている

turn sth 'up [句動] (機器の制御装置を動かして音[熱, 光]を)上げる, 強める ◇Could you *turn* the TV *up*? テレビの音量を上げていただけますか ◇The music was *turned up* loud. 音楽の音量が大きくされた [反意] **turn sth down** (REDUCE), ☞ **turn sth on** (TURN STH ON)

incredible [形] ☞ UNLIKELY 2

incredible・unbelievable・beyond belief
物事が非常に信用ならないこと
【類語訳】信じられない, 信じがたい

【文型&コロケーション】
▶ incredible/ unbelievable **to** sb
▶ to be incredible/ unbelievable/ beyond belief **that**...
▶ incredible/ unbelievable **as it may seem**...
▶ to find sth incredible/ unbelievable
▶ almost incredible/ unbelievable/ beyond belief
▶ **completely/ totally/ just/ quite/ simply** incredible/ unbelievable

incredible 信じられない, 信じがたい ◇The speed of her recovery seems almost *incredible*. 彼女の回復の早さはほとんど信じられないほどに思える ◇It's just *incredible* to me that only one person was hurt. 一人しかけがをしなかったとは私にはまったく信じられない ◇It's *incredible* to think that the affair had been going on for years. その情事が何年も続いていたなんて信じられない [反意] **credible** (POSSIBLE 2)
▷ **incredibly** [副] ◇ *Incredibly*, a year later the same thing happened again. 信じられないことに, 一年後同じ事がまた起こった

unbelievable (疑わしく)信じられない, 信じがたい ◇It's all so *unbelievable*! それはまったく信じがたい ◇It seemed *unbelievable*, but it was true. それは信じがたく思えたが, 事実だった ◇I found the ending of the novel a bit *unbelievable*. 私にはその小説の結末は少し信じがたいものに思えた [反意] **believable** (POSSIBLE 2)
▷ **unbelievably** [副] ◇It was published, *unbelievably*, almost fifty years ago. それがほぼ半世紀前に出版されたとは信じがたい

【ノート】 **incredible** と **unbelievable** の使い分け: incredible は非常に信じがたいと思っていても, 真実であることを受け入れている場合に用いられる(文脈で信じていないことが明らかな場合は例外). ◆ You surely don't believe this *incredible* accusation against him? (まさか彼へのこのとんでもない非難を信じちゃいないだろうね) unbelievable は真実[可能]であるとはまったく信じていない場合に用いられることが多い.

beyond be'lief [行外] (あまりに大きくて[難しくて, 衝撃的で])信じられない[信じがたい] ◇It is *beyond belief* that anyone could commit such a crime. そんな犯罪を犯すことができる人間がいるなんて信じられない ◇Dissatisfaction with the government has grown *beyond belief*. 政府に対する不満は信じがたいほど大きくなっている ❶ beyond belief は特に否定的な感情や意見を表現[修飾]する場合に用いられる.

independence [名]

independence・autonomy・sovereignty・self-determination・self-government
他国から政治的に支配されずに, 国家や地域が有する自己統治の自由
【類語訳】独立, 自立, 自治, 主権, 自決権, 自主運営

【文型&コロケーション】
▶ independence/ autonomy/ sovereignty/ self-determination/ self-government **for** sb
▶ **complete/ full** independence/ autonomy/ sovereignty
▶ **national** independence/ autonomy/ sovereignty/ self-determination
▶ **local/ regional** autonomy/ self-determination/ self-government
▶ **political** independence/ autonomy/ sovereignty/ self-determination
▶ **to achieve** independence/ autonomy/ sovereignty/ self-determination/ self-government
▶ **to have/ enjoy/ give sb/ grant sb/ recognize sth's** independence/ autonomy/ sovereignty
▶ **the principle/ right of** autonomy/ sovereignty/ self-determination/ self-government

independence [U] (他国からの)独立; (国家の政治的)自立 ◇Cuba gained *independence from* Spain in 1898. キューバは1898年にスペインから独立した ◇There has been international recognition for the island's *declaration of independence*. その島の独立宣言は国際的に承認されている ◇Namibia became a full member of the UN *at independence* (= when it became independent). ナミビアは独立時に正式に国連に加盟した ◇Malaysia celebrates its *independence day* on 31st August. マレーシアは8月31日に独立記念日を祝う ☞ **independence** (FREEDOM)
▷ **independent** [形] ◇Mozambique became *independent* in 1975. モザンビークは1975年に独立した

indifferent, industry

autonomy [U]《ややフォーマル, 書き言葉》(国家[地域]の)自治(権) ◇There has been a campaign for greater *autonomy* for the region. その地域の自治権の拡大を求める運動が続いている ☞ **autonomy** (FREEDOM)
▸ **autonomous** 形 ◇an *autonomous* republic/state/province 自治共和国/州/省

> ノート **independence** と **autonomy** の使い分け：この意味では, independenceはふつう外部からの政治的支配を離れた((非))独立)国家全体にとっての完全な自由を指し, autonomyはふつう完全な独立に満たない段階の自由を指す。

sovereignty [U]《書き言葉》(国家の)主権 ◇The declaration proclaimed the full *sovereignty* of the republic. その宣言は共和国の完全な主権を謳っていた ◇She has strong views on preserving national *sovereignty*. 彼女は国家の主権維持に関して強硬な意見を持っている
▸ **sovereign** 形 ◇a *sovereign* state 主権国家

,self-de,termi'nation [U]《ややフォーマル, 書き言葉》(国家・国民の)自決権 ◇All nations have the right to *self-determination*. すべての国家は自決権を有する

,self-'government [U]（国民[構成員]による国家[組織]の）自治, 自主運営 ◇There have been demands for a wider measure of regional *self-government*. より大きな単位の地方自治体を望む声が湧き起こっている

indifferent 形

indifferent・lukewarm・unimpressed・half-hearted・uninterested・detached・apathetic・tepid
関心[熱意]を示さない人[態度]を表す
【類語訳】無関心な, 無頓着な, 熱意のない, 冷めた, 気のない, 気乗りしない, 超然とした, 淡々とした

> 文型&コロケーション
> ▸ indifferent/ lukewarm/ half-hearted/ apathetic **about** sth
> ▸ indifferent/ lukewarm/ apathetic **towards** sb/ sth
> ▸ lukewarm/ half-hearted/ uninterested **in** sth
> ▸ an indifferent/ a lukewarm/ a detached/ an apathetic **attitude**

indifferent 《名詞の前はまれ》無関心な, 無頓着な ◇Public opinion remained largely *indifferent to* the issue. 世論はその問題についてほぼ無関心のままだった
▸ **indifference** 名 [U, 単数で] ◇What she said is *a matter of complete indifference* to me. 彼女が言ったことは, 私にとってはどうでもいいことである

lukewarm 関心[熱意]のない ◇Union leaders were at best *lukewarm* in their response. 労働組合のリーダーたちの反応は無関心もいいところであった ◇He was disappointed by the *lukewarm* support from Washington. 彼はワシントンからの熱意のない支持にがっかりした 反意 **enthusiastic** (EAGER)

unimpressed 《名詞の前はまれ》感動しない, 感銘を受けない, 冷めた ◇The city remained *unimpressed by* the chancellor's speech. 市民は首相の演説にも冷めたままだった ◇Voters are *unimpressed with* his performance so far. 有権者たちはこれまでの彼の仕事ぶりには感銘を受けていない ◇She looked distinctly *unimpressed*. 彼女は明らかに冷めているように見えた 反意 **impressed** ◇I must admit I am *impressed*. (感動した ことを認めざるをえません). ☞ **impress** (IMPRESS)

,half-'hearted 気のない, 気乗りしない, 中途半端な, 生半可な ◇He made a *half-hearted* attempt to justify the decision. 彼は気乗りしないもののその決定を正当化しようと試みた

uninterested《名詞の前はまれ》関心[興味]のない；知りたがらない ◇They were totally *uninterested* in politics. 彼らは政治にまったく興味がなかった 反意 **interested** (INTERESTED), ☞ **uninteresting** (BORING)

detached《特に書き言葉》超然とした, 淡々とした ◇He was able to talk about it in a cold, *detached* manner. 彼はそれについては冷静に淡々と話すことができた ◇She spoke in a normal, *detached* tone. 彼女はいつもの淡々とした口調で話した
▸ **detachment** 名 [U] ◇He answered with an air of *detachment*. 彼は超然として答えた

apathetic《ややフォーマル, 特に書き言葉》関心[熱意]のない ◇She became *apathetic* and withdrawn. 彼女は熱意を失って引っ込みがちになった
▸ **apathy** 名 [U] ◇There is widespread *apathy* among the electorate. 有権者の間には無関心が広がっている

tepid《特にビジネス》熱意のない, 気のない ◇The play was greeted with *tepid* applause. そのプレー[劇]は気の抜けた拍手で迎えられた ◇The deal drew a *tepid* response from shareholders. その取り引きに対して株主から気のない反応が返ってきた

industry 名

industry・trade・business・service
商品の生産[サービスの提供]を伴う活動の一種
【類語訳】産業, 工業, …業, 業界, サービス業

> 文型&コロケーション
> ▸ to be **in** a particular industry/ trade/ business/ service
> ▸ the **book/ tourist/ car/ catering/ hotel/ construction** industry/ trade/ business
> ▸ the **timber/ fur/ wool/ wine/ motor/ building** industry/ trade
> ▸ the **energy/ oil/ food/ computer/ advertising/ insurance/ entertainment/ music/ film/ hospitality** industry/ business
> ▸ **computer/ insurance/ catering** services
> ▸ to **work in** a particular industry/ trade/ business/ service
> ▸ to **enter/ dominate** the industry/ trade/ business

industry [C] (特定の物の生産[サービスの提供]を行う)産業, 工業 ◇Thousands of jobs were lost in the steel *industry*. 鉄鋼業で何千もの職が失われた ◇We need to develop local *industries*. 地元産業を発展させる必要があります ◇Weaving and knitting were traditional *cottage industries* (= small businesses in which the work is done by people in their homes). 機織りと編み物は伝統的な家内工業だった ❶ industryは特に工場における商品の生産について用いる。サービスについて用いる場合は, ふつう非常に成功したものが対象となる。◆the film/entertainment/tourist/advertising/insurance *industry* (映像/娯楽/観光/広告/保険産業) ☞ **industry** (PRODUCTION)

trade [C] (特定の種類の)産業, …業, 業界 ◇Employment in the building *trade* is notoriously irregular. 建設業における雇用は不定期であるという悪評がある ◇He

↳industry

works in the retail *trade* (= selling goods in shops). 彼は小売業界で働いている ◆*trade*は, the building/motor/construction *trade* (建設業/自動車産業/建築業) などの, 高水準の正規教育を必要としない活動, または, the book/retail/car *trade* (書籍販売業/小売業/自動車販売業) などの, 特定の売買活動について用いられることが多い. trade [単数＋単数・複数動詞] は, 特定の産業[商業]分野とそれに関わる人々[会社] を指す. ◆They offer discounts to the *trade* (= to people who are working in the same business). (彼らは同業者に割引を提供している). ◆You should advertise in newspapers and *trade* magazines. (新聞と業界誌に広告を出したほうがいいよ). ☞ **trade** (TRADE), **trade** (WORK 名 1)

business [C] (利益の追求を目的とした商品[サービス]の製造[売買, 提供] を行う) 産業, …業, 業界 ◇She works in the computer *business*. 彼女はコンピュータ業界で働いている ◇Falling prices are wreaking havoc in the oil *business*. 価格の下落は石油業界に大損害を与えている ❶ *business*は活動に伴う肉体労働よりも産業やサービスに関わる経営活動を強調する. 特にサービス産業について用いられる. ◆the catering/hotel/entertainment/advertising/insurance *business* (賄い/ホテル/娯楽/広告/保険産業). *business*はジャーナリズムで用いられ, 極めて基礎的な製品や原料を製造[売買] する巨大な産業についても用いられるが, industryよりもいくぶんフォーマルである. ◆the energy/oil/food *business* (エネルギー/石油/食品産業).
☞ **business** (COMPANY), **business** (TRADE)

service [C, ふつう複数形] (顧客のための) サービス業 ◇They are offering special incentives to the financial *services* sector. 彼らは金融サービス部門に特別な刺激となる材料を提供している ◇The *service* industries were most affected by the recession. サービス産業は景気後退の影響を一番に受けた ❶ *service*は形容詞[名詞] の後で複数形で用いられることが多い. ◆computer/catering/financial/insurance/marketing/freight/accommodation *services* (コンピュータ/賄い/金融/保険/マーケティング/貨物運送/宿泊サービス業). *service*はふつう単独で用いられることはなく, 前出のように形容詞[名詞] の後で用いられない場合は, company, industry, sectorを後ろに伴うのが一般的である.

ineffective 形

ineffective・inefficient・unproductive・counterproductive・ineffectual・self-defeating
求められ[意図され] ていることを達成しないことや, 大した成果を上げないことを表す
【類語訳】役に立たない, 無能な, 無力な, 効果のない, 能率の悪い, 生産性のない

文型&コロケーション

▶ineffective/ inefficient/ counterproductive **for** sb/ sth
▶ineffective/ ineffectual **as** sth
▶ineffective/ inefficient **in/ at doing** sth
▶**to be** ineffective/ inefficient/ counterproductive/ self-defeating **to do** sth
▶**largely** ineffective/ unproductive/ ineffectual/ self-defeating
▶**rather** ineffective/ inefficient/ ineffectual
▶**relatively** ineffective/ inefficient/ unproductive
▶**entirely** ineffective/ unproductive/ counterproductive

ineffective (目的を達成できずに) 役に立たない, 無能な, 無力な; 効果[効力] のない, 無駄な ◇It has been criticized as an unfair and *ineffective* system. それは不公平で役に立たない制度として批判されてきた ◇The missiles are totally *ineffective against* tanks. そのミサイルは戦車に対してまったく無力である ◇High interest rates proved to be *ineffective* in reducing inflation. 高い金利はインフレを軽減する上で効果がないとわかった 反意 **effective** (SUCCESSFUL 1)
▷**ineffectively** 副 ◇Why is this crime dealt with so *ineffectively*? なぜこの犯罪の対処はそれほどに実効が上がらないのか 反意 **effectively** (SUCCESSFUL 1)

inefficient (仕事を十分にせずに) 役に立たない, 無能な, (時間[お金, エネルギー] などを最大限に利用せずに) 能率[効率] の悪い ◇The regime was both *inefficient* and corrupt. その政権は無能かつ腐敗していた ◇The boss thinks the new secretary is *inefficient*. 上司は新しい秘書は役立たずだと思っている ◇This method of data storage is an *inefficient* use of memory. このデータの蓄積方法はメモリーの非効率的使用の一例だ 反意 **efficient** (EFFICIENT)
▷**inefficiency** 名 [U, 複数で] ◇The measures encouraged *inefficiency* and waste. その対策は非効率と浪費を助長した ◇*inefficiencies* in the system システムに内在する非効率性 反意 **efficiency** (EFFICIENCY)
▷**inefficiently** 副 ◇The firm was *inefficiently* run. その会社の経営は能率が悪かった 反意 **efficiently** (EFFICIENT)

unproductive 生産性[成果] のない, 不毛な; 無駄な ◇I've spent yet another *unproductive* day. 私は不毛な日をさらにもう一日費やした ◇We had a series of *unproductive* meetings. 私たちは無駄な会議を続けた 反意 **productive** (PRODUCTIVE)

counterproductive [名詞の前はまれ] 逆効果の ◇Increases in taxation would be *counterproductive*. 増税は逆効果となるだろう ◇It would be *counterproductive* to act hastily at this stage. この段階で性急に行動するのは逆効果だろう

ineffectual (《フォーマル》) (人が大した成果を上げずに) 無能な, 無力な, (行動が目的を達成できずに) 無駄な, 無益な ◇The president is seen as weak and *ineffectual*. 社長は無力で無能だと見られている ◇She made an *ineffectual* grab at the book. 彼女はその本をつかもうとしたが無駄だった ❶ *ineffectual*は特に弱さ[必要な能力の欠如] から大した成果を上げられないときに用いられ, 特に何かを行おうとする人やその試みが「無力」「無駄」であると言うときに用いられる.
▷**ineffectually** 副 ◇He struggled *ineffectually* to get out from behind the wheel. 彼は運転席から抜け出そうともがいたが無駄だった

,**self-de'feating** (解決する代わりに問題[困難] をさらに引き起こして) 自滅する; 逆効果の ◇Paying children too much attention when they misbehave can be *self-defeating*. 子どもの行儀が悪いときに注意しすぎるのは逆効果になることもある

inequality 名

inequality・injustice・unfairness・inequity
社会に存在する人々の間の公平さの差, それによって他人よりもお金[権力, 機会] を持つ人がいること
【類語訳】不平等, 不公平

inevitable, in favour

文型&コロケーション
- inequality/ injustice/ unfairness/ inequity **in** sth
- inequality/ inequity **between** sb/ sth
- injustice/ unfairness **to** sb/ sth
- **social/ economic/ racial** inequality/ injustice/ inequity
- **great/ gross** inequality/ injustice/ inequity
- to **fight/ tackle/ struggle against** inequality/ injustice
- to **redress/ rectify/ remedy** inequality/ injustice/ inequity

inequality [U, C] (人々の間における)不平等 ◇There is generally some *inequality* between men and women within the family. ふつう家庭内の男女の間には不平等がいくつかある ◇Inequalities in health tend to reflect *inequalities* in income. 健康の不平等は収入の不平等を反映する傾向にある 反意 **equality** (JUSTICE), ☞ **unequal** (WRONG 3)

injustice [U, C] (相応の対価が得られない)不公平；不公平な行為[扱い] ◇I did not really see myself as a victim of *injustice*. 私は不公平な扱いの犠牲者という自覚はあまりなかった ◇Perhaps I'm *doing you an injustice* (= being unfair to you). 私は君を不公平に扱っているかもしれない ◇The report exposes the *injustices* of the system. その報告書は制度の不公平を暴いている 反意 **justice** (JUSTICE), ☞ **unjust** (WRONG 3)

unfairness [U] (正当な理由もなく相応の対価が得られない)不公平 ◇There are several examples of *unfairness* in the recruitment system. 採用制度にはいくつか不公平な点がある ◇She was still raging about the *unfairness* of it all. 彼女はそのことすべての不公平さにまだ腹を立てていた 反意 **fairness** (JUSTICE), ☞ **unfair** (WRONG 3)

inequity [C, U] 《フォーマル》(異なる人々[集団]に対して異なる扱いをする)不公平 ◇There are huge *inequities* in funding for schools. 学校向けの予算には大きな不公平がある ◇The new government sought to justify social *inequity* by promoting ideals of self-help. 新政府は自助の理念を推進することで社会的不公平を是認しようとした 反意 **equity** (JUSTICE)

inevitable 形

inevitable • necessary • unavoidable • inescapable • inexorable
物事が避けられない[防げない]ことを表す
【類語訳】避けられない, 不可避の, 必然的な, 必要な, 必須の, 不可欠な, 免れえない

文型&コロケーション
- an inevitable/ a necessary/ an unavoidable **consequence**
- an inevitable/ a necessary/ an inescapable **conclusion/ fact**
- an inevitable/ unavoidable **delay/ problem**
- an inevitable/ inescapable **fact**
- the inevitable/ inexorable **slide** into/ towards war, fascism, mediocrity, etc.
- the inevitable/ inexorable **decline/ rise** (of sth)
- **seemingly** inevitable/ unavoidable/ inescapable/ inexorable
- **almost** inevitable/ unavoidable/ inescapable

inevitable (不快な物事が)避けられない, 不可避の, 必然的な, 当然の ◇It was an *inevitable* consequence of the decision. それはその決定がもたらす必然的な結果だった ◇*It was inevitable that* there would be job losses. 失業が出るのは避けられなかった ◇A rise in interest rates seems *inevitable*. 利率の上昇は避けられないように思える

▸ **the inevitable** 名 [単数で] ◇You have to accept *the inevitable*. やむをえないとあきらめなくちゃね

▸ **inevitably** 副 ◇*Inevitably*, the press exaggerated the story. 当然, 報道機関はその話を誇張した

necessary [名詞の前で]《ややフォーマル, 書き言葉》(存在・発生が)必要な, 必須の, 不可欠な, 避けられない, 不可避の, 必然的な, 当然の ◇A *necessary* condition for a steep fall in demand is a widespread collapse in confidence. 需要の急落が起こる必要条件として広範囲に及ぶ信用の失墜がある ◇This is a *necessary* consequence of progress. これは進歩の必然的な帰結である ❶この意味でのnecessaryは, 特定の物事が起こる以前に存在せねばならないconditions, prerequisites, または特定の状況で[特定の出来事の後に]必ず起こるresults, outcome, consequenceを表すのに用いられる。 ☞ **necessary** (NECESSARY)

▸ **necessarily** 副 ◇The number of places available is *necessarily* limited. 利用できる場所の数は必然的に限られている

unavoidable (不快な物事が)避けられない, 不可避の, 必然的な, 当然の ◇All dates are approximate and are subject to *unavoidable* delays. すべての日付はおよその見通しであって止むを得ない事情で遅れるのは避けられない 反意 **avoidable**

▸ **unavoidably** 副 ◇I was *unavoidably* delayed. 遅れるのは避けられなかった

ノート inevitable と unavoidable の使い分け: inevitable は unavoidable よりもはるかに頻繁に用いられ, 連語の種類もずっと多い。 unavoidable は常に不快な物事, 特に delays や consequences と用いられる。 inevitable も不快な物事を表すことが多いが, 不快であるとは限らない。 連語には change, comparison, conclusion, development, effect, outcome, part, product, question, response, result, tendency, conflict, tension, disappointment が挙げられる。

inescapable (事実・状況が)避けられない, 不可避の, 免れえない ◇It is an *inescapable* fact that how we eat affects how we feel. 食生活が健康状態に影響を与えるのは避けようのない事実である

▸ **inescapably** 副 ◇Despite its remodelling, the building remains *inescapably* linked to the past. 改築したにもかかわらず, その建物は是非もなく過去と結びついている

inexorable 《フォーマル》(過程が)止められない, 変えられない；(論理が)反論できない ◇What is the reason for the *inexorable* rise in crime? 犯罪が増加の一途をたどっている原因は何ですか ◇This is where the *inexorable logic* of the theory breaks down. こここそ, その理論の反論できない論理の破綻しているところです

▸ **inexorably** 副 ◇Pressure of population is leading *inexorably* towards a crisis. 人口の圧迫は容赦なく危機につながっていっている

(be) in favour (of sb/sth) 《英》
《米》(be) in favor (of sb/sth) フレーズ ☞ SUPPORT

(be) in favour (of sb/sth) • approve • believe in sth/in doing sth • subscribe to sth • be all for sth/for doing sth

↳ in favour

物事が好ましい[受け入れられる, 適切である]との考えを表す
【類語訳】賛成で, 支持して, 賛成する, 同意する, 承諾する, 認める, 支持する

文型&コロケーション

- to be in favour of/ approve of/ believe in/ subscribe to/ be all for a(n) **idea/ view**
- to be in favour of/ approve of/ be all for a **plan/ course of action/ policy/ strategy/ suggestion**
- to approve/ believe in sth/ subscribe to sth **wholeheartedly**
- to **fully** approve/ subscribe to sth
- to **strongly** approve/ believe in sth
- to be **wholeheartedly/ fully/ strongly/ very much/ thoroughly** in favour (of sb/ sth)
- to **wholeheartedly/ fully/ strongly/ very much/ thoroughly** approve (of sth)

(be) in favour (of sb/sth) 《英》 《米》 **(be) in favor (of sb/sth)** [フレーズ] (多くの人々に影響を与える人・方針・計画に)賛成で(ある), 支持して(いる) ◇He argued *in favour of* a strike. 彼はストライキに賛成論を唱えた ◇There were 247 votes *in favour of* (the motion) and 152 against. (その動議に対し)賛成247票, 反対152票だった ◇I'm *all in favour of* (= completely support) equal pay for equal work. 私は同一労働一賃金に全面的に賛成です ◇Most of the 'don't knows' in the opinion polls came down *in favour of* (= eventually chose to support) the Democrats. 世論調査における態度保留者のほとんどは結局民主党を支持した [反意] **opposed** (AGAINST SB/STH)

approve [動] [自]《進行形なし》 (物事が好ましい[受け入れられる, 適切である]と考えて)賛成[同意, 承認]する ◇I told my mother I wanted to leave school but she didn't *approve*. 私は退学したいと母に告げたが, 承諾しなかった ◇Do you *approve of* my idea? 私の考えに賛成してくれますか ◇She doesn't *approve* of me leaving school this year. 彼女は今年私が退学することに同意しない [反意] **disapprove** (DISAPPROVE), ☞ **approval** (PRAISE [名]), **approving** (GOOD 6)

ノート (be) in favour (of sb/sth)とapproveの使い分け: in favourは人々が票決する物事, 例えば政府の政策[ビジネス戦略]などに用いられることが多い. ◆All those *in favour*, please raise your hand. (賛成の方は皆さん, 挙手願います). ✕In the class vote, three *approved* of the idea, four didn't. ▶ approveは, 行動や物事に影響を与えるより個人的な問題, 例えば両親[教師, 上司]などが自分たちの子ども[生徒, 従業員]などの行動・計画・考えなどをどう考えるかについて用いられる. ◆I don't think your mother would *approve* of this behaviour, do you? (お母様はこの行動をお認めにはならないでしょう). ✕My mother wasn't *in favour of* my behaviour.

bel**ieve in sth/in doing sth** [動詞]《進行形なし》 (やり方・振る舞いについて)賛成する, 認める ◇I don't *believe in* hitting children. 私は子どもを殴ることに賛成しない ◇Do you *believe in* capital punishment? あなたは死刑を認めますか ❶believe in sthは信条・生き方を理由に賛[反]成[しない]場合に用いられる. ☞ **belief** (FAITH)

sub'**scribe to sth** [動詞句]《フォーマル》 (意見・理論などに)賛成[同意, 支持]する ◇The authorities no longer *subscribe to* the view that disabled people are unsuitable as teachers. 障害者は教師に不向きだとする見解に, 当局はもはや同意しない ❶subscribe to sthはviewと結びつくことが最も多い. その他の一般的な連語には, opinion, theory, idea, beliefが挙げられる.

be all for sth/for doing sth [フレーズ] 《インフォーマル》 (当然のこととして)大賛成である ◇They're *all for* saving money where they can. 彼らは可能なところで節約することに大賛成 ◇What's the matter? You *were all for it* yesterday! どうしたの. 昨日は大賛成だったじゃない ❶この表現は時に, 密接に関わり合う[初めからずっと抱き続けている]考え・提案などに賛成しない場合に用いられる. ◆I'm *all for giving* people a second chance, but I'm afraid he's missed up too many times. I can't take him back. (人にやり直しの機会を与えることには大賛成だけど, 彼の場合は残念ながらもううんざりだわ. 元のさやには戻せないのよ).

influence [名]

influence • force • example • lead
他人がまねる[他人の振る舞い方や考え方に影響を与える]対象である人[行為]
【類語訳】実力者, 有力者, 原動力, 手本, 模範, 先例, 先導

文型&コロケーション

- an influence/ example **for** sb
- an influence/ a force **for** sth
- a **great** influence/ force/ example
- a **bad** influence/ example
- a **decisive/ positive/ strong** influence/ force/ lead
- a **moral** influence/ force/ lead
- to **follow** sb's example/ lead

influence [C] (振る舞い方・考え方に)影響力を持つ人[物事], 実力者 ◇She was by far the biggest *influence on* my writing. 彼女は私の著作に断然大きな影響力を持つ人だった ◇Those friends are a bad *influence* on her. あの友人たちが彼女に悪い影響を与えている ◇Who were your early *influences*? あなたが若い頃影響を受けた人は誰ですか ◇There seem to be several *influences* at work in his paintings. 彼の絵に影響を与えているものがいくつかあるようだ

force [C] (出来事・振る舞い方・考え方に)大きな影響力を持つ人[物事], 原動力, 勢力[有力, 立役]者 ◇The expansion of higher education was a powerful *force* for change. 高等教育の拡大は変革の大きな原動力であった ◇Many social and economic *forces* contributed to this trend. 社会や経済における様々な影響力がこうした動きの一因となった ◇They see the world as a battleground between the *forces* of good and evil. 彼らは世界を善と悪の勢力の戦場だと捉えている ◇Ron is the *driving force* (= the person who has the most influence) behind the project. ロンはそのプロジェクトの陰の立役者である

example [C, ふつう単数で] (他人がまねる良い[悪い])手本, 模範 ◇You're *setting a bad example to* the children. あなたは子どもたちの悪い手本になっている ◇It would be a mistake to follow his *example*. 彼を模範とするのは間違いだろう ☞ **example** (EXAMPLE 2)

lead [単数で] (人がまねる)先例, 手本, 先導 ◇If one bank raises interest rates, others will follow their *lead*. 一つの銀行が利率を上げれば, 他行もその先例に従うでしょう ◇Intellectuals *took the lead* in criticism of the

influence, informal, information

government. 知識人たちが政府批判を先導した ◇You go first, I'll *take my lead from* you. 君が先にやってくれ、君の手本に従うから

influence 動 ☞ AFFECT

influence・sway・prejudice・sour・poison・bias
人の考え方[振る舞い方]に影響を与えたり、人の意見を否定的方向[不公平]に変えさせたりする
【類語訳】影響を与える、感化する、偏見を抱かせる、険悪になる、険悪にする、悪くする、偏らせる

文型&コロケーション
▸ to influence/ sway/ prejudice/ poison/ bias sb/ sth **against** sb/ sth
▸ to influence/ sway/ bias sb/ sth **in favour of** sb/ sth
▸ to influence/ bias sb/ sth **towards/ toward** sb/ sth
▸ to influence/ sway/ bias the **result** of sth
▸ to influence/ prejudice the **outcome** of sth
▸ to influence/ sway a **decision**
▸ to sour/ poison **relations/ the atmosphere**
▸ to be **easily** influenced/ swayed (by sth)

influence [他] (模範を示して)影響を与える、感化する ◇His writings have *influenced* the lives of millions. 彼の著作は何百万もの人の人生に影響を与えてきた ◇Her parents tried to *influence her in* her choice of career. 両親は彼女が職業を選択する際に自分たちの意見も聞かせようとした ◇The wording of the question can *influence how* people answer. 質問の言い回しは人々の答え方に影響を与えることがある ☞ **influence** (AFFECT)

sway [他、しばしば受身で] (意見をまとめる[決定を下す]際に)影響を与える、感化する、動かす ◇The panel was not *swayed* by his arguments. 陪審団は彼の主張に動かされなかった ◇Don't allow yourself to be *swayed* by emotion. 感情に流されないようにしなさい ◇The speech was important in *swaying* public opinion. 演説は世論を動かす上で重要だった

prejudice [他] (不公平[不合理]な形で)偏見を抱かせる ◇Some argued that the media attention had *prejudiced* the jury. メディアの関心が陪審に偏見を持たせたと主張する人もいた ◇Poor handwriting might *prejudice* people against the applicant. 字が下手だと人々が志願者を色メガネで見かねない ☞ **prejudiced** (BIASED)

sour [自、他] 《書き言葉》(関係・態度・状況・人々が)こじれる、険悪になる;(物事を)こじらせる、険悪にする ◇The atmosphere in the house had *soured*. 家の中の雰囲気が険悪になってしまった ◇The disagreement over trade tariffs *soured* relations between the two countries. 貿易関税に関する意見の相違で二国間の関係はこじれた

poison [他] 《書き言葉》(関係・状況・意見を)悪くする、毒する、害する ◇She succeeded in *poisoning their minds* against me. 彼女は彼らに私に対する憎しみを抱かせることに成功した ◇His comment served only to *poison* the atmosphere still further. 彼の発言は雰囲気をさらに悪くしただけだった

ノート **sour** と **poison** の使い分け: poison はふつう sour よりも意味が強い。sour は関係・状況が以前よりも好ましく[友好的]でなくなることを表す。poison は関係・状況が非常に不快[非友好的]になり、怒りや嫌悪などの強い感情を伴う場合に用いられることが多い。

bias [他] (人の決定[意見]に不当な)影響を与える、偏見を抱かせる;(物事の結果を不正確に)偏らせる ◇The newspapers have *biased* people against her. 新聞は人々に彼女に対する偏見を植えつけてきた ◇The use of faulty equipment may have *biased* the result. 欠陥のある機器を使ったことで結果に偏りが生じたのかもしれない ☞ **biased** (BIASED)

informal 形

informal・relaxed・casual
振る舞い方[その場に適した服装]の厳しいルールに従う必要のない場面[場所]を表す
【類語訳】非公式の、普段着の、略装の、和やかな、カジュアルな

文型&コロケーション
▸ an informal/ a relaxed **atmosphere**
▸ informal/ casual **dress**

informal (好ましい[友好的な]形での)非公式の;(衣服が)普段着の、略装の ◇Discussions are held on an *informal* basis within the department. 部内での非公式の段階で話し合いが行われている ◇Dress is *informal*, and storage space often limited, so you'll be more comfortable travelling light. 服装は普段着ですし、収納スペースは限られていることが多いので、身軽に旅行するほうが快適でしょう 反意 **formal** (FORMAL), **formal** (OFFICIAL) 形
▸ **informally** 副 ◇They told me *informally* (= not officially) that I had got the job. その仕事を私がもらえたと彼らは非公式に教えてくれた ◇to dress *informally* 平服を着る

relaxed (場所が)和やかな ◇It's a family-run hotel with a *relaxed* atmosphere. そこは和やかな雰囲気の家族経営の旅館だ

casual (衣服が)普段着の、カジュアルな ◇She felt comfortable in *casual* clothes and wore them most of the time. 彼女はカジュアルな服装でいると心地よく、ほとんどの時間それを着ていた 反意 **formal** (FORMAL)

ノート **informal** と **casual** の使い分け: 衣服について言う場合、casual は informal よりも頻繁に用いられる。普段着全般を意味するときは、informal/casual dress と言えるが、特定の服装について言う場合には casual を用いる。◆ *casual* shirt/jacket (カジュアルなシャツ/ジャケット). ◆ *casual* shoes (カジュアルな靴). ◆ *casual* trousers ((英)カジュアルなズボン). ◆ *casual* pants ((米)カジュアルなズボン). ✗ *informal* shirts/jackets/shoes/trousers/pants.

information 名 ☞ FIGURE, SITUATION

information・data・detail・fact・point・material・intelligence・particular・info
状況[人]などに関して知っている[わかっている、真実である]中身
【類語訳】情報、知らせ、案内、データ、資料、些細、事実、素材、謀報、情報機関、謀報部

文型&コロケーション
▸ information/ data/ a detail/ a fact/ a point/ material/ intelligence/ particulars/ info **about/ relating to** sb/ sth
▸ information/ data/ material/ intelligence/ info **on** sb/ sth
▸ information/ intelligence/ the fact/ the point **that**...
▸ (an) **important** information/ data/ detail/ fact/ point/ ma-

↳**information**

terial/ intelligence/ particular/ info
▸**accurate/ precise** information/ data/ details/ facts/ intelligence/ info
▸(a) **detailed** information/ data/ facts/ point/ material/ intelligence/ particulars
▸**hard** information/ data/ facts/ intelligence
▸(a/ an) **further/ additional** information/ data/ details/ fact/ point/ material/ intelligence/ particulars/ info
▸to **have** information/ data/ details/ the facts/ intelligence/ particulars/ info
▸to **collect/ gather** information/ data/ details/ facts/ material/ intelligence/ info
▸to **get/ receive** information/ data/ details/ intelligence/ info
▸to **record** information/ data/ details/ facts/ info
▸to **give** (sb) information/ data/ details/ the facts/ particulars/ info
▸to **provide** information/ data/ details/ material/ particulars/ info
▸a **piece** of information/ data/ intelligence

information [U] (人・物事に関する)情報, 知らせ, 案内 ◇Do you have any *information* about local buses? 地元のバスについて何か情報はありますか ◇He is accused of giving false *information* to the police. 彼は警察に虚偽の情報を与えた容疑で起訴されている ◇*Information* is stored on their computerized databases. 情報は電子化されたデータベースに蓄積されている ◇For further *information*, contact us at the above address. 詳細につきましては, 上記のアドレスまでお問い合わせください ◇You can go to the *information desk* for help. お困りのことがありましたら案内デスクまでどうぞ ◇This letter is *for information only*. この手紙はお知らせだけのものです ☞ **in-form** (TELL 1)
data [U] (物事を解明する[決定を下す]ために調査[使用]される)データ, 情報, 資料 ; (コンピュータに蓄積される)データ ◇They are not allowed to hold *data* on people's private finances. 人々の個人財産に関するデータを保持することは許されていない ◇What methods are you using to interpret the *data*? データの解釈にどんな方法を使っていんですか ◇There is no hard *data* to support this theory. この理論を支持する確かな[ハード]データはない ◇This is just *raw data* (= data that has not been examined). これは未加工のデータにすぎません ◇One vital item of *data* was missing. 重要なデータ項目が一つ欠けていた ❶*data*はふつう不可算名詞として扱われるが, 専門的な言い回しでは複数名詞として用いられ, その場合, 単数形は *datum* となる. ◆These *data* were collected over a period of several months. (《専門的》これらのデータは数か月間にわたって収集された).
detail [C] 詳細な情報, 細部, 項目 ; 些細なこと ◇The expedition was planned down to the last *detail*. その探検旅行の計画は徹底して細部に至るまで詰められた ◇He stood still, absorbing every *detail* of his surroundings. 彼はじっと立って, 周囲の細かな状況をすべて把握した ◇Oh that's *just a detail* — we can deal with it later. ああ, それは些細なことだ—後で処理すればいい ◇Sharon will fill you in on the *details* (= tell you them). シャロンが詳細について聞かせてくれるだろう ❶*details* [複数形]は情報, 特に出来事, サービスなどについての実用的な情報, または出来事についての完全な情報を指す. ◆Our personnel officer will *take your details* (= take in-

informative

formation about you). (うちの人事部長があなたの情報を限なく調べるでしょう). ◆'We had a terrible time.' 'Oh, *spare me the details*(= I do not want to know all the details)!' (「ひどい目に遭ったよ」「あら, でも細かい話はいいからよ」). ☞ **detail** (LIST 動), **detailed** (DETAILED)
fact [C] (立証可能な)事実 ◇First, let's look at some basic *facts* about healthy eating. まず, 健康的な食事に関する基本的な事実をいくつか見ていきましょう ◇I've asked to see all the *facts and figures* before I make a decision. 結論を出す前に正確な情報をすべて理解するようお願いした ◇I wish you'd *get your facts right*! あなたが事実をきちんと把握していればなあ ◇The judge ordered both lawyers to *stick to the facts*. 裁判官は双方の弁護士に事実から離れないよう命じた ◇It's time you learnt to *face the facts* (= accept reality). 君は現実を受け入れることを学んでいい頃だ ◇*I know for a fact* that he's involved in something illegal. 私は彼が何か違法なことに関わっていることを事実として知っている ☞ **fact** (FACT), **factual** (RELIABLE 2)
point [C] (詳細情報)の特定の)項目, 点 ◇Here are the main *points* of the news. ここにニュースの主な項目があります ◇Could you explain that *point* again? その点をもう一度ご説明いただけますか ◇There are one or two *points* that aren't yet clear. まだはっきりしない点が一つ二つある
material [U] (書物などに用いられる)資料, 素材, 題材 ◇She's collecting *material* for her next novel. 彼女は次の小説のための題材を集めている
intelligence [U] (敵[犯罪者]に関する機密の)情報, 諜報 ; 情報機関, 諜報部 ◇They had obtained secret *intelligence* about enemy plans. 彼らは敵の計画に関する機密情報を得ていた ◇*Intelligence* sources (= people who give this information) report that a terrorist attack is highly probable. 情報筋ではテロ攻撃が起こる可能性が高いと伝えている ◇He's head of military *intelligence*. 彼は軍の諜報部長である
particular [C, ふつう複数形で] 《フォーマル》 (公式に記録された)事項, 点, 詳細, 明細 ◇The police officer took down all the *particulars* of the burglary. その警察官は強盗の詳細をすべて書き留めた ◇The new contract will be the same in every *particular* as the old one. 新しい契約はすべての点で古いものと同じになるだろう ❶*particulars* [複数形]は財産や取引, 仕事などに関する記述情報[詳細]を指す. ◆We asked for the *particulars* of the house. 私たちはその家の詳細な情報を請求した.
info [U] 《インフォーマル》 情報, 知らせ, 案内 ◇Have you had any more *info* about the job yet? その仕事についてさらに詳しい情報をもう入手しましたか ❶*info*はインフォーマルな語で, 仕事・課程・出来事などの詳細について用いられることが多く, しばしば印刷物の中で用いられる. *info-* は *infosheet* や *infopack* などの単語の接頭辞として用いられることもある. ◆We send all potential clients an *infopack*. (私どもはご依頼人となる可能性のある人すべてにインフォパックをお送りします).

informative 形

informative • **revealing** • **instructive** • **illuminating** • **telling** • **enlightening**
物事や情報を与えてくれることを表す
【類語欄】有益な, ためになる, 明らかにする, 合点のいく

informed, injure

文型&コロケーション
- informative/ revealing/ instructive/ illuminating/ enlightening **about** sth
- to be instructive/ illuminating/ enlightening **to do sth**
- an informative/ a revealing/ an illuminating/ a telling/ an enlightening **insight/ account**
- a revealing/ an illuminating/ a telling/ an enlightening **comment**
- a revealing/ an instructive/ an illuminating/ a telling **example**
- to **find sth** informative/ instructive/ illuminating/ enlightening
- **very** informative/ revealing/ instructive/ illuminating/ telling/ enlightening
- **highly/ extremely/ particularly/ most** informative/ revealing/ instructive/ illuminating/ enlightening
- **not very** informative/ revealing/ instructive/ illuminating/ enlightening

informative (文書[口頭]による情報源が)有益な，ためになる ◇The talk was both entertaining and *informative*. その講演は面白くまた有益だった ◇The book is not very *informative* about local customs. その本は地方のしきたりに関してはあまり役に立たない 反意 **uninformative** ❶ uninformative は物事が十分な情報を与えてくれないことを表す． ◆The reports of the explosion were brief and *uninformative*. (その爆発に関する報告書は短くて役に立たなかった)． ☞ **inform** (TELL1)

revealing (興味深い未知の情報を)暴露する，明らかにする ◇The answers the students gave were extremely *revealing*. 学生たちが出した答えは実情がよくわかるものだった ◇It was a most *revealing* remark. それは最も多くの情報を明かしてくれる発言だった ❶ revealing は，話し手(の考え[態度])について，実際には話し手が考える以上のことがわかる発言[答え]について用いられる． ☞ **reveal** (REVEAL)

instructive (経験・活動が)有益な，ためになる ◇It was a most *instructive* experience. それはきわめて有益な経験だった ◇He said he had found the meeting 'extremely *instructive*'. その会議について「非常に得るところが大きい」と感じたと彼は述べた

ノート informative と instructive の使い分け：informative は読んだり聞いたりする物事について，instructive は行ったり経験したりする物事について言うことが多い．

illuminating (物事を明確に[理解しやすく]して)合点のいく ◇The examples he used weren't particularly *illuminating*. 彼の用いた実例はとりわけ問題点がはっきりするというものではなかった

telling (意図せずに人・物事の実情を)よく物語る ◇The number of homeless people is a *telling* comment on the state of society. 路上生活者の数は社会の状態をよく物語っている

enlightening (未知の情報を与えて物事をより理解する手助けとなり)ためになる，有意義な ◇A visit to her partner proved most *enlightening*. 彼女のパートナーの元を訪れてきわめて有益だとわかった ☞ **enlighten** (TELL1)

informed 形

informed • educated • knowledgeable • thinking • well read

物事について多くの知識[情報]を持っている[示す]ことを表す

【類語訳】情報を持っている，知らされている，見聞の広い，博識な，情報に基づいた，教育を受けた，教養のある

文型&コロケーション
- informed/ educated/ knowledgeable **about** sth
- informed/ educated/ knowledgeable/ thinking/ well-read **people**
- **very/ extremely** educated/ knowledgeable/ well read

informed [ふつう名詞の前で] 情報を持っている，知らされている，見聞の広い，博識な；(特定のテーマ[状況]に関する)情報に基づいた ◇The newspaper's readership is generally *well informed* and intelligent. その新聞の読者層は概して博識で聡明である ◇They are not *fully informed* about the changes. 彼らはその変更について十分知らされていない ◇*Keep me informed of* any developments. 進展があればどんなことでも逐次報告してください ◇*Informed* sources say that the president may have received hospital treatment last year. 情報筋によれば，大統領は昨年入院治療を受けた可能性があるようだ ◇It was a serious and *informed* debate. それは真剣かつ内容をよく理解した上での議論だった ❶ informed は人が下す決定について用いられることが多い．一般的な連語には，decision, choice, discussion, debate, opinion, advice, consent が挙げられる． 反意 **uninformed** (IGNORANT)

educated [ふつう名詞の前で] 教育を受けた，教養[学識]のある；知識[経験]に基づいた[を示す] ◇She's an *educated* and articulate spokeswoman. 彼女は教養があり発言が歯切れよいスポークスウーマンだ ◇He spoke in an *educated* voice. 彼は教養ある人にふさわしい声で話した ◇Let's make an *educated guess* (= a guess that is based on some degree of knowledge, and is therefore likely to be correct). 知識に基づいて推測しよう 反意 **uneducated** (IGNORANT)

knowledgeable 見聞の広い，博識な；(特定の主題に)精通した ◇Bill was nice enough and seemed extremely *knowledgeable* too. ビルは十分に感じがよく，また非常に博識であるように思えた ◇She's very *knowledgeable* about all kinds of music. 彼女はあらゆる種類の音楽にとても精通している 反意 **ignorant** (IGNORANT)

thinking [名詞の前で] 思慮深い ◇*Thinking* people agreed on the need for radical reform. 思慮深い人たちは抜本的な改革の必要性に賛同した ◇She is known as the *thinking* person's crime writer. 《ややインフォーマル》彼女は考え深い読者がファンにつく犯罪小説家として知られている ❶ thinking はややインフォーマルな文章，特にジャーナリズムで，the thinking person/man/woman's... のように，人気はあるが愚かではない人や物事について言う場合にごく普通に用いられる．

well 'read (本をたくさん読んでいて)博識な，造詣の深い ◇He became *well read in* French and German literature. 彼はフランス文学とドイツ文学に造詣が深くなった ◇She was *better read* than her husband. 彼女は夫よりも博識だった

injure 動

injure • wound • hurt • bruise • maim • sprain • pull • tear • twist • strain

事故で自分自身[他人]を身体的に傷つける
【類語訳】痛める，負傷させる，けがをさせる，痛みを与える，あざができる，くじく，捻挫する

↪injure

文型&コロケーション
- to injure/ hurt/ strain **yourself**
- to injure/ hurt/ sprain/ pull/ tear/ strain a **muscle**
- to injure/ hurt/ sprain/ twist your **ankle/ foot/ knee**
- to injure/ hurt/ sprain your **wrist/ hand**
- to injure/ hurt/ strain your **back/ shoulder/ eyes**
- to injure/ hurt your **spine/ neck**
- to be **badly** injured/ wounded/ hurt/ bruised/ maimed/ sprained/ torn
- to be **severely** injured/ wounded/ hurt/ bruised/ sprained
- to be **seriously** injured/ wounded/ hurt/ bruised
- to be **slightly** injured/ wounded/ hurt/ bruised/ sprained
- to **accidentally** injure/ wound/ hurt sb/ sth

injure [他] (事故で自分自身[他人]を身体的に)痛める，負傷させる，けがをする ◇He *injured* his knee playing hockey. 彼はホッケーをしていて膝を痛めた ◇Three people were killed and five *injured* in the crash. その衝突事故で3人が死亡，5人が負傷した ◇She *injured* herself during training. 彼女はトレーニング中にけがをした

wound [他，しばしば受身] (ややフォーマル) (武器によって体の部位[皮膚]に)外傷を負わせる ◇He was *wounded* in the arm. 彼は腕に傷を負った ◇About 50 people were seriously *wounded* in the attack. その攻撃で約50人が重傷を負った ❶ *wound* は戦争や多くの人々に影響を及ぼす攻撃で人々が負傷する場合に用いられることが多い．

hurt [他，自] (他人[自分自身]に身体的な)痛みを与える；(他人[自分自身]に)痛める，負傷させる，けがを負わせる ◇He *hurt* his back playing squash. 彼はスカッシュをしていて背中を痛めた ◇Did you *hurt* yourself? けがしたの ◇Stop it. You're *hurting* me. やめろ．痛いよ ◇My back is really *hurting* me today. 今日は背中がすごく痛む ◇Strong light *hurts* my eyes. 強い光を見ると目が痛い ◇My shoes *hurt* — they're too tight. 靴が痛い — きつすぎるんだ ☞ **hurt** (HURT 2)

ノート **hurt** と **injure** の使い分け：両語とも事故で体の部位にけがを負うことについて言うことができる．**hurt** は引き起こされる身体的な痛みを強調し，**injure** は何らかの形で体の部位を痛めることを強調する．

bruise [他，自] (転倒[殴打]によって)あざをつける；あざができる ◇She had slipped and badly *bruised* her face. 彼女は滑って顔にひどいあざを作った ◇Careful: I *bruise* easily. 注意：私は傷つきやすい (のでお手やわらかに)
▸**bruising** [名] [U] ◇She suffered severe *bruising*, but no bones were broken. (ややフォーマル) 彼女はあざができたが，骨は折れていなかった

maim [他] (ややフォーマル) (人を)不具にする，体に障害を残す ◇Hundreds of people are killed or *maimed* in car accidents every week. 何百という人々が毎週自動車事故で死亡したり体に障害を残したりしている

sprain [他] (足首[手首，膝]を)くじく，捻挫する ◇I stumbled and *sprained* my ankle. 私はつまずいて足首を捻挫した
▸**sprain** [名] [C] ◇a bad ankle *sprain* 足首のひどい捻挫

pull [他] (伸ばしすぎて筋肉などを)痛める，違える ◇She has *pulled* her Achilles tendon. 彼女はアキレス腱を痛めている

tear [他] (伸ばしすぎて筋肉などを)切る，断裂する ◇She's *torn* a ligament in her right hand. 彼女は右手のじん帯を切ってしまった

ノート **pull** と **tear** の使い分け：筋肉を pull することと tear することは原理的に同じだが，torn muscle (肉離れ) は pulled muscle (筋違い) よりも重傷である．injury や tear は筋肉の深くに及ぶものである．a badly torn muscle とは言えるが，✕a badly *pulled* muscle とは言えない．

twist [他] (足首[手首，膝]を)ひねる，ねじる ◇She fell and *twisted* her ankle. 彼女は転んで足首をひねった

ノート **sprain** と **twist** の使い分け：sprain は痛みと腫れを引き起こす足首[手首，膝]のけがを指す．つまり，sprain your ankle/wrist/knee は，「足首/手首/膝をくじく[捻挫する]」ことを表す．twist your ankle/wrist/knee は，捻挫を引き起こす動作(突然無理にひねる[ねじる]こと)を指す．

strain [他] (酷使して自分自身[体の部位]を)痛める，体を壊す ◇Don't *strain* your eyes by reading in poor light. 暗がりで読書して目を悪くしないように ◇Are you sure you can carry all that? Don't *strain* yourself. 本当にそれ全部運べるの．体を痛めないようにね
▸**strain** [名] [C, U] ◇a calf/groin/leg *strain* ふくらはぎ/股間/脚を痛めること ◇muscle *strain* 筋挫傷

injury [名]

injury・wound・cut・bruise・scratch・gash・graze
皮膚を引き裂いた状態を表す語
【類語訳】傷害，けが，外傷，傷，切り傷，すり傷，裂傷

文型&コロケーション
- an injury/ a wound/ cuts/ a bruise/ a gash **to** a part of the body
- (a) **severe** injuries/ wound/ bruise
- a **deep** wound/ cut/ scratch/ gash
- **minor** injuries/ wounds/ cuts/ bruises
- to **suffer** an injury / a wound/ cuts/ bruises/ scratches/ a gash
- to **sustain** an injury/ a wound/ cuts/ bruises
- to **clean** a wound/ cut
- a wound/ cut/ bruise **heals**
- **cuts and** bruises/ scratches/ grazes

injury [C, U] (事故などによる人・動物の)傷害，けが ◇As a result of the accident, several passengers sustained serious head *injuries*. その事故の結果，数人の乗客が頭に重傷を負った ◇She escaped with only minor *injuries*. 彼女は軽傷だけですんだ ◇Two players are out of the team because of *injury*. 二人の選手がけがでチームを離れている ❶ このグループに属する他の類義語は，ふつう皮膚の外傷を指すが，injury は骨・筋肉を初めとする他の体の部位に影響を及ぼす傷害を指すことができる．

wound [C] (武器による体の部位[皮膚]の)外傷，傷，けが ◇She survived, despite receiving severe *stab wounds*. 彼女は，ひどい刺し傷を負ったにもかかわらず，生き延びた ◇He proudly showed us his *war wounds*. 彼は戦争でもらった傷を私たちに誇らしげに見せた ❶ wound は外傷をもたらす武器の名前と結びつくことが多く，bullet/gunshot/knife/shrapnel wound (銃弾/発砲/ナイフ/榴散弾による傷) が挙げられる．

cut [C] (鋭利な物による皮膚の)切り傷 ◇He came home covered in *cuts* and bruises. 彼は切り傷とあざだらけで帰宅した ◇Blood poured from the deep *cut* on his arm. 彼の腕の深い傷口から血があふれ出た

bruise [C] (転倒[殴打]による皮膚の)あざ ◇He had a huge *bruise* over his eye. 彼は目の上に大きなあざがあった ◇His legs were covered in *bruises*. 《英》彼の両脚はあざだらけだった ◇She was treated for minor *cuts and bruises*. 彼女は小さな切り傷とあざの手当てをしてもらった

scratch [C] (ほとんど[まったく]血の出ない)すり傷, 引っかき傷 ◇Her hands were covered in *scratches* from the brambles. 彼女の手はいばらでできた引っかき傷だらけだった ☞ **scratch** (SCRATCH)

gash [C] (長く深い皮膚の)裂傷 ◇He had a nasty *gash* across his chest. 彼は胸に醜い裂傷があった

graze [C] (肌がわずかに傷ついた小さな)すり傷 ◇Paul had a *graze* on his knee from where he had fallen over on the concrete. ポールはコンクリートの上で転んでぶつけた膝をすりむいた ☞ **graze** (SCRATCH)

in love 形

in love・crazy about sb・smitten・besotted・infatuated

人に対して恋愛感情を抱いている[魅力を感じている]ことを表す
【類語訳】恋して, 恋仲で, 恋した, ほれ込んだ, 心を奪われた, のぼせ上がった

▶文型&コロケーション
▶ in love/ smitten/ besotted/ infatuated **with** sb
▶ **completely/ totally** in love/ crazy about sb/ smitten/ besotted/ infatuated

in love フレーズ (人に)恋して, 恋仲で ◇We're *in love*! 私たちは恋仲です ◇She was madly *in love* with him. 彼女は彼に首ったけだった ◇They *fell in love* with each other. 彼らは互いに恋に落ちた[相思相愛の仲になった] ☞ **love** (LOVE 名 1)

crazy about sb フレーズ 《インフォーマル》(人に)夢中になっった, 熱を上げた ; (人に)恋した ◇I've been *crazy about* him since the first time I saw him. 私は初めて彼に会ったときから彼に夢中です

smitten [名詞の前はまれ] 《しばしばおどけて》(突然人に)ほれ込んだ, 心を奪われた ◇From the moment they met, he was completely *smitten by* her. 出会った瞬間から, 彼は彼女にすっかり惚れ込んだ

besotted (理性を失うほど人に)夢中になった ◇He was so *besotted* with her that he forgave her for everything. 彼は彼女に夢中で, 何でも許した

infatuated (理性を失うほど人に)熱を上げた, のぼせ上がった ◇He's behaving like an *infatuated* teenager. 彼はのぼせ上がったティーンエイジャーのように振る舞っている ☞ **infatuation** (LOVE 名 1)

ノート besotted と infatuated の使い分け: 両語とも理性的に考える[行動する]妨げとなる強い感情を表すが, infatuated のほうが長く続かず, よく知らない人に対して抱くことが多い。besotted with の対象はふつう彼氏・彼女・連れ合いなどである。◆She is still *besotted* with him after all these years. (何年経った後も彼女はまだ彼に夢中だ) ✕She is still *infatuated* with him after all these years. ◆They've just got married, and are *besotted* with each other. (彼らは結婚したばかりで, 互いに夢中になっている)。 ✕They've just got married and are *infatuated* with each other.

innocent 形

innocent・not guilty・in the clear・blameless

人が邪悪[違法]なことを一切していないことを表す
【類語訳】無実の, 潔白な, 罪のない, 無罪の, 容疑が晴れて

▶文型&コロケーション
▶ to be innocent/ not guilty **of** sth
▶ to **plead** innocent/ not guilty
▶ to **find sb** innocent/ not guilty

innocent 無実の, 潔白な, 罪[悪意, 悪気]のない ◇They have imprisoned an *innocent* man. 彼らは無実の人を投獄している ◇She was found *innocent of* any crime. 彼女はいかなる罪も犯していないと判明した ◇He was the *innocent* party (= person) in the breakdown of the marriage. 彼にはその結婚生活の破綻において罪はなかった ◇There must be an *innocent* explanation for her behaviour. 彼女の行動については悪意のない説明があってもいいはずだ 反意 **guilty** (GUILTY)
▶ **innocence** 名 [U] ◇She *protested her innocence* (= said repeatedly that she was innocent). 彼女は自分の身の潔白を主張した 反意 **guilt** (FAULT)

‚not 'guilty フレーズ 《法律》無罪の ◇The jury found the defendant *not guilty* of the offence. 陪審はその罪に関して被告を無罪と評決した ❶違法なことをしていない人々はその罪に対して plead not guilty (無罪を主張する). be found not guilty (無罪となる) 人もいれば, 陪審員が return a verdict of not guilty (無罪の評決を下す) こともある。反意 **guilty** (GUILTY)

in the 'clear フレーズ 《ややインフォーマル》容疑[嫌疑]が晴れて ◇It seems that the original suspect is *in the clear*. 最初の容疑者は嫌疑が晴れたようだ

blameless 《ややフォーマル, 書き言葉》非[罪]のない ◇None of us is entirely *blameless* in this matter. 私たちは誰一人としてこの問題にまったく非がないわけではありません ☞ **blame** (FAULT)

insensitive 形

insensitive・unsympathetic・uncaring・thoughtless・tactless・unthinking・inconsiderate

人が他人(の気持ち)を考えず[気遣わず]しばしば相手の気分を害することを表す
【類語訳】無神経な, 鈍感な, 思いやりのない, 気配りのない, 思慮のない, 気の利かない

▶文型&コロケーション
▶ insensitive/ unsympathetic **to** sb/ sth
▶ thoughtless/ tactless/ inconsiderate **of** sb to do sth
▶ an unsympathetic/ uncaring/ tactless **attitude**
▶ an insensitive/ a thoughtless/ a tactless **remark**
▶ thoughtless/ unthinking **words**

insensitive 《けなして》(相手の気分を害するほど)無神経な, 鈍感な ◇Many of the institutions were *insensitive* to the needs of their patients. 多くの施設が患者の要望に鈍感だった ◇It was a really *insensitive* thing to say. それを口にするとは実に無神経だった 反意 **sensitive** (SENSITIVE 1)

unsympathetic 《けなして》同情[思いやり]のない ◇I

↪**insensitive**

told him about the problem but he was totally *unsympathetic*. 私は彼にその問題を話したが、彼には思いやりがまったくなかった 反意 **sympathetic** (SENSITIVE 1)
uncaring 《けなして》(他人の問題[苦悩]を)気に留めない、思いやりのない ◇He was so totally *uncaring of* anyone's feelings. 彼は誰の気持ちもまったく気に留めなかった ◇We seem to be living in an increasingly *uncaring* society. 私たちは思いやりがどんどん薄れていく社会に暮らしているようだ 反意 **caring** (LOVING)
thoughtless 《けなして》(自分の言動が他人に与える影響を顧みず)不注意な、不親切な、思いやりのない ◇It was *thoughtless* of him to take the car without checking first. 最初に確かめもせずその車にするとは彼は不注意だった 反意 **thoughtful** (KIND 形)
tactless 《けなして》(他人をいら立たせる[怒らせる]言動をして)無神経な、気配りのない ◇It had been *tactless* of her to mention it. そのことに触れるとは彼女は気配りに欠けていた ◇It was so obviously a *tactless* question. それが無神経な質問であることは明々白々だった 反意 **tactful** (TACT)
unthinking 《書き言葉》(自分の言動が与える影響を顧みず)思慮のない、無分別な、軽率な ◇*Unthinking*, he started to cross the road. 軽率にも彼は道路を渡り始めた ◇She blushed at being caught out in such *unthinking* prejudice. 彼女はそんな浅はかな偏見にとらわれていることを見破られて赤面した

┌─ ノート **thoughtless**と**unthinking**の使い分け：thoughtlessは他人に悪影響を及ぼす可能性のある行動・発言を表し、このような言動をする人は他人にもっと注意を払うべきだということを示唆する。unthinkingは行為の悪影響がそれを行う当人にのみ及ぼされる場合に用いられることが多い。この場合、その行為は単に愚かで適切だと思えないものである。─┘

inconsiderate 《ややフォーマル, けなして》(他人の気持ち[要望]を十分に考えず)配慮のない、思いやりのない、気の利かない ◇It was *inconsiderate* of you not to call. 電話しないとは気が利かなかったね 反意 **considerate** (KIND 形)

inspection 名

inspection・observation・check・examination・audit・surveillance・survey・scan・check-up
すべてが満足のいくものであるか確認するために注意深く見ること
【類語訳】調査、検査、点検、視察、査察、検閲、診察、監視、検診、監査

文型&コロケーション

▸ (a) **detailed** inspection/ observation/ check/ examination/ audit/ survey
▸ (a) **close** inspection/ observation/ check/ examination/ surveillance
▸ (a) **thorough** inspection/ check/ examination/ audit/ survey/ check-up
▸ (a) **careful** inspection/ observation/ check/ examination
▸ (a) **regular** inspection/ observation/ check/ examination/ audit/ surveillance/ check-up
▸ (a/ an) **routine** inspection/ check/ examination/ surveillance/ scan/ check-up
▸ a **medical** inspection/ check/ examination/ check-up
▸ to **carry out/ do** an inspection/ an observation/ a check/ an examination/ an audit/ surveillance/ a survey/ a scan
▸ to **conduct** an inspection/ a check/ an examination/ an audit/ surveillance/ a survey

inspection

▸ to **give sb/ sth** an inspection/ a check/ an examination/ a scan/ a check-up
▸ to **have** an inspection/ a check/ an examination/ a scan/ a check-up
▸ an inspection/ observation/ a check/ an examination/ an audit/ a survey/ a scan/ a check-up **reveals/ shows** sth
▸ an inspection/ observation/ a check/ an examination/ a survey **confirms** sth

inspection [U, C]《すべてが満足のいくものであるかを確認するための》調査、検査、点検、視察、査察、検閲、閲覧 ◇The documents are available for public *inspection*. その文書は一般の閲覧が可能である ◇*On closer inspection*, the notes proved to be forgeries. さらに詳しく調べてみると、そのメモは偽物だとわかった ◇The principal went on a *tour of inspection* of all the classrooms. 校長はすべてのクラスの巡回監視に出かけた ◇Council officials made one site *inspection* of the property. 郡幹部たちはその物件を現地視察した ☞ **inspect** (CHECK 1)
observation [U, C]《物事を発見するための》観察、観測、診察、偵察、監視 ◇Most of the information was collected by direct *observation* of the animals' behaviour. ほとんどの情報は動物の行動を直接観察して集められた ◇We managed to escape *observation* (= we were not seen). 私たちはどうにか監視の目を免れた ◇The report is based on scientific *observations*. その報告書は科学的観測に基づいている ☞ **observe** (LOOK 動 1)
check [C]《安全[正確, 良い状態]であるかを確認するための》調査、検査、点検 ◇Could you give the tyres a quick *check*? タイヤをさっと点検していただけますか ◇Regular safety *checks* are conducted *on* the equipment used in the factory. 工場で使われている設備に対しては定期的な安全点検が行われている ◇In a series of *spot checks* (= checks made without warning), police searched buses crossing the border. 警察は一連の抜き打ち検査で国境を越えるバスを調べた ☞ **check** (CHECK 1)
examination [U, C]《物事を発見する[問題があるかどうかを確認する]ための》調査、検査、診察、検診 ◇Careful *examination* of the ruins revealed an even earlier temple. 入念な遺跡調査で、さらに古い寺院が見つかった ◇Doctors gave him a thorough medical *examination*. 医師たちは彼に対して徹底的な診察を行った ☞ **examine** (CHECK 1)
audit [C]《特にビジネス》(取引・財務記録に対する公式の)監査; (物の品質[基準]に対する公式の)検査 ◇a tax *audit* 税務監査 ◇Environmental *audits* are being carried out by many companies, showing the environmental impact of their activities. 環境検査が多くの会社によって実施され、自らの企業活動の環境に及ぼす影響が明らかにされている ☞ **audit** (CHECK 1)
surveillance [U]《犯罪の容疑者[犯行現場]に対する》監視、偵察 ◇The police are keeping the suspects *under* constant *surveillance*. 警察は容疑者を常に監視している
survey [C]《地図[計画]を作成するための土地に対する》調査、測量 ◇They carried out an aerial *survey* (= made by taking photographs from an aircraft) of the mountains. その山脈の航空測量が実施された ◇A geological *survey* revealed the presence of oil beneath the ground. 地質調査で地下に石油があることが明らかになった ❶《英》では surveyは建物の状態に対する入念な調査も指し、ふつう購入を検討している人のために行われる。◆We

paid for a detailed structural *survey*, which identified two areas of dry rot in the attic. (私たちは詳しい構造調査の代金を支払って、屋根裏に乾燥腐敗部分が2か所あることが明らかになった)

scan [C] (医学検査でX線[超音波]を用いてコンピューター画面に体内映像を写し出す)スキャン ◇The brain *scan* revealed no signs of injury. 脳スキャンでは何の損傷の形跡も示されなかった

'check-up [C] 《ややインフォーマル》(健康を確認するための)健診 ◇I *went for* my regular *check-up*. 私は定期健診に出かけた

inspector 名

inspector・regulator・observer・watchdog・
examiner・consumer group・monitor
規則が遵守されているかどうか確認する仕事をする人
【類語訳】調査官、検査官、監査委員、監督機関、傍聴人、立会人、監視機関、試験官、消費者団体、監視員

【文型&コロケーション】
▸ a **government/ federal** inspector/ regulator/ observer/ watchdog/ examiner
▸ an **independent** inspector/ regulator/ observer/ watchdog/ examiner
▸ an **official** inspector/ regulator/ observer/ watchdog
▸ a **local** inspector/ regulator/ observer/ watchdog/ consumer group
▸ a **safety** inspector/ regulator/ watchdog
▸ an **industry** regulator/ observer/ watchdog
▸ to **call** an inspector/ a regulator/ an examiner
▸ to **send** an inspector/ an observer/ an examiner/ a monitor

inspector [C] (学校・工場などへの)調査[検査、査察]官 ◇a school *inspector* 視学官 ◇UN weapons *inspectors* have been called in to verify the government's claims. その政府の主張を実証するために国連武器査察官らが招致されている ☞ **inspect** (CHECK 1)

regulator [C] (ビジネス・産業などへの)監査委員、監査機関 ◇Federal banking *regulators* have raised concerns about high levels of consumer debt. 連邦金融監査委員たちは高水準の消費者負債に関し懸念の声を上げた ☞ **regulate** (REGULATE)

observer [C] (会議・授業などへの)傍聴[立会]人 ◇A team of British officials were sent as *observers* to the conference. イギリスの官僚チームがその会議に傍聴人として送り込まれた

watchdog [C] 《ややインフォーマル、特にジャーナリズム》(会社への)監視機関 ◇She is a member of the consumer *watchdog* for transport in London and Southern England. 彼女はロンドン及びイングランド南部における輸送に関する消費者監視機関の一員である

examiner [C] 《特に米》(公認の)調査[検査、審査、試験]官 ◇He was the official *examiner* of electronic voting systems for Pennsylvania and Texas for 20 years. 彼は20年間にわたり、ペンシルバニア州とテキサス州の電子投票システムの公式検査官だった ☞ **examine** (CHECK 1)

con'sumer group [C] (権利保護の確認をする)消費者団体 ◇*Consumer groups* said lax safety measures and overcrowded trains were the underlying cause of the crash. ずさんな安全対策と超満員の電車がその事故の根本原因であると消費者団体は述べた

【ノート】regulator, watchdog, consumer group の使い分け: regulator は公的立場にあり、ふつう政府に任命される。その目的は会社間の競争が公正であるか[すべて法律の範囲内で運営され人々の権利を尊重しているか]を確認することである。watchdog は人である場合も集団である場合もある。watchdog は regulator を表すインフォーマルな語としてジャーナリズムで用いられることが多い。また、watchdog は公的機関である必要はなく、個々の会社の権利よりも、サービスの利用者の権利保護を監視の対象とする。consumer group は非公式の watchdog を指す。

monitor [C] (外国での)監視員 ◇UN *monitors* declared the referendum fair. 国連監視員たちは国民投票は公正であると宣言した

inspiration 名

inspiration・creativity・vision・ingenuity・
originality・imagination・inventiveness
刺激的な新しい考え[物事]を生み出す能力を表す肯定的な語
【類語訳】インスピレーション、ひらめき、創造性、先見の明、洞察力、発明の才、創意、工夫、独創性

【文型&コロケーション】
▸ **great** inspiration/ creativity/ vision/ ingenuity/ originality/ imagination/ inventiveness
▸ to **have** inspiration/ ingenuity/ originality/ imagination
▸ to **lack/ be lacking in** inspiration/ vision/ ingenuity/ originality/ imagination
▸ to **show** creativity/ ingenuity/ originality/ imagination/ inventiveness
▸ to **use** your ingenuity/ imagination

inspiration [U] (美術・音楽・文学における)インスピレーション、ひらめき ◇Looking for *inspiration for* a new dessert? Try this recipe. 新しいデザートのアイデア(になるもの)を探しているの。このレシピを試してごらん ◇Both poets drew their *inspiration from* the countryside. 両詩人とも田園からインスピレーションを引き出していた ◇Dreams can be a rich *source of inspiration* for an artist. 夢は芸術家にとってインスピレーションの宝庫となりえる

creativity [U] (新しい物事[芸術作品]を生み出す)創造性[力] ◇My job does not give me much scope for *creativity*. 私の仕事はあまり創造力を発揮する機会を提供してくれない ☞ **creative** (CREATIVE)

vision [U] (将来を考える[計画する])先見の明、洞察力 ◇a leader of great *vision* 先見の明豊かな指導者 ◇He's a competent politician but he lacks *vision*. 彼は有能な政治家だが洞察力に欠ける ☞ **visionary** (VISIONARY) 名

ingenuity [U] (物事を発明する[問題を解決する])発明の才、創意、工夫 ◇There is always a solution, so long as you are prepared to use your *ingenuity*. 工夫を凝らす気がある限り、常に解決策はある ☞ **ingenious** (CREATIVE)

originality [U] (既存のものとは異なる)独創性[力] ◇His *originality* as a painter lies in his representation of light. 画家としての彼の独創性はその光の表現にある ◇Creativity and *originality* are more important than technical skill. 創造性と独創性は技巧よりも重要である ☞ **original** (CREATIVE), **individuality** (IDENTITY)

imagination [U] (刺激的な新しい考えを生み出す)想像力 ◇His writing lacks *imagination*. 彼の著作は想像力

に欠ける ◇With a little *imagination* you can create a delicious meal from yesterday's leftovers. ちょっと想像力を働かせれば、昨日の残り物からおいしい食事を作ることができます ☞ **imaginative** (CREATIVE)

inventiveness [U] (新しい物事[考え]を生み出す)発明の才, 創意；創造性, 独創性 ◇the *inventiveness* of modern advertising 現代広告の独創性 ☞ **inventive** (CREATIVE)

inspire 動

inspire・motivate・fire sb up・stimulate
人に物事をしたいと思わせる[物事に関して興奮させる]
【類語訳】奮い立たせる, 鼓舞する, 希望を与える, 意欲を起こさせる, 刺激する, 励ます

| motivate | inspire | fire sb up |
| stimulate | | |

⟶

文型&コロケーション
▶ to be fired up/ inspired **with** sth
▶ to inspire/ motivate/ stimulate sb **to** sth
▶ to inspire sb/ motivate sb/ fire sb up/ stimulate sb **to do** sth
▶ to inspire sb/ motivate sb/ fire sb up **by doing** sth

inspire [他] (人にうまく[新たに]物事を行うよう)奮い立たせる, 鼓舞する, 希望[元気]を与える ◇The actors *inspired* the kids with their enthusiasm. 俳優たちは熱意を込めて子どもたちを奮い立たせた ◇His superb play *inspired* the team to a thrilling 5-0 win. 彼の華麗なプレーがチームを鼓舞し, 5対0でスリル満点の勝利に導いた ◇The actors visit schools and hope to *inspire* the children to put on their own productions. 俳優たちは自分たちの学校訪問が, 子どもたちが自らの作品を上演するきっかけになることを願っている ☞ **inspiration** (EXAMPLE 2), **inspiration** (INCENTIVE)
▷**inspired** 形 ◇an *inspired* performance 見事な演技
▷**inspiring** 形 ◇an *inspiring* teacher やる気を起こさせる教師

motivate [他] (人に勤勉に[努力して]物事を行うよう)意欲[やる気]を起こさせる ◇She's very good at *motivating* her students. 彼女は学生たちをやる気にさせるのが非常に得意だ ◇The plan is designed to *motivate* employees to work more efficiently. その計画の目的は従業員にもっと効率的に働く意欲を起こさせることだ ☞ **motivation** (INCENTIVE)
▷**motivated** 形 ◇a highly *motivated* student (= one who is very interested and works hard) 意欲的な学生

.**fire sb 'up** 句動詞 [しばしば受身で] (人にうまく物事を行う[試合に勝つ]よう)火をつける, 燃え上がらせる ◇He's all *fired up* about his new job. 彼は新しい仕事にすごく燃えている

stimulate [他] 《ややフォーマル, 特に書き言葉》(人に多少困難な物事を学ぶ[行う]よう)刺激[激励]する ◇Parents should give children books that *stimulate* them (= interest them and mentally challenge them). 親は子どもたちに頭の刺激となる本を与えるべきである ◇*Stimulate* the patient to activity but don't push him too hard. その患者を励まして活動的な生活をするようにさせなさい, で

も限度は超えないように ☞ **stimulating** (INTERESTING), **stimulus** (INCENTIVE)
▷**stimulation** 名 [U] ◇Children need intellectual *stimulation*. 子どもたちには知的な刺激が必要です

instinct 名

instinct・intuition・sixth sense
言われず[教えられず, 訓練されず]とも物事を知る[行う]ことができる生まれつきの能力
【類語訳】本能, 直観, 直感, 勘, 第六感

文型&コロケーション
▶ an instinct/ an intuition/ a sixth sense **for** sth
▶ an instinct/ intuition **that**...
▶ to do sth **by** instinct/ intuition
▶ to **have** an instinct/ an intuition/ a sixth sense
▶ to **rely on** your instinct/ intuition
▶ your instinct/ intuition/ sixth sense **tells** you
▶ your instinct/ sixth sense **warns** you

instinct [U, C] (人・動物の)本能 ◇His first *instinct was to* run away. 彼がまず本能的に考えたことは, 逃げることだった ◇Children do not know the difference between right and wrong by *instinct*. 子どもは本能的には善悪の区別がつかない ◇I acted purely *on instinct*. 私は純粋に本能のままに行動した ◇Most people have a well-developed survival *instinct* (= the instinct of trying to protect yourself from danger). ほとんどの人には非常に発達した生存本能が備わっている ☞ **instinctive** (NATURAL)

intuition [U] 直観, 直感, 勘 ◇*Intuition* told her that he was telling the truth. 彼女は直観で彼が真実を語っているとわかった ◇Call it *women's intuition* if you like, but I knew he was up to something. 女の勘とでもいうのかしらね, でも彼には下心があるとわかっていたわ ☞ **intuitive** (NATURAL)

.**sixth 'sense** [単数で] 第六感, 直感, 勘 ◇Some kind of *sixth sense* warned me not to stay there. ある種の第六感がそこにいてはいけないと私に警告した

insulting 形 ☞ OFFENSIVE

insulting・derogatory・disparaging・pejorative
人の反感を買う恐れのある非難を込めた言い方を表す
【類語訳】侮辱的な, 侮蔑的な, 失礼な, 無礼な, けなすような, 名誉を傷つけるような, 中傷的な, 見くびるような

文型&コロケーション
▶ insulting/ derogatory **to** sb
▶ an insulting/ a derogatory/ a disparaging **remark/ comment**
▶ an insulting/ a derogatory/ a disparaging/ a pejorative **term/ word**

insulting 侮辱的な, 侮蔑的な, 失礼な, 無礼な ◇He denies charges of *insulting* behaviour to a police officer. 彼は警官に対する侮辱行為の容疑を否認している ◇She was really *insulting* to me. 彼女は私に対して実に無礼だった ☞ **insult** (OFFEND)
▷**insultingly** 副 ◇He behaved *insultingly* towards her and should apologize. 彼は彼女に失礼な態度をとった

のだから謝罪すべきだ

derogatory (人に対して)けなすような、名誉を傷けるような ◇He complained that the supervisor had made *derogatory* remarks about him. 監督に名誉を傷つけるような発言をされたと彼は苦情を言った

disparaging 《フォーマル》(人・物事に対して)中傷的な、見くびる[さげすむ]ような ◇She made some *disparaging* remarks about standards in education. 彼女は教育水準について中傷的な発言をした

【ノート】**derogatory** と **disparaging** の使い分け：これらの語は意味的に非常に近い. derogatory はふつう人・集団に向けられる不公平な発言を表す. disparaging は公平・不公平を問わず、人・物事に向けられる発言を表す. ×She made some *derogatory* remarks about standards in education.

pejorative 《フォーマル》(言葉・発言が)軽蔑的な(意味の) ◇I'm using the word 'academic' here in a *pejorative* sense. 私はここではacademicという語を軽蔑的な意味で使っています
▸**pejoratively** 副 ◇These days the term 'chauvinist' is always used *pejoratively*. 最近ではchauvinistという言葉は常に軽蔑的に用いられる

integrity 名

integrity・honesty・honour・probity
道徳性や美徳に関わるような人がもつ個人的資質を表す
【類語訳】高潔、清廉潔白、正直、誠実、名誉、道義心

【文型&コロケーション】
▸a man/ woman of integrity/ honour
▸absolute/ complete/ total integrity/ honesty
▸sb's personal integrity/ honesty/ honour/ probity
▸sb's professional integrity/ honour/ probity

integrity [U] 高潔、清廉潔白 ◇She behaved with absolute *integrity*. 彼女は徹底して清廉潔白に振る舞った ◇They preserved their *integrity* throughout the trial. 公判中彼らは高潔を保っていた

honesty [U] 正直、誠実 ◇I always expect total *honesty* from my employees. 私は全面的な誠実さを常に従業員に求めている ◇At least he had the *honesty* to admit he was wrong. 少なくとも彼には間違いを認める正直さがあった 反意 dishonesty (FRAUD 1)
▸**honest** 形 ◇an *honest* man/woman 正直な男/女

honour 《英》《米》**honor** [U] 名誉、道義心 ◇He would always fight to defend the **family honour**. 彼はいつも一族の名誉を守るために闘ったものだ ◇Proving his innocence was a **matter of honour**. 彼の潔白を証明することは名誉の問題だった ◇Many schoolchildren have a very strong **code of honour**. 多くの学童は非常に強い道義的規範を備えている ◇I give you my **word of honour** (= a solemn promise) that I will not forget what I owe you. 私は受けた恩義を忘れないと名誉にかけて約束します 反意 dishonour (DISGRACE), ☞ honourable (RESPECTABLE 1)

【ノート】**integrity** と **honour** の使い分け：integrity は主に自分が自分自身をどのように見るかを強調し、自分自身の人格と行動を認めることができるように善良で正直であることを指す. honour は他人が自分をどのように見るかを強調し、共同体における自分の評判を維持するために善良で正直であることを指す. integrity はたいてい個人的なものだが、integrity of the company/profession と言うこともある. honour は個人にも集団にも用いられる. ×to defend the family *integrity*. ×a strong code of *integrity*. ×I give you my word of *integrity*.

probity [U] 《フォーマル》(ビジネスにおける)誠実、高潔 ◇They have very high standards of **financial probity**. 彼らは金融取引における誠実さを高い水準で持ち合わせている

intellectual 形

1 intellectual・theoretical・psychological・mental・abstract・philosophical・academic・conceptual
物事が物理的世界ではなく思想[精神]に関連することを表す
【類語訳】知的な、理論的な、心理的な、精神的な、抽象的な、哲学的な、学問的な、学術的な、概念的な

【文型&コロケーション】
▸an intellectual/ a theoretical/ a psychological/ sb's mental/ an abstract/ a philosophical/ an academic/ a conceptual approach
▸an intellectual/ a theoretical/ a philosophical/ an academic/ a conceptual framework
▸intellectual/ theoretical/ psychological/ abstract/ philosophical/ conceptual terms
▸an intellectual/ a theoretical/ a psychological/ a mental/ an abstract/ a philosophical concept
▸intellectual/ abstract/ philosophical/ academic/ conceptual thought/ thinking
▸intellectual/ theoretical/ abstract/ philosophical/ academic discussion/ argument/ debate
▸an intellectual/ a theoretical/ a psychological/ a mental/ a philosophical/ a conceptual problem
▸theoretical/ psychological/ philosophical/ academic study
▸purely intellectual/ theoretical/ psychological/ mental/ abstract/ philosophical/ academic/ conceptual
▸highly/ largely intellectual/ theoretical/ abstract/ academic

intellectual [ふつう名詞の前で] 知性[知力]に関する[を用いる]、知的な ◇It can be very difficult to measure *intellectual* ability. 知力を測定することは非常に難しいこともある ◇You can't really appreciate art from a purely *intellectual* standpoint. 純粋に知的な観点からは本当の意味で芸術を鑑賞することはできない
▸**intellectually** 副 ◇The party carries no weight *intellectually*. その政党は知的な意味では影響を失っている ◇It's an *intellectually* demanding job. それは知性を要する仕事です

theoretical [ふつう名詞の前で] (実践[実験]ではなく)理論に関する、理論上の、理論的な ◇We aim to provide you with both *theoretical* and practical knowledge of your subject. 我々はあなたのテーマについての理論的・実践的両面の知識を提供することを目指しています ◇The emphasis of his lectures is on *theoretical* physics. 彼の講義は理論物理学に重点を置いている 反意 practical, experimental, ☞ theory (THEORY 1)
▸**theoretically** 副 ◇Travelling faster than the

↳intellectual

speed of light is *theoretically* impossible. 光速より速く移動することは理論的に不可能である ◇*Theoretically*, education is free in this country. 理論上、この国では教育は無償である

psychological [ふつう名詞の前で] 心理[精神]に関する、心理[精神]的な ◇*Victory* in the previous game should give them a ***psychological advantage*** over their opponents. 前回の試合に勝利したことで、彼らは敵に対して心理的に有利に立つはずだ ◇Her latest movie is a tense *psychological* drama. 彼女の最新映画は緊迫した心理ドラマである ◇I think his illness is more *psychological* (= caused by the mind) than physical. 彼の病気は肉体的というより精神的なものだと思います

▶**psychologically** 副 ◇Some of these so-called therapies can actually be *psychologically* harmful. これらのいわゆるセラピーの中には、実際には心理的に有害となるものもある

mental [ふつう名詞の前で] 精神[心]に関する[の中で起こる]、精神[心]的な；思考を伴う ◇The experience caused her huge amounts of *mental* suffering. その経験は彼女に多大な精神的苦痛をもたらした ◇Do you have a ***mental picture*** of the scene (= Can you imagine what it looks like?)? その光景を心に思い描けますか ◇I made a ***mental note*** to call her as soon as I got home. 私は帰宅したらすぐに彼女に電話することを心に刻んだ ◇I have a complete ***mental block*** (= I cannot learn or remember) when it comes to physics. 私は物理学のこととなると、まったく思考が働かなくなる ◇Are you any good at ***mental arithmetic*** (= mathematical calculations that you do in your mind rather than on paper)? 多少なりとも暗算はできますか

▶**mentally** 副 ◇The team were outplayed, physically and *mentally*. そのチームは物理的にも精神的にも敗北を喫した ◇You need to be *mentally* prepared for the race. レースに向けて心の準備をする必要があります

abstract 抽象的な；観念的な ◇Freedom is more than a purely *abstract* notion. 自由は単に抽象的な概念にとどまらない ◇We may talk of beautiful things but beauty itself is *abstract*. 我々は美しいものについて語ることは可能だが、美そのものは観念的である 反意 **concrete** (FINAL)、☞ **abstraction** (IDEA 1)

▶**the abstract** [単数で] ◇Legal questions rarely exist *in the abstract*; they are based on real cases. 法律問題は抽象的に存在することは稀であり、実際の事件に基づいている

philosophical [ふつう名詞の前で] 哲学に関する、哲学的な ◇The level of *philosophical* debate is usually quite high. 哲学的論争の水準は通常きわめて高い

▶**philosophically** 副 ◇She is right-wing both politically and *philosophically*. 彼女は政治的にも哲学的にも右翼である

academic [ふつう名詞の前で] 学問的な、学究的な、学術的な ◇I wasn't sure I could cope with the *academic* demands of the course. 私はその課程の学究的な要求に対処できるか確信が持てなかった ◇She had very few *academic* qualifications. 彼女は学術的な資格をほとんど持っていなかった

▶**academically** 副 ◇They are all well qualified *academically*, but have little practical experience. 彼らは皆高学歴だが、実践経験はほとんどない

conceptual (フォーマル) 概念に関する[基づく]、概念的な ◇She presents a *conceptual* framework for the analysis of educational processes. 彼女は教育課程の分析のための概念的枠組を提示している ☞ **concept** (IDEA 1)

▶**conceptually** 副 ◇*conceptually* similar/distinct 概念的に類似した/異なる

2 intellectual・cultured・literary・studious・learned・scholarly・highbrow・bookish
書物や学術研究、文化などに本格的な興味を示す人を表す
【類語訳】知性のある、知的な、教養のある、洗練された、博学な、高尚ぶった、学者ぶった

文型&コロケーション
▶an intellectual/ a cultured/ a literary/ a studious young/ a learned/ a scholarly/ a bookish **man/ woman**
▶(a/ an) intellectual/ cultured/ literary/ learned/ scholarly/ highbrow **readers/ readership**
▶an intellectual/ a cultured/ a literary/ a scholarly **elite**
▶**highly** intellectual/ cultured/ literary

intellectual 知性のある、知的な ◇His works were popular among the *intellectual* elite of the time. 彼の作品は当時の知的エリートの間で人気があった ◇Don't imagine that all college students are highly *intellectual*! 大学生が皆非常に知的だなどと考えるな

cultured (ほめて) 教養のある、洗練された ◇She was a deeply *cultured* woman who had travelled a great deal. 彼女は多くの旅行経験を持つ教養の高い女性だった ◇He spoke with a *cultured* accent (= the accent of a cultured person). 彼は洗練された口調で話した

literary 文学に通じた、文学を専門とする、文筆を業とする ◇She was one of the great *literary* figures of her age. 彼女は当時の文豪の一人だった ◇He was a *literary* man and had dreamed of becoming the Shakespeare of the movies. 彼は文士で、映画界のシェイクスピアになるのを夢見ていた

studious 勉強[学問]好きな ◇She was a quiet, *studious* girl. 彼女は物静かで勉強好きな少女だった ◇He liked to wear glasses, which he thought made him look *studious*. 彼は眼鏡をかけるのが好きで、眼鏡をかければ賢そうに見えると思っていた

learned [ふつう名詞の前で] (フォーマル) 学問[学識]のある、博学な ◇The lecture was given by an elderly *learned* professor. 講義は年配の博学な教授によって行われた ☞ **learning** (KNOWLEDGE)

scholarly (ややフォーマル) 学者的な、学問好きな ◇He was a very *scholarly* young man. 彼はとても学者肌の若者だった

ノート studious, learned, scholarly の使い分け：
studious は研究の習慣とどのくらいの時間を研究に費やしているかを強調する場合に用いられる。studious はふつう若者に用いられる。learned は人がどれほど知っているか、特に生涯にわたる研究に基づく知識を強調する場合に用いられる。learned はふつう年配者に用いられる。scholarly は研究の習慣と研究から得た知識の両方を強調する場合に用いられる。scholarly は若者・年配者の両方に用いられる。

highbrow (時にけなして)(芸術[文化]的思想に関心が高く)知識人の、教養のある、知的[高尚]ぶった ◇The journal is aimed at a *highbrow* readership. その新聞は教養のある読者層に狙いを定めている ❶ highbrow はふつう新聞・テレビ番組・その読者[視聴者]を指し、連語には readers, papers,

intelligence, intelligent

press, television (programmes)が挙げられる。
bookish《時にけなして》読書好きな、学者ぶった ◇Quiet and *bookish*, he was sometimes teased by the other boys. 彼は物静かで読書好きだったので、時々他の少年たちにからかわれた

intelligence 名

intelligence・mind・genius・intellect・wits・brain・smarts
人の思考[学習, 理解]する能力
【類語訳】知能, 知性, 知力, 天分, 機転, 知恵, 才覚, 頭脳

文型&コロケーション
▸ (a) **great** intelligence/ mind/ genius/ intellect/ brain
▸ (a) **sharp** intelligence/ mind/ intellect/ wits/ brain
▸ (a) **keen** intelligence/ mind/ intellect/ brain
▸ (a/ an) **creative/ artistic/ musical** intelligence/ mind/ genius/ intellect
▸ to **have** intelligence/ a ...mind/ genius/ intellect/ ... wits/ a ...brain/ smarts
▸ to **have** (the) intelligence/ wits/ smarts **to do sth**
▸ to **use** your intelligence/ mind/ wits/ brain/ smarts
▸ a **man/ woman of** intelligence/ genius/ intellect

intelligence [U]《学習[理解, 論理的に思考]する》知能, 知性, 知力；知能の高さ ◇Most people of average *intelligence* would find this task quite difficult. 平均的知能を持つほとんどの人はこの作業をかなり困難だと思うだろう ◇Each child had to do an *intelligence test*. 子どもは一人一人知能検査を受けなければならなかった ◇Don't *insult my intelligence* (= treat me as if I were stupid). 私の知性をばかにするなよ
mind [C, ふつう単数で]《論理的に思考する》知性, 知力；(人に特有の)考え方, 心的傾向, 心理, 気質 ◇His *mind* is as sharp as ever. 彼の知性は相変わらず鋭い ◇Did you know you have a nasty suspicious *mind*? ご自分がひどく疑い深い気質であることを自覚していましたか ◇I've no idea how her *mind* works. 私は彼女の考え方がよくわからない ◇He has the body of a man but the *mind* of a child. 彼は体は大人だが考え方は子どもだ ◇Their evidence might give us some insight into the criminal *mind*. 彼らの証言から犯罪者心理を洞察できるかもしれない
genius [U] 非凡な知能[技術, 芸術的才能], (資質としての)天才, 天分 ◇the *genius* of Shakespeare シェイクスピアの非凡な芸術的才能 ◇She was at the peak of her creative *genius*. 彼女は創造的才能の頂点にあった ◇It's undoubtedly a work of *genius*. それは紛れもない天才技だ ◇That was a stroke of *genius*. それは天才的ひらめきだった
intellect [U, C]《高度に論理的に思考する》知性, 知力 ◇A teacher recognized his outstanding *intellect*. 教師は彼のずば抜けた知性に気づいた ◇She was a brilliant scholar with a formidable *intellect*. 彼女は素晴らしい知性を備えた優れた学者だった
wits [複数で]《迅速かつ明瞭に思考し的確な決定を下す》機転, 知恵, 知力, 才覚 ◇He needed all his *wits* to get out of that situation. 彼にはその状況から抜け出すための知恵が必要だった ◇This will be your chance to *pit your wits against* (= compete with, using your intelligence) our reigning champion. これは現チャンピオンと知恵比べをする機会となるでしょう ◇The game was a long *battle of wits*. その試合は長い知力戦だった

◇*Keep your wits about you.* This could be tricky. 抜かりなく立ち回りなさい。これには罠があるかもしれない
brain [U, C, ふつう複数で]《ややインフォーマル》《学習[理解, 論理的に思考]する》頭脳；頭の良さ ◇It doesn't take much *brain* to work out that both stories can't be true. 大して頭を使わなくとも両者の話が真実たりえるわけではないことはわかる ◇She must have inherited her mother's *brains*. 彼女は母親の頭の良さを受け継いだに違いない
smarts [U]《米, インフォーマル》《学習[理解, 論理的に思考]する》知能, 知力；頭の切れ, 利口さ ◇She made it to the top on her *smarts* and hard work. 彼女はその知性と懸命な努力でトップに上りつめた ◇You'll have to use all your *smarts* to figure this one out. これを解くためには知力を使い果たすことになるよ

intelligent 形

intelligent・smart・clever・brilliant・bright
人が学習[理解, 思考]に長けていること
【類語訳】知能の高い, 聡明な, 利口な, 頭の切れる, 賢い, 抜け目のない, 如才ない, 気の利いた, 才気あふれる, 優秀な

文型&コロケーション
▸ clever/ brilliant **at sth**
▸ an intelligent/ a smart/ a clever/ a brilliant/ a bright **child/ boy/ girl/ man/ woman**
▸ an intelligent/ a smart/ a clever/ a brilliant **thing to do/ move**
▸ **really/ quite** intelligent/ smart/ clever/ brilliant/ bright
▸ **pretty/ very/ extremely/ incredibly** intelligent/ smart/ clever/ bright

intelligent《学習[理解, 論理的に思考]に長けて》知能の高い, 聡明な, 利口な；頭の良さを示す ◇He's a *highly intelligent* man. 彼は非常に聡明な人だ ◇She asked a lot of *intelligent* questions. 彼女は頭の良さを示す質問をたくさんした 反意 **stupid** (STUPID)
smart《特に米》《学習[理解]が速く》頭の切れる, 賢い, 利口な；(取引[個人的決断]において)抜け目のない, 如才ない ◇She's *smarter* than her brother. 彼女は兄より頭が切れる ◇If you're *smart*, you'll take my advice. もしあなたが賢いならば、私の忠告を受け入れるでしょう ◇That was a *smart* career move. それは抜け目ない転職だった ◇OK, I admit it was not the *smartest* thing I ever did (= it was a stupid thing to do). わかった、私がばかだったよ 反意 **dumb, stupid** (STUPID)
clever《特に英, 時にけなして》《学習[理解]が速く》頭の切れる, 賢い, 利口な；頭の良さを示す, 気の利いた ◇*Clever girl!* すごいぞ ◇How *clever* of you to work it out! それを解いてしまうとは何て君は賢いんだ ◇He's *too clever by half*, if you ask me. 私に言わせれば、彼は才を鼻にかけるんだよね ◇This book is clever, without being merely *clever*. この本は気が利いている、いや気が利いているなんてもんじゃない ◇That wasn't a very *clever* thing to do (= that was a rather stupid thing to do). そんなことをするのはあまり賢いとは言えなかった ❶ *clever*は以下の句で用いられる。◆ *Clever* boy/girl!《すごいぞ》は幼い子に対して物事をよく覚えた[やった]ことを伝えるために用いる。大人に用いる場合は、cleverはけなしたり(too clever, merely cleverの形で)、皮肉ったり、見下したりする場合に用いる。 反意 **stupid** (STUPID)
brilliant 才気あふれる, 優秀な, 素晴らしい ◇He's a *bril-*

liant young scientist. 彼は才気あふれる若き科学者だ ◇She has one of the most *brilliant* minds in the country. 彼女は国内で最も優秀な知性の持ち主の一人だ ◇This is a *brilliant* and fascinating piece of writing. これは素晴らしく読者の心をつかんで離さない文学作品だ
bright 頭のよい, 聡明な, 利口な; 物覚えの速い ◇She's probably the *brightest* student in the class. 彼女はおそらくクラスで一番頭のいい生徒だろう ◇Some *bright spark* (= stupid person) left the tap running all night. 《英, インフォーマル, 皮肉で》どこかのお偉いさんが一晩中水を出しっぱなしにしておいたんだ 反意 **dumb** (STUPID), ☞ **bright** (CHEERFUL)

intend 動

intend・mean・plan・aim・have sb/sth in mind・propose
物事を行うときに頭の中に計画[結果, 目的]を持つ
【類語訳】(…する)つもりである, 意図する, 予定する, つもりで言う, 計画する, 目指す, 考えている, 心当たりがある, もくろむ

文型&コロケーション

▶ to intend/ mean/ plan/ aim/ have in mind/ propose **to do sth**
▶ to intend/ propose **doing sth**
▶ sb **originally** intended/ meant/ planned sth
▶ to **clearly/ directly** intend/ aim to do sth

---

intend [自, 他] (…する)つもりである, (…しようと), (…することを)意図[予定]する ◇We finished later than *intended*. 予定したより終わるのが遅かった ◇I *fully intended* (= definitely intended) to pay for the damage. 私は必ず損害を賠償するつもりだった ◇The writer clearly *intends* his readers to identify with the main character. 作家が読者を主人公になったつもりにさせようと意図しているのは明らかだ ◇I don't *intend* staying long. 《英》長居するつもりはありません ◇*It is intended that* production will start at the end of the month. 生産は月末に開始される予定です ◇The company *intends* a slowdown in expansion. 会社は拡大を減速させる予定です ❶ intend はしばしば将来の計画について現在形で用いられる.
◆ He *intends* to retire at the end of this year. 彼は今年末に引退するつもりだ ◆ What do you *intend* to do now? 今度は何をしようとしてるの 過去の出来事について用いられる場合, 計画した[望んだ]にもかかわらず起こらなかった出来事を表すことが多い. ◆ They stayed much longer than they'd originally *intended*. 彼らは初めに予定していたよりずっと長居をした ◆ She *didn't intend* to kill him (= but she did). 彼女は彼を殺すつもりはなかった
☞ **intended** (DELIBERATE), **intention** (PURPOSE)
mean [他] 《特に話し言葉》(…する)つもりである, (…しようと)思う, (冗談[賛辞]などの)つもりで言う, (対象に)向ける, (必然的に物事を)引き起こす ◇I've *been meaning to* call her, but I've been so busy lately. 彼女に電話しようとずっと思っていたんだ, 最近とても忙しくて ◇I'm sorry I hurt you. I *didn't mean to*. 傷つけてごめんね. そんなつもりはなかったんだ ◇*You're meant to* (= you are supposed to) pay before you go in. 《特に英》入る前に支払いをしなければならない ◇Don't be upset — I'm sure he *meant it as* a compliment. 怒るなよ—きっと彼は褒め言葉のつもりだったんだよ ◇Don't laugh! *I mean it* (= I am serious). 笑うな. 本気なんだ ◇He *means what he*

---

says (= is not joking, exaggerating, etc.). 彼は真面目に言ってるんだ ◇He *means trouble* (= to cause trouble). 彼はトラブルの元だ ◇The chair was clearly *meant for* a child. その椅子は明らかに子ども用だった ❶ mean は人が意図したことを実際にはできなかった場合や, 意図したとおりに物事が起こらなかった場合に用いられることが多い.
plan (-nn-) [自, 他] (細部かに…することを)予定[計画]する ◇We hadn't *planned on* going anywhere this evening. 私たちは今晩どこへも出かける予定はなかった ◇They *plan* to arrive some time after three. 彼らは3時すぎには到着する予定です ◇We're *planning* a trip to France in the spring. 私たちは春にフランス旅行を計画しています ☞ **plan** (PURPOSE)
aim [自] (特定の目標を)目指す ◇The government is *aiming at* a 50% reduction in unemployment. 政府は失業率を50%下げることを目指している ◇We should *aim for* a bigger share of the market. 我々は市場のシェア拡大を目標とすべきです ◇We *aim* to be there around six. 私たちも6時ごろの到着を目指しています ☞ **aim** (PURPOSE)
have sb/sth in 'mind [行成] (特定の目的[仕事, 活動]のために人・物事のことを)考えている, 心当たりがある, (…する)つもりである, (…しようと)思う, (…することを)意図[予定]する ◇Do you *have* anyone *in mind for* the job? その仕事に向いた人に誰か心当たりはありますか ◇Watching TV all evening wasn't exactly what I *had in mind*! 一晩中テレビを見ることは必ずしも考えていたことではなかった ◇I *had* (it) *in mind* to give you an overview first of all. まず最初にあなたに概要を説明しようと思った
propose [自] 《ややフォーマル》(…する)つもりである, (…することを)もくろむ[企てる] ◇What do you *propose* to do now? 今度は何をするつもりなの ◇How do you *propose* getting home? どうやって帰宅するつもりですか

intense 形

intense・passionate・fierce・heated・emotional・violent・fiery・ardent・fervent
人や行動に非常に強い感情が示されている状況を表す
【類語訳】真剣な, 熱心な, 集中的な, 熱烈な, 情熱的な, 猛烈な, 白熱した, 感情的な, 激しやすい

文型&コロケーション

▶ intense/ passionate/ fierce/ heated/ emotional **about** sth
▶ an intense/ a passionate/ a fierce/ a heated/ an emotional/ a fiery **debate**
▶ a passionate/ a fierce/ a heated/ an emotional/ a violent **argument**
▶ an intense/ a passionate/ a fierce/ a heated/ a violent **controversy**
▶ a fierce/ heated/ fiery **exchange/ dispute**
▶ intense/ fierce/ violent **opposition**
▶ a passionate/ fierce/ violent/ fiery **temper**
▶ intense/ passionate/ fierce/ fervent **devotion/ conviction**
▶ a passionate/ an ardent/ a fervent **supporter**

---

intense 真剣な, 熱心な; (短期間にわたって)激しい, 強い, 集中的な ◇He's very *intense* about everything. 彼は何に対してもとても真剣だ ◇She met his *intense* gaze. 彼女は彼からの熱い視線を受けた ◇There was an *intense* relationship between mother and son. 母と息子の間には張りつめた関係があった ◇There has been *intense*

speculation about divisions in the party. 党内の不和について盛んに憶測がなされている
▶**intensely** 副 ◇She disliked him *intensely*. 彼女は彼を激しく嫌っていた
▶**intensity** 名 [U, 単数で] ◇*intensity* of feeling 感情の激しさ ◇He was watching her with an *intensity* that was unnerving. 彼は相手を不安にさせるほど熱心に彼女を見ていた
passionate 熱心な, 熱烈な, 情熱的な, 激しい, 強い ◇She is *passionate* about her work. 彼女は仕事に熱心だ ◇He has a ***passionate interest*** in music and opera. 彼は音楽とオペラに熱烈な関心を抱いている ◇She was a *passionate* defender of civil liberties. 彼女は市民の自由の熱烈な擁護者であった ❶*passionate* は人の信念や情熱だけでなく, 人・物事を強く支持する人々にも用いられる. ◆a *passionate* speech/sincerity/attachment/belief/commitment/conviction (熱のこもった演説／強い誠意／強い愛着／強い信念／強い情熱／強い確信). ◆a *passionate* supporter/defender of sth (物事の熱烈な支持者／擁護者). ☞ **passion** (EMOTION), **passion** (TASTE)
▶**passionately** 副 ◇She believes *passionately* in education and hard work. 彼女は教育と勤勉を強く信奉している
fierce (行動・感情が)猛烈な, 激烈な, 激しい, 過酷な ◇He launched a *fierce* attack on the Democrats. 彼は民主党に対して猛攻撃を開始した ◇His wife is his ***fiercest critic***. 妻が彼の最大の批判者だ ◇Competition from abroad became *fiercer* in the 1990s. 1990年代に海外からの競争が激化した
▶**fiercely** 副 ◇*fiercely* competitive/independent/proud 競争の激しい／独立心の旺盛な／自尊心むき出しの
heated (人・議論が怒り[興奮]で)熱くなった, 白熱した ◇We all seem to be getting very *heated* about this. 私たちは皆このことで非常に熱くなっているように思える ◇Their voices rose in *heated* argument. 白熱した議論で彼らの声は大きくなった ☞ **heat** (EMOTION)
▶**heatedly** 副 ◇'You had no right!' she said *heatedly*. 「あなたに権利はなかったでしょ」と彼女は熱くなって言った
emotional (時にけなして) (他人には不要と思えるほど)感情的な, 切実な ◇an *emotional* outburst/response/reaction 感情的な爆発／返答／反応 ◇They made an *emotional* appeal for help. 彼らは援助を求めて切実に訴えた ◇He tends to get *emotional* on these occasions. 彼はこういった場面で感情的になりがちだ ☞ **emotion** (EMOTION)
violent (感情的に)猛烈な, 激しい ◇There was a *violent* reaction from the public. 世間から猛反発が起こった
▶**violence** 名 [U] ◇The *violence* of her feelings surprised him. 彼は彼女の感情の激しさに驚いた
▶**violently** 副 ◇They are *violently* opposed to the idea. 彼らはその考えに猛烈に反対している
fiery [ふつう名詞の前で] 激しやすい; (怒って)熱烈な, 激しい ◇He's a big strong lad with a *fiery* temper. 彼は激しやすい気性の大柄で頑強な男だ ◇John Wesley preached his *fiery* sermons to large crowds. ジョン・ウェスレーは大勢の群衆に熱烈な説教をした
ardent [ふつう名詞の前で] 《ややフォーマル, 特に書き言葉》(強い賞賛[敬意]を持って[示して])熱狂的な, 熱心な, 熱烈な ◇He was one of the president's most *ardent* admirers. 彼は大統領の最も熱狂的な崇拝者の一人だった
▶**ardently** 副 ◇They were *ardently* anti-Communist. 彼らは熱烈な反共主義者だった

interest 401

fervent [ふつう名詞の前で] 《ややフォーマル, 特に書き言葉》(強く偽りのない感情[信念]を持って[示して])熱心な, 熱烈な, 切実な ◇It is my *fervent* hope that she will find success in her chosen career. 彼女が選んだ職業で成功を収めることが私の切なる願いです ◇She was a *fervent* Catholic. 彼女は熱心なカトリック教徒だった ☞ **fervour** (EMOTION)
▶**fervently** 副 ◇She prayed *fervently* for his complete recovery. 彼女は彼の全快を切実に祈った

ノート **passionate, ardent, fervent の使い分け**: 多くの場合, これらの語は入れ替え使用可能. ◆a *passionate/ardent/fervent* supporter of sb/sth (人・物事の熱烈な支持者). *passionate* は特に人の信念について, *fervent* は特に人の願い[祈り]について, *ardent* は特に人・物事の崇拝者[ファン]である人について用いられる.

interest 名

1 interest・attraction・appeal・glamour・magic・charm・spell・fascination
人に魅力的だ[興味深い, 刺激的だ]と思わせる特徴[特性]
【類語訳】興味を引く特性, 趣, 面白さ, 魅力, 魅惑, 魔力, 魔法

文型&コロケーション

▶an interest/ an attraction/ an appeal/ a fascination **for** sb/sth
▶a **special** interest/ attraction/ appeal/ magic/ charm/ fascination
▶**great/ considerable** interest/ attraction/ appeal/ charm/ fascination
▶**obvious/ growing** interest/ attraction/ appeal/ fascination
▶a **powerful** attraction/ appeal/ spell
▶sth **loses** its attraction/ appeal/ glamour/ magic/ charm/ fascination
▶to **have** an interest/ an attraction/ an appeal/ glamour/ a magic/ charm/ a fascination
▶to **hold** an interest/ an attraction/ an appeal/ a magic/ a charm/ a fascination
▶to **exert** an attraction/ an appeal/ a spell/ a fascination
▶the attraction/ appeal/ fascination (of sth) **lies in** sth
▶to be **part of** the attraction/ appeal/ magic/ charm/ fascination

interest [U, 単数で] 興味[関心]を引く特性, 趣, 面白さ ◇There are many places of *interest* around Oxford. オックスフォード周辺には名所がたくさんある ◇The subject is *of no interest* to me at all. そのテーマには私はまったく興味がない ◇These plants will add *interest* to your garden. これらの植物は庭に趣を加えるでしょう ◇His books have a special *interest* for me. 彼の本は私にとっては特別に面白い

attraction [U, C] 興味[関心]を引く特徴[特性, 人], 魅力 ◇I can't *see the attraction* of sitting on the beach all day. 私は一日中浜辺に座っていることに魅力を感じません ◇And there's the *added attraction* of free champagne on all flights. それから, すべての便にシャンパンの無料サービスというあの特典も付いております ◇She is the *star attraction* of the show. 彼女はそのショーの花形の人気だ ☞ **attractive** (POPULAR)

appeal [U, 単数で] (興味を引く人・物事の)魅力, 面白さ

◇We are trying to **broaden the appeal** of classical music. 私たちはクラシック音楽の魅力を広げようとしています ◇Her stories have a universal *appeal*. 彼女の話には普遍的な魅力がある ☞ **appealing** (POPULAR)
glamour [U] （人・仕事・場所（に関わる財産・地位ゆえ）の）魅力, 魅惑 ◇Hopeful young actors are drawn by the *glamour* of Hollywood. 前途に夢をもつ若い俳優たちがハリウッドの魅惑に惹きつけられる ☞ **glamorous** (FASHIONABLE)
magic [U] （人・物事に備わる神秘的で素晴らしい）魔力, 魅力, 魔法 ◇The show is three hours of pure *magic*. そのショーはまったく魔法にかかったような3時間です ◇Like all truly charismatic people, he can **work his magic** on both men and women. すべてのカリスマ性のある人たちのように, 彼は男女どちらもとりこにすることができる
charm [U, C, ふつう複数で] （場所[物事]が備えるいくぶん古風な）魅力 ◇The hotel is full of *charm* and character. そのホテルは魅力と特色にあふれている ◇The route certainly had its *charms*. そのルートには確かに魅力があった ☞ **charming** (BEAUTIFUL 2)
spell [単数で] （人・物事が備える）魅力 ◇Since last century, the *spell* of the pyramids has drawn tourists to Egypt. 前世紀より, ピラミッドの魅力がエジプトに観光客を惹きつけている ◇I completely **fell under her spell**. 私はすっかり彼女のとりこになった
fascination [C, ふつう単数で] （物事が備える）魅力 ◇Water holds a *fascination* for most children. 水はほとんどの子どもたちを魅了する

2 interest・hobby・game・pastime・entertainment・amusement
余暇に楽しむために行う活動
【類語訳】趣味, 遊び, 娯楽, 遊戯, ゲーム, 気晴らし, 催し物, 余興, 演芸

【文型&コロケーション】
▶a **popular** interest/ hobby/ pastime/ entertainment/ amusement
▶to **have/ share** interests/ hobbies
▶to **take up/ pursue** an interest/ a hobby

interest [C] （[活動[研究テーマ]としての）趣味 ◇Her main *interests* are music and gardening. 彼女の主な趣味は音楽とガーデニングです ◇He was a man of wide *interests* outside his work. 彼は仕事以外で多趣味な人だった ☞ **passion** (TASTE)
hobby [C] （活動としての）趣味 ◇Her *hobbies* include swimming and cooking. 彼女の趣味には水泳や料理などがある ◇I only play jazz **as a hobby**. 私は趣味でジャズ演奏をしているだけです
game [C] （子どもの）遊び；娯楽, 遊戯, ゲーム ◇The children invented a new *game*. 子どもたちは新しい遊びを考案した ◇He was playing *games* with the dog. 彼は犬とゲームをして遊んでいた
pastime [C] 気晴らし, 娯楽, 遊戯 ◇Eating out is the national *pastime* in France. フランスでは外食が国民的な気晴らしである

[ノート] **interest, hobby, pastime** の使い分け：hobby は interest よりも活動的なものであることが多い。◆His main *hobby* is football (= he plays football). 彼の一番の趣味はサッカー（をすること）です ◆His main *interest* is football (= he watches and reads about football, and may or may not play it). 彼の一番の趣味はサッカー（をするしないは別にして, 観戦したり見聞きしたりすること）です. *pastime* は人々の一般的な「気晴らし」について言う場合に用いられる。自分自身や個人について言う場合は, interest か hobby を用いるほうがふつう。×Eating out is the national *interest/hobby* in France. ×Do you have any *pastimes*?

entertainment [C] （映画・ショーなどの）催し物, 娯楽, 余興, 演芸 ◇Local *entertainments* are listed in the newspaper. 地元で行われる催し物は新聞に載っています
amusement [C, ふつう複数で] 娯楽(施設) ◇traditional seaside *amusements* including boats, go-karts and a funfair ボート・ゴーカート・遊園地を含む, 海辺にある伝統的な娯楽施設

interest [動] ☞ DELIGHT

interest・appeal・attract・fascinate・intrigue・absorb・rivet・grip
注意を引いたり, 引きつけておいたりすることを表す
【類語訳】興味を引く, 好奇心を抱かせる, 興味をそそる, 心に訴える, 魅了する, 熱中させる, 没頭させる, 釘付けにする

interest	absorb	fascinate
appeal		rivet
attract		grip
intrigue		

【文型&コロケーション】
▶to attract/ rivet/ grip sb's **attention**
▶a **question/ subject** interests/ fascinates/ intrigues sb
▶to **really** interest sb/ appeal to sb/ attract/ fascinate/ intrigue sb

interest [他] 興味[関心]を引く, 関心を抱かせる ◇Politics just doesn't *interest* me. 私はただ単に政治に関心が持てないだけだ ◇The musuem has something to *interest* everyone. その美術館には万人を引きつける何かがある ◇*It may interest you to know* that he didn't accept the offer. 彼がその申し出を受けなかったと知ることに興味があろうかと思います ◇She has always *interested herself in* (= given her attention to) helping younger musicians. 彼女は若いミュージシャンを支援することにずっと興味を持っている
appeal [自] （物事が）興味をそそる, 受ける, 心に訴える ◇The prospect of a long wait in the rain did not *appeal*. 雨の中で長く待つかと思うと気が乗らなかった ◇It's a book that *appeals to* people of all ages. それはあらゆる年齢の人に受ける本です
attract [他, ふつう受身で] （物事が注意・興味などを）引きつける；（人が）魅了する ◇That was what first *attracted me to* the place. それが私の関心をその場所に最初に引きつけたことだった ◇I had always been *attracted by* the idea of working abroad. 私は海外で働くという考えにずっと魅力を感じていた ◇What first *attracted* me about her was her sense of humour. 私が彼女に最初に魅了されたのはそのユーモアのセンスだった [反意] **repel** (SHOCK [動])
fascinate [他, 自] （学ぶことが多い[不思議である]と感じるため）興味をそそる, 魅了する ◇China has always *fasci*-

interested, interesting

nated me. 私はずっと中国に魅了されてきた ◇The private lives of the rich and famous never fail to *fascinate*. 金持ちや有名人の私生活には必ず興味をそそられる

intrigue [他] (珍しく[不思議に]思えるため)興味をそそる ◇There was something about him that *intrigued* her. 彼には彼女の興味をそそるものがあった

absorb [他] (他のものにまったく注意を払わないほど)熱中[没頭]させる ◇The work had *absorbed* him for several years. 彼は数年間その仕事に熱中していた ◇She was completely *absorbed in* the task. 彼女はその仕事にすっかり没頭していた

rivet [他, ふつう受身で] (目を離すことができない[他のことを考えられない]ほど)釘付けにする ◇I was absolutely *riveted* by her story. 私は彼女の話にすっかり釘付けにされた ◇My eyes were *riveted on* the figure lying in the road. 私の目は路上に横たわっている人影に釘付けになっていた

grip (-pp-) [他] 心をつかんで離さない;(人の注意を)引きつけて離さない ◇The book *grips* you from the first page to the last. その本は最初のページから最後のページまであなたの心をつかんで離しません ◇The atmosphere of the World Cup *gripped* the nation. ワールドカップの雰囲気は国中の関心を引きつけた

interested [形]

interested・fascinated・absorbed・engrossed・attentive・rapt
物事にすべての注意を払っている人を表す
【類語訳】興味がある, 面白がった, 興味深げな, 熱中した, うっとりした, 心を奪われた

| interested | absorbed | fascinated |
| attentive | engrossed | rapt |

【文型&コロケーション】
▶ **interested/ absorbed/ engrossed/ rapt in** sth
▶ **interested/ absorbed/ engrossed in doing** sth
▶ **interested/ fascinated to do** sth
▶ an **interested/** a **fascinated/** an **attentive/** a **rapt expression**
▶ an **interested/** an **attentive/** a **rapt audience**
▶ **utterly** fascinated/ absorbed/ rapt
▶ **completely/ totally** absorbed/ engrossed

interested 興味[関心]がある;面白がった, 興味深げな ◇I'm very *interested* in history. 私は歴史にとても興味があります ◇Anyone *interested* in joining the club should contact us at the address below. クラブへの参加に関心のある方はどなたでも下記のアドレスにお問い合わせください ◇We would be *interested* to hear your views on this subject. このテーマについてのあなたの意見をお伺いしたい ◇He's not the least bit *interested* in girls. 彼は女の子にはさらさら興味がない ◇She was watching with a politely *interested* expression on her face. 彼女は社交辞令的に顔に興味深げな表情を浮かべて見ていた 〖反意〗 **uninterested, bored**

fascinated 非常に興味[関心]のある ◇I've always been *fascinated by* his ideas. 私は彼の考えにはいつも興味がある ◇The children watched, *fascinated*, as the picture began to appear. 絵が見え始めると, 子どもたちは興味津々にじっと見ていた

absorbed [名詞の前はまれ] 熱中[没頭]した ◇She seemed totally *absorbed* in her book. 彼女はすっかり本に熱中しているようだった ◇He was too *absorbed in* watching the game to notice. 彼は試合の観戦に熱中していて気づかなかった

engrossed [名詞の前はまれ] 熱中[没頭]した ◇She was *engrossed* in conversation. 彼女は会話に熱中していた ◇Dawn was *engrossed* in stuffing clothes into a bag. ドーンはバッグに服を詰め込むのに没頭していた

attentive 注意深い ◇He listened, quiet and *attentive*. 彼は静かに注意深く耳を傾けた ◇Never before had she had such an *attentive* audience. 彼女はそれまでこれほど集中してくれる聴衆を前にしたことはなかった 〖反意〗 **inattentive** ❶ inattentiveは人が人や物事に注意を払っていないことを表す. ◆an *inattentive* pupil (不注意な生徒). ◆*inattentive* to the needs of others (他人の要求に気を配らない).

▷ **attentively** [副] ◇The children listened *attentively* to the story. 子どもたちは注意深く話を聞いた

rapt 《書き言葉》うっとりした, 心を奪われた ◇He watched her with a *rapt* expression. 彼女はうっとりとした表情で彼女を見ていた ◇Jill stared at them blankly, *rapt* in thought. ジルは考えに心を奪われて彼らをぽかんと見つめた

〖ノート〗**absorbed, engrossed, rapt**の使い分け: rapt はこの3つの語の中で最も意味の強い語で, ぽかんとして目の前のものが目に入らないときの, 人の表情を表すのに用いられる. absorbedの対象となるのは, 本当に興味を引くものだけで, 特に物を読んだり見たりする場合に用いられる. engrossedの対象となるのは, 行われているもののうち, 格別面白くはないかもしれないが, それでも注意を向けるものである. ✕Dawn was *absorbed* in stuffing clothes into a bag.

interesting [形]

interesting・fascinating・compelling・stimulating・gripping・riveting・absorbing
人や物事が刺激的である[珍しい, 素晴らしい発想にあふれている]ので注意を引く[引きつけておく]ことを表す
【類語訳】面白い, 興味深い, 目が離せない, 刺激的な, 発奮させる, 魅惑的な, 釘付けになるような, 熱中させる, 没頭させる

interesting	compelling	fascinating
stimulating	absorbing	gripping
		riveting

【文型&コロケーション】
▶ **interesting/ fascinating/ stimulating for** sb
▶ **interesting/ fascinating to** sb
▶ **interesting/ fascinating that**...
▶ **interesting/ fascinating to see/ hear/ find/ learn/ know**...
▶ an **interesting/** a **fascinating/** a **compelling/** a **gripping story/ read/ book**
▶ an **interesting/** a **fascinating/** a **stimulating experience/ discussion/ idea**
▶ an **interesting/** a **fascinating example**
▶ a **compelling/ riveting performance**
▶ to **find** sth **interesting/ fascinating/ compelling/ stimulating/ gripping/ riveting/ absorbing**
▶ **very interesting/ fascinating/ compelling/ stimulating/ gripping**

↳interesting　　　　　　　　　　international

▶**really** interesting/ fascinating/ stimulating/ gripping
▶**especially/ particularly** interesting/ fascinating/ compelling
▶**absolutely** fascinating/ gripping/ riveting

interesting (刺激的な[珍しい, 素晴らしい発想にあふれた]ものであるため)面白い, 興味深い ◇That's an *interesting* question, Daniel. ダニエル, それは面白い質問だね ◇You seem to know a lot of very *interesting* people. 君はとても面白い人を大勢知っているようだね ◇It would be *interesting* to know what he really believed. 彼が本当に信じていることがわかれば面白いだろうね ◇I find it *interesting* that she claims not to know him. 彼女が彼のことを知らないと主張するのは興味深い ◇Can't we do something more *interesting*? もっと面白いことができませんか ◇Our survey produced some *interesting* results. 我々の調査で興味深い結果がいくらか出ました　[反意] **boring, dull, uninteresting** (BORING)
▷**interestingly** 副 ◇*Interestingly*, there are very few recorded cases of such attacks. 面白いことに, そういった攻撃の記録例はほとんどありません
fascinating 非常に興味深い[魅力的な] ◇It's *fascinating* to see how different people approach the problem. 異なる人々が問題にどうアプローチするかを見るのは非常に興味深い ◇The book provides a *fascinating* glimpse into Moroccan life. この本を通して, 心ときめくモロッコの生活を垣間見ることができます ◇I fail to see what women find so *fascinating* about him. 女性が彼のどんなところをそれほど魅力的に思うのかわからない
compelling 《書き言葉》(読む[見る]ことをやめられないほど)やみつきになる, 目が離せない ◇Her latest book makes *compelling* reading. 彼の最新の本は読んだらやみつきになる ◇His eyes were strangely *compelling*. 不思議なことに彼は目をそらすことができなかった
stimulating 《やや硬い》(興味深い考えであふれていて)刺激的な; (人々を)発奮させる ◇Thank you for a most *stimulating* discussion. 大変刺激的な議論をありがとうございました ◇She was a very *stimulating* teacher who got the best out of her students. 彼女は非常に生徒を発奮させその能力を最大限に引き出す教師だった ☞ **stimulate** (INSPIRE)
gripping (完全に注意を引きつけて)人の心をとらえて離さない, 魅惑的な ◇The film is a *gripping* account of the early days of the revolution. その映画は革命初期についての人々をとらえて離さない物語である
riveting 《特に書き言葉》(完全に注意を引きつけて)釘付けになるような ◇As usual, she gave a *riveting* performance. 例によって彼女は人をとりこにするような演技をした
absorbing (注意を引きつけて)熱中[没頭]させる ◇Chess can be an extremely *absorbing* game. チェスは人をとても夢中にさせるゲームかもしれない

[ノート] **compelling, gripping, riveting, absorbing** の使い分け：これらの語はすべて物事が注意を引く場合に用いられる. gripping と riveting は compelling や absorbing よりも意味が強く, 特に刺激的で劇的な物語や映画, パフォーマンスに用いられる. compelling は本にも用いられるが, ふつう, それは事実に基づく[その筋がとても素晴らしい]として注意を引く本である. absorbing はより控えめに注意を引く本やテーマ, 活動に用いられる.

international 形

international・global・worldwide・multinational・cosmopolitan・intercontinental・multiracial

世界の二つ以上の国[地域]に関連することを表す
【類語訳】国際の, 国際的な, グローバルな, 世界的規模の, 世界的な, 地球上の, 多国籍の, 多国間の, 世界主義的な, 国際人の, 大陸間の, 多民族の

[文型&コロケーション]

▶international/ global/ worldwide **attention/ campaigns/ influence/ issues/ markets**
▶an international/ a global/ a worldwide **campaign/ reputation**
▶an international/ a global/ a multinational **company/ corporation**
▶an international/ a cosmopolitan/ a multiracial **society/ community**
▶an international/ a global/ a cosmopolitan **outlook**
▶**truly** international/ global/ cosmopolitan

international [ふつう名詞の前で] 国際(上)の, 国際的な ◇the importance of preserving *international* peace and security 国際的な平和と安全を守ることの重要性 ◇In crucial areas of *international* relations the nation state still dominates. 国際関係にきわめて重要な地域では, 依然として民族国家が支配している ◇She is a professor of *international* law. 彼女は国際法の教授である ◇He plays *international* rugby. 彼はラグビーの国際試合でプレーする ◇The island now has an *international* airport (= one with flights to and from foreign countries). その島には現在, 国際空港がある [反意] **national** (NATIONAL)
▷**internationally** 副 ◇He was *internationally* famous. 彼は国際的に有名だった
global [ふつう名詞の前で] グローバルな, 世界的規模の, 世界的な, 地球上の ◇The commission is calling for a *global* ban on whaling. 委員会は世界的規模の捕鯨禁止を提唱している ◇the company's domestic and *global* markets その会社の国内市場と世界市場 ◇a conference on *global* warming (= the increase in temperature of the earth's atmosphere that is caused by the increase of particular gases, especially carbon dioxide) 地球温暖化会議 [反意] **local** ❶ local は一つの特定の場所に属する[関連する]ことを表す. ◆ a *local* newspaper/radio station (地方紙/地元ラジオ局). ◆ decisions made at a *local* rather than national level (全国レベルではなく地方レベルで下された決定).
▷**globally** 副 ◇*globally* accepted standards 世界的に認められた基準
worldwide [ふつう名詞の前で] 世界中に及ぶ, 世界的な ◇The company has a *worldwide* sales force. その会社には世界中に広がる販売網がある ◇She soon gained *worldwide* fame as a dancer. 彼女はやがてダンサーとして世界的な名声をつかんだ ◇There was a danger of a *worldwide* recession. 世界的な景気後退の危険があった ◇a *worldwide* flu epidemic 世界中に及ぶインフルエンザの流行
▷**worldwide** 副 ◇We have 2,000 members *worldwide*. 私どもには世界中に2千人の会員がいます

interrupt, intervene

ノート global と worldwide の使い分け：多くの場合、両語とも使用可能。◆global/worldwide attention/campaigns/influence/issues/markets（世界的な注目/運動/影響/問題/市場）。global はいくぶんより政治的な文脈で用いられ、関心や問題を共有する大きな一つの共同体としての世界を強調する。worldwide はいくぶんよりビジネス的な文脈で用いられ、独自の関心や問題を持つ、広範にわたる異なる共同体の集まりであることを強調する。

multinational [ふつう名詞の前で]《特にビジネス or ジャーナリズム》（ビジネスが）多国籍の、多国間の ◆the huge profits made by *multinational* drug manufacturers 多国籍製薬会社が上げた莫大な利益 ◆A *multinational task force* is being sent to the trouble spot. 多国籍の機動部隊がその紛争地域に送られる予定だ
▶ **multinational** 名 [C] ◆one of the world's leading *multinationals* (= multinational companies) 世界有数の多国籍企業の一つ

cosmopolitan 《ほめて》（場所が）国際的な；（人が）世界主義的な、国際人の ◆She liked the *cosmopolitan* atmosphere of the city. 彼女はその都市の国際的な雰囲気が好きだった ◆people with a truly *cosmopolitan* outlook 真に世界主義的な見解を持った人々
▶ **cosmopolitan** 名 [C] ◆She's a real *cosmopolitan*. 彼女は紛れもない国際人だ

intercontinental [ふつう名詞の前で] 大陸間の ◆*intercontinental* flights/missiles/travel/trade 大陸を結ぶ航空便/大陸間ミサイル/大陸をまたぐ旅行/大陸間貿易

multiracial 多民族の ◆We live in a *multiracial* society. 我々は多民族社会に暮らしている

interrupt 動

interrupt・disturb・bother・intrude・cut in・chip in・trouble・barge in

他の人が話し[何かをやり]続けるのを妨げる
【類語訳】さえぎる、中断させる、話の腰を折る、割り込む、口を挟む、邪魔をする、首を突っ込む

文型&コロケーション
▶ to interrupt/ disturb sb/ bother sb/ cut in/ chip in/ trouble sb **with** sth
▶ intrude/ cut in/ chip in/ barge in **on** sth
▶ to be **sorry to** interrupt sb/ disturb sb/ bother sb/ intrude/ cut in/ trouble sb
▶ to **suddenly** interrupt/ intrude/ barge in

interrupt [自, 他]（話して[何かをして]いる最中に）さえぎる、中断させる、話の腰を折る、割り込む、口を挟む、邪魔をする ◆Please stop *interrupting* all the time! 年がら年中話の腰を折らないでください ◆They were *interrupted* by a knock on the door. 彼らはドアのノックで話を中断させられた ◆'What's his name?' John *interrupted*.「彼の名前は」とジョンは言葉をさえぎった ◆I hope I'm not *interrupting* you. 君の邪魔をしていないといいんだけど
▶ **interruption** 名 [C, U] ◆He ignored her *interruptions*. 彼は彼女の割り込みを無視した ◆She spoke for 20 minutes **without** *interruption*. 彼女はぶっ通しで20分間話した

disturb [他]（話しかけて[物音を立てて]）邪魔をする、起こす ◆If you're up early, try not to *disturb* the others. もし早く起きたら、他の人を起こさないようにしなさい ◆Don't *disturb* her when she's working. 彼女が仕事をしているときは邪魔をするな

bother [他]《ややインフォーマル、特に話し言葉》（話しかけて[質問をして]）煩わせる、邪魔をする、面倒[迷惑, 手数]をかける ◆Sorry to *bother* you, but there's a call for you on line two. お手数をかけて申し訳ありませんが、2番にお電話が入っております ◆Please stop *bothering* me with all these questions! こんな質問で私を煩わせないでください ◆Let me know if he *bothers* you again. 彼がまたご迷惑をおかけするようなことがあれば、知らせてください

ノート interrupt, disturb, bother の使い分け：interrupt はふつう人が話している最中に自分も話すこと。disturb と bother は話しかけたり[質問したり]して、何かをしようとしている人の「邪魔をする」こと。disturb は人が休もうとしている最中に物音をしきりに立てて「邪魔をする」ときにも用いられるが、bother と interrupt は不可。✕Don't *disturb/bother* me when I'm speaking. ✕Stop *interrupting* me when I'm working. ✕If you're up early, try not to *interrupt/bother* the others.

intrude 《ややフォーマル》（呼ばれていない[いるべきでない]場所に）押しかける、首を突っ込む、邪魔する、立ち入る、侵害する ◆He didn't wish to *intrude* at such a sensitive time. 彼はこんな微妙なときに首を突っ込みたくなかった ◆They must be prevented from *intruding into* the family's private grief. 彼らにその家族の私的な悲しみに立ち入らせるわけにはいかない
▶ **intrusion** 名 [U, C] ◆She apologized for the *intrusion* but said she had an urgent message. 彼女は邪魔になって申し訳ないけれども、緊急の伝言があると言った ◆They claim the noise from the airport is an *intrusion on* their lives. 彼らは空港の騒音は生活への侵害だと主張している ◆This was another example of press *intrusion into* the affairs of the royals. これは王室事情の過剰報道のもう一つの例だった

,cut 'in 句動詞（話している最中に）割り込む、口を挟む ◆She kept *cutting in* on our conversation. 彼女は私たちの会話に口を挟み続けた ◆'What on earth are you talking about?' Maria *cut in*.「いったい何の話をしてるの」と言ってマリアは割り込んだ

,chip 'in 句動詞 (-pp-)《インフォーマル》（他人の会話に意見[提案, 質問]を）差し挟む、割り込ませる ◆Pete and Ann *chipped in* with a few suggestions. ピートとアンはいくつか提案を差し挟んだ

trouble [他]《ややフォーマル》（頼みごとをしようと思って）煩わせる、邪魔をする、面倒[迷惑, 手数]をかける ◆Sorry to *trouble* you, but could you read this document through for me? お手数かけて申し訳ありませんが、この書類に目を通していただけませんか ◆I didn't want to *trouble* the doctor with such a small problem. 彼はこんなささいな問題で医者を煩わせたくなかった ❶この意味の trouble は丁寧な依頼で用いられることが多く、bother よりもフォーマル

barge in 句動詞《ややインフォーマル》（話して[何かをして]いる最中に無作法に）押しかける、立ち入る、口を挟む ◆I hope you don't mind me *barging in* like this. こんなふうに押しかけてご迷惑でなければいいのですが ◆He just *barged in* on us while we were having a meeting. 私たちが会議を開いている最中に彼はまさに押しかけてきた

intervene 動

intervene・mediate・intercede・arbitrate

↳intervene

他人に代わって口論をやめさせ[合意に至らせ]ようとする
【類語訳】調停する, 仲裁する, 介入する, 干渉する, 仲に入る, 仲を取り持つ

文型&コロケーション
▶to intervene/ mediate/ intercede **on behalf of** sb
▶to intervene/ mediate/ intercede **with** sb
▶to intervene/ mediate/ arbitrate **between** A and B
▶to intervene/ mediate/ arbitrate **in** sth
▶to **ask sb to** intervene/ mediate/ intercede

intervene [自]《ややフォーマル》(改善[援助]を試みて)調停[仲裁, 介入, 干渉]する ◇He *intervened* with the authorities on the prisoners' behalf. 彼は囚人たちを代表して当局との調停に入った ◇The EU refuses to *intervene to* control the trade. EUは貿易統制のための介入を拒んでいる ◇She might have been killed if the neighbours hadn't *intervened*. 隣人が仲裁しなければ, 彼女は殺されていたかもしれない
▷**intervention** [名][U, C] ◇There have been calls for government *intervention* to save the steel industry. 鉄鋼業を救うために政府の介入の要請がなされてきた ◇People resented his repeated *interventions* in the debate. 人々は彼の再三にわたる討議の妨害に憤れた
mediate [自, 他]《ややフォーマル》(合意に向けて)調停[仲裁]する, (調停[仲裁]によって)成立させる ◇An independent body was brought in to *mediate* between workers and management. 労使間の仲裁のために独立機関が加わった ◇The UN attempted to *mediate* a solution to the conflict. 国連はその紛争の解決策を講じようとした ☞ **mediator** (NEGOTIATOR)
intercede [自]《フォーマル》(同情すべき事情を考慮させ[口論をやめさせ]ようと)仲[仲間]に入る, 仲を取り持つ ◇I prayed that she would *intercede for* us. 私は彼女が私たちの仲裁に入ってくれることを祈った ◇Their father made no attempt to *intercede*. 彼らの父は仲を取り持とうとしなかった

ノート **intervene** と **intercede** の使い分け: intervene のほうが一般的な語で, 行動だけでなく話し合いを指すこともあり, 何らかの形で援助できると考えられるあらゆる状況に用いられる. intercede はしばしば一方の人[集団]がもう一方の人[集団]に対して権力を持っている状況において, 権力のある人[集団]に語りかけて, もう一方の人[集団]を優しく[同情をもって]扱うよう説得しようとする場合に用いられる.

arbitrate [自, 他]《ややフォーマル》(公式に口論[意見の相違]を)調停[仲裁]する ◇A committee was created to *arbitrate* between management and the unions. 経営陣と労働組合の間の調停をするために委員会が設けられた ◇He is the official responsible for *arbitrating* the case of disputed trades. 彼は係争中の取り引きの問題を仲裁する責任を負う役人である
▷**arbitration** [名][U] ◇Both sides in the dispute have agreed to *go to arbitration*. 論争の両陣営は調停を依頼することに同意した

interview [名]

1 interview・interrogation・audience・consultation
人が意見や助言を求められたり, 質問されたりする場
【類語訳】インタビュー, 記者会見, 取材, 面談, 尋問, 取り調べ,

interview

公式会見, 謁見, 診察, 相談

文型&コロケーション
▶an interview/ an audience/ a consultation **with** sb
▶an **in-depth** interview/ consultation
▶a **police** interview/ interrogation
▶to **have/ request** an interview/ an audience/ a consultation
▶to **give/ grant sb** an interview/ an audience/ a consultation
▶to **carry out/ conduct** an interview/ interrogation
▶interview/ interrogation **procedures/ techniques**

interview [C] (ジャーナリストによる公式の)インタビュー, 記者会見, 取材; (質疑応答がなされる私的な)面談 ◇He's a very private man and rarely gives *interviews* (= agrees to answer questions). 彼は非常に引っ込みがちで, めったにインタビューに応じない ◇The survey team carried out over 200 *interviews* with retired people. 調査チームは200人以上の退職者との面談を行った ☞ **interview** (QUESTION [動])
interrogation [U, C] (情報を得るための強引な)尋問; (尋問による)取り調べ ◇He confessed after four days *under interrogation*. 彼は4日間尋問を受けた後で白状した ◇She hated her parents' endless *interrogations* about where she'd been. 彼女はどこにいたのかについて両親に延々と問いただされるのをひどく嫌がった ☞ **interrogate** (QUESTION [動])
audience [C] (要人との)公式会見, 謁見 ◇The Pope granted her a private *audience*. 法王は彼女に内謁を授けた
consultation [C] (助言・治療を受けるための医者・専門家の)診察, 相談 ◇A 30-minute *consultation* will cost £50. 30分の相談料は50ポンドになります ☞ **consult** (ASK 1)

2 interview・audition・trial・tryout・screen test
自分が特定の職[劇や映画などの役, チームの選手]に適していることを示そうとする場
【類語訳】面接, オーディション, トライアル, 試験, 選考会, 予選, トライアウト, スクリーンテスト, 撮影審査

文型&コロケーション
▶an interview/ an audition/ trials/ tryouts/ a screen test **for** sth
▶an interview/ an audition/ a trial/ a tryout/ a screen test **with** sb
▶**in** an interview/ an audition/ trials/ tryouts
▶**at** an interview/ audition
▶**Olympic/ international/ national/ club** trials/ tryouts
▶to **have** an interview/ an audition/ a trial/ a tryout/ a screen test
▶to **go for** an interview/ an audition/ a screen test
▶to **hold** interviews/ auditions/ trials/ tryouts
▶to **do/ pass/ fail** an audition/ a screen test

interview [C] (特定の職・大学の科目履修などに適性を見るための公式の)面接 ◇I've got a *job interview* tomorrow. 明日私は就職面接があります ◇She's been called for (an) *interview*. 彼女は面接に呼ばれていた
▷**interview** [動][他, 自] ◇We *interviewed* ten people for the job. 我々はその仕事を求める10人に面接をした

introduce

◇The deadline for applications is 15 October and we will be *interviewing* early in November. 応募の締め切りは10月15日で、11月初めに面接が予定されています

audition [C] 《劇・コンサートなどの俳優・歌手などを選出する》オーディション ◇He went for an *audition* with the Royal Ballet. 彼はロイヤル・バレエのオーディションを目指した ▶**audition** 動《自, 他》◇I *auditioned* and was given the part. 私はオーディションを受けてその役を手に入れた ◇We *auditioned* over 200 children for the role. 私たちはその役のために200人以上の子どもたちをオーディションにかけた

trial [C, ふつう複数で]《英》《スポーツのチーム作り[重要な大会]に向けて最も優秀な選手を選出する》トライアル, 試験, 選考会 ◇She just missed selection when she came third in the *trials*. 彼女は代表選考会で3位になってたった今選考から外れたところだ

tryout [C, ふつう複数で]《米》《スポーツのチーム作り[大会]のための》予選, トライアウト ◇He's now focusing on next week's Olympic *tryouts*. 彼は今, 来週のオリンピック予選に焦点を合わせている

'screen test [C] 《映画出演の適性を見るための俳優に対する》スクリーンテスト, 撮影審査 ◇He asked Redford to read the script and *take a screen test*. 彼は脚本を読んで撮影審査を受けるようレッドフォードに頼んだ

introduce 動 ☞ BEGIN

introduce • launch • initiate • institute • instigate • set/put sth in motion • bring sth in • phase sth in
人々に新しいシステム[法律]を使い始めさせること, 措置を講じ始めること
【類義訳】売り出す, 発表する, 導入する, 取り入れる, 開始する, 実施する, 立ち上げる

【文型&コロケーション】
▶to introduce/ launch/ initiate/ institute/ instigate/ set in motion/ bring in/ phase in a **scheme/ reform**
▶to introduce/ launch/ initiate/ institute/ instigate/ bring in/ phase in a **system**
▶to introduce/ launch/ initiate/ institute/ instigate/ bring in a **policy**
▶to introduce/ launch/ initiate/ institute/ instigate a **programme**
▶to introduce/ launch/ initiate/ institute/ instigate/ set in motion/ bring in/ phase in **changes**
▶to introduce/ initiate/ bring in (a) **legislation/ law**
▶to introduce/ initiate/ institute a **practice**
▶to launch/ initiate/ institute/ instigate (a/ an) **campaign/ enquiry/ investigation/ proceedings**
▶to launch/ initiate/ set in motion a **plan**
▶to introduce/ launch/ initiate/ institute sth **formally**

introduce [他]《製品・法律・システム・考えなどを初めて》売り出す, 発表する, 導入する, 取り入れる, 付け加える ◇The company is *introducing* a new range of products this year. 今年その会社は新シリーズの製品を売り出す予定だ ◇We want to *introduce* the latest technology *into* schools. 私たちは学校にその最新技術を導入したい ◇We are going to *introduce* a few changes to the system. 私たちはそのシステムに少し変更を加えるつもりだ

launch [他]《特にビジネス or ジャーナリズム》《組織的な活動を公式に》開始する ◇The Duchess of Cornwall, president of the charity, will *launch* the appeal in London. 慈善事業の会長であるコーンウォール公爵夫人はロンドンで呼びかけ運動を開始します ◇Police have *launched* a murder enquiry. 警察は殺人事件の捜査を開始した ◇A massive attack was *launched* in the spring of 1918. 1918年の春に大規模な攻撃が開始された ❶ビジネスの文脈において, launchの典型的な連語には appeal, bid, campaign, enquiry, initiative, investigation, operation, plan, project, programmeが挙げられる。軍事的な文脈では, attack, assault, raid, invasionが挙げられる。また, 新製品を目的語にとることもある。

initiate [他]《フォーマル》《システム・方針・措置を》開始[実施]する, 立ち上げる, 起こす ◇The government has *initiated* a programme of economic reform. 政府は経済改革計画を立ち上げた ◇He *initiated* a national debate on reform. 彼は改革に関する国民的議論を開始した ◇The organization may *initiate* legal action against you. その組織はあなたに対して訴訟を起こすかもしれない

institute [他]《フォーマル》《システム・方針・措置を》開始[実施]する, 立ち上げる, 起こす ◇The new management intends to *institute* a number of changes. 新経営陣はいくつかの変革を実施するつもりだ ◇They could *institute* criminal proceedings against you. 彼らならあなたに対して刑事訴訟を起こすことができるだろう

【ノート】**initiate と institute の使い分け**: これらの語に意味による違いはほとんどない。initiateにはinstituteよりも幅広い連語があり, 法的手段などの公式の措置にも, 討論・議論などのよりインフォーマルな措置にも用いられる。instituteはよりフォーマルな措置についてのみ用いられる。×He *instituted* a national debate on reform.

instigate [他]《特に英, フォーマル》《措置・行動を公式に》開始[実施]する, 起こす, 扇動する, 《措置・行動の》発端となる ◇We will *instigate* a comprehensive review of defence policy. 我々は防衛政策の包括的な見直しを実施します ◇It was Rufus who *instigated* the whole thing. そもそもすべての発端はルーファスだった ❶instigateは誰が物事を起こさせたかについて議論する[とられた行動が関係者全員に受けが悪い]場合に用いられることが多い。
▶**instigation** [名] [U] ◇An appeal fund was launched *at the instigation of* the President. 義援金は大統領の肝入りで始められた ◇It was done *at his instigation*. それは彼にそそのかされて行われた

set/put sth in 'motion [句動]《特に書き言葉》《措置を》開始[実施, 発動]する, 起こす ◇The wheels of change have been *set in motion*. 改革が次々に実施されている ❶set/put sth in motionはふつういくつかの段階から成る措置を開始することを指す。◆to *set in motion* preparations/a chain of actions/steps/a procedure/measures (準備/措置/一連の行動/一連の手段/手順/手段を開始する[起こす])

,bring sth 'in [句動]《新法・議案を》導入する, 取り入れる, 提出する ◇They want to *bring in* a bill to limit arms exports. 彼らは武器輸出を制限する議案を提出したいと思っている ❶bring sthinのsthには主にact, bill, law, regulation, legislationが用いられる。

,phase sth 'in [句動]《特にビジネス》《一定期間にわたって物事を》段階的に導入する[取り入れる, 利用する] ◇The new tax will be *phased in* over two years. 2年にわたって新税が段階的に導入されるだろう [反意] **phase sth out** ❶phase sth outは一定期間にわたって段階的に物事の利用をやめることを表す。

introduction 名

introduction・preface・preamble・prologue・foreword
後に続くことの概要を伝える書物[演説]の最初の部分
【類語訳】序文, 前置き, はしがき, 前文, 前口上, 序章

文型&コロケーション
▶ the introduction/ preface/ preamble/ prologue/ foreword **to** a book, etc.
▶ **in** the introduction/ preface/ preamble/ prologue/ foreword
▶ to **read/ write** the introduction/ a preface/ a preamble/ a prologue/ a foreword

introduction [C, U] (書物の)序文, (演説の)前置き ◇This book has an excellent *introduction* and notes. この本には素晴らしい序文と注釈がついている ◇*By way of introduction*, let me give you the background to the story. 前置きとして, 話の背景を説明いたします ☞ **introductory** (FIRST)

preface [C] (著者の意図を説明するための)序文, はしがき ◇In his *preface* he claimed that he had created a new kind of music. 彼は序文で, 新しい種類の音楽を生み出したと主張した ❶ **preface** は書物の目的・テーマの範囲・種々の制約を扱う. ふつう著者によって書かれ, introduction の前に置かれる.

▶ **preface** [動] [他] ◇He *prefaced* the diaries with a short account of how they were discovered. 彼はそうした日記が発見された経緯の短い説明をその日記集の序文とした

preamble [C, U] 《フォーマル》(書物・文書の)序文, 前文 ;(話す際の)前置き ◇the *Preamble* to the US Constitution アメリカ合衆国憲法の前文 ◇She gave him the bad news *without preamble*. 彼女は前置きなしに彼に悪い知らせを伝えた ❶記述される preamble はふつう小説などの文学作品ではなく公式文書[事実に基づいた書物]に付けられる.

prologue [C] (劇・小説などの)前口上, 序章 ◇the *Prologue* to Chaucer's 'Canterbury Tales' チョーサーの『カンタベリー物語』の序章 ◇ prologue はふつう読者が読むか読まないか選択できるような別仕立ての文章ではなく, 物語の一部を構成するものである.

foreword [C] (書物の)序文 ◇He was asked if he would consider writing a *foreword* for her book. 彼女の本に序文を書くことを考えてくれるかどうかを彼は訊ねられた ❶ foreword はふつう著者以外の人によって書かれる. foreword の書き手は時に自分と著者との関係やその本の内容について説明する. foreword は introduction の前に付けられる.

invade 動 ☞ ATTACK 動 2

invade・occupy・seize・capture・annex・take・conquer
軍事力を用いて場所を抑えこむ
【類語訳】侵攻する, 侵略する, 占領する, 制圧する, 奪取する, 掌握する, 攻略する, 攻め落とす, 併合する, 支配する, 征服する

文型&コロケーション
▶ to invade/ occupy/ seize/ annex/ conquer a **country/ region**
▶ to invade/ occupy/ seize/ capture/ take/ conquer a **town/ city**
▶ to occupy/ seize/ capture/ take a **building**
▶ to seize/ take **control** of a place
▶ **troops/ soldiers** invade/ occupy/ seize/ capture/ take a place
▶ a **country** invades/ occupies/ annexes/ conquers a place

invade [自, 他] (軍事力を用いて国に)侵攻[侵略]する ◇Troops *invaded* on August 9th that year. 軍隊はその年の8月9日に侵攻した ◇When did the Romans *invade* Britain? ローマ人がイギリスを侵略したのはいつですか ☞ **invasion** (ATTACK 1)

occupy [他] (大集団で場所を)占領[占拠]する ◇The capital has been *occupied* by the rebel army. 首都は反乱軍によって占領されている ◇Protesting students *occupied* the TV station. 抗議する学生たちはテレビ局を占拠した

▶ **occupation** 名 [U] ◇The military *occupation* has created anger and resentment. 軍隊による占拠は怒りと敵意を生んでいる

seize [他] (突然かつ暴力的に場所[状況]を)制圧[占領, 占拠]する, 奪取[掌握]する ◇They *seized* the airport in a surprise attack. 彼らは奇襲で空港を制圧した ◇The army has *seized* control of the country. 軍が国を掌握している ◇He *seized power* in a military coup. 彼は軍事クーデターで権力を奪取した

▶ **seizure** 名 [U] ◇The invasion began with the *seizure* of the country's largest southern city. 侵略は国内最大の南部の都市の占拠から始まった

capture [他] (戦争において軍事力を用いて)獲得[奪取]する, 攻略する, 攻め落とす ◇The city was *captured* in 1941. その都市は1941年に攻略された ◇He led the party that *captured* the enemy's flag. 彼は敵の旗を奪い取った部隊を率いていた

▶ **capture** 名 [U] ◇The *capture* of enemy territory followed the defeat of their air force. 空軍撃破の後敵地攻略が続いた

annex [他] (隣接する国[国の一部]を)併合する ◇Germany *annexed* Austria in 1938. ドイツは1938年にオーストリアを併合した

▶ **annexation** 名 [U, C] ◇The *annexation* of Texas was one of the causes of the Mexican War. テキサス併合がメキシコ戦争の一因だった

take [他] (戦争で場所を)攻略する, 攻め落とす ;(物事を)支配[掌握]する ◇The rebels succeeded in *taking* the town. 反乱軍はその町を攻め落とすのに成功した ◇The state has *taken* control of the company. 国がその会社を掌握している

conquer [他] (歴史において軍事力を用いて国[都市]及び国民[市民]を)征服する ◇In 330 BC Persia was *conquered* by Alexander the Great. 紀元前330年, アレキサンダー大王によってペルシャは征服された

▶ **conquest** 名 ◇The Norman *Conquest* of England in 1066 led to changes in the system of government. 1066年のノルマン人によるイングランド征服は統治体制に変化をもたらした

investigate 動

investigate・explore・look into sth・research・probe・enquire into sth・delve into sth

investigation

物事をより詳しく解明する
【類語訳】捜査する, 調査する, 取り調べる, 調べる, 研究する, 究明する, 探る, 検討する, 準備をする, 尋ねる, 詮索する

文型&コロケーション

- to look/ research/ probe/ enquire/ delve **into** sth
- to investigate/ explore/ look into/ research/ enquire into **what/ why/ how/ whether...**
- to investigate/ explore/ look into/ research/ enquire into a **problem/ matter**
- to investigate/ explore/ look into/ research/ delve into a **subject**
- to investigate/ look into/ probe/ enquire into an **allegation**
- to investigate/ explore/ probe **further**
- to look/ enquire/ delve **further** into sth
- to **carefully** investigate/ explore/ research sth
- to enquire **carefully** into sth
- to look/ probe/ enquire/ delve **deep/ deeper/ deeply** into sth
- to investigate/ explore/ probe sth **in detail**

investigate [自, 他] (状況・出来事・犯罪を)捜査[調査]する, 取り調べる;(人の性格・行動を)調べる;(テーマ・問題を)研究[調査]する, 究明する ◇The FBI has been called in to *investigate*. 捜査のためにFBIが呼ばれた ◇'What was that noise?' 'I'll go and *investigate*.'《インフォーマル》「あの音は何だったの」「調べてくるよ」 ◇Police are *investigating* possible links between the two murders. 警察はその2件の殺人事件の関連性を捜査している ◇This is not the first time he has been *investigated* by the police for fraud. 彼が詐欺の件で警察の取調べを受けたのはこれが初めてではない ◇The research *investigates* how foreign speakers gain fluency. その研究では外国人話者がどのようにして流暢さを獲得するかが調査されている ☞ **investigation** (REPORT 1)

explore [他] (考え・問題・可能性を)掘り下げる, 探る, 調査[検討]する ◇These ideas will be *explored* in more detail in chapter 7. これらの考えについては, 第7章でもっと詳しく掘り下げます ◇The study *explores* the differences between the way girls and boys talk. その研究では女の子と男の子の話し方の違いを調べている ◇We need to *explore* every possible *avenue* (= every possibility). 我々はあらゆる可能な手段を探る必要があります ☞ **exploration** (RESEARCH)

look 'into sth [句動] (より詳しく解明する[可能性を見極める]ために)物事を)調べる, 調査する ◇A working party has been set up to *look into* the problem. その問題を詳しく調べるために作業グループが立ち上げられた ◇He was asked to *look into* the feasibility of a trial. 彼は裁判の実行可能性を調査するよう頼まれた

research [他, 自] (新事実を発見するために)研究[調査]する, (執筆の)準備をする ◇She's in New Zealand *researching* her new book. 彼女はニュージーランドで新しい本の執筆準備をしている ◇The book has been *poorly researched*. その本の内容は調査不十分だった ◇They're *researching* into new ways of improving people's diets. 彼らは人々の食事を改善する新たな方法を研究している ❶ research は特に本の執筆・新製品[方法]の開発・新事業の立ち上げのために行われる. ☞ **research** (RESEARCH)

probe [自, 他] (特にジャーナリズム》(質問によって人・物事に関する秘密[隠された情報]を)探る, 調査する ◇Jim changed the subject before she could *probe* any further. ジムは彼女にそれ以上探りを入れられる前に話題を変えた ◇He didn't like the media *probing* into his past. 彼は自分の過去を探るマスコミが好きでなかった ◇Scotland Yard to *probe* fraud allegations (= in a news headline)《新聞の見出し》ロンドン警視庁, 詐欺疑惑で取り調べ

en'quire into sth (または特に米で **inquire into sth**) [句動詞] (質問によって物事を)調べる, 尋ねる, 取り調べる ◇He was instructed to *enquire into* where responsibility for the conflict lay. 彼は紛争の責任がどこにあるかを調べるよう指示された ◇Jack knew not to *enquire* too closely into the affairs of his uncle. ジャックは伯父の事はあまり詳しく尋ねてはならないとわかっていた ☞ **enquiry** (RESEARCH)

delve into sth [句動詞]《ややインフォーマル》(複雑[解明の困難]な物事を)徹底的に調査する, 掘り下げて研究する, 詮索する ◇She had started to *delve into* her father's distant past. 彼女は父親の遠い過去を詮索し始めた

investigation [名]

investigation・survey・poll・enquiry・case・probe・inquest・check

事実[原因]のすべてを知る[解明する]ために行う調査[分析]
【類語訳】捜査, 調査, 取り調べ, 世論調査, 検死, 反省会, 原因の究明

文型&コロケーション

- an investigation/ a survey/ an enquiry/ a probe/ an inquest **into** sth
- a survey/ an inquest/ a check **on** sth/ sb
- **in** a survey/ a poll/ an enquiry
- a **full** investigation/ survey/ enquiry/ inquest/ check
- an **independent** investigation/ survey/ poll/ enquiry/ probe/ inquest/ check
- an **official** investigation/ survey/ enquiry/ probe
- a **public** investigation/ survey/ enquiry/ inquest
- a **murder** investigation/ enquiry/ case/ probe
- a **police** investigation/ enquiry/ probe/ check
- to **carry out** an investigation/ a survey/ a poll/ an enquiry/ a check
- to **conduct** an investigation/ a survey/ a poll/ an enquiry/ an inquest/ a check
- to **order** an investigation/ an enquiry/ a probe/ an inquest
- to **launch** an investigation/ a survey/ an enquiry/ a probe
- an investigation/ a survey/ a poll/ an enquiry/ an inquest/ a check **reveals/ shows** sth
- an investigation/ a survey/ a poll/ an enquiry/ an inquest **finds** sth
- the **results/ findings of** an investigation/ a survey/ a poll/ an enquiry/ an inquest

investigation [C, U] (犯罪・事故などに関する公式の)捜査, 調査, 取り調べ ◇The police have completed their *investigations* into the accident. 警察はその事故の捜査を完了した ◇These are the same methods used in criminal *investigations*. これらは犯罪捜査で使われるのと同じ手法です ◇She is currently *under investigation* for possessing illegal drugs. 彼女は現在, 不法薬物所持で取り調べを受けている

survey [C] (質問による特定集団の意見[言動]に関する)調

↪**investigation**　　　　　　　　　　　　**investment**

査 ◇*According to the survey*, many young adults have experimented with drugs. その調査によると、若い成人の多くが麻薬を試したことがある ◇The charity *did a survey* of people's attitudes to the disabled. その慈善団体は人々の障害者に対する姿勢に関する調査を実施した ☞ **survey** (SURVEY)

poll [C]（大集団の代表者への質問による）世論調査 ◇Nelson has a clear lead in the *opinion polls*. ネルソンは世論調査で明らかにリードしている ◇A nationwide *poll* revealed differences in food preferences between the North and South. 全国的な世論調査で南北間の食べ物の好みの違いが明らかになった ☞ **exit poll, straw poll** (ELECTION), **poll** (SURVEY)

enquiry（特に米でまた **inquiry**）[C]（原因・情報に関する公式の）調査 ◇There will be a public *enquiry* into the impact of the proposed new road. 新道路案の影響に関する公的調査が行われるだろう ◇The director has been suspended on full pay *pending an* internal *enquiry*.《フォーマル》その重役は内部調査を待つ間給料の全額支給を受けながら休職扱いになっている

case [C]（警察によって公式に捜査される）事件 ◇A detective is *on the case* at the moment. 一人の刑事が現在その事件を捜査している ◇Four police officers are *investigating the case*. 4人の警官がその事件を捜査している ◇They never *solved* the Jones murder *case*. ジョーンズ殺人事件は解決されなかった

probe [C]《ジャーナリズム》（違法の可能性のある事柄に関する）調査、捜査 ◇There is to be a police *probe* into the financial affairs of the company. 会社の財務問題に警察による調査が入る予定である ◇Arson *probe* after three die in blaze (= in a news headline)《新聞の見出し》3人死亡の火災への放火捜査

inquest [C]（死因を特定するための公式の）検死；（失敗した事柄に関する）反省会、原因の究明 ◇There will be a coroner's *inquest* into his death. 彼は検死に回されるだろう ◇There will inevitably be an *inquest* into the team's poor performance. チームの成績不振の原因究明は不可避であろう

check [C]《ややインフォーマル》（物事を解明するための）調査 ◇Was any *check* made *on* Mr Morris when he applied for the job? 仕事に応募した際、モリス氏は何か調査を受けましたか ◇The police *ran a check* on the registration number of the car. 警察はその車の登録番号を調べた

investment 名

investment・grant・funding・subsidy・backing・sponsorship・endowment
援助のために政府[会社]が人[会社、組織]に支払う金
【類語訳】投資、助成金、補助金、財政支援、支援、後援、資金提供、寄付金、寄付

[文型&コロケーション]

▸ investment/ a grant/ funding/ a subsidy/ backing/ sponsorship/ an endowment **from** sb/ sth
▸ investment/ a grant/ funding/ a subsidy/ backing/ sponsorship/ an endowment **for** sth
▸ a grant/ a subsidy **to** sb/ sth
▸ a grant/ funding **to do** sth
▸ (a) **substantial** investment/ grant/ funding/ backing/ sponsorship

▸ (a) **generous** grant/ funding/ subsidy/ sponsorship/ endowment
▸ (a) **government** investment/ grant/ funding/ subsidy/ backing/ sponsorship
▸ (a) **public** investment/ funding/ subsidy/ backing
▸ (a) **business/ commercial/ corporate** investment/ funding/ backing/ sponsorship
▸ (an) **annual** investment/ grant/ funding/ subsidy
▸ to **get** investment/ a grant/ funding/ a subsidy/ backing/ sponsorship
▸ to **receive/ increase** investment/ a grant/ funding/ a subsidy/ sponsorship/ an endowment
▸ to **cut** investment/ funding/ a subsidy
▸ to **attract** investment/ funding/ sponsorship
▸ to **apply for/ be eligible for/ qualify for** a grant/ funding/ a subsidy

investment [C, U]（会社・政府・人の不動産・事業・サービスへの）投資 ◇We made an initial *investment* of $10,000. 我々は1万ドルの初期投資を行った ◇I'm hoping for a good return on my *investment*. 私は投資に対して相当の収益を見込んでいる ◇We bought the house as an *investment* (= to make money). 私たちは投資としてその家を購入した ◇The country needs massive government *investment in* education. この国は教育への大規模投資が必要だ

grant [C]（政府・組織による）助成金、補助金 ◇She has been awarded a research *grant* by Liverpool University. 彼女はリバプール大学から研究助成金を与えられた ◇The hospital has applied for a government *grant* to buy a new scanner. その病院は新しいスキャナーを購入するため政府補助金の申請を出した

funding [U]（政府・組織による）助成金、補助金；財政支援 ◇There have been large cuts in government *funding* for scientific research. 科学研究のための政府補助金は大幅に削減された ◇the current debate on the *funding* of higher education 高等教育に対する財政支援についての目下の議論 ☞ **fund** (FUND 動), **funds** (MONEY 1)

[ノート] **grant** と **funding** の使い分け：**grant** はしばしば特定事業のための、特定の人・組織に与えられる個々の多額の金を指す。**funding** は個々の金額・原資について用いることもできるが、額はより多く、はっきりとは定まっておらず、より一般的な目的のために、一般的な人々[組織]に与えられる。◆public *funding* for the arts（芸術のための公的補助金）×public *grants* for the arts.

subsidy [C, U]（低価格維持のためコスト削減に政府[組織]によって支払われる）助成金、補助金 ◇The EU spends billions on *subsidies* to farmers every year. EUは毎年、農業経営者に助成金に莫大な金を費やしている ◇They want to reduce the level of government *subsidy*. 彼らは政府補助金の水準を下げたいと思っている ☞ **subsidize** (FUND 動)

backing [U]（人・組織・計画に与えられる財政的な）支援 ◇The museum has always received limited financial *backing* from the local authority. その美術館は常に地方自治体から限られた財政支援を受けてきた ◇The police gave the proposals their full *backing*. 警察はその計画を全面支援した ☞ **back** (SUPPORT)

sponsorship [U]（広告の見返りにコンサート・スポーツイベント・人の教育などへの会社・人からの）後援、資金提供 ◇The race organizers are trying to attract *sponsorship* from local firms. レースの主催者たちは地元企業からの後援を誘致しようとしている ☞ **sponsor** (SPONSOR), **sponsor** (FUND 動)

endowment [C, U] 《フォーマル》 (学校・大学などの施設への)寄付金;寄付 ◇The purpose of the fund was to provide *endowments* for houses of historic interest that were threatened with sale. 基金の目的は売却の恐れがある歴史的に重要な邸宅に寄付金を出すことであった ☞ **endow** (FUND 動)

involvement 名

involvement・role・part・contribution・participation・interest・input・stake・engagement・hand
出来事[状況]において積極的であるという事実を表す
【類語訳】関わり、関与、参加、従事、熱中、没頭、役割、貢献、寄与、利害、関心、影響力

文型&コロケーション
▸ involvement/ a role/ a part/ an interest/ a stake/ engagement/ a hand **in** sth
▸ involvement/ a contribution/ participation/ input **from** sb
▸ a contribution/ input **to** sth
▸ (a) **direct** involvement/ role/ part/ contribution/ participation/ interest/ input/ stake/ engagement
▸ (a) **greater** involvement/ role/ part/ contribution/ participation/ interest/ input/ stake
▸ (a) **full** involvement/ contribution/ participation
▸ (a/ an) **major/ considerable/ substantial/ significant** involvement/ role/ part/ contribution/ interest/ input/ stake
▸ (a) **positive** involvement/ role/ part/ contribution/ participation/ interest
▸ (an) **active** involvement/ role/ part/ participation/ interest/ engagement
▸ (an) **alleged** involvement/ role/ part/ participation
▸ (a) **valuable/ useful/ crucial/ essential/ important/ key/ constructive** role/ part/ contribution/ input
▸ (a) **personal** involvement/ role/ part/ contribution/ participation/ interest/ input/ stake/ engagement
▸ (a) **public/ limited** involvement/ role/ part/ contribution/ participation
▸ (a) **parental/ political/ military** involvement/ role/ participation/ input
▸ to **encourage/ increase** involvement/ participation
▸ to **need/ get/ receive** a contribution/ input
▸ to **have** a role/ part/ an interest/ an input/ a stake/ a hand in sth
▸ to **play** a role/ part in sth
▸ to **have** a role/ part **to play**

involvement [U, C, ふつう単数で] (出来事・状況への)関わり、関与、参加;(関心の対象となる物事への)従事、熱中、没頭 ◇The success of the venture may lead to *involvement by* other foreign companies. その事業の成功は他の諸外国の企業の参加につながるかもしれない ◇The new album came out of her growing *involvement with* contemporary music. 新しいアルバムは彼女が現代音楽にますます関わることによって生まれた ◇Nurses usually try to avoid *emotional involvement* with patients. 看護師はふつう患者に感情移入するのを避けようとする ◇He was found to have a deep *involvement* in drug dealing. 彼は麻薬取引に深く関わっていることが判明した ☞ **involve** (INCLUDE), **involved** (BUSY 1), **be/get involved** (JOIN)

role [C] (状況・活動での)役割 ◇He stressed the *role* of diet in preventing disease. 彼は病気の予防における食事の役割を強調した ◇The media play a major *role* in influencing people's opinions. マスコミは世論に影響を与える上で大きな役割を果たしている ◇Regional managers have a crucial *role* in developing a strategic framework. 地方担当のマネージャーは戦略的枠組みの形成において重要な役割を担っている

part [C] (物事での[への])役割、関与、参加 ◇She plays an active *part* in local politics. 彼女は地方政治に積極的に関与している ◇He had no *part* in the decision. 彼は決定にまったく関与していなかった ◇How many countries *took part in* the last Olympic Games? 前回のオリンピック大会には何か国が参加したのですか

ノート **role** と **part** の使い分け:この意味では**part**は主に、以下の句で用いられる。◆ have a *part* to play (果たすべき役割がある)。◆ have/play a *part* in sth (…に関与する/…の役割を果たす)。◆ have/play/take no *part* in/of sth (物事に関与しない/何の役割も果たさない/に参加しない)。◆ take *part* (in sth) (…に参加する)。**role**はいくぶんフォーマルで、ビジネスや経済の文脈で一般的に用いられる。特に key, important, essential, crucial, central, fundamental, major, pivotal, prominent, primary のような形容詞と共に用いられる。

contribution [C, ふつう単数で] (物事の発生・増加を助ける)貢献、寄与 ◇She has *made* a significant *contribution* to scientific knowledge. 彼女は科学知識に大きな貢献をしてきた ◇These measures would make a valuable *contribution towards* reducing industrial accidents. これらの対策は労働災害の減少に向けて貴重な貢献をするだろう

participation [U] (活動・行事への)参加 ◇It's a show with lots of audience *participation*. それは視聴者の参加が多い番組です ◇A back injury prevented active *participation* in any sports for a while. 背中のけがでしばらくの間、何のスポーツにも積極的に参加できなかった ☞ **participate** (JOIN)

ノート **involvement** と **participation** の使い分け:involvementの「関わり」は積極的なものではないが、participationの「関わり」は積極的なものである。

interest [C, U] 利害(関係)、関与 ◇Organizations *have an interest in* ensuring that employee motivation is high. 組織は従業員の意欲を確実に高めることに関与している ◇I should, at this point, *declare my interest*. 現時点では、私の関与を認めなければなりません

input [U, C] (仕事・事業を成功させるための)時間[情報、尽力]の投入 ◇I'd appreciate your *input* on this. これについての情報提供に感謝します ◇There has been a big *input* of resources *into* the project from industry. 産業界からその事業に多大な資金が投入された

stake [単数で] (in を伴って) (事業・計画などへの)利害(関係)、関与、関心 ◇She has a personal *stake* in the success of the play. 彼女はその芝居の成功に個人的な関心を抱いている ◇Many young people no longer feel they have a *stake* in society. 多くの若者はもはや自分たちが社会に関わりがあるとは感じていない

engagement [U] 《フォーマル》 (人・物事を理解しようとす

ることへの)従事, 熱中, 没頭 ◇Her views are based on years of *engagement* with the problems of the inner city. 彼女の意見は何年にもわたる都心部の問題への取り組みに基づいている

hand ［単数で］《in を伴って》《特にジャーナリズム》(人・物事が特定の状況で果たす)役割, 関与；(状況での人の)影響力 ◇Several of his colleagues had a *hand* in his downfall. 同僚の数人が彼の失脚に関与していた ◇This appointment was an attempt to *strengthen her hand* in policy discussions. この任命は政策論議における彼女の影響力を強めることが狙いだった

ironic 形

ironic・sarcastic・wry・sardonic・satirical・dry
意味することと反対の言葉を用いて, 露骨[直接的]でない形で物事がこっけいであったり, 人を笑いものにしたりすること
【類語訳】皮肉を含んだ, 皮肉な, 嫌みな, 風刺的な, 冷笑的な, 嘲笑的な, さりげない

| wry | ironic | sarcastic |
| dry | satirical | sardonic |

▶ 文型&コロケーション
- an ironic/ a sarcastic/ a wry/ a sardonic/ a satirical/ a dry **comment**
- ironic/ wry/ sardonic/ satirical/ dry **humour**
- a sarcastic/ wry/ satirical/ dry **wit**
- an ironic/ a sarcastic/ a wry/ a sardonic/ a dry **tone/ smile**
- a sarcastic/ wry/ sardonic/ dry **look**
- an ironic/ a sarcastic/ a sardonic/ a dry **voice**
- ironic/ wry/ sardonic **amusement**

ironic 皮肉を含んだ；(状況が期待と裏腹で)皮肉な ◇He was greeted with *ironic* cheers from opposition MPs. 彼は野党の下院議員に皮肉の歓声で迎えられた ◇*It's ironic that* she became a teacher — she used to hate school. 彼女が教師になったのは皮肉だ―彼女は昔は学校を嫌っていたんだから
▷**ironically** 副 ◇He smiled *ironically*. 彼は皮肉っぽくほほ笑んだ ◇*Ironically*, the book she felt was her worst sold more copies than any of her others. 皮肉にも, 最悪だと思った自著は, 他のどれよりたくさんの部数を売り上げた
▷**irony** 名 [U, C] ◇His writing is rich in *irony*. 彼の著述は皮肉が満載だ ◇*The irony is that* when he finally got the job, he found he didn't like it. 皮肉なことに, ようやく仕事にありついたとき彼はそれが好きでないことに気づいた ◇It was one of life's little *ironies*. それは人生におけるちょっとした皮肉な出来事の一つだった

sarcastic 《ふつうけなして》(不快感を与えて[からかって])嫌みな ◇Her tone was faintly *sarcastic*. 彼女の口調はわずかに嫌みっぽかった ◇There's no need to be *sarcastic*. 嫌みを言う必要はない
▷**sarcasm** 名 [U] ◇Her voice was heavy with *sarcasm*. 彼女の声は嫌みたっぷりだった

wry ［ふつう名詞の前で］《書き言葉, ふつうほめて》(面白かって[がっかりして, むかついて])顔をゆがめた；(皮肉的な面白さがあって)風刺的な ◇'At least we got one vote,' she said with a *wry* smile. 「少なくとも一票は入ったわよ」と彼女は苦笑しながら言った ◇The film takes a *wry* look at the British class system. その映画は英国の階級制度を風刺的に捉えている
▷**wryly** 副 ◇to grin/smile *wryly* 苦々しくにっこり笑う/ほほ笑む

sardonic 《書き言葉, けなして》(他人より優れていると思って)冷笑的な, 嘲笑的な ◇He looked at her with *sardonic* amusement. 彼はあざけるように面白がって彼女に視線を向けた

satirical (短所・弱点を面白おかしく批判して)風刺的な ◇The cartoon appeared in a popular *satirical* magazine. その漫画は人気のある風刺雑誌に載った ◇He is a sharp, *satirical* observer of the London social scene. 彼はロンドンの社交界の動きに鋭く風刺的な目を向ける人物だ
▷**satire** 名 [U, C] ◇There is a strong tradition of political *satire* in this country. この国には政治風刺の根強い伝統がある ◇The novel is a stinging *satire on* American politics. その小説はアメリカ政治への辛辣な風刺だ
▷**satirize** (英でまた **-ise**) ［他］◇The cartoon *satirizes* middle-aged, middle-class liberals. 《ややフォーマル》その漫画は中産階級の中高年の自由主義者たちを風刺している

dry 《ほめて》(非常に気が利いていて愉快な皮肉を交えて)さりげない ◇He was a man of few words with a delightful *dry* sense of humour. 彼は愉快でさりげないユーモアのセンスを持った口数の少ない男だった

irrational 形 ☞ UNOFFICIAL

irrational・illogical・unfounded・groundless・unconfirmed・unsubstantiated・unsupported・unscientific
もっともな理由[証拠]にまったく基づかないことを表す
【類語訳】不合理な, 筋の通らない, 理性を失った, 非論理的な, 根拠のない, 事実無根の, 根も葉もない, 証拠のない, 裏づけのない

▶ 文型&コロケーション
- an irrational/ illogical **fear**
- an unfounded/ a groundless/ an unsubstantiated/ an unsupported **claim/ allegation/ assertion**
- an unfounded/ a groundless/ an unsubstantiated **accusation/ charge**
- an unfounded/ an unconfirmed/ an unsubstantiated **rumour**
- an unfounded/ an unconfirmed/ an unsubstantiated **story/ report**
- totally irrational/ illogical/ unfounded/ groundless/ unsubstantiated/ unsupported/ unscientific
- completely irrational/ unfounded/ groundless/ unsubstantiated/ unsupported
- largely unfounded/ groundless/ unsupported

irrational 不合理な, 筋の通らない, 理性を失った ◇These are just *irrational* fears. これらはただばかげた不安にすぎない ◇You're being *irrational*. 君はいま理性を失っているんだ 反意 **rational** (RATIONAL)
▷**irrationally** 副 ◇to behave *irrationally* 理性を失した振る舞いをする

illogical 非論理的な, 不合理な, 筋の通らない ◇From all this evidence he drew a strange and *illogical* con-

clusion. このすべての証拠から, 彼は訳のわからない非論理的な結論を出した 反意 **logical** (RATIONAL)
▶**illogically** 副 ◇He felt *illogically* that somehow he was responsible for the disaster. 彼はどういうわけか自分にその災害の責任があるとのばかばかしい思いを抱いた

ノート **irrational** と **illogical** の使い分け：場合によって, 両語とも使用可能. ◆ an *irrational/illogical* fear of insects (愚かなまでの虫に対する恐怖). irrational は物事にもっともな理由がないことを強調する. illogical は実際には推論の裏づけとはならない事実から誤った論理の道筋を人が使用していることを示唆する. irrational は人を主語にできるが, illogical は不可. ×You're being *illogical*.

unfounded 根拠のない, 事実無根の ◇I was pleased to discover that my fears were *unfounded*. 私の恐怖は根拠がないとわかってうれしかった ◇I dismissed the story as *unfounded* speculation. 私はその話を事実無根の憶測として退けた

groundless 根拠のない, 根も葉もない ◇Most of his worries proved to be *groundless*. 彼の不安のほとんどは根拠のないものとわかった ◇They denied what they called completely *groundless* allegations. 彼らはいわゆるまったく根も葉もない主張を否定した

ノート **unfounded** と **groundless** の使い分け：多くの場合, 両語とも使用可能. ◆ *unfounded/groundless* claims/allegations/accusations/fears/worries (根拠のない主張/申し立て/非難/恐怖/不安). しかしながら groundless は, 理屈ではなく事実に基づいているべき事柄には用いられない. ×*groundless* stories/reports/rumours/speculation.

unconfirmed (事実として)確認されていない ◇*Unconfirmed* reports stated that at least six people had died. 未確認の情報によれば, 少なくとも6人の人が亡くなったとのことだ

unsubstantiated 《フォーマル》証拠のない ◇There were *unsubstantiated* rumours of abuse at the prison. 証拠はないものの刑務所で虐待があるとの噂があった
unsupported (証拠による)裏づけのない ◇Their claims are *unsupported* by any research findings. 彼らの主張は何の研究成果にも裏づけられていない

ノート **unsubstantiated** と **unsupported** の使い分け：これらの語に実質的な意味の違いはない. unsubstantiated はよりフォーマルで, 名詞の前で用いられることが多い. unsupported は連結動詞の後で用いられ, sth is unsupported by the evidence/findings などの句で用いられることが多い.

unscientific 《しばしばなして》非科学的な ◇Their approach to the problem was very *unscientific*. 彼らのその問題へのアプローチは非常に非科学的だった 反意 **scientific** (RATIONAL)

irrelevant 形

irrelevant・immaterial・extraneous・beside the point・inapplicable
物事が大したことはない[状況と関連のない]ことを表す
【類語訳】関係のない, 見当外れの, 的外れの, 重要でない, 取るに足らない, 当てはまらない

文型&コロケーション
▶*irrelevant/ immaterial/ extraneous/ inapplicable* **to** sth
▶to be *irrelevant/ immaterial/ beside the point* **whether**...
▶to be *irrelevant/ immaterial* **that**...
▶**quite** *irrelevant/ immaterial/ beside the point*

irrelevant (状況・テーマと)関係[関連]のない, 見当違いの, 的外れの ◇It's totally *irrelevant* whether I'm married or not. 私が未婚か既婚かはまったく関係ない ◇Many people consider politics to be *irrelevant* to their lives. 多くの人々が政治は自分の生活に無関係だと考えている ◇Please keep all *irrelevant* remarks to yourself. 論点に無関係の発言はすべてお控えください 反意 **relevant** (RELEVANT)
▶**irrelevance** 名 [U, C, ふつう単数で] ◇the *irrelevance* of the curriculum to children's daily life そのカリキュラムの子どもたちの日常生活との関連性の欠如 ◇His idea was rejected as an *irrelevance*. 彼の考えは的外れだとして却下された

immaterial [名詞の前にはまれ]《ややフォーマル》(特定の状況において)重要でない, 取るに足らない, 関係[関連]のない ◇The cost is *immaterial*. 経費は問題ではない ◇It is *immaterial* to me whether he stays or goes. 彼がいるかいないか私には関係ない 反意 **material** (RELEVANT)

extraneous 《フォーマル》(状況・テーマと)関係[関連]のない, 的外れの ◇We do not want any *extraneous* information on the page. そのページの関係のない情報は一切要りません ◇We shall ignore factors *extraneous* to the problem. その問題に無関係な要因は無視します

ノート **irrelevant, immaterial, extraneous** の使い分け：いくつかの場合, どの語も使用可能. ◆ factors *irrelevant/immaterial/extraneous* to the case その事件と関連のない要因. しかしながら extraneous はふつう to を後に伴わない限り, 連結動詞の後で用いられることはない. ◆The cost is *irrelevant/immaterial*. (経費は重要ではない). ×The cost is *extraneous*. extraneous は特に特定の文脈において, 重要でない[不要な]factors, variables, considerations, information, material, matter について用いられる. irrelevant と immaterial はどちらも, It is irrelevant/immaterial whether/that... という構文で用いられることが多い. immaterial のほうがいくぶん意味が強く, 比較的強い, もう問題にしたくないと思う気持ちを表すことがある. immaterial はふつう名詞の前では用いられない. ×*immaterial* remarks/thoughts.

beside the 'point フレーズ 《特に話し言葉》(状況・テーマと)関係[関連]がなくて, 見当違いで, 的外れで ◇'He's been married before.' 'That's *beside the point*.' 「彼は以前結婚していた」「それは無関係だ」 反意 **to the point** (RELEVANT)

inapplicable [名詞の前では用いない]《ややフォーマル, 特に書き言葉》(特定の状況において)当てはまらない, 適用できない ◇These regulations are *inapplicable* to international students. これらの規則は留学生には適用されない 反意 **applicable** (RELEVANT)

irritable 形

irritable・sullen・bad-tempered・grumpy・morose・sulky・petulant
人が機嫌が悪い[腹を立てている, 口をききたくない気分である]ことを表す
【類語訳】怒りっぽい, いらいらした, 気難しい, 短気な, 不機嫌

な、むっつりした、すねた、だだをこねた

文型&コロケーション
- an irritable/ a sullen/ a bad-tempered/ a grumpy/ a morose **man**
- a sulky/ petulant **child**
- to **look** sullen/ grumpy/ morose/ sulky/ petulant

irritable 怒りっぽい；いらいらした ◇He was tired and *irritable*. 彼は疲れていて怒りっぽかった ◇She waved him away with an *irritable* gesture. 彼女はいらいらした仕草で手を振って彼を追い払った ☞ **irritate** (ANNOY), **irritated** (ANNOYED), **irritating** (ANNOYING), **irritation** (FRUSTRATION)

sullen《けなして》(他人が理不尽だと思うほど不機嫌で)口を利かない ◇*sullen* teenagers 口を利かないティーンエイジャーたち ◇He lapsed into a *sullen* silence. 彼はぶすっとして黙り込んだ

‚bad-'tempered 気難しい、短気な；不機嫌な ◇Her husband was a *bad-tempered* man. 彼女の夫は気難しい人だった ◇What's making her so *bad-tempered*? 彼女はどうしてそんなに機嫌が悪いの

grumpy《インフォーマル、しばしばけなして》(他人をいら立たせるほど文句が多くて)気難しい ◇Pay no attention to his moods — he's just a *grumpy* old man. 彼の機嫌なんか気にするな—彼はただの気難しい爺さんにすぎん

morose《書き言葉》(不機嫌で)むっつりした ◇She just sat there looking *morose*. 彼女はただむっつりした顔つきでそこに座っていた

sulky《けなして》(他人が理不尽だと思うほど不機嫌で)口を利かない ◇Sarah had looked *sulky* all morning. サラは午前中ずっとぶすっとしていた ☞ **sulk** (TEMPER)

> **ノート** sullenとsulkyの使い分け：一般的にsulkyは子どもに用いられる。大人に用いる場合は、それが子どもじみた振る舞いであることを示唆する。sullenはsulky以上に人をけなして用いられる語で、一時的にそうである場合にも、性格的にそうである場合にも用いられる。

petulant《書き言葉、けなして》(したいことができなくて[ほしいものが手に入らなくて])すねた、だだをこねた ◇He behaved like a *petulant* child and refused to cooperate. 彼はだだっ子のように振る舞い、協力を拒んだ

isolate 動

isolate・cut sb/sth off・part・quarantine・divide・segregate
人や物事を他の人や物事から別々にしておく
【類語訳】引き離す、隔離する、孤立させる、切り離す、分離する

文型&コロケーション
- to isolate/ cut off/ part/ divide/ segregate sb/ sth **from** sb/ sth else
- to isolate **yourself**/ cut **yourself** off
- to isolate/ quarantine/ segregate a **patient**
- a **community** is isolated/ cut off/ segregated
- **completely**/ **totally** isolated/ cut off
- **socially** isolated/ divided/ segregated

isolate [他、しばしば受身で] (物理的・社会的に)引き離す、隔離する、孤立させる ◇Patients with the disease should be *isolated*. その病気の患者は隔離されるべきだ ◇He was immediately *isolated* from the other prisoners. 彼は他の囚人たちから即座に引き離された ☞ **isolation** (DIVISION 1)

‚cut sb/sth 'off [句動詞] [しばしば受身で] (場所・人から)切り離す、分離する、孤立させる ◇The army was *cut off* from its base. 軍隊は基地から切り離された ◇She feels very *cut off* living in the country. 彼女はお国での暮らしに非常に孤立感を覚えている ◇He *cut* himself *off* from all human contact. 彼はすべての人間との接触を断った

part [他、しばしば受身で]《フォーマル》(他の人から)引き離す ◇I hate being *parted* from the children. 私は子どもたちと離れたくない ◇The puppies were *parted* from their mother at birth. 子犬たちは生まれたときに母犬から引き離された

quarantine [他] (病気の蔓延防止のために動物・人を)隔離する ◇Animals brought into the country are automatically *quarantined*. 国に持ち込まれる動物は自動的に隔離されます ❶ quarantineは名詞として用いるほうが一般的である。☞ **quarantine** (DIVISION 1)

divide [他]《フォーマル》(二人[二つの物事]を)引き離す、分ける ◇Can it ever be right to *divide* a mother from her child? 母親を子どもから引き離すのが適切であることなどありえますか 反意 **unite** (COMBINE)

segregate [他、しばしば受身で]《フォーマル》(人種・宗教・性別の異なる人々を)差別[分離、隔離]する ◇It is a culture in which women are *segregated* from men. それは女性が男性から差別されている文化である ◇This is perhaps the most racially *segregated* city in the United States. ここはおそらく米国で最も人種差別が激しい都市であろう 反意 **integrate** (COMBINE), ☞ **segregation** (DIVISION 1)

issue 名 ☞ SUBJECT

issue・matter・question・concern・item
人々が議論している[対策を講じる必要のある]こと
【類語訳】問題、論点、争点、事柄、関心事、事項、項目

文型&コロケーション
- an issue/ a matter/ a question/ an item **relating to**/ **concerning** sth
- **on** an issue/ a matter/ a question
- an **important** issue/ matter/ question/ concern/ item
- a **vital**/ **key**/ **major**/ **serious**/ **general**/ **complex** issue/ matter/ question/ concern
- a **controversial**/ **contentious**/ **sensitive** issue/ matter/ question/ item
- a **difficult**/ **delicate** issue/ matter/ question
- the **basic**/ **fundamental**/ **underlying** issue/ question/ concern
- a/ an **political**/ **moral**/ **technical**/ **economic**/ **ethical**/ **practical** issue/ matter/ question/ concern
- to **discuss**/ **consider**/ **deal with**/ **tackle**/ **raise** an issue/ a matter/ a question/ a concern/ an item
- to **examine**/ **explore**/ **focus on**/ **address** an issue/ a matter/ a question/ a concern
- to **debate** an issue/ a matter/ a question/ an item
- to **look at**/ **touch on**/ **bring up**/ **broach**/ **debate**/ **clarify**/ **decide**/ **settle** an issue/ a matter/ a question
- an issue/ a matter/ a question **arises**

issue [C] (議論される)問題(点), 論点, (係)争点 ◇The union plans to raise the *issue* of overtime. 労働組合は時間外労働の問題を取り上げるつもりです ◇This is a *big issue*; we need more time to think about it. これは大問題だ, もっと考える時間が必要だ ◇She usually writes about environmental *issues*. 彼女はふだん環境問題について執筆している ◇You're just *avoiding the issue*. 君は問題を回避しているだけよ ◇Don't *confuse the issue*. 問題を曖昧にするな ◇What you say is interesting, but it does not affect the point *at issue* here. あなたの言うことは興味深いが, ここでの論点には影響がないね

matter [C] (議論しなければ[対策を講じなければ]ならない)事柄, 問題 ◇It's a private *matter*. それは個人的な問題です ◇I always consulted him on *matters* of policy. 私はいつも政策に関わる問題について彼に助言を求めた ◇The incident is definitely a *matter for* the police. その事件は明らかに警察が扱う問題だ ◇That's a *matter* for you to take up with your boss. それはあなたが上司に相談すべき問題です ◇I don't have much experience *in* these *matters*. 私はこれらの問題にはあまり経験がない ◇I wasn't prepared to *let the matter drop* (= stop discussing it). 私はその問題を棚上げにするつもりなんかなかった ❶ a matter [単数形] は何かに影響を与えたり, 影響されたりする「問題」に用いられる. ◆That's not a problem. It's *simply a matter of* letting people know in time. (そんなの問題じゃない. ゆくゆく人々の耳に入るような問題にすぎないのだから). ◆She resigned over *a matter of principle*. (彼女は信条に関わる問題をめぐって辞任した). ◆Just *as a matter of interest* (= because it is interesting, not because it is important), how much did you pay for it? (興味本位で聞くだけなんだけど, それにいくら払ったの). ◆'I think this is the best so far.' 'Well, that's *a matter of opinion*' (= other people may think different-

ly). (「今までのところ, これが最善だと思うな」「まあ, それは意見の分かれる問題だね」).

question [C] (熟考する[対策を講じる]必要のある)問題, 事柄 ◇Let's look at the *question* of security. 安全に関わる問題を調べてみましょう ◇This raises fundamental *questions about* the nature of our society. これは我々の社会の本質に関する根本的な問題を提起している ◇Which route is better remains *an open question* (= it is not decided). どちらのルートがいいかは未決定のままだ

ノート **matter** と **question** の使い分け: 多くの場合, 両語とも使用可能. matter は対策を講じる必要のある実際的な「問題」を指すことが多い. 典型的な連語に, talk about, look at, discuss, debate, refer, pursue, deal with, handle, investigate, resolve, settle が挙げられる. question は実際的な「問題」である場合もあるが, 何の結論に達しなくともただ考えるのが面白い, より哲学的な「問題」に用いられることが多い. 典型的な連語に, think about, focus on, raise, address, ponder が挙げられる. しかしながら, これらの連語はすべて, どちらの語とも使用可能.

concern [C] (人・組織・社会にとっての)関心事, 問題, 事柄 ◇What are your main *concerns* as a writer? 作家としてのあなたの主な関心事は何ですか ◇The overriding *concern* of the organizers is the safety of the participants. 主催者の最優先事項は参加者の安全である ◇Environmental *concerns* have been thrust to the head of the party agenda. 環境問題が党の政治課題の筆頭に押し上げられた ☞ **consideration** (FACTOR)

item [C] (購入する[行う, 話し合う]次の)事項, 項目 ◇What's the next *item* on the agenda? 次の議題は何ですか ◇Check the list carefully, *item* by item. リストを項目別に入念にチェックしてください

J j

jail 動

jail・detain・hold・imprison・lock sb up/away・intern・send sb to prison・incarcerate
人をある場所に引き止めて、そこから去らせなくすることを表す
【類語訳】投獄する、留置する、勾留する、引き止めておく、拘留する、刑務所に入れる、収容する、監禁する、抑留する

文型&コロケーション
▶ to jail sb/ detain sb/ hold sb/ imprison sb/ lock sb up/ intern sb/ send sb to prison **for** sth
▶ to jail/ detain/ hold/ imprison/ lock sb up/ incarcerate sb **in** sth
▶ to jail/ detain/ hold/ imprison sb **without** trial/ charge

jail [他、ふつう受身で]《特にジャーナリズム》投獄する、留置する ◇He was *jailed* for life for murder. 彼は殺人罪で終身刑を受けた

detain [他]《ややフォーマル》勾留する、留置する ◇One man has been *detained* for questioning. 一人の男性が尋問のために勾留されている
▶ **detention** 名 [U] ◇police powers of arrest and *detention* 逮捕と勾留の警察権

hold [他] 引き止めておく、拘留する ◇Police are *holding* two men in connection with last Thursday's bank raid. 警察は先週木曜日の銀行強盗の絡みで二人の男を拘留している ◇He was **held prisoner** for two years. 彼は2年間、捕虜になった

imprison [他、しばしば受身で]《ややフォーマル》投獄する、刑務所に入れる；閉じ込める ◇They were *imprisoned* for possession of drugs. 彼らは麻薬所持により投獄された ◇Some young mothers feel *imprisoned* in their own homes.《比喩的》自宅にいると閉じ込められているように感じる若い母親もいる
▶ **imprisonment** 名 [U] ◇He was sentenced to **life imprisonment** for murder. 彼は殺人罪で終身刑を言い渡された

lock sb 'up/a'way 句動詞《インフォーマル》収容する、監禁する ◇You ought to be *locked up*! お前なんか刑務所へ行きな ◇After what he did, they should *lock* him *up* and throw away the key. そんなことをしたのだから、彼を収容して、鍵を投げ捨てるべきだ

intern [他、しばしば受身で]《戦時下・政治的理由で》抑留する、拘禁する ◇They were *interned* by the government for the duration of the war. 彼らは戦時中ずっと政府によって抑留されていた
▶ **internment** 名 [U] the *internment* of suspected terrorists テロリストの嫌疑による拘禁 ◇an *internment* camp 捕虜収容所

,send sb to 'prison 句動詞 （判決によって）投獄する ◇The judge *sent* her *to prison* for seven years. 判決により彼女は7年間投獄された

incarcerate [他、ふつう受身で]《フォーマル》《理不尽に》投獄する、監禁する ◇Thousands were *incarcerated* in labour camps. 何千人もの人たちが強制労働収容所に監禁された

jealousy 名

jealousy・envy
他人が持っている物事をほしがる気持ち
【類語訳】嫉妬、焼きもち、ねたみ、羨望

文型&コロケーション
▶ jealousy/ envy **of** sb
▶ **extreme** jealousy/ envy
▶ to **feel/ arouse** jealousy/ envy
▶ a **feeling/ pang/ stab/ twinge of** jealousy/ envy

jealousy [U, C] （好きな[愛する]人の関心が他に向けられて起こる）嫉妬、焼きもち、（他人が持っている物事に対する）ねたみ、羨望；嫉妬からの言動 ◇He felt a sudden stab of pure sexual *jealousy*. 彼は突然ただ単なる性的な嫉妬に駆られた ◇Her promotion aroused intense *jealousy* among her colleagues. 彼女の昇進は同僚から激しいねたみを買った ◇I'm tired of her petty *jealousies*. 彼女のつまらない焼きもちにはうんざりだ
▶ **jealous** 形 She's *jealous* of my success. 彼女は私の成功をねたんでいる ◇Children often feel *jealous* when a new baby arrives. 赤ちゃんが新しく生まれると、子どもはよく焼きもちを焼く
▶ **jealously** 副 ◇She eyed Natalia *jealously*. 彼女はナタリアを羨望の目で見た

envy [U] （他人の境遇[他人が持っている物事]への）うらやみ、羨望、嫉妬 ◇She felt a pang of *envy* at the thought of his success. 彼は彼の成功を思うと激しい羨望を覚えた ◇Her colleagues were **green with envy** (= they had very strong feelings of envy). 彼女の同僚たちはひどく嫉妬した
▶ **envious** 形 ◇Everyone is so *envious* of her having the chance to study abroad. 皆彼女が海外留学する機会を持つことをとてもうらやましがっている
▶ **enviously** 副 ◇They look *enviously* at the success of their European counterparts. 彼らはヨーロッパ勢の活躍をうらやましそうに眺めている
▶ **envy** 動 [他] ◇He *envied* her — she seemed to have everything she could possibly want. 彼は彼女をうらやんだ―彼女は望みさえすればすべてを手にできるように思えた ◇I don't *envy* Ed that job (= I am pleased I do not have it). 私はエドのその仕事をうらやましいとは思わない

ノート jealousyとenvyの使い分け：jealousyはしばしばenvyよりも不快な感情を指し、人を不親切な[愚かな]行動に駆り立てることがある。人は envious（うらやましい）であることは認めても、jealous（ねたんだ）であることを認めるのはまれである。また、時に人は他人に inspire/arouse envy（羨望を抱かせること）に喜びを感じるが、ふつう cause/provoke jealousy（嫉妬を買うこと）は嫌がる。

job, join

job 名 ☞ WORK 名 1

job・position・post・vacancy・opening・appointment・posting
定期的に給与が得られる仕事上の立場
【類語訳】仕事, 職, 地位, 空き, 欠員, 空席, 空位, 任命, 配属, 職務, 任務

文型&コロケーション

▶ a vacancy/ an opening for sb
▶ a **temporary** job/ position/ post/ vacancy/ appointment/ posting
▶ a **permanent/ full-time/ part-time** job/ position/ post/ vacancy/ appointment
▶ a **good/ top** job/ position/ post/ appointment
▶ a **well-paid/ highly-paid** job/ position/ post
▶ to **have/ have got** a job/ a position/ a post/ a vacancy/ an opening/ an appointment/ a posting
▶ to **apply for** a job/ a position/ a post/ a vacancy/ a posting
▶ to **hold/ seek** a job/ a position/ a post/ an appointment
▶ to **look for/ give sb** a job/ position/ post/ posting
▶ to **find** a job/ position/ post
▶ to **get** a job/ a position/ a post/ an appointment/ a posting
▶ to **offer sb/ take** a job/ a position/ a post/ an appointment/ a posting
▶ to **fill** a job/ position/ post/ vacancy
▶ to **land/ resign from/ leave/ quit/ keep/ lose** a job/ position/ post
▶ to **create/ provide** jobs/ positions/ posts/ vacancies/ openings

job [C] (定期的に給与が得られる)仕事, 職 ◇He's trying to get a *job in* teaching. 彼は教職を得ようと努めている ◇I'm *only doing my job* (= I'm doing what I'm paid to do). 私は自分の仕事をしているだけです ◇He certainly *knows his job* (= is very good at his job). 彼は確かに自分の仕事に通じている ◇We provide training *on the job* (= while sb is actually doing the job). 私たちは実地研修を行います ◇She's been *out of a job* (= unemployed) for six months now. 彼女は今で6か月間失業中だ ◇She's never had a *steady job* (= a job that is not going to end suddenly). 彼女は定職に就いたことが一度もない ◇Her *job title* is Senior Advisor. 彼女の職位は上級顧問である ◇*Job satisfaction* (= being happy with the job you do) is very important to me. 働きがいは私にとってとても重要なことです

position [C] 《ややフォーマル》(定期的に給与が得られる)職, 地位 ◇She holds a senior *position* in a large corporation. 彼女は大企業の上級職に就いている ◇I would like to apply for the *position* of sales director. 私は営業部長の職に志願したいと思います ❶ position はふつう組織内の特定の職(位), 特に上級職を指し, ふつう仕事全般には用いられない。また, しばしば求職, 職務説明書, 求人広告で用いられる

post [C] 《特に英》(大組織内の重要な)職, 地位 ◇Ideally I'm looking for an academic *post*. 理想を言えば, 私は研究職を求めています ◇She was offered a key *post in* the new government. 彼女は新政府における要職への誘いを受けた ❶《米》では post は実際の政府内の任命職のみに用いるものを指し, それ以外の《英》で post を用いるものには,

《米》では position を用いる。◆ a Cabinet *post*(大臣の職).
◆ an academic *position*(研究職).

vacancy [C] (職の)空き, 欠員, 空席, 空位 ◇We have several *vacancies* for casual workers. 当社は数名の臨時従業員の欠員があります ◇We'll let you know if any more *vacancies* come up. 今後また欠員が生じたらお知らせします

opening [C] (職の)空き, 欠員, 空席, 空位 ◇There are several *openings* in the sales departments. 営業部に数名の空きがある

ノート **vacancy** と **opening** の使い分け:これらの語の意味は同じで使い方の違いもほとんどない。vacancy のほうが特に《英》でよく用いられる。opening のほうがいくぶんインフォーマルで,《米》および金融ジャーナリズムで用いられることが多い

appointment [C] 《特に英, ややフォーマル》(責任のある)職, 地位 ◇This is a permanent *appointment*, requiring commitment and hard work. これは常勤の職であり, 職務専念と精力的勤務が求められます ☞ **appoint** (APPOINT)

posting [C] 《特に英》(期限付きの派遣場所への)任命, 配属;(任命を受けた)職務, 任務 ◇He asked for a *posting to* the Middle East. 彼は中東への配属を志願した ◇Staff will work abroad on 2-5 year *postings*. 職員は2〜5年間の海外勤務を任命されます ❶ posting は《米》でも用いられるが, ふつうは政府内の任命職のみを指す。

join 動

join・be/get involved・participate・take part・engage in sth・enter・join in (sth)・have/play a part・share・enter into sth
事に携わったり, 他の人と共に事を行ったりする
【類語訳】加わる, 加入する, 入会する, 従事する, 参加する, 関与する

文型&コロケーション

▶ to join sb/ get involved/ participate/ take part/ engage/ play a part/ share **in** sth
▶ to get involved/ join in/ share sth/ enter into sth **with** sb/ sth
▶ to **fully** participate/ take part/ engage in sth/ enter into sth
▶ to **actively/ directly** participate/ take part/ engage in sth
▶ to be **fully/ actively/ directly** involved in sth

join [他, 自] (組織・会社・クラブに)加わる;(他の人に)合流する ◇She *joined* the company three months ago. 彼女は3か月前にその会社に入った ◇I've *joined* an aerobics class. 私はエアロビクスの教室に入会している ◇It costs £20 to *join*. 入会費は20ポンドだ ◇Will you *join* us for lunch? 私たちとお昼を一緒に食べませんか ◇Members of the public *joined* the search for the missing boy. 一般の人たちが行方不明の少年の捜索に加わった

be/get involved [フレーズ] (特定の活動に)従事する;(集団・クラブ・団体に)参加[関与]する ◇I *got involved* in politics when I was at college. 私は大学に在学しているときに政治に携わるようになった ◇She *is* very much *involved* with several local charitable groups. 彼女はとても熱心に地元のいくつかの慈善団体に参加している ☞ **involvement** (INVOLVEMENT)

participate [自] 《ややフォーマル》(活動・行事に)参加[関与]する ◇She didn't *participate* in the discussion. 彼

↪join

女はその議論に参加しなかった ◇We want to encourage students to *participate* fully in the running of the college. 本学としては学生たちに大学の運営に本格的に参加するよう促したい ☞ **participation** (INVOLVEMENT), **participant** (PARTICIPANT)

take 'part フレーズ (活動・行事に)参加[関与]する ◇He had *taken part* in a demonstration several years earlier. それより数年前彼はあるデモに関わったことがあった ◇How many countries *took part* in the last Olympic Games? 何か国が前回のオリンピック大会に参加しましたか ☞ **part** (INVOLVEMENT)

en'gage in sth 句動詞 《ややフォーマル》 (特定の活動に)参加[関与]する ◇Even in prison, he continued to *engage in* criminal activities. 刑務所に入っていても、彼は犯罪活動に関与し続けた ☞ **engagement** (INVOLVEMENT)

ノート be/get **involved, participate, take part, engage in sth**の使い分け:**participate**と**take part**は特定の活動・行事に参加[関与]することで、**participate**のほうが**take part**よりもフォーマルである。**be/get involved**は自分の時間を特定の活動や興味のある分野に向けることを表す一般的な言い方。したがって、**be involved in politics** (政治に携わる)と言うのに対し、**participate/take part in a political debate** (政治討論に参加する)と言う。**engage in sth**は特に(常にではないが)何らかの形で好ましくない[非難を引き起こすような]活動について用いられる。

enter [他、受け身も] 《ややフォーマル》 (機関に)入会する;(組織・会社に)加入する、(専門的職業に)就く;(活動・状況に)参加[関与]する ◇I *entered* politics late in life. 私は晩年になって政界に入った ◇She *entered* Parliament (= became an MP) in 1998. 彼女は1998年に下院議員になった ◇It was his aim to *enter* the Church (= become a priest). 聖職者になるのが彼の目標だった ◇When did the US *enter* the conflict? いつアメリカはその紛争に突入したのですか ◇Several new firms have now *entered* the market. 現在いくつかの新会社がその市場に参入している

▶ **entry** 名 [U] ◇countries seeking *entry* into the European Union EUへの加盟を求めている国々 ◇the American *entry* into the war アメリカの参戦

ノート **join**と**enter**の使い分け:**join**は組織やクラブの一員になることを表す一般的な語。**enter**は政治、弁護士・医者などの専門的職業、大学・議会・キリスト教会などの機関に関わる場合に用いられる。

,join 'in, ,join 'in sth 句動詞 (他の人の行動に)加わる、合流する ◇She listens but she never *joins in*. 彼女は聴いてはいるが決して参加しない ◇I wish he would *join in* with the other children. 彼も他の子たちの輪に入ってくれたらいいのに ◇He didn't dare to *join in* the singing. 彼はあえて一緒に歌おうとしなかった

have/play a 'part フレーズ (活動・状況に)参加[関与]する、役割[一翼]を担う ◇She *plays an* active *part* in local politics. 彼女は地方政治に積極的に参加している ◇We all *have a part* in the making of this decision. 私たちは皆この決定に一役買っている ☞ **part** (INVOLVEMENT)

share [自, 他] (他の人と仕事・責任を)分担する ◇I try to get the kids to *share* in the housework. 私は子どもたちに家事を分担させようと思う ◇Don't try to do everything yourself: you will need to *share the load* with your partner. 自分で全部やろうとしないでください、パートナーと仕事量を分担する必要があります ❶この意味の**share**と結びつく語には work, load, burden, responsibilities が挙げられる。☞ **share** (SHARE 名)

'enter into sth 句動詞 《ややフォーマル》(正式な[商取引の]関係を)結ぶ;(積極的に)参加[関与]する ◇Read the small print before you *enter into* any agreement. いかなる契約も結ぶ前に細字部分を読みましょう ◇I refuse to *enter into* correspondence with such people. 私はそのような人々と連絡を取り合う関係になりたくありません

joke 名

joke • quip • prank • pun • gag • one-liner • wisecrack
ふざけて[人を笑わせようとして]行う言動
【類語訳】冗談、しゃれ、おどけ、ふざけ、いたずら、地口、駄じゃれ、語呂合わせ、ギャグ、ジョーク、皮肉

文型&コロケーション
▶ a joke/ quip/ gag/ wisecrack **about** sb/ sth
▶ to do sth **as** a joke/ prank
▶ to **make** a joke/ quip/ pun/ wisecrack
▶ to **tell (sb) crack** a joke/ gag
▶ to **laugh at** a joke/ pun/ gag

joke [C] (言動に見られる)冗談、しゃれ、おどけ、ふざけ ◇I can't tell *jokes*. 私は冗談が言えない ◇I didn't *get the joke* (= understand it). 私はそのしゃれがよくわからなかった ◇I wish he wouldn't tell *dirty jokes* (= about sex). 彼が下ネタの冗談をやめてくれたらいいんだけど ◇He's always playing *practical jokes* on people (= tricks that are played on people to make them look stupid and to make other people laugh). 彼はいつも人に悪ふざけばかりしている ◇The trouble with Ruby is she can't *take a joke* (= she isn't able to laugh at a joke against herself). ルビーの厄介なところは冗談を笑って受け流すことができないことだ ❶**joke**はしばしば面白い落ちのある話を指す。話の登場人物・出来事・言葉までもがかなり固定されていて、ほとんど、あるいはまったく変えられることなく人から人へと伝えられる。同じことが後出の**gag**, 時に**one-liner**にも言える。その他の語は特定の状況や他の人の発言に応じて作り出されるようなものを指す。

quip [C] (即席に考える)気の利いたしゃれ ◇The senator made several *quips* during the interview, which got the audience laughing. その議員は記者会見中にいくつか気の利いたしゃれを言って聴衆を笑わせた

prank [C] (冗談としての)いたずら、ふざけ ◇It was just a childish *prank* — don't take it so seriously. あれはただ子どもじみたいたずらだったんだよ—そんなにまじめに取らないでね ◇a silly/stupid *prank* 悪ふざけ ◇a *prank* call/ phone call いたずら電話 ☞ **trick** (TRICK)

pun [C] (多義語[同音異義語]を用いた)地口、駄じゃれ、語呂合わせ ◇We're banking on them lending us the money — no *pun* intended! 私たちは彼らがそのお金を貸してくれることを当てにしている—駄じゃれじゃないよ(ここは banking と lending の語呂合わせ) ❶ 人は **pun** を聞くと、笑う代わりによくなることがある。forgive the pun, excuse the pun, pardon the pun (駄じゃれで失礼), の句は、(偶然にせよ故意にせよ)駄じゃれを言ったことを謝るときに用いられる。◆ So you collect pins? But what's the point in that, you'll *forgive the pun*? (じゃあピンを集めてるんだね。そんなことしてどうするの。駄じゃれで失礼)。 (ここは pin と point の語呂合わせ)

gag [C] 《インフォーマル》(プロのコメディアンによる)ギャグ ◇He was a non-stop comedian, cracking *gags* by

the dozen. 彼はひっきりなしにギャグを飛ばしまくるコメディアンだった ◇a ***running gag*** (= one that is regularly repeated during a performance) 連発されるギャグ
,**one-'liner** [C]《インフォーマル》(短く1文にまとめた)気の利いたジョーク, 寸言 ◇He came out with some good *one-liners*. 彼はいくつかなかなか気の利いたジョークを言った
wisecrack [C]《インフォーマル》(人の気にさわることのある)皮肉 ◇He promised not to make any *wisecracks* during the dinner. 彼は夕食中は一言も皮肉は言わないことを約束した

joy 〘名〙 ☞ SATISFACTION

joy・delight・ecstasy・bliss・euphoria
とても幸せな気持ち
【類語訳】喜び, うれしさ, 楽しさ, 恍惚, 有頂天, 至福

〘文型&コロケーション〙
▶ sb's joy/ delight/ euphoria **at** sth
▶ **sheer/ pure** joy/ delight/ ecstasy/ bliss
▶ to **feel/ be filled with** joy/ delight/ ecstasy

joy [U] 喜び, うれしさ, 楽しさ ◇the pure *joy* I felt at being free again また自由になれて私が感じた純粋な喜び ◇I literally ***jumped for joy*** (= was very happy and showed it) when I heard the news. 私はその知らせを聞いて, まさに飛び上がって喜んだ 〘反意〙 **grief** (GRIEF), ☞ **joyful** (HAPPY)
delight [U] 大喜び, うれしさ, 楽しさ ◇Alex squealed with *delight* when he saw the monkeys. アレックスはサルを見るととても喜んでキャッキャッと声を上げた ◇She takes great *delight* in proving others wrong. 彼女は他人が間違っていることを証明することに大きな喜びを感じる ☞ **delight** (DELIGHT)
ecstasy [U, C] 恍惚(状態), 有頂天 ◇Kate closed her eyes ***in ecstasy*** at the thought of a cold drink. ケイトは冷たい飲み物のことを考えてうっとりと目を閉じた ☞ **ecstatic** (EXCITED)
bliss [C] 無上の喜び, 至福 ◇The first six months of marriage were sheer *bliss*. 結婚生活の最初の6か月は本当にこの上なく幸せだった ☞ **blissful** (HAPPY)

〘ノート〙 **joy, delight, bliss** の使い分け：**joy** と **delight** は **bliss** よりも活発な感情を指す。dance/jump/sing/weep for joy (小躍りして/飛び跳ねて/歌って/泣いて喜ぶ) こともあれば, scream/squeal/whoop with delight (叫んで/キャッキャッと声を上げて/歓声を上げて喜ぶ) こともある。bliss はより静かな幸福感を指す。 ◆ married/wedded/domestic bliss (結婚生活の/家庭を持つ幸せ)

euphoria [U] (短い間の)喜び, 幸福感 ◇I was in a state of *euphoria* all day. 私は一日中喜びの状態にあった ◇*Euphoria* soon gave way to despair. 喜びも束の間, 絶望に陥った ☞ **euphoric** (EXCITED)

judge 〘名〙

judge・referee・examiner・umpire・arbiter・moderator・ref
決定を下す[意見を述べる]仕事[役目]を果たす人
【類語訳】審判員, 審査員, 鑑定家, 目利き, レフェリー, 試験官, アンパイア

〘文型&コロケーション〙
▶ an **independent** judge/ examiner
▶ a **neutral** referee/ umpire/ arbiter
▶ the **ultimate/ sole/ final** judge/ arbiter
▶ to **act as** (a) judge/ (a) referee/ (an) arbiter/ (a) moderator
▶ a judge/ a referee/ an umpire **decides/ awards** sth
▶ the judge's/ referee's/ umpire's/ ref's **decision**

judge [C](競技・コンテストなどの)審判[審査, 判定]員；(人・物事の価値・性質を見極める)鑑定[評論, 専門]家, 目利き ◇The *judges'* decision is final. 審査員の決定が最終的なものです ◇The winner was chosen by a ***panel of judges***. 受賞者は審査委員会によって選ばれた ◇She's a good *judge* of character. 彼女は人を見る目がある ◇You are the best *judge* of what your body needs. あなたの体のことはあなたが一番よく知っている ◇The last singer was the best — not that I'm any *judge* (= I do not know much about the subject). 最後の歌手が一番よかった──専門家じゃないからよくわからないけど
referee [C](サッカー・バスケットボール・ボクシングなどのスポーツ競技の)審判員, レフェリー ◇He was sent off for arguing with the *referee*. 彼は審判と口論して退場になった ◇Graham is a qualified ***football referee***. グレアムはサッカーの審判員の資格を持っている ⓘ *referee* には「論文審査員」(刊行前の論文を査読する人) の意味もある。 ◆ All papers are sent out to external *referees*. (論文はすべて外部の論文審査員に送付される)
▶ **referee** 〘動〙〘自, 他〙a *refereeing* decision 審判の判定 ◇Who *refereed* the final/this paper? 誰が決勝戦の審判[この論文の査読]をしたのですか
examiner [C]《英》(試験問題の作成・採点を行う)試験官 ◇She was a member of the **board of examiners** of the college. 彼女はその大学の試験官委員会の一員だった ◇He is a former senior driving *examiner*. 彼は運転免許の元上級試験官だ ☞ **examine** (TEST 〘動〙2)
umpire [C](テニス・クリケット・野球などのスポーツ競技の)審判員, アンパイア ◇He received an official warning from the *umpire* for his conduct. 彼は自分の行為について審判から正式な警告を受けた
▶ **umpire** 〘動〙〘自, 他〙We need someone to *umpire*. 誰かに審判をしてほしい ◇to *umpire* a baseball game/a cricket match 野球/クリケットの試合で審判を務める
arbiter [C]《フォーマル》(影響力のある)決定[権威]者 ◇The law is the final *arbiter* of what is considered obscene. その法律こそが何がわいせつだと見なされるかを最終的に決定する ◇This style would be dismissed as too ornate by contemporary ***arbiters of taste***. このスタイルは現代の審美的権威なら, 派手すぎだと言って却下するだろう
moderator [C]《特に米》(議論・討論の)議長, 司会者 ◇The *moderator* of this week's quiz is Professor Edmund James. 今週のクイズ番組の司会者はエドマンド・ジェームズ教授です
ref [C]《インフォーマル》(サッカー・バスケットボールなどのスポーツ競技の)審判員, レフェリー ◇The game isn't over until the *ref* blows his whistle. 審判が笛を吹くまで試合は終わらない

judge 〘動〙

judge・assess・evaluate・rate・gauge・size sb/sth up
情報に基づいて人や物事に関する意見を持つ

↳judge

【類語訳】判断する, 評価する, 審査する, 診断する

【文型&コロケーション】
▶ to judge/ assess/ evaluate/ rate sb/ sth **as** sth
▶ to judge/ assess/ evaluate/ rate sb/ sth **on/ according to** sth
▶ to judge/ assess/ evaluate/ gauge sb/ sth **by** sth
▶ to judge/ assess/ gauge sb/ sth **from** sth
▶ to judge/ assess/ evaluate/ rate/ gauge **how...**
▶ to judge/ assess/ evaluate/ gauge **what/ whether...**
▶ to judge/ assess/ evaluate/ gauge the **extent/ significance/ success/ effectiveness/ effect/ impact** of sth
▶ to judge/ assess/ evaluate/ gauge sth's **progress/ performance/ quality/ merits/ potential**
▶ to judge/ assess/ evaluate/ gauge/ size up the **situation**
▶ to judge/ assess/ gauge the **mood/ reaction**
▶ to judge/ assess/ evaluate/ gauge sb/ sth **accurately/ correctly**
▶ to judge/ assess/ evaluate/ rate sb/ sth **fairly/ accordingly**
▶ to judge/ assess/ evaluate sb/ sth **properly/ objectively**

judge [自, 他] (人・物事を)判断[評価]する ◇As far as I can *judge*, they are all to blame. 私が判断するに、彼ら全員に非がある ◇*Judging* from what he said, he was very disappointed. 彼の発言から判断すると、彼はとてもがっかりしていた ◇I don't really think that you're *in a position to judge*. 本当にあなたは評価する立場にないと思います ◇You shouldn't *judge by appearances* (= form an opinion about sb/sth from the way they look). 見た目で判断すべきではない ◇You shouldn't *judge* her too harshly. 彼女をあまり厳しく評価すべきではない ◇They *judged it wise* to say nothing. 彼らは何も言わないことが賢明だと判断した ☞ **judgement** (VIEW 1), **judgemental** (CRITICAL)

assess [他] (本質・能力・性質を専門的に)審査[評価, 診断]する ◇The new patient is *assessed* by the nursing staff. 新患は看護職員の診断を受けます ◇I'd *assess* your chances of winning as pretty low. 私はあなたの勝算はかなり低いと見なします ◇The committee *assesses* whether a building is worth preserving. 委員会が建物を保存する価値があるかどうかを審査します ☞ **assess** (TEST 動 2), **assessment** (ASSESSMENT)

evaluate [他] (量・価値・性質を)審査[評価, 診断]する ◇Our research attempts to *evaluate* the effectiveness of the different drugs. 私たちは研究によってさまざまな薬の効果を審査しようとしている ◇We need to *evaluate* how well the system is working. 私たちはその制度がどの程度機能しているかを審査する必要がある ☞ **evaluation** (ASSESSMENT)

【ノート】**assess** と **evaluate** の使い分け：assess はふつう判断を下す(しばしば特定の基準に照らして, 人・事物が基準を満たしているかどうかを見る)ために審査すること. evaluate はふつうよりよく理解する(そしてより多くの情報に基づいて決定を下す)ために審査すること. 時に両語とも使用可能. ◆ Candidates are *assessed/evaluated* on their ability to think independently. (志願者は独自の考え方ができるかどうかを審査される). この例では, ある判断がなされるが, evaluate はより肯定的な響きがあるので, しばしば仕事での人の成績について用いられ, 試験や授業での学生の成績についてはふつう assess が用いられる. ☞ **assess** (TEST 動 2)

---

jump

rate [他]《進行形なし》(特定の水準の性質・価値をもっているかを)判断[評価]する ◇How did you *rate* her speech? 君は彼女の演説をどう思った ◇The university is highly *rated for* its research. その大学は研究を高く評価されている ◇Voters continue to *rate* education high on their list of priorities. 有権者は引き続き教育を優先順位の高い位置に挙げている ☞ **rate** (RANK), **rating** (CLASS 3)

gauge (米でまた **gage**) [他] (感情・態度等を)判断[評価]する ◇He tried to *gauge* her mood. 彼は彼女の機嫌を推し測ろうとした ◇It was difficult to *gauge* whether she was angry or not. 彼女が怒っているかどうかを判断するのは困難だった ☞ **gauge** (CRITERION)

size sb/sth 'up 句動詞《ややインフォーマル》(人・物事を)判断[評価]する ◇He *sized up* the situation very quickly. 彼は状況を即座に判断した ◇The children looked at each other warily, as if *sizing* each other *up*. その子たちは互いを品定めするかのように, 用心深く見合った

jump 動

jump・leap・hop・vault・bounce・hurdle
両脚[足]を伸ばして体を地面から離す
【類語訳】跳ぶ, 飛び跳ねる, 跳び越える, 跳躍する

【文型&コロケーション】
▶ to jump/ leap/ hop/ vault/ hurdle **over** (sth)
▶ to jump/ leap/ hop/ bounce **up and down**
▶ to jump/ leap/ hop **about/ around**
▶ to jump/ leap/ hop/ vault/ hurdle a **fence/ hedge/ wall**
▶ to jump/ leap/ hop **3 feet/ 2 metres, etc.**

jump [自, 他] (両脚[足]で)跳ぶ, 飛び跳ねる；(物を)跳び越える ◇I held my nose and *jumped* into the water. 私は鼻をつまんで水に飛び込んだ ◇Can you *jump* over that fence? あの柵を跳び越えられるかい ◇The dog kept *jumping* up at me. 犬は私に向かって飛び跳ね続けた ◇'Quick! *Jump!*' she shouted. 「急いで, ジャンプして」と彼女は叫んだ ◇He can *jump* over two metres. 彼は2m以上跳べる ◇Her horse fell as it *jumped* the last fence. 最後の障害物を跳び越える際に彼女の馬は転倒した ▶ **jump** 名 [C] ◇She managed a *jump* of 1.6 metres. 彼女は何とか1.6mを跳ぶことができた

leap [自, 他]《副詞や前置詞と共に》《書き言葉》(高く・遠くまで)跳ぶ, 飛び跳ねる, 跳躍する ◇A dolphin suddenly *leapt* out of the water. 1頭のイルカが突然水から飛び跳ねた ◇The horse galloped on, *leaping* fences and hedges as it came to them. 馬は柵や垣根の障害物に近づくたびにそれらを跳び越えて全速力で走り続けた ▶ **leap** 名 [C] ◇She took a flying *leap* and landed on the other side of the stream. 彼女は大きく跳躍して小川の向こう岸に着地した

hop (**-pp-**) [自] (人が片脚[足]で)跳ぶ；片足で跳んで[びっこを引いて]歩く；(動物・鳥が両脚[足]で)ぴょんぴょんと跳び回る ◇I couldn't put any weight on my ankle and had to *hop* everywhere. 私は足首に体重をまったくかけることができず, どこへ行くにも片足でぴょんぴょんと歩くしかなかった ◇A robin was *hopping* around on the path. 1匹のコマドリがぴょんぴょんと小道の上を跳ね回っていた ▶ **hop** 名 [C] ◇He crossed the hall with a *hop*, skip and a jump. 彼はホールをホップ・スキップ・ジャンプで横切った

vault [自, 他]《ややフォーマル》(手足・棒で)跳び越える ◇She

vaulted over the gate and ran up the path. 彼女は門を跳び越えて道を駆け上がった ◇There's no way he could have *vaulted* the fence with that injury. 彼があんなけがでその柵を飛び越えられたわけないだろう

bounce [自, 他]（物の上で）ぴょんぴょんと飛び跳ねる；（子どもを）ひざの上でぴょんぴょんと飛び上がらせる ◇She *bounced* up and down excitedly on the bed. 彼女はベッドの上で興奮してぴょんぴょん飛び跳ねた ◇I *bounced* the baby on my knee while Pat did the dishes. パットが皿洗いをしている間、私は赤ちゃんをひざの上でぴょんぴょん飛び上がらせていた

hurdle [他, 自]（走りながら物を）跳び越える ◇He *hurdled* two steel barriers in an attempt to escape from the police. 警官から逃げようとして彼は二つの鋼鉄製の柵を跳び越えた ◇She had to *hurdle* over three fences to reach the finishing line. 彼女はゴールするために三つの障害物を跳び越えねばならなかった ☞ **hurdle** (BARRIER)

justice 名

justice・equality・fairness・fair play・equity
すべての人がえこひいきなく扱われている状況
【類語訳】正義, 公正, 公平, 平等, 均等, フェアプレー

▸文型&コロケーション
▸ justice/ equality/ fairness/ fair play/ equity **for** sb
▸ justice/ equality/ fairness/ fair play **in** sth
▸ **strict** justice/ equality/ fairness
▸ **social/ economic** justice/ equality/ fairness/ equity
▸ to **ensure** justice/ equality/ fairness/ fair play/ equity
▸ to **guarantee** justice/ equality/ fairness/ equity
▸ a **sense of** justice/ equality/ fairness/ fair play

justice [U]（社会全般における）正義, 公正, 公平 ◇Our laws must be based on the principles of *justice*. 我が国の法律は正義の原則に基づくものでなければならない ◇Sometimes I feel that there's no *justice* in the world. ときどき私は世の中に神も仏もあったもんじゃないと感じることがある 反意 **injustice** (INEQUALITY), ☞ **just** (REASONABLE)

equality [U]（社会における権利・身分・利益の）平等, 均等 ◇Sexual *equality* is an ideal that we have not yet achieved. 男女平等はまだ達成されていない一つの理想である ◇The people were demanding full *equality with* their former masters. 国民はかつての支配者との完全な平等を要求していた ◇*Equality of opportunity* is our priority. 我々は機会均等を優先する ◇We need to ensure *equality of opportunity* in all areas of work. あらゆる職場で機会均等が保障される必要がある 反意 **inequality** (INEQUALITY), ☞ **equal** (REASONABLE)

fairness [U]（人の扱いにおける）公正[公平]さ ◇The system needs to be changed in the interests of *fairness to* genuine refugees. その制度は正真正銘の難民に公平さを期するために修正される必要がある ❶ in (all) fairness (to sb) の句は, 今まさに批判されている人を弁護する際や, 筋が通っていないとされかねない他の発言を説明する際の導入部に用いられる. ◆ *In all fairness to* him, he did try to stop her leaving.（彼に対して公正な立場で言うならば、彼は彼女が出て行くのを止めようとしたのだ）反意 **unfairness** (INEQUALITY), ☞ **fair** (REASONABLE)

,fair 'play [U]（試合などでの）フェアプレー, 公正な[正々堂々とした, 公明正大な, 規則にかなった]行為 ◇As a player, he was always admired for his sense of *fair play*. 一選手として, 彼は持ち前のフェアプレー感覚をいつもたたえられていた ☞ **fair** (REASONABLE)

equity [U]《フォーマル》（人の扱いにおける）公正[公平]さ ◇They envisaged a society in which justice and *equity* prevailed. 彼らは正義と公正さが広く行き渡った社会を心に描いていた 反意 **inequity** (INEQUALITY)

K k

keep 動

1 keep・store・hoard・stock up・stash・stockpile
後で使えるように物をどこかに置いておく
【類語訳】保管する、貯蔵する、保存する、収納する、蓄える、貯め込む、秘密する、買いだめする、買い込む、備蓄する

文型&コロケーション
- to store/ stash sth **away**
- to keep/ store/ hoard/ stock up on/ stockpile **food** (somewhere)
- to keep/ store/ stockpile **weapons** (somewhere)
- to keep/ hoard/ stash **money** (somewhere)

keep [他] (特定の場所に)保管する、しまって[置いて、取って]おく ◇*Keep* your passport in a safe place. パスポートは安全な場所に保管しましょう ◇Where do you *keep* the sugar? 砂糖はどこにしまってあるの ◇The documents are all *kept under lock and key* (= locked up safely somewhere). 書類はすべて鍵をかけて安全に保管されています

store [他] (長期間)保管[貯蔵、保存、収納]する、蓄えておく ◇The squirrels are *storing up* food for the winter. リスは冬に備えて食べ物を蓄えている ◇You can *store* coffee beans in the freezer to keep them fresh. 鮮度を保つためにコーヒー豆は冷凍庫で保存しておくことができる ◇He hoped the electronic equipment was safely *stored* away. 彼は電子機器が安全に保管されていることを願った ☞ **store** (SUPPLY)

▶**storage** 名 [U] ◇tables that fold flat for *storage* 収納のための折りたたみ式テーブル ◇There's lots of *storage* space in the attic. 屋根裏に収納スペースがたくさんある

hoard [他] (大量の食べ物・お金などをひそかに)蓄える、貯め込む、秘蔵する、隠しておく ◇The prisoners used to *hoard* scraps of food in secret places. 以前囚人たちは秘密の場所に残飯を貯め込んだものだった ☞ **hoard** (SUPPLY)

stock 'up 句動詞 (大量に)まとめ買いしておく、買いだめする、買い込む ◇We ought to *stock up on* film before our trip. 旅行の前にフィルムをまとめ買いしておかないといけないな ◇I go shopping once a week to *stock up with* essentials. 私は週に1回買い物に行って生活必需品をまとめ買いしておきます ◇The store was full of families *stocking up for* Christmas. 店はクリスマスに備えてまとめ買いをする家族でいっぱいだった ☞ **stock** (SUPPLY)

stash [他] (《ややインフォーマル》) (安全な[秘密の]場所に)しまって[取って、隠して]おく ◇She's probably got loads of cash *stashed* away. おそらく彼女はへそくりをたっぷり隠しているんだろう ☞ **stash** (FUND) 名

stockpile [他] (大量の武器・食べ物・燃料などを)備蓄[貯蔵]する ◇Consumers began to *stockpile* fuel amid fears of a shortage. 不足が懸念される中で、消費者は燃料を備蓄し始めた ☞ **stockpile** (SUPPLY)

2 keep・retain・hold on to sth・save
何かを維持する

【類語訳】持ち続ける、保持する、保つ、保有し続ける、取っておく

文型&コロケーション
- to keep/ retain **control** (of sth)
- to retain/ hold on to **your lead**
- to **still** keep/ retain/ hold on to sth

keep [他] 持ち続ける、保持する ◇She handed me a ten dollar bill. 'Here — *keep the change*.' 彼女は私に10ドル札を手渡して、「ほら、お釣りはいりません」と言った ◇I've *kept* all her letters. 彼女からの手紙はすべて取ってある

retain [他] 《フォーマル》保つ、保持する ◇Please *retain* your ticket stub during the event. イベント開催中は切符の半券を捨てないでください ◇The house *retains* much of its original charm. その家は建てられた頃の魅力を多く保ったままだ ◇She has *retained* her *title* (= won the competition again) for the third year. 彼女は3年目もチャンピオンを保持した

> ノート **keep**と**retain**の使い分け: retainはフォーマルに公式文書で用いられ、話し言葉で使われることはほとんどない。持ち続けている物が将来必要になる[役に立つ]ことが時に示唆される。keepはより一般的な語で、ほとんどすべての状況で用いることができる。

,hold 'on to sth, ,hold 'onto sth 句動詞 《受身なし》 (有利に働く物を)保持し続ける ◇You should *hold on to* your oil shares. 石油株は保持し続けたほうがいいよ ◇She took an early lead in the race and *held onto* it for nine laps. 彼女はレース序盤から先頭に立っていたが、10周目で初めてリードを奪われた

save [他] (将来のために)取っておく ◇He's *saving* his strength *for* the last part of the race. 彼はレースの終盤のために体力を温存している ◇We'll eat some now and *save* some for tomorrow. ぼくたちは今は少し食べて、あしたのために少し残しておこう

3 keep・hold・store・retain
特に情報のようなものを持ち続ける

【類語訳】記入する、記録する、持っている、保持している、保存する、蓄積する、保つ、保持する

文型&コロケーション
- to keep/ hold/ store/ retain **information/ data**
- to keep/ hold **a record/ records**
- to store/ retain **facts**
- to hold/ retain **land/ territory**
- to **still/ no longer** keep/ hold/ store/ retain sth

keep [他] 記入する、記録する ◇She *kept a diary* for over twenty years. 彼女は20年以上も日記を付けていた ◇*Keep a note* of where each item can be found. 各品目がどこにあるかを記録しておきなさい ◇Separate *accounts* must be *kept* for each different business activity. 会計記録は事業活動ごとに個々に行われるべきだ

hold [他] (書類などを後で使うために)持っている、保持している ◇Employees do not have access to personal records *held* on computer. 従業員はコンピューターに保存されている個人記録にアクセスはできない ◇Our solicitor *holds* our wills. 事務弁護士が我々の遺言状を持っている

store [他] (情報・事実を)保存する, 蓄積する ◇Each department has a different system for *storing* and retrieving data. 各部署はデータ保存・検索用に異なるシステムを持っている ◇We are conducting research into how information is *stored* in the brain. 私たちはどのように情報が脳に蓄積されるか研究している

retain [他] 《フォーマル》 保つ, 保持する ◇These plants will need a soil that *retains* moisture during the summer months. これらの植物は夏の数か月間は湿気を保つ土壌を必要とするだろう ◇This information is no longer *retained* within the computer's main memory. この情報はこれ以上はコンピューターの主記憶装置に残ることはない

4 keep・breed・rear・raise
動物を所有して世話をする
【類語訳】飼う, 飼育する, 栽培する, 養殖する

[文型&コロケーション]
▶to keep/ breed/ rear sth **for** sth
▶to keep/ breed/ rear/ raise **animals/ cattle/ horses/ sheep**
▶to keep/ breed/ raise **chickens**
▶to keep/ breed/ rear/ raise sth **in captivity**

keep [他] (家庭で[小規模に]動物を)飼う ◇Residents are not allowed to *keep* pets. 居住者はペットを飼うことを許可されていない ◇to *keep* bees/goats 蜂/山羊を飼う

breed [他] (繁殖させるために動植物を)飼育[栽培, 養殖]する ◇Greyhounds were originally *bred* as hunting dogs. グレーハウンドはもともと猟犬として飼育されていた

rear [他] (飼育[養殖]場などで動物・鳥を)飼育[養殖]する ◇The young crocodiles were *reared* indoors at a constant temperature of 32℃. 子どものクロコダイルが室温32度のもとで飼育されていた ☞ **rear** (BRING SB UP)

raise [他] (販売などの目的で特定の家畜・作物を)飼育[栽培, 養殖]する ◇Farmers cleared the land in order to *raise* cattle. 農夫たちは牛を飼育するために土地を切り開いた ☞ **raise** (BRING SB UP)

[ノート] rear と raise の使い分け：《米》では raise のほうが rear よりも頻繁に用いられるが, 強調する点においてもわずかな違いがある. rear はしばしば動物の扱い方・飼育環境に関する情報を強調する場合に用いられ, raise はしばしば生産物としての家畜・作物について用いられる.

kidnap [動]

kidnap・seize・abduct
人を連れ去って拘束する
【類語訳】誘拐する, 拉致する, 捕らえる, 逮捕する, 拘束する

[文型&コロケーション]
▶to kidnap/ seize/ abduct sb's/ your **son/ daughter/ child**

kidnap (-pp-, 米でまた -p-) [他] (身代金などの目的で人を)誘拐[拉致]する ◇Two businessmen have been *kidnapped* by terrorists. ビジネスマンが二人, テロリストに拉致された

▶**kidnapping** (または **kidnap**) [名] [C, U] ◇No group has yet claimed responsibility for the *kidnappings*. 拉致の犯行声明はまだどのグループからも出されていない ◇He admitted the charge of *kidnap*. 彼は誘拐の容疑を認めた

seize [他] 《特にジャーナリズム》 (合法的[違法]に人を)捕らえる, 逮捕[拘束]する ◇A Briton has been *seized* by border guards and jailed for eight years. 英国人1人が国境警備隊に捕らえられ, 8年間拘置された ◇Terrorists have *seized* his wife and children. テロリストは彼の妻と子どもたちを拘束している

abduct [他] (力ずくで人を)誘拐[拉致]する ◇He had attempted to *abduct* the two children. 彼は二人の子どもを誘拐しようとしていた ❶ **abduct** は法律用語として用いられ, ふつう政治的理由や身代金目的ではなく性的な動機から女性・子どもを連れ去る行為を指す.

▶**abduction** [名] [U, C] ◇child *abduction* 子どもの誘拐

kill [動]

kill・murder・execute・assassinate・slay・bump sb off・take sb/sth out・eliminate・finish sb/sth off
人や動植物を消滅させる
【類語訳】殺す, 枯らす, 殺害する, 処刑する, 暗殺する, ばらす, 破壊する

[文型&コロケーション]
▶to kill/ murder/ assassinate sb **in cold blood**
▶to **brutally** kill/ murder/ slay sb

kill [他, 自] (人・動物を)死なせる, 殺す, (植物を)枯らす ◇Cancer *kills* thousands of people every year. 毎年何千人もの人ががんで亡くなっている ◇Three people were *killed* in the crash. その衝突事故で3人が死亡した ◇He tried to *kill* himself with sleeping pills. 彼は睡眠薬で自殺を図った ◇I bought a spray to *kill* the weeds. 私は除草スプレーを買った ◇Excessive tiredness while driving can *kill*. 過度の疲労を感じながらの運転は死亡事故につながることがある ☞ **killing** (MURDER)

murder [他] (意図的[違法]に人を)殺害する ◇He denies *murdering* his wife's lover. 彼は妻の愛人の殺害を否認している ☞ **murder** (MURDER), **murderous** (VIOLENT)

execute [他, ふつう受身で] (刑罰として人を)死刑に処する, 処刑する ◇He was *executed* for treason. 彼は反逆罪で死刑に処された ◇The prisoners were *executed* by firing squad. 囚人は銃殺隊に処刑された

assassinate [他, しばしば受身で] (政治的理由で要人・有名人を)暗殺する ◇The prime minister was *assassinated* by extremists. 首相は過激派によって暗殺された ☞ **assassination** (MURDER)

slay [他] 《特に米, 特にジャーナリズム》 (意図的[違法]に人を)殺害する ◇Two passengers were *slain* by the hijackers. 乗客二人がハイジャック犯に殺害された ❶ 《英》《米》の古風・文語的な言い回しでは, slay は「(戦争[戦闘]で人・動物を)殺す」ことを意味する. ◆St George *slew* the dragon. (聖ジョージはドラゴンを殺した). ☞ **slaying** (MURDER)

,bump sb 'off [句動詞] 《インフォーマル, おどけて》 (意図的[違法]に人を)殺す, ばらす ◇She'd had three husbands and *bumped* them all *off* for the insurance money. 彼女には3人の夫がいたが, 彼らは皆保険金目当てで彼女に殺された

,take sb/sth 'out 句動詞 《インフォーマル》(害を与える人・敵・動物などを)殺す、破壊する ◇They *took out* two enemy bombers. 彼らは敵の爆撃機2機を撃墜した

eliminate [他]《ややフォーマル、書き言葉》(敵・敵対者を)殺害する ◇Most of the regime's left-wing opponents were *eliminated*. その政権に敵対する左派の大多数が殺害された ☞ **eliminate** (REMOVE)

,finish sb/sth 'off 句動詞 《ややインフォーマル》(重傷/損傷)を負った人・動物などに)とどめを刺す ◇The hunter moved in to *finish* the animal *off*. 猟師はその動物に近寄ってとどめを刺した

kind 名 ☞ CATEGORY

kind・sort・type・form・version・variety・style・genre・nature・brand
人や物事が何らかの形で同一のグループであることを表す
【類語訳】種類、型、タイプ、版、バージョン、ジャンル

文型&コロケーション

▶ a kind/ sort/ type/ form/ version/ variety/ style/ genre/ brand **of** sth
▶ **of** a/ the ... kind/ sort/ type/ form/ version/ variety/ style/ nature
▶ **in** kind/ type/ form/ style/ nature
▶ **different** kinds/ sorts/ types/ forms/ versions/ varieties/ styles/ genres
▶ **various** kinds/ sorts/ types/ forms/ versions/ styles/ genres
▶ a **different** kind/ sort/ type/ form/ version/ variety/ style/ nature/ brand
▶ **another** kind/ sort/ type/ form/ version/ variety/ style/ brand
▶ the **same** kind/ sort/ type/ form/ version/ variety/ style/ genre/ nature/ brand
▶ **all** kinds/ sorts/ types/ forms/ varieties/ styles/ brands (of sth)
▶ **every/ any** kind/ sort/ type/ form/ style/ nature
▶ **some** kind/ sort/ type/ form/ variety/ nature (of sth)
▶ a **particular** kind/ sort/ type/ form/ version/ variety/ style/ genre/ nature/ brand
▶ the **best/ worst** kind/ sort/ type/ form
▶ a/ the/ that kind/ sort/ type **of thing**
▶ **of this/ that** kind/ sort/ type
▶ **of every** kind/ sort/ type/ form/ variety/ style/ nature

kind [C, U] 種類、部類 ◇They play music of all *kinds*. 彼らはあらゆる種類の音楽を演奏する ◇The school is the first of its *kind* in the UK. この学校はこの種のものとしてはイギリスで最初のものだ ◇She does the same *kind* of work as me. 彼女は私と同じような仕事をしている ◇She isn't that *kind* of person. 彼女はそんな類の人じゃないよ ◇I miss him, in a funny *kind* of way. 私は彼がいなくて何だか妙に寂しい ◇They sell all *kind* of things. そこではあらゆる種類の品が売られている ◇You're going to need some *kind* of cover to protect it from the rain. それを雨から守るために何らかのカバーが必要になるだろう ◇'I was terrible!' 'You were ***nothing of the kind***!' 「とてもひどかったな」「全然そんなことなかったよ」

sort [C]《特に英》種類、部類 ◇What *sort* of music do you like?' 'Oh, all *sorts*.'「どんな種類の音楽が好きなの」「うん、どんな種類のものでも」 ◇This *sort* of problem is quite common. この種の問題はこの辺にはある ◇He's the *sort* of person who only cares about money. 彼はお金のことしか頭にない種類の人間です ◇Most people went on training courses of one *sort* or another. たいていの人たちは何らかの研修コースを受け始めた ◇What *sort* of price are you willing to pay (= approximately what price)? 《話し言葉》いくらくらいなら払っていいとお思いですか ☞ **sort** (CLASSIFY)

type [C] 種類、部類、型、タイプ ◇He mixes with all *types* of people. 彼はあらゆるタイプの人と交流がある ◇What *type* of car do you drive? どんな型の車を運転していますか ◇How much do you charge for this *type* of work? この種の仕事の請求額はどのくらいですか ◇This is the oldest existing shrine of its *type*. これは現存するその種の神殿の中で最古のものです ◇You can divide his novels into three main *types*. 彼の小説は大きく3つの種類に分けられる ◇She has a very rare **blood *type***. 彼女の血液型は非常に珍しい ◇This is a new formula for all skin *types*. これは全肌質に向けた新製法です

ノート **kind, sort, type** の使い分け: この意味では kind が最も使用頻度が高い。sort も使用頻度は高いが、kind よりもいくぶんインフォーマルで、《米》よりも《英》において、書き言葉より話し言葉で用いられることが多い。type は他の2語よりもいくぶんフォーマルで、例えば公的[科学的、学問的]な文脈において、客観的にはっきりと分類できる物事について用いられる傾向がある。

form [C] (異なる物理的特性を持つ)形態 ◇We need to look for an alternative *form* of energy. 代替エネルギーを探す必要がある ◇This is one of the most common *forms* of cancer. これはがんの最も一般的な形態の一つです ◇Will we ever discover intelligent **life *forms*** on other planets? いったい他の惑星に知的生命体が見つかることはあるのでしょうか ◇Music is not like other **art *forms***. 音楽は他の芸術形態とは異なる ❶ types (種類) は物理的特性が異なる必要はないが、forms (形態) はふつう物理的特性が異なる。✕ He mixes with all *forms* of people. ✕ Are there intelligent life *types* on other planets?

version [C] (元の製品を別の形に作り変えた)版、型、バージョン ◇the latest *version* of the Volkswagen Golf フォルクスワーゲン・ゴルフの最新型 ◇the de luxe/luxury *version* デラックス/豪華版 ◇The English *version* of the novel is due for publication next year. その小説の英語版は来年出版される予定です

variety [C] (植物・言語などの)種類 ◇Apples come in a great many *varieties*. リンゴは非常に多くの品種が入荷する ◇The *variety* of English that they speak is closer to American than British. 彼らが話す英語はイギリス英語よりもアメリカ英語に近い ◇They stock over 200 *varieties* of cheese. 200種類以上のチーズが売られている

style [C, U] (書物・絵画・建築物などの)様式、形式、スタイル ◇This is a fine example of the Gothic *style*. これはゴシック様式の適例です ◇The city contains many different *styles* of architecture. その都市には多種多様な様式の建築物がある ◇They were told to write the passage in the *style* of Hemingway. 彼らはヘミングウェイの文体で文章を書くように言われた

genre [C, U]《フォーマル》(文学・芸術・音楽・映画の)形式、様式、ジャンル ◇Crime fiction is a *genre* which seems likely to stay with us for many years. 推理小説は永年にわたってすたれずに残りそうなジャンルだ ◇His essay discusses theories of style and *genre*. 彼はそのエッセイにスタイルとジャンルの理論を論じている

nature [単数で]《ややフォーマル》特有の種類, 性質, 特質 ◇His books were mainly of a scientific *nature*. 彼の著作の大部分には科学的な特質が見られた ◇Don't worry about things of that *nature*. その種のことによくよするな ◇Decisions of this *nature* often take a long time. この種の決定にはしばしば時間がかかる ❶この意味では *nature* はふつう *of a ... nature* の句で用いられる.

brand [C]（行動・思考の）特有の種類 ◇She has her own unique *brand* of humour. 彼女には独特のユーモアが備わっている

kind 形 ☞ NICE 2

kind・good・generous・benign・benevolent・considerate・sweet・thoughtful
人が他人を気づかい, 手助けをいとわず, 必要としていることや気持ちに思いをはせること
【類語訳】優しい, 親切な, 寛大な, 寛容な, 温和な, 慈悲深い, 奇特な

〖文型&コロケーション〗
▶ kind/ good/ generous/ benevolent/ considerate **to**/ **towards**/ **toward** sb
▶ to be kind/ good/ generous/ considerate/ sweet/ thoughtful **of** sb (to do sth)
▶ a kind/ generous/ benevolent/ considerate/ sweet/ thoughtful **man**/ **woman**/ **person**
▶ a kind/ generous/ considerate/ thoughtful **gesture**
▶ **very** kind/ good/ generous/ considerate/ sweet/ thoughtful
▶ **extremely** kind/ good/ generous/ considerate

kind（人・行為・表情が）優しい, 親切な, 思いやりのある ◇They were taught to be *kind* to animals. 彼らは動物に優しくするよう教えられた ◇It was really *kind* of you to help me. 親切に手伝ってくれて本当にありがとう ◇She may seem quite stern at times, but she has a *kind* heart. 彼女は時々とても厳しそうに見えることがあるかもしれないが, 心は優しい ◇Thanks for your card ― it was a very *kind* thought. 葉書をくれてありがとう―とても優しい心づかいだったよ 反意 **cruel** (CRUEL), **unkind** (MEAN 形)；☞ **caring** (LOVING)
▶ **kindly** 副 ◇She *kindly* agreed to give me a ride home. 彼女は親切にも私を家まで車で送ることを了解してくれた
▶ **kindness** 名 [U] ◇She wanted to thank him for his *kindness*. 彼女は彼の思いやりにお礼を言いたかった

good [名詞の前にまれ]《ややインフォーマル, 特に話し言葉》優しい, 親切な, 思いやりのある ◇He was very *good* to me when I was ill. 私が病気のときとてもよくしてくれた ◇It was *good* of you to come. 来てくれてありがとう ◇He had a lot of time off work, but my boss was very *good* **about** it. 私は仕事をよく休んだが, 上司はそのことにとても理解があった ❶話し言葉では *good* はこれらの類語の中で最も使用頻度が高い. この意味ではふつう人間への表現で, より広い意味を持っており,「善良な男性[女性]（節操を持って道徳的に正しい生活を送る人）」を表す. 親切であることはこの意味の一部でしかない. ☞ **good** (GOOD 5)

generous（人の扱い方において）優しい, 心の温かい；（人・物事に対して）心の広い, 寛大な [寛容] な ◇Her *generous* spirit shone through in everything she did. 心の温かさが彼女の一挙一投足から伝わってきた ◇He wrote a very *generous* assessment of my work. 彼は私の仕事［作品］に対してとても寛大な評価を書いてくれた 反意 **mean** (MEAN 形)

benign《フォーマル》優しい, 温和な；害のない, 良性の ◇Her face was gentle and *benign*. 彼女は穏やかな優しい顔をしていた ◇The presence of women and children had a *benign* influence on the soldiers. 女性と子どもの存在は兵士たちの心を和らげる効果があった
▶ **benignly** 副 ◇She smiled *benignly* as the students entered the room. 生徒たちが部屋に入ると彼女は優しくほほ笑んだ

benevolent《フォーマル》（権力者が）慈悲［情け］深い, 奇特な ◇The colonel was *benevolent*, but not stupid. その大佐は慈悲深かったが愚かではなかった ◇She took a *benevolent* interest in her nieces' education. 彼女は奇特にも姪の教育に関心を寄せた

considerate（他人の感情・願望に対して）思いやり［理解］のある；（他人の気持ちを傷つけないように）気づかいのある, 察しのよい ◇Try to be a bit more *considerate*. もう少し思いやりを持つようにしなさい ◇Louis was a kind, caring and *considerate* young man. ルイスは優しくて, 思いやりも気づかいもできる青年だった 反意 **inconsiderate** (INSENSITIVE)
▶ **consideration** 名 [U] ◇You should show a little more *consideration* towards other people. あなたはもう少し他人に思いやりを見せるべきだ

sweet《ややインフォーマル, 特に話し言葉》（性格的に）優しい, 親切な ◇It was *sweet* of them to offer to help. 彼らは親切にも援助を申し出てくれた ◇She gave him her *sweetest* smile. 彼女は彼にとても優しくほほ笑んだ

thoughtful（他人に対して）思いやり［心づかい］のある ◇It was very *thoughtful* of you to send the flowers. 花を届けていただいたお心づかい本当に感謝します 反意 **thoughtless** (INSENSITIVE)

ノート **considerate** と **thoughtful** の使い分け：**thoughtful** は他人のために頼まれなくても特定の事を行う場合に用いることが多く, **considerate** は人の全般的な性格や他人に対する態度について言うことが多い.

knock 動

knock・tap・drum・rap
物を強く打って音を立てる
【類語訳】たたく, ノックする

〖文型&コロケーション〗
▶ to knock/ tap/ rap **at** sth
▶ to knock/ tap/ drum/ rap **on** sth
▶ to knock/ tap/ drum/ rap **with** sth
▶ to knock/ rap **loudly**
▶ to knock/ tap **hard**/ **gently**

knock [自]（人の注意を引くためにドアなどを）トントン［コツコツ］とたたく, ノックする ◇He *knocked* three times and waited. 彼は3回ノックして待った ◇Somebody was *knocking* on the window. 誰かが窓をトントンとたたいていた ☞ **knock** (HIT 1)

tap (-pp-) [自, 他]（指・足などで軽快に物を）トントン［コツコツ］とたたく ◇He was busy *tapping* away at his computer. 彼は忙しそうにコンピュータに向かってカチャカチャやっていた ◇The music set everyone's feet *tapping*. そ

→knock

の音楽が流れると皆足でトントンと音を立て始めた ◇He kept *tapping* his fingers on the table. 彼はテーブルを指でコツコツとたたき続けた
tap 图[C] ◇a *tap* at/on the door ドアをトントンとたたく音
drum (**-mm-**) [他, 自] (低い音を立てて繰り返し表面を)ドンドン[トントン]とたたく ◇Impatiently, he *drummed* his fingers on the table. 落ち着かない様子で彼はテーブルを指でタタタとたたいた ◇His fingers *drummed* on the door frame. 彼は指でドアの枠をタタタとたたいた
rap (**-pp-**) [自, 他] (突然に音を立てて素早く何回か物を)ドンドン[トントン]とたたく ◇She *rapped* angrily on the door. 彼女は腹立たしげにドアをドンドンとたたいた ◇He *rapped* the table with his pen. 彼はペンでテーブルをトントンとたたいた

know 動

know・realize・appreciate
物事を理解する[に通じている]
【類語訳】知っている、わかっている、気づく、悟る、認識する、察知する

📦文型&コロケーション
▸ without knowing/ realizing/ appreciating sth
▸ to know/ realize/ appreciate that...
▸ to know/ realize/ appreciate what/ how/ why...
▸ to know/ realize where...
▸ to begin/ come to know/ realize/ appreciate sth
▸ hope sb knows/ realizes/ appreciates sth
▸ should have known/ realized/ appreciated sth

know [他]《進行形なし》(特定の事実・状況を)知って[わかって]いる ◇He *knew* he was dying. 彼は自分が死にかけていることを知っていた ◇I *know* exactly how you feel. 君の気持ちはよくわかるよ ◇You *know* perfectly well what she meant. あなたは彼女が言ったことの意味を本当によくわかっているんですね ◇'He's feeling really down.' '*I know*.'「彼は本当に落ちこんでいるね」「そうなんだよ」 ◇If only we'd *known* you were having so many problems! 君がそんなに多くの問題を抱えていたことを私たちが知ってさえいたらなぁ ◇This case is hopeless *and he knows it* (= although he will not admit it). この事態はどうしようもないが、そのことは彼も内々わかっているよ ☞ **knowledge** (AWARENESS)
realize [英でまた **-ise**] [他]《進行形なし》(特定の事実・状況)に気づく、悟る、知って[わかって]いる ◇I didn't *realize* (that) you were so unhappy. 君がそんなにも悲しい思いをしているなんて気づかなかった ◇I don't think you *realize* how important this is to her. 君のこのことが彼女にとってどれほど大切かわかっていないと思う ◇She soon *realized* her mistake. 彼女はすぐに自分の勘違いに気づいた ◇We make assumptions all the time without *realizing* it. 私たちはそれと気づかずに始終憶測でものを言っている ◇They managed to leave without any of us *realizing*. 私たちの誰も気づくこともなく彼らはまんまと出て行った ☞ **realization** (AWARENESS)

📝 **know**と**realize**の使い分け: この意味では know はふつう目的語に名詞を取らない。 ×She soon *knew* her mistake. realizeは「気づいている」だけでなく「気づく」を意味することもある。knowは瞬時に理解する場合には、「気づく」を意味することもある。 ◆As soon as/The moment

know, knowledge

I walked in the room I *knew*/*realized* something was wrong. (部屋に入ったとたん私は何かがおかしいことに気づいた)。 ◆Suddenly/All of a sudden/At once I *knew*/*realized* what he meant. (突然/瞬時に/ただちに私は彼の言ったことの意味がわかった)。 しかしながら、理解する過程にたとえ短くても時間がかかる場合には realize を用いる。 ◆I soon/quickly/gradually/slowly *realized* what he meant. (私はまもなく/すぐに/徐々に/ゆっくりと彼の言ったことの意味がわかった)。 ×I soon/quickly/gradually/slowly *knew* what he meant.

appreciate [他]《進行形なし》《ややフォーマル》(他人にとって状況が困難であると)認識する[察知]する ◇You have to *appreciate* the difficulties we are facing. あなたは我々が直面している窮地を認識する必要がある ◇I don't think you *appreciate* how expensive it will be. どれだけ費用がかかることになるかあなたはわかっていないと思う ◇As you'll *appreciate*, the task has not always been easy. これからわかると思うけど、この仕事はこれまでだって必ずしも容易だったわけではない ☞ **appreciation** (UNDERSTANDING)

knowledge 名

knowledge・experience・literacy・scholarship・learning・enlightenment・wisdom・lore
教育[経験]を通して学ぶ情報、理解、技能
【類語訳】知識、学識、理解、精通、経験、識字能力、学問、学術、教え、啓蒙、啓発、教化、知恵、英知

📦文型&コロケーション
▸ knowledge/ learning/ enlightenment/ wisdom about sth
▸ great knowledge/ experience/ scholarship/ learning/ enlightenment/ wisdom
▸ ancient/ traditional/ folk knowledge/ wisdom/ lore
▸ human knowledge/ experience/ enlightenment/ wisdom
▸ academic knowledge/ scholarship/ learning
▸ practical knowledge/ experience/ wisdom
▸ to acquire knowledge/ experience/ literacy/ learning/ wisdom
▸ to gain knowledge/ experience/ enlightenment/ wisdom
▸ to increase your knowledge/ experience/ learning

knowledge [U, 単数で] (研究・実践から得た)知識、学識、理解、精通 ◇You do not need to have specialist *knowledge* to express an opinion about language. 言葉について意見を述べるために専門知識を持っている必要はない ◇There will be a test of your *general knowledge* (= your knowledge about things generally). 一般常識のテストがあります ◇He has a wide *knowledge* of music and painting. 彼には音楽と絵画に関して幅広い知識がある 反意 **ignorance** (IGNORANCE), ☞ **know** (LEARN)
experience [U] (一定期間にわたる実際的な)経験、体験、(経験から得た)知識、能力；経験[体験]する過程 ◇I have over ten years' teaching *experience*. 私は人を教えた経験が10年以上あります ◇Do you have any *previous experience* of this type of work? この種の仕事を少しでも以前経験されたことはありますか ◇She didn't get paid much but it was all *good experience*. 彼女の給料は多くなかったが、すべてよい経験だったとは言える ◇We all *learn by experience*. 私たちは皆経験から学ぶものだ ℹ️

knowledge

の意味では experience は特に仕事・経歴に関する文脈で用いられる. work experience (実務経験) はこれまでの人生において携わってきた仕事・職業を指す. ◆The opportunities available will depend on your previous ***work experience*** and qualifications. (どんな働き口があるかはこれまでの実務経験と取得資格によります。) 反意 **inexperience** (IGNORANCE) ☞ **experience** (EVENT 1), **experience** (LIFE 3), **experienced** (EXPERIENCED), **experienced** (SOPHISTICATED), SKILL 1

literacy [U] 読み書きの能力, 識字能力 ◇The government is running a campaign to promote ***adult literacy*** (= the ability of adults to read and write). 政府は成人の識字率を高めるキャンペーンを行っている 反意 **illiteracy**

scholarship [U] （人文学に関する）学問, 学識, 学術 ◇Oxford became one of the great centres of medieval *scholarship*. オックスフォードは中世の学問の大きな中心地の一つになった ☞ **scholarly** (EDUCATIONAL)

learning [U] （読書・研究から得た）知識, 学識 ◇He is a teacher of great intellect and *learning*. 彼は偉大な知性と学識のある教師だ ☞ **learned** (INTELLECTUAL 2)

enlightenment [U] 《フォーマル》知識, 理解, 教え；啓蒙, 啓発, 教化 ◇Seeking *enlightenment*, I asked one of my professors about the matter. 教えを請おうと私は教授の一人にそのことについて質問した ◇Mankind has long been on a quest for spiritual *enlightenment*. 人類はこれまで長い間霊的悟りの境地を探求してきた ☞ **enlighten** (TELL 1)

wisdom [U] （長い時間をかけて培われた社会・文化の）知恵, 英知 ◇We need to combine ancient *wisdom* and modern knowledge. 古代の知恵と現代の知識を組み合わせる必要がある ☞ **wise** (WISE)

lore [U] （特定のテーマに関する明文化されていない）知識；（特定の人の集団に伝わる）言い伝え, 伝説, 伝承 ◇Women with an understanding of herbal *lore* were often regarded as witches. 薬草に精通した女性はしばしば魔女とみなされた ◇an expert in ancient Celtic *lore* 古代ケルトの伝説の専門家

L l

lack 名

lack・absence・deficit・shortage・shortfall・deficiency・scarcity
物事が十分にない[存在しない]ことを表す
【類語訳】不足、欠乏、欠如、ないこと、いないこと、不在、劣勢

文型&コロケーション
- ▶ a shortage/ shortfall/ deficiency **in** sth
- ▶ a **serious** lack/ deficit/ shortage/ deficiency
- ▶ a **major/ severe** lack/ deficit/ shortage/ deficiency
- ▶ to **have/ suffer from** a lack/ absence/ deficit/ shortage/ deficiency
- ▶ to **face** a lack/ deficit/ shortage/ shortfall
- ▶ **There is no** lack/ shortage/ deficiency/ scarcity **of** sth.

lack [U, 単数で]（物事の）不足、欠乏、欠如、ないこと ◇*a lack* of food/money/skills 食糧不足／金欠／技術不足 ◇There was no *lack* of volunteers. ボランティアには事欠かなかった ◇They haven't won a game yet, but it isn't *for lack* of trying. 彼らはまだ試合に勝ったことがないが、それは努力不足のためではない ◇The trip was cancelled *through lack of* (= because there was not enough) interest. その旅行は人々の関心があまりないという理由で中止された ☞ **lacking** (INADEQUATE)
▶**lack** 動 [他、受身なし] ◇Some houses still *lack* basic amenities such as bathrooms. まだ浴室など基本設備のない家もある ◇He *lacks* confidence. 彼には自信がない

absence [U]（人・物事の）不在、欠如、いない[ない]こと ◇The case was dismissed *in the absence of* any definite proof. その申し立ては確かな証拠がなく却下された ◇I was surprised by the *absence* of any women on the board of directors. 私は取締役会に女性が一人もいないことに驚いた 反意 **presence** ❶ presenceは特定の場所[物]に誰か[何か]が存在する事実を指す。◆The test can identify the *presence* of abnormalities in the unborn child. (そのテストで胎児の異常の確認ができる)

deficit [C]（量・金額などの）不足(分/額)、劣勢 ◇There's a *deficit* of $3 million in the total needed to complete the project. その事業の完成には総額で3百万ドル不足している ◇The team has come back from a 2-0 *deficit* in the first half. そのチームは前半2-0から挽回した ❶経済学では、deficitは使われた[借りた]金のほうが特定の期間にわたって得られた金よりも多いことを指す。◆You cannot cut a budget *deficit* simply by raising taxes. (増税だけでは財政赤字を減らすことはできない) ◆The trade balance has been *in deficit* for the past five years. (貿易収支は過去5年間赤字である) 反意 **surplus** (EXCESS)

shortage [C, U]（必要な人・物事の）不足、欠乏 ◇The government must address the current acute *shortage* of teachers. 政府は現在の深刻な教員不足に取り組まねばならない ◇The recent heavy rains have helped to ease the water *shortage*. 最近の大雨は水不足の解消の一助となっている ◇There is no *shortage* of (= there are plenty of) things to do in the town. その町ではいろんなことが体験できる 反意 **surplus** (EXCESS), ☞ **short** (SCARCE)

shortfall [C]（供給・金額の）不足(分/額) ◇Last year there was a *shortfall* of over 500,000 tonnes in the grain supply. 昨年穀物供給は50万トン以上不足した ◇The estimated *shortfall* for this financial year is $1.2 million. 今会計年度の推定不足額は120万ドルである

ノート **shortage** と **shortfall** の使い分け：shortfallは例えば会社が一定期間に見込む収益など、物事に見込まれる「不足」について用いられる。shortageは人にも用いられるが、shortfallは不可。×a *shortfall* of people.

deficiency [U, C]（健康などに不可欠な物の）不足、欠乏、欠如、ないこと ◇Vitamin *deficiency* in the diet can cause illness. 食事におけるビタミン不足で病気になることがある ◇The condition is caused by a *deficiency* of calcium. その疾患はカルシウム不足によって引き起こされる ☞ **deficient** (INADEQUATE)

scarcity [U, C]（食糧・資源などの）不足、欠乏 ◇We must ensure that the animals are given food in times of *scarcity*. 食糧難のときに確実に動物に餌が与えられるようにしなければならない ◇The job was made more difficult because of a *scarcity* of data. その仕事はデータ不足によって一層難しくなった ☞ **scarce** (SCARCE)

land 名

1 land・estate・real estate・farmland
人が所有する地面の一区域
【類語訳】土地、地所、所有地、不動産、農地、耕地

文型&コロケーション
- ▶ **on** land/ an estate/ real estate/ farmland
- ▶ (a) **private** land/ estate/ real estate/ farmland
- ▶ **prime** land/ real estate/ farmland
- ▶ to **own/ buy/ sell** land/ an estate/ real estate/ farmland
- ▶ a **piece of** land/ real estate/ farmland

land [U]（またはフォーマル **lands** [複数で]）（売買可能な資産として人が所有する）土地、地所、所有地 ◇The price of *land* is rising rapidly. 地価が急騰している ◇During the war their *lands* were occupied by the enemy. 戦時中彼らの土地は敵に占領されていた ☞ **land** (COUNTRY 2), **land** (SOIL)

estate [C]（田舎にある個人[一家]が所有する広大な）地所、所有地 ◇The house is set on a 200-acre *estate* near the Black Mountains. その家はブラック山地付近の200エーカーの所有地に位置している

'real estate [U]《特に米》（土地・建物のような）不動産 ◇My father sold *real estate*. 父は不動産を売った ◇He bought a piece of *real estate* several years ago for $50,000. 彼は数年前5万ドルで不動産物件を一件購入した

farmland [U, 複数で] 農地、耕地 ◇The United States loses over 4,000 acres of *farmland* every day. アメリカ合衆国では毎日4千エーカー以上の農地が失われている

language, large

2 ☞ SOIL
land・lot・ground・space・plot
特定の目的に使用される地面の一区画
【類語訳】土地, 用地, 敷地, 場所, 広がり

【文型&コロケーション】
- (an) **open** land/ ground/ space
- (a/ an) **empty/ vacant** land/ lot/ ground/ plot
- **waste/ derelict** land/ ground
- a **burial** ground/ plot

land [U] (または **lands** [複数で]) (特定目的に使用される)土地, 用地, 敷地 ◇The valley provides some rich grazing *land* for farmers. その盆地は農家に肥沃な牧草地を提供している ◇It's an attractive village in the heart of the county's agricultural *lands*. そこは郡の農耕地域の中心にある魅力ある村です ☞ **land** (SOIL)

lot [C] 《米》 (特定目的に使用(予定)の)一区画の)土地, 用地, 敷地 ◇Some kids were playing ball in a vacant *lot*. 何人かの子どもたちが空き地で野球をしていた ◇Building *lots* will cost between $100,000 and $500,000. 建設用地は10万〜50万ドルかかるだろう ◇He backed the car into the parking *lot*. 彼は駐車場に車をバックで入れた ❶《英》では parking lot の代わりに car park が用いられる.

ground [C] (特定目的に使用(予定)の)土地, 用地, 敷地 ◇The kids were playing on waste *ground* near the school. 子どもたちが学校の近くの空き地で遊んでいた ◇They're building a new *football ground* in the town. 《英》その町に新しいサッカー場が建設されている ◇We visited the site of an ancient burial *ground*. 私たちは古代墓地の遺跡を訪ねた

[ノート] **land, lot, ground** の使い分け: land は特に農業用の, 田舎にある広大な開けた土地を表す. lot は特に建設[駐車]用の, 町[都市]にある小区画の土地を指すことが多い. ground[U]はあらゆる種類の開けた土地を表し, a ground[C] は特定の目的[活動]に予定[使用]される土地を指す.

space [U, C] (建物の立っていない広大な)土地, 場所, 広がり ◇The city has fine buildings and plenty of open *space*. その都市には見事な建物群とたくさんの開けた空間がある ◇the *wide open spaces* of the Canadian prairies カナダの大草原の広大な広がり

plot [C] (特定目的に使用(予定)の)小区画の)土地, 用地, 敷地 ◇She bought a small *plot of land* to build a house. 彼女は家を建てるために小区画の土地を購入した ◇He was buried in the family *plot* at the cemetery. 彼はその共同墓地にある一族の墓に埋葬された ◇At the back of the house was a small vegetable *plot*. その家の裏には小さな菜園があった

[ノート] **lot** と **plot** の使い分け: 両語とも建設用地に用いられる. また, plot のみ人の埋葬[野菜の栽培]用の土地に用いられることもある.

language 名

language・vocabulary・terms・wording・terminology・usage
人々が話したり書いたりするときに用いる単語や語句, または話したり書いたりするときの特別なスタイルを表す
【類語訳】言葉, 語彙, 用語, 専門用語, 術語, 言い方, 文言, 語法, 用法

【文型&コロケーション】
- **in**... language/ vocabulary/ terms/ terminology/ usage
- **formal/ informal/ everyday** language/ vocabulary/ terms/ usage
- **simple** language/ vocabulary/ terms
- **sophisticated/ business/ scientific/ technical/ specialized** language/ vocabulary/ terminology
- **to use** ... language/ vocabulary/ terms/ wording/ terminology
- **to be couched in** ... language/ vocabulary/ terms
- A word **enters** the language/ the vocabulary/ ...usage...

language [U] 言葉, 言葉づかい ◇Give your instructions in everyday *language*. 日常語で指示をしてください ◇the *language* of the legal profession 法曹界における専門用語 ◇They were shouting and using *bad/foul language*. 彼らは罵り/汚い言葉を使って叫んでいた

vocabulary [C, U] 語彙, 用語 ◇to have a wide/limited *vocabulary* 幅広い/限られた語彙を持つ ◇your active *vocabulary* (= the words that you use) 自分が使う語彙 ◇your passive *vocabulary* (= the words that you understand but don't use) 自分が使わない語彙 ◇Reading will increase your *vocabulary*. 読書は語彙を増やす ◇When did the word 'bungalow' first enter the *vocabulary*? 「バンガロー」という語が語彙に取り入れられたのはいつですか ◇The word has become part of advertising *vocabulary*. その語は宣伝用語の一部となっている

terms [複数で] 言い方 ◇I'll try to explain in simple *terms*. 簡単な言葉で説明するように努めます ◇She spoke of you in *glowing terms* (= expressing her admiration of you). 彼女はあなたのことをほめそやした ◇We wish to protest **in the strongest possible terms** (= to say that we are very angry). 《ややフォーマル》我々としてはできる限り強い口調で抗議の意思を表した

wording [U, C, ふつう単数で] 文言 ◇It was the standard form of *wording* for a consent letter. それは同意書では標準的な表現形式だった ◇What was the exact *wording* of the message? その伝言は正確にはどのような文言だったのですか

terminology [U, C] 《ややフォーマル》 術語, 専門用語 ◇The article avoids using too much medical *terminology*. その記事は医学用語を使いすぎないようにしている ◇Scientists are constantly developing new *terminologies*. 科学者たちは絶え間なく新しい専門用語を造り続けている ❶ literary/poetic terminology (文学/詩学用語)は, 文学や詩について語る際の用語のことで, literary/poetic language (文学の/詩学の言葉)は, 文学的・詩的な文体で書くのに用いる言葉である.

usage [U, C] 語法, 用法 ◇It's not a word in common *usage*. それはよく用いられる単語ではない ◇The dictionary focuses on the more usual words of the language and avoids rare *usages* of these words. その辞書はその言語のより一般的な語に的を絞り, これらの語のまれな用法には触れていない

large 形 ☞ HUGE

large・big・great・substantial・considerable・extensive・hefty・sizeable・bumper・handsome

↪**large**

サイズ[程度, 数量]が平均をはるかに超えていることを表す
【類語訳】大きい, 広い, 広大な, 広範囲にわたる, 多い, 多額の, 莫大な, 大いなる, かなりの, たっぷりの, 立派な

文型&コロケーション
- a large/ a big/ a great/ a substantial/ a considerable/ an extensive/ a sizeable/ a handsome **amount**
- a large/ big/ great/ substantial/ considerable/ hefty/ sizeable/ handsome **sum/ profit**
- a large/ a big/ a great/ a substantial/ a considerable/ an extensive/ a sizeable **area**
- a large/ big/ great/ substantial/ considerable/ sizeable/ handsome **majority**
- a large/ big/ great/ substantial/ considerable/ hefty/ sizeable **increase**
- a large/ a big/ a great/ a substantial/ a considerable/ an extensive/ a bumper/ a handsome **collection**
- a large/ big/ great/ substantial/ sizeable **crowd/ army**
- a large/ big/ substantial **meal/ breakfast**
- a large/ big/ bumper **crop/ harvest**
- a large/ great/ substantial/ considerable **size**
- a big/ a great/ a substantial/ a considerable/ an extensive **change/ improvement/ gain/ loss/ influence**
- **very** large/ big/ great/ substantial/ considerable/ extensive/ hefty/ sizeable
- **really** large/ big/ substantial/ extensive/ hefty
- **quite/ fairly** large/ big/ great/ substantial/ considerable/ extensive/ hefty/ sizeable
- **rather** large/ big/ great/ substantial/ extensive/ hefty

large (サイズ・程度・数量が)大きい, 広い, 多い ◇Some of the clothes looked very *large*. その何着かの服は非常に大きく見えた ◇I grew up in a *large* family. 私は大家族の中で育った ◇There were some very *large* sums of money involved. かなり膨大な金額の金が絡んでいた ◇Brazil is the world's *largest* producer of coffee. ブラジルは世界最大のコーヒー生産国である ◇Who is the rather *large* (= fat) lady in the hat? 帽子をかぶっているやや大柄な女性は誰ですか ❶large (略語はL)は衣服・食品・家庭用製品などのさまざまなサイズの中の一つを指すこともある. ◆Would you like small, medium or *large*? (S, M, L のうちどれがよろしいですか). 反意 **small, little** (SMALL).

big (サイズ・程度・数量が)大きい, 広い, 多い ◇This house is too *big* for us now. この家は今の私たちには大きすぎる ◇This shirt isn't *big* enough. このシャツはあまり大きくない ◇He was a *big* man — tall and broad-shouldered. 彼は大柄な男だった—背が高く肩幅が広かった ◇There's been a *big* increase in prices. 物価が大きく上昇している ◇It's the world's *biggest* computer company. それは世界最大のコンピュータ会社です ◇He had this *great big* grin on his face. 《インフォーマル》彼は例の大きな満面の笑みを浮かべていた ◇They were earning *big* money. 彼らは大金を稼いでいた 反意 **little, small** (SMALL).

great [ふつう名詞の前で] (サイズ・程度・数量が)大きい, 広い, 多い; 大いなる, 非常な, 大変な ◇A *great* crowd had gathered. 大群衆が集まっていた ◇He must have fallen from a *great* height. 彼は非常に高い所から落ちたに違いない ◇She lived to a *great* age. 彼女は長生きした ◇The concert had been a *great* success. コンサートは大成功を収めていた ◇Her death was a *great* shock to us all. 彼女の死は私たち皆にとって大きな衝撃だった ◇It gives me *great* pleasure to welcome you here today. 本日ここにあなたをお迎えできて非常に光栄に存じます ◇Take *great* care of it. よく面倒を見てあげてね ◇You've been a *great* help. 大変助かりました ❶インフォーマルな言い回しでは, *great* は大きさ・数量を表す形容詞を強めるために用いられることがある. ◆There was a *great big* pile of books on the table. (テーブルの上に非常に大きな本の山があった).

ノート **large, big, great** の使い分け: これらの形容詞は以下の名詞と共に用いられることが多い. ◆a *big* man/house/car/boy/dog/smile/problem/surprise/question/difference (大きな男/家/車/男の子/犬/笑い/問題/驚き/疑問/違い). ◆(a) *large* numbers/part/area/room/company/eyes/family/volume/population/problem (多数/大部分/広域/広い部屋/大会社/大きな目/大家族/大部/多くの人口/大問題). ◆(a) *great* success/majority/interest/importance/difficulty/problem/pleasure/beauty/surprise (大成功/大多数/大きな関心/重大性/大変な困難/大問題/大きな喜び/大きな美しさ/大きな驚き).

large は **big** よりもフォーマルで, 文章がインフォーマルな文体でないならば, 書き言葉ではふつう **large** を用いるべきである. また, **large** は fat の使用を避けるため以外は, 人つうに用いられない. **great** は大きさだけでなく質を表すことが多い. しかしながら, ふつう物・人の物理的な大きさを表すことはない. ×a *great* house/boy/dog. a great man は「背の高い[大柄な]男性」ではなく, 感心に値する「素晴らしい[善良で分別のある]男性」を意味する. 以下の句にも注意. ◆a *large* amount of sth (大量[多量]の物). ◆a *large* number of sth (多数の物). ◆a *large* quantity of sth (大量[多量]の物). ◆a *great* deal of sth (大量[多量]の物). ◆in *great* detail (極めて詳細に). ◆a person of *great* age (長寿者).

substantial 《ややフォーマル》(数量[大きさ, 重要性]が)相当な, かなりの, たっぷりの; 立派な, 重大な ◇There were *substantial* sums of money involved. 相当な額の金が絡んでいた ◇We were able to see a *substantial* improvement. 私たちはかなりの改善を見ることができた ◇He ate a *substantial* breakfast. 彼は朝食をたっぷりとった ◇Their share of the software market is *substantial*. ソフトウェア市場におけるその会社の占有率は相当なものである

considerable 《ややフォーマル》(数量・程度・重要性が)相当な, かなりの, 重大な ◇The project wasted a *considerable* amount of time and money. その事業はかなりの時間と金を無駄にした ◇Damage to the building was *considerable*. その建物の損害は相当なものだった ◇*Considerable* progress has been made in finding a cure for the disease. その病気の治療法を発見する上でかなりの進歩がもたらされている ◇Caring for elderly relatives requires *considerable* moral courage. 高齢の身内の介護には, 道徳上の勇気がかなり必要とされる

ノート **substantial** と **considerable** の使い分け: **considerable** は食事・建物など物質については用いない. **substantial** は怒り・関心・勇気・効率など感情[個性]については用いない.

extensive 広い, 広大な, 広範囲にわたる; (数量が)大きい, 広い, 多い ◇The house has *extensive* grounds. その家の敷地は広大だ ◇The fire caused *extensive* damage. その火事は広範囲にわたる被害をもたらした ◇*Extensive* repair work is being carried out. 大がかりな修復作業が行われています ◇They have an *extensive* range of wines. そこはワインを幅広くそろえている

hefty (金額が通常[予想]より)高[多]額の, 莫大な ◇They sold it easily and made a *hefty* profit. 彼らはそれをどんどん売りさばき, 莫大な利益を上げた ◇Interest rates have gone up to a *hefty* 12%. 利率は12%の高水準まで上昇している

sizeable (または **sizable**) 《ややフォーマル》相当な[かなりの]大きさ[広さ, 多さ]の ◇The town has a *sizeable* Sikh population. その町には相当な数のシーク教徒が住んでいる ◇Income from tourism accounts for a *sizeable* proportion of the area's total income. 観光収入がその地域の総収入のかなりの比率を占める

bumper [名詞の前で]《ほめて》並外れて大きい, 特大の; 並外れて大量の, 大豊作《漁》の ◇Don't miss next month's *bumper* Christmas issue (= of a magazine, etc.). 来月のクリスマス特大号をお見逃しなく ◇Farmers have been celebrating *bumper* crops this year. 農家の人たちは今年の大豊作を祝っている

handsome [名詞の前で]《ほめて》(数量・金額が)相当な, かなりの, 高[多]額の ◇They sold the house two years later at a *handsome* profit. 彼らは2年後にその家を売って, 相当な利益を得た ◇I enjoyed the job, and was paid a *handsome* salary too. 私は仕事を楽しみ, 給料もかなりもらっていた

▶**handsomely** 副 ◇to be paid/rewarded *handsomely* 手厚い給料をもらう/報酬を受ける

last 限定詞 形

1 last・final・closing・later・eventual・ultimate・latter

物事がすべての後で生じたり, 人がすべての人々の後から来たりすることを表す

【類語訳】最後の, 最終の, 最後に残った, 最終的な, 結果的な, 終わりの, 結びの, 後期の, 後半の, 晩年の

[文型&コロケーション]
▶the last/ final/ closing/ later/ ultimate/ latter **stage/ phase**
▶the last/ final/ later/ eventual/ ultimate **aim/ goal/ outcome**
▶eventual/ ultimate **success/ failure/ victory/ defeat**
▶sb/ sth's last/ final/ closing/ later/ latter **years**
▶sb's last/ final/ closing **speech/ address**
▶the last/ final/ closing **remark/ chapter/ minutes**

last 限定詞 形 (同類の物事・人々の中で)最後の, 最終の, ;(物事・人が)最後に残った ◇We caught the *last* bus home. 私たちは帰りの最終バスに間に合った ◇It's the *last* house on the left. それが左手一番奥の家です ◇She was *last* to arrive. 彼女は最後に到着した ◇I wouldn't marry you if you were the *last* person on earth! あなたが地球上に残った最後の人でも, 私はあなたとは結婚しません ◇He knew this was his *last* **hope** of winning. 彼には勝ちが望めるのはこれが最後だとわかっていた 反意 **first** (FIRST)

▶**lastly** 副 ◇*Lastly*, I'd like to ask you about your plans. 最後に, あなたの計画についてお尋ねします
▶**at last** フレーズ ◇We're home *at last*! やれやれ, やっと帰ってきた ◇*At long last* the cheque arrived. やっとのことで小切手が届いた

final [名詞の前で] (一連の出来事[行動, 発言]の中で)最後の, 最終の, ;(特定の過程の中で)最終[結果]的な ◇His *final* act as president was to pardon his predecessor. 大統領としての彼の最後の行為は前任者に恩赦を与えることであった ◇The referee blew the *final* whistle. 審判は試合終了のホイッスルを吹いた ◇I'd like to return to the *final* point you made. あなたが言われた最後の論点に立ち戻りたいのですが ◇No one could have predicted the *final* outcome. 誰にも最終結果を予測できなかっただろう 反意 **initial** (FIRST)

▶**finally** 副 ◇*Finally*, stir in the fruit and walnuts. 最後に, 果物とクルミを入れてよくかき混ぜてください ◇The performance *finally* started half an hour late. 30分遅れてようやく公演が始まった

closing 形 [名詞の前で] (一つの話[活動, 期間]の中で)終わり[結び]の; 閉会[店]の ◇The *closing* ceremony proved to be a spectacular and memorable affair. その閉会式は壮観で記憶に残る出来事となった 反意 **opening** (FIRST)

later 形 (一定期間の中で)後[末]期の, 晩年の ◇the *later* part of the seventeenth century 17世紀末期 ◇She found happiness in her *later* years. 彼女は晩年に幸せを見つけた 反意 **earlier**

▶**later** 副 ◇His father died *later* that year. 彼の父はその年の暮れに亡くなった ◇We're going to Rome *later* in the year. 私たちは年末にローマに出かける予定です

eventual 形 [名詞の前で] (一つの期間[過程]の中で)最終[結果]的な ◇The school may face *eventual* closure. その学校は結果的に閉鎖になるかもしれない ◇the *eventual* winner of the tournament トーナメントの最終的な勝者

▶**eventually** 副 ◇She hopes *eventually* to attend medical school and become a doctor. 彼女は最終的に医学部に通って医者になることを希望している ◇I'll get round to mending it *eventually*. 最後にはその修理に取りかかるよ

ultimate 形 [名詞の前で] (計画[予定]されているなかで)最終的な ◇our *ultimate* goal/aim/objective/target 我々の最終目標 ◇The *ultimate* decision lies with the parents. 最終決定をするのは両親である ◇We will accept *ultimate* responsibility for whatever happens. 何が起ころうとも最終的な責任は我々が負うつもりです

▶**ultimately** 副 ◇The campaign was *ultimately* successful. そのキャンペーンは最終的にうまくいった ◇*Ultimately*, you'll have to make the decision yourself. 最終的には, 君が自分で決断を下さなければならないだろう

latter 形 (一定期間の中で)後半の, 晩年の ◇The *latter* half of the twentieth century saw huge growth in air travel. 20世紀後半は飛行機の旅行に目覚しい発展が見られた

▶**latterly** 副 ◇Her health declined rapidly and *latterly* she never left the house. 《フォーマル》彼女の健康は急激に衰え, 晩年は家からまったく出なかった

2 last・past・previous・preceding

物事がほんの少し前や, 特定の時間[出来事, 対象]の前に起こった[存在した]ことを表す

【類語訳】この前の, 先の, 昨…, 最近の, 最新の, 過ぎ去ったばかりの, 終わったばかりの

[文型&コロケーション]
▶the last/ past/ previous/ preceding **few days/ week/ month/ year/ decade/ century**
▶the last/ past/ previous **weekend/ season/ hundred years**
▶the last/ past **hour**

↳ last　　　　　　　　　　　　　late, laugh

▶ the previous/ preceding **day**
▶ last/ the previous **night/ Friday/ July/ summer**
▶ the last/ previous/ preceding **paragraph/ section**
▶ the last/ previous **page/ chapter/ time/ visit/ meeting/ war**
▶ sb's last/ previous **album/ appearance**
▶ the previous/ preceding **discussion/ argument/ analysis/ example**

last 限定詞　この[すぐ]前の，先の，先[昨]…，最近の，最新の　◇He got home late *last* night. 彼は昨夜遅くに帰宅した　◇*Last* summer we went to Greece for a month. 昨夏私たちは1か月間ギリシャに行った　◇The critics all hated her *last* book. 批評家たちは皆彼女の最新本をひどく嫌った　◇This *last* point, that Hamish has mentioned, is crucial. ハミッシュが挙げたこの最後の点は非常に重要です　反意 **first** (FIRST), **next** (NEXT)

past 形　[名詞の前で]（一定期間が）過ぎ去ったばかりの，この［ここ]…；終わったばかりの　◇I haven't seen much of her in the *past* few weeks. 私はここ数週間彼女をあまり見かけていない　◇**next** (NEXT)

ノート **last** と **past** の使い分け：past は過ぎ去ったばかりの一定期間，特に長い［おおよその]期間についてのみ用いることができる．◆These *past* months have been terribly stressful for everyone.（ここ何か月間かは皆にとってひどくストレスの多い期間だった）．past は形容詞であるが，the または these などの限定詞と共に用いなければならず，単独での使用は不可．（先週は非常に忙しかった）．◆The *past* week has been very busy.（ここ1週間は非常に忙しかった）．past は特定の日［時点]・物事については用いられない．✗He got home late *past* night. ✗The critics hated her *past* book.

previous ［名詞の前で]（言及している時・物事より）直前の，前の，先の　◇He went jogging on Friday, despite the doctor's warnings the *previous* day (= the day before the time mentioned). 前日に医者から警告を受けたにもかかわらず，彼は金曜日にジョギングに出かけた　◇We dealt with this in the *previous* chapter. 私たちは前章でこれを取り上げた　反意 **the following** (NEXT)

preceding ［名詞の前で]（フォーマル）（言及している時・物事より）直前の，前の，先の　◇This policy was pursued less vigorously in the 1880s than in the *preceding* decade (= the 1870s). この政策は1880年代になると，その前の70年代ほど強力には推進されなかった　◇The reasoning in the *preceding* paragraph applies equally to a number of other cases. 前段落の論証は数ある他の場合にも同様に当てはまる　反意 **the following** (NEXT)

late 形

late・slow・overdue・belated
人や物事が予定[通常]の時間の後に到着する[起こる，行われる]ことを表す
【類語訳】遅れた，遅刻した，遅延した，遅い時間の，遅くなった，遅まきの，期限を過ぎた，延び延びになった

文型&コロケーション
▶ late/ overdue **for** sth
▶ late/ slow **in doing** sth
▶ late/ overdue **payment**
▶ overdue/ belated **recognition**

▶ two weeks/ a year late/ overdue
▶ very/ extremely/ rather/ slightly late/ slow/ belated

late ［名詞の前はまれ]　遅れた，遅刻[遅延]した，遅い時間（まで）の，遅くなった，遅まきの　◇I'm sorry I'm *late*. 遅れてごめん　◇She's *late* for work every day. 彼女は毎日仕事に遅れて来る　◇My flight was an hour *late*. 私の乗る便は1時間遅れだった　◇Some children are very *late* developers. 子どもたちの中には発育が非常に遅れている子もいる　◇Because of the cold weather the crops are *later* this year. 今年は寒波のせいで穀物が遅れている　反意 **early, on time, punctual**
▶**late** 副　◇Can I stay up *late* tonight? 今夜は遅くまでかしててもいいかな　◇The big stores are open *later* on Thursdays. 毎週木曜日は大型店舗はさらに遅くまで営業している　◇She married *late*. 彼女は晩婚だった　◇The birthday card arrived three days *late*. 誕生日カードが3日遅れで届いた

slow …するのが遅い[時間のかかる]；なかなか…しない　◇She wasn't *slow to* realize what was going on. 彼女は何が起きているのかすぐに気づいた　◇His poetry was *slow* in achieving recognition. 彼の詩は認められるのに時間がかかった　◇They were very *slow* paying me. 彼らは私になかなか支払いをしてくれなかった　反意 **quick** (QUICK), ☞ **slow** (SLOW)

overdue （支払い・実行・返却の)期限を過ぎた，延滞の；遅れた，遅延した，延び延びになった　◇2% interest will be charged on *overdue* payments. 支払い延滞分には2%の利子がかかります　◇My library books were *overdue*. 私が図書館から借りている本は返却期限を過ぎていた　◇Her baby is two weeks *overdue*. 彼女の出産は予定より2週間遅れている　◇This car is *overdue* for a service (= has needed a service for a long time). この車の保守点検の期限は切れている　◇A book like this is **long overdue**. この種の本の出版はかなり延び延びになる

belated ［書き言葉]（行動・返答が)遅れた，遅くなった，遅まきの　◇Many apologies for sending you such a *belated* birthday present. 誕生日プレゼントをお送りするのがこんなに遅くなり大変申し訳ありません　◇The government has been criticized for its *belated* response to the report. 政府はその報告書に対する返答が遅れたことで批判されている
▶ **belatedly** 副　◇He apologized *belatedly*. 彼は遅まきながら謝罪した

laugh 動

laugh・giggle・chuckle・crack up・snigger・snicker・roar・be/have sb in stitches・titter
声や表情で面白いと思っていることを表す
【類語訳】笑う，くすくすと笑う，ほくそえむ，独り笑いをする，にやにや笑う，大笑いする，爆笑させる，忍び笑いをする

文型&コロケーション
▶ to laugh/ giggle/ chuckle/ snigger/ snicker/ roar/ titter **at** sth
▶ to laugh/ giggle/ chuckle/ snigger/ snicker/ titter **about/ over** sth
▶ to laugh/ giggle/ chuckle/ snigger/ snicker/ roar **with pleasure/ amusement,** etc.
▶ to **make sb** laugh/ giggle/ chuckle/ crack up/ snigger/ snicker/ roar/ titter

- to giggle/ chuckle **to yourself**
- to giggle/ chuckle **softly/ quietly**
- to giggle/ titter **nervously**

laugh [自] (うれしくて[面白くて]声を立てて)笑う ◇It was so funny I *laughed out loud*. それがとてもおかしくて私は声を上げて大笑いした ◇You never *laugh* at my jokes! 私の冗談には決して笑わないのね ◇He *burst out laughing* (= suddenly started laughing). 彼は突然ふき出した
▶ **laugh** [名] [C] ◇to give a short/harsh/bitter/nervous *laugh* 短く笑う/きつい笑い方をする/苦笑する/落ち着きなく笑う ◇His first joke got the biggest *laugh* of the night. 彼の最初のジョークはその晩で一番大きな笑いを取った
▶ **laughter** [名] [U] ◇He threw back his head and *roared with laughter*. 彼は頭をのけぞらせて大笑いした
giggle [自] (面白くて[恥ずかしくて、はにかんで])くすくす[キャッキャッ、フフフ、イヒヒ]と笑う ◇The girls *giggled* at the joke. 女の子たちはその冗談にキャッキャッと笑った ◇She *giggled* with delight. 彼女はうれしくてキャッキャッと笑った
▶ **giggle** [名] [C] ◇She gave a nervous *giggle*. 彼女は不安げに笑った
chuckle [自] 《特に書き言葉》(黙って)ほくそえむ, 独り[含み]笑いをする ◇George *chuckled* at the memory. ジョージは思い出し笑いをした
▶ **chuckle** [名] [C] ◇She gave a *chuckle* of delight. 彼女はうれしくてほくそえんだ
,crack 'up [句動詞] 《インフォーマル》 大笑い[爆笑]し出す ◇He walked in and everyone just *cracked up*. 彼が入ってきたとたんに皆大笑いした
snigger [自] 《特に英, ややインフォーマル》(下品な事[人の間違い]などに対して)にやにや[にたにた]笑う ◇What are you *sniggering* at? 何にやにやしてるの
snicker [自] 《米, ややインフォーマル》(下品な事[人の間違い]などに対して)にやにや[にたにた]笑う ◇Although his friends *snickered*, they were still impressed. 彼の友人たちはにたにた笑っていたが, それでも感動はしていた
roar [自] 《ややインフォーマル》大笑い[爆笑]する ◇It made them *roar with laughter*. それに対して彼らは爆笑した ◇He looked so funny, we all *roared*. 彼は見た目がとてもおかしくて, 私たちは皆大笑いした ❶ *roar* は大いに笑うことについて用いられることが多い. *roar with laughter* の句で用いられるよりも, 単独で用いられるほうがインフォーマルである.
▶ **roar** [名] [C] ◇The crowd burst into *roars of laughter*. 群衆は突然大笑いし出した
be/have sb in 'stitches [句動] 《ややインフォーマル》大笑い[爆笑]する;(人を)大笑い[爆笑]させる ◇We were all *in stitches* from the beginning to the end of the play. 私たちは皆その芝居の初めから終わりまで大笑いしていた ◇The play *had us in stitches*. 私たちはその芝居に大笑いだった
titter [自] (恥ずかしくて[はにかんで])忍び笑いをする ◇There was an embarrassing pause on stage and the audience began to *titter*. 舞台上で気まずい間があいて, 観客は忍び笑いをし始めた

laugh at sb/sth [句動詞]

laugh at sb/sth・mock・tease・ridicule・sneer・make fun of sb/sth・poke fun at sb/sth
人や物事について冗談を言って取るに足らないものとしたり, ちゃかしたりする
【類語訳】笑う, からかう, ばかにする, あざ笑う, 揶揄する

[文型&コロケーション]
- to laugh/ mock/ sneer/ poke fun **at** sb/ sth
- to laugh at/ mock/ tease/ ridicule/ sneer at sb/ sth **for** sth
- to laugh at/ poke fun at **yourself**
- to mock/ tease/ ridicule sb/ sth **mercilessly**
- to mock/ tease sb/ sth **gently/ a little**

'**laugh at sb/sth** [句動詞] (ばかにして[ちゃかして])人・物事を笑う ◇Everybody *laughs at* my accent. 皆私の訛りを笑うんだ ◇She is not afraid to *laugh at herself* (= not be too serious about herself). 彼女は自分のことを笑い飛ばすことができる ❶ *laugh at* sb/sth は自分を笑っていると人を責める[疑う]場合, または人々が自分を笑うだろうと予想する場合に用いられることが多い. ◆Are you *laughing at me*? (私のことを笑っているのか). ◆I'm not wearing that hat; everyone will *laugh at me*! (あの帽子はかぶらないよ, 皆に笑われちゃうね).
mock [他, 自] 《特に書き言葉》(言動をまねて意地悪く人・物事を)からかう, ばかにする ◇He's always *mocking* my French accent. 彼ったら, 私のフランス訛りをまねてからかってばかりいるの ◇The other children *mocked* her, laughing behind their hands. 他の子どもたちは彼女をばかにしては陰で笑っていた ◇You can *mock*, but at least I'm willing to have a try! ばかにしてもいいけど, 一応挑戦してみようとは思うんだ ☞ **mockery** (CONTEMPT)
tease [自, 他] (打ち解ける[悩ませる, 恥ずかしがらせる]ために人を)からかう ◇Don't get upset — I was only *teasing*. 怒るなって—からかってただけだよ ◇I used to get *teased about* my name. 私はよく名前のことでからかわれたものだ
ridicule [他] 《ややフォーマル, 特に書き言葉》(意地悪く人・物事を)あざ笑う, ばかにする ◇At first, his theory was *ridiculed* and dismissed. 最初は彼の理論は嘲笑されて退けられた ◇She suspected him of trying to *ridicule* her. 彼女は彼が自分をばかにしようとしていると疑った ☞ **ridicule** (CONTEMPT)
sneer [自] 《特に書き言葉》(顔の表情[話し方]で人を)あざ[せせら]笑う ◇He *sneered* at people who liked pop music. 彼はポピュラー音楽好きの人たちをせせら笑った ◇'You? A writer?' she *sneered*. 「あなたが, 作家なの」と彼女はあざけるような調子で言った ❶ 名詞の a *sneer* は嫌な感じのほほ笑み・表情・発言を指す.
make 'fun of sb/sth [句動] (意地悪く人・物事を)からかう, ばかにする ◇It's cruel to *make fun of* people who stammer. 吃音(きつおん)の人をからかうのは残酷だ
poke 'fun at sb/sth [句動] (やんわりと打ち解けて人・物事を)からかう, 揶揄する ◇Her novels *poke fun at* the upper class. 彼女の小説は上流社会を揶揄している ❶ *poke fun at* sb/sth は個人ではなく, 人の集団・組織・慣習について冗談を言うことを指す.

law [名]

law・legislation・constitution・code・charter
国家を統治したり, 組織を管理したりする制度や一連の規則[原則]
【類語訳】法律, 法典, 憲法, 規約, 決まり, 憲章

[文型&コロケーション]
- legislation/ a charter **on** sth

- ▶ **under/ in** the legislation/ constitution/ code/ charter
- ▶ (a) **draft** legislation/ constitution/ code/ charter
- ▶ (the) **civil/ criminal** law/ legislation/ code
- ▶ (the) **state/ federal** law/ legislation/ constitution
- ▶ to **draw up/ draft/ adopt/ approve/ amend** legislation/ a constitution/ a code/ a charter
- ▶ to **break** the law/ a code
- ▶ to **contravene** legislation/ a constitution/ a code
- ▶ to **be enshrined in** law/ legislation/ the constitution/ a charter
- ▶ the law/ legislation/ the constitution **forbids** sth
- ▶ legislation/ the constitution/ a charter **guarantees** sth

law (または **the law**) [U] (国家・社会の)法律；(特定分野の)法律, …法 ◇In Sweden it is **against the law** to hit a child. スウェーデンでは子どもをたたくことは法律違反である ◇Defence attorneys can use any means **within the law** to get their client off. 弁護人たちは依頼人を無罪にするために法律の範囲内であらゆる手段を用いることができる ◇British schools are now required **by law** to publish their exam results. 現在英国の学校では試験結果を公表するよう法律で義務づけられている ◇The reforms have recently **become law**. その改革は最近法令化された ◇He specializes in international law. 彼は国際法を専攻している ☞ **law** (RULE 名)

legislation [U] (議会が可決した)法律 ◇The civil rights campaign resulted in **legislation against** segregation. 公民権運動が人種差別を取り締まる法律をもたらした ◇There were calls for **legislation to** ban smoking in public places. 公共の場での喫煙を禁止する法律を求める声が上がった ◇The government is trying to push through a controversial **piece of legislation**. 政府は異論の多い法律を押し通そうとしている ☞ **legislate** (RULE 動) 2)

constitution [C] (国家・組織の)憲法, 規約 ◇These rights are established in the federal *constitution*. これらの権利は合衆国憲法で規定されている ◇A two-thirds majority is needed to amend the club's *constitution*. そのクラブの規約を改正するには3分の2の大多数が必要である

code [C] (組織・国家の)決まり, 規約, 法典, 法規 ◇The company has drawn up a new disciplinary *code*. 会社は新しい懲戒規約を策定した ◇The law includes amendments to the **penal code**. その法律には刑法の改正条項が含まれている

charter [C] (特定の人の集団の権利[組織の原理と目的]を明記した)憲章 ◇He fought for a social *charter* of workers' rights. 彼は労働者の権利の社会憲章を求めて闘った ◇Minority rights are protected by the UN *charter*. 少数民族の権利は国連憲章で保護されている

lawyer 名

lawyer・attorney・solicitor・counsel・barrister・the Bar・advocate
人に法的助言を行ったり、法廷で人の代理人を務めたりする資格を有する人
【類語訳】弁護士, 弁護団, 弁護士業

- ▶ a lawyer/ an attorney/ a solicitor/ counsel/ a barrister/ an advocate **for** sb
- ▶ a **good/ practising** lawyer/ attorney/ solicitor/ barrister/ advocate
- ▶ (an) **experienced** lawyer/ attorney/ solicitor/ counsel/ barrister/ advocate
- ▶ the **chief** lawyer/ attorney/ counsel/ advocate
- ▶ a **defence** lawyer/ attorney/ solicitor/ counsel/ barrister/ advocate
- ▶ (a) **prosecuting/ prosecution** lawyer/ attorney/ solicitor/ counsel/ barrister
- ▶ to **appoint/ hire/ instruct/ consult** a lawyer/ an attorney/ a solicitor/ counsel/ a barrister
- ▶ a lawyer/ an attorney/ a solicitor/ counsel/ a barrister/ an advocate **represents** sb
- ▶ a lawyer/ an attorney/ a solicitor/ an advocate **acts for** sb
- ▶ a lawyer/ an attorney/ a solicitor/ counsel **advises** sb
- ▶ a lawyer/ an attorney/ a solicitor/ counsel **argues/ claims/ submits** sth
- ▶ a lawyer/ an attorney/ a solicitor/ counsel/ a barrister **cross-examines** sb

lawyer [C] (法的助言を行う[法廷で代理人を務める, 法律文書を作成する])弁護士 ◇*Lawyers* for the families said they were pleased with the decision. それらの家族の弁護士たちは家族は判決に満足していると述べた ◇You'll be hearing from my *lawyer*. 私の弁護士から話を聞いてください ◇You would be wise to consult a *lawyer*. 弁護士に相談されるのが賢明でしょう

attorney [C] (《特に米》)(法廷で代理人を務める)弁護士 ◇Acting on the advice of his *attorney*, he remained silent. 弁護士の助言に従って, 彼は黙秘を続けた

solicitor [C] (《英》)土地[建物]の売却などの法律文書を作成する[法的助言を行う, 時に法廷で代理人を務める])事務弁護士 ◇Her first step was to contact a *solicitor* for advice. 彼女の最初の行動は事務弁護士に連絡を取って助言を求めることだった

counsel [U] (《法律》)(法廷で代理人を務める)弁護士, 弁護団 ◇The court then heard *counsel* for the dead woman's father. 裁判官らは死亡した女性の父親の弁護団の話を聞いた ◇Williams is the **leading counsel** for the victims' groups (= the main lawyer in the group representing them). 《英》ウィリアムズは被害者団体の主任弁護士である ◇the **lead counsel** 《米》主任弁護士

barrister [C] (イングランド・ウェールズで上級裁判所で代理人を務める)法廷弁護士 ◇The solicitor must instruct a *barrister* to appear before the court. 事務弁護士は法廷弁護士に出廷するよう指示を与えなければならない

the Bar [単数で] (法廷)弁護士業 ◇She studied law and **was called to the Bar** (= was allowed to work as a qualified barrister) in 2004. 彼女は法律を勉強し, 2004年に法廷弁護士になった ◇The changes were met with opposition from **members of the Bar**. その改正は弁護士たちからの反対に遭った ❶《英》では the Bar は barrister (法廷弁護士)のみを指す. 《米》ではあらゆる種類の弁護士に用いられる

advocate [C] (法廷で代理人を務める)弁護士；(スコットランドで上級裁判所で代理人を務める)法廷弁護士 ◇Those charged should be represented by trained, qualified legal *advocates*. 被告人は訓練を受け資格を有する弁護士に代理を務めてもらうべきである

ノート lawyer, attorney, solicitor, counsel, barrister, advocate の使い分け：lawyer は法的助言を行う

[法律文書を作成する，法廷で代理人を務める]資格を有する人を表す一般的な語。《米》では lawyer の代りに attorney が用いられる。イングランド・ウェールズでは上級裁判所で代理人を務める資格を有する弁護士に barrister と呼ばれ，スコットランドでは advocate と呼ばれる。counsel は法廷で代理人を務める弁護士を表す正式な法律用語。solicitor は《英》の用語で，法的助言を行う[法律文書を作成する，時に(特に下級)裁判所で代理人を務める]権利を有する弁護士を表す。

lead 動

lead・head・preside・chair・spearhead・captain
責任ある，または指導的立場にあることを表す
【類語訳】率いる，先導する，先頭に立つ，(…の)長を務める，議長を務める，主宰する，陣頭に立つ，先陣を切る

文型&コロケーション
- to lead/ head/ captain a **team**
- to lead/ captain a (sports) **side**
- to lead/ head a (political) **party/ the government**
- to lead/ head/ preside over/ chair a/ an **commission/ committee/ enquiry**
- to lead/ preside over/ chair a **meeting/ debate**
- to lead/ spearhead a **campaign/ fight**
- to head/ preside over a (legal) **case**
- to **jointly** lead/ head/ chair sth

lead [他，自] 率いる，先導する，(…の)長を務める ◇Who will *lead* the party into the next election? 誰がその党を率いて次の選挙に突入するのですか ◇He *led* the first *expedition* to the North Pole. 彼が初めて北極探検を率いた ◇Top management should be seen to *lead by example* (= to set a good example for others to copy). 経営陣のトップが率先して範を垂れるのが当然だ ☞ **leadership** (GOVERNMENT 2)

head [他] 率いる，先頭に立つ ◇She has been appointed to *head* the research team. 彼女は研究チームのリーダーに指名されている ◇The committee will be jointly *headed* by two men. 委員会は二人の男性が連携して率いることになる

ノート lead と head の使い分け：これら二つの動詞の使い方はとてもよく似ている。しかし，何かを head する人は，その公職におけるリーダーである。例えば，政府を率いるのは総理大臣であり，審理の指揮を執るのは判事というように，head の主語は個人である。一方，何かを lead する人は，その公職におけるリーダーである場合もあるが，lead はリーダーとしての質を強調するので，重要な計画の立案や決定をしたり，他の人たちが従うような人である。lead の主語は，組織や国といった人々の集団の場合もありうる。

preside [自]《フォーマル》議長[座長，司会]を務める，主宰する ◇A tribunal, *presided over* by Lord Haskin, was established to investigate the allegations. それらの申し立てを調査する裁判機関がハスキン卿を座長にして設置された ◇The Archbishop *presided at* a special mass in the city's cathedral. 大司教がその市の大聖堂で特別ミサを執り行った

chair [他] 議長[司会]を務める ◇Who's *chairing* the meeting? 誰がその会議の議長になっているのですか ◇Lord Stansfield will *chair* the committee. スタンス

フィールド卿がその委員会の議長を務めることになっている

spearhead [他]《特にジャーナリズム》先頭[陣頭]に立つ，先陣を切る ◇He is *spearheading* a campaign for a new stadium in the town. 彼はその町の新しいスタジアム建設運動の陣頭指揮を執っている ◇Gardner *spearheaded* Britain's challenge at this year's World Championships. ガードナーは今年の世界選手権で英国の挑戦の先頭に立った

captain [他] 主将[船長]を務める ◇He played in the West Indies team *captained* by Clive Lloyd. 彼はクライヴ・ロイドが主将を務める西インド諸島チームでプレーをした ◇He told us about the ship he had *captained* during the war. 彼は戦時中に自分が船長をしていた船について私たちに語ってくれた

leader 名

1 ☞ MANAGER

leader・chairman・head・president・chief executive・chief・managing director・boss・governor・chair
会社[組織，委員会など]を管理している人を表す
【類語訳】指導者，統率者，長，首長，会長，社長，総長，部長，最高経営責任者，委員長，議長

文型&コロケーション
- a **deputy** leader/ chairman/ head/ president/ chief executive/ chief/ managing director/ boss/ governor/ chair
- a **vice** chairman/ president/ chair
- an **acting** chairman/ head/ president/ chief executive/ governor/ chair
- the **honorary** chairman/ president/ chair
- a **joint** leader/ head/ president/ managing director
- a **party** leader/ chairman/ president/ chief/ boss/ chair
- a **union** leader/ chairman/ president/ chief/ boss
- a **company/ club** chairman/ president/ chief executive/ chief/ managing director/ boss
- a **council** leader/ chairman/ chief/ boss/ chair
- an **industry** leader/ chairman/ chief/ boss
- to be **appointed (as)** leader/ chairman/ head/ president/ chief executive/ chief/ managing director/ governor/ chair
- to be **elected (as)** leader/ chairman/ head/ president/ chair
- to **nominate sb as** leader/ chairman/ president
- to **take over as** leader/ chairman/ head/ president/ chief executive/ managing director/ chair
- to **serve as** chairman/ head/ president/ governor/ chair
- to **resign/ stand down/ step down as** leader/ chairman/ head/ president/ chief executive/ chief/ managing director/ governor/ chair

leader [C] (国家・組織の)指導[統率，指揮]者，首長 ◇He resigned as *leader* of the Democratic Party. 彼は民主党の党首を辞任した ◇Discuss any problems with your *team leader*. どんな問題でもチームリーダーと話し合ってください ◇A *strong leader* is one who is not afraid of listening to people. 強い指導者とは人々の話を聞くのを恐れない人のことである ◇She's a *born leader* (= she has the skills needed to be a good leader). 彼女には指導者の素質がある ◇He was not a *natural leader*. 彼は根っからの指導者ではなかった ☞ **leadership** (GOVERNMENT 2)

chairman [C] (委員会・会社の)委員長, 社長；(会議の)議長 ◇The *chairman* of the company presented the annual report. その会社の社長は年次報告書を提出した ◇Sir Herbert took it upon himself to *act as chairman*. ハーバート卿は議長を務めることを引き受けた ❶*chairman* はほとんど常に男性である。この地位にある女性は *chairwoman* と呼ばれるが, あまり頻繁には用いられない。*chair* (下記参照)は男性にも女性にも用いるが, ふつう会社の社長ではなく委員会の委員長[会議の議長]を指す。◆the committee/council/party *chair* (委員長／諮問委員長／党委員長) ×the company/industry/union/club *chair*.

head [C] (人の集団・組織の)長 ◇The Bishop is *head* of the Church in Kenya. その主教はケニアの英国国教会の長である ◇She resigned as *head of department*. 彼女は学科長を辞任した ◇It is a parliamentary democracy with a president as *head of state*. それは大統領を国家の元首とする議会民主主義である ☞ *headship* (MANAGEMENT)

president (または **President**) [C] (複数の組織[企業, クラブ, 大学]を管理する)会長, 部長, 総長 ◇She was elected *president* of the student's union. 彼女は学生自治会の会長に選ばれた ◇He was appointed as vice *president* of business development the following year. 翌年彼は営業開発の副部長に任命された ❷商業団体における長や上級管理者としての *president* の肩書は,《英》よりも《米》においてより頻繁に用いられる。

chief e'xecutive [C] (会社・組織の)最高(経営)責任者 ◇The *chief executive* addressed the board. 最高責任者は理事会で演説した

chief [C] (会社・組織の)長 ◇We spoke to a former CIA *chief* of European operations. 我々は中央情報局の元ヨーロッパ作戦部長と話した ◇Virgin *chief*, Richard Branson, may take legal action against the newspaper. ヴァージン・グループの会長であるリチャード・ブランソンはその新聞社に対して訴訟を起こすかもしれない ❶*chief* は特に《米》で, 公職名の肩書として用いられることがある。◆the police/fire *chief* (《特に米》警察署長／消防署長) ◆the *chief* of staff (参謀長). 警察・保安局など政府省庁を始めとする公共団体の長の役職名として一般的である。《英》ではジャーナリズムにおいて, ややインフォーマルに用いられることが多い。◆Health *chiefs* say waiting times are down. (《英, ややインフォーマル, ジャーナリズム》)保健局の長たちは待ち時間は減っていると述べている。

managing di'rector [C] 《英》(事業の日常的運営と会社(の部署)を管理する)最高(経営)責任者 ◇The firm's *managing director* is now under investigation for corruption. その会社の最高経営責任者は現在, 汚職で取調べを受けている ☞ **manager, director** (MANAGER)

ノート **chairman, president, chief executive, managing director** の使い分け：会社の *chairman* はふつう役員の中で最も上級の役員を指す。*president* は複数の会社を統括する最も上位の地位に与えられる肩書きである。*chief executive* や *managing director* はいかに企業[企業の部門]を運営するかに関する決定を任された人である。*chief executive* や *managing director* は *chairman* であることも多い。

boss [C] (《インフォーマル, ジャーナリズム》) (会社・組織の)長 ◇There's been criticism of bonuses paid to top oil company *bosses*. 一流の石油会社の社長たちに支払われるボーナスに対して批判が起こっている

ノート **chief** と **boss** の使い分け：両語とも特にジャーナリズムで用いられ, 組織[公共事業]を管理する人を指す。*industry chiefs/bosses* (産業界の長／実力者). *chief* は特に政府[公共事業]を管理する人について用いられる。*Health Service chiefs* (保健局の長たち). *boss* は特定の会社[スポーツクラブ]を管理する人を指すことが多い。*a record label boss/the Sheffield United boss* (レコード会社社長／シェフィールド・ユナイテッドの会長). *boss* のほうが *chief* よりもインフォーマルである。

governor [C] 《英》(刑務所・銀行などの機関の)長 ◇He is a former *governor* of the Bank of England. 彼はイングランド銀行の元総裁である ◇A copy of the report was sent to the *prison governor*. 彼の報告書のコピーは刑務所長に送られた ☞ **governor** (MANAGER)

chair [単数で] (会議・委員会の)議長[委員長]の座；(会議・委員会の)議長, 委員長 ◇She *takes the chair* in all our meetings. 彼女は我々の全会議で議長を務めている ◇Who is *in the chair* today? 今日は誰が議長を務めていますか ◇All remarks should be addressed to the *chair*. すべての発言は議長に向けられるべきである ◇He was elected *chair* of the city council. 彼は市議会議長に選出された ❶☞ **chairman** (上記)の❶を参照。

2 leader · pioneer · market leader · innovator · front runner

活動や競技会において最も優秀[重要]な人, または他者が追随する事を最初に行う人

【類語訳】先頭者, 首位, トップ, 先駆者, 草分け, 革新者, 業界最大手, 主力商品, 売れ筋商品, 最有力候補

文型&コロケーション
▸ a leader/ a pioneer/ a market leader/ an innovator/ a front runner **in** sth
▸ **among** the leaders/ pioneers/ front runners
▸ an **early** leader/ pioneer/ front runner
▸ a **great** pioneer/ innovator
▸ a **clear/ world** leader/ market leader

leader [C] (レース・競技会・ビジネスでの)先頭者, 首位, トップ ◇She was among the *leaders* of the race from the start. 彼女はスタートからレースの先頭集団にいた ◇The company is a world *leader* in electrical goods. その会社は電気製品の分野で世界をリードしている ◇They are the *brand leader* (= most successful brand) for herbs and spices in the UK. それらは英国において香草や香辛料のトップ銘柄である

pioneer [C] (特定分野の知識・文化の)先駆者, 草分け ◇He is known as a *pioneer* in veterinary surgery. 彼は獣医外科の先駆者として知られている ◇She later became a *pioneer* of education for women. 彼女は後に女性教育の草分けとなった ☞ **pioneer** (DEVELOP 2)

market 'leader [C] (特定の種類の製品の)業界最大手；(同種の製品の中での)主力[売れ筋]商品 ◇We are the *market leader* in hi-fi. 当社はハイファイ装置の業界最大手です ◇The system is the *market leader* in the home PC market. そのシステムは家庭用パソコン市場における主力製品です

innovator [C] (新しい物事[考え, 方法]を導入する)革新者 ◇The company is a global *innovator* in science and technology. その会社は科学技術における世界の革新の担い手である ◇She is one of the great *innovators* of contemporary dance. 彼女は現代舞踊の偉大なる革新者の一人である ☞ **innovation** (DEVELOPMENT), **innovative** (CREATIVE)

▸**front 'runner** [C] （レース・競技・契約などにおいて勝利が見込まれる）最有力候補, 最右翼 ◇France and England are *front runners for* semi-final places. フランスとイングランドがベスト4の最有力候補である ◇Auckland is still the *front runner* in the bid to host the event. オークランドは依然としてその大会の開催招致における最有力候補である

leaflet 名

leaflet・brochure・booklet・pamphlet・circular・handout・flyer
物事に関する情報が記載された一枚の紙[薄い本]
【類語訳】ちらし, ビラ, 小冊子, リーフレット, パンフレット, 案内状, 通知書, 配布資料

文型&コロケーション
▸in a/ the leaflet/ brochure/ booklet/ pamphlet/ circular/ handout/ flyer
▸a free leaflet/ brochure/ booklet/ pamphlet/ handout
▸a promotional/ publicity leaflet/ brochure/ pamphlet
▸to produce a leaflet/ brochure/ booklet/ pamphlet/ circular/ handout/ flyer
▸to issue/ publish a leaflet/ brochure/ booklet/ pamphlet/ circular
▸to distribute a leaflet/ brochure/ booklet/ pamphlet/ circular/ handout/ flyer
▸to give out leaflets/ brochures/ handouts/ flyers
▸to hand out leaflets/ brochures/ flyers
▸a leaflet/ brochure/ booklet/ pamphlet/ circular explains sth
▸a leaflet/ brochure/ flyer advertises sth

leaflet [C] （宣伝・案内・説明のための1枚[数頁]の）ちらし, 小冊子, リーフレット ◇We picked up a few *leaflets* on local places of interest. 私たちは地元の名所に関するちらしを数枚手に取った ☞ **notice** (POSTER)
brochure [C] （商品・サービスの宣伝のための）小冊子, パンフレット ◇a travel *brochure* 旅行パンフレット ◇Send for your free colour *brochure* today! 無料のカラーカタログを今日お取り寄せください
booklet [C] （案内・説明のための）小冊子, パンフレット,（チケット・商品券の）一綴り ◇I had to refer to the instruction *booklet*. 私は取扱説明書を参照しなければならなかった ◇a *booklet* of tickets/vouchers/coupons 一綴りのチケット／商品券／クーポン
pamphlet [C] （案内用の）小冊子, パンフレット ◇The government provides a *pamphlet* for all immigrants, outlining their rights. 政府はすべての移民向けに彼らの権利についての概略を記したパンフレットを提供している

ノート **booklet** と **pamphlet** の使い分け：booklet は pamphlet よりも厚いことがある。pamphlet はチケットの綴りには用いられない。歴史的に見ると, pamphlet には特に政治に関する意見・主張が記されることもあった。◇He dismissed claims published in *pamphlets* that the King's powers had been usurped. 彼は国王の権力が不当に奪われたとの小冊子に載せられた主張を退けた。

circular [C] （多数の人に送付される通知・宣伝の）案内状, 通知書, ちらし ◇The company will dispatch a *circular* to its shareholders giving details of the takeover. 会社は株主たちに対して企業買収の詳細を記した通知書を発送する予定だ
handout [C] （催し物[公益に関する事柄, 政策など]の案内のための）配布資料 ◇The party's press *handout* was largely ignored by journalists. その党のマスコミ用の配布資料はジャーナリストたちの大半に無視された ☞ **hand sth out** (DISTRIBUTE)
flyer （または **flier**）[C] （製品[催し物]の宣伝のための）街頭で配られるちらし, ビラ ◇We were asked to hand out *flyers* for the new club. 私たちは新しいクラブのビラを配るよう依頼された

ノート **handout** と **flyer** の使い分け：handout はふつう大きな組織によって作成され, ジャーナリスト[顧客に渡すために店・企業]に配られる。flyer は小さな企業によって作成され, 街頭で人々に配られる。

lean 動

lean・tilt・tip・angle・slant・slope・bank
人や物が動いて[動かされて]垂直[まっすぐ]でなくなることを表す
【類語訳】上体を傾ける, 傾く, 傾ける, 向きを変える, 斜向かいに置く

文型&コロケーション
▸to lean/ tilt/ tip/ angle/ slant/ slope (sth) **towards/ away from** sth
▸to lean/ angle/ slant (sth) **across** sth
▸to tilt/ tip/ angle/ slant/ slope (sth) **up/ down**
▸to lean/ tilt/ tip (sth) **forwards/ back/ backwards/ to one side**
▸to lean/ tilt/ tip / angle/ slant/ slope/ bank (sth) **slightly**
▸to tilt/ tip/ angle your **head**

lean [自] 《ふつう副詞や前置詞と共に》(人が)上体を傾ける;（通常は垂直に立っている物が）傾く ◇I *leaned* back in my chair. 私は自分の椅子に背をもたせかけた ◇A man was *leaning* out of the window. 一人の男が窓から身を乗り出していた ◇He *leaned* closer, lowering his voice. 彼は声をひそめて身を寄せた ◇The tower is *leaning* dangerously. その塔は危険なまでに傾いている
tilt [自, 他] 《ふつう副詞や前置詞と共に》（一方の端がもう片方の端よりも高くなって）傾く;（物を）傾ける ◇The seat *tilts* forward, when you press this lever. このレバーを押すと, シートは前に傾きます ◇His hat was *tilted* slightly at an angle. 彼の帽子は少し斜めに傾いていた ◇She *tilted* her head back and looked up at me. 彼女は頭を後ろに反らして私を見上げた
tip (-pp-) [自, 他] 《ふつう副詞や前置詞と共に》（一方の端がもう片方の端よりも高くなって）傾く;（物を）傾ける ◇Suddenly the boat *tipped* to one side. 突然ボートは片側に傾いた ◇She *tipped* her head back and laughed loudly. 彼女は頭を後ろに反らして大声で笑った ◇He *tipped* the wheelbarrow on its side. 彼は手押し車を片側に傾けた

ノート **tilt** と **tip** の使い分け：tilt のほうが tip よりも小さ[緩やかな, 控えめな]動きに用いられる。◆The train *tilts* to one side when it goes round bends. (列車はカーブを曲るとき片方に傾く) ×The train *tips* to one side when it goes round bends. ◆While trying to sit

↳lean

down, I *tipped* the tray and my entire dinner went onto the rug. (座ろうとしたとき, 私はお盆を傾けてしまって料理を全部敷物の上にこぼした). ×While trying to sit down, I *tilted* the tray and my entire dinner went onto the rug.

angle [他] (物を[の])傾ける, 向きを変える, (人・物の正面ではなく)斜向かいに置く ◇He *angled* his chair so that he could sit and watch her. 彼は座って彼女を見られるように椅子の向きを変えた

slant [他, 自] 《副詞や前置詞と共に》(物を)傾ける;(水平[垂直]ではなく)傾く ◇*Slant* your skis a little more to the left. スキー板をもう少し左に傾けてください ◇The sun *slanted* through the window. 《文語》日差しが窓から斜めに差し込んだ

slope [自] 《ふつう副詞や前置詞と共に》(通常は垂直に立っているものが)傾く ◇His handwriting *slopes* backwards. 彼の筆跡は右下がりだ ◇It was a very old house with *sloping* walls. それは壁の傾いた非常に古い家だった

bank [自, 他] (飛行機が旋回の際に)傾く;(飛行機を)傾ける ◇The plane *banked* steeply to the left. 飛行機は左に急角度に傾いた ◇The pilot *banked* the plane to give passengers a better look at the mountain. パイロットは乗客に山がもっとよく見えるように機体を傾けた

learn [動]

learn・study・know・acquire・do・memorize・
pick sth up・master・get the hang of sth・revise・
learn/know sth by heart・review

学習[経験, 教授]によって知識[技術]を習得する

【類語訳】学ぶ, 勉強する, 研究する, 教わる, 習う, 習得する, 身につける, 記憶する, 暗記する, 覚えている, わかる

[文型&コロケーション]
▸ to learn/ know/ pick up sth **from** sb/ sth
▸ to study/ revise/ review (sth) **for** sth
▸ to learn/ know/ memorize/ pick up/ master/ get the hang of **what...**
▸ to learn/ know/ master/ get the hang of **how...**
▸ to learn/ study **to be** sth
▸ to learn/ study/ know/ do/ pick up/ master a **language**
▸ to learn/ study/ know/ do/ pick up/ master **French/ Arabic, etc.**
▸ to learn/ study/ know/ do/ master/ revise/ review a **subject**
▸ to learn/ study/ do/ revise/ review **geography/ biology, etc.**
▸ to learn/ acquire/ pick up/ master a **skill**
▸ to learn/ do/ memorize a **poem/ speech**
▸ to memorize a **number**
▸ to learn/ know a **poem/ speech/ number** (off) by heart
▸ to **quickly** learn/ pick up/ master sth
▸ to **thoroughly** learn/ study/ master/ revise/ review sth
▸ to study/ revise **hard**

learn [他, 自] (学習・経験・教授によって知識・技術を)学ぶ, 勉強する, 習う, 身につける;(繰り返し読んで)記憶する, 覚える ◇I've forgotten most of what I *learned* at school. 私は学校で習ったことをほとんど忘れてしまっている ◇She's still quite young and she's got a lot to *learn*. 彼女はまだかなり若いし学ばなければならないことがたくさんある ◇She's very interested in *learning* more *about* Japanese culture. 彼女は日本文化についてもっと学ぶことに非常に興味がある ◇I'll need to *learn* how to use the new software. 私は新しいソフトウェアの使い方を学ぶ必要があるだろう ◇He *learned to* ride when he was about three years old. 彼は3歳くらいのときに乗馬を覚えた ◇You'll have to *learn* your lines (= for an acting part) by next week. あなたは来週までに台詞を覚えなければならないでしょう ◇Most of the kids here are eager to *learn*. この子どもたちの大半は勉強熱心です ◇All children *learn* through play (= by playing). 子どもは皆遊びを通して学ぶ ◇We have to *learn* one of Hamlet's speeches for school tomorrow. 私たちは明日の授業のためにハムレットの台詞の一つを覚えなければならない ☞ **learning** (EDUCATION)

study [自, 他] (読書・研究・学校[大学]への通学によってあるテーマについて)学ぶ, 勉強[研究]する ◇Michael *studied* at Sussex University. マイケルはサセックス大学で学んだ ◇He sat up very late that night, *studying*. 彼はその夜非常に遅くまで起きて勉強していた ◇As a young composer he *studied under* Nadia Boulanger (= Nadia Boulanger taught him to be a composer). 若き作曲家時代に, 彼はナディア・ブーランジェに師事して学んだ ◇Did you ever *study* any sciences? 何か科学を学んだことはありますか ◇She's *studying* to be an architect. 彼女は建築家になるべく勉強している ❶《米》では*study*はテスト[試験]のために勉強することについて用いられる一般的な語。 ◆I have two tests tomorrow, and I've barely had time to *study*. (明日テストが二つあるので, 勉強する時間はわずかしかなかった). ◆I was up late *studying* for my biology final. (私は夜遅くまで生物の期末試験の勉強をしていた). 《英》ではこの意味の*study*の代わりにふつう*revise*が用いられる。 ☞ **study** (EDUCATION)

know [他] (技術・言葉を学んで)知っている, わかる; (物事について)知っている ◇Do you *know* how to use spreadsheets? スプレッドシートの使い方を知っていますか ◇Do you *know* any Japanese? 何か日本語を知っていますか ◇He *knows* this city better than anyone. 彼はこの町のことを誰よりもよく知っている ☞ **knowledge** (KNOWLEDGE)

acquire [他] 《フォーマル》(知識・技術を)習得する, 身につける ◇She has *acquired* a good knowledge of English. 彼女は英語の知識を十分身につけた ◇He decided to put his newly *acquired* skills to the test. 彼は新たに身につけた技術を試すことに決めた ☞ **acquire** (GET 1)
➢ **acquisition** [名] [U] ◇theories of child language *acquisition* 子どもの言語習得理論

do [他] (学校[大学]の授業でテーマ・主題・書物などを)勉強する ◇I'm *doing* physics, chemistry and biology. 私は物理と化学と生物を勉強しています ◇Have you *done* any (= studied anything by) Keats? いくらかキーツを勉強したことはありますか

memorize 《英でまた **-se**》[他] (正確に)記憶[暗記]する, 覚える ◇She had *memorized* his phone number. 彼女は彼の電話番号を暗記してしまっていた ◇Each night I tried to *memorize* long lists of verbs. 毎晩私は動詞の長い一覧表を覚えようとした ☞ **memory** (MEMORY)

,pick sth 'up [句動] 《ややインフォーマル》(努力することなく偶然に情報・知識を)覚える, 教わる ◇I *picked up* one or two words of Thai while I was on vacation. 私は休暇中にタイ語を一つ二つ覚えた ◇This is a tip I *picked up* from my mother. これは母から教わったコツです

master [他]（物事を完全に）習得する，身につける ◇Once you've *mastered* the basics, you can begin to experiment a little. いったん基礎を習得したら，実験を少し始めることができます

get the 'hang of sth [仕れ]《インフォーマル》（物事のやり方・使い方を）つかむ，わかる ◇It seems tricky at first but you'll soon *get the hang of* it. 最初は難しく思えますが，すぐにコツがつかめるでしょう ◇I never quite *got the hang of* riding a bike. 私は自転車の乗り方が今一つつかめなかった

revise [自,他]《英》（習ったことを復習して）試験勉強をする ◇I can't come out tonight — I'm *revising*. 今夜は出て行けないんだ—試験勉強してるから ◇She's *revising* for her exams at the moment. 彼女は今試験勉強をしている ◇Have you *revised* geography yet? もう地理の試験勉強をしたの

▶**revision** [名][U] ◇Have you started your *revision* yet? もう試験勉強を始めたの

learn/know sth by 'heart [仕れ]（詩・事実などを正確に）暗記する，覚える ◇He was told to *learn* the passage *by heart*. 彼はその一節を暗記するよう言われた ◇I had dialled the number so often that I *knew* it *off by heart*.《英》私はごく頻繁にその番号に電話していたので，そらで覚えていた

review [他,自]《特に米》（試験勉強に備えるために習ったことを）復習する，見直す ◇Take a little time to *review* your notes the evening before. 前の晩に少し時間を取って自分のノートを見直しなさい ❶個々の学生が「復習する」場合，reviewは目的語が必要となる。✕I need to *review* for my math final. この場合は代わりにstudyを用いること。✓I need to *study* for my math final. （私は数学の期末試験の勉強をしなければならない）。しかしながら，復習に関する授業を指導する先生が言う場合，目的語の有無にかかわらずreviewを用いることが可能。◆I think it would be a good idea to *review* the material in chapter 10. （その教材の第10章を復習するのはいい考えだと思う）。◆Next week we're going to be *reviewing* for the final. （来週は期末試験に備えて復習をします）。

▶**review** [名][C, U] ◇I should have time for a quick *review* of my notes before the test. テスト前にはノートをざっと見直す時間を取るほうがいいと思う ◇We'll have time at the end of class for *review*. 私たちは授業の最後に復習の時間を取ります

leave [動]

1 leave・go・exit・depart・be off・part

人や場所から立ち去る

【類義訳】出る，出て行く，出かける，去る，出発する，離れる，別れる，退出する，いなくなる

> [ノート] **leave**と**go away**の使い分け：親見出し leave の類語は，人や物事から去る行為や物事を強調する。親見出し**go away**の類語は，話し手が別の場所にいたい「他の人に別の場所にいてほしい」という欲求や願望を強調する。☞ **GO AWAY**

[文型&コロケーション]

▶ to leave/ go/ exit/ depart/ part **from** sb/ sth
▶ to leave/ depart **for** sth
▶ to leave/ go/ depart **at** 9 a.m., midnight, etc.
▶ to be ready/ about/ going to leave/ go/ depart

▶ to be forced to leave/ go/ depart/ part
▶ let's go/ be off
▶ to leave/ go/ depart/ be off **now/ soon/ at once**
▶ to leave/ go/ depart **quickly/ immediately**
▶ to leave/ go/ be off **in a hurry**

leave [自,他]（場所から）出る，出発する，去る，離れる ◇Come on — it's time we *left*. さあ—もう出る時間だ ◇The plane *leaves* for Dallas at 12.35. その飛行機はダラスに向けて12時35分に発ちます ◇They got into an argument and were asked to *leave*. 彼らは口論になり，出て行くように求められた ◇John says he *left* the restaurant at around midnight. ジョンは夜の12時くらいにそのレストランを出たと言っている ◇I hate *leaving* home. 私は外出するのが嫌いだ [反意] **arrive** (ARRIVE), **enter** (ENTER)

go [自]（場所から）出て行く，出発する，去る，離れる ◇I must be *going* now. もう行かなくちゃ ◇Has she *gone* yet? 彼女はもう行ってしまったの ◇Don't *go* — I want to talk to you. 行かないでくれ—話があるんだ ◇He's been *gone* an hour (= he left an hour ago). 彼は1時間前に出て行った ◇The train *goes* in a few minutes' time. 列車はあと数分で出ます ❶ goは旅に出る[休暇を過ごす，違うことをする]ために人が場所から去ることについて，onと共に用いられることが多い。◆to *go on* a journey/tour/trip/cruise（旅行/周遊/旅/クルージングに出かける）．◆to *go on* holiday/vacation（休暇に出かける）．[反意] **stay** (STAY 1), ☞ **go** (GO 1, 2)

exit [自,他]《フォーマル》（建物・部屋・舞台・乗り物から）退出[退場]する，出る ◇The bullet entered his chest and *exited through* his back. 弾丸は彼の胸部から入って背中から抜けた ◇We *exited* via a fire door. 私たちは防火扉から出た ◇*Exit* Hamlet (= used in the text of a play to say who should come off the stage) ハムレット退場 ◇Passengers *exited* the aircraft through the rear door. 乗客たちは後部扉から飛行機を降りた [反意] **enter** (ENTER)

depart [自,他]《ややフォーマル》（旅行[移動]のため）出発する，いなくなる ◇Flights for Amsterdam *depart* from Terminal 3. アムステルダム行きの便は3番ターミナルから出発します ◇You must *depart* for England immediately. あなたは即刻イングランドに向けて発たねばなりません ◇The train *departs* Amritsar at 4.20 p.m.《米》その列車は午後4時20分にアムリッツァルから出発します ◇She waited until the last of the guests had *departed*. 彼女は最後の客がいなくなるまで待った ❶日常会話では，departはフォーマルだが，飛行機・列車などの発着には一般的に用いられる公式用語である。[反意] **arrive** (ARRIVE)

be 'off [フレーズ]《特に英，インフォーマル，話し言葉》（場所から）出かける，出発する，去る ◇It's time we *were off*. そろそろ出かける時間です ◇He's *off to* Rome in the morning. 午前中彼はローマに出かけている ◇And they're *off*! (= used by sb describing the start of a race) さあスタートしました

part [自]《フォーマル》（人々が）別れる；（人と）別れる ◇We *parted* at the airport. 私たちは空港で別れた ◇He has recently *parted* from his wife (= they have started to live apart). 彼は最近妻と別れた ◇I never forgot his *parting words* (= what he said as he left). 私は彼の別れの言葉を決して忘れなかった

2 leave・move・move out・emigrate・relocate・migrate・quit

↳leave

一つの場所に住むこと[一つの集団に所属すること、一つの場所で勉強することなど]をやめる
【類語訳】退く、辞める、立ち退く、引っ越す、転勤する、転勤させる、移転する、移転させる、異動する、転職する、移住する

文型&コロケーション

▶ to move/ move out/ emigrate/ relocate/ migrate **from**...
▶ to move/ move out/ emigrate/ relocate/ migrate **to**...
▶ to leave/ quit your **home/ school/ college/ job**
▶ to leave/ quit **town**
▶ to **threaten to** leave/ move out/ quit
▶ to **decide/ plan/ want to** leave/ move/ move out/ emigrate/ relocate/ quit

leave [他, 自] (住む場所・所属団体・学校などから)退く、辞める、立ち退く、離れる ◇She *left* school at 14 with no qualifications. 彼女は何の資格ももたずに14歳で学校を辞めた ◇He had *left* the organization some years before. 彼は何年か前にその組織を抜けていた ◇Too many teachers are *leaving* the profession for higher-paid jobs. あまりにも多くの教員がより給料の高い仕事を求めて教職を退いている ◇Hundreds of villagers have already *left* to seek work in the towns. すでに何百人もの村人たちが町で仕事を探すために村を離れている [反意] **stay on** ❶ *stay on* は予想以上に長く[他の人々がやめた後も]、ある場所で勉強[仕事など]を続けることを指す。◇How can we encourage more 16-year-olds to *stay on* at school? (もっと多くの16歳に学校に残ることを勧めるにはどうしたらいいでしょうか).

move [自, 他] (住む[働く、商売の]場所を変えて)引っ越す、転居する、転勤[異動、転職]する、移転する ◇*Moving* (= moving home) can be an extremely stressful experience. 引っ越しは非常にストレスの多い経験となることもある ◇All her family have *moved* away so she's on her own. 家族が皆引っ越したので、彼女は一人で生活している ◇The company is *moving* to Scotland. その会社はスコットランドに移転予定である ◇He worked as a sales rep before *moving* to the marketing department. 彼はマーケティング部に異動になるまでは、営業マンとして働いていた ◇They've *moved house* three times in the past year. 彼らはこの一年で3回引っ越している ◇I'm being *moved* to the New York office. 私はニューヨーク支社に異動になる予定です

,move 'out [句動詞] (元の家から)引っ越す、立ち退く ◇They're *moving out* next week. 彼らは来週引っ越す予定です ◇Local people were forced to *move out* when the new settlers arrived. 新たな入植者がやって来ると、地元の人たちは立ち退かされた [反意] **move in**

emigrate [自] (自国から他国へ)移住する ◇My grandparents *emigrated* from Vietnam to the US in the 1980s. 私の祖父母は1980年代にベトナムから米国へ移住した [反意] **immigrate (REFUGEE)**, ☞ **emigrant (REFUGEE)**

▶ **emigration** [名] [U, C] the mass *emigration* of Jews from eastern Europe 東欧からのユダヤ人の集団移住

relocate [自, 他] (会社・社員が)移転[転勤]する、(会社・社員を)移転[転勤]させる ◇A lot of people were unwilling to *relocate*. 多くの人たちが転勤したがらなかった ◇The company *relocated* its head office to Sacramento. その会社は本社をサクラメントに移転させた ☞ **locate (BASE)**

▶ **relocation** [名] [U] ◇Most workers will get pay rises if they agree to *relocation*. 転勤に合意すれば、ほとんどの従業員は昇給する ◇We will pay all your *relocation costs/expenses*. 会社が転勤費用を全額負担します

migrate [自] (鳥・動物などが季節ごとに)移動[回遊]する、渡る ; (人が集団で町[国]から)移住する ◇Swallows *migrate* south in winter. ツバメは冬になると南方へ渡る ◇Thousands were forced to *migrate* from rural to urban areas in search of work. 何千人もの人々が仕事を求めて農村から都会へ移住せざるをえなかった ☞ **migrant (REFUGEE)**

▶ **migration** [名] [U, C] ◇seasonal *migration* 季節移動[回遊] ◇mass *migrations* 集団移住

quit [他, 自] 《インフォーマル》(住んでいる場所・学校などを)退く、辞める、立ち退く、離れる ◇He was forced to *quit* college and find work. 彼は大学を辞めて仕事を探さざるをえなかった ◇I decide to *quit* town and lie low for a while. 私は町を離れてしばらく身を隠すことにする ◇The family has been given *notice to quit* (= told to leave their home). その家族は立ち退きの通知を受けている ❶ quit には「仕事を辞める」の意味もある。

---

3 leave・retire・resign・quit・step down・give in/hand in your notice・depart・stand down

被雇用者として働くことや、これまで成果を収めてきた活動から退くことを表す
【類語訳】退職する、引退する、辞任する、辞職する、退任する、退陣する、辞表を提出する、身を引く、辞退する

文型&コロケーション

▶ to retire/ resign/ quit/ step down/ depart/ stand down **as** director, chief executive, etc.
▶ to leave/ resign/ quit **over** pay, conditions, etc.
▶ to leave/ retire from/ resign from/ quit/ step down from/ depart/ stand down from a **post/ position**
▶ to leave/ retire from/ resign from/ depart a **job**
▶ to **decide to** leave/ retire/ resign/ quit/ step down/ hand in your notice/ stand down
▶ to **have/ be forced to** leave/ retire/ resign/ quit/ step down/ depart/ stand down
▶ to **be ready/ going to** leave/ retire/ resign/ quit/ step down/ stand down
▶ to **ask sb to** leave/ retire/ resign/ quit/ step down/ stand down
▶ to **refuse to** leave/ retire/ resign/ quit/ step down
▶ to **threaten to** leave/ resign/ quit

leave [自, 他] 退職する ◇My assistant is threatening to *leave*. 私の助手は辞めるぞと脅している ◇She claims she was forced to *leave* her job after she became pregnant. 彼女は妊娠してやむなく退職させられたと主張している [反意] **stay on** ❶ *stay on* は、勉学、勤務などを、予想外に長く、あるいは他の人々がやめた後でも継続することを表す。◆Fewer than half of the employees chose to *stay on* when the company was taken over. (会社が買収されたとき、会社に残ることを選んだ従業員は半分にも満たなかった).

retire [自] (定年・病気で)退職する、引退する ◇He is *retiring* next year after 30 years with the company. 彼は来年、30年間勤務した会社を退職する ◇My dream is to *retire to* a villa in France. 私の夢は退職後にフランスの別荘で暮らすことだ ◇The company's official *retir-*

ing age is 65. その会社の定年[正式な退職年齢]は65歳だ ◇She has decided to *retire* from international tennis. 彼女はテニスの国際試合から引退することを決めた

▶**retirement** 名 [U, C] ◇to *take early retirement* 早期退職する ◇This year we have seen the *retirements* of several senior personnel. 今年、我が社では数人の古参社員が退職した

resign [自, 他]《ややフォーマル》(正式に)辞任する, 辞職する, 退任する ◇Two members *resigned* from the board in protest. 二人が抗議して役員を退任した ◇My father *resigned* his directorship last year. 父は昨年、管理職を退いた

▶**resignation** 名 [U, C] ◇a letter of *resignation* 辞表 ◇Further *resignations* are expected. さらに辞職者が出ることが見込まれる

quit [自, 他]《インフォーマル》(仕事を)やめる, 辞職する ◇If I don't get more money I'll *quit*. 収入が増えないのなら私はやめます ◇He *quit* the show last year because of bad health. 彼は昨年、健康を損ねて番組を降りた

,**step 'down** 句動詞 (-pp-) (後任に譲って)退陣する, 辞職する ◇He *stepped down* as party leader a week ago. 彼は1週間前に党首の地位を退いた

,**give in/,hand in your 'notice** 句動 辞表を提出する ◇She decided that she would *hand in her notice* and go travelling. 彼女は辞表を出して旅に出る決心をした

depart [自, 他]《米 or ビジネス》退職する, (職を)去る ◇Giving a large pay-off to a *departing* executive may be seen as rewarding failure. 退職する重役に高額な退職金を支払うことは失敗に報いる行為だと見なされるかもしれない ◇He *departed* the troubled firm after less than a year in the post. 彼はその職に1年もいないでその経営難の会社を退職した

▶**departure** 名 [C] ◇His *departure* leaves the board without a leader. 彼の退職で役員会はリーダー不在となる

,**stand 'down** 句動詞 (後任に譲って)身を引く, 退く ◇He *stood down* to make way for someone younger. 彼は若手に道を譲るために退いた

ノート step down と stand down の使い分け：stand down は have to, be obliged to, be asked to, refuse to などと共に使われることが多く、人が必ずしも自ら重要な地位を辞退するわけではないことを表す。step down は冷静で個人的な決断に基づく行動であることを表すことが多い。

4 leave・abandon・dump・desert・strand・turn your back on sb/sth・neglect・walk out

人を受けつけない, 助け[支え]ようとせずに人の元を去る
【類語訳】別れる, 振る, 見捨てる, 見放す, 放置する, 取り残す, 背を向ける

文型&コロケーション
▶ to leave/ dump/ desert sb **for** sb else
▶ to leave/ abandon/ dump/ desert/ neglect/ walk out on a **husband/ wife**
▶ to leave/ abandon/ dump/ desert a **lover**
▶ to abandon/ desert/ neglect a **child**
▶ sb's **husband/ wife** leaves/ abandons/ dumps/ deserts/ neglects/ walks out on them
▶ sb's **lover** leaves/ abandons/ dumps/ deserts them
▶ sb's **boyfriend/ girlfriend** leaves/ dumps them
▶ sb's **mother/ father** abandons/ deserts/ neglects them

leave [他] (妻・夫・連れ合いと永久に)別れる ◇She's *leaving* him for another man. 彼女は彼と別れて別の男の元へ行くつもりだ

abandon [他, しばしば受身で](世話する責任のある人・動物を)見捨てる, 見放す ◇People often simply *abandon* their pets when they go abroad. 人は国外へ行くとき、簡単にペットを見捨てることがよくある ◇The study showed a deep fear among the elderly of being *abandoned to* the care of strangers. 高齢者の間に見捨てられて知らない人の世話になるという根強い不安があることが、その研究でわかった

dump [他]《インフォーマル》(恋愛関係にある人を)振る ◇Did you hear he's *dumped* his girlfriend? 彼が恋人を振ったってこと聞いた

desert [他](助け[支え]ようとせずに人を)見捨てる, 見放す ◇She was *deserted* by her husband. 彼女は夫に見捨てられた ◇Don't worry — I won't *desert* you. 心配するな — 君を見捨てたりしないよ

ノート abandon と desert の使い分け：abandon は自助の不可能な人の元を去ることについて用いられることが多い。desert は助けようとせずに友人の元を去ることを含め、不誠実な行為を表すのに用いられることが多い。

strand [他, ふつう受身で](身動きのとれない場所に人を)取り残す ◇The strike left hundreds of tourists *stranded* at the airport. そのストライキで何百人もの旅行客が空港に取り残された ❶ strand はほとんどの場合、旅行中の人々(例えば空港で飛行機を待つ[故障した車・列車の中にいる]人々)について用いられる。

turn your back on sb/sth 句動 (以前に関係のあった人・物事に)背を向ける, 無視する, 見捨てる, 見放す ◇She *turned her back on* them when they needed her. 彼女は彼らが自分を必要としているときに彼らを見捨てた ◇Some newspapers have *turned their backs on* discussion and argument. 新聞の中には話し合いや議論を無視したものもある ☞ **reject** (REJECT)

neglect [他]《ややフォーマル》(世話をせずに人を)放置する ◇She denies *neglecting* her baby. 彼女は赤ちゃんを放置したことを否定している ☞ **neglect** (IGNORE)

▶**neglect** 名 [U] ◇The law imposed penalties for the *neglect* of children. その法律は子どもの放置に対して罰金を科した

,**walk 'out** 句動詞《インフォーマル》(世話する責任のある人を)見捨てる, 見放す, 蒸発する ◇How could she *walk out on* her kids? 彼女はどうして自分の子どもを見捨てることができたのか ◇I was just seven when my dad *walked out*. 父が蒸発したとき、私はやっと7歳になったばかりだった

lecturer 名 ☞ TEACHER

lecturer・professor・fellow・don

(総合)大学で教える人
【類語訳】教授, 講師, 教師, 会員

文型&コロケーション
▶ lecturer/ professor/ fellow/ don **at** sth
▶ lecturer/ professor **in** sth
▶ a **university** lecturer/ professor/ fellow/ don
▶ a **college** lecturer/ professor/ fellow
▶ a/ an **Cambridge/ Harvard/ Oxford, etc.** professor/ fellow/ don
▶ a **chemistry/ history etc.** lecturer/ professor/ fellow/ don
▶ a **senior** lecturer/ professor/ fellow

↳lecturer　　　　　　　　　　　　　　　**legal, leisure**

▸ a **distinguished** lecturer/ professor/ fellow
▸ an **honorary** lecturer/ professor/ fellow
▸ to be **made/ appointed** lecturer/ professor/ fellow

lecturer [C] (英国の大学の)講師 ◇He's a *lecturer* in French at London University. 彼はロンドン大学でフランス語の講師をしている

professor [C] (米国の大学の)教授 ◇She was my *professor* when I was a grad student. 彼女は私が大学院生だったときの指導教授だった ❶(英)では, professor は最高位の大学教授についてのみ用いられる.

fellow [C] (学会の)会員 ◇He's a *fellow* of the Royal College of Surgeons. 彼は英国外科医師会の会員です ❶(英)では, fellow は大学の上級メンバーを指す. ◇She's a *fellow* of New College, Oxford. (彼女はオックスフォード大学のニューカレッジの評議員です). 《米》では, fellow は(時に講義を受け持つ)特別研究員の資格を有する大学院生も指す. ◆ He became a teaching *fellow* at the University of Texas. (彼はテキサス大学の教育助手になった).

don [C] 《英》(オックスフォード[ケンブリッジ]大学の)教師 ◇an Oxford *don* オックスフォード大学の教師

legal 形

legal・statutory・legitimate・valid・lawful・constitutional
物事が法的に許されたり, 求められたり, 関わったりしていること
【類語訳】法律に関する, 法的な, 憲法に関する, 規約に関する, 法律で認められた, 合法の, 適法の, 法律で定められた, 法定の, 法的に有効な

▸ a legal/ statutory/ legitimate/ valid/ lawful/ constitutional **claim**
▸ legal/ statutory/ legitimate/ valid/ lawful/ constitutional **means**
▸ a legal/ statutory/ legitimate/ lawful **owner**
▸ a legal/ legitimate/ lawful **heir**
▸ **perfectly** legal/ legitimate/ lawful

legal 法律に関する, 法的な; 法律で認められた, 合法の, 適法の, 法律で定められた, 法定の ◇We were advised to take *legal* advice. 私たちは法的助言を受けるようアドバイスされた ◇They are facing a long *legal* battle in the US courts. 彼らはアメリカの裁判所で長期にわたる法廷論争に直面している ◇Should euthanasia be made *legal*? 安楽死は合法化すべきですか 反意 **illegal** (ILLEGAL)
▸**legally** 副 ◇a *legally binding* agreement 法的拘束力のある契約 ◇It's an important case both *legally* and politically. それは法的にも政治的にも重要な訴訟である

statutory [ふつう名詞の前で] 法律で定められた, 法定の; 制定法で義務付けられた ◇When you buy foods you have certain *statutory* rights. 食品を購入する場合, 購入者は制定法で定められた権利を有する ◇The authority failed to carry out its *statutory* duties. 当局は制定法上の義務を果たさなかった

legitimate 法律で認められた, 合法の, 適法の ◇The *legitimate* government was reinstated after the uprising. 合法政府は反乱後に復権した ◇Is his business strictly *legitimate*? 彼の商売は厳密には適法ですか 反意 **illegitimate** (ILLEGAL)

valid 法的に有効[正当]な ◇Do you have a *valid* passport? 法的に有効なパスポートをお持ちですか ◇He bought a bus pass *valid* for one month. 彼は1か月間有効なバスの定期券を購入した ◇They have a *valid* claim to compensation. 彼らには補償金を要求する正当な権利がある 反意 **invalid** ◇invalid は法的に無効[不当]であることを表す. ◆ The treaty was declared *invalid* because it had not been ratified. (その条約は批准されておらず, 無効であると宣告された).
▸**validity** 名 [U] ◇The period of *validity* of the agreement has expired. 契約の有効期限が切れている

lawful 《フォーマル》 法律で認められた, 合法の, 適法の ◇Can an act that causes death ever be *lawful*? 死を招く行為は合法となることがありうるであろうか ◇She is his *lawful* wife, and so is entitled to inherit the money. 彼女は彼の正妻であり, その金を相続する資格を有する 反意 **unlawful** (ILLEGAL)
▸**lawfully** 副 ◇The jury agreed that the doctor had acted *lawfully*. 陪審団はその医師が合法的に行動したということで意見の一致を見た

ノート **legal** と **lawful** の使い分け: 両語とも「法律で認められた」を意味する. ◆ by *legal/lawful* means (合法的な手段によって). lawful は専門的な[文語的]文脈で用いられる傾向にある. 同じことが反意語である unlawful と illegal についても言えるが, illegal は特に犯罪活動について用いられる. legal には「法律に関する」の意味もある. ◆ the US *legal* system (アメリカの法体系).

constitutional (国家・組織の)憲法[規約]に関する[認められた, 定められた] ❶ constitution は国家・組織を統治するための法体系および基本原則である. ◆ She had long advocated *constitutional* reform. (彼女は憲法改正を長らく主張してきた). ◆ They can't pass this law. It's not *constitutional*. (彼らにはこの法律は通過させられない. 合憲ではないからだ). ◆ a *constitutional* monarchy (= a country with a king or queen, whose power is controlled by a set of laws and basic principles) (立憲君主制[政体]). 反意 **unconstitutional** (ILLEGAL)

leisure 名

leisure・spare time・free time
働いて[勉強して]いない時間
【類語訳】余暇, レジャー, 空き時間, 自由時間, 暇

▸ **in** your spare/ free time
▸ to **have** (more/ no) leisure/ spare time/ free time
▸ to **spend** your spare time/ free time doing sth
▸ to **give up** your spare time/ free time

leisure [U] 《ややフォーマル》余暇, レジャー ◇These days we have more money and more *leisure* to enjoy it. 近頃私たちが持てるお金とそれを享受できる余暇が増えている ◇*leisure* activities/interests/pursuits 余暇の活動/興味/楽しみ ◇the growth of the *leisure* industry レジャー産業の発展

ˌspare ˈtime [U] 空き時間, 暇 ◇In her *spare time* she managed to complete her Master of Education degree. 彼女は空き時間を使って教育学修士の学位を何とか修得した ◇He spent most of his *spare time* watching television. 彼は暇があればたいていテレビを見て過ごした
☞ **spare** (FREE 形 3)

,free 'time [U] 自由時間, 暇 ◇It's wonderful the way the students give up their *free time* to help these children. 学生たちが自分たちの自由時間をこの子たちの援助に割く様子は素晴らしい ☞ **free** (FREE 形 3)

ノート leisure, spare time, free time の使い分け：
leisure は特にビジネスの文脈で、世間一般の人々[社会全般]について用いられる。自分自身[個人]について言う場合は、spare time または free time が用いられる。×What do you do in your *leisure*? ×the *spare/free time* industry. spare time は free time よりも、my, your, his, her, their などの所有代名詞と共に用いられることがはるかに多い。◆What do you do in your *spare time*? (暇なときは何をしてるの？) ◆In my *spare time* I write stories. (空き時間に私は物語を書きます). free time はどの程度仕事 [勉強] をしていない時間があるかについて用いられることが多い。◆I don't have much *free time*. (私にはあまり暇な時間はない).

let sb in 句動詞

let sb in/into sth・accept・admit・welcome・enrol・receive
人がある場所に入る[ある組織に加わる]ことを許す
【類語訳】招き入れる、中に入れる、受け入れる、迎え入れる、入会させる、入学させる、入場させる、歓迎する、登録する

文型&コロケーション

▸ to let/ accept/ admit/ welcome/ enrol/ receive sb **into** sth
▸ to accept/ admit/ enrol sb **as** sth
▸ to let in/ admit/ welcome/ receive a **visitor**
▸ to let in/ welcome/ receive a **guest**
▸ to let in/ accept/ admit/ welcome **immigrants**
▸ to accept/ admit/ welcome/ enrol a **candidate/ member/ student**
▸ to accept/ admit/ welcome **applicants**
▸ to accept/ admit/ welcome/ receive sb **formally/ officially**
▸ to accept/ welcome/ receive sb **with open arms**

,let sb 'in, let sb into sth 句動詞 《特に話し言葉》(人を場所に)招き入れる、中に入れる ◇He *let* her *into* the house. 彼は彼女を家の中に入れた ◇I'll give you a key so that you can *let yourself in*. 鍵を渡すから入っていいよ 反意 **keep sb/sth out** (EXCLUDE 2)

accept [他] (申し込みを受けて人を組織・機関・施設に)受け入れる、入会[入学]させる ◇The college he applied to has *accepted* him. 志願した大学に彼は入学できた ◇She was disappointed not to be *accepted* into the club. そのクラブに入会できず彼女はがっかりした ◇The landlord was willing to *accept* us as tenants. 大家は私たちを借家人として受け入れることをいとわなかった ◇She was *accepted to* study music. 彼女は音楽専攻で入学できた ❶ *accept* は特に大学への入学[組織への入会]を許可するかどうかについて用いられる。反意 **reject** (REFUSE), ☞ **accept** (GREET)

admit (-tt-) [他] 《フォーマル》(人を)入場させる；(人をクラブ・学校・組織に)入会[入学]させる ◇Each ticket *admits* one adult and one child. 各チケットで大人一人と子ども一人が入場できます ◇You will not be *admitted to* the theatre after the performance has started. 上演が始まってからの劇場への入場は許されません ◇The society *admits* all US citizens over 21. その協会には21歳以上の全米国市民が入会できる ❶ *admit* は特に公共の場所への入場を許可するかどうかについて用いられる。反意 **exclude** (EXCLUDE 2)
▸**admittance** [名] [U] ◇Hundreds of people were unable to *gain admittance* to the hall. 何百人もの人々がそのホールへの入場を許可してもらえなかった ☞ **admission** (ACCESS)

welcome [他] (人の来場を)歓迎する、(人を組織・活動に)喜んで迎え入れる ◇They *welcomed* the new volunteers with open arms (= with enthusiasm). 彼らは新しいボランティアの人たちを心から歓迎した ☞ **welcome** (GREET)

enrol 《特に英》(米でふつう **enroll**) -ll- [他] (学校・大学・教育課程に正式に)登録する、入学させる ◇The centre will soon be ready to *enrol* candidates for the new-style programme. センターはまもなくその新しい形式の教育課程に志願者を入学させる準備ができるだろう

receive [他] 《フォーマル》(人を集団の一員として正式に)迎え入れる ◇Three young people were *received* into the Church at Easter. 復活祭のときに3人の若者が教会に迎え入れられた ❶ この意味の receive はほとんどの場合、教会の一員になることについて用いられる。☞ **receive** (GREET)

letter 名

letter・message・email・mail・note・memo・fax・text・post・communication・correspondence
意思の疎通を図るために人に書いて送る物
【類語訳】手紙、書簡、通信文、投書、伝言、メッセージ、Eメール、メール、郵便物、メモ、連絡票、ファックス、連絡

文型&コロケーション

▸ a **letter**/ a **message**/ an **email**/ **mail**/ a **note**/ a **memo**/ a **fax**/ a **text**/ **post**/ a **communication**/ **correspondence from/ to** sb
▸ (a) **personal/ private letter**/ **message**/ **email**/ **mail**/ **note**/ **communication**/ **correspondence**
▸ a **brief letter**/ **message**/ **email**/ **note**/ **memo**/ **communication**
▸ (a) **business letter**/ **email**/ **mail**/ **memo**/ **correspondence**
▸ a **thank-you letter**/ **message**/ **email**/ **note**
▸ to **send/ receive** a **letter**/ a **message**/ an **email**/ **mail**/ a **note**/ a **memo**/ a **fax**/ a **text**/ **post**/ a **communication**/ **correspondence**
▸ to **write** a **letter**/ a **message**/ an **email**/ a **note**/ a **memo**
▸ to **open** a **letter**/ a **message**/ an **email**/ the **mail**/ the **post**
▸ a **letter**/ a **message**/ an **email**/ the **mail**/ a **fax**/ the **post arrives**

letter [C] 手紙、書簡、書状 ◇You should include a covering *letter* with your CV. 履歴書に添え状を同封したほうがいいよ ◇They wrote a *letter* of complaint to the television network. 彼らはそのテレビ局に苦情の手紙を書いた ◇You will be notified by *letter*. 書簡で通知いたします ◇to post a *letter* 《英》手紙を投函する ◇to mail a *letter* 《米》手紙を郵送する

message [C] 伝言、メッセージ ◇I left a *message* on her answering machine. 私は彼女の留守番電話に伝言を残した ◇Victoria's not here at the moment. Can I take a *message*? ヴィクトリアは今こちらにはおりません。お言付けいたしましょうか ◇The computer displays an error

↳**letter**

email (または **e-mail**) [C, U] Eメール ◇I got an *email* from Andrew last week. 私は先週アンドリューからEメールを受け取った ◇I have to check my *email*. 私は自分のEメールをチェックしなければならない
▶**email** (または **e-mail**) [動] [他] ◇David *emailed* me yesterday. デービッドは昨日私にメールを送ってきた ◇I'll *email* the documents to her. 私は彼女にその文書をEメールで送ります

mail [U] (手紙・小包などの)郵便物;(コンピューターで送受信される)メール ◇There isn't much *mail* today. 今日はあまり郵便物がない ◇Is there a letter from them in the *mail*? 彼らから手紙が郵送されてきていますか ◇You've got *mail*. あなたにメールが届いています ❶(英)では、人から送り届けられる手紙・小包を指すのに、mail の代わりに post が用いられることが多い。☞ **mail** (SEND)

note [C] (短い非公式の)メモ、手紙 ◇Just a quick *note* to say thank you for a wonderful evening. 素晴らしい夜への、取り急ぎの感謝の手紙です ◇I left a *note* for Judith on her desk. 私はジュディスの机の上にメモを残した ◇It is suspicious that he did not leave a suicide *note*. 彼が遺書を残さなかったのは疑問だ

memo (またはフォーマル **memorandum**) (複 **memoranda**) [C] (同じ組織内で交わされる正式な)回覧状、連絡票 ◇The confidential *memo* was leaked to the press. 極秘の連絡票が報道機関に漏れた

fax [U, C] ファックス(送信);ファックス(文書) ◇a *fax* machine ファックス(機) ◇Can you send it to me *by fax*? それをファックスで送っていただけますか ◇What is your *fax* number? ファックス番号は何ですか ◇Did you get my *fax*? 私のファックスは届きましたか
▶**fax** [動] [他] ◇Can you *fax* me the latest version? 最新版を私にファックスしていただけますか ◇Can you *fax* it to me? それを私にファックスしていただけますか

text (または '**text message**) [C] (携帯電話で送る)メール ◇Send a *text* to this number to vote. 投票にはこの電話番号にメールを送ってください
▶**text** (または '**text-message**) [動] [他] ◇I *texted* him to say we were waiting at the hotel. 私たちがホテルで待っていることを伝えるために、私は彼に(携帯)メールを送った

post [U] (英) (手紙・小包などの)郵便物 ◇The book arrived in the morning *post*. その本は午前の配達便で届いた ☞ **post** (SEND)

communication [C] (フォーマル)(伝言・手紙・電話での)連絡 ◇If you no longer wish to receive *communications* from us, follow the instructions at the bottom of the email. もう私どもからの連絡をご希望でない場合は、Eメールの最後にある指示に従ってください ☞ **communication** (COMMUNICATION), **communicate** (CONVEY), **communicate** (TALK)

correspondence [U] (ややフォーマル) (人から送り届けられる)通信文、投書、往復書簡 ◇The editor welcomes *correspondence* from readers on any subject. 編集部はあらゆるテーマに関する読者からの投書を歓迎いたします ◇the *correspondence* column/page (= in a newspaper) 投書欄/面 ☞ **correspondence** (COMMUNICATION)

licence

licence (英) (米 **license**) [名] ☞CERTIFICATE, PERMISSION

licence・franchise・warrant・permit・charter・authorization・pass
事を行う許可を与える正式文書
【類語訳】許可証、免許証、ライセンス、フランチャイズ、特権、特許、免許、特許状、令状、出入許可証、入場券、乗車券

|文型&コロケーション|
▶**under** (a) licence/ franchise/ charter
▶a licence/ franchise/ warrant/ permit/ charter **to do sth**
▶the **necessary** licence/ permit/ authorization
▶to **have** a licence/ a franchise/ a warrant/ a permit/ a charter/ an authorization/ a pass
▶to **get/ obtain** a licence/ a franchise/ a warrant/ a permit/ a charter/ an authorization/ a pass
▶to **give** (sb) a licence/ franchise/ permit/ charter/ pass
▶to **grant** (sb) a licence/ a franchise/ a warrant/ a permit/ a charter
▶to **issue** (sb) a licence/ warrant/ permit/ charter/ pass
▶to **apply for** a licence/ a franchise/ warrant/ permit/ charter/ pass
▶to **renew** a licence/ franchise/ permit/ charter/ pass
▶to **revoke** sb's licence/ permit/ charter
▶to **see/ check** sb's licence/ permit/ authorization/ pass
▶a licence/ franchise/ permit/ charter/ pass **expires**
▶a licence/ franchise/ permit/ pass **holder**

licence (英) (米 **license**) [C] (事を行う[物を所有・使用する]ための)許可[認可、免許]証、ライセンス ◇You need a *licence* to fish in this river. この川で釣りをするには許可書が必要です ◇The beer is brewed under *licence* in the UK. 英国ではビールは認可を受けて醸造される ◇Do you have a valid *driving licence*? (英) 有効な運転免許証を持っていますか ◇a *driver's license* (米) 運転免許証 ◇She *lost* her *licence* (= had her driving licence taken away) for six months. 彼女は6か月間運転免許証を停止された ◇a marriage *licence* 結婚許可証 ◇a liquor *licence* (= giving permission to sell alcoholic drinks) 酒類販売許可証 ◇an export *licence* (= a licence to export goods) 輸出許可証 ◇Is there a *licence fee*? ライセンス料がかかりますか ☞ **license** (ALLOW)

franchise [C] (会社が与える)一手販売権、フランチャイズ;(政府が与える公共事業運営の)特権、特許、免許 ◇a catering *franchise* in the fast-food industry ファストフード産業における料理提供の一手販売権 ◇In the reorganization, Southern Television lost their *franchise*. 再編成においてサザンテレビは特許を失った ◇They operate the business under *franchise*. 彼らは特許を受けてその商売を行っている
▶**franchise** [動] [他、ふつう受身で] ◇The catering has been *franchised (out) to* a private company. 料理提供する民間企業に一手販売権が与えられている

warrant [C] (警察に判事から与えられる)令状 ◇They issued a *warrant for* her arrest. 彼女に逮捕状が出された ◇Police arrived with a *search warrant*. 警察が捜索令状を持って到着した ◇Federal agents tried to serve *arrest warrants* on him for firearms offences. 連邦捜査官たちは武器取扱い違反容疑で彼に逮捕状を執行しようとした

permit [C]（期限付きの）許可[認可, 免許]証 ◇I asked to see his *permit*. 私は彼の許可証を見せるよう求めた ◇His 30-day *permit* expires on Tuesday. 彼の30日間の許可証は火曜日に期限が切れる ◇a **work** *permit* (= giving you permission to work in a foreign country) 就労許可証 ◇a residence *permit* 居住許可証 ☞ **permit** (ALLOW)

charter [C]（組織・町・大学の設立に関する主権者[政府]からの）特許[勅許, 免許]状 ◇The BBC's *charter* was due to be renewed. BBCの特許状は更新されることになっていた ◇The university received its **Royal Charter** in 1946. その大学は1946年に勅許を受けた ❶（英）ではcharterは時に, 特別の権利を与えることで犯罪者の手助けになると思われる法律[政策] を皮肉的に表すこともある. ◆The new law will be a *charter for* unscrupulous financial advisers.（その新法は恥知らずな財務顧問に対する特許状となるだろう）.

authorization（英でまた **-isation**）[C]（事を行うための）許可[認可]証 ◇Can I see your *authorization* please? 許可証を拝見できますか ☞ **authorize** (ALLOW)

pass [C]（場所に出入りする[バス・列車などに乗る]ための）出入[通行]許可証, 入場[乗車, 搭乗]券 ◇You can buy a three-day *pass* that gives you entry to all the major sights. すべての主な名所に3日間有効の入場券を購入できます ◇a bus *pass* バスの乗車券 ◇You will need a boarding *pass* to get onto the plane. 飛行機に乗り込むには搭乗券が必要となるでしょう

lie 图 ☞ NONSENSE

lie・story・fiction・perjury・fabrication・falsehood・fib
真実でないことを知っている人による発言
【類語訳】嘘, 虚言, 作り話, でたらめな話, 偽証罪, 虚偽

文型&コロケーション
- (a) **complete** lie/ fiction/ fabrication/ falsehood
- **pure** fiction/ fabrication
- a **little** lie/ story/ fiction
- a **plausible/ convincing** lie/ story
- a **malicious** lie/ story/ fabrication/ falsehood
- to **tell (sb)** a lie/ a story/ a falsehood/ a fib
- to **spread** lies/ stories
- to **believe** a lie/ a story/ a fiction

lie [C] 嘘, 虚言 ◇I couldn't tell her a *lie*. 私は彼女に嘘をつけなかった ◇The whole story is nothing but *a pack of lies*. その話はすべて嘘八百以外の何物でもない ◇What's the harm in telling a little *white lie* (= a harmless or small lie)? ちょっとした罪のない嘘をついたっていいじゃないか
▶**lie** 動［自］◇Don't *lie* to me! 私に嘘をつくな ◇She *lies* about her age. 彼女は歳をごまかしている ◇You could see from his face that he was *lying*. 顔の表情から彼が嘘をついていることがわかるでしょう

story [C, ふつう複数で]（ややインフォーマル）（大げさに[人に関する悪意な]）作り話, でたらめな話, 嘘 ◇She knew the child had been telling *stories* again. 子どもがまた作り話をしていたことは彼女にはわかっていた ◇He's been spreading malicious *stories* about you. 彼が君に関する意地悪な話を広めているよ ❶（英）**tall story**（米）**tall tale**）は, 誇張されているもしくは, 真実ではありそうにないこと

信じがたいような話を指す. ◆Sounds like another one of his *tall stories* to me.（また彼の大ぼらみたいには聞こえるけれど）.

fiction [C, U]（ややフォーマル）（でっち上げられた［人をだますための］）作り話, 嘘 ◇For years he managed to keep up the *fiction* that he was not married. 何年もの間彼は自分は結婚していないという嘘を何とかつき続けていた ◇*Fact and fiction* became all jumbled up in his report of the robbery. 強盗に関する彼の報告書では, 事実と虚言がすべてごたまぜになっていた 反意 **fact** (FACT)

perjury [U]（法律）（法廷における）偽証(罪) ◇She was found guilty of *perjury*. 彼女は偽証罪で有罪になった
▶**perjure yourself** ◇She admitted that she had *perjured herself*. 彼女は偽証していたことを認めた

fabrication [C, U]（ややフォーマル）（人をだますための［でっち上げられた］）嘘, 作り話；話をでっち上げること ◇Her story was a complete *fabrication* from beginning to end. 彼女の話は最初から最後まで真っ赤な嘘だった ◇Much of the 'evidence' is rumour and conjecture; some of it is pure *fabrication*.「証言」のほとんどはうわさと憶測であり, そのいくつかはまったくのでっち上げである ☞ **fabricate** (INVENT)

ノート **fiction** と **fabrication** の使い分け：fiction はふつう事実として述べられる真実でない単独の話. fabrication はふつう完全な物語に組み立てられた一連の虚言を指す.
×For years he managed to keep up the *fabrication* that he was not married. ×Her story was complete *fiction* from beginning to end.

falsehood [U, C]（フォーマル）虚偽；偽ること；嘘, 虚言 ◇He needed to test the truth or *falsehood* of her claims. 彼は彼女の主張が真実か虚偽かを調べる必要があった ◇It is an offence to deliberately publish a serious *falsehood*. ゆゆしき偽りを故意に出版することは犯罪である 反意 **truth**

fib [C]（インフォーマル）（ささいな）嘘 ◇Stop telling *fibs*. 嘘をつくのはやめなさい
▶**fib** 動［自］◇Come on, don't *fib*! Where were you really last night? おい, 嘘をつくな. 昨晩は本当はどこにいたんだ

life 图

1 life・existence・survival
生きている［存在している］状態［事実］
【類語訳】生命, 命, 人命, 寿命, 存在, 現存, 生存, 存続, 生き残り

文型&コロケーション
- sb/ sth's **very/ continued/ day-to-day** existence/ survival
- to **threaten** sb/ sth's life/ existence/ survival
- to **fight for** your life/ survival
- a **struggle for** existence/ survival

life [U, C]（人・動物・植物の）生命；（人の）命, 人命；（個人の）生存, 寿命 ◇The body was cold and showed *no signs of life*. その死体は冷たく何の生体反応も示さなかった ◇In spring the countryside bursts into *life*. 春になると田舎は一気に生命にあふれる ◇The floods caused a massive *loss of life* (= many people were killed). その洪水で多くの人命が失われた ◇He *risked his life* to save his daughter from the fire. 彼は命がけで娘を火事から救い出した ◇The operation *saved her life*. その手術で彼女の命は助かった ◇My grandfather *lost his life* (= was killed) in the Second World War. 私の祖父は第二次世界大戦で命を落とした ◇You mustn't let anyone know — *it's a matter of life and death* (= sb's life depends on it). 誰にも知られてはならない—これは死活問題なんだ ❶life は物について用いられる場合, 存在[機能]する期間を指す. ◆The International Stock Exchange *started life as* a London coffee shop. (国際証券取引所はロンドンのコーヒー店として発祥した). ◆The product has a guaranteed *shelf life* (= the length of time that food or other items can be kept before it is too old to be sold) of 60 days. (その製品は60日間の陳列期限が保証されている). 反意 **death** (DEAD), ☞ **live** (SURVIVE)

existence [U] 存在, 現存, 生存, 存続 ◇I was unaware of his *existence* until today. 私は今日まで彼の存在に気づかなかった ◇This is the oldest Hebrew manuscript *in existence*. これは現存するヘブライ語の写本で最も古いものです ◇Pakistan *came into existence* as an independent country after the war. パキスタンはその戦争後に独立国家として誕生した ◇The crisis threatens the industry's continued *existence*. その危機はその産業の存続を脅かしている

survival [U] (困難[危険]な状況における)生き残り, 生存, 存続 ◇His only chance of *survival* was to make his own way down the mountainside. 彼が唯一生き残るチャンスは山腹を下ることだった ◇Rhino poaching is now threatening the *survival* of the species. サイの密猟は今や種の生存を脅かしている ◇Exporting is necessary for our economic *survival*. 我々が経済的に生き残るためには輸出が必要である 反意 **extinction** ❶extinction は植物・動物・生活様式などが生存[存続]しなくなることを指す. ◆The mountain gorilla is in danger of *extinction*. (マウンテンゴリラは絶滅の危機にある). ☞ **survive** (SURVIVE)

2 life・career・lifetime・in sb's day
人が生きている[特定の物事を行っている]期間
【類語訳】一生, 人生, 生涯, 経歴, 存続期間, 寿命, 全盛期に, 若かりし頃に

▸ 文型&コロケーション
▸ in/ of sb's life/ career/ lifetime/ day
▸ during sb's life/ career/ lifetime
▸ sb's entire/ whole life/ career/ lifetime
▸ sb's school life/ career
▸ a life/ career/ lifetime of doing sth

life [C, U] (生まれてから死ぬまでの人の)一生, 人生, 生涯; (人生の)一時期 ◇He's lived here *all his life*. 彼は人生のすべてをここで過ごしてきた ◇He will spend *the rest of his life* in a wheelchair. 彼は残りの人生を車椅子で過ごすことになる ◇My mother took up tennis *late in life*. 私の母は晩年にテニスを始めた ◇There's no such thing as a job *for life* any longer. 一生を懸ける仕事なんてものはもはや存在しない ◇She is a *life member* of the club. 彼女はそのクラブの終身会員である ◇He spent his entire adult *life* in France. 彼は大人になってからはずっとフランスで過ごした

career [C] (仕事[特定の活動]を通じての)人生, 経歴 ◇She started her *career* as an English teacher. 彼女は英語教師としての道を歩み始めた ◇He is playing the best tennis of his *career*. 彼はテニス人生最高のプレーをしている ◇Her stage *career* spans sixty years. 彼女の舞台経歴は60年に及ぶ

lifetime [C, ふつう単数で] (人の)一生, 人生, 生涯, (物事の)存続[有効]期間, 寿命 ◇Only two volumes of his poetry were published during his *lifetime*. 彼の詩集は生涯でたった2巻しか出版されなかった ◇He has nothing to look forward to but a *lifetime* of misery. 彼は苦難の一生以外に期待できるものは何もない ◇These spending commitments are not achievable in the *lifetime* of the present government. これらの予算注入の公約は現政権の存続期間中には達成できない ◇For *the chance of a lifetime* (= a wonderful opportunity that you are not likely to get again) fill in the coupon below and send it to the following address. この千載一遇のチャンスを生かすために, 下の申込み券に記入の上, 下記の住所にお送りください

in sb's day [行礼] (人の経歴の)全盛期に; (人の)若かりし頃に ◇*In her day* she was one of the most famous dancers in Britain. 彼女は全盛期には英国で最も有名なダンサーの一人だった ◇It was different *in my day*, there were plenty of jobs when you left school. 私の若い頃は(今とは)違っていて, 卒業したら仕事がたくさんあった ❶of sb's/the day は人が生きた特定の期間や過去の特定の期間について用いられる. ◆He was regarded as the greatest architect *of his day*. (彼は同時代で最も偉大な建築家とみなされていた). ◆The event attracted all the great names and popular artists *of the day*. (その出来事は当時の偉人や人気アーティストすべての目を引いた). ☞ **day** (PERIOD)

3 life・experience・lifestyle・way of life・living・existence
人々の生き様を表す
【類語訳】生活, 暮らし, 人生, 経験, 体験, 生活様式, 生き方, 暮らし方

▸ 文型&コロケーション
▸ (sb's) day-to-day life/ experience/ living/ existence
▸ (sb's) daily/ everyday life/ experience/ existence
▸ a comfortable/ busy life/ lifestyle/ existence
▸ a miserable/ communal life/ existence
▸ a traditional lifestyle/ way of life
▸ to have/ lead/ enjoy a ... life/ lifestyle/ existence

life [C] (生涯における)生活, 暮らし; (特定の時期の)人生; (すべての人に特徴的な)生活, (特定の)暮らし方, 生活様式, 生き[暮らし]方 ◇He has had a hard *life*. 彼はつらい生活を送ってきた ◇She led a *life* of luxury. 彼女はぜいたくな生活を送った ◇Many of these children have led very *sheltered lives* (= they have not had many different experiences). この子たちの多くは非常に過保護な生活を送ってきた ◇He doesn't like to talk about his *private life*. 彼は私生活について話したがらない ◇She has a full *social life*. 彼女は充実した社会生活を送っている ◇They emigrated to *start a new life* in America. 彼らはアメリカで新生活を始めるために移住した ◇She has been an accountant all her *working life*. 彼女は職業人生のすべてを会計士として過ごしてきた ◇They were very happy throughout their *married life*. 彼らは結婚生活を通してずっととても幸せだった ◇He is young and has little experience of *life*. 彼は若くて、人生経験がほとんどない ◇We bought a dishwasher to ***make life easier***. 私たちは家事を楽にするために食器洗い機を購入した ◇In ***real life*** (= when she met him) he wasn't how she had imagined him at all. 実際会ってみると、彼は彼女が想像していた彼とはまったく違っていた ◇She enjoyed political *life*. 彼女は政治家としての人生を楽しんだ ◇How do you find *life* in America? アメリカでの生活をどう思いますか

experience [U] (考え[振る舞い]方に影響を与える)経験, 体験 ◇*Experience* has taught me that life can be very unfair. 私は経験から人生には非常に不公平なこともあるのだということを学んだ ◇It is important to try and ***learn from experience***. 経験から学ぼうとすることは大切である ◇***In my experience***, very few people really understand the problem. 私の経験からすると、ごくわずかな人しかその問題を本当には理解していない ◇She knew ***from past experience*** that Ann would not give up easily. 彼女は過去の経験から、アンは簡単にはあきらめないだろうとわかっていた ◇The book is based on ***personal experience***. その本は個人的な経験に基づいている ◇He has had ***direct/first-hand experience*** of poverty. 彼は貧困をじかに体験したことがある ☞ **experience** (EVENT 1), **experience** (KNOWLEDGE), **experience** (HAVE 3)

lifestyle [C, U] (人・人の集団の)生活様式, 生き[暮らし]方 ◇She has had to curb her lavish *lifestyle* after losing millions in legal fees. 彼女は裁判費用で何百万も失ってから、そのぜいたくな暮らしぶりを抑えざるをえなくなった ◇Many people are trying to adopt a healthy *lifestyle* these days. 最近多くの人々が健康的な生活様式を採り入れようとしている

a/the/sb's way of 'life [フレーズ] (人・人の集団の典型的な)生活様式, 生き[暮らし]方 ◇Making small adjustments to your *way of life* can allow you to find more time. 生活の仕方を少し正せば、使える時間が増えますよ ◇The expansion in tourism is seen as a threat to *the islanders'* traditional *way of life*. 観光事業の拡大は島民の伝統的な生活様式に対する脅威とみなされている

[ノート] **lifestyle**と **way of life** の使い分け：しばしば両語とも使用可能。 ◆to change/make adjustments to your *lifestyle/way of life* (生き方/生活様式を変える[正す]) しかしながら、lifestyle は概して、way of life よりも現代的で個人的なものである。個人的であれば、busy/hectic lifestyle (忙しい/多忙な生活) を送ったり、modern/healthy/alternative lifestyle (現代的な/健康的な/新しいタイプの生活様式)を採り入れたりするだろう。way of life は伝統的な[古い]ものであったり、イギリス的な[西洋風の]ものであったり、地域社会全体で共有されるものであったりする傾向が強い。

living [U] 《特に複合語や成句で》 生活様式, 生き[暮らし]方 ◇The classes are about helping children make informed choices about healthy *living*. それらの授業は子どもが健康的な生活について十分な情報を得た上での選択ができるように手助けするものだ ◇The prisoners' ***living conditions*** were appalling. 囚人たちの生活環境はぞっとするようなものだった ◇Their ***standard of living*** is very low. 彼らの生活水準は非常に低い ◇The ***cost of living*** has risen sharply. 生活費は急激に上がっている

existence [C] (困難[退屈]な)生活様式, 生き[暮らし]方 ◇The family endured a miserable *existence* in a cramped and noisy apartment. 家族は狭苦しく騒々しい

アパートでの惨めな暮らしに耐えた ◇They eke out a precarious *existence* (= they have hardly enough money to live on). 彼らはかろうじて生計を立てている ◇The peasants depend on a good harvest for their ***very existence*** (= in order to continue to live). 農民たちはまさにその生活が豊作にかかっている

like [動] ☞ LOVE [動]

like・love・be fond of sth・be keen on sth・adore・go for sb/sth
物事を愉快[魅力的, 満足]だと感じること, 物事を享受すること
【類語訳】好む, 好きである, 大好きである, 気に入る, 楽しむ, 大いに楽しむ, 惹かれる, 好みである

→

like　　　　　　　love　　　　　　adore
be fond of sth
be keen on sth
go for sb/sth

[文型&コロケーション]
▶ to like/ love/ be fond of/ be keen on/ adore *doing sth*
▶ to like/ love **to do sth**
▶ to like/ love sth **very much**
▶ I like/ love/ adore **it here/ there/ when...**
▶ to like/ love/ adore **the way** sb does sth
▶ to **really** like/ love/ go for sb/ sth
▶ to be **really** fond of/ keen on sth
▶ to **just/ simply/ absolutely/ clearly/ obviously** love/ adore sth

like [他]《進行形はまれ》 好きである, 気に入る；楽しむ ◇Which tie do you *like* best? どのネクタイが一番好きですか ◇How did you *like* Japan (= did you find it pleasant)? 日本はどうでしたか ◇You've got to go to school, whether you *like* it or not. 好むと好まざるにかかわらず、学校へは行かねばなりません ◇I didn't *like* him taking all the credit. 私は彼が手柄を独り占めにしたのが気に入らなかった ◇I *like* to see them enjoying themselves. 私は彼らが楽しんでいるのを見るのが好きです ◇I *like* it in Spain (= I like the life there). スペインでの暮らしが好きです [反意] **dislike** (HATE), ☞ **liking** (TASTE)

love [他]《進行形はまれ》 大好きである, 大いに好きである ◇I just *love* it when you bring me presents! 私はあなたがプレゼントを持ってきてくれるのがほんとに嬉しいの ◇He *loved* the way she smiled. 彼は彼女の笑い方が大好きだった ◇My dad *loves* going to football games. 私の父はサッカー観戦に出かけるのがとても好きです ◇I *love* to go out dancing.《特に米》私はダンスに出かけるのが大好きです ◇I'm *loving* every minute of this.《インフォーマル》私にはこの瞬間瞬間がもうたまらないのよ ◇***You're going to love this***. They've changed their minds again.《皮肉》あなたこれは気に入りますよ。彼らもまた気が変わったんだから [反意] **hate** (HATE), ☞ **love** (TASTE), **lover** (FAN)

be fond of sth [フレーズ] (長期間にわたって)好きである, 楽しむ ◇I'm particularly *fond of* music. 私は特に音楽が好きです ◇We *were fond of* the house and didn't want to leave. 私たちはその家が好きで、出たくなかった ☞ **fond** (LOVING)

be keen on sth [フレーズ] 《英, インフォーマル, 特に話し言葉》(し

↳like

like, likely

しばしば否定的な文で》好きである, 楽しむ ◇I'm not *keen on* spicy food. 私は辛い食べ物が好きではない ◇She's not *keen on* being told what to do. 彼女は指図されるのが嫌いだ ◇He's very *keen on* golf. 彼はゴルフがとても好きだ
☞ **keen** (EAGER)

adore /他》《進行形なし》《インフォーマル》大好きである, 大いに楽しむ ◇Don't you just *adore* that dress! あのドレス, 惚れ惚れしない ◇She *adores* working with children. 彼女は子どもを扱う仕事が大好きだ 反意 **loathe** (HATE)

ノート love と adore の使い分け：adore は love よりもインフォーマルで, より強い感情を表現する.

'**go for sb/sth** 句動詞《進行形なし》《インフォーマル》〈人・物事に〉惹かれる, 好みである；〈人・物事(のほう)を〉好む ◇She *goes for* tall slim men. 彼女はすらっと背の高い男性が好き ◇I don't really *go for* modern art. 私はあまりモダンアートは好きではない

like 前 形

like • similar • close • alike
他の人や物事とほとんど変わらないことを表す
【類語訳】似て, よく似て, 酷似して, 同じように, ほとんど同じで, …ふうに, 似た, よく似た, 同じような, 近い

文型&コロケーション
▶ similar/ close **to** sb/ sth
▶ like sth/ similar/ close/ alike **in** size, amount, etc.
▶ like/ similar **age**/ **circumstances**/ **kind**/ **manner**
▶ a like/ similar **case**/ **situation**
▶ **to look** like sth/ similar/ alike
▶ **to feel**/ **sound**/ **taste** like sth/ similar
▶ **very**/ **quite** like sth/ similar/ close/ alike
▶ **rather**/ **remarkably**/ **basically** like sth/ similar/ alike
▶ **exactly** like sth/ alike

like 前 似て, 同じようで；…のようなやり方で, …ふうに ◇She's wearing a dress *like* mine. 彼女は私と同じようなドレスを着ている ◇He's *very like* his father. 《特に英》彼は父親そっくりだ ◇She looks *nothing like* (= not at all like) her mother. 彼女は母親とまったく似ていない ◇Students were angry at being treated *like* children. 生徒たちは子ども扱いされて腹を立てていた ◇You do it *like* this. こんなふうにやりなさい ◇Don't look at me *like* that. そんなふうに私を見ないで ❶《フォーマル》な言い回しでは, like は形容詞として名詞の前で用いられることもあり,「もう一方の人[物事]と似た性質を持つ」ことを意味する. ◆You'll get a chance to meet people of *like mind* (= with similar interests and opinions). 《フォーマル》うまの合う人と出会う機会があるでしょう. ◆She responded in *like* manner. 彼女は同じような態度で答えた. 反意 **unlike** (DIFFERENT), ☞ **likeness** (SIMILARITY)
▶ **like** 名 [単数で] ◇I enjoy jazz, rock *and the like* (= similar types of music). 私はジャズやロックなどの音楽が好きです ◇I let the apartment to students, backpackers *and such like*. 私は学生やバックパッカーといった類の人たちにアパートを貸している ◇They experienced a period of expansion *the like of which* the world had rarely seen. 彼らは世界でもめったに見られないような発展期を経験した ◇You're not *comparing like with like*. 君は鳶(とんび)と鷹を比べているようなものだ[似た者同士の間じゃないと比較にならないよ]

similar 形 似た, 同じような ◇We have very *similar* interests. 私たちは興味が非常によく似ている ◇My teaching style is *similar* to that of most other teachers. 私の指導方法は他のほとんどの先生たちと同じようなものです ◇The two houses are *similar* in size. その2軒の家は同じくらいの大きさである ◇The brothers look very *similar*. その兄弟は非常によく似ている ◇Stir the paint with a piece of wood or something *similar*. 木材かその手の物で塗料をかき混ぜてください 反意 **different, dissimilar** (DIFFERENT), ☞ **similarity** (SIMILARITY)
▶ **similarly** 副 ◇Husband and wife were *similarly* successful in their chosen careers. 夫婦はそれぞれが選んだ職業で同じくらいの成功を収めた

close よく似た, 近い ◇There's a *close* resemblance between them (= they look very similar). 彼らはよく似ている ◇His feeling for her was *close* to hatred. 彼の彼女に対する感情は憎しみに近いものだった ◇We tried to match the colours, but this was the *closest* we could get. その色と同じ色のものを見つけようとしたが, 手に入る一番近いものだった
▶ **closely** 副 ◇She *closely* resembled her mother at the same age. 彼女は母親の同じ年頃のときとよく似ていた

alike [名詞の前では用いない] よく似た, 酷似した；ほとんど同じで ◇My sister and I do not look *alike*. 姉と私は似ていません ◇The two towns are very much *alike* in size and population. その2つの町は大きさも人口もほとんど同じである ❶ alike は pretty much alike, so (much) alike, very (much) alike, look alike の句で用いられることが多い.
▶ **alike** 副 ◇They tried to treat all their children *alike*. 彼らは子どもたちを皆同じように扱おうとした

likely 形

likely • possible • potential • prospective • probable
物事に蓋然性があることを表す
【類語訳】可能性のある, ありそうに思われる, 起こりうる, 見込みのある, 予想される, 潜在的な, …しそうな

→

| possible | prospective | likely |
| potential | | probable |

文型&コロケーション
▶ **to be** likely/ possible/ probable **that**…
▶ a likely/ possible/ potential/ prospective/ probable **site**
▶ a likely/ possible/ potential/ probable **cause**/ **effect**/ **consequence**/ **outcome**
▶ a likely/ possible/ probable **explanation**
▶ the likely/ possible/ probable **cost**
▶ a likely/ possible/ potential/ prospective **candidate**
▶ a potential/ prospective **husband**/ **wife**/ **parent**
▶ **quite** likely/ possible/ probable
▶ **hardly** likely/ possible
▶ **very**/ **extremely**/ **highly** likely/ probable

likely 可能性のある, あり[起こり]そうに思われる, 有力な ◇What is the most *likely* cause of the infection? 最も有力な感染源は何ですか ◇Tickets are *likely to* be expensive. チケットは高価なものになりそうだ ◇It's *more than likely that* the thieves don't know how much it is worth. 泥棒たちがどれくらいの価値があるか知らないのはほぼ間違いない ◇They might refuse to let us do it, but it's hardly *likely*. 彼らが私たちにそうさせまいとする可能性はあるが、まずそうはならないだろう 反意 **unlikely** (UNLIKELY 1), ☞ **likelihood** (POSSIBILITY), **most likely** (PROBABLY)

possible 可能性のある、あり[起こり]うる、有力な ◇They spoke of her as a *possible* future president. 彼らは彼女のことを将来の大統領候補だと言った ◇With the *possible* exception of the Beatles, no other band has become so successful so quickly. ビートルズのような例外はあるかもしれないが、他のバンドでこれほど速くこれほどの成功を収めているものはない ◇It's just *possible* that I gave them the wrong directions. 私が彼らに間違った指示を与えた可能性はないとは言えない ◇'You might be wrong, of course!' 'It's *possible*, but I doubt it.'「もちろん、あなたが間違っているかもしれないよね」「そうかもしれないけど、それはどうかな」 反意 **impossible** (IMPOSSIBLE), ☞ **possibility** (POSSIBILITY)

potential [名詞の前で] 見込みのある、予想される、潜在的な ◇First we need to identify actual and *potential* problems. 初めに私たちに実際に起こる、そして起こりうる問題を特定する必要があります ◇What are the *potential* benefits of these proposals? これらの計画にはどのような利益が見込めますか ❶ *potential* はいくつかの形の連語で用いられる。製品を購入[サービスを利用]する可能性のある人々について: ◆a *potential* audience/buyer/client/consumer/customer （潜在的な視聴者/購入者/依頼人/消費者/顧客）悪い方向に進む可能性のある物事について: ◆a *potential* complication/danger/disaster/drawback/embarrassment/hazard/pitfall/risk/threat（予想される面倒（な問題）/危険/災害/障害/困難/危険/落とし穴/リスク/脅威）人々が享受する可能性のある物事について: ◆a *potential* advantage/benefit/improvement/saving （見込まれる利点/利益/改良点/節減） 反意 **actual** (REAL), ☞ **potential** (POTENTIAL)

▷ **potentially** 副 ◇a *potentially* dangerous situation 潜在的に危険な状況

prospective [名詞の前で]《ややフォーマル》見込みのある、…し[になり]そうな ◇I had a phone call from a *prospective* client today. 今日依頼人になりそうな人から電話があった ❶ *prospective* は主に人について用いられる。◆a *prospective* buyer/client/customer/applicant/candidate/employee/employer/husband/wife/parent （購入者/依頼人/顧客/志願者/候補者/従業員/雇い主/夫/妻/親になる見込みのある人）☞ **prospect** (POSSIBILITY), **prospects** (POTENTIAL)

ノート **potential** と **prospective** の使い分け: 両語とも購入者[従業員]などになる見込みのある人に用いられるが、**prospective** はすでに製品[サービス]に関心を示している人に用いられることが多い。**potential** は、例えば会社の広告対象となりうる一般的な人々に用いられることが多い。

probable 《ややフォーマル、特に書き言葉》可能性のある、あり[起こり]そうに思われる、有力な ◇The *probable* cause of the fire was an electrical fault. 火事の原因と思われるものは電気の故障だった ◇It is quite *probable* that they will call an election next spring. 来春選挙が行われる可能性が極めて高い 反意 **improbable** (UNLIKELY 1), ☞ **probability** (POSSIBILITY), **probably** (PROBABLY)

ノート **likely** と **probable** の使い分け: likely は probable よりも幅広い構文や言語使用域で用いられる。◆It is *likely/probable* that... （…という可能性がある）◆sb/sth is *likely* to do sth （人・物事が…する可能性がある）✗sb/sth is *probable* to do sth. probable は話し言葉よりも書き言葉において10倍は頻繁に用いられる。likely は書き言葉でも話し言葉でも非常に頻繁に用いられる。

limit 名

1 limit・restriction・control・constraint・restraint・limitation・ceiling・curb・check
行動の幅や生じる可能性のあるものに限度を設けること
【類語訳】範囲、限度、制限、制約、規制、規定、統制、抑制、抑止、防止、自制、節度、遠慮、最高限度

文型＆コロケーション

▶ limits/ restrictions/ controls/ constraints/ restraints/ limitations/ a ceiling/ curbs/ checks **on** sth
▶ limits/ limitations/ checks **to** sth
▶ **without** limits/ restrictions/ controls/ constraints/ restraints/ limitations/ checks
▶ **severe** limits/ restrictions/ controls/ constraints/ restraints/ limitations/ checks
▶ **tight** limits/ restrictions/ controls/ constraints
▶ **effective** limits/ restrictions/ controls/ constraints/ restraints
▶ an **artificial** limit/ restriction/ constraint
▶ to **impose** limits/ restrictions/ controls/ constraints/ restraints/ limitations/ a ceiling/ curbs/ checks
▶ to **place** limits/ restrictions/ controls/ constraints/ restraints/ limitations/ a ceiling/ checks
▶ to **introduce** limits/ restrictions/ controls/ constraints/ limitations/ curbs/ checks
▶ to **remove**/ **accept** limits/ restrictions/ controls/ constraints/ restraints/ limitations
▶ to **lift** restrictions/ controls/ constraints/ restraints/ the ceiling
▶ to **tighten**/ **relax** restrictions/ controls/ constraints
▶ to **act as** a control/ constraint/ restraint/ limitation/ ceiling/ curb/ check

limit [C] （許される最大[最小]の）範囲、限度、制限 ◇The EU has set strict *limits* on pollution levels. EUは汚染レベルに厳しい制限を設けている ◇He admitted that he had broken the speed *limit*. 彼は制限速度を破ってしまったことを認めた ◇You can't drive — you're **over the limit** (= you have drunk more alcohol than is legal when driving). 運転はできませんよ—法定許容アルコール量を超えています ◇It is our job to keep government spending within acceptable *limits*. 政府支出を許容範囲内に保つことが我々の任務である

restriction [C] 《ややフォーマル》（規則[法律]上の）制限、制約、規制、規定 ◇Speed *restrictions* are in operation on the M4 due to poor visibility. 視界の悪さから、高速幹線道路4号線ではスピード制限が実施されている ◇The government has agreed to lift *restrictions* on press freedom. 政府は報道の自由に対する制約を解除することに合意した ◇There are no *restrictions* on the amount of money you can withdraw. 引き出し可能な金額に制限はありません

control [U, C] 《しばしば複合語で》（管理上の）規制、統制、抑制、防除、蔓延防止；規制[防除]の方法 ◇traffic *control* 交通規制 ◇talks on arms *control* 軍縮交渉 ◇A new advance has been made in the *control* of malaria. マラリアの蔓延防止策において新しい進歩が遂げられた ◇*government controls* on trade and industry 通商・産業に関する政府統制 ◇Price *controls* on food were ended. 食品に対する価格統制は終了した ◇A pest *control* officer was called in to deal with the rat problem. ネズミ問題に対処するために有害生物防除官が呼ばれた

constraint [C]《ややフォーマル》《事実上の[決定された]》制限, 制約, 規制 ◇We have to work within severe *constraints* of time and money. 我々は時間と金の厳しい制約の中で働かなければならない ◇This decision will impose serious financial *constraints* on all schools. この決定により,すべての学校に深刻な財政的制約が課せられるだろう

restraint [C, ふつう複数形, U]《ややフォーマル》《決定された[規則上の,考えの上での]》制限, 制約, 規制, 抑制 ;《必要[良識]から生まれる》自制, 節度, 遠慮 ◇The government has imposed export *restraints* on some products. 政府はいくつかの製品に対して輸出制限を課している ◇There are certain social *restraints* on drinking alcohol. 飲酒については一定の社会的制約がある ◇The unions are unlikely to accept any sort of wage *restraint*. 労働組合はいかなる種類の賃金抑制も受け入れそうにない ◇They said that they would fight without *restraint* (= completely freely) for what they wanted. 彼らはほしいものを手に入れるためにはとことん闘うと述べた

limitation [U, C] 制限[行為[過程]] ;（規則[事実]上の[条件としての]）制約, 規制 ◇They would resist any *limitation* of their powers. 彼らは自分たちの権力に対するどんな制約にも抵抗するだろう ◇Disability is a physical *limitation* on your life. 障碍(がい)とは人生に物理的制約がつきまとうことだ ◇There should be no *limitations* to progress in the talks. 交渉の進展に制約があってはならない

[ノート] **restriction, constraint, restraint, limitation**の使い分け: これらの語はすべて可能な行動を制限することを指す. restrictionは権限のある者によって作られるもの規則[法律]によるものを指す. constraintは作られるというよりは,すでに存在するものを指し,それは外部からもたらされる「制約」である. restraintもすでに存在するものだが,外部からの「制約」でもあるし,自らに課せる「制約」でもある. ◆ moral/social/cultural/conventional *restraints*（道徳的/社会的/文化的/慣習的制約）. limitationはより一般的で,人によって作られる場合もある, 事実[条件]として存在する場合もある.

ceiling [C]（価格・賃金などに対する）最高限度, シーリング ◇They have put a *ceiling* on the price of fuel. 燃料価格に対して最高限度が設けられている ◇The government has decided to lift price *ceilings* on bread and milk. 政府はパンと牛乳に対する最高価格を引き上げることを決定した

curb [C]（水準・数量・程度の）制限, 制約, 規制, 抑制 ◇We are in favour of strict *curbs* on government spending. 我々は政府支出を厳しく抑制することに賛成する ◇Counselling acted as a *curb* on his violent behaviour. カウンセリングは彼の暴力行為を抑制する役割を果たした

check [C]《ややフォーマル》（進展を鈍化させる[悪化を妨げる]）抑制, 抑止, 防止 ◇A cold spring will provide a natural *check* on the number of insects. 春が寒いと昆虫の数は自然に抑制されるだろう ◇The House of Commons became the most fundamental *check* to the power of the British monarchy. 下院は英国の君主制が持つ権力の最も基本的な抑止機関となった

2 limit・line・boundary・parameter・bounds・frontier・confines・borderline
思考[行動, 可能性]の領域のへり, 一つの思考などの領域とも一方の領域との間を分け隔てるもの
【類語訳】範囲, 限界, 境界, 限度, 最前線, 空間

[文型&コロケーション]
▶the line/ boundary/ borderline **between** sth and sth else
▶**beyond** the limits/ boundaries/ parameters/ bounds/ frontiers/ confines of sth
▶**within** the limits/ boundaries/ parameters/ bounds/ confines of sth
▶**outside** the limits/ parameters/ bounds/ confines of sth
▶**at** the limits/ boundaries/ frontiers/ borderline of sth
▶**on** the boundary/ borderline between/ of sth
▶to **extend** the limits/ boundaries/ parameters/ bounds/ frontiers of sth
▶to **set/ define/ establish** the limits/ boundaries/ parameters/ bounds of sth
▶to **cross** the boundary/ borderline between/ of sth

limit [C]（可能で[存在し]なくなる）限界(点) ◇There is *a limit to* the amount of pain we can bear. 我々が耐えられる痛みには限界がある ◇There is *no limit to* what we can achieve. 私たちが達成できることに限界はない ◇Our finances have been stretched *to the limit*. 我々の融資は限界に達している ◇She pushed me *to the limit of* my abilities. 彼女は私を能力の限界まで押し上げてくれた ◇She knew the *limits* of her power. 彼女は自分の力の限界を知っていた

line [C]（思考[行動]領域の）境界(線), 限界 ◇We want to cut across *lines* of race, sex and religion. 私たちは人種・性別・宗教の境界を越えたいと思っています ◇There is a *fine line* between showing interest in what someone is doing and interfering in it. 人がしていることに関心を示すこととそれに干渉することは紙一重の差だ ◇There is no clear *dividing line* between what is good and what is bad. 良いことと悪いことの間にははっきりした境界線はない

boundary [C]（思考[行動]領域の）境界(線), 限界 ◇It is up to the teacher to set the *boundary* between acceptable and unacceptable behaviour. 許容できる行動と許容できない行動の間に境界を設けるのは教師の責任だ ◇Scientists continue to push back the *boundaries* of human knowledge. 科学者は人間の限界を広げ続けている

[ノート] **line**と**boundary**の使い分け: lineは二つの思考[行動]領域の間の「境界」で, しばしば慎重に判断する必要のあるものを指す. boundaryは人によって決められる「境界」である. ×no clear dividing *boundary*. ×a fine *boundary* between. ×It is up to the teacher to set the *line*... boundaryの内にあるものには注意が向けられ, それは考慮の対象となる. push back/extend the boundaries of sth（物事の限界を広げる）とは言えるが, lineは不可. ×push/back extend the *lines*.

parameter [C, ふつう複数で]《フォーマル》（考慮が必要な）範囲, 限界, 境界 ◇We need to define the *parameters* of this debate. 私たちはこの議論の範囲を限定する必要がある ◇We had to work within the *parameters* that had already been established. 私たちはすでに設定された範囲

内で作業を進めるほかなかった

bounds [複数で]《ややフォーマル》(受け入れられる[最大限の])範囲, 限界, 境界, 限度 ◇Public spending must be kept within reasonable *bounds*. 公共支出は妥当な範囲内にとどめなければならない ◇It was not *beyond the bounds of possibility* that they would meet again one day. 彼らがいつか再び会うことはありえないことではなかった ◇His enthusiasm *knew no bounds* (= was very great). 彼の熱意はとどまることを知らなかった

frontier [C, ふつう複数で] (知識[できること]の)範囲, 限界, 境界, 最前線 ◇This research programme aims to push back the *frontiers* of science. この研究プログラムは科学の最前線を推し進めることを目指している

confines [複数で] (壁などの障害物で囲まれた)空間；(知識[許されること, 可能性]の狭い)範囲, 限界, 境界 ◇He spent three years within the narrow *confines* of the prison. 彼は刑務所の狭い空間の中で3年間を過ごした ◇She wanted to experience things outside the close *confines* of family life. 彼女は家庭生活の密接で狭い関係から外に出ていろんな事を経験したいと思った

[ノート] **frontiers** と **confines** の使い分け：confines は空間[知識]などの狭さを強調する. frontiers は知識の広さや広がりを強調する.

borderline [C] (二つの性質[状態]の間の)境界線 ◇The biography sometimes crosses the *borderline* between fact and fiction. 伝記は時として事実と虚構の境界線を越える ☞ **borderline** (VAGUE)

limited [形]

1 ☞ SCARCE
limited・narrow・restricted
数量や程度があまり大きくないことを表す
【類語訳】限られた, 制限された, 乏しい, 狭い, 狭量な, 偏狭な

[文型&コロケーション]
▶ limited/ narrow/ restricted **in** scope
▶ a limited/ narrow/ restricted **range/ scope/ vocabulary**
▶ a limited/ narrow **objective**
▶ limited/ narrow **horizons**
▶ the limited/ narrow **confines** of sth
▶ a limited/ restricted **franchise**

limited (数量[程度]が)限られた, 乏しい ◇We are doing our best with the *limited* resources available. 我々は利用できる限られた資源で最善を尽くしている ◇This animal's intelligence is very *limited*. この動物の知能は非常に限られている ◇These are issues that go beyond the *limited* confines of this book. これらはこの本が対象とする限られた範囲を超える問題である ❶ *limited* は物や能力などについて用いられる. ◆*limited* resources/funds/ supplies (限られた資源/資金/供給). ◆a *limited* ability/ capability/ capacity/ ability/ intelligence/ intellect/ knowledge/ understanding (乏しい能力/才能/(潜在的)能力/知能/知性/知識/理解力). 反意 **unlimited** ❶ *unlimited* は制限がないことを表す. ◆The ticket gives you *unlimited* travel for seven days. (そのチケットで7日間無制限に旅行できます). ◆You will be allowed *unlimited* access to the files. (そのファイルには無制限にアクセスすることが許されます).

narrow 《ふつうなしで》(種類・数が)限られた, 狭い；(他人の意見[重要な問題]を無視するほど)狭量な, 偏狭な ◇She only has a *narrow* circle of friends. 彼女の交友関係はほんの狭いものに過ぎない ◇The exhibition is disappointingly *narrow* in scope. その展覧会はがっかりするほど視野が狭い ◇She has a very *narrow* view of the world. 彼女の世界観は非常に偏狭だ 反意 **wide, broad** (WIDE 1)

restricted (数量・種類が)限られた, 制限された ◇There is only a *restricted* range of goods available. 限られた品ぞろえの商品しかない ◇He has a severely *restricted* diet. 彼は厳しく食事を制限している

2 limited・restricted・controlled
物事が規則[法律]の一部として設定された特定領域内にある[とどまるべき]ことを表す
【類語訳】制限された, 限られた, 限定の, 専用の, 規制された

[文型&コロケーション]
▶ to be limited/ restricted **to** sth
▶ limited/ restricted/ controlled **access**
▶ highly/ tightly restricted/ controlled
▶ strictly limited/ controlled

limited (数・時間などが)制限された, 限られた, 限定の ◇The number of passengers is *limited* to fifteen. 乗客数は15人に制限されている ◇This offer is for a *limited* period only. この特価は期間限定です ◇Places are strictly *limited*, so you should apply as soon as possible. 席はかなり限られているから, できるだけ早く申し込んだほうがいい

restricted (行動が)制限された；(特定の集団に)限られた, 専用の ◇In those days women led fairly *restricted* lives. 当時女性はかなり制限された生活を送っていた ◇They are closely guarded and severely **restricted in** their movements. 彼らはぴったりと監視され, 行動を厳しく制限されている ◇The tournament is *restricted* to players under the age of 23. そのトーナメントは23歳未満の選手に限られている

controlled (法律[規則]によって)規制[統制, 管理]された ◇In many countries the production of the drug is illegal or tightly *controlled*. 多くの国でその麻薬の製造は違法であるか, または厳しく規制されている ◇He was charged with possessing a *controlled* drug. 彼は規制薬物所持の罪で起訴された

list [名]

list・index・table・catalogue・directory・register・inventory・roll・checklist・listing
順に書き記される[印刷される]一連の名前[項目, 数字]
【類語訳】リスト, 表, 一覧表, 目録, 名簿, 索引, カタログ, 電話帳, 住所氏名録, 商工名鑑, 記録簿, 出席簿, チェックリスト

[文型&コロケーション]
▶ **in** a list/ an index/ a table/ a catalogue/ a directory/ a register/ an inventory/ a listing
▶ **on** a list/ a register/ an inventory/ a roll/ a checklist
▶ a **comprehensive/ complete/ full** list/ index/ table/ catalogue/ register/ inventory/ listing
▶ a **detailed** list/ index/ catalogue/ directory/ register/ inventory/ listing
▶ an **alphabetical** list/ index/ catalogue/ directory/ listing

- ▶to **compile** a list/ an index/ a table/ a directory/ a register/ an inventory/ a checklist
- ▶to **draw up** a list/ a table/ a catalogue/ a register/ an inventory/ a checklist
- ▶to **create** a list/ an index/ a table/ a directory/ a register/ an inventory
- ▶to **produce** a list/ a table/ a catalogue/ a directory/ an inventory/ a checklist/ a listing
- ▶to **keep** a list/ an index/ a register/ an inventory
- ▶to **list sth in** an index/ a table/ a catalogue/ the directory/ an inventory
- ▶to **include sth in** a list/ a table/ a catalogue/ an inventory/ a checklist/ a listing
- ▶to **consult/ look (sth up) in** an index/ a table/ a catalogue/ a directory
- ▶an index/ a table/ a catalogue/ a directory/ an inventory **lists** sth

list [C] (名前・項目・数字の)リスト, 表, 一覧表, 目録, 名簿 ◇Is your name on the *list*? あなたの名前は名簿にありますか ◇Make a *list* of all the places you've visited. あなたが訪れたことのあるすべての場所の一覧表を作ってください ◇This issue is pretty low on their *list of priorities*. この問題は彼らの優先順位ではかなり低い ◇What's on your *shopping list*? 買い物リストには何が載っていますか ◇There's a long *waiting list* to get treatment. 治療を受ける長い順番待ちリストがある ◇Do you want to be put on our *mailing list*? 当社のメーリングリスト[郵送先名簿]への登録をご希望ですか ◇Over 200 people are on our *guest list*. 200人以上の方々が私どもの来賓名簿に載っています ◇Her name was at *the top of the list*. 彼女の名前は名簿の一番上にあった

index [C] 索引, 目録 ◇Look it up in the *index*. それを索引で調べてください ◇It's a general *index to* the whole work. それはその作品全体の総索引である
 ▷**index** [他, ふつう受身で] ◇The reports are *indexed by* subject and name. それらの報告書にはテーマと名前別の索引が付けられている ◇The article was *indexed* under 'Parliament' and 'Law'. その記事は「議会」と「法律」の索引項目に載っていた

table [C] (横[縦]行に並べられた事実・数字の)表, 一覧表, 目録 ◇a *table of contents* (= a list of the main points or information in a book, usually at the front of the book) 目次 ◇*Table* 2 shows how prices and earnings have increased over the last 20 years. 表2では過去20年間で価格と所得がいかに増加しているかが示されている

catalogue (米また **catalog**) [C] (商品などの)カタログ, 目録 ◇She consulted the museum *catalogue*. 彼女はその美術館のカタログを調べた ◇Please take a look at our online *catalogue*. 当社のオンライン・カタログをご覧ください ◇a mail-order *catalogue* 通信販売カタログ
 ▷**catalogue** (米また **catalog**) [動] [他] ◇She painstakingly *catalogued* all the photographs in the museum. 彼女はその美術館にあるすべての写真の目録を苦労して作った ◇The collection had never been properly *catalogued*. そのコレクションはそれまでまともに作られたことがなかった

directory [C] 電話帳, 住所氏名録, 商工名鑑 ◇You can get some useful contacts from a trade *directory*. 商工名鑑から役に立つ連絡先を得ることができます ◇They are listed in the *telephone directory*. 《フォーマル》彼らの電話番号は電話帳に載っている ❶電話帳は日常の話し言葉ではふつう **phone book** と呼ばれる.

register [C] (名前・項目の正式な)一覧表, 目録, 名簿; 記録[登録, 出席]簿 ◇Could you *sign* the hotel *register* please? 宿泊者名簿に記入していただけますか ◇The teacher *called the register* (= checked that all the students on a class register were present by calling out their names). 《英》その教師は出席を取った ❶《米》では roll と呼ばれる. ☞ **register** (RECORD)

inventory [C] (特定建物内の品目の)目録 ◇She compiled an *inventory* of all the museum's contents. 彼女はその美術館のすべての所蔵品の目録を一冊にまとめた

roll [C] 名簿, 出席簿 ◇You can check that you are on the *electoral roll* by calling this number. この番号に電話すればあなたが選挙人名簿に載っていることが確認できます ◇Who would appear on your personal *roll of honour* (= a list of people who you think deserve special praise)? あなたが個人的に尊敬する人には誰がいますか ◇The teacher *called the roll* (= checked that all the students on a class register were present by calling out their names). 《米》その教師は出席を取った ❶出席簿は《英》では register と呼ばれる. ❶ **payroll** は会社に雇われている人々の給与の額を示す名簿を指す. ◆We have 500 people on the *payroll*. (当社の給与支払名簿には500人が記載されている).

checklist [C] 照合表, チェックリスト ◇She ticked off the items on the *checklist*. 彼女は照合表の項目に✓印をつけた ◇I ran through my mental *checklist* of items. 私は頭の中のチェックリストの項目をざっと点検した

listing [C] (アルファベット順に正式に記載された[発表された])リスト, 表, 一覧表, 目録, 名簿 ◇The agency provides a comprehensive *listing* of all airlines. その代理店は全航空会社の一覧表を提供している

list [動]

list • define • specify • detail • state • itemize
物事を一覧にして[特定の順序で]示す
【類語訳】表にする, 一覧表を作る, 列挙する, 記載する, 明確に述べる, 明示する, 明記する, 詳述する, 指定する

【文型&コロケーション】
- ▶to list/ define/ specify/ detail/ state/ name/ itemize sth **as** sth
- ▶to list/ define/ specify/ detail/ state/ name/ itemize sth **in** sth
- ▶to list/ define/ specify/ detail/ itemize sth **under** sth
- ▶to define/ specify/ detail/ state **what/ how/ where/ who...**
- ▶to specify/ state **that...**
- ▶to list/ define/ specify/ detail **tasks**
- ▶to list/ specify/ state/ itemize **details**
- ▶to list/ define/ specify/ detail/ name/ enumerate **items**
- ▶to **fully/ carefully** list/ define/ specify/ detail/ itemize sth
- ▶to **clearly** define/ specify/ state sth
- ▶to list/ define/ specify/ itemize sth **separately**

list [他] (名前を特定の順序で)表にする, 一覧表[リスト]を作る, 列挙する ;(一覧表[リスト]に)記載する ◇We were asked to *list* our ten favourite songs. 私たちは好きな歌曲を10曲列挙するように求められた ◇Towns in the guide are *listed* alphabetically. 旅行案内にある町はアルファベット順に記載されている ◇Articles may be *listed* under more than one heading. 記事は一つ以上の見出しの下に

live, lively

記載されているかもしれない ◇The names are *listed below*. 名前は以下に記載されています

define [他]（物事を）明確に述べる[記す]，明示する，はっきりと規定する ◇We need to *define* the task ahead very clearly. 私たちは前もって職務をはっきりと規定する必要がある ◇The difficulty of a problem was *defined in terms of* how long it took to complete. ある問題の困難さは完了までどのくらい時間がかかるかという観点から明確に示された ◇It is difficult to *define* what makes him so popular. どうして彼がそれほどまでに人気があるのかを明確に説明するのは難しい ☞ **definition** (DEFINITION)

specify [他]（ややフォーマル）（測定・時期・指示などを）明細に述べる[記す]，指定[明記]する，明示する，はっきり[仕様]を示す ◇Forms must be returned by the *specified* date. 用紙は指定期日までに必ずご返送ください ◇The contract clearly *specifies* who can operate the machinery. その契約書には誰が機械を操作できるかがはっきりと明記されている ◇The regulations *specify* that calculators may not be used in the examination. その規則には試験で計算機は使えないことが明記されている
▶ **specification** [名] [C, U] ◇the technical *specifications* of the new model (= of car) 新型モデルの技術仕様[明細]書 ◇The house has been built exactly *to our specification*. その家は私たちの仕様に正確に合わせて建築された

detail [他]（事実[入手可能な全情報]を）詳細に[記す]，列挙する ◇The brochure *details* all the hotels in the area and their facilities. パンフレットにはその地域にあるすべてのホテルとその設備が列挙されている ☞ **detail** (INFORMATION)

state [他，ふつう受身で]（文書で）詳述[明記]する，詳細[明確]に提示する[定める] ◇This is not one of their *stated* aims. これは彼らが明示している目標の一つではない ◇You must arrive at the time *stated*. あなたは定められた時刻に到着しなければならない

name [他]（正確に）指定する，列挙する；はっきり決める ◇*Name your price*. 価格を指定してください ◇They're engaged, but they haven't yet *named the day* (= fixed a date for the wedding). 彼らは婚約しているが，まだ結婚式の日取りをはっきり決めていない ◇Activities available include squash, archery and swimming, *to name but a few*. 利用可能な活動には，ほんのいくつか例を挙げると，スカッシュ，アーチェリー，水泳が含まれます ◇Chairs, tables, cabinets — *you name it*, she makes it (= she makes anything you can imagine). 椅子にテーブルに戸棚に—どんなものでも，彼女は作ります
❶ name は specify ほどフォーマルではないが，たいていの場合のいくつかの定型句で用いられる

itemize [英でまた **-ise**] [他]（物事を）項目別[箇条書き]に述べる[記す]，列挙する，明細[仕様]を示す ◇The report *itemized* over 25 different faults. 報告書には25を超える種類の欠陥が列挙されていた ◇You can ask for an *itemized* phone bill (= one which gives details of each call). 項目別に記載された電話代の請求書を求めることができます

live [動]

live・inhabit・occupy・reside・people
特定の場所に自分の家を持つ
【類語訳】住む，生息する，占有する，居住する，暮らす

文型&コロケーション
▶ to live/ reside **in**/ **among**/ **near** sth
▶ to live in/ inhabit/ occupy/ reside in a **house**
▶ to live in/ inhabit/ occupy a **building**
▶ to live in/ inhabit/ people the **world**
▶ to live in/ inhabit in a **region**

live [自]（副詞や前置詞と共に）（特定の場所に）住む ◇I *live* in an old farmhouse. 私は古い農家に住んでいる ◇We used to *live* in London. 私たちは昔ロンドンに住んでいた ◇Where do you *live*? あなたはどこに住んでるの ◇She needs to find somewhere to *live*. 彼女はどこか住む場所を見つける必要がある

inhabit [他]（特定の（種類の）地域[区域]に）住む，生息する ◇Some of the rare species that *inhabit* the area are under threat. その地域に棲息するいくつかの珍種は危機に瀕している ◇The island used to be *inhabited* (= have people living there). その島にはかつて人が住んでいた ☞ **inhabitant** (RESIDENT)

occupy [他]（フォーマル）（生活する[働く]目的で部屋[建物]を[に]）占有[使用]する，居住する，構える ◇He *occupies* an office on the 51st floor. 彼は51階にオフィスを構えている ☞ **occupant** (TENANT)

reside [自]（副詞や前置詞と共に）（フォーマル）（特定の場所に）住む ◇Do you still *reside* at 56 Elm Road? まだエルム街56番地に住んでるの ◇Their passports do not give them the right to *reside* in the United Kingdom. 彼らのパスポートでは英国に住む権利は得られない ☞ **residence** (HOME), **resident** (RESIDENT)

people [他，ふつう受身で]（書き言葉）（場所に）住む，（環境の中で）暮らす，（場所・環境を人々で）一杯にする ◇The town was *peopled* largely by workers from the car factory and their families. その町は主に自動車工場の従業員とその家族が住んでいた ◇Her novels are *peopled* with interesting, complex characters. 彼女の小説には面白い複雑な登場人物がたくさん出てくる

lively [形] ☞ ENERGETIC

lively・spirited・exuberant・hearty・ebullient・animated・vivacious・bubbly
人が活力にあふれていることを表す
【類語訳】元気な，活発な，快活な，陽気な，はつらつとした，生き生きとした，活気に満ちた，生気に満ちた，にぎやかな，はしゃいだ，意気揚々とした

文型&コロケーション
▶ a lively/ an exuberant/ an ebullient/ a vivacious/ a bubbly **personality**
▶ a lively/ spirited/ vivacious **young woman**
▶ a lively/ vivacious/ bubbly **girl**
▶ a lively/ an exuberant/ an ebullient **mood**
▶ a lively/ a spirited/ an exuberant **performance**

lively （ほめて）元気な，活発な，快活な，はつらつとした；生き生きとした，活気[生気]に満ちた，にぎやかな，熱心な ◇She's an intelligent and *lively* young woman. 彼女は聡明で活発な若い女性である ◇He showed a *lively* interest in politics. 彼は政治に強い関心を示した ◇Her eyes were bright and *lively*. 彼女の目は生き生きと輝いていた
▶ **liveliness** [名] [U] ◇Her *liveliness* and wit impressed him. 彼女の快活さと機知が彼の印象に残った

↪lively

spirited [ふつう名詞の前で]《ほめて》元気な、活発な、快活な、猛烈な、勇気のある ◇She was an attractive and *spirited* young woman. 彼女は魅力的で快活な若い女性だった ◇He put up a *spirited* defence in the final game. 彼は決勝で猛烈なディフェンスを示した ☞ **spirit** (DETERMINATION)

exuberant [特に書き言葉] 元気[熱意、喜び]に満ちあふれた ◇A noisy bunch of *exuberant* youngsters were gathered outside. 元気一杯の騒がしい若者の一団が外に集められた ◇She gave an *exuberant* performance. 彼女は熱意あふれる演奏を行った

▸ **exuberance** [名] ◇Nothing will curb his natural *exuberance*. 彼の生まれつきの元気のよさを止められるものはないだろう

hearty [時にけなして] 元気一杯の、熱烈な、うるさい、遠慮のない、はしゃいだ ◇'I'll do it!' he said in a *hearty* voice. 「僕やります」と彼は元気一杯の声で言った ◇Her laugh was far too *hearty* to be genuine. 彼女の笑い方は元気一杯すぎて心からの笑いには思えなかった

ebullient [書き言葉] 意気揚々とした、威勢のよい ◇The Prime Minister was in *ebullient* mood. 首相は意気揚々とした気分だった ◇The *ebullient* Mr Clarke was not to be discouraged. 威勢のよいクラーク氏ががっかりするようなことはなかった

▸ **ebullience** [名] [U] ◇I put her remarks down to youthful *ebullience*. 私は彼女の発言を若気の至りであると見なした

animated (人の見た目・話し方が)生き生きとした、元気な、活発な、活気[生気]に満ちた ◇Her face suddenly became *animated*. 彼女の顔が突然生き生きとしてきた ◇Sounds of *animated* conversation and laughter came from the next room. 活気に満ちた会話や笑い声が隣の部屋から聞こえてきた [反意] **impassive**

▸ **animation** [名] [U] ◇His face was drained of all colour and *animation*. 彼の顔から血色と生気が失われた

vivacious 《ほめて》(女性が)元気な、活発な、快活な、陽気な ◇He had three pretty, *vivacious* daughters. 彼には可愛くて快活な娘が3人いた

▸ **vivacity** [名] [U] ◇He was charmed by her beauty and *vivacity*. 彼は彼女の美しさと快活さに惹かれた

bubbly (ややインフォーマル、ほめて)(少女・女性が)元気な、活発な、快活な、陽気な ◇Anna has a bright, *bubbly* personality. アンナは明るく陽気な性格だ

loan [名]

loan・credit・mortgage・advance・overdraft
個人や銀行などの組織が人に貸与する金
【類語訳】ローン、貸付金、融資、信用貸し、クレジット、抵当、前払い金、当座借越額

【文型&コロケーション】
▸ a loan/ credit/ a mortgage/ an advance/ an overdraft from sb/ an organization
▸ a mortgage/ an advance on sth
▸ a large/ huge loan/ mortgage/ advance/ overdraft
▸ (a) low-interest loan/ credit/ mortgage/ overdraft
▸ (a) cheap loan/ credit/ mortgage
▸ (an) interest-free loan/ credit/ overdraft
▸ a temporary loan/ mortgage/ overdraft
▸ (a) bank loan/ credit/ mortgage/ overdraft
▸ to have a loan/ a mortgage/ an advance/ an overdraft

loan, logic

▸ to get a loan/ credit/ a mortgage/ an advance
▸ to obtain/ arrange/ apply for/ refuse sb/ deny sb (a) loan/ credit/ a mortgage
▸ to take out/ request/ pay off/ repay a loan/ mortgage

loan [C] (銀行などからの)ローン、貸付金、融資 ◇I'm going to have to take out a bank *loan* (= to borrow money from a bank) to pay for the car. 私は車の代金を支払うために近く銀行から融資を受けなければならないだろう ◇It took three years to repay my *student loan* (= money lent to a student). 私は学生ローンを返すのに3年かかった ◇He ran up massive debts borrowing from *loan sharks* (= people who lend money at very high rates of interest). 彼のもとには高利貸しから借りた借金が多大にたまった

credit [U] (購入代金を後払いする)信用貸し、クレジット; (銀行からの)貸付金 ◇We bought the dishwasher *on credit*. 私たちは食器洗い機をクレジットで買った ◇We offer two months' interest-free *credit*. 弊社は2か月間無利子の信用貸しを提供しております ◇Your *credit limit* is now £2,000. あなた様の信用限度額は現在2千ポンドです ◇The bank refused further *credit* to the company. 銀行はその会社への追加貸付を断った ☞ **debit** (DEBT)

[ノート] **loan** と **credit** の使い分け：loan はある金額の金を借りて、後から返済する特定の取り決めを指す。credit は銀行が顧客に提供する金を指す一般的な語で、そのとき顧客には自分の口座にそれだけの金額の預金はない。

mortgage [C] (不動産購入のための)ローン、抵当; 貸付金 ◇Do you have a *mortage* on this house? この家は抵当に入っていますか ◇Fortunately we've already paid off our *mortgage*. 幸運なことに、私たちはすでにローンを完済している ◇*Mortgage rates* (= of interest) are up again this month. 住宅ローンの利率は今月再び上昇している

▸ **mortgage** [動] [他] ◇He had to *mortgage* his house to pay his legal costs. 彼は家を抵当に入れて訴訟費用を支払わなければならなかった

advance [C, ふつう単数で] (給与・代金などの)前払い金 ◇They offered an *advance* of £5,000 after the signing of the contract. 契約を結んだ後で、彼らは5千ポンドの前払い金を渡した ◇She asked for an *advance* on her salary. 彼女は給料の前払いを頼んだ

overdraft [C] (口座預金以上の銀行への)当座借越額; 当座借越[貸越] ◇She had *run up an overdraft* of £3,000. 彼女の当座借越額は3000ポンドに達していた ◇I had to arrange an *overdraft* to pay for the car. 私は車の代金を支払うために当座借越の手続きをしなければならなかった

▸ **overdraw** [動] [他] ◇Customers who *overdraw* their accounts will be charged a fee. 《特に英》当座借越には手数料がかかります

▸ **overdrawn** [形] ◇I'm *overdrawn* by £100. 私は100ポンドの借越がある ◇Your account is £200 *overdrawn*. あなたの口座は200ポンドの借越になっています

logic [名]

logic・rationality・reason
感情よりも筋道の通った思考に基づく考え方[説明の仕方]を表す
【類語訳】論理、理屈、正当な理由、道理、筋、説得力、合理性

logo, lonely

文型&コロケーション
- the logic/ rationality/ reason in sth
- strict logic/ rationality
- commercial/ economic/ scientific logic/ rationality
- to see (the) logic/ reason
- to defy logic/ reason
- a lack of logic/ rationality/ reason

logic [U, 単数で] (思考[説明]上の)論理, 理屈;(事を行う上での)正当な理由, 道理, 筋, 説得力 ◇I fail to see the *logic behind* his argument. 私には彼の主張の背後にある論理がわからない ◇There is a compelling *logic to* her main theory. 彼女の主な理論には抵抗しがたい説得力がある ☞ **logical** (RATIONAL)

rationality [U]《ややフォーマル》(感情[気持ち]よりも論理的思考に基づいた)合理性 ◇The concept of scientific *rationality* is crucial to modern thinking. 科学的合理性の概念は現代的思考にとって非常に重要である ☞ **rational** (RATIONAL)

reason [U] (分別があり論理的な)正当な理由, 道理 ◇I can't get her to **listen to reason**. 彼女を道理に従う気にさせることができない ◇I'm willing to do anything — *within reason* — to get my case heard. 私は何をすることもいといません—理にかなった範囲でですが, 事件を審理してもらうためならば ◇It stands to reason (= any sensible person would agree) that people leave if you don't pay them enough. 十分な報酬を支払ってやらないと人は去るというのは理の当然です ☞ **reasonable** (REASONABLE)

logo 名

logo・trademark・arms・seal・emblem・stamp・colours・insignia・crest
組織や集団が特別な印として用いる名前[意匠, 象徴]
【類語訳】ロゴ, 商標, 紋章, 印章, 記章, 象徴, 旗, 刻印, 証印, 検印

文型&コロケーション
- the royal arms/ seal/ emblem/ colours/ insignia/ crest
- an official seal/ stamp
- to bear/ carry a logo/ the arms/ a seal/ an emblem/ a stamp/ the colours/ an insignia/ a crest
- to display a logo/ the arms/ an emblem/ the colours/ a crest
- to feature a logo/ the arms/ an emblem/ a crest

logo(複 -os)[C](会社・組織の特別な印として用いられる)ロゴ ◇All over the world there are red and white paper cups bearing the company *logo*. 世界中にその会社のロゴの付いた赤と白の紙コップがあります

trademark (略 TM) [C](製品用の他社が使用できない)商標 ◇'Big Mac' is McDonalds' best-known *trademark*. 「ビッグマック」はマクドナルドの最も有名な商標です

arms (複数形)[または, **coat of arms**で[C])(複 **arms**, **coats of arms**) (一族[都市]など組織の象徴的としての)紋章 ◇The royal *arms* appear on the door of the Queen's carriage. 女王の馬車のドアには王室の紋章が付いている

seal [C] (公文書用の)印章, 印 ◇The letter bore the president's *seal*. その手紙には大統領の印章が押されていた

emblem [C] (国家・組織の象徴的)記章;(代表・主義の)象徴 ◇America's national *emblem*, the bald eagle 米国の国章たる白頭鷲 ◇The dove is an *emblem* of peace. 鳩は平和の象徴である

stamp [C] (物の表面に押印される)刻印, 証印, 検印 ◇The passports, with the visa *stamps*, were waiting at the embassy. 大使館ではビザの証印が押されたパスポートが待ち受けていた

ノート **stamp** と **seal** の使い分け:**stamp** は **seal** よりも一般的な語である。**stamp** には日付・語・記号などが添えられることがある。**seal** はより公式的で, 法的文書に付けられる傾向にある。両語とも物事が承認されていることを比喩的に表すこともある。 ◆The project has the government's *seal/ stamp of approval*.(《比喩的》この事業は政府の太鼓判を押されている)

colours《英》(《米》**colors**)[複数で]《特に英》(チーム・国家・船舶などを象徴する)旗, 記章 ◇Most buildings had a flagpole with the national *colours* flying. ほとんどの建物には旗ざおに国旗がはためいていた

insignia [U+単数・複数動詞](地位[集団]・組織の一員であること]を示す)記章 ◇His uniform bore the *insignia* of a captain. 彼の制服には大尉の記章が付いていた

crest [C] (一族・組織を象徴する長い歴史のある)紋章 ◇The family *crest* consists of a crown and an eight-pointed star. その家紋は王冠と八芒星からなっている

ノート **arms**, **emblem**, **crest** の使い分け:**coat of arms** は盾に付けられ, 立ち上がった獅子や大きな鳥類など特定の意匠で表されることが多い。**crest** は伝統的に **coat of arms** の上に付けられるが, 現在は単独で用いられることもあり, 所有者は高い評価を得ていて, 多大の尊敬を集めていることを示唆する。**emblem** はより一般的な語で, **coat of arms** や **crest** も **emblem** と見なされることもあるが, **emblem** はふつう組織を象徴する比較的小さなものを指す。

lonely 形

lonely・alone・isolated・homesick・forlorn・bereft・desolate
人に友人がいなくて[他人との接触がほとんどなくて]不幸であることを表す
【類語訳】孤独な, 一人ぼっちの, 寂しい, わびしい, 孤立した, 疎外感を感じた, 郷愁にかられた, ホームシックにかかった

lonely	alone	desolate
isolated	forlorn	
homesick	bereft	

文型&コロケーション
- to feel lonely/ alone/ isolated/ homesick/ forlorn/ bereft/ desolate
- utterly alone/ isolated/ bereft/ desolate
- desperately/ terribly lonely/ homesick

lonely (友人[話しかける人]がいないために)孤独な, 寂しい ◇She lives alone and often feels *lonely*. 彼女は独り住まいで, 孤独に思うことが多い ◇The support they give to *lonely* old people is invaluable. 孤独な高齢者に対して行われる彼らの支援は非常に貴重である

alone [名詞の前では用いない]《ややインフォーマル》(友人[話しかける人, 助けてくれる人]がいないために)孤独な, 一人ぼっちの, 寂しい ◇I've been so *alone* since you went away.

↳**lonely**

あなたが立ち去ってしまってから私はとても寂しいです ◇Carol felt **all alone** in the world. キャロルは世界中でまったくの一人ぼっちだと感じた

ノート lonelyとaloneの使い分け: aloneはlonelyよりもいくぶんインフォーマルで、名詞の前で用いることはできない。aloneは人が孤独を感じているだけでなく、ある意味で傷つきやすいことも意味することがある。

isolated (他人とあまり接触を持たないために)孤立した,疎外感を感じた ◇I felt very *isolated* in my new job. 私は新しい仕事でとても疎外感を感じた ◇Elderly people easily become **socially isolated**. 高齢者は社会的に孤立してしまいがちだ

homesick (家を離れていて家族[友人]がいなくて)郷愁にかられた, 故郷を恋しがった, ホームシックにかかった ◇I felt *homesick for* Scotland. 私はスコットランドが恋しかった ◇Seeing other families together made him terribly *homesick*. 他の家族が一緒にいるのを見て彼はひどく郷愁にかられた

▸**homesickness** 名 [U] ◇She soon got over her *homesickness*. 彼女はすぐに望郷の念[ホームシック]を克服した

forlorn (書き言葉) (孤独なために)惨めな, 哀れな ◇She looked so *forlorn*, standing there in the pouring rain. 彼女は土砂降りの雨の中でそこに立っているととても惨めに見えた

bereft [名詞の前では用いない] (ややフォーマル) (人・物を失って)喪失感を感じた ◇He was utterly *bereft* when his wife died. 彼は妻が死んだとき, ひどい喪失感に包まれた

desolate [名詞の前はまれ] (非常に孤独なために)寂しい, わびしい ◇The thought that her husband did not want the baby made her feel utterly *desolate*. 夫がその子を望んでいないことを考えると, 彼女はたまらなく寂しかった

long 形

long・prolonged・lengthy・protracted・long-lasting・extended
物事が長く続くことを表す
【類語訳】(時間的に)長い, 長期間かかる, 長期的な, 延長した

文型&コロケーション
▸a long/ prolonged/ lengthy/ extended **period**
▸a long/ prolonged/ lengthy/ protracted **delay/ dispute/ illness**
▸a long/ lengthy/ protracted/ extended **process**
▸long/ prolonged/ lengthy/ protracted/ extended **negotiations**
▸**very/ relatively** long/ prolonged/ lengthy/ protracted/ long-lasting
▸**quite** long/ prolonged/ lengthy/ long-lasting/ extended

long (時間的に)長い, 長時間[期間]続く[かかる]; (多忙[不手際]などの理由で)長く続く[かかる] ◇I haven't seen him **for a long time**. 私は彼と長いこと会っていない ◇There was a *long* silence before she spoke. 彼女が口を開くまで長い沈黙があった ◇I like it now the days are getting *longer* (= in spring). 最近, 日が長くなってきているのがうれしい ◇a *long* book/film/list (= taking a lot of time to read/watch/deal with) 分厚い本/長い映画/長いリスト ◇Nurses have to work *long* hours (=

long, look

for more hours in the day than is usual). 看護師たちは長時間働かなければならない ◇He stared at them **for the longest time** (= for a very long time) before answering. 《米》彼は答える前に非常に長い間彼らを見つめた ◇I'm tired. **It's been a long day**. 疲れたよ。長い一日だった ◇We were married for ten *long* years. 私たちは10年もの長い間結婚生活を送っていた ❶ *long*は特定の時間[期間]について尋ねたり話したりする場合にも用いられる
◆ **How long** is the film? (映画はどのくらいの長さですか)
◆ I think it's only about two hours *long*. (ほんの2時間くらいだと思うよ) 反意 **short, brief** (SHORT 1), **short** (SHORT 3)

prolonged [名詞の前で] (特に書き言葉) 長時間[期間]続く ◇There were *prolonged* spells of dry weather. 何も雨が降らないことが繰り返しあった ◇The drug becomes less effective after *prolonged* use. その薬は長期間使用するとあまり効かなくなります ☞ **prolong** (MAINTAIN)

lengthy (ややフォーマル, 特に書き言葉) (過度に)長時間[期間]かかる, 長たらしい ◇I had to go through the *lengthy* process of obtaining a visa. 私はビザをもらうのに長たらしい手続きを踏まなければならなかった ◇A court case will be expensive and *lengthy*. 裁判は費用がかかるし長期にわたるでしょう

protracted (フォーマル) (予想[通常]より)長時間[期間]続く ◇There followed a *protracted* series of legal wrangles. その後, 一連の法律論争が長期間続いた ◇A *protracted* strike carries a high risk of violence. ストライキが長引けば暴力の危険性が高くなる

long-ˈlasting (効果が)長時間[期間]持続する, 長期的な ◇The change brought about *long-lasting* improvements. その変革は長期にわたる改善をもたらした ◇The experience made an immediate and *long-lasting* impression on me. その経験で私は直接的でありながら長く残る印象を得た 反意 **short-lived** (SHORT 1), ☞ **lasting** (PERMANENT)

extended [名詞の前で] (ややフォーマル, 特に書き言葉) (予想[通常]より)長い, 長く続く; (以前より)延長[増補]した ◇They are going to publish an *extended* version of the report. その報告書の増補版が発行される予定です ◇More staff will be needed when the *extended* opening hours are introduced. 営業時間が延長されれば, もっとスタッフが必要になるでしょう ☞ **extend** (MAINTAIN)

look 名

look・glance・sight・gaze・stare・glimpse・glare
特定の方向に目を向けて見る行為
【類語訳】見ること, 見えること, 見つめること, にらむこと, 一見, 一瞥, 一目, 視線, 目線, 凝視

文型&コロケーション
▸a look/ glance **at** sb/ sth
▸a **hard** look/ glance/ gaze/ stare/ glare
▸a **cold/ penetrating/ piercing/ curious/ quizzical** look/ glance/ gaze/ stare
▸an **angry** look/ glance/ gaze/ glare
▸a **suspicious/ withering** look/ glance/ stare/ glare
▸a **long/ disapproving** look/ glance/ stare
▸a **brief/ fleeting/ momentary/ quick** look/ glance/ glimpse
▸a **sharp/ questioning/ searching/ admiring/ anxious**

look / glance / gaze
- to **have/ get/ take** a look/ glance/ glimpse
- to **fix sb with** a look/ stare/ glare
- to **send/ shoot/ throw sb** a look/ glance/ glare
- to **catch** sight/ a glimpse **of** sb/ sth
- to **draw** a/ sb's look/ glance/ gaze
- to **avoid** sb's glance/ gaze/ stare

look [C, ふつう単数で] 見ること, 一見, 視線, 目線 ◇Here, have a *look* at this. ほら, これを見てごらん ◇It's an interesting place. Do you want to take *a look around*? そこは面白い場所だよ. 見物に行きたいかい ◇I had a brief *look* through the report before the meeting. 私は会議の前に報告書にざっと目を通した ◇Make sure you get a *good look* at their faces. 彼らの顔をよく見るのを忘れないで ◇She threw him a *dirty look*. 彼女は彼にさげすむような視線を投げかけた ◇A *look* passed between them (= they looked at each other). 彼らは視線を交わした ☞ **look at sth (CHECK 1)**

glance [C] (ちらっと)見ること, 一瞥, 一目 ◇I had a *glance* at the newspaper headlines as I waited at the counter. 私はカウンターで待ちながら新聞の見出しをちらっと見た ◇She shot him a sideways *glance*. 彼女は彼を横目でちらっと見た ◇The sisters exchanged *glances* (= looked at each other). その姉妹は視線を交わした ◇He could tell what was wrong *at a glance* (= with only a quick look). 彼は一目で何が悪いかわかった

sight [U] 見ること, 見えること ◇After ten days at sea, we had our first *sight* of land. 海上で10日間過ごした後, 私たちは陸を初めて目にした ◇She caught *sight* of a car in the distance. 彼女は遠くに1台の車を見つけた ◇She kept *sight* of him in her mirror. 彼女は鏡越しに彼から目を離さなかった ◇I always faint *at the sight of* blood. 私は血を見るといつも気を失う ◇He looked at first *sight* like an English tourist. 彼は一見するとイギリス人観光客のように見えた ◇The soldiers were given orders to *shoot on sight* (= as soon as they saw sb). 兵隊には見つけ次第銃撃するよう命令が下された ◇I *know her by sight* (= can recognize her but do not know her well). 私は彼女の顔だけは見ればわかる ☞ **sight (SIGHT), sight (SEE)**

gaze [C, ふつう単数で] (じっと)見る[見つめる]こと, 凝視, 視線, 目線 ◇She felt embarrassed *under his* steady *gaze*. 彼女は彼にじっと見つめられて戸惑いを感じた ◇He *met her gaze* (= looked at her while she looked at him). 彼女は彼と目と目を合わせた ◇She *dropped her gaze* (= stopped looking). 彼女は目線をそらした ◇I followed her *gaze* and spotted a new arrival at the far side of the room. 私は彼女の視線を追っていくと部屋の向こう側にいる新たな来訪者に気づいた ☞ **gaze (STARE)**

stare [C] (敵意・驚きを示してじっと[じろじろ]にらむこと, 見つめる)こと ◇She gave the officer a blank *stare* and shrugged her shoulders. 彼女はその職員をぽかんと見つめ, 肩をすくめた ◇He fixed the interviewer with a hard *stare*. 彼は厳しい視線で面接官を凝視した ☞ **stare (STARE)**

glimpse [C] ちらっと見ること, 一瞥, 一目 ◇He caught a *glimpse* of her in the crowd. 彼は群衆の中に彼女をちらっと見かけた ◇I came up on deck to get my first *glimpse* of the island. 私は甲板に上がってその島を初めて一瞥した ☞ **glimpse (SEE)**

glare [C] (怒りを示してじっと)にらむこと ◇She fixed her questioner with a hostile *glare*. 彼女は敵意に満ちた目つきで質問者をにらみつけた ☞ **glare (STARE)**

look 動

1 ☞ NOTICE, SEE, STARE
look・watch・see・view・check sth out・observe・regard・catch・contemplate
特定の方向に目をやる
【類語訳】目を向ける, 見る, 眺める, 見守る, 注視する, 観察する, 見物する, 調べる, 見に行く, 熟視する

【文型&コロケーション】
- to look/ watch/ view/ observe/ regard/ contemplate (sb/ sth) **from** somewhere
- to look/ watch **for** sb/ sth
- to watch/ observe **what/ who/ how**...
- to look/ watch/ view/ observe/ regard/ contemplate (sb/ sth) **with** amazement/ surprise/ disapproval, etc.
- to look/ see/ view/ catch a **film/ movie/ show/ programme**
- to watch/ see/ catch a **match/ game/ fight**
- to look/ watch/ observe sb/ sth/ regard sb/ sth **closely**
- to look/ watch/ observe sb/ sth **carefully**
- to look/ watch/ regard sb/ sth **intently/ thoughtfully/ suspiciously/ expectantly/ warily/ impassively**

look [自] (特定の方向に)目を向ける, 見る, 眺める ◇If you *look* carefully you can just see our house from here. 注意して見れば, ここから私たちの家がすぐ見えます ◇She *looked at* me and smiled. 彼女は私を見てほほ笑んだ ◇'Has the mail come yet?' 'I'll *look and see*.' 「もう郵便届いた」「見てくるよ」 ◇*Look*! I'm sure that's Brad Pitt! 見てよ. あれ, 絶対ブラッド・ピットだよ ◇*Don't look* now, but there's someone staring at you! 今は見るなよ, でも君をじっと見てる奴がいる

watch [他, 自] (注意を払いながらじっと)見ている, 見守る, 注視[観察, 見物]する ◇I only let my kids *watch* television at the weekends. 私は子どもたちには週末だけテレビを見させている ◇*Watch* what I do, then you try. 私がやるのを見ておけ, その後で君がやるんだ ◇She *watched* the kids playing in the yard. 彼女は子どもたちが庭で遊んでいるのを見守った ◇They *watched* the bus disappear into the distance. 彼らはバスが遠くに消えて行くのを見つめていた ◇'Would you like to play?' 'No thanks — I'll just *watch*.' 「君もプレーしたい」「いや, 結構—見てるだけにするよ」 ◇She stood and *watched* as the taxi drove off. 彼女はタクシーが走り去るのを立って見ていた ◇We *watched* to see what would happen next. 私たちは次に何が起こるか見るために注視していた

see [他] 《進行形まれ》(試合・テレビ番組・演技などを)見る, 見物する ◇Did you *see* that documentary about Brazil last night? 昨夜のブラジルについてのドキュメンタリーを見た ◇Fifty thousand people *saw* the game. 5万人の人々がその試合を観戦した

view [他] 《フォーマル》(注意深く)見る；(テレビ番組・映画などを)見る, 見物する ◇People came from all over the world to *view* her work. 彼女の作品を見るために世界中から人々がやって来た ◇The eclipse should only be *viewed* through a special lens. 日食は特別なレンズを通してしか見てはいけません ◇The show has a *viewing* audience of six million (= six million people watch it). その番組は600万人の視聴者がいる ☞ **view** (SIGHT)

> ノート **watch, see, view** の使い分け：see/view a film/movie/TV show（映画／テレビ番組を見る）とは言えるが、×see/view television とは言えない。view は see よりもフォーマルで、特にビジネスの文脈で用いられる。

,check sth 'out [句動詞]《インフォーマル、特に話し言葉》（面白そうな人・物事を）見る、調べる ◇*Check out* the prices at our new store! 私どもの新店舗で価格をご覧ください ◇Hey, *check out* that car! おい、あの車見てみろよ

observe [他, 自]《進行形は不可》《フォーマル》（知識を深めるために注意深く）注視［観察］する ◇The patients were *observed* over a period of several months. 患者たちは数か月間にわたって注意深く見守られた ◇He *observes* keenly, but says little. 彼は観察力は鋭いが、口数は少ない ☞ **observation** (INSPECTION), **observe** (NOTICE)

regard [他]《フォーマル》（特定の態度で）見る ◇He *regarded* us suspiciously. 彼は私たちを疑わしげに見た

catch [他]《特に米、インフォーマル》（映画・試合・行事などを）見［聴き］に行く、見る ◇Let's eat now and maybe we could *catch* a movie later. さあ食べよう、そうすればたぶん後で映画を見に行けるよ［見られるよ］

contemplate [他]《フォーマル》（注意深く）見る、熟視する ◇She *contemplated* him in silence. 彼女は黙って彼をじっと見た ◇He sat there, *contemplating* his fingernails. 彼はそこに座って自分の爪をじっと見ていた

---

2 look・search・seek・hunt・forage・scout・cast about/around for sth
物を見つけようとする
【類語訳】探す、探索する、捜索する、検索する、検査する、調べる、捜し求める、捜し回る、捜し出す

文型&コロケーション
▸ to look/ search/ seek/ hunt/ forage/ scout **for** sth
▸ to look/ search/ hunt/ forage/ scout **around** (for sth)
▸ to look/ search/ hunt **through** sth
▸ to look/ search/ hunt/ forage **in** sth
▸ to look for/ search for/ seek/ cast around for a/ an **alternative/ way**
▸ to look/ search/ seek/ hunt for **clues**
▸ police/ detectives look for/ search for/ seek/ hunt sb/ sth
▸ to look/ search/ seek/ hunt/ cast around **desperately** (for sth)
▸ to look/ search/ seek/ cast around **in vain**
▸ to look/ search/ hunt **everywhere**

look [自] 探す、捜す ◇I can't find my book — I've *looked* everywhere. 本が見つからないんだ—あらゆる場所を捜したんだけど ◇Are you still *looking* for a job? まだ仕事を探しているの ◇We're *looking* for someone with experience for this position. 我々はこの職に経験がある人を探しています ◇We're *looking* around for a house in this area. 私たちはこの地域で家を捜しています ◇I was just about to come *looking* for you. ちょうどあなたを捜しに行こうとしていたところなのよ ☞ **look** (SEARCH)

search [自, 他]（人・物を）捜す［探す、探索（検索）］する；（人・物を見つけるために特定の場所を）調べる；（警察が衣服などを）検査［捜索］する ◇She *searched* in vain for her passport. 彼女はパスポートを捜したが無駄だった ◇The customs officers *searched* through her bag. 税関職員たちは彼女のかばんをくまなく調べた ◇I found out more about the company by *searching online*. 私はオンライン検索でその会社についてさらに多くのことがわかった ◇Firefighters *searched* the building for survivors. 消防士は生存者を求めてその建物を捜索した ◇Visitors are regularly *searched* as they enter the building. 来訪者は決まって、その建物に入る際に検査を受けます ☞ **search** (SEARCH)

seek [他, 自]《フォーマル》（人・物を）捜し［探し］求める［出す］ ◇Drivers are advised to *seek* alternative routes. ドライバーは代わりとなるルートを探すよう言われている ◇Police are *seeking* witnesses to the accident. 警察はその事故の目撃者を捜している ◇He admired her ability to *seek out* bargains (= to look for and find them). 彼はお買い得品を探し出す彼女の能力に感心した ◇They *sought* in vain for somewhere to shelter.《英》彼らは避難場所を探したが見つからなかった ☞ **seek** (ASK 2), **seek** (TRY 1)

hunt [他, 自]（見つけにくい［捕まえる／傷つける］目的で人・物を）捜す、捜し求める、追う ◇I've *hunted* everywhere, but I can't find it. 私はあらゆる場所を捜したのだが、それを見つけられないんだ ◇She was *hunting* through her bag for her keys. 彼女は鍵を見つけようとかばんをくまなく捜していた ◇Police are *hunting* an escaped criminal. 警察は脱走犯を追っている ☞ **hunt** (SEARCH)

forage [自]《書き言葉》（動物が餌を［人が両手を使って物を］）捜す［探す］、捜し［探し］回る ◇The female only leaves the young to *forage for food*. この動物はメスが子どもを残して餌を探しに出るのです ◇Her assistant was *foraging* in a drawer for some envelopes. 彼女の助手は封筒がないかと引き出しの中をかき回していた

scout [自, 他]（物を見つけるために1か所［いろいろな地域］を）捜す［探す］、捜し［探し］回る ◇The kids were *scouting* around for wood for the fire. 子どもたちはたき火に使う薪を探し回っていた ◇They *scouted* the area for somewhere to stay the night. 彼らは夜を過ごす場所を求めてその地域を探した

,cast a'bout/a'round for sth [句動詞]《書き言葉》（厄介な事柄の答えを）捜す［探す］、見つけようとする ◇She *cast around* desperately *for* a safe topic of conversation. 彼女は差し障りのない話題を必死に探した ◇The authorities are clearly *casting about for* someone to blame. 当局は責任を押しつけるべき相手を誰にするか明らかに思案中だ

---

look after sb [句動詞]

look after sb・take care of sb・care for sb・tend・attend to sb/sth
人に必要とする物を与えてあげて、その人の健康［安全］に責任を持つことを表す
【類語訳】世話をする、面倒を見る、健康を管理する、介護する、看病する、手当てをする、番をする、手入れをする

文型&コロケーション
▸ to tend/ attend **to** sb/ sth
▸ to look after/ take care of/ care for/ tend to **the sick**
▸ to look after/ take care of/ care for **the children/ the elderly/ an elderly relative**
▸ to look after/ take care of **yourself**
▸ to care for/ tend sb **lovingly**

,look 'after sb 句動詞 《特に英》(病[けが]人・子ども・高齢者の)世話をする、面倒を見る ◇My daughter was sick so I took the day off to *look after* her. 娘が病気だったので、私はその日は休んで世話をした ◇Who's going to *look after* the children while you're away? あなたがいないときは、誰が子どもたちの面倒を見るの ☞ **look after yourself** (TAKE CARE OF YOURSELF)

,take 'care of sb フレーズ (病[けが]人・子ども・高齢者の)世話をする、面倒を見る、健康を管理する ◇Who's *taking care of* the kids while you're away? あなたがいないときは、誰が子どもたちの面倒を見るの ◇You should *take better care* of yourself. あなたはもっと自分の健康管理をしたほうがいいよ ◇Don't you worry. I'll *take care of* you. 心配するな。俺が世話してやるわ ☞ **take care of yourself** (TAKE CARE OF YOURSELF)

▶ **care** 名 [U] medical/patient *care* 医療/患者の治療 ◇How much do men share housework and the *care* of the children? 男性はどのくらい家事や子どもの世話を分担してやっていますか

'care for sb 句動詞 《ややフォーマル、特に書き言葉》(重傷[重病]患者・高齢者を)介抱[介護、看護、看病]する、(身の回りの)世話をする ◇She does some voluntary work, *caring for* the elderly. 彼女はボランティア活動でお年寄りの介護をしている ◇He gave up work to *care for* his wife. 彼は仕事をやめて妻の介護に回った

> ノート **look after sb, take care of sb, care for sb** の使い分け：look after sb は短期間《人が病気の間、ふだん面倒を見ている人がいない間》に用いられることが多い。take care of sb も同じように用いられるが、《米》では look after sb よりも頻繁に用いられる。両表現ともに言えるが、特に take care of sb は単に義務からではなく、それに対する愛情や心遣いからそうするのである。care for sb はしばしば長期にわたる常勤の職業として行うことを指す。care for sb も人に対する愛情からそうすることがある。☞ **care for sb** (LOVE 動)

tend [他, 自] 《ややフォーマル》(動物・植物の)番をする、手入れをする、(病[けが]人の)世話をする[看病、手当て] ◇a shepherd *tending* his sheep 羊の番をする羊飼い ◇We looked out of the window at the well-*tended* gardens. 私たちは窓から手入れの行き届いた庭を見た ◇Ambulance crews were *tending* to the injured. 救急隊員たちが負傷者の手当てをしていた

at'tend to sb/sth 句動詞 《ややフォーマル》(人・物事の[に])世話[看病、手当て]をする、応対する ◇A nurse *attended to* his needs constantly. 看護師が絶えず彼の要求に応対した

loser 名

1 loser・runner-up・also-ran
競技[レース, 試合, 選挙]で勝てない[成功しない]人
【類語訳】負けた人、負けたチーム、敗者、2位になる人、2位になるチーム、落選者、落後者

▸ 文型&コロケーション
▸ a loser/ runner-up/ also-ran **in** sth
▸ a loser/ runner-up **to** sb
▸ winners and losers/ runners-up

loser [C] (競技で)負けた人[チーム]、敗者 ◇Sweden will now play the *losers* of the other semi-final for the bronze medal. スウェーデンは今度は、もう一方の準決勝で負けたチームと銅メダルをかけて戦います ◇He's extremely competitive and a ***bad*** *loser* (= does not react well to losing). 彼は非常に競争心が旺盛で、負けっぷりが良くない 反意 **winner**

,runner-'up (複 **runners-up**) [C] (レース[競技]で)2位になる人[チーム]；上位入賞者 ◇She was last year's *runner-up* to Sarah Jones. 彼女は昨年、サラ・ジョーンズに敗れて2着だった ◇They finished *runners-up behind* Italy. 彼らはイタリアに次いで2位に終わった ◇Twenty *runners-up* will receive a $50 book voucher. 上位入賞者20名には50ドルの図書券がもらえます ◇There are three *runners-up prizes* of club shirts. 上位入賞者3名には賞品としてクラブのシャツが用意されています

'also-ran [C] 《しばしばけなして》(競技・選挙などでの)敗者、等外者、落選者、落後者 ◇The campaign transformed him from an *also-ran* in the polls to front-runner. 選挙運動により彼は世論調査での落選予定者から最有力候補へと一変した

2 loser・failure・incompetent・has-been・no-hoper・underachiever・disappointment・disaster
以前[本来]のようにうまくいかない人
【類語訳】負け犬、失格者、不適格者、過去の人、役立たずの人、落ちこぼれの人、期待はずれの人、どうしようもない人

▸ 文型&コロケーション
▸ to be a failure/ disappointment/ disaster **as** sth
▸ a **complete** failure/ no-hoper/ disaster
▸ a **group/ bunch of** losers/ incompetents/ no-hopers

loser [C] 《しばしばけなして》(評価の低い)負けてばかりの人、負け犬 ◇She's one of life's *losers*. 彼女は人生の負け組の一人さ ◇He's a ***born*** *loser*. 彼は生まれつきの負け犬だ 反意 **winner** (SUCCESS)

failure [C] 失格者 ◇He was a *failure* as a teacher. 彼は教師として失格だった ◇I felt a **complete** *failure*. 私はまったく失格だと思った 反意 **success**, ☞ **fail** (FAIL 2)

incompetent [C] 《けなして》(仕事・職務を行う技術・能力のない)無能者、不適格者 ◇The whole thing is being led by a bunch of *incompetents*. そのすべてのことが無能な人間どもの手に握られつつある ☞ **incompetent** (INCOMPETENT)

'has-been [C] 《インフォーマル、けなして》過去の人、盛りを過ぎた人 ◇She's just an old *has-been*. 彼女は年老いた過去の人にすぎない ◇He's very much a political *has-been*. 彼はまさしく盛りをとっくに過ぎた政治家だ

,no-'hoper [C] 《インフォーマル、けなして》(使い物にならない[勝利・成功の可能性が非常に低い])役立たずの人、弱小チーム、大穴の馬 ◇They were written off as a bunch of *no-hopers*. 彼らは役立たずの集まりだとして見限られた ◇He backed an apparent *no-hoper* at odds of 100-1. 彼はオッズ100対1という明らかな大穴の馬に賭けた

underachiever [C] (学業において)落ちこぼれの人 ◇At school he was a *classic underachiever*. 彼は学校では典型的な落ちこぼれだった

disappointment [C] (業績を残せず[不品行から])期待はずれの人 ◇I always felt I was a *disappointment to* my father. 父にとっての私は期待はずれの存在だといつも感じていた

disaster [C] 《インフォーマル、けなして》(技術[能力]不足のため)どうしようもない人 ◇He was a competent accountant, but as a manager he's a *disaster*. 彼は有能な会計士だったが、経営者としてはどうしようもない人だ

lose your temper 〖行れ〗

lose your temper・get angry・get mad・go mad・lose patience・go berserk
話し方や振る舞いに現れる(非常に)立腹している様子を表す
【類語訳】頭にくる、かっとなる、キレる、腹を立てる、怒る、むっとする、怒り狂う、しびれを切らす、我慢の限界を超える

| lose patience | lose your temper
get angry
get mad | go mad
go berserk |

〖文型&コロケーション〗
▶ to lose your temper/ get angry/ get mad/ lose patience **with** sb
▶ to lose your temper/ get angry/ get mad/ go mad **at** sth
▶ to lose your temper/ get angry **over** sth

lose your 'temper 〖行れ〗 頭にくる、かっとなる、キレる ◇She *lost her temper* with a customer and shouted at him. 彼女は客に頭にきてどなりつけた ◇Try to ignore it. It's not worth *losing your temper* over. そんなことは無視するようにしなさい。キレるほどのことじゃないです 〖反意〗 **keep your temper, ☞ temper** (TEMPER)

get 'angry 〖行れ〗 腹を立てる、怒る、むっとする ◇Please don't *get angry* with me. I'm trying my best. 私に腹を立てないでね。精一杯努力してるんだから

〖ノート〗 **lose your temperとget angryの使い分け**: lose your temperは人をどなりつけるなどして、怒りを言動に表す場合。get angryはどなることもあるかもしれないが、感情のほうが強調され、言動はそれほど強調されない。

get 'mad 〖行れ〗 《米、インフォーマル》腹を立てる、怒る、むっとする ◇Please don't *get mad* at me. 私に腹を立てないでください ◇He *got mad* and walked out. 彼は怒って出て行った

go 'mad 〖行れ〗 《英、インフォーマル》怒り狂う、かんかんになって怒る ◇She *went mad* when I told her. 私が打ち明けると彼女は怒り狂った

〖ノート〗 **get madとgo madの使い分け**: get madは《米》でインフォーマルに用いられ、「腹を立てる」ことを表す一般的な表現。go madは《英》で、どなるなどして激怒を言動に表す場合に用いられるより強い表現である。go madには「気が狂う」「非常に興奮する」の意味もある。

lose 'patience 〖行れ〗 いら立つ、しびれを切らす、我慢の限界を超える ◇People have *lost patience* with the slow pace of reform. 人々は改革の遅れにしびれを切らしている

go berserk 〖行れ〗 怒り狂う、逆上する ◇He *went berserk* when he found out where I'd been. 私がどこにいたかを知ると彼は逆上した

loss-making 〖形〗

loss-making・unprofitable・non-profit・uneconomic
企業[組織、活動]が利益を上げていないことを表す
【類語訳】赤字の、採算の取れない、損をする、業績の悪い、利益の上がらない、儲からない、非営利の、不経済な

〖文型&コロケーション〗
▶ to be unprofitable/ uneconomic **for** sb
▶ to be unprofitable/ uneconomic **to do** sth
▶ a loss-making/ an unprofitable/ a non-profit **company**
▶ loss-making/ unprofitable/ uneconomic **industries**
▶ loss-making/ unprofitable **routes/ years**
▶ **increasingly** unprofitable/ uneconomic

'loss-making (会社・事業活動が)赤字の、採算の取れない；損をする ◇The publisher sold its *loss-making* magazine business. その出版社は不採算の雑誌事業を売却した 〖反意〗 **profit-making** (SUCCESSFUL 2), ☞ **loss** (DEBT)

unprofitable (会社・事業活動・製品が)業績の悪い、利益の上がらない、儲からない ◇It became *unprofitable* to sell large electrical goods in high street stores. 大通りにある店舗での大型電気製品の販売は儲からなくなった 〖反意〗 **profitable** (SUCCESSFUL 2)

ˌnon-'profit ［ふつう名詞の前で］(組織が)非営利の ◇The Arthritis Foundation is a *non-profit organization* which helps sufferers. 関節炎財団は患者を援助する非営利団体である ❶《英》では non-profit-making も用いられるが、いくぶん古風である。特に《米》では、その組織の法的[税的]立場に関連して not-for-profit も用いられ、non-profit より明確な意味を持つ 〖反意〗 **commercial, profit-making** (SUCCESSFUL 2)

uneconomic (企業・工場が零細[老朽化]のため)不経済な ◇The plant had become *uneconomic* to run. その工場は経営する上で不経済となっていた 〖反意〗 **economic** (SUCCESSFUL 2)

loud 〖形〗

loud・noisy・deafening・roaring・ear-splitting
人や物が立てる音が強力であることを表す
【類語訳】うるさい、やかましい、騒々しい、騒がしい、耳をつんざくような

〖文型&コロケーション〗
▶ a loud/ a deafening/ a roaring/ an ear-splitting **noise**
▶ the loud/ deafening **sound** of sth
▶ loud/ deafening/ roaring **applause**
▶ a loud/ deafening **crash/ roar**
▶ loud/ deafening **music**
▶ a loud/ deafening **cheer**
▶ a loud **voice**

loud (音・声が)大きい ◇There was a *loud* bang and a big puff of smoke. 轟音が響き、大量の煙が噴き上がった ◇That music's too *loud* — please turn it down. その音楽は大きすぎます―音量を下げてください 〖反意〗 **quiet, soft** (QUIET 2)
▶**loud** 〖副〗 ◇Do you have to play that music so *loud*? 《ややインフォーマル》その音楽はそんなに大きな音でかけなくちゃいけないの ◇You'll have to speak *louder* — I can't hear you. もっと大きい声で話さなくちゃ一聞こえないよ
▶**loudly** 〖副〗 She screamed as *loudly* as she could. 彼女はできるかぎり大声で叫んだ

noisy 《しばしばけなして》(人・物・場所が)うるさい、やかましい、騒々しい、騒がしい ◇The field was full of *noisy* chil-

dren running around. 広場は走り回る騒々しい子どもたちであふれていた ◇The engine is very *noisy* at high speed. そのエンジンは高速になると非常にうるさい ◇A *noisy* classroom is a poor learning environment. 騒がしい教室は学習環境としては劣っている 反意 **quiet** (QUIET 1)
▶**noisily** 副 ◇The children were playing *noisily* upstairs. 子どもたちが2階で騒がしく遊んでいた
deafening (他の音が聞こえないほど大きな音で)耳をつんざくような ◇The team was greeted by *deafening* applause from the audience. チームは観衆から割れんばかりの拍手で迎えられた ◇The noise of the machine was *deafening*. その機械の騒音は耳をつんざくほどだった
roaring (絶え間ない低い音で)うなるような、ゴーゴーという ◇All we could hear was the sound of *roaring* water. 聞こえるのは、ゴーゴーという水の音だけだった
'ear-splitting 《ややインフォーマル》(大きな[かん高い]音で)耳をつんざくような ◇The *ear-splitting* noise made him feel quite light-headed. その耳をつんざくような騒音で、彼は頭がくらくらした

love 名

1 love・desire・passion・romance・lust・attraction・crush・infatuation
恋愛感情を持った[性的に]人を好きであるという強い気持ち
【類語訳】愛情、恋愛、恋心、性欲、情欲、激情、熱情、欲情、魅力、魅惑、熱中、夢中、心酔

【文型&コロケーション】
▶love/ desire/ passion/ lust/ attraction/ infatuation **for** sb
▶love/ passion/ romance/ attraction **between** A and B
▶to kiss sb, look at sb, etc. **with** love/ desire/ passion
▶**sexual/ physical/ mutual** love/ desire/ passion/ lust/ attraction
▶**great** love/ desire/ passion/ romance
▶**overwhelming** love/ desire/ passion/ attraction
▶to **be consumed with** desire/ passion/ lust
▶to **find** love/ romance
▶love/ desire/ passion/ attraction **grows**
▶love/ desire/ passion **dies**

love [U] (異性に対する)愛情、恋愛 ◇We're *in love*! 私たちは恋仲だ ◇She was madly/deeply *in love with him*. 彼女は彼にぞっこんだった ◇They *fell in love with* each other. 彼らは互いに恋に落ちた ◇It was *love at first sight* (= they were attracted to each other the first time they met). それは一目ぼれだった ◇At last she had found *true love*. ついに彼女は真実の愛を見つけた ◇a *love* song/story ラブソング/恋愛小説 ☞ **in love** (IN LOVE)
desire [C, U] 性欲、肉欲、色欲、情欲 ◇She felt a surge of love and *desire* for him. 彼女は彼に対して恋心と情欲の高まりを感じた ◇He felt he was nothing more to her than an *object of desire*. 自分は彼女にとって性欲の対象にすぎないのだと彼は感じた
passion [U] (性愛の)激情、熱情、欲情 ◇His *passion* for her had made him blind to everything else. 彼女に対する激しい欲情で、彼は他に何も見えなくなった ◇They kissed with *passion*. 彼らは熱っぽくキスした
▶**passionate** 形 ◇*passionate* love/feelings 性愛/欲情 ◇a *passionate* kiss/embrace/affair/lover 情熱的なキス/抱擁/情事/愛人

ノート **love, desire, passion** の使い分け: **love** は非常に一般的な語で、あらゆる文脈で用いられる。時として、セックスを指すことがある。◆ physical/sexual *love* (肉体的恋愛/性愛)、◆ to make *love* (= to have sex) (セックスする)。しかし、感情や振る舞いについて用いられることのほうが多い。◆ romantic *love* (熱烈な恋愛)。**desire** と **passion** はより意味の強い語で、肉体的恋愛やセックスについて用いられることのほうがはるかに多い。◆ to burn with/be filled with *desire*/*passion* (情欲/欲情を強く感じる/に満ちる)。**desire** も **passion** もセックスしたいという感情を指すことがあるが、**passion** のみ性行為を指すことができる。◆ a night of *passion* (情交の夜)。

romance [U] (感情・行動としての)恋愛 ◇How can you put the *romance* back into your marriage? どうしたら結婚生活に恋心を取り戻せますか ◇People find *romance* in strange places. 人は思いもよらない所で恋を見つけるものだ ☞ **romance** (RELATIONSHIP 2)
▶**romantic** 形 ◇a *romantic* candlelit dinner ロマンチックなキャンドルライト・ディナー ◇*romantic* stories/fiction/comedy 恋物語/恋愛小説/恋愛コメディ
lust [U] 《しばしばけなして》(愛情を伴わない)性欲、肉欲、色欲、情欲 ◇Their affair was driven by pure *lust*. 彼らの情事は純然たる色欲に突き動かされていた
attraction [U, 単数で] (性的な)魅力、魅惑 ◇Sexual *attraction* is a large part of falling in love. 性的な魅力は恋が始まる大きな要因だ ◇She felt an immediate *attraction* for him. 彼女はたちまち彼の魅力の虜となった
crush [C] (長く続かない)恋心、熱中、のぼせ上がり ◇It's only a schoolgirl *crush*, it'll pass. それは女子生徒ののぼせだけのことで、すぐ冷めるだろう ◇I *had a huge crush on* her when I was younger. 私は若かった頃、彼女にすごく熱を上げていたんだ ❶**crush** はふつう若者が抱く感情を指し、その相手は年上の[付き合えないとわかっている]人であることが多い。
infatuation [C, U] (現実離れした[長く続かない])心酔、夢中、のぼせ上がり ◇It isn't love, it's just a passing *infatuation*. それは愛じゃない、単なる一時的なのぼせ上がりにすぎない ◇My *infatuation with* her continued to grow. 私の彼女への憧れはふくらみ続けた ❶infatuation は活動[物事]に対しても用いられることがある。◆ the current *infatuation* with popular culture (ポップカルチャーに現在夢中であること). ☞ **infatuated** (IN LOVE)

2 love・affection・tenderness・attachment・devotion・liking
人を非常に好きで大切に思う感情
【類語訳】愛情、大切に思う気持ち、親愛の情、優しさ、思いやり、愛着、献身的な愛、好きであること、好意

liking	love	devotion
	affection	
	tenderness	
	attachment	

【文型&コロケーション】
▶love/ affection/ tenderness/ liking **for** sb
▶attachment/ devotion **to** sb
▶affection/ tenderness **towards** sb
▶love/ affection/ tenderness/ devotion **between** A and B
▶to do sth **with** love/ affection/ tenderness/ devotion

▶ **genuine/ real** love/ affection/ tenderness/ devotion
▶ **great/ mutual** love/ affection/ tenderness/ devotion/ liking
▶ **deep** love/ affection/ attachment/ devotion
▶ **undying/ eternal** love/ devotion
▶ **to show** love/ affection/ tenderness/ devotion
▶ **to feel** love/ affection/ tenderness/ an attachment
▶ **to have** love/ affection/ an attachment/ a liking
▶ **to develop** an affection/ an attachment/ a liking for sb
▶ **a feeling of** love/ affection/ tenderness/ attachment/ devotion

love [U] (家族・友人に対する)愛情, (挨拶として)よろしくとの伝言 ◇People say there is nothing greater than a mother's *love* for her children. 母親の子どもに対する愛情ほど大きなものはないと言われている ◇He seems incapable of *love*. 彼は人を愛せないように思える ◇Bob sends his *love*. ボブがよろしくって言ってるよ 反意 **hatred, hate** (HATRED)

affection [U, 単数で] (頼りにしてくれる人への)愛情, 大切[大事]に思う気持ち, 親愛の情, かわいがり ◇Children need lots of love and *affection*. 子どもは大いに愛され, 大事にされる必要がある ◇Open displays of *affection* always embarrassed her. 愛情を素直に表現されると彼女はいつも恥ずかしがった ◇He'll be remembered with genuine *affection*. 彼のことは心からの親愛の情と共に記憶されるだろう

> ノート **love** と **affection** の使い分け: love はこの類義語の中で最も一般的な語で, ごく軽い感情から非常に強い感情までどんなものでも表すことができる。以下, 比較のこと。
> ◆ Bob sends his *love*. (ボブがよろしくって言ってるよ)
> ◆ Bob sends his best wishes/regards. (ボブがよろしくって言ってるよ) ここでは love のほうがいくぶん意味が強い。以下, 比較のこと。
> ◆ There is nothing greater than a mother's *love* for her children. (母親の子どもに対する愛情ほど大きなものはない) × There is nothing greater than a mother's *affection* for her children. affection はこの場合, love ほど意味が強くなく, 人に話しかける[目を向ける, 触れる]ときに表す優しさを指す。 ◆ She spoke/treated him/looked at him/hugged him with great *affection*. (彼女は親しみを込めて彼に話しかけた/彼をもてなした/彼を見た/彼を抱きしめた)。また, affection は, 大人が自分より年下またはずっと年上の人に対して抱く愛情であり, 特に自分が何らかの形で彼らに頼られているような場合に用いる。

tenderness [U] 優しさ, 思いやり ◇She spoke with loving *tenderness*. 彼女は愛情を込めて優しく話した ◇There was *tenderness* in his face as he looked at her. 彼女を見るときの彼の顔には優しさがあった

attachment [C] (離れたくないと思う)愛着 ◇The children have a strong *attachment* to their parents. その子どもたちは親に対して強い愛着を抱いている ◇Prisoners can develop *attachments* to their warders. 囚人は看守に対する愛着を深めることがある

devotion [U, 単数で] 献身的な愛情 ◇His *devotion* to his wife and family is touching. 妻と家族に対する彼の献身的な心は心動かされる ◇He cared for his mother with great *devotion*. 彼はとても献身的に母親を介護した ❶ devotion はこの類義語の中で最も意味が強い語であり, 変わることのない完全な情を表す。 ◆ her total/undying/lifelong *devotion* to her husband (全面的な/尽きることのない/生涯にわたる夫に対する彼女の献身的な愛情)。
☞ **devotion** (DEVOTE)

liking [単数で, U] 好きであること, 好意 ◇She had **taken a liking to** him on their first meeting. 彼女は初めて会ったときから彼のことが好きだった ◇They have little *liking* for each other. 彼らはお互いにほとんど好意を持っていない 反意 **dislike** (HATRED)

love 動 ☞ LIKE 動

love・like・be fond of sb・adore・be devoted to sb・care for sb・idolize・dote on/upon sb
人に対して愛情[親愛の情]を抱く
【類語訳】愛する, 大切に思う, 好きである, 好意を抱く, 献身的に愛する, 愛情をささげる, 崇拝する, 心酔する, 溺愛する

→

like	love	adore
be fond of	care for sb	be devoted to sb
		idolize
		dote on/upon sb

文型&コロケーション

▶ to love/ like/ be fond of/ adore/ be devoted to/ care for/ dote on your **children**
▶ to love/ like/ be fond of/ adore/ be devoted to/ care for your/ sb's **husband/ wife/ mother/ father**
▶ to **really** love/ like/ adore/ care for/ idolize/ dote on sb
▶ to be **really/ genuinely** fond of/ devoted to sb
▶ to love/ like/ care for sb **very much**
▶ to love/ care for sb **deeply**
▶ to **clearly/ obviously** love/ adore/ idolize/ dote on sb

love [他]《進行形なし》愛する, 大切[大事]に思う ◇I *love* you. あなたを愛しています ◇If you *love* each other, why not get married? 愛し合っているなら, 結婚したらどう ◇He had become a well-*loved* and respected member of the team. 彼はとても愛され尊敬されるチームの一員となっていた ◇Relatives need time to grieve over *loved ones* they have lost. 身内においては失った故人を悼む時間が必要だ 反意 **hate, loathe, detest** (HATE), ☞ **lovable** (SWEET)

like [他]《進行形なし》好きである, 好意を抱く ◇She's nice. I *like* her. 彼女はすてきだ。彼女のことが好きだよ ◇He never did *like* me much, did he? 彼は私にあまり好意を抱いてなかったよね 反意 **dislike** (HATE), ☞ **likeable** (NICE 2)

be 'fond of sb 伝he (長い付き合いの人を)好きである, 大切[大事]に思う ◇Over the years, I have **grown** quite *fond* of him. 年月を重ねるにつれて, 私はますます彼のことを大切に思うようになった

adore [他]《進行形なし》非常に愛する, 大好きである ◇It's obvious that she *adores* him. 彼が彼女のことを大好きなのは明らかだ 反意 **loathe** (HATE), ☞ **adorable** (SWEET)

be de'voted to sb 伝he (人を[に])献身的に愛する, 愛情をささげる ◇They are *devoted to* their children. 彼らは子どもたちに愛情をささげている

'care for sb 句動詞《進行形なし》(親愛の情[守ってあげたいと思う感情]に基づいて人を)愛する, 大切[大事]に思う ◇He *cared for* her more than she realized. 彼女が気づいている以上に彼は彼女のことを愛していた ❶ care for は人が自分の気持ちを誰にも話さない[自分の気持ちに気づき始める]場合に用いられることが多い。また, 愛情を求める[疑う]場合にも用いられる。 ◆ What if he realized she was beginning to *care for* him? (彼女が自分のことを愛し始め

ていることに彼が気づいたらどうなるだろう). ◆If he really *cared for* you, he wouldn't behave like that. (彼があなたをほんとに大切に思っているなら、そんなふうには振る舞わないだろう) ☞ **care for sb** (LOOK AFTER SB)
idolize (英でまた**-ise**) [他]《進行形なし》崇拝[心酔]する ◇He longed to be a pop star, *idolized* by millions of fans. 彼はポップスターになって何百万ものファンに崇拝されることに憧れた
'dote on/upon sb [句動詞]《進行形なし》(人を)溺愛する、猫かわいがりする ◇He *dotes on* his children. 彼は子どもたちを溺愛している

> [ノート] **idolize**と**dote on sb**の使い分け: **idolize**は若者がポップスター・サッカー選手などの有名人や教師・親などの権威者を崇拝すること。**dote on**は両親・祖父母・おじ・おばなどが家族の子どもを溺愛すること。

loving [形]

loving・caring・devoted・affectionate・romantic・tender・fond・adoring

人や物事に対して愛の気持ちを抱く[示す]ことを表す
【類義訳】愛情を抱いた、愛情を示した、優しい、思いやりのある、献身的な、愛情をささげた、懐かしい、愛情に満ちた

[文型&コロケーション]
▸ loving/ affectionate/ tender **towards** sb/ sth
▸ a loving/ a caring/ a devoted/ an affectionate/ a fond/ an adoring **mother/ father/ parent**
▸ a loving/ a caring/ a devoted/ an affectionate/ an adoring **husband/ wife/ family**
▸ a loving/ a caring/ a devoted/ an affectionate **friend**
▸ a loving/ a devoted/ an affectionate **son/ daughter/ brother/ sister**
▸ a loving/ a caring/ an affectionate/ a romantic **man/ woman/ person**
▸ a loving/ an affectionate **child/ boy/ girl**
▸ a loving/ caring/ affectionate/ tender **relationship**
▸ a loving/ caring **attitude**
▸ loving/ romantic/ tender/ fond **feelings**
▸ a loving/ an affectionate/ a tender **kiss**
▸ a loving/ a tender/ a fond/ an adoring **look**
▸ an affectionate/ a tender **smile**

loving (家族への)愛情を抱いた[示した] ◇He came from a warm and *loving* family. 彼は温かく愛情に満ちた家庭の出だった ◇She chose the present with *loving* care. 彼女は愛情を込めた心遣いでプレゼントを選んだ
▸ **lovingly** [副] ◇He gazed *lovingly* at his children. 彼は愛情深く子どもたちを見つめた
caring [ふつう名詞の前で] (人を気遣い守ろうとするような) 思いやりのある ◇She's a very *caring* person. 彼女は非常に思いやりのある人だ ◇Children need a *caring* environment. 子どもには思いやりのある環境が必要である [反義] **uncaring** (INSENSITIVE)、**kind** (KIND) [形]
devoted 献身的な、愛情をささげた They are *devoted to* their children. 彼らは子どもたちに愛情をささげている ◇She has left behind a *devoted* son and many good friends. 彼女は孝行息子と多くの親友のもとを後にしていた ☞ **faithful** (RELIABLE 1)
affectionate (抱擁・キスなどをして)愛情[愛情の情]を示した ◇He is very *affectionate* towards his children. 彼

は子どもたちを非常に愛している ◇She gave him an *affectionate* kiss. 彼女は愛情のこもったキスを彼にした
▸ **affectionately** [副] ◇She kissed him *affectionately* on the cheek. 彼女は彼の頬に親しみを込めてキスをした
romantic 愛情[恋愛感情]を示した ◇Why don't you ever give me flowers? I wish you'd be more *romantic*. どうして一度もお花をくれないの。もっと愛情を示してほしいわ ❶ **romantic**はこの類義語の他のどの語以上に性的な愛情(例えば夫婦[恋人]間などの愛情)を表す。☞ **romance** (RELATIONSHIP 2)
tender (人を気遣って)優しい、思いやりのある ◇I listened to his *tender* words, and started to feel better. 彼の思いやりのある言葉に耳を傾けて、私は気分がよくなり始めた ◆What he needs now is a lot of *tender loving care* (= sympathetic treatment). 彼に今必要なのは優しく愛情のこもった気遣いだ
▸ **tenderly** [副] ◇He smiled *tenderly* down at her. 彼は彼女に優しくほほ笑みかけた
fond [名詞の前で] (人・物事に対して)愛情[親愛の情]を示した、優しい、懐かしい ◇She waved a *fond* farewell to her parents and sister. 彼女は手を振って両親と妹に愛情のこもった別れを告げた ◇I have very *fond memories* of my time in Spain (= I remember it with affection and pleasure). 私にはスペインで過ごしたとても懐かしい思い出があります ❶ **fond**は人を修飾することがある。◆a *fond* father/mother (優しい父/母)。しかし、人の感情に起因する事柄・行動を修飾することのほうが多い。◆a *fond* look/smile/memory (愛情深いまなざし/優しいほほ笑み/懐かしい思い出) ☞ **be fond of sth** (LIKE [動])
▸ **fondly** [副] ◇He looked at her *fondly*. 彼は彼女を優しく見つめた ◇She is still *fondly* remembered by her former students. いまだに彼女は元生徒たちの懐かしい記憶として残っている
adoring [ふつう名詞の前で] (人に対して)愛情に満ちた、熱烈な ◇She was looking at him with large, *adoring* eyes. 彼女は愛のこもった大きな瞳で彼を見つめていた ◇He waved to the *adoring* crowds. 彼は熱烈な群衆に手を振った
▸ **adoringly** [副] ◇She sat there, gazing *adoringly* at him across the table. 彼女はそこに座って、テーブルを挟んで彼を愛情をこめて見つめた

luck [名]

luck・chance・coincidence・accident・fortune・fate・destiny・providence

物事がたまたま起こる現象、物事を引き起こす力
【類義訳】運、幸運、偶然、偶然の一致、同時発生、巡り合わせ、偶然の出来事、椿事、運命、宿命、摂理、神意

[文型&コロケーション]
▸ **by** ...luck/ chance/ coincidence/ accident
▸ **It's no** coincidence/ accident **that**...
▸ **pure/ sheer** luck/ chance/ coincidence/ accident
▸ **good/ bad/ ill** luck/ fortune
▸ a/ an **happy/ unfortunate/ strange** chance/ coincidence/ accident
▸ to **bring sb** good/ bad luck/ fortune
▸ to **have the ...** luck/ fortune **to do sth**
▸ to **leave sth to** chance/ fate/ providence
▸ to **believe in** luck/ coincidences/ fate/ destiny/ providence

▶ to **tempt** fate/ providence
▶ sb's luck/ fortune **changes/ turns**
▶ fate/ providence **decides/ decrees**...
▶ a **stroke of** luck/ fortune/ fate

luck [U] (幸[不])運, つき ◇*The best of luck with your exams.* 試験がうまくいくことを祈ってます ◇*Bad luck, Helen, you played very well.* ついてなかったね, ヘレン, でもすごくよくやった ◇*Never mind — better luck next time.* 気にするな―次はうまくいくよ ◇*It was his hard luck that he wasn't chosen.* 彼が選ばれなかったのは運が悪かったね ◇*It's hard luck on him that he wasn't chosen.* 《英》彼が選ばれなかったのは運が悪かったね ◇*Just my luck to arrive after they had left* (= used to show you are not surprised sth bad has happened to you, because you are not often lucky). 彼らがいなくなってから着くなんて, 案の定, ついてないわ ☞ **lucky** (TIMELY)

chance [U, 単数形] 偶然, 運, 成り行き ◇*We met by chance at the airport.* 私たちは空港で偶然出会った ◇*Chess is not a game of chance.* チェスは出たとこ勝負[運次第]のゲームではない ◇*We'll plan everything very carefully and leave nothing to chance.* 私たちはすべてを非常に入念に計画し, 何事も運[成り行き]に任せたりするつもりはありません ◇*By a happy chance he bumped into an old friend on the plane.* 幸運にも彼は飛行機の中で旧友にばったり出くわした

coincidence [C, U] (2つの物事の驚くべき)偶然の一致, 同時発生, 巡り合わせ ◇*They met through a series of strange coincidences.* 不思議な巡り合わせが重なって彼らは出会った ◇*It's not a coincidence that none of the directors is a woman.* 女性監督が一人もいないのは偶然ではない ◇*It was pure coincidence that they were both in Paris on the same day.* 彼らが二人とも同じ日にパリにいたのは単なる偶然の一致だった

▶ **coincidental** 形 ◇*I suppose your presence here today is not entirely coincidental.* あなたが今日ここにいるのはまったくの偶然ではないのでしょうね

▶ **coincidentally** 副 ◇*Coincidentally, they had both studied in Paris.* 偶然の一致で, 彼らもまたパリで学ぶ体験をしていたのだ

accident [C, U] 偶然(の出来事), 椿事, 運, 巡り合わせ ◇*It is no accident that men fill most of the top jobs in the profession.* 男性がこの専門職の最高職位の多くを占めているのは偶然ではない ◇*an accident of birth/fate/history* (= describing facts and events that are due to chance or circumstances) 生まれ合わせ/運命のいたずら/歴史上の椿事 ◇*It happened, whether by accident or design* (= by accident or on purpose), *that Steve and I were the last two people to leave.* 偶然か故意か, スティーヴと私の二人が最後まで残ることになった

▶ **accidental** 形 ◇*I didn't think our meeting was accidental — he must have known I would be there.* 私たちが出会ったのは偶然だとは思わなかった―彼は私がそこにいることを知っていたに違いない

fortune [U] 《ややフォーマル》(人々の生活に影響を与える)運, 運命, 巡り合わせ ◇*I have had the good fortune to work with some brilliant directors.* 私は幸運にも数名の素晴らしい監督たちと仕事をすることができた ◇*The team had a dramatic reversal of fortune in the second half.* そのチームは後半に運命の大逆転劇を演じた ☞ **fortunate** (TIMELY)

fate [U, 単数形] (定められた)運, 巡り合わせ, 運命, 宿命 ◇*Fate was kind to me that day.* その日, 運は私に味方した ◇*By a strange twist of fate, Andy and I were on the same plane.* 不思議な運命の巡り合わせで, アンディと私は同じ飛行機に乗っていた ◇*She felt it would be tempting fate* (= being too confident in a way that might bring her good luck to an end) *to try the difficult climb a second time.* 彼女はその難しい登攀(註)に2度目の挑戦をすることは大胆極まる賭けに出ることだと感じていた ◇*He believed that the universe was controlled by the whims of a cruel fate.* 森羅万象は無慈悲な運命の気まぐれによって支配されていると彼は信じていた

destiny [U] (定められた)運命, 宿命 ◇*I believe there's some force guiding us — call it God, destiny or fate.* 私は何か私たちを導く力が存在していると信じています―それが神であれ, 運命であれ, 宿命であれ ◇*She was spurred on by a strong sense of destiny.* 彼女は運命を強く感じて鼓舞された ☞ **destined** (CERTAIN)

providence (または**Providence**) [U] 《フォーマル》(神[見えない力]の)摂理, 神意 ◇*He trusted in divine providence.* 彼は神の摂理を信じていた ◇*She believed her suffering was sent by providence.* 彼女は自分の苦しみは神意によってもたらされているのだと信じていた

> ノート fate, destiny, providenceの使い分け: providenceはふつう情け深いものとみなされている。たとえ苦しみをもたらす場合でも, それは神の計画の一部として受け入れられる. fateは情け深いものであることもあるが, それは思いがけない偶然である。また fateはしばしば無慈悲で, 人々に無力感を与えるものである. destinyは人々に運命の力を感じさせる場合に用いられる傾向が強い. a strong sense of destiny (運命を強く感じること)を持つ人はふつう, 自分は偉大である[偉大なことを行うことになっている]と信じているのである.

M m

mad 形

mad・crazy・nuts・batty・out of your mind・(not) in your right mind

人が正常ではないことを表すインフォーマルな語
【類語訳】正気ではない、気が狂った、頭のおかしい、いかれた

batty	mad	out of your mind
	crazy	
	nuts	
	not in your right mind	

【文型&コロケーション】
- to be mad/ crazy/ nuts/ out of your mind/ not in your right mind **to do sth**
- to **go** mad/ crazy/ nuts/ batty
- to **drive sb** mad/ crazy/ nuts/ batty/ out of their mind
- to **think sb (must be)** mad/ crazy/ nuts/ batty/ out of their mind
- **completely** mad/ crazy/ nuts/ batty/ out of your mind

mad（比較・最上級はまれ）《特に英、インフォーマル、時に侮蔑的》正気ではない、気が狂った、頭のおかしい ◇The local people all thought he was *mad*. 地元の人々は皆、彼は気が狂っていると思った ◇She seemed to have gone *stark raving mad*. 彼女はまったくの狂乱状態になってしまったように見えた ❶多くは極度の精神的圧迫から振る舞いがとても奇妙であることを示すときに用いられるインフォーマルな語。本当の精神病を患う人を表すのに用いると侮蔑的なので、代わりに **mentally ill** を用いる。《米》では通常この意味で用いられることはなく、代わりに **crazy** を用いる。☞ANGRY

crazy《特に米、インフォーマル、時に侮蔑的》正気ではない、気が狂った、頭のおかしい ◇A *crazy* old woman rented the upstairs room. 頭のおかしい婆さんが上の部屋を借りていた ◇She was driven half-*crazy* by the thought of him in prison. 彼女は獄中にいる彼のことを考えると半ば気が狂ったようになった ◇Do you think I'm *crazy*? 私をおかしいと思いますか ❶mad と同様に、crazy は本当の精神病患者を表すのに用いると侮蔑的。

nuts《名詞の前では用いない》《インフォーマル、話し言葉》気が狂った、いかれた ◇That noise is driving me *nuts*! あの騒音で気が狂いそうだ ◇You guys are *nuts*! 君たちはいかれている

batty《インフォーマル、特に英》（実害はないが）ちょっと頭がおかしい ◇Her mum's completely *batty*. 彼女の母親は完全にいかれている

out of your 'mind 伝わ《インフォーマル》（ショック・不安から）正気を失った ◇He almost went *out of his mind*, waiting for news of his son. 息子の消息を待っている間に彼は正気を失いかけていた ◇She was *out of her mind* with grief. 彼女は悲しくて正気を失っていた

(not) in your right 'mind 伝わ《インフォーマル》正気で（ない） ◇*No one in their right mind* would choose to work there. そこで働こうなんて正気の沙汰ではない

magnificent 形 ☞ BEAUTIFUL 2, WONDERFUL

magnificent・impressive・spectacular・grand・glorious・majestic・imposing

非常に魅力的で感嘆させられることを表す
【類語訳】荘厳な、見事な、感動的な、印象的な、壮観な、盛大な、壮大な、燦然たる、壮麗な

impressive	grand	magnificent
imposing	majestic	spectacular
		glorious

【文型&コロケーション】
- a magnificent/ an impressive/ a spectacular/ a glorious/ a majestic **sight**
- a magnificent/ an impressive/ a spectacular/ a glorious **display/ array**
- magnificent/ impressive/ spectacular/ grand/ glorious/ majestic **scenery/ views**
- magnificent/ spectacular/ glorious **countryside**
- a magnificent/ an impressive/ a spectacular **waterfall**
- a magnificent/ spectacular/ glorious **coastline/ sunset**
- magnificent/ spectacular/ majestic **mountains**
- a magnificent/ an impressive/ a grand/ a majestic/ an imposing **building**
- a magnificent/ a grand/ a majestic/ an imposing **castle**
- a magnificent/ a grand/ an imposing **palace/ staircase**
- glorious/ majestic **beauty**
- **quite** magnificent/ impressive/ spectacular/ grand
- **truly/ rather** magnificent/ impressive/ spectacular/ grand/ glorious
- **absolutely** magnificent/ spectacular/ glorious
- **very** impressive/ spectacular/ grand/ majestic/ imposing

magnificent 驚くほど美しい、荘厳な、見事な ◇The Taj Mahal is a *magnificent* building. タージ・マハルは荘厳な建造物だ ◇She looked *magnificent* in her wedding dress. ウェディングドレスを着た彼女は息をのむほど美しかった ◇It was an absolutely *magnificent* performance. まったく見事な演奏だった

▷**magnificence** 名 [U] ◇the *magnificence* of the scenery 景色の壮大さ

▷**magnificently** 副 ◇The city boasts a wealth of *magnificently* preserved temples and palaces. その街は見事に保存された多くの神殿や建物を誇っている

impressive 感心させられる、感動的な、印象的な ◇A large portico provides a suitably *impressive* entrance to the chapel. 大きなポルチコがあって、いかにも教会にふさわしい印象的なエントランスになっている ◇This is one of the most *impressive* novels of recent years. これは近年、最も印象に残る小説の一つだ ❶場所や物に対して深く感動したときにしばしば用いられるが、美しいとは限らない。☞ **impressive (IMPRESSIVE)**

spectacular（景色・実演などが）とても美しく感動的な、目

↪ **magnificent**　　　　　　　　　　　　　　　　　　　**main**

を見張らせるような ◇The coastal road has *spectacular* scenery. その湾岸道路は壮観だ ◇In the evening, there will be a *spectacular* display of fireworks. 夜には盛大な花火の打ち上げがある ☞ **spectacular (IMPRESSIVE), breathtaking (AMAZING)**

grand 感動的で大きい[重要な]、壮大な、盛大な ◇It's not a very *grand* house. たいして豪華な家ではないね ◇The wedding was a very *grand* occasion. その結婚式はとても盛大だった ❶ふつう建物(家、別荘、ホテル、城、宮殿、階段や玄関など)について用いられる。行事を表すときは通常金持ちの人が参加したり、大金が費やされているものに関して使われる。

glorious とても美しく感動的な、燦然たる ◇We sat on the beach and gazed at the *glorious* sunset. 私たちはビーチに座って燦然たる日没を眺めていた ◇Both her daughters had *glorious* red hair. 彼女の二人の娘たちは麗しい赤毛の髪をしていた ❶特に夏や太陽に関係する黄色、オレンジ色、赤色に輝く物に用いられる。

majestic (大きさ・美しさが)感動的な、壮麗な ◇The college is close to Edinburgh's *majestic* castle. その大学はエディンバラの壮麗な城の近くにある ◇The Rockies are *majestic* in size. ロッキー山脈は壮大だ ❶ふつう城、邸宅、ホテルなどの建物、または山や崖といったそびえ立つ自然を表すのに用いる。

▷**majestically** 副 ◇The cliffs rise *majestically* from the ocean. 壮大な絶壁が海にそびえ立っている

imposing 印象的な、人目を引く ◇The Tower House is not a particularly grand or *imposing* building. その城館はとりわけ壮大でもいかめしいというわけでもない ◇She was a tall *imposing* woman. 彼女は背が高く、人目を引く女性だった ❶*imposing*な人や物は、人に敬意を抱かせながらも、少し気おくれさせることもありうる。

main 形 ☞ TOP

main・major・key・central・principal・chief・prime・primary・number one・predominant
人や物事が同種類の中で最大、あるいは最も重要であること
【類語訳】最重要な、主要な、中心的な、第一の、際立った

> 文型&コロケーション

▶to be key/ central **to** sth
▶a/ the main/ major/ key/ central/ principal/ chief/ prime/ primary/ number one/ predominant **concern**
▶a/ the main/ major/ key/ central/ principal/ chief/ prime/ primary/ predominant **purpose/ source/ factor**
▶a/ the main/ major/ key/ central/ principal/ chief/ prime/ primary **aim/ focus/ function/ objective/ task/ reason/ consideration**
▶a/ the main/ major/ principal/ chief/ prime/ primary **object**
▶a/ the main/ major/ key/ principal/ chief/ prime/ primary/ number one **cause**
▶a/ the main/ major/ principal/ chief/ primary/ predominant **effect**
▶a/ the main/ major/ key/ central/ principal/ chief/ prime **attraction**
▶a/ the main/ major/ key/ central/ principal/ chief/ primary/ predominant **theme**
▶a/ the main/ major/ key/ central/ principal/ primary/ predominant **role**
▶a/ the main/ major/ principal/ prime/ number one **contender**
▶the main/ chief/ prime/ number one **suspect**
▶a/ the main/ major/ principal **road/ town/ city**
▶the main/ key **thing** is to...
▶to be **of** major/ key/ central/ prime/ primary **importance**

main [名詞の前で] 最大の、最も重要な、主要な ◇Be careful crossing the *main* road. 大通りを渡るときは気をつけなさい ◇We have our ***main* meal** at lunchtime. 私たちのメインの食事は昼食です ◇The ***main* course** was roast lamb. メインコースは子羊のローストだった ◇Reception is in the *main* building. 受付は本館にございます ◇Please use the *main* entrance. 正面玄関をご使用ください ◇Poor housing and unemployment are the *main* problems. 住宅不足と失業が最重要課題だ ◇The *main* thing is to remain calm. 《話し言葉》最も重要なのは冷静さを保つことだ

▷**mainly** 副 ◇They eat *mainly* fruit and nuts. 彼らは主に果実と木の実を食べる ◇The population almost doubles in August, *mainly* because of the film festival. 8月は人口がほぼ2倍になるが、その最大の理由は映画祭だ

major [ふつう名詞の前で] とても大きい、とても重要な ◇A *major* road runs right through the centre of the town. 幹線道路がその街の中心部を通っている ◇He played a *major* role in setting up the system. 彼はそのシステムの構築に重要な役割を果たした ◇We have encountered *major* problems. 私たちは重大な問題に出くわした ❶しばしば冠詞 a の後で単数名詞と、または冠詞なしで複数名詞と共に用いられる。定冠詞 the あるいは my, your など代名詞の所有格と共に用いられる場合は「最大の、最も重要な」を意味する。◆ Our *major* concern here is combatting poverty. (ここで私たちにとって最大の関心事は貧困を克服することだ)。この意味では、物ではなく人々の考えや不安にのみ使われる。また、main よりもフォーマルな語。×Be careful crossing the *major* road. ×The *major* thing is to remain calm. 反意 **minor (MINOR)**

key [ふつう名詞の前で] 最も重要な ◇The *key* issue here is taxation. ここでの最重要問題は税制だ ◇'Caution' is the *key* word in this situation. この状況では「警戒」が最も重要な言葉だ ◇Attitude is a *key* concept in social psychology. 社会心理学において態度が最も重要な概念だ ❶ビジネスや政治の文脈で最も頻繁に用いられる。物ではなく、考えや、ある状況における人の役割について用いられる。特に名詞や連結動詞の後で用いられるときは major よりややインフォーマルな感じになる。◆ Speed is *key* at this point. (《ややインフォーマル》この段階ではスピードが最も肝心だ)

central 《ややフォーマル》最重要な；主要な、中心的な ◇The *central* issue is that of widespread racism. 中心的課題は人種差別の蔓延だ ◇She has been a *central* figure in the campaign. 彼女は選挙運動で中心的な人物だった ◇Reducing inflation is *central* to (= is an important part of) the government's economic policy. インフレの抑制が政府の経済政策の要だ ◇the *central* committee (= of a political party) 中央委員会 ◇The organization has a *central* office in New York. その団体は本部をニューヨークに置いている ❶key と同じように用いられるが、よりフォーマルな語。sth is central to sth else の言い回しで最も頻繁に使用され、key よりも名詞との連語がやや少ない。連語となる名詞は character, component, feature, figure, motif, part, role, theme, topic といった役割や部分、aim, focus, issue, preoccupation, problem, recommendation といった達成しようとする事柄、belief, concept, doctrine, truth など、あることに抱く考えに関するものがほとんどである。

principal [名詞の前で]《ややフォーマル》最重要の ◇New roads will link the *principal* cities. 新しい道路は主要都市を結ぶ予定だ ◇Tourist revenue is now our *principal* source of wealth. 観光収入は今や我が国の主要な財源になっている ◇My *principal* concern is to get the job done fast. 私の一番の関心事は早くその仕事を終わらせることだ ❶たいてい議論の余地のない事実に関して用いられる. 意見を述べたり, 事実を人に説明するときには, ふつうkeyやcentralを使う. ◆The *key/central* issue here is... (ここでの最重要問題は…)

▶**principally** [副] ◇The tax was very unpopular, *principally* because it hit the poor hardest. その税金が大変不人気だった最大の理由は貧困層をもろに直撃したためだ ◇The farms are *principally* arable. その農場はおおむね耕作に適している

chief [名詞の前で]《特に書き言葉》最重要の, 主要な ◇Unemployment was the *chief* cause of poverty. 失業が貧困の主たる原因だった ◇Her *chief* rival for the gold medal is Jones of the USA. 金メダルを争う彼女の一番のライバルはアメリカのジョーンズだ ❶職位の「最高の地位の」の意味もある.「最重要の」の意味では, さまざまに異なる役割の人々についてもよく用いられる. ◆sb's *chief* enemy/rival/opponent (最大の敵). ◆the *chief* architect/exponent of sth (…の主要な建築家/提唱者).

▶**chiefly** [副] ◇Defence spending was cut, *chiefly* by reducing national service by six months. 主に徴兵期間を6か月減らすことで防衛費は削減された ◇The scientists cannot be held solely or even *chiefly* to blame. 科学者たちにすべて, あるいはほとんどの責めを負わせることはありえない

prime [名詞の前で]《ややフォーマル》最重要な; 第一の ◇My *prime* concern is to protect my property. 私の一番の関心事は自分の財産を守ることだ ◇The care of the environment is of *prime* importance. 環境の保護はきわめて最重要である ◇He's the police's *prime* suspect in this case. 彼は警察からこの事件の第一容疑者とされている

primary [ふつう名詞の前で]《ややフォーマル》最重要な; 第一の ◇The *primary* aim of this class is to improve your spoken English. この授業の第一の目的は口語英語を上達させることです ◇Our *primary* concern must be the children. 我々の一番の関心事は子どもたちでなければならない

▶**primarily** [副] ◇In the 1790s Britain was still *primarily* an agricultural country. 1790年代, イギリスはまだ農業中心の国だった ◇History is after all *primarily* about people. 歴史とは結局は主に人間に関することなのだ

> **ノート** **prime**と**primary**の使い分け: 多くの場合どちらも使用可能. ◆your *prime/primary* concern/purpose/aim/object/objective/task (あなたの一番の関心事/目的/課題) ◆to be of *prime/primary* importance (最重要である). しかしながら, **primary**が使用できない決まった結びつきもある. ◆the *prime* (×*primary*) attraction/contender/suspect (第一の目玉/候補者/容疑者). **primary**は「最初の」の意味もある. ☞ **primary** (FIRST)

number one [名詞の前で]《インフォーマル》最重要の, 最良の ◇Our *number one* priority is to find larger office space. 我々の最優先事項は事務所でもっと広いスペースを見つけることだ ◇I just love your work! I'm your *number one fan*. あなたの作品が本当に好きです. あなたの一番のファンです

predominant《ややフォーマル》最も目立つ, 際立った ◇A *predominant* feature of his work is the use of natural materials. 彼の作品の際立った特徴は自然素材を使用している点です ◇Yellow is the *predominant* colour this spring in the fashion world. この春はファッション界で黄色が主流です

▶**predominantly** [副] ◇The firm has a *predominantly* female workforce. その会社は大部分が女性労働者で占められている ◇Ours is a *predominantly* Buddhist country. 我が国は圧倒的に仏教国です

maintain [動]

---

maintain • preserve • sustain • extend • prolong • keep up • keep sth going • perpetuate • prop sth up

物事を同じ水準で続けることを表す
【類語訳】維持する, 保つ, 持続する, 長引かせる, 延長する, 長続きさせる

〖文型&コロケーション〗

▸to maintain/ preserve/ sustain/ keep up **standards/ a relationship**
▸to maintain/ sustain/ keep up **levels/ rates/ morale/ interest/ growth/ the momentum**
▸to keep the **momentum** going
▸to maintain/ preserve/ sustain/ perpetuate a **system/ myth**
▸to maintain/ preserve/ sustain a/ an **balance/ illusion**
▸to maintain/ preserve/ keep up a **tradition**
▸to keep a **tradition** going
▸to maintain/ sustain/ keep up a **pretence**
▸to maintain/ preserve **anonymity/ confidentiality/ order/ the status quo/ your heritage**
▸to maintain/ preserve/ sustain/ extend/ prolong (sb's) **life**
▸to extend/ prolong a **visit/ stay**
▸to **still** maintain sth/ preserve sth/ sustain sth/ keep sth up/ keep sth going/ perpetuate sth/ prop sth up
▸to maintain/ preserve/ sustain/ prolong sth/ keep sth going **indefinitely**
▸to maintain/ extend/ prolong sth **deliberately**

maintain [他]《ややフォーマル》(同水準に)維持する ◇Our principle task is to *maintain* law and order. 我々の信条は法と秩序を維持することにある ◇The two countries have always *maintained* close relations. その2か国は常に密接な関係を保っている ◇She *maintained* a dignified silence.《フォーマル》彼女は毅然として沈黙を守った

preserve [他]《ややフォーマル》(特定の性質・特徴を)保つ ◇He was anxious to *preserve* his reputation. 彼は自分の評判を落としたくなかった ◇Efforts to *preserve* the peace have failed. 平和維持の努力は報われなかった ◇She managed to *preserve* her sense of humour under very trying circumstances. 彼女はとてもつらい状況においてもユーモアのセンスだけは失わなかった

sustain [他]《ややフォーマル》(同水準にしばらく)保つ, 持続する ◇We are experiencing a period of *sustained* economic growth. 持続的な経済成長の時期を迎えている ◇She had been the victim of a *sustained* attack. 彼女は絶え間ない攻撃の犠牲者となっていた ◇She managed to *sustain* everyone's interest until the end of her speech. 彼女はなんとかスピーチの最後まで皆の興味を持たせた

↳maintain　　　　　　　　　　　　　make

▶**sustainable** 形 ◇*sustainable* economic growth 持続的経済成長 反意 **unsustainable**

ノート **maintain** と **sustain** の使い分け：どちらも使用できる場合がある。◆to *maintain/sustain* a balance/ a pretence/people's interest/life（バランス/見せかけ/人々の興味/生活を維持する）。maintain は無期限に普段の水準を保つときに用いられる。◆They believe that the role of the state is to *maintain* the status quo, rather than to promote major economic and social change.（国家の役割は現状を維持することであり、大きな経済的かつ社会的な変革を促進することではないと信じられている）。sustain は無期限ではないが長い間、通常より高い水準を保つときに用いられる。◆How long can this level of growth be *sustained*?（この水準の成長はどのくらい持続するでしょうか）。

extend [他]《ややフォーマル》長続きさせる, 長引かせる, 延長する ◇They've agreed to *extend* the deadline. 彼らは期限を延長することに合意した ◇The show has been *extended* for another six weeks. そのショーはもう6週間延長されることになった ◇Careful maintenance can *extend* the life of your car by several years. 丁寧に手入れをすればあなたの車の寿命は数年は伸びます ☞ **extended** (LONG)

▶**extension** 名 [C] ◇He's been granted an *extension* of the contract for another year. 彼は契約延長をもう1年認められた

prolong [他]《ややフォーマル》 長続きさせる, 長引かせる ◇The operation could *prolong* his life by two or three years. その手術をすれば彼は2、3年寿命が延びるかもしれない ◇Don't *prolong the agony* (= of not knowing sth) — just tell us who won! もったいぶるのはやめて、誰が勝ったかちょっと教えてよ ☞ **prolonged** (LONG)

ノート **extend** と **prolong** の使い分け：extend は特にビジネスの文脈で用いられる。◆to *extend* a deadline/an overdraft/a trip/a visa/a right/a mandate（期限/当座貸越/出張/ビザ/権利/任期を延ばす）。prolong は経験を長続きさせることを表す。◆to *prolong* your stay/visit/life/survival/agony/misery （滞在/旅行/寿命/生存/苦痛/苦難を延ばす）。

,**keep sth 'up** 句動詞 （物事を高い水準に）保つ；（物事を使用・実行し）続ける ◇The high cost of raw materials is *keeping* prices *up*. 原料のコスト高で物価が上がったままだ ◇They sang songs to *keep* their spirits *up*. 元気を保つため彼らは歌を歌った ◇We try to *keep up* the old customs. 我々は古いしきたりを守ろうとしている ◇Do you still *keep up* your Spanish? まだ君のスペイン語はさびついていないの

,**keep sth 'going** フレーズ 《ややインフォーマル, 特に話し言葉》（進行・活動・伝統などを努力して）存続させる ◇We have a chance of winning the championship as long as we can *keep* the momentum *going* (= keep playing at the same high level). この勢いを保てば優勝のチャンスはある

perpetuate [他]《フォーマル》（よくない状況・信念を長い間）維持する, 長続きさせる ◇This new law just serves to *perpetuate* inequality. この新法は不平等の存続につながるだけだ ◇This system *perpetuated itself* for several centuries. 数世紀もの間この制度は存続した ◇Comics and books for children tend to *perpetuate* the myth that 'boys don't cry'. 子ども向けの漫画と本は「男の子は泣かないものだ」という虚構を維持しようとする ❶ inequality, myth, stereotype, system と結びつくことが多い。

,**prop sth 'up** (-pp-)《しばしばしなしで, 特にビジネス》（資金を使って）支える,（苦境に陥らないように）援助する ◇The government was accused of *propping up* declining industries. 政府は衰退産業にてこ入れしたことで非難された ❶ 金融関係の文脈で最も頻繁に用いられる。◆to *prop up* the economy/exchange value of sterling [pound/dollar]/stockmarket（景気/スターリング[ポンド, ドル]の交換価値/株式市場を下支えする）。

make 動

1 ☞ DEVELOP 2, MANUFACTURE
make・do・create・produce・build・generate・form
部品や原料から物を生成したり、事を存在させたり、生じさせたりすることを表す
【類語訳】作る, 発生させる, 創造する, 生み出す

文型&コロケーション

▶to make/ create/ produce/ build/ generate/ form sth **from/ out of** sth
▶to make/ form sth **into** sth
▶to make/ do/ create/ produce a **drawing/ painting**
▶to make/ do/ produce a **sketch**
▶to make/ create/ produce **a meal**
▶to make/ produce **wine**
▶Who made/ created the **universe/ world**?
▶to create/ produce/ generate **income/ profits/ wealth**
▶to produce/ generate **electricity/ heat/ power**
▶to make/ create/ produce a/ an **noise/ impression**
▶to make/ create a **fuss/ mess**
▶to create/ build/ form a **picture** of past societies

make [他]（材料・部品で物を）作る；（事を）起こす ◇She *makes* her own clothes. 彼女は自分で服を作る ◇Wine is *made* from grapes. ワインは葡萄から作られる ◇The grapes are *made* into wine. その葡萄はワインになる ◇What's your shirt *made* of? 君のシャツは何の材料でできているの ◇She *made* us all coffee. 彼女は私たち全員にコーヒーを入れてくれた ◇He has *made* (= directed or acted in) several movies. 彼はいくつかの映画を作っている ◇She tried to ***make a good impression*** on the interviewer. 彼女は面接官によい印象を与えようとした ☞ **making** (PRODUCTION)

do [他]《ややインフォーマル, 特に話し言葉》（芸術的なもの, 料理を）作る ◇He *did* a beautiful drawing of a house. 彼はある家をきれいにスケッチした ◇Who's *doing* the food for the party? パーティー用の食事は誰が作るの ◇Does this pub *do* (= provide) lunches? このパブは昼食を出すの ◇I'll *do* a copy for you. 君にコピーをしてあげるよ ◇I'll *do* you a copy. 君にコピーをしてあげるよ

create [他]（新しい物事を）起こさせる, 創造する ◇Scientists disagree about how the universe was *created*. どのように宇宙が生まれたか、科学者たちの意見は分かれている ◇The government plans to *create* more jobs for young people. 政府は若い人にもっと職を創出しようと計画している ◇*Create* a new directory and put all your files into it. 新しいディレクトリーを作って君のファイルを全部入れなさい ☞ **creation** (DEVELOPMENT), **creative** (CREATIVE)

maker

ノート make と create の使い分け：make の方がより一般的な語で、物についてしばしば用いられる。例えば通常 table/dress/cake には make を使い、job/wealth には create を用いる。物についても、そのオリジナリティーや珍しさを強調するときには create を使用することも可能。◆Try this new dish, *created* by our head chef. (料理長が創作した私の新しい料理を試食してみてください。) ☞ **CAUSE**

produce [他] (技術を駆使して物を)作り出す；(力・お金を)生み出す ◇She *produced* a delicious meal out of a few leftovers. 彼女は少しの残り物でおいしい食事を作った ◇He argued that wealth is *produced* by the labour power of the workers. 富は労働者の労働力によって生み出されると彼は主張した ☞ **produce** (MANUFACTURE)

build [他] (長い時間をかけて生活様式・印象を)築く ◇She's *built* a new career for herself. 彼女は自力で新たなキャリアを築いた ◇This information will help us *build* a picture of his attacker. この情報は彼を襲った人物像を確立するのに役立つだろう

generate [他] (力・金・アイデアを)生み出す、発生させる ◇The wind turbines are used to *generate* electricity. その風力タービンは電気を生み出すために使用されている ◇The lottery is expected to *generate* substantial funds for charity. その宝くじはチャリティーのためにかなりの資金を生むと期待されている ◇Brainstorming is a good way of *generating* ideas. ブレインストーミングはアイデアを生む良い方法だ

form [他、しばしば受身で] (別の物から物を)作る ◆Rearrange the letters to *form* a new word. 文字を並べ替えて新しい単語を作りなさい ◇Do you know how to *form* the past tense? 過去形の作り方を知ってますか ◇The chain is *formed* from 136 links. その鎖は136の環からできている

---

2 make・earn・profit・net・bring (sb) in sth・gross・pocket・pull sth in・rake sth in
仕事によってお金を手にすることを表す
【類語訳】稼ぐ、利益を得る、収益を上げる、儲ける

文型&コロケーション
▶to make/ earn/ net/ bring in/ gross/ pocket/ pull in/ rake in **$100,000 a year**
▶to make/ earn **money/ a living/ a fortune**

make [他] (仕事の報酬として金を)得る、(貸付・投資の利益として金を)稼ぐ ◇He *makes* a living as a stand-up comic. 彼はお笑いタレントとして生計を立てている ◇She *made* a fortune on the stock market. 彼女は株で大儲けした ◇A movie with big name stars in it should *make* money. 大物スターが出演する映画は儲かるはずだ ◇Did they *make any money out of* their invention? 彼らの発明は金になったのですか

earn [他、自] (仕事の報酬として金を)得る、(貸付・投資の利益として金を)稼ぐ ◇She *earns* about £25,000 a year. 彼女は年間に約2万5千ポンドを稼ぐ ◇His victory in the tournament *earned* him $50,000. その試合での勝利で5万ドルを稼いだ ◇Your money would *earn* more in a high-interest account. 高利回りの口座ならもっと利益が出るだろう ◇He was willing to **earn his keep** (= do useful things in return for being allowed to live somewhere). 彼は住まわせてもらっている分くらいは役に立とうと思った ◇All her children are *earning* now (=

working for their living). 今はもう彼女の子どもたちは皆自活している

ノート make と earn の使い分け：両語とも money, living, fortune を目的語として取ることが可能。earn はお金が入る元となる仕事を強調する。お金を利息として得て、主語が人の場合には make を使用する。×She *earned* a fortune on the stock market. 主語が会社や工場どちらでも使用できる。◆The plant will *make/earn* £950 million for the UK. (そのプラントは9億5千万ポンドをイギリスにもたらすだろう)。主語が money の場合 earn を使用する。×Your money would *make* more in a high-interest account.

profit [自] (ややフォーマル) (活動から)お金を得る、利益を得る ◇The private sector will *profit by* selling the surplus electricity abroad. その民間企業は余剰電力を海外に売ることで利益を生むだろう ◇Convicted criminals should not be allowed to *profit from* their crimes. 有罪となった犯罪者がその犯行から利益を得ることなど許してはならない ☞ **profit** (PROFIT)

net (-tt-) 純益を得る ◇The sale of paintings *netted* £17,000. 絵画の販売で1万7千ポンドの純益を上げた

,bring sb 'in sth, ,bring 'in sth [句動詞] お金を稼ぐ ◇His freelance work *brings* him *in* about £20,000 a year. 彼はフリーランスの仕事で年間約2万ポンド稼ぐ ◇New taxes are expected to *bring in* $12 billion in extra revenue. 新税で120億ドルの追加歳入が見込まれている

gross [他] 総収益を上げる ◇The tour *grossed* a massive £20 million at the box office. そのコンサートツアーは2千万ポンドもの総興行収益を上げた

pocket [他] (ややインフォーマル、時にけなして) (金を)儲ける ◇Last year, she *pocketed* over $1 million in advertising contracts. 昨年、彼女は広告契約で100万ドル以上儲けた ☞ **pocket** (FUND [名]), **bank** (SAVE 3)

,pull sth 'in [句動詞] (インフォーマル) (大金を)稼ぐ ◇She must be *pulling in* over $100,000 a year. 彼女は年間10万ドル以上稼いでいるに違いない

,rake sth 'in [句動詞] (インフォーマル、しばしばけなして) (簡単に大金を)稼ぐ、ぼろ儲けする ◇The movie *raked in* more than $300 million. その映画は3億ドル以上稼いだ ◇She's been *raking it in* since she started her new job. 新しい仕事を始めてから彼女は荒稼ぎしている

---

maker [名]

maker・manufacturer・producer・builder・craftsman
物を作る人や会社を表す
【類語訳】製作者、製造業者、メーカー、製造機械、生産者、建設者、建造者、職人

文型&コロケーション
▶a **big/ large/ leading/ major** manufacturer/ producer
▶a **local** manufacturer/ producer/ builder/ craftsman
▶a **car** maker/ manufacturer/ producer
▶a **computer** maker/ manufacturer
▶a **steel/ wine** maker/ producer
▶a **chemical** manufacturer/ producer

maker [C] (しばしば複合語で) 製作者、製造業者、メーカー、製造機械 ◇His father was a watch*maker* and jeweller. 彼の父親は時計と宝石の職人だった ◇a new movie

↪maker　　　　　　　　　　　　　　　　　　　　　　　　　　man

from the *makers* of 'The Matrix' 「The Matrix」の製作者たちによる新作映画 ◇an electric coffee-*maker* 電動コーヒーメーカー ◇a decision/law/policy *maker* 意思決定者/立法者/政策立案者

manufacturer [C] （大量の商品を作る）製造者, 製造会社, メーカー ◇the daughter of a rich textile *manufacturer* 財力のある繊維メーカーの娘 ◇Always follow the *manufacturer's* instructions. 必ずメーカーの使用説明書の指示に従ってください ◇Faulty goods should be returned to the *manufacturers*. 不良品はメーカーに返品したほうがよい ☞ **manufacture** (MANUFACTURE)

producer [C] （食物・原料・商品の）生産者, 生産会社, 生産国 ◇British milk *producers* イギリスの牛乳生産者 ◇The country is one of the world's largest oil *producers*. その国は世界最大の石油産出国の一つだ ☞ **produce** (MANUFACTURE)

ノート **maker, manufacturer, producer** の使い分け：どの語も会社またはその経営者を指すことが可能。特に maker と manufacturer は部品を組み立てて車やコンピューターといった商品を作る会社に用いる。producer は食物や石油など天然資源の生産に用いられる。鉄鋼やワインなど質や技術が重要と思われる製品に関しては maker も頻繁に使用される。

builder [C] （しばしば複合語で）（建物を建てたり修理したりする）建設者, 建造者 ◇We got a local *builder* to do the work for us. その仕事は地元の建設業者にやってもらった ◇a ship*builder* 造船技師[会社] ◇Going on the course was a real confidence-*builder* for me. その道に進んだことは本当の自信になった ☞ **build** (BUILD)

craftsman [C] （しばしばほめて）（手で物を作る）職人 ◇rugs handmade by local *craftsmen* 地元の職人による手作りの敷物 ❶あまり一般的ではないが、女性形は craftswoman、男女ともに craftsperson を使う。性別がわからない場合は女性の可能性があっても craftsman をふつう使用する。

man 名

1 man・guy・gentleman・male・bloke・dude
大人の女性ではない性を表す
【類語訳】男性, 男, 男の人, 奴

文型&コロケーション
▶ a/ an **young/ old** man/ guy/ gentleman/ male/ bloke/ dude
▶ a/ an **middle-aged/ older** man/ guy/ gentleman/ male/ bloke
▶ a/ an **elderly** man/ gentleman/ male
▶ a **big/ little** man/ guy/ bloke/ dude
▶ a **black/ white** man/ guy/ male/ dude
▶ an **ordinary** man/ guy/ bloke
▶ a **handsome** man/ guy/ gentleman/ dude
▶ a **good-looking** man/ guy/ dude
▶ a **nice** man/ guy/ gentleman/ bloke/ dude
▶ a **good/ great/ funny** man/ guy/ bloke/ dude
▶ a **decent** man/ guy/ bloke
▶ a **cool** guy/ dude

man [C] （大人の）男性 ◇He's a good-looking young *man*. 彼は顔立ちのよい若者だ ◇He's a family *man* who rarely goes out with his friends. 彼はマイホームパパで、めったに友達と外出しない ◇Over 150 *men*, women and children were killed. 150人以上もの男性, 女性と子どもが殺害された 反意 **woman** (WOMAN)

guy [C] 《インフォーマル》男 ◇He seemed like a nice *guy*. 彼はいい奴のように思えた ◇It was made by a *guy* called Alan Webster. それはアラン・ウェブスターという男が作った ◇At the end of the film, the *bad guy* gets shot. その映画の最後で悪役が銃で撃たれる 反意 **girl** (GIRL)

gentleman [C] 《フォーマル》男の人[方] （特に見知らぬ男性を指す丁寧な語） ◇There's a *gentleman* here to see you. 男の方が面会に見えています ❶ *gentlemen* は二人以上の男性を指す丁寧な語。◆ *Ladies and gentlemen*! Can I have your attention, please? （皆さん、ご静聴お願いします）◆ Can I help you, *gentlemen*? （いらっしゃいませ、皆様）❶一人の男性にこのように呼びかけるは sir を使う。◆ Can I help you, *sir*? （いらっしゃいませ）❶よりインフォーマルな表現だと ◆ Can I help you? （いらっしゃい）◆ There's someone to see you. （誰かお見えですよ）反意 **lady** (WOMAN)

male [C] 《フォーマル or 専門語》男性 ◇The body is that of a white *male* aged about 40. その死体は40歳くらいの白人男性のものです ◇Haemophilia is a condition that mostly affects *males*. 血友病は主に男性がかかる病気だ ❶フォーマル、公的、科学的、医学的な文脈で主に用いられる。特に女性に対比して用いられる。反意 **female** (WOMAN)

bloke [C] 《英、インフォーマル》男, 奴 ◇I got chatting to a *bloke* in the pub. パブで一人の男とおしゃべりし始めた ◇He was ever such a nice *bloke*. 彼は本当にいい奴だった

dude [C] 《特に米、インフォーマル》男, 奴 ◇He's a real cool *dude*. 彼は本当にいかす奴だ ◇Hey, *dude*, what's up? よー、元気か

ノート **guy, bloke, dude** の使い分け：bloke は《英》でのみ、dude は特に《米》で、guy は《英》《米》両方で用いられる。bloke はいい人で普通の男を指す。dude は魅力的でおしゃれな人を意味することもある。guy はどちらの意にも用いられる。

2 man・humanity・mankind・the human race・humankind
ひとまとまりとしての人を表す
【類語訳】人間, 人類

文型&コロケーション
▶ to **save** humanity/ mankind/ the human race/ humankind
▶ to **destroy** humanity/ mankind/ the human race
▶ to **belong to** humanity/ mankind/ the human race
▶ **all (of)/ the whole of** humanity/ mankind/ humankind
▶ the **rest of** humanity/ mankind/ the human race/ humankind

man [U] 人間, （特定の時代の）人類 ◇In *man* the brain is highly developed. 人類の脳は高度に発達している ◇This is the most poisonous substance known to *man*. これは人類が知る最も毒性の強い物質です ◇They uncovered tools used by *prehistoric man*. 先史時代の人類が使用していた道具が発見された

humanity [U] 人間 ◇He was found guilty of *crimes against humanity* (= very serious and cruel crimes against many people). 彼は非人道的犯罪を犯したとして有罪になった ◇All the streets around the temple were just a *mass of humanity* (= filled with people). その神殿の周囲の道路はすべて大勢の人でごった返していた

mankind [U] 人類, 人間 ◇Some described it as 'the

greatest disaster in the history of *mankind*. それを「人類史上最大の天災」だと言う者もいた ◇These objects date back to *the dawn of mankind*. これらの物は人類の黎明期までさかのぼる

the ˌhuman ˈrace [単数で] 人類 ◇Twenty-five percent of *the entire human race* could be affected by this disease. 全人類の25％がこの病気にかかっていることも考えられる ◇They are perhaps some of the most vulnerable *members of the human race*. 彼らは人類の中でも最も傷つきやすい人たちかもしれない ☞ **race** (PEOPLE)

humankind [U] 人類, 人間 ◇This could provide new clues about the origins of *humankind*. これは人類の起源に関する新たな手がかりになるかもしれない

|ノート| *man* は最も一般的な語。動物と対比して人を指すことも可能。 ◆ the relationship between *man* and nature (人間と自然の関係)。歴史を通じて人類の発展を表す場合に用いられる。 ◆ early/Stone Age/modern *man* (古代人/石器時代人/現代人)。また世界中の人, 社会, 文化について言う。 ◆ all diseases known to *man* (人間に知られたあらゆる病気)。この最後の用法は古風で, 主に文学的文脈で用いられる。 humanity, mankind, humankind は特に社会や文化に属する人間について言う。 humanity はしばしば一般的な道徳, 倫理, 原則を扱う際に用いられる。 ◆ crimes against *humanity* (非人道的犯罪)。 mankind と humankind はしばしば社会やその発展を扱う際に用いられる。次は月に降り立った時の有名なニール・アームストロングの言葉からの引用。 ◆'That's one small step for a man, one giant leap for *mankind*.' (「一人の人間にとっては小さな一歩が, 人類にとっては大きな飛躍だ」)。the human race は特に動物と対比したり歴史を通じての種としての人間を指す。 *man* と *mankind* は元来「すべての男と女」を意味しているが, *man* を含まない humanity や humankind といった性に関して中立的な語を好む人もいる。

management [名]

management・leadership・executive・administration・captaincy・directorate・directorship・headship
会社やチームなどの組織を運営する人やグループ, またはその在任期間
【類語訳】経営者, 運営者, 経営陣, 指導部, 幹部

|文型&コロケーション|
▸ **under** the management/ leadership/ captaincy/ directorship/ headship **of** sb
▸ the **new/ current/ existing** management/ leadership/ executive/ administration
▸ the **central** management/ leadership/ executive/ administration/ directorate
▸ the **local** management/ leadership/ executive/ administration
▸ the **national** leadership/ executive/ administration/ directorate
▸ the **college/ hospital** management/ administration
▸ the **party/ union** leadership/ executive

management [U＋単数・複数動詞, C] 経営者, 運営者, 経営陣 ◇Union leaders are seeking talks with *management* over the proposed layoffs. 提示された一時解雇案に関して労働組合の幹部が経営側との話し合いを要求している ◇It is a one-day workshop for *senior* and *middle management*. それは上級管理職と中間管理職のための1日研修なのです ◇The store is now *under new management*. その店は今新しい経営者になっている ◇Most *managements* are keen to avoid strikes. たいていの経営者はストライキを避けたがる ☞ **management** (GOVERNMENT 2), **manage** (RUN 2)

leadership [C＋単数・複数動詞] (組織・政党・国の)指導部 ◇The party *leadership* is divided. その政党の執行部は分裂している ◇There have been disagreements within the *leadership* of the union. 労働組合の幹部の間で意見の相違がある ❶国の指導者について言う場合, 通例, 選挙によって選ばれていない, あるいは非民主的な政府を指す。 ◆ the Communist/East German/military *leadership* (共産党/東ドイツ/軍首脳部)。 × the British/Australian/Indian *leadership*. ☞ **regime** (GOVERNMENT 1)

executive [C＋単数・複数動詞] (会社・組織の)幹部 ◇She is a member of the party's national *executive*. 彼女はその政党の全国組織の幹部だ ◇She was *on the executive* of the Women's Social and Political Union. 彼女は女性社会政治連合の執行部の一員だった ❶《米》では通常, 他の名詞の前で用いられる。 ◆ There are still too few women in top *executive* positions. (最高幹部の地位には未だに女性がほとんどいない)。 ◆ the *executive* board/ committee (執行理事会/委員会)。☞ **executive** (EXECUTIVE)

administration [C] (官公庁・企業・組織の)経営陣 ◇The prison *administration* is working hard to improve the service. 刑務所当局は業務を改善しようと努力している ◇He has been in dispute with the New Zealand cricket *administration*. 彼はニュージーランドのクリケット協会幹部と論争を続けてきている ☞ **administer** (RUN 2), **administrator** (ORGANIZER)

|ノート| **management, executive, administration** の使い分け: 会社の management には executive よりはるかに多くの人がいる。 top [senior, middle, junior] management とさまざまな職位があるが, management 単体で用いる場合は, top または senior management (最高/上級管理職)のどちらかである。会社の executive は top management (最高管理職)のみを指し, 特に会社経営を議論する執行理事会 (executive board) のメンバーを指す。また, 政党や労働組合の executive は, 特に任命されるあるいは選出された幹部にも用いる。 administration は公共事業を提供したり活動を組織したりする機関を運営する人々を指す。 ◆ the school/college/university/prison/hospital *administration* (学校/大学/刑務所/病院の理事会)。

captaincy [C, ふつう単数で, U] チームの主将の地位[在任期間] ◇The team won the league under the *captaincy* of Martin Jones. 主将マーチン・ジョーンズの下, チームはリーグ優勝を果たした ◇In 2006 he *took over the captaincy* from Vaughan. 2006年, 彼はヴォーンからキャプテンを引き継いだ

directorate [C] 《ややフォーマル》(会社の)経営陣 ◇He is the longest-standing member of the bank's permanent *directorate*. 彼はその銀行の常任取締役会の中でも最古参だ

directorship [C] (会社の)重役(の在任期間) ◇He was forced to resign his *directorship* of the company. 彼はその会社の重役を辞任せざるをえなかった ◇Since leaving politics, he has *held directorships* of various

→management

financial companies. 政界を離れてからは彼はいろいろな金融会社の重役を務めている

headship [C]《英》(組織・大学の学部・学校などの)責任者の地位(の在任期間) ◇He has just retired from the *headship* of the Diplomatic Service. 彼は外交部の長を辞めたばかりだ ◇She applied for the *headship* of a small, rural primary school. 彼女は田舎の小さな小学校の校長職に志願した ❶headshipは校長, 局長, 官公庁の長といった長の付く地位のことを指す. ☞ **head (LEADER 1)**

manager 名 ☞ LEADER 1

manager・director・employer・boss・supervisor・governor・superintendent・foreman
会社または部局の経営, 運営責任者を表す
【類語訳】責任者, 雇用主, 上司, 上役, 職長, 現場監督

〔文型&コロケーション〕
▸ to work **for** a manager/ a director/ an employer/ a boss
▸ to work **under** a manager/ supervisor/ superintendent/ foreman
▸ a **good** manager/ director/ employer/ boss/ supervisor/ governor
▸ a **company** manager/ director/ boss
▸ to **have** a manager/ a director/ an employer/ a boss/ a supervisor/ a governor/ a foreman
▸ to **act as** manager/ director/ supervisor/ governor
▸ to **work as** a manager/ director/ supervisor/ foreman
▸ to **assist** the manager/ director/ supervisor/ governor/ superintendent
▸ to **appoint** a manager/ director/ supervisor/ governor/ superintendent
▸ to **become/ make sb** a manager/ director/ supervisor/ governor

manager [C] (会社・店などの)経営責任者; (会社内の事業・部局の)責任者 ◇a bank/hotel *manager* 銀行の支店長/ホテルの支配人 ◇Sales *manager* Chris Jones says, 'We're thrilled with the results'. 営業部長クリス・ジョーンズは「その結果にわくわくしている」と述べている ◇There's a meeting of area *managers* next Tuesday. 来週の木曜日, エリアマネージャーの会合がある ❶《英》ではline managerは直属の上司のことで, 部下の仕事に直接責任を持つ. line managerまたはmanagerはbossよりもフォーマルな語. ♦I'll ask my *manager* if I can leave early. (早退できるか課長に尋ねてみます) ☞ **management (GOVERNMENT 2), managing director (LEADER 1)**

director [C] (会社を経営する)上級管理職; (会社・大学などでの仕事・部署の)責任者 ◇She's on the board of *directors*. 彼女は取締役会のメンバーだ ◇He was musical *director* at the National Theatre from 1976 to 1997. 彼は1976年から1997年まで国立劇場の音楽監督だった ☞ **managing director (LEADER 1), direct (RUN 2), direction (GOVERNMENT 2)**

〔ノート〕**managerとdirectorの使い分け**: どちらの語も会社内の仕事や部署の責任者を指すことが可能. ♦a sales/ marketing/finance/personnel/technical *manager/ director* (営業/マーケティング/財務/人事/技術部長). しかしながら, 大会社におけるdirectorは何人かのmanagerを管理していることが多い.

employer [C] 雇用主 ◇They're very good *employers* (= they treat the people that work for them well). 彼らはとてもよい雇用主だ ◇They're one of the largest *employers* in the area. 彼らはその地域内で最大の会社の一つだ ☞ **employ (EMPLOY)**

boss [C]《ややインフォーマル, 特に話し言葉 or ジャーナリズム》上司, 上役 ◇I'll ask my *boss* if I can have the day off. 休日を取れるか上司に尋ねてみます ◇I like being *my own boss* (= working for myself and making my own decisions). 私は誰の指図も受けずに生きたい ◇Who's the *boss* (= who's in control) in this house? この家を仕切っているのは誰ですか ❶代名詞の所有格と一緒に用いられることが多い. 上司を表すかなりインフォーマルな語. ある状況や関係において支配的な立場にある人についておどけて用いることもある.

supervisor [C] 管理者, 監督者 ◇I have a meeting with my *supervisor* about my research topic. 研究テーマに関して指導教官と面談します ◇All work is done under the guidance of a *supervisor*. すべての作業が監督者の指導の下で行われます ☞ **supervise (REGULATE), supervision (GOVERNMENT 2)**

governor [C]《特に英》(学校・大学・病院などの)管理責任者 ◇One way of getting things changed is to become a school *governor*. 状況を変える一つの方法は学校理事になることだ ❶《英》では刑務所や銀行の一人しかいない管理者を指すこともある. ☞ **governor (LEADER 1)**

superintendent [C] (大きな権限を持つ)指導[管理]監督者 ◇In 1945 he became *superintendent* of schools in Dallas. 1945年に彼はダラスで教育長になった ❶主として病院, 鉄道, 学校を管理する人を指す. ☞ **superintend (REGULATE)**

foreman [C] 職長, 現場監督 ◇He got a job as *foreman* of a building site. 彼は建設現場の現場監督の仕事に就いた ❶男性にも女性にも用いられる. forewomanという女性形もあるが, あまり一般的ではない

manufacture 動 ☞ MAKE 1

manufacture・produce・turn sb/sth out・churn sth out・mass-produce
売るために物を大量に作る
【類語訳】製造する, 生産する

〔文型&コロケーション〕
▸ a **factory** that manufactures/ produces **cars/ mainframes/ microchips**
▸ to manufacture/ produce/ turn out/ churn out **900 cars a week**
▸ manufactured/ mass produced **goods**
▸ to produce/ turn out/ churn out **books/ articles**

manufacture [他]《機械を用いて大量に》生産する, 製造する ◇This company *manufactures* the equipment used to make contact lenses. この会社はコンタクトレンズを作る装置を製造している ❶商品を大量に生産するという意味で最も頻繁に使用されますが, より広義のmakeもしばしばこの意味で用いられる. ♦a factory that *makes* cars/mainframes/microchips (車/大型汎用コンピューター/マイクロチップの製造工場). ☞ **manufacturer (MAKER), manufacturing, manufacture (PRODUCTION)**

produce [他] (大量に)製造する, 生産する ◇a factory that *produces* microchips マイクロチップを製造する工場 ◇the wine-*producing* regions of France フランスの

map, mark

ワインの生産地域 ◇The country *produces* more than two million barrels of oil per day. その国は1日に200万バレルの石油を生産している ☞ **produce** (MAKE 1), **producer** (MAKER), **product** (PRODUCT), **production** (OUTPUT), **production** (PRODUCTION)

> ノート **manufacture** と **produce** の使い分け：**produce** は **manufacture** より広義で、商品以外に原料の採集や植物の栽培、書物の執筆などにも用いられる。**manufacture** はビジネスの文脈で用いられ、商品の製造過程や機械の使用を強調するのに対し、**produce** はできあがった製品を強調する。

,turn sb/sth 'out 句動詞《ややインフォーマル》(大量に商品を)生産する、(本を)執筆する、(食事を)用意する、(人を)育成する ◇If we can *turn out* plenty of work between us, we should manage. 私たち二人で十分に作業がこなせるようなら、何とかなりそう ◇We turned the kitchen into a production line, *turning out* hot meals for the servicemen. 私たちはその台所を製造ラインに変えて、温かい食事を軍人に提供した ◇The school has *turned out* some first-rate students. その学校は第一級の学生をかなり輩出している

,churn sth 'out 句動詞《インフォーマル、けなして》(粗悪品を速く大量に)生産する ◇She *churns out* novels at the rate of three a year. 彼女は1年に3冊のペースで小説を乱作する ◇the second-rate movies *churned out* by the studios そのスタジオによって量産された二流映画

,mass-pro'duce 他、しばしば受身で》(機械を使って)大量生産する ◇Because the coins were *mass-produced* they can often be accurately dated. その硬貨は大量生産されたので製造時期が正確に突き止められることが多い
▸ **,mass-pro'duced** 形 ◇He was wearing a cheap, *mass-produced* suit. 彼は安物の量産型スーツを着ていた

map 名

map・plan・atlas・chart・globe
地球の表面またはその一部の図面で、国、町、川などを表示するもの
【類語訳】地図、地図帳、海図、地球儀

> 文型&コロケーション
> ▸ **on** a map/ plan/ chart/ globe
> ▸ a/ an **detailed/ accurate** map/ plan/ chart
> ▸ a **simple/ rough** map/ plan
> ▸ a **large-scale/ small-scale** map/ plan/ atlas/ chart
> ▸ a **street/ route** map/ plan/ atlas
> ▸ a **road/ world** map/ atlas
> ▸ to **look at/ consult** a map/ a plan/ an atlas/ a chart
> ▸ to **read** a map/ chart
> ▸ to **find sth on** a map/ a plan/ a chart/ the globe
> ▸ to **draw** a map/ plan/ chart
> ▸ a map/ a plan/ an atlas/ a chart **shows** sth

map [C] 地図 ◇a *map* of the world 世界地図 ◇I'll draw you a *map* of how to get to my house. 私の家までの地図を描いてあげます

plan [C] 《建物内・都市の》詳細地図 ◇Do you have a *plan* of the museum? 博物館の見取り図を持っていますか ◇We asked for a *street plan* of the city. 私たちはその都市の市街地図を求めた

atlas [C] 地図帳 ◇Do you have a road *atlas* of the UK? イギリスの道路地図帳を持っていますか

chart [C] 海図 ◇There are no *charts* available for this part of the ocean. この辺りの海で使える海図はありません

globe [C] 地球儀 ◇Find Laos on the *globe*. 地球儀でラオスを探しなさい

mark 名

mark・stain・fingerprint・streak・speck・blot・smear・blemish・smudge・spot
表面に泥などが小さく付いた部分
【類語訳】跡、染み、指紋、すじ、斑点、汚れ

> 文型&コロケーション
> ▸ a mark/ stain/ fingerprint/ streak/ speck/ blot/ smear/ blemish/ smudge/ spot **on** sth
> ▸ a streak/ speck/ blot/ smear/ smudge/ spot **of** sth
> ▸ a **greasy** mark/ stain/ smear
> ▸ an **ink** mark/ stain/ blot/ spot
> ▸ a **grease** mark/ stain/ spot
> ▸ to **leave** a mark/ stain/ fingerprint/ streak/ speck/ blot/ smear/ smudge
> ▸ to **remove** a mark/ stain/ fingerprint/ speck/ smear/ blemish/ smudge/ spot

mark [C] (見栄えの悪い)跡 ◇The kids left dirty *marks* all over the kitchen floor. 子どもたちは台所の床いっぱいに汚れ跡を残した ◇There were **burn marks** on the carpet. カーペットの上に焼け焦げた跡があった ◇A faint *pencil mark* showed where the house was on the map. 地図上にその家のありかを示すかすかな鉛筆跡があった

stain [C] (液体による)染み ◇I couldn't get the *stains* out of my jeans. ジーンズの染みは取り除くことができなかった ◇A dark *stain* spread over the patterned carpet. 柄物のカーペットに黒ずむ染みが広がっていた ◇blood/coffee/wine *stains* 血/コーヒー/ワインの染み ☞ **stained** (DIRTY)

fingerprint [C] 指紋 ◇His *fingerprints* were all over the gun. 彼の指紋がその銃の至る所に付いていた ◇The police **took their fingerprints** (= made them leave the mark of their fingerprints as a record). 警察は彼らの指紋を採取した
▸ **fingerprint** 動 [他] ◇I was booked, *fingerprinted* (= my fingerprints were taken) and locked up for the night. 私は調書と指紋を取られ、その晩は拘留された

streak [C] 筋 ◇There was a *streak* of blood on his face. 彼の顔には一筋の血が流れていた ◇She had *streaks* of grey in her hair. 彼女の髪には白髪の筋があった ◇The sooty rain left dirty *streaks* on the window. すすで汚れた雨で窓に汚い筋が残った

speck [C] 小さな斑点 ◇There isn't a **speck of dust** anywhere in the house. その家にはどこにも塵一つない ◇The bird has reddish *specks* on its breast. その鳥の胸部には赤みがかった小さな斑点がある

blot [C] (インク・ペンキの)汚れ ◇There were ink *blots* all over the paper. その紙の至る所にインク汚れがあった

smear [C] (オイル・ペンキなどの)汚れ ◇There was a *smear* of paint on his cheek. 彼の頬にペンキ汚れが付いていた

blemish [C] 《特に書き言葉》(肌の)染み、(外観を損なう表面の)傷 ◇Cover up unsightly *blemishes* with our new liquid make-up. 気になる染みは当社の新しい液状化粧品でお手入れしましょう ☞ **imperfection** (DEFECT)

smudge [C] （ペンキ・インクなどの）ぼやけた汚れ ◇There was a *smudge* of lipstick on the cup. カップに口紅の跡が付いていた

spot [C] (小さな)汚れ ◇His jacket was covered with *spots* of mud. 彼の上着の一面に泥が跳ねた跡があった ◇There were grease *spots* all over the walls. そこらの壁一面に油が飛び散った跡があった

marked 形 ☞ CLEAR 形 1, VISIBLE

marked・striking・distinct・conspicuous・unmistakable・sharp・pronounced・definite・decided
普通でなかったり、他と違ったりしていることを表す
【類語訳】目立つ、目を引く、はっきりした、紛れもない、明白な、議論の余地のない

▶ 文型&コロケーション

▸ a marked/ striking/ distinct/ sharp/ pronounced/ definite **difference**
▸ a marked/ striking/ distinct/ sharp **contrast**
▸ a marked/ striking/ distinct **resemblance**
▸ a marked/ striking/ distinct/ sharp/ definite/ decided **improvement**
▸ a marked/ striking/ sharp/ pronounced/ definite **increase**
▸ a marked/ striking/ pronounced/ definite **effect**
▸ a marked/ striking/ conspicuous **success**
▸ a marked/ striking/ distinct/ conspicuous/ pronounced **feature**
▸ a distinct/ an unmistakable/ a pronounced **flavour**
▸ quite marked/ striking/ distinct/ unmistakable/ sharp/ pronounced/ definite
▸ very marked/ striking/ distinct/ conspicuous/ sharp/ pronounced/ definite
▸ fairly distinct/ sharp/ pronounced/ definite

marked 《特に書き言葉》目立つ ◇The recent advertising campaign has had a *marked* effect on sales. 最近の広告活動で売り上げ面で目覚ましい効果が出ている ◇She is quiet and studious, in *marked* contrast to her sister. 姉とは好対照で彼女は物静かで勉強熱心だ
▹ **markedly** 副 ◇Her background is *markedly* different from her husband's. 彼女の育ってきた環境は夫とはまったく違う ◇This year's sales have risen *markedly*. 今年の売り上げは著しく伸びている

striking 《興味深くて[珍しくて]》人目を引く ◇She bears a *striking* resemblance to her older sister. 彼女はお姉さんとはっとするほどよく似ている ◇What is immediately *striking* is how resourceful the children are. すぐに目を引くのはその子どもたちが才能に溢れているかという点である ☞ striking (BEAUTIFUL 1)
▹ **strikingly** 副 ◇The two polls produced *strikingly* different results. 二つの世論調査は著しく異なる結果になった

distinct (五感に)はっきりとわかる ◇There was a *distinct* smell of gas. 明らかにガスの臭いがした ◇His voice was quiet but every word was *distinct*. 彼の声は小さかったが一言一言はっきりしていた 反意 **indistinct** (VAGUE)
▹ **distinctly** 副 ◇I *distinctly* heard someone calling my name. 誰かが私の名前を呼んでいるのがはっきり聞こえた

conspicuous 目立つ；(普通でなくて[違っていて])目を引く ◇I felt very *conspicuous* in my new car. 新車に乗るととても目立っている気がした ◇Bay windows are a *conspicuous* feature of his architecture. 出窓は彼の建築の際立った特徴となっている 反意 **inconspicuous**
▹ **conspicuously** 副 Women were *conspicuously* absent from the planning committee. 実行委員会では女性たちの欠席が目立った

unmistakable （または頻度は低いが **unmistakeable**）間違えようのない、紛れもない ◇Her accent was *unmistakable*. 彼女の訛りは独特だった ◇The main symptom is a scarlet rash that's quite *unmistakable*. その主な症状は明らかにそれとわかる緋色疹である ◇the *unmistakable* sound of gunfire 紛れもない発砲音
▹ **unmistakably** His accent was *unmistakably* British. 彼の発音は明らかにイギリス英語だった

sharp [ふつう名詞の前で] 鮮明に見える、明快な ◇The sky was dark, with only the outlines of dockside warehouses standing *sharp* on the skyline. 空は暗く、波止場の倉庫の輪郭だけがくっきりと浮かび上がっていた ◇She drew a *sharp* distinction between domestic and international politics. 彼女は内政と外交を明確に区別した ◇The issue must be brought into *sharper* focus. その問題はさらに詳しく究明されなければならない ❶ この意味では、異なる考えや問題の対比や、景色や絵画の中の異なる物の対比を表すのに用いられる。☞ **stark** (PLAIN 2)

pronounced 《特に書き言葉》目立つ、明白な ◇He walked with a *pronounced* limp. 彼は明らかに足をひきずって歩いていた ◇She had a *pronounced* Scottish accent. 彼女は明らかにスコットランド訛りだった

definite [ふつう名詞の前で] 目立つ、明白な ◇The look on her face was a *definite* sign that something was wrong. 彼女の顔の表情は明らかに何かがおかしいという兆候だった ◇There was a *definite* feeling that things were getting worse. 状況がさらに悪化しているとはっきりと感じられた

ノート **marked, pronounced, definite** の使い分け：
変化や違いについて言うときには多くの場合どの語も使用可能。marked はほとんどの場合に使われるが、特にビジネスの文脈で使われる。pronounced は話し言葉よりも書き言葉で用いられ、身体的特徴または性格に用いられる傾向がある。definite は見たり感じたりすることができる物について使われる。

decided [名詞の前で] 明確な、議論の余地のない ◇Her recent work has shown a *decided* improvement. 彼女の最近の作品は確実によくなっている ◇His height was a *decided* advantage in the game. 彼の身長は試合では明らかに有利だった
▹ **decidedly** 副 ◇Things were looking *decidedly* gloomy. すべての物がまったく陰気くさく見えた

market 名

1 market・audience・public・clientele
商品を購入する、または購入すると思われる特定の地域、国、特定の階層の人
【類語訳】市場（しじょう）、観衆、読者、視聴者、顧客

▶ 文型&コロケーション

▸ a market/ an audience **for** sth
▸ a **wide** market/ audience/ public/ clientele
▸ a/ an **large/ small/ international** market/ audience/ clientele

match

▶to **serve** a market/ an audience/ the ...public/ a clientele
▶to **reach** a market/ an audience/ a wide public
▶to **attract/ build up** a market/ an audience/ clientele
▶to **establish** a market/ an audience

market [C] 市場 ◇The jacket is designed for the Japanese *market*. そのジャケットは日本市場向けに作られている ◇They supply beef to the domestic *market*. 彼らは国内市場に牛肉を供給している ❶the *market* (単数形) 価格や商品供給が購買によって左右される経済システムとしての市場を指す。◆The *market* will decide if the TV station has any future. (市場がそのテレビ局の今後を決定するだろう)。◆We now have an unprotected, *market-led economy*. (現在あるのは保護されていない市場主導型の経済である)。the *market* は購入希望者数を表すこともできる。
☞ **market** (DEMAND) 名

audience [C] 観衆, 読者, 視聴者 ◇An *audience* of millions watched the wedding on TV. 何百万もの視聴者がその結婚式をテレビで見た ◇The target *audience* for this advertisement was mainly teenagers. この広告が対象とする視聴者は主に十代の若者である

public [単数+単数・複数動詞] 特定の興味を共有する [同じ活動に従事している] 集団 [層, 人] ◇The show drew 12% of the viewing *public*. その番組の視聴率は12％だった ◇She knows how to keep her *public* (= for example, the people who buy her books) satisfied. 彼女は自分の読者をつかまえて離さない術を知っている ❶この意味では、しばしば特定の活動を示す形容詞の後に置かれる。◆the book-buying/reading/sporting/theatre-going/travelling/viewing *public* (書籍購入者／読者／スポーツ愛好家／芝居好き／旅行者／視聴者)

clientele [単数+単数・複数動詞] (店・レストラン・組織の) 顧客 ◇The facilities appeal to an international *clientele*. それらの施設は外国からの顧客に受けている ☞ **client** (CUSTOMER)

2 market・mall・shopping centre・farmers' market・strip mall
人々が集まって商品を売り買いする場所を表す
【類語訳】市場(ぱ), 市, 商店街, ショッピングモール, ショッピングセンター

文型&コロケーション
▶**at** the market/ mall/ shopping centre
▶a/ an **covered/ indoor** market/ shopping centre
▶to **go to** the market/ mall/ shopping centre

market [C] 市場 ◇We buy our fruit and vegetables at the *market*. 果物と野菜をその市場で買っています ◇Thursday is *market day* in Poitiers. ポワティエでは木曜日は市の立つ日です ◇a fruit *market* 青果市場 ◇a *market* stall 市場の店 ◇It's a busy *market town* (= a town in Britain where a regular market is or was held). そこはにぎやかな市場町です

mall (または '**shopping mall**) [C] (特に米) ショッピングモール (一つ屋根の下に店が立ち並ぶ車両通行止めの商店街) ◇'Where'd you get those earrings?' 'At the *mall*.' 「どこでそのイヤリングを買ったの」「ショッピングモールよ」◇Let's go to the *mall*. ショッピングモールに行こう ❶(英) でもますます一般的になっている。しばしばレストランや映画館をはじめ他の公共娯楽施設が入っている。

'**shopping centre** (英) (米 **shopping center**) [C] ショッピングセンター (一つ屋根の下に店が並ぶこともある) ◇The two children were left unattended in the main *shopping centre*. 子どもが二人ショッピングセンター本館に置き去りにされていた ❶(米) では shopping center はふつう一つ屋根の下に並んでいないものを言い、一つ屋根の下に並んでいるものは mall と言う。

'**farmers' market** [C] (特に米) 直売所 (栽培者から直接新鮮な食品を買うことができる市場) ◇I bought some delicious strawberries at the *farmers' market*. おいしい苺を直売所で買った

'**strip mall** [C] (米, 時にけなして) 小規模なショッピングセンター (店が一列に並び、専用の駐車場がある) ◇It's just another of the many *strip malls* that are taking over the landscape. それは景観を占領しているストリップモール [道路沿いの商店街] のありふれた一つにすぎない

match 動

1 match・correspond・fit・correlate・tie in・coincide・agree
同じかまたは似ている、何らかの形で密接に結びついている
【類語訳】同じである、そっくりである、一致する、相互に関係する

文型&コロケーション
▶A corresponds/ correlates/ ties in/ coincides/ agrees **with** B
▶A and B correspond/ correlate/ coincide/ agree
▶**figures** match/ correspond/ correlate/ coincide/ agree
▶sb's **account/ version** matches/ corresponds/ coincides/ agrees with sb else's
▶to match/ fit/ correlate/ tie in **well**
▶to **almost** match/ correspond/ correlate/ coincide
▶to **not quite** match/ fit/ correlate

match [自, 他]《進行形なし》同じである, そっくりである ◇The two sets of figures don't *match*. その2組の数字は一致しない ◇Her fingerprints *match* those found at the scene of the crime. 彼女の指紋が犯行現場で見つかったものと一致している ◇The dark clouds *matched* her mood. 暗い雲は彼女の気分にぴったり合っていた ▷**match** 名 [C] ◇I've found a vase that is an exact *match of* the one I broke. 壊したものとまったくそっくりな花瓶を見つけた ◇The paint is a close enough colour *match to* the original. その塗料は元の色の代わりに使えるくらい近い色だ

correspond [自]《進行形なし》《ややフォーマル》一致する ◇Your account of events does not *correspond* with hers. 事件についてのあなたの説明は彼女のものと一致していない ◇Your account and hers do not *correspond*. あなたと彼女の説明は一致していない ◇The written record of the conversation doesn't *correspond to* (= is different from) what was actually said. その対話の文書記録は実際に話されたことと一致していない ◇The British job of Lecturer *corresponds* roughly to the US Associate Professor. イギリスでの講師という地位は大雑把に言ってアメリカでの准教授に相当する ❶厳密には同じでないことを言うときは to しか使えないが、まったく同じであることを言うときは to でも with でも使うことができる。☞ **correspondence** (SIMILARITY), **corresponding** (EQUIVALENT)

fit [自, 他]《進行形なし》当てはまる, 適合する, (説明・考え方が) 一致する ◇His pictures don't *fit into* any category. 彼の絵はどのカテゴリーにも当てはまらない ◇Something doesn't quite *fit* here. ここにはあまりふさわしくない物もある ◇The facts certainly *fit* your theory. それらの事実はあなたの理論に確かに当てはまる ◇The punishment ought to *fit* the crime. その刑はその犯罪に適合すべきだ ◇We should *fit* the punishment *to* the crime. その犯罪にはその刑を当てはめるべきだ

▶**fit** [名] [C] ◇We need to work out the best *fit between* the people required and the people available. 求められている人材と求めに応じられる人材をできる限り一致させる必要がある

correlate [自] 《フォーマル or 専門用語》《事実・数字が》相互に関係する, 依存する ◇The figures do not seem to *correlate*. それらの数字は相互に関係しているようには思えない ◇A high-fat diet *correlates* with a greater risk of heart disease. 高脂肪の食事は心臓病のリスクの増加と相互に関係がある ☞ **correlation** (RELATION)

,tie 'in [句動詞] 《ややインフォーマル, 特に書き言葉》《別の一連の事柄と》一致する ;（同じテーマ・考えを扱うことで）結びつく ◇This evidence *ties in* closely with what we already know. この証拠は私たちがすでに知っていることと密に結びついている ◇The concert will *tie in* with the festival of dance taking place the same weekend. そのコンサートは同じ週末に開催されるダンス大会と抱き合わせで行われる

coincide [自] 《ややフォーマル, 特に書き言葉》《意見が》一致する, 非常に似ている ◇The interests of employers and employees do not always *coincide*. 雇用主と被雇用者の利益はいつも一致するとは限らない ◇Our views on this issue *coincide* closely with those of the Countryside Council. この問題に対する我々の見解は地方評議会のそれと非常に近い

agree [自] 《ややフォーマル, 特に書き言葉》 （説明・数字が）一致する ◇The figures do not *agree*. 数字が合わない ◇Your account of the accident does not *agree* with hers. その事故に対するあなたの説明は彼女のものと一致しない

2 match・blend・go・mix・coordinate
魅力的または効果的に組み合わさる［組み合わせる］
【類語訳】調和する, 調和させる, 一緒にする

《文型&コロケーション》
▶ to blend/ go/ mix/ coordinate **with** sth
▶ to blend/ go **together**
▶ sth matches/ goes with/ coordinates with the **curtains/ decor**
▶ sth matches/ goes with sb's **dress**
▶ to match/ coordinate **colours**
▶ **colours** match/ blend/ go with each other/ coordinate
▶ to match/ blend/ go with sth/ coordinate **perfectly/ well**
▶ to **not** quite match/ go with sth

match [他, 自] 《色・柄・様式が［を］》調和する［させる］ ◇The doors were painted blue to *match* the walls. 壁と調和するようにドアは青色に塗られていた ◇I've got her a scarf with gloves *to match*. 彼女にスカーフとそれに合う手袋を買ってあげた ◇None of these glasses *match* (= they are all different). これらのグラスはどれも揃ってはいない ☞ **matching** (EQUIVALENT)

▶**match** [名] [単数で] ◇The curtains and carpet are a *good match*. そのカーテンとカーペットはよく調和している ◇Jo and Ian are a perfect *match for* each other. ジョーとイアンはぴったりお似合いの二人だ

blend [自, 他] 《特に書き言葉》調和する；調和させる ◇The old and new buildings *blend* together perfectly. 古い建物と新しい建物が完璧に調和している ◇The colour of the carpet doesn't *blend in*. カーペットの色が調和していない ◇Their music *blends* traditional and modern styles. 彼らの音楽は伝統的スタイルと現代的スタイルを融合させている ❶色や音（特に音楽）, 香りや建築様式の調和によく使われる

go 《ややインフォーマル, 特に話し言葉》《服・色が》調和する ◇Does this jacket *go* with this skirt? このジャケットはこのスカートに合うかしら ◇Those colours don't really *go* (together). それらの色はあまり合わない

mix [自] 《ふつう否定文で》（問題・危険を起こすような形で）一緒にする ◇Children and fireworks don't *mix*. 子どもと花火を一緒にすると危険だ

coordinate 《英でまた **co-ordinate**》 [自, 他] 《ややフォーマル》（色・衣服・生地が）調和する；コーディネートする ◇This shade *coordinates* with a wide range of other colours. この色調は他のさまざまな色と調和する ◇The company has extended its *coordinated* clothing range. その会社はコーディネートされた衣料品の品揃え幅を拡大している ❶衣料産業や繊維産業, 服飾に関するコメントや広告によく使われる

▶**coordination** 《英でまた **co-ordination**》 [名] [U] ◇advice on colour *coordination* カラーコーディネートについてのアドバイス

material [名]

material・substance・chemical・gas・fluid・stuff・matter・solid・element
物を作る原料を表す
【類語訳】材料, 物, 物質, 化学物質, 気体, 液体, 流体, 固体, 元素

《文型&コロケーション》
▶ a **natural** material/ substance/ chemical/ gas
▶ a **chemical** substance/ element
▶ **organic** material/ substances/ chemicals/ liquid/ matter/ elements
▶ **radioactive** material/ substances/ chemicals/ gas/ liquid/ matter/ elements
▶ a **toxic** material/ substance/ chemical/ gas/ liquid/ element
▶ a **flammable** material/ substance/ gas/ liquid
▶ (a) **sticky** substance/ stuff/ liquid/ fluid/ solid
▶ **waste** material/ chemicals/ gas/ matter

material [C, U] 原材料 ◇Toxic chemicals and other *materials* have been found. 有毒化学物質その他の物質が検出された ◇There were bricks, sand and other *building materials* in the courtyard. 煉瓦や砂や他の建築資材が中庭にあった ◇Oil is the *raw material* for plastic. 石油はプラスチックの原料です

substance [C] （特別な性質を持つ）物質 ◇Psychoactive drugs are chemical *substances* that act on the brain. 向精神薬は脳に作用する化学物質である ◇*Substances* can be divided into elements, compounds and mixtures. 物質は元素, 化合物と混合物に分けられる

chemical [C] 化学物質 ◇This *chemical* is often used to make cleaning products. この化学物質は洗浄剤を作るのによく使用される ◇Hormones are *chemicals* that are released in the body and control many important functions. ホルモンは体内で分泌される化学物質で, 多くの重要な機能を制御している

gas [C, U] 気体 ◇Air is a mixture of *gases*. 空気は気体の混合物である ◇Producing methane *gas* from organic waste is another extremely practical use of resources. 有機廃棄物からメタンガスを作り出すのも非常に実用的な資源の使い方である

liquid [C, U] 液体 ◇She offered me a cup containing a dark brown *liquid*. 彼女は濃褐色の液体が入ったコップを私に差し出した ◇As the air became warmer the droplets of *liquid* turned to invisible water vapour. 空気が温まるにつれ水滴は目に見えない水蒸気に変化した
▶ **liquid** Water is *liquid* at room temperature. 水は室温では液体である ◇The samples were frozen in *liquid* nitrogen. その標本は液体窒素で凍らされていた 反意 **solid** (SOLID)

fluid [C, U] 《フォーマル or 専門語》液体;流体 ◇The doctor told him to drink plenty of *fluids*. 医者は十分に流動食を取るよう彼に言った ◇The attacker's DNA pattern was identified from a sample of body *fluid*. 加害者のDNAパターンが体液のサンプルから確認された ❶ふつう液体を指すが, 細かい固体を含む気体や液体を指すこともある.

stuff [U] 《インフォーマル》物, 材料(その名前を知らないときや名前は重要でないとき, あるいは話の中で明白なときに用いる) ◇What's all that sticky *stuff* on the carpet? カーペットに付いたあのべたべたした物は何なの ◇The chairs were covered in some sort of plastic *stuff*. それらの椅子はある種のプラスチックで覆われていた ◇This wine is **good** *stuff*. このワインは上物だ ◇I don't know how you can eat that *stuff*. 《けなして》どうしてあんな物を食べられるのかわからない ☞ **stuff** (THING 2), **thing** (THING 1)

matter [U] 《フォーマル or 物理》 (精神に対比して)物質, (特定の)物 ◇The soil is rich in organic *matter*. その土壌は有機物質が豊富である ◇She didn't approve of their choice of **reading** *matter*. 彼女は彼らの読み物の選び方には賛成しなかった ◇The behaviour of *matter* can be quantified by measures such as weight. 物質の挙動は例えば重量などの単位で定量化できる

solid [C] 《化学》固体 ◇Is calcium carbonate normally a *solid* or a liquid? 炭酸カルシウムは通常は固体ですか液体ですか ◇The baby is not yet on *solids* (= eating solid food). その赤ちゃんはまだ固形食は食べられない ☞ **solid** (SOLID)

element [C] 《化学》元素 ◇All chemical substances, whether *elements*, compounds or mixtures, are made up of three types of particles. すべての化学物質は, 元素, 化合物, 混合物のどれであれ, 3種類の粒子で構成されている

mean 動

1 mean・mark・signal・signify・denote
物事が存在する印, または発生する兆しを表す
【類語訳】意味する, 兆候となる

文型&コロケーション
▶ to mean/ signify sth **to** sb
▶ to mean/ signify **that**...
▶ to mean/ mark/ signal/ signify/ denote a **change** in sth
▶ to mean/ mark/ signal/ signify/ denote the **beginning/ start/ arrival/ end** of sth
▶ to **clearly** mean/ mark/ signal/ signify/ denote sth

mean [他]《進行形なし》意味する ◇What does this sentence *mean*? この文は何を意味していますか ◇**What is** *meant* **by 'batch processing'**? 「バッチ処理」ってどういう意味ですか ◇Does the name 'David Berwick' *mean* **anything to you** (= do you know who he is)? 「デイヴィッド・ベリック」という名前に心当たりはありませんか ◇The flashing light *means* (that) you must stop. 点滅ライトは止まれを意味します ◇Mr President, does this *mean* an end to the current conflict? 大統領, これは現在の紛争の終結を意味するのですか

mark [他]《進行形なし》《特に書き言葉, ジャーナリズム》兆候となる ◇The agreement *marks* a new phase in international relations. その協定は国際関係における新たな局面に入ったことを示す

signal (-ll-, 米 -l-) [他]《進行形なし》《ややフォーマル, 特に書き言葉, ジャーナリズム》兆候となる ◇The scandal surely *signals* the end of his political career. そのスキャンダルは確かに彼の政治活動の終焉を予兆させる

ノート **mean, mark, signal** の使い分け : これらの語はすべて「物事が発生した印または発生する兆候になる」ことを意味する. 話し言葉では mean が最も一般的. 書き言葉, 特に報道では mark と signal のほうがよく使われる.

signify [他]《進行形なし》《ややフォーマル》印になる ;(特定の)意味を持つ ◇This decision *signified* a radical change in their policies. この決定は急激な政策変更を意味した ◇This mark *signifies* that the products conform to an approved standard. このマークは定められた基準に製品が適合していることを示す

denote [他]《進行形なし》《フォーマル》印になる ;(特定の)意味を持つ ◇A very high temperature often *denotes* a serious illness. 大変な高熱はしばしば重い病気の印となる

ノート **signal, signify, denote** の使い分け : signal は物事を人々に理解させることを示し, signify と denote は公的にまたは一般に認められた特定の意味を持つことを表す.
♦ The white belt *signifies/denotes* that he's an absolute beginner. (白帯は彼がまったくの初心者であることを示している). しかしながら, signify は denote 以上に複雑な意味を示す場合にも用いられる. ♦ What does the term 'patrician' *signify* (= what does it mean and what might it suggest)? (「patrician」という言葉はどのような意味を持つのでしょうか). ♦ The Hebrew term used here simply *denotes* a young girl (= it does not mean or suggest anything more than that). (ここで使われているヘブライ語の単語は単に幼い少女を指しています)

2 ☞ **SUGGEST**
mean・suggest・hint・imply・intend・what sb is getting/driving at・insinuate
…のことを言う, 示唆する
【類語訳】(…の)つもりで言う, 遠回しに言う, ほのめかす

文型&コロケーション
▶ to mean/ intend sth **by/ as** sth
▶ to mean/ suggest/ hint/ imply/ insinuate **that**...
▶ to suggest/ imply **agreement/ acceptance**
▶ to suggest/ imply an **intention**
▶ to **seem/ appear** to mean/ suggest/ hint/ imply sth
▶ to (not) **mean/ intend** to suggest/ imply sth
▶ to suggest/ hint/ imply sth **clearly/ strongly**

mean [他]《進行形なし》《特に話し言葉》(…の)つもりで言う ◇What did he *mean* by that remark? あんなこと言って彼はどういうつもり ◇'Perhaps we should try another approach.' '*What do you mean?* (= I don't understand what you are suggesting.)'「たぶん別のアプローチを試したほうがいい」「どういう意味」◇*What do you mean,* you thought I wouldn't mind? (= of course I mind and I am very angry.) どういうつもりなの. 私が気にしないとでも思ったの ◇*I know what you mean* (= I understand and feel sympathy). I hated learning to drive too. 君の言いたいことはわかるよ. 私も運転の教習は嫌いだった ◇*I see what you mean* (= I understand although I may not agree), but I still think it's worth trying. 言いたいことはわかるが, まだ私は試す価値があると思う ◇'But Pete doesn't know we're here!' '*That's what I mean!* (= that's what I have been trying to tell you.)' 「だけどピートは私たちがここにいることを知らないよ」「だから言ってんじゃないか」◇Did he *mean* (that) he was dissatisfied with our service? 彼は私たちのサービスが不満だと言いたかったのですか ◇*You mean* (= are you telling me) we have to start all over again? 最初からやり直すべきだと言いたいのかい

suggest [他]《特に否定的な文と疑問文で》遠回しに言う ◇Are you *suggesting* (that) I'm lazy? 私が怠惰だと言いたいの ◇I would never *suggest* such a thing. 決してそんなことは言わないだろう ☞ **suggestion** (SUGGESTION)

hint [自, 他]《真実である可能性を》ほのめかす ◇What are you *hinting at*? 何を言いたいんだい ◇They *hinted* (that) there might be more job losses. さらに人員を削減する可能性のあることが示唆された ☞ **hint** (SUGGESTION)

ノート suggestとhintの使い分け: suggestは特に疑問文や否定的な文で用いられる. hintは事実や可能性を暗に示すときに用いられる.

imply [他]《ややフォーマル》《真実である可能性[自分の考え]を》ほのめかす ◇His silence seemed to *imply* agreement. 彼の沈黙は同意をほのめかしているように思えた ◇I disliked the *implied* criticism in his voice. 彼の非難めいた口調が私は嫌だった

intend [他]《進行形なし》《ややフォーマル》…のつもりで言う ◇What exactly did you *intend* by that remark? あんな発言をしたのは一体どういうつもりなの ◇He *intended* it as a joke. 彼は冗談のつもりでそう言った

what sb is 'getting/'driving at 行例《インフォーマル, 話し言葉》人が何かを言おうとしている ◇I'm partly to blame? *What* exactly *are you getting at*? 私にも一部責任があると言うの. 一体何が言いたいの

insinuate [他]《ややフォーマル, けなして》《不快なことを》ほのめかす ◇The article *insinuated* that he was having an affair with his friend's wife. その記事は彼が友人の妻と浮気していることをほのめかしていた ◇What are you trying to *insinuate*? 何が言いたいの

mean [形]

mean・nasty・unkind・obnoxious・objectionable・hurtful・unpleasant
人が親切ではないことを表す
【類語訳】意地の悪い, 不親切な, 不愉快な, 無礼な, 中傷的な

unkind	mean	obnoxious
objectionable	nasty	
unpleasant	hurtful	

文型&コロケーション

▶ to be mean/ nasty/ unkind/ obnoxious/ objectionable/ hurtful/ unpleasant **to** sb
▶ to be mean/ nasty **about** sb
▶ to be mean/ nasty/ unkind **of** sb (to do sth)
▶ to be mean/ nasty/ unkind **to do** sth
▶ a mean/ a nasty/ an unkind/ a hurtful **thing to say/ do**
▶ a mean/ an unkind/ a hurtful **remark**
▶ a nasty/ an obnoxious/ an unpleasant **little man**
▶ **very** mean/ nasty/ unkind/ objectionable/ hurtful/ unpleasant
▶ **really** mean/ nasty/ obnoxious/ objectionable/ unpleasant
▶ **rather** mean/ nasty/ unkind/ hurtful/ unpleasant

mean《ややインフォーマル, 特に話し言葉》意地の悪い(人に何かを与えなかったり, させなかったりする場合) ◇Don't be so *mean* to your little brother! 自分の弟にそんな意地悪なことしないで ◇I thought it was really *mean* of him not to let her use the car. 彼女に車を使わせないなんて彼は本当に意地悪だと思った ◇He has a *mean streak* in him (= an unpleasant side to his character). 彼には意地悪なところがある 反意 **generous** (KIND 形)

nasty《ややインフォーマル, 特に話し言葉》《発言が》意地の悪い ◇She's always making *nasty* remarks about people. 彼女はいつも人の悪口ばかり言っている ◇She was *nasty* about (= said nasty things about) everyone. 彼女は皆の悪口を言った ◇He has a *nasty* temper. 彼には意地悪なところがある 反意 **nice** (NICE 2)

unkind 不親切な ◇He was never actually *unkind* to them. 実際のところ彼は彼らに対して不親切では決してなかった ◇It would be *unkind* to go without him. 彼を連れて行かないというのは薄情だろう ◇She never said anything *unkind* about anyone. 彼女は人のことを決して悪く言わなかった ❶unkindはmeanやnastyよりソフトな表現 反意 **kind** (KIND 形), ⇔ **cruel** (CRUEL 1)

▶ **unkindly** [副] ◇I'm sure it wasn't meant *unkindly*. 意地悪でそう言ったつもりがないことは確かだ

obnoxious《無礼[不親切]な》非常に不愉快 ◇What an *obnoxious* little man! 何て感じの悪い小男なんだ

objectionable《ややフォーマル》《人・態度が》不愉快な, 無礼な ◇His views on race are quite *objectionable*. 彼の人種に関する意見ははなはだ不愉快だ

hurtful《言葉が》人を傷つける, 中傷的な ◇I cannot forget the *hurtful* things he said. 彼が言ったひどいことが忘れられない ⇔ **hurt** (DISTRESS), **hurt** (HURT 1)

unpleasant《ややフォーマル》不親切な, 無礼な ◇He was very *unpleasant* to me. 彼は私にとても感じが悪かった ◇She said some very *unpleasant* things about you. 彼女は君のことをすごく悪く言っていたよ ❶人の態度が無礼であることや発言が侮辱的であることを表す 反意 **pleasant** (FRIENDLY 1)

meaning [名]

meaning・sense・significance
語や語句, 記号が表しているもの

meet

【類語訳】意味, 目的, 意図

文型&コロケーション
- the **original/ exact/ precise/ general/ true** meaning/ sense/ significance
- a **special/ symbolic** meaning/ sense/ significance
- the **accepted/ wide/ narrow/ literal/ figurative/ metaphorical/ legal/ technical** meaning/ sense of sth
- the **real/ hidden** meaning/ significance
- to **have** a meaning/ sense/ significance
- to **grasp/ understand** the meaning/ significance of sth
- to **acquire/ take on/ gain** meaning/ significance

meaning [C, U] (語・語句・記号が表す)意味；(言動によって伝えようとする)事柄, 考え；(作家・芸術家の作品を通じての)目的, 意図 ◇Words often have several *meanings*. 単語はしばしばいくつかの意味を持つ ◇I don't quite *get your meaning* (= understand what you mean to say). おっしゃっていることの意味がよくわからないのですが ◇What's the *meaning* of this? I explicitly told you not to leave the room. これはどういうつもりなの. 部屋を出ないようにってはっきり言ったでしょ ◇The text manages to convey multiple layers of *meaning*. その文章は重層的な意味をなんとか伝えている

sense [C] (語・語句が持つ)意味 ◇The word 'love' is used in different *senses* by different people. 「愛」という語は人によってさまざまな意味で用いられる ◇He was a true friend, *in every sense of the word* (= in every possible way). 彼はあらゆる意味で親友だった ◇The medical care was excellent, in a technical *sense*. その診療は技術的な意味で素晴らしかった ◇*In a sense* (= in one way) it doesn't matter any more. ある意味で, それはもはやどうでもいい

> ノート **meaning** と **sense** の使い分け：どちらも語の「意味」として用いることができるが, sense はより専門的またはフォーマルな文脈で用いられる.

significance [U, C] (ややフォーマル) (言動の)意味, 意義；(記号の)意味 ◇She couldn't grasp the full *significance* of what he had said. 彼女は彼が言ったことの意味をすべては理解できなかった ◇Do these symbols have any particular *significance*? これらの印には何か特別な意味があるのですか ❶しばしば隠された特別な意味について用いられる.

meet 動

1 meet • meet with sb • gather • get together • assemble • mass • rally • convene • meet up
何かの目的で集う
【類語訳】会う, 集まる, 会合する

文型&コロケーション
- to meet/ meet with sb/ gather/ get together/ assemble/ mass/ rally/ convene/ meet up **for** sth
- to meet/ get together/ meet up **with** sb
- **crowds/ supporters** gather/ assemble/ rally
- **people** gather/ assemble/ mass
- to meet/ meet with sb/ gather/ get together/ convene **regularly**

meet [自, 他, 受身なし] (議論のために公式に)集まる；(予定して打ち解けて)集まる ◇The committee *meets* on Fridays. 委員会は毎週金曜日に開かれる ◇Let's *meet* for a drink after work. 仕事の後会って飲もう ◇The Prime Minister *met* other European leaders for talks. 首相は他のヨーロッパ諸国の首脳と会談した ◇We're *meeting* them outside the theatre at 7. 7時に映画館の外で彼らと会う予定だ

'meet with sb 句動詞 《特に米》(話し合いのために)人と会う ◇The President *met with* senior White House aides. 大統領はホワイトハウスの上級補佐官と会った

gather [自] 一箇所に集まる ◇A crowd soon *gathered*. 群集がすぐに集まった ◇Can you all *gather* round? I've got something to tell you. みんな周りに集まってくれるかい. 少し話したいことがあるんだ ◇His supporters *gathered* in the main square. 彼のサポーターたちが中央広場に集まった

,get to'gether 句動詞 (ややインフォーマル)(打ち解けて)集まる, (会合のために)会う ◇We must *get together* for a drink sometime. ぜひいつか集まって飲みましょう ◇We all *get together* every year at Christmas. 私たちは皆毎年クリスマスに集まる ◇Management should *get together* with the union. 経営陣は労働組合と会合すべきだ ❶get together は meet よりもややインフォーマルな表現で, ふつうあまりはっきりした取り決めをせずに集まること ✕The committee *gets together* on Fridays. ✕We're *getting together* outside the theatre at 7. ☞ **get-together** (EVENT 2)

assemble [自] (ややフォーマル) 集まる ◇The students were asked to *assemble* in the hall. 生徒たちはホールに集まるように言われていた

mass [自] (大ぜいで)集まる ◇Demonstrators had *massed* outside the embassy. デモの参加者が大使館の外に大集結していた ◇Dark clouds *massed* on the horizon. 暗い雲が地平線に集まっていた

> ノート **gather, assemble, mass** の使い分け：gather が最も一般的な語で規模に関係なく集まることを意味する. assemble は比較的フォーマルな語で, 予定の上で開かれる正式な会合に用いられる. mass は参加者が多いことを強調するときに用いられる.

rally [自] (援助のために)集まる ◇The cabinet *rallied behind* the Prime Minister. 閣僚は首相の下に結束した ◇Many national newspapers *rallied to* his support. 多くの全国紙が彼を支持して集まった ❶物理的に1箇所に集まるではなく, 支援のために結束することを表す.

convene [自] (フォーマル) (正式に)会合する ◇The committee will *convene* at 11.30 next Thursday. 委員会は来週の木曜日の11時30分に招集される

,meet 'up 句動詞 (ややインフォーマル) (約束して)会う ◇I *met up* with him later for a drink. 私は後で彼と会って飲みに行った

2 meet • run into sb • encounter • bump into sb
誰かと偶然に同じ場所にいて, その人と言葉を交わすことを表す
【類語訳】会う, 出会う, 出くわす, 遭遇する, 偶然発見する

文型&コロケーション
- to meet/ run into/ bump into **a friend**

meet [自, 他, 受身なし] (偶然)会う, 出会う ◇I hope we'll *meet* again soon. また近いうちにお会いしたいものです ◇Did you *meet* anyone in town? 町で誰かに会いましたか

,run 'into sb [句動詞]《ややインフォーマル》(知り合いと)偶然出会う, 出くわす ◇Guess who I *ran into* today! 今日, 誰に出会ったと思う

encounter [他]《フォーマル》(新しい『珍しい』物・人と)偶然出会う, 遭遇する, 偶然発見する ◇She was the most remarkable woman he had ever *encountered*. 彼女は彼がこれまで出会った中で最も注目すべき女性だった ◇Walruses were commonly *encountered* in the Shetland Islands until quite recently. セイウチはごく最近までシェトランド諸島でふつうに見られた ☞ **come across sb/sth** (FIND 2)

,**bump 'into sb** [句動詞]《インフォーマル》(知り合いと)偶然出会う, ばったり出くわす ◇I *bumped into* Tina this morning. けさティナにばったり出会った

[ノート] **run into** と **bump into** の使い分け: この二つの動詞句の意味や使用範囲にさほど違いはない。**bump into** のほうがよりインフォーマルで, 《米》では使用頻度はやや低い。

3 meet・get to know sb・make sb's acquaintance
初めて会って言葉を交わすことを表す
【類語訳】知り合いになる, 親しくなる, 知己を得る

[文型&コロケーション]
▶ to **first** meet/ get to know/ make the acquaintance of sb

meet [他, 受身なし] 知り合いになる, 紹介される ◇Where did you first *meet* your husband? ご主人に初めて会われたのはどこでしたか ◇There's someone I want you to *meet*. あなたに会っていただきたい方がいます ◇I don't think we've *met*. これまでにお会いしたことはありませんね ◇*Pleased to meet you*. 《特に英》お会いできてうれしいです ◇*Nice to meet you*. 《特に米》お会いできてうれしいです ❶正式に誰かに紹介されたときはすぐに Pleased to meet you. か Nice to meet you. と言うのが普通である。初めて会った人と別れるときには《英》《米》で Nice meeting you. と言えるが, 《米》では Nice to meet you. とも言える。しかしながら別れるときに Pleased to meet you. と言うのは《米》でも《英》でも不自然である。

,**get to 'know sb** [フレーズ] (徐々に) 親しくなる ◇She's very nice when you *get to know* her. 彼女と親しくなると彼女はとても親切だよ ❶この意味での know を用いた表現が他にもいくつかある。◆Do you two *know* each other (= have you met before?). あなたたち二人はお知り合いですか。◆I've *known* David for 20 years. (デイヴィッドと知り合って20年になります)。◆She was a secretary when I first *knew* her. (初めて彼女と知り合ったときは彼女は秘書をしていた)。

make sb's acquaintance, make the acquaintance of sb [フレーズ] 《フォーマル》 知り合いになる, 知己を得る ◇I am delighted to *make your acquaintance*, Mrs Phillips. フィリップスさん, お近づきになれてうれしいです ◇I *made the acquaintance of* several musicians around that time. 私はその頃に数人の音楽家と知り合いになった ☞ **acquaintance** (FRIEND), **acquaintance** (FRIENDSHIP)

4 meet・suit・satisfy・fulfil・serve
十分間に合う, 要求されていることに沿う
【類語訳】満たす, 好都合である, 満足させる, 役に立つ

[文型&コロケーション]
▶ to meet/ suit/ satisfy/ fulfil/ serve a **requirement**/ **need**/ **purpose**
▶ to suit/ satisfy/ fulfil/ serve sb/ sth's **interests**
▶ to meet/ suit/ satisfy/ fulfil a **demand**/ **condition**
▶ to meet/ satisfy/ fulfil a/ an **standard**/ **obligation**
▶ to meet/ satisfy/ fulfil the **terms**/ **criteria**

meet [他] (要求を) 満たす ◇Until these conditions are *met* we can't proceed with the sale. これらの条件が満たされるまで販売を始めることはできない ◇50% of the candidates failed to *meet* the standard required. 応募者の50%が必要基準を満たしていなかった ◇I can't possibly *meet* that deadline. その締め切りに合わせることはとうていできない

suit [他, 受身なし]《進行形なし》好都合である ◇Choose a computer to *suit* your particular needs. 君自身のニーズに合うコンピューターを選びなさい ◇If you want to go by bus, that *suits me fine*. バスで行きたいなら私も好都合だ ◇*It suits me to* start work at a later time. 後で仕事に取りかかるほうが私には好都合だ

satisfy [他]《ややフォーマル》(要求を) 満たす; 満足させる ◇It seemed that no amount of information would *satisfy* their curiosity. どんなに情報量が多くても彼らの好奇心を満たすことはないように思えた ◇Our hunger *satisfied*, we continued our journey. 空腹を満たして旅を続けた ◇She failed to *satisfy* all the requirements for entry to the college. 彼女はその大学の入学条件すべてを満たすことはできなかった

fulfil《英》《米 **fulfill**》(-ll-) [他]《フォーマル, 特にビジネス》(要求を) 満たす ◇Failure to *fulfil* the terms of the agreements may result in legal action. 契約条件を満たさない場合, 法的手段を取ることがあります ◇He had *fulfilled* his promise to his father. 彼は父親との約束を実現していた

serve [他]《ややフォーマル》(物事を達成する[要求を満たす]のに)役に立つ ◇These experiments *serve* no useful purpose. これらの実験は何の役にも立たない ◇His linguistic ability *served him well* in his chosen profession. 彼の言語能力は彼が選んだ仕事でとても役に立った

meeting [名]

1 meeting・conference・session・summit・assembly・gathering・convention・caucus
特定の目的で大勢の人が集まる行事
【類語訳】会議, 会合, 協議会, 会期, 集会

[文型&コロケーション]
▶ an **annual** meeting/ conference/ session/ summit/ gathering/ assembly/ convention
▶ an **international** meeting/ conference/ summit/ gathering/ assembly/ convention
▶ a **public** meeting/ gathering/ assembly/ session
▶ a **two-day**/ **three-day** conference/ session/ summit/ convention
▶ a **bilateral**/ **multilateral** meeting/ session/ summit/ convention
▶ an **illegal** meeting/ gathering/ assembly
▶ to **hold** a meeting/ a conference/ a session/ a summit/ a gathering/ an assembly/ a convention/ a caucus
▶ to **host** a meeting/ a conference/ summit/ gathering/ convention

meeting

481

- ▶to **call** a meeting/ a conference/ a session/ a summit/ an assembly/ a caucus
- ▶to **attend** a meeting/ a conference/ a session/ a summit/ a gathering/ an assembly/ a convention
- ▶to **chair** a meeting/ a conference/ a session/ a summit/ an assembly
- ▶to **address** a meeting/ a conference/ a session/ a gathering/ an assembly/ a convention
- ▶a meeting/ conference/ session/ summit/ gathering/ convention **takes place**
- ▶**delegates to** a conference/ a session/ a summit/ an assembly/ a convention

meeting [C] 会議, 会合 ◇a committee/staff *meeting* 委員会/スタッフ会議 ◇What time is the *meeting*? 会議は何時だっけ ◇Helen will chair the *meeting* (= be in charge of it). ヘレンはその会議の議長を務める予定だ ◇I'll be *in a meeting* all morning — can you take my calls? 午前中いっぱい会議に出る予定だ. 代わりに電話に出てもらえますか ◇A *meeting* of the United Nations Security Council was called. 国連安全保障理事会が招集された ❶the meeting (単数形) は会議に出席している人を指す. ◆The *meeting* voted to accept the pay offer. (会議出席者はその支払い案を受け入れることを(投票で)決めた.
conference [C, U] (大規模な公式)会議, 協議会 ◇She is attending a three-day *conference on* AIDS education. 彼女はエイズ教育に関する3日間にわたる会議に出席する予定だ ◇The AIDS *conference* will be held in Glasgow. エイズ会議はグラスゴーで開かれる予定だ ◇He was *in conference* with his lawyers all day. 彼は弁護士たちと一日中協議していた ❶記者会見は《英》で press conference,《米》で news conference.
session [C] (議会・国会などでの)会議, (の期間) ◇a *session* of the UN General Assembly 国連総会 ◇The court is now *in session*. 裁判所は今開廷中です ◇The committee met *in closed session* (= with nobody else present). 委員会は非公開の会議であった
summit [C] 首脳会議 ◇The conference will form part of the European *summit* in Rome next month. その協議会はローマで来月開催されるヨーロッパ首脳会議の一環として行われる ◇The President of Costa Rica will chair the *summit meeting*. コスタリカの大統領がその首脳会議の議長を務める予定だ
gathering [C] (特定の目的を持つ人々の)会合 ◇a social/ family *gathering* 親睦会/家族会議 ◇He was asked to speak at a *gathering* of religious leaders. 彼は宗教指導者の集まりでスピーチを求められた
assembly [C, U] (ややフォーマル) (特定の目的を持つ人々の)会合 ◇He was to address a public *assembly* on the issue. 彼はその問題に関して市民集会で講演する予定だった ◇Laws governing *freedom of assembly* were gradually being relaxed. 集会の自由を規制する法律は徐々に緩和されていった ❶学校でしばしば一日の始まりに行われる先生と生徒の集会を表すこともある. その際連絡事項を伝えたり, 学校行事の話し合いをしたり, 一緒にお祈りをしたりする. ◆There is a whole school *assembly* every Friday morning. (毎週金曜日の朝に全校集会がある). ◆I'm playing the flute in *assembly* tomorrow morning. (明日の朝, 集会でフルートを演奏します).

ノート gathering と assembly の使い分け：gathering は assembly よりもインフォーマルな語で, 社交的な集まりや共通の関心事について話し合う集まりを指すことが多い. assembly は政府や当局によって適切に処理されていない重要な問題を議論するために招集される会合を指すことが多い.

convention [C] (職業団体・政党・ファンクラブなどの)集会 ◇The party's annual *convention* will be held on April 6. その政党の年次党大会は4月6日に開かれる予定だ
caucus [C]《特に米》党員集会, 党幹部会議；(集合的に)党員, 党幹部 ◇20 states will hold precinct *caucuses* on Tuesday to choose delegates to the parties' national conventions. 全国党大会に参加する代表者を選ぶため, 20の州で選挙区党員集会が火曜日に開催される予定だ ◇the dean of the Black Congressional *Caucus* 黒人議員連盟の長

2 meeting・appointment・encounter・date・engagement・introduction
二人以上の人々が会うこと
【類語訳】出会い, 約束, 予約, 遭遇, 衝突, 紹介

文型&コロケーション

- ▶a meeting/ an appointment/ an encounter/ a date/ an engagement **with** sb
- ▶a meeting/ an encounter **between** people
- ▶(a) **formal** meeting/ appointment/ encounter/ engagement/ introduction
- ▶an **important** meeting/ appointment/ date/ engagement/ introduction
- ▶a **casual** meeting/ encounter/ introduction
- ▶a **dinner** appointment/ date/ engagement
- ▶to **have** a meeting/ an appointment/ an encounter/ a date/ an engagement
- ▶to **arrange** a meeting/ an appointment/ a date/ an introduction
- ▶to **keep** an appointment/ a date/ an engagement
- ▶to **make** an appointment/ a date/ introductions
- ▶to **cancel** a meeting/ an appointment/ a date/ an engagement

meeting [C] (約束して[偶然に])会うこと ◇At our first *meeting* I was nervous. 初めて会った時, 私は緊張していた ◇It was a *chance meeting* that would change my life. それは私の人生を変えるような偶然の出会いだった
appointment [C] (仕事上の理由で[特定の時間に]会う)約束, 予約 ◇She made an *appointment* for her son to see the doctor. 彼女は息子をその医者に診てもらうため予約を取った ◇I've got a dental *appointment* at 3 o'clock. 3時に歯医者の予約がある ◇He had failed to keep the *appointment*. 彼は会う約束を守らなかった ◇Viewing is *by appointment* only (= only at a time that has been arranged in advance). 鑑賞は予約でのみ可能です
encounter [C] (突然の予期せぬ)出会い, 遭遇, 衝突 ◇Three of them were killed in the subsequent *encounter* with the police. その後の警察との衝突で彼らのうち3人が亡くなった ◇I've had a number of *close encounters* (= situations that could have been dangerous) with bad drivers. 悪質なドライバーに何度もひやっとさせられた ◇It was his first sexual *encounter* (= his first experience of sex). それは彼にとって初の性体験となった
date [C] デート ◇I've got a *date* with Lucy tomorrow night. 明日の夜ルーシーとデートするんだ ◇I can't believe

you set me up on a **blind date** (= a date with sb you have not met before). 会ったこともない人とのデートを仕組むなんて信じられない ☞ **date** (GO OUT)
engagement [C] （特定の時間に何かをする）約束, 用务 （特に公式［仕事上］のものを指す） ◇He has a number of social *engagements* next week. 来週彼には（社交上の）予定がたくさんある ◇It was her first official *engagement*. それが彼女にとって初めての公務だった ◇I had to refuse because of a *prior engagement*. 先約があって断らなければならなかった ☞ **engaged** (BUSY 1)
introduction [C, U] 紹介 ◇*Introductions* were made and the conversation started to flow. 紹介があって, 会話が始まった ◇Our speaker today **needs no introduction** (= he is already well known). 今日お話しくださる方は紹介する必要はありません

memory 名

memory・mind・recollection・recall・reminiscence・remembrance
物事を覚えておく能力, 覚えておくこと, 覚えている事柄
【類語訳】記憶力, 思い出, 思い出話, 回想録, 追憶, 追憶

文型&コロケーション
▸ a memory/ recollection/ reminiscence **of** sb/ sth
▸ **in** memory/ remembrance **of** sb/ sth
▸ a **vague/ vivid/ clear** memory/ recollection
▸ to **have a** ... memory/ recollection/ recall
▸ to **have no** memory/ recollection of sb/ sth

memory [C, U] 記憶力, 思い出 ◇I have a bad *memory for* names. 私は名前の記憶力が悪い ◇People have **short memories** (= they soon forget). 人間はすぐに忘れる ◇He had a **long memory** for people who had disappointed him. 彼は失望した相手のことをずっと忘れなかった ◇She can recite the whole poem *from memory*. 彼女はその詩を全部暗唱できる ◇There hasn't been peace in the country *in/within my memory*. 私の記憶ではその国が平和だったことはない ◇This hasn't happened *in living memory* (= nobody alive now can remember it happening). これが起きたことを覚えている人はもはや生存していない ◇childhood *memories* 子どもの頃の記憶 ◇I have vivid *memories* of my grandparents. 私は祖父母のことを鮮明に覚えている ◇The photos **bring back** lots of good *memories*. それらの写真はたくさんのいい思い出を思い出させてくれる ◇He founded the charity in *memory* of his late wife. 彼は亡くなった妻を追悼してその慈善団体を設立した ☞ **memorize** (LEARN)
mind [C, ふつう単数で] 記憶(力) ◇When I saw the exam questions my *mind* just *went blank* (= I couldn't remember anything). 試験問題を見たときに私の頭は真っ白になった ◇Sorry — your name has gone right out of my *mind*. ごめんなさい. お名前を失念してしまいました ☞ **bear sb/sth in mind** (REMEMBER)
recollection [U, C] 《ややフォーマル》想起；思い出 ◇I have no *recollection* of meeting her before. 彼女と以前会った記憶がない ◇My *recollection* of events differs from his. 私と彼の記憶には食い違いがある ◇*To the best of my recollection* (= if I remember correctly) I was not present at that meeting. 覚えている限りでは私はその会合に出席していませんでした ◇his early *recollections* of his father 彼の幼い頃の父親の思い出 ☞ **recol-**

lect (REMEMBER)
recall [U] 記憶力 ◇She has amazing powers of *recall*. 彼女は驚くほど記憶力がよい ◇to have *instant recall* (= to be able to remember sth immediately) 即座に覚える ◇to have *total recall* (= to be able to remember all the details of sth) 一部始終記憶している ☞ **recall** (REMEMBER)
reminiscence [C, ふつう複数で, U] 思い出話, 回想録；回想 ◇The book is a collection of his *reminiscences about* the actress. その本はその女優についての彼の回想録である ◇The role of *reminiscence* in family history research should never be underestimated. 家系調査において回想の役割を見くびるべきではない ☞ **reminisce** (REMEMBER)
remembrance [U] 《ややフォーマル》追悼, 追憶 ◇A service was held in *remembrance* of local soldiers killed in the war. 戦争で命を落とした地元兵士を追悼して礼拝式が行われた ◇a *remembrance* service 追悼礼拝 ◇a chapel/garden of *remembrance* (= in memory of people who have died) 記念の礼拝堂/庭園 ❶フォーマルでは可算名詞としての remembrance は「思い出を引き起こす物」を指す. ◆The cenotaph stands as a *remembrance* of those killed in the war. （その慰霊碑は戦死者を記念して立っている）. ☞ **remember** (REMEMBER)

mention 動

mention・refer to sb/sth・speak・cite・quote・allude to sb/sth
例を挙げたり証明したりするために, 書いたり口にしたりする
【類語訳】言及する, 触れる, 引用する, 引き合いに出す, ほのめかす

文型&コロケーション
▸ to mention/ refer to/ speak of/ cite/ quote/ allude to/ sth **as** sb/ sth
▸ to mention/ refer to/ cite/ quote a/ an **example/ case/ instance** of sth
▸ sth is **frequently/ often** mentioned/ referred to/ spoken of/ cited/ quoted/ alluded to
▸ to mention/ refer to/ speak of/ quote/ allude to sb/ sth **briefly**
▸ the example mentioned/ referred to/ cited/ quoted/ alluded to **above/ earlier/ previously**

mention [他] （詳細は省いて）言及する, 触れる ◇Nobody *mentioned* anything to me about it. 誰もそのことについて何も私に言わなかった ◇*Now that you mention it*, she did seem to be in a strange mood. そう言われれば彼女は確かに妙な雰囲気だったような気がする ◇Did she *mention* where she was going? どこに行くか彼女は言いましたか ◇He failed to *mention that* he was the one who started the fight. 彼は自分が喧嘩を始めた張本人であることを言いそびれた ☞ **mention** (REFERENCE)
re'fer to sb/sth 句動詞 **(-rr-)** 《ややフォーマル》…について言及する［話す］ ◇I promised not to *refer to* the matter again. 私はその件にはもう二度と触れないと約束した ◇She always *referred to* Ben as 'that nice man'. 彼女はいつもベンのことを「あのいい人」と呼んだ ◇The victims were not *referred to* by name. 犠牲者の名は伏せられた ☞ **reference** (REFERENCE)
speak [自] 話す, 言及する ◇She still *speaks about* him with great affection. 彼女は未だに大いなる親しみ

を込めて彼のことを話す ◇Witnesses **spoke of** a great ball of flame. 目撃者たちは大きな火の玉のことを話した ◇**Speaking of** travelling, (= referring back to a subject just mentioned) are you going anywhere exciting this year? 旅行と言えば、今年はどこか楽しい所に行く予定ですか

cite [他]《フォーマル》(理由[例]として)引用する、引き合いに出す ◇He *cited* his heavy workload as the reason for his breakdown. 彼は神経衰弱の理由として仕事の多さを挙げた ◇She *cited* the case of Leigh v. Gladstone. 彼女はリー対グラッドストンの判例を引用した ☞ **cite** (QUOTE), **citation** (REFERENCE)

quote [他]（例として）引用する、引き合いに出す ◇He *quoted* one case in which a person had died in a fire. 彼は人が一人火事で亡くなった事例を引き合いに出した ☞ **quote** (QUOTE), **quotation** (REFERENCE)

ノート **cite** と **quote** の使い分け：cite は理由や例を引き合いに出すことができるが、quote は例のみ。×He *quoted* his heavy workload as the reason for his breakdown. cite は quote よりフォーマルで、判例などを述べるときにしばしば用いられる。

al'lude to sb/sth [句動詞]《フォーマル》…のことを暗にほのめかす ◇The problem had been *alluded to* briefly in earlier discussions. その問題は前の議論で簡単に触れられていた ☞ **allusion** (REFERENCE)

mess [名]

1 mess・clutter・jumble・disorder・muddle
場所[物の集まり]が整然としていない様子を表す
【類語訳】散乱、散乱物、ごちゃごちゃ、ごちゃ混ぜ、乱雑

文型&コロケーション
▶ a mess/ clutter/ jumble/ muddle **of** sth
▶ to be **in** a mess/ a jumble/ disorder/ a muddle
▶ (a) **complete** mess/ jumble/ disorder
▶ to be a mess/ jumble/ muddle
▶ a **bit of a** mess/ jumble

mess [C, ふつう単数で]《時にけなして》物が散らかった状態 ◇The room was in a *mess*. その部屋は散らかっていた ◇Sorry, this place is a bit of a *mess*. ごめんなさい。この場所は少し散らかっています ◇The kids **made a mess** in the bathroom. 子どもたちはバスルームを散らかした ◇**What a mess!**' she said, surveying the scene after the party. パーティー後の現場を見渡して「なんていう散らかりようなの」と彼女は言った ◇My hair's a real *mess*! 髪が本当にぼさぼさだわ ☞ **messy** (DIRTY), **messy** (UNTIDY)
▶, **mess sth 'up** [句動詞] ◇I don't want you *messing up* my nice clean kitchen. きれいですてきな私のキッチンを散らかさないでね

clutter [U, 単数で]《ややインフォーマル、けなして》(いらない[使っていない]物の)散乱物 ◇There's always so much *clutter* on your desk! いつも君の机は物が散乱してるね ◇There was a *clutter* of bottles, glasses and ashtrays on the table. テーブルの上には瓶やグラス、灰皿が散乱していた ❶しばしば人が片付けようとしている物を指して言う。よく結びつく語句に avoid, get rid of, shed, free sth from, clear sth of がある。☞ **cluttered** (UNTIDY)
▶ **clutter** [動][他] ◇Don't *clutter* the page with too many diagrams. 図を入れすぎでページをごちゃごちゃにしな

いように ◇I don't want all these boxes *cluttering* up the place. そこに散乱している箱はすべていらないよ

jumble [単数で] ごちゃ混ぜ(の物) ◇The room was a *jumble* of books, toys and sports equipment. 部屋には本や玩具、スポーツ用品がごちゃ混ぜに置かれてあった ☞ **jumbled** (UNTIDY)

ノート **clutter** と **jumble** の使い分け：clutter のほうがより強い非難を表す。jumble は単に説明的な語。

disorder [U]《ややフォーマル》乱雑 ◇The room was in a state of *disorder*. その部屋は乱雑な状態だった ◇He loves tidying up, making order out of *disorder*. 彼は乱雑な状態を整理整頓するのが好きだ [反意] **order** (EFFICIENCY), ☞ **disordered** (UNTIDY)

muddle [C, ふつう単数で, U] (物が見つからないくらいの)乱雑な状態 ◇My papers are all in a *muddle*. 私の書類は全部乱雑に置いてある ◇My desk was the usual *muddle* of books, files and papers. 私の机は相変わらず本やファイル、書類が散らかっていた

2 mess・dilemma・plight・predicament・vicious circle・corner・straits
困難な状況を表す
【類語訳】混乱、板挟み、ジレンマ、苦境、窮地、悪循環、困窮、窮乏

文型&コロケーション
▶ **in** a mess/ a dilemma/ a plight/ a predicament/ a vicious circle/ a corner/ … straits
▶ a **real**/ **terrible** mess/ dilemma
▶ (a) **dire** predicament/ straits
▶ (a) **financial** mess/ dilemma/ plight/ predicament/ straits
▶ a **moral**/ **personal** dilemma/ predicament
▶ to **find yourself in** a dilemma/ a predicament/ … straits
▶ to **put sb in** a dilemma/ predicament
▶ to **be caught in** a dilemma/ vicious circle

mess [C, ふつう単数で]《ややインフォーマル》(組織化されていないこと[人のミス]による)混乱 ◇The economy is in a *mess*. 経済は混乱している ◇The whole situation is a *mess*. 全体の状況が混乱している ◇I feel I've **made a mess of** things. 事を台なしにしたように感じる ◇Let's try to **sort out** the *mess*. この厄介な問題を整理してみよう
▶ **messy** [形] ◇The divorce was painful and *messy*. 離婚は痛みを伴い厄介だった

dilemma [C] 板挟みの状態 ◇She faced a *dilemma* **about** whether to accept the offer or not. その申し出を受け入れるか否かで彼女はジレンマに直面した ◇This poses a difficult *dilemma* **for** teachers. これによって教師たちは難しい板挟みにあう ◇I could see no way of *resolving* this moral *dilemma*. この道徳的なジレンマを解決する方法は見つからなかった

plight [単数で]《特に書き言葉》苦境 ◇He has expressed deep concern about the *plight* of the flood victims. 彼は洪水の被害者の苦境について強い懸念を表明した ◇A neighbour heard of her *plight* and offered to help. 近所の人が彼女の苦境を聞いて援助を申し出た

predicament [C]《ややフォーマル》(どうしていいかわからないような)窮地 ◇Other companies are in an even worse *predicament* than ourselves. 他の会社は我々よりもさらに厳しい窮地に陥っている

,**vicious 'circle** [単数で] 悪循環 ◇He was trapped in

a *vicious circle* of addiction and petty crime. 彼は麻薬の常習と軽犯罪の悪循環に陥っていた
corner [C, ふつう単数で]（ややインフォーマル）(脱することが困難な)窮地 ◇She was used to talking her way out of *tight corners*. 何だかんだ言って窮地から抜け出すことに彼女は慣れていた ◇He had her *backed into a corner* a couple of times with new facts she didn't know. 彼女の知らない新事実を突きつけ，彼は彼女を何度か窮地に追いやった
straits [複数で]《形容詞の後で》（金欠による）困窮，窮乏 ◇The factory is *in dire straits*. その工場はひどく困窮している ◇She found herself in desperate financial *straits*. 彼女はどうしようもなく経済的に困窮していた

message 名

message・content・substance・subject matter・the thrust・thread・gist
文書やスピーチ，会話のポイント
【類語訳】メッセージ，内容，要旨，主題，要点，筋道，脈絡，大意

文型&コロケーション
▸ the **main** message/ content/ substance/ subject matter/ thrust/ thread of sth
▸ the **general** message/ content/ thrust/ gist of sth
▸ (a) **common** message/ content/ thread
▸ to **convey** a message/ the gist
▸ to **get/ understand** the message/ gist of sth
▸ to **follow** the thread/ gist of sth
▸ to **lack** content/ substance

message [C, ふつう単数で] メッセージ《書物・演説・運動・芸術作品が伝えようとする道徳的・社会的・政治的な考え方》◇This is a film with a strong religious *message*. これは宗教的なメッセージの強い映画です ◇The campaign is trying to *get the message across* to young people that drugs are dangerous. その運動は若者に薬物は危険だというメッセージを伝えようとしている
content [単数で, U]《ややフォーマル，特に書き言葉》内容《書物・演説・研究計画に含まれる考え》◇Your tone of voice is as important as the *content* of what you have to say. 話し方は話すべき内容と同じくらい重要です ◇Her poetry has a good deal of political *content*. 彼女の詩には政治的内容がかなり含まれている
substance [U]《ややフォーマル》（書物・演説・計画・政治網領における）要旨 ◇I agree with what he said *in substance*, though not with every detail. 彼が言ったことに大筋は賛成だが，細部では反対だ ◇The party's manifesto is good on style but lacks real *substance*. その政党のマニフェストは格好はよいが実質的内容に欠けている
'subject matter [U]《ややフォーマル》（書物・演説・芸術作品の）主題 ◇She's searching for *subject matter* for her new book. 彼女はこれから書く本のテーマを探している ◇The artist was revolutionary in both *subject matter* and technique. その芸術家は題材と技法の両面において革新的だった ☞ **subject** (SUBJECT)

ノート content, substance, subject matter の使い分け: content は特に文章，演説，研究計画の内容を指す。substance は主たる内容部分のみ（要旨）を指し，重要［考慮に値するもの］でなければ lack substance（内容がない）

欠ける) と言うことができる。subject matter は作家や芸術家による書物や芸術作品における題材に用いられる。
the thrust [単数で]《ややフォーマル》（主張・政策の）要点 ◇*The thrust* of his argument was that change was needed. 彼の主張の要点は変革が必要だということだった ◇She explained *the broad thrust* of the party's policies. 彼女はその党の政策の大まかな骨子を説明した ❶人による argument や proposal, 政府など組織による strategy, initiative, plan, policy の要点を指すときに用いられる。
thread [C]（全体を流れる）特徴；筋道，脈絡 ◇A common *thread* runs through these discussions. 共通の特徴がこれらの議論に一貫している ◇The author skilfully draws together the different *threads* of the plot. 著者は話の筋の異なった脈絡を巧みに結び合わせている ◇*lost the thread* of the argument (= I could no longer follow it). 私は議論の筋道を見失った ❶central/main/common/connecting thread や follow/keep the thread, draw together/pick up/pull together the threads のように言う。
gist [単数で, U]《特に話し言葉》(話・文章の)趣旨，大意 ◇Just try to get (= understand) the *gist* of the argument. 議論の趣旨を理解するよう努めてごらん ◇I'm afraid I don't quite follow your *gist* (= what you really mean). 申し訳ありませんが話の趣旨がよくわかりません ◇Students are taught the skill of reading for *gist*. 学生たちは大意をつかむ術(￤)を教わっている

mind 名

mind・brain・head・soul・spirit・ego・the/your subconscious
見たり触ったりすることはできないが，物事を考えたり，感じたりしたりする体の部分
【類語訳】頭，脳，精神，心，魂，自我，潜在意識

文型&コロケーション
▸ the **human** mind/ brain/ soul/ spirit
▸ a thought **enters** sb's mind/ head
▸ **deep in** your mind/ the brain/ your subconscious

mind [C, U] 頭，心，精神 ◇There were all kinds of thoughts running through my *mind*. さまざまな想念が私の頭を駆け巡っていた ◇There was no doubt in his *mind* that he'd get the job. 自分はその仕事に就くものと彼は信じて疑わなかった ◇She was in a disturbed *state of mind*. 彼女の心はかき乱されていた ◇I could not have complete *peace of mind* before they returned. 彼らが戻って来るまで私の心の平穏は完全には取り戻せなかった
brain [C] 脳 ◇The scan apparently showed no damage to the *brain*. スキャンでは見たところ脳に損傷はなかった ◇*brain* cells 脳細胞 ◇She died of a *brain* tumour. 彼女は脳腫瘍で死んだ ◇Electrodes were used to measure *brain* activity during sleep. 電極が寝ている間の脳の活動を測定するために用いられた
head [C] 頭 ◇I sometimes wonder what goes on in that *head* of yours. 時々あなたのその頭の中で何が起こっているのかしらと思う ◇I wish you'd *use your head* (= think carefully before doing or saying sth). 頭を使ってほしいな ◇I can't work it out *in my head* — I need a calculator. それは暗算ではできないです。計算機が必要です ◇I *can't get* that tune *out of my head*. その曲を

minor

思い出せない ◇When will you **get it into your head** (= understand) that I don't want to discuss this any more! このことについてこれ以上話し合いたくないってことがいつになったらわかってもらえるの ◇For some reason she's **got it into her head** (= believes) that the others don't like her. なぜだか彼女はほかの人に嫌われていると思い込んでいる

> [ノート] **mind** と **head** の使い分け：この意味においては head のほうが mind よりややインフォーマルな感じで、特に考えなどに言及するときには get into your head や you can't get out of your head の形で用いられる。

soul [C]（肉体に対して）精神, 心；（死後残るとされる）魂 ◇There was a feeling of restlessness deep in her *soul.* 彼女は心の奥底で不安を感じていた ◇He believed his immortal *soul* was in peril. 彼は自分の不滅の魂が危機にあると信じていた ◇His poetry deals with the dark side of the human *soul.* 彼の詩は人間性の暗部をえぐっている

spirit [C] 精神, 心；魂 ◇He felt a kind of lightness in his *spirit* as the sun came up. 太陽が昇るにつれて彼は心の中である明るさを感じていた ◇He is dead, but his *spirit* lives on. 彼は死んだが、彼の魂は生き続けている ◇You are underestimating the power of the human *spirit* to overcome difficulties. 君は困難を克服する人間の精神力を見くびっている

> [ノート] **soul** と **spirit** の使い分け：spirit は soul よりもしばしば肯定的な意味で用いられる。soul の連語としては lost/tormented/troubled souls, the dark side of the human soul. 一方の spirit の連語は indomitable spirit, the power of the human spirit などがある。また、魂について言うとき、spirit はしばしば生きている人から離れた、特に死者の魂を指すのに対し、soul はしばしば生きている人の魂を意味する。

ego [複 **-os**] [C]《心理》自我 ◇Freud introduced the idea that a part of the *ego* is unconscious. フロイトは自我の一部は無意識的であるという考えを提唱した ☞ **self** (IDENTITY)

the/your subconscious [単数で] 潜在意識 ◇She buried the guilt deep in her *subconscious.* 彼女は罪悪感を意識下深くに葬り去った ◇Delving into *the subconscious* can be helpful in working through psychological problems. 潜在意識を究明することは精神的問題を克服するのに有用かもしれない ☞ **subconscious** (UNCONSCIOUS)

minor [形] ☞ SLIGHT

minor・trivial・petty・insignificant・peripheral・light・unimportant
人や物事があまり注目に値しないことを表す
【類語訳】重要でない、取るに足らない、些細の、末梢的の、周辺的の

> [文型&コロケーション]
> ▶ minor/ trivial/ petty/ peripheral/ unimportant **things**
> ▶ a minor/ trivial/ petty **problem**
> ▶ minor/ trivial/ insignificant/ unimportant **details**
> ▶ a minor/ a trivial/ an insignificant **matter/ incident**
> ▶ minor/ trivial/ petty **offence**
> ▶ minor/ petty **crime/ theft/ criminals**
> ▶ a minor/ trivial **ailment**

> ▶ a trivial/ an insignificant/ an unimportant **fact**
> ▶ **very** minor/ trivial/ petty/ insignificant/ light/ unimportant
> ▶ **apparently/ seemingly** minor/ trivial/ insignificant/ unimportant

minor [ふつう名詞の前で] あまり大きくない、重要でない、深刻でない ◇The new plan involves widening a *minor* road through the valley. その新計画には谷間を走る小さな道路の拡張が含まれる ◇There may be some *minor* changes to the schedule. スケジュールに小さな変更がいくつかあるかもしれません ◇Women played a relatively *minor* role in the organization. 女性はその組織の中で比較的小さな役割を果たしていた ◇The CD contains a number of delightful short pieces by *minor* composers. そのCDには有名ではない作曲家による軽快な小品がたくさん入っている ◇Both the driver and the passenger suffered *minor* injuries. ドライバーも通行人も軽傷を負った ◇You may need to undergo *minor* surgery. 簡単な手術を受ける必要があるかもしれない [反意] **major** (MAIN), **serious, severe** (SERIOUS 1)

trivial《しばしばけなして》取るに足らない、些細の ◇I didn't want to bother you with such a *trivial* matter. こんな些細なことで君に迷惑をかけたくない ◇I know it sounds *trivial*, but I'm worried about it. それは取るに足らないことのように聞こえるだろうが、私は心配なんだ ❶特に incident, matter, detail と結びつき、また too trivial to bother about/ worry about/mention/make a fuss about の形でもよく使われる。

> ▶ **triviality** [名] [C, U] ◇I don't want to waste time on *trivialities.*《けなして》つまらないことに時間を使いたくないんだ ◇His speech was one of great *triviality.* 彼のスピーチは大変つまらないものだった

petty [ふつう名詞の前で]《ふつうけなして》（小さくて）取るに足らない、些細の ◇I don't want to hear any more about your *petty* squabbles. 君のたわいのない喧嘩の話はもうそれ以上聞きたくないよ ◇There are plenty of *petty* bureaucrats (= who do not have much power or authority) who would report you for that. その件で君のことを告げ口しそうな下級官僚がたくさんいる ◇The removal of *petty* restrictions has made life easier. つまらない制限を取り除いたら生活が楽になった ❶特にそれほど重大ではない犯罪や対立について用いられる。◆ *petty* **crime/theft/ corruption/tyranny**（軽犯罪／些細な窃盗／違法行為／暴力行為）◆ a *petty* **criminal/thief/tyrant**（軽犯罪者／こそ泥／狭量な暴君）◆ *petty* **squabbles/jealousies/feuds**（些細な喧嘩／嫉妬心／争い）

insignificant《ややフォーマル、特に書き言葉》取るに足らない ◇These results are statistically *insignificant.* これらの結果は統計学的には無意味だ ◇The levels of chemicals in the river are not *insignificant.* その川の化学物質の濃度は軽視できない ◇He made her feel *insignificant* and stupid. 彼は彼女がつまらなく愚かな者であることを感じさせた ❶not insignificant は「非常に重要である」思ったより重要である」ことを表すややフォーマルな表現. insignificant は「重要でない[影響力がない]」ように思われる」人についても用いられる。[反意] **significant** (IMPORTANT)

> ▶ **insignificance** [名] [U] ◇Her own problems **paled into insignificance** beside this terrible news. この恐ろしいニュースを前にすれば彼女自身の問題は影が薄くなった [反意] **significance** (IMPORTANCE)

peripheral《フォーマル、特にビジネス》 末梢的な、周辺的な ◇The experiment looks at subjects' ability to take

↪minor

light 軽い ◇Do you need some *light* reading for the beach? ビーチでの読書に軽い読み物がいりますか ◇a concert of *light* classical music 軽いクラシック音楽のコンサート ❶特に娯楽について用いられる。◆*light* reading/fiction/entertainment/comedy/music/opera（軽い読み物/軽い小説/軽い娯楽/軽喜劇/軽音楽/軽歌劇）.

in *peripheral* information. その実験は被験者の周辺情報を取り込む能力を調べている ◇Fund-raising is *peripheral to* their main activities. 資金調達は彼らの主な活動にとって重要ではない ❶特に information, details, activities, developments を修飾する。☞ **periphery**（EDGE）

unimportant 《特に書き言葉》重要でない；特に注意を払う必要がない ◇Don't worry about these *unimportant* details. こんなどうでもいい細かな事に気をもむな ◇They dismissed the problem as *unimportant*. 彼らはその問題を取るに足らないものとして退けた 反意 **important**（IMPORTANT）

minute 名

minute・moment・second・bit・instant・sec・split second
非常に短い時間を表す
【類語訳】分, 瞬間, ちょっとの間, 秒, あっという間

instant	moment	minute	bit
split second	second		
	sec		

文型&コロケーション
▶ **in** a minute/ a moment/ a second/ a bit/ an instant/ a sec
▶ **for** a minute/ a moment/ a second/ a bit/ an instant/ a sec/ a split second
▶ **after** a minute/ moment/ second/ bit
▶ **at/ from that** minute/ moment/ second/ instant
▶ **within** minutes/ moments/ seconds
▶ **just a** minute/ moment/ second/ sec
▶ **this** minute/ moment/ second/ instant
▶ **a brief/ fleeting** moment/ second/ instant
▶ **one/ a single** minute/ moment/ second/ instant
▶ **to hang on/ hold on/ wait** a minute/ moment/ second/ sec
▶ **to have/ spare/ give sb** a minute/ moment/ second
▶ **to last/ take** a minute/ moment/ second
▶ **a** minute/ moment/ second/ a bit/ an instant/ a split second **later**
▶ **a** minute/ a moment/ a second/ a bit/ an instant **longer**

minute [C] 分 ◇It's four *minutes* to six. 6時4分前です ◇I'll be back in a few *minutes*. 2,3分で戻ります ◇It's only a ten-*minute* bus ride into town. 町までバスでたったの10分です ◇I enjoyed every *minute* of the party. そのパーティーはずっと楽しかった ❶単数形の minute は特に話し言葉で「非常に短い時間」を表す。◆Hang on (= Wait) a *minute* — I'll just get my coat.（ちょっと待って、コートを取って来るだけだから）. ◆I just have to finish this — I won't be a *minute*.（これだけは終えないといけない、すぐに戻って来るよ）. ◆Could I see you for a *minute*?（ちょっとお会いできますか）. ◆Don't leave everything till the last *minute*.（何でもぎりぎりまで残しておくのはやめなさい）.

moment [C] 瞬間, ちょっとの時間 ◇Could you wait a *moment*, please? 少しお待ちいただけますか ◇One *moment*, please (= Please wait a short time). 少しお待ちください ◇He thought for a *moment* before replying. 彼は一瞬考えて返事をした ◇I'll be back in a *moment*. すぐに戻ります ◇*Moments* later, I heard a terrible crash. 少したって凄まじく大きな音が聞こえた ◇We arrived *not a moment too soon* (= almost too late). 私たちはぎりぎりで到着した

second [C] 秒 ◇She can run 100 metres in just over 11 *seconds*. 彼女は100mを11秒ちょっとで走ることができる ◇The light flashes every 5 *seconds*. そのライトは5秒毎に光ります ◇The water flows at about 1.5 metres per *second*. その水は秒速約1.5mで流れている ❶特に話し言葉では「非常に短い時間」を表す。◆Hang on (= Wait) a *second* while I find my keys.（鍵を探す間ちょっと待ってて）. ◆I'll be finished with this in a couple of *seconds*.（すぐにこれを終わらせます）.

ノート **minute, moment, second** の使い分け：多くの場合どの語も同じように使用できる。◆Wait/Hang on/Just a *minute/moment/second*.（ちょっと待ってください）. minute は話し言葉では最も使用頻度が高く, 書き言葉では moment が一般的。✕He thought for a *minute/second* before replying.

bit [単数で]《特に英, インフォーマル》ちょっとの間 ◇Wait a *bit*! ちょっと待って ◇Greg thought for a *bit* before answering. グレッグは一瞬考えて答えた

instant [C, ふつう単数で]《特に書き言葉》あっという間 ◇It was all over in an *instant*. あっという間にすべて終わった ◇Just for an *instant* I thought he was going to refuse. 彼は断るつもりかと私はほんの一瞬考えた ❶instant は minute, moment, second よりもさらに短い時間を表す。主に書き言葉で用いられる。

sec [単数で]《インフォーマル, 話し言葉》ちょっとの間；1秒 ◇Stay there. I'll be back in a *sec*. そこにいて。すぐに戻るから ◇Hang on (= Wait) a *sec*. ちょっと待ってて

split 'second [C]《インフォーマル》ほんの一瞬 ◇Their eyes met for a *split second*. 彼らはほんの一瞬目が合った
▶ **'split-second** 形 ◇She had to make a *split-second* decision. 彼女は瞬時に決断しなければならなかった ◇The success of the raid depended on *split-second* timing. 奇襲の成功はほんの一瞬のタイミングにかかっていた

miracle 名

miracle・wonder・phenomenon・marvel・fluke
驚嘆させられる物事や人
【類語訳】奇跡, 偉業, 驚異, 成功者, 大成功, まぐれ

文型&コロケーション
▶ **It's** a miracle/ wonder/ fluke (that)...
▶ a miracle/ wonder/ phenomenon/ marvel **of** sth
▶ a **natural** wonder/ phenomenon/ marvel
▶ **to do** wonders/ marvels **(for sb/ sth)**
▶ **to work/ perform** a miracle/ wonders
▶ a miracle/ wonder **cure/ drug**

miracle [C]《インフォーマル》奇跡；偉業 ◇It's a *miracle* that nobody was killed. 誰も殺されなかったのは奇跡だ ◇It would take a *miracle* to make this business profitable. 奇跡でも起こらない限りこの商売で収益を出すの

難しいだろう ◇You shouldn't expect the treatment to work *miracles*. その治療法は奇跡を起こすことは期待すべきではない ◇The car is a *miracle* of engineering. その車は工学技術の奇跡だ ☞ **miraculous** (AMAZING)

wonder [C] 驚嘆[称賛]に値する人[物事, 性質] ◇The Grand Canyon is one of the natural **wonders of the world**. グランド・キャニオンは世界の自然の驚異の一つだ ◇It's all become possible, thanks to the *wonders* of modern technology. 現代の驚異的な科学技術のおかげで, それはすっかり可能になった ◇The news **did wonders for** (= had a very good effect on) our morale. その知らせに我々の士気は大いに上がった ◇It's a *wonder* (= it's surprising) more people weren't injured. 負傷者がそれ以上出なかったのは驚きだ ◇**No wonder** you're tired! You didn't get any sleep last night. 君が疲れているのも無理はない. 昨晩まったく寝られなかったのだから ◇The club's new **boy wonder** scored two goals in the second half. そのクラブの新人の天才少年は後半に2ゴールを上げた ☞ **wonderful** (WONDERFUL)

phenomenon (複 英 **phenomena**, 米 **phenomenons**) [C] 成功者, 大成功 ◇This young pianist is a *phenomenon*. この若いピアニストは天下の逸材だ ◇Harry Potter was the greatest book publishing *phenomenon* ever. ハリー・ポッターは出版界にかつてない大成功を収めた ☞ **phenomenal** (REMARKABLE)

marvel [C] 驚異的な人[物事] ◇The design is a *marvel* of elegance and simplicity. そのデザインは驚くほど優雅でシンプルだ ❶複数形のmarvelsは驚異的な結果や偉業を表す. ♦The doctors have done *marvels* for her. (その医者たちは彼女のために驚くべきことをやってのけた). ☞ **marvellous** (WONDERFUL)

fluke [C, ふつう単数で]《インフォーマル》まぐれ ◇They are determined to show that their last win was no *fluke*. 彼らは前回の勝利がまぐれではなかったことを証明しようと決意している

misleading 形

misleading・ambiguous・deceptive・spurious

間違った考えや印象を与え, 真実でないことを信じさせること
【類語訳】誤解を招く, 紛らわしい, あいまいな, 見せかけの

文型&コロケーション
▶a misleading/ an ambiguous **statement**
▶a misleading/ spurious **argument/ claim/ impression**
▶a misleading/ deceptive **advertisement**
▶**rather** misleading/ ambiguous/ deceptive/ spurious
▶**highly/ very/ dangerously** misleading/ ambiguous/ deceptive

misleading 誤解を招く, 紛らわしい, 人を惑わす ◇They face prosecution if they provide false or *misleading* information. 虚偽または誤解を招く恐れのある情報を提供すれば彼らは起訴される ◇It would be seriously *misleading* to suggest that television has no effect on children. テレビは子どもに影響を与えないなどと示唆すれば深刻な誤解を招くだろう

▶**misleadingly** 副 ◇These bats are sometimes *misleadingly* referred to as 'flying foxes'. これらのコウモリは時に「flying foxes」と紛らわしい名で呼ばれることがある

ambiguous 《ややフォーマル》あいまいな, 両義に取れる ◇Her account was deliberately *ambiguous*. 彼女の説明はわざとあいまいなものになっていた ◇It is for the jury to decide what an *ambiguous* statement was intended to mean. あいまいな供述の裏にどのような意図があったのかを判断するのは陪審員である 反意 **unambiguous** (CLEAR 形 2), ☞ VAGUE

▶**ambiguously** 副 ◇an *ambiguously* worded agreement あいまいな言葉で表現された協定

deceptive 《ややフォーマル》人をごまかすような ◇*Appearances can be deceptive* (= things are not always as they seem). 見かけは当てにならない

▶**deceptively** 副 ◇a *deceptively* simple idea (= an idea that seems simple but is not really) 一見単純そうな着想

ノート misleading と deceptive の使い分け：misleading は嘘は言わずに, 意図的に間違った考えを与える場合. deceptive はふつう意図せずに誤った印象を与える場合. 最もよく結びつくのは appearances である. しかしながら, よりフォーマルな文脈では故意にだますことについて用いられることもある.

spurious 《ややフォーマル》見せかけの ◇He had managed to create the entirely *spurious* impression that the company was thriving. 彼は会社がうまくいっていると見せかけるためにあれこれ小細工を弄していた ❶典型的に結びつくのは argument, claim, grounds, impression, logic など.

mistake 名

1 mistake・error・omission・blunder・gaffe・oversight

行いや考え, 発言が正しくないこと
【類語訳】間違い, 誤解, ミス, エラー, 脱落, 抜け, 失態, へま, 見落とし

文型&コロケーション
▶sth happens **due to** a mistake/ an error/ an omission/ a blunder/ an oversight
▶a **major** mistake/ error/ omission/ blunder/ gaffe
▶a/ an **serious/ glaring** mistake/ error/ omission
▶a/ an **simple/ stupid/ dreadful/ terrible/ fatal/ tragic** mistake/ error/ blunder
▶an **unfortunate** mistake/ error/ oversight
▶to **make** a mistake/ an error/ a blunder/ a gaffe
▶to **realize/ admit (to)** a mistake/ an error/ a blunder
▶to **correct** a mistake/ an error/ an omission/ a blunder
▶to **rectify/ remedy** a mistake/ an error/ an omission

mistake [C] 間違い, 誤解, ミス ◇Don't worry, we all make *mistakes*. 気にするな, 皆ミスを犯すものだ ◇I made the *mistake* of giving him my address. 彼に住所を教えるという過ちを私は犯してしまった ◇You must try to learn from your *mistakes*. 君は過ちから学ぼうとしなければならないよ ◇Leaving school so young was the biggest *mistake* of my life. そんなにも若くして退学したのは私の人生で最大の過ちだった ◇I took your bag instead of mine **by mistake** (= accidentally; without meaning to). あなたのバッグと私のを取り違えてしまいました ◇Children may eat pills **in mistake for** sweets. 子どもはお菓子と間違えて錠剤を口にしてしまうかもしれない ☞ **mistaken** (WRONG 1)

error [C, U] 《ややフォーマル》(問題を引き起こす[結果を左右

する]) 間違い, エラー, ミス ◇No payments were made last week because of a computer *error*. 先週コンピューターのエラーで支払いがなされなかった ◇I think you have made an *error* in calculating the total. 君の合計の計算が間違っていると思うよ ◇He accused the prime minister of committing a serious ***error of judgement***. 重大な判断ミスを犯したとして彼は首相を非難した ◇The delay was due to ***human error*** (= a mistake made by a person rather than a machine). その遅延は人的ミスによるものだった ◇The computer system was switched off ***in error*** (= by mistake). そのコンピューターシステムの電源が誤って切られた ◇Children learn to use computer programs by ***trial and error*** (= by trying various methods until they find one that is successful). 子どもたちは試行錯誤しながらコンピュータープログラムの使い方を学ぶ

omission [C] 《ややフォーマル》脱落, 抜け ◇There were a number of errors and *omissions* in the article. その記事には誤りと抜けがたくさんあった

blunder [C] (ばかげた) 失態, (不注意による) へま ◇After a series of political *blunders* he finally resigned. 度重なる政治的失態の後, 彼はついに辞職した ❶公の要職にある人による過ちについてしばしば用いられる. **administrative, bureaucratic, economic, political** といった形容詞とよく結びつく.

gaffe [C] (公の場[社交上]の) 失態, 失策, へま ◇He made some real *gaffes* early in his career. 彼は駆け出しの頃いくつかの大失態を演じた ◇Most people will politely look the other way if you commit some social *gaffe*. もし誰かが公の場で何か失態をしでかしたら, たいていの人は礼儀として見て見ぬふりをするだろう

oversight [C, U] 《ややフォーマル》見落とし ◇I didn't mean to leave her name off the list; it was an *oversight*. 彼女の名前をリストから外すつもりはなかった. 見落としていた ◇You can never entirely eliminate human error and *oversight*. 人間の誤りと見落としを完全に排除することは決してできない

2 mistake・error・inaccuracy・slip・howler・misprint
正しく言われて[書かれて, タイプされて]いないこと
【類語訳】誤り, 言い間違い, 書き間違い, ミスプリント, 誤植

▷文型&コロケーション◁

▶a mistake/ an error/ an inaccuracy/ a slip/ a howler/ a misprint **in** sth
▶a **simple** mistake/ error/ slip/ misprint
▶to **make** a mistake/ an error/ a slip/ a howler
▶to **contain**/ **be full of** mistakes/ errors/ inaccuracies/ howlers/ misprints
▶to **find**/ **point out** a mistake/ an error/ an inaccuracy

mistake [C] (語・数字の) 間違い ◇The waiter made a *mistake* in adding up the bill. そのウェイターは勘定書の合計を間違った ◇Her essay is full of spelling *mistakes*. 彼女のエッセイにはスペルミスがたくさんある

error [C] 《やや改まって》(語・数字の) 間違い ◇There are too many *errors* in your work. 君の仕事には間違いが多すぎる

inaccuracy [C, U] 《ややフォーマル》(情報の) 誤り ◇The article is full of *inaccuracies*. その記事には誤りがたくさんある ◇The writer is guilty of bias and *inaccuracy*. そのライターは偏見と情報の誤りがあるのが欠点だ ☞ **inaccurate** (WRONG 1)

slip [C] (ちょっとした) 誤り, うっかりミス ◇He recited the whole poem without making a single *slip*. 彼は一言も間違えずにその詩を全部暗唱した ◇a ***Freudian slip*** (= sth you say by mistake but which is believed to show your true thoughts) フロイト的失言

howler [C] 《インフォーマル, 特に英》ばかげた言い間違い[書き間違い] ◇The report is full of *howlers*. その報告書にはばかげた書き間違いがたくさんある ❶ふつう無知を露呈するような恥ずかしい間違いについて言う.

misprint [C] ミスプリント, 誤植 ◇The book was reprinted with a few *misprints* corrected. その本はいくつか誤植を訂正して再版された

misunderstand 動

misunderstand・misinterpret・get sth wrong・get sb wrong・mistake・misread・misjudge
正しく理解していない
【類語訳】誤解する, 勘違いする, 見誤る

▷文型&コロケーション◁

▶to misunderstand/ misinterpret/ mistake/ misread sth **as** sth
▶to misunderstand/ misinterpret/ mistake/ misjudge **what**...
▶to misunderstand/ misinterpret/ mistake sb's **meaning**/ **intentions**
▶to misunderstand/ misinterpret/ misread/ misjudge a **situation**
▶to get a **situation** wrong
▶to **badly** misunderstand/ mistake/ misread/ misjudge sb/ sth
▶to **seriously** misunderstand/ misinterpret/ misread/ misjudge sb/ sth
▶to **completely** misunderstand/ misinterpret/ mistake/ misread/ misjudge sb/ sth
▶to **totally** misunderstand/ mistake/ misread sb/ sth
▶to get sb/ sth **badly**/ **seriously**/ **totally**/ **completely** wrong
▶to **deliberately** misunderstand/ misinterpret sb/ sth
▶to be **easily** misunderstood/ misinterpreted/ mistaken/ misread/ misjudged

misunderstand [自, 他] 誤解する, 勘違いする ◇I thought he was her husband — I must have *misunderstood*. 彼が彼女の旦那だと思ってた. 勘違いしてたよ ◇Don't *misunderstand* me — I'm grateful for everything you've done. 誤解しないで. あなたがしてくれたことすべてに感謝しています ◇She must have *misunderstood* what I was trying to say. 私が何を言おうとしていたか彼女は誤解していたに違いない 反意 **understand** (UNDERSTAND 1), ☞ **misunderstanding** (ILLUSION)

misinterpret [他, しばしば受身で] 誤解する, 間違って解釈する ◇His comments were *misinterpreted* as a criticism of the project. 彼のコメントはその事業計画に対する批判だと誤解された ☞ **misinterpretation** (ILLUSION)

get sth 'wrong 仔用 《ややインフォーマル, 話し言葉》(状況を) 誤解する, 勘違いする ◇No, you've *got it all wrong*. She's not his wife. いや, 君はまったく勘違いしてる. 彼女は彼の奥さんじゃないよ ◇Trust you to *get it all wrong*! 間

modern, moisture, money

解すると思ったよ

get sb 'wrong [行イディ] 《ややインフォーマル, 話し言葉》(発言・真意を)誤解する ◇*Don't get me wrong* (= don't be offended by what I am going to say), I think he's doing a good job, but... 誤解しないでね、彼はいい仕事をしてるとは思うけど…

mistake [他] (人の振る舞い・状況を)誤解する、思い違いをする ◇He *mistook* the other man's offer as a threat. 彼は相手の申し出を脅しと誤解した ◇*There was no mistaking* (= it was impossible to mistake) the bitterness in her voice. 彼女の口調は明らかに辛辣なものだった
☞ **mistaken** (WRONG 1)

misread [他] (状況を)読み違える ◇She had seen the warning signs but she had *misread* them. 彼女は警告サインを見たが、勘違いしていた

misjudge [他] 不当に評価する、評価を誤る、見誤る ◇She was beginning to realize that she had *misjudged* him. 彼女は彼を間違って評価していたことに気づき始めていた ◇They had seriously *misjudged* the mood of the electorate. 彼らは有権者の気持ちをひどく見誤っていた

modern [形] ☞ EXPERIMENTAL

modern・advanced・up to date・state of the art
技術や方法が最も新しいこと
【類語訳】最新の, 先進の, 最先端の

```
modern                                      state of the art
advanced              up to date
```

《文型&コロケーション》
▶ modern/ advanced/ up-to-date/ state-of-the-art **design/ technology/ techniques**
▶ **very** modern/ advanced/ up to date
▶ **fairly/ quite/ relatively** modern/ advanced/ up to date

modern 《ふつうほめて》(技術・方法・デザイン・素材が)最新の ◇The company needs to invest in a *modern* computer system. その会社は最新式のコンピューターシステムに投資する必要がある ◇It is the most *modern*, well-equipped hospital in the country. そこは国内で最新の設備がよく整った病院だ ◇*Modern* methods of farming are destroying the countryside. 最新の農法が田園地方を破壊しつつある 反意 **old-fashioned** (OLD-FASHIONED)

advanced (技術・方法・デザインが)最新式の, 先進の ◇Even in *advanced* industrial societies, poverty persists. 先進の産業社会においても貧困はなくならない ◇It is a technologically *advanced* society. そこは科学技術面で先進社会だ 反意 **primitive** ❶ primitive は「産業のない簡素な社会に属する」ことを表す. ◆ *primitive* societies/ tribes/ beliefs (原始的な社会/部族/信仰).

《ノート **modern** と **advanced** の使い分け:多くの場合どちらの語も使用可能. ◆ **modern/advanced** technology/ techniques/designs (最新の科学技術/技術/デザイン). ◆ a **modern/** an **advanced** society/economy/civilization/nation (現代社会/経済/文明/国). **advanced** は特に科学技術や経済の文脈で用いられる. **advanced society** は複雑な経済構造を持ち、科学技術に多くを頼っている社会を指し, **modern society** はもっと広い意味で社会的関係や文化を含む現在の生活を言うときに用いられる. mod-

ern は芸術やファッション, 思想に関しても用いることができる.
☞ **modern** (EXPERIMENTAL), **modern** (RECENT)

,up to 'date (設備・技術・方法が)最新式の, 最先端の ◇We need to spend at least half a million on getting the most *up-to-date* equipment. 最新の設備を導入するのに最低でも50万ドルを費やす必要がある ◇This technology is *bang up to date* (= completely modern). この技術は最先端を行っている 反意 **out of date** (OLD-FASHIONED)

,state of the 'art (ほめて)(設備・技術・方法が)最先端の ◇He spent thousands on a *state-of-the-art* sound system. 彼は最先端の音響システムに大金をはたいた

moisture [名]

moisture・damp・humidity・condensation・spray・dew
大気中や物の表面に付いたごく小さな水滴
【類語訳】水蒸気, 露, 水分, 湿気, 湿度, 蒸し暑さ, 結露, 水しぶき, 水煙

《文型&コロケーション》
▶ condensation/ dew **forms**
▶ **drops of** moisture/ dew

moisture [U] 水蒸気, 露, 水分 ◇Trees need *moisture* in order to maintain their growth. 樹木は生長し続けるために水分が必要だ ◇Beads of *moisture* were forming on his forehead. 汗の玉が彼の額に浮かんでいた
☞ **moist** (WET)

damp [U] 《英》湿った状態, 湿気; 湿った所 ◇The house smells of *damp*. その家は湿気臭い ◇One wall of my house is affected by *rising damp*. 我が家の壁の一つが上昇湿気の影響を受けている ☞ **damp** (WET)

humidity [U] 湿気, 湿度; 蒸し暑さ ◇Instruments constantly monitor temperature and *humidity*. 機器が常に温度と湿度を測定している ◇The *humidity* was becoming unbearable. 蒸し暑さは我慢できないほどになっていた ☞ **humid** (HUMID)

condensation [U] 結露 ◇The window was misty with *condensation*. 窓は結露で曇っていた

spray [U, C] 水しぶき, 水煙 ◇A cloud of fine *spray* came up from the waterfall. 細かな水しぶきが雲のように滝から昇ってきた

dew [U] 露, 夜露 ◇The grass was wet with early morning *dew*. 草は朝露で濡れていた

money [名]

1 money・cash・funds・capital・finance・means
物を購入するために使う金銭
【類語訳】お金, 資金, 資本, 財源, 収入, 資力

《文型&コロケーション》
▶ **government/ public** money/ cash/ funds/ capital/ finance
▶ **to have/ lack** (the) money/ cash/ funds/ capital/ finance/ the means (**to do sth**)
▶ **to be short of** money/ cash/ funds/ capital
▶ **to raise/ provide/ put up** money/ cash/ funds/ capital/ finance (**for sth**)

↪**money**

▶to **get/ obtain** money/ cash/ funds/ finance (**for** sth)
▶to **spend/ borrow/ invest** money/ cash/ funds/ capital
▶to **lend** money/ cash/ funds
▶to **pay/ save** money/ cash

money [U] お金 ◇He hoped the project would **make money**. 彼はその事業がお金になることを期待した ◇He returned the new TV to the store and got his **money** back. 彼は新しく買ったそのテレビを店に返品して、お金を返してもらった ◇This desk is worth a lot of **money**. この机は高いだけのことはある ◇The **money** (= the pay) is great in my new job. 新しい仕事は給料がいい ☞ **income** (IN-COME)

cash [U]《インフォーマル》お金, 資金 ◇She refused to part with her **hard-earned cash**. 彼女は苦労して稼いだ金を手放したくなかった ◇The company is **strapped for cash** (= without enough money). その会社は資金繰りに困っている

funds [複数で] 資金 ◇The hospital is trying to raise **funds** for a new kidney machine. その病院は新型の腎臓透析機の購入のため資金を調達しようとしている ☞ **fund** (FUND 名), **fund** (FUND 動), **funding** (INVESTMENT)

|ノート| **cash** と **funds** の使い分け：cash のほうが funds よりくだけているが、両方とも個人の物にも組織の物にも用いることができる。◆I'm/The government is short of *cash/funds*. (私/政府は資金不足である)。funds は不可だが、cash は他の名詞の前で形容詞的に用いられることがある。◆The company is having *cash* (✗*funds*) flow problems. (その会社は資金繰りに苦しんでいる)。

capital [U, 単数で]（会社・個人の所有する）元金, 資産, 資本 ◇We don't have enough *capital* to buy new premises. 私たちには新たな土地を購入するのに十分な資金がない ◇Our *capital* is all tied up in property. 我々の資本はすべて不動産に投資されている ◇*capital* assets/ goods/stock (= wealth in the form of buildings, equipment, etc.) 資本資産/資本財/資本金

finance [U]《ややフォーマル》資金, 財源, 財政 ◇*Finance* for education comes from taxpayers. 教育財源は納税者からのものである ◇[複数形の *finances* は個人、組織、の資金、またはその金の運用の仕方を意味する]。◆Moving house put a severe strain on our *finances*. (引っ越しで我が家の財政は危機に) ◆The firm's *finances* are basically sound. (その会社の財務状況は基本的には健全だ)。☞ **finance** (FINANCE), **finance** (FUND 動)

means [複数で] 収入, 資力 ◇People should pay *according to their means* (= according to what they can afford). 収入に応じて支払いをするのがいい ◇Private school fees are **beyond the means of** most people (= more than they can afford). 私学の授業料はほとんどの人の資力を超えている ◇Try to live **within your means** (= not spend more money than you have). 身分相応の生活をしなさい

2 money・cash・change
硬貨や紙幣の形態のお金
【類語訳】貨幣, 通貨, 現金, 釣り銭, 小銭

|文型&コロケーション|

▶to **draw out/ get out/ take out/ withdraw** money/ cash
▶**ready** money/ cash (= money that you have available to spend immediately)

money [U] 貨幣, 通貨 ◇I counted the *money* carefully. 私はそのお金を注意して数えた ◇Where can I change my *money* into dollars? どこでお金をドルに交換できますか ◇*paper money* (= money that is made of paper, not coins) 紙幣

cash [U] 貨幣, 現金 ◇How much *cash* do you have on you? 現金の持ち合わせはどれくらいですか ◇Payments can be made by cheque or **in cash**. お支払いは小切手または現金が可能です ◇Customers are offered a 10% discount if they **pay cash**. 現金で支払えば、客は10%の割引きを受けられる ◇*petty cash* (= a small amount of money kept in an office for small payments) 小口現金 ☞ **cash** (CASH)

|ノート| **money** と **cash** の使い分け：現金の場合と現金以外の金銭形態の対比が重要な場合は cash を用いる。◆How much *money/cash* do you have on you? (あなたの持ち合わせはいくらですか)。✗Payments can be made by cheque or in *money*. ✗Customers are offered a discount if they pay *money*.

change [U] 釣り銭；小銭 ◇That's 40p *change*. 40ペンスのお釣りです ◇The ticket machine doesn't give *change*. その券売機はお釣りが出ません ◇Do you have any *change* for the ticket machine? 券売機用の小銭を持ってますか ◇a dollar **in change** (= coins that together are worth one dollar) 小銭での1ドル ◇Can you give me **change for** a ten pound note (= coins or notes that are worth this amount)? 10ポンド紙幣を細かくしてもらえますか ◇I didn't have any *small change* (= coins of low value) to leave as a tip. チップとして置いて帰る小銭をまったく持っていなかった ☞ **change** (CASH)

3 money・wealth・fortune・prosperity・riches・affluence
裕福な人や組織、社会が持つ大量の金や資産
【類語訳】財産, 富, 富裕, 裕福, 大金, 繁栄

|文型&コロケーション|

▶(a) **great** wealth/ fortune/ prosperity/ riches/ affluence
▶**growing/ increasing/ rising** wealth/ prosperity/ affluence
▶(a) **personal/ family** money/ wealth/ fortune/ prosperity
▶(a) **private** money/ wealth/ fortune/ affluence
▶**public** money/ prosperity
▶**national** wealth/ prosperity
▶to **have/ possess/ accumulate/ acquire/ inherit** money/ wealth/ a fortune/ riches
▶to **bring** money/ wealth/ prosperity/ riches/ affluence
▶to **create** money/ wealth/ prosperity/ affluence
▶to **make** money/ a fortune (on/ out of sth)

money [U]（人の所有する）財産, 富 ◇He lost all his *money* in the 1929 stock market crash. 1929年の株式市場の暴落で彼は全財産を失った ◇The family made their *money* in the 18th century. その一族は18世紀に富を築いた

wealth [U]（人・組織・国が所有する）財産, 富；裕福, 裕福 ◇She called for a redistribution of *wealth* and power in society. 彼女は社会における富と権力の再分配を訴えた ◇The purpose of industry is to create *wealth*. 産業の目的は富を生むことだ |反意| **poverty** (POVERTY), ☞ **wealthy** (RICH)

mood, moral

fortune [C, ふつう単数で] 財産, 富, 大金 ◇She inherited a share of the family *fortune*. 彼女は家の財産の分け前を相続した ◇You don't have to spend a *fortune* to give your family tasty, healthy meals. 家族においしくて健康的な食事を与えるために大金を使う必要がない ◇That ring must be worth a *fortune*. その指輪は大変な値打ち物に違いない ◇A car like that costs **a small fortune** (= a lot of money). あのような車はかなり値が張る

prosperity [U] 《しばしばほめて》繁栄, 富裕 ◇The future *prosperity* of the region depends on economic growth. その地域の将来の繁栄は経済成長次第である ◇The country is enjoying a period of *peace and prosperity*. その国は平和と繁栄の時代を享受している ☞ **prosper** (DO WELL), **prosperous** (RICH)

riches [複数扱い]《文語》財産, 富 ◇He embarked on a business career that eventually brought him fame and *riches*. 最終的に名声と富をもたらすビジネス界に彼は乗り出した ☞ **rich** (RICH)

affluence [U]《時にけなして》繁栄, 富裕 ◇The 1950s were an age of *affluence* in America. 1950年代はアメリカの繁栄の時代だった ☞ **affluent** (RICH)

| ノート | **prosperity** と **affluence** の使い分け：affluence は人や社会についての富裕と貧困を対比し, 常によい意味とは限らない. ◆the city's mixture of private *affluence* (×*prosperity*) and public squalor (富める個人と公共のみすぼらしさが混在する町). prosperity はこのようには用いられず, 常によい意味で, 人のために望ましい場合である. ◆Please drink to the health and *prosperity* (×*money/×wealth/×fortune/×riches/×affluence*) of the bride and groom. (新郎新婦の健康と繁栄を願って飲みましょう). 他人のためであっても prosperity ではなく money や wealth などを願うことは欲深いことと考えられている.

mood 名

mood・morale・spirits・frame of mind
ある時の気持ちのありようを表す
【類語訳】気分, 機嫌, 士気, 意気

| 文型&コロケーション |
- **in** (a) (good/ better, etc.) mood/ spirits/ frame of mind
- **in the mood/ frame of mind for** sth
- **in the mood/ frame of mind to do** sth
- (a) **good/ better** mood/ morale/ spirits/ frame of mind
- a **happy/ confident/ cheerful/ calm/ determined/ positive/ relaxed** mood/ frame of mind
- the **right/ wrong** mood/ frame of mind
- sb's **morale is/ spirits are high/ low**
- **to get into/ put sb in** a (good/ positive, etc.) mood/ frame of mind
- **to lift/ raise** sb's morale/ spirits
- sb's **mood/ morale/ spirits improve/ improves**
- sb's **mood/ spirits lift/ lifts**

mood [C] 気分, 機嫌 ◇She's in a good *mood* today. 今日は彼女は機嫌がいい ◇I'm just not in the *mood* for a party. パーティーに行く気分じゃないだけさ ◇The news had put Michelle in a foul *mood*. そのニュースを聞いてミシェルの機嫌は悪くなった ◇Some addicts suffer violent ***mood swings*** (= changes of mood) if deprived of the drug. 常習者の中には麻薬が切れると激しい気分変動

を催す者がいる ☞ **mood** (TEMPER)

morale [U] 士気, 意気 ◇*Morale* amongst the players is very high at the moment. 現在のところ選手の士気は非常に高い ☞ **demoralize** (DISCOURAGE 2), **demoralized** (DEPRESSED)

spirits [複数形で] よい[悪い]気分 ◇She isn't in the best of *spirits* today. 彼女は今日は上機嫌とは言えない ◇She was tired and her *spirits* were low. 彼女は疲れて意気消沈していた

| ノート | **morale** と **spirits** の使い分け：両方ともふつう high であるか low であるかで表され,「高める」か「低める」を表す語と結びつく. ◆**to lift/raise** sb's *morale/spirits* (人の士気/やる気などを高める). ◆sb's *spirits* **lift/rise/soar** (人のやる気が高まる). ◆The competition will **boost** children's *morale* and self-esteem. (競争は子どもたちの意欲と自尊心を高めるだろう). ◆We sang songs to **keep our spirits up**. (私たちは士気を保ち続けるために歌を歌った). ◆My *spirits* **sank** at the thought of starting all over again. (一からやり直すことを考えると私の気分は沈んだ).

,frame of 'mind [単数で] 気分, 機嫌, 心の状態 ◇We'll discuss this when you're in a better *frame of mind*. 君の機嫌がいい時にこのことについて話し合おう

moral 形

moral・ethical
善悪の規準に関することを表す
【類語訳】道徳上の, 倫理上の

| 文型&コロケーション |
▸ a moral/ an ethical **question/ issue/ problem/ dilemma**
▸ moral/ ethical **ideals/ values/ standards/ principles/ practices**

moral [名詞の前で]（法的な権利・義務に基づくものではなく）道徳上の ◇The basic *moral* philosophies of most world religions are remarkably similar. 世界の宗教の大半が持つ基本的な道徳哲学は著しく似通っている ◇He's a deeply religious man with a highly developed *moral* sense. 彼は敬虔な男で非常に道徳意識が高い ◇British newspapers were full of ***moral outrage*** at the weakness of other countries. イギリスの新聞は他国の腰抜けぶりに対する道徳的な怒りに満ちあふれていた ◇The job was to call upon all her skills of diplomacy and ***moral courage*** (= the courage to do what you think is right). 《英》その仕事には彼女の外交手腕と正しいことを行う真の勇気が必要だった ☞ **moral** (GOOD 5), **morals, morality** (PRINCIPLE 1)

▸**morally** 副 ◇Was the attack *morally* justified? その攻撃は道徳的に正当だったのですか

ethical [名詞の前で]（ビジネス・政治・社会の場で）倫理上の ◇There's an overwhelming *ethical* argument for the protection of the environment. 環境保護に賛成する倫理的主張が圧倒的だ ☞ **ethical** (GOOD 5), **ethics** (PRINCIPLE 1), **ethic** (VALUES)

▸**ethically** 副 ◇Paying workers less than a living wage is *ethically* unacceptable. 労働者への賃金が生活賃金を下回るのは倫理的に受け入れられない

↳moral

morality, movement, murder

ノート moral と ethical の使い分け：moral は特に日常生活における行為や個人の規範について用いられる。特に義務や感情に関連する duty, obligation, imperative, sense, indignation, outrage, panic, courage などと結びつく。ethical はふつう特定の職業や社会における原則やしきたりについて用いられる。moral よりもフォーマルであるが、強い表現ではない。また、義務や感情ではなく、さまざまな論点に関連する guideline, criterion, proposition などと結びつく。

morality 名 ☞ PRINCIPLE 1

morality・right・good・goodness・purity・virtue・righteousness
善悪の基準、道徳的によい性質
【類語訳】道徳、正義、善、善行、善良、純潔、清純、美徳、高潔、貞操、正当性

文型&コロケーション
▶to **do** right/ good

morality [U] 道徳 ◇He seems to have no *personal morality* at all. 彼はまったく徳性を持ち合わせていないようだ ◇Do you think *standards of morality* are falling? 道徳的基準が下がりつつあると思いますか **反意** **immorality** (EVIL 名)

right [U, C, ふつう複数で] 正義、正当、善 ◇She doesn't understand the difference between *right and wrong*. 彼女は善悪の区別がわからない ◇You did *right* to tell me about it. 君が私にそれについて話してくれたのは正しいことだった ◇They both knew he was *in the right* (= had justice on his side). 二人とも彼が正しいとわかっていた ◇It was difficult to establish *the rights and wrongs* (= the true facts) of the matter. その問題の善悪を定めるのは困難だった **反意** **wrong** (EVIL 名)

good [U] 善行 ◇Do they know the difference between *good and evil*? 彼らは善悪の区別がつくのだろうか ◇Schools can definitely be seen as a *force for good* in this area. 学校はこの地域で間違いなく善を促進する力だと見なされている ◇Look for an opportunity to do *good* whenever you can. できる時にはいつも善行をする機会を探しなさい **反意** **evil** (EVIL 名), ☞ **good** (GOOD 5)

ノート right と good の使い分け：right and wrong は正義に関わり人々を扱う際に「公平」か「不公平」かを問う。good and evil は人々を扱う際に「優しい」か「残酷である」かを問う。

goodness [U] 善良さ ◇We like to think that *goodness* exists in everyone. すべての人に善良さはあると考えたい ☞ **good** (GOOD 5)

purity [U] (性的な)純潔さ、清純さ ◇The veil was regarded as a symbol of the bride's *purity*. ヴェールは花嫁の純潔のシンボルと考えられていた

virtue [U] 《ややフォーマル》美徳、高潔、貞操 ◇a woman of *easy virtue* (= a sexually immoral woman) ふしだらな女 ◇He was convinced of the inherent *virtue* of hard work. 彼は勤勉は本来的に美徳であると確信していた **反意** **vice** (EVIL 名), ☞ **virtuous** (GOOD 5)

righteousness [U] 《フォーマル、特に宗教》正当性 ◇the *righteousness* of God 神の正当性 ◇They had absolute faith in the *righteousness* of their cause. 彼らは自らの信念の正当性をすっかり信じ込んでいた

movement 名

movement・motion・move・gesture・wave
動いたり動かしたりすること
【類語訳】動き、動作、移動、身振り、しぐさ、ジェスチャー

文型&コロケーション
▶a **little/ slight** movement/ motion/ gesture/ wave
▶a **hand** movement/ gesture
▶to **make** a movement/ motion/ move/ gesture
▶to **give** a gesture/ wave
▶a movement/ motion/ gesture **with your hand**
▶a movement/ motion/ wave **of your hand**
▶sb's **every** movement/ move

movement [C, U] 体の動き、動作 ◇Don't make any sudden *movements*. 急に動かないように ◇She observed the gentle *movement* of his chest as he breathed. 彼女は彼の胸が呼吸する際に穏やかに動くのを観察した ◇Choose loose clothes that give you greater *freedom of movement*. 動きやすいゆったりした服を選びなさい ❶*movement* は他の語と違って、downward, upward, forward, backward, horizontal, vertical, lateral といった方向を表す形容詞の後に用いることが可能。◆Power comes from the forward *movement* of the entire body. (力は体全体の前方向への動きから生じる)

motion [U, C] 《ややフォーマル》動作；(手・腕の)動き ◇The swaying *motion* of the ship was making me feel sick. 船の揺れる動きで私は気分が悪くなった ◇He wound the key and set the toy in *motion*. 《フォーマル》彼はねじを巻いてその玩具を動かした ◇Rub the cream in with a circular *motion*. 円を描くようにクリームを塗り込んでください

move [C, ふつう単数で] 移動 ◇He made a *move* towards the door. 彼はドアの方へ動いた ◇She felt that he was watching her every *move*. 彼女は彼が自分の一挙一動を見ているような気がした

gesture [C, U] 身振り、しぐさ、ジェスチャー ◇He made an obscene *gesture* with his hand. 彼は手で卑猥なジェスチャーをした ◇Expression and *gesture* are both forms of non-verbal communication. 表情としぐさは共に非言語(的)コミュニケーションの形態である

wave [C, ふつう単数で] (手を)振ること ◇She sent him away with a *wave* of her hand. 彼女は手を振って彼を追い払った

murder 名

murder・killing・suicide・assassination・homicide・slaying・manslaughter・euthanasia
人を殺すこと
【類語訳】殺人、自殺、殺害、暗殺、故殺、安楽死

文型&コロケーション
▶a **double/ mass** murder/ killing/ suicide/ slaying
▶(a) **premeditated** murder/ killing/ homicide
▶an **unsolved** murder/ killing/ slaying
▶(an) **attempted** murder/ suicide/ assassination/ homicide/ manslaughter
▶a **brutal** murder/ killing/ slaying
▶to **commit** murder/ suicide/ homicide/ manslaughter

murder

- ▸ to **carry out** a murder/ a killing/ an assassination/ euthanasia
- ▸ to **prevent** a murder/ a killing/ suicide/ an assassination
- ▸ to **witness** a murder/ a killing/ a suicide/ an assassination/ a slaying
- ▸ a murder/ a suicide/ an assassination **attempt**

murder [U, C] (故意の)殺人(犯罪) ◇He was found guilty of *murder*. 彼は殺人の罪で有罪判決を受けた ◇She has been charged with the attempted *murder* of her husband. 彼女は夫に対する殺人未遂の容疑をかけられている ◇What was the *murder weapon*? (殺害の)凶器は何でしたか ◇The play is a *murder mystery*. その劇は殺人ミステリーです ☞ **murder** (KILL), **murderous** (VIOLENT)

killing [C, ふつう複数で]《特にジャーナリズム》(故意の)殺人 ◇Refugees from the war-torn country brought accounts of mass *killings*, rape and torture. 戦争で荒廃した国からの難民によって大量殺人、強姦、拷問の話がもたらされた ☞ **kill** (KILL)

> ノート murderとkillingの使い分け：killingは戦時中の、または過激な政治組織や犯罪組織による行為について通常複数形で用いられる。murderは一人の人間の殺害を言うことが多い。

suicide [U, C] 自殺 ◇It was a case of attempted *suicide* (= one in which the person survives). それは自殺未遂事件だった ◇He hadn't left a *suicide note* (= written before sb tries to commit suicide). 彼は自殺の遺書を残していなかった ◇The attack had been carried out by a *suicide bomber*. その攻撃は自爆犯によって実行された

assassination [U, C] (政治的な理由による)暗殺 ◇The president survived a number of *assassination* attempts. 大統領は数々の暗殺未遂を切り抜けた ☞ **assassinate** (KILL)

homicide [U, C]《特に米, 法律》殺人(罪) ◇He has been arrested on *homicide* and assault charges. 彼は殺人と暴行の容疑で逮捕された ❶法律用語ではhomicideはmurderより意味の範囲が広く、manslaughterやjustifiable homicide (罪に問われない正当殺人)を含む。☞ **homicidal** (VIOLENT)

slaying [C]《特に米, ジャーナリズム》殺人, 殺害 ◇The papers told of the drug-related *slayings* of five people. 新聞に麻薬絡みの5人の殺害記事が載った ☞ **slay** (KILL)

manslaughter [U]《法律》故殺(罪), (故意のない)殺人 ◇The charge has been reduced to *manslaughter*. 容疑は故殺罪に減刑された

euthanasia [U] 安楽死 ◇They argued in favour of legalizing voluntary *euthanasia* (= people being able to ask for euthanasia for themselves). 彼らは患者の意思による安楽死を合法化することに賛成の方向で論じ合った

N n

naive

naive (または **naïve**) [形]

naive・inexperienced・innocent・trusting・gullible・impressionable
人が世間に疎く、他人のことを信じ[受け入れ]すぎること
【類語訳】世間知らずの、うぶな、未熟な、無垢な、信じやすい、だまされやすい、多感な

▶ an inexperienced/ a trusting/ a gullible/ an impressionable **person**
▶ an innocent/ impressionable **child**
▶ a naive/ an innocent **belief**
▶ very naive/ inexperienced/ innocent/ trusting/ impressionable
▶ politically naive/ inexperienced/ innocent
▶ sexually inexperienced/ innocent
▶ young and inexperienced/ innocent/ impressionable

naive (または **naïve**)《けなして》(人生経験・知識・的確な判断がなく)他人の言うことを信じすぎる、世間知らずの、うぶな ◇He made some particularly *naive* remarks. 彼はずいぶんぶなことをいくつか述べた ◇It would be *naive* of us to think that football is only a game. サッカーをただのゲームだと考えるのは世間知らずというものだろう ❶ *naive* は、さほど頻繁ではないが、人やその行動を表す際に「純真な」という肯定的な意味でも用いられる。◆Their approach to life is refreshingly *naive*. (彼らの人生に取り組む姿勢はさわやかと言っていいほど純真である) [反意] **sophisticated** (SOPHISTICATED), ☞ **naivety** (IGNORANCE).
▶ **naively** [副] ◇I *naively* assumed that I would be paid for the work. 私は何もせずにその仕事で報酬をもらえるものと思いこんでいた

inexperienced《特に書き言葉》知識[経験]不足の、未熟な、不慣れな ◇*Inexperienced* drivers can expect to pay higher insurance premiums. 経験の浅いドライバーは高めの保険料支払いを求められることもある ◇Some of the older teachers are *inexperienced* in modern methods. 年配の教師の中には、今風のやり方に不慣れな者もいる ◇A child of his age is too young and *inexperienced* to recognize danger. 彼くらいの年齢の子どもは、危険を見極めるにはあまりにも幼く未熟である [反意] **experienced** (SOPHISTICATED), ☞ **inexperience** (IGNORANCE).

innocent (性的[邪悪、不快]な物事について)経験がほとんどない、汚れを知らない ◇He prefers to see his teenage daughter as an *innocent* young child. 彼はティーンエイジャーである自分の娘を無垢な子どもだと見ている ☞ **innocence** (IGNORANCE), **childlike** (CHILDISH).

trusting《しばしばほめて》(人を善良[真面目、素直]であると)信じやすい ◇There is a need for a *trusting* relationship between client and consultant. 依頼人とコンサルタントの間には、信頼し合える関係が必要である ◇If you're too *trusting*, other people will take advantage of you. あまりに人を疑わないと、人に利用されますよ ☞ **trust**

(FAITH), **trust** (TRUST).

gullible《けなして》(他人が言うことを真にうけすぎて)だまされやすい ◇The advertisement is aimed at *gullible* young women worried about their weight. その広告は、体重が気になるだまされやすい若い女性をターゲットにしている

impressionable《特に書き言葉》(人・若者が)感化[影響]されやすい、多感な ◇He was a bad influence on the child, who was at an *impressionable* age. 彼は多感な年齢のその子どもに悪い影響を与える人物だった

naked

naked [形]

naked・bare・nude・undressed・in the nude
人が何も服を身に着けていないことを表す
【類語訳】裸の、むき出しの、ヌードの

▶ sb's naked/ bare **skin/ flesh/ shoulder/ thigh/ torso**
▶ **completely/ almost** naked/ bare/ nude

naked 何も服を身に着けていない、裸の ◇She was clutching the sheet around her *naked* body. 彼女は裸の体に巻いたシーツを握りしめていた ◇The prisoners were *stripped naked*. 囚人たちは裸にされた ◇They often wandered around the house *stark naked* (= completely naked). 彼らはしばしば、素っ裸で家をうろうろした ◇*buck naked* (= completely naked)《米》素っ裸の ◇They found him *half naked* and bleeding to death. 彼らは彼が半裸で失血死しているのを見つけた ❶ *naked* は、人、体の部分のいずれも指すことができる。体の部分を指す時に性的なことを言う場合が多い。

bare 何の服にも覆われていない、裸の、むき出しの ◇She likes to walk around in *bare feet*. 彼女は裸足で歩き回るのが好きだ ◇When she stood up she was completely *bare*. 立ち上がった時、彼女は素っ裸だった ❶ *bare* は、人より体の部分を指すのに用いられることが多い。体の部分を指す時は、性的なことを言うとは限らない。人を指すのに用いられる時は、ふつう名詞、連結動詞、completely や totally といった副詞の後に置かれる。

nude (芸術において人間が)何の服も身に着けていない、裸の、ヌードの;裸の人を含んだ ◇He asked me to pose *nude* for him. 私は裸でポーズを取ってくれるよう彼に頼まれた ◇Are there any *nude* scenes in the movie? その映画にヌードシーンはありますか ◇Some of the resorts allow *nude* sunbathing on the beaches. ビーチで全裸で日光浴するのを許可しているリゾートもある

undressed [名詞の前はまれ] 何も服を身に着けていない ◇She began to *get undressed* (= remove her clothes). 彼女は服を脱ぎ始めた ◇He said he felt *undressed* (= felt that he wasn't completely dressed) without a hat. 帽子がないと服を着ていない気分だと彼は言った ◇He was half *undressed* when he answered the door. 戸口に応対に出た時、彼は半裸だった ❶ *undressed* はほぼ常に、get, feel の後で用いられる。be と共に用いられる時はふつう、totally, completely, half といった副詞を伴う。

in the 'nude [フレーズ] 何も服を身に着けていない、裸で、ヌードで ◇She refuses to be photographed *in the nude*. 彼女はヌード写真は撮られたくない ◇He always slept *in the nude*. 彼はいつも裸で眠った ❶*in the nude* は主に、服を何も身に着けていないで人々が活動する時に用いられる。

narrow [形]

narrow・thin・fine
一方からもう他方までの距離が短いことを表す
【類語訳】狭い、細い、薄い

文型&コロケーション
▶ a narrow/ thin/ fine **crack/ strip**
▶ narrow/ thin **shoulders**
▶ (a) thin/ fine **hair/ thread/ layer**
▶ **very/ extremely** narrow/ thin/ fine
▶ **quite** narrow/ thin

narrow (一方からもう他方までの長さが)狭い ◇I love walking down the *narrow* streets in the old city. 古都の狭い通りを歩くのが大好きです ◇I sat next to him on the *narrow* bed. 狭いベッドの上で彼の隣に座った ◇The jacket looked very large across his *narrow* shoulders. そのジャケットは、彼の幅の狭い肩にはかなり大きく見えた ◇There was only a *narrow* gap between the bed and the wall. ベッドと壁の間にはわずかな隙間しかなかった [反意] **wide, broad** (WIDE 2), ☞ **narrow** (SHRINK)
thin (両側[両面]の)間隔が)狭い、細い、薄い ◇Cut the vegetables into *thin* strips. 野菜を千切りにしてください ◇A number of *thin* cracks appeared in the wall. 壁に多くの細い亀裂が現れた ◇The body was hidden beneath a *thin* layer of soil. 死体は薄く土をかけて隠されていた ◇The wind blew cold through his *thin* shirt. 彼の薄いシャツを通して風が冷たく吹きつけた [反意] **thick** (WIDE 2)

ノート narrow と thin の使い分け : narrow は幅の狭さを強調する。thin は幅の薄さ・細さを強調する。◆ *narrow*/*thin* shoulders/strips/cracks (狭い[薄い]肩/細片/ひび)。× *thin* streets. × a *thin* bed/gap. × a *narrow* layer/shirt.

fine とても薄い[細い] ◇His *fine* blond hair came down almost to his shoulders. 彼の細い金髪はほぼ肩まで垂れ下がっていた ◇You could see the sweat in the *fine* hairs above his upper lip. 彼の上唇の上の細い毛に汗が見えるでしょう ◇Acupuncture uses *fine* needles inserted into the patient's skin. 鍼治療は、患者の皮膚に差し込む細い針を用いる ◇I need a brush with a *fine* tip. 先の細い刷毛がいる

national [形]

national・domestic・civil・nationwide・internal・home
外国ではなく特定の国に関連していることを表す
【類語訳】国の、国内の、市民の、全国的な、自国の

文型&コロケーション
▶ national/ domestic/ home **news**
▶ domestic/ internal/ home **affairs**
▶ national/ domestic **politics/ law**
▶ the national/ domestic/ internal/ home **market**
▶ national/ domestic/ internal **security**
▶ domestic/ civil/ internal **unrest/ conflict**
▶ a domestic/ an internal **flight/ crisis**
▶ domestic/ internal **trade**
▶ a national/ civil **emergency**
▶ national/ civil **defence**
▶ a national/ nationwide **campaign/ survey/ strike**
▶ **on** the domestic/ home **front**

national [ふつう名詞の前で] (特定の)国の;特定の国のすべての地域で起こる[を含む]、全国的な ◇He has won medals in both *national* and international competitions. 彼は国内外どちらの競技会でもメダルを獲得した ◇The country has a *national* debt of 80% of GNP. その国は国民総生産の80%に当たる負債を抱えている ◇The state of our hospitals is a *national* disgrace. 我が国の病院の状況は国の恥だ ◇Decide whether it would be better to advertise in a *national* or a local newspaper. 広告を打つのは全国紙、地方紙どちらがよいか決めください [反意] **international** (INTERNATIONAL), **local** ❶*local* は、話題にしている特定の場所[地域]に属する[関連した]物事や住んでいる場所に関連した物事を指すのに用いられる。◆ A *local* man was accused of the murder. (地元の男が殺人容疑で起訴された)。◆ *decisions* made at a *local* rather than national level (全国レベルというより地方レベルでなされる決定)。☞ **nation** (COUNTRY 1)
▶ **nationally** [副] ◇He's a talented athlete who competes *nationally* and internationally. 彼は国内外で競い合う才能ある運動選手である ◇The programme was broadcast *nationally*. その番組は全国放送された
domestic [ふつう名詞の前で] (特定の)国の、国内の ◇The company has made losses in both its *domestic* and international operations. その会社は、国内事業と国際事業の双方で損失を出してきた ◇He was a chief White House adviser on *domestic* policy. 彼は国内政策に関するホワイトハウスの主席顧問であった [反意] **foreign, overseas** (FOREIGN)
▶ **domestically** [副] ◇*domestically* produced goods 国内生産された商品

ノート national と domestic の使い分け : national は、international、local と対照を成す。domestic は、international (または foreign) とは対照を成すが、local とは対照を成さない。domestic は、ビジネスや政治関連で用いられることがほとんどで、national はさらに使用範囲が広い。

civil [名詞の前で] (特定の国に居住する)市民の ◇Both are veterans of the country's long *civil war* (= between groups of people in the same country). 二人とも、その国の長い内戦を戦った人たちである ◇Some groups have been calling for a non-violent *civil disobedience* campaign. 市民の非暴力不服従運動を求めつづけているグループがいくつかある ❶*civil* は特に、国内の一般人を巻き込む問題[暴力]を指すのに用いられる。war, unrest, conflict, disorder, disturbance, disobedience などと結びつく。
nationwide [ふつう名詞の前で] 特定の国の全地域で起こる[に存在する] ◇The study uses data from a *nationwide* survey of 5,000 people. その研究では5千人の全国調査のデータが用いられる ◇The police conducted a *nationwide* hunt for the missing girl. 警察は行方不明の少女の全国的な捜索を実施した
▶ **nationwide** [副] ◇The company has over 500

stores *nationwide*. その会社は全国に500以上の店舗を所有している

ノート **national** と **nationwide** の使い分け：*nationwide* は特に，全国的に人々が参加する[全国を移動する]活動[イベント]に用いられる．campaign, drive, strike, survey, tour, hunt, search などと結びつく．*national* は，全国的なサービスをする組織[機関]に用いられることが多いが，*nationwide* はこの形では用いられない．×a *nationwide* health service．×*nationwide* radio.

internal [名詞の前で] (特定の)国の，国内の ◇Nations should be left to resolve their own *internal* difficulties. 国内問題の解決は国家に委ねるべきである ◇The civil war led to considerable *internal* migration (= people moving to different areas within a country). 内戦で大量の人々が国内をさ迷うことになった 反意 **external** (FOREIGN)

ノート **domestic** と **internal** の使い分け：2語の間に意味・用法の違いはほとんどない．*domestic* のほうが頻繁に用いられ，特に，ビジネス・政治における一般的な状況で，currency, demand, service, economy, policy, issue, law などと結びつく．*internal* は紛争状態の話に用いられることがやや多く，conflict, strife, division, self-government, security などと結びつく．

home [名詞の前で] (特に英) 自国の ◇The newspaper has different sections for *home* news, international and foreign news. その新聞は，国内ニュース，国際及び国外ニュースに対して異なる欄を設けている ◇The *Home* Secretary has drawn up national guidelines. 《英》内務大臣は国としての指針を策定した ❶ (英) において *home* は，Home Office (内務省)，Home Secretary (内務大臣) など，国内問題を扱う政府の省庁や大臣の名称に用いられるが．反意 **foreign, overseas** (FOREIGN)

natural 形

natural・genetic・intuitive・instinctive・innate・congenital・hereditary
人や動物の特徴や能力，病気が先天性のものであることを表す
【類語訳】生まれつきの，生来の，生得の，遺伝的な，本能的な，先天的な，根っからの

文型&コロケーション
▸ a natural/ a genetic/ an innate **characteristic**
▸ natural/ intuitive/ instinctive/ innate **ability**
▸ natural/ intuitive/ instinctive/ innate **understanding**
▸ natural/ intuitive/ innate **sense** (of sth)
▸ natural/ intuitive/ innate **intelligence**
▸ natural/ instinctive/ innate **knowledge**
▸ natural/ instinctive/ innate **desires/ needs**
▸ natural/ innate **instinct**
▸ a natural/ an intuitive/ an instinctive/ an innate **response**
▸ a natural/ an intuitive/ an instinctive **reaction**
▸ a genetic/ congenital/ hereditary **disease/ condition/ disorder**
▸ purely natural/ intuitive/ instinctive

natural (人[動物]の)行動・性質・感情が)生まれつきの，生来の，生得の ◇Hunting is one of a cat's *natural* instincts. 狩猟は猫の生来の本能の一つである ◇His *natural* gifts as a preacher meant he was in great demand. その説教師としての天分により，彼は引く手あまたとなった ◇It's only *natural* to worry about your children. 子どものことを心配するのはごく自然である ❶ *natural* は，名詞の前に置いて特定の種類の性質[能力]を持って生まれた人を表すのに用いられる．◆He's a *natural* rebel/leader. (彼は生まれついての反逆者[指導者]である).

▸**naturally** 副 ◇She was *naturally* gifted when it came to music. 音楽に関して言えば，彼女は生まれつきの才能があった

genetic 遺伝子によって引き起こされる，遺伝的な ❶ gene (遺伝子) は生物の細胞を構成するもので，身体的特徴を支配し親から子どもへ伝えられる．◆A person's intelligence is based on both *genetic* and environmental factors. (人の知性は，遺伝と環境両方の因子に基づいている). ◆There are about 4,000 inherited human *genetic* diseases. (人間が受け継ぐ遺伝病は約4千名よ)

▸**genetically** 副 ◇*genetically* determined characteristics 遺伝的に決定された特質

intuitive (考えが)直観的な；(人が)直観力のある，直観的にわかる ◇Our approach to the subject can be strictly rational or wholly *intuitive*. そのテーマに対する我々のアプローチは，厳密に理詰めであるかもしれないし完全に直観的であるかもしれない ◇I don't think that women are necessarily more *intuitive* than men. 女性が必ずしも男性より直観的だとは思わない ☞**intuition** (INSTINCT), **intuition** (IDEA 2)

▸**intuitively** 副 ◇*Intuitively*, she knew that he was lying. 彼女は直観的に彼が嘘をついているとわかっていた

instinctive 本能的な ◇A bird's knowledge of its migratory route is partly learnt and partly *instinctive*. 渡りのルートに関する鳥の知識は，一部分は学んだものであり，一部分は本能的なものである ◇My *instinctive* reaction was to deny everything. 私の本能的な反応はすべてを否定することだった ☞**instinct** (INSTINCT), **instinct** (IDEA 2)

▸**instinctively** 副 ◇I knew *instinctively* that something was wrong. 何かが間違っていると，私には本能的にわかっていた

innate 《ややフォーマル》(人[動物]の)行動・性質・感情が)生まれつきの，生来の，生得の ◇Many children seem to have an *innate* sense of justice. 多くの子どもたちは，生まれながらに正義感を持っているように思える

▸**innately** 副 ◇Some philosophers viewed human nature as *innately* good. 哲学者の中には，人間の本質が性善であるとみる者もいた

ノート **natural** と **innate** の使い分け：これらの語の間に，意味・用法の違いはほとんどない．*natural* はより頻繁に用いられ，フォーマル度は低い．*innate* は，*natural* の他の意味と混同される可能性がある場合に用いられることがある．たとえば，*innate* response は，人・物事の生来の反応を指す．*natural* response は，人の自然な反応を指す傾向が強い．◆Anxiety at a perceived threat is an *innate* response in any animal. (知覚した脅威に対する不安は，あらゆる動物における生来の反応である). ◆It's a *natural* response to keep your troubles quiet. (トラブルを内密にしておくことは自然な反応である). ☞**natural** (OBVIOUS)

congenital (病気・症状が)先天的な；(性質が)根っからの ◇*Congenital* abnormalities can occur in babies whose mothers drink heavily. 先天性異常は，母親が大酒飲みの赤ん坊に起こる可能性がある ◇He's a *congenital* liar! 彼は根っからの嘘つきだ

hereditary (病気が)遺伝性の ◇It's a *hereditary* disorder that can cause abnormal growth. それは異常な発育を招きかねない遺伝性疾患である

nature 名

1 nature・character・essence・stuff・spirit
物事の基本的な[最も重要な]質を表す
【類語訳】本質, 本性, 性質, 特質, 特色, 根本, 根幹, 素質

▸文型&コロケーション
▸ **in** nature/ character/ essence/ spirit
▸ the **very** nature/ character/ essence/ stuff/ spirit of sth
▸ the **real/ true** nature/ character/ essence/ spirit of sth
▸ the **individual/ fundamental** nature/ character/ essence of sth
▸ to **preserve/ capture/ convey/ reflect** the nature/ character/ essence of sth
▸ to **consider/ understand/ reveal/ define** the nature/ character/ essence of sth

nature [単数で] 本質, 本性, 性質 ◇It's difficult to define the exact *nature* of the problem. その問題の正確な本質を定義するのは難しい ◇My work is very specialized in *nature*. 私の仕事は本質的に非常に専門化されたものだ ◇The future **by its very nature** is uncertain. 未来は, まさにその性質上不確かなものである ☞ **nature** (PERSONALITY)

character [C, ふつう単数で, U] (他とは異なる)特質, 特色 ; (物事・場所の)性質 ◇The *character* of the neighbourhood hasn't changed at all. 近隣の特徴は全く変わっていない ◇I love the delicate *character* of the light in the evening. 夜の灯りの優美なところが大好きです ☞ **character** (PERSONALITY)

> ノート **nature** と **character** の使い分け : nature は特に, problem, work, society, strategy, risks, future といった抽象的な事柄の基本的な性質について用いる。character は, 場所・建物などの物理的な性質・特徴, 特に, 自分の感覚・感情に訴え, 他とは異なるものや特別なものに見せる性質・特徴について用いることが多い。

essence [U] 最も重要な性質[特徴], 根本, 根幹, 本質 ◇Like so many peasant foods, the *essence* of pasta is its simplicity. 数多くの農民の食べ物同様に, パスタの本質はその簡素さにある ◇In *essence* (= when you consider the most important points), your situation isn't so different from mine. 本質において, あなたの状況は私の状況とあまり違わない ☞ **essential** (FUNDAMENTAL)

stuff [U] 最も重要な特徴, 本質 ; 素材, 素質 ◇Parades and marches were the very *stuff* of politics in the region. パレードと行進はその地域における政治のまさに本質だった ◇Let's see what *stuff* you're made of (= what sort of person you are). あなたにどんな素質があるか見てみましょう

spirit [単数で, U] 意図, 真意 ◇The referee should try to obey the *spirit* as well as the letter (= the narrow meaning of the words) of the law. 裁定人は, 法の文言だけでなくその精神も守るようにしなければならない

2 nature・the environment・wildlife・life・ecosystem・the wild・the natural world
世界およびそこに棲む動植物

【類語訳】自然界, 自然環境, 野生動物, 生物, 生態系

▸文型&コロケーション
▸ **in** nature/ the environment/ an ecosystem/ the wild
▸ (a/ an/ the) **marine/ terrestrial/ aquatic** environment/ wildlife/ life/ ecosystem
▸ to **protect** the environment/ wildlife/ ... life/ the natural world
▸ to **damage** the environment/ wildlife/ ... life
▸ to **benefit/ preserve/ save/ affect/ destroy** the environment/ wildlife

nature (または **Nature**) [U] (人によって作られたものではない)自然界 ; (人によってコントロールされていない)自然のままの状態 ◇Take time to appreciate the beauties of *nature*. 時間をかけて自然の美観を味わいなさい ◇**The forces of nature** are constantly reshaping our world. 自然の力は常に世界を作り変えている ◇It seemed against **the laws of nature** that such a creature could even exist. そんな生物の存在さえありうるとは自然の法則に反するように思えた ◇Just let *nature* take its course. 自然はただ成り行きに任せたままにしておきなさい ◇Her illness was *Nature*'s way of telling her to do less. 彼女の病気は, 自然が彼女に頑張りすぎないよう伝えているのだった ❶動植物や自然界について語る場合, 定冠詞を付けて the nature とすることはできない。×the beauties of *the nature*. また, 自分を取り巻く環境について言う場合は, 別の語を用いるほうがよい。×They stopped to admire *nature*. ◆They stopped to admire the scenery/countryside. (彼らは景色/田園地方をめぐるために立ち止まった). ☞ **countryside, scenery** (COUNTRY 2)

▸ **natural** 形 ◇a country's *natural* resources (= its coal, oil, forests, etc.) 国の天然資源
▸ **naturally** 副 ◇*naturally* occurring chemicals 自然に存在する化学物質

the environment [単数で] (人間の活動によって脅かされたり損なわれたりする)自然環境 ◇There is increasing public concern about pollution of *the environment*. 環境汚染への社会的関心が高まっている
▸ **environmental** 形 ◇the *environmental* impact of pollution 公害の環境への影響
▸ **environmentally** 副 ◇an *environmentally* sensitive area (= one that is easily damaged or that contains rare animals, plants, etc.) 環境保全地域

wildlife [U] 野生動物 ◇Development of the area would endanger *wildlife*. その地域の開発で野生動物は危険にさらされるだろう ◇The area is an important *wildlife* habitat. その地域は野生動物の重要な生息環境である

life [U] 生物 ◇pond *life* 池の生物 ◇Yet more species of plant and animal *life* die out as their very specialized habitat is disturbed. 非常に特殊化した生息環境が乱されるにつれ, さらに多くの動植物の種が絶滅する ◇Is there intelligent *life* on other planets? 他の惑星には知的生命体はいるのか

ecosystem [C] 生態系, エコシステム ◇Islands often support delicate *ecosystems* that evolved without any need for defence. 島はしばしば, 防御をまったく必要とせずに発達した脆弱な生態系を支えている

the wild [C, 単数で] (人によってコントロールされていない)自然環境, 野生 ◇The bird is too tame now to survive in *the wild*. その鳥は今あまりに飼いならされており, 自然の中で生き延びることができない ◇The animals were released back into *the wild* when they had recovered. その動物たちは回復すると、野生に戻された

the ˌnatural ˈworld [C, 単数で]（人間の手の入っていない）自然界 ◇Many medicines are made from ingredients found in *the natural world*. 多くの薬は自然界で発見される原料から作られる

neat 形

neat・tidy・ordered・orderly・uncluttered
すべてが注意深く整えられ、物があるべき場所にあるような状態
【類語訳】整然とした、整頓された、整った、きちんとした、秩序のある、すっきりとした、さっぱりとした

文型&コロケーション
▶neat/ tidy/ orderly **rows**
▶a neat/ a tidy/ an orderly **arrangement**
▶a neat/ a tidy/ an uncluttered **house/ room**
▶to **look/ keep** sth neat/ tidy
▶to **leave** sth neat/ tidy/ uncluttered
▶a **nice** neat/ tidy...
▶**clean/ nice and** neat/ tidy

neat 《ほめて》整然とした、整頓された、整った、きちんとした ◇She was wearing a *neat* black suit. 彼女はきちんとした黒のスーツを着ていた ◇You've got very *neat* handwriting! あなたの筆跡はとてもきれいだね ◇He sorted his papers into a *neat* pile. 彼は書類を分類してきちんと積み重ねた ◇This hairstyle is easy to keep *neat and tidy*. この髪型はきちんとまとめておきやすい ☞ neat (EFFICIENT)
▶**neatly** 副 ◇The tools were *neatly* arranged on the bench. 道具は作業台の上にきちんと並べられていた

tidy 《特に英, ほめて》（場所が）整頓された ◇Someone needs to keep the place *tidy*. 誰かがその場所を整頓しておく必要がある ◇The house is much *tidier* now. お家(うち)は前にもましてずいぶん片付いていますね ◇The room was clean and *tidy*. 部屋はきれいに片付いていた 反意 **untidy** (UNTIDY), ☞ **tidy** (EFFICIENT), **tidy** (TIDY)
▶**tidily** 副 ◇Tubes of paint were set out *tidily*. チューブ入りの絵具がきちんと並べられていた

ordered [ふつう名詞の前で] 注意深く整えられた、整然とした、秩序のある ◇She tried not to think about the turmoil he had caused in her *ordered* existence. 彼女は、規則正しい自分の生活の中で引き起こされた騒ぎについて考えないようにした ◇a well-*ordered* society 秩序だった社会 ❶ordered はふつう物理的な物[場所]ではなく、人の生活[社会, 制度]が整えられていることを表す. life, existence, society, universe, structure などと結びつく. 反意 **disordered** (UNTIDY), ☞ **order** (EFFICIENCY)

orderly [ふつうほめて] きちんと論理的に整えられた、整然とした ◇The vegetables were planted in *orderly* rows. 野菜は整然と列をなして植えられていた ☞ **order** (EFFICIENCY)

ノート neat, tidy, orderly の使い分け：neat が最も一般的で、人の外見、場所、rowやpileといった物の配置に用いることができる. tidy はふつう、roomやdeskといった場所に用いられる. orderly はふつう、物が列をなして[積み重ねて]整頓された状態を表す.

uncluttered 《ほめて》すっきりとした、さっぱりとした ◇Keep the work area *uncluttered* and clean. 作業区域はすっきりときれいにしておきなさい 反意 **cluttered** (UNTIDY)

necessary 形 ☞ ESSENTIAL

necessary・compulsory・mandatory・requisite・obligatory・forced・involuntary
人がしなければならない[備えなければならない]ことを表す
【類語訳】必要な、必須の、義務的な、強制的な、強いられた

文型&コロケーション
▶it's necessary/ compulsory/ mandatory/ obligatory **for** sb **to do** sth
▶it's necessary/ compulsory/ mandatory/ obligatory **to do** sth
▶forced/ involuntary **repatriation**
▶**almost/ legally** compulsory/ obligatory

necessary （目的[理由]のために）必要な ◇It may be *necessary* to buy a new one. 新しいものを買う必要があるかもしれない ◇Only use your car when absolutely *necessary*. 絶対に必要な時にだけ車を使うようにしなさい ◇*If necessary*, you can contact me at home. 必要なら、自宅にご連絡ください ◇I'll make the *necessary* arrangements. 必要な手配をしましょう 反意 **unnecessary**, ☞ **necessary** (INEVITABLE)

compulsory 《ややフォーマル》（法律[規則]上）必須の、義務的な ◇It is *compulsory* for all motorcyclists to wear helmets. ヘルメットをかぶるのは、バイクに乗るすべての人の義務である ◇English is a *compulsory* subject at this level. 英語はこのレベルでは必須科目である 反意 **voluntary, optional** (VOLUNTARY 1), ☞ **compulsion** (PRESSURE 2)

mandatory 《フォーマル》（法律[規則]上）義務的な、強制的な ◇It is *mandatory* for blood banks to test all donated blood for the virus. 献血された血液をすべてウィルス検査することは、血液銀行の義務である ◇The offence carries a *mandatory* life sentence. その犯罪には強制的に終身刑が伴う

requisite [名詞の前で]《フォーマル》（特定の目的のために）必要な ◇She lacks the *requisite* experience for the job. 彼女にはその仕事に必要な経験が欠けている

obligatory 《フォーマル》（法律[規則]上）必須の、義務的な ◇It is *obligatory* for all employees to wear protective clothing. すべての従業員は防護服を着用することが義務づけられている ❶obligatory は時として、しばしば存在する[行われる]が実際には全く必要ない物事について、名詞の前に置いておどけて用いられる. ◆The hotel has a terrace with comfy chairs for that *obligatory* cocktail. （そのホテルには、お決まりのカクテルのために快適な椅子を備えたテラスがある.）反意 **optional** (VOLUNTARY 1)

ノート compulsory, mandatory, obligatory の使い分け：compulsory は特に、教育・ビジネス・雇用に関して用いられる. ◆*compulsory* education/schooling/reading/subjects（義務教育／(通信教育の)義務的スクーリング／必須の読み物／必須科目）. ◆*compulsory* insurance/liquidation/purchase/redundancy/retirement（強制保険／強制清算／強制収用／強制解雇／定年退職）. mandatory は特に、法律関係で用いられる. ◆a *mandatory* sentence/penalty/duty/requirement（強制的な判決／強制的刑罰／必須の義務／必須条件）. obligatory は、

need

たとえばスポーツ[職場]において,安全に関する規則・法律について用いられることが多い. ◆Recently safety regulations have made it *obligatory* for all competitors to wear fist protectors. (最近,安全規則で,すべての出場選手に拳のプロテクターの着用が義務づけられた.)

forced [ふつう名詞の前で] 強制的な,強いられた ◇Many are unhappy about the *forced* repatriation of the refugees. 多くの人が難民の本国への強制送還について不満に思っている ◇I hope there will be no need for the *forced* sale of any property. いかなる財産であれ競売処分の必要がないことを望んでいます

involuntary [ふつう名詞の前で]《ややフォーマル,書き言葉》強制的な,強いられた ◇The distinction between voluntary and *involuntary* unemployment is often blurred. 自発的失業とやむえない失業の区別はしばしば不鮮明である 反意 **voluntary** (VOLUNTARY 1)

ノート **forced**と**involuntary**の使い分け: forcedはしばしば,人が誰かに強制的に何かを行わせることを表す. involuntaryは強制するのが別の誰かではなく,周りの状況であることを表す. ×*forced* unemployment. しかし, involuntaryはまた,よりフォーマルな直接的でない言い方として,人が誰かに強制的に何かを行わせたり,決断させたりする場合に用いられることがある. ◆the *forced/involuntary* repatriation of the refugees (難民の強制送還)

need 名

need・requirement・necessity・essential・want
自分が必要とする物,その物が必要とされる状況
【類語訳】必要,必要性,要求物,必然性,必需品

文型&コロケーション
▸ a need/ requirement/ necessity **for** sth
▸ **basic** needs/ requirements/ necessities/ essentials
▸ a/ an **pressing/ urgent/ immediate/ absolute/ fundamental** need/ requirement/ necessity
▸ a **political/ social/ physical** need/ requirement/ necessity
▸ **human/ bodily** needs/ wants
▸ the **bare** necessities/ essentials
▸ to **have** a need/ a requirement/ wants
▸ to **meet/ satisfy** sb's needs/ requirements/ wants
▸ to **understand/ be aware of/ remove/ reduce** the need/ requirement/ necessity for sth

need [単数で, U] 必要(性) ◇There is an urgent *need* for qualified teachers. 資格を持った教師の必要に迫られている ◇There is *no need* for you to get up early tomorrow. あなたは明日は早起きしなくてもいいですよ ◇I *had no need to* open the letter — I knew what it would say. その手紙を開ける必要はなかった — 何と書いてあるかわかっていたから ◇The house is *in need of* a thorough clean. その家は徹底的に掃除する必要がある ❶ needs [複数形で] (快適に生活する[ほしい物を手に入れる]ために備えなければならない物を指す. ◆First we will assess your financial *needs*. (まず,財政的なニーズを査定します.) ◆Your role will be to support children with special educational *needs*. (あなたの役割は,特別な教育的ニーズのある子どもたちの支援ということになります.) ☞ **need** (DESIRE)

requirement [C]《フォーマル》必要な物,要求物 ◇Our immediate *requirement* is extra staff. 我々が緊急に求めるのはスタッフの増員である ◇These goods are *surplus to requirements* (= more than we need). これらの商品は過剰なものです

necessity [C]《ややフォーマル》必要,必要性; 必需品 ◇There had never been any *necessity* for her to go out to work. 彼女は働きに出る必要があった試しはなかった ◇Many people cannot even afford basic *necessities* such as food and clothing. 多くの人々が食糧や衣類といった基本的な必需品を買う余裕さえない ◇Air-conditioning is an absolute *necessity* in this climate. この気候では,エアコンが絶対必需品である

essential [C,ふつう複数で] (特定の状況で[特定の物事を行うために])なくてはならないもの ◇I only had time to pack the bare *essentials* (= the most necessary things). 最低限必要なものを詰め込む時間しかなかった ◇The studio had all the *essentials* like heating and running water. そのスタジオには暖房や水道のような必要なものはすべてあった ❶ essentialsはしばしば, bare, basicと結びつく. ☞ **essential** (ESSENTIAL)

want [C,ふつう複数で] (生きるために)必要なもの ◇The snail does not need to travel far to satisfy all its bodily *wants*. カタツムリは,身体上必要なものをすべて充足させるのに遠方まで移動する必要はない ☞ **want** (DESIRE)

ノート **necessities, essentials, wants**の使い分け: wantsはふつう,これらの中で最も基本的かつ身体的なもので,生き続けるために体が必要とするものを指す. human, bodilyと結びつくことが多い. essentialsはより実際的であり,特定の物事・活動を行うために基本的なものを指すのがふつうである. necessitiesは,より一般的な単語で,身体的に必要なもの・実際的に必要なものの両方に用いられる.

need 動

need・require・rely on/upon sb/sth・want・call for sth・demand
不可欠な[非常に重要な]人や物事を欲することを表す
【類語訳】必要とする,依存する

文型&コロケーション
▸ to **really** need/ require/ want/ call for/ demand sth
▸ to **just** need/ require/ want sth
▸ to **still** need/ require/ rely on/ call for sth
▸ to **urgently** need/ require/ want sb/ sth
▸ to **clearly/ obviously** need/ require/ call for/ demand sth

need [他]《進行形はまれ》(不可欠[非常に重要]なため)必要とする ◇Do you *need* any help? 何かお手伝いしましょうか ◇Don't go — I might *need* you. 行かないでくれ — 君が必要になるかもしれない ◇They badly *needed* a change. 彼らは大いに変化を必要としていた ◇Food aid is urgently *needed*. 食糧援助が緊急に必要である ◇This shirt *needs* washing. このシャツは洗う必要がある ◇I *need to* get some sleep. 少し眠らなくちゃ ☞ **need** (DESIRE)

require [他]《進行形はまれ》《フォーマル》必要とする; (人・物事に)依存する ◇This condition *requires* urgent treatment. この状態は緊急治療が必要である ◇These lentils do not *require* soaking before cooking. これらのヒラマメは調理前に水にひたす必要はありません ◇The situation *required that* he be present. 彼がいなくてはいけない状況だった

re'ly on/upon sb/sth 句動詞 《何かをし続けるために人・ものを[に])必要とする[依存する]》◇As babies, we *rely* entirely *on* others for food. 赤ん坊の頃は、私たちは食べ物についてはまったく他人頼りである ◇These days we *rely heavily on* computers to organize our work. 今日では仕事をまとめる上で我々はコンピュータに大きく依存している ◇The industry *relies on* the price of raw materials remaining low. その産業は低く留まっている原材料価格に依存している ❶ rely upon sb/sth は、rely on sb/sth よりフォーマルである。☞ **rely on/upon sb/sth** (TRUST)

want [他] 《進行形はまれ》《ややインフォーマル、特に話し言葉》必要とする ◇What this house *wants* is a good clean. この家には十分な清掃が必要である ◇The plants *want* watering daily. それらの植物には毎日の水やりが必要だ ❶ どこかで人が *want* される場合、その場所[目的のため]にいることが求められている。◆ She's *wanted* immediately in the director's office. (彼女はすぐ重役のオフィスにくるよう求められた) ◆ Excuse me, you're *wanted* on the phone. (すみません、お電話が入っています)

'call for sth 句動詞 《進行形なし》《状況が物事を)必要とする、(人に物事を)必要とさせる ◇The situation *calls for* prompt action. 状況は迅速な行動を求めている ◇I've been promoted. 'This *calls for* a celebration!' 「昇進したよ」「これはお祝いしなくちゃね」 ❶ call for sth は主に、This calls for a celebration/a drink/patience/new ways of thinking. (これはお祝い/一杯飲む/がまん/新しい考えでなくちゃね) という句で、特定の状況で必要とされるものについて語る場合に用いる。

demand [他] 《進行形なし》《ややフォーマル》(首尾よく行われるために)必要とする ◇This sport *demands* both speed and strength. このスポーツにはスピードと力の両方が求まれる ❶ *demand* は一般的に、力・勤勉・高い道徳水準に関する人間の質を必要とする状況について用いられる。 ◆ This *demands* commitment/skill/courage/mental effort/maturity/respect/honesty. (これには、献身/スキル/勇気/精神的努力/成熟/敬意/誠実さが要求される)

negative 形

negative・bleak・gloomy・depressing・dark・pessimistic・miserable・downbeat・black
将来に対して希望や熱意がなく、悪い物事が起こることを予想する人や態度を表す
【類語訳】悲観的な、後ろ向きの、消極的な、見通しの暗い、憂鬱な、意気消沈させる、陰鬱な、暗い、悲惨な、希望のない

downbeat	negative	miserable
	bleak	dark
	gloomy	black
	depressing	
	pessimistic	

文型&コロケーション

▸ negative/ pessimistic/ miserable **about** sth
▸ a negative/ bleak/ gloomy/ pessimistic **outlook**
▸ negative/ gloomy/ depressing/ dark/ black **thoughts**
▸ a negative/ bleak/ gloomy/ pessimistic **view**
▸ a negative/ gloomy/ depressing/ pessimistic **conclusion**
▸ a negative/ gloomy/ pessimistic **report**

▸ to **paint** a negative/ bleak/ gloomy/ depressing/ pessimistic **picture** (of sb/ sth)
▸ to **sound** negative/ gloomy/ pessimistic/ downbeat
▸ to **look** bleak/ gloomy/ pessimistic/ black
▸ **very** negative/ bleak/ gloomy/ depressing/ dark/ pessimistic/ miserable/ black
▸ **extremely** negative/ bleak/ depressing/ dark/ pessimistic
▸ **rather** negative/ bleak/ gloomy/ depressing/ pessimistic/ miserable

negative 悲観的な、後ろ向きの; 希望[熱意]のない、消極的な ◇He's been rather *negative* about the idea. 彼はずっとその考えにかなり否定的だ ◇Scientists have a fairly *negative attitude* to the theory. 科学者たちはその理論に対してかなり否定的な態度を取っている ◇We try to pinpoint the cause of any *negative* feelings. 私たちはあらゆる後ろ向きな感情の原因を特定しようとしている ◇'He probably won't show up.' 'Don't be so *negative*.' 「たぶん彼は来ないだろう」「そんなに悲観的になるな」 反意 **positive** (OPTIMISTIC), **positive** (GOOD❻), ☞ **negative** (HARMFUL)

bleak (状況が改善の)見込みがない、見通しの暗い ◇The future looks *bleak* for the fishing industry. 漁業の将来は暗い ◇The report paints an unnecessarily *bleak* picture of the town. その報告書は町の未来を必要以上に暗く描いている
▸ **bleakly** 副 ◇'There seems no hope,' she said *bleakly*. 「希望はないみたい」と彼女は暗い調子で言った

gloomy (態度・状況が改善の)見込みがない、見通しの暗い ◇The committee's view was in fact far from *gloomy*. 委員会の見解は実際、決して悲観的なものではなかった ◇We're quietly confident despite the *gloomy* predictions. 暗い予測にもかかわらず、私たちはひそかに自信を持っている ☞ **gloom** (GLOOM)

ノート bleak と gloomy の使い分け：多くの場合、どちらの単語も用いることができる。 ◆ Suddenly, the future didn't look so *bleak/gloomy* after all. (突然、将来の見通しは結局のところそこまで暗く/陰鬱なものではないように思えた)。 ◆ to paint a *bleak/gloomy* picture of the situation (見通しの暗い状況を描く)。だが、bleak は特に、将来の状況を表すのに用いられる。 ◆ The future/outlook is/looks *bleak*. (将来/前途は暗い/暗く映る)。gloomy はこのように用いることもできるが、将来[状況]に対する見解を表すのに用いられるほうが多い。 ◆ a *gloomy* forecast/prognosis (暗い予想)。 ◆ *gloomy* predictions/prospects/thoughts (暗い予測/見通し/考え)。

depressing (状況が)憂鬱な、意気消沈させる ◇Looking for a job these days can be very *depressing*. 近頃の職探しは非常に気がめいることもある ◇He found the whole visit a *depressing* experience. 彼はその訪問全体に憂鬱なものを感じた ☞ **depress** (DISCOURAGE❷), **depressed** (DEPRESSED), **depression** (GLOOM)
▸ **depressingly** 副 ◇a *depressingly* familiar experience 情けなくなるほどありきたりの体験

dark (態度・時が)陰鬱な、暗い ◇The film is a *dark* vision of the future. その映画は暗い未来像である ◇The theatre stayed open even in the *darkest days* of the war. その劇場は戦時中の最も暗い時期でさえ開業していた

pessimistic 悲観的な ◇They appeared surprisingly *pessimistic* about their chances of winning. 彼らは勝算については驚くほど悲観的なようだった ◇He seems to

take a rather *pessimistic* view of human nature. 彼は人間の本質をかなり悲観的に捉えているようだ [反意] **optimistic** (OPTIMISTIC)
▶**pessimism** [名] [U] ◇a mood of *pessimism* 悲観的な雰囲気 [反意] **optimism** (HOPE [名] 1)

miserable (状況が)非常に不幸[不快]に感じさせる, 悲惨な ◇I spent a *miserable* weekend alone at home. 家で一人で惨めな週末を過ごした ◇What a *miserable* day (= cold and wet)! 何て嫌な天気なんだ ◇The play was a *miserable failure*. その芝居は悲惨なほどの失敗だった ☞ **misery** (DISTRESS)
▶**miserably** [副] ◇He *failed miserably* as an actor. 彼は俳優としては無残にも失敗した

[ノート] **depressing** と **miserable** の使い分け: depressing は特に, 他人が抱えている問題や悪い一般的世界情勢に対する感情を示すのに用いられる. miserable はふつう, 自分自身の状況について, 情けない気持ちを表すのに用いられる. ◆The report on the state of water pollution paints a *depressing* picture. (水質汚染の状況に関する報告書は憂鬱な実態を表している). ✗The report on the state of water pollution paints a *miserable* picture. ◆My school days were thoroughly *miserable*. (私の学生時代はまったく悲惨だった). ✗My school days were thoroughly *depressing*.

downbeat 《ややインフォーマル》(活気がなく)憂鬱な; (将来に対して)希望のない ◇The overall mood of the meeting was *downbeat*. 会議の雰囲気は全体的に重苦しかった ◇Their assessment of the UK's economic prospects is *downbeat*. 英国の経済見通しに対する彼らの評価は悲観的だ [反意] **upbeat** (OPTIMISTIC)

black 《ややインフォーマル》希望のない; 非常に憂鬱な ◇The future looks pretty *black*, I'm afraid. 残念だが, お先真っ暗だ ◇It's been another *black* day for the northeast with the announcement of further job losses. さらなる雇用喪失の発表で, 今日もまた北東部では陰鬱な日であった

negotiate [動]

negotiate • deal with sb/sth • hold talks • bargain • do a deal • haggle
合意に達するために人と話すことを表す
【類語訳】交渉する, 協議する, 取り決めをする

[文型&コロケーション]
▶to negotiate/ deal/ hold talks/ bargain/ do a deal/ haggle **with** sb/ sth
▶to negotiate/ hold talks/ do a deal **on** sth
▶to deal with sb/ hold talks/ bargain/ do a deal/ haggle **over** sth

negotiate [自] (合意・紛争解決のために)交渉する, 協議する ◇The government will not *negotiate* with terrorists. 政府はテロリストたちとは交渉しないだろう ◇We are *negotiating for* the release of the prisoners. 我々は囚われている人たちの解放に向けて交渉を行っている ◇They have refused to *negotiate* on this issue. 彼らはこの問題についての協議を拒んでいる ◇Her financial adviser is *negotiating on her behalf*. 彼女の財務顧問が彼女に代わって交渉をしている ◇Are the employers really willing to *negotiate*? 雇用者側には本当に交渉の用意があるんですか

▶**negotiation** [名] [C, ふつう複数で, U] ◇peace/trade/wage *negotiations* 和平/貿易/賃金交渉 ◇They begin another *round of negotiations* today. 今日, 再度一連の交渉が始まる ◇The rent is a *matter for negotiation* between the landlord and tenant. 賃貸料は家主と賃借人との交渉で決める ◇The issue is still *under negotiation*. その問題は依然として交渉中です

'deal with sb/sth [句動詞] (人・会社・組織と)商取引を行う[交渉する] ◇We *deal with* companies all over Europe. 我々はヨーロッパ中の会社と取り引きしています ◇He had *dealt with* Mr Simpson on several occasions. 彼はシンプソン氏と何度か交渉を持っていた ☞ **dealings** (COMMUNICATION)

,hold 'talks [フレーズ] (政府・組織(の指導者たち)が合意・問題解決のために)交渉する, 協議する ◇The two governments *held* secret *talks* on the nuclear threat. その二か国の政府は核の脅威について秘密裏に会談を持った
▶**talks** [名] [複数で] ◇arms/pay/peace *talks* 軍備/賃金/和平交渉

bargain [自] (価格・条件などについて)交渉する ◇He said he wasn't prepared to *bargain*. 彼は交渉の用意はないと言った ◇In the market dealers were *bargaining* with growers over the price of coffee. 市場では, 販売業者たちがコーヒーの価格に関して栽培業者たちと交渉をしていた ☞ **bargain** (AGREEMENT)

,do a 'deal [フレーズ] (ビジネス・政治において特定条件について)取り決めをする ◇We *did a deal* with the management on overtime. 我々は時間外労働について経営陣と取り決めを行った ☞ **deal** (AGREEMENT)

haggle [自] (価格について)やり合う ◇I left him in the market *haggling* over the price of a shirt. シャツの価格についてやり合う彼を市場に置いてきた

negotiator [名]

negotiator • mediator • intermediary • arbitrator • go-between • peacemaker • liaison officer
紛争を解決するために, 人やグループの間の意思疎通を手助けしようとする人を表す
【類語訳】交渉人, 仲介者, 調停者, 仲立ち, 仲裁人, 渉外係

[文型&コロケーション]
▶a mediator/ an intermediary/ a peacemaker **between** A and B
▶**through**/ **via** a mediator/ an intermediary
▶an **independent** mediator/ intermediary/ arbitrator
▶to **act as** (a) mediator/ (an) intermediary/ (a) go-between/ (a) peacemaker/ (a) liaison officer

negotiator [C] (仕事として行う政治・財務に関する)交渉人 ◇The chief union *negotiator* indicated that they would reject the pay award. 組合の交渉責任者は賃金裁定の拒絶をほのめかした ◇She has an image as a tough *negotiator*. 彼女にはしたたかな交渉人という印象がある ❶ *negotiator* は, 人[グループ]の間の紛争を解決しようとしたり, 人[組織]に代わって商取引[契約, 合意]の条件を協議し決めよう[交渉しよう]としたりする人を指す一般的な語.

mediator [C] 《ややフォーマル》(意見の異なる人[グループ]の)仲介者[組織] ◇A Swedish diplomat acted as *mediator* between the government and the rebels. 一人のスウェーデンの外交官が政府と反乱軍の間の仲介者の役

目を務めた ☞ **mediate** (INTERVENE)
intermediary [C]《ややフォーマル》(人[グループ]の間の意思疎通役である)仲介者[組織] ◇All talks have so far been conducted through an *intermediary*. これまで、交渉はすべて仲介者を通じて行われてきた

> **ノート mediator と intermediary の使い分け**：mediator や intermediary は、似たような役割を果たす。mediator はふつう、対立する人々[グループ]が紛争を解決しようとする話し合いにかかわる。mediator の役割は、話し合いの手助けをすることである。intermediary は、二人の人間[二つのグループ]が会合を持ちたがらない状況で介入し、双方にメッセージを伝える中立的人物としての役割を持つ。

arbitrator [C]《ややフォーマル》(紛争を解決するための)調停者 ◇Where no agreement can be reached, the matter will be referred to an independent *arbitrator*. 何の合意にも至らなければ、問題は独立した立場の調停者に委ねられることになります
'go-between [C] (人[グループ]の間に立って双方の意見を伝える)仲立ち, 仲介者 ◇A number of local church leaders have acted as *go-betweens* with the paramilitaries. 地元の多数の教会指導者たちが, 準軍事的組織との橋渡しの役目を果たしてきた
peacemaker [C] (人・国家に和解をうながす)仲裁人, 調停者 ◇She always acted as the *peacemaker* when family arguments boiled over. 家族の議論が収拾がつかなくなると, 彼女はいつも仲裁の役割を務めた
li'aison officer [C] (二つの集団[組織]が良好な関係であるように)渉外係 ◇The council has a number of community *liaison officers*. 協議会には数多くの共同体の渉外係がいる

new [形]

1 new・fresh・novel
物事が以前存在しなかったため馴染みがなく興味深いことを表す
【類語訳】新しい, これまでにない, 真新しい, 最新の, 斬新な

> 文型&コロケーション
> ▶ a new/ fresh/ novel **idea/ approach/ way**
> ▶ a new/ novel **concept/ design/ feature/ form/ method**
> ▶ **completely/ entirely/ totally/ relatively** new/ fresh/ novel

new 新しく作られた[発明された, 導入された], 新しい；これまでにない ◇Have you read her *new* book? 彼女の新しい本を読みましたか ◇This idea isn't *new*. この考えは新しいものではない ◇The latest model has over 100 *new* features. 最新モデルは100以上の新機能を備えている 反意 **old** (OLD 1)
▶**the new** [名] [U] ◇The songs are a good mix of the old and *the new* (= ones that are new). それらの歌曲は古いものと新しいものとをうまく取り混ぜている
fresh [ふつう名詞の前で] (追加した[取り替えた]ため)新しい；最近作られた[経験した], 真新しい, 最新の ◇The defence have found *fresh* evidence that could form the basis of an appeal. 被告側は上訴の基礎となりうる新たな証拠を見つけた ◇*Fresh* towels are provided every day. 新しいタオルが毎日提供されます ◇This is the opportunity he needs to *make a fresh start* (= to try sth new after not being successful at sth else). これは再出発をするのに彼に必要なチャンスです ◇There were *fresh* tracks through the snow. 雪の中に新しい足跡があった ◇Let me write it down while it's still *fresh in my mind* (= clearly remembered because recently experienced). まだ記憶に新しいうちに書き留めさせてください
▶**freshness** [名] [U] ◇I like the *freshness* of his approach to the problem. 彼のその問題に対するアプローチの新鮮さがいい
novel《しばしばほめて》これまでにない, 斬新な；奇抜な ◇It was an American who came up with the *novel* idea of drive-in restaurants. ドライブインレストランという斬新なアイデアを思いついたのはアメリカ人だった ☞ **original** (CREATIVE)
▶**novelty** [名] [U] ◇It was fun working there at first but *the novelty soon wore off* (= it became boring). そこで働くのは初めは楽しかったが, 目新しさはまもなく消えてなくなった ◇There's a certain *novelty value* in this approach. このアプローチにはある種の目新しさがある

2 new・brand new・untried
最近購入した, あるいはこれまで誰も使わなかった[試さなかった, 所有しなかった]物事のことを表す
【類語訳】買ったばかりの, 新しい, 新品の, 真新しい

> 文型&コロケーション
> ▶ new/ brand new/ untried **technology**
> ▶ a new/ brand new **product/ computer/ house**
> ▶ **relatively** new/ untried

new 買ったばかりの, 新しい；新品の ◇Let me show you my *new* dress. 新しいドレスを見てちょうだい ◇A secondhand car costs a lot less than a *new* one. 中古車は新車よりはるかに値段が安い 反意 **old** (OLD 1)
,brand 'new 真新しい, 新品の ◇We just spent a thousand pounds on a *brand new* computer. 新品のコンピューターに千ポンド使ったばかりだ ◇She bought her car *brand new*. 彼女は車を新車で買った
untried《書き言葉》まだ試されていない, うまくいくかわからない ◇This is a new and relatively *untried* procedure. これは割と試されていない新しい方法です

3 new・unfamiliar with sth・unused to sth・unaccustomed to sth
人が経験がないために物事に馴染みがないことを表す
【類語訳】不慣れな, 新参の, 不案内の, よく知らない

> 文型&コロケーション
> ▶ new/ unused/ unaccustomed **to sth**
> ▶ unused/ unaccustomed **to doing sth**
> ▶ **totally/ quite** new/ unfamiliar/ unused/ unaccustomed to sth
> ▶ **completely/ relatively** new/ unfamiliar

new 不慣れな, 新参の ◇I was fairly *new* to teaching at the time. 当時, 私は教えることにかなり不慣れだった ◇You're *new* in this town, aren't you? この町は初めてですね ◇We offer intensive training to all *new recruits*. 新人全員を集中トレーニングすることにします ◇*New arrivals* should have their passports ready for inspection. 新たに到着した人たちはパスポートのチェックを受ける準備をしなければなりません
unfamiliar with sth [名詞の前では用いない] (物事について)何の知識[経験]もない, よく知らない, 不案内の ◇The

crew were *unfamiliar with* the safety procedures. 乗組員たちは安全手順を知らなかった ◇Those *unfamiliar with* the area should bring a good guide book with them. その地域をよく知らない人たちは、よいガイドブックを持ってきてください [反意] **familiar with sth** (USED TO STH)

unused to sth [名詞の前では用いない]《ややフォーマル、書き言葉》(物事に)不慣れな ◇If you are *unused to* exercise, start off gently. 運動になじみがないなら、徐々に始めてください ◇I was *unused to* speaking in public. 私は人前で話すのに慣れていなかった ◇He was so *unused to* people questioning his authority that he didn't know how to react. 彼は自分の権威に対して疑いを持つ人たちにはとても不慣れだったので、どう反応していいか分からなかった [反意] **used to sth** (USED TO STH)

unaccustomed to sth [名詞の前では用いない]《フォーマル、書き言葉》(物事に)不慣れな ◇He was *unaccustomed to* hard work. 彼は重労働に慣れていなかった ◇I am *unaccustomed to* being told what to do. 何をすべきか命じられるのには不慣れです [反意] **accustomed to sth** (USED TO STH)

[ノート] **unused to sth** と **unaccustomed to sth** の使い分け：unaccustomed は、unused よりフォーマルである。だが、特に話し言葉では、これらの単語をどちらも使わず、not used to sth や not used to doing sth と言うほうがずっと普通である。◆ He was *not used to* hard work/exercise/speaking in public/being told what to do/people questioning his authority. 彼は重労働/運動/人前で話すこと/何をすべきか命じられること/自分の権威について疑いを持つ人たちに慣れていなかった

next [形]

next・the following・future・subsequent・coming・later・forthcoming・upcoming・prospective
物事が他の物事の後や現在より後に起きる[存在する、言及される]ことを表す
【類語訳】次の、隣の、将来の、未来の、来るべき、後の、間近の

[文型&コロケーション]
▶ the next/ following **month/ decade/ generation**
▶ future/ subsequent/ coming/ later **months/ decades/ generations**
▶ the next **event**
▶ future/ subsequent/ coming/ later/ forthcoming/ upcoming **events**
▶ the next/ a future/ a subsequent/ a later/ the forthcoming/ the upcoming **meeting/ trial**
▶ sb's next/ future/ subsequent/ later/ forthcoming/ upcoming **book/ books**
▶ sb's next/ subsequent/ forthcoming/ upcoming **album**
▶ the next/ the following/ a future/ a subsequent/ a later **stage/ chapter**
▶ the next/ a future/ a subsequent/ a later **time**
▶ sb's next/ future/ subsequent/ later/ forthcoming/ upcoming **marriage**

next [名詞の前で] (時間的・順序的・空間的で)次の、隣の ◇The *next* train to Baltimore is at ten. 次のボルティモア行きの列車は10時発です ◇The *next* six months will be the hardest. 今後半年は最も厳しいものとなるだろう ◇The *next* chapter deals with the post-war situation. 次章では戦後の状況を扱います ◇Who's *next*? 次の方は ◇The woman in the *next* room was talking in a very loud voice. 隣の部屋の女性は非常に大声で話していた ◇I fainted and *the next thing I knew* I was in the hospital. 私は失神し、次に気づいたことは自分が病院にいることだった ❶ next は、曜日・季節・週・月・年などと副詞的に用いられる場合、the は不要。◆ I'm going away *next* month (= the month after this one). (来月退去する予定です)。◆ *Next* Thursday (= the Thursday after this one) is 12 April. (次の木曜は4月12日です)。◆ *Next* time I'll bring a book. (次の時には本を持ってきますよ)。
[反意] **last, past** (LAST2)

▶**next** [副] ◇What happened *next*? 次に何が起こったの ◇*The next best thing* to flying is gliding. 飛ぶ次に 最もいいのは滑空だ

▶**next** [名] [単数で] ◇One moment he wasn't there, the *next* he was. ある時には彼はそこにいなくて、次にはいた ◇the week *after next* 再来週

the following (時間的)次の；次に言及される ◇We set off on Monday evening and arrived in New Zealand *the following* afternoon. 私たちは月曜の夜出発し、次の日の午後にニュージーランドに到着した ◇Answer *the following* questions. 以下の質問にお答えください
[反意] **previous, preceding** (LAST2)

future [名詞の前で] 将来の、未来の ◇Climate change will be a very serious issue for *future* generations. 気候変動は将来の世代にとって非常に深刻な問題となろう ◇We try to predict *future* developments in computer software. 我々はコンピューターソフトの未来の発達を予測しようとしている ◇He met his *future* wife at law school. 彼はロースクールで妻となる人と出会った [反意] **ex-, former** (FORMER), **past, previous** (PREVIOUS)

subsequent《ややフォーマル》(他の物事の)後に起こる[やってくる] ◇*Subsequent* events confirmed our doubts. 続いて起こった出来事が私たちの疑念を裏づけた ◇Developments on this issue will be dealt with in a *subsequent* report. この問題に関する進展は次の報告書で扱われることになります

▶**subsequently** [副] ◇The original interview notes were *subsequently* lost. インタビューのオリジナルメモがそのあとなくなった

coming [名詞の前で] (期間が)まもなく起こる、来るべき；次の ◇The building work may cause some disruption in the *coming* months. その建築工事は次の数か月かも混乱を引き起こすことになるかもしれない ◇This *coming* Sunday is her birthday. この次の日曜日は彼女の誕生日です

later [名詞の前で] もっと後に起こる、後の ◇This is discussed in more detail in a *later* chapter. これは後の章でもっと詳しく論じられます ◇The game has been postponed to a *later* date. 試合は後日に延期された [反意] **earlier**

▶**later** [副] ◇See you *later*. じゃあまた ◇I'm going out *later on*. 後で出かけるよ

[ノート] **future** と **later** の使い分け：どちらの単語も用いることができる場合がある。◆ The Committee will reconsider these proposals at a *future*/*later* date. (委員会ではこれらの提案を後日再考することにします)。だが、future は特に、将来の状況[進展]について用いられる。◆ *future* plans/prospects/prosperity/earnings/benefits/trends/growth/directions (将来の計画/見通し/

↳next

繁栄/収入/利益/動向/成長/方向). **later**は特に, 出来事[過程, 説明]における後の段階について用いられる. ◆a *later* stage/phase/chapter/section/addition/modification/alteration/age (もっと後の段階/局面/章/項/追加/修正/変更/年代).

forthcoming [名詞の前で]《ややフォーマル》(出版などが) まもなく起こる, 来るべき, 間近の ◇Three main parties will contest the *forthcoming* elections. 主要3政党が来る選挙で競い合うだろう ◇The band have added an extra date to their *forthcoming* UK tour. そのバンドは今度の英国ツアーに一日日程を追加した

upcoming [名詞の前で]《(特に米)》(出版などが) まもなく起こる, 来るべき, 間近の ◇No one knows what the outcome of the *upcoming* presidential election will be. 来る大統領選の結果がどうなるか誰にもわからない ◇This is a single from the band's *upcoming* album. これは近く発表されるバンドのアルバムからのシングル曲です

prospective [ふつう名詞の前で]《ややフォーマル》まもなく起こると予想される ◇They are worried about *prospective* changes in the law. 彼らは法律について予想される改正について憂慮している

ノート **coming, forthcoming, upcoming, prospective**の使い分け：これらの単語はすべて, まもなく起こるであろう[かもしれない]物事について用いられる. 他の物事の後に起こる単独の物事には用いない. ☞Answer the *coming/forthcoming/upcoming/prospective* questions. **coming**はふつう, 期間を表すのに用いられる. ◆Media attention will be focused on the Prime Minister in the *coming* weeks. (マスコミの注目は, 首相の今後数週間に向けられるだろう). まもなく起こることになっている事柄すのには, **forthcoming**や**upcoming**を用いる. ◆He is understandably nervous about his *forthcoming/upcoming* trial. (無理もないが, 彼は来る裁判に対して神経質になっている). まもなく起こると予想される[可能性の高い]出来事を表すには, **prospective**も用いる. ◆On learning of a *prospective* sale, the lawyer should call the client as soon as possible. (売却の可能性の情報をつかんだら, 弁護士は依頼人にできるだけ早く電話するべきである).

nice 形

1 ☞ SATISFYING, WONDERFUL
nice・good・pleasant・enjoyable・pleasurable
喜びを与えてくれる経験[活動, 出来事]を表す
【類語訳】楽しい, うれしい, 魅力的な

文型&コロケーション
- a nice/ a good/ a pleasant/ an enjoyable/ a pleasurable **experience/ thing (to do)**
- a nice/ a good/ a pleasant/ an enjoyable **time/ evening/ party**
- a nice/ a good/ a pleasant/ a pleasurable **feeling/ sensation**
- nice/ good/ pleasant **weather**
- a pleasant/ an enjoyable/ a pleasurable **task**
- It's nice/ good/ pleasant **to be/ feel/ find/ have/ know/ meet/ see...**
- It would be nice/ good/ pleasant **if...**
- It's nice/ good **that...**
- very nice/ good/ pleasant/ enjoyable

nice 《ややインフォーマル》楽しい; うれしい; 魅力的な ◇Have a *nice* day (= enjoy yourself today)! よい一日を ◇If it's a *nice* day tomorrow (= if the weather is good), shall we go out? 明日天気が良ければ, 出かけようか ◇The *nicest* thing about her is that she never criticizes us. 彼女の一番いいところは, 私たちをけっして批判しないことです ◇'Do you want to come too?' 'Yes, *that would be nice*.'「君も来たいかい」「ああ, いいね」◇*Nice to meet you!* お会いできて光栄です ◇*It's been nice meeting you.* お目にかかれてよかったです ◇You look *nice*. すてきですね ❶ **nice**は, 物事がいかに好ましいかを強調するために, 形容詞[副詞]の前で用いることができる. ◆a *nice* hot bath (いい湯加減の風呂). ◆Everyone arrived *nice* and early. (みんないずぶん早く到着した). 別の形容詞を伴った**nice**と, 名詞の前では用いることができない. ✗a *nice* and quiet place. 反意 **nasty** (BAD)

good 《ややインフォーマル, 特に話し言葉》楽しい; うれしい; 魅力的な ◇Did you have a *good* time in America? アメリカで楽しく過ごしましたか ◇This is very *good news*. これはとてもよい知らせだ ◇It would be *good* if he moved to London. 彼がロンドンに引っ越すなら, それはよいことだが ◇We are still friends though, which is *good*. でも私たちは今も友達なんです, いいことですよね 反意 **bad** (BAD), **terrible** (TERRIBLE 1)

pleasant 《ややフォーマル》うれしい; 魅力的な ◇It was *pleasant* to be alone again. 再び一人になることは楽しかった ◇It's nice to live in *pleasant* surroundings. 気持ちのよい環境で生活することは素晴らしい 反意 **unpleasant** (BAD)

▶ **pleasantly** 副 ◇a *pleasantly* cool room 涼しくて気持ちのいい部屋 ◇I was *pleasantly* surprised by my exam results. 自分の試験結果はうれしい驚きでした

ノート **nice, good, pleasant** の使い分け：これらの単語はすべて, 時間・出来事・感情・天気を表すことができる. **nice** と **pleasant** は場所を表すこともできるし, **nice** は人の外見を表すこともできる.

enjoyable 楽しい ◇I always try to make my lessons *enjoyable*. 私はいつもレッスンを楽しいものにするよう努めています ◇Swimming is a very *enjoyable* way of staying in shape. 泳ぐのは体型を保つのに非常に楽しいやり方です

pleasurable 《フォーマル》楽しい ◇She had the *pleasurable* sensation of being swept off her feet. 彼女は心を奪われるよう心地よい喜びを覚えた

ノート **enjoyable** と **pleasurable** の使い分け：**pleasurable** は, **enjoyable** よりフォーマルな語で, 特に, 肉体的な喜びや感情を表すのに用いられる.

2 ☞ FRIENDLY 1, KIND 形, SWEET
nice・wonderful・lovely・charming・charismatic・engaging・likeable・personable
人なつっこく感じのよい性格で好まれやすい人を表す
【類語訳】素晴らしい, すてきな, カリスマ的な, 引きつける, 感じのよい, 好ましい, 人好きのする

nice	charming	wonderful
engaging	charismatic	lovely
likeable		
personable		

night

文型&コロケーション

- a nice/ a wonderful/ a lovely/ a charming/ a charismatic/ an engaging/ a likeable/ a personable **man**
- a nice/ a wonderful/ a lovely/ a charming/ an engaging/ likeable **person**
- a nice/ a wonderful/ a lovely/ a charming/ an engaging **woman**
- a nice/ a wonderful/ a lovely/ a charming/ a charismatic/ an engaging/ a likeable **character/ personality**
- **very** nice/ charming/ charismatic/ engaging/ likeable/ personable
- **extremely** nice/ charming/ engaging/ likeable/ personable
- **really** nice/ wonderful/ lovely/ charming/ engaging/ likeable
- **rather** nice/ wonderful/ lovely/ charming/ engaging
- **quite** (= rather) nice/ likeable/ personable
- **quite** (= very) wonderful/ charming

nice《ややインフォーマル、特に話し言葉、ほめて》(親切で人なつっこく一緒にいて楽しいので)素晴らしい、すてきな ◇Our new neighbours are very *nice*. 新しい隣人は非常に感じがよい ◇He's a really *nice* guy. 彼は実にいいやつです ◇Be *nice to* me. I'm not feeling well. 優しくしてよ。気分が悪いんだから ◇It was *nice of them to* invite us. 彼らは親切にも私たちを招いてくれた ◇I complained to the manager and he was very *nice about* it. 部長に文句を言ったが、彼はそのことに対してとても寛大だった ❶ nice は非常に広い意味を持ち、特にインフォーマルな話し言葉の場合には、とても頻繁に用いられる。書き言葉やフォーマルな場合には、このグループに属する他の語のような、より正確な語を用いる方がよいであろう。 反意 **nasty** (MEAN 形)
- **nicely** 副 ◇If you ask her *nicely* she might say yes. うまく頼めば、彼女はイエスと言うかもしれません

wonderful《特に英、ややインフォーマル、特に話し言葉、ほめて》(とても親切かつ人なつっこいので)素晴らしい、すてきな ◇She's a truly *wonderful* person. 彼女は実に素晴らしい人物です ◇You've all been absolutely *wonderful*! あなた方はみな実にすてきだった

lovely《特に英、ややインフォーマル、特に話し言葉、ほめて》(とても親切かつ寛容で人なつっこいので)素晴らしい、すてきな ◇Her mother was a *lovely* woman. 彼女の母親は素晴らしい女性だった

> ノート **wonderful**と**lovely**の使い分け：ふつう、いずれの語も用いることができる。lovelyは《英》の話し言葉で頻繁に用いられる。《米》では、wonderfulが話し言葉・書き言葉の両方で頻繁に用いられる。

charming《ふつうほめて》(非常に礼儀正しく人なつっこいので)魅力的な ◇She's a *charming* person. 彼女はチャーミングな人です ❶ *charming* は、人の感じのよい態度と礼儀正しさを強調する。このため、人々は彼らを好きになり、彼らのために物事を行う。しかし、charming な人が負の性質も持っていることもある。 ◆ He was certainly *charming*, but he was also ruthless and ambitious. (彼は確かに魅力的だが、非情で野心的でもある) ◆ What is she really like behind that *charming* facade? (その魅力的なうわべの裏の、実際の彼女はどんなでしょう) ☞ **charm**（CHARM），**charm**（DELIGHT）
- **charmingly** 副 ◇She smiled *charmingly* at me. 彼女は私に感じよくほほ笑んだ

charismatic《しばしばほめて》(男性が)カリスマ的な ◇the *charismatic* leader of a religious sect ある宗派のカリスマ的な指導者 ☞ **charisma** (CHARM)

engaging（人を）引きつける、感じのよい ◇She had an *engaging* smile, which charmed everyone. 彼女は誰をも魅了する感じのよいほほ笑みを浮かべた

likeable《特に英》（または **likable**《米、英》）好ましい、人好きのする ◇He's a very *likeable* man. 彼は非常に好感の持てる人間である ☞ **like** (LIKE 動)

personable《ややフォーマル》(男性の外見[性格、振る舞い]が)感じがよい ◇Her assistant seemed a very *personable* young man. 彼女の助手は非常に感じのよい若者に見えた ❶ **personable** は特に、よく知らない人に対する自分の印象を表すのに用いる。

night 名

1 night・midnight・the early hours・the middle of the night・night-time・the small hours

ある日と翌日の間の暗い時間、あるいはその時間の一部を表す
【類語訳】夜、夜間、真夜中、早朝、未明、夜更け、深夜

文型&コロケーション

- **in** the night/ early hours/ middle of the night/ night-time/ small hours
- **at** night/ midnight/ night-time
- **until** midnight/ the early hours/ the small hours
- **(well) into** the night/ early hours/ small hours
- the early hours/ small hours **of the morning**

night [U, C] (人々が眠る)夜、夜間 ◇They sleep by day and hunt *by night*. 彼らは昼間は眠り、夜は狩りを行う ◇The accident happened on Friday *night*. その事故は金曜の夜に起きた ◇Did you hear the storm *last night*? ゆうべ嵐の音を聞きましたか ◇I lay awake *all night*. 一晩中まんじりともせず横になっていた ◇Where did you *spend the night*? その夜はどこで過ごしていたの ◇You're welcome to *stay the night* here. どうぞこちらにお泊まりください ◇What is he doing calling *at this time of night*? 夜のこんな時間に電話するなんて彼はどうなっているの ◇The hotel costs €65 per person *per night*. そのホテルは一泊一人当たり65ユーロです 反意 **day**
- **nights** 副 ◇She works *nights* (= at night). 彼女は夜働いている

midnight [U] 夜中の12時、真夜中 ◇The ship set sail shortly after *midnight*. 船は真夜中をすぎてすぐに出帆した ◇She heard the clock strike *midnight*. 彼女は時計が夜の12時を打つのを聞いた ◇The law comes into effect *on the stroke of midnight* (= at midnight exactly) tomorrow. その法律は明日の夜12時きっかりに発効される 反意 **midday**

the 'early hours フレーズ 早朝、未明 ◇The raid was carried out in *the early hours* of 25 May. 手入れは5月25日未明に行われた

the ,middle of the 'night フレーズ (ほとんどの人々が眠っている)真夜中 ◇He always calls me in *the middle of the night*. 彼はいつも真夜中に電話してくる

'night-time [U] (暗い)夜間 ◇It was *night-time*, but no one was asleep. 夜間だが、誰も眠っていなかった ◇A *night-time* curfew will be imposed throughout the country. 国中に夜間外出禁止令が敷かれるでしょう 反意 **daytime**

↳night

nonsense

ノート night, the middle of the night, night-timeの使い分け：nightは、ひとまとまりの夜間全体としても、継続しているある一定の時間としても捉えることができる。night-timeは継続しているある一定の時間を指し、夜間全体を指すことはない。the middle of the nightは、夜の時間帯の一時点を指す。◆during the night/night-time (に)。×during the middle of the night. ◆I lay awake all night. (一晩中まんじりともせず横になっていた)。何かをするには普通でない時間帯であることを強調する場合にもthe middle of the nightを用いる。◆Go back to bed — it's the middle of the night! (ベッドに戻りなさい—真夜中ですよ)。night-timeは特に、複合語で用いられる。◆a night-time curfew/raid/visit (夜間外出禁止令/夜襲/夜間の訪問)。◆night-time entertainment (夜間の楽しみ)。

the 'small hours 《ややインフォーマル》夜更け, 深夜 ◇We worked well into the small hours. 私たちは夜更けまでよく働いた

ノート the early hoursとthe small hoursの使い分け：the early hoursは、ofと日(付)の前で用いられることが多く、公的な報告書やジャーナリズムで用いられる。◆The robbery took place in the early hours of Monday morning. (強盗事件は月曜の未明に起きた)。the small hoursはかなりインフォーマルで、こうした文脈では用いない。夕暮れに始まり真夜中すぎまで続く物事について用いることが多い。

2 night・evening・sunset・dusk・twilight・nightfall・sundown
一日のうち暗くなる[暗くなった後の]時間を表す
【類語訳】夜, 晩, 日没, 日暮れ, 夕暮れ, 薄暮, たそがれ

文型&コロケーション
▶ at night/ sunset/ dusk/ twilight/ nightfall/ sundown
▶ in the evening/ dusk/ twilight
▶ after/ before/ by/ until/ till sunset/ dusk/ nightfall/ sundown
▶ tomorrow/ yesterday/ Monday night/ evening
▶ a beautiful night/ evening/ sunset
▶ night/ evening/ dusk falls

night [U, C]（午後の終わりから就寝時間までの）夜, 晩 ◇She doesn't like to walk home **late at night**. 彼女は夜遅くに歩いて帰宅するのを好まない ◇**My mother-in-law came for dinner last night**. 昨晩, 私の義母が夕食を食べにきた ◇I saw her in town **the other night** (= a few nights ago). この前の夜, 町で彼女を見かけた 反意 morning

evening [U, C]（午後の終わりから就寝時間までの）夜, 晩 ◇I'll come and see you **this evening**. 今晩あなたに会いに行きます ◇The evening performance begins at 7.30. 夜の部は7時半に開演です ◇We spent the long winter evenings inside by the fire. 私たちは冬の夜長を屋内の炉辺で過ごした 反意 morning
▷ **evenings** 副 ◇He works evenings (= in the evenings). 彼は夜働いている

ノート nightとeveningの使い分け：いくつかの場合, どちらの語も用いることができる。◆Let's go out on Saturday night/evening. (土曜の夜に出かけよう)。eveningは, 6時くらいからの早い時間帯を強調する。nightは, 夜の後半を意味

調し, 翌日の未明を含むことができる。◆We were up late last night — I didn't get to bed until two o'clock. (私たちは昨晩夜更かしをしてて—2時まで寝なかった)。nightは, 翌朝明るくなるまでの時間すべてを意味することもできる。意味がはっきりしている場合のみ, nightをeveningの意味で用いることができる。◆I'm going to my sister's for the evening (= and coming back later in the evening). (夜姉の家に行きます(夜のうちに戻ります))。
◆I'm going to my sister's for the night (= and not coming back until the morning). (夜姉の家に行きます(朝まで戻りません))。

sunset [U, C] 日没, 日暮れ；夕焼け ◇After sunset the temperature drops. 日没後気温は下がります ◇We sat by the river and **watched the sunset**. 私たちは川辺に座り, 夕焼けを見ていた 反意 **sunrise**

dusk [U] 夕暮れ ◇We arrived in town as dusk was falling. 私たちは夕闇が迫る頃町に着いた ◇She works from **dawn to dusk** and sometimes at night. 彼女は明け方から夕暮れまで, 時には夜も働く 反意 **dawn**

twilight [U] 薄暮, たそがれ(時) ◇It was hard to see him clearly in the thickening twilight. 夕闇が迫ると彼の姿ははっきりとは見えなくなった ◇We went for a walk along the beach at twilight. 私たちはたそがれ時に浜辺を散歩に出かけた
▷ **twilit** 形 ◇She hurried out into the twilit street. 《文語》彼女は大急ぎで薄明かりの通りに出た

nightfall [U]《フォーマル or 文語》日暮れ, 夕暮れ ◇He wanted to be home before nightfall. 彼は日の暮れないうちに帰宅していたかった 反意 **daybreak**

sundown [U]《特に米, 特に書き言葉》日没 ◇The celebration begins at sundown. 祝典は日没時に始まります

nonsense 名 ☞ LIE

nonsense・bullshit・rubbish・crap・bull・garbage・B.S.・gibberish
ばかげている[明らかに事実と違う]と思われる事
【類語訳】たわごと, ナンセンス

文型&コロケーション
▶ nonsense/ bullshit/ rubbish/ crap/ bull/ garbage/ B.S. about sth
▶ pure nonsense/ rubbish/ garbage
▶ absolute/ total nonsense/ rubbish/ crap/ garbage
▶ complete/ utter nonsense/ rubbish/ garbage
▶ to talk nonsense/ bullshit/ rubbish/ crap/ gibberish
▶ to believe that nonsense/ bullshit/ rubbish/ crap/ bull/ garbage/ B.S.
▶ a load/ lot of nonsense/ bullshit/ rubbish/ crap/ bull/ garbage/ B.S.
▶ What nonsense/ bullshit/ rubbish/ bull/ garbage!

nonsense [U, 単数で]《しばしばなしで》たわごと, ナンセンス；意味をなさない言葉 ◇'I heard he's resigning.' 'That's nonsense.'「彼は辞任するって聞いたよ」「ばかしい」 ◇What's all this nonsense about you getting married? 君が結婚するなんて, これは一体何の冗談だい ◇**It's nonsense to** say they don't care. 彼らが気にもしないなんて言うのはばかげている ◇The idea is an economic nonsense. その考えは経済的には無意味だ ◇a book of **nonsense poems** (= poems that seem not to make sense) 滑稽詩の本 反意 **sense**

bullshit [U]《単語, 俗語, 話し言葉, けなして》くだらないこと, たわごと ❶bullshitは話し言葉で非常に一般的で, 特に, なされたばかりの発言がnonsenseであると言うときに用いられる. インフォーマルな場面で, 年齢・地位が自分と同等の人に対してのみ用いるべきである. 年上の人, あるいは目上の人に対して用いた場合, 感情をひどく害することもある. ◆Don't give me that *bullshit* (= stop talking nonsense)! (そんなたわごとはやめなさい) ◆Don't listen to him — he's full of *bullshit*. (彼の言うことなんか聞くな—でたらめばっかりだから).

rubbish [U]《英, インフォーマル, 特に話し言葉, けなして》くだらないこと, たわごと ◇*Rubbish*! You're not fat! ばかばかしい. 君は太ってなんかいないよ ◇We were told a lot of *rubbish* about 'leadership' and 'bonding'. それら我々は「リーダーシップ」と「絆」についてくだらないことを山ほど聞かされた ❶rubbishは, nonsenseよりインフォーマルで, 敬意がかなり欠落している場合に用いられ,《英》でしか用いられない.

crap [U]《卑語, 俗語, 話し言葉, けなして》くだらないこと, たわごと ❶crapは, 年齢・地位が自分と同等の人に対し, インフォーマルな場面でしか用いるべきではない. 年上の人, あるいは目上の人に対して用いた場合, ひどく感情を害することもある. ◆Let's just *cut the crap* (= stop talking nonsense) and get down to business. (もうくだらない話はやめて, 本題に入りましょう). ◆You're talking a load of *crap*. (《英》よくそんなでたらめを). ◆What a *bunch of crap*. (《米》何とまあくだらないことばかり).

bull [U]《特に米, 俗語, 話し言葉, けなして》くだらないこと, たわごと ❶bullは, bullshitよりは相手に与える不快感が弱い. ◆That's just *bull* and you know it. (それはただの話だとわかってるだろ).

garbage [U]《特に米, インフォーマル, けなして》くだらないこと, たわごと ◇That's complete *garbage*! そいつはまったくのたわごとだ ◇Don't believe all that *garbage* the government tells you. 政府が吹き込むそんなたわごとは一切信じるな

B.S. 略《米, 卑語, 俗語》くだらないこと, たわごと (bullshitの略語) ◇That guy's full of *B.S.* その男はでたらめばかり並べる

gibberish [U] 意味のない[理解できない]言葉 ◇He speaks *gibberish* all the time. He's mad. 彼はしょっちゅうわけのわからないことを話している. 頭がおかしいんだ

normal 形

normal・ordinary・average・common・typical
特別ではない[異なっていない]人[物, 出来事]を表す
【類語訳】普通の, 通常の, 平均的な, 並みの, ありふれた, 平凡な, 典型的な, 標準的な, 一般的な

〚文型&コロケーション〛
▶ to be normal/ common **for sb to do sth/ for sth to happen**
▶ the normal/ ordinary/ average/ common **man**
▶ a normal/ an ordinary/ the average **person**
▶ the normal/ ordinary/ common **sort**
▶ a normal/ an ordinary/ an average/ a typical **working day**
▶ **in the** normal/ ordinary **course of events/ business/ things**
▶ pretty/ fairly normal/ ordinary/ average/ typical
▶ quite normal/ ordinary/ typical

normal (ほとんどの場合に起こるので)普通の, 通常の ◇Her temperature was *normal*. 彼女の体温は平熱だった ◇The help desk is available during *normal* office hours. 問い合わせの窓口は通常の営業時間にご利用できます ◇He should be able to **lead a** perfectly **normal life**. 彼はまったく普通の暮らしを送れるはずだ ◇*It's normal to* feel tired after such a long journey. そんな長旅の後に疲れを感じるのは当然です ◇Life continued *as normal*. 生活はいつものように続いた ◇The skin surface is resistant to infection **under normal circumstances**. 皮膚の表面は, 通常の状況下ならば, 感染に対して抵抗力がある 反意 **exceptional** (SPECIAL), **strange, odd, weird** (STRANGE 1)

▶**normality** 名 [U] ◇They are hoping for a **return to normality** now that the war is over. 戦争が終わり, 平常の状態への復帰が望まれている

▶**normally** 副 ◇The exercise *normally* takes twenty minutes. その運動はふつう20分かかる ◇His heart is beating *normally*. 彼の心臓は正常に鼓動している

ordinary [ふつう名詞の前で] (あらゆる点で異常[特別]ではないので)普通の, 通常の ◇We were an *ordinary* family. 私たちは普通の家族だった ◇The images can be printed on *ordinary* paper. その画像は普通紙に印刷できます ◇It began as an *ordinary* sort of day. その日は普通の一日として始まった ◇This was no *ordinary* meeting. これは通常の会議ではなかった ◇He was not a nervous person *in the ordinary way* (= usually).《英》彼はふだんは神経質な人間ではなかった 反意 **extraordinary** (REMARKABLE), **special** (SPECIAL)

〚ノート〛 **normalとordinaryの使い分け**: normalなことは, あるべき[思ったとおりの]ことを指す. ×Her temperature was *ordinary*. ×It's *ordinary* to feel tired after such a long journey. abnormalなこととは本来そうあるべきではないことを指す. ordinaryは, 物事がいかにあるべきかについてではなく, 善し悪しにかかわらず物事がどうなのかについて述べる. extraordinaryな人々[物事]は, ある点で特別[異例]であり, よい場合も指せば悪い場合も指す.
☞ **ordinary** (AVERAGE)

average 平均的な, 並みの ◇An entrance fee of £5 is about *average*. 5ポンドという入場料はまあ普通だ ◇The route is for walkers of *average* ability. そのルートは平均的な体力の歩行者向きである ☞ **average** (AVERAGE)

common [名詞の前で] (あらゆる点で異常[特別]ではないので)ありふれた, 平凡な; 普通の, 通常の ◇I wanted a recording of the *common* cuckoo. ごく普通のカッコウの鳴き声を録音したものがほしかった ◇Oats were the staple food of *the common people* (= the majority of the population, who are not rich). えん麦は庶民の主食だった ◇In most people's eyes she was nothing more than a *common criminal*. ほとんどの人から見て, 彼女はよくいる犯罪者にすぎなかった ◇Polite letters of rejection are a matter of *common courtesy*. 断りの手紙を丁重に書く礼儀に関わる問題だ ❶commonは, ordinaryと意味は同じだが, 決まったいくつかの形で用いられることが多い. commonは, 最も一般的な種類の, あらゆる点で珍しくない[まれでない]動物[植物]に用いられる. ◆ *common* gulls/frogs/ragwort (一般種のカモメ/カエル/サワギク). commonは, 特別な地位[立場]にない人々を指すのにも用いられる. ◆ *common* people/soldiers/criminals (庶民/兵卒/よくいる犯罪者). また, ほとんどの人々が備えていると思われる種類[水準]のよい性質を指すのにも用いられる. ◆ *common* courtesy/decency (一般的な礼儀/品位).

typical (ふつうの形で起こる[ふつうの姿を示す]ので)典型的な, 標準的な, 一般的な ◇Each woman was asked to describe a *typical* working day. 女性はそれぞれ, 通常の就業日について述べるよう求められた ◇*Typical* interview questions are 'Why do you want to study law?' or 'Why did you choose this college?' よくある面接の質問は「どうして法律を勉強したいと思うのですか?」とか「なぜこの大学を選んだのですか?」といったものである 反意 **atypical (UNUSUAL)**

▶**typically** 副 ◇The factory *typically* produces 500 cars a week. その工場は通常, 週に500台の車を製造する ◇*Typically*, the contracts were for five years. 通例, 契約期間は5年だった

notice 動 ☞ LOOK 動 1, SEE

notice・note・detect・observe・witness・perceive・take sth in
特に細心の気遣いをして物事を見ることを表す
【類語訳】目にする, 耳にする, 気づく, 注意を払う, 注目する, 発見する, 感知する, 目撃する, わかる

【文型&コロケーション】
▶ to notice/ note/ detect/ observe/ perceive **that**...
▶ to notice/ note/ detect/ observe/ perceive **how/ what/ where/ who**...
▶ to notice/ observe/ witness **sth happen/ sb do sth**
▶ to **quickly** notice/ note/ detect/ take in sth
▶ to **immediately/ suddenly/ soon** notice/ detect/ perceive sth
▶ to **just** notice/ note/ observe sth

notice [他, 自]《進行形はまれ》目にする, 耳にする, 気づく; 注意を払う, 注目する ◇The first thing I *noticed* about the room was the smell. その部屋について最初に気づいたのはにおいだった ◇I couldn't help *noticing* that she was wearing a wig. 彼女がかつらを着けていることに着目せずにはいられなかった ◇I *noticed* them come into the room. 彼らが部屋に入ってくるのに気づいた ◇I didn't *notice* him leaving. 彼が出て行くのに気づかなかった ◇My husband hardly seems to *notice* me any more. 夫はもはやほとんど私のことを気にも留めないようだ ◇She wears those strange clothes just to **get herself noticed**. 人目を引くためだけに, 彼女はそういう風変わりな服装をしている ◇People were making fun of him but he didn't seem to *notice*. 人々は彼のことをからかっていたが, 彼は気づいていないようだった ☞ **notice (ATTENTION), noticeable (VISIBLE)**

note [他]《進行形はまれ》《ややフォーマル》気づく, 細心の注意を払う ◇*Note* the fine early Baroque altar inside the chapel. チャペル内にあるバロック様式初期の見事な祭壇にご注目ください ◇*Note* how these animals sometimes walk with their tails up in the air. これらの動物が時々しっぽを宙に向けて歩くさまに注目してください ◇**It should be noted** that dissertations submitted late will not be accepted. 提出遅れの論文は受け付けてもらえないことに注意しなければなりません ❶ note はビジネス英語において非常に一般的である. ◆We *note* your concerns regarding an increase in costs. (コストの上昇に関するご懸念はうかがります). ◆*Note* that the prices are inclusive of VAT. (価格は付加価値税込みだということにご留意ください).

detect [他]《進行形はまれ》《ややフォーマル》(見聞きするのが容易でない物事を)発見する, 気づく, 感知する ◇The tests are designed to *detect* the disease early. 検査はその病気を早期発見するためのものだ ◇This is an instrument that can *detect* very small amounts of radiation. これはごく少量の放射線を検知できる器械である ◇Do I *detect* a note of criticism in your voice? あなたの言い分に非難がましいものを感じるんですか

observe [他]《進行形はまれ》《ややフォーマル》目にする, 気づく, 注意を払う, 注目する ◇Have you *observed* any changes lately? 最近何か変化に気づきましたか ◇He was *observed* to enter the bank. 彼は銀行に入るのを監視されていた ◇All the characters in the novel are closely *observed* (= seem like people in real life). その小説の登場人物は全員如実に描き出されている ❶すぐ上のような例では受動態でしか用いられない. ☞ **observe (LOOK 1), observer (WITNESS)**

witness [他]《ややフォーマル》(現場に居合わせて)目撃する ◇She was shocked by the violent scenes she had *witnessed*. 彼女は目撃した暴力的な光景にショックを受けた ◇Police have appealed for anyone who *witnessed* the incident to contact them. 警察は事件を目撃したあらゆる人に連絡してくれるよう呼びかけた ◇The last century *witnessed* an unprecedented increase in violent crime (= It happened during that period).《フォーマル》前世紀には凶悪犯罪の未曾有の増加があった ☞ **witness (WITNESS)**

perceive [他]《進行形なし》《フォーマル》(明らかでない物事に)気づく, わかる ◇I *perceived* a change in his behaviour over those months. その数か月間, 彼の行動の変化に気づいた ◇The patient was *perceived* to have difficulty in breathing. その患者は呼吸困難な状態であると見られた ❶すぐ上のような例ではふつう, 受動態で用いられる. ☞ **perception (AWARENESS)**

,take sth 'in 句動詞 (物事に目で見て)気づく ◇He took in every detail of her appearance. 彼は彼女の外見を隅々まで見て取った

number 名

number・amount・volume・sum・quantity
人や物の集まり具合を表す
【類語訳】数, 額, 量, 金額, 分量, 数量

【文型&コロケーション】
▶ **the** number/ amount/ volume/ quantity **of** sth
▶ **a/ an** number/ amount/ quantity **of** sth
▶ a number/ quantity of **people/ things**
▶ an amount/ a volume/ a quantity of **information**
▶ an amount/ a sum of **money**
▶ a/ an **reasonable/ considerable/ significant/ large/ substantial/ great/ huge/ enormous/ vast/ small** number/ amount/ volume/ sum/ quantity
▶ **record/ sufficient** numbers/ amounts/ volumes/ sums/ quantities
▶ a **limited** number/ amount/ volume/ quantity
▶ a **tiny** number/ amount/ sum/ quantity
▶ **growing/ increasing** numbers/ amounts/ volumes/ quantities
▶ the **total/ sheer** number/ amount/ volume/ quantity

number [C] 数 ❶ number は人[物]がどれだけいるか[あ

number

るか]を話題にするときによく用いられる。◆The *number* of homeless people has increased dramatically. (ホームレスの人たちの数が劇的に増えた。) ◆Huge *numbers* of (= very many) animals have died. (途方もない数の動物が死んだ。) ◆A *number* of (= some) problems have arisen. (いくつかの問題が持ち上がった。) ◆I could give you ***any number of*** (= a lot of) reasons for not going. (私が行かない理由ならいくらでも挙げられよう。) ◆We were eight ***in number*** (= there were eight of us). (我々は総勢8人だった。) ◆***Sheer weight of numbers*** (= the large number of soldiers) secured them the victory. (圧倒的な数の力で彼らの勝利を揺るぎなかった。) ❶複数名詞と共に用いられるのでa (large, small, etc.) number of... の後は動詞も複数形に呼応した形にする必要がある。◆*A number of* people *were* late for the meeting. (何人もの人が会議に遅刻した。)

amount [C, U] 額;量 ◇You will receive a bill for the full *amount*. 全額分の請求書をお送りします ◇Small *amounts* will be paid in cash. 少額は現金で支払われます ◇The server is designed to store huge *amounts* of data. サーバーは膨大な量のデータが保存できるように設計されている ◇There's been ***any amount of*** (= a lot of) research into the subject. そのテーマに関して多くの研究がされてきている ❶amountはふつう不可算名詞と共に用いられる。

volume [U, C]《ややフォーマル》量, 数 ◇We had to work hard to keep up with the sheer *volume* (= large amount) of business. 膨大な量の仕事を遅れずにこなすために私たちは懸命に働かなくてはならなかった ◇New roads are being built to cope with the high *volumes* of traffic. 激しい交通量に対処するために新しい道路が建設中である ◇Sales *volumes* fell 0.2% in June. 6月には売上数が0.2%落ちた ❶volumeは物の量や数に関して用いられる。この意味においては、形容詞または節で修飾しないで単にa volume of sthと言うことはできない ◆He managed to get through a considerable *volume* of work. (彼はなんと

か相当量の仕事をこなした。) ◆We were attracting a *volume* of business that, frankly, we could not handle. (私たちには、正直なところ、手に負えない量の仕事が舞い込んできていた。)

sum [C] 金額 ◇You will be fined the *sum* of £200. あなたには合計200ポンドの罰金が科されるだろう ◇She inherited a large *sum* of money when her father died. 彼女は父親が死んで多額の財産を引き継いだ ◇He is now earning a six-figure *sum*. 彼は今や数10万ポンドの金を稼いでいる ◇Huge *sums* have been invested in this project. 巨額のお金がこの計画に投資されてきている ◇She was given a ***lump sum*** (= an amount paid at once rather than on separate occasions). 彼女は一括払い金を手にした

quantity [C, U] 分量, 数量 ◇A substantial *quantity* of jewellery was taken during the burglary. 強盗が押し入っている間に相当量の宝石類が盗まれた ◇It is a product that is cheap to produce ***in large quantities***. それは大量生産すると安上がりになる製品だ ◇There is a discount for goods bought ***in quantity***. 大量に買っていただいた品物は割り引きが利きます ◇Is the medicine available in sufficient *quantity*? その薬の在庫は十分ですか ◇The data is limited in terms of both quality and *quantity*. そのデータは質的にも量的にも十分ではない

> **ノート number, amount, quantity の使い分け:**
> number は可算名詞の複数形と共に用いられる。◆a *number* of books/dogs/people (数冊の本/数匹の犬/数人の人々) ×a *number* of money/rain/wood. amountはふつう不可算名詞と共に用いられる。◆a large *amount* of time/money/information (膨大な時間/金額/情報) ×a large *amount* of coins/dogs/girls. quantityは可算・不可算のどちらの名詞にも用いることができる。◆a large *quantity* of wine/food/books (大量のワイン/食料/書籍) とは言えるが、ややフォーマルな語であるため使用頻度はそれだけ低い。

O o

objective 形

objective・impartial・neutral・disinterested・non-partisan・unbiased

人や物事が個人的な意見[感情]に影響を受けないことを表す
【類語訳】事実に基づいた、客観的な、偏りのない、中立的な、私欲のない、第三者的な、不偏不党の、偏見のない

【文型&コロケーション】
- objective/ neutral about sb/ sth
- an objective/ an impartial/ a neutral/ a disinterested/ an unbiased **observer**
- an objective/ an impartial/ a neutral/ an unbiased **opinion/ assessment/ analysis**
- objective/ impartial/ disinterested/ unbiased **advice**
- to **remain** objective/ impartial/ neutral
- **completely/ totally** objective/ impartial/ disinterested/ non-partisan/ unbiased
- **quite** objective/ impartial/ neutral/ disinterested
- **fairly** objective/ impartial/ neutral
- **truly** objective/ impartial/ neutral/ unbiased
- **strictly** objective/ impartial/ neutral/ non-partisan

objective 事実に基づいた、客観的な ◇There's little *objective* evidence to suggest that he is guilty. 彼が有罪であることを示す客観的証拠はほとんどない ◇It's hard for parents to be *objective* about their own children. 両親にとって、自分の子どもについて個人的な感情を交えないことは難しい 反意 **subjective** (OWN)
➤ **objectively** 副 ◇Try to weigh up the issues as *objectively* as you can. 問題をできるだけ客観的に評価するよう努めなさい
➤ **objectivity** 名 [U] ◇The survey's claims to scientific *objectivity* are highly dubious. その調査が客観的であるという主張は、きわめて疑わしい

impartial 偏りのない、公平な ◇Teenagers need access to confidential and *impartial* advice. ティーンエイジャーには内密に公平なアドバイスを受けられる機会が必要だ ◇As chairman, I must remain *impartial*. 私は議長として公平を保たねばなりません
➤ **impartiality** 名 [U] ◇The BBC is supposed to maintain strict *impartiality* in its broadcasts. BBCは放送における厳しい公平性を保つことになっている
➤ **impartially** 副 ◇There are fears that the matter will not be investigated *impartially*. その問題が公平に調査されない恐れがある

neutral (争い・競争・論争において)中立的な ◇Very few journalists are politically *neutral*. 政治的に中立なジャーナリストはほとんどいない ◇The UN are sending six *neutral* observers to the talks. 国連はその協議に中立的なオブザーバーを6人派遣している
➤ **neutrality** 名 [U] ◇I'm afraid we cannot guarantee the *neutrality* of the courts. 残念ながら、我々は法廷の中立性を保証することはできないと思う

disinterested 私心のない、私欲のない、第三者的な ◇I was merely a *disinterested* spectator in the whole affair. その事件全般において、私は第三者的な傍観者にすぎなかった 反意 **interested** ❶ *interested* な人とは、ある状況に利害関係のある立場にいる人のことである。◆As an *interested party*, I was not allowed to vote. (私は当事者だったので、投票を許されなかった)

non-parti'san 不偏不党の、無党派の ◇Our work has always been non-violent and *non-partisan*. 我々の仕事は常に非暴力かつ不偏不党であり続けてきた 反意 **partisan** (BIASED)

unbiased (または **unbiassed**) 偏見のない、不偏の ◇We'd like an *unbiased* opinion, if possible. できるなら、偏見のない意見がほしい 反意 **biased** (BIASED)

obsession 名

obsession・preoccupation・mania・neurosis・hang-up・fixation・complex

人が異常に考えたり心配したりするような精神状態を表す
【類語訳】強迫観念、没頭、執心、熱中、…熱

【文型&コロケーション】
- an obsession/ a preoccupation/ a neurosis/ a hang-up/ a fixation/ a complex **about** sb/ sth
- an obsession/ a preoccupation/ a mania/ a fixation **for** sb/ sth
- an obsession/ a preoccupation/ a fixation **with** sb/ sth
- sb's **current** obsession/ preoccupation/ fixation
- a **new** obsession/ preoccupation/ mania
- to **become** an obsession/ a preoccupation
- to **develop** an obsession/ a neurosis/ a complex

obsession [U, C] 《ふつうけなして》強迫観念；頭から離れないこと ◇Her devotion to him bordered on *obsession*. 彼女の彼に対する献身は強迫観念といっていいものだった ◇She has an unhealthy *obsession* with her diet. 彼女のダイエットへのとらわれようは不健全だ
➤ **obsess** 動 [他、ふつう受身で、自] ◇She's completely *obsessed* with him. 彼女は彼のことで頭が一杯だ ◇I think you should try to stop *obsessing about* food. あなたは食べ物にばかり神経を使うのをやめるべきだと思います

preoccupation [U, C] (心配ゆえの)没頭、執心；気がかりなこと ◇She found his *preoccupation* with money irritating. 彼女は彼のお金への執心に苛立ちを覚えた ◇Their chief *preoccupation* was how to feed their families. 彼らの心を主に占めていたのは、いかに家族を養うかということであった
➤ **preoccupied** 形 ◇He was too *preoccupied* with his own thoughts to notice anything wrong. 彼は自分の考えであまりに頭が一杯で何かがおかしいことなど気づかなかった

mania [C, ふつう単数で, U] 熱中、…熱 ◇He had a *mania* for fast cars. 彼は高速車マニアだった ◇Football *mania* is sweeping the country. サッカー熱が国中を席巻してい る

neurosis (複 **neuroses**) [C, U]《医学》神経症, ノイローゼ ◇Those of anxious temperament are more likely to develop anxiety *neurosis*. 心配症の人たちは不安神経症を患う傾向が強い ❶*neurosis*は深刻な病状である。しかし医学的な用法でなければ、あらゆる強い恐怖心・心配に用いられる。◆This obsession with time is a modern *neurosis* and one we all have to live with. (このように時間にとらわれるのは現代のノイローゼであり、我々みなそれと付き合って暮らしていかなければならないものである)。

'hang-up [C]《インフォーマル, ふつけなして》悩み ◇He's got a real *hang-up* about his height. 彼は自分の身長のことを本当に悩んでいる
▶**,hung 'up** [形]《名詞の前では用いない》◇You're not still *hung up on* that girl? もうあの子にこだわってはいないだろう

fixation [C]《ふつけなして》(病的な)執着, 固執 ◇He's got this *fixation* with cleanliness. 彼にはこの病的にきれい好きというのがあってね
▶**fixated** [形]《名詞の前では用いない》◇He is *fixated on* things that remind him of his childhood. 彼は自分が子ども時代を思い起こさせる物事にとりつかれている

complex [C] 異常心理；コンプレックス ◇He suffers from a *guilt complex*. 彼は罪責コンプレックスに苛まれている ◇Don't mention her weight — she has a *complex* about it. 彼女の体重のことに触れるなよ—コンプレックスを持ってるんだから

obstacle [名]

obstacle・barrier・hurdle・stumbling block・impediment・roadblock・handicap・hindrance
人が事を行う［達成する］のを困難にする物事を表す
【類語訳】障害, 邪魔, 障壁, 困難, 問題, 不和, 支障, ハンディキャップ, 邪魔者

〔文型&コロケーション〕

▶an obstacle/ a barrier/ a stumbling block/ an impediment/ a handicap/ a hindrance **to** sb/ sth
▶**without** obstacles/ impediment/ hindrance
▶**despite** the obstacles/ barriers/ handicap
▶a **major** obstacle/ barrier/ hurdle/ stumbling block/ impediment/ roadblock/ handicap/ hindrance
▶a **big** obstacle/ hurdle/ stumbling block/ roadblock/ handicap
▶a **real** obstacle/ barrier/ stumbling block/ handicap/ hindrance
▶the **main** obstacle/ barrier/ hurdle/ stumbling block/ impediment/ roadblock
▶a **legal** obstacle/ barrier/ impediment/ roadblock/ handicap
▶a **financial** obstacle/ barrier/ hurdle/ roadblock
▶to **face** an obstacle/ a barrier/ a hurdle/ a roadblock
▶to **remove** an obstacle/ a barrier/ a stumbling block/ an impediment/ a roadblock
▶to **overcome** an obstacle/ a barrier/ a hurdle/ a handicap

obstacle [C]《実行・達成を困難にする》障害, 邪魔 ◇The huge distances involved have proved to be an *obstacle* to communication. 非常な距離の隔たりがあるとコミュニケーションの障害となることがわかっている ◇So far, we have managed to overcome all the *obstacles* placed in our path. 今のところ, 行く手にあるあらゆる障害を何とか克服してきた

barrier [C]《実行を妨げる[物事を不可能にする]》障害, 障壁 ◇Cost should not be a *barrier* to the use of legal services. 費用が司法サービスの利用の障害であってはならない ◇There has been a gradual reduction in subsidies and trade *barriers*. 助成金や貿易障壁が徐々に減少してきた

〔ノート〕**obstacle**と**barrier**の使い分け：**obstacle**は, 事を行うことを困難にするが, ふつう多大な努力をすることで可能になる。**barrier**は, 人が試みない［試みることができない］ことを意味し, 実際に人が事を行うのを妨げるものを指す。

hurdle [C]《物事の達成のために解決しなければならない》障害, 困難 ◇Well, we've **cleared** the first *hurdle*; let's see what happens next. さあ, 第一関門を突破したぞ。次に何が起こるか見てみようじゃないか ◇The next *hurdle* will be getting her parents' agreement. 次の障害は彼女の両親の同意を得ることだろう ❶*hurdle*はしばしば, 一連の問題・困難の一つと見なされる。

'stumbling block [C]《特にジャーナリズム》(達成・進展を妨げる)問題, 不和, 障害 ◇The peace process encountered another *stumbling block* in mid-June. 和平プロセスは6月中旬に別の障害に見舞われた

impediment [名][C]《フォーマル》(実行・進展を困難にする)障害, 支障 ◇There are no legal *impediments* to their appealing against the decision. 決定を不服として訴える上で法的障害はない

roadblock [C]《米, 特にジャーナリズム》(計画の進展の)障害 ◇The project faces legal *roadblocks*. そのプロジェクトは法の壁に直面している

handicap [C]《技術・知識・経験の欠如などの》ハンディキャップ, 障害 ◇Not speaking the language proved to be a bigger *handicap* than I'd imagined. その言語を話さないことは, 想像以上に大きな障害であることがわかった ☞**handicap** (BLOCK 1)

hindrance [C, ふつう単数で]《ややフォーマル》(物事の実行・発生を困難にする)障害, 邪魔者 ◇To be honest, she was *more of a hindrance than a help*. 正直言うと, 彼女は助けというより邪魔だった〔反意〕help, ☞**hinder** (BLOCK 1)

obvious [形]

obvious・natural・logical・understandable
物事が普通であり予期されるものであることを表す
【類語訳】明白な, 自明の, 当然の, 理にかなった, もっともな, 無理もない

〔文型&コロケーション〕

▶obvious/ natural/ logical/ understandable **that**...
▶natural/ logical **to do sth**
▶natural/ logical **for sb to do sth**
▶the obvious/ natural/ logical **thing to do/ choice/ conclusion/ solution**
▶the obvious/ a natural/ an understandable **temptation**
▶a natural/ a logical/ an understandable **reaction/ response**
▶**perfectly/ quite** obvious/ natural/ logical/ understandable

obvious (ほとんどの人にとって)明白な；自明の ◇There's an *obvious* question that no one has asked. 誰も訊ねたことのない一つの明白な疑問がある ◇The solution was

obvious. 解決策は明らかだった ◇'What should we do?' 'It's *obvious*, isn't it?' 「どうしましょう」「わかりきってるよね」 ◇It's *obvious* that she'd be upset. 彼女が狼狽するのは目に見えている
▸**obviously** 副 ◇*Obviously* we don't want to spend too much money. 言うまでもなく、私たちはあまりお金を使いたくありません

natural ふつうの、自然な；当然の ◇It's *natural* that he would want to see his own son. 彼が自分の息子に会いたがるのは当然だ ◇It's perfectly *natural* for you to feel annoyed. あなたが不愉快になるのもごく当たり前だ ◇Children have a *natural* desire for affection and security. 子どもは愛情と安心感を自然に求める ◇The man died of *natural causes* (= not by violence). その男は自然死した ◇He thought inequality was all part of the *natural order* of things. 不平等はごく当たり前のことだと彼は考えた ☞ **natural** (NATURAL)
▸**naturally** 副 ◇*Naturally*, I get upset when things go wrong. 当然ながら、物事がうまく行かない時は私だって機嫌は悪くなります ◇This leads *naturally* to my next point. このことは当然、次に私が言いたいことにつながります

ノート **obvious** と **natural** の使い分け：**obvious** は特に、決定・選択・行動方針について用いられる。**natural** も、同様に用いることができるが、感情についてより頻繁に用いられる。◆ a *natural* feeling/desire/fear/concern/anxiety/reluctance（自然に抱く感情／願望／恐怖／関心／不安／不本意）。**obvious** がこれらの単語と共に用いられる場合、容易に気づく「露骨な、隠さない」といった意味で用いられる。✕ Children have an *obvious* desire for affection. ◆ George ignored Lucy's *obvious* wish to be left alone.（ジョージは放っておいてもらいたいというルーシーの明白な願望を無視した）。**obvious** も **natural** も、it's obvious/natural that sb would... の形で行動を表すのに用いることができるが、it's natural for sb to do sth の形で用いられるのは **natural** だけである。✕ It's perfectly *obvious* for you to feel annoyed.

logical（行動方針・論理の道筋が）当然の、理にかなった、もっともな ◇It was a *logical* thing to do in the circumstances. そうした状況ではそうするのが当然のことだった ◇It seemed *logical* to try and contact the child's mother. 子どもの母親に連絡しようとするのはもっともだと思えた 反意 **illogical** ❶ *illogical* な物事は、分別がない、あるいは論理的に考えられていないものである。◆ *illogical* behaviour/arguments（筋の通らない行動／議論）
▸**logically** 副 ◇The problem is that you can never trust them to act *logically*. 問題は、彼らが論理的に行動することを決して当てにできないことである

understandable（特定の状況での感情・行動・反応が）無理もない、もっともな ◇Their attitude is perfectly *understandable*. 彼らの態度はしごくもっともだ ◇It was an *understandable* mistake to make. それは無理もない誤りだった
▸**understandably** 副 ◇They were *understandably* disappointed by the result. 彼らが結果にがっかりしたのは無理もない

occasional 形

occasional・the odd…・sporadic・intermittent
あまり頻繁[定期的]ではなく起こる[現れる]ことを表す
【類語訳】時折の、たまの、時々の、時多の、散発的な、まばらな、断続的な、間欠的な

文型&コロケーション
▸ occasional/ sporadic/ intermittent **bursts** of sth
▸ on an occasional/ a sporadic/ an intermittent **basis**
▸ occasional/ sporadic/ intermittent **contact/ attacks**
▸ the occasional/ odd **bit/ bout/ spot** of sth

occasional [名詞の前で] 時折の、たまの ◇He makes *occasional* references in the letters to the planned autobiography. 彼は手紙の中で時折、計画された自叙伝に触れている ◇She found *occasional* work on television. 彼女は時折テレビに出る仕事を見つけた ◇You have to expect a few difficulties and the *occasional* setback. 君はいくらかの困難と時折の挫折を覚悟しなければならない 反意 **regular, frequent** (FREQUENT), ☞ **occasionally** (SOMETIMES)

the odd… [名詞の前で]《ややインフォーマル、特に話し言葉》時々の、時たまの ◇It doesn't matter on *the odd* occasion, but it's occurring regularly. 時々なら問題ないが、それは何度となく起きている ◇I love the long bare hills with just *the odd* clump of trees. 私は所々にしか木の茂みのないその長いはげ山が大好きです ❶悪い［間違った］物事について *the odd…* を用い、それがあまり重要だと思っていないことを表す。◆You have to expect *the odd* mistake.（たまに起こるミスを予想しなければならない）。◆He did take *the odd* afternoon off.（彼は時々午後に休みをとった）.

sporadic《書き言葉》散発的な；まばらな ◇*Sporadic* gunfire was reported each night. 散発的な銃砲のことが毎晩報道された ◇Planning controls protect the countryside from *sporadic* development. 建築計画規制が散発的な開発から地方を保護している ❶ *sporadic* はふつう、暴力・病気といった不快な物事に用いられる。
▸**sporadically** 副 ◇Fighting continued *sporadically* for two months. 戦闘は2か月間散発的に続いた

intermittent 断続的な、間欠的な ◇A day of *intermittent* rainstorms followed. 断続的な暴風雨の一日があとに続いた ◇There had been twenty years of *intermittent* warfare. 20年間武力衝突が断続的に続いていた 反意 **continuous** (CONTINUOUS)
▸**intermittently** 副 ◇The protests continued *intermittently*. 断続的に抗議が続いた

odour (英) (米 odor) 名 ☞ SMELL

odour・stench・smell・stink・reek
不快に嗅覚を刺激するもの
【類語訳】におい、悪臭、異臭、嫌なにおい

odour	stink	stench
smell		reek

文型&コロケーション
▸ an odour/ a stench/ a smell/ a stink/ a reek **of** sth
▸ an **acrid** odour/ stench/ smell/ stink
▸ a **foul/ putrid/ powerful** odour/ stench/ smell
▸ a **pungent** odour/ smell/ reek
▸ to **give off** an odour/ a stench/ a smell
▸ an odour/ a stench/ a smell/ a reek **fills** sth
▸ an odour/ a stench/ a smell/ a stink **comes from** sth

offend, offensive

odour《英》(米 **odor**) [C]《ややフォーマル, 特に書き言葉》(強烈な)におい, 悪臭 ◇There was an *odour* of decay in the house. 家の中で腐敗臭がした ◇Use this spray to remove everyday household *odours*. ふだんの家の中のにおいを取り除くにはこのスプレーをお使いください ◇He suffers badly from *body odour*. 彼は体臭にひどく悩んでいる

stench [単数で]《特に書き言葉 or 文語》(強烈な)悪臭, 異臭 ◇The *stench* of rotting fish filled the hut. 腐りかけの魚の悪臭が小屋に充満した ◇The *stench* of death and decay hung in the air. 死臭と腐敗臭が漂っていた
❶ stench はおそらく, ここであげるにおいの中で最も強烈で最も不快なものである。stench は特に, 体や死と結びついたにおいを表すために文学的作品で用いられる。blood, death, decay, fear, sweat, urine, rotting meat/flesh/fish/vegetables などと結びつく.

smell [単数で]《ややインフォーマル, 特に話し言葉》(嫌な)におい ◇What's that *smell*? あのにおいは何だ ◇Yuk! What a *smell*! うっ, 何ていうにおいだ ◇See if you can get rid of that *smell*. そのにおいを消せるかどうかやってみて
▶**smell** 動 [自] *It smells* in here, can you open a window? ここは臭いね, 窓開けてもらえる

stink [単数で]《インフォーマル》悪臭 ◇What a *stink*! Open the window! 臭い, 窓開けて ◇The room was filled with the *stink* of sweat and urine. 部屋は汗と尿のにおいが立ち込めていた
▶**stink** 動 [自] Her breath *stank* of garlic.《インフォーマル》彼女の息はニンニク臭かった ◇*It stinks* of smoke in here. ここはタバコ臭い

reek [単数で](強烈な)悪臭 ◇The *reek* of gunpowder and smoke grew stronger. 火薬と煙の強烈なにおいがだんだん強くなった ❶ reek は stench とほぼ同じくらい強烈だが, 死とはさほど関連がない.
▶**reek** 動 [自] ◇His breath *reeked* of tobacco. 彼はタバコ臭かった

offend 動

offend・insult・shock・abuse
自分の言動のために人の気分を害することを表す
【類語訳】機嫌を損ねる, 不快にさせる, 侮辱する, ショックを与える, 暴言を吐く, ののしる

〔文型&コロケーション〕
▶to feel offended/ insulted/ shocked
▶deeply offended/ insulted/ shocked

offend [他, しばしば受身で, 自](無礼な[困惑させるような]言動で)人の気分を害する, 機嫌を損ねる, 不快にさせる ◇They'll be *offended* if you don't go to their wedding. 結婚式に出ないと彼らの気分を害するよ ◇Some people found his jokes funny but others were deeply *offended*. 彼の冗談を面白いと思う人たちもいたが, ひどく不快に思う人もいた ◇A TV interviewer must be careful not to *offend*. テレビのインタビュアーは不快感を与えないように注意しなければならない
▶**offence** 名 [U] ◇I'm sure he *meant no offence* when he said that. そう言った時, 彼には悪気はなかったと思う ◇The photo on the cover of the book may *cause offence* to some people. その本の表紙の写真に不快感を抱く人もいるかもしれない ◇No one will *take offence* (= feel offended) if you leave early. あなたが早

insult [他, しばしば受身で](無礼な言動で)侮辱する ◇I have never been so *insulted* in all my life! これほど侮辱されたことは私は今まで一度もない ◇She felt *insulted* by the low offer. 彼女は低い額を提示されて侮辱されたように感じた ◇Do you really expect me to believe that? Don't *insult my intelligence*! 本当にそれを信じろって言うわけ. ばかにしないで ☞ **insulting** (INSULTING)
▶**insult** 名 [C] ◇The crowd was shouting *insults* at the police. 群衆は警察を大声で罵っていた ◇His comments were seen as an *insult to* the president. 彼の発言は大統領に対する侮辱とみなされた

〔ノート〕**offend** と **insult** の使い分け：insult は, ふつう故意に, 人に対して無礼なことを言う[行う]ことである. offend は, 人を侮辱したり, その人にとって大切な人・物事に関して無礼[軽率]であったりすることで, 気分を害することである.

shock [自, 他](故意にひどい言動で)気分を害させる, 不快にさせる, ショックを与える ◇These movies deliberately set out to *shock*. これらの映画はわざとショックを与えることを狙っている ◇She enjoys *shocking* people by saying outrageous things. 彼女はひどいことを言って人が嫌な思いをするのを楽しんでいる ☞ **shocking** (OUTRAGEOUS)

abuse [他](人に対して[について])暴言を吐く, ののしる ◇Journalists covering the case have been threatened and *abused*. その事件を扱うジャーナリストたちは脅迫とののしりを受けてきた
▶**abuse** 名 [U] ◇to scream/hurl/shout *abuse* 罵詈雑言を声を張り上げて言う/浴びせる/叫ぶ ◇a *stream/torrent of abuse* 立て続けの暴言/暴言の連発

offensive 形 ☞ INSULTING

offensive・abusive・bad・filthy・rude・foul・coarse
言葉や人が無礼でひどいことを表す
【類語訳】不快な, 腹立たしい, 侮辱的な, いらいらさせる, ののしりの, 口汚い, 卑猥な, 無作法な, 下品な, 汚い

〔文型&コロケーション〕
▶offensive/ abusive to sb
▶offensive/ abusive/ bad/ filthy/ rude/ foul language
▶an offensive/ an abusive/ a filthy/ a rude/ a coarse word
▶an offensive/ an abusive/ a rude gesture/ remark/ comment
▶an offensive/ a filthy/ a rude joke
▶very/ quite offensive/ abusive/ rude/ foul/ coarse
▶rather offensive/ rude/ foul/ coarse

offensive《ややフォーマル》不快な, 腹立たしい, 侮辱的な, いらいらさせる ◇I've had enough of her *offensive* remarks. 彼女の不快な発言にはうんざりだ ◇His comments were deeply *offensive* to a large number of single mothers. 彼の発言は数多くのシングルマザーに対して極めて侮辱的だった ◇This job is stressful enough even without clients being *offensive*. この仕事は依頼人が不愉快な人でなくてもストレスがたまる 〔反意〕**inoffensive** ❶ inoffensive は, 誰の気分も害さない[も怒らせない]ことを表す.
◆a shy, *inoffensive* young man (内気で当たり障りのない若者)

abusive《ややフォーマル》(非常に)侮辱的な; ののしりの, 口汚い ◇He was fined for making *abusive* comments to the referee. 彼は審判員に対して口汚い発言をしたとし

↪**offensive**　　　　　　　　　　　　　**offer**

て罰金を科された　◇He became *abusive* when he was drunk. 彼は酔うと口汚くなった
bad [ふつう名詞の前で] 不快な, 腹立たしい, 侮辱的な, いらいらさせる　◇Most of the complaints received were about *bad* language. 受けたほとんどの苦情は不適切な言葉に関するものだった　❶この意味では, bad は常に bad language という句で用いられる.
filthy 卑猥(%)な　◇That's enough of your *filthy* language! 君の下品な言葉はもうたくさんだ　◇He's got a *filthy* mind (= is always thinking about sex). 彼はみだらなことばかり考えている
rude (特に英) 無作法な, (卑猥で)下品な　◇The joke is too *rude* to repeat. そのジョークはあまりに下品で2度と口にできない　◇Someone made a *rude* noise. 誰かが無作法な物音を立てた
foul [ふつう名詞の前で] (言葉が)汚い, 下品な　◇He called her the *foulest* names imaginable. 彼は彼女のことを考えられる限り最も下品にののしった　◇I'm sick of her *foul* mouth (= habit of swearing). 彼女の口汚さにはうんざりだ
coarse (ややフォーマル) (卑猥で)下品な, 下卑た　◇He constantly made *coarse* jokes about his girlfriend. 彼は始終自分のガールフレンドに関する下品な冗談を言った

offer 名

1　offer・approach・overture・advances・proposal
人のために物事を行う[物事を一緒に行う]のはどうかと言う行為
【類語訳】申し出, 提供, 働きかけ, 申し入れ, 提案, 言い寄り, 口説き

文型&コロケーション
▶an offer/ an approach/ overtures/ advances/ a proposal **to** sb
▶an offer/ overtures/ a proposal **of** sth
▶an offer/ a proposal **of marriage**
▶(a) **friendly** offer/ approach/ overtures
▶to **make/ receive** an offer/ an approach/ overtures/ advances/ a proposal
▶to **reject** sb's offer/ approach/ overtures/ advances/ proposal
▶to **respond to/ spurn** sb's offer/ overtures/ advances/ proposal
▶to **accept/ decline/ refuse/ turn down** an offer/ a proposal

offer [C] (人への)申し出, 提供　◇Thank you for your kind *offer* of help. ご親切な援助の申し出に感謝します　◇I accepted her *offer* to pay. 支払いをしてくれるという彼女の申し出を受けた　◇I took him up on his *offer* of a loan. 私は彼の融資の申し出を受けた　◇You can't just turn down *offers* of work like that. そういった仕事の提示をむげに断ってはいけません
approach [C] (ややフォーマル) (申し出・頼みごとをする際の言葉による)働きかけ　◇The club has made an *approach* to a local company for sponsorship. そのクラブは後援を求めて地元企業に働きかけを行ってきた　◇She resented his persistent *approaches*. 彼女は彼がしつこく言い寄ってくるのに憤慨した
▶**approach** 動 [他]　◇We have been *approached* by a number of companies that are interested in our product. 我々の製品に関心のあるいくつかの会社から打診がありました

overture [C, ふつう複数で] (親交・ビジネス・話し合いにむけての)申し出, 申し入れ, 提案　◇He began making *overtures* to a number of merchant banks. 彼はいくつかのマーチャントバンクに打診をし始めた　◇Maggie was never one to reject a friendly *overture*. マギーは親切な申し出を断るような人間では決してなかった

ノート approach と overture の使い分け: approach は, 人への事務的な働きかけついて用いることが多い. overture は, むしろ人を説いて自分を好きにさせよう[自分とビジネスを行わせよう]とすることを表す.

advances [複数形で] (ややフォーマル) (性的関係を求めての)言い寄り, 口説き　◇He had made *advances* to one of his students. 彼は自分の学生の一人に言い寄っていた　◇She rejected his sexual *advances*. 彼女は彼の性的な口説きをはねつけた　❶ advances は amorous や sexual と共に用いられることが多いが, なんの形容詞がつかなくても性的な意味合いを帯びる.
proposal [C] (正式な)結婚の申し込み, プロポーズ　◇She had been hoping for a sweet old-fashioned *proposal* of marriage. 彼女はすてきな古風な結婚の申し込みを期待していた　❶ proposal には, 「正式な提案[計画]」というずっと頻度が高い一般的な意味もある. ☞ **proposal** (PROPOSAL)
▶**propose** 動 [自, 他]　◇He was afraid that if he *proposed* she might refuse. プロポーズしたら彼女に断られるかもしれないと, 彼は心配した　◇She *proposed to* me! 彼女が僕にプロポーズしたんだよ　◇to *propose* marriage 求婚する

2　offer・bid・tender
購入[仕事, サービスの報酬]のために特定の金額を示す行為
【類語訳】提示額, 付け値, 入札

文型&コロケーション
▶an offer/ a bid/ a tender **for** sth
▶a **competitive** offer/ bid/ tender
▶to **put in/ receive/ accept** an offer/ a bid/ a tender
▶to **invite** offers/ bids/ tenders
▶to **make/ withdraw** an offer/ a bid

offer [C] 提示額　◇I've had an *offer* of £2,500 for the car. その車に2千5百ポンドの提示があった　◇They made me an *offer* I couldn't refuse. 彼らは私には断れない額を提示してきた　◇The original price was $3,000, but I'm *open to offers* (= willing to consider offers that are less than that). 元値は3千ドルですが, 提示いただいた額で検討いたします
bid [C] (特にビジネス or ジャーナリズム) (買い手の)付け値; (仕事の請負[商品・サービスの提供]への)入札　◇The company mounted a hostile *takeover bid* for its rival. その会社はライバル会社に対し敵対的株式公開買い付けをしかけた　◇At the auction (= a public sale where things are sold to the person who offers most), the highest *bid* for the picture was £200,000. オークションでは, その絵に対する最高入札額は20万ポンドだった　◇Any more *bids*? 他にご入札は　◇The company *submitted a bid* for the contract to clean the hospital. その会社は病院の清掃契約の入札を行った　◇a *bid on* the contract 契約への入札
▶**bid** 動 [自, 他]　◇They successfully *bid* for the contract. 彼らは首尾よく契約を落札した　◇They successfully *bid on* the contract. 彼らは首尾よく契約を落札した

◇Which other cities are *bidding* to host the 2016 Olympics? 他にどの都市が2016年のオリンピック開催に立候補していますか

tender [C]《特に英、ややフォーマル、ビジネス》(仕事の請負[商品・サービスの提供]への)入札 ◇The local authority has invited *tenders* for the supply of school meals. 地方自治体は学校給食供給への入札を募った ◇Cleaning and laundry services have been *put out to tender* (= companies have been asked to make offers to supply these services). 清掃・洗濯サービスが入札にかけられている

▶**tender** 動［自］◇Local firms were invited to *tender* for the building contract. 地元企業に向け建設契約入札の募集が行われた

official 名

official・officer・councillor・councilman/councilwoman・mayor・commissioner・civil servant・secretary・bureaucrat

政府省庁[大組織]において、特に権能のある地位で働く人
【類語訳】幹部職員、官僚、評議員、議員、首長、委員、理事、公務員、幹事、官吏、役員、お役人

▸ 文型&コロケーション

▶ a **senior** official/ officer/ councillor/ civil servant/ bureaucrat
▶ a **chief** official/ officer/ commissioner/ civil servant/ secretary
▶ a **junior** official/ officer/ civil servant
▶ a **deputy** officer/ mayor/ commissioner/ secretary
▶ a **local** official/ officer/ councillor/ councilman/ mayor/ commissioner/ civil servant/ bureaucrat/ secretary
▶ a **regional/ district** official/ officer/ commissioner/ secretary
▶ a **city/ town** official/ councillor/ councilman/ mayor
▶ a **public** official/ officer/ servant
▶ a **government** official/ officer/ bureaucrat/ servant
▶ a **party** official/ bureaucrat/ secretary
▶ a **union** official/ officer/ secretary
▶ to **appoint** an official/ an officer/ a commissioner
▶ to **elect (sb as)** a councillor/ mayor/ councilman
▶ to **serve as** an officer/ a councillor/ a councilman/ mayor/ a commissioner/ secretary

official [C]（大組織の）幹部職員、官僚 ◇A senior *official* in the State Department issued a statement. 国務省高官は声明を出した

officer [C]《しばしば複合語で》（大組織の）幹部職員、官僚 ◇The charity has a full-time *press officer* working with the national newspapers. その慈善団体には、全国紙と連携する専任の広報主任がいる ◇the company's Chief Executive/Financial *Officer* (= CEO/CFO) 会社の最高経営責任者/最高財務責任者

▸ ノート **official** と **officer** の使い分け：official は、権能ある地位にいるあらゆる人を指すことができる一般的な語。◆ government/bank/Olympic *officials*（官吏／銀行幹部／オリンピック役員）. *officer*は、特定の地位に対する肩書きの一部であることが多い。◆ an environmental health *officer*（環境衛生官）. ◆ the chief medical *officer*（医部部長）.

councillor（米でまた **councilor**）[C] 評議員、議員 ◇*Councillor* Bob Harris. ボブ・ハリス議員 ◇Talk to your *city councillor* about the problem. その問題に関して市会議員と話しなさい ◇She served as a Conservative *councillor for* Harwich for many years.《英》彼女は長年、ハリッジの保守党市会議員として働いた

'councilman, 'councilwoman（または **Councilman, Councilwoman**）[C]《米》'This is a first for the city,' said *Councilman* Wallis.「これは市としては初めてです」とウォリス議員は言った

mayor（または **Mayor**）[C]（町・自治都市・州の議会の）長；（町・市の）首長 ◇He became the first directly elected *mayor* of London in 2000. 彼は2000年に、直接選挙された最初のロンドン市長となった

commissioner（または **Commissioner**）[C] 委員、理事 ◇a *commissioner* for the Central Collegiate Hockey Association 大学ホッケー中部協会の委員 ◇The merger has been referred to the *European* Competition *Commissioner*. 合併はEU競争法委員に委ねられてきた

ˌcivil 'servant [C] 公務員 ◇The committee will question a number of ministers and high-ranking *civil servants*. 委員会では何名かの大臣と上級公務員に質問することになっている

secretary [C]（書状作成・記録保管・ビジネス協定の締結を担当する）幹事；《英》大臣［大使］補佐 ◇She served as *club secretary* for 25 years. 彼女は25年間クラブの幹事を務めた ◇Anyone interested in joining the society should contact *membership secretary* Bob Barwood. 協会への入会に関心のある方はどなたでも、会員担当総務のボブ・バーウッドにお問い合わせください ◇He had talks with the Chief *Secretary to* the Treasury. 彼は大蔵副大臣と会談した

bureaucrat [C]《しばしばけなして》（厳格すぎるほどに規則を守る）官吏、役員、お役人 ◇He was just another *faceless bureaucrat*. 彼はよくいる主体性なき官僚にすぎなかった ☞ **bureaucracy** (AUTHORITIES), **bureaucracy** (BUREAUCRACY).

official 形

official・formal・authorized・licensed・accredited

権能ある地位にある人と関連していること、およびその許可のもとで行われることを表す
【類語訳】公務上の、職務上の、公式の、公認の、正式の、認可された

▸ 文型&コロケーション

▶ to be authorized/ licensed/ accredited **by** sb/ sth
▶ to be authorized/ licensed **to do** sth
▶ official/ formal/ authorized/ licensed **institutions**
▶ an official/ a formal/ an authorized **body**
▶ an official/ a formal/ an accredited **programme**
▶ an official/ a formal **announcement/ request/ enquiry/ complaint/ protest/ apology/ agreement**
▶ an authorized/ accredited **practitioner/ representative/ supplier**
▶ the official/ authorized **biography** of sb

official [ふつう名詞の前で] 公務上の、職務上の；公式の、公認の ◇The minister was in Berlin on *official* business. 大臣は公務でベルリンにいた ◇She attended *in her*

↪**official**

official capacity as mayor. 彼女は市長としての公的立場で出席した ◇The news is not yet *official*. そのニュースはまだ公式のものではない ◇The country's *official* language is Spanish. その国の公用語はスペイン語です ◇The report revealed *official* corruption (= corrupt behaviour by officials) in relation to road building. その報告書は道路建設に関連した公務員の汚職を暴いた ❶出来事についての *official* な談話とは、権威ある人たちによって一般に向けて語られるものである。それは真実であることもないこともある。◆That was the ***official version*** of events but nobody believed it. (それは出来事についての公式見解だったが、誰もそれを信じなかった)。◆The ***official line*** is that the date for the election has not yet been decided. (表向きには、選挙日はまだ決定していないとのことである)。 反意 **unofficial** (UNOFFICIAL)

▶**officially** 副 ◇The library will be *officially* opened by the local MP. その図書館は地元の国会議員によって正式に開館されます ◇*Officially*, he resigned because of ill health. 表向きには、彼は体調不良のために辞任した

formal (合意に則した)正式の ◇Once the loan has been approved we'll send a *formal* agreement for you to sign. いったん融資が承認されれば、署名していただく正式契約書をお送りします ◇*Formal* diplomatic relations between the two countries were re-established in December. 2か国間の正式な外交関係が12月に再構築された ◇What this announcement does is put the arrangement on a *formal* basis. この発表は取り決めを正式なものとするためのものである 反意 **informal** (INFORMAL)

▶**formally** 副 ◇The accounts were *formally* approved by the board. その収支計算書は委員会によって正式に認められた

authorized (英でまた **-sed**) 認可された、公認の ◇The family agreed to an *authorized* biography of the artist. 家族はそのアーティストの公認の伝記であることに同意した ◇There was a notice on the door: *Authorized* Personnel Only. ドアには「関係者以外立入禁止」という張り紙があった 反意 **unauthorized** (UNOFFICIAL)

licensed 認可された；免許を受けた ◇There aren't enough *licensed* taxis in the city. その都市には認可タクシーが十分にない ◇The handgun had been bought from a *licensed* dealer. その拳銃は認可を受けた販売業者から購入されていた ◇There are only two companies *licensed* to produce the vaccine. そのワクチン製造を許可された会社は2社しかない 反意 **unlicensed** (UNOFFICIAL)

accredited [ふつう名詞の前で] (正式に)承認[許可]された；(正式な)許可を得た ◇Only *accredited* golfing journalists were allowed near the players. 許可を得たゴルフジャーナリストだけが選手に近づくのを許された ◇The former business school is now a fully *accredited* British university. そのかつてのビジネススクールは現在、れっきとした認可を受けた英国の大学である

▶**accreditation** 名 [U] ◇the *accreditation* of engineering qualifications 工学技能の認定

often 副

often・frequently・a lot・routinely・habitually
繰り返し行われる[起きる]ことを表す
【類語訳】何度も、しばしば、頻繁に、しょっちゅう、習慣的に

often, oil

文型&コロケーション
▶often/ routinely **available**
▶frequently/ routinely/ habitually **used**
▶to **happen** often/ frequently/ a lot
▶to **occur** often/ frequently
▶to **wear sth** often/ frequently/ a lot/ habitually
▶how **often**/ frequently?
▶quite **often**/ frequently/ a lot
▶fairly/ very **often**/ frequently

often 何度も、しばしば ◇I've *often* wondered what he looked like. しばしば、私は彼がどんなふうだったかと思う ◇The dog *often* went missing for days. その犬はしょっちゅう、何日も行方不明になった ◇How *often* does it happen? それはどのくらいよく起こるのですか ◇You should come and see us more *often*. もっと頻繁に私たちに会いに来なさいよ ◇She likes to get out of the city as *often* as possible. 彼女は暇さえあれば町から抜け出したがる ◇It's *not often* that I receive fan letters. ファンレターをもらうことはしょっちゅうではない 反意 **rarely, seldom** (RARELY), ☞ **often** (USUALLY)

frequently (ややフォーマル) 何度も、しばしば、頻繁に ◇It was a word he used *frequently*. それは彼がよく使う言葉だった ◇Passengers complained that trains were *frequently* cancelled. 列車がよく運休になると、乗客は苦情を言った ◇It's the most ***frequently asked question*** these days. それは最近最も多い質問です 反意 **infrequently** (RARELY) ☞ **frequent** (FREQUENT)

ノート **often** と **frequently** の使い分け：多くの場合、どちらの語も用いることができる。frequentlyは、oftenよりフォーマルで、特に一般大衆に影響を与える[によって行われる]物事について用いられる。oftenは、自分が行う[自分個人に影響を与える]物事についてより頻繁に用いられる。

a lot 《インフォーマル、特に話し言葉》何度も、しばしば、しょっちゅう ◇We used to go out quite *a lot*. 私たちはしょっちゅう出かけたものだ ◇They worry about it *a lot*. 彼らはよくそのことを心配している 反意 **not much** ❶反意語は not much である。◆We didn't go out *much*. (私たちはあまり出かけなかった)

routinely 日課として、定期的に；非常に頻繁に；(悪事を行うことが)ごく普通に ◇A red blood cell count and blood pressure were *routinely* recorded. 赤血球の数と血圧は定期的に記録された ◇He is *routinely* cited as one of America's best businessmen. 彼は決まって、米国で最高のビジネスマンの一人に挙げられる ◇The regime was accused of *routinely* torturing prisoners. その政権は囚人を日常的に拷問していたとして告発された ☞ **routine** (USUAL)

habitually 習慣的に；(非常に)頻繁に ◇She was without the steel-framed glasses she *habitually* wore. 彼女はいつものスチールフレームのメガネをかけていなかった ◇The rules were *habitually* broken. 規則は常に破られた ☞ **habitual** (FREQUENT), **habitual** (USUAL)

oil 名

oil・gas・fuel・coal・petrol・gasoline・petroleum・diesel・fossil fuel
燃焼時に熱[光]エネルギーを生む物質を表す
【類語訳】石油、ガス、燃料、石炭、原油、ディーゼル油、化石燃料

| 文型&コロケーション |

- ▸unleaded fuel/ gas/ petrol/ gasoline
- ▸sth runs on oil/ gas/ (a particular kind of) fuel/ petrol/ gasoline/ diesel
- ▸to fill the car up with gas/ petrol/ diesel
- ▸to run out of oil/ gas/ fuel/ petrol/ diesel
- ▸the oil/ gas/ fuel/ coal/ petroleum industry
- ▸oil/ gas/ fuel/ coal/ petrol/ gasoline/ petroleum/ diesel prices
- ▸oil/ gas/ fuel/ coal/ petrol/ gasoline/ petroleum/ diesel/ fossil fuel consumption
- ▸oil/ gas/ fuel/ coal/ petroleum/ fossil fuel reserves
- ▸an oil/ a gas/ a fuel/ a petrol/ a gasoline/ a diesel tank
- ▸an oil/ a gas/ a fuel leak
- ▸an oil/ a gas/ a petrol/ a gasoline/ a diesel engine
- ▸an oil/ a gas/ a fuel/ a petrol/ a gasoline tanker
- ▸gas/ petrol/ gasoline/ diesel fumes

oil [U] 石油 ◇Several companies are *drilling for oil* in the region. 数社がその地域で石油目当ての掘削を行っている ◇*oil* wells 油井 ◇At the time, *oil* was trading at around $18 per barrel. 当時,石油は1バレル約18ドルで取引されていた ❶ **crude** oil (または crude). は,化学薬品で処理される前の天然状態の原油である。だがふつう,処理されていないことを強調したいのでなければ,単に oil と呼ばれる。

gas [U] (燃料として用いられる)(混合)ガス ◇Much of Britain's energy is supplied by *natural gas* from the North Sea. 英国のエネルギーの多量の部分が,北海の天然ガスによって供給される ◇All the apartments are fitted with *gas* central heating. アパートの全室には,ガスによる集中暖房設備が設置されている ❶《米》では, gas はまた, petrol/gasoline (下記参照)を表すふつうの語でもある。 ◆He still had plenty of *gas* in the tank. (彼のタンクには,まだガソリンを一杯だった). ◆We need to find a *gas* station. (ガソリンスタンドを見つけなくちゃ).

fuel [U, C] (熱・動力を生み出す)燃料 ◇Most of the houses are heated with *solid fuel* (= wood or coal). ほとんどの家庭は固形燃料で暖房している ◇Domestic *fuel* bills are set to rise again this winter. 国内の燃料代は,この冬また値上がりすることになっている

coal [U] 石炭 ◇Put some more *coal* on the fire. 火にもう少し石炭をくべなさい ◇a *lump of coal* 石炭の塊 ◇a *coal mine* 炭鉱

petrol [U] 《英》(原油から得られる)ガソリン ◇Does your car run on *unleaded petrol*? あなたの車は無鉛ガソリンで走行するの ❶《米》ではふつう gas あるいは gasoline が用いられる。

gasoline [U]《米, ややフォーマル》ガソリン ◇They bought a ten-gallon can of *gasoline*. 彼らは10ガロン缶のガソリンを購入した ❶《米》ではほとんどの話し言葉・書き言葉において, gasoline の代わりに gas が用いられる。

petroleum [U] 原油 ◇The government suspended its supplies of *petroleum* to the country as a result of the crisis. 政府はその危機の結果として,その国への原油の供給を一時停止した

diesel ディーゼル油 ◇The *diesel* engine burns its fuel much more efficiently. ディーゼルエンジンは燃料をはるかに効率的に燃焼する

'fossil fuel [C, U] (石炭・石油・天然ガスなどの)化石燃料 ◇Carbon dioxide is produced in huge amounts when *fossil fuels* are burnt. 化石燃料が燃焼する際に, 二酸化炭素が大量に発生する

old

old 形

1 old・ancient・long-standing・antique
物事が長く存在してきたことを表す
【類語訳】古い,古来の,古代の,長年に及ぶ,年代ものの,骨董の

| 文型&コロケーション |

- ▸an old/ an ancient/ a long-standing tradition/ belief/ method/ problem
- ▸an old/ ancient/ antique chair/ clock/ coin
- ▸an old/ ancient custom/ way/ ritual/ city/ civilization

old 古い ◇This carpet's getting pretty *old* now. このカーペットはかなり古くなってきている ◇It's not easy to break *old* habits. 古い習慣を捨てるのは容易ではない ◇He always gives the *same old* excuses. 彼はいつもお決まりの言い訳をする ◇It's one of the *oldest* remaining parts of the church. それは,その教会の最も古い残存部分の一つである 反意 **new** (NEW 1, 2)

ancient 古来の;古代の ◇The area is still covered by huge *ancient* forests. その地域はいまだに広大な太古の森林に覆われている ◇This philosophy dates back to *ancient* Greece. この哲学は古代ギリシャに遡る ◇He's *ancient* — he must be at least fifty!《おどけて》彼は古代人だよ—少なくとも50はいってるね 反意 **modern** (RECENT), ☞ **historic** (FAMOUS)

long-'standing 《ふつう名詞の前で》《ややフォーマル》長年存在してきた,長年に及ぶ ◇The country's *long-standing* relationship with the US was finally under strain. その国の長年にわたる米国との関係は,ついに緊張状態に入った ◇*Long-standing* grievances were aired at the meeting. 会議で積年の不満がぶちまけられた ❶ *long-standing* は,関係・慣習・感情に用いることができるが,物体・場所・人には用いることはできない。 反意 **recent** (RECENT)

antique 《ふつう名詞の前で》(家具・宝飾品などの)年代ものの,骨董の ◇It's an *antique* mahogany desk that belonged to my great-grandfather. それは私の曾祖父が所有していた時代もののマホガニーの机である

2 old・elderly・aged・long-lived・mature
長年生きてきた[生きている]ことを表す
【類語訳】年取った,年老いた,年配の,高齢の,老齢の,長寿の,長命の,熟年の

| 文型&コロケーション |

- ▸an old/ an elderly/ an aged/ a long-lived/ a mature man/ woman
- ▸an old/ an elderly/ an aged/ a mature gentleman/ lady/ couple
- ▸sb's old/ elderly/ aged father/ mother/ aunt/ uncle/ relative

old 年取った;年老いた ◇She's getting *old* — she's 75 next year. 彼女は年老いてきている—来年75歳だ ◇The *old* man lay propped up on cushions. その老人はクッションにもたれて横になっていた ◇These are some of the *oldest* trees in the world. これらは世界で最も年を経た樹木の類です 反意 **young** (YOUNG)

▸**the old** 名《複数扱い》◇*The old* (= old people) feel the cold more than the young. 高齢者は若者より寒さを感じやすい

↪old

old-fashioned, operate

elderly《ややフォーマル》年配の、高齢の（oldの丁寧語）◇She is very busy caring for two *elderly* relatives. 彼女は二人の年配の親戚の世話で非常に忙しい 反意 **young (YOUNG)**
▸**the elderly** 名 [複数扱い] ◇caring for *the elderly* 高齢者介護

aged《フォーマル》老齢の ◇Having *aged* relatives to stay in your house can be quite stressful. 老齢の親類を自分の家に泊めるのは、かなりストレスがかかることもある ◇I'm not sure if my *aged* car can make it up that hill.《インフォーマル、おどけて》私のよぼよぼの車ではあの坂を無事に上れるかどうかわかりません 反意 **young (YOUNG)**
▸**the aged** 名 [複数扱い] ◇The authorities have a duty to provide services for the sick and *the aged*(= very old people). 当局は、病人と老齢者に対してサービスを提供する義務がある

,long-'lived 長寿の、長命の；長い間続く ◇Trout are a *long-lived* species. マスは長命の種である ◇Everyone in my family is exceptionally *long-lived*. うちの一族はみな、ことのほか長生きだ ◇Good management was essential to the creation of a *long-lived*, successful business. 息が長く業績の上がる企業を作り上げるにはよい経営は不可欠だ

mature 熟年の（若くないことの丁寧[滑稽]な表現）◇The shop specializes in clothes for the *mature* woman. その店は熟年女性向けの服を専門にしている ◇He's a man of *mature* years. 彼は熟年だ ☞ **mature (ADULT)**

old-fashioned 形

old-fashioned・obsolete・out of date・outdated・antiquated・dated
人や物事が今ふうでないことを表す
【類語訳】現代的でない、昔ふうの、流行遅れの、昔かたぎの、古臭い、保守的な、時代遅れの、旧弊な、旧式の

文型&コロケーション
▸an old-fashioned/ obsolete/ outdated/ antiquated **system**
▸old-fashioned/ outdated/ antiquated/ dated **attitudes/ ideas/ views**
▸an old-fashioned/ outdated **method/ style**
▸an old-fashioned/ obsolete **word**
▸old-fashioned/ dated **clothes/ furniture**
▸to **become** old-fashioned/ obsolete/ out of date/ outdated/ dated
▸to **look** old-fashioned/ out of date/ dated
▸**rather** old-fashioned/ out of date/ outdated/ antiquated/ dated
▸a **bit/ little** old-fashioned/ out of date/ dated
▸**very** old-fashioned/ out of date/ outdated/ dated
▸**now** obsolete/ out of date/ outdated/ dated
▸**already** obsolete/ out of date/ outdated/ antiquated

,old-'fashioned《時にけなして》現代的でない、昔ふうの；流行遅れの；（人が）昔かたぎの、古臭い；保守的な ◇The bedroom was full of heavy *old-fashioned* furniture. 寝室は重い流行遅れの家具で一杯だった ◇My parents are *old-fashioned* about marriage and relationships. うちの両親は結婚や恋愛関係についての考えが古い ❶ old-fashionedは時として、現代的な物事や姿勢を好む人々が用いて、少し非難めいた語となる。だが、過去への思い入れを示すよい意味で用いられることもある。◆It was a lovely little *old-fashioned* cafe.《ほめて》それは美しく古風な小さなカフェだった。反意 **modern (EXPERIMENTAL), modern (MODERN)**

obsolete《時にけなして》（新しいものが考案されたため）廃れた ◇Factories cannot compete if they are using *obsolete* technology. 工場は時代遅れとなった技術を用いているなら、競争に勝てない ◇With technological changes many traditional skills have become *obsolete*. 技術変化に伴って、多くの伝統的な技術が廃れた

,out of 'date《時にけなして》（最新の情報がなく役に立たないほど）古い、時代遅れの ◇These figures are several years *out of date*. これらの数字は数年古い ◇an *out-of-date* map/dictionary 古くさい地図/辞書 ◇Suddenly she felt old and *out of date*.《比喩的》突然彼女は、自分が年老いて時代においていかれていると感じた 反意 **up to date (MODERN)**

outdated《ふつうけなして》（最新の情報・考え・技術がなく役に立たないほど）古い、時代遅れの ◇It is an *outdated* and inefficient system. それは時代遅れで非効率的なシステムである ◇The college was struggling with *outdated* equipment and facilities. その大学は旧式の備品と施設で苦労していた

ノート **out of date** と **outdated** の使い分け：時として、どちらの語も用いることができる。◆These figures are *out of date/outdated*.（これらの数字は古い）。out of date は特に、情報（源）について用いられ、outdated は特に、設備・考え・やり方について用いられる。

antiquated《ふつうけなして》（物事・考えが）時代遅れの、旧弊な ◇The committee has recommended that all *antiquated* legal procedures should be simplified. 委員会があらゆる旧弊な法的手続きは簡素化すべきだと勧告してきた ◇The *antiquated* heating system barely heats the larger rooms. 時代遅れの暖房システムでは広めの部屋をかろうじて温めるだけだ

dated《けなして》時代遅れの；旧式の ◇Those TV comedies were OK in their day but seem incredibly *dated* now. それらのTVコメディーは当時ならOKだったが、今では途方もなく時代遅れに思える

operate 動 ☞ WORK 動 2

operate・run・control・work・manipulate
機械[装置]を使うこと、それを機能させることを表す
【類語訳】操作する、動かす、稼働させる、作動させる、制御する

文型&コロケーション
▸to operate/ run/ control/ work a **machine**
▸to operate/ run/ control a/ an **engine/ motor**
▸to operate/ run **machinery**
▸to operate/ manipulate the **controls/ levers**

operate [他]《ややフォーマル》（機械を）操作する、動かす ◇What skills are needed to *operate* this machinery? この機械類を操作するにはどんな技術が必要ですか ☞ **operate (WORK 動 2)**
▸**operation** 名 [U] ◇*Operation* of the device is extremely simple. その装置の操作はきわめて単純である

run [他]（機械・装置・エンジン・コンピュータープログラムを）稼働させる、作動させる、動かす ◇Could you *run* the engine for a moment? 少しの間エンジンをかけたままにしていただけますか ◇What applications were you *running*

when the problem occurred? その問題が発生した時、どのアプリケーションを実行していましたか ☞ **run** (WORK 動2)
control (-ll-) [他] (機械・システムを)操作する, 稼働させる, 制御する ◇This knob *controls* the volume. このつまみは音量を調節します ◇The traffic lights are *controlled* by a central computer. 交通信号は中央コンピューターで制御されている ☞ **control** (BUTTON 1)

【ノート】**operate, run, control**の使い分け：人は機械をoperateしたりrunしたりする。機械は, computer, knob, button, switch, leverといった制御装置でcontrolされることが多い。

work [他]《ややインフォーマル, 話し言葉》(機械・装置・家庭用機器を)動かす, 動作させる ◇Do you know how to *work* the coffee machine? コーヒーメーカーの作動の仕方を知っていますか ☞ **work** (WORK 動2)
manipulate [他]《ややフォーマル》巧みに操作する[扱う] ◇I had to learn to *manipulate* the gears and levers of the machine. 機械のギアとレバーの操作を学ばなければならなかった ◇Computers are very efficient at *manipulating* information. コンピューターは情報の取り扱いに非常に効果的である
▶ **manipulation** 名 [U] ◇data *manipulation* データ操作

opportunity 名

opportunity・chance・turn・possibility・moment・occasion・break・start・window・go
物事を行う[達成する]のを可能にする特定の状況を表す
【類語訳】機会, 好機, チャンス, 順番, 時機, 頃合い, スタート, 門出

【文型&コロケーション】
▶ the opportunity/ a chance/ your turn **to do** sth
▶ an opportunity/ possibilities/ an occasion **for** sth
▶ a **suitable** opportunity/ occasion/ moment
▶ the **last** opportunity/ chance/ moment
▶ to **have** an opportunity/ a chance/ a turn/ a break/ a window/ a moment/ a go
▶ to **get/ give** sb an opportunity/ a chance/ a turn/ a break/ a start/ a window/ a moment/ a go
▶ to **wait for** an opportunity/ a chance/ your turn/ the moment/ an occasion
▶ to **take advantage of** an opportunity/ a chance/ the possibilities/ a window
▶ to **take** the opportunity/ your chance/ turns
▶ to **seize** an opportunity/ a chance/ the moment
▶ to **miss** an opportunity/ your chance/ a turn/ a go

opportunity [C, U]《ややフォーマル》機会, 好機 ◇I'd like to *take this opportunity to* thank my colleagues for their support. この機会をお借りして同僚の支援に感謝したいと思います ◇He is rude to me *at every opportunity* (= whenever possible). 彼は事あるごとに私に対して失礼な態度をとる ◇There are more *job opportunities* in the south. 南部には雇用の機会がもっとある ◇Our company promotes *equal opportunities* for women (= women are given the same jobs, pay, etc. as men). わが社は女性に対しての機会均等を進めています ◇There'll be plenty of *opportunity* for relaxing once the work is done. その仕事が終われば, ゆっくり

ラックスできる機会があるだろう
chance [C] 機会, 好機, チャンス ◇Please give me a *chance* to explain. どうか説明の機会をください ◇We won't get another *chance of* a holiday this year. 《英》今年はもう休暇をとるチャンスはないだろう ◇We won't get another *chance at* a vacation this year. 《米》今年はもう休暇をとるチャンスはないだろう ◇Jeff deceived me once already — I won't give him a *second chance*. ジェフはすでに一度私を騙している―二度目はありえない ◇This is your *big chance* (= opportunity for success). これはあなたにとって大きなチャンスです

【ノート】**opportunity**と**chance**の使い分け：多くの場合, どちらの語も用いられることができる。◆You'll have the *opportunity/chance* to ask questions at the end. (最後に質問がある機会があります。opportunityはchanceよりフォーマルな文脈で用いられる傾向が強く, いくつかの句では, どちらか一方の語しか用いることができない。×job/equal *chances*. ×I won't give him a second *opportunity*.

turn [C]《特に話し言葉》(物事を行う)順番, 番 ◇Please *wait your turn*. ご自分の順番をお待ちください ◇*Whose turn* is it to cook? 料理担当は誰の番かな ◇The male and female birds *take turns* sitting on the eggs. 鳥の雄と雌が代わりばんこに卵の上に座る ◇We *take it in turns* to do the housework. 《英》私たちは交代で家事をしています
possibility [C, ふつう複数で] (物事を達成するための)可能性, 機会 ◇The class offers a range of exciting *possibilities* for developing your skills. そのクラスは自分の技術向上心を刺激してくれる様々な可能性を与えてくれる ◇Career *possibilities* for women are much greater than they were fifty years ago. 女性の就職の機会は, 50年前よりずっと大きくなっている ❶この意味では, possibilitiesはしばしば, 仕事に関連した状況で用いられる。◇career/employment/development/commercial/design *possibilities* (就職/雇用/発展/商業上/設計上の可能性[機会])。また, 肯定的な響きのある形容詞の後で用いられることも多い。◆excellent/interesting/exciting/creative *possibilities* (素晴らしい/興味深い/刺激的な/創造の可能性)。×a/the *possibility* to do sthとは言えないことに注意。×I had the *possibility* to spend a year in Paris while I was a student. これらの場合は, opportunity, あるいはchanceを用いる。◆I had the *opportunity/chance* to spend a year in Paris. (パリで一年を過ごす機会があった)。☞ **possible** (POSSIBLE 1)
moment [C]《特に話し言葉》(特定の)機会, 時機；(物事を行うための)時 ◇I'm waiting for the right *moment* to tell him the bad news. 彼に悪い知らせを告げる頃合いを見計らっているんです ◇Have I caught you at a bad *moment*? ご都合の悪い時に来ちゃいましたか
occasion [単数で]《ややフォーマル》(物事を行う)頃合い, 好機 ◇It should have been an *occasion* for rejoicing, but she could not feel any real joy. 喜んでいいはずだったが, 彼女は本当の喜びは何も感じることができなかった ◇I'll speak to him about it *if the occasion arises* (= if I get a chance). 機会があれば, そのことを彼に話します
break [C]《インフォーマル》(ほしい物事・成功を手に入れるための)機会, チャンス ◇I got my *lucky break* when I won a 'Young Journalist of the Year' competition. 「ヤング・ジャーナリスト・オブ・ザ・イヤー」コンテストで優勝するという幸運を得た
start [C, ふつう単数で] (首尾よく物事を始めるための)機会,

スタート, 門出 ◇They worked hard to give their children a good *start in life*. 彼らは子どもたちに人生の素晴らしいスタートを切らせるために一生懸命働いた ◇The job gave him his *start* in journalism. 彼はその仕事でジャーナリストとしてスタートを切った ☞ **start** (START 名)

window [C] 《特にビジネス》(長くは続かない可能性もある) 機会, チャンス ◇We now have a small *window of opportunity* in which to make our views known. 今我々には、自らの見解を知ってもらうささやかなチャンスがある

go (複 **goes**) [C] 《英, 話し言葉》(ゲーム・活動での)順番 ◇Whose *go* is it? 誰の番 ◇It's your *go*. あなたの番よ ◇'How much is it to play?' 'It's 50p a *go*.' 「プレーするのはいくら」「一回50ペンスです」 ◇Can I have a *go* on your new bike? あなたの新しいバイクに乗ってみてもいいですか ❶《米》では, turnを用いる.

oppose 動

oppose・resist・fight・combat・defy・rebel・
go against sb/sth・disobey・stand up to sb・flout
意にそぐわないことに対抗して発言[行動]することを表す
【類語訳】反対する, 抵抗する, 奮闘する, 立ち向かう, 逆らう, 反抗する, 反発する, 反逆する, 従わない

〖文型&コロケーション〗
▶to fight/ rebel **against** sb/ sth
▶to oppose/ resist/ fight a **plan**/ **proposal**
▶to oppose/ fight/ defy/ flout a **ban**
▶to oppose/ fight/ defy/ stand up to **the government**
▶to defy/ disobey your **parents**
▶to oppose/ defy/ disobey/ flout the **law**
▶to defy/ rebel against/ disobey/ flout **authority**
▶to oppose/ defy/ go against/ flout sb's **wishes**
▶to fight/ combat **crime**/ **disease**/ **pollution**/ **inflation**
▶to defy/ disobey/ flout a/ an **rule**/ **order**
▶to **fiercely**/ **bitterly**/ **strongly** oppose/ resist sth

oppose [他] (人・計画・方針に)反対する ◇This party would bitterly *oppose* the re-introduction of the death penalty. この党は死刑の再導入に激しく反対するだろう ◇He found himself *opposed* by his own deputy. 彼は気づいた時には自分の代理人その人に反対されていた ◇I would *oppose* changing the law. その法律を変えるのには反対します 反意 **support** (SUPPORT), **propose** (PROPOSE), ☞ **opposition** (OPPOSITION), **opponent** (ENEMY)

resist [他] (変化[人がしたいこと]に)抵抗する ◇They are determined to *resist* pressure to change the law. 彼らは法律改正の圧力に抵抗しようと固く決意している ◇The bank strongly *resisted* cutting interest rates. その銀行は利下げに強く抵抗した ☞ **resistance** (OPPOSITION)

fight [他, 自] (決定・計画・悪事に反対して)闘う, 奮闘する ◇Workers are *fighting* the decision to close the factory. 労働者たちは工場閉鎖の決定に反対して闘っている ◇We are committed to *fighting* poverty. 私たちは貧困との闘いに身を投じている ◇We will *fight* for as long as it takes. 我々は闘いが続くかぎり闘うつもりだ ☞ **battle** (COMPETE)

combat (**-t-**, **-tt-**) [他] 《ややフォーマル》(悪事と)闘う, 立ち向かう ◇He announced new measures to *combat* crime in the inner cities. 彼は都心部の犯罪と闘うための新しい対策を発表した ◇The country has appealed for aid to *combat* serious shortages of foodstuffs. その国は深刻な食糧不足と闘うために援助を訴えた

〖ノート〗 **fight**と**combat**の使い分け：fightはcombatより幅広い語と結びつき、しばしば個人的に反対する場合に用いられる。◆to *fight* a decision/plan/ban (決定/計画/禁止に反対する). ◆to *fight* against sth (物事に反対して闘う). ×to *combat* a decision/plan/ban. ×to *combat* against sth. fightもcombatも, poverty, crime, unemployment, inflation など経済的・社会的状況に対処する公的な努力について用いることができる. fightはふつうshortagesと共には用いない. ×to *fight* serious shortages of foodstuffs.

defy [他] (権威・法律・規則・決定)に逆らう, 反抗する ◇I wouldn't have dared to *defy* my teachers. 先生たちに公然と逆らう気など私にはなかった ◇Hundreds of people today *defied* the ban on political gatherings. 今日何百人もの人々が政治集会禁止を無視した

▷**defiance** 名 [U] ◇Nuclear testing was resumed in *defiance* of an international ban. 核実験は国際的な禁止を無視する形で再開された ◇She held up a clenched fist in a gesture of *defiance*. 彼女は服従拒否の意思表示として、握り締めた拳を突き上げた

rebel [自] (権威)に反抗する, 反逆する, 逆らう ◇He later *rebelled* against his strict religious upbringing. 彼は後に、自分の受けた厳しい宗教的教育に逆らった ◇Most teenagers find something to *rebel* against. ほとんどのティーンエイジャーは反発すべき対象を見つけるものだ

▷**rebellion** 名 [U, C] ◇Some members are in *rebellion* against proposed cuts in spending. メンバーの中には、支出削減の提案に反発している者もいる ◇Teenage *rebellion* often starts in the home. 十代の反逆は家庭内で始まることが多い

.go a'gainst sb/sth 句動詞 (規則・人の願望に)逆らう ◇He would not *go against* his parents' wishes. 彼は両親の願いに逆らおうとはしなかった

disobey [他, 自] (法律・命令などに)従わない, そむく ◇He was punished for *disobeying* orders. 彼は命令にそむいて罰せられた ◇How dare you *disobey* me! 私に逆らうなんて 反意 **obey** (FOLLOW 3)

,stand 'up to sb 句動詞 (力のある人・組織からのひどい扱いに)反抗する, 立ち向かう ◇It was brave of her to *stand up to* those bullies. その暴漢たちに立ち向かったとは彼女も勇敢だ

flout [他] (法律・規則・慣習を)軽んじる, (公然と)無視する ◇She likes *flouting* convention and doing her own thing. 彼女はしきたりなどおかまいなしに思い通りに行動するのを好む

opposite 名

opposite・the contrary・the reverse・contrast・
antonym
人や物事が他とは可能なかぎり異なることを表す
【類語訳】正反対, 逆, 反対, 反意語, 反対語

〖文型&コロケーション〗
▶a/ the **complete** opposite/ reverse/ contrast
▶the **exact**/ **very** opposite/ reverse
▶to **be** the opposite/ the reverse/ a contrast
▶to **represent** the opposite/ a contrast
▶to **do** the opposite/ contrary/ reverse

▶ **quite the** opposite/ contrary/ reverse
▶ **quite a** contrast

opposite [C] (人・物事が)反対 ◇Hot and cold are *opposites.* hot(暑い)とcold(寒い)は反対です ◇What is the *opposite* of heavy? heavy(重い)の反対は何ですか ◇I thought she would be small and blonde but she's the complete *opposite.* 彼女は小柄でブロンドかと思っていたが、まったく反対だ ◇'Is it better now?' 'Quite the *opposite,* I'm afraid.' 「これでよくなった」「残念ながら、まったくその反対だね」

the contrary [単数で]《ややフォーマル》(言った[示唆した]ことの)正反対、逆 ◇In the end *the contrary* was proved true: he was innocent and she was guilty. 最後には正反対のことが真実であると証明された。彼が潔白で、彼女が有罪だったのだ ◇'You're not rejecting them?' '*On the contrary,* I plan to give them special status.'「彼らを拒絶しないということですか」「それどころか、特別な地位を与えるつもりです」 ◇I don't find him funny at all. Quite *the contrary.* 彼のことは全然面白いと思わない。まったく逆さ ◇I will expect to see you on Sunday unless I hear anything *to the contrary* (= showing or proving the opposite). 何か変更がなければ、日曜日にお会いいたしましょう ❶ **the contrary** は、**on the contrary, quite the contrary, to the contrary** という句で最も頻繁に用いられる。

the reverse [単数で]《ややフォーマル、特に書き言葉》(言われている事実・出来事・状況の)反対、逆 ◇Although I expected to enjoy living in the country, in fact *the reverse* is true. 田舎暮らしを楽しもうと期待していたが、実際はまったく楽しむどころではない ◇This problem is *the reverse* of the previous one. この問題は以前の問題と逆だ ❶ **the reverse** は、次の句で最も頻繁に用いられる。 ♦*The reverse* is true/holds/is the case/happens. (逆のことが真実である/続く/事実である/起きる) ♦A is *the reverse* of B. (AはBの反対である) ♦Quite *the reverse.* (その正反対だ)

contrast [C] (人・物事の)対照 ◇The work you did today is quite a *contrast* to (= very much better/ worse than) what you did last week. 今日君がした仕事は、先週したこととまったく対照的だ ➡ **contrast (COMPARE 1), contrast (CONFLICT 動), contrasting (DIFFERENT)**

antonym [C]《専門語》反意語、反対語 ◇'Old' has two possible *antonyms*: 'young' and 'new'. oldには二つの反意語が考えられる。youngとnewである

opposite 形

opposite・reverse・contrary・inverse・opposed
物事が他とは可能なかぎり異なる状態を表す
【類語訳】反対の、逆の

━━━━━━━━━━━━━━━━━━━━━━━━

文型&コロケーション
▶ the opposite/ reverse **direction/ side**
▶ the opposite/ reverse **order/ effect**
▶ an opposite/ a contrary **view/ opinion**
▶ Their **views/ opinions** are opposed.
▶ **completely/ directly/ entirely/ quite** contrary/ opposed

━━━━━━━━━━━━━━━━━━━━━━━━

opposite [ふつう名詞の前で](性質・方向が)反対の、逆の ◇She tried calming him down but it seemed to be having the *opposite* effect. 彼女は彼を落ち着かせようとしたが、逆効果になっているように見えた ◇I'm trying to teach students at *opposite* ends of the ability range. 能力の幅の両極端にいる生徒たちを教えようとしています ◇Clothes are often used as a way of attracting *the opposite sex.* 服装はしばしば、異性をひきつける手段として用いられる

reverse [名詞の前で]《ややフォーマル》(方向が)逆の、反対の ◇The winners were announced *in reverse order* (= the person in the lowest place was announced first). 入賞者たちは順位の下から発表された ◇Iron the garment on the *reverse* side (= on the back or inside). 《フォーマル》衣服の裏側にアイロンをかけてください

ノート **opposite** と **reverse** の使い分け： **reverse** は **opposite** よりフォーマルな文脈で用いられることがほとんどで、結びつきの幅はずっと狭い。**opposite** は、物理的あるいは抽象的な意味で、性質にも方向にも用いることができる。**reverse** は、ふつう物理的な意味で、方向にしか用いられない。二人の人[二つのもの]が **opposite directions** に移動するということは、同じ場所から出発して互いに離れる、あるいは異なる場所から出発して互いに向かって進むことのいずれも指す。**the reverse direction** に移動するとは、通常とは逆向きに進むことを指す。 ♦I watched them leave and then drove off in the *opposite* direction. (彼らが別れて反対方向へ車で走り去るのを見た) ♦He hit a truck travelling in the *opposite* direction. (彼は対向して走るトラックと衝突した) ♦One year later she made the same journey in the *reverse* direction. (一年後、彼女は同じ旅行を逆になぞった) 地域・物体の **opposite sides** にある人々や物はふつう、互いに向き合っている。物体の **reverse sides** は、背中合わせで互いに向き合っていない。 ♦He waved at me from the *opposite side* of the road. (彼は道路の反対側から私に手を振った) ♦On the *reverse side* of the medal is a coat of arms. (メダルの裏面には紋章がついている)

contrary [名詞の前で]《ややフォーマル》(性質が)反対の ◇Despite all the *contrary* evidence, they still believed that the Earth was flat. すべての反証にもかかわらず、彼らはなお地球は平面であると信じていた ◇The *contrary* view is that prison provides an excellent education — in crime. 反対意見は、刑務所は素晴らしい教育を提供している—犯罪についての、というものだ

ノート **opposite** と **contrary** の使い分け： **contrary** は **opposite** よりフォーマルな語で、結びつきの幅はずっと狭い。**opposite** は、物体・地域の反対側といった物理的なものや、反対意見といった抽象的なものにも用いることができる。**opposite** は、**direction, side, end, corner, extreme, effect, sex** などと結びつく。**contrary** は抽象的なものにしか用いられず、**opinion, view, intention, argument, evidence** などと結びつく。

inverse [名詞の前で]《ややフォーマル》(量・位置が)逆の、反比例の ❶ **inverse** はふつう、一つの要素が増加するにつれ他の要素が減少するというような、二つの物事の関係を表す。 ♦A person's wealth is often in *inverse proportion to* their happiness (= the more money they have, the less happy they are). (人の財産はしばしば、その幸福と反比例する) ♦There is often an *inverse relationship* between the power of the tool and how easy it is to use. (道具の力とその使いやすさは反比例の関係にあることが多い)

▶ **inversely** 副 ◇Can we assume that the demand

for bank lending is *inversely* related to the rate of interest charged? 銀行の貸出への需要は, 付加される金利と反比例すると考えられますか

opposed [名詞の前はまれ]《ややフォーマル》(考え・意見が)反対の ◇Our views are *diametrically opposed* on this issue. この件に関して我々の見解は正反対である

opposition 名

opposition・protest・resistance・objection・hostility
人や物事と全く意見が合わないことを表す
【類語訳】反対, 抵抗, 抗議, 異議, 敵対

▸ 文型&コロケーション
▸ opposition/ resistance/ objection/ hostility **to** sth
▸ **in** opposition/ protest/ objection
▸ **without** opposition/ resistance/ hostility
▸ **widespread/ strong/ fierce** opposition/ protests/ resistance/ objections/ hostility
▸ **growing** opposition/ resistance/ hostility
▸ to **provoke/ meet with/ face** opposition/ protests/ resistance/ objections/ hostility
▸ to **arouse** opposition/ resistance/ hostility
▸ to **express** your opposition/ protest/ resistance/ objections/ hostility
▸ to **voice** your opposition/ protest/ resistance/ objections

opposition [U]《口論・闘いによる》反対, 抵抗 ◇Delegates expressed strong *opposition* to the plans. 代表団は計画に強い反対を表明した ◇The army met with fierce *opposition* in every town. 軍隊はどの町でも激しい抵抗に遭った ◇*Opposition* forces have seized control of the airport. 反対勢力が空港を占拠した ☞ **oppose (OPPOSE), opposed (AGAINST SB/STH)**

protest [U, C] (賛成できないものへの)抗議 ◇The director resigned in *protest* at the decision. 監督はその決定に抗議して辞任した ◇The announcement raised a ***storm of protest***. その発表は抗議の嵐を巻き起こした ◇The building work will go ahead, despite *protests* from local residents. 地元住民の抗議にもかかわらず, 建設作業は進行するでしょう ❶ *protest* はまた, 抗議する組織的な市民集会も指す. ☞ **protest (COMPLAIN)**

resistance [U, 単数で] (考え・計画・法律に対する)抵抗 ; (力を使っての)抵抗 ◇*Resistance* to change has nearly destroyed the industry. 変化に対してかたくなに抵抗したため, その産業はほとんど壊滅してしまった ◇The demonstrators offered little or no *resistance* to the police. デモ隊は警察にほとんどもしくはまったく抵抗しなかった ◇armed *resistance* 武力抵抗 ☞ **resist (OPPOSE), resist (RESIST), resistant (AGAINST SB/STH)**

objection [U, C] 反対理由 ; 異議 ◇I *have no objection* to him coming to stay. 彼が泊まりに来ることはかまいません ◇Because an *objection* was raised we decided to look at the matter again. 異議が唱えられたので, その問題を見直すことにしました ☞ **object (COMPLAIN)**

hostility [U] (考え・計画・状況に対する)敵対, 敵意 ◇There is still considerable public *hostility towards* nuclear power. 原子力に対して民衆の反発がまだかなりある ☞ **hostile (AGAINST SB/STH), hostility (TENSION)**

optimistic 形

optimistic・hopeful・positive・bullish・upbeat・expectant
物事がおそらく[確実に]望む形で起きるだろうと思っている人のことを表す
【類語訳】楽観的な, 楽天的な, 肯定的な, 前向きな, 明るい, 陽気な

▸ 文型&コロケーション
▸ optimistic/ hopeful/ positive/ bullish/ upbeat **about** sth
▸ optimistic/ hopeful **that**...
▸ an optimistic/ a positive/ a bullish/ an upbeat/ an expectant **mood**
▸ an optimistic/ a positive/ a bullish/ an upbeat **note**
▸ an optimistic/ a hopeful/ a positive/ a bullish **view**
▸ an optimistic/ a positive/ a bullish **attitude/ outlook**
▸ an optimistic/ a bullish **prediction/ forecast**
▸ to **feel** optimistic/ hopeful/ positive/ bullish
▸ to **remain** optimistic/ hopeful/ positive/ bullish/ upbeat

optimistic 楽観的な, 楽天的な ◇She's not very *optimistic* about the outcome of the talks. 彼女は交渉の成り行きにあまり楽観的ではない ◇They are *cautiously optimistic* that the reforms will take place. 彼らは改革が起きるだろうと慎重ではあるが楽観的に見ている ◇I think you are being a little *over-optimistic*. あなたは少し楽観しすぎていると思う 反意 **pessimistic (NEGATIVE)**, ☞ **optimism (HOPE 名 1)**

▸ **optimistically** 副 ◇He spoke *optimistically* about better relations between the two countries. 彼は2か国の関係がよりよいものになろうと楽観的に語った

hopeful [名詞の前はまれ] 希望[期待]をもった ◇I feel *hopeful* that we'll find a suitable house very soon. 私たちに適当な家がすぐに見つかると期待しています ◇He is not very *hopeful* about the outcome of the interview. 彼は面接の結果にあまり期待していない 反意 **hopeless,** ☞ **hopeful (PROMISING), hope (HOPE 名 1)**

positive (状況について)肯定的な ; (将来に対して)前向きな ◇She tried to be more *positive* about her new job. 彼女は新しい仕事に対してもっと前向きになろうとした ◇On the *positive* side, profits have increased. 肯定的な面を見れば, 利益は増加した 反意 **negative (NEGATIVE)**

bullish《特にビジネス》(将来に対して)前向きな ◇Fraser was in (a) *bullish* mood about the future of his company. フレーザーは自分の会社の将来について強気に見ていた

upbeat《ややインフォーマル, 特にビジネス》楽天的な, 明るい, 陽気な ◇The tone of the speech was *upbeat*. 演説の語調は明るいものだった ◇The presentation ended on an *upbeat* note. プレゼンテーションは明るい調子で終わった 反意 **downbeat (NEGATIVE)**

expectant《特に書き言葉》(刺激的なよいことを)期待している, 待望している ◇A sudden roar came from the *expectant* crowd. 待ちかねた群衆から突然大声が上がった ◇An *expectant* hush came over the room. 期待に満ちた静けさが部屋中を包んだ ❶ *expectant* は主に, 人々が刺激的なことが起こるのを今か今かと待っていることが表され, その際 crowd (群衆), faces, a look (表情), hush, silence (静けさ) の語と結びつく. ☞ **expectancy (HOPE 名 1)**

▸ **expectantly** 副 ◇She looked at him *expectantly*. 彼女は期待を込めて彼を見つめた

option

option・choice・alternative・possibility・best/good/safe bet
物事を特定の状況で選ぶことを表す
【類語訳】選択肢, 選択の自由, 最善の方策

文型&コロケーション
▶ with/ without the option/ choice/ possibility of sth
▶ (a/ an) real/ realistic/ viable/ practical/ obvious option/ choice/ alternative/ possibility
▶ (a/ an) good/ acceptable/ reasonable/ healthy/ available/ possible/ preferred/ cheap/ expensive option/ choice/ alternative
▶ the only option/ choice/ alternative/ possibility open to sb
▶ to have/ give sb/ offer (sb) several options/ choices/ alternatives/ possibilities
▶ to have a/ an/ the option/ choice of doing sth
▶ to have no option/ choice/ alternative (but to do sth)
▶ to look at/ limit the options/ choices/ alternatives/ possibilities
▶ a number/ range of options/ choices/ alternatives/ possibilities

option [C, U] 選択肢；選択の自由 ◇As I see it, we have two *options*... 私の見るところでは,我々には二つの選択肢があります… ◇We are currently studying all the *options* available. 私たちは現在,可能なすべての選択肢を検討しています ◇Going to college was not an *option* for me. 大学進学は私の選択肢になかった ◇Students have the *option* of studying abroad in their second year. 学生は2年生の時に留学を選択できます ◇It is important at this stage to *leave your options open* (= avoid making a decision so that you still have a choice in the future). この段階では,選択の自由を留保しておくことが大切です ❶ *option* はまた,コンピュータープログラムを使用する際に選択可能な候補の一つを指すコンピューター用語でもある. ◆Choose the 'Cut' *option* from the Edit menu. (編集メニューで「切り取り」を選んでください). ☞ **opt** (CHOOSE), **optional** (VOLUNTARY 1)

choice [U, C, ふつう単数で] 選択の自由；選択肢 ◇If I had the *choice*, I would stop working tomorrow. 選べるんだったら明日にも働くのをやめます ◇She's going to do it. She doesn't have much *choice*, really, does she? 彼女はそれをするでしょう. 実際選択の余地はありませんね ◇*The choice is yours*: a quiet drink in the bar, the late night disco or a stroll along the beach. バーで静かに飲む, 深夜のディスコ, 浜辺の散歩, どれにするかはあなた次第です ◇There is a wide range of *choices* open to you. あなたには幅広い選択の余地があります ☞ **choice** (CHOICE 1, 2), **choose** (CHOOSE), **choose** (DECIDE)

alternative [C] (二つ(以上)の可能性からの)選択肢 ◇You can be paid in cash weekly or by cheque monthly: those are the two *alternatives*. 現金で週給を受け取ることも, 小切手で月給を受け取ることもできます. その二つが選択肢です ◇We had no *alternative* but to (= we had to) fire Gibson. ギブソンを解雇するより仕方なかった ◇There is a vegetarian *alternative* on the menu every day. メニューには毎日, ベジタリアンの方がお選びいただけるものがあります

ノート option, choice, alternative の使い分け:
choice は option より少しインフォーマルで, alternative は少しフォーマルである. 「選択の自由」を表す上で, 時には option も用いることができる (ふつうは alternative は用いない) が, choice が最も頻繁に用いられる. ◆We had no *choice/option/alternative* but to... (我々には…する他に選択肢がなかった). ◆If I had the *choice/option*, I would... (選択できるなら, …するだろう). ◆She doesn't have much *choice/option*. (彼女にはあまり選択肢がない). ×If I had the *alternative*, I would... ×She doesn't have much *alternative*. ◆ parental *choice* in education (教育における親の選択). ◆The *choice* is yours. (選ぶのはあなたです). ×parental *option/alternative* in education. ×The *option/alternative* is yours. options, choices, alternatives は選択できる物事を指す. だが alternative は, いくつかの物事の選択についてより頻繁に用いられる.

possibility [C] (特定の状況で)実行可能な事柄, 可能性のあること ◇I think we've exhausted all the *possibilities*. 我々はあらゆる手立てが尽きてしまったと思う ◇Selling the house is just one *possibility* that is open to us. 家の売却が, 私たちにできる唯一のことだ ◇The *possibilities* are endless. やれることはいくらでもある ◇ possibility は, option, choice, alternative と似た形で用いることができるが, 選択する必要性にはさほど強調を置かず, 何が選択可能かをより強調する. ☞ **possible** (POSSIBLE 1)

the/your 'best bet, a 'good/'safe bet 佰 (インフォーマル)(望む結果を得るための)最善の方策 ◆If you want to get around London fast, the Underground is *your best bet*. ロンドン内を素早く移動したいなら, 地下鉄が一番です ◆Clothes are *a safe bet* as a present for a teenager. ティーンエイジャーへのプレゼントには服が一番です
反意 **gamble** (RISK 2)

order 動

1 ☞ RULE 動 2
order・tell・instruct・direct・command
権限のある地位を利用して人に事を行わなければならない旨を告げることを表す
【類語訳】命じる, 命令する, 指示する

文型&コロケーション
▶ to order/ tell/ instruct/ direct/ command sb to do sth
▶ to order/ tell/ instruct/ direct/ command sb that...
▶ to order/ instruct/ direct/ command that...
▶ to do sth as ordered/ told/ instructed/ directed/ commanded
▶ to specifically/ expressly order/ tell/ instruct/ direct/ command (sb to do sth)

order [他] (権限をもって)命じる, 命令する ◇The officer *ordered* them to fire. 将校は彼らに発砲を命じた ◇The government has *ordered* an investigation into the accident. 政府はその事故の調査を命じた ◇They were *ordered* out of the class for fighting. 彼らはけんかをしたので教室から出るよう命じられた ◇Come here at once! she *ordered*. 「すぐにここへ来なさい」と彼女は命じた ◇Stop trying to *order* me *around*! いちいち指図しようとするのはやめて

tell [他] …するようにと言う, 命じる ◇He was *told* to sit

↪**order**

down and wait. 彼は座って待つよう言われた ◇There was a sign *telling* motorists to slow down. ドライバーに減速するよう促す標識があった ◇I kept *telling* myself to keep calm. 平静を保つよう自分に言い聞かせ続けた ◇The doctor *told* me (that) I should lose some weight. 医者に減量するように忠告された ◇Don't *tell* me what to do! 私に指図しないで ◇*Do as you're told*! 言われたとおりにしなさい

instruct [他]《ややフォーマル》(正式[公式]に)指示する ◇The letter *instructed* him to report to headquarters immediately. その書簡は、すぐに本部に出頭するよう彼に指示していた ◇You will be *instructed* where to go as soon as the plane is ready. 飛行機の準備ができ次第、行き先が指示されるでしょう ◇She arrived at ten o'clock as *instructed*. 彼女は指示どおり10時に到着した

direct [他]《フォーマル》(正式に)命令を出す ◇The judge *directed* the jury to return a verdict of not guilty. 判事は陪審団に無罪評決を出すよう命じた

command [他] (権限をもって)命じる,命令する ◇He *commanded* his men to retreat. 彼は部下に退却を命じた ◇She *commanded* the release of the prisoners. 彼女は囚人の解放を命じた ☞ **command** (CONTROL)

┃**ノート** order と command の使い分け:order は, command よりも一般的な語で, 人に物事を行うよう告げる。親・教師・政府など権限がある者すべてが発する場合に用いることができる。command は order より少し意味が強い。command は, 命令を出す軍の将校が発したり, あるいは一方的に命令を下すのがふつうであるような文脈で通常用いられる。親・教師が用いる傾向は少ない。

2 order・book・hire・rent・charter・reserve
物事を後に利用できるよう頼む[一時的に物事を利用するためにお金を支払う]ことを表す
【類語訳】注文する, 取り寄せる, 発注する, 予約する, 賃借りする, レンタルする, チャーターする

┃**文型&コロケーション**
▶ to order/ book/ hire/ rent/ charter/ reserve sth for sb
▶ to book/ reserve a **place/ seat/ table/ ticket**
▶ to book/ hire/ rent/ reserve a **room/ hall**
▶ to book/ rent a **DVD/ video**
▶ to book/ charter a **flight**
▶ to hire/ rent **a bicycle/ a boat/ a car/ equipment/ a movie/ a van/ a vehicle**
▶ to hire/ charter a **plane/ vessel/ yacht**
▶ to order/ book/ reserve sth **for eight o'clock/ this evening/ midday**, etc.

order [他,自] (商品を)注文する, 取り寄せる, 発注する ; (飲食物を)注文する ◇The furniture can be *ordered* direct from the manufacturer. その家具はメーカーから直接取り寄せられます ◇I'd like to *order* some books, please. 本を数冊注文したいんですが ◇I'll *order* you a taxi. タクシーを呼んであげますよ ◇I've *ordered* some sandwiches. サンドイッチを注文した ◇The waiter asked if we were ready to *order*. 注文が決まったかどうかウェイターに訊かれた ☞ **order** (REQUEST)

book [他,自]《特に英》(ホテルの部屋・劇場の席を)予約する ; (飛行機・列車・船の席を人のために)予約してやる ◇The hotel is *fully booked* that weekend. その週末は, ホテルは予約で埋まっている ◇The seminars get quickly *booked up* (= have no more places available). それらのセミナーはすぐに予約で一杯になる ◇I've *booked* you on the 9.30 flight. 9時半の便で予約を取っておきました ◇*Book* early to avoid disappointment. 込み合いますのでご予約はお早めに

hire [他]《英》(短期間)賃借りする, レンタルする ◇There's a place where you can *hire* bikes for the day. 一日単位で自転車を借りられる場所があります ◇They *hired* a room above a pub for the wedding reception. 彼らはパブの上の部屋を結婚披露宴用に借りた
▶ **hire** [名] [U] ◇bicycles *for hire*, £4 an hour 貸し自転車, 一時間4ポンド ◇The costumes are *on hire from* the local theatre. 衣装は地元の劇場からのレンタルです

rent [他]《特に米》(短期間)賃借りする, レンタルする ◇She *rented* a car at the airport. 彼女は空港でレンタカーを借りた ◇He had a list of movies they had *rented* from the local video store. 彼は彼らが地元のビデオ店から借りた映画のリストを持っていた

┃**ノート** hire と rent の使い分け:《英》では, 乗り物・部屋・道具には hire を用い, DVD・ビデオには rent を用いる。《米》では, これらすべてのものに rent を用いる。だが, 通常お金を払って乗客を運ぶ大型の乗り物には charter を用いる。

charter [他] (飛行機・船・バス・列車を)賃借りする, チャーターする ◇The club *chartered* a special flight from Manchester to Turin. クラブはマンチェスターからトリノへの特別便をチャーターした
▶ **charter** [名] [U] ◇a yacht available for *charter* チャーターできるヨット

reserve [他]《ややフォーマル》(座席・テーブル・部屋・講座の席を)予約する ◇They had *reserved* seats on the train. 彼らは列車の座席を予約してあった ◇Please *reserve* a place for me on the software training day. ソフトウェアのトレーニング日の席の予約をとらせてください

┃**ノート** book と reserve の使い分け:book はふつう, しばしば予約と同時に支払いを行う場合やキャンセル料の請求を伴う場合のように, 確実な手配がなされるときに用いられる。reserve は, 列車の座席の場合を除き, ふつう前払いを必要とせずに物事を確保してもらうよう頼むときに用いられる。make a reservation と言うこともでき, 《米》ではこの意味を表す最もふつうの言い方である。◆I'd like to *make a reservation* for August 14. (8月14日に予約を入れたいんです) ☞ **reservation** (REQUEST)

organization (英でまた -isation) [名] ☞ UNION

organization・centre・institution・institute
教育や研究, ビジネスなど, 特定の目的のために共同する人々の集団, あるいはそういった目的のために用いられる場所を表す
【類語訳】組織, 団体, 中心地, 拠点, 機関, 協会, 学会

┃**文型&コロケーション**
▶ an organization/ a centre/ an institution/ an institute **for sth**
▶ a **private** organization/ institution
▶ a **government** organization/ institution/ institute
▶ a **research/ training** organization/ centre/ institution/ institute

organization (英でまた -isation) [C] (会社・クラブ・政府省庁などの)組織, 団体 ◇There need to be changes *throughout the organization*. 組織全体にわたって改変の必要がある ◇***Voluntary organizations*** working with the homeless are against the proposal. ホームレスと活動するボランティア団体がその提案に反対している ◇The World Health *Organization* has called for $10 million to purchase medical supplies. 世界保健機関は医療用品の購入に1千万ドルの寄金を要請した ❶or-ganizationは, 企業・クラブ・協会・政府省庁・政党・労働組合・圧力団体・慈善団体を表す一般的な語として用いることができる. ふつう, 学校・大学には用いない. ☞ **foundation** (CHARITY)

centre 《英》《米**center**》 [C] (特定の目的・活動のための)センター; (特定の活動の)中心地, 拠点 ◇They've set up a local *centre* for people with epilepsy. てんかん患者のための地方の総合施設が設立された ◇The classes are run by the *Centre* for Languages and Literature. その講座は言語・文学センターによって運営されている ◇The university is recognized as an international *centre of excellence* for training dentists. その大学は歯科医療成のためのすぐれた国際的な拠点とみなされている ❶centreは複合語で用いられることが多い. ◆ a sports/leisure/community/shopping/conference/business *centre* (スポーツ/レジャー/コミュニティ/ショッピング/カンファレンス/ビジネスセンター).

institution [C] (大学・銀行などの)機関 ◇The deal is backed by one of the country's largest *financial institutions*. その取引は, その国最大の金融機関の一つに支援されている ◇The system is targeted mainly at academic and research *institutions*. そのシステムは主に, 学術研究機関を対象としている ☞ **foundation** (CHARITY)

institute [C] (教育・特定の職業と関連する)協会, 学会, 機関; 協会 [学会, 機関] の建物 ◇He is a member of the *Institute* of Chartered Accountants. 彼は勅許会計士協会の一員である

┃**ノート institution と institute の使い分け**: institutionは, 銀行・政府省庁といった幅広い組織を指すことができる. institutionもinstituteも, 学術研究機関を指す語である. instituteはふつう, ある種の組織を表すのに用いられる. ◆ many research *institutions* (多くの研究機関). instituteはふつう, 特定の組織(の建物)を指し, その名称の一部となる. ◆ the Dundee *Institute* of Technology (ダンディー工科大学).

organize 《英でまた -ise》 [動]

organize・arrange・plan・operate・run・sort sth out・mount・orchestrate
物事を起こすのに必要なことを行う
【類義訳】手配する, 主催する, 手はずを整える, 段取りをつける, 計画する, 予定を立てる, 提供する, 運営する, 展開する

▸ 文型&コロケーション
▸ to arrange/ plan **for** sth
▸ to arrange/ plan **to do** sth
▸ to arrange/ plan **that**...
▸ to arrange/ plan/ sort out **how/ who/ when/ where**...
▸ **as** arranged/ planned
▸ to organize/ plan/ operate/ run/ mount/ orchestrate a **campaign**
▸ to organize/ plan/ run/ mount an **operation**
▸ to organize/ arrange/ plan/ mount an **exhibition**
▸ to organize/ plan/ run/ mount an **event**
▸ to organize/ plan/ mount a **raid**
▸ to organize/ arrange/ operate/ run/ mount/ orchestrate sth **successfully**
▸ to organize/ plan/ operate/ run sth **efficiently/ effectively/ well**
▸ to organize/ plan/ run sth **badly**
▸ to **jointly** organize/ arrange/ plan/ operate/ run/ mount sth

organize 《英でまた **-ise**》 [他] (活動・供給などを)手配する, 主催する ◇I've *organized* a lot of school trips. 私は多くの修学旅行の手配を行ってきた ◇The committee will *organize* the food for the reception. 委員会がレセプション用の食べ物の手配をします ☞ **organization** (PLANNING)

arrange [他, 自] (物事を行う(日時の))手はずを整える, 手配する, 段取りをつける ◇A news conference was hastily *arranged*. 記者会見がにわかに準備された ◇I'll *arrange* for a car to meet you at the airport. 空港でのお迎え用に車を手配します ◇We met at six, as *arranged*. 私たちは予定どおり6時に出会った ☞ **arrangement** (AGREEMENT), **arrangement** (PLANNING)

plan (-nn-) [他, 自] (詳細に)計画する, 予定を立てる; 予定する ◇It took six months to *plan* the expedition. 探検旅行の計画に半年かかった ◇Everything went exactly as *planned*. すべてが計画どおりに進んだ ◇I've been *planning* how I'm going to spend my last week here. ここでの最後の週をどう過ごすか予定を立てているところです ◇It's always a good idea to ***plan ahead***. 常に前もって計画することはよい考えです ☞ **plan** (PLAN 1), **planning** (PLANNING)

operate [他]《ややフォーマル》(サービスを)運営する; (システム・プロセスを)運用する ◇The airline *operates* flights to 25 countries. その航空会社は25か国へ運航している ◇France *operates* a system of subsidized loans to dairy farmers. フランスは酪農家たちに助成金付き貸付の制度を運用している ☞ **in operation** (ACTIVE)

run [他] (サービス・イベントを)提供する, 運営する ◇The college *runs* several English classes for adults. その大学は成人向けの英語の講座を設けている ◇Volunteer counsellors *run* a 24-hour helpline. ボランティアのカウンセラーが, 24時間サービスの相談回線を提供している

,sort sth 'out [句動詞]《ややインフォーマル, 特に話し言葉》(物事をうまく)解決する ◇If you're going to the bus station, can you *sort out* the tickets for tomorrow? バスの発着所に行くなら, 明日のチケットをなんとかしてもらえますか ◇Paula *sorted out* all the travel arrangements for us. ポーラが, 私たちのために旅行のお膳立てをすべてやってくれた

mount [他]《書き言葉》(イベント・一連の計画活動を)展開する, 執り行う ◇The party successfully *mounted* a campaign to change the law. 党はその法律を改正するための運動を成功裏に展開した ◇The National Gallery *mounted* a major exhibition of her work. ナショナルギャラリーは彼女の作品の大展示会を開催した

orchestrate [他]《書き言葉》(複雑な計画・イベントを)練り上げる, ひそかに準備する ◇The party was accused of *orchestrating* violence at demonstrations. その党はデモにおける暴力行為を画策したとして非難を受けた

organizer (英でまた -iser) 名

organizer・administrator・planner
物事を手配[計画、管理]する人、計画[手配]に長けた人
【類語訳】主催者、組織者、まとめ役、管理者、理事、計画者、立案者

文型&コロケーション
- an organizer/ administrator **for** sth
- a **good** organizer/ administrator/ planner
- a/ an **area/ local/ regional** organizer/ administrator/ planner

organizer (英でまた -iser) [C] 主催者、組織者；まとめ役 ◇Police had a number of meetings with the *organizers* of the race to discuss safety. 警察は安全性を話し合うためにレースの主催者と何度か会合を持った ◇She was an excellent *organizer* and fund-raiser for the club. 彼女はクラブにとっての優秀なまとめ役であり資金調達係であった ❶ the organizers of an event でイベントを計画し開催に必要な物事をすべて手配したグループ・会社を表すことが多い。

administrator [C] (会社・機関の業務の)管理者、理事；まとめ役 ◇Such organizational decisions are made by the hospital *administrators*. そういった組織の意思決定は、病院管理者たちによってなされます ☞ He is known as a good manager and an efficient *administrator*. 彼はよい経営者かつ有能な管理者として知られている ☞ **administer** (RUN 2), **administration** (GOVERNMENT 2), **administration** (MANAGEMENT)

planner [C] (仕事としての特定の活動の)計画を立てる人、計画者、立案者 ◇Emergency *planners* are keeping a close eye on forecasts. 緊急対策立案者は予報を注意深く監視している ◇The oil crisis gave *economic planners* a jolt. 石油危機は経済政策立案者にショックを与えた

output 名

output・production・productivity・yield
生み出される物事の総量を表す
【類語訳】生産高、生産量、生産力、生産性、収穫高

文型&コロケーション
- a **high/ low** output/ productivity/ yield
- **agricultural** output/ production/ productivity/ yields
- **industrial/ manufacturing** output/ production/ productivity
- to **boost/ improve/ increase/ raise** output/ production/ productivity/ yields
- to **reduce** output/ production/ productivity/ yields

output [U, 単数で] (国・会社・機械・人の)生産高、生産量 ◇Manufacturing *output* has increased by 8%. 製造業生産高は8%増加した

production [U] (国・会社の)生産高、生産量 ◇*Production* will drop by 60,000 next year. 生産量は来年6万減少するだろう ☞ **production** (PRODUCTION), **produce** (MANUFACTURE)

> ノート **output** と **production** の使い分け: output はこの意味では、production より幅広く用いられる。output は、国・会社・機械・人が「生み出す」ものである。◆the country's/company's total *output* (国/会社の総生産高). ◆her prodigious literary *output* (彼女の膨大な執筆量). production は、所有格と共には用いられない。×the country's/company's total *production*. ×her prodigious literary *production*.

productivity [U] (会社・国・労働者の商品の)生産力；(時間・仕事量・費用に比した)生産性 ◇Wage rates depend on levels of *productivity*. 賃金率は生産性のレベルによって決まる ◇If you want to stay in this job you'll need to get your *productivity* up. この仕事に留まりたければ、生産性を高める必要があるね

yield [C, U] (穀物・牛乳の)生産量、収穫高 ◇This method of cultivation gives a higher *yield*. この栽培法でより高い収穫が得られる ◇a reduction in milk *yield* 牛乳の生産量の減少 ☞ **yield** (PROVIDE)

outrageous 形

outrageous・shocking・disgraceful・shameful・criminal・scandalous・deplorable・unforgivable
行為[振る舞い、状況]が衝撃を与え、受け入れがたいことを表す
【類語訳】けしからぬ、とんでもない、ショッキングな、恥ずべき、みっともない、嘆かわしい、許しがたい、容赦できない

文型&コロケーション
- to be outrageous/ shocking/ disgraceful/ shameful/ scandalous/ deplorable/ unforgivable **that**...
- outrageous/ shocking/ disgraceful/ shameful/ criminal/ scandalous/ deplorable **behaviour**
- an outrageous/ a shocking/ a disgraceful/ a shameful/ a criminal/ a scandalous **waste**
- an outrageous/ a shocking/ a scandalous **story**
- a shocking/ disgraceful/ shameful/ scandalous/ deplorable **situation/ condition**
- a shocking/ disgraceful/ shameful/ criminal/ deplorable **state**
- **quite** outrageous/ shocking/ disgraceful/ deplorable/ unforgivable
- **utterly** outrageous/ disgraceful/ scandalous/ deplorable
- **absolutely** outrageous/ shocking/ disgraceful/ scandalous

outrageous (道徳的に間違っているので)けしからぬ、とんでもない ◇'That's *outrageous*!' he protested. 「そいつはとんでもない」と彼は抗議した ◇She thought it absolutely *outrageous* that he should be promoted over her. 彼が自分よりも上位に昇進するのはまったく言語道断だと彼女は思った ☞ **outrage** (ANGER 名), **outrage** (ANGER 動), **outraged** (FURIOUS)

➤ **outrageously** 副 ◇They behaved *outrageously*. 彼らは傍若無人に振る舞った ◇The meal was *outrageously* expensive. 食事はべらぼうに高価だった

shocking (道徳的に間違っている[非常に深刻である]ので)ショッキングな、けしからぬ ◇What a *shocking* waste of money! 何てけしからぬ金の無駄だ ◇Today we reveal the *shocking* truth about heroin addiction among the young. 私たちは今日、若者のヘロイン中毒に関するショッキングな真実を明らかにします ☞ **shock** (OFFEND)

➤ **shockingly** 副 ◇a *shockingly* high mortality rate 衝撃的な高い死亡率

ノート outrageous と shocking の使い分け：道徳的に間違っていると考えられる行動・活動について言う場合には、どちらの語を用いることもできる。◆ *outrageous/shocking* behaviour （けしからぬ行動）・ a/an *outrageous/shocking* act/waste/story/suggestion （けしからぬ行為/無駄/話/提案）．物事が自分にとって不公平に思えるために気分を害した場合、outrageous を用いる。× She thought it *shocking* that he should be promoted over her. 非常に深刻[危険]な状況に対しては、shocking を用いる。× the *outrageous* truth about heroin addiction.

disgraceful （受け入れがたいほど）とてもひどい；恥ずべき、みっともない ◇It's *disgraceful* that none of the family tried to help her. 家族の誰一人として彼女を助けようとしなかったのは恥ずべきことだ ☞ **disgrace** (DISGRACE)
▶**disgracefully** 副 ◇He considered that Liza was behaving *disgracefully*. ライザはみっともない行動をとっていると彼は思った

shameful 《ややフォーマル》（受け入れがたいほど）とてもひどい；恥ずべき、みっともない ◇It was *shameful* the way she was treated. 彼女の扱われ方はひどいものだった ◇We reveal one of the most *shameful* secrets of modern US history. 我々は米国の現代史の最も恥ずべき秘密の一つを暴きます ☞ **shame** (DISGRACE)
▶**shamefully** 副 ◇The buildings have been *shamefully* neglected. 情けないことにそれらの建物は放置されてきた

ノート shameful と disgraceful の使い分け：disgraceful は、特に《英》において、shameful より頻繁に話し言葉で用いられる。秘密や人の秘めた思いに対して、shameful は用いられるが、disgraceful は用いられない。

criminal （道徳的に間違っているので）けしからん、嘆かわしい ◇This is a *criminal* waste of resources. これは嘆かわしい資源の無駄遣いである

scandalous （道徳的に間違っているので）けしからん、とんでもない ◇It is *scandalous* that he has not been punished. 彼が罰せられなかったとはけしからん ◇The decision is nothing short of *scandalous*. その決定は不愉快以外の何ものでもない ❶ *scandalous* は、道徳的に、自分にとって不公平というよりは、不道徳と考えられるものである。他人よりずっとよい待遇を受けている権力や財産を持った人に関係することも多い。
▶**scandalously** 副 ◇*scandalously* low pay 恥ずかしいほどに低い賃金

deplorable 《フォーマル》（衝撃的なほど）ひどい、嘆かわしい、悲しむべき ◇They were living in the most *deplorable* conditions. 彼らは最も嘆かわしい条件下で暮らしていた ◇The acting was *deplorable*. その演技はひどかった ☞ **deplore** (DISAPPROVE)
▶**deplorably** 副 ◇They behaved *deplorably*. 彼らは嘆かわしい振る舞いをした

unforgivable （人の行動が）許しがたい、容赦できない ◇It was an *unforgivable* thing to say. それは言うに許しがたいことだった ◇He had committed the *unforgivable* sin ─ he had betrayed his friends. 彼は許されない罪を犯していた ─ 友を裏切ったのだ 反意 **forgivable** ❶ *forgivable* な行動は、理解でき許すことのできる行為の意。◆ His rudeness was *forgivable* in the circumstances. （彼の無礼はその状況下では致し方ないものだった）
▶**unforgivably** 副 ◇She was *unforgivably* rude. 彼女は許せないほど失礼だった

own 形

own・personal・individual・private・subjective・exclusive
物事が一人の特定の人に属する[関連した]ものであることを表す【類語例】自身の、自分自身の、個人の、個人的な、一個人の、個人用の、専用の、私用の、私有の

文型&コロケーション
▶sb's own/ personal/ individual/ private/ subjective **experience**
▶sb's own/ personal/ private/ subjective **opinion**
▶sb's own/ personal/ private/ exclusive **property**
▶sb's own/ personal/ individual **needs/ requirements/ objectives/ freedom**

own 自身（について）の、自分の；自分で行った[生み出した] ◇It was her *own* idea. それは彼女自身の考えだった ◇I saw it with my *own* eyes (= I didn't hear about it from sb else). 私はこの目でそれを見たんだ ◇Our children are grown up and have children *of their own*. うちの子どもたちは成長し、自分の子どもがいる ◇*For reasons of his own* (= special reasons that perhaps only he knew about) he refused to join the club. 彼は自分なりの理由からクラブに加入するのを断った ◇The accident happened *through no fault of her own*. その事故は彼女自身のせいではなかった ◇He wants to come into the business *on his own terms*. 彼は自分の思うままにビジネスを行いたいと望んでいる ◇I need a room *of my own*. 私には自分の部屋が必要です ◇I have my *very own* room at last. やっと自分だけの部屋をもらえたよ ◇She makes all her *own* clothes. 彼女は自分の服はすべて手作りです ❶ own は冠詞の後で用いることはできない。◆ I need my *own* room.（自分の部屋が必要です）× I need an *own* room. ◆ It's good to have your *own* room.（自分の部屋を持つことはいいことです）× It's good to have a room of the *own*.

personal [名詞の前で] 自分自身の；個人の、個人的な ◇They packed up their *personal* belongings and left. 彼らは私物を荷造りして立ち去った ◇The receptionist asked for my *personal* details (= my name, age, etc.). 受付係は私に個人的な情報を訊ねた ◇Of course, this is just a *personal* opinion. もちろん、これは個人的な意見に過ぎません ◇The novel is written from *personal* experience. その小説は個人的な体験から書かれている ◇All hire cars are for *personal* use (= not business use) only. レンタカーはすべて個人使用に限ります ◇Use stencils to add a few *personal touches* to walls and furniture. ステンシルを使って、壁や家具に少し独自のタッチを加えてください ◇He has run a *personal best* of just under four minutes. 彼は4分をわずかに切る自己最高記録で走った
▶**personally** 副 ◇*Personally*, I prefer the second option. 個人的には、二つ目の選択肢がいいです

individual [名詞の前で] 一個人の、個人の；個人用の ◇Respect for *individual* freedom is a cornerstone of our culture. 個人の自由の尊重は我々の文化の礎である ◇Try to measure in *individual* portions how much people will eat. 人がどれだけ食べるか個人の量から計ってみなさい 反意 **communal** (COMMON), ☞ **individual** (PARTICULAR), **individual** (PERSON)

➤**individually** 副 ◇The manager spoke to them all *individually*. その経営者は彼ら全員と個別に話した
private [ふつう名詞の前で] (特定の人・グループ)専用の；私用の, 私有の ◇The sign said, '*Private* property. Keep out.' 看板には「私有地. 立入禁止」と書いてあった ◇Those are my father's *private* papers. それらは父の私文書です ◇The hotel has 110 bedrooms, all with *private* bathrooms. ホテルには110の寝室があり、それにはすべて専用のバス・トイレが付いています 反意 **public** (COMMON)

ノート **personal** と **private** の使い分け：personal な物・事柄は、実際のところ、ある特定の一個人の持ち物で、他の人のものではないことを表し、private な物・事柄は、ある特定の人やグループのものであるか、または彼らが使うためのものであり、一般の人向けでないことを表す. また, personal property は, ある特定の人に帰属する小さな品目からなるのが普通だが, private property は, ある特定の人・集団が所有する土地のことである.

subjective 《時にけなして》主観的な ◇a highly *subjective* point of view 非常に主観的な観点 ◇Everyone's opinion is bound to be *subjective*. 人の意見というものは確実に主観的なものになるはずだ 反意 **objective** (OBJECTIVE)
➤**subjectively** 副 ◇People who are less *subjectively* involved are better judges. 人は主観的な関わりが少ないほど、よい判断ができる
exclusive (特定の人・集団)専用の；(特定の人・集団)独占の ◇The hotel has *exclusive* access to the beach. そのホテルからは専用のビーチに出入りできる ◇*exclusive* rights to televise the World Cup ワールドカップの独占放映権 ◇His mother has told 'The Times' about his death in an ***exclusive interview*** (= not given to any other newspaper). 彼の母は『タイムズ』の独占インタビューで彼の死について語った

P p

pack 動

pack・cram・stuff・squeeze・jam・wedge
人や物を狭い空間に押して入れる
【類語訳】埋め尽くす, 詰め込む, 押し込む

文型&コロケーション
- to pack/ cram/ stuff/ squeeze/ jam/ wedge sb/ sth **in/ into** sth
- to pack/ cram/ stuff/ squeeze/ jam/ wedge sb/ sth **between** sth and sth else
- to pack/ cram/ stuff sth **with** sth
- to be packed/ crammed/ squeezed/ jammed/ wedged **together**
- to be packed/ crammed/ stuffed/ squeezed/ jammed/ wedged **tightly**

pack 〖自, 他〗《ふつう副詞や前置詞と共に》(人が)ぎゅうぎゅう詰めに入る, 埋め尽くす;(物を)ぎゅうぎゅうに入れる, きっしり詰め込む ◇We all *packed* together into one car. 私たちは皆で一緒に1台の車にぎゅうぎゅう詰めになって乗り込んだ ◇Fans *packed* the hall to see the band. ファンがそのバンドを見ようと会場を埋め尽くした ◇*Pack* wet shoes with newspaper to help them dry. ぬれた靴の乾きがよくなるように新聞紙を詰めましょう ☞**packed** (FULL)

cram (-mm-) 〖他, 自〗(人・物を)ぎゅうぎゅうに入れる, きっしり[無理やり]押し[詰め]込む;(人が)ぎゅうぎゅう詰めに入る, 埋め尽くす ◇I managed to *cram* down a few mouthfuls of food. 私は何とか無理やり食べ物を数回に分けて口の中に押し込んだ ◇Supporters *crammed* the streets. サポーターが通りを埋め尽くした ◇We all managed to *cram* into his car. 私たちは全員何とか彼の車にぎゅうぎゅう詰めで乗り込んだ ☞**crammed** (FULL)

ノート pack と cram の使い分け:多くの場合, 両語とも使用可能。◆We all managed to *pack/cram* into the car. (私たちは全員何とかその車にぎゅうぎゅう詰めで乗り込んだ)。しかしながら, pack は人・物ができるだけ多く入るように, きちんと[うまく]押し[詰め]込まれることを表すのに対して, cram はしばしば乱雑で, 無理やり押し[詰め]込まれるという意味合いが強い。✕I managed to *pack* down a few mouthfuls of food.

stuff 〖他〗(無造作[乱雑]に物を)ぎゅうぎゅうに入れる, ぎっしり[無理やり]押し[詰め]込む ◇She had 500 leaflets to *stuff* into envelopes. 彼女には封筒に詰めるちらしが500枚あった ◇The closet was *stuffed* to bursting. クローゼットは物ではち切れそうだった ◇All the drawers were *stuffed* full of letters and papers. すべての引き出しが手紙や書類であふれ返っていた

squeeze 〖他, 自〗《副詞や前置詞と共に》(人・物を)ぎゅうぎゅう詰めに入れる, きっしり[無理やり]押し[詰め]込む ◇We managed to *squeeze* six people into the car. 私たちは何とか6人をその車にぎゅうぎゅう詰めで押し込めることができた ◇They were able to *squeeze* through a gap in the fence. 彼らはフェンスのすき間を身をよじって通り抜けることができた

▷**squeeze** 〖名〗[単数で] ◇It was *a tight squeeze* but we finally got everything into the case. その箱ははんぱんだったが, ついに私たちはすべてを中に入れた

jam (-mm-) 〖他, ふつう受身で〗《副詞や前置詞と共に》(人・物を)ぎゅうぎゅう詰めに入れる, ぎっしり[無理やり]押し[詰め]込む ◇We were *jammed* together like sardines in a can. 私たちは缶詰の中のイワシのようにぎゅうぎゅう詰めだった

ノート pack, stuff, jam の使い分け: pack はしばしば正当な理由があって, どれだけきっしりと物が空間に押し込まれているかを強調する。◆*Pack* wet shoes with newspaper to help them dry. (ぬれた靴の乾きがよくなるように新聞紙を詰めましょう)。この文では stuff を用いることも可能だが, jam は不可。stuff はしばしば物が素早く[無造作に, 乱雑に]空間に入れられていることを表す。◆All the drawers were *stuffed* full of letters and papers. (すべての引き出しが手紙や書類であふれ返っていた)。この文では jam を用いることも可能だが, pack は不可。jam はしばしば受動態で用いられ, 人・物が誰かのよくの考えた行動からというよりはその場の状況で, 意思に反して空間に押し込まれていることを表す。

wedge 〖他〗《副詞や前置詞と共に》(物を動かないように)押し[詰め]込む ◇The phone was *wedged* under his chin. 電話は彼のあごの下にはさみ込まれていた

pain 名

pain・ache・suffering・discomfort・agony
けがをした[病気になった]ときに身体に感じる感覚
【類語訳】苦痛, 痛み, うずき, 不快感, 激痛

discomfort　　　pain　　　　　　　　agony
　　　　　　　　ache
　　　　　　　　suffering

文型&コロケーション
- **in** pain/ discomfort/ agony
- (a) **back/ stomach** pain/ ache
- to **cause** pain/ suffering/ discomfort
- to **inflict** pain/ suffering
- to **suffer** pain/ discomfort/ agony
- to **relieve/ ease** the pain/ suffering/ discomfort/ agony

pain [U, C] (けが・病気による身体的な)苦痛, 痛み ◇She was clearly in a lot of *pain*. 彼女は明らかにひどく痛そうだった ◇He felt a sharp *pain* in his knee. 彼は膝に鋭い痛みを感じた ◇He went to the doctor with chest *pains*. 彼は胸が痛くて医者に行った ◇The booklet contains information on *pain relief* during labour. この小冊子には分娩時の鎮痛に関する情報が載っています ❶ pain は心的感情を指すこともある。☞**pain** (DISTRESS), **pain** (HURT 1)

ache [C] (体の部位の継続的な)痛み, うずき ◇You get more *aches and pains* as you get older. 年をとればとるほど, あちこち痛くなるよ ❶ ache はしばしば複合語で用いられる。◆Mummy, I've got a tummy *ache*. (ママ, お

なかが痛いよ). ◆to have a stomach*ache*/head*ache*/back*ache*/tooth*ache* (おなか/頭/背中/歯が痛い)。《英》ではこれらの複合語の中には不可算で用いられる語もある。◆to have back*ache*/tooth*ache* (《英》背中/歯が痛い) ☞ **ache** (HURT 2)

suffering [U, 複数で] (全身を冒す長期にわたる)苦痛 ◇Death finally brought an end to her *suffering*. 死ぬことでついに彼女は苦痛から解放された ◇The hospice aims to ease the *sufferings* of the dying. ホスピスは末期患者の苦痛を和らげることを目的としている ❶ *suffering* は感情的苦痛を指すこともある。☞ **suffering** (DISTRESS)
▸**suffer** 動 [自] ◇I hate to see animals *suffering*. 私は動物が苦しむのを見たくない

discomfort [U] (ややフォーマル) (身体的な)不快感 ◇You will experience some minor *discomfort* during the treatment. 治療中はわずかながらある種の不快感があると思います

agony [U, C] (身体的な)激しい苦痛, 激痛 ◇Jack collapsed in *agony* on the floor. ジャックは激痛で床の上に倒れ込んだ ◇The animal writhed in its death *agonies*. その動物は死の苦しみにのたうち回った ❶ *agony* は感情的苦痛を指すこともある。☞ **agony** (DISTRESS)

painful 形

1 painful・sore・raw・inflamed・excruciating・burning・itchy
身体的苦痛を表す
【類語訳】痛い, 苦しい, 炎症を起こした, ひりひりする, かゆい, むずむずする

itchy	painful	excruciating
	sore	burning
	raw	
	inflamed	

文型&コロケーション
▸ sore/ inflamed/ itchy **eyes**
▸ raw/ inflamed/ itchy **skin**
▸ a painful/ an excruciating **death**
▸ a painful/ a burning **sensation**
▸ excruciating/ burning **pain**

painful (身体的に)痛い, 苦しい, 痛み[苦痛]を伴う ◇Is your knee still *painful*? 膝はまだ痛いの ◇Ulcers can be unbearably *painful*. 潰瘍は耐えられないほどの苦痛を伴うことがある ◇I had to undergo a series of *painful* injections. 私は一連の痛い注射を受けねばならなかった ◇It was a slow and *painful* death. その死はゆっくりと苦しみを伴うものだった ❶ *painful* は体の部位・病気・けが・治療・死に用いられる。反意 **painless** ❶ *painless* は「苦痛を引き起こさない」ことを表す。◆a *painless* death (安楽死)。◆The treatment is *painless*. (その治療は苦痛を伴わない)。
▸**painfully** 副 ◇He limped *painfully* to the door. 彼はドアのところまで痛そうにびっこを引いて行った

sore (感染症・筋肉痛で体の部位が赤くなって)痛い ◇He had a high temperature and a ***sore throat***. 彼は熱があってのどが痛かった ◇Their feet were *sore* after hours of walking. 何時間も歩いた後, 彼らは足が痛くなった ☞ **sore** (TUMOUR)
▸**soreness** 名 [U] ◇an ointment to reduce soreness and swelling 痛みと腫れを和らげる軟膏

raw (感染症・肌荒れなどで体の部位が)赤むけした, ひりひり[ちくちく]痛い ◇His throat was *raw* and painful. 彼はのどがひりひり痛かった ◇The skin on her feet had been rubbed *raw*. 彼女の足の皮膚はこすれて赤むけしていた

inflamed (感染症・けがで体の部位が)炎症を起こした ◇Her finger was swollen and *inflamed*. 彼女の指は腫れ上がって炎症を起こしていた ◇The wound had become *inflamed*. 傷が炎症を起こしてしまった ☞ **inflammation** (TUMOUR)

excruciating 激しく[耐えがたいほど]痛い[苦しい] ◇The pain in my back was *excruciating*. 背中の痛みは激しかった ◇The process is painful, but not *excruciating*. その処置は痛みを伴いますが, 耐えがたいほどではありません ◇She groaned at the memory, suffering all over again the *excruciating* embarrassment of those moments. 彼女はその時の耐えがたいほどの恥ずかしさにもう一度襲われ, 思い出してうめき声を上げた ❶ *excruciating* は感覚・治療・死に用いられるが, 体の部位には用いられない。✕ an *excruciating* throat/back/knee。また, 身体的苦痛だけでなく精神的苦痛をも表すことがある。
▸**excruciatingly** 副 ◇an *excruciatingly* painful death 耐えがたいほどの苦痛を伴う死

burning 焼けるようにひりひりする; 燃えるように熱い ◇She felt a *burning* sensation in her throat. 彼女はのどが焼けるようにひりひりした ◇The boy's forehead was *burning*. その少年のおでこは燃えるように熱かった ❶ *burning* は感覚・体の部位に用いられる。

itchy かゆみを伴う[引き起こす]; かゆい, むずむずする ◇The skin on my legs broke out in an *itchy* rash. 私の脚の皮膚にかゆみを伴う発疹が現れた ◇I feel *itchy* all over. 私は全身がかゆい

2 ☞ SAD, STRESSFUL, WORRYING
painful・traumatic・distressing・upsetting・harrowing・agonizing
動揺したり心配したりすることを表す
【類語訳】嫌な, 苦しい, つらい, 痛ましい, 悲惨な, ひどい, 苦渋の, 苦悶に満ちた

painful	traumatic	harrowing
upsetting	distressing	agonizing

文型&コロケーション
▸ to be painful/ traumatic/ distressing/ upsetting **for sb**
▸ to be painful/ distressing/ upsetting **to do sth**
▸ to be distressing/ upsetting **that...**
▸ a painful/ a traumatic/ a distressing/ an upsetting/ a harrowing **experience**
▸ a painful/ a traumatic/ a harrowing/ an agonizing **time**
▸ a painful/ distressing/ harrowing **scene**
▸ a distressing/ harrowing **sight**
▸ a painful/ an agonizing **decision**
▸ rather painful/ traumatic/ distressing/ pathetic/ upsetting/ harrowing
▸ very/ extremely/ deeply/ particularly painful/ distressing/ upsetting

painful 嫌な, 苦しい, つらい, 痛ましい ◇Seeing her again brought back *painful* memories. もう一度

paint, pale

彼女に会って嫌な思い出がよみがえった ◇Their efforts were *painful* to watch. 彼らの努力は見るも痛ましかった ☞ **pain** (DISTRESS)

traumatic (経験が)心に深い傷として残る ◇a *traumatic* childhood 心に深い傷として残る幼年時代 ◇Divorce can be *traumatic* for everyone involved. 離婚は関わりのある全員の心に深い傷として残ることがある ☞ **traumatize** (FRIGHTEN)

distressing (他人の苦難について)悲惨な、痛ましい ◇The divorce was extremely *distressing* for the children. 親の離婚はその子たちにとってきわめて悲惨なことだった ◇What could be more *distressing* than the death of their only child? たった一人の子を亡くすことほど痛ましいことがあろうか ☞ **distress** (DISTRESS), **distress** (HURT 1), **distressed** (UPSET)

upsetting つらい、苦しい、ひどい ◇I could see that it had been an *upsetting* experience for him. 彼にとってそれはつらい経験だったことだろう ◇It's always *upsetting* to lose a patient. 患者に死なれることはいつもながらつらいことだ ☞ **upset** (UPSET), **upset** (HURT 1)

harrowing (きわめて)悲惨な、痛ましい ◇There were *harrowing* scenes at the airport as relatives heard news of the crash. 近親者たちが空港でその墜落事故の知らせを聞く光景は何とも痛ましかった ◇You've had a *harrowing* experience and a lucky escape. 君は悲惨な経験をしたけど、九死に一生を得たね

agonizing (英でまた **-sing**) ひどい苦痛を伴う、苦渋の、苦悶に満ちた ◇his father's *agonizing* death 彼の父親のひどい苦しみを伴う死 ◇It was the most *agonizing* decision of her young life. それは彼女の短い人生の中で最も苦渋に満ちた決断だった

paint 動

paint・dye・colour・tint・stain
物に色を加える、材料を用いて物の色を変える
【類語訳】ペンキを塗る、塗装する、染める、着色する、染色する

文型&コロケーション
▶ to paint/ dye/ colour/ tint/ stain sth **with** sth
▶ to paint/ dye/ colour/ tint/ stain sth **red/ yellow/ green**, etc.
▶ to paint/ stain **wood**
▶ to dye/ colour your **hair**

paint [他] (表面・物体に)ペンキを塗る、塗装する ◇We've decided to have the house *painted*. 私たちは家を塗装してもらうことに決めた ◇*Paint* the shed with weather-resistant paint. 小屋に耐候性のペンキを塗りましょう ◇a brightly *painted* barge 鮮やかな色で塗装された屋形船 ◇The walls were *painted* yellow. その壁は黄色に塗装されていた ☞ **paint** (DRAW)
▷ **paint** 名 [U] ◇The woodwork has recently been given a fresh **coat of paint**. その木材品は最近塗装されたばかりだ ◇The *paint* is starting to peel off. ペンキがはがれ始めている

dye [他] (髪・織物を)染める、着色[染色]する ◇to *dye* clothes/fabric/wool 衣服/織物/ウールに着色する ◇She *dyed* her hair blonde. 彼女は髪をブロンドに染めた ◇*dyed* black hair 黒染めされた髪
▷ **dye** 名 [U, C] ◇hair *dye* 毛髪染料 ◇natural/chemical/vegetable *dyes* 自然/化学/植物染料

colour 《英》(米では **color**) [他] (髪を)染める、着色[染色]する ◇How long have you been *colouring* your hair? 髪を染めてどのくらいになりますか ☞ **colour** (DRAW)
▷ **colour** 《英》(米では **color**) 名 [C, U] ◇a semi-permanent hair *colour* that lasts around six washes 約6回髪を洗っても持続する半永久的な毛髪染料

tint [他、ふつう受身で] (物を薄く)染める、着色[染色]する ◇She's having her eyelashes *tinted*. 彼女はまつげを薄く染めている ◇*tinted* windows/lenses 着色ガラスの窓/レンズ

stain [他] (物を)染める、着色[染色]する ◇The floors had been *stained* dark brown. 床はこげ茶色に着色されていた ◇He *stained* the specimen before looking at it under the microscope. 彼は顕微鏡で見る前にその標本を染色した
▷ **stain** 名 [U, C] ◇Apply two coats of white *stain*. 白の染料を2度塗りましょう ◇a wood *stain* 木材染料

ノート **dye** と **stain** の使い分け：髪・織物を染めるには dye を、木材には stain を用いる。

pale 形

pale・light・soft・dull・pastel・subtle・dusky・neutral・cool
光や色が明るく[強く]ないことを表す
【類語訳】薄い、淡い、鈍い、つやのない、ぼんやりとした、パステル調の、ほのかな、ほの暗い、くすんだ、涼しげな、寒色の

文型&コロケーション
▶ a pale/ light/ soft/ dull/ pastel/ subtle/ neutral/ cool **colour**
▶ a pale/ light/ soft/ dull/ pastel/ subtle/ neutral/ cool **shade**
▶ pale/ light/ soft/ pastel/ subtle/ neutral **tones**
▶ pale/ light/ soft/ dull/ pastel/ subtle/ dusky **pink**
▶ pale/ light/ soft/ dull/ pastel/ subtle/ cool **green**
▶ pale/ light/ soft/ dull/ dusky **red**
▶ pale/ light/ soft/ dull/ pastel/ cool **blue**
▶ pale/ light/ soft/ dull/ cool **grey**
▶ pale/ light/ soft/ dull/ brown/ yellow
▶ pale/ light/ dull/ dusky **orange**
▶ a pale/ soft/ dull/ dusky **light**
▶ a pale/ soft/ dull **glow**
▶ a pale/ dull **sky**
▶ pale/ soft/ cool **blue eyes**
▶ sth is pale/ light/ neutral **in colour**

pale (色・光が)薄い、淡い ◇The bedroom walls are *pale* green. 寝室の壁は淡い緑色だ ◇The rooftops and chimneys stood out against the *pale* sky. 屋根と煙突が淡い色の空に映えていた ◇The flowers were *pale* and wilted. 花々が色あせてしおれていた 反意 **dark, deep** (DARK 2)

light (色が)薄い、淡い ◇He's got *light* blue eyes. 彼は薄い青の目をしている ◇*Lighter* shades suit you best. 君には薄い色合いが一番似合う ◇People with pale complexions should avoid wearing *light* colours. 肌の色が白い人は薄い色の服を着るのは避けるべきです 反意 **dark** (DARK 2)

ノート **pale** と **light** の使い分け：色について用いる場合は、両語とも使用可能。◆*pale/light* blue/green/yellow/or-

↪**pale**

ange/red/pink/purple/grey/brown（薄い青色／緑色／黄色／オレンジ色／赤色／ピンク色／紫色／グレー／茶色）。
◆**pale/light** colours/shades/tones（薄い色／色合い／色調）。paleは特にあまり明るくなく白みがかった色についても用いられる。◆ a *pale* light/glow/sky（淡い光／輝き／空）。× a *light* light/glow/sky.

soft ［ふつう名詞の前で］やわらかな、やさしい ◇ a colour scheme of *soft* pink and cream やわらかなピンク色とクリーム色の配色 ◇ the *soft* glow of candlelight ろうそくのやさしい光 [反意] **harsh**

dull 鈍い、つやのない、ほんやりとした ◇ The blood stained the grass a *dull* red colour. 血で草が鈍い赤色に染まった ◇ The fire died down to a *dull* glow. 火は衰えてほんやりと輝いた [反意] **bright** (BRIGHT)

pastel ［名詞の前で］（色が）淡い、パステル調の ◇ The white walls were repainted in *pastel* shades. その白壁は淡い色調に塗り直された
▶ **pastel** ［名］ [C] ◇ The whole house was painted in soft *pastels*. 家全体がやわらかなパステル調に塗装された

subtle ［ふつう名詞の前で］《ほめて》（色が）ほのかな ◇ Her paintings are characterized by sweeping brush strokes and *subtle* colours. 彼女の絵は大胆な筆遣いとほのかな色遣いに特徴がある

dusky ［ふつう名詞の前で］《文語》（色が）ほの暗い、くすんだ、黒ずんだ ◇ The setting sun tinged the sky with a *dusky* orange. 太陽が沈むにつれ空はほの暗いオレンジ色に染まった

neutral （グレー・ライトブラウンのような）中間色の ◇ a *neutral* colour scheme 中間色の配色 ◇ *Neutral* tones will give the room a feeling of space. 中間色を使えば部屋が広く感じられるだろう

cool （ふつうほめて）（色が）涼しげな、寒色の ◇ a room painted in *cool* greens and blues 涼しげな緑と青で塗装された部屋 [反意] **warm** (DARK 2)

panic ［動］

panic・freak out・lose your nerve・take fright・chicken out
愚かな[危険な]行動をする、意思どおりに行動できないほど怖がる
【類語訳】パニックになる、うろたえる、慌てふためく、びびる、おじけづく、気後れする、おびえる

[文型&コロケーション]
▶ to **just** panic/ freak out/ lose your nerve

panic (-ck) ［自］（恐怖で）パニックになる、うろたえる、慌てふためく ◇ I *panicked* when I saw smoke coming out of the engine. 私はエンジンから煙が出ているのを見てパニックになった ◇ Don't *panic*! We need to try and stay calm. 慌てるな、落ち着かないといけない ☞ **panic** (FEAR), **panicky, panic-stricken** (HYSTERICAL)

,**freak 'out** [句動] 《インフォーマル》〔衝撃・恐怖・驚きで〕びびる、びっくりする ◇ I could hear her downstairs, and I was *freaking out*, hiding under the bed. 彼女が下りてくるのが聞こえて、私はびびってベッドの下に隠れていた

,**lose your 'nerve** [書れ]（…しようとして恐怖で）おじけづく、気後れする ◇ I tried to go parachuting once, but I *lost my nerve* at the last minute and didn't jump. 私は一度スカイダイビングに挑戦しようとしたが、直前になっておじけづいて飛び出せなかった [反意] **keep/hold your nerve**

take 'fright [書れ]《書き言葉》（逃げ出したくなるほど）おびえる、びっくりする ◇ The birds *took fright* and flew away. 鳥たちはびっくりして飛び去った ◇ Investors *took fright at* the falling market. 投資家たちは下降市場におびえた

,**chicken 'out** （インフォーマル、けなして）おじけづいてやめる、びびって…しない ◇ She *chickened out of* telling him what really happened. 彼女はびびって実際に起きたことを彼に話すのをやめた

paper ［名］☞ ARTICLE, ASSIGNMENT

paper・essay・thesis・dissertation・monograph・treatise・tract
特定のテーマに関する学術的な書き物
【類語訳】論文、小論文、作文、評論、随筆、エッセイ、卒業論文、学位論文

[文型&コロケーション]
▶ a **paper**/ an **essay**/ a **thesis**/ a **dissertation**/ a **monograph**/ a **treatise**/ a **tract on** sth
▶ a **paper**/ an **essay**/ a **thesis**/ a **dissertation**/ a **monograph**/ a **treatise about** sth
▶ a **short** paper/ essay/ thesis/ monograph/ treatise/ tract
▶ a **long** paper/ essay/ dissertation/ treatise/ tract
▶ a **research** paper/ essay/ thesis/ dissertation/ monograph
▶ a **recent** paper/ essay/ dissertation/ monograph
▶ a **scholarly** paper/ essay/ monograph/ treatise
▶ to **write/ read** a paper/ an essay/ a thesis/ a dissertation/ a monograph/ a treatise/ a tract
▶ to **publish** a paper/ an essay/ a thesis/ a monograph/ a treatise/ a tract
▶ to **submit** a paper/ an essay/ a thesis/ a dissertation

paper [C]（学術的な）論文 ◇ a recent *paper* in the Journal of Medicine『ジャーナル・オブ・メディスン』に発表された最近の論文 ◇ She was invited to *give a paper* (= a talk) on the results of her research. 彼女は研究結果に関する発表を行うために招かれた ❶《米》では a paper は学生の課題としての「レポート」を指すこともある。◆ Your grade will be based on four *papers* and a final exam. (成績は4回のレポートと期末試験に基づいて決められます)。

essay [C]（学生の課題としての短い）小論文、作文；（出版目的で書かれる短い）小論、評論、随筆、エッセイ ◇ We have to write an *essay* on the causes of the First World War. 私たちは第一次世界大戦の原因についての小論文を書かなければならない ◇ The book contains a number of interesting *essays* on women in society. その本には社会における女性の立場に関する興味深いエッセイが数多く含まれている

thesis (複 **theses**) [C]（学位を取得するための）学位論文 ◇ Students must submit a *thesis* on an agreed subject within four years. 学生は4年以内に決められたテーマに関して卒業論文を提出しなければならない ◇ a doctoral/PhD *thesis*《英》博士論文 ◇ a *thesis* for a master's degree《米》修士論文 ☞ **thesis** (THEORY 2)

dissertation [C]（学位を取得するための）卒業[学位]論文 ◇ She is writing her *dissertation* on the history of the Knights Templar. 彼女はテンプル騎士団の歴史に関する学位論文を書いている

[ノート] **thesis** と **dissertation** の使い分け：これらの語はしばしば大学によって用いられ方が違う。例えば、博士号との

parallel, parody

関連でthesisを用いる大学もあれば, dissertationを用いる大学もある。一般的には, thesisはその論文に書き手が特定の理論・考えを擁護するために行う独自の研究が含まれることを強調する。

monograph [C]《専門語》(限定されたテーマに関する短い)論文 ◇He has published several books on Cubism and numerous *monographs* on individual artists. 彼はキュービズムに関する本を数冊と個々の画家に関する論文を多数出版している

treatise [C]《フォーマル》(特定のテーマに関する長い)論文 ◇Any of these questions would deserve a lengthy *treatise*, perhaps even a small book. これらの疑問に答えるとすればどれも非常に長い論文に, 場合によっては小さな本にさえなるだろう

tract [C]《時にけなして》(人を感化するための宗教[道徳, 政治]的テーマに関する短い)小論, 小冊子 ◇He wrote several *tracts* on the dangers of alcohol. 彼はアルコールの危険性に関する小論をいくつか書いた ◇socialist/feminist *tracts* 社会主義/女権拡張論に関する小冊子

parallel 形

parallel・side by side・simultaneous・concurrent
物事が他の物事と同時に発生[存在]することを表す
【類語訳】似たような, 同様の, 並行した, 共に, 一緒に

▶文型&コロケーション
▸ side by side/ simultaneous/ concurrent **with** sth
▸ a parallel/ simultaneous/ concurrent **change**
▸ a parallel/ simultaneous **increase/ operation/ process**
▸ parallel/ concurrent **development**

parallel 似たような, 同様の; 同時に発生[存在]する, 並行した ◇Two poisonings have been reported recently in London and now there has been a *parallel* case in the Netherlands. 最近2件の中毒事件がロンドンで報告されているが, 現在オランダでも似たような事例が起きている ◇Though still a committed painter, in 1978 she launched a *parallel* career as a photographer. 彼女は画家としてなお熱意を傾注しているが, 1978年には並行して写真家としての道を歩み始めた
▸ **parallel** 副 ◇The grammar classes **run parallel to** the literature class. 文法の授業は文学の授業と並行して行われます
▸ **in 'parallel with sth** フレーズ ◇The city has grown *in parallel with* the growth of its industries. その都市は産業の成長と共に発展している

,side by 'side 行刑 (困難なく)共に, 一緒に, 並行して ◇We have been using both systems, *side by side*, for two years. 私たちは両システムを2年間にわたり並行して使用している ◇The two communities exist happily *side by side*. その二つの共同体は平和的に共存している

simultaneous 同時に発生する[行われる] ◇There were several *simultaneous* attacks by the rebels. 反逆者たちによって複数か所に対する同時攻撃が行われた ◇They will provide *simultaneous translation* of the President's speech into English. 大統領演説は英語に同時通訳される予定です
▸ **simultaneously** 副 ◇The game will be broadcast *simultaneously* on TV and radio. その試合はテレビとラジオで同時放送される予定です

concurrent 《フォーマル》同時に発生[存在]する, 並行した ◇He was imprisoned for two *concurrent* terms of 30 months and 18 months. 彼は30か月と18か月の二つの刑期のため同時拘留された
▸ **concurrently** 副 ◇The prison sentences will run *concurrently*. 実刑判決が同時に下される予定です

parody 名

parody・caricature・impersonation・spoof・impression・imitation
人や物事を意図的に模倣した公演や映画, 文学作品など
【類語訳】パロディー, 風刺, 戯画, 物まね, 扮装, もじり

▶文型&コロケーション
▸ a parody/ a caricature/ an impersonation/ a spoof/ an impression/ an imitation **of** sb/ sth
▸ a **brilliant** parody/ caricature
▸ a **grotesque** parody/ caricature/ imitation
▸ a **passable** impersonation/ impression/ imitation
▸ a **convincing** impersonation/ impression
▸ a **poor** impersonation/ imitation
▸ an **Elvis Presley/ Marilyn Monroe,** etc. impersonation/ impression/ imitation
▸ to **do** a parody/ an impersonation/ a spoof/ an impression/ an imitation
▸ to **write** a parody/ spoof

parody [C, U] (娯楽のための文学作品・音楽・演技などの)パロディー ◇He's currently working on a *parody* of a horror film. 現在彼はホラー映画のパロディーに取りかかっている ◇His personality made him an easy subject for *parody*. その人柄から彼は格好のパロディーの標的となった
▸ **parody** 動 [他] ◇Her work *parodies* genres such as the thriller and the spy novel. 彼女の作品はスリラーやスパイ小説などのジャンルをパロディー化している

caricature [C]《時にけなして》(特徴を誇張して面白おかしくする)風刺(画), 戯画 ◇He had unfairly presented a *caricature* of my views. 彼は私の意見の風刺画を不当に発表してしまった
▸ **caricature** 動 [他, しばしば受身で] ◇She was unfairly *caricatured* as a dumb blonde. 彼女は不当にも頭の悪いブロンドの女性として風刺的に描かれた

impersonation [C, U] (人を楽しませる[だます]ための)物まね, 扮装, 振りをする[声色を使う]こと ◇He did an extremely convincing *impersonation* of the singer. 彼はすごくもっともらしくその歌手の物まねをした

spoof [C]《インフォーマル》(映画・テレビ番組の特徴を誇張した)もじり ◇It's a *spoof on* horror movies. その作品はホラー映画のもじりです ◇They did a very clever game show *spoof*. 彼らは非常に巧妙にクイズ番組をもじった

impression [C] (余興のための)物まね ◇She did her Marilyn Monroe *impression*. 彼女はマリリン・モンローの物まねをした

imitation [C] (余興のための)物まね ◇He does a hilarious *imitation* of George W Bush. 彼はジョージ・W・ブッシュのすごく面白い物まねをする

▶ノート **impersonation, impression, imitation** の使い分け: impersonation は impression や imitation よりも真面目なものである。impression と imitation は (と, おどけて用いられる場合の impersonation) は人々が即座にそれと

わかる人の声・振る舞いの最も顕著な特徴だけを余興のためにまねることを指す。impersonation は相手に本人であるとすっかり信じ込ませて人をだますためにも, 真面目な演劇の役柄としても, 人の全体的な外見・性格を真剣にまねようとすることを指す. impression と imitation はほとんど同じ意味だが, impression のほうがより上手で成功している可能性が高いことを表す. ◆ a convincing *impression* (ピンとくる物まね). ◆ a poor *imitation* (下手な物まね).

participant 名 ☞ CANDIDATE

participant・contender・challenger・contestant・competitor
スポーツや競技会, 選挙などに参加する人
【類語訳】参加者, 出場者, 関係者, 協力者, 候補者, 競争相手, 挑戦者, 対立候補者, 選手

文型&コロケーション
- a contender/ challenger/ contestant/ competitor for sth
- a participant/ contender/ challenger/ contestant/ competitor in sth
- a likely/ possible participant/ contender
- a main/ major participant/ contender/ challenger
- a serious/ strong contender/ challenger/ competitor
- a Democratic/ Republican/ presidential contender/ challenger
- to take on a contender/ challenger
- a contestant/ competitor enters sth

participant [C] (活動・行事の)参加[出場]者, 関係[協力]者 ◇Enrolment will be limited to 35 *participants*. 参加者の制限人数は35人までとなります ◇She was an ***unwilling participant*** in his downfall. 彼女は彼の失脚にしぶしぶ関係した人物だった ☞ **participate** (JOIN)

contender [C] (競技会などで勝つ見込みの高い)候補[出場]者, 競争者[相手] ◇She is a strong *contender* for the party leadership. 彼女はその党首の有力候補である ◇Germany last night emerged as a *contender* to stage next year's event. 昨夜ドイツが来年の大会を主催する候補地として浮かび上がった

challenger [C] (スポーツ・政治でタイトル[職位]を争う)挑戦者, 対立候補者 ◇These two teams are the main *challengers* for the European title. これら2チームがヨーロッパ選手権の有力優勝候補です ◇He has been tipped as a potential ***challenger to*** the prime minister. 彼は首相と争える対立候補として有力視されてきた

contestant [C] (クイズ大会などの)出場者, 競争者[相手] ◇Please welcome our next *contestant*. 次の出場者を迎えましょう ☞ **contest** (COMPETITION 1)

competitor [C] (スポーツ・競技などの)出場者, 選手, 競争者[相手] ◇Over 200 *competitors* entered the race. 200人を超える出場者がその競技に参加した ◇She is one of the sport's top *competitors*. 彼女はそのスポーツのトップ選手の一人だ ☞ **competition** (COMPETITION 1, 2)

particular 形

particular・certain・separate・specific・individual・single・respective・distinct
複数の人々や物事ではなく一人の人や一つの物事を表す
【類語訳】特定の, 特別の, ある種の, 独立した, 単独の, 別々の, ばらばらの, 分かれた, 別個の, 異質の, 関連のない, 具体的な, 明確な, 特殊な, 個別の, 個々の

文型&コロケーション
- sth is separate/ distinct from sth else
- a particular/ certain/ specific/ individual person
- a particular/ a certain/ a separate/ a specific/ an individual/ a single/ a distinct category/ region
- respective categories/ regions
- a particular/ certain/ separate/ specific/ single event/ incident/ occasion
- a particular/ certain/ separate/ specific location
- particular/ certain/ separate/ individual/ single/ distinct components
- particular/ certain/ specific/ individual/ respective/ distinct needs/ requirements
- a particular/ certain/ specific/ single/ distinct context
- respective contexts
- a particular/ certain/ specific/ single/ distinct objective/ purpose
- a particular/ certain/ specific date
- respective dates
- a particular/ a separate/ an individual/ a single/ a distinct strand
- a separate/ individual/ single/ distinct entity
- a particular/ a certain/ a separate/ a specific/ an individual/ a distinct type of sth
- a particular/ certain/ specific/ distinct kind of sth
- quite separate/ specific/ distinct

particular [名詞の前で] (複数ではないことを強調して)特定の, 特別の, …だけの ◇There is one *particular* patient I'd like you to see. 私があなたに診てもらいたいある特定の患者がいます ◇The policy seems to discriminate against *particular* groups of people. その政策は特定の人の集団を差別するように思える ◇Here, ***in no particular order*** (= the order is not important and has not been deliberately chosen), is a selection of readers' comments. ここに, 順不同で, 読者の意見が載っています
> **particularly** 副 ◇Traffic is bad, *particularly* on the way into town. 車が混むんだ, 特に町に入るときにね ◇I enjoyed the play, *particularly* the second half. あの劇は楽しかった, 特に後半がね

certain [名詞の前で] (詳述せずに)ある, ある種の ◇*Certain* people might disagree with this. ある人々がこれに賛成しない可能性がある ◇They refused to release their hostages unless *certain* conditions were met. ある条件が満たされない限り, 彼らは人質の解放を拒んだ ❶フォーマルな言い回しでは, certain は名前を挙げるが, よく知らない人について用いられることがある. ◇It was a *certain* Dr Davis who performed the operation. (手術を行ったのはデービス先生とかいう人だった).

separate 独立した, 単独の, 別々の; ばらばらの, 分かれた, 別個の; 異質の, 関連のない ◇They sleep in *separate* bedrooms. 彼らは別々の寝室で寝る ◇Raw meat must be ***kept separate*** from cooked meat. 生肉は調理済みの肉と分けて保存しなければいけません ◇Write a list of names on a *separate* piece of paper. 別紙に名前の一覧表を書いてください ◇It happened on three *separate* occasions. それは三つの異なる場面で起こった ◇For the past three years they have been leading totally *separate* lives. この3年間彼らはまったく別々の生活を送ってい

る 反意 **joint, communal** (COMMON)
▶**separately** 副 ◇They were photographed *separately* and then as a group. 彼らは別々に写真を撮られ、その後でグループ写真を撮られた ◇That matter will be considered *separately* from the main agenda. その問題は主要議題と別個に検討されるだろう

specific [ふつう名詞の前で] 個別的な、具体的な、明確な、特殊な ◇Each debate will focus on a *specific* political issue. 各討論は個別の政治問題が中心となるでしょう ◇The money was collected for a *specific* purpose. そのお金はある明確な目的で集められた
▶**specifically** 副 ◇a magazine aimed *specifically* at working women 働く女性向け専用雑誌

ノート **particular** と **specific** の使い分け：a particular は他ならぬ一人[一つ]の人・集団・物事(例えば、メアリーではなくジョン、ドイツ人ではなくフランス人、これではなくあのもの)を表す。a specific は全般的な集団・物事の種類ではなく、厳密に特定される一つの集団・物事(例えば、児童全般ではなく〈学習障害(児)のある児童、失業問題全般ではなく衰退する産業中心地における長期失業問題など)を表す。

individual [名詞の前で] (集団の一部ではなく) 個別の、個々の ◇We interviewed **each individual** member of the community. 私たちは地域住民の一人一人にインタビューした ◇The minister refused to comment on *individual* cases. 大臣は個々の問題に関するコメントを拒否した
反意 **collective** (COMMON), ☞ **individual** (OWN)
▶**individually** 副 ◇*individually* wrapped chocolates 個別包装されたチョコレート

single [名詞の前で] (特定の一人[一つ]の人・物事を強調して) 唯一の、個々の ◇Unemployment is the **single most important** factor in the rising crime rates. 失業こそが犯罪率の高まりの唯一にして最大の要因である ◇We eat rice **every single day**. 私たちは毎日毎日お米を食べる
▶**singly** 副 ◇The stamps are available *singly* or in books of ten. このスタンプは一個ずつまたは10個一綴りでご利用できます

respective 《ふつう複数名詞の前で》《ややフォーマル》(既述の人・物事について) 各自[個々]の、めいめい[それぞれ]の ◇They are each recognized as specialists in their *respective* fields. 彼らはおのおのそれぞれの分野における専門家と認識されている
▶**respectively** 副 ◇Julie Wilson and Mark Thomas, aged 17 and 19 *respectively* それぞれ17歳と19歳のジュリー・ウィルソンとマーク・トーマス

distinct 異なる、別種の ◇The results of the survey fell into two *distinct* groups. その調査結果は明確に異なる二つのグループに分かれた ◇Jamaican reggae music is quite *distinct* from North American jazz or blues. ジャマイカのレゲエ音楽は北アメリカのジャズやブルースとはまったくの別物だ ◇We are talking about rural areas, **as distinct from** major cities. 私たちは主要都市とは異なる、農村地域について話している

partly 副 ☞ QUITE 1

partly・in part・partially・half・to some extent・somewhat・moderately・up to a point
完全ではなくある段階までであることを表す
【類訳語】ある程度、部分的に、一部分が、半分、いくぶん

ノート 親見出し quite 1 の類語と比較のこと。quite 1 の類語は一般に partly より肯定的で、物事の良さ[成功、難しさ]などの程度を強調する。この partly の類語は quite 1 の類語ほどは肯定的でないが、物事がどれほど真実[成功]などから離れているかいないかや、物事がどれほど完全な真実[成功]などからかけ離れているかを強調する傾向がある。

文型＆コロケーション
▶partly/ partially/ moderately **successful**
▶partly/ partially/ half **true**
▶to some extent/ somewhat **arbitrary**
▶partly/ in part/ partially/ to some extent **because...**
▶partly/ in part/ to some extent **due to** sth
▶**only** partly/ partially/ half/ to some extent/ moderately/ up to a point

partly ある程度は、少しは；部分的には、一部分は ◇The measure was popular, *partly* because it was a way of avoiding tax. その措置はそれが一部税金逃れの方法の一つであったため広く行き渡っていた ◇The result is partly a matter of skill and *partly* of chance. 結果は一部は手腕の問題であり、一部は運の問題である ◇He was only *partly* responsible for the accident. 彼にはその事故の責任の一部があるだけだった ◇It was *partly* my fault. それはある程度は私にも責任があった 反意 **completely** (QUITE 2)

in ˈpart 《ˈフォーマル、特に書き言葉》ある程度、少しは；部分的には、一部分は ◇Her success was due *in part* to luck. 彼女の成功のある部分は運のおかげだった ◇The money was at least *in part* provided by the families. そのお金の少なくとも一部はそれらの家族から提供されたものだった

partially ある程度は、少しは；部分的には、一部分は ◇The road was *partially* blocked by a fallen tree. その道路は倒木によって部分的に通行止めになっていた ◇Machines replaced, at least *partially*, the skills of human workers. 少なくとも部分的には、機械が人間の作業技術に取って代わった ◇She teaches blind and *partially sighted* children. 彼女は全盲の子どもたちと弱視の子どもたちを教えている

ノート **partly, in part, partially** の使い分け：これらの表現はすべて「完全ではなく」を意味する。◆The road is *partly/partially* finished. (その道路は部分的に完成している)。partly と in part は特に理由について用いられ、because of や due to を伴うことが多い。◆I didn't enjoy the trip very much, *partly* because of the weather. (天気のこともあり、その旅行はあまり楽しくなかった)。◆Health problems attributed to air pollution may *in part* be due to heavy smoking. (空気汚染に起因するとされる健康問題は、ある程度はたばこの吸いすぎによるのかもしれない)。in part は partly よりもフォーマルで、たいていの場合書き言葉で用いられる。永久的な身体状況について言う場合は、partially を用いるべきである。◆The accident left her *partially* blind/deaf/disabled. (その事故で彼女は一部失明した/難聴になった/体の一部に障害(*s*)を負った)。

half 半分は；ある程度は、少しは；部分的には、一部分は ◇The bottle was only *half* full. その瓶は中身が半分しかなかった ◇I was still *half* asleep. 私はまだ半分眠っていた ◇He felt *half* afraid, *half* excited. 彼は恐怖と興奮が相半ばした ◇She is *half* Italian. 彼女は半分イタリア系だ ◇I *half* expected them to follow us. 私は彼らが私たちに従

うことをある程度は期待した ◇The result was not *half* as (= not nearly as) bad as expected. 結果は予想していたほどひどく悪くなかった

to some extent [フレーズ] 《ややフォーマル, 特に書き言葉》(真実性・妥当性について)ある程度は ◇*To some extent*, this is still the case. ある程度は, これはいまだに言えることです ◇By this time, animals were, *to some extent* at least, tamed if not domesticated. この時までに動物は, 少なくともある程度は, 家畜化されていなくとも人に慣れていた

somewhat 《米 or ややフォーマル, 英》ある程度は；やや, いくぶん, 少し ◇Her version of what happened was *somewhat* different. 起こったことに関する彼女の説明はいくぶん違っていた ◇He was *somewhat* taken aback by the girl's directness. 彼はその女の子の率直さに少し驚いた

moderately 《ややフォーマル》平均的に, 並に；適度に, ほどよく ◇The plan was only *moderately* successful. その計画はまずまずうまくいったという程度にすぎなかった ◇Cook in a *moderately* hot oven. 適度に熱したオーブンで調理しましょう

up to a 'point [フレーズ] ある程度(まで)は ◇I agree with you *up to a point*. 私はある程度まではあなたに賛成します ◇That is true only *up to a point*. それはある程度まで当てはまるにすぎない ◇I was successful *up to a certain point*. 私はある程度まではうまくいった ❶ up to a point はこの見出し語の類義語の中で, 最も肯定的要素が弱い表現. 実際, 人が賛成しない[物事が真実でない]程度が強調される.

partner [名]

1 [FRIEND]
partner・colleague・associate・contact・ally・classmate・co-worker・collaborator・workmate・teammate
一緒に働く[勉強する, 活動する]人
【類語訳】パートナー, 共同経営者, 共同事業者, 相棒, 相方, 同僚, 提携者, 仲間, 知人, つて, 盟友, 同級生, クラスメート, チームメート

[文型&コロケーション]
- a **business** partner/ colleague/ associate/ contact/ ally
- a **political** colleague/ associate/ contact/ ally
- a **junior/ senior** partner/ colleague/ associate
- a **former** partner/ colleague/ associate/ ally/ classmate/ co-worker/ collaborator/ workmate/ teammate
- an **old** colleague/ associate/ ally/ classmate
- a **new** partner/ colleague/ associate/ contact/ ally/ classmate
- a **long-term** partner/ associate/ collaborator
- a **close** partner/ colleague/ associate/ contact/ ally/ collaborator

partner [C] (企業を所有[利益を共有]する)パートナー, 共同経営[事業]者(の一人)；(ダンス・ゲーム・競技などの)パートナー, 相棒, 相方, ペアを組む相手 ◇He has recently been made a junior *partner* in the family business. 最近彼は家業で准経営者の一人に任命された ◇Choose a *partner* for the next activity. 次の活動のためにペアを組む相手を選びましょう ◇My regular dancing *partner* has broken her ankle. 私のダンスのいつもの相手が足首を骨折した ☞ **partnership** (GROUP 3), **partnership** (RELATIONSHIP 1)
- **partner** [動] [他] ◇Gerry offered to *partner* me (=

colleague [C] (専門的職業・企業で一緒に働く)同僚 ◇I'd like you to meet a *colleague* of mine from the office. あなたに私の職場の同僚に会ってもらいたい ◇the Prime Minister and his Cabinet *colleagues* 首相と閣僚たち

associate [C] 《ややフォーマル》同僚, 提携者, 共同経営者, (一緒に多くの時間を過ごす)仲間 ◇The company is called Landor *Associates*. その会社はランダー・アソシエイツという名だ ◇He was known to be one of the convicted man's *associates*. 彼は有罪の男の仲間[共犯者]の一人として知られていた ☞ **association** (RELATIONSHIP 1)

[ノート] **colleague** と **associate** の使い分け：colleague のほうが associate よりもはるかに頻繁に用いられ, 特に職場・学校・政府などで一緒に働く人を表す一般的な語である. associate は, 例えば一緒に事業を行った[行っている]など, 仕事上の関係にある人を指すことが多い.

contact [C] (仕事上の助けになる)知人, つて ◇I've made some useful *contacts* in journalism. 私には報道関係に有力なつてができたところだ ◇It takes time to build up good *contacts*. 頼りになるつてを増やすには時間がかかる

ally [C] (窮地にある人を援助[支援]する政治家などの)盟友, 協力者, 味方 ◇He's a close friend and *ally* of the prime minister. 彼は首相の親友であり盟友である ◇His sister was his *ally against* their grandparents. 彼にとって姉は祖父母に一緒に対抗してくれる味方であった [反意] **enemy** (ENEMY)

classmate [C] (学校・大学での)同級生, クラスメート ◇Are you curious to know where your former *classmates* are now? 昔の同級生たちが今どこにいるか知りたいかい

'co-worker [C] (同種の仕事をする)同僚, 仕事仲間 ◇He is worried about his job after seeing his *co-workers* laid off. 彼は同僚が一時解雇されるのを見て, 自分の職に不安を感じている

collaborator [C] (書籍などを一緒に生み出す)共同制作者, 協力者 ◇He is working on a new series with his long-time *collaborator* Michel Baudin. 彼は長年の共同制作者であるミシェル・ボーダンと新シリーズに取りかかっている

workmate [C] 《特に英》(職場・工場などで一緒に同じ仕事をする)同僚, 仕事仲間 ◇Her *workmates* organized a leaving party for her last day in the office. 最後の日に同僚が彼女のために職場で送別会を開いてくれた

[ノート] **co-worker** と **workmate** の使い分け：workmate は《英》で, co-worker は《米》で用いられることが多い. また, workmate はいくぶんインフォーマルで, 非常に仲のよい同僚であることを示唆する.

teammate [C] チームメート ◇He was determined not to let his *teammates* down. 彼は自分のチームメートの期待に背かないよう決心していた

2 partner・girlfriend・boyfriend・man・date・fiancée・fiancé・sweetheart・suitor・admirer
恋愛関係にある男性[女性]
【類語訳】パートナー, 連れ合い, 伴侶, 彼女, 恋人, 彼氏, 夫, 男, フィアンセ, 求婚者

[文型&コロケーション]
- a **steady/ serious** girlfriend/ boyfriend

▶sb's **new** partner/ girlfriend/ boyfriend/ man/ admirer
▶sb's **ex-** partner/ girlfriend/ boyfriend/ fiancée/ fiancé
▶sb's **former/ current** partner/ girlfriend/ boyfriend
▶sb's **old** girlfriend/ boyfriend
▶to **have** a partner/ a girlfriend/ a boyfriend/ a man/ a date/ a fiancée/ a fiancé/ an admirer
▶to **get** a girlfriend/ boyfriend/ man
▶to **find** a partner/ girlfriend/ boyfriend/ man

partner [C]（真剣な恋愛[性的]関係にあって同棲している）パートナー、連れ合い、伴侶 ◇This is my *partner*, Mark. こちらは私の連れ合いのマークです ❶ *partner* の場合、一組の男女が結婚しているか否かはわからない[重要でない]。ふつう結婚はしていないが一緒に住んでいる人について用いられる。しかし、夫[妻]を指すこともある。◆ Come to the New Year disco and bring your *partner*. (新年のディスコパーティーにはパートナーと一緒にお越しください). また、*partner*は人の連れ合いの性別がわからない[に興味のない]場合にも用いられる

girlfriend [C] 彼女、恋人 ◇He's got a new *girlfriend*. 彼には新しい彼女がいる

boyfriend [C] 彼氏、恋人 ◇I just ran into my ex-*boyfriend*. 私、たった今、元彼と出くわしたところなの

ノート **partner** と **girlfriend/ boyfriend** の使い分け：
partner は girlfriend や boyfriend よりも真剣で長い付き合いであることを示唆する。girlfriend はふつう同棲している人を指す。girlfriend や boyfriend は同棲している場合もそうでない場合もある。また、partner はより成熟した関係を示唆することもあり、十代や若者には partner というより boyfriend や girlfriend がいることになる。しかしながら、このことは彼らの関係が長くは続かない[より真剣な交際に発展しない]ことを示唆するわけではない。◆ I've been going out with my *girlfriend* for seven years and she wants us to get married. (私は彼女と7年付き合っていて、彼女は結婚を望んでいる)

man [C] 夫、彼氏、男 ◇What's her new *man* like? 彼女の新しい男[彼氏]はどんな人 ◇I now pronounce you *man* and wife (= you are now officially married). ここにあなた方が夫婦であることを宣言します

date [C]《特に米》(恋人に発展しそうな)デートの相手 ◇My *date* is meeting me at seven. デートの相手と7時に会うんだ ☞ **date** (GO OUT)

fiancée [C] 婚約中の彼女、フィアンセ ◇Paul and his *fiancée* were there. ポールと婚約中の彼女がそこにいた

fiancé [C] 婚約中の彼氏、フィアンセ ◇Linda and her *fiancé* were there. リンダと婚約中の彼氏がそこにいた

sweetheart [C]《やや古風》恋人 ◇They were *childhood sweethearts*. 彼らは幼なじみの恋人同士だった ❶ sweetheart は childhood sweethearts という句の形以外では、現在ではやや古風な語である。特に幼い子ども同士の純粋無垢な関係を表し、恋愛感情や友情を伴うがふつうセックスは伴わない

suitor [C]《フォーマル or 古風》(女性への)求婚者 ◇In the play, the heroine has to choose between three *suitors*. その劇でヒロインは3人の求婚者の中から選ばねばならない ❶ suitor は主に昔の人・時代小説[劇]に出てくる人について用いられる

admirer [C] (女性に)愛慕する男性 ◇She never married but had many *admirers*. 彼女は一度も結婚しなかったが、彼女を慕う男性はたくさんいた

party

party 名

1 party・faction・camp・lobby
政治の世界において同じ目的[考え]を持ち、異なる目的[考え]を持つ人々に反対する集団
【類語訳】政党、派閥、党派、グループ、陣営、圧力団体

文型&コロケーション
▶**rival/ opposing** parties/ factions/ camps
▶the **socialist** party/ camp
▶to **belong to** a party/ faction/ camp

party (または **Party**) [C+単数・複数動詞] 政党 ◇the Democratic and Republican *Parties* in the United States 合衆国の民主党と共和党 ◇the ruling/opposition *party* 与党/野党 ◇the *party* leader/manifesto/policy 党首/政党のマニフェスト/政策

faction [C+単数・複数動詞] (集団内部の)派閥、党派 ◇There are rival *factions* within the administration. 政府内に対抗し合う派閥がある

camp [C+単数・複数動詞] (同じ考えをもつ)グループ、陣営 ◇The scientists split into two *camps* over the validity of animal studies. その科学者たちは動物実験の正当性をめぐって、二つのグループに分裂した

lobby [C+単数・複数動詞] (政治家に影響を与えようとする)圧力団体 ◇The gun *lobby* is against any change in the law. 銃器の圧力団体がその法律のいかなる改正にも反対している ☞ **lobby** (CAMPAIGN 動)

2 ☞ GROUP 2, TEAM 1
party・gang・band・contingent・company・pack
一つの場所で事を一緒に行う[共有する]人々の集団
【類語訳】一団、一行、一隊、一味、暴力団、ギャング、集団、仲間、非行グループ、族、代表団、派遣団

文型&コロケーション
▶a **party**/ gang/ band/ contingent/ pack **of** sth
▶**in** a party/ gang/ band/ company/ a pack
▶a **small/ large** party/ gang/ band/ contingent
▶a **10-strong/ 20-strong, etc.** party/ gang/ band/ contingent
▶a **growing/ strong** band/ contingent
▶to **join** a party/ gang/ band
▶a party/ gang/ pack **leader**
▶a **member of** a party/ gang/ band/ contingent/ pack

party [C+単数・複数動詞] (旅行・訪問などの)団体、一団[行]；(同じ任務の)一隊 ◇The theatre gives a 10% discount to *parties* of more than 10. その劇場は10人以上の団体に対して10%の割引を行っている ◇a *coach party* of German tourists 観光バスのドイツ人旅行客の一団 ◇It was decided to send out a *search party* to look for the missing climbers. 行方不明の登山者を捜すために捜索隊が派遣されることが決まった

gang [C+単数・複数動詞] (犯罪組織の)一団[味]、暴力団、ギャング；(他のグループともめごと[けんか]を起こす若者の)集団、仲間、非行グループ、族 ◇The robbery was carried out by an *armed gang*. その強盗事件は武装集団によって行われた ◇a *criminal gang* 犯罪集団 ◇We were in the same *gang*. 私たちは同じ非行グループにいた ◇Fights had ensued between rival *gangs* of football fans.

→party

path, patience

敵対し合うサッカーファンの集団の間で続いてけんかが生じた
☞ ring, gang (TEAM 1)
band [C+単数・複数動詞](物事を一緒に行う[共通の興味・特徴・達成を共有する])団体, 一団[行, 隊] ◇She persuaded a small *band* of volunteers to help. 彼女は小さなボランティア団体に援助を促した ◇They are members of a growing *band* of enthusiasts. 彼らは大きくなりつつあるファン集団の一員だ
contingent [C+単数・複数動詞](同じ地域から会議[行事]に参加する)代表[派遣]団 ◇The largest *contingent* was from the United States. 最大の代表団はアメリカ勢だった ◇A strong *contingent* of local residents were there to block the proposal. 地元住民から成る強力な派遣団がその企画案を阻止するためにそこに来ていた
company [U]《フォーマル》(会議・パーティーなどに参加する)人の集まり, 一同[団, 行] ◇Those children don't know how to behave *in company* (= in a group of people). あの子たちは人が集まるところでの振る舞い方を知らないんだ ◇It's not the type of joke you'd tell *in mixed company* (= with men and women present). 君の冗談は男女同席のところで言うことじゃないよ ◇She told *the assembled company* what had happened. 彼女は呼び集められた一同に何が起こったかを話した
pack [C+単数・複数動詞]《しばしばけなして》(好感のもてない人々・作物等の)集まり, 一団[群] ◇We avoided a *pack* of journalists waiting outside. 私たちは外で待ち構える記者の一団を避けた

path 名

path・trail・pavement・sidewalk・track・footpath
人が歩くための細長い場所
【類語訳】道, 小道, 歩道

📘 文型&コロケーション
▸ a path/ trail/ track/ footpath **through** sth
▸ a path/ trail/ track/ footpath **to** sth
▸ a **long** path/ trail/ track
▸ a **narrow** path/ trail/ pavement/ sidewalk/ track
▸ a **dusty** pavement/ trail/ track
▸ a **muddy** path/ trail/ track/ footpath
▸ to **follow** a path/ trail/ track/ footpath
▸ to **keep to** the path/ pavement/ sidewalk
▸ to **leave** the path/ track
▸ to **step off/ mount** the pavement/ sidewalk
▸ a path/ track **forks/ divides**
▸ a path/ trail/ track/ footpath **leads to** sth

path [C] (敷設された[踏みならされてきた])道, 小道 ◇a garden *path* 園路 ◇They took the cliff *path* as far as the lighthouse. 彼らは灯台まで崖道をつたった ◇They have cleared a *path* (= made one by cutting down plants) through the forest. 彼らは森を通り抜ける道を切り開いた ◇He walked down the garden *path* to the front gate. 彼は庭の道を通って正門まで歩いて行った
trail [C] (田園地方の[特定の目的で造られた]長距離の)道, 小道 ◇We set off to walk the *trail* that winds along the Colorado River. 私たちはコロラド川沿いに曲がりくねる道を歩き始めた ◇They have made a new *nature trail* (= a path where you can see interesting plants and animals) through the woods. 森を通る自然遊歩道が新しく造られた

pavement [C]《英》(車道わきの舗装されて一段高くなった)歩道 ◇A parked car was blocking the *pavement*. 駐車中の一台の車が歩道を妨害していた ◇A bus mounted the *pavement* and hit her. 一台のバスが歩道に乗り上げ, 彼女をはねた
sidewalk [C]《米》(車道わきの舗装されて一段高くなった)歩道 ◇The crowd filled the church and spilled onto the *sidewalk* outside. その教会は群衆でいっぱいになり, 外の歩道に人があふれていた ◇We stopped for coffee at a *sidewalk* cafe. 私たちはコーヒーを飲みに歩道にあるカフェに立ち寄った
track [C]《特に英》(人・動物・乗り物で踏みならされてできたでこぼこの)道, 小道 ◇The path joins a *farm track* (= one used by tractors) near a barn. その道は家畜小屋の近くで農道とつながっている ❶この意味のtrackは主に《英》で用いられる. 《米》では複数形で用い, ふつう人・物が残す「足跡, わだち」を意味するだけである.
footpath [C]《特に英》(人が歩くための田舎の)道, 小道 ◇Follow the marked *footpath*. 標識の付いた道を通ってください ◇A *public footpath* (= one that everyone has the right to use) crosses his land. 公道の小道が彼の土地を横切っている

patience 名

patience・tolerance・resignation
いら立たせる[厄介な]人や物事を文句を言わずに受け入れる能力[意欲]
【類語訳】忍耐力, 我慢強さ, 辛抱強さ, 寛容, 寛大, 容認

📘 文型&コロケーション
▸ patience/ tolerance **for** sb/ sth
▸ **with** patience/ tolerance/ resignation
▸ **great/ infinite/ little** patience/ tolerance
▸ to **have/ lack/ require/ show/ exercise/ learn** patience/ tolerance

patience [U] (遅延・いら立たせる事に対する)忍耐力, 我慢[辛抱]強さ ◇People have *lost patience with* the slow pace of reforms. 人々は改革の遅いペースにしびれを切らしている ◇I have *run out of patience* with her. 私は彼女に我慢できなかった ◇The children were beginning to *try my patience* (= make it hard for me to remain patient). 子どもたちは私をいらいらさせ始めていた 反意 **impatience** (RESTLESS), ☞ **patient** (CALM)
tolerance [U] (賛成できない意見[行為]・好感がもてない人に対する)忍耐, 我慢[辛抱]強さ, 寛容, 寛大, 容認 ◇She had no *tolerance for* jokes of any kind. 彼女はどんな冗談も許さなかった ◇She showed greater *tolerance towards* her younger sister than before. 彼女は以前よりも妹に対して寛大になった ◇He was a strong advocate of *religious tolerance*. 彼は宗教的に寛容であることを強く提唱した ◇Howard County has a *zero tolerance* policy on alcohol use by teenagers. ハワード・カウンティーは十代の若者の飲酒に対して一切容赦しないという政策を取っているものである 反意 **intolerance** (DISCRIMINATION), ☞ **tolerant** (TOLERANT), **tolerate** (STAND 2)
resignation [U] (変え[避け]られない厄介[不快]な状況に対する)甘受, 忍従 ◇They accepted their defeat with *resignation*. 彼らは自分たちの敗北を甘んじて受け止めた

patient 名

patient・case・victim・sufferer・the sick・invalid・the dying
体調がすぐれず医療の助けを必要とする人々
【類語訳】患者,病人,病状,容態,症状,症例,末期患者

文型&コロケーション
▶ a/ the **long-term** patient/ victim/ sufferer/ sick
▶ a **chronic** patient/ case/ sufferer/ invalid
▶ a/ an **cancer/ AIDS** patient/ case/ victim/ sufferer
▶ an **asthma** patient/ sufferer
▶ a **stroke** patient/ victim
▶ to **care for** a patient/ a sufferer/ the sick/ an invalid/ the dying
▶ to **treat** a patient/ a case/ a victim/ a sufferer/ the sick

patient [C] (病院・(歯)医者にかかっている)患者,病人 ◇He made friends with another *patient* on the ward. 彼はその病室のもう一人の患者と仲良くなった ◇She's one of Dr Shaw's *patients*. 彼女はショー先生の患者の一人です
case [C] (病気・けがの)病状,容態,症状,症例;(病気・けがの)患者,病[けが]人 ◇Over 500,000 *cases* of cholera were reported in 1991. 50万件を超えるコレラの症例が1991年に報告された ◇The most serious *cases* were treated at the scene of the accident. 最も重傷のけが人はその事故現場で処置を受けた
victim [C] (病気・病状の)患者 ◇AIDS *victims* are prone to pick up infections. エイズ患者は感染症にかかりやすい
sufferer [C] (病気・病状の)患者 ◇Local services provide residential care for dementia *sufferers*. 地方行政が認知症患者のための介護住宅施設を提供している ◇She received many letters of support from fellow *sufferers*. 彼女は同じ境遇にある患者たちから励ましの手紙をたくさんもらった ☞ **suffer from sth** (SUFFER FROM STH)

ノート **victim** と **sufferer** の使い分け:これらの語はふつう病名を表す名詞の後で用いられ,多くの場合,両語とも使用可能。◆ cancer/AIDS/leukaemia *victims/sufferers* (がん/エイズ/白血病患者)。この場合, **victim** のほうが頻繁に用いられ,その病気の響きが深刻に聞こえることがある。**sufferer** はよりさまざまな病気,特に長期的なものと共に用いられる。◆ dementia/asthma/arthritis/sclerosis *sufferers* (認知症/ぜんそく/関節炎/硬化症患者)。**victim** は犯罪・事故の結果としてけがを負った人についても用いられる。

the sick [複数扱い] (重度の)病人 ◇He healed *the sick* and comforted the broken-hearted. 彼は病人を治し,心に傷を負った人々を元気づけた ☞ **sick** (SICK 1)
invalid [C] (長期的な)看護[介護]が必要な)病人 ◇She had been a delicate child and her parents had treated her as an *invalid*. 彼女はひ弱な子どもで,両親は彼女を病人として扱っていた
the dying [複数扱い] 瀕死の人,末期患者 ◇Volunteer nurses were tending to the sick and *the dying*. ボランティアの看護師たちが病人と末期患者の世話をしていた

pause 名

pause・break・interruption・lull・gap
再開まで物事が停止している時間[期間]

【類語訳】中断,休止,一息,間(ま),途切れ,休憩,コマーシャル,中止,停止,遮断,邪魔,静止,静けさ,途絶え,合間

文型&コロケーション
▶ a pause/ a break/ an interruption/ a lull/ a gap **in** sth
▶ **after** a pause/ a break/ an interruption/ a lull/ a gap
▶ **without** pause/ a break/ interruption
▶ a **short** pause/ break/ interruption/ lull/ gap
▶ a **long** pause/ break/ gap
▶ a **sudden** pause/ break/ lull
▶ to **fill** a pause/ gap

pause [C] 《特に書き言葉》(話・物事が再開するまでの)中断,休止,間,途切れ,お知らせ ◇There was a long *pause* before she answered. 彼女が答えるまで長い間があった ◇After a brief *pause*, they continued climbing. 少し休んでから,彼らはまた登り続けた
break [C] (物事が再開するまでの)中断,休止,休憩;(テレビ・ラジオ番組などの)コマーシャル,お知らせ ◇I need a *break* in my daily routine. 私は日課を中断する必要がある ◇She wanted to take a *career break* in order to have children. 彼女は子どもを産むために産休を取りたいと思った ◇More news after the *break*. お知らせをはさんで,さらにニュースが続きます ◇a *commercial break* コマーシャルを流すための中断 ❶ **break** は一定期間仕事を休止することについて用いられることが多い。
interruption [C] (活動・状況の一時的な)中止,停止,休止;(活動が再開するまでの)中断,途切れ,遮断,邪魔 ◇The birth of her son was a minor *interruption to* her career. 息子が生まれても,彼女は少し仕事を休止しただけだった ◇There's been an *interruption* in the power supply. 電力の供給の遮断が起こっている ◇I managed to work for two hours without *interruption*. 私は何とか中断せずに2時間働くことができた ❶ *interruption to/in the power supply/normal service/sb's career/activities/output/production* は「電力の供給/通常業務/人の仕事/活動/生産が(一定期間にわたって)中止されること」を表す。しばしば発表・声明の中で用いられる。
lull [C, ふつう単数形] 《特に書き言葉》(活動の間に生じる)静止,静けさ,途切れ ◇There was a *lull* in the conversation. 会話が途絶えた ◇Just before an attack everything would go quiet, but we knew it was just *the lull before the storm* (= before a time of noise or trouble). 攻撃の直前は静まりかえるだろうが,私たちはそれが単に嵐の前の静けさであることはわかっていた ❶ **lull** はしばしばビジネスの文脈で用いられ,人々があまり製品・サービスの購入をしない一定期間を指す。◆ There will probably be a *lull* over the winter, followed by a resurgence of activity next spring. (冬の間はおそらく冬枯れが起こり,その後来春は活気が戻るだろう)
gap [C] 《特に話し言葉》(物事が再開するまでの[二つの出来事の間の])合間,途切れ ◇I waited for a *gap* in the conversation. 会話が途切れるのを待っていた ◇They met again after a *gap* of twenty years. 彼らは20年ぶりに再会した

ノート **break, lull, gap** の使い分け: **break** はしばしば計画的なもので,休憩や別のことをするために活動を休止する必要のある場合。**lull** は会話・戦闘・商業活動中に,計画的にではなく単に偶然に起こる中断。**gap** もふつう計画的にではなく偶然に起こるものを指すが,ふつう会話中の途切れ[二つの出来事の間の合間]について用いられる。

payment 名

payment・premium・contribution・subscription・repayment・deposit・settlement・instalment
払う[払いを求められる]金額、払う行為
【類語訳】支払い、保険料、追加料金、割増金、賦課金、分担金、負担金、寄付、返済、頭金、清算

文型&コロケーション

▶ a payment/ premium/ subscription/ repayment/ deposit/ settlement **for** sth
▶ a payment/ a premium/ a repayment/ a deposit/ an instalment **on** sth
▶ to pay sth **by** subscription/ instalments
▶ (a/ an) **monthly/ annual** payment/ premium/ contributions/ subscription/ repayment/ deposit/ settlement/ instalment
▶ (a) **regular** payment/ premium/ contributions/ subscription/ repayment/ deposit/ instalment
▶ (a) **cash** payment/ premium/ deposit/ settlement/ instalment
▶ (an) **immediate** payment/ repayment/ deposit/ settlement
▶ (a) **final** payment/ repayment/ settlement/ instalment
▶ (a) **full** payment/ premium/ subscription/ repayment/ deposit/ settlement
▶ payment/ repayment/ settlement **in full**
▶ to **pay** a premium/ contributions/ a subscription/ a deposit/ a settlement/ an instalment
▶ to **make** a payment/ repayment/ deposit/ settlement
▶ to **meet/ keep up (with)** the payments/ premiums/ repayments/ instalments
▶ to **accept** payment/ repayment/ a deposit/ settlement
▶ (a/ an) payment/ premium/ subscription/ repayment/ settlement/ an instalment **is due**
▶ a payment/ a subscription/ a repayment/ a settlement/ an instalment **plan**

payment [C, U] 支払い金額；支払い ◇They are finding it difficult to meet the *payments* on the new car. 彼らは新車の購入代金の支払いは容易ではないと思っている ◇There will be a penalty for late *payment* of bills. 請求金額の滞納に対しては罰金が科せられます
premium [C] (英)保険料、追加料金、割増金 ◇We pay a monthly *premium* of £6.25 for home contents insurance. 私たちは家財保険に毎月6.25ポンドの保険料を支払っている ◇You have to pay a high *premium* for express delivery. 速達便には高い追加料金を支払わねばならない ◇Daytime calls are charged at *premium* rate. 日中の電話には割増金が課せられる
contribution [C] (雇用主・政府に支払う健康保険・年金などの)賦課金、分担金、負担金 ◇You can increase your monthly *contributions* to the pension plan. 年金プランでの月々の賦課金を増額することが可能です
subscription [C, U] (新聞・雑誌などの定期)購読料、寄付金；(定期)購読、寄付 ◇Do you think we should get a *subscription* to 'Newsweek'? 『ニューズウィーク』を定期購読したほうがいいと思う ◇to cancel/renew a *subscription* 定期購読を解約/更新する ◇A statue in his memory was erected by public *subscription*. (英) 彼を追悼して肖像が公募寄付で建てられた ❶(英)ではsub-

scriptionはクラブの会員になるために支払うお金を指すこともある。◆Club *subscriptions* are due annually by the end of January. (クラブの会費は毎年1月末までの支払いです)。《米》では、会費はduesまたはmembership feeと呼ばれる。☞ **fee, dues** (RATE)
➢**subscribe** 動 [自] ◇Which journals does the library *subscribe* to? 図書館が購入しているのはどの新聞[雑誌]ですか
repayment [C, ふつう複数で, U] (銀行などへの)返済金；返済 ◇We were unable to keep up the *repayments* on the loan. 私たちはローンの返済を続けることができなかった ◇The loan is due for *repayment* by the end of the year. ローンの返済期限は年末までです
deposit [C, ふつう単数で] 頭金 ◇We've put down a 5% *deposit* on the house. 私たちは家の購入代金の5%を頭金として支払った ❶*deposit*は物を賃借りする際に支払い、その借りた物をなくさ[傷つけ]なければ戻ってくる金額を指すこともある。◆The car costs $50 per day in rental, plus a $200 *deposit* which you will get back at the end of the week. (この車はレンタル料1日50ドルに加えて、週末に返却される200ドルの保証金がかかります。
settlement [U] (負債の)清算 ◇She had to pay over $5,000 *in settlement of* her debts. 彼女は借金の清算に5千ドル以上を支払わねばならなかった ◇*Settlement* is made monthly by direct debit. 清算は毎月自動引き落としによってなされます
instalment (特に英) (米でふつう **installment**) [C] 分割払いの1回分 ◇We paid for the car by/in *instalments*. 私たちはその車の代金を分割で支払った

peace 名

peace・order・law and order・the rule of law・calm
国[地域]において戦争[暴力]がなく、人々が法律に従っている状況[期間]
【類語訳】平和、和平、講和、治安、秩序、公安、法治、平穏

文型&コロケーション

▶ an **uneasy** peace/ calm
▶ **relative/ comparative** peace/ calm
▶ to **maintain/ establish/ preserve** peace/ order/ law and order/ the rule of law
▶ to **restore** peace/ order/ law and order/ the rule of law
▶ to **enforce** peace/ order/ law and order/ the rule of law
▶ peace/ order/ law and order/ the rule of law/ calm **prevails**
▶ order/ law and order/ the rule of law **breaks down**
▶ the **breakdown of** order/ law and order/ the rule of law

peace [U, 単数で] 平和、講和、和平、治安 ◇Any hopes of *peace between* the two nations seem to have faded. その2国間の和平への望みはすべて潰えてしまったように思える ◇The two communities now live together *in peace*. その二つの地域社会は今では平和に共存している ◇England and France were once again *at peace with* each other. イングランドとフランスは再度、相互に平和な関係にあった ◇*Peace* finally returned to the city streets. 治安がようやくその街の通りに戻った ◇The negotiators are trying to *make peace* between the warring factions. 交渉調停者たちが敵対し合う勢力を仲裁しようと努めている ◇Troops were brought in to *keep the peace*. 軍隊が平和を維持するために投入された ◇Obviously ***world peace*** is our ultimate goal. 当然ながら、世界平和が我々の最終目標である ◇After years of war, the people longed for a ***lasting peace***. 何年もの戦争の後で、国民は永久の平和を切望した 反意 **war (WAR)**

order [U] 秩序, 規律, 治安, 公安 ◇The army had been brought in to maintain *order* in the capital. 軍隊が首都の治安を維持するために投入されていた ◇Some teachers find it hard to ***keep order*** in their classes. 教師の中には自分の授業で規律を保つことに困難を覚える者もいる ◇Some teachers find it difficult to ***keep*** their classes ***in order***. 教師の中には自分の授業で規律を守らせることに困難を覚える者もいる ◇It is our duty to preserve ***public order***. 公の秩序を守ることが我々の義務である 反意 **disorder (TROUBLE 1)**

,law and 'order 行和 法と秩序, 治安 ◇They regarded the ***forces of law and order*** (= the police and the courts) as their enemy. 彼らは司法機関と警察を敵とみなした

the rule of 'law 行和 《ややフォーマル》 法治, 法の支配 ◇It is our duty to ***uphold the rule of law***. 法の支配を守ることが我々の義務です

calm [U, 単数で] 平穏, 沈静 ◇The police ***appealed for calm***. 警察は事態の沈静化を求めた ◇An uneasy *calm* descended on the streets. 通りには不穏な空気が立ちこめた ☞ **calm (QUIET 1)**

peak 名

peak・top・height・highlight・climax・high・culmination・prime・heyday・high point
人や物事が最高の[最も成功した, 最強の, 最も高いレベルの]位置にあることを表す
【類語訳】頂点, 絶頂, 最盛期, ピーク, 最高位, 首席, 首位, 首脳部, ハイライト, 山場, 最高潮, クライマックス, 全盛期

文型&コロケーション
▶ **the** peak/ top/ height/ highlight/ climax/ culmination/ prime/ heyday/ high point **of** sth
▶ **a** peak/ high/ high point **of** $40 a barrel
▶ **at** its peak/ the top/ its height/ its climax/ a high/ its culmination/ a high point
▶ **in** your/ its prime/ heyday
▶ **a new** peak/ height/ high/ high point
▶ **to reach** its peak/ the top/ its height/ its climax/ a high/ its culmination/ a high point
▶ **to represent** the peak/ climax/ culmination/ high point of sth
▶ **to mark** the climax/ culmination/ high point of sth
▶ **to pass/ be past** its peak/ prime/ heyday

peak [C, ふつう単数で] (人・物事の)頂点, 絶頂, 最盛期, 最高[大]限度, ピーク ◇She's at the *peak* of her career. 彼女は自分の職歴の中でいま最盛期にある ◇Membership of the club has fallen from a *peak* of 600 people in 2005. そのクラブの会員数は2005年の最高600人から低下している ◇Economic life moves in cycles of ***peaks and troughs***. 経済生活は好不調を繰り返している ◇***Peak-rate*** phone calls cost more. ピーク時間帯の電話料金は高くなる ◇You want your hair to look in *peak* condition. 髪を最もよい状態の時のようにしたいですね 反意 **trough (RECESSION)**
▶ **peak** 動 [自] ◇North Sea oil production *peaked* in 1999. 北海の石油生産の最盛期は1999年だった ◇Unemployment *peaked* at 17%. 失業率は最高で17%に達した

top [単数で] (地位・順位における)最高[上]位, 首席, 頂点, 首脳部 ◇He's at the *top* of his profession. 彼は仕事の頂点にいる ◇She is determined to make it to the *top* (= to achieve the highest level of fame or success). 彼女は一番になる[トップに昇り詰める]ことを決心している ◇This decision came from the *top*. この決定は首脳部からのものだった ◇They finished the season at the *top* of the league. 彼らはシーズンをリーグ首位で終えた ◇We have a lot of things to do, but packing is at ***the top of the list***. 私たちはやることがたくさんあるが, 荷造りが最優先事項だ ◇This printer is a ***top of the range*** model (= the best it is possible to buy). このプリンターは最上位機種だ 反意 **bottom** ❶ bottom は階級・順位などの中で最も低い地位・順位(にいる人・チームなど)を表す. ◆a battle between the teams at the *bottom* of the league (リーグの最下位チーム同士の争い). ◆You have to be prepared to start at the *bottom* and work your way up. (あなたは最底辺から始めてじっくりのし上がる覚悟でいなければならない). ◆I was always ***bottom of the class*** in English. (私はいつも英語ではクラスの最下位にいた).

height [単数で] (物事の)頂点, 絶頂, 最盛期, 最高[大]限度, ピーク ◇She is still at the *height* of her powers. 彼女は依然として権力の絶頂期にある ◇The fire reached its *height* at around 2 a.m. その火事は午前2時くらいに最大に達した ◇I wouldn't go there in the ***height of summer***. 私は夏の暑い盛りにそこへ行きたくない ❶ *heights* [複数形では]成功・幸せがよい[大きい]水準にあることを指す. ◆Their success had reached new *heights*. (彼らの成功は新たな高みに達していた). ◆She dreamed of reaching the ***dizzy heights*** of stardom. (彼女はスターダムのはるかな高みに駆け上がる夢を見た).

ノート **peak** と **height** の使い分け: *peak* は *height* より も使用頻度が高く, より一般的な語. 人を主語にして at the peak/height of their career/powers (キャリア/権力の絶頂にあって)と用いられるが, *height* は人については用いられない. ◆She seems to be reaching her *peak* after a great three-set victory over Henin-Hardenne. (エナンをアーデンを3セットで見事に下し彼女は頂点に昇りつつあるようだ). ✗She seems to be reaching her *height*... the peak/height of sth, または物事を主語にしてa peak of の後に特定の数・水準を用いることはできるが, a height of の後では不可(a high of が可能→下記の high を参照). *peak* は複合語または他の名詞の前でpeak hours/period/season/time/year/demand/rate/level/efficiency/performance/fitness/form/conditionのように用いられるが, *height* は不可. しかし, ✗the *peak* of summer とは言えない.

highlight [C] (物事の)圧巻, 目玉, 見もの, ハイライト ◇One of the *highlights* of the trip was seeing the Taj Mahal. その旅行の目玉の一つはタージマハルの見学だった ◇The *highlights* of the game will be shown later this evening. その試合のハイライトは今晩後ほどお見せします

climax [C] (出来事・時点・物語・映画・楽曲の)最大の山場, 最高潮, クライマックス ◇The team's 3-1 victory in the final provided a fitting *climax* to a great season. 決勝戦における3対1でのそのチームの勝利は素晴らしいシーズンのクライマックスにふさわしかった ◇The story builds up to a powerful *climax* with the murder of Nancy by her

↳peak people, perfect

lover Bill Sikes. その物語は恋人ビル・サイクスによるナンシーの殺害で強烈な山場を迎える 反意 **anticlimax**
▸**climax** [動] [自] ◆The festival will *climax* on Sunday with a gala concert. 《ややインフォーマル》その記念祭は日曜日の祝賀演奏会でクライマックスを迎えます ❶《米》では *climax*は目的語と共に用いられることもある. ◆The sensational verdict *climaxed* a six-month trial. (その裁判の)沸かせた評決は6か月間の裁判の最大の山場となった.

high [C] 《ビジネス or ジャーナリズム》(価格・売上高などの)最高(水準[数値]); (特定の日・週などにおける)最高気温 ◆Profits reached an all-time *high* last year. 収益は昨年史上最高額に達した ◆Oil prices hit a *high* of $70 a barrel yesterday. 石油価格は昨日1バレルあたり70ドルの最高値をつけた ◆*Highs* today will be in the region of 25℃. 今日の最高気温は25℃前後になるでしょう 反意 **low** ❶反意語は low. ◆The dollar has fallen to an all-time *low* against the pound. (ドルはポンドに対して史上最安値まで下げている). ◆The government's popularity has hit a new *low*. (政府の支持率は最低記録を更新した).

culmination [単数で] 《ややフォーマル, 特に書き言葉》(長期間にわたる物事の)絶頂, 最高潮, 成就, 達成 ◆The reforms marked the successful *culmination* of a long campaign. それらの改革は長きにわたる運動の成功を印すものだった
▸**culminate** [動] [自] ◆Months of hard work *culminated* in success. 何か月にもわたる懸命の作業が日の目を見た

prime [単数で] (人生における)最[全]盛期, 盛り ◆She was then a great artist in her *prime*. 彼女はその当時偉大な芸術家として全盛期にあった ◆He was barely 30 and *in the prime of (his) life* when he had the accident. 彼がその事故に遭ったとき、まだ30歳になったばかりで人生の盛りであった

heyday [C, ふつう単数で] (人・物事の)最[全]盛期, 盛り, 人気の絶頂 ◆In its *heyday* in the 1820s, 80 horse-drawn coaches passed through the town each day. 1820年代の最盛期には、80台の馬車が毎日その町のあちこちを駆け回っていた ◆This is a fine film from the *heyday* of Italian cinema. これはイタリア映画の最盛期に生まれた素晴らしい映画だ

'high point [C] (物事が最も面白い[成功している]状態の)絶頂, 最高潮, 山場 ◆It was the *high point* of the evening. それがその晩の最大の山場だった ◆From a *high point* of nearly 140,000 in the 1950s, the workforce had fallen to 74,000 by 1984. 全従業員数が1950年代の14万人近くの高水準から、1984年には7万4千にまで低下していた ❶ high point はふつう肯定的な意味を持つ. ◆The violence reached its *peak/height* in the summer of that year. (暴力事件はその年の最高件数に達した). ✕The violence reached a *high point* in the summer of that year. 反意 **low point**

people [名]

people・race・nationality・tribe・clan・ethnic group
同じ場所の出身であったり、同じ国家[人種, 文化]に属したりする人々の集団
【類語訳】住民, 国民, 民族, 人種, 部族, 氏族

文型&コロケーション
▸a race/ tribe/ clan **of** sth
▸**from** a race/ a tribe/ a clan/ an ethnic group
▸**between** peoples/ races/ nationalities/ tribes/ clans/ ethnic groups
▸**among** peoples/ races/ ethnic groups
▸**different/ other** peoples/ races/ nationalities/ tribes/ clans/ ethnic groups
▸a **minority** people/ nationality/ tribe/ ethnic group
▸a **local** people/ tribe/ clan/ ethnic group
▸to **belong to** a race/ a nationality/ a tribe/ a clan/ an ethnic group

people [C] (特定の国家・人種・文化に属する)住民, 国民, 民族 ◆The organization campaigns for the rights of *tribal peoples*. その団体は部族民の権利を求める運動を行っている ◆The book contains translations of folk poetry of the Slav *peoples*. その本にはスラブ民族の民謡の歌詞の訳が載っている ◆We should strive for peace among the *peoples of the world*. 私たちは世界人民の平和のために努力すべきだ

race [C, U] (肌の色などで分類される)人種 ◆This custom is found in people of all *races* throughout the world. この風習は世界中のあらゆる人種の人々に見られる ◆Black and *mixed race* (= with parents of different races) employees complained of harassment. 黒人と混血の従業員が嫌がらせに関する苦情を述べた ◆There is legislation against discrimination on the grounds of *race* or sex. 人種や性別に基づく差別を禁じる法律がある ◆Immigration and *race relations* were key political issues at the time. 移民と人種関係が当時の重要な政治問題だった ☞ **the human race** (MAN 2), **racial** (CULTURAL), **racism** (RACISM)

nationality [C] (同じ言語・文化・歴史を共有する)国民 ◆The city is home to more than a hundred *nationalities*. その都市に住む人の国籍は100か国以上にわたる

tribe [C] 《時に侮蔑的》(発展途上国・過去の時代における)部族 ◆She went to live with a nomadic *tribe* in Mongolia. 彼女はモンゴルの遊牧民との生活をしに行った ❶ tribe という語はかつて、ほとんど[まったく]産業のない素朴な社会に住む人々の集団を指すために用いられた. いまだに時として発展途上国において、特に伝統的な様式で、しばしば他の人々と離れて生活を続けている部族を指すこともある. 文明化されていない素朴な民族であることを示唆するため、侮蔑的と捉える人もいる. 代わりに ethnic group が現在ではより頻繁に用いられるようになっている. ☞ **tribal** (CULTURAL)

clan [C+単数・複数動詞] (スコットランドにおける過去の時代の)氏族 ◆His grandfather was a descendant of the Guthrie *clan* in Scotland. 彼の祖父はスコットランドのガスリー一族の末裔だった

,ethnic 'group [C] (同じ人種・部族・国家出身の)民族 ◆The school has a large number of students from different *ethnic groups*. その学校には多数の異なる民族出身の生徒が学んでいる ❶ ethnic group は人の人種・国籍を指す一般的な語として用いられることが多い. ある地域に住む人々が、他の大部分の人々とは違う人種や国家である場合、しばしば minority ethnic group とか ethnic minority (少数民族)という語で呼ばれることがある. ☞ **ethnic** (CULTURAL)

perfect [形]

perfect・impeccable・exemplary・unspoiled・pristine・flawless・immaculate・faultless
欠陥や欠点のまったくないことを表す
【類語訳】完璧な, 完全な, 理想的な, 申し分のない, 非の打ち

performance

所のない, 手本とすべき, 新品同様の

文型&コロケーション
▶ perfect/ impeccable/ exemplary **behaviour**
▶ a perfect/ an impeccable/ an exemplary/ a flawless/ an immaculate/ a faultless **performance**
▶ a perfect/ an impeccable/ an exemplary/ an immaculate **record**
▶ perfect/ impeccable/ pristine/ immaculate **condition**
▶ perfect/ impeccable/ flawless/ faultless **English/ French**
▶ perfect/ pristine/ immaculate **hair/ make-up**
▶ almost perfect/ flawless/ faultless

perfect　(欠陥・欠点がなくて)完璧な, 完全な；(可能な限り完璧で)理想的な, 申し分のない ◇He smiled, revealing a *perfect* set of teeth. 完璧な歯並びを見せて彼は笑った. ◇Well, I'm sorry, but *nobody's perfect* (= used when sb has criticized you). まあ, 残念だけど完璧な人なんていないからね ◇*In a perfect world* no one would need to pay for health care. 理想的な世界なら, 誰も医療に金を支払う必要はないだろう 反意 **imperfect** ❶ imperfect は欠陥・間違いを含むことを表す. ◆ an *imperfect* world (不完全な世界). ◆ an *imperfect* understanding of English (不十分な英語の理解). ◆All our sale items are slightly *imperfect*. (この特売商品にはすべて少し欠陥があります).

▶**perfection** 名 [U] ◇The fish was cooked *to perfection* (= perfectly). その魚は完璧に調理されていた ◇We were encouraged to strive for *perfection* (= try to achieve perfection). 私たちは完璧を求めて努力するよう促された

▶**perfectly** 副 ◇The dress fitted *perfectly*. そのドレスはまったくぴったりだった

impeccable　《ややフォーマル》(欠陥・間違いがなくて)完璧な, 非の打ち所のない ◇*impeccable* manners/taste 非の打ち所のない作法/味 ◇She came to the company with *impeccable credentials* (= a perfect record, perfect qualifications, very highly recommended by previous employers, etc.). 彼女は非の打ち所のない信用証明書をもってその会社に入った

▶**impeccably** 副 ◇They behaved *impeccably*. 彼らは完璧に振る舞った ◇She was always *impeccably* dressed. 彼女は常に非の打ち所のない服装をしていた

exemplary　《ややフォーマル》手本とすべき, 模範的な ◇He was known as a man of *exemplary* character. 彼は模範的人物として知られていた

unspoiled　《英でまた **unspoilt**》(田舎地方が美しくて)自然のままの, 手つかずの；(子供が)甘やかされていない ◇It's a country of stunning landscapes and *unspoiled* beaches. その地方には驚くほど美しい風景と自然のままの海浜がある ◇She was an affectionate child and remarkably *unspoiled*. 彼女は情愛の深い子供で, 珍しく甘やかされていなかった 反意 **spoiled** ❶ spoiled 《英》では spoilt とも言う) は欲しいものをすべて与えられて, しつけが悪い・行儀が悪い子供について用いられる. ◆ a *spoiled* brat (甘やかされた悪がき). ◆He's *spoilt rotten* (= very spoiled). (彼はすごく甘やかされている).

pristine　新品同様の, ぴかぴかの ◇The car is in *pristine* condition. その車は新車のような状態です ◇All the tables were covered with *pristine* white linen. すべてのテーブルは純白のリネンで覆われていた

flawless　《ややフォーマル》(人[物事]の外見[状態]が)完璧な, 非の打ち所のない ◇She has a *flawless* complexion. 彼女の顔の色つやは非の打ち所がない ◇It's a demanding piece to play and requires a *flawless* technique. それは演奏の難しい曲で, 完璧な技術を要する

immaculate　《ややフォーマル》(人[物事]の外見[状態]が)清潔な, きちんとした；(人の記録・出来栄えが)完璧な, 非の打ち所のない ◇She always looks *immaculate*. 彼女はいつも清潔にしているように見える ◇The incident ruined an otherwise *immaculate* safety record. その事件でこれさえなければ無傷の安全記録が台無しになった

faultless　(出来栄え・論理が)完璧な, 非の打ち所のない ◇He gave a *faultless* performance. 彼は完璧な演技を披露した ◇Her logic was always *faultless*. 彼女の論理は常に完璧だった

performance 名

performance • show • production • display • act • spectacle
劇やコンサートなどの催し物を表す
【類語訳】上演, 演奏, ショー, 芝居, 制作, 展示, 出し物

文型&コロケーション
▶ **in** a performance/ a show/ a production/ a display/ an act/ a spectacle
▶ **at** a performance/ show/ production/ display/ spectacle
▶ **during** a performance/ a show/ a display/ an act
▶ a **great** performance/ show/ display/ spectacle
▶ a **brilliant/ superb** performance/ show/ production/ display
▶ a **magnificent** performance/ display/ spectacle
▶ a **live** performance/ show/ production/ act
▶ a **stage** performance/ show/ production
▶ a **public** performance/ display/ spectacle
▶ a/ an **amateur/ professional** performance/ show/ production
▶ a **musical** performance/ show/ production/ act
▶ to **do** a performance/ a show/ a production/ an act
▶ to **put on/ stage** a performance/ show/ production/ display
▶ to **perform** a show/ an act
▶ to **see** a performance/ a show/ a production/ a display/ an act
▶ to **watch** a performance/ show/ production/ display

performance [C] (劇・コンサートなどの)上演, 演奏 ◇They gave a magnificent *performance* of Ravel's String Quartet. ラベルの弦楽四重奏曲の素晴らしい演奏が行われた ◇Please refrain from talking during the *performance*. 上演中は私語をお控えください ☞ **perform** (PLAY 動 2)

show [C] (歌や踊りが含まれる劇場での)ショー, 芝居 ◇This one-man *show* had the audience falling about with laughter. この独り芝居に観客は笑い転げた ◇She's the *star of the show*! 彼女はショーの花形だ

production [C] (映画・劇・放送番組の)上演(作品), 制作 ◇She's currently performing in a new *production* of 'King Lear'. 彼女は現在『リア王』の新作に出演している ❶ production はほとんどの場合, 劇・ミュージカルについて用いられる. ☞ **produce** (PLAY 動 2)

display [C] (娯楽のための)見せ物, 展示, ショー ◇Most of the local people attended the firework *display*. 地

元住民の大半がその花火大会を見に行った ◇We watched a breathtaking *display* of aerobatics. 私たちは息をのむような曲芸飛行のショーを見ていた
act [C] (ショーの中の)出し物 ◇The show includes clowns and other circus *acts*. そのショーにはピエロをはじめとするサーカスの出し物が含まれています
spectacle [C, U] (見ごたえのある)見せ物, ショー ◇The carnival parade was a magnificent *spectacle*. そのカーニバルのパレードは壮大なショーだった ☞ **spectacular** (IMPRESSIVE)

period 名

period・century・decade・day・time・era・age・generation・epoch

時間の長さ, とりわけ特定の人物の生涯や特定の国の歴史における期間を表す

【類語訳】期間, 時期, 時代, 世紀, 10年間, 治世, 時世, 時代区分, 世代

文型&コロケーション

- **in** a period/ the ... century/ a decade/ ...day(s)/ the time of.../ ...times/ an era/ the age of.../ a generation/ an epoch
- **during** the period/ century/ decade/ days/ era/ age/ epoch
- **a new** period/ century/ decade/ era/ generation/ epoch
- **(the) present** period/ century/ decade/ day/ time/ era/ generation/ epoch
- **(the) modern** period/ day/ time/ era/ age
- **(the) medieval/ Victorian/ post-war, etc.** period/ days/ time/ era
- **to enter** a period/ a century/ a decade/ an era/ an age
- **to usher in** a period/ an era/ an age
- **a period/ a century/ a decade/ an era/ an age begins/ ends**
- **the beginning/ end of** a period/ a century/ a decade/ an era/ an age/ an epoch

period [C] 期間, 時期, 時代 ◇Which *period* of history would you most like to have lived in? 歴史上どの時代にいちばん生きてみたかったと思いますか ◇This textbook covers the post-war *period*. この教科書は戦後の時期を扱っています ◇The picture was painted by Picasso during his blue *period*. その絵はピカソが「青の時代」に描いた物です ◇Most teenagers go through a *period* of rebelling. 十代の若者の多くは反抗期を体験する ❶ period は歴史教科として学ぶ, 国の歴史における時代区分に使われることが多い

century [C] 世紀 ◇A *century* ago, weavers and bricklayers in this working class district won some of the earliest strikes for the ten-hour day. この労働者階級居住区の機織りやレンガ職人は, 1世紀前に1日10時間労働を要求した最初期のストでいくつか勝利を収めた ◇the 20th *century* (= AD 1901-2000 or 1900-1999) 20世紀 ◇eighteenth-*century* writers 18世紀の作家たち

decade [C] 10年間 ◇The effects of climate change have been increasingly apparent over the last *decade*. 気候変動の影響はここ10年間でますます顕著になってきている ◇The nineties was a *decade* of rapid advances. 90年代は急速な進歩を遂げた10年間であった

day [C, ふつう複数で] (ある一定の際立った)時代, 時期, 治世 ◇Dickens gives us a vivid picture of poverty in Queen Victoria's *day*. ディッケンズはヴィクトリア女王治世下の貧困ぶりを私たちに鮮やかに伝えている ◇Most women stayed at home in *those days* (= in the past). その当時, ほとんどの女性は家庭に閉じこもっていた ◇Kids grow up so quickly *these days* (= in the present). 最近の子どもたちの成長は大変早い ◇This book is a study of European drama, from Ibsen to the *present day*. この本はイプセンから今日に至るまでのヨーロッパ演劇の研究書である ◇Slavery continues to exist, even in *this day and age* (= in the present). 奴隷制度は今日この時代においてさえ存続している ☞ **in sb's day** (LIFE 2)

time [U, 複数で] (特定の事柄と関連する)時代, 時世 ◇The movie is set at the *time* of the Russian revolution. その映画はロシア革命の時代に設定されている ◇The Industrial Revolution took place in Victorian *times*. 産業革命はヴィクトリア朝時代に起こった ◇The violence of *our times* (= the present period of history) is nothing new. 今日の暴力も取り立てて変わりばえはしない ◇*Times* are hard for the unemployed. 失業者には過酷な時世だ ◇*Times have changed* since Grandma was young. おばあちゃんが若かった頃とは時代が変わってしまった

era [C] (ややフォーマル) (ある特徴のみられる長い)時代, 時代区分 ◇It is one of the most famous churches built in the Victorian *era*. それはヴィクトリア時代に建てられた最も有名な教会の一つである ◇When she left the firm, it was *the end of an era* (= things were different after that). 彼女が会社を去ったことは, 一つの時代の終わりを告げる出来事であった ◇This is the start of a new *era* of peace and prosperity. 今こそ平和と繁栄の新時代の幕開けだ

age [C] (技術・道具の発展段階で表される)時代, 時期 ◇Are the laws of war still relevant in the nuclear *age*? 戦時国際法は核の時代にあっても妥当だろうか ◇This is the *age* of the computer. 現代はコンピュータの時代である ◇They dug up several examples of *Bronze Age* pottery. 彼らは青銅器時代に特徴的ないくつかの陶器を掘り出した ◇The *golden age* of cinema was in the 1950s. 映画の黄金期は1950年代だった ◇The museum is putting on an exhibition of spinning *through the ages*. その博物館は紡績の歴史の展示を催している

generation [C] 世代 ◇Divorce is much more common now than it was a *generation* ago. 離婚は今や1世代前に比べてはるかに一般的だ ◇My family have lived in this house *for generations*. 私の家族は何世代にもわたってこの家に住んでいます

epoch [C] (フォーマル) (重大な出来事のあった)時代 ◇The death of the emperor marked the end of an *epoch* in the country's history. 皇帝の死はその国の歴史において一つの時代の終焉を画するものだった

> **ノート** day, time, era, age, epoch の使い分け: era, age, epoch は歴史上のある期間を指すのに用いられる. day と time は, 特に複数形の場合, 現在のことについて用いられる. ◆ these *days* (最近). ◆ modern *times* (現代). day または time が歴史上のある期間を指す場合, 人名の後に来ることが多い. ◆ The battle happened in King Alfred's *day*. (その戦闘はアルフレッド王の時代に起こった). ◆ The family was very poor in my great grandmother's *time*. (一族は私の曾祖母の時代にはとても貧しかった).

permanent 形

permanent・eternal・lasting・enduring・immortal
将来的に長期間にわたって[とわに]続くことを表す
【類語訳】永久の, 恒久的な, 一生残る, 常にある, 常設の, 果てしない, 永遠の, 長続きする, 持続的な, 不死の, 不滅の

▸ permanent/ eternal/ lasting/ enduring **value**
▸ a permanent/ a lasting/ an enduring **relationship/ solution/ legacy**
▸ eternal/ lasting/ enduring **love/ friendship**

permanent 永久の, 恒久的な, 一生残る; 常にある, 常設の ◇No *permanent* damage was done. 修復不能の傷はつかなかった ◇The sheds were replaced with a *permanent* brick building. その小屋は恒久的なれんがの建物に取って代わられた ◇She was unable to find a *permanent* job. 彼女は一生の仕事を見つけることができなかった ◇I'm not planning to move in here **on a permanent basis**. 私はここに永住するつもりはない ◇The house is in a *permanent* state of chaos. その家は常にカオス状態だ 反意 **temporary** (SHORT 1)
▸ **permanently** 副 ◇She had decided to settle *permanently* in France. 彼女はフランスに永住することに決めていた ◇The stroke left his right side *permanently* damaged. その一撃で彼の右側面に一生残る傷が残った 反意 **temporarily** (SHORT 1)

eternal 果てしない; 永遠の, 永久の ◇The two heroes swore *eternal* friendship. その二人の英雄は永遠の友情を誓った ◇She's the *eternal* optimist (= she always expects that the best will happen). 彼女はどこまでも楽天的だ ◇The story is about a woman who is offered the elixir of *eternal* youth. それは永遠に若さをもたらす秘薬を勧められる一人の女性についての物語である
▸ **eternally** 副 ◇I would be *eternally* grateful if you could help me with this matter. このことで助けていただけたら一生感謝いたします ◇He is *eternally* optimistic about the country's political future. 彼はその国の政治の行く末についてどこまでも楽天的だ

lasting [ふつう名詞の前で] (存在・効果について)長続きする, 持続的な ◇Few of the songs made any *lasting* impact. ほとんどの歌が長続きしなかった ◇It's a solution that could bring *lasting* peace. それは持続的な平和をもたらす解決策だ 反意 **short-lived** (SHORT 1), ☞ **long-lasting** (LONG)

enduring (質の高さによって)長続きする ◇What is your most *enduring* memory of her? 最も忘れ難い彼女の思い出は何ですか ◇What is the reason for the game's *enduring* appeal? その試合が長く人の心に訴える理由は何ですか 反意 **short-lived** (SHORT 1)

immortal 不死の, 不滅の ◇He believed himself *immortal*. 彼は自分は不死身であると信じた ◇She believed that her *immortal* soul was in danger. 彼女は自分の不滅の魂が危機に瀕していると信じていた 反意 **mortal ❶** mortalは生き物が永遠に生きることはできず, 必ず死ぬ運命にあることを表す. ♦We are all *mortal*. (我々は皆死ぬべき運命にある)

permission 名 ☞APPROVAL, LICENCE

permission・consent・authorization・authority・clearance・the go-ahead・leave
事が生じたり, 人が何かしたりするのを許すことを表す
【類語訳】許可, 承諾, 同意, 認可, 権限

▸ permission/ consent/ authorization/ authority/ clearance **for** sth
▸ **without** sb's permission/ consent/ authorization/ authority/ leave
▸ **with** sb's permission/ consent/ authorization/ authority/ leave
▸ permission/ consent/ authorization/ authority/ clearance/ the go-ahead/ leave **to do** sth
▸ **formal** permission/ consent/ authorization/ authority/ clearance
▸ **special** permission/ consent/ authorization/ leave
▸ **official** permission/ authorization/ clearance
▸ **prior/ written** permission/ consent/ authorization/ authority
▸ **to give** (sb) permission/ consent/ authorization/ authority/ clearance/ the go-ahead/ leave
▸ **to get** permission/ consent/ authorization/ authority/ clearance/ the go-ahead/ leave
▸ **to receive** authorization/ clearance/ the go-ahead
▸ **to have** (sb's) permission/ consent/ authorization/ authority/ clearance/ leave
▸ **to require** permission/ consent/ authorization/ authority/ leave
▸ **to refuse** (sb) permission/ consent/ authorization/ clearance/ leave

permission [U] (権威者による)許可, 承諾 ◇I asked *permission* to photograph the house. 私はその家を撮影する許可を求めた ◇Who gave *permission* for this? この許可は誰が与えたのか ◇He had taken the car without his father's *permission*. 彼は父親の許可なくその車を持ち出していた ◇The portrait is reproduced **by kind permission of** the artist. その肖像画は作者の寛大なる許可によって複製されている ◇The council refused **planning permission** (= official permission for new buildings or changes to existing ones). 自治体は建築許可を与えなかった ☞ **permit** (ALLOW)

consent [U] (ややフォーマル)(個人・家族・私財に関連する)同意, 承諾, 許可 ◇He was accused of taking a vehicle without the owner's *consent*. 彼は所有者の同意なしに車を持ち出した容疑で起訴された ◇The written *consent* of a parent is required. 親の同意書が必要です ◇Children under sixteen cannot give *consent to* medical treatment. 16歳未満の子どもは医療処置に同意を与えることはできません ◇The girl was under the **age of consent** (= the age at which sb is legally old enough to agree to have sex). その女の子は性交同意年齢未満だった 反意 **refusal** (REFUSAL), ☞ **consent** (AGREE)

ノート **permission** と **consent** の使い分け: permissionはしばしば(常にではないが)公式の許可で, 権威者によって与えられる. 人がやりたいと思うことに与えられる重要な許可にはpermissionが用いられ, 動詞はhaveまたはgetを用い

↪permission

◆Have you got *permission* to do that? (それをする許可を得ていますか). ✕Have you got *consent* to do that? consentはより個人的で、人の私有財産や身体の扱いに関連して用いられる。しばしば医療や性交渉に関する文脈で用いられる。事を行うことに関して人に与えられる重要な許可にはconsentが用いられ、動詞はgiveを用いる。 ◆Children under sixteen cannot give *consent* to medical treatment. (16歳未満の子どもは医療処置に同意を与えることはできません). ✕Children under sixteen cannot give *permission* for medical treatment. しかしながら、それほどフォーマルでない文脈では、consentの代わりにpermissionが用いられることもある。 ◆You need written *permission* from your parents. (両親からの文面による許可が必要です). 逆によりフォーマルな文脈ではpermissionの代わりにconsentが用いられることもある。 ◆They had planning *consent* for a hotel and conference centre on the site. (彼らはその用地にホテルと会議場を建てる建築許可を受けていた).

authorization [英でまた -isation] [U, C] (ややフォーマル) (公式の)認可, 許可 ; (行為としての)認可, 許可 ◇You may not enter the security area without *authorization*. 許可なく警備区域に立ち入ることはできません ◇The order was, in effect, an *authorization* to plan a coup. その命令は、事実上、クーデターの計画を認めるものだった ◇The department is responsible for the *authorization* of spending. その部局が支出の認可を担当している ☞ **authorize (ALLOW)**

authority [U] (ややフォーマル) (公式の)認可, 許可, 権限 ◇The government was accused of selling the land without formal *authority*. 政府は正式な権限なしにその土地を売却したことで非難された ◇The minister must answer to Parliament for anything his officials have done *under his authority*. 大臣は役人たちが彼の権限の下で行ったことすべてについて国会で答弁しなければならない

[ノート] authorizationとauthorityの使い分け：これらの語に意味による大きな違いはない。authorizationはほとんど常に特定の行為に対する許可(を与える行為)を指す。authorityはより一般的で、「許可を与える権限」を意味し、物事が行われる際に、under sb's authority (人の権限の下で)とは言えるが、under sb's authorizationとは言えない。

clearance [U, C] (ややフォーマル) 許可, 就労許可, 情報の使用許可 ; (人・乗り物に対する)通関手続き, 出入国許可, 離着陸許可 ◇It is safest to seek advance *clearance* from the tax office. 税務署に事前に決済を求めるのが一番安全だ ◇Allow a minimum of six weeks to obtain the necessary *clearances*. 必要な許可を得るには少なくとも6週間かかります ◇The aircraft received *clearance* to taxi out for take-off. その航空機は離陸に向けて誘導滑走の許可を受けた ☞ **clear (ALLOW)**

the 'go-ahead [単数で] (ややフォーマル, 特にジャーナリズム) (人が事を始める)許可 ◇The company hopes to get *the go-ahead* for the new service. その会社は新サービスの開始許可を得たいと望んでいる ◇Councils were given *the go-ahead* to spend more on housing. 評議会には住宅に対する支出を増やす許可が与えられた ❶ *the go-ahead* はほとんど常に、動詞getまたはgiveと共に用いられる。

leave [単数で] (フォーマル) (公式の)許可 ; (告訴・上訴の)許可 ◇In May the officer went *absent without leave*. 5月に、その士官は無断欠勤した ◇The school gave him *leave of absence* (= permission to be away) to play in the final. 決勝戦に出場するため彼は学校から欠席許可を与えられた ◇An application for *leave to appeal* (= against a decision in court) must be made within four weeks. 控訴の申請は4週間以内に行わねばならない

persist 動

persist・keep going・hang on・persevere・keep at sth・struggle along/on

困難にもかかわらず物事をやり続けることを表す
【類語訳】固執する, 頑張る, 我慢する, 辛抱する, 耐える

[文型&コロケーション]
▶ to persist/ persevere with/ in sth

persist [自, 他] (ややフォーマル) (困難な状況において[反対を押し切って])固執する, やり続ける, あくまでも…する, しつこく繰り返す ◇Why do you *persist* in blaming yourself for what happened? なぜ起こったことに対して自分を責め続けるのですか ◇He *persisted* with his questioning. 彼はしつこく質問を繰り返した ◇'So, did you agree or not?' he *persisted*. 「それで、賛成したのしなかったの」と彼はしつこく繰り返した ☞ **persistence (DETERMINATION)**

,keep 'going [フレーズ] (特に話し言葉) (困難な状況において[大きな苦難を乗り越えて])前進し続ける ; やり続ける, そのまま頑張る ◇You just have to keep yourself busy and *keep going*. ひたすら身を入れて前進あるのみだ ◇*Keep going*, Sarah, you're nearly there. そのまま頑張れ, サラ, もう少しだ (人を励ますときに用いられる)

,hang 'on [句動詞] (ややインフォーマル, 特にジャーナリズム) (困難な状況において成し遂げようと)やり続ける, 頑張る ◇The team *hung on* for victory. チームは勝利のために頑張った

persevere [自] (ややフォーマル, ほめて) (困難な状況において成し遂げようと)やり続ける, 頑張る, 我慢[辛抱]する, 耐える, 耐え続ける ◇Despite a number of setbacks, they *persevered* in their attempts to fly around the world in a balloon. 何度もの挫折にもめげることなく, 彼らは気球での世界一周に挑戦し続けた ◇You have to *persevere* with difficult students. 扱いにくい生徒には辛抱しなければなりません ☞ **perseverance (DETERMINATION)**

,keep 'at sth [句動詞] (ややインフォーマル, 特に話し言葉) (成し遂げようと)やり続ける ; (人にやり続けるよう励まして)頑張る ◇Encouraged by his confidence in us, we *kept at it*. 私たちに対する彼の信頼に励まされ, 私たちはそれをやり続けた ◇Come on, *keep at it*, you've nearly finished! さあ, 頑張って, もうほとんど終わりじゃない (やり続けるように人を励ますときに用いられる)

,struggle a'long/'on [句動詞] (困難な状況において)何とかやっていく ◇The business *struggled along* for some time. その業務はしばらくの間何とか持っていた ◇Life is hard but we all have to *struggle on*. 人生はつらいが, 皆何とかやっていかねばならない ❶ *struggle along/on* では物事を成し遂げようとする大きな熱意や強い欲求は感じられず, 疲労や困難を感じていることが示唆される。

person 名

person・individual・figure・human・human being・mortal・type・character・soul・thing

男性や女性や子どものことを表す
【類語訳】人, 人間, 人物, 個人, タイプ, 変わり者

personality

文型&コロケーション

▶a/ an **average/ normal/ ordinary** person/ individual/ human/ human being/ mortal
▶a **rational** person/ individual/ human being
▶an **intelligent** person/ human/ human being
▶a **sad** person/ individual/ figure/ character
▶a **brave/ kind** person/ soul
▶a **mere** human/ mortal
▶a/ an **key/ powerful/ independent** person/ individual/ figure
▶the person/ individual **concerned/ responsible**

person [C] (男性・女性・子どもを含めた) 人, 人間, 人物, …好みの人; (誰か不特定の) 人 ◇What sort of *person* would do a thing like that? どんな人があんなことをするんだろう ◇He's a fascinating *person*. 彼は魅力的な人物だ ◇What is she like **as a person**? 彼女は人としてどんな感じなの ◇He's just the *person* we need for the job. 彼はまさに我々がその仕事に必要とする人物だ ◇I had a letter from the *person* who used to live next door. 私はかつて隣に住んでいた人から手紙をもらった ◇I'm not really a city *person* (= I don't like cities). 私は実は都会向きじゃないんです ◇The price is $40 **per person**. 価格は一人につき40ドルです ☞ *person* の複数形はふつう people だが, フォーマルな言い回しでは persons が用いられることが多い. ◆This vehicle is licensed to carry 4 *persons*. (この車の乗車定員は4名です). ◆The verdict was murder by a *person* or *persons* unknown. (《法律》単独または複数犯による殺人だとの評決が下された).

individual [C] 個人 ◇The competition is open to both teams and *individuals*. 競技会にはチーム・個人の両方で出場できます ◇The teacher should *treat* each student **as an individual**. 教師は各生徒をひとりの人間として扱うべきだ ◇Each course has to be tailored to ***the needs of the individual***. 各コースは個々人のニーズに合わせる必要があります ◇The school's reputation is being ruined by the bad behaviour of a few *individuals*. その学校の評判は数人の不品行によって傷つけられている ☞ *individual* は特定のタイプの人, 特に奇妙あるいは不快な人を指すこともある. ◆This scruffy-looking *individual* wandered into the office. (この薄汚い格好をした奴が事務室にふらりと入ってきたんだ). ☞ **individual** (OWN)

figure [C] (公に言及される) 人, 人間, 人物 ◇He's a leading *figure* in the music industry. 彼は音楽業界の大物だ ◇a cult/public/political *figure* 崇拝される人物/著名人/政界の大立物 ◇a *figure* of authority 権威(者) ◇When she last saw him he was a sad *figure* — old and tired. 彼女が彼に最後に会ったとき, 彼は惨めな姿になっていた一年老いてくたびれて ☞ **public figure** (STAR)

human [C] (動物・機械・SFの地球外生物に対する) 人, 人間 ◇Dogs can hear much better than *humans*. 犬は人間よりも聴覚がはるかに優れている ◇More work is needed on the interface between *humans* and machines. 人間と機械の間の意思疎通にはより一層の研究が必要です

▶**human** 形 ◇the *human* body/brain 人体/人の脳 ◇a terrible loss of *human* life 悲惨にも人命が奪われること ◇Contact with other people is a basic *human* need. 他の人との触れ合いは人間の基本的欲求だ

▶**,human 'being** [C] 人, 人間 ◇That is no way to treat another *human being*. それは人を扱うやり方でない ◇He was just a normal *human being* with faults like the rest of us. 彼は私たちの大分にもれず欠点のあるただふつうの人間だった

ノート human と human being の使い分け: human は動物・機械・SFの地球外生物と対比させて, 人間の生物学的特性を指すことが多い. ◆Pigs are biologically very similar to *humans*. (豚は生物学的に人間と非常によく似ている). また, human は人類の進化の異なる段階を指すことにも用いられる. ◆early/primitive/modern *humans* (古代/原始/現代人). human being は動物と対比させて, 人間の思考力・感情・社会性をとりあげて言うときに用いられることが多い. ◆She was not behaving like a rational *human being*. (彼女は理性ある人間のようには振る舞っていなかった).

mortal [C] (おどけて) (力・影響力・技能をもたないふつうの) 人, 人間 ◇She can deal with complicated numbers in her head, but we *lesser mortals* need calculators! 彼女は複雑な数字を頭の中で処理できるが, 私たち凡人には計算機が必要だ

type [単数で] (インフォーマル) (特定の気質・性質を備えた) 人, 人間, タイプ ◇She hangs around with all those artistic *types*. 彼女はあのようなあらゆる芸術家タイプの人たちと付き合っている ◇He's not the *type* to be unfaithful. 彼は不実を働くような人間ではない ◇She's **not my type** (= not the kind of person I am usually attracted to). 彼は私のタイプではない

character [C] (ふつう形容詞と共に) (ややインフォーマル) (奇妙な[不快な, 個性の強い]) 人, 変わり者 ◇There were some really strange *characters* hanging around the bar. すごい変わり者が何人かバーにたむろしていた ◇She's a *reformed character* nowadays. 彼女は最近まともになった ◇She's quite a *character*! 彼女はまったくの変わり者だ ❶ character で奇妙[不快]な人を表せる. ◆a/an unsavoury/undesirable/suspicious/shady *character* (嫌な/不快な/うさん臭い/怪しい奴). また, 過去に悪事を働いたが改心した人をも表せる. ◆a reformed *character* (改心した人). さらに, 単に個性が強い人をも表せる. ◆a tough/determined/shrewd *character* (頑固な/意志の強い/抜け目のない人).

soul [C] (特定のタイプの) 人, 人間 ◇It means bad news for some *poor soul* (= an unlucky person that you feel sympathy for). それはかわいそうな立場にある人にとって悪い知らせだ ◇A few brave *souls* queued all night to get tickets for centre court. 数人の勇敢な人たちがセンターコートのチケットを入手するために徹夜で並んでいた ◇There *wasn't another soul in sight* (= no one around). 他に人っ子一人見えなかった (このように特に否定文で用いられる) ❶ soul は主にいくつかの決まった句, 特に否定文で用いられる. ◆There was not a *soul* about/in sight/to be seen. (人っ子一人見えなかった). ◆I won't tell a *soul*. (誰にも言わない). ◆She's completely exhausted, poor *soul*! (彼女はまったく疲れ果てている, かわいそうに). 他の用法は古風になりつつあるか, 文学的な文脈でのみ用いられる.

thing [C] (形容詞と共に) (話し言葉) (人・動物に対して何らかの気持ちを込めて) 人, 者, 奴 ◇You silly *thing*! このばか者め ◇You must be starving, you poor *things*. 腹ぺこなんだ, かわいそうな奴らめ ◇The cat's very ill, poor old *thing*! この猫は重病だ, かわいそうに年とって

personality 名

personality・nature・character・temperament・self・persona・make-up・disposition

人をその人たらしめ、他人と異ならせている性質や特性
【類語訳】個性, 性格, 気質, 性分, 本性, 特性, 人格

文型&コロケーション
- by nature/ temperament
- in sb's nature/ character
- a **violent** personality/ nature/ character/ temperament
- a/ an **outgoing/ charming** personality/ character/ disposition
- a **sunny** personality/ nature/ disposition
- a **generous** nature/ character/ disposition
- sb's **real/ true** nature/ character/ self
- sth **reflects** sb's personality/ nature/ character
- an **aspect of** sb's personality/ nature/ character/ temperament/ disposition
- a **side of** sb's personality/ nature/ character
- a **part of** sb's personality/ character/ make-up

personality [C, U] (他人と異なる)個性, 性格 ◇The children all have very different *personalities*. その子どもたちは皆それぞれ非常に異なる個性を持っている ◇His wife has a strong *personality*. 彼の奥さんは個性が強い ◇He maintained order by sheer *force of personality*. 彼はまさに[他でもなく]強い人柄でもって秩序を維持した ◇There are likely to be tensions and *personality clashes* in any social group. いかなる社会集団においても緊張関係と性格の不一致[個性の衝突]は起こりうる

nature [C, U] (個性の一部としての)気質, 性格, 本性 ◇He has an inquisitive *nature*. 彼は好奇心旺盛な性格だ ◇It's *not in her nature* to be unkind. 彼女は不親切にできない性分だ ◇It was *against his nature* to tell lies. 嘘をつくことは彼の性分に反していた ◇She is very sensitive by *nature*. 彼女は生まれつき非常に繊細だ ◇It's only *human nature* to want more money. より多くのお金を欲しがるのは人情の常だ ◇People are always taking advantage of her *good nature* (= her kindness). いつも彼女は人の良さにつけ込まれてばかりいる ☞ **nature** (NATURE 1)

character [C, ふつう単数で] (他人と異なる)気質, 性格, 性質, 特性, 人格 ◇She revealed her true *character* when anyone disagreed with her. 誰かに反対されると彼女は本性を現した ◇The lawyer argued that his client's violent behaviour was *out of character*. 弁護士は依頼人の暴力行為は彼の人格からは考えられないと主張した ◇Generosity is part of the American *character*. 気前の良さはアメリカ人気質の一部だ ☞ **character** (NATURE 1)

temperament [C, U] (振る舞い・反応に現れる)気質, 気性, 性分, 性質, 気立て ◇To become a champion, you have to have the right *temperament*. チャンピオンになるためには、それにふさわしい気質をもたなくてはならない ◇She was fiery by *temperament*. 彼女は気性が激しかった

📝 **personality, nature, character, temperament** の使い分け: personality は特に他人と一緒にいるときの人の振る舞い方(例えば、活発な[物静かな]、自信に満ちた[内気な]、陽気な[気難しい]など)について用いられる。nature は時に人のふだんの行いに見られ、しばしばふだんと異なる振る舞いと対比する場合に用いられる。character は nature と似ているが、人の道徳的振る舞い[いかに誠実である[気が強い]か]に関連して用いられることが多い。temperament はほとんどの場合、例えば、怒る[悲しむ、冷静である]状況で示される感情について用いられる。

self (複**selves**) [C, ふつう単数で] (普段の振る舞い[見た目, 感じ方]に表れる)性質, 本性, 性分, 自分 ◇He's not his usual happy *self* this morning. 今朝の彼はいつものような幸せな本人ではない ◇Only with a few people could she be her real *self*. ごく限られた人にしか彼女は本当の自分を見せられなかった ◇You'll soon be feeling *your old self* again (= feeling well or happy again). すぐにまた本来の自分を取り戻せますよ ◇Her private and public *selves* were vastly different. プライベートでの彼女と人前での彼女はまるっきり違った ☞ **self** (IDENTITY)

persona (複 **personae, personas**) [C] 《フォーマル》(他人に示す本性とは異なる)性質, 性格, 本性 ◇His *public persona* is quite different from the private family man described in the book. 彼の人前での性格は、その本で描かれているプライベートな家庭人とはまったく違う

'make-up [単数で] 《ややインフォーマル》(人格を形成するさまざまな)性格, 気質, 性質, 性分 ◇Jealousy is not part of his *make-up*. 嫉妬深さは彼の性格の一部とは言えない ◇The report studies the *psychological make-up* of a serial killer. その報告書では連続殺人犯の気質が心理学的に調べられている

disposition [C, ふつう単数で] 《フォーマル》(振る舞い・反応に現れる)気質, 性分, 性質, 気立て, 性格 ◇Tom was everybody's favourite with his bouncy, cheerful *disposition*. トムはその活発で陽気な性格で皆から好かれていた ◇Some scenes aren't recommended for viewers *of a nervous disposition*. いくつかの場面は神経質な気質の視聴者にはお勧めできない

persuade 【動】 ☞ CONVINCE

persuade・get・convince sb to do sth・win sb over・coax・talk sb into sth・cajole・get round/around sb・convert

人になぜそうすべきなのかもっともな理由を言い聞かせて同意に至らせる

【類語訳】説得する, 納得させる, 支持を得る, 賛同を得る, なだめすかす, おだてる, 甘言で釣る, 改心させる, 転向させる

文型&コロケーション
- to persuade sb/ get sb/ convince sb/ be coaxed/ be cajoled **to do sth**
- to persuade/ coax/ talk/ cajole sb **into** (doing) sth
- to **try to** persuade sb/ get sb to do sth/ convince sb to do sth/ win sb over/ coax sb/ talk sb into sth
- to **manage to** persuade sb/ get sb to do sth/ convince sb to do sth/ win sb over/ coax sb
- to **finally** persuade sb/ convince sb to do sth/ win sb over

persuade [他, 自] (人を)説得する, 説得して…してもらう[させる] ◇Can you *persuade* him to come? 彼を説得して来させることはできますか ◇Please try and *persuade* her. 彼女を説得してみてください ◇He was fairly *easily persuaded*. 彼はいとも簡単に説得された ◇I allowed myself to be *persuaded* into entering the competition. 私はその大会に出場するよう説得されるにまかせた 〖反意〗 **dissuade** (DISCOURAGE 1)

▶**persuasion** [名] [U] ◇After a little gentle *persuasion*, he agreed to come. 少し優しく説得されて、彼は来ることに同意した ◇She has great powers of *persuasion*. 彼女は説得力がとてもある

get [他] 《インフォーマル》(人に)…してもらう, …させる, (…する

よう)説得する ◇He got his sister to help him with his homework. 彼は妹に自分の宿題を手伝ってもらった ◇We had trouble getting enough people to sign up. 私たちはたくさんの人に参加してもらうのに苦労した ◇It's not hard to get him talking — the problem is stopping him! 彼に話をしてもらうのは難しいことではない―問題はどう話を止めるかだ

convince sb to do sth [他] (人を)説得して…してもらう[させる], (…するよう)説得する ◇I've been trying to convince him to see a doctor. 私は医者に診てもらうよう彼を説得しようとしてきた

ノート persuade と convince の使い分け: to 不定詞が後に続く場合, 両語とも発言[行動]に促されて人が…することを意味する。persuade sb to do sth にはさまざまな方法があり, 例えば物事が正しいことであると信じ込ませたり, それをすれば何かを得られると示したり, 見返りに物事を与えたりする方法がある。◆Nothing would persuade them to go back again. (何があっても彼はまた戻ることはしないだろう) ◆Subsequently he was persuaded by bribes to reverse his judgement. (その後, 彼は賄賂を受けて自分の判断を覆す結果になった) convince sb to do sth はふつうそうすることが正しい[最善である]と信じ込ませてさせることを表す。◆He convinced me to get legal advice. (彼は法的助言を得るように私を説得した)。convince をこの意味で使用するようになったのはかなり最近になってからで,(米)で一般的である。(英)では多くの場合, persuade が使われる。convince は「物事が真実であると人に確信[納得]させる」という意味でのみ用いられる。◆He convinced me that he was right. (彼は自分が正しいのだと私に納得させた)。
☞ **convince** (CONVINCE)

,win sb 'over [句動詞] (反対者を)納得させる, 支持[賛同]を得る ◇She's against the idea but I'm sure I can win her over. 彼女はその考えに反対しているが, きっと納得させられると思う ◇They were immediately won over by his famous charm. 彼の名うての魅力によって彼らは即座に賛同にまわった

coax [他] 《ふつう副詞や前置詞と共に》(…するよう人を優しく)説得する, なだめすかす; (…するよう動物・機械を)うまく扱う ◇He was coaxed out of retirement to help the failing company. 業績が悪化している会社を助けるために, 引退しないよう彼は説得された ◇Police managed to coax him down from the ledge. 警察は何とか彼をなだめすかして, 建物の出っ張りから身を降ろさせた ◇She coaxed the horse into coming a little closer. 彼女はその馬をなだめてもう少し近くに寄らせた

,talk sb 'into sth [句動詞] 《ややインフォーマル》(気の進まない事をするよう人を)説得し, 説得して…してもらう[させる] ◇I didn't want to go, but Bill talked me into it. 私は行きたくなかったが, ビルが私を説得した ◇She tried to talk him into staying a bit longer. 彼女は彼を説得してもう少しくいてもらおうとした 反意 **talk sb out of sth** (DISCOURAGE 1)

cajole [他, 自] (…するよう人を)おだてる, 甘言で釣る, うまく言って…させる ◇He didn't like the microphone and had to be cajoled into using it. 彼はマイクが好きではなかったので, うまく言って使わせる必要があった ◇He pleaded, cajoled, even offered bribes, but it was too late. 彼は懇願し, おだて, 賄賂さえも贈ったが, 遅すぎた

ノート coax と cajole の使い分け: 多くの場合, 両語とも使用可能。◆He was coaxed/cajoled out of retire-

ment. (彼は引退しないよううまく説得された)。しかしながら, coax のほうが cajole よりも親切で優しい行為を示唆し, 自分だけでなく相手にとってもよいことを説得してさせることを指す。×Police managed to cajole him down from the ledge. cajole は他人に自分の意のとおりのことをさせるために, 親切な振りをしているだけであることを示唆し, 時にいじめ・脅迫・脅し・賄賂など優しくない方法で他人を扱う場合に用いられる。

,get 'round sb 《英》(または特に米で **get a'round sb**) [句動詞] 《ややインフォーマル》(人を)おだてる, (人に)うまく言って…させる ◇She knows how to get round her dad. 彼女は自分の父親をうまく扱う方法を知っている

convert [他] 《ややインフォーマル》(意見・癖を変えるよう人に)改心[転向]させる ◇I've never liked opera but you might convert me! 私はオペラが好きではなかったが, 君なら私を変えられるかもね ❶ convert は人の宗教・信念を変えさせる場合にも用いられる。説得して考え・癖を変えさせることについて言う場合は, いくぶんインフォーマルでしばしばどぎ味を伴い言う場合は, 例えば物事に対して嫌悪から熱狂に変わるなど, その変化がかなり劇的で驚くべきものであることを示唆する。

picture [名]

picture • painting • drawing • portrait • graphics • print • sketch • image • artwork • cartoon
紙の上で表現される風景・人物・静物
【類語訳】絵, 絵画, 肖像画, 線画, デッサン, グラフィックス, 画像, 複製画, スケッチ, 像, 図版, 風刺漫画

文型&コロケーション

▶ to draw a picture/ portrait/ sketch/ cartoon
▶ to paint a picture/ portrait
▶ to make a painting/ a drawing/ a portrait/ a print/ a sketch/ an image
▶ to do a painting/ drawing/ portrait/ sketch
▶ to show/ display/ exhibit a picture/ painting/ drawing/ portrait/ print
▶ to frame/ hang a picture/ painting/ portrait/ print
▶ a picture/ painting/ drawing/ portrait/ print/ sketch/ cartoon **shows** sb/ sth

picture [C] (鉛筆・ペン・絵の具で描かれる)絵, 絵画, 肖像画 ◇The children were drawing pictures of their pets. 子どもたちが自分たちのペットの絵を描いていた ◇She got a famous artist to paint her picture (= a picture of herself). 彼女は有名な画家に自分の肖像画を描いてもらった ◇He likes books with lots of pictures in them. 彼はたくさん絵が載っている本が好きだ

painting [C] (絵の具で描かれる)絵, 絵画 ◇a collection of paintings by American artists アメリカ人画家による絵画集 ◇cave paintings 洞窟壁画 ☞ **paint** (DRAW)

drawing [C] (鉛筆・ペンで描かれる)線画, デッサン ◇a pencil/charcoal drawing 鉛筆画/木炭画 ◇a drawing by Paul Klee パウル・クレーによる線画 ◇He did a drawing of a yacht. 彼はヨットのデッサンを描いた ☞ **draw** (DRAW)

portrait [C] (絵画・線画・写真による)肖像画 ◇Vermeer's 'Portrait of the artist in his studio' フェルメールの『画家のアトリエ』◇She had her portrait painted. 彼女は自分の肖像画を描いてもらった ◇a self-portrait (= a painting that you do of yourself) in pen and ink ペンとイ

→**picture**

ンクによる自画像 ◇a *portrait* painter 肖像画家 ☞ **por-trait (DESCRIPTION)**

graphics [複数で] (本・雑誌・テレビ・コンピューターでの) グラフィックス, 画像 ◇computer *graphics* コンピューター・グラフィックス ◇Text and *graphics* are prepared separately and then combined. テキストと画像は別々に用意されてから組み合わされる

print [C] (写真撮影による絵画の) 複製画 ◇a Renoir *print* ルノアールの複製画 ◇a framed set of *prints* 額縁付きの複製画セット

sketch [C] (素早く線で描いた) スケッチ ◇I usually do a few very rough *sketches* before I start on a painting. 私はふつう絵の具で描き始める前に非常に大ざっぱなスケッチをいくつか描く ◇He drew me a quick *sketch*. 彼は私に素早くスケッチを描いてくれた ☞ **sketch (DRAW)**

image [C] (フォーマル) (絵画・彫像の形で複製された) 絵, 像 ◇*Images* of deer and hunters decorate the cave walls. 鹿と猟師の絵が洞窟の壁を飾っている ◇a wooden *image* of the Hindu god Ganesh ヒンドゥー教の神ガネーシャの木像 ❶ *image* はテレビやコンピューター画面上の人物・静物の画像を指すこともある。

artwork [U] (本・広告・雑誌用の挿絵・画像などの) 図版 ◇Can you let me have the finished *artwork* by Friday? 金曜日までに仕上げた図版をお送りいただけますか

┃ノート┃ **graphics** と **artwork** の使い分け: **artwork** は画像 (例えば絵画・線画) を制作する過程を強調し, **graphics** は出来上がった実物を強調する。**artwork** は絵・写真を指し, **graphics** はデザイン・図・表も指す。

cartoon [C] (新聞・雑誌に掲載される政治・出来事に関する) 風刺漫画 ◇a political *cartoon* 政治風刺漫画 ❶ *cartoon* はストーリーのある一連の線画も指す。◆a strip *cartoon* (続き漫画). ◆a full-length Disney *cartoon* (ノーカットのディズニー漫画).

piece [名] ☞ **BIT, FRAGMENT**

piece • lump • block • slice • loaf • slab • bar • chunk • length • cube • wedge • hunk • rasher
食べ物や材料などの量を表す
【類語訳】一片, 一切れ, 断片, 切れ端, 一かたまり, ブロック, 薄切り, 厚板, 厚切り, 角切り, さいの目

┃文型&コロケーション┃
▸ a piece/ lump/ slice/ chunk/ wedge/ hunk of **cheese**
▸ a piece/ lump/ slice/ slab/ chunk/ hunk of **meat**
▸ a piece/ slice/ loaf/ chunk/ hunk of **bread**
▸ a piece/ lump/ block/ slab of **ice**
▸ a piece/ lump/ block of **wood**
▸ a piece/ block/ slab of **stone**/ **marble**
▸ a piece/ lump/ slab of **concrete**
▸ a piece/ lump of **coal**
▸ a piece/ slice of **cake**/ **ham**/ **pizza**/ **pie**
▸ a piece/ slab/ bar of **chocolate**
▸ a piece/ slice/ wedge of **lemon**
▸ **lemon** slices/ wedges
▸ a **big** piece/ lump/ slice/ loaf/ slab/ chunk of sth
▸ a **thick** piece/ slab/ slice of sth
▸ a **great** lump/ slab/ chunk/ wedge of sth
▸ to **cut** sth **into** pieces/ slices/ chunks/ lengths/ cubes/ wedges

piece

piece [C] (特にof+不可算名詞と共に) (切り分けられた) 一片, 一切れ, 断片, 切れ端; (標準量としての) 一つ, 一本 ◇She wrote something on a small *piece* of paper. 彼女は小さな紙の切れ端に何か書いた ◇He cut the pizza into bite-sized *pieces*. 彼はピザを一口大に切った ◇I've got a *piece* of grit in my eye. ほこりが目に入った ◇You should have at least two good portions of vegetables and two *pieces* of fruit a day. 1日に少なくとも十分な量の野菜2皿に果物2切れを食べるべきです ❶ 少量の材料について言う場合は, さまざまな類語が使用可能。言及する材料によって正しいものを選ばねばならない。*piece* はこれらすべての類語の中で最も使用頻度が高く, 多くの異なる材料・物に用いられる。その中には bread, cake, cardboard, cheese, chocolate, fabric, glass, land, meat, paper, plastic, string が含まれる。☞ **piece (BIT)**

lump [C] (硬い[固形の]物の) 一かたまり, だま ◇He put a few more *lumps* of coal on the fire. 彼は炉に石炭のかたまりをもう少しくべた ◇This sauce has *lumps* in it. このソースにはだまがある ◇She gave the pony a *sugar lump*. (英) 彼女は角砂糖を1つポニーに与えた ❶ sugar lump は (米) では sugar cube と呼ばれる。

block [C] (四角い固形物の大きな) 一かたまり; 角材, ブロック ◇The wall was made from massive *blocks* of stone. その壁は大きな石のブロックで作られていた

slice [C] (切り分けられた食べ物の) 薄切り, 一切れ ◇Cut the meat into thin *slices*. 肉を薄切りにしましょう ◇Another *slice* of cake, anyone? 誰かケーキをもう一切れいかがですか ☞ **slice (CUT 2)**

loaf [C] (パンの) 一かたまり ◇He cut several thick slices from a *loaf of bread*. 彼は一かたまりのパンから何枚か厚切りにした ◇Two white *loaves*, please. 白パンを2かたまり下さい

slab [C] (石・氷の) 厚板; (食べ物の) 厚切り ◇The road was paved with smooth stone *slabs*. その道路は滑らかな石の厚板で舗装されていた ◇paving *slabs* 舗装板 ◇They were sitting at the table, tucking into great *slabs* of meat. 彼らは食卓に着いて, 大きな肉の厚切りをがつがつ食べていた

bar [C] (チョコレート・石けんなどの) 棒状のかたまり, バー ◇a *bar* of soap 石けん一個 ◇a chocolate *bar* (特に英) チョコバー1本 ◇a candy *bar* (米) キャンディーバー1本

chunk [C] (切り分けられた[割られた] 固形物の) 厚切り, 大きなかたまり ◇*Chunks* of masonry lay in the grass around the ruined building. 石角のかたまりが廃墟の周りの草地にあった ◇He bit a great *chunk* out of the apple. 彼はリンゴを大きくひと口かじった

length [C] (of を伴って) (長いものの) 1本 ◇Carry a whistle and a spare *length* of rope. 笛と予備のロープを1本持って行きましょう ◇The timber is sold in *lengths* of 2, 5 or 10 metres. その木材は1本2, 5, 10メートル単位で売られている

cube [C] (食べ物の立方体状の) 角切り, さいの目 ◇Cut the meat into *cubes*. お肉をさいの目に切りましょう ◇She put some ice *cubes* into her lemonade. 彼女は氷水をいくつかレモネードに入れた ◇She offered the pony a *sugar cube*. (米) 彼女は角砂糖を一つポニーにやった ❶ sugar cube は (英) では sugar lump と呼ばれる。

wedge [C] (切り分けられた食べ物の) くさび形の一切れ ◇Serve the fish with salad and *wedges* of lemon. 魚にサラダとくし形に切ったレモンを添えて出しましょう ◇He cut a great *wedge* out of the cake and began to eat it. 彼はケーキを大きくくさび形に切って食べ始めた

hunk [C] (切り分けられた[割られた]食べ物の)厚切り, 大きなかたまり ◇He offered me a *hunk* of bread with some cheese. 彼はパンの大きな一切れにチーズを添えて私にくれた

rasher [C]《英》(ベーコンの)薄切り ◇I'd like a fried egg and two *rashers* of bacon, please. 目玉焼きとベーコンの薄切り2枚を下さい

place 名

place・site・area・position・point・location・scene・spot・venue・whereabouts

特定の目的に用いられたり, 事が生じたりする所を表す

【類語訳】場所, 用地, 敷地, 現場, 区域, 範囲, 領域, 部分, 居所, ありか, 地点, 開催地, 会場

▶文型&コロケーション

▶ a (good, etc.) place/ site/ position/ location/ spot/ venue **for** sth
▶ **at** a place/ site/ position/ point/ location/ scene/ spot/ venue
▶ **in** a place/ an area/ a position/ a location/ a venue
▶ the place/ site/ point/ location/ spot/ venue **where...**
▶ a/ an **good/ ideal/ suitable** place/ site/ position/ location/ spot/ venue
▶ a/ an **interesting/ beautiful/ convenient/ remote** place/ site/ position/ location/ spot
▶ the **right** place/ site/ position/ location/ spot/ venue
▶ a **central** site/ position/ location/ venue
▶ a **prime** site/ position/ location
▶ the/ sb/ sth's **exact/ precise** site/ position/ point/ location/ spot/ whereabouts
▶ the/ sb/ sth's **current/ present** site/ position/ location/ whereabouts

---

place [C] 場所, 所 ◇Is this the *place* where it happened? ここがそれが起こった場所ですか ◇This would be a good *place* for a picnic. ここはピクニックにうってつけの場所だろう ◇I can't be in two *places* at once. 私は同時に二つの場所には居られない ◇The police searched the *place*. 警察はその場所を捜索した ◇These streets are no *place* for a child to be out alone at night. こちらの通りは子どもが夜一人で外出する所ではない ◇We're looking for a *place to eat*. 私たちは食べる場所を探しています ◇There was no *hiding place*. 隠れ場所はなかった ◇Please write your full name, date and *place of birth*. フルネームと生年月日, 出生地を書いてください

site [C] (建物の)用地, 敷地, 遺跡; 場所, 現場 ◇We visited the *site* of a 16th century abbey. 私たちは16世紀の大修道院のある遺跡を訪れた ◇All the materials are **on site** so that work can start immediately. あらゆる材料が現場にありますので, 作業を即座に開始することができます ◇a building *site*《英》建設用地 ◇a construction *site*《米, 英》建設用地 ◇This was the *site* of a great battle. ここは激しい戦闘があった場所だ ◇They say it's an ancient *burial site*. ここは古代の墓地遺跡だそうだ ◇a camp/camping/caravan *site* キャンプ場 ◇The kids used to play on an old *bomb site* (= a place that had been bombed in the past). 子どもたちは昔の爆撃被災地でよく遊んだものだ ☞ *site* (BASE).

area [C] (特別な目的に用いられる)場所, 区域, 用地, 敷地 ; (物の特定の)範囲, 領域, 部分 ◇the hotel reception *area* ホテルの受付のある所 ◇a play/parking/dining *area* 遊び場/駐車場/食堂 ◇Move the cursor to a blank *area* on the screen. カーソルを画面上の空白部分に移動させましょう ◇The tumour had not spread to other *areas* of the body. その腫瘍は体の他の部位に広がってはいなかった ☞ *area* (AREA 1).

position [C, U] (人・物の)位置, 居所, ありか ; (人・物のいる[ある]べき)場所, 所定の位置 ◇From his *position* at the top of the hill, he could see the harbour. 丘のてっぺんにいる彼の位置から, 港が見えた ◇Radars determine the aircraft's *position*. レーダーで航空機の位置を特定します ◇Is everybody **in position**? 全員所定の位置についていますか ◇The dancers all got **into position**. ダンサーたちは皆所定の位置についた ◇She **took up her position** by the door. 彼女はドアの脇に陣取った ❶ *position* は一時的であることが多く, 特定の時間に人・物がいる[ある]場所を指す. ☞ *position* (POSITION), *position* (PUT).

point [C] (物事が発生する(と思われる)特定の)地点, 場所 ◇I'll wait for you at the meeting *point* in the arrivals hall. 到着ロビーにある待合所でお待ちしてます ◇the *point* at which the river divides 川の分岐点 ◇No parking beyond this *point* この先, 駐車禁止

location [C] (名称のない[不明の])位置, 場所, 居所, ありか ◇Please tell us your exact *location*. あなたがいる正確な位置を教えてください ◇The company is moving to a new *location*. その会社は新たな場所に移転する予定だ ◇They got married at a secret *location* in Scotland. 彼らはスコットランドの秘密の場所で結婚した ❶ *location* は映画の場面が撮影されるスタジオ外の場所も指す. ◆A mountain in the Rockies became the *location* for a film about Everest. (ロッキー山脈にある山がエベレスト山の映画の撮影地になった). ◆The movie was shot entirely **on** *location* in Italy. (その映画は全編イタリアの撮影地で撮られた). ☞ **locate** (BASE), **locate** (FIND 4).

scene [C, ふつう単数で] (不快な物事が発生する)場所, 現場 ◇Several onlookers gathered at the *scene of the accident*. 数人の野次馬がその事故現場に集まった ◇The *scene of the crime* is being investigated by the police. その犯行現場は警察によって捜査中です ◇Firefighters were **on the scene** immediately. 消防隊員が即座に現場に到着していた

spot [C] (特徴のある[物事が発生する])場所, 地点, 地域 ◇She stood **rooted to the spot** (= unable to move) with fear. 彼女は恐怖のあまりその場に立ち尽くした ◇The lake is one of the local *beauty spots*. その湖は地元の景勝地の一つです ◇He has reported from several of the world's major *trouble spots* (= places where trouble often happens, especially violence and war). 彼はいくつかの主な紛争地域から報道している

venue [C] (催し物・スポーツ大会などの)開催地, 会場 ◇The band will be playing at several different *venues* in the UK. そのバンドはイギリスのいくつかの異なる会場で演奏する予定です ◇Please note the change of *venue* for this event. このイベントの開催地の変更にご注意ください

whereabouts [U+単数・複数動詞] (人・物の[ある])位置, 場所, ありか ◇Her *whereabouts* is/are still unknown. 彼女の居場所はまだわかっていない ◇They were forced to reveal the *whereabouts* of the ship. 彼らはその船の位置[ありか]を明かさざるをえなかった ❶ *whereabouts* は所在のわからない人・物について言うときに用いられることが多い.

plain 形

1 **plain**・**simple**・**bare**・**stark**・**severe**・**austere**
飾りがなく、余分な物がないことを表す
【類語訳】無地の、簡素な、質素な、平易な、単純な、簡略な、むき出しの、殺風景な、地味な、飾り気のない

plain	stark
simple	severe
bare	austere

文型&コロケーション
- a plain/ a simple/ an austere **design**
- a plain/ simple/ bare **interior**
- the simple/ stark/ austere **lines** of sth
- a plain/ simple/ bare/ stark **white**...
- a plain/ simple/ stark/ severe **black**...
- **very** plain/ simple/ bare/ austere
- **rather** plain/ stark/ severe/ austere
- **almost** bare/ severe/ austere

plain (飾り・模様・マークなどがない) 無地の、簡素な、質素な；(香辛料が) 無添加の；(複雑でなく) 平易な、わかりやすい ◇Wear it with a *plain* white shirt. 無地の白のシャツと一緒にそれを着ましょう ◇Patterned carpet shows the dirt less than a *plain* colour. 柄のカーペットのほうが無地の色物よりも汚れが目立ちません ◇Do you want *plain* or lined paper？ 無地の紙ですか、それとも線入りの紙をお求めですか ◇*plain* food/cooking 質素な食べ物/料理 ◇*plain* yogurt (= without sugar or fruit) プレーン・ヨーグルト 反意 **fancy**, ☞ **plain** (UGLY)
▶**plainly** 副 ◇She was *plainly* dressed and wore no make-up. 彼女は質素ななりをして、すっぴんだった

simple 《特に書き言葉、ふつうほめて》 (余分な物がなくて) 簡素な、質素な；(部品・要素が少なくて) 単純な；(構造的に) 単純の、単一の ◇The best gowns are *simple* and elegant. 最高のガウンとは簡素で上品なものなんです ◇We had a *simple* meal of soup and bread. 私たちはスープとパンという質素な食事をとった ◇The accommodation is *simple* but spacious. そこの宿泊設備は簡素だが広々としている ◇It's quite a *simple* machine (= one that is not complicated and has only a few parts). それはかなり単純な機械です ◇a *simple* sentence (= one with only one verb) 《文法》単文 反意 **fancy**
▶**simplicity** 名 [U] ◇the *simplicity* of the architecture 《ほめて》その建築の簡素さ
▶**simply** 副 ◇The rooms were *simply* furnished. 部屋の家具の備え付けは簡素だった ◇They live *simply* (= they do not spend much money). 彼らは質素に暮らしている

bare 《特に書き言葉》(表面が) むき出しの、打ちっぱなしの；裸の、がらんとした ◇*bare* wooden floorboards 打ちっぱなしの木製の床板 ◇The walls were *bare* except for a small mirror. 壁は小さな鏡が付いている以外は打ちっぱなしだった ◇They found themselves in a huge *bare* hall. 彼らは自分たちががらんとした巨大な広間にいることに気づいた

stark 《特に書き言葉、しばしばけなして》(色・飾り・快適性がなくて) 荒涼[殺伐]とした、殺風景な、がらんとした ◇The corridors were *stark* and uncarpeted. 廊下はがらんとしていて、絨毯は敷かれていなかった ◇The hills stood *stark*

against the winter sky. 丘は冬の空を背景に荒涼としていた

severe 《ふつうけなして》(穏やかさ・美しさがなくて) 地味な、飾り気のない ◇Her hair was cut in a very short, *severe* style. 彼女の髪型はとても短く、飾り気がなかった ◇She was wearing a *severe* dark grey jacket. 彼女は地味なダークグレーの上着を着ていた
▶**severely** 副 ◇Her hair was tied *severely* in a bun. 彼女は髪を飾り気なく束ねていた

austere 《特に書き言葉、ふつうほめて》飾り気のない、簡素な、渋い (ふつうこういう状態を好んでいる場合に用いられる) ◇the *austere* simplicity of the building 飾り気のない簡素な建物 ◇the lonely, *austere* beauty of his painting of a station in the snow 雪の中の駅を描いた彼の絵のわびしく飾り気のない美しさ

2 ☞ HONEST
plain・**simple**・**stark**・**bare**・**unequivocal**・**bald**
ある程度不快であるものの、非常に明白かつ直接的であること
【類語訳】ありのままの、率直な、あからさまな、歯に衣着せぬ、はっきりとした、明確な

文型&コロケーション
- the plain/ simple/ stark/ bare/ unequivocal/ bald **truth**
- a plain/ a simple/ a stark/ a bare/ an unequivocal/ a bald **fact/ statement**
- a plain/ a simple/ an unequivocal **answer**

plain (事実を表しているので) ありのままの、まったくの；(他の人が不快感を覚えるほど) 率直な、あからさまな、歯に衣着せぬ ◇The *plain* fact is that nobody really knows. 誰も本当のことを知らないというのがありのままの事実だ ◇He's a politician with a reputation for *plain speaking*. 彼は歯に衣着せぬ発言で知られる政治家だ ◇*Let's be plain* about this: we will need to make some difficult choices. 率直に言って、私たちはいくつか難しい選択をせねばなりません ◇He was a *plain*, straightforward sort of man. 《特に米》彼は率直で、正直な類の男だった ☞ **plain** (AVERAGE), **plain** (CLEAR 形 2)
▶**plainly** 副 ◇To put it *plainly*, he's a crook. 率直に言って、彼はペテン師です

simple [名詞の前で] (事実を表しているので) 純然たる、まったくの；(非常に明らかで複雑でないので) はっきりとした、単なる ◇The *simple* truth is that we just can't afford it. 私たちにそんな余裕がまったくないことは純然たる事実だ ◇I had to do it *for the simple reason that* (= because) I couldn't trust anyone else. 私は単に他の誰も信用できないという理由でそうせざるをえないだけだった ◇It's *a simple matter of* giving them enough to eat. 単に彼らに十分な食べ物を与えればいいというだけのことだ
▶**simply** 副 ◇I don't want to be rude, *it's simply that* we have to be careful who we give this information to. 失礼なことは言いたくないが、ただこの情報を誰に伝えるかは注意する必要があるよ ◇He was loud, vulgar and arrogant — quite *simply* the rudest man I've ever met! 彼はうるさくて、低俗で横柄で—はっきり言って私が今まで会った中で一番下品な男だった

ノート plain と simple の使い分け：他の人が聞きたくない事実を強調する場合、plain はふつう the plain fact/truth is that... の形で用いられる。simple もこのように用いられるが、もっとさまざまな構文や連語 (reason, matter など) で

plan

◆The problem was due to the *simple* fact that... (その問題は単に…という事実によるものだった)。×The problem was due to the *plain* fact that... ×for the *plain* reason that... ×It's a *plain* matter of... *simple*を用いた表現はしばしば他人の振る舞いに我慢できないことを示唆する。◆Nobody wanted to believe the *simple* truth (= it was easy to see and understand the true facts; people just didn't want to believe them). (誰もそうした純然たる事実を信じたがらなかった)。

stark 《特に書き言葉, ふつうほめて》(不快な事実・明らかな相違に直面して) 厳然たる, まったくの, はっきりした ◆The government faced a stark choice between civil war and martial law. 政府は内戦か戒厳令かの厳しい選択に直面した ◆Social divisions in the city are *stark*. その都市には社会的区分が厳然としてある ◆The good weather was *in stark contrast to* the storms of previous weeks. その週の好天は前の週の嵐とはまったく対照的だった ☞ **sharp** (MARKED)
▶ **starkly** 副 ◆These theories contrast *starkly* with the reality of everyday life. これらの理論は日常生活の現実とまったく対照的だ

bare 《名詞の前で》最低限の…しかない ◆She gave me only the *bare* facts of the case. 彼女はその事件に関して最低限の事実しか私に伝えなかった ◆The family was short of even the *bare necessities* of life. その家族には最低限の生活必需品さえ不足していた ◆We only had the *bare essentials* in the way of equipment. 私たちには必要最低限の装備しかなかった ◆He did the *bare minimum* of work but still passed the exam. 彼は最低限の勉強しかしなかったが, 試験に合格した

unequivocal 《フォーマル》(意見・意図の表し方が)明確な, はっきり [きっぱり] とした ◆She gave a typically *unequivocal* answer. 彼女はいつものようにに明確に答えた ◆The reply was an *unequivocal* 'no'. 返事ははっきりと「No」だった 反意 **equivocal** ❶ an equivocal statement とははっきりとした [明確な] 意味を持たず, 複数の解釈が可能な発言を指す。
▶ **unequivocally** 副 ◆He stated *unequivocally* that he knew nothing about the document. 彼はその書類については何も知らないとはっきりと述べた

bald (十分な説明・詳細を伝えずにやや不快な事実・発言を表しているので) ありのままの ◆The *bald* fact is that we don't need you any longer. ありのままの事実を言えば, 我々はあなたをこれ以上必要としていないということだ ◆The letter was a *bald* statement of our legal position. その書状には我々の法的立場がありのままに書かれていた ❶ a bald fact はふつう a plain/simple fact よりも不快な事実であるが, a stark fact ほど不快ではない。

plan 名

1 ☞ PROPOSAL

plan・programme・policy・scheme・strategy・initiative・platform・manifesto
物事を達成するために事前によく考えて行う一連の事柄
【類語訳】計画, 案, プログラム, 政策, 方針, 制度, 戦略, 方策, 綱領, マニフェスト

文型&コロケーション

▶ a plan/ a programme/ a policy/ a scheme/ a strategy/ an initiative/ a platform/ a manifesto **for** sth
▶ a policy/ a strategy/ an initiative **on** sth
▶ a plan/ a programme/ a policy/ a scheme/ a strategy/ an initiative **to do** sth
▶ a **comprehensive/ coherent** plan/ programme/ policy/ scheme/ strategy
▶ a **detailed** plan/ programme/ strategy/ manifesto
▶ a **major** programme/ scheme/ strategy/ initiative
▶ a **long-term/ short-term** plan/ programme/ policy/ strategy
▶ an **economic** plan/ programme/ policy/ strategy/ initiative
▶ a **political** programme/ strategy/ initiative/ platform/ manifesto
▶ a **government** programme/ policy/ scheme/ strategy/ initiative
▶ a **training** programme/ policy/ scheme/ strategy/ initiative
▶ to **have/ propose/ adopt** a plan/ policy/ scheme/ strategy
▶ to **develop** a plan/ a programme/ a policy/ a strategy/ an initiative
▶ to **draw up** a plan/ a programme/ a scheme/ strategy/ manifesto
▶ to **approve/ announce** a plan/ a policy/ a scheme/ an initiative
▶ to **implement** a plan/ a programme/ a policy/ a scheme/ a strategy/ manifesto
▶ to **launch** a plan/ a programme/ a scheme/ an initiative/ a manifesto
▶ to **carry out** a plan/ a programme/ a policy/ a scheme/ a strategy

plan [C] (事前に細かく練り上げられる)計画, 案 ◆The government has announced *plans* to create 50,000 new training places. 政府は5万か所の訓練所を新設する計画を発表した ◆You will need a clear and realistic *business plan*. あなたには明確で現実的な事業計画が必要になるだろう ◆an *action plan* 行動計画 ◆a *plan* of action/ campaign 行動/活動計画 ◆We need to *make plans* for the future. 私たちは将来の計画を立てる必要がある ◆Let's hope everything goes *according to plan*. 計画どおりにすべて事が運ぶことを願おう ☞ **plan** (PURPOSE), **plan** (ORGANIZE)

programme 《英》《米 program》 [C] (一定期間にわたる[開発に関わる])計画, プログラム ◆We were asked to devise a training *programme* for new employees. 私たちは新入社員の研修プログラムを考案するよう求められた ◆The new *programme* is designed to encourage investment in the region. 新計画にはその地域への出資を促す狙いが込められている

policy [C, U] (政府・政党・企業による)政策, 方針 ◆The party's new *policy* on education has yet to be revealed. その党の教育に関する新たな政策はまだ明らかになっていない ◆We should not let such concerns influence our economic *policies*. このような懸念が経済政策に影響を与えるようなことがあってはならない ◆We operate a strict no-smoking *policy*. 私たちは厳しい禁煙方針をとっている ◆What aspects of *foreign policy* would you like to see changed? 外交政策のどのような面に変化を望みますか

scheme [C] 《特に英》(人々にサービスを提供する行動に関わる)計画, 制度 ◆Over 10,000 people joined the training *scheme*. 1万人以上の人々がその訓練計画に参加し

↳plan ... planning

た ◇Under the new *scheme* only successful schools will receive extra funding. 新たな制度の下では、成功を収めている学校のみが追加助成金を受け取れることになっている ❶主に《英》では、schemeは政府・大組織による公式の計画についても用いられる。《米》では、うまくいきそうにない[いくぶん不正な]計画を示唆することが多い。◆Is this just another of your crazy *schemes*? (これはまた君のばかげた計画か)

strategy [C, U] (特定の目的を達成するための長期的な)戦略、方策；(巧みな)策略 ◇What *strategies* will you use to achieve this goal? この目標を達成するためにどんな方策を用いるつもりですか ◇Agreeing to meet the rebels is obviously a high-risk *strategy*. 反乱軍との会談に応じることは明らかにリスクの高い戦略だ ◇Poor marketing *strategy* was blamed for the failure of the service to catch on. マーケティング戦略のまずさがそのサービスの不人気の原因だった ☞ **tactic** (TACTIC)

initiative [C] (特定の問題を扱う[目的を達成する]ための)新たな案 ◇Government leaders are meeting to discuss the latest peace *initiative*. 政府首脳が最新の和平案を議論するために会談する予定だ

platform [C] (政党の)綱領 ◇She campaigned *on a platform of* zero tolerance towards racist behaviour. 彼女は人種差別主義的言動を一切許さないとする綱領に則して選挙運動を行った

manifesto (複 **manifestos**) [C] (政党の)マニフェスト、宣言[声明](書) ◇You should stick to the promises in your party *manifesto*. あなたはご自身の党のマニフェストで約束したことをやり通すべきです

2 plan・draft・design・blueprint
物がどのように建設、製造、配置されるかを示す線図
【類語訳】設計図、見取り図、下書き、図面、青写真

[文型&コロケーション]
▶ a plan/ draft/ design/ blueprint **of** sth
▶ a plan/ design/ blueprint **for** sth
▶ a **detailed/ rough** plan/ draft/ design
▶ the **final** plan/ draft/ design/ blueprint
▶ the **original/ first** plan/ draft/ design
▶ an **initial** draft/ design
▶ an **early** draft/ blueprint
▶ to **draw up/ produce** a plan/ draft/ design

plan [C] (建物・機械などの)設計図；(配置を示す)見取り図 ◇Enemy spies stole the *plans* for the new aircraft. 敵のスパイが新型航空機の設計図を盗んだ ◇Who was responsible for the *seating plan* (= a plan of where people will sit)? 誰が座席図を担当していたのですか ◇The *floor plan* (= showing how furniture etc. is arranged in a room) is very simple. その間取り図は非常に簡潔だ

draft [C] (原稿・建設・製造に関する大ざっぱな)下書き、図面 ◇This is only the first *draft* of my speech. これは私のスピーチの最初の下書きにすぎない ◇The original *drafts* for the new building are with the architects. その新しい建物の最初の図面は建築家たちが持っている ❶*draft* はふつうまだ最終的な形ではなく、変更が加えられる可能性があるものを言い、特に手紙・スピーチ・本のような書き物の初期の版を指す。☞ **draft** (PREPARE 1)

design [C] (製造に関する)設計図 ◇The *design* for the new model is top secret. 新型モデルの設計図は極秘だ

◇The original *designs* were stolen. 元の設計図が盗まれた

blueprint [C] (建物・機械の)青写真 ◇The watch was designed according to a 19th century *blueprint*. その腕時計は19世紀の青写真に従って設計された

planning 名

planning・arrangement・preparation・provision・organization・coordination・logistics
物事の計画を立てる行為や過程を表す
【類語訳】準備、用意、手配、手はず、備え、段取り、調整、協調

[文型&コロケーション]
▶ planning/ arrangements/ preparations/ provision/ organization **for** sb/ sth
▶ planning/ arrangements/ preparations/ provision **to do** sth
▶ **careful/ detailed/ meticulous** planning/ preparation/ organization
▶ **adequate/ proper** arrangements/ preparation/ provision/ coordination
▶ the **essential/ necessary** planning/ arrangements/ preparation/ provision/ coordination
▶ **final** planning/ arrangements/ preparations
▶ **financial/ economic** planning/ arrangements/ provision
▶ to **make** arrangements/ preparations/ provision
▶ to **need/ require** planning/ preparation/ provision/ coordination
▶ to **do** the planning/ preparation/ organization/ coordination
▶ to **complete/ finalize** the planning/ arrangements/ preparations
▶ a **lack of** planning/ preparation/ provision/ organization/ coordination

planning [U] (行為・過程としての)計画を立てること ◇*Planning* for the future makes some people nervous. 将来の計画を立てることで心配になる人もいる ◇Sensible *planning* will minimize disruption to the schedule. 理にかなった計画を立てることで、スケジュールの混乱を最小限に抑えられるでしょう ◇The project is still at the early *planning* stage. その事業はまだ計画の初期段階にある ☞ **plan** (ORGANIZE)

arrangement [C, ふつう複数で] (物事が行われるために必要な)準備、用意、手配、手はず ◇I made *arrangements* for him to be met at the airport. 私は彼を空港で出迎える手配をした ◇I'll leave the practical *arrangements* to you. 実際的な手はずはあなたにお任せします ◇Have you finalized your travel *arrangements* yet? 旅行の準備はもうでき上がったの ☞ **arrange** (ORGANIZE)

preparation [U, C, ふつう複数で] (行為・過程としての)準備、用意、備え ◇*Preparation* for the party started early. パーティーの準備は早くから始まった ◇The third book in the series is currently *in preparation*. その本のシリーズ三作目は現在準備中です ◇The team has been training hard *in preparation* for the big game. チームは大きな試合に備えて激しい練習をしている ◇The gallery is making *preparations* to celebrate the artist's centenary. 美術館はその画家の百周年を祝う準備をしている ☞ **preparatory** (FIRST), **prepare** (PREPARE 1, 2)

provision [U, C] (将来起こるかもしれないことへの)備え、準

備, 用意 ◇You need to make adequate *provision* for your retirement. 退職に備えて十分な準備をする必要があります ◇The company had made *provisions against* falls in land prices. その会社は地価の下落に備えてあった
☞ **provide for sth** (PREPARE 2)
organization (英でまた -isation) [U] (行為としての)準備, 用意, 備え, 手配, 手はず, 段取り ◇An event on this scale takes a lot of *organization*. この規模の行事には多くの準備がいる ◇They blamed the government for the poor *organization* of the election. 政府は選挙の段取りのまずさを非難された ☞ **organize** (ORGANIZE)
coordination (英でまた co-ordination) [U] (行為としての)調整, 協調, 協同 ◇There's a need for greater *co-ordination between* departments. 部局間でのさらなる協調が必要である ◇The job requires a lot of *coordination with* others. その仕事では他人との協調性が大事だ ◇The pamphlet was produced *in coordination with* residents' groups. そのパンフレットは住民団体と協同で作成された
logistics [U＋単数・複数動詞] (複雑な計画を成功させるための)実際的な)準備, 用意, 備え, 手配, 手はず, 段取り ◇We have the aid money, but the *logistics* of getting it to those in need are daunting. 我々のところに義援金が寄せられているが, その義援金を必要としている人々のところにどのようにして届けたらよいかその段取りを思うと気が重い

play 名

play・drama・comedy・tragedy・sketch・farce
娯楽として上演される目的で書かれる作品
【類語訳】劇, 芝居, ドラマ, 喜劇, コメディー, 悲劇, 寸劇, 笑劇, 茶番劇, 脚本, 上演

文型&コロケーション
▶ a play/ drama/ comedy/ tragedy/ sketch/ farce **by** sb
▶ a play/ drama/ comedy/ tragedy/ sketch/ farce **about** sth
▶ a **Shakespearean** play/ drama/ comedy/ tragedy
▶ a **television/ radio** play/ drama/ comedy
▶ a **historical** play/ drama
▶ to **write** a play/ drama/ comedy/ tragedy/ sketch/ farce
▶ to **perform** a play/ drama/ sketch
▶ to **do** a play/ sketch
▶ to **see** a play/ drama/ comedy/ sketch

play [C] (劇場・テレビでの)劇, 芝居 ◇Kate's class decided to put on (= organize and perform) a *play* for the school. ケイトのクラスは学校で劇を上演することに決めた ◇The theatre was refused permission to stage the *play*. その劇場はその芝居の上演許可が下りなかった ☞ **playwright** (WRITER)
drama [C] (刺激的・感情的な)劇, ドラマ ◇The story easily fits into the standard mould of a courtroom *drama*. その物語は紛れもなく法廷ドラマの典型に属するものだ ◇It is a lavish *costume drama* (= a film, especially on television, about a period in the past) set in the early twentieth century. それは20世紀初頭を想定した豪華な時代劇映画だ ☞ **drama** (DRAMA), **dramatist** (WRITER)
comedy [C, U] (ハッピーエンドで終わる劇・映画などの)喜劇, コメディー; (集合的に)喜劇 ◇It's a romantic *comedy* starring Meg Ryan and Tom Hanks. その映画はメグ・ライアンとトム・ハンクス主演の恋愛コメディーだ ◇They spent hours watching *comedy* on television. 彼らは何時間もテレビで喜劇を見て過ごした
tragedy [C, U] (主人公が死んで悲しい結末で終わる)悲劇; (集合的に)悲劇 ◇Revenge *tragedies* were very popular in Elizabethan England. 復讐悲劇はエリザベス朝のイングランドでとても人気があった ◇In Greek *tragedy* the main character usually identifies himself upon entering the stage. ギリシャ悲劇では主人公はふつう舞台に上がるとすぐに自分の素性を明らかにする
sketch [C] (劇場・テレビ・ラジオでの長い劇の一部としての)面白おかしい)寸劇 ◇The drama group did a *sketch* about a couple buying a new car. その劇団は新車を購入する夫婦の寸劇を行った
farce [C, U] (ばかばかしくてありそうもないことを扱う劇場での)笑劇, 茶番劇; 脚本, 上演 ◇Feydeau's classic *bedroom farce* (= a funny play about sex) is set in turn-of-the-century Paris. フェドーの第一級の寝室笑劇は世紀末前後のパリが舞台である ◇*Farce* is often looked down upon by serious theatre goers. 茶番劇はシリアスな芝居好きの人たちからしばしば見下されている

play 動

1 play・celebrate・have fun・enjoy yourself・have a good/great time・party・live it up
何かを行って楽しむことを表す
【類語訳】遊ぶ, 祝う, 楽しむ, 楽しく過ごす, どんちゃん騒ぎをする

文型&コロケーション
▶ **Let's** play/ celebrate/ have fun/ enjoy ourselves/ have a good time/ party/ live it up

play [自, 他] 遊ぶ ◇A group of kids were *playing with* a ball in the street. 子どもの一団が通りでボール遊びをしていた ◇You'll have to *play* inside today. 今日は家の中で遊ばないといけないね ◇I haven't got anybody to *play* with! 一緒に遊ぶ子が誰もいないんだ ◇There's a time to work and a time to *play*. 仕事をする時間と遊ぶ時間がある ◇Let's *play* a different game. 違うゲームで遊ぼう ☞ **play** (ENTERTAINMENT)
celebrate [自, 他] 祝う ◇Jake's passed his exams. We're going out to *celebrate*. ジェイクが試験に合格したから, 外出してお祝いをするのさ ◇We *celebrated* our 25th wedding anniversary in Florence. 私たちは銀婚式[結婚25周年記念]をフィレンツェで祝った ◇How do people *celebrate* New Year in your country? あなたの国では正月をどのように祝うのですか
▷ **celebration** 名 [U] ◇Her triumph was a *cause for celebration*. 彼女の大成功が盛大な祝宴の大義名分であった ☞ **celebration** (EVENT 2)
have 'fun フレーズ 《インフォーマル, 特に話し言葉》 楽しむ, 楽しく遊ぶ ◇*Have fun!* 楽しんでね ◇The kids were *having fun* in the water. 子どもたちが水の中で楽しく遊んでいた ◇You can *have* a lot of *fun* with a cheap digital camera. 安いデジカメですごく楽しめますよ ☞ **fun** (FUN), **fun** (ENTERTAINMENT)
en'joy yourself フレーズ 楽しむ ◇*Enjoy yourselves!* 楽しんでください ◇The kids all seemed to *enjoy themselves* at the party. 子どもたちは皆パーティーで楽しそうにしていた ☞ **enjoyment** (FUN)
have a good 'time, have a 'great time フレーズ 《インフォーマル, 特に話し言葉》 (すごく)楽しむ, 楽しく過ごす

→ **play**

◇Did you *have a good time* in Spain? スペインは楽しかったかい ◇Yes, we *had a great time*. うん、すごく楽しかったよ ❶ have a great time は疑問文では用いられない. ×Did you *have a great time*?

ノート have fun, enjoy yourself, have a good time の使い分け：have fun と have a good time は enjoy yourself よりもインフォーマルで,特に話し言葉で用いられる. have fun は楽しめそうもないことをしようとしている人に対して皮肉交じりに用いられることがある. ◆Oh, is it your exam today? *Have fun*! (ああ,今日は試験かい.楽しんで）.

party [自]《インフォーマル》どんちゃん騒ぎをする ◇They were out *partying* every night. 彼らは毎晩外でどんちゃん騒ぎをしていた

live it 'up フレーズ《インフォーマル》ぜいたく三昧をする ◇They had this great win on the lottery and now they're *living it up* in Hawaii. 彼らは宝くじで大金を当てて,今はハワイでぜいたく三昧をしている

2 play・perform・stage・do・produce・act・put sth on・present
観客を楽しませるために楽器を奏でる[歌を歌う,劇を行う,など]
【類語訳】演奏する,演じる,上演する,公演する,演技する,開催する,制作する,出演する

文型&コロケーション
▶ to play/ perform/ do a **piece**
▶ to play/ act a **role/ part**
▶ to perform/ stage/ do/ produce/ act in/ put on/ present a **play/ show**
▶ to perform/ stage/ do/ act in/ put on a **production**
▶ to stage/ do/ put on/ present a/ an **performance/ concert/ exhibition**
▶ a band/ musician plays/ performs/ does sth
▶ a company stages/ does/ produces/ puts on/ presents a play/ show
▶ to play/ perform/ stage/ act/ present sth **well**
▶ to play/ perform/ stage/ present sth **brilliantly**
▶ to play/ perform/ act sth **together**
▶ to play/ perform/ do sth **live/ in public**

play [他,自]（楽器を)演奏する；（劇・映画で)…の役を演じる ◇I'm learning to *play* the piano. 私はピアノを習っています ◇*Play* us that new piece. その新しい曲を私たちに演奏して ◇In the distance a band was *playing*. 遠くでバンドが演奏していた ◇The part of the Queen was *played* by Helen Mirren. 女王の役はヘレン・ミレンによって演じられた ◇He had always wanted to *play* Othello. 彼はいつもオセロの役を演じたがっていた

perform [他,自]（劇・音楽などを)上演[公演]する,演技[演奏]する ◇The play was first *performed* in 1987. その劇は1987年に初演された ◇I'd like to hear it *performed* live. 私はそのライブ公演が聴きたい ◇I'm looking forward to seeing you *perform*. あなたの演技を見るのを楽しみにしてます ☞ **performance** (PERFORMANCE), **performer** (ACTOR)

stage [他]《特に書き言葉》（劇・催し物を)上演[開催]する ◇The local theatre group is *staging* a production of 'Hamlet'. 地元の劇団が『ハムレット』を上演している ◇They're *staging* an exhibition in the church hall. 教会のホールで展覧会が開催されている ◇Birmingham has bid to *stage* the next national athletics champi-

please

onships. バーミンガムが次の全国陸上選手権大会の開催地に名乗りを上げている ☞ **stage** (DRAMA)

do [他]《ややインフォーマル,特に話し言葉》（劇・オペラ・コンサートなどを)上演[公演]する ◇The local dramatic society is *doing* 'Hamlet' next month. 地元の劇団が来月『ハムレット』を上演する予定です

produce [他]（劇・映画・テレビ番組を)制作[上演]する ◇She *produced* a TV series about adopted children. 彼女は養子に関するテレビのシリーズ番組を制作した ☞ **production** (PERFORMANCE)

act [自,他]（劇・映画で役を[に])演じる,演技[出演]する ◇Most of the cast *act* well. 出演者のほとんどが好演している ◇He just can't *act* (= acts very badly). 彼はまったく演技ができない ◇The play was well *acted*. その劇は好演された ◇She is *acting* the role of Juliet. 彼女はジュリエットの役を演じている ☞ **acting** (DRAMA), **actor** (ACTOR)

ノート play と act の使い分け：この意味では,act は目的語と共に (act a part/role) 用いることも,目的語なし (He just can't act.) で用いることも可能. play は目的語を必ず必要とする. ある役柄を演じることを言う場合は act よりも play のほうが一般的で,act はふつう日常生活において特定のタイプの人を装うことを指す. ◆I found myself *acting* the part of the happy newly-married wife. (私は自分が幸せな新妻を装っていることに気づいた）. 劇・映画の一作品全体を「演じる」ことを言う場合は act が用いられ,play は不可. ◆The play/film was well *acted*. (その劇/映画は好演された) ×The play/film was well *played*. ☞ **act** (PRETEND)

,put sth 'on 句動詞 （劇・催し物を)上演[開催]する ◇The local drama club is *putting on* 'Macbeth' at the Playhouse. 地元の劇団がプレーハウス劇場で『マクベス』を上演している

present [他]《書き言葉》（劇・催し物を)上演[提供]する ◇Compass Theatre Company *presents* a new production of 'King Lear'. コンパス・シアター社が『リア王』の新作を上演している ◇We plan to *present* the film uncensored and without commercial breaks. 当社はその映画を無検閲,コマーシャルなしでお届けする予定です

ノート stage, put sth on, present の使い分け：どの語もライブによる performance, show, play, concert, exhibition について用いることが可能. present は film または収録番組に用いることができるが,stage と put on は film に不可. put on は特にアマチュアによる上演について用いられる.

please [動] ☞ DELIGHT

please・satisfy・make sb's day・gratify
人をハッピーな気持ちにさせることを表す
【類語訳】喜ばせる,満足させる,納得させる,うれしがらせる

satisfy　　please　　　　　　make sb's day
　　　　　gratify

文型&コロケーション
▶ It pleased/ satisfied/ gratified **sb that...**
▶ It pleased/ gratified **sb to** find/ hear/ know/ see/ think...
▶ to really please sb/ make sb's day/ gratify sb
▶ You can't please/ satisfy **everybody/ everyone**.
▶ Nothing pleases/ satisfies sb.

please [他, 自]（人を）喜ばせる ◇I did it to *please* my parents. 私は両親を喜ばせるためにそうした ◇There's just *no pleasing* some people (= some people are impossible to please). なかなか喜んでくれない人もいる ◇She's always very *eager to please*. 彼女はいつも人を喜ばせたがっている [反意] **displease** (ANNOY), ☞ **pleased** (GLAD), **pleasing** (SATISFYING)

satisfy [他]《進行形では用いない；しばしば否定文で》（望みを叶えて人を）満足［納得］させる ◇Nothing *satisfies* him — he's always complaining. 彼を満足させるものは何もない — いつも不平ばかり言っている ◇The proposed plan will not *satisfy* everyone. その提案では皆は納得しないだろう ☞ **satisfied** (HAPPY), **satisfying** (SATISFYING)

[ノート] **please** と **satisfy** の使い分け：please はしばしば satisfy よりも意味が強く肯定的である. satisfy は単に申し分なく十分であることを表すだけだが、please は非常に喜ばしいことを表す. ◆The result *pleased* us enormously. (その結果に私たちはとても喜んだ) ✗The result *satisfied* us enormously. 両語とも否定文で用いることが可能で、物事に不服・不満であることを表す. ◆The planning policy failed to *please/satisfy* anyone. (その政策立案には誰も満足しなかった)

make sb's 'day [句他]《ややインフォーマル、特に話し言葉》(特定の日に人を)非常に喜ばせる、幸せな気分にさせる ◇The phone call from Mike really *made my day*. マイクからのその電話で私は(その日)とても幸せな気分になった

gratify [他]《ややフォーマル、書き言葉》(上手である[好かれている、大切にされている]と感じさせて人を)喜ばせる、うれしがらせる ◇It *gratified* him to think that it was all his work. 彼はすべて自分の仕事だと考えると彼はうれしかった ◇I was *gratified* by their invitation. 彼らに招待されて私はうれしかった ☞ **gratifying** (SATISFYING)

pleasure [名]

pleasure・delight・joy・privilege・treat・honour・pride
物事が喜ばせて［楽しませて］くれることを表す
【類語訳】喜び、楽しみ、名誉、光栄

pleasure	delight
privilege	joy
treat	honour
	pride

[文型&コロケーション]
▶ the pleasures/ delights/ joys **of** sth
▶ It's a great pleasure/ joy **to me that**...
▶ It's a pleasure/ delight/ joy/ privilege/ treat/ honour **to do sth**
▶ It's a pleasure/ delight/ joy **to see/ find**...
▶ a pleasure/ delight/ joy **to behold/ watch**
▶ a **real** pleasure/ delight/ joy/ privilege/ treat
▶ a **great** pleasure/ joy/ privilege/ honour
▶ a **rare** joy/ privilege/ treat/ honour

pleasure [C] 喜び、楽しみ ◇the *pleasures* and pains of everyday life 日常生活における苦楽 ◇Chocolate is one of life's little *pleasures*. チョコレートは暮らしの上での小さな楽しみの一つだ ◇It's *been a pleasure* meeting you.《話し言葉》お会いできて光栄です ◇'Thanks for doing that.' '*It's a pleasure./My pleasure.*' 「そうしてくれて感謝します」「どういたしまして」 [反意] **pain** (DISTRESS)

delight [C] (大きな)喜び、楽しみ ◇the *delights* of living in the country 田舎の国で暮らせる大きな喜び ◇Savour the culinary *delights* of Morocco. モロッコ料理のごちそうを味わいましょう ◇It was a *delight* to see him so fit and healthy. 彼があんなにも元気で健やかでいるのを見てとてもうれしかった ☞ **delight** (DELIGHT [動])

joy [C] (大きな)喜び、楽しみ ◇the *joys* and sorrows of childhood 幼年時代の喜びと悲しみ ◇a dancer who is a *joy* to watch. 見ていて楽しいダンサー [反意] **grief, sorrow** (GRIEF)

[ノート] **pleasure, delight, joy** の使い分け：delight と joy は pleasure よりも大きな喜び［楽しみ］を表す. 人、特に子どもは delight や joy となりえるが、pleasure は不可. joys はしばしば sorrows と対比されるが、delights は対比されない.

privilege [単数で]《ややフォーマル》（ある機会を与えられる）名誉、光栄 ◇I hope to have the *privilege* of working with them again. また彼らと一緒に仕事ができたら光栄に存じます ◇It was a great *privilege* to hear her sing. 彼女の歌を聴けるなんてすごく名誉なことだった

▶ **privileged** [形][名詞の前では用いない] ◇We are *privileged* to welcome you as our speaker this evening. 今晩の講演者にあなたをお迎えできて光栄です

treat [C]《インフォーマル、特に話し言葉》喜び、楽しみ ◇You've never been to this area before? Then you're *in for a* real *treat*./Then you *have a* real *treat in store*. この地域に以前来たことがないんですね. それならこれからすごく楽しめますよ ◇If you have never seen one of these fish then you have *missed a treat*.《特に英》これらの魚を見たことがないなんて、それはついてなかったね

honour [C]《英》(米では **honor**) [単数で]《フォーマル》(多大な尊敬を得る)名誉、光栄 ◇It was a great *honour* to be invited here today. 本日ここにお招きいただき大変光栄でした

▶ **honoured**《英》(米では **honored**) [形][名詞の前では用いない] ◇I felt *honoured* to have been mentioned in his speech. 私のことを彼のスピーチで触れてもらって光栄に思った

pride [単数で] 誇り、自慢 ◇The new sports stadium is *the pride of* the town. 新しい競技場はその街の誇りだ ◇He loves that boat, it's his *pride and joy*. 彼はそのボートをすごく大事にしている. それは彼の自慢であり喜びなのだ

plot [動]

plot・conspire・scheme・collude・connive
不法[有害]な行為をひそかに計画する
【類語訳】たくらむ、共謀する、陰謀を企てる、陥れる、結託する

[文型&コロケーション]
▶ to plot/ conspire/ scheme **against** sb
▶ to plot/ conspire/ collude/ connive **with** sb
▶ to plot/ conspire/ collude **together**
▶ to plot/ conspire/ scheme/ collude/ connive **to do sth**
▶ to **secretly** plot/ conspire/ scheme/ connive

plot [自, 他] (政府・首相・大統領への危害を[の])ひそかに計画する、たくらむ、陰謀を企てる ◇They were accused of *plotting* against the state. 彼らは国家に対して陰謀を企てた容疑で起訴された ◇She spends every waking hour *plotting* her revenge. 彼女は起きている時間はずっと復

↳**plot**

の計画をひそかに立てているのだ ◊They were *plotting* to overthrow the government. 彼らは政府の転覆をたくらんでいた ☞ **plot** (CONSPIRACY)

conspire [自]《フォーマル》(不法[有害]な行為を[の])共謀する, 陰謀を企てる ◊They were accused of *conspiring* against the king. 彼らは国王に対して陰謀を企てた容疑で起訴された ◊She admitted *conspiring* with her lover to murder her husband. 彼女は夫を殺害するために愛人と共謀したことを認めた ☞ **conspiracy** (CONSPIRACY)

scheme [自, 他] (他人への危害を[の])ひそかに計画する, たくらむ, 陰謀を企てる, 計略を練る;(他人を)陥れる ◊She seemed to feel that we were all *scheming* against her. 彼女は私たち全員が自分を陥れようとしていると感じているようだった ◊His colleagues, meanwhile, were busily *scheming* to get rid of him. 同僚たちは, 一方で, 彼を排除する陰謀を熱心に企てていた ❶*scheme* はふつう前置詞と共に用いられるか, または scheme to do sth の句で用いられ, 名詞句を目的語に取ることはない. ×to *scheme* a coup/your revenge. また *scheme* は, 人に対するある特定の陰謀を言うのではなく, ある人の活動全般を示唆する. ☞ **scheme** (CONSPIRACY)

collude [自] (不法[有害]な行為を他の人と)共謀[結託]する ◊Several people had *colluded in* the murder. 数人がその殺人に共謀していた ◊The president accused his opponents of *colluding* with foreigners. 大統領は対立候補を外国人と結託していると非難した ☞ **collusion** (CONSPIRACY)

connive [自]《フォーマル》(不法[有害]な行為を他の人と)共謀[結託]する ◊The government was accused of having *connived* with the security forces to permit murder. 政府は公安と結託して殺害を容認したと非難された

ノート **conspire, collude, connive の使い分け**:
conspire はふつう同じ目的を持つ同一組織に所属する人々による行為. collude と connive はふつう異なる組織に所属する[異なる目的を持つ]人々による行為だが, 全員何らかの形でその陰謀から利益を得る. conspire が最も積極的な関与を示唆し, connive は最も消極的なものを指す. connive はふつう他人が不当なことをするのに手を貸すことを意味する.

point [名]

point・core・heart・body・crux・nucleus
物事の最も重要な考え[部分]を表す
【類語訳】要点, 重点, 論旨, 核心, 問題点, 本文, 核

文型&コロケーション
▶at the core/ heart/ crux of sth
▶the main point/ core/ body of sth
▶the very core/ heart/ crux of sth
▶to form the core/ heart/ body/ nucleus of sth
▶to make up the core/ body of sth
▶to get to the point/ core/ heart/ crux (of sth)
▶to lie at/ go to the core/ heart of sth
▶the heart/ crux of the matter

point [単数で] (発言・行為の)要点, 重点, 論旨, 肝心な点, 核心, 問題点 ◊*The point is* you shouldn't have to wait so long to see a doctor. 重要なのは医者に診てもらうためにそれほど長く待つ必要はないということです ◊I'll *come straight to the point*: we need more money. いきなり核心を突くけれど, もっとお金が必要だ ◊Do you

point, point sth out

see my point (= understand)? 私の言いたいこと[論旨]がわかりますか ◊I think I *missed the point* (= did not understand). よく要点がつかめませんでした ◊You *have a point* (= your idea is right) — it would be better to wait till this evening. 的を射てるね[言えてるね]—今晩まで待つほうがよさそうだ ◊'There won't be anywhere to park.' 'Oh, *that's a (good) point.*' (= I had not thought of that)「どこにも車を止められないだろう」「ああ, その通りだ」◊It just isn't true. That's *the whole point* (= the only important fact). それはまったくのうそです. このところが重要な点です ◊I know it won't cost very much but *that's not the point*. 大して費用がかからないことはわかってるけど, そんなことは問題じゃない ☞ **to the point** (RELEVANT)

core [単数で] (問題・活動・考えの)核心, 主要[中心]部分 ◊This report goes to the *core* of the argument. この報告書は議論の核心を突いている ◊Maths, English and science are the *core subjects* (= subjects that all the students have to do). 数学と国語, 理科が主要科目です ◊What are the *core* activities of the job? その仕事の中心となる活動は何ですか

heart [単数で] (問題の)核心 ◊Cost is at the *heart* of the matter for the Government. コストの件が政府にとってその問題の核心となっている ◊The committee's report went to the *heart* of the government's dilemma. 委員会のその報告書は政府がおかれている難局の核心を突いていた

ノート **core と heart の使い分け**:heart は問題, 特に道徳心・感情が絡む問題の最も重要な部分を指し, **the heart of the matter/problem** の句で用いられる. core は問題がより論理的・理知的な観点で捉えられる場合に用いられる. また, core は教育・ビジネスにおける最も重要な科目・活動のことも指し, 他の名詞の前で形容詞的に用いられることもある.
◆the *core* subjects/curriculum/activities/business (主要な科目/カリキュラム/活動/事業). ×the *heart* subjects/curriculum/activities/business.

body [単数で] (建物・乗り物の)主要部分, 本体, 胴体, (本・記事の)本文, ボディー ◊the *body* of the plane (= the central part where the seats are) 飛行機の胴体 ◊There are some references in the main *body* of the text. そのテキストの本文にはいくつか参照事項がある

crux [単数で] (ある状況の)核心 ◊Now we come to the *crux* of the matter. それではその問題の核心に迫ります

nucleus [単数で] 中心部分, 核(他の部分は周囲に位置して[集められて]いる) ◊These paintings will form the *nucleus* of a new collection. これらの絵画が新コレクションの核となるだろう ◊It was this cluster of houses which formed the *nucleus* of the village. 村の中心部を形成していたのがこの集落だった ❶ nucleus はほとんどの場合, 場所・展示の最も重要な部分, または集団内の最も重要な人物について用いられる.

point sth out [句動詞] ☞ STRESS

point sth out・highlight・draw attention to sb/sth・point sth up
何かについて話して[何かを明らかにして]人々に目を向けさせる
【類語訳】指摘する, 強調する, 浮き彫りにする, 挙げる

文型&コロケーション
▶to point out/ highlight/ point to **how**...
▶to point out/ highlight/ draw attention to/ point to/ point up

policeman

- the fact that...
  ▶ to point out/ highlight/ draw attention to/ point to/ point up the **importance/ difference**
  ▶ to point out/ highlight/ draw attention to/ point to a/ an **need/ aspect**
  ▶ to highlight/ draw attention to/ point up an **issue**
  ▶ to point out/ highlight/ draw attention to the **weaknesses/ inadequacy** in/ of sb/ sth
  ▶ to **clearly** point out/ highlight/ point to/ point up sth
  ▶ to **further** point out/ highlight/ point to sth

,point sth 'out 句動詞 （人に情報を与えて）指摘する
◇She tried in vain to *point out to* him the unfairness of his actions. 彼女は彼にその行為が不当であることを指摘しようとしたが無駄だった ◇He *pointed out* the dangers of driving alone. 彼は一人で運転することの危険性を指摘した ◇I should *point out that* not one of these paintings is original. これらの絵画のうちのどれ一つとして原作ではないことを指摘せねばなりません ◇'It's not very far,' she *pointed out*. 「そこはあまり遠くありません」と彼女は指摘した

highlight 〔他〕《特にジャーナリズム》（人々に注意を喚起するために）問題に）強調する, 浮き彫りにする ◇The report *highlights* the major problems facing society today. その報告書は今日の社会が直面している主要な問題を強調している ◇The earthquake *highlighted* the vulnerability of elevated highways. その地震で高架道路のもろさが浮き彫りとなった ❶highlightは主語に reports, studies, surveys, figuresを, 目的語に problem, need, issue, danger, difficultyを取る場合がほとんどである. 人々に注意を喚起するために人が問題を意図的に強調することもあれば, 出来事が人々に問題に目を向けさせてその問題を浮き彫りにする効果をもたらすこともある. ☞ **underline, underscore** (STRESS)

,draw a'ttention to sb/sth フレーズ （人・物事に注意を向けさせる, 注意を喚起する）We need to *draw* people's *attention to* the dangers of this approach. 我々にこの取り組みに伴う危険性に対して人々の注意を喚起する必要がある ◇He took care to avoid *drawing attention to himself*. 彼は自分に注意が向けられないように気をつけた ❶フォーマルな言い回しでは, call attention to sthも用いられる. ♦ He *called* their *attention to* the fact that many files were missing. 彼は多くのファイルが紛失している事実に対して彼らの注意を喚起した)

point to sth 句動詞 （重要事項・特定の状況の存在理由を）指摘する, 挙げる ◇The board of directors *pointed to* falling productivity to justify their decision. 取締役会は自らの決定を正当化するために生産性の下降を挙げた

,point sth 'up 句動詞 《フォーマル》（人々に目を向けさせて物事を）浮き彫りにする ◇The conference merely *pointed up* divisions in the party. その会議では党内の分裂が浮き彫りになっただけだった ❶point sth upは組織内の不和・諸問題に人々の目を向けさせる場合に用いられることが多い.

policeman 名

policeman・officer・detective・police officer・cop・constable・PC/WPC・policewoman・trooper
警察の職員
【類義訳】警官, 巡査, 刑事, 警察官

文型&コロケーション
▶ a **uniformed** policeman/ officer/ police officer/ cop/ policewoman
▶ a **plain-clothes** policeman/ officer/ detective/ police officer/ cop/ policewoman
▶ an **undercover** policeman/ officer/ detective/ police officer/ cop
▶ an **off-duty** policeman/ officer/ detective/ police officer/ policewoman/ cop
▶ a **senior** policeman/ officer/ detective/ police officer/ policewoman
▶ a policeman/ an officer/ a detective/ a police officer/ a cop/ a constable **arrests sb/ investigates sth**
▶ a policeman/ an officer/ a police officer/ a cop/ a constable **patrols** sth

policeman [C]（男性の）警官 ◇A *policeman* was called to the house just after midnight. 一人の警官が真夜中を過ぎた直後にその家に呼び入れられた

officer [C] 巡査, お巡りさん, 警官（しばしば呼びかける場合に用いられる）◇Yes, *officer*, I saw what happened. はい, お巡りさん, 私が起こったことを見ました ◇We spoke to the *duty officer* at the police station. 私たちは警察署で当直の警官に話しかけた ◇I tried to find out who was the *officer in charge* of the case. 私はその事件の担当官は誰であるか調べようとした ❶《米》ではofficerは Officer Dibble（ディブル巡査）のように, 警察官の階級を表す肩書きの一つとしても用いられる.

detective [C]（犯罪捜査の）刑事 ◇*Detective Sergeant* John Nelson 刑事巡査部長ジョン・ネルソン ◇*Detectives* investigating the case are appealing for witnesses to the attack. その事件を捜査している刑事たちは襲撃の目撃者からの通報を呼びかけている ❶detectiveは犯罪を捜査する警察官の階級の一つであり, Detective Inspector（警視）や Detective Constable（刑事巡査）のように, しばしば肩書きの一つとして用いられる.

po'lice officer [C] 警官 ◇The plans were drawn up at a meeting of senior *police officers*. その計画は上級警察官の会議で作成された

ノート policeman, officer, police officerの使い分け： policemanは特に一般の人の会話において, 警察の職員を表す最も使用頻度の高い語である. officerとpolice officerはニュース報道などのよりフォーマルな文脈や警察の職員の性別に言及することを避けるために, 警察によって用いられる語である. officerは文脈から, 警察官について話していることが明らかな場合にpolice officerの代わりに用いられる. ✕We spoke to the duty *police officer* at the police station.

cop [C]《インフォーマル》警官 ◇The film is based on the true story of a New York *cop*. その映画はニューヨークの一人の警官の本当の話に基づいたものだ ◇Somebody call the *cops*! 誰か警察を呼んでください ❶the *cops*は「警察（全体）」を表す the policeの意でしばしば用いられる.

constable [C] 巡査, 警官《英》などでは最下位の警察官を指す）◇Have you finished your report yet, *Constable*? 巡査, 報告書はもう書き終わったのか ◇The children were taken out of the room by a woman *police constable*. 子どもたちは女性巡査によってその部屋から連れ出された ◇*Special constables* provide part-time assistance for the regular police force. 特別巡査は正規警察官の補佐を非常勤で務める ❶constableは一つの階級を指し, 肩書きとしても, この階級に属する特定の警察官を指す［に呼びかける］場合にも主に警察内で用いられる. ♦ *Consta-*

↳ **policeman**

ble Quinn（クイン巡査）. constable は警察(官)全体を指す場合には用いられない.《英》ではa chief constable は特定地域の「警察長官」を指す.

PC, WPC [C]《英》巡査, 警官；(肩書きが)巡査(police constable と woman police constable の略) ◇*PC Jason Adams is a community policeman patrolling the estate.* ジェイソン・アダムズ巡査はその住宅地をパトロールする地域警官です ◇*WPC Karen Mills was praised for her swift action.* カレン・ミルズ巡査はその迅速な行動を称えられた

policewoman [C] 女性警官 ◇*A plain-clothes policewoman waited at the entrance to her office.* 私服の女性警官がその事務所の玄関で待っていた

trooper [C]《米》州警察官 ◇*The teenager was shot by a state trooper during a drugs raid.* その十代の若者は麻薬の強制捜査中の州警察官によって撃たれた

polite 形

polite・civil・gracious・respectful・courteous・gentlemanly・deferential
人が行儀正しく, 敬意を示して振る舞うさまを表す
【類語訳】礼儀正しい, 丁寧な, 丁重な, 儀礼的な, 社交辞令の, 親切な, 優しい, 紳士的な, 敬意を示す

【文型&コロケーション】
- polite/ civil/ gracious/ respectful/ courteous/ deferential **to** sb
- a polite/ civil/ respectful/ courteous/ gentlemanly **manner**
- a polite/ gracious/ respectful/ gentlemanly **way**
- a polite/ gracious/ courteous/ gentlemanly **man**
- a polite/ gracious/ courteous **smile**
- polite/ courteous **behaviour**
- **extremely/ perfectly** polite/ civil/ courteous

polite（ふつうほめて）礼儀正しい, 丁寧[丁重]な；儀礼的な, 社交辞令の ◇*Please be polite to our guests.* お客さんには丁重に振る舞ってください ◇*In Western culture, it is polite to maintain eye contact during conversation.* 西洋文化では, 会話中は人の目を見続けるのが礼儀です ◇*We all stood around making polite conversation.* 私たちは皆立ったまま社交辞令的な会話をした ◇*The performance was greeted with polite applause.* その演技は儀礼的な喝采を受けた 反意 **rude, impolite** (RUDE), ☞ **politeness** (RESPECT 名)
➤**politely** 副 ◇*The receptionist smiled politely.* その受付係は丁重にほほ笑んだ

civil（ともすれば親しみがなくて）礼儀正しい, 丁寧[丁重]な ◇*The less time I have to spend being civil to him the better!* 彼にはあまり礼儀正しくしないほうがいいんだ 反意 **uncivil** ❶ civil の反意語は uncivil だが, あまり用いられない. ☞ **civility** (RESPECT 名)
➤**civilly** 副 ◇*She greeted him civilly but with no sign of affection.* 彼女は彼に礼儀正しく挨拶したが, 気持ちはこもっていなかった

gracious（ややフォーマル, ほめて）（社会的地位の低い人に対して）親切な, 優しい, 礼儀正しい, 丁寧[丁重]な ◇*Lady Caroline was gracious enough to accept our invitation.* キャロライン夫人は丁重にも我々のお招きをお受けくださった ◇*He has not yet learned how to be gracious in defeat.* 彼は負けたときの礼儀がまだわかっていない 反意 **ungracious** ❶ gracious の反意語は ungracious だが, あまり

polite, politician

用いられない. ☞ **grace** (RESPECT 名)
➤**graciously** 副 ◇*She graciously accepted our invitation.* 彼女は丁重に我々のお招きをお受けくださった

respectful（ややフォーマル, ほめて）敬意を示す, 丁寧[丁重]な ◇*We were brought up to be respectful of authority.* 私たちは権威を尊重するよう育てられた ◇*We all stood in respectful silence.* 私たちは皆うやうやしく沈黙して立っていた 反意 **disrespectful** (RUDE), ☞ **respect** (RESPECT 動), **respect** (RESPECT 名)
➤**respectfully** 副 ◇*He listened respectfully.* 彼は敬意をもって耳を傾けた

courteous（ほめて）（知らない人々に対して）礼儀正しい, 丁寧[丁重]な ◇*The hotel staff were friendly and courteous.* ホテルのスタッフは親切で礼儀正しかった ◇*I wrote him a short letter and received a courteous reply.* 私は彼に短い手紙を書き, 丁寧な返事をもらった 反意 **discourteous** (RUDE), ☞ **courtesy** (RESPECT 名)
➤**courteously** 副 ◇*'I don't think we have met,' said the chairman courteously.* 「お会いしたことはございませんね」と委員長は丁重に言った

gentlemanly（ほめて）（男性が）礼儀正しい；紳士的な, 紳士らしい ◇*So far, the election campaign has been a very gentlemanly affair.* 今までのところ, この選挙戦はとても紳士的である

deferential（ややフォーマル, 特に書き言葉）（社会的地位の高い人に対して）敬意を示す, 礼儀正しい, 丁寧[丁重]な ◇*Older people tend to be more deferential to medical authorities.* お年寄りのほうが医学の権威者に対してより丁重な態度をとる傾向がある
➤**deference** 名 [U] ◇*The women wore veils in deference to the customs of the country.* 女性たちはその国の慣習に敬意を表してベールをかぶっていた

politician 名

politician・MP・senator・Congressman/Congresswoman・Representative・lawmaker・legislator・Member of Parliament・statesman
政治に関わる仕事を持つ人
【類語訳】政治家, 国会議員, 下院議員, 上院議員, 立法者

【文型&コロケーション】
- the MP/ Member of Parliament **for** an area
- the senator/ Congressman/ Representative **from** an area
- a **great** politician/ senator/ legislator/ statesman
- a **leading** politician/ senator/ lawmaker/ statesman
- an **influential** politician/ senator/ Congressman/ lawmaker
- a **local** politician/ MP/ Congressman/ lawmaker/ Member of Parliament
- a **state** senator/ Representative/ lawmaker/ legislator
- a **Conservative/ Labour, etc.** politician/ MP/ Member of Parliament
- a **Republican/ Democratic, etc.** senator/ Congressman/ Representative/ lawmaker/ legislator
- an **opposition** politician/ MP/ lawmaker/ legislator/ Member of Parliament
- to **elect** a politician/ an MP/ a senator/ a Congressman/ a Representative/ a Member of Parliament

politician [C]（国会議員などの）政治家 ◇*The affair led to the resignations of three leading politicians.* この一件で3人の主要な政治家が辞任するに至った

poor

MP [C] 国会議員, 下院議員(Member of Parliamentの略) ◇You should write to your *MP* about it. 国会議員にそれについて手紙を書くべきだ ◇A number of *back-bench MPs* (= MPs who do not have senior positions) have expressed doubts about the bill. 下院の平の議員の多くがその法案に関して疑問を表明した ❶MPは話し言葉でも書き言葉でも, Member of Parliamentという形でよりもはるかに頻繁に用いられる.

senator (または **Senator**) [C] 上院議員;(肩書きとしての)上院議員 ◇He was elected *senator* for Pennsylvania in 2004. 彼は2004年にペンシルベニア州選出の上院議員に選ばれた ◇I would like to thank *Senator* Kelman for his warm welcome. 温かく歓迎していただきケルマン上院議員に感謝したいと思います

'Congressman, 'Congresswoman [C]（米）の連邦議会議員, 下院議員;(肩書きとしての)連邦議会議員, 下院議員 ◇*Congressmen* from energy-producing states have opposed the deal. エネルギー生産州の下院議員らがその政策に反対している ◇*Congresswoman* Barbara Lee バーバラ・リー下院議員

Representative [C]（（米）の連邦議会の）下院議員;（（米）の州議会の）下院議員 ◇He was elected state *Representative* in 1989. 彼は1989年に州議会の下院議員に選ばれた ◇*Representative* Harris ハリス下院議員

lawmaker [特に米, 特にジャーナリズム]（国・州の）立法者 ◇State *lawmakers* have been arguing over the new healthcare reform bill for months. 州議会議員が何か月にもわたって保健医療の新たな改革案に関して議論している

legislator [C]（（フォーマル）立法者 ◇Seven of the state's 90 *legislators* have been indicted. その州の90人の立法権者のうち7人が起訴されている

ノート **lawmaker** と **legislator** の使い分け: legislator はフォーマルな語で, lawmaker は特に(（米）で主にジャーナリズムで用いられ, しばしば politician の代わりに用いられる.

,Member of 'Parliament [C]（ややフォーマル）（（英）・カナダなどの）国会議員, 下院議員 ◇Phil Wilson, *Member of Parliament* for Sedgefield セッジフィールドの下院議員であるフィル・ウィルソン

statesman [C]（賢明で経験豊富な尊敬すべき）政治家 ◇Power still resided with the party's *elder statesman*. 権力はいまだに党の長老政治家の手中にあった ◇He has a reputation as a *world statesman*. 彼は世界的な政治家との評価を得ている

poor 形

1 ☞ BANKRUPT

poor・disadvantaged・needy・impoverished・deprived・penniless・destitute・hard up

ほとんど[まったく]お金がなく, 基本的な必要を満たすことができないことを表す

【類語訳】貧しい, 貧乏な, 貧困の, 無一文の, 極貧の, 金に困った

disadvantaged → poor → penniless
　　　　　　　 needy　　 destitute
　　　　　　　 impoverished
　　　　　　　 deprived
　　　　　　　 hard up

文型&コロケーション

▷ poor/ disadvantaged/ needy/ impoverished/ deprived/ destitute/ hard-up **people/ families**
▷ poor/ disadvantaged/ needy/ impoverished/ destitute **children**
▷ poor/ disadvantaged/ needy/ impoverished/ penniless/ hard-up **students**
▷ poor/ disadvantaged/ needy/ impoverished/ deprived **groups**
▷ poor/ disadvantaged/ needy/ impoverished/ deprived **areas**
▷ poor/ disadvantaged/ impoverished/ deprived **regions**
▷ poor/ disadvantaged/ impoverished **countries**
▷ a poor/ a disadvantaged/ an impoverished/ a deprived **background**
▷ a poor/ an impoverished/ a deprived **childhood**
▷ **very** poor/ disadvantaged/ needy/ impoverished/ deprived/ hard up
▷ **really** poor/ needy/ hard up
▷ **relatively** poor/ disadvantaged/ impoverished/ deprived

poor 貧しい, 貧乏な;（必需品に事欠いて）貧困の ◇They were too *poor* to buy shoes for the kids. 彼らはあまりに貧乏で子どもの靴を買うことができなかった ◇They always treated me like a *poor* relation. 私はいつも貧しい親戚のように扱われた ◇We aim to help the *poorest* families. 我々は最貧家庭を援助することを目的としている ◇It's among the *poorer* countries of the world. その国は世界の貧困国の中に数えられる ◇I may be *dirt poor*, but I have my pride.（米, ややインフォーマル）私は極貧かもしれないが, プライドはある [反意] **rich, wealthy, affluent** (RICH), ☞ **poverty** (POVERTY)

▷ **the poor** 名 [複数扱い] ◇They provided food and shelter for *the poor* (= people who are poor). 彼らは貧しい人々のために食料と住む場所を提供した

disadvantaged [ふつう名詞の前で]（社会の大半の人に比べて）恵まれない ◇socially *disadvantaged* sections of the community その地域の社会的に恵まれない階層 ◇the issues facing farmers in *disadvantaged* rural areas of Europe ヨーロッパの恵まれない農村地域に住む農家が直面している諸問題

▷ **the disadvantaged** 名 [複数扱い] ◇helping the poor and *the disadvantaged* 貧しくて恵まれない人々への援助

needy 貧しい, 貧乏な, 貧困の ◇It's a charity that provides help and comfort for *needy* children. それは貧しい子どもたちへ援助と慰めを与える慈善事業だ [反意] **wealthy** (RICH), ☞ **need** (POVERTY)

▷ **the needy** 名 [複数扱い] ◇They provide shelter and a hot meal to the homeless and *the needy*. 彼らはホームレスや貧しい人々に(*) と温かい食事を提供している

impoverished《ジャーナリズム》貧しい, 貧乏な, 貧困な ◇Thousands of *impoverished* peasants are desperate to move to the cities. 何千もの貧窮にあえぐ零細農民が都市への移住を切望している [反意] **prosperous, affluent** (RICH)

ノート **poor, needy, impoverished** の使い分け: poor がこれらの語の中で最も一般的で, 自分自身・個人・人の集団・国・地域に用いられる. needy はほとんどの場合, 集団として見なされる人々に用いられ, 自分自身・個人には用いら

れない。♦*poor/needy* children/families（貧しい子どもたち/家庭）．×They were too *needy* to buy shoes for the kids． impoverishedは特にジャーナリズムで用いられ、貧困国とそこで暮らす人々について用いられる。ちなみに富裕国にある貧困地域についてはdeprivedを用いる。

deprived ［ふつう名詞の前で］（必要なあらゆるものがなくて）恵まれない ◇It's a very *deprived* area, with no amenities. そこは公共サービスがなく非常に恵まれない地域だ ◇We try to identify and provide support for emotionally *deprived* children. 我々は愛情に恵まれない子どもたちを見つけて支援しようとしている ［反意］**privileged** (RICH)，☞ **deprivation** (POVERTY)

ノート disadvantaged と deprived の使い分け：disadvantagedはお金を稼ぎ、教育を受けて生活をよりよくする機会がないことに重点を置き、deprivedはもっと直接的に十分な食料・住宅などの物質的な快適さがないことに重点を置く。emotionally deprivedは十分な愛情や感情面での心地良さを得られない人々を指して用いられる。

penniless ［文語］無一文の；極貧の ◇She arrived in 1978 as a virtually *penniless* refugee. 彼女は1978年に事実上無一文の難民としてたどり着いた ◇He died *penniless* in Paris. 彼はパリで極貧のうちに死んだ

destitute ［名詞の前はまれ］《ややフォーマル》（生活必需品に事欠いて）貧困の，貧窮の ◇When he died, his family was left completely *destitute*. 彼が死んで、家族はまったく貧窮した状態で残された ☞ **destitution** (POVERTY)
▶ **the destitute** 图［複数扱い］◇homes and refuges for *the destitute* 貧困者のための家と避難所

hard up 《インフォーマル》（一時的に）貧乏な，金に困った ◇After he lost his job he was so *hard up* he couldn't afford the price of a beer. 彼は仕事を失ってからというもの、とても金に困って、ビール一杯買い求めることすらできなかった ◇A couple of *hard-up* students came looking for part-time jobs. 数人の貧乏学生がアルバイトを探しに来た ［反意］**well off** (RICH)

2 poor・bad・cheap・low・dismal・crap・inferior・shit・hopeless・second-rate
物事の水準や質が低いことを表す
【類語訳】悪い、不良の、お粗末な、劣った、ひどい、下手な、安物の、下手くそな、情けない、劣等な、どうしようもない、二流の

文型&コロケーション
▶ a poor/ a bad/ a cheap/ an inferior/ a second-rate **copy/ imitation**
▶ poor/ bad/ low/ inferior/ second-rate **quality**
▶ poor/ bad/ low **visibility**
▶ a poor/ bad/ low **opinion** of sb/ sth
▶ a poor/ a bad/ a crap/ an inferior/ a shit **performance**
▶ a poor/ bad/ dismal **result/ record**
▶ a poor/ a bad/ a crap/ an inferior/ a shit **design**
▶ poor/ bad/ inferior/ second-rate **service**
▶ poor/ bad/ inferior **workmanship**
▶ a poor/ a low/ a dismal/ an inferior **standard**
▶ a bad/ a cheap/ a crap/ an inferior/ a shit/ a second-rate **product**
▶ very poor/ bad/ low/ inferior/ second-rate

poor （水準・質の面で）悪い，不良の，お粗末な，振るわない，劣った ◇We discussed the party's *poor* performance in the election. 私たちは選挙におけるその党の失態について話し合った ◇She's been in *poor* health for some time now. 彼女はもうしばらく前から体調不良が続いている ◇On the whole he had a *poor* opinion of human nature. 全体的に彼は人間性についてお粗末な意見を持っていた ◇It was raining heavily and visibility was *poor*. その日は大雨が降っていて、視界が悪かった ［反意］**fine** (GOOD 1)
▶ **poorly** 副 ◇The job is relatively *poorly* paid. その仕事は比較的給料が安い ◇Our candidate *fared poorly* in the election (= did not get many votes). 我々の候補者は選挙で振るわなかった

bad 《ややインフォーマル》（水準・質の面で）悪い、ひどい、不良の、お粗末な、下手な ◇I thought it was a very *bad* article. それはとてもひどい記事だと私は思った ◇That's not a *bad* idea. それは悪い考えじゃないね ◇This isn't as *bad* as I thought. これは私が思ったほど悪くはない ［反意］**good** (GOOD 1)
▶ **badly** 副 ◇She sang two songs, very *badly*. 彼女は2曲歌ったが、とてもひどいものだった ◇The whole thing was *badly* organized. 全体的にうまくまとまってなかった

ノート poorとbadの使い分け：この意味において、書き言葉ではpoorのほうが使用頻度は高いが、話し言葉ではbadのほうがより頻繁に用いられる。また、poorかbadの一方としか結びつかない語もある。♦They have a *poor* standard of living.（彼らの生活水準は低い）．×a *bad* standard of living. ♦I don't think it's a *bad* school.（そこが悪い学校だとは私は思わない）．×I don't think it's a *poor* school.

cheap （価格および質が低くて）安価な、安物の ◇The room was filled with the smell of *cheap* perfume. その部屋は安物の香水のにおいが充満していた ◇The market has been flooded with *cheap* imports. その市場は安価な輸入品であふれている ［反意］**cheap** (CHEAP)
▶ **cheaply** 副 ◇The leaflet had been *cheaply* produced and photocopied. そのちらしは安っぽく作られコピーされていた

low （水準・質の面で）低い，劣った ◇Much of the work was of a very *low* standard. その作品の多くはとても低水準だった ◇These measures will lead to a *lower* quality of life for many older people. これらの措置は多くの高齢者の生活水準の低下につながるだろう ［反意］**high** (HIGH 1)

dismal 《インフォーマル》下手くそな；（非常に低水準で）ぶざまな、情けない ◇The singer gave a *dismal* performance of some old songs. その歌手はいくつか昔の歌を歌ったが下手くそだった ◇Their recent attempt to increase sales has been a *dismal failure*. 売上を伸ばそうとする彼らの最近の試みはぶざまにも失敗に終わった ❶dismalはほとんどの場合、failure, performance, result, record, weatherと結びつく。
▶ **dismally** 副 ◇I tried not to laugh but *failed dismally* (= was completely unsuccessful). 私は笑うまいとしたが、情けないことにうまくいかなかった

crap 《英》《米 **crappy**》《卑語, 俗語》（質・水準が非常に低くて）くそみたいな ❶crapは年齢・地位が対等の人に対してインフォーマルな状況でのみ用いるべき。年上の人［自分よりも偉いと思われる人］に対して用いると、非常に気分を害してしまう原因になるだろう。♦I used to be in this really *crap* band.（私は以前この本当にくそみたいなバンドにいたことがある）．♦a *crappy* movie/apartment（くそみたいな映画/アパート）

▶**crap** 副 ◇The team played *crap* yesterday. (英) 昨日チームはくそみたいなプレーをした
inferior (ややフォーマル)(同種の他のものよりも)劣等な,下等な,粗悪な ◇The cracks in the structure were due to the poor-quality materials and *inferior* workmanship. その構造物のひび割れは質の悪い材料と粗悪な技術のためであった ◇Modern music is often considered *inferior to* that of the past. 現代音楽はしばしば過去のものよりも劣っていると見なされる 反意 **superior** (BETTER), **superior** (GOOD 1)
shit (英) (米 **shitty**)(単語,俗語)(質・水準が非常に低くて)くそみたいな ❶ shit は年齢・地位が対等の人に対してインフォーマルな状況でのみ用いるべき。年上の人[自分より目上である人]に対して用いると、非常に気分を害してしまう原因になるだろう。crap よりさらに意味が強く、侮辱的である。 ◆I was a *shit* player. (私はくそみたいな選手だった)。 ◆They're a *shitty* team. (彼らはくそみたいなチームだ).
hopeless (英,インフォーマル)(サービスなどの質・水準が非常に低くて)どうしようもない ◇The buses are absolutely *hopeless* these days. この頃のバスはまったくどうしようもないね
▶**second-'rate** (同種の他のものよりも劣っていて)二流の,二級の ◇Why do we only produce *second-rate* films? なぜ私たちは二流の映画しか制作しないの 反意 **first-rate** (EXCELLENT)

popular 形

popular・attractive・desirable・hot・appealing・in demand・enviable
人や物事が大勢の人々に好まれる[ほしがられる]ことを表す
【類語訳】人気のある,魅力的な,興味をそそる,面白い,手に入れたい,望ましい,好ましい,ホットな,受けのよい

文型&コロケーション
▸ **attractive/ appealing to** sb
▸ an **attractive/ appealing idea/ prospect**
▸ **very popular/ attractive/ desirable/ appealing/ enviable**
▸ **highly popular/ attractive/ desirable**
▸ **immediately/ enormously popular/ attractive/ appealing**

popular (人・物事・活動が)人気のある ◇He was a hugely *popular* singer. 彼はものすごく人気のある歌手だった ◇This is one of our most *popular* designs. これは私どもの最も人気のあるデザインの一つです ◇These policies are unlikely to prove *popular with* middle-class voters. これらの政策が中産階級の有権者に人気はなさそうだ ◇These designs are *popular among* young people. これらのデザインは若者の間で人気がある 反意 **unpopular** (UNWANTED)
▶**popularity** 名 [U] ◇Their music still enjoys widespread *popularity* among teenagers. 彼らの音楽はいまだに十代の若者の間で広く人気がある
attractive (ややフォーマル)(物事が)魅力的な,興味そそる,面白い ◇They are able to offer *attractive* career opportunities to graduates. 彼らは卒業生たちに魅力的な就職の機会を提供することができる ❶ *attractive* は検討中の考え・可能性について用いられることが多い。 ◆an *attractive* idea/theory/proposition/option/prospect/package/offer (魅力的な考え/理論/企画/選択肢/見込み/組み合わせ商品/申し出). 反意 **unattractive**, ☞ **attraction** (INTEREST 名 1)

desirable (フォーマル) ほしい,手に入れたい;(持つ[する]価値があるので)望ましい,好ましい ◇It is *desirable that* interest rates be reduced. 金利は引き下げられることが望ましい ◇It is no longer *desirable for* adult children to live with their parents. 成人した子どもたちが親元で暮らすことはもはや好ましいことではなくなっている ◇She chatted for a few minutes about the qualities she considered *desirable in* a secretary. 彼女は少しの間秘書に望ましいと自分が思う資質についておしゃべりした ❶ *desirable* は特に不動産の販売で用いられることが多い。 ◆a *desirable* home/feature/residence/property/area (望ましい家/特徴/住居/不動産/地域). 反意 **undesirable** (UNWANTED)
▶**desirability** 名 [U] ◇No one questions the *desirability* of cheaper fares. 低運賃が望ましいことに誰も異論はない
hot (インフォーマル) 最新の,ホットな,熱烈な人気のある,アツい ◇They are one of this year's *hot new* bands on the rock scene. 彼らはロック界で今年のホットな新バンドの一つだ ◇The couple are Hollywood's *hottest property*. その夫婦はハリウッドで最も熱烈な人気がある ❶ *hot* の典型的な連語には talent, fashion, trend, band, new product, name が挙げられる。人や物事は the hottest thing in America/Japan などのようにも表される。この意味の *hot* は広告やジャーナリズムで用いられることが多い。
appealing 魅力的な,面白い,受けのよい;ほしい,手に入れたい,望ましい,好ましい ◇Spending the holidays in Britain wasn't a prospect that I found particularly *appealing*. イギリスで休暇を過ごすのが見通しとして特段魅力的には思えなかった ◇Brightly coloured packaging made the pens especially *appealing* to children. 明るい色で包装されたペンは子どもたちに特別受けがよかった 反意 **unappealing**, ☞ **appeal** (INTEREST 名 1)
in demand フレーズ 需要が高い ◇Good secretaries are always *in demand*. よい秘書は常に需要が高い ❶ *in demand* はほとんどの場合、多くの人々が購入したがる製品や多くの人々[雇い主]が使いたいと思う技術を持つ人について用いられる。よく always, constantly, greatly, increasingly, much と共に用いられる。
enviable (ややフォーマル)(人がもつ物事が)うらやましがられる ◇He is in the *enviable* position of having two job offers to choose from. 彼には選べる仕事のオファーが二つあって、うらやましがられる立場にある ❶ *enviable* は人の position, reputation, record と共によく用いられる。
unenviable ❶ unenviable (嫌な、気乗りしない)は行い[持ち]たくない不快[困難]な仕事・物事について用いられる。 ◆She was given the *unenviable task* of informing the losers. (彼女は不合格者に通知するという嫌な仕事を与えられた).

position 名

position・stance・posture・pose
人が立って[座って]いる様子
【類語訳】姿勢,体位,配置,状態,構え,ポーズ

文型&コロケーション
▸ a **sitting position/ posture**
▸ an **upright position/ stance**
▸ a **relaxed position/ stance/ posture/ pose**
▸ a **comfortable position/ posture**
▸ a **stiff posture/ pose**

↱position

possibility

▶ a **good** stance/ posture
▶ the **correct** stance/ posture
▶ to **adopt/ take up** a position/ stance/ posture/ pose
▶ to **keep/ maintain** a position/ stance/ posture
▶ to **change** your position/ stance/ posture/ pose

position [C, U]（人が座って[立って]いる）姿勢, 体位；（物の）配置, 状態 ◇Can you get into a kneeling *position*? 立てひざの姿勢がとれますか ◇My arms were aching so I shifted (my) *position*. 両腕が痛くて姿勢を変えた ◇The soldiers had to stand for hours without changing *position*. 兵士たちはじっと姿勢を変えず何時間も立っていなければならなかった ◇Keep the box in an upright *position*. 箱を垂直の状態にしておいてください ☞ **position** (PLACE), **position** (PUT)

stance [C]（スポーツでの人の）構え ◇Widen your *stance* (= move your feet wider apart) for greater stability when hitting the ball. ボールを打つときは安定感を増すため脚をもっと開いて構えなさい

posture [U, C]（ややフォーマル）（立って[座って]いるときの）姿勢 ◇Try to maintain an upright *posture* and keep your voice low and clear. 姿勢はまっすぐに保ち, 声は低くはっきりを心がけましょう ◇Back pains can be the result of bad *posture*. 背中の痛みは姿勢の悪さの結果であることもある ❶ *posture* は特定の姿勢が健康によいか悪いか[人の姿勢・身振りがどのような感情を伝えているか]について考える場合に用いられる。

pose [C]（絵に描かれる[写真に撮られる]ときの）姿勢, ポーズ ◇He adopted a dramatic *pose* for the camera. 彼はカメラに向かって決めポーズを取った ◇I can't *hold this pose* much longer! これ以上あまり長くはこのポーズを維持できません

▷ **pose** 動 [自] ◇The delegates *posed for* a group photograph. 使節の者たちはグループ写真のためにポーズを取った

possibility 名

possibility • chance • probability • odds • prospect • likelihood
物事の発生の程度を表す
【類語訳】可能性, 見込み

possibility	prospect	probability
chance		likelihood
odds		

文型&コロケーション

▶ a **possibility/** a **chance/** a **probability/** the **odds/** the **prospect/** the **likelihood** **of** sth
▶ a **possibility/** a **chance/** the **probability/** the **odds/** the **prospect/** the **likelihood** **that**...
▶ a **real/ reasonable** possibility/ chance/ probability/ prospect/ likelihood
▶ a **strong** possibility/ chance/ probability/ likelihood
▶ a **high** chance/ probability/ likelihood
▶ a **realistic/ serious/ remote** possibility/ chance/ prospect
▶ **every** possibility/ chance/ probability/ prospect/ likelihood
▶ **little** chance/ prospect/ likelihood

▶ **There is (no)** possibility/ chance/ prospect/ likelihood of sth.
▶ **The** chances/ probability/ odds/ likelihood **is/ are that**...
▶ to **have** the possibility/ a chance/ a ... probability/ the prospect/ a ...likelihood
▶ to **increase/ reduce** the possibility/ chance/ probability/ odds/ likelihood
▶ to **calculate** the probability/ odds/ likelihood

possibility [U, C]（存在・発生の）可能性 ◇He refused to rule out the *possibility* of a tax increase. 彼は増税の可能性を排除することを拒否した ◇It is not *beyond the bounds of possibility* that we'll all meet again one day.《特に英》私たちが皆でいつか再会する可能性がないわけではない ◇What had seemed impossible now seemed a *distinct possibility*. 不可能と思われたことが今やはっきりと可能性があるように思えた ◇There is a remote *possibility* that we might have got it wrong. 私たちが誤解していたかもしれない可能性はわずかながらありうる ☞ **possible** (LIKELY)

chance [C, U]（望ましいことの存在・発生の）可能性, 見込み ◇Is there any *chance* of getting tickets for tonight? 今夜のチケットが手に入る見込みはありますか ◇The operation has a *fifty-fifty chance* of success. その手術が成功する可能性は五分五分だ ◇As long as there is an *outside chance* (= a slight chance) we'll go for it. 見込みが少しでもあるのなら, 私たちはそれをやってみるつもりです ◇She has only a *slim chance* of passing the exam. 彼女が試験に合格する見込みはわずかしかない ◇There is *no chance* that he will change his mind. 彼の気が変わる可能性はない

probability [U, C]（発生することの高い）可能性 ◇The *probability* is that prices will rise rapidly. 物価が急騰する可能性が高い ◇A fall in interest rates is a strong *probability* in the present economic climate. 現在の経済状況では金利が低下する可能性は高い ❶数学では probability は特定の物事が発生する可能性を示す比率を指す。 ◆There is a 60% *probability* that the population will be infected with the disease.（60%の確率で住民はその病気に感染するだろう）. ☞ **probable** (LIKELY)

odds《ふつう the odds》[複数で]（発生することの高い）可能性；（実現[達成]不可能な）可能性 ◇*The odds are* very much *in our favour* (= we are likely to succeed). 勝算は我々にある ◇*The odds are* heavily *against him* (= he is not likely to succeed). 彼に勝算はまずない ◇*What are the odds* (= how likely is it) he won't turn up? 彼が現れない可能性はどれくらいですか ◇*Against all (the) odds*, he made a full recovery. まったく思いがけないことに, 彼は全快した ❶賭け事でodds は賭けに勝った場合に人が受け取る金額を二つの数字で示す場合に用いられる。 ◆I put £10 on Middlesbrough to beat Manchester at *odds* of three to one (= three times the amount of money that has been bet by sb will be paid to them if they win).（私は3対1のオッズでミドルズブラがマンチェスターに勝つほうに10ポンド賭けた）. ◆They are offering *long/short odds* (= the winnings will be high/low because there is a high/low risk of losing) on the defending champion.（ディフェンディング・チャンピオンのオッズは高い/低い）.

prospect [U, 単数で]（ややフォーマル）（好ましいことの発生の）可能性, 見込み ◇There is no immediate *prospect* of peace. 即座に平和が実現する見込みはない ◇A place

possible

in the semi-finals is *in prospect* (= likely to happen). 準決勝進出の可能性はありそうだ ☞ **prospective** (LIKELY)

likelihood [U, 単数で] (好ましいことの発生の)可能性, 見込み；(発生することの高い)可能性 ◇There is very little *likelihood* of that happening. それが起こる可能性はほとんどない ◇The *likelihood* is that (= it is likely that) unemployment figures will continue to fall. 失業率は下がり続けそうだ ◇*In all likelihood* (= very probably) the meeting will be cancelled. 会議が中止になる可能性は非常に高い ☞ **likely** (LIKELY)

> ノート **probability** と **likelihood** の使い分け：probability は科学的・技術的な文脈で用いられることが多く, likelihood はビジネスの文脈で用いられることが多い。しかしながら, 両語とも日常会話でも使用可能。

possible 形

1 possible・viable・practical・realistic・feasible・workable・achievable
成功しそうなので実行[実現, 挑戦]する価値があることを表す
【類語訳】可能な, 実際的な, 現実的な, 実現可能な, 達成可能な

文型&コロケーション
- to be possible/ realistic/ feasible **to do sth**
- a viable/ practical/ realistic/ feasible/ workable **solution/ policy/ plan**
- a viable/ practical/ realistic/ feasible **means**
- a viable/ practical/ realistic/ workable **alternative**
- a realistic/ an achievable **goal/ objective/ target**
- **perfectly** possible/ viable/ practical/ feasible
- **quite** possible/ practical/ realistic/ feasible
- **very** practical/ realistic/ feasible/ achievable
- **reasonably** practical/ realistic/ achievable

possible [名詞の前はまれ] (実行[実現])可能な, できる ◇It is *possible* to get there by bus. そこへはバスで行くことが可能です ◇This would not have been *possible* without you. これは君なしでは実現不可能だっただろう ◇Try to avoid losing your temper *if (at all) possible* (= if you can). できることなら, 腹を立てるのは避けるようにしましょう ◇Travel by bus *whenever possible* (= when you can). できるだけバスで移動しなさい ◇Do *everything possible* to get it finished on time. 時間どおりに終わらせるために, できることはすべてやりなさい ◇New technology has *made it possible* to communicate more easily. 新技術のおかげで, コミュニケーションはより容易になった [反意] **impossible** (IMPOSSIBLE), ☞ **possibility** (OPPORTUNITY), **possibility** (OPTION), **possibilities** (POTENTIAL)

viable 《ややフォーマル, 特にビジネスで》(実行)可能な；(成功しそうで)検討[支持]に値する ◇There is no *viable* alternative. 実行可能な代替案はない ◇If there was any delay then the rescue plan would cease to be *viable*. 少しでも遅れがあれば, その救済策は効力を失うだろう ❶ **commercially/economically/financially viable** (商業的に/経済的に/財政的に持続可能な)会社・計画・事業は利益を生むことができる。

practical 有用な, 適切な；(うまくいきそうなので)現実的な ◇It wouldn't be *practical* for us to go all that way just for the weekend. 私たちが週末の間だけ, はるばるそ

ちらに出向くのは実際的ではあるまい ◇It was difficult to find a *practical* solution to the problem. その問題の実際的な解決策を見つけるのは困難だった ❶この意味では practical は考え・一連の行動・物事の行い方について用いられる。
◆ a *practical* alternative/approach/measure/method/option/possibility/proposition (実際的な代替案/アプローチ/方策/手段/選択肢/可能性/企画) [反意] **impractical**

realistic 有用な, 適切な；現実的な ◇We must set *realistic* goals. 我々は現実的な目標を設定しなければならない ◇If you want to retain good employees, you have to pay a *realistic* salary. よい従業員を逃したくなければ, 実際に見合った給料を支払わねばならない ❶ **realistic** はビジネス・仕事で実現したいことについて用いられることが多い。 ◆ a *realistic* alternative/demand/estimate/goal/hope/option/plan/solution/target (現実的な代替案/要求/見積もり/目標/願い/選択肢/計画/解決策/対象) [反意] **unrealistic**

> **realistically** 副 ◇*Realistically*, there is little prospect of a ceasefire. 現実的に考えて, 停戦の可能性はほとんどない ◇How many can you *realistically* hope to sell? 実際のところいくつ売れると見込めるのですか

feasible 実現可能な ◇It's just not *feasible* to manage the business on a part-time basis. 時間給基準で企業を経営することはまったく実現不可能だ

workable 実現可能な, うまくいきそうな ◇Gradually, through discussion, a *workable* plan emerged. 議論を通して次第に実現可能な計画が浮かび上がった ◇I'm sure we can come to some *workable* arrangement. 私はきっと何らかの実行可能な取り決めを交わせるものと思う ❶ **workable** はしばしばビジネスに関連する文脈で用いられ, システム・考えなどと共に用いられる。 ◆ a *workable* arrangement/framework/plan/programme/proposal/solution/system (実現可能な取り決め/枠組み/計画/プログラム/提案/解決策/システム)

achievable 《ややフォーマル》実現[達成]可能な ◇Profits of $20m look *achievable*. 2千万ドルの利益は達成可能に思える ◇Setting *achievable* goals will help to build confidence in your staff. 実現可能な目標を設定することは, 職員が自信をつけるのに役立つだろう ❶ **achievable** はほとんどの場合, goal, objective, target, standard と結びつく。

2 possible・plausible・credible・conceivable・imaginable・believable
物事が理にかなっているように思える[真実でありそうである]こと
【類語訳】ありうる, 考えうる, もっともらしい, まことしやかな, 信じられる, 信用できる, 想像できる

文型&コロケーション
- possible/ plausible/ credible/ conceivable/ imaginable/ believable **that**...
- a possible/ plausible/ credible/ believable **explanation/ excuse**
- a possible/ plausible/ credible **solution/ answer**
- a plausible/ credible/ believable **story/ account**
- to sound possible/ plausible/ credible/ believable
- **entirely/ perfectly/ quite** possible/ plausible/ credible/ conceivable
- **barely/ hardly/ scarcely** possible/ credible/ conceivable/ imaginable/ believable
- **every** possible/ conceivable/ imaginable...

possible (特定の状況において)ありうる, 考えうる ◇There are several *possible* explanations. 考えられる理由がいくつかある ◇It's scarcely *possible* that he knew nothing about it. 彼がそれについて何も知らなかったなんてことはほとんどありえない 反意 **impossible** (IMPOSSIBLE)

plausible (ややフォーマル) (弁解・釈明が)もっともらしい, まことしやかな ◇Her story sounded perfectly *plausible*. 彼女の話は完璧にもっともらしく聞こえた ◇The only *plausible* explanation is that he forgot. 唯一もっともらしい釈明は彼が忘れていたということだけだ 反意 **implausible** (UNLIKELY 2), ☞ **reasonable** (REASONABLE)
  ▸**plausibly** 副 ◇He argued, very *plausibly*, that the claims were untrue. 彼はその主張は事実に反すると, いかにももっともらしく主張した

credible 信じられる, 信頼[信用]できる ◇It's just not *credible* that she would cheat. 彼女が人をだますなんてまったく信じられない ◇There's only one *credible* witness in the case. その事件の信用できる目撃者は一人しかいない 反意 **incredible** (INCREDIBLE)
  ▸**credibility** 名 [U] ◇The prosecution did its best to undermine the *credibility* of the witness. 検察側は全力で目撃者の信頼性を弱めようとした

conceivable 考えられる, 想像[信用]できる ◇It's not *conceivable* that she didn't know what was going on. 彼女が何が起こっているかを知らなかったとは考えられない ◇We've examined the problem from every *conceivable* angle. 私たちは考えられるあらゆる角度からその問題を調べている 反意 **inconceivable** (IMPOSSIBLE)
  ▸**conceivably** 副 ◇He might *conceivably* go on to win the finals. もしかすると彼がこのまま優勝するかもしれない

imaginable 考えられる, 想像できる ◇What those prisoners went through is hardly *imaginable*. その囚人たちがどんな目に遭ったかほとんど想像できない ❶ *imaginable*しばしば最上級, all, everyなどと共に用いられ, 想像できる[考えられる]あらゆる物事が最善[最悪など]であることを強調する. ◆The house has the most spectacular views *imaginable*. (その家からは想像できる最も壮大な景色が見える). ◆They stock every *imaginable* type of music. (考えるあらゆるタイプの音楽が店に置かれている). 反意 **unimaginable** ❶ *unimaginable*は物事が考え[想像]つかないことを表す. ◆ *unimaginable* wealth/possibilities (考え[想像]もつかない富/可能性). ◆This level of success would have been *unimaginable* just last year. (このレベルの成功はつい昨年には想像もつかなかっただろう).

believable 信じられる, 信頼[信用]できる ◇The characters in the play are simply not *believable* (= you cannot believe they represent real people). その劇の登場人物は実在するとはまったく信じられないような人物 反意 **unbelievable** (INCREDIBLE)

potential 名

potential・prospects・promise・possibilities
首尾よく物事が生じる[進展する, 用いられる]確率が高いこと
【類語訳】可能性, 将来性, 潜在能力, 有望性, 見込み, 展望, 見通し, 有望

文型&コロケーション
▸ potential/ prospects/ possibilities **for** sth
▸ sb/ sth **with** potential/ prospects/ promise/ possibilities
▸ **real/ great** potential/ prospects/ promise/ possibilities
▸ **exciting/ future** potential/ prospects/ possibilities
▸ **commercial/ development/ economic** potential/ prospects/ possibilities
▸ to **have** potential/ prospects/ promise/ possibilities
▸ to **offer** potential/ prospects/ possibilities
▸ to **show** potential/ promise
▸ to **fulfil** sb/ sth's potential/ promise
▸ to **assess/ examine/ consider/ discuss/ explore** sb/sth's potential/ prospects/ possibilities

potential [U] (物事の)可能性, 将来性；(人・物事に存在する)潜在能力 ◇It is clear that the *potential* for change is there. そこに改革の可能性があることは明らかだ ◇She has great *potential* as an artist. 彼女は芸術家としての潜在能力が大いにある ◇All children should be encouraged to realize their **full** *potential*. すべての子もたちにその全潜在能力を発揮するよううながすべきだ ❶ 人々・物事に発揮する資質がある場合, 一般的にhave/show potentialと表現される. それらの資質が首尾よく発揮される場合には, fulfil/reach/realize one's potentialと表現される.
☞ **potential** (LIKELY)

prospects [複数で] (仕事上の)有望性, 見込み, 展望, 見通し ◇They want a reasonable salary and good *career prospects*. 彼らは妥当な給料と仕事の上でのよき見通しを求めている ◇At 25 he was an unemployed musician with no *prospects*. 25歳にして, 彼は仕事にあぶれた見込みのない音楽家だった ◇What are the *prospects* of promotion in this job? この仕事での昇進の見込みはどんなものでしょうか ☞ **prospective** (LIKELY)

promise [U] (人・物事の成功する)見込み, 展望；有望 ◇Her work shows great *promise*. 彼女の作品を見れば将来は大いに有望だ ◇Their future was **full of** *promise*. 彼らの将来は前途有望だった ☞ **promising** (PROMISING)

possibilities [複数で] (物事の)可能性, 将来性 ◇The house is in a bad state of repair but it has *possibilities*. その家は修理段階としてひどい状態だが修復可能性はある ☞ **possible** (POSSIBLE 1)

ノート **potential** と **possibilities** の使い分け：potentialは人・物事, 特に人が持つ可能性・将来性. possibilitiesは物事の可能性・将来性で, ふつう人は不可.

poverty 名

poverty・need・deprivation・privation・destitution
基本的な必要を満たすための十分なお金をほとんど持っていない状態
【類語訳】貧乏, 貧困, 貧窮, 窮乏, 不自由, 極貧, 赤貧

文型&コロケーション
▸ **in** poverty/ need/ destitution
▸ poverty/ need/ deprivation **among**...
▸ **great** poverty/ need/ deprivation/ privation
▸ **extreme/ real** poverty/ need/ deprivation
▸ **rural/ inner-city/ urban** poverty/ deprivation
▸ **economic** poverty/ need/ deprivation/ privation
▸ **material** poverty/ need/ deprivation
▸ to **endure/ suffer** poverty/ deprivation/ privation

poverty [U] 貧乏, 貧困, 貧窮 ◇Thousands of families are living in *abject/dire poverty* in the shanty towns. その貧民街では何千もの家庭が赤貧の暮らしをしている ◇There are millions living on incomes below **the poverty line** (= who are too poor to afford necessary items). 貧困線を下回る収入で暮らす人々が何百万人といる 反意 **wealth** (MONEY 3), ☞ **poor** (POOR 1), **hardship** (TROUBLE 2)

need [U] (十分な食料・金・支援のない)困窮, 窮乏 ◇The charity aims to provide assistance to people in need. この慈善事業は困窮している人々への援助を提供することが目的である ◇He helped me in my **hour of need**. 彼は困っているまさにその時に私を助けてくれた ☞ **needy** (POOR 1)

deprivation [U] (ややフォーマル)(十分な生活必需品のない)不自由, 窮乏 ◇In the inner cities you will find neglected children suffering from social deprivation. 大都市スラムに踏み入ると社会的窮乏にあえぐ放置された子どもたちに出会うだろう ☞ **deprived** (POOR 1)

privation [C, ふつう複数で, U] (フォーマル)(十分な生活必需品のない)不自由, 窮乏 ◇They suffered all the privations of poverty. 彼らは皆貧困の不自由さを味わっていた ◇They endured years of suffering and privation. 彼らは何年もの苦難と窮乏に耐えた

destitution [U] (金・食料・家などのない)極貧, 赤貧 ◇Help from local charities meant that the degree of deprivation stopped short of actual destitution. 地元の慈善事業からの援助によって窮乏の程度は実際的には極貧状態寸前で止められた ☞ **destitute** (POOR 1)

> ノート deprivation, privation, destitution の使い分け: privation と deprivation は適切な食料・衣類など基本的必需品が欠如していることを意味する. deprivation は例えば大人の子どもへの保護の欠如も指す. destitution は仕事・金・家がないときに経験する状況を指す.

powerful 形

powerful・dominant・strong・influential・important・great・instrumental・high-powered
人が人[出来事]に対して権力[影響力]を持っていることを表す 【類語訳】強力な, 強大な, 有力な, 支配的な, 優位な, 優勢な, 影響力のある, 重要な, 偉大な, 助けになる

文型&コロケーション

▶ dominant/ influential/ important/ instrumental **in** (doing) sth
▶ a powerful/ a dominant/ a strong/ an influential/ a great/ an important **figure/ leader/ position**
▶ a powerful/ a dominant/ an influential/ an important **individual/ group**
▶ a powerful/ strong/ influential **lobby**
▶ a powerful/ a dominant/ a strong/ an influential/ an important/ an instrumental **role**
▶ a powerful/ a dominant/ a strong/ an important/ a great **influence**
▶ **very** powerful/ dominant/ strong/ influential/ important/ high-powered
▶ **economically** powerful/ dominant/ strong/ important

powerful (人々・集団が)強力な, 強大な, 有力な, 実力[影響力]のある ◇He is one of the most **powerful** directors in Hollywood. 彼はハリウッドで最も実力のある監督の一人だ ◇This extremist movement has become increasingly powerful in recent years. この過激派の運動は近年ますます強大になってきている ◇Why are there still so few women in politically powerful positions? なぜいまだに政治的に有力な地位に女性がほとんど就いていないのですか

dominant (人々・集団・考えが)支配的な, 優位な, 優勢な, 主要な ◇The firm has achieved a dominant position in the world market. その会社は世界市場において支配的な地位を獲得している ◇The state of the economy has been the dominant theme of the election. 経済状態が選挙の主要テーマとなっている

➤ **dominance** 名 [U] ◇The firm soon achieved dominance in the marketplace. その会社はすぐに市場での優位性を確立した ◇Ex-colonial countries began to challenge the cultural dominance of Europe. 元植民地の国々はヨーロッパの文化的支配に対して疑念を向け始めた

strong (ほめて)(人々・集団が)強力な, 強大な, 有力な, 実力[影響力]のある ◇Will this damage his image as a **strong** leader? このことで彼の強力な指導者というイメージは損なわれるのでしょうか ◇What the country needs right now is a **strong government**. その国にとって目下必要なのは強い政府である 反意 **weak** ❶ weak は大した力がなく, 影響力を受けやすい人・集団について用いられる. ◆ a weak and cowardly man ((けなして)力がなく臆病な男). ◆ **In a weak moment** (= when I was easily persuaded) I said she could borrow the car. (気弱になって私は彼女にその車を貸してあげようと言った).

influential (人々・集団・考えが)(特定の範囲内で)影響力のある[強い] ◇The committee was influential in formulating government policy on employment. その委員会は雇用に対する政府の政策の策定に影響力を及ぼした ◇This was a **highly influential** book. これは非常に影響力の強い本だった

important (人々・集団が)有力な, 影響力のある, 重要な, 偉大な ◇He likes to **feel important**. 彼は自分が偉いと思いたがる ◇Many disabled people do now hold important jobs in industry. 実際今多くの障碍(がい)を持つ人々が産業界の重要な職に就いている

> ノート powerful, strong, influential, important の使い分け: これらの語はすべて多大な権力・影響力を持つ人々・集団に用いられる. powerful は最も一般的な語で, 特に地位により権力を持ち, 人々・出来事を支配することができる人を指すのに用いられる. 指導者・政治家・最高位の経営者はしばしば powerful と形容される. strong は特に権力のある地位にあり, その権力を効果的に行使するのに必要な技術・素質を持つ人を指すのに用いられる. 指導者はその立場上 powerful であるかもしれないが, a strong leader は度胸があり, 指導者としての素質を持っている人のことを指す. influential は人々が尊敬する[耳を傾ける, 注目する]人・物事に用いられ, 人々の意見[振る舞い]に影響を及ぼす. important はしばしば尊敬されている[その人の行動が他の人々の行動よりも影響力がある]ため, 人々・出来事に対して多大な影響力を及ぼす場合に用いられる.

great 偉大な, 影響力の強い ◇the great powers (= important and powerful countries) 列強 ◇We can make this country great again. 我々はこの国をもう一度強くすることができるのです ◇Alexander the Great アレクサンダー大王

instrumental ((ややフォーマル))(物事の[に])助けになる, 一役買う ◇He was instrumental in bringing about an end to the conflict. 彼はその紛争の終結に一役買った

↪ powerful

practise, praise

,high-'powered (政治家・経営者が)有力な、影響力のある；(仕事・活動が)重要な、責任重大な ◇She's a *high-powered* executive with a salary to match. 彼女は力のある経営幹部でそれ相当の給与をもらっている ◇He has a very *high-powered* job and a hectic schedule. 彼は非常に責任の重い仕事をしていて、スケジュールは過密だ

practise 《英》《米 **practice**》動 ☞ TRAIN 2

practise・rehearse・go over sth・run through sth
技や技術を上達させるために繰り返す、物事を学ぶ
【類語訳】練習する、稽古する、リハーサルする、稽古をつける、通し稽古をする、おさらいする

〔文型&コロケーション〕
▸ to practise/ rehearse **for** sth
▸ to practise/ rehearse/ go over sth/ run through sth **again**
▸ to practise/ rehearse **regularly**

practise 《英》《米 **practice**》［自, 他］練習する、稽古する ◇You need to *practise* every day. 毎日練習しなきゃね ◇She's been *practising* hard for her piano exam. 彼女はピアノの試験に向けて一生懸命稽古している ◇I've been *practising* my tennis serve for weeks. 私は何週間もテニスのサーブを練習している ◇He usually wants to *practise* his English **on** me. 彼は私を使って英語の練習をしたがることが多い ◇*Practise* reversing the car into the garage. ガレージに車をバックで入れる練習をしなさい ☞ **practice** (TRAINING), **practised** (EXPERIENCED)

rehearse ［自, 他］(公演に向けて劇・楽曲などを)稽古する、リハーサルする、(人に)稽古をつける、リハーサルさせる；(頭の中で[非公式に]人に言う[やろうとしている])ことを)復唱［暗唱］する、練習［予行］する ◇We were given only two weeks to *rehearse*. 私たちには稽古する期間がたったの2週間しか与えられなかった ◇Today, we'll just be *rehearsing* the final scene. 今日は、最後の場面をリハーサルするだけにしましょう ◇The actors were poorly *rehearsed*. 俳優たちはあまり稽古していなかった ◇She *mentally rehearsed* what she would say to Jeff. 彼女はジェフに言おうと思うことを頭の中で復唱した ☞ **rehearsal** (TRAINING)

,go 'over sth ［句動詞］(勉強・説明を)繰り返す、反復する ◇Let's not *go over* all this again. これをもう一度初めから繰り返すのはやめよう ◇Can we just *go over* those instructions one more time? その指示をもう一度だけ繰り返していただけますか ◇He *went over* the events of the day in his mind (= thought about them carefully). 彼はその日の出来事を頭の中で思い返した ☞ **repeat** (REPEAT)

,run 'through sth ［句動詞］(素早く)通し稽古をする、通しで練習[リハーサル]する、おさらいする、繰り返す ◇Can we *run through* Scene 3 again? もう一度第3場を通しでリハーサルしようか ◇Could we *run through* your proposals once again? もう一度あなたの提案にざっと目を通せていただけますか
▸ **'run-through** ［名］［C］ ◇Can we have just one more *run-through*? もう一度だけ練習できますか

praise 名

praise・credit・approval・acclaim・flattery・adulation・a pat on the back
人の行動・功績・外見をほめ称える気持ち[言葉]
【類語訳】称賛、賞賛、礼賛、是認、賛成、賛同、喝采、お世辞

〔文型&コロケーション〕
▸ praise/ credit/ approval/ acclaim/ a pat on the back **for** sth/ doing sth
▸ praise/ approval/ acclaim/ adulation/ a pat on the back **from** sb
▸ **great** praise/ credit/ acclaim
▸ **public** praise/ approval/ acclaim/ adulation
▸ **universal/ widespread** praise/ approval/ acclaim
▸ to **deserve** praise/ credit/ acclaim/ a pat on the back
▸ to **earn/ win** praise/ approval/ acclaim
▸ to **get** praise/ credit/ approval/ a pat on the back
▸ to **receive** praise/ credit/ approval/ acclaim
▸ to **give** sb praise/ credit/ approval/ a pat on the back

praise ［U］(または頻度は低いが **praises** ［複数で］) (人(の行い)・物事を)ほめること、称賛、賞辞、礼賛 ◇His teachers are *full of praise for* the progress he's making. 先生方は彼の進歩をとてもほめている ◇She wrote poems *in praise of* freedom. 彼女は自由を礼賛する詩を書いた ◇His latest movie has won *high praise* from the critics. 彼の新作映画は評論家から高い称賛を得ている ◇They always *sing his praises* (= praise him very highly). 彼はいつもほめそやされている

credit ［U］(好ましい結果をもたらしたことで人を)ほめること、称賛 ◇I can't *take* all *the credit* for the show's success — it was a team effort. このショーの成功に対して私がすべての称賛を受けることはできない、これはチームの努力のおかげだったからだ ◇We did all the work and she gets all the *credit*! 私たちがその仕事をすべてしたのに、彼女が称賛のすべてを受けているんだ ◇At least give him *credit* for trying (= praise him because he tried, even if he did not succeed). 挑戦したことに対して少なくとも彼をほめるべきだ 反義 **blame** (FAULT)

〔ノート〕**praise** と **credit** の使い分け：praise は実際に述べる言葉を指す。例えば、◆Well done! (よくやった)。◆You did a great job. (すごいじゃないか)。◆I think he's a wonderful cook. (彼は素晴らしい料理人だと思う)。credit は実際に述べる言葉ではなくて、称賛する意見・感情を指すことが多い。◆We should give due *credit* to the organizers of this event (= we think they did a good job). (このイベントの主催者にしかるべき称賛を送るべきだ)。credit はよい行いに対して与えられることをも示唆する。◆*Credit* will be given in the exam for good spelling and grammar (= you will get extra marks). (試験では正しい綴りと文法が評価されます)

approval ［U］(人・物事に対する)是認、賛成、賛同、(人・物事に対する)肯定的な意見、称賛 ◇Do the plans *meet with your approval*? その計画にご賛同願えますか ◇Several people nodded *in approval*. 幾人かの人々が賛同してうなづいた 反義 **disapproval** (CRITICISM), ☞ **approve** (IN FAVOUR)

acclaim ［U］(ややフォーマル)(芸術的偉業に対しての公からの)喝采 ◇Her latest novel has received widespread critical *acclaim*. 彼女の新作小説は評論家から広く喝采を浴びている ◇The play opened last week to universal *acclaim*. その劇は先週封切られて世界中から喝采を浴びた

flattery ［U］(人からの)お世辞 ◇You're too intelligent to fall for his *flattery*. あなたは利口だから、彼のお世辞に

praise

だまされないだろうね ◇***Flattery will get you nowhere*** (= it will not get you what you want). お世辞を言っても無駄だよ

adulation [U]《フォーマル》(有名人に対する)多大な称賛 ◇The band enjoy the *adulation* of their fans wherever they go. そのバンドはどこへ行ってもファンから多大な称賛を受けている ❶ adulationはしばしば過度の称賛を示唆する. ◆He found it difficult to cope with the *adulation* from those around him. 彼は周囲からのもてはやしに対応するのに苦労した.

a ˌpat on the ˈback [行為] 《ややインフォーマル》(よくやったことを[への])ほめること, 称賛 ◇He deserves *a pat on the back* for all his hard work. 彼の頑張りすべては称賛に値する ◇Give yourself *a pat on the back*! 自分をほめてあげよう

praise [動]

praise・congratulate・hail・applaud・celebrate acclaim・commend・glorify・compliment・rave

人や物事に感心したり, 賞賛したりする
【類語訳】ほめる, 称賛する, 称える, 祝福する, お祝いを言う, 是認する, 賛美する

praise	hail	glorify
congratulate	applaud	rave
commend	celebrate	
compliment	acclaim	

《文型&コロケーション》

▸ to praise/ congratulate/ applaud/ commend sb **for (doing) sth**
▸ to congratulate/ commend/ compliment sb **on** sth
▸ to praise/ hail/ acclaim sb/ sth **as** sth
▸ to praise/ hail/ applaud/ commend a **decision/ plan**
▸ to praise/ applaud/ commend sb's **effort/ courage**
▸ to praise/ congratulate/ applaud/ commend sb **warmly**
▸ to be **highly/ widely/ universally** praised/ acclaimed/ commended
▸ sb **is to be/ should be** congratulated/ applauded/ commended

praise [他] (人・物事を)ほめる, 称賛する, 称える ◇He *praised* his team for their performance. 彼は自分のチームのパフォーマンスを称えた ◇They were *praised* by police for reporting the theft. 彼らは窃盗を通報したとで警察から表彰された ◇Critics *praised* the work as highly original. 評論家たちはその作品を極めて独創性が高いと称賛した [反意] **criticize** [BLAME]

congratulate [他] (成功・功績について人に[を])祝福する, お祝いを言う ◇I *congratulated* them all on their results. 私は彼ら全員にその結果に対しお祝いを言った ◇The authors are to be *congratulated* on producing such a clear and authoritative work. これほど文句なしに権威ある作品を生んだ作者は祝福されるべきだ
▸ **congratulations** [名]《複数で》◇*Congratulations* on your exam results! 試験に合格おめでとう

[ノート] **praise**と**congratulate**の使い分け: praiseの目的語は人・素質・能力・功績であるが, congratulateの目的語は人でなければならない. ◆I *praised/congratulated* him. (私は彼を称賛[祝福]した). ×I *praised* his ability to stay calm under pressure. (私はプレッシャーにも平静を保つ彼の能力を称賛した). ×I *congratulated* his ability to stay calm. praiseの対象は子ども・従業員など自分が面倒を見ている[管理下にある]人であり, ふつう友人・パートナー・上司などの目上の人[管理者]に対しては用いられない. ◆He *praised/congratulated* his son/class/ team. (彼は自分の息子/クラス/チームを称賛した). ◆He *congratulated* his colleague. (彼は自分の同僚にお祝いを言った). ×He *praised* his colleague. congratulateは特定の状況での功績, 特に明確な結果について人を祝福する場合に用いられる. ◆She *congratulated* me on passing my driving test. (彼女は私に運転試験に合格のお祝いを言ってくれた). ◆She *praised* me for the way I deal with difficult customers. (彼女は扱いにくい客への私の対応の仕方をほめてくれた).

hail [他, ふつう受身で]《特にジャーナリズム》(人・物事を公然と)称賛する, 称える ◇The conference was *hailed* as a great success. その会議は大成功だと称えられた ◇Teenager Matt Brown is being *hailed* a hero for saving a young child from drowning. 十代の若者マット・ブラウンは溺れかけている幼い子どもを救ったヒーローとして称えられている

applaud [他]《進行形はまれ》《フォーマル》(人・物事を)是認[称賛]する ◇We *applaud* her decision. 我々は彼女の決定を是認します ◇I *applaud* her for having the courage to refuse. 私は彼女の断る勇気を称賛します ❶ applaudの一般的な連語としてdecision, effort, attitude, determination, courageが挙げられる.

celebrate [他]《フォーマル》(映画・歌・芸術作品において人・物事を公然と)称える, 称賛[賛美]する ◇songs that *celebrate* the joys of romantic love 恋愛の喜びを賛美する歌 ◇It was a movie *celebrating* the life and work of Martin Luther King. それはマーティン・ルーサー・キング牧師の人生と業績を称える映画だった

acclaim [他, ふつう受身で]《ややフォーマル》(本・映画・パフォーマンス・作家・演技者などを公然と)称賛[喝采]する, 歓呼して迎える ◇Mario Vargas Llosa, the internationally *acclaimed* novelist 国際的に称賛を受けている作家, マリオ・バルガス・リョサ ◇The work was *acclaimed* as a masterpiece. その作品は傑作と称えられた

commend [他]《フォーマル》(公然と・公式に)人・物事を)称賛する ◇She was *commended* on her handling of the situation. 彼女はその状況処理の仕方が称賛された ◇His designs were highly *commended* by the judges (= they did not get a prize but they were especially praised). 彼のデザインは審査員から別格で称賛された

glorify [他]《しばしばけなして》美化する ◇He denies that the movie *glorifies* violence. 彼はその映画は暴力を美化してはいないと言っている ❶ glorifyは正確には「称賛する」のではなく, 暴力・犯罪・麻薬使用・戦争などを肯定的に描いて, 人々にそれらが好ましい[許容できる]と考えさせるようにすることを指す. この語はほとんどの場合, 映画・テレビ・本の中で暴力などの描写について用いられる.
▸ **glorification** [名] [U] ◇the *glorification* of war 戦争の美化

compliment [他] (功績・振る舞い・外見について人に)賛辞を述べる, 称賛する, ほめる ◇She *complimented* him on his excellent German. 彼女は彼を素晴らしいドイツ語だと言ってほめた ❶ complimentはほとんどの場合, 公然と[公式に]称賛を表明するのではなく, 個々人が互いにほめ合うことを

↪praise

表す. ☞ **complimentary** (GOOD 6)
rave [自]《ややインフォーマル, 特にジャーナリズム》(口頭・文書で)激賞する ◇The critics *raved about* his performance in 'Hamlet'. 評論家たちは『ハムレット』での彼の演技を激賞した ❶rave は特に新聞や雑誌で, 映画・本・劇などへの人の反応について用いられることが多い.

precaution 名

precaution・defence・shield・safeguard・screen・buffer
人や物を害や危険から守ることを表す
【類語訳】対策, 予防, 備え, 防備, 防御, 盾, 隠れもの, 遮蔽物

文型&コロケーション

▶a precaution/ defence/ shield/ safeguard/ buffer **against** sth
▶**as** a precaution/ defence/ shield/ safeguard/ screen/ buffer
▶an **adequate** precaution/ defence/ safeguard
▶to **provide** a defence/ shield/ safeguard/ screen/ buffer

precaution [C]《ややフォーマル》(問題の防止[危険の回避]のための)対策, 予防(策), 備え ◇Serious injury can occur if proper *safety precautions* are not followed. 適切な安全対策に従わなければ, 大けがを起こす可能性がある ◇You must *take* all reasonable *precautions* to protect yourself. 自分自身を守るために適切な備えをすべて整えておかねばならない
defence〈英〉《米 **defense**》[C, U] (敵・天候・病気などに対する)防衛, 防御 ◇The town walls were built as a *defence* against enemy attacks. その街壁は敵の攻撃に対する防衛策として建設された ◇The harbour's sea *defences* are in poor condition. その港の防波堤はひどい状態だ ◇The body has natural *defence mechanisms* to protect it from disease. 体には病気から身を守る生まれながらの防御機構が備わっている ☞ **defend** (PROTECT)
shield [C] (防壁を形成する人・物事の)盾 ◇The gunman used the hostages as a *human shield*. 銃を持った男が人質を人間の盾として使った ◇She hid her true feelings behind a *shield* of cold indifference. 彼女は冷淡な無関心を装い本当の気持ちを隠した ☞ **shield** (PROTECT)
safeguard [C] (人々を害・危険から守るための)防衛(対)策 ◇The measures have been introduced as a *safeguard* against fraud. その措置は詐欺に対する防衛策として導入されている ◇Stronger legal *safeguards* are needed to protect the consumer. 消費者保護のため, より強力な法的防衛措置が求められている ☞ **safeguard** (PROTECT)
screen [C] (見え[気づか]ないように)隠すもの, 遮蔽物 ◇All the research was conducted behind a *screen* of secrecy. すべての調査は秘密のベールに包まれて行われた ◇We planted a *screen* of tall trees. 私たちは遮蔽のための高い木々を植えた
buffer [C] (衝撃・反対などの)緩衝[盾]となる物[人] ◇Support from family and friends acts as a *buffer* against stress. 家族や友人からの応援はストレスを和らげてくれる ◇Peacekeepers have been sent in to establish a *buffer zone* (= an area that keeps two other areas distant from one another) between the rival forces. 平和維持軍が敵対し合う勢力の間に緩衝地帯を設けるために送り込まれている

predict 動

predict・forecast・say・foresee・project・prophesy
将来起こると思うことを言う
【類語訳】予報する, 予測する, 予想する, 予知する, 予言する, 推定する

文型&コロケーション

▶to predict/ forecast/ foresee/ prophesy **that**...
▶to predict/ forecast/ say/ foresee/ prophesy **what/ how/ when/ where/ who/ whether**...
▶to be predicted/ forecast/ projected **to do sth**
▶to predict/ forecast/ foresee/ prophesy **the future**
▶to predict/ forecast/ foresee **a trend/ the outcome**
▶to predict/ foresee/ prophesy **war/ danger/ sb's death**
▶to be **difficult/ impossible to** predict/ forecast/ say/ foresee/ project
▶sth was **originally** predicted/ forecast/ foreseen/ projected
▶to predict/ forecast/ say sth **in advance**

predict [他] 予報[予測, 予想, 予知, 予言]する ◇a reliable method of *predicting* earthquakes 地震を予知する確かな方法 ◇It is impossible to *predict* with any certainty what effect this will have. 確信をもってこれがどのような影響を及ぼすか予測することは不可能だ ◇She *predicted* (that) the election result would be close. 彼女は選挙結果は接戦になるだろうと予測した ◇The trial is *predicted* to last for months. 裁判は何か月も続くと予想されている ☞ **prediction** (EXPECTATION)
forecast [他] 予報[予測, 予想, 予知]する ◇Experts are *forecasting* a recovery in the economy. 専門家たちは景気の回復を予測している ◇Snow is *forecast* for tomorrow. 明日は雪が降るとの予報だ ◇The costs were higher than those originally *forecast*. コストは当初の予想よりも高くなった ☞ **forecast** (EXPECTATION)

ノート **predict**と**forecast**の使い分け：predictは手元にある情報・知識・意見に基づいて, または宗教的な[不思議な]力を用いて, 起こることを予測すること. forecastはふつう手元にある情報に基づいて, しばしば科学的方法を用いて予測すること.

say [他, 自]《特に否定文と疑問文で》《ややインフォーマル, 特に話し言葉》(将来起こるだろうと思うことを)言う ◇*Who can say* what will happen between now and then? 今後何が起こるか誰が言えようか ◇'*When will it be finished?*' 'I couldn't *say*.'「それはいつ終わりますか」「何とも言えませんね」
foresee [他] (物事が将来起こるだろう)予測[予想]する；(物事が起こる前に)予知する ◇No one could have *foreseen* that things would turn out this way. 事態がこのような結果になることを誰も予測できなかっただろう ◇We do not *foresee* any problems. 私たちはいかなる問題も起こらないだろうと思っている ☞ **foresight** (EXPECTATION)
project [他, ふつう受身で]《特にビジネス》(現在起こっていることに基づいて将来の物事の大きさ・コスト・量を)予想[推定]する ◇A growth rate of 4% is *projected* for next year. 来年は4%の成長率が予想されている ◇The unemployment rate has been *projected* to fall. 失業率は低下すると推定されている ☞ **projection** (EXPECTATION)
prophesy [他] (宗教的な[不思議な]力を用いて将来起こることを)予言する ◇He *prophesied* that a flood would cover the Earth's surface. 彼は洪水で地球の表面が水没

predictable, prefer, prepare

するだろうと予言した ◇He experienced visions and later *prophesied* his own death. 彼は幻覚を体験して、後に自分自身の死を予言した ☞ **prophecy** (EXPECTATION)

predictable 形

**predictable・foreseeable・unsurprising・
to be expected**
物事が予測できる[起こりそうである]ことを表す
【類語訳】予測可能な, 予想どおりの, 予知できる, 予想される

文型&コロケーション

▸ predictable/ foreseeable/ unsurprising/ to be expected that...
▸ a predictable/ a foreseeable/ an unsurprising **result**
▸ predictable/ foreseeable **consequences**

predictable 予測可能な, 予想どおりの ◇He asked whether this was *predictable from* previous performances. これはこれまでのパフォーマンスから予想できることかどうか彼は聞いた ◇The disease follows a highly *predictable* pattern. その病気にはかなり予測可能なパターンが伴う ◇In March and April, the weather is much less *predictable*. 3月と4月は天気が予想するのがはるかに難しい 反意 **unpredictable**
➢**predictably** 副 ◇Prices were *predictably* high. 物価は予想どおり高かった ◇*Predictably*, the new regulations proved unpopular. 予想どおり, 新規制は不評であることが証明された

foreseeable 《ややフォーマル, 特に書き言葉》予測可能な, 予知できる ◇The statue will remain in the museum for *the foreseeable future* (= the period of time when you can predict what is going to happen, based on present circumstances). 当面の間, その彫像は博物館に残る予定です ◇Some of these problems were not *foreseeable* or preventable. これらの問題のうちいくつかは予測不可能または不可避であった 反意 **unforeseeable** (SURPRISING)

unsurprising 予想される, 予想どおりの; 驚くことでない, 当たり前の ◇Her failure to win the leadership race is *unsurprising*. 主導権争いでは彼女が敗北したも驚くに当たらない ◇It is *unsurprising* that people with dogs walk more than others. 犬を連れた人が他の人たちよりもたくさん歩くのは当たり前だ 反意 **surprising** (SURPRISING)
➢**unsurprisingly** 副 ◇Perhaps *unsurprisingly*, she refused to talk to the press. 予想どおりかもしれないが, 彼女は記者会見を拒否した

to be ex'pected フレーズ (特定の状況で起こると)予想される; 当たり前の ◇A little tiredness after taking these drugs is *to be expected*. これらの薬を服用すると少しだるくなると思っていてください ◇Of course, it's *only to be expected* that people will moan about paying tax. もちろん, 人々が税金の支払いに不満を言うのはごく当たり前のことだ ☞ **expect** (EXPECT)

prefer 動

prefer・favour・would rather...
一方より他方を取ることを表す
【類語訳】好む, 選ぶ

prefer (-rr-) [他]《進行形なし》(一方の物事を)好む, 選ぶ

…のほうがよい ◇I *prefer* jazz *to* rock music. 私はロックよりもジャズが好きだ ◇I *would prefer it if* you didn't tell anyone. 誰にも言わないでくれるとありがたいのですが ◇A local firm is *to be preferred*. 現地企業のほうがいいですね ◇I *prefer* my coffee black. コーヒーはブラックのほうがいい ◇The donor *prefers to* remain anonymous. ドナーは匿名でいたいとの御希望です ◇I *prefer* not to think about it. 私はそのことについて考えたくない ◇Would you *prefer* me to stay? 私はいたほうがいい ◇I *prefer* playing in defence. 私はディフェンスでプレーしたい ☞ **preference** (CHOICE 2), **preference** (TASTE), **preferred** (FAVOURITE)

favour 《英》《米 **favor**》[他]《ややフォーマル》(一方の制度・計画・行い方などを)好む, 選ぶ ◇Many countries *favour* a presidential system of government. 多くの国が大統領制を採っている ◇It's a resort *favoured* by families with young children. そこは小さな子どもがいる家庭に好まれる行楽地です ☞ **favourite, favoured** (FAVOURITE)

would rather... フレーズ《特に話し言葉》《ふつう'd ratherと短縮して》…するほうがよい ◇I'd *rather* die *than* give a speech. スピーチするくらいなら死んだほうがましです ◇'Do you want to come with us?' 'No, I'd *rather* not.'「私たちと一緒に行きませんか」「いいえ, 私は結構です」 ◇Would you *rather* walk or take the bus? 歩くかバスに乗るかどっちがいいですか ◇'Do you mind if I smoke?' 'Well, I'd *rather* you didn't.'「たばこを吸っても構いませんか」「うーん, 吸わないでくれたほうがいいな」

prepare 動

**1 prepare・draw sth up・draft・put sth together・
get sb/sth ready**
使用[実行]に備えて心構えをする, 人に…する心構えをさせる
【類語訳】準備をする, 用意をする, 作成[策定]する, 起草する

文型&コロケーション

▸ to prepare sth/ draw sth up/ draft sth/ put sth together/ get sth ready **for** sth
▸ to prepare/ draw up/ draft/ put together a **list/ report/ paper/ plan/ programme/ strategy**
▸ to prepare/ draw up/ draft a/ an **document/ contract/ agenda/ budget/ constitution/ treaty/ petition/ will**
▸ to prepare/ put together a **show/** to get a **show** ready
▸ to prepare sth/ draw sth up/ draft sth/ put sth together **carefully**

prepare [他]《ややフォーマル》(使用に備えて物事の)準備[用意]をする, (人に…する)準備[用意]をさせる ◇I've asked her to *prepare* a report for the meeting. 私は会議に向けて報告書を用意するよう彼女に頼んでいる ◇A hotel room is being *prepared* for them. 彼らのためにホテルの部屋が用意されている ◇The college *prepares* students for a career in business. その大学は学生に実業界への道に進む教育を施します ☞ **preparation** (PLANNING), **preparatory** (FIRST)

,draw sth 'up 句動詞 (文書・計画などを)作成[策定]する ◇Let's *draw up* a list of possible guests. 考えられる客のリストを作成しよう ❶draw sth up は公文書を用意することについて用いられることが多い. ◆to *draw up* a contract/ lease/ document/ treaty/ charter/ will (契約書/ 賃貸借契約書/ 文書/ 条約/ 憲章/ 遺言書を作成する). また, いろいろ他のビジネスの文脈でも用いられる. ◆to *draw up* an agenda/a memorandum/a report/a shortlist/a strategy (議事日程/回報/報告書/選抜候補者リスト/戦略を作成[策定]する).

draft 〜（または特に英で **draught**）［他］（書状・スピーチ・本などの）下書き［草稿］を書く, 起草する ◇I'll *draft* a letter for you. あなたのために手紙の下書きを書きましょう ◇Some of the clauses in the contract had been very poorly *drafted*. その契約書の条項のいくつかは非常に粗末な起草ぶりになっていた ☞ **draft** (PLAN 2)

ˌput sth toˈgether 句動詞 （要素をまとめ合わせて）組み立てる ◇I think we can *put together* a very strong case for the defence. 我々は被告側を弁護する非常に強力な主張を組み立てることができると思う

get sb/sth ˈready フレーズ 《ややインフォーマル》（使用に備えて物事の）準備［用意］をする, （人に…する）準備［用意］をさせる ◇Can you help me *get* everything *ready* for the party? パーティーの準備をいっさい切り盛りするのを手伝ってくれるかい ◇I'm just *getting* the kids *ready* for school. ちょうど子どもたちに学校へ行く準備をさせているところです

2 prepare・get ready・provide for sth・gear (yourself) up
しようとしている［起こることが予想される］ことに対して構える
【類語訳】準備をする, 用意をする, 備える

〔文型&コロケーション〕
▶ to prepare/ get ready/ provide/ gear up **for** sth
▶ to prepare/ get ready/ gear up **to do** sth
▶ to prepare **yourself**/ gear **yourself** up

prepare ［自, 他］《ややフォーマル》（しようとしていることの）準備［用意］をする,（起こることが予想されることに）備える ◇I had no time to *prepare*. 私は準備する時間がまったくなかった ◇The whole class is *preparing* for the exams. そのクラス全体で試験に備えての勉強をしている ◇I had been *preparing* myself for this moment. 私はこの瞬間に備えていた ◇I was *preparing* to leave. 私は出かける用意をしていた ☞ **preparation** (PLANNING), **preparatory** (FIRST)

get ˈready フレーズ 《ややインフォーマル, 特に話し言葉》（日常生活ですることの）準備［用意］をする ◇I have to *get ready* for work. 仕事の準備をしなきゃ ❶work以外の典型的な連語に school, dinner, supper が挙げられる.

proˈvide for sth 句動詞 《フォーマル》（将来起こるかもしれないことに）備える ◇It is impossible to *provide* for every eventuality. あらゆる不測の事態に備えることは不可能だ ☞ **provision** (PLANNING)

ˌgear ˈup, ˌgear yourself ˈup 句動詞 《ややインフォーマル, 特にジャーナリズム》（特別な行事・挑戦に備えて）準備をする ◇Cycle organizations are *gearing up* for National Bike Week. 自転車協会は全国自転車週間の準備をした ◇The supermarkets have been *gearing themselves up* to meet increased customer demand. スーパーは増加する顧客の需要を満たすために準備をしている

present 動

1 present・show・display・produce・unveil・launch
人に物事を見えるようにする
【類語訳】発表する, 公開する, 展示する, 出品する, 上映する, 上演する, 陳列する, 見せる, 提示する, 売り出す

〔文型&コロケーション〕
▶ to present/ show/ display/ unveil/ launch a new **product/ model**
▶ to present/ show/ display **your wares**
▶ to present/ show/ display **plans**
▶ to show/ display **a painting/ your work/ a collection/ a trophy**
▶ to present/ show/ display sth **proudly**

present ［他］（新製品・計画を）発表する, 公開する ◇They are going to *present* the new model at the trade fair. 展示会でそのニューモデルが発表される予定だ

show ［自, 他］（物事を［が］）公開［発表, 展示, 出品, 上映, 上演］する［される］ ◇The film is being *shown* now. その映画は現在上映中です ◇She plans to *show* her paintings early next year. 彼女は来年早々に絵画を発表する予定だ ☞ **show** (EXHIBITION)

display ［他］（ある場所に物を）展示する, 陳列する ;（人に物を）見せる ◇The exhibition gives local artists an opportunity to *display* their work. その展覧会は地元の芸術家に彼らの作品を展示する機会を与えている ◇She *displayed* her bruises for all to see. 彼女は皆に見えるようにあざを見せた ☞ **display** (EXHIBITION)

〔ノート〕**show** と **display** の使い分け：show のほうがインフォーマルで一般的. 芸術家自身が作品を展示する場合, ふつう display が用いられる. display は物ができる限り多くの人に見える場所に置かれ, ふつう魅力的に並べられていることを強調する

produce ［他］（物をある場所から）見せる,（見えるように）取り出す, 提示する ◇He *produced* a letter *from* his pocket. 彼は一通の手紙をポケットから取り出した ◇At the meeting the finance director *produced* the figures for the previous year. 会議で財務部長が前年の数字を提示した

unveil ［他］《ジャーナリズム》（新製品・計画を）発表する, 初公開する ◇They will be *unveiling* their new models at the Motor Show. モーターショーでは新型車が初公開される予定です ◇The government has *unveiled* plans for new energy legislation. 政府は新エネルギー法の計画を発表した

launch ［他］（新刊書・新製品を）売り出す ◇The book was *launched* amid a fanfare of publicity. その本は派手な宣伝と共に売り出された ◇The new model will be *launched* in July. 新モデルは7月に売り出される予定です

〔ノート〕**unveil** と **launch** の使い分け：unveil/launch a product/model（製品/モデルを初公開する［売り出す］）, unveil plans（計画を発表する）, launch a book（本を出版する）と言えるが, ×*launch* plans または ×*unveil* a book とは言えない.

2 ☞ DESCRIBE
present・show・portray・depict・represent
人や物事がどのようであるか［どのように人や物事を見てもらいたいか］を表す
【類語訳】見せる, 示す, 表現する, 描写する, 演じる, 描く

〔文型&コロケーション〕
▶ to present/ show/ portray/ depict/ represent sb/ sth **as** sth
▶ to present/ show/ portray/ depict/ represent sb/ sth **accurately**

▶to present/ show/ portray/ depict sb/ sth **clearly**
▶to present/ show/ portray/ depict sth **vividly**

present [他]《進行形まれ》(特定の観点から[方法で])見せる, 示す, 表現[描写]する ◇The company has decided it must *present* a more modern image. その会社はもっと現代的なイメージを示さねばならないとの結論を出した ◇You need to *present* yourself better. 君は自分をよりよく見せる必要がある ◇The article *presents* these proposals as misguided. その記事はこれらの提案が見当違いであるように描いている

show [他]《進行形まれ》(絵画・写真が)描いている, 写している ◇She had objected to a photo *showing* her in a bikini. 彼女はビキニ姿で写っている自分の写真に不服を申し立てていた ◇The picture *shows* St George slaying the dragon. その絵は聖ジョージが竜を殺している場面を描いている

portray [他]《進行形まれ》《ややフォーマル》(絵画・文章で)表現[描写]する;(不完全[不正確]な印象を与えるように)演じる ◇His war poetry vividly *portrays* life in the trenches. 彼の戦争詩は塹壕での生活を生き生きと描いている ◇Throughout the trial, he *portrayed* himself as the victim. 裁判の間中ずっと彼は被害者を演じた ☞ **portrayal** (DESCRIPTION)

depict [他]《進行形まれ》《ややフォーマル》(芸術作品の中で特定の方法で)表現[描写]する ◇The panels *depict* scenes from the life of St Ursula. そのパネル画は聖ウルスラの生涯の場面を描いている ◇The advertisements *depict* smoking as glamorous and attractive. その広告は喫煙を妖艶かつ魅惑的なものとして描いている ☞ **depiction** (DESCRIPTION)

represent [他]《進行形まれ》《フォーマル》(絵画の中で)表現[描写]する, 示す;(不当に)描く ◇The results are *represented* in fig 3 below. 結果は下の図3で示されている ◇The risks were *represented* as negligible. そのリスクは取るに足りないと述べられていた ☞ **representation** (DESCRIPTION)

📝 **portray, depict, represent** の使い分け: represent はこれらの語の中で最もフォーマルだが最も一般的な語で, 報告書やフォーマルなジャーナリズムなどで用いられる. depict は portray よりもいくぶん専門的な語で, 単なる絵・絵画ではない形態の芸術について用いられることが多い. 典型的な主語に work, scene, panel, mosaic, tapestry, fresco が挙げられる. portray はメディアにおける物事の描かれ方について用いられることが多い. 典型的な目的語に character, image, idea, view, society が挙げられる.

---

3 present・submit・file・hand sth in・lodge・table・send sth in・register・put sth in

検討[処理]用に物事を差し出すことを表す
【類語訳】提出する, 提示する, 申し立てる, 届け出る, 送付する, 表明する

📋 文型&コロケーション

▶to present/ submit/ hand sth in/ send in/ put in sth **to** sb
▶to present/ submit/ file/ lodge/ send in/ register/ put in an **application**
▶to present/ submit/ file/ lodge/ register/ put in a **claim/ complaint**
▶to present/ submit/ file/ lodge an **appeal**
▶to submit/ file/ lodge/ register a/ an **objection/ protest**
▶to present/ submit/ put in a **proposal/ request**
▶to present/ submit/ table a **bill/ motion/ resolution**
▶to present/ submit/ register/ send in your **views**
▶to present/ submit/ file/ send in a **report**
▶to **formally** present/ submit/ file/ table/ register sth

present [他] (検討用に)提出[提示]する ◇Eight options were *presented for* consideration. 検討する材料として8つの選択肢が提示された ◇Are you *presenting* a paper at the conference? 学会で論文を発表するつもりですか ◇He *presents* a convincing case. 彼は説得力のある主張を展開している

▶**presentation** [名] [U] ◇The trial was adjourned following the *presentation* of new evidence to the court. 法廷に新証拠が提出された後, その裁判は休廷になった

submit (-tt-) [他]《ややフォーマル》(権威者向けに文書・提案を)提出[提示]する ◇They have *submitted* an application for planning permission to build an extension. 彼らは建物の増築許可の申請を提出した ◇Completed projects must be *submitted* by 10 March. 研究課題が完成したら3月10日までに提出のこと

▶**submission** [名] [U] ◇When is the date for the *submission* of proposals? 提案の提出期限はいつですか

file [他, 自] (法的文書・請求を正式に)提出する, 申し立てる;(ジャーナリストが新聞に原稿を)送る ◇He *filed a lawsuit* against the company for $100,000 in damages. 彼は10万ドルの損害賠償を求めてその会社を相手取って訴訟を起こした ◇She decided to *file for* divorce. 彼女は離婚を申し立てることに決めた ◇More than one correspondent *filed* a story describing the spectacle of a cruise missile travelling up the street. 複数の通信者がその通りの上空を巡航ミサイルが移動するすごい光景を描いた話を送った ❶file の目的語には suit, claim, petition, appeal, application, charges, for bankruptcy も用いられる.

hand sth 'in [句動] (権威者に課題・紛失物を)提出する, 届け出る ◇You must *hand in* this homework by the end of the week. この宿題は週の終わりまでに提出すること ◇I *handed* the watch *in* to the police. 私はその腕時計を警察に届け出た ◇I advise you to *hand in your notice* (= formally tell your employer that you want to stop working for them). 辞表を提出することを勧めます

lodge [他]《フォーマル》(公的機関・当局に正式に発言を)提出する, 申し立てる ◇They *lodged* a compensation claim against the factory. 彼らは工場に対して賠償請求書を提出した ◇Portugal has *lodged* a complaint with the International Court of Justice. ポルトガルは国際司法裁判所に提訴した ❶lodge の目的語には appeal, application, objection, protest も用いられる.

table [他]《英》(議論のために正式に)提出する ◇They have *tabled* a motion for debate at the next Party Conference. 彼らは次回の党会議での議論のための動議を提出した ❶table の目的語には amendment, motion, question, resolution も用いられる. ☞ **propose** (PROPOSE)

send sth 'in [句動] (郵送で)送付する, 提出する ◇Have you *sent in* your application yet? 願書はもう送付したのか

register [他]《フォーマル》(意見を正式に[公然と])表明する ◇China has *registered* a protest over foreign intervention. 中国は外国からの干渉に対して抗議を表明している ❶register の目的語には view, opinion, disapproval, complaint も用いられる. opinion を目的語に取る場合, ふつう既知の事柄に反対の意を表明することを指す.

put sth 'in [句動] (正式に請求書・要請書を)提出する

↳**present**

◇The company has *put in* a claim for damages. その会社は損害賠償を請求している ❶*put in*の目的語にはbid, offer, request, proposalも用いられる。

4 present・host・introduce
テレビ[ラジオ]番組に出演して、番組や出演者の詳細を伝える
【類語訳】司会を務める、紹介する

文型&コロケーション
▶to present/ host/ introduce a **programme/ show**

present [他]《英》(テレビ・ラジオ番組の)司会を務める ◇She used to *present* a gardening show on TV. 彼女は昔テレビでガーデニング番組の司会をよく務めていた
host [他] (テレビ・ラジオ番組の)司会を務める ◇Charlie Rose will *host* tonight's show. チャーリー・ローズが今夜の番組の司会を務めます ❶《米》ではhostは番組の司会を務めることを表す一般的な語で、《英》でも用いられるが、そのほとんどの場合、ゲスト・観客を招く番組に用いられる
introduce [他]《特に話し言葉》(テレビ・ラジオ番組で出演者を)紹介する ◇May I *introduce* my first guest on the show tonight... それでは今夜の番組の最初のゲストをご紹介します…

presentation [名]

presentation・demonstration・demo
人々の集団に物事が説明[提示]される場[行為]を表す
【類語訳】発表、プレゼンテーション、実演、デモンストレーション

文型&コロケーション
▶a **sales/ product** presentation/ demonstration/ demo
▶to **give/ watch** a presentation/ demonstration/ demo

presentation [C, U] (新しい考え・製品・作品に関する)発表[説明](会);(行為としての)プレゼンテーション ◇The sales manager will give a *presentation on* the new products. 営業部長による新製品の説明会が行われる予定です ◇The main emphasis of the training will be on *presentation* skills. 研修の主な力点はプレゼンの技術に置かれるでしょう
demonstration [C] (使い[やり]方に関する)実演、デモンストレーション ◇We were given a brief *demonstration* of the computer's functions. 私たちはそのコンピューターの機能について短い実演を見せてもらった

> **ノート presentation と demonstration の使い分け:**
> presentationは物・考えに関する説明で、demonstrationは常に実地による物・技術に関する説明を指す。◆Candidates have to give a short *presentation* on a subject of their choice.(候補者は自分が選んだテーマに関して短い説明をしなければならない)◆Can you give me a practical *demonstration*?(実演をしてもらえますか)

demo [C]《インフォーマル》(使い[やり]方に関する)実演、デモンストレーション ◇Look, I'll give you a *demo*. 見て、私が実演します

presenter [名]☞REPORTER

presenter・announcer・host・anchor/anchorman/anchorwoman・broadcaster・commentator・newscaster・newsreader

テレビ[ラジオ]番組で司会[話]をする人
【類語訳】司会者、アナウンサー、アンカー、キャスター、コメンテーター、ニュースキャスター

文型&コロケーション
▶a **radio/ television/ TV** presenter/ announcer/ host/ anchor/ anchorman/ anchorwoman / broadcaster/ commentator/ newscaster/ newsreader
▶a **news** anchor/ anchorman/ anchorwoman
▶a **sports** presenter/ announcer/ anchor/ anchorman/ anchorwoman/ broadcaster/ commentator

presenter [C]《英》(ラジオ・テレビ番組の)総合司会者 ◇Jenni Murray, *presenter* of 'Woman's Hour'「女性の時間」の総合司会者、ジェニー・マレー ❶《米》ではこの仕事を務める人はannouncerと呼ばれる
announcer [C]《米》(ラジオ・テレビ番組の)総合司会者、アナウンサー ◇The continuity *announcer* advertised a few forthcoming programmes. 番組紹介のアナウンサーがこれから放送される番組をいくつか宣伝した
host [C]《特に米》(テレビ・ラジオ番組でゲストと話をする)司会者 ◇a TV game show *host* テレビのクイズ番組の司会者
anchor《特に米》(または **anchorman, anchorwoman**《英、米》)[C] (ラジオ・テレビ番組の)総合司会者、アンカー ◇ABC news *anchor* Peter Jennings ABCニュースのアンカー、ピーター・ジェニングズ ❶《米》ではnews anchorがニュース記事を司会し、sports anchorがスポーツ記事を司会する。《英》ではanchorman, anchorwoman, news anchorがニュース記事を司会するが、sports anchorはふつう用いられない
broadcaster [C]《ややフォーマル》(テレビ・ラジオ番組で司会[話]をする)キャスター ◇She is a writer and *broadcaster* on environmental matters. 彼女は環境問題に関する記者でありキャスターでもある

> **ノート presenter, announcer, host, anchor, broadcaster の使い分け:** anchorはニュース番組の司会を務める人。presenter(《英》)とannouncer(《米》)はテレビ・ラジオのあらゆる番組の司会を務める人。《英》ではhostはゲスト・観客を迎える娯楽番組の司会者で、《米》ではより真面目な番組の司会者も指すことがある。broadcasterはさまざまな番組で司会・話をするが、特定の番組を担当していない人のことを指す。✕Jenni Murray, *anchor/broadcaster* of 'Woman's Hour'

commentator [C]《特に英》(テレビ・ラジオ番組の)コメンテーター ◇He's one of the great sports *commentators* of our time. 彼は現代の素晴らしいスポーツ・コメンテーターの一人だ
newscaster [C]《フォーマル》(テレビ・ラジオのニュース番組の)ニュースキャスター ◇She was named *newscaster* of the year. 彼女はその年のニュースキャスターに指名された
newsreader [C]《英》(テレビ・ラジオのニュース番組の)ニュースキャスター ◇The *newsreader* reported that the man had not yet been named. ニュースキャスターはその男はまだ特定されていないと報じた

press [動]

1 press・push・squeeze
装置の一部に指[手、足]で作動のための圧力をかける
【類語訳】押す、引く、しぼる

pressure

文型&コロケーション
▶to press/ push/ squeeze **on** sth
▶to press/ push a **bell/ button/ key/ bell/ switch**
▶to press/ push/ squeeze (sth) **hard/ gently**

press [他, 自] (装置・機械の一部を)押す ◇*Press* any key to restart your computer. どれかキーを押してコンピューターを再起動させましょう ◇She *pressed* the gas pedal gently. 彼女はアクセルをそっと踏んだ ◇*Press* here to open. ここを押して開けてください
push [他] (機械のボタン・スイッチなどを)押す ◇*Push* the red button to open the doors. 赤いボタンを押してドアを開けてください ❶この意味ではpushはふつうbuttonと共に用いられるが、switchやbellなど他のとも用いられる
squeeze [他, 自] (指・手で)引く, しぼる ◇He slowly *squeezed the trigger* (= of a gun). 彼はゆっくりと引き金をしぼった ◇She *squeezed* on the reins and the cart came to a halt. 彼女が手綱を引くと, 荷馬車は止まった

ノート **press, push, squeeze の使い分け**: press が最も一般的な語で, 指・手・足を使って押すことを指す. push はほとんどの場合, button と共に用いられる. squeeze は一本 [すべて]の指を物に引っ掛けて曲げる動作に用いられる.

2 press・push・pressure・coerce・pressurize・twist sb's arm
必死に説得して[無理やり]人にやりたくないことをさせようとする
【類語訳】迫る, せき立てる, 押しつける, 強制する, 強要する

push   press   pressure   coerce
                 pressurize
                 twist sb's arm

文型&コロケーション
▶to press/ push/ pressure/ coerce/ pressurize sb **into** (doing) sth
▶to press sb/ push sb/ pressure sb/ coerce sb/ pressurize sb/ twist sb's arm **to do** sth
▶to press/ push sb **for** sth

press [他] 迫る, せき立てる, 押しつける, 強制する, 強要する ◇The bank is *pressing* us for repayment of the loan. 銀行がローンの返済を我々に迫っている ◇They are *pressing* us to make a quick decision. 彼らは私たちに即決を迫っている ◇I did not *press* him further on the issue (= ask him more questions about it). 私はその問題についてそれ以上彼を問い詰めなかった ❶press は例えば, 記者が繰り返し質問することで政治家から回答・情報を得ようとするなど, しばしば人に発言[質問に対する回答]を迫るのに用いられる. ◆When *pressed* by journalists, he refused to comment. (記者に迫られても, 彼はコメントを拒否した)
☞ **press for** sth (DEMAND 動)
push [他] 迫る, せき立てる, 押しつける, 強制する, 強要する ◇My teacher *pushed* me into entering the competition. 先生が私にその大会に出場するようせっついた ◇No one *pushed* you to take the job, did they? 誰もその仕事を引き受けるようあなたに迫りませんでしたよね

ノート **press と push の使い分け**: 多くの場合, 両語とも使用可能. ◆They were *pressing/pushing* the minister for a decision. (大臣は決定を迫られていた) しかしながら, press のほうが push よりも強制的であることがある. press は相手に自分がしてほしい[してもらう必要がある]ことを迫る場合. push は相手が楽しめる[利する]と思うことを迫る場合に用いられる. ✕My teacher *pressed* me into entering the competition.

pressure [他, しばしば受身で] (特に米) (人に)…しなければならないと思わせる, 強制[強要]する ◇Don't let yourself be *pressured* into making a hasty decision. 早急に決定を下さねばならないとは思わなくていいですよ ◇No one has the right to *pressure* you. You can always say no. 誰もあなたに強制する権利はないよ. いつでも拒否できるからね ❶(英)では pressure の代わりに pressurize を用いるほうが一般的だが, pressure も用いられる
coerce [他]《ややフォーマル》(人を)脅迫して…させる, 無理やり…させる ◇They were *coerced* into negotiating a settlement. 彼らは無理やり和解への協議の席に着かされた ◇She hadn't *coerced* him in any way. 彼女は一切彼に強制していなかった
pressurize (英ではまた **-ise**) [他, しばしば受身で]《英》(人に)…しなければならないと思わせる, 強制[強要]する ◇Stop trying to *pressurize* me! 私に強制しようとするのはやめて
twist sb's 'arm [行为]《インフォーマル》(友好的に)強制する ◇No one *twisted my arm*. I wanted to come. 誰かに強制されたんじゃないよ. 私が来たかったんだよ

pressure 名

1 pressure・stress・tension・strain・demands・heat
実生活において諸問題が引き起こす不安な気持ち
【類語訳】プレッシャー, 重圧, ストレス, 緊張, 負担, 緊迫

文型&コロケーション
▶to be **under** pressure/ stress/ strain
▶pressure/ stress/ demands/ heat **on** sb
▶**considerable** pressure/ stress/ tension/ strain/ demands
▶**social/ economic/ financial** pressure/ stress/ demands
▶to **cause** stress/ tension/ strain
▶to **cope with** the pressure/ stress/ tension/ strain/ demands
▶to **deal with/ handle** the pressure/ stress/ tension/ demands
▶to **relieve/ release** the pressure/ stress/ tension/ strain
▶to **feel** the pressure/ tension/ strain/ heat
▶to **take** the pressure/ strain/ heat
▶to **suffer from** stress/ tension

pressure [U] (または **pressures** [複数で]) (達成の必要性[特定の振る舞い]に伴う)プレッシャー, 重圧 ◇She was unable to attend because of the *pressure* of work. 彼女は仕事が忙しくて出席することができなかった ◇How can anyone enjoy the *pressures* of city life? 都会生活のプレッシャーをどうすれば楽しめようか ☞ **under pressure** (TENSE)
stress [U, C, ふつう複数で] (実生活において諸問題が引き起こす)ストレス ◇emotional/mental *stress* 心理的/精神的ストレス ◇*stress*-related illnesses ストレスから引き起こされる病気 ◇*Stress* is often a factor in the development of long-term sickness. ストレスはしばしば長期的な病気を進行させる要因となる ◇She failed to withstand the *stresses and strains* of public life. 彼女は公人とし

↳pressure

ての生活のストレスと重圧に耐えられなかった ☞ **stressful** (STRESSFUL), **stressed** (TENSE)

|ノート| **pressure** と **stress** の使い分け：suffer from stress という表現が一般的。pressure は stress を引き起こすもの。

tension [U, C, ふつう複数で] （くつろぐことのできない）緊張 ◇She was suffering from nervous *tension*. 彼女は神経の緊張に悩まされていた ◇Walking and swimming are excellent for releasing *tensions*. 散歩と水泳は緊張をほぐすのに最適です ☞ **tense** (STRESSFUL), **tense** (TENSE)

strain [U, C] （する[管理する]ことが多すぎることによる）重圧, 圧迫；負担 ◇Their marriage is under great *strain* at the moment. 彼らの結婚生活は今, 多大な重圧下にある ◇These repayments are *putting a strain on* our finances. これらの返済のために私たちの財政は逼迫している ◇Relax, and let us take the *strain* (= do things for you). リラックスしてね, 私たちがその負担を引き受けるから ☞ **strained** (STRESSFUL), **strained** (TENSE)

demands [複数で] （困難な[疲れさせる, 心配させる]）ことによる）負担 ◇the *demands* of children/work 子ども/仕事がもたらす負担 ◇Flying makes enormous *demands* on pilots. 飛行はパイロットに大きな負担となる

heat [U] （ややフォーマル, 特にジャーナリズム）（…する[…を成し遂げる]ための）重圧, 緊迫 ◇*The heat is on* now that the election is only a week away. 選挙が1週間後に控えているのでいま緊迫している ◇Can she take the *heat* of this level of competition? 彼女はこのレベルの大会の重圧には耐えられますか

2 pressure・force・coercion・compulsion
脅しや力ずくで人に…させようとすること
【類語訳】圧力, 強制, 暴力, 無理強い, 義務

pressure — coercion / compulsion — force →

|文型&コロケーション|
▸pressure/ compulsion **on** sb
▸**under** pressure/ coercion/ compulsion
▸**by** force/ coercion/ compulsion
▸pressure/ compulsion **to do sth**
▸**physical** pressure/ force/ coercion
▸**legal** pressure/ compulsion
▸**to use** force/ coercion

pressure [U] （人に…させようとする）圧力, 強制, 強い要求 ◇The *pressure for* change continued to mount. 改革を求める強い要求は高まり続けた ◇My parents never *put any pressure on* me to work in the family business. 両親は私に家業を手伝うよう強いることは決してない ◇Teenagers may find it difficult to resist *peer pressure* (= pressure to behave in the same way as others of your age). 十代の若者は同年代の人と同調しなければならないという圧力に耐えるのに苦労するかもしれない

force [U] （人に…させようとする）暴力 ◇We will achieve much more by persuasion than by *brute force*. 暴力よりも説得によるほうがずっと多くのことが達成できるでしょう ◇There were plans to seize power by *force of arms* (= by military action). 武力によって政権を握る計画があった ☞ **force** (FORCE 動)

coercion [U] 《フォーマル》（脅し・暴力による）強制, 無理強い ◇His defence was that he was *acting under coercion*. 自分は強制されて行っていたと彼は弁明した

compulsion [U, C] 《ややフォーマル》（法律・規則・契約による）強制, 義務 ◇You are *under no compulsion* to pay. あなたに支払う義務はありませんよ ◇There are no *compulsions* on students to attend classes. 生徒に授業に出席するよう強制力をかけてはいない ☞ **compel** (FORCE 動), **compulsory** (NECESSARY)

pretend 動

pretend・act・feign・put sth on・adopt・fake・bluff・assume
物事が真実であると人々に信じ込ませるために特定の方法で振る舞う
【類語訳】振りをする, 装う, 見せかける, 演じる

|文型&コロケーション|
▸to pretend/ feign/ assume **interest/ indifference**
▸to feign/ fake **illness/ injury**
▸to put on/ adopt/ assume an **accent**
▸to put on/ adopt/ assume **an air of** concern/ indifference, etc.

pretend [自, 他] 振りをする, 装う, 見せかける ◇I'm tired of having to *pretend* all the time. 私は常にうわべをつくろわねばならないことに疲れている ◇Of course it was wrong; it would be hypocritical to *pretend otherwise*. もちろんそれは間違いだった, しかしそうでない振りをすれば偽善的だろう ◇I *pretended to be* asleep. 私は寝た振りをした ◇He *pretended* not to notice. 彼は気づかない振りをした ◇She *pretended (that)* she was his niece. 彼女は彼の姪を装った ◇He *pretended to* his family that everything was fine. 彼は家族にすべて順調である振りをした ◇Why hurt her by *pretending* an interest he did not feel? 《フォーマル》彼がもともとない興味がある振りをしたらどうして彼女を傷つけることになるの ❶ pretend はフォーマルな文脈では一つの名詞しか伴わない.

act [自] 《名詞補語や形容詞補語と共に》（特定のタイプの人を）演じる ◇He's been *acting* the devoted husband all day. 彼は一日中献身的な夫を演じていた ◇I decided to *act* dumb. 私はばかを演じることにした ☞ **act** (PLAY 動 2)

feign [他] 《ややフォーマル, 書き言葉》（病気・けがなどの[を]）振りをする, 装う ◇He survived the massacre by *feigning* death. 彼は死んだ振りをして虐殺を免れた ◇'A present for me?' she asked with *feigned* surprise. 「私にプレゼント」と彼女は驚いた振りをして聞いた

put sth 'on [句動詞] 《ややインフォーマル》（考えて[感じて]いる）振りをする；（特定の話し方を）装う ◇I don't think she was hurt. She was just *putting it on*. 彼女は傷ついてなかったと思うよ. 彼女はただ傷ついた振りをしていただけさ ◇He *put on* an American accent. 彼はアメリカ人なまりを装った

adopt [他] 《フォーマル》（特定の態度・表情・話し方を）取る ◇She *adopted* an air of indifference. 彼女は無関心な振りをした ◇He smiled and *adopted* a more casual tone of voice. 彼はほほ笑み, より気さくな口調に切り換えた

fake [他, 自] 《ややインフォーマル》（病気・けがなどを[の]）装う, 振りをする ◇She's not really sick — she's just *faking* it. 彼女は本当は病気じゃないよ — その振りをしてるだけさ ◇He *faked* a yawn. 彼はあくびをした振りをした ◇Do you think she's *faking*? 彼女, 仮病を使ってると思う ❶ fake

prevent, previous

は目的語なしで用いられる場合、ふつう否定的な文[疑問文]で faking の形で用いられる。◆But what if he wasn't *faking*? (しかし彼が仮病を使ってなかったらどうなる).

bluff [自, 他]《する[知っている]》振りをする ◆I don't think he'll shoot — I think he's just *bluffing*. 彼は撃つつもりはないと思う─ただ振りをしているだけだと思うよ ◆She successfully *bluffed her way* through the interview (= by pretending to be sb she was not or know things that she did not know). 彼女は知ったかぶりでうまく面接を切り抜けた ☞ **bluff** (TRICK)

assume [他]《フォーマル, 時にけなして》(考えて[感じて])いる振りをする;(特定の話し方を)装う ◆She *assumed* an air of concern. 彼女は関心のある振りをした ◆He had *assumed* a stage Southern accent. 彼は芝居で使われるような南部訛りをまねていたことがある

> ノート **put sth on, adopt, assume** の使い分け：**put sth on** はややインフォーマルで, **adopt** と **assume** はフォーマル。**assume** は **adopt** よりもけなして用いられ, 人の振る舞いが見せかけであることを示唆する。

prevent 動

prevent・stop・avoid・keep sb from sth・avert・preclude・rule sb/sth out・restrain
何かが起こらないようにしたり、人が何かをしないようにしたりする
【類語訳】防ぐ、妨げる、止める、やめる、避ける、させないようにする、回避する、不可能にする、除外する、排除する、やめさせる

> 文型&コロケーション
> ▶ to prevent/ stop/ keep/ preclude/ restrain **sb from doing sth**
> ▶ to prevent sb/ stop/ avoid/ preclude **doing sth**
> ▶ to prevent/ stop/ avoid/ avert a/ an **crisis/ accident**
> ▶ to prevent/ avoid/ avert a **disaster/ catastrophe/ tragedy/ conflict**
> ▶ to prevent/ stop the **spread** of sth
> ▶ to prevent/ avoid/ preclude/ rule out the **possibility** of sth
> ▶ to prevent/ avoid/ preclude the **need/ necessity** for sth/ to do sth
> ▶ to **forcibly/ physically** prevent/ stop/ restrain sb/ sth
> ▶ to **narrowly** avoid/ avert sth
> ▶ to prevent/ avoid sth **altogether/ at all costs**

prevent [他] 防ぐ, 妨げる ◆These strategies are aimed at *preventing* crime. こうした方策は犯罪防止が目的だ ◆He is *prevented* by law from holding a licence. 彼は法律で免許を持つことを禁じられている ◆Nothing would *prevent* him from speaking out against injustice. 彼が声高に不正を追及することを何物も止められないだろう
▶ **prevention** 名 [U] ◆accident/crime *prevention* 事故/犯罪防止 ◆the *prevention* of disease 病気の予防

stop (-pp-) [他] 止める, やめる ◆I want to go and you can't *stop* me. 私は行きたいしあなたには止められない ◆The activists failed to *stop* the tests from going ahead. 活動家たちは実験が進行するのを阻止できなかった ◆There's nothing to *stop you* from accepting the offer. あなたがその申し出を受けようとご自由です

> ノート **prevent** と **stop** の使い分け：**stop** のほうがよりインフォーマルであるが, 多くの場合どちらの語も用いられることができ

る。**prevent** のほうが、何も起きないように誰かが事前に計画する行動を示唆する傾向が強い。**stop** は、すでに進行中の物事を止めるために人が取る緊急の行動について用いられることが多い。

avoid [他]《よくないことを》避ける ◆The accident could have been *avoided*. その事故は避けられたかもしれない ◆They narrowly *avoided* defeat in the semi-final. 彼らは準決勝で危うく負けるところだった ◆Getting involved in a court case is something to be *avoided* at all costs. 裁判沙汰に巻き込まれることだけは何としても避けたいところだ

'keep sb from sth 句動 (人に事を)させないようにする ◆I hope I'm not *keeping* you *from* your work. お仕事のお邪魔でなければいいのですが ◆The church bells *keep* me *from* sleeping. 教会の鐘の音のせいで眠れない

avert [他]《書き言葉》(差し迫った危機などを)避ける, 防ぐ, 回避する ◆A disaster was narrowly *averted*. かろうじて災害は回避された ◆He did his best to *avert* suspicion. 彼は嫌疑をかけられないよう何でもした ◆Talks are taking place in an attempt to *avert* a strike. ストライキ回避のための話し合いが行われているところだ

preclude [他]《フォーマル》妨げる, 不可能にする ◆Lack of time *precludes* further discussion. 時間が足りないのでこれ以上は議論できません ◆His religious beliefs *precluded* him serving in the army. 彼は宗教的信条から兵役を拒否した ❶ *preclude* の主語は, その場の状況や出来事であって, 人ではない。

,rule sb/sth 'out 句動 《規定・考慮によって人・物事を》除外する, 排除する ◆His age effectively *ruled* him *out* as a possible candidate. 彼は事実上, 年齢制限により候補者とはなりえなかった ◆Common sense and logistics *ruled out* this option. 常識と事業計画に鑑みてこの選択肢は除外された

restrain [他]《ややフォーマル, 書き言葉》(力ずくで)やめさせる, 抑える, 抑制する ◆I had to *restrain* her from hitting out at passers-by. 彼女が通行人たちに殴りかかろうとするのを制止しなければならなかった

previous 形

previous・old・former・past・prior・distant・remote・bygone
物事がもっと早い時期に帰属することを表す
【類語訳】以前の、前の、先立つ、先の、昔の、過去の、過ぎ去った、元の、以前…、事前の

> 文型&コロケーション
> ▶ (a) previous/ former/ past/ distant/ remote/ bygone **era/ times**
> ▶ a previous/ past/ distant/ remote/ bygone **age**
> ▶ a previous/ former/ past/ prior **existence**
> ▶ (a) previous/ past **experience/ history/ life**
> ▶ a previous/ former/ past **owner/ president/ prime minister**
> ▶ a previous/ prior **engagement**
> ▶ previous/ prior **knowledge**
> ▶ former/ past **glories**
> ▶ the distant/ remote **past**
> ▶ a distant/ remote **ancestor**
> ▶ **very/ fairly** old/ distant/ remote

↪**previous**

previous [名詞の前で] 以前の, 前の, 先立つ, 先の ◇No *previous* experience is necessary for this job. 以前の経験はこの仕事に必要ありません ◇The car has only had one *previous* owner. この車の前のオーナーは一人しかいません ◇She is his daughter from a *previous* marriage. 彼女は彼の前妻との間にできた娘です ◇We had met on two *previous* occasions. 私たちは以前に2度会う機会があった 反意 **current** (RECENT), **future** (NEXT)
▸**previously** 副 ◇The building had *previously* been used as a hotel. その建物は以前ホテルとして使用されていた 反意 **currently** (RECENT)

old [名詞の前で] (時代・人生の中での)昔の, 過去の ◇Things were different in **the old days**. 昔は状況は違っていた ◇I went back to visit my *old* school. 私は母校を訪れるために戻った

former [名詞の前で] 《ややフォーマル》 過ぎ去った, 昔の, 過去の; 前の, 元の, 旧… ◇This fine ruin was, in *former* times, a royal castle. この素晴らしい遺跡は, 昔, 国王の城だった ◇The historic quarter of the city has been restored to **its former glory**. その都市の歴史地区はかつての見事な姿に復元されている ◇It is one of the countries of the *former* Soviet Union. それは旧ソビエト連邦諸国の一つだ
▸**formerly** 副 ◇I learned that the house had *formerly* been an inn. 私はその家が元々宿屋だったことを知った

past [ふつう名詞の前で] 過ぎ去った, 昔の, 過去の; 前の, 元の ◇In *past* years the industry received large subsidies. 過去にその産業は莫大な助成金を受けた ◇The book is a celebration of working class life in times *past*. その本は昔の労働者階級の生活を賛美したものだ ◇The time for discussion is *past*. 話し合いの時間は終わった ◇From *past* experience I'd say he'd probably forgotten the time. 過去の経験から, 彼はおそらくその時のことを忘れてしまっていたんでしょうね ◇The reunion is for *past* and present students of the college. その再会のつどいは大学の卒業生と在校生のためのものです ◇Let's forget about who was more to blame — it's all *past history*. 誰により責任があるかについては忘れよう—それはもうすべて過去のことだ 反意 **present** (RECENT), **future** (NEXT)

ノート **old, former, past** の使い分け: **old** は特に自分自身の人生の事柄について用いられる. ◆my *old* school/teacher/colleagues (私の母校/恩師/昔の同僚). **former** もこのような場合に用いられるが, ややフォーマルな響きがあり, **past** は使用不可. ✕my *past* school/teacher/colleagues. ◆old *friends* (昔からの友達) は長年知っている友人を指し, former *friends* (昔の友達) はもはや友人ではない人を指す. **old** は **the old days** の句以外では, 過ぎ去った時代については用いられない. ✕an *old* age/era. ✕in *old* times/years/centuries. これらの場合, **former** も **past** も使用可能. **former** のほうがよりフォーマルな響きがあり, **past** のほうが個人的・文学的な響きがある. 自分自身の過去 experience (過去の経験) のように用いることが可能で, 過去において自分に起こった出来事[出来事から学んだこと]を指す. **previous** experience (以前までの経験) はふつう特定の仕事での経験を指す. ◆your *old/former/past* experience. **former** はもはや存在しない[変わってしまっている] 国・組織を修飾することがある. ◆the *former* Yugoslav republic (旧ユーゴスラビア共和国). ✕the *old/past* Yugoslav republic.

price

prior [名詞の前で] 《フォーマル》 以前の, 前の, 先立つ, 先の, 事前の ◇Visits are by *prior* arrangement. ご来訪は事前に予約願います ◇This information must not be disclosed without *prior* written consent. この情報は書面による事前承諾なしに公開してはなりません ◇They have a ***prior claim*** (= already existing and therefore more important) to the property. 彼らはその財産の優先権を持っている ❶ **prior** は **previous** よりフォーマルな表現で, 特に予約をする[許可を与える, 二人[二つ]の人・物事のうちどちらが重要かを決定する]ことについて用いられる. 連語には **arrangement, engagement, commitment, notice, notification, warning, consent, approval, authorization, permission, claim** が挙げられる.

distant [ふつう名詞の前で] (時間的に)遠い(昔[未来])の ◇The time we spent together is now a *distant* memory. 私たちが一緒に過ごした時間は今では遠い昔の思い出だ ◇We will be moving house in the ***not too distant future*** (= quite soon). それほど遠くない将来, 私たちは家を引っ越す予定だ

remote [名詞の前で] (時間的に)はるか遠い(昔[未来])の ◇a *remote* ancestor (= one who lived a long time ago) はるか遠い昔の祖先

ノート **distant** と **remote** の使い分け: **distant** past/future は必ずしも **remote** past/future ほど遠く離れてはいない. 「それほど遠くない過去/将来」の意味で **not too distant** past/future と言うことができるが, ✕the not too *remote* past/future とは言えない.

bygone [名詞の前で] 《書き言葉》 昔の, 過去の ◇The horse and cart belongs to a *bygone* era. その馬車は過去の時代のものだ

price 名 ☞RATE

price・cost・value・expense・worth
物に対して支払わねばならないお金
【類義訳】値段, 価格, 金額, 費用, 価値, 出費

文型&コロケーション
▸the **high** price/ cost/ value
▸the **considerable/ enormous** cost/ value/ expense
▸the **real/ true** price/ cost/ value/ worth
▸the **market/ net** price/ cost/ value/ worth
▸to **put/ set** a price/ value **on** sth
▸to **increase/ reduce** the price/ cost/ value/ expense
▸to **raise/ double/ lower** the price/ cost/ value
▸to **cut** the price/ cost

price [C, U] (商品・サービスの)値段, 価格, 金額 ◇house/retail/oil/share *prices* 住宅価格/小売価格/石油価格/株価 ◇The *price* includes dinner, bed and breakfast. その値段は夕食, 宿泊, 朝食込みです ◇He was charging a very high *price* for it. 彼はそれに対し非常に高い金額を請求していた ◇How much are these? They don't have a *price* on them. これらはいくらですか. 値段がついていませんけど ◇I can't afford it **at that price**. その価格では私には買う余裕はない ◇It's amazing how much computers have ***come down in price*** over the past few years. ここ数年でのコンピューターの価格の下がりようには驚かされる ◇to pay ***half/full price*** for sth 物の半額/全額を支払う

cost [C, U] (購入・製造・実行に伴う)値段, 価格, 費用 ◇A

new computer system has been installed at a *cost* of £80,000. 新しいコンピューターシステムが8万ポンドの価格で導入された ◇Allow $25 per day to *cover the cost* of meals. 食費にあてられるように1日あたり25ドルは取っておきましょう ◇Consumers will have to *bear* the full *cost* of these pay increases. 消費者がこれらの賃上げの全費用を負担せねばならないだろう ◇The total *cost to* you (= the amount you have to pay) is £3,000. あなたにかかる全費用は3千ポンドです ◇The plan had to be abandoned on grounds of *cost* (= it was too expensive). その計画は費用が理由で断念せざるをえなかった ◇sharp rises in *the cost of living* (= the amount of money that people need to pay for food, clothing and somewhere to live) 生活費の急激な上昇

value [U, C] (お金・商品と交換可能な)価値, 価格 ◇The winner will receive a prize *to the value of* £1,000. 受賞者には1千ポンド相当の賞品が贈られます ◇Sports cars tend to *hold their value* well. スポーツカーの価格は下がらない傾向にある ◇Tickets were changing hands at three times their *face value* (= the value shown on the front). チケットは額面価格の3倍で取り引きされていた ◇London property *values* are rising fast. ロンドンの不動産価格が高騰している ☞ **valuable** (VALUABLE 1)

ノート price, cost, value の使い分け：price は人に求める商品・サービスの支払い額を指す。◆to ask/charge a high *price*（高い金額を要求／請求する）, ×to ask/charge a high *cost/value*。物事の取得・実行については cost が用いられ, value は人がいとわずに支払う金額を指す。◆house *prices*（住宅価格）. ◆the *cost* of moving house（引っ越しの費用）. ◆The house now has a market *value* of twice what we paid for it.（その家の今の市場価値は私たちが支払った価格の2倍だ）

expense [U, C, ふつう単数形で] (物に費やす)費用, 出費；出費の対象 ◇The garden was transformed *at great expense*. 庭は莫大な費用をかけて作り変えられた ◇We were taken out for a meal *at the company's expense* (= the company paid). 私たちは会社の費用で食事に連れて行ってもらった ◇He's arranged everything; *no expense spared*. 彼は必要なだけお金を使って可能なだけ用意した 彼は必要なだけお金を使ってすべてを用意した ◇They *went to* all *the expense of* redecorating the house and then they moved. 彼らは家の改装にさんざんお金を使って, 引っ越した ◇Their visit *put us to* a lot of *expense*. 彼らが来ると出費がかさむ ◇Running a car is a big *expense*. 車の維持に多額の費用がかかる ☞ **expenses** (COSTS), **expensive** (EXPENSIVE)

worth [U] (人・物の財務的な)価値, 価格 ◇He has a personal *worth* of $10 million. 彼は正味1千万ドルの価値のある動産を所有している ❶名詞としての worth は, 物の実際的な[道徳上の]価値を意味することが多い。☞ **worth** (VALUE)

▷**worth** 形 ◇Our house is *worth* about $300,000. 私たちの家はおよそ30万ドルの価値があります ◇How much is this painting *worth*? この絵の価格はいくらですか ◇to be *worth a bomb/packet/fortune* (= a lot of money) 大変な値打ちがある ◇It isn't *worth* much. それは大して価値はないよ

▷**worthless** 形 ◇Shares in the company are now almost *worthless*. その会社の株は今やほとんど価値がない 反意 **valuable** (VALUABLE 1)

pride, principle 579

pride 名

pride・arrogance・vanity・egoism・hubris・conceit
他の人よりも優れている[偉い]と思う気持ち
【類語訳】傲慢, うぬぼれ, 優越感, プライド, 自尊心, 尊大, 虚栄心, 独りよがり, 利己心, 思い上がり

文型&コロケーション
▶to **appeal to** sb's **pride**/ **vanity**

pride [U] 《けなして》傲慢, うぬぼれ, 優越感, プライド, 自尊心 ◇Male *pride* forced him to suffer in silence. 男のプライドから彼は黙って耐えるしかなかった ◇You're going to have to *swallow your pride* and ask for your job back. プライドを捨てて仕事を返してもらうように頼まないといけなくなるよ 反意 **modesty**, ☞ **proud** (PROUD 2)

arrogance [U] 《けなして》傲慢, 横柄, 尊大 ◇He has a reputation for rudeness and intellectual *arrogance*. 彼は無礼で知性を鼻にかけているという評判だ 反意 **humility**, ☞ **arrogant** (PROUD 2)

vanity [U] 《けなして》(外見・能力・功績に対する)うぬぼれ, 虚栄心 ◇She had no *personal vanity* (= about her appearance). 彼女は自分の外見にうぬぼれてはいなかった ◇The invitation to head the committee flattered his *vanity* and he agreed. 委員長への誘いに彼の虚栄心は満たされ, 同意した 反意 **modesty**, ☞ **vain** (PROUD 2)

egoism (または **egotism**) [U] 《けなして》エゴ, うぬぼれ, 独りよがり, 利己心 ◇His *egoism* prevented him from really loving anyone but himself. 彼は利己心から自分以外の誰も心からは愛せなかった ☞ **ego** (DIGNITY)

hubris [U] 《フォーマル or 文語, けなして》(後々失敗・事故・死亡によって罰が下されるような)過信, 思い上がり ◇He thought he was above the law and was ultimately punished for his *hubris*. 彼は法律には縛られないと思ったが, その思い上がりで極刑に処せられた

conceit [U] 《ややフォーマル, 特に書き言葉, けなして》(能力・功績に対する)うぬぼれ, 思い上がり ◇Can you believe the *conceit* of the man? その男のうぬぼれときたら, 信じられるかい ☞ **conceited** (PROUD 2)

principle 名

1 ☞ MORALITY, VALUES
principle・ethics・ideal・standards・morals・morality
人の行動に影響を与える道徳的規範や強い信念
【類語訳】主義, 信条, 倫理, 道徳, 理想, モラル

文型&コロケーション
▶**high** principles/ ideals/ standards
▶**personal** principles/ ethics/ standards/ morality
▶**public** ethics/ morals/ morality
▶**moral** principles/ ideals/ standards
▶**religious** principles/ ideals/ morality
▶**political** principles/ ethics/ ideals/ morality
▶**professional** ethics/ standards
▶**have** (no/ high etc.) principles/ ideals/ standards/ morals
▶**compromise** your principles/ ideals/ standards
▶**betray** your principles/ ideals
▶**a matter/ question of** principle/ ethics/ morality

principle

principle [C, ふつう複数で, U]（行動に影響を与える）主義, 信条 ◇I refuse to lie about it — it's *against my principles*. それについて嘘をつきたくはありません—それは私の主義に反します ◇*Stick to your principles* and tell him you won't do it. 自分の信条を貫いて, 彼にそうするつもりはないと言いなさい ◇He doesn't invest in the arms industry *on principle*. 彼は主義に基づいて軍需産業には投資しません ☞ **unprincipled** (CORRUPT)

ethics [複数で]（行動に影響を与える）倫理；倫理性, 道徳性 ◇Their professional body is drawing up a *code of ethics* (= a statement of acceptable principles for a particular group). 彼らの職業団体は倫理規定を作成中である ◇He began to question the *ethics* of his position. 彼は自分の地位の倫理性に疑問を持ち始めた ❶ ethics は特定の分野の活動, 特に経済[職業]活動における主義について用いられる. 連語には professional, business, medical が挙げられる. ☞ **ethical** (GOOD 5), **ethical** (MORAL), **ethic** (VALUES)

ideal [C] 理想 ◇His followers sometimes found it hard to live up to his high *ideals*. 彼の信徒は時に彼の高い理想に従って行動することに難しさを感じた ◇Is true love an unattainable *ideal* (= one that can never be achieved)? 真の愛とは達成不可能な理想なのですか

standards [複数で] 道徳基準 ◇*Standards* aren't what they used to be. 道徳基準は以前とは異なる ◇We intend to uphold *standards of behaviour* throughout the college. 我々は大学内全体において行動規範を維持するつもりです

morals [複数で]（性的問題における）道徳, モラル ◇He thinks that young people these days have no *morals*. 彼は最近の若者は道徳感がないと考えている ◇The play was considered an affront to public *morals*. その劇は公共のモラルを傷つけるものと考えられた ☞ **amoral** (CORRUPT), **moral** (GOOD 5), **moral** (MORAL)

morality [U]（特定の人・集団が従う）道徳律；道徳性, 倫理性 ◇Whatever her personal *morality*, she has no right to judge others. 彼女の個人的な道徳律が何であれ, 彼女には他人を裁く権利はない ◇There is a continuing debate on the *morality* of abortion. 妊娠中絶の道徳性に関する議論が続いている ☞ **moral** (GOOD 5), **moral** (MORAL)

---

2 principle・rule・law・tenet
人が行動すべき方法と取るべき行動に対する信念
【類語訳】原則, 理念, 通則, 決まり, 規律, 作法

〔文型&コロケーション〕
- the principle/ rule/ law/ tenet that …
- a basic/ fundamental principle/ rule/ law/ tenet
- a moral principle/ rule/ law
- a religious principle/ law
- to accept a principle/ rule/ tenet
- to apply a principle/ rule

principle [C, U]（特定の方法で行動・思考するための）原則, 理念 ◇Their policy is based on the *principle* that free education should be available for all children. 彼らの政策は無償教育がすべての子どもに与えられるべきだという原則に基づいている ◇The order to show no mercy was contrary to the most basic *principles* of their religion. 情け容赦を見せてはいけないとするその命令は彼らの宗教の最も基本的な原則に反していた ☞ **principle** (THEO-RY 1)

rule [C]（特定の状況での）通則, 決まり, 規律 ◇I've *made it a rule* not to talk to the press. 私は報道陣には話さないことにしている ◇There are no *hard and fast rules* for planning healthy meals. 健康的な食事の献立作りにはきちんとした決まりはない ◇The *golden rule* (= most important rule) of teaching is to remember that all children learn at different rates. 教えることの黄金律として子どもによって学習のペースは異なるものであるということを覚えておくとよい ☞ **rule** (HABIT), **rule** (RULE 名), **rule** (THEORY 1), **as a rule** (USUALLY)

law [C, U]（特定の状況におけるよい行い(方)の）決まり, 作法, 規律 ◇He frequently behaved as though moral *laws* did not exist. 彼はたびたびまるで道徳律なんて存在しないかのように振る舞った ☞ **law** (RULE 名), **law** (THEORY 1)

tenet [C]《フォーマル》（理論・教義が基づく）原則, 理念 ◇Underlying Leninism was the *tenet* that revolution was inevitable. レーニン主義の基本理念は革命は不可避であるということだった

priority 名

priority・emphasis・stress・precedence
物事に特別の重要性を与えること
【類語訳】優先, 重要視, 重点, 強調

〔文型&コロケーション〕
- priority/ precedence **over** sb/ sth
- (a) **particular/ special/ equal** priority/ emphasis/ stress
- the **main** priority/ emphasis
- **great/ undue** emphasis/ stress
- to **have** priority/ a … emphasis/ precedence
- to **take** priority/ precedence
- to **give sb/ sth** priority/ emphasis/ precedence
- to **put** emphasis/ stress on sb/ sth
- to **lay/ place** emphasis/ stress on sb/ sth
- **in order of** priority/ precedence

priority [C, U] 優先事項；優先(権)[順位] ◇a *high/ low priority* 最優先事項/優先順位の低い事柄 ◇Education is a *top priority*. 教育は最優先事項だ ◇You need to *get your priorities right* (= decide what is important to you). 《特に英》あなたは正しい優先順位を確立する必要がある ◇You need to *get your priorities straight*. 《米》あなたは正しい優先順位を確立する必要がある ◇Club members will be given *priority*. クラブの会員には優先権が与えられます ◇Her family takes *priority* over her work. 彼女は仕事より家族を第一に考えている ◇List the tasks in order of *priority*. やるべきことを優先度順に表にしてください ◇*Priority* cases, such as homeless families, get dealt with first. ホームレスの家庭など優先度の高い事例が最初に扱われます ☞ **prioritize** (STRESS)

emphasis (複 **emphases**) [U, C] 重要視, 重点, 強調 ◇The *emphasis* is very much on learning the spoken language. 話し言葉を学ぶことが非常に重要視されている ◇There has been a *shift of emphasis* from manufacturing to service industries. 製造業からサービス業に重点が置き変わってきている ◇The classes have a vocational *emphasis*. それらの授業は職業指導に重点を置いている ☞ **emphasize** (STRESS)

stress [U] 重要視, 重き, 強調 ◇She lays great *stress*

probably, problem

on punctuality. 彼女は時間厳守にとても重きを置いている ◇I think the company places too much *stress* on cost and not enough on quality. その会社はコストに重きを置きすぎて、品質を軽んじていると私は思う ☞ **stress** (STRESS)

ノート **emphasis** と **stress** の使い分け：これらの語に意味による違いはほとんどない。emphasisのほうがはるかに使用頻度が高く、いくぶんフォーマル。stressはしばしば個人的で、例えば議論・運動・サービスなどに焦点を置くのではなく、特定の人物が重要であると考えるような場合に用いられる。

precedence [U]《ややフォーマル》(他の人・物事よりも)優先されること ◇She had to learn that her wishes did not take *precedence* over other people's needs. 彼女は自分の希望が他の人の要求より優先されないことを学ばされた ◇The speakers came on to the platform in order of *precedence*. 演説者たちが偉い順に壇上に上がった

ノート **priority** と **precedence** の使い分け：場合によって両語とも使用可能。◆Her wishes did not take *priority/precedence* over other people's needs.(彼女の希望が他の人が必要としていることより優先されることはなかった)。しかしながら、precedence は年上である[社会的地位が高い、上級の地位にある]ことを理由に、優先される場合を指し、priority はふつう必要性に基づいて優先される場合を指す。✕The speakers came on to the platform in order of *priority*. ✕Homeless families will be given *precedence*.

probably 副

probably・presumably・no doubt・doubtless・(the) chances are...・most likely・in all probability...
物事が起こりそう[事実でありそう]であることを表す
【類語訳】たぶん、おそらく、十中八九

probably the chances are...	presumably most likely in all probability...	no doubt doubtless

probably《特に話し言葉》たぶん、おそらく ◇You're *probably* right. たぶんそうでしょうね ◇It'll *probably* be OK. おそらく問題ないでしょう ◇Is he going to be there?' 'Probably.' 「彼は来るの」「たぶんね」 ◇Do we need the car?' '*Probably not*.' 「車は必要かな」「おそらく必要ないでしょう」 ☞ **probable** (LIKELY)

presumably《特に話し言葉》(証拠に基づいて)たぶん、おそらく ◇*Presumably* this is where the accident happened. おそらくここが事故が起こった場所なんだろう ◇I couldn't concentrate, *presumably* because I was so tired. たぶんすごく疲れていたので、集中できなかったんだ ☞ **presume** (SUPPOSE)

ノート **probably** と **presumably** の使い分け：どちらの語も確信を示さないにしても、probably はおよそ事実でありうることに基づいて結論を表す場合に、presumably は特定の証拠に基づくはずの事柄に用いられることがある。◆*Presumably* you'll be leaving the children at home. (おそらく子どもは家に置いて行くことになるだろう)。✕*Probably* you'll be leaving the children at home. また、すでに自分が

信じていることを他人に念を押して確認する場合にも用いられる。◆You'll be taking the car, *presumably*?（確か君が車を出してくれるんだよね）✕You'll be taking the car, *probably*? probably は人に同意するときに用いられることがある。◆You're *probably* right.（たぶんそうでしょうね）✕You're *presumably* right. また、人を慰める場合にも用いられる。◆It'll *probably* be OK.（おそらく問題ないでしょう）✕It'll *presumably* be OK.

no 'doubt《ややフォーマル》(ふつうに考えて)たぶん、おそらく ◇*No doubt* she'll call us when she gets there. きっと彼女はそこに着いたら私たちに電話するだろう

doubtless《ややフォーマル、書き言葉》まず間違いなく ◇He would *doubtless* disapprove of what Kelly was doing. 彼はケリーがしていたことをまず間違いなくけなすだろう

(the) chances are... 行語《ややインフォーマル》たぶん、おそらく ◇*(The) chances are* you won't have to pay. たぶんあなたは支払わなくていいだろう

most likely 十中八九、まず間違いなく ◇The illness was caused, *most likely*, by a virus. その病気は十中八九ウイルスによって引き起こされたのだろう ☞ **likely** (LIKELY)

in ,all proba'bility... フレーズ《書き言葉》十中八九、まず間違いなく ◇*In all probability* he failed to understand the consequences of his actions. まず間違いなく、彼は自分の行動の結果を理解していなかったのだろう

problem 名

problem・difficulty・issue・challenge・trouble・the matter・complication
処理[理解]の難しい物事や状況を表す
【類語訳】問題、課題、難点、不具合、困難、難題、窮地、障害、挑戦、もめごと、トラブル

文型&コロケーション
▸ a problem/ a difficulty/ an issue/ trouble/ the matter/ a complication **with** sth
▸ a problem/ an issue/ a challenge/ trouble **for** sb
▸ **further** problems/ difficulties/ issues/ challenges/ troubles/ complications
▸ the **main** problem/ difficulty/ issue/ challenge/ trouble
▸ (a) **serious/ real** problem/ difficulties/ issue/ challenge/ trouble
▸ **basic** problems/ difficulties/ issues/ trouble
▸ **endless/ severe** problems/ difficulties/ trouble
▸ (a) **major/ minor** problem/ difficulty/ issue/ challenge/ complication
▸ (a) **big** problem/ issue/ challenge/ trouble
▸ to **have** problems/ difficulties/ issues/ trouble
▸ to **cause/ avoid** problems/ difficulties/ trouble/ complications
▸ to **create/ bring/ run into** problems/ difficulties/ trouble
▸ to **make** difficulties/ an issue of sth/ trouble
▸ a problem/ a difficulty/ an issue/ a complication **arises/ exists**
▸ the problem/ difficulty/ trouble **lies in** sth

problem [C] 問題、課題、難点、不具合 ◇Most students face the *problem* of funding themselves while they study. たいていの学生は勉強しながら学資を得るという問題に直面します ◇Unemployment is a very real *prob-*

lem for graduates now. 失業は今、新卒者にとって非常に現実的な問題となっている ◇There's no history of heart *problems* (= disease connected with the heart) in our family. 私たちの家系に心臓疾患の病歴はない ◇It's a nice table. *The only problem is* it's too big for the room. すてきなテーブルだね。唯一の難点はその部屋には大きすぎることだね ◇But what am I supposed to do now?' 'Don't ask me — *it's not my problem/that's your problem* (= I don't care and you must deal with it yourself). 「で、今度は何をすればいいかな」「私に聞かないでよ—私の知ったことじゃないわ」 ◇'Can I pay by credit card?' 'Yes, *no problem*.' 「クレジット・カードで支払えますか」「はい、結構です」 ☞ **problematic** (SENSITIVE 2)

difficulty [C, ふつう複数で, U] 困難, 難題, 窮地, 障害 ◇We've run into *difficulties* with the new project. 私たちはその新プロジェクトで難題にぶつかっている ◇He *got into difficulties* while swimming and had to be rescued. 彼は泳ぐのが困難になり、救助されることになった ◇She works with children with *learning difficulties*. 彼女は学習障害児にかかわる仕事をしている ◇The bank is *in difficulty* at the moment. その銀行は現在、窮地に陥っている ☞ **difficult** (DIFFICULT 1, 2)

ノート **problem** と **difficulty** の使い分け：処理の難しい一つの特定の物事については problem を用いる。◆The *problem* first arose in 2003. (その問題は2003年に初めて生じた)。処理の難しい多数の物事をまとめて言う時は、problems も difficulties も使用可能。◆The project has been fraught with *problems/difficulties* from the start. (その事業はのっけから課題/難題をはらんでいる)。問題の多い状況では difficulties か difficulty を用いる。◆What should you do if you see someone in *difficulties/difficulty* in the water? (水の中で溺れている人を見つけたらどうすべきだと思いますか)。

issue [C]《ややインフォーマル》(人が抱えている)問題 ◇Money is not an *issue*. お金は問題ではありません ◇I don't think my private life is the *issue* here. 私の私生活はここでは関係ないと思います ◇I'm not bothered about the cost — you're the one who's making an *issue* of it. 私は費用に関しては気にしてないよ—それを問題にしているのは君のほうだよ ◇She's always on a diet — she *has issues about/with* food.《特に米》彼女はいつもダイエットしている—彼女は食べ物に問題があるみたい

challenge [C]《ふつうほめて》(人の能力・技量を試す)課題, 難題, 挑戦 ◇The role will be the biggest *challenge* of his acting career. その役は彼の役者人生で最大の挑戦となるだろう ◇She has taken on some exciting new *challenges* with this job. 彼女はこの仕事で新たな刺激的な課題にいくつか取り組んでいる ❶このグループの他の類語と異なり、challenge はふつう肯定的に捉えられる。◆*an exciting/interesting challenge* (刺激的な/面白い課題)。しかしながら、積極的に処理することを決意している深刻な問題にも用いられる。◆Destruction of the environment is one of the most serious *challenges* we face. (環境破壊は我々が直面している最も深刻な難題の一つである)。☞ **challenging** (DIFFICULT 1)

trouble [U, C]《けなして》問題, 困難, 窮地, もめごと, トラブル ◇We've never had much *trouble* with vandals around here. 私たちはこのあたりの暴徒どもと大したトラブルになったことはない ◇He could make *trouble* for me if he wanted to. 彼が望めば私を窮地に陥れることもできるだろう ◇She was on the phone for an hour telling me all her *troubles*. 彼女は電話で1時間もの間、私に困っていることをすべて話した ◇*The trouble with you is* you don't really want to work. あなたのいけないところは、本当は働きたくないと思っている点だ

the matter [単数で]《特に話し言葉》問題, 困難 ◇*What's the matter?* Is there something wrong? どうしましたか。何かおかしいのですか ◇Is *anything the matter*? どうしましたか ◇Is *something the matter* with Bob? He seems very down. ボブはどうしたの。すごく元気がないように見えるけど ◇'We've bought a new TV.' 'What was *the matter* with the old one?' 「新しいテレビを買ったんだ」「古いやつに何か問題でもあったの」 ◇*What's the matter with you* today (= why are you behaving like this)? 今日はどうしたんだい

complication [C, U] 面倒な事態, 混乱の種 ◇The bad weather added a further *complication* to our journey. 悪天候でさらに私たちの旅行は混乱した ☞ **complicated** (COMPLEX)

product 名

product・goods・commodity・merchandise・produce
販売するために製造される物
【類語訳】製品, 生産物, 商品, 品物, 農産物

文型&コロケーション
▶ consumer/ industrial products/ goods/ commodities
▶ household products/ goods
▶ farm products/ produce
▶ perishable products/ goods/ commodities/ produce
▶ durable products/ goods
▶ luxury products/ goods/ commodities
▶ to sell/ market a product/ goods/ a commodity/ merchandise
▶ to export a product/ goods/ a commodity/ merchandise
▶ to buy/ purchase a product/ goods/ a commodity/ merchandise/ produce

product [C, U] (販売用に製造・飼育・栽培される)製品, 生産物 ◇meat/pharmaceutical *products* 肉製品/医薬品 ◇to create/develop/launch a new *product* 新製品を生み出す/開発する/売り出す ◇We need new *product* to sell (= a range of new products).《ビジネスで》販売用に多様な新製品がほしい ☞ **produce** (MANUFACTURE)

goods [複数で] (販売用に製造される)商品, 製品, 用品, 品物 ◇cotton/leather/paper *goods* 綿花/皮革/紙製品 ◇electrical/sports *goods* 電気製品/スポーツ用品 ◇factories which produce luxury *goods* for the export market 輸出市場に向けた高級品を製造する工場 ◇*consumer goods* (= goods such as food and clothing that are bought by individual customers) 消費財 ◇increased tax on *goods and services* 商品とサービスに対する増税

commodity [C]《経済》(国家間で売買される)生産物, 製品, 商品 ◇rice, flour and other basic *commodities* 米、小麦粉をはじめとする基本的生産物 ◇Crude oil is the world's most important *commodity*. 原油は世界で最も重要な生産物である

merchandise [U] (売買される)商品, 製品；(特定のイベント・組織に関連する[を広告する])商品 ◇These tokens can be exchanged for *merchandise* in any of our

production, productive

stores. これらの商品券は全店で商品と交換できます ◇official Olympic *merchandise* 公式オリンピック商品

ノート goods と merchandise の使い分け: 製品が何でできている[用途が何である]かを強調する場合, goods を用いる。◆leather/household *goods*（皮革製品/日用品）。製品自体よりもブランド[売買行為]を強調する場合, merchandise を用いる。

produce [U]（飼育・栽培・製造される）農産物 ◇We sell only fresh local *produce*. 私たちは新鮮な地元の農産物しか売っていません ◇It says on the label '*Produce* of France'. ラベルには「フランス産」と書かれている

production 名

production • construction • industry • manufacturing • building • making • manufacture • assembly
物を作る[建てる]過程
【類語訳】生産, 産出, 製造, 製作, 建設, 建築, 工業, 製造業

【文型&コロケーション】
- ▸ **commercial/ industrial** production/ construction/ manufacturing/ building/ manufacture
- ▸ **local** production/ construction/ industry/ manufacturing/ building/ manufacture
- ▸ **large-scale/ small-scale** production/ industry/ manufacturing/ manufacture
- ▸ **car/ textile/ food** production/ manufacture
- ▸ **house/ road** construction/ building
- ▸ production/ construction/ manufacturing/ building/ assembly **methods/ processes/ systems/ techniques**
- ▸ construction/ manufacturing/ building **companies/ costs/ firms/ jobs/ materials/ work**
- ▸ the construction/ (a/ the) manufacturing/ the building **industry**
- ▸ a production/ construction/ manufacturing/ building/ assembly **worker**
- ▸ a production/ an assembly **line**

production [U]（商品・原料・食べ物の大量）生産, 産出, 製造, 製作 ◇*Production* of the new aircraft will start next year. 新型航空機の生産は来年開始される予定だ ◇The new model will be **in production** by the end of the year. 新モデルは年末までに生産される予定だ ◇**to go into production** 生産に入る ◇The car **went out of production** in 2005. その車は2005年に製造中止になった ◇the **mass production** of consumer goods (= production of goods in large quantities, using machinery) 消費財の大量生産 ☞ **production** (OUTPUT), **produce** (MANUFACTURE)

construction [U]（道路・建物・橋などの）建設, 建築, 建造, 架設 ◇Work has begun on the *construction* of the new airport. 新空港の建設工事が始まった ◇Our new offices are still **under construction**. 我が社の新社屋はまだ建設中です 反意 **demolition** (DEMOLISH), ☞ **construct** (BUILD), **construction** (STRUCTURE)

industry [U]（工場で原料に加工[商品に製造]する）工業 ◇Pollution from the country's **heavy industry** is probably the worst in Europe. その国の重工業による汚染はおそらくヨーロッパの中で最悪であろう ◇It is the home of **light industry**, with several small businesses based in the town. いくつかの中小企業が拠点を置き、

この町は軽工業の本拠地になっている ◇On leaving college she got a job in *industry*. 大学卒業するとすぐに彼女は工業関係の仕事に就いた ☞ **industry** (INDUSTRY)

▸ **industrial** 形 ◇*industrial* output 工業生産高 ◇*industrial* chemicals 工業化学物質 ◇the world's leading *industrial* nations 世界主要工業国

manufacturing [U]（工場で商品を大量に製造する）製造業 ◇Many jobs in *manufacturing* were lost during the recession. 不景気で製造業での多くの職が失われた ◇The company has established its first *manufacturing* base in Europe. その会社は製造拠点を初めてヨーロッパに置いた ☞ **manufacture** (MANUFACTURE)

building [U] 建設[建築][工事] ◇the *building* of the new stadium 新スタジアムの建設 ◇There's *building* work going on next door. 隣で建築工事が行われている 反意 **demolition** (DEMOLISH), ☞ **build** (BUILD)

ノート construction と building の使い分け: 多くの場合, 両語とも使用可能。construction はより専門的な語で, ビジネス・工業の文脈で用いられることが多い。building はより日常的な語で, 小規模な建築工事について用いられることが多い。

making [U]《しばしば複合語で》（物の）製造, 製作, 作成 ◇film-*making* 映画制作 ◇dress*making* 婦人服の仕立て ◇tea and coffee *making* facilities 紅茶とコーヒーをいれる設備 ◇the *making* of social policy 社会政策の策定 ◇This model was two years **in the making** (= being made). このモデルは2年かけて製造された ❶ making は非常に一般的な語で, 作る物であればどんな物についても用いることができるが, 建てる物には用いられない。✗house *making*. ☞ **make** (MAKE 1)

manufacture [U]（商品の大量）生産, 製造 ◇cloth/vehicle *manufacture* 布/自動車の製造 ◇What is the date of *manufacture*? 製造日はいつですか ☞ **manufacture** (MANUFACTURE)

ノート production, manufacturing, manufacture の使い分け: production と manufacture は実際に商品を製造する過程に重点が置かれる。◆car/steel *production/manufacture*（自動車/鉄鋼の生産/製造）。manufacturing は大量に商品を製造する事業を強調する。◆*manufacturing* industry（製造業）。✗*production/manufacture* industry。production は商品の製造だけではなく, 食べ物の飼育・栽培や原料の産出についても用いられるが, manufacture は商品・食べ物の製造についてのみ用いられ, 飼育・栽培は不可。✗oil/meat/wheat *manufacture*.

assembly [U]（自動車・家具などの部品の）組み立て（作業）◇the correct *assembly* of the parts 部品の正しい組み立て方 ◇a car *assembly* plant 自動車組み立て工場 ◇Some *assembly* of the equipment is required. その装置はいくらか組み立て作業が必要だ ☞ **assemble** (BUILD)

productive 形

productive • fertile • fruitful • prolific • rich
多くの物[よい結果]を生み出すことを表す
【類語訳】生産的な, 有意義な, 肥沃な, 効果的な, 実りの多い, 多作の, 多産の, 豊かな

↪productive

profit, progress

【文型&コロケーション】
- productive/ fertile/ rich **land/ soil**
- a productive/ fruitful **collaboration/ discussion/ meeting**
- a fertile/ fruitful **source** of sth
- **highly** productive/ fertile

productive (商品・穀物の)生産[産出]力のある, 生産性の高い; 生産的な, 有意義な ◇highly *productive* farming land/manufacturing methods 生産性の非常に高い農地／製造方法 ◇*productive* farmers/workers 生産性の高い農家／労働者 ◇My time spent in the library was very *productive*. 図書館で過ごした時間は非常に生産的だった 反意 unproductive (INEFFECTIVE)
➤**productively** 副 ◇We need to use the land more *productively*. その土地をもっと生産的に利用する必要がある ◇It's important to spend your time *productively*. 時間を有意義に過ごすことが大切だ

fertile (土地・土壌・が)肥沃な; 有意義な ◇a *fertile* region/valley 肥沃な地域／盆地 ◇a *fertile* source of argument/dispute よく論争の種となること ◇The region at the time was ***fertile ground*** for revolutionary movements (= there were the necessary conditions for them to develop easily). 《比喩的》当時その地域は革命運動の醸成に最適の環境だった

fruitful 効果的な, 実り[収穫]の多い ◇The research has proved extremely *fruitful*. その調査は非常に収穫が多かった 反意 **fruitless** (USELESS), ☞ **VALUABLE** 2

prolific (本・芸術作品に関して)多作の, 多くの作品を残す, (果物・子どもに関して)多産の, 多くの実を結ぶ, (ゴールを多く生み出して)得点力の高い ◇a *prolific* author/writer/composer 多作の著者／作家／作曲家 ◇He was noted for his *prolific* output — ten books a year was normal. 彼は多作で有名だった一年10冊が普通だった ◇a *prolific* scorer/striker 得点力の高い選手／ストライカー ◇The kiwi fruit is known for its *prolific* yield and good export price. キーウィフルーツは多くの実を結び, 輸出価格が高いことで知られている

rich (土壌が)肥沃な, 豊かな ◇*rich* farming land 肥沃な農地 ◇a *rich* well-drained soil 豊かで水はけのよい土壌 反意 **poor**

profit 名

profit・interest・earnings・dividend・return・surplus・gain
会社や人が物を販売して[投資によって]得るお金で, 関連する経費を差し引いたもの
【類語訳】利益, 利潤, 収益, 利子, 利息, 配当, 剰余, 黒字, 儲け

【文型&コロケーション】
- (a) profit/ interest/ earnings/ dividend/ return/ surplus/ gain **on** sth
- (a) profit/ interest/ earnings/ dividend/ return/ surplus/ gain **from** sth
- to do sth **for** profit/ gain
- to be **in** profit/ surplus
- (a) **good** profit/ interest/ earnings/ dividend/ return/ gains
- (a) **record** profit/ interest/ earnings/ dividend/ return/ surplus/ gains
- (a) **high/ low** profit/ interest/ earnings/ dividend/ return/ gains
- (a) **large/ huge/ small** profit/ dividend/ return/ surplus/ gains
- (a) **net** profit/ earnings/ interest/ dividend/ return/ surplus/ gains
- (a) **gross/ taxable** profit/ earnings/ interest/ dividend/ return/ gains
- (an) **annual** profit/ earnings/ interest/ dividend/ return/ surplus
- to **generate** a profit/ earnings/ interest/ a return/ a surplus
- to **make/ produce** a profit/ return/ surplus/ gain
- to **pay** interest/ a dividend
- a **rate** of interest/ return

profit [C, U] (ビジネス・販売で得る)利益, 利潤, 収益 ◇The company made a healthy *profit* of $106m last year. その会社は昨年1億6百万ドルの堅調な利益を上げた ◇We should be able to sell the house ***at a profit***. 我々はその家を売って利益を出せるはずだ ◇The agency is voluntary and not run for *profit*. その機関はボランティアで営利団体ではない 反意 **loss** (DEBT), ☞ **profit** (MAKE 2), **proceeds** (REVENUE)

interest [U] 《金融》利子, 利息 ◇They're paying 16% *interest* on the loan. 彼らはそのローンに16%の利息を支払っている ◇The Gold Account pays monthly *interest* of 5.5%. ゴールド・アカウントは月々5.5%の利息がつく ◇The money was repaid ***with interest***. その金は利子と共に返済された ◇***Interest rates*** have risen by 1%. 金利は1%上昇している

earnings [複数形]《金融》(会社の)利益, 利潤, 収益 ◇The company's *earnings* per share have fallen to 29p. その会社の一株当たりの収益は29ペンスまで下がっている ◇Whisky accounts for a large percentage of Scotland's export *earnings*. ウイスキーがスコットランドの輸出利益の大きな割合を占めている ☞ **earnings** (INCOME)

dividend [C]《金融》(株主への)配当(金) ◇Shareholders will receive an interim *dividend* payment of 50 cents a share. 株主には一株当たり50セントの中間配当が支払われる

return [U, C]《金融》(投資による)利益, 利潤, 収益 ◇The bank offers a higher rate of *return* on investments over $10,000. その銀行は1万ドル以上の投資に対してはより高い利率を提供している ◇The capital she invested failed to generate much of a *return*. 彼女が投資した資本は大した利益を生まなかった

surplus [C, U]《金融》(経費を差し引いた)剰余(金), 黒字 ◇Britain at that time enjoyed a trade *surplus* of £400 million. 当時イギリスは4億ポンドの貿易黒字を享受していた ◇The balance of payments was in *surplus* last year (= the value of exports was greater than the value of imports). 昨年の国際収支は黒字だった

gain [U, C, ふつう複数形で]《しばしばけなして》(ビジネス・販売で得る)利益, 儲け ◇She only seems to be interested in personal *gain*. 彼女は個人の利益にしか興味がないように思える ◇He spent his ***ill-gotten gains*** on fast cars and women. 彼は不正な手段で得た金をスポーツカーや女に使った

progress 名

progress・development・advance・rise・promotion・progression・advancement

物事が進み、拡がり、育まれていくことを表す
【類語訳】進歩, 上達, 発展, 発達, 向上, 進展, 発育, 成長, 拡張, 台頭, 勃興, 繁栄, 出世, 昇進, 昇格, 振興, 促進

文型&コロケーション

▶ progress/ development/ an advance/ advancement **in** sth
▶ sb/ sth's rise/ promotion/ progression/ advancement **to** sth
▶ sth is **in** progress/ development
▶ (a) **rapid** progress/ development/ advance/ rise/ promotion/ progression/ advancement
▶ (a) **steady** progress/ development/ advance/ progression
▶ (a) **slow/ gradual/ smooth** progress/ development/ progression
▶ **further** progress/ development/ advances/ promotion/ advancement
▶ **scientific/ technical/ technological/ economic/ political/ social** progress/ development/ advances/ advancement
▶ **personal/ individual** development/ advancement
▶ **career** development/ progression/ advancement
▶ to **achieve** progress/ development/ advances/ promotion/ progression
▶ to **make** progress/ advances
▶ to **chart/ halt** the progress/ development/ rise/ progression of sth
▶ to **assist** the progress/ development/ rise/ advancement of sth

progress [U]《しばしばほめて》進歩, 上達, 発展, 発達, 向上, (達成[完成]へ向けた)進行, 進展, 進捗, 経過 ◇We have made great *progress* in controlling inflation. 我々はインフレ抑制に大きな成果を上げた ◇Technological *progress* is changing the demand for labour. 科学技術の進歩が労働需要に変化をもたらしている ◇Work on the new offices is now in *progress*. 新社屋の工事は現在進行中です ◇I have one file for completed work and one for **work in progress**. 私が完了した作業用のファイル一つと進行中の作業用のファイル一つを持っている ◇They asked for a **progress report** on the project. 彼らはその事業の経過報告書を求めた ❶ *progress* は特に科学技術の変化が社会に対して悪影響を及ぼしていると考える人がいる場合に, しばしば肯定的に用いられる. ☞ **progress** (DEVELOP 1), **progressive** (RADICAL)

development [U] (漸進的な)発育, 成長, 発達, 拡張, 開発 ◇a baby's *development* in the womb 子宮での赤ちゃんの発育 ◇the *development* of basic skills such as literacy and numeracy 識字能力や計算能力などの基本的技能の発達 ◇The company can offer a number of opportunities for career *development*. その会社はキャリア開発の機会を数多く提供することができます ❶ *development* は(子どもなどの)成長や(生涯を通じての)学習について用いられる. ☞ **develop** (DEVELOP 1)

advance [C, U] (特定の活動・技能における)進歩, 上達, 発展, 発達 ◇recent *advances* in medical science 最近の医学における進歩 ◇This represents an *advance on* existing techniques. これは既存の技術に積み上げられた発展を象徴するものだ ◇We live in an age of rapid technological *advance*. 我々は急速な科学技術の発達の時代に暮らしている ❶ *advance* と *advances* は特に科学的[科学技術的, 医学的]分野での達成について用いられる. ☞ **advance** (DEVELOP 1)

rise [単数で] 台頭, 勃興, 繁栄, 隆盛, 出世 ◇The film traces the *rise* of fascism in Europe. その映画はヨーロッパにおけるファシズムの台頭をたどっている ◇the **rise and fall** of the Roman Empire ローマ帝国の興亡 ◇His eventual fall was as fast as his **meteoric rise** to power. 彼の最終的な失脚は権力の座への流星のような出世と同じくらい速かった ❶ *rise* はふつう政党・社会階級・地位・宗教・政治体制がしばしばいかに突然に重要性を増すか, または, 特に sb's **rapid/swift/spectacular/meteoric rise to power/fame** の句で, 人がいかに突然に力を持つように[有名に]なるかを表す. 反義 **fall**

▶ **rise** 動 [自] ◇She *rose to power* in the 70s. 彼女は70年代に権力の座に就いた ◇He *rose* to the rank of general. 彼は大将の階級まで出世した

promotion [U, C] (会社・組織内での)昇進 ; (スポーツチームの上級リーグへの)昇格 ◇Her *promotion* to Sales Manager took everyone by surprise. 彼女の営業部長への昇進は皆を驚かせた ◇The new job is a *promotion* for him. 新しい職務は彼にとっては昇進だ ◇The players were paid bonuses for winning *promotion* to the First Division. 1部リーグへの昇格を勝ち取ったことで選手たちにはボーナスが支給された 反義 **demotion, relegation** ❶ *demotion* はよりよい職へ昇進することとは反対の語だが, あまり頻繁には用いられない. スポーツチームの降格には *relegation* を用いる.

▶ **promote** 動 [他] ◇She worked hard and was soon *promoted*. 彼女は一生懸命働いて, すぐに昇進した ◇They were *promoted* to the First Division last season. 昨シーズン彼らは1部リーグへ昇格した

progression [U, C] 《ややフォーマル》(ある段階[状態]から別の段階[状態]への)進行, 発達, 進展, 進歩 ◇What are the opportunities for career *progression*? キャリアアップの見込みはどうですか ◇The medication halts the rapid *progression* of the disease. その薬物療法は病気の急速な進行を止めます ◇This is all part of the natural *progression* from childhood to adolescence. これはすべて子どもから青年期への自然な成長の一環です ☞ **progress** (DEVELOP 1)

advancement [U, C]《フォーマル》振興, 促進, 増進 ; 進歩, 発展, 発達, 向上, (職・社会階級における)昇進, 出世 ◇the *advancement* of knowledge/education/science 知識の増進/教育の発展/科学の振興 ◇There are good opportunities for *advancement* if you have the right skills. 適切な技術を持っていれば, 昇進できるよい機会があります ❶ *advancement* は個人の生活分野での達成について用いられることが多い. ◇ career/material/personal/individual/social *advancement* (キャリアアップ/物質的豊かさの向上/個人的な昇進/個人的な進歩/社会的出世). ☞ **advance** (DEVELOP 1)

project 名

project • activity • operation • venture • exercise • enterprise • pursuit • undertaking • occupation

特定の目標を達成するために時間と気力を注ぎ込む対象
【類語訳】計画, 課題, 事業, プロジェクト, 活動, 作戦, 作業, 開発事業, 大仕事, 楽しみ, 企て, 気晴らし

文型&コロケーション

▶ a **major/ successful/ joint** project/ activity/ operation/ venture/ exercise/ enterprise/ undertaking
▶ a **big/ difficult** project/ operation/ exercise/ enterprise/

↳ **project**

undertaking
▶ an **ambitious** project/ operation/ venture/ exercise/ enterprise/ undertaking
▶ an **expensive** project/ activity/ operation/ venture/ exercise/ undertaking
▶ a **profitable** activity/ venture/ exercise/ enterprise
▶ a **worthwhile** project/ activity/ venture/ exercise/ pursuit/ undertaking/ occupation
▶ a **dangerous** activity/ operation/ exercise/ enterprise/ undertaking
▶ a **risky** project/ activity/ operation/ venture/ enterprise/ undertaking
▶ a/ an **business/ commercial/ industrial** project/ activity/ operation/ venture/ enterprise/ undertaking
▶ to **set up/ run/ support** a project/ an activity/ an operation/ a venture/ an enterprise
▶ to **launch** a project/ an operation/ a venture/ an enterprise
▶ to **carry out/ supervise** a project/ an activity/ an operation/ an exercise
▶ to **be involved in** a project/ an activity/ an operation/ a venture/ an exercise/ an enterprise
▶ a project/ a venture/ an enterprise **fails/ succeeds**

project [C] 計画, 課題, 事業, プロジェクト ◇He's working on a research *project* in the department of social sciences. 彼は社会科学部で研究課題に取り組んでいる ◇We want to set up a ***project to*** computerize the library system. 我々は図書館システムのコンピューター化の企画を立ち上げたいと思う

activity [C] （興味を満たす[楽しむ, 特定の目標を達成する]ための）活動 ◇The club provides a wide variety of *activities* including tennis, swimming and squash. そのクラブはテニスや水泳, スカッシュなど, さまざまな活動を提供している ◇The book contains plenty of ideas for classroom *activities*. その本には教室での活動のためのアイデアがたくさん載っている

operation [C] 《ややフォーマル》（組織的な）活動, 作戦, 作業 ◇A major rescue *operation* was launched after two divers were reported missing. ダイバー二人が行方不明との通報を受け, 大掛かりな救助活動が開始された ◇It was a ***tricky operation*** to get all the barrels safely down on to the road. 《英》すべての樽を安全に道路に降ろすのは慎重を要する作業だった

venture [C] （投機的な）事業, 開発事業 ◇The project is a joint *venture* between the public and private sectors. そのプロジェクトは官民両セクターによる共同開発事業である

exercise [C] （特定の結果を達成するための）活動 ◇Staying calm was an ***exercise in*** self-control. 平静を保つことは自己制御の行為だった ◇In the end it proved a pointless *exercise*. 結局それは徒労に終わった ◇As a ***public relations exercise*** the festival was clearly a success. 広報活動としては, その祭典は明らかに成功だった ❶この意味でのexerciseはしばしば人や組織に対する人々のイメージを操作したり見つけ出したりする意味合いで用いられる. したがって連語としてmarketing, publicity, public relations, propaganda, damage limitation, consultation, evaluation, researchが挙げられる.

enterprise [C] （大規模で困難な）事業, 大仕事 ◇The music festival is a new *enterprise* which we hope will become an annual event. その音楽祭は我々が今年

promise

行事になってほしいと願う新事業です

pursuit [C, ふつう複数で]《ややフォーマル》（仕事以外で興味を満たす[楽しむ]ための）活動, 楽しみ ◇She has time now to follow her various artistic *pursuits*. 彼女にはさまざまな芸術活動を追求する時間が今はある

undertaking [C]《ややフォーマル》（重要[困難]な）事業, 企て ◇He is interested in buying the club as a commercial *undertaking*. 彼は営利目的でそのクラブを買収することに興味を持っている ◇In those days, the trip across country was a dangerous *undertaking*. 当時はその国を横断する旅行は危険な企てだった

|ノート| **enterprise** と **undertaking** の使い分け: undertaking は問題になっている仕事が困難・複雑であるという印象を与える. 典型的な連語に major, large, massive が挙げられる. enterprise は大規模な[重要な]事業についても用いられるが, その仕事の目的が何か新しい[異なる]物事を生み出すことであるという印象を与える.

occupation [C]《ややフォーマル》（仕事以外で興味を満たす[楽しむ]ための）活動, 気晴らし ◇Her main *occupation* seems to be shopping. 彼女の一番の気晴らしは買い物のようだ

|ノート| **activity, pursuit, occupation** の使い分け: activity はこれらの語の中で最も一般的で, ビジネス・政府・軍・教育・スポーツ・余暇に関連する幅広い連語と結びつく.
◆ business/commerical/trading/training *activities* （ビジネス／商業／貿易／訓練活動）, ◆ government/economic/political/military/guerrilla/terrorist *activities* （政府／経済／政治／軍事／ゲリラ／テロ活動）.
◆ classroom/cultural/extra-curricular/educational/learning *activities* （教室／文化／課外／教育／学習活動）. ◆ leisure/outdoor/recreational/social/sporting *activities* （余暇／アウトドア／レクリエーション／社会／スポーツ活動）. occupation はこの意味では, favourite と共に用いられることが多く, 編み物, 夕日の観察, 田園での散歩, ベンチに座っての人間観察, 美術館へ行くことなど気晴らしに楽しめる穏やかな活動について用いられる. pursuit は文書で用いられることが多く, より体系的なスポーツ・文化・知的活動について用いられる.

promise 名

promise • commitment • word • pledge • guarantee • oath • assurance • vow
必ず実行するかしないか, あるいは必ず何かが起こる意思を表す
【類義訳】約束, 公約, 言質, 保証, 誓約, 宣誓, 請け合い, 誓い

|文型&コロケーション|
▶ a promise/ a commitment/ your word/ a pledge/ a guarantee/ an oath/ a vow **to do** sth
▶ a promise/ your word/ a pledge/ a guarantee/ an oath/ an assurance/ a vow **that...**
▶ a/ your **solemn** promise/ word/ oath/ assurance/ vow
▶ a **firm** promise/ commitment/ pledge/ guarantee/ assurance
▶ a **formal** commitment/ guarantee/ oath/ assurance
▶ a **written** promise/ commitment/ guarantee/ assurance
▶ to **give** a promise/ a commitment/ your word/ a pledge/ a guarantee/ an assurance
▶ to **make** a promise/ commitment/ pledge/ guarantee/ vow
▶ to **take** a pledge/ an oath/ a vow

▶to **have** sb's promise/ commitment/ word/ assurance
▶to **honour** your promise/ commitment/ word/ pledge/ assurance
▶to **keep** your promise/ commitment/ word/ vow
▶to **break** a promise/ a commitment/ your word/ a pledge/ a vow

promise [C] 約束 ◇I try not to make *promises* that I can't keep. 私は自分が守れない約束はしないようにしている ◇He simply broke every single *promise* he ever made me. 彼は私との約束をあっさりとことごとく破った ◇She had obviously forgotten her *promise* to call me. 私に電話する約束を彼女は明らかに忘れてしまっていた ◇You haven't gone back on your *promise* to me, have you? 私との約束を破ったわけじゃないでしょうね ◇I won't be late. That's a *promise*! 遅れたりはしません。約束だ

commitment [C, U]《ややフォーマル》約束, 公約, 言質 ◇She doesn't want to make a big emotional *commitment* to Steve at the moment. 彼女はまだスティーブに重大な気持ちを打ち明けたいとは思っていない ◇The company's *commitment* to providing quality at a reasonable price has been vital to its success. お得な価格で上質な物を提供するというその会社の約束が成功に不可欠だった ◇He questioned the government's *commitment* to public services. 彼は公的サービスに関する政府の公約に疑問を投げかけた ☞ **committed** (RELIABLE 1)

word [単数で]（約束の）言葉, 約束, 保証 ◇I give you my *word* that it won't happen again. 二度とそんなことにはならないとお約束します ◇I never *doubted her word*. 私は彼女の言葉を疑ったことなど決してなかった ◇They claimed that the minister had *gone back on her word* (= broken her promise). 彼らはその大臣が約束を果たさなかったと主張した ◇We only have his *word* for it that he wasn't there that night. 彼はその晩そこにはいなかったと言っていますが, 果たして真偽の程はどうでしょうかね ◇She won't go to the police. You can *take my word for it* (= believe me). 彼女は警察には行かないだろう。誓ってね

pledge [C]《特にジャーナリズム》誓約, 公約 ◇The new leader demanded a *pledge* of loyalty from each of his allies. 新しい指導者は同士の個々人に忠誠の誓いを求めた ◇Will the government honour its election *pledge* not to raise taxes? 政府は増税をしないという選挙公約を守るだろうか

guarantee [C] 保証 ◇The union wants cast-iron *guarantees* that there will be no job losses. 労組は雇用喪失はないという確固たる保証を欲している

ノート **promise, pledge, guarantee** の使い分け：promise が最も使用頻度が高く, 最も一般的で, 3語の中で人間関係の文脈で用いることのできる唯一の語である。×She had obviously forgotten her *pledge/guarantee* to call me. pledge は特に政治と政党公約の文脈で用いられる。◆election/campaign/manifesto *pledges*（選挙公約/キャンペーン公約/マニフェスト公約）◆spending *pledges* given by the government（政府による支出公約）。guarantee は会社や組織に関わるビジネス関連の事柄に特に用いられる。

oath [C]《ややフォーマル》宣誓, 誓約 ◇All the barons were called on to *swear an oath* of allegiance to the king. 国王への忠誠を誓わせるために男爵全員が召集された ◇Before giving evidence, witnesses in court have to *take the oath* (= promise to tell the truth). 証言をする前に証人たちは法廷で宣誓をしなければならない ❶on/under oath とは, 法廷で真実を述べる正式な約束をしたことを表す。◆The judge reminded the witness that he was still *under oath*.（裁判官は証人がまだ宣誓下にあるという自覚を促した）

assurance [C]《ややフォーマル》（安心のための）保証, 請け合い ◇They asked for *assurances on* the safety of the system. 彼らはそのシステムの安全性の保証を求めた ◇Despite *assurances to the contrary* the birds are still being sold as pets. そうしてはならないと言われているもかかわらず, それらの鳥は今なおペットとして売られている

vow [C] 誓い, 誓約, 誓願 ◇The monks take a *vow* of silence. その僧侶たちは沈黙の誓いを立てる ◇She would not be unfaithful to her *marriage vows*. 彼女は自分の結婚の誓約に背くことはないだろう

promise 動

promise・guarantee・swear・pledge・commit・assure・vow・undertake

必ず…する[物事が起こる]と人に言う
【類語訳】約束する, 保証する, 保障する, 宣誓する, 誓う, 断言する, 誓約する, 確約する, 公約する

文型＆コロケーション
▶to swear/ vow **to sb** (that...)
▶to promise/ guarantee/ swear/ pledge/ vow/ undertake **to do sth**
▶to promise/ guarantee/ swear/ pledge/ vow **that...**
▶to promise/ guarantee/ pledge your **support**
▶to swear/ pledge **allegiance/ loyalty**
▶to swear/ vow **revenge/ eternal friendship/ undying love**
▶to **solemnly** promise/ swear/ vow/ undertake sth

promise [他, 自] 約束する ◇'*Promise* not to tell anyone!' 'I *promise*.'「誰にも言わないと約束して」「約束するよ」 ◇I'll see what I can do but I *can't promise anything*. 私に何ができるか考えてみるけど, 何も約束はできないよ ◇You *promised* me (that) you'd be home early tonight. 今夜は早く帰るって私に約束したじゃない ◇'I'll be back soon,' she *promised*.「すぐに戻るわ」と彼女は約束した ◇He *promised* the money to his grandchildren. 彼はそのお金のことを孫たちに約束した

guarantee [他] 保証[保障]する, 約束する ◇Basic human rights, including freedom of speech, are now *guaranteed*. 言論の自由を含めた基本的人権が今は保障されている ◇The ticket will *guarantee* you free entry. このチケットで無料で入場いただけます ◇We *guarantee* to deliver your goods within a week. 品物は1週間以内にお届けすることをお約束いたします

ノート **promise** と **guarantee** の使い分け：promise は話をしている相手に, ふつう…することを個人的に約束すること。guarantee はそれほど個人的ではなく, 物事が起こることを請け合うこと。promise は約束したことを行う道徳的義務はあるが, 法的な強制力はない。guarantee は請け合ったことを行う法的義務があるが, 実際には法的義務を認めず, promise の強意語として用いられることが多い。

swear [他, 自, 受身なし]（法廷などで）宣誓する, 誓う, 断言する ◇She made him *swear* not to tell anyone. 彼女

彼に誰にも言わないと誓わせた ◇He *swore* revenge on the man who had killed his father. 彼は父親を殺した男に対する復讐を誓った ◇I *swear to God* I had nothing to do with it. 私は神に誓ってそれとは無関係だったのだ ◇Witnesses were required to *swear on* the Bible. 証人は聖書に手をのせて宣誓することを求められた ◇I think I put the keys back in the drawer, but I couldn't *swear to it* (= I'm not completely sure).《話し言葉》鍵は引き出しの中に戻したと思うけど、断言はできないな

pledge [他] 誓約[確約, 公約]する ◇Japan *pledged* $100 million in humanitarian aid. 日本は1億ドルの人道支援を確約した ◇Politicians of all parties *pledged* their support for the idea. 全政党の政治家がその考えに対して支持を約束した ◇The government has *pledged* that it will not raise taxes. 政府は増税しないと公約している

commit (-tt-) [他]《協約・取り決めを守ることを》誓約[確約, 公約]させる;《意見・決定を》表明[明言]させる ◇Several countries were reluctant to *commit themselves* to the treaty. いくつかの国々がその条約に縛られるようになることをしぶった ◇The party was *committed* to reforming the electoral system. その党は選挙制度を改革すると公約した ◇You don't have to *commit* yourself now, just think about it. 今明言する必要はありません、ただそれについて考えておいてください ☞ **committed** (RELIABLE 1)

assure [他]《間違いなく真実である[必ず起こる]ことを》断言する, 約束する, 保証する ◇We were *assured* that everything possible was being done. 私たちはできることはすべてやっていると断言された ◇She's perfectly safe, I can *assure* you. 彼女は完全に無事です, 私が保証します ◇We *assured him of* our loyal support. 私たちは彼に忠実な支持を約束した

vow [他]《ややフォーマル, 特に書き言葉》(…することを正式[真剣]に)宣誓する, 誓う ◇She *vowed* never to speak to him again. 彼女は二度と彼と口をきかないと誓った ◇They *vowed* eternal friendship. 彼らは永遠の友情を誓い合った

ノート **swear**と**vow**の使い分け: swearは物事が真実である[であった, であろう]ことについて用いられるが, vowは将来的に必ず…することについて用いられることが多い.

undertake [他]《フォーマル or ビジネス》(…することを)同意する, 約束する ◇They *undertook* to finish the job by Friday. 彼らはその仕事を金曜日までに終わらせると約束した

promising [形] ☞ TIMELY

promising・encouraging・bright・rosy・heartening・auspicious・hopeful
物事が成功し[よい結果を与えてくれ]そうであることを表す
【類語訳】前途有望な, 希望の持てる, 見込みのある, ばら色の, 元気づけられる, 励みになる, さい先のよい

文型&コロケーション

▶ to be/ look promising/ encouraging/ bright/ rosy/ auspicious/ hopeful **for** sb/ sth
▶ to be encouraging/ heartening **to find/ know/ see**...
▶ a promising/ an encouraging/ a bright/ an auspicious/ a hopeful **start**
▶ a promising/ an encouraging/ a bright/ a rosy/ a hopeful **future/ prospect/ outlook/ picture**
▶ a promising/ an encouraging/ an auspicious/ a hopeful **sign**
▶ encouraging/ heartening/ hopeful **news**
▶ **very** promising/ encouraging/ bright/ reassuring/ rosy/ heartening/ auspicious/ hopeful
▶ **extremely** promising/ encouraging/ bright/ reassuring/ hopeful
▶ **highly** promising/ encouraging/ auspicious/ hopeful

promising 前途有望な, 希望の持てる, 見込みのある ◇At that time, I had a *promising* career in TV. その当時, 私は前途有望なテレビの仕事を抱えていた ◇The weather doesn't look very *promising*. 天気はあまりよくなりそうにない 反意 **unpromising** ❶ unpromisingは物事が成功しそうにないことを表す. ◆The first attempt was *unpromising*. (その最初の試みは見込みのないものだった). ☞ **promise** (POTENTIAL)

encouraging 前途有望な, 希望の持てる, 明るい材料になる ◇Last year's results were very *encouraging*. 昨年の結果には大いに期待を持てた ◇The response we got from our readers was extremely *encouraging*. 読者からの反応は非常に明るい材料になるものだった 反意 **discouraging** (DISAPPOINTING)

ノート **promising**と**encouraging**の使い分け: 多くの場合, 両語とも使用可能. ◆a *promising*/an *encouraging* sign/result/start/prospect (希望の持てる徴候/結果/スタート/見通し). promisingは人の職業について用いられるが, encouragingは不可. ◆a *promising* young player/newcomer/candidate/career (前途有望な若手選手/新人/候補者/職業). ×an *encouraging* young player/newcomer/candidate/career. encouragingは他の人の反応について用いられるが, promisingは不可. ×The response we got from readers was extremely *promising*.

bright《特にジャーナリズム or ビジネス》(成功しそうで)明るい; 前途有望な, 希望の持てる, 見込みのある ◇This young musician has a *bright* future. この若い音楽家には明るい未来がある ◇Prospects for the coming year look *bright*. 来年の見通しは希望が持てそうだ ◇**Look on the bright side** (= be cheerful about a bad situation by thinking only of the advantages and not the disadvantages). You managed to do more than I did. 明るい面に目を向けなさい. 私よりも多くをなし遂げたのだから

rosy《ジャーナリズム or ビジネス, 時にけなして》(よさ[成功]について)明るい, 前途有望な;(実際にはよさ[成功]そうでなくても)明るく見せる, ばら色の ◇The future is looking *rosy* for our company. 我が社の未来はばら色のようだ ◇She painted a *rosy picture* of what their life in Italy would be like (= made it appear to be very good, and perhaps better than it really would be). 彼女はイタリアでの彼らの生活がどんなものになるかばら色の未来を描いた

heartening 元気づけられる, 励みになる, 希望の持てる ◇It is *heartening* to see the determination of these young people. これらの若者の決意には元気づけられる

auspicious《フォーマル》さい先のよい, 前途有望な ◇It seemed an *auspicious* start to the new year. さい先のよい新年のスタートのように思えた ❶ auspiciousはふつう時間・出来事を修飾し, 連語にはday, moment, time, occasion, start, beginningが挙げられる.

hopeful 前途有望な, 希望の持てる, 見込みのある ◇This is the first *hopeful* sign that the hostages might be

proposal, propose

released soon. これは人質がまもなく解放されるかもしれないという初めての希望の持てる徴候だ ◇The future did not seem very *hopeful*. 未来は前途有望であるとはあまり思えなかった 反意 **hopeless** (USELESS), ☞ **hopeful** (OPTIMISTIC), **hope** (HOPE 名 1)

proposal 名 ☞ PLAN 1

proposal・recommendation・suggestion・proposition・motion
他の人に検討してもらうように示される考えや計画
【類語訳】提案, 提言, 勧告, 提示, 申し出, 動議

文型&コロケーション
▶ a proposal/ recommendation/ suggestion/ motion **for/ on** sth
▶ a recommendation/ suggestion **about** sth
▶ a proposal/ recommendation/ suggestion/ proposition/ motion **that**...
▶ a **practical/ specific** proposal/ recommendation/ suggestion
▶ to **accept/ support/ reject/ discuss** a proposal/ recommendation/ suggestion/ proposition/ motion
▶ to **make/ consider** a proposal/ recommendation/ suggestion/ proposition
▶ to **submit/ put forward/ oppose** a proposal/ recommendation/ suggestion/ motion
▶ to **put** a proposal/ motion/ submission **to** sb
▶ to **welcome** a proposal/ recommendation/ suggestion
▶ to **adopt** a recommendation/ suggestion/ motion
▶ to **approve** a proposal/ recommendation/ motion

proposal [C, U] 提案; 提案すること ◇I welcome the *proposal to* reduce taxes for the low-paid. 低所得者のために減税する提案を私は歓迎します ◇His *proposal* that the system be changed was rejected. 制度を変えるべきだという彼の提案は退けられた ◇They judged the time was right for the *proposal* of new terms for the trade agreement. 彼らはその貿易協定の新たな条項を提案するのに適した時期であると判断した ☞ **proposal** (OFFER 1)

recommendation [C] (報告書に含まれる正式な)提言, 勧告 ◇The committee made *recommendations to* the board on teachers' pay and conditions. 委員会は教員の給与と労働環境に関して教育委員会に提言を行った ◇The major *recommendation* is for a change in the law. 提言の主旨はその法律の改正を支持するというものである ◇I had the operation *on the recommendation of* my doctor. 私は医者の勧めで手術を受けた ☞ **recommend** (RECOMMEND 1)

suggestion [C] (他の人が考えるための)提案 ◇Can I make a *suggestion*? 提案してもよいですか ◇Do you *have any suggestions*? 何か提案はありますか We need to get it there by four. *Any suggestions*? 私たちは4時までにそこに到着する必要がある. 何か提案はあるかい ◇We are *open to suggestions* (= willing to listen to ideas from other people). 私たちは他人に耳を傾ける用意があります ☞ **suggest** (RECOMMEND 2)

proposition [C] (ビジネスでの)提案, 提示, 申し出 ◇I'd like to put a *business proposition* to you. あなたに仕事上の提案があるのですが ◇He was trying to make it look like an *attractive proposition*. 彼はそれが魅力

的な提示であるように見せようとしていた ◇Is that a *viable proposition*? それは実行可能な提案ですか

motion [C] (会議で議論[票決]される)動議 ◇The *motion was carried* by six votes to one. その動議は6票対1票で可決された ◇He proposed a *motion of no confidence* in the government (= to show that there is no longer any support for government). 彼は政府への不信任動議を提出した

propose 動 ☞ RECOMMEND 1

propose・suggest・put sth forward・move・advance・moot
人々が議論[検討]するために計画や考え, 理論について話す
【類語訳】提案する, 提議する, 発議する, 提出する, 説明する, 提唱する

文型&コロケーション
▶ to propose/ suggest/ put forward/ advance/ moot sth **as** sth
▶ to propose/ suggest/ be put forward/ move/ be mooted **that**...
▶ to propose/ suggest/ put forward/ advance/ moot an **idea**
▶ to propose/ put forward/ advance/ moot a **plan**
▶ to propose/ suggest/ put forward/ moot a **scheme**
▶ to propose/ suggest/ put forward/ advance a **solution**
▶ to propose/ put forward/ advance a **theory**
▶ to put forward/ advance/ moot a **proposal**
▶ to propose/ suggest/ put forward a/ an **change/ measure/ alternative**
▶ to propose/ put forward/ advance a **view**

propose [他]《ややフォーマル》(計画・考えを)提案する; 提議[発議]する, 提出する; 説明する ◇The measures have been *proposed* as a way of improving standards. その方策は基準を改善する一つの方法として提案されている ◇He *proposed* changing the name of the company. 彼は会社名を変更することを提案した ◇It *was proposed that* the president be elected for a period of two years. 大統領を2年任期で選出することが発議された ◇It *was proposed to* pay the money from public funds. 公的資金からそのお金を支払うことが発議された ◇He will *propose a motion* (= be the main speaker in support of an idea) in tomorrow's debate. 彼は明日の討論会では動議を提出するだろう ◇She *proposed* a possible solution to the mystery. 彼女はその謎を解く可能性のある答えを提示した ◇**oppose** (OPPOSE), **second** (SUPPORT), **table** (PRESENT 3)

suggest [他] (計画・考えを)提案する, 提議する, 提唱する ◇I *suggest* (that) we go out to eat. 外食するというのはどうですかね ◇I *suggested* going in my car. 私は私の車で行くことを提案した ◇He *suggested to* the committee that they should delay making a decision. 彼は委員会に決定を延期すべきだと提案した ◇It *has been suggested that* bright children take their exams early. 聡明な子どもには早期に試験を受けるようにすることが提案されている ◇The report *suggested* a two-stage process. その報告書では2段階のプロセスが提唱された

,put sth 'forward 句動詞 《ややフォーマル》(計画・考えを)提出する, 提議する, 提唱する ◇Several suggestions were *put forward* for possible venues. 開催候補地の提案がいくつか出された ◇He *put forward* some very

→propose　　　　　　　　　　　　　　protect

convincing arguments. 彼はいくつか非常に説得力のある主張をした

ノート propose, suggest, put sth forward の使い分け: suggest は propose や put sth forward ほどフォーマルでない状況で用いられることが多く、特に個人的な提案・取り決めをする場合に用いられる. ◆I *suggest* that we go out to eat. (外食するというのはどうですかね). I propose that we go out to eat. とも言えるが、非常にフォーマルな響きがある. put sth forward はこのようには用いられない. ×I *put forward* that we go out to eat. suggest は時に propose や put sth forward より確信の度合いが弱く、自分の提案がどれほど歓迎されるか分からないので参考程度に[穏やかに]提案することを指す. propose や put sth forward は自信を持って提案する傾向にあり、自分の考えが確実に受け入れられることを望む場合に用いられる. 物事が正式な過程を経て検討される場合は、propose か put sth forward を用いるのが一般的. ◆They are ready to discuss plans *proposed/put forward* by the UN. (彼らは国連から提出された計画を議論する用意がある). ×They are ready to discuss plans *suggested* by the UN. put forward は suggestion や argument を目的語に取ることができるが、propose と suggest は不可.

move [他]《フォーマル》(国会・正式な会議などで)提議[発議]する, 動議として提出する ◇I *move* that a vote be taken on this. 私にこれについて採決を行うことを提議します ◇The Opposition *moved* an amendment to the Bill. 野党はその法案の修正を動議として提出した

advance [他]《フォーマル》(考え・理論・計画を)提出する, 提議する, 提唱する ◇The article *advances* a new theory to explain changes in the climate. その記事は気候変動を説明する新理論を提示している ❶ advance は put sth forward のフォーマルな表現で、特に理論的な文脈で idea, theory, thesis, explanation, argument と共に用いられるが、実際的な文脈で計画・解決法についても用いられる.

moot [他, ふつう受身で]《フォーマル》(計画を)提案する, 提出する, 提議する ◇The idea was first *mooted* at last week's meeting. その考えは先週の会議で初めて提議された ◇It had been *mooted* that there should be a study period after school. 放課後, 自習時間を設けることが提案されていた ❶ moot はふつう詳細がすべて明確な提案に練り上げられる前の、かなり早い検討段階での考えを提案することを指す.

protect [動] ☞ SAVE 1

protect • defend • guard • preserve • safeguard • shield • shelter • secure
絶対に人や物が傷つけられないようにする
【類語訳】守る, 保護する, 防ぐ, 防御する, 防衛する, 護衛する, 警備する, 保存する, 遮蔽する, かくまう

文型&コロケーション
▶ to protect/ defend/ guard/ preserve/ safeguard/ shield/ shelter/ secure sb/ sth from sth
▶ to protect/ defend/ guard/ safeguard/ secure sth against sth
▶ to protect/ defend **yourself**
▶ to protect/ preserve/ safeguard **jobs**
▶ to protect/ preserve a **species**
▶ **heavily** protected/ defended/ guarded

protect [他, 自] (傷つけられないように人・物を)守る, 保護する, 防ぐ ◇They huddled together to *protect* themselves from the wind. 彼らは風から身を守るために身を寄せ合った ◇Each company is fighting to *protect* its own commercial interests. 会社はそれぞれ自社の営業利益を守ろうと闘っている ◇The paint helps *protect* against rust. その塗料はさびを防ぐのに役立つ ☞ **protection** (SECURITY)

defend [他, 自] (攻撃から人・物を)守る, 防御[防衛]する ◇All our officers are trained to *defend* themselves against knife attacks. すべての警官はナイフによる攻撃から身を守る訓練を受けている ◇Troops have been sent to *defend* the borders. 国境を防衛するために軍隊が派遣された ◇It is impossible to *defend* against an all-out attack. 全面攻撃を防ぐことは不可能だ ☞ **defence** (PRECAUTION)

guard [他] (攻撃・危険から財産・場所・人々を)守る, 護衛する, 警備する ◇Delegates at the conference were *guarded* by the police. 会議に出席した代表者たちは警察に護衛された ◇You can't get in; the whole place is *guarded*. 中には入れません, この場所全体が警戒中です ◇The recipe is a closely *guarded* secret. 《比喩的》そのレシピは極秘です ☞ **guard** (GUARD)

preserve [他]《ややフォーマル》(危害・危険から人・物の生命・存在・安全を)守る, 保護する, 保存する ◇To *preserve* life should always be the goal. 生命を守ることが常に目標であるべきだ ◇The society was set up to *preserve* endangered species from extinction. その協会は絶滅危惧種を絶滅から保護するために設立された ◇She was determined to *preserve* her independence and way of life. 彼女は自分の自立と生き方を守ろうと決めていた

▶ **preservation** [名] [U] ◇The central issue in the strike was the *preservation* of jobs. ストライキの中心的課題は職の保護だった

safeguard [他, 自]《フォーマル》(損失・危害・損害から物を)守る, 保護する, 防ぐ ◇It is hoped that the order will *safeguard* jobs at the plant. その注文で工場の仕事が守られることが期待されている ◇The leaflet explains how to *safeguard* against dangers in the home. そのチラシには家庭での危険を防止する方法が説明されている ☞ **safeguard** (PRECAUTION)

shield [他] (間に何かを置いて危険・危害・不快な物事から人・物を)守る, 遮蔽する, かくまう, 隠す ◇I *shielded* my eyes against the glare. 私はまぶしい光から目を守った ◇Police believe that somebody is *shielding* the killer. 警察は何者かが殺人犯をかくまっていると考えている ◇You can't *shield* her from the truth forever. 永遠に彼女に真実を隠しておくことはできない ☞ **shield** (PRECAUTION)

shelter [他] (天候・危険から避難する場所を与えて人・物を)守る, 保護する, かくまう ◇Trees *shelter* the house from the wind. 木々がその家を風から守っている ◇Perhaps I *sheltered* my daughter too much (= protected her too much from unpleasant or difficult experiences). たぶん私は娘に過保護だったのだろう ☞ **shelter** (SHELTER)

secure [他] (安全に物を)守る, 保護する, 防ぐ; 安全にする ◇No home can be completely *secured* against intruders. いかなる家も侵入者を完全には防ぐことはできない ◇The windows were *secured* with locks and bars. 窓はロックとかんぬきで厳重に閉鎖されていた ◇The government has deployed 35,000 troops in an effort to *secure* the border. 政府は国境を守るために3万5千もの兵を配備している ☞ **security** (SECURITY)

protester 名

protester・opponent・demonstrator・dissident・rebel
人や物事に反対の意を表明する人
【類語訳】抗議者, 反対者, 対抗者, 敵対者, 反体制派, 造反者

文型&コロケーション
- a protester/ demonstrator/ rebel **against** sth
- **angry/ peaceful** protesters/ demonstrators
- an **anti-government** protester/ demonstrator/ rebel
- a **political** opponent/ demonstrator/ dissident
- protesters/ opponents/ demonstrators/ rebels **call for/ demand** sth

protester [C] 抗議者 ◇Police arrested more than 200 anti-nuclear *protesters* at the military base. 警察は軍事基地で200人以上の反核の抗議者を逮捕した ☞ **protest** (COMPLAIN)

opponent [C] 反対者, 対抗者, 敵対者 ◇He has emerged as a leading *opponent* of the reforms. 彼はその改革の主要な反対者として登場した ◇The regime has been accused of torturing and killing its *opponents*. その政権は敵対者を拷問し殺害したとして非難されている 反意 **supporter,** ☞ **oppose** (OPPOSE)

demonstrator [C] デモ参加者 ◇Troops opened fire on a crowd of pro-democracy *demonstrators*. 軍隊は民主化を要求するデモ隊に発砲した

ノート protester と demonstrator の使い分け: 行進する人を指す場合は, demonstrator のほうが protester よりも繁繁に用いられる。◆A procession of 30,000 *demonstrators* marched to the parliament building. (3万人のデモ参加者の列が国会議事堂の建物へ向けて行進した)。protester は他の方法で反対の意を表明する人を指すことが多い。◆Two anti-war *protesters* climbed the clock tower at the Houses of Parliament. (反戦の抗議者二人が国会議事堂の時計台に登った)。

dissident [C] (統制の厳しい国において政府を批判する)反体制派の人 ◇*Dissidents* were often imprisoned by the security police. 反体制派の人々がしばしば公安警察によって投獄された

rebel [C] (組織内において権威者に反抗する)造反者 ◇A number of Labour *rebels* are planning to vote against the government. 数多くの労働党の造反者が政府に反対票を投じる計画を立てている

proud 形

1 proud・dignified・self-respecting
自らを尊敬している[尊敬に値すると思っている]人のことを表す
【類語訳】誇り高い, 自尊心のある, 威厳のある, 貫禄のある, 堂々とした

文型&コロケーション
- a proud/ dignified/ self-respecting **man/ woman**

proud 《しばしばほめて》誇り高い, 自尊心のある ◇They were a *proud* and independent people. 彼らは誇り高く自立した人々だった ◇Don't be too *proud* to ask for advice. アドバイスを求めることができないほどの自尊心を持ってはならない ☞ **pride** (DIGNITY), **proud** (GLAD)

dignified 《ほめて》威厳[貫禄]のある, 堂々とした ◇They left quietly in an orderly and *dignified* manner. 彼らは規律正しく威厳ある物腰で静かに退出した ◇Throughout his trial he maintained a *dignified* silence. 審理の間ずっと彼は威厳ある沈黙を守った 反意 **undignified,** ☞ **dignity** (DIGNITY)

self-re'specting [名詞の前で]《特に否定文で》(自分の行動が正しいと信じていて)自尊心のある, 誇り高い ◇No *self-respecting* journalist would ever work for that newspaper. 自尊心のあるジャーナリストならその新聞社では働かないだろう ☞ **self-respect** (DIGNITY)

2 proud・arrogant・pompous・vain・cocky・haughty・self-important・high-handed・conceited・boastful
他の人よりも優れている[偉い]と思って振る舞う人のことを表す
【類語訳】傲慢な, 高慢な, 尊大な, 横柄な, もったいぶった, 鼻にかける, 生意気な, 思い上がった, 偉ぶった, うぬぼれた

文型&コロケーション
- arrogant/ vain/ cocky/ conceited **about** sth
- a proud/ an arrogant/ a pompous/ a vain/ a haughty/ a self-important/ a conceited **man**
- a proud/ an arrogant/ a vain/ a haughty/ a conceited **woman**
- an arrogant/ a pompous/ a haughty/ a high-handed **way/ manner**
- an arrogant/ a cocky/ a haughty/ a high-handed **attitude**
- arrogant/ self-important/ high-handed **behaviour**

proud 《けなして》傲慢な, 高慢な, 尊大な ◇She was too *proud* to admit she could be wrong. 彼女は高慢で自分の非を認められなかった ◇He was too *proud* now to be seen with his former friends. 彼は今や尊大になっていて昔の友人たちと一緒にいるところを見せることはなくなっていた 反意 **humble,** ☞ **pride** (PRIDE), **proud** (GLAD)

arrogant 《けなして》(他人の気持ち・意見を考えずに)横柄な, 傲慢な, 尊大な ◇He was a rude, *arrogant* young man. 彼は無礼で横柄な若者だった ◇The chief inspector disliked his *arrogant* manner. 主任警部は彼の横柄な態度が気に入らなかった ☞ **arrogance** (PRIDE)

➤ **arrogantly** 副 ◇Luke was *arrogantly* confident. ルークは傲慢なほど自信たっぷりだった

pompous 《けなして》(長々と堅苦しい言葉を並べ立てて)もったいぶった, 尊大な, 気取った, 仰々しい ◇a *pompous* official 尊大な役人 ◇She made a long, *pompous* speech. 彼女は長々ともったいぶったスピーチをした

➤ **pomposity** 名 [U] ◇The prince's manner was informal, without a trace of *pomposity*. 王子は尊大さのかけらも見せず打ち解けた態度だった

vain 《けなして》(自分の外見・能力・業績について)うぬぼれた[虚栄心]の強い, 鼻にかける ◇She's too *vain* to wear glasses. 彼女は虚栄心が強く眼鏡が掛けられない ◇I don't think it's *vain* to care about how you look. 私は見た目を気にすることはうぬぼれが強いのだとは思わない 反意 **modest,** ☞ **vanity** (PRIDE)

cocky 《インフォーマル, けなして》(他の人をいら立たせるほど)生意気な, 気取った, 思い上がった ◇Don't get *cocky* with me! 私に生意気な口を利くな

haughty 《特に書き言葉, けなして》横柄な, 傲慢な, 高慢な, 尊大な ◇She threw him a look of *haughty* disdain.

彼女は彼に高慢な軽蔑の眼差しを投げかけた
▷**haughtily** 副 ◇She looked *haughtily* at me, waiting for me to leave. 彼女は偉そうに私を見て、私が出て行くのを待っていた

,**self-im'portant** 《けなして》尊大ぶった、偉ぶった ◇He was a *self-important* little man. 彼は尊大ぶった小人物だった 反意 humble

,**high-'handed** 《けなして》(他人の意見を考えずに権力を不当にふるって)高圧的な、横暴な ◇Customers are angry over the bank's *high-handed* attitude. 顧客たちは銀行の高圧的な態度に怒っている

conceited 《けなして》(自分に)うぬぼれた、思い上がった ◇It's very *conceited* of you to assume that your work is always the best. 常に自分の作品が一番だと思うのは大いにうぬぼれだよ ☞ conceit (PRIDE)

boastful 《けなして》自慢する、自慢げな ◇I tried to emphasize my good points without sounding *boastful*. 私は自慢に聞こえないようにして自分の長所を強調しようとした
反意 **modest**, ☞ **boast** (BOAST)

provide 動

---

provide・give・supply・yield・issue・lend・put sth up
人が物を使えるようにすることを表す
【類語訳】用意する、提供する、与える、供給する、生じる、生む、もたらす、発行する、支給する

文型&コロケーション
▶ to provide/ supply/ put up sth **for** sb
▶ to give/ supply/ issue/ lend sth **to** sb
▶ to provide/ supply/ issue sb **with** sth
▶ to provide/ give/ supply/ issue **equipment/ details/ information**
▶ to provide/ give/ supply/ put up **funds**
▶ to provide/ give/ supply/ lend **protection**
▶ to provide/ give/ supply a **service**
▶ to provide/ give/ supply **housing/ assistance**
▶ to provide/ give/ lend **support/ credibility/ weight/ credence**
▶ to provide/ give/ yield/ issue a **dividend**
▶ to provide/ give/ yield a/ an **improvement/ profit/ result/ return/ revenue**
▶ to provide/ give/ supply an **alibi/ alternative/ answer**
▶ to provide/ give/ supply/ issue sth **free (of charge)**

provide [他]《ややフォーマル, 特に書き言葉》用意する、提供する ◇The hospital has a commitment to *provide* the best possible medical care. 病院は考えられる最善の医療を提供する責任がある ◇Please answer questions in the space *provided*. 与えられた空欄で質問に答えてください ◇The report was not expected to *provide* any answers. 報告書から何らかの解答が得られるとは期待されていなかった
▷**provision** 名 [U, C, ふつう単数で] ◇educational/housing *provision* 教育/住宅の提供 ◇The *provision* of specialist teachers is being increased. 専門教員の人員供給は増えつつある

give [他] 与える ◇They were all thirsty so I *gave* them a drink. 彼らはみんな喉が渇いていたので、彼らに飲み物を与えた ◇*Give* me your name and address. あなたの名前と住所を教えてください ◇I was hoping you would *give* me a job. あなたから仕事がいただけるものと期待していました ◇She wants a job that *gives* her more responsibility. より責任の重い仕事を彼女は欲しています ◇He was *given* a new heart in a five-hour operation. 彼は5時間に及ぶ手術で新しい心臓を移植された ◇They couldn't *give* me any more information. 彼らは私にそれ以上の情報を与えることができなかった ◇I'll *give* you (= allow you to have) ten minutes to prepare your answer. 10分あげるから返事の準備をしてください ◇He *gives* Italian lessons to his colleagues. 彼は同僚たちにイタリア語のレッスンをしている

> **ノート provideとgiveの使い分け**: provideはgiveよりもフォーマルで、特に書き言葉で使われる。provideは、物事が一般の人々[不特定の人]に利用される場合にしばしば用いられる。giveは、特定の人に利用される場合により頻繁に用いられる。◆The hospital aims to *provide* the best possible medical care. (病院は考えられる最善の医療を提供することを目指している)。◆We want to *give you* the best possible care. (私たちはあなたに考えられる最高の介護を提供したいと思います)。

supply [他]《ややフォーマル》(必要なものを大量に)供給する ◇Foreign governments *supplied* the rebels with arms. 外国政府は反抗者たちに武器を供与した ◇Here is a list of foods *supplying* our daily vitamin needs. ここに我々が日々必要とするビタミンを与えてくれる食料のリストがあります ◇She was jailed for *supplying* drugs. 彼女は薬物提供のかどで拘留された ◇This one power station keeps half the country *supplied* with electricity. この発電所一つで国の半分の電力をまかなっている ☞ **supply** (SUPPLY)
▷**supply** 名 [U] ◇the electricity *supply* 電力供給 ◇The UN has agreed to allow the *supply* of emergency aid. 国連は緊急援助の供与を認めることに同意した

yield [他]《ややフォーマル, 特にビジネス》(利益・結果などを)生じる、生む、もたらす ◇Higher-rate deposit accounts *yield* good returns. 高率の預金口座は大きな利益を生む ◇The research has *yielded* useful information. その調査から有益な情報が得られた ☞ **yield** (OUTPUT)

issue [他, しばしば受身で]《ややフォーマル》(公式に)発行する、支給する ◇We can *issue* a passport within a day. ここではその日のうちにパスポートを交付できます ◇New members will be *issued* with a temporary identity card. 新規メンバーたちには仮の身分証明書が支給されるでしょう ◇Work permits were *issued* to only 5% of those who applied for them. 就労許可が下りたのは申請者のわずか5%だった

lend [他] (支援を)与える ◇I was more than happy to *lend* my support to such a good cause. そのような立派な目的に支援できるとはこの上なく幸せだった ◇He came along to *lend* me moral support. 私を精神的に援助するために彼はやって来た

,**put sth 'up** 句動詞 《ややインフォーマル, 特にビジネス》(金を)提供する ◇A local businessman has *put up* the £500,000 needed to save the club. 地元のあるビジネスマンがそのクラブを救うのに必要な50万ポンドを出した

public 形

---

public・state・national・federal
一国の政府、特に財政支出[行政]に関連する事柄を表す
【類語訳】公の、公務の、国の、国事の、公共の、公営の、公立の、

公設の, 国有の, 国営の, 国立の, 連邦政府の, 中央政府の

【文型&コロケーション】
▶public/ state/ national/ federal **authorities/ funding/ expenditure/ investment**
▶public/ state/ federal **power/ control/ regulation/ institutions/ officials/ employees/ funds/ money/ finance/ spending**
▶public/ state **education/ hospitals/ enterprise/ ownership**
▶the public/ state **sector**
▶the national/ federal **government**

public [名詞の前で] (政府・行政に関連していて)公の, 公務の, 国(事)の, 公共の, 公営の, 公立の, 公設の ◇Their tax plans would hit *public services*. 彼らの税制計画は公共事業に打撃を与えるだろう ◇There has been massive investment in *public housing*. 公営住宅に莫大な投資がなされている ◇He spent much of his career in *public office* (= working for the government). 彼は職歴の大半を官公庁で過ごした ❶アメリカ・オーストラリア・スコットランドなどの国々では, *public school* (公立学校) は政府によって支払われる無料の地域の学校を指すが, イングランドでは, *state school*と呼ばれる. イギリス, 特にイングランドでは *public school* (パブリックスクール) は13～18歳の生徒が通う, しばしば全寮制の私立学校を指し, 親によって教育費が支払われる. また, *public company* または *public limited company* (《英》公開会社), *public corporation* (《米》公開会社) も政府による所有ではなく, 一般の人々に自社株を販売する会社を指す. しかしながら, 《英》では *public corporation* は政府によって所有され, 国務に従事する組織を指す. 反意 **private**. ❶ *private* は政府ではなく, 個人・独立系企業によって所有・運営される業務・施設を表す. ◆*private companies/ schools* (民間企業/私立学校). ◆a programme to return many of the state companies to *private* ownership (国有企業の多くを民間に戻す計画).
▶**publicly** 副 ◇a *publicly* owned company 公営企業
state [名詞の前で] (政府によって提供・管理されていて)国(事)の, 国家の ◇The law applies only to schools within the *state system*. その法律は国家制度下の学校にのみ適用される ◇There needs to be an increase in the basic *state pension*. 基本的な国民年金の増額が必要とされている ◇Many local families are dependent on *state benefits* (= in Britain, government money given to people who are poor). 地域の多くの家庭が国からの給付金に依存している 反意 *private*, ☞ *state* (COUNTRY 1)
national [ふつう名詞の前で] (政府によって所有・管理・財政援助されていて)国家の, 国有の, 国営の, 国立の ◇The collection is housed at the *national* museum. そのコレクションは国立美術館に所蔵されている ◇The Romanian *national* airline has ordered seven of the new aircraft. ルーマニアの国営航空会社がその新型航空機を7機発注している
federal (地方政府ではなくて)連邦[中央]政府の ◇On 15th February a *federal* judge ruled in their favour. 2月15日に連邦判事が彼らの訴えを認める判決を下した ◇We will continue *federal* funding for the arts. 我々はそうした芸術のために連邦の補助金を継続する ❶ *federal* は個別に自治権を持つ州が存在し, 国家の決定が中央政府が管理する国, 特にアメリカについて言う.
▶**federally** 副 ◇*federally* funded health care 連邦政府資金による保健医療

publish

publish 動

1 publish・issue・release・advertise・print・publicize・circulate
一般の人々に情報を知らせる
【類語訳】掲載する, 発表する, 公表する, 公開する, 広告を出す, 宣伝する, 回覧する

【文型&コロケーション】
▶to issue/ release/ circulate sth **to sb**
▶to publish/ issue/ release/ print/ circulate a **report/ details**
▶to publish/ issue/ release/ print a **document/ statement/ description**
▶to publish/ issue/ print an **apology**
▶to publish/ print a/ an **picture/ photo/ article**
▶to publish/ advertise/ publicize/ circulate sth **widely**
▶to publish/ issue/ release/ advertise sth **formally**
▶to publish/ issue/ release sth **officially**

publish [他] (新聞・雑誌に手紙・記事・写真などを)掲載する, 発表する, 公表する;(インターネット上で)公開する ◇The editors *published* a full apology in the following edition. 編集部は全謝罪文を次の版に載せた ◇The report will be *published* on the Internet. その報告書はインターネット上で公開される予定です ❶フォーマルな言い回しでは, *publish* には「(公的情報を一般の人々に)発表[公表]する」という意味もある. ◆The findings of the committee will be *published* on Friday. (委員会の調査結果は金曜日に公表される予定です).
▶**publication** 名 [U] ◇The newspaper continues to defend its *publication* of the photographs. その新聞社はその写真の掲載の正当性を主張し続けている
issue [他] (ややフォーマル)(情報を正式に)発表する, 公表する ◇They *issued* a joint statement denying the charges. 彼らは容疑を否認する共同声明を発表した ◇The police have *issued* an appeal for witnesses. 警察は目撃者情報の公募を発表した
▶**issue** 名 [U] ◇the *issue* of a joint statement by the French and German governments フランス・ドイツ両政府による共同声明の発表
release [他] (ややフォーマル)(情報を正式に)発表する, 公表する ◇Police have *released* no further details about the accident. 警察はその事故に関してそれ以上詳しい情報を公表していない

📝 *publish, issue, release* の使い分け:これらの語はすべて説明・報告書・公文書・声明などを一般の人々に正式に発表することについて用いられるが, この意味では *issue* が最も幅広い連語と結びつき, *summons, warrant, writ* などの法的通達だけでなく, 例えば *declaration, proclamation, joint/public statement, notice, communiqué* などの発表に関連する語と共に用いられることが多い. *publish* は手紙・記事についても用いられるが, *issue* と *release* は不可.

advertise [自, 他] (行事・求人などの)広告を出す, 宣伝する;(自分自身について)公表する ◇We are currently *advertising for* a new sales manager. 当社では現在新たに営業部長の求人広告を出しております ◇We should have *advertised* the concert much more widely. もっとずっと広くそのコンサートを宣伝するべきだった ◇If I were you, I wouldn't *advertise the fact that* you don't have a

↪ **publish**

work permit. 私が君の立場なら、君が就労許可を持っていない事実を公言したりはしないだろうね ☞ **advertise** (ADVERTISE)
▶**advertisement** [名] [U] ◇We are employing an assistant to help with the *advertisement* of the group's activities. 我々はそのグループの活動の宣伝を手伝うアシスタントを雇っている

print [他] (印刷物の形態で)掲載する、発表する、公表する ◇The photo was *printed* in all the national newspapers. その写真はすべての全国紙に掲載された ◇The magazine was sued for *printing* a libellous article about her family. その雑誌は彼女の家族に関する中傷的な記事を掲載したかどで訴えられた

publicize (英でまた -ise) [他] (一般の人々に)発表する、公表する ◇They flew to Europe to *publicize* the plight of the refugees. 彼らは難民の窮状を広く伝えるためにヨーロッパへ飛んだ ◇In a much *publicized* speech (= that has received a lot of attention on television, in newspapers, etc.) she condemned the government for its inactivity. 報道陣の前で、彼女は政府の怠慢さを非難した

┌─ノート─ **advertise** と **publicize** の使い分け: **advertise** はふつう求人・行事を印刷物・新聞・看板・インターネットで広告・宣伝すること。**publicize** は行事・情報を公の場で盛んに話題にしたり、特別な催しを開いて、その後それらをテレビ・新聞・インターネットで報道されること。

circulate [他] 《ややフォーマル》(集団内の全員に情報を)回覧する ◇The document will be *circulated* to all members. その書類は全員に回覧します

2 publish・issue・print・release
本や雑誌、CDなどを作って一般の人々に販売する
【類語訳】出版する、刊行する、発行する、公開する、売り出す

┌─文型&コロケーション─
▶to publish/ issue/ print/ release a **book**
▶to publish/ issue/ print a **booklet/ brochure/ newsletter/ leaflet/ pamphlet**
▶to publish/ issue/ release a new **title/ edition**
▶to issue/ release a/ an **CD/ single/ album**
▶to issue/ print **banknotes**
▶to publish/ release sth **on CD-ROM**
▶to issue/ release sth **on CD**
▶to be **newly/ recently** published/ issued/ released
▶to be **privately** published/ printed

publish [他、自] (本・雑誌・CD-ROMなどを)出版[刊行、発行]する;(作家が)作品を出版してもらう ◇He works for a company that *publishes* reference books. 彼は参考図書を出版している会社に勤めている ◇Most of our titles are also *published* on CD-ROM. 当社の出版物のほとんどCD-ROMでも発行されています ◇She hasn't *published* anything for years. 彼女は何年も作品を出していない ◇University teachers are under pressure to *publish*. 大学の教員は自分の本を出すことが求められている
▶**publication** [名] [U] ◇the *publication* of his first novel 彼の処女小説の刊行

issue [他] 《ややフォーマル》(雑誌・新刊書・CDなどを)刊行[発行]する;(切手・硬貨・会社株を新たに)発行する ◇We *issue* a monthly newsletter. 当社は月刊で会報を発行しています ◇The Royal Mail *issued* a special set of stamps to

pull

mark the occasion. ロイヤル・メールはその行事を記念して特別切手を一組発行した
▶**issue** [名] [U] ◇I bought a set of the new stamps on the date of *issue*. 私は発売日にその新しい切手を一組買った

┌─ノート─ **publish** と **issue** の使い分け: **publish** は一般の人々に販売する本を作ることを表す一般的な語。 ◆ a company that *publishes* reference books (参考図書を出版している会社). × a company that *issues* reference books. しかしながら、特定の本、特に新刊書について言う場合は、両語とも使用可能。 ◆ They have just *published/ issued* a new edition. (新版が刊行されたばかりです)。 **issue** は組織によって作られる booklet, newsletter, leaflet, pamphlet などの小規模な出版物を表す語と共に用いられることが多い。もっとも、**publish** もこれらの語と用いられることもある。

print [他] (本・新聞などを大量に)出版[刊行、発行]する ◇They *printed* 30,000 copies of the book. その本は3万部発行された ◇The firm specializes in *printing* calendars. その会社はカレンダーの発行を専門にしている

release [他] (映画・本・CDなどを)公開する、売り出す ◇When was the film first *released*? その映画はいつ初公開されましたか ◇There have been a lot of new products *released* onto the market. たくさんの新製品が市場に売り出されている
▶**release** [名] [U] ◇The movie *goes on* general *release* (= will be widely shown in cinemas) next week. その映画は来週一般公開されます

pull [動]

1 pull・drag・draw・haul・tow・trail・tug
特定の方向、特に自分の方や後ろで物を動かす
【類語訳】引っ張る、牽引する、引き寄せる、引きずる

┌─文型&コロケーション─
▶to pull/ drag/ draw/ haul/ tow/ trail/ tug sb/ sth **along/ down/ towards** sth
▶to pull/ drag/ draw/ haul/ tow/ trail sb/ sth **behind you**
▶to pull/ drag/ draw/ haul a **cart/ sledge/ sled**
▶to pull/ draw a **coach/ carriage**
▶to pull/ haul/ tow a **truck**
▶**horses** pull/ draw/ haul sth
▶**dogs** pull/ drag/ haul sth

pull [他] (特定の方向に)引いて動かす、引っ張って行く;(乗り物につかまって[つないで]物を)引っ張る、牽引する ◇*Pull* the chair nearer to the table. 椅子をテーブルの近くに引いて ◇She took his arm and *pulled* him along roughly. 彼女は彼の腕をつかんで乱暴に引っ張って行った ◇I quickly *pulled* on my sweater. 私は素早くセーターを着た ◇They use oxen to *pull* their carts. 彼らは牛を使って荷車を引っ張っている [反意] **push** (PUSH 1)

drag (-gg-) [他] (特定の方向に[自分の後ろで]苦労して)引きずって動かす、引っ張って行く ◇I *dragged* the chair over to the window. 私は椅子を窓のほうへ引きずって動かした ◇Police *dragged* protesters away from the embassy entrance. 警察は大使館の入り口から抗議者たちを引きずって移動させた ◇The sack is too heavy to lift — you'll have to *drag* it. この袋は重すぎて持ち上げられない—引きずるしかないよ ◇Dogs *drag* the sledges for hundreds of miles across the snow. 犬たちは雪の中を何百マイルもそりを引っ張って行く

draw [他]《書き言葉》(優しく)引いて動かす、引き寄せる；(車などの)乗り物を)引っ張る、牽引する ◇He *drew* the cork out of the bottle. 彼は瓶からコルクを引き抜いた ◇I *drew* my chair closer to the fire. 私は椅子を暖炉の近くに引き寄せた ◇I tried to *draw him aside* (= for example in order to talk to him privately). 私は彼を脇に引き寄せようとした ◇a *horse-drawn* carriage 馬車

haul [他] (特定の場所へ非常に苦労して)引きずって動かす、引っ張って行く ◇He reached down and *hauled* her up onto the ledge. 彼は下方の彼女に手を伸ばして岩棚に引き上げた ◇Fishermen were *hauling* in their nets. 漁師たちが網を引き上げていた ◇The trucks were *hauled* by steam locomotives. 貨車が蒸気機関車に引かれていた

> [ノート] **drag** と **haul** の使い分け：drag はふつう自分の後ろで地面から離さずに物を引きずって動かすことで、haul はふつう自分の方、しばしば上方に物を引きずって動かすことを指す。
> × He reached down and *dragged* her up onto the ledge.　drag はしばしば努力を要するが、haul は常に努力を要する。I hauled the chair over to the window. と言うことはできるが、これは動かすのが大変な非常に重い椅子の場合のみである。

tow [他] (別の乗り物の後ろにロープ[鎖]でつないで車・ボート・軽飛行機を)引っ張る、牽引する ◇Our car was *towed* away by the police. 私たちの車は警察に牽引されて行った

trail [他、自] (後ろで)引きずって動かす、引っ張って行く；引きずられる ◇She *trailed* her hand in the cool water as the boat moved along. ボートが進んでいる間、彼女は手を冷たい水に浸けたままにしていた ◇The bride's dress *trailed* behind her. 花嫁はドレスのすそを引きずって歩いた

tug (-gg-) [他] (特定の方向に強く)ぐいと引いて動かす[引っ張って行く] ◇He *tugged* his hat down over his head. 彼は帽子を頭の上からぐいと引っ張ってかぶった ◇Annie appeared, *tugging* her little sister by the arm. アニーが妹の腕をぐいぐい引いて現れた

---

2 pull・yank・tug・jerk

物を強く握って、腕力を使って自分のほうに動かす
【類語訳】引く、引っ張る、引き寄せる

> [文型&コロケーション]
> ▸ pull/ yank/ tug **on/ at** sth
> ▸ pull/ yank/ tug sb/ sth **toward/ towards/ out of** sth
> ▸ pull/ yank/ tug/ jerk sth **open**
> ▸ pull/ tug (at) sb's **hair/ elbow/ arm**
> ▸ pull/ yank/ jerk sb **to their feet**
> ▸ pull/ yank/ tug/ jerk (sth) **hard**

pull [自、他] (自分のほうに物を)引く、引っ張る、引き寄せる ◇You push and I'll *pull*. 君は押して、私は引っ張るから ◇Don't *pull* so hard or you'll break it. そんなに強く引っ張らないで、壊しちゃうよ ◇I *pulled* on the rope to see if it was secure. 私はロープを引っ張ってそれが大丈夫かどうか確認した ◇He keeps *pulling* my hair! 彼が私の髪の毛を引っ張ってばかりいるの ◇She *pulled* him gently towards her. 彼女は自分のほうに彼を優しく引き寄せた ◇Mary *pulled* the blanket up over her head. メアリーは毛布を引っ張り上げて顔を隠した ◇*Pull* the door shut. ドアを引いて閉めてください [反] **push** (PUSH 2)
▸ **pull** [名] [C] ◇I gave the door a sharp *pull*. 私はドアを

勢いよく引っ張った ◇One last *pull* on the rope should do it. 最後に一度ロープを引っ張るとそうなるはずだ

yank [他、自]《ふつう副詞や前置詞と共に》《インフォーマル》(人・物を強く[素早く、突然])ぐいと引く[引っ張る] ◇The man grabbed her hair and *yanked* her head back. その男は彼女の髪をつかむと、頭を後ろにぐいと引っ張った ◇Liz *yanked* at my arm. リズは私の腕をぐいと引っ張った
▸ **yank** [名] [C] ◇She gave the rope a *yank*. 彼女はロープをぐいと引っ張った

tug (-gg-) [自、他](物を強く)ぐいぐい引く[引っ張る] ◇She *tugged* at his sleeve to get his attention. 彼女は注意を引こうと彼の袖をぐいぐい引っ張った ◇The baby was *tugging* her hair. 赤ちゃんは彼女の髪の毛をぐいぐい引っ張っていた
▸ **tug** [名] [C] ◇I felt a little *tug* on my arm. 私は腕が少しぐいと引っ張られるのを感じた

jerk [他]《ふつう副詞や前置詞と共に》(突然物を短く勢いよく)ぐいと引く[引っ張る] ◇She grabbed his hand and *jerked* him back from the kerb. 彼女は彼の手をつかむと、縁石から彼をぐいと引き戻した

---

pump [動]

pump・extract・drain・squeeze・siphon・draw
液体や気体をある場所から別の場所へ移動させる
【類語訳】くむ、抽出する、流し出す、抜き出す、排出する、流れ出る、流出する、搾り出す

> [文型&コロケーション]
> ▸ to pump/ extract/ drain/ squeeze/ siphon/ draw sth **from** sth
> ▸ to pump/ drain/ squeeze/ siphon/ draw sth **out of** sth
> ▸ to pump/ drain/ squeeze/ siphon sth **into** sth
> ▸ to pump/ drain/ siphon sth **away**
> ▸ to drain/ siphon sth **off**
> ▸ to pump/ extract/ drain/ squeeze/ siphon/ draw **water** from sth
> ▸ to pump/ extract/ drain/ squeeze/ siphon **oil/ a liquid** from sth
> ▸ to pump/ extract/ siphon **gas** from sth

pump [他、自]《ふつう副詞や前置詞と共に》(液体・空気・気体を特定の方向に)ポンプなどで送る[くむ] ◇The engine is used for *pumping* water out of the mine. このエンジンは採掘坑から水をくみ出すのに使用されている ◇The lungs *pump* oxygen into the bloodstream. 肺は酸素を血流に送っている ◇His heart *pumped* harder as he held his breath. 息を止めると彼の心臓の鼓動は激しくなった

extract [他]《ややフォーマル》(物から物質を)抽出する ◇They developed a machine that can *extract* harmful gases from the air. 彼らは空気から有害ガスを抽出することのできる機械を開発した ◇Animals take in food and *extract* nutrients from it. 動物は食べ物を摂取して、そこから栄養素を抽出している ☞ **obtain** (GET 1)
▸ **extraction** [名] [U] ◇oil/mineral/coal *extraction* 油/ミネラル/石炭の抽出 ◇the *extraction* of salt from the sea 海からの塩の抽出

drain [他、自]《ふつう副詞や前置詞と共に》(物から液体を)流し出す、抜き出す、排出する；(液体が)流れ出る、抜け出る、流出する ◇*Drain* off the excess fat from the meat. 肉から余分な油分を抜きましょう ◇She pulled out the plug and the water *drained* away. 彼女が栓を抜くと水が流れ出た

squeeze [他]《副詞や前置詞と共に》（物から液体を）搾り出す ◇*Squeeze* the juice of half a lemon over each fish. それぞれの魚の上にレモン半分から汁を搾り出しましょう ◇He took off his wet clothes and *squeezed* the water out. 彼は濡れた服を脱いで、水を搾り出した ❶squeeze は目的語に orange や lemon など、または物から搾り出される juice, water, liquid を取ることができる。

siphon（または **syphon**）[他]《ふつう副詞や前置詞と共に》（容器から容器へ）サイフォンで移す ◇I *siphoned* some petrol into a can. 私はサイフォンでガソリンを缶に移した ◇The waste liquid needs to be *siphoned* off. 廃液をサイフォンでくみ出す必要がある

draw [他]《書き言葉》（場所から液体・気体を）送る、引く、くむ ◇She *drew* water from the well, and splashed her hands and face. 彼女は井戸から水をくみ上げて、手や顔にかけた ◇The device *draws* water along the pipe. その装置はパイプに水を引くものです ❶この意味では、draw は主に well, stream, river, canal などの場所から水を引くことについて用いられる。

purpose [名] ☞ TARGET

purpose・aim・intention・plan・point・idea・intent
人や物事がもくろむことを表す
【類語訳】目的、目標、意図、意向、つもり、計画、予定

〔文型&コロケーション〕
▶ with the purpose/ aim/ intention/ idea/ intent of doing sth
▶ sb's purpose/ aim/ intention/ plan/ intent that...
▶ sb's intention/ plan/ intent to do sth
▶ sb/ sth's original purpose/ aim/ intention/ plan/ idea/ intent
▶ a specific purpose/ aim/ intention/ plan/ intent
▶ the whole point/ idea
▶ to have a purpose/ an aim/ an intention/ a plan/ a point/ an intent
▶ to state your purpose/ aim/ intention
▶ to declare your aim/ intention/ intent
▶ to achieve/ fulfil a purpose/ an aim

purpose [C]（達成すべき）目的；（人が達成しようとする）目標 ◇The main *purpose* of the campaign is to raise money. その運動の主な目的は資金を集めることです ◇A meeting was called *for the purpose of* appointing a new treasurer. 新たに経理部長を任命する目的で会議が開かれた ◇He did not want anything to distract him from his *purpose*.《ややフォーマル》彼は何かによって目標から気をそらされたくなかった

aim [C]（人が達成しようとする）目標；（達成すべき）目的 ◇She went to London with the *aim* of finding a job. 彼女は仕事を探すためにロンドンに行った ◇Our main *aim* is to increase sales in Europe. 我々の主な目的はヨーロッパの売上を増やすことだ ◇She set out the company's *aims* and objectives in her speech. 彼女はスピーチの中で会社の目標を設定した ☞ aim (INTEND)

〔ノート〕**purpose** と **aim** の使い分け：purpose は何かを行う際の理由であって、aim は達成したい物事である。aim はただ単に達成しようとしているものに対して、purpose は確実に達成するという意味合いが強い。aim は sb's aim や the aim of sth という形で、purpose は the purpose of sth という形で用いられるのが一般的で、sb's purpose とも言えるが、フォーマルである。

intention [C]（…する）意図、意向、つもり ◇I have no *intention of* going to the wedding. 私は結婚式に出るつもりは一切ない ◇He has announced his *intention* to retire. 彼は引退する意向を表明した ◇I *have every intention* of paying her back what I owe her. 私は彼女からの借金を返済する意向を固く抱いている ◇She's full of *good intentions* but they rarely work out. 彼女は善意に満ちているが、それでうまくいったためしはない ☞ intend (INTEND)

plan [C]（…する[を達成する]）計画、予定、つもり ◇Do you have any *plans for* the summer? 夏は何か予定はありますか ◇There are no *plans* to build new offices. 新社屋建設の予定はありません ◇There's been *a change of plan*. 計画の変更があった ◇We can't change our *plans* now. 今となっては計画は変更できません ☞ plan (PLAN 1), plan (INTEND)

〔ノート〕**intention** と **plan** の使い分け：intention は特に近い将来にやりたいこと、plan はしばしば（常にではないが）より長期的にやろうと決めて[準備して]いることに用いられる。

point [U, 単数で]《ややインフォーマル、ふつけなして》（物事の）目的、意義 ◇*What's the point* of all this violence? こんな暴力をふるっていったい何のつもり ◇There's *no point in* getting angry. 怒っても無駄だ ◇I *don't see the point of* doing it all again. それをもう一度初めからやる意味がよくわからない

idea [単数で]《ややインフォーマル》（物事・人の）目的、意図 ◇The whole *idea* of going was so that we could meet her new boyfriend. 行く目的はもっぱら彼女の新しい彼氏に会うためだけだった ◇*What's the idea* of all this? このことすべての目的は何ですか ◇My original *idea* was to use amateur actors. 私の元々の意図はアマの俳優を使うことだった

〔ノート〕**point** と **idea** の使い分け：point は idea よりも否定的な語で、What's the point...? と言う場合、無駄であることを示唆する。What's the idea...? と言う場合は、純粋に質問をしているのである。point はいら立ち・不満の対象にも用いられ、idea は不可。×There's no *idea* in... ×I don't see the *idea* of... また、miss the point of sth（物事がよくわからない）と言ったり、get the idea（わかる）と言ったりする。the point/idea of sth（物事の目的）や sb's idea（人の目的）とは言うが、sb's point とは言わない。×My original *point* was to use amateur actors.

intent [U]《フォーマル or 法律》（…する）意図、意向、つもり ◇She denies possessing the drug with *intent* to supply. 彼女は人に与えるつもりでその麻薬を所持していたのではないと主張している ◇He was charged with wounding with *intent*. 彼は故意による傷害の罪で告発された

push [動]

1 push・thrust・force・shove・stick・ram・drive・poke・press
手[腕、体]を使って人や物を前方へ[自分から離そうと]動かす
【類語訳】押す、伸ばす、突き進む、押しやる、押し込む、突き刺す、打ち込む、小突く、つつく、押しつける

〔文型&コロケーション〕
▶ to push/ thrust/ force/ shove/ stick/ ram/ drive/ poke/ press sth into sth
▶ to push/ thrust/ force/ shove/ stick/ drive/ poke sth

put

through sth
▶ to push/ thrust/ force/ shove sb/ sth **away**
▶ to thrust/ force/ shove/ press sth **into sb's hands/ arms**
▶ to push/ thrust/ force/ shove sth **open/ shut**
▶ to push/ thrust/ force/ shove/ ram/ drive (sth) **hard** (into/ down, etc. sth)
▶ to push/ poke/ press (sth) **gently**
▶ to push/ thrust/ drive sth **deep** (into sth)

push [他, 自]《しばしば副詞や前置詞と共に》(手・腕・体を使って人・物を自分から離そうと)押す；(体の部位を特定の位置に)伸ばす ◇He walked slowly up the hill, *pushing* his bike. 彼は自転車を押しながら坂をゆっくりと歩いて上がった ◇Marty tried to kiss her but she *pushed* him away. マーティーは彼女にキスしようとしたが、彼女は彼を押しのけた ◇Stop *pushing* me! 私を押すのはやめて ◇*Push* hard when I tell you to. 私が「押して」と言ったら、強く押して ◇You *push* and I'll pull. 君は押して、私は引っ張るから 反意 **pull** (PULL 1)

thrust [他, 自]《ふつう副詞や前置詞と共に》《書き言葉》(特定の方向に)人・物を突然[乱暴]にぐいと押す[突く]；(特定の方向に素早く)さっと動く、突き進む ◇He *thrust* the baby into my arms and ran off. 彼は赤ちゃんを私の腕に押しつけて走り去った ◇She *thrust* her hands deep into her pockets. 彼女は両手をポケットに深く突っ込んだ ◇Mike *thrust* her towards the staircase. マイクは彼女を階段のほうへぐいと押した ◇She *thrust* past him angrily. 彼女は怒って彼のそばをさっと素通りした

force [他]《しばしば副詞や前置詞と共に》(腕力を使って人・物を特定の位置に)押しやる ◇She *forced* her way through the crowds. 彼女は人込みを押し分けて進んだ ◇He *forced* the lid of his suitcase shut. 彼はスーツケースのふたを無理やり閉めた ◇Someone had tried to *force an entry* (= enter a building using force). 誰かが力ずくで押し入ろうとしていた ◇We had to *force the lock* (= break it open using force). 私たちは無理やり鍵をこじ開けねばならなかった ☞ **force** (FORCE 名)

shove [他]《ふつう副詞や前置詞と共に》《インフォーマル》(物を乱暴[無造作]に)突っ込む、押し込む、放り込む ◇She *shoved* the book into her bag and hurried off. 彼女は本をバッグの中に突っ込んで、急いで立ち去った ◇Just *shove* your suitcase under the bed. スーツケースをベッドの下に押し込むだけでいいよ

stick [他, 自]《副詞や前置詞と共に》(鋭利な物を物に)突き刺す；(物に)突き刺さる ◇The nurse *stuck* a needle into my arm. 看護師が私の腕に針を突き刺した ◇The little boy had *stuck* his head through the railings. その小さな男の子が頭を手すりの間から突き出していた ◇I found a nail *sticking* in the tyre. 私はタイヤに釘が突き刺さっているのを見つけた

ram (**-mm-**) [他]《副詞や前置詞と共に》(腕力を使って物をどこかに)押しやる、押し込む ◇She *rammed* the key into the lock. 彼女は鍵を錠にぐいと押し込んだ ◇He *rammed* his foot down hard on the brake. 彼は足でブレーキを思い切り踏んだ

drive [他]《副詞や前置詞と共に》(特定の方向・位置に物を)押し[打ち]込む ◇He took a wooden peg and *drove* it into the ground. 彼は木製の杭を手にしてそれを地面に打ち込んだ

poke [他]《副詞や前置詞と共に》(小さく素早い動きで物をどこか[特定の方向]に)小突く、つつく、突っ込む ◇He *poked* his head around the door. 彼は頭でドアを小突いた

◇Someone had *poked* a message under the door. 誰かがドアの下にメモを突っ込んでいた

press [他]《(物を物の中[上]に)しっかりと)押し込む[つける] ◇He *pressed* a coin into her hand. 彼はコインを彼女の手にしっかりと握らせた

2 push・shove・jostle・barge・shoulder・elbow
手[腕, 体]を使って人や物を無理やり脇へ動かして進む
【類語訳】押し分ける, 押しのける, 肩で押す

文型&コロケーション

▶ to push/ shove/ barge/ shoulder/ elbow **past** sb
▶ to push/ barge/ elbow **through** sb/ sth
▶ to push/ shove/ shoulder/ elbow sb **aside/ out of the way**
▶ to push/ shove/ jostle/ barge/ shoulder/ elbow **your way through/ into/ past,** etc. (sb/ sth)
▶ to push/ shove/ shoulder sb **roughly**

push [自, 他]《ふつう副詞や前置詞と共に》(手・腕・体を使って人・物を無理やり脇へ)押し分け[のけ]て進む ◇There's no need to *push*! 押しのける必要はないでしょ ◇Please don't *push in front* of other customers. 他のお客様の前に割り込まないでください ◇A woman *pushed* her way through the crowd. 一人の女性が人込みを押しのけて進んだ 反意 **pull** (PULL 2)

shove [自, 他]《進もうとして人・物を乱暴に)押し分ける[のける] ◇The crowd was *pushing and shoving* to get a better view. 群衆はよりよい景色を見ようと押し合いへし合いしていた ◇They *shoved* the guard aside. 彼らは警備員を脇へ押しのけた ❶ **shove** は目的語と共に用いられる場合、常に副詞または前置詞を伴う。

jostle [他, 自]《(前に出ようとして人込みを乱暴に)押し分け[のけ]て進む ◇The Senator was *jostled* by angry demonstrators. その上院議員は怒ったデモ参加者に押しのけられた ◇Anxious refugees *jostled for* a place in the line. 不安を覚えた難民たちが列に入ろうとして割り込んだ

barge [自, 他]《副詞や前置詞と共に》(無理やり構わずに)押し分け[のけ]て進む ◇He *barged* past me to get to the bar. 彼は私を押しのけてカウンターに向かった ◇They *barged* their way through the crowds. 彼らは人込みの中を突き進んだ

shoulder [自, 他]《副詞や前置詞と共に》(どこかへ行くために)肩で押しのけて進む；(人を)肩で押す ◇She *shouldered* past a woman with a screaming baby. 彼女は泣き叫ぶ赤ん坊を抱いた女性を押しのけて進んだ ◇He *shouldered* the younger man aside. 彼はその自分より若い男を肩で押しのけた

elbow [他]《ふつう副詞や前置詞と共に》(進もうとして人を)肘で押しのける ◇She *elbowed* me out of the way. 彼女は私をじゃまにならないように肘で押しのけた ◇He *elbowed* his way past the other shoppers. 彼は他の買い物客を肘で押しのけて進んだ

put 動

put・place・lay・set・position・stuff・pop・dump・stick・settle・plant
特定の場所[位置]に物を移す
【類語訳】置く, 載せる, 据える, 寝かせる, 配置する, 押し込む, 突っ込む, 放り込む, 投げ出す, 立てる

↳**put**

文型&コロケーション
- to put/ place/ lay/ set/ position/ pop/ dump/ stick sth **on** sth
- to put/ place/ set/ stuff/ pop/ dump/ stick sth **in/ into** sth
- to put/ lay/ set sth **down**
- to put/ place/ lay sth **carefully**

put [他]《副詞や前置詞と共に》(特定の場所・位置に物を)動かす, 置く, 載せる, 上げる, 入れる ◇*Put* the cases down there, please. 箱はそこに置いてください ◇*Put* that knife down (= stop holding it) before you hurt somebody! 誰かを傷つけないうちにそのナイフを下に置きなさい ◇*Put* your hand up if you need more paper. 紙がもっと必要なら, 手を上げなさい ◇Did you *put* sugar in my coffee? 私のコーヒーに砂糖を入れた

place [他]《副詞や前置詞と共に》(特定の場所に物を慎重[故意]に)置く ◇He *placed* his hand on her shoulder. 彼は彼女の肩に手を置いた ◇A bomb had been *placed* under the seat. 爆弾が座席の下に置かれていた

lay [他]《ふつう副詞や前置詞と共に》(特定の位置に人・物を優しく[慎重に])置く, 据える, 寝かせる ◇She *laid* the baby down gently on the bed. 彼女はベッドの上に赤ちゃんをそっと寝かせた ◇He *laid* a hand on my arm. 彼は私の腕に手を添えた ◇Relatives *laid* wreaths on the grave. 近親者たちが墓の上に花輪を置いた

ノート **place**と**lay**の使い分け:多くの場合, 両語とも使用可能。しかしながら, **place**のほうがふつうより意図的で, **lay**のほうが優しい。**place**は目的語に物を取るが, 人は不可。**lay**は物も人も可能。×A bomb had been *laid* under the seat. ×She *placed* the baby on the bed.

set [他]《副詞や前置詞と共に》(他の場所から運んできて特定の場所・位置に人・物を)置く ◇She *set* a tray down on the table. 彼女はトレーをテーブルの上に置いた ◇They ate everything that was *set* in front of them. 彼らは前に置かれているものを全部平らげた ◇When she fell he picked her up and *set* her on her feet again. 彼女が転ぶと, 彼は彼女を抱き上げて, 彼女をもう一度自分の足で立たせた

position [他]《ふつう副詞や前置詞と共に》(準備するために特定の場所に人・物を)置く, 配置する ◇Large television screens were *positioned* at either end of the stadium. 大きなテレビ画面がスタジアムの両端に配置されていた ◇She quickly *positioned* herself behind the desk. 彼女は素早く机の向こう側の定位置についた ☞ **position** (**PLACE**), **position** (**POSITION**)

stuff [他]《副詞や前置詞と共に》(狭い空間の中に素早く[無造作に]物を)押し込む, 突っ込む ◇She *stuffed* the money under the pillow. 彼女はお金を枕の下に押し込んだ ◇His hands were *stuffed* in his pockets. 彼は両手をポケットに突っ込んでいた

pop (**-pp-**) [他]《副詞や前置詞と共に》《特に英, インフォーマル》(物を素早く[突然に, 短い間])ひょいと置く, 放り込む ◇He *popped* his head around the door and said hello. 彼は頭をドアからひょいとのぞかせて, あいさつした ◇I'll *pop* the books in (= deliver them) on my way home. 私が家に帰る途中にその本を持って行くよ

dump [他]《ふつう副詞や前置詞と共に》(床・テーブルなどの上に物を無造作に[だらしなく])どさっと置く, 投げ出す ◇Just *dump* your stuff over there — we'll sort it out later. 荷物はそこら辺に置くだけでいいから—私たちが後で整理するわ

stick [他]《副詞や前置詞と共に》《インフォーマル》(物を素早く[無造作に])どさっと置く, 貼る ◇*Stick* your bags down there. バッグはそこに置いておいて ◇Can you *stick* this on the noticeboard? これを掲示板に貼ってもらえますか

settle [他]《副詞や前置詞と共に》(ある位置に動かないように慎重に)置く, 据える ◇She *settled* the blanket around her knees. 彼女は毛布を膝に掛けた

plant [他]《副詞や前置詞と共に》(特定の場所・位置に物・自分自身をしっかりと)置く, 据える, 立てる ◇They *planted* a flag on the summit. 彼らは頂上に旗を立てた ◇He *planted* himself squarely in front of us. 彼は私たちの真正面に立ちはだかった

Q q

quality 名

quality・standard・level・grade・calibre
ある物が他の物と比較してどれだけよいか悪いかを表す
【類語訳】質, 基準, 標準, 水準, レベル, (品質)等級

文型&コロケーション
▶ to **be of** (a/ the) ...quality/ standard/ level/ grade/ calibre
▶ **high/ highest/ low** quality/ standard/ level/ grade/ calibre
▶ **poor** quality/ standard/ level/ grade
▶ **top** quality/ level/ grade
▶ to **raise/ improve** the quality/ standard/ level/ calibre of sth
▶ to **maintain** the quality/ standard/ level of sth
▶ to **reach** a standard/ level

quality [U, C] 質 ◇Most of the goods on offer are of very poor *quality*. 売りに出ている品物の多くは大変に質が悪い ◇Use the highest *quality* ingredients you can find. 探しうる最高品質の材料を使いなさい ◇There's been a serious decline in *air quality* recently. 最近, 大気汚染が著しく高くなってきている ◇Their *quality of life* improved dramatically when they moved to the US. 合衆国に移住して彼らの生活の質は劇的に改善した

standard [C, U] 基準, 標準, 水準 ◇There are real concerns about falling *standards* in schools. 学力水準の低下が現実的に懸念されている ◇A number of Britain's beaches fail to *meet* European *standards* on cleanliness. 英国の浜辺の何か所かは清浄度の面でヨーロッパ基準を満たしていない ◇Who *sets the standard* for water quality? 水質基準を定めるのは誰ですか ◇sb's *standard of living* 人の生活水準 ◇This *living standards* 生活水準 ◇Her work is not *up to standard* (= of a good enough standard). 彼女の仕事は合格点に達していない

level [C, U] 水準, レベル ◇Most of these students have a high *level* of language ability. これらの学生の多くは高度の言語能力を持っている ◇This computer game has fifteen *levels*. このコンピュータゲームには15レベルがある ◇She studied psychology at *degree level*. (英) 彼女は心理学を学位レベルで学んだ

grade [C] (品質)等級 ◇All the materials used were of the highest *grade*. 使われた原料はどれも最高級品だった ◇a piece of *top grade* beef (英) 最高級ビーフの一切れ ◇*Grade A beef* (米) A級のビーフ

calibre (英) (米 **caliber**) [U] 能力レベル ◇The company needs more people of your *calibre*. その会社はあなた並の能力ある人をもっと必要としている

question 名

question・enquiry・query
情報を求めることを表す
【類語訳】質問, 問い, 問題, 問い合わせ, 疑問

文型&コロケーション
▶ a question/ an enquiry/ a query **about/ as to/ concerning/ on** sth
▶ a question/ an enquiry/ a query **from** sb
▶ a **specific/ further** question/ enquiry/ query
▶ **detailed/ routine/ preliminary** questions/ enquiries
▶ a **customer/ general** enquiry/ query
▶ to **address/ direct** a question/ an enquiry/ a query to sb
▶ to **have/ deal with/ handle/ reply to/ respond to/ answer** a question/ an enquiry/ a query
▶ to **raise/ send (in)/ put** a question/ query

question [C] 質問, 問い, 問題 ◇She refused to answer *questions* about her private life. 彼女は私生活に関する質問には答えようとはしなかった ◇In the exam there's sure to be a *question* on energy. 試験にはエネルギーに関する問題があるにちがいない ◇*Question* 3 was quite difficult. 問3は実に難しかった ◇I hope the police don't *ask* any awkward *questions*. 警察が厄介な質問をしないことを望まです ◇*The question is*, how much are they going to pay you? 問題は彼らがあなたにいくら支払ってくれるかだ

enquiry (特に米でまた **inquiry**) [C] (情報・詳細を[の]) 尋ねること, 問い合わせ ◇We received over 300 *enquiries* about the job. その仕事について300件以上のお問い合わせをいただきました ◇I'll have to *make* a few *enquiries* (= try to find out about it) and get back to you. 少し問い合わせをしてみる必要があり, その上でお返事いたします ◇After the disaster, the police had a *flood of enquiries* about missing relatives. 災害の後, 警察には行方不明の親族についての問い合わせが殺到した ☞**enquire** (ASK 1)

query [C] (情報・正否を問う)質問, 疑問 ◇If you have a *query* about our policy, contact our helpline. 我々のポリシーについてご質問があれば, 電話相談サービスにご連絡ください ◇Our assistants will be happy to answer your *queries*. 我々のアシスタントが喜んでご質問にお答えいたします ❶自分が的確に理解したかどうか定かでない時, あるいはもっと明確に説明してほしい時, 人(特に組織)に対して query を投げかける.

question 動

question・interview・interrogate・quiz・cross-examine・grill・debrief
人に物事に関して尋ねること
【類語訳】質問する, 問う, インタビューする, 面談する, 面接する, 問いただす, 尋問する, 問い詰める, 報告を求める

文型&コロケーション
▶ to question/ interview/ interrogate/ quiz/ cross-examine/ grill/ debrief sb **on** sth
▶ to question/ interview/ interrogate/ quiz/ cross-examine/ grill sb **about** sth
▶ to question/ interview/ quiz sb **in connection with** sth
▶ to question/ interview/ interrogate/ cross-examine a **wit-**

ness
▶ to question/ interview/ interrogate a **suspect**
▶ to be questioned/ interviewed/ interrogated/ quizzed/ grilled **by police/ detectives**
▶ a **journalist** questions/ interviews sb
▶ to question/ interview sb **further/ in depth**

question [他] (正式に)質問する, 問う ◇A man is being *questioned* in connection with the robbery. その強盗事件に関連して, ある男が尋問を受けている ◇Over half of those *questioned* said they rarely took any exercise. 質問を受けた人の半数以上が, めったに運動しないと答えた

interview [他] (ラジオ・テレビ・新聞・雑誌で)インタビューする; (正式に)面談する, 面接する ◇Next week, I will be *interviewing* Spielberg about his latest movie. 来週, その最新の映画についてスピルバーグにインタビューする予定です ◇The police are waiting to *interview* the injured man. 警察はそのけがをした男を聴取しようと待ち構えている
☞ **interview** (**INTERVIEW 1**)

interrogate [他] (強い調子で長時間数多く)質問する, 問いただす, 尋問する ◇He was *interrogated* by police for over 12 hours. 彼は12時間以上警察の取調べを受けた ◇Soon after we arrived, I was *interrogated* about my parents and our home life. 私たちが到着するとすぐ, 私は両親と家庭生活についてあれこれ質問された ☞ **interrogation** (**INTERVIEW 1**)

quiz (**-zz-**) [他] (特にジャーナリズムで)質問する, 問い詰める, 尋問する ◇Two men *quizzed* over betting shop killings (= in a newspaper headline). 馬券売り場殺人で二人の男性に尋問(新聞の見出し) ◇More than half the people *quizzed* in a poll said they would not use the new service. 世論調査で質問を受けた人の半数以上が, 新サービスを利用しないだろうと答えた

,cross-e'xamine [他] (法廷で)反対尋問する ◇The witness was *cross-examined* for over two hours. 証人は2時間以上にわたって反対尋問を受けた

▶ **,cross-exami'nation** [名] [U, C] ◇He broke down *under cross-examination* (= while he was being cross-examined) and admitted his part in the assault. 彼は反対尋問を受けている最中に取り乱し, 暴行への関与を認めた

grill [他] (ややインフォーマル)(不快な形で)きびしく質問する, 質問攻めにする ◇They *grilled* her about where she had been all night. 彼らは, 彼女が一晩中どこにいたのかあれこれ追及した ◇He was *grilled* by detectives for several hours. 彼は数時間にわたって刑事たちから厳しく尋問を受けた

▶ **grilling** [名] [C, ふつう単数で] ◇The minister faced a tough *grilling* at today's press conference. 大臣は今日の記者会見で厳しく問い詰められた

debrief [他] (完了したばかりの仕事について正式に)報告を求める ◇He was taken to a US airbase to be *debriefed* on the mission. 彼は米国空軍基地に連れていかれ, 遂行任務について報告を求められた

quick [形] ☞ **FAST, SHORT 1**

quick・rapid・fast・speedy・hasty・swift・hurried
物事が短い時間ですんだり[続いたり, 生じたり]することを表す
【類語訳】短時間の, 迅速な, 素早い, 急速な, 速やかな, 性急な, 慌ただしい, 即座の, 大急ぎの

文型&コロケーション
▶ a quick/ rapid/ fast/ hasty/ swift/ hurried **exit**
▶ a quick/ rapid/ speedy/ hasty/ hurried **departure**
▶ a quick/ rapid/ fast/ hasty/ swift **change**
▶ quick/ rapid/ fast/ speedy/ swift **service**
▶ a quick/ rapid/ fast/ hasty/ swift **decision**
▶ a quick/ rapid/ speedy **result**
▶ a quick/ rapid/ fast/ speedy **rate**
▶ a quick/ rapid/ fast **pulse/ heartbeat**
▶ a quick/ rapid/ fast/ swift **movement**
▶ a quick/ rapid/ swift **look/ glance**
▶ a quick/ rapid/ swift **answer/ reply/ assessment/ calculation/ rise/ descent**
▶ in quick/ rapid/ swift **succession**
▶ **very/ fairly** quick/ rapid/ fast/ speedy/ swift
▶ **really/ extremely/ quite/ pretty** quick/ rapid/ fast

quick 時間がかからない, 短時間の; 迅速な, 素早い ◇She gave him a *quick* glance. 彼女は彼をちらっと見た ◇Would you like a *quick* drink? 軽く一杯いかがですか ◇These cakes are very *quick* and easy *to* make. これらのケーキはとても手早く簡単に作れます ◇It's *quicker* by train. 列車の方が早い ◇Are you sure this is the *quickest* way? これが最も早い方法だというのは確かですか ◇Have you finished already? That was *quick*! もう済んだの. それは早い ◇His *quick* thinking saved her life. 彼の素早い判断が彼女の命を救った ◇We need to make a *quick* decision. 我々は即断する必要がある ◇There isn't a *quick* answer to this problem. この問題に即決の答えは出せない ❶ 「(遅れることなく)迅速な, 素早い」を意味する際, quick は名詞の前でしか用いられない. ×Their decision was *quick*. 反意 **slow** (LATE)

▶ **quickly** [副] ◇How *quickly* can you get here? どのくらい早くここに来られますか

rapid [ふつう名詞の前で] (ややフォーマル) 短期間に起きる; 急速な ◇There has been a *rapid* rise in sales. 売上げが急増している ◇The patient made a *rapid* recovery. 患者は急速に快復した ◇The disease is spreading at a *rapid* rate. 病気は急速に広まっている ◇The guard fired four shots in *rapid* succession. 護衛兵は続けざまに4発撃った ❶ *rapid* は, 物事が変化する速度を表すのに最も頻繁に用いられる. 反意 **slow** (SLOW), ☞ **rapidity** (SPEED)

▶ **rapidly** [副] ◇a *rapidly* growing economy 急成長する経済 ◇Crime figures are rising *rapidly*. 犯罪件数が急増している

fast 短期間に起きる, 迅速な, 素早い ◇We've recorded the *fastest* rate of increase for several years. 我々は数年間で最も速い増加率を記録した ◇We can guarantee a *fast* response time. 私どもは迅速な対応を保証いたします 反意 **slow** (SLOW)

▶ **fast** [副] ◇Children grow up so *fast* these days. 近年, 子どもの成長はとても速い

ノート **quick** と **fast** の使い分け: **quick** は, 短時間しかかからない物事について最も頻繁に用いる語である. **fast** は, quick 同様に, 変化 (recovery, rate, rise) やサービス (delivery, response, repair) に関連する語と共に用いることができるが, 食事 (breakfast, snack, lunch) や人がする行為 (hug, kiss, wash, bath) に関連する語と共には用いることができない. しかし **fast** は, 高速で移動する人・物事については頻繁に用いられる. ☞ **FAST**

speedy [ふつう名詞の前で] (ややインフォーマル) 迅速な, 速

やかな ◇We wish you a *speedy* recovery (= from an illness or injury). 早く回復されることを願っております ◇They wanted to bring the war to a *speedy* end. 彼らは戦争を速やかに終わらせたかった ❶ *speedy* はふつう, 人が特定の結果を願う[望む]文脈で用いられる. ☞ **speed** (SPEED), **speed** (ACCELERATE)

▶**speedily** 副 ◇All enquiries will be dealt with as *speedily* as possible. すべての問い合わせにできるだけ迅速に対応します

hasty 《しばしばけなして》(悪い結果を招くほど)性急な, 慌ただしい ◇Let's not make any *hasty* decisions. どんな性急な判断も下さないようにしましょう ◇She regretted her *hasty* words the moment she'd spoken. 彼女は口にした途端に自分の性急な言葉を後悔した ◇The army beat a *hasty* retreat. 《書き言葉》軍隊は慌ただしく退却した ☞ **haste** (SPEED)

▶**hastily** 副 ◇She *hastily* changed the subject. 彼女はあわてて話題を変えた

swift 《特に書き言葉, 特にジャーナリズム》迅速な, 速やかな; 即座の ◇*Swift* action was taken to recover the money. 金を取り戻すために迅速な措置がとられた ◇The White House was *swift to* deny the rumours. ホワイトハウスは即座に噂を否定した

▶**swiftly** 副 ◇Surprise was *swiftly* followed by outrage. 驚きに続いてすぐに憤りがこみ上げてきた

hurried 〖ふつう名詞の前で〗(十分な時間がないため)大急ぎの, 慌ただしい ◇I ate a *hurried* breakfast and left. 大急ぎで朝食をとって出かけた ◇She wrote a few *hurried* lines to him on the back of an envelope. 彼女は封筒の裏面に彼への数行の走り書きをした 反意 **unhurried** (EASY 2), ☞ **hurry** (HURRY)

▶**hurriedly** 副 ◇I *hurriedly* got up and dressed. 私は飛び起きて着替えをした

quiet 形

1 quiet・peaceful・silent・tranquil・calm・sleepy
ある場所や期間に物音や活動がない状態を表す
【類語訳】静かな, 活気のない, 邪魔されない, 平穏な, しんとした, 音を立てない, のどかな, 穏やかな

〖文型&コロケーション〗
▶a quiet/ peaceful/ silent/ tranquil/ sleepy **place/ village/ town**
▶a quiet/ peaceful/ tranquil/ calm **day/ night/ morning/ afternoon/ evening**
▶a quiet/ peaceful/ tranquil/ calm/ sleepy **atmosphere**
▶a quiet/ peaceful/ tranquil **life/ setting**
▶quiet/ peaceful/ tranquil **countryside/ surroundings**

quiet (人が多くなくて)静かな, 活気のない; 邪魔されない ◇The house was *quiet* except for the sound of the television. テレビの音以外, 家は静かだった ◇They had a *quiet* wedding. 彼らは静粛に結婚式を行った ◇Business is usually *quieter* at this time of year. 一年のこの時期, ふつう商売は比較的暇になる ◇I was looking forward to a *quiet* evening at home. 私は家での静かな夜を心待ちにしていた 反意 **busy** (BUSY 2), **noisy** (LOUD)

peaceful 平穏な; 静かで落ち着いた ◇I fell into a deep, *peaceful* sleep. 私は深く安らかな眠りに落ちた ◇It's so *peaceful* out here in the country. ここ田舎ではとても平穏です ☞ **peace** (SILENCE)

▶**peacefully** 副 ◇He died *peacefully* in her arms. 彼は彼女の腕の中で安らかに息を引き取った

silent (ほとんど[まったく])音のない, しんとした (ほとんど[まったく])音を立てない ◇The streets were *silent* and deserted. 通りは人けがなく静まり返っていた ◇As darkness began to fall, the cannon *fell silent*. 夜の帳が下りはじめ, 砲声がやんだ ☞ **silence** (SILENCE)
◇She crept *silently* out of the room. 彼女は部屋からこっそり抜け出した

tranquil 《ややフォーマル, 書き言葉》(リラックスさせるような)静かで穏やかな, のどかな ◇It is a *tranquil* place of quiet beauty. そこは静かな美しさをたたえたのどかな景勝地である ☞ **tranquillity** (SILENCE)

calm (海が)大波のない, 穏やかな; (天気が)風のない; (雰囲気が)平穏な ◇a *calm*, cloudless day 穏やかで雲一つない一日 ◇The city is *calm* again (= free from trouble and fighting) after yesterday's riots. 昨日の暴動の後, その都市は再び平穏を取り戻している 反意 **rough** (ROUGH) ❶反意語であるroughは, 海・天気にのみ用いられ, 時・場所には用いられない. ☞ **calm** (PEACE), calm (SILENCE)

sleepy (町・村が)活気のない ◇It was a *sleepy* little town before it became popular with tourists. 観光客に人気になる前は, そこは活気のない小さな町だった

2 quiet・soft・faint・inaudible・silent・hushed・dull・muffled
ほとんど[まったく]音[声]を立てないために容易に聞こえないこと
【類語訳】静かな, 沈黙した, 穏やかな, かすかな, 聞こえない, はっきりしない, 鈍い

〖文型&コロケーション〗
▶a quiet/ a soft/ a faint/ an inaudible/ a hushed/ a muffled **voice**
▶quiet/ soft/ hushed **tones**
▶a quiet/ hushed/ muffled **conversation**
▶quiet/ soft/ silent/ muffled **laughter**
▶a quiet/ a soft/ a faint/ an inaudible/ a hushed **whisper**
▶a soft/ faint/ silent/ muffled **cry**
▶a quiet/ soft/ faint/ dull/ muffled **sound**
▶a quiet/ soft/ faint/ dull **click**
▶a soft/ faint/ dull/ muffled **noise/ thud/ thump**

quiet ほとんど物音を立てない, 静かな ◇We could hear *quiet* footsteps in the corridor. 廊下から静かな足音が聞こえた ◇How would you like a *quieter*, more efficient engine? もっと静かで効率的なエンジンはいかがですか ◇Could you *keep* the kids *quiet* while I'm on the phone? 電話している間, 子どもたちを静かにさせておいてもらえますか ◇'*Be quiet*,' said the teacher. 「静かに」と先生は言った ◇He went very *quiet* (= did not say much) so I knew he was upset. 彼の口数がとても少なくなったので, 怒っているのだとわかった 反意 **loud** (LOUD)

▶**quietly** 副 ◇I can't hear you — you're speaking too *quietly*. 聞こえません—話す声が小さすぎます

soft (声・音が大きくなく)穏やかな ◇He chose some *soft* background music and lit the candles. 彼は穏やかなBGMを選び, ろうそくに火をつけた 反意 **loud** (LOUD), **sharp** (HIGH 5)

▶**softly** 副 ◇She closed the door *softly* behind her. 彼女はうしろ手にドアをそっと閉めた

faint (離れているため音が弱い)はっきり聞こえない, かすかな

→quiet

◇We could hear their voices growing *fainter* as they walked down the road. 彼らが道路を歩いていくにしたがって、その声は聞こえにくくなった
▶**faintly** 副 ◇'Does it matter?' she said *faintly*. 「それって、重要なのでしょうか」と彼女は力なく言った
inaudible (音が)聞こえない ◇She spoke in an almost *inaudible* whisper. 彼女はほとんど聞き取れないささやき声で話した ◇The whistle was *inaudible to* the human ear. その笛の音は人間の耳にはほとんど聞こえなかった 反意 **audible** ❶ *audible* な音は、あまり大きくなくても「聞き取れる」ことを指す。◆Her voice was **barely** *audible* above the noise. (彼女の声は騒音の中でもかろうじて聞こえた; barely は「かろうじて[どうにか]…である」の肯定的意味合い) ◆The alarm must be clearly *audible* in all bedrooms (= in fire safety regulations). (警報はすべての寝室ではっきり聞こえなければならない)
silent [名詞の前で]沈黙した、無言の ◇She closed her eyes to say a *silent* prayer. 彼女は目を閉じて黙祷を捧げた ◇They nodded in *silent* agreement. 彼らは無言のまま了解してうなずいた
▶**silently** 副 ◇She prayed *silently*. 彼女は黙祷を捧げた
hushed [ふつう名詞の前で](話し声が)非常に静かな ◇They spoke in *hushed* tones. 彼らは声をひそめて話した ◇They were deep in *hushed* conversation. 彼らはひそひそと話しこんでいた ❶ *hushed* conversation とは、他人には決して聞かれたくない当事者同士の会話のこと。
dull [名詞の前で]《書き言葉》(音が)はっきりしない、大きくない、鈍い ◇The gates shut behind him with a *dull* thud. 門は彼の後ろで、ドンと鈍い音を立てて閉まった
▶**dully** 副 ◇The gates clanged *dully* behind him. 門は彼の後ろでガチンと鈍い音を立てた
muffled (さえぎるものがあるため音が)はっきり聞こえない ◇*Muffled* voices could be heard coming from the next room. 隣の部屋からくぐもった声が聞こえてきた

3 ☞ SHY, SOLITARY
quiet・reserved・reticent・taciturn・silent
あまり話をしない人のことを表す
【類語訳】口数の少ない、無口な、引っ込み思案な、控えめな、口の重い、寡黙な

[文型&コロケーション]
▶a quiet/ reserved/ reticent/ silent **person/ man**
▶He's the quiet/ silent **type**.
▶**very** quiet/ reserved/ reticent/ silent
▶**strangely** quiet/ reticent/ silent

quiet (人が)口数の少ない、無口な ◇She was *quiet* and shy, and never spoke up in class. 彼女は口数が少なく内気で、授業中は決して発言しなかった
▶**quietly** 副 ◇She sat *quietly* in the corner. 彼女は隅のほうに黙って座っていた
reserved (感情・意見を出すのに)引っ込み思案な、控えめな Neighbours described him as a *reserved* man who didn't mix much. 隣人は彼を、あまり人付き合いをしない控え目な人だと言った ◇I think in her day people were more *reserved*. 彼女の若い頃は人々はもっと引っ込み思案だったと思う
reticent 《フォーマル》口の重い、寡黙な ◇He was extremely *reticent* about his personal life. 彼は自分の私生活については口が重かった 反意 **forthcoming**

taciturn 《フォーマル》(陰気で)口数の少ない、むっつりした ◇He was a *taciturn* and serious young man. 彼は無口で真面目な若者だった
silent [名詞の前で](男性が)あまり話をしない、寡黙な ◇He's the strong, *silent* type. 彼は力強く、寡黙なタイプだ

ノート a quiet man と a silent man の使い分け: quiet man は、かなり穏やかだが、あまり自信がないのだろうとみられる。silent man も寡黙な人だが、その寡黙さは強さのしるしであり、余計なおしゃべりで時間を無駄にしたくないということだと思われている。

quite 副

1 ☞ PARTLY
quite・rather・pretty・fairly・reasonably
相当な程度であることを表す
【類語訳】かなり、ずいぶん、なかなか、まあまあ

ノート 親見出し partly であげている類語と比較のこと。これらの語は一般にはっきりと、完全には good, successful, difficult ではないが、それに程度が相当することを強調する。親見出し partly にある類語はその感じがやや弱い。

reasonably　　fairly　　　　quite　　　　rather
　　　　　　　　　　　　　pretty

[文型&コロケーション]
▶quite/ rather **a/ an**...
▶quite/ rather/ pretty/ fairly/ reasonably **good/ successful/ high/ large/ quiet/ common/ easy/ pleased/ confident**
▶quite/ rather/ pretty/ fairly/ reasonably **well/ soon/ quickly/ easily**
▶quite/ rather/ pretty/ fairly **bad/ big/ heavy/ new/ tired/ dull/ difficult/ rare/ expensive/ dangerous**
▶quite/ rather/ pretty/ fairly **recently/ frequently**
▶quite/ rather/ pretty **annoyed/ exciting/ nice/ ill**
▶rather/ pretty/ fairly/ reasonably **harmless**
▶rather/ pretty/ fairly **narrow/ obvious**
▶pretty/ fairly/ reasonably **certain/ accurate/ happy/ safe/ sure**
▶I quite/ rather **like** sth

quite 《特に英》《否定文では用いない》 かなり、ずいぶん ◇I went to bed *quite* late last night. 昨晩かなり遅く就寝した ◇I see him *quite* often. 結構頻繁に彼に会います ◇I think it's *quite* likely we'll win. 我々が勝つ可能性はかなりあると思います ◇He plays *quite* well. 彼のプレーは相当うまい ◇He's *quite* a good player. 彼はかなりの実力の選手です ◇Her children are still *quite* young. 彼女の子どもたちはまだかなり幼い ◇Even *quite* young children can manage it. こく幼い子どもでも、それをやってのけられる ◇I *quite* like opera. オペラがとても好きなんです ❶ quite が形容詞を伴って名詞の前で用いられる時、a [an] の前にくる。◆It's *quite* a small room. (それはかなり小さな部屋です) ◆The room is *quite* small. (部屋はかなり小さい) ✕It's a *quite* small room. ☞ **quite** (VERY 副)
rather 《特に英》 かなり、ずいぶん ◇The rules are *rather* complicated. その規則はかなり複雑である ◇I didn't fail

quite

the exam; in fact I did *rather* well! 試験に失敗しなかった。実際のところ、かなりできたんだよ ◇He looks *rather* like his father. 彼はずいぶん父親に似ている ◇I'm sorry, I've got *rather* a lot on my mind. ごめん、気になっていることがいっぱいあるんだ ◇It's ***rather a*** difficult question. それは相当難しい質問ですね ❶*rather*は、批判・落胆・驚きをわずかに表すのに用いられることが多い。

pretty 《米 or インフォーマル、英》 かなり、ずいぶん ◇I was *pretty* sure I'd seen the coin before. まず間違いなく、以前にそのコインを見たことがあった ◇I'm afraid we're going to have to go *pretty* soon. 残念だけど、すぐにでも行かなくちゃならないよ

fairly なかなか、まあまあ ◇The software is *fairly* easy to use. そのソフトはかなり使いやすい ◇That's a *fairly* typical reaction. それはまあまあよくある反応だ

reasonably なかなか、まあまあ ◇I was *reasonably* happy with the situation. その状況にはまあまあ満足だった ◇The hostages had been *reasonably* well cared for. 人質たちはそこそこよい待遇を受けていた ☞ **reasonable (ADEQUATE)**

[ノート] **fairly** と **reasonably** の使い分け:どちらの語も、quite, rather, prettyほど強い意味はない。fairly は、reasonably より肯定的で、物事が最高ではないが許容できる水準にあることを示すことが多い。

2 quite・completely・totally・absolutely・fully・entirely・perfectly・utterly

最大限可能な程度であることを表す(語[句]の強調にも用いる)
【類語訳】まったく、実に、あらゆる点で、間違いなく、本当に、全面的に、全然、すごく、断然

[文型&コロケーション]

▸ quite/ completely/ totally/ absolutely/ fully/ utterly **sure/ convinced**
▸ quite/ completely/ totally/ absolutely/ entirely/ perfectly **normal**
▸ quite/ completely/ not totally/ not entirely/ utterly **irrelevant**
▸ quite/ completely/ totally/ absolutely/ perfectly/ utterly **absurd**
▸ quite/ completely/ totally/ entirely/ utterly **different**
▸ quite/ completely/ totally/ absolutely **exhausted**
▸ quite/ totally/ absolutely/ perfectly/ utterly **miserable**
▸ quite/ completely/ totally/ perfectly **honest**
▸ quite/ completely/ absolutely/ perfectly **still**
▸ quite/ absolutely/ perfectly **awful**
▸ quite/ completely/ not totally/ not entirely/ perfectly/ utterly **happy**
▸ to quite/ completely/ totally/ absolutely/ fully **agree**
▸ to quite/ completely/ totally/ fully/ perfectly **understand**
▸ to quite/ completely/ totally/ entirely **forget**
▸ to completely/ totally/ entirely/ utterly **destroy** sth
▸ **not** quite/ completely/ totally/ fully/ entirely

quite 《特に英》 まったく、実に ◇*quite* delicious/amazing/perfect 実においしい/驚嘆すべき/申し分のない ◇This is *quite* a different problem. これはまったく違う問題です ◇It wasn't *quite* as simple as I thought it would be. それは思ったほど単純ではなかったよ ◇***Quite frankly***, I couldn't care less. ごく率直に言えば、どうでもよかったんだ ◇By then I had done *quite enough*. その時にはまあ

いたところまで終わらせてあった ◇The bottle is not *quite* (= almost) empty. その瓶はすっかり空というわけではない ◇It's like being in the Alps, but not *quite*. アルプスにいるみたいな感じだがもちろん文字通りとはいかない ◇I don't *quite* know what to do next. 次に何をすべきかまったくわからない ◇'I'm sorry to be so difficult.' '***That's quite all right.***' 「お手間をおかけして申し訳ない」「まったく問題ないよ」 ◇Flying is ***quite the best*** way to travel. 飛行機に乗ることは本当に最高の移動方法です ◇It's too risky, ***quite apart from*** the cost. 経費の点はまったく別にしても、それは危険すぎる ◇'I almost think she prefers animals to people.' '***Quite right too***,' said Bill. 「彼女は人間より動物が好きと言っても過言じゃないね」「まったく同感だ」とビルは言った ☞ **quite (VERY)** 副

completely 《後に続く語や句を強調して》あらゆる点で;実に、実に ◇The technique is *completely* new. その技術はまったく新しい ◇We were ***completely and utterly*** broke. 私たちはまったくの文なしだった [反義] **partly (PARTLY)**, **part (COMPLETE)**

totally あらゆる点で;まったく、実に ◇His behaviour is *totally* unacceptable. 彼の行動はとても容認できない ◇I'm still not *totally* convinced that he's right. 私はまだ、彼が正しいとすっかり確信してはいない ◇The flight was *totally* awesome! 《特に米、インフォーマル、話し言葉》空の旅はとてもすばらしかった ◇'She's so cute!' '*Totally* (= I agree)!' 《特に米、インフォーマル、話し言葉》「彼女はとても可愛いね」「ほんと」 ❶*totally*のインフォーマルな例は、若者の会話に特有である。☞ **total (COMPLETE)**, **full (WHOLE)**

absolutely 《特に話し言葉》間違いなく、(同意を強調して)本当に[全面的に];(否定的に強調して)全然、(強い感情[極端な性質]を表す形容詞[動詞]と共に用いて)すごく、断然 ◇You're *absolutely* right. まったく君の言うとおりだ ◇They should have told me earlier, shouldn't they? '*Absolutely.*' 「彼らはもっと早く私に話すべきだったろ」「そうだとも」 ◇There's ***absolutely nothing*** more the doctors can do for him. 医者が彼にしてやれることはもうまったく何もない ◇That man does ***absolutely no*** work! その男は全然何の仕事もしない ◇'Are you happy with the decision?' 'No, ***absolutely not***.' 「その決定に満足ですか」「いや、とんでもない」 ◇I was *absolutely* furious with him. 彼にはこの上なく腹が立った ◇She *absolutely* adores you! 彼女は君のことがほんとに大好きなんだ ☞ **absolute (COMPLETE)**

fully 《ややフォーマル》あらゆる点で;まったく、実に ◇She had not yet *fully* recovered from the operation. 彼女はまだ手術からすっかり回復してはいなかった ◇We are *fully* aware of the dangers. 私たちは危険を百も承知している ❶フォーマルな言葉では、*fully*は総量を強調するのにも用いられる。 ◆The disease affects *fully* 30 per cent of the population. 《《フォーマル》人口の優に30%がその病気にかかる ☞ **full (WHOLE)**

entirely 《ややフォーマル》あらゆる点で;まったく、実に ◇I'm not *entirely* happy about the decision. その決定にすっかり満足していると言うわけではない ◇The audience was almost *entirely* made up of children. 観衆はすべてが子どもだった ☞ **entire (WHOLE)**

perfectly 《特に話し言葉》あらゆる点で;まったく、実に ◇To be *perfectly* honest I don't like the colour. 本当に包み隠さず言えば、その色は好きじゃない ◇It's *perfectly* OK as it is (= it doesn't need changing). そのままでまったく大丈夫です ◇You know *perfectly well* I can't help you. あなたは私が助けてあげられないのをちゃんとわかっている

◇'Do you understand?' 'Perfectly.'「わかりますか」「それはもう」☞ **perfect (COMPLETE)**

utterly あらゆる点で；まったく，実に ◇We're so *utterly* different from each other. 私たちはお互い相手とはまったく違います ◇She *utterly* failed to convince them. 彼女は彼らをまったく説得できなかった ☞ **utter (COMPLETE)**

> これらの語の大きな違いは、言語使用域においてであって意味においてではない。quite は，《英》の話し言葉ではきわめて頻繁に用いられるが，《米》ではこの意味であまり用いられない。totally は，《米》の話し言葉で最も頻繁に用いられる。書き言葉で最も頻繁に用いられるのは completely。よりフォーマルな文脈なら fully である。entirely もかなりフォーマルで，特に，否定文や almost entirely という句で用いられる。perfectly は，さほどフォーマルではなく，特に話し言葉で用いられる。utterly はふつう，否定文では用いられないが，示される考えが駄目なものだったり不可能なものだったりする時に用いられることが多い。

quote 動

quote・cite・repeat・say・recite・narrate・dictate
他の人が言った[書いた]言葉を繰り返すことを表す
【類語訳】引用する，復唱する，唱える，朗唱する，ナレーションを入れる，口述する，書き取らせる

文型&コロケーション
▶ to quote/ cite/ repeat/ recite/ dictate a **passage**
▶ to quote/ repeat/ say/ recite a **line**
▶ to quote/ recite (a) **poem/ speech/ poetry**
▶ to narrate/ dictate a **story**

quote [他，自] 引用する ◇He *quoted* a passage from the prime minister's speech. 彼は首相の演説から一節を引用した ◇The figures *quoted* in this article refer only to Britain. この記事に引用された数字は，英国に限ったものだ ◇Don't *quote me on* this (= this is not an official statement), but I think she is going to resign. これはオフレコでお願いするけど，彼女は辞めることになると思います ◇*Quote* this reference number in all correspondence. すべての通信文書にこの参照番号を付けてください ◇They said they were *quoting from* a recent report. 最近の報告書から引用していると彼らは言った ☞ **quote (MENTION), quotation (REFERENCE)**

cite [他]《フォーマル》（論文・レポートの権威づけのために著者の言葉をそのまま）引用する ◇She *cited* a passage from the President's speech. 彼女は大統領の演説の一節を引用した ☞ **cite (MENTION), citation (REFERENCE)**

repeat [他]（覚えるために他の人が言ったことを）復唱する ◇Listen and *repeat* each sentence after me. 各文を聞き，私の後について復唱してください ◇Can you *repeat* what I've just said word for word? 私が言ったことを一語一語復唱してもらえますか

say [他]（祈り・演説の言葉を）繰り返す，復唱する，唱える ◇He *said* a quiet prayer to himself. 彼は心の中で祈りの言葉を唱えた ◇Try to *say* that line with more conviction. もっときっぱりとそのせりふを言ってみてください

recite [他]（覚えた詩・文学作品などを聴衆に向かって）朗唱する ◇Each child had to *recite* a poem to the class. 子どもはひとりひとりクラスの生徒たちに向かって詩を朗唱しなければならなかった

narrate [他]（ドキュメンタリー映画・番組に）ナレーションを入れる ◇The film was *narrated* by Andrew Sachs. その映画はアンドルー・ザックスがナレーターを務めた

dictate [他，自] 口述する，書き取らせる ◇She *dictated* a letter to her secretary. 彼女は手紙を秘書に書き取らせた ◇OK, you write, I'll *dictate*. いいかね，君が書いて，僕が口述する

R r

racism 名 ☞ DISCRIMINATION

racism・nationalism・patriotism・sexism・bigotry・ageism・chauvinism・xenophobia・sectarianism
人種や国籍、性別、年齢に基づいてある人々の集団が他の集団より優れている[重要である]とする信念を表す
【類語訳】人種差別、民族主義、民族主義、愛国心、性差別、偏見、外国人嫌い、派閥主義、宗派主義、党派主義

【文型&コロケーション】
▶ rampant racism/ nationalism/ sexism
▶ overt/ blatant racism/ sexism
▶ to combat racism/ sexism/ ageism
▶ a form of racism/ nationalism/ patriotism/ sexism/ bigotry/ ageism/ chauvinism

racism [U]《けなして》人種差別;(暴力的な)人種差別的行為;(ある人種が他の人種より優れているとする)人種(差別)主義 ◇a victim of *racism* 人種差別の犠牲者 ◇ugly outbreaks of *racism* 忌まわしい人種差別の発生 ◇irrational *racism* 理不尽な人種主義 ☞ race (PEOPLE)
▶ **racist** 名 [C] ◇He's a *racist*. 彼は人種差別主義者である
▶ **racist** 形 ◇*racist* thugs 人種差別主義者の暴漢 ◇*racist* attitudes/attacks/remarks 人種差別的な態度/攻撃/発言

nationalism [U]《同じ人種・文化・言語などを共有する人々による独立国家樹立を目指す》民族主義;民族意識、愛国心 ◇Scottish *nationalism* スコットランドの民族主義 ❶ *nationalism* はふつう否定的な語ではない。しかし、自国に対する誇りが他国よりも優れているという感情になると、否定的に用いられることもある。◆The war was fuelled by aggressive *nationalism* and feelings of cultural superiority.《けなして》その戦争は侵略的な国粋主義と文化的優越感にあおられたものだ.
▶ **nationalist** 名 [C] ◇Scottish *nationalists* スコットランドの民族主義者
▶ **nationalist** 形 ◇*nationalist* sentiments 愛国心、民族主義的感情

patriotism [U]《ふつうほめて》愛国心 ◇The early war poems promoted *patriotism*, justice and principle. 昔の戦争詩は愛国心や正義、大義を鼓舞した
▶ **patriot** 名 [C] ◇I wouldn't say I'm a great *patriot*, but I would never betray my country. 自分が熱烈な愛国者だと言うつもりはありませんが、決して祖国を裏切るようなことはしません
▶ **patriotic** 形 ◇a *patriotic* man who served his country well 祖国のために立派に尽くした愛国者 ◇*patriotic* songs 愛国的な歌

sexism [U]《けなして》(特に女性に対する)性差別;性差別主義 ◇legislation designed to combat *sexism* in the workplace 職場における性差別に対処する法律 ◇a study of *sexism* in language 言語における性差別の研究
▶ **sexist** 形 ◇a *sexist* attitude 性差別的な態度 ◇*sexist* language 性差別語

bigotry [U]《けなして》(宗教・人種に関連した)偏狭な考え[態度、行為]、偏見 ◇When religious people show *bigotry* and intolerance, they are in fact betraying the religion they uphold. 信心深い人たちが偏狭な態度や不寛容を示すとき、彼らは実際には自分たちが支持する宗教を裏切っていることになる
▶ **bigot** 名 [C] ◇a religious/racial *bigot* 宗教的な/人種的な偏見を持つ人
▶ **bigoted** 形 ◇a *bigoted* man 偏狭な男

ageism（または **agism**）[U] 高齢者差別、年齢差別 ◇This form of *ageism* deprives older people of social status and role. この種の高齢者差別が年配者から社会的な地位と役割を奪うのです

chauvinism [U]《けなして》(祖国が他国より優れているという)好戦的で不合理な)盲目的[狂信的]愛国主義;男性優位主義、女性差別主義 ◇national/cultural *chauvinism* 国民的な/文化的な盲目的愛国主義 ◇*Male chauvinism* was rife in the medical profession in those days. 当時の医療界には男性優位主義がはびこっていた
▶ **chauvinist** 名 [C] ◇She denounced him as a *male chauvinist pig*. 彼女は彼のことを男性優位主義のブタ野郎だと非難した

xenophobia [U]《けなして》(猛烈な)外国人嫌い、外国人恐怖 ◇a campaign against racism and *xenophobia* 人種差別と外国人嫌いに反対する運動

sectarianism [U]《けなして、特にジャーナリズム》(分派間の抗争につながる宗教・政治上の)派閥主義、宗派[党派]主義 ◇reports of a rise in religious and ethnic *sectarianism* 宗教的かつ民族的な派閥主義の高まりに関する報道 ◇victims of *sectarianism* 宗派主義の犠牲者たち
▶ **sectarian** 形《ふつう名詞の前で》◇*sectarian* attacks/violence 宗派間の攻撃/暴力 ◇attempts to break down the *sectarian* divide in Northern Ireland 北アイルランドの宗派間の溝をなくそうとする試み

radical 形

radical・revolutionary・progressive・extreme
(政治の世界での)非常に新しい[異なった]考え方や見方を表す
【類語訳】急進的な、革新的な、過激な、先鋭的な、革命的な、進歩的な、極端な

progressive　　radical　　extreme　　revolutionary

【文型&コロケーション】
▶ radical/ revolutionary/ progressive/ extreme **ideas/views**
▶ radical/ revolutionary **proposals/ solutions**
▶ a radical/ revolutionary **leader**

radical [ふつう名詞の前で]（考えが）急進的な、革新的な、過激な;（人・意見が）急進派の、過激派の、先鋭的な ◇He proposed a *radical* solution to the problem. 彼はその問題に抜本的な解決策を提案した ◇the *radical* wing of the party 党の急進派 ◇*radical* politicians/students/

writers 急進派の政治家/過激派の学生/先鋭的な作家
[反意] **conservative** (CONSERVATIVE), ☞ **radical** (FUNDAMENTAL)

revolutionary 革命的な;(政治的な)革命の ◇It was a time of rapid and *revolutionary* change. 急速に革命的な変化の時代だった ◇At the time this idea was *revolutionary*. この考え方はその当時は革命的だった ◇*revolutionary* uprisings 革命による反乱 ☞ **revolution** (REVOLUTION), **revolutionary** (GUERRILLA)

progressive 《ふつうほめて》(新しい考え・現代的な方法・変革を支持して)進歩的な, 進歩主義の ◇*progressive* schools 進歩的な教育を行う学校 ◇Are you in favour of *progressive* teaching methods? 進歩的な教授法に賛成ですか [反意] **conservative** (CONSERVATIVE), ☞ **progress** (PROGRESS)

extreme 《ふつうけなして》(人・政治団体・意見が)極端な, 過激な ◇*extreme* left-wing/right-wing views 極左的な/極右的な見方 [反意] **moderate**
➤ **extremism** 名 [U] ◇political/religious *extremism* 政治上の/宗教上の過激主義

rain 動

rain・fall・pour・come down・drizzle
空から水滴が落ちて来ることを表す
【類語訳】雨が降る

drizzle → rain fall come down → pour

[文型&コロケーション]
▶ to pour/ come **down**
▶ it's raining/ pouring/ drizzling
▶ the **rain** falls/ pours/ comes down
▶ to rain/ fall **heavily/ lightly/ steadily**

rain [自]《itと共に》雨が降る ◇Is it *raining*? 雨は降っていますか ◇It had been *raining* all night. 一晩中雨が降っていた ◇It hardly *rained* at all last summer. 去年の夏はほとんど雨が降らなかった ◇It started to *rain*. 雨が降り始めた

fall [自]《ふつう副詞や前置詞と共に》(雨・雪が)降る ◇The snow was *falling* steadily. 雪は絶え間なく降っていた ◇70 millimetres of rain *fell* in just a few hours. わずか数時間で70ミリの雨が降った

pour [自] (雨が)激しく降る ◇The rain continued to *pour* down. 雨は激しく降り続いた ◇It's *pouring* outside. 外は雨が激しく降っている ◇**It's pouring with rain.**《英》雨が激しく降っている ❶《米》ではIt's pouring rainとも言えるが, 単にIt's pouringと言うのがふつうである.

,come 'down 句動 (雨・雪が)降る ◇The rain *came down* in torrents. 土砂降りの雨だった

[ノート] **rain, fall, come down** の使い分け: rainは最も頻繁に使う動詞で, itを主語にして用いられる. fallとcome downは, 雨や雪などを主語にして用いられる. fallは正確な降水量を述べるときに用いられる. ◆70 millimetres of rain *fell* in just a few hours. (わずか数時間で70ミリの雨が降った). ✕70 millimetres of rain *came down* in just a few hours. ✕It *rained* 70 millimetres of rain in just a few hours. come downは雨の降り方の描写と共に用いられることが多い. ◆The rain was *coming down* in a solid curtain. (雨は分厚いカーテンのように降っていた).

drizzle [自]《ふつう進行形で, it を主語として》霧雨[小雨]が降る ◇It was *drizzling* outside. 外は霧雨が降っていた

random 形

random・haphazard・indiscriminate・disorganized・untidy・unsystematic
物事の準備[計画]がなされていないことを表す
【類語訳】成り行き任せの, 無作為の, 任意の, 行き当たりばったりの, でたらめな, 手当たり次第の

[文型&コロケーション]
▶ the random/ indiscriminate/ random **use of sth**
▶ a random/ haphazard **approach**
▶ random/ indiscriminate **attacks**
▶ a haphazard/ an indiscriminate **method**
▶ **in** a random/ haphazard **fashion/ manner**
▶ **in** a random/ a haphazard/ an unsystematic **way**
▶ **totally** random/ haphazard/ disorganized
▶ **very** haphazard/ disorganized/ untidy/ unsystematic
▶ **rather** haphazard/ disorganized/ untidy
▶ **seemingly/ apparently** random/ haphazard/ indiscriminate

random [ふつう名詞の前で] 成り行き任せの, 無作為の, 任意の, 行き当たりばったりの ◇The group to be studied was selected on a *random* basis. 研究対象のグループは無作為に選ばれた ◇There's no motive for this kind of *random* killing. この種の無差別殺人には動機がない ◇*Random* numbers are generated by the computer. 乱数はコンピューターによって作り出される ◇The names are listed in *random* order. 名前は順不同で記載されている ❶ randomは統計や調査に関連して用いられることが多い. allocation, distribution, effects, fluctuations, numbers, sampleなどと結びつく.
➤ **at 'random** [行れ] ◇She opened the book *at random* (= not at any particular page) and started reading. 彼女は適当に本を開いて読み始めた
➤ **randomly** 副 ◇The winning numbers are *randomly* selected by computer. 当選番号はコンピューターによって無作為に選ばれます

haphazard《けなして》計画性のない; よく準備されていない, でたらめな, 手当たり次第の ◇It was the result of rather *haphazard* planning. それはかなりでたらめな計画の結果だった ◇In the early years training was *haphazard*. 初期の訓練は行き当たりばったりだった
➤ **haphazardly** ◇She started packing, throwing things *haphazardly* into the case. 彼女は手当たり次第に物をケースにほうり込んで荷造りを始めた

indiscriminate《けなして》(危害を及ぼす行動が)結果を考えずに行われる, 無差別な, 手当たり次第の; (人が)慎重な判断なしに行動する, 見境のない ◇*indiscriminate* violence/killing/slaughter 無差別暴力/殺人/虐殺 ◇The newspaper denounced the *indiscriminate* firing by the police. 新聞は警察による無差別発砲を糾弾した ◇She's always been **indiscriminate in** her choice of friends. 彼女はいつも誰かれ見境なく友達を選んできた

▶**indiscriminately** 副 ◇The soldiers fired *indiscriminately* into the crowd. 兵士たちは群衆に向けて手当たり次第に発砲した

disorganized (英でまた **-sed**) 《けなして》(人が)計画性のない;(出来事が)よく計画されていない、まとまりのない ◇They are lazy and *disorganized*. 彼らは怠惰で計画性がない ◇It was a dismal, *disorganized* weekend. 何も計画のない憂鬱な週末だった 反意 **organized** (EFFICIENT)

untidy (人が)整理整頓しない、だらしない ◇Why do you have to be so *untidy*? どうしてそんなにだらしなくする必要があるのよ 反意 **tidy** (EFFICIENT)

▶**untidiness** 名 [U] ◇Their arguments were usually about his *untidiness*. 彼らの言い争いはたいてい彼のだらしなさに関するものだった

unsystematic 体系的でない、組織だっていない ◇Training for volunteers is patchy and *unsystematic*. ボランティアの訓練は不完全で組織だっていない 反意 **systematic** (EFFICIENT)

range 名

1 range・variety・choice・diversity・array・selection・assortment
さまざまな種類の特定の物があることを表す
【類語訳】範囲、幅広さ、選択肢、品ぞろえ、多様性、勢ぞろい、取り合わせ

文型&コロケーション

▶ a **wide** range/ variety/ choice/ diversity/ array/ selection/ assortment
▶ a **great/ huge/ vast** range/ variety/ choice/ diversity/ array/ selection
▶ a **rich** range/ variety/ choice/ diversity/ array/ selection/ assortment
▶ a **wonderful** range/ variety/ diversity/ array/ selection
▶ a/ an **good/ interesting** range/ variety/ choice/ selection
▶ a **limited** range/ variety/ choice/ selection
▶ an **odd** range/ array/ selection/ assortment
▶ to **have** a range/ a variety/ a choice/ diversity/ an array/ a selection/ an assortment (of sth)
▶ to **offer/ provide** a range/ a variety/ choice/ diversity/ an array/ a selection/ an assortment (of sth)
▶ to **choose from** a range/ a variety/ an array/ a selection/ an assortment of sth
▶ to **stock** a range/ variety/ selection of sth
▶ the range/ variety/ choice/ selection/ assortment **includes...**

range [C、ふつう単数で] さまざまな種類、(種類の)幅、範囲 ◇The hotel offers a wide *range* of facilities and services. そのホテルは多様な施設とサービスを提供しています ◇There is *a full range of* activities for children. 子ども向けのあらゆる種類の活動がございます ◇This material is available in a huge *range* of colours. この素材にはありとあらゆる色をご用意しています ◇*range* は *a large/wide/full range of sth* といった句で、ビジネスやマーケティングで用いられることが多い. ☞ **range** (DIFFER)

variety [単数で] さまざまな種類、(種類の)幅広さ ◇There is a wide *variety* of patterns to choose from. さまざまな柄の中からお選びいただけます ◇He resigned for a *variety* of reasons. 彼は(理由に)いろいろあって辞任した ◇This tool can be used in a *variety* of ways. この道具はさまざまな使い方ができます ◇I was impressed by the *variety* of dishes on offer. メニューにある料理の幅広さに感心した ☞ **vary** (DIFFER), **varied** (DIVERSE)

ノート **variety** と **range** の使い分け: variety は種類の違いの多さを強調する. range は利用できる数(の多さ)を強調する.

choice [単数で、U] 選択の幅[種類]、選択肢、品ぞろえ ◇The menu has a good *choice* of desserts. メニューには豊富に品ぞろえしたデザートが載っています ◇There *wasn't much choice* of colour. あまり色の選択肢がなかった ☞ **choose** (CHOOSE)

diversity [C、ふつう単数で、U] 《ややフォーマル》多種多様な人[物事]；多様性、多様さ ◇There was a great *diversity* of opinion. 非常に多種多様な意見が出た ◇the biological *diversity* of the rainforests 熱帯雨林の生物の多様性 ◇There is a need for greater *diversity* and choice in education. 教育にはさらなる多様性と選択肢が必要である ☞ **diverse** (DIVERSE)

array [C、ふつう単数で] 《ややフォーマル》(印象的な)物事[人]の集まり、勢ぞろい ◇On the shelf was a vast *array* of bottles of different shapes and sizes. 棚にはさまざまな形や大きさの無数の瓶がずらりと並んでいた ◇I was amazed by the dazzling *array* of talent. まばゆいばかりの逸材の勢ぞろいに唖然となった ❶ *array* はふつう、人に強い印象を与えることを表す形容詞と共に用いられる. ◆ a vast/huge/rich/impressive/fascinating/colourful/glittering/bewildering/confusing/dazzling/wonderful *array* of sth (無数の/膨大な/豊富な/印象的な/魅力的な/多彩な/きらめくような/まごつくほどの/混乱するほどの/まばゆいばかりの/すばらしい…の集まり)

selection [C] 《ややフォーマル》選択の幅[種類]、品ぞろえ ◇The showroom has a wide *selection* of kitchens. そのショールームはキッチンの品ぞろえが豊富である ❶ *selection* は choice よりフォーマルで、特にマーケティングで用いられる. ☞ **select** (CHOOSE)

assortment [C、ふつう単数で] 《ややフォーマル》さまざまな物[種類]の集まり、取り合わせ ◇He was dressed in an odd *assortment* of clothes. 彼は風変わりな服を取り合わせて着ていた ❶ *assortment* はふつう一緒に見られるのが珍しい物の寄せ集めについて用いられることが多い. ◆ a/an odd/ strange/mixed/motley/random *assortment* of objects/people/clothes (風変わりな/奇妙な/各種の/雑多な/でたらめな物[人、服]の取り合わせ). ☞ **assorted** (DIVERSE)

2 range・scope・spectrum・reach・breadth
一定の制限内におけるばらつきの程度を表す
【類語訳】範囲、距離、射程距離、限度

文型&コロケーション

▶ **within/ beyond/ outside** the range/ scope/ reach of sb/ sth
▶ a/ the **entire/ full/ whole** range/ scope/ spectrum/ breadth
▶ the **complete** range/ scope/ spectrum/ breadth
▶ a **wide/ good/ limited** range/ scope/ spectrum/ breadth
▶ the **broad/ narrow** range/ scope/ spectrum of sth
▶ a/ the **geographical/ global/ political/ social** range/ scope/ spectrum/ reach
▶ to **expand/ extend/ increase/ widen/ limit/ narrow/ reduce/ restrict/ define/ determine** the range/ scope/

↪range

rank, rare

spectrum/ reach/ breadth
▶to **broaden** the range/ scope/ spectrum/ reach
▶to **cover/ include** a range/ spectrum/ breadth

range [C, ふつう単数で, U]（ばらつきの）範囲；(見る[聞く]ことのできる)距離, 範囲；(銃などの兵器の)射程距離 ◇Most of the students are in the 17-20 age *range*. 学生のほとんどは年齢が17歳から20歳です ◇The students in Class 4 have a very wide *range* of abilities. 4組の学生の能力は非常に広範囲に渡っています ◇It's difficult to find a house in our *price range* (= that we can afford). 私たちが支払える範囲内で家を見つけるのは難しい ◇This was outside the *range* of his experience. これは彼が経験したことのないことだった ◇The child was now out of Penny's *range of vision* (= not near enough for Penny to see). その子はもうペニーには見えない所にいた ◇These missiles have a *range* of 300 miles. これらのミサイルの射程距離は300マイルである

scope [U]（テーマ・組織・活動が扱う）範囲 ◇Our powers are limited in *scope*. 我々の権限は範囲が限られている ◇These issues were outside the *scope* of the article. これらの問題はその条項の適用範囲外だった ◇The police are broadening the *scope* of their investigation. 警察は捜査の範囲を広げつつある

spectrum [C, ふつう単数で]《ややフォーマル》(関連のある考え・意見・性質の十分な[幅広い])範囲 ◇We shall hear views from across the political *spectrum*. あらゆる政治的側面から意見を伺います ◇The policy has the support of a broad *spectrum* of opinion. その政策は幅広い世論の支持を受けている

reach [U]（影響力の）限度,（手の届く）範囲 ◇Such matters are beyond the *reach* of the law. そうした問題は法律の範囲外にある ◇Victory is now out of her *reach*. 現在, 勝利は彼女の手の届かない所にある ◇The basic model is priced well within the *reach* of most people. 基本モデルはほとんどの人が十分手が届く価格だ

breadth [U, 単数で]《ややフォーマル》(知識・感心の)広範囲なこと, 幅広い ◇He was surprised at her *breadth* of reading. 彼は彼女の読書の幅広さに驚いた ◇The party needs a new leader with a *breadth of vision* (= willingness to accept new ideas) that can persuade others to change. 党は他人に対して説得力のある広い視野を持った新しい指導者を必要としている ☞ **broad** (WIDE 1)

rank 動

rank・rate・grade・place・put・order
(その性質によって)特定の順序付けすることを表す
【類語訳】ランク付けする, 格付けする

文型&コロケーション
▶to rank/ rate/ grade/ order sb/ sth **according to** sth
▶to rank/ grade (sb/ sth) **as** sb/ sth
▶to rank/ grade/ order sb/ sth **by** sth
▶to rank/ rate/ place/ put/ order sb/ sth **above/ below** sb/ sth
▶to rank/ rate/ grade/ place/ put/ sth **in order of** sth
▶to rank/ rate (sb/ sth) **with** sb/ sth
▶to rank/ rate/ grade sb/ sth **for** sth

rank [他, 自]《進行形なし》(性質・大きさ・成績によって)位置付ける, ランク付ける；(ある地位に)位置する ◇The criteria are *ranked* in order of importance. それらの基準は重要順位に並べられている ◇They both lost to *top-ranked* American players. 彼らは二人ともトップランクのアメリカ人選手に負けた ◇The collection *ranks* among the finest in the country. そのコレクションは国内で最も素晴らしい物の一つに数えられる ◇It now *ranks* as Japan's fourth largest market. 現在それは日本にとって4番目に大きな市場に位置付けられている ☞ **ranking** (CLASS 3)

rate [他, ふつう受身で]《進行形なし》(比較して)格付けする, ランク付けする ◇The schools are *rated* according to their exam results. 学校は試験の結果によって格付けされます ◇She is currently *rated* number two in the world. 彼女は現在, 世界ナンバー2にランクされている ☞ **rate** (JUDGE 動), **rating** (CLASS 3)

grade [他, しばしば受身で]（共有する性質によって）グループ別にする, 等級[段階]に分ける ◇Eggs are *graded* from small to extra large. 卵は小から特大までの等級に分けられている ◇Responses were *graded* from 1 (very satisfied) to 5 (not at all satisfied). 回答は1(非常に満足している)から5(まったく満足していない)までの段階に分けられた ◇The grammar exercises are *graded* for difficulty. 文法の練習問題は難易度で分類されている

place [他]（副詞や前置詞と共に）(比較してある順位・地位と)する ◇I would *place* him among the top five tennis players in the world. 私なら彼を世界でトップ5に入るテニス選手の一人にします ◇Nursing attracts people who *place* relationships high on their list of priorities. 看護の仕事は人間関係を優先リストの上位に置く人たちを引きつけます

put [他]（副詞や前置詞と共に）(ある地位・順位に)置く ◇I'd *put* her in the top rank of modern novelists. 私なら彼女を現代作家のトップランクに位置付けます

ノート **place** と **put** の使い分け：これらの単語には意味や用法の違いはほとんどない. place は put よりも入念に考えられた行為であることを示す場合もある.

order [他, ふつう受身で]《フォーマル》(物をある順序に)並べる ◇The books are *ordered* alphabetically by title. 本は書名のアルファベット順に並べられています ◇In the periodic table elements are *ordered* according to atomic number. 周期表では元素は原子番号順に配置されている ☞ **order** (SERIES)

rare 形

rare・uncommon・infrequent
物事が頻繁には見つからない[起こらない]ことを表す
【類語訳】珍しい, まれな, めったにない, 希少の

文型&コロケーション
▶rare/ uncommon/ infrequent **in** sth
▶rare/ uncommon **among** sb
▶rare/ (not) uncommon (**for** sb/ sth) **to do** sth
▶rare/ uncommon/ infrequent **words**
▶a rare/ an uncommon **experience/ feature/ occurrence**
▶a rare/ no uncommon **thing**
▶rare/ infrequent **occasions/ use**
▶a rare/ an infrequent **visitor**
▶**fairly/ rather/ relatively/ very** rare/ uncommon/ infrequent
▶**not** uncommon/ infrequent

rare (あまり行われず[見られず,起こらず]に)珍しい,まれな,めったにない;(少数しかないために)珍しい,希少な ◇It is *rare* for a prison sentence to be imposed for a first offence. 初犯で実刑を科されるのは珍しい ◇This is a *rare* sight: badgers are normally active only at night. これはめったにない光景です.穴熊はふつう夜しか活動しない ◇He suffers from a *rare* bone disease. 彼は珍しい骨の病気を患っている ◇The library has a collection of *rare* books and manuscripts. その図書館は稀覯本や写本を収蔵している ◇The farm specializes in *rare* breeds. その農場では珍しい品種を専門に扱われている 反意 **common** (GENERAL)
▸**rarity** 名 [U] The value of antiques will depend on their condition and *rarity*. 骨董の価値はその状態と希少性によって決まるものです
uncommon (数多く[多くの場所に]なくて)珍しい,まれな ◇Side effects from the injection are *uncommon*. その注射による副作用はまれです ◇It is not *uncommon* to find 30 different species on one tree. 1本の木に30の異なる種(しゅ)が見つかるのは珍しいことではない 反意 **common** (GENERAL)
infrequent (頻繁には起こらずに)たまの,少ない ◇Examinations need to be carried out only at *infrequent* intervals. 試験はほんのたまに実施するだけでよい ◇American trains are *infrequent* and the network is patchy. アメリカの列車は本数が少なく,鉄道網は未発達だ 反意 **frequent** (FREQUENT)

rarely 副

rarely・seldom・hardly ever・infrequently
物事が頻繁に[ほとんど]起こらない[行われない]ことを表す
【類語訳】めったに…ない,まず…ない,ほとんど…ない,まれに

文型&コロケーション
▸ *rarely*/ *seldom*/ *hardly ever*/ *infrequently* **used**
▸ *rarely*/ *seldom*/ *hardly ever* **available**/ **the case**
▸ **to** *rarely*/ *seldom*/ *hardly ever* **happen**/ **speak**
▸ **only**/ **relatively**/ **very** *rarely*/ *seldom*/ *infrequently*

rarely めったに…ない,まれにしか…ない ◇He *rarely* spoke. 彼はめったには話さなかった ◇That's something I very *rarely* do. それは私がこくまれにしかしないことです ◇Finding a hotel is *rarely* a problem. ホテルを見つけるのが難しいことはまれだ 反意 **often** (OFTEN)
seldom 《ややフォーマル》めったに…ない,まず…ない ◇She *seldom* smiled. 彼女はめったに笑わなかった ◇He had *seldom* been happier in his life. 彼は人生でそれほど幸せだったことはなかった ◇Revenge was *seldom*, if ever, the motive in these cases. その事件で復讐が動機だったことはまずなかった 反意 **often** (OFTEN)

ノート **rarely** と **seldom** の使い分け: **rarely** は **not often** よりもややフォーマルで,**seldom** は **rarely** よりもややフォーマルである.文頭に **rarely** や **seldom** を置いて後ろに助動詞を続ける用法は,文語的ないし非常にフォーマルである.
◆ *Rarely* has a debate attracted so much media attention. (《フォーマル》論争がそれほど大きくマスコミの注目を引くことはめったになかった)
◆ *Seldom* have I come across such vindictive reviews. (そんなに悪意に満ちた批評に出くわすことはめったになかった)

hardly ever ほとんど…ない,めったに…ない ◇We *hard-ly ever* see him. 私たちは彼をめったに見かけない ◇The room was *hardly ever* used. その部屋はほとんど使われなかった
infrequently 《ややフォーマル》まれに ◇The satellites are launched only *infrequently*. それらの衛星はまれにしか打ち上げられない ◇The charges made for the drugs are **not** *infrequently* (= very often) excessive. 薬の請求額が法外なことは往々にしてある ❶ *infrequently* は **seldom** と同じくらいフォーマルな語だが,公式文書で受身の文で用いられることが多い. **seldom** は文芸作品で個人的な感情や習慣を語るのに用いられることが多い 反意 **frequently** (OFTEN)

rate 名 ☞ PRICE

rate・charge・fee・rent・fine・fare・terms・dues・toll・rental
請求される[支払われる]金額を表す
【類語訳】料金,給料,報酬,費用,手数料,授業料,入会金,会費,入場料,賃貸料,家賃,罰金,運賃,通行料,使用料

文型&コロケーション
▸ a **rate**/ a **charge**/ a **fee**/ **rent**/ a **fine**/ the **fare**/ the **terms**/ **dues**/ a **toll**/ the **rental for** sth
▸ a **rate**/ a **charge**/ a **fee**/ **rent**/ a **toll**/ the **rental on** sth
▸ **at** a **rate**/ **charge**/ **fee**/ **rent**/ **fare**/ **rental** of…
▸ **for** a **charge**/ **fee**
▸ (**a**/ **an**) **annual**/ **monthly rate**/ **charge**/ **fee**/ **rent**/ **dues**/ **rental**
▸ (**a**) **daily rate**/ **charge**/ **fee**/ **rent**/ **rental**
▸ (**a**) **reasonable rate**/ **charge**/ **fee**/ **rent**/ **fare**/ **terms**/ **toll**/ **rental**
▸ (**a**) **high**/ **low rate**/ **charge**/ **fee**/ **rent**/ **fare**/ **toll**/ **rental**
▸ (**a**) **fixed rate**/ **charge**/ **fee**/ **rent**/ **fare**/ **terms**/ **rental**
▸ (**a**) **flat rate**/ **charge**/ **fee**/ **fare**
▸ the **full rate**/ **charge**/ **fee**/ **rent**/ **fare**/ **toll**/ **rental**
▸ **to pay** a **rate**/ a **charge**/ a **fee**/ **rent**/ a **fine**/ a **fare**/ your **dues**/ a **toll**/ the **rental**
▸ **to charge** a **rate**/ a **fee**/ **rent**/ a **dues**/ a **toll**/ the **rental**
▸ **to increase**/ **reduce** the **rate**/ **charge**/ **fee**/ **rent**/ **fine**/ **fare**/ **dues**/ **toll**

rate [C] (請求される[支払われる]一定の)金額,料金,給料 ◇The job has a very low hourly *rate* of pay. その仕事の時間給は非常に安い ◇We offer special reduced *rates* for students. 私どもでは学割がききます ◇What is the **going rate** (= the usual level of payment) for bar work? バーの仕事の給料相場はいくらですか ◇We were forced to borrow the money at an extortionately high *rate of interest*. 私たちは法外に高い金利で金を借りざるをえなかった ◇The bank has announced a cut in **interest** *rates*. その銀行は金利引き下げを発表した ☞ **rates** (TAX)
charge [C] (商品・サービスの)料金 ◇We have to make a small *charge* for refreshments. 軽食の料金を少しいただかなければなりません ◇Delivery is **free of charge** (= costs nothing). 配達は無料です ◇The museum has introduced a £3 admission *charge*. 《英》その美術館は3ポンドの入場料を導入した ☞ **charge** (CHARGE 動)
fee [C] 《ややフォーマル》(専門家のアドバイスに対する)報酬,料金,費用,手数料,(学校・大学の)授業料,(組織の)会費,(ある場所への)入場料 ◇The fami-

↳rate

ratio, rational

ly spent over £20,000 on legal *fees*. その家族は訴訟費用に2万ポンド以上使った ◇Does the bank charge a *fee* for setting up the account? その銀行では口座の開設に手数料がかかりますか ◇Club members pay an annual membership *fee* of £775. クラブの会員年会費は775ポンドです ◇There is no entrance *fee* to the gallery. (特に英)そのギャラリーは入場無料です ◇an admission *fee* (特に米)入場料 ☞ **subscription** (PAYMENT)

ノート chargeとfeeの使い分け: feeは, 特に legal fees (訴訟費用)やschool fees (授業料)といった組み合わせでは, chargeより多い金額を表す. charge は, さほどフォーマル[専門的]でない文脈で, 小規模なサービスについて用いられる. ×We have to charge a small *fee* for refreshments. 美術館などの入場料は, (英)ではadmission charge, entrance feeと呼ばれ, (米)ではadmission fee, (やや頻度が少ないが) entrance feeと呼ばれる(×entrance *charge*とは言わない).

rent [U, C] (建物・部屋の)賃貸料, 家賃, 部屋代 ◇The landlord charged them a month's *rent* in advance. 家主は彼らにひと月分の家賃を前もって請求した ◇They began falling behind with their *rent* (= paying it late or not at all). (英)彼らは家賃を滞納しだした ◇They began falling behind in their *rent*. (米)彼らは家賃を滞納しだした ◇*Rents* are rising in the business district. ビジネス街では賃貸料が上昇している

fine [C] 罰金 ◇a parking *fine* 駐車違反の罰金 ◇Offenders will be liable to a ***heavy fine*** (= one that costs a lot of money). 違反者は重い罰金が科されます ◇She has already paid over $2,000 in *fines*. 彼女はすでに2000ドル以上の罰金を払っている ☞ **fine** (CHARGE 動)

fare [C] (バス・飛行機・タクシーなどの)運賃, 料金 ◇*Fares* have been increased by 10%. 運賃が10パーセント値上げされた ◇a bus/taxi/rail/air *fare* バス運賃/タクシー料金/電車賃/航空運賃 ◇How much is the ***return/single fare***? (英)往復/片道運賃はいくらですか ◇*Round-trip fare* from New York to Cincinnati is $229. (米)ニューヨークからシンシナティの往復運賃は229ドルです ◇one-way *fare* (米)片道運賃

terms [複数で] (購入・販売・支払い時の)条件;価格, 値段 ◇to buy sth ***on easy terms*** (= paying for it over a long period) 分割払いで…を購入する ◇My *terms* are £20 a lesson. 私の料金は1レッスン20ポンドです ☞ **terms** (CONDITION)

dues [複数で] (組織の)会費 ◇He had not paid his trade union *dues* for six months. 彼は労働組合費を半年間払っていなかった ☞ **subscription** (PAYMENT)

toll [C] (道路・橋の)通行料, 料金 ◇She took enough money to pay for motorway *tolls* and ferry tickets. 彼女は高速道路料金とフェリー代を払える分のお金は持った ◇a *toll* road/bridge 有料道路/橋 ❶(米)ではtollは市外通話の電話料金も指す. ◆Is San Jose to San Mateo a *toll call*? (= Do I have to pay extra for this call? Is it not a local call?) (米)サンノゼからサンマテオまでは市外通話になりますか.

rental [U, C, ふつう単数で] 使用料, レンタル料金, 賃貸料 ◇Telephone charges include line *rental*. 電話料金には回線使用料が含まれます ◇The weekly *rental* on the car was over £200. (英)車の1週間のレンタル料に200ポンド以上かかった

ノート rentとrentalの使い分け: rentは建物や部屋の使用に支払う料金を指す. 他のものにはrentalやrateを用いる. (米)では動詞rentは車のレンタルに用いられるが, 名詞はふつうrateである. ◆It costs us $300 a week to *rent* a car. (車のレンタルするのに1週間で300ドルかかる). ◆The *rate* on the car was $300 a week. (車のレンタル料金は1週間で300ドルだった).

ratio 名

ratio・proportion・scale
他と比較した場合の数量や大きさを表す
【類語訳】比率, 比, 釣り合い, バランス, 縮尺

文型&コロケーション
▸ the ratio/ proportion **of** A **to** B
▸ a ratio/ scale **of** 1:25, etc.
▸ **out of** proportion/ scale
▸ a **high/ low** ratio/ proportion

ratio (複 -os) [C] (2つのグループの)比率, 比 ◇What is the *ratio* of men to women in the department? その部署の男女比はどのくらいですか ◇The school has a low student-teacher *ratio* (= there are few students for each teacher). その学校の教師一人当たりの学生数は少ない ◇The *ratio* of applications to available places currently stands at 100:1. 志願数と定員の空きとの比率は現在100対1である

proportion [U, 複数で] (大きさ・数量などの)比率;釣り合い, バランス ◇The room is very long ***in proportion to*** (= relative to) its width. その部屋は横幅に比べてすごく縦長だ ◇You haven't drawn the figures in the foreground ***in proportion***. あなたが前景に描いた人物は釣り合いが取れていない ◇The head is ***out of proportion*** with the body. 頭と体が不釣り合いだ ◇Always try to keep a ***sense of proportion*** (= of the relative importance of different things). いつもバランス感覚を保つようにしなさい ◇It is an impressive building with fine *proportions*. その建物はよく均斉が取れていて印象的だ
☞ **proportional, proportionate** (RELATIVE)

scale [C, U] (地図・図・模型の大きさにおける)比率, 縮尺 ◇The map is ***drawn to*** a ***scale*** of 1:25000. その地図は2万5000分の1に縮尺して描かれている ◇Engineers have built a *scale model* of part of the coast. 技師たちは海岸の一部の縮尺模型を作った ◇Is this diagram ***to scale*** (= are all the parts the same size and shape in relation to each other as they are in the thing represented)? この図は一定の比率で縮小されたものですか

rational 形 ☞ GOOD 3

rational・coherent・logical・scientific・reasoned
行動や考え方が道理や事実, 思慮に基づいていることを表す
【類語訳】合理的な, 理にかなった, 筋の通った, 論理的な, 系統的な

文型&コロケーション
▸ to be rational/ scientific **about** sth
▸ a rational/ coherent/ logical/ scientific/ reasoned **argument/ explanation**
▸ rational/ coherent/ logical/ scientific/ reasoned **thought**

- a rational/ coherent/ logical/ scientific **approach**
- a rational/ logical/ scientific/ reasoned **choice/ decision/ conclusion**
- rational/ logical/ scientific/ reasoned **thinking**
- **perfectly** rational/ coherent/ logical

rational （行動・考え方が）合理的な，理にかなった ◇There's no *rational* explanation for his actions. 彼の行動に対しては合理的な説明がつかない ◇In some ways their behaviour is perfectly *rational*. いくつかの点で彼らの行動はまったく理にかなっている 反意 **irrational** (IRRATIONAL), ☞ **rationality** (LOGIC)
- ➤**rationally** 副 ◇Scientific training helps you to think *rationally*. 科学的トレーニングによって合理的な思考が培われる

coherent （考え・システム・説明が）筋の通った；明瞭な ◇She gave a clear, *coherent* account to the court. 彼女は法廷で明瞭で筋の通った説明をした ◇They have yet to come up with a *coherent* policy on this issue. 彼らはこの件に関してまだはっきりした方針を打ち出していない ❶ coherent は特に計画や組織［構造］について用いられる. approach, framework, pattern, picture, plan, policy, programme, scheme, strategy, structure, system, theory, whole と結びつくことが多い. 反意 **incoherent**, ☞ **coherence** (EFFICIENCY)

logical 論理的な ◇The problem can be solved using a process of *logical* reasoning. その問題は論理的な推論法を用いて解くことができる ◇A contradiction is a *logical impossibility*. 矛盾とは論理的にありえないことである 反意 **illogical** (IRRATIONAL), ☞ **logic** (LOGIC)
- ➤**logically** 副 ◇If you look at it *logically* his argument makes no sense. 論理的に見て彼の主張は筋が通っていない

scientific （方法・考え方が）系統立った，系統的な ◇He took a very *scientific* approach to management. 彼は経営に非常に系統立った手法を取り入れた ◇We need to be more *scientific* about this problem. この問題に対してはもっと系統的な取り組みをする必要がある 反意 **unscientific** (IRRATIONAL)
- ➤**scientifically** 副 ◇We should try to approach this *scientifically*. これには系統的に取り組む努力をすべきだ

reasoned ［名詞の前で］（主張・意見が）筋の通った ◇They refused the appeal without offering any *reasoned* argument. 彼らはなんら筋の通った論拠も示さずにその訴えを退けた ☞ **reason** (REASON), **reason** (CONCLUDE)

read 動

read・flick through sth・look through sth・leaf through sth・dip into sth・scan・skim・plough through sth
印刷された［書かれた］言葉を見てその意味を理解する
【類語訳】読む，読み上げる，目を通す，ぱらぱらめくる，拾い読みする，ざっと読む

文型&コロケーション
- to read/ flick/ look/ leaf/ scan/ skim/ plough **through** sth
- to read/ flick through/ look through/ leaf through/ dip into/ plough through a **book**
- to read/ flick through/ look through/ leaf through/ scan/ skim a **newspaper/ paper**
- to read/ flick through/ look through/ leaf through a **magazine**
- to read/ look through/ plough through a **report**
- to flick through/ look through/ leaf through/ scan/ skim **the pages of** sth
- to **quickly** read/ flick through/ look through/ leaf through/ scan/ skim sth

read ［自, 他］（本などを）読む；（本などを）読み上げる，（人に）読んであげる ◇He learned to *read* when he was three. 彼は3歳のときに読めるようになった ◇Just *read* through what you've written before you send it off. 送る前に書いたことをひととおり読んでみなさい ◇What are you *reading* at the moment? (= what book?) 今何を読んでいるのですか ◇Can you *read* music? 楽譜は読めますか ◇I'm trying to *read* the map. 地図を読もうとしているところです ◇I used to *read to* my younger brothers at bedtime. 寝る前に弟に本を読んでやったものだ ◇Will you *read* me a story? お話を読んでくれますか ◇I *read* the words out loud (= spoke them). その言葉を大きな声に出して読んだ ❶ read は読んで知ることも意味する. ◆I *read about* it in today's paper.（今日の新聞でそのことを知った）. ◆I *read that* he'd resigned.（彼が辞任したことを読んで知った）.

,flick 'through sth 句動詞 ［受身なし］（本・雑誌などを）ぱらぱらめくって見る，ざっと目を通す ◇She was *flicking through* the pages of a magazine. 彼女は雑誌のページをぱらぱらめくって見ていた ◇I've only had time to *flick through* your report but it seems to be fine. その報告書にはざっと目を通す時間しかなかったけど，いいんじゃないかな

'look through sth 句動詞 ［受身なし］（本・雑誌などを）めくって見る，目を通す ◇I caught him *looking through* my confidential files. 彼が私の機密ファイルに目を通しているところを見つけた ◇She *looked through* her notes before the exam. 彼女は試験前にノートに目を通した

> **ノート** flick through sth と look through sth の使い分け：flick through sth と look through sth よりもすばやい．後者のほうは通例じっくり行う．報告書をさほど注意して読む必要がないと思えば，ただ look through a report でよいが，こうしたからと言って謝ることはない．◆I've *looked through* your report and it's fine.（君の報告書に目を通したが問題ないよ）. × I've only had time to *look through* your report.

'leaf through sth 句動詞 ［受身なし］（本のページを）ぱらぱらめくる ◇She *leafed through* the guide book until she found the page she wanted. 彼女は読みたいページを見つけるまでそのガイドブックをぱらぱらめくった

dip into sth 句動詞 (**-pp-**)［受身なし］（本・雑誌の）部分的に読む，拾い読みする ◇It's a good book to *dip into* now and again. それは時々拾い読みするにはいい本です

scan (**-nn-**) ［他, 自］（特定の情報を見つけるために）ざっと読む，ざっと目を通す ◇I *scanned* the list quickly, looking for my name. 自分の名前を探すために急いでリストにざっと目を通した ◇She *scanned* through the newspaper over breakfast. 彼女は朝食を取りながら新聞をざっと読んだ ◇You should teach students to *scan for* essential information. ざっと目を通して必要な情報を探すように学生に教えるべきです

skim (**-mm-**) ［他, 自］（（必）要点を見つけるために）ざっと読む，ざっと目を通す ◇I always *skim* the financial section of the newspaper. いつも新聞の金融欄にざっと目を

↳read

real, realistic

通します ◇He *skimmed* through the article trying to find his name. 彼は自分の名前を見つけようと記事にざっと目を通した

> ノート **scan と skim の使い分け**：時にはどちらの語も用いることができる。◆I *scanned/skimmed* the list until I found my name. (私は自分の名前を見つけるまでリストに目を通した). しかし、scanはふつう特定の情報を探しているときに用いられ、skimは情報の大体の中身をつかみたいときに用いられることが多い. skim for sthとは言わない. ×Teach students to *skim* for essential information.

,plough 'through sth 〈英〉 (〈米〉 **plow through sth**) 句動詞 [受身なし] (難しい[退屈な]本・書類などを)苦労しながら読み進む ◇I had to *plough through* dozens of legal documents. 何十冊もの法律文書を苦労しながら読み進まざるをえなかった

real 形

real・actual・true・genuine・authentic・proper
架空[偽物、模造]でないことを表す
【類語訳】実在の、実物の、本物の、本当の、真の、実際の

> 文型&コロケーション
> ▶ a real/ the actual/ the true/ genuine/ a proper **reason**
> ▶ the real/ actual/ true **cost** of sth
> ▶ a real/ a true/ a genuine/ an authentic **work of art**
> ▶ real/ genuine **leather/ silk/ gold**
> ▶ real/ genuine/ authentic **enough**

real [ふつう名詞の前で] 実在の、実物の、本物の、本当の、真の ◇It wasn't a ghost; it was a *real* person. それは幽霊ではなく実在の人物だった ◇pictures of animals, both *real* and mythological 実在する動物と神話上の動物の両方の絵 ◇Marilyn Monroe's *real* name was Norma Jean Baker. マリリン・モンローの本名はノーマ・ジーン・ベイカーだった ◇See the *real* Africa on one of our walking safaris. 私どもの徒歩による冒険旅行で本物のアフリカをご覧ください ◇I do my best to hide my *real* feelings from others. 何としてでも私の本心は隠すようにします ◇Are those *real* flowers? あれらは本物の花ですか ◇She never had any *real* friends at school. 彼女は学校で本当の友達が一人もいなかった 反意 **imaginary, pretend** (FICTIONAL)

▶ **really** 副 ◇Tell me what *really* happened. 本当は何があったのか教えてください

actual [名詞の前で] 実際の ◇What were his *actual* words? 彼が実際に言った言葉は何だったのですか ◇The *actual* cost was much higher than we had expected. 実際の費用は我々の予想よりずっと高かった ◇James looks younger than his wife but **in actual fact** (= really) he is several years older. ジェームズは妻より若く見えるが、実際は何歳か年上である 反意 **hypothetical, notional** (SUPPOSED), **potential** (LIKELY)

▶ **actually** 副 ◇Well, what did she *actually* say? では、実際に彼女は何と言ったの

true 本当の、まさにその；本物の、真の ◇the *true* face of socialism (= what it is really like rather than what people think it is like) 社会主義の本当の姿 ◇He reveals his *true* character to very few people. 彼はごくわずかな人にしか本性を見せない ◇It was *true love* between them. それは彼らの間の真の愛だった ◇He's a *true*

gentleman. 彼は本物の紳士だ ◇The painting is a masterpiece *in the truest sense* of the word. その絵画はまさに真の意味で傑作である

▶ **truly** 副 ◇He started the first *truly* international ballet company. 彼は真に国際的な最初のバレエ団を立ち上げた

> ノート **real と true の使い分け**：多くの場合、どちらの語も用いることができる。◆You're a *real/true* friend. (君は真の友人だ). ◆He's a *real/true* gentleman. (彼は本物の紳士だ). しかし、realは備えているべき性質をより現実的な見方でとらえるのに対し、trueはより理想化した見方でとらえる。否定文ではrealのほうがtrueよりよく用いられる。希少さや独特さを強調するにはtrueのほうがよく用いられる。×She never had any *true* friends at school. ×It was *real* love between them.

genuine (見た目どおり模造ではなく)本物の、本当の ◇Is the painting a *genuine* Picasso? それは本物のピカソの絵ですか ◇Fake designer watches are sold at a fraction of the price of *the genuine article*. デザイナーブランドの時計の偽物は本物の値段よりかなり安く売られている ◇Only *genuine* refugees can apply for asylum. 本当の難民しか保護を求めることはできない 反意 **fake, imitation** (ARTIFICIAL)

authentic (複製ではなく)本物の ◇I don't know if the painting is *authentic*. その絵が本物かどうかわからない

> ノート **genuine と authentic の使い分け**：この2語は意味や使用範囲が非常に近い。genuineは同じ種類の物のグループに属するので「本物」と言える場合に用いられる。authenticは作り[生み]出されたものが「本物」と言える場合に用いられる。このことは時にはどちらの語も使えることがあるということを意味する。◆a *genuine/an authentic* Picasso (本物のピカソ).

proper [名詞の前で] 《英、話し言葉》 本当の、まともな、ちゃんとした ◇Eat some *proper* food, not just toast and jam! ジャムトーストだけではなく、まともな物を食べなさい ◇When are you going to get a *proper* job? いつになったらちゃんとした仕事に就くの ❶《米》ではrealを用いる。

realistic 形

realistic・pragmatic・practical・no-nonsense・down-to-earth・level-headed・matter-of-fact
人が感情に左右されずに冷静に分別を持って状況に対処すること
【類語訳】現実的な、実際的な、事務的な、気取らない、分別のある、冷静な、淡々とした、ドライな

> 文型&コロケーション
> ▶ to be realistic/ pragmatic/ practical/ down-to-earth/ matter-of-fact **about** sth
> ▶ a realistic/ pragmatic/ practical/ no-nonsense/ down-to-earth/ level-headed/ matter-of-fact **approach**
> ▶ a realistic/ pragmatic/ practical/ no-nonsense/ down-to-earth/ matter-of-fact **attitude**
> ▶ a realistic/ pragmatic/ practical **solution**
> ▶ a no-nonsense/ practical/ matter-of-fact **manner/ way**
> ▶ a no-nonsense/ matter-of-fact **tone/ voice**
> ▶ a down-to-earth/ practical/ level-headed **person**
> ▶ **very** realistic/ pragmatic/ practical/ down-to-earth/ level-headed/ matter-of-fact
> ▶ **quite** realistic/ pragmatic/ practical/ matter-of-fact

realistic 《ふつうほめて》（特定の状況において）現実的な，現実的に考えて［対処して］ ◇This report takes a much more *realistic* view of the situation. この報告書ではずっとより現実的な見方で状況がとらえられている ◇We have to be *realistic* about our chances of winning. 我々が勝つ可能性については現実的であるべきだ ◇It is not *realistic* to expect people to spend so much money. 人がそんな大金を使うだろうと考えるのは現実的ではない 反意 **unrealistic**
▶ **realistically** 副 ◇How many can you *realistically* hope to sell? 実際のところいくつ売れたらいいと思ってるの
pragmatic 《ふつうほめて，特に書き言葉》（確たる考え・理論によらず）現実的な，実際的な ◇We take a *pragmatic* approach to management problems. 我々は経営問題に対して現実的な取り組みをしています ❶ *pragmatic* であることは，伝統的な慣行に従わない解決策を見つけることを意味することが多い. *pragmatic* はふつう行動の指針を表すのに用いられる.
♦ a *pragmatic* response/solution/approach/attitude（現実的な対応/解決策/取り組み/態度）
▶ **pragmatically** 副 ◇The company responded *pragmatically* to local conditions. その会社は地域の状況に現実的に対応した
practical 《ふつうほめて》（問題解決に）現実的な，実際的な ◇Let's be *practical* and work out the cost first. まず実際に費用を割り出そう 反意 **impractical**, ☞ **practicalities** (BASICS)
,no-'nonsense ［名詞の前で］（人の気持ちを考えず）現実的な，事務的な ◇We adopt a *no-nonsense* approach to unpaid bills. 我々は未払いの請求書に対しては現実的に対処しています ◇She was a tough, *no-nonsense* leader. 彼女はタフで現実的な指導者だった
,down-to-'earth 《ほめて》（協力的・友好的で）気取らない，実際的な ◇She was friendly and *down-to-earth*, and quickly put me at my ease. 彼女は人当たりがよくて気取りもなく，すぐに私を和ませてくれた ❶ *down-to-earth* は自分が実際［他人］より偉くない［教養がない］と考えている人について用いられることが多い.
,level-'headed 《ほめて》（落ち着いて）分別のある，（困難な状況でも）冷静な ◇This position requires a *level-headed* person with experience in managing risk. この職にはリスク管理にたけた分別のある人物が必要だ
,matter-of-'fact（感情を表さずに）事務的な，淡々とした，ドライな ◇She told us the news of his death in a very *matter-of-fact* way. 彼女は私たちに彼の訃報をごく事務的に伝えた ◇He was very *matter-of-fact* about the breakdown of his marriage. 彼は自分の結婚生活が破綻したことに非常に淡々としていた

reason 名 ☞ ARGUMENT 2

reason・explanation・grounds・basis・excuse・motive・need・justification・cause・pretext
なぜ起こったのか［事を起こしたのか］を述べることを表す
【類語訳】理由，わけ，根拠，言い訳，弁解，口実，動機

文型&コロケーション
▶ a reason/ an explanation/ grounds/ a basis/ an excuse/ a motive/ a need/ justification/ cause/ a pretext **for** sth
▶ the reason/ motive **behind** sth
▶ **on** the grounds/ basis/ pretext **of/ that**...
▶ the reason/ grounds/ basis/ excuse/ justification/ pretext **that**...

▶ (an) **obvious** reason/ explanation/ grounds/ excuse/ motive/ need/ justification/ cause/ pretext
▶ (a) **clear/ legitimate** reason/ grounds/ excuse/ motive/ need/ justification/ cause/ pretext
▶ (a) **logical/ personal/ no apparent** reason/ explanation/ grounds/ excuse/ motive/ need/ justification/ cause
▶ (a) **good/ valid** reason/ explanation/ grounds/ excuse/ motive/ justification/ cause
▶ (a) **convincing** reason/ explanation/ grounds/ excuse/ motive/ justification/ pretext
▶ (a) **reasonable** explanation/ grounds/ excuse/ motive/ need/ justification/ cause/ pretext
▶ the **real** reason/ explanation/ grounds/ motive/ justification/ cause
▶ to **have** a reason/ an explanation/ grounds/ an excuse/ a motive/ a justification/ cause/ a pretext
▶ to **give/ offer** (sb) a reason/ an explanation/ an excuse/ a justification/ a pretext
▶ to **suggest** a reason/ an explanation/ grounds/ a motive/ a justification
▶ to **see/ understand/ explain** (the/ sb's) reasons/ grounds/ motive/ justification

reason [C, U]（事が起こった［人が何かをした］）理由，わけ；（事を行う）もっともな理由 ◇I'd like to know *the reason why* you're so late. あなたがそんなに遅刻した理由を知りたい ◇He said no but he didn't give a *reason*. 彼はノーと言ったが，理由は述べなかった ◇We aren't going for the *simple reason* that we can't afford it. 私たちは単に金銭的に余裕がないという理由で行かないだけです ◇*For some reason* (= one that I don't know or don't understand) we all have to come in early tomorrow. 何らかの理由で明日はみんな早く来ないといけない ◇*For reasons of* security the door is always kept locked. 警備上の理由でドアにはいつも鍵がかかっている ◇They have *reason* to believe that he is lying. 彼らには彼が嘘をついていると信じるだけの理由がある ◇She complained, *with reason* (= rightly), that she had been underpaid. ずっと薄給だったと彼女が不平を言うのももっともだった
☞ **reason** (CONCLUDE), **reasoned** (RATIONAL)
explanation [C, U]（事が起こった）説明；理由 ◇The most likely *explanation* is that his plane was delayed. いかにももっともらしい理由としては彼が乗った飛行機が遅れたということだ ◇I can't think of any possible *explanation* for his absence. どう考えても彼が欠席した理由が見当たらない ◇The book opens with an *explanation* of why some drugs are banned. その本はいくつかの薬物が禁止されている理由についての説明から始まっています ◇She left the room abruptly *without explanation*. 彼女は理由も言わずに突然部屋を出て行った ☞ **explain** (EXPLAIN 2)
grounds ［複数で］《ややフォーマル》（正当な［本当の］）理由，根拠 ◇You have no *grounds* for complaint. 不平を言う理由など君にはないよ ◇He retired from the job on health *grounds*. 彼は健康上の理由で退職した ◇Employers cannot discriminate on *grounds* of age. 雇用主は年齢を理由に差別してはいけない
basis ［単数で］《ややフォーマル》（人がある行動を取る）理由，根拠 ◇She was chosen for the job on the *basis* of her qualifications and ideas. 彼女は持っている資格と着想力に基づいてその仕事の担当者に選ばれた ◇On what *basis* will this decision be made? 何を根拠にこの決定が下さ

れるのですか ❶ basis はふつう, on the basis of/that..., On what basis...? の句で用いられる。

excuse [C] (自分の行動を説明・弁護するための)言い訳, 弁解; もっともな理由, 口実 ◇Late again! What's your *excuse* this time? また遅刻か. 今度はどんな言い訳をするんだ ◇There's no *excuse* for such behaviour. そんな態度を取って弁解の余地はないよ ◇You don't have to **make excuses** for her (= try to think of reasons for her behaviour). 彼女を弁護してやる必要はない ◇It gave me an *excuse* to take the car. それでその車を利用する口実ができた ☞ **excuse** (FORGIVE)

motive [C] (人の行動を説明する)理由, 動機 ◇There seemed to be no *motive* for the murder. その殺人には動機がないように思えた ◇I'm suspicious of his *motives*. 私は彼の動機を不審に思っている ◇I have an *ulterior motive* in offering to help you. 君を手助けしようと申し出るのはちょっとした思惑があってのことなんだ ☞ **motivation** (INCENTIVE)

need [単数で, U] 《ふつう否定的な文で》(事を行う)もっともな理由, 必要(性) ◇There is no *need* for you to get up early tomorrow. 君が明日早起きする必要はないよ ◇I had no *need* to open the letter — I knew what it would say. 手紙を開ける必要はなかった. 何が書かれているかわかっていたから ❶ この意味では, need はほぼ常に There is/was no need (for sb) to do sth., have no need to do sth の句で用いられる。

justification [U, C] 《ややフォーマル》(事が存在する[行われる])正当な理由 ◇I can see no possible *justification* for any further tax increases. さらなる増税を行う正当な理由らしきものは何一つない ◇The government is struggling to find a *justification* for this war. 政府はこの戦争を正当化する理由を見つけようと躍起になっている ☞ **justify** (EXPLAIN 2)

> [ノート] **grounds** と **justification** の使い分け : justification は行動の理由を見つける[理解する]場合や, 事を行うよい理由を説明しようとする場合に用いられ, little, no, some, every, without, not any のような語句が添えられることが多い。grounds はすでに存在する理由, (例えば法律などで)すでに定められた理由についてよく用いられる。moral/economic/constitutional/environmental/ethical/medical/legal grounds (道徳的な/経済上の/憲法上の/環境上の/倫理的な/医学的な/法的な理由).

cause [U]《ややフォーマル》(特定の感情を抱く[特定の行動に出る])理由 ◇There is no *cause for alarm/concern*. 不安になる/心配するには及ばない ◇If your child is absent without good *cause* (= without a good reason), you may receive a warning from the school board. お子さんがもっともな理由なしに欠席すれば, 教育委員会から注意を受けることもあります

pretext [C, ふつう単数で]《ややフォーマル》(悪事に対する)偽りの理由, 口実 ◇The incident was used as a *pretext* for intervention in the area. その事件は地域への介入の口実に使われた ◇He left the party early on the *pretext* of having work to do. やるべき仕事があると偽って彼はパーティーを早めに切り上げた

reasonable 形

reasonable・fair・equal・just・equitable・even-handed
適切かつ一様に人に対処することを表す

【類語訳】分別のある, 理にかなった, もっともな, 妥当な, 適正な, 公正な, 公明正大な

[文型&コロケーション]
▸ to be reasonable/ fair/ just/ equitable **that**...
▸ to be reasonable/ fair/ just **to do sth**
▸ a reasonable/ a fair/ an equal/ a just/ an equitable **division/ distribution/ share** of sth
▸ a reasonable/ a fair/ a just/ an equitable **system/ settlement/ solution**
▸ a reasonable/ fair/ just **law/ punishment/ sentence/ judgement/ person/ man/ woman**
▸ perfectly reasonable/ fair/ just

reasonable 分別のある, 理にかなった, もっともな, 妥当な ◇It is *reasonable* to assume that she knew beforehand that this would happen. 彼女がこうなることを事前に知っていたと考えるのが理にかなっている ◇It seems a perfectly *reasonable* request to make. そのような要請はしごく当然だと思われる ◇Any *reasonable* person would have done exactly as you did. 分別のある人なら誰でも, あなたがやったとおりにしたでしょう ◇Be *reasonable!* We can't work late every night. 無理を言わないでください. 毎晩遅くまで働けません 【反意】 **unreasonable** (UNACCEPTABLE), **reasonable** (FINE), **reason** (LOGIC), **plausible** (POSSIBLE 2)
▸ **reasonably** 副 ◇He couldn't *reasonably* be expected to pay back the loan all at once. 彼が一度に借金を返すなんて思えないのももっともだった

fair 適正な, 妥当な, 理にかなった,；(規則・法律に従って扱われ)公平な ◇All we're asking for is a *fair* wage. 私たちが求めているのは適正賃金にすぎません ◇It's not *fair to* the students to keep changing the schedule. 時間割を変更してばかりいるのは学生に悪い ◇It's not *fair on* the students... 《英ではまた》…は学生に悪い ◇It's fair to say *that* they are pleased with the latest offer. 彼らは最新のオファーに満足していると言ってもいいだろう ◇**To be fair**, she behaved better than we expected. 公平を期すために言えば, 彼女は私たちの予想以上にうまく振る舞った ◇It seems *only fair* that they should give us something in return. 彼らがお返しに何かをくれるのはごく当然のことのように思われる ◇It's *not fair!* He always gets more than me! 《話し言葉》不公平よ. 彼はいつも私よりたくさんもらってるじゃない 【反意】 **unfair** (WRONG 2), ☞ **fair** (FINE), **fairness, fair play** (JUSTICE)
▸ **fairly** 副 ◇He's always treated me very *fairly*. 彼はいつも私をとても公平に扱ってくれる ◇Her attitude could *fairly* be described as hostile. 彼女の態度はまるで敵対的だと評していいだろう

equal (人種・宗教・性別などの面で)平等な, 均等な ◇*equal rights/pay* 平等な権利/賃金 ◇The company has an *equal opportunities* policy (= gives the same chances of employment to everyone). その会社は機会均等の方針を採っている ◇the desire for a more *equal* society (= in which everyone has the same rights and chances) より平等な社会への願望 【反意】 **unequal** (WRONG 2), ☞ **equality** (JUSTICE)

just [ふつう名詞の前で]《ややフォーマル》(道徳的に)正しい, 公平な, 公正な ◇I think it was a *just* decision. それは正しい決定だったと思う ◇Of course we all strive for a *just* and humane society. 私たちがみな公平で人道的な社会を目指して努力するのは当然です ◇He was known to be a *just* man. 彼は公平な人物として知られていた ◊The law must be seen to be *just*. 法律は公正であると見なされなければならない ❶ *just* は法律関係や社会のあるべき姿に関する文脈で用いられることが多い. ふつう, インフォーマルな[私的な]文脈では用いられない. 反意 **unjust** (WRONG 3), ☞ **justice** (JUSTICE)

equitable 《フォーマル》(制度・方法・税などが)公平で理にかなった, 公正な; (誰にでも)公平な ◊We need to construct an *equitable* and efficient method of local taxation. 公平かつ効率的な地方税のシステムを構築する必要がある 反意 **inequitable** (WRONG 3)

even-'handed (誰にでも)公明正大な, 公平な ◊They took an *even-handed* approach to industrial relations. 彼らは労使関係に公明正大な取り組み方をした ◊He is *even-handed in* his criticism of the various political parties. 彼はさまざまな政党を公平に批判する ❶ even-handed は問題の扱い方について用いられ, 人には用いられない. ✗ an *even-handed* person/man/woman.

recent 形

recent • current • latest • present • modern • new • contemporary • present-day • modern-day

今起こっている[ほんの少し前に起こった]ので現在に属していることを表す

【類語訳】最近の, 現在の, 今の, 最新の, 現代の, モダンな, 新しい, 今日の

文型&コロケーション
▸ recent/ modern **times**/ the present **time**
▸ recent/ current/ present/ contemporary/ present-day **events**
▸ the current/ latest/ present/ contemporary/ present-day **situation**
▸ recent/ current/ the latest/ present/ modern/ contemporary **trends**
▸ the recent/ current/ latest/ present/ modern/ new/ contemporary/ modern-day **version**
▸ recent/ current/ the latest/ present/ modern/ new/ contemporary/ present-day **forms**/ **theories**
▸ the current/ modern/ contemporary **scene**
▸ current/ modern/ new/ contemporary **politics**
▸ modern/ a new/ contemporary/ present-day/ modern-day **society**
▸ modern/ contemporary/ present-day **life**
▸ the modern/ a new/ the contemporary **world**
▸ (a) recent/ modern/ new/ contemporary/ present-day **literature**/ **writer**
▸ (a) modern/ new/ contemporary/ present-day **art**/ **artist**/ **music**

recent [ふつう名詞の前で] (ほんの少し前に起こって[始まって])最近の ◊The next chapter summarizes *recent* developments in the field. 次の章ではその分野の最近の進展を要約している ◊The Prime Minister discussed the issue during his most *recent* visit to Poland. つい最近のポーランド訪問中に首相はその問題を話し合った ◊There have been many changes *in recent years*. 近年, 多くの変化があった 反意 **long-standing** (OLD 1)
➤ **recently** 副 ◊We received a letter from him *recently*. 私たちは最近, 彼から手紙をもらった ◊I haven't seen them *recently* (= It is some time since I saw

them). 彼らに近頃会っていません

current [名詞の前で] (今起こって[存在して]いて)現在の, 今の ◊The necklace would be worth over $5,000 at *current* prices. そのネックレスは時価で5000ドル以上はするでしょう ◊Ask your *current* employer to give you a reference. 今の雇い主に頼んで人物証明書を出してもらってください ◊Our *current* financial situation is not good. 私たちの現在の財政状況はよくない 反意 **former, then, ex-** (FORMER), **previous** (PREVIOUS)
➤ **currently** 副 ◊This matter is *currently* being discussed by the Board. この問題は現在, 役員会で審議中です 反意 **previously** (PREVIOUS)

latest [名詞の前で] (つい)最近の, 最新の ◊She always wears the *latest* fashions. 彼女はいつも最新ファッションに身を包んでいる ◊Her *latest* novel has been shortlisted for a literary prize. 彼女の小説の最新作はある文学賞の最終候補に挙がっている ◊Have you heard the *latest* news? 最新情報を聞きましたか
➤ **the latest** 名 [単数で] ◊This is *the latest* in robot technology. 《ややインフォーマル》これはロボット技術の最新のものである ◊Have you heard *the latest*? 最新情報を聞きましたか

present [ふつう名詞の前で] 現在の, 今の ◊The *present* owner of the house is a Mr T. Grant. その家の現在の所有者はT.グラント氏である ◊This is a list of all club members, *past and present*. これは過去と現在のクラブ会員の全リストです ◊We do not have any more information *at the present time*. 現在のところ我々はさらなる情報は何も得ていません 反意 **past** (PREVIOUS)
➤ **at present** フレーズ ◊The council has no plans *at present* to develop this site. 《ややフォーマル》地方議会にはこの用地を開発する計画が現在のところない
➤ **presently** 副 ◊The crime is *presently* being investigated by the police. 《特に米》その犯罪は現在, 警察が捜査中である

ノート **current** と **present** の使い分け: 多くの場合, どちらの語も用いることができる. ◆ the *current/present* situation/state/position/climate/trend/practice/arrangement/value/level/generation/crisis (現在の状況/状態/立場/天候/動向/慣行/協定/価値/水準/世代/危機) **current** は特に金融関連で用いられる. ◆ *current* spending/expenditure (現在の支出/歳出), the *current* surplus/deficit/yield (経常黒字/経常赤字/現行収益). また, **current affairs** (時事問題) の句でも特に用いられる. **present** は時間の長さを表す語と共に用いられることが多い. ◆ the *present* day/century/moment/time (現代/今世紀/現時点/現在). ただし, 金融関連では用いられない. ◆ What's the budget for the *current* year? (本年度の予算はいくらですか).

modern [名詞の前で] 現代の; (美術・音楽・ファッションなどの様式が)現代の, モダンな ◊*Modern* European history 現代ヨーロッパ史 ◊Stress is a major problem of *modern* life. ストレスは現代の生活における大きな問題である ◊Shakespeare's language can be a problem for *modern* readers. シェークスピアの言語は現代の読者には手に負えないかもしれない ◊The gallery has regular exhibitions of *modern* art. その美術館は現代美術の常設展を行っている 反意 **ancient** (OLD 1), ☞ **modern** (MODERN)

new 《しばしば the と共に》現代の; 最新型の, 新しい ◊He couldn't stand the *new* breed of career politicians. 彼は新しいタイプの政治家に我慢がならなかった ◊Comedy is the *new* rock and roll. 喜劇は現代のロックンロールだ ◇They called themselves the *New* Romantics. 彼らは自らをニューロマンティックスと称した

contemporary《ややフォーマル》(生活・社会・文化などの)現代の ◇The film paints a depressing picture of life in *contemporary* Britain. その映画は現代英国での生活の苦しい状況を描いている ◇She is one of the great innovators of *contemporary* dance. 彼女は現代舞踊の偉大な革新者の一人である

[ノート] **modern と contemporary の使い分け**: 多くの場合, 特に芸術・文化・社会について言う際は, どちらの語も用いることができる. ◆ *modern/contemporary* art/architecture/dance/fiction/literature/music/painting/culture/society/politics/history (現代美術/建築/舞踊/小説/文学/音楽/絵画/文化/社会/政治/史). ◆ the *modern/contemporary* world/scene (現代の世界/事情). modernは科学・技術についても用いられるが, contemporaryは用いられない. ◆ *modern* technology/physics/medicine/warfare/equipment/machinery/techniques (現代技術/現代物理学/現代医学/近代戦/現代的な設備/現代的な機械/近代技術). ☞ **modern** (MODERN)

,present-'day [名詞の前で]《特に書き言葉》現在の, 今日(ミ)の ◇His theories have no relevance to *present-day* society. 彼の理論は現代社会となんら関連性がない ◇Serbia at that time already included *present-day* Macedonia. 当時のセルビアにはすでに今日のマケドニアが含まれていた ❶present-dayは特に, 今の形態が過去の形態と異なる物事について用いられる. ◆ *present-day* society/English/Russia (現代社会/英語/ロシア)
▶ **the ,present 'day** [名][単数形で] ◇a study of European drama, from Ibsen *to the present day* イプセンから現代までのヨーロッパ演劇の研究

'modern-day [名詞の前で] 現代の ◇*modern-day* America 現代アメリカ ❶modern-dayは過去に存在した(ふつう悪い[嫌な])人や物事の現代版を表すのに用いることが多い. ◆ It has been called *modern-day* slavery. (それは現代版の奴隷制度と呼ばれてきた)

recession 名

recession・depression・slump・slowdown・trough
ビジネスや経済の厳しい時期を表す
【類語訳】不況, 景気後退, 恐慌, 不景気

slowdown — slump — recession — depression
　　　　　　trough

[文型&コロケーション]
▶ **in** recession/ a depression/ a slump/ a trough
▶ a **major/ serious/ severe** recession/ depression/ slump
▶ an **economic** recession/ depression/ slump/ slowdown
▶ a **worldwide** recession/ depression/ slump/ slowdown
▶ to **cause** a recession/ slump/ slowdown
▶ to **go into** recession/ depression

recession [C, U] 不況, 景気後退 ◇How do you assess the impact of the current *recession* on manufacturing? 現在の不況が製造業に与える影響をどう評価しますか ◇We need active policies to pull the country out of *recession*. 我々には国を不況から脱却させる積極的な政策が必要です ◇These industries have been hit hard by the *recession*. これらの産業は景気後退によって大きな打撃を受けています

depression [C, U] 不況, 恐慌 ◇The country was in the grip of (an) economic *depression*. その国は経済不況に陥っていた ◇He grew up during the Great *Depression* of the 1930s. 彼は1930年代の大恐慌の時代に育った
▶ **depressed** [形] ◇They have made little attempt to bring jobs to economically *depressed* areas. 経済不況の地域に仕事をもたらそうとする試みはほとんどなされていなかった

slump [C]《特にジャーナリズム or ビジネス》不景気, (景気)不振 ◇Housing sales are finally coming out of a three-month *slump*. 住宅販売は3か月間の不振からようやく抜け出しつつある ◇The toy industry is in a *slump*. おもちゃ業界は不景気の最中(ᣞ)にある 反意 **boom** (DO WELL), **slump** (REDUCTION)

slowdown [C]《特にビジネス》減速, 景気後退 ◇There has been a *slowdown* in economic growth in recent months. ここ数か月, 経済成長が減速してきた

trough [C]《特にビジネス》停滞期, (景気の)谷 ◇There have been *peaks and troughs* in the long-term trend of unemployment. 失業が長期化する傾向にあって景気の山と谷があった 反意 **peak** (PEAK)

[ノート] これらの中でslowdownが最も深刻でなく, depressionが最も深刻なものである. slowdown, slump, troughは, 国の経済全般に, またはある特定のビジネスや産業だけに影響を与えるものである. ふつう数か月間続き, 時に通常の景気循環の一部とも見なされる. recessionは産業全体または国の経済全体に影響を与え, 何年も続くこともあり, ふつう通常の景気循環の一部とは見なされない. しかし, それでもrecessionは主にビジネスや経済に対する影響という角度からとらえられる. これに対しdepressionは, 不況が一般市民の生活に与える影響, 特に非常に多くの人に影響を与え, 貧困や失業による厳しい状況を考慮する際に用いられる. the Great Depressionは1929年の米国株式市場の大暴落に続く世界的な経済不況のことである.

reckless 形 ☞CRAZY

reckless・irresponsible・premature・unwise・rash・hasty
自分の行動が元で生じる可能性のある結果に配慮や用心が欠けることを表す
【類語訳】無謀な, 向こう見ずな, いい加減な, 無責任な, 時期尚早の, 無分別な, 軽率な, 軽はずみな, 早まった, 性急な

[文型&コロケーション]
▶ It would be reckless/ irresponsible/ premature/ unwise/ rash **to do sth**.
▶ You would be unwise **to do sth**.
▶ a reckless/ a premature/ an unwise/ a rash/ a hasty **decision**
▶ **rather/ somewhat** reckless/ irresponsible/ premature/ rash/ hasty
▶ **extremely/ very** reckless/ irresponsible/ unwise/ rash

reckless《ふつうけなして》(危険・結果に配慮せず)無謀な, 向こう見ずな ◇He showed a *reckless disregard* for

his own safety. 彼は無謀にも自分の身の安全を顧みなかった ◇She had always been ***reckless with*** money. 彼女はいつも見境なくお金を使った ☞ ***impulsive*** (SPONTANEOUS)
▶***recklessly*** 副 ◇She had fallen hopelessly and *recklessly* in love. 彼女はどうしようもないほど向こう見ずな恋に落ちてしまっていた
▶***recklessness*** 名 [U] ◇an act of sheer *recklessness* まったく無謀な行為

irresponsible (けなして) (影響を顧みず)いい加減な;責任感のない, 無責任な ◇He's fun but totally *irresponsible*. 彼はおもしろいけど, まったくいい加減な ◇This was highly *irresponsible* behaviour. これは極めて無責任な行動だった ❶ *irresponsible* は, 特に behaviour (行動), action (行為), conduct (行い), attitude (態度), way of doing things (物事のやり方) について用いられる。また, 問題を無視するなど, ある危険を冒すことが無責任だということを it is/would be irresponsible to で表せる。◆ It would be *irresponsible* to carry on if there really was a problem. (本当に問題があるのなら続行するのは無責任だろう)。反意 ***responsible*** (RELIABLE 1)

premature (ややフォーマル, 特にビジネス, 時にけなして) (起こる[行われる]のが)早すぎる, 時期尚早の ◇The incident brought the game to a *premature* conclusion. その事件で試合は早すぎる結末を迎えることになった ◇It is *premature* to talk about success at this stage (= because it may not happen). この段階で成功について論じるのは時期尚早だ

unwise (ややフォーマル, 特に書き言葉, ふつうけなして) (将来起こりうる問題を考えずに)無分別な, 賢明でない, 愚かな ◇It would be *unwise* to comment on the situation without knowing all the facts. 事実をすべて把握せずに状況についてとやかく言うのは賢明ではなかろう ◇He made some very *unwise* investments and lost a lot of money. 彼は非常に愚かな投資をして大金を失った 反意 **wise** (BEST), ☞ **foolish** (CRAZY)
▶***unwisely*** 副 ◇Perhaps *unwisely*, I agreed to help. おそらく無分別だっただろうが, 手を貸すことに同意してしまった

rash (ふつうけなして) (結果を顧みず)軽率な, 軽はずみな;軽率になされた ◇This is what happens when you make *rash* promises. 安請け合いをするとこういうことが起こるのです ◇It would be *rash* to assume that everyone will agree with you on this. このことについて誰もがあなたに賛成してくれると思うのは軽率だろう ◆ Think twice before doing anything *rash*. よく考えて軽はずみなことはしないようにしなさい ❶ 人は通例, *rash* の promises (約束) / decisions (決断) / statements (発言) をする。It is/would be rash to... は, assume, expect, state, conclude, say といった意見を述べたり結論を出したりする意味の動詞と共に用いられることが多い。
▶***rashly*** 副 ◇She had *rashly* promised to lend him the money. 彼女は軽率にも彼に金を貸す約束をしてしまっていた ◇I see now that I may have acted *rashly*. 今では軽はずみな行動をしでかしたかもしれないと思う

hasty (しばしばけなして) (行動・決定が)早まった, 性急な;(言動が)早まげ, 軽率な ◇Perhaps I was too *hasty* in rejecting his offer. たぶん彼の申し出を断るのが性急すぎたのだろう ◇Let's not make any *hasty* decisions. 性急な決定をしないようにしよう
▶***hastily*** 副 ◇Perhaps I spoke too *hastily*. おそらくあまりに軽率に話してしまったのだろう

recommend 617

recommend 動

1 ☞ PROPOSE
recommend・advise・advocate・urge
特定の状況でなすべきだと思うことを人が告げることを表す
【類語訳】勧める, 推奨する, 希望する, 忠告する, アドバイスする, 奨励する

recommend　　　advise　　　urge
advocate

文型&コロケーション
▶ to recommend/ advise/ advocate/ urge **that**...
▶ **It is** recommended/ advised/ advocated/ urged **that**...
▶ to recommend/ advise/ urge **sb to do sth**
▶ to recommend/ advise/ advocate **doing sth**
▶ to recommend/ advise/ advocate/ urge **caution**
▶ to advise/ advocate/ urge **restraint**
▶ to **strongly** recommend/ advise/ advocate **sb/ sth**

recommend [他] (すべきことを)勧める;(価格・レベルを)推奨する, 希望する ◇I *recommend* (that) he see a lawyer. 彼は弁護士に相談するといいと思います ◇It is strongly *recommended* that the machines be checked every year. 機械を毎年点検することを強くお勧めします ◇He *recommended* reading the book before seeing the movie. 彼はその映画を見る前に原作を読むことを勧めた ◇It is dangerous to exceed the *recommended* dose. 薬の推奨用量を超えて過度に服用することは危険である ◇a *recommended* price of $50 希望価格50ドル ☞ **recommendation** (PROPOSAL)

advise [他, 自] (すべきことを)勧める, 忠告する, アドバイスする ◇Her mother was away and couldn't *advise* her. 彼女の母親は出かけていたので忠告できなかった ◇I'd *advise* extreme caution. 細心の注意を払うことをお勧めします ◇I'd *advise* you not to tell him. 彼には言うべきではありませんね ◇I would strongly *advise against* going out on your own. 一人で外出ならないよう強くお勧めします ☞ **advice** (ADVICE)

ノート **recommend** と **advise** の使い分け: advise は recommend より意味の強い語で, アドバイスする側が高い[権威ある]地位にある場合に用いられることが多い。◆ Police are *advising* fans without tickets to stay away. (警察はチケットのないファンには来ないよう忠告している)。×Police are *recommending* fans without tickets to stay away. I advise you... は自分がアドバイスを与える相手よりよく知っている立場にあることを示すので, 相手が同等あるいは上位である場合, 相手の感情を害することもある。I recommend... は主に役立とうとしていることを示し, 相手の感情を害することはありません。recommend はありえる利益について述べる前向きな勧告に用いられることが多いが, advise はありえる危険について警告する, より否定的な忠告に用いられることが多い。×He *advised* reading the book before seeing the movie. ×I would *recommend* against going out on your own. 単に recommend sb には sth (to sb) と言わねばならない。×Her mother was away and couldn't *recommend* her.

advocate [他] 《フォーマル》 (公然と)支持する, 奨励する ◇The group does not *advocate* the use of violence.

R

その団体は暴力の行使を奨励してはいない ☞ SUPPORT

urge [他] 強く勧める, 強く促す ◇The situation is dangerous, but the UN is *urging* caution. 状況は危険だが, 国連は警戒は怠らないように強く促している ◇The report *urged* that all children be taught to swim. その報告書はすべての子どもに水泳を教えることを強く勧告した

2 recommend・suggest・nominate・endorse

人にいいことを教えたり, 特定の仕事や地位などにふさわしい人を提案したりすることを表す
【類語訳】推薦する, 薦める, ノミネートする

文型&コロケーション
▶ to recommend/ suggest/ nominate sb/ sth **for/ as** sth
▶ to recommend/ suggest sb/ sth **to** sth
▶ to recommend/ suggest/ nominate **sb to do** sth
▶ to recommend/ suggest/ nominate a **candidate**
▶ to recommend/ endorse a **product**

recommend [他] (人・物事を)推薦する, 薦める;(人・物事を)魅力ある[優れている]ものに(思えるように)する ◇Can you *recommend* a good hotel? いいホテルを推薦していただけますか ◇I *recommend* the book to all my students. その本を自分のすべての学生に薦めています ◇They were invited to *recommend* likely candidates for the two new positions. 彼らはその二つの新しい職にふさわしい候補を推薦するよう要請された ◇The hotel's new restaurant comes **highly** *recommended*. そのホテルの新しいレストランはたいへんお薦めです ◇The system has **much to** *recommend* **it**. 《ややフォーマル, 書き言葉》 そのシステムには魅力[優れた点]がたくさんある ❶人や物をrecommendする場合, ふつう推薦している人や物事についてよく知っていることを表す. 例えば, 人を個人的に知ってる場合しかその人をある仕事に推薦できないだろうし, 自分で実際に読んだことがある場合にしかその本を人に推薦できないだろう. ☞ **recommendation** (ENDORSEMENT)

suggest [他] (人・物事・方法などを)推薦する, 薦める ◇Who would you *suggest* for the job? あなたならその仕事に誰を推薦しますか ◇She *suggested* Paris as a good place for the conference. 彼女は会議に適した場所としてパリを推した ◇Can you *suggest* how I might contact him? 彼と連絡を取るよい方法をあげてもらえませんか ❶suggestはrecommendとは異なり, 確信がない場合に用いられる. 人や物事について自分の経験があるとは限らず, その人や物事について他人から聞いたことがあるだけの場合や, 試してみる価値はあるだろうと思っている場合に「薦める」のである. ☞ **suggestion** (PROPOSAL)

nominate [他, 自] (役割・賞・地位の)候補として推薦[指名]する, ノミネートする ◇He was *nominated* as best actor. 彼は最優秀男優賞にノミネートされた ◇Each office will *nominate* a representative to sit on the committee. 各営業所は委員会の一員となる代表候補を指名することになっている ◇Ten critics were asked to *nominate* their Book of the Year. 10人の批評家たちがそれぞれのブック・オブ・ザ・イヤー[年間最優秀図書]候補を挙げるよう依頼された ☞ **nomination** (CHOICE 1), **nominee** (CANDIDATE)

endorse [他] (広告で)推薦する, 宣伝する ◇I wonder how many celebrities actually use the products they *endorse*. 自分が宣伝している製品を実際に使っている有名人はどれほどいるのかしら ☞ **endorsement** (ENDORSEMENT)

record [動]

record・register・enter・document・chart・log・minute

情報をリストに載せたり, 出来事を文書などの永久的な形で残すことを表す
【類語訳】記録する, 登録する, 届け出る, 記入する, 記載する, 入力する

文型&コロケーション
▶ to record/ register/ enter/ document/ log/ minute sth **as** sth
▶ to record/ register/ enter/ document sth **in** sth
▶ to record/ document/ chart **how**...
▶ to record/ document/ minute **that**...
▶ to record/ register/ document/ chart the **history/ progress** of sth
▶ to record/ register/ enter/ log the **details** of sth
▶ to record/ register/ enter **names**
▶ to record/ enter/ log **data**
▶ to **carefully** record/ enter/ document/ log sth
▶ to **accurately** record/ document/ chart sth

record [他] (文書・フィルムなどの形で)記録する ◇The discussion was *recorded* in detail in his diary. その話し合いの内容は彼の日記に詳細に記録されていた ◇The figures *recorded* for 2007 show an increase of 23 per cent. 2007年に記録された数字は23%の増を示すものである ◇As a war artist she *recorded* the work of female volunteers. 戦争画家として彼女は女性ボランティアの仕事ぶりを記録に残した ◇Examples can be found in every era of *recorded history*. 有史以来のどの時代にも例が見られる

register [他, 自] (名前を公式に)登録する, 届け出る ◇The company's logo has not yet been *registered* as a trademark. その会社のロゴはまだ商標登録されていません ◇All students must be *registered with* a local doctor. すべての学生が地元の医師の下で登録されていなければなりません ◇You need to go to the Registrar's Office to *register* the death. 死亡届けを出すには登記所に行く必要があります ◇Many older people have *registered for* a postal vote. 多くの高齢者が郵便投票ができるように登録している ☞ **register** (LIST [名])

enter [他] (情報をリスト・本に)記入する, 記載する, (コンピューターに)入力する ◇He *entered* the details of the case *into* a file. 彼は訴訟の詳細をファイルに記載した ◇*Enter* your name and age in the boxes (= on a form). 枠の中に名前と年齢を記入してください ◇The notebook window is where you can *enter* and display data. ノートブックウィンドウはデータを入力・表示できる場所です

document [他, ふつう受身で] (詳細を文書で)記録する, 記載する ◇His exploits have been well *documented* by the national press. 彼の偉業は全国紙に何度も取り上げられてきた ◇The 790s are one of the best *documented* decades in Anglo-Saxon history. 790年代はアングロサクソン史上最もよく記録が残っている10年間の一つである

chart [他] (進行を)記録する, (跡を)たどる ◇The exhibition *charts* the development of modern Irish painting. その展覧会では現代アイルランド絵画の発展の跡をたどっている

log (-gg-) [他] (情報を公式に)記録に残す, 記録する ◇The

crimes were *logged* but not investigated. それらの犯罪は記録に残されたが捜査はされなかった ◊The call was *logged* at 16.20. その通話は16時20分と記録されていた

minute [他] 《特に英, ややフォーマル》(発言・決定事項を)議事録に記録する ◊I'd like that remark to be *minuted*. その発言は議事録に残してもらいたい ◊Meetings must be *minuted* and the minutes approved at the following meeting. 会議は議事録に記録され,その議事録は次の会議で承認されなければならない

recover [動] ☞ SURVIVE

recover • get better • heal • recuperate • get well • convalesce • shake sth off • pull through
病気やけがの苦しみがなくなることを表す
【類語訳】回復する, 立ち直る, よくなる, 治る

文型&コロケーション

▶ to recover/ recuperate **from** sth
▶ to **gradually** recover/ get better/ heal
▶ to **completely/ partially** recover/ heal

recover [自] (人が病気・けがに)回復する;(通常の状態に)回復する, 立ち直る ◊He's still *recovering* from his operation. 彼はまだ手術からの回復途上にある ◊Mother and baby are *recovering* well. 母親と赤ん坊は順調に回復している ◊It can take many years to *recover* from the death of a loved one. 愛する人の死から立ち直るには長い年月がかかることがある ◊The economy is at last beginning to *recover*. 経済はようやく回復し始めている 反意 **relapse** (WORSEN)
➤**recovery** [名] [C, ふつう単数で, U] ◊My father has made a full *recovery* from the operation. 父は手術からすっかり回復した ◊The economy is showing signs of *recovery*. 経済は回復の兆しを見せている

get 'better [フレーズ] (人・体の部位が病気・けがに)回復する, よくなる ◊I hope you're *getting better*. We'll need you at work tomorrow! あなたが回復しつつあるならいいんだけど. 明日には出勤してほしいんだ ◊My wrist is *getting better* — I'll be able to play tennis again soon. 手首はよくなってきている. すぐにまたテニスができるようになるよ
☞ **get better** (IMPROVE 2)

heal [自, 他] (傷に)治る;(傷・けがを)治す ◊It took a long time for the wounds to *heal*. 傷が治るのには時間がかかった ◊The cut *healed up* without leaving a scar. 《英》その切り傷は傷跡を残すことなく治った

recuperate [自] 《フォーマル》(病気・疲労・けがから時間をかけて)健康[体力, 元気]を取り戻す, 回復する ◊He's still *recuperating* from his operation. 彼はまだ手術からの回復途上にある ◊After an exhausting few weeks I needed some time to *recuperate*. 数週間くたくたで, 体力を取り戻す時間が必要だった

get 'well [フレーズ] (人が病気から)元気になる, 回復する ◊*Get well* soon! 早く元気になってね(例えばカードに書く文句として) ◊Now all she had to do was *get well*. 彼女は今やるべきことは病気を治すことだった ◊get well は特に人に回復してもらいたいという願いや欲求を表す場合に用いられる. 過去時制ではあまり用いられない.

convalesce [自] 《フォーマル》(時間をかけて)健康を取り戻す, 快方に向かう ◊She is *convalescing* at home after her operation. 彼女は休養し, 自宅で快方に向かいつつある

shake sth 'off [句動詞] 《ややインフォーマル》(風邪のような軽い病気を)治す ◊I can't seem to *shake off* this cold. この風邪はなかなかしつこいようだ

pull 'through [句動詞] 《ややインフォーマル》(重病・手術から)回復する ◊The doctors think she will *pull through*. 彼女は回復するだろうと医師たちは考えている

recruit [名] ☞ BEGINNER

recruit • trainee • apprentice • cadet • intern
仕事や活動を始めたばかりで経験がわずかしかない人を表す
【類語訳】新兵, 新人, 研修生, 実習生, 見習い, 訓練生

文型&コロケーション

▶ a trainee/ an apprentice/ an intern **with** a company
▶ to join a company **as** a trainee/ an apprentice
▶ a **young/ 19-year-old** recruit/ trainee/ apprentice/ cadet/ intern
▶ a **management** recruit/ trainee
▶ to **have/ become** a recruit/ a trainee/ an apprentice/ a cadet/ an intern
▶ to **work as** a trainee/ an apprentice
▶ to **train** a recruit/ an apprentice

recruit [C] (軍隊の)新兵,(警察の)新米警官;(会社・組織の)新人 ◊Army *recruits* are all trained in first aid. 軍の新兵は全員が応急処置の訓練を受けている ◊They are stepping up attempts to attract *recruits* to the nursing profession. 彼らは看護の仕事に新人を引きつける努力を強化している ◊All members were urged to go out and try to gain *new recruits* for the party. 全党員が外回りをして新党員の獲得に励むよう勧告を受けた ◊He spoke of us scornfully as *raw recruits* (= people without training or experience). 彼は私たちのことをあざけって新米と呼んだ ☞ **recruit** (EMPLOY)

trainee [C] (仕事のやり方の)訓練を受けている人, 研修生, 実習生, 見習い ◊She joined the company as a management *trainee*. 彼女は経営研修生[管理職見習い]としてその会社に入社した ❶ trainee は通例, apprentice に求められるよりも高い教育水準を必要とする仕事を学んでいる人について用いられる. 《英》では他の名詞の前で用いられることが多い. ◆ a *trainee* teacher/pilot/nurse/journalist (《英》)教育実習生/パイロット訓練生/看護実習生/見習い記者).(《米》)では student を用いる. ◆ a *student* teacher/pilot/nurse/journalist (《米》)教育実習生/パイロット訓練生/看護実習生/見習い記者)

apprentice [C] (仕事に必要な技術を学ぶために一定期間雇い主の下で働く)見習い ◊She joined us as an *apprentice* chef in 1990. 彼女は1990年に見習いシェフとして私たちの所に入社した ❶ apprentice は通例, 学力よりも実践的な技術を必要とする仕事について用いられる. 他の名詞の前で用いられることが多い. ◆ an *apprentice* electrician/plumber/bricklayer/jockey/chef (見習い電気工/配管工/レンガ職人/騎手/シェフ)

cadet [C] (警察の)訓練生,(軍隊の)士官候補生 ◊army *cadets* 陸軍士官候補生

intern [C] 《米》(実践経験を積む)医学研修生, 研修医;(実践経験を積む学生・新卒者の)研修生, 実習生 ◊*Interns* in hospitals learn how to act professionally in the most dire emergencies. 病院の研修医は最も深刻な緊急事態にプロとしてどう行動すべきかを学ぶ ◊a summer *intern* at a law firm 法律事務所の夏期研修生

reduce ☞ CUT 1

reduce・lower・minimize・decrease・bring sth down・turn sth down
サイズや量，程度を大きく[多く]しないことを表す
【類語訳】小さくする，減らす，削減する，最小限にする，落とす

文型&コロケーション

- to reduce sth/ lower sth/ bring sth down **from** 10 **to** 5
- to reduce/ lower/ decrease sth **by** half, 50, etc.
- to reduce/ lower/ minimize/ decrease/ bring down the **number/ amount/ level/ cost** of sth
- to reduce/ lower/ minimize/ decrease the **risk/ chance/ rate** of sth
- to reduce/ lower/ decrease/ bring down the **price** of sth
- to reduce/ lower/ turn down the **volume/ sound**
- to reduce/ lower/ decrease sth **significantly/ gradually**
- to reduce sth/ turn sth down **slightly**

reduce [他] (大きさ・量・数・水準を)小さくする，減らす，削減する ◇The number of employees was *reduced* from 40 to 25. 従業員数は40人から25人に削減された ◇Costs have been *reduced* by 20% over the past year. 経費はここ1年で2割削減された ◇Giving up smoking *reduces* the risk of heart disease. 禁煙によって心臓病のリスクが減る ◇*Reduce* speed now (= on a sign). (標識に)スピード落とせ 反意 **increase** (INCREASE 動).

lower [他] (水準を)下げる ◇This drug is used to *lower* blood pressure. この薬は血圧を下げるのに使われる ◇The company may be forced to *lower* prices in order to stay competitive. その会社は競争力を維持するために価格を下げざるをえないかもしれない ◇He *lowered* his voice to a whisper. 彼は声をひそめてささやき声になった ❶ lower は特に健康・金融関連で用いられる．◆ to *lower* blood pressure/cholesterol levels (血圧/コレステロール値を下げる)．◆ to *lower* prices/interest rates (価格/利率を下げる)．reduceもこれらの場合に用いることができるが，人の声の大きさについて言う場合はlowerしか用いることができない．✕He *reduced* his voice to a whisper. 反意 **raise** (INCREASE 動).

minimize (英でまた **-ise**) [他] (悪い事柄を)できるだけ少なくする，最小限にする ◇Good hygiene helps to *minimize* the risk of infection. よい衛生状態は感染リスクを最小限にするのに役立ちます ◇They worked at night in order to *minimize* the disruption. 彼らは混乱を最小限に抑えるために夜間作業をした 反意 **maximize** (INCREASE 動).

decrease [他] 《ややフォーマル》(量・水準を)減らす，下げる ◇People should *decrease* the amount of fat they eat. 人が摂取する脂肪分は減らしたほうがいい ◇The dose was gradually *decreased* after eight weeks. 8週間後からは服用量が徐々に減らされた 反意 **increase** (INCREASE 動). ❶decrease は，increaseよりフォーマルで，increaseほど頻繁ではないが，特に健康・医療関係で用いられる．increaseのより一般的な反意語はreduceである.

,bring sth 'down 句動詞 (価格・数・水準を)下げる，減らす ◇We aim to *bring down* prices on all our computers. 我が社ではすべてのコンピューターの価格を下げることを目標にしています ◇The economic recovery will *bring down* unemployment. 景気回復によって失業者が減るだろう

,turn sth 'down 句動詞 (音・熱・光を)下げる，落とす ◇Please *turn* the volume *down*. 音量を下げてください ◇He *turned* the lights *down* low. 彼は照明を落として暗くした 反意 **turn sth up** (INCREASE 動), ☞ **turn sth off** (TURN STH OFF)

reduction 名

reduction・cut・decline・fall・drop・downturn・decrease・slump・cutback
量や数，水準，大きさが減る[下がる，小さくなる]状況を表す
【類語訳】削減，割引，減少，引き下げ，低下，衰退，下落，後退

文型&コロケーション

- a reduction/ cut/ decline/ fall/ drop/ downturn/ decrease/ slump/ cutback **in** sth
- a reduction/ cut/ decline/ fall/ drop/ decrease/ cutback **of** 20%
- a 20% reduction/ cut/ decline/ fall/ drop/ decrease in sth
- (a) **sharp** reduction/ cuts/ decline/ fall/ drop/ downturn/ decrease/ slump/ cutbacks
- (a) **large/ significant** reduction/ cuts/ decline/ fall/ drop/ downturn/ decrease/ cutbacks
- (a) **big/ huge/ massive/ major** reduction/ cuts/ decline/ fall/ drop/ downturn/ slump/ cutbacks
- (a) **dramatic** reduction/ cuts/ decline/ fall/ drop/ downturn/ slump
- (a) **drastic** reduction/ cuts/ decline/ fall/ drop/ downturn/ cutbacks
- a **sudden** reduction/ decline/ fall/ drop/ downturn/ decrease/ slump
- a **slight** reduction/ decline/ fall/ drop/ downturn/ decrease
- to **lead to/ result in/ cause** a reduction/ cut/ decline/ fall/ drop/ decrease
- to **see** a reduction/ decline/ fall/ drop/ downturn/ decrease
- to **make** reductions/ cuts/ cutbacks

reduction [C, U] 少なく[小さく]すること，削減，割り引き；少なく[小さく]なった状態，減少 ◇This year has seen a 33% *reduction* in the number of hospital beds available. 今年，病院の空きベッド数は33%減少した ◇The report recommends further *reductions* in air and noise emissions. その報告書は排気音放出のさらなる削減を勧告している ◇There are *reductions* (= in the price) for children sharing a room with two adults. 大人2名と相部屋のお子様には割り引きがあります ◇There has been some *reduction* in unemployment. 失業者数がやや減少してきた 反意 **increase** (INCREASE 名).

cut [C] (量・大きさ・供給を)減らす[小さくする]こと，削減，引き下げ ◇They had to take a 20% *cut* in pay. 彼らは賃金を20%引き下げなければならなかった ◇The company has announced a new round of job *cuts*. その会社は新たな雇用削減を発表した ◇The proposed tax *cuts* will come into effect next May. 減税案は来年5月から実施に移されます 反意 **increase** (INCREASE 名), ☞ **cut** (CUT 1), **lay-off** (UNEMPLOYMENT)

ノート reduction と cut の使い分け：reduction はひとりでに少なく[小さく]なる，あるいは人によって意図的に少なく[小さく]される場合に用いることができる．cut はひとりでに起こる

ことはなく、必ず人によってなされる。cut は（常にではないが）否定的なことが多い。◆ job/salary/pay **cuts**（雇用／給与／賃金削減）。また、reduction は時間をかけて起こることがあるが、cut はそうではない。◆ a gradual **reduction**（段階的な減少）。× a gradual **cut**。

decline [C, ふつう単数で, U]（数・価値・質の継続的な）減少、低下；（場所・伝統・制度の段階的な）衰退 ◇These measures have failed to reverse the country's economic *decline*. これらの対策では国の経済の衰退を逆転させることができなかった ◇His book charts the *decline and fall* of a great civilization. 彼の著作は偉大なる文明の衰亡の跡をたどっている ◇The town *fell into (a) decline* (= started to be less busy, important, etc.) after the mine closed. 鉱山が閉鎖されたあと、その町は衰退した ◇Industry in Britain has been *in decline* since the 1970s. 英国の産業は1970年代以降下り坂にある 反意 **rise** (INCREASE 名), ☞ **decline** (FALL1), **decline** (WORSEN)

fall [C]《特にビジネス》（大きさ・数・価格・水準の）低下、減少、下落 ◇Share prices suffered a slight *fall* yesterday. 株価は昨日少し下落した ◇This figure represents a *fall* of 23% on the same period last year. この数字は昨年同期比23%減を示している 反意 **rise** (INCREASE 名), ☞ **fall** (FALL1)

drop [C, ふつう単数で]《特にジャーナリズム》（大きさ・数・価格・水準の）減少、低下 ◇If you want the job, you must be prepared to take a *drop* in salary. その仕事に就きたいのなら、給与が下がるのを覚悟しなければならない ◇The restaurant has suffered a 10% *drop* in trade. そのレストランは売り上げが10%減少した 反意 **rise** (INCREASE 名), ☞ **drop** (FALL1)

ノート **decline, fall, drop** の使い分け：これらの語はどれも、人の意図的な行為ではなく、減少・低下が起こる過程を表す。decline は過程が早かろうが遅かろうが、その過程を強調する。◆ a steady/sharp *decline* in profits（利益の徐々の／急激な減少）。◆ a civilization in terminal *decline*（衰退の一途をたどる文明）。fall と drop は過程の結果を強調する。◆ a *fall/drop* of 30% (30%の減少)。fall は decline と同様に時間をかけて起こるが、drop はそうではない。◆ a gradual *decline/fall*（段階的な減少）。× a gradual *drop*.

downturn [C, ふつう単数で]（商取引の）減少；（景気の）後退(期) ◇The building industry is experiencing a severe *downturn* in its workload. 建設業界は仕事の深刻な減少にある ☞ **upturn** (INCREASE 名)

decrease [C, U]（量・水準・数の）減少 ◇There has been a *decrease* of nearly 6% in the number of visitors to the museum. 美術館の来館者数は6%近く減少した ◇Marriage is still on the *decrease*. 結婚は依然として減少傾向にある ☞ **increase** (INCREASE 名), ☞ **decrease** (FALL1) ❶ decrease は increase のまったく正反対の語のように思えるが、increase ほど頻繁に用いられることはない。意図的な減少や削減には reduction, cut を用いる。発生した減少や低下には、特にビジネス関連で fall や drop が好まれることが多い。

slump [C]（売り上げ・価格・価値の）急な落ち込み、急減 ◇The recession led to a *slump* in consumer spending. 不景気で消費者支出が急に落ち込んだ ◇The present *slump* has hit manufacturing hard. 現在の不景気は製造業に大打撃を与えている ☞ **slump** (RECESSION), **slump** (SLUMP)

ノート **downturn** と **slump** の使い分け：どちらの語もビジネス・経済関連で用いることができる。◆ a *downturn/ slump* in demand/trade/business/profits（需要／取引／商取引／利益の減少／急減）。しかし、slump は、ふつう赤字を出しているビジネスの観点から見た、より大きく、より急激な減少を指す。

cutback [C, ふつう複数で]（経費・人員・給付金などの）削減 ◇Many theatres are having to make major *cutbacks*. 多くの劇場が大幅な経費削減を迫られている ☞ **cut sth back** (CUT 1)

reference 名

reference・mention・quote・quotation・citation・allusion
他の人や物事に言及する[を繰り返す]発言[記述]を表す
【類語訳】言及、引用句、引用、ほのめかし

文型&コロケーション
▸ a quote/ quotation/ citation (**taken**) **from** sb/ sth
▸ **in** a reference/ an allusion **to** sb/ sth
▸ a **brief** reference/ mention/ allusion
▸ the **earliest** reference to/ mention of sb/ sth
▸ to **make no** reference to/ mention of sb/ sth
▸ to be **full of** references/ allusions to sth
▸ This quote/ quotation/ citation **comes from**...

reference [C, U]（口頭・文書での）言及；言及する[触れる]こと ◇In an obvious *reference* to the president, she talked of corruption in high places. 明らかに大統領に言及しながら、彼女は上層部の腐敗について語った ◇She made no *reference* to her illness, but only to her future plans. 彼女は自分の病気のことはさておき、今後の予定だけに触れた ◇*With reference to* your letter of 22 July...《フォーマル、書き言葉》7月22日付けのお手紙に関して… ☞ **refer to sb/sth** (MENTION)

mention [U, C, ふつう単数で] 言及する[触れる]こと；（口頭・文書での）言及 ◇He went white *at the mention of* her name. 彼女の名前が出ると、彼は青ざめた ◇We have several other products *worthy of mention*. 他にもご注目いただきたい製品がいくつかございます ◇The concert didn't even *get a mention* in the newspapers. そのコンサートは新聞に取り上げられることさえなかった ☞ **mention** (MENTION)

ノート **reference** と **mention** の使い分け：reference はふつう可算名詞。不可算名詞用法は主にフォーマルな書き言葉の定型表現で用いられる。mention は不可算名詞で用いられる場合が多い。可算名詞扱いの場合は get a mention のような句で用いられ、ややインフォーマルになる。

quote [C]《インフォーマル》（本・演劇・人の発言からの）引用句[文]◇This *quote* comes from a poem by Robert Browning この句はロバート・ブラウニングの詩からの引用です ◇The article included *quotes* from detectives who worked on the case. 記事にはその事件を手がけた刑事たちの言葉が引用されていた

quotation [C, U]《フォーマル or 書き言葉》（本・演劇・演説からの）引用句[文]；引用(すること) ◇The book began with a *quotation* from Goethe. その本はゲーテからの引用文で始まっていた ◇The writer illustrates his point by *quotation* from a number of sources. 著者はいくつ

↪reference

かの出典を引用して自らの論点を説明している

ノート quoteとquotationの使い分け：これらの語はどちらも、文章やフォーマルな話し言葉から引用された言葉を表すことができる。◆a *quote/quotation* from Shakespeare（シェイクスピアからの引用文）。しかし、インフォーマルな話し言葉の引用に用いられるのはquoteだけである。×*quotations* from detectives who worked on the case. ☞ quote (MENTION), quote (QUOTE)

citation [C, U]《フォーマルor書き言葉》(学術的な書物・作品・文章・著者からの)引用句[文]；引用 ◇The report contained several *citations* taken from her PhD thesis. その報告書には彼女の博士論文から取られた引用文がいくつか含まれていた ◇Space does not permit the *citation* of examples. スペースの関係で例を引用することができません ☞ cite (MENTION), cite (QUOTE)

allusion [C, U]《ややフォーマル》(口頭・文書による)間接的な言及、ほのめかし、引喩 ◇His statement was seen as an *allusion* to the recent drug-related killings. 彼の発言は薬物に絡んだ最近の殺人をほのめかすものと見なされた ◇Her poetry is full of obscure literary *allusion*. 彼女の詩はあいまいな文学的引喩にあふれている ☞ allude to sb/sth (MENTION)

refuge 名

refuge • shelter • sanctuary • haven • hiding place • retreat • hideout • safe house

人や動物などが保護してもらえる[隠れる]ことのできる場所を表す
【類語訳】逃げ場、保護施設、保護区、避難所、安息の地、隠れ家、隠し場所、静養地、アジト

文型&コロケーション

▶ a refuge/ shelter/ sanctuary/ haven/ hiding place/ retreat/ hideout/ safe house for sb/ sth
▶ a refuge/ sanctuary/ haven/ hiding place/ retreat from sth
▶ a secret refuge/ hiding place/ retreat/ hideout
▶ an animal refuge/ shelter/ sanctuary
▶ a wildlife refuge/ sanctuary
▶ a mountain refuge/ retreat/ hideout
▶ an island refuge/ retreat
▶ a refuge/ shelter for the homeless

refuge [C] (害・危険から逃れられる)避難場所、逃げ場；(保護を必要としている人の)保護施設 ◇He regarded the room as a *refuge* from the outside world. 彼はその部屋を外界からの逃げ場所と見なした ◇The marshes are a wetland *refuge* for seabirds, waders and wild fowl. その沼地は海鳥や渉禽、水鳥にとって湿地帯の避難場所になっている ◇The best option for a female victim of domestic abuse is to contact a *women's refuge*.《特に英》家庭内暴力の女性被害者にとって最善の選択肢は女性向け保護施設に連絡することです ❶これは(米)ではふつうwomen's shelterと呼ばれる。☞ refuge (SHELTER)

shelter [C] (慈善団体が所有する)保護施設、宿泊所[施設] ◇a night *shelter* for the homeless ホームレスの夜間宿泊所 ◇We adopted a rescue dog from an animal *shelter*. 私たちは動物保護施設から救助犬を1匹引き取った ☞ shelter (SHELTER)

sanctuary [C] (鳥獣[野生動物])保護区；(追われている[暴力を受けている]人向けの)安全な場所、避難所 ◇The island was declared a wildlife *sanctuary* in 1969. その

島は1969年に野生動物保護区に指定された ◇The church became a *sanctuary* for the refugees. その教会は難民たちの避難所になった ☞ sanctuary (SHELTER)

haven [C]《ややフォーマル》(休息する[保護を受ける]ための)避難所、安息の地 ◇The hotel is a *haven* of peace and tranquillity そのホテルは平穏で静寂の安息の地だ ◇We have a duty to offer a *safe haven* to all refugees. 我々にはすべての難民に安全な避難所を提供する義務がある

'hiding place [C] 隠れ場所、隠れ家、隠し場所 ◇They used the cave as a *hiding place* for their weapons. 彼らはその洞窟を武器の隠し場所に使った ◇As darkness fell, she emerged from her *hiding place*. 日が暮れると彼女は隠れ家から出てきた

retreat [C]《ややフォーマル》(日常生活から抜け出すための)個人の)隠れ家、静養地 ◇She bought the cottage as a weekend *retreat*. 彼女は週末を過ごす隠れ家としてその小さな別荘を購入した ❶go on a retreatとは、通常の活動を一定期間やめて、祈りや瞑想のために静かな場所に行くことを指す。◆He went on a Buddhist *retreat*.（彼は仏教の瞑想会に参加した。

hideout [C] (警察の手から隠れる)隠れ家、アジト ◇Several terrorist *hideouts* were discovered in the area. その地域でテロリストのアジトがいくつか見つかった

'safe house [C] (人をかくまうための)隠れ家、(人を保護するための)安全な場所 ◇He is under heavy police guard in a *safe house* after receiving death threats. 殺害の脅しを受けてからは、彼は安全な場所で警察の厳重な警護の下に置かれている

refugee 名

refugee • immigrant • migrant • expatriate • exile • emigrant • asylum seeker • evacuee

住んでいた場所を去って新たに住む[滞在する]場所を見つけに行く[行った]人を表す
【類語訳】難民、移民、移住者、外国人居住者、亡命者、疎開者、避難民

文型&コロケーション

▶ a would-be refugee/ immigrant/ migrant/ emigrant/ asylum seeker
▶ a genuine/ bogus refugee/ asylum seeker
▶ an illegal immigrant/ migrant/ emigrant
▶ a political refugee/ exile/ asylum seeker
▶ an economic refugee/ migrant
▶ refugees/ migrants/ expatriates/ exiles/ emigrants/ asylum seekers/ evacuees return
▶ immigrant/ migrant workers
▶ a flow/ flood of refugees/ immigrants/ migrants/ emigrants
▶ an influx of refugees/ immigrants/ migrants

refugee [C] (戦争や政治的[宗教的、社会的]理由で国・故郷を去る)難民 ◇There has been a steady flow of *refugees* from the war zone. 紛争地帯から絶え間なく難民たちが流出している ◇a *refugee* camp 難民キャンプ ☞ refuge (SHELTER)

immigrant [C] (母国でない国に永住する)移民、移住者 ◇Illegal *immigrants* are to be sent back to their country of origin. 不法移民は母国へ送り返されることになっている ◇*immigrant* communities/families/work-

ers 移民の共同体/家庭/労働者
▶**immigrate** 動 [自] ◇About 6.6 million people *immigrated* to the United States in the 1970s. 《特に米》1970年代にはおよそ660万人が米国へ移住した ▷反意 **emigrate** (LEAVE 2)
▶**immigration** 名 [U] ◇laws restricting *immigration* into the US 米国への移住を制限する法律 ◇an *immigration* officer 入国審査官

migrant [C] (仕事を見つけるための)移住者, 移民 ◇They claimed they were political refugees and not economic *migrants*. 彼らは経済移民ではなく政治亡命者だと主張した ▷☞ migrate (LEAVE 2)

expatriate [C] (母国以外の国に住む)国外居住者, 外人居住者 ◇FUSAC is a magazine for American *expatriates* in Paris. FUSACはパリのアメリカ人居住者向けの雑誌である ❶インフォーマルでは, *expatriate* は時として *expat* と短縮される. ◇There are more than two million British *expats* down under (= in Australia). (オーストラリアには200万人以上のイギリス人居住者がいる).
▶**expatriate** 形 [名詞の前で] ◇*expatriate* Britons in Spain スペインの英国人居住者 ◇*expatriate* workers 国外在住の労働者

📝 **immigrant** と **expatriate** の使い分け: immigrant は他国に永住するために去っていく人だが, expatriate はふつう, 数か月[数年]後に戻って来るつもりの人である.

exile [C] (ややフォーマル)(母国を離れることを選ぶ[強いられる])亡命者 ◇A general amnesty was granted, allowing political *exiles* to return freely. 大赦が行われ, 政治亡命者が自由に帰国することが許された ◇a tax *exile* (= a rich person who moves to another country where taxes are lower) (税金の安い国へ移住する)税金逃れの国外脱出者 ☞ **exile** (EXPEL)

emigrant [C] 《ややフォーマル》(外国で永住する)移民 ◇My grandparents were Italian *emigrants* who settled in New York in the 1920s. 私の祖父母は1920年代にニューヨークに移住したイタリア系移民だった ☞ **emigrate** (LEAVE 2)

📝 **immigrant** と **emigrant** の使い分け: immigrant は(特に政治的・社会的な現在問題になっていると考えられる場合に)入国してくる人を指す. emigrant は(特に歴史と絡めて考えた場合に)出国していく人を指す.

a'sylum seeker [C] (政治的理由による)亡命希望者 ◇Genuine *asylum seekers* should not be denied entry to the country. 真に亡命を希望している者の入国を拒否してはならない ☞ **asylum** (SHELTER)

evacuee [C] (戦時中の)疎開者, 避難民 ◇During 1942 *evacuee* families started to arrive in the town. 1942年に疎開者の家族がその町に到着し始めた

refusal 名

refusal • veto • rejection • denial • rebuff • no
受け入れない[許可するつもりはない]と言う[示す]ことを表す
【類語訳】拒否, 拒絶, 拒否権, 不採用, 不合格, 否定, ノー, 反対票

文型&コロケーション
▶a refusal/ rejection/ rebuff/ no **from** sb
▶a refusal/ veto/ rejection/ rebuff **by** sb
▶a rebuff/ no **to** sb/ sth

▶a/ an **outright/ firm/ blanket** refusal/ rejection/ no
▶a **complete** refusal/ veto/ rejection
▶to **receive/ be met with** a refusal/ rejection/ rebuff
▶to **give** (sb) a refusal/ rejection/ no

refusal [U, C] (依頼・申し出などの)拒否, 拒絶 ◇There were a number of reasons given for the *refusal* of the application. その申請を拒否する理由がいくつか示された ◇His *refusal to* discuss the matter is very annoying. 彼がその問題について話し合いを拒んでいて非常に困っている ◇What do you do in the case of a *refusal* by a patient to accept treatment? 患者が治療の受け入れを拒否した場合はどうしますか ▷反意 **agreement, acceptance** (APPROVAL), **consent** (PERMISSION)

veto (複 -oes) [C, U] (法案通過・決定に対する)拒否権 ◇The president has a *veto* on/over all political appointments. 大統領にはあらゆる官職の任命に対して拒否権がある ◇The British government used its *veto* to block the proposal. 英国政府はその提案を阻止するために拒否権を行使した ◇The Ministry of Defence has the power of *veto* over all arms exports. 国防省にはあらゆる武器輸出に対する拒否権がある ☞ **veto** (BAN 名)

rejection [U, C] (受け入れ・使用・考慮の)拒否, 不採用, 不合格 ◇It takes a very buoyant personality to cope with constant *rejection*. 何度拒絶されても切り抜けるには非常に楽天的な性格を要する ◇Eventually, after months of *rejections*, she was offered a job. 彼女は何か月も不採用が続いたが, ついに仕事が決まった ◇Another *rejection letter* arrived this morning. 今朝, また不採用[不合格]通知が届いた ▷反意 **acceptance** (APPROVAL)

denial [C, U] (権利を持つことへの)拒否, 否定 ◇This advertising ban is a *denial* of freedom of speech. この広告禁止令は言論の自由の否定である ◇Pressure groups have drawn attention to the *denial* of human rights in some areas. 圧力団体がいくつかの地域における人権の否定に対して注意を喚起している

rebuff [C] 《ややフォーマル》(好意的な申し出・要請・提案に対する冷たい)拒絶 ◇In a *rebuff* to the president, Congress voted against the bill. 大統領の言うことには耳を貸さず, 議会は法案に反対の票を投じた ◇Her offer has met with a sharp *rebuff*. 彼女の申し出はきっぱりと拒絶された

no (複 **noes**) [C] 《ややインフォーマル》(同意しない[受け入れない]ことを示す)否定の答え, ノー, 反対票 ◇I think that's a *no* to the first question. それは最初の質問にはノーだということだと思う ◇Can you give me *a straight yes or no*? イエスかノーか率直に言ってもらえますか ◇When we took a vote there were nine yesses and 3 *noes*. 採決したら賛成9票, 反対3票だった ▷反意 **yes**

refuse 動

refuse • reject • deny • decline • turn sb/sth down • veto • throw sth out • rebuff • disallow
申し出や提案, 要請などを受け入れない[考慮しない]と決める[言う]ことを表す
【類語訳】拒む, 断る, 辞退する, 与えない, 拒絶する, 却下する, 拒否する, はねつける

文型&コロケーション
▶to reject/ turn down sth **in favour of** sth else
▶to refuse/ reject/ decline/ turn down/ veto/ throw out a **proposal**

↪refuse

- to refuse/ reject/ decline/ turn down/ rebuff a/ an **offer/ request**
- to refuse/ reject/ decline/ turn down a/ an **chance/ opportunity/ invitation**
- to refuse/ reject/ turn down/ throw out/ disallow an **appeal**
- to refuse/ reject/ turn down/ veto/ throw out a **plan**
- to refuse/ reject/ decline/ turn down/ veto/ disallow an **application**
- to refuse/ reject/ veto/ rebuff a **suggestion**
- to reject/ veto/ throw out a **bill**
- to refuse/ deny sb **access** to sth
- to **politely** refuse/ reject/ decline sth

refuse [自, 他] (依頼・申し出を)拒む, 断る, 辞退する;(受け入れる[考慮する]のを)拒む;(人がほしい[必要とする]物を)与えない ◇Go on, ask her. She can hardly *refuse*. ほら, 彼女に頼みなよ. 彼女はまず断れないたちだから ◇She *refused to* accept that there was a problem. 彼女は問題があることを認めようとしなかった ◇He *flatly refused* to discuss the matter. 彼はその問題について話し合うことをきっぱりと断った ◇We invited her to the wedding but she *refused*. 私たちは彼女を結婚式に招待したが, 彼女は辞退した ◇The job offer was simply too good to *refuse*. その仕事の話はいいことだらけでとても断れなかった ◇The government has *refused* all demands for a public enquiry. 政府は公的な調査を求める要求をすべて拒んだ ◇They *refused* him a visa. 彼はビザを発給されなかった ◇She would never *refuse* her kids anything. 彼女は自分の子どもたちの欲求を何一つ拒もうとはしなかった [反意] **agree** (AGREE), **accept** (TAKE 4), ☞ **refusal** (REFUSAL)

reject [他] (受け入れる[考慮する]のを)拒む, 拒絶する, 認めない;(仕事・地位などに人を)受け入れない, 不採用にする, 不合格にする ◇He urged the committee to *reject* the plans. 彼は委員会に計画を認めないよう強く迫った ◇The proposal was *rejected as* too costly. その提案は費用がかかりすぎるとして拒絶された ◇I've been *rejected* by all the colleges I applied to. 出願した大学が全部不合格になってしまった [反意] **approve** (AGREE), **accept** (LET SB IN)

deny [他] 《フォーマル》(人がほしい[必要とする]物を)与えないのを拒む, 与えない ◇They were *denied* access to the information. 彼らはその情報へのアクセスを認められなかった ◇Access to the information was *denied to* them. その情報へのアクセス権は彼らに与えられなかった

decline [他, 自] 《フォーマル》(受け入れる[行う]のを)(丁寧に)断る ◇Their spokesman *declined to* comment on the allegations. 彼らのスポークスマンはその申し立てについてコメントを断った ◇We politely *declined* her invitation. 私たちは彼女の招待を丁重に断った [反意] **accept** (TAKE 4)

turn sb/sth 'down 句動詞 (申し出・提案・申し出る人を)拒絶する, 断る, 却下する ◇His appeal against conviction was *turned down*. 彼の有罪判決に対する上訴は却下された ◇He has been *turned down for* ten jobs so far. 彼はこれまで10の仕事を断られた ◇He asked her to marry him but she *turned* him *down*. 彼は彼女に求婚したが, 彼女は断った [反意] **take sth up** (TAKE 4)

veto [他] (拒否権を行使して)拒否する;(提案を受け入れ[実行]するのを)拒む ◇Plans for the dam have been *vetoed* by the Environmental Protection Agency. ダ

ム計画は環境保護庁によって拒否されてきた ◇I wanted to go camping but the others quickly *vetoed* that idea. 私はキャンプに行きたかったが, 他の人たちはすぐにその案を却下した ❶ふつう veto するのは権威ある地位にいる人である. veto される決定や計画はすでに他の人々の同意を得ていることが多い. ☞ **veto** (BAN 名)

throw sth 'out 句動詞 (票決後に提案・考え・訴訟を受け入れる[考慮する]のを)拒否する, 却下する ◇The case was *thrown out* for lack of evidence. その訴訟は証拠不十分で却下された ◇The recommendation was *thrown out* by an overwhelming majority. その勧告は圧倒的多数で拒否された

rebuff [他] 《書き言葉, しばしばはなして》(好意的な申し出・要請・提案を冷たく)拒絶する, はねつける ◇They *rebuffed* her request for help. 彼らは彼女の支援要請を拒否した ◇The offer was immediately *rebuffed* by union leaders. その申し出は労働組合の指導者たちによって即座にはねつけられた

disallow [他, しばしば受身で] (誤った行為・ルール違反のために正式に)認めない. 2点目のゴールは認められなかった ◇Her claim for unfair dismissal was *disallowed*. 彼女の不当解雇への賠償請求は却下された

regard 動 ☞ THINK

regard・call・find・consider・describe・see・view・ count・reckon・look at sth

特別な方法で人や物について考えたり, 話題にしたりすること 【類語訳】見なす, 評する, 思う

文型&コロケーション

- to regard/ consider/ describe/ see/ view/ count/ look at sb/ sth **as** sth
- to regard/ consider/ see/ view/ look at sb/ sth **from** a particular point of view
- to regard/ see/ view/ look at sb/ sth **with** sth
- to find/ consider/ see/ reckon sb/ sth **to be** sth
- to consider/ reckon **that**...
- to regard/ consider/ describe/ see/ view/ count/ reckon **yourself** (as) sth
- **generally/ widely/ usually/ still** regarded/ considered/ seen/ viewed/ reckoned as sth
- **no longer** regarded/ considered/ seen/ viewed as sth
- to regard/ consider/ describe/ see/ view/ look at sb/ sth **differently**
- to consider/ describe/ see/ view/ look at sb/ sth **objectively**
- to regard/ consider/ view sb/ sth **favourably/ positively**

regard [他] 《ややフォーマル》《進行形なし》(…だと)見なす ◇Her work is very *highly/well regarded*. 彼女の仕事は非常に高く評価されている ◇Capital punishment was *regarded* as inhuman and immoral. 死刑は非人道的で社会倫理に反する行為と見なされた ◇I had come to *regard* him as a close friend. 私は彼を親友と見なすようになっていた ◇They *regarded* people outside their own village with suspicion. 彼らは自分たち村民以外は疑いの目で見た

call [他] (特定の性質があると)評する, 見なす(と言う) ◇I wouldn't *call* German an easy language. ドイツ語が易しい言語とは思わない ◇Are you *calling* me a liar? 私

が嘘つきだと言う。◇He was in the front room, or the lounge, or whatever you want to *call* it. 彼は居間というか応接間というか、まあそんな所にいた ◇Would you *call* it blue or green? それは青、それとも緑と思いますか ◇I make it ten pounds forty-three you owe me. Let's *call* it ten pounds. 君に10.43ポンドの貸しがあるはずだ。でも端数は省いて10ポンドでいいよ

find [他] (…だと)思う ◇You may *find* your illness hard to accept. 君は自分の病気がなかなか受け入れられないと思うかもしれない ◇You may *find it hard* to accept your illness. 君は自分の病気を受け入れるのが難しいと思うかもしれない ◇I *find* it amazing that they're still together. 彼らがまだ別れないでいるとは驚きだね ◇She *finds it a strain* to meet new people. 彼女は初めての人たちに会うのは負担だと思っている

consider [他]《進行形なし》《ややフォーマル》(…だと)見なす ◇Who do you *consider* (to be) responsible for the accident? その事故の責任者は誰だと思うかね ◇*Consider yourself lucky* you weren't fired. 首にならずに済んでついていると思いなさい ◇These workers are *considered* (as) a high-risk group. これらの労働者たちは高危険分子と見なされている ☞ **consider** (CONSIDER)

|ノート| **regard** と **consider** の使い分け:これらの語は意味は同じだが、使われるパターンや文型が異なる。considerは補語や節と共に用いて、consider sb/sth to be sthや consider sb/sth as sthと言うことができ、to beとasがしばしば省略される。◆He *considers* himself an expert. (彼は自分を専門家だと思っている)。◆They are *considered* a high-risk group. (彼らは高危険分子と見なされている)。また consider that sb/sth is sthと言うこともできて、ここでも that は省略できる。◆The Home Secretary will release prisoners only if he *considers* it is safe to do so. (内相は因人を釈放しても問題なしと見なせばそうするだろう)。一方、regardは限られた文型で用いられる。最もよく使われるのは regard sb/sth as sthで、ここでは asは省略できない。×I *regard* him a close friend. また以下のように言うこともできない。×*regard* sb/sth to be sth. また ×*regard* that sb/sth is sth. しかしながら regard は(この点は considerは不可)に、名詞か形容詞の補語がなくても用いることができる。ただし目的語と副詞(句)を伴わなければならない。◆sb/sth is highly *regarded* (人/物事は高く評価されている)。◆*regard* sb/sth with suspicion/jealousy/admiration (人/物事を疑いの目で/嫉妬して/賞賛の目で見る)。

describe [他]《asと共に》(…だと)評する ◇Jim was *described* by his colleagues as 'unusual'. ジムは同僚たちには「変わっている」と評されていた ◇The man was *described* as tall and dark, and aged about 20. その男は背が高くて、浅黒く、20歳くらいと考えられていた ☞ **describe** (DESCRIBE)

|ノート| **call** と **describe** の使い分け:この2語は意味は同じだが、使われるパターンが異なる。call は、asなしで名詞補語か形容詞補語と共に用いる。×I wouldn't *call* German an easy language. call では、名詞補語か形容詞補語よりもずっと頻繁に用いられる、I wouldn't *call* German easy. と言うこともできるが、an easy language という名詞句を用いるほうが普通であろう。一方、describe は、asに続いて形容詞か名詞句と共に用いる。◆Jim was *described* by his colleagues as an unusual man. (ジムは同僚たちに変わっている奴だと評されていた)。×Are you *describing* me as a liar?

see [他]《進行形なし》(…だと)考える ◇I *see things* differently now. 今では物の見方が変わってしまっている ◇Try to *see* things from her point of view. 物事を彼女の観点から見てみなさい ◇Lack of money is the main problem, *as I see it* (= in my opinion). 私が見るところでは資金不足が主たる問題だね ◇*The way I see it*, you have three main problems. 私が思うに君には主に問題点が3つある

view [他]《進行形なし》(…だと)見なす ◇When the car was first built, the design was *viewed* as highly original. その車が初めて製造されたとき、デザインはきわめて独創的だと見なされた ◇How do you *view* your position within the company? 社内における自分の立場をどう見ているの ◇You should *view* their offer with a great deal of caution. 彼らからの申し出は念には念を入れて検討したほうがいいですよ ❶ viewはregardやconsiderと同じ意味だが、やや使用頻度が低く、いくぶんインフォーマルである。主な文型はview sb/sth as sb/sth (ここではasを省略してはならない)とview sb/sth with sthである。「どう思いますか」と全般的な質問をする場合には、How do you *view*...?やviewを用いるのが最も自然である。How do you regard...?と言えないこともないが、頻度は低い。ふつうの意味では×How do you *consider*...? とは言わない。

count [他, 自]《進行形なし》(…だと)見なす, 見なされる ◇I *count* him among my closest friends. 彼を最高の親友の一人だと思っている ◇I *count myself lucky* to have known him. 彼と知り合えて幸運だと考えている ◇For tax purposes that money *counts/is counted* as income. 課税の面からはその金は収入と見なされる

reckon [他, ふつう受身で]《進行形なし》《特に英、ややインフォーマル》(…だと)見なす ◇Children are *reckoned* to be more sophisticated nowadays. 今日では子どもたちはより洗練されていると考えられている ◇It was generally *reckoned* a success. それはおおむね成功と見なされた ☞ **reckon** (THINK)

look at sth [句動詞] (物事を…だと)見なす ◇*Looked at* from that point of view, his decision is easier to understand. その観点から見ると彼の決心はより理解しやすい ◇It all depends on how you *look at* it. それはすべて君の見方次第だ ◇*Look at* it this way:... こう考えてみてください:… ❶ look at sthは、ある状況をさまざまな観点から考える場合に特に用いられる。☞ **look at sth** (CONSIDER)

regulate [動]

regulate・supervise・oversee・administer・police・superintend
管理者[責任者]として物事が正しく行われる[規則が遵守される]ようにすることを表す
【類語訳】規制する, 取り締まる, 監督する, 見守る, 責任がある, 司る, 監視する

|文型&コロケーション|
▶ to regulate/ supervise/ oversee/ administer the **affairs** of sb/ sth
▶ to supervise/ oversee/ superintend **work**
▶ to be **properly** regulated/ supervised/ administered/ policed
▶ to be **well** regulated/ supervised/ policed
▶ to be **effectively** regulated/ supervised/ administered/ policed

regulate [他]（ビジネス活動を）規制する，取り締まる ◇The activities of credit companies are *regulated by law*. 信販会社の活動は法律によって規制されている ◇The Council was set up to *regulate* the fishing industry. その審議会は水産業界の規制のために設置された ◇The trade in these animals is highly *regulated*. これらの動物の取り引きは厳しく規制されている ☞ **regulation** (GOVERNMENT 2), **regulator** (INSPECTOR)

supervise [他，自]（仕事・活動が正しく[安全に]行われるように）監督する，見守る ◇I will *supervise* the work personally. 私が自分でその仕事の監督をします ◇She *supervised* the children playing near the pool. 彼女はプールのそばで遊んでいる子たちを見守った ◇Jenny decided to stay and *supervise*. ジェニーは留まって見守ることにした ☞ **supervision** (GOVERNMENT 2), **supervisor** (MANAGER)

oversee [他]（仕事・活動が正しく行われるように）監督する ◇The director made regular visits to personally *oversee* operations. その重役は業務を自ら監督するために定期的に訪れた

> **ノート** supervise と oversee の使い分け：supervise, oversee のどちらも，仕事や活動が正しく行われるように監督する場合に用いられる．◆ to *supervise/oversee* building work/an election （建設作業/選挙を監督する）．oversee は主に高い地位にある人が監督する場合に用いられる．supervise は安全の確保，援助，問題への対処のために，子どもや未熟な労働者などを見守る[監視する]場合にも用いられる．

administer [他，しばしば受身で]《フォーマル》（法律・規則・試験の）（管理）責任がある，監督する，司る ◇The team is responsible for *administering* the tests and marking the papers. チームには試験監督と答案採点の責任がある ◇It is the function of the courts to *administer* the laws which Parliament has enacted. 議会が制定する法を司ることが裁判所の役目である

police [他]（特定の規則が遵守されるように）監視する，規制する ◇The government has called on newspapers to *police themselves*. 政府は新聞社に自主規制を求めてきた ◇These sort of regulations are very difficult to *police*. こうした種類の規則違反を取り締まるのは非常に難しい

superintend [他]《フォーマル》（仕事・活動が正しく行われるように）監督する ◇He *superintended* the building work. 彼は建設作業の監督をした ☞ **superintendent** (MANAGER)

reject [動]

reject・disown・disinherit・wash your hands of sb/sth
これ以上は関係[保護]責任を持ちたくないと決心すること
【類語訳】拒絶する，縁を切る，関係を断つ，手を切る，手を引く

▸文型&コロケーション
▸ His **father/ family** rejected/ disowned/ disinherited him.
▸ Her **friends/ mother** rejected/ disowned her.
▸ to **virtually** disown/ disinherit sb

reject [他]（人・動物を）受け入れない，拒絶する ◇The lioness *rejected* the smallest cub, which died. 雌ライオンは一番小さい子を受け入れず，その子は死んだ ◇He was only three when his father left and I think he still *feels rejected*. 父親が出て行ったとき彼はわずか3歳で，彼はいまだに自分が拒絶された存在だと感じているのだと思う ［反義］ **accept** (GREET), ☞ **turn your back on sb/sth** (LEAVE 4)
▸**rejection** [名] [U] ◇painful feelings of *rejection* つらい拒絶感

disown [他]（怒り・非難を示すために）縁を切る，関係を断つ ◇Her family *disowned* her for marrying a foreigner. 彼女が外国人と結婚するというので，家族は彼女との縁を切った ◇Later he *publicly disowned* the rebellion. 後に彼は反乱との関わりをきっぱり断った

disinherit [他]（息子・娘から）相続権を剥奪する ◇He threatened to *disinherit* his eldest son. 彼は長男に相続権を取り上げるぞと脅した

wash your 'hands of sb/sth [イディオム]（援助・関わりをやめて）手[縁]を切る，手を引く ◇When her son was arrested again she *washed her hands of* him. 息子が再び逮捕されたとき，彼女は息子との縁を切った ◇I've *washed my hands of* the whole sordid business. 私は下劣な商売からすっかり手を引いた

relate [動]

relate・associate・link・match・connect
2つまたはそれ以上の物事が関わる[を関わらせる]ことを表す
【類語訳】関連づける，結びつける，連想する，組み合わせる

▸文型&コロケーション
▸ to **relate/ link/ match/ connect** sth **to** sth
▸ to **associate/ link/ match/ connect** sth **with** sth
▸ to **relate/ associate/ link/ match/ connect** (sth) **directly**
▸ to **relate/ associate/ link/ connect** sth **specifically**
▸ to **relate/ associate/ link** sth **explicitly**
▸ to **associate/ link/ connect** sth **firmly**

relate [他]《ややフォーマル》（物事を）関連づける，結びつける ◇I found it difficult to *relate* the two ideas in my mind. 頭の中でその2つの考えを関連づけるのは難しかった ◇In future, pay increases will be *related* to productivity. 将来，賃上げは生産性と連動するだろう ❶ *relate* はビジネス関連で用いられることが多く，ある物事が他の物事の変化の仕方によってどう変化するかを表す場合に用いられる．◆ performance-*related* pay（能力給）．◆ income-*related* benefits（収入に応じた給付金）．◆ an earnings-*related* pension scheme（所得に応じた年金制度）．

associate [他]《ややフォーマル》（人・物事に）結びつけて考える，連想する ◇I always *associate* the smell of baking with my childhood. パンを焼くにおいがするといつも子どもの頃が思い浮かぶ ◇He is closely *associated* in the public mind with horror movies. 世間の人たちは彼と言えばすぐにホラー映画を連想する

link [他]《特にジャーナリズム》（人・物事に）関連があると言う，結びつける ◇Detectives have *linked* the break-in to a similar crime in the area last year. 刑事たちはその不法侵入と昨年その地域で起きた類似の犯罪に関連があると言った ◇Newspapers have *linked* his name with the singer. 新聞各紙は彼の名前とその歌手との関連性を取り上げている ❶ *link* はある犯罪に関わっている可能性のある人や誰が関わっているのかを知っている人について新聞で用いられることが多い．

match [他]（人・物事を）組み合わせる，そろえる ◇The aim of the competition is to *match* the quote to the person who said it. そのコンテクストの趣旨は、引用句とそれを言った人物とを組み合わせることにあります ◇The control group in the experiment was *matched for* age and sex. その実験の対照群は年齢と性別がマッチしていた

connect [他]《ややフォーマル》(人・物事を)結びつけて考える、結びつける ◇There was nothing to *connect* him with the crime. 彼とその犯罪を結びつけるものは何もなかった ◇I was surprised to hear them mentioned together; I had never *connected* them before. 彼らの名前が一緒に挙がっているのを聞いて驚いた。私はそれまで彼らを結びつけて考えたことはなかったからだ

[ノート] **relate, associate, connect の使い分け**: 頭の中で2つの物事を associate するのは、しばしば自分の経験から、自然に起こることである。頭の中で2つの物事を relate または connect する場合、関連性がそれほど明白[自然]でないため、より多くの努力を要する。◆I always *associate* the smell of baking with my childhood. (パンを焼くにおいがするといつも子どもの頃が思い浮かぶ). ×I always *relate/connect* the smell of baking with/to my childhood. ◆I found it hard to *relate/connect* the two ideas in my mind. (頭の中で2つの考えを関連づけるのは難しかった). ×I found it hard to *associate* the two ideas in my mind. relate はまた、2つの物事を意図的に相互に関連づける場合にも用いられる。◆Pay increases will be *related* to productivity. (賃上げは生産性と連動するだろう). ×Pay increases will be *associated* with/connected with productivity. connect はまた、物事を関連づける事実や証拠の有無についても用いることができる。◆There was nothing to *connect* him with the crime. (彼とその犯罪を結びつけるものは何もなかった). ×There was nothing to *relate/associate* him to/with the crime.

related [形]

related・associated・resulting・attendant・consequent・ensuing・resultant・connected

ある点で二つの物事が関わっていることを表す
【類語訳】関連した、付随する、伴う、後に続く、その後の

[文型&コロケーション]

▶ associated/ connected **with** sth
▶ attendant/ consequent **on/ upon** sth
▶ related/ associated/ resulting/ attendant/ consequent/ ensuing/ resultant **problems/ changes**
▶ a related/ an associated/ a resulting/ a consequent/ a resultant **increase**
▶ related/ associated/ attendant/ consequent/ resultant **costs/ effects**
▶ an associated/ a resulting/ a consequent/ the ensuing/ a resultant **loss**
▶ an associated/ a resulting/ a consequent **reduction**
▶ associated/ attendant/ consequent **risks**
▶ **closely** related/ associated/ connected

related (人・物事が)関連[関係]した、関連[関係]がある ◇Much of the crime in this area is *related to* drug abuse. この地域の犯罪の多くは薬物乱用と関連がある ◇These two problems are closely *related*. これら二つの問題には密接な関連がある ◇He was suffering from a stress-*related* illness. 彼はストレス性の病気を患っていた

[反意] **unrelated** (INDEPENDENT)

associated 《ややフォーマル, 特にビジネスで》(人・事が)関連[関係]した ◇Salaries and *associated* costs have risen substantially. 給与およびその関連手当はかなり増えた ◇Young people need to be made aware of the risks *associated* with taking drugs. 若者には麻薬の使用に関連する危険を知らせておく必要がある

[ノート] **related と associated の使い分け**: related は associated より一般的に用いられる。◆a *related* issue/ question/problem/field/area/subject/matter/theme (関連した問題点/質問/問題/分野/領域/話題/事柄/テーマ). associated は特にビジネス関連や risk と共に用いられる。×the risks *related* to taking drugs.

resulting (損失・変化が)結果として生じる ◇The major problem here is soil erosion and the *resulting* loss in crop productivity. ここでの大きな問題は土壌の浸食と、その結果生じる作物の生産性の低下である ◇The benefits would include greater publicity and the *resulting* increase in funding. 利点としては知名度アップと、それがもたらす資金増が挙げられるだろう ☞ **result** (RESULT), **result** (FOLLOW 2), **result in sth** (CAUSE)

attendant [ふつう名詞の前で]《フォーマル》(大きな[重要な]物事の影響として)付随する、(…に)伴う ◇She wanted to avoid the awards ceremony and all its *attendant* publicity. 彼女としては授賞式とそれに伴うさまざまな注視の目は避けたかった ◇We had all the usual problems *attendant* upon starting a new business. 我々は新会社の立ち上げに伴うよくある問題をすべて抱えていた

consequent (または頻度は低いが **consequential**)《ややフォーマル》(損失・変化が)結果として生じる ◇the lowering of taxes and the *consequent* increase in spending 減税とその結果生じる支出増 ◇the responsibilities *consequent* upon the arrival of a new child 新たな子どもの誕生で生じる責任 ☞ **consequence** (RESULT)
▶ **consequently** [副] ◇She failed her exams and was *consequently* unable to start her studies at college.《ややフォーマル, 書き言葉》彼女は試験に落ち、その結果大学に進学できなかった

ensuing (戦い・奮闘・混乱が)続いて起こった；(時期が)続く、その後の ◇He had become separated from his parents in the *ensuing* panic. 続いて起こったパニック状態の中で彼は両親からはぐれてしまったのだ ◇He married in 1782, and in the *ensuing* years produced a wealth of new music. 彼は1782年に結婚し、その後数年にわたって新しい曲を数多く作った ❶ *ensuing* は週(week), 月(month), 年(year) といった期間を表す語の前に用いることが多い。 ☞ **ensue** (FOLLOW 2)

resultant [名詞の前で]《フォーマル》結果として生じる、それに伴う ◇We deplore the use of force and the *resultant* loss of life. 我々は武力行使とその結果生じた人命の損失を遺憾に思う ◇the growing economic crisis and *resultant* unemployment 高まる経済危機とそれに伴う失業状態 ☞ **result** (RESULT), **result** (FOLLOW 2), **result in sth** (CAUSE)

[ノート] **resulting, consequent, resultant の使い分け**: 多くの場合、損失や変化を表すどの語も用いることができる。◆the war and the *resulting/consequent/resultant* loss of life (戦争とその結果生じる人命の損失). ◆lower taxation and the *resulting/consequent/resultant* increase in spending (減税とその結果生じる支

↪related **relation, relationship**

出).resultingとresultantはまた、ある過程の結果について用いることもできる。◆The *resulting* product will be marketed by IBM. (その結果できる製品はIBMによって市販されることになっています). ◆The *resultant* chemical structure is flexible. (その結果生じる化学構造は柔軟である). ✕the *consequent* product/structure. resultingとresultantはよい結果にも悪い結果にも用いることができるが、consequentはふつう、ある点で問題を引き起こす結果について用いられる。resultantはresultingよりフォーマルで使用頻度は低い。

connected (事実・出来事が)関連がある;(相互に)関連した ◇Do these sentences describe a *connected* sequence of events? これらの文章は一連の関連した出来事を描写しているのですか 反意 unconnected (INDEPENDENT)

relation 名

relation・connection・relationship・correlation・link・association・interdependence
類似の物事の結びつき(方)を表す
【類語訳】関連、関係、相互関係、相関関係、相互依存

文型&コロケーション
▶the relation/ connection/ relationship/ correlation/ link/ association/ interdependence **between** A and B
▶a connection/ a relationship/ a correlation/ a link/ an association **with** sb/ sth
▶a connection/ link **to** sth
▶the relation/ relationship **of** sth **to** sth
▶**in** connection/ association **with** sb/ sth
▶a **close/ significant** relation/ connection/ relationship/ correlation/ link/ association
▶a **direct/ clear/ strong/ definite/ possible** relation/ connection/ relationship/ correlation/ link/ association
▶a **complex** relation/ connection/ relationship/ association/ interdependence
▶a **simple** relation/ connection/ relationship/ correlation
▶a **causal** connection/ relationship/ link/ association
▶a **positive** relation/ connection/ relationship/ correlation/ link
▶a **negative** relation/ relationship/ correlation/ link
▶to **have** a relation/ a connection/ a relationship/ a correlation/ a link/ an association
▶to **show/ examine** the relation/ connection/ relationship/ correlation/ link/ association
▶to **find** a relation/ a connection/ a relationship/ a correlation/ a link/ an association
▶to **prove** the relation/ connection/ relationship/ link/ association
▶to **see** the connection/ relationship/ correlation/ link

relation [U, C] 《ややフォーマル》(二つ以上の物事の)関連(の仕方)、関係 ◇The fee they are offering bears no *relation* to the amount of work involved. 彼らが提示している料金はそれに関わる仕事量とは関係がない ◇Its brain is small *in relation to* (= compared with) its body. それの脳は体に比べて小さい ◇I have some comments to make *in relation to* (= concerning) this matter. 《フォーマル》 この問題に関して言っておきたいことがいくつかあります ◇The study shows a close *relation* between poverty and ill health. その研究は貧困と不健康の間に密接な関連があることを示している

connection [C] (二人・二つ以上の人・物事の)関連(性)、関係 ◇Scientists have established a *connection* between cholesterol levels and heart disease. 科学者によってコレステロール値と心臓病との関連性が立証されている ◇The union did not have a direct *connection* with any political party. その労働組合はどの政党とも直接的な関係はなかった ◇How did you **make the connection** (= realize that there was a connection between two facts that did not seem to be related)? どうしてその関係に気づいたのですか

relationship [C, U] (二つ以上の物事の)関連(の仕方)、関係 ◇the *relationship* between mental and physical health 心の健康と肉体の健康との関係 ◇People alter their voices in *relationship* to background noise. 《ややフォーマル》 人は周りの音の程度に応じて声を変えます ◇There is an *inverse relationship* between disability and social contact (= the greater sb's disability, the less social contact they have). 《ややフォーマル》体の障害と人付き合いの間には反比例の関係がある

ノート **relation** と **relationship** の使い分け：relation は、in relation to sth, bear no/little relation to sthといった表現で用いられることが最も多い。二つまたはそれ以上の物事の間のrelation/relationshipについて言う場合、より専門的な文脈ではrelationを用いることが多い。

correlation [C, U] 《ややフォーマル》(物事の)相互関係、相関関係 ◇There is a direct *correlation* between exposure to sun and skin cancer. 日光にさらされることと皮膚がんとの間には直接的な相関関係が見られる ◇the *correlation* of social power with wealth 社会的影響力と富との相互関係 ☞ **correlate** (MATCH 1)

link [C] (二人・二つ以上の人・物事の)関連(性)、関係 ◇Police suspect there may be a *link* between the two murders. 警察はその2件の殺人に関連があるかもしれないとにらんでいる ◇The report failed to prove a causal *link* between violence on screen and in real life. その報告書は映画の暴力シーンと現実世界の暴力との因果関係の証明にまでは至らなかった

ノート **connection** と **link** の使い分け：両語に実質的な意味の違いはない。make the connectionという句では、linkを代わりに用いることはできない。✕How did you make the *link*? linkはconnectionよりややインフォーマルで、新聞で用いられることが多い。

association [C] 《ややフォーマル》(物事の)関連(性) ◇Is there a proven *association* between passive smoking and cancer? 受動喫煙とがんとの間に確かな関連性があるのですか

interdependence [U, C] 《フォーマル》(人・物事の)相互依存 ◇The report stresses the *interdependence* of teaching and research in universities. その報告書では大学における教育と研究の相互依存の関係が力説されている

relationship 名

1 relationship・relations・partnership・tie・link・association・contact・affiliation
二人の人[二つの集団・国]の結びつきを表す
【類語訳】関係、間柄、協力関係、きずな、つながり、関連

relationship

[文型&コロケーション]
- a relationship/ relations/ a partnership/ ties/ a link/ an association/ contacts/ an affiliation **with** sb/ sth
- a relationship/ relations/ a partnership/ ties/ links/ an association/ an affiliation **between** A and B
- (a) **close** relationship/ relations/ partnership/ ties/ links/ association/ contacts
- (a) **strong** relationship/ partnership/ ties/ links
- **economic/ diplomatic/ family** relations/ ties/ links
- **trade** relations/ links/ contacts
- (a) **business/ professional** relationship/ relations/ partnership/ ties/ links/ association/ contacts
- (a) **political** relationship/ relations/ partnership/ ties/ links/ association/ affiliation
- (a) **personal** relationship/ relations/ ties/ links/ association/ contacts/ affiliation
- **international** relations/ partnership/ ties/ links/ contacts
- to **have** a relationship/ relations/ a partnership/ ties/ a link/ an association/ contacts/ an affiliation
- to **build/ establish/ foster** a relationship/ relations/ a partnership/ ties/ links/ contacts
- to **develop** a relationship/ relations/ a partnership/ ties/ links/ an association/ contacts
- to **improve/ strengthen** a relationship/ relations/ a partnership/ ties/ links
- to **sever/ break off** relations/ ties/ links

relationship [C, U] (人・集団・国の)関係；(家族・親類の中での)関係, 間柄 ◇The *relationship* between the police and the local community has improved. 警察と地域社会の関係は改善されてきた ◇I have established a good *working relationship* with my boss. 私は職場で上司とよい関係を築いている ◇She has a *love-hate relationship* with her job (= her feelings for her job are a mixture of love and hatred). 彼女は自分の仕事に愛憎相半ばする気持ちを抱いている ◇a father-son/mother-daughter *relationship* 父と息子[母と娘]の関係 ◇I'm not sure of the exact *relationship* between them ─ I think they're cousins. 彼らの正確な間柄はよくわからないけど, いとこ同士だと思うよ

relations [複数で] (人・集団・国の)関係 ◇US-Chinese *relations* 米中関係 ◇*Relations* with neighbouring countries are under strain at present. 現在, 隣国との関係は緊迫している ◇The change of government led to improved *industrial relations* (= relations between employers and employees). 政権交代が労使関係の改善につながった

[ノート] **relationship** と **relations** の使い分け：relations という語は, 人・集団・国の関係の善し悪しについて用いられることが多い. ◆ strained/difficult *relations* (緊張/面倒な関係). ◆ cordial/harmonious/improved *relations* (心温まる/友好的な/改善された関係). relationships は relations よりも個人的な関係に用いられる場合が多い. ◆ international/race/cultural *relations* (国際/人種間の/文化間の関係). ◆ interpersonal/one-to-one/parent-child *relationships* (対人/一対一の/親子関係)

partnership [C, U] (人・集団などの)関係；協力関係 ◇Marriage should be an equal *partnership*. 婚姻は対等の相互関係であるべきだ ◇the school's *partnership* with parents 学校と親との協力関係 ◇a *partnership* be-

tween the United States and Europe 米国とヨーロッパとの協力関係 ☞ **partner** (PARTNER 1)

tie [C, ふつう複数で] (人・組織の)(強力な)関係, きずな ◇The firm has close *ties* with an American corporation. その会社は米国の企業と緊密な関係にある ◇The community was bound by *family ties* and a strong church. その共同体は家族のきずなと教会の力によって結束していた ◇Although he was raised as a Roman Catholic, he has *cut his ties* with the Church. 彼はローマカトリック教徒として育てられたが, 教会との関係は断っている ◇the *ties* of friendship/kinship 友情の/親族のきずな

link [C] (人・国・組織の)関係, つながり ◇They were keen to establish trade *links* with Asia. 彼らはアジアとの貿易関係を築くことに熱心だった ◇Social customs provide a vital *link* between generations. 社会のしきたりは世代に必要なつながりをもたらす

[ノート] **tie** と **link** の使い分け：ties は links より関係が強く, 人・集団が密接な関係にあることや, ある意味で相互依存していることを示唆する. ties は感情的な面が強い関係を言う場合には links よりよく用いられる. ◆ trade/business *ties/ links* (貿易/ビジネス関係). ◆ *family ties* (家族のきずな). ◆ the *ties* of friendship (友情のきずな). × *family links*. × the *links* of friendship.

association [C, U] (ややフォーマル) (ビジネスにおける人・組織の)関連, 関係 ◇He was questioned about his alleged *association* with terrorist groups. 彼はテロ集団との関連の容疑で尋問を受けた ◇The book was published *in association with* (= together with) British Heritage. その本はブリティッシュ・ヘリティジと共同で出版された ☞ **associate** (PARTNER 1)

contact [C, ふつう複数で] (特にビジネス) (人と会う[意思を通じ合う])機会；(人との)関係 ◇We have good *contacts* with the local community. 私たちは地域社会とよい関係にあります ◇The company has maintained trade *contacts* with India. その会社はインドとの貿易関係を維持している

affiliation [U, C] (フォーマル) (集団・組織の公的[政治的, 宗教的]な)関係, つながり ◇Trade unions have a long history of *affiliation* to the Labour Party. 労働組合は労働党との長い歴史的関係があります ◇the diverse religious *affiliations* of Ghanaian Americans 多様な宗教的つながりを持つガーナ系アメリカ人

2 relationship • affair • romance • love affair • courtship • liaison

恋人関係を表す
【類語訳】恋愛関係, 関係, 性的関係, 不倫, 恋愛, ロマンス, 情事, 求愛, 密通

[文型&コロケーション]
- a relationship/ an affair/ a romance/ a love affair/ a liaison **with** sb
- a relationship/ an affair/ a romance/ a love affair/ a liaison **between** A and B
- a **brief/ long** relationship/ affair/ romance/ love affair/ courtship
- a **passionate** relationship/ affair/ romance/ love affair
- a **secret** relationship/ affair/ romance/ love affair/ liaison
- to **have** a relationship/ an affair/ a romance/ a love affair/ a liaison
- to **start/ begin/ embark on** a relationship/ an affair/ a

love affair
▶a relationship/ an affair/ a romance/ a love affair **is over**

relationship [C] 恋愛関係, (性的)関係 ◇He was not married but he was *in* a stable *relationship*. 彼は結婚はしていなかったが, 恋愛関係はずっと続けていた ◇She's had a series of miserable *relationships*. 彼女はいくつもの惨めな恋愛を経験してきた ◇Money problems have put a strain on their *relationship*. 金銭問題が彼らの関係に重くのしかかっている

affair [C] (双方[一方]が結婚している場合の)性的関係, 不倫(関係) ◇She is having an *affair* with her boss. 彼女は上司と不倫している

romance [C] (激しく短い)恋愛(関係), ロマンス ◇They married after a *whirlwind romance*. 彼らはあっと言う間の恋愛の末に結婚した ◇a holiday *romance*《英》(休暇中の)旅先のロマンス ◇a summer *romance*《特に米》(休暇中の)ひと夏の恋 ☞ **romance** (LOVE 名 1), **romantic** (LOVING)

'**love affair** [C] (結婚していない二人の)恋愛(関係), 情事 ◇So you're not going to tell me when your *love affair* with Sam ended? じゃあサムとの恋がいつ終わったのか言う気はないんだね

ノート **affair** と **love affair** の使い分け: **love affair** はふつう **affair** よりロマンチックなもので, セックスを伴う必要はなく, 二人とも独身の場合もある。

courtship [C, U]《古風》(結婚前の)交際期間; 求愛 ◇They married after a short *courtship*. 彼らは短い交際期間の末に結婚した ◇Mr Elton's *courtship* of Harriet エルトン氏のハリエットへの求愛 ❶ **courtship** は今ではかなり古風な語だが, 過去の人たちについては今でも用いられる。
☞ **court** (GO OUT)

liaison [C]《フォーマル》(双方[一方]が既婚の場合の)密通 ◇He finally admitted to several sexual *liaisons*. 彼はついにいくつかの性的関係を認めた

relative 形 ☞ EQUIVALENT

relative・proportional・proportionate
位置[立場]や関係に応じた考え方をする
【類語訳】比較して, 相対的な, 比較的な, 比例した, 見合った

文型&コロケーション
▶relative/ proportional/ proportionate **to** sth
▶a relative/ proportional/ proportionate **increase**

relative [形] (位置・関係を)比較して;(考慮・判断について)比較したうえでの; 相対的な, 比較的な ◇the position of the sun *relative* to the earth 地球に対する太陽の位置 ◇You must consider the *relative* **merits** of the two plans. その二つのプランの優劣を考えなければなりません ◇They now live in *relative* comfort (= compared with how they lived before). 彼らは今では比較的楽な生活をしている ◇*It's all relative* though, isn't it? We never had any money when I was a kid and $500 was a fortune to us. やはりすべてが相対的なものじゃないかな。子どもの頃は全然お金がなくて, 500ドルといったら私たちには大金だったもの
▶**relatively** [副] ◇At first glance the poem seems to be *relatively* straightforward. 一見したところでは, この詩は比較的わかりやすく思える ◇The colleges had become, *relatively speaking*, short of funds. 相対的に

言って, それらの大学は資金不足に陥っていた

proportional 《ややフォーマル》(大きさ・量・程度が)比例した, 見合った ◇Salary is directly *proportional* to years of experience. 給与は経験年数に正比例する ◇The number of teachers appointed is *proportional* to the total number of students. 任命される教師の数は学生の総数に見合ったものだ ☞ **proportion** (RATIO)
▶**proportionally** [副] ◇Families with children spend *proportionally* less per person than families without children. 子どものいる家庭は子どものいない家庭より一人当たりの出費が相対的に少ない

proportionate《フォーマル》(公正さ・妥当性の点から)比例した, 見合った ◇Inner cities have more than a *proportionate* share of social problems. 都心部では妥当な線を越えた社会問題を抱えている ◇Penalties should be *proportionate* to the gravity of the offence. 刑罰は犯罪の重大性に見合って然るべきだ 反義 **disproportionate** (EXCESSIVE)
▶**proportionately** [副] ◇Prices have risen but wages have not risen *proportionately*. 物価は上がったが, それに比例するほど賃金は上がっていない

ノート **proportional** と **proportionate** の使い分け:
多くの場合, どちらの語も用いることができる。◆Salary is *proportional/proportionate* to experience. (給与は経験に比例する). ◆*proportional/proportionate* increases in costs (引き起こされたコストの増加). これらの場合, **proportionate** は **proportional** よりフォーマルで使用頻度が低い。しかし, **proportionate** は単に二つの量を比較するのではなく, 二つの行動や決定を評価し, 考慮したうえでどちらが公正[妥当]かを決めることが問題である場合によく用いられる。◆The police response should be *proportionate* to the level of risk posed. (警察の対応は引き起こされる危険のレベルに見合ったものにすべきだ). 反義語 **disproportionate** は, 他の行動や状況に応じた反応や判断が公正[妥当]でない場合に用いられる。**proportional** の反意表現は *inversely proportional* である。◆The amount of force needed is *inversely proportional* to the rigidity of the material (= the more rigid the material, the less force is needed). (必要な力の量は材料の硬さに反比例する).

release 動

release・let sb go・free・liberate・set sb/sth free・ransom・emancipate・let sb/sth loose
引き止められて[閉じ込められて]いた場所から出て行かせること
【類語訳】釈放する, 解放する, 放つ, 自由にする

文型&コロケーション
▶to release/ free/ liberate/ set free/ emancipate sb **from** sth
▶to release/ let go/ free/ liberate/ set free/ ransom **a prisoner/ hostage**
▶to **finally** release sb/ let sb go/ free sb/ liberate sb
▶to release/ free sb **on bail**
▶to release/ free an animal/ a bird **into the wild**

release [他] (刑務所から)釈放する, (人・動物などを)解放する, 放つ ◇The kidnappers have agreed to *release* the hostages by 12 noon. 誘拐犯たちは正午までに人質を解放することに同意した ◇He was *released* without *charge* (= not charged with committing a crime) after questioning by police. 彼は警察の尋問を受けてから無罪放免された ◇She was *released* on bail (= after paying a sum of money to make sure she would return) by the New York police. 彼女はニューヨーク警察から保釈された ◇The birds were cleaned and fed and *released* again into the wild. 鳥たちはきれいにされ、餌を与えられ、再び野に放たれた ☞ **release** (FREE 動)

▶**release** 名 [U, 単数любо] ◇The government has been working to secure the *release* of the hostages. 政府は人質の解放を保証するために尽力している ◇She can expect an early *release* from prison. 彼女は早期の出所が見込める

,let sb 'go フレーズ《ややインフォーマル》(人を)自由にさせる，解放する，放す ◇He was beaten up quite badly before they *let* him *go*. 彼は解放されるまでに実にひどい暴力を受けていた ◇*Let* me *go*! You're hurting me! 放して，痛いわよ ❶ let sb go はふつう通常の犯罪者を刑務所から釈放することには用いられず，不法に捕らわれた人質を解放することに用いる ☞ **let go** (FREE 動)

free [他] (刑務所から) 釈放する，(人・奴隷を)解放する ◇Over 2,000 political prisoners were *freed* as a gesture of good will. 善意の証として2000人以上の政治犯の解放が行われた ◇The starting point for emancipation was the *freeing* of children of slaves born after a certain date. 解放の第一歩は，特定の日以降に生まれた奴隷の子どもたちから始まった ☞ **free** (FREE 形 1), **free** (FREE 動)

liberate [他]《ややフォーマル》(他者の支配から国・人などを)解放する ◇The city was *liberated* by the advancing army. その都市は進軍する軍隊によって解放された

▶**liberation** 名 [U, 単数love] ◇He took part in the *liberation* of the occupied countries. 彼は被占領国の解放運動に参加した

,set sb/sth 'free フレーズ (刑務所から)釈放する，(人を)自由にする，(捕らわれた[かご・おりに入れられた]動物・鳥を)自由にする ◇Police were forced to *set* him *free* because of a lack of evidence. 警察は彼を証拠不十分で釈放せざるをえなかった ◇Dozens of laboratory animals were *set free* by animal rights activists. 数十頭の実験動物が動物の権利活動家の手で自由になった

ノート **release, free, set free** の使い分け：free は人を解放する決定を強調，release は人を解放する行為を強調する。裁判所や政府は囚人や捕虜などを free することになろうが，警察や刑務所は彼らを release するだろう。set free は，特に権力ではなく武力や暴力で解放する行為を強調する。
  ♦ Rioters stormed the prison and *set* all the prisoners *free*. (暴徒たちは刑務所を襲撃して，すべての囚人を解放した)

ransom [他] (身代金などを払って拘束されている人を)解放させる，受け戻す ◇The hostages were *ransomed* and returned home unharmed. 捕虜たちは解放され，無事帰国した

▶**ransom** 名 [C, U] ◇The kidnappers demanded a *ransom* of £50,000 from his family. 誘拐犯たちは彼の家族に5万ポンドの身代金を要求した ◇They are refusing to pay *ransom* for her release. 彼らは彼女を解放するための身代金の支払いを拒んでいる

emancipate [他，しばしば受身]《(法的，政治的，社会的)制約から》◇Slaves were not *emancipated* until 1863 in the United States. 米国では奴隷たちは

1863年まで解放されなかった

▶**emancipation** 名 [U] ◇the struggle for the *emancipation* of women 女性解放闘争

let sb/sth 'loose 行フレ (危険になる[問題を起こす]可能性のある人・物を)自由にする，放す ◇Who *let* the dogs *loose*? 誰がその犬を放したのですか ◇How did such a violent criminal get to be *let loose* in the community? どうしてその地域ではそんな凶悪犯が野放し状態になったのですか ☞ **loose** (FREE 形 1)

relevant 形

relevant・applicable・pertinent・to the point・material
議論[検討]していることに直接関わっていたり，人々の生活や仕事にまさにぴったりであることを表す
【類語訳】関連した，関係のある，当てはまる，適用できる，要を得た，適切な

文型&コロケーション
▸ relevant/ applicable/ pertinent/ material **to** sb/ sth
▸ relevant/ applicable/ pertinent/ material **for** sb/ sth
▸ relevant/ pertinent **to do** sth
▸ a relevant/ pertinent/ material **point/ fact/ factor**
▸ **particularly/ directly** relevant/ applicable/ pertinent
▸ **very** relevant/ pertinent/ material
▸ **highly/ extremely** relevant/ pertinent

relevant (問題・状況に密接に)関連した，関係のある；(生活・仕事が)意義のある ◇I don't think that question is really very *relevant*. その問題は本当はあまり関連はないと思う ◇They are looking for someone with *relevant* experience in childcare. 彼らは保育関係の経験がある人を探している ◇These comments are not directly *relevant* to this enquiry. これらのコメントはこの調査に直接関係はありません ◇Her novel is still *relevant* today. 彼女の小説は今日でもまだ意義がある 反意 **irrelevant** (IRRELEVANT)

▶**relevance** 名 [U] ◇I don't see the *relevance* of your question. あなたの質問の妥当性が見いだせません ◇It's a classic play of contemporary *relevance*. それは現代に通じるものがある古典劇です

▶**relevantly** 副 ◇She has experience in teaching and, more *relevantly*, in industry. 彼女には指導経験と，さらに実際の事業経験がある

applicable [名詞の前before はまれ]《ややフォーマル》(人・物事に)直接関連した，(人・物事に)当てはまる，適用できる ◇Many of the questions on the form were not *applicable* (= did not apply) to me. その用紙に書かれた質問の多くは私に向けられたものではなかった ◇Give details of children where *applicable* (= if you have any). 該当する場合[お子さんがいらっしゃる場合]はお子さんについて詳しくお書きください ◇His rules are not universally *applicable* (= they do not apply to everyone or everything). 彼の決めたルールは誰にでも，またあらゆる場合に適用できるわけではない 反意 **inapplicable** (IRRELEVANT)

pertinent《フォーマル》(特定の状況に)関連した ◇I reminded him of a few *pertinent* facts. 私は彼にいくつかの関連した事実を思い起こさせた ◇Please keep your comments *pertinent* to the topic under discussion. コメントは討議中のテーマに関連したものに留めておいてください

to the 'point 行フレ (ほめて) (関連があって)要を得た，適切

↪relevant

な, 的を射た ◇Her speech was brief and *to the point*. 彼女のスピーチは簡潔で要を得ていた ◇That remark was not really *to the point*. その発言はあまり的を射てはいなかった 反意 **beside the point** (IRRELEVANT), ☞ **point** (POINT), **concise** (SHORT 3)

material 《フォーマル or 法律》(特定の状況で)重要な, 重大な ◇She omitted information that was *material* to the case. 彼女はその事件にとっての重要な情報を省いた 反意 **immaterial** (IRRELEVANT)

▶ **materially** ▷Their comments have not *materially* affected our plans (= in a noticeable or important way). 彼らのコメントが我々の計画に著しく影響を与えたということはない

reliable 形

1 reliable・loyal・dedicated・faithful・committed・true・trusted・staunch・responsible・trustworthy
人や物事が頼みにできることを表す
【類語訳】当てにできる, 忠実な, 献身的な, 熱心な, 誠実な, 専念した, 傾倒している, 信頼できる

文型&コロケーション

▶ loyal/ dedicated/ faithful/ committed/ true **to** sb/ sth
▶ a reliable/ loyal/ faithful/ true/ trusted/ staunch/ trustworthy **friend**
▶ a reliable/ loyal/ faithful/ trusted/ staunch **ally**
▶ a reliable/ loyal/ faithful/ committed/ staunch **supporter**
▶ a loyal/ dedicated/ faithful/ true **fan/ follower**
▶ a loyal/ dedicated/ faithful/ committed/ trusted/ staunch/ responsible **member** (of sth)
▶ reliable/ loyal/ dedicated/ committed/ trustworthy **staff**
▶ a loyal/ dedicated/ faithful **following**
▶ reliable/ loyal/ faithful **service**
▶ totally reliable/ loyal/ dedicated/ trustworthy

reliable 《しばしばほめて》(人・物事が)当てにできる; 頼りになる ◇We are looking for someone who is *reliable* and hard-working. 私たちは頼りになり, よく働いてくれる人を探している ◇My car's not as *reliable* as it used to be. 私の車は以前ほどは頼りにならない ◇There is no *reliable* supply of electricity or running water. 電気や水道の安定供給に欠ける 反意 **unreliable** ❶ unreliable な人や物事は当てにできない[頼りにならない]. ◆The trains are notoriously *unreliable*. (列車は当てにならないとの評判が付きまとっている). ☞ **rely on/upon sb/sth** (TRUST)
▶ **reliability** 名 [U] ◇The incident cast doubt on her motives and *reliability*. その出来事は彼女の動機と信頼性に疑いを投げかけた
▶ **reliably** 副 ◇You need to show that you can work *reliably* and be trusted to handle responsibility. 君は仕事を任せられ, 責任をこなせる人物であることを示す必要がある

loyal 《ほめて》(特定の人・組織・信条に)忠実な, 忠実な ◇She has always remained *loyal* to her political principles. 彼女は常に自らの政治信条に忠実だった ◇He is one of the president's most *loyal* supporters. 彼は大統領の最も忠実な支持者の一人である 反意 **disloyal**
▶ **loyally** 副 ◇He *loyally* supported the government through the crisis. 彼は危機の間も忠実に政府を支援した
▶ **loyalty** 名 [U, C] ◇They swore their *loyalty* to the king. 彼らは王に忠誠を誓った ◇a case of **divided loyal-**ties (= with strong feelings of support for two different people or causes) 二股をかけた忠誠心の事例 反意 **disloyalty**

dedicated 《ほめて》(物事に)打ち込んでいる, 献身的な, 熱心な ◇She is *dedicated* to her job. 彼女は仕事に打ち込んでいる ◇The workforce is small but highly *dedicated*. 従業員は少ないが非常に熱心だ ◇The ship was painstakingly rebuilt by a *dedicated* team of engineers. 船は献身的な技術者チームによって苦心の末に再建された ☞ **dedicate** (DEVOTE)
▶ **dedication** 名 [U] ◇I really admire Gina for her *dedication* to her family. ジーナの家族への献身ぶりに私は心から感謝している ◇The job requires total *dedication*. その仕事には全身全霊で打ち込む必要がある

faithful 《ほめて》(特定の人・組織・信条に)忠実な, 誠実な; (人・物事が)頼りになる ◇He remained *faithful* to the ideals of the party until his death. 彼は死ぬまでずっとその党の理念に忠実だった ◇His *faithful* old dog sat by his feet. 彼の忠実な老犬が彼の足元に座っていた ◇a *faithful* worker/correspondent 誠実な労働者/記者 ◇my *faithful* old car 古いが頼りになる私の車 ☞ **devoted** (LOVING), **faith** (FAITH)
▶ **the faithful** 名 [複数扱い] ◇The president will keep the support of *the* party *faithful*. 大統領は熱心[忠実]な党の支持者の支援を受け続けるだろう
▶ **faithfully** 副 ◇He had supported the local team *faithfully* for 30 years. 彼は30年間, 地元チームを忠実に応援し続けてきた ◇She promised *faithfully* not to tell anyone the secret. 彼女は秘密を誰にも言わないと固く約束した

ノート **loyal** と **faithful** の使い分け:多くの場合, どちらの語も用いることができる. ◆a *loyal/faithful* friend/ally/supporter/fan/follower/servant (忠実な友人/同盟国/支持者/ファン/信奉者/召し使い). しかし, 強調の違いが多少ある場合もある. **loyal** friend/servant は信条から忠実であり続けるが, **faithful** friend/servant は情愛から忠実であり続ける.

committed 《ほめて》(時間・精力をいとわずに)打ち込んでいる, 専念した, 献身的な;(物事を)強く信じる, (物事に)傾倒している ◇The government remains *committed* to protecting Green Belt areas. 政府はグリーンベルト地域の保護に引き続き力を注いでいる ◇They are *committed* socialists. 彼らは筋金入りの社会主義者だ ◇We have a highly-motivated, trained and *committed* staff. 我々には非常に意欲的で, 訓練を積んだ献身的なスタッフがいる ☞ **commit** (DEVOTE), **commit** (PROMISE) 動, **commitment** (PROMISE) 名

true 《ほめて》(特定の人・信条に)忠実な, 誠実な ◇Many were executed for remaining *true* to their principles. 自分の主義に忠実であり続けたために多くの人が処刑された ◇He was *true to his word* (= did what he promised to do). 彼は約束を守る人だった ◇Through that difficult period he proved to be a *true* friend. あのつらい時期を通して彼は誠実な友であることがわかった

trusted 《ほめて》(人が)頼りにできる, 信頼できる ◇As time went on he became a *trusted* adviser to the king. 時が経つにつれて彼は王の信頼できる相談相手となった ☞ **trust** (FAITH), **trust** (TRUST)

staunch 《しばしばほめて》(意見・態度が)忠実な, 断固とした ◇a *staunch* Catholic 忠実なカトリック教徒 ◇She is one of the president's *staunchest* allies. 彼女は大統領の最

も忠実な盟友の一人である
▶**staunchly** 副 ◇She *staunchly* defended the new policy. 彼女は断固として新方針を擁護した ◇The family was *staunchly* Protestant. その一家は忠実なプロテスタントだった

responsible (人・行動・態度が)信頼できる、頼りになる ◇Clare has a mature and *responsible* attitude to work. 仕事に対するクレアの態度は分別があり信頼に足る 反義 **irresponsible** (RECKLESS)

trustworthy 《ほめて》(善良さ・正直さ・誠実さを)頼りにでき、信頼できる ◇Women were seen as more *trustworthy* and harder working. 女性のほうが信頼に足る勤勉な働き手だと見なされた 反義 **untrustworthy**

2 ☞ TRUE
reliable・factual・authoritative・real-life・verifiable・authentic
情報(源)が真実で、正確であることを表す
【類語訳】信頼できる、確かな、実在の、現実の、立証できる、実証できる

文型&コロケーション
▶a reliable/ a factual/ an authoritative/ a real-life/ an authentic **account** (of sth)
▶reliable/ factual/ authoritative/ verifiable **evidence**/ **information**
▶a reliable/ an authoritative/ a verifiable/ an authentic **source** (of information)

reliable (情報(源)が)信頼できる、確かな ◇These tests are a *reliable* indicator of future performance. これらのテストは将来の成績を占う確かな指標となるものです ◇Prosecution lawyers tried to show that she was not a *reliable* witness. 検事たちは彼女が信頼に値しない証人であることを立証しようとした 反義 **unreliable** ●信頼できない人[物事]が信頼できない[信用できない] ◇He's totally *unreliable* as a source of information. (彼は情報源としてまったく信頼できない) ☞ **accurate** (EXACT)
▶**reliability** 名 [U] ◇The *reliability* of these results has been questioned. これらの結果の信頼性は疑問視されてきた
▶**reliably** 副 ◇I am *reliably* informed (= told by sb who knows the facts) that the company is being sold. 《ややフォーマル》その会社は売却されようとしているという情報を信頼できる筋から得ている

factual 事実に基づく、事実を含む ◇He fails to distinguish *factual* information from opinion. 彼は事実に基づく情報と意見とを区別できない ◇The essay contains a number of *factual* errors. そのエッセイにはいくつかの事実誤認が含まれている 反義 **fictitious** (FICTIONAL), ☞ **fact** (FACT), **fact** (INFORMATION)
▶**factually** 副 ◇It was *factually* correct, but I don't think it was fair. その事実関係は正しかったが、それが公平だったとは思わない

authoritative (真実かつ正確であり)信頼できる ◇He is credited with writing the most *authoritative* and up-to-date book on the subject. その問題に関して最も信頼できる最新情報を盛り込んだ本を執筆したのは彼だとされている ☞ **authority** (EXPERT)
▶**real-'life** [名詞の前で] (本・物語・映画などで)実際に起こった、実在の、現実の ◇The novel is a political thriller based on *real-life* events. その小説は現実の出来事に基

づいた政治スリラーである ◇The local press has been referring to them as a *real-life* Romeo and Juliet. その地元紙は彼らのことを実在のロミオとジュリエットと呼んできた 反義 **fictional** (FICTIONAL)

verifiable 立証できる、実証できる ◇That's just your opinion, not a *verifiable* fact. それは単なる君の意見で、立証できる事実ではない ☞ **verify** (CHECK 2)

authentic (正確かつ現実的に描写していて)本当の ◇He is the *authentic* voice of the poor, white working class. 彼は貧しい白人労働階級の真の代弁者である

relief 名 ☞ SYMPATHY

relief・comfort・reassurance・consolation
悲しみや苦痛などが少ない時の気持ち、悲しみや苦痛などが減らされること
【類語訳】安堵、安心、緩和、安らぎ、慰め

文型&コロケーション
▶a relief/ comfort/ consolation **to** sb
▶relief/ comfort/ reassurance/ consolation **in** sth
▶the comfort/ reassurance/ consolation **that**...
▶(a) **great** relief/ comfort/ reassurance/ consolation
▶to **seek**/ **find**/ **bring**/ **offer** (sb) relief/ comfort/ reassurance/ consolation
▶to **give** sb comfort/ reassurance
▶to **take** comfort/ consolation
▶It's a relief/ comfort/ consolation **to** know/ have/ be, etc.

relief [U, 単数で] (不快なことが少なくなったときの)ほっとした気持ち、安堵、安心 ; (痛み・不安・苦痛の)除去、緩和 ◇We all *breathed a sigh of relief* when he came back safely. 彼が無事に戻ってきたとき、私たちはみな安堵のため息をついた ◇Much *to my relief* the car was not damaged. 私が大いに安心したのは車に損傷がなかったことだ ◇It was a *relief* to be able to talk to someone about it. そのことを人に話せてほっとした ◇*What a relief!* ああよかった ◇modern methods of *pain relief* 現代の鎮痛法 ◇the *relief* of poverty/misery/suffering 貧困/苦しみ/苦痛の緩和 ☞ **relieve** (EASE), **relieved** (GLAD)

comfort [U, 単数で] (悲しみ・苦痛・不安が少なくなったときの)安らぎ、安心、慰め ; (苦痛な[不安な、不幸な]ときに)慰めになる人[物事]、安心をもたらす人[物事] ◇I *drew comfort* from his words. 彼の言葉に慰められた[安らぎを覚えた] ◇I tried to offer a few words of *comfort*. 慰めの言葉を二言三言かけようとした ◇The children have been a great *comfort* to me through all of this. この間ずっと子どもたちは私にとって大きな慰めであった ◇It's a *comfort* to know that she is safe. 彼女が無事だと知って安心した

reassurance [U, C] (恐怖・疑いを取り除いて)安心させること、安心感を与えること ; (恐怖・疑いを取り除くための)安心させる言葉[行為] ◇Teenagers need love, encouragement and *reassurance* from their parents. ティーンエイジャーは親からの愛情、励まし、安心感を与えてもらうことを必要としている ◇We have been given *reassurances* that the water is safe to drink. その水は飲んでも大丈夫だとずっと安心させられてきた

consolation [C, U] (悲しい[がっかりしている]ときに)慰めになる人[物事] ; (不安・悲しみが少なくなったときの)安らぎ、慰め ◇If it's any *consolation*, she didn't get the job either. 慰めにもならないけど、彼女もその仕事には

ありつけなかったんだよ ◇When things went wrong, she found *consolation* in her religious beliefs. 物事がうまくいかないときに彼女は信仰に安らぎを見いだした

ノート **comfort** と **consolation** の使い分け：これらの語は同じパターンで用いることができる。◆ If it's any *comfort/consolation to you...* (慰めになるかわからませんが…). ◆ It's a great *comfort/consolation that...* (...は大いに慰めとなる). ◆ to seek/find/take *comfort/consolation* (安らぎを求める/見いだす/得る). しかし、意味にわずかな違いがある。競争に負ける、就職できないといった落胆のあとでは consolation を見いだすことになるだろうが、あることでとても悲しく[不安に]なっているというより深刻な状況では comfort を見いだすことになるだろう。◆ Chocolate is a great *comfort food* (= it makes you feel better). (チョコレートは心がとても安らぐ食べ物だ). ◆ Six runners-up will get a *consolation prize* of a disposable camera (= a small prize, even though they did not win the competition). (二位以下の6名には残念賞で使い捨てカメラを差し上げます).

reluctant 形

reluctant・unwilling・grudging
人が何かをしたがらない状況を表す
【類語訳】しぶしぶの、いやいやながらの、不本意ながらの

文型&コロケーション
▶ reluctant/ unwilling **to do sth**
▶ reluctant/ unwilling/ grudging **acceptance**
▶ a reluctant/ grudging **admiration/ admission**
▶ a reluctant/ an unwilling **participant**

reluctant （する前にためらって）なかなか…しようとしない、しぶしぶの、いやいやながらの ◇She was *reluctant* to admit she was wrong. 彼女は自分が間違っていることをしぶしぶ認めた[なかなか認めようとしなかった] ◇They nodded in *reluctant* agreement. 彼らは不承不承同意してうなずいた ◇He finally gave a *reluctant* smile. 彼はやっといやいやながらほほ笑んだ 反意 **EAGER**
▶ **reluctance** 名 [U, 単数で] ◇There is still some *reluctance* on the part of employers to become involved in this project. 今でも雇用者側にはこのプロジェクトに関わることにいくらかためらいがある
▶ **reluctantly** ◇We *reluctantly* agreed to go with her. 私たちは彼女と一緒に行くことにいやいや同意した
unwilling （するのを拒んで）…したがらない、…するのをしぶる；（強制されて）いやいや[不本意]ながらの ◇They are *unwilling* to invest any more money in the project. 彼らはこれ以上その事業に投資するのをしぶっている ◇He became the *unwilling* object of her affection. 彼は不本意にも彼女の愛情の対象になった 反意 **willing (HELPFUL)**
▶ **unwillingly** ◇*Unwillingly* she raised her eyes to his. 彼女はいやいや彼の目を見上げた
▶ **unwillingness** 名 [U, 単数で] ◇the government's *unwillingness* to reform 政府が改革をしぶること
grudging [ふつう名詞の前で] 不本意に与えられる[行われる]、いやいやながらの ◇There was *grudging* admiration in his voice. 彼の声にはいやいや賞賛している響きがあった
▶ **grudgingly** ◇She *grudgingly* admitted that I was right. 私が正しいと彼女はしぶしぶ認めた

remain 動

remain・keep・stay・last・continue・be left・linger・live・stand
ずっと同じ状態にいることを表す
【類語訳】（…の）ままでいる、（…で）あり続ける、継続する、持ちこたえる、留まる、残っている、残存している、生き長らえる

文型&コロケーション
▶ to linger/ live **on**
▶ to remain/ keep/ stay **awake/ calm/ cheerful/ cool/ dry/ fine/ healthy/ quiet/ silent**
▶ to remain/ stay **alert/ alive/ asleep/ loyal/ safe/ the same/ a secret/ shut/ sober/ upright**
▶ to keep/ stay **close/ still/ warm**
▶ sb's **memory** remains/ lingers/ lives (on)

remain [自, 他]《進行形はまれ》《フォーマル》（…の）ままでいる；残っている ◇For a long time he *remained* motionless. 彼は長いこと動かないままでいた ◇Train fares are likely to *remain* unchanged. 鉄道運賃は改定されない見通しだ ◇It *remains* true that sport is about competing well, not winning. スポーツは勝つことではなく堂々と競うことだということに変わりはない ◇In spite of their quarrel, they *remain* the best of friends. いさかいがあっても彼らはずっと無二の親友である ◇Very little of the house *remained* after the fire. 火事でその家はほとんど跡形もなかった ◇There were only ten minutes *remaining*. 残っている時間は10分しかなかった ◇Much *remains* to be done. やるべきことがたくさん残っている ◇I feel sorry for her, but **the fact remains (that)** she lied to us. 彼女には同情するが、彼女が我々に嘘をついたという事実は残ったままだ ◇**It remains to be seen** (= it will only be known later) whether you are right. あなたが正しいかどうかはまだわからない ◇**There remained** one significant problem. 一つの重大な問題が残ったままだった ☞ re-main (STAY 1)
keep [自, 他]（…で）あり続ける、あり続けさせる ◇We huddled together to *keep* warm. 我々は寒くならないように身を寄せ合った ◇The notice said '*Keep* off (= Do not walk on) the grass'. 看板には「芝生に入るべからず」と書いてあった ◇She *kept* the children amused for hours. 彼女は子どもたちを何時間も楽しませた ◇He *kept* his coat on. 彼はコートを着たままだった ◇Don't *keep us in suspense* — what happened next? もったいぶらないで — で、その後どうなったの ◇She had trouble *keeping her balance*. 彼女はバランスを保つのに苦労した ◇I'm very sorry to *keep you waiting*. お待たせしていて大変恐縮です
stay [自, 他]（…の）ままでいる ◇I can't *stay* awake any longer. これ以上眠らずにはいられない ◇Inflation *stayed* below 4% last month. インフレ率は先月は4%以下にとどまった ◇The store *stays* open until late on Thursdays. その店は毎週木曜日には遅くまで開いている ◇I don't know why they *stay* together (= remain married or in a relationship). 彼らがどうして別れずにいるのかわからない ◇We promised to *stay* friends for ever. 私たちは永遠に友達でいようねと約束した ❶ この意味では stay は remain よりインフォーマルで、日常会話で用いられる。stay は明らかに関連した形容詞を後ろに従えることが多い。◆ to *stay* awake/alive/afloat/cool/healthy/dry/sober/calm/

sane/constant/faithful/alert（目が覚めて/生きて/浮かんで/冷静で/健全で/ぬれないで/しらふで/平静で/正気で/変わらないで/忠実で/警戒している）．☞ **stay** (STAY 1)

last ［自，他］《進行形なし》続く，継続する，持ちこたえる ◇This weather won't *last*. この天気は長持ちしないだろう ◇He's making a big effort now, and I hope it *lasts*. 彼は今大いに努力しているところで，私としては長続きしてほしい ◇These shoes should *last* you till next year. この靴なら来年まで持つはずだ

continue ［自］《ややフォーマル，特に書き言葉》（職・地位に）留まる ◇I want you to *continue* as project manager. プロジェクト管理者として引き続き任務に当たってほしい ◇She will *continue* in her present job until a replacement can be found. 彼女は代わりの人が見つかるまで今の仕事に留まるだろう

be left ［他，受身で］（使われず・売れずに）残っている，残存している ◇Is there any coffee *left*? コーヒーは残ってるかい ◇How many tickets do you have *left*? チケットは何枚残っていますか ◇They are fighting to save what *is left* of their business. 《比喩的》彼らは残された仕事を人がいなくてもいいように奮闘している ◇The only course of action *left to* me was to notify her employer. 私にできることと言えば，彼女の雇用主に知らせることだけだった

linger ［自］《書き言葉》なかなかなくならない，長引く ◇The faint smell of her perfume *lingered* in the room. 彼女の香水のかすかな匂いが部屋に残っていた ◇The civil war *lingered* on well into the 1930s. 内戦は優に1930年代まで長引いた

live ［自］《副詞や前置詞と共に》《特に書き言葉》生き続ける ◇She died ten years ago but her memory *lives* on. 彼女は10年前に亡くなったが，その思い出は生き続けている ◇Her words have *lived with* me all my life. 彼女の言葉は私の中で終生生き続けてきた ❶この意味では live in my/our/their heart(s)/mind(s)/memory のような表現，または特に大変長期にわたる表現の方が従うことが多い
◆to *live* (on) for decades/many years/all my life/the rest of my life（何十年も/多年にわたって/終生/一生生き続ける）.

stand ［自］（依然として）有効である ◇My offer still *stands*. 私の申し出はまだ有効です ◇The world record *stood* for 20 years. その世界記録は20年間破られなかった

remains ［名］

remains・ruin・debris・wreckage・rubble・wreck
破壊された［ひどい損害を受けた］物の残った部分を表す
【類語訳】遺物，遺跡，残骸，廃墟，破片，がれき，難破船

〘文型&コロケーション〙
▶ the remains/ ruins/ wreckage/ wreck **of** a building/ vehicle, etc.
▶ the debris/ rubble **from** a building, etc.
▶ **in/ amid/ among/ amongst** the remains/ ruins/ debris/ wreckage/ rubble
▶ **ancient/ Roman** remains/ ruins
▶ to **reduce** sth to ruins/ rubble
▶ to **clear (away)** the debris/ wreckage/ rubble
▶ to **be trapped in** the wreckage/ the rubble/ a wreck
▶ to **sift through** remains/ debris/ wreckage
▶ a **piece/ pile of** debris/ wreckage

remains ［複数で］（古代の物・建物の）遺物，遺跡 ; （物の）

remains, remarkable

残った部分，残骸 ◇The museum has an impressive collection of prehistoric *remains*. その博物館には先史時代の遺物の見事なコレクションがある ◇They have found the *remains* of a Roman settlement on the land. 彼らはその土地でローマ時代の集落の遺跡を発見した ◇The mangled *remains* of a bicycle were sticking out of the windscreen. めちゃくちゃになった自転車の残骸がフロントガラスから突き出ていた

ruin ［C］（または **ruins** 複数で）（建物の）残存部分，廃墟，跡 ◇The old mill is now little more than a *ruin*. その古い工場は今では廃墟にすぎない ◇We visited the *ruins* of a Norman castle. 私たちはノルマン人の城の跡を訪れた ◇Years of fighting have left the area **in ruins**. 何年にもわたる戦いでその地域は荒廃した
▷ **ruined** ［形］ ◇a *ruined* castle 廃墟と化した城

debris ［U］（木材・金属・れんがなどの）破片，残骸 ◇Emergency teams are still clearing the *debris* from the plane crash. 緊急救助隊はまだ飛行機墜落事故の残骸を片づけている ◇A man of 76 was fatally injured by flying *debris* (= a piece of material flying through the air after an explosion). 76歳の男性が（爆発で）飛び散った破片で致命傷を負った

wreckage ［U］（乗り物・建物の）残存部分，残骸 ◇An elderly man was cut from the *wreckage* by firefighters. 一人の年配の男性は消防士によって残骸を切り分けて救出された ◇Pieces of *wreckage* were found several miles away from the scene of the explosion. 残骸のかけらが爆発現場から数マイル離れた所で見つかった

rubble ［U］（建物・壁の）砕けた石［れんが］，がれき ◇A bomb reduced the house next door to *rubble*. 爆弾で隣家は瓦礫と化してしまった

wreck ［C］沈没船，難破船，大破した船 ; （事故で）大破した車［飛行機など］，残骸 ◇A new search of the *wreck* of the Titanic has been launched. 難破したタイタニック号の捜索が新たに始まった ◇She was pulled from the burning *wreck* by firefighters. 彼女は大破して燃えている車の中から消防士によって運び出された ☞ **wreck** (CRASH)

remarkable ［形］☞ AMAZING

remarkable・unique・extraordinary・incredible・exceptional・unbelievable・phenomenal・unusual
注目されるほど非常に優れている［よい，悪い］こと
【類語訳】並外れた，驚くべき，非凡な，際立った，比類ない，途方もない，抜群の，ものすごい，ひどい，すばらしい

unusual	remarkable	unique
	exceptional	extraordinary
		incredible
		unbelievable
		phenomenal

〘文型&コロケーション〙
▶ a remarkable/ an extraordinary/ an incredible/ an exceptional/ an unbelievable/ a phenomenal/ an unusual **amount**
▶ a remarkable/ a unique/ an extraordinary/ an incredible/ an exceptional **achievement**
▶ a remarkable/ a unique/ an extraordinary/ an incredible/ an exceptional/ an unbelievable/ a phenomenal **perform-**

↪remarkable

ance
▶remarkable/ extraordinary/ incredible/ exceptional/ unbelievable/ phenomenal/ unusual **speed**
▶remarkable/ unique/ extraordinary/ incredible/ exceptional/ unbelievable **beauty**
▶remarkable/ extraordinary/ incredible/ exceptional/ phenomenal/ unusual **strength**
▶a unique/ an extraordinary/ an incredible/ an exceptional **opportunity**
▶a remarkable/ an extraordinary/ an incredible/ a phenomenal/ an unusual **success**
▶remarkable/ unique/ extraordinary/ incredible/ exceptional/ unusual **talent/ skill**
▶a remarkable/ an extraordinary/ an incredible/ an exceptional **career**
▶**of** remarkable/ extraordinary/ exceptional/ unusual **quality**
▶**quite** remarkable/ unique/ extraordinary/ incredible/ exceptional/ unbelievable/ phenomenal
▶**really** remarkable/ extraordinary/ incredible/ exceptional/ unbelievable/ phenomenal
▶**just** extraordinary/ incredible/ unbelievable/ phenomenal

remarkable 〖(人々の注目を引くほど)〗並外れた, 驚くべき, 非凡な, 際立った ◇She was a truly *remarkable* woman. 彼女は実に非凡な女性だった ◇The interior of the house was *remarkable for* its beauty. 家の内装がその美しさで際立っていた ◇It was *remarkable that* the body had not been found sooner. 遺体をもっと早くに見つけられなかったのには驚いた ◇What is even more *remarkable* about the whole thing is... そのすべてに関してさらに驚くべきことは… 反意 **unremarkable** (AVERAGE)
▶**remarkably** 副 ◇She looked *remarkably* fit for an eighty-year-old. 彼女は80歳にしては並外れてセクシーに見えた

unique 〖(同種の人・物事とは異なり)〗非常に特殊な, 比類ない, めったにない ◇The museum is of *unique* historical importance. その美術館は歴史的に比類なく重要である ◇I have had a *unique* opportunity to observe the problems faced by the police in this city. この都市の警察が直面している問題を観察するめったにない機会を得た
❶ unique には「その種の中で唯一のものである」という意味もあり, この意味では, very unique, more unique と言うことはできない。「非常に特殊な」という意味では, very unique, more unique と言うえるが, これはかなりインフォーマルに響くこともあり, フォーマルな書き言葉ではよいとは言えない。☞ **unique** (UNIQUE)
▶**uniquely** 副 ◇He was a *uniquely* gifted teacher. 彼は比類ない才能に恵まれた教師だった

extraordinary 普通でない, 並外れた, ;(普通より優れていて[よくて])非凡な ◇They went to *extraordinary* lengths to obtain a copy of the report. 彼らはその報告書のコピーを手に入れるために並々ならぬ努力をした ◇I found an *extraordinary* number of errors in the document. その書類にはけた外れに多いミスが見つかった ◇She is a truly *extraordinary* woman. 彼女は実に非凡な女性だ 反意 **ordinary** (AVERAGE), **ordinary** (NORMAL), ☞ **extraordinary** (SURPRISING)
▶**extraordinarily** 副 ◇She was an *extraordinarily* attractive girl. 彼女は外れて魅力的な少女だった

incredible 〖(インフォーマル)〗すごく大きい[多い, よい], すさまじい, 途方もない ◇The prize money is an *incredible* $6 million. 賞金は600万ドルという途方もないものである ◇The demand for the new product has been quite *incredible*. その新製品の需要はまったくすさまじい状態だ ◇I felt an *incredible* sense of relief. 私はすごい安堵感を覚えた
▶**incredibly** 副 ◇*incredibly* attractive/boring ものすごく魅力的な/退屈な

exceptional 並外れてよい[優れた], 抜群の ◇*Exceptional* students are given free tuition. 並外れて優秀な学生は授業料が無料になります ◇He was a man of *exceptional* personal warmth and charm. 彼は並外れた人間的優しさと魅力を持つ人だった
▶**exceptionally** 副 ◇an *exceptionally* gifted child 抜群の才能に恵まれた子ども

unbelievable 〖(インフォーマル)〗ものすごい；すごく悪い[よい], ひどい, すばらしい ◇The pain was *unbelievable*. 痛みはひどかった ◇I've had three *unbelievable* years with the team. 私はチームとすばらしい3年間を過ごしてきた ◇It's *unbelievable that* (= very shocking) he was allowed to escape. 彼が逃げおおせたなんて実にけしからんことだ
▶**unbelievably** 副 ◇*unbelievably* beautiful/loud/painful ものすごく美しい/うるさい/痛い

phenomenal 非常に優れた[印象的な], 並外れた, ものすごい, 驚くべき ◇There was a *phenomenal* response to the appeal. 呼びかけにはすごい反応があった ◇He has a *phenomenal* memory for facts and figures. 彼は事実と数字の記憶力が並外れていい ◇Exports have been *phenomenal* this year. 今年の輸出額は並外れている ☞ **phenomenon** (MIRACLE)
▶**phenomenally** 副 ◇*phenomenally* successful ものすごく成功した

unusual 〖名詞の前で〗〖(書き言葉)〗並外れて優れた[よい], 驚くような ◇He's a man of *unusual* strength and courage. 彼は並外れた体力と勇気のある人だ ◇The conference has generated an *unusual* degree of interest. その会議は驚くほどの関心を呼んでいる
▶**unusually** 副 ◇an *unusually* talented designer 並外れた才能を持ったデザイナー

> ノート **exceptional** と **unusual** の使い分け：exceptional は unusual より程度が強い。exceptional な人・物事は非常に unusual である。

remember 動

remember・recall・bear sb/sth in mind・look back・recollect・think back・reminisce
事実や出来事を忘れていないことを表す
【類語訳】記憶している, 覚えている, 思い出す, 念頭に置く, 思い起こす

文型&コロケーション
▶to remember/ recall/ bear in mind/ recollect **that**...
▶to remember/ recall/ bear in mind/ recollect **how/ what/ where/ when**...
▶It should be remembered/ borne in mind **that**...
▶to remember/ recall/ bear in mind the **facts**
▶to remember/ recall sb's **name**
▶to **vaguely/ vividly** remember/ recall sth
▶**as far as I can** remember/ recall/ recollect

remember [他, 自]《進行形まれ》(過去の出来事・人・場所のイメージを)記憶している，忘れずにいる；(事実・情報を)覚えている，思い出す；忘れずに…する◇This is Carla. Do you *remember* her? こちらはカーラです．彼女のこと覚えてますか◇I don't *remember* my first day at school. 登校初日のことは覚えていません◇Do you *remember* switching the lights off before we came out? 外に出る前に電気消したっけ◇As far as I can *remember*, this is the third time we've met. 私の記憶ではお会いしたのはこれで3度目ですね◇I'm sorry — I can't *remember* your name. ごめんなさい．お名前が思い出せないのですが◇Can you *remember* how much money we spent? 私たちがいくら使ったか思い出せますか◇You were going to help me with this. *Remember*? これ手伝ってくれるんだったよね．覚えてるかい◇*Remember* that we're going out tonight. 今夜出かけるのを忘れないでね◇It should be *remembered* that the majority of accidents happen in the home. 事故の大半が家庭で起こることを肝に銘じておくべきだ◇*Remember* to call me when you arrive! 着いたら忘れずに電話してね◇Did you *remember* your homework (= to bring it)? 宿題を忘れずに持って来ましたか ❶ remember doing sth と remember to do sth の違いに注意． ◆ I *remember* posting the letter (= I have an image in my memory of doing it). (その手紙を出した記憶がある)． ◆ I *remembered* to post the letter (= I didn't forget to do it). (その手紙を忘れずに出した). [反意]forget (FAIL1), ☞ remembrance (MEMORY)

recall [他, 自]《進行形なし》《フォーマル》(事実・出来事を)思い出す◇She could not *recall* his name. 彼女は彼の名前を思い出せなかった◇I can't *recall* meeting her before. 彼女に以前会った覚えがない◇If I *recall* correctly, he lives in Boston. 記憶に間違いがなければ，彼はボストンに住んでるよ ☞ **recall** (MEMORY)

bear sb/sth in 'mind, bear in 'mind that… [句動]《進行形まれ》(重要な事実を)忘れずにいる，覚えておく，念頭に置く◇*Bear in mind that* money is one of the main causes of marriage break-up. お金が結婚生活の破綻の主因の一つであることを覚えておいてください ◇*Bearing in mind* the rapid population growth of recent years, these figures look optimistic. 近年の急激な人口増を念頭に置くと，これらの数字は見通しが甘いようだ ☞ **mind** (MEMORY)

,look 'back [句動]《進行形まれ》(自分の)過去の(ある時)を振り返る◇When I *look back on* my childhood, it seems as if it was always sunny. 子どもの頃を振り返ると，いつも晴れていたように思われる◇If there's one thing I've learnt from this: never *look back*. 私が学んだことが一つあるとすればこのことです．過去を振り返るな

recollect [他, 自]《進行形なし》《フォーマル》(思い出そうと努力して出来事・事実を)思い出す◇She could no longer *recollect* the details of the letter. 彼女はもはやその手紙の細かいところまでは思い出せなかった◇I *recollect* him saying that it was dangerous. 彼がそれは危険だと言ったことを思い出す◇As far as I can *recollect*, she wasn't there on that occasion. 思い出せる限りでは，彼女はそこにいなかった ☞ **recollection** (MEMORY)

,think 'back [句動]《進行形なし》(過去にあったことを)思い出す，思い起こす，振り返る◇I keep *thinking back to* the day I arrived here. ここに着いた日のことを振り返ってばかりいる◇Lying in bed, she *thought back over* the conversation. 彼女はベッドに横たわってその会話を思い出した

ノート **look back** と **think back** の使い分け：**look back (on)** は，今では過ぎ去った幸せな［悲しい］時を思い出して悲喜こもごもの思いに浸るために，あるいは単に物事がどう変わったかを考えるために，過去のある時を振り返る場合に用いる．**think back (to/over)** は，遠い［近い］過去の出来事に関することに今でも関心があって［悩まされていて］忘れられないために，その出来事を振り返る場合に用いられる．

reminisce [自]《ややフォーマル》(過去の幸せな時について考えて［話して，書いて］)思い出にふける◇We spent a happy evening *reminiscing about* the past. 私たちは過去の思い出にふけりながら楽しい夕べを過ごした ☞ **reminiscence** (MEMORY)

remove [動] ☞ ABOLISH, CUT 1

remove • get rid of sb/sth • eliminate • dispose of sb/sth • discard • dump • throw sth away/out • shed • dispense with sb/sth • scrap
望まない［必要としない］人や物事をいなくする［なくす］ことを表す
【類語訳】取り除く，消す，除去する，なくす，捨てる，排除する，除く，処分する，処理する，投棄する，削減する，廃棄する

文型&コロケーション
▸to remove/ get rid of/ eliminate sth **from** sth
▸to remove/ get rid of/ eliminate/ dispose of/ discard/ dump **waste**
▸to remove/ discard/ dump/ dispose of/ throw away **rubbish/ garbage/ trash**
▸to remove/ get rid of/ dispose of/ dump a **(dead) body**
▸to remove/ get rid of/ eliminate/ dispose of a **problem**
▸to eliminate/ shed/ scrap **jobs**
▸to remove/ discard/ shed your **jacket/ clothes,** etc.
▸to remove/ eliminate/ discard/ dispense with/ scrap sth **altogether**
▸to **entirely** remove/ eliminate/ dispose of/ discard/ dispense with sth
▸to **completely** remove/ eliminate/ discard/ dispense with/ scrap sth
▸to **quickly** remove/ get rid of/ eliminate/ dispose of/ discard/ shed/ dispense with sth
▸to **easily** remove/ eliminate/ dispose of/ discard

remove [他] (物事が不快で［汚い，厄介な］ので)取り除く，消す，除去する◇the best way to *remove* stains しみを取る最善の方法◇She has **had** the tumour *removed*. 彼女は腫瘍を除去してもらった◇A subsequent agreement *removed* the major obstacles to negotiations. その後の協定によって交渉の大きな障害が取り除かれた◇The news *removed* any doubts about the company's future. そのニュースで会社の将来に対するあらゆる疑念が消えた
▸**removal** [名][U] ◇stain *removal* しみ抜き◇the *removal* of trade barriers 貿易障壁の撤廃

get 'rid of sb/sth [フレーズ]《ややフォーマル》(厄介な［望まない］人・物事を)いなくする，なくす，取り除く，捨てる◇Try and *get rid of* your visitors before I get there. 私がそっちへ着く前にお客さんを追い払っておいてね◇*Get rid of* weed seedlings before they grow into plants. 雑草は大きくなる前に抜いてしまってください◇I can't *get rid of* this headache. この頭痛が治まらないのです◇We got rid of all the old furniture. 古い家具は全部捨てました

eliminate [他]《ややフォーマル》(問題となる人・物事を)いなくする, なくす, 除去する, 排除する ◇Credit cards *eliminate* the need to carry a lot of cash. クレジットカードがあれば現金をたくさん持ち歩く必要がなくなる ◇This diet claims to *eliminate* toxins from the body. この食事療法は体から毒素を除去するという触れ込みだ ◇They attempted to *eliminate* him as a political rival. 彼らは彼を政敵として排除しようとした

> ノート **eliminate**と**get rid of sb/sth**の使い分け: これら2つの表現の主な違いは使用域である。**get rid of sb/sth**はふつう, よりインフォーマルで私的な文脈で用いられる。**eliminate**はややフォーマルで, 物理的に物を捨てることについては用いられない。×We *eliminated* the old furniture. 人について用いる場合, **get rid of**は人を去らせることを表す。**eliminate a person as sth**は強制的にある役割をやめさせることを表す。単に**eliminate sb**の場合は殺害することを表す。☞ **eliminate** (KILL)

▷ **elimination** [名] [U] ◇the *elimination* of disease/poverty/crime 病気/貧困/犯罪の除去

dispose of sb/sth [句動]《ややフォーマル》(望まない「維持できない」人・物事を)除く, 処分する, 処理する ◇the difficulties of *disposing of* nuclear waste 核廃棄物の処理の問題点 ◇Markets such as these are often used by thieves to *dispose of* stolen property. このような市場は窃盗犯が盗品の処分に使うことが多い

▷ **disposal** [名] [U] ◇a bomb *disposal* squad 爆弾処理班 ◇sewage *disposal* systems 下水処理システム

discard [他]《フォーマル》(望まない[必要としない])物事を)捨てる, 処分する ◇The floor was littered with *discarded* newspapers. 床には打ち捨てられた新聞が散らかっていた ◇He had *discarded* his jacket because of the heat. 彼は暑くて上着を脱ぎ捨てていた ◇Most of the data was *discarded* as unreliable. データのほとんどが信頼できないとして処分された

dump [他, 自]《ややインフォーマル, けなして》(適当ではない場所にいらない物を)捨てる, 投棄する ◇Too much toxic waste is being *dumped* at sea. あまりにも多くの有毒廃棄物が海に投棄されている ◇The dead body was *dumped* by the roadside. 死体は道端に投げ捨てられていた ◇Any vessel *dumping* at sea without a licence will be prosecuted. 無許可で海に投棄すれば, どの船舶も起訴されます

,throw sth a'way/'out [句動] (いらない物をごみ箱に入れて)捨てる ◇I don't need that — you can *throw* it *away*. それはいらない。捨てていいよ ◇The fish was off — I had to *throw* it *out*. その魚は腐っていて, 捨てなくてはならなかった

shed [他]《ややインフォーマル, 特にジャーナリズム》(どうなってもいい場合にいらない物事を)取り除く, なくす, 削減する ◇The defence industry is in decline and *shedding* jobs. 軍需産業は衰退しており, 雇用削減が進んでいる ◇It's a quick way to *shed pounds* (= lose extra weight or fat on your body) but it won't make you healthier. それは減量するには手っ取り早い方法だが, 健康によくないだろう ◇Museums have been trying hard to *shed* their stuffy image. 美術館は堅苦しいイメージを払拭しようと懸命に努力してきた ◇Her mother had *shed* ten years since her marriage to Douglas (= looked ten years younger). 彼女の母はダグラスと結婚してから10歳若返った ❶この意味では, **shed**はふつうweight, pounds, jobs, staff, workers, employees, image, responsibility, bur-

den, yearsと結びつく。

di'spense with sb/sth [句動]《フォーマル》(必要でないために人・物事を)使うのをやめる, …なしで済ませる ◇Debit cards *dispense with* the need for cash altogether. デビットカードがあればまったく現金なしで済む ◇The company now has no choice but to *dispense with his services* (= to fire him). 会社はもはや彼を解雇するしかない ◇I think we can *dispense with the formalities* (= speak openly and naturally with each other). 堅苦しい物の言い方はやめましょうよ

scrap (-pp-) [他, しばしば受身で] (役に立たない乗り物・機械などを)処分する, 廃棄する ◇The oldest of the aircraft should be *scrapped*. 最も古い航空機は廃棄すべきである ☞ **scrap** (WASTE)

repair [動]

repair・fix・mend・overhaul・patch・darn
再びよい状態になる[正しく機能する]ように損傷した[破れた, 壊れた]物に手を施すことを表す
【類語訳】直す, 修繕する, 修復する, 修理する, 整備する, オーバーホールする, 継ぎを当てる, 繕う

文型&コロケーション
▶ to repair/ fix/ mend a **road/ fence/ roof/ bike/ puncture**
▶ to repair/ fix/ overhaul an **engine**
▶ to repair/ fix a **car/ television/ fault/ defect/ leak**
▶ to repair/ fix the **heating/ damage**
▶ to repair/ mend/ patch **shoes/ clothes**
▶ to **have/ get** sth repaired/ fixed/ mended/ overhauled

repair [他] (物を)直す, 修繕する, 修復する ◇We'll need to get someone to *repair* the roof. 誰かに屋根を修繕してもらわなければならない ◇The damage to the ship had been *repaired*. 船の損傷は修復されていた ◇Are you going to get the television *repaired*? テレビを直してもらうつもりかい ◇The human body has an amazing capacity to *repair* itself. 人体には驚くべき自己修復能力がある ☞ **repair** (STATE)

fix [他] (物を)直す, 修理する ◇I had to take the car into the garage to get it *fixed*. 自動車修理工場に車を持って行って修理してもらわなければならなかった ◇We're not moving in until the heating's *fixed*. 私たちは暖房装置が直るまで入居しません ◇Mommy, can you *fix* my toy? ママ, 僕のおもちゃ直して

> ノート **repair**と**fix**の使い分け:《英》では, **repair**は最も一般的な語。**fix**は少しインフォーマルで, 特に機械や装置の修理について用いられる。《米》では, **fix**は最も普通の語で, 壊れた[損傷した]どんな物でもその修理について用いられ, **repair**はややフォーマルな響きがある。

mend [他]《特に英》(物を)直す, 修繕する ◇He *mended* shoes for a living. 彼は靴の修繕で生計を立てていた ◇Could you *mend* my bike? 《英》私の自転車を直してもらえますか ❶《米》では, **mend**は修繕が必要な衣類や装身具などにしか用いられない。

overhaul [他] (機械・システムを)整備する, オーバーホールする ◇The engine has been completely *overhauled*. エンジンは完全にオーバーホールされた ◇The company was called in to *overhaul* the railroad system. その会社は鉄道網を整備するために呼ばれた

patch [他] (布地などの素材で)継ぎを当てる, 修繕する

◇He was wearing *patched* jeans. 彼は継ぎの当たったジーンズをはいていた ◇We need to *patch* that hole in the roof. 屋根のその穴を修繕する必要がある ❶ **patch sth up** は,特に一時的に新たな素材を足して物を直すことを言う.
◆Just to *patch* the boat *up* will cost £10,000. (ボートの応急修理だけで1万ポンドかかります). **patch sb up** は,特に迅速[一時的]に人のけがを治療することを指す. ◆The doctor will soon *patch* you *up*. (医師がすぐに応急手当をしてくれます).

darn [他, 自] (針で縫い合わせて衣類に空いた穴を)繕う
◇He was sitting *darning* his socks. 彼は腰かけて靴下を繕っていた

repeat [動]

repeat・echo・reiterate・restate
もう一度[二度以上]言う[書く]ことを表す
【類語訳】繰り返し書く,繰り返し言う,言い直す

【文型&コロケーション】
▶to repeat/ reiterate/ restate that...
▶to repeat/ echo/ reiterate a **warning**/ **sentiment**
▶to repeat/ reiterate a **request**
▶to reiterate/ restate your **commitment**/ **support**/ **opposition**
▶to **merely**/ **simply** repeat/ echo/ reiterate/ restate sth

repeat [他] もう一度言う[書く], 二度以上言う[書く], 繰り返し言う[書く] ◇I'm sorry — could you *repeat* that? すみません. もう一度言ってもらえませんか ◇She kept *repeating* his name softly over and over again. 彼女は優しい口調で彼の名前を何度も繰り返し言った ◇The president's opponents have been *repeating* their calls for his resignation. 大統領に敵対する人たちが辞任を繰り返し求めてきている ◇Do say if I'm *repeating myself* (= if I have already said this). 私が同じことを繰り返していたら言ってくださいね ☞ **repeat** (CONVEY), **go over sth** (PRACTISE)
▶**repetition** [名] [U, C] ◇learning by *repetition* 反復学習

echo [他] 《特に書き言葉》(考え・意見を)繰り返し述べる;(驚いて相手の言葉を)繰り返し言う ◇This is a view *echoed* by many on the right of the party. これは党の右派に属する多くの人が繰り返し述べる見解だ ◇'He's gone!' Viv *echoed* incredulously. 「彼はもういないんだって」と, ヴィヴは信じられないといった様子で繰り返し言った
▶**echo** [名] [C] ◇The speech *found an echo* in the hearts of many of the audience (= they agreed with it). 演説は聴衆の多くの共感を得た

reiterate [他] 《フォーマル》(強調のためすでに言ったことを)繰り返し述べる ◇The government has *reiterated* its commitment to economic reform. 政府は経済改革を断行する約束を繰り返し述べた ◇Let me *reiterate* that we are fully committed to this policy. 我々がこの政策に全力で取り組んでいることを改めて述べさせていただきたい ❶ **reiterate** の目的語には, commitment, support, willingness, determination, opposition などがある.
▶**reiteration** [名] [単数で, U] ◇a *reiteration* of her previous statement 彼女の以前の発言の繰り返し

restate [他] 《フォーマル》(もっとはっきり[強く]示すために)再び述べる, 言い直す ◇They *restated* their belief in the existence of a 'hidden agenda'. 彼らは「裏の動機

があるとの思いを再び述べた ❶ **restate** の目的語には一般に beliefs, commitment, intentions, opposition, support がある.

replace [動]

1 replace・stand in for sb/sth・fill in for sb/sth・substitute for sb/sth・cover for sb・deputize・relieve
特定の役割を交代したり, 特定の状況で入れ替わったりすること
【類語訳】取って代わる, 後任となる, 代わりをする, 代用となる, 代理をする, 代わる, 交替する

【文型&コロケーション】
▶to stand in/ fill in/ substitute/ cover/ deputize **for** sb
▶to stand in/ fill in/ cover for a **colleague**

replace [他] (人・物事に)取って代わる, (人の)後任[後継者]となる ◇The new design will eventually *replace* all existing models. 新しいデザインが最終的にはすべての現行モデルに取って代わるでしょう ◇Teachers will never be *replaced* by computers in the classroom. 教室では教師がコンピュータに取って代わられることは決してないだろう ◇She *replaced* her husband as the local doctor. 彼女は地元の医師として夫の後を継いだ

ˌstand ˈin for sb/sth [句動詞] (重要な[有名な]人・物事の)代わりをする, 代理[代役]を務める, 代用となる ◇My assistant will *stand in for* me while I'm away. 私が不在の間は助手が代理を務めます ◇The scenes were filmed in North Wales, which had to *stand in for* the North West Frontier. それらのシーンのロケ地は北ウェールズであったが, やむをえず(パキスタンの)ノースウエスト・フロンティア(州)の代わりとしたものだった

ˌfill ˈin for sb/sth [句動詞] 《特に米》(人・物事の)代わりをする, 代理[代役]を務める, 代用となる ◇He called me one Saturday morning and asked me to *fill in for* him. 彼からある土曜の朝に電話があって, 代役を務めるように頼まれた ◇Most of the locations *filling in for* Venezuela are really in the United States. ベネズエラの代わりとなるロケ地のほとんどが実際には米国内にある

【ノート】**stand in for sb/sth** と **fill in for sb/sth** の使い分け:この二つの句動詞は同じように用いられるが, **stand in for sb/sth** は《英》で多く用いられ, **fill in for sb/sth** は《米》で多く用いられる.

substitute for sb/sth [句動詞] 《ややフォーマル》(人・物事の)代わりをする, 代理を務める ◇Nothing can *substitute for* the advice your doctor is able to give you. 担当医師にもらえる助言に代わるものはない ◇One of her colleagues agreed to *substitute for* her at the last minute. 彼女の同僚の一人がぎりぎりになって彼女の代理を務めることに同意した ☞ **substitution** (EXCHANGE)

cover for sb [句動詞] (不在の人の)代わりに仕事をする, 代理をする ◇I'm *covering for* Jane while she's on leave. ジェーンが休暇の間は私が彼女の代理をします ◇You may be asked to *cover for* employees who are off sick. 病気欠勤の従業員の代わりをあなたが頼まれるかもしれません

【ノート】**stand in for sb/sth, fill in for sb/sth, cover for sb** の使い分け:**cover for** は, 職場の同僚, 特に自分と同様の仕事をしている同じ地位の人の代わりをすることを

表す。stand/fill in forは、組織で自分より上位の人、自分より有名で人気のある俳優や演奏者などの代わりをすることを表す。cover for sbの場合、その人のために代わってやると見なされ、stand/fill in for sbの場合、代わりの人は次善の人と見なされることが多い。

deputize (英でまた **-ise**) [自] [フォーマル] (自分より地位の高い人の)代理を務める ◇**Ms Green has asked me to** *deputize* **for her at the meeting.** グリーン女史から会議で代理を務めるよう依頼されている

relieve [他] (勤務中の人と)代わる、交替する ◇**to** *relieve* **a driver/sentry** 運転手/歩哨と交替する ◇**You'll be** *relieved* **at 6 o'clock.** あなたは6時に交替になります

2 replace・switch・change・exchange・substitute・swap・trade・reverse・barter
一方を取り除いて代わりに他方を置くことを表す
【類義訳】取り替える、交換する、入れ替える、替える、両替する、代用する、交替する、物々交換する

▶ to switch/ change/ exchange/ substitute/ swap/ trade/ barter A **for** B
▶ to replace/ substitute/ switch B **with** A
▶ to switch/ exchange/ swap/ reverse A **and** B
▶ to replace/ change a **battery/ bulb/ fuse/ tyre/ wheel**
▶ to switch/ exchange/ swap/ reverse **roles**
▶ to change/ exchange/ swap/ trade **places**
▶ to change/ swap **seats/ clothes**
▶ to exchange/ swap/ trade **stories/ jokes**
▶ to exchange/ swap **experiences/ news/ phone numbers**
▶ to exchange/ trade **insults**
▶ to **simply** replace/ switch/ change/ exchange/ substitute/ reverse sth
▶ to **easily** replace/ switch/ change/ substitute/ swap sth

replace [他] 《ややフォーマル》 (人・物事を)取り替える、交換する ◇**He will be difficult to** *replace* **when he leaves.** 彼が辞めた後任を置くのは難しいだろう ◇**All the old carpets need** *replacing*. 古いカーペットは全部取り替える必要がある ◇**She had an operation to** *replace* **both hips.** 彼女は両(人工)股関節の置換手術を受けた ☞ **replacement (EXCHANGE)**

switch [他] 《ややインフォーマル》 (物事を)取り替える、入れ替える ◇**The dates of the last two exams have been** *switched*. 最後の二つの試験の日付が入れ替わった ◇**Do you think she'll notice if I** *switch* **my glass with hers?** 私のグラスと彼女のグラスを取り替えたら、彼女は気づくと思いますか ◇**I see you've** *switched* **the furniture** *around* (= changed its position). 家具の配置を変えたでしょう

change [他] (物事・人・サービスを)交換する、替える、変える;(立場・場所を)交換する、替わる ◇**Marie** *changed* **her name when she got married.** マリーは結婚して名前が変わった ◇**That back tyre needs** *changing*. その後ろタイヤは交換する必要がある ◇**At half-time the teams** *change* **ends.** ハーフタイムになると両チームはサイドチェンジをする ◇**Can I** *change* **seats with you?** 座席を替わっていただけますか ◇**I want to** *change* **my doctor.** 医者を替えようと思ってるんだ ❶同種のものよりよいものを得るために替えることについて言う場合、《米》で普通の語はexchangeである。これ

は《英》ではややフォーマルな響きがある。◆**We** *changed* **the car for a bigger one.**(《英》車をもっと大きな物に替えた)。◆**We** *exchanged* **the car for a bigger one.**(《米》車をもっと大きな物に替えた)。

exchange [他] (同種の物事を)交換する、交わす;(持っている物を)交換する、両替する ◇**We use the forum to** *exchange* **ideas.** 私たちはフォーラムを利用して意見を交換します ◇**I shook hands and** *exchanged* **a few words with the manager.** 支配人と握手をして言葉を二言三言交わした ◇**Juliet and David** *exchanged glances* (= they looked at each other). ジュリエットとデイヴィッドは視線を交わした ◇**The two men** *exchanged blows* (= hit each other). その二人の男は殴り合った ◇**You can** *exchange* **your currency for dollars in the hotel.** ホテルで通貨をドルに両替できます ◇**If it doesn't fit, take it back and the store will** *exchange* **it.** サイズが合わない場合、返品すれば店は交換してくれます ☞ **exchange (EXCHANGE), exchange (DISCUSSION)**

substitute [他] (人・物事を)代わりに使う、代用する、交替する ◇**Margarine can be** *substituted* **for butter in this recipe.** このレシピではバターの代わりにマーガリンも使えます ◇**Butter can be** *substituted* **with margarine in this recipe.** このレシピではバターをマーガリンで代用できます ◇**Gerrard was** *substituted* **in the second half after a knee injury** (= sb else played instead of Gerrard in the second half). ジェラードは膝をけがして後半交替した ❶ substitute A for Bとも substitute B with Aとも言える。どちらの場合も、BのためにAを使うことを表す。また、単に substitute sthとも言えるが、この場合は「物事」が何かの代わりに使われるのか、何かに取って代わるのかが文脈からはっきりわかるようにする必要がある。☞ **substitution (EXCHANGE)**

swap (または **swop**) (**-pp-**) [自、他] (人・物事を)交換する、取り替える、交わす ◇**I've finished this magazine. Can I** *swap* **with you?** この雑誌は読み終わった。君のと交換してくれないか ◇**I** *swapped* **my red scarf for her blue one.** 私の赤いスカーフと彼女の青いスカーフを交換した ◇**We spent the evening in the bar** *swapping* **stories** (= telling each other stories) **about our travels.** 私たちはバーでお互いの旅の話をしながら夕べを過ごした ◇**Can we** *swap* **places? I can't see the screen.**《特に英》場所を替わってもらえるかな。スクリーンが見えないんだ ❶特に《英》では、swapは持っている物を与えて[返して]代わりに別の[よりよい]物を手に入れることも表せる。◆**I think I'll** *swap* **this sweater for one in another colour.**(このセーターを別の色の物と交換しようと思う)。☞ **swap (EXCHANGE)**

trade [他] 《特に米 or ジャーナリズム》(人・物事を)交換する ◇**She** *traded* **her posters for his CD.** 彼女はポスターを彼のCDと交換した ◇**I wouldn't mind** *trading* **places with her for a day.** 彼女と一日入れ替わっても構いません ◇**Cabinet colleagues** *traded* **insults over the future of the pound.** 閣僚たちはポンドの将来をめぐってののしり合った

ノート switch, exchange, swap, trade の使い分け: switchは頼みもせずに[知らないうちに]、ある物が別の物と取り替えられる場合に用いられることが多い。◆**The two babies had been** *switched* **at birth.**(二人の赤ん坊は生まれたときに取り違えられていた)。×**The two babies had been** *exchanged/swapped/traded* **at birth.** exchangeはswapやtradeよりフォーマルで、互いに見たり話したりする場合の定型句で用いられることが多い。◆**to** *exchange* **glances/a few words**(視線/言葉を二言三言

replacement, report

交わす). ×to swap/trade glances/a few words. また, exchange information/ideas (情報/意見を交換する) とも言える. swapは, swap stories/jokes (話/冗談を交わす) とも言えるが, 物質的な物により多く用いる. tradeは,《米》では物や品物（立場・場所), stories (話), jokes (冗談), insults (侮辱) に用いられるが,《英》では物質的な物ではなく, 主にstories, jokes, insultsだけに用いられる.《英》ではchange/swap placesと言う.

reverse [他]（立場・役割を）交換する, 逆転させる　◇It felt as if we had *reversed* our roles of parent and child. 私たちはまるで親と子の立場が逆転したような感じだった　◇She used to work for me, but our situations are now *reversed*. 昔は彼女が私の下で働いていたが, 今では状況が逆転している　❶この意味では, reverseはroles, situations, positionsと結びつく. ☞ **reversal** (EXCHANGE)

barter [他, 自]（商品・財産・サービスを）交換する, 物々交換する, 交換取引をする　◇The local people *bartered* wheat for farm machinery. 地元民は小麦を農業機械と物々交換した　◇The prisoners tried to *barter* with the guards for items like writing paper and books. 囚人たちは看守と物々交換して便箋や本のような品物を手に入れようとした ☞ **barter** (EXCHANGE)

replacement [名]

▸ replacement・substitute・reserve・surrogate・relief・understudy・stand-in・cover・proxy
ふだん使う「持つ」代わりの人や物
【類語訳】後任, 代用品, 控え選手, 交替要員, 代役, 代理

[文型&コロケーション]

▸ a replacement/ a substitute/ a surrogate/ an understudy/ a stand-in/ cover/ a proxy/ a stopgap **for** sb/ sth
▸ (an) **adequate** replacement/ substitute/ stand-in/ cover
▸ a/ an **good/ satisfactory/ appropriate/ suitable/ likely/ possible/ ideal/ poor** replacement/ substitute
▸ to **act as** a replacement/ a substitute/ surrogate/ understudy/ stand-in/ proxy
▸ to **get** a replacement/ a substitute/ cover
▸ to **appoint** a replacement/ substitute/ proxy
▸ to **go on as/ use sth as** a replacement/ substitute

replacement [C]《しばしば形容詞として》（古い/壊れた）物の代わりになる物；（仕事/組織内）での代わりの人, 後任（者）　◇a hip *replacement*（人工）股関節置換　◇*replacement* windows 交換窓　◇If your passport is stolen you should apply for a *replacement* immediately. パスポートを盗られたら, すぐに代わりのパスポートを申請すべきです　◇We need to find a *replacement* for Sue. 我々はスーの後任を見つける必要があります ☞ **replacement** (EXCHANGE)

substitute [C]（人・物の）代わりの人[物], 代用品；（スポーツなどの）控えの選手, 交替選手　◇a meat/milk *substitute* 肉の代用品/代用乳　◇The book will teach you the theory but **there's no substitute for** practical experience. 本理論は教えてくれるだろうが, 実際の経験に代わるものはない　◇The local bus service was a poor *substitute* for their car. 地元バスの運行状況は車の代わりにしてはお粗末だった　◇I regarded them as a *substitute* family. 私は彼らのことを家族の代わりと見なした　◇He was brought on as a *substitute* after half-time 彼はハーフ

タイム過ぎに交替選手として出場した　❶インフォーマルな言葉では, スポーツのsubstituteはsubとも言える. ☞ **substitution** (EXCHANGE)

reserve [C]《特に英》（スポーツの）控え選手　◇The team consists of three competitors plus one *reserve*. チームは3人の出場選手と1人の控え選手から成る　❶the reserves [複数名詞]《特に英》の場合は, 通常の出場選手ではなく必要な時にはプレーする控えチームを指す. the reserve [単数名詞]/the reserves [複数名詞]（《英》・《米》）は国の正規軍に含まれないが, 必要な時には出動できる控えの軍隊[警官隊]を指す.　◆The missile landed on a US army *reserve* barracks.（ミサイルは米国陸軍の予備軍の兵舎に着弾した).

surrogate [C]《しばしば形容詞として》《ややフォーマル》（人・物に（の）代わる人[物], 代用品　◇She saw him as a sort of *surrogate* father. 彼女は彼を父親代わりのような人と見なしていた　◇For these people, television is a *surrogate* for real life. この人たちにとってテレビは実生活の代わりとなるものである　❶日常英語では, surrogateは実の親の代わりをする人について用いられることが最も多い. しかし, surrogate motherはふつう自分で子を産めない他の女性のために実際に子どもを産む女性（代理母）である. surrogateが物事に用いられる場合, substituteよりフォーマルな言い方である.

relief [C＋単数・複数動詞]《しばしば形容詞として》（人・グループ）の交替要員[班]　◇The next crew *relief* comes on duty at 9 o'clock. 次の交替の乗組員は9時に勤務に就きます　◇We have a pool of *relief* drivers available to us. 私どもには動員できるドライバーの交替要員がそろっております

understudy [C]（俳優の）代役, アンダースタディー　◇She worked as an ***understudy** to* Elaine Page. 彼女はエレイン・ペイジの代役を務めた

'stand-in [C]《ややインフォーマル》（仕事の）代理；（映画の危険なシーンでの俳優の）代役　◇I acted as Tom's *stand-in* when he was away. 私はトムが不在の時にトムの代役を務めた　◇Most of the stunts are performed by *stand-ins*. スタントのほとんどは代役がこなします

cover [U]（不在[人手不足]の時に仕事の）代わりをすること　◇It's the manager's job to organize *cover* for employees who are absent. 欠勤の従業員の代わりを手配するのは管理職の務めである

proxy [C, U]《フォーマル or 法律》（権限を与えられた）代理人　◇Your *proxy* will need to sign the form on your behalf. あなたの代わりに代理人がその用紙に署名する必要があるでしょう

report [名]

1 report・study・investigation・review・survey
特定の状況や問題を調査した人[グループ]が作成する公式文書
【類語訳】調査, 研究, 調査報告, 概説

[文型&コロケーション]

▸ a report/ an investigation/ a survey **into** sth
▸ a report/ a study/ an investigation/ a review/ a survey **by** sb
▸ a/ an **new/ recent/ important/ major/ comprehensive/ wide-ranging/ extensive** report/ study/ investigation/ review/ survey
▸ the **latest** report/ study/ investigation/ review/ survey
▸ a/ an **government/ official/ public/ independent** report/ study/ investigation/ review/ survey
▸ to **do** a report/ a study/ an investigation/ a review/ a survey

▶ to **undertake** a study/ an investigation/ a review/ a survey
▶ to **order** a report/ a study/ an investigation/ a review
▶ to **commission** a report/ study/ review/ survey
▶ to **call for** a report/ an investigation/ a review
▶ to **publish/ release/ read** a report/ study/ review/ survey
▶ a report/ study/ investigation/ review/ survey **finds/ shows/ reveals/ suggests** sth
▶ a report/ study/ review **calls for/ proposes/ recommends** sth

report [C]（公式の）調査報告書 ◇The committee will publish their *report on* the health service in a few weeks. 委員会は数週間のうちに公共医療サービスに関する調査報告書を発表する予定です ◇We will have to wait until they deliver their *report* before we can come to any conclusions. 彼らが調査報告書を提出するまで待たなければ、いかなる結論も出すこともできません

study [C]（勧告するための）調査, 研究 ◇A recent *study* revealed an unacceptable level of air pollution in the city. 最近の調査でその都市の大気汚染が許容できないレベルであることが明らかになった ◇The company undertook an in-depth *feasibility study* (= a study into whether it is possible and how it could be done) before adopting the new system. その会社は新システムの採用前に徹底的な予備調査を行った ◇A *comparative study* (= a study comparing two things) was carried out into the environmental costs of different energy sources. 異なるエネルギー源の環境コストについて比較研究が行われた ❶ case *study* は, ある期間にわたる人・グループ・状況に関する「事例研究」を指す。☞ **study** (RESEARCH), **study** (EXAMINE)

investigation [C, U]（正式な[学術的な]）調査 ◇The government has ordered an official *investigation* into the matter. 政府はその問題の公式調査を命じた ◇Closer *investigation* showed this idea to be untenable. より綿密な調査でこの考えは批判に耐えられないことが明らかになった ☞ **investigate** (INVESTIGATE)

review [C]（ある問題[一連の出来事]についての）調査報告(書) ◇The first chapter presents a critical *review* of the existing preschool education system. 第1章では, 現在の幼児教育システムについての批判的な調査報告が取り上げられている ❶ *review* は, ある期間の問題や出来事に関して, あらゆる研究や文献を考慮に入れた調査報告書について用いることが多く, 現状やわかったことについて意見を述べるものである。☞ **review** (EXAMINE)

survey [C]（全般的な）調査; 概説 ◇They are carrying out a *survey* of small businesses in London. 彼らはロンドンの中小企業の調査を行っているところだ ☞ **survey** (EXAMINE)

2 ☞ DESCRIPTION
report・story・account・version・commentary・item
出来事の文書[口頭]による説明
【類義語】報告, 情報, 報道, レポート, 記事, ニュース, 実況放送, 実況解説

文型&コロケーション
▶ a report/ a story/ an item **about** sth
▶ a report/ commentary **on** sth
▶ a report/ a story/ an account/ a version/ an item **is based on** sth
▶ a **brief/ short** report/ story/ account/ item

▶ a **full** report/ story/ account/ version/ commentary
▶ a **true/ false/ conflicting** report/ story/ account/ version
▶ a **news** report/ story/ item
▶ the **lead** story/ item in a newspaper
▶ to **give** a report/ an account/ your version/ a commentary

report [C]（文書・口頭による）説明, 報告(書), 情報,（新聞・ニュースなどの）報道, レポート ◇Are these newspaper *reports* true? これらの新聞報道は本当ですか ◇And now over to Jim Muir, for a *report* on the South African election. さて次はジム・ミューアの南アフリカの選挙に関するレポートです ◇I've asked Jen for a full *report* of the meeting. ジェンに会議の詳細な報告書を書くよう頼んだ ◇Police received *reports* of drug dealing in the area. 警察はその地域における麻薬取引の情報をつかんだ ☞ **report** (DESCRIBE)

story [C]（口頭による）説明, 話;（新聞・雑誌の）記事,（放送の）ニュース ◇The police didn't believe her *story*. 警察は彼女の話を信じなかった ◇We must stick to our *story* about the accident. その事故に関する我々の説明を変えないようにしなければならない ◇I can't decide until I've heard **both sides of the story** (= two different people's account of the same event). 双方の話を聞くまでは決められません ◇the front-page/cover *story* 一面/特集記事 ◇Now for a summary of the day's main *stories*. さて次は今日の主なニュースの概要です ◇He was *covering the story* (= reporting on the events) for the 'Glasgow Herald'. 彼は『グラスゴーヘラルド』紙に記事を書いていた ☞ **story** (STORY)

account [C]（文書・口頭による）説明, 話 ◇The diaries contained detailed *accounts* of the writer's experiences in China. 日記にはその作家の中国での経験談が詳細に綴られていた ◇I've never been there, but it's a lovely place **by all accounts** (= according to what people say). そこに行ったことはないが, みんなの話ではすばらしい所だということだ

ノート **report** と **account** の使い分け: report は必ず最近の出来事, 特にニュース性の高いものである。account はその出来事が最近のものの場合も過去のものの場合もある。

version [C]（特定の人・グループの視点からの）説明, 見解 ◇She gave us her *version* of what had happened that day. 彼女はその日あったことについて自分なりの見解を私たちに述べた ◇Their *versions* of how the accident happened conflict. 事故が起きた様子に関する彼らの説明は一致していない

commentary [C, U]（特に英）（ラジオ・テレビの）実況放送[中継], 実況解説 ◇a sports *commentary* on the radio ラジオでのスポーツ実況放送 ◇BBC1 will give a live *commentary* on the election results. BBC第一放送は選挙結果を生で実況中継いたします ◇He kept up a *running commentary* on everyone who came in. 彼は入場者全員の実況解説を続けた ❶（米）ではふつう commentary という語を用いずに他の言い方で表す。◆We'll be bringing you all the action live beginning at 8 o'clock.（8時から完全生放送いたします）。◆We'll have all the play-by-play from the Superbowl.（スーパーボウルをすべて実況放送いたします）。しかし, running commentary は（英）（米）どちらでもよくある結びつきである。

item [C]（新聞・テレビなどの一つの）ニュース, 記事 ◇There was an *item* on the radio about women engineers. ラジオで女性技師に関するニュースがあった

reporter

PRESENTER, WRITER

reporter・journalist・editor・correspondent・columnist・reviewer・contributor・hack
新聞や雑誌の記事を書く仕事をする人を表す
【類語訳】記者、ジャーナリスト、編集長、通信員、コラムニスト、批評家、評論家、寄稿者、ライター

文型&コロケーション
- a **newspaper/ magazine/ news/ sports/ financial** reporter/ journalist/ editor/ correspondent/ columnist
- an **investigative** reporter/ journalist
- to **tell** reporters/ journalists

reporter [C] (新聞・ラジオ・テレビの)記者 ◇I spoke to a *reporter* from the 'New York Times'. 私は『ニューヨークタイムズ』の記者と話をした ◇He's chief *reporter* on the 'Daily Herald'. 彼は『デイリーヘラルド』の主任記者である ☞ **report** (DESCRIBE)

journalist [C] (新聞・雑誌・ラジオ・テレビの)記者、ジャーナリスト ◇He's had more than three decades of experience as a broadcast *journalist*. 彼には放送ジャーナリストとして30年以上の経験がある

ノート reporterとjournalistの使い分け：reporter は、事件の報道のために現場を訪れることが仕事の一部である人について特に用いられる。journalistは、編集者、カメラマン、芸術家、デザイナーなども含めた、ジャーナリズムで働く人に広く用いることができる。

editor [C] (新聞・雑誌の)編集長、編集者 ◇She's the *editor* of a national magazine. 彼女はある全国誌の編集者である ◇the fashion/industrial/economics *editor* ファッション/産業/経済担当編集者
- **edit** [動] [他] ◇She used to *edit* a women's magazine. 彼女はかつて女性誌の編集をしていた

correspondent [C] (定期的に報道するために新聞社・テレビ局・ラジオ局に雇われている)(通信)記者、通信員 ◇She's the BBC's political *correspondent*. 彼女はBBCの政治担当記者である ◇Now, a report from our Hong Kong *correspondent*. さて、香港通信員からのレポートです ◇a foreign/legal *correspondent* 海外特派員/法律担当記者

columnist [C] (特定のテーマについて新聞・雑誌に定期的に記事を書く)コラムニスト ◇The gossip *columnists* ran the story as fact without checking the source. ゴシップ記者たちは情報源をチェックせずにこの記事を実話として掲載した ☞ **column** (ARTICLE)

reviewer [C] (本・映画・演劇の)批評家、評論家 ◇The movie was enthusiastically received by the *reviewers*. その映画は批評家に絶賛された ◇a book *reviewer* for The Guardian 『ガーディアン』紙の書評家 ☞ **review** (ASSESSMENT)

contributor [C] (雑誌・本に記事を書く)寄稿者、(ラジオ・テレビの番組や会議への)発言者 ◇She continues to be a regular *contributor* to the journal. 彼女はその雑誌に定期的に寄稿し続けている
- **contribute** [動] [他, 自] ◇She *contributed* a number of articles to the magazine. 彼女はその雑誌に記事をいくつか寄稿した ◇He *contributes* regularly to the magazine 'New Scientist'. 彼は『ニューサイエンティスト』誌に定期的に寄稿している

hack [C] 《ややインフォーマル、けなして》(質の低い仕事をたくさんこなす新聞記者の)ライター ◇His comments triggered nervous laughter from the assembled tabloid *hacks*. 集まったタブロイド紙のライターの間で彼のコメントに対して不安の混じった笑いが起こった

represent [動]

1 represent・constitute・pose・amount to sth・come down to sth・add up to sth
…と考えられる[…の結果になる]といったことを表す
【類語訳】(…で)ある、(…に)相当する、(…を)もたらす、(…も)同然である、結局…になる

文型&コロケーション
- to represent/ constitute/ pose/ amount to a **challenge/ threat**
- to represent/ constitute/ pose a **problem/ danger/ risk**
- to represent/ constitute/ amount to a/ an **failure/ increase/ breach**
- to represent/ constitute an **achievement/ improvement**
- a/ an **result/ activity/ action** represents/ constitutes sth
- **It all** amounts to/ comes down to/ adds up to sth.

represent [連結動] 《進行形なし》《ややフォーマル、書き言葉》…である、…に相当する；…の結果である ◇This contract *represents* 20% of the company's annual revenue. この契約は会社の年間収入の20%に相当する ◇These results *represent* a major breakthrough in AIDS research. これらの結果はエイズ研究の大躍進を物語るものである ◇The peace plan *represents* (= is the result of) weeks of negotiation. その和平案は何週間にもわたる交渉の産物である

constitute [連結動] 《進行形なし》《フォーマル》…である；…と考えられる ◇Does such an activity *constitute* a criminal offence? そうした活動は犯罪行為になりますか ◇The increase in racial tension *constitutes* a threat to our society. 人種間の緊張の高まりは我々の社会にとって脅威である

ノート representとconstituteの使い分け：represent は特に変化に関連する語と共に用いられる。◆This *represents* a change/a break/a shift/a departure/a turning point/an improvement/an increase/a reduction/a decline. (これは変化/急変/転換/新展開/転機/改善/増加/減少/下落である). constitute は危険な[悪い]状況や行為についてよく用いられる。◆This *constitutes* a threat/danger/crime/breach/nuisance/weakness/refusal. (これは脅威/危険/犯罪/違反/迷惑/弱点/拒絶である).

pose [他] (対処しなければならない問題・脅威)である、…をもたらす ◇The task *poses* no special problems. その作業で特別な問題がもたらされることはない ◇Pollutants in the river *pose* a real risk to the fish. 川の汚染物質は魚にただならぬ危険をもたらす

a'mount to sth [自動詞] [受身なし] [進行形なし] 《ややフォーマル》…に等しい、…も同然である ◇Her answer *amounted to* a complete refusal. 彼女の返事は完全な拒絶に等しかった ◇Their actions *amount to* a breach of contract. 彼らの行動は契約違反も同然である ◇We were jailed for a week — well, confined to quarters, but it *amounted to the same thing*. 我々は1週間投

↪represent / repression

獄された．まあ，部屋に監禁されたんだけど，同じようなものだ ◆This *amounts to* sth は法律違反や犯罪に関して用いられることが多い．◆This *amounts to* dismissal/contempt of court/abuse/discrimination/obstruction/assault. (これは解雇/法廷侮辱罪/虐待/差別/妨害/暴行に等しい)．

,come 'down to sth 句動詞 [受身なし][進行形なし]（ややインフォーマル）結局…(の問題)になる ◇What it *comes down to* is, either I get more money or I leave. 結局のところは，もっとお金をもらうか辞めるかです

,add 'up to sth 句動詞 [受身なし][進行形なし] 結局…になる；…を示す ◇These clues don't really *add up to* very much (= give us very little information). これらの手がかりは結局のところほとんど役に立たない

---

2 represent・embody・symbolize・exemplify・typify・epitomize
一つの例[表現]であることを表す
【類語訳】一例である，象徴する，体現する，代表する，典型である

文型&コロケーション

▶ to be embodied/ exemplified/ typified/ epitomized/ encapsulated **in** sth
▶ to represent/ embody/ symbolize/ epitomize/ encapsulate/ personify the **spirit/ essence** of sth
▶ to represent/ embody/ exemplify/ encapsulate/ personify an **idea/ ideal**
▶ to represent/ embody/ exemplify a **principle**
▶ to exemplify/ typify/ epitomize a/ an **problem/ approach**
▶ to **clearly** represent/ embody/ symbolize/ exemplify/ typify/ encapsulate sth

represent [他，受身なし]（ややフォーマル）（考え・性質・意見の[を]）一例である，表す，象徴する ◇The project *represents* all that is good in the community. そのプロジェクトにはその地域社会のよいところがすべて表れている ◇Those comments do not *represent* the views of us all. それらのコメントは我々全員の意見を反映してはいない ◇The artist uses doves to *represent* peace. その画家は平和の象徴に鳩を使う ☞ **representation** (DESCRIPTION)

embody [他]《進行形まれ》（ややフォーマル）（人が考え・性質・感情を）目に見える形で表す，体現する ◇a politician who *embodied* the hopes of black youth 黒人の若者の希望を体現した政治家 ◇We want to build a national team that *embodies* competitive spirit and skill. 我々は競争心と技術を体現するナショナルチームを作りたい ☞ **embodiment** (EXAMPLE 2)

symbolize [英でまた **-ise**] [他]《進行形まれ》（人・物・性質・出来事・行動がより一般的な性質・状況を）表す，象徴する ◇The use of light and dark *symbolizes* good and evil. 光と闇を使って善と悪を象徴する ◇He came to *symbolize* his country's struggle for independence. 彼は自国の独立を目指す闘争の象徴となった ☞ **symbol** (SIGN 1)

ノート **represent, embody, symbolize** の使い分け：特に人については，これらのどの語を用いてもいい場合がある．◆He came to *represent/embody/symbolize* his country's struggle for independence. (彼は自国の独立を目指す闘争を象徴[体現]するようになった)．**embody** はこれらの語の中で最も物理的か視覚的で，他の人たちの希望の礎になる現実の人について用いられる．**embody** によって表される性質は常によいものである．**symbolize** はより抽象的な場合が多く，平和の概念を表すのに用いられる鳩など，事物に用いることもできるが，この場合は鳩の絵や概念であって，実在する特定の鳩ではない．**represent** はこれらの語の中で最も一般的なもので，**embody** や **symbolize** の意味でも，単に express（表現する）の意味でも用いることができる．◆The comments *represent* the views of the majority. (その発言は大多数の意見を代弁している)．

exemplify [他，しばしば受身で]《進行形まれ》（フォーマル）（物事の[を]）よい例である，典型的に示す ◇Her early work is *exemplified* in her book, 'A Study of Children's Minds'. 彼女の初期の頃の研究はその著書『子どもの心の研究』に典型的に示されている ◇His food *exemplifies* Italian cooking at its best. 彼の料理は最高のイタリア料理の典型だ ☞ **example** (EXAMPLE 2)

typify [他]《進行形まれ》（ややフォーマル）（物事の）典型例である，代表する；（物事の）典型的な特徴である ◇These are clothes that *typify* the 1960s. これらは1960年代の典型的な衣装である ◇There's a new style of politician, *typified* by the Prime Minister. 首相によって代表される，政治家の新しいスタイルがある

epitomize [英でまた **-ise**] [他]《進行形まれ》（ややフォーマル）（物事の）完璧な例である，典型である，まさしく代表する ◇The fighting qualities of the team are *epitomized* by the captain. チームの戦う姿勢はまさしくキャプテンに代表されている ◇These movies seem to *epitomize* the 1950s. これらの映画は1950年代をまさしく代表しているように思える ☞ **epitome** (EXAMPLE 2)

ノート **exemplify, typify, epitomize** の使い分け：**exemplify** は考え・仕事・研究などの典型例を示す場合に用いられる．**typify** は（特に特定の時期・場所の）風潮・スタイル・雰囲気などの典型例を示す場合に用いられる．**epitomize** はこれ以上の典型例が思いつかないことを示唆する．**typify** はより中立的で，ある時期・場所やある種の人・事物がふつう持っている性質・特徴を，示された例がすべて備えていることを示唆する．

---

repression 名

repression・dictatorship・oppression・persecution・tyranny・bullying
権力者による人や集団への無慈悲な[不当な]扱いを表す
【類語訳】弾圧，独裁政権，独裁国家，迫害，横暴さ，専制政治，専制国家，いじめ

文型&コロケーション

▶ repression/ oppression/ persecution **against** sb
▶ to be/ live **under** a dictatorship/ tyranny
▶ **brutal** repression/ dictatorship/ oppression
▶ **political/ religious** repression/ dictatorship/ oppression/ persecution
▶ **state/ police** repression/ oppression/ persecution
▶ to **suffer** repression/ oppression/ persecution/ tyranny
▶ to **face** repression/ oppression/ persecution
▶ to **fight/ protest against** repression/ oppression/ tyranny
▶ to **escape** persecution/ tyranny
▶ to **overthrow** a dictatorship/ tyranny
▶ a **form of** repression/ dictatorship/ oppression/ tyranny/ bullying
▶ a **victim of** repression/ oppression/ persecution/ bullying

repression [U]《ややフォーマル》(集団への)不正な権力の行使, 弾圧 ◇There was a campaign of *repression* against minorities in the north. 北部の少数民族に対する一連の弾圧があった ☞ **repress** (SUPPRESS 1)

dictatorship [C, U] 独裁権[政治]; 独裁国家 ◇They had lived for almost 50 years under a fascist *dictatorship*. 彼らはほぼ50年間ファシズムの独裁政権下で暮らしていた ◇a military *dictatorship* 軍事独裁政権 ◇The commission will investigate the atrocities which took place *during* his *dictatorship*. 委員会は彼の独裁政権下で行われた残虐行為を調査することになる ☞ **dictator** (DICTATOR)

oppression [U]《ややフォーマル》(権利・自由を与えない)無慈悲な[不当な]扱い, 迫害 ◇He spoke out against the *oppression* of women. 彼は女性への迫害に反対の声を上げた ☞ **oppress** (SUPPRESS 1)

persecution [U]《ややフォーマル》(人種・宗教・政治信条を理由とした)無慈悲な[不当な]扱い, 迫害 ◇The organization helps refugees fleeing from *persecution*. その団体は迫害から逃れる難民を支援している ☞ **persecute** (SUPPRESS 1)

> ノート **repression, oppression, persecution** の使い分け: repression は, 特に意見の表明, 自由な行為, 権力者への抗議などができないように自由を制限することによって, 権力者が人々(例えば労働組合や政治的に対立する団体)を支配すること, それに不当に権力を行使することを指す。oppression は, ある人々の集団(例えば女性や特定の人種に属する人々など)が他の人たちと同じ権利や自由を持てなくするために, 不正な権力を行使することを指す。persecution は, 特に人種, 宗教, 政治信条が異なるという理由で, ある人々の集団が他の人たちや権力者から腹立たしいと思われて受ける, 危害や死さえも含めた不当な扱いを指す。

tyranny [U, C] 横暴さ; 専制政治; 専制国家 ◇The children had no protection against the *tyranny* of their father. その子どもたちには横暴な父親から守ってくれる人が誰もいなかった ◇Any political system refusing to allow dissent becomes a *tyranny*. 異議申し立てを認めないどんな政治体制も専制政治になる ☞ **tyrant** (DICTATOR)

bullying [U] (人に嫌がらせを行うための)力[権力]の行使, 横暴さ;(より弱い人を脅かす[傷つける])いじめ ◇He was suspended from his position when several members accused him of *bullying*. 彼は数人のメンバーに横暴さを非難されて停職になった ◇Teenagers talk about their experiences of *playground bullying*. ティーンエイジャーたちは遊び場でのいじめ体験を語りあう

repressive 形

repressive・oppressive・totalitarian・undemocratic・dictatorial・autocratic・tyrannical
人や政府が絶対的権力を持ったり, 人々を不当な形で支配したりすること
【類語訳】弾圧的な, 抑圧的な, 圧制的な, 全体主義の, 非民主的な, 独裁的な, 専制の

文型&コロケーション

▶a repressive/ an oppressive/ a totalitarian/ an undemocratic/ a dictatorial/ an autocratic/ a tyrannical **regime**
▶a repressive/ a totalitarian/ a dictatorial/ an autocratic/ a tyrannical **government**
▶a repressive/ a totalitarian/ an autocratic **state**
▶repressive/ oppressive/ totalitarian/ dictatorial/ autocratic/ tyrannical **power**
▶repressive/ oppressive/ undemocratic/ autocratic/ tyrannical **rule**
▶a repressive/ an oppressive/ a totalitarian/ an autocratic **system/ structure**
▶a repressive/ an oppressive/ a totalitarian **society**
▶the repressive/ oppressive/ undemocratic **nature of** sth

repressive (制度・政府が)弾圧的な, 抑圧的な ◇The government used the incident to justify more *repressive* measures against the unions. 政府はその事件を利用して, これまで以上に抑圧的な組合に対する方策を正当化した

oppressive (権力の座にある人々が)圧制的な, 暴虐な ◇The refugees were fleeing from *oppressive* social and political conditions. 難民たちは圧制的な社会や政治状況から逃れて来ていたのだ

totalitarian (国・政治・団体が)一党独裁主義の, 全体主義の ◇The country was closed to outsiders for many years under a *totalitarian* dictatorship. その国は一党独裁政権下にあって長年, 部外者に門戸を閉ざしていた
▶**totalitarianism** 名 [U] ◇to oppose dictatorship and *totalitarianism* 独裁制と全体主義に反対する

undemocratic (政府・政治行動が)非民主的な ❶ democracyは国民が自分たちの代表を投票で選挙できる統治制度を指す。◆The system is fundamentally *undemocratic*. (その制度は基本的に非民主的である)。◆It is *undemocratic to* govern an area without an electoral mandate. (選挙による権限の付与なしに一定地域を治めるのは非民主的である)。 反意 **democratic** ❶democraticな国・政府・組織・社会・行動は, すべての人々が政治の選択[組織運営など]に関わる同等の権利を有するという原則に基づいている。◆a *democratic* country/government/system/ society (民主国家/政府/制度/社会) ◆a *democratic* decision (民主的な決定)

dictatorial 独裁者の, 独裁的な ◇The military leader gradually assumed more and more *dictatorial* powers. その軍事指導者は徐々に独裁的な権力を掌握するようになった ☞ **dictator** (DICTATOR)

autocratic (制度・政府が)専制の, 独裁的な ◇The measures were seen as evidence of a more *autocratic* style of government. それらの方策はより独裁的な政治スタイルの証拠と見なされた ☞ **autocrat** (DICTATOR)

tyrannical (人・指導者・政府が)専制君主の, 専制の ◇His reputation as a *tyrannical* captain made it hard to find a crew. 船長が横暴だとの評判が立ち, 乗組員を見つけるのが難しくなった ☞ **tyrant** (DICTATOR)

reputation 名 ☞ STATUS

reputation・image・profile・name・honour・stature・character
人や物事について一般大衆が持つ意見
【類語訳】評判, 噂, 名声, 信望, イメージ, 印象, 知名度, 名誉, 面目, 尊敬, 敬意, 威信

文型&コロケーション

▶sb's reputation/ image/ name/ stature **as** sth
▶**by** reputation/ repute
▶**of** considerable reputation/ stature
▶a **bad** reputation/ image/ name

→reputation　　　　　　　　　　　　　　　　request

▶ (an) **international** reputation/ image/ profile/ stature
▶ sb's **professional** reputation/ image/ honour/ stature
▶ to **gain** a reputation/ an image/ a name as/ for sth
▶ to **damage** sb's reputation/ image/ character
▶ to **blacken** sb's reputation/ name/ character
▶ to **protect** sb's reputation/ image/ name
▶ to **defend/ restore** sb's reputation/ image/ honour

reputation [C, U]（人・物事に対する）評判, 噂, 名声, 信望 ◊The restaurant has an excellent *reputation*. そのレストランは素晴らしい評価を得ている ◊He acquired a dubious *reputation* for dealing in stolen goods. 彼には盗品を扱っているという, いかがわしい評判が立っていた ◊He had *staked his reputation* on the success of the play. 彼は自分の名声をその劇の成功に賭けていた ◊The weather in England is *living up to its reputation* (= is exactly as expected). イングランドの天候は噂どおりである ☞ **reputable** (RESPECTABLE).

image [C, U]（人・組織・製品などに対する）イメージ, 印象 ◊His public *image* is very different from the real person. 彼に対する世間のイメージは実際とはかなり異なる ◊The advertisements are intended to improve the company's *image*. それらの広告は会社のイメージ改善を図る意図が込められている ◊the stereotyped *images* of women in children's books 児童書における型にはまった女性のイメージ ◊*Image* is very important in the music world. 音楽の世界ではイメージが非常に大切である

profile [C]（人・物事に対する）注目（度）, 知名度 ◊The deal will certainly *raise* the company's international *profile*. 確かにその取り引きで会社の国際的知名度は上がるだろう ◊This issue has had a *high profile* (= a lot of public attention) in recent months. この問題はここ数か月高い注目を浴びてきた ◊I advised her to *keep a low profile* (= not to attract attention) for the next few days. 私は口の先数日は目立たないように彼女に忠告した ❶人・物事のprofileはふつう高さの観点から考えられる. have a high/low profile（知名度が高い/低い）とも言えるし, raise/ lower the profile of sb/sth（人・物事の注目度を上げる/下げる）とも言える.

name [C, ふつう単数で]（人・集団・組織の）名声, 評判 ◊She *made her name* as a writer of children's books. 彼女は児童書作家として名を成した ◊These practices give the industry a bad *name*. こうした慣行はこの産業の評判を落とす ◊We must avoid anything that might damage the *good name* of the firm. 我々は会社のよい評判を落とすようなことは避けなければならない ☞ **make a name for yourself** (SUCCEED).

honour [《英》, 《米では honor》] [U]（高い道徳規範ゆえの）名誉, 信望, 面目 ; （他人からの）尊敬, 敬意 ◊She felt that she had to defend the *honour* of her profession. 彼女は自分の職業の名誉は守らなければならないと思った ◊The family *honour* is at stake. 家族の面目が失われかけている ◊She *brought honour* to her country by winning an Olympic gold medal. 彼女はオリンピックの金メダルを獲得することで自国に名誉をもたらした [反意] **dishonour** (DISGRACE), **honourable** (RESPECTABLE), **honourable** (WORTHY).

stature [U]《ややフォーマル》（能力・実績から人・集団が抱く）威信 ◊The orchestra has *grown in stature*. そのオーケストラは威信を高めた ◊The election result enhanced the party's *stature*. 選挙結果で党の威信が高まった

character [C, U]《ややフォーマル》（信頼できる[頼りにでき

る]かどうかに関する）評判, 名声, 信望 ◊He had been discharged without a *stain on* his *character*. 彼は名声を汚すようなこともなかったのに解雇されてしまった ◊My teacher agreed to be a *character witness* (= sb who says that a person can be trusted) for me in court. 私の先生は私のために法廷で性格証人になることに同意してくれた

request 名

request・order・application・claim・demand・call・petition・plea・appeal・reservation
人に正式（かつ丁寧）に物事を依頼する行為
【類語訳】依頼, 要望, 要請, 請求, 注文, 要求, 嘆願, 懇願, 呼びかけ, 訴え, 予約

[文型&コロケーション]
▶ a **request**/ an **order**/ an **application**/ a **claim**/ a **demand**/ a **call**/ a **petition**/ a **plea**/ an **appeal for** sth
▶ **on** request/ order/ application/ demand
▶ a request/ demand **that**...
▶ **repeated** requests/ demands/ calls/ pleas/ appeals
▶ a **formal** request/ application/ claim/ demand/ petition/ appeal
▶ a **personal** request/ application/ plea/ appeal
▶ an **urgent** request/ order/ demand/ plea/ appeal
▶ a/ an **successful/ unsuccessful** application/ claim/ demand/ petition/ appeal
▶ to **make** a request/ an application/ a claim/ a demand/ a plea/ an appeal/ a reservation
▶ to **put in** a request/ an order/ an application/ a claim/ a demand
▶ to **file/ lodge** an application/ a claim/ a petition
▶ to **withdraw** a request/ an application/ a claim/ a demand/ a petition
▶ to **receive** a request/ an order/ an application/ a demand/ a petition/ a plea/ an appeal
▶ to **meet** a request/ an order/ a claim/ a demand
▶ to **grant** a request/ an application/ a claim/ a petition
▶ to **refuse/ reject** a request/ an application/ a claim/ a demand/ a petition

request [C]《ややフォーマル》（正式かつ丁寧な）依頼, 要望, 要請, 請求 ◊They made a *request* for further aid. 彼らはさらなる援助を要請した ◊He was there *at his manager's request* (= because his manager had asked him to go). 彼は上司の要望でそこにいた ◊Catalogues are available on *request*. カタログはご請求いただければご用意します ☞ **request** (ASK 2), **request** (WISH).

order [C]（商品の製造・供給の）注文 ; （レストラン・バーでの飲食物の）注文 ;（飲食物などの）注文の品 ◊I would like to place an *order* for ten copies of this book. この本を10冊注文したいのですが ◊The machine parts are still on *order* (= they have been ordered but have not yet been received). 機械部品はまだ注文中である ◊These items can be made *to order* (= produced especially for a particular customer). これらの品目は受注生産できます ◊May I *take your order*? ご注文はお決まりですか ◊a *side order* of fries (= that you eat with your main dish) サイドメニューとしてのフライドポテトの注文 ☞ **order** (ORDER 2).

application [C]（文書による仕事などへの）申込書, （許可を得る）申請書, （大学への入学）願書 ◊We put in our planning *application* about six weeks ago. 我々は6週間ほど前に計画の申請書を提出した ◇We received over 100 *applications* for the job. 我々はその仕事に対して100件以上の申し込みを受け付けた ◇Where can I get an *application form* (= a piece of paper on which to apply for sth)? どこで申込用紙を手に入れることができますか ☞ apply (ASK 2)

claim [C] 《会社・政府への権利のある金額の》請求, 要求 ◇You can make a *claim on* your insurance policy. 保険契約に関して支払いの請求を行うことができます ◇Nurses have put in a three per cent *pay claim*. 看護師たちは3%の賃上げ要求を行った ☞ claim (ASK 2)

demand (ASK 2) [C] 《物事への非常に断固とした》要求, 請求；要求[請求]物 ◇Their *demand* for higher pay was ignored. 彼らの賃上げ要求は無視された ◇Our firm is constantly striving to satisfy customers' *demands* (= to give them what they are asking for). 当社は絶えずお客様のご要望にお応えするよう努めております ☞ demand (DEMAND 動)

call [C] 《特にジャーナリズム》《人への》要求 ◇There have been *calls* for the minister to resign. その大臣に対して辞任要求が出ている ◇This is the last *call* for passengers travelling on British Airways flight 199 to Rome. 英国航空199便ローマ行きについて, ご搭乗の最終案内をいたします ☞ call for sth (ASK 2)

petition [C] 《権威を有する人への》嘆願書 ◇Would you like to sign our *petition against* experiments on animals? 動物実験に反対する嘆願書に署名いただけますか ☞ petition (ASK 2)

plea [C] 《フォーマル》《急を要する切実な》嘆願, 懇願 ◇She made an impassioned *plea* for help. 彼女は助けを求めて必死に懇願した

appeal [C] 《ややフォーマル, 特に書き言葉》《慈善団体・警察の金・支援・情報への》嘆願, 懇願, 呼びかけ, 訴え ◇They've just launched a TV *appeal* for donations to the charity. 彼らはテレビでその慈善団体への寄付の呼びかけを始めたばかりだ ◇The police made an *appeal* to the public to remain calm. 警察は大衆に対して冷静さを保つよう訴えた ☞ appeal (ASK 2)

reservation [C] 《ややフォーマル》《飛行機[列車]の座席・ホテルの部屋などの》予約 ◇I'll call the restaurant and make a *reservation*. レストランに電話して予約しますね ◇We have a *reservation* in the name of Grant. グラントの名前で予約してあります ☞ reserve (ORDER 2)

research 名

research・analysis・exploration・scrutiny・examination・study・discussion・enquiry
物事についてさらに検討[解明]する過程, またはその過程の結果
【類語訳】研究, 調査, 分析, 探検, 探査, 探究, 精査, 審査, 議論, 論考, 聞き込み調査, 問い合わせ

文型&コロケーション
▸ research/ enquiry **into** sth
▸ **detailed** research/ analysis/ exploration/ scrutiny/ examination/ study/ discussion/ enquiry
▸ **close** analysis/ scrutiny/ examination/ study
▸ **scientific** research/ analysis/ exploration/ scrutiny/ examination/ study/ enquiry
▸ **historical** research/ analysis/ exploration/ examination/ study/ enquiry

▸ to **carry out/ conduct/ undertake** research/ analysis/ exploration/ an examination/ a study
▸ to **do** research/ analysis/ a study
▸ research/ analysis/ exploration/ scrutiny/ examination/ the study **reveals** sth
▸ research/ analysis/ examination/ the study **shows/ suggests** sth

research [U] 《または **researches** [複数で]》《新情報を発見するための》研究, 調査 ◇He's done a lot of *research* into renewable energy sources. 彼は再生可能なエネルギー源についてかなりの調査を行ってきた ◇I've done some *research* to find out the cheapest way of travelling there. そこへ旅行に行く最も安い方法を見つけるために少し調べてみました ◇Recent *research on* deaf children has yielded some interesting results. 聴覚障害の子どもたちについての最近の研究で, いくつか興味深い結果が得られた ◇We're trying to raise money for cancer *research*. 我々はがん研究のために資金を調達しようと努力しています ◇This is a *piece of research* that should be taken very seriously. これは非常に深刻に受け止めなければならない一つの調査です ◇James is a 24-year-old *research student* from Iowa. ジェームズはアイオワ出身の24歳の研究生である ◇They pour millions of dollars into *research and development* (= researching and creating new products). 彼らは研究開発に何百万ドルもの金を注ぎ込んでいる ◇I work for a *market research* organization (= an organization that finds out what people buy and why). 私は市場調査機関で働いています ◇In the course of my *researches*, I came across some of my grandfather's old letters. 調査の過程で数通の祖父の古い手紙を偶然見つけました ☞ research (INVESTIGATE)

analysis [U, C] 《理解を深めるための》分析；分析結果 ◇Most of the information we have so far is based on statistical *analysis*. 私たちがこれまでに入手している情報のほとんどは統計分析に基づいている ◇The book is an *analysis* of poverty and its causes. その本は貧困とその原因についての分析結果を扱っている ☞ analyse (EXAMINE)

ノート research と analysis の使い分け：research は新情報を見つけようとする努力を指し, analysis は理解を深めるためにすでに持っている情報をより詳細に調べることを指す.

exploration [U, C] 探検, 探査；探究, 調査 ◇The film is a chronicle of man's *exploration* of space. その映画は人類の宇宙探査の歴史を扱っている ◇Extensive *oil exploration* was carried out using the latest drilling technology. 広範囲に及ぶ石油探査が最新の掘削技術を使って行われた ◇This was the time of Humboldt's *explorations* in South America. これはフンボルトの南アメリカ探検の時代のことでした ☞ explore (INVESTIGATE)

scrutiny [U] 《フォーマル》《よいかどうか確かめる[決定する]ための》精査, 厳しい調査 ◇Her argument doesn't really stand up to *scrutiny*. 彼女の主張は精査されればすぐに崩れる ◇The documents should be available for public *scrutiny*. その手の書類は市民が精査できるようにしておくべきである ◇Foreign policy has *come under* close *scrutiny* recently. 最近, 外交政策は厳しく監視されている

examination [U, C] 《理解を深める[決定をする, 判断を下す]ための》調査, 審査 ◇Your proposals are still *under examination*. あなたの企画はまだ審査中である ◇On

↪research   **resident, resist**

closer examination, her story did not seem to stand up. さらに詳しく調べてみると、彼女の話は説得力がないように思えた ◇The chapter concludes with a brief *examination* of what causes family break-up. その章は家族の崩壊の原因についての簡単な調査で終わっている
☞ **examine** (EXAMINE)
study [U, C] (さらなる理解・発見のための)研究, 調査 ◇The scientific *study* of American dialects began in 1889. アメリカ方言の科学的研究は1889年に始まった ◇A detailed *study* of the area was carried out. その地域についての詳しい研究が行われた ☞ **study** (REPORT 1), **study** (EXAMINE)

ノート examination と study の使い分け： *examination* は *study* より幅広い意味を持つ。*study* はふつうテーマについてさらに発見するためのもので、より学術的である。*examination* は物事の決定を下すためのもので、より実際的である。

discussion [C, U] (テーマに関する)議論, 論考 ◇Her article is a *discussion* of the methods used in research. 彼女の論文では調査に用いる方法について論じられている ◇There will be further *discussion* of these issues in the next chapter. 次章では、これらの問題についてさらに議論します ☞ **discuss** (EXAMINE)
enquiry (または **inquiry**) [U] (人・物事についての)研究, 聞き込み調査, 問い合わせ ◇Some regimes have tried to stifle scientific *enquiry*. 政権の中には科学研究を阻害しようとしたものがある ◇We are following several lines of *enquiry*. 我々はいくつかの研究方法を追い求めている
☞ **enquire into sth** (INVESTIGATE)

resident 名 ☞ TENANT

resident・citizen・inhabitant・dweller・householder・local・native
特定の場所に住む人
【類語訳】居住者, 在住者, 在留者, 住人, 住民, 市民, 町民, ネイティブ

文型&コロケーション
▸ **local** residents/ citizens/ inhabitants/ householders
▸ **rural** residents/ inhabitants/ dwellers/ householders
▸ **city/ urban** residents/ dwellers
▸ **permanent** residents/ inhabitants
▸ **private** citizens/ householders

resident [C] 居住者, 在住者, 在留者, 住人, 住民 ◇There were confrontations between local *residents* and the police. 地元住民と警察は対立していた ◇Japan has more than 1.1 million registered *foreign residents*. 日本には登録している在留外国人が110万人以上います
☞ **reside** (LIVE)
citizen [C] 居住者, 住人, 住民, 市民, 町民 ◇She is a *prominent citizen* of the town. 彼女はその町の有名人です ◇The king was visiting France as a private *citizen* (= not as a head of state). 王は私人としてフランスを訪れていた ❶ *citizen* は特に共同体の一員としての人々の特性や地位について論評を加えるために用いられる。◆This terrible crime has shocked all *law-abiding citizens*. (この凶悪犯罪は法を遵守する全市民に衝撃を与えた) ◆When you're old, people treat you like a *second-class citizen* (= with fewer rights than other people). (年を取ると人から二級市民のように扱われるよ) ☞ **citizen** (CITI-ZEN)
inhabitant [C] 居住者, 住人, 住民, 生息動物 ◇It is a town *of* about 10,000 *inhabitants*. そこは人口約1万人の町です ◇He is Brixham's oldest *inhabitant*. 彼はブリクサムで最高齢の住人だ ◇The island's earliest *inhabitants* came from India. その島の最古の住民はインドからやって来た ☞ **inhabit** (LIVE)

ノート resident と inhabitant の使い分け： *resident* は最も一般的な語で、文字どおり町・地域・国に住む人すべてに言及することができる。また、例えば納税など、公的な目的のために特定の場所に家を構える人々を指すこともできる。*resident* はふつう村・町・市の家・アパートで生活する現代社会の一員である。*inhabitant* は同様に用いられることもあるし、過去に、または広い環境においてより簡素な生活を送る人々や動物を指すこともある。◆the *inhabitants* of the rainforest/tundra/remote islands (多雨林／ツンドラ／離島の住人)

dweller [C] (特に複合語)(ややフォーマル, 書き言葉) 居住者, 住人, 住民, 生息動物 ◇The disease spread quickly among the poor *slum dwellers* of the city. 病気は都市の貧困なスラム住民たちの間にすぐ広がった ◇Almost all Asian hornbills are *forest dwellers*. アジア産のサイチョウはほとんどすべて森林地帯に生息している
householder [C] (フォーマル) 世帯主 ◇Single *householders* receive a 20% discount on their council tax. 独身の世帯主たちは20%の地方議会税割引を受ける
local [C, ふつう複数で] 地元住民 ◇*The locals* are very friendly. 地元住民は非常に好意的である ◇Tensions have been growing between students and *locals* in the area. その地域の学生と地元住民の間には緊張が高まってきている
native [C] 現地住民, ネイティブ ◇You can always tell the difference between the tourists and the *natives*. 必ず観光客と現地の人との見分けはつきますよ ◇She speaks Italian *like a native*. 彼女はネイティブのようにイタリア語を話す ❶ 過去には *native* という語は、白人が到来する前に元々ある場所に住んでいた人を表すために、ヨーロッパ人によって用いられた。この語のこの用法は現在、攻撃的と見なされ、避けるべきものである。文字どおり長い間ある場所に住んできた人を意味するために *native* を用いる場合、比較の対象は、白人や西洋人ではなく、(特に異なる言語を話す)観光客や外国人であることを明確にすること。多くの場合、代わりに *local* を用いるほうがよいかもしれない。◆You can always tell the difference between the tourists and the *locals*. (必ず観光客と地元住民との見分けはつきますよ) 　だが、言語に関する文脈では *native* を用いること。×She speaks Italian like a *local*.
☞ **native** (CITIZEN), **native** (CULTURAL)

resist 動

resist・struggle・hold/keep sb/sth at bay・hold/stand your ground・hold out against sb
自分に攻撃を仕掛けている[脅威を与えている, 反対している]人や物事と争う
【類語訳】抵抗する, 阻止する, 闘う, 食い止める, こらえる

文型&コロケーション
▸ to struggle/ hold your ground **against** sb/ sth
▸ to resist/ hold out against an **attack**
▸ to resist/ hold out against **pressure**

resist [自, 他]（攻撃を受けた際に）抵抗する；（武力を行使して）阻止する ◇He tried to pin me down, but I *resisted*. 彼は私を拘束しようとしたが、私は抵抗した ◇She was charged with *resisting arrest*. 彼女は逮捕の際に抵抗したとして起訴された ◇He gathered forces to *resist* the invasion. 彼は勢力を結集して侵略を阻止した 反意 **give in, submit** (GIVE WAY), ☞ **resistance** (OPPOSITION)

struggle [自]（悪い状況[結果]を防ぐために）闘う ◇He *struggled* against cancer for two years. 彼は2年間がんと闘った ◇We should all *struggle* against injustice. 私たちはみな不正に対して闘うべきである ◇Lisa *struggled* with her conscience before talking to the police. リサは警察に話す前に自分の良心との葛藤があった ☞ **struggle** (CAMPAIGN 名)

hold/keep sb/sth at 'bay [句動]（敵の接近[問題が悪影響を及ぼすのを]）防ぐ、寄せつけない、食い止める、こらえる ◇I'm trying to *keep* my creditors *at bay*. 私は債権者たちを寄せつけないようにしている ◇Charlotte bit her lip to *hold* the tears *at bay*. シャーロットは涙をこらえようと唇をかみ締めた

hold/stand your 'ground [句動]（人の反対に）自分の意見を守る；（状況に直面して）自分の立場を守る ◇Don't let him persuade you — *stand your ground*. 彼に説得されてはいけない―自分の意見を守るように ◇It is not easy to *hold your ground* in front of someone with a gun. 銃を持った人を前にして自分の立場を守るのは容易ではない

,hold 'out against sb/sth [句動]（危険な[困難な]状況で）…に抵抗する、…に屈しない ◇British troops *held out against* constant attacks. 英国軍は絶え間ない攻撃に屈しなかった ◇The Prime Minister *held out against* pressure to speed up the reforms. 首相は改革を促進せよとの圧力に最後まで抵抗した

resolve [動]

resolve・settle・repair・mend・patch sth up
不一致に終止符を打つ、問題の解決策を見つける、悪い関係を改善する
【類語訳】解決する、修復する、仲直りする

文型&コロケーション
▶ to settle/ patch up sth with sb
▶ to resolve/ settle/ mend/ patch up your differences
▶ to resolve/ settle a/ an dispute/ argument/ crisis/ matter/ issue
▶ to resolve/ mend matters
▶ to repair/ mend/ patch up a rift/ the damage/ relations
▶ to mend/ patch up a relationship/ marriage

resolve [他]《ややフォーマル》（納得のゆく形で問題・議論を）解決する ◇Where can ordinary people get help with *resolving* family problems? 家族の問題を解決してもらうにはふつうどこに行けばいいの ◇The matter has never really been satisfactorily *resolved*. その問題は実際のところ満足のいく解決を見ていない ☞ **resolution** (SOLUTION)

settle [他, 自]（議論・不一致を）解決する ◇Talks will be held in an attempt to *settle* the dispute. 論争の解決を目指して交渉が行われることになっている ◇I want this thing *settled*. この問題を解決したい ◇The company agreed to *settle out of court* (= come to an agreement without going to court). 会社は示談で解決することに同意した ☞ **settlement** (AGREEMENT)

repair [他]（悪い状況・関係を）修復する ◇They moved quickly to *repair* relations between themselves and the US. 彼らは米国との関係を修復するために迅速に行動した ◇It was too late to *repair* the damage done to the relationship. 傷ついた関係を修復するには遅すぎた

mend [他]（不一致を）解決する、（悪い状況・関係を）修復する ◇They met in an attempt to *mend* their differences. 彼らは意見の不一致を埋めようとして会合を持った ◇Is it too late to *mend fences* with your ex-wife (= settle your disagreement with her)? 前妻とよりを戻すには遅すぎるのでは

,patch sth 'up [句動]《ややインフォーマル》（人と）仲直りする ◇Have you managed to *patch things up* with him? 彼とうまく仲直りできましたか

respect [名]

respect・manners・courtesy・formality・politeness・etiquette・grace・civility
礼儀正しい[正当]と考えられる行動
【類語訳】敬意、尊重、礼儀、マナー、儀礼、堅苦しさ、丁寧さ、丁重さ、作法、エチケット、上品さ、気品

文型&コロケーション
▶ with respect/ courtesy/ politeness/ grace/ civility
▶ out of respect/ courtesy/ politeness
▶ great respect/ courtesy/ formality/ politeness/ civility
▶ good manners/ grace
▶ exaggerated respect/ courtesy/ politeness/ formality
▶ to show respect/ manners/ courtesy/ politeness
▶ to treat sb with respect/ courtesy/ politeness/ civility

respect [U, 単数で]（人・物事に対する）敬意、尊重 ◇They show a lack of *respect for* authority. 彼らは権威に対して敬意を示さない ◇He has no *respect* for her feelings. 彼は彼女の気持ちを尊重していない ◇Everyone has a right to be treated with *respect*. 誰も大切に扱われる権利がある 反意 **disrespect, contempt** (CONTEMPT), ☞ **respect** (ADMIRATION), **respect** (FOLLOW 3), **respectful** (POLITE)

manners [複数で]（特定の社会・文化における）礼儀、マナー ◇It is *bad manners* to talk with your mouth full. 口に物をほおばったままで話すのは無作法だ ◇He has *no manners* (= behaves very badly). 彼は礼儀を知らない ◇She could at least *have the good manners to* let me know she isn't coming. 彼女は少なくとも来るつもりはないことを知らせる礼儀ぐらいはわきまえていてもいいのに ◇Those kids have no *table manners*. その子たちのテーブルマナーはなっていない ❶ manners は食事をする際にどう振舞うか[他人をどう扱うか]といった文脈で用いられることが多い.

courtesy [U, C, ふつう複数で]《ややフォーマル》（他人に対する）礼儀；（正式な場面での）儀礼的な言動 ◇It's only common *courtesy* to tell the neighbours that we'll be having a party. パーティーの予定を隣人に伝えるのはごく当たり前の礼儀です ◇We asked them as *a matter of courtesy*. 私たちは礼儀として彼らに声をかけた ◇The prime minister was welcomed with the usual *courtesies*. 首相はいつもどおりうやうやしく出迎えられた ☞ **courteous** (POLITE)

formality [U]（意図的にくつろぎすぎ[友好的すぎ]ことを避ける）儀礼、堅苦しさ ◇She greeted him with stiff

↳respect

formality. 彼女は彼に非常に堅苦しく挨拶をした ◇Different levels of *formality* are appropriate in different situations. 状況が異なれば適切な儀礼のレベルも異なる ☞ **formal** (FORMAL)

politeness [U] (他人に対する)丁寧さ, 丁重さ, 礼儀正しさ ◇He stood up out of *politeness* and offered her his seat. 彼は礼儀正しく立ち上がって自分の席を譲った 反意 **rudeness** (RUDE), ☞ **polite** (POLITE)

etiquette [U] (社交界における[特定の職業の間の])礼儀, 作法, エチケット ◇What's the correct *etiquette* when addressing a judge? 判事に話しかけるのにふさわしい礼儀って, どんなの ◇She is an expert on matters of *etiquette*. 彼女は作法の専門家である

grace [U, 単数で] 上品さ, 気品, 感じのよさ ◇He conducted himself with *grace* and dignity throughout the trial. 彼は公判中終始, 気品と威厳をもって振る舞った ◇She didn't even *have the grace* to look embarrassed. 彼女は恥ずかしそうな顔をするしみさえ持ち合わせていなかった ◇We will simply have to accept the situation *with a good grace*. 私たちはただただ快くその状況を受け入れなければならないだろう ☞ **gracious** (POLITE)

civility [U] 《フォーマル》丁寧さ, 丁重さ, 礼儀正しさ ◇Staff members are trained to treat customers with *civility* at all times. 職員たちは常に礼儀正しく顧客を扱うよう訓練される ❶ *civilities* は礼儀正しく, 無礼になるのを避けるためだけに口にされる言葉を指す. ◆She didn't waste time on *civilities*. (彼女は丁寧な言葉遣いに時間を割きはしなかった). ☞ **civil** (POLITE)

respect 動

respect・admire・esteem・be/stand in awe of sb/sth・look up to sb
よい性質[立派な業績]ゆえに高く評価する
【類語訳】尊敬する, 尊重する, 賞賛する, 感嘆する, 感心する, 感服する

| respect | admire | be/stand in awe of sb/sth |
| esteem | look up to sb | |

文型&コロケーション

▶ to respect/ admire/ esteem/ look up to sb **as** sth
▶ to respect/ admire/ esteem/ look up to sb **for** sth
▶ to respect/ admire **the way** sb does sth
▶ a respected/ an esteemed **writer/ teacher/ scientist**
▶ **greatly/ much** respected/ admired/ esteemed
▶ **highly** respected/ esteemed
▶ to **really** respect/ admire/ look up to sb/ sth

respect [他]《進行形なし》(人・物事を)尊敬する, 尊重する ◇She is always honest with me, and I *respect* her for that. 彼女はいつも私には誠実なので, それゆえ尊敬しています ◇She was a much loved and highly *respected* teacher. 彼女は大変に愛され, 尊敬される教師だった ◇I *respect* Jack's opinion on most subjects. 私はほとんどの問題についてジャックの意見を尊重します ☞ **respect** (ADMIRATION), **respectful** (POLITE)

admire [他]《進行形なし》(人・物事を)賞賛する, 感嘆する, 感心する, 感服する ◇I really *admire* your enthusiasm. あなたの熱意には本当に感服します ◇The school is widely *admired* for its excellent teaching. その学校は優れた教育内容が広く賞賛されている ◇You have to *admire* the way he handled the situation. 彼の状況対処の仕方は賞賛すべきだ ☞ **admiration** (ADMIRATION), **admirer** (FAN), **admiring** (GOOD 6)

ノート **respect** と **admire** の使い分け: admire は respect より強い感情を表現する. 人を admire することはふつう, その人に賛同する[同意し彼らのようになりたいと思う]ことを意味する. admire は, 人(のよい性質)を目的語に取るが, ふつう人の意見は目的語としない. ◆I really *admire* her for her courage. (彼女の勇気に心底感服している). ◆I really *admire* her courage. (彼女の勇気に心底感服している). ✕I *admire* Jack's opinion on most subjects. 人を respect する場合, その人に賛同していない[のようになりたいと思わない]かもしれないが, それでもなおそのよい性質は認めている. ◆These academics may be *respected* as experts in their field, but they can also be quite arrogant. (この学者たちは, その分野の専門家として尊敬されているかもしれないが, 実に傲慢なこともある). ◆I *respect* him for his honesty. (誠実さゆえに彼を尊敬しています). ✕I *respect* his honesty.

esteem [他, ふつう受身で]《進行形なし》《フォーマル》(人・物事を)尊敬する, 尊重する, 高く評価する ◇He was *esteemed* as a dedicated and imaginative scholar. 彼は熱心で想像力に富んだ学者であると高く評価されていた ◇Many of these qualities are *esteemed* by managers. これらの品質の多くは経営者たちに高く評価されている ☞ **esteem** (ADMIRATION)

be/stand in 'awe of sb/sth 仔細 《進行形なし》(人・物事に)畏敬の念を抱いている ◇She was tall, confident and beautiful, and all the other girls *were in awe of* her. 彼女は長身で, 自信にあふれ, 美しく, 他の少女全員が畏敬の念を抱いていた ☞ **awe** (ADMIRATION)

,look 'up to sb 句動詞《進行形なし》(年上の[権威の地位にある]人を)尊敬する ◇He's good with the kids, who really *look up to* him. 彼は子どもの扱いがうまく, 子どもたちは彼をとても尊敬しています 反意 **look down on sb** ❶ look down on sb は, 自分が人より優れていると思っていることを意味する. ◆She *looks down on* people who haven't been to college. (彼女は大学を出ていない人を見下している).

respectable 形

respectable・decent・reputable・honourable・law-abiding
人や物事が世間から優れていて, 道徳的に受け入れられると見なされていることを表す
【類語訳】立派な, 堅気の, まともな, きちんとした, しかるべき, ふさわしい, 正当な, 高潔な

文型&コロケーション

▶ a respectable/ a decent/ an honourable/ a law-abiding **man/ woman**
▶ respectable/ decent/ honourable/ law-abiding **people**
▶ a respectable/ decent/ law-abiding **citizen/ member of the community**
▶ respectable/ decent/ law-abiding **folk**
▶ a respectable/ reputable **firm/ organization**
▶ to **do** the decent/ honourable **thing**
▶ **perfectly/ very** respectable/ decent/ reputable/ honourable

respectable 尊敬に値する, 立派な, 社会的地位のある, 堅気の ◇This is a *respectable* neighbourhood. ここは社会的地位のある人々が住む地域である ◇I'm a *respectable* married woman. 私はまともな既婚女性です ◇It's about time you got yourself a *respectable* job. 君もそろそろ堅気の仕事に就くべきだよ 反意 **disreputable** ❶ disreputable は respectable の反意語であり, reputable の反意語ではない.

▶ **respectability** 名 [U] ◇middle-class notions of *respectability* 中流階級の考える市民的価値観

▶ **respectably** 副 ◇Mrs Wilson dressed quietly and *respectably* in grey or black. ウィルソン夫人は地味で, グレーというか黒っぽい服をきちんと着ていた

decent [ふつう名詞の前で] (人・行動が)まともな, 適正な, きちんとした, しかるべき, ふさわしい ◇These are ordinary, *decent*, hard-working people. こういう人たちはふつうに, まともに, よく働きます ◇The chairman must now do the *decent* thing and resign. 議長は今やいさぎよく責任を取って辞任しなければならない

▶ **decency** 名 [U] ◇We need to restore values of *decency*, caring and understanding to our society. 良識, 思いやり, 理解といった価値基準を我々の社会に取り戻す必要があります

▶ **decently** 副 ◇We always try to treat prisoners *decently*. 私たちは常に囚人を適正に扱おうとしています

reputable (誠実でよいサービスを提供していて)評判のよい ◇Buy your car from a *reputable* dealer. 評判のよいディーラーから車を買いなさい ❶ reputable はふつうビジネスや商取引に携わる会社や人々に用いられる. ☞ **reputation** (REPUTATION)

honourable 《英》《米 **honorable**》 (高い道徳規範を示して)正直な, 高潔な, 立派な; 名誉[面目]が保てる ◇He was an *honourable* man who could not lie. 彼は嘘をつかない高潔な人物だった ◇The only *honourable* thing to do is to resign. 唯一の立派なやり方は辞めることだ 反意 **dishonourable** (DESPICABLE), ☞ **honour** (INTEGRITY), **honour** (REPUTATION), **honourable** (WORTHY)

▶ **honourably** 《英》《米では **honorably**》 副 ◇He served *honourably* during his 44 years in office. 彼は44年間, 立派に勤め上げた

ノート decent と honourable の使い分け: 時に両語も使用可能. ◆It's time she did the *decent*/*honourable* thing and resigned. (彼女はいさぎよく責任を取って辞めるべき時だ). しかし, honourable は decent よりも重い道徳的選択を含むことが多い. decent な人々はふつうの日常生活で勤勉で, 他人を敬意をもって扱う. honourable な人々は, 非常に困難[危険]である場合か, または他人が嘘をついている[だましている]場合に, 事実を話し, 金銭に関しては誠実で, 他人や国家に対しては忠実である. live decently (まともな暮らしをする), die honourably (立派な死に方をする) と言えるが, 以下のようには言えない. ×live *honourably*. ×die *decently*.

law-abiding 法律を遵守する ◇The police have been preventing ordinary *law-abiding* citizens from going about their own business. 法を遵守する一般市民がいつもどおりに自分の仕事をするのを警察は妨げてきている ❶ law-abiding はふつう, 普段から法を遵守する人が, 法を犯した場合のように扱われる場合や, 法を犯した人々と比較される場合に用いられる

responsibility 名

responsibility・duty・charge・obligation・burden・liability・job・commitment・accountability

しなければならない物事, 物事をやらなければならない状態
【類語訳】責任, 義務, 義務, 本分, 職務, 管理, 負担, 重荷, 苦労, 仕事, 約束, 公約

文型&コロケーション

▶ a duty/ an obligation/ a burden/ a commitment/ accountability **to** sb/ sth
▶ a responsibility/ duty **towards** sb
▶ responsibility/ liability/ accountability **for** sth
▶ (a) **heavy** responsibility/ obligations/ burden/ commitments
▶ (a) **greater** responsibility/ obligation/ burden/ liability/ accountability
▶ (a) **personal** responsibility/ duty/ charge/ obligation/ commitment/ accountability
▶ **collective/ public** responsibility/ duty/ accountability
▶ (a) **professional/ social** responsibility/ duty/ obligation/ commitment/ accountability
▶ (a) **financial** responsibility/ duty/ obligation/ burden/ commitment/ accountability
▶ (a) **moral** responsibility/ duty/ obligation/ accountability
▶ (a) **legal** responsibility/ duty/ obligation/ liability/ accountability
▶ (a) **family** responsibility/ duty/ obligations/ commitments
▶ to **have** a responsibility/ a duty/ a charge/ an obligation/ liability/ the job/ a commitment
▶ to **accept** responsibility/ a duty/ an obligation/ the burden/ liability
▶ to **bear/ shoulder** the responsibility/ burden
▶ to **fulfil/ meet** a responsibility/ a duty/ an obligation/ a commitment
▶ a responsibility/ a duty/ the burden **falls on** sb

responsibility [U, C] 《ややフォーマル》(仕事[立場]上の)責任, 責務, 義務 ◇It is their *responsibility* to ensure that the rules are enforced. 規則[法律]が施行されるよう取り計らうのが彼らの責任だ ◇I'm not ready to be in a *position of responsibility*. 私は責任ある立場に就く覚悟ができていません ◇I don't feel ready to take on new *responsibilities*. 新たな責務を引き受ける心構えが私にはできていないように思います ◇I think we have a moral *responsibility* to help these countries. 我々にはこれらの国を支援する道徳的義務があると思います ❶ responsibility のある人とは, 何かがうまく行かなくなった場合に非難を受けるべき人のことを指す. ☞ **be responsible for sb/sth** (RUN 2)

duty [C, U] (道徳[法的]な)義務, 本分, 職務 ◇It is my *duty* to report it to the police. 警察にそのことを通報するのは私の義務だ ◇I supposed we'd better *do our duty* and report the accident. 私たちは義務を果たして事故の通報をするほうがよいと思った ◇I'll have to go I'm afraid — *duty calls*. 残念だけど行かなくちゃ—用があってね ◇The time he put in helping new recruits went *beyond the call of duty*. 新入社員の手助けに費やす時間は, 職務を上回るものであった

charge [U] (人・物事に対する)管理 ◇She *has charge of* the day-to-day running of the business. 彼女は

日々の事業運営を管理している ◇He ***took charge of*** the farm after his father's death. 彼は父親の死後、農場の管理を引き受けた ◇They left the nanny ***in charge of*** the children for a week. 彼らは一週間、子どもを子守に預けた ❶have/take charge of sb/sth (人・物事の管理を引き受ける)、be in charge of sb/sth (人・物事を管理している)、leave/put sb in charge of sb/sth (人・物事の管理を人に任せる) という表現が可能である。☞ **be in charge** (RUN 2)

obligation [U, C] 《ややフォーマル》《特に書き言葉》(義務[法律、規則、約束]上の)義務 ◇You are ***under no obligation*** to buy anything. あなたに何も買う義務はない ◇She did not feel ***under any obligation*** to tell him the truth. 彼女は彼に真実を話さなくてはならない義務をまったく感じなかった ◇We will send you an estimate for the work ***without obligation*** (= you do not have to accept it). 私どもは仕事の見積もりをお送りしますが、ご納得いただけなくても構いません ◇You must fulfil your legal *obligations*. 法的義務は果たさなければなりません ☞ **oblige** (FORCE 動)

burden [C] 《ややフォーマル》(心配・困難・重労働を招く)負担、重荷、苦労 ◇The main *burden* of caring for old people falls on the state. 高齢者介護の大きな負担は国家に振りかかる ◇I don't want to become a *burden* to my children when I'm old. 年老いて子どもに負担はかけたくない ◇How can we reduce the heavy ***tax burden*** on working people? どうしたら勤労者の重い税負担を軽減できるだろうか
▶**burden** [動] [他] ◇They have ***burdened themselves*** with a large mortgage. 彼らは多額の住宅ローンの負担を負うことになった ◇I don't want to ***burden*** you with my worries. 私の心配事であなたを苦しめたくない

liability [U] 《ややフォーマル、特にビジネス or 法律》(法的な)責任 ◇The company cannot accept *liability* for any damage caused by natural disasters. 会社は自然災害によって引き起こされるどんな損害の責任も負うことはできません
▶**liable** [形] ◇You will be ***liable for*** any damage caused. 引き起こされるあらゆる損害の責任を負うことになります

job [C, ふつう単数で] 《ややインフォーマル、特に話し言葉》仕事、責務、義務 ◇It's not my *job* to lock up! 戸締まりをするのは私の仕事じゃないよ ◇It's the *job* of the press to expose wrongdoing. 悪行を暴くのは報道機関の責務である ❶この意味では job はふつう、It's my/your/his/her, etc. job to do sth や、it's the job of sb/sth to do sth の表現で用いられる。

commitment [C] 《特にビジネス》(仕事・家族に関わる)約束(事)、公約、用事;(定期的にある金額を払わなければならない)義務、責務、責任 ◇He's busy for the next month with filming *commitments*. 撮影の用件で来月、彼は手がふさがっている ◇Women very often have to juggle work with their family *commitments*. 女性は家事と仕事を両立させなければならないことがあまりに多い ◇Buying a house is a big financial *commitment*. 家の購入は大きな経済的負担になる

accountability [U] 《フォーマル》(自分の決定・行動に対する)説明義務[責任] ◇There have been proposals for greater police *accountability*. より大きな説明義務を警察に求める提案が出ている ◇the *accountability* of a company's directors to the shareholders 会社の重役たちの株主たちへの説明義務
▶**accountable** [形] [名詞の前まれ] ◇Politicians are ultimately ***accountable to*** the voters. 政治家たちは究極的には有権者への説明責任がある ◇Someone must be held ***accountable for*** the killings. 誰かがその一連の殺

人事件の説明責任を果たさなければならない

rest 動

rest • relax • hang out • take it/things easy • sit back • unwind • chill out • potter • put your feet up
一定期間の活動[病気]の後、寝たり、ほとんど何もしなかったり、ただ楽しんだりすること
【類語訳】休む、休息する、休憩する、休養する、くつろぐ、のんびりする、ぶらぶらする

〖文型&コロケーション〗
▶to **try to/ help sb (to)** rest/ relax/ unwind
▶to **just** rest/ relax/ hang out/ take it easy/ sit back/ unwind/ potter
▶to rest/ relax/ sit back **a little/ bit**

rest [自, 他] (一定期間の活動・病気の後で)休む、休息[休憩、休養]する;(体の部位を)休ませる、医者は私に休養するように言った ◇*Rest* your eyes every half an hour. 30分ごとに目を休ませなさい ◇I awoke feeling *rested* and refreshed. 目覚めると体が休まり、元気を取り戻せた気がした

relax [自] (仕事・努力の後で)くつろぐ、のんびりする ◇When I get home from work I like to *relax* with a glass of wine. 仕事から帰宅したらワインを1杯飲んでのんびりするのがいい ◇Just *relax* and enjoy the movie. まあ、くつろいで映画を楽しんでください ☞ **relaxation** (ENTERTAINMENT)

,hang 'out [句動詞] 《特に米、インフォーマル》のんびりする;(特定の場所で)(特定の人の集団と)ぶらぶらする ◇Do we have to rush around today? I'd rather just *hang out*. 今日は飛び回らなくちゃいけないの。ぼくはちょっとのんびりしていたいんだけどなあ ◇The local kids *hang out* at the mall. 地元の子どもがショッピングモールをぶらぶらする

,take it/things 'easy [句動] 《ややインフォーマル》(働く[頑張り]すぎをやめて)無理しない、気楽にする ◇The doctor told me to *take it easy* for a few weeks. 医者に数週間無理しないように言われた

,sit 'back [句動詞] 《ややインフォーマル》(没頭[心配]しすぎをやめて)手を出さない、何もしない ◇She's not the kind of person who can *sit back* and let others do all the work. 彼女は何もしないで仕事はすべて他人に任せられるようなタイプの人間ではない ❶sit back は人が休んで他人が仕事をするのを見ていることを意味する。

unwind [自] (問題について心配する[考える]のをやめて)くつろぐ ◇Listening to music helps me *unwind* after a busy day. 忙しい一日の後、音楽を聴くと、くつろいだ気分になれます

,chill 'out [句動詞] (または **chill**) 《インフォーマル》(仕事の後で他人と一緒に)ぶらぶらする ◇They like to *chill out* and listen to music after work. 彼らは仕事の後で好んでゆったりと音楽に耳を傾けます

potter [自] 《副詞や前置詞と共に》《英》《米 **putter**》(楽しんで)のんびり過ごす、ぶらぶらする ◇I spent the day *pottering around* the house. その日、家でのんびりして過ごした

put your 'feet up [句動] 《ややインフォーマル》足を台に載せてくつろぐ ◇After a hard day's work, it's nice to get home and *put your feet up*. 一日働き詰めの後は、家に帰って足を台に載せてくつろぐと気持ちいいよ

restless 形 ☞ WORRIED, HYSTERICAL

restless・impatient・agitated・flustered・unsettled
人が退屈[神経質]でくつろげないこと表す
【類語訳】そわそわした、いらいらした、じりじりした、じれったい、もどかしい、興奮した、慌てた

文型&コロケーション
- to **become** restless/ impatient/ agitated/ flustered/ unsettled
- to **get** restless/ impatient/ agitated/ flustered
- to **feel/ look** restless/ impatient/ agitated/ flustered/ unsettled

restless (退屈で)落ち着きのない、じっとしていられない、そわそわした、満足していられない ◇The audience was becoming *restless*. 観客はじっとしていられなくなっていた ◇After five years in the job, he was beginning to feel *restless*. その仕事について5年経ち、彼は落ち着かない気持ちになりかけていた
➤**restlessly** 副 ◇He moved *restlessly* from one foot to the other. 彼は落ち着きなく動き回った
impatient (長時間待たなければならなくて)いらいらした、じりじりした、我慢しきれない、せっかちな、もどかしい ◇I'd been waiting for twenty minutes and I was getting *impatient*. 20分待たされて我慢できなくなってきた ◇Try not to be too *impatient with* her. 彼女にあまりいらいらしないようにしなさい 反意 **patient** (CALM)
➤**impatience** 名 [U] ◇She was bursting with *impatience* to tell me the news. 彼女は私にその知らせを伝えたいじれったさを抑え切れなくなっていた 反意 **patience** (PATIENCE)
➤**impatiently** 副 ◇We sat waiting *impatiently* for the movie to start. 私たちは席に着いて映画が始まるのを今か今かと待っていた
agitated (心配[神経質]で)いらいらした、興奮[動揺]した ◇She's *agitated about* getting there on time. 彼女は時間どおりにそこに着けるかといらいらしている ◇Calm down! Don't get so *agitated*. 落ち着け。そんなに興奮するな 反意 **calm** (CALM), **agitation** (CONCERN)
➤**agitation** 名 [U] ◇Jen arrived in a state of great *agitation*. ジェンは非常に興奮した状態で到着した
flustered (しなければならないことがたくさんあるために)慌てた ◇She arrived late, looking hot and *flustered*. 彼女は遅れて到着し、興奮して慌てた様子だった 反意 **composed** (CALM)
unsettled [名詞の前のまれ] (変化[不安]で)落ち着きのない、精神的に不安定な ◇They all felt restless and *unsettled*. 彼らは皆、気分が落ち着かず精神的に不安定だった
☞ **unsettling** (WORRYING)

result 名 ☞ EFFECT

result・consequence・outcome・implication・product・the fruit/fruits of sth・repercussion・upshot
他から引き起こされる一つの事柄
【類語訳】結果、成果、影響、産物、波紋、飛び火、結末

文型&コロケーション
- to have consequences/ implications/ repercussions **for** sb/ sth
- **with** the result/ consequence/ outcome that...
- **as** a result/ consequence...
- (a/ an) **important** result/ consequences/ outcome/ implications/ repercussions
- the **possible** result/ consequences/ outcome/ implications/ repercussions
- the **likely** result/ consequences/ outcome/ implications
- the **inevitable** result/ consequences/ outcome/ product
- (a/ an) **immediate/ direct/ negative/ positive** result/ consequences/ outcome/ implications/ repercussions
- (a) **long-term/ far-reaching/ serious** results/ consequences/ implications/ repercussions
- the **final** result/ outcome/ product
- (a/ an) **unfortunate** results/ consequences/ outcome/ implications
- (a/ an) **disastrous** results/ consequences/ outcome
- to **have** a result/ consequences/ an outcome/ implications/ repercussions
- to **lead to** (a)... result/ consequences/ outcome/ repercussions
- to **show/ observe/ assess/ examine/ measure** the results/ consequences/ outcome
- to **achieve/ get/ obtain** a result/ an outcome

result [C, U] 結果、成果 ◇She died as a *result* of her injuries. 彼女はけがが元で亡くなった ◇The farm was flooded, with the *result* that most of the harvest was lost. 農場は冠水し、その結果、収穫のほとんどが失われた ◇This book is the *result* of 25 years of research. この本は25年にわたる研究の成果です ☞ **resulting, resultant** (RELATED), **result in sth** (CAUSE)
consequence [C]《ややフォーマル》(悪い)結果 ◇This decision could have serious *consequences* for the future of the industry. この決定は産業の将来に重大な結果をもたらすかもしれない ◇Two hundred people lost their jobs as a direct *consequence* of the merger. 合併の直接的な結果として200人の人々が失業した ◇At some point you will have to *face the consequences* of your actions. ある時点で自分の行動の結果に面と向かわなければならないでしょう ❶ *consequences* は、否定的な結果について最も頻繁に用いられる。ふつう、adverse, dire, disastrous, fatal, harmful, negative, serious, tragic, unfortunate と共に用いられる。形容詞を伴わなくても、consequences は否定的な結果を示唆することが多い。 ◆Fearing the *consequences*, she left the company. 彼女はまずいことになりそうだと思って会社を辞めた ☞ **consequent** (RELATED)
➤**consequently** 副 ◇This poses a threat to agriculture and the food chain, and *consequently* to human health. これは農業や食物連鎖、ついには人間の健康を脅かします
outcome [C] (行動・過程の)結果 ◇These costs are payable whatever the *outcome* of the case. これらの経費は裁判の結果がどうであれ支払うべきものです ◇We are confident of a successful *outcome*. 我々はよい結果が出ることに自信を持っています ◇Four possible *outcomes* have been identified. 起こりうる4つの結果が明らかとなった

ノート **result** と **outcome** の使い分け：result は、他から直接引き起こされる「結果」について用いられることが多い。◆Aggression is often the *result* of fear. (攻撃はしば

しば恐怖の結果である). outcome は, 正確な因果関係があまりはっきりしない場合に, 一つの過程の最後に起こる「結果」について用いられることが多い. ×Aggresssion is often the *outcome* of fear. result は, 一つの出来事の後に起こった「結果」について用いられることが多い. outcome は, 行動・過程の前に起こる可能性が高い「結果」について用いられることが多い.

implication [C, ふつう複数で] (行動・決定が与えうる)影響 ◇The development of the site will have *implications* for the surrounding countryside. その用地開発は周囲の田舎に影響を及ぼすことになろう ◇They failed to consider the wider *implications* of their actions. 彼らは自分たちの行動の今まで以上に幅広い影響について考えが及ばなかった

product [C] (ややフォーマル) (物事の結果としての)産物, 生産物, 生成物 ◇The child is the *product* of a broken home. その子は家庭崩壊の申し子だ ◇A complicated string of chemical reactions leads to the end *product*. 一連の複雑な化学反応によって最終生成物ができる

the fruit/fruits of sth [行い] (ややフォーマル) (活動・状況のよい)結果, 成果 ◇Allow yourself to enjoy the *fruits* of your labour (= the rewards for your hard work). 労働の成果を享受したらいい ◇The book is the *fruit of* years of research. その本は何年にもわたる研究の成果である

repercussion [C, ふつう複数で] (書き言葉) (行動・出来事の間接的な悪い)影響, 波紋, 飛び火 ◇The collapse of the company will have *repercussions* for the whole industry. その会社の破綻は産業全体に飛び火するだろう

upshot [ふつう the upshot に] [単数で] (ややインフォーマル) (一連の出来事の最終的な)結果, 結末, 結局 ◇The *upshot* of it all was that he left college and got a job. そのすべての結末は彼が大学を辞めて仕事に就くというものだった ❶ the upshot は話し言葉ではふつう用いられない. 文脈で, 特に The upshot (of ...) is/was that... という表現で用いられることが最も多い.

return 動

1 return・come back・go back・get back・turn back
ある場所から別の場所へ再び来る[行く]
【類語訳】戻る, 帰る, 引き返す

〘文型&コロケーション〙
▶ to return/ come back/ go back/ get back **to/ from/ with** sth
▶ to return/ come back/ go back/ get back/ turn back **again**
▶ to return/ come back/ go back/ get back **home/ to work**
▶ to return/ come back/ get back **safely**

return [自] (ややフォーマル) (ある場所から別の場所へ)戻る, 帰る ◇I waited a long time for him to *return*. 私は彼が戻って来るのを長いこと待った ◇They were forced to *return* to their country of origin. 彼らは祖国へ帰らざるをえなかった ◇He finally *returned* with the drinks. 彼はやっと飲み物を持って戻って来た
➤ **return** 名 [単数で] ◇He was met by his brother *on his return* from Italy. 彼はイタリアから戻って来たとき兄の出迎えを受けた ◇on the *return* flight/journey/trip 帰りの飛行機で/帰路で/帰路で

come 'back 句動詞 (ある場所から別の場所へ)戻って[帰って]来る ◇*Come back* and visit again soon! またのお越しをお待ちしています ◇I asked her to *come back* to Japan with me. 一緒に日本へ戻ってくれるよう彼女に頼んだ ❶ come back はふつう人が戻ろうとしている先の人や場所の視点から用いられる. 反義 **go away** (GO AWAY)

,go 'back 句動詞 (最近[もともと, 以前]いた場所へ)戻って[帰って]行く ◇Do you ever want to *go back* to China? 中国に帰りたいと思うことがありますか ◇John shrugged and *went back* downstairs. ジョンは肩をすくめて階下へ降りて戻った ◇She's *gone back* to her husband (= to live with him again). 彼女は夫の元へ戻った ◇This toaster will have to *go back* (= to the shop) — it doesn't work. このトースターは返品しないとな―壊れてるもん ❶ go back はふつう戻ろうとしている人の視点から用いられる

,get 'back 句動詞 (家・滞在場所へ)戻る, 帰る ◇What time did you *get back* last night? 昨晩は何時に戻ったの ◇We only *got back* from our trip yesterday 私たちは旅から昨日戻ったばかりです ◇Oh, well. I must be *getting back* = going back home, back to work, etc.). (話し言葉)あらあら. 帰らなくちゃ

,turn 'back 句動詞 (進めなくてやって来た道を)引き返す ◇The weather got so bad that we had to *turn back*. 天気がひどく悪くなって引き返さざるをえなかった

2 return・put sth back・give sth back・take sth back・replace・hand sth back・restore
以前持っていた人に物を渡す, 以前あった場所に物を置く
【類語訳】返す, 戻す, 返却する, 返送する, 返品する, 返還する

〘文型&コロケーション〙
▶ to return sth/ give sth back/ take sth back/ restore sth/ hand sth back **to** sb/ sth
▶ to put sth back/ replace sth **on** sth
▶ to return/ put back/ give back/ replace/ hand back **money**
▶ to return/ put back/ give back/ take back/ replace a **book**
▶ to return/ take back **faulty/ unwanted goods**
▶ to put back/ replace a **lid**
▶ to put back/ replace the **(telephone) receiver**
▶ to return sth/ put sth back/ replace sth **quickly/ soon**
▶ to put sth back/ replace sth **firmly/ gently/ carefully**

return [他] (ややフォーマル) (以前持っていた人[以前あった場所]に物を)返す, 戻す, 返却する, 返送する, 返品する ◇We had to *return* the hairdryer to the store because it was faulty. 欠陥があったためドライヤーを店に返品しなければならなかった ◇Completed questionnaires should be *returned* to this address. 記入済みのアンケート用紙はこの住所に返送してください ◇I *returned* the letter unopened. 手紙は未開封のまま送り返した
➤ **return** 名 [U, 単数で] ◇We would appreciate the prompt *return* of books to the library. 本を図書館に迅速にご返却ください

,put sth 'back 句動詞 (通常[移動の前]の場所に物を)戻す ◇If you use something, *put it back*! 何か使ったら戻しておいてね ◇I *put* the book *back* on the shelf. 本を棚に戻した

,give sth 'back, ,give sb 'back sth 句動詞 (所有者に物を)返す; (人が物を持つのを)可能にする ◇*Give me back* my pen! 私のペンを返して ◇*Give* me my pen *back*! 私のペンを返して ◇I picked it up and *gave* it *back* to him. それを拾って彼に返してやった ◇The opera-

tion gave him *back* the use of his legs. 彼は手術のおかげでまた両脚を使えるようになった
- **,take sth 'back** 句動詞 （サイズ間違い[動かない]）などのために物を）返品する；（店が返金[交換]して）返品に応じる ◇Don't worry. If you decide you don't like it, you can always *take it back*. ご心配なく。お気に召さなければいつでもご返品いただけます ◇The store refused to *take the jacket back*, claiming that it had already been worn several times. すでに何回か着用されていたと主張して、店はジャケットの返品を断った
- **replace** [他]《ややフォーマル》（以前あった場所に物を）戻す ◇I *replaced* the cup carefully in the saucer. カップを慎重に受け皿に戻した
- **,hand sth 'back** 句動詞 （所有する人に手渡して物を）返す、返還する ◇She picked up the wallet and *handed it back* to him. 彼女は財布を拾って、彼に手渡してあげた ◇Control of the territory was *handed back* to China. その領土の統治権は中国に返還された
- **restore** [他]《フォーマル》（失った[盗まれた]物を）返す、返還する ◇The police have now *restored* the painting to its rightful owner. 警察はその絵を正当な権利を有するその所有者に返却済みだ

reveal [動]

reveal・disclose・expose・uncover・leak・betray・divulge・give sb/sth away・bring sth to light
情報の秘密が保たれると思われる場合に、その情報を人に与える
【類語訳】明らかにする、発表する、開示する、暴く、暴露する、漏洩する、ばらす

文型&コロケーション
- ▶to reveal/ disclose/ expose/ leak/ betray/ divulge/ give away sth **to** sb
- ▶to reveal/ disclose/ expose/ uncover sb/ sth **as** sb/ sth
- ▶It was revealed/ disclosed that...
- ▶to reveal/ disclose/ betray/ divulge **what/ how/ who/ where/ whether**...
- ▶to reveal/ disclose/ uncover/ leak/ betray/ divulge/ give away a **secret**
- ▶to reveal/ disclose/ expose/ uncover/ give away the **truth**
- ▶to reveal/ disclose/ leak/ divulge/ give away **details** of sth
- ▶to **fully/ publicly** reveal/ disclose/ expose sth

reveal [他] （秘密事項を）明らかにする ◇Her expression *revealed* nothing. 彼女の表情からは何もわからなかった ◇The report *reveals* (that) the company made a loss of £20 million last year. 報告書によると、その会社は昨年2000万ポンドの損失を出している ◇Officers could not *reveal* how he died. 警察官たちは彼がどのようにして亡くなったのか明らかにできなかった ◇Salted peanuts were recently *revealed* as the nation's favourite snack. 塩を振ったピーナッツは最近、国民の大好きなスナックであるとわかった ☞ **reveal** (SHOW 2), **revealing** (INFORMATIVE)
▷**revelation** [名] [C, U] ◇He was dismissed after *revelations* that confidential files were missing. 機密ファイルがなくなっていることが発覚して彼は解雇された ◇The company's financial problems followed the *revelation* of a major fraud scandal. 重大な詐欺スキャンダルの発覚に続いて、会社の財源問題が浮かび上がった

disclose [他]《ややフォーマル》（秘密事項を）明らかにする、発表する、開示する ◇The spokesman refused to *disclose* details of the takeover to the press. スポークスマンは企業買収の詳細を報道陣に発表するのを拒んだ ◇It was *disclosed* that two women were being interviewed by the police. 二人の女性が警察で事情聴取されていることが明らかとなった ☞ **undisclosed** (SECRET)
▷**disclosure** [名] [C, U] ◇There were some startling *disclosures* about his private life.《フォーマル》彼の私生活について驚愕すべきことがいくつか発覚した ◇The bank will need full *disclosure* of your financial situation and assets. その銀行はあなたの資金と資産の全面開示を求めるだろう

ノート reveal と **disclose** の使い分け：これらの語の間に実質的な意味の違いはないが、**disclose** は常にややフォーマルである。**reveal** は大衆的な新聞・雑誌で、フォーマルな文脈でもそれほどフォーマルでない文脈でも用いられる。✕Salted peanuts were recently *disclosed* as the nation's favourite snack.

expose [他] （人・状況が悪[違法]であることを）暴く、暴露する ◇She was *exposed* as a liar and a fraud. 彼女が嘘つきで詐欺師であることが暴かれた ◇He threatened to *expose* the racism that existed within the police force. 彼は警察内部に存在する人種差別を暴露すると脅した ☞ **expose** (SHOW 2)
▷**exposé** [名] [C] ◇The magazine contained a damning *exposé* of police corruption.《ジャーナリズム》その雑誌には警察汚職を証明する暴露記事が載っていた

uncover [他] （秘密事項を）暴く、暴露する ◇Police have *uncovered* a plot to kidnap the President's son. 警察は大統領の息子を誘拐しようとする陰謀を暴いた

leak [他]《ジャーナリズム》（機密情報を大衆に）漏らす、流す、漏洩する ◇The contents of the report were *leaked* to the press. 報告書の内容がマスコミに漏れた ◇He obtained a *leaked* document containing the views of some officials. 彼は数人の役人の見解を含む流出文書を入手した ☞ **leak out** (TURN OUT)
▷**leak** [名] [C] ◇There will be an enquiry into the alleged security *leaks*. その機密漏洩の疑惑は調査されることになるでしょう

betray [他] （うっかり情報・感情を）表す ◇His voice *betrayed* the worry he was trying to hide. 彼が隠そうとしている気苦労は声に表れた ◇She was terrified of saying something that would make her *betray herself* (= show her feelings or who she was). 彼女は本性が表れてしまうようなことを口にするのを恐れていた

divulge [他]《フォーマル》（秘密であると思われる情報を）明らかにする ◇Police refused to *divulge* the identity of the suspect. 警察は容疑者の身元を明かすのを拒んだ ❶ *divulge* は否定文で[否定的な意味を持つ動詞と共に]用いられることが多い。

,give sb/sth a'way 句動詞 （秘密事項を）漏らす、ばらす ◇She *gave away* state secrets to the enemy. 彼女は国家機密を敵に漏らした ◇His voice *gave him away* (= showed who he really was). 声で彼の身元がばれた ◇It was supposed to be a surprise but the children *gave the game away*.《特に英》それはサプライズであったのだが、子どもたちが口をばらした ☞ **betray** (TELL 2)

ノート divulge と **give sth away** の使い分け：**give sth away** する人は、本当は情報を秘密にしておくべきである。情報を **divulge** する人は、そうする権利を持っている可能性が高い。

↪reveal

bring sth to 'light [行] (新情報を)明らかにする, 明るみに出す ◇These facts have only just been *brought to light*. これらの事実が明るみに出たばかりだ

revenge [名]

revenge • retaliation • vengeance • reprisal
自分がされたことを人にも行うこと
【類語訳】復讐, 報復, 仕返し, 雪辱

retaliation   revenge   vengeance
               reprisal

【文型&コロケーション】
▶ revenge/ retaliation/ vengeance/ reprisals **for** sth
▶ retaliation/ vengeance/ reprisals **against** sb
▶ to take revenge/ vengeance **on** sb
▶ **in** revenge/ retaliation/ vengeance/ reprisal
▶ **in** revenge/ retaliation/ reprisal **for** sth
▶ to **take/ seek** revenge/ vengeance/ reprisals
▶ to **fear** retaliation/ vengeance/ reprisals
▶ to **want/ vow/ swear/ exact/ wreak** revenge/ vengeance

revenge [U] (危機・苦痛への)復讐, 報復, 仕返し, 雪辱 ◇The team wanted to get their *revenge* for their defeat earlier in the season. チームはシーズン初期の敗北に対して雪辱を果たしたがっていた ◇He swore to take *revenge* on his political enemies. 彼は政敵に対する復讐を誓った ◇His death set off a series of *revenge killings*. 彼の死から一連の報復殺人が始まった

retaliation [U] 《ややフォーマル》(自分にされた悪への)復讐, 報復, 仕返し ◇The shooting may have been in *retaliation* for the arrest of the terrorist suspects. その銃撃はテロの容疑者たちの逮捕に対する報復であったかもしれない

vengeance [U] 《フォーマル》(殺害・傷害などの暴力的な)復讐 ◇*Vengeance* was swift and brutal. 復讐は即座にかつ残酷に行われた ◇He swore *vengeance* on his child's killer. 彼は自分の子供を殺害した犯人に対して復讐を誓った

reprisal [C, U] 《書き言葉》(軍隊・政治団体による暴力的[攻撃的]な)報復 ◇They were frightened to talk publicly *for fear of reprisals*. 彼らは報復を恐れて人前で話すのを怖がっていた ◇A dozen hostages were shot in *reprisal* for the killing of an army officer. 陸軍将校の殺害に対する報復として, 十数人の人質が射殺された

【ノート】revenge はこれらの語の中で最も一般的な語で, ゲームで最初に打ち負かされた後に人を打ち負かしたいと思うことから, 愛する人を殺されたために人を殺害することまで, すべての範囲の行動を含む. 個人的にされたことに応えて行う, 実に私的で個人的な行為を指すことが多い. retaliation と reprisals は, 軍隊などによる他の集団により他の集団に対して行われる行為を指すことが多い. その相手方の集団が, 実際には最初の犯罪に責任があるかもしれないし, そうでないかもしれない. ◆They fear *retaliation* against US troops and aid workers (= for example, because of sth that the US government has done). (彼らは米軍や支援活動家への報復を恐れている). vengeance はこれらの行動の中で最も過激なものである. しばしば個人的なもので, 復讐対象の元の犯罪よりずっと激しいものである場合もある.

revenue [名] ☞ INCOME

revenue • income • turnover • proceeds • receipts • takings • take
税の徴収[商品の販売, サービスの提供]で得られるお金
【類語訳】税収, 収入, 収益, 歳入, 売上高

【文型&コロケーション】
▶ the **revenue**/ income/ turnover/ proceeds/ receipts/ takings/ take **from** sth
▶ the **gross/ net/ total** revenue/ income/ turnover/ proceeds/ receipts/ takings/ take
▶ the **expected/ annual** revenue/ income/ turnover/ proceeds/ receipts/ takings
▶ the **potential/ overall** revenue/ income/ turnover
▶ a **large/ substantial/ low/ small** revenue/ income/ turnover
▶ to **increase/ boost/ reduce** (your) revenue/ your income/ turnover
▶ to **spend/ use** your revenue/ your income/ the proceeds
▶ to **bring in/ generate/ produce** revenue/ an income
▶ revenue/ income/ turnover/ receipts **is/ are up/ down**

revenue [U, C] 《ややフォーマル》(政府の)税収, (会社・国の)収入, 収益, 歳入 ◇The government is currently facing a shortfall in tax *revenue*. 政府は現在, 税収不足に直面している ◇Advertising *revenue* finances the commercial television channels. 広告収入が民間のテレビ番組に資金を提供している ◇The company's annual *revenues* rose by 30% last year. 《ビジネスで》その会社の年間収益は昨年3割増加した

income [C, U] (会社・国の)収入, 収益, 歳入 ◇The company has an *income* of around $10 million a year. その会社は年に約1000万ドルの収益がある ◇Tourism is the island's main source of *income*. 観光業はその島の大きな収入源である

【ノート】**revenue** と **income** の使い分け：税収については revenue を用いる. それ以外の場合は, 両語とも使用可能だが, revenue のほうがフォーマルである. income はまた個人が稼ぐお金についても用いられる. ☞ INCOME

turnover [C, ふつう単数で, U] 《ビジネスで》(会社の)売上高 ◇The firm has an annual *turnover* of $75 million. その会社は年間7500万ドルの売上高がある ◇A 10% rise in *turnover* would increase company profits by $3.3 million. 売り上げが1割増えれば, 会社の利益は330万ドル増加する

proceeds [複数で] (費用の支払い後に使うことのできる人・会社の)収入, 収益 ◇She sold her car and bought a piano with the *proceeds*. 彼女は車を売り, その金でピアノを買った ◇The *proceeds* of the concert will go to charity. コンサートの収益は慈善団体に寄付される ☞ PROFIT

receipts [複数で] 《ビジネスで》(会社・銀行・政府の)収入, 収益, 歳入 ◇The accounts department is predicting net *receipts* of £750,000 for the summer season. 会計課は夏季に75万ポンドの純利益を予想している

takings [複数で] (店・レストラン・劇場などの)売上高, 収入 ◇Burglars forced open the safe containing the weekend *takings*. 強盗一味が週末の売上金の入った金庫をこじ開けた

> **ノート** receipts と takings の使い分け：receipts のほうがフォーマルな語で、比較的大きなビジネスの長い期間にわたる《収入》に用いられることが多い。どちらの語も、特に《英》において、劇場・映画・映画産業が売り上げるお金に用いられる。《米》のインフォーマルな言い回しでは、take という語が用いられる。 ◆ He estimated the film's box-office *receipts/takings* at £15 million. (特に《英》)彼は映画の興行収入を1500万ポンドと見積もった。 ◆ the movie's box-office *take* (《米、ややインフォーマル》)映画の興行収入》

take [C、ふつう単数で]《特に《米、ややインフォーマル、ビジネス》》《特定の収入源・ビジネスから得られる》売上高、収入 ◇ Last year's *take* totaled $10.2 million. 昨年の売上高は合計1020万ドルとなった

revolution [名]

revolution・coup・riot・uprising・revolt・rebellion・rioting・insurgency・mutiny
人々が権威に対抗して一緒に行動すること
【類語訳】革命、クーデター、暴動、蜂起、反乱、動乱、反発、反逆、謀反、造反

> 文型&コロケーション
> ▸ a revolution/ a coup/ an uprising/ a revolt/ a rebellion **against** sb/ sth
> ▸ a **successful** revolution/ coup/ revolt
> ▸ a **major/ full-scale** riot/ revolt/ rebellion
> ▸ a **military** coup/ uprising/ rebellion/ mutiny
> ▸ a **popular** revolution/ uprising/ revolt/ rebellion
> ▸ an **armed** coup/ uprising/ revolt/ rebellion/ insurgency
> ▸ (a) **violent** revolution/ riot/ uprising/ rebellion/ rioting
> ▸ to **plan** a revolution/ coup/ rebellion
> ▸ to **provoke** a riot/ an uprising/ a revolt/ a rebellion
> ▸ to **stage/ lead** a revolution/ coup/ revolt/ rebellion/ mutiny
> ▸ to **quell** a riot/ an uprising/ a revolt/ a rebellion/ rioting
> ▸ to **crush** an uprising/ a revolt/ a rebellion
> ▸ to **put down** a revolt/ rebellion
> ▸ a revolution/ a riot/ a revolt/ a rebellion/ rioting **breaks out**

revolution [C, U]《統治体制を変えるための国民による》革命 ◇ The French *Revolution* brought about great changes in the society and government of France. フランス革命はフランスの社会と政治に大きな変革をもたらした ◇ The country appears to be on the brink of *revolution*. その国は今にも革命が起きそうに見える ☞ **revolutionary** (GUERRILLA), **revolutionary** (RADICAL).

coup [C]《指導者・政府を変えるための軍事【強力】グループによる不法な》クーデター、政変 ◇ The regime was overthrown in a bloodless *coup* led by young army of officers. 政権は若い陸軍将校たちが指揮する無血クーデターによって転覆した ◇ Months of unrest in the company led to a *boardroom coup* (= a sudden change of power among senior managers in a company) that saw four directors voted out. 《比喩的》何か月にもわたって会社の不穏な状態が続き、役員室で4人の重役が投票で解任されるというクーデターが起こった **i** *coup* は *coup d'état* の短縮形だが、*coup* のほうがずっと頻繁に用いられる。

riot [C]《抗議としての群衆による公共の場での》暴動 ◇ Food *riots* resulted in two deaths and looting throughout the city. 食糧暴動で二人の死者が出て、町中で略奪行

為が行われた ◇ The demonstrators were held back by 6,000 *riot police* using tear gas and water cannon. デモ隊は催涙ガスと放水銃を使う6000人の機動隊によって阻止された
▸ **riot** [動][自] ◇ The fans *rioted* after their team lost. ファンたちはひいきのチームが負けた後で暴動を起こした

uprising [C]《国・地域・都市で権力の座にある人々に対する》蜂起、一揆、反乱、動乱 ◇ He used his troops to crush a popular *uprising* in the north. 彼は軍隊を使って北側での民衆蜂起を鎮圧した **i** *uprising* は歴史に残る特定の反乱の名称に用いられる。 ◆ the 1956/Hungarian *uprising* (1956年蜂起/ハンガリー動乱). *uprising* は、しばしば強烈な暴力によって打ち破られるのが常であるが、成功した場合には *revolution* と呼ばれる。

revolt [C, U]《政府に対する》反乱、暴動、蜂起、一揆、《権威に対する》反発 ◇ 27 members of the Bohemian nobility led the *revolt* against Ferdinand II. 27人のボヘミア人貴族がフェルディナント2世に対する暴動を指揮した ◇ A shareholders' *revolt* against the chairman led to senior management changes. 会長に対する株主の反発で、上級管理職が交替することになった ◇ The people rose in *revolt*. 民衆が蜂起した

rebellion [C, U]《国・組織の一部による政府[主たる権力]に対する暴力的な》反乱、反逆、謀反、造反 ◇ The army put down the *rebellion*. 軍が反乱を鎮圧した ◇ After years of protest, much of the country was now in open *rebellion* against the president. 何年にも及ぶ抗議の後、国の大部分の地域でもはや公然と大統領に反旗が翻っていた ☞ **rebel** (GUERRILLA).

> **ノート** revolt と rebellion の使い分け：revolt は rebellion よりも小規模[限定的]である可能性がある。 ◆ The English Tudors faced six major *rebellions* and countless minor *revolts*. (英国のチューダー朝は、6度の大反乱と無数の小さな暴動に直面した)。 *rebellion* は時に大きな集団・組織の内部の人々の反対を指す。 ◆ The prime minister faces a *rebellion* from junior members of his party. (首相は自党の若手による造反に直面している)。

rioting [U]《抗議の間に行われる群衆による公共の場での》暴動 ◇ Serious *rioting* broke out in the capital. 首都で深刻な暴動が起きた

insurgency [U, C]《フォーマル》《長期間にわたる武装集団による政治的主導権を握るための》反乱、暴動 ◇ The government faces continuing *insurgency* in the northeast. 政府は引き続き北東部における反乱に直面している ◇ The 23-year *insurgency* had cost an estimated 21,000 lives. 23年に及ぶ暴動で推定2万1千人の命が失われてしまった ☞ **insurgent** (GUERRILLA).

mutiny [U, C]《兵士・水兵による》反乱、暴動、謀反 ◇ Discontent among the ship's crew finally led to the outbreak of *mutiny*. 船の乗組員たちの不満はついに爆発して反乱に至った ◇ The famous *mutiny* on the British Navy ship Bounty took place in 1789. 有名な英国海軍船バウンティ号の反乱は1789年に起きた

rich [形]

rich・wealthy・prosperous・affluent・well off・privileged・comfortable・loaded
大金[多くの財産、貴重品]を持っていることを表す
【類語訳】金持ちの、裕福な、富裕の、繁栄した、羽振りのよい

文型&コロケーション

- a rich/ a wealthy/ a prosperous/ an affluent/ a well-off/ a privileged **family**
- a rich/ wealthy/ prosperous/ well-off **man/ woman**
- a rich/ a wealthy/ a prosperous/ an affluent **country/ city/ suburb**
- very rich/ wealthy/ prosperous/ affluent/ well off/ comfortable
- quite/ fairly/ reasonably/ relatively rich/ wealthy/ prosperous/ affluent/ well off/ comfortable
- newly rich/ wealthy/ prosperous/ affluent

rich (人が)金持ちの, 裕福な; (国・都市が)富裕な ◇She's one of the *richest* women in the world. 彼女は世界で最も裕福な女性の一人である ◇He's *stinking/filthy rich*. (=extremely) 《俗語》彼は有り余るほどの大金持ちだ ◇*Rich* countries can afford to spend more on the environment. 富裕国は環境関連支出を増やすゆとりがある 反意 **poor** (POOR 1), ☞ **riches** (MONEY 3)
▶ **the rich** [複数で] ◇It's a favourite resort for *the rich and famous* (= people who are rich and famous). そこは金持ちの有名人がお気に入りのリゾートである

wealthy (人が)裕福な; (国・都市が)富裕な ◇She comes from a very *wealthy* family. 彼女は非常に裕福な家庭の出だ ◇They live in a *wealthy* suburb of Chicago. 彼らはシカゴの富裕層がいる郊外に住んでいる 反意 **poor, needy** (POOR 1), ☞ **wealth** (MONEY 3)
▶ **the wealthy** [名][複数で] ◇He promised tax cuts for *the wealthy* (= people who are wealthy). 彼は富裕層に対する減税を約束した

ノート rich と wealthy の使い分け: これら二つの語の間に実質的な意味の違いはないが, 非常に頻繁に用いられるが, rich のほうがより頻繁に用いられ, wealthy を用いることができない定型句でも用いることができる. ✗He's stinking/filthy *wealthy*. ✗It's a favourite resort for the *wealthy* and famous.

prosperous 《ややフォーマル》繁栄した, 羽振りのよい ◇These countries became *prosperous* through trade, not aid. こうした国々は援助でなく貿易によって繁栄してきた ◇The 1960s were *prosperous* years for the company. 1960年代はその会社にとって繁栄の時代だった 反意 **impoverished** (POOR 1), ☞ **prosper** (DO WELL), **prosperity** (MONEY 3)

affluent 《ややフォーマル》裕福な, 富裕な ◇The *affluent* Western countries are better equipped to face the problems of global warming. 富裕な西欧諸国は地球温暖化問題に取り組むより優れた備えができている 反意 **poor, impoverished** (POOR 1), ☞ **affluence** (MONEY 3)

ノート prosperous と affluent の使い分け: prosperous も affluent も人や場所について用いられる. prosperous は, 時間や期間について, affluent より以上に頻繁に用いられる. affluent は, 必ずしもよいとは限らないと示唆する形で, 裕福な人々や社会と貧困な人々や社会とを比較する形で用いられることが多い. prosperous であるとは, よいことと見なされることがほとんどである. ◆It's good to see you looking so *prosperous*. (豊かな暮らし向きを拝見して嬉しいです). ✗It's good to see you looking so *affluent*.

well 'off 《しばしば否定文で》(人が)裕福な, 金持ちの; (国・都市が)富裕な ◇His parents are not very *well off*. 彼の両親はあまり裕福ではない ◇The less *well-off* families are finding it hard to survive on what they get. さほど裕福でない家庭は, 手に入るもので生き延びるのは難しいと感じている 反意 **hard up** (POOR 1)

privileged 《(けなして)》特権階級に属する ◇She comes from a *privileged* background. 彼女は特権階級の出である 反意 **deprived** (POOR 1)
▶ **privilege** [名][U] ◇As a member of the nobility, his life had been one of wealth and *privilege*. 《(けなして)》貴族の一員として, 彼の生活は富と特権に恵まれたものだった

comfortable 暮らし向きの楽な, 不自由のない ◇They're not millionaires, but they're certainly very *comfortable*. 彼らは大富豪ではないが, 暮らし向きが非常に楽なのは明らかである ◇He makes a *comfortable* living. 彼は不自由のない生活を送っている
▶ **comfortably** [副] ◇You should be able to live *comfortably* on your allowance. あなたは手当だけで不自由なく暮らせるはずだ

loaded [名詞の前では用いない] 《インフォーマル》大金持ちの ◇Let her pay — she's *loaded*. 彼女に払わせろよ—大金持ちなんだから

ridiculous [形]

ridiculous・absurd・silly・ludicrous・foolish・laughable

分別[道理]のないことを表す
【類語訳】ばかげた, ばかばかしい, 笑える, おかしな, こっけいな, 不合理な, くだらない

silly	ridiculous	ludicrous
foolish	absurd	
laughable		

文型&コロケーション

- ridiculous/ absurd/ silly/ ludicrous **that...**
- It would be ridiculous/ absurd/ silly/ ludicrous/ foolish **to do sth**.
- a ridiculous/ an absurd/ a silly/ a ludicrous/ a foolish **idea/ notion**
- a ridiculous/ an absurd/ a silly/ a foolish **question**
- a ridiculous/ an absurd/ a ludicrous **suggestion/ situation**
- a silly/ a foolish **comment/ remark/ smile/ grin**
- quite/ pretty ridiculous/ absurd/ silly/ ludicrous/ foolish/ laughable
- rather ridiculous/ absurd/ silly/ ludicrous/ foolish
- completely/ totally/ utterly/ downright ridiculous/ absurd/ silly/ ludicrous
- simply ridiculous/ absurd/ ludicrous/ foolish

ridiculous ばかげた, ばかみたいな, とんでもない; ばかばかしい, 笑える, おかしな, こっけいな ◇You look *ridiculous* in that hat! その帽子をかぶるとばかみたいに見えるよ ◇Don't be so *ridiculous*! そんなばかげたことはやめろ ◇It's *ridiculous* to suggest that she was involved in anything illegal. 彼女が何か不法なことに関わってるって言い出すなんてばかげている ◇That's the most *ridiculous* thing I've ever heard. そんなおかしなことは今まで聞いたことがない ◇They ate and drank a *ridiculous* amount. 彼らは途方もなく大量に飲み食いした ☞ **ridicule** (CONTEMPT)

▸**ridiculously** 副 ◇The food there is *ridiculously* expensive. そこの食べ物は途方もなく高い

absurd ばかげた、ばかみたいな、とんでもない；ばかばかしい、おかしな；不合理な、理屈に合わない ◇What an *absurd* idea! 何てばかげた考えなんだ ◇He has a good sense of the *absurd* (= things that are absurd). 彼にはなかなかこっけいさのセンスがある
▸**absurdity** 名 [U] ◇She failed to appreciate the *absurdity* of her position. 彼女は自分の立場のばかばかしさに気づかなかった
▸**absurdly** 副 ◇I was offered an *absurdly* large amount of money. 途方もなく多額のお金を提示された

ノート **ridiculous** と **absurd** の使い分け：これらの語の間にはほとんど意味の違いはない。ridiculous な物事はridicule（あざけり）を招く、absurd な物事は、まったく非論理的な[その場にそぐわない]ので、しばしば笑いを招く。absurd は《米》よりも《英》で頻繁に用いられ、ridiculous よりもいくぶんフォーマルである。

silly （子どもが）ばかげた、ばかみたいな、ばかばかしい、くだらない、面倒 ◇I feel really *silly* in these clothes. こんな服を着てると本当に間抜けな感じがする ◇She had a *silly* grin on her face. 彼女はばかみたいなニヤニヤした笑顔を浮かべていた ◇This is getting *silly*! I think we had all better calm down. こいつは面倒なことになってきた。ぼくたちみんな落ち着いたほうがいいと思う

ludicrous まったくばかげた、とんでもない、こっけいな ◇That's a *ludicrous* suggestion! それはまったくばかげた提案だ ◇This is *ludicrous*! Of course no one's going to murder you! こいつはこっけいだね。もちろん、誰も君を殺そうとなんかしないよ
▸**ludicrously** 副 ◇Everything here is *ludicrously* expensive. ここではすべてが途方もなく高額だ

foolish 《ややフォーマル》ばかげた、ばかみたいな、恥ずかしい；ばかみたいな思いにさせる、恥ずかしくさせるような ◇He didn't want to look *foolish* in front of his friends. 彼は友人たちの前でばかみたいに見られたくなかった ◇She spoke as though to a child who had asked a *foolish* question. 彼女はばかげた質問をする子どもに向かって話すかのように話した ☞ **fool** (FOOL)

laughable 《名詞の前まれ》ばかばかしい、笑える、おかしな、こっけいな ◇The whole incident would be *laughable* if it wasn't so serious. その事件全体がそんなに深刻なものでないなら、笑い飛ばせるのに ◇He's so wrong it's almost *laughable*. 彼がそこまで間違っているとなるとほとんどお笑い種（の）だ

right 名

right・power・privilege・claim・authority・liberty・entitlement・title・due
法的[道徳的]に持つ[行う]ことが許されている物事
【類語訳】権利，権力，権限，特権，請求権，所有権，職権，資格

文型&コロケーション
▸sb's right/ power/ claim **over** sb/ sth
▸a right/ a claim/ an entitlement/ a title **to** sth
▸the right/ power/ authority/ entitlement **to do** sth
▸a/ an **special, exclusive** right/ power/ privilege/ claim
▸a/ the **legal** right/ power/ claim/ authority/ entitlement/ title
▸**personal** rights/ freedoms/ claims/ liberties

▸**have** a/ the right/ the power/ the privilege/ a claim/ the authority/ an entitlement/ title
▸**use/ exercise** your right/ powers/ privilege/ authority/ entitlement
▸**give sb** a right/ the power/ a privilege/ title/ their due
▸**grant sb** rights/ powers/ privileges/ liberties
▸**revoke** a right/ the power/ a privilege/ the authority
▸**lose** your right/ powers / privilege/ entitlement
▸**forfeit** your right/ privilege/ claim/ entitlement/ title
▸**give up** your right/ powers/ privilege/ claim/ title
▸**renounce** your right/ privilege/ claim/ title
▸**waive** your right/ privilege/ claim
▸**respect** sb's right/ claim/ liberties

right [C] （法的[道徳的]な）権利 ◇Everyone has the *right* to a fair trial. 誰もが公正な裁判を受ける権利を持っている ◇What gives you the *right* to do that? 何の権利があってそれをするの ◇You're *quite within your rights* to ask for your money back (= you definitely have a right to do it). あなたがお金を返してもらうよう求めるのはまったく当然のことだ ◇She *had every right* to be angry. 彼女が怒るのももっともだった ◇*By rights* (= according to sb's rights) half the money should be mine. 権利として、そのお金の半分は私の物であるはずだ ◇This is a fundamental *human right* (= a right that all people should have). これは基本的人権である ◇They have always fought hard for *equal rights* (= the right of all people in society to be treated fairly and equally). 彼らは常に平等の権利を求めて懸命に闘ってきた

power [U, C, ふつう複数で]（人・集団が行使する）権力，権限 ◇The Secretary of State has the *power* to approve the proposals. 国務長官には提案を承認する法的権限がある ◇The president has the *power* of veto over all new legislation. 大統領にはすべての新法に対する拒否権がある ◇The *powers* of the police must be clearly defined. 警察の権限は明確に規定されなければならない

privilege [C]（特定の人・集団が持つ）特権 ◇Education should be a universal right and not just a *privilege*. 教育は単なる特権ではなく、普遍的な権利であるはずだ ◇Club members have special *privileges*, like being allowed to use the swimming pool. クラブのメンバーたちにはプールの使用許可などの特権がある ❶privilege は「社会において裕福[有力]な人が持つ権利と利点」を意味するために批判的に用いられる。◆ His life had always been one of wealth and *privilege*. (けなして) 彼の生活は常に富と特権に甘えたものだった

claim [C, U]（財産・土地などの）要求[請求]権，所有権 ◇The court ruled that they had no *claim* on the land. 彼らにはその土地の所有権はないとの裁定を裁判所が下した ◇The princess was forced to renounce her *claim* to the throne. 王女は王位継承権を放棄せざるをえなかった ◇He went back to *lay claim to* his inheritance. 彼は相続権を主張するために戻った
▸**claim** 動 [他] ◇A lot of lost property is never *claimed*. 多くの遺失物が（持ち主から）請求もされない ◇The family arrived in the UK in the 1990s and *claimed* political asylum. その家族は1990年代に英国にやって来て政治亡命を申請した

authority [U]（組織の上級職が持つ）権限，職権 ◇Only the manager has the *authority* to sign cheques. 経営者だけが小切手に署名する権限を持っている

↳right

ノート powerとauthorityの使い分け：この意味ではauthorityはふつう(have) the authority to do sthの句で用いられる。このauthorityはふつう会社などの組織内部の地位ある人によってもたらされ、許可が与えられる。powerやspecial powersは、裁判所・政府・政体によってもたらされることが多く、国の法律・政体に則って許可が与えられる。×Only the manager has the *power* to sign cheques. ×The *authority* of the police must be clearly defined.

liberty [C]（法的な）自由，権利 ◇The right to vote should be a *liberty* enjoyed by all. 選挙権はすべての人が享受できる権利であるべきだ ◇This is a gross infringement of our *civil liberties* (= the right of people to be free to say or do what they want while respecting others and staying within the law). これは紛れもなく我々市民の自由を侵害するものである ❶この意味でlibertyは特にpersonal/civil libertiesの句で用いられる。

entitlement [U, C]《特に英，フォーマル》（支払いを受け取る[財産を所有する]）公的な）資格，権利；（公的権利のある）給付金 ◇This may affect your *entitlement* to compensation. これは補償を受けるあなたの資格に影響を与えるかもしれない ◇Your contributions will affect your pension *entitlements*. 掛け金次第で受け取れる年金の給付金は変わります ❶entitlementの上記の意味は《米》ではあまり頻繁に用いられない。しかし特に《米》では，a sense of entitlementの句で、実際には物事に貢献せずに、それに対する権利を持っていると思っている人々について、批判的に用いられる。◆The only child of very wealthy parents, she embodies the spoiled brat with *a sense of entitlement*. 《特に米，けなして》彼女は非常に裕福な両親を持つ一人っ子で、権利意識を持つ甘やかされた子どもの典型だ ☞entitle (ALLOW)

title [U, C]《法律》（財産・土地などの）所有権；（所有権の）権利証書 ◇He claims he has *title* to the land. 彼の主張はその土地の所有権があるとのことだ ◇Who holds the *title deed* (= the legal document proving that sb is the owner of a particular property or piece of land)? 誰が権利証書を持っているんですか

due [U]（自らの行動によって獲得したので）当然受けるべきもの，当然の評価 ◇He received a large reward, which was no more than his *due* (= what he deserved). 彼は大きな報酬を手にしたが、それはもらって当然のものにすぎなかった ◇She's a slow worker, but to *give her her due* (= be fair to her) she is very thorough. 彼女は仕事は遅いが、公平を期して言うなら、非常に行き届いてはいる ❶この意味でdueは常に，my/your/his/her/our/their dueの句で用いられる。

right 形

1 right・correct・proper
信念や意見，決定，方法が特定の状況で妥当[最善]であること
【類語訳】正しい，間違いのない，適切な，ふさわしい，しかるべき

文型&コロケーション
- right/ correct **about** sb/ sth
- right/ correct **to do sth**
- right/ correct **in thinking/ believing/ saying** sth
- the/ a right/ correct/ proper **decision/ judgement/ conclusion**
- the right/ correct/ proper **way/ method/ approach**
- **absolutely/ quite/ undoubtedly** right/ correct

right（ある状況において）正しい，間違いのない，適切な，ふさわしい ◇She was *right* about Tom having no money. トムにはお金がないという点については、彼女は間違っていなかった ◇You're *right* to be cautious. 君が用心深くなるのは間違っていないよ ◇Am I *right* in thinking we've met before? 確か以前会ったことがありますよね ◇He's made the *right* decision. 彼は適切な判断を下した ◇'It's not easy.' 'Yeah, you're *right*.'「そいつは簡単じゃないよ」「ああ、そのとおりだ」 反意 **wrong** (WRONG 1)

▶ **rightly** 副 ◇She believed, quite *rightly*, that he had let her down. 彼女は彼が期待を裏切ったと思っていたが、まったくそのとおりだった

correct《ややフォーマル》（方法・信念・意見・決定が特定の状況において）正しい，間違いのない，適切な，ふさわしい ◇What's the *correct* way to shut the machine down? どうやって機械の電源を正しく切るの ◇Am I *correct* in thinking that you know a lot about wine? ワインのことはお詳しいと考えてもいいですか 反意 **incorrect** ❶反意語はincorrectだが、この意味では非常にフォーマルであまり頻繁に用いられない。

▶ **correctly** 副 ◇Make sure the letter is *correctly* addressed. 手紙の宛名が正しく書かれているか確かめなさい

proper《名詞の前で》《特に英》正しい，間違いのない，適切な，ふさわしい；（規則に従って）しかるべき ◇We should have had a *proper* discussion before voting. 我々は投票前にしかるべき議論をすべきだった ◇Please follow the *proper* procedures for dealing with complaints. 苦情を処理する際にはしかるべき手順を踏んでください ◇Nothing is in its *proper* place. あるべき所にある物が何もない

▶ **properly** 副 ◇How much money do we need to do the job *properly*? その仕事を間違いなく行うにはいくらいりますか

ノート right, correct, proper の使い分け：correctは、right, properよりもフォーマルである。properは《米》ではあまり用いられない。また、correctは人を修飾できるが、properは不可。×You're *proper* to be cautious. ×Am I *proper* in thinking...? correct, properは方法について用いられることが多く、rightは信念・意見・決定について用いられることが多い。

2 right・acceptable・proper・due・justified・decent・justifiable
道徳的に優れていること，社会的に受け入れられていること
【類語訳】正しい，正当な，当然の，適切な，適当な，しかるべき，まともな，きちんとした

文型&コロケーション
- right/ acceptable/ proper/ justified/ justifiable **to do sth**
- right/ justified **in doing sth**
- right/ acceptable/ proper **that...**
- acceptable/ proper/ decent **behaviour**
- **to do** the right/ proper/ decent **thing**
- **scarcely/ hardly/ not really** right/ acceptable/ proper/ justified
- **perfectly** right/ acceptable/ proper/ justified/ decent/ justifiable
- **entirely** right/ acceptable/ proper/ justified/ justifiable
- **morally** right/ acceptable/ justified/ justifiable
- **only** right/ proper

rise

right [名詞の前はまれ]（道徳的に）正しい、正当な；（法律・義務に照らして）当然の ◇You were quite *right* to tell me. 私に君が話してくれてまったく正解だったよ ◇It's *right* that he should be punished. 彼が罰されるのは当然だ ◇Hunting may be legal, but that doesn't make it *right*. 狩りは合法かもしれないが、だからと言って正当ということにはならない ◇I hope we're doing the *right* thing. 私たちが間違ったことをしていなければいいのだが 反意 **wrong** (WRONG 3)

▶**rightly** 副 ◇*Rightly or wrongly*, he was released early from prison. 事の是非はさておき、彼は早期に釈放された ◇Politicians are asked to declare any business interests, *and rightly so*. 政治家はあらゆるビジネス関連の収益について公表することが求められるが、それは当然のことだ

acceptable （振る舞い・行動が社会的に）受け入れられる ◇Children have to learn what is *acceptable* behaviour and what is not. 子どもたちは何が受け入れられる行動で何がそうでないかを学ばなければならない ◇Divorce is much more *socially acceptable* than it used to be. 離婚は以前よりずっと社会的に受け入れられている 反意 **unacceptable** (UNACCEPTABLE)

proper 《ややフォーマル》（社会的）適切な、当然の ◇It is *right and proper* that parents take responsibility for their children's behaviour. 両親が子どもの行動に責任を持つのは至極当然のことだ ◇I'll do whatever I think *proper*. 適切と思えることは何でもやります ◇The development was planned without *proper regard* for the feelings of the local residents. その開発は地元住民の感情にまともな配慮もせずに計画された 反意 **improper**

▶**properly** 副 ◇You acted perfectly *properly* in approaching me first. 私に初めて声をかけてきたときのあなたの振る舞いは申し分がなかった

[ノート] **acceptable** と **proper** の使い分け：acceptable は proper より幅広い意味を持つ。物事が socially/morally acceptable とは言えない。なぜなら social/moral の意味合いが proper の意味の中に含まれているからである。proper は acceptable よりフォーマルで、《米》よりも《英》でよく使われる。proper はまた承認の度合いが強いことを暗示する。つまり、proper である行動は、認められた行動であるが、acceptable である行動は、認められていないわけではない行動である。

due [名詞の前で]《フォーマル》（ある状況において）適当な、当然の ◇After *due* consideration we have decided to appoint Mr Davis to the job. 我々はしかるべき考慮をした上で、その仕事にデイヴィス氏を任命することに決めた ◇Your request will be dealt with *in due course* (= at the right time and not before). 適切な時期が来れば、あなたの要望は取り上げられるであろう

justified [名詞の前はまれ]（もっともな理由があり）正当な、当然の；（もっともな理由があり）正当化された ◇She felt fully *justified* in asking for her money back. 返金を求めるのはまったく当然と彼女は感じていた ◇I don't think the death penalty is ever *justified*. 死刑は決して正当化されないと思います 反意 **unjustified**

decent [名詞の前はまれ]《ややフォーマル》（特定の状況で人々に受け入れられる）まともな、きちんとした、しかるべき ◇Local people made sure the soldiers were given a *decent* burial. 地元住民は兵士たちがきちんと埋葬されることを確認した ◇I think he should do the *decent* thing and resign. 彼はいさぎよく辞めるべきだと思います ◇She should have waited *a decent interval* before marrying again. 彼女は再婚する前にしかるべき期間を空けるべきだった 反意 **indecent**

justifiable （もっともな理由があり）正当な、当然の ◇She took a *justifiable* pride in her son's achievements. 彼女が息子の出来栄えを誇りに思うのももっともであった ◇There were no *justifiable* grounds for sending him to prison. 彼を投獄する正当な理由はなかった 反意 **unjustifiable**

▶**justifiably** 副 ◇The college can be *justifiably* proud of its record. その大学が自らの歴史に誇りを持つとは当然のことと言えよう

[ノート] **justified** と **justifiable** の使い分け：justified は人や行動に、justifiable は行動、感情、理由に用いられる。×She felt *justifiable* in asking for her money back. ×There were no *justified* grounds for sending him to prison.

rise 動 ☞ SOAR

rise・grow・increase・climb・go up・escalate
量[水準、数]が大きく[高く]なることを表す
【類語訳】上がる、上昇する、増える、増加する、高まる、強まる、発展する、伸びる、拡大する、急上昇する、激化する

[文型&コロケーション]

▶to rise/ grow/ increase/ go up **in** price, number, etc.
▶to rise/ grow/ increase/ climb/ go up **by** 10%, 2,000, etc.
▶to rise/ grow/ increase/ climb/ go up/ escalate **from** 2% **to** 5%
▶the **price/ number** rises/ increases/ climbs/ goes up/ escalates
▶the **level/ cost** rises/ increases/ goes up/ escalates
▶the **size/ amount** grows/ increases
▶to rise/ grow/ increase/ climb/ go up/ escalate **sharply**
▶to rise/ grow/ increase/ climb/ go up **slightly/ steadily/ slowly/ rapidly/ dramatically**
▶to rise/ grow/ increase/ escalate **suddenly**
▶to rise/ increase/ climb/ go up **steeply**

rise [自]（数・水準・量が）上がる、上昇する、高くなる、増える ◇*rising* fuel bills/divorce rates 上昇する燃料代/離婚率 ◇The price of gas has *risen* by 3%. ガス代が3%上昇した ◇Gas *rose* sharply in price. ガス代が急上昇した ◇Interest rates are expected to *rise* from 4.5% to 5% in the next six months. 利率はこの先半年で4.5%から5%に上がることが予想される 反意 **fall, drop, sink** (FALL 1), ☞ **rise** (INCREASE 名)

grow [自]（大きさ・数・強さが）大きくなる、増す、増加[増大]する、高まる、強まる、発展する ◇The company profits are expected to *grow* by 5% next year. その会社では来年は5%の利益増が期待されている ◇She is *growing* in confidence all the time. 彼女は常に自信を深め続けている ◇Their performance improved as their confidence *grew*. 自信が増すにつれて、彼らの業績は改善した ◇There is *growing* opposition to the latest proposals. 最新の提案に反対の声が高まっている ◇The company is *growing* bigger all the time. その会社は常に発展し続けている 反意 **shrink** (SHRINK), ☞ **growth** (INCREASE 名), **expand** (EXPAND)

increase [自]（量・水準・数・程度・価値・大きさ）大

↪ rise

きくなる, 増す, 増加[増大]する, 高まる, 強まる ◇The population has *increased* from 1.2 million to 1.8 million. 人口は120万人から180万人に増加した ◇Demand is expected to *increase* over the next decade. 次の10年の間には需要の増加が見込まれる ◇Disability *increases* with age (= the older sb is, the more likely they are to have a disability). 機能障害は年齢と共に増える 反意 **decrease, decline** (FALL1), ☞ **increase** (INCREASE 名), **increase** (INCREASE 動)

ノート **rise, grow, increase** の使い分け: rise はこれらの動詞の中で最も頻繁に用いられるが, 数や水準について用いられることが一番多い. grow と increase は, 大きさや強さについても用いることができる. ◆ Profits/Numbers have *risen/grown/increased*. (利益/数が増えた). ◆ Her confidence/fear *grew/increased*. (彼女の自信/恐怖心が増した). × Her confidence/fear *rose*. increase は rise, grow よりもいくぶんフォーマルである.

climb [自] (数字・温度・お金の価値が)上がる, 上昇する, 高くなる, 伸びる ◇The dollar/temperature has been *climbing* all week. 一週間の間ずっとドル/温度は上昇し続けている ◇The paper's circulation continues to *climb*. その新聞の発行部数は上昇し続けている ◇Membership is *climbing* steadily. 会員数は堅調に伸びている ❶ climb はふつう量より数について用いられる. ◆ Unemployment (= the number of unemployed people) is still *climbing*. (失業者数は依然上昇を続けている). × The pollution/mess is *climbing*. 反意 **drop** (FALL1)

go up 句動詞《ややインフォーマル, 特に話し言葉》(水準・価値が)上がる, 高くなる ◇The price of cigarettes is *going up*. タバコの価格は上昇している ◇Do you think interest rates will *go up* again? 金利はまた値上がりすると思いますか 反意 **come down** (FALL1)

escalate [自]《ややフォーマル》拡大する, 増大する, 急上昇する, 激化する, 発展する ◇The fighting *escalated* into a full-scale war. その戦闘は全面戦争に発展した ◇the *escalating* costs of health care 増大する医療費

risk 名

1 risk・danger・threat・fear

悪い[不快な]事が起こる可能性
【類語訳】危険, リスク, 危機, 脅威, 恐れ

文型&コロケーション
▸ the risk/ danger/ threat **of** sth happening
▸ the risk/ danger/ threat **that** sth will happen
▸ (a) **real/ great/ serious/ grave** risk/ danger/ threat
▸ to **pose** a risk/ danger/ threat
▸ to **put** sth **at risk/ in danger/ under threat**

risk [C, U] (悪い事が起こる)危険(性), リスク ◇There is still a *risk* that the whole deal will fall through. 依然として取り引きが全体として不成立に終わる危険性がある ◇We don't want to *run the risk* of losing their business. 私たちは彼らとの仕事を失うリスクを負いたくない ◇We could probably trust her with the information but it's just not *worth the risk*. その情報を彼女に与えても大丈夫だとは思うが, それでも危ない橋を渡ってまでもやることではない ◇*At the risk of* showing my ignorance, how exactly does this system work? 自分の無知をさらけ出すことになるのですが, このシステムはどういう仕組みになっているのですか ◇He dived in to save the dog *at considerable risk to* his own life. 彼は自分の命をかなり危険にさらしてまでその犬を助けようと頭から水中に飛び込んだ ☞ **risk** (THREAT), **risk** (DARE), **risky** (DANGEROUS), **at risk** (VULNERABLE)

danger [U, C] (傷害・危害・殺害・損害・破壊が伴う)危険, 危機 ◇*Danger*! Keep Out! (= written on a sign) (標識で)危険. 立入禁止 ◇Children's lives are *in danger* every time they cross this road. 子どもたちの命はこの道路を渡るたびに危険にさらされている ◇The building is in *danger* of collapsing. その建物は崩壊の危険性がある ◇Doctors said she is now *out of danger* (= not likely to die). 彼女はもう危険を脱していると医者は言った ◇There is a *danger* that the political disorder of the past will return. 過去の政治の混乱が再燃する危険性がある ☞ **danger** (THREAT), **dangerous** (DANGEROUS)

threat [U, C, ふつう単数で] (悪い事が起こる)脅威 ◇These ancient woodlands are *under threat* from new road developments. これらの古代からの森林地帯は新しい道路開発の脅威にさらされている ◇There is a real *threat* of war. 現実に戦争の脅威がある ☞ **threat** (THREAT), **threaten** (THREATEN)

fear [U] (事が起こる)恐れ ❶ この意味で fear は, 「事が起こる危険を回避する」ことを意味する for fear of sth/of doing sth, for fear that... の表現でしか用いられない. ◆ We spoke quietly *for fear of* waking the guards. (私たちは護衛が目を覚まさないように小声で話した). ◆ I had to run away *for fear that* he might one day kill me. (彼にいつか殺されるかもしれないと恐れて私は逃げる必要があった).

2 risk・gamble・chance・lottery

悪い結果を招くかもしれないことを承知したうえで成功することを望んで事を行うこと
【類語訳】賭け, 冒険, 運, 巡り合わせ

文型&コロケーション
▸ to take a risk/ gamble/ chance **on** sth
▸ to take a risk/ chance **with** sth
▸ a **big** risk/ gamble/ chance
▸ a **huge/ major/ calculated** risk/ gamble
▸ **something of/ a bit of** a risk/ gamble/ lottery
▸ to **take** a risk/ gamble/ chance
▸ a risk/ gamble **pays off**

risk [C] 《ふつう take a risk の形で》賭け, 冒険, 危険を冒す[危険にさらす]こと ◇That's a *risk* that I'm not prepared to take. その賭けに出る覚悟はまだできていません ◇You have no right to *take risks with* other people's lives. 他人の命を危険にさらす権利はありませんよね ◇Thankfully the *risk* paid off (= the action was successful). ありがたいことに危険を冒した甲斐があった ☞ **risk** (DARE), **risky** (DANGEROUS)

gamble [単数で] 賭け, 冒険 ◇It was the biggest *gamble* of his political career. それは彼の政治家としての経歴の中で最も大きな賭けだった ◇She knew she was taking a *gamble* but decided it was worth it. 彼女には一か八かの賭けだとわかっていたが, 賭けるだけの価値があると判断した 反意 **safe bet** (OPTION)

▸ **gamble** [他, 自] ◇He *gambled* his reputation *on* this deal. 彼はこの取り引きに自分の名声を賭けた ◇It was wrong to *gamble with* our children's future. 自

分たちの子どもの将来に夢を賭けるのは間違いだった

chance [C] ((take a chance/take no chances の形で)) 賭け, 冒険, 危険を冒すこと ◇The manager **took a chance on** a young, inexperienced player. 監督は一人の未熟な若い選手に賭けてみた ◇The police were **taking no chances with** the protesters. 警察は抗議デモの参加者に万全の警備態勢を敷いていた

ノート **risk, gamble, chance** の使い分け：risk は特に自分や人の命(安全)を危険にさらす場合に用いられる。gamble はふつう危険がさほど大きくない(金銭リスクを冒している)場合に用いられる機会を人に与える, 与えないという判断をする場合に用いられることが多い。

lottery [単数形] ((しばしばけなして)) 運, 巡り合わせ ◇Politicians have acknowledged that it is a bit of a *lottery* who gets funding. 誰が資金提供を受けるかはちょっとした巡り合わせみたいなものだと政治家たちは認めている

road 名

road・street・alley・lane・avenue・boulevard・row・terrace
両側に家などの建物があり, 乗り物がその上を移動するために造られた堅い表面
【類型訳】道, 道路, 車道, 街路, 通り, 大通り, 路地, 裏通り, 田舎道

文型＆コロケーション
- in the road/ street/ alley/ lane/ avenue
- on a road/ street
- a wide/ broad road/ street/ avenue/ boulevard
- a narrow road/ street/ alley/ lane/ terrace
- a main road/ street/ avenue/ boulevard
- a back/ side road/ street/ alley
- a straight road/ street/ avenue/ terrace
- a tree-lined road/ street/ avenue/ boulevard
- to cross the road/ street
- to turn into a road/ a street/ an alley/ a lane/ an avenue/ a boulevard
- to turn off a road/ a street/ an avenue/ a boulevard

road [C] (車が通る)道, 道路, 車道 ◇A man's body was lying in the *road*. 男の死体が道路に横たわっていた ◇She lives on a very busy *road*. 彼女は非常に交通量の多い道路に面した所に住んでいる ◇My mother lives down the *road*. 母はその道の先に住んでいます ◇Take the first *road* on the left. 最初の道を左に進んでください ◇It's a quiet residential *road*. そこは静かな住宅街の道路です ◇It would be better to go **by road**. 道路で行くほうがいいでしょう ◇The aim is to reduce the number of **road accidents**. 目的は交通事故の件数を減らすことにある ◇The children learn about **road safety** (= ways to avoid road accidents). 子どもたちは交通安全について学びます

ノート このグループの語はすべて, 通りの名称にも用いられ, 大文字で書かれる。◆53 York *Road* (ヨーク街53番地). ◆Oxford *Street* (オックスフォード街). ◆Ocean *Boulevard* (オーシャン大通り). 短縮形の Rd., St., Ave., Blvd. は住所に用いられることが多い。(英)では, これらはふつうピリオドなしで用いられ, (米)では The letter was addressed to:

Margaret Willis, 14 Hamilton *Rd*, London W3. (その手紙の宛先はロンドン市W3地区ハミルトン街14番地マーガレット・ウィリス様だった)

street [C] (片側[両側]に家々・建物がある)街路, 通り ◇I met him by chance in the *street*. 偶然その通りで彼に出会った ◇I walked up the *street* as far as the post office. 郵便局までその通りを歩いて行った ◇It's a medieval town, with narrow cobbled *streets*. そこは丸石を敷き詰めた狭い街路のある中世の町です ◇There are several banks in the **high street** (= the main street in a town). 《英》本通りにはいくつか銀行があります

ノート **road** と **street** の使い分け：町や市の street は, 片側[両側]に建物のある道路を表す最も一般的な語である。◆a *street* map of London (ロンドンの市街地図). street は町同士をつなぐ道路については用いられず, 特に《英》では *road* も Road と称されることが多い。◆a *road* map of Britain (イギリスの道路地図). ◆Woodstock *Road* (ウッドストック街). 《米》では street が road より頻繁に用いられる。

alley [C] (建物の裏[間]・古い家並みの間にある狭い)路地, 裏通り ◇It is a medieval city of courtyards and twisting *alleys*. そこは中庭と曲がりくねった路地のある中世風の都市である ◇An *alley* ran along the side of the house. 裏通りが家の側面に沿って走っていた ◇We walked up what turned out to be a **blind alley** (= one that is blocked at the end). 私たちが歩いて行った路地は行き止まりだった ☞ **passage** (CORRIDOR)

lane [C] (狭い)田舎道 ◇We walked down the quiet country *lane* towards the riverbank. 私たちは川岸に向かって静かな田舎道を歩いた ❶ lane はまた, 町や市の通りの名称, 特に非常に古い通りの名称にも用いられる。◆The address is 53 Chancery *Lane*. (住所はチャンセリー通り53番地です).

avenue [C] (町・市の)街路, 通り ◇We stayed at a hotel on Lexington *Avenue*. 私たちはレキシントン街のホテルに泊まった ❶《英》では avenue はまた, 両側に並木のある広くまっすぐな道路について用いられる。◆They drove along a broad, tree-lined *avenue*. (彼らは広い並木道に沿って車を走らせた).

boulevard [C] 《米》大通り ◇A police car sped down the crowded *boulevard*. パトカーが1台混雑した大通りを駆け抜けた ❶《英》で boulevard は, しばしば両側に並木のある広い市街を意味し, ふつう外国の都市についてしか用いられない。◆A number of little cafes lined the sunny *boulevard*. (たくさんの小さなカフェが日当たりのよい大通りに沿って並んでいた). ◆We visited the world-famous Hollywood *Boulevard*. (私たちは世界的に有名なハリウッド大通りを訪れた).

row [C] 《米》(1ブロックごとに結合した似たような家並みの)テラス式住宅街, 通り ◇They live in a **row house** in Washington's Mount Pleasant neighborhood. 彼らはワシントンのマウントプレザント近隣にあるテラスハウスに住んでいる ❶《英》で row は, いくつかの道路の名称に用いられ, 一直線に並んだ集合住宅を指す一般的な語は terrace である。◆I live at 22 Western *Row*. (私はウェスタン通り22番地に住んでいる).

terrace [C] 《英》(1ブロックごとに結合した似たような家並みの)テラス式住宅街, 通り ◇The houses were in long *terraces*, built in the nineteenth century. その家々は19世紀に建てられた長く続くテラス式住宅にあった ◇They

↪road

rob, rotten

sold their house in Brunswick *Terrace*. 彼らはブランズウィック通りの家を売却した

rob 動 ☞ STEAL

rob・loot・break into sth・raid・plunder・ransack・burgle・burglarize・hold up sb/sth
ある場所からお金[財産]を盗む
【類語訳】奪う、略奪する、強奪する、押し入る、あさる、泥棒に入る

文型&コロケーション
▶ to be robbed/ plundered **of** sth
▶ to rob/ loot/ break into/ raid/ ransack/ burgle/ burglarize a **building/ shop/ store**
▶ to rob/ break into/ raid/ ransack/ burgle/ burglarize a **house**
▶ to rob/ hold up a **bank**
▶ to loot/ plunder a **town/ city**
▶ to rob/ raid a **tomb**

rob (-bb-) [他] (人・場所から金・財産を)奪う、略奪[強盗]する、強盗を働く ◇An armed gang *robbed* a bank in Main Street last night. 昨晩メイン通りの銀行に武装した一味が強盗に入った ◇The gang had *robbed* and killed the drugstore owner. ギャングが強盗を働き、ドラッグストアの経営者を殺害してしまった ◇He was accused of *robbing* the company's pension funds. 彼は会社の年金基金を横領したとして起訴された ◇The tomb had been *robbed* of all its treasures. その墓からはすべての財宝が奪われてしまっていた ☞ **robber** (THIEF), **robbery** (THEFT)
loot [他、しばしば受身で、自] (爆撃・火事・騒ぎの後に店・建物から物を)略奪[強奪]する、荒らす ◇Most of the stores in the town had been *looted*. 町のほとんどの店が略奪されていた ◇The invaders rampaged through the streets, *looting* and killing. 侵略者たちは略奪や人殺しをしながら街中を暴れ回った ☞ **looter** (THIEF)
break 'into sth 句動詞 (力ずくで建物・車に[を])押し入る、荒らす ◇Thieves *broke into* the store and got away with $50,000. 泥棒たちが店に押し入り5万ドルを奪って逃げた ◇Our car got *broken into* last night. 昨晩、私たちは車上荒らしに遭った ☞ **break-in** (THEFT)
raid [他] (力ずくで場所に押し入って物を)略奪[強奪]する、荒らす、あさる ◇Many treasures were lost when the tombs were *raided* in the last century. 前世紀には墓が荒らされ、多くの財宝が失われた ◇I caught him *raiding* the fridge again (= taking food from it). 《おどけて》彼がまた冷蔵庫をあさっているのを見つけた ☞ **raid** (THEFT), **raider** (THIEF)
plunder [自、他]《フォーマル》(戦時中に力ずくで場所・地域から物を)略奪[強奪]する、荒らす ◇The troops crossed the country, *plundering* and looting as they went. 軍隊は進軍のたびに略奪や強奪を繰り返しながら国を横断した ◇Delhi was captured and *plundered* in 1739. デリーは1739年に攻略され、略奪に遭った
ransack [他] (物を盗むために場所を散らかしながら)荒らす、あさる、くまなく捜す ◇The house had been *ransacked* by burglars. 強盗が家を荒らし回っていた ◇Police completely *ransacked* the offices in their search for the missing files. 警察は紛失したファイルを求めて事務所を隅から隅までくまなく捜した

burgle [他]《英》(力ずくで建物に)泥棒に入る ◇Her house has been *burgled* five times. 彼女の家は5度泥棒に入られている ◇We were *burgled* while we were away (= our house was burgled). 私たちは留守中に泥棒に入られた ☞ **burglary** (THEFT)
burglarize 《米》(居)場所に力ずくで)泥棒に入る ◇The doctor's office is frequently *burglarized* by drug addicts. その医院はしばしば麻薬常用者に泥棒に入られる

ノート raid と burgle/burglarize の使い分け：burgle/burglarize は建物、特に人々の住宅についてしか用いられない。raid はあらゆる場所について用いることができるが、特に店や企業について、や、tombs といった語と共に用いられる (rob しか目的語に取ることができない graves は不可)。

,hold up 'sb/sth 句動詞 (武器を用いて銀行・店・車に[を])強盗を働く、荒らす ◇Masked men *held up* a security van in South London yesterday. 覆面をした男たちが昨日、ロンドン南部で警備会社のバンを襲った ◇They were *held up* at gunpoint. 彼らは強盗に遭って銃を突きつけられた

rotten 形

rotten・stale・sour・mouldy・bad・off
食べ物がもはや新鮮でないことを表す
【類語訳】腐った、腐敗した、干からびた、臭い、かびた、かび臭い、ほろほろの、傷んだ

文型&コロケーション
▶ rotten/ stale/ mouldy **food**
▶ rotten/ bad **eggs**
▶ stale/ mouldy **bread**
▶ to **go** rotten/ stale/ sour/ mouldy/ bad/ off

rotten (食べ物・木材などが)腐った、腐敗した ◇The *fruit* is starting to go *rotten*. 果物が腐り始めている ◇They pelted him with *rotten eggs*. 彼らは彼に腐った卵を投げつけた ◇He stepped on a *rotten* floorboard and felt it give way. 彼は腐りかけた床板を踏み、床が抜けるのではと思った
stale (食べ物・パン・ケーキが)干からびた ◇There was one piece of *stale* chocolate *cake* left in the tin. 缶の中には干からびたチョコレートケーキが1個残っていた
sour (牛乳が)酸っぱくなった、(人の息が)酸っぱいにおいがして)臭い ◇The *milk* had turned *sour*. 牛乳は酸っぱくなっていた ◇He smelled a *sour* whiff on the old man's breath. 彼はその老人が吐く息に臭さを感じた
mouldy 《英》《米 **moldy**》かびた、かび臭い；(古くてよい状態ではなく)ほろほろの ❶ mould は、古びた食べ物[暖かく湿った空気にさらされた物]の上で生長する、柔らかい粒子の細かい緑色[灰色、黒色]のかびのような物体を指す。◆The potatoes went *mouldy* before we'd had a chance to use them. (そのじゃがいもは使う機会がないままかびてしまった) ◆We threw away all the *mouldy* old furniture. (ほろほろの古い家具は全部捨てました)
bad (食べ物が)腐った ◇The meat had gone *bad*. その肉は腐ってしまっていた ◇There was a smell of *bad* eggs. 卵の腐った臭いがした
off [名詞の前では用いない]《英》(食べ物が)傷んだ、新鮮でない ◇The fish had gone *off*. 魚は傷んでしまっていた ◇The milk smells *off*. その牛乳は傷んだにおいがする

rough 形

rough・violent・stormy・turbulent・raging・choppy
天候[海]が強い風[大きな波]の状態であることを表す
【類語訳】荒れた, しけた, 激しい, 猛烈な, 荒れ狂う, 嵐の, 暴風雨の, 波立つ

choppy	rough	violent
	stormy	raging
	turbulent	

【文型&コロケーション】
- a rough/ violent/ stormy/ turbulent/ raging/ choppy **sea**
- rough/ violent/ stormy/ turbulent/ choppy **conditions**
- rough/ stormy/ turbulent/ choppy **waters**
- rough/ turbulent/ choppy **water**
- rough/ violent/ stormy **weather**

rough (海が)荒れた, しけた; (海上の天候が)荒れた ◇It was too *rough* to sail that night. その夜, 海があまりに荒れていて出帆できなかった ◇There's no way he could have swum ashore in such *rough* weather. こんな荒れた天気に彼が岸に泳ぎ着くなんて到底不可能だっただろう 反意 **calm** (QUIET 1)

violent (天気・海が)激しい, 猛烈な, 強暴な, 荒れ狂う, 大しの ◇The islands were hit by a *violent* cyclone. その島々は激しいサイクロンに襲われた ◇Members of the lifeboat crew were presented with bravery awards for launching in *violent* seas. 救命艇の乗員たちが荒海に乗り出した勇気に対して栄誉賞が授与された

stormy 嵐の, 暴風雨[雪]の ◇She visited me one dark and *stormy* night in November. 彼女は11月のある暗い嵐の夜に私を訪ねて来た

turbulent [ふつう名詞の前で] (大気・水流が)荒れ狂う, 乱流の ◇The aircraft is designed to withstand *turbulent* conditions. 飛行機は乱気流の条件に耐えるよう設計されている

raging [名詞の前で] (風・水流・火などが)激しい, 荒れ狂う, 猛威を振るう ◇The stream had become a *raging torrent*. その流れは荒れ狂う奔流と化していた ◇The building was now a *raging inferno* (= the fire was out of control). その建物はもはや燃え盛る火の海にあった

choppy (海・水流が)波立つ ◇The *choppy* waters caused some of the boats to capsize. 波立つ海で数隻の船が転覆した

rude 形

rude・cheeky・irreverent・insolent・disrespectful・impolite・impertinent・churlish・discourteous
人が他人に対する敬意の欠如を示すこと
【類語訳】失礼な, 無礼な, 無作法な, ぶしつけな, 生意気な, 厚かましい, ずうずうしい, 不敬な, 横柄な, 傲慢な

cheeky	rude	insolent
irreverent	disrespectful	
	impolite	
	impertinent	
	churlish	
	discourteous	

【文型&コロケーション】
- rude/ cheeky/ disrespectful/ impolite/ discourteous **to sb**
- rude/ impolite/ impertinent/ churlish **to do sth**
- very rude/ cheeky/ impolite/ impertinent/ discourteous

rude 《けなして》(他人・人の感情に対して)失礼な, 無礼な, 無作法な, ぶしつけな, 思いやりのない ◇He made a *rude* comment. 彼は失礼なコメントをした ◇She was very *rude* about my driving. 彼女は私の運転をこき下ろした ◇Why are you so *rude* to your mother? どうしてお母さんにそんなに思いやりがないの ◇It's *rude* to speak when you're eating. 食べながら話すのは無作法です 反意 **polite** (POLITE)

▶ **rudely** 副 ◇They brushed *rudely* past us. 彼らは失礼にも私たちをかすめて通った ◇'What do you want?' she asked *rudely*. 「何か用」と彼女はぶしつけに尋ねた

▶ **rudeness** 名 [U] ◇She was critical to the point of *rudeness*. 彼女は無礼とも言えるほど批判的だった ◇I want to apologize for my *rudeness* the other day. 先日の無礼に対して謝罪したいのです 反意 **politeness** (RESPECT 名)

cheeky 《英, 特に話し言葉, 時にけなして》(子どもが面白い[気に障る]ほど)生意気な, こしゃくな, 厚かましい, ずうずうしい ◇You *cheeky* monkey! なんて生意気なお猿さん ◇He's got a *cheeky* grin. 彼ったら, えらそうににやけやがって ◇You're getting far too *cheeky*! あまりにずうずうしすぎるよ

▶ **cheek** 名 [U, 単数で] ◇He had the cheek to ask his ex-girlfriend to babysit for them.《英, インフォーマル, ふつうけなして》彼は厚かましくも自分たちの子どものベビーシッターを元の彼女に頼んだ ◇I think they've got a cheek making you pay to park the car. 彼らはよくも君に駐車料金を支払わせたものだと思うよ

▶ **cheekily** 副 ◇He grinned *cheekily*. 彼はにやりと不敵な笑みを浮かべた

irreverent [しばしばほめて](他人が尊敬する人・物事に対して)不敬[不遜]な ◇He was famous for his *irreverent* wit. 彼は非礼な冗談を飛ばすことで有名だった ◇She has an *irreverent* attitude to tradition. 彼女は伝統に対して不遜な態度を取る ❶ **irreverent** は特にコメディアン・作家・キャスターが公にする言行に用いられる

insolent 《ややフォーマル, けなして》(年上の[自分より偉い]人に対して)失礼な, 無礼な, 横柄な, 傲慢な ◇He was always an *insolent* child. 彼はいつも不遜な子どもだった ❶ **insolent** は特に大人に対する子どもたちの振る舞いについて用いられる

▶ **insolence** 名 [U] ◇Her *insolence* cost her her job. 彼女はその横柄な態度で仕事を失った

▶ **insolently** 副 ◇'Well?' he queried *insolently*. 「それで」と彼は傲慢な態度で尋ねた

disrespectful 《ややフォーマル, けなして》(人・物事に対して)敬意を示さない, 失礼な, 無礼な ◇Some people said he had been *disrespectful* to the Queen in his last speech. 彼の最後の演説が女王に対して礼節を欠くものであったという人もいた 反意 **respectful** (POLITE), ☞ **disrespect** (CONTEMPT)

impolite 《ややフォーマル, けなして》失礼な, 無礼な, 無作法な ◇Some people think it is *impolite* to ask someone's age. 人の年齢を聞くのは無作法だと考える人々もいる ❶ **impolite** は It seems/would be impolite (to...) の表現で用いられることが多い ◆Refusing to eat what was offered would be *impolite*. (出されたものを食べようとしないのは失礼に当たるでしょう) 反意 **polite** (POLITE)

↪rude

ruin, rule

impertinent 《ややフォーマル，けなして》（年上の[自分より偉い]人に対して）失礼な，無礼な，生意気な，偉そうな ◇Don't ask such *impertinent* questions! そんな無礼な質問はするな ❶*impertinent* は、子どもたちの無礼さに腹を立てているということを伝えるときに、両親や教師といった人々が用いることが多い。◆Don't be *impertinent*!（生意気なこと言うな）。
▷**impertinence** 名 [U, C, ふつう単数で] ◇She had the *impertinence* to ask my age! 彼女は失礼にも私に歳を聞いたのよ
churlish 《ややフォーマル，けなして》 失礼な，無礼な，無作法な，無愛想な ◇It would be *churlish* to refuse such a generous offer. そんな寛大な申し出を断るのは失礼でしょう ❶*churlish* はほとんどの場合、It would be/seems churlish to...の表現で用いられる。
discourteous 《フォーマル，けなして》失礼な，無礼な，無作法な ◇He didn't wish to appear *discourteous*. 彼は無作法に見られたくなかった 反意 **courteous** (POLITE)

ruin 動

ruin・spoil・mar・wreck
物事がよい状態であったのに、それを失敗に[不快，役に立たなく]する
【類語訳】台無しにする，めちゃくちゃにする，駄目にする，損なう，壊す，傷つける，ぶち壊す，害する

spoil   ruin
mar   wreck

文型&コロケーション
▶to ruin/ spoil/ wreck sth **for** sb
▶to ruin/ spoil/ mar/ wreck sb's **career**
▶to ruin/ spoil/ wreck **things/ everything**
▶to ruin/ spoil/ wreck sb's **plans/ day/ evening/ life/ chances/ hopes**
▶to ruin/ mar/ wreck sb's **happiness**
▶to ruin/ wreck **sb's health/ sb's marriage/ the economy**
▶to **completely/ totally/ almost/ nearly** ruin/ spoil/ mar/ wreck sth
▶to **effectively** ruin/ spoil/ wreck sth

ruin ［他］台無しにする，めちゃくちゃにする，駄目にする，損なう ◇The bad weather completely *ruined* our trip. 悪天候で私たちの旅は台無しになった ◇You've *ruined* my whole life! あなたが私の人生をすべてめちゃくちゃにしたのよ ◇Years of drinking had *ruined* his health. 何年にもわたる飲酒で彼は健康を損なってしまった ◇My shoes got totally *ruined* in the mud. 泥で靴がすっかり駄目になった ◇The crop that year was *ruined* by drought. その年、農作物は日照りで駄目になった
spoil ［他］台無しにする，駄目にする，損なう，壊す，そぐ ◇Don't let him *spoil* your evening. 彼なんかにあなたの夜を台無しにさせないでね ◇Why do you always have to *spoil* everything? どうしてあなたはいつもすべてを台無しにしないと気が済まないの ◇I don't want to *spoil* your fun, but it's nearly time to go home. あなたの楽しみをそぎたくないけど、そろそろ帰宅する時間よ ◇I won't tell you what happens in the last chapter — I don't want to *spoil* it for you. 最終章で何が起きるか話さないでおくよ—あなたの楽しみを損ないたくないから

ノート **ruin** と **spoil** の使い分け：ruin のほうが spoil よりも意味が強い。ruin された物事はすっかり spoil されている。spoil された物事は、ruin されているか，単にあるべき姿ほどはよくない状態であろう。

mar (-rr-) ［他，しばしば受身で］《ややフォーマル》台無しにする，損なう，傷つける ◇A few violent incidents *marred* the celebrations. いくつかの暴力沙汰で祭典が台無しになった ◇A frown *marred* his handsome features. しかめ面で彼の端麗な容貌が損なわれた ❶*mar* はある一つの物事が別の物事の良さを異なる形に壊すこと。しばしばインフォーマルな話し言葉で用いられる。×Why do you always have to *mar* everything?
wreck ［他］（すっかり）ぶち壊す，台無しにする，めちゃくちゃにする，損なう，害する ◇A serious injury in 2006 threatened to *wreck* his career. 2006年に負った重傷で彼の経歴が台無しになる恐れがあった ◇His affair *wrecked* our marriage. 彼の浮気が私たちの結婚生活をぶち壊した ❶*wreck* は特に人々の生活において重要な物事について用いられる。主な連語として life, career, marriage, health, happiness が挙げられる。

rule 名

rule・law・regulation・act・statute・commandment
特定の状況において行ってもよい[行わなければならない，行ってはならない]ことに関する公式の定め
【類語訳】規則，決まり，ルール，法，法律，規定，条例，法令，定款，戒律

文型&コロケーション
▶the rules/ laws/ regulations **on** sth
▶a rule/ law **against** sth
▶**under** a rule/ the regulations/ an act/ a statute
▶**within** the rules/ law/ regulations/ act/ statute
▶**against** the rules/ law/ regulations
▶**strict** rules/ laws/ regulations
▶to **pass** a law/ a regulation/ an act/ a statute
▶to **obey** a rule/ a law/ the regulations/ a commandment
▶to **comply with** a rule/ a law/ the regulations/ a statute
▶to **break** a rule/ a law/ a regulation/ commandment
▶to **contravene/ be in breach of** a rule/ a law/ the regulations/ an act/ a statute
▶to **repeal** a law/ a regulation/ an act/ a statute
▶to **tighten up** a rule/ a law/ the regulations
▶a rule/ a law/ a regulation/ an act/ a statute **governs/ prohibits/ forbids** sth
▶a rule/ a law/ a regulation/ an act **allows (for)** sth
▶a rule/ a law/ a regulation/ an act **comes into force**

rule ［C］規則，決まり，約束事，ルール ◇Tackling a player without the ball is against the *rules*. ボールを持っていない選手にタックルすることはルール違反である ◇He was punished for breaking *school rules*. 彼は校則を破ったとして罰せられた ◇You and your room-mates should establish some *ground rules*. あなたとルームメイトたちは基本的な決まりをいくつか作っておくべきです ◇Without *unwritten rules* civilized life would be impossible. 不文律なしの文明生活などありえないだろう ◇Couldn't they just *bend the rules* and let us in without a ticket? 彼らはちょっと規則を曲げて、チケットなしで私たちを入れてくれることはできないの ☞ **rule** (PRINCIPLE 2)

law [C] (国・社会の)法, 法律 ◇The government has introduced some tough new *laws* on food hygiene. 政府は食品衛生に関する厳しい新法をいくつか導入した ◇There ought to be a *law* against it! それを禁じる法律があるべきだ ◇The country has very strict gun *laws*. その国には非常に厳しい銃規制法がある ☞ **law** (LAW), **law** (PRINCIPLE 2)

regulation [C, ふつう複数で] (公式の)規則, 規定, 条例 ◇It's against safety *regulations* to eat or drink in the laboratory. 実験室で飲食するのは安全規則に違反している ◇There are too many *rules and regulations*. 規則や規定があまりにも多い ☞ **regulation** (GOVERNMENT 2)

act (しばしば **Act**) [C] (議会で可決された)制定法, 法律, 法令 ◇an *Act* of Parliament/Congress 国会制定法 ◇the Higher Education *Act* 1965 1965年制定の高等教育法 ◇The *Act* was passed by a majority of 175 votes to 143. その法令は175対143の過半数で可決された

statute [C] (議会・評議会などで可決された)制定法, 法律, 法令;(組織・機関の正式な)規則, 定款 ◇Penalties are laid down *in* the *statute*. 処罰は法律に定められている ◇Corporal punishment was banned *by statute* in 1987. 体刑は1987年に法令によって禁じられた ◇It is not yet *on the statute book* (= it has not yet become law). それはまだ法令集に載っていない ◇Under the *statutes* of the university they had no power to dismiss him. 大学の規則によれば, 彼らには彼を解任する権限はなかった

commandment [C] 戒律(聖書においてユダヤ人に与えられた十戒のうちの一つ) ◇You shall *keep the commandments* of the Lord your God. 神である主の戒律を守るべし

rule 動

1 rule・govern・be in power・reign
国[地域]とそこに住む人々を治める
【類語訳】統治する, 支配する, 君臨する

▶ 文型&コロケーション

▶ to rule/ reign **over** sth
▶ to rule/ govern a **country**
▶ a (political) **party** rules/ governs/ is in power
▶ a **king/ queen/ monarch** rules/ reigns
▶ a ruling/ governing **party/ coalition/ class/ elite**

rule [他, 自] (国・地域・人々を)統治する, 支配する ◇The country was *ruled* by a brutal dictatorship. その国は残忍な独裁政権によって統治されていた ◇The family *ruled* London's gangland in the sixties. 一族は1960年代のロンドンの暗黒街を支配していた ◇Charles I *ruled* for eleven years. チャールズ1世は11年間統治した ◇She once *ruled* over a vast empire. 彼女はかつて広大な帝国を支配していた ☞ **rule** (CONTROL)

govern [他, 自] (合法的に国・地域を)統治する ◇The PCP had *governed* the province for 23 years. パレスチナ共産党がその地域を23年間統治していたのだ ◇He accused the opposition party of being *unfit to govern*. 彼は野党には統治資格がないとして非難した ☞ **government** (GOVERNMENT 1, 2)

> ノート **rule** と **govern** の使い分け: 国や地域を govern する政府や党が, 法的[政治]支配力を有し, ふつう選挙によっ

て選ばれる. rule は, 王, 女王, 皇帝, 独裁者, 軍事指導者など, 政治力を有するが選出されてはいない個人について用いられることが多い. また rule は, 時としてあまり直接的でない形で, 支配する国の少数グループについても用いることができる. この意味では, 形容詞的に用いられることが多い. the ruling party/coalition/classes/elite (与党/連立与党/支配階級/支配層のエリート)

be in power フレーズ (国・地域の)政権の座にある ◇The present regime has *been in power* for two years. 現政権は2年間政権の座にある

reign [自] (王・女王・皇帝として国を[に])統治する, 支配する, 君臨する ◇Queen Victoria *reigned* from 1837 to 1901. ヴィクトリア女王は1837年から1901年まで君臨した ◇It was the first visit by a British *reigning monarch* to Russia. それは現役の英国君主による初のロシア訪問だった ☞ **reign** (RULE 動 1)

2 ☞ ORDER 1
rule・prescribe・lay sth down・decree・order・legislate・dictate
物事について公式に決定を下す, 物事が起こるべきだと公言する
【類語訳】裁定する, 制定する, 定める, 規定する, 宣言する, 命じる, 命令する, 指示する, 立法する, 指図する

▶ 文型&コロケーション

▶ to rule/ legislate **on/ against** sth
▶ to rule/ prescribe/ lay down/ decree/ order/ legislate/ dictate **that**...
▶ to rule/ prescribe/ lay down/ decree/ order/ dictate **how/ what/ who**...
▶ It is prescribed/ laid down/ decreed/ ordered **that**...
▶ to do sth **as** prescribed/ laid down/ ordered/ dictated
▶ to **officially** rule/ prescribe/ lay down/ decree/ order/ legislate (that...)

rule [自, 他] (裁判官・法廷が)判決[裁決]を下す, 裁定[判定]する ◇The high court will *rule* on the legality of the action. 最高裁判所はその訴訟の合法性について裁決を下すだろう ◇The judge *ruled in favour of* the plaintiff. 裁判官は原告に有利な判決を下した ◇The court *ruled* that the women had been unfairly dismissed. 裁判所は女性たちが不正に解雇されたとの裁定を下した ◇The deal may be *ruled* illegal. その取り引きは違法と下される可能性がある ☞ **ruling** (CONCLUSION)

prescribe [他] 《ややフォーマル》(規則が)定めている, 規定している ◇The syllabus *prescribes* precisely which books should be studied. シラバスにはどの本で学べばいいかが正確に指示されている

,lay sth 'down 句動詞 (特定の規則・法律・原則を)制定する, 定める, 規定する ◇You can't always *lay down* hard and fast rules. 常に非常に厳重な規則が定められるわけではない ◇You should follow the regulations as *laid down* in the handbook. 手引書に定められているとおりに規則を守らなければなりません

decree [他] (権限を行使して公式に)定める, 宣言する ◇The government *decreed* a state of emergency. 政府は非常事態を宣言した ◇It was *decreed* that the following day should be a holiday. 翌日は休日と定められた

order [他] (権限のある立場から)命じる, 命令する, 指示する ◇They *ordered* that for every tree cut down two more be planted. 伐採される木1本につき、もう2本植えるべしと命じられた ◇The Justice Minister has *ordered* an investigation into the matter. 司法大臣はその問題の調査を命じた

legislate [自]《フォーマル》(物事に影響を与える)法律を制定する、立法する ◇The government has been urged to *legislate* against discrimination in the workplace. 政府は職場における差別を禁じる法律の制定を迫られている ◇The King restricted Parliament's power to *legislate*. 王は議会の立法権限を制限した ☞ **legislation** (LAW)

dictate [他]《気に障る形で人に》指図する、命令する、指示する ◇What right do they have to *dictate* how we live our lives? 彼らに私たちがどのような生活を送るべきか指図する権利なんてないだろ ◇I refuse to be *dictated* to. 私に指図されたくない ◇They are in no position to *dictate terms*. 彼らは条件を指示できる立場にない

run [動]

1 run・race・jog・tear・sprint・charge・gallop・trot・bound・pound・stampede
両脚を使って速く移動する
【類語訳】走る、駆ける、ジョギングする、突進する、疾走する、早足で歩く、小走りする、暴走する

jog	run	race
trot	bound	tear
	pound	sprint
		charge
		gallop
		stampede

文型&コロケーション

▶ to run/ race/ jog/ sprint/ charge/ gallop/ trot/ bound/ pound **towards** sb/ sth
▶ to run/ race/ sprint/ charge/ gallop/ trot/ bound/ pound **after** sb/ sth
▶ to run/ race/ tear/ sprint/ gallop/ trot/ bound/ pound **along** (sth)
▶ to run/ race/ tear/ sprint/ gallop/ bound **off**
▶ to run/ race/ sprint/ bound **away**
▶ to run/ race/ tear/ sprint/ bound **back**
▶ to run/ race/ tear/ charge **around/ round**
▶ to **come** running/ racing/ tearing/ sprinting/ charging/ galloping/ trotting/ bounding

run [自, 他] 走る、駆ける;(特定の距離を)走って行く ◇Can you *run* as fast as Mike? マイクと同じくらい速く走れますか ◇The boy went *running* off to get the ball. その少年はボールを取りに走って行った ◇I had to *run* to catch the bus. バスに乗るために走らなければならなかった ◇Alan was *running* for a bus when he slipped on some ice. アランはバスに乗ろうと走ったら氷で滑って転んだ ◇I like to *go running* (= run as a form of exercise) in the mornings before work. 朝の出勤前にランニングに出かけるのはいいよ ◇I *ran* four miles today. 今日は4マイル走った ◇Terrified, he *ran* all the way home. 彼は怖がって家までずっと走って帰った

▶ **run** [名] [C] ◇I go for a *run* every morning. 毎朝ランニングに出かける ◇He *broke into a run* (= started running). 彼は急に走り出した

▶ **running** [名] [U] ◇to *go running* ランニングに出かける ◇*running* shoes ランニングシューズ

race [自]《副詞や前置詞と共に》《書き言葉》(早く着くことが重要で)急いで走る、駆ける ◇Peter *raced* ahead to be the first to tell his mother the news. ピーターはそのニュースを母親に一番に知らせようと先頭に立って走った ◇We all *raced* back to the camp. 私たちはみんなキャンプ地に走って戻った

jog (または **go jogging**) [自](運動のために)ジョギングする ◇I *go jogging* every evening. 毎晩ジョギングに出かけます ◇He *jogged* down the path and into the lane. 彼は細道をジョギングで駆け下りて小道に出た

▶ **jog** [名] [単数で] ◇I like to go for a *jog* after work. 仕事の後のジョギングはいいね

▶ **jogging** [名] [U] ◇He decided to take up *jogging*. 彼はジョギングを始めることにした

tear [自]《副詞や前置詞と共に》(興奮して[急いで])走って[駆けて]行く ◇The girls looked at each other and *tore* off towards the house. 少女たちは互いに顔を見合わせて、その家に向かって走って行った

sprint [自, 他]《ふつう副詞や前置詞と共に》(短距離を)全速力で走る ◇He *sprinted* towards the finishing line. 彼はゴールに向かって全速力で走った ◇I *sprinted* the last few metres. 私は最後の数メートルを全速力で走った ❶レースの出場者が *sprint* し始めるとは、特にレース終盤に全速力で走り出すことを指す

▶ **sprint** [名] [C] ◇a 100-metre *sprint* 100メートル走 ◇It was a *sprint* for the finishing line. それはゴールに向かっての全力疾走だった

charge [自]《副詞や前置詞と共に》(音を立てながら[不用意に]特定の方向に)走って[駆けて]行く、突進する ◇The kids were *charging* around outside. 子どもたちは外で走り回っていた ◇He came *charging* into my office and demanded an explanation. 彼は私のオフィスに駆け込んできて説明を求めた

gallop [自, 他]《ふつう副詞や前置詞と共に》(馬(に似た動物)が)疾走する;(人が)馬に乗って疾走する、(馬を)疾走させる;(興奮して[騒がしい足取りで]人が)走る、駆ける ◇The horse neighed and *galloped* off across the field. 馬はいなないて野原を疾走して横切った ◇The cavalry *galloped* past in a cloud of dust. 騎兵隊が砂ぼこりを上げて疾走して行った ◇She *galloped* her horse all the way home. 彼女は家に着くまでずっと馬を疾走させた ◇The kids came *galloping* along the street. 子どもたちが通りを駆けて来た

▶ **gallop** [名] [単数で] ◇Diane urged her horse into a *gallop*. ダイアンは馬を駆って疾走させた

trot (-tt-) [自, 他] (馬が)速歩で駆ける;(人が)馬に乗って速歩で駆ける、(馬を)速歩で駆けさせる;(人が)早足で歩く、小走りする ◇I could hear the sound of several horses *trotting* along in the lane. 数頭の馬が小道を速歩で駆けている音が聞こえた ◇Bob *trotted* his pony around the field. ボブは野原でポニーを速歩で駆けさせた ◇The dog *trotted* obediently at her heels. 犬は彼女のすぐ後ろを従順に小走りで付いて行った ◇He *trotted* off to greet the other guests. 彼は他の客に挨拶をするために早足で去った

▶ **trot** [名] [単数で] ◇She slowed her horse to a *trot*. 彼女は馬の速度を速歩にまで落とした ◇She moved at a brisk *trot*. 彼女はきびきびと早足で移動した

bound [自]《副詞や前置詞と共に》(熱狂して)飛び跳ねて行く ◇The dogs *bounded* ahead. 犬たちは前方へ飛び跳ねて行った

pound [自]《ふつう副詞や前置詞と共に》(騒々しく重い足取りで)ドタドタ走る ◇A group of men on horseback came *pounding* across the field. 馬に乗った男の一団が野原をドドッと走ってきた

stampede [自]《大きな動物・人々の一群が》暴走する, どっと走る ◇The cattle started to *stampede*, as if they could sense the danger. 牛が危険を察知したかのように暴走し始めた ◇A bunch of kids came *stampeding* down the corridor. 子どもたちの一団が廊下をどっと走って来た

2 run・manage・control・be responsible for sb/sth・be in charge・direct・administer・command

商売[組織, 事業, 状況]の責任を背負っていることを表す
【類語訳】経営する, 運営する, 管理する, 監督する, 統制する, 担当している, 仕切っている, 指導する, 司る, 指揮する

[文型&コロケーション]
▶ to run/ manage/ control a/ an **company/ business/ organization**
▶ to run/ manage/ be responsible for a **department**
▶ to run/ manage a **hotel/ store/ club**
▶ to run/ manage/ control/ be responsible for/ direct/ administer a **project**
▶ to run/ manage/ be responsible for/ administer a **service**
▶ to run/ manage/ administer a **school**
▶ to manage/ control/ be responsible for/ be in charge of/ direct **operations**
▶ to manage/ administer a **fund**
▶ to be **properly/ efficiently** run/ managed/ administered
▶ to be **well/ badly** run/ managed
▶ to be **tightly** run/ managed/ controlled
▶ to be **centrally** run/ managed/ controlled/ directed/ administered
▶ to be **jointly** run/ managed/ controlled/ administered by/ with sb

run [他]《商売・組織・事業》を経営する, 運営する, 管理する ◇The shareholders want more say in how the company is *run*. 株主たちは会社の経営に関してより大きな発言権を求めている ◇The programme will be jointly *run* with NASA in the US. その計画は米国航空宇宙局と合同で展開されることになるだろう ◇It is a small, *privately run* (= not owned or controlled by a large organization) hotel. それは個人経営の小さなホテルだ ◇Stop trying to *run my life* (= organize it) for me. 私の生活にあれこれ指図するのはやめてくれません

manage [他, 自]《商売・組織・事業・チーム》を経営する, 運営, 管理する ◇Organizers are looking for someone to *manage* the project. 主催者はその企画を取り仕切れる人を探している ◇We need a new approach to *managing* our hospitals. 我々の病院経営には新しい取り組みが必要だ ◇We need people who are good at *managing*. 私たちは管理に長けている人々を必要としている
☞ **management** (GOVERNMENT 2), **management** (MANAGEMENT)

[ノート] **run** と **manage** の使い分け: これら二つの動詞はしばしば同じように用いることができる. ◆The hotel is *run/ managed* by two brothers. (そのホテルは兄弟によって経営されている). **run** は, 事業(計画, 株の注文, 商品輸送の編成など)の運営に関わる仕事を強調する, (従業員のいない)

小企業, 企業の一部, 部門, 大組織が **run** の対象となりうる. **manage** は労働者を組織することを指すことが多い. **manager** は, 企業や部門などがどのように **run** されるかについて決定を下すが, 彼らは自分で行うより他人に何をすべきかを伝えるのがふつうである.

control (-II-) [他]《企業・組織・事業・国》を管理[監督, 統制, 操作]する ◇The whole territory is now *controlled* by the army. 領土全体が現在は軍に支配されている ◇By the age of 21 he *controlled* the company. 彼は21の歳になるまでに会社を掌握した

be responsible for sb/sth [フレーズ]《人・物事に》責任を負っている, 担当している ◇Mike *is responsible for* designing the entire project. マイクはプロジェクト全体の設計を担当している ◇Even where parents no longer live together, they each continue to *be responsible for* their children. 一緒に住んでいない場合でも両親はそれぞれ引き続き子どもに対して責任がある ☞ **responsibility** (RESPONSIBILITY)

be in charge [フレーズ]《人・物事を》管理[担当]している, 仕切っている ◇I've usually been the one *in charge of* the petty cash. 私はふだん小口現金を管理する立場にある ◇Who's *in charge* here? ここを仕切っているのは誰ですか ☞ **charge** (RESPONSIBILITY)

direct [他]《計画・過程》を指導する, 管理する, 監督する ◇He was asked to take command and *direct* operations. 彼は業務を指導監督するよう依頼された ☞ **direction** (GOVERNMENT 2), **director** (MANAGER)

administer [他, しばしば受身で]《業務・会社・組織・国》を統治する, 司る, 管理する, 運営する ◇The country has to face up to the high cost of *administering* medical services. 国は医療サービスの高い運営費用に直面するはずだ ◇The pension funds are *administered* by commercial banks. 年金基金は市中銀行によって管理されている ☞ **administration** (GOVERNMENT 2), **administration** (MANAGEMENT), **administrator** (ORGANIZER)

command [他]《陸軍・海軍・空軍の人間集団》を指揮する ◇He was the officer *commanding* the *troops* in the Western region. 彼は西部地区の部隊を指揮する将校だった ◇The squadron was *commanded* by Major Frank Broad. その戦隊はフランク・ブロード少佐によって指揮された ☞ **command** (CONTROL)

ruthless [形] ☞ CRUEL, STERN

ruthless・hard・callous・unmoved・heartless・merciless・cold-blooded・brutal

人が他人に対して優しさ[憐れみ, 同情]を示さないことを表す
【類語訳】無慈悲な, 非情な, 無情な, 情け容赦のない, 冷たい, 無神経な, 冷淡な, 薄情な, 冷酷な, 血も涙もない, 残酷な

unmoved	hard	ruthless
	callous	cold-blooded
	heartless	
	merciless	
	brutal	

[文型&コロケーション]
▶ a ruthless/ hard/ callous/ heartless **man/ woman**
▶ a ruthless/ merciless/ cold-blooded **attack**
▶ a ruthless/ hard/ brutal **side**

▶ruthless/ brutal **honesty**
▶a callous/ cold-blooded **murder**
▶totally ruthless/ callous/ unmoved

ruthless《ふつうけなして》無慈悲な、非情な、無情な、情け容赦のない；(他人を傷つけることを気にせずに)断固とした ◇He's a violent, *ruthless* man who will stop at nothing. 彼はどんなことにも躊躇しない、凶暴で無慈悲な男である ◇He has a *ruthless* determination to succeed. 彼は成功への断固とした決意を持っている ◇Like all great survivors, she has a ***ruthless streak***. 逆境を見事に生きのびたすべての人々と同様、彼女にも情け容赦がないところがある ❶ruthlessであることは一般に非常に悪いと考えられるが、人がほしい物を手に入れる必要があるとの決意の下に明らかによい意味合いで用いられることもある。◆We'll have to be *ruthless* if we want to make this company more efficient. (この会社をより効率的にしたいならば我々は無情にならざるをえないだろう)。
▶**ruthlessly** 副 ◇The regime *ruthlessly* crushed all opposition. 政権はすべての反対勢力を容赦なく押さえ込んだ

hard《ふつうけなして》非情な、冷たい、ひどい ◇My father was a *hard* man. 父は非情な人間だった ◇She gave me a *hard* stare. 彼女は私に冷たい視線を向けた ◇He said some very *hard* things to me. 彼は私に対してとてもひどいことを言った 反意 **soft** (SENSITIVE 1)

callous《けなして》(他人の感情[苦しみ]を気にせず)無情な、無神経な、冷淡な、平然とした ◇The troops showed a ***callous disregard*** for life and property. 軍隊は命や財産を平然と無視した

unmoved [名詞の前では用いない] (心を動かされる状況で)平然とした、冷静な ◇Alice seemed totally ***unmoved by*** the whole experience. アリスはあらゆる経験にまったく平然としているように見えた ☞ **move** (IMPRESS)

heartless《けなして》(他人が言う[する]ことに)薄情な、不人情な、無慈悲な、冷酷な ◇How can you be so *heartless*! どうしたらそんなに不人情でいられるの ◇The decision does seem a little *heartless*. その決定は確かに少しばかり無慈悲に思える

merciless《ややフォーマル、特に書き言葉》無慈悲な、非情な、無情な、情け容赦のない ◇He was left reeling after a *merciless* attack by the opposition. 彼は反対勢力に容赦ない攻撃を受けてから動揺したままの状態が続いた ◇It brought relief from the *merciless* summer heat. それで容赦ない夏の暑さが和らいだ 反意 **merciful**

cold-'blooded《けなして》(恐ろしいことを行う間の)冷酷な、血も涙もない ◇a *cold-blooded* killer 血も涙もない殺人者 ◇There was something very *cold-blooded* about the way he used his father's death. 父親の死を利用した彼のやり方には非常に冷酷なところがあった

ノート unmovedな人とは、他人に悲しみを現にもたらす人でなく、人の悲しみや怒りに反応しない人を指すがゆえに、これらの語の中で最も意味が弱い。hard, callous, heartlessな人とは人の悲しみに同情せずに反応する[与える影響を気にせずに人を傷つけることを積極的に行う]人を指す。ruthless, cold-bloodedはさらにいっそう強い意味を持つ。ruthlessな人はほしい物を手に入れるために何でもするだろう。cold-bloodedな人は、何の同情も感じないばかりか、残酷な振る舞いの原因かもしれない(怒りなどの)感情さえもまったく感じない。

brutal《ふつうけなして》(不快な物事に対してずばり)残酷な；(人の感情を考えず)情け容赦のない ◇With *brutal* honesty she told him she did not love him. 彼女は残酷なまでに正直に、彼に愛していないと告げた ☞ **brutal** (CRUEL)
▶**brutally** 副 ◇Let me be *brutally* frank about this. このことについては情け容赦なく率直に申し上げましょう

S s

sad 形 ☞ UNHAPPY 1, PAINFUL 2

sad・tragic・pathetic・heartbreaking
惨めであったり、残念であったりする思いを表す
【類語訳】悲しむべき、悲惨な、悲劇的な、痛ましい、哀れな、不憫な、悲痛な

→
sad　　　　tragic　　　　　　heartbreaking
pathetic

文型&コロケーション
▶ to be sad/ tragic/ heartbreaking **for** sb
▶ to be sad/ heartbreaking **to do** sth
▶ to be sad/ tragic **that**...
▶ a sad/ tragic/ pathetic/ heartbreaking **story**
▶ a sad/ pathetic **sight**

sad (人・物事について)悲しむべき, 悲しませる ◇It was *sad* to see them go. 彼らが去るのを見るのは悲しかった ◇It is *sad* that so many of his paintings have been lost. こんなにも多くの彼の絵が失われてしまったのは悲しむべきことだ ◇We had some *sad* news yesterday. 私たちは昨日, 悲しい知らせを聞いた ◇The *sad* truth is, he never loved her. 悲しい事実だが, 彼は彼女を愛していなかった ☞ **sadness** (GRIEF), **sad** (UNHAPPY)
▶ **sadly** 副 ◇*Sadly*, after eight years of marriage they had grown apart. 悲しいことに, 彼らは8年の結婚生活の後, 心が離れてしまっていた

tragic (人の死・多大な苦しみゆえに)非常に悲しむべき, 悲惨な, 悲劇的な ◇He was killed in a *tragic* accident at the age of 24. 彼は24歳という年齢で, 悲惨な事故死を遂げた ◇Cuts in the health service could have *tragic* consequences for patients. 医療サービスの削減は, 患者たちに悲劇的な結果をもたらすかもしれない ◇It would be *tragic* if her talent remained unrecognized. 彼女の才能が認められないままなら, それは非常に悲しむべきことだ ☞ **tragedy** (CRISIS)
▶ **tragically** 副 ◇*Tragically*, his wife was killed in a car accident. 悲劇的にも, 彼の妻は自動車事故で亡くなった ◇He died *tragically* young. 彼は若くして非業の死を遂げた

pathetic 痛ましい, 哀れな, 不憫な ◇The starving children were a *pathetic* sight. 飢えた子どもたちの姿は痛ましいものだった ◇She thought he looked a *pathetic* figure of a man. 彼女は彼が哀れな風采の男に見えると思った

heartbreaking 胸の張り裂けるような, 悲痛の, 心の痛む ◇It's *heartbreaking* to see him wasting his life like this. 彼がこんなふうに人生を浪費しているのを見ると心が痛む ☞ **heartbreak** (GRIEF), **heartbroken** (UNHAPPY 1)

ノート **tragic** と **heartbreaking** の使い分け: **tragic** な出来事は, **heartbreaking** な出来事よりも深刻であることが多く, 苦しんでいる[死にかけている]人に関連して用いられることが非常に多い. しかし, **heartbreaking** はふつう, 比較的程度の強い個人的な悲しみに用いられる. **tragic** は他人に起こる悲惨な出来事を表す場合に, **heartbreaking** は自分自身に個人的な影響が及ぼされるような出来事を表す場合に用いられる.

safe 形

safe・OK・all right・in one piece・unharmed・out of harm's way・unscathed・unhurt・alive and well・secure・uninjured
危険[危害]から保護されている, 危害[損害, 傷害]を受けていない
【類語訳】安全な, 無事な, 大丈夫な, 無傷の, 元気な, 健在で

文型&コロケーション
▶ safe/ secure **from** sth
▶ unharmed/ unscathed/ unhurt **by** sth
▶ **to remain** safe/ OK/ all right/ in one piece/ unharmed/ unscathed/ alive and well/ secure
▶ **to escape** unharmed/ unscathed/ unhurt/ uninjured
▶ **apparently/ completely** safe/ unharmed/ unscathed/ secure
▶ **perfectly** safe/ OK/ all right/ secure
▶ **otherwise** OK/ all right/ unharmed/ unhurt/ secure

safe [名詞の前はまれ] (危険・危害から保護されており)安全な, 危険のない, 守られた ; (危害・危険を受けておらず[行方不明でなくて])無事な, 大丈夫な ◇The children are quite *safe* here. ここなら子どもたちはとても安全です ◇Will the car be *safe* parked in the road? 道路に車を駐車しておいて大丈夫ですか ◇They aim to make the country *safe* from terrorist attacks. 彼らの目的はテロ攻撃から国を守ることである ◇The girl was eventually found *safe and well*. その少女は結局, 無事で元気な状態で発見された ◇They turned up *safe and sound* (= with no harm done to them). 彼らは無事な状態で姿を現した ☞ **safety** (SHELTER)
▶ **safely** 副 ◇Let me know you've arrived *safely*. 無事に着いたことを知らせてください ◇The money is *safely* locked in a drawer. お金は引き出しに鍵を掛けて安全に保管されている

OK (または **okay**) [名詞の前はまれ]《インフォーマル, 話し言葉》安全な ; (けが・病気をしておらず)無事な, 大丈夫な ◇Are you *OK*? 大丈夫かい ◇Write and let me know you're *OK*. 手紙で無事を知らせてください ◇She worries too much — I'll be perfectly *OK*. 彼女は心配しすぎなんだ—私はこれからもまったく大丈夫だから
▶ **OK** ◇Did they get there *OK*? 《インフォーマル, 話し言葉》彼らは無事にそこに着いたの

all right [名詞の前はまれ]《ややインフォーマル, 話し言葉》安全な ; (けが・病気をしておらず)無事な, 大丈夫な ◇I hope the kids are *all right*. 子どもたちの無事を願っています ◇He'll be perfectly *all right*, you'll see. 彼はまるで問題なしになるさ, 今にわかるよ
▶ **all right** 副 ◇Did they get there *all right*? 《ややインフォーマル, 話し言葉》彼らはちゃんとそこに着いたの

ノート OKとall rightの使い分け：これらの語に実質的な意味の違いはない。どちらかなりインフォーマルだが、OKのほうがいくぶんall rightよりもインフォーマルである。☞ WELL

in one 'piece 仔細 《ややインフォーマル》（旅行・危険な経験の後で）無事に ◇She's had a bit of a shock, but she seems to be *all in one piece*. 彼女は少しショックを受けていたが、無傷なようだ

unharmed [名詞の前はまれ]［比較・最上級で］（危険な［恐ろしい］経験の後で）無傷の ◇He was released *unharmed* after being held hostage for three weeks. 彼は3週間人質にとられた後、無傷で解放された

out of harm's 'way 仔細 ［傷害・損傷を受けることのない［危害を加えることのできない］］安全な場所に ◇They sent the children to stay with their grandmother, where they would be *out of harm's way*. 彼らは祖母の家に滞在するよう子どもたちを送ったが、そこなら彼らは安全だろう ◇She put the knife in a drawer, *out of harm's way*. 彼女は安全な引き出しにナイフをしまった

unscathed [名詞の前では用いない]［比較・最上級で］《ややフォーマル、書き言葉》（危険な［恐ろしい］経験の後で）無傷の ◇Not many European cities survived the war *unscathed*. その戦争を無傷で生き延びたヨーロッパの都市は多くはなかった

unhurt [名詞の前には用いない]［比較・最上級で］（経験の後で）無傷の ◇He was bruised but otherwise *unhurt*. 彼にはあざができていたが、そのほかは無傷だった 反意 hurt

a,live and 'well ［危険な状況の後で［人に何が起こったかわからない場合に］］もしれない状況の後で［人に何が起こったかわからない場合に］元気で、健在で ◇He turned up *alive and well* on my doorstep, after an absence of ten years. 彼は10年ぶりに元気な姿で私の家の玄関先に現れた ◇She's *alive and well and living in* Detroit. 《ややインフォーマル》彼女は健在でデトロイトで暮らしている

secure 《ややフォーマル》[重要［貴重］な物の状態][在り場所]が]安全な、びくともしなくて ◇Information must be stored so that it is *secure* from accidental deletion. 情報は誤って削除される危険のないように保存されなければならない ◇The roof was *secure against* the coming winter rains. その屋根は間近に迫る冬の雨にもびくともしない造りだった

uninjured [名詞の前はまれ]（危険にさらされた後で）無傷の ◇They were shocked but otherwise *uninjured*. 彼らはショックを受けていたが、そのほかは無傷だった ❶ uninjured は、片方の腕などが傷ついていてもう片方が傷ついていない場合に、arm, hand, leg, footなどの名詞の前で用いられるが、その他の名詞の前では用いられない。◆He grasped the rope with his *uninjured* hand. 彼は傷を負っていないほうの手でロープをつかんだ）反意 injured

ノート unharmed, unscathed, unhurt, uninjured の使い分け：これらの語はすべて何かを経験した後に「無傷である」ことを意味する。unharmed, unscathed はいずれも、その経験が危険である［恐ろしい、不快である］ことを強調する。unhurt と uninjured は「無傷である」という事実を強調する。unharmed は人が捕虜になり解放されたときに用いられることが多い。unharmed, unscathed は人がどうにか生き残った［逃れた］場合に用いられる。

salesman 名

salesman/saleswoman/salesperson • rep • representative • auctioneer • assistant • clerk

商品を売ることを仕事とする人
【類語訳】販売員, 外交員, 競売人, 店員

文型&コロケーション
▶ a **sales** rep/ representative/ assistant/ clerk
▶ a **company** rep/ representative
▶ a **car/ computer** salesman/ saleswoman/ salesperson
▶ a salesman/ a saleswoman/ a salesperson/ a rep/ a representative/ an auctioneer/ an assistant/ a clerk **sells** sth

salesman, saleswoman, salesperson [C] （店頭での［会社・組織・住宅を回る］）販売員, 外交員 ◇He began his career as an insurance *salesman*. 彼は保険の外交員としての道を歩み始めた ◇a travelling *salesman* 販売外交員 ◇A *saleswoman* came out from behind the counter and asked if she could help. 女性販売員がカウンターの後ろから出てきて、御用を承りましょうかと尋ねた ◇The *salesperson* should adopt a question-and-listen procedure. 販売員は質問をしてから用件を聞くという手順を踏むべきです ❶ salesperson という語は特に商品を売ることが仕事である人向けの訓練教材で用いられる。salespersonは男性である場合も女性である場合もあるが、物を売ることを仕事とする特定の男性［女性］を指すのにはあまり用いられない。というのも、いまだに salesmanや（あまり頻繁ではないが）saleswomanが用いられているからである。× He began his career as an insurance *salesperson*. × A *salesperson* came out from behind the counter.

rep （または **'sales rep**）[C] 《ややインフォーマル》販売外交員 ◇She's a *sales rep* for a recording company. 彼女はレコード会社の販売外交員である

representative [C] 《フォーマル》販売外交員 ◇He works as a sales *representative* for an insurance company. 彼は保険会社の外交員として働いている ◇She's our *representative* in France. 彼女はフランスで当社の販売外交員を務めている

auctioneer [C] 競売人 ❶ auction は最高金額の値を付ける人に物を売る公共イベントである。 ◆ 'Yours for £200,' said the *auctioneer*. 「200ポンドで落札です」と競売人が言った。

assistant （または **'shop assistant, 'sales assistant**）[C]《英》店員 ◇She's a *sales assistant* in a department store. 彼女はデパートの販売担当の店員です ◇Maybe one of our *assistants* can help you make your choice? なんでしたら、当店の店員の一人に選ぶお手伝いをさせましょうか

ノート salesman/woman/person と assistantの使い分け：salesman/woman/person はふつう、assistantやshop/sales assistantよりも高度な訓練を受けた人、販売商品についてより特殊な知識を持つ人について用いられる。

clerk （または **'sales clerk**）[C]《米》店員 ◇The *sales clerk* answered all our questions. その店員は私たちの質問すべてに答えてくれた

satisfaction 名 ☞ JOY

satisfaction • happiness • pride • contentment • fulfilment

うれしいときや、何かをやり遂げたときに抱くよい感情
【類語訳】満足（感）, うれしさ, 幸せ, 幸福, 誇り, やりがい, 達成感, 充実感

satisfying, save

文型&コロケーション
- satisfaction/ happiness/ pride/ contentment/ fulfilment in sth
- with satisfaction/ pride/ contentment
- great satisfaction/ happiness/ pride
- real satisfaction/ happiness/ pride/ contentment/ fulfilment
- true satisfaction/ happiness/ contentment/ fulfilment
- deep satisfaction/ happiness/ contentment
- quiet satisfaction/ pride/ contentment
- to feel satisfaction/ happiness/ pride/ contentment
- to bring sb satisfaction/ happiness/ pride/ contentment/ fulfilment
- to give sb satisfaction/ happiness
- to find satisfaction/ happiness/ contentment/ fulfilment
- to take satisfaction/ pride in sth
- to sigh with satisfaction/ happiness/ contentment

satisfaction [U] (物事を達成した[望みどおりになった]ときの)満足(感) ◇He derived great *satisfaction* from knowing that his son was happy. 彼は息子が幸せだと知ってとても満ち足りた気分になった。 ◇She had the *satisfaction* of seeing her book become a bestseller. 彼女は自分の本がベストセラーになるのを目にして満足だった。 ◇The company is trying to improve *customer satisfaction*. その会社は顧客満足度を向上させる努力をしている。 ◇How would you rate your level of *job satisfaction*? どうやって仕事の満足度を評価するつもりですか。 反意 regret (GRIEF), dissatisfaction (UNHAPPY 2) ❶ regret は自分が望みどおりにすべてを達成できなかった場合、dissatisfaction は望みどおりに物事が起こらない[他の人々が物事を行わない]場合に用いられる. dissatisfaction はややフォーマルである. ◆Many people have expressed their *dissatisfaction* with the arrangement. (多くの人々がその取り決めに不満を表している). ◆ **satisfied** (HAPPY)

happiness [U] うれしさ, 幸せ, 幸福 ◇Her eyes shone with *happiness*. 彼女の目はうれしさで輝いた ◇Money can't buy you *happiness*. お金では幸福は買えない 反意 **sadness, unhappiness** (GRIEF), ◆ **happy** (HAPPY)

pride [U, 単数で] (物事を成功させた[他人が賞賛するようなことを手に入れた]ときの)誇らしい気持ち, 誇り ◇The sight of her son graduating filled her with *pride*. 息子が卒業するのを目にして, 彼女は誇らしい気持ちで一杯になった ◇Success in sport is a source of national *pride*. スポーツにおける勝利は国の誇りの源である ◇I take (a) *pride* in my work. 私は仕事に誇りを持っている 反意 **shame** (GUILT), ◆ **proud** (GLAD), **pride yourself on sth** (BOAST)

contentment [U] 《ややフォーマル》(現状に対する)満足(感) ◇They found *contentment* in living a simple life. 彼らは質素な生活を送ることに満足感を覚えた ◆ **content, contented** (HAPPY)

fulfilment 《英》《米 **fulfillment**》 [U] やりがい, 達成感, 充実感 ◇her search for personal *fulfilment* 個人的達成感の彼女の追求

ノート satisfaction, happiness, contentment, fulfilment の使い分け: 事の大小にかかわわらず, ほとんど何であれ達成すれば, satisfaction (満足感)を覚える. 生活に役立つ楽しい事を行う場合には, fulfilment (充実感)を感じる. happiness は物事に喜びを感じる際に抱く感情であり, 非常に快活な感情を指す. contentment は物事を喜びを見出せるようになったときに抱く穏やかな感情を指す.

satisfying 形 ☞ NICE 1, WONDERFUL

satisfying・rewarding・pleasing・gratifying・fulfilling
経験[活動, 事実]が必要とする[ほしい]物事を提供してくれて, 喜びを与えてくれることを表す
【類語訳】満足のゆく, やりがいのある, 心地よい, 楽しい, 喜ばしい

文型&コロケーション
- to be satisfying/ rewarding/ pleasing/ gratifying to do sth
- a satisfying/ rewarding/ gratifying/ fulfilling experience
- (a) satisfying/ rewarding/ fulfilling job/ career/ work
- to find sth satisying/ rewarding/ pleasing/ gratifying
- very/ extremely/ particularly satisfying/ rewarding/ pleasing/ gratifying
- immensely satisfying/ rewarding/ gratifying

satisfying (必要とする[ほしい]物事を提供してくれて)満足のゆく ◇a *satisfying* meal 満足のゆく食事 ◇It's *satisfying* to play a game really well. 本当にいい試合ができると満ち足りた気持ちになる ◇It's hard work, but very *satisfying*. きつい仕事ですが, とても満足です ☞ **satisfy** (PLEASE)

rewarding (経験・活動が有用[重要]なので)やりがい[報い]のある ◇Nursing can be a very *rewarding* career. 看護とはとてもやりがいのある職業かもしれない ◇Teaching is not very financially *rewarding* (= is not very well paid). 教職は金銭的にあまり報われない 反意 **unrewarding** ❶ unrewarding な活動・仕事は, 満足[達成]感をもたらさない.

pleasing 《ややフォーマル》(見て[聞いて, 考えると])心地よい, 楽しい, 喜ばしい ◇It was a simple but *pleasing* design. それは簡素だが心地よいデザインだった ◇You can create a very *pleasing* effect with pale colours on a dark background. 黒っぽい背景に淡い色を使うと, とても心地よい効果を生み出せる ☞ **please** (PLEASE)

gratifying 《フォーマル》(うまくできて)満足のゆく, 喜ばしい ◇It is *gratifying* to see such good results. こんなよい結果を目の当たりにできることはうれしい ☞ **gratify** (PLEASE)

fulfilling (技術・才能が発揮できて)やりがいのある, 達成[充実]感を与えてくれる ◇I'm finding the work much more *fulfilling* now. 今は, この仕事に一段とやりがいを感じています

ノート satisfying, rewarding, fulfilling の使い分け: 重要な[非常に短期間の]経験はほとんど何であれ, satisfying となりうる. rewarding は仕事・職業について, より長期的で真剣な活動について用いられる. ◆What is the most *satisfying* moment in your career so far? (これまでの職歴で最も満足感を覚えた瞬間は何ですか). ◆All in all, it's been an extremely *rewarding/fulfilling* career. (全体としてみれば, それはきわめてやりがいのある職業であった). satisfying と fulfilling は, 個人的な満足[幸福]感について用いられることが多い. rewarding は重要な物事を行っている[他人の役に立っている]という気持ちについて用いられることが多い.

save

1 ☞ PROTECT
save・rescue・bail sb out・redeem
死ぬ[消滅する, 何かを失う, 危害を受ける, 困惑する]のを防ぐこ

↪save

say

とを表す
【類語訳】救う, 保つ, 救出する, 救助する, 助け出す, 救済する

文型&コロケーション
▶to save/ rescue/ redeem sb/ sth **from** sth
▶to save/ rescue/ redeem a **situation**
▶to save/ redeem **sinners/ mankind**
▶to rescue sb/ bail sb out **financially**

save [他] (死・消滅・危害・破壊・喪失などから人・物事を)救う, 保つ ◇Doctors were unable to *save* him. 医師たちは彼を救うことができなかった ◇Money from local businesses helped *save* the school from closure. 地元企業からの金のおかげで, その学校を閉鎖から救えた ◇We made one last attempt to *save* our marriage. 私たちは結婚生活を破綻させまいとする最後の試みを行った ◇There's no doubt that the firefighters *saved* my daughter's *life* (= prevented her from dying). 消防士たちが娘の命を救ってくれたのは間違いない

rescue [他] (危険[有害]な状況から人・物事を)救う, 救出[救助]する ◇He was drowned in an attempt to *rescue* the child. 彼は子どもを救助しようとして溺れた ◇They were *rescued* by a passing cruise ship. 彼らは通りがかりのクルーズ船に救出された ◇You *rescued* me from a very embarrassing situation. あなたが私を非常に厄介な状況から救い出してくれたのです

▷**rescue** 名 [U, C] ◇A wealthy benefactor *came to their rescue* with a generous donation. 裕福な後援者が寛大な寄付によって彼らに救いの手を差し伸べてくれた ◇Ten fishermen were saved in a daring sea *rescue*. 勇敢な海難救助により10人の漁人が救われた

,bail sb 'out 句動詞 (資金提供によって困難な状況から人・物事を)救い[助け]出す, 救済する ◇Don't expect me to *bail* you *out* if it all goes wrong. 仮にすべてがうまくいかなくっても, 私に助けてもらうことなど期待しないで ◇The government had to *bail* the company *out of* financial difficulty. 政府は財政難のその会社を救済する必要があった

redeem [他] (《フォーマル, 宗教》)(キリスト教において悪の力から)救う, 救済する ◇He was a sinner, *redeemed* by the grace of God. 彼は罪人だったが, 神の恩寵によって救われた ❶ redeem はまた(「悪心から」状況を立て直す)」を意味する redeem a situation の句で, 非宗教的な言い回しでも用いられる. ◆In an attempt to *redeem* the situation, Jed offered to help sell tickets. (状況を立て直そうと, ジェドはチケットを売る手伝いを申し出た)

▷**redemption** 名 [U] ◇the *redemption* of the world from sin 罪からの世界の救済

2 ☞ CUT 1
save・budget・economize・tighten your belt・skimp
お金をあまり使わないようにする
【類語訳】貯金する, 予算を組む, 節約する, 倹約する, けちる

文型&コロケーション
▶to save up/ budget **for** sth
▶to economize/ skimp **on** sth

save [自] (特定の物を買うために)貯金する ◇I'm not very good at *saving*. 私は貯金が得意ではない ◇I'm *saving* for a new bike. 新しい自転車を買うために貯金しています ◇We've been *saving up* to go to Australia. 私たちはオーストラリアに行くために貯金してきています ☞ **savings**

budget [自, 他] 予算を組む;(ある金額を)予算に計上する, (特定の目的の)予算を立てる ◇If we *budget* carefully we'll be able to afford the trip. 慎重に予算を組めば, 私たちはその旅行の費用を捻出できるでしょう ◇I've *budgeted* for two new assistants. 新たに二人のアシスタントを雇う予算を立てた ◇Ten million euros has been *budgeted* for the project. その事業には1000万ユーロの予算が計上された ◇The project has been *budgeted* at ten million euros. その事業に1000万ユーロの予算が組まれた
☞ **budget** (FUND) 名

economize 《英でまた **-ise**》[自] (お金・時間などを)節約[倹約]する ◇Old people often try to *economize* on heating, thus endangering their health. 高齢者はしばしば暖房費を節約しようとして健康を危険にさらす ◇Managers have been ordered to *economize*. 部長たちは節約するよう命じられた

tighten your 'belt 成句 《ややインフォーマル》(手元金がないので)倹約する ◇With price increases on most goods, we are all having to *tighten our belts*. ほとんどの商品が値上がりして, 私たちは皆, 倹約しなければならなくなっている

skimp [自] (必要以上にお金・時間を)節約[倹約]する, けちる, 渋る ◇Older people should not *skimp* on food or heating. 高齢者は食べ物や暖房をけちるべきではない

3 save・deposit・put/set sth aside・bank
お金を使う代わりにとっておく
【類語訳】貯蓄する, 貯金する, 預金する, 貯めておく, 蓄えておく

文型&コロケーション
▶to save/ deposit/ put aside/ set aside/ bank **money/ £100, etc.**
▶to save/ deposit **cash**
▶to deposit/ bank a **cheque**

save [他] 貯蓄[貯金]する ◇You should *save* a little each week. 毎週少しずつ貯金すべきです ◇I've *saved* almost £100 so far. 今のところ100ポンド近く貯まっている ☞ **savings** (FUND) 名

deposit [他] (銀行口座に)預金する ◇Millions were *deposited* in Swiss bank accounts. 多額の金がスイスの銀行口座に預金されていた ◇You can withdraw and *deposit* money in any of our branches. 当行のどの支店でもお金の出し入れができます

,put/set sth a'side 句動詞 《特に話し言葉》(特定の目的のためにお金を)貯めておく, 蓄えておく ◇How much have you got *put aside*? 蓄えはいくらありますか ◇We ought to *set* some money *aside* for emergencies. 急場に備えていくらかお金を貯めておくべきです ❶ put sth aside は《英》で, set sth aside は《米》で用いられることがいぶん多い

bank [他] (銀行口座に給与・報酬などを)預金する, 預ける ◇She is believed to have *banked* (= been paid)$10 million in two years. 彼女は2年間で1000万ドルを銀行に預けていたと考えられている

say 動

1 say・speak・talk
言葉で表現するために声を使う
【類語訳】言う, 口に出す, 話す, しゃべる

文型&コロケーション
- to say sth/ speak/ talk **to** sb
- to say sth/ speak/ talk **about** sth
- They were speaking/ talking **(in)** French.

say [他] 言う, 口に出す ◇She *said* nothing to me about it. 彼女はそれについて私に何も言わなかった ◇That's a terrible **thing to *say*.** そんなことを言うなんて, それはひどい ◇I didn't believe a word she *said*. 私は彼女が言った言葉をひと言も信じなかった ◇He *said* (that) his name was Sam. 彼は自分の名前はサムだと言った ◇She finds it hard to *say what* she feels. 彼女は感じていることを口に出すのが苦手だ ◇'Why can't I go out now?' 'Because I *say so*.' 「どうして今出かけられないの」「言うからにしなさい」 ◇He *said* to meet him here. 彼はここで会おうと言った ❶物語の中では, 話された実際の言葉に続く場合, 主語は代名詞でなければ, said, says, say の後にくることが多い. ◆'Hello!' she *said*. (「あら」と彼女は言った). ◆'That was marvellous,' *said* Daniel. (「そいつは素晴らしかったね」とダニエルは言った).

speak [自] 話す, しゃべる ◇He can't *speak* because of a throat infection. 彼はのどの感染症でしゃべることができない ◇Please *speak* more slowly. どうかもっとゆっくり話してください ◇Without *speaking*, she stood up and went out. 何も言わずに, 彼女は立ち上がって出て行った ◇What language are they *speaking* in? 彼らが話しているのは何語ですか ◇He *speaks* with a strange accent. 彼は変なアクセントで話す ❶*speak* にはまた「特定の言語を使うことができる」の意味もある. この意味では進行形では用いられない. ◇She *speaks* several languages/a little Urdu/ an unusual dialect. (彼女は数か国語を/ウルドゥー語を少し/珍しい方言を話せる). ◆Do you *speak* English? (英語は話せますか). ☞ **speak (TALK)**

talk [自, 他] 話す, しゃべる ◇Alex can't *talk* yet — he's only just one year old. アレックスはまだしゃべれないんだ—彼はたった一歳だものね ◇Are they *talking* Swedish or Danish? 彼らはスウェーデン語とデンマーク語のどちらを話しているのですか ☞ **talk (TALK)**

ノート **speak** と **talk** の使い分け：talk は, 話し言葉で speak よりもずっと頻繁に用いられる. 人が speak できない場合は, 病気・障害・感情が原因である. まだしゃべれるようになっていない赤ん坊について言う場合は, talk を用いる.

2 ☞ DECLARE, SHOW 2
say・talk・express・put・voice・air・phrase

どのように感じて[何を考えて]いるかを人々に知らせる行為を表す
【類語訳】言う, 述べる, 断言する, 主張する, 話す, 語る, 表現する, 表明する, 口に出す, 公表する, 言い表す

文型&コロケーション
- to express/ voice/ air your **thoughts/ opinions/ views/ concerns**
- to express/ put/ phrase sth **clearly**
- to talk/ express yourself/ air sth **openly**
- to talk/ express yourself **freely**

say [他, 自] (意見を)言う, 述べる, 断言[主張]する ◇*Say what you like* (= although you disagree) about her, she's a fine singer. あなたは彼女のことを何と言おうと, 彼女は素晴らしい歌手だ ◇*I'll say this for them*, they're a very efficient company. 彼らのよいところとしてこれだけは言えます, 非常に効率的な会社だとね ◇Anna thinks I'm lazy — **what do you say** (= what is your opinion)? アンナは僕のことを怠け者だと思ってるんだ—君はどう思う ◇*It's hard to say* what caused the accident. なぜその事故が起きたかについては何とも言えない ◇*I can't say I blame* her for resigning (= I think she was right). 彼女が辞めたのは間違っていないと思う ◇*I wouldn't say* they were rich (= in my opinion they are not rich) 私は彼らが金持ちだとは思わない ◇When will it be finished?' *'I couldn't say* (= I don't know).' 「それはいつ終わるの」「わからないなあ」

talk [自, 他] (感情・思いをこめて)話す, 語る；(分別のある[ない]ことを)言う ◇Stop *talking* and listen! 話をやめて聴きなさい ◇He *talked* excitedly of his plans. 彼は自らの計画を興奮して語った ◇She *talks* a lot of sense. 彼女はとても意味があることを話す ◇You're *talking* nonsense! あなたはたわ言ばっかり ☞ **TALK**

express [他]《ややフォーマル》(言葉・表情・行動で感情・意見・考えを)表現する, 述べる ◇Teachers have *expressed* concern about the emphasis on testing. 教師たちはテストを重要視することに懸念を示した ◇Perhaps I have not *expressed* myself very well. もしかしたら自分の意見があまりうまく言えていないのかもしれない ◇She *expresses* herself most fully in her paintings. 彼女は絵でとても豊かに自己表現をする ❶*express* には気持ち・感情を表す部分に続くことが多い. ◆to *express* (your, my, etc.) dissatisfaction/fear/horror/gratitude/desire ((あなた[私など])の不満/恐怖感/戦慄/謝意/願望を表す). *say* と *talk* はこの形で用いることができない. 人々が理解できるように, 考えて[感じて]いることを述べることについて言う場合には, *express yourself* を, また, 芸術・詩などを通じて特定の形で自分の感情を表現することについて言う場合には, by, through, in と共に用いること. ☞ **expression (EXPRESSION)**

put [他]《副詞や前置詞と共に》(特定の形で)表現する, 述べる ◇She *put it* very tactfully. 彼女はそれをとても巧みに表現した ◇*Put simply*, we accept their offer or go bankrupt. 端的に言えば, 我々は彼らの申し出を受け入れるか倒産するかだ ◇I was, **to put it mildly**, annoyed (= I was extremely angry). 控え目に言うが, いら立ってはいたんだ ◇He was too trusting — or, **to put it another way**, he had no head for business. 彼はあまりに人を信じすぎた—別の言い方をすれば, 彼には商才がなかったのだ ◇She had never tried to *put* this feeling *into words*. 彼女は決してこの気持ちを言葉で表そうとしたことはなかった

voice [他]《ややフォーマル》(感情・意見を)表明する, 述べる, 口に出す ◇A number of parents have *voiced* concern about their children's safety. 数多くの親が子どもの安全に関して懸念を口にしている

air [他]《ややフォーマル》(意見を)公表[発表]する ◇The weekly meeting enables employees to *air their grievances*. 週一度の会議のおかげで, 従業員たちは不満を吐き出すことができる

ノート **voice** と **air** の使い分け：意見を一人の人に向けて voice できるが, 意見を air する場合は, ふつう会議などで多くの人々とその意見を共有していることを意味する.

phrase [他] (口頭・文面で)表現する, 言い表す, 述べる ◇I agree with what he says, but I'd have *phrased* it differently. 彼の言っていることに賛成だが, 私だったら違う言い方で表現していたところだ

3 say・suppose・speculate・presume・postulate・presuppose

一つの可能性として持ち出したり[挙げたり]、確かな証拠がないにもかかわらず真実であるかのように受け止めたりする
【類語訳】例えば…、仮定する、推測する、憶測する、推定する、前提とする、想定する

【文型&コロケーション】
▶ to say/ suppose/ speculate/ presume/ postulate/ presuppose **that**...
▶ to suppose/ presume/ postulate/ presuppose the **existence** of sth
▶ let's (just)/ let us say/ suppose (that...)

say [他, 受身なし]《特に話し言葉》(例・可能性として挙げて)例えば…、…だとしておく ◇You could learn the basics in, let's *say*, three months. 例えば3か月で、基本は身につけることができるでしょう ◇Take any writer, *say* (= for example) Dickens... 例えばディケンズなど、どんな作家でもいいから選びなさい ◇*Say* you lose your job. What then? 君が失業したとしよう。そうしたらどう

suppose [他]《真実だと》仮定する ◇*Suppose* all the flights are booked on that day. Which other day could we go? その日は全便が満席だと仮定しましょう。その日以外ならいつ行けますか ◇Let us *suppose*, for example, that you are married with two children. 例えば、あなたが結婚していて子どもが二人いるとしましょう ◇*Suppose* him dead — what then? 彼が死んでいると仮定しよう―そうしたらどう

speculate [他]《詳細・事実を知らずに》推測[憶測]する ◇Everyone *speculated* wildly *about* the reasons for her resignation. 皆が彼女の辞任理由についてあれこれ憶測した ◇It's useless to *speculate* why he did it. 彼がそうした理由を憶測しても無駄だ ☞ **speculation** (SPECULATION), **speculative** (SUPPOSED)

presume [他]《ややフォーマル》(法廷などで反証が出るまで真実だと)推定[仮定]する ◇Twelve passengers are *missing, presumed dead*. 12名の乗客が行方不明で、生存が絶望視されている ◇In English law, a person is *presumed innocent* until proven guilty. 英国法では、人は有罪が立証されるまでは無罪と推定される ☞ **presumption** (SPECULATION), **presume** (SUPPOSE)

postulate [他]《フォーマル》(理論・議論の基礎として真実だと)仮定する、前提とする ◇Some linguists have *postulated* a change in English pronunciation from around 1600. 言語学者の中には、1600年頃からの英語の発音における変化を前提とする者もいる

presuppose [他]《フォーマル》(証明される前に真実だと)仮定[想定]する；(議論・理由において他が真実であることを)前提とする ◇Teachers sometimes *presuppose* a fairly high level of knowledge on the part of the students. 教師は時に学生の側にかなり水準の高い知識を前提とすることがある ◇This argument *presupposes* that all children start off life with equal advantages. この主張はすべての子どもたちが平等に恵まれた生活を送り始めることを前提としている ☞ **presupposition** (SPECULATION)

scarce 形 ☞ LIMITED 1

scarce・low・in short supply・short・few and far between

多くの場所に存在しないこと、大量には存在しないことを表す
【類語訳】不足した、少ない、乏しい、希少な

【文型&コロケーション】
▶ **resources** are scarce/ low/ in short supply/ short
▶ **food** is scarce/ low/ in short supply/ short
▶ **time/ money** is scarce/ short

scarce 不足した、足りない；(必要量に満たず)少ない、乏しい、希少な ◇Land suitable for building on is *scarce*. 建設に適した土地が不足している ◇This is a criminal waste of *scarce resources*. これは希少資源の法外な浪費である ◇*scarce*はある特定の地域に少数しか存在しない動物・鳥・植物を指して言う場合にも用いられる。ふつう動物などがいかに興味深いかよりも、この変化がいかに深刻であるかを示唆するために、getting/becoming scarce/scarcerの句で用いられる。◆Butterflies are *getting scarcer and scarcer* in industrialized areas. (工業地域ではチョウがだんだん希少になってきている) ×This species is extremely *scarce*. [反意] **plentiful** ❶plentifulは大量に[多数]利用できる[存在する]ことを表す。◆There was always a *plentiful* supply of food. (常に大量の食糧供給があった). ◆In those days jobs were *plentiful*. (当時、仕事はたくさんあった). ☞ **scarcity** (LACK)

low [名詞の前では用いない](量的に)少ない、不足した、乏しい ◇The reservoir was *low* after the long drought. 長い干ばつの後貯水池は水位が低くなっていた ◇Our supplies are *running low* (= we have only a little left). 我々への支給品は残り少なくなっている ◇They were *low on* fuel. 彼らの燃料は乏しかった

in ˌshort supˈply [叙述] 不足して、足りなくて ◇Basic foodstuffs were *in short supply*. 日常的な食料品が不足していた ◇Shelter and warm clothing are *in very short supply*. 住まいと暖かい衣類が非常に不足している

short [名詞の前では用いない] 不足した、足りない ◇When food was *short* they used to pick berries in the woods. 食糧が不足しているときは、彼らは森でベリーを摘むのだった ◇He felt his time was *running short* (= becoming short). 彼は時間が足りなくなってきていると感じた ☞ **shortage** (LACK)

ノート scarce, low, in short supply, short の使い分け：shortは特に時間・お金について用いられる。lowは特に自分が持っている残り少ない補給品について用いられる。scarceとin short supplyは手に入りづらい資源について用いられる。scarceは名詞の前で用いることのできる唯一の語である。×a waste of *low/short* resources.

ˌfew and ˌfar beˈtween [叙述] (数的に)ごく少ない；(頻度について)ごくまれな ◇Well-paid acting jobs are *few and far between*. ギャラの高い芝居の仕事はごく少ない ◇There were some inspired moments in the performance, but these were *few and far between*. 演技ではインスピレーションを受ける瞬間があったが、それはごくまれであった ❶few and far betweenはふつう、もっとたくさんある[頻繁に起こる]ことを願う場合に用いられるが、まれだが満足する場合にも用いられる。◆Disappointments were *few and far between*. (幻滅することはごくまれだった).

scepticism 《英》《米 skepticism》名

scepticism・disbelief・suspicion・distrust・cynicism

信じる[信頼する]ことができない態度や感情を表す
【類語訳】懐疑, 不信, 不信仰, 疑念

文型&コロケーション
- scepticism/ suspicion/ distrust/ cynicism **towards** sth
- scepticism/ suspicion/ cynicism **about** sth
- scepticism/ suspicion **over** sth
- **with** scepticism/ disbelief/ suspicion/ cynicism
- scepticism/ disbelief **that**...
- **deep/ growing** scepticism/ suspicion/ distrust
- **healthy/ widespread** scepticism/ suspicion/ distrust/ cynicism
- to **express** scepticism/ disbelief/ suspicion/ distrust
- to **greet** sb/ sth **with** scepticism/ disbelief/ suspicion/ cynicism
- to **regard** sb/ sth **with** scepticism/ suspicion/ distrust

scepticism 《英》**skepticism**《米》[U] (主張・言説の真実性[物事の発生]に対する)懐疑 ◇Other scientists have expressed *scepticism* about these results. 他の科学者たちはこれらの結果に懐疑の念を表している ☞**sceptical** (SUSPICIOUS 1)
▶**sceptic**《英》《米では**skeptic**》[名][C] ◇He was unable to convince the *sceptics* in the audience. 彼は聴衆の中の懐疑的な人たちを納得させることができなかった

disbelief [U] 信じられないこと, 不信(感), 不信仰 ◇He stared at me *in disbelief*. 彼は信じられないという様子で私を見つめた ◇*Disbelief in God* was her way of rebelling against her strict religious upbringing. 神を信じないのは, 宗教上の厳しいしつけに対する彼女なりの反抗であった ◇To enjoy the movie you have to *suspend your disbelief* (= pretend to believe sth, even if it seems very unlikely). その映画を楽しむためには, 嘘だとわかっていても信じようとしないといけない ☞**disbelieve** (SUSPECT), **disbelieving** (SUSPICIOUS 1)

suspicion [U] (誠実[善良]さに対する)疑念, 不信(感) ◇Their offer was greeted with some *suspicion*. 彼らの申し出は少々不信感を持って迎えられた ☞**suspicion** (DOUBT 名 2), **suspect** (SUSPECT), **suspicious** (SUSPICIOUS 1)

distrust [U, 単数で] 疑念, 不信(感) ◇They looked at each other with *distrust*. 彼らは互いに疑いの目で見た ◇He has a deep *distrust* of all modern technology. 彼は現代技術すべてに対して深い不信感を抱いている ☞**distrust** (SUSPECT)

cynicism [U] (しばしばけなして) (人間)不信(人間は善良[誠実]な理由からではなく利己的にしか行動しないという気持ち) ◇In a world full of *cynicism* she was the one person I felt I could trust. 不信だらけの世の中で, 彼女は私が唯一信用できると思える人だった ☞**cynical** (SUSPICIOUS 1)
▶**cynic**[名][C] ◇Don't be such a *cynic*! そんな人間不信に満ちたこと言わないで

schedule [名]

schedule・agenda・timetable・calendar・programme・diary・itinerary
将来行われる[起こる]特定の活動[出来事]
【類語訳】予定, 計画, スケジュール, 番組表, 議事日程, カレンダー, 予定表, プログラム, 手帳

文型&コロケーション
- the schedule/ agenda/ timetable/ calendar/ programme/ diary/ itinerary **for** tomorrow/ next week
- to be/ put sth **in** the schedule/ the timetable/ the programme/ your calendar/ your diary/ the itinerary
- to be/ put sth **on** the schedule/ agenda/ timetable/ programme/ calendar/ itinerary
- a **busy/ full/ packed** schedule/ agenda/ timetable/ calendar/ programme/ diary/ itinerary
- a **detailed** schedule/ agenda/ timetable/ programme/ itinerary
- a/ an **realistic/ ambitious** schedule/ agenda/ timetable/ programme
- a **hectic/ demanding** schedule/ timetable/ programme
- a **daily/ weekly** schedule/ timetable/ programme/ itinerary
- to **look at** the schedule/ the agenda/ the timetable/ the calendar/ the programme/ your diary
- to **check/ consult** the schedule/ the agenda/ the calendar/ your diary
- to **agree (on)/ draw up** a schedule/ an agenda/ a timetable/ a programme/ an itinerary
- to **follow/ change** the schedule/ agenda/ timetable/ programme/ itinerary
- to **keep/ stick/ adhere to** the schedule/ agenda/ timetable/ programme

schedule [C, U] (仕事上の)予定, 計画, スケジュール; (テレビ・ラジオの)番組表, 放送予定 ◇We're working to a tight *schedule* (= we have a lot of things to do in a short time). 我々はぎっしり詰まったスケジュールで働いています ◇Filming began *on schedule* (= at the planned time). 撮影は予定どおり始まった ◇The new bridge has been finished two years *ahead of schedule*. 新しい橋は予定より2年早く完成した ◇The tunnel project has already fallen *behind schedule*. トンネル事業はすでに予定より遅れている ◇The show trebled ratings for the channel's afternoon *schedule*. その番組は同チャンネルの午後の放送時間帯の視聴率を3倍にした ❶《米》では, schedule はバス・航空便や列車の発車の時刻表や学校の時間割も表す. ◆a bus/flight/train *schedule* (バス/航空便/列車の時刻表). ◆What's your *schedule* like next semester? (君の来学期の時間割はどうなっているの). 《英》では timetable が用いられる.

agenda [C] (会議用の)議事日程; 重要課題 ◇The next item on the *agenda* is the publicity budget. 次の協議事項は広報予算についてです ◇For the government, education is now *at the top of the agenda* (= most important). 政府にとって, 教育は今や最重要課題である ◇Newspapers have been accused of trying to *set the agenda* for the government (= decide what is important). 新聞が政府に代わって協議事項を決めようとしていると非難されている ❶ agenda は diary (手帳) や calendar (予定表) の意味で用いてはいけない. ×Let me just check my *agenda*.

timetable [C] (待ち望む)予定[計画](表) ◇I have a busy *timetable* this week (= I have planned to do many things). 今週は予定がびっしり詰まっている ◇The government has set out its *timetable* for the peace talks. 政府は和平交渉の計画を発表した ❶《英》では, timetable はまたバス・列車の発着の時刻表や学校の時間割も表す. ◆a bus/flight/train *timetable* (バス/航空便/列車の時

↪ **schedule**

刻表). ◆ We have a new *timetable* each term. (私たちは各学期に新しい時間割がある). 《米》では schedule が用いられる.

ノート schedule と timetable の使い分け: 両語とも使用可能な場合が多い. ◆ I have a busy *schedule/timetable* this week. (今週は予定がびっしり詰まっている). しかし, schedule はふつう, 行われなければならない予定を指し, 仕事について用いられることが多い. ◆ work/production *schedules* (勤務/生産予定). × work/production *timetables*. また work (仕事) を主語にする場合, on/ahead of/behind schedule (予定どおりである/より早い/より遅い) と言える. × on/ahead of/behind *timetable*. timetable は, 計画に従って事が進行することを望む場合に用いられることが多いが, これは管轄外の物事に部分的に左右されることもある. ◆ the government's *timetable* for the peace talks (政府の和平交渉の計画表). × the government's *schedule* for the peace talks.

calendar [C] (壁に掛ける) カレンダー; (電子形態の) 予定表; (重要行事 [日程] が示された) 年間予定表 ◇ Did you get a *calendar* for 2008/a 2008 calendar? 2008年のカレンダーは買ったかい ◇ I think I'm free on that day — let me check my *calendar*. その日は空いていると思うよ — 予定表をチェックしてみるよ ◇ This is one of the biggest weeks in the racing *calendar*. 今週は競馬の年間予定表の中で最も重要な週の一つである ◇ It is a major festival in the church's *calendar*. それは教会の年間予定表の中での大きな祭典である

programme 《英》《米 **program**》 [C] (公演・催し物の) プログラム, 予定表 ◇ We have an exciting musical *programme* lined up for you. 皆さんのために心躍る音楽プログラムをご用意しました ◇ What's the *programme* for (= what are we going to do) tomorrow? 《話し言葉》明日の予定はどうなってるの

diary [C] 《英》(予定を書き留める) 手帳 ◇ I'll just make a note of that date in my *diary*. すぐ手帳にその日付を書き留めます ◇ I'm afraid my *diary* is full (= I have no available time) for this week, but I could see you next Monday. 残念ながら今週は予定が詰まっていますが, 来週の月曜日ならお目にかかれると思います 《米》では, calendar か schedule を用いる. また, 例えばコンピュータなどの電子形態の「予定表」には, 《英》《米》ともに calendar を用いる. diary はまた思ったことや起こったことを記録する「日記」も指す.

itinerary [C] (道順・訪問場所を含む) 旅行計画 ◇ He drew up a detailed *itinerary*. 彼は詳細な旅行計画を作成した ◇ Visits to four different countries are included in your *itinerary*. あなたの旅行計画には4か国別々に訪問することが含まれています

scold

scold [動] ☞ BLAME

scold • lecture • tell sb off • rebuke • reprimand • chide • castigate • berate • reproach

人にその行為を認めないと告げる
【類語訳】叱る, 説教をする, どなりつける, 怒る, 非難する, 叱責する, たしなめる, 酷評する, 責める

文型&コロケーション

▸ to scold/ tell sb off/ rebuke/ reprimand/ chide/ castigate/ berate/ reproach sb **for** sth

▸ to scold/ rebuke/ chide/ castigate/ berate/ reproach **yourself**

▸ to scold/ tell sb off/ rebuke/ reprimand/ castigate/ berate sb **severely**

▸ to scold/ rebuke/ reprimand/ chide sb **gently**

▸ to **publicly** rebuke/ reprimand/ castigate/ berate sb

scold [他]《書き言葉》(子どもを) 叱る ◇ Rose *scolded* the child gently for her behaviour. ローズはその子の振る舞いを優しくとがめた ◇ 'Don't be such a baby!' he *scolded*. 「そんな駄々っ子みたいなことを言っちゃ駄目だよ」と彼は叱った
▸ **scolding** [名] [C, ふつう単数形] ◇ She got a *scolding* from her mother. 彼女は母親に叱られた

lecture [他]《けなして》(迷惑な形で人に) 説教をする ◇ Don't start *lecturing* me! 私に説教なんか始めないでくれ ◇ He's always *lecturing her about* the way she dresses. 彼はいつも彼女に服装のことで説教ばかりしている
▸ **lecture** [名] [C] ◇ I know I should stop smoking — don't give me a *lecture* about it. タバコをやめるべきなのはわかってるよ — だからそのことで説教しないでくれ

tell sb 'off [句動]《特に英, 話し言葉》(悪いことをしたとして人に) どなりつける, 怒る ◇ I *told* the boys *off* for making so much noise. 大騒ぎしている少年たちをどなりつけてやった ◇ Did you **get told off**? 怒られたのかい
▸ **telling-'off** [名] [C, ふつう単数形] ◇ The nurse gave him a *telling-off* for smoking in the hospital.《英, インフォーマル》その看護師は病院でタバコを吸ったことで彼をどなりつけた

ノート scold と tell sb off の使い分け: 人にその行動を不可とすることを告げることを表す動詞に, フォーマルもインフォーマルもない. scold はこれらの動詞の中で最も頻繁に書き言葉, 特に物語で用いられるが, 話し言葉ではあまり用いられない. tell sb off は話し言葉で群を抜いて頻繁に用いられるが, 書き言葉や《米》ではあまり用いられない.

rebuke [他, しばしば受身で]《フォーマル》(悪いことをしたとして公的 [私的] に人を) 非難する, 叱責する ◇ The company was publicly *rebuked* for having neglected safety procedures. その会社は安全手順を軽んじてきたことで公に非難された ◇ She *rebuked* herself for her stupidity. 彼女は自分の愚行について自戒した
▸ **rebuke** [名] [C, ふつう単数で, U] ◇ He was silenced by her stinging *rebuke*. 彼は彼女の辛辣な非難に沈黙していた

reprimand [他]《フォーマル》(規則・法律を破ったとして公式に人を) 非難する, 叱責する ◇ The judge *reprimanded* him for using such language in court. 裁判官は法廷でそのような言葉を使ったことに対して彼を叱責した
▸ **reprimand** [名] [C, U] ◇ He received a severe *reprimand* for his behaviour. 彼はその行動で厳しい非難を受けた

ノート rebuke と reprimand の使い分け: rebuke には幅広い意味があり, ふつう reprimand の代わりに用いることができる. reprimand は必ずしも rebuke の代わりに用いることができるわけではない. × She *reprimanded* herself for her stupidity.

chide [他]《フォーマル》(人を優しく) たしなめる, 言い聞かせる ◇ She *chided* herself for being so impatient with the children. 彼女は子どもたちに対してとても短気な自分自身をたしなめた

castigate [他]《フォーマル》(失敗した [悪いことをした] と して人・物事を) 厳しく非難する, 酷評する ◇ The minister *castigated* schools for falling standards in educa-

tion. 大臣は教育水準の低下について諸学校を厳しく非難した ❶castigate は人の落ち度を人に伝える場合や、そこをスピーチなどで公的に話す場合に用いられる。
berate [他]《フォーマル》(不賛成を表して人を)激しく非難する、怒号する ◇The minister was *berated* by angry demonstrators as he left the meeting. 大臣は会議を後にする際、憤慨したデモ参加者から怒号を浴びせられた ❶ berate は、非難が公的なものである場合にも、(文書によるものではなく)直接本人に向けられる場合にも用いられることが多い。×The minister was *scolded/told off/rebuked/reprimanded/chided/castigated/reproached* by angry demonstrators.
reproach [他]《フォーマル》(悪いことをしたとして人を)非難する、責める；(自分を責めて)後悔する ◇She was *reproached* by colleagues for leaking the story to the press. 彼女はその話を報道陣に漏らしたとして同僚から非難された ◇He *reproached* himself for not telling her the truth. 彼は彼女に真実を話さなかったことを後悔した ❶このグループの語のいくつかは、人が自分自身に対して罪の意識を示すために、yourself/himself/herselfなどと共に用いることができるが、reproach はこのパターンで最も頻繁に用いられる。
▶**reproach** [名][U, C, ふつう単数で] ◇His voice was full of *reproach*.《フォーマル》彼の声には非難の響きがあふれていた ◇He listened to his wife's bitter *reproaches*. 彼は妻の厳しい非難に耳を傾けた

scratch [動]

scratch・scrape・rub・scuff・graze
とがった硬い物を動かして、表面を傷つけたり、物を取り去ったりすること
【類語訳】引っかく、かく、すりむく、する、すり減る

▣ 文型&コロケーション
▶to scratch sth/ scrape sth/ rub/ scuff sth/ graze sth **on** sth
▶to scrape/ graze your **knee/ knuckles/ elbow/ shin**
▶to scratch/ scrape/ graze a **surface**
▶to scratch/ scuff/ graze sth **badly**

scratch [他] (誤って物の表面を)かき[すり]傷をつける；(とがった物で皮膚を)引っかく、かく ◇Be careful not to *scratch* the furniture. 家具にかき傷をつけないように注意しなさい ◇The car's paintwork is badly *scratched*. 車の塗装面にはひどいすり傷がある ◇I'd *scratched* my leg and it was bleeding. 脚を引っかいて、血が出ていた ◇She *scratched herself* on a nail. 彼女は爪で体をかいた ☞ **scratch** (INJURY)
scrape [他] (誤ってざらざらした物で物を)こすって傷つける、すりむく ◇I *scraped* the side of my car on the wall. 車の側面を壁にこすって傷つけちゃった ◇Sorry, I've *scraped* some paint **off** the car. ごめん、車をこすって塗装がはがれちゃった ◇She fell and *scraped* her knee. 彼女は転んで膝をすりむいた ◇The wire had *scraped* the skin **from** her fingers. 彼女はワイヤーで指の皮がむけてしまった

▣ ノート **scratch** と **scrape** の使い分け：表面を scratch した場合、その表面には細長い線ができる。表面を scrape した場合、ふつう scratch よりも幅の広い跡がつく。体の部位を scratch する場合、その傷はあまりひどくないが、scrape した際の傷はふつう少し大きめである。

rub [-bb-] [自] (表面に痛み・傷を引き起こすほど何度も前後に)すれる、すり減る ◇The back of my shoe is *rubbing*. 靴の裏がすり減ってるんだ ◇The wheel is *rubbing* on the mudguard. 車輪が泥除けにすってる ◇The horse's neck was *rubbed* raw (= until the skin came off) where the rope had been. その馬の首の手綱のところがすれて肉が露出していた
scuff [他] (ざらざらした物で物の滑らかな表面に)こすって傷つける、すり減らす ◇I *scuffed* the heel of my shoe on the stonework. 石畳で靴のかかとをすり減らした
graze [他] (ざらざらした物で皮膚を)すりむく ◇I fell and *grazed* my knee. 転んで膝をすりむいた ◇He *grazed* his elbow on a sharp piece of rock. 彼は角ばった岩でひじをすりむいた ☞ **graze** (INJURY)

▣ ノート **scrape** と **graze** の使い分け：graze は体の部位についてしか用いられない。scrape はさまざまな表面を傷つけることについて用いられ、行為に重点が置かれる。graze はすりむいた後のけがに重点が置かれる。

scream [動] ☞ SHOUT

scream・cry out・screech・wail・squeal・shriek・howl・yelp
大きな高い叫び声を上げる、大きな高い物音を立てる
【類語訳】叫ぶ、悲鳴を上げる、金切り声を上げる、絶叫する、わめく、大笑いする

▣ 文型&コロケーション
▶to scream/ cry out/ screech/ wail/ squeal/ shriek/ howl/ yelp **at** sb
▶to scream/ cry out/ screech/ wail/ squeal/ shriek/ howl/ yelp **in/ with** pain/ terror, etc.
▶**brakes/ tyres** scream/ screech/ squeal/ shriek
▶a **dog** howls/ yelps
▶to **almost** scream/ cry out/ wail/ shriek
▶to screech/ squeal/ shriek **to a halt**

scream [自] (人が苦痛・恐怖・興奮などで)叫ぶ、悲鳴[金切り声]を上げる、絶叫する；(物が)甲高い音を立てる[立てて動く]、キーッと鳴る ◇He covered her mouth to stop her from *screaming*. 彼は彼女の口を抑えて叫ぶのを止めさせた ◇The kids were *screaming* with excitement. 子どもたちは興奮して金切り声を上げていた ◇Lights flashed and sirens *screamed*. ライトが点滅し、サイレンが甲高い音で鳴った ❶scream はふつう目的語なしで用いられるが、scream yourself hoarse/silly/to death の句では目的語を取ることができる。◆The baby was *screaming itself hoarse*. (赤ん坊が声をからして泣いていた)。scream はほとんどの場合、女性や少女について用いるが、男性が scream する場合は、特に極度の苦痛・恐怖を示唆することが多い。scream はまた発話動詞としても用いられる。☞ **scream** (SHOUT)
▶**scream** [名][C] ◇She let out a *scream* of pain. 彼女は苦痛の悲鳴を上げた ◇He drove off with a *scream* of tyres. 彼はタイヤをキーッときしらせて走り去った
cry 'out [句動詞] (人が苦痛・恐怖・興奮などで)叫ぶ、絶叫する ◇He *cried out* in fear. 彼は恐怖のあまり絶叫した ◇She *cried out* loud with the pain. 彼女は痛みで大声で叫んだ ❶cry out はまた発話動詞としても用いられる。
▶**cry** [名][C] ◇He gave a loud *cry* of despair. 彼は絶望のあまり大声で叫んだ
screech [自] (人・動物が)悲鳴[金切り声]を上げる、キー

↪ **scream**

キーと鳴る;(乗り物が動いたり止まったりするときに)鋭い音を立てる,キーッと鳴る ◇He *screeched* with pain. 彼は痛みに悲鳴を上げた ◇Monkeys were *screeching* in the trees. 猿が森の中でキーキー鳴いていた ◇The car *screeched* to a halt outside the hospital. その車は病院の外でキーッと音を立てて止まった ❶ *screech* はまた発話動詞としても用いられる. ◆'No, don't!' she *screeched*. (「いや,やめて」と彼女は悲鳴を上げた). ◆He *screeched* something at me. (彼は私に向かって何かを甲高い声で叫んだ).

➤**screech** 名 [C] ◇She suddenly let out a *screech*. 彼女は突然悲鳴を上げた ◇The car came to a halt with a *screech* of brakes. その車はキーッとブレーキ音を立てて止まった

wail [自] (人・動物が悲しみ・苦痛で長く)(泣き)叫ぶ;(物が長く)物悲しい音を立てる ◇The little girl was *wailing* miserably. その幼い女の子は惨めな様子で泣き叫んでいた ◇The cat was *wailing* to be let out. その猫は外に出たくて悲しげに鳴いていた ◇Ambulances raced by with sirens *wailing*. 救急車はサイレンを鳴り響かせて駆け抜けた ❶ *wail* はまた発話動詞としても用いられる. ◆'It's broken!' she *wailed*. (「壊れてる」と彼女は泣き叫んだ).

➤**wail** 名 [C] ◇He let out a *wail* of anguish. 彼は苦痛の叫び声を上げた ◇She could hear the distant *wail* of sirens. 彼女は遠くにサイレンの鳴り響く音が聞こえた

📝 **scream と wail の使い分け**: **wail** は **scream** より長い間続くが, **scream** ほど力強くもはなはだしくもない. **wail** は音が高いことも低いこともあるが, **scream** は常に高い.

squeal [自] (豚・興奮した子ども・乗り物が長く)キーキーと鳴く,キャッキャッと奇声を上げる,悲鳴を上げる,キーッと鳴る ◇The pigs were *squealing*. 豚がキーキーと鳴いていた ◇Children were running around *squealing* with excitement. 子どもたちは興奮してキャッキャッと奇声を上げながら走り回っていた ◇The car *squealed* to a halt. その車はキーッと音を立てて止まった ❶ *squeal* はまた発話動詞としても用いられる. ◆'Don't!' she *squealed*. (「やめて」と彼女は悲鳴を上げた).

➤**squeal** 名 [C] ◇a *squeal* of pain/delight 苦痛の悲鳴/喜びの歓声 ◇The car stopped with a *squeal* of brakes. その車はキーッとブレーキ音を立てて止まった

shriek [自] (興奮・驚き・苦痛などで)叫ぶ,悲鳴[金切り声]を上げる,絶叫する ◇She *shrieked* in fright. 彼女は恐怖で金切り声を上げた ◇The audience was *shrieking* with laughter. 観衆はキャーキャーと笑い声を上げていた ❶ *shriek* はまた発話動詞としても用いられる. ◆'Look out!' she *shrieked*. (「気をつけて」と彼女は叫んだ).

➤**shriek** 名 [C] ◇She let out a piercing *shriek*. 彼女は耳をつんざくような金切り声を上げた

howl [自] (苦痛・怒り・おかしみなどで)(泣き)わめく,大笑いする ◇The child *howled* in pain. その子は痛くてわめいた ◇We *howled* with laughter. 私たちは大笑いした ◇The baby was *howling* (= crying loudly) all the time I was there. 赤ん坊は私がそこにいる間ずっと泣きわめいていた ❶ *howl* は,狼や時に犬の悲しげな「遠吠え」に用いられる.また発話動詞としても用いられる. ◆'Ouch!' *howled* Ricky. (「痛い」とリッキーはわめいた).

➤**howl** 名 [C] ◇The suggestion was greeted with *howls* of laughter. その提案は大爆笑で迎えられた

yelp [自] (苦痛で突然短く)叫ぶ,悲鳴を上げる,キャンと鳴く ◇The dog *yelped* with pain and surprise. その犬は痛みと驚きでキャンと鳴いた

sea 名

sea・ocean・waters
地球表面を覆う塩水
【類語訳】海, 大海, …洋, 水域, 領海

📋 文型&コロケーション
▶ **by/ on/ across/ beneath/ under** the sea/ ocean
▶ **in** the sea/ the ocean/ ... waters
▶ **to cross/ sail** the sea/ ocean

sea [U, C] (しばしば **the sea**) 海;…海 ◇The waste is dumped in the *sea*. 廃棄物は海に投棄されている ◇The goods were sent *by sea*. 商品は船便で送られた ◇Her husband was in the navy and spent a lot of time away *at sea*. 彼女の夫は海軍所属で,多くの時間を海上で過ごした ◇She stood on the cliff, *looking out to sea*. 彼女は崖に立って海に視線を向けていた ◇I asked for a room with a *sea* view. 私は海の見える部屋を頼んだ ◇They live in a cottage by the *sea*. 《英》彼らは海辺の小さな家に住んでいる ◇the North *Sea* 北海 ❶複数形の *seas* が文学的文脈で用いられることもある. ◆the cold *seas* of the Antarctic (南極圏の冷たい海). ◆They sailed the *seven seas* in search of adventure. (彼らは冒険を求めて7つの海を航海した). 反義 **land**

ocean [C] (しばしば **the ocean**) 海, 大海;(大海を5つに分割した)…洋 ◇*Ocean* levels are rising. 海面が上昇している ◇The plane hit the *ocean* several miles offshore. 《米》その飛行機は沖合い数マイルの海に墜落した ◇Our beach house is just a few miles from the *ocean*. 《米》私たちのビーチハウスは海からほんの数マイルのところにあります ◇the Antarctic/Arctic/Atlantic/Indian/Pacific *Ocean* 南極海/北極海/大西洋/インド洋/太平洋

📝 **sea と ocean の使い分け**: 《英》では, 地球表面を覆う「海」を表す一般的な語は **sea** であり, 《米》では, ふつう **ocean** である. ◆a cottage by the *sea* (《英》海辺の小さな家). ◆a house on the *ocean* (《米》海辺の家). また 《英》では a week at the seaside, 《米》では a week at the beach と言うのも一般的である. 5つの大洋の一つについて言う場合は **ocean** (名称の一部となるときは Ocean)が用いられる. ◆the Pacific *Ocean* (太平洋). *ocean* の中[陸地の間]の特定の海域について言う場合は **sea** (名称の一部となるときは Sea)が用いられる. ◆the Mediterranean *Sea* (地中海). ☞ **COAST**

waters [複数で] (特定の国に属する)水域, 領海 ◇British/international *waters* 英国の領海/国際水域〔公海〕 ◇The treaty prohibited the use of the country's navy outside its own *territorial waters*. その条約で領海外でのその国の海軍の使用権が禁じられた

search 名

search・pursuit・quest・hunt・look
人や物事を探す[見つけようとする]行為
【類語訳】捜索, 探索, 追求, 探求, 追跡, 検索

📋 文型&コロケーション
▶ a **search/ quest/ hunt/ look for** sb/ sth
▶ **in search/ pursuit/ quest of** sth
▶ the **search/ hunt is on** (for sb/ sth)
▶ a/ an/ the **successful/ relentless/ endless** search/ pur-

suit/ quest
▶a **major/ massive/ nationwide/ police** search/ hunt
▶to **begin/ launch/ help in** a search/ quest/ hunt
▶to **abandon/ be involved in** the search/ pursuit/ hunt
▶to **be engaged in** the search/ pursuit/ quest
▶to **mount/ lead/ join (in)/ call off** a search/ hunt

search [C] （人・物事を）捜すこと，捜索，探索 ◇After a long *search* for the murder weapon, the police found a knife. 殺人の凶器を長い時間をかけて捜索した結果，警察はナイフを発見した ◇Detectives carried out a thorough *search* of the building. 刑事たちはそのビルの徹底的な捜索を行った ◇She went into the kitchen in *search* of (= looking for) a drink. 彼女は飲み物を探しに台所に行った ☞ **search** (LOOK 動 2)

pursuit [U] 《書き言葉》（目標・達成・幸福などの）追求 ◇She travelled the world in *pursuit* of her dreams. 彼女は夢を追い求めて世界を旅した ◇The purpose of the award is to encourage the *pursuit* of excellence. その賞の目的は優れたものの追求を奨励することである

quest [C] 《書き言葉》（名誉のための長期にわたる大切な物事の）追求，探求 ◇The team will continue its *quest* for Olympic gold this afternoon. 今日の午後，チームは引き続きオリンピックの金メダルを目指す ◇This is an important stage in their *quest* for the truth. 今が真実を追求する重要な段階です ◇The initiative aims to foster the province's *quest to* reinforce its distinct cultural identity. 住民発議が目指すのは明確な文化的アイデンティティーを強化しようとする州の追求を促進することである

ノート **pursuit**と**quest**の使い分け：場合によって，両語も使用可能．◆He set off in *pursuit/quest* of adventure. （彼は冒険を追い求めて出発した）．しかし，pursuitは人が特定の目標・目的を達成しようとしている場合，特に金儲け［個人的な充実感］と関連する場合に用いられる．◆the *pursuit* of wealth/profit/self-interest/a career/love/happiness（富／利益／私利／出世／愛／幸福の追求）．questはふつう，より精神的で，決して完全にはつかみ取ることのできない普遍的な特質について用いられることが多い．◆to be on an endless/a spiritual *quest*（果てしなく／精神的に追求している）．◆the *quest* for truth/knowledge/perfection（真実／知識／完璧さの追求）．pursuitは可算でも不可算でもthe pursuit of sthの形をとるが，questは可算でa quest for sthの形をとることに注意．また両語とも，in pursuit/quest of sthの形で用いることができる．

hunt [C, ふつう単数で]《ややインフォーマル，特にジャーナリズム》（発見の困難な人・物事の）捜索，探索，追跡，追求，追究 ◇The *hunt* is on for a suitable candidate. ふさわしい候補者を探し求めている ◇Police forces in five counties are now involved in the **murder hunt**. 現在，その殺人犯の追跡には5つの州警察が関わっている ☞ **hunt** (LOOK 動 2)

look [C, ふつう単数で]《ややインフォーマル》（人・物事を）探すこと，検索 ◇I had a *look* for websites on Egyptian music. 私はエジプト音楽に関するウェブサイトを探した ◇We've had a good *look around* downstairs, but can't find your keys. 下の階をよく探したけれど，君の鍵は見つからないよ ☞ **look** (LOOK 動 2)

secret 形

secret・private・confidential・personal・undisclosed・intimate・classified

情報が他人に知られていない[知られることを意図されていない]ことを表す
【類語訳】秘密の，機密の，内緒の，個人的な，親展の，内輪の，内密の，私的な，某…，非公開の，秘めた

文型&コロケーション
▶secret/ private/ confidential/ personal/ undisclosed/ classified **information**
▶secret/ private/ confidential/ personal/ classified **documents**
▶a secret/ confidential/ personal **file**
▶a private/ confidential/ personal **letter**
▶secret/ confidential/ classified **material**
▶(a) secret/ private **talks/ meeting**
▶a secret/ an undisclosed **location**
▶sb's private/ personal **life**
▶to **remain** secret/ private/ confidential/ undisclosed/ classified
▶to **keep sth** secret/ private/ confidential
▶**highly** secret/ confidential/ personal/ classified
▶**entirely** secret/ private/ confidential

secret 秘密の，機密の，内緒の ◇The ceasefire was agreed following *secret* talks between the two leaders. 二人の指導者間の秘密交渉の後，停戦が合意された ◇There's a *secret* passage leading to the beach. 浜辺に通じる秘密の通路がある ◇He tried to keep it *secret* from his family. 彼はそれを家族に内緒にしようとした ◇This information has been classified *top secret* (= completely secret, especially from other governments). この情報は極秘扱いにされている 反意 **open**
➤**secrecy** 名 [U] ◇the need for absolute *secrecy* in this matter この問題における極秘扱いの必要性 ◇Everyone involved was *sworn to secrecy*. 関係者は皆，口外しないことを誓わされた
➤**secret** 名 [C] ◇Can you *keep a secret*? 秘密を守れるかい ◇trade/official/State *secrets* 企業秘密／職務上の秘密／国家機密
➤**secretly** 副 ◇The police had *secretly* recorded the conversations. 警察によりその会話は秘密裏に録音済みであった

private （一般向けでなくて）個人的な，親展の ; （他人に知られたくなくて）内輪の，内密の，秘密の ; （仕事［公的］立場）と関連しておらず）私的な ◇You shouldn't listen in on other people's *private* conversations. 他人の個人的な会話に聞き耳を立てるべきではありません ◇They were sharing a *private* joke. 彼らは内輪で冗談を披露しあっていた ◇She was scared of revealing her *private* thoughts and feelings. 彼女は私的な考えや感情を明かすのを怖がっていた ◇The media is obsessed with the star's *private* life. マスコミはそのスターの私生活に取りつかれている状態だ 反意 **public** (**FAMOUS**)
➤**privately** 副 ◇Can we speak *privately*? 内密に話せるかな

confidential 秘密の，機密の，内密の，親展の ◇Your medical records are *strictly confidential* (= completely secret). 医療記録は極秘にされています ◇The envelope says it is *private and confidential*. その封筒には親展と書かれている
➤**confidentiality** 名 [U] ◇They signed a *confidentiality* agreement. 彼らは秘密保持契約に署名した
➤**confidentially** 副 ◇She told me *confidentially*

that she is going to retire early. 彼女は早期退職するつもりだと内密に教えてくれた

personal （仕事[公的立場]と関連しておらず）個人的な、私的な、親展の ◇The letter was marked '*Personal*'. 手紙には「親展」と記されていた ◇I'd like to talk to you about a *personal* matter. 個人的な問題についてお話したいのですが ◇I try not to let work interfere with my *personal* life. 仕事で私生活を左右されないように努めます ◇She's a *personal* friend of mine (= not just sb I know because of my job). 彼女は私の個人的な立場での友人です

> **ノート private と personal の使い分け**：仕事[公的立場]と関連していないことを表すには、ふつう両語とも使用可。 ◆your *private/personal* life （あなたの私生活）. ◆a *private/personal* matter （個人的な問題）. ◆a letter marked '*Private/Personal*' （「親展」と記された手紙）. しかし、×a *private* friend of mine (= not just sb I know because of my job). 有名人や重要人物の「私生活」については、*private life* を用いるほうが普通だが、自分自身や一般の人々の「私生活」については両語とも使用可能。

undisclosed ［ふつう名詞の前で］《ややフォーマル》秘密の、某…、非公開[公表]の ◇The painting was sold for an *undisclosed* sum to a private collector. その絵は非公開の金額で個人収集家に売られた ◇Several inmates were moved to an *undisclosed* location in the south. 何人かの囚人が南部にある秘密の場所に移動させられた ☞ **disclose** (REVEAL)

intimate （性的な意味で）秘めた、秘め事の ◇The article revealed *intimate* details about his private life. その記事は彼の私生活について詳細な秘め事で暴露した ◇the most *intimate* parts of her body 彼女の体の最も秘めた部分

classified ［ふつう名詞の前で］《ややフォーマル》（情報が公式に）秘密の、機密の ◇The magazine printed a controversial article based on *classified* material. その雑誌は機密事項に基づいた議論をかもす記事を掲載した ◇We are not in a position to divulge that information: it is *classified*. 私たちはその情報を明かせる立場にない。それは機密なのだ 反意 **unclassified** ❶ unclassified な情報は、秘密ではなく誰でも入手できる。

security 名

security・protection・defence・cover
人や物事が守られている状況を表す
【類語訳】安全、治安、警備、保護、防護、防御、防衛、弁護、擁護、援護

▸文型&コロケーション
▸ protection/ defence **from/ of/ against** sth
▸ **adequate** security/ protection/ defence
▸ **effective** protection/ defence
▸ to **provide** security/ protection/ defence/ cover

security [U] （攻撃・危険からの国・建物・人の）安全、治安、警備 ◇The incident has provoked calls to tighten airport *security*. その事件で空港警備強化の要請が誘発された ◇The government claimed that the organization posed a threat to **national *security*** (= the defence of a country). 政府はその組織は国家の安全保障に脅威を及ぼすものであると主張した ◇The visit took place amidst **tight *security*** (= the use of many police of-

ficers). その訪問は厳重な警備の中で行われた ◇The demonstrations were brutally broken up by the ***security* forces** (= the police, army, etc.). デモは治安部隊によって容赦なく解散させられた ◇Investigations are continuing into a ***security* alert** in the city yesterday. 昨日の都市の安全警備態勢に関する調査が継続中である ☞ **secure** (PROTECT)

protection [U] 《ややフォーマル》（けが・損傷・攻撃・危険・誤った使用法からの人・物への）保護、防護 ◇Remember to bring clothes that provide adequate *protection* against the wind and rain. 雨風をうまく避けられる服を持参するのを忘れないように ◇He asked to be put **under** police ***protection***. 彼は警察に保護してくれるように頼んだ ◇She acknowledged that much work needs to be done to improve data *protection* laws. 彼女は情報保護法を改正するには多くの作業が必要であることを認めた ☞ **protect** (PROTECT)

defence 《英》（*米* **defense**）[U] （攻撃・批判からの人・物事の）防御、防衛、弁護、擁護 ◇He paid tribute to all those who had died **in *defence* of** their country. 彼はお国のために亡くなった人すべてに敬意を表した ◇What points can be raised in *defence* of this argument? この主張を支持するとしてどんな点が上げられますか ◇When her brother was criticized she **leapt to his *defence***. 彼女は兄が批判を受けたとき、即刻兄の弁護に回った ◇He has shown courage in **coming to the *defence*** of the embattled president. 彼は四面楚歌の大統領を擁護する勇気を示している ❶ **self-defence** は攻撃[批判]されたときに、自分を守るために行う[言う]行為を指す。 ◇The man later told police that he was acting **in *self-defence***. （後にその男は警察に対して、自分は自己防衛の行動をとっていたと話した）. ☞ **defend** (EXPLAIN 2)

cover [U] （攻撃を行う[受ける]さいの）援護 ◇The ships needed air *cover* (= protection by military planes) once they reached enemy waters. 船舶がひとたび敵国の領海に到達すると、空からの援護が必要であった

see 動 ☞ LOOK 動 1, NOTICE

see・spot・catch・glimpse・sight
突然[見えにくい場合に]、両目を使って人や物に気づく
【類語訳】見る、見つける、見分ける、見きわめる、見抜く、見出す、ちらっと見る、認める

▸文型&コロケーション
▸ to see/ spot **that/ how/ what/ where/ who...**
▸ to **just** see/ spot/ catch/ glimpse sb/ sth
▸ to **suddenly** see/ spot/ catch/ glimpse sb/ sth

see ［他］《進行形なし》（人・物（が…しているの）を）見る、見かける ◇She looked for him but couldn't *see* him in the crowd. 彼女は彼を探したが、群衆の中に彼の姿を見つけることはできなかった ◇He could *see* (that) she had been crying. 彼には彼女がずっと泣いていたのがわかった ◇Did you *see* what happened? 何が起こったかわかりましたか ◇I hate to *see* you unhappy. 不幸でいるあなたを見るのは嫌です ◇She was *seen* running away from the scene of the crime. 彼女は犯行現場から逃走するところを見られた ◇I *saw* you put the key in your pocket. あなたがポケットに鍵を入れるのを見ました

spot (**-tt-**) ［他］《進行形なし》（突然[見えにくい場合に]）人・物を）見つける、見分ける、見きわめる、見抜く ◇I've just *spotted* a mistake on the front cover. 表紙に間違いを見つけたところよ ◇Can you *spot* the difference between these two pictures? この二つの絵の違いが分かりますか ◆Her modelling career began when she was *spotted* by an agent at the age of 14. 彼女のモデルとしての経歴は14歳のエージェントに見出されたときに始まった

catch [他] (はっきりと[完全に]ではないが物が(…している)の)を見る, 見つける ◇She *caught sight* of a car in the distance. 彼女は遠くに1台の車を見つけた ◇He *caught a glimpse* of himself in the mirror. 彼には鏡に映った自分がちらっと見えた ◇I *caught* a look of surprise on her face. 彼女の顔に驚きの表情を見てとった

glimpse [他]《書き言葉》(はっきりと[完全に]ではないが人・物を)ちらっと見る ◇He'd *glimpsed* her through the window as he passed. 彼は通りすがりに窓越しに彼女をちらっと見てしまった ☞**glimpse** (LOOK 名)

sight [他]《書き言葉》(ずっと探していた物を突然)見つける, 認める ◇After twelve days at sea, they *sighted* land. 海上で12日間過ごした後, 彼らは陸地を見つけた ☞**sight** (LOOK 名)

seem [連結動詞]

seem・look・appear・sound・feel・come across・strike・come over
…である[する]という感じを与える
【類語訳】思える, 見える, 似ている, 聞こえる, 印象を与える

《文型&コロケーション》
▶ to seem/ look/ appear/ sound/ feel odd/ OK/ nice, etc.
▶ to come across/ strike sb/ come over as (being) odd, etc.
▶ to seem/ look/ appear to be sth
▶ to seem/ look/ sound/ feel like sth
▶ to seem/ look/ sound/ feel as if/ as though…
▶ It seems/ appears/ strikes sb that…
▶ It would seem/ appear that…

seem [連結動詞]《進行形なし》(印象として…である[する]ように)思える, …らしい ◇Do whatever *seems* best to you. 自分に最善だと思えることなら何でもしなさい ◆He *seems* a nice man. 彼はいい人のようだ ◆It *seemed* like a good idea at the time. それは当時はいい考えのように思えた ◆It always *seemed* as though they would get married. 彼らは結婚するようにいつも思われていた ◇They *seem* to know what they're doing. 彼らは自分たちがしていることがわかっているらしい ◇'He'll be there, then?' '*So it seems* (= people say so).' 「じゃあ, 彼は来るね」「そうらしいよ」❶*seem* は自分の考え・感情・行動について言うときの印象を弱めたり, 確信がない[丁寧でありたいと思う]ことを示唆したりする場合に用いられることが多い ◆I *seem* to have left my book at home. (本を家に置いてきたようだ) ◆I can't *seem* to (= I've tried, but I can't) get started today. (今日は始められないようだ) ◆It *seems* only reasonable to ask students to buy a dictionary. (学生に辞書を買うよう求めるのはごく当然のことだと思う) ◆It would *seem* that we all agree. (《ややフォーマル》どうやら我々はみな同じ意見のようだ) ☞**seeming** (APPARENT)

look [連結動詞]《進行形が稀》(見た様子から…のように)見える; (外観が)似ている; (外観が)…らしい, しそうだ; …そうだ ◇You *look* tired. お疲れのようだね ◇That photograph doesn't *look* like her at all. その写真は全然彼女に似ていない ◆It *looks* like rain (= it looks as if it's going to rain). 雨が降りそうだ ◇That *looks* an interesting book.《特に英》それは面白そうな本だ ❶《米》では, 名詞句と共に *look like* を用いるほうが一般的である ◆That *looks like* an interesting book. 《米, 英》それは面白そうな本だ ❶特に《米》では, 話し言葉では, *as if, as though* の代わりに *like* を用いることが多い ◆You *look as though* you slept badly. (よく眠れなかったようだね) ◆It doesn't *look as if* we'll be moving after all. (結局私たちは引越ししないらしいね) ◆You *look like* you slept badly. (話し言葉, 特に《米》)よく眠れなかったようだね ◆It doesn't *look like* we'll be moving after all. (結局私たちは引越ししないらしいね) これは《英》の書き言葉では誤用であると考えられている ❶*seem* とは異なり, *look* は特定の時, 特に普段の様子と異なる場合に, 人・物事がどのように見えるかを表すのに進行形で用いられることがある ◆I thought she was *looking* rather tired last night. (彼女は昨晩かなり疲れているように見えたんだが) ☞**look** (APPEARANCE)

appear [連結動詞]《進行形なし》《ややフォーマル》(見た様子から…のように)見える ◇She didn't *appear* at all surprised at the news. 彼女はその知らせにあまり驚いていないようだった ◇They *appeared* not to know what was happening. 彼らは何が起きているのかわかっていないように見えた ❶*appear* は *look* よりもフォーマルで, 自分や相手が人・物事を実際に見たままであるとは信じていないことを示唆する ◆He *appears* to be a perfectly normal person (= but there is still some reason to suppose that he might not be). (彼はまったく普通の人のように見える) ◆It would *appear* that this was a major problem (= although I don't really understand why it should be). (これが大きな問題だったようだ) また, 物事について確信がないときや, または人の誤りをあまり直接的に非難したくないときに, *seem* のように用いられることもある ◆There *appears* to have been a mistake. (間違いがあったようだ) 《英》では, *appear* + 名詞句の形で用いることができる 《米》では, *appear to be* + 名詞句《英》でも容認される)の形で用いる必要がある ◆He *appears* a perfectly normal person.《英》彼はまったく普通の人のように見える ☞**apparent** (APPARENT), **appearance** (APPEARANCE)

sound [連結動詞]《進行形なし》(口頭・文面の印象として…のように)聞こえる, 思える, 印象を与える ◇His voice *sounded* strange on the phone. 彼の声は電話では変な印象だった ◇Her explanation *sounds* reasonable to me. 彼の説明は私には理にかなっているように思える ◇Leo **made it *sound*** so easy. But it wasn't. レオの口振りだととても簡単そうに聞こえた。だが, そうではなかったのだ ◆She *sounds* like just the person we need for the job. 彼女はまさに我々がその仕事に必要としている人物のように思える ◇You *sounded* just like your father when you said that. そう言った時の君は, お父さんとまったく同じように聞こえたよ ◇I hope I don't *sound* as if I'm criticizing you. 君を批判しているような印象を与えていないといいのだが

feel [連結動詞]《進行形なし》(…のような)感じを与える, 気がする; (…という)感触を与える ◇It *felt* strange to be back in my old school. 母校に戻ると妙な感じがした ◆The interview only took ten minutes, but it *felt* like hours. インタビューは10分しかかからなかったが, 何時間にも感じた ◆It *feels like rain* (= seems likely to rain). 雨が降りそうな気がする ◆Her head *felt* as if it would burst. 彼女は頭が爆発しそうな感じがした ◆It *felt* as though he had run a marathon. 彼はひとマラソン走り終えたかのように感じた ◆How does it *feel* to be alone all day? 一日中一人でいるとどんな感じがするのだろう ◇The water *feels* warm. そ

↪seem

の水は温かく感じる ◇This wallet *feels* like leather. この財布は革のような感触だ ☞ **feeling, feel** (ATMOSPHERE), **feeling** (SENSE)

[ノート] **sound** と **feel** の使い分け：人・物事の声・音を聞いて受ける印象については sound, 自分自身 [他人] の本心については feel を用いる. ◆He *sounded* happy, but I don't think he *felt* it. (彼は嬉しそうだったが, 実際はそうではなかったと思う). 話し言葉において, 特に《米》では, 両語とも as if, as though の代わりに like を用いることが多いが, これは《英》の書き言葉では誤用とみなされる. ◆You *sound* like you're ready to give up. (あなたはもうあきらめようとしているような口振りだね). ◆He *felt* like he'd run a marathon. (彼はひとマラソン走ったような気分だった).

,**come a'cross** [句動詞] (…のような) 印象を与える ◇She *comes across* well in interviews. 会見での彼女はよい印象を与えます

strike [他] (人に…のような) 印象を与える ◇His reaction *struck* me as odd. 私には彼の反応が奇妙に思えた ◇She *strikes* me as a very efficient person. 彼女は非常に有能な人物のように私には思えます ◇How does the idea *strike* you? その考えにどのような印象をお持ちですか

,**come 'over** [句動詞] (…のような) 印象を与える ◇He *came over* as a sympathetic person. 彼は思いやりのある人物だとの印象だった

[ノート] **come across** と **come over** の使い分け：come across はふつう後に副詞を伴うことが多い. come over はふつう後に as a/an... を伴うことが多い.

selfish [形]

selfish • self-centred • self-serving • egotistical • egocentric
自分のことしか考えない人を表す
【類語訳】利己的な, 自分本位の, 自分勝手な, わがままな, 自己中心的な, 独善的な

[文型&コロケーション]
▶ a selfish/ a self-centred/ an egotistical **person**
▶ a selfish/ a self-centred/ an egotistical/ an egocentric **man**
▶ a selfish/ a self-centred/ egocentric **nature**
▶ a selfish/ a self-serving/ an egotistical **way**

selfish 《けなして》利己的な, 自分本位の, 自分勝手な, わがままな ◇It was *selfish of him to* leave all the work to you. 仕事を君に丸投げするとは彼は自分勝手な人間だったんだ ◇Do you think I'm being *selfish* by not letting her go? 彼女を行かせないのは私のわがままだと思うすか ◇What a *selfish* thing to do! 何て自分勝手なことをするんだ ◇He did it for purely *selfish* reasons. 彼はまったく自分本位の理由でそうした [反意] **unselfish, selfless** ❶ unselfish, selfless な人は, 自分の欲求などよりも他人の欲求・幸せのことを考える. selfless は unselfish よりも文語的な語である. ◆His motives were completely *unselfish*. (彼の動機にはまったく利己的なところはなかった). ◆a life of *selfless* service to the community (共同体に対する無私の奉仕の生活).

▷**selfishly** [副] ◇She looked forward, a little *selfishly*, to a weekend away from her family. 彼女は少し身勝手にも, 家族から離れる週末を楽しみにしていた

▷**selfishness** [名] [U] ◇He was the victim of his own greed and *selfishness*. 彼は自分の強欲と身勝手さの犠牲者だった

,**self-'centred** 《英》,**self-'centered** 《けなして》自己中心的な, 自分本位の, 自分勝手な ◇Your father's too *self-centred* to care what you do. あなたのお父様はあまりにも自己中心的で, あなたがすることなど気にかけないんだね

,**self-'serving** 《けなして》利己的な, 自分本位の, 自分勝手な ◇He was portrayed as a *self-serving* careerist. 彼は利己的な立身出世主義者として描かれた

egotistical 《特に書き言葉, けなして》利己的な, 自分本位の, 独善的な ◇For all his charm, he was arrogant and *egotistical*. 彼はあれだけの魅力があるにもかかわらず, 傲慢で利己的だった

egocentric 《特に書き言葉, けなして》自己中心的な, 自分本位の, 自分勝手な ◇In the film he appears *egocentric* and opinionated. その映画では, 彼は自己中心的で独善的であるように見える

sell [動]

1 **sell • sell sth off • auction • sell up • liquidate • auction sth off**
お金と引き換えに物事を人に与える
【類語訳】売る, 売却する, 競売にかける, 売り払う, 現金化する, 換金する

[文型&コロケーション]
▶ to sell sth/ sell sth off/ auction sth/ auction sth off **to** sb/ a place
▶ to sell sth/ auction sth/ auction sth off **for** £100, $47,000, etc.
▶ to sell/ sell off/ auction/ liquidate **property/ assets**
▶ to sell/ sell off/ liquidate **shares/ a company**
▶ to sell/ sell off/ auction/ auction off a **collection**
▶ to sell/ sell off/ auction **land**
▶ to sell/ auction a **house**

sell [他, 自] (お金と引き換えに物事を人に) 売る, 売却する ◇I *sold* my car to James for £800. 私は車をジェームズに800ポンドで売った ◇I *sold* James my car for £800. 私はジェームズに800ポンドで車を売った ◇They *sold* the business at a profit/loss (= they gained/lost money when they sold it). 彼らはその事業を利益を上げた上で [損失を出して] 売却した ◇We offered them a good price but they wouldn't *sell*. 我々は彼らによい値を申し出たが, 彼らは売ろうとしなかった

,**sell sth 'off** [句動詞] (処分したい [お金が必要な]) ので物事を) 安く売り払う；(事業・会社・土地のすべて [一部] を) 売却する ◇The Church *sold off* the land for housing. 教会は住宅建設のためにその土地を安く売り払った ◇In the nineties most state-owned industries were *sold off*. 90年代には, ほとんどの国有産業が売却された

auction [他, ふつう受身で] 《特に英》(物事を) 競売にかける ◇The costumes from the movie are to be *auctioned* for charity. その映画の衣装は慈善事業のために競売にかけられることになっている ❶《米》では, auction sth off と言うほうが一般的である.

,**sell 'up** [句動詞] (国を出る [退職する]) ので家・財産・会社などを) 売り払う ◇They *sold up* and moved to France. 彼らは家・財産を売り払ってフランスへ引っ越した

liquidate [他] 《金融》(物事を) 現金化する, 換金する

◇The shares are easy to sell, should you wish to *liquidate* your assets. 資産を現金化したいのなら、株は売却しやすい ❶ liquidate の典型的な連語には、assets, endowment, share portfolio, company, firm, debts が挙げられる。

,auction sth 'off 句動詞 (不必要[不用]な物を)競売で売り払う ◇The Army is *auctioning off* a lot of surplus equipment. 軍は余剰となった備品を競売で大量に売り払っている

2 sell・trade・export・import・do business・deal in sth・stock・carry・handle・deal・retail
人々に購入する物事を提供する
【類語訳】販売している、売買する、取り引きする、交易する、輸出する、輸入する、商売する、取り扱う、密売する、小売りする

文型&コロケーション
▸ to trade/ do business **with** sb
▸ to sell/ trade/ export/ import/ deal in/ stock/ handle/ retail **goods**
▸ to sell/ trade/ deal in **shares/ futures/ stocks/ bonds/ securities**
▸ to sell/ deal in **furniture/ antiques/ property**
▸ to sell/ import/ deal in/ deal **drugs**
▸ to sell/ stock/ carry/ retail a **range/ line** of goods

sell [他] 販売している ◇Most grocery stores *sell* a range of organic products. ほとんどの食料品店でさまざまな有機製品が販売されている ◇Do you *sell* stamps? 切手を売っていますか ◇He works for a company that *sells* insurance. 彼は保険を販売している会社に勤めている

trade [自, 他] 売買する, 取引する, 交易する;(企業・会社として)商売を営む, 営業する ◇After settling in Madeira they began ***trading*** in flour, sugar and leather. マデイラ諸島に定住してから、彼らは小麦粉・砂糖・革の売買を始めた ◇Early explorers *traded* directly with the Indians. 初期の探検家たちはアメリカ先住民族と直接取引した ◇Our products are now *traded* worldwide. 我々の製品は現在、世界中で取引されている ◇The firm has now *ceased trading*. その会社はもう営業していない ☞ **trade, trading** (TRADE)

export [他] 輸出する ◇The islands *export* sugar and fruit. その島々は砂糖と果物を輸出している ◇90% of the engines are *exported* to Europe. エンジンの90%はヨーロッパに輸出される 反意 **import**
▸**export** 名 [U, C, ふつう複数] ◇Then the fruit is packaged *for export*. その後、果物は輸出向けに包装される ◇the country's major *exports* その国の主要な輸出品 反意 **import**

import [他] 輸入する, 持ち込む ◇The country has to *import* most of its raw materials. その国は原材料のほとんどを輸入しなければならない ◇goods *imported from* Japan *into* the US 日本から米国に輸入される商品 ◇customs *imported* from the West 西欧から持ち込まれた慣習 反意 **export**
▸**import** 名 [U, C, ふつう複数] ◇The report calls for a ban on the *import* of hazardous waste. その報告書では、有害廃棄物の輸入禁止が求められている ◇food *imports* from abroad 海外からの輸入食品 反意 **export**

,do 'business フレーズ 商売する, 取引する, 営業する ◇It's been a pleasure to *do business* with you. 御社と取引できて光栄です ◇I don't like his way of *doing busi-*

ness. 彼の商売のやり方が気に食わない ☞ **business** (TRADE)

'deal in sth 句動詞 (特定の製品を)取り扱う, 取引する ◇The company *deals in* computer software. その会社はコンピューターソフトを扱っている ☞ **dealing** (TRADE)

ノート **trade in sth** と **deal in sth** の使い分け: **trade in sth** はほとんどの場合、生地・絹などの織物だけでなく、動物・石炭・砂糖・革・毛皮・象牙といった品物の売買に用いられる。**deal in sth** は車・骨董品・家具・電子機器などの工業製品について用いられることが多い。**deal in sth** はまた犯罪となる売買についてもよく用いられる。典型的な連語に、drugs (薬物), guns (銃), stolen goods (盗品) が挙げられる。**trade in sth, deal in sth** はいずれも、例えば、shares (株式), futures (先物), stocks (確定利付き証券), bonds (公債), securities (有価証券)など、金融市場の品目の売買について用いられる。

stock [他] 《ややフォーマル、特にビジネスで》(店が特定の種類の商品を)取り扱っている, 置いている ◇We *stock* a wide range of camping equipment. 当店はさまざまなキャンプ用品を取り扱っております ☞ **stock** (SUPPLY)

carry [他] 《米 or フォーマル》(店が特定の種類の商品を)取り扱っている, 置いている ◇We *carry* a range of educational software. 当店は多様な教育ソフトを取り扱っております

ノート **stock** と **carry** の使い分け: これらの語は、《英》と《米》で言語使用域が異なる。《英》では両語とも特に店で働く人々によって[店の宣伝で]用いられる。**carry** は **stock** よりもフォーマルである。《英》の日常会話では、ほとんどの人が sell を用いる。◆Do you *sell* green tea? 《英》緑茶は売っていますか。×Do you *stock/carry* green tea? しかし《米》では、**carry** は **stock** ほどフォーマルではなく、日常会話でも用いられることがある。◆We do *carry* green tea, but we don't have any (in stock) right now. 《米》当店では緑茶を扱っておりますが、ただ今(在庫を)切らしております

handle [他] (違法に)密売する ◇They were arrested for ***handling** stolen goods*. 彼らは盗品売買で逮捕された ❶ この意味では handle はふつう stolen goods (盗品) と共に用いられる。

deal [自, 他] (違法薬物を)密売[取引]する, 麻薬を売買する ◇You can often see people *dealing* openly on the streets. 人々が街頭でおおっぴらに麻薬を売買するのが頻繁に見かけられる ◇He was sent to jail for *dealing* drugs to his friends. 彼は友人に麻薬を売ったとして投獄された ❶ 《英》では、人を主語にして、deal drugs, deal in drugs と言うことができる。《米》では、(in を用いずに) deal drugs と言うほうが普通である。《英》《米》のいずれにおいても、drug よりインフォーマルな dope や、cocaine, heroin など薬物の名称と共に用いる場合、(in を用いずに) deal dope/cocaine/heroin と言うほうが普通である。

retail [他] 《ビジネスで》小売りする ◇The firm manufactures and *retails* its own range of sportswear. その会社は、スポーツウェアを独自の品揃えで製造・小売販売しています

send 動

send・mail・post・address・forward・dispatch・send sth on
郵便で物をある場所へ持って行くことを表す

↪**send**

【類語訳】送る, 郵送する, 投函する, 宛名を書く, 転送する, 発送する

文型&コロケーション
- to send/ mail/ post/ address/ forward/ dispatch/ send on sth **to** sb
- to send/ mail/ post/ address/ forward/ dispatch/ send on a **letter**
- to send/ mail/ post/ address/ forward a **message**
- to send/ mail/ post/ forward/ dispatch a **document**
- to send/ mail/ post/ address a/ an **invitation/ package/ parcel/ postcard/ reply**
- to send/ post/ address/ forward **mail**
- to send/ address/ forward **correspondence**
- to send/ forward an **email**
- to send/ dispatch **goods**

send [他] (郵便・eメール・ファクス・無線で)送る ◇Have you *sent* a postcard to your mother yet? もう葉書きをお母さんに送ったの ◇Have you *sent* your mother a postcard yet? もうお母さんに葉書きを送ったの ◇A radio signal was *sent* to the spacecraft. 無線信号が宇宙船に送られた ◇The CD player was faulty so we *sent* it *back* to the manufacturers. そのCDプレーヤーには欠陥があったので, 製造元に送り返した

mail [他] (特に米) 郵送する; 投函する ◇The company intends to *mail* 50,000 households in the area. 会社は地域の5万世帯に郵便を送る予定だ ◇Don't forget to *mail* that letter. その手紙を投函するのを忘れないでね ☞ **mail** (LETTER)

post [他] (英) 郵送する; 投函する ◇Is it OK if I *post* you the cheque next week? 来週小切手を郵送してもよろしいですか ◇Could you *post* this letter for me? この手紙を出しておいてもらえますか ☞ **post** (LETTER)

address [他, ふつう受身で] (封筒・小包に[を])宛名を書く, …宛にする ◇The letter was correctly *addressed*, but delivered to the wrong house. その手紙には正確に宛名が書かれていたが, 間違った住所に配達された ◇*Address* your application to the Personnel Manager. 願書は人事部長宛てに送ってください ☞ **address** (HOME)

forward [他] (旧住所に送られた手紙を新住所に[eメールを他の人に])転送する ◇Could you *forward* any mail to us in New York? 郵便物はどれもニューヨークの私どもに転送していただけますか ◇I'm *forwarding* you this email that I had from Jeff. ジェフからもらったこのeメールを転送します ❶ この用法では, forward は商品・情報を人に「送る」という意味のみで用いる。 ◆We will be *forwarding* our new catalogue to you next week. (来週私どもの新しいカタログをお送りいたします).

dispatch [英でまた **despatch**] [他] (フォーマル, 特にビジネス) (手紙・メッセージ・商品・情報を)送る, 発送する ◇Goods are *dispatched* within 24 hours of your order reaching us. ご注文が私どもに届いてから24時間以内に商品は発送されます

,send sth 'on [句動] (物を)前もって送る; (旧住所に送られた手紙を新住所に[ある場所から別の場所に])転送する ◇We *sent* our furniture *on* by ship. 家具は前もって船便で送りました ◇They promised to *send on* our mail when we moved. 私たちが引っ越したとき, 郵便物は転送してくれる約束だった ◆They arranged for the information to be *sent on* to us. 彼らが私たちに情報が転送されるように手配してくれたのです

sense [名]

sense・feeling・impression・idea・sensation

心[感覚]を通じて感じる[思う]こと
【類語訳】感じ, 気持ち, 印象, 観念, 概念, 認識, 見当, 感覚

文型&コロケーション
- a **strong** sense/ feeling/ impression/ idea/ sensation
- an **overwhelming** sense/ feeling/ impression/ sensation
- a **good/ definite/ distinct/ vague** sense/ feeling/ impression/ idea
- a **strange** sense/ feeling/ impression/ idea/ sensation
- a/ an **wonderful/ warm/ uncomfortable** sense/ feeling/ sensation
- to **have** a sense/ a feeling/ an impression/ an idea/ a sensation
- to **have the** sense/ feeling/ impression/ sensation **that**...
- to **get/ give** sb**/ leave** sb **with/ convey** a sense/ a feeling/ an impression/ an idea

sense [C] (しばしば of を伴って) (重要な事柄に関する)感じ, 気持ち ◇He felt an overwhelming *sense* of loss. 彼は抗しがたい喪失感を覚えた ◇Doesn't she have any *sense* of guilt about what she did? 彼女は自分がしたことに何の罪悪感も感じていないのですか ◇Helmets can give cyclists *a false sense of security*. ヘルメットは自転車に乗る人たちに間違った安心感を与えることがある ◇I had the *sense* that he was worried about something. 彼が何かを心配しているという感じがした ☞ **sense** (FEEL)

feeling [C] (心・感覚を通じての)感じ, 気持ち ◇There was a *feeling* of sadness in the room. その部屋には悲しみの思いが漂っていた ◇You need to stop having these guilty *feelings*. こうした罪悪感を抱くのはやめたほうがいい ◇I've got a tight *feeling* in my stomach. 胃が締めつけられるような感じがする ◇I really resent the way he treated me.' '*I know the feeling*.' (= I know how you feel.) 《話し言葉》「彼の私に対する扱いには本当に腹が立つ」「気持ちはわかるよ」 ❶ 複数形の feelings は「感情」を意味する。☞ **feeling** (EMOTION) ☞ **feel** (FEEL), **feel** (SEEM)

impression [C] (人・物事に抱く[人・物事が与える])印象, 感じ ◇My *first impression* of him was favourable. 彼に対する私の第一印象はよかった ◇I *get the impression* there are still a lot of problems. まだ問題が山積しているという印象だ ◇She *gives the impression* of being very busy. 彼女は非常に忙しいという印象だ ◇Try and smile. You don't want to give people the *wrong impression* (= that you are not friendly). 笑顔を作ってみて。人に嫌な印象を与えたくないでしょ ❶ impression は特に初めて人に会う[物事を体験する]ときの思いについて用いられる。

idea [単数で, U] (人・物事に抱く)観念, 概念, 印象, 認識, 見当 ◇The brochure should give you a good *idea* of the hotel. そのパンフレットを見ればどんなホテルかということがよくわかるはずです ◇If this is your *idea* of a joke, then I don't find it very funny. これがあなたの考える冗談というものなら, 私はあまり面白いとは思いませんね ◇I had *some idea of* what the job would be like. 私にはその仕事がどのようなものであるかいくらか見当はついていた

sensation [C] 《ややフォーマル》(身体に覚える)感覚, 感じ, 気持ち ◇You may get a tingling *sensation* in your fingers. 指がちくちくする感じがするかもしれません ◇I had a

sensitive

sensation of falling, as if in a dream. まるで夢の中にいる時のように、落ちていく感覚があった

> **ノード feeling と sensation の使い分け**: feeling は身体的であることも精神的であることもある。sensation は身体的な感覚である。sensation は特にすぐには認識[理解]できない感覚について用いられる。◆ a *sensation* of falling/floating/movement/nausea/sinking（落ちていく感覚/浮いている感覚/運動感覚/吐き気/沈む感覚）

sensitive 形

1 sensitive・sympathetic・gentle・humane・compassionate・understanding・soft
人が他人に対して優しさと理解を示すことを表す
【類語訳】敏感な、繊細な、気の利く、思いやりのある、同情的な、共感的な、親身の、おとなしい、物わかりのよい、情にもろい

▶文型&コロケーション
▶ sensitive/ sympathetic/ gentle/ compassionate/ understanding **towards** sb
▶ sensitive/ sympathetic **to** sb/ sth
▶ a sensitive/ sympathetic/ gentle/ humane/ compassionate **manner/ man**
▶ (in) a sensitive/ sympathetic/ gentle/ humane/ compassionate **way**
▶ (a) sensitive/ sympathetic/ gentle **handling/ approach**
▶ sensitive/ sympathetic/ humane **treatment**
▶ a humane/ compassionate **society**

sensitive （ほめて）(他人の(気持ち)に)敏感な、繊細な、気のきく、心遣いの細やかな ◇a *sensitive* and caring man 気がきいて面倒見のよい人 ◇She is very *sensitive* to other people's feelings. 彼女は他人の気持ちにとても敏感だ ◇This type of situation requires a *sensitive* approach by doctors. この種の状態には医師による心遣いの細やかな取組みが必要である 反意 **insensitive** (INSENSITIVE), ☞ **sensitivity** (TACT).
▷**sensitively** 副 ◇She handled the matter *sensitively* and effectively. 彼女はその問題を細やかな心配りをして効果的に取り扱った
sympathetic （ほめて）(傷ついている[動揺している]人に)思いやりのある、(傷ついている[動揺している]人の問題に)同情的な、共感的な、親身の ◇a *sympathetic* friend/listener/employer 思いやりのある友人/聞き手/雇い主 ◇I did not feel at all *sympathetic* towards Kate. 私はケイトに対してはまったく同情しなかった ◇I'm here if you need a *sympathetic ear* (= sb to talk to about your problems). 親身になって話を聞いてくれる人が必要になれば私がここにいますからね 反意 **unsympathetic** (INSENSITIVE), ☞ **sympathy** (SYMPATHY), **sympathize** (SORRY FOR SB), **sorry** (UPSET)
▷**sympathetically** 副 ◇to nod/look/smile at sb *sympathetically* 共感して人にうなずく/を見る/にほほ笑む
gentle （ほめて）(心が)優しい、おとなしい；(行いが)優しい、穏やかな ◇Be *gentle* with her! 彼女には優しくしなさい ◇She agreed to come, after a little *gentle* persuasion. 彼女は穏やかに少し説得を受けた後、行ってもいいと言った ◇He looks scary, but he's really a *gentle giant*. 彼はこわもてだが、実際は心の優しい大男である 反意 **rough** (VIOLENT)
▷**gently** 副 ◇She held the baby *gently*. 彼女は赤ん

坊を優しく抱いた ◇'You miss them, don't you?' he asked *gently*. 「彼らがいなくて寂しいんでしょ」と彼は優しく尋ねた
humane （ややフォーマル、ほめて）(人・動物に対して)人間[人情]味のある、思いやりのある、慈悲深い ◇a caring and *humane* society 思いやりと人情味のある社会 ◇The animals must be reared in *humane* conditions. 動物は思いやりのある状況で育てねばならない 反意 **inhumane, cruel** (CRUEL), ☞ **humanity** (SYMPATHY)
▷**humanely** 副 ◇The dog was *humanely* destroyed. その犬の殺し方は慈悲深いものであった
compassionate （ややフォーマル、ほめて）(苦しんでいる人に)同情的な、思いやりのある、哀れみ深い ◇Are these the actions of a *compassionate* and caring society? これらが哀れみ深く思いやりのある団体の活動なのですか ◇He was granted *compassionate leave* to visit his mother in hospital. 彼は入院中の母親を見舞うために特別休暇をもらった ☞ **compassion** (SYMPATHY)
understanding （ほめて）(他人に)物わかりのよい、理解のある ◇She has very *understanding* parents. 彼女には非常に物わかりのよい両親がいる ☞ **understand** (UNDERSTAND 2), **understanding** (SYMPATHY)
soft （ふつうほめて）心の優しい、思いやりのある；情にもろい ◇Julia's *soft heart* was touched by his grief. 情にもろいジュリアは彼の深い悲しみに心を動かされた 反意 **hard** (RUTHLESS)

2 sensitive・tricky・problematic・awkward・delicate・emotive
取り扱いが難しく、注意深い扱いが必要であることを表す
【類語訳】扱いにくい、微妙な、際どい、厄介な、不確実な、困った、難しい、デリケートな

▶文型&コロケーション
▶ a sensitive/ a tricky/ a problematic/ an awkward/ a delicate **matter/ situation**
▶ a sensitive/ a tricky/ an awkward/ a delicate/ an emotive **question/ subject**
▶ a sensitive/ a tricky/ an awkward/ a delicate **problem**
▶ a sensitive/ a tricky/ a problematic/ an emotive **issue**
▶ a sensitive/ tricky/ problematic/ delicate **business**
▶ a sensitive/ a problematic/ an awkward/ a delicate **relationship**
▶ the sensitive/ problematic/ delicate/ emotive **nature** of sth
▶ **very/ rather** sensitive/ tricky/ problematic/ awkward/ delicate/ emotive
▶ **extremely/ somewhat** sensitive/ tricky/ problematic/ awkward/ delicate
▶ **highly** sensitive/ problematic/ emotive

sensitive （気分を害する[怒らせる]かもしれなくて）扱いにくい、慎重な対処を要する、微妙な ◇It might be better to avoid such a *sensitive* topic. そういう扱いにくい話題は避けたほうがいいかもしれない ◇She is currently involved in highly *sensitive* negotiations. 彼女は現在、非常に慎重な対処を要する交渉に関わっています ◇Health care is a *politically sensitive* issue. ヘルスケアの問題は政治的には扱いにくいものです ◇The exact figure has not been released because it is judged to be *commercially sensitive* information. 正確な数字は営業的に慎重な対処を要する情報であると判断されるため、発表されていません
tricky （ややインフォーマル）(特別な注意・技術が必要で)扱

いにくい, 手際のいる, 際どい ◇The incident has raised some *tricky* questions about the future of the project. その出来事で事業の将来に関していくつかの際どい問題が提起された ◇Getting it to fit exactly is a *tricky* business. それをぴったり適合させるのは手際のいる仕事だ ◇The equipment can be *tricky* to install. その設備は据え付けるのに注意を要するかもしれない

problematic (扱いにくくて[理解しがたくて])厄介な, 解決の難しい；問題の多い[ある]；不確実な ◇The situation is more *problematic* than we first thought. 状況は我々が当初考えていた以上に厄介だ ◇Providing the necessary care for elderly people can be *problematic*. 高齢者に必要な介護の提供ということに関しては問題が多いかもしれない [反意] **unproblematic**, ☞ **problem** (PROBLEM)

awkward (状況・人の行動が)人を困らせる, 困った, 厄介な, 扱いにくい, 難しい ◇Don't ask *awkward* questions. 答えにくい質問はしないでください ◇You've put me in an *awkward position*. 君はこの私を困った立場に追い込んでくれたね ◇It makes things *awkward* for everyone when you behave like that. そんなふうに行動されると, 皆が困るんだよ

delicate 細心の注意[手際]を要する, 扱いにくい, 際どい, 微妙な, デリケートな ◇The *delicate* surgical operation took five hours. その細心の注意を要する外科手術に5時間かかった ◇I wasn't sure how to approach the *delicate* matter of pay. 扱いにくい賃金問題にどう取り組むべきかわからなかった

emotive (問題・人の言葉が)感情を喚起する[逆なでする] ◇Capital punishment is a highly *emotive* issue. 死刑は非常に感情的な問題である ◇Try to keep your report factual and avoid using *emotive language*. 報告書は常に事実に基づくようにして, 感情を逆なでするような言葉の使用は避けるよう努めなさい

3 sensitive・touchy・prickly
人が動揺しやすい[気分を害しやすい]ことを表す
【類語訳】神経過敏な, 神経質な, 敏感な, 傷つきやすい, 繊細な, 短気な, 怒りっぽい, ぴりぴりした

[文型&コロケーション]
▸ to be sensitive/ touchy/ prickly **about** sth
▸ **very** sensitive/ touchy/ prickly

sensitive (時にけなして)神経過敏な, 神経質な, 敏感な, 傷つきやすい, 繊細な, すぐ気にする[怒る] ◇You're far too *sensitive*. あなたはあまりに神経過敏だ ◇She's acutely *sensitive to* criticism. 彼女は批判に対してひどく敏感である ◇He's depicted as an insecure and *sensitive soul*. 彼は臆病で傷つきやすい人物として描かれている

touchy [名詞の前はまれ] (ややインフォーマル, しばしばけなして)(過度に)神経質な, 短気な, 怒りっぽい, ぴりぴりした ◇He's a little *touchy* about his weight. 彼は自分の体重に少し神経質だ ◇She gets very *touchy* if you mention the divorce. あなたが離婚の話を出すと, 彼女はとてもぴりぴりする

prickly (英, インフォーマル, しばしばけなして)神経過敏な, 神経質な, 敏感な, すぐ気にする[怒る] ◇She's still a bit *prickly* about the whole incident. 彼女は依然として, この件全体について少々敏感だ ◇He could be very *prickly* with journalists. 彼はジャーナリストに対しては非常に神経質かもしれない

[ノート] **sensitive, touchy, prickly** の使い分け：sensitive, touchy な人は, 動揺し[泣き]やすい. どちらの語も少し非難的であるが, touchy はふつう sensitive よりも強い非難を示唆する. prickly な人は, 泣くというよりは少し攻撃的になる可能性が高い.

series 名

series・sequence・order・chain・string・succession・catalogue・chronology・line
数多くの同種の出来事[物事, 人々]が次々と現れること
【類語訳】連続, 一続き, 一連, 続発, 配列, 順序, 順番, 順位, 連鎖, 系列, 系統, チェーン, 一列, 一群, 一覧表, 年表

[文型&コロケーション]
▸ a series/ sequence/ chain/ string/ succession/ catalogue/ chronology/ line **of** sth
▸ **in a/ an** (...) series/ sequence/ order/ string
▸ **in** sequence/ order (of sth)/ succession
▸ **out of** sequence/ order
▸ **a whole** series/ sequence/ string/ succession/ catalogue
▸ **a/ an long/ endless/ continuous/ unbroken** series/ sequence/ chain/ string/ succession/ line
▸ **a random** series/ sequence/ order/ string
▸ a series/ sequence/ chain/ string/ succession/ chronology **of events**
▸ a series/ string/ catalogue **of errors**
▸ a series/ sequence/ string **of numbers/ letters**
▸ **the first/ last/ latest in** a series/ sequence/ string/ succession/ line

series (複 series) [C] (of を伴って) (同種の出来事・物事の)連続, 一続き, 一連 ◇This is the first in a *series* of articles about rock 'n' roll legends. これはロックンロール伝説に関する一連の記事の最初のものです ◇The shooting was the latest in a *series* of violent attacks in the city. その発砲は, この都市での一連の激しい攻撃の最新のものだった

sequence [C, U] (特定の結果をもたらす出来事・行動・数字の)連続, 続発, 配列；(出来事・行動などが発生する(べき))順序 ◇The novel contains a long *dream sequence* (= describing a dream). その小説では長い夢の続きが描かれている ◇Put these numbers into the correct *sequence*. これらの数字を正しい順序に並べなさい ◇The computer generates a random *sequence* of numbers. コンピューターは無作為の数列を生み出します ◇The papers were all out of *sequence*. 書類の並べ方がまったくばらばらだった

[ノート] **series** と **sequence** の使い分け：series はふつう一連の個別項目を指す. それぞれの項目はある点では似ているが, 他のものとは異なる別個のものである. series の順序は論理的である必要はないが, sequence の方は多分に論理的である. sequence はふつうそれぞれの出来事・行動・数字がある意味で, その前の出来事・行動・数字と関連していることを示唆する.

order [U, C] (関連し合う数多くの中の)順序, 順番, 順位 ◇The names are listed in alphabetical *order*. 名前はアルファベット順に挙げられています ◇We will deal with cases in *order* of importance. 重要度の順番に事例を取り扱うことにします ◇Winners are announced *in re-*

verse order. 入賞者たちは逆の順番で[下位から]発表されます ◇The information is given in no particular *order.* 情報は特定の順序で提供されるわけではない ❶ **order**は一連の物事自体ではなく物事の配列に用いられる方式に重点が置かれる。☞ **order** (RANK)

chain [C] (特定の結果をもたらす)連続、一連、連鎖、系列、系統、チェーン(組織) ◇I was next in the ***chain of command*** (= a system by which instructions are passed from one person to another). 私は指揮系統の次の順位にいた ◇Middlemen are important ***links in the chain.*** 仲買人はチェーン組織を結びつける重要な存在である ◇Volunteers formed a ***human chain*** to pass buckets of water to each other. ボランティアが人間の鎖を作って水をバケツリレーした ❶この意味での **chain** の連語は、この語の文字どおりの意味(「鎖」)を思い起こさせる、link、break、unbroken が挙げられる。

string [C] (次々と現れる[密接し合う]同種のものの)連続、一続き、一連、一列、一群 ◇He retired after a *string* of chart hits in the 1980s. 彼は1980年代に次々にヒットチャートに登場した後、引退した ◇The company owns a *string* of casinos in Nevada. その会社はネヴァダ州に一連のカジノを所有している ❶物事がたくさんあることを強調するために、a string of が用いられる。

succession [C, ふつう単数で, U] (時間[順序]的な)連続、一続き、一連 ;(規則的な)連続 ◇She was cared for by a *succession* of nannies. 彼女は次々にベビーシッターに面倒を見てもらった ◇The team lost the final six years in *succession*. そのチームは6年連続で決勝で敗れた ◇They won several games *in quick succession*. 彼らは立て続けに数試合の勝利を得た ❶ある物事が絶え間なく[一気に]別の物事に続くことを強調するため、a succession of が用いられる。

catalogue [米でまた **catalog**] [C, ふつう単数で] (of を伴って) (特に英) (長期的に発生する悪い事の)連続、一続き、一連 ◇What followed was a whole *catalogue* of disasters. その後に起こったのは、あらゆる災害の連続であった ◇Child protection officers uncovered a *catalogue* of cruelty and abuse. 児童保護官たちは一連の残虐行為や虐待を暴いた

chronology [U, C] (一連の出来事の発生した)順序、年代順配列; (順に並んだ出来事の)一覧表、年表 ◇Historians seem to have confused the *chronology* of these events. 歴史家たちがこれらの出来事の年代順配列をかく乱させたように思える ◇At the front of the book is a *chronology* of the artist's life. その芸術家の生涯の年表は本の冒頭にある ❶ *chronology* はそれぞれの出来事が他の出来事に関連して、いつ発生したかに重点が置かれる。

line [C, ふつう単数で] (時間的な)連続、一続き、一連、系列 ◇She came from a long *line* of doctors (= there were many doctors in her family in the past). 彼女は医者だらけの家系の出だった ◇Property was passed down through the male *line* (= through the males in the family). 財産は男系に継承された ◇The novel is the latest in a long *line* of thrillers that he has written. その小説は彼が書いた多くの一連のスリラー本のうち最新のものです ☞ **lineage** (FAMILY 3)

serious 形

1 serious・severe・extreme・critical・grave・drastic・desperate・dire・acute・bad・life-threatening

人や物事に影響[危害、損害]が与えられた場合の状況を表す【類語ная】重大な、深刻な、ゆゆしい、重度の、厳しい、極端な、極度の、危険な、重篤な、憂慮すべき、抜本的な、急激な、思い切った、必死の

serious	severe	extreme
critical	grave	drastic
bad	acute	desperate
		dire
		life-threatening

文型&コロケーション

▶ a serious/ a severe/ a critical/ a grave/ an acute/ a desperate/ a bad/ a life-threatening **problem**
▶ a serious/ a severe/ an extreme/ a critical/ an acute/ a desperate/ a dire **shortage**
▶ serious/ severe/ extreme/ grave/ acute **danger**
▶ a serious/ a severe/ a grave/ a dire **threat**
▶ serious/ severe/ extreme/ acute/ desperate/ dire **poverty**
▶ a serious/ an extreme/ a critical/ an acute/ a desperate/ a dire **need**
▶ serious/ grave/ drastic/ dire/ bad **consequences**
▶ a serious/ a severe/ a critical/ a grave/ an acute/ a life-threatening **illness**
▶ a serious/ a severe/ an acute/ a life-threatening **disease**
▶ a serious/ a severe/ a grave/ an acute/ a bad/ a life-threatening **injury**
▶ a serious/ a severe/ an acute/ a life-threatening **infection**
▶ a serious/ a severe/ an acute/ a bad **attack/ bout**
▶ **particularly** serious/ severe/ extreme/ grave/ acute/ dire/ bad
▶ **very/ extremely** serious/ severe/ grave/ acute/ bad

serious 重大な、深刻な、ゆゆしい ◇The storm caused *serious* damage to farm buildings. 嵐が農舎に深刻な打撃を与えた ◇They pose a *serious* threat to security. それらは安全面に深刻な脅威をもたらす ◇The consequences could be *serious*. 結果は深刻なものとなるかもしれない 反意 **minor** (MINOR), ☞ **seriousness** (IMPORTANCE)
▶ **seriously** 副 ◇Smoking can *seriously* damage your health. 喫煙は著しく健康を害することがある
severe 重大な、重度の、深刻な、厳しい、ひどい ◇The victim suffered *severe* brain damage. その被害者は重度の脳障害を被った ◇The bridge has been closed due to *severe* weather conditions. その橋はひどい悪天候のため閉鎖されている ◇Strikes are causing *severe* disruption to all train services. ストですべての列車の運行に重大な混乱をきたしている 反意 **minor** (MINOR)、**mild** (GENTLE)
▶ **severely** 副 ◇Anyone breaking the law will be *severely* punished. 法を破るものは厳しく処罰されるだろう
▶ **severity** 名 [U] ◇The chances of a full recovery will depend on the *severity* of her injuries. 全快の見込みは彼女のけがのひどさ次第だろう

ノート **serious** と **severe** の使い分け: severeはほとんどの場合、病状や気象状況を表すのに用いられる。seriousは気象状況を表すのには用いられない。×*serious* weather. ×a *serious* winter. seriousは日常会話で病状を表すのに

↪**serious**

に用いられるが、医療用語ではsevereが用いられる。◆a *serious* illness（重病）. ◆*severe* learning difficulties（重度の学習障害）.

extreme (状況・行動が)極端な、尋常でない；極度の、極限の ◇Children will be removed from their parents only **in extreme circumstances**. 子どもたちは極端な状況下でしか両親から引き離されることはないだろう ◇Don't go doing anything *extreme* like leaving the country. 祖国を捨てるような極端な行動に走ってはならない ◇It was the most *extreme example* of cruelty to animals I had ever seen. それは今まで見たこともないような尋常ではない動物虐待の例だった ◇*extreme* weather conditions 極限の気象条件

critical (ややフォーマル) 重大な、危険な、重篤な ◇The first 24 hours after the operation are the most *critical*. 術後最初の24時間が最も危険である ◇One of the victims of the fire remains **in a critical condition**. 《英》 その火事の犠牲者の一人は依然として重体のままである ◇One of the victims remains **in critical condition**. 《米》犠牲者の一人は依然として重体のままである ◇This is a *critical* moment in our country's history. 今が我が国の歴史における重大な局面を迎えている ❶*critical*はillness, conditionと共に用いられることが多く、患者が生存しない可能性のある病状を表す。また、moment, period, phase, point, stage, time, yearsなどの時間に関連する語と共に用いられることも多く、重要な状況が失敗[成功]に終わる時を表す。
▶**critically** 副 ◇He is *critically* ill in hospital. 彼は重病で入院中だ

grave (フォーマル) 重大な、深刻な、憂慮すべき、ゆゆしい ◇I fear you are making a very *grave* mistake. あなたは非常に重大なミスを犯しているのではないかと思う ◇The police have expressed *grave* concern about the missing child's safety. 警察はその行方不明の子どもの安全について深刻な懸念を表明していた ◇We were in *grave* danger. 我々は重大な危機に瀕していた ❶*grave*はerror, mistake, offence, violationなどの語と共に用いられ、人々の誤った行動を表す。また、concern, doubt, misgivings, reservations, suspicions, worriesなどの語と共にも用いられ、物事を心配しているときに人々が抱く強い感情を表す。状況について用いられる場合は、consequences, danger, implications, problems, risk, threatなどの語と共に用いられることが多い。☞**gravity** (IMPORTANCE)
▶**gravely** 副 ◇Local people are *gravely* concerned. 地元の人々は重大な懸念を抱いている

drastic (行動が)徹底的な、抜本的な、急激な、思い切った ◇The government is threatening to **take drastic action**. 政府は抜本的な措置を講じると脅しに出ている ◇Talk to me before you do anything *drastic*. 何か思い切ったことをする前に私に話してください
▶**drastically** 副 ◇Output has been *drastically* reduced. 生産高が急激に減っている ◇Things have started to go *drastically* wrong. 事態は急激に悪い方向に進み始めた

desperate きわめて深刻[危険]な、必死の、絶望的な ◇The children are in *desperate* need of love and attention. その子どもたちには愛情と心づかいがどうしても必要だ ◇They face a *desperate* shortage of clean water. 彼らはきわめて深刻な清浄水の不足に直面している ❶*desperate*は人々が物事を必要とする状況に置かれているときに用いられる。
▶**desperately** 副 ◇She felt *desperately* in need of

serious

human company. 彼女は無性に人恋しくなった

dire (ふつう名詞の前で) (特に英、フォーマル) きわめて深刻な ◇They were living in *dire* poverty. 彼らは赤貧の生活を送っていた ◇The firm is **in dire straits** (= in a very difficult situation) and may go bankrupt. その会社は非常に苦しい状況にあり、倒産するかもしれない ❶*dire*は病状については用いられない。《米》では、in dire straitsの句でしか用いられない。

acute (ややフォーマル) 重大な、深刻な、厳しい、激しい ◇The scandal was an *acute* embarrassment for the President. そのスキャンダルは大統領にとって深刻な困惑の種だった ◇Competition for jobs is *acute*. 就職競争が熾烈である ❶*acute*な病気は急速に重篤になる病気である。◆He was suffering from *acute* chest pains. (彼は急性の胸の痛みに苦しんでいた). 反意 **chronic** ◆*chronic* bronchitis/arthritis/asthma （慢性気管支炎/関節炎/喘息）. ◆the country's *chronic* unemployment problem （その国の慢性的な失業問題）
▶**acutely** 副 ◇She suddenly felt *acutely* embarrassed. 彼女は突然激しく狼狽した

bad (ややインフォーマル、特に話し言葉) 重大な、深刻な；厳しい、ひどい ◇The engagement was a *bad* mistake. その取り決めは大きな誤りだった ◇It was a very *bad* winter that year. その年はひどい厳冬だった ◇My headache is getting *worse*. 頭痛がひどくなってきている ❶*bad*は多くの深刻な状況を表すのに用いられるが、危険・緊急事態を表すのには用いられない。ややインフォーマルで、特に話し言葉で用いられる。フォーマルな場面や書き言葉では多くの場合、このグループの他の語を選ぶほうがよい。
▶**badly** 副 ◇The building is *badly* in need of repair. その建物は修繕が大いに必要だ

life-threatening 命を脅かす、生死に関わる ◇His heart condition is not *life-threatening*. 彼の心臓の状態は生死に関わるものではない ◇Aid workers are having to deal with very difficult, sometimes *life-threatening* situations. 救援隊員たちは、非常に困難で時に生死に関わる状況に対処しなければならなくなりつつある ❶*life-threatening*は症状・事故が起こるかもしれない危険な状況に置かれているときに用いられる。

2 serious・grave・earnest・sombre・solemn・sober・humourless
喜びや笑いを伴わないことが多く、人が慎重にかつ賢く考えて行動することを表す
【類語訳】まじめな、厳粛な、重々しい、真剣な、本気の、熱心な、重苦しい、暗たんたる、まじめくさった

文型&コロケーション
▶a serious/ a grave/ an earnest/ a sombre/ a solemn/ a sober **expression**
▶a serious/ a grave/ an earnest/ a solemn/ a sober **face**
▶a serious/ sombre/ solemn/ sober **mood/ atmosphere**
▶on a serious/ sombre/ sober **note**
▶very serious/ grave/ earnest/ sombre/ solemn/ sober

serious まじめな、厳粛な、重々しい；まじめに考える、本気の ◇He's not really a very *serious* person. 彼は実際にはあまりまじめな人間ではない ◇Suddenly the conversation turned *serious*. 会話は突然重々しくなった ◇**Be serious** for a moment; this is important. ちょっとはまじめに考えて。これは大切なの 反意 **light-hearted** (FUNNY)

service, shake

▶**seriously** 副 ◇You need to think *seriously* about your next career move. あなたは次の身を立てる道について真剣に考える必要がある ◇They're no help at all — they're refusing to *take* the problem *seriously*. 彼らはまったく役に立たない—彼らは問題をまじめに受け止めようとしていない

grave 《ややフォーマル, 書き言葉》 (悲しい [重要な, 心配な] 事が起こったかのように) まじめな, 厳粛な, 重々しい ◇He looked very *grave* as he entered the room. 彼は部屋に入るとき, 厳粛な顔つきだった

▶**gravely** 副 ◇He nodded *gravely* as I poured out my troubles. 私が自分の問題を吐露すると, 彼はまじめにうなずいてくれた

earnest 《ややフォーマル》 熱心な, 真剣な, 本気の ◇The *earnest* young doctor answered all our questions. その熱心な若いお医者さんは私たちの質問にすべて答えてくれた ◇I could tell that she spoke *in earnest* (= seriously and sincerely). 彼女は真剣に語っていると見てとれた

sombre 《英》《米 **somber**》《書き言葉》 悲しそうな, 重苦しい, 暗たんたる ◇The year had ended on a *sombre* note (= in a sombre way). その年は暗たんたる雰囲気で幕を閉じたのだ ◇Her expression grew *sombre*. 彼女は悲しそうな表情になった

solemn 《ややフォーマル》(表情・口調が) まじめくさった, 重々しい；(行動・発言が) 真剣な, 本気の, 厳粛な ◇She looked at the *solemn* faces of the children. 彼女は子どもたちのまじめくさった顔を見た ◇You have all taken a *solemn oath* of loyalty to your country. 皆さんは, 母国に対し厳粛に忠誠を誓われました ◇I made a *solemn promise* that I would return. 私は戻ってくると本気で約束した

▶**solemnly** 副 ◇He nodded *solemnly*. 彼はまじめくさってうなずいた

sober 《ややフォーマル, 書き言葉》(思慮深く) まじめな ◇*On sober reflection* (= after thinking about it seriously) I have decided to drop the case. 真剣によく考えて, その訴訟を取り下げることにした

humourless 《英》《米 **humorless**》(けなして)(ユーモアがなく)くそまじめな ◇He gave a short, *humourless laugh* (= a laugh that does not express any amusement). 彼はおかしくもなげに短く笑った

service 名

service・agency・office・bureau・ministry
公衆にサービスを提供する政府の組織や団体
【類語訳】機関, 部門, 部局, 代理店, 事務所, 事務局, 省庁

▶文型&コロケーション
▶to do sth **through** a service/ an agency/ an office/ a bureau
▶a **government/ federal/ public/ state** service/ agency/ office/ bureau/ ministry
▶a/ an **local/ employment/ press/ information/ intelligence/ security/ advisory** service/ agency/ office/ bureau
▶a/ an **private/ international/ counselling/ police/ recruitment/ travel** service/ agency/ office
▶a/ an **independent/ outside/ commercial/ news** service/ agency/ bureau

service [C] 機関, 部門, 部局 ◇She works for the prison *service*. 彼女は刑務局に勤めている ◇The news was reported on the BBC World *Service* last night. そのニュースは昨晩, BBCワールドサービスで報道された ❶*service* は政府部門の名称に用いられることが多い. ◆the Diplomatic *Service*《英》外交部)．◆the Foreign *Service*《米》外交官)

agency [C] 代理店；(米)で政府の)機関, 部門, 部局 ◇He works for an advertising *agency*. 彼は広告代理店に勤めている ◇International aid *agencies* are caring for many of the refugees. 国際援助機関は多くの難民の世話をしている ◇the Central Intelligence *Agency* 中央情報局 (CIA)

office [C] 《ふつう複合語で》(情報・サービスを提供する) 事務所, 事務室, 仕事場 ◇You should be able to get a map at the local tourist *office*. 地元の観光案内所で地図を入手できるはずです ◇There was a long wait at the ticket *office*. チケット売り場で長時間待った ❶*office* は英国政府のいくつかの部門の名称に用いられる. ◆the Foreign *Office*（外務省）．◆the Home *Office*（内務省）．◆the *Office* of Fair Trading（公正取引局）.

bureau [C] (情報を提供する)事務所, 事務局；《米》で政府の)部局 ◇She works for an employment *bureau*. 彼女は職業安定所に勤めている ◇the Federal *Bureau* of Investigation 連邦捜査局 (FBI)

ministry [C] 《英》で政府の)省庁 ◇The *Ministry* of Defence has issued the following statement. 国防省は次のような声明を出した ◇A *ministry* spokesperson defended the measures. 省報道官はその措置について弁明した

shake 動

1 shake・wave・wag・swish・flap・beat
左右 [上下] に体の一部を動かす
【類語訳】振る, 握手する, 突き上げる, 手を振る, 羽ばたく, ばたつく

▶文型&コロケーション
▶to shake your head/ shake your fist/ wave/ wag sth **at** sb
▶sth **waves/ wags/ swishes** its **tail**
▶sth **flaps/ beats** its **wings**
▶to shake your head/ shake sb's hand/ wave/ wag sth **vigorously**

shake [他] (首を横に) 振る；(人の手をとって) 握手する；(拳を上下に) 突き上げる ❶shake your head は「いいえ」と言う方法として, または悲しみ・不同意・疑念を示す方法として用いられる. ◆'Drink?' he offered. She *shook her head*. (「飲み物は」と彼は勧めたが, 彼女は首を振った).◆She *shook her head* in disbelief. (彼女は信じられないといった様子で首を振った). ❶shake hands with sb, shake sb's hand は挨拶として, または人と合意したことを示すために用いられる. ◆The captains *shook hands* before the game commenced. (主将同士が試合前に握手した). ◆He *shook my hand* warmly. (彼は私と温かい握手をかわした). ◆She refused to *shake hands with* him. (彼女は彼と握手しようとしなかった). ◆They *shook hands on* the deal (= to show that they had reached an agreement). (彼らは話がまとまって握手をした). shake sb *by the hand* は特に熱狂・賞賛を示すために用いられる. ◆If I met him I'd *shake* him *by the hand* and congratulate him. (彼に会ったら, 握手してお祝いを言ってあげるのに). ❶shake your fist at sb は人に腹を立てていることを示すた

↪**shake**

め、または人を脅すために用いられる。◆The man *shook his fist at* the court after he was sentenced.（その男は判決を受けた後、法廷に対してこぶしを振りかざした）
▶**shake** 图 [C, ふつう単数で] ◇He dismissed the idea with a firm *shake* of his head. 彼はきっぱりと首を振って、その考えを退けた
wave [自, 他]（注意を引くために［挨拶として、さよならを言うために］手・腕を）振る、手を振る ◇The people on the bus *waved* and we waved back. バスに乗っている人々は手を振り、私たちは手を振り返した ◇The man in the water was *waving* his arms around frantically. 水中にいる男性は、半狂乱で腕を振り回していた ◇***Wave** goodbye* to Daddy. パパに手を振ってバイバイして ◇My mother was crying as I *waved* her goodbye. 私が別れの挨拶に手を振ると、母は泣いていた
▶**wave** 图 [C, ふつう単数で] ◇He gave us a *wave* as the bus drove off. バスが走り出すと共に、彼は私たちに手を振った
wag (**-gg-**) [他, 自]（犬が尻尾を）振る、（犬の尻尾が）振られる；（人が不同意を表して指・首を左右［上下］に）振る ◇The dog bounded forwards, *wagging* its tail excitedly. その犬は興奮して尾を振りながら、前の方に飛び出した ◇The dog bounded forwards, its tail *wagging*. その犬は尾を振りながら、前の方に飛び出した ◇'Just remember what I said,' she repeated, *wagging* her finger at him.「私が言ったことをとにかく忘れないように」と、彼女は彼に向かって指を振りながら繰り返した
▶**wag** 图 [C, ふつう単数で] ◇Flossie managed a feeble *wag* of her tail. フロッシーは弱々しげに何とか尾を振った
swish [自, 他]（動物の尻尾が）シュッシュッと音を立てて振られる、（物を）シュッシュッと音を立てて動かす ◇The pony's tail *swished* from side to side. ポニーの尻尾がシュッシュッと音を立てて左右に振られた ◇The cows were *swishing* their tails lazily. 牛たちが物憂げに尻尾をシュッシュッと振り動かしていた ◇She *swished* her racket aggressively through the air. 彼女は威嚇するかのようにラケットをシュッシュッと音を立てて空中で振り動かした
▶**swish** 图 [C, ふつう単数で] ◇She turned away with a *swish* of her skirt. 彼女はシュッとスカートの衣擦れの音を立たせてそっぽを向いた
flap (**-pp-**) [他, 自]（鳥が翼を）羽ばたかせる、（鳥の翼が）羽ばたく；（人が腕を上下に）振る ◇The bird *flapped* its wings and flew away. その鳥は翼を羽ばたかせて飛び去った ◇The gulls flew off, wings *flapping*. カモメは翼を羽ばたかせて飛び去った ◇She walked up and down, *flapping* her arms to keep warm. 彼女は体を暖かくしておくために腕を上下に振って、行ったり来たりした
▶**flap** 图 [C, ふつう単数で] ◇With a *flap* of its wings the bird was gone. 翼を羽ばたかせて、その鳥は飛び去った
beat [他, 自]（鳥が翼を音を立たせて）はたつかせる、（鳥の翼が音を立てて）はたつく ◇The bird was frantically *beating* its wings. その鳥は必死に翼をはたつかせていた ◇Its wings *beat* feebly against the window. その翼が窓を弱々しくたたいた

2 shake・rattle・vibrate・clatter・wobble・shudder・jolt・rock・jiggle・jar・bump
左右［上下］に小刻みに素早く動く［動かす］
【類語訳】揺れる、振動する、ガタガタと鳴る、ぐらぐらする、そわそわする、衝撃を与える、ぶつかる

文型＆コロケーション
▶to shake/ rattle/ vibrate/ shudder/ rock/ jar **with** sth
▶to rattle/ clatter/ shudder/ jolt/ bump **along**
▶to rattle/ clatter/ wobble/ jiggle/ bump **around/ about**
▶to shake/ rattle/ vibrate/ shudder/ rock (sth) **violently**
▶to shake/ vibrate/ rock/ bump (sth) **gently**
▶to shake/ shudder/ rock (sth) **suddenly**

shake [自, 他] 揺れる、振動する；揺する、振動させる；（特定の方向に）振り動かす ◇The whole house *shakes* whenever a train goes past. 列車が通り過ぎるたびに、家全体が揺れる ◇*Shake* the bottle well before use. 使用前に瓶をよく振ってください ◇He *shook* her violently by the shoulders. 彼は彼女の肩を激しく揺すった ◇Tom bent down to *shake* a pebble out of his shoe. トムはかがみこみ、靴を振って小石を出した
▶**shake** 图 [C, ふつう単数で] ◇Give the bottle a good *shake*. 瓶をよく振ってください
rattle [自, 他] ガタガタ［ガラガラ、カタカタ］と鳴る；ガタガタ［ガラガラ、カタカタ］といわせる；（乗り物が）ガタガタと音を立てて動く ◇Every time a bus went past, the windows *rattled*. バスが通り過ぎるたびに、窓がガタガタと鳴った ◇She stood there, *rattling* the collecting tin. 彼女はそこに立って寄付を募る缶をガラガラいわせた ◇A convoy of trucks *rattled* past. トラックの一団がガタガタと音を立てて通り過ぎた
▶**rattle** （または **rattling**）图 [C, ふつう単数で] ◇the *rattle* of gunfire 発砲音 ◇From the kitchen came a *rattling* of cups and saucers. 台所からカップとお皿のガチャガチャ鳴る音が聞こえてきた
vibrate [自, 他] 揺れる、振動する；揺する、振動させる ◇The ground beneath their feet began to *vibrate*. 彼らの足下で地面が揺れ始めた ◇The male spider will *vibrate* one of the threads of the female spider's web. オスグモはメスグモの巣の一本の糸を揺らのです
▶**vibration** 图 [C, U] ◇We could feel the *vibrations* from the trucks passing outside. 私たちは外を通過するトラックの振動を感じることができた ◇Is it possible to reduce the level of *vibration* in the engine? エンジンの振動レベルを下げることは可能ですか
clatter [自]（硬い物がぶつかり合って）ガタガタ［ガラガラ、ガチャガチャ］と鳴る；ガタガタと音を立てて動く ◇He dropped the knife and it *clattered* on the stone floor. 彼はナイフを落とし、ナイフがガチャンと石の床で音を立てた ◇The cart *clattered* over the cobbles. 荷車は丸石を敷いた道路の上をガタガタと音を立てて動いた
▶**clatter** （または **clattering**）图 [単数で] ◇the *clatter* of horses' hooves 馬の蹄のパカパカという音
wobble [自, 他]（不安定な形で左右に）ぐらぐら［がたがた］する；ぐら［がた］つかせる ◇This chair *wobbles*. この椅子はぐらぐらする ◇The vase *wobbled* and then crashed to the ground. 花瓶はぐらついて、それから床にガチャンと落ちた ◇Don't *wobble* the table — I'm trying to work. テーブルをがたがたさせないで—仕事しようとしてるんだから
shudder [自]（乗り物・機械が）激しく振動する ◇The boat's engines *shuddered*, and it began to leave the shore. 船のエンジンが激しく振動し、船は岸から離れ始めた ◇The bus *shuddered to a halt*. バスは激しく揺れて止まった
▶**shudder** 图 [C, ふつう単数で] ◇The elevator rose with a *shudder*. エレベーターは大きく一揺れして上昇した
jolt [自, 他] 激しく揺れる；（人・物を）激しく揺さぶる ◇The truck *jolted* and rattled over the rough ground. トラックは激しく揺れながら、でこぼこの地面をガタガタと音を立て

shape

て走った ◇He was *jolted* forward as the train moved off. 列車が走り出すと, 彼は前方へ激しく揺さぶられた
▶**jolt** [名] [C, ふつう単数で] ◇The plane landed with a *jolt*. 飛行機は激しく揺れて着陸した
rock [自, 他] 《ややインフォーマル, 特にジャーナリズム》激しく揺れる[振動する]; (物を)激しく揺さぶる[振動させる] ◇The whole house *rocked* when the bomb exploded. 爆弾が爆発して, 家全体が激しく揺れた ◇The town was *rocked* by an earthquake. その町は地震で激しく揺れた ◇The raft was *rocked* by a huge wave. いかだは大波で激しく揺さぶられた
jiggle [自, 他] 《インフォーマル》(上下[左右]に小刻みに)揺れる, そわそわする; (軽い小物を)揺する ◇Stop *jiggling* around! そわそわ歩き回るのはやめなさい ◇She *jiggled* with the lock. 彼女は錠を揺すった ◇He stood *jiggling* his car keys in his hand. 彼は手に持っている車の鍵束をガチャガチャ揺らしながら立っていた
jar (-rr-) [他, 自] (突然痛みを伴う)衝撃を与える[受ける]; ぶつける[当たる] ◇The jolt seemed to *jar* every bone in her body. その衝撃で彼女の体中の骨に痛みが走るようだった ◇The spade *jarred on* something metal. 鋤が金属性の何かにぶち当たった
bump [自, 他] (でこぼこの表面を特定方向に)ガタガタと揺れながら進む; (物を)ドシンドシンとぶつけながら進む ◇The jeep *bumped* along the dirt track. ジープは未舗装の道路をガタガタ揺れながら進んだ ◇She entered the subway, *bumping* her bags down the step. 彼女はかばんをドシンドシンと階段にぶつけながら地下鉄に入って行った

3 shake・tremble・shudder・twitch・shiver・convulse
恐怖や寒さで, 制御できないくらい小刻みに素早い動きをする
【類語訳】震える, 身震いする, そくっとする, ぴくっと動く, 痙攣(れん)する

文型&コロケーション
▶to shake/ tremble/ shiver/ be convulsed **with fear**
▶to shake/ tremble/ shiver **with cold**
▶to tremble/ shudder/ shiver **at** a thought/ memory, etc.
▶sb's **whole body** shakes/ trembles/ shudders/ twitches/ shivers/ convulses
▶sb's **hands** shake/ tremble/ twitch
▶sb's **legs** shake/ tremble
▶sb's **mouth/ lip** trembles/ twitches
▶to shake/ tremble/ shudder/ twitch/ shiver **slightly**
▶to shake/ tremble/ shudder/ twitch/ shiver/ convulse **violently**
▶to shake/ shudder/ shiver **suddenly**

shake [自] (恐怖・寒さなどで)震える ◇I was *shaking like a leaf*. 私は葉のように震えていた ◇Her hands started to *shake*. 彼女の両手が震え始めた ☞**shaking** (SHIVER)
tremble [自] (緊張・興奮・恐怖で)震える ◇He opened the letter with *trembling* hands. 彼は震える手で手紙を開けた ◇I *trembled* at the thought of making a speech. スピーチすることを考えると体が震えた ☞**tremble** (SHIVER)
shudder [自] 《進行形はまれ》(恐怖・寒さ・強い嫌悪で)身震いする, ぞくっとする ◇Alone in the car, she *shuddered* with fear. 車に一人でいて, 彼女は恐怖で身震いした ◇I *shudder to think* what might have happened. 起

きていたかもしれないことを考えるとぞっとする ☞**shudder** (SHIVER)

ノート **tremble** と **shudder** の使い分け: **tremble** は繰り返し震える動きを表す. **shudder** はふつう一回だけの震えである. ◆He *trembled* (= he was shaking). (彼は(ぶるぶると)震えていた). ◆He *shuddered* (= he shook once). (彼は(ぞくっと)身震いした).

twitch [自, 他] (体の一部が)ぴくっと動く; (体の一部を)ぴくっと動かす ◇Her lips *twitched* with amusement. 彼女の唇は喜びでぴくっと動いた ◇The dog *twitched* its ears and looked very intently. その犬は耳をぴくっと動かして一点を見つめた ☞**twitch** (SHIVER)
shiver [自] (寒さ・病気・恐怖・興奮でわずかに)震える ◇Don't stand outside *shivering* — come in and get warm. 外で震えて立ってないで一中に入って温まりなさい ❶ **shiver** は恐怖よりも寒さ・病気で震えることを表すことが多い. ☞**shiver** (SHIVER)
convulse [他, 自] 身震いさせる, 痙攣(れん)させる; 身震いする, 痙攣する ◇She was *convulsed* by a bout of sneezing. 彼女はひとしきりくしゃみをして身を震わせた ◇His whole body *convulsed*. 彼の体全体が痙攣した ☞**convulsion** (SHIVER)

shape [名]

shape・figure・form・shadow・outline・profile・silhouette・line・contour
人や物の物理的な見た目, 人や物の外側の様子
【類語訳】形, 形状, 姿形, 影, 人影, 体つき, 輪郭, 横顔, シルエット, 影法師

文型&コロケーション
▶**in** shape/ form/ outline/ profile/ silhouette
▶a **tall** shape/ figure/ form/ shadow/ silhouette
▶a **slender** shape/ figure/ form
▶a **black/ dark** shape/ figure/ shadow/ outline/ profile/ silhouette
▶a **shadowy** shape/ figure/ form/ outline
▶a **ghostly** shape/ figure/ form/ shadow
▶(a) **sleek** shape/ outline/ profile/ lines
▶(a) **sharp** outline/ lines/ contours
▶to **make out/ see** a shape/ a figure/ a form/ an outline/ a silhouette
▶to **trace** a shape/ an outline/ the line/ the contours

shape [C, U] 形, 外形, 形状; (特定の例としての)…形; (はっきりとはわかりにくい人・物の)姿形, 影 ◇The building has a rectangular *shape*. そのビルは長方形をしている ◇The pool was *in the shape of* a heart. プールはハート形をしていた ◇The island was originally circular in *shape*. その島は元々丸い形をしていた ◇Candles come in *all shapes and sizes*. ろうそくはあらゆる形と大きさのものがそろっています ◇You can recognize the fish by the *shape* of their fins. ひれの形でその魚を見分けることができます ◇This old T-shirt has completely lost its *shape*. この古いTシャツはすっかり型崩れしている
figure [C] (遠くから見える[はっきりわからない])人影 ◇There before him stood a tall *figure* in black. 彼の前には黒い服を着た背の高い人影が立っていた
form [C] 形, 姿形, 体つき; (ほんやりとした人・物の)影 ◇Her slender *form* and graceful movements entranced

↪**shape**

him. 彼女のすらりとした体つきと優雅な物腰に彼はうっとりした ◇The human *form* has changed little over the last 30,000 years. 人間の姿形は過去3万年にわたってほとんど変化していない ◇They made out a shadowy *form* in front of them. 彼らの目の前であるはっきりしない形のものが見分けられた

shadow [C]（地面などにできる黒い）影 ◇The children were having fun, chasing each other's *shadows*. 子どもたちは互いの影を追いかけて楽しんでいた ◇The ship's sail *cast a shadow* on the water. 船の帆が水面に影を落とした ◇The *shadows* lengthened as the sun went down. 太陽が沈むにつれ、影が長くなった

outline [C] 輪郭 ◇At last we could see the dim *outline* of an island. ついにぼんやりした島の輪郭が見えた
☞ **outline** (SUMMARY)

profile [C] 横顔 ◇He turned his head so his strong *profile* was facing the camera. 彼が後ろを振り向いたので、際立ったその横顔がカメラに向かっていた ◇The portrait shows her in *profile*. その写真は彼女の横顔を写している

silhouette [C, U]（明るい背景に浮かぶ黒い）シルエット，影法師；（人・物の）形，姿形，体つき ◇The trees were black *silhouettes* against the pale sky. 木々は薄暗い空を背景に黒いシルエットになっていた ◇The mountains stood out in *silhouette*. 連山がくっきりとシルエットをなしていた ◇The dress is fitted to give you a flattering *silhouette*. そのドレスは君の体つきが引き立つように合わせてあるね

line [C]（設計された［作り出された］物の）輪郭（線），外形 ◇With its sleek *lines* and powerful engine, the XK8 is the definition of a luxury sports car. 流線形と強力なエンジンを備えたXK8は、まさしく高級スポーツカーである ◇He traced the *line* of her jaw with his finger. 彼は彼女のあごの輪郭を指でなぞった

contour [C]（書き言葉）（物の）形、外形；輪郭（線）◇The road follows the natural *contours* of the coastline. その道路は海岸線の自然の輪郭に沿って走っている

share 名

share・quota・allocation・commission・allowance・ration・cut・percentage
与えられる物事の量
【類語訳】分け前，取り分，市場占有率，シェア，負担，分担分，割当分，定員，支給，手当，歩合，手数料，配当

〘文型&コロケーション〙
▸ a share/ quota/ allocation/ allowance/ ration/ cut/ percentage **of** sth
▸ a **full** share/ quota/ allocation/ commission/ allowance/ ration
▸ a **large** share/ quota/ allocation/ commission
▸ a **small** share/ quota/ allocation/ commission/ percentage
▸ an **annual** quota/ allocation/ allowance
▸ a **fixed** share/ quota/ commission/ percentage
▸ to **get** your share/ your quota/ an allocation/ a commission/ a cut/ a percentage
▸ to **receive** a share/ an allocation/ a commission/ a percentage
▸ to **take** a share/ commission/ cut/ percentage
▸ to **have** your share/ quota/ ration
▸ to **be entitled to** a share/ an allocation/ a commission

share [C, ふつう単数で] 分け前，取り分；役割，貢献；市場

share

占有率，シェア；負担，分担分，割当分 ◇How much was your *share* of the winnings? その賞金のあなたのシェアはいくらでしたか ◇Next year we hope to have a bigger *share of the market*. 来年は市場でより大きなシェアを占めることを我々は望んでいます ◇I'm hoping for a *share in* the profits. 利益の分け前を期待しています ◇We all *did our share* of the work. 私たちは皆、自分の仕事の分担をこなした ◇Everyone must accept their *share* of the blame. 皆、それぞれ自分で責任を取らなければいけない
☞ **share** (JOIN)

quota [C]（公式の）定員，割当数［量］；（期待される［必要とされる］）分担分，割当分 ◇They are bringing in a *quota* system for accepting refugees. 難民の受け入れに割当制度が導入されようとしている ◇The show is good fun and yields its full *quota* of laughs. その番組はとても面白く、十分な笑いをとっている

allocation [C]（特定の目的のための）支給（額），手当（金）◇We have spent our entire *allocation* for the year. 私たちは年間の支給額のすべてを費やしてしまった

commission [U, C]（売上げに従って支払われる）歩合；（銀行などが取る）手数料 ◇In this job you work *on commission* (= are paid according to the amount you sell). この仕事は、歩合制です ◇You get a 10% *commission on* everything you sell. 売るものすべてに関して、10%の歩合が得られます ◇One per cent *commission* is charged for cashing traveller's cheques. トラベラーズチェックの現金化には1%の手数料がかかります

allowance [C]（特定の状況下での）制限［許容］量 ◇There is a maximum *baggage allowance* of 20 kilos. 最大20キロの手荷物制限があります

ration [C]（戦時中などでの）食糧の）配給［割当］量 ◇I gave him my butter *ration* at breakfast one morning. ある朝、私は朝食で配給されるバターを彼にあげた ◇a *ration* book/card/coupon (= allowing you to claim a certain amount of sth) 配給手帳／カード／クーポン ❶単数形の *ration* には「一人分とされる標準［許容］の量」の意味もある．◆As part of the diet, allow yourself a small daily *ration* of sugar.（食事の一部として毎日少量の砂糖を取ってかまいません．
▸**ration** 動 〔他, しばしば受身で〕◇Eggs were *rationed* during the war. 卵は戦時中は、配給制だった ◇The villagers are *rationed to* two litres of water a day. 村人たちには1日2リットルの水が配給される

〘ノート〙 **share, quota, ration** の使い分け：いずれも「一人分とされる標準［許容］の量」の意味で用いられる．share と quota は luck, laughs, work, blame など好ましい［好ましくない］事柄についても用いることができるが，share のほうが一般的であり，quota がこの意味で用いられるのはフォーマルまたは書き言葉においてである．ration は食べ物について、あるいはあまり欲張ってはいけない何かすてきなことについて用いられる．

cut [C, ふつう単数で]（ややインフォーマル）（利益の）分け前，取り分，配当 ◇They were rewarded with a *cut* of 5% from the profits. 彼らには利益の5%の配当が与えられた ◇There wasn't much left after his agents took their *cut*. 代理人が取り分を受け取った後には、大した額は残っていなかった

percentage [C, ふつう単数で]（利益の）歩合 ◇He gets a *percentage* for every car sold. 彼には販売した車1台ごとに歩合が入る

〘ノート〙 **cut** と **percentage** の使い分け：percentage は特に仕事に対してお金が人［例えば従業員］に支払われる状況において

おいて用いられる。cutは人々がお金の総額を自分たちで分ける場合に用いられることが多い。百分率で表される数字が示される場合はcutを用いる。◆Our manager gets a *cut* of 10%. (私たちの主任は10%の配当を受け取っている)。×Our manager gets a *percentage* of 10%.

share 動

share・divide・split・pool・carve sth up
分けた[集めた]ものの一部を持ったり、使ったりする
【類語訳】共有する、共用する、分け与える、分配する、割り当てる、割り振る、振り分ける、持ち寄る、出し合う、分割する

文型&コロケーション
▶ to share sth/ divide sth/ split sth/ carve sth up **between/ among** different people
▶ to share/ split/ pool sth **with** sb
▶ to share/ divide/ split the **money/ work**
▶ to share/ divide the **spoils/ booty**
▶ to divide/ split your **time**
▶ to share/ divide/ split sth **equally/ evenly**

share [他, 自] (他人と)共有する、共用する；(自分のものを)分け与える；(二人以上の人々に)分配する、分担する、割り当てる ◇She *shares* a house with three other students. 彼女は他の3人の学生と同居している ◇There isn't an empty table. Would you mind *sharing*? 空いているテーブルがございません。ご相席していただけませんか ◇Tom *shared* his chocolate with the other kids. トムは他の子どもたちと自分のチョコレートを分け合った ◇The conference is a good place to *share* information and exchange ideas. その会議は情報を共有し意見を交換するのにいい場所です ◇The old man *shared* his money *out* among his six grandchildren. その老人は6人の孫にお金を分け与えた

divide [他] 分配する、分担する；(異なる活動・目的に)割り振る、振り分ける ◇The story is about a father who *divides* his property among his sons. それは自分の財産を息子たちに分配する父親の物語である ◇Jen *divided up* the rest of the cash. ジェンは残りの現金を分配した ◇He *divides* his energies between politics and business. 彼は政治とビジネスにエネルギーを振り分けている ☞ **division (DIVISION 1)**

split [他] 《ややインフォーマル》 (異なる人々・物事・場所の間に)分配する、分担する、割り当てる ◇She *split* the money she won with her brother. 彼女は勝ち取ったお金を弟と分けた ◇Four of us live here and we *split* all the bills *four ways*. 私たち4人はここで暮らしていて、請求金額はすべて4人で分担している ◇His time is *split* between the London and Paris offices. 彼は自分の時間をロンドン支店とパリ支店に振り分けている ☞ **split (DIVISION 1)**

ノート **share, divide, split**の使い分け: shareは人々の間での分配。divideは人々・用途・場所の間の分配。splitは人々・物事・場所の間の分配。divideは土地・大金などの非常に重要とみなされるものについて用いられることが多い。あまり重要でないものについてはshareを用いる。◆He *shared* his sweets out among his four friends. (彼は4人の友だちに自分のデザートを分け与えた) ×He *divided* his sweets among his four friends. splitはお金・仕事について、それほどフォーマルでない文脈で用いられる。

pool [他] (お金・情報などを)持ち寄る、出し合う ◇The students work individually, then *pool* their ideas in groups of six. 学生たちは個々に作業して、その後6人のグループになって意見を出し合います ◇Police forces across the country are *pooling* resources in order to solve this crime. 国中の警察がこの犯罪を解決するための方策を持ち寄っている ❶poolは、ある共通の目的が成功する機会を増やすために行われる。一般的な連語としては、お金(fundsなど)、情報(knowledge, ideas, resultsなど)、他の有用な[望ましい]物事(talent, efforts, resourcesなど)が挙げられる。☞ **pool (SUPPLY)**

carve sth 'up 句動詞 《けなして》 (会社・土地などを小集団の人々・会社・国々で)分割する ◇They have been accused of *carving up* the industry for their own benefit. 彼らは自分たちの利益のために産業を分割したとして非難されてきた ◇The territory was *carved up* by the colonizing powers. その領土は植民地化を進める列強によって分割された

shelter 名

shelter・asylum・safety・cover・refuge・sanctuary
守りが得られる場所[こと]
【類語訳】家、宿、すみか、保護、避難、亡命、聖域

文型&コロケーション
▶ shelter/ asylum/ refuge/ sanctuary **from** sth
▶ **temporary** shelter/ asylum/ refuge/ sanctuary
▶ to **seek/ find** shelter/ asylum/ refuge/ sanctuary
▶ to **take** cover/ refuge/ sanctuary
▶ to **run for** shelter/ cover
▶ **a place of** safety/ refuge/ sanctuary

shelter [U] (人が身を守る)家、宿、すみか；(天候・危険・攻撃からの)隠れ場、保護、避難(所) ◇They were anxious to find *shelter* for the night. 彼らはその夜の宿を見つけるのに躍起だった ◇He took *shelter* from the rain under a bridge. 彼は橋の下で雨宿りをした ◇The fox ran for the *shelter* of the trees. 狐は隠れ場を求めて森を目指した ☞ **shelter (REFUGE), shelter (PROTECT)**

asylum [U] (政治的な)保護、亡命 ◇She was granted *political asylum* by Canada in 2003. 彼女は2003年にカナダへの政治亡命が認められた ☞ **asylum seeker (REFUGEE)**

safety [U] (危険にさらされない)安全な場所 ◇I managed to swim *to safety*. 私は何とか安全な場所に泳ぎ着いた ◇We watched the lions *from the safety of* the car. 私たちは安全な車の中からライオンを見た ☞ **safe (SAFE)**

cover [U] (悪天候・攻撃からの)隠れ場 ◇After the explosion the street was full of people running for *cover*. 爆発の後、通りは隠れ場所を求めて走る人々であふれていた

refuge [U] (危険・トラブル・問題からの)保護、避難(所) ◇A further 300 people have taken *refuge* in the embassy. さらに300人の人々が大使館に保護された ◇As the situation at home got worse she increasingly *took refuge in* her work. 家の状況が悪化するにつれ、彼女はますます仕事に逃避した ☞ **refuge (REFUGE), refugee (REFUGEE)**

sanctuary [U] 《フォーマル》 (追っ手・攻撃からの)聖域、保護、避難(所) ◇During the uprising the royal family took *sanctuary* in an abbey. 暴動の間、王室は大修道院に避難した ☞ **sanctuary (REFUGE)**

shine 動

shine・gleam・glow・sparkle・glisten・shimmer・glitter・twinkle・glint
光を生み出す[反射する]
【類語訳】輝く、光る、照る、きらめく、ゆらめく

文型&コロケーション

▶ to shine/ gleam/ sparkle/ glisten/ shimmer/ glitter/ glint **on** sth
▶ to shine/ gleam/ glow/ sparkle/ glisten/ shimmer/ glitter/ twinkle/ glint **with** sth
▶ to shine/ gleam/ sparkle/ glisten/ shimmer/ glitter/ glint **in the sunlight**
▶ to shine/ gleam/ glisten/ shimmer/ glitter/ glint **in the moonlight**
▶ to shine/ gleam/ glow/ glitter/ twinkle **in the dark**
▶ a **light** shines/ gleams/ glows
▶ the **stars** shine/ glitter/ twinkle
▶ sb's **eyes** shine/ gleam/ glow/ sparkle/ glisten/ glitter/ twinkle/ glint
▶ the **water/ river/ sea** gleams/ sparkles/ glistens/ shimmers/ glitters
▶ to shine/ gleam/ glow/ glitter **brightly**
▶ to shine/ gleam/ glow/ shimmer **softly**
▶ to shine/ gleam/ glow **faintly**

shine [自] （光を生み出して[反射して]明るく）輝く、光る、照る、きらめく ◇The sun was *shining* and the sky was blue. 太陽は輝いていて、空は青かった ◇They could see a faint light *shining* in the distance. 彼らには遠くにかすかな光が輝くのが見えた ◇The polished wood *shone* like glass. 磨き上げられた木材はガラスのように光った ◇Their faces *shone* white in the moonlight. 彼らの顔は月の光を浴びて青白く光った
▷ **shine** [名][単数で, U] ◇Use a buffer to bring a natural *shine* to your nails. 爪磨きを使って爪に自然な輝きを与えなさい ◇the *shine* of the polished wood 磨き上げられた木材の輝き
▷ **shiny** [形] ◇A *shiny* red car was parked in the drive. ぴかぴかの赤い車が敷地内の車道に停めてあった ◇His face was red and *shiny*. 彼の顔は血色がよく輝いていた

gleam [自] （光を反射して明るく[淡く]）輝く、光る、きらめく ◇Moonlight *gleamed* on the water. 月光が水面にきらめいた ◇The house was *gleaming* with fresh white paint. その家は塗りたての真っ白なペンキで光り輝いていた ◇Laughter *gleamed* in his eyes. 彼の目は笑みできらりと輝いた
▷ **gleam** [名][C, ふつう単数で] ◇We could see the *gleam* of moonlight on the water. 私たちは水面に月光の輝くのが見えた

glow [自] （熱い[温かい]物が鈍く安定して）輝く、光る、照る ◇The embers still *glowed* in the hearth. 燃えさしはまだ炉床で赤く燃えていた ◇He has a watch that *glows* in the dark. 彼は暗闇で光る時計を持っている
▷ **glow** [名][単数で] ◇Now the city was just a red *glow* on the horizon. その都市は今や、地平線上の単なる赤い光にすぎなかった

sparkle [自] （小さな閃光を発して明るく）輝く、きらめく、光る ◇Her necklace *sparkled* in the can-

dlelight. 彼女のネックレスがろうそくの灯りできらきら光った ◇Her eyes *sparkled* with excitement. 彼女の目は興奮で輝いた
▷ **sparkle** [名][C, U] ◇the *sparkle* of light on the water 水面にきらめく光

glisten [自] （濡れた物が）輝く、きらきらと光る、きらめく ◇Her eyes were *glistening* with tears. 彼女の目は涙できらきら輝いていた ◇Sweat *glistened* on his forehead. 汗が彼の額できらきら光った

shimmer [自] 《書き言葉》（柔らかい光で）ゆらめく、淡く光る ◇Everything seemed to *shimmer* in the heat. 何もかもが熱で揺らめいているようだった
▷ **shimmer** [名][単数で, U] ◇the *shimmer* of silk in the candlelight ろうそくの灯りで淡く照らされた絹

glitter [自] （光を反射して無数の小さな閃光を発して明るく）輝く、きらきらと光る、きらめく ◇The water *glittered* in the sunlight. 水は日光に照らされてきらきら光った
▷ **glitter** [名][単数で] ◇the *glitter* of diamonds ダイヤモンドのきらめき

▎**ノート sparkleとglitterの使い分け**：これら二語に意味の違いはほとんどない。glitterはほぼ常に、絶えず動いて変化している表面からの反射光について用いられるが、特に名詞として比喩的に用いられる場合は、深みに欠けることを示唆することにも用いられることがある。◆the superficial *glitter* of show business（《比喩的》ショービジネスのうわべだけのきらびやかさ）。sparkleも表面からの反射した光について用いられることが多いが、光を生み出す物にも用いられる。◆Stars *sparkled* in the sky.（星々が空に輝いた）。

twinkle [自] （光を強弱させて）きらきら[ちらちら, ぴかぴか]と輝く[光る]、きらめく ◇Stars *twinkled* in the sky. 星々が空にきらきら輝いた ◇His eyes *twinkled* with laughter. 彼の目が笑みで輝いた

glint [自] （光を反射して小さな閃光を発する）きらきらと光る、きらめく ◇A flash of a blade *glinted* in the darkness. 刃の閃光が闇の中できらめいた ◇Amusement *glinted* in his eyes. 彼の目は楽しさに輝いた
▷ **glint** [名][単数で] ◇He saw the *glint* of a knife and froze. 彼はナイフのきらめきを見て、血の気が引いた ◇There was a *glint* of admiration in her eyes. 彼女の目にはちらっと賞賛の輝きが見えた

shiver 名

shiver・tremor・twitch・tremble・shudder・spasm・convulsion・tic・shaking・quiver
制御できない、絶え間ない[突然の]震える動き[感情]
【類語訳】身震い、震え、痙攣、引きつり、ひきつけ、チック

文型&コロケーション

▶ **a slight** shiver/ tremor/ twitch/ tremble/ shudder/ spasm/ convulsion/ quiver
▶ **a little** shiver/ tremor/ shudder/ spasm/ quiver
▶ **a small** shiver/ tremor/ shudder/ spasm
▶ **a faint** tremor/ tremble/ shudder/ quiver
▶ **a violent** tremor/ shudder/ spasm/ convulsion
▶ **a nervous** tremor/ twitch/ tic
▶ to **cause** a shiver/ tremor/ shudder/ spasm/ convulsion
▶ to **feel** a shiver/ tremor/ twitch/ tremble/ shudder/ spasm/ quiver
▶ to **send** a shiver/ tremor/ shudder/ spasm/ quiver down, through, etc. sth

shock

▶ to have a tremor/ a twitch/ convulsions/ a tic
▶ a shiver/ tremor/ shudder/ quiver goes/ runs through sb/ sth

shiver [C]（寒さ・病気・恐怖・興奮による突然の）身震い，震え，ぞくっとすること ◇She gave a little *shiver* as she walked into the cold room. その寒い部屋に入ると，彼女は少し身震いした ◇He felt a cold *shiver* of fear run through him. 彼は恐怖で冷たい震えが体に走るのを感じた ◇The sound *sent shivers down her spine* (= was very frightening). その音に彼女は背筋がぞくっとした ☞ **shiver** (SHAKE 3)

tremor [C, U]（寒さ・恐怖などによる体の部位の）震え ◇An uncontrollable *tremor* shook his mouth. 彼はどうしようもなく口元が震えた ◇She could hear the *tremor in his voice* (= his voice was shaking with emotion). 彼女は彼の声が震えているのが聞こえた ◇Large doses of the drug produce *tremor* and rigidity.《専門的》その麻薬の大量摂取で震えと硬直が生じる

twitch [C]（筋肉の突然の）痙攣, 引きつり, ぴくっと動くこと,（突然の）身震い, 震え, ぞくっとすること ◇He has a nervous *twitch* in his cheek. 彼の頬はぴくぴく引きつる ◇I felt a *twitch* of anxiety. 不安で体が震えるのを感じた ❶ふつう目・唇など顔の部位の *twitch* を生じる. ☞ **twitch** (SHAKE 3)

tremble [C, ふつう単数で]（極度の緊張・興奮・恐怖などによる）震え ◇The only sign of fear was a slight *tremble* in his legs. 恐怖の唯一の徴候として彼の脚にわずかな震えが見られた ☞ **tremble** (SHAKE 3)

shudder [C, ふつう単数で]（寒さ・恐怖・嫌悪などによる突然の）身震い, 震え, ぞくっとすること ◇a *shudder* of fear 恐怖の身震い ◇She gave an involuntary *shudder*. 彼女は無意識に震え上がった ☞ **shudder** (SHAKE 3)

spasm [C, U]《ややフォーマル》(筋肉の突然の痛みを伴う)痙攣, ひきつけ ◇Cholera reduces heartbeat and causes muscle *spasms*. コレラでは心拍が減り, 筋肉に痙攣が起きる ◇The injection sent his leg into *spasm*. 注射で彼の脚が痙攣した

convulsion [C, ふつう複数で]《フォーマル》(突然の激しい)痙攣, ひきつけ ◇The child went into *convulsions*. その子は痙攣を起こした ◇She started to have *convulsions* again. 彼女はまたひきつけを起こし始めた ☞ **convulse** (SHAKE 3)

tic [C]（顔面・頭部が突然痙攣する）チック ◇He has a nervous *tic* around his left eye. 彼は左の目の周りに神経性チックが起きる

shaking [U]（恐怖・寒さなどによる）震え ◇The *shaking* got less as the boy calmed down. 少年は落ち着くにつれ, 前より震えが治まってきた ☞ **shake** (SHAKE 3)

quiver [C]《特に書き言葉》(強い感情による体・声の)震え ◇He felt a *quiver* of anticipation run through him. 彼は胸の知らせに震えが体を駆け抜けるのを感じた ◇She couldn't help the *quiver* in her voice. 彼女は声の震えを止めることができなかった

shock 名

shock・horror・dismay
不快な不意打ちを受けて抱く感情
【類語訳】ショック, 衝撃, 驚き, 恐怖, 戦慄, 嫌悪, 失望, 落胆, 幻滅

| dismay | shock | horror |

文型&コロケーション
▶ shock/ horror/ dismay at sth
▶ in/ with shock/ horror/ dismay
▶ to sb's horror/ dismay
▶ to fill sb with horror/ dismay

shock [U]（予期せぬ事が起こったときの）ショック, 衝撃, 驚き ◇He's still in *shock*. 彼はまだショックを受けている ◇The team suffered a *shock* defeat in the first round. そのチームは1回戦で衝撃的な敗北を喫した ❶ *shock* はふつう不可算だが, そうでなければならないわけではない. ◆ Since winning the competition, we've all been a state of *shock*.（競技会で優勝して以後, 私たちは皆, 放心状態だ）

horror [U] 恐怖, 戦慄, 嫌悪, ぞっとする思い ◇She recoiled in *horror* at the sight. 彼女はその光景に恐れをなして後ずさりした ◇His eyes were wide with *horror*. 彼の目は恐怖で大きく見開いていた ◇There was a terrible look of *horror* on his face. 彼は顔に恐怖によるひどい表情を浮かべていた

dismay [U]（不快な驚きを受けるときの）失望, 落胆, 幻滅 ◇She could not hide her *dismay* at the result. 彼女はその結果に落胆を隠すことができなかった ◇I felt a jolt of *dismay*. 私は急に失望感を覚えた ☞ **dismayed** (UPSET)

shock 動

shock・appal・horrify・disgust・rock・scandalize・sicken・repel・dismay
人に大きく不意打ちをかけたり, 動揺させたりする
【類語訳】ショックを与える, びっくりさせる, 愕然とさせる, 震撼させる, ぞっとさせる, 怖がらせる, 憤慨させる, 失望させる

shock	disgust	appal
rock		horrify
scandalize		sicken
repel		
dismay		

文型&コロケーション
▶ shocked/ appalled/ horrified/ disgusted/ scandalized/ dismayed at sb/ sth
▶ to shock/ appal/ horrify/ disgust/ scandalize sb that...
▶ to shock/ appal/ horrify/ disgust/ scandalize/ sicken/ dismay sb to think/ see/ hear/ find/ learn...
▶ It shocks/ appalls/ horrifies/ disgusts/ sickens me that...
▶ a thought shocks/ appals/ horrifies/ sickens sb
▶ an idea shocks/ appals/ horrifies/ disgusts sb
▶ sb's behaviour shocks/ appals/ scandalizes sb
▶ violence shocks/ appals/ horrifies/ disgusts sb
▶ deeply shocked/ disgusted/ dismayed

shock [他, しばしば受身で]《進行形なし》ショック[衝撃]を与える, びっくりさせる ◇It *shocks* you when something like that happens. あんなことがあれば, だれでもびっくりするよ ◇We were all *shocked* at the news of his death. 私たちは皆, 彼の死の知らせに衝撃を受けた ◇I was *shocked* to hear that he had resigned. 彼が辞めたと聞

→shock

いて、ショックだった☞ **shock** (OFFEND)
▶**shocked** [形] ◇I was deeply *shocked* when she told me what had happened. 何が起きたか彼女が話してくれたとき、深い衝撃を受けた

appal 《英》《米 **appall**》(-ll-) [他]《進行形なし》愕然とさせる、震撼させる、ぞっとさせる ◇The brutality of the crime has *appalled* the public. その犯罪の残忍性は世間を震撼させた ◇It *appalled* me that they could simply ignore the problem. 彼らがその問題をあっさり無視できるのには愕然とした
▶**appalled** [形] ◇We watched *appalled* as the child ran in front of the car. 私たちは子どもが車の前を走るのを見てぞっとした

horrify [他]《進行形なし》衝撃を与える、びっくりさせる、ぞっとさせる、怖がらせる ◇The whole country was *horrified* by the killings. 国中がその殺人事件に衝撃を受けた
▶**horrified** [形] ◇She stared at him in *horrified* disbelief. 彼女はびっくりして信じられないといった様子で彼を見つめた

disgust [他]《進行形なし》（あまりに不快なため）吐き気を催させる、気分を悪くさせる ◇The level of violence in the film really *disgusted* me. その映画の凶暴性に本当に吐き気を催した ◇The feel of it, all cold and slimy, *disgusted* him. その感触がとても冷たくぬるぬるしていて、彼は気持ち悪くなった ☞ **disgusting** (DISGUSTING 1, 2)

rock [他、しばしば受身で]《ややインフォーマル》（国・地域社会に）衝撃を与える、揺るがす ◇The country was *rocked* by a series of political scandals. その国は一連の政治スキャンダルに揺れ衝撃を受けた ◇The news *rocked* the world. そのニュースに世界が衝撃を受けた

scandalize 《英でまた **-ise**》[他]（衝撃的なことをして）憤慨させる、あきれさせる ◇She *scandalized* her family with her extravagant lifestyle. 彼女の贅沢三昧のライフスタイルに家族は憤慨した

sicken [他]《進行形なし》《英》（あまりに不快なため）吐き気を催させる、気分を悪くさせる ◇The public is becoming *sickened* by these continual images of violence and death. こうした絶え間なく続く暴力と死の映像に大衆は不快感を募らせている

repel (-ll-) [他、しばしば受身で]《進行形なし》《やや フォーマル》不快〔嫌悪〕感を抱かせる、嫌がらせる ◇I was *repelled* by the smell of drink on his breath. 彼の息の酒臭さが嫌だった ◇Her heartlessness *repelled* him. 彼は彼女の無情さに嫌悪感を抱いた [反意] **attract** (INTEREST [動]), ☞ **repulsive** (DISGUSTING 1)

dismay [他、しばしば受身で] 失望〔落胆、幻滅〕させる ◇Their reaction *dismayed* him. 彼は彼らの反応にがっかりした ◇He was *dismayed* at the change in his old friend. 彼は旧友の様変わりに失望した ◇They were *dismayed* to find that the ferry had already left. フェリーがすでに出てしまったと知って、彼らは落胆した ❶ *dismay* は状況・人の振る舞いに対する反応について用いられる ◆I was *dismayed* to find that he was still there when I arrived home. （帰宅したときに彼がまだそこにいたとわかってがっかりした）×He *dismayed* me. ☞ **dismayed** (UPSET)

short [形]

1 ☞ QUICK
short・temporary・brief・short-lived・fleeting・momentary・passing

物事が少しの時間続くことを表す
【類語訳】短い、一時的な、つかの間の、臨時の、短期の、一瞬の、短命の、はかない

[文型&コロケーション]
▶a short/ brief/ fleeting/ passing **moment**
▶a short/ temporary/ brief **stay**
▶a short/ brief/ fleeting **visit**
▶a short/ brief/ momentary **silence/ pause**
▶a temporary/ short-lived/ momentary/ passing **interest**
▶a temporary/ brief/ short-lived **success**
▶a brief/ fleeting/ momentary/ passing **glance/ glimpse**
▶a brief/ fleeting/ momentary **look/ smile**
▶a brief/ fleeting/ passing **reference**
▶very/ relatively short/ temporary/ brief/ short-lived
▶only temporary/ brief/ fleeting/ momentary

short 短い、短時間［短期間］の ◇I'm going to France next week for a *short* break. 来週、短い休暇でフランスへ行く予定です ◇Which is the *shortest* day of the year? 1年のうちで昼間が最も短いのはいつですか ◇It's quite a *short* book (= that takes a short time to read). それはかなり薄い［短時間で読める］本です ◇She has a very *short* memory (= remembers only things that have happened recently). 彼女はとても記憶力が悪い ❶ *short* は また、「短く感じられる」時間を表す ◆Just two *short* years ago he was the best player in the country. （つい2年前までは、彼は国内最高の選手だった）[反意] **long** (LONG), ☞ **shorten** (SHRINK)

temporary 一時的な、つかの間の、臨時の、仮の、短期の ◇25,000 households are living in *temporary* accommodation. 2万5千世帯が仮の宿泊施設で暮らしている ◇The job's only *temporary*, while their secretary's on maternity leave. その仕事は秘書が産休の間の一時的なものに過ぎません ◇More than half the employees are *temporary*. 従業員の半数以上が臨時雇いである [反意] **permanent** (PERMANENT)
▶**temporarily** [副] ◇We regret that this service is *temporarily* unavailable. 申し訳ありませんが、このサービスは一時的にご利用できません [反意] **permanently** (PERMANENT)

brief 《特に書き言葉》 短い、短時間［短期間］の、一瞬の、つかの間の ◇The prime minister is due to make a *brief* visit to South Korea. 首相は韓国へ短期訪問をする予定である ◇Sean gave a *brief* glance at the screen. ショーンはちらっとスクリーンに目をやった ◇There was a *brief* silence after I made my announcement. 私がその発表をした後、短い沈黙があった ◇Mozart's life was *brief*. モーツァルトの人生は短かった [反意] **long** (LONG)
▶**briefly** [副] ◇He had spoken to Emma only *briefly*. 彼はほんの短い間エマに話しかけたことがあった

[ノート] **short と brief の使い分け**：short はインフォーマルな言い回しや話し言葉で、brief よりも頻繁に用いられる。×I'm going to France for a *brief* break. ◆The Dutch prime minister is making a *short/brief* visit. （オランダの首相が短期訪問中です）. short は読む［扱う、完了する］のに短時間しかかからない本・リスト・事業などを表すのに用いられる。brief は不可。brief は、look (一見)、glance (一瞥)、glimpse (一目)、smile (笑み)、sigh (ため息) を表す上で、short よりも頻繁に用いられる。

short-'lived （好ましい［楽しい］物事が）短命の、一時的

short

な, つかの間の, はかない ◇The benefits are likely to be *short-lived*. その給付金は一時的なもののようだ ◇It was a very *short-lived* government. それは非常に短命の政府だった ◇The stars enjoyed an intense but *short-lived* romance. スターたちは情熱的だがつかの間の恋を楽しんだ
反意 long-lasting (LONG), lasting, enduring (PERMANENT)

fleeting [ふつう名詞の前で]《書き言葉》(好ましい[楽しい]物事が)一瞬の, つかの間の ◇A *fleeting* smile touched his lips. 一瞬, 笑みが彼の唇に浮かんだ ◇Alone on deck, I experienced a *fleeting* moment of happiness. 甲板に一人出て, つかの間の幸せを味わった
▶**fleetingly** 副 ◇She smiled *fleetingly*. 彼女はほんの一瞬, 笑みを浮かべた

ノート **short-lived**と**fleeting**の使い分け: 両語とも特にほんの短時間しか続かない好ましい[楽しい]物事について用いられる。fleetingのほうがshort-livedよりも文語的で, ふつうより短い行為[経験]に用いられる。fleetingは楽しい物事を表すが, ごく短時間しか続かないために悲しみの感情を生み出すこともある。

momentary《特に書き言葉》一瞬の, つかの間の ◇There was a *momentary* flicker of pain in his face. 彼の顔には一瞬苦悩の色が浮かんだ ◇The accident was the result of a *momentary* lapse of concentration. その事故は一瞬の集中力の途切れによって生じた ❶ *momentary* は特に, 疑念・過失の瞬間を表すのに用いられ, doubt (疑念), hesitation (ためらい), pause (間), silence (沈黙), confusion (困惑), unease (不安), panic (パニック), lapse (途切れ), aberration (出来心) と結びつく。

passing [名詞の前で]一時的な, つかの間の, はかない, 少しだけの ◇My son is very jealous at the moment, but I think it's just a *passing* phase. 息子は目下のところ, とても嫉妬深いのが, でも, 一時的なものだと思う ◇He makes only a *passing* reference to the theory in his book. 彼の著書の中でその理論はほんの少し言及されているだけだ ❶ *passing* は特に時間・言及・興味の続く期間を表すのに用いられる。連語に phase (段階), fashion (流行), fad (熱中), craze (大流行), interest (興味), mention (言及), reference (論及) が挙げられる。

2 short • diminutive • petite • stubby • stunted • dumpy

人が平均より背が高くない, 体の部位が通常より小さいこと
【類語訳】背の低い, 短い, 小さい, 小柄の, ずんぐりした

文型&コロケーション
▶a short/ diminutive/ petite/ dumpy **woman**
▶a short/ diminutive **man**
▶a short/ petite/ dumpy **girl**
▶a short/ diminutive/ petite/ dumpy **figure**

short (人が)背の低い; (体の部位が)短い ◇He was a *short*, fat little man. 彼は背の低い小太りの男だった ◇I'm slightly *shorter* than you. 私はあなたより少し背が低い ◇The little boy ran as fast as his *short* legs could carry him. その小さな少年は, 短い脚でできる限り速く走った 反意 **tall, long**

diminutive 《フォーマル》(人が)小さい, 小柄の ◇She was a *diminutive* figure beside her husband. 彼女は夫と並ぶと小柄だった

petite 《ほめて》(少女・女性・体つきが魅力的に)小さい, 小柄

の ◇She was fair-haired and *petite*. 彼女は金髪で小柄だった ◇With her slim, *petite* figure, she could have been any age from 13 to 30. 彼女はほっそりとした小柄な体つきで, 13歳から30歳の間の年齢だったのかもしれない

stubby (指などの体の部位が)短くて太い, ずんぐりした ◇He pointed with his *stubby* finger to the page. 彼はずんぐりした指でそのページを指した

stunted 発育[成長]の遅れた ◇Instead of grass, there was a strip of thin scrub and *stunted* trees. 草の代わりに, 細い低木と生長の遅れた木々の一帯があった ◇Lack of adequate nutrition often leads to *stunted* growth in children. 栄養不足はしばしば子どもの発育不全につながる

dumpy 《けなして》(人が)背が低くて太った, ずんぐりした ◇That skirt makes you look *dumpy*. そのスカートをはくとずんぐりして見えるよ

3 short • brief • concise • abbreviated • succinct • economical • pithy

少ししか言葉[文字]を使わないことを表す
【類語訳】簡潔な, 手短な, 縮約された, 短縮形の, 経済的な

文型&コロケーション
▶a short/ a brief/ a concise/ an abbreviated/ a succinct **account**
▶a short/ a brief/ a concise/ an abbreviated **version**
▶a short/ brief/ concise/ succinct **summary/ answer/ statement**
▶a brief/ pithy **comment**
▶a concise/ a succinct/ an economical/ a pithy **style**
▶very short/ brief/ concise/ succinct/ economical
▶relatively short/ brief/ succinct

short (言葉が[を])簡潔な, 手短な, 縮約した; (名前・単語の)短縮形の ◇The *short* answer to your query is that he has acted completely illegally. あなたのご質問に手短にお答えすれば, 彼は完全なる違法行為を行ったということです ◇Try to keep your sentences *short*. 文を簡潔にするように努めなさい ◇I've only read the *shorter* version of the report. その報告書の縮約版しか読んでいません ◇Call me Jo — it's *short for* Joanna. ジョーと呼んでください — ジョアンナの短縮形です ◇file transfer protocol or FTP *for short* ファイル転送プロトコル, または省略形でFTP 反意 **long** (LONG), ☞ **shorten** (SHRINK)

brief (言葉が)簡潔な, 手短な ◇The author makes only a *brief* mention of the role of Japan in this period. その作家はこの時期の日本の役割については簡単にしか触れていない ◇Please *be brief* (= say what you want to say quickly). どうぞ手短にお願いします ◇Now the rest of the news *in brief*. では, 残りのニュースを大急ぎでお伝えします
▶**briefly** 副 ◇*Briefly*, the argument is as follows... 手短に言えば, 論拠は次のとおりです

ノート **short**と**brief**の使い分け: 多くの場合, 両語とも使用可能。◆a *short*/*brief* account/version/description/summary/statement/answer (簡潔[手短]な)説明/見解/描写/概要/声明/回答)。briefはしばしば文章などなく発言について用いられる。×Please be *short*... しかし, mention には, 発言・文章のいずれにおいても, brief を用いるのが普通だが, answer には, 発言においても short を用いる傾向にある。

concise 《ややフォーマル》(必要で重要な情報しか与えず)簡潔な, 手短な ◇She gave us clear and *concise* instructions. 彼女は私たちに明確で簡潔な指示を出した ❶ *concise* は元となる原典よりも薄い本を表すのに用いられる。この意味で, 連結副詞の後でなく, 名詞の前でしか用いられない。◆This is just a *concise* dictionary — you should get yourself something bigger. (これは簡略版の辞書だ—もっと大きなものを手に入れるべきです)。☞ **to the point** (RELEVANT)
➢ **concisely** 副 ◇He spoke clearly and *concisely*. 彼ははっきりと簡潔に話した
abbreviated (単語・句・名前が)短縮[省略]形の ◇On the map, *abbreviated* forms such as USA and UK are consistently used. 地図では, USAやUKなどの短縮形が常に用いられる
➢ **abbreviate** 動 [他] ◇Et cetera is usually *abbreviated to* etc. et ceteraはふつう, etc. と短縮される
succinct 《ほめて》(論評・文章が)簡潔な ◇Keep your answers as *succinct* as possible. 答えはできるだけ簡潔にしてください 反意 **long-winded** ❶ long-winded な発言・文章は, あまりに長く続いて退屈で, 理解しにくい可能性がある。
➢ **succinctly** 副 ◇You put that very *succinctly*. あなたは非常に簡潔にそのことをおっしゃいました
economical 《ややフォーマル》(必要以上に言葉・空白・エネルギーを使わず)簡潔な, 経済的な ◇He uses an *economical* prose style. 彼は簡潔な散文体を用いる ◇an *economical* use of land/space 土地/空間の経済的な利用
➢ **economically** 副 ◇She writes elegantly and *economically*. 彼女は優雅に, 簡潔に書きながら

> ノート **concise, succinct, economical** の使い分け: concise, succinct は事実をどのように提示するかを言う場合に用いられることが多い。economical は人の話し方・書き方を言う場合に用いられることが多い。succinct は明快で言葉をまったく無駄に使っていないことから, 表現の仕方を肯定していることを示唆する。concise は肯定的でも否定的でもない。

pithy 《ほめて》(論評・文章が)簡潔な, 簡にして要を得た ◇a *pithy* advertising slogan 簡にして要を得た宣伝文句

shout 動 ☞ SCREAM

shout・yell・cry・scream・cheer・bellow・raise your voice・roar・holler・bawl
非常に大きな声をあげることを表す
【類語訳】叫ぶ, どなる, わめく, 悲鳴を上げる, 絶叫する, 喝采する, 声援する, うなる

〘文型&コロケーション〙
▶ to shout/ yell/ cry/ raise your voice/ holler **to** sb
▶ to shout/ yell/ scream/ bellow/ roar/ holler/ bawl **at** sb
▶ to shout/ yell/ cry out/ scream/ bellow/ roar/ holler **in** pain/ anguish/ rage, etc.
▶ to shout/ cry out/ scream **for** joy/ excitement/ delight etc.
▶ to shout/ yell/ cry out/ scream/ roar **with** excitement/ triumph, etc.
▶ to shout/ yell/ scream/ bellow/ roar/ holler/ bawl at sb **to do sth**
▶ to shout/ yell/ scream/ bellow/ holler **that**...
▶ to shout/ yell/ cry/ scream/ roar/ bawl **out**
▶ to shout/ yell/ bellow/ bawl **orders/ instructions**
▶ to shout/ yell/ scream **abuse**
▶ to shout/ yell/ cry/ scream **for help**
▶ to shout/ cry/ scream/ holler **out loud**
▶ to shout/ yell/ scream **at the top of your voice/ lungs**

shout [自, 他] 大声で言う, 叫ぶ; どなりつける ◇Stop *shouting* and listen! 大声で話すのをやめて聞きなさい ◇He started *shouting* and swearing at her. 彼は彼女をどなりつけ, ののしり始めた ◇Protesters threw stones and *shouted* abuse at the Senator. 抗議者たちはその上院議員に対し, 石を投げ罵声を浴びせた ◇'Run' he *shouted*. 「走れ」と彼は叫んだ 反意 **whisper** (WHISPER)
➢ **shout** 名 [C] ◇We heard angry *shouts* coming from the apartment below. アパートの下の部屋からどなり声が聞こえてきた
yell [自, 他] (怒り・興奮・恐怖・苦痛で)大声で言う, 叫ぶ, どなる, わめく ◇She *yelled* at the boy to get down from the wall. 彼女は少年に向かって, 壁から降りるように大声で言った ◇I had to *yell* at the top of my voice to make myself heard. 《特に英》私は声が届くように力の限り叫ばねばならなかった ◇I had to *yell* at the top of my lungs. 《特に米》私は力の限り叫ばねばならなかった ◇The crowd *yelled* encouragement to the team. 群衆は大声でチームを激励した ◇'Watch out!' he *yelled*. 「危ない」と彼は叫んだ
➢ **yell** 名 [C] ◇He let out a *yell* of delight. 彼は歓喜の叫びを上げた
cry [自, 他] 《書き言葉》大声で言う, 叫ぶ ◇She ran over to the window and *cried* for help. 彼女は窓に走り寄って, 助けを求めて叫んだ ◇'You're safe!' Tom *cried* with delight. 「無事だったんだね」とトムは歓喜の叫び声を上げた ◇He bit his lip, trying not to *cry* out in pain. 彼は痛くても大声を上げないように唇をかんだ
➢ **cry** 名 [C] ◇Her answer was greeted with *cries* of outrage. 彼女の答は怒号の嵐に迎えられた
scream [自, 他] (恐怖・怒り・興奮で)金切り声で言う, 叫ぶ, 悲鳴を上げる, 絶叫する ◇He *screamed* at me to stop. 彼は立ち止まるよう, 私に向かって叫んだ ◇'Help!' he *screamed*. 「助けてくれ」と彼は金切り声を上げた
☞ **scream** (SCREAM)
cheer [自, 他] (大勢の人々が)喝采[歓呼]する, 声援[応援]する ◇We all *cheered* as the team came onto the field. そのチームがグラウンドに出てくると, 私たちは皆で声援を送った ◇The spectators *cheered* the runners *on*. 観客は走者たちに声援を送った ◇The crowd *cheered* the president as he drove slowly by. 群衆は車でゆっくり通過する大統領に歓呼の声を送った
➢ **cheer** 名 [C] ◇A great *cheer went up* from the crowd. 群衆から大歓声が上がった ◇**Three cheers for** the winners! (= used when you are asking a group of people to cheer three times, in order to congratulate sb, etc.) 勝者たちに万歳三唱を
bellow [自, 他] どなる, うなる ◇He fell to the floor, *bellowing* with pain and rage. 彼は床に転倒し, 痛みと怒りでうめき声を上げた ◇'Quiet!' the teacher *bellowed*. 「静かに」と先生はどなった
➢ **bellow** 名 [C] ◇He let out a *bellow* of rage. 彼は怒りでうなり声を上げた
ˌraise your ˈvoice 〘行止〙 (怒りで)声を荒げる ◇She never once *raised her voice* to us. 彼女は私たちに向かって, ただの一度も声を荒げたことがなかった ◇'Just you get in here,' he said, *raising his voice*. 「君だけここに入りなさい」と彼は声を荒げて言った

show

roar [自, 他]《書き言葉》(怒り・苦痛・興奮で)大声で言う, 叫ぶ, どなる, わめく ◇The crowd *roared* with excitement. 群衆は興奮してわめいた ◇Fans *roared* their approval. ファンたちは大声で賛同した ◇'Stand back,' he *roared*.「後ろに下がっていろ」と彼は叫んだ

holler [自, 他]《米, インフォーマル》大声で言う, 叫ぶ ◇Don't *holler* at me like that! 私に向かってそんなふうに大声を上げないで ◇'Look out,' I *hollered*.「気をつけて」と私は叫んだ

bawl [自, 他]《けなして》大声で言う, どなる ◇She *bawled* at him in front of everyone. 彼女は皆の前で彼にどなった ◇He sat in his office *bawling* orders at his secretary. 彼はオフィスに座って, 大声で秘書に命令していた

show [動]

1 show・prove・indicate・demonstrate・illustrate
物事をはっきりさせる, 物事が真実であることを示す
【類語訳】示す, 証明する, 教える, 伝える, 立証する, 裏づける, 明示する

indicate	show	prove
	demonstrate	
	illustrate	

▶文型&コロケーション
▶to show/ prove/ indicate/ demonstrate sth **to** sb
▶to show/ prove/ indicate/ demonstrate/ illustrate **that/ what/ how**...
▶**figures/ studies** show/ prove/ indicate/ demonstrate/ illustrate sth
▶**research** shows/ proves/ indicates/ demonstrates/ illustrates sth
▶to show/ prove/ indicate/ demonstrate/ illustrate sth **clearly**
▶to show/ prove/ demonstrate sth **conclusively/ beyond doubt**

show [他](事実・証拠を使ってはっきりと)示す, 証明する, 教える, 伝える ◇The government's popularity is declining rapidly, as the opinion polls *show*. 世論調査が示すとおり, 政府の人気は急落している ◇Let me *show* you exactly what this will mean. これが厳密には何を意味することになるのかお教えしましょう ◇They have published a report *showing* the company's current situation. 彼らは会社の現状を伝える報告書を発表した ◇He has *shown* himself to be a caring father. 彼は自ら面倒見のよい父親であることを証明した ◇They think I can't do it, but I'll *show* them!《インフォーマル》私にはそれができないと彼らは思っているが, 目に物見せてやるわ

prove [他](事実・証拠を使って真実であることを)証明する, 立証する, 裏づける, 示す ◇This *proves* (that) I was right. これは私が正しかったことを証明している ◇She was determined to *prove* everyone wrong. 彼女は皆の間違いを証明する覚悟だった ◇They hope this new evidence will *prove* her innocence. 彼らはこの新しい証拠が彼女の無実を証明してくれることを願っている ◇'I know you're lying.' '*Prove* it!'「君が嘘をついているのはわかってるよ」「証明してみろよ」◇He felt he needed to *prove his point* (= show other people that he was right). 彼は自らの主張を裏づける必要があると思った ◇Are you just do-ing this to *prove a point*? 言い分を証明するためだけにこれをやっているわけ 反意 **disprove** (DISPROVE), ☞**proof** (EVIDENCE), **proven** (FINAL)

ノート **show**と**prove**の使い分け: proveは正義が行われるという意味をより強く与えるために, showよりも好まれることが多い.

indicate [他]《ややフォーマル》(真実である[存在する]ことを)示す ◇Record profits in the retail market *indicate* a boom in the economy. 小売市場における記録的収益は, 経済のにわか景気を示すものである ◇Kingston-upon-Thames, as the name *indicates*, is situated on the banks of the Thames. その名が示すとおり, キングストン・アポン・テムズはテムズ川岸に位置している ☞**indication, indicator** (SIGN1), **indicate** (DECLARE), **indicate** (SUGGEST)

demonstrate [他]《ややフォーマル》(真実である)ことを示す, 証明する ◇These results *demonstrate* convincingly that our campaign is working. これらの結果は, 我々の活動が功を奏していることを納得いく形で示している ◇The theories were *demonstrated* to be false. それらの理論が間違っていることが証明された ☞**demonstration** (EVIDENCE)

illustrate [他]《ややフォーマル》(真実である[存在する]ことを)明示する ◇The incident *illustrates* the need for better security measures. その事件はよりよい安全対策の必要性があることを明示している ☞**illustrate** (EXPLAIN1), **illustration** (EXAMPLE1)

ノート **indicate, demonstrate, illustrate**の使い分け: これらの語の中で, demonstrateが最も意味の強い語で, indicateは最も意味の弱い語である. この意味では indicateとillustrateは主語と目的語に物事を取る. これらの語は人を主語に取ることはできないが, demonstrateはできる.
◆Let me *demonstrate* to you some of the difficulties we are facing. (我々が直面している困難のいくつかをお示ししましょう). ✗Let me *indicate/illustrate* to you the difficulties we are facing.

2 show・reveal・expose
人に物がわかるようにする
【類語訳】見せる, 現す

▶文型&コロケーション
▶to show/ reveal sth **to** sb

show [他](人に物を)見せる ◇If there's a letter from France please *show* it to me. フランスからの手紙があれば, 私に見せてください ◇You have to *show* your ticket as you go in. 入るときにチケットを見せなければなりません ◇Have you *shown* your work to anyone? あなたの作品を誰かに見せましたか ◇Have you *shown* anyone your work? 誰かにあなたの作品を見せましたか

reveal [他]《ややフォーマル》(それまで見えなかった物を)見せる, 現す ◇He laughed, *revealing* a line of white teeth. 彼は白い歯並びを見せて笑った ◇X-rays *revealed* a fracture. X線で骨折がわかった ◇She crouched in the dark, too frightened to *reveal* herself. 彼女は怖くて姿を見せることができずに暗がりにうずくまった ☞**reveal** (REVEAL)

expose [他]《ややフォーマル》(ふだん隠れている物を)見せる, 現す ◇Miles of sand are *exposed* at low tide. 引き潮

ときには何マイルにもわたる砂地が現れる ◇He did not want to *expose* his fears and insecurity to anyone. 彼は恐怖心と不安感を誰にも見せたがらなかった ☞ expose (REVEAL)

ノート reveal と expose の使い分け：場合によって、両語とも使用可能。 ◆He laughed, *revealing/exposing* a line of white teeth. (彼は白い歯並びを見せて笑った). reveal は物が現れるまで、人々はその存在さえ知らなかったことを示唆する. expose は単に現れるまで物を見ることができなかったことを示唆する. ✗ X-rays *exposed* a fracture. ✗ Miles of sand are *revealed* at low tide.

shrewd 形

shrewd・perceptive・astute・incisive・canny・discriminating・discerning
人や状況を鋭く、的確に判断することができることを表す
【類語訳】鋭敏な、明敏な、頭の切れる、抜け目のない、的確な、痛烈な、辛辣な、目の肥えた

文型&コロケーション
▸ a shrewd/ an astute/ a canny **businessman/ politician**
▸ a shrewd/ a perceptive/ an astute **observer**
▸ a perceptive/ an astute/ an incisive **analysis**
▸ a shrewd/ a perceptive/ an astute **observation**
▸ a shrewd/ a perceptive/ an incisive **comment**
▸ a shrewd/ astute/ canny **move**

shrewd《しばしばほめて》(状況判断が)鋭敏な、明敏な、頭の切れる、洞察力のある、抜け目のない；(判断が)的確な ◇My mother was a *shrewd* judge of character. 母には人の性格を鋭く見抜く力があった ◇I could take a pretty *shrewd guess* at who had sent the letter. 私は手紙の送り主をかなり鋭く言い当てることができた ◇She had a *shrewd idea* of what their motives were. 彼女は彼らの動機が何であるか鋭く見抜いていた

perceptive《ほめて》(明白でない物事に対して)洞察力のある、鋭敏な ◇It was very *perceptive* of you to notice that. それに気づくとは君の洞察力は素晴らしい ◇The article gives a *perceptive* analysis of the way bureaucracies work. その記事は官僚制の機能の仕方を鋭く分析している

astute《ほめて》(いかに優位に立つかについて)抜け目のない、鋭敏な ◇An *astute* politician, he understood the need to get them on his side. 彼は抜け目のない政治家だったので、彼らを味方につける必要性がわかっていた

incisive《ほめて》(明晰な思考力[十分な理解力]があり)鋭敏な、明敏な、痛烈な、辛辣な ◇He had a clear, *incisive* mind. 彼は明晰かつ鋭敏な頭脳を備えていた ◇She is an *incisive* critic of the current education system. 彼女は現在の教育制度を痛烈に批評している

canny（ビジネス・政治の世界において）抜け目のない ◇It was a *canny* move, which brought Palmer in on their side. 彼らは抜け目ない手段でパーマーを味方につけた ❶ canny はこのグループのほとんどの語とは違いほめて用いられず、時に人が自分に対して如才なさすぎることを示唆する。 ◆Her opponent proved to be more *canny* than she'd thought. (彼女の敵は彼女が考えていたよりも抜け目のないことがわかった)

discriminating《ほめて》(相対的に質について)良さのわかる、見る目[眼識]のある、目の肥えた[高い] ◇They are very *discriminating about* what restaurants they go to. どのレストランに行くか、彼らの目は非常に肥えている
▸ **discrimination** 名 [U] ◇The president has been criticized for his lack of *discrimination* in his choice of political allies. 大統領は政治的同盟国の選択において見る目がないと批判されている

discerning [ふつう名詞の前で]《ほめて》(物事の質について)違いのわかる、見る目[眼識]のある、目の利く ◇There is growing demand for the product from *discerning* customers. 違いのわかる顧客からのその製品に対する需要が高まっている ◇To the *discerning eye* (= to sb who is discerning), the quality may seem quite poor. 目の利く人には、その品質はかなり劣ると思われるかもしれない
▸ **discernment** 名 [U] ◇She saw herself as a woman of taste and *discernment*. 彼女は自分のことを、センスがあって違いのわかる女だと思っていた

ノート discriminating と discerning の使い分け：discriminating な人々は、どちらがよりよい質であるかがわかるので、物が選べる. discerning な人々は、個々の物事の質が判断できる. discerning は discerning eye などのように名詞を修飾して用いられる. ◆*discerning* clients/customers/collectors/travellers（眼識のある依頼人／顧客／収集家／旅行者）

shrink 動

shrink・narrow・contract・shorten
大きさ[広さ、長さ]が減ることを表す
【類語訳】縮む、収縮する、小さくなる、縮小する、細くなる、狭まる、短縮する、短くなる

文型&コロケーション
▸ to shrink/ narrow/ contract/ shorten (sth) **to** a particular size
▸ to shrink/ narrow/ contract/ shorten (sth) **by** a particular amount
▸ **a market/ the economy** shrinks/ contracts
▸ shrink/ narrow/ contract (sth) **slightly**
▸ to shrink/ narrow/ contract/ shorten (sth) **considerably**
▸ to narrow/ contract **sharply**

shrink [自, 他]（大きさ・量が[を]）縮む、収縮する、小さくなる；縮める、収縮させる、縮小する ◇The tumour had *shrunk* to the size of a pea. 腫瘍はエンドウ豆の大きさにまで縮んでいた ◇The market for their products is *shrinking*. それらの製品の市場は縮小している ◇Households have been *shrinking* in size but increasing in number. 世帯規模は小さくなりつつあるが、数は増えてきている ◇In some ways, the Internet has *shrunk* the world. いくつかの点で、インターネットは世界を縮めた ❶ shrink は熱湯で洗濯された衣服・生地が小さくなる場合にも用いられる. ◆My sweater *shrank* in the wash.（私のセーターは洗濯で縮んだ）反意 **grow** (RISE)
▸ **shrinkage** 名 [U] ◇the *shrinkage* of heavy industry 重工業の縮小 ◇She bought a slightly larger size to allow for *shrinkage*. 彼女は縮む分の余裕をみて少し大きめのサイズを買った

narrow [自, 他] 狭く[細く]なる、狭まる、狭まる；狭く[細く]する、狭める、狭まる ◇This is where the road *narrows*. ここで道路が狭くなります ◇Her *eyes narrowed* (= almost closed) to slits. 彼女は目を細め状態に細めた

◇The *gap* between the two teams has **narrowed** to three points. その2チームの点差は3点まで縮まった ◇We need to *narrow* the health divide between rich and poor. 私たちは貧富の健康格差を狭める必要がある 反意 **widen, broaden** (EXPAND), ☞ **narrow** (NARROW)

contract [自, 他]《ややフォーマル》《大きさ・量が[を]》収縮する, 縮まる; 収縮させる, 縮小する, 短縮する ◇Glass *contracts* as it cools. ガラスは冷えると収縮する ◇The electrical market is forecast to *contract* by 2% this year. 電気製品市場は今年, 2%縮小すると予測されている ◇The heart muscles *contract* to expel the blood. 心筋は血液を送り出すために収縮する ◇'I will' and 'I shall' are usually *contracted* to 'I'll' (= made shorter). 「I will」や「I shall」はふつう, 「I'll」に短縮される 反意 **expand** (EXPAND)

▶**contraction** [名] [U] ◇the expansion and *contraction* of the metal 金属の膨張と収縮 ◇The sudden *contraction* of the markets left them with a lot of unwanted stock. 突然の市場の縮小で, 彼らは多くの不要な在庫を抱えた

ノート **shrink** と **contract** の使い分け：衣服・生地は **shrink** する。ガラス・金属など他の物質は特に冷えると, **contract** する。market (市場), economy (経済) は, **shrink**, **contract** できるが, **contract** のほうがフォーマルである。muscle (筋肉) は **contract** し, word (単語) はより短い形に **contract** される。他のほとんどの物は **shrink** する。**shrink** の反意語は **grow** で, **contract** の反意語は **expand** である。

shorten [他, 自] 短くする, 短縮する; 短くなる, 短縮される ◇Injury problems could *shorten* his career. けがの問題で彼の経歴は縮められるかもしれない ◇They performed a *shortened* version of the play in just 40 minutes. その劇の短縮版がわずか40分で演じられた ◇Katherine generally *shortens* her name to Kay. キャサリンという名は一般的に, ケイと短縮される ◇In November the temperature drops and the days *shorten*. 11月には, 気温が下がり日は短くなる 反意 **lengthen** (EXPAND), ☞ **short** (SHORT 1), **short** (SHORT 3)

shy [形] ☞ QUIET 3, SOLITARY

shy・**insecure**・**timid**・**coy**・**diffident**・**inhibited**
人が他人に会うことや話しかけることに自信のない[緊張する, 恥ずかしがる]ことを表す
【類語訳】恥ずかしがりの, 内気な, 引っ込み思案な, はにかんだ, 臆病な, 自信のない, 気の小さい, おどおどした, 控えめな

文型&コロケーション
▶shy/ insecure/ timid/ coy/ diffident/ inhibited **about** sth
▶a shy/ an insecure/ a timid (**young**) **man**/ **woman**/ **child**
▶a shy/ timid **girl**/ **boy**/ **creature**/ **animal**
▶a shy/ coy/ diffident **smile**/ **manner**

shy (人が) 恥ずかしがりの, はにかみ屋の, 内気な, 引っ込み思案な; 恥ずかしそうな, はにかんだ; (動物が) 臆病な ◇Don't be *shy* — come and say hello. 恥ずかしがらないで一来てご挨拶しなさい ◇He gave a *shy* little smile. 彼はわずかにはにかんだ笑みを浮かべた ◇The panda is a *shy* creature. パンダは臆病な動物である

▶**shyly** [副] ◇She smiled *shyly*. 彼女は恥ずかしそうにはにかんで笑んだ
▶**shyness** [名] [U] ◇He tried to overcome his *shy-*

ness. 彼は引っ込み思案を克服しようとした

insecure (自分自身[他人との関係]に)自信のない, 不安な ◇He's very *insecure* about his appearance. 彼は自分の外見にあまり自信がもてないのだ 反意 **confident** (CONFIDENT)

▶**insecurity** [名] [U, C, ふつう複数で] ◇feelings of *insecurity* 不安な感じ ◇We all have our fears and *insecurities*. 私たちは皆, 心配や不安の種を持っている

timid 《特に書き言葉》(人・動物が)臆病な, 気の小さい, おどおど[びくびく]した ◇I was too *timid* to ask anyone. 私はあまりにも臆病なもので誰にも訊けなかった ◇They're pretty *timid* creatures who will run away at the slightest noise. 彼らはほんのちょっとした物音でも逃げてしまうような, かなり臆病な生き物である 反意 **bold** (BOLD)

coy (恋愛・セックスに対して)恥ずかしがりの, はにかみ屋の, (人の気を引くために)純情ぶった, うぶなふりをした ◇She gave him a *coy* smile. 彼女は彼にうぶな笑みを投げかけた

diffident 《特に書き言葉》自信のない, 臆病な; (自分について語りたがらず)控えめな, 遠慮がちな ◇He was modest and *diffident* about his own success. 彼は自らの成功については控えめで多くを語りたがらなかった ◇Greg was the quiet, *diffident* type. グレッグは物静かで遠慮がちなタイプだった

▶**diffidence** [名] [U] ◇She overcame her natural *diffidence* and spoke with great frankness. 彼女は生来の臆病さに打ち勝ち, ざっくばらんに大いに話した

inhibited (リラックスする[感情を表現する]ことができず)内気な, 引っ込み思案な ◇Boys are often more *inhibited* than girls about discussing their problems. 男の子は自分たちの問題を話し合うのに女の子以上に引っ込み思案なことが多い 反意 **uninhibited** (SOCIABLE)

▶**inhibition** [名] [C, U] ◇The children were shy at first, but soon lost their *inhibitions*. 子どもたちは初めははにかんでいたが, すぐに打ち解けた

sick [形]

1 sick・**ill**・**not (very) well**・**bad**・**ailing**・**unwell**・**unfit**・**sickly**・**unhealthy**
人の健康状態がよくないことを表す
【類語訳】病気にかかっている, 体調の悪い, 故障した, 病弱な, 病気がちの, 不健康な

文型&コロケーション
▶sick/ ill/ unwell **with** flu, a fever, etc.
▶a sick/ an ailing **mother**/ **father**/ **parent**/ **husband**/ **wife**
▶sick/ seriously ill/ sickly/ unhealthy **children**
▶to **look** sick/ ill/ not (very) well/ bad/ unwell/ sickly/ unhealthy
▶to **feel** ill/ not (very) well/ bad/ unwell
▶to **become**/ **get**/ **fall** sick/ ill
▶**very** sick/ ill/ unwell

sick 病気にかかっている; 体調[具合]の悪い ◇Her mother's very *sick*. 彼女の母親は重い病気にかかっている ◇Don't ask a babysitter to look after a *sick* child. ベビーシッターに病気の子どもの面倒を見させないように ◇Peter has **been off sick** (= away from work because he is sick). ピーターはずっと病欠だ ◇Emma has just **called in sick** (= phoned to say she will not be coming to work because she is sick). エマが電話で病欠を伝えてきた 反意 **well** (WELL), ☞ **sickness** (ILLNESS), the

sick (PATIENCE)

ill [名詞の前はまれ]《特に英》病気にかかっている；体調[具合]の悪い ◇Her father is ***seriously ill*** in St Luke's hospital. 彼女の父親は重病でセント・ルーク病院に入院中だ ◇Uncle Harry is ***terminally ill*** with cancer. ハリー伯父さんは末期がんを患っている ◇We both started to feel *ill* shortly after the meal.《英》私たちは二人とも、食事の直後に具合が悪くなり始めた 反意 **well** (WELL), ☞ **illness** (DISEASE), **illness** (ILLNESS)

ノート **sick** と **ill** の使い分け：特に重病について《英》では、ill のほうが一般的． ×He is seriously *sick* in hospital. しかし、病気のために仕事を休むような場合は sick を用いる． ×Peter has been off *ill*. ×Emma has just called in *ill*. また、ill はふつう副詞の後に置かれない限り、名詞の前では用いられない．名詞の前で用いる場合、名詞はふつう複数形である． ♦ an *ill* child. ♦ terminally *ill* children（末期症状の子どもたち）．《米》で一般的な語は sick である． ill はよりフォーマルで、かなりの重病にしか用いられない．《英》では、sick の一般的な意味は「吐き気を催して」である． ☞ **sick** (SICK 2)

not (very) well 体調[具合]の悪い ◇I wasn't feeling *very well* so I decided not to go to the concert. あまり具合がよくなかったので、コンサートには行かないことにした ◇I'm a bit worried — she's *not well*.《特に英》少し心配なんだ—彼女の具合が悪いんだ ❶ not (very) well はほとんどの場合、それほど重くない病気について、特に問題が何であるか正確にわからない場合に用いられる．《米》ではふつう動詞の feel と共に用いられる．

bad《ややインフォーマル，特に話し言葉》体調[具合]の悪い ◇I'm afraid I'm feeling pretty *bad*. どうもかなり具合が悪いようなんだ ❶ この意味では、bad は常に、feel, look の後で用いられる. 反意 **good** (WELL)

ailing《フォーマル》病気にかかっている ◇She cares for her *ailing* father. 彼女は病気の父親の世話をしている

unwell [名詞の前では用いない]《ややフォーマル》体調[具合]の悪い ◇She said she was feeling *unwell* and went home. 彼女は体調が優れないと言って帰宅した 反意 **well** (WELL)

unfit [名詞の前はまれ]《英》（けが・病気で）故障した；（運動していなかったので）体力の衰えた ◇The captain is still *unfit* and will miss tonight's game. キャプテンはまだ故障していて、今夜の試合には出ないだろう ◇I'm so *unfit* — I'm out of breath just from walking up the steps! かなり体力が落ちてるな一階段を上っただけで息が切れたよ ❶ unfit は《英》《米》のどちらでも、「病気・けがのために…(すること)に耐えられない」ことを意味する unfit for sth, unfit to do sth の句で用いられる． ♦ He's still *unfit for* work.（彼はまだ仕事に戻れない） ♦ The company's doctor found that she was *unfit to* carry out her normal work.（会社の医師は彼女は通常業務の遂行に耐えられないと判断した） 反意 **fit** (WELL)

sickly 病弱な，病気がちの；病弱そうな，病人のような ◇He was a *sickly* child. 彼は病気がちの子どもだった ◇She looked *pale and sickly*. 彼女は青白く病弱そうに見えた 反意 **healthy** (WELL)

unhealthy [名詞の前はまれ] 不健康な；不健康そうな，不健康を示す ◇They looked poor and *unhealthy*. 彼らは貧しく不健康そうに見えた 反意 **healthy** (WELL)

2 sick・nauseous・queasy

人々が吐き気を覚えることを表す

【類語訳】吐き気を催して，酔って

文型&コロケーション
▸ sick/ nauseous/ queasy **with** fear
▸ **to feel** sick/ nauseous/ queasy
▸ **to make sb** sick/ nauseous/ queasy
▸ **a bit/ a little/ slightly/ very** sick/ nauseous/ queasy

sick [名詞の前はまれ] 吐き気を催して，酔って ◇Whenever I think about my exams I feel *physically sick*. 試験のことを考えるたびに吐き気を催すんだ ◇I had a *sick* feeling in my stomach. 胃に吐き気を感じていた ❶ 接尾語の -sick は、乗り物での移動の結果、吐き気を感じることを意味する複合語で用いられることが多い． ♦ I was feeling sea*sick* so I went up on deck for some fresh air.（船酔いしたので、新鮮な空気を吸いに甲板に上がった） ♦ air*sick*（飛行機酔って） ♦ car*sick*（車酔いして） ♦ travel-*sick*（乗り物酔いして）
▸ **sickness** 名 [U] ◇After a few minutes the *sickness* subsided.《特に英》数分したら吐き気が治まった

nauseous [名詞の前はまれ]《フォーマル》吐き気を催して ◇She felt dizzy and *nauseous*. 彼女はめまいを催して吐き気を催した ☞ **nauseating** (DISGUSTING 1)
▸ **nausea** 名 [U] ◇A wave of *nausea* swept over me. 吐き気が襲ってきた

queasy [名詞の前はまれ]（少し）吐き気を催して，酔って ◇Travelling by boat makes me *queasy*. 船での移動だと酔うんです

sight 名

sight・view・vision
特定の位置から見える地域[広がり]
【類語訳】視野，視界

文型&コロケーション
▸ **in/ out of** sight/ view
▸ **in/ within** sight/ view **of** sth
▸ **in full/ plain** sight/ view
▸ **to come into/ disappear from** sight/ view/ sb's vision
▸ **to come in** sight/ view of sb/ sth
▸ **to block** sb's view/ vision
▸ sb's **line of** sight/ vision
▸ sb's **field of** view/ vision

sight [U] 視野，視界，見えること，見える所 ◇He looked up the street, but there was no one in *sight*. 彼は通りの先に目をやったが、視界に入る人は誰もいなかった ◇He strode by, in full *sight* of the guards. 彼は警備員のまん前を堂々と通り過ぎた ◇At last we came in *sight* of a few houses. ついに私たちは数軒の家が見える所にやってきた ◇A bicycle came into *sight* on the main road. 幹線道路上に一台の自転車が見えてきた ◇Leave any valuables in your car out of *sight*. 貴重品はいずれも車の中の見えない所に置きなさい ◇Don't let him out of your *sight* (= Make sure that you can always see him, wherever he goes). 彼をあなたの目の届かない所に決して行かせないように ☞ **sight** (LOOK 名), **sight** (VIEW 2)

view [U, 単数で]《特に書き言葉》視野，視界，見えること，見える所 ◇The sun disappeared from *view*. 太陽は視界から消えた ◇The carriage was put *on view* for the public to see. その馬車は大衆に見えるように公開された ◇The knife was in plain *view* on the kitchen table. ナイフは台所のテーブルの上の目につく所にあった ◇I didn't have a good *view* of the stage. 舞台がよく見えなかった ☞ **view** (VIEW 2), **view** (LOOK 動 1)

vision [U] 視野, 視界, 見えること, 見える所 ◇The couple moved outside her field of *vision* (= total area you can see from a particular position). そのカップルは彼女の視界の外に移動した ◇He glimpsed something on the edge of his *vision*. 彼は視界の端にちらりと何かを見た

ノート sight, view, vision の使い分け：view は, sight と vision よりも文語的である。view はどの程度よく見えるかについて言うことのできる唯一の語。×I didn't have a good *sight*/*vision* of the stage. vision は常に所有代名詞と共に用いなければならない。◆ my/his/her (field of) *vision* (私/彼/彼女の視界)　また vision は, sight や view と共に非常によく用いられる in, into, out of などの前置詞とは一緒に用いられない。×There was nobody in *vision*. ×A tall figure came into *vision*.

sign 名

1 ☞ SUGGESTION
sign・indication・symptom・symbol・indicator・signal・trace・mark・hallmark
物事が存在する[起こり始めている, 将来起こるかもしれない]ことを示す出来事[行動, 事実]
【類語訳】兆候, 前兆, 表れ, しるし, きざし, 指示, 証, 症状, 象徴, シンボル, 指標, シグナル, 痕跡, 形跡, 足取り, 特徴, 特質

文型&コロケーション
▸ a **sign**/ an **indication**/ a **symptom**/ a **symbol**/ an **indicator**/ a **signal**/ a **trace**/ a **mark**/ a **hallmark of** sth
▸ a **sign**/ an **indication**/ a **symptom**/ an **indicator**/ a **signal that**...
▸ a **clear sign**/ **indication**/ **symptom**/ **symbol**/ **indicator**/ **signal**/ **trace**
▸ an **obvious sign**/ **indication**/ **symptom**/ **symbol**/ **indicator**/ **trace**
▸ a **good**/ **reliable sign**/ **indication**/ **indicator**/ **signal**
▸ a **powerful sign**/ **symbol**/ **indicator**/ **signal**
▸ an **early sign**/ **indication**/ **symptom**/ **indicator**/ **signal**
▸ an **outward sign**/ **indication**/ **symbol**/ **mark**
▸ to **have** (the) **signs**/ **symptoms**/ **traces**/ **marks**/ **hallmarks of** sth
▸ to **bear** (the) **signs**/ **traces**/ **marks**/ **hallmarks of** sth
▸ to **give** a **sign**/ an **indication**/ a **signal**
▸ a **sign**/ an **indication**/ a **symptom**/ an **indicator shows**/ **suggests** sth
▸ **no**/ **any sign**/ **indication**/ **trace of** sth

sign [C, U] (物事の)兆候, 前兆, 表れ, きざし ◇Headaches may be a *sign* of stress. 頭痛はストレスの兆候かもしれない ◇Call the police *at the first sign of* trouble. トラブルの兆候が出た時点で警察を呼びなさい ◇The fact that he didn't say 'no' immediately is a good *sign*. 彼がすぐに「ノー」と言わなかったのは良いきざしだ ◇The gloomy weather *shows no sign of* improving. 天気はどんよりとしていて一向に回復のきざしを見せない ◇There was *no sign of life* in the house (= there seemed to be nobody there). その家にはひと気がなかった

indication [C, U] 《ややフォーマル》(物事が)起こり始めている

[人が考え[感じ]始めている]ことの)兆候, 前兆, 表れ, しるし, 指示 ◇They gave no *indication as to* how the work should be done. 仕事のやり方について何の指示も与えられなかった ◇All the *indications* are that the deal will go ahead as planned. あらゆる兆候から見て, 取引は計画どおりに進展するだろう ◇He shows *every indication* (= clear signs) of wanting to accept the post. 彼がその職を受け入れたがっているのが丸わかりだ ☞ **indicate** (DECLARE), **indicate** (SHOW 1), **indicate** (SUGGEST)

ノート sign と indication の使い分け：indication は人の発言という形で現れることが多い。sign はふつう出来事や人の行動に見られる。

symptom [C] (身体・精神的)症状;(悪い)兆候, 前兆, 表れ, しるし ◇cold/flu *symptoms* 風邪/インフルエンザの症状 ◇*Symptoms* include a headache and sore throat. 症状には頭痛と喉の痛みが含まれます ◇The rise in inflation was just one *symptom* of the poor state of the economy. 物価上昇率の高まりは, 困窮した経済状態の一つの兆候にすぎなかった

symbol [C] (一般的な性質・状況を表す)象徴, シンボル ◇The dove is a universal *symbol* of peace. 鳩は全世界共通の平和のシンボルである ◇The company car is an outward *symbol* of the employee's status. 社用車は従業員の地位を対外的に象徴するものである ◇A stressful job can actually be a *status symbol*. ストレスの多い仕事は意外にもステイタスシンボルになりうる ☞ **symbolize** (REPRESENT 2)

indicator [C] 《ややフォーマル》(物事・状況の)指標 ◇The economic *indicators* for the end of the year are better than expected. 年末に向けての経済指標は予想以上によい ☞ **indicate** (SHOW 1), **indicate** (SUGGEST)

signal [C] (物事の)兆候, 前兆, 表れ, しるし, シグナル ◇Chest pains can be a warning *signal* of heart problems. 胸の痛みは心臓病を警戒しなければならない前兆であることがある ◇Reducing prison sentences would send the wrong *signals* to criminals. 懲役刑の減刑は犯罪者に誤ったシグナルを送ることになりうる

ノート sign と signal の使い分け：signal は人に物事を行うべきであることを示唆する出来事[行動, 事実]について用いられることが多い。sign はふつうそのようには用いられない。◇Reducing prison sentences would send the wrong *signs* to criminals.

trace [C, U] (人・物事の)痕跡, 形跡, 跡形, 足取り ◇It's exciting to discover *traces* of earlier civilizations. もっと早い時期の文明の痕跡を発見することは刺激的である ◇Police searched the area but found no *trace* of the escaped prisoners. 警察はその地域を捜索したが, 脱獄囚の足取りは見つけられなかった ◇The ship had vanished *without (a) trace*. その船は跡形もなく消えてしまった ❶ *trace* は, no trace of, disappear/vanish without (a) trace の句で用いられることが多い。☞ **trace** (FIND 4)

mark [C] (特質・感情の)しるし, 証 ◇On the day of the funeral businesses remained closed as a *mark of respect*. その葬儀の日, 各企業は弔意を表すため休業にした ◇Such coolness under pressure is the *mark* of a champion. プレッシャーがかかる場面でのそうした冷静さはチャンピオンであることの証である

hallmark [C] 《ジャーナリズム》(人・物事に典型的な)特徴, 特質 ◇Police said the explosion bore all the *hallmarks* of a terrorist attack. その爆発にはテロ攻撃の顕著

な特徴のすべてが見られると警察は述べた

2 sign・board・plaque・notice・plate・noticeboard・bulletin board
情報[指示, 警告]を与える言葉[図]が記された一枚の金属片[木材, 石]
【類語訳】標識, 看板, 貼り紙, 掲示板, 黒板, 飾り板, 銘板, プレート

【文型&コロケーション】
▶ **on** a sign/ board/ plaque/ notice/ plate/ noticeboard/ bulletin board
▶ to **put up/ see/ read** a sign/ board/ plaque/ notice/ plate/ noticeboard/ bulletin board
▶ a sign/ board/ plaque/ notice **appears/ goes up**
▶ a sign/ plaque/ notice **says/ reads** sth

sign [C] 標識, 看板, 貼り紙 ◇All the road *signs* are in both languages. すべての道路標識は両方の言語で書かれている ◇A *sign* on the wall said 'Now wash your hands'. 壁の貼り紙には「さあ、手を洗いましょう」と書いてあった ◇Follow the *signs* for the Performing Arts Centre. パフォーミング・アーツ・センターへの標識に従ってください

board [C]（しばしば複合語で）黒[白]板 ◇The exam results went up on the *board*. 試験結果が掲示板に貼り出された ◇I'll write it up on the black*board*/white*board*. 私は黒板/白板にそれを清書します

plaque [C]（人・出来事を記念する金属[陶器]製の）飾り板, 銘板 ◇A bronze *plaque* marks the house where the poet was born. 一枚のブロンズの銘板がその詩人が生まれた家であることを示しています

notice [C] 掲示(板), 看板 ◇There was a *notice* saying 'Keep off the Grass'.「芝生立ち入り禁止」と書かれた掲示があった

【ノート】**sign**と**notice**の使い分け：noticeは言葉で情報・指示・警告を与えるのが普通である。この意味ではsignのほうがより頻繁に広い文脈で用いられる。◆a road/traffic/street/shop/pub *sign*（道路標識／交通標識／通りを示す標識／店の看板／パブの看板）×a road/traffic/shop/pub *notice*。しかし, noticeにはまた「情報が記載[印刷]された紙」という意味もある。

plate [C]（人の名前・車の登録番号などが記された）プレート ◇A brass *plate* beside the door said 'Dr Alan Tate'. ドアの脇にある真鍮のプレートには「アラン・テート博士」と書かれてあった ◇A name*plate* was fitted to the side of the boat. ネームプレートが船の側面に取り付けられていた ◇a vehicle's **number plates**《英》車のナンバープレート ◇a vehicle's **license plates**《米》車のナンバープレート

noticeboard [C]《英》掲示板 ◇Please check the *noticeboard* by the library for news of future events. 図書館脇の掲示板で、これからの催し物の情報をチェックしてください

'bulletin board [C]《米》掲示板 ◇Please keep an eye on the *bulletin board* for further details. さらなる詳細については, 掲示板に気をつけておいてください

signal 名

signal・sign・cue
人に情報を与える[人に事を行うよう伝える]ための動き[音, 出来事]
【類語訳】信号, 合図, 身振り, サイン, きっかけ

【文型&コロケーション】
▶ a signal/ sign/ cue **for** sb/ sth
▶ a signal/ sign/ cue (for sb) **to do sth**
▶ a **clear** signal/ sign/ cue
▶ a **warning** signal/ sign
▶ to **wait for/ miss a/** your signal/ sign/ cue
▶ to **understand/ misunderstand** a/ sb's signal/ sign
▶ to **give sb** a signal/ sign/ cue
▶ to **make** a signal/ sign

signal [C]（人に情報・指示・警告などを与える）信号, 合図 a danger/distress *signal* 危険／遭難信号 ◇At an agreed *signal* they left the room. 決めておいた合図で, 彼らは部屋を出た ◇The siren was a *signal* for everyone to leave the building. そのサイレンは全員が建物から出るようにとの合図だった ◇When I give the *signal*, run! 俺が合図したら走れ ◇All I get is a **busy signal** when I dial his number (= his phone is being used).《米》彼の電話番号にかけると, いつもお話し中だ

sign [C]（人に事を行うよう伝える）合図, 身振り, サイン ◇He gave a thumbs-up *sign*. 彼は親指を立てる身振りをした ◇She nodded as a *sign* for us to sit down. 彼女は私たちに着席を促す合図としてうなずいた

【ノート】**signal**と**sign**の使い分け：signはふつう手の動きであり, かなり定着していて一般の人に理解できる可能性が高いことが多い。signalはより範囲が広く, 特定の状況下で個人によって考案された可能性がある。◆*sign* language (= a system of communicating with people by using hand movements rather than spoken words)（身振り言語）◆a V-*sign* (= a sign that you make by holding up your hand and making a V-shape with your first and second fingers)（Vサイン）◆We agreed on a *signal* to mean 'stop'.（私たちは「止まれ」を意味する合図を決めた）。

cue [C]（人が事を行うための）きっかけ, 合図 ◇Jon's arrival was a *cue* for more champagne. ジョンの到着はシャンパンのお代わりのきっかけとなった ◇I think that's my *cue* to explain why I'm here. それはなぜ私がここにいるか説明せよとの合図ですね ◇'Where is that boy?' As if **on cue**, Simon appeared in the doorway (= as if sb had given him a signal).「あの少年はどこだ」とすると, まるで合図であるかのように, サイモンが戸口に現れた ◇Investors are **taking their cue from** the big banks and selling dollars (= taking what other people do as a sign for them to do the same).《比喩的》投資家たちは大手銀行に見習ってドルを売っている

silence 名

silence・peace・quiet・tranquillity・hush・calm
物音のないことを表す
【類語訳】静けさ, 静寂, 安らぎ, 平穏, 平静, 平安

【文型&コロケーション】
▶ **in** silence/ peace/ tranquillity
▶ **absolute/ total** silence/ peace/ quiet/ tranquillity/ calm
▶ **relative** silence/ peace/ quiet/ tranquillity/ calm
▶ a **sudden** silence/ quiet/ hush/ calm
▶ to **break** the silence/ peace/ quiet/ calm

silent, similarity

▶silence/ quiet/ a hush **falls** on sth

silence [U]（物音のない）静けさ, 静寂 ◇Their footsteps echoed in the *silence*. 彼らの足音が静寂の中で鳴り響いた ◇A scream broke the *silence* of the night. 叫び声が夜のしじまを破った ☞ **silent** (QUIET 1)

peace [U]（物音・問題・心配・不要な動きのない）静けさ, 静寂, 安心, 平穏, 平安 ◇She lay back and enjoyed the *peace* of the summer evening. 彼女は仰向けになって, 夏の夕べの静けさを楽しんだ ◇He never felt really *at peace* with himself. 彼は一人でいて決して本当に気持ちが安らぐことがなかった ◇He just wants to be *left in peace* (= not to be disturbed). 彼はそっとしておいてほしいと思っているだけだ ◇I need to check that she is all right, just for my own *peace of mind* (= so that I do not have to worry). 私はただ自分の安心のために, 彼女が無事だと確かめる必要がある ☞ **peaceful** (QUIET 1)

quiet [U]（あまり物音のない）静けさ, 静寂 ◇He seemed to prefer the *quiet* of his own room. 彼は自分の部屋の静けさのほうがいいようだった ◇I go to the library for a little *peace and quiet*. 私はちょっとした静けさを求めて図書館に出かける

tranquillity《特に英》《米でふつう tranquility》 [U]《ややフォーマル, 書き言葉》静けさ, 静寂, 静穏, 平安, 平穏, 平静 ◇It is the perfect place to relax in an atmosphere of peace and *tranquillity*. そこは静かで平穏な雰囲気の中でリラックスするには最適の場所である ☞ **tranquil** (QUIET 1)

hush [単数で]（騒ぎ・騒音の後の[人々の期待に反する]）静けさ, 静寂 ◇There was a *deathly hush* in the theatre. 劇場は死んだような静けさに包まれていた ◇A *hush* fell over the landscape. その景色に静寂が訪れた

calm [U, C] 静けさ, 静寂, 平穏, 平静 ◇We sat together for a while in the *calm* of the evening. 私たちはしばらくの間, 夜の静けさの中で共に腰掛けていた ☞ **calm** (QUIET 1)

silent 形

silent・speechless・dumb・mute・inarticulate
人が話をしない[話せない]こと, 行動が言葉で表されないこと
【類語訳】黙った, 唖然とした, 無言の, 口の利けない, はっきりしない, 歯切れの悪い

文型&コロケーション
▶speechless/ dumb/ inarticulate **with** rage/ anger

silent（人が）物を言わない, 口を利かない, 黙った ◇They huddled together in *silent* groups. 彼らは何人かずつ黙って身を寄せ合った ◇As the curtain rose, the audience *fell silent*. 幕が上がると, 観客は静かになった
▶**silently** 副 ◇They marched *silently* through the streets. 彼らは無言で通りを行進した

speechless（激怒・驚愕して）物が言えない, 口が利けない, 唖然とした ◇Laura was *speechless* with rage. ローラは激しい怒りで口が利けなかった ◇His words left her *speechless*. 彼の言葉に彼女は唖然とした

dumb（人が）黙った, 唖然とした ◇We were all struck *dumb* with amazement. 私たちは皆驚いて唖然とした ◇We all sat there in *dumb* silence. 私たちは皆無言でそこに座っていた ❶ *dumb* はまた「口の利けない」という意味もある. ◆She was born deaf and *dumb*. (聾唖の状態で生まれた). しかし, この *dumb* の意味は古風で, 侮蔑的となりうる.
▶**dumbly** 副 ◇'Are you all right?' Lucy nodded *dumbly*. 「大丈夫かい」するルーシーは黙ってうなずいた

mute《文語》黙った, 音を立てない；(言葉・声を出さずに) 無言の；口の利けない ◇The child sat *mute* in the corner of the room. その子は部屋の隅に黙って座っていた ◇She gave him a look of *mute* appeal. 彼女は彼に無言で訴える表情をした ◇The film concerns a *mute* Scottish widow and her passion for music. それは, ある口の利けないスコットランドの未亡人の音楽に対する情熱に関わる映画だ
▶**mutely** 副 ◇He nodded *mutely*. 彼は黙ってうなずいた

ノート **dumb** と **mute** の使い分け:「口の利けない」という意味では, dumb と mute はかなり古風で, dumb は侮蔑的になりうる. 受け入れられる代替語として speech-impaired があるが, これは常用されるものではなく, 代わりに unable to speak の句が用いられることが多い. ◆The 2nd Duke of Montrose was deaf and *unable to speak*. (モントローズ公爵二世は耳が不自由で話せなかった).

inarticulate《ややフォーマル》(人々が) はっきり意見の言えない[感情を表現できない], はっきり口が利けない；(発言が) はっきりしない, 歯切れの悪い ◇You can't expect an *inarticulate* young child to defend himself in court. はっきり意見の言えない幼い子どもに, 法廷での自己弁護を期待することはできません ◇She was *inarticulate* with rage. 彼女は激しい怒りで口が利けなかった ◇He gave a particularly *inarticulate* reply. 彼はとりわけ歯切れの悪い返事をした

similarity 名

similarity・resemblance・uniformity・equivalence・likeness・parallel・affinity・correspondence・there's no comparison
似ている[同じ]状態を表す
【類語訳】類似, 共通点, 同一, 同等, 同値, 同量, 類縁, 関連

文型&コロケーション
▶a similarity/ a resemblance/ an equivalence/ a likeness/ a parallel/ an affinity/ a correspondence/ no comparison **between** A and B
▶a similarity/ a resemblance/ an equivalence/ a likeness/ a parallel **to** sth
▶similarity/ uniformity/ equivalence/ a parallel **in** sth
▶a similarity/ equivalence/ a parallel/ an affinity/ a correspondence/ no comparison **with** sth
▶a **close** similarity/ resemblance/ likeness/ parallel/ affinity/ correspondence
▶a **strong** similarity/ resemblance/ likeness/ parallel/ affinity
▶(a) **remarkable** similarity/ resemblance/ uniformity/ parallel/ affinity/ correspondence
▶(a) **great** similarity/ resemblance/ uniformity/ affinity
▶**broad** similarity/ uniformity/ equivalence
▶a **direct** equivalence/ parallel/ correspondence
▶a **superficial/ physical** similarity/ resemblance/ likeness
▶to **bear** a similarity/ a resemblance/ a likeness/ an affinity/ no comparison
▶to **have** similarities/ uniformity/ a parallel/ an affinity/ a correspondence
▶to **show** a similarity/ a resemblance/ uniformity/ a like-

ness/ an affinity/ a correspondence
▶to see a similarity/ resemblance/ likeness/ parallel

similarity [U, C] (人・物事が[の]) 似ていること、類似；(物事・人々が備える) 類似点、共通点 ◇There is some *similarity* in the way they sing. 彼らの歌い方はいくらか似ている ◇They are both doctors but that is where the *similarity* ends. 彼らは二人とも医者だが、共通点はそこまでだ ◇We carried out a study of the *similarities* and differences between the two countries. 我々はその2か国の類似点と相違点について研究した 【反意】 **difference** (DIFFERENCE), ☞ **similar** (LIKE 前形)

resemblance [C, U] 《やや formal》 (人・物事が[の]) 似て見える[似ている]こと、類似(点) ◇The *resemblance* between the two signatures was remarkable. その二つの署名が似ていることは注目に値した ◇She bears a striking *resemblance* to the Queen. 彼女は女王に驚くほど似ている ◇The movie bears little *resemblance* to the original novel. その映画には原作小説とほとんど類似点がない ❶*resemblance* はほとんどの場合、外見について用いられる。

uniformity [U, 単数で] 《やや formal》 (あらゆる点における) 同一[統一、均一、画一](性) ◇They tried to ensure *uniformity* across the different departments. 彼らは異なる部門にわたって統一性を確保しようとした ◇The drab *uniformity* of the houses depressed me. 家々の単調な画一性にはがっかりした ☞ **uniform** (EQUAL)

equivalence [U, C] 《フォーマル》 (価値・量・意味・重要性における) 同等[等価](性)、同値、同量 ◇There is no straightforward *equivalence* between economic progress and social well-being. 経済発展と社会福祉とは直接イコールではない ☞ **equivalent** (EQUIVALENT)

likeness [C, U] (人・物事が) 似て見えること ◇There's a superficial *likeness*, but they're really very different. 外見上は似て見えるが、実際にはそれらは非常に異なる ◇I can't see any *likeness* between her children. 彼女の子どもたち同士はまったく似ているように見えない ☞ **like** (LIKE 前形)

ノート **resemblance** と **likeness** の使い分け：resemblance のほうがはるかに頻繁に用いられる一般的な語である。likeness は特に同じ家族の外見について用いられることがほとんどである。一般的には、physical や family などと結びつく。likeness はまた絵画・素描が本人に酷似しているときにも用いられる。 ♦ The drawing is said to be a **good *likeness*** of the girl's attacker. (その線画は少女を襲った犯人によく似ているそうだ)

parallel [C, ふつう複数で] 《やや formal》 類似(点) ◇There are interesting *parallels* between the 1960s and the first decade of this century. 1960年代と今世紀の最初の10年間には、興味深い類似点が見られる ◇It is possible to ***draw a parallel*** between (= find similar features in) their experience and ours. 彼らの経験と我々の経験の類似性を指摘することは可能である

affinity [U, C] 《フォーマル》 (人・物事の性質・構造・特徴の) 類似[類縁](性) ◇There is a close *affinity* between Italian and Spanish. イタリア語とスペイン語の間には密接な類縁性がある

correspondence [C, U] 《やや formal》 (物事の) 関連(性)；(物事の) 類似(性) ◇There is a close *correspondence* between the two extracts. その二つの抽出物の類似点にある ❶この意味では、correspondence は特に、a/an close/direct/exact/one-to-one correspondence between A and B の句で用いられる。☞ **correspond** (MATCH 1), **corresponding** (EQUIVALENT)

there's no com'parison フレーズ (比較される人々・物事の違いを強調して) 比べものにならない ◇In terms of price *there's no comparison* (= one thing is much more expensive than the other). 価格の観点から言えば、比べものにならない ◇The education system ***bears no comparison*** with that in many Eastern European countries (= it is not as good). その教育制度は、多くの東ヨーロッパ諸国の教育制度とは比べものにならない

single 形

single・divorced・unmarried・lone・estranged・widowed・separated
結婚していない[恋愛関係を持っていない]ことを表す
【類語訳】独身の、離婚した、未婚の、別居した

文型&コロケーション
▶to be divorced/ estranged/ separated from sb
▶a single/ a divorced/ an unmarried/ a lone/ a widowed/ a separated **man/ woman/ parent/ mother/ father**
▶a divorced/ an unmarried/ a separated **couple**

single 結婚していない、独身の；恋人のいない ◇The apartments are ideal for *single* people living alone. そのアパートは一人暮らしの独身者には最適である ◇Are you still *single*? まだ恋人はいないの[独身なの] ❶*single* parent/mother/father とは、夫・妻・パートナーなしで子育てをする人を指す。♦ Marriage breakdown is common and there are a large number of ***single-parent families***. (結婚生活の破綻はよくあることで、片親の家族がたくさんある)

divorced 離婚した ◇Many *divorced* people remarry and have second families. 離婚者の多くは再婚し、2度目の家族を持つ ◇My parents are *divorced*. 私の両親は離婚している ◇Are they going to ***get divorced***? 彼らは離婚するつもりなの

unmarried 結婚していない、未婚の ◇He remained *unmarried* all his life. 彼は生涯結婚しないままだった ◇*Unmarried* couples do not have the same rights as married couples. 未婚のカップルには既婚夫婦と同じ権利はない 【反意】 **married**

lone [名詞の前で] 《特に英、やや formal、特に書き言葉》 片親家庭の ◇Nine out of ten *lone* parents are women. 片親家庭の親の10人に9人が女性である ◇*Lone* fathers tend to be older than *lone* mothers. 片親家庭の父親は片親家庭の母親よりも年齢が高い傾向にある ❶*lone* は、普段の話し言葉ではそれほど頻繁に用いられないが、ジャーナリズムや公式報告では一般的である。

estranged 《フォーマル》 (夫[妻]と同居しておらず) 別居した ◇He is being questioned in connection with the death of his *estranged* wife. 彼は別居した妻の死に関する尋問を受けているところだ ◇She has been *estranged* from her husband since 1999. 彼女は1999年から夫と別居している ☞ **estrangement** (DIVISION 2)

widowed 夫[妻]と死別した、(男)やもめになった ◇She was *widowed* by the time she was 35. 彼女は35歳の時には夫と死別していた ◇She spent twenty years looking after her *widowed* father. 彼女は男やもめの父親の面倒を20年見た

sit, situation

separated [名詞の前のみ] (夫[妻, パートナー]と同居しておらず)別居した ◇Her parents are *separated* but not divorced. 彼女の両親は別居しているが離婚はしていない ◇He's *separated* from his wife. 彼は妻と別居している

ノート **estranged** と **separated** の使い分け：estrangedの夫婦は結婚しているが、もはや同居していない、またはいかなる関係も持って[連絡も取って]いない. separatedの夫婦はもはや同居していないが、例えば子どもの世話をするなど、依然として連絡を取っている可能性もある. また, separatedは結婚していないカップルが以前は同居していたことも表す.

sit 〔動〕☞ STAND 1

sit・sit down・be seated・take a seat・perch
椅子などの上で、背中を起こしてしてお尻に体重を載せる
【類語訳】座る、腰掛ける、腰を下ろす、着席する

文型&コロケーション
▶to sit/ sit down/ be seated/ take a seat/ perch **on** sth
▶to sit/ sit down/ be seated/ take a seat **in** sth

sit [自] (椅子などに)座る, 腰掛ける ◇May I *sit* here? ここに座ってもいいですか ◇I was *sitting* at my desk, gazing out of the window. 机に向かって座り、窓の外を見つめていた ◇*Sit* still, will you! じっと座ってろ ◇*Sit up* straight — don't slouch. 背筋を伸ばして座りなさい―前かがみにならないこと ◆She *sat back* and stretched out her legs. 彼女は深く腰掛けて両脚を伸ばした ❶ sit はふつう人がどこに[どのように]座っているかを示す副詞・前置詞句と共に用いられるが、時に座っている間に人が行うことを示すために他の句・節が用いられる. ◆We *sat* talking for hours. (私たちは座って何時間も話した). ◆He *sat* and stared at the letter in front of him. (彼は腰掛けて目の前の手紙を見つめた). 背もたれがまっすぐで肘掛けのない椅子には sit on が、またソファも sit on、肘掛け椅子には sit in が用いられる. [反意] **stand, stand up** (STAND 1)

,sit 'down, ,sit yourself 'down 〔句動詞〕 (立っている姿勢から)腰を下ろす、着席する ◇Please *sit down*. どうぞお掛けください ◇He *sat down* on the bed. 彼はベッドの上に腰を下ろした ◇Come in and *sit yourselves down*. 入って着席してください [反意] **get up, stand up** (STAND 1)

be seated [他] (《フォーマル》) 座っている、着席している ◇She *was seated* at the head of the table. 彼女はテーブルの上座に座っていた ◇Wait until all the guests *are seated*. すべてのお客様がご着席されるまでお待ちください ❶ be seated は人に座るよう促すフォーマルな表現として用いられることが多い. ◆Please *be seated*. (お座りください).

,take a 'seat 〔フレーズ〕(立っている姿勢から)腰を下ろす、着席する ◇Please *take a seat*. I'll be with you shortly. ご着席ください、すぐにご一緒いたします ◇He *took a seat* at the opposite end of the table. 彼はテーブルの反対側に腰を下ろした ❶ take a seat は特に人に座るよう促す丁寧な表現として用いられる.

perch [自, 他] (《副詞や前置詞と共に》) (ややインフォーマル) (物(の端)に)座る, 腰掛ける ◇We *perched* on a couple of high stools at the bar. 私たちはバーで二つの丈の高いスツールに座った ◇She *perched* herself on the edge of the bed. 彼女はベッドの端に腰掛けた

situation 〔名〕☞ INFORMATION

situation・circumstance・position・conditions・things・the case・state of affairs
有り様や様子を表す
【類語訳】状況、事態、情勢、局面、立場、境遇、状態、事情、環境、暮らし向き、条件、実情

文型&コロケーション
▶**in** (a) particular situation/ circumstances/ position/ state of affairs
▶the **general/ current/ present/ real** situation/ circumstances/ position/ conditions/ state of affairs
▶the/ sb's **economic/ financial/ social** situation/ circumstances/ position/ conditions
▶(a/ an) **normal/ unusual/ ideal** situation/ circumstances/ position/ conditions/ state of affairs
▶(a/ an) **favourable/ difficult/ exceptional/ desperate** situation/ circumstances/ position/ conditions
▶(a) **healthy/ satisfactory** situation/ position/ conditions/ state of affairs
▶(a/ an) **happy/ unhappy** situation/ circumstances/ position/ conditions/ state of affairs
▶to **create** a situation/ circumstances/ conditions
▶to **describe/ explain** the situation/ circumstances/ position/ things/ state of affairs
▶to **look at/ review** the situation/ circumstances/ conditions/ things

situation [C] (特定の時・場所での)状況, 事態, 情勢, 局面, 立場, 境遇, 状態 ◇You need to consider the present economic *situation*. いまの経済情勢を考慮する必要があるよ ◇In your *situation*, I would look for another job. あなたのような立場に置かれれば、私は別の仕事を探すでしょうね ◇He could see no way out of the *situation*. 彼にはその局面から抜け出す方法がわからなかった ◇You could get into *a situation where* you have to decide immediately. 即断せねばならない事態に陥るかもしれません

circumstance [C, ふつう複数で] (影響が及ぶ)事情, 状況, 環境 ; (人の)境遇, 暮らし向き[ぶり] ◇Police said there were no **suspicious** *circumstances* surrounding the boy's death. その少年の死を取り巻く不審な状況はないと警察は述べた ◇*Under the circumstances* (= considering the facts of the situation), it seemed better not to tell him about the accident. 事情が事情だから、事故については彼に教えないほうがいいと思えた ◇*Under no circumstances* should you lend Paul any money. 事情がどうあれ、ポールに金など貸してはならない ◇Grants are awarded according to your financial *circumstances*. 経済的状況に応じて助成金[奨学金]が与えられます ❶ circumstance [U] は「生活に影響を与えどうすることもできない状況・出来事」を指すフォーマルな語である. ◆a *victim of circumstance* (= a person who has suffered because of a situation that they cannot control) (状況の犠牲者、とばっちりを受ける人). ◆He had to leave the country through *force of circumstance* (= events or the situation made it necessary). (彼は成り行き上、祖国を離れなければならなかった).

position [C, ふつう単数で] (できること[できないこと]を左右する)立場, 境遇, 状態 ◇This put him and his colleagues in a difficult *position*. このことで彼と彼の同僚

→situation

は困難な境遇に置かれることとなった ◇The company's financial *position* is not certain. その会社の財政状況は不明だ ◇I'm afraid I am ***not in a position*** to help you. あいにく私はあなたを手助けする立場にはありません

conditions [複数で]（生活・労働・行動の）状況，環境，条件；（物理的な）状態，条件 ◇These neglected children are living ***under*** the most appalling *conditions*. 放置されたこの子たちは最もひどい環境下で生活している ◇They held a one-day strike to demand improvements in ***pay and conditions***. 彼らは賃金と労働条件の改善を求めて全日ストライキを行った ◇Beware of treacherous ***driving conditions***. 危険の潜む走行条件には注意すること

ノート **circumstances** と **conditions** の使い分け：
circumstances は人の経済状態を指す．conditions は人が食べる食べ物の質・量や住まい，または休日・疾病手当・快適な労働環境または，雇用主から与えられるものを指す．出来事が影響が及ぶ circumstances は，その出来事を取り巻く事実を指す．conditions はふつう天候などの物理的な事実を指して言う．

things [複数で]《ややインフォーマル，特に話し言葉》（一般的な）状況，事情，事態 ◇*Things* haven't gone entirely to plan. 全面的に計画されて生じた事態ではない ◇Hi, Jane! How are *things*?《インフォーマル》やあ，ジェーン．調子はどう ◇Think *things* over before you decide. 決定する前に状況をじっくり考えなさい ◇***As things stand*** at present, he seems certain to win. 現状では，彼が間違いなく勝つように思える ◇***All things considered*** (= considering all the difficulties or problems), she's done very well. すべての事情を考慮すれば，彼女はとてもよくやった ◇Why do you make *things* so difficult for yourself? あなたはどうして自分で事態をそんなに難しくするの ❶ things は，書き言葉より話し言葉で，また特に（政治・経済などよりも）個人的な生活について，いくぶんインフォーマルな文脈で，用いられることが多い．● *Things* are rather difficult at home.（家庭の事情はかなり苦しい）．● the political *situation*（政治情勢）．× political *things*．

the case [単数で] 実情，事情 ◇If that is *the case* (= if the situation described is true), we need more people. もしそれが事実なら，私たちはもっと人手が必要です ◇It is simply not ***the case that*** prison conditions are improving. 刑務所の環境が改善しつつあるなどということはまったくない ☞ **fact** (FACT)

state of af'fairs [単数で]（特定の時・場所での）状況，事態，情勢，局面，立場，境遇 ◇How did this unhappy *state of affairs* come about? どうしてこの不幸な事態が生じたのか ☞ **state** (STATE)

ノート **situation** と **state of affairs** の使い分け：state of affairs はほとんどthis と共に用いられる．state of affairs はまた present, current などの時間と関連する形容詞だけでなく，desirable, happy, sorry, shocking, sad, unhappy など，状況がいかに（よい[悪い]）かを表す形容詞と共にも用いられる．situation のほうがはるかに広い範囲で用いられる．

skill 名

1 skill・ability・talent・art・gift・flair・knack・aptitude
人が事を行う際のうまさを表す
【類語訳】能力，技量，力量，手腕，腕前，才能，素質，技術，技

法，術，要領，こつ，わざ，適性

文型&コロケーション
▶ a talent/ a gift/ a flair/ a knack/ an aptitude **for** (doing) sth
▶ (a) **great** skill/ ability/ talent/ gift/ flair/ aptitude
▶ a **useful** skill/ talent/ gift
▶ (a) **rare** skill/ ability/ talent/ gift
▶ a **special** skill/ ability/ talent/ gift/ aptitude
▶ (a) **natural** skill/ ability/ talent/ gift/ flair/ aptitude
▶ (an) **artistic** skill/ ability/ talent/ gift/ flair
▶ (a) **musical** skill/ ability/ talent/ gift
▶ (an) **entrepreneurial/ organizational** skill/ ability/ talent/ flair
▶ to **have** a skill/ an ability/ a talent/ the art/ a gift/ flair/ the knack/ the aptitude
▶ to **need/ lack** a skill/ an ability/ a talent/ a gift/ flair
▶ to **show** a skill/ an ability/ a talent/ a gift/ flair/ an aptitude
▶ to **demonstrate** a skill/ an ability/ a talent/ flair/ an aptitude
▶ to **acquire** a skill/ an ability/ the knack
▶ to **develop** a skill/ an ability/ a talent/ the art/ a gift/ a flair/ the knack/ the aptitude
▶ to **master/ perfect** a skill/ the art
▶ to **lose** a skill/ an ability/ a talent/ the art/ the knack

skill [C]（経験を通じて身につけた）能力，技量，力量，手腕，腕前 ◇We need people with practical *skills* like carpentry. 我々は大工職のような実用的な技術を備えた人を必要としている ◇The course focuses on management *skills* and customer service. その講座では，経営技術と顧客サービスが重点的に取り上げられます ❶ skill(s) は特定の種類の能力を表す形容詞・名詞の後にくることが多い．skill(s) はふつう経験や訓練の結果によって得られるものである．
☞ **skilled, skilful** (GOOD 4), **experience** (KNOWLEDGE)

ability [U, C]（技術的[知的]）能力；（生まれつきの）技量，力量，手腕，腕前 ◇Almost everyone has some musical *ability*. ほとんどすべての人が何らかの音楽的能力を持っている ◇Are you used to teaching students of mixed *abilities*? 能力混成クラスの生徒を教えることに慣れていますか ◇This programme is about discovering the natural *abilities* of each child. このプログラムは子どもたち一人一人の生まれ持った能力を発掘するためのものです ☞ **able** (GOOD 4)

talent [U, C]（生まれつきの）才能，素質 ◇Hard work is important but it is no substitute for raw *talent*. 努力は重要だが，手つかずの素質に代わるものではない ◇She showed considerable *talent* for getting what she wanted. 彼女は欲しいものを手に入れるのにかなりの才能を示した ◇He's a man of many *talents*. 彼は多才な人である
☞ **talented** (GOOD 4)

art [C, U]《特に書き言葉》（訓練・練習で得られる）技術，技術 ◇Painting is ***the art of*** reaching the soul through the eyes. 絵画は目を通して魂に行き着く芸術である ◇Letter-writing is a lost *art* nowadays. 手紙を書くことは，最近では失われた技能なのだ ◇Appearing confident at interviews is ***quite an art*** (= rather difficult). 面接で堂々としているにはかなりの技量がいる

ノート **skill** と **art** の使い分け：skill は両手を使ったり，人々・物事を管理[組織]する実際的・専門的な能力を指す．art は自己表現や他人との関わりに用いられる技術を指すことが多い．

◆ the *art* of fiction/poetry/painting/film (小説/詩/絵画/映画の技法). ◆ the *art* of conversation/communication/persuasion/negotiation/compromise/healing/listening/love (会話/コミュニケーション/説得/交渉/妥協/治癒/傾聴/恋愛術).

gift [C]《特に書き言葉》(生まれつきの)才能, 素質 ◇She has a great *gift* for music. 彼女には優れた音楽の才能がある ◇He has the *gift* of making friends easily. 彼には簡単に友だちを作る才能がある ☞ **gifted** (GOOD 4)

ノート talent と gift の使い分け: gift は人間関係における才能や人の役に立つ才能だけでなく, 特に人の芸術的能力について, 比較的文語的な文脈で用いられることが多い. ◆a *gift* for drawing/painting/writing/drama/improvisation/languages/music (デッサン/絵画/執筆/演劇/即興/言語/音楽の才能). ◆a *gift* for friendship/teaching/humour/calming people down/bringing people together/healing (交友の/教授の/ユーモアの/人を落ち着かせる/人々を団結させる/癒しの才能). talent は話し言葉では gift よりも頻繁に用いられる. talent はまた人々の芸術的才能についても用いられるが, ビジネスの腕前について用いるほうが一般的である. ◆a *talent* for business/computing/diplomacy/leadership/figures/governing/management/organization (ビジネスの/コンピューター操作の/外交の/統率の/数字を扱う/管理の/経営の/組織化の手腕).

flair [単数で, U]《特に書き言葉》(生まれつきの)才能, 素質;(流行・想像力を駆使する)センスのよさ ◇He has a natural *flair* for languages. 彼には語学の才能がある ◇She dresses with real *flair*. 彼女は服のセンスが本当にいい

knack [《ややインフォーマル》(生まれつきの[習得可能な])要領, こつ, わざ ◇It's easy, once you've got the *knack*. 一度こつをつかんでしまえば, それは簡単だ ◇He had a *knack* for picking winners. 彼は勝者を当てるこつを心得ていた

aptitude [U, C]《ややフォーマル, 特に書き言葉》(生まれつきの)才能, 素質, 適性 ◇She showed a natural *aptitude* for the work. 彼女はその仕事に生まれながらの才能を示した ◇They may ask you to do an *aptitude test* (= one designed to show whether sb has the natural ability for a particular job or educational course). あなたは適性検査を受けるよう求められるかもしれません

2 skill・expertise・competence・technique・know-how・prowess・proficiency・dexterity・artistry
長期間にわたる学習・練習を通じて, 物事をうまく行う力を表す
【類語訳】技術, 技能, 熟達, 熟練, 専門知識, 能力, 適性, 技法, 術, ノウハウ, 器用さ, …さばき, 巧妙さ, うまさ, 技巧

文型&コロケーション
▶ skill/ expertise/ competence/ know-how/ prowess/ proficiency **in** sth
▶ skill/ prowess **as** sb/ sth
▶ **to do** sth **with** skill/ expertise/ competence/ dexterity/ artistry
▶ **great** skill/ expertise/ competence/ technique/ proficiency/ dexterity
▶ **remarkable** skill/ expertise/ prowess
▶ the **necessary** skill/ expertise/ competence
▶ **practical** skill/ expertise/ technique/ know-how
▶ **technical** skill/ expertise/ competence/ know-how/ prowess/ proficiency

▶ **scientific/ technological** skill/ expertise/ competence/ know-how/ prowess
▶ **to have** the skill/ expertise/ competence/ technique/ know-how/ dexterity
▶ **to need/ lack** the skill/ expertise/ competence/ technique/ know-how
▶ **to demonstrate/ show** your skill/ expertise/ competence/ technique/ prowess/ proficiency
▶ **to use** your skill/ expertise/ know-how
▶ **to acquire** skill/ expertise/ competence/ technique/ the know-how/ proficiency
▶ **to develop** your skill/ expertise/ competence/ technique/ proficiency

skill [U] (訓練・練習で上達する)技術, 技能, 熟達, 熟練 ◇The job requires *skill* and an eye for detail. その仕事には技能と細部を見る目が必要である ◇She is a negotiator of considerable *skill*. 彼女はかなり熟練した交渉人である ☞ **skilled, skilful** (GOOD 4)

expertise [U]《特定のテーマ・活動・仕事における》専門知識[技術] ◇They have considerable *expertise* in dealing with oil spills. 彼らには石油流出処理のかなりの専門技術がある ◇We have the *expertise* to help you run your business. 私どもにはお宅の企業経営に役立つ専門知識がございます ❶ expertise は特に仕事・ビジネスの文脈で用いられる. ☞ **expert** (EXPERT), **expert** (IMPRESSIVE)

competence [U]《ややフォーマル》(特定の仕事に向くレベルの)能力, 適性 ◇She gained a high level of *competence* in English. 彼女は高い水準の英語能力を身につけた ◇The course is aimed at developing professional *competence* in language teachers. その講座は, 語学教師の専門的能力の開発を目的としている ☞ **competent** (GOOD 4)

technique [U, 単数で] (実際的な)技術, 技能, 技法, 術 ◇Her *technique* has improved a lot over the past season. 彼女の技術は昨シーズン大幅に向上した ◇He needs to work on his interview *technique* if he's going to get a job. 彼は就職するつもりなら, 面接技術に取り組む必要があるね

'know-how [U]《インフォーマル》(特定のテーマ・活動・仕事における)専門知識[技術], ノウハウ ◇We need skilled workers and technical *know-how*. 私たちは熟練した労働者と技術的なノウハウを必要としている

prowess [U]《フォーマル》優れた能力[腕前] ◇academic/athletic/sporting *prowess* 優れた学究能力/運動競技能力/スポーツ能力 ◇He was complimented on his *prowess* as an oarsman. 彼は競漕選手としての優れた能力を賞賛された ❶ prowess はほとんどの場合, 特に男性の身体的[知的]能力について用いられる.

proficiency [U]《ややフォーマル》(訓練・練習で上達する)技術, 技能, 熟達, 熟練 ◇The exercise is aimed at developing *proficiency*. その練習は技術の向上を目指している ◇A high level of oral *proficiency* in English is required for the job. その仕事には高い水準の英会話技能が必要です ☞ **proficient** (GOOD 4)

dexterity [U]《ややフォーマル》(手先の)器用さ, …さばき;巧妙さ, うまさ ◇You need manual *dexterity* to be good at video games. テレビゲームがうまくなるには手先の器用さが必要です ◇Desirable qualities for this type of career include charm, verbal *dexterity* and charisma. この種の職業に望ましい資質には, 魅力・言葉の巧みさ・カリスマ性が含まれる

↳skill

artistry [U]《特に書き言葉》(芸術家の)技術, 技能, 技巧
◇He played the piece with effortless *artistry*. 彼は卓越した技巧で難なくその曲を演奏した ◇They showed an appreciation of the beauty and *artistry* of the painting. その絵画の美しさと芸術的技巧が賞賛された

sleep [動]

sleep・doze・nap・snooze
目を閉じて精神と肉体の動きを活発にせず休息をとる
【類語訳】眠る, 寝る, 泊まる, うたた寝する, 仮眠をとる, 居眠りする, 昼寝する

文型&コロケーション
▶ to sleep/ doze **lightly**/ **fitfully**
▶ to doze/ snooze **gently**

sleep [自] 眠る, 寝る, 睡眠をとる;泊まる ◇Did you *sleep* well? よく眠れた ◇No, I *slept* pretty badly. いや, ろくろく眠れなかったよ ◇How did you *sleep*? よく眠れましたか ◇I couldn't *sleep* last night. ゆうべは眠れなかった ◇She hardly *slept* at all the following night. 彼女は次の日の夜, ほとんど眠れなかった ◇He *slept* soundly (= very well) that night. 彼はその夜, ぐっすり眠った ◇Let her *sleep* — it'll do her good. 彼女を寝かせておいてやれ—で元気になれるよ ◇She *slept* at her sister's house last night (=spent the night there). 彼女は昨晩, 妹の家に泊まった ◇I *slept* late (= into the morning), and didn't hear the news till midday. 私は遅くまで寝ていて, 正午になって初めてそのニュースを耳にした ❶sb is sleepingと言うよりもsb is asleepと言うほうがふつうである。しかし, どのように眠っているかを表す副詞を用いるときは, sleepingを用いる。◆'What's Ashley doing?' 'Sh! She's *asleep*.'(「アシュリーは何をしているの」「しっ. 眠っているよ」)◆The baby was *sleeping* peacefully. (その赤ん坊はすやすや寝ていた). ×The baby was *asleep* peacefully. また sleep が受動態で用いることができるのは, in や on などの前置詞が続く場合である。◆Her bed hadn't *been slept in*. (彼女のベッドには寝ていた形跡がなかった).
▶**sleep** [名] [U, 単数で] ◇I need to **get some sleep**. 私はちょっと睡眠をとる必要がある ◇I can't **get to sleep**. 眠れない ◇**Go to sleep** — it's late. 寝なさい—もう遅いから ◇He cried out *in his sleep*. 彼は睡眠中に大声を上げた ◇Did you have a good *sleep*? ぐっすり眠れましたか ◇I'll feel better after a **good night's sleep**. 夜ぐっすり眠れば気分はよくなるだろう

doze [自] (ベッドに入らずに)うたた寝する, 仮眠をとる ◇I *dozed* fitfully until dawn. 夜明けまで途切れがちにうたた寝した ◇She would often *doze off* in the armchair after lunch. 彼女はしばしば昼食後に肘掛け椅子でうたた寝することがあった
▶**doze** [名] [単数で] ◇I had a *doze* on the train. 電車でうたた寝した

nap (-pp-) [自] (日中に)うたた寝する, 居眠りする ◇Try not to *nap* during the day. 日中, 居眠りしないようにしなさい
▶**nap** [名] [単数で] ◆to have/take a *nap* 昼寝する

snooze [自]《インフォーマル》(日中にベッドに入らず)うたた寝する, 居眠りする, 仮眠をとる ◇My brother was *snoozing* on the sofa. 弟はソファで居眠りをしていた
▶**snooze** [名] [単数で] ◇I often have a *snooze* after lunch. 昼食後はよく仮眠をとります

slight [形] ☞ MINOR

slight・small・modest・little・marginal・minimal・negligible
程度がそれほど重大[深刻]でないことを表す
【類語訳】軽い, 取るに足らない, 些細な, ちょっとした, わずかの, 小さな, 適度の, 程よい, 妥当な, 手ごろな, 控えめな

文型&コロケーション
▶a slight/ small/ modest/ little/ marginal/ minimal **change**/ **difference**/ **improvement**
▶a small/ modest/ minimal/ negligible **amount**
▶a slight/ small/ little **error**/ **mistake**/ **defect**/ **accident**/ **problem**
▶a slight/ small/ minimal **chance**
▶a modest/ marginal/ minimal/ negligible **effect**/ **impact**
▶a small/ modest/ minimal **investment**/ **outlay**/ **sum**/ **charge**

slight (重大[深刻]ではなく)軽い, 大したことのない, 取るに足らない, 些細な;(程度が)少しの, ちょっとした, わずかの ◇I woke up with a *slight* headache. 軽い頭痛がして目が覚めた ◆The picture was at a *slight* angle. その写真は少し斜めになっていた ◇A *slight* breeze was blowing. そよ風が吹いていた ◇The damage was *slight*. 被害は大したことなかった ◇She takes offence at the *slightest* thing (= is very easily offended). 彼女はちょっとしたことで腹を立てる ◇There was *not the slightest* hint of trouble. 少しもトラブルの気配はなかった
▶**slightly** [副] 少し, ちょっと, わずかに ◇This author takes a *slightly* different approach. この作家は少し異なるアプローチの仕方をする ◇It will make the cost *slightly* higher. その分費用は少し高くなるでしょう ◇The door was *slightly* ajar. ドアがわずかに開いていた

small [ふつう名詞の前で] (重大[深刻, 困難]ではなく)取るに足らない, 些細な;少しの, 小さな, ちょっとした, わずかの ◇I made only a few *small* changes to the report. 私はその報告書に, ほんの少し, わずかな変更を加えた ◇Can I ask you a *small* favour? あなたにちょっと頼みがあるんですが ◇Everything had been planned down to the *smallest* detail. 小さな細かい部分に至るまですべて計画が詰められていた ◇It was *no small* achievement getting her to agree to the deal. 彼女から取引の合意を取りつけるなんて大した功績だったよ

> **ノート slight と small の使い分け**:両語とも変更・問題について用いられる。◆a *slight*/*small* adjustment/alteration/amendment/change/improvement/reduction/rise/variation (わずかな調整/変更/修正/変更/改良/縮小/上昇/変化)。◆a *slight*/*small* mistake/error/defect/flaw/blemish/discrepancy/problem/snag/accident (ちょっとしたミス/誤り/欠陥/欠点/汚点/矛盾/問題/障害/事故). 疾患・感情・感覚に影響を与えるものについては, small ではなく slight を用いること. ◆a *slight* cold/headache/movement/noise/touch (軽い[少しの]風邪/頭痛/動き/物音/接触), ◆*slight* discomfort/embarrassment (ちょっとした不快感/恥ずかしさ). 量・数については, slight ではなく small を用いる. ◆a *small* amount/number/quantity/degree/proportion/minority (少量/少数/わずかな量/少しの程度/少しの割合/ごく少数). 両語とも最上級で用いられることが多いが, 特に **slightest**

は否定文で用いられることが多い．◆He is, without the *slightest* doubt, the greatest living novelist. (彼は，まず間違いなく，現存の最も優れた小説家である). ◆I did not feel the *slightest* inclination to hurry. (私はまったく急ぐ気になれなかった).

modest (大きく[高価で, 壮大で]なく)適度の, 程よい, 妥当な, 手ごろな, 控えめな, 質素な, まずまずの, いくぶんな ◆There has been a *modest* improvement in the situation. 状況はいくぶん改善されてきた ◆He charged a relatively *modest* fee. 彼は比較的控え目の料金を請求した ◆She grew up in a *modest* little house in the suburbs. 彼女は郊外の質素な小さな家で育った ◆The research was carried out on a *modest* scale. 適度な規模での調査が実行された ❶ *modest*は特に目的・達成について用いられる. ◆a *modest* aim/achievement/ambition/goal/success (控えめな[まずまずの]目的/業績/野心/目標/成功). また，人々が使う[稼ぐ]金額について，◆a *modest* contribution/expenditure/fee/gain/investment/outlay/profit/sum (適度[妥当]な寄付/費用/料金/利益/投資/支出/収益/総額). 大して費用のかからない[壮大でない]建物について，◆a *modest* house/flat/villa (質素な家/アパート/田舎家). ◆*modest* premises (まずまずの敷地). 物事の大きさについて，◆a *modest* size/amount/quantity/scale/share/proportion (程よい大きさ/量/量/規模/分担/割合).
▶**modestly** 副 ◇*modestly* priced goods 手ごろな価格の商品

little [ふつう名詞の前で] 《ややインフォーマル, 特に話し言葉》(重大[深刻]ではなく)取るに足らない, 些細な；少しの, 小さな, ちょっとした, わずかの ◇I can't remember every *little* detail. 小さなこまごましたことまですべてを思い出せるわけではない ◇You'll soon get used to these *little* difficulties. こうしたちょっとした困難にはすぐに慣れるよ ◇We had a *little* adventure yesterday. 私たちは昨日, ちょっとした冒険をした ❶ *little*はそれほど深刻[重大]でない問題・出来事・謎について用いられることが多い. ◆a *little* error/mistake/defect/problem/argument/accident/incident/adventure/mystery/quirk/secret (ちょっとした誤り/ミス/欠陥/問題/議論/事故/事件/冒険/謎/奇抜さ/秘密).

marginal 《ややフォーマル》ほんの少しの[わずかの, 些細な] ◇The story will only be of *marginal* interest to our readers. その物語はほんのわずかの程度にしか読者の興味を引かないだろう ◇The difference between the two estimates is *marginal*. その二つの評価の違いはほんの些細なものだ
▶**marginally** 副 ◇He's in a new job but he's only *marginally* better off. 彼は新しい仕事に就いているが, 暮らし向きは大してよくなっていない

minimal (大きさ・量が)ほんの小さな[少しの, わずかの]；最小の, 最少の, 最低限の, 最小限の ◇The work was carried out at *minimal* cost. その仕事は最低限の費用で行われた ◇The damage to the car was *minimal*. 車の損傷はごく些細なものだった

negligible 《特に書き言葉》(考慮に値するほど)無視してよいほどの, 取るに足らない, ほんの小さな[少しの, わずかの] ◇The cost was *negligible*. その費用は無視してよいほど少ない ◇Tests found only a *negligible* amount of the chemical in the product. 試験の結果, その製品にはごく化学物質はごく少量しか見つからなかった ❶ *negligible*を用いる場合, ある程度の量は存在するが, 影響が出るほど十分ではないことを意味する.

slogan, slow

slogan 名

slogan・formula・motto・mantra・catchphrase
覚えやすく, 人々に考えを提唱するのにしばしば繰り返される語や短い句
【類語訳】スローガン, 標語, 宣伝文句, 決まり文句, モットー, 座右の銘, 呪文, 経, はやり言葉, キャッチフレーズ

【文型&コロケーション】
▶to **come up with** a slogan/ formula
▶to **coin/ adopt** a slogan/ motto
▶to **use** a slogan/ motto/ mantra/ catchphrase
▶to **chant** a slogan/ mantra

slogan [C] (政党・広告で用いられる)スローガン, 標語, 宣伝文句 ◇The crowd began chanting anti-government *slogans*. 群衆は反政府スローガンを唱え始めた ◇They came up with a catchy new advertising *slogan*. 彼らは受けそうな新しい宣伝文句を思いついた

formula (複 **formulas, formulae**) [C] 《ややフォーマル》(特定の状況で用いられる)定式文句, (定)式文, 決まり文句 ◇What are the correct legal *formulae* for this kind of letter? この種の手紙に適した正しい定式文句は何ですか ◇The prime minister keeps coming out with the same tired *formulas*. 首相は同じ陳腐な決まり文句を相も変わらず並べている
▶**formulaic** 形 ◇Traditional stories make use of *formulaic* expressions like 'Once upon a time...' 《ややフォーマル》 昔話では「むかしむかし…」のような定式表現が用いられる

motto (複 **mottoes, mottos**) [C] (人・グループ・機関の目的・信条を表現する)モットー, 標語, 座右の銘 ◇The school's *motto* is: 'Duty, Honour, Country'. その学校のモットーは「義務, 名誉, 国家」である ◇'Live and let live.' That's my *motto*. 「人は人, 自分は自分」これが私のモットーだ

mantra [C] (祈り・瞑想で繰り返し唱えられる)呪文, 真言, 経 ◇He was chanting a Buddhist *mantra*. 彼は仏教のお経を唱えていた

catchphrase [C] (政治家・芸能人が使って有名な)はやり言葉, キャッチフレーズ ◇It was PC Dixon who gave us the *catchphrase* 'Evening all!'. 「皆さん, こんばんは～」というキャッチフレーズをはやらせたのは, ディクソン巡査だった

slow 形 ☞EASY 2

slow・gradual・sluggish・measured
長時間かかる[続く]ことを表す
【類語訳】遅い, のろい, ゆっくりした, 緩慢な, ゆるやかな, 徐々の, 鈍行の, 徐行の, 漸次の, 鈍い, 気だるい

【文型&コロケーション】
▶a slow/ gradual **improvement/ change/ acceptance**
▶slow/ sluggish **progress**
▶(a) slow/ measured **pace/ steps**

slow (動作・行動が)遅い, のろい, ゆっくりした, 緩慢な；時間のかかる, ゆるやかな, 徐々の；(走行が)ゆっくり進む, 鈍行の, 徐行の ◇a *slow* driver/walker/reader 運転の/歩くのが/読むのが遅い人 ◇Oh you're so *slow*; come on, hurry up! まあ, 君はとてもゆっくりだねえ, さあさあ, 急いで ◇Progress was *slower* than expected. 進行具合

→slow

は予想よりも遅かった ◇Collecting data is a painfully *slow* process. データ収集はひどく時間がかかる作業です ◇She gave a *slow* smile. 彼女はおっとりとほほ笑んだ ◇I missed the fast train and had to get the *slow* one (= the one that stops at all the stations). 急行列車に乗り損なって、鈍行列車に乗らなければならなかった 反意 **fast, quick (FAST), rapid, fast (QUICK),** ☞ **slow (LATE)**
▶**slowly** 副 ◇Please could you speak more *slowly*? もっとゆっくり話していただけませんか ◇*Slowly* things began to improve. ゆっくりと事態は改善し始めた

gradual (長い時間がかかるので)ゆるやかな、徐々の、漸次の ◇a *gradual* change in the climate 気候のゆるやかな変化 ◇Recovery from the disease is very *gradual*. その病気からの快復には非常に時間がかかる 反意 **sudden**
▶**gradually** 副 ◇The weather *gradually* improved. 天気は徐々に回復した ◇*Gradually*, the children began to understand. 次第に子どもたちは理解し始めた

sluggish (書き言葉、しばしばけなして)(動作・反応・機能が)遅い、鈍い、のろのろとした、ゆっくりとした、緩慢な、けだるい ◇*sluggish* traffic 交通渋滞 ◇the *sluggish* black waters of the canal ゆっくりと流れる用水路の黒い水 ◇He felt very heavy and *sluggish* after the meal. 彼は食後、けだるく非常に重たい気分になった ❶ *sluggish* はまた、あまり活発でない[活気のない、繁栄していない]ビジネス・経済などに用いられる。◆a *sluggish* economy ((ビジネス))低迷する経済). ◆ Sales were *sluggish*. (売上げは低調だった).
▶**sluggishly** 副 ◇Traffic moved *sluggishly* along the London Road. 通行車両はロンドン通りをのろのろ動いた

measured [名詞の前で](制御されていて)ゆっくりとした ◇She replied in a *measured* tone to his threat. 彼女は彼の脅しに慎重に対応した ◇He walked down the corridor with *measured* steps. 彼はゆっくりとした足どりで廊下を歩いた ❶ *measured* はふつう人の話し方・歩き方に用いられる。

slump 動 ☞FALL1

slump・plunge・tumble・plummet
価値や水準が突然下がることを表す
【類語訳】急落する、続落する、暴落する

文型&コロケーション
▶to slump/ plunge/ tumble/ plummet **by** 100, 25%, a half, etc.
▶to slump/ plunge/ tumble/ plummet **from** 15,000 **to** 1,000
▶to plunge/ plummet **in** value
▶prices/ profits/ sales slump/ plunge/ tumble/ plummet
▶rates plunge/ tumble/ plummet
▶to slump/ plunge **dramatically/ suddenly**
▶to plunge/ tumble **sharply**

slump [自]((進行形はまれ))((ビジネスで))急落する ◇Profits *slumped* by over 50%. 利益は50%以上急落した 反意 **jump, surge (SOAR),** ☞ **slump (REDUCTION)**
plunge (特にビジネス) 急落する ◇Stock markets *plunged* at the news of the coup. 株式市場がクーデターのニュースで急落した 反意 **leap (SOAR)**
▶**plunge** 名 [単数形で] ◇a dramatic *plunge* in profits 利益の劇的な急落
tumble (特にビジネス) 急落する、続落する ◇The price of oil is still *tumbling*. 石油価格は依然として急落である

slump, small

反意 **soar (SOAR)**
▶**tumble** 名 [単数形で] ◇Share prices *took a tumble* following news of the merger. 株価はその合併のニュースの後で急落した
plummet (特にビジネス)暴落する ◇Share prices *plummeted* to an all-time low. 株価は最安値まで暴落した ◇Her spirits *plummeted* at the thought of having to meet him again. 彼にまた会わなければならないと思うと、彼女は気分が落ち込んだ 反意 **soar, rocket (SOAR)**

ノート ビジネスの文脈では、このグループの類語間にほとんど意味の違いはない。それ以上維持する材料がないために、価格は slump する。出来事がきっかけとなり、価格は plunge する。価格は tumble すると言う場合は、slump(進行形では用いられない)のように一度で大きく下落するというより、数回に分けて急速に低下する。×The price of oil is still *slumping*. plummet は最も急速ではないが、最も高い水準から最も低い水準への大きな下落を示唆することが多い。

small 形

small・little・tiny・miniature・compact・minute・microscopic
大きさ[数、程度、量]が大きくない[多くない]ことを表す
【類語訳】小さい、狭い、少ない、わずかの、小型の、ミニチュアの、こぢんまりした、微小の、微細の、微量の

small　　　　　tiny　　　　　minute
little　　　　　　　　　　　　microscopic
miniature
compact

文型&コロケーション
▶a small/ little/ tiny/ miniature **house/ town/ room**
▶a small/ little/ tiny/ miniature/ compact **car**
▶a small/ little/ tiny/ minute/ microscopic **detail**
▶a small/ little/ tiny **baby/ child**
▶a small/ little/ tiny **boy/ girl/ man/ woman**
▶small/ little/ tiny/ minute/ microscopic **particles/ organisms/ creatures**
▶a small/ little/ tiny **bit** (of sth)
▶a small/ tiny/ minute **amount/ quantity/ trace/ fraction**
▶**very/ quite/ relatively/ comparatively** small/ little/ tiny/ compact
▶**extremely/ really** small/ little/ tiny
▶**rather** small/ little/ compact

small (大きさ・数・程度・量が)小さい、狭い、少ない、わずかの;(同種のものに比べて)小型の、小柄の、ささやかな ◇Their apartment's pretty *small*. 彼らのアパートはかなり狭い ◇That dress is too *small* for you. そのドレスは君には小さすぎる ◇They're having a relatively *small* wedding. 彼らは比較的ささやかな結婚式を挙げる予定 ◇These shoes are too big. Do you have some in a *smaller size*? この靴は大きすぎます。もっとサイズの小さいのはありますか 反意 **large, big (LARGE)**
little [ふつう名詞の前で](比較・最上級はまれ) (大きさ・数・程度・量が)小さい、狭い、少ない、わずかの;(同種のものに比べて)小型の、小柄の、ささやかな ◇A *little* boy was standing on the doorstep. 小さな少年が戸口に立っていた ◇What a cute *little* baby! 何て可愛い小さな赤ちゃんなの ◇She

smell, smile

gave a *little* laugh. 彼女は少し笑った ◇I was a *little* bit afraid of him. 彼のことが少し心配だった ◇Here's a *little something* (= a small present) for your birthday. これはあなたへのお誕生日のささやかなプレゼントです 反意 **big**, **large** (LARGE)

> ノート **small** と **little** の使い分け：small は big, large の最も一般的な反意語である。little は特に ugly, nice, cute などの他の形容詞の後で、人・物事についてどう感じるかを示すために用いられることが多い。little はまた人・物事が大したことないと考えるときにも用いることができる。◆You'll feel a *little* sting. (少しちくっとします) ◆What a horrible *little* man! (何て恐ろしい小男なんだ)。littler, littlest の形はまれで、smaller, smallest を用いるほうが一般的である。

tiny (大きさ・量が)とても小さい、ほんの少しの ◇His room is absolutely *tiny*. 彼の部屋はほんとに小さい ◇She held the *tiny* baby in her arms. 彼女は腕にそのとても小さな赤ん坊を抱いた ◇Only a *tiny* minority hold such extreme views. ほんのわずかな人だけがそうした極端な意見を持つのだ ◇We come from a *tiny little* town in up-state New York. 私たちはニューヨーク州北部のちっぽけな町の出身です ◇There's only one *little tiny* problem with the booking. 帳簿の記入に、唯一ごく小さな問題点があります 反意 **huge**, **enormous** (HUGE)

miniature [名詞の前で] 《比較・最上級なし》(同種のものに比べて)ミニチュアの、小型の ◇It belongs to a rare breed of *miniature* horses. それは分類上小型馬の珍しい品種に属します ◇In the centre of the table was a bowl filled with *miniature* roses. テーブルの真ん中にミニバラで一杯のボウルが置かれていた ◇They expect their children to behave like *miniature* adults. 彼らは自分たちの子どもに、小さな大人のように振る舞うよう期待している ❶ miniature の型の植物・動物はふつう故意に小さく品種改良されている。

compact (小さくて運びやすくて)コンパクトな；(空間が狭くて)こぢんまりした ◇a *compact* camera コンパクトカメラ ◇The kitchen was *compact* but well-equipped. そのキッチンはこぢんまりしているが、設備は整っている

minute きわめて小さい、ほんの少しの、微小の、微細の、微量の ◇There were *minute* traces of the drug present in his blood. 彼の血液は微量の麻薬が検出されていた ◇The kitchen on the boat is *minute*. その船のキッチンはきわめて小さい

microscopic [ふつう名詞の前で] 顕微鏡でしか見えない、微小の、微細の、ミクロの ◇It is claimed that the fumes contain *microscopic* particles of carbon. そのガスには炭素の微細粒子が含まれていると言われている

smell 名 ☞ ODOUR

smell・scent・aroma・fragrance・whiff
人や動物が鼻を通じて感じることのできる主に心地よい物質
【類語訳】におい、香り、芳香

文型&コロケーション
▶a smell/ the scent/ an aroma/ the fragrance/ a whiff **of** sth
▶a **faint** smell/ scent/ aroma/ fragrance/ whiff
▶a **strong** smell/ scent/ aroma/ whiff
▶a/ an **pungent/ heady** smell/ scent/ aroma
▶a **fresh** smell/ scent/ fragrance
▶to **have/ give off** a smell/ a scent/ an aroma/ a fragrance/ a whiff
▶to **be filled/ fill** sth with a smell/ a scent/ an aroma/ a fragrance
▶to **catch** the smell/ the scent/ a whiff of sth
▶a smell/ a scent/ an aroma **hangs/ lingers/ comes/ wafts somewhere**

smell [C, U] におい、香り ◇There was a musty *smell* in the attic. 屋根裏部屋はかび臭いにおいがした ◇What a terrible *smell*! 何てひどいにおいなんだ ◇Do you like the *smell* of coffee? コーヒーの香りはお好きですか
  ▷**smell** 動 [他、受身なし]《進行形では用いない；しばしば can や could と共に》:Can you *smell* something burning? 何か燃えてるにおいがしない ◇I bent down to *smell* the flowers. 私はかがんでその花のにおいをかいだ

scent [U, C] (心地よいほのかな)におい、香り、芳香 ◇The air was filled with the *scent* of wild herbs. 大気には野生のハーブの香りが溢れていた
  ▷**scented** 形 ◇*Scented* soap いい香りのする石けん

aroma [C] (コーヒーなど飲食物の心地よい強烈な)におい、香り、芳香 ◇The *aroma* of fresh coffee wafted towards them. 淹れたてのコーヒーの香りが彼らのいるほうに漂ってきた
  ▷**aromatic** 形 ◇*aromatic* oils/herbs かぐわしいオイル/薬草

fragrance [U, C] (花・果物などの心地よい)におい、香り、芳香 ◇The flowers are chosen for their delicate *fragrance*. その花は繊細な香りが理由で選ばれている ◇The bath oils come in various *fragrances*. バスオイルはさまざまな香りのものが売られている
  ▷**fragrant** 形 ◇*fragrant* herbs/flowers/oils かぐわしい薬草/花々/オイル

whiff [C] 《ふつう of を伴って》(短い間しか続かない)におい、香り ◇He caught a *whiff* of her perfume as she passed. 彼女が通り過ぎるとき、香水の香りを彼は嗅ぎとった ◇She can't bear the slightest *whiff* of tobacco smoke. 彼女はタバコの煙のかすかなにおいにも耐えられない

smile 動

smile・grin・beam・smirk・simper
口角を上げて顔にうれしそうな表情を浮かべる
【類語訳】ほほ笑む、にこにこしている、にっこり笑う、満面の笑みを浮かべる、にやにや笑う

smirk   smile   grin
simper   beam

文型&コロケーション
▶to smile/ grin/ beam/ smirk/ simper **at** sb/ sth
▶to smile/ grin/ beam/ smirk **with** sth
▶to smile/ grin/ smirk **to yourself**
▶to smile/ grin/ beam **broadly/ widely/ happily/ cheerfully/ from ear to ear**
▶to smile/ grin/ smirk **slightly/ maliciously**

smile [自, 他, 受身なし] ほほ笑む、にこにこしている；ほほ笑んで…を言う [表す] ◇She *smiled* at him and he *smiled* back. 彼女は彼にほほ笑みかけたので、彼はほほ笑み返した ◇I had to *smile* at (= was amused by) his optimism. 彼の楽観主義にはほほ笑むしかなかった ◇The memory still made her *smile*. そのことを思い出すと彼女はやはりほほ笑みが出た ◇She *smiled* a smile of dry amusement. 彼

↪smile

女はちょっとおどけたような笑みを浮かべた ◇'Perfect,' he smiled.「完璧だ」と言って彼ははほ笑んだ
▶**smile** 图 [C] ◇He had a big *smile* on his face. 彼は顔に満面の笑みを浮かべていた ◇She gave a wry *smile*. 彼女は苦笑した

grin (-nn-) [自, 他, 受身なし] にっこり [にやり, にたり] と笑う；にっこり [にやり, にたり] と笑って…を言う [表す] ◇He was *grinning* from ear to ear. 彼は口を大きく開けてにっこり笑っていた ◇'Don't be daft,' he *grinned*.「ばかなことを言うな」と言って彼はにやにや笑った
▶**grin** 图 [C] ◇She gave a broad *grin*. 彼女は顔に満面の笑みを浮かべた ◇Take that *grin* off your face! そのにたに笑いはやめろ

beam [自, 他, 受身なし] 満面の笑みを浮かべる；満面の笑みを浮かべて…を言う [表す] ◇She was positively *beaming* with pleasure. 彼女は本当にうれしそうに満面の笑みを浮かべていた ◇'I'd love to come,' she *beamed*.「私も行きたい」と彼女は満面の笑みを浮かべて言った

ノート **grin** と **beam** の使い分け：人が beam するのは常にうれしい [楽しい] ときである。grin もうれしさ [楽しさ] を表すが，愚かに思って，恥ずかしがって，面白がって，さらには多少意地悪い人をからかってgrinすることもある。◆ to *grin* inanely/sheepishly/apologetically/ruefully/wryly/cheekily/wickedly/maliciously（うつろに/おずおずと/弁解がましく/悲しげに/顔をしかめて/生意気に/いたずらっぽく/意地悪くにやにや笑う）。

smirk [自]（けなして）（自分で満足して [人を密かにばかにして，他人が知らないことを知っていて]）にやにや [にたにた] 笑う ◇What are you *smirking* at? 何をにやにや笑っているの ◇He *smirked* unpleasantly when we told him the bad news. その悪い知らせを伝え聞くと，彼は嫌そうに笑った
▶**smirk** 图 [C] ◇She had a self-satisfied *smirk* on her face. 彼女は顔に自己満足の笑みを浮かべた

simper [自, 他]（書き言葉, けなして）間の抜けた笑い方をする；にやにや [にたにた] 笑う ◇She was nothing like the silly, *simpering* village girls back home. 彼女は故郷にいるばかで間の抜けた笑い方をする村の少女たちとはまるで違っていた ◇'You're such a darling,' she *simpered*.「あなたは本当にかわいい人ね」と彼女はにたにたしながら言った

soak 動

---

soak・dip・drench・wet・flood・moisten・dampen・douse・immerse
物を濡らす

【類義訳】ずぶ濡れにする，浸す，つける，濡らす，水浸しにする，湿らす，浴びせる，沈める

---

dip	wet	soak	flood
moisten		drench	
dampen		douse	
		immerse	

文型&コロケーション

▶to soak/ drench/ wet/ moisten/ dampen/ douse sth **with** sth

▶to soak/ dip/ drench/ douse/ immerse sth **in** sth

▶to soak/ drench/ douse/ immerse **yourself** in sth

▶to dip/ wet/ moisten/ dampen a **brush** (in sth)

▶to wet/ moisten **your lips**

---

soak

▶**rain** soaks/ drenches/ floods sb/ sth
▶to be soaked/ drenched sth with **blood/ sweat**
▶to soak/ douse sth in/ with **petrol**
▶to be soaked/ drenched **to the skin**
▶to **completely/ totally** soak/ drench/ immerse sth
▶to **thoroughly** soak/ drench/ wet/ moisten/ dampen sth
▶to **slightly** wet/ moisten/ dampen sth

soak [他, 自]（人・物を完全に）ずぶ [びしょ, ぐしょ] 濡れにする；（物を液体にしばらくの間）浸す，つける；浸る，つかる ◇A sudden shower of rain *soaked* the spectators. にわか雨で観客はずぶ濡れになった ◇His shirt was *soaked* with blood. 彼のシャツには血がぐっしょりついていた ◇If you *soak* the tablecloth before you wash it, the stains should come out. テーブルクロスを洗う前に液に浸せば，染みが浮き出るはずです ◇I'm going to go and *soak in the bath*. 風呂につかってくるよ ☞ **soaked** (WET)

dip (-pp-) [他]（物を液体にちょっとの間）浸す，つける，くぐらせる ◇He *dipped* the brush into the thick white paint. 彼はその刷毛をどろどろした白いペンキにつけた ◇*Dip* your hand in to see how hot the water is. 手をつけて，お湯がどれくらい熱いか確かめなさい

drench [他, しばしば受身で]（人・物を完全に）ずぶ [びしょ, ぐしょ] 濡れにする ◇We were caught in the storm and got *drenched* to the skin. 私たちは嵐に遭ってびしょ濡れになった ◇His face was *drenched* with sweat. 彼の顔は汗びっしょりだった ◇She *drenched* herself in perfume. 《比喩的》彼女は香水を浴びるほど付けた
☞ **drenched** (WET)

ノート **soak** と **drench** の使い分け：場合によって，両語とも使用可能。drench は特に大量の水が人・物に落ちてくる [押し寄せる] 場合に用いられる。soak は液体が物の下から上がってきてすっかり濡らす場合に用いられることが多い。物を意図的に水に浸す場合は，drench ではなく soak が用いられる。

wet [他]（物を）濡らす ◇*Wet* the brush slightly before putting it in the paint. 筆を絵の具につける前に，少し濡らしてください ◇He *wet* his finger to test the wind. 彼は指を濡らして風向きを確かめた ☞ **wet** (WET)

flood [他]（場所を）水浸しにする；（川が周囲の土地に）氾濫して浸水 [冠水] させる ◇If the pipe bursts it could *flood* the whole house. パイプが破裂すれば，家中が水浸しになるかもしれない ◇The river *flooded* the valley. 川が氾濫して谷間は水に埋没した ☞ **flood** (FLOOD 图1), **flood** (FLOOD 動)

moisten [他]（物を少し）湿らす ◇He *moistened* his lips before he spoke. 彼は話をする前に唇を湿らせた ◇Wash the wound gently with a piece of *moistened* cotton wool. 湿らせた脱脂綿で傷を優しく洗浄してください ☞ **moist** (WET)

dampen [他]（物を少し）湿らす ◇He *dampened* his hair to make it lie flat. 彼は髪をおさえるために湿らせた ◇Perspiration *dampened* her face and neck. 汗で彼女の顔と首は湿っていた ☞ **damp** (WET)

ノート **moisten** と **dampen** の使い分け：moisten のほうが dampen よりもいくぶん肯定的な語である。唇・土などのように濡らしたい物・本来濡れている物には moisten を用いる。紙・布・ブラシなどのように本来乾いている物には dampen を用いる。また物を主語にして be dampened by water/rain/sweat のように言うこともできる。

douse [他]（人・物に大量の液体を)浴びせる；(人・物に引火して燃えやすい液体を)かける ◇The horses are *doused* with buckets of cold water. 馬たちはバケツに入れた冷たい水を浴びせられる ◇The car was *doused* in petrol and set alight. その車はガソリンをかけられ，火をつけられた

immerse [他]《フォーマル》(完全に人・物を液体に)浸す，つける，沈める ◇The seeds will swell when *immersed* in water. 水に浸すと，種は膨らむだろう
▶**immersion** [名] [U] *Immersion* in cold water resulted in a rapid loss of heat. 冷水に浸すと，急激に熱が失われる結果になった

soar [動] ☞ RISE

soar・jump・surge・spiral・rocket・leap・shoot up
量[水準，数]が急速に増えることを表す
【類語訳】急上昇する，急騰する，急増する，跳ね上がる

文型&コロケーション
▶ to soar/ jump/ shoot up **in** price, number, etc.
▶ to soar/ jump/ surge/ rocket/ leap/ shoot up **(by) 10%, 2,000**, etc.
▶ to soar/ jump/ rocket/ leap/ shoot up **from 2% to 5%**
▶ **the price** soars/ jumps/ surges/ spirals/ rockets/ leaps/ shoots up
▶ **the cost** soars/ jumps/ surges/ spirals/ rockets
▶ **profits** soar/ jump/ surge/ leap
▶ **the number/ level** soars/ jumps/ shoots up
▶ to soar/ jump/ surge/ leap/ shoot up **suddenly**
▶ to jump/ surge/ leap/ shoot up **dramatically**

soar [自]《書き言葉》(価値・量・水準が)急上昇する，急増する ◇*Soaring* costs have made progress difficult. コストの急増で進行が妨げられた ◇Air pollution is set to *soar* above safety levels. 大気汚染は安全レベルを大幅に上回ろうとしている 反意 **tumble, plummet** (SLUMP)

jump [自]《特にジャーナリズム》跳ね上がる，急騰する，急増する ◇Prices *jumped* by 60% last year. 物価は昨年，6割急騰した 反意 **slump** (SLUMP)

surge [自]《特にビジネス》(価格・利益・率の水準が)急上昇する，急増する ◇Profits from cigarettes *surged* to $225m last year. タバコの利益は昨年，2億2500万ドルまで急増した 反意 **slump** (SLUMP), ☞ **surge** (INCREASE [名])

spiral [–ll–, 米でふつう –l–] [自]《けなして》(水準・量が)急上昇する，急増する ◇Prices are *spiralling out of control*. 物価が統制できないほど急騰しつつある ❶ *spiral* はほぼ常に否定的な意味合いで用いられる. *spiralling* debt/price/budget deficit (急増する負債/価格/財政赤字). *spiral down/downward* は，急激に減少することを指す. ◆Shares in the company continued to *spiral downwards*. (その会社の株は急落し続けた.)

rocket [自] (量・率が)急上昇する，急増する ◇They were forced to move out because of the *rocketing* crime rate. 急上昇する犯罪率のせいで，彼らは引っ越さざるを得なかった 反意 **plummet** (SLUMP)

leap [自]《しばしばほめて》 跳ね上がる，急騰する，急増する ◇The company saw pre-tax profits *leap* to £14.5 million in 2004. その会社は2004年に，税引前利益の1450万ポンドまでの急増を見た 反意 **plunge** (SLUMP)

,shoot 'up [句動詞]《ややインフォーマル，しばしばほめて》急上昇する，急騰する，急増する ◇Ticket prices *shot up* last year. チケットの価格は昨年，急騰した

ノート **jump, leap, shoot up** の使い分け：**leap** はふつう増加が肯定的なものとみなされる場合に用いられる．利益・株・価格は leap, jump すると言えるが，費用は jump するとしか言えない．**leap** はふつうより劇的な（驚くべき，著しい）増加を示唆する．◆Raw material costs *jumped* 1 per cent last month. (原材料費は先月，1%急増した．) ×Raw material costs *leaped* 1 per cent last month. **shoot up** は特に増加が否定的なものとみなされる場合に，よりインフォーマルな文脈で用いられる．◆Prices/charges/interest rates have *shot up*. (価格/手数料/利率が急上昇した．)

sociable [形]

sociable・social・outgoing・uninhibited・extrovert・gregarious・demonstrative
人が他人との時間を楽しむこと，堂々と他人に自分の感情を示すことを表す
【類語訳】社交的な，人付き合いのよい，愛想のよい，和やかな，外向的な，遠慮のない，無礼講の

文型&コロケーション
▶ a sociable/ a social/ an outgoing/ an extrovert/ a gregarious **person**
▶ a sociable/ a social/ an outgoing/ a gregarious **nature**
▶ an outgoing/ extrovert **personality/ character**

sociable《ほめて》社交好きな，社交的な，人付き合いのよい，愛想のよい，和やかな ◇She's a *sociable* child who'll talk to anyone. 彼女は誰にでも話しかける愛想のいい子どもだ ◇I'm not feeling very *sociable* this evening. 今夜はあまり人と付き合いたい気分じゃないの ◇We had a very *sociable* weekend (= we did a lot of things with other people). 私たちはとても社交的な週末を過ごした 反意 **unsociable, antisocial** (SOLITARY)

social《特に米，ほめて》社交好きな，社交的な，人付き合いのよい，愛想のよい，和やかな ◇He's not very *social* tonight, he just got dumped. 今夜は彼はあまり愛想がよくない，ふられたばかりだもの

outgoing 社交的な，外向的な ◇She was always cheerful and *outgoing*. 彼女はいつも陽気で社交的だった ◇I think the role needs a more *outgoing* personality. その役にはもっと外向的な個性がいると思う 反意 **introverted** (SOLITARY)

uninhibited 遠慮のない，無礼講の ◇His friends were a lively, *uninhibited* crowd. 彼の友人たちはにぎやかで遠慮のない連中だった ◇It was an evening of *uninhibited* fun. その夜は無礼講で楽しんだ 反意 **inhibited** (SHY)

extrovert 社交的な，外向的な ◇Ray was a much more *extrovert* character. レイははるかに外向的な人物でした 反意 **introverted** (SOLITARY)

gregarious《ややフォーマル，特に書き言葉》社交好きな，社交的な，人付き合いのよい ◇Hugh was a popular and *gregarious* man. ヒューは評判のいい社交的な人だった 反意 **solitary** (SOLITARY)

ノート **sociable** と **gregarious** の使い分け：sociable は好ましい意味合いの語で，人の性格・行動・気分に用いられる．sociable の反意語は，非常階的な語であるunsociableである．gregarious は中立的な語でその反意語は solitary である．これらの語は人の性格・行動に用いられる，人の気分

↳ sociable

social, soft, soil

には用いられない。×I'm not feeling very *gregarious* this evening.

demonstrative 愛情をはっきり表に出す ◇We were a very physically *demonstrative* family, giving lots of hugs and kisses. 私たちは、よくハグをしキスをする、体で愛情を非常にはっきりと表す家族だった

social 形

social・public・popular・civic
世間と一般の人々に関わることを表す
【類語訳】社会の, 社会的な, 公の, 公共の, 公衆の, 大衆の, 市民としての

[文型&コロケーション]
▸ social/ public/ popular awareness/ pressure/ support/ unrest
▸ social/ public/ civic responsibility
▸ social/ public issues/ values/ policy/ welfare
▸ public/ popular opinion
▸ a public/ popular outcry

social [名詞の前で] 社会の, 社会的な, 社会に関する；社会的地位に関する, 社会の中における ◇*social* changes/ problems 社会改革/問題 ◇Applicants should have a degree in the *social sciences* (= the study of people in society). 志願者は社会学の学位を有すること ◇The study found that health was strongly affected by *social class*. その研究で健康が社会階級の強い影響下にあることがわかった
▹ **socially** 副 ◇The reforms will bring benefits, *socially* and politically. そうした改革で社会的・政治的に利益がもたらされるだろう ◇a *socially* disadvantaged family (= one that is poor and from a low social class) 社会的に恵まれない家族

public [名詞の前で] 公の, 公共の, 公衆の, 大衆の, 一般の ◇Levels of waste from the factory may be a danger to *public health*. 工場廃棄物のレベルは公衆衛生への脅威である可能性がある ◇Why would the closure of hospitals be *in the public interest* (= useful to ordinary people)? 病院の閉鎖がなぜ公共の利益になるのだろうか

popular [名詞の前で] 公の, 公共の, 公衆の, 大衆の, 一般の ◇They won the largest share of the *popular vote*. 彼らは一般投票では最大の票数を獲得した ◇The regime was overthrown by a *popular uprising*. その政権は大衆が蜂起して打倒された
▹ **popularly** 副 ◇a *popularly* elected government 公選された政府

[ノート] **public**と**popular**の使い分け：多くの場合, 両語とも使用可能. ◆*public/popular* pressure/awareness/ opinion （大衆からの圧力/大衆の意識/世論）. **popular**はふつう一般の人々から出てくる考え・行動などに用いられる. ◆*popular* support （大衆の支持）, a *popular* movement/uprising （大衆運動/蜂起）. **public**はより一般的に, すべての人のための[についての, に関わる]事柄に用いられることもある. ◆*public* health （公衆衛生）. ◆the *public* interest （公共の利益）.

civic [ふつう名詞の前で] 《ややフォーマル》（町・都市に暮らす）市民（として）の, 市民に関する ◇The competition would be an opportunity to foster *civic pride* (= pride that people feel for their town or city). その競技会は市民としての誇りを育む機会となるだろう ◇Voting should be a matter of *civic duty*. 投票行為は市民の義務に関わる問題であるはずだ

soft 形 ☞ WET

soft・soggy・gooey・spongy・slimy・mushy・squishy
物や物質が濡れているために硬くないことを表す
【類語訳】柔らかい, しなやかな, ふわふわした, 柔軟な, ねばねばした, ぬるぬるした, どろどろした

[文型&コロケーション]
▸ a soft/ soggy/ gooey/ spongy mass
▸ a soft/ gooey/ slimy substance
▸ a soggy/ gooey/ slimy mess
▸ a soft/ spongy texture
▸ soft/ soggy ground/ bread
▸ soft/ slimy mud
▸ to go (all) soft/ soggy/ gooey/ mushy

soft （圧力で簡単に形が変わるほど）柔らかい, しなやかな；ふわふわした, ；（標準よりも）柔軟な ◇*Soft margarine* is better for you than butter or hard margarine. ソフトマーガリンのほうが, バターやハードマーガリンより体によい ◇He sank back gladly into the *soft* feather pillows. 彼はうれしそうにふわふわの羽毛枕に頭を沈めた ◇*Soft rocks* such as limestone are easily eroded. 石灰岩のような軟らかい岩は容易に浸食されます ◇It is a *soft cheese* with a hard rind. それは硬い表皮に覆われた柔らかいチーズだ 反意 firm, hard (SOLID).

soggy 《ややインフォーマル, ふつうけなして》（不快に濡れて柔らかく）びちゃびちゃ[ぐしょぐしょ, べちゃべちゃ]した ◇We squelched over the *soggy* ground. 私たちは水浸しの地面をピチャピチャと音を立てて歩いた ◇I hate it when cornflakes go all *soggy*. コーンフレークがすっかりべちゃべちゃになっているのは我慢ならない

gooey 《インフォーマル, ふつうけなして or ほめて》（非常に不快に[心地よく]）ねばねば[どろどろ]した, べっとり[ねっとり]した ◇The chocolate had gone all *gooey* in the heat. チョコレートは熱ですっかりどろどろになってしまっていた ◇He bought them a couple of lovely *gooey* Danish pastries. 彼はかわいらしいねっとりのデニッシュペストリーを二つ, 彼らに買ってやった

spongy （スポンジのように）ふわふわした ❶ **sponge**は洗い物・掃除に用いられる, 穴がたくさんあいた人工[天然]素材を指す. ◆This bread has a *spongy* texture. （このパンはふわふわした生地です）.

slimy 《けなして》ぬるぬる[どろどろ]した ◇The walls were black, cold and *slimy*. 壁は黒く冷たくぬるぬるしていた

mushy 《ややインフォーマル, しばしばけなして》（お粥のように）どろどろした ◇Cook until the fruit is soft but not *mushy*. その果物を柔らかくなるまで煮てください, でもどろどろにしちゃ駄目ですよ

squishy 《インフォーマル》（少し濡れて柔らかくて）ぐしょぐしょした ◇The leaves were soft and *squishy* underfoot. 足元の葉っぱは濡れて柔らかかった

soil 名 ☞ LAND 2

soil・mud・dust・clay・land・earth・dirt・ground・peat

solid

植物が育つ, 大地の上層部にある物を表す
【類語訳】土, 土壌, 泥, ぬかるみ, 砂煙, 土ほこり, 粘土, 地面

文型&コロケーション
- ▶ **dry** soil/ mud/ dust/ clay/ land/ earth/ dirt/ ground/ peat
- ▶ **wet/ soft** soil/ mud/ clay/ earth/ dirt/ ground/ peat
- ▶ **damp/ moist** soil/ earth/ clay/ dirt/ ground/ peat
- ▶ **heavy** soil/ mud/ clay/ land/ dirt/ ground
- ▶ **marshy** soil/ land/ ground
- ▶ **sandy** soil/ earth/ dirt/ ground
- ▶ **good/ rich** soil/ land/ earth/ peat
- ▶ **fertile/ infertile/ poor** soil/ land/ ground
- ▶ to **dig** the soil/ mud/ clay/ earth/ ground/ peat
- ▶ to **cultivate/ till/ fertilize/ drain** the soil/ ground

soil [U, C] (植物が育つ)土, 土壌 ◇Plant the seedlings in damp *soil*. 湿った土に苗木を植えなさい ◇Cutting down forest trees can lead to serious *soil* erosion. 森林の木々の伐採は深刻な土壌浸食を招くことがある ◇the study of rocks and *soils* 岩石と土壌の研究

mud [U] 泥, ぬかるみ ◇The car wheels got stuck in the *mud*. 車の車輪がぬかるみにはまり込んだ ◇Your boots are covered in *mud*. あなたのブーツは泥まみれだよ ◇They live in *mud* huts with grass roofs. 彼らは草で屋根をふいた泥壁の小屋で暮している ☞ **muddy** (DIRTY)

dust [U] 砂煙, 土ほこり ◇A cloud of *dust* rose as the truck set off. トラックの出発と共に砂煙が舞い上がった ◇They rolled in the *dust*, fighting. 彼らは土煙の中を転がりながら戦った ◇The workers wear masks to stop them from inhaling the *dust*. 労働者たちは砂ぼこりを吸い込むのを防ぐためにマスクを着用している
▶ **dusty** 形 ◇They plodded along the *dusty* road. 彼らは土ぼこりの上がる道をとぼとぼ歩いた

clay [U] 粘土 ◇Not much can grow in the wet *clay* here. ここの濡れた粘土で育つものはあまりありません ◇She moulded the *clay* into the shape of a head. 彼女は粘土で頭の形を作った

land [U] (特定の種類の)土地 ◇an area of rich, fertile *land* 肥沃で豊作をもたらす土地 ◇His family had worked the *land* for generations (= grown crops or raised animals on it). 彼の家族は代々その土地を耕してきた ◇They own a small plot of *land*. 彼らは狭い区画の土地を所有している ☞ **land** (LAND 1, 2)

earth [U] (植物が育つ)土, 土壌 ◇She put a couple of handfuls of *earth* into the pot. 彼女は数握り分ほどの土を鉢に入れた ◇In the air was the smell of freshly dug *earth*. 掘り返されたばかりの土の匂いが漂っていた ❶ *earth* は庭の[園芸用の]土を指すことが多い.
▶ **earthy** 形 ◇*earthy* colours/smells 土色/土のにおい

dirt [U] 《特に米》(固まっていないほろほろの)土, 土壌 ◇He picked up a handful of dry *dirt*. 彼は一握りの乾いた土を拾い上げた ◇Pack the *dirt* firmly around the plants. 植物の周りを土でしっかり固めなさい ◇They lived in a shack with a *dirt* floor. 彼らは土の床の丸太小屋で暮した

ground [U] 地面 ◇Dig a hole in the *ground* about ten inches across. 直径約10インチの穴を地面に掘りなさい ◇There was a small patch of *ground* at the side of the cottage. 田舎家の脇に小さな空き地があった ❶ *ground* は, 固まっていないほろほろの土については用いられない. ×a handful of dry *ground*.

peat [U] (涼しく湿り気の多い地域にある)泥炭, ピート(地表のすぐ下で腐りかけている植物から形成される柔らかい黒い[茶色い]物質で, 庭園の土壌を改良するのに使ったり, 燃料として燃やすことができる) ◇Dig some *peat* into the soil before planting. 植える前に泥炭を土に混ぜましょう ◇a *peat* bog (= the place where peat is naturally formed) 泥炭(湿)地
▶ **peaty** 形 ◇*peaty* soils 泥炭地

solid 形

solid・stiff・rigid・firm・hard
物が触れても柔らかくないこと, 曲げる[壊す, 動かす]のが難しいことを表す
【類語訳】固体の, 固形の, 硬い, 固い, 堅い

文型&コロケーション
- ▶ solid/ stiff/ rigid **material**
- ▶ a solid/ firm/ hard **surface**
- ▶ firm/ hard **ground**
- ▶ to **go** stiff/ hard

solid 固体の, 固形の ;(柔らかくなくて)硬い, 固い ;(曲げる[壊す, 動かす])のが難しくて)堅い ◇It was so cold that the stream had *frozen solid*. とても寒くて小川は固く凍ってしまっていた ◇The boiler uses *solid fuel* (= not oil or gas). ボイラーは固形燃料を使う ◇She had refused all *solid food* (= would not eat, only drink). 彼女は固形食をすべて拒んでいた ◇The door was *solid* as rock. ドアは岩のように堅かった 反意 **liquid** (MATERIAL), ☞ **solid** (MATERIAL)

stiff (容易に折れず[形を変えられず])堅い ◇a sheet of *stiff* black cardboard 一枚の堅い黒いボール紙 ◇Scrub away any residue with a *stiff* brush. 堅いブラシでかすをこすり取りなさい ❶人々[体の部位]は, しばしば寒さのために, 動かしてその筋肉が傷つくと, stiff になることがある. ◆I felt *stiff* all over. (私全いにたるところで凝っていた). ◆I've got a *stiff* neck from sleeping in a draught. (隙間風の通るところに寝ていて肩が凝った). ◆My fingers had gone *stiff* with cold. (寒さで指がかじかんでしまった). ☞ **stiff** (TIGHT)

rigid (曲げる[押して形を崩す])のが難しくて)堅い ◇Sandwiches are best packed in a *rigid* container. サンドイッチは堅い容器にとても上手に詰められていますね ◇The material is *rigid* and brittle. その原料は堅く砕けやすい ❶人々は, 恐怖・怒りなどで rigid になることがある. ◆His body suddenly went *rigid with fear*. (彼の体は突然, 恐怖で固まった). 反意 **flexible** (FLEXIBLE 2)

firm (ほめて) (柔らかくなくて)硬い, 固い ;(押して容易に別の形にできなくて)堅い ◇It was good to feel the *firm* ground underfoot. 足の下に固い地面が感じられてよかった ◇four large tomatoes, ripe but *firm* 熟しているが硬い4個の大きなトマト ◇Bake the cakes until they are *firm* to the touch. 手触りが堅くなるまでケーキを焼いてください 反意 **soft** (SOFT), ☞ **firm** (FIRM), **firm** (TIGHT)

hard (柔らかくなくて)硬い, 固い ;(押して容易に別の形にできなくて)堅い ◇Wait for the concrete to go *hard*. コンクリートが固まるまで待ちなさい ◇a *hard* bench/chair 堅いベンチ/椅子 ◇The ground is still *rock-hard*. 地面はまだ岩のように堅い 反意 **soft** (SOFT)

ノート **firm** と **hard** の使い分け: hard のほうが firm よりかたい. そこで, hard は「very hard (非常にかたい)」ことを意味することもある. ◆Diamonds are the *hardest* known

↳solid

mineral. (ダイヤモンドは最も硬い鉱物である)。また、hardは「too hard (かたすぎる)」ことを意味することもある。◆a *hard* mattress (硬すぎるマットレス)。firmは常に肯定的な語である。hard mattressは望ましくないが、firm mattressは好ましい。

solitary 形 ☞ QUIET 3, SHY

solitary・introverted・reclusive・withdrawn・antisocial・unsociable
人が他人と一緒にいるよりも、一人で時間を過ごすのを好むこと
【類語訳】内向的な、引きこもりがちな、無口、内気な、非社交的な、無愛想な

文型&コロケーション
▸ a solitary/ reclusive **figure/ man**
▸ to feel antisocial/ unsociable
▸ **rather** solitary/ introverted/ withdrawn/ antisocial/ unsociable

solitary (人・動物が)孤独癖のある; 独りでする ◇He was a *solitary* child. 彼は孤独癖のある子どもだった ◇Tigers are *solitary* animals. 虎は単独動物だ 反意 **gregarious (SOCIABLE)**

introverted 内向的な ◇His teachers perceived him as shy and *introverted*. 教師たちは彼のことを恥ずかしがり屋で内向的だと受けとめていた 反意 **outgoing, extrovert (SOCIABLE)**

reclusive 隠遁生活を好む、引きこもりがちな ◇They lived a *reclusive* life and were hardly ever seen. 彼らは隠遁生活を送り、ほとんど見かけることはなかった
▸**recluse** 名 [C] ◇He led the life of a *recluse* (= a reclusive person). 彼は隠遁生活を送った

withdrawn 無口な;(身に起こった出来事の結果として)内気、内向的な ◇The doctor noticed how *withdrawn* she had become. 医者は彼女がどれほど内向的になっていたかに気づいた

ノート **solitary, introverted, reclusive, withdrawn の使い分け**: solitaryとintrovertedはふつう人の性格を表す。それは人のタイプである。reclusiveとwithdrawnは人の行動を表す。そうせざるを選択したり、身に起こった出来事によってそうせざるを得なかったりする。

antisocial 《ふつうけなして》社交嫌いな、非社交的な、人付き合いの悪い ◇They'll think you're *being antisocial* if you don't go. 行かなければ、人付き合いが悪いと思われるよ 反意 **sociable (SOCIABLE)**

unsociable 社交嫌いな、非社交的な、人付き合いの悪い; 無愛想な ◇I was feeling very *unsociable*, so I didn't go to the party. あまり人に会いたい気分じゃなかったので、私はパーティーには行かなかった 反意 **sociable (SOCIABLE)**

ノート **antisocialとunsociableの使い分け**: これらの語は非常に似ていて、人の性格よりも行動を表す。しばしば特定の人に[特定の状況で]期待することとに対比して、一時的な振る舞い方を指して用いられる。◆We've got guests. Why are you being so *antisocial/unsociable*? (お客さんが来てるのよ。どうしてそんなに無愛想なの) ✕an *antisocial/ unsociable* man. antisocialは、人が故意にそのように振る舞っていて自分がそれに悩まされていることを示唆して、より否定的な語となりうる。

solution 名

solution・answer・key・resolution・remedy・way out・fix
問題を解く[困難な状況を処理する]方法
【類語訳】解決、解答、答え、対処法、秘訣、手がかり、鍵、救済策、逃げ道

文型&コロケーション
▸ the solution/ answer/ key/ resolution/ remedy/ fix **to** sth
▸ the solution/ answer/ remedy/ fix **for** sb/ sth
▸ a **simple** solution/ answer/ resolution/ remedy/ fix
▸ an **easy** solution/ answer/ remedy/ way out
▸ a **quick** solution/ answer/ resolution/ fix
▸ a **satisfactory** solution/ answer/ resolution/ remedy
▸ to **look for** a solution/ an answer/ the key/ a fix
▸ to **seek** a solution/ an answer/ a resolution/ a remedy/ a fix
▸ to **find/ provide** a solution/ an answer/ the key/ a resolution/ a remedy
▸ to **offer** a solution/ an answer/ the key/ a fix
▸ to **arrive at** a solution/ an answer/ a resolution

solution [C] (問題・難局の)解決策;(問題の)解決;(難問に対する正しい)解答 ◇Do you have a better *solution*? よりよい解決策がありますか ◇Will this lead to a peaceful *solution* of the conflict? これは紛争の平和的解決につながりますか ◇The *solution* to last week's quiz is on page 81. 先週のクイズの解答は81ページにあります

answer [C] (テスト・練習問題・クイズの)答え; 解答;(問題の)解決策、対処法 ◇Write your *answers* on the sheet provided. 与えられた紙に答えを書きなさい ◇The sender of the first correct *answer* to be drawn will receive £100. 最初に正答を引き出して送った人は100ポンドがもらえます ◇Do you know the *answer* to question 12? 第12問の答はわかりますか ◇The *answers* are at the back of the book. 解答は巻末にあります ◇This could be the *answer* to all our problems. これが私たちの問題すべての解決策になるかもしれません ◇The obvious *answer* would be to cancel the party. どう見ても対処法としてはパーティーを中止することだろう

key [C、ふつう単数で] (理解・達成・処理のための)秘訣、手がかり、鍵 ◇The *key* to success is preparation. 成功の秘訣は準備にある ◇The driver of the car probably *holds the key* to solving the crime. おそらくその車の運転手が犯罪解決の鍵を握っているだろう ◇*The key is*, how long can the federal government control the inflation rate? (特に米)鍵は連邦政府がいかに長くインフレ率を抑制できるかである

resolution [単数で、U] 《ややフォーマル》(問題・論争の)解決 ◇The government is pressing for an early *resolution* of the hostage crisis. 政府は人質事件の早期解決を迫っている ◇Hopes for a peaceful *resolution* to the conflict were fading. 紛争の平和的解決の望みは薄らぎつつあった ☞ **resolve (RESOLVE)**

remedy [C] 《ややフォーマル》(不快な[困難な]状況の)救済策 ◇There is no simple *remedy* for unemployment. 簡単に失業を救済する策はない ◇They advised him to exhaust all other *remedies* before applying to court. 裁判にかける前に、彼らは彼に他のあらゆる対策を検討し尽くすように助言した ☞ **remedy (CORRECT)**

,way 'out [C, ふつう単数で] 《ややインフォーマル》(困難な[不快な]状況からの)脱出方法, 逃げ道 ◇A local agreement is the only *way out of* the current crisis. 地域協定が現在の危機を脱する唯一の方法である ◇She had *taken the easy way out* by returning the keys without a message. 彼女は伝言なしに鍵を戻すという安易な策に出ていた

fix [C] 《インフォーマル》(安易な[一時的]な問題の)解決策 ◇There is no quick *fix* for the steel industry. 製鉄業のための手っ取り早い解決策はない ◇This is nothing other than a short-term political *fix*. これは短期的な政治的解決策でしかない ☞ **fix** (CORRECT)

sometimes 副

sometimes・occasionally・at times・from time to time・now and again/then・on occasion(s)・once in a while・every so often・off and on/on and off
あまり頻繁ではないが, 二度, 三度以上行われる[起こる]ことを表す 【類語訳】ときどき, 時には, 場合によって, 折にふれて, 時折, 断続的に

[文型&コロケーション]

▶to **appear** sometimes/ occasionally/ at times/ from time to time
▶to **seem** sometimes/ occasionally/ at times/ on occasion
▶to **happen** sometimes/ occasionally/ at times/ from time to time/ now and again
▶to **crop up** occasionally/ from time to time
▶to **wonder** sometimes/ occasionally/ at times/ from time to time
▶to **think** sometimes/ at times/ from time to time that...
▶to **stop** sometimes/ from time to time/ now and again/ every so often
▶**only** sometimes/ occasionally/ from time to time/ now and then/ on occasion
▶**every** now and again/ once in a while/ so often

sometimes ときどき, 時には; いくつかの場合, 場合によって ◇They played tennis and golf and *sometimes* went swimming. 彼らはテニスとゴルフをやり, 時には泳ぎに行った ◇*Sometimes* I look at him and wonder what is going on in his mind. ときどき彼を見て, 何を考えているのだろうと思う ◇It is *sometimes* difficult to know where to begin. どこから手をつけるべきか判断に迷うことがある

occasionally (定期的ではないが)ときどき, 折にふれて; いくつかの場合, 場合によって ◇We *occasionally* meet for a drink after work. 私たちは折にふれ, 仕事の後会って一杯やります ◇Only *occasionally* was there any doubt that they would succeed. ほんのたまに, 彼らが成功しないかもしれないという疑念が生じた ◇This type of allergy can very *occasionally* be fatal. この種のアレルギーはごくまれに致命的になる場合がある ☞ **occasional** (OCCASIONAL)

at 'times [フレーズ] ときどき, 時には; いくつかの場合, 場合によって ◇The work is difficult and *at times* dangerous. その仕事は難しく, 時として危険である ◇He could be quite maddening *at times*. 彼は時々かなりしゃくに障ることがある ◇*At times* (= in places) the road is little better than a forest track. 道路は所々, 森林の小道とほとんど変わらない

from ,time to 'time [フレーズ] (必ずしも定期的ではないが)ときどき, 時折 ◇The payment will be reviewed *from time to time* in the light of inflation. 報酬はときどき, インフレの観点から見直されることになります

now and a'gain/'then [フレーズ] (必ずしも定期的ではないが)ときどき, 時折 ◇He still rings me *now and again*. 彼はまだ, ときどき電話をかけてくる ◇*Every now and then* things happen to you in life that put everything else into perspective. 人生においては時折, 他のすべての事柄を大局的に見る事態が起こる

on oc'casion(s) [フレーズ] (普通にではなく)ときどき, 時折 ◇He has been known *on occasion* to lose his temper. 彼は時折, かっとなることで知られている ◇*On occasions* hospital doctors have to manage with little or no sleep. 病院勤務医はときどき, ほとんど, あるいは, まったく眠らずに事態を切り抜けなければならないときがある

,once in a 'while [フレーズ] (定期的ではなく)ときどき, 折にふれて; いくつかの場合, 場合によって ◇I feel I need to get away *every once in a while*. ときに休暇をとって出かける必要があるように思う

,every so ,often [フレーズ] (それほど定期的ではなく)ときどき, 折にふれて ◇He paced up and down, pausing *every so often* to look at his watch. 彼はときどき時計を見て立ち止まりながら, 行ったり来たりしていた

,off and 'on, ,on and 'off [フレーズ] (常にではないが)ときどき, 時折; 断続的に, 途切れ途切れに ◇It rained *on and off* all day. 雨は一日中降ったり止んだりしていた ◇She'd been learning Italian for about ten years, *off and on*. 彼女は約10年の間, 途切れ途切れにイタリア語を学んでいました

sophisticated 形

sophisticated・experienced・suave・urbane
世事にたけ, 社交上の振る舞い方を知っていることを表す 【類語訳】洗練された, 教養のある, 世慣れた, あか抜けた, 経験豊富な, 上品な, 都会風の, 丁重な, 礼儀正しい

[文型&コロケーション]

▶a sophisticated/ an experienced/ a suave/ an urbane man/ manner

sophisticated 《しばしばほめて》洗練された, 教養のある, 世慣れた, あか抜けた ◇Ben did his best to look *sophisticated*. ベンは洗練されて見えるように最善をつくした ◇Students have more *sophisticated* tastes nowadays. 今日の学生たちは, 比較的洗練された趣味を持っている 反意 **naive** (NAIVE)

experienced 経験豊富な, 経験を積んだ ◇She's very young and not very *experienced*. 彼女はとても若く, あまり経験を積んでいない ◇an *experienced* traveller (= sb who has travelled a lot) 経験豊富な旅行者 ❶ *experienced*は, 比較的好ましい意味合いのこのグループの他の語に比べて中立的である. 反意 **inexperienced** (NAIVE), ☞ **experienced** (EXPERIENCED), **experience** (KNOWLEDGE)

suave 《しばしばほめて》(男性が)洗練された, 上品な, 人当たりのよい(時に誠実とは思えない形での態度なども指す) ◇He gave his usual *suave* performance. 彼はいつもの洗練された演技をした ◇He plays a *suave and sophisticated* detective. 彼は人当たりのよいあか抜けた刑事を演じている

urbane 《書き言葉, しばしばほめて》(男性が社交上の言動を心

↳ **sophisticated**　　　　　　　　　　**sorry, sorry for sb**

得ていて)都会風の, 洗練された, 上品な, あか抜けた ；(くつろいで自信のあるように見えて)丁重な, 礼儀正しい ◇He was charming and *urbane*, full of witty conversation. 彼は魅力的で都会風で, 会話は気が利いていた

sorry 形

sorry・I'm afraid・bad・guilty・apologetic・ashamed
人々が過ちを不快で[失望させられるような]事のために, 悲しい気持ちを抱いていることを表す
【類語訳】後悔して, 残念ながら…, あいにく…, 後ろめたく思って, やましい, 恥じて

| I'm afraid | sorry | guilty |
| apologetic | bad | ashamed |

文型&コロケーション

▶ sorry/ bad/ guilty/ apologetic/ ashamed **about** sth
▶ to feel sorry/ bad/ guilty/ apologetic/ ashamed **that**…
▶ I'm sorry/ afraid **that**…
▶ to **feel** bad/ guilty/ apologetic/ ashamed
▶ to **look** guilty/ apologetic/ ashamed
▶ **very** sorry/ bad/ guilty/ apologetic/ ashamed
▶ **deeply** sorry/ apologetic/ ashamed
▶ **really/ quite/ rather** sorry/ bad/ guilty/ ashamed
▶ **almost/ slightly** guilty/ apologetic/ ashamed

sorry [名詞の前では用いない]《特に話し言葉》(過ちについて)すまないと[申し訳ない]と思って, 後悔して, 残念に思う(遺憾)に思う ◇We're very *sorry* about the damage to your car. あなたの車を傷つけてしまってとても申し訳なく思っています ◇She was *sorry* that she'd lost her temper. 彼女は短気を起こしたことを後悔した ◇If you *say you're sorry* we'll forgive you. 謝るなら, 許してあげましょう ❶*I'm/ We're sorry* は, 自分の過ちを認め, 人に許してもらいたいと思っていることを意味する. 謝るべきだと人に告げる場合の「謝る」は say sorry を使う. また, sb is sorry that… と表現する場合は, 起こったことについて, 人がそれを残念に思って, それが終わったことを意味する.

I'm afraid フレーズ 話し言葉 (不快な[失望させるような, すまないと思っている]ことを丁寧に伝えて)残念ながら…, あいにく… ◇I can't help you, *I'm afraid*. 残念だけど, 手を貸してあげられないんだ ◇*I'm afraid* we can't come. 悪いけど, 行けないよ ◇Is there any left?' *'I'm afraid not.*'「何か残ってる？」「あいにくと」 ◇'Will it hurt?' *'I'm afraid so.*'「痛くなりそうなの」「そのようだ」

bad〔動詞feelの後で〕(ややインフォーマル, 特に話し言葉)(過ちを)後悔して ◇She felt *bad* about leaving him. 彼女は彼を捨てたことを後悔した ◇Why should I want to make you feel *bad*? どうして私があなたを後悔させたいなどと思うだろうか

guilty (過ちについて)罪の意識のある, 後ろめたく思って, やましい ◇I felt *guilty* about not visiting my parents more often. もっと頻繁に両親を訪ねなかったことを後ろめたく思った ◇I had a *guilty conscience* and could not sleep. 良心がとがめられなかった ☞ **guilt** (GUILT)

apologetic (過ち・問題について)すまない[申し訳ない]と思って, 申し訳なさそうな ◇'Sorry,' she said, with an *apologetic* smile. 「ごめんなさい」と言って, 彼女は申し訳なさそうな笑みを浮かべた ◇They were very *apologetic* about the trouble they'd caused. 彼らは自分たちが引き

起こしたトラブルについてとても申し訳なさそうだった
➤ **apologetically** 副 ◇'I'm sorry I'm late,' he murmured *apologetically*. 「遅れてすまない」と彼は申し訳なさそうにつぶやいた

ashamed [名詞の前では用いない] (人・行為を)恥じて, 恥ずかしく思って ◇She was deeply *ashamed of* her behaviour at the party. 彼女はパーティーでの自分の振る舞いを深く恥じていた ◇You should be *ashamed of yourself* for telling such lies. そんな嘘をついた自らを恥じるべきです 反意 **shameless, unabashed, unashamed**, ☞ **shame** (GUILTY)

be/feel **sorry for sb** 動

be/feel sorry for sb・pity・sympathize・commiserate・feel for sb
他人の問題に悲しみの思いを向ける
【類語訳】気の毒に思う, 哀れむ, 同情する

文型&コロケーション

▶ to sympathize/ commiserate **with** sb
▶ to **really** feel sorry for/ sympathize (with sb)/ feel for sb
▶ **It's easy/ difficult/ hard (not) to** feel sorry for sb/ sympathize (with sb).

be/feel 'sorry for sb フレーズ (人のことを)気の毒[かわいそう]に思っている ◇*I'm sorry for* those poor boys, working in that horrible place. あんなひどい場所で働いているあの貧しい少年たちが気の毒だ ◇He decided to help Jan as he *felt sorry for* her. 彼はジャンのことをかわいそうに思ったので, 助けてやることにした ❶be/feel sorry for sb は, 特に日常会話や話し言葉で, このグループの他の動詞よりもずっと頻繁に用いられる. very/extremely/so sorry for sb とも, quite/rather sorry for sb とも, a bit/slightly sorry for sb とも言える. また, feel sorry for yourself とも言える. これは, インフォーマルで非難的な表現である. ◆ Stop *feeling sorry for yourself* and think about other people for a change. (自分を哀れむのはやめて, たまには他人のことに思いをはせなさい).

pity [他] (進行形なし) 気の毒[かわいそう]に思う, 哀れむ ◇I *pity* her having to work such long hours. 彼女がそんなに長い時間働かなければならないのはかわいそうだ ◇Compulsive gamblers are more *to be pitied* than condemned. ギャンブルから離れられない人は, 非難すべきというより哀れむべきである ☞ **pity** (SYMPATHY)

sympathize (英でまた -**ise**) [自] 気の毒[かわいそう]に思う, 同情する；同情を表す ◇I find it very hard to *sympathize* with him. 彼に同情するなんてとても無理だと思う ◇I think we can all *sympathize* with her dilemma. 彼女のジレンマには我々は皆同情できると思う ☞ **sympathy** (SYMPATHY), **sympathetic** (SENSITIVE 1), **empathize** (UNDERSTAND 2)

ノート **pity** と **sympathize** の使い分け：pity のほうが意味の強い語で, より深刻な状況で用いられる. ◆ 'I've got a terrible headache.' 'I can *sympathize*. I had one yesterday.' (「ひどい頭痛がするんだ」「わかるよ, 僕も昨日そうだったんだ」) ◆ I *pity* that poor child, left all alone without her parents. (両親もいなくてまったく一人でいるあの貧しい子がかわいそう). 人に sympathize する場合, その人がどう感じているかを理解し, 同じ状況にいる自分を想像できる. pity はこういった理解を示唆せず, 人に対する尊

敬の欠如や人よりも優っているという感情を示唆する。◆He *pitied* people who were stuck in dead-end jobs (= and was pleased with himself because he was not stuck in a dead-end job). (彼は将来性のない仕事に従事している人たちを哀れに思った。) I sympathize with you. と言う場合, 人々は感謝するだろうが, I pity you. と言う場合, 人々は嬉しくはないだろう。◆He lied to you again and again and you just kept on forgiving him. *I pity you*. (彼は君に何度も嘘をついたのに, 君はひたすら許し続けただけだ。哀れだね。)◆She gave me a *pitying* look, which just made me feel even worse. (彼女は哀れむような眼差しを向けてきたが, それで私はさらに惨めな気分になっただけだった。) pity は人を目的語にとるが, sympathize は sympathize with で人 (の置かれている状況) を目的語にとることができる。◆I can really *sympathize*. (よくわかります。)◆I can really *sympathize with* her. (彼女の気持ちがよくわかります。)◆I can really *sympathize with* what she's going through. (彼女が味わっている苦痛がよくわかる気がします。)

commiserate [自] (動揺・失望している人に) 同情する ◇She *commiserated* with the losers on their defeat. 彼女は敗北を喫した人たちに同情した ❶ commiserate with sb と言う場合は, ふつう I'm sorry. (お気の毒に), Bad luck! (あいにくだったね) など, 人に対して優しい [思いやりのある] 言葉をかけることを意味する。
▶ **commiseration** [名] (U, C) ◇I offered him my *commiseration*. 私は彼に同情の言葉をかけた ◇Commiserations to the losing team! 敗戦チームにねぎらいの言葉を

'feel for sb [句動詞] (ややインフォーマル) (人に) 心から同情する ◇I really *felt for* her when her husband died. ご主人を亡くした彼女に心から同情した ◇I do *feel for* you, honestly. 心よりお悔やみ申し上げます

source [名]

source・cause・origin・root・starting point・beginnings
物事が始まる点, もとを表す
【類義訳】根源, 源, 原因, 起源, 発端, 由来, 発祥, 原産, 根本, 根底, 本質, ルーツ, 起点, 出発点, 始まり, 起こり

文型&コロケーション
▶ (a) **common** source/ cause/ origin/ roots/ starting point
▶ a **possible/ natural** source/ cause/ origin/ starting point
▶ the **real** source/ cause/ origin/ roots/ beginnings
▶ the **true/ obscure** source/ cause/ origin/ beginnings
▶ a/ an **known/ unknown** source/ cause/ origin
▶ to **have** a source/ a cause/ origins/ roots/ a starting point/ beginnings
▶ to **identify** the source/ cause/ origin/ starting point/ beginnings of sth
▶ to **find** the source/ cause/ origin/ root/ starting point of sth
▶ to **locate/ discover/ investigate/ trace** the source/ cause/ origin/ roots of sth

source [C] (物事を手に入れる)根源, 源 ◇We need to obtain more energy from renewable *sources*. 私たち再生可能な資源からもっとエネルギーを得る必要がある ◇Your local library will be a useful *source* of in-formation. お住まいの地域の図書館は有用な情報源となるでしょう ◇The tiny window was the only *source* of light. ちっぽけな窓が唯一の光源だった

cause [C] (物事を起こさせる)原因 ◇Unemployment is a major *cause* of poverty. 失業が貧困の主因である ◇There was discussion about the fire and its likely *cause*. 火事とその推定原因に関して議論があった ◇He died of natural *causes*. 彼は自然死した ☞ **cause** (CAUSE)

origin [C, U] (または **origins** [複数形]) (特に書き言葉) (物事が始まる)起源, 源, (考え・兆候・段階の)発端, 由来, 発祥, 原産, 原因 ◇The *origin* of the word remains obscure. その語源ははっきりしないままである ◇Most coughs are viral *in origin* (= caused by a virus). ほとんどの咳はウイルスが原因である ◇Bottles are labelled by country *of origin*. ボトルには原産国によってラベルが貼られている ◇The TV series examines the *origins* of life on earth. そのテレビシリーズでは地球上の生命の起源が検証されている ◇This particular custom has its *origins* in Wales. この独特の慣習はウェールズに端を発している

root [C] (特に書き言葉) (問題・困難な状況などの)根源, 原因; (物事の)起源, 根本, 根底, 本質, ルーツ ◇We have to get to *the root of the problem*. 我々はその問題の根本に行き着かねばならない ◇What *lies at the root of* his troubles is a sense of insecurity. 彼の悩みの根源にあるのは不安感だ ◇What would you say was the *root cause* of the problem? 問題の根本的な原因は何だったとお思いですか ◇The two languages share a common *root*. その二つの言語は同じ起源を持つ ◇Flamenco has its *roots* in Arabic music. フラメンコはアラビア音楽にその起源がある

ノート **origins** と **root** の使い分け：場合によって両語も使用可能。◆The custom has its *origins/roots* in Wales. (その慣習はウェールズに端を発する)。両語とも cause (原因) を意味することができるが, 少し用法が異なる。問題の原因については root を用いること。✕We have to get to the *origin* of the problem. 物事がいつ, どこで, どのように始まったかについては origin を用いる。◆the *origin* of life/species/the universe (生命/種/宇宙の起源)。✕the *roots* of life/species/the universe. root はしばしば, 情緒的[文化的]な愛着を示唆する。origin はより科学的である。ふつう人の cultural roots (文化的起源) 以外は, 人の social origins (社会的起源) のように用いられる。☞ **origin, roots** (FAMILY 3)

'starting point [C] (議論・過程の)起点, 出発点 ◇The TV documentary served as a useful *starting point* for our discussion. そのテレビドキュメンタリー番組は, 我々の議論の有益な出発点として役立った ◇They reached the same conclusion from different *starting points*. 彼らは異なる出発点から始めて同じ結論に達した ❶ *starting point* は, convenient, good, suitable, useful といった肯定的な形容詞の後で用いられることが多い。

beginnings [複数で] (特に書き言葉) (考え・兆候・段階の) 起源, 始まり, 起こり, 発端, 由来, 発祥, 原産 ◇Did democracy have its *beginnings* in ancient Greece? 民主主義の発祥は古代ギリシャだったのですか ◇From these small *beginnings* it grew into the vast company we know today. こうした小さな始まりから, この会社は, 今日我々が知る大会社に成長した ❶ *beginnings* はふつう, sth had its beginnings in... の形で用いられる。また humble, modest, simple, small の後に置いて物事がどのように変化したかを言うような場合に用いられる。

special 形 ☞ UNIQUE

special・exceptional・particular・extraordinary
物事や出来事が通常[普通]ではないことを表す
【類語訳】特別の, 特殊な, 特異な, 例外的な, 異例の, 際立った, 格別の, 臨時の

▷文型&コロケーション
- a special/ an exceptional **case/ situation**
- special/ exceptional **circumstances**
- exceptional/ extraordinary **costs/ losses/ profit/ items**
- a special/ an extraordinary **meeting**
- a special/ particular **threat**
- of special/ particular **concern/ importance/ interest**
- to take special/ particular **notice** of sb/ sth

special [ふつう名詞の前で] 特別の, 特殊な; 尋常でない, 特異な ◇*Journalists were given no special privileges.* ジャーナリストには何の特権も与えられなかった ◇*The oil industry was treated as a special case.* 石油産業は特例として扱われた ◇*There really is something special about the place.* その場所には何か本当に特別なものがある 反意 **ordinary** (NORMAL), ➡ **special** (UNIQUE)
exceptional 例外的な, 異例の, 尋常でない; (費用・収入が)特別の ◇*The deadline can be extended only in exceptional circumstances.* 締め切りは例外的な状況下でしか延長される可能性はありません ◇*Exceptional items in the last financial year increased profits by $25 million.* 前営業年度における特別項目は, 利益を2500万ドル押し上げた 反意 **normal** (NORMAL)
➤ **exceptionally** 副 ◇*There was an exceptionally high tide.* 異例の高さの高潮が生じた ◇*Exceptionally, the director may override the decision of the committee.* 異例ですが, その理事は委員会の決定を無視するかもしれません
particular [名詞の前で] いつも[ふだん]以上の, 際立った, 格別の, 特別の ◇*The high inflation rates were of particular concern.* 高いインフレ率がいつも以上に懸念された ◇*The chemicals pose a particular threat to water quality.* これらの化学物質は水質に際立った脅威を及ぼす
➤ **particularly** 副 ◇*Traffic is bad, particularly in the downtown area.* 車は, 特に繁華街の地域で混んでいる ◇'Did you enjoy it?' 'No, *not particularly* (= not very much).' 「楽しみましたか」「いや, 特に」 ◇*The lecture was not particularly interesting.* 講義は格別面白いものではなかった
extraordinary [名詞の前で] 《フォーマル》臨時の ◇*The club convened an extraordinary general meeting.* そのクラブは臨時総会を開催した

speculation 名 ☞ CONCLUSION

speculation・assumption・guess・presumption・presupposition・conjecture・guesswork
必ずしもすべてが事実に基づいてはいない考え
【類語訳】憶測, 推測, 想定, 仮定, 前提, 推量, 当て推量, 推定

▷文型&コロケーション
- speculation/ an assumption/ a guess/ a presumption/ presupposition/ conjecture/ guesswork **about** sth
- speculation/ the assumption/ a guess/ the presumption/ the presupposition/ the conjecture **that**...
- (a) **general** speculation/ assumption/ presumption/ conjecture
- (a) **mere** speculation/ guess/ presumption/ conjecture/ guesswork
- **pure/ sheer** speculation/ conjecture/ guesswork
- a **basic** assumption/ presumption/ presupposition
- to **make** an assumption/ a guess/ a presumption/ a conjecture
- to **base sth on** an assumption/ a guess/ a presumption/ presupposition

speculation [U, C] (事実を知らずに行う)憶測, 推測 ◇*There has been increasing speculation over the future of the monarchy.* 君主制の将来に関する憶測が高じてきている ◇*She dismissed the newspaper report as pure speculation.* 彼女はその新聞報道を単なる憶測だとしてはねつけた ◇*Speculation was rife* (= there was a lot of speculation) *that he was having an affair.* 彼が浮気をしているという憶測が広まっていた ◇*Our speculations proved correct.* 我々の推測が正しいとわかった ☞ **speculate** (SAY 3)
assumption [C] (証拠のない)憶測, 想定, 仮定, 前提 ◇*There is a general but false assumption that intelligent people do better in life.* 頭のよい人は人生で成功を収めるという広く誤った憶測がなされている ◇*We are working on the assumption that about 50 people will turn up.* 私たちは, 約50人がいらっしゃるという想定のもとで作業しています ☞ **assume** (SUPPOSE)
guess [C] (事実を確かめずに行う)推測, 推量, 憶測, 当て推量 ◇*Go on! Have a guess!* 《英》ほら. 当ててごらん ◇*Take a guess!* 《米》当ててごらん ◇*Who do you think I saw yesterday? I'll give you three guesses.* 昨日, 誰に会ったと思う. 3回で当ててごらん ◇*My guess is that not many people will turn out today.* 私の推測では, 今日はあまり多くの人は集まらないだろうと思います ◇*At a guess, there were about 40 people there.* 推測では, 約40人がそこにいたとのことです ◇*It's probably about 300 kilometres away, but that's just a rough guess.* たぶん約300キロは離れているでしょうが, それは大ざっぱな推測にすぎません ☞ **guess** (ESTIMATE 動)
presumption [C] 《ややフォーマル》 (真実であるとの)推定, 仮定, 推測 ◇*The general presumption is that the doctor knows best.* 一般的な推測だが, その医師は最善策を心得ているね ❶法律英語では, presumption [U, C]は, まだ証明されていない[確かではない]が, 物事を真実であると仮定する行為を指す. ◆*Everyone is entitled to the presumption of innocence until they are proved guilty.* (《法律》有罪と立証されるまで, 誰もが推定無罪の権利がある). ☞ **presume** (SAY 3), **presume** (SUPPOSE)
presupposition [C, U] 《フォーマル, しばしばけなして》 (議論の根拠として用いる)前提; (真実であるとの)仮定 ◇*Try to clear your mind of any presuppositions.* 頭からいかな前提もなくすようにしなさい ◇*These theories are based on presupposition and guesswork.* これらの説は仮定と当て推量に基づいている ☞ **presuppose** (SAY 3)
conjecture [C, U] 《ややフォーマル》 (確実な知識に基づかない)推測, 推量, 憶測 ◇*The truth of this conjecture was confirmed the next day.* この推測が正しかったことの確証が翌日得られた ◇*What was going on in the killer's mind is a matter for conjecture.* その殺人犯の胸中に去来していたことは推測の域を出ない事柄である

guesswork [U]（確信のない）当て推量 ◇A combination of *guesswork* and luck led them to the right address. 運とあてずっぽうの両者が合わさって、彼らは正しい住所にたどり着いた

speech 名

speech・lecture・address・talk・sermon
聴衆相手のしゃべりを表す
【類語訳】スピーチ、演説、講演、講義、式辞、話、談話、説教、訓話

[文型&コロケーション]
- a **long/ short** speech/ lecture/ address/ talk/ sermon
- a **public** speech/ lecture/ address/ talk
- a/ an **inaugural/ farewell/ keynote** speech/ lecture/ address
- a **formal** speech/ lecture/ talk
- an **informal** lecture/ talk
- to **give/ deliver** a speech/ a lecture/ an address/ a talk/ a sermon
- to **hear** a speech/ a lecture/ an address/ a talk/ a sermon
- to **attend/ go to** a lecture/ talk
- to **write/ prepare** a speech/ a lecture/ an address/ a talk/ a sermon

speech [C]（正式な）スピーチ、演説、講演 ◇Several people made *speeches* at the wedding. 数人の人たちが結婚式でスピーチをした
lecture [C]（特定のテーマに関する）講義、演義 ◇He gave a very interesting and informative *lecture* on the Roman army. 彼はローマ軍に関する非常に興味深く有益な講演を行った ◇a series of *lectures* 一連の講義 ◇a lecture room/hall 講義室／講堂 ◇a *lecture* theatre《英》階段講堂 ☞ **lecture** (TEACH)
address [C]（正式な）演説、式辞、講演 ◇a televised presidential *address* テレビ放送された大統領演説

ノート **speech** と **address** の使い分け：speech は公的あるいは私的な場で行われる。address は常に公的なものである。✕He gave an *address* at the wedding.

talk [C]（あるテーマに関するインフォーマルな）話、談話 ◇She gave an interesting *talk* on her visit to China. 彼女は自分の中国訪問の面白い話をした
sermon [C]（宗教指導者による）説教、訓話 ◇He preached a long *sermon* against the war. 彼は戦争に反対する長い説教を行った

speed 名

speed・velocity・haste・rapidity
物事の生起［移動、実行］の敏速さを表す
【類語訳】速さ、速度、急ぎ、焦り

[文型&コロケーション]
- **increasing** speed/ velocity/ rapidity
- **great** speed/ haste/ rapidity
- **maximum/ constant** speed/ velocity
- **reckless** speed/ haste
- **alarming/ amazing/ bewildering/ remarkable** speed/ rapidity
- to **measure** speed/ velocity

speed [U]（スピードの）速いこと；高速、速さ ◇The accident was due to excessive *speed*. その事故はスピードの出しすぎによるものであった ◇She was overtaken by the *speed of events* (= things happened more quickly than she expected). 彼女は出来事の起こる速さについて行けなかった ◇The car flashed past them *at speed*.《フォーマル》その車は高速であっという間に彼らのそばを通過した ☞ **speedy** (QUICK)
velocity [U, C]《専門語 or フォーマル》（特定の方向に向かう）速さ、速度；高速 ◇to gain/lose *velocity* 速度を増す／失う ◇Light travels at a constant *velocity*. 光は等速で移動する ◇Jaguars can move with an astonishing *velocity*. ジャガーは驚くほどの速さで走れます
haste [U]《フォーマル》（十分な時間がないことによる）急ぎ、焦り ◇In her *haste* to finish on time she made a number of mistakes. 時間どおりに終わらせようと急いで、彼女はいくつもミスを犯した ◇The letter had clearly been written *in haste*. その手紙が慌てて書かれたのは明らかだった ☞ **hasten** (HURRY), **hasty** (QUICK)
rapidity [U]（生起・変化の）速いこと、急速さ、速さ ◇These changes happen with extreme *rapidity*. これらの変化の速度はきわめて速い ☞ **rapid** (QUICK)

spin 動

spin・turn・circle・rotate・revolve・roll・orbit・whirl・go around/round (sth)・swivel・twist・twirl
中心点の周りを動く［動くようにする］
【類語訳】回転する、回る、旋回する、転がる、ぐるぐる回る、渦を巻く

[文型&コロケーション]
- to spin/ turn/ circle/ rotate/ revolve/ roll/ orbit/ whirl **around/ round** (sth)
- to spin/ turn/ rotate/ revolve/ swivel **on** sth
- to spin/ turn/ rotate/ whirl **faster (and faster)**
- to spin/ turn/ rotate **rapidly/ quickly**
- to spin/ turn/ circle/ rotate/ revolve/ orbit/ twist/ twirl (sth) **slowly**

spin［自, 他］（素早く）回転する、回る；回転させる、回す ◇The dancers *spun* round and round. ダンサーたちはぐるぐる回った ◇The Earth *spins* around a central axis. 地球は中心軸の周りを回転する ◇My *head was spinning* (= it felt as if it was spinning round). 頭がくらくらしているような感じだった ◇She *spun* the roulette wheel one last time. 彼女は最後にもう一度ルーレット盤を回した ◇*Spin* your partner around (= in dancing). パートナーを回転させてあげて踊ってください ❶ spin やこのグループの他の動詞と共に、特に《英》では round が、《米》では around が用いられる。
▶**spin** 名 [C, U] ◇The dance was full of twists and *spins*. そのダンスには、ひねりやスピンがいっぱいあった ◇He lost everything on the *spin* of a roulette wheel. 彼はルーレット盤のその一回転ですべてを失った

turn［自, 他］（中心点の周りを）回転する、回る；回転させる、回す ◇The blades of the helicopter were *turning* slowly. ヘリコプターの翼はゆっくり回転していた ◇He *turned* the key in the lock. 彼は鍵穴に鍵を差し込んで回した ◇She *turned* the steering wheel as far as it would go. 彼女はハンドルを切れるかぎりいっぱいに切った
▶**turn** 名 [C] ◇Give the handle a few *turns*. 取っ手

↪spin

を2度, 3度回してください ◇Rotate the image through a quarter turn. 画像を90度回転させてください

circle [自, 他]（空中で円を描いて）旋回する,（周りを）回る ◇Seagulls circled around the boat. カモメたちが船の周りを旋回した ◇A small aircraft was circling overhead. 小さな航空機が頭上を旋回していた ◇The bell rang and the two boxers began circling each other. ゴングが鳴り, 二人のボクサーは互いの周りを回り始めた

rotate [自, 他]（固定した中心点の周りを）回転する, 回る；回転させる, 回す ◇Make sure that the propellor can rotate freely. プロペラが自在に回転するかどうか確かめてください ◇The earth takes 24 hours to rotate on its axis. 地球は24時間かけて地軸を中心に回転する ◇Rotate the wheel through 180 degrees. ハンドルを180度回してください

▶**rotation** 名 [U, C] ◇The length of a day is based on the rotation of the earth on its axis. 1日の長さは地軸を中心にした地球の回転に基づいている ◇This switch controls the number of rotations per minute. このスイッチは毎分の回転数を調整するものです

revolve [自]（ややフォーマル）（中心点の周りを）回転する, 回る ◇People used to think that the sun revolved around the earth. かつて人々は太陽が地球の周りを回ると考えていた ◇She saw him heading towards the revolving door. 彼女は彼が回転ドアに向かって歩いていくのを見た ◇The world doesn't revolve around you, you know.（比喩的）世界は君を中心に回ってはいないことはわかってるだろ

▶**revolution** 名 [C, U] ◇The disk rotates at up to 500 revolutions per minute. このディスクは毎分最大500回転する ◇The revolution of the earth around the sun takes one year. 太陽の周りを地球が回るのに1年かかる

ノート **rotate** と **revolve** の使い分け：物が rotate する場合, ふつうそれ自体の中心[軸]の周りを移動する. 物が revolve する場合, ふつうそれの外にある点の周りを移動するが, rotate と同じように用いられる場合もある. ●The ceiling fan rotated/revolved slowly overhead.（天井の扇風機が頭上でゆっくり回転していた）

roll [自, 他]（同じ場所で何度も）転がる, ぐるぐる回る；転がす, ぐるぐる回す ◇A dog was rolling in the mud. 犬が泥の中で転がっていた ◇Her eyes rolled. 彼女の目は（びっくりして）ぐるぐる回った ◇He was rolling a pencil between his fingers. 彼は指にはさんだ鉛筆を回していた

orbit [他, 自]（ややフォーマル）（惑星・恒星の）軌道を描いて回る ◇The earth takes a year to orbit the sun. 地球は1年をかけて太陽の周囲を軌道を描いて回る ◇Stars near the edge of the galaxy orbit more slowly. 銀河系の端近くにある恒星はほかよりゆっくりと軌道周回する ☞**orbit**（WAY 3）

whirl [自, 他]《書き言葉》（円を描いて非常に素早く）ぐるぐる回る, 渦を巻く；ぐるぐる回す, 渦を巻かせる ◇Leaves whirled in the wind. 葉っぱが風で渦をまいた ◇He whirled her around the dance floor. 彼は彼女をくるくる回しながらダンスフロア中を踊った

go a'round/'round, go around/round sth
句動詞 《特に話し言葉》（円を描いて）ぐるぐる回る ◇The wheel was going round and round. 車輪はぐるぐる回っていた ◇He didn't even know that the earth goes around the sun! 彼は地球が太陽の周りを回ることさえ知らなかったのだ

---

sponsor

swivel (-ll-, 米 -l-) [自, 他]（固定した中心点の周りを）回転する, 回る；回転させる, 回す ◇The ball should be able to swivel freely in the socket. ボールがソケットの中で自由に回転できていないといけない ◇She swivelled her chair around to face them. 彼女は椅子を回転させて彼らのほうに向いた

ノート **rotate, revolve, swivel** の使い分け：物が rotate, revolve する場合, 常に同じ方向に, 円を描いてぐるぐると回転する. 物が swivel する場合, しばしば方向を変えながら, 中心点の周りを前後に回転する.

twist [他]（手で）回す, 回転させる ◇Try twisting the handle to the right. 取っ手を右に回してみなさい ◇She was nervously twisting the ring on her finger. 彼女ははめている指輪を神経質に回していた

twirl [他]《書き言葉》（素早くかつ軽快に）ぐるぐる回す ◇He twirled his hat in his hand. 彼は手で帽子をくるくると回した

sponsor 名

sponsor・donor・patron・promoter・backer・contributor・benefactor・philanthropist
お金などの生活の糧を与える人[組織]
【類語訳】スポンサー, 出資者, 保証人, 後援者, 寄付者, 寄贈者, ドナー, 提供者, パトロン, 主催者, 興行主, 後ろ盾, 慈善家

文型&コロケーション

▶ a donor/ contributor/ benefactor **to** sth
▶ the **main/ principal** sponsor/ donor/ patron/ promoter/ backer/ contributor/ benefactor
▶ a **major/ potential** sponsor/ donor/ patron/ backer/ contributor/ benefactor
▶ a **generous** sponsor/ donor/ patron/ contributor/ benefactor
▶ a **wealthy** donor/ patron/ backer/ benefactor/ philanthropist
▶ a **great** patron/ promoter/ benefactor/ philanthropist
▶ a **private** sponsor/ donor/ patron/ benefactor
▶ an **anonymous** donor/ patron/ benefactor
▶ to **look for/ seek/ find/ get** a sponsor/ donor/ patron/ backer
▶ a sponsor/ donor/ benefactor/ philanthropist **gives** sth
▶ a sponsor/ benefactor/ philanthropist **donates** sth
▶ a sponsor/ donor/ promoter/ backer/ philanthropist **supports** sb/ sth

sponsor [C]（ラジオ[テレビ]番組・コンサート・スポーツ大会の）スポンサー；（慈善事業への）出資者；（訓練・教育の資金を提供する）後援者；（身元・債務などの）保証人 ◇The race organizers are trying to attract sponsors. レースの主催者たちはスポンサーを引きつけようと努めている ◇I'm collecting sponsors for next week's charity run. 来週のチャリティー競走のスポンサーを集めているところです ◇Unless he can find a sponsor he'll be forced to retire from athletics. 後援者を見つけられなければ, 彼は陸上競技を辞めざるを得ないだろう ☞**sponsor** (FUND 動), **sponsorship** (INVESTMENT)

donor [C]（お金・衣服・食べ物などの慈善団体への）寄付者, 寄贈者；（血液・体の部位の）ドナー, 提供者 ◇She is one of the charity's main donors. 彼女はその慈善団体への主たる寄付者の一人である ◇a blood/an organ donor 献

血者/臓器提供者 ☞ **donate** (GIVE 3)
patron [C] (芸術家・作家の)後援者, パトロン；(慈善団体などの)後援者 ◇He was a great ***patron of the arts*** and helped to establish the Baltimore Museum. 彼は芸術の偉大な後援者で, ボルチモア美術館の設立を支援した ◇The Duchess of Cornwall is to be ***patron*** of the new Unicorn Theatre for Children. コーンウォール公爵夫人は, 新しいユニコーン・シアター・フォー・チルドレンの後援者となることになっている
▶**patronage** [名] [U] ▷***Patronage*** of the arts comes from businesses and private individuals. 芸術への支援は企業や匿名の私人からもたらされる
promoter [C] (芸術的な催し物・スポーツイベントなどの)主催者, 興行主 ◇The boxing ***promoter*** expects a full house when the World Champion defends his title. そのボクシングの興行主は, 世界チャンピオンがタイトルを防衛するときには満席になることを期待しています ❶***promoter*** は, このグループにおける他の種類のほとんどの人々より商業的である. ***promoter*** はふつうスポーツ・芸術などを支援するためにお金を使うというよりは, お金儲けのためにスポーツ・芸術を利用する.
backer [C] (特にビジネス) (金銭的な)後援者, 後ろ盾 ◇The project receives its money from European ***backers***. その事業はヨーロッパの後援者からお金を受けている ☞ **supporter** (SUPPORTER)
contributor [C] (ややフォーマル, 特にビジネスで) (支払い・事業の援助への)貢献者, 寄与者 ◇Older people are important ***contributors*** to the economy. 高齢者たちは経済に重要な貢献をしている ◇Which country is the largest net ***contributor*** to EU funds? ヨーロッパ連合の基金への最大の純益貢献国はどこですか ❶***contributor*** は, お金を払う[物を購入する]ことによって組織[経済]にお金をもたらす人[国, 顧客]の数を問題にする場合に用いられることが多い. ☞ **contribute** (GIVE 3)
benefactor [C] (フォーマル) (学校・慈善団体などへの)寄付者, 寄贈者, 後援者 ◇He was a generous ***benefactor***, providing schools and churches throughout the region. 彼は地域中の学校や教会に必要品を寄贈する気前のよい篤志家だった ❶***benefactor*** は一般的に, generous, kind, great, wealthy と結びつく. また, mysterious, anonymous, unknown であることも多い.
philanthropist [C] (ややフォーマル) (貧民・困窮者を支援する裕福な)慈善家 ◇He was a wealthy businessman and ***philanthropist***. 彼は裕福な実業家であり慈善家であった

spontaneous [形]

spontaneous・impromptu・impulsive・off-the-cuff
物事が準備[計画]されていなかったこと, 人が最初に計画せずに[考えずに]事を行うことを表す
【類義訳】自発的な, のびのびした, 即興の, 衝動的な, 直情的な, ぶっつけ本番の

▶ 文型&コロケーション
▸ a spontaneous/ an impulsive **gesture/ reaction/ act**
▸ a spontaneous/ an off-the-cuff **remark**

spontaneous (行動が計画されずに)自然に起こる；(強いられずに[訓練されずに])自発的な, のびのびした ◇The audience burst into ***spontaneous*** applause. 観客から, 自然と拍手が巻き起こった ◇It was a wonderfully ***spontaneous*** performance of the piece. それはその曲の素晴ら

しくのびのびとした演奏だった
▶**spontaneously** [副] ◇We ***spontaneously*** started to dance. 私たちは自然と踊りだした
impromptu (準備なしで)即興で[即席]の ◇She gave an ***impromptu*** speech. 彼女は即興でスピーチした ◇They often held ***impromptu*** meetings in their house. 彼らはよく思いつきで自宅で会議を持つことがあった ❶***impromptu*** はふつう前もって準備されずに起こる lecture, meeting, press conference, speech などの情報公開の場を表す語と共に用いられる.
impulsive (結果を注意深く考えずに)衝動的な, 直情的な ◇He told me not to be ***impulsive*** but to think it over. 私に衝動的にならずそのことをよく考えるように彼は忠告してくれた ◇She has a generous and ***impulsive*** nature. 彼女は気前がよく後先を考えない性格です ❶***impulsive*** にならないようにしなさいと人への忠告として使うことができるが, 人を impulsive だと表現しても, 常に批判的であるとは限らない. むしろその人への愛情やその人の短所に対する理解を示唆していることが多い. こうした振る舞いをより批判的に言いたければ, rash や reckless を使うとよい. ☞ **RECKLESS**, ☞ **impulse** (DESIRE)
▶**impulsively** [副] ◇***Impulsively*** he reached out and took her hand. 彼は衝動的に手を伸ばして彼女の手を取った
off-the-'cuff (ややインフォーマル) (話が)即興[即席]の, ぶっつけ本番の, 準備なしの ◇He was embarrassed when a journalist's microphone picked up an ***off-the-cuff*** remark. ジャーナリストのマイクに出まかせの発言を拾われて, 彼はうろたえた
▶**off the 'cuff** [副] ◇I'm just speaking ***off the cuff*** here — I haven't seen the results yet. ここではただ非公式に話しているだけです—まだ結果はわかっておりません

sport [名]

sport・exercise・PE・workout・aerobics
健康でいる[体力を増強する]ために行う活動
【類義訳】スポーツ, 運動, 体操, 練習, 体育, エアロビクス

▶ 文型&コロケーション
▸ to do **sport/ exercises/ PE/ a workout/ aerobics**

sport [U] (英) (米では **sports** [複数形で]) (楽しみの[健康を保つ]ために行う)スポーツ, 運動 ◇I'm not interested in ***sport***. 私はスポーツに興味がありません ◇Do you do a lot of ***sport***? (英) よく運動をしますか ◇We played ***sports*** together when we were kids. (米) 私たちは, 子どもの頃, 一緒に運動した ❶複数形の ***sports*** は他の名詞の前にくる場合, (英)でも(米)でも用いられる. ◆***sports*** shoes (運動靴). ◆ a ***sports*** club (スポーツクラブ).
exercise [U, C] (健康でいる[体力を増強する]ために行う)運動, 体操；(健康でいる[技術を磨く]ために行う)練習 ◇Swimming is good ***exercise***. 水泳はよい運動である ◇I don't **get** much ***exercise*** sitting in the office all day. 私は一日中オフィスに座っていてあまり体を動かさない ◇Remember to **take** regular ***exercise***. (英) 定期的に運動することを忘れないで ◇The mind needs ***exercise*** as well as the body. 肉体と同様, 精神にも鍛錬が必要だ ◇vigorous/gentle ***exercise*** 激しい/軽い運動 ◇breathing/relaxation/stretching ***exercises*** 呼吸/弛緩/ストレッチ運動 ◇Repeat the ***exercise*** ten times on each leg. それぞれの脚に10回ずつその運動を繰り返してください

↳sport

☞ **exercise** (TRAIN 2), **training** (TRAINING)
PE《英》《米》**P.E.**〔U〕（学校の）体育(physical educationの短縮形) ◇a *PE* lesson/class/teacher 体育の指導／授業／教師
workout〔C〕（健康を保つために行う）運動、体操 ◇She does a 20-minute *workout* every morning. 彼女は毎朝20分間、運動をする ☞ **work out** (TRAIN 2)
aerobics〔U〕エアロビクス ◇I go to *aerobics* (= to an aerobics class) every Monday. 毎週月曜日エアロビクスをしに行きます
▶**aerobic** 形 ◇*aerobic* exercise エアロビクス体操

spread 動

spread・lay sth out・lay・unfold・open・unroll
紙や布地のような平べったい物をより広い範囲を覆うように開く
【類語訳】広げる、覆う、開く、広がる、ほどく、ほどける

文型&コロケーション
▶to spread/ lay/ lay out/ open sth **on** sth
▶to spread/ lay sth **over** sth
▶to spread/ lay/ open sth **out**
▶to spread out/ lay out/ unfold/ open a **map**
▶to spread/ lay/ unfold a **cloth/ tablecloth**
▶to unfold/ open your **arms**

spread〔他〕広げる ◇Tom *spread* the map out on the floor. トムは床の上にその地図を広げた ◇The bird *spread* its wings and flew away. その鳥は羽を広げて飛び去った
,lay sth 'out 句動（平らなところに）広げる ◇*Lay* the material *out* flat. その材料を平らに広げてください
lay〔他〕《ふつう副詞や前置詞と共に》広げる、覆う ◇Before they started they *laid* newspaper on the floor. 始める前に彼らは新聞紙を床に広げた ◇The grapes were *laid* to dry on racks. ぶどうは乾かすために棚にびっしりと並べられた
unfold〔他, 自〕（折り畳んである物を[が]）広げる、開く; 広がる ◇She *unfolded* the letter and read it yet again. 彼女はその手紙を開いてさらにもう一度読んだ ◇He *unfolded* his arms and stood up. 彼は両腕を広げて立ち上がった ◇The collapsible ladder *unfolds* quickly and locks into place for added safety. その折り畳み式はしこはすぐに組み立てられ、安全性を高めるよう、場所に固定できる 反意 **fold**
open〔自, 他〕（畳まれて[閉じて]いた物を[が]）開く、広げる ◇What if the parachute doesn't *open*? 万一パラシュートが開かなければどうしよう ◇The flowers *open* in the morning and close again in the evening. それらの花は朝開いて、夕方また閉じる ◇He *opened* his arms wide to embrace her. 彼は彼女を抱きしめようと両腕を大きく広げた
unroll〔他, 自〕（巻いた物を[が]）ほどく、ほどける ◇We *unrolled* our sleeping bags. 我々は寝袋をほどいた 反意 **roll**

staff 名 ☞ WORKER 1

staff・personnel・workforce・manpower・sales force・human resources
組織のために働く（ことが可能な）人々、その人々が提供する技術と力
【類語訳】スタッフ、職員、部員、人員、従業員、労働人口、人力、人手、販売員、営業部員、人材

文型&コロケーション
▶(a/ an) **female/ male/ skilled/ unskilled/ qualified/ trained/ experienced** staff/ personnel/ workforce
▶(a/ an) **10-strong/ 2,000-strong**, etc. staff/ workforce/ sales force
▶to **join** the staff/ workforce/ sales force
▶to **train/ reduce/ increase** staff/ personnel/ the workforce

staff〔C, ふつう単数で〕（会社・組織の）スタッフ、職員、部員 ◇All medical *staff* are tested for the virus. すべての医療スタッフにそのウィルス検査が実施されます ◇We have 20 part-time **members of** *staff*.《英》我々は20人の非勤職員を抱えている ◇Three *staff* **members** were suspended after the incident.《米》その事件後、3人の職員が停職となった ◇He's a lawyer **on the** *staff* of the Worldwide Fund for Nature.《特に英》彼は世界自然保護基金に勤務する弁護士です ❶《英》では staff は、単数扱いでも複数扱いでも用いられる。◆ a *staff* of ten (= a group of ten people) (10名の職員). ◆ I have ten *staff* working for me. (10人の職員が部下にいる). 動詞の主語になる場合、staff は複数扱いとなり動詞は複数形となる。◆ The *staff* in this shop are very helpful. (この店の店員はとても力になってくれる).《米》では、staff は単数扱いでしか用いない。◆ a *staff* of ten (10名の職員). × ten *staff*. ◆ The *staff* in this store is very helpful. (この店の店員はとても力になってくれる). 複数形の staffs は、あまり頻繁に用いられないが、二つ以上の人々の集団に言及するために《英》《米》いずれでも用いられる。◆ the senator and his *staff* (上院議員とそのスタッフ). ◆ senators and their *staffs* (上院議員たちとそのスタッフ). ☞ **staff member, member of staff** (WORKER 1), **staff** (WORKER 2)
personnel〔複数扱い〕（ビジネスで）（会社・組織・国軍の）人員、職員 ◇There is a severe shortage of skilled *personnel*. 熟練した人員がひどく不足している ◇The bomb killed 28 military *personnel*. 爆弾で28人の兵士が死亡した ❶ personnel は特に、administrative, civilian, computer, key, medical, military, security, technical, skilled, trained などの語の後で用いられる。personnel はまたビジネスの文脈では staff の代わりに用いられることも多い。personnel [U + 単数・複数動詞] はまた、人々の採用・教育を担当する会社の部門を指す。◆ the *personnel* department (人事部). ◆ *Personnel* is currently reviewing pay scales. (人事部は現在、給与体系を見直している).
workforce〔C + 単数・複数動詞〕（会社・組織の）従業員；（国・地域の）労働人口 ◇The factory will have to lose half of its 1,000-strong *workforce*. その工場は総勢1000人の従業員の半数を失わざるをえないだろう ◇A quarter of the local *workforce* is unemployed. 地元の労働人口の4分の1が失業している ❶ workforce は特に組織で働く人々の数やその数の増減について用いられる。
manpower〔U〕（特定の仕事に必要な[が可能な]）人力、人手, 有効総員[労働力] ◇We need to ensure best use of the available *manpower*. 我々は活用できる人手が最大限どれだけかを確かめる必要がある
'sales force〔C + 単数・複数動詞〕（製品販売をする）販売員、営業部員 ◇The company has a 500-strong nationwide *sales force*. その会社には全国に500人の営業部員がいる
,human re'sources〔複数で〕（ビジネスで）（会社・組織が活用できる）人的資源、人材 ◇She's responsible for making the best use of *human resources*. 彼女は人材

stage, stall, stand

を最大限に活用する責任がある ❶human resources と HR [U＋単数・複数用法]はまた、人々の採用・教育を担当する会社の部門を指す. ◆the *human resources* director (取締役人事部長). ◆She works in *human resources*. (彼女は人事部で働いている). ☞ **resource** (SUPPLY)

stage 名

stage・phase・step・round・leg
進行期間や過程の一部を表す
【類語訳】段階, 局面, ステップ, 一回, 一区間

文型&コロケーション
- a stage/ phase/ step/ round/ leg **of** sth
- the **first/ second/ third/ next/ final/ last** stage/ phase/ step/ round/ leg
- the **initial/ preliminary/ opening** stage/ phase/ step/ round
- the **early** stages/ phases/ steps/ rounds
- the **opening/ current/ latest** stage/ phase/ round
- **successive** stages/ phases/ steps/ rounds
- a/ an **important/ critical/ crucial/ key/ difficult** stage/ phase/ step
- to **begin/ enter/ reach/ finish** a stage/ phase/ round/ leg

stage [C] 段階 ◇The product is *at* the design *stage*. その製品は設計の段階だ ◇The children are at different *stages* of development. その子どもたちは異なった成長段階にある ◇*At one stage* it looked as though they would win. ある時点では彼らが勝つかのように見えた ◇The pay increase will be introduced *in stages* (= not all at once). 賃上げは段階的に導入されるだろう ◇We can take the argument one *stage* further. 私たちはもう一段階議論を深めることができる

phase [C] 段階, 局面 ◇We are now entering a critical *phase* of the campaign. 我々は今やそのキャンペーンの重要な局面に入ろうとしている ◇His anxiety about the work was just *a passing phase*. 彼の仕事の不安はほんの一時的なものだった ◇Most teenagers go through a difficult *phase*. ティーンエージャーの多くが難しい時期を経る

> ノート **stage** と **phase** の使い分け: phase には常に始めと終わりがあり、phase を目的語にして、enter, go through, finish の動詞が用いられる. また、during を共に用いて、phase の中で起こることや、phase がいつまで last するかを言うこともできる. phase は、特に企画の計画段階や人生のさまざまな情緒的局面についても用いられる. stage も同様に用いることができるが、より長い期間内の特定の状態や瞬間についても用いられ、ある特定の段階で ... stage で表すことができるが、phase は不可. ×The product is at the design *phase*. ×At one *phase* it looked as though they would win.

step [C] (一連の事の中での) 段階, ステップ ◇Having completed the first stage, you can move on to *step* 2. 第1段階を終了して第2段階に進んでもよい ◇I'd like to take this idea a *step* further. 私はこの考えをさらに一歩進めてみたいと思います ◇The promotion was a big *step up* (= move to a better position) in his career. その昇進は彼の経歴における大きなステップアップだった ◇I'll explain it to you *step by step*. 段階を追ってそれを説明しましょう

round [C] (一連の行事の) 一回 ◇The party did very well in the final *round* of voting. その党は最終投票で大いに健闘した

leg [C] (行程の) 一部, 一区間 ◇At last we were on the homeward *leg* of our journey. 我々はついに旅の帰途に差しかかっていた

stall 名

stall・booth・stand・kiosk
前方が開いた物を売るテーブル[小さな店]
【類語訳】露店, 売店, 屋台, 陳列台, 模擬店, ブース, 売り場, 売り台, キオスク

文型&コロケーション
- a **hot-dog** stall/ stand
- a **food/ refreshment** stall/ kiosk
- a/ an **information/ ticket** booth/ kiosk
- a **newspaper** stand/ kiosk
- to **have/ run** a stall/ booth/ stand/ kiosk
- to **set up/ man** a stall/ stand

stall [C] (市場にある) 露店, 売店, 屋台, 陳列台 ◇He works on a market *stall* in the Square. 彼は広場にある市場の露店で働いている

booth [C] (市場・展示会・催事会場などの) 売店, 屋台, 露店, 模擬店, ブース ◇The stalls and *booths* were doing a brisk trade. 売店や露店は活況を呈していた ❶booth は一般的に、海水浴場・海辺・道端にある露店を指し、そこでは物を購入したり占ってもらったりする. また booth は、情報提供・チケット販売・料金の受け取りが行われる、一人の人がちょうど座れる空間のある場所も指す. ◆an information/a ticket/a toll *booth* (案内所/チケット売り場/料金所).

stand [C] (街頭の) 売店, 売り場, 屋台, 売り台 ◇A crowd lined up outside her newspaper *stand*. 彼女の新聞売り場の外で、大勢の人が行列を作った ❶stand は一般的には、hot-dog, doughnut, hamburger, newspaper, news と結びつく. 特に《英》ではまた、例えば展示会における、物が陳列される[宣伝される]テーブル・直立型の構造物も指す. ◆People crowded round Oxford University Press's *stand* at the book fair. (書籍市では人々はオックスフォード大学出版局の売り場のまわりに群がった).《米》では、booth を用いる.

kiosk [C] 《特に英》(新聞・飲み物などが売られる) キオスク ◇She stopped at a newspaper *kiosk* to pick up a copy of 'Private Eye'. 彼女は新聞売り場に立ち寄って、『プライベート・アイ』を一冊手に入れた ❶kiosk はふつう、簡単に解体[移動]できる stand のような直立型の構造物というより、小さな建物を指す.

stand 動

1 ☞ SIT
stand・get up・stand up・rise・get to your feet・be on your feet・pick yourself up
体を足にかけた直立の姿勢にあること/をその姿勢をとることを表す
【類語訳】立つ, 立ち上がる, 起き上がる, 起立する

文型&コロケーション
- to get up/ stand up/ rise/ pick yourself up **from** sth

stand [自] 立っている; 立つ, 立ち上がる ◇She was too

weak to *stand*. 彼女は弱すぎていて立っていられなかった ◇He was *standing* on a chair, trying to change a light bulb. 彼は椅子の上に立って、電球を取り替えようとしていた ◆***Stand still*** when I'm talking to you! 人が話しかけているときはじっと立っていなさい ◇The kids were ***standing around*** chatting. 子どもたちはぼんやりと突っ立っておしゃべりしていた ◇Everyone *stood* when the president entered the room. 大統領が部屋に入ると、全員立ち上がった ❶ stand はふつう人がどこに[どのように]立っているかを示す副詞[前置詞句]と共に用いられるが、時に立っているときに人が何をするかを示すために別の句[節]が用いられる。
◆We *stood* talking for a few minutes. (私たちは2,3分立ち話をした)。◆He *stood* and looked out to sea. (彼は立って海に目をやった)。反意 sit

,get 'up 句動詞 (座っている[ひざまずいている、横になっている]姿勢から)立ち上がる、起き上がる ◇He *got up* and strolled over to the window. 彼は立ち上がって窓辺に歩み寄った ◇Please don't *get up*! どうか立ち上がらないでください 反意 **sit down** (SIT)

,stand 'up 句動詞 立っている;(座った後に)立ち上がる、起立する ◇***Stand up*** straight! 真っすぐに立ちなさい ◇He *stood up* and put on his coat. 彼は立ち上がってコートを着た 反意 **sit, sit down** (SIT)

ノート **stand, get up, stand up の使い分け: stand** はふつう「立っている姿勢にある」ことを意味するが、「立っている姿勢になる」ことをも意味する。これら二つの意味のいずれかで用いられるが、その用法は限定されている。**stand up** は特に人(々)に立つように命じる際に用いられる。**get up** は、「立っている姿勢になる」ことを表す最も頻度の高い言い方で、座っている[ひざまずいている、横になっている]姿勢を起点とする。**stand up** する場合、それは以前に立っていた(椅子、床に)座った後である。椅子から移動する必要がないことを人に丁寧に伝えたい場合、**get up** を用いる。× Please don't *stand up*!

rise [自] 《フォーマル》(座っている[ひざまずいている、横になっている]姿勢から)立ち上がる、起き上がる ◇They *rose* from the table. 彼らはテーブルを立った ◇She *rose to her feet*. 彼女は立ち上がった

,get to your 'feet フレーズ 《書き言葉》(座った[ひざまずいた、横になった]後に)立ち上がる、起き上がる ◇I helped her to *get to her feet*. 私は彼女が立ち上がるのを手助けした

be on your' feet フレーズ 立っている ◇I've been on my *feet* all day. 私は一日中立ちっぱなしだった

,pick yourself 'up 句動詞 (転んだ後に再び)立ち上がる ◇He just *picked himself up* and went on running. 彼はすぐに立ち上がって、走り続けた ◇She *picked herself up* off the dusty ground. 彼女はほこりっぽい地面から立ち上がった

---

2 stand・endure・take・bear・put up with sb/sth・tolerate
不快[迷惑]な事を受け入れる[に対処する]
【類語訳】我慢する、辛抱する、耐える、甘受する

文型&コロケーション
▶ (can't/ not) stand/ endure/ bear **doing sth**
▶ (can't/ not) stand/ bear/ put up with **sb/ sth doing sth**
▶ to stand/ endure/ bear/ put up with **pain**
▶ to not stand/ take/ tolerate any **nonsense**
▶ to take/ tolerate **criticism**

▶ sb **can't** stand/ bear sth
▶ sb **has to** endure/ bear/ put up with/ tolerate sth
▶ sb can **no longer** stand/ endure/ bear/ tolerate sth
▶ sb can **hardly** stand/ bear sth

stand [他、受身なし]《進行形では用いない;否定文および疑問文で can/could と共に》(不快な事に)我慢[辛抱]する、耐える ◇I can't *stand* his brother. 私は彼の兄に我慢できない ◇I ***can't stand it*** when you do that. あなたにそれをされると、私は我慢ができないんだ ◇She couldn't *stand* being kept waiting. 彼女は待ち続けることに耐えられなかった ◇I can't *stand* people interrupting all the time. 私はいつも邪魔する人に我慢がならない ◇How can you *stand* it here? こんなところでどうして我慢ができるのだ

endure [他]《フォーマル》(不平を言わずに骨の折れる[不快な]事に)じっと我慢[辛抱]する、耐える ◇He had to *endure* the racist taunts of the crowd. 彼は群衆の人種差別的なあざけりにじっと耐えなければならなかった ◇She could not *endure* the thought of parting. 彼女は別離の思いに耐えられなかった

take [他、受身なし]《進行形では用いない;特に否定文で》(不快な事を)甘受する、我慢[辛抱]する、耐える ◇She can't *take* criticism. 彼女は批判を受け入れることができない ◇I don't think I can *take* much more of this heat. この暑さにこれ以上あまり耐えられないと思う ◇I find his attitude a little hard to *take*. 彼の態度には少々我慢がならないんだ

bear [自、他]《進行形では用いない;特に否定文および疑問文で can/could と共に》(不快な事に)我慢[辛抱]する、耐える ◇The pain was almost more than he could *bear*. 痛みはほとんど彼が耐えられる限界を越えていた ◇How can you *bear* to eat that stuff? どうしてそんなものを食べる我慢ができるのか ◇She *bore* it all with her usual patience. 彼女は持ち前の忍耐でそんなあれこれに耐え抜いた

ノート **stand と bear の使い分け:** 多くの場合、両語とも使用可能だが、**bear** のほうが **stand** よりもいくぶん意味が強く、少しフォーマルである。**stand** は決して肯定的な文では用いられない。× She *stood* it all with her usual patience. ☞ HATE

,put 'up with sb/sth 句動詞 《ややインフォーマル、特に話し言葉》(不平を言わずに迷惑[不快]な人・物事に)じっと我慢[辛抱]する、耐える ◇I don't know how she *puts up with* him. 彼女がどうして彼に我慢しているのかわからない

tolerate [他]《ややフォーマル、特に書き言葉》(不平を言わずに迷惑[不快]な人・物事に)じっと我慢[辛抱]する、耐える ◇There is a limit to what one person can *tolerate*. 一人の人間が耐えられることには限界がある ☞ **tolerance** (PATIENCE)

---

star 名

star・celebrity・name・personality・superstar・legend・public figure・great
エンターテインメントやスポーツの分野において有名で成功した人
【類語訳】スター、花形、有名人、著名人、名士、芸能人、セレブ、タレント、スーパースター、大物、大御所、巨匠

celebrity　　　　star　　　　　　superstar
name　　　　　　　　　　　　　　legend
personality　　　　　　　　　　　great
public figure

stare, start

文型&コロケーション
- a famous/ top star/ celebrity/ name/ personality
- a leading/ prominent name/ personality/ public figure
- a big star/ celebrity/ name
- an international star/ celebrity/ name/ superstar
- a television/ TV/ media star/ celebrity/ personality
- a showbiz star/ celebrity/ personality/ legend
- a film/ movie/ pop/ rock star/ superstar/ legend
- a screen star/ legend/ great
- a Hollywood star/ superstar/ legend
- a sporting/ sports star/ celebrity/ personality/ legend
- to make sb a star/ celebrity/ superstar/ legend/ public figure

star [C]（俳優・歌手・スポーツ選手などの）スター, 花形 ◇I wanted to be a pop *star* when I was a teenager. 私はティーンエイジャーの頃、ポップスターになりたかった ◇She acts well but she hasn't got *star quality*. 彼女は演技はうまいが、スターの資質はない ☞ **stardom** (FAME)

celebrity [C]（よくテレビに登場する）有名人, 著名人, 名士, 芸能人, セレブ ◇She was the first TV *celebrity* he had met in the flesh. 彼女は彼が生で初めて会ったテレビに出ている有名人だった ◇The show's success made her an overnight *celebrity*. そのショーの成功で彼女は一夜にして有名になった ☞ **celebrity** (FAME)

name [C]（文化・スポーツの分野の）有名人, 著名人, 名士 ◇Some of the biggest *names* in the art world were at the party. 芸術界における超有名人が数人そのパーティーに出席していた ◇The event attracted many famous *names* from the past. そのイベントは往年の多くの著名人を一堂に集めた ❶ *name* はイベントに招待される有名人, 大衆の関心を集めるために雇われる人々について用いられることが多い。

personality [C]《特に書き言葉》（芸能・スポーツ界で働く）有名人, 名士, タレント, 芸能人 ◇Various *personalities* from the world of music were invited. 音楽界からさまざまな名士が招待された ◇In a viewers' poll he was voted TV *Personality* of the Year. 彼は視聴者投票で年間最優秀テレビタレントに選出された

superstar [C]《ややインフォーマル》（俳優・歌手・スポーツ選手などの）スーパースター ◇The movie made her an international *superstar*. その映画で彼女は世界的スーパースターになった

legend [C]（スポーツ・音楽・演技の分野での）伝説(的人物) ◇She was a legend in her own lifetime. 彼女は生きている時から伝説的存在だった ◇Many of golf's *living legends* were playing. 多くのゴルフ界の生きる伝説がプレーしていた ❶ *legend* は、他の有名人よりも高い水準の名声と地位を持つ人を指す。legend は長いキャリアを通じて人が真の才能を示してきたこと、外見・人格による以上に有名であることを示唆する。☞ **legendary** (FAMOUS)

public 'figure [C]《ややフォーマル》（政治的[社会的]に多大な影響を及ぼす）有名人, 著名人 ◇He is an important *public figure* with a significant influence on public policy. 彼は公共政策に重大な影響を及ぼす大物の著名人である ☞ **public** (FAMOUS), **figure** (PERSON)

great [C, ふつう複数で]《インフォーマル》大物, 大御所, 巨匠 ◇He was one of boxing's *all-time greats*. 彼は史上最高のボクサーの一人だった ❶ *great* は主に過去に非常に人気のあった人々に用いられる。人々は一般に、movie/Hollywood/all-time *greats*（映画界/ハリウッド/史上最大の大物たち）とか, one of the greats of British comedy/the game（英国のコメディー界/その競技界の大物の一人）と表される。☞ **great** (GREAT 2)

stare 動 ☞ LOOK 動 1

stare・gaze・peer・glare・squint・gawk
人や物に長い間目を向ける
【類語訳】じろじろ見る, じっと見る, 凝視する, にらみつける, のぞく

文型&コロケーション
- to stare/ gaze/ peer/ glare/ squint/ gawk at sb/ sth
- to stare/ gaze/ gawk in surprise/ amusement, etc.
- to stare/ gaze/ peer/ glare/ squint for a moment
- to stare/ gaze/ peer/ glare suspiciously
- to stare/ gaze/ peer anxiously/ intently
- to stare/ gaze/ glare wildly/ fiercely

stare [自]（驚き・恐怖・思いなどから人・物を）じっと見つめる, じろじろ見る ◇I screamed and everyone *stared*. 私が叫ぶと, 皆がじろじろ見た ◇Peter *stared* in disbelief at the message on the screen. ピーターは信じられないといった様子でスクリーン上のメッセージをじっと見つめた ◇He sat for hours just *staring into space* (= looking at nothing). 彼は何時間も座ってただ宙をじっと見つめていた ☞ **stare** (LOOK 名)

gaze [自]《特に書き言葉》（驚き・愛情・思いなどから人・物を）じっと見つめる, じろじろ見る ◇We all *gazed* at Marco in amazement. 私たちは皆驚いてマルコをじっと見た ◇She *gazed* adoringly into his eyes. 彼女は崇めるように彼の目をじっと見つめた ☞ **gaze** (LOOK 名)

peer [自]（はっきり見えない場合に物を）じっと見る, 凝視する, 目を凝らして見る ◇We *peered* into the shadows. 私たちはその影の中をじっと見た ◇She kept *peering* over her shoulder. 彼女は振り返ってじっと見続けた

glare [自]（怒って人・物に）にらみつける ◇I looked at her and she *glared* stonily back. 私が彼女を見ると, 彼女は冷酷な目でにらみ返してきた ☞ **glare** (LOOK 名)

squint [自, 他]（まぶしそうに[もっとよく見ようとして]人・物を）目を細めて見る, 細目で見る, のぞく ◇She was *squinting* through the keyhole. 彼女は鍵穴をのぞいていた ◇When he *squinted* his eyes, he could just make out a house in the distance. 彼は目を細めると, 何とか遠くにある家を見分けることができた

gawk [自]《インフォーマル》（無作法に[ばかげた様子で]人・物に）ぽかんと見とれる ◇Stop *gawking* like that! そんなふうにぽかんと見とれてないの

start 名

start・beginning・opening・outset・onset・birth・dawn・kick-off
物事の初頭の部分[段階]
【類語訳】始まり, 最初, 初め, 開始, 出発, スタート, 初期, 冒頭, 発症, 誕生, 起源, 夜明け, 黎明, 試合開始, キックオフ

文型&コロケーション
- the start/ opening to sth
- at the start/ beginning/ opening/ outset/ onset/ birth/ dawn (of sth)
- from the (very) start/ beginning/ outset
- a new start/ beginning/ opening/ birth/ dawn

- ▶a **slow** start/ beginning/ onset
- ▶a/ an **early/ late** start/ onset/ kick-off
- ▶a **delayed** start/ opening/ onset
- ▶a **promising** start/ beginning/ opening
- ▶to **mark** the start/ beginning/ opening/ onset/ birth/ dawn (of sth)
- ▶to **herald** the start/ beginning/ opening/ onset/ dawn (of sth)
- ▶to **see** the start/ beginning/ opening/ birth/ dawn (of sth)
- ▶to **delay** the start/ opening/ onset/ kick-off (of sth)

start [C, ふつう単数で] 始まり, 最初, 初め；開始, 出発, スタート ◇What a perfect *start* to the day! 何て完璧な一日の始まりなんだ ◇If we don't hurry, we'll miss the *start* of the game. 急がないと, 試合開始に間に合わないよ ◇We've had problems (right) from the *start*. 我々には(まさに)最初からさまざまな問題があった ◇The meeting **got off to a good/bad start** (= started well/badly). 会議はよい／悪いスタートを切った ◇The trip was a disaster **from start to finish**. 旅は最初から最後まで最悪だった ◇I'll paint the ceiling if you **make a start on** the walls. 君が壁から始めるなら, 僕は天井を塗ろう ◇She's moving abroad to make a **fresh start** (= to begin a new life). 彼女は再出発するために海外へ移住するつもりだ 反意 **finish** (END 動), ☞ **start** (BEGIN), **start** (OPPORTUNITY)

beginning [C, ふつう単数で] 初めの頃, 初期, 最初の部分, 冒頭；始まり, 最初, 初め ◇We're going to Japan at the *beginning* of July. 私たちは7月初めに日本に出かけるつもりです ◇We missed the *beginning* of the movie. 私たちはその映画の冒頭を見逃した ◇Let's start again from the *beginning*. もう一度最初から始めましょう ◇I've read the whole book **from beginning to end**. 最初から最後までその本を全部読んでしまった ❶at the beginning は, 物事が始まる場所・時間に用いられる. in the beginning は「最初は」を意味し, 後半の状況との対比を示唆する 反意 **end, ending** (END 名), ☞ **begin** (BEGIN)

ノート **start** と **beginning** の使い分け：これらの語はほぼ同じ意味を持つが, 少し異なった形で用いられる傾向がある. 試合・会議といった行事にはふつう, start (開始)が用いられる. 物語・本・映画にはふつう, beginning (冒頭)が用いられる. さらに, start はふつう beginning よりも時間的には短い. ◆We'll miss the *start* of the game (= the moment when it starts; the kick-off). (試合開始に間に合わないよ). ◆We missed the *beginning* of the movie (= the first few scenes). (私たちは映画の冒頭を見逃した). ふつう from start to finish, from beginning to end とは言うが, ✗from start to end. ✗from beginning to finish とは言わないことに注意. ふつう特定の月・季節・10年間に関しては at the beginning of と言う. ✗*at the start of* July/ summer/ the 90s. 両語とも他の期間と共にも用いられることができるが, ふつう beginning のほうが使われる. ◆the *beginning/start* of the day/week/year/century/a new era (一日／一週間／一年／新しい時代の初め[始まり]). start のみ「物事を始める行為［過程］」を意味することができる. ✗I want to make an early *beginning*.

opening [C, ふつう単数で] (特に書き言葉)(劇・本・映画・試合などの)冒頭, 開始 ◇The movie has an exciting *opening*. 映画の冒頭はわくわくするものだ ◇The New Zealanders quickly lost control after a promising *opening*. ニュージーランドチームは, 勝つ見込みのあった試合開始後

ぐ大きく崩れた 反意 **ending** (END 名), ☞ **open** (BEGIN), **opening** (FIRST)

outset [単数で]《*at/from the outset* の形で》(ややフォーマル) 最初, 初め ◇I made it clear right from the *outset* that I disapproved. 不賛成だと最初からはっきり言った

onset [単数で]《特に書き言葉》(不快な物事の) 始まり, 開始, 到来, 発症 ◇An active and healthy lifestyle can delay the *onset* of disease in later life. 活動的で健全なライフスタイルにより, 人生後半の病気の発症を遅らせることができる ❶ onset は病気・体の変化の初期段階について用いられることが多い. ◆the *onset* of illness/infection/disease/depression/AIDS/symptoms/shock/menstruation/puberty (不健康の始まり／感染症の発症／病気の発症／うつ病の発症／エイズの発症／症状の始まり／卒中の発症／月経の始まり／思春期の始まり). 他の典型的な連語に天候に関連した語が挙げられる. ◆the *onset* of winter/cold weather (冬／寒波の到来).

birth [単数で]《特に書き言葉》(新しい状況・考え・場所の)始まり, 誕生, 起源 ◇This declaration marked the *birth* of a new society in South Africa. この宣言によって南アフリカにおける新しい社会の誕生が記された

dawn [単数で]《文語》(新しい状況・考え・場所の)始まり, 夜明け, 黎明 ◇That's been going on since the *dawn* of civilization. 文明の夜明け以来, そうしたことは繰り返されてきた ◇Peace marked the new *dawn* in the country's history. 平和がその国の歴史の新たな始まりを印した

'kick-off [C, U] (サッカー・ラグビー・アメフト の)試合開始, キックオフ ◇*Kick-off* is at 3. キックオフは3時です

start 動 ☞ BEGIN

start・begin・start off・kick off・commence・open
物事が初期から起こる, 人々が物事の最初の部分を行う
【類語訳】始まる, 始める

文型&コロケーション
- ▶to start/ begin/ start off/ kick off/ commence/ open **with** sth
- ▶to start/ begin/ start off/ kick off/ commence/ open **by** doing sth
- ▶to start/ begin/ start off/ commence **as** sth
- ▶a **campaign/ season/ tour/ competition/ match/ festival/ meeting** starts/ begins/ starts off/ kicks off/ commences/ opens
- ▶a **film/ book/ chapter** starts/ begins/ starts off/ opens
- ▶an **enquiry/ investigation** starts/ begins/ commences/ opens
- ▶**work/ production** starts/ begins/ starts off/ kicks off/ commences
- ▶**proceedings** start/ begin/ kick off/ commence/ open
- ▶a **period** starts/ begins/ commences/ opens
- ▶to have **just** started/ begun/ started off/ kicked off/ commenced/ opened
- ▶to start/ begin/ start off/ kick off/ commence/ open **immediately**

start [自] 始まる；始める ◇When does the class *start*? 授業はいつから始まるの ◇There are a lot of small businesses *starting up* in that area. その地域で多くの小規模事業が起こっている ◇She *started* as a secretary but ended up running the department. 彼女は秘書に始まり, 最後にはその部門の経営者となった ◇The company *started out* with 30 employees. 会社は従業員30人で創業した ◇The evening *started* badly when the speaker failed to turn up. 演説者が姿を見せず、そのイベントはすべり出しからよくなかった ◇The trail *starts* just outside the town. 登山道の登り口は町のすぐ外にある ◇Hotel prices *start* at £65 a night for a double room. ホテルの宿泊料金は、ダブルの部屋で一泊65ポンドからです 反意 **finish** (END 動), ☞ **start** (BEGIN)

begin [自] 始まる;始める;話し始める ◇When does the concert *begin*? コンサートはいつから始まるの ◇The evening *began* well. その夜はいい出だしだった ◇Use 'an' before words *beginning* with a vowel. 母音で始まる単語の前には「an」を使いなさい ◇'Ladies and gentlemen,' he *began*, 'welcome to the Town Hall.'「紳士淑女の皆さん、タウンホールへようこそ」と彼は話し始めた 反意 **end** (END 動), ☞ **begin** (BEGIN)

ノート **start** と **begin** の使い分け：これらの語に意味の違いはあまりない。**start** は、話し言葉やビジネスの文脈でより頻繁に用いられる。**begin** は書き言葉でより頻繁に用いられ、一連の出来事を表そうとする場合に用いられることが多い。◆The story *begins* on the island of Corfu. (物語はコルフ島から始まる)。**start** は「話し始める」ことを意味するためには用いられない。×'Ladies and gentlemen,' he *started*.

,start 'off 句動《ややインフォーマル》始まる;始める ◇The discussion *started off* mildly enough. 話し合いはすこぶる穏やかに始まった ◇The leaves *start off* green but turn red later. 葉は始めは緑で、後に赤くなる ◇I *started off* working quite hard, but it didn't last. かなり精を出して仕事し始めたが、続かなかった 反意 **finish up** ❶《英》は finish up...は、一連の出来事の後で特定の状態になる［場所にいる］ことを表す。◆If you're not careful, you could *finish up* seriously ill. (《英》大事にしないと、結局重い病気を患うかもしれないよ).

,kick 'off 句動《インフォーマル》(行事・活動を)始める;(行事・活動・映画・物語が)始まる ◇Tom will *kick off* with a few comments. トムがいくつかのコメントで(番組の)口火を切ってくれます ◇The festival *kicks off* on Monday, September 13. フェスティバルは、9月13日月曜日に始まります 反意 **wind up** (END 動)

commence [自]《フォーマル》始まる ◇The meeting is scheduled to *commence* at noon. 会議は正午に始まる予定です ◇I will be on leave during the week *commencing* 15 February. 2月15日から始まる週に休暇をとるもりです ☞ **commence** (BEGIN)

open [自](行事・活動を)始める;(行事・映画・物語が)始まる ◇He *opened* with a version of Elvis's 'Can't Help Falling in Love.' 彼はエルヴィス・プレスリーの『好きにならずにいられない』で(番組を)始めた ◇The story *opens* with a murder. その物語は人殺しから始まる ◇**open** は、kick off よりフォーマルな表現である。しかし、ふつう人々が比較的短時間の[インフォーマルな]活動を始める場合については用いられない。◆What time do we *kick off*? (何時に始めるの). ×What time do we *open*? **open** は比較的長期間で時間のかかる行事の期日と時間に用いられる。◆The Annual General Meeting *opens* at 1pm on March 15th. (年次総会は3月15日午後1時に始まります). 反意 **close** (END 動), ☞ **open** (BEGIN)

state 名

state • condition • shape • repair

物事が特定のときに帯びる性質を表す
【類語訳】状態、事態、調子、手入れ

文型&コロケーション

▶ **in** (a) ... state/ condition/ shape/ repair
▶ (a) **good** state/ condition/ shape/ (state of) repair
▶ (a) **fine** state/ condition/ shape
▶ **excellent** condition/ shape/ repair
▶ (a) **reasonable** condition/ shape/ (state of) repair
▶ (a) **poor/ bad** state/ condition/ shape/ (state of) repair
▶ sth's **general** state/ condition/ state of repair
▶ sth's **physical** state/ condition/ shape
▶ sb's/ sth's **financial/ economic** state/ condition/ shape
▶ to **keep sth in** (a) ... state/ condition/ shape/ repair
▶ to **get (sth) into** (a) ... state/ condition/ shape

state [C] (特定の)状態、事態 ◇There are serious concerns about the current *state* of the economy. 経済の現状が深刻に懸念されている ◇His teeth were in an appalling *state*. 彼の歯はひどい状態になっていた ◇Look at the *state* of this room (= look how messy, dirty, etc. it is)! この部屋の状態を見てごらん ◇The government has declared a **state of emergency** in the flooded regions. 政府は冠水地域に非常事態宣言を出した ☞ **state of affairs** (SITUATION)

condition [U, 単数で] (物理的な)状態 ◇The car was in perfect *condition*. その車の状態は申し分なかった ◇The poor *condition* of our schools should be of concern to all of us. 私たちの学校の劣悪な状態には、私たちはみんな、関心を持つべきだ

ノート **state** と **condition** の使い分け：**state** のほうが一般的な語であり、特定のときの状態について用いられる。世話が行き届いていない[取り散らかった]状態には、**state** を用いる。**condition** は、しばしば物が使い古されている場合の外観・機能の状態について用いられる。

shape [U]《ややインフォーマル》(影響が予想される)状態、調子 ◇What sort of *shape* was your car in after the accident? 事故後あなたの車はどんな状態でしたか ◇The economy is still in pretty good *shape*. 経済はまだかなり好調である

repair [U] 手入れ(された状態) ◇Try to keep your vehicle in good *repair*. 車の手入れをよくしておくように ◇The old clock tower is in a **poor state of repair**.《特に英》その古い時計台は手入れが行き届いていない ❶この意味では repair は、in good repair, in a poor state of repair の句で用いられるのが普通である。

statement 名

statement • comment • announcement • remark • declaration • observation

言われた[書かれた]ものを表す
【類語訳】声明、発言、陳述、供述、見解、意見、所見、発言、論評、コメント、告示、発表、公表、宣言、布告、言明、告知、告白

文型&コロケーション

▶ a statement/ a comment/ an announcement/ a remark/ a declaration/ an observation **about** sth
▶ a statement/ a comment/ an observation **on** sth
▶ an announcement/ a declaration **of** sth
▶ a **brief** statement/ comment/ announcement/ remark/ ob-

servation
- a/ an **public/ official** statement/ comment/ announcement/ declaration
- a **formal** statement/ announcement/ declaration
- a **casual** comment/ remark/ observation
- to **make** a statement/ a comment/ an announcement/ a remark/ a declaration/ an observation
- to **issue** a statement/ an announcement/ a declaration

statement [C] (口頭・文書による正式な)声明, 発言, 陳述, 供述 ◇A government spokesperson made a brief *statement* to the press. 政府の報道官は記者団に向けて短い声明を出した ◇She made one of her sweeping *statements* about young people. 彼女は若者についても例によって粗っぽい発言をした ◇The police asked me to make a *statement* (= a written account of facts about a crime, used in court if legal action follows). 私は警察に供述してくれるように頼まれた ☞ **state** (DECLARE)

comment [C, U] (特定の状況に関する質問への口頭・文書による)見解, 意見, 所見, 発言, 論評, コメント ◇She made helpful *comments* on my work. 彼女は私の仕事に有益な意見を言ってくれた ◇He handed me the document *without comment*. 何も言わずに彼は私に書類を手渡した ◇When asked about the rumours, the chairman replied, '*No comment.*' 噂について尋ねられると, 議長は「ノーコメント」と答えた ☞ **comment** (COMMENT)

announcement [C, U] (口頭・文書による)声明, 告示; 発表, 公表 ◇Today's *announcement* of a peace agreement comes after weeks of discussion. 和平協定に関する今日の発表は数週間の議論の後に出されるものである ◇I have a few *announcements* to make. 発表することが2,3あります ◇The *announcement* of the verdict was accompanied by shouts and cheers. 評決の発表と共に歓声と喝采が起きた ☞ **announce** (DECLARE)

remark [C] (口頭・文書による)見解, 意見, 所見, 発言, 論評 ◇He made a number of rude *remarks* about the food. 彼は食べ物に関して数々の失礼な発言をした ◇What exactly did you mean by that last *remark*? あの先週の論評では正確には何を言いたかったのですか ☞ **remark** (COMMENT)

declaration [C, U] (ややフォーマル)(口頭・文書による意図・信念・感情・情報を伝える公式の[正式な])宣言, 布告, 声明, 言明, 告知, 告白 ◇a *declaration* of love/support 愛の告白/支援の告知 ◇We were asked to sign a *declaration* to the effect that we were UK citizens. 私たちは英国市民であるという旨の宣言書に署名するよう求められた ◇The summit has been postponed due to the *declaration* of war. 首脳会談は宣戦布告のために延期された ◇The *Declaration of Independence* was signed on 4 July 1776 by representatives of the US states. 米国独立宣言は合衆国各州代表によって1776年7月4日に署名された ☞ **declare** (DECLARE)

observation [C] (ややフォーマル)(見た[聞いた, 読んだ]事に基づく口頭・文書による)見解, 意見, 所見, 発言, 論評 ◇He began by making a few general *observations* about the report. 彼はその報告書に関していくつか一般的な所見を述べることから始めた ☞ **observe** (COMMENT)

📝 **comment, remark, observation** の使い分け: comment は公式にも私的にも出される。 remark は公に私的にもなされるが、常に非公式であり、話す側もよく考えて発したとは言えないかもしれない。 observation も非公式だが、ふつう remark よりも熟考されたものである。

status 名 ☞ REPUTATION

status • honour • prestige • glory
多くの人々に尊敬されて[崇拝されて, 重要だと考えられて]いる状態を表す
【類語訳】身分, 地位, 敬意, 称賛, 威信, 名声, 信望, 名誉, 栄誉, 光栄, 栄光

文型&コロケーション
- **personal/ national** honour/ prestige/ glory
- **social** status/ prestige
- to **gain/ bring/ lose/ seek** status/ honour/ prestige/ glory
- to **enjoy** status/ prestige
- status/ honour/ prestige **is attached to** sth

status [U, C, ふつう単数で] (高い[社会的])身分, 地位; (物事に与えられる)地位 ◇The job brings with it *status* and a high income. その仕事と共に地位と高収入がもたらされます ◇The Chanel suit was the number one fashion *status symbol*. シャネルのスーツはファッションとして比類なき地位の象徴であった ◇This reflects the *high status* accorded to science in our culture. これは我々の文化において科学に与えられている高い地位を反映している ◇In the teaching of literature, Shakespeare is given a *special status*. 文学教育において, シェークスピアは特別な地位を与えられている

honour 《英》(米では **honor**) [U] (人に対する)敬意, 称賛 ◇The arch was built *in honour of* the Emperor. そのアーチ型の門は皇帝への敬意を表して建てられた ◇They organized a party *in his honour*. 彼を称えるパーティーが計画された ◇The president was the *guest of honour* at the banquet. 大統領は晩餐会の主賓だった

prestige [U] (社会的地位・行いによって人・物事に付される)威信, 名声, 信望 ◇The post carried great *prestige* within the civil service. 役人の世界ではそのポストが大きな威信をもたらすものだった ◇The jobs are accorded different levels of *prestige*. 仕事それぞれには異なる評価が与えられるものだ ☞ **prestigious** (GREAT 2)

glory [U] (重要な物事の達成によって人に与えられる)名誉, 栄誉, 光栄, 栄光 ◇I do all the work and he gets all the *glory*. 仕事はすべて私がやって, 名誉はすべて彼が手にしている ◇She basked in the *reflected glory* of her daughter's success. 彼女は娘の成功がもたらした栄誉に浴した ◇She wanted to enjoy her *moment of glory*. 彼女は栄光の時を楽しみたいと思った ☞ **glorious** (FAMOUS)

stay 動

1 stay • remain • hang around • stop • stick around • stay put • linger • loiter
立ち去ることなく一定期間特定の場所に居続ける
【類語訳】留まる, いる, 居残る, ぶらつく, じっとしている, うろつく

文型&コロケーション
- to stay/ remain/ hang around/ stop/ stick around/ linger **for** a few minutes/ weeks/ years, etc.
- to stay/ stop **for** sth
- to stay/ remain/ hang around/ stop/ stick around/ linger

here
▶to stay/ remain/ hang around/ linger **there**
▶to stay/ remain/ stop **at home**
▶to stay/ remain/ stop **behind/ indoors**
▶to stay/ hang/ stick **around**

stay [自] (特定の場所に)留まる, いる ◇I just want to *stay* in bed today. 今日はただ寝ていたい ◇*Stay* there and don't move! そこにいて動かないで ◇'Do you want a drink?' 'No thanks, I can't *stay*.'「飲み物, いる」「いや, 結構, ゆっくりできないんだ」◇We ended up *staying* for lunch. 私たちは昼食まで居座ることになった ◇I'm *staying late* at the office tonight. 今夜は遅くまで職場にいるつもりです ◇She *stayed* at home (= did not go out to work) while the children were young. 彼女は子どもたちが幼いうちは働きに出ず家にいた ◇My hat won't *stay* on! 帽子がすぐに脱げちゃうんだ ◇We *stayed to* see what would happen. 我々は何が起きるのか確かめるために留まった ❶話し言葉では, stay は目的を示す[人にすべきことを伝える]ために, to不定詞の代わりに, and +別の動詞と共に用いることができる ◆I'll *stay* and help you. (お手伝いするために私はここに残りましょう) 反語 go (LEAVE 1), ☞ **stay** (REMAIN)

remain [自] 《ふつう副詞や前置詞と共に》《ややフォーマル》(同じ場所で)留まる, 居残る ◇They *remained* in Mexico until June. 彼らは6月までメキシコに居残った ◇The plane *remained* on the ground. 飛行機は地上に留まったままだった ◇She left, but I *remained* behind. 彼女は去ったが, 私は後に残った ☞ **remain** (REMAIN)

,**hang a'round** [句動詞] 《インフォーマル》(何もせずある場所の近くで)ぶらつく ◇You *hang around* here in case he comes, and I'll go on ahead. 彼が来るといけないから, あなたはこのあたりをぶらついていて. 私は先に行くから

stop (-pp-) [自] 《英, インフォーマル》(人の家に短い時間)留まる ◇I'm not *stopping*. I just came to give you this message. すぐ帰るよ. この伝言を伝えに来ただけなので ◇Can you *stop* for tea? お茶でも飲んでいきませんか
☞ **stop by** (VISIT 動)

,**stick a'round** [句動詞] 《インフォーマル》(物事が起こる[人が到着する]のを待って)近くにいる ◇*Stick around* ─ we'll need you to help us later. ここにいてよ ─ 後で私たちの手伝いをしてもらわなきゃならないから

stay 'put [行句] 《ややインフォーマル》(人・物が)じっとしている ◇He chose to *stay put* while the rest of us toured the area. 他の人たちがその地域を見て回る間, 彼は動かずじっとしていることにした ❶stay put はふつう動かない[どこかへ行かない]と下した決定について用いられる.

linger [自] 《ふつう副詞や前置詞と共に》《特に書き言葉》(去りたくないために)居残る; (行為に)いつまでもふける ◇She *lingered* for a few minutes to talk to Nick. 彼女は数分居残ってニックと話した ◇We *lingered* over breakfast on the terrace. 私たちはテラスでだらだら時間をかけて朝食を取った

loiter [自] 《時にけなして》(明白な理由なしに)ぶらつく, うろつく ◇Teenagers were *loitering* in the street outside. ティーンエイジャーたちが外の通りをうろついていた

〔ノート〕**hang around** と **loiter** の使い分け: hang around は, 大したこともせずある場所にただ留まっていることだが, 待っている理由があるかもしれないし, そこに批判の気持ちが実際に表れているわけではない. 一方, loiter の場合は, そこにいるべき理由もないし, 早く立ち去るべきなのにという気持ちが表れていることが多い.

2 stay・visit・stop over・do
短期間ある場所へ行く[で暮らす]
【類語訳】滞在する, 泊まる, 立ち寄る, 見物する

[文型&コロケーション]
▶stay/ visit/ stop over **for** two nights, a week, etc.
▶stay/ stop over **in/ at** a place
▶to **come/ go to** stay/ visit

stay [自] (客・訪問者として一時的に)滞在する, 泊まる ◇I'm *staying* at a hotel near the beach. 浜辺に近いホテルに泊まる予定です ◇She's *staying with* her sister. 彼女は妹と一緒に滞在している ◇He *stayed* for over a week. 彼は一週間以上滞在した ◇Come and *stay* any time! いつでも泊まりに来いよ ☞ **stay** (VISIT 名)

visit [自, 他] (短期間)滞在する, 泊まる ◇We don't live here. We're just *visiting*. 私たちはここに住んではいません. 単なる訪問者です ◇Next time you *visit* the States you'll have to come and see us. 次にアメリカに滞在する時は, ぜひ私たちに会いに来てね ☞ **visit** (VISIT 名), **visitor** (TOURIST)

,**stop 'over** [句動詞] (-pp-) (長旅の間に少しの間)立ち寄る, 滞在する, 泊まる ◇We had to *stop over* in Kuala Lumpur for a night. クアラ・ルンプールに一泊しなくてはならなかった ☞ **stopover** (VISIT 名), **stop by** (VISIT 動)

do [他] 《インフォーマル》(観光客として)見物する ◇We *did* Tokyo in three days. 私たちは3日間で東京を見物した

steady

steady [形]

steady・stable・regular・constant・consistent・static・even・unchanging
物事がパターンに従って変わらないことを表す
【類語訳】着実な, 堅実な, 不変の, 安定した, 一定の, 揺るぎない, 正常な, 規則的な, 定期的な, 静止した, 変わらない

[文型&コロケーション]
▶a steady/ a stable/ a constant/ an even **temperature**
▶a steady/ constant/ consistent **trend/ rate**
▶a steady/ constant **speed/ stream/ trickle**
▶a steady/ a constant/ an even **flow**
▶a consistent/ an unchanging **pattern**
▶steady/ stable/ regular **employment**
▶steady/ regular/ constant **supply**
▶steady/ regular/ even **breathing**
▶a steady/ stable/ regular **relationship**
▶to **remain** steady/ stable/ constant/ consistent/ static/ even/ unchanging
▶**more or less** steady/ stable/ constant/ consistent/ static/ even
▶**fairly** steady/ stable/ constant/ consistent/ static/ even
▶**very** steady/ stable/ consistent/ static/ even

steady (徐々にかつ規則正しく)着実な, 堅実な; (変わることなく[中断されずに])不変の, 安定した, 一定の, 絶え間ない, 定まった, 決まった ◇We are making slow but *steady* progress. 我々はゆっくりだが着実に進歩している ◇The castle receives a *steady* stream of visitors. その城にはひっきりなしに観光客が訪ねてくる ◇She drove at a *steady* 50 mph. 彼女は時速50マイルの一定の速度で車を走らせた ◇She's got a *steady boyfriend* (= with

↪**steady**

whom she has a serious relationship or one that has lasted a long time). 彼女には決まったボーイフレンドがいる ☞ **steady** 《FIRM》
▶**steadily** 副 ◇The company's exports have been increasing *steadily*. その会社の輸出は堅実に伸びてきている ◇The situation got *steadily* worse. 状況はじりじりと悪化した

stable 《ふつうほめて》（変わり/失敗じ）そうになく）安定した、揺るぎない ◇He was not married, but he was in a *stable* relationship. 彼は結婚していなかったが、ずっと付き合っている相手がいた ◇The industry should do everything it can to keep prices *stable*. その産業界は価格を安定させるためにあらゆる手を打つべきだ ◇The patient's condition is *stable* (= it is not getting worse). 患者の容態は安定している ❶この意味では stable は特に、人々の私生活・家庭生活について用いられる。◆a *stable* mind/relationship/family/home（揺るぎない精神/関係/家族/家庭）。また、経済的[政治的]状況に用いられる。◆a *stable* situation/environment/government/population（安定した状況/環境/政府/人口）。◆*stable* employment（安定雇用）。stable は悪化はしていない重症患者の状態についても用いられる。 反意 **unstable**, ☞ **stable** 《FIRM》

regular（物事が）正常な、規則的な、一定の；（仕事・供給・関係が）定期的な、定まった、決まった ◇a *regular* pulse/heartbeat 正常な脈拍/鼓動 ◇There is a *regular* bus service to the airport. 空港までバスの定期便があります ◇A light flashed *at regular intervals*. 光が一定間隔で点滅していた ◇The equipment is checked *on a regular basis*. 設備は定期的に点検される ◇She couldn't find any *regular* employment. 彼女は定職を見つけられなかった ◇This breed of dog benefits from a *regular* supply of green vegetables in its diet. この種の犬に、餌に青野菜を定期的に与えるとよい 反意 **irregular** 《VARIABLE》, ☞ **regular** 《FREQUENT》

ノート **steady と regular の使い分け**：steady と regular は長い期間続き、当てになる仕事・務め・雇用・収入・供給・関係について用いることができる。意味の違いはないことが多いが、regular job（定職）は、regular でない他の仕事と対比して用いられることがある。◆I decided to give up the freelance work and concentrate on my *regular job*.（フリーランスの仕事を辞めて、定職に専念することにした）。steady はこのようには用いられない。

constant 《ややフォーマル or 専門語》（一定期間にわたって水準・速度が）不変の、一定の ◇The samples need to be stored at a *constant* temperature. サンプルは一定温度で保管しておく必要がある ❶constantは一般的に、flow, rate, rhythm, speed, state, improvement, temperature と結びつく。

consistent 《ややフォーマル》（一定期間同じように起こり続けて）着実な、堅実な、安定した ◇There has been a pattern of *consistent* growth in the economy. 着実な経済成長には一定のパターンが見られる ❶consistent は一般的に、evidence, findings, results, quality, standards, growth, performance, success, failure と結びつく。反意 **inconsistent** 《VARIABLE》
▶**consistently** 副 ◇Her work has been of a *consistently* high standard. 彼女の仕事は一貫して高い水準にある

static《時にけなして、特にビジネス》（動かず[変わらず、発展せず]）不変の、動きの、静止した ◇Sales were up 5% on last year, but pre-tax profits remained *static*. 売り上げは昨年5%増加したが、税込利益は変化なしのままであった ❶ static はこのグループの他の語と違い、特にビジネスの文脈で、変化の欠如がよいというより悪いと見なされる場合に用いられることが多い。反意語 dynamic は好ましい意味合いの語である。反意 **dynamic**《VARIABLE》

even（一定期間にわたって水準・速度が）一定の ◇Children do not learn at an *even* pace. 子どもたちは一定のペースで学ぶということをしない 反意 **uneven**《VARIABLE》

unchanging《書き言葉》（基本的なパターン・原則の観点から）変わらない、不変の ◇The days went by, *unchanging*. 変わらない日々が過ぎて行った ◇The party stood for certain *unchanging* principles. 党はいくつかの不変的な原則を支持した

steal 動 ☞ ROB

steal・take・shoplift・poach・embezzle・nick
許可を得ず、また返す[支払いする]意図もなく、人[店など]から物を取る
【類語訳】盗む、持ち去る、（盗み）取る、万引きする、引き抜く、横取りする、横領する、着服する

文型&コロケーション
▶ to steal/ take/ shoplift/ poach/ embezzle/ nick (sth) from sb/ a place
▶ to steal/ take/ embezzle/ nick sb's **money**
▶ to steal/ take/ embezzle sb's **property/ funds**
▶ to steal/ take/ nick sb's **bag/ purse/ passport**
▶ to steal/ take **food/ goods/ items**
▶ to steal/ take/ poach/ nick sb's **ideas**

steal ［自, 他］（人・店などから物を）盗む ◇We found out he'd been *stealing* from us for years. 彼が何年にもわたって私たちから盗みを働いていたことを知った ◇I *had* my wallet *stolen*. 私は財布を盗まれた ◇Thieves *stole* jewellery worth over $10,000. 窃盗団は1万ドル以上の価値がある宝石類を盗んだ
▶**stealing** 名 [U] ◇You can't just take one! That's *stealing*! をそをほんとに持ってっちゃ駄目！盗みになるよ

take ［他］（許可なく[誤って]）物を持ち去る、（盗み）取る ◇Someone has *taken* my scarf. 誰かが私のスカーフを持ち去った ◇Did the burglars *take* anything valuable? 泥棒は何か高価な物を取っていきましたか ❶take は、「誤って持ち去る」の意味で使う場合や、また、文脈から盗難についてであることがはっきりわかる場合に、steal の代わりに用いられる。

shoplift ［自］（店から）万引きする ◇What do you do if you suspect a customer may be *shoplifting*? お客が万引きしているかもしれないと思ったらどうする ☞ **shoplifter**《THIEF》, **shoplifting**《THEFT》

poach（特に英）（内密[不正, 不当]に人・考え・物を）盗む、引き抜く、横取りする ◇She accused him of *poaching* her ideas. 彼女はアイデアを盗んだとして彼のことを非難した ◇Several of our employees have been *poached* by a rival firm. 私どもの数人の従業員が競争会社に引き抜かれたのです ❶ poach はもっぱらビジネスの文脈で、従業員の引き抜き、アイデアの盗用などの意味で用いられる。

embezzle ［他, 自］（金を）横領［着服］する ◇He was found guilty of *embezzling* $150,000 of public funds. 彼は15万ドルの公金を横領したとして有罪判決を受けた ☞ **embezzlement**《THEFT》

nick ［他］《英, インフォーマル》（簡単に動かせる物を）盗む ◇Who *nicked* my pen? 私のペンを盗んだのは誰だい

step

step・footstep・pace・stride
歩く[どこかへ移動する]ために、足を上げて再びそれを下ろす行為
【類語訳】歩み、一歩、歩幅、足音、一またぎ

文型&コロケーション
- to take a (few) step(s)/ pace(s)/ stride(s) back/ forward/ to/ towards (sth)
- to take a step/ pace backwards
- quick steps/ footsteps/ strides
- light/ heavy steps/ footsteps
- to take a step/ pace
- to hear (sb's) steps/ footsteps

step [C] 歩み、一歩；一歩の距離、歩幅；足音 ◇the baby's first **steps** 赤ん坊の最初の歩み ◇He took a **step** towards the door. 彼はドアに向かって一歩歩んだ ◇I could hear his **steps** coming closer. 彼の足音が近づいてくるのが聞こえた ◇He turned and **retraced his steps** (= went back the way he had walked). 彼は向きを変え、来た道を戻った ◇The hotel is only **a short step** (= short way to walk) from the beach. 《英》そのホテルは浜辺からほんのちょっとのところにある ◇The hotel is only **steps away** from the beach. 《米》そのホテルは浜辺のすぐそばにある ☞ **step** (WALK 2)

footstep [C, ふつう複数で] (歩く[走る]ときの)足音 ◇I could hear her **footsteps** echoing in the hall. 彼女の足音がホールに鳴り響くのが聞こえた

pace [C] 歩み、一歩；一歩の距離、歩幅 ◇She took two **paces** forward. 彼女は2歩前進した ◇Jean followed a few **paces** behind. ジーンは2,3歩遅れて後に続いた ☞ **pace** (WALK 1)

stride [C] 大股の一歩、一またぎ；大股の一歩の距離、一またぎの歩幅 ◇He crossed the room *in* two **strides**. 彼は2歩の大股で部屋を横切った ◇She **lengthened** her **stride** to try and keep up with him. 彼女は彼に遅れまいと歩幅を広げた ☞ **stride** (WALK 1)

stern 形 ☞ RUTHLESS

stern・grim・severe・steely・unforgiving・dour
人がまじめでよそよそしく[恐ろしく聞こえる]ことを表す
【類語訳】険しい、厳しい、痛烈な、容赦のない、断固たる、いかめしい、近寄りがたい、頑固な、冷酷な、非情な、無慈悲な、気難しい

文型&コロケーション
- a stern/ grim/ severe/ steely **look/ voice**
- a stern/ grim/ severe/ dour **expression/ face**
- a stern/ grim/ severe **warning**
- rather stern/ grim/ severe/ dour

stern 険しい、厳しい；痛烈な、容赦のない ◇Her mother appeared, looking very **stern**. 彼女の母は険しい表情で現れた ◇His voice was suddenly **stern**. 彼の声は突然厳しくなった ◇She was one of the government's **sternest** critics. 彼女は政府を最も容赦なく批判する人物の一人だった

▷**sternly** 副 ◇'Don't be stupid,' Marie told herself **sternly**. 「ばかなまねはやめなきゃ」とマリーは厳しい調子で自分に言い聞かせた

grim (表情・口調が)険しい、厳しい、断固たる ◇Archer's expression was **grim**. アーチャーの表情は険しかった ◇They clung on to the edge of the boat with **grim** determination. 彼らは断固意を決してボートの端にしがみついていた

▷**grimly** 副 ◇'It won't be easy,' he said **grimly**.「それは簡単ではないだろう」と彼は厳しい調子で言った ◇**grimly** determined 断固決意した

severe 《特に書き言葉》(優しくて[同情的で]なく)厳しい、いかめしい、怖い、近寄りがたい ◇She fixed them with a very **severe** look. 彼女は非常にいかめしい表情で彼らをじっと見据えた ◇She was a **severe** woman who seldom smiled. 彼女はめったに笑わない近寄りがたい女性だった

▷**severely** 副 ◇a **severely** critical report きわめて手厳しい報告書

▷**severity** 名 [U] ◇He frowned with mock **severity**. 彼はいかめしさを装って眉をひそめた

steely 《特に書き言葉》(表情・口調が)頑固な、冷酷な、非情な ◇She saw the look of **steely** determination in his eyes. 彼女は彼の目に頑とした決意のまなざしを見て取った ◇Her eyes narrowed into a **steely** glare. 彼女は目を細め、冷酷そうににらみつけた

unforgiving 《けなして》(間違いに)情け容赦のない、無慈悲な ◇I wonder what makes a man so **unforgiving** and hard? どうして人はそんなにまで情け容赦なく冷酷になれるのかしら 反義 **forgiving**

dour 《けなして》気難しい、むっつりした ◇They were barely acknowledged by a **dour** receptionist. 彼らは気難しそうな受付係になんとか気づいてもらえた

still 形

still・motionless・stationary・inert・immobile・at a standstill
人や物が移動していないことを表す
【類語訳】静止した、静まり返った、止まった、固定された、動かない、停止して

文型&コロケーション
- a motionless/ an inert **body/ figure**
- to **remain** still/ motionless/ stationary/ inert/ immobile
- to **stay/ lie** still/ motionless/ inert/ immobile
- to **sit/ stand** still/ motionless/ immobile
- to **hold sb/ sth** still/ motionless/ immobile
- **perfectly/ quite** still/ motionless/ immobile
- **almost** motionless/ stationary/ immobile/ at a standstill

still 静止した、じっと動かない、静まり返った ◇**Stand** *still* when I'm talking to you! 私が話しかけている時にじっと立ってろ ◇I wish you'd **keep** *still*. じっとしててほしいんだけど ◇**Hold** the ladder *still* while I try to get over the wall. 壁を乗り越えようとしてる間、はしごを動かないように持ってて ◇**Keep** your head *still*. 頭を動かさないよう ◇The surface of the lake was calm and *still*. 湖面は穏やかに静まり返っていた ❶ *still* は、これらの語の中で最も一般的で、個々の人・動物・物体にだけでなく、水や空気のようなものについて言う場合にも用いられる。

motionless 《ややフォーマル、書き言葉》(人・動物が)静止した、じっと動かない ◇She sat *motionless* as the verdict was announced. 彼女は評決が下されているとき、身じろぎも

↳still　　　　　　　stimulate, stir, stop

せずに座っていた

stationary [（ややフォーマル）（乗り物・機械が）止まった, 動いていない ; 固定された ◇The car collided with a *stationary vehicle*. その車は止まっている車にぶつかった ◇a *stationary* exercise bike 室内固定式のエアロバイク

inert [（フォーマル）（ぐったりと）動かない ; (力がなくて)動けない ◇He lay *inert* with half-closed eyes. 彼は半分目を閉じてぐったりと横になっていた ◇They dragged the *inert* body out of the river. 彼らは動くことのない死体を川から引きずり上げた

immobile [名詞の前にまれ]《ややフォーマル, 書き言葉》（人・体の部位が）静止した, じっと動かない ; 動けない, 動かせない ◇She stood *immobile* by the window. 彼女はじっと窓際に立ちつくしていた ◇The cast is used to keep the leg *immobile*. そのギプスは脚を固定するために用いられます

at a 'standstill 行列（交通・列車が）動かないで, 停止して ◇Traffic was *at a* complete *standstill* for over two hours. 車両の通行は2時間以上にわたって完全に止められていた ◇Trains were *at a standstill* yesterday as drivers went on strike. 昨日は運転士たちがストライキに突入して, 列車は停止していた ❶ *at a standstill* は, 動いているべきだが止められてしまっている物について用いられる.

stimulate 動 ☞ CAUSE

stimulate・arouse・stir・inspire・excite
人に特定の感情を感じさせる[特定の形で反応させる]
【類語訳】刺激する, 活性化させる, 喚起する, 興奮させる, 感動させる, かき立てる

文型&コロケーション
▶ to stir/ inspire/ excite sth in sb
▶ to stimulate/ arouse/ stir/ excite (sb's) **interest**
▶ to arouse/ stir/ inspire/ excite **feelings** (of sth)
▶ to arouse/ stir/ inspire **emotions**
▶ to stimulate/ arouse/ excite **curiosity/ speculation**

stimulate [他]《ほめて》（成長・関心・議論・感情・考えなどを）刺激する, 活性化する ◇A newspaper article can be used to *stimulate* discussion among students. 新聞記事は学生間の議論を活性化させるのに使うことができる ◇Any increase in industrial activity will *stimulate* demand for electricity. 産業がいくらかでも活気づくと電気需要が高まるだろう ◇The first workshop is intended to *stimulate* ideas. 第一回目のワークショップではアイデアを活性化することが意図されています

arouse [他]（特定の感情・態度・反応を）起こさせる, 喚起する ◇Her strange behaviour *aroused* our suspicions. 彼女の奇行は我々の疑念を生んだ ◇The book *aroused* a lot of adverse criticism. その本は敵意のこもった批判を招いた ◇The issue succeeds in *arousing* a great deal of controversy. その問題は大いに物議をかもすことに成功しています ❶ この意味では arouse の目的語は感情・態度・反応となる. 人が arouse の目的語である場合は, 「人を性的に興奮させる」ことを意味する ◇He began to feel *aroused* (= sexually excited). 彼は性的に興奮し始めた 反義 **suppress** (SUPPRESS 2)

stir (-rr-) [他]《特に書き言葉》（人を）興奮させる, 感動させる, (感情を)かき立てる, 起こさせる ◇It's a book that really *stirs* the imagination. それは想像力をかき立てる本です ◇This brutal killing has *stirred* the nation's conscience. この殺人の残酷さに国民の良心は呼び覚まされた ◇He was *stirred* by the child's sad story. 彼はその子の悲しい身の上話に強く心を動かされた

inspire [他]（行動・振る舞い方が特定の感情を）抱かせる, 起こさせる ◇As a general, he *inspired* great **loyalty** in his troops. 将軍として彼は兵士たちに大いなる忠誠心を抱かせた ◇Henry did not *inspire* **confidence** as a figure of authority. 権力の座にある人物としてのヘンリーには信頼が寄せられなかった

excite [他]《ややフォーマル》（興味・反応を）起こさせる, かき立てる, 喚起する ◇This story *excited* some **comment** (= made people talk about it). この話は何かと物議をかもした ◇The move *excited* more criticism abroad than at home. その動きに自国よりも外国で批判が巻き起こされた

stir 動

stir・beat・whip・whisk
スプーンなどの道具で液体[物質]を混ぜる
【類語訳】かき回す, かき混ぜる, 撹拌する, 泡立てる

文型&コロケーション
▶ to stir/ beat/ whisk sth **into** sth
▶ to stir/ beat/ whisk sth **in**
▶ to stir/ beat/ whisk A and B **together**
▶ to stir/ beat/ whisk **ingredients/ a mixture**
▶ to beat/ whip/ whisk **cream/ eggs/ egg whites**
▶ to stir/ beat/ whisk sth **thoroughly**

stir (-rr-) [他]（スプーン状の物で液体・物質を）かき回す, かき混ぜる ◇She *stirred* her tea. 彼女はお茶をかき混ぜた ◇*Stir* the paint before you use it. ペンキは使用前によくかき混ぜなさい ◇The vegetables are *stirred* into the rice while it is hot. 炊いているお米に野菜を入れて混ぜ合わすのです
▶ **stir** 名 [C, ふつう単数で] ◇Could you give the rice a *stir*? 米をかき混ぜてもらえますか

beat [他]（フォーク状の物で液体の食べ物を）かき混ぜる, 撹拌する ◇*Beat* the eggs to a frothy consistency. 卵をもったりとした泡状になるまで強くかき混ぜてください

whip (-pp-) [他]（きめ細かくなるまでクリーム・卵白を）泡立てる ◇Serve the pie with *whipped cream*. パイに泡立てた生クリームを添えて出してください

whisk [他]（フォーク・泡立て器で液体の食べ物を）泡立てる ◇*Whisk* the egg whites until stiff. 卵白が固まるまで泡立ててください

ノート **beat, whip, whisk** の使い分け : これらは非常に似た行為である. beat は食べ物をいかに素早く強くかき混ぜるかを強調する. whip は特にクリームについて用いられる. whisk は特に手回しの[電動]泡立て器を使う時に用いられる.

stop 動

stop・give sth up・cease・drop・abandon・quit・discontinue・leave off・knock off (sth)・pack sth in
もうこれ以上何かを行い続けない[続けさせない]ことを表す
【類語訳】やめる, 止める, あきらめる, 放棄する, 終わる, 途絶える, 停止する, 中止する, 断念する, 捨てる, 中断する

文型&コロケーション
▶ to stop/ give up/ cease/ quit/ leave off **doing** sth
▶ to stop/ give up/ cease/ drop/ abandon/ quit/ leave off

what you are doing
- to **stop**/ give up/ cease/ abandon/ quit/ leave off **work**
- to **give up**/ abandon/ quit/ pack in your **job**
- to **give up**/ abandon **hope**
- to **give up**/ quit **smoking**
- **work** stops/ ceases
- to **soon**/ finally stop/ give up/ cease/ abandon/ discontinue
- to **suddenly**/ immediately/ almost/ simply/ never stop/ give up/ cease/ abandon/ quit
- to **stop**/ cease/ quit/ leave off **for a moment**

stop (-pp-) [他, 自]（…することを)やめる；やめさせる、止める ◇That phone never *stops* ringing! その電話、全然鳴りやまないんだ ◇He couldn't *stop* thinking about her. 彼は彼女のことを考えずにはいられなかった ◇Mike immediately *stopped* what he was doing. マイクはやっていたことをすぐにやめた ◇*Stop* me (= Make me stop talking) if I'm boring you.《話し言葉》うるさかったら言ってね ◇*Stop it!* You're hurting me. やめてくれ。気分を害するよ ◇Can't you just *stop*? ちょっとやめられないの ❶ stop doing sth と stop to do sth の違いに注意。◆We *stopped* taking pictures.（私たちは写真を撮るのをやめた）。これは「私たちはもはや写真を撮っていなかった」ことを意味する。◆We *stopped to* take pictures.（私たちは写真を撮るために立ち止まった）。これは「写真を撮り始められるように、私たちはしていたことをやめた」ことを意味する。

give sth 'up [句動詞]《受身なし》(…する[を持つ]ことを)やめる、あきらめる、放棄する ◇She didn't *give up* work when she had the baby. 彼女は赤ん坊ができても、仕事を辞めなかった ◇We'd *given up* hope of ever having children. 子どもをいつか持つ望みは捨てていた ◇You ought to *give up* smoking. あなたはタバコをやめるべきだ ◇He *gave up* medicine for a career in show business. 彼はショービジネスの道を進むために医学の道をあきらめた [反意] **take sth up** (BEGIN)

cease [自, 他]《フォーマル》(発生・存在が)終わる、やむ、途絶える；停止する、中止する、やめる ◇Welfare payments *cease* as soon as an individual starts a job. 個人が仕事を始めるや、生活保護費の支払いは途絶える ◇You never *cease* to amaze me! 君にはいつも驚かされるよ ◇The company *ceased* trading in June. その会社は6月に営業を停止した ◇He ordered his men to *cease fire* (= stop shooting). 彼は部下に発砲をやめるように命じた

drop (-pp-) [他]《ややインフォーマル, 特に話し言葉》(行い・議論を)やめる；中止する ◇I *dropped* German (= stopped studying it) when I was 14. 14歳の時、ドイツ語を学ぶのをやめた ◇*Drop everything* and come at once. 全部やめてすぐに来てください ◇Look, can we just *drop it* (= stop talking about it)? なあ、その話やめないか ◇I think we'd better *drop the subject*. その話題はやめたほうがいいと思う ◇The police decided to *drop* the charges against her. 警察は彼女への告訴を取り下げることにした

abandon [他]《ややフォーマル》(終了の前に)やめる、断念する；(持ち物を)あきらめる、捨てる、放棄する ◇They were forced to *abandon* the game because of rain. 彼らは雨のため試合を断念せざるをえなかった ◇We had to *abandon* any further attempt at negotiation. 我々は交渉でこれ以上の試みを一切あきらめざるをえなかった

quit [他, 自]《特に米, インフォーマル》(行いを)やめる ◇I'm still trying to *quit* smoking. 依然として私は禁煙しようと努めている ◇Just *quit it!* いいからやめろ ◇We only just started. We're not going to *quit* now. たった今始めたばかりなんだ。だから今やめるつもりはない

discontinue [他]《フォーマル》(定期的行い・使用・提供を)やめる、停止する、中止する ◇It was decided to *discontinue* the treatment after three months. 3か月後にその治療を中止することが決定された

leave 'off [句動詞]《インフォーマル》(一時的に行いを)やめる、中断する ◇Start reading from where you *left off* last time. この前やめたところから読み始めてください

knock 'off, knock 'off sth [句動詞]《インフォーマル》(仕事を)やめる、切り上げる ◇Do you want to *knock off* early today? 今日は早く仕事を切り上げたいのかい ◇What time do you *knock off* work? 何時に仕事を終えるの

pack sth 'in [句動詞]《インフォーマル》(行いを)やめる ◇She decided to *pack in* her job. 彼女は仕事を辞めることにした ◇*Pack it in* (= stop behaving badly or annoying me), you two! 《特に英》そこの二人、いい加減にしないか

[ノート] give sth up, quit, leave off, knock off (sth), pack sth in はすべて、「行いをやめる」ことを意味するインフォーマルな表現である。knock off はふつう一日の終わりに[短時間]作業をやめる場合に用いられる。leave off は一時的にやめて後でもう一度始めるつもりでいる場合にも用いられる。give up/quit work する場合、仕事を辞めて別の仕事もしない場合に用いられる。×pack in work とは言えない。しかし、仕事を辞めて別の仕事に就く、あるいは仕事を始める[世界中を旅行する]など、他の事をする場合、give up/quit/pack in your job と言うことができる。一つのプロジェクトに取り組んでいるグループの全員が、やめることを決定する[やめるように命じられる]場合、その仕事は cease, be abandoned する。◆Work on redeveloping the site has *ceased/been abandoned*.（用地再開発の仕事は中止された/打ち切られた）。仕事が cease する場合、それは再び始まるかもしれないが、be abandoned の場合は、おそらく再開されないだろう。stop はこれらのどの用法においても、work と共に用いることができる。◆What time do you *stop/knock off* work today?（今日は何時に仕事を切り上げるの）◆She *stopped/gave up/quit* work when she had the baby.（彼女は子どもができたとき、仕事を辞めた）◆Work on the project has *stopped/ceased/been abandoned*.（その事業に関わる仕事は中止になった）

story [名]

story・tale・plot・narrative・anecdote・saga・storyline
人々を楽しませることを意図した本当[想像上]の出来事について描写したもの
【類語訳】物語、話、筋、構想、逸話、秘話

[文型&コロケーション]
- a **story**/ a tale/ a plot/ a narrative/ an anecdote/ a saga/ a storyline **about** sb/ sth
- a **long** story/ tale/ narrative/ anecdote/ saga
- a/ an **good**/ amusing story/ tale/ plot/ anecdote/ storyline
- a **simple** story/ tale/ plot/ narrative
- a **dramatic**/ romantic/ complicated story/ tale/ plot/ saga

↳story / strange

- a **popular/ traditional/ fictional** story/ tale/ narrative
- a/ an **interesting/ entertaining/ humorous/ charming/ wonderful/ apocryphal** story/ tale/ anecdote
- a/ an **epic/ extraordinary/ sad/ sorry/ terrible** story/ tale/ saga
- a **great** story/ plot/ narrative/ saga
- a **historical** story/ narrative/ saga
- to **tell (sb)** a story/ a tale/ a plot/ an anecdote
- to **recount/ relate** a story/ a tale/ an anecdote
- to **read (sb)/ write** a story/ tale/ narrative/ saga
- a story/ tale/ narrative/ saga **begins/ unfolds/ ends**

story [C] （創作した）物語，話 ◇a/an adventure/detective/ghost/love story 冒険物語/探偵物語/怪談/恋物語 ◇a book of short *stories* 短編集 ◇a *story* about time travel タイムトラベルに関する話 ◇It's the epic *story* of a family's escape from war. それは戦争からの家族の脱出についての壮大な物語だ ◇Shall I tell you a *story*? お話をしてあげましょうか ◇I always read the children a bedtime *story*. 私は寝るときにいつも子どもたちに物語を読んで聞かせています ☞ **story** (REPORT 2)

tale [C]《特に書き言葉》（想像上の）物語；（口頭による）話 ◇I love listening to his *tales* of life at sea. 私は彼の海の上での生活の話を聞くのが大好きだ ◇I've heard *tales* of people seeing ghosts in that house. その家で幽霊を見た人々の話を聞いたことがある ◇Her experiences provide a *cautionary tale* (= a warning) for us all. 彼女の経験は私たちみんなの教訓になります ❶moral tale, cautionary tale は人に善悪について考えさせる話を指す．

plot [C, U]（小説・劇・映画などの）筋，構想 ◇a conventional *plot* about love and marriage 恋愛と結婚を扱った月並みな話の筋 ◇The novel is well organized in terms of *plot*. その小説は話の筋という点からはよく仕上がっている

narrative [C]《フォーマル》（小説における）物語，話 ◇She has written a gripping *narrative* of their journey up the Amazon. 彼女はアマゾン川をさかのぼる旅についての, 人の心を捉えて放さない物語を書いた ☞ **narrate** (DESCRIBE)

anecdote [C, U]（実在の人物・実際の出来事に関する短い［興味深い，面白い］）逸話；（出来事に関する個人的な）秘話 ◇He has lots of amusing *anecdotes* about his brief career as an actor. 彼には俳優としての短い経歴の中で楽しい逸話がたくさんある ◇This research is based on *anecdote*, not fact. この研究は事実ではなく秘話に基づいているのだ

saga [C]（長編の）歴史物語 ◇She has written a compelling family *saga*. 彼女は思わず読み入ってしまう家族の歴史物語を書いた

storyline [C]（小説・劇・映画などの基本的な）筋 ◇Her novels always have the same basic *storyline*. 彼女の小説にはいつも同じ基本的な話の筋がある

strange 形

1 ☞ UNUSUAL

strange・odd・weird・curious・mysterious・funny・bizarre・peculiar・uncanny

人や物事が理解が普通でない［驚かされる］ことを表す
【類語訳】奇妙な，変な，異様な，不思議な，変わった，奇怪な，不気味な，おかしな，不可解な，奇抜な，とっぴな

文型&コロケーション

- **strange/ odd/ weird/ curious/ funny/ bizarre/ peculiar/ uncanny that**...
- **strange/ odd/ weird/ curious/ funny/ peculiar/ uncanny how/ what**...
- a **strange/ an odd/ a weird/ a curious/ a mysterious/ a funny/ a bizarre/ a peculiar/ an uncanny way**
- a **strange/ an odd/ a weird/ a curious/ a mysterious/ a funny/ a bizarre/ a peculiar thing**
- a **strange/ an odd/ a weird/ a curious/ a mysterious/ a funny/ a peculiar place**
- a **strange/ an odd/ a curious/ a funny/ a bizarre/ a peculiar situation**
- a **strange/ an odd/ a curious/ a funny/ a bizarre/ a peculiar/ an uncanny feeling**
- a **strange/ an odd/ a curious/ a funny/ a peculiar smell**
- **strange/ odd/ curious/ mysterious/ bizarre/ peculiar behaviour**
- a **strange/ an odd/ a mysterious/ a peculiar person/ man/ woman**
- **something strange/ odd/ weird/ curious/ mysterious/ funny/ bizarre/ peculiar/ uncanny**
- **very strange/ odd/ weird/ curious/ mysterious/ funny/ peculiar**
- **really strange/ odd/ weird/ funny/ bizarre/ uncanny**
- **rather strange/ odd/ weird/ curious/ mysterious/ funny/ bizarre/ peculiar/ uncanny**
- **slightly strange/ odd/ weird/ curious/ mysterious/ bizarre**

strange（理解しがたいほど）奇妙な，変な，異様な，不思議な ◇A *strange* thing happened this morning. 妙なことが今朝起こった ◇It's *strange* (that) we haven't heard from him. 彼からの便りがないのはおかしい ◇That's *strange* — the front door's open. おかしいな—玄関のドアが開いている ◇There was something *strange* about her eyes. 彼女の目はどこか異様だった 反意 **normal** (NORMAL)

▶ **strangely** 副 ◇She's been acting very *strangely* lately. 彼女の行動は最近, どうもおかしい ◇*Strangely* enough, I don't feel at all nervous. 不思議と, 私はまったく緊張しないんです

odd（理解しがたいほど）奇妙な，変わった，異様な，奇怪な ◇They're very *odd* people. 彼らは非常に変わっている ◇The *odd* thing was that he didn't recognize me. 妙なことに, 彼は私のことがわからなかった ◇She had the *oddest* feeling that he was avoiding her. 彼女は彼が彼女を避けているというまったく途方もない思いを抱いた 反意 **normal** (NORMAL)

▶ **oddly** 副 ◇She's been behaving very *oddly* lately. 彼女の行動は最近, どうもおかしい ◇He looked at her in a way she found *oddly* disturbing. 彼女には妙に気になる見方で彼は彼女を見つめた

ノート **strange** と **odd** の使い分け：strange は時に人・物事がある意味で神秘的である［恐ろしい］ことを示唆する可能性がある． ◆*Strange* things have been happening round here. (このあたりで妙なことが起きている). ◆A *strange*/an *odd* thing happened this morning. (妙なことが今朝起きた). これは普通ではないが, 恐ろしいことではないだろう. odd は人・物事がある意味で理解しがたい［正しくない］と思われることを示唆する可能性がある. そこで, odd people に危害を加えられることはおそらくないだろうが, strange people には危害を加えられるかもしれない.

weird《ややインフォーマル，特に話し言葉，時にけなして》変わった，異様な，不気味な，おかしな ◇I had a really *weird* dream last night. ゆうべほんとに不気味な夢を見たんだ ◇She's a very *weird* girl. 彼女はとても風変わりな少女だ ◇It's *weird* seeing yourself on television. テレビで自分を見ると変な気がする ❶ *weird* が他人(の考え)を表す場合，判断[非難]の要素が含まれることが多い． ◆ He's got some *weird* ideas (= ideas that I do not agree with at all). (彼はおかしな考え方をする). 反意 **normal** (NORMAL)
▶ **weirdly** 副 ◇The town was *weirdly* familiar. その町は不気味に見覚えがある気がした

curious《ややフォーマル》(理解しがたいほど)奇妙な，変な，異様な，不思議な ◇It was a *curious* feeling, as though we were floating on air. それは私たちが宙に浮いているような不思議な感覚だった ◇It was *curious* that she didn't tell anyone. 彼女が誰にも語らなかったのは妙だった ❶ この意味の *curious* は人について述べることはない．a *curious person/man/woman* は「(ある事柄に)好奇心のある人」であって，「奇妙な[変な]人」ではない．
▶ **curiously** 副 ◇His clothes were *curiously* old-fashioned. 彼の服は不思議なくらい流行遅れだった ◇*Curiously* enough, a year later exactly the same thing happened again. 奇妙なことに，ちょうど一年後，同じことがまた起きた

mysterious 不可解な，奇怪な，不思議な ◇He died in *mysterious* circumstances. 彼は不可解な状況で亡くなった ◇A *mysterious* illness is affecting all the animals. 奇病があらゆる動物に蔓延している
▶ **mysteriously** 副 ◇My watch had *mysteriously* disappeared. 不思議なことに，私の腕時計がなくなってしまっていた

funny《ややインフォーマル，特に話し言葉》奇妙な，変な，不思議な，おかしな ◇That's *funny* — he was here a moment ago and now he's gone. それは変だね—彼は少し前までここにいたのに，もういない ◇The engine's making a very *funny* noise. エンジンがとても変な音を立てている ◇I'm pleased I didn't get that job, in a *funny* sort of way. その仕事もらえなくて妙な具合によかったと思っている ❶ この意味での *funny* は，*strange* のよりインフォーマルな言い方だが，*strange* とは異なり，物事が少し恐ろしいということを示唆しない．
▶ **funnily** 副 ◇*Funnily* enough, I met her only yesterday. おかしな話だが，昨日初めて彼女に会ったんだ

bizarre《非常に》奇妙な，異様な，突飛な，とっぴな ◇What a *bizarre* story! 何て奇怪な話なんだ ◇He was exhibiting some very *bizarre* behaviour. 彼はとてもとっぴな行動を見せていた
▶ **bizarrely** 副 ◇She was *bizarrely* dressed, in a sort of tent thing. 彼女は一種のテント素材の，奇抜な服を着ていた

peculiar《英 or ややフォーマル》(不快[厄介]なほど)奇妙な，変わった，異様な，奇怪な ◇I had a *peculiar* feeling we'd met before. 私たちが以前に会ったことがあるような奇妙な感覚を抱いた ◇He died in very *peculiar* circumstances. 彼は非常に異様な状況で亡くなった ❶ *peculiar* は，《米》ではかなりフォーマルであるが，《英》ではそうではない．
☞ **peculiar** (UNIQUE)

uncanny 不可解な，不気味な，不思議な ◇It was *uncanny* really, almost as if she knew what I was thinking. それは，もうまるで彼女は私が考えていることがわかっているようで，実に不思議だった ◇He has an *uncanny* knack of being able to see immediately where the problem lies. 彼は問題がどこにあるかをすぐに見出せる，不思議な能力を持っている ❶ *uncanny* は主に，(特に通常の科学的な説明のつかない)状況・能力に用いられる．

2 strange・unknown・unfamiliar・alien
人々[場所，物事]が見[聞き]覚えのないことを表す
【類語訳】知らない，未知の，不明の，なじみのない，異質の，無縁の

文型&コロケーション
▶ strange/ unknown/ unfamiliar/ alien **to** sb
▶ a strange/ an unknown/ an unfamiliar/ an alien **place**
▶ a strange/ an unknown/ an unfamiliar/ an alien **environment**
▶ a strange/ an unfamiliar **situation/ feeling**

strange 知らない，未知の，見[聞き]慣れない，見[聞き]覚えのない ◇Never accept rides from *strange* men. 知らない男の車に絶対乗らないように ◇She woke up in a *strange* bed in a *strange* room. 彼女は見知らぬ部屋の見知らぬベッドで目覚めた ◇At first the place was *strange* to me. 最初はその場所に見覚えがなかった

unknown 知られていない，未知の，不明の ◇a species of insect previously *unknown* to science これまで科学的に知られていない種の昆虫 ◇He was trying, *for some unknown reason*, to count the stars. 何か測り知れない理由で，彼はその星々を数えようとしていた ◇The man's identity remains *unknown*. その男の身元は不明のままである

unfamiliar よく知らない，なじみのない，見[聞き]慣れない，見[聞き]覚えのない ◇An *unfamiliar* sound came from the hall. 聞き慣れない音がホールから聞こえてきた ◇Please highlight any terms that are *unfamiliar* to you. よく知らないどんな用語もマーカーで強調してください 反意 **familiar** ❶ *familiar* な人・場所・物事は，以前に見た[会った]ことなどがあってよく知られていることを表す． ◆ to look/sound/ taste *familiar* (見/聞き/味わった覚えがある). ◆ He's a *familiar* figure in the neighbourhood. (彼は近所ではよく知られた人物だ).

ノート **strange** と **unfamiliar** の使い分け：この意味では *strange* は特に人々・場所を表すのに用いられる．*word, term, name, face, voice, sound, feeling* などに用いられる場合，「奇妙な」を意味することが多い．「知らない」ことを明確に意味する場合は，*unfamiliar* を用いる．

alien《書き言葉》異質の；無縁の ◇In a world that had suddenly become *alien* and dangerous, he was her only security. 突然異質で物騒になってしまった世界に入り込んで，彼女には彼だけが頼りだった

stress 動 ☞ POINT STH OUT

stress・emphasize・underline・underscore・weight・prioritize
注目されるように人や物事に特定の重要性を与える
【類語訳】重点を置く，強調する，力説する，強勢を置く，際立たせる，優先順位をつける

文型&コロケーション
▶ to stress/ emphasize/ underline **that/ how...**
▶ to stress/ emphasize/ underline/ underscore **the fact that...**
▶ to stress/ emphasize/ underline/ underscore the **impor-**

↪stress

tance/ extent/ necessity of sth
▶to stress/ emphasize/ underline/ underscore/ prioritize a **need**
▶to stress/ emphasize/ ❶underline/ underscore a **point**
▶to stress/ emphasize/ underline the **difference**
▶to stress/ emphasize/ underline an **aspect** of sth
▶to stress/ emphasize a **word/ syllable/ phrase**
▶to **clearly** stress/ emphasize/ underline/ underscore/ weight sth
▶to **heavily** stress/ emphasize/ weight sth
▶to **further** stress/ emphasize/ underline/ underscore sth
▶to **just** stress/ emphasize/ underline sth

stress [他] (物事に)重点を置く;強調[力説]する;(単語・音節に)強勢[アクセント]を置く ◇She *stressed* the importance of a good education. 彼女はよい教育の重要性を強調した ◇*I must stress* that everything I've told you is strictly confidential. お話したことはすべて極秘であるということを強調しておかなければなりません ◇*It must be stressed that* this disease is very rare. この病気は非常にまれであるということを強調しなければなりません ◇I want to *stress* how important this work is. この仕事がいかに重要であるかを強調したい ◇You *stress* the first syllable in 'happiness'. 「happiness」は第一音節にアクセントを置きます ☞ **stress** (PRIORITY)

emphasize (英 **-ise**) [他] (ややフォーマル) (重要性を)強調[力説]する;(単語・句を)強めて言う ◇The report *emphasizes* the need for economic stability. その報告書は経済が安定することの必要性を強調している ◇*It should be emphasized that* this is only one possible explanation. これが唯一可能な説明であることを強調しなければなりません ◇He *emphasized* how little was known about the disease. 彼はその病気についてはほとんど何も知られていないことを強調した ◇'Let nothing... nothing,' he *emphasized* the word, 'tempt you.' 「何事にも…何事にも」と彼はnothingという語を強調し、「そそのかされないように」と続けた ☞ **emphasis** (PRIORITY)

ノート **stress** と **emphasize** の使い分け：事実・問題に特定の重要性を与えることについては、両語とも使用可能。stressはいくぶんインフォーマルで、特に主語が人間のとき(I must stress ... など)に、話し言葉やジャーナリズムで用いられることが多い。emphasizeは少しフォーマルで、特に主語が人間でないとき(The report emphasize...など)に、書き言葉や学術的文脈で用いられることが多い。単語を強調する場合、音節の強勢についてはstressを用い、単語に特定の重要性を与えることには、stress, emphasizeを用いることができる。

underline [他] (ややフォーマル) (重要・真実であることを)強調[力説]する、際立たせる ◇The report *underlines* the importance of pre-school education. その報告書は就学前教育の重要性を強調している ◇Her question only *underlined* how little she understood him. 彼女の質問はかえって、彼女が彼のことをほとんど理解していないことを際立たせただけだった ❶報告書や陳述は、事実・必要性・要点を underlineすることが多い。人は物事を行う決意・約束を underlineすることもある。

underscore [他] (特に米, 特にビジネス) (重要性を)強調[力説]する ◇His speech *underscored* the need for a clear policy. 彼は演説で明確な政策の必要性を力説した

ノート **underline** と **underscore** の使い分け：(英)では underlineは、人・物事が物事を意図的に強調する場合にしか

stressful

用いられない underscoreよりも使用範囲が広い。意図せず物事が重要・真実であることを示す場合にはunderlineを用いる。(米)ではunderscoreもこのように用いられるが、(英)では用いられない。◆Her question only *underlined* how little she understood him. (彼女の質問はかえって、彼女が彼のことをほとんど理解していないことを際立たせただけだった). ◆Her question only *underscored* how little she understood him. ((米でも)彼女の質問はかえって、彼女が彼のことをほとんど理解していないことを際立たせただけだった). (英)(米)の双方において、物事に特定の注意を引きたいときには、highlightを用いることもできる。☞ **highlight** (POINT STH OUT)

weight [他, ふつう受身で] (専門語) (比較して)重みを与える ◇Each of these factors should be *weighted* according to their relative importance. これらの要素はそれぞれ、その相対的な重要性に従って重みを与えられるべきだ

prioritize (英でまた **-ise**) [他, 自] (ややフォーマル) (仕事・問題に)優先順位をつける、重要な順に処理する ◇You should make a list of all the jobs you have to do and *prioritize* them. しなければならない仕事をすべてリストアップして、それらに優先順位をつけたらいい ◇You have to learn to *prioritize*. 重要な順に処理することを学ばなければなりません ☞ **priority** (PRIORITY)

stressful 形 ☞ PAINFUL 2

stressful • tense • strained • fraught • anxious • nerve-racking
状況[出来事, 時]が気がかりであることを表す
【類語訳】ストレスの多い, 張り詰めた, 緊迫した, 不安な, 心配な

文型&コロケーション

▶a stressful/ tense/ fraught/ anxious **time**
▶a stressful/ tense/ fraught **meeting/ situation**
▶a tense/ strained/ fraught **atmosphere/ silence/ relationship**
▶a tense/ an anxious **wait**
▶**emotionally** stressful/ tense/ fraught

stressful ストレスの多い, 張り詰めた ◇a *stressful* job/ lifestyle ストレスの多い仕事/生活様式 ◇It was a very *stressful* time for all of us. それは私たち全員にとって非常に張り詰めた時間だった ☞ **stress** (PRESSURE 1), **stressed** (TENSE)

tense 張り詰めた, 緊迫した ◇I spent a few *tense* weeks waiting for the results of the tests. 私は試験の結果を待ちながら、張り詰めた数週間を過ごした ◇The atmosphere in the meeting was getting more and more *tense*. 会議の雰囲気はますます緊迫していた ☞ **tense** (TENSE), **tension** (PRESSURE 1), **tension** (TENSION)

strained 緊迫した;張り詰めた ◇Relations between the two countries remain *strained*. その2か国間の関係は緊迫したままだ ◇The game was played in an atmosphere of *strained* silence. 試合は張り詰めて沈黙した雰囲気の中で行われた ☞ **strained** (TENSE), **strain** (PRESSURE 1)

fraught (特に英) 緊迫した, 張り詰めた, 思い悩んだ ◇His relationship with his mother had always been *fraught*. 彼の母親との関係はつねに張り詰めていた ◇She looked *fraught*. 彼女は思い悩んでいるように見えた

ノート tense, strained, fraught の使い分け：これらの語はすべて雰囲気・関係を表すことができる。tense と strained はどちらも、特にジャーナリズムで、(外見上は儀礼的に)正式な[公式の]関係を表すのに用いられる。fraught はより個人的で情緒的な関係を表す。

anxious (時が)不安[心配]な；(表情が)不安[心配]そうな ◇There were a few *anxious* moments during the game. 試合中には不安な瞬間が2,3度あった ◇There was an *anxious* expression on her face. 彼女の顔には心配そうな表情が浮かんでいた ☞ **anxious** (WORRIED)

'nerve-racking (または **'nerve-wracking**)(経験が)神経をすり減らす ◇My first visit was rather *nerve-racking*. 私の最初の訪問はかなり神経をすり減らすものだった ☞ **nervous** (WORRIED)

strict 形

strict・tough・harsh・rigid・stringent・punitive・firm・severe
従わなければならないような人や、守らなければならないような一連の規則を指し示す
【類語訳】厳しい、厳格な、きつい、過酷な、無慈悲な、厳正な、柔軟性のない、融通の利かない、懲罰的な、断固たる

firm	strict	harsh
	tough	punitive
	stringent	severe

文型&コロケーション

▶ strict/ tough/ harsh/ firm/ severe **with** sb/ sth
▶ strict/ tough/ harsh/ severe **on** sb/ sth
▶ strict/ tough/ harsh/ rigid/ firm/ severe **discipline**
▶ a tough/ harsh/ severe **penalty/ sentence**
▶ strict/ tough/ rigid/ stringent/ firm **controls**
▶ strict/ tough/ rigid/ stringent/ severe **restrictions**
▶ strict/ rigid/ stringent/ severe **limits**
▶ strict/ tough/ rigid/ stringent **rules/ standards**
▶ strict/ tough/ harsh/ stringent **conditions/ legislation**
▶ a strict/ harsh/ punitive **regime**
▶ tough/ harsh/ stringent/ punitive/ firm **measures**
▶ tough/ punitive/ firm **action**
▶ harsh/ stringent/ severe **criticism**
▶ **increasingly** strict/ tough/ harsh/ stringent/ punitive/ severe
▶ **extremely** strict/ tough/ harsh/ rigid/ severe
▶ **excessively/ unnecessarily** strict/ harsh/ rigid

strict (規則・指示が)厳しい；(人が)厳格な ◇She left *strict* instructions that she must not be disturbed. 彼女は自分を起こさないようにとの厳しい指示を残した ◇She's on a very *strict* diet. 彼女は非常に厳しい食事制限中である ◇They were always very *strict* with their children. 彼らは常に自分の子どもたちにとても厳しかった ◇She's very *strict about* things like homework. 彼女は宿題などの事柄には非常に厳しい ◇I had a very *strict* upbringing. 私は非常に厳しくしつけられた 反意 **lenient**
▶ **strictly** 副 ◇The industry is *strictly* regulated. その産業は厳重に規制されている ◇She was brought up very *strictly*. 彼女は非常に厳しく育てられた

tough (ややインフォーマル)(規則に)厳しい ◇Don't be too *tough* on him — he was only trying to help. 彼にあまり厳しくするな—彼は手助けしようとしていただけなんだから ◇The government has promised to *get tough on* crime. 政府は犯罪を厳しく取り締まることを約束した ◇The school *takes a tough line on* (= punishes severely) cheating. 学校ではカンニングに対して厳しい態度がとられます ◇There will be *tough* new controls on car emissions. 車の排ガスに関する厳しい規制が新しく出るだろう ◇Courts are imposing *tougher* penalties for street crime. 裁判所は路上犯罪に対してより厳しい罰を科しつつある ❶ tough は、規則を作る[施行する]人々[規則自体、規則を守らないことに対する罰]を表すのに用いられる。反意 **soft**

harsh (ふつうけなして)(判決・罰・状況が適切でなく)厳しい、きつい、過酷な、無慈悲な ◇It may seem a bit *harsh* to criticize him after his death. 彼の死後彼を批判することは少々過酷と思えるかもしれない ◇He later regretted his *harsh* words. 彼は後できつい言葉を放ったことを後悔した ◇He accused her of being *unduly harsh*. 彼は過度に無慈悲だとして彼女を責めた ◇We had to face up to the *harsh realities* of life sooner or later. 私たちは遅かれ早かれ、人生の厳しい現実に立ち向かわなければならなかった 反意 **lenient**
▶ **harshly** ◇Don't judge him too *harshly*. 彼をあまり厳しく評するな

rigid (しばしばけなして)(規則・方法が)厳しい、厳正な、融通の利かない、柔軟性のない ◇His *rigid* adherence to the rules made him unpopular. それらの規則に固執して、彼は人気を落とした ◇The warriors were governed by a *rigid* code of ethics. 戦士たちは厳しい倫理規定によって支配されていた
▶ **rigidly** 副 ◇The speed limit must be *rigidly* enforced. 速度制限は厳正に実施されなければならない

stringent (フォーマル)(規則・手続きが)厳しい、厳正な ◇There are *stringent* quality control procedures. 厳正な品質管理手順がある ◇Safety standards were less *stringent* in those days. 当時、安全基準はさほど厳しくなかった

punitive [ふつう名詞の前で](フォーマル)処罰[罰則]のための、懲罰的な；(税・料金が)過酷な、報復のための ◇*Punitive* action will be taken against the hooligans. フーリガンに対して懲罰措置がとられるだろう ◇They could impose *punitive tariffs* of up to 100% on imports.《米》輸入品に対して最大100%までの報復関税が課されるかもしれない ❶ punitive は taxes (税), tariffs (関税), charges (料金), damages (損害賠償), sanctions (制裁) は、人を罰する[不利な状況に置く]ことを意図している(ように見える)。例えば、政府は貿易紛争の一部として、特定の国からの商品に関して punitive tariff (報復関税)を課すかもしれない。

firm (しばしばほめて)(行動が)確固たる、断固たる、きっぱりした ◇People are looking towards him for *firm* leadership. 人々は彼に確固たる指導力を期待している ◇Parents must be *firm* with their children. 両親は子どもたちに対して断固たる態度でいなければならない
▶ **firmly** 副 ◇'I can manage,' she said *firmly*. 「何とかやれます」と彼女はきっぱりと言った

severe (規則違反に)厳しい、過酷な、情け容赦のない ◇He received a *severe reprimand* for his behaviour. 彼はその素行で厳しく叱責された ◇The courts are becoming more *severe* on young offenders. 裁判所は若い犯罪者たちに対して厳しくなりつつある
▶ **severely** 副 ◇Anyone breaking the law will be *severely* punished. 法を犯す者は誰でも、厳しく罰せられるだろう

strong 形

1 strong・powerful・muscular
人や動物が体力の旺盛なことを表す
【類語訳】力持ちの, 強靭な, 筋骨隆々の

文型&コロケーション
▶ (a) strong/ powerful/ muscular **build/ body/ arms/ legs**
▶ strong/ powerful **muscles/ jaws**

strong (人・動物が)力持ちの ◇He's *strong* enough to lift a car! 彼は車を持ち上げるほどの力持ちなんだ ◇She wasn't a *strong* swimmer (= she could not swim well). 彼女はあまりうまく泳げなかった 反意 **weak**, ☞ **strength** (FORCE 名)

powerful 《特に書き言葉、ふつうほめて》(人・動物が)強靭な ◇He was lithe and *powerful* as an athlete. 彼は運動選手として柔軟で強靭だった ☞ **power** (FORCE 名)

ノート **strong** と **powerful** の使い分け: この意味では strong は、最も普通に用いられる平易な語である。powerful は特により文語的な記述で用いられるほめ言葉である。

muscular 筋骨隆々の ◇He was tall, lean and *muscular*. 彼は背が高く細身で筋骨隆々だった

2 strong・spicy・savoury・hot
食べ物や飲み物の風味が強いことを表す
【類語訳】強烈な, 濃い, 香辛料の利いた, 塩味の利いた, 辛い

文型&コロケーション
▶ a strong/ spicy/ savoury/ hot **flavour**
▶ a strong/ spicy/ savoury **taste**
▶ (a) spicy/ savoury **food/ dish/ sauce**
▶ strong/ hot **mustard**
▶ a spicy/ hot **curry**

strong (食べ物が)風味の強い, 強烈な;(飲み物が)濃い ◇*strong* cheese 風味の強いチーズ ◇a cup of *strong* black coffee 一杯の濃いブラックコーヒー 反意 **mild** (MILD), **weak** ❶ strong でないチーズ・香辛料は mild である。strong でない茶・コーヒー(などの飲み物)は weak である。◆a cup of sweet, *weak* tea (一杯の甘く薄い紅茶).

spicy (食べ物が)香辛料の利いた ◇a plate of *spicy* chicken wings 一皿の香辛料の利いた鶏の手羽肉

savoury 《英》《米 **savory**》塩味の利いた ◇a *savoury* snack 塩味の利いたスナック ◇What's in the pastry? Is it sweet or *savoury*? ペストリーの中身は、甘いの、それとも塩味の 反意 **sweet** 甘い食べ物には、砂糖が入っている[の味がする]。◆I had a craving for something *sweet*. (すごく甘い物が欲しかった). ◆This wine is too *sweet* for me. (このワインは私には甘すぎる).

hot (コショウ・香辛料が入っていて)辛い ◇You can make a curry *hotter* simply by adding chillies. チリを加えるだけでもカレーをもっと辛くできるよ 反意 **mild**

structure 名 ☞ SYSTEM

structure・framework・form・composition・construction・fabric・make-up
部分部分が組み合わされてできている形
【類語訳】構造, 構成, 機構, 体系, 枠組み, 形式, 構図, 組成

合成, 造り, 体制

文型&コロケーション
▶ the **basic** structure/ framework/ form/ composition/ construction/ fabric of sth
▶ a **simple/ complex/ coherent/ rigid/ flexible** structure/ framework/ form
▶ the **economic/ political/ social** structure/ framework/ composition/ fabric/ make-up of sth
▶ the **chemical/ genetic** structure/ composition/ make-up of sth
▶ to **create/ devise/ establish/ provide** a structure/ framework for sth

structure [C] (異なる層から成る)構造, 構成, 機構, 体系 ◇the *structure* of the building/human body 建物/人体の構造 ◇a career/salary/tax *structure* 職歴体系/給与体系/税体系 ◇the grammatical *structures* of a language 言語の文法構造 ◇Students study the *structure* of human societies throughout history. 学生たちは歴史を通して人間社会の構造を勉強するのです ☞ **structure** (EFFICIENCY)

framework [C] (信条・考え・規則の)枠組み ◇They established a basic *framework* of ground rules for discussions. 彼らは話し合いの基本原則の基礎的な枠組みを確立した ◇The report provides a *framework for* further research. その報告書はさらなる調査のための枠組みを提供するものです

form [U] (芸術作品・文学作品における)形式, 形の構成, 構図 ◇The photographer always said that shape and *form* were more important to him than colour. その写真家はいつも、自分にとって形と構図は色彩よりも大切だと言っていた ◇The *form* of the poem is of great significance. その詩の形式は非常に重要である

composition [C] 《ややフォーマル》(異なる部分・人々から成る)構造, 構成, 組成, 合成;[構造(構成, 組成, 合成)]物 ◇recent changes in the *composition* of the workforce 労働力の構成における最近の変化 ◇The two drugs are nearly identical in *composition*. その二つの薬物の組成はほぼ同一である

construction [U] (建造物の)構造, 造り ◇ships of steel *construction* 鉄骨構造の船 ◇The earliest Greek temples were small buildings, simple in *construction*. 最古のギリシャ寺院は簡単な構造の小さな建物だった ☞ **construction** (PRODUCTION), **construct** (BUILD)

fabric [単数で] 《ややフォーマル》(社会・組織の)構成 ◇This is a worrying trend which threatens *the very fabric of society*. これは社会の体制そのものを脅かす厄介な流れである

'make-up [単数で] 《ややインフォーマル, 特に話し言葉 or ジャーナリズム》(異なる部分・人々から成る)構造, 構成, 組成, 合成;[構造(構成, 組成, 合成)]物 ◇the genetic *make-up* of plants and animals 動植物の遺伝子構造 ◇Ireland did show up a number of flaws in the England team's *make-up*. アイルランドはイングランドのチーム構成の弱点をいくつも浮き彫りにした

ノート **composition** と **make-up** の使い分け: composition は科学的[専門的]な文脈で用いられることが多い。make-up は講演・ジャーナリズムで用いられることが多い。

stubborn 形

stubborn・obstinate・wilful・headstrong・strong-willed
人が意見[振る舞い]は変えないと決め、忠告には耳を傾けようとしないことを表す
【類語訳】頑固な、強情な、不屈な、揺るぎない、意固地な、わがままな、意志の強い

[文型&コロケーション]
▶a stubborn/ an obstinate/ a wilful **child**
▶a stubborn/ an obstinate **man/ woman**
▶a stubborn/ an obstinate/ a wilful **refusal**

stubborn 《しばしばけなして》頑固な、強情な、不屈な、揺るぎない ◇He was too *stubborn* to admit that he was wrong. 彼はあまりにも頑固で、自分が間違っていることを認めなかった ◇She has inherited her mother's *stubborn streak*. 彼女は母親の強情な性格を受け継いでいる ◇He started out with nothing but raw talent and *stubborn* determination. 《ほめて》彼は磨けば光る才能と不屈の決意以外何もないままスタートした
▶**stubbornly** 副 ◇She *stubbornly* refused to pay. 彼女は頑なに支払いを拒んだ

obstinate 《ふつうけなして》(説得に対して)頑固な、強情な ◇He can be very *obstinate* when he wants to. 彼はなろうと思えば非常に強情にもなれる ◇Their position remains one of *obstinate* denial, even in face of the new evidence. 新しい証拠を目の前にしても、彼らの態度は頑なに否認したままだ
▶**obstinately** 副 ◇She *obstinately* refused to consider the future. 彼女は頑として将来のことを考えようとしなかった

wilful 《特に英》《米でふつう**willful**》《けなして》(やりたいと思って)意固地な、強情な；(他人の思いを気にかけず)わがままな ◇He was an aggressive, often selfish and *wilful* child. 彼は攻撃的で、しばしば自分勝手でわがままな子どもだった

headstrong 《けなして, 特に書き言葉》(好きなようにやりたくて)頑固な、強情な ◇She is too wild and *headstrong* to be guided by me. 彼女はあまりに奔放、強情で私の指導など及ばない

,strong-'willed 《しばしばけなして》(望みどおりやろうと思って)頑固な、意志の強い ◇She was a fiercely independent and *strong-willed* woman. 彼女は非常に自立した意志の強い女性だった

[ノート] wilful と headstrong は常に非難的な言葉である。wilful, headstrong な人は常に間違っていて、その人に反対・助言しようとする人のほうが常に正しい。strong-willed な人は、正しいかもしれないし間違っているかもしれないが、助言を聞かない。obstinate は、単に他人にとって扱いにくく、問題を引き起こすだけで、振る舞いを変えようとはしない人に用いられる。stubborn もこれを示唆するが、stubborn determination（不屈の決意）の句などで、称賛したり賛成したりする場合にも用いられる。

stupid 形

stupid・dumb・thick・obtuse
人が頭のよくないことを表す
【類語訳】ばかな、頭の悪い、頭の鈍い

[文型&コロケーション]
▶to **look** stupid/ dumb/ thick
▶**very/ really/ rather/ pretty** stupid/ dumb
▶**a bit** stupid/ dumb/ thick/ obtuse
▶**totally/ completely** stupid/ dumb/ thick
▶**Don't be so/ How can you be so** stupid/ dumb/ obtuse!

stupid 《ややインフォーマル、特に話し言葉》ばかな、頭の悪い ❶人を stupid と呼ぶのは失礼である。◆He'll be OK — he's not *stupid*. (彼は大丈夫だろう—ばかじゃないんだから). ◆I felt completely *stupid*. (ほんとにばかになったような気がした). ◆You *stupid* idiot! Put that gun down! (ばか野郎。その銃を下ろせ). [反意] **intelligent, smart, clever** (INTELLIGENT) ❶intelligent の直接的な反意語は、unintelligent であるが、これはあまり頻繁には用いられない。stupid はかなりインフォーマルな語で、書き言葉よりも話し言葉で用いられることが多い。フォーマルな言い回しや書き言葉では、unintelligent は人をあまり頭がよくないと評する上で、より普通に用いられ、丁寧である。
▶**stupidity** 名 [U] ◇He faked *stupidity* to try to escape punishment for the crime. 彼は犯罪の処罰を逃れようとしてばかをよそおった
▶**stupidly** 副 ◇She stared *stupidly* at the screen. 彼女はばかみたいにスクリーンをじっと見つめた

dumb 《特に米, インフォーマル》ばかな、頭の悪い ❶人を dumb と呼ぶのはふつう無礼だが、stupid ほど侮辱的ではない。◆If the police question you, act *dumb* (= pretend you do not know anything). (警察に尋問されたら、ばかをよそおいなさい). ◆She's going out with some *dumb* jock from her high school. (彼女は同じ高校出身のあるスポーツばかとデートすることになっている). ◆His new girlfriend is a classic *dumb blonde*. 《侮蔑的》彼の新しい恋人は、典型的に頭が空っぽのブロンドの髪の女性だ). [反意] **smart, bright** (INTELLIGENT)

thick 《英, インフォーマル》ばかな、頭の悪い ❶人を thick と呼ぶのは無礼である。◆Are you *thick* or what? (君はばかでなけりゃ何なんだ). ◆I'm not completely *thick*, you know. (いいかい、僕はまったくのばかというわけじゃないんだ). しかし stupid とは違い、人はふつうは自分自身については thick を用いない。×I felt completely *thick*.

obtuse 《フォーマル》頭の鈍い ◇Are you being deliberately *obtuse*? わざと頭の鈍いふりをしているの ❶sb is being *obtuse* と言う場合、故意にわからないふりをしていることを示唆することが多い。

style 名 ☞ FASHION

style・elegance・flair・class・grace・glamour
物事を見たり、行ったりする際の魅力的で想像力に富んださまを表す
【類語訳】手際の良さ、上品さ、気品、優雅さ、センスの良さ、品格、高級、優秀さ、一流、艶やかさ

[文型&コロケーション]
▶to do sth **with** style/ elegance/ flair/ grace
▶**great** style/ elegance/ flair/ class/ grace
▶**sheer** style/ elegance/ class/ grace
▶**real** style/ elegance/ flair/ class
▶**natural** style/ elegance/ flair/ grace
▶**a certain** style/ elegance/ flair/ class/ grace/ glamour

↪**style**

▶to **give** sb/ sth style/ elegance/ class/ grace/ glamour
▶to **lend** sb/ sth style/ elegance/ grace/ glamour
▶to **have/ lack** style/ elegance/ flair/ class/ grace/ glamour
▶to **add** style/ elegance/ flair/ class/ glamour
▶a **touch of** style/ elegance/ class/ glamour

style [U]《ほめて》(物事を行う)手際の良さ;(魅力的で高水準の)上品さ,気品 ◇She does everything with *style* and grace. 彼女は何でも手際よく優雅にこなす ◇The hotel has been redecorated but it's lost a lot of its *style*. ホテルは改装されたが,その気品をだいぶ失った ☞**stylish** (ELEGANT)

elegance [U]《ほめて》(外見・衣服・振る舞いの)優雅さ;(場所・物事に見られる心地よい)上品さ,気品 ◇She dresses with casual *elegance*. 彼女はさりげなく優雅に着こなしている ◇His writing combines *elegance* and wit. 彼の文章には気品とウィットの両方が備わっている ☞**elegant** (ELEGANT)

flair [U]《ほめて》(物事を行う際の)センス[趣味]の良さ ◇She dresses with real *flair*. 彼女の服装は実に趣味がいい ◇His designs are all right, but he lacks artistic *flair*. 彼のデザインは申し分ないが,芸術的センスには欠けるんだよね

class [U]《ほめて》気品,品格,高級,優秀さ,一流 ◇She has *class* all right — she looks like a model. 彼女には十分な気品がある—モデルみたいだ ◇There's a real touch of *class* about this team. このチームにはほんと品格が漂っている ❶class は特に a touch of class の句で用いられる。印象的で永続的上質感を感じさせる物は add a touch of class to sth の句としばしば結びつく。 ◆A real parquet floor will *add a touch of class to* the room. (本物の寄木細工の床は,その部屋に気品を与えるだろう)。 ☞**classy** (FASHIONABLE), **classic** (ELEGANT)

grace [U]《ほめて》優雅さ,上品さ,気品 ◇She moves with the natural *grace* of a ballerina. 彼女の動きはバレリーナらしい自然な優雅さがある ☞**graceful** (ELEGANT)

glamour [U]《ほめて》(富・成功をも暗示する)艶やかさ ◇Add a cashmere scarf under your jacket for a touch of *glamour*. 上着の下にカシミアのスカーフを足して艶やかさを出しなさい ❶glamour は有名人に関連したファッション・優雅さについて用いられることが多い。 ☞**glamorous** (FASHIONABLE)

subject 名 ☞ ISSUE

subject・theme・topic・motif・keynote
話し合われる[描かれる]物事[人,考え]
【類語訳】主題,話題,議題,題材,テーマ,論題,楽想,モチーフ,基調,基本方針

文型&コロケーション
▶**on** a subject/ theme/ topic
▶a/ an **important/ key/ major/ serious/ general** subject/ theme/ topic
▶a **central** theme/ topic/ motif
▶to **discuss/ consider/ deal with/ examine/ explore/ look at/ focus on/ touch on/ tackle** a subject/ theme/ topic

subject [C] (話し合われる[描写される,扱われる])主題,話題,議題,題材 ◇I have nothing more to say on the subject. その話題についてこれ以上言うことはない ◇Nelson Mandela is the *subject* of a new biography. ネルソン・マンデラが新しい伝記の題材である ◇I wish you'd *change the subject* (= talk about sth else). 話題を変えてほしいなあ ◇How did we *get onto the subject* of marriage? 何で結婚の話になったんだっけ ◇We seem to have *got off the subject* we're meant to be discussing. 話し合うことになっている議題からそれたようです ◇The *subject* of gambling has *come up* several times lately. ギャンブルの問題は最近何度か話にのぼっている ☞**subject** (AREA 2), **subject matter** (MESSAGE)

theme [C] (話・文学作品・芸術作品の)主題,話題,テーマ ◇North American literature is the main *theme* of this year's festival. 北米文学が今年のフェスティバルのメインテーマである ◇Several familiar *themes emerged* from the discussion. 討論を通じておなじみのテーマがいくつか出てきた ◇The stories are all *variations on the theme* of unhappy marriage. それらの物語はすべて,不幸な結婚をテーマに形を変えたものだ

topic [C] (語る[書く,学ぶ])主題,話題,議題,論題 ◇The *topic for* tonight's discussion is... 今夜の議題は…である ◇It might be better to avoid such a controversial *topic*. そうした物議をかもすような話題は避けたほうがいいかもしれない ◇The main *topic of conversation* was Tom's new girlfriend. 話題はもっぱらトムの新しい恋人のことだった

motif [C] (文学作品・楽曲で繰り返し展開される)主題,題材,楽想,モチーフ ◇Alienation is a central *motif* in her novels. 疎外ということが彼女の小説の中心的なモチーフである

keynote [C, ふつう単数で]《特にジャーナリズム or 政治》(本・演説などの)基調,基本方針 ◇Choice is the *keynote* of the new education policy. 選択の自由ということが新しい教育方針の要(かなめ)である ◇a *keynote speech/speaker* (= a very important one, introducing a meeting or its subject) 基調演説/演説者

succeed 動

succeed・make it・make your/a mark・achieve・arrive・make a name for yourself・conquer・get on
仕事が[特定の活動分野で]うまくいっていることを表す
【類語訳】成功する,有名になる,制覇する

文型&コロケーション
▶to succeed/ make it/ make your mark/ make a name for yourself/ get on **in** sth
▶to succeed/ make it/ make your mark/ arrive/ make a name for yourself **as** sth
▶to make your mark/ make a name for yourself **by doing** sth

succeed [自] (金・権力・尊敬を手に入れて仕事で)成功する ◇You will have to work hard if you are to *succeed*. 成功したいのなら,懸命に働かなければならないよ ◇She doesn't have the ruthlessness to *succeed* in business. 彼女はビジネスで成功するための非情さに欠ける 反意 **fail** (FAIL 2), ☞**succeed** (ACHIEVE)

'make it 〈ややインフォーマル〉(仕事で)成功する ◇You can *make it* if you believe in yourself. 自分を信じれば成功できる ◇He never really *made it* as an actor. 彼は俳優としては決して成功しなかった

successful

,**make your/a 'mark** [行礼] 《ややインフォーマル》(特定の分野で有名になって)成功する ◇She has already *made her mark on* the music industry. 彼女は音楽業界ですでに成功している

achieve [自] (自分の研究で)成功する ◇Their background gives them little chance of *achieving* at school. 彼らはその生い立ちのせいで、学校で学業を修める機会がほとんど得られない ☞ *achieve* (ACHIEVE)

arrive [自] 《ふつう sb has/had arrived の形で》《ややインフォーマル》(特定の分野で)成功する ◇He knew he had *arrived* when he was shortlisted for the Booker Prize. ブッカー賞の選考候補者リストに入った時、彼は自分が成功したと思った

make a name for yourself [行礼] 《ややインフォーマル》有名になる ◇She's *made* quite *a name for herself*. 彼女はすっかり有名になった ☞ *name* (REPUTATION)

conquer [他] 《ややインフォーマル》(特定の場所で)成功を収める、制覇する ◇The band is now setting out to *conquer the world*. そのバンドは現在、世界制覇を目指しているところだ ◇This is a British film which could *conquer the US market*. これは米国市場を席巻するかもしれない英国映画だ

,**get 'on** [句動] 《英、ややインフォーマル》(仕事で)成功する ◇Parents are always anxious for their children to *get on*. 両親はいつも子どもたちの成功を願っている ◇I don't know how he's going to *get on in life*. 彼がどうやって人生を切り開いていくつもりなのかわからない

> [ノート] **make it** と **get on** の使い分け : **make it** は人の経歴において、成功したかどうかがわかる重大な局面があることを示唆したり、成功は才能と自信次第であることを示唆したりする。**get on** は勤勉さによる成功という比較的緩やかな段階を踏む過程があることを示唆する。

successful [形]

1 successful・effective・winning・victorious・triumphant
人が競技で勝っている[物事が目的を達成した]状態を表す
【類語訳】成功した、合格した、当選した、効果的な、有効な、勝利した、決勝の

[文型&コロケーション]
▶ successful/ effective/ victorious/ triumphant **in** sth
▶ successful/ effective/ victorious **in doing** sth
▶ a successful/ an effective/ a victorious/ a triumphant **campaign/ challenge**
▶ a successful/ victorious/ triumphant **conclusion/ return**
▶ a successful/ winning/ victorious **team**
▶ the successful/ winning **side**
▶ a successful/ triumphant **outcome**
▶ a successful/ victorious **opponent**
▶ to **emerge/ return** victorious/ triumphant
▶ **eventually/ ultimately** successful/ victorious/ triumphant

successful (目的・意図の達成で)成功した、合格した、当選した ◇The *successful* candidate will be responsible for a large research project. 当選した候補者は大きな研究プロジェクトを担当することになります ◇He had a phenomenally *successful* period as manager. 彼には経営者としてめざましい成功を収めた時期があった ◇The experiment was entirely *successful*. 実験は完全に成功だった ◇He had been *successful at* every job he had done. 彼は手を染めた仕事すべてに成功を収めてきた [反意] **unsuccessful, failed,** ☞ **succeed** (ACHIEVE)
▶ **successfully** [副] ◇The operation was *successfully* completed. その手術は首尾よく完了した

effective (望まれる[意図された]結果を生んで)効果的な、有効な ◇Aspirin is a simple but highly *effective* treatment. アスピリンは単純だが非常に効果的な治療薬である ◇drugs that are *effective against* cancer がんに有効な薬 ◇I admire the *effective* use of colour in her paintings. 彼女の絵の効果的な色使いには感心させられます [反意] **ineffective** (INEFFECTIVE)
▶ **effectively** [副] ◇The company must reduce costs to compete *effectively*. 会社が競争に打ち勝つためには、コストを削減しなければならない [反意] **ineffectively** (INEFFECTIVE)

winning [名詞の前で](レース・競技会などで)勝利した、決勝の ◇Next week we will publish the *winning* entry in the short story competition. 来週私たちは、短編コンテストの優勝者を正式発表します ◇He scored the *winning* goal in the final. 彼は決勝戦で決勝のゴールを決めた ◇They had fought on the *winning* side. 彼らは勝利チームになったことがあった [反意] **losing**

victorious 《ややフォーマル、特に書き言葉》(戦い・選挙・スポーツで)勝利を収めた；勝利に終わる ◇The *victorious* army entered the city. 勝利を収めた軍隊が町に入場した ◇Canada was *victorious over* Australia at the start of the World Championships. カナダは世界選手権の初戦でオーストラリアに勝った

triumphant 《特に書き言葉》(大いに満足をもたらす形で)勝利[成功]を収めた ◇He had steered the campaign through to its *triumphant* conclusion. 彼はそのキャンペーンを成功裡に展開し終えていた ◇She rose above all the problems and emerged *triumphant*. 彼女はすべての問題を克服して成功を収めた

2 successful・profitable・commercial・lucrative・buoyant・thriving・economic・profit-making
人がお金を稼いだり、物事がお金になることを表す
【類語訳】成功した、繁栄した、輝かしい、儲かる、商業的な、営利の、実入りのよい

[文型&コロケーション]
▶ a successful/ profitable/ lucrative/ thriving/ profit-making **business**
▶ a successful/ profitable/ lucrative/ profit-making **enterprise**
▶ a successful/ profitable/ lucrative **investment/ career/ year**
▶ a profitable/ lucrative/ buoyant/ thriving **market**
▶ **very/ particularly/ extremely/ fairly/ quite** successful/ profitable/ lucrative/ buoyant
▶ **highly/ immensely** successful/ profitable/ lucrative
▶ **relatively** successful/ profitable/ buoyant

successful (評判を得て)成功した、繁栄した、輝かしい ◇The play was very *successful* on Broadway. その芝居はブロードウェーで大成功した ◇She has had a long and *successful* career in television. 彼女はテレビで長く輝かしい経歴を持つ

profitable 利益の上がる、儲かる ◇She runs a highly *profitable* business. 彼女は高収益の会社を経営している ◇It is usually more *profitable* to sell direct to the

public. 一般人に直接販売するほうがふつう儲かります 反意 **unprofitable** (LOSS-MAKING)
➤ **profitability** 名 [U] ◊Downsizing is one way to increase *profitability*. 人員削減は収益率を上げる一つの方法である
➤ **profitably** 副 ◊This is no way to run a business *profitably*. これは利益の上がる事業経営のやり方ではない
commercial [名詞の前で] 利益の上がる, 儲かる, 商業的な, 営利の ◊The movie was not a *commercial* success (= made no profit). その映画は商業的には不成功だった ◊They are an educational charity, not a *commercial* publisher. 彼らは営利目的の出版者ではなく教育慈善団体である 反意 **non-profit** (LOSS-MAKING)
➤ **commercially** 副 ◊His invention was not *commercially* successful. 彼の発明は商売的には結びつかなかった
lucrative (ビジネス・仕事が)利益の上がる, 儲かる；大儲けする, 実入りのよい ◊The firm has a *lucrative* business contract with the Scottish Executive. その会社はスコットランドの行政府と利益率の高い事業契約を結んでいる ◊Many of the engineers left the service for more *lucrative* jobs abroad. 技師の多くが海外でのもっと実入りのよい仕事を求めてその業務を離れた
buoyant (ビジネスで)(価格・ビジネス活動が)上昇傾向にある ◊Car sales have remained *buoyant*. 自動車売上げは上昇傾向を維持してきた ❶ buoyantは一般に, market, economy, trading, sales, demandと結びつく.
thriving (ビジネス・地域が)繁栄した ◊Twenty years ago London Road was a *thriving* commercial centre thronged with shoppers. 20年前のロンドン街道は, 買い物客たちでこった返す繁栄を誇る商業中心地だった ❶ thrivingは一般に, company, business, industry, trade, market, economy, centre, town, portと結びつく. ☞ **thrive** (DO WELL)
economic 《しばしば否定文で》(利益・ビジネス・活動が)利益の上がる, 儲かる ◊It's simply not *economic* for these small farmers to start buying large amounts of expensive fertilizer. 高価な肥料の大量購入を始めることは, これらの小規模農家にとってまったく採算が取れない 反意 **uneconomic** (LOSS-MAKING)
'profit-making [ふつう名詞の前で] (ビジネス・活動が)利益の上がる, 儲かる, 営利の ◊I believe that public transport should be run as a service, not as a *profit-making* enterprise. 公共交通は営利企業としてではなくサービス事業として走らせるべきだと私は思う 反意 **loss-making**, **non-profit** (LOSS-MAKING)

suffer from sth 動

suffer from sth・have・get・develop・catch・contract・come down with sth
病気である, または病気になることを表す
【類語訳】苦しむ, (病気に)かかる, 患う, (問題を)生じる, 感染する

文型&コロケーション
▶ to suffer from/ have/ get/ develop/ catch/ contract a/ an **disease/ illness**
▶ to suffer from/ have/ get/ catch/ come down with a **bug**
▶ to suffer from/ have/ get/ develop/ contract **cancer/ AIDS**
▶ to suffer from/ have/ get/ catch/ contract **a virus/ HIV/ malaria**
▶ to suffer from/ have/ get/ catch/ contract/ come down with the **flu**
▶ to suffer from/ have/ get/ catch/ come down with a **cold**
▶ to suffer from/ have/ get a **headache**
▶ to suffer from/ have/ get/ develop **a condition/ arthritis/ diarrhoea**
▶ to suffer from/ have/ develop a/ an **allergy/ disorder**

suffer from sth 句動詞 [他, 受身なし] (心身の痛み・不足に)苦しむ, (病気に)かかっている, 患う ◊The driver was taken to hospital *suffering from* shock. ドライバーはショック状態になって病院に運び込まれた ◊Many companies are *suffering from* a shortage of skilled staff. 多くの会社が熟練したスタッフの不足に困っている ☞ **sufferer** (PATIENT)
have (または **have got**) [他, 受身なし]《進行形なし》(病気に)かかっている, (痛みを)負う ◊I *had* a cold yesterday and I couldn't come to work. 昨日は風邪を引いて仕事に来れなかった ◊I've got a headache. 頭が痛い ◊He found out that he *had* HIV just last year. 彼はまさに去年, HIV感染が判明した
get [他, 受身なし] (病気に)かかる, なる, (痛みを)生じる ◊I *got* this cold off (= from) you! この風邪は君からもらったんだよ ◊I think I'm *getting* a cold. どうやら風邪気味です ◊She *gets* (= often suffers from) really bad headaches. 彼女はすごい頭痛持ちだ ☞ **pick sth up** (GET 1)
develop [他, 受身なし] (病気に)なる, (問題を)生じる ◊She *developed* lung cancer at the age of sixty. 彼女は60歳で肺がんを発症した ◊The car *developed* engine trouble and we had to stop. その車がエンジントラブルを起こし, 私たちは立ち止まらざるをえなかった
catch [他, 受身なし] 感染する, (病気を)移される ◊I think I must have *caught* this cold from you. この風邪は君から移されたに違いないと思う
contract [他, 受身なし]《ややフォーマル》(重病に)かかる ◊He *contracted* malaria while abroad. 彼は外国滞在中にマラリアにかかった
,come 'down with sth 句動詞 [他, 受身なし] (軽めの病気に)かかる ◊I think I'm *coming down with* something. 何か体がおかしいなあ

suggest 動 ☞ MEAN 動 2

suggest・imply・indicate・point
人に何かの可能性があると思わせる
【類語訳】示す, 示唆する, 暗示する, ほのめかす, におわせる, 兆候となる, 指し示す

文型&コロケーション
▶ to suggest/ imply/ indicate sth **to sb**
▶ to suggest/ imply/ indicate **that...**
▶ to suggest/ imply/ indicate/ point to a **meaning**
▶ to suggest/ imply/ indicate an **idea**
▶ to suggest/ indicate/ point to a **feeling**
▶ to suggest/ imply/ indicate/ point to a **great deal/ high degree/ lack of** sth
▶ the **results/ facts** suggest/ imply/ indicate/ point to sth
▶ sb/ sth's **behaviour** suggests/ implies/ indicates sth
▶ the **evidence** suggests/ indicates/ points to sth
▶ the **signs/ symptoms** suggest/ indicate/ point to sth
▶ to **strongly** suggest/ imply/ indicate/ point to sth

suggestion, summary

suggest [他] （考えを）示す，連想させる；（真実であると）示唆する，暗示する，ほのめかす ◇All the evidence *suggests* (that) he stole the money. すべての証拠が彼がその金を盗んだことを示唆している ◇The symptoms *suggest* a minor heart attack. 軽度の心臓発作を示す症状が出ている ◇The stage lighting was used to *suggest* a beach scene. 浜辺の場面を連想させるために舞台照明が用いられた

imply [他]《ややフォーマル》（真実である[存在する可能性がある]と）暗示する，ほのめかす，におわせる ◇The survey *implies* (that) more people are moving house than was thought. その調査では予想していた以上に多くの人々が引越しを考えていることが示されている ◇The fact that she was here *implies* a degree of interest. 彼女がここにいたという事実は，彼女の関心の高さを意味している

ノート suggestとimplyの使い分け：しばしば両語とも使用可能。しかし，suggestは調査・報告書・証拠がいかに事柄の関連性・関係性・類似性があるかを示す場合に用いられることが多い。◆ Research *suggests* a link between a person's outlook and the immune system. (調査は人のものの見方と免疫システムとの間に関連性があることを示している). implyはふつうデータ・事実がいかに事柄の必要性・存在性・可能性などがあるかを示す場合に用いられることが多い。◆ Campaigners said the data *implies* the existence of 'a pressing social need'. (運動家たちは，データは「差し迫った社会的ニーズ」が存在することを示唆していると言った)

indicate [他]《ややフォーマル》（物事の）兆候[しるし]となる；（可能性が高いことを）示す ◇A red sky at night often *indicates* fine weather the next day. 赤い夜空はしばしば，翌日の好天の兆しである ◇Early results *indicate* that the government will be returned to power. 序盤の結果によればその政権が返り咲くことになるだろう ☞ **indication, indicator** (SIGN 1), **indicate** (DECLARE), **indicate** (SHOW 1)

point [自，他]《副詞や前置詞と共に》（可能性が高いことを）示す，（特定の展開[論理的な議論]へと）向かわせる，指し示す ◇All the signs *point* to a successful year ahead. すべての兆候が一年先の成功を指し示している ◇The evidence seems to *point* in that direction. 証言はその方向に向かれているようだ ◇The fans are looking to the new players to ***point the way*** to victory. ファンたちは新しい選手たちが勝利への道を指し示してくれることを待ち望んでいる

suggestion [名] ☞ SIGN 1

suggestion・clue・hint・pointer
間接的に与えられる，物事の解明を手助けする情報
【類語訳】示唆，手がかり，糸口，気配，しるし，兆候

文型&コロケーション
▸ a **suggestion/ clue/ hint/ pointer as to** how/ what/ why, etc.
▸ a **suggestion/ hint that**...
▸ a/ an **useful/ valuable/ obvious** suggestion/ clue/ hint/ pointer
▸ an **important** suggestion/ clue/ pointer
▸ to **give sb/ provide** a clue/ hint/ pointer

suggestion [U, C, ふつう単数で]《ややフォーマル》（望ましくない事が真実であるとする）示唆 ◇A spokesman dismissed any *suggestion* of a boardroom rift. スポークスマンは重役会で意見の食い違いがあるのではとのどんな示唆をもはねつけた ◇There was no *suggestion* that he was doing anything illegal. 彼が何か違法なことをしていることを示唆するものは何もなかった ☞ **suggest** (MEAN 動 2)

clue [C] （犯罪・問題解決のための）手がかり，糸口 ◇The police think the videotape may ***hold some*** vital *clues* to the identity of the killer. 警察はそのビデオテープに殺人犯の身元の重要な手がかりがあるかもしれないと考えている ◇Diet may hold the *clue* to the causes of migraine. 食事が偏頭痛の原因究明の糸口を握っているかもしれない

hint [C] （何かが起こる）気配，兆候 ◇At the first *hint* of trouble, they left. トラブルの兆候があるとすぐに，彼らは立ち去った ◇That was the first *hint* we had that things were going wrong. それは私たちが受けた，事態が悪い方向に向かっているという最初の兆候だった ☞ **hint** (MEAN 動 2)

pointer [C] （存在の）しるし；（発展の）兆候 ◇The surge in car sales is an encouraging ***pointer to*** an improvement in the economy. 車の売上げの急増は経済の改善への有望な兆しである

ノート hintとpointerの使い分け：pointerはふつうhintよりも専門的な文脈で見られる。hintの後には，of, thatが続き，pointerの後にはふつうtoが続く。

summary [名]

summary・outline・overview・sketch・synopsis・abstract・rundown
長いものを短くした文書や解説
【類語訳】要約，概要，摘要，梗概，概略，大要，粗筋

文型&コロケーション
▸ a summary/ an outline/ an overview/ a sketch/ a synopsis/ an abstract/ a rundown **of** sth
▸ **in** summary/ outline
▸ a **brief** summary/ outline/ overview/ sketch/ synopsis
▸ a **quick/ short/ general** summary/ outline/ overview
▸ a **full** summary/ outline/ overview/ rundown
▸ to **give sb** a summary/ an outline/ an overview/ a sketch/ a synopsis/ a rundown
▸ to **provide** a summary/ an outline/ an overview/ a sketch/ a synopsis/ an abstract

summary [C] 要約，概要，摘要 ◇The following is a *summary* of our conclusions. 以下が我々の結論の概要である ◇a news *summary* ニュースの概要 ◇a two-page *summary* of a government report 政府の報告書の2ページにわたる梗概

outline [C] 概略，概要 ◇This is a brief *outline* of the events. これらはそれらの出来事の簡単な概要である ◇The article describes in *outline* the main findings of the research. その記事は調査の主たる成果をかいつまんで述べている ☞ **outline** (SHAPE)

overview [C] 概観，大要 ◇The second chapter will provide an *overview* of the issues involved. 第2章では関連する諸問題の概観を示します ◇My main concern is to get an *overview* of the main environmental problems facing the area. 私の主な関心事は，地域が直面している主な環境問題の概観を得ることにあります

summary

ノート summary, outline, overview の使い分け:
summary は常に本文・解説などの完全版が書かれた[記録された]後に、書かれる[作られる]もの。outline は、完全版が作られる[仕上げられる]前に書かれる[与えられる]可能性がある。◆You should draw up an *outline* for the essay before you start writing. (書き始める前に、エッセーの概要を作成すべきです) ◆The *outline agreement* about the country's transition to full democracy still has to be discussed at a multi-party forum. (完全なる民主主義への移行に関するその国の合意の枠組みは、依然として多党によるフォーラムで議論し合う必要がある) overview は、outline に似ているが、詳細はこれから取り決められるということよりも、求められているのは広範囲にわたる一般的傾向であるということを強調する。summary, outline は、人によって与えられる[提供される]もの。overview は与えられることができるが、人は自分自身のために overview を get, take, gain することもある。

sketch [C] 概略、概要 ◇The first few pages give a biographical *sketch* of the author. 最初の数ページは作家の略歴を伝えている

synopsis (複 **synopses**) [C] 《ややフォーマル》(本・劇の)粗筋 ◇The programme gave a complete *synopsis* of the play. その番組は劇の粗筋を完全に伝えていた

abstract [C] 《ややフォーマル》(公式の[学術的な]文書の)要約、摘要 ◇*Abstracts* of about 300 words should be submitted to the conference committee who will decide which papers to accept. 約300語の摘要が採択すべき論文を決定する協議委員会に提出されなくてはならない

rundown [C, ふつう単数で] 《ややインフォーマル、特に話し言葉》要約、概要 ◇Shall I give you a brief *rundown* of each of the job applicants? 就職希望者各人について簡単に説明いたしましょうか

sunny 形

sunny • dry • clear • good • temperate • fine • mild • glorious
天気がよいことを表す
【類語訳】晴れた、乾燥した、快晴の、温暖な、好天の、晴れ上がった

文型&コロケーション
▶sunny/ dry/ clear/ good/ fine/ mild/ glorious **weather**
▶a sunny/ dry/ clear/ fine/ mild/ glorious **day/ morning/ evening/ afternoon**
▶sunny/ dry/ clear/ good/ fine **(weather) conditions**
▶a sunny/ dry/ mild **spell**
▶a dry/ temperate/ mild **climate**
▶to **remain/ stay** sunny/ dry/ fine/ mild

sunny 《ほめて》晴れた、日が照った ◇It was a brilliantly *sunny* day in June. 6月の明るい日の光にあふれた日であった ◇The outlook for the weekend is warm and *sunny*. 週末の見通しは暖かく、晴れ間も多い ◇These plants grow best in a *sunny* spot. これらの植物は日当たりのよい場所で最もよく育つ ❶ sunny は陽光が心地よいときに用いる肯定的な語である。日光が不快なほど暑いときには用いられない。
反意 cloudy (CLOUDY), shady (DARK 1)

dry 雨の降らない、乾燥した ◇weeks of hot *dry* weather 数週間にわたる暑くて乾燥した天気 ◇the *dry* season 乾季 ◇I hope it stays *dry* for our picnic. ピクニックの時は雨が降らないといいわね ◇Rattlesnakes occur in the warmer, *drier* parts of North America. ガラガラヘビは北アメリカの比較的温暖で乾燥した地域に生息している **反意 wet**

clear (雲・霧がなくて)晴れた、快晴の ◇The weather was bright and *clear*. 天気は明るく、晴れていた ◇a *clear* blue sky 青く晴れ渡った空 ◇On a *clear* day, you can see the mountains in the distance. 晴れた日には遠くに山並みが見えます **反意 cloudy, misty, foggy (CLOUDY)**

good 《ほめて》(天気が)望ましい ◇Let's hope we have *good* weather tomorrow. 明日はいい天気だといいね **反意 bad**

temperate [ふつう名詞の前で]《専門語》(暑すぎず・寒すぎず)温暖な、穏やかな ◇a country with a *temperate* climate 温和な気候の国 ◇In winter, the birds fly from the Arctic to more *temperate zones*. 冬には鳥たちは北極圏からより温暖な地帯へと飛んで行く

fine 《特に英、ほめて》晴れた、好天の ◇The next morning *turned out fine* again. その翌日はまた晴れた ◇That summer saw weeks of *fine* dry weather. その夏には雨の降らない好天が数週間続いた

mild (寒くなく)温暖な、穏やかな ◇That winter was exceptionally *mild*. その冬は珍しく暖かだった ◇Most of the birds seek out *milder* climates during the winter months. 大半の鳥たちは冬の数か月間はもっと穏やかな土地を探し出す ❶ mild は、特に当然寒いと思われる天候、例えば冬の天候について、あるいはより寒い地域とある地域を比較するときに用いられる。 **反意 cold (COLD 1), harsh, ☞ mild (GENTLE)**

glorious 《ほめて》晴れ上がった、(太陽がふりそそいで)暑い ◇They had three weeks of *glorious* sunshine. 3週間にわたって太陽が燦々とふりそそいだ

supply 名

supply • resource • stock • reserve • pool • hoard • bank • store • arsenal • stockpile
必要なときに使える物事の量
【類語訳】供給、資源、財源、資金、在庫、蓄え、備蓄、予備、埋蔵量、貯蔵、秘蔵、蓄積

文型&コロケーション
▶a supply/ a stock/ a reserve/ a pool/ a hoard/ a bank/ a store/ an arsenal/ a stockpile **of** sth
▶to **be/ have** sth **in** supply/ stock
▶a supply/ stocks/ an arsenal/ a stockpile **of weapons**
▶a supply/ bank/ store **of information**
▶a supply/ a stock/ stores **of food**
▶a supply/ reserves/ a store **of water**
▶supplies/ stocks/ reserves/ stockpiles **of coal**
▶(a) **vast** supply/ resources/ stock/ reserve/ hoard/ bank/ store/ arsenal/ stockpile
▶(a) **large** supply/ resources/ stock/ reserve/ hoard/ store/ arsenal/ stockpile
▶(a) **dwindling** supplies/ resources/ stocks/ reserves/ pool/ stockpiles
▶a **secret** supply/ stock/ hoard/ store
▶(a) **food** supply/ stocks/ reserves/ store/ stockpile
▶**weapons** supplies/ stocks/ stores
▶**coal** supplies/ stocks/ reserves
▶**oil/ gas** supplies/ reserves
▶to **build up** a supply/ resources/ a stock/ reserves/ a

support

bank/ a store/ an arsenal/ a stockpile
▶to **reduce** the supply/ resources/ stock/ reserves/ pool/ stores
▶to **use up/ exhaust** the supply/ resources/ stock/ reserves/ store

supply [C] 供給(量) ◇The water *supply* is unsafe. 給水量が不安定である ◇*Supplies* of food are almost exhausted. 食糧供給はほとんど枯渇している ◇We cannot guarantee adequate *supplies* of raw materials. 我々は十分な原材料の供給を保証できない ☞ **supply** (PROVIDE)

resource [C, ふつう複数で] (国・組織・人が持つ)資源, 財源, 資金 ◇the exploitation of minerals and other *natural resources* 鉱物やその他の天然資源の開発 ◇We do not have the *resources* (= money) to update our computer software. 我々にはそのコンピューターソフトを更新する資金がない ◇We agreed to *pool our resources* (= so that everyone gives sth). 私たちは金を出し合うことに同意した ☞ **human resources** (STAFF)

stock [U, C] (店の商品の)在庫;(使える物の)蓄え, 備蓄 ◇That particular model is not currently in *stock*. そのモデルに限って現在, 在庫がありません ◇I'm afraid we're temporarily *out of stock*. あいにく, 一時的に品切れなのですが ◇We don't carry a large *stock* of pine furniture. 松材の家具は在庫はあまりございません ◇I've built up a good *stock* of teaching materials over the years. 私は長年かけて教材を相当量蓄えてきた ◇Food *stocks* are running low. 食糧の備蓄は乏しくなってきている ☞ **stock** (SELL 2), **stock** (EQUIP), **stock up** (KEEP 1)

reserve [C, ふつう複数で] (将来[必要にとき]に使える物の)蓄え, 備蓄, 埋蔵量 ◇The country is thought to have huge untapped oil and gas *reserves*. その国は, 未開発の石油とガスが多量に埋蔵されていると考えられる ◇He discovered unexpected *reserves of strength*. 彼は予想外に余力が残っていることに気づいた ◇The report calls for *reserve* funds to be established. その報告書では積立基金の設立が提唱されている

pool [C] (一団の人々が必要なときに使える)共同利用の資材, 共同基金 ◇There is a *pool* of cars used by the firm's salesmen. その会社には販売員が共同利用できる車がある ◇a *pool* car 《英》共同利用の車 ◇The purpose of an insurance company is to provide a *pool* of funds from which to meet claims made by its customers. 保険会社の目的は顧客の請求に応じられる資金をプールすることにある ☞ **pool** (SHARE 動)

hoard [C] (お金・食べ物などの金銭的価値のある物の)貯蔵[秘蔵](物) ◇They dug up a *hoard* of Roman coins. 彼らはローマ時代の秘蔵物である硬貨を掘り起こした ◇Police have uncovered a *hoard* of stolen goods which may help to trace the fugitives. 警察は逃亡者を追跡するのに役立つかもしれない秘蔵の盗品の山を発見した ☞ **hoard** (KEEP 1)

bank [C] 蓄え, 蓄積;(物事が使える状態で蓄えられている所)バンク ◇They intend to establish a *bank* of information which will be accessible to the public. 彼らは一般人が利用できる情報バンクを設立するつもりでいる ◇a blood/sperm *bank* 血液/精子バンク

store [C] (持っていて必要な時のものの)蓄え, 蓄積 ◇her secret *store* of chocolate 彼女がひそかにしているチョコレート ◇This is vital information to add to your *store* of knowledge. これはあなたの知識を広げるのに不可欠の情報です ☞ **store** (KEEP 1)

arsenal [C] (銃・爆薬などの兵器の)備蓄(量) ◇The treaty requires them to reduce their nuclear *arsenal* by 30%. その条約では核兵器の30%の削減が求められている

stockpile [C] (将来必要なら使える)備蓄(量);(使用[破棄]しにくい)貯蔵(量) ◇*Stockpiles* of coal have reached a critically low level. 石炭の備蓄量は危機的低水準に達している ◇The growing *stockpile* of used tyres is a worldwide problem. 古タイヤの蓄積量の増大は世界的な問題である ☞ **stockpile** (KEEP 1)

support 動 ☞ IN FAVOUR

support・vote・back・stand for sth・second・champion・side with sb

人[考え, 政策など]に賛同して助成することを表す
【類語訳】支持する, 投票する, 後押しする, 擁護する, 賛成する, 味方する

文型&コロケーション

▶to support/ vote for/ back/ side with sb **in** sth
▶to vote/ side with sb **against** sb/ sth
▶to support/ back/ stand for/ champion an **idea**
▶to support/ back/ champion a **measure**
▶to support/ back/ champion **reform**
▶to support/ vote for/ back/ second a **proposal/ plan/ motion/ resolution**
▶to support/ vote for/ back a **move/ scheme**
▶to support/ back/ champion a **cause**
▶to support/ back/ stand for a **policy**
▶to **openly/ publicly** support/ back/ side with sb/ sth
▶to **overwhelmingly/ unanimously** support/ vote for/ back sth

support [他] (人・物事を)支持する ◇If you raise it at the meeting, I'll *support* you. あなたがそれを会議で提案するなら, 私は支持します ◇These measures are strongly *supported* by environmental groups. これらの対策は環境保護団体から強い支持を得ている 反意 **oppose** (OPPOSE), ☞ **advocate** (RECOMMEND 1)
▶**support** 名 [U] There is strong public *support* for the change. 変革に対して大衆の強い支持がある ◇Only a few people spoke *in support of* the proposal. 数人からしかその支持の発言がなかった ◇The idea has met with widespread *support*. その考えには幅広い支持が寄せられている

vote [自, 他] (賛成票を)投票する, 投じる ◇They all *voted for* the new tax. 彼らはみな新税に賛成票を投じた ◇Over 60% of members *voted in favour of* the motion. 6割以上のメンバーが, その動議に賛成票を投じた ◇We'll listen to the arguments on both sides and then *vote on* it. 私たちは双方の主張を聞いてから, それに関して投票するつもりです ◇We *voted* Democrat in the last election. 我々は前回の選挙では民主党員に投票した

back [他] (人・物事を)後押しする, 擁護する ◇Her parents *backed* her in her choice of career. 両親が彼女の職業選択の後押しをしてくれた ◇Doctors have *backed* plans to raise tax on cigarettes. 医師たちはタバコの増税案を擁護した ❶ back は, 支持する人が影響力をもつ[有力な, 上位の]地位にあるときに用いられることが多い.
▶**backing** 名 [U] ◇The police gave the proposals

their full *backing*. 警察はその提案を全面的に支持した
☞ **backing** (INVESTMENT)

'stand for sth 句動詞 (組織が特定の考え・信条・政策を)支持する ◇I hated the organization and all it *stood for* (= the ideas that it supported). 私はその組織とその組織が唱えるすべての考えが嫌いだった

second [他] (提案を[に]) 支持する, 賛成 (表明) する ◇Any proposal must be *seconded* by two other members of the committee. いかなる提案も, 他に二人の委員の賛意表明を受けなければならない ☞ **propose** (PROPOSE)

champion [他] (人々・信条を)支持する, 擁護する ◇He has always *championed* the cause of gay rights. 彼は常に同性愛者の言い分を擁護してきた

'side with sb 句動詞 (議論において一人[一つの集団]の)側につく, 味方する ◇The kids always *sided with* their mother against me. 子どもたちはいつも私に反対して母親の側についた

suppose 動

suppose・assume・guess・suspect・imagine・expect・presume・take it・I dare say
手元の情報に基づいて, 物事が真実である[可能である]と見なす
【類語訳】思う, 考える, 想定する

文型&コロケーション

▶ to suppose/ assume/ guess/ suspect/ imagine/ expect/ presume/ take it/ dare say that...
▶ to be supposed/ assumed/ suspected/ imagined/ presumed **to be** sth
▶ Let's/ Let us suppose/ assume/ imagine/ presume/ take it...
▶ **can only** suppose/ assume/ imagine/ presume/ take it (that)...
▶ to **reasonably** suppose/ assume/ suspect/ presume
▶ to **rightly** suppose/ assume/ suspect
▶ to be **widely** supposed/ assumed/ suspected/ presumed
▶ to be **commonly/ generally** supposed/ assumed/ imagined/ presumed
▶ **always** supposing/ assuming/ presuming that...
▶ I suppose/ assume/ guess/ suspect/ imagine/ expect/ presume **so**.

suppose [他] 《進行形なし》(手元の情報に基づいて)思う, 考える ◇Getting a visa isn't as easy as you might *suppose*. ビザを手に入れるのは思うほど簡単ではない ◇Prices will go up, I *suppose*. 価格は上昇すると思う ◇I *suppose* you think that's funny! それはおかしいと思っているだろ ◇Why do you *suppose* he resigned? どうして彼は辞めたと思う ◇I don't *suppose* for a minute that he'll agree (= I'm sure that he won't). 彼が賛成するなんてこれっぽっちも思ってないよ ❶ *suppose* はまた, 陳述・要望・提案をより直接的ではない[ソフトな]ものにするために用いられる. ◆I could take you in the car, I *suppose* (= but I don't really want to). (車で連れて行ってあげないでもないけど) ◆'Can I borrow the car?' 'I *suppose* so (= Yes, but I'm not very happy about it).' (「車借りていい」「いいと言えばいいけど」) ◆ *Suppose* we take a later train? (もっと後の列車に乗ったらどうかな)

assume [他] (証拠もなく)思う, 考える, …ということにしておく, 想定する ◇Let's *assume* for a moment that the plan succeeds. 一応, 計画は成功するということにしておきしょう ◇I think we can *safely assume* that this situation will continue. この状況が続くと考えて差し支えないと思う ◇It's generally *assumed* that stress is caused by too much work. 一般的には, ストレスは働きすぎによって引き起こされると考えられている ◇Don't always *assume* the worst (= think that the worst thing will happen). 必ずしも最悪の事態を想定することはない ☞ **assumption** (SPECULATION)

guess [他] 《ふつう I guess の形で》《特に米, 話し言葉》思う, 考える ◇I *guess* I'm just lucky. 単に運がいいんだと思う ◇He didn't see me, I *guess*. 彼は私を見なかったと思う ❶ I guess so は, 陳述・招待・要望に賛成するのに用いられるが, 躊躇を示す形での賛成である. ◆'Can I have another cookie?' 'I *guess so*.' I guess so, that's the last one.' (「もう一枚クッキーもらえる」「いいけど, それ最後の一枚だよ」)

suspect [他] 《進行形なし》(望ましくないことを確たる証拠なく) 思う, 考える ◇If you *suspect* a gas leak, call the emergency services immediately. ガス漏れだと思うなら, すぐに緊急事態に電話しなさい ◇As I *suspected* all along, he was not a real policeman. 最初からずっと思っていたとおり, 彼は本当の警官ではなかった ☞ **suspicion** (DOUBT 名 2), **suspicion** (IDEA 2)

imagine [他] 思う, 考える ◇'Will we still be allowed in?' 'I *imagine* so.' 「まだ入れるのかな」「たぶんね」 ◇I don't *imagine* he'll get here now, do you? 彼がここにもう着くなんて思わないよ, だろ ◇He's always *imagining* that we're talking about him behind his back. 彼はいつも, 私たちが隠れて彼の話をしていると思っているんだ

expect [他] 《進行形なし》《特に英, 話し言葉》思う, 考える ◇'Will Bill be there?' 'I *expect* so.' 「ビルはそこに行くの」「そう思う」 ◇'Are you going out tonight?' 'I don't *expect* so.' 「今夜出かける」「いや, 出かけないと思う」 ◇I *expect* he'll be late, as usual. いつものように彼は遅刻すると思うよ

presume [他] 《フォーマル》(証拠もなく)思う, 考える ◇I *presumed* that he understood the rules. 彼は規則を理解しているなと思った ◇Little is known of the youngest son; it is *presumed* that he died young. 末の息子についてはほとんど知られていない. 彼は若死にしたと考えられている ❶ *presume* は assume よりもフォーマルである. 物事について, それが実際には真実であるかどうかを調べるほどの十分な関心がないときに用いられることが多い. ◆'Is he still abroad?' 'I *presume* so (= but I don't actually know and I don't really care either).' (「彼はまだ海外なの」「そうじゃないかな」). ☞ **presume** (SAY 3), **presumably** (PROBABLY), **presumption** (SPECULATION)

'take it フレーズ 《ややインフォーマル》思う, 考える ◇I *take it* you won't be coming to the party. パーティーには来るつもりないんだね ❶ take it は常に, 実際には that が省略されている形を伴う.

I dare say (または **I daresay**) フレーズ 《特に英, 話し言葉》思う, 考える ◇I *dare say* he'll cope. おそらく彼はなんとか切り抜けるだろう ❶ I dare say は常に, 後に that 節を伴う. 実際には that が省略されていることもある.

supposed 形

supposed・alleged・hypothetical・assumed・notional・speculative・theoretical
確実に真実[本当]とは言えないが, 可能な状況[考え(方)]に基づいていることを表す

【類語訳】仮想された, 仮定された, 仮定上の, 架空の, 想像上の, 推論的な, 思弁的な, 理論上の

文型&コロケーション
- purely hypothetical/ speculative/ theoretical
- entirely hypothetical/ theoretical
- highly/ rather speculative/ theoretical

supposed [名詞の前で]《ふつうけなして》（主張・陳述・表現が）…と思われている, …とされる ◇This is the opinion of the *supposed* experts. これは専門家とされる人たちの意見です ◇When did this *supposed* accident happen? この事故と思われることはいつ起きたの
- **supposedly** 副 ◇The novel is *supposedly* based on a true story. その小説はおそらく実話に基づいています

alleged [名詞の前で]《フォーマル》（証明されていない場合に）人・物事が）…と思われている, …とされる ◇the *alleged* attacker/victim/killer (= that sb says is one) 襲撃者/犠牲者/殺人犯と思われる人物 ◇the *alleged* attack/offence/incident (= that sb says has happened) 襲撃/違反/紛争と思われる事件 ◇The girl gave evidence in court against her *alleged* attacker. その少女は裁判所で, 彼女を襲ったとみられる容疑者に不利な証言をした ☞ **allege** (CLAIM)
- **allegedly** 副 ◇crimes *allegedly* committed during the war 戦時中に犯したとされる犯罪

hypothetical 《ややフォーマル》（状況・考えに基づいていて）仮想[仮定]された, 仮定上の ◇Let us take the *hypothetical* case of Sheila, a mother of two... 二人の母親であるシーラの仮想症例を取り上げてみよう… ◇I wasn't asking about anybody in particular — it was a purely *hypothetical* question. 特に誰のことについて尋ねていたんじゃないよ—まったくの仮定の質問だったんだ ❶要点を解説する[問題の解決策を打ち出す手助けをする]ために, hypothetical example/question/situation がよく用いられる. 反意 **actual** (REAL), ☞ **hypothesis** (THEORY 2)

assumed [名詞の前で]《ややフォーマル, 特に書き言葉》（真実だ[存在する]と）仮定された ◇The report takes into account the *assumed* differences between the two states. その報告書では二つの国家間にあるとされる違いが考慮されている

notional 《フォーマル》推測[見積もり, 仮説]に基づいた；架空の, 想像上の ◇My calculation is based on *notional* figures, since the actual figures are not yet available. 実際の数字がまだ使えないので, 私の計算は仮の数字に基づいています 反意 **actual** (REAL), ☞ **notion** (IDEA 1)

speculative 《ややフォーマル, 特に書き言葉, しばしばけなして》（推測・見積もり, 仮説に基づいて）推論的な, 思弁的な ◇The report is highly *speculative* and should be ignored. その報告書は推測に基づくところが大きく, 無視していい ☞ **speculate** (SAY 2)

ノート hypothetical, notional, speculative の使い分け: 数字・考え・話が speculative であると言う場合, それが十分にできず信頼できないことを意味することが多い. notional は, 実際の数字がない場合, 量・数・時間についてできるかぎり最善の見積もりをするような場合に, より専門的な文脈で用いられる. hypothetical は, 要点を解説する[問題の解決策を打ち出す]ために実例として想像上の人物・物事を挙げるような場合に用いられる.

theoretical [ふつう名詞の前で]《ややフォーマル》（見込みは薄い）理論上の ◇It's a *theoretical* possibility. それは理論

上の可能性である
- **theoretically** 副 ◇It is *theoretically* possible for him to overrule their decision, but highly unlikely. 彼が彼らの決定を却下することは理論的には可能だが, まずそうにないことだ

suppress 動

1 suppress・persecute・quell・crush・put sth down・disenfranchise・subdue・oppress・repress
人々の集団を[の, が]管理下に置く[権利と自由を制限する, 当局に反対することを妨げる]ために政治力[軍事力]を使う
【類語訳】鎮圧する, 弾圧する, 迫害する, 奪う, 剥奪する

disenfranchise	suppress	persecute
subdue	quell	crush
	put sth down	
	oppress	
	repress	

文型&コロケーション
- to suppress/ quell/ crush/ put down/ repress a **rebellion**
- to suppress/ quell/ crush/ put down a/ an **uprising**/ **revolt**
- to suppress/ quell/ crush **opposition**
- to suppress/ quell/ put down a **riot**
- to quell/ crush/ subdue **rebels**
- a persecuted/ a disenfranchised/ an oppressed **minority/ people**
- the **army/ troops/ police** (are used/ called in, etc. to) suppress/ quell/ crush/ put down/ subdue sb/ sth
- a **government** suppresses/ quells/ crushes sb/ sth
- to **brutally** suppress/ crush/ put down/ repress sb/ sth
- to **ruthlessly** suppress/ crush/ repress sb/ sth

suppress [他]《ややフォーマル, 書き言葉, けなして》（政府・統治者が団体・活動を）鎮圧する, 弾圧する ◇The regime ruthlessly *suppresses* all dissent. その政権は手段を選ばずすべての反対意見を弾圧する ◇Trade union rights were *suppressed* and casual work became the norm. 労働組合権が弾圧され, 臨時の仕事が普通となった
- **suppression** 名 [U] the *suppression* of a rebellion/free speech 反乱の鎮圧/言論の自由の弾圧

persecute [他, しばしば受け身]《ややフォーマル, けなして》（権力者が人種・宗教・政治信条を理由に人を）迫害する ◇Throughout history, people have been *persecuted for* their religious beliefs. 歴史を通して, 人々はその宗教的信条ゆえに迫害されてきた ☞ **persecution** (REPRESSION)

quell [他]《けなして, ジャーナリズム》（政府・統治者が暴力的行為[抗議]などを）鎮圧する ◇Extra police were called in to *quell* the disturbances. 騒動を鎮めるために, 予備の警察官が召集された

crush [他]《けなして, ジャーナリズム》（政府・統治者が人々を）鎮圧する, 弾圧する ◇The army was sent in to *crush* the rebellion. 反乱を鎮圧するために軍隊が送り込まれた

,put sth 'down 句動詞《けなして》（政府・当局が集団・活動などを）鎮圧する, 弾圧する ◇Troops loyal to the president *put down* an attempted coup. 大統領に忠実な軍隊がクーデターを未遂で鎮圧した

disenfranchise [他]《フォーマル》(人の選挙権を)奪う, 剥奪する ◇Many disabled people were effectively *dis-*

enfranchised because of lack of access. 多くの障碍〔(比)〕者が事実上選挙権を行使できないという理由でその権利を剥奪された

subdue [他]《フォーマル、けなして》(政府・当局が集団・活動などを)鎮圧する、弾圧する ◇Troops were called in to *subdue* the rebels. 反乱軍を鎮圧するために軍隊が召集された

ノート **suppress, quell, crush, put sth down, subdue の使い分け**：これらの語はすべて、非難的に用いられ、不当な権力の行使を示唆する。**suppress** は最も一般的な語である。**suppress** は政治的な圧力から肉体的な暴力まで、異なる方法により、さまざまな集団・活動を押さえることを指す。**quell** はふつう暴力・抗議・暴動などを押さえることを指す。**quell** は政治的な抗議・反乱、サッカーのフーリガンの暴力を押さえる場合にも用いられる。**crush** と **put sth down** はどちらも、反乱・抗議・暴動を押さえる力を行使することを指す。**crush** は、暴力的な手段の行使を示唆し、特にジャーナリズムで用いられる。**subdue** は、例えば警察・軍によって、緊急措置として[一定期間にわたって]反対勢力を押さえることを指すフォーマルな語である。

oppress [他]《ややフォーマル、書き言葉、けなして》(権力者が権利・自由を与えないで人を)迫害する、弾圧する ◇The regime is accused of *oppressing* religious minorities. その政権は宗教的少数派を迫害したとして非難されている ☞ **oppression** (REPRESSION)

repress [他、しばしば受身で]《ややフォーマル、書き言葉、けなして》(政府・当局が人々を)弾圧する ◇The government was quick to *repress* any opposition. 政府は素早くいかなる抵抗をも弾圧した ☞ **repression** (REPRESSION)

ノート **persecute, disenfranchise, oppress, repress の使い分け**：**persecute** は、これらの動詞の中で最も極端なもので、他人・権力者が一団の人々を傷つけ、さらには殺害することも含みうる残酷な扱い方を指す。例えば、第二次世界大戦中のユダヤ人迫害など、特に人種・宗教・政治的信条を理由に、人々は **persecute** される。**disenfranchise** は、感情抜きの最も説明的な語で、人々の権利(特に投票権)を奪うことを意味する。**oppress** と **repress** は意味の強弱の点で、上の二つの単語の間に位置し、意見を表明できない[望むとおりに行動できない、権力の座にある人たちに要求できない]など、人々の自由を制限することを意味する。通例、**oppress** の目的語は人であり、**repress** の目的語はその人の活動である。

2 suppress • control • stifle • contain • restrain • keep (yourself) from sth • repress • hold sth back • check • curb
感情の表出を自らやめる
【類語訳】抑える、こらえる、拭い去る、抑制する、我慢する

文型&コロケーション
▶ to control/ contain/ restrain/ check **yourself**
▶ to restrain/ keep yourself **from doing sth**
▶ to suppress/ control/ contain/ restrain/ repress/ hold back/ check your **anger**
▶ to suppress/ control/ stifle/ restrain/ repress/ check/ curb an **impulse**
▶ to suppress/ control/ stifle/ contain/ repress an **urge**
▶ to suppress/ control/ stifle/ restrain/ repress check a/ an **feeling/ emotion**
▶ to suppress/ control/ check/ curb an **instinct**
▶ to control/ contain/ restrain/ curb your **impatience**
▶ to suppress/ control/ contain your **excitement**
▶ to control/ contain/ curb your **temper**
▶ to suppress/ control/ contain/ restrain/ hold back **tears**
▶ to suppress/ control/ stifle/ restrain a **smile**
▶ to **barely** suppress/ control/ contain/ restrain/ repress/ hold back sth
▶ to **hardly** suppress/ control/ contain/ keep from sth

suppress [他] (感情・考えを)抑える、こらえる、拭い去る ◇She was unable to *suppress* a giggle. 彼女は忍び笑いをこらえることができなかった ◇He had *suppressed* the painful memories of his childhood. 彼は子どもの頃の辛い思い出を拭い去り切っていた ◇Her face was charged with barely *suppressed* anger. 彼女の顔にはかろうじて抑えてはいるが怒りがあふれ出ていた 反意 **arouse** (STIMULATE)
➢ **suppression** [名] [U] ◇the *suppression* of emotion/feelings 感情/気持ちの抑制

control [-ll-] [他] (怒って[動転して]いても)抑制する ◇I was so furious I couldn't *control* myself and I hit him. 怒り狂って、自制できずに彼を殴った ◇The clerk could scarcely *control* his excitement. 店員は興奮をほとんど抑え切れなかった

stifle [他] (笑い・泣き・あくびなどを)抑える、こらえる、かみ殺す ◇He *stifled* the urge to laugh. 彼は笑いたい衝動をこらえた ◇She managed to *stifle* a yawn. 彼女は何とかあくびをかみ殺した ❶ 失礼に見られたくないために、笑い・あくびを *stifle* するのである。

contain [他]《書き言葉》(感情を)抑制する ◇I was so furious I just couldn't *contain* myself. どうしても自分を抑えることができないほど腹が立っていた ◇She could hardly *contain* her excitement. 彼女はほとんど興奮を抑えきれなかった

restrain [他] (感情・行動を)抑制する、我慢する ◇I *restrained* the urge to punch him. 私は彼を殴りたい衝動を抑え込んだ ◇I was tempted to answer back, but I *restrained* myself. 言い返したくなったが我慢した

'keep from sth, 'keep yourself from sth 句動詞 (感情の表出を)こらえる、我慢する ◇She could hardly *keep herself from* laughing out loud. 彼女は爆笑をこらえるのはとても無理だった ◇Caroline bit her lip to *keep from* telling him how wrong he was. キャロラインは唇をかんで、いかに彼が間違っているか口にするのをこらえた

repress [他]《ややフォーマル》(感情を)抑制する ◇He burst in, making no effort to *repress* his fury. 彼は激情を抑えようとはまったくせずに、口をはさんだ ◇They tend to hide their emotions and *repress* their desires. 彼らは感情を隠し欲望を抑える傾向にある
➢ **repression** [名] [U] ◇sexual *repression* 性的抑制

ノート **suppress** と **repress の使い分け**：**repress** は、**suppress** ほど頻繁に用いられず、よりフォーマルである。**suppress** は自分の感情を他人に悟られまいと意識的に努めていることがより表現される。一方 **repress** は **suppress** より若干意味が強く、内に秘めた自分の感情を(たとえ自分に対しても)いっさい表に出したくないという思いが示唆される。

,hold sth 'back 句動詞 (笑い・泣きを)抑える、こらえる、我慢する ◇He bravely *held back* his tears. 彼は気丈くもって涙をこらえた ◇At times he could barely *hold back* his impatience. 時たま彼はどうにかいら立ちを我慢が

sure, surprise

できた
check [他]《書き言葉》(言動・感情の表出を突然)抑える、こらえる、我慢する ◇She wanted to tell him the whole truth but she *checked* herself. 彼女はすべての真実を彼に語りたかったがこらえた ◇She made no effort to *check* her tears and just let them run down her face. 彼女は涙をこらえようとはまったくせず、ただ頬を伝うに任せた

curb [他]《望ましくない自分の性格の一面を》抑制する ◇He needs to learn to *curb* his temper. 彼はかんしゃくを抑えることを学ぶ必要がある ◇She has to *curb* her natural exuberance. 彼女は自然と感情があふれ出るのを抑える必要がある

sure [形]

sure・confident・convinced・certain・positive・clear・satisfied
人が物事が真実である[起こる]ことを疑いもなく知っていること
【類語訳】確信して、自信があって、納得して

→
clear	sure	confident
satisfied	certain	convinced
		positive

【文型&コロケーション】

▸ sure/ confident/ convinced/ certain/ positive/ clear **about** sth
▸ sure/ confident/ convinced/ certain/ satisfied **of** sth
▸ sure/ confident/ convinced/ certain/ positive/ clear/ satisfied **that**...
▸ sure/ certain/ clear/ satisfied **who/ what/ how**, etc.
▸ to **feel** sure/ confident/ convinced/ certain/ positive/ satisfied
▸ **quite/ absolutely/ completely/ fairly/ pretty** sure/ confident/ convinced/ certain/ positive/ clear/ satisfied
▸ **fully** confident/ convinced/ satisfied
▸ **not altogether** sure/ confident/ convinced/ certain/ clear/ satisfied
▸ **(not) very** sure/ confident

sure [名詞の前では用いない] 確信して、自信があって ◇'Is that John over there?' 'I'm not *sure*.' 「あそこにいるのはジョンかな」「さあ」 ◇You don't sound very *sure*. あまり自信はないようだね ◇Are you *sure* about that? それは確かですか ◇England must win this game to be *sure* of qualifying. 予選通過を確実にするためには、イングランドはこの試合に勝たなければなりません ◇Are you *sure* you don't mind? 本当に気にしない ◇Ask me if you're not *sure* how to do it. そのやり方がわからなければ聞いてください ❶ sure は事柄に対していくらかの疑念・不安があるために、否定的な発言や疑問文で用いられることが多い。疑念がない場合、quite sure がよく用いられる。◆I'm *quite sure* (that) I left my bag here (= I have no doubt about it). (確かに、ここにカバンを置いたんだ) ◆I'm *pretty sure* (that) he'll agree (= but it is still just possible that he won't). (彼が同意するのはまず間違いない) 反意 **unsure** (UNSURE)
▸**surely** [副] ◇*Surely* you don't think I was responsible for this? まさかその責任は私にあるとは思っていないでしょうね ◇'They're getting married.' '*Surely not*!' 「彼らは結婚するよ」「まさか」

confident (望み[期待]どおりであることを[に])確信して、自信があって ◇I'm quite *confident* that you'll get the job. 君がその仕事に就けると心から確信している ◇The team feels *confident* of winning. そのチームには勝つ自信がある ❶ confident は、sure より意味が強く確信に満ちた語であり、不安のないときに、肯定的な発言で用いられることが多い。
◆She was *quietly confident* that everything would go as planned. (彼女は予定どおり運ぶだろうとひそかに自信を持っていた) ✕She was quietly *sure* that... ☞ **confidence** (FAITH)
▸**confidently** [副] ◇The report asserts *confidently* that the industry will grow. 報告書はその産業の成長を確信をもって断言している

convinced [名詞の前では用いない]（証拠・説明により）確信して、納得して ◇I'm totally *convinced* of her innocence. 彼女の無罪を全面的に確信している ◇I'm *convinced* that she's innocent. 彼女は無実だと確信しています ◇Sam nodded but he didn't look *convinced*. サムはうなずいたが、納得しているようには見えなかった 反意 **unconvinced** ❶ unconvinced of sthと言う場合、相手が言ったことに関わらず、信じない[確信がもてない]ことを意味する。◆I remain *unconvinced of* the need for change. (私は引き続き、変革の必要性を確信できないでいる) ◆She seemed *unconvinced by* their promises. (彼女は彼らの約束に納得していないようだった) ☞ **convince** (CONVINCE)

certain [名詞の前はまれ] 確信して、自信があって ◇Are you absolutely *certain* about this? これは絶対に確かですか ◇She wasn't *certain* (that) he'd seen her. 彼女は彼が自分を見かけたことがあるということに確信が持てなかった 反意 **uncertain** (UNSURE), ☞ **certainty** (FAITH)

> ノート **sure** と **certain** の使い分け：sureと同様、certainも否定的な発言や疑問文で用いられることが多い。certainは、sureよりもいくぶんフォーマルである。sureは特に話し言葉でより頻繁に用いられる。

positive [名詞の前では用いない]《ややインフォーマル、特に話し言葉》確信して、自信があって ◇She was *positive* that he'd been there. 彼女には彼がそこに行ったことがあったという確信があった ◇'Are you sure?' '*Positive*.'「確かですか」「間違いありません」

clear 《しばしば否定文および疑問文で》（疑い・不明瞭さがなく）確信して、はっきりわかって ◇My memory isn't really *clear on* that point. その点については、私の記憶はあまりはっきりしていません ◇I'm still not *clear* what the job entails. その仕事では何をやることになるのかまだはっきりわかっていません ◇We need a *clear understanding* of the problems involved. 我々は関連する問題について明確に理解する必要がある 反意 **vague** (VAGUE)

satisfied [名詞の前では用いない] 確信して、納得して ◇Police were *satisfied* that the death was accidental. 警察はその死が不慮によるものであることを確信していた ☞ **satisfy** (CONVINCE)

surprise [動]

surprise・startle・amaze・stun・astonish・take sb aback・bowl sb over・astound・stagger
人に意外感を与えることを表す
【類語訳】驚かす、びっくりさせる、仰天させる、唖然とさせる、面食らわせる

surprise	amaze
startle	stun
take sb aback	astonish
	bowl sb over
	astound
	stagger

文型&コロケーション

▶It surprises sb/ startles sb/ amazes sb/ stuns sb/ astonishes sb/ takes sb aback/ bowls sb over/ astounds sb/ staggers sb
▶What surprises/ startles/ amazes/ stuns/ astonishes/ astounds/ staggers sb is...
▶to surprise/ startle/ amaze/ stun/ astonish/ astound sb that...
▶to surprise/ amaze sb what/ how...
▶to surprise/ startle/ amaze/ stun/ astonish/ astound sb to know/ find/ learn/ see/ hear...
▶to be surprised/ startled/ stunned into (doing) sth
▶to really surprise s/ startle sb/ amaze sb/ stun sb/ astonish sb/ take sb aback/ bowl sb over/ astound/ stagger sb
▶to absolutely amaze sb/ stun sb/ stagger sb

surprise [他] (予想しない[理解できない]物事で)驚かす, びっくりさせる ◇The outcome didn't *surprise* me at all. その結果に私はまったく驚かなかった ◇It's always *surprised* me how popular he is. 彼の人気ぶりにはいつも驚かされます ◇**It wouldn't *surprise* me** if they got married soon. 彼らがすぐに結婚しても私は驚きはしないよ
▷**surprise** [名] [C] ◇What a nice *surprise*! 素晴らしい, 驚いた ◇a *surprise* attack/announcement/visit 奇襲/電撃発表/電撃訪問 ◇There are few *surprises* in this year's budget. 今年の予算にはサプライズがほとんどない ◇Her letter **came as a** complete *surprise*. 彼女の手紙にはまったく不意をつかれた
▷**surprised** [形] ◇a *surprised* look びっくりした顔つき ◇She looked *surprised* when I told her. 彼女に伝えたとき, 彼女は驚いた様子だった ◇I was *surprised* at how quickly she agreed. 彼女がすぐに同意したのには驚いた ◇They were *surprised* to find (that) he'd already left. 彼らは彼がすでに立ち去ったと知って驚いた

startle [他] (少し衝撃を与える[怖がらせる]形で)驚かす, びっくりさせる ◇Sorry, I didn't mean to *startle* you. ごめんよ, びっくりさせるつもりじゃなかった ◇The explosion *startled* the horse. 馬はその爆発に驚いた ☞ **startled** (AFRAID), **alarm** (FRIGHTEN)

amaze [他] (大いに)驚かす, びっくりさせる, 仰天させる ◇Just the huge size of the place *amazed* her. まさにその場所の巨大さに彼女は驚いた ◇What *amazes* me is how long she managed to hide it from us. 私がびっくりするのは, 彼女がどうやって長い間それを私たちから隠しおおせたのかという点だ ☞ **amazing** (AMAZING)
▷**amazed** [形] ◇an *amazed* silence あっけにとられた沈黙 ◇I was *amazed* at her knowledge of French literature. 彼女のフランス文学に関する知識に仰天した ◇She was *amazed* how little he had changed. 彼女は彼がほとんど変わっていないことに驚いた
▷**amazement** [名] [U] ◇**To my** *amazement*, he was able to recite the whole poem from memory. 驚いたことに, 彼はその詩をすべて暗唱してみせた ◇She looked at him **in** *amazement*. 彼女は呆然と彼を見つめた

stun (-nn-) [他] 《ややインフォーマル, 特にジャーナリズム》(はっきり考えられない[口が利けない]ほど)驚かす, びっくりさせる, 唖然とさせる ◇Her words *stunned* me — I had no idea she felt that way. 彼女の言葉にはびっくりした—彼女がそんなふうに感じているとは知らなかった ◇The company *stunned* investors with its third profits warning in five months. その会社は5か月間で3度目となる業績の下方修正をして, 投資家たちは唖然とした ☞ **stunning** (AMAZING)

astonish [他] (大いに)驚かす, びっくりさせる, 仰天させる ◇You *astonish* me! びっくりしたよ ◇The news *astonished* everyone. その知らせにみんな驚いた ☞ **astonishing** (AMAZING)
▷**astonished** [形] ◇He was *astonished* to learn (that) he'd won the competition. 競技会で自分が優勝したと知って, 彼はひどく驚いた ◇My parents looked *astonished* at my news. 両親は私の知らせにかなり驚いた様子だった
▷**astonishment** [名] [U] ◇**To my utter** *astonishment*, she remembered my name. まったく驚いたことに, 彼女は私の名前を覚えていたのです ◇He stared **in** *astonishment* at the stranger. 彼は驚いてその見知らぬ人をじっと見つめた

ノート amaze と astonish の使い分け：ほとんどの場合, 両語とも使用可能. 驚かせもするし恥ずかしい思いもさせる物事については astonish を用いること. ♦He was *astonished* by his own stupidity. (彼は自分の愚かさに驚いた).

take sb a'back [句動詞] 《ふつう受身で》《書き言葉》(否定的な物事で人を)面食らわせる, 驚かせる ◇We were rather *taken aback* by her hostile reaction. 私たちは彼女の敵意ある反応にかなり面食らった

bowl sb 'over [句動詞] 《しばしば受身で》(大いに人を)驚かす, びっくりさせる, 仰天させる ◇She was *bowled over* by his charm. 彼女は彼の魅力に大いに驚いた

astound [他] (大いに)驚かす, びっくりさせる, 仰天させる ◇His arrogance *astounded* her. 彼は彼の傲慢さにびっくり仰天した

stagger [他] 《ややインフォーマル》(否定的な物事で)驚かす, びっくりさせる, 仰天させる ◇The inspectors were *staggered* at the level of incompetence among senior staff. 調査官たちは, 上級職員の無能ぶりに仰天した ☞ **staggering** (AMAZING)

surprising [形] ☞ AMAZING

surprising・unexpected・unpredictable・extraordinary・unforeseen・unforeseeable

事態が予想していなかったことなので, 驚かされることを表す
【類語訳】驚くべき, 意外な, 思いもよらない, 予期せぬ, 不測の, 異常な

文型&コロケーション

▶surprising/ unexpected/ unpredictable/ extraordinary/ unforeseen/ unanticipated **events**
▶surprising/ unexpected/ unpredictable/ extraordinary/ unforeseen **effects/ changes**
▶surprising/ unexpected/ unpredictable/ extraordinary **results**
▶a surprising/ an unexpected/ an extraordinary/ an unforeseen **development**
▶unexpected/ unpredictable/ extraordinary/ unforeseen **demand/ problems**
▶unexpected/ unforeseen/ unforeseeable **circumstances**

survey, survive

- ▶quite surprising/ unexpected/ unpredictable/ extraordinary/ unforeseen
- ▶totally unexpected/ unpredictable/ unforeseen
- ▶very/ rather surprising/ unexpected/ unpredictable/ extraordinary

surprising 驚くべき、意外な ◇It is not *surprising (that)* they lost. 彼らが負けたのは驚くにあたらない ◇It is *surprising how* quickly rumours spread. 噂が広まるのがどれほど速いか驚くべきものがある ◇It's *surprising what* people will do for money. 人はお金のためなら何をしでかすか、驚くに値する ◇The *surprising thing* is how little it costs. 驚くべきことは、費用がいかに少なくて済むかということだ ◇I find that rather *surprising*. それはかなり驚きだと思う ◇Quite a *surprising* number of people turned up. 実に驚くべき人数の人々がやってきた ❶ surprising は、これらの語の中で最も頻繁に用いられる一般的な語であり、驚きを引き起こすあらゆる事実・出来事に用いることができる。
反意 **unsurprising** (PREDICTABLE)
▶**surprisingly** 副 ◇The event was *surprisingly* popular. そのイベントは意外にも人気があった ◇*Not surprisingly*, the request was refused. 驚くことではないが、その依頼は拒絶された

unexpected 思いもよらない、予期せぬ、意外な、不測の ◇We had an *unexpected* visitor this morning. 私たちは今朝、不意の訪問客を迎えた ◇Although not *unexpected*, his death had still come as a shock. 意外ではなかったが、それでも彼の死は衝撃ではあった ◇The following day something quite *unexpected* happened. その翌日、全く予期せぬことが起きた ❶ unexpected は、起きると予想していなかった出来事に用いられるし、予想していなかったことを行う人にも用いられる。
▶**the unexpected** 名 [単数扱い] ◇Police officers must be prepared for *the unexpected*. 警察官は不測の事態への備えを怠ってはならない
▶**unexpectedly** 副 ◇The plane was *unexpectedly* delayed. 飛行機は思いのほか遅れていた ◇They encountered an *unexpectedly* high level of demand. 彼らは予想外に高い需要水準に直面した

unpredictable (変化するために) 予測できない、不測の ◇The result is entirely *unpredictable*. 結果はまったく予測できない ◇The *unpredictable* weather in the mountains can make climbing extremely hazardous. 予測できない山の天気が、登山をきわめて危険なものにすることがある 反意 **predictable** (PREDICTABLE)

extraordinary 尋常でない、異常な、驚くべき ◇It's *extraordinary* that he managed to sleep through the party. 彼がパーティーの間中眠りおおせたなんて異常だ ◇What an *extraordinary* thing to say! 何て驚くべき言い草だ (REMARKABLE)

unforeseen 《ややフォーマル》思いもよらない、予期せぬ、意外な、不測の ◇We reserve the right to alter the timetable in the event of *unforeseen* circumstances. 万一不測の状況では、私たちは計画表を変更する権利を留保する

ノート **unexpected** と **unforeseen** の使い分け：unforeseen は、unexpected よりフォーマルで、人ではなく出来事にしか用いられない。 ✗an *unforeseen* visitor.

unforeseeable 《ややフォーマル》予測できない、不測の ◇You need to allow for any *unforeseeable* expenses. 予測できない出費を考慮する必要があります 反意 **foreseeable** (PREDICTABLE)

survey 動

survey・poll・sample・canvass・ballot
人々に質問することによって何かについて解明する
【類語訳】調査する、世論調査をする、投票を求める

文型&コロケーション
- ▶to poll/ ballot sb **on** sth
- ▶to canvass/ ballot sb **for** sth
- ▶to survey/ canvass **opinion**
- ▶to poll/ ballot your **members**

survey [他] (意見・行動を) 調査する ◇We *surveyed* 500 smokers and found that over three quarters would like to give up. 500人の喫煙者を調査して、4分の3以上の人が禁煙したがっていることがわかった ◇The aim of the project is to *survey* public attitudes to disability. そのプロジェクトの目的は、身体障碍(がい)に対する一般市民の意識を調査することにあります ☞ **survey** (INVESTIGATION)

poll [他、ふつう受身で] 世論調査をする ◇Over 50% of those *polled* were against the proposed military action. 世論調査の対象者の半数以上が、その軍事行動案に反対した ☞ **poll** (INVESTIGATION)

sample [他]《専門語》(残りがどうかを見出すために一部を) 調査する ◇The survey was done using a group of 100 children *randomly sampled* from the school population. 調査は全児童から無作為に選んだ100人の子供の集団を使って行われた
▶**sample** 名 [C] ◇*Samples* of the water contained pesticide. サンプルの水に殺虫剤が含まれていた ◇The interviews were given to a *random sample* of students. インタビューは学生を無作為に選んで行われた

canvass [他] (意見を) 求める ◇I quickly *canvassed* opinion on the issue among my colleagues. 私はすぐに、その問題点について同僚に意見を求めた ◇People are being *canvassed* for their views on the proposed new road. その新道路案に関する人々の見解が求められているところです

ballot [他] (意見を見出すために) 投票を求める ◇The union *balloted* its members on the proposed changes. 組合はその変更案について組合員に投票を求めた ☞ **ballot** (ELECTION)

survive 動 ☞ RECOVER

survive・live・live on sth・make it・weather・live through sth・come through (sth)
生命を維持する
【類語訳】生き残る、生き延びる、存続する、残存する、生き長らえる、食べていく、切り抜ける、乗り切る、耐え抜く

文型&コロケーション
- ▶to survive/ live **on** (a diet of) sth
- ▶to survive/ live **for** a few days/ many years, etc.
- ▶to survive/ make it / live/ come **through** sth
- ▶to survive/ live **without** food/ money, etc.
- ▶to survive/ weather a **storm/ crisis/ recession**
- ▶to survive/ come through an **operation**

survive [自、他] 生き残る、生き続ける、存続する；(危険な出来事[時代]にもかかわらず) 生き残る、生き延びる、残存する

↪ survive

◇She was the last *surviving* member of the family. 彼女はその家族のうちで最後まで生き残った ◇Of the six people injured in the crash, only two *survived*. その墜落で負傷した6人のうち、生き残ったのは2人だけだった ◇I can't *survive* on £40 a week (= it is not enough for my basic needs). 週40ポンドでは私はとてもやっていけない ◇The children had to *survive by* begging and stealing. その子たちは物乞いと盗みで生き延びねばならなかった ◇Some strange customs have *survived from* earlier times. いくつかの風変わりなしきたりが昔から存続している ◇He *survived as* party leader until his second election defeat. 彼は2度目の選挙で敗北するまで党首の座を守り続けた ◇Many birds didn't *survive* the severe winter. 多くの鳥たちが厳しい冬を越せなかった ◇Few buildings *survived* the war intact. 無傷で戦争をかいくぐった建物はほとんどなかった ☞ **survival** (LIFE 1)

live [自] 生きる、生き長らえる ◇The doctors said he only had six months to *live*. 医師たちは彼の命は半年しかもたないと言った ◇Spiders can *live* for several days without food. クモは餌なしに数日生きることができる ◇She *lived to see* her first grandchild. 彼女は生き長らえて初孫との対面を果たした ☞ **life** (LIFE 1)

'**live on sth** [句動] (特定の種類の食べ物)を常食とする、食べて生きている；(生きるのに必要な基本的な物を買うための金で)食べていく、生活する ◇Small birds *live* mainly *on* insects. 小鳥たちは主に昆虫を食べて生きている ◇My salary isn't enough for us to *live on*. 私の給料は私たちが食べていくには十分でない ◇You don't want to end up *living on benefits* (= money from the state). 福祉手当を頼りにの生活をする羽目になりたくないでしょう ❶ live on sthはまた、「特定の種類の食べ物だけを[食べ物を大量に]食べる」を意味して非難的に用いることもある。◆She seems to *live on* burgers. (彼女はハンバーガーばかり食べているようだ).

'**make it** [他動] (ややフォーマル) (大病・重大事故の後で)助かる；(難しい体験を)切り抜ける ◇The doctors think he's going to *make it*. 彼は助かるだろうと医師たちは考えている ◇I don't know how I *made it* through the week. 私はその週をどう切り抜けたかわからない

weather [他] (ビジネス・政治において)乗り切る、切り抜ける ◇The company just managed to *weather* the recession. その会社は不況を何とか乗り切ったところだった ◇She refuses to resign, intending to *weather the storm* (= wait until the situation improves again).《比喩的》彼女は危機を切り抜けるつもりで辞職を拒んでいる

,**live 'through sth** [句動] (災難などを)生き抜く ◇He *lived through* two world wars. 彼は二度の世界大戦を生き抜いた

,**come 'through sth**, ,**come 'through** [句動] (大病・手術の)を耐え抜く；(負傷・困難を)切り抜ける ◇With such a weak heart she was lucky to *come through* the operation. そんな虚弱な心臓で手術を耐え抜いたとは、彼女は幸運だった ◇If you've ever done something dangerous and *come through unscathed*, you'll know what I mean about this feeling. 何か危険なことをして無傷で切り抜けたことがあるなら、私のこの気持ちがわかるだろう

suspect [動]

suspect・disbelieve・distrust・doubt
人の言うことや物事を本当だと思わない
【類語訳】疑う、容疑をかける、信じない、信用しない

suspect, suspicious

【文型&コロケーション】
▶ to suspect/ distrust sb's **motives**
▶ to **still/ never** suspect/ disbelieve/ distrust/ doubt sb
▶ to **have (no) reason to** suspect/ disbelieve/ distrust/ doubt sb

suspect [他]《進行形なし》疑う；容疑をかける ◇He resigned after being *suspected of* theft. 彼は盗みの容疑をかけられて辞めた ◇The drug is *suspected of* causing over 200 deaths. その薬物は200人以上の死を招いたとの疑いをかけられている ◇He dealt through a broker whose honesty he had no reason to *suspect*. 誠実さを疑いようもないあるブローカーを通じて彼は取引した ☞ **suspicion** (SCEPTICISM)

disbelieve [他]《進行形なし》《フォーマル》信じない ◇Why should I *disbelieve* her story? どうして彼女の話は信じないほうがいいの 【反意】**believe** (FAITH), ☞ **disbelief** (SCEPTICISM)

distrust [他] (ややフォーマル、書き言葉) 疑う；信用しない ◇She *distrusted* his motives for wanting to see her again. 彼女は自分にもう一度会いたいという彼の動機を疑った 【反意】**trust** (TRUST), ☞ **distrust** (SCEPTICISM)

[ノート] suspect と distrust の使い分け： suspect sb's motives, suspect sb of doing sth とは言えるが、単に suspect sb とは言えない。distrust はより概括的である。distrust sb's motives や、単に distrust sb/sth (一般的にある人・物事を信用できないと感じる)と言えるが、特定の行動や犯罪を of で受けて distrust sb of... と言うことはできない。

doubt [他] (人の言うことを)疑う ◇I had no reason to *doubt* him. 彼を疑う理由がなかった ☞ **doubt** (DOUBT [名] 2)

suspicious [形]

1 suspicious・sceptical・cynical・incredulous・disbelieving
人は真実を話していない[物事は真実でない]と人が感じている[信じている]ことを表す
【類語訳】疑って、怪しんで、疑い深い、懐疑的な、冷笑的な、世をすねた

【文型&コロケーション】
▶ suspicious/ sceptical/ cynical/ incredulous **about** sth
▶ suspicious/ sceptical/ incredulous **of** sb/ sth
▶ suspicious/ sceptical **as to** sth
▶ a suspicious/ a sceptical/ a cynical/ an incredulous/ a disbelieving **look**
▶ **very/ deeply** suspicious/ sceptical/ cynical

suspicious (証拠なしに)疑って、怪しんで；(人・物事に対して)疑い深い ◇They became *suspicious* of his behaviour and contacted the police. 彼らは彼の行動を疑うようになり、警察に連絡した ◇She cast a *suspicious* glance at him. 彼女は彼に疑いのまなざしを投げかけた ◇You have a very *suspicious* mind (= you always think that people are behaving in an illegal or dishonest way). あなたって、とっても疑い深い人ですね ◇Many were *suspicious* of reform. 大勢の人が改革に疑念を抱いていた ☞ **suspicion** (SCEPTICISM), **suspicion** (DOUBT [名] 2)
▶ **suspiciously** [副] ◇The man looked at her *suspiciously*. その男は彼女を怪訝そうに見つめた

sweet

sceptical《英》(米 **skeptical**)（主張・発言が）懐疑的な、疑って、疑い深い ◇I am *sceptical* about his chances of winning. 私は彼が勝つ見込みについて疑ってかかっている ◇The public remain *sceptical* of these claims. 大衆はこういう主張にはずっと懐疑的でいる ◇She looked highly *sceptical*. 彼女は強く疑っているようだった ☞**scepticism** (SCEPTICISM)
▶**sceptically**《英》(米では **skeptically**)副 ◇The announcement was greeted *sceptically* by the press. その発表は報道陣に疑いの目で迎えられた

cynical 冷笑的な、人を信じない、世をすねた ◇Do you have to be so *cynical* about everything? そんなに何でも疑う必要があるの ◇Her lips curled into a *cynical* smile. 彼女の唇はゆがんで冷笑へと変わった ☞**cynicism** (SCEPTICISM)

incredulous 疑い深い；疑うような ◇'Here?' said Kate, *incredulous*. 「ここなの」とケイトは怪しむように言った ◇She shot him an *incredulous* look. 彼女は彼に疑うような視線を投げかけた
▶**incredulously** 副 ◇He laughed *incredulously*. 彼は疑い深げに笑った

disbelieving 不審そうな ◇She gave him a *disbelieving* look. 彼女は彼に不審そうな視線を投げかけた ☞**disbelief** (SCEPTICISM)
▶**disbelievingly** 副 ◇She stared *disbelievingly* at the alarm clock. 彼女は不審そうに目覚まし時計を見つめた

ノート **incredulous** と **disbelieving** の使い分け：多くの場合、両語とも使用可能. incredulous は物事について信じるにはあまりに奇妙で驚くべきということを示唆することが多い. disbelieving は物事について話す人を信用していないために、その物事も信じないということを示唆することが多い.

2 suspicious・suspect・questionable・dubious・dodgy・shifty・shady・fishy
人や行動が間違っている[違法である、不正である]との感じを表す
【類語訳】怪しい、不審な、疑わしい、いかがわしい、ずるそうな、うさんくさい

文型&コロケーション
▶a suspicious/ suspect/ questionable/ dubious/ shifty/ shady **character**
▶a suspicious/ questionable/ dubious **circumstances**
▶a suspicious/ shifty **look/ manner**
▶a suspicious/ suspect **package**
▶a dodgy/ shady **deal/ past**
▶a dodgy/ fishy **business**
▶There's **something** suspicious/ suspect/ shifty/ shady/ fishy **about** sb/ sth.
▶There's **something** suspicious/ shady/ fishy **going on**.
▶**very** suspicious/ suspect/ questionable/ dubious/ dodgy/ shifty/ shady/ fishy
▶**a bit** suspicious/ suspect/ questionable/ dubious/ dodgy/ shifty/ fishy
▶**rather/ pretty** suspicious/ suspect/ questionable/ dubious/ dodgy/ shifty
▶**highly/ slightly/ somewhat** suspicious/ suspect/ questionable/ dubious

suspicious 怪しい、不審な ◇Didn't you notice anything *suspicious* in his behaviour? 彼の行動の何か怪しいところに気づかなかったの ◇Police are not treating the death as *suspicious*. 警察はその死を不審死だとは見ていない ◇It might look *suspicious* if we arrived together. 私たちが一緒に到着したら、怪しいと思われるかもしれない ☞**suspicion** (DOUBT 名2)
▶**suspiciously** 副 ◇Let me know if you see anyone acting *suspiciously*. 誰か怪しげな行動をとっている人を見たら私に知らせてください ◇Everything was *suspiciously* quiet. すべてが静まりかえっていてどうもおかしかった

suspect《特にジャーナリズム》（間違っているかもしれず[当てにできず]）疑わしい、怪しい、不審な ◇Some of the evidence they produced was highly *suspect*. 彼らが提出した証拠のいくつかはかなり疑わしかった ◇The police have been informed of the discovery of a *suspect* package (= that may contain drugs, a bomb, etc.). 警察が不審な小包を発見したとの通報を受けた

questionable《ややフォーマル》（不正であるために[道徳的に間違っていて]）疑わしい、怪しい、不審な ◇Her motives for helping are *questionable*. 助けようという彼女の動機は疑わしい 反意 **unquestionable**

dubious《ややフォーマル》（不正であるために[道徳的に間違っていて]）疑わしい、怪しい、不審な ◇The man who sold it to him was known to be of *dubious* character. それを彼に売った男は不審人物として知られていた

ノート **questionable** と **dubious** の使い分け：questionable は、人々の行動・動機について用いられることが最も多い. dubious は、物事[人々]の価値・人々の行状について用いられることが多い. 以下は典型的なパターンである. ◆**of** *dubious* character/nature/provenance/quality/reputation/value (怪しげな特徴/性質/由来/品質/評判/価値の)

dodgy《英, インフォーマル》（ビジネス活動が）いかがわしい ◇Travel websites that offer *dodgy* deals have been uncovered in a worldwide investigation. いかがわしい取引を提供している旅行サイトが世界規模の調査で発覚している

shifty《インフォーマル》いかがわしい、ずるそうな；うさんくさい ◇I don't trust him — he's got *shifty* eyes. 彼のことは信用していない—彼はずるそうな目をしているもの ◇He was trying not to look *shifty*. 彼はうさんくさそうに見えないようにに努めていた ❶ shifty は、人々の目(つき)について用いられることが最も多い.

shady［ふつう名詞の前で］《インフォーマル》いかがわしい、うさんくさい、怪しい ◇He's a bit of a *shady* character. 彼はちょっといかがわしい人物だ ◇I don't want anything to do with your *shady* deals. あなたの怪しげな取引には関わりたくない

fishy《インフォーマル》いかがわしい、うさんくさい、怪しい ◇There's something *fishy* going on here. ここでは何かいかがわしいことが進行中だ ◇I don't know what they're up to. It sounds a distinctly *fishy* business. 彼らが何をたくらんでいるかわからない. どうも実にうさんくさいものに思える ❶ *fishy* は, fishy business, something fishy, sth sounds fishy の句で用いられるのがほとんどである.

sweet 形 ☞ NICE 2

sweet・cute・adorable・lovable・dear old/little…・endearing・cuddly
人[子ども、動物]が魅力的で好きになりやすいことを表す
【類語訳】かわいい、すてきな、愛すべき、憎めない、いとしい…

文型&コロケーション
▶a sweet/ a cute/ an adorable/ a lovable/ a dear/ an endearing **little**…

↪sweet
switch, sympathy

▶ a sweet/ a cute/ an adorable/ a cuddly **baby**
▶ a sweet/ a cute/ an adorable **girl/ boy/ child/ kid**
▶ an endearing/ a cuddly **animal/ creature**
▶ a sweet/ cute/ lovable **way**

sweet 《特に英, 特に話し言葉, ほめて》(子ども・動物・小さな物が)かわいい(らしい) ◇His sister's a *sweet* young thing. 彼の妹はかわいいねえ ◇You look *sweet* in this photograph. 君, この写真はかわいらしく写ってるね ◇What a *sweet* little dog! 何てかわいい小犬なの
▷ **sweetly** 副 ◇She smiled *sweetly* at him. 彼女はかわいらしく彼にほほ笑みかけた

cute 《特に話し言葉, ほめて》(子ども・動物・小さな物が)かわいい(らしい) ◇You were such a *cute* baby. あなたって, とってもかわいい赤ん坊だったのよ ◇She had a *cute* little nose. 彼女のお鼻は小さくてかわいらしかった

> ノート **sweet**と**cute**の使い分け：ふつう両語とも使用可能。 ◆ How *sweet/cute*! (何てかわいいの). ◆ What a *sweet/cute* (little) baby, picture, dress! (何てかわいい(小さな)赤ちゃんに絵にドレスなの). **sweet**は《英》でよく用いられ, **cute**は《米》でよく用いられる.

adorable 《特に米, 特に話し言葉, ほめて》すてきな, かわいらしい ◇Isn't he just *adorable*? 彼って, ちょっとすてきじゃない ◇What an *adorable* child! 何てかわいらしい子なの ☞ **adore** (LOVE 動)

lovable (または **loveable**)《ほめて》(欠点があるにもかかわらず)愛すべき, 憎めない ◇People saw him as a *lovable* rogue. 人々は彼を憎めないいたずらっ子と見なしていた ☞ **love** (LOVE 動)

dear old/little... 《英, ほめて》(愛情を示して)かわいい…, いとしい… ◇*Dear old* Sue! I knew she'd help. いとしのスー. 彼女なら助けてくれると思ってたわ ◇Their baby's a *dear little* thing. 彼らの赤ちゃん, ちっちゃくてかわいらしいの

endearing 《ほめて》人の心を引きつける, 人に慕われる ◇I like his honesty. It's one of his most *endearing* qualities. 私は彼の誠実さが好きなの. それって, 彼が最も人に慕われる性質の一つなのよ
▷ **endearingly** 副 ◇an *endearingly* old-fashioned idea 人の心を引きつけるほど古風な考え
▷ **endear sb/yourself to sb** 句動詞 ◇She was a talented teacher who *endeared herself to* (= made herself popular with) all who worked with her. 彼女は一緒に働いている人全員に慕われている才能ある教師だった

cuddly 《インフォーマル, ほめて》抱きしめたくなるような ◇a tiny, *cuddly* kitten 小さくて抱きしめたくなるような子猫 ❶ **cuddly**は, 《特に, 柔らかい毛をした若い》動物に用いられることが多い. **cuddly**な人は, ぽっちゃり柔らかそうに見える. それゆえに, **fat** (太った)と評されるような大人よりも, 赤ん坊を表すのによく用いられる. ☞ **cuddle** (HUG)

switch 動

switch・change (sth) over・convert・swap
ある物事から別の物事に変わる[変える]
【類語訳】切り換える, 変更する, 転換する, 変換する, 交代する, 交代する

> 文型&コロケーション

▶ to switch over/ change over/ convert **from** sth **to** sth
▶ to switch/ change/ swap **over**
▶ to switch/ convert/ swap **easily**

switch 〔自, 他〕《ややインフォーマル》切り換[替]わる；切り換[替]える, 変更する, 転換する ◇Press these two keys to *switch between* documents on screen. 画面上のドキュメントを切り換えるには, この二つのキーを押してください ◇The meeting has been *switched* to next week. 会議は来週に変更された ◇When did you *switch* jobs? いつ転職したの ☞ **switch** (CHANGE 名 2)

,change 'over, ,change sth 'over 句動詞 (別のシステム・位置に)切り換[替]わる；切り換[替]える ◇The farm has *changed over* to organic methods. その農場では有機農法に切り替えた ◇We've *changed* the farm *over* to organic production. 私たちは農場を有機生産に切り替えた ☞ **change** (CHANGE 名 2)

> ノート **switch**と**change over**の使い分け：**switch**は**change over**よりインフォーマルで, ジャーナリズムで用いられることが多い. **change over**は**from**よりも**to**と共に用いられることが多い. ◆ to *change over to* nicotine gum/ dairy farming/a nuclear policy (ニコチンガムに/酪農に/核政策に切り替える). **switch**は正反対の位置に移動すること, 時代遅れのシステムから新しいシステムに移行することについて用いられることが多い. ◆ to *switch over* from recovery to relapse (快復から再発に転じる). ◆ to *switch over* to a metric standard/electronic mail (メートル規格/電子メールに切り替わる).

convert 〔自〕《ややフォーマル》(習慣・意見を)変換する, 切り換[替]える ◇I've *converted* to organic food. 自然食品に切り替えた ☞ **conversion** (CHANGE 名 2)

swap (または **swop**) (-pp-) 〔自〕(仕事などを)交換する, 交代する ◇I'll drive there and then we'll *swap* over on the way back. そこへは私が運転して行き, その後帰り道では運転を交代します ☞ **swap** (EXCHANGE)

sympathy 名 ☞ RELIEF

sympathy・concern・compassion・pity・understanding・condolence・humanity
不幸な[苦しんでいる]人を気の毒に思うときに抱く気持ち
【類語訳】同情, 哀れみ, お悔やみ, 共感, 心配, 気遣い, 思いやり, 哀悼, 弔意, 慈悲, 人情

> 文型&コロケーション

▶ sympathy/ concern/ compassion/ pity **for** sb/ sth
▶ to do sth **out of** sympathy/ concern/ compassion/ pity
▶ to do sth **with** sympathy/ concern/ compassion/ understanding/ humanity
▶ **without** sympathy/ compassion/ pity
▶ **great** sympathy/ concern/ compassion/ understanding/ humanity
▶ **deep** sympathy/ concern/ compassion/ understanding
▶ **real/ genuine** sympathy/ concern/ compassion/ pity/ understanding/ humanity
▶ to **feel/ be full of** sympathy/ concern/ compassion/ pity
▶ to **have** sympathy/ compassion/ pity (for sb/ sth)
▶ to **express** (your) sympathy/ concern/ condolences
▶ to **show** (sb) sympathy/ concern/ compassion/ pity/ understanding/ humanity
▶ to **offer** (sb) (your) sympathy/ understanding/ condolences
▶ to **give** sb (your) sympathy/ compassion/ pity/ understanding/ condolences

sympathy 〔U, C, ふつう複数で〕(人を気の毒に思う)同情, 哀

れみ、お悔やみ；(人の問題に対する)共感 ◇I have no *sympathy* for Jan; it's all her own fault. ジャンには同情しません。全部彼女自身の責任だもの ◇He didn't get much *sympathy* from anyone. 彼は誰からもあまり共感されなかった ◇Their plight aroused considerable public *sympathy*. 彼らの窮状はかなり世間の同情を引いた ◇May we offer our deepest *sympathies* on the death of your wife. 《フォーマル》奥様の死に対し心からのお悔やみを申し上げます ☞ **sympathetic** (SENSITIVE 1), **sympathize** (SORRY FOR SB)

concern [U] (人・物事を守り助けたいとの)心配、気遣い ◇She forgot her own worries in her *concern* for her children. 彼女は子どもたちを気遣ううちに自分自身不安に思っていることは忘れた ◇I appreciate everyone's *concern* and help at this difficult time. この難局での、皆様のお気遣いとご支援に感謝いたします ❶人々は、例えば家族や友人など、責任がある[を感じる]人々に対して concern を感じることが多い。

compassion [U] 《ややフォーマル》(苦しんでいる人への)思いやり、同情、哀れみ ◇He was filled with overwhelming love and *compassion* for his wife. 彼は妻に対する絶大な愛と思いやりにあふれていた ◇She was known as a hard woman with no *compassion*, no emotion. 彼女は哀れみも感情も表に出さない厳しい女性として知られていた ☞ **compassionate** (SENSITIVE 1)

pity [U] (人の苦しみ・問題に対する)同情、哀れみ ◇I could only feel *pity* for what they were enduring. 彼らの苦しみに対しては同情することしかできなかった ◇I *took pity on* her and lent her the money. 彼女を気の毒に思い、お金を貸してあげた ◇I beg you to *have pity on* him. 《フォーマル》どうか彼に哀れみを ☞ **pity** (SORRY FOR SB)

🗒 **compassion** と **pity** の使い分け: compassion は pity より強い気持ちを表す。compassion は他人が感じていることを理解していること、ある意味で彼らの苦しみを共有していることを示唆する温かく優しい気持ちである。pity を感じる場合、必ずしもそういった理解はなく、同情を抱いた相手に対し、等しく尊敬の念を抱かない[示さない]かもしれない。この理由から人は、◆I don't want your *pity*! (同情はいらない)とは言うかもしれないが、×I don't want your *compassion*! とはまず言わない。pity は、have/take pity on sb の句で用いられることが多い。

understanding [U、単数で] (特定の行動に対する)共感、思いやり ◇Please try to show a little more *understanding*. もう少しご理解いただけますように ◇We are looking for a better *understanding* between the two nations. 我々は二か国間にさらに十分な理解が得られることを期待しています ☞ **understanding** (SENSITIVE 1)

condolence [C、ふつう複数で、U] 《ややフォーマル》(亡くなった人に対して表す)お悔やみ、哀悼、弔意 ◇Our heartfelt *condolences* go out to his wife and family. 私たちは彼の奥様とご家族に心からの哀悼の意を捧げます ◇a letter of *condolence* お悔やみ状 ❶ my/his/her/our, etc. condolences は、例えばスピーチ・手紙など、正式な[公式の]文脈で用いられる。

humanity [U] (必要以上に傷つかないことを確かめる)慈悲、人情 ◇The judge was praised for his courage and *humanity*. その裁判官の勇気と慈悲が称賛された 反意 **inhumanity** (CRUEL), ☞ **humane** (SENSITIVE 1)

system 名 ☞ STRUCTURE

system • network • organization • web • apparatus • workings

物事が組織される形、物事の異なる部分が互いに結びつく形 【類語訳】組織、制度、機構、体制、系統、装置、システム、ネットワーク、編成、構成、機能

文型&コロケーション
▶ a system/ a network/ an apparatus **for** sth
▶ **in/ within** a system/ a network/ a web/ the apparatus
▶ the **whole** system/ network/ web/ apparatus
▶ a/ the **complex** system/ network/ organization/ web/ apparatus/ workings
▶ a **social** system/ network/ organization
▶ an **administrative** system/ network/ apparatus
▶ to **create** a system/ network/ web
▶ to **set up/ establish** a system/ network
▶ to **improve** a system/ the organization of sth
▶ to **understand/ explain** a system/ the organization of sth/ the workings of sth

system [C] 組織、制度、機構、体制；(接続[連携]する物[設備]の)系統、装置、システム ◇the educational/justice *system* 教育/司法制度 ◇a heating/computer *system* 暖房/コンピューターシステム ◇Their existing *system* of government seems to work reasonably well. その国の現行の行政組織は、適度によく機能しているように見える ◇The *alarm system* had been switched off. 警報システムのスイッチが切られていた

network [C] (互いに情報を交換し合う密接に結びついた)網状組織、ネットワーク ◇She has a supportive *network* of close friends. 彼女には支援してくれる親友のネットワークがある ◇The company has a *network* of regional offices. その会社には支社同士をつなぐネットワークがある ◇They have one of the most efficient distribution *networks* in Europe. 彼らはヨーロッパで最も効率的な流通網の一つを備えている

organization (英でまた **-isation**) [U] (社会・機関における)組織、編成、構成、体制 ◇The report studies the *organization* of labour within the civil service. その報告書では行政事務における労働者の組織化が検討されている ◇They experimented with new forms of social *organization*. 彼らは新しい形態の社会組織の実験を行った

web [C] (扱い[理解]の困難な)もつれ合った関係[事態]、わな ◇An increasingly complex *web* of legislation has been considered. ますます複雑な法律体系が検討されている ◇We were caught in a *tangled web* of relationships. 私たちは人間関係のもつれた網に捕らわれた ◇She discovered a *web of intrigue* (= secret activities). 彼女は入り組んだ陰謀に気づいた ◇a *web* of deceit/lies 策略のわな/嘘八百 ❶ この意味でのwebという語の連語の多くは、文字どおりクモの巣を連想させる。tangled, caught (up) in, entangled in, drawn into, spin, weave, centre of と結びつく。

apparatus [C、ふつう単数で] (政府[政党]の)組織、機関 ◇Under the new system there was to be no all-powerful central state *apparatus*. 新体制の下では、全権を有する中央集権組織を置かないことになっていた ◇the *apparatus* of government 政府機関

workings [複数で] (組織の)機能、働き ◇The classes give an introduction to the *workings* of Congress. これらの授業では議会の機能に関する概論を講じます ◇In the book he tries to give a complete description of the *workings* of the human mind. その本の中で、彼は人間の精神の働きをまるごと説明しようとしています ❶ workingsはふつうthe workings (of sth), sth's workingsの句で用いられる。

T t

tact 名

tact・sensitivity・discretion・diplomacy
難なく人を扱う術
【類語訳】機転, 臨機応変の才, 気配り, 感受性, 敏感さ, 思いやり, 慎重さ, 用心深さ, 外交術

文型&コロケーション
- to do sth **with** sensitivity/ discretion/ diplomacy
- **great** sensitivity/ discretion/ diplomacy
- **the utmost** tact/ sensitivity/ discretion
- to **require/ need/ call for** sensitivity/ discretion/ diplomacy
- to **have/ show** sensitivity/ diplomacy

tact [U]《ほめて》機転, 臨機応変の才, 気配り ◇Settling the dispute required great *tact* and diplomacy. 紛争解決のために機転と外交術が大いに必要とされた ◇She is not exactly known for her *tact*. 彼女に必ずしも臨機応変の才が備わっているというわけではない ❶*tact* には, 人を怒らせたり, 気分を害するようなことを「言わない」という意味を含む。人を困惑させたり, 気分を害するような話題を持ち出す人は, tactless と見なされるだろう。
▸**tactful** 形 ◇That wasn't a very *tactful* thing to say! あれはあまり機転の利いた発言ではなかったね 反意 **tactless** (INSENSITIVE)

sensitivity [U]《ほめて》感受性, 敏感さ, 思いやり ◇*Sensitivity* to the needs of children is the main requirement for the job. 子どもの要求に敏感であることがその仕事の主たる必要条件である ◇She pointed out with tact and *sensitivity* exactly where he had gone wrong. 彼がどこで間違った方向に進んだかを, 彼女は臨機応変に, かつ思いやりを持って正確に指摘した ☞ **sensitive** (SENSITIVE 1)

discretion [U]《特に書き言葉, ほめて》慎重さ, 用心深さ, 気配り ◇This is confidential, but I know that I can rely on your *discretion*. ここだけの話, あなたの気配りに頼れるものと思っています 反意 **indiscretion** (IMPROPER)
▸**discreet** 形 ◇He was always very *discreet* about his love affairs. 彼は常に自分の情事には非常に用心深かった ◇You ought to make a few *discreet* enquiries before you sign anything. 何かに署名する前には少し慎重に問い合わせるべきです 反意 **indiscreet**

diplomacy [U]《ややフォーマル, 特に書き言葉》外交術[手腕] ◇She handled the situation with her usual quiet *diplomacy*. 彼女はいつもの落ち着いた外交手腕で事態を処理した
▸**diplomatic** 形 ◇a *diplomatic* answer 角立たない返事

> ノート **tact** と **diplomacy** の使い分け: tact は他人を怒らせないようにするときに用いられる性質であり, ある人々に生まれつき備わっているものである。diplomacy は実践を通して学ばれる術を指し, 他人を助けるためだけでなく, 自分が優位に立つためにも用いられる。

tactic 名 ☞ TRICK

tactic・device・ploy・manoeuvre
ほしいものを手に入れる[ある状況において優位に立つ]ための特定の賢明な術
【類語訳】戦術, 作戦, 方策, 工夫, 方法, 策略, 戦略

文型&コロケーション
- a tactic/ device/ ploy **for** (doing) sth
- a tactic/ device/ ploy/ manoeuvre **to do sth**
- a **clever** device/ ploy/ manoeuvre
- an **effective** tactic/ device/ ploy
- a **marketing** tactic/ device/ ploy
- a **political** tactic/ device/ manoeuvre
- to **use** a tactic/ device/ ploy/ manoeuvre
- to **resort to** a tactic/ device/ ploy
- a tactic/ device/ ploy/ manoeuvre **works**
- a tactic/ ploy/ manoeuvre **succeeds/ fails**

tactic [C, ふつう複数で]《物事を達成するための》戦術, 作戦, 方策 ◇The manager discussed *tactics* with his team. 監督は自分のチームと作戦を練った ◇Confrontation is not always the best *tactic*. 対決が必ずしも最善の方策とは限らない ◇This was just the latest in a series of *delaying tactics*. これが一連の引き延ばし作戦のまさに最新のものだった ◇They were desperate enough to try *shock tactics*. 彼らは自暴自棄に陥り奇襲作戦に打って出るとした ☞ **strategy** (PLAN 1)

device [C]《ややフォーマル》《特定の結果・効果を生むための》工夫, 方法 ◇We use a range of *devices* for testing children's numerical ability. 私たちはさまざまな方法を使って子どもたちの計算能力をテストします ❶このように, device は物事を行う巧みで有効な方法を指すが, 不正な計画や策略を指すこともある。☞ **device** (TRICK)

ploy [C]《しばしばけなして》《人をだまして優位に立つ[何かをさせる]ための》策略, 戦略 ◇a clever marketing *ploy* 賢いマーケティング戦略 ◇It was all a *ploy* to distract attention away from his real aims. それはすべて彼の本当の目的や注意をそらすための策略だった ☞ **scheme** (CONSPIRACY)

manoeuvre《英》《米**maneuver**》[C, U]《人をだまして誰かを優位に立たせるための》策略, 戦略 ◇It can be seen as a tactical *manoeuvre* to gain some time. それは時間を稼ぐための抜け目ない策略と見なされるかもしれない ◇The agreement was a result of weeks of diplomatic *manoeuvre*. その合意は数週間にわたる外交戦略の結果だった

take 動

1 take・bring・deliver・ship・carry・transport・fly・ferry・leave
ある場所から別の場所へ物を移動させる
【類語訳】持って行く, 連れて行く, 持って来る, 連れて来る, 持参する, 配達する, 送り届ける, 輸送する

take

文型&コロケーション

- to take/ bring/ deliver/ ship/ carry/ transport/ fly/ ferry sb/ sth **to/ from** sb/ sth
- to take/ bring/ ship/ carry/ transport/ fly/ ferry sb/ sth **back/ home**
- to take/ bring sb/ sth **with** you
- to take/ bring/ deliver/ carry/ transport/ ferry/ sb/ sth **by car/ rail/ truck, etc.**
- to take/ bring/ deliver/ transport sb/ sth **by air/ sea/ land**

take [他] (物を)持って行く, 運ぶ ◇*Take* this to the bank for me, would you? 私の代わりにこれを銀行に持って行っていただけますか ◇My things had already been *taken* to my room. 私の持ち物はもう部屋に運んでもらいました ◇Think about what you need to *take* for the trip. 旅行に持って行く必要のある物について考えなさい ◇All she had *taken* was her passport and driving licence. 彼女が持って行ったのはパスポートと運転免許証だけだった ◇Should I *take* him a gift? 彼に手土産を持って行くべきかな ❶ *take* は人をどこかへ連れて行く場合にも用いられる。 ☞ **take** (TAKE 2)

bring [他] (人・物を)持って[連れて]来る, 持って[連れて]行く, 持参する, 運ぶ ◇Remember to *bring* your books with you. 自分の本を忘れずに持参してください ◇The ferries *brought* tourists in their hundreds. そのフェリーは大勢の観光客を運んで来た ◇I've *brought* something to show you. 君に見せる物を持って来たんだ ◇*Bring* a present for Helen. ヘレンにプレゼントを持って来てね ◇*Bring* Helen a present. ヘレンにプレゼントを持って来てね

ノート take と bring の使い分け: take はどこかへ物を持って行こうとしている人の視点から用いられ, bring はその人が行こうとしている場所にすでにいる人の視点から用いられる。

deliver [他, 自] (商品・手紙などを)配達する, 送り届ける; (人を)連れて行く ◇Leaflets have been *delivered* to every household. ちらしは各家庭に届けられている ◇to have groceries/flowers/packages *delivered* 食糧雑貨類/花/小包を配達してもらう ◇She *delivered* the kids on time at their father's house. 彼女は子どもたちを彼らの父親の家に時間どおりに送り届けた ◇We promise to *deliver* within 24 hours. 私どもは24時間以内に配達することをお約束します ☞ **delivery** (DELIVERY)

ship (-pp-) [他] (船などで人・物を)輸送[出荷]する ◇The company *ships* its goods all over the world. その会社は世界に商品を出荷している ◇He was arrested and *shipped* back to the UK for trial. 彼は逮捕され, 裁判を受けるためにイギリスに送還された ☞ **shipment, shipping** (DELIVERY)

carry [他] 《しばしば進行形で》 (乗り物で人・物を)運ぶ, 輸送する ◇The boat can *carry* up to five people. そのボートは5人まで乗れます ◇The truck was *carrying* illegal drugs worth up to $2 million. そのトラックは200万ドル相当に上る違法薬物を運んでいた

transport [他, しばしば受身で] (乗り物で人・物を)運ぶ, 輸送する ◇Too many goods are currently being *transported* by road. 現在, あまりにも多くの商品が陸路で輸送されている ◇The animals are *transported* in trucks, often without being fed or watered for days. しばしば何日も餌も水も与えられずに, 動物がトラックで輸送されている ☞ **transport** (DELIVERY)

ノート carry と transport の使い分け: carry は特に人について用いられ, transport は特に商品について用いられる。transport が人・動物について用いられる場合, 商品のように扱われていることを示唆することがある。

fly [他] 《副詞や前置詞と共に》 (商品・乗客を)飛行機で運ぶ, 空輸する ◇The stranded tourists were finally *flown* home. 足止めを食らった観光客たちはようやく飛行機で帰国した ◇He had flowers specially *flown* in for the ceremony. 彼は式典のために花を特別に空輸してもらった

ferry [他] 《ふつう副詞や前置詞と共に》(ボートなどで人・商品を短い距離[定期便]で)渡す, 運ぶ, 輸送する, 連れて行く ◇He offered to *ferry* us across the river in his boat. 彼はボートで川向こうに私たちを渡すことを申し出た ◇You really don't have to *ferry* us around while we're in town. 私たちが町にいる間, あちこち連れ回ってくれる必要は本当にないからね

leave [他] (送り届けて物を)残して行く ◇Someone *left* this note for you. 誰かがこのメモを君に残して行ったよ ◇Someone *left* you this note. 誰かが君にこのメモを残して行ったよ ❶ この意味では leave は一般的に, letter, note, card, parcel, package, present/gift などと結び付く。

2 take・lead・escort・drive・show・walk・guide・usher・direct

ある場所から別の場所へ人と一緒に行く
【類語訳】連れて行く, 送る, 案内する, 先導する, 護衛する, 付き添う

文型&コロケーション

- to take/ lead/ escort/ drive/ show/ walk/ guide/ usher/ direct sb **to/ out of/ into** sth
- to take/ lead/ escort/ drive/ walk/ guide/ usher/ direct sb **there/ somewhere**
- to take/ lead/ escort/ drive/ show/ walk/ guide sb **around/ round**
- to take/ lead/ escort/ drive/ walk sb **home**
- to take/ lead/ escort/ show/ guide/ usher sb **in/ out**
- to take/ lead/ escort/ guide sb **to safety**
- to lead/ show **the way**

take [他] (人を)連れて行く, 送る, 案内する ◇It's too far to walk — I'll *take* you by car. 歩くには遠すぎます — 車で連れて行ってあげますよ ◇The boy *took* us to our rooms. その少年は私たちを部屋に案内してくれた ◇I asked them if they'd *take* me **with** them. 私も一緒に連れて行ってくれるかどうか彼らに尋ねた ◇I'm *taking* the kids swimming later. 私が後で子どもたちを泳ぎに連れて行くよ

lead [他, 自] (人・動物を)先導[誘導]する, 連れて行く, 案内する ◇She *led* the horse back into the stable. 彼女は馬を厩舎に引き戻した ◇Firefighters *led* the survivors to safety. 消防隊は生存者たちを安全な場所に誘導した ◇If you *lead*, I'll follow. 君が案内してくれるなら付いて行くよ
[反意] follow (FOLLOW 1)

escort [他] (人を[に])護衛する, 付き添う, 送る ◇The president arrived, *escorted* by twelve guards. 大統領は12人の警備員に護衛されて到着した ◇The prisoners were *escorted* back to their cells. 囚人たちは付き添われて独房に戻った

drive [他] (車・タクシーなどで人を)送る, 連れて行く ◇My mother *drove* us to the airport. 母が私たちを車で空港まで送ってくれた

show [他] (人を)案内する、道を教える ◇They'll need someone to *show* them the way. 彼らには道案内をしてくれる人が必要になるでしょう ◇There's a Mr Smith here to see you.' '*Show* him in.'「スミスとかいう人が面会に来られました」「通しなさい」

walk [他] (徒歩で人を安全に)送る、連れて行く；(犬などを)散歩に連れて行く、歩かせる ◇He always *walked* her home. 彼はいつも彼女を家まで歩いて送った ◇She *walks* the dog every day at about two o'clock. 彼女は毎日2時頃犬を散歩に連れて行く ◇He *walked* the pony up and down the yard. 彼はポニーに庭のあちこちを歩かせた

guide [他] (同行して人を[に])案内する、道を教える；(よく知っている場所で人を)案内する ◇She *guided* us through the busy streets. 彼女が私たちを繁華街に案内してくれた ◇We were *guided* around the museums. 私たちは美術館周辺を案内してもらった

usher [他]《ややフォーマル、特に書き言葉》(建物内で人を丁寧に)案内する ◇The secretary *ushered* me into her office. その秘書は彼女のオフィスに私を案内してくれた ◇She *ushered* her guests to their seats. 彼女は客を席まで案内した

direct [他]《ややフォーマル》(人に[を])道を教える、案内[誘導]する ◇A young woman *directed* them to the station. 一人の若い女性が彼らに駅への道を教えてあげた ◇A police officer was *directing* the traffic. 一人の警官が交通整理に当たっていた ◇He was *directed* to a table beside the window. 彼は窓際のテーブルに案内された

☞ **direction** (WAY 3)

3 take・grab・snatch・catch・seize
手で、急に、しっかり、手荒くつかむことを表す
【類語訳】手に取る、つかむ、抱く、ひっつかむ、ひったくる、強奪する、捕まえる、捕らえる

▸ 文型&コロケーション

▸ to take/ grab/ snatch/ seize sth **from** sb
▸ to grab/ snatch **at** sth
▸ to take/ grab/ catch/ seize **hold of** sb/ sth
▸ to take/ grab/ snatch/ catch/ seize sth **suddenly/ quickly**
▸ to take/ grab/ catch/ seize sth **immediately**

take [他] 手に取る、つかむ、抱く ◇I passed him the rope and he *took* it. 彼にロープを渡し、彼はそれを手に取った ◇Free newspapers: please *take* one. 無料の新聞：どうぞお取りください ◇Can you *take* (= hold) the baby for a moment? ちょっと赤ちゃんを抱っこしてくれる ◇He *took* her hand/took her by the hand (= held her hand, for example to lead her somewhere). 彼は彼女の手を取った

grab (-bb-) [他、自] つかむ、ひっつかむ ◇She *grabbed* the child's hand and ran. 彼女はその子どもの手をつかんで走った ◇He *grabbed* hold of me and wouldn't let go. 彼は私をしっかりつかんで離そうとしなかった ◇Someone *grabbed* me from behind. 誰かが背後から私をひっつかんだ ◇Don't *grab* — there's plenty for everyone. つかみ取らないで。みんなに行き渡るようにたくさんあるんだから ◇She *grabbed* at (= tried to grab) the branch, missed and fell. 彼女はその枝につかまろうとしたが、失敗して落ちた

snatch [他]《ふつう副詞や前置詞と共に》ひったくる、奪い取る ◇She managed to *snatch* the gun from his hand. 彼女はどうにか彼の銃をひったくった ◇He *snatched* at (= tried to take hold of) the steering wheel. 彼は車のハンドルを奪い取ろうとした

> **ノート grab と snatch の使い分け**：snatch は、誰かの手から何かを直接奪い取るときに最もよく用いられる。grab はそれよりも広い範囲で用いられる。

catch [他] (動いている物を)捕まえる、捕らえる、キャッチする ◇She managed to *catch* the keys as they fell. 彼女は落ちる鍵束をキャッチした ◇'Throw me over that towel, will you?' 'OK. *Catch*!'「そのタオル、こっちに投げてくれる」「いいよ、受け止めて」 ◇The dog *caught* the stick in its mouth. その犬は棒を口でキャッチした ◇He *caught* hold of her arm as she tried to push past him. 彼は彼女の腕をつかんで彼女を捕まえた ❶ *catch* できるのは、落下中の物や投げられた物である。このグループの他の語と違って、catch sth from sb の表現は不可。
◆ I threw the bag in the air and she *caught* it. (私がそのかばんを空中に放り投げ、彼女がそれを捕まえた). ✗ She *caught* the bag from me and ran away.

seize [他]《ややフォーマル、特に書き言葉》(急に強く)つかむ、握る ◇She tried to *seize* the gun from him. 彼女は彼からその銃をつかみ取ろうとした ◇He *seized* her by the arm. 彼は彼女の腕をグイッとつかんだ ◇She *seized* hold of my hand. 彼女は私の手をぎゅっと握った

4 take・accept・take sb/sth on・take sth up
申し出[招待、要求]に対して「はい」と言う
【類語訳】受ける、受け入れる、応じる、受け取る、引き受ける

▸ 文型&コロケーション

▸ to take/ accept/ take on a **job/ post/ position/ role/ responsibility**
▸ to take/ accept/ take on **new clients**
▸ to take/ accept/ take up an **offer**
▸ to accept/ take up a/ an **invitation/ suggestion**
▸ to accept/ take on/ take up a **challenge**
▸ to take/ accept sth **gratefully/ reluctantly**
▸ to accept/ take sth on **gladly**

take [他] (申し出・要求を[に])受ける、受け入れる、応じる；(物を)受け取る ◇If they offer me the job, I'll *take* it. 彼らが仕事を提供してくれたら、引き受けるつもりです ◇Does the hotel *take* credit cards? そのホテルではクレジットカードが使えますか ◇I'll *take* the call in my office. オフィスで電話を受けることにします ◇If you *take* my advice you'll have nothing more to do with him. 私の忠告を聞けば、彼とはこれ以上関わりを持たなくて済むよ ◇Will you *take* $10 for the book (= will you sell it for $10)? その本を10ドルにしてくれますか ◇The store *took* (= sold goods worth) $100,000 last week. その店は先週10万ドルの売り上げがあった ❶ この意味では、take はしばしばビジネスの文脈で用いられる。 ◆ *take* a job（仕事に応じる）. ◆ *take* a cheque/credit card/£50 note（小切手/クレジットカード/50ポンド札が使える）. ◆ *take* a particular amount of money for sth（…の代金として特定の金額を受け取る）.

accept [自、他]《ややフォーマル》(申し出・要求・招待を[に])受ける、受け入れる、応じる；(物を快く)受け取る ◇He asked me to marry him and I *accepted*. 彼からの結婚の申し込みを受け入れた ◇Please *accept* our sincere apologies. 心よりお詫び申し上げます ◇She's decided not to *accept* the job. 彼女はその仕事を引き受けないこと

にした ◇She said she'd *accept* $15 for it. 彼女はその代金として15ドルを受け取ったと言った 反意 **refuse, decline (REFUSE)**
➤**acceptance** 名 [U, C] ◇Please confirm your *acceptance* of this offer in writing. この申し出の受諾を文書でご確認ください ◇So far we have had one refusal and three *acceptances*. 今のところ、1件は断られて、3件は承諾されている

,**take sb/sth 'on** 句動詞 (人・物事・責任を)引き受ける ◇I can't *take on* any extra work. 余分な仕事は一切引き受けられません ◇We're not *taking on* any new clients at present. 現在のところ、我々は新たな依頼人を引き受ける予定はありません ❶ take sb/sth on は人が主語の場合、典型的な目的語として work, chores, tasks や、特定の job, position, role, responsibility, challenge が挙げられる。会社が主語の場合、staff, clients が目的語になることがある。

,**take sth 'up, ,take sb 'up on sth** 句動詞 (申し出・招待を[に])受ける、受け入れる、応じる ◇He urged us to *take up* the challenge. 彼は我々にその挑戦に応じるよう迫った ◇She *took* him *up on* his offer of a drink. 彼女は彼から飲み物の申し出を受けた ❶ take sth up はほとんどの場合、invitation, offer, challenge と共に用いられる。 反意 **turn sb/sth down (REFUSE)**

take care of yourself 動

take care of yourself • look after yourself • fend for yourself • stand on your own (two) feet
人の助けを借りずに、自身[自分の世話、安全]に責任を持つ
【類語訳】自己管理する、自活する、自立する

文型&コロケーション
▶to **be able to** take care of yourself/ look after yourself/ fend for yourself/ stand on your own feet
▶to **be capable of** taking care of yourself/ looking after yourself/ fending for yourself
▶to **learn to** fend for yourself/ stand on your own feet

take care of yourself フレーズ 自己管理する、自分の面倒を見る、自分の身を守る、自分の体を大事にする、自分の外見に気を遣う ◇He's old enough to *take care of himself*. 彼は十分に自己管理できる年齢だ ◇You should *take better care of yourself*. あなたはもっと自己管理するべきだ ☞ **take care of sb (LOOK AFTER SB)**

,**look 'after yourself** 句動詞 《特に英》自己管理する、自分の面倒を見る、自分の身を守る、自分の体を大事にする ◇Don't worry about me — I can *look after myself* (= I don't need any help). 私のことは気にしないで—自分の面倒は自分で見られるから ☞ **look after sb (LOOK AFTER SB)**

,**fend for your'self** 句動詞 自活する、自力で生きていく ◇His parents agreed to pay his rent but otherwise *left him to fend for himself*. 彼の両親は彼の家賃を払ってやることにしたが、それ以外は自活をさせた ◇The pups have been weaned and are now learning to *fend for themselves*. 子犬たちはすでに乳離れしていて、今は自力で生きていくことを学んでいる

ノート take care of yourself, look after yourself, fend for yourself の使い分け: take care of yourself と look after yourself は、人の助けを借りずに、自分自身の世話・健康・安全に責任を持つ人について用いられ

ることが多い。どちらの語句も、特に人の健康に対する気遣いを表すために用いられる。 ◆ *Take* good *care of yourself*. (お大事になさってください)。 ◆ You *look after yourself* and make sure you eat properly. (自らの体を気遣って、必ずきちんとした食事を取りなさい)。 take care of yourself はまた、外見に気を遣い、できるだけ若く魅力的に見えるよう努力する人にも用いられる。 ◆ It is natural for a woman to *take* good *care of herself*. (女性が外見に気を遣うのは当然だ)。 fend for yourself は食糧・お金・住む場所を見つけるといった、より実際的な状況に対処する場合に用いられる。人だけでなく動物にも用いられる。難しい状況・環境に自力で対処しなければならない人・動物に用いられることが多い。

stand on your own (two) 'feet 行[口] (金銭的に)自立する ◇When his parents died he had to learn to *stand on his own two feet*. 両親が死んで、彼は自立することを学ばなければならなかった

take sth off 句動詞

take sth off • strip • remove • undress • get undressed
自分[人]の体から衣類を取り去る
【類語訳】脱ぐ、脱がせる、裸になる、服を脱ぐ、裸にする、(眼鏡などを)外す

文型&コロケーション
▶to take off/ strip off/ remove your **clothes/ jacket/ coat/ shirt/ sweater/ jeans/ gloves**
▶to **quickly** take sth off/ strip off/ remove sth/ undress/ get undressed

,**take sth 'off** 句動詞 (衣類などを)脱ぐ；脱がせる ◇Please, *take off* your coat. コートをお脱ぎください ◇He *took off* my wet boots and made me sit by the fire. 彼は私の濡れたブーツを脱がせ、炉辺に座らせてくれた 反意 **put sth on (WEAR)**

strip (-pp-) [自, 他] 裸になる、服を脱ぐ；裸にする、服を脱がせる ◇I *stripped* and washed myself all over. 私は裸になって体中を洗った ◇We *stripped off* and ran down to the water. 私たちは服を脱いで走って水に入った ◇She *stripped down to* her underwear. 彼女は下着姿になった ◇He stood there *stripped to the waist* (= the upper part of his body was bare). 彼は上半身裸になってそこに立っていた ◇He was *stripped naked* and left in a cell. 彼は全裸にされて独房に残された

remove [他]《ややフォーマル、書き言葉》(衣類などを)脱ぐ；脱がせる、外す ◇She *removed* her glasses and rubbed her eyes. 彼女は眼鏡を外して両目をこすった ❶ remove はふつう肌の上に着用している衣類ではなく、hat, scarf, shoes, boots, glasses, coat, jacket などを[外す]ことについて用いられる。

undress [自, 他] 裸になる、服を脱ぐ；裸にする、服を脱がせる ◇She *undressed* and got into bed. 彼女は裸になってベッドにもぐった ◇to *undress* a child/doll 子ども/人形の服を脱がせる 反意 **dress (WEAR)**

get undressed フレーズ 裸になる、服を脱ぐ ◇He *got undressed* and fell into bed. 彼は裸になってベッドに倒れ込んだ 反意 **get dressed (WEAR)**

ノート strip, undress, get undressed の使い分け: strip は体を洗いたい[薄着になってもっと心地よくなりたい、(例

えば武器・麻薬の検査のために）人に命じられた]ため、服を脱ぐことを指す。就寝の準備をしている場合は、ふつう undress か get undressed を用いる。strip は比較的素早い手荒な行為を指す。看守が囚人に対して命じるような場合は strip を、医者が患者に対して求めるような場合は undress か take sth off を用いる。

talk 動

talk・discuss・speak・communicate・debate・consult・confer
ほかの人にしゃべってニュース[情報, 考え, 感情]を共有する
【類語訳】話す、話し合う、相談する、話をする、伝える、連絡する、意思を疎通する、議論する、意見を聞く

文型&コロケーション
- to talk/ discuss sth/ speak/ communicate/ debate/ consult/ confer **with** sb
- to talk/ speak **to** sb
- to talk/ speak to sb/ consult sb/ confer **about** sth
- to consult sb/ confer **on** sth
- to talk/ speak **of** sth
- to discuss/ debate **what/ how/ whether/ when/ who...**
- to talk/ discuss sth/ speak/ communicate/ debate sth **openly**
- to talk/ discuss sth/ speak/ debate sth **at length**
- to talk/ discuss sth/ speak/ confer **briefly**

talk [自] 話す ◇We *talked* on the phone for over an hour. 私たちは電話で1時間以上話した ◇Who were you *talking* to just now? 今さっき誰に話しかけていたの ◇When they get together, all they *talk* about is football 彼らが集まると、サッカーの話しかしない ◇Mary is *talking* of looking for another job. メアリーが別の仕事を探すことについて話している ❶ talk が「(物事に関する)考えを共有する」ことを意味するのに用いられる場合、深刻[重要]な物事を指すことが多い。◆This situation can't go on. We need to *talk*. (こんな状況は続くはずがない。話し合う必要があるね) ◆*Talk* to your doctor if you're still worried. (まだ心配なら医者と相談しなさい) この意味では目的語と共に用いられることもある。◆They spent the whole evening *talking* business (= talking about business). (彼らは一晩中商談をして過ごした). ☞ **talk (DISCUSSION), talk (SAY 1, 2)**

discuss [他] 《ややフォーマル》話し合う、相談する ◇Have you *discussed* the problem with anyone? その問題について誰かと話し合ったことはありますか ◇I'm not prepared to *discuss* this on the phone. このことについて電話で話し合う準備などできていません ◇They briefly *discussed* buying a new car. 彼らは新車の購入について手短に相談した ❶discuss about sthと言うことはできない。×I'm not prepared to *discuss about* this on the phone. ☞ **discussion (DISCUSSION)**

speak [自] (人に)話す；(人と)話をする ◇We *spoke* briefly on the phone. 私たちは電話で手短に話した ◇I've *spoken* to the manager about it. 私はそのことについて支配人に話をした ◇Can I *speak* with you for a minute? 《特に米》ちょっと話せますか ◇'Can I *speak* to Susan?' 'Speaking.' (電話で)「スーザンさんをお願いします」「私です が」 ☞ **speak (SAY 1)**

ノート **talk** と **speak** の使い分け：speak は talk よりもフォーマルなコミュニケーションであることを示唆する。talk は仲良くなる[助言を求める]ために話す[相談する]ことを指す。speak は特定の目的を達成する[何かを指示する]ために、人に話すことを指す。◆'What were you two *talking* about?' 'Oh, this and that.'(「お二人は何を話していたの」「ああ、あれとかね」). ◆Have you *talked* to your parents about the problems you're having? (抱えている問題についてご両親に相談したことはあるの). ◆I've *spoken* to Ed about it and he's promised not to let it happen again. (私がそのことをエドに話したら、彼は二度とそんなことは起きないと約束したわ).

communicate [自, 他] 《ややフォーマル》(情報[考え]を)伝える、連絡する、意思を疎通する ◇We only *communicate* by email. 私たちはeメールでしか連絡しない ◇Dolphins use sound to *communicate* with each other. イルカは音を使ってお互いに意思の疎通を行う ◇Nobody had *communicated* the information to us. 《フォーマル》誰も私たちにその情報を伝えてくれていなかった ❶communicate は使用されるコミュニケーションの手段に話し手が注目したい場合に用いられることが多い。communicate sth to sb は tell sb sth (人に物事を伝える)のフォーマルな表現である。☞ **communication (COMMUNICATION), communication (LETTER)**

debate [他] (決定を下す[解決策を見つける]前に正式に)議論[討論]する ◇Politicians will be *debating* the bill later this week. 政治家たちは今週後半、その法案について議論することになっている ◇The question of the origin of the universe is still *hotly debated* (= strongly argued about) by scientists. 宇宙の起源に関する疑問は依然として科学者たちによって熱く議論されている ☞ **debate (DISCUSSION)**

consult [他, 自] 《ややフォーマル》(許可を得る[決定を下す参考にする]ために人に)意見を聞く、相談する ◇You shouldn't have done it without *consulting* me. あなたは私の意見を聞かずにそれを行うべきではなかった ◇I need to *consult* with my colleagues on the proposals. 私はその提案について同僚と相談する必要がある ❶consult sb は物事に対する許可を求めることを指す。consult with sb (人と相談する) は discuss sth with sb のよりフォーマルな表現である。☞ **consultation (DISCUSSION)**

confer (**-rr-**) [自] 《ややフォーマル》(意見を交換する[助言を得る]ために人と)相談する ◇He wanted to *confer* with his colleagues before reaching a decision. 決論に至る前に彼は同僚と相談したかった

target 名 ☞ PURPOSE

target・objective・goal・object・end
達成しようとしている物事
【類語訳】目標, 目的, 対象

文型&コロケーション
- targets/ objectives/ goals **for** sth
- to work **towards** a target/ an objective/ a goal
- a **worthwhile** target/ objective/ goal/ object/ end
- the **main/ primary/ prime/ principal** target/ objective/ goal/ object
- the **ultimate** target/ objective/ goal/ object/ end
- a **common** target/ objective/ goal/ end
- a/ an **ambitious/ major/ long-term/ short-term/ future** target/ objective/ goal

- ▶ **economic/ financial/ business** targets/ objectives/ goals
- ▶ to **define** a target/ an objective/ a goal/ an object
- ▶ to **set/ agree on/ identify/ reach/ meet/ exceed** a target/ an objective/ a goal
- ▶ to **achieve** a target/ an objective/ a goal/ an end
- ▶ to **promote/ pursue/ accomplish/ attain** an objective/ a goal/ an end

target [C] （達成しようとする）目標, 目的, 対象 ◇Set yourself *targets* that you can reasonably hope to achieve. 達成したいと思う無理のない目標を設定しなさい ◇We're aiming to meet a *target* date of April 2009. 我々は2009年4月の目標期日に間に合わせることを目指している ◇Write a plan that sets out your business *goals and targets*. ビジネスの目的と目標を設定する計画書を作成しなさい ◇The new sports complex is *on target* to open in June. 新しいスポーツ複合施設は6月オープンを目指している ◇Our *target audience* (= the particular audience that the programme is aimed at) is men aged between 18 and 35. 我々の視聴者の対象は18～35歳の男性である ◇What's the *target market* for this product? この製品が狙っている市場は何ですか

objective [C] 《ややフォーマル》（達成しようとしている）目標, 目的 ◇What is the main *objective* of this project? このプロジェクトの主な目的は何ですか ◇You must set realistic *aims and objectives* for yourself. 自分で現実的な目的と目標を設定しなければなりません

goal [C] （達成したいと望む）目標, 目的 ◇He continued to pursue his *goal* of becoming a photographer. 彼はカメラマンになるという目標を追求し続けた ◇Their *goal* was to eradicate malaria. 彼らの目的はマラリアを根絶することだった

ノート **target, objective, goal の使い分け**：target はふつう, 例えば雇用主・政府委員会によって, 何らかの方法で公式に記録されているものを指し, しばしば具体的で, 売上高［試験の合格者数, 日付など］の数字の形で表される。objective は自分で設定することが多く, しばしば事業・話し合いの一環として, 達成したいと願うものを指す。goal はしばしば長期的で, 人々の生活・キャリア計画・会社［組織］の長期計画に関連するものを指す。

object [C] 《ややフォーマル》（物事の）目的 ;（達成する予定の）目標 ◇The *object* is to educate people about road safety. 目的は道路の安全について人々を教育することである ◇The whole *object of the exercise* is to get people to listen to each other. その行動の目的とするところは人々に互いに耳を傾けさせることである

end [C] 《フォーマル》（達成する予定の）目標, 目的 ◇She is exploiting the current situation for her own *ends*. 彼女は現在の状況を自分の目的のために利用している ◇He joined the society for political *ends*. 彼は政治目的でその協会に入会した ◇*With this end in view* (= in order to achieve this) they employed 50 new sales reps. この目標を目指して新たに50人の販売員が雇われた ◇We are willing to make any concessions necessary *to this end* (= in order to achieve this). 私たちはこの目標に必要なあらゆる譲歩をいといません ◇That's only OK if you believe that *the end justifies the means* (= bad methods of doing sth are acceptable if the final result is good). 目的が手段を正当化すると信じているなら, それでいい ❶end はふつう複数形や定型表現で用いられる。

task

task 名 ☞ ASSIGNMENT

task・work・duty・mission・job・business・housework・chore・errand・commission
人がしなければならない務め
【類語訳】仕事, 作業, 職務, 義務, 任務, 使命, 用事, 家事, 雑用, 日課

文型&コロケーション
- ▶ (a) **routine** task/ work/ duties/ mission/ job/ business/ chore
- ▶ (a) **daily/ day-to-day** task/ work/ duties/ job/ business/ chore
- ▶ (a/ an) **easy/ difficult** task/ work/ mission/ job
- ▶ (a) **challenging** task/ work/ job
- ▶ (a) **dangerous** task/ work/ mission/ job
- ▶ (a) **household/ domestic** task/ work/ duties/ job/ chore
- ▶ to **do** a task/ your work/ a job/ business/ the housework/ a chore/ an errand
- ▶ to **have** a task/ work/ job/ the housework/ a chore/ an errand **to do**
- ▶ to **get** the task/ work/ job/ housework/ chores **done**
- ▶ to **get on with** a task/ your work/ a job/ the housework/ a chore
- ▶ to **carry out** a task/ the work/ your duties/ a mission/ a job/ a commission
- ▶ to **finish** a task/ the work/ a mission/ a job/ your business/ the housework/ the chores
- ▶ to **take on/ undertake** a task/ the work/ your duties/ a mission/ a job
- ▶ to **tackle/ approach** a task/ the work/ a job
- ▶ to **give sb** a task/ some work/ their duties/ a mission/ a job/ a chore/ a commission
- ▶ to **set (sb)** a task/ their duties
- ▶ to **accept** a task/ a mission/ a commission
- ▶ to **be on** a mission/ a job/ business/ an errand

task [C] （困難[不快]な）仕事 ◇Our first *task* will be to set up a communications system. 私たちの最初の難題はコミュニケーション・システムの構築ということになろう ◇She had the unenviable *task* of talking to the missing girl's parents. 彼女には行方不明の少女の両親に話をするという気乗りのしない仕事があった ◇The *task* eventually fell to me (= I had to do it). その仕事は結局私の肩のしかかってきた ◇Getting hold of the information was *no easy task* (= it was difficult). その情報を手に入れることは決して簡単な仕事ではなかった

work [U] （職の一環としての）仕事 ;（終わらせる必要のある）作業 ◇Police *work* is mainly routine. 警察の仕事は大部分が型どおりだ ◇I have some *work* for you to do. あなたにしてもらいたい仕事がいくつかあります ◇Stop talking and get on with your *work*. おしゃべりをやめてどんどん作業を進めなさい

duty [U] （または **duties** [複数で]）職務, 義務 ;（職の一環としての）仕事 ◇*Report for duty* at 8 a.m. 義務として午前8時に出勤しなさい ◇He was accused of neglecting his professional *duties*. 彼は職務怠慢で告発された ◇Your *duties* will include setting up a new computer system. 新しいコンピューター・システムを使える状態にするのもあなたの仕事です ◇The suspect was charged with obstructing an officer *in the course of his duties* (= while doing what his job requires). その容疑者には警

↳task

官への業務妨害の嫌疑がかけられていた

ノート workとdutiesの使い分け：両語とも職の一環として行う事柄を指すが、workのほうがdutiesよりも幅広い意味を持つ。dutiesは義務であるために、しなければならない仕事で、怠れば非難[処罰]されるものを指す。workは勤務中に行うあらゆる活動を指し、義務であるのと同様、力を発揮する機会と見なされるものを指す。

mission [C] (他国に派遣される際の重要かつ公式の)任務、使命 ◇a trade *mission* to China 中国への貿易使節団 ◇The *mission* ended in failure. その任務は失敗に終わった ◇They undertook a *fact-finding mission* in the region. 彼らはその地域における実情調査の使命を負った

job [C] (しなければならない)仕事 ◇I've got various *jobs* around the house to do. 私には家周りの仕事がたくさんある ◇Sorting these papers is going to be a long *job*. これらの書類の整理は時間のかかる仕事になるだろう ◇Bringing up kids is a full-time *job*. 子育てはかかりきりの仕事である ◇He spends his time doing *odd jobs* (= various jobs in the home). 彼は家事雑事に時を取られている

ノート taskとjobの使い分け：taskはjobよりも困難で、どのように行うかについて慎重に考えることを求められるもの。jobは特に家庭でしなければならない細々とした仕事のうちの一つを指すが、時間がかかり、かなりの忍耐を必要とするものである場合もある。

business [U] (商談・取引に伴う職の一環としての)仕事、用事 ◇a *business* trip/lunch 出張旅行/商談を兼ねた昼食 ◇Is the trip to Rome *business or pleasure*? ローマへの旅行は仕事ですか、遊びですか ◇She's away *on business*. 彼女はいつも商用で出かけている 反意 **pleasure** (ENTERTAINMENT)

housework [U] 家事 ◇I spent all morning doing *housework*. 私は午前中ずっと家事をして過ごした

chore [C] (定期的に家庭でしなければならない不快[退屈]に感じる)雑用、日課 ◇Of all the household *chores*, I hate ironing most. すべての家事の中で私はアイロンがけが一番嫌いです ◇I find shopping a *real chore* (= a boring and unpleasant job). 買い物は本当に退屈な雑用だと思う

errand [C] (人のためにする)使い(走り) ◇He often *runs errands* for his grandmother. 彼はしばしば祖母のお使いをする

commission [C] (建物の設計・塗装などの仕事を正式に依頼する)委託 ◇Who won the *commission* to design the new town hall? 新しい町役場の設計を受注できたのは誰ですか ◇The work will be done *by commission* (= sb will be formally asked to do it). その仕事は委託によってなされる予定だ

taste 名

taste • preference • love • passion • liking • weakness
特定の物事[活動]を好む感情
【類語訳】好み、ひいき、選択、優先、大のお気に入り、熱中、熱中の対象、愛好、嗜好

→
taste　　　　　love　　　　　passion
preference
liking
weakness

taste

文型&コロケーション
▸a taste/ preference/ passion/ liking/ weakness **for** sth
▸a **great** love/ passion/ liking for/ of sth
▸to **have** a taste/ preference/ love/ passion/ liking/ weakness for/ of sth
▸to **develop** a taste/ preference/ love/ passion/ liking/ weakness for/ of sth
▸to **share** a taste/ preference/ love/ passion/ liking for/ of sth
▸to **show** a preference/ liking for sth
▸sth is **to** sb's taste/ liking
▸**too** big, small, sweet, crowded, etc. **for** sb's taste/ liking

taste [C, U] 好み、愛好、嗜好 ◇That trip gave me a *taste* for foreign travel. 私はその旅で外国旅行が好きになった ◇She has a very expensive *taste in* clothes. 彼女は服装に関してはとても高級品好きである ◇Art is *an acquired taste* — no one is born knowing that Michelangelo is wonderful. 芸術は後天的に獲得される嗜好である—ミケランジェロが素晴らしいことを知って生まれる人は誰もない ◇The colour and style is a matter of personal *taste*. 色やスタイルは個人的な好みの問題である ❶ have a taste for sthと言う場合、物事を好む[楽しむ]ことを指す。◆She *has* a real *taste for* adventure/designer clothes. 彼女は冒険/デザイナーズ・ブランドの服が大好きだ。◆ taste in clothes/music/booksはどのような種類の服・音楽・本を好むかを表す。◆He has an unusual *taste in music*. (彼の音楽の好みは変わっている[並のものではない]).

preference [U, 単数形] 好み、ひいき、選択、優先 ◇It's a matter of personal *preference*. それは個人の好みの問題である ◇Many people expressed a *strong preference* for the original plan. 多くの人々が原案のほうを強く望んだ ◇I can't say that I have any particular *preference*. 何か特に好きだということはない ◇Let's make a list of possible speakers, *in order of preference*. 優先順に演説者の候補のリストを作りましょう

ノート tasteとpreferenceの使い分け：preferenceは常に二つ以上の物事・場所・人々などからの選択を指す。tasteにはこの選択の概念は含まれない。 ◆a *taste* for French bread (フランスパン好き)。◆a *preference* for brown bread (= rather than white bread) (黒パン好み)。
☞ **preference** (CHOICE 2), **prefer** (PREFER), **preferred** (FAVOURITE)

love [U, 単数形] 《ほめて》 大好きであること、大のお気に入り、愛好、愛着 ◇I *fell in love* with the house. 私はその家がとても気に入った ◇They share a *love* of classical music. 彼らはともにクラシック音楽が大好きである ☞ **love** (LIKE 動)

passion [C] 《ほめて》 熱中、夢中；熱中の対象 ◇The English have a *passion* for gardens. イギリス人は庭好きだ ◇Music is a *passion* with him. 音楽に彼は夢中だ ☞ **passionate** (INTENSE), **interest** (INTEREST 名 2)

ノート loveとpassionの使い分け：passionのほうがloveよりも意味が強く、その関心が生活様式や仕事選びに影響を与えるかもしれないことを示唆する。◆The royal family had a *passion* for art, it seems, for the palace was full of paintings and sculptures. (宮殿が絵画や彫刻であふれていたところからすると、王室は芸術に熱を上げていたようだ)。◆He knew he was going to be a musician and eventually stopped attending high school. Music was the only thing he ever had a *passion* for. (彼は自分がミュージシャンになって、いずれ高校を退学することがわかっていた。音楽は彼が夢中になった唯一のものだったからだ).

liking [単数で] 好きであること, 好み, 愛好, 嗜好 ◇The town was too crowded for my *liking* (= I would prefer it less crowded). 私の好みからするとその町は混雑しすぎだった ◇Is the coffee to your *liking*, sir? そのコーヒーはお好みですか ☞ **like** (LIKE 動)

weakness [C, ふつう単数で] (自分に好ましくないのに)目がないこと, 大好きであること ◇He worries a lot about his weight, but can't overcome his *weakness* for fatty foods. 彼は自分の体重を大いに気にしているが, 脂肪分の多い食べ物の誘惑には勝てない

tax 名

tax・duty・customs・tariff・rates
政府に支払わなければならないお金
【類語訳】税, 税金, 関税, 地方(財産)税

〔文型&コロケーション〕
▶ (a) tax/ (a) duty/ a tariff/ rates **on** sth
▶ to **pay** an amount of money **in** tax/ duty/ customs/ rates
▶ to **pay** tax/ duty/ customs/ a tariff/ rates
▶ to **collect** taxes/ duties/ rates
▶ to **increase/ raise/ reduce** taxes/ duty/ tariffs/ rates
▶ to **cut** taxes/ duties/ rates
▶ to **impose** a tax/ duty/ a tariff
▶ to **levy** a tax/ duty/ rates
▶ to **put** a tax/ duty **on** sth

tax [C, U] (政府に支払う)税, 税金 ◇The government had to raise *taxes* to pay for the war. 政府は戦争の代価を支払うために増税しなければならなかった ◇The middle classes are demanding *tax* cuts. 中産階級は減税を求めている ◇There's no *tax* on cigarettes in some countries. いくつかの国ではタバコは無税だ ◇The business makes £750,000 **after** *tax*. その企業は税引き後収益は75万ポンドだ ❶ 人々は所得に応じてtaxを支払い, 企業は利益に応じてtaxを支払う。また, しばしばtaxは商品やサービスに対してもかかる。 ◇ income/sales/road/property *tax* (所得/売上/道路/固定資産税).
▶**tax** 動 [他] ◇Any interest payments are *taxed* as part of your income. いかなる利払いも所得の一部として課税される ◇His declared aim was to *tax* the rich. 彼が掲げた目標は富裕層に税金をかけることだった

duty [C, U] (国内に持ち込まれる購入物に対して支払う)関税 ◇The company has to pay customs *duties* on all imports. 会社はすべての輸入品にかかる関税を支払わなければならない ◇*Duty* on wine and beer has been increased. ワインとビールにかかる関税が高くなっている ❶ duty-free はduty を支払わずに国内に持ち込むことのできる商品に用いられる。 ◆ *duty-free* cigarettes (免税のタバコ).

customs [複数で] (商品が他国から持ち込まれる際に支払う)関税 ◇You must pay *customs* on all imports of alcohol. 輸入アルコール飲料すべてに関税を支払わなければならない ◇Imports from non-EU countries are subject to *customs* duty of 20 per cent. 非EU加盟国からの輸入品には20%の関税がかかります ❶ *customs* は, 国内に持ち込まれる商品を検査し, それにかかる税金を徴収する政府省庁または入国時に荷物が検査される港・空港の場所を意味する。 ◆ *Customs* have seized a large quantity of smuggled heroin. (税関は大量の密輸ヘロインを押収した). ◆ We had to go through *customs* before we could leave the airport. (私たちは空港を後にする前に税関を通らなければならなかった).

tariff [C] (産業保護のための輸出入品に対して支払う)関税 ◇A general *tariff* was imposed on foreign imports. 一般関税が国外輸入品に課せられた

rates [複数で] ((英)で)土地・建物に企業が支払う)地方(財産)税 ◇Business *rates* are very high in the city centre. 都心では法人に対する地方税は非常に高い ☞ **rate** (RATE)

teach 動 ☞ TRAIN 1

teach・educate・lecture・prepare・tutor
人が学ぶのを手助けすることを表す
【類語訳】教える, 教育する, 講義をする, 個人教授をする, 家庭教師をする

〔文型&コロケーション〕
▶ to teach/ lecture (sb) **about** sth
▶ to teach/ educate/ lecture/ prepare/ tutor (sb) **effectively**

teach [自, 他] (学校・大学などで)教える ◇She *teaches* at our local school. 彼女は私たちの地元の学校で教師をしている ◇He *teaches* English to advanced students. 彼は上級クラスの生徒に英語を教えている ◇He *teaches* them English. 彼は彼らに英語を教えている ◇to *teach* school (= teach in a school) (米) 教師をする ☞ **teach** (TRAIN 1), **teaching** (EDUCATION)

educate [他, しばしば受身で] (《ややフォーマル》(学校・大学などで)教育する ◇She was *educated* in the US. 彼女はアメリカで教育を受けた ◇He was *educated* at his local comprehensive school and then at Oxford. 彼は地元の総合中学校で, その後はオックスフォード大学で教育を受けた ❶ この意味では, ecucate はふつう国・町・学校・大学の名前と共に用いられる。 ☞ **education** (EDUCATION)

lecture [自] (大学で)講義をする ◇She *lectures* in Russian literature. 彼女はロシア文学の講義をしている ☞ **lecture** (SPEECH)

prepare [他] (《ややフォーマル》(生徒に)準備させる ◇The college *prepares* students **for** a career in business. 大学では学生たちに就職の準備をさせます ◇to *prepare* students for exams 生徒に試験の準備をさせる

tutor [他, 自] (生徒個人 [少人数のグループ] に)個人教授をする; 家庭教師をする ◇He *tutors* students in mathematics. 彼は学生たちに数学の個人教授をしている ◇Her work was divided between *tutoring* and research. 彼女の仕事は個別指導と研究に分かれていた ☞ **tutoring** (EDUCATION)

teacher 名 ☞ LECTURER

teacher・tutor・educator・schoolteacher・governess・educationalist
教えることが仕事である人
【類語訳】教師, 教員, 先生, 家庭教師, 教育者, 学校教師, 教育専門家

teacher

文型&コロケーション
- a teacher/ tutor/ governess **to** sb
- a **former** teacher/ tutor/ schoolteacher/ governess
- a/ an **qualified/ experienced/ good/ excellent** teacher/ tutor
- a **private** teacher/ tutor
- a **full-time/ part-time** teacher/ tutor
- a/ an **history/ music/ English, etc.** teacher/ tutor

teacher [C] (学校の)教師, 教員, 先生 ◇Who's your favourite *teacher*? 君が好きな先生は誰だい ◇We are looking for qualified and experienced English *teachers*. 私たちは資格と経験のある英語教師を探している ☞ **teaching** (EDUCATION)

tutor [C] (生徒個人[少人数のグループ]に教える)家庭教師 ◇He worked as a *tutor* to the family's three young children. 彼はその家族の幼い3人の子どもたちの家庭教師をして働いた ◇Children who miss a lot of schoolwork through illness are usually allowed a **home tutor**. 病気で学校を多く休む子どもたちにはふつう家庭教師が認められている ❶《英》では, tutor は大人に教える[学校・大学で特別な役割を持つ]教師も指す. ◆ She's a part-time adult education *tutor*. (《英》彼女は成人教育の非常勤講師である). ◆ Who's your form *tutor*? (あなたのクラス担任は誰ですか). ☞ **tutorial** (CLASS 2), **tutoring** (EDUCATION)

educator [C] 《フォーマル》(仕事としての)教育者 ◇The video is being used by health *educators* in remote areas. そのビデオは辺ぴな地域の保健教育者に用いられている ◇We have a wealth of resources for teacher *educators* (= people who teach people to be teachers). 私たちには教師への指導者のための資金が潤沢にある ❶《米》では, educator は educationalist の代わりに用いられる一般的な語でもある. ◆ Modern *educators* prefer a different approach to the teaching of reading. (現代の教育専門家たちは読む教育とは異なる教授法を好む). ☞ **education** (EDUCATION)

schoolteacher [C] 《やや古風》学校教師, 学校の先生 ◇An elderly *schoolteacher* rented the apartment upstairs. 年配の学校教師がアパートの2階を賃借りしていた

governess [C] (裕福な家庭の子どもを住み込みで教える)女性家庭教師 ◇She was educated at home by a series of *governesses*. 彼女は女性家庭教師たちによってずっと家庭で教育を受けた

educationalist (または **educationist**) [C] 《特に英》(教育理論と教育法の)教育専門家 ◇Some leading *educationalists* have been cautious about this theory. 一流の教育専門家たちの中にはこの理論に慎重な者もいる ❶《米》では, ふつう educator と呼ばれる.

team 名

1 ☞ PARTY 2, GROUP 2

team • crew • squad • ring • detachment • corps • shift • gang
共同で働く人々の集まり
【類語訳】チーム, 団, 班, 乗組員, 搭乗員, 乗務員, 隊, 分隊, 暗殺部隊, 組織, 一味

文型&コロケーション
- a team/ crew/ squad/ detachment/ corps/ gang **of** sth
- **in** a team/ crew/ squad/ gang
- a **5-strong, 100-strong, etc.** team/ crew/ squad
- a **small** team/ crew/ squad/ corps
- a **large** team/ crew/ squad/ corps
- to **join** a team/ crew/ corps
- a team/ squad/ ring/ gang **leader**
- a **member of** a team/ crew/ squad/ ring/ corps/ gang
- **part of** a team/ squad/ ring/ detachment

team [C+単数・複数動詞] (仕事での)チーム, 団, 班 ◇A *team* of experts has been called in to investigate. 調査のために専門家チームが呼ばれた ◇He was part of a research *team* under Professor James. 彼はジェームズ教授の下で研究班の一員だった ◇They need to learn to work together **as a team**. 彼らはチームとして共同で働くことを学ぶ必要がある ◇It took a ***team effort*** to finish the project on time. その事業を予定どおりに終わらせるにはチームの努力が必要だった

crew [C+単数・複数動詞] 《特に複合語》(船・飛行機の)乗組員, 搭乗員, 乗(務)員; (特殊技能を持った)団, 班, 隊 ◇None of the passengers or *crew* were injured. 乗客乗員誰一人として負傷しなかった ◇Two *crews* of six men carried out the work in shifts. 6人からなる2班が交代でその作業を遂行した ❶ *crew* は特に映画の撮影・救急サービス・技術サポートの文脈で複合語として用いられる. ◆ a TV/film/camera *crew* (テレビ取材班/映画制作班/カメラ撮影班). ◆ an ambulance/a fire *crew* (救急隊/消防隊). ◆ a maintenance/support *crew* (整備班/サポート班). 航空機の文脈では, 機内で働く aircrew, flight crew, cabin crew や, 空港で働き, 地上で航空機や乗客の面倒を見る ground crew がいる.

squad [C+単数・複数動詞] (警察・兵士の)分隊, 班; (政治的理由で敵対者を殺害する)暗殺部隊 ◇He was deputy head of the force's serious ***crime squad***. 彼は警察の重大犯罪捜査班の副班長だった ◇A ***squad*** of soldiers had arrived to arrest him. 兵士の分隊が彼を逮捕するために到着していた ◇People lived in fear of the regime's notorious ***death squads***. 人々はその政権の悪名高き暗殺隊に怯えて暮らしていた ❶警察にはさまざまな種類の犯罪を扱う squad がある. ◆ the drugs/vice/anti-terrorist/bomb/riot/fraud *squad* (麻薬捜査班/風俗犯罪取締班/テロ対策班/爆弾処理班/機動隊/企業詐欺捜査班). また, death squad は hit squad, assassination squad とも呼ばれる.

ring [C] (秘密裏[違法]に働く)組織, 一味 ◇The four men are accused of running a ***drug smuggling ring***. その4人の男は麻薬密輸組織を指揮したとして起訴されている ◇a ***spy ring*** スパイ組織 ☞ **gang** (PARTY 2)

detachment [C] (特殊任務遂行のための)派遣隊, 分遣艦隊, 班 ◇A *detachment* of marines was left to guard the site. 海兵隊の派遣隊が現場警護のために残された ◇The attack wiped out the entire twelve-man *detachment*. その攻撃で12人の派遣隊は全滅した ☞ **unit** (ARMY)

corps [C+単数・複数動詞] (特定の仕事・活動に関わる)団体, 団 ◇Local people worked alongside an international *corps* of volunteers. 地元住民は国際的なボランティア団体と行動を共にした ◇the press *corps* 記者団 ◇the diplomatic *corps* 外交団

shift [C+単数・複数動詞] (特定の時間働く労働者の)勤務組 ◇The drama began at 5.15 am as the ***day shift*** was going on duty. その劇的な事件は日勤者たちが勤務に就こうとする午前5時15分に始まった ◇Most of the ***night shift*** had already left. 夜勤者のほとんどはもう帰っていた ◇As I

left the next *shift* was settling in for the day. 私が帰る頃，次の勤務組がその日の仕事に就き始めていた
gang [C＋単数・複数動詞]（肉体労働を行う労働者・囚人の）集団 ◇The work was done by convicts working in *gangs*. その作業は集団で働く服役囚たちによって行われた ◇a prison/work *gang* 服役囚/労働者の集団 ☞ **gang** (PARTY 2)

2 team・club・side・squad・line-up
他のグループに対抗してスポーツを共同で行う人々の集団
【類語訳】チーム，組，団体，クラブ，陣容，メンバー

文型&コロケーション
▶ a **successful/ local/ top** team/ club/ side
▶ the **junior/ senior/ youth/ under-19/ national** team/ side/ squad
▶ a/ an **Irish/ French, etc.** team/ club/ side/ squad
▶ the **England/ Ireland, etc.** team/ side/ squad/ line-up
▶ a **football/ rugby/ cricket** team/ club/ side/ squad
▶ to **join** a team/ club/ squad/ line-up
▶ to **play for/ sign for** a team/ club/ side
▶ to **name** a team/ side/ squad/ line-up
▶ to **field** a team/ side/ line-up
▶ a team/ club/ side **plays/ wins/ loses** (a game/ match)
▶ a **member of** a team/ club/ side/ squad/ line-up

team [C＋単数・複数動詞]（ゲーム・スポーツの）チーム，組，（種目としての）団体 ◇Whose *team* are you *in*? 《英》どのチームに入っているの ◇After two years out with injury, he's back *on* the *team*. 《米》けがで2年間戦列を離れた後，彼はチームに復帰している ◇You didn't *make the team* (= weren't chosen to play) I'm afraid. 君がチームのメンバーに選ばれなかったのは残念だね ◇What *team* do you support? どのチームを応援しているの ◇We want to encourage *team sports* in schools. 私たちは学校で団体競技を奨励したいと思います

club [C＋単数・複数動詞]《英》(選手・監督・オーナー・団員を含むプロのスポーツ団体である)クラブ ◇He is expected to sign for a Premier League *club* next season. 来シーズン彼はプレミアリーグのクラブと契約することが予想される ◇Athletico Madrid Football *Club* アトレティコ・マドリード・サッカー・クラブ ☞ **club** (UNION)

side [C＋単数・複数動詞]《英》(スポーツの)チーム，組，側，陣，軍 ◇As captain, Pryce is credited with leading his *side* to victory. プライスは主将として自らのチームを勝利に導く自信がある ◇The French have a very strong *side*. フランスには非常に強いチームがある

ノート **team, club, side** の使い分け：**club** はその歴史を通じて選手・監督・オーナーを含む団体を指す．選手・監督・オーナーが変わることがあっても，クラブ自体は変わることはない．**team** と **side** はふつう選手を指す意味合いが強く，特に **side** はクラブ史上の特定時期[特定の試合]における選手を指すことが多い．◆This *team* is arguably even better than the Welsh *side* of the seventies. (このチームはまず間違いなく70年代のウェールズ・チームよりもずっと素晴らしい).

squad [C＋単数・複数動詞]（特定の試合に選出されるチームに所属する選手から成る）チーム，顔ぶれ，陣容 ◇He has named a *squad* of 16 from which to pick the side for the two one-day games. 1日2試合のために彼は16人の陣容を発表した

'line-up [ふつう単数形で]（特定の試合・競技に出場が予定されている選手の）顔ぶれ，陣容，メンバー ◇The team returns this season with a new car and a new *line-up* of drivers. そのチームは今シーズン，新型車と新ドライバーの陣容で復帰する ◇He was named in the *starting line-up* for the game against Chelsea. 彼は対チェルシー戦の先発メンバーに指名された

tear 動

tear・rip・split・shred・pull sth apart
異なる方向に引っ張って[鋭利な物で細かく切断して]物に損傷を与える
【類語訳】引き裂く，切り裂く，破る，ちぎる，裂ける，破れる，ちぎれる，空ける，割れる

split   tear   rip   shred
                                             pull sth apart

文型&コロケーション
▶ to **tear/ rip** sth **from/ out of** sth
▶ to **tear/ rip/ pull** sth **apart**
▶ to **tear/ rip** sth **up/ open**
▶ to **tear/ rip/ shred** paper
▶ to **tear/ rip** your **clothes**
▶ to **tear/ rip/ split** your **trousers/ pants/ jeans**
▶ to **tear/ rip** a **hole** in sth
▶ to **tear/ rip** sth **in two/ to shreds/ to pieces**

tear [他, 自]（引っ張って[鋭利な物で切断して]物を[が]）引き[切り]裂く，破る，ちぎる；裂ける，破れる，ちぎれる；(無理やりに裂いて物に穴を)空ける ◇I *tore* my jeans on the fence. ジーンズをフェンスで破いちゃった ◇He *tore* the package open. 彼は小包を破いて開けた ◇She *tore* a page from her notebook. 彼女はノートから1ページを破り取った ◇She *tore* up the letter (= tore it into small pieces). 彼女はその手紙をびりびりに破いた ◇His jacket had been *torn* to shreds on the barbed wire. 彼の上着は有刺鉄線でずたずたに裂けてしまった ◇The dogs *tore* the fox apart. 犬たちは狐を噛みちぎった ◇He *tore at* the meat with his bare hands. 彼は素手で肉を引きちぎった ◇Careful — this fabric *tears* very easily. 気をつけて—この生地はすごく破れやすいから ◇I *tore* a hole in my shirt. シャツに穴を空けちゃった
▶**tear** [C] ◇This sheet has a *tear* in it. このシーツに破れている

rip (-pp-) [他, 自]（突然手荒く）物を[が]引き[切り]裂く，破る，ちぎる；破れる，ちぎれる；(裂いて物に穴を)空ける ◇The flag had been *ripped* in two 旗が二つに裂かれた ◇I heard the tent *rip*. 私はテントが裂ける音を聞いた ◇A bullet *ripped into* his shoulder. 銃弾で彼の肩に穴が空いた ◇The nail *ripped* a hole in my jacket. 釘で私の上着に穴が空いた
▶**rip** 图 ◇The jacket had a *rip* in the sleeve. そのジャケットは袖が破れていた

ノート **tear** と **rip** の使い分け：**rip** はふつう **tear** よりも手荒い動作を示す．両動詞ともよく，特に **rip** は物が裂かれる[破られる]際の激しい動作を示す前置詞[副詞]と共に用いられることが多い．

split [自, 他]（生地・木材が一直線に）裂ける，割れる，（物を一直線に）裂く，割る ◇Her dress had *split* along

↪tear

the seam. 彼女のドレスは縫い目に沿って裂けていた ◇The cushion *split* open and sent feathers everywhere. 座布団がぱっくり裂けて、羽毛があちこちに飛んだ ◇I was put to work *splitting* wood for the fire. 私は火にくべる薪割りをさせられた

shred (-dd-) [他] 《紙・生地・野菜を細かく》裂く、破る、ちぎる、刻む ◇Serve the fish on a bed of *shredded* lettuce. 細かく刻んだレタスの上に魚を載せて出してください ◇He was accused of *shredding* documents relating to the case. 彼は事件の関係書類をシュレッダーにかけたかどで告訴された ❶紙をshredする場合は、ふつうshredder, shredding machineと呼ばれる機械で行われる。手で行う場合は、tear/rip sth upと言う。☞ **shred** (FRAGMENT)

‚pull sth a'part [句動詞]《異なる方向に引っ張って物を》引き裂く ◇The wolves will *pull* the carcass *apart*. 狼たちがその死骸をバラバラにするだろう ◇It is wise to *pull* the gearbox *apart* only when absolutely necessary. 絶対に必要なときにだけギアボックスを分解するようにするのが賢明だ ❶pull sth apartは本来、力や激しさを伴って「引き裂く」ことだが、必ずしもそうでなくてもよい。

tell [動]

1 ☞ CONVEY

tell・report・inform・notify・brief・alert sb to sth・fill sb in・enlighten
口頭[文面]で人に情報を与える
【類語訳】伝える、教える、知らせる、報告する、通知する、通報する、届け出る

〖文型&コロケーション〗
▸ to tell sb/ report/ inform sb/ notify sb/ brief sb **that**…
▸ to tell/ inform/ notify sb **of** sth
▸ to inform/ brief/ enlighten sb **about** sth
▸ to report/ brief sb/ fill sb in/ enlighten sb **on** sth
▸ to tell sb/ report sth/ inform sb/ notify sb **officially**
▸ to tell sb/ report sth/ notify sb **formally**
▸ to tell/ inform sb/ notify sb **in writing**
▸ to tell/ inform/ brief sb **personally**
▸ to tell sb/ report sth/ inform sb/ notify sb **immediately**
▸ to report sth/ inform sb/ brief sb **regularly**
▸ to be **fully** informed/ briefed

tell [他]《口頭・文面で情報を》伝える、教える;《文書・計器・記号などが情報を》知らせる ◇Why wasn't I *told* about the accident? どうしてその事故について教えてもらえなかったの ◇Did she *tell* you her name? 彼女はあなたに名乗りましたか ◇*Tell* me where you live. どこに住んでいるか教えて ◇'I'm ready to go now,' he *told* her. 「もう行く準備はできたよ」と彼は彼女に伝えた ◇The advertisement *told* us very little about the product. その広告を見ただけでは製品についてほとんどわからなかった ◇This gauge *tells* you how much fuel you have left. この計器で後どのくらい燃料が残っているかがわかります ☞ **tell** (DESCRIBE)

report [自、他]《情報を》報告する、伝える ◇The committee will *report* on its research next month. 委員会は来月その調査について報告します ◇The crash happened seconds after the pilot *reported* engine trouble. パイロットがエンジントラブルを報告した数秒後に墜落した ◇The house was *reported* to be in excellent condition. その家は素晴らしい状態にあるとの報告があった

inform [他]《ややフォーマル》《正式[公式]に》知らせる、通報

[通報]する ◇Please *inform* us of any changes of address. 住所変更があればお知らせください ◇The leaflet *informs* customers about healthy eating. そのちらしは健康的な食事について顧客に教えてくれている ◇Have the police been *informed*? 警察に通報はありましたか ◇I have been *reliably informed* (= sb I trust has told me) that the couple will marry next year. 私はこのカップルは来年結婚するという情報を信頼できる筋から得ています ☞ **information** (INFORMATION), **informative** (INFORMATIVE)

notify [他、しばしば受身で]《フォーマル》《正式[公式]に》事実[状況]について)知らせる、通知[通報]する、届け出る ◇Competition winners will be *notified* by post. 競技会の優勝者は郵便で通知されます ◇The police must be *notified* of the date of the demonstration. デモの日程を警察に届け出なければならない

📝 **inform** と **notify** の使い分け: notify は当局・世間が知る必要のある重要な事実について用いられる。より個人的[一般的]な情報については用いられない。×I have been reliably *notified* that the couple will marry next year. ×The leaflet *notifies* customers about healthy eating.

brief [他]《ややフォーマル》《情報の[を]》概要[要点]を伝え、手短に話す[説明する] ◇The officer *briefed* her on what to expect. 役人は予想なることを彼女に手短に話した ◇I expect to be kept fully *briefed* at all times. 私は常に十分に概要を把握しておこうと思います

a'lert sb to sth [句動詞]《しばしば受身で》《ややフォーマル》《物事を人に》気づかせる、注意を喚起する、警告する ◇They had been *alerted to* the possibility of further price rises. さらなる物価上昇の可能性が警告されていた ❶be alerted to sthは誰かから教えられて[物事が起こって]気づかせる場合に用いられる。

‚fill sb 'in [句動詞]《ややインフォーマル》《起こった物事について人に》伝える、教える、知らせる ◇Can you *fill* me *in* on what's been going on while I've been away? 私が不在の間に何が起きていたのか聞かせてもらえますか

enlighten [他]《特に書き言葉 or おどけて》《物事をよりよく理解できるように情報を》伝える、教える、知らせる ◇She didn't *enlighten* him about her background. 彼女は自分の生い立ちについて彼には教えなかった ☞ **enlightening** (INFORMATIVE), **enlightenment** (KNOWLEDGE)

2 tell・betray・stab sb in the back・blow the whistle on sb/sth・turn King's/Queen's/State's evidence・grass・blab・inform on sb・finger
人に秘めていることを知らせ、敵に情報を与える
【類語訳】秘密を漏らす、他言する、口外する、密告する、告げ口する、内部告発する、共犯証言をする、たれ込む

〖文型&コロケーション〗
▸ to tell/ blow the whistle/ grass/ inform **on** sb
▸ to betray sb/ grass/ blab **to** sb
▸ to tell on/ betray/ inform on a **friend**
▸ to betray/ blow the whistle on/ inform on a **colleague**
▸ to betray/ blow the whistle on **your partner/ husband/ employer/ wife/ master**

tell [自]《インフォーマル、特に話し言葉、しばしばけなして》秘密を漏らす、他言[口外]する、告げ口する ◇Promise you won't *tell*. 他言しないと約束してください ◇'Who are you going out with tonight?' 'That would be *telling*!' (= it's a secret) 「今夜は誰とデートするの」「言えないわ」 ◇Don't *tell* on me, will you? (= Don't tell anyone in authority what I have done.) 私のこと告げ口しないよね

betray [他]《ややフォーマル、けなして》(敵に情報を)漏らす, 密告する, 売る ◇For years they had been *betraying* state secrets *to* Russia. 何年もの間、彼らは国家機密をロシアに漏らし続けていた ◇He was offered money to *betray* his colleagues. 彼は金を受け取って同僚たちを売った
☞ **give sb/sth away** (REVEAL), **betray** (CHEAT 動)

stab sb in the 'back [行れ] (-bb-)《インフォーマル》(信頼してくれている人を)中傷する ◇It was very competitive and everyone was *stabbing* everyone else *in the back*. 競争が激しく、誰もがそれぞれ中傷し合っていた

blow the 'whistle on sb/sth [行れ]《インフォーマル、しばしばほめて、特にジャーナリズム》(不正[違法]行為を権威者に)内部告発する ◇It is getting more difficult for people to *blow the whistle on* their employers. 自分の雇用主を内部告発することはますます難しくなってきている

turn King's/Queen's 'evidence《英》《米 turn State's 'evidence》[行れ] (刑罰を軽くしてもらうために)共犯証言をする、共犯者に不利な証言をする ◇Two of the prisoners agreed to *turn Queen's evidence*. 二人の囚人が共犯証言をすることに同意した

grass [自]《英、俗語、けなして》(犯罪行為について警察に)たれ込む, 売る ◇Who *grassed* on us? 誰が俺たちをたれ込んだんだ ◇You wouldn't *grass up* your mates, would you? 仲間を売ったりしないだろうね

blab (-bb-) [自, 他]《インフォーマル、けなして》(秘密にしておくべきことを)うっかり漏らす ◇Someone must have *blabbed* to the police. 誰かが警察に秘密を漏らしたに違いない ◇Try not to *blab* the whole story. 事のてん末をペラペラしゃべらないように

in'form on sb [句動詞]《ややフォーマル、しばしばけなして》(犯罪行為について警察・権威者に)密告する ◇He *informed on* his own brother. 彼は自分の兄を密告した

finger [他]《特に米、インフォーマル》(違法行為を告発して警察に)たれ込む ◇Who *fingered him for* the burglaries? 誰が彼の住居侵入をたれ込んだんだ

temper [名]

temper・tantrum・rage・mood・sulk・huff
短い間の怒りに満ちた振る舞いを表す
【類語訳】癇癪(かんしゃく)、腹立ち、いら立ち、怒り、激怒、憤慨、不機嫌、すねること、むくれること、むっとすること

		→
mood	temper	rage
sulk	tantrum	
huff		

文型&コロケーション
▶ to be in a temper/ rage/ huff at/ about/ over sth
▶ in a temper/ rage/ mood/ sulk/ huff
▶ a **violent** temper/ tantrum/ rage
▶ to **have** a temper/ a tantrum/ the sulks
▶ to **get in** a temper/ rage/ huff
▶ to **fly into** a temper/ rage

temper [C, ふつう単数で, U] 癇癪, 腹[いら]立ち, 怒り ◇He has a *short/quick temper* (= gets angry very easily). 彼は短気だ ◇You must learn to control your *temper*. 怒りが抑えられるようにならなくてはなりません ◇After an hour of waiting *tempers began to fray* (= people began to get angry). 1時間も待たされて、人々はいら立ち始めた ◇She broke the plates in a *fit of temper*. 彼女はカッとなって皿を割った ❶ *temper* はまた短い時間の激怒している状態をも指す ◆ She says awful things when she's in a *temper*. (彼女は腹立ちまぎれにひどいことを口にする).
☞ **lose your temper** (LOSE YOUR TEMPER)

tantrum [C]《子どもの突然で一時的な》癇癪 ◇They claimed she *threw tantrums* and was difficult to work with. 彼女が癇癪を起こすので一緒に働きづらいと彼らは言い張った ◇Young children often have *temper tantrums*. 幼い子どもはしばしば癇癪を起こす

rage [C]《抑えがたい》激怒, 憤慨 ◇Sue stormed out in a *rage*. スーはカッとなってけたたましく飛び出した ◇She attacked him in a jealous *rage*. 彼女は嫉妬に怒り狂って彼を非難した ☞ **rage** (ANGER 名)

mood [C] 不機嫌 ◇I wonder why he's in such a *mood* today. 彼って今日、どうしてあんなに不機嫌なのかしら ◇She was *in one of her moods* (= one of her regular periods of being angry or impatient). 彼女は虫の居どころが悪かった ◇to be in a bad/foul/filthy/terrible *mood* 非常に機嫌が悪い ☞ **mood** (MOOD)

sulk [C]《英でまた **the sulks**》《複数形で》(いら立って黙り込んで)すねる[ふてる, むっつりする]こと ◇Jo was in a *sulk* upstairs. ジョーは2階ですねていた ◇Ed's got the *sulks* again. エドがまたふてくされている ☞ **sulky** (IRRITABLE)

huff [C]《インフォーマル》(いら立って腹を立てて)むくれる[むっとする]こと ◇She went home in a *huff*. 彼女はむくれて家に帰った

tenant [名] ☞ RESIDENT

tenant・occupant・guest・resident・lodger
特定の家で生活[宿泊]する人を表す
【類語訳】賃借人、借家人、借地人、テナント、居住者、占有者、宿泊客、下宿人

文型&コロケーション
▶ a **new** tenant/ occupant/ lodger
▶ the **previous/ current/ sole** tenant/ occupant

tenant [C] 賃借人, 借家[地]人, テナント ◇They had evicted their *tenants* for non-payment of rent. 彼らは家賃の不払いにより借家人を立ち退かせた

occupant [C]《ややフォーマル、特に書き言葉》居住[占有]者, 賃借人, 借家[地]人;(乗り物・座席などに)乗って[座って]いる人 ◇All outstanding bills will be paid by the previous *occupants*. 未払い勘定はすべて以前の居住者の支払いとなります ◇The car was badly damaged but the *occupants* were unhurt. その車はひどく損傷していたが、乗っていた人たちにけがはなかった ☞ **occupy** (LIVE)

guest [C]《ホテルなどの》宿泊客 ◇*Guests* should vacate their rooms by 10.30 a.m. 宿泊客は午前10時半までに部屋を出なければなりません ◇The accommodation secretary has a list of families who take *paying guests* (= people who are living in a private house, but paying as if they were in a hotel). 宿泊担当者が短期の下宿人を受け入れる家庭のリストを持っている

resident [C]《フォーマル》《ホテルなどの》宿泊客 ◇The hotel

↪tenant

restaurant is open to non-*residents*. そのホテルのレストランは宿泊客以外にも開放されている ☞ **resident** (RESIDENT)

lodger [C]《特に英》(部屋代と食事代を支払って他人の家で生活する)下宿人 ◇Many people take in a *lodger* because they need the income. 収入を当てに下宿人を受け入れる人が多い

tendency 名

tendency・orientation・bias・propensity・bent
人や物事の頻繁な振る舞いの様式を表す語
【類語訳】性向, 傾向, 志向, 指向, 態度, 姿勢, 偏見, 好み

文型&コロケーション
▶ a tendency/ an orientation/ a bias **toward/ towards** sth
▶ a tendency/ a propensity **to do** sth
▶ a tendency/ an orientation **to** sth
▶ a propensity/ bent **for** sth
▶ a **natural** tendency/ bias/ propensity/ bent
▶ an **innate** tendency/ propensity
▶ to **have** a tendency/ an orientation/ a bias/ a propensity/ a bent

tendency [C] (人・物事の)性質, 性向, 傾向 ◇This material has a *tendency* to shrink when washed. この生地には洗うと縮む性質がある ◇There is a *tendency* for this disease to run in families. この病気は家庭内で広まる傾向がある ◇Several patients admitted to suicidal *tendencies*. 数人の患者が自殺志向があることを認めた ☞ **tendency** (TREND)

▷**tend** 動 [自] Women *tend* to live longer than men. 女性は男性より長生きする傾向にある ◇When I'm tired, I *tend* to make mistakes. 私は疲れるとミスを犯しがちです ◇It *tends* to get very cold here in the winter. ここでは冬になるととても寒くなる傾向があります ◇People *tend to think* that the problem will never affect them. 人々はその問題からは決して影響を受けないと考えがちだ

orientation [U, C]《ややフォーマル》(人・組織の目的・関心の)志向(性);(特定のテーマに関する基本的な信念・感情の)方向(性), 指向, 態度, 姿勢 ◇The classes are essentially theoretical *in orientation*. 授業は本質的に理論指向です ◇He belonged to a group with a specific religious and political *orientation*. 彼は特定の宗教的・政治的志向を持つグループに属していた ◇legislation forbidding discrimination on the grounds of *sexual orientation* (= whether sb is attracted to men, women or both) 性的指向による差別を禁じている法律

bias [C, ふつう単数で] (ある物事への)偏見, 好み ◇In British universities there was a *bias* towards pure science. 英国の大学には純粋科学を好む傾向があった ◇These classes have a strong practical *bias*. これらの授業は実習的な事柄に強く偏っています

propensity [C, ふつう単数で]《フォーマル》(特定の種類の行動を取る)傾向, 性向 ◇There is an increased *propensity* for people to live alone. 人々が一人暮らしをする傾向が高まっている ◇They all knew about his *propensity* for violence. 彼らは皆, 彼の暴力的性向について知っていた

bent [C, ふつう単数で] (生まれながらの)傾向, 性向, 好み ◇Some students have no natural *bent* for literature at all. 学生の中には生まれつき文学をまったく好まない者もいる

tense 形

tense・strained・stressed・under pressure・uptight
人が心配しすぎてリラックスできないことを表す語
【類語訳】緊張した, 張り詰めた, ぴりぴりした, いらいらした

文型&コロケーション
▶ to **look/ sound/ seem** tense/ strained/ uptight
▶ to **get** tense/ uptight
▶ sth **makes sb** tense/ uptight

tense (神経質・心配で)緊張した, 張り詰めた, ぴりぴりした ◇Try to relax. Are you always this *tense*? リラックスしてごらん. いつもこんなに緊張してるの ❶ *tense* は自分の置かれている状況あるいは性格から起こる場合に用いられる. ◆She sounded *tense* and angry. (彼女はぴりぴりして怒っているように思えた). ◆He's a very *tense* person. (彼は非常に神経質な人だ). ☞ **tense** (STRESSFUL), **tense** (TIGHTEN), **tension** (PRESSURE 1)

strained (心配・重圧で)緊張した, 張り詰めた, ぴりぴりした ◇Her face looked *strained* and weary. 彼女の顔は緊張して疲れ果てているように見えた ◇He spoke in a low, *strained* voice. 彼は低い張り詰めた声で話した ☞ **strain** (PRESSURE 1), **strained** (STRESSFUL)

stressed (またはインフォーマル **stressed out**) (心配・疲労で)ストレスを受けた, くたびれた ◇He was feeling very *stressed* and tired. 彼はストレスと疲労をすごく感じていた ◇*Stressed* out? Take a break in the sun. くたびれたの. 日なたで一休みしなさい ◇*stressed* business executives ストレスがたまった管理職たち ☞ **stress** (PRESSURE 1), **stressful** (STRESSFUL)

under 'pressure フレーズ (しなければならないことで)重圧を受けて ◇The team performs well *under pressure*. そのチームはプレッシャーを受けながらも素晴らしいプレーをします ◇I don't want to **put** you *under pressure*, but… あなたにプレッシャーをかけたくはないが… ☞ **pressure** (PRESSURE 1)

uptight 《インフォーマル》(心配・怒りで)いらいら[ぴりぴり]した ◇She felt too *uptight* to do any work. 彼女はあまりにもいらいらして仕事が手に着かなかった ❶ *uptight* は自分の置かれている状況の結果あるいは性格から起こる場合に用いられる. ◆Relax! You're getting too *uptight* about this. (力を抜いて. 君はこのことでぴりぴりしすぎだ). ◆He's a very *uptight* person. (彼はとても神経質な人だ). 反意 **easygoing** (CALM)

tension 名

tension・aggression・hostility・antagonism・animosity・antipathy・enmity
人々の間の敵対的な状況や感情
【類語訳】緊張関係, 攻撃性, 敵意, 敵対行為, 敵対感情, 憎悪, 反感, 恨み

文型&コロケーション
▶ tension/ hostility/ antagonism/ animosity/ antipathy/ enmity **between** A and B
▶ aggression/ hostility/ antagonism/ animosity/ antipathy/ enmity **towards** sb/ sth
▶ **mutual/ personal** hostility/ antagonism/ animosity/ antipathy/ enmity

- ▶ open aggression/ hostility
- ▶ natural antagonism/ antipathy
- ▶ to feel the tension/ hostility/ antagonism/ animosity/ antipathy
- ▶ to arouse hostility/ antagonism

tension [U, C, ふつう複数で]（人々が互いに信用せず[敵意を抱いて]攻撃し合う）緊張関係 ◇There is mounting *tension* along the border. 国境沿いに緊張が高まっている ◇*international/racial/political tensions* 国際的な/人種間の/政治的な緊張 ◇*Family tensions and conflicts may lead to violence.* 家庭内の緊張と言い争いは暴力につながることもある ☞ **tense** (STRESSFUL)

aggression [U]（怒り・憎しみによって引き起こされる）攻撃性 ◇*Nowadays our aggression is channelled into sports.* 今日では、我々の攻撃性はスポーツに向けられる ☞ **aggressive** (AGGRESSIVE 1)

hostility [U, 単数で]（人・物事に対する）敵意、敵対行為 ◇*There was open hostility between the two schools.* その二つの学校の間にはむき出しの敵対心があった ◇*The talk lasted well over an hour and he sensed a growing hostility from his audience.* 話し合いは優に1時間以上にも及び、彼は聴衆が敵意を募らせているのを感じた ☞ **hostile** (AGGRESSIVE 1), **hostility** (OPPOSITION)

antagonism [U, C, ふつう複数で]《書き言葉》（人々・集団間の）敵意、敵対感情 ◇*The gap between rich and poor is widening and class antagonism is growing.* 貧富の格差は広がりつつあり、階級間の反目が高まっている ◇*Natural antagonisms and rivalries between the communities became worse.* 地域社会間に自然と生まれた敵意と対抗意識は深刻化した ☞ **antagonize** (ANGER 動)

animosity [U, C, ふつう複数で]（人への個人的な）敵意、憎悪 ◇*He felt no animosity towards his critics.* 彼は批評家たちに対してまったく敵意を覚えなかった ◇*Personal animosities between the leaders have made negotiations difficult.* 指導者間の個人的な憎悪が交渉を難しくしている

antipathy [U, C]《フォーマル》（物事・考え・人に対する）反感、嫌悪 ◇*Growing antipathy to the government has led to a low voter turnout in local elections.* 政府に対する反感の高まりは地方選挙における低投票率につながった ◇*His professional judgement was coloured by his personal antipathies.* 彼の専門家としての判断は個人的な嫌悪に影響されていた

ノート antagonism, animosity, antipathy の使い分け：antagonism は人々の集団・階級全体に対して抱かれることが多い。◆ *class/racial antagonism*（階級間の/人種間の敵対感情）。animosity は主義や伝統ではなく、人の個人的な悪い関係に基づく感情を表す。antipathy は考えや理屈ではなく、本能に基づく感情を表す。

enmity [U, C]（長期的な人への強い）敵意、恨み ◇*Her action earned her the enmity of two or three colleagues.* 彼女の行動は2, 3人の同僚から恨みを買った ◇*Personal enmities and conflicts have soured relations within the department.* 個人的な恨みと対立が部内の人間関係を気まずくさせている

terrible [形]

1 ☞ BAD, DISGUSTING 1
terrible・awful・horrible・dreadful・vile・horrendous

物事が非常に不快であることを表す
【類語訳】ひどい、嫌な、つらい、残念な、悲惨な、恐ろしい、気分の悪い、最悪な、がっかりな、惨めな、むかつく、悪質な

文型&コロケーション

- ▶ terrible/ awful/ horrible/ dreadful for sb
- ▶ a terrible/ an awful/ a horrible/ a dreadful/ a vile thing
- ▶ a terrible/ an awful/ a horrible/ a vile smell
- ▶ a terrible/ an awful/ a horrible/ a dreadful/ a vile business
- ▶ a terrible/ an awful/ a horrible/ a dreadful/ a horrendous time
- ▶ a terrible/ an awful/ a horrible/ a dreadful noise/ thought/ feeling/ shock
- ▶ the terrible/ awful/ horrible/ dreadful truth
- ▶ terrible/ awful/ dreadful/ vile/ horrendous conditions
- ▶ terrible/ awful/ dreadful/ vile weather
- ▶ terrible/ awful/ dreadful news
- ▶ really/ pretty terrible/ awful/ horrible/ dreadful/ vile/ horrendous
- ▶ rather terrible/ awful/ horrible/ dreadful/ vile
- ▶ absolutely/ truly terrible/ awful/ horrible/ dreadful/ horrendous

terrible ひどい、嫌な；つらい、残念な、悲惨な、恐ろしい、たまらない、どうしようもない、気分の悪い、後悔した、最悪な ◇*What terrible news!* 何てひどいニュースなんだ ◇*How terrible for you!* まあお気の毒に ◇*It was a terrible thing to happen to someone so young.* そんな若い人に起こるとは悲惨だったね ◇*That's a terrible thing to say!* ひどいこと言うね ◇*I feel terrible — I think I'll go to bed.* 気分が悪い─寝ようと思う ◇*I feel terrible: it could so easily have ended in tragedy and I just didn't think.* たまらないなあ。そんなにあっけなく悲劇に終わるなんて私は考えなしなかった 反意 **good** (NICE 1)

awful《特に話し言葉》ひどい、嫌な；がっかりな、気分の悪い、後悔した、最悪な ◇*That's an awful colour.* それはひどい色だね ◇*I feel awful — maybe it was something I ate.* 気分が悪い─たぶん食べた物だと思う ◇*I feel awful about forgetting her birthday.* 彼女の誕生日を忘れるなんて最悪だ ◇*The awful thing is, it was my fault.* 申し訳ないことに、それは私のせいだった ◇*'They didn't even offer to pay.' 'Oh that's awful.'*「彼らは支払おうとさえしなかった」「いやあ、そいつはひどい」

horrible《特に話し言葉》ひどい、嫌な；悲惨な、惨めな、むかつく ◇*What a horrible child!* 何て嫌な子なの ◇*The coffee tasted horrible.* そのコーヒーはひどい味だった ◇*It was horrible sitting there all on my own.* 一人っきりでそこに座っているのは惨めだった

dreadful《特に英、特に話し言葉》ひどい、嫌な、むかつく、惨めな ◇*What dreadful weather!* 何てひどい天気なんだ ◇*What a dreadful thing to say!* 何てひどい言い草 ◇*It's dreadful the way they treat their employees.* 彼らの従業員の扱い方はひどい ◇*How dreadful!* 何てひどい

vile《インフォーマル》ひどい、嫌な、悪質な、汚い ◇*There was a vile smell coming from the locked room.* 鍵のかかった部屋からひどい臭いがしていた ◇*It was a vile business from beginning to end.* それは終始悪質な取り引きだった

horrendous《ややインフォーマル》ひどい、むちゃくちゃな ◇*The traffic around the city was horrendous.* その都

↪terrible

市の交通量ときたら，ひどかった

2 terrible・awful
人や物事がいかに悪い[極端]かを強調する語
【類語訳】すさまじい，ものすごい，ひどい，とんでもない

【文型&コロケーション】
▶a terrible/ an awful mistake/ mess/ nuisance/ disappointment
▶a terrible/ an awful fool/ snob
▶a/ an really/ truly/ absolutely/ pretty/ rather terrible/ awful...

terrible [名詞の前で]《インフォーマル，特に話し言葉》(人・物事がいかに悪い[極端]かを強調して)すさまじい，ものすごい，ひどい，とんでもない ◇The room was in a *terrible* mess. 部屋はすごく散らかっていた ◇I had a *terrible* job (= it was very difficult) to persuade her to come. 私は彼女を説得して来させるというひどく厄介な仕事を抱えていた ◇You'll be in *terrible* trouble if you're late again. 今度遅れたらとんでもなく面倒なことになるよ

awful [名詞の前で]《インフォーマル，特に話し言葉》(量・質・物事がいかに悪いかを強調して)すさまじい，ものすごい，ひどい，とんでもない ◇It's going to cost *an awful lot of* money. それには莫大なお金がかかりそうだ ◇The whole thing has been an *awful* nuisance. すべてがとんでもなく厄介になっている ❶awfulが量を強調する場合，必ずしも悪い物事を表すとは限らない．◆I feel an *awful* lot better than I did yesterday. (昨日よりもはるかに気分がいい)．

3 terrible・awful・appalling・horrible・dreadful・horrific・horrifying・gruesome
物事が極めて衝撃的である[恐ろしい，多大な害を及ぼす]ことを表す
【類語訳】ものすごい，激しい，ひどい，甚大な，並々ならない，恐ろしい，すさまじい，ぞっとする，陰惨な，身の毛もよだつ

【文型&コロケーション】
▶a terrible/ an awful/ an appalling/ a horrible/ a dreadful/ a horrific/ a horrifying/ a gruesome scene/ sight
▶a terrible/ an awful/ an appalling/ a horrible/ a dreadful/ a horrific crime
▶terrible/ appalling/ horrible/ dreadful/ horrific injuries
▶terrible/ awful/ appalling/ horrible/ dreadful/ horrific pain/ suffering
▶a terrible/ an awful/ an appalling/ a horrible/ a dreadful/ a horrific nightmare
▶a terrible/ an awful/ an appalling/ a horrible/ a dreadful tragedy
▶terrible/ appalling/ dreadful consequences
▶a terrible/ an appalling/ a horrible/ a dreadful/ a horrific/ a horrifying accident/ incident
▶a terrible/ an awful/ a horrible/ a dreadful/ a horrific/ a horrifying/ a gruesome death
▶a terrible/ an awful/ a horrible/ a dreadful/ a gruesome fate
▶a terrible/ an awful/ an horrible/ a dreadful cry/ scream
▶a terrible/ an awful/ a horrible/ a horrific/ a horrifying/ a gruesome ordeal
▶a terrible/ a dreadful/ horrific/ gruesome attack
▶a terrible/ horrible/ dreadful/ horrific/ gruesome murder
▶a terrible/ a horrible/ a horrific dreadful/ slaughter/ massacre

terrible

▶to be in a terrible/ an awful/ an appalling/ a dreadful state
▶absolutely/ quite terrible/ awful/ appalling/ horrible/ dreadful/ horrific/ horrifying
▶truly terrible/ awful/ appalling/ horrible/ dreadful/ horrific/ gruesome
▶really terrible/ awful/ appalling/ horrible/ dreadful/ horrific
▶particularly terrible/ awful/ horrible/ dreadful/ horrific/ horrifying/ gruesome
▶pretty terrible/ awful/ horrible/ dreadful/ horrific/ gruesome
▶It's terrible/ awful/ horrible/ dreadful/ horrific/ horrifying to see/ think...

terrible (非常に有害[深刻]で)ものすごい，激しい，ひどい；(多大な害・損傷を伴って)甚大な，並々ならない ◇He had suffered *terrible* injuries. 彼はものすごいけがを負った ◇It was the night of that *terrible* storm. それはあの激しい嵐の夜のことだった ◇I'll have to stay with her — she's in a *terrible* state. 彼女のそばにいてやらなくちゃ — 彼女はひどい状態なんだ

▷**terribly** 副 ◇They suffered *terribly* when their son was killed. 息子が殺されて彼らはひどく苦しんでいた ◇The experiment went *terribly* wrong. 実験はまったくうまくいかなかった

awful (非常に有害[衝撃的]で)恐ろしい，すさまじい；(多大な苦しみを伴うほど)激しい，ひどい ◇He had never known the *awful* horrors of war. 彼は戦争のすさまじい恐怖をまったく知らなかった ◇I woke from the most *awful* nightmare. 最も恐ろしい悪夢から目覚めた 反意 **great** (GREAT 1)

appalling (英 or フォーマル，米)(非常に有害[衝撃的]で)恐ろしい，ぞっとする；(多大な苦しみ・残酷さを伴うほど)ひどい ◇The prisoners were living in *appalling* conditions. 囚人たちはぞっとするような状況で生活していた ◇The regime has an *appalling* record on human rights. その政権は人権に関して恐るべき記録がある

▷**appallingly** 副 ◇They had to work under *appallingly* difficult circumstances. 彼らはぞっとするような厳しい環境で働かなければならなかった

【ノート】**terrible，awful，appalling**の使い分け：awfulは出来事・経験を表すのに用いられることが多い．一般的には，dream, event, experience, happening, nightmareと結びつく．appallingは悪い社会的状況だけでなく，事故・犯罪およびそれらの結果を表すのに用いられることが多い．一般的には，accident, atrocity, tragedy, attack, crash, injuries, conditions, deprivation, hardship, human rights record, povertyと結びつく．appallingはほとんど《英》で用いられる．terribleはappallingよりも少し意味が弱いが，上記の用例のすべてにおいて《英》《米》どちらでも用いられる．

horrible 恐ろしい，すさまじい ◇She woke from a *horrible* nightmare. 彼女は恐ろしい夢から覚めた ❶horribleがこの意味で用いられる場合，murder, mutilation, nightmare, injuries, slaughter, screamingなどの語や，It was horribleという句で用いられるのがふつうである．

▷**horribly** 副 ◇The experiment went *horribly* wrong. 実験は大失敗だった

dreadful [ふつう名詞の前で] (非常に有害[深刻]で)ものすごい，激しい，ひどい ◇There's been a *dreadful* accident.

ものすごい事故があった ▶**dreadfully** 副 ◇They suffered *dreadfully* during the war. 彼らは戦争中ひどく苦しんだ

ノート **terrible** と **dreadful** の使い分け：terrible は個人的体験によって動揺していることを示唆することが多い。dreadful を用いると、若干の嫌悪感はあるが、個人的にはその体験にあまり思い入れがないことを表す。

horrific 恐ろしい、ぞっとする ◇There's been a *horrific* murder. 恐ろしい殺人事件があった ◇Her injuries were *horrific*. 彼女のけがはぞっとするほどのものだった ◇She's been through a *horrific* ordeal. 彼女は恐ろしい苦難を経てきた

horrifying 恐ろしい、ぞっとする ◇It was a *horrifying* experience. それはぞっとするような体験だった ◇It's *horrifying* to see such poverty. そんな貧困を目にするのは恐ろしいことだ

ノート **horrific** と **horrifying** の使い分け：horrific は injuries, wounds, burns, death など、直接人々に影響を与える物事について用いられることが多い。horrifying は accident, dream, event, incident, ordeal, sight, story など、出来事・体験を表す語と共に用いられることが多い。また、it's horrifying to see/think sth という表現でも用いられる。×It's *horrific* to see such poverty.

gruesome (死・けがに関わっていて)恐ろしい、陰惨な、身の毛もよだつ ◇a particularly *gruesome* murder とりわけ陰惨な殺人 ◇We were shown *gruesome* pictures of dead bodies. 私たちは陰惨な死体写真を見せられた

territory 名

territory・colony・enclave・possession・dominion・satellite
他国によって占領[支配]されている国や地域を表す
【類語訳】領土、領地、統治領、属領、植民地、衛星都市[国]

文型&コロケーション
▶(a) **British/ Spanish**, etc. territory/ colony/ enclave/ possession
▶a **self-governing** territory/ colony/ dominion
▶(a) **former** territory/ colony/ possession
▶**overseas** territory/ possessions

territory [U, C] (特定の国・統治者の支配下にある)領土、領地、統治領、属領 ◇They have refused to allow UN troops to be stationed in their *territory*. 彼らは国連軍が自分たちの領土に駐屯するのを拒否した ◇The killings had set off widespread rioting in the occupied *territories*. その殺害事件は占領地での広範囲に及ぶ暴動を誘発した
▶**territorial** 形 ◇*territorial* gains/disputes/claims 領土獲得／領土紛争／領土権の主張

colony [C] (他の強国に統治されている)植民地、属領、属国 ◇East Timor was a former Portuguese *colony*. 東チモールは旧ポルトガル植民地だった
▶**colonial** 形 ◇Western *colonial* attitudes 西欧の植民地に対する態度

enclave [C] 《ややフォーマル》(異なる宗教・文化を持つ国・都市に囲まれる)包領、飛び地、居住地 ◇The northern part of the city is a Christian *enclave*. その都市の北部はキリスト教徒の居住地である

possession [C, ふつう複数で]《フォーマル》(他国に所有[統治]される)属領、属国 ◇The former colonial *possessions* are now independent states. その旧植民地国家は現在では独立国家になっている

ノート **colony** と **possession** の使い分け：colony は特に新たな永住の地を求めて、多くの人々が移住した国について用いられる。colony はふつう宗主国から遠く離れにいて用いられる。possession は強国の帝国を形成するすべての国と地域について、複数形で用いられることが多い。

dominion [C] 《フォーマル》(一人の統治者に支配される)領土、領地 ◇He ruled over the vast *dominions* of the Holy Roman Empire. 彼は神聖ローマ帝国の広大な領土を支配した

satellite [C] (他の大国・強国に支配され依存する)衛星都市[国]、付属機関 ◇Following the Second World War it became a *satellite* state of the Soviet Union. 第二次世界大戦後、そこはソビエト連邦の衛星国となった

test 名

1 test・experiment・testing・trial・pilot study
物事を解明する[物事が機能するかを確認する]ために行われる手順
【類語訳】検査、試験、調査、実験、実地試験、試し、試用期間、試験的研究

文型&コロケーション
▶a test/ an experiment/ testing/ a trial **on** sth
▶an experiment/ testing/ a trial **with** sth
▶**in/ during** a test/ an experiment/ testing/ a trial
▶a test/ an experiment/ testing/ a trial/ a pilot study **to do** sth
▶**successful** tests/ experiments/ testing/ trials/ pilot studies
▶**extensive/ rigorous** tests/ experiments/ testing/ trials
▶**scientific/ practical/ field/ laboratory/ pilot/ clinical/ medical** tests/ experiments/ testing/ trials
▶to **do** a test/ an experiment
▶to **carry out/ conduct** a test/ an experiment/ testing/ a trial/ a pilot study
▶to **set up/ design** a test/ an experiment/ a trial/ a pilot study
▶to **undergo** tests/ testing/ trials
▶tests/ experiments/ testing/ trials/ pilot studies **show** sth
▶a test/ an experiment/ a trial/ a pilot study **demonstrates/ indicates** sth
▶a test/ an experiment/ a trial **suggests/ proves/ finds** sth

test [C] (人の健康状態を調べるための)検査(方法)；(物事がうまく機能するかを調べるための)試験、検査、調査 ◇a/an eye/blood/pregnancy *test* 視力／血液／妊娠検査 ◇He developed a simple *test* for diabetes. 彼は糖尿病の簡単な検査方法を開発した ◇The hospital is doing some *tests*. その病院ではいくつかの検査を行っている ◇Rigorous safety *tests* are being carried out on the new jet. 新しいジェット機に関する厳密な安全性テストが行われている ◇Three athletes were sent home after failing drugs *tests*. 3人の運動選手が薬物検査に引っかかって帰国させられた ◇*Tests* have shown high levels of pollutants in the water. 一連の検査によって水中における高レベルの環境

汚染物質が検出された

experiment [C, U] （科学的な）実験；実地試験, 試し ◇Many people do not like the idea of *experiments* on animals. 多くの人々は動物実験という考え方が好きではない ◇Facts can be established *by* observation and *experiment*. 事実は観察と実験によって立証することができる ◇The school decided to try an *experiment in* single-sex education. その学校は男女別教育の実地試験を試みることに決めた ◇I've never cooked this before so it's a bit of an *experiment*. 今までこんなの料理したことが一度もないから, ちょっとした実験みたいなものだ

testing [U] （物事がうまく機能するかを確認するための）実験, 試験 ◇All our cosmetics are produced without animal *testing*. 私どもの化粧品はすべて動物実験なしに製造されます ◇He announced a moratorium on all nuclear *testing*. 彼はあらゆる核実験の一時停止を宣言した

trial [C, U] （薬などに対する）試験；（物事・人に関わる）試用期間, 試し ◇The new drug is undergoing clinical *trials*. その新薬は臨床試験を受けているところだ ◇She agreed to employ me for a *trial period*. 彼女は私を試用期間中に雇用することに同意した ◇The system was introduced *on a trial basis*. そのシステムは試験的に導入された ◇We had the machine *on trial* for a week. 我々はその機械を1週間試してみた ◇They are treating the trip as a *trial run* for their 500-mile sponsored ride later this month. 彼らはその旅を, 今月後半に資金集めのために行う500マイル走行のための試乗として捉えている

pilot study [C] （小規模な）試験的研究 ◇The Mayor's office has agreed to fund a *pilot study into* the plan. 市長室はその計画の試験的研究に資金を提供することに同意した

2 ☞ ASSESSMENT

test・exam・examination・paper・quiz・oral・practical
教科についての知識を確認するために人が答える[行う]一連の質問[活動]
【類義訳】テスト, 試験, 試験問題, 答案, 小テスト, 口頭試験, 実習

〖文型&コロケーション〗
▶ a test/ an exam/ an examination/ a quiz **on** sth
▶ a test/ an exam/ an examination **in** sth
▶ a **written** test/ exam/ examination/ paper/ quiz
▶ a **practical** test/ exam/ examination/ paper
▶ a/ an **difficult/ easy/ important/ final/ end of year** test/ exam/ examination
▶ a **chemistry/ geography, etc.** test/ exam/ examination/ paper/ quiz/ practical
▶ to **pass/ fail** a test/ an exam/ an examination/ a paper/ a quiz/ an oral/ a practical
▶ to **take** a test/ an exam/ an examination/ a paper/ a quiz/ a practical
▶ to **do** a test/ an exam/ an examination/ a paper/ a quiz
▶ to **set/ mark** a test/ an exam/ an examination/ a paper
▶ to **grade** a test/ an exam/ an examination/ a paper/ a quiz
▶ test/ exam/ examination/ quiz **questions**

test [C] （教科に関する）テスト, 試験 ◇There are end of year *tests* in English, maths and science. 英語, 数学, 理科の学年末試験があります ◇a good mark in the *test*《英》テストのよい点数 ◇a good grade on the *test*《米》テストのよい成績 ◇Is this a fair *test* of students' skills? これは公平な学力試験ですか ◇I took my driving *test* last week. 《英》先週, 私は運転免許試験を受けた ◇my driver's *test*《米》私の運転免許試験

exam [C] （学校・大学における教科に関する筆記・口頭・実地による正式な）試験 ◇She did well in her *exams*.《英》彼女は試験でよい点を取った ◇She did well on her *exams*.《米》彼女は試験でよい点を取った ◇to mark an *exam*《英》試験の採点をする ◇to grade an *exam*《米》試験の採点をする ◇I got my *exam* results today.《英》今日, 私は試験の成績をもらった ◇I got my *exam* grades/ scores today.《米》今日, 私は試験の成績をもらった ◇He's practising hard for his piano *exam*.《英》彼はピアノの試験に向けて懸命に練習している

examination [C] （フォーマル）（学校・大学における教科に関する筆記・口頭・実地による正式な）試験 ◇Students may *enter for* both *examinations*. 学生たちは両方の試験に受験の申し込みをするかもしれない ◇There has been a fall in the number of *examination candidates*. 受験者数は減少してきている

┏━━━━━━━━━━━━━━━━━━━━━━━━━━━━━┓
┃〖ノート〗**test, exam, examination** の使い分け：exam は学校・大学における筆記・口頭・実地による試験で, ふつう学年[学期, 課程]末に行われる重要なものを指す。《米》では, final exams, または単に finals と呼ばれることも多い。《英》では finals は学位課程の最終試験のみを指す。examination は試験を表すかなりフォーマルな語である。test は学年・学期・課程の途中で学生が受けることもあり, 教材の一部のみから出題されるものを指す。test はふつう試験内容が学問知識ではなく, 実技・身体能力・知能である場合に用いられる。◆an endurance *test*（耐久試験）。◆an IQ *test*（知能テスト）。◆a driving *test*（《英》運転免許試験）。◆a driver's *test*（《米》運転免許試験）。
┗━━━━━━━━━━━━━━━━━━━━━━━━━━━━━┛

paper [C]《英》（教科に関する）試験問題；（筆記による）答案 ◇The geography *paper* was hard. 地理の試験問題は難しかった ◇She spent the evening marking *exam papers*. 彼女は試験の答案を採点してその晩を過ごした

quiz （複 **quizzes**）[C]（特に米）（学生が受ける短い非公式の）小テスト ◇After reading a book, students take a short reading comprehension *quiz*. 1冊, 本を読み終わると学生たちは読解力の小テストを受けます ◇We had a *pop quiz* (= one that we were not told about in advance) in math class today. 今日, 数学の授業で抜き打ちテストがあった

oral [C] 口頭試験[試問] ◇I've got my French *oral* on Tuesday. 私は火曜日にフランス語の口頭試験がある ◇He passed the written exam, but failed the *oral*. 彼は筆記試験に通ったが, 口頭試験で落ちた ❶《英》では, oral はふつう会話力を試すための外国語の試験を指す。《米》では, oral はふつうすべての科目において学生が問題に答える大学での口頭試問を指す。

practical [C]《英, ややインフォーマル》（理科・技術の）実習 ◇The course involves lectures, demonstrations and *practicals*. そのコースには講義, 公開授業, 実習が含まれる ◇The second part of the exam is a three-hour *practical*. 試験の第二部は3時間の実習です

test 〖動〗

1 ☞ TRY 2
test・experiment・try sb/sth out・pilot・put sb/sth to the test・screen

thanks

うまく機能するか確認する[問題を調べる]
【類語訳】試験する, 検査する, 調査する, 実験する, 試す, 試用する, 試験的に使う, 吟味する

文型&コロケーション
- ▶ to test (sb/ sth)/ try sth out/ screen sb **for** sth
- ▶ to test sth/ experiment/ try sth out **on** sb/ sth
- ▶ to test/ screen **patients**
- ▶ to test a **theory**
- ▶ to put a **theory** to the test
- ▶ to **fully/ thoroughly** test/ pilot sth
- ▶ to test/ screen (sb/ sth) **regularly/ routinely**
- ▶ to **rigorously** test sth/ put sth to the test

test [他] (機械・製品・物質を)試験[検査, 調査]する；(健康状態を)検査する ◇Our beauty products are not *tested* on animals. 私どもの美容製品については動物実験はしていません ◇The water is regularly *tested* for purity. 水は定期的に純度の検査を受けています ◇You should have your hearing *tested*. 聴力検査をしてもらうほうがいいよ ◇Two athletes *tested positive* for steroids. 二人の運動選手はステロイド検査で陽性反応が出た

experiment [自] (科学的に)実験する；(新しい物事・考え・方法を)試す ◇Some people feel that *experimenting* on animals causes unnecessary suffering. 動物実験は不要な苦痛をもたらすと思う人々もいる ◇He wanted to *experiment* more *with* different textures in his paintings. 彼は絵の異なる質感をもっと試してみたかった ◇I *experimented* until I got the recipe just right. レシピどおりにきちんとやれるまで試しました

,try sb/sth 'out [句動詞] (人・物事を)試用する, 試す ◇They're *trying out* a new presenter for the show. 彼らはそのショーの新しい司会者を試用しているところだ ◇I've got an idea I'd like to *try out*. 試してみたい考えがある ☞ **try** (TRY 2)

pilot [他] (少ない人数[狭い地域]で新しい製品・システム・考えを)試験的に使う[行う], 試す ◇The recycling boxes have been successfully *piloted* in a number of areas. リサイクルボックスは多くの地域での試用に成功している

put sb/sth to the 'test [フレーズ] (人・物事を)試験[吟味]する, 試す ◇His theories have never really been *put to the test*. 彼の理論は実際には一度も試されていない ◇He took her out on the ski slopes to *put* her skills *to the test*. 彼は彼女をスキー場に連れ出して, 彼女の腕前を試した

screen [他, しばしば受身で] (特定の病気[疾患]の検査)をする ◇Men over 55 should be regularly *screened for* prostate cancer. 55歳以上の男性は前立腺がんの検査を受けるほうがいい

2 test・examine・quiz・assess

人の知識[能力]を調べる
【類語訳】テストする, 試験する, 小テストをする, 評価する

文型&コロケーション
- ▶ to test/ examine/ quiz/ assess sb **on** sth
- ▶ to test/ examine sb **in** sth

test [他, 自] テスト[試験]する ◇All students are *tested* in English and mathematics. すべての学生に英語と数学のテストが課せられます ◇We *test* your English before deciding which class to put you in. クラス分けの前にあなたの英語力をテストをします ◇Schools use various methods of *testing*. 学校ではさまざまなテスト方法を用います

examine [他]《フォーマル》(正式[公式]に)試験する ◇The students will be *examined* in all subjects at the end of term. 学生は学期末にすべての教科の試験を受けることになります ◇You are only being *examined* on this semester's work. 今学期に学んだことについて試験するだけです ☞ **examiner** (JUDGE 名)

quiz [-zz-] [他]《米》(学生に短い非公式の)小テストをする ◇You will be *quizzed* on chapter 6 tomorrow. 明日第6章の小テストを受けてもらいます

assess [他] (課題・テスト・実習で学生を)評価する ◇Students will be *assessed* on their use of these skills. 学生たちはこれらの技能の活用について評価を受けることになります ◇The tests are used to *assess* individual students' ability and knowledge. テストは学生の能力と知識を個別に評価するために用いられます ☞ **assess** (JUDGE 動), **assessment** (ASSESSMENT)

thanks 名

thanks・gratitude・appreciation

何かに対してありがたい気持ちを表す言葉, 行動, 感情
【類語訳】感謝(の言葉), 謝意, 感謝の念

文型&コロケーション
- ▶ thanks/ gratitude **for** sth
- ▶ **in/ with** thanks/ gratitude/ appreciation
- ▶ **heartfelt/ sincere** thanks/ gratitude/ appreciation
- ▶ **real/ deep** gratitude/ appreciation
- ▶ to **express/ show/ deserve** thanks/ gratitude/ appreciation
- ▶ to **get/ accept/ earn** sb's thanks/ gratitude
- ▶ to **nod/ smile** your thanks/ appreciation
- ▶ a **word of** thanks/ gratitude/ appreciation
- ▶ a **token of** your thanks/ gratitude/ apreciation

thanks [複数で] 感謝(の言葉), 謝意 ◇*Thanks* are due to all those who worked so hard for so many months. 何か月にもわたってご尽力くださったすべての皆様に御礼を申し上げます ◇She murmured her *thanks*. 彼女は感謝の言葉をぼそぼそと口にした ◇We *gave thanks* to God for all our blessings. 我々は我々へのあらゆる恵みに対して神に感謝の気持ちを捧げた ☞ **thankful** (GRATEFUL)

gratitude [U] 感謝の念, 謝意 ◇She was presented with the gift *in gratitude for* her long service. 彼女の永年勤続に対する感謝の気持ちとして贈り物が授与された ◇I feel a deep sense of *gratitude* to her. 私は彼女に対して深い感謝の念を抱いている [反意] **ingratitude** ❶反意語はingratitudeである。◆She accused him of *ingratitude*. (感謝の気持ちがないと彼女は彼を非難した) ☞ **grateful** (GRATEFUL)

appreciation [U]《ややフォーマル》感謝の念 ◇Please accept this gift *in appreciation of* all you've done for us. 私たちのためにご尽力くださったことに対する感謝の気持ちとして, この贈り物をお受け取りください ☞ **appreciative** (GRATEFUL)

ノート gratitude と appreciation の使い分け：gratitudeは, より一般的に感謝の気持ちを表す語である。appreciationは, 誰かがしてくれた特定の事柄を評価し, それに感

⤴thanks

謝の気持ちを表す語である。×I feel a deep sense of *appreciation* to her.

theft 名

theft・robbery・burglary・raid・break-in・embezzlement・shoplifting・larceny・heist
人[場所]から物を盗む犯罪
【類語訳】窃盗, 盗み, 強盗, 略奪, 住居侵入, 押し込み, 押し込み強盗, 不法侵入, 押し入り, 横領, 着服, 万引き

文型&コロケーション
- ▶ (an) **attempted** theft/ robbery/ burglary/ break-in/ larceny
- ▶ a **bank** robbery/ raid/ heist
- ▶ **grand/ petty** theft/ larceny
- ▶ to **commit** (a) theft/ robbery/ burglary/ larceny
- ▶ to **carry out** a theft/ robbery/ burglary/ raid
- ▶ to **take part in/ foil** a robbery/ burglary/ raid
- ▶ to **report/ investigate** a theft/ robbery/ burglary/ raid/ break-in
- ▶ a theft/ robbery/ burglary/ raid/ break-in **happens/ takes place**

theft [U, C] 窃盗(罪[事件]), 盗み ◇Police are investigating the *theft* of computers from the company's offices. 警察は会社の事務所からコンピューターが盗まれた事件を捜査している ◇There has been a reduction in the number of car *thefts*. 盗難車数は減少してきている ☞ **thief** (THIEF)

robbery [U, C] (暴力[脅迫]による)強盗(罪[事件]), 略奪 ◇He already had a conviction for *armed robbery* (= using a gun, knife, etc.). 彼にはすでに武装強盗の前科があった ◇There has been a spate of *robberies* in the area recently. 最近その地域では多数の強盗事件が起きている ☞ **rob** (ROB), **robber** (THIEF)

ノート **theft**と**robbery**の使い分け：**theft**は盗まれた物を強調する。◆car/computer *theft* (自動車/コンピューターの窃盗)。×car/computer *robbery*。**robbery**は物が盗まれた場所, 特に銀行などの企業を強調し, 暴力が用いられたことを示唆することが多い。◆bank *robbery* (銀行強盗)。◆armed *robbery* (武装強盗)。×bank *theft*。×armed *theft*。

burglary [U, C] 住居侵入窃盗(罪), 押し込み ◇The youth was charged with three counts of *burglary*. その青年は3件の押し込みで起訴された ◇There has been a rise in the number of *burglaries* committed in the area. その地域で起こった押し込みの件数は増加している ❶ burglaryはふつう人の家から物を盗む行為を指す。人の留守[就寝]中に発生し, 脅迫[暴力]を伴わないのがふつうである。☞ **burgle, burglarize** (ROB), **burglar** (THIEF)

raid [C] (犯罪を犯す[物を盗む]目的での建物・場所・乗り物への)襲撃, 押し込み強盗 ◇He had once been involved in a bank *raid*. 彼はかつて銀行強盗に巻き込まれたことがあった ◇She was shot during an armed *raid on* a security van. 警護車に対する武装襲撃の最中に彼女は撃たれた ☞ **raid** (ROB), **raider** (THIEF)

'break-in [C] (物を盗む目的で暴力を用いて建物に侵入する)不法侵入, 押し込み ◇Police were called to three *break-ins* in the same area last night. 警察は昨晩, 同じ地域内で3件の不法侵入の通報を受けた ☞ **break into** sth (ROB)

embezzlement [U] (お金の)横領, 着服 ◇She was found guilty of *embezzlement*. 彼女は横領で有罪判決を受けた ☞ **embezzle** (STEAL)

shoplifting [U] 万引き ◇She was convicted of *shoplifting*. 彼女は万引きで有罪となった ☞ **shoplift** (STEAL), **shoplifter** (THIEF)

larceny [U, C] 《米 or 古風, 英, 法律》(人から物を盗む)窃盗罪；窃盗 ◇The couple were charged with grand/petty *larceny* (= stealing things that are valuable/not very valuable). そのカップルは重[軽]窃盗罪で起訴された

heist [C] 《特に米, インフォーマル》(銀行・店から高価な物を盗む)強盗 ◇It's a tense thriller about a diamond *heist* that goes badly wrong. それは, 失敗に終わるが, ダイヤモンド強盗を描くハラハラドキドキのスリラーだ ◇a *heist* movie 強盗映画

theory 名

1 theory・principle・law・rule・theorem
なぜある物事が起こる[存在する]のかを説明する(一連の)考え
【類語訳】理論, 原理, 法則, 本能, 規則, 定理

文型&コロケーション
- ▶ a theory/ law/ rule/ theorem **about** sth
- ▶ the theory/ principle **behind** sth
- ▶ **in** theory/ principle
- ▶ the theory/ principle/ law/ rule/ theorem **that**...
- ▶ a **basic/ fundamental** theory/ principle/ law/ rule/ theorem
- ▶ a **mathematical** theory/ principle/ law/ rule/ theorem
- ▶ a **scientific** theory/ principle/ law/ rule
- ▶ to **prove** a theory/ principle/ law/ rule/ theorem
- ▶ to **define** a law/ rule
- ▶ to **apply** a theory/ principle
- ▶ a theory/ principle/ law/ rule/ theorem **states that**...

theory [C, U] (正式な)理論；(特定のテーマの)理論, 原理 ◇There are conflicting *theories* as to the very early origins of mankind. 人類のごく初期の起源に関しては, 相対立する考え方がある ◇According to Einstein's *theory of relativity*, nothing can travel faster than light. アインシュタインの相対性理論によれば, 光より速く進めるものはない ◇He wrote a number of books on political *theory*. 彼は政治理論に関する本を数多く執筆した ◇In *theory*, all children get an equal chance at school. 理屈の上では, すべての子どもは学校で平等な機会を得る ☞ **theoretical** (INTELLECTUAL 1)

principle [C, U] 原理；(一般的[科学的]な)原理, 法則 ◇The *principle* behind it is very simple. その背後にある原理は非常に単純です ◇We must get back to *first principles* (= the basic principles of sth). 我々は第一原理に立ち戻らなければならない ◇It is based on the *principle* that heat rises. それは温度が上昇する原理に基づいている ◇A tidal current turbine is similar in *principle* to a windmill. 潮流タービンは原理上, 風車に似ている ☞ **principle** (PRINCIPLE 2)

law [C] (物事が常に同じ形で起こる)法則；(自然の作用を説明する科学的な)法則, 本能 ◇The usual *laws* of supply and demand do not seem to apply in this case. 需要と供給の通常の法則はこのケースには当てはまらないようだ ◇Do you remember anything about Ohm's *Law*? オームの法則について何か覚えていますか ☞ **law** (PRINCIPLE 2)

rule [C] (文法などの)規則 ◇He's a writer who doesn't seem to know the most basic *rules* of English grammar. 彼は英文法の最も基本的な規則を知らないように思える作家だ ☞ **rule** (PRINCIPLE 2)

theorem [C] 《専門語》(数学での証明可能な)定理 ◇Work out the answer using Pythagoras's *Theorem*. ピタゴラスの定理を用いて答えを出してください

2 theory・hypothesis・premise・thesis・proposition
他の考え[提案]の根拠として用いられ, 人によって信じられているがまだ証明されていない考え
【類語訳】説, 仮説, 前提, 命題

▶文型&コロケーション

▶ a theory/ hypothesis/ thesis/ proposition **about** sth
▶ a theory/ hypothesis/ thesis **on** sth
▶ a theory/ hypothesis/ premise/ thesis/ proposition **that**...
▶ to **have** a theory/ hypothesis/ premise/ thesis
▶ to **formulate** a theory/ hypothesis/ thesis
▶ to **support** a theory/ hypothesis/ premise/ thesis/ proposition
▶ to **test** a theory/ hypothesis/ premise/ proposition
▶ to **prove** a theory/ hypothesis/ thesis/ proposition
▶ to be **based on** a theory/ hypothesis/ premise/ thesis/ proposition
▶ a theory/ hypothesis/ premise/ thesis/ proposition **is based on** sth

theory [C, U] (真実であると信じられている)説, 仮説 ◇I have this *theory* that most people prefer being at work to being at home. 私の説ではたいていの人が自宅よりも職場を好む ◇This is all *theory* so far...you'll need to back it up with facts. 今のところこれは仮説にすぎない, あなたはこれを事実で裏付ける必要がある

hypothesis (複 -theses) [C] 《ややフォーマル》(周知の事実に基づく)仮説 ◇His *hypothesis* about what dreams mean provoked a lot of debate. 夢がどんな意味を持つかに関する彼の仮説は多くの論争を巻き起こした ◇This economic model is really a *working hypothesis* (= sth that people are using as if it were true or correct but which may yet be proved wrong). この経済モデルは実際には作業仮説である ☞ **hypothetical** (SUPPOSED)

premise [C] 《フォーマル》(正当な理論のための根拠となる)前提 ◇The basic *premise* of this argument is deeply flawed. この議論の基本前提には大きな欠陥がある ◇The argument rests on a *false premise*. その主張は虚偽の前提に基づいている

thesis (複 **theses**) [C] 《ややフォーマル》(論理的に真実である証拠となる)命題 ◇The basic *thesis* of the book is fairly simple. その本の基本的な命題はかなり単純である ☞ **thesis** (PAPER)

proposition [C] 《フォーマル》(意見・主張の根拠となる)命題 ◇Her argument is based on the *proposition* that power corrupts. 彼女の論は権力は腐敗するという命題に基づいている

thief 名

thief・burglar・robber・pirate・raider・bandit・poacher・looter・pickpocket・highwayman・shoplifter

人[場所]から物を盗む人
【類語訳】泥棒, 盗人, 住居侵入者, 強盗犯, 略奪者, 海賊, 襲撃者, 盗賊, 密漁者, すり, 追いはぎ, 万引き犯

▶文型&コロケーション

▶ a **professional** thief/ burglar/ robber/ poacher/ pickpocket
▶ a **suspected** thief/ burglar/ robber/ poacher/ looter/ shoplifter
▶ a **would-be** thief/ burglar/ robber/ poacher/ looter/ pickpocket/ shoplifter
▶ **armed** robbers/ raiders/ bandits
▶ to **catch** a thief/ burglar/ robber/ poacher/ looter/ pickpocket/ shoplifter
▶ a thief/ burglar/ robber/ pirate/ raider/ looter/ pickpocket/ highwayman/ shoplifter **takes/ steals** sth
▶ a thief/ burglar/ robber/ looter **escapes/ gets away/ makes off** with sth
▶ a thief/ burglar/ robber **strikes** somewhere
▶ thieves/ burglars/ robbers/ pirates/ looters **raid** somewhere
▶ pirates/ raiders/ bandits **attack** sb
▶ a **gang** of thieves/ robbers/ raiders/ looters/ pickpockets/ shoplifters

thief [C] (人・場所から物を盗む)泥棒, 盗人 ◇A car *thief* made off with a top director's BMW last night. 昨晩, 自動車泥棒が代表取締役のBMWを盗んだ ❶*thief* は一般的な語で, この見出し内のあらゆる語の代わりに用いることができる。 ☞ **theft** (THEFT)

burglar [C] (物を盗む目的で不法に建物に侵入する)泥棒, 住居侵入者 ◇*Burglars* broke into the gallery and stole dozens of priceless paintings. 泥棒は画廊に押し入り, 値段を付けられないほど高価な絵画を多数盗んだ ☞ **burglary** (THEFT)

robber [C] (暴力・脅迫を用いて人・場所から物を盗む)強盗(犯), 略奪者 ◇The prison sentence ended his career as a bank *robber*. 銀行強盗としての彼のキャリアは実刑判決で終わった ◇an armed *robber* 武装強盗(犯) ☞ **rob** (ROB), **robbery** (THEFT)

> **ノート** burglar と robber の使い分け: burglar は物を盗む目的でこっそりと建物に侵入し, robber はふつう物を盗む目的で店・銀行などの建物に押し入り, そこにいる人々に対して暴力[脅迫]を用いる。

pirate [C] 海賊 ◇There were reports that a *pirate* ship had come looking for treasure in the cove. 海賊船が入り江の宝を探しにやって来たという報告があった

raider [C] (犯罪を犯す場所が限定される)強盗(犯), 襲撃者 ◇A gang of armed *raiders* held up a bank in the city today. 今日, 武装強盗団の一味がその都市の銀行を襲撃した ☞ **raid** (THEFT), **raid** (ROB)

bandit [C] (旅行者を襲撃する)盗賊 ◇Buses driving through the mountains have been attacked by *bandits*. その山地を通るバスは盗賊に襲われてきた ❶*bandit* はふつう特に貧困国において, 町・市街から遠く離れた地域で襲撃を仕掛ける。

poacher [C] (不法に鳥・動物・魚を狩る[獲る])密漁[猟]者 ◇The measures are designed to protect the fish from *poachers*. その対策は密漁者たちから魚を守るために講じられた

looter [C] (火事・暴動などの後に店・建物から物を盗む)略

↪thief

奪者 ◇*Looters* carried clothes and electrical equipment out of shop windows. 略奪者たちは店の窓から服や電気機器を運び出した ☞ **loot** (ROB)

pickpocket [C] すり ◇Watch out for *pickpockets*, especially at the train station. 特に鉄道の駅ではすりに用心しなさい

highwayman [C] (馬に乗り銃を携えて公道で旅行者から物を略奪する)追いはぎ ◇Lady Sybil's coach was held up by *highwaymen* on the Plymouth road. シビル卿夫人の馬車はプリマスの路上で追いはぎに遭った

shoplifter [C] 万引き犯 ◇*Shoplifters* will be prosecuted. 万引き犯は起訴されます ☞ **shoplifting** (THEFT)

thin [形]

thin・slim・slender・lean・skinny・slight・underweight
人にあまり肉が付いていないことを表す
【類語訳】やせた、細い、やせこけた、ほっそりした、スリムな、すらりとした、体の引き締まった、やせぎすな、きゃしゃな

〔文型&コロケーション〕
▸ a thin/ slim/ slender/ lean/ skinny/ slight **woman/ man/ boy**
▸ a thin/ slim/ slender/ skinny/ slight **girl**
▸ sb's thin/ slim/ slender/ lean/ skinny/ slight **body/ figure**
▸ sb's thin/ slim/ slender/ slight **build**
▸ thin/ slender/ lean/ skinny **arms/ legs/ fingers**
▸ a slim/ slender **waist**
▸ **very** thin/ slim/ slender/ lean/ skinny/ underweight
▸ **quite** thin/ slim/ slender

thin (人・体が)やせた、細い、やせこけた ◇He was tall and *thin*, with dark hair. 彼は黒髪で背が高くやせていた ◇She pinched her *thin* lips together. 彼女は薄い唇を固く結んだ ❶《米》では、thin は slim と同じようによい意味合いの語として用いられることがある.《英》では、人・体がやせすぎている [細すぎである]ことを示唆し、中立的にも悪い意味合いでも用いられる. 反意 **fat** (FAT)

slim 《ほめて》(人・体が魅力的に)ほっそりした、スリムな ◇He put his arms around her *slim* waist. 彼は彼女のほっそりした腰に両腕を回した ◇How do you manage to stay so *slim*? どうしたらそんなにスリムな体型を維持できるの ❶ slim はほとんどの場合、女性や少女に用いられるが、男性や少年に用いられることもある. 反意 **plump** (FAT)

slender 《書き言葉、ほめて》(人・体が魅力的で[優美]に)ほっそりした、すらりとした ◇The dress flattered her *slender* figure. そのドレスは彼女のほっそりした体つきを引き立てた ◇Her long *slender* fingers paused over the keyboard. 彼女のすらりと長い指がキーボードの上で少し止まった ❶ slender はほとんどの場合、女性や少女に用いられる. 男性について用いられる場合、書き手・話し手がその男性が女性的な性質を備えていることを示唆していることが多い.

lean 《書き言葉、ふつうほめて》(人・体が)ほっそりした; 体の引き締まった ◇He had a *lean*, muscular body. 彼はほっそりした筋肉質の体をしていた ◇He's tall, *lean* and handsome 彼は背が高くて、体が引き締まっていて、ハンサムだ ❶ lean はふつう男性(の体)や数種類の動物に用いられる.

skinny 《インフォーマル、ふつうけなして》(人・体が不快に[醜く])やせこけた、やせすぎな、骨と皮ばかりの ◇She had wild hair and long *skinny* arms. 彼女の髪は乱れ、腕は長く、やせこけていた ◇He was such a *skinny* kid. 彼は骨と皮

ばかりの子どもだった 反意 **chubby** (FAT)

slight (人が小さくて)きゃしゃな、やせた ◇He was of *slight* build. 彼の体つきはきゃしゃだった ◇She was smaller and *slighter* than I had imagined. 彼女は想像していたよりも小さくてやせていた ❶ slight はふつう体の部位を表すのには用いられないが、build, figure, physique などの人の全体的な体型を表す語とは用いられることが多い.

underweight [名詞の前はまれ]《しばしばけなして》(人が)標準体重に満たない ◇She's dangerously *underweight*. 彼女は危険なほど体重が不足している ◇She is a few pounds *underweight* for (= in relation to) her height. 彼女は身長の割には標準体重に数ポンド満たない 反意 **overweight** (FAT)

thing [名]

1 thing・object・whole・item・entity・artefact・commodity・thingy
見たり触ったりできるが、生きておらず、名前で呼べないもの
【類語訳】物、物体、完全な物、(完)全体、物品、品物、品目、工芸品、実用品、何とかいう人[物]、あの人

〔文型&コロケーション〕
▸ a **precious/ valuable** thing/ object/ item/ artefact/ commodity
▸ an **expensive** thing/ item/ artefact/ commodity
▸ a **rare** thing/ object/ item/ artefact/ commodity
▸ a **single** thing/ object/ whole/ item/ entity
▸ a **physical** thing/ object/ item/ entity
▸ a **basic** thing/ object/ item/ entity/ commodity
▸ a **separate** thing/ object/ item/ entity
▸ **everyday/ household** objects/ items
▸ a **historical** object/ item/ artefact
▸ to **produce/ manufacture** a thing/ an object/ an item/ an artefact/ a commodity

thing [C] (名前で呼べない)物; (生きていない)物、物体 ◇Can you pass me that *thing* over there? あそこにあるれを取ってもらえますか ◇She's very fond of sweet *things* (= sweet foods). 彼女は甘い物がとても好きだ ◇He's just bought one of those exercise *things*. 彼はあれらの運動器具の一つを買ったばかりだ ◇Turn that *thing* off while I'm talking to you! 私があなたに話しかけている間は あれを止めておいてください ◇Don't treat her like that — she's a person, not a *thing*! そんなふうに彼女を扱わないで—彼女は人だよ、物じゃないよ ◇He's good at making *things* with his hands. 彼は自分の手で物を作るのが得意だ ☞ **stuff** (MATERIAL)

object [C] (生きていない)物、物体 ◇He uses everyday *objects* to teach basic scientific principles to the kids. 彼は身の回り品を使って科学の基本的な法則を子どもたちに教えている ◇Glass and plastic *objects* lined the shelves. ガラス製とプラスチック製の物が棚に並んでいた

〔ノート〕**thing** と **object** の使い分け: thing のほうが object よりもはるかに一般的な語. object はふつう三次元の(平べったくない)かなり硬い物で、すぐには使い切れない物を指す. 紙製の物は object とは言えないかもしれないが、食べ物・飲み物は object ではない. object は特にその物が何であるかを正確に知らない場合に用いられる. ◆This looks a very unusual *object*. What is it exactly? (これは非常に珍しい物のようだ. 正確には何だね) また特に、個別的な語で呼べ

thing

れることのない物を総称して用いられる。◆Furniture and other household *objects* were piled up outside the house. (家具や家庭用品が家の外に山積みされていた)。この用例では、**objects**には照明器具・座布団・掃除機など、**furniture**という語の部類に入らない家庭内で用いられる物が含まれる。

whole [C] (それ自体で)完全な物、(完)全体 ◇Four quarters make a *whole*. 4分の1が4つで完全になる ◇The subjects of the curriculum form a coherent *whole*. カリキュラムの科目がそろって統一性のある全体を形作っている ◇The festival will be great for our city and for the country *as a whole* (= as one thing, not as separate parts or regions). その祭典は我々の都市と国全体にとって素晴らしいものとなるでしょう

item [C] (個別的な)物品、品物、品目 ◇Can I pay for each *item* separately? 品物ごとに別々に支払うことができますか ◇The computer was my largest single *item of expenditure*. そのコンピューターは私にとって単独では最も高価な品目でした ◇This clock is a *collector's item* (= because it is rare and valuable). この時計はマニアにとっての逸品です

entity [C] 《フォーマル》(独立した)存在[実在](物) ◇The unit has become part of a larger department and no longer exists as a separate *entity*. その部署は、より大きな部門の一部となり、もはや独立した存在ではない ◇Each subsidiary of the company will be treated as a single *entity*. その会社の各子会社は個別の存在として扱われることになる

artefact (または特に米で **artifact**) [C] 《専門語》(人が作った歴史[文化]的に重要な)工芸品 ◇The museum has a superb collection of ancient *artefacts* from Nubia. その博物館には古代ヌビアの工芸品の素晴らしいコレクションがある

commodity [C] 《ややフォーマル》(有用な)実用[日用、必需]品 ◇Water is a precious *commodity* that is often taken for granted in the West. 水は西洋では当たり前とされることの多い貴重な必需品である

thingy [C] 《インフォーマル、話し言葉》(名前を知らない[忘れた、挙げたくない]人・物を指して)何とかいう人[物]、あれ、あの人 ◇This new multimedia *thingy* means you can research things a lot more easily. この新しいマルチメディアの何かやつで、物事がずっと簡単に調べられるということだ

2 ☞ EQUIPMENT
things・stuff・property・asset・possession・holding・junk・belongings・goods・valuables
特定の時に所有[携帯]する品
【類語例】持ち物、衣服、衣類、用具、用品、物、荷物、財産、所有物、資産、所持品、所蔵品、株、がらくた、物品、貴重品

文型&コロケーション

▸ **personal** things/ stuff/ property/ assets/ possessions/ holdings/ belongings
▸ **private** property/ assets/ possessions/ holdings/ belongings/ goods
▸ to **collect/ gather/ pack** your things/ stuff/ possessions/ belongings
▸ to **search** sb's/ your/ the things/ stuff/ property/ belongings
▸ to **go through** sb's/ your/ the things/ stuff/ belongings

▸ to **buy** things/ stuff/ property/ assets/ a holding/ goods
▸ to **acquire** things/ stuff/ property/ assets/ possessions/ your holdings/ goods
▸ to **sell** your things/ stuff/ property/ assets/ possessions/ holdings/ belongings/ goods/ valuables

things [複数形] 《特に英、ややインフォーマル》(特定の目的で所有[使用]する)持ち物、衣服、衣類、用具、用品 ◇Shall I help you pack your *things*? 持ち物の荷造りを手伝いましょうか ◇Bring your swimming *things* with you. 水着類は持参してください ◇I'll just clear away the breakfast *things*. 朝食の食器類をちょうど片づけるところです ◇Put your *things* (= coat, etc.) on and let's go. 服を着なさい、それから出かけよう ❶《米》では、**stuff**を用いるほうが一般的であるが、《英》でも《米》でも、**things**は形容詞を伴って、「特定の方法で表すことのできる物すべて」に用いられるが、この用法は比較的フォーマルである。◆She loves all *things* Japanese. (彼女は日本的なものすべてが大好きだ)

stuff [U] 《インフォーマル》(荷物、用具[名前を知らない[名前が重要ではない、指しているものが明らかである]ときに用いられる) ◇Where's all my *stuff*? 私の全部の荷物はどこ ◇They sell stationery *and stuff (like that)*. そこでは文房具などが売られている ◇Could you move all that *stuff* off the table? (けなして)そこにある物全部をテーブルからどかしていただけますか ❶**stuff**は物質や材料を表すこともある。☞ **stuff** (MATERIAL)

property [U] 《ややフォーマル》財産、所有物 ◇This building is government *property*. この建物は国有財産である ◇Be careful not to damage other people's *property*. 他人の所有物を傷つけないよう気をつけなさい ◇The youths were convicted of defacing *public property*. 若者たちは公共の財産の外観を損なったとして有罪判決を受けた ◇I rang the *lost property* office at the station to see if my bag had been handed in. 《英》私は自分のかばんが届いているか確認するために、駅の遺失物取扱所に電話をかけた ❶《米》では遺失物取扱所は lost and found と呼ばれる。

asset [C、ふつう複数形で] 《特にビジネス》(人・会社の負債返済用の)資産、財産 ◇Her *assets* include shares in the company and a house in France. 彼女の資産には会社の株やフランスの邸宅が含まれています ◇What is the *net asset value* of the company? その会社の純資産価値はどのくらいですか ◇financial/capital *assets* 金融/固定資産 ◇income from *fixed asset* investments 固定資産投資からの収入 [反意] **liability** (DEBT)

possession [C、ふつう複数形で] (持ち運びできる)所有物、所持品 ◇The ring is one of her most *treasured/prized possessions*. その指輪は彼女の最も貴重な所有物の一つです ◇Prisoners were allowed no personal *possessions*. 囚人には個人的な所持品は認められなかった ☞ **possess** (HAVE 1)

holding [C] 《フォーマル or ビジネス》(人・美術館・図書館などが所有する)所有財産、所蔵品；(人が所有ある会社の)株 ◇one of the most important private *holdings* of Indian art インドの芸術作品の中で最も重要な個人所有財産の一つ ◇She has a 40% *holding* in the company. 彼女はその会社の40%の株を所有している

junk [U] がらくた ◇I've cleared out all that old *junk* from the attic. 私は屋根裏部屋から古いがらくたをすべて処分した ◇This china came from a *junk shop*. この磁器はがらくた屋で手に入れたものだ ◇Is this all your *junk* (= are these all your things)? 《インフォーマル、けなして》これ全部君のがらくたかい ☞ **WASTE**

belongings [複数で] (《携帯できる[持ち運びできる]》所持品) ◇She packed her few *belongings* in a bag and left. 彼女はかばんに少しの所持品を詰め込んで出て行った ◇Please make sure you have all your *belongings* with you when leaving the plane. 飛行機を降りる際にご自分の所持品をすべてお持ちかご確認ください

goods [複数で] 《特に書き言葉 or 法律》(持ち運びできる)財産, 所有物, 物品 ◇He was found guilty of ***handling stolen goods***. 彼は盗品を扱ったかどで有罪となった ◇The plastic bag contained ***all her worldly goods*** (= everything she owned). そのビニール袋には彼女の全財産が入っていた

valuables [複数で] (宝石類・カメラなどの)貴重品 ◇Never leave cash or other *valuables* lying around. 現金やその他の貴重品を絶対に出しっぱなしにしておかないように

think 動 ☞REGARD

think・believe・feel・hold・reckon・make sth of sb/sth・be under the impression
物事が真実である[ありうる]との考えを持つ, 人や物事に関して特定の考えを持つ
【類語訳】思う, 考える, 感じる, 意見を持つ, 理解する, 判断する, 思い込んでいる

［文型&コロケーション］
▶ to think/ believe/ feel/ hold/ reckon/ be under the impression that...
▶ It is thought/ believed/ reckoned that...
▶ to be thought/ believed/ felt/ held/ reckoned to be sth
▶ to think/ believe/ feel/ make sth of sb/ sth
▶ to think/ believe/ feel sth about sb/ sth
▶ to sincerely/ honestly think/ believe/ feel/ hold
▶ to personally think/ believe/ feel/ reckon
▶ to really/ seriously/ mistakenly think/ believe/ feel
▶ to firmly believe/ hold/ be under the impression

think [他] 《進行形なし》(物事が真実であると)思う; (人・物事に関して)考える ◇Do you *think* (that) they'll come? 彼らは来ると思うかい ◇I didn't *think* you liked sports. 君がスポーツ好きだとは思わなかった ◇I *think* this is their house, but I'm not sure. これが彼らの家だと思うけど, 確かじゃない ◇We'll need about 20 chairs, ***I should think***. 20脚くらい椅子が必要になるのではないでしょうか ◇It was once *thought* that the sun travelled around the earth. かつて太陽は地球の周りを回っていると考えられていた ◇What did you *think* about the idea? その考えについてどう思いましたか ◇Well, I like it. What do you *think*? まあ, 僕は好きだね. 君はどう思う ◇'Will we make it in time?' '*I think so*.' 「間に合うかな」「間に合うと思うよ」 ◇'Is he any good?' 'I ***don't think so***.' 「彼は役に立つかな」「立たないと思うよ」

believe [他] 《進行形なし》(物事を)思う, 考える ◇Police *believe* (that) the man may be armed. その男は武装しているかもしれないと警察は考えている ◇It is *believed* that the couple have left the country. その男女は国を出たと思われている ◇The paintings are *believed* to be worth over $20,000 each. その絵画はそれぞれ2万ドル以上の価値があると思うよ ◇'Where does she come from?' 'Spain, I *believe*.' 「彼女はどこの出身だい」「スペインだと思うわ」 ◇Does he still work there?' 'I *be-lieve so/not*.' 「彼はまだそこで働いてるの」「そう/違うと思う

よ」◇She *believes* that killing animals for food or fur is completely immoral. 食糧や毛皮のために動物を殺すのはまったく倫理に反すると彼女は考えている ☞ **belief** (VIEW 1)

|ノート| think と believe の使い分け: 物事が真実である[ありうる]と自分[他人]が考える場合, believe は think よりもフォーマルで, 特に他人が抱いている考えについて用いられる. think は自分の考えについて用いられることが多い. ◆Police *believe*... (警察は…と考えている). ◆I *think*... (私は…と思う). I *believe*... という場合, 他の人から信じさせられた上での考えであり, 情報が間違っていると責任を負わないことを示唆することがある. 意見を表明する場合, believe は think よりも意味が強く, 特に主義の問題について用いられる. think は実際的な[個人的好みの]問題について用いられることが多い. ◆I *believe* that we have a responsibility towards the less fortunate in society. (我々は社会であまり幸運でない人に対して責任があると思います). ◆I *think* we should reserve seats in advance. (私たちは前もって席を予約すべきだと思う). ◆I don't *think* he's funny at all. (彼が面白いとはまったく思わない).

feel [他, 自] 《進行形なし》(起こった物事[自分・他人がすべきこと]に関して)感じる, 思う, 考える ◇We all *felt* (that) we were unlucky to lose. 私たちは皆, 負けたのは運が悪かったと思った ◇I *felt* (that) I had to apologize. 私は謝らなければならないと感じた ◇She *felt* it to be her duty to tell the police. 彼女は警察に話すことが自分の義務だと考えた ◇I *felt* it advisable to do nothing. 何もしないのが賢明だと思った ◇This decision is, *I feel*, a huge mistake. この決定は大きな誤りだと思う ◇This is something I *feel* strongly about. これは私が強く感じていることです ☞ **feeling** (VIEW 1)

hold [他] 《進行形なし》《ややフォーマル》(人・物事に関する)意見[信条]を持つ; (物事が真実であると)思う, 考える ◇She *holds* strange views on education. 彼女は教育に関し一風変わった意見を持っている ◇He has very firmly-*held* religious beliefs. 彼は宗教的信条を固持している ◇She is ***held in high regard*** by her students (= they have a high opinion of her). 彼女は学生たちから敬意を払われている ◇Parents will be ***held responsible*** (= will be considered to be responsible) for their children's behaviour. 両親は自分の子どもたちの行動に責任を問われます

reckon [他, 自] 《特に英, インフォーマル, 特に話し言葉》(真実である[ありうる]と)思う, 考える ◇I *reckon* (that) I'm going to get that job. その仕事に就くことになると思います ◇He'll be famous one day. ***What do you reckon*** (= Do you agree)? 彼はいつか有名になるでしょう. あなたはどう思いますか ◇It's worth a lot of money, I *reckon*. それは大金に見合う価値があると思うよ ◇They'll never find out.' '*You reckon*?' (= I think you may be wrong about that.) 「彼らには解明できないだろう」「そう思ってるのかい」❶ reckon は受動態で It is reckoned that... の句で用いられる. ◆*It* is generally *reckoned that* about half of all job vacancies are never advertised publicly. (仕事の欠員の半分くらいは絶対に公表されないと一般的には思われている). この受動態での用法は, I reckon... ほどインフォーマルではなく, 書き言葉で用いられるが, それでもなおややインフォーマルであると言える. ☞ **reckon** (REGARD)

'make sth of sb/sth 句動詞 《ふつう否定的な文と疑問文で》(人・物事の意味・性質を)理解する; (人・物事に関して)意見を持つ, 判断する ◇I can't *make* anything *of* this

note from Petra. 私にはペトラからのこのメモがまったく理解できない ◇I don't know **what to make of** the new manager. 新しい経営者をどう判断すべきかわからない
be ,under the im'pression that... 〔仔his〕（物事が真実であると）思い［信じ］込んでいる ◇I *was under the impression that* the work had already been completed (= but I have just learnt that it had not). 私は仕事はもう完了しているものと思い込んでいた

threat 〔名〕

threat・risk・danger・hazard・menace
危険となる［問題をもたらす］可能性のある人や物事を表す
【類語訳】脅威となる人，脅威となる物事，危険な人，危険な物事，危険分子，危険要因［因子］

〔文型&コロケーション〕
▶ a threat/ risk/ danger/ hazard/ menace **to** sb/ sth
▶ a **great/ serious** threat/ risk/ danger/ hazard/ menace
▶ a **major/ possible** threat/ risk/ danger/ hazard
▶ the **main** threat/ risk/ danger/ hazard
▶ a **potential** threat/ risk/ danger/ hazard/ menace
▶ to **pose** a threat/ risk/ danger/ hazard/ menace
▶ a threat/ risk/ danger/ hazard to **health**
▶ a threat/ risk/ danger to **the public**
▶ a threat/ danger/ menace to **society**

threat [C, ふつう単数で] （損害・危険・問題をもたらす可能性の）脅威となる人［物事］ ◇Drug abuse poses a major *threat* to the fabric of our society. 薬物の乱用は我々の社会組織にとって重大な脅威となる ◇He could be a real *threat* to the Spanish player in the final. 彼は決勝でスペインの選手にとって本当に脅威となるでしょう ☞ **threat** (RISK 1)
risk [C] （問題・危険をもたらす可能性のある）危険な人［物事］，危険分子 ◇The group was considered to be a *risk* to national security. その集団は国の安全保障にとって危険分子と見なされていた ◇Tuberculosis threatens to become a major health *risk* worldwide. 結核は世界的に健康被害をもたらす主要な病気となる恐れがある ☞ **risk** (RISK 1)
danger [C] （危険をもたらす可能性のある）危険な人［物事］，危険要因［因子］ ◇Smoking is a serious *danger* to health. 喫煙は健康にとって深刻な危険要因である ◇There are many hidden *dangers* for small children in the home. 家庭には小さな子どもにとって多くの危険因子が潜んでいる ☞ **danger** (RISK 1), **dangerous** (DANGEROUS)
hazard （損害をもたらす可能性のある）危険な物事，危険因［因子］ ◇Avoid foam-filled sofas — they are a serious fire *hazard*. 発泡材を詰め込んだソファは避けなさい—火災の重大要因ですから ◇Getting injured is an occupational *hazard* for athletes (= a hazard caused by their job). 負傷はスポーツ選手にとって職業上の危険である ☞ **hazardous** (DANGEROUS)

〔ノート〕**threat, risk, danger, hazard** の使い分け：
threat はふつう起こりうることであり，risk, danger, hazard は考えられなくもないことである。threat は **a threat to sth** という句で用いられることが多い。threat 自体は，重大である(a major threat to the fabric of society)場合も，さほど重大でない(a real threat to the Spanish player)場合もある。
hazard は特に人の健康・安全にとっての身体的危険の可能性を意味し，その危害をもたらすのは人でなく物事である。danger は身体［道徳］的危険の可能性（すなわち健康・社会にとっての危険）を指し，その危害をもたらすのは物事および人である。risk は特に複合語で，hazardと同じように用いられることが多い。a health/fire/safety risk (健康被害をもたらす可能性/火災をもたらす危険/安全を脅かす危険)。しかし risk には，risk to national/personal security (国家安全保障/個人の安全を脅かす危険) や security risk (危険人物) など幅広い用法があり，人・集団・物事・活動に対して用いられる。

menace [C, ふつう単数で] （（危害・損害をもたらす可能性のある））脅威となる人［物事］ ◇The government's new initiative is aimed at beating the *menace* of illegal drugs. 政府の新戦略は違法薬物の脅威に打ち勝つことを目指している ◇The protesters remain a potential *menace* to the stability of the government. その抗議団体は政治の安定にとって潜在的な脅威であり続ける

threaten 〔動〕

threaten・endanger・risk・jeopardize
人や物事に対して危険要因となることを表す
【類語訳】脅かす，脅威を与える，危険にさらす，危うくする，懸ける，賭ける

〔文型&コロケーション〕
▶ to threaten/ endanger/ risk sb's/ your **life/ health**
▶ to threaten/ risk/ jeopardize sb's/ your **job/ career**
▶ to threaten/ endanger/ jeopardize the **survival** of sth
▶ a **threatened/ endangered species**
▶ to **seriously** threaten/ endanger/ jeopardize sth

threaten [他] （人・物事を［に］）脅かす，脅威を与える ◇She claimed that the conflict was *threatening* stability in the region. 彼女は紛争がその地域の安定を脅かしていると主張した ◇Many species are now *threatened with* extinction. 現在，多くの種が絶滅の危機にさらされている ◇Our marriage was constantly *threatened* by his other women. 私たちの結婚生活は常に彼の不倫相手たちから脅かされていた ☞ **threat** (RISK 1)
endanger [他] （人・物事を）危険［危機］にさらす，危うくする ◇The health of our children is being *endangered* by exhaust fumes. 私たちの子どもの健康は排ガスによって危険にさらされている ◇That one mistake seriously *endangered* the future of the company. その一つのミスが会社の将来をひどく危ういものにした ◇The sea turtle is an *endangered* species (= it may soon no longer exist). そのウミガメは絶滅危惧種である ☞ **endangered** (VULNERABLE)
risk [他] （貴重［重要］な物事を）危険にさらす，懸［賭］ける ◇He *risked* all his money on a game of cards. 彼は有り金全部をカードゲームに賭けた ◇She has been willing to *risk life and limb* (= risk being killed or injured) to get a good close-up shot of the nesting birds. 巣作りをする鳥の素晴らしいクローズアップ写真を撮るためなら，彼女は命を懸けることなどいとわない ◇He had no desire to *risk his neck* (= risk being killed, especially by being executed) for the king and his favourites. 王やその寵臣たちのために命を懸ける気など彼には毛頭なかった
❶risk はふつう life, health, money, job, career (生命，健康，金，仕事，経歴) など自分自身の物事を懸［賭］けて他の物事を手に入れようとする場合に用いられる。しかしながら，その

選択は時にそれほどじっくりと考え抜かれたものではないことがある。◆In ignoring the warnings, she was *risking* her own and her children's health. (彼女は警告を無視して自分と子どもの健康を危険にさらしていた) ▪ *risk* は人の手の及ばない物事については用いられない。×The health of our children is being *risked* by exhaust fumes.

jeopardize [英でまた **-ise**] [他] [書き言葉] (人の将来を) 危険にさらす, 危うくする ◇She would never do anything to *jeopardize* her career. 彼女は自分の経歴を危うくするようなことは決してしないだろう ◇This scandal could seriously *jeopardize* his chances of being re-elected. このスキャンダルで彼の再選のチャンスは非常に危うくなるかもしれない

throw 動

throw・toss・hurl・fling・chuck・lob・bowl・pitch
手で空中に物を放つ
【類語訳】投げる, 放り投げる, 投げつける, 投げ上げる, 投球する

[文型&コロケーション]
▶ to throw/ toss/ hurl/ fling/ chuck/ lob/ bowl/ pitch sth **at/ to** sb/ sth
▶ to throw/ toss/ fling/ chuck sth **aside/ away**
▶ to throw/ toss/ hurl/ fling/ chuck/ lob/ bowl/ pitch a **ball**
▶ to throw/ toss/ hurl/ fling/ chuck **stones/ rocks/ a brick**
▶ to throw/ toss/ fling/ chuck sb a **towel**
▶ to throw/ toss/ hurl/ fling sth **angrily**
▶ to throw/ toss sth **casually/ carelessly**

throw [他, 自] (片手・両手で空中に物を)投げる ◇Some kids were *throwing* things at the window. 窓に物を投げている子どもたちもいた ◇The body had been *thrown* into the river. その死体は川に投げ込まれていた ◇Can you *throw* me that towel? そのタオルを投げてもらえますか ◇They had a competition to see who could *throw* the furthest. 誰が一番遠くに投げられるかを見るための競技会が開かれた
▶ **throw** [C] ◇a well-aimed *throw* 十分に狙いをつけた投球[発射] ◇It's your *throw* (= it's your turn to throw the dice). 君が投げる番さ

toss [他] (物を軽く[無造作に])放り投げる ◇I got up, *tossing* aside my book. 本をわきへ放り投げて私は起きあがった ◇He *tossed* the ball to Anna. 彼はボールをアンナに放り投げた ◇He *tossed* Anna the ball. 彼はアンナにボールを放り投げた

hurl [他] (特定の方向に物を乱暴に)投げつける ◇Rioters *hurled* a brick through the car's windshield. 暴徒たちはれんがを投げつけて車のフロントガラスを割った

fling [他] (怒って[急いで][人・物を力いっぱい])放り投げる ◇He *flung* her to the ground. 彼は彼女を地面に放り出した ◇I *flung* a few clothes into a bag. 服を数着かばんに放り込んだ

chuck [他] 《特に英, インフォーマル》(物を無造作に)投げる ◇*Chuck* me that newspaper, can you? その新聞を私に投げてもらえる

lob (**-bb-**) [他] 《インフォーマル》(空中高く物を)投げ[放り]上げる ◇They were *lobbing* stones over the wall. 彼らは壁越しに石を投げ上げていた

bowl [自, 他] (クリケットで打者に対して)投球する, (球)を投げる ◇It was Peter's turn to *bowl*. ピーターが投球する番だった ◇He *bowled* him a gentle first ball. 彼は彼に向

けてゆるやかに第一球を投げた

pitch [自, 他] (野球で打者に対して)投球する, (球)を投げる ◇He *pitched* against UCLA last week. 彼は先週UCLA戦に登板した ◇The pitcher *pitched* the ball right down the middle of the plate. ピッチャーはホームベースのど真ん中にボールを投げた

tidy 動

tidy・clean (sth) up・clear (sth) up・sort sth out
いろいろな物を本来あるべき所に置き, ごみやほこりを取り除いてきれいに見せることを表す
【類語訳】整頓する, 片づける, 清掃する, 整理する, 整える

[文型&コロケーション]
▶ to tidy up/ clean up/ clear up **after** sb
▶ to tidy/ clear up/ sort out a **house/ room**
▶ to tidy/ sort out a **cupboard/ your desk**
▶ to tidy up/ clean up/ clear up the **mess**

tidy [他, 自] (特に英) (元どおりに)整頓する, 片づける ◇She wanted to *tidy* herself up before the appointment (= comb her hair, etc.). 彼女は面会の約束前に身だしなみを整えたいと思った ◇She was always cleaning and *tidying*. 彼女はいつも掃除と整頓に明け暮れていた ◇When you use the kitchen please *tidy up* after yourself. 台所を使ったら自分で後片づけをしてね ☞ **tidy** (NEAT), **freshen up** (WASH)

ˌclean ˈup, ˌclean sth ˈup [句動詞] (場所などを)清掃する ◇He always expected other people to *clean up* after him (= when he had made the place dirty or untidy). 自分が汚したあとは他の人が清掃してくれるものとばかり彼は思っていた ◇Who's going to *clean up* this mess? 誰がこの散らかりをきれいにするのですか ◇to *clean up* beaches after an oil spillage 原油流出のあとの砂浜を清掃する ☞ **clean** (CLEAN 動)
▶ˈclean-up [名] [ふつう単数で] ◇a massive *clean-up* operation 大規模掃討作戦 ◇the *clean-up* of the river その川の清掃

ˌclear ˈup, ˌclear sth ˈup [句動詞] (ごみを捨てて元どおりに)片づける, 整頓する ◇Start *clearing up* now. 今から片づけに入りなさい ◇Let him *clear up* his own mess! 自分が散らかした跡は彼に片づけさせなさい ◇They were still *clearing up* the debris after the accident. 彼らは事故の残骸をいまだに片づけていた

ˌsort sth ˈout, ˈsort through sth [句動詞] 《インフォーマル》(中にある物を)整理する, 整える ◇We'll need to *sort out* the contents of the house. 私たちは家の中を整理する必要があるだろう ◇He was *sorting through* his desk and throwing away old papers. 彼は机の中を整理し, 昔の書類を投げ捨てているところだった

tight 形

tight・firm・stiff・taut
物がある位置に強く固定されている[可能な限り引き伸ばされている]ことを表す
【類語訳】しっかりした, 堅い, ぴんと張った

firm　　　　　tight　　　　　taut
　　　　　　　stiff

tighten, time

> 文型&コロケーション
> ▶a tight/ firm **grip**/ **hold**
> ▶a **rope**/ **wire** is tight/ taut

tight （強く固定されて）しっかりした ;（動かす［ほどく, 外す］のが難しくて）堅い ;（最大限に引き伸ばされて）ぴんと張った ◇He kept a *tight* grip on her arm. 彼は彼女の腕をしっかりつかんでいた ◇She twisted her hair into a *tight* knot. 彼女は髪を編んで堅く結んだ ◇The screw was so *tight* that it wouldn't move. スクリューはとても堅くて動きそうになかった ◇The rope was stretched *tight*. ロープがぴんと張られていた 反意 **loose** ❶loose は物がしっかりと固定されていないことを表す. ◆ a *loose* button/tooth （外れそうなボタン/ぐらぐらの歯）. ◆ Check that the plug has not *come loose*.（栓が緩んでいないか調べて）.
▶**tight** 副 ◇Hold *tight*! しっかり持て ◇His fists were clenched *tight*. 彼の両拳は堅く握り締められていた
▶**tightly** 副 ◇Her eyes were *tightly* closed. 彼女の両目はしっかりと閉じられていた ◇He held on *tightly* to her arm. 彼は彼女の腕をしっかりつかんでいた

firm （しばしばほめて）（人の手の動きが）しっかりした, 堅い ◇His handshake was cool and *firm*. 彼は落ち着いてしっかりと握手した ◆ Close the hatches with a *firm* push on the lever. レバーをしっかり押してハッチを閉めて ☞ **firm** (FIRM), firm (SOLID)
▶**firmly** 副 ◇He held her *firmly* but gently. 彼は彼女をしっかりと, だが優しく抱いた

stiff （しばしばけなして）（動かすのが難しくて）堅い ◇The windows were *stiff* and she couldn't get them open. 窓は堅くて彼女には開けることができなかった ❶この意味では *stiff* は窓・ドア・ふた・人の膝［脚］など, 開く［曲がる］はずのものについて用いられる. ☞ **stiff** (SOLID)

taut ぴんと張った ◇Keep the rope *taut*. ロープをぴんと張っておきなさい 反意 **slack** ❶slack は物がぴんと張っていないことを表す. ◆ The rope suddenly went *slack*.（ロープが突然緩んだ）.

tighten 動

tighten・clench・tense・grit your teeth・screw your eyes/face up
物を（さらに）堅くする
【類語訳】しっかり締まる［締める］, 堅く締まる［締める］, 握り締める, 食いしばる, 緊張させる, 緊張する, 歯を食いしばる

> 文型&コロケーション
> ▶to tighten/ clench/ tense/ grit your teeth/ screw your eyes up **with**/ **in** pain, irritation, etc.
> ▶to tighten/ clench your **hand**/ **fist**/ **jaw**
> ▶to tighten/ tense your **muscles**
> ▶to clench/ grit your **teeth**
> ▶your **jaw**/ **hand** tightens/ clenches/ tenses
> ▶your **fist**/ **stomach** tightens/ clenches
> ▶your **muscles** tighten/ tense
> ▶to tighten/ clench/ tense (sth) **involuntarily**
> ▶to clench/ grit your teeth/ screw your eyes up **tight**/ **tightly**

tighten ［自, 他］（物が）しっかり締まる ;（物を）しっかり［堅く］締める ◇His mouth *tightened* into a thin line. 彼の口は真一文字にきゅっと結ばれていた ◇This tool is for *tightening* screws. この工具はねじを締めるためのものです ◇She *tightened* her grip on his arm. 彼女は彼の腕をしっかりつかんだ ◇The brake cable needs *tightening up*. ブレーキケーブルはしっかり締めておく必要がある 反意 **relax, loosen, slacken**

clench ［他, 自］（怒り・決意・動揺で両手・歯・腹筋を［が］）握り締める, 食いしばる, 堅く引き締める ;（握り締められる, 堅く引き締まる ◇He *clenched* his fists in anger. 彼は怒って拳を握り締めた ◇Through *clenched* teeth she told him to leave. 彼女は歯を食いしばって, 彼に出て行くように言った ◇His fists *clenched* slowly until his knuckles were white. 彼はゆっくり拳を握り締めてついに指関節が白くなった

tense ［自, 他］（筋肉を）緊張させる ;（筋肉が）緊張する ◇She *tensed*, hearing the strange noise again. 妙な音を再び耳にして, 彼女は緊張した ◇He *tensed himself*, listening to see if anyone had followed him. 彼は緊張して, 誰かが後をつけているかどうか確かめようと耳を澄ました ◇Expecting a blow, she *tensed* every muscle in her body. 殴られるのかと思って, 彼女は体中の筋肉が緊張した 反意 **relax**, ☞ **tense** (TENSE)

grit your 'teeth 行止 -tt- 歯を食いしばる ;（困難[不快]な状況で物事をやり続けようと）意を決する ◇She *gritted her teeth* against the pain. 彼女は歯を食いしばって痛みに耐えた ◇It started to rain harder, but we *gritted our teeth* and carried on. 雨が激しくなったが我々は意を決して続行した

> ノート grit your teeth と clench your teeth の使い分け: grit your teeth は特に決意を表す場合に用いられる. clench your teeth は怒って［痛くて］叫ぶなど声を立てるのを避けるために, また, 寒くて［怖くて］歯がガチガチ鳴るのを防ぐために, 口をしっかり閉じておく場合に用いられることが多い.

,screw your 'eyes/'face up 行止 （苦痛などに）目を細める, 顔をしかめる[ゆがめる] ◇He took a sip of the medicine and *screwed up his face*. 彼は薬を一口飲んで顔をゆがめた

time 名

time・moment・point・occasion・hour・date・instant
特に何かが起きる, または何かの発展段階が到達する時間軸上の一点を表す
【類語訳】時刻, 時点, 瞬間, 時, 機会, 時間, 時限, 日付, 刹那

> 文型&コロケーション
> ▶a time/ a moment/ the point/ sb's hour **of** sth
> ▶**at** the time/ the moment/ that point/ that instant
> ▶**on** that occasion/ date
> ▶**from**/ **until** that time/ moment/ point/ date
> ▶**for** the time/ moment/ occasion
> ▶at/ on **(any) given**/ **one** time/ moment/ point/ occasion/ instant
> ▶the **very**/ **precise** time/ moment/ hour/ instant
> ▶a/ an **memorable**/ **emotional** time/ moment/ occasion
> ▶to **choose**/ **pick** a/ your time/ moment
> ▶the time/ moment/ hour **comes**/ **arrives**

time [U, C] 時刻, 時点 ◇What *time* do you finish work? 何時に仕事を終えますか ◇It's *time for* lunch. 昼食の時間です ◇I think it's *time to* go to bed. 寝る時間だと思うよ ◇It's *time* the kids were in bed. 子どもたちが

は寝ているはずの時間だ ◇**By the time** you get there the meeting will be over. 君がそこに着く頃には会議は終わっているだろう ◇You'll feel differently about it **when the time comes** (= when it happens). その時になれば思いも違っているでしょう ◇The train arrived right **on time** (= at exactly the correct time). 列車はまさに定刻に到着した ◇A computer screen shows arrival and departure *times*. コンピューター画面に発着時刻が表示されている ◇I want to fix a *time* for a meeting next month. 来月の会議の時間を決めたい ◇Have I called at a bad *time*? 都合の悪い時に電話を差し上げましたか ◇**Every time** I hear that song I feel happy. その歌を聞くたびに幸せになる ◇**Next time** you're here let's have lunch together. 今度お見えのときは昼食をご一緒しましょう ◇He failed the test three *times*. 彼は試験に三度落第した ◇He's determined to pass **this time**. 彼は今度こそ合格するつもりでいる ◇When was the **last time** you saw her? 彼女を最後に見かけたのはいつでしたか ◇I remember **one time** (= once) we had to abandon our car in the snow. 《米》私はかつて雪に埋もれて車を置き去りにせざるをえなかった記憶がある

moment [単数で] 瞬間, たった今 ◇We're busy **at the moment** (= now). ただ今私たちは手が離せないのですが ◇**At that very moment**, the phone rang. まさにその瞬間に電話が鳴った ◇I agreed **in a moment** of weakness. ふと弱気になって同意した ◇From that *moment* on, she never felt really well again. その時を境に彼女は二度と体調が戻ることはなかった ❶ *moment* は, ある特定の気持ちを抱いている時, または特定のことをするのによい時か悪い時を表すこともある. ◆That was one of the happiest *moments* of my life. (それは私の人生で最も幸せな瞬間の一つだった。) ◆Have I caught you at a bad *moment*? (今はご都合が悪かったでしょうか? (販売員が自分の押しつけがましさを和らげるための前置き))

point [C] (進展の中の)時点, 段階 ◇The climber was **at the point of** death when they found him. その登山者は発見時には息を引き取る間際だった ◇We were **on the point of** giving up. 我々はまさに断念しようとしていたところだった ◇Many people suffer from mental illness **at some point** in their lives. 人生のある時期で精神疾患を患う人は多い ◇We had reached the *point* when there was no money left. 私たちはお金がもう残っていないという段階に達してしまっていた ◇**At this point in time** (= Now) we just have to wait. この時点では我々はただ待つしかない ❶ *point* は, 出来事や過程における特定の時点や段階を意味する多くの複合語の一部を成す. ◆the high *point*/low *point* of the trip (旅の最高の時期/最悪の時期). ◆to reach boiling/freezing/melting/saturation *point* (沸点/氷点/融点/飽和点に達する). ◆This could be the sticking *point* in the negotiations. (ここが交渉の行き詰まりかもしれない)。

occasion [C] (何かが起きる)時, 場合, 機会 ◇They have been seen together on two separate *occasions*. 彼らは二度別々の機会に一緒にいるところを目撃されている ◇He used the *occasion* to announce further tax cuts. 彼はその機会を利用してさらなる減税を発表した ◇He has even been known to go shopping himself **on occasion** (= only a few times). 彼はたまに自ら買い物に行くとまで知られている ☞ **occasion** (OPPORTUNITY)

hour [単数で] (特定の)時間, 時期 ◇You can't turn him away **at this hour of the night**. 夜のこんな時に彼を追い返すわけにはいかないでしょう ◇She thought her **last**

hour had come. 彼女は自分の臨終の時が来たのだと思った ◇Don't desert me in my **hour of need**. 助けが必要なときに私を見捨てないで

date [単数で, U] (一般に)日, 年代 ◇The details can be added at a later *date*. 詳細は後日付け加えればいい ◇The coins are all of late Roman *date*. その硬貨はすべてローマ時代後期のものだ

instant [単数で] 瞬間, 刹那 ◇**At that (very)** *instant*, the door opened. まさにその瞬間にドアが開いた ◇I recognized her **the instant (that)** (= as soon as) I saw her. 私は見たとたんに彼女であることがわかった ◇Come here **this instant** (= immediately)! 今すぐここに来なさい

timely 形 ☞ PROMISING

timely・lucky・happy・fortunate
物事が適切な時に起こることを表す語
【類語訳】時を得た, 適時の, 折よい, 運のよい, 幸運な

[文型&コロケーション]
▶to be timely/ lucky/ fortunate **for** sb/ sth
▶to be timely/ lucky/ fortunate **that**...
▶a lucky/ happy/ fortunate **coincidence/ chance**
▶in a happy/ fortunate **position**
▶a lucky/ fortunate **escape**
▶**very** timely/ lucky/ happy/ fortunate
▶**extremely/ particularly** timely/ lucky/ fortunate

timely [ふつう名詞の前で] 時を得た, 適時の, 折よい ◇A nasty incident was prevented by the *timely* arrival of the police. 折よく警察が到着して不快な事件は防がれた ◇This has been a *timely* **reminder** to us all. これは私たち皆にとって折よい合図であった

lucky 運のよい, 幸運な ◇It was *lucky* for us that he didn't see us. 運よく私たちは彼に見られなかった ◇That was the *luckiest* escape of my life. それは私の生涯からの願ってもない逃避であった ◇I didn't know he was there — it was just a *lucky* **guess**. 彼がそこにいるなんて知らなかった—単にまぐれ当たりだったんだ 反意 **unlucky** (UNFORTUNATE 1), ☞ **luck** (LUCK)

▶**luckily** 副 ◇We were late, but *luckily* for us that plane had been delayed. 私たちは遅れて着いたが, 運よく飛行機は遅れて出発していた

happy [名詞の前で] (折よく[望みどおりに, 偶然に]起こって)運のよい, 幸運な ◇**By a happy coincidence**, John was in London at that time too. 運よく偶然の一致でジョンもそのときロンドンにいた ◇He is now in the *happy* **position** of never having to worry about money. 彼は現在, 金の心配のいらない幸運な地位にいる

fortunate (ややフォーマル) (利益・機会を得て)運のよい, 幸運な ◇It was *fortunate* for us that the guard was looking the other way. 警備員が向こうを見ていたなんて, 私たちは運がよかった ◇He was in a relatively *fortunate* **position** as far as work was concerned. 彼は仕事に関する限り, かなり幸運な立場にいた 反意 **unfortunate** (UNFORTUNATE 2), ☞ **fortune** (LUCK)

▶**fortunately** 副 ◇I was late, but *fortunately* the meeting hadn't started. 私は遅刻したが, 運よく会議は始まっていなかった

tired 形

tired・exhausted・drained・weary・sleepy・drowsy・worn out・shattered・pooped・fatigued

人が眠る[休む]必要のある状態を表す
【類語訳】疲れた, 疲れ果てた, へとへとになった, 疲労困憊の, 眠い, 眠そうな, うとうとした, 眠気を催させる

tired	drained	exhausted
sleepy	weary	shattered
drowsy	worn out	pooped
	fatigued	

文型&コロケーション

▸ tired/ exhausted/ weary/ sleepy/ drowsy/ worn out/ pooped **from** sth
▸ tired/ worn/ pooped **out**
▸ to **feel** tired/ exhausted/ drained/ weary/ sleepy/ drowsy/ worn out/ shattered/ fatigued
▸ to **look** tired/ exhausted/ drained/ weary/ sleepy/ worn out/ shattered/ pooped/ fatigued
▸ to **sound** tired/ exhausted/ weary/ sleepy
▸ to **leave** sb tired/ exhausted/ drained
▸ to **make** sb sleepy/ drowsy
▸ **very/ a little** tired/ weary/ sleepy/ drowsy
▸ **quite** tired/ sleepy/ drowsy/ worn out
▸ **completely/ totally/ utterly** exhausted/ drained
▸ **physically/ mentally** exhausted/ drained

tired (眠り[休み]たいと感じるほど)疲れた ◇I'm too *tired* even to think. あまりに疲れていて考える気にさえなれない ◇They were cold, hungry and *tired* out (= very tired). 彼らは寒くて, 空腹で, 疲れ切っていた ◇The words danced on the page before his *tired* eyes. 彼の疲れた目の前でページの文字が揺らいでいた

exhausted (極度に)疲れ果てた, へとへとになった ◇I'm *exhausted*! へとへとだ ◇The *exhausted* climbers were rescued by helicopter. 疲れ果てた登山者たちはヘリコプターで救助された

▸ **exhaustion** 名 [U] ◇Her face was grey with *exhaustion*. 彼女の顔は疲労困憊で青ざめていた

drained [名詞の前はまれ](体力・精神力・活力を使い果たし)疲れ果てた, へとへとになった ◇He suddenly felt totally *drained*. 彼は突然, 極度の疲労感を覚えた ◇The experience left her physically and emotionally *drained*. その体験で彼女は肉体的にも感情的にも疲れ果てた

weary 《ややフォーマル》(重労働などで)疲れ果てた, 疲労困憊の ◇She suddenly felt old and *weary*. 彼女は突然, 年を取ったと感じて疲労感を覚えた ◇He gave a long, *weary* sigh. 彼は長い疲れ切ったようなため息をついた

▸ **wearily** 副 ◇He closed his eyes *wearily*. 彼は疲れて目を閉じた

sleepy 眠い; 眠そうな ◇The heat and the wine made him *sleepy*. 暑さとワインのせいで彼は眠くなった

▸ **sleepily** 副 ◇She yawned *sleepily*. 彼女は眠そうにあくびをした

drowsy [名詞の前はまれ] うとうとした; 眠気を催させる ◇The tablets may make you feel *drowsy*. その錠剤が眠気を催すかもしれません ◇She lay in the sun all through the long, *drowsy* afternoon. 彼女は眠気を誘う長い午後の間ずっと日光浴をしていた

▸ **drowsiness** 名 [U] ◇The drugs tend to cause *drowsiness*. その薬は眠気を催させる傾向があります

,worn 'out [名詞の前はまれ]《ややインフォーマル》(重労働[激しい運動]で)疲れ果てた, へとへとになった ◇Can we sit down? I'm *worn out*. ぼくたち座ってもいいかい. ぼくはへとへとなんだ

shattered [名詞の前はまれ]《英, インフォーマル》(極度に)疲れ果てた, へとへとになった ◇By the end of the day I was absolutely *shattered*. その日の終わりまでには私はすっかりへとへとになっていた

pooped (または **,pooped 'out**) [名詞の前はまれ]《米, インフォーマル》(極度に)疲れ果てた, へとへとになった ◇I'm *pooped*! へとへとだ

fatigued [名詞の前はまれ]《フォーマル》(肉体的にも精神的にも)疲れ果てた, 疲労困憊の ◇The troops were already *fatigued* from the long forced march. 軍隊は長い行軍を強いられ, すでに疲労困憊だった

▸ **fatigue** 名 [U] ◇Driver *fatigue* was to blame for the accident. その事故が起こったのは運転手の過労のせいだった

toilet 名

toilet・bathroom・lavatory・loo・restroom・potty・latrine・ladies' room・men's room・urinal

体から老廃物を取り除くために行く部屋[建物]
【類語訳】トイレ, 便所, お手洗い, 公衆便所, 便器, おまる

文型&コロケーション

▸ a **public** toilet/ bathroom/ lavatory/ loo/ restroom/ latrine/ urinal
▸ the **men's** toilet/ bathroom/ loo/ restroom/ urinal
▸ the **ladies'** toilet/ bathroom/ loo/ restroom
▸ to **use** the toilet/ bathroom/ lavatory/ loo/ restroom/ latrine/ ladies' room/ men's room/ urinal
▸ to **go to** the toilet/ bathroom/ lavatory/ loo/ restroom/ ladies' room/ men's room
▸ to **need** the toilet/ bathroom/ lavatory/ loo
▸ toilet/ lavatory/ loo **paper**

toilet [C] (大便・小便用の)便器, トイレ ◇Have you flushed the *toilet*? 便器の水を流したかい ◇a *toilet* seat 便座 ◇*Toilet* facilities for the disabled are available. 身障者向けのトイレ設備が利用できます ❶《英》では, toiletは便器を備えた部屋のみを指す ◆Every flat has its own bathroom and *toilet*. 《英》各アパートにはバスルームとトイレが付いています ◆Who's in the *toilet*? (誰がトイレに入ってるの). また《英》では, toilet, toilets [複数形]は, 例えば大きな建物[公共の場]にある, いくつかの便器を備えた部屋[小さな建物]を指す ◆The *toilets* are located in the entrance area. (トイレは入口のところにあります.)

bathroom [C]《特に米》(バス・シャワー付きで便器を備えた)便所, トイレ, お手洗い ◇I have to go to the *bathroom* (= use the toilet). トイレに行かなくちゃ ◇Where's the *bathroom*? (= for example in a restaurant) お手洗いはどこですか (= レストランなどで尋ねる言い方)

📝 toiletとbathroomの使い分け:《英》では, bathroomはバスとシャワーの付いた部屋(浴室)を指し, toilet (便器)が付いていることもある.《米》では, bathroomはバスとシャワーが付いていなくても, 便器の付いた部屋を指すことが多い.

↪**toilet**

lavatory [C]《英, フォーマル》便器, 便所, トイレ；公衆便所, お手洗い ◇There's a bathroom and a *lavatory* upstairs. 2階に浴室とトイレがあります ◇The nearest public *lavatory* is at the station. 一番近い公衆便所は駅にあります ❶《米》では, lavatoryは飛行機内のトイレについてのみ用いられる.
loo [C]《英, インフォーマル》便器, 便所, トイレ ◇I just need to pop to the *loo*. すぐトイレに行かなくちゃ
restroom [C]《米》(劇場・レストランなど公共の場にある)公衆便所, お手洗い ◇The gas station *restroom* was locked. ガソリンスタンドのトイレは鍵がかかっていた
potty [C]《ややインフォーマル》(幼児用の)おまる, 便所, トイレ ◇I have to go *potty*.《米》トイレに行かなくちゃ ❶《英》では幼児は次のように言うだろう. ◆I need a wee/poo. (おしっこ/うんちしたい).
latrine [C](地面に穴を掘って作られる野営地・屋外の)便所 ◇We put up the tents and dug a *latrine* pit. 我々はテントを張って便所の穴を掘った
'ladies' room [C]《米》(公共の建物・場所にある)女性用トイレ ◇Could you tell me where the *ladies' room* is? 女性用トイレはどこにあるか教えていただけますか
'men's room [C]《米》(公共の建物・場所にある)男性用トイレ ◇The *men's room* is located in the foyer. 男性用トイレはロビーにあります
urinal [C] (壁に取り付けられた男性用の)小便器 ◇Modern waterless *urinals* can help to save the environment. 現代の無水小便器は環境保護の一助となりうる

tolerant 形

tolerant・liberal・enlightened・permissive・open-minded・indulgent
他人の意見[行動]が自分の意見[行動]と異なっていても受け入れることを表す語
【類語訳】寛容な, 開放的な, 自由主義の, 見識のある, 進んだ, 自由放任の, 心を開いた, 頭の柔軟な, 甘やかす

文型&コロケーション
▶tolerant/ liberal/ permissive **in** sth
▶tolerant/ open-minded/ indulgent **towards** sb/ sth
▶tolerant/ indulgent **with** sb
▶a tolerant/ a liberal/ an enlightened/ a permissive/ an open-minded **attitude**
▶a tolerant/ a liberal/ an enlightened/ a permissive **approach**
▶tolerant/ liberal/ enlightened **views**
▶a tolerant/ a liberal/ a permissive **atmosphere**
▶a tolerant/ a liberal/ an enlightened/ an open-minded **person/ man/ woman**
▶liberal/ permissive/ indulgent **parents**
▶a tolerant/ a liberal/ an enlightened/ a permissive **society**
▶**very** tolerant/ liberal/ enlightened/ permissive/ open-minded
▶**remarkably** tolerant/ liberal/ enlightened

tolerant 《ほめて》(同意せずとも他人を受け入れて)寛容な ◇She was becoming less quick to condemn and more *tolerant of* others. 彼女は他人をすぐにとがめたりせず, 他人により寛容になってきていた ◇There is little chance of a *tolerant* democratic system emerging. 寛容な民主制度が出現する可能性はほとんどない 反意 **intolerant** (BIASED), ☞**tolerance** (PATIENCE), **easy-going** (CALM)
liberal 《ふつうほめて》(他人を進んで理解・尊敬して)寛容な, 開放的な；自由主義の(人は自分の行動を選択できるべきであるとする考え) ◇Her parents are very *liberal* and allow her a lot of freedom. 彼女の両親は非常に開放的で, 彼女に多くの自由を認めている ◇His later films reflect the more *liberal* values of the 1960s. 彼の後期の映画は1960年代のより自由主義的な価値観を反映している
enlightened [ふつう名詞の前で]《ほめて》(人々の欲求・状況を理解していて)見識のある；(古風な態度・偏見に基づいておらず)進んだ ◇More *enlightened* companies provided education for the workforce. より見識ある会社は全従業員に対して教育を施した ◇My mother had more *enlightened* opinions than my father. 母は父よりも進んだ考えを持っていた
permissive (性的問題について)自由放任の ◇Even in the most *permissive* times fidelity in marriage is important to many. 最も自由放任の時代でも, 結婚生活における貞節は多くの人にとって大切である ◇He grew up before *the permissive society*. 彼は自由放任社会以前に大人になっていた (「自由放任社会」とは1960年代, 70年代を指す)
open-'minded 《ほめて》(異なる考えに)心を開いた, 頭の柔軟な ◇I encourage the children to be *open-minded about* new ideas and experiences. 子どもたちには新しい考えや体験に心を開くように勧めています
indulgent 《ふつうけなして》(望めば何でも持たせて[やらせて])甘やかす ◇Mothers are sometimes less *indulgent* towards daughters. 母親は時に娘に対してそれほど甘くない

tool 名

tool・device・aid・instrument・gadget・implement・utensil
仕事をする[物事を達成する]手助けとなる物
【類語訳】道具, 用具, 工具, 手段, ツール, 装置, 補助器具, 器具, 機器

文型&コロケーション
▶a **useful** tool/ device/ aid/ gadget
▶a **little/ special** tool/ device/ instrument/ gadget
▶a **basic** tool/ device/ aid
▶a **simple/ crude** tool/ device/ instrument
▶a **sharp/ metal** tool/ instrument/ implement
▶a **mechanical/ hi-tech** device/ aid/ gadget
▶an **electrical/ electronic** device/ gadget
▶a **teaching/ training/ research** tool/ device/ aid
▶a **measuring/ navigation/ navigational** tool/ device/ instrument
▶a **drawing/ writing** tool/ aid/ instrument/ implement
▶a **medical/ surgical** device/ instrument/ implement
▶a **kitchen/ household** gadget/ implement/ utensil

tool [C] (物を作る[修理する]ために手に持つ)道具, 用具, 工具；(仕事の手助けをする)手段, ツール ◇First prize is this beautiful set of garden *tools*. 一等賞はこの美しい園芸用具のセットです ◇You will need a good-quality, sharp *cutting tool*. 高品質でよく切れる切削工具が必要になるでしょう ◇Always select the right *tool* for the job. 常に仕事に適したツールを選びなさい ◇a *tool* kit (= a set of tools in a box or bag) 工具一式 ◇We make use of various research *tools* such as questionnaires. 我々

はアンケートなどさまざまな調査手段を活用しています

device [C]《ややフォーマル》(特定の仕事用に設計された)装置 ◇This *device* enables pilots to navigate with pinpoint accuracy. この装置のおかげでパイロットは寸分たがわぬ正確さで航行できます ◇The twentieth century saw the introduction of labour-saving *devices* around the home. 20世紀は家庭の省力装置の導入の場となった ❶ *device*はふつう小型の電気機器を指す.

aid [C]《特に複合語》補助器具 ◇You may need a *hearing aid*. あなたは補聴器が必要かもしれません ◇Photographs make useful teaching *aids*. 写真は有用な補助教材となります ❶*aid*はhearing aid (補聴器)などの小型装置や授業で用いられるあらゆる種類の教材に用いられる. ◆ a classroom/teaching/visual *aid* (教室の/補助/視覚教材)

instrument [C]《細心の注意を要する仕事/科学的研究》に用いられる)器具, 機器 ◇surgical *instruments* 外科用具 ◇This pen is the ideal *precision instrument* for all your graphic needs. このペンはあらゆる図画の要望に適した理想的な精密器具だ ◇medieval *instruments* of torture 中世の拷問器具

gadget [C]《便利な》小型器具[機器] ◇Modern *gadgets* like these make a huge difference to home life. これらのような現代の小型機器は家庭生活に大きな影響を及ぼします ❶ *gadget*はふつう現代的な物, 特に電子機器を指す.

implement [C]《ややフォーマル》(非常に簡素な屋外用の)道具, 用具, 器具 ◇Various local crafts and agricultural *implements* are represented in the exhibition. さまざまな地元工芸品や農機具が展示会に出品されています

utensil [C]《ややフォーマル》(家庭用の)道具, 用具, 器具 ◇Wash your hands and all cooking *utensils* after preparing raw meat. 生肉で下ごしらえをしたら, 手と調理器具を洗ってください ❶ *utensil*は一般的に台所で用いられ, 特に手に持つことのできる道具を指す.

top 形 ☞ MAIN

top・senior・chief・leading・high・first・high-ranking・premier・foremost・superior・elite

人や物事が最も高い位置[順位, 程度]にあることを表す【類義訳】最高位の, 最高級の, 首位の, 首席の, 最高の, 高位の, 高級の, 上位の, 第一級の, 一流の, エリートの, 精鋭の

〖文型&コロケーション〗
▶ a top/ senior/ chief/ leading/ high-ranking/ superior **officer**
▶ a top/ senior/ chief/ leading **adviser/ aide/ economist/ lawyer**
▶ a top/ senior/ chief/ high-ranking **executive**
▶ a top/ senior/ leading/ high-ranking **official**
▶ a senior/ leading/ top-ranking **figure/ member**
▶ the chief/ leading/ foremost **exponent** of sth
▶ the leading/ foremost **authority/ expert** on sth
▶ a top/ senior **grade/ appointment/ job**
▶ the top/ first/ premier **division/ prize**
▶ top/ high **grades/ marks**

top [ふつう名詞の前で](位置・階級・程度が)最も高い, 最高位[上位]の, 最高級[上級]の, 首位の, 首席の, 最高の, 最大の ◇He lives on the *top* floor. 彼は最上階に住んでいる ◇She's one of the *top* players in the country. 彼女は国内のトッププレイヤーの一人です ◇The car was travelling at *top* speed. その車は全速力で走っていた ◇This is

top quality silk. これは最高品質の絹(織物)です ❶ *top*は《英》においてのみ, 連結動詞の後で用いることができる. ◆ He finished *top* in the exam. (《英》彼は試験を首席で終えた). ◆ They're *top* of the league. (彼らはリーグ首位である).

▶**top** 名 [C] ◇She was standing *at the top* of the stairs. 彼女は階段のてっぺんに立っていた ◇Write your name at the *top*. 一番上に名前を書きなさい ◇He's at the *top* of his profession. 彼は自分の職業の世界で頂点にいる ◇This decision came from the *top* (= the most important person in an organization). この決定は首脳陣によってなされた 反意 **bottom** (BOTTOM)

senior (階級・地位が)高位の, 高級の, 上位の, 上級の, ; (他人より)身分の高い, 先輩の ◇She's a *senior* lecturer at the university. 彼女は大学の上級講師である ◇I'm looking for a more *senior* position. 私はもっと上級職を探しています ◇He is *senior to* me. 彼は私の先輩です 反意

junior ❶*junior*は階級・地位が下位・下級の地位にある, または他人より身分の低い[後輩の]人を表す. ◆ *junior* employees (準社員). ◆ She is *junior* to me. (彼女は私の後輩です).

chief (しばしば Chief) [名詞の前で](階級が)最高位の, 長である ◇Who is the new *Chief* Education Officer? 新しい教育長は誰ですか ◇The *chief* financial officer of the company paid us a visit. 会社の財務総責任者が我々を訪問した ◇Detective *Chief* Inspector Williams 主任警部ウィリアムズ ❶*chief*は主に地位の名称に用いられる.

leading [名詞の前で](最も重要なので[成功しているので])第一級の, 一流の, 主役の ◇She was offered the *leading* role in the new TV series. 彼女は新しいテレビの連続番組で主役をオファーされた ◇He's a *leading* business analyst. 彼は一流の経済アナリストだ ❶*leading*は製品を製造する[サービスを提供する]会社の宣伝で用いられることが多い. ◆ a *leading* brand/manufacturer/supplier (一流ブランド/メーカー/納入業者). ☞ **prominent** (FAMOUS)

high [ふつう名詞の前で](階級・地位が)高位の, 高級の, 高等の, 上位の, 上級の, 上流の ◇She has held *high* office under three prime ministers. 彼女は3人の首相の下で高位の役職に就いてきた ◇The case was referred to a *higher* court. その訴訟は上級裁判所に送られた ◇He has friends *in high places* (= among people of power and influence). 彼には上層部に友達がいる ❶この意味では, *high*はかなり限られた連語関係で用いられる. ◆ *high* status/rank/position/office (高い地位/階級/職位/役職). また, いくつかの非常に重要な人々・物事のより特定の名称に用いられる. ◆ a *high* court/magistrate/commissioner/priest (最高裁判所/最高治安判事/高等弁務官/司祭長).

first [限定詞] 最も重要な, 一位の ◇Your *first* duty is to your family. あなたの最も重要な義務はご自分の家族に対するものです ◇She won *first* prize in the competition. 彼女は競技会で一等賞を獲った ❶ *first*が「最も重要な」を意味する場合, 典型的な連語に duty, importance, consideration が挙げられる. *first*が「競技会で一位の」を意味する場合, 典型的な連語に prize, place が挙げられる.

high-'ranking [ふつう名詞の前で](階級・地位が)高位の, 高級の, 上位の, 上級の ◇He's a *high-ranking* officer in the army. 彼は軍の高級将校である ◇She's been offered a *high-ranking* post in the police force. 彼女は警察組織で高位のポストを与えられた ❶*high-ranking*は政治・軍に関わる地位について用いられることが多い. 典型的な連語に officer, bureaucrat, official, (party) member が挙げられる.

⇨top　　　　　　　　　touch, tourist

premier [名詞の前で]《特に書き言葉 or ジャーナリズム》最も重要な, (最も有名なので[成功しているので])最高(級)の, 第一級の, 一流の ◇The new Institute of Contemporary Art is one of Boston's *premier* attractions. 新しい現代美術館はボストンの第一級の呼び物の一つです ◇They've just moved up to the *Premier* League (= in football). 《英, スポーツ》彼らはプレミアリーグに上がってきたばかりです ❶ *premier* はジャーナリズム・広告で用いられることが多く, 国・場所と, 人気のある大当たりのイベント・場所とを結びつけて用いられる. ◆Scotland's *premier* resort/hotel/exhibition/tourist attraction (スコットランドの最高級リゾート地/最高級ホテル/人気展示会/一級の観光地).

foremost 《ややフォーマル, 特に書き言葉》最も重要な, (最も有名なので[成功しているので])第一級の, 一流の, ; 先頭の, 第一線の ◇I'd like to introduce you to the world's *foremost* authority on the subject. このテーマに関する世界的な第一人者をご紹介したいと思います ◇The President was *foremost among* those who condemned the violence. 大統領は第一線に立って暴力を非難した ◇This question has been *foremost* in our minds recently. 最近, この問題が私たちの頭の中で最も重要な位置を占めている

[ノート] **premier** と **foremost** の使い分け: *premier* は場所・イベントに用いられることが多い. *foremost* は人々に用いられることが多い. *foremost* はフォーマルな語で, 重大であることを示唆する. *premier* は人気のあることを示唆する. ◆ the world's *foremost* authority on/expert on/exponent of sth (…に関する世界的な第一人者/一流の専門家/一流の演奏家). ◆ Britain's *premier* chef (英国の一流シェフ).

superior (階級・地位が)高位の, 高級の, 上位の, 上級の ◇I'll need to check with my *superior* officer. 高官に相談しなければならないだろう ❶ この意味では, *superior* の典型的な連語に officer, status, position, power が挙げられる. [反意] **inferior** ❶ inferior は階級・地位が下位・下級の役人・職位であることに用いられる.

[ノート] **senior** と **superior** の使い分け: *superior* は例えば軍隊などの組織における地位に関しては, *senior* よりも頻繁に用いられる. 日常の職場・仕事においては, *senior* colleague/manager/adviser/clerk/editor/designer/teacher (上位の同僚/上級管理者/相談役/先任書記/上役の編集者/上級デザイナー/上級教師) のように用いるほうが一般的.

elite [名詞の前で](富・能力・縁故で)エリートの, 精鋭の ◇The secret was known only by an *elite* group of senior executives. その秘密は上級管理者のエリート集団のみに知られていた ◇He was trained at an *elite* military academy. 彼はエリートの陸軍士官学校で訓練を受けた ❶ *elite* は軍部・教育に関連する文脈で用いられることが多い. ◆ *elite* troops/force/corps (精鋭部隊/軍/軍団). ◆ an *elite* force/corps (精鋭軍/軍団). ◆ an *elite* education/private school (エリート教育/名門私立学校). また, *elite* は特別な知識・技能を共有する人々の集団について用いられることが多い. ☞ *elite* (ELITE).

touch 動

touch・feel・brush・graze
人や物に手[指]を置く
【類語訳】触る, 触れる, 触って調べる, 触ってみる, 軽く触れる, かする, かすめる

[文型&コロケーション]
▶ to touch/ feel/ brush/ graze sb/ sth **with** sth
▶ to touch/ brush sb/ sth **gently**/ **lightly**
▶ to **accidentally** touch/ brush sb/ sth

touch [他] (手・指で人・物に)触る, 触れる ◇Don't *touch* that plate — it's hot! その板に触るな—熱いよ ◇Can you *touch* your toes (= bend and reach them with your hands)? つま先に触れられますか ◇I *touched* him lightly on the arm. 私は彼の腕にそっと触れた
▶ **touch** [名][C, ふつう単数形, U] ◇The gentle *touch* of his hand on her shoulder made her jump. 彼の手が肩に優しく触れると彼女は跳び上がった ◇She has learnt to recognize the raised patterns of Braille by *touch*. 彼女は浮き上がった点字模様を手探りで認識することを覚えた

feel [他] (指で慎重に)触って調べる, 触ってみる ◇Can you *feel* the bump on my head? 私の頭のこぶに触ってわかりますか ◇Try to tell what this is just by *feeling* it. 触るだけでこれが何か当ててみなさい ◇*Feel* how rough this is. これがどのくらいざらざらしているか触ってみなさい

brush [自, 他] (近づきながら人・物に)軽く触れる, かする, かすめる ◇She *brushed past* him. 彼女は彼のそばをかすって通り過ぎた ◇His hand accidentally *brushed against* hers. 彼の手が偶然に彼女の手に軽く触れた ◇The leaves *brushed* her cheek. 葉っぱが彼女の頬をかすめた

graze [他]《書き言葉》(通り過ぎながら)軽く触れる, かする, かすめる ◇The bullet *grazed* his cheek. 弾丸が彼の頬をかすめた

[ノート] **brush** と **graze** の使い分け: *brush* はふつう他の物にそっと触れる柔らかい物について用いられる. *graze* はふつう他の物にそっと触れる硬い物について用いられる.

tourist 名

tourist・visitor・pilgrim・holidaymaker・vacationer・sightseer・backpacker
楽しみ[興味]のために場所へ旅する[を訪れる]人
【類語訳】観光客, 旅行者, 見物客, 訪問客, 巡礼者, 行楽客, バックパッカー

[文型&コロケーション]
▶ tourists/ visitors/ holidaymakers/ vacationers/ sightseers **from**...
▶ **foreign** tourists/ visitors
▶ a **seasoned** tourist/ pilgrim/ backpacker
▶ to **attract** tourists/ visitors/ pilgrims/ holidaymakers/ vacationers/ sightseers
▶ to **cater for** tourists/ visitors
▶ tourists/ visitors/ pilgrims/ sightseers **flock** to a place

tourist [C] (楽しみのためにある場所を訪れる)観光客, 旅行者 ◇A busload of *tourists* arrived at the village. バスいっぱいの観光客がその村に到着した ◇The temple is a major *tourist attraction*. その寺は主要な観光名所である ◇Local people rely on the *tourist industry* for employment. 地元の人たちは雇用を観光産業に依存している ☞ **tour** (TRIP), **tourism** (TRAVEL)

visitor [C] (ある場所を訪れる)観光客, 見物客, 訪問客 ◇The palace is **open to visitors** from April to September. 宮殿は4月から9月まで見物客に公開されている ◇They publish a guide to Europe for overseas *visi-*

tors. 海外からの観光客向けにヨーロッパの旅行案内書が出版されている ☞ **visit** (VISIT 名), **visit** (STAY 2)

pilgrim [C] (宗教的な理由で聖地へ旅行する)巡礼者 ◇Millions of *pilgrims* travel to Mecca. 何百万もの巡礼者たちがメッカに旅する ◇They were following one of the great medieval *pilgrim* routes. 彼らは中世の大巡礼ルートの一つをたどっていた ☞ **pilgrimage** (TRIP)

holidaymaker [C] 《英》(休暇にある場所を訪れる)行楽客 ◇The resort attracts thousands of British *holidaymakers.* そのリゾート地は何千もの英国の行楽客を魅了します

vacationer [C] 《米》(休暇にある場所を訪れる)行楽客 ◇Millions of *vacationers* come every year for the beaches and casinos. 毎年、多くの行楽客がビーチとカジノを求めやってくる

sightseer [C] (休暇に興味深い建物・場所を訪れる)観光客、見物客 ◇Crowds of *sightseers* throng the streets in summer. 夏には観光客の群れが通りに押し寄せる ☞ **sightseeing** (TRAVEL)

backpacker [C] (衣類・備品をバックパックで持ち歩いて旅する)バックパッカー ◇A couple of *backpackers* were trying to hitch a ride to Chiang Mai. バックパッカーの二人連れはチェンマイまで車に乗せてもらおうとしていた

trade 名

trade・business・market・operation・trading・commerce・marketplace・trafficking・enterprise・dealing

お金と交換で商品[サービス]を購入[販売, 供給]する行為, あるいは販売される商品[サービス]の量
【類語訳】商売, 商い, 取り引き, 交換, 貿易, 通商, 取引高, 事業, 市場, 売買, 営業, 操業, 密売

文型&コロケーション

▶ a trade/ the market **in** sth
▶ trade/ business/ trading/ commerce/ trafficking/ enterprise/ dealing **between** people/ countries
▶ trade/ business/ trading/ commerce/ dealing **with** sb/ a country
▶ (the) **foreign/ international/ global** trade/ business/ market/ operations/ trading/ commerce/ marketplace
▶ (the) **domestic/ internal** trade/ business/ market/ operations/ trading/ commerce
▶ (a/ the) **local** trade/ business/ market/ operations/ trading/ marketplace/ enterprise
▶ **illegal** trade/ business/ operations/ trading/ trafficking/ enterprise/ dealings
▶ (a) **profitable** trade/ business/ market/ operations/ trading
▶ (a) **free** trade/ market/ trading/ enterprise
▶ to **engage in** trade/ business/ trading/ commerce/ enterprise
▶ to **encourage/ promote** trade/ business/ commerce/ enterprise
▶ trade/ business/ the market/ an operation **expands/ grows/ increases**
▶ trade/ business/ the market **is booming/ picks up/ declines/ falls**

trade [U, C] (人々・国々の間での)商売, 商い, 取り引き, 交易, 貿易, 通商 ;(販売される商品・サービスの)取引高 ◇*Trade* between the two countries has increased. 2国間の貿易は増加している ◇The international *trade* in oil has been massively affected. 石油の国際貿易は甚大な影響を受けている ◇*Trade* was very good last month. 先月の取引高は非常によかった ◇Stores are doing a **brisk trade in** wizard accessories and vampire kits. 《特に英》店は魔法使いのアクセサリーと吸血鬼グッズで盛況だ ❶ 《米》では, doing brisk business in sthと用いるほうが一般的である. ☞ **trade** (SELL 2), **trader** (DEALER)

business [U] (お金もうけの)商売, 取り引き, 事業, 仕事 ;(会社の)取引高 ;商売[仕事]の調子 ◇It's been a pleasure to **do business with** you. お宅と取り引きできて光栄に思っています ◇She has **set up in business** as a hairdresser. 彼女は美容師として商売を始めた ◇When he left school he **went into business** with his brother. 彼は学校を卒業すると, 兄と事業を始めた ◇What **line of business** are you in? どんな業種に就いているのですか ◇There are strong links between politics and **big business** (= large companies that have a lot of power and influence). 政治と大企業には強いつながりがある ◇How's *business*? 仕事の調子はどうだい ◇If we close down for repairs, we'll lose *business*. 修繕のために店を閉めたりしたら, 商売できなくなるだろう ◇Stores are **doing brisk business in** wizard accessories and vampire kits. 《特に米》店は魔法使いのアクセサリーと吸血鬼グッズで盛況だ ❶ 《英》では, doing a brisk trade in sthと言うほうが普通である. ☞ **business** (COMPANY), **business** (INDUSTRY), **do business** (SELL 2)

ノート **trade**と**business**の使い分け : tradeはサービスよりも商品の売買について用いられることがやや多い. businessは商品・サービスを供給する上で, 互いに連絡を取り, 話し合い, 合意し, 協同するといった活動の, より個人的な側面を強調する場合に用いられることが多い.

market [単数で] (特定の種類の商品の)市場, 売買, 取り引き ◇They have 20% of the world *market* in coffee. 彼らはコーヒーの世界市場の2割を占めている ◇We have increased our **share of the market** by 10%. 我々の市場シェアは10%増加した ◇There has been a downturn in the property *market* (= the number and type of houses that are available). 不動産市場は沈滞してきた ◇They have **cornered the market** in sportswear (= they sell the most). 彼らはスポーツウェア市場を独占してきた

operation [C, ふつう複数で] (ビジネス・産業の領域で行われる)事業, 営業, 操業, 業務 ◇The firm's banking *operations* overseas have been affected by the disaster. その会社の海外での銀行業務は災害で影響を受けている

trading [U] (店・株式市場における)取り引き ◇Stores everywhere reported excellent *trading* in the run-up to Christmas. どの店もクリスマス商戦に向けて抜けた取り引きを報告した ◇Shares worth $8 million changed hands during a day of hectic *trading*. 一日の活発な取り引きの間に800万ドル相当の株式の株主が変わった ☞ **trade** (SELL 2), **trader** (DEALER)

commerce [U] (ややフォーマル) (国家間の)商業, 通商, 貿易 ◇Leaders of industry and *commerce* met at the summit in Paris. 産業および通商の指導者たちがパリの首脳会談で会合した ☞ **commercial** (ECONOMIC)

marketplace [単数で] (商品・サービスの売買のために他と競合する)市場 ◇They have successfully adapted to the demands of the global *marketplace*. 彼らは首尾

↪trade

〈世界市場の需要に順応した〉

trafficking [U] 不正[不法]取引, 密売 ◇She was accused of drug *trafficking*. 彼女は麻薬密売で起訴された ❶ *trafficking*は drug (麻薬) と最も頻繁に結びつく。他には illegal, heroin, narcotic と結びつく。

enterprise [U] (国民主導による)企業経営 ◇They provide grants to encourage *enterprise* in the region. 地域における企業経営を奨励するための助成金が出されます ◇The culture of dependency was replaced by an *enterprise culture* (= in which people are encouraged to develop small businesses). 他人に依存する文化から自ら起業する文化に取って代わられた

dealing [U, C] 取り引き；売買 ◇We have a reputation for honest *dealing*. 我々は公正な取り引きで定評がある ◇Drug *dealing* on our streets is becoming a growing problem. 路上で行われる麻薬取引はますます深刻な問題となってきている ◇Sales plummeted just after *dealings* in shares began. 《特に英》株取引の開始直後に売り上げが急落した ☞ **deal in sth** (SELL 2), **dealer** (DEALER)

ノート **trading** と **dealing** の使い分け：trading は店で物を売ることについて用いられ, dealing は不法に, 特に麻薬を売ることについて用いられる。また, 両語とも会社の株式の売買について用いられるが,《米》では trading のほうが一般的。

tradition 名

tradition・practice・custom・convention・norms
あるグループや社会にいつもどおりに受け入れられている行動
【類語訳】伝統, 慣習, 慣例, 慣行, 習慣, 風習, しきたり, 因習, 規範

文型&コロケーション
▸ **by** tradition/ custom/ convention
▸ **a** tradition/ custom/ convention **that** ...
▸ **(an) established** tradition/ practice/ custom/ convention/ norms
▸ **accepted** practice/ conventions/ norms
▸ **social** practice/ custom/ convention/ norms
▸ **cultural** tradition/ practice/ convention/ norms
▸ **a local/ British** tradition/ practice/ custom
▸ **traditional** practices/ customs/ norms
▸ **to follow** a tradition/ a practice/ a custom/ convention/ ... norms
▸ **to break with** a tradition/ practice/ convention
▸ tradition/ custom/ convention **demands** sth

tradition [C, U] 伝統 ◇Germany has a *tradition* of good quality newspapers. ドイツは伝統的に新聞の質が高い ◇There is a *tradition* in our family that one of our ancestors was a Cherokee Indian. 我が家では先祖の一人がチェロキー・インディアンだったということが脈々と流れている ◇The bride's parents are *by tradition* expected to pay for the wedding. 伝統的に花嫁の両親が婚礼費用を負担するものとされている ◇He is *in the* great *tradition of* British travel writers. 彼は英国の紀行作家たちの偉大な伝統を受け継いでいる ◇This year there will be *a break with tradition* (= something different will be done). 今年は新機軸が打ち出されるだろう ◇Brittany has a lively and very distinctive sense of *tradition*. ブルターニュ地方には生き生きとした, 実に独特な伝統感覚がある

tradition, traditional

practice [U, C] (組織・状況における)慣例, 慣習, 慣行 ◇It is *standard practice* not to pay bills until the end of the month. 月末まで請求書に対する支払いをしないのは当たり前のことだ ◇They have produced a guide to *best practice* for employers. 彼らは雇用主向けに最優良事例の手引きを作った ◇Members have to abide by the federation's *code of practice*. 会員は連盟の行動規約に従わなければならない ◇They have been studying Japanese business *practices*. 彼らは日本の商慣習を勉強してきている ❶ practicesはビジネス慣習についてよく用いられ, business, corrupt, discriminatory, employment, management, recruitment, restrictive, trading, working などと連語を構成する。

custom [C, U] (特定の社会・場所・時代における)習慣, 風習, 慣行 ◇They were unfamiliar with local *customs* and culture. 彼らは地元の慣習や文化に通じていなかった ◇*It is the custom* here to put flowers on the graves at Easter. ここでは復活祭に墓所に花を供えるのが習慣です ◇They poured wine round the trees in accordance with local *custom*. 彼らは地元の習慣に従って木々の周りにワインを注いだ

convention [C, U] (適切なものとされている)しきたり, 因習, 慣習；伝統的手法 ◇The handshake is a social *convention*. 握手は社会的慣習である ◇She is a lively young woman who enjoys flouting *convention*. 彼女はしきたりを軽視して楽しむ, 陽気で若い女性だ ◇The novel conforms to the *conventions* of nineteenth-century realism. その小説は19世紀リアリズムの伝統表現法に準拠している

norms [複数で] (特定の集団における)規範, 模範 ◇*Norms* of dress vary from society to society. 服装に関する規範は社会によってまちまちだ ◇She considered people to be products of the values and *norms* of the society they lived in. 彼女は人々を自分たちが暮らしている社会の価値観と規範の産物と見なしていた

traditional 形 ☞ CONSERVATIVE

traditional・conventional・mainstream・classical・orthodox
過去に起こった[受け入れられた]ことに基づいていることを表す
【類語訳】伝統的な, 従来の, 旧来の, 考え方の古い, 慣習的な, 従来型の, 主流の, 古典派の, 正統派の

文型&コロケーション
▸ **the** traditional/ conventional/ mainstream/ classical/ orthodox **view**
▸ traditional/ conventional/ mainstream/ classical/ orthodox **theories/ methods/ approaches/ economics**
▸ traditional/ conventional/ mainstream/ classical **ideas/ thinking/ education**
▸ traditional/ conventional/ mainstream/ orthodox **politics**
▸ traditional/ conventional/ orthodox **medicine**
▸ tradtional/ mainstream/ orthodox **parties**
▸ **fairly** traditional/ conventional/ mainstream/ orthodox
▸ **very** traditional/ orthodox

traditional 《時にけなして》伝統に従った, 伝統的な, 従来の, 旧来の, 考え方の古い ◇*Traditional* attitudes to divorce were changing. 離婚に対する従来の意識は変わりつつあった ◇I'm a very *traditional* guy. 私は非常に考え方の古い男です 反意 **modern** (EXPERIMENTAL)

▶**traditionally** 副 ◇Housework has *traditionally* been regarded as women's work. 家事は伝統的に女性の仕事だと見なされてきた
conventional [ふつう名詞の前で] 従来の, 慣習的な；従来型の, 通常型の ◇It's not a hotel *in the conventional sense*, rather a whole village turned into a hotel. それは月並みな意味での旅館ではなく, むしろ村全体が旅館に変わったのです ◇You can use a microwave or cook it in a *conventional* oven. 電子レンジでも従来型のオーブンでもそれは調理できます 反意 **alternative** ❶ alternative は通常とは異なるやり方を表す場合に用いられる. ◆ *alternative comedy/lifestyles/values* (新しい形のコメディー/まったく新しい生活様式/従来とは異なる価値観) ◆ *alternative energy* (= electricity or power that is produced using the sun, wind, water, etc.) (代替エネルギー).
▶**conventionally** 副 ◇Cooperatives perform at least as well as *conventionally* organized businesses. 協同組合は少なくとも従来の企業組織と同様に機能している

ノート **traditional** と **conventional** の使い分け：traditional は方法や考えがいかに古いかを強調する. conventional は現在広く用いられているかを強調する. conventional medicine (従来の医療) は, 現代的かつ科学的な方法や薬を用いて, 多くの人々に現在利用されている医療の一種である. traditional medicine (伝統的な医療) はずっと古い方法や植物などの天然原料から調合された薬を用いる. この医療は科学的に試験されたことはないかもしれないが, 多くの人々が効果的であると信じている. それは alternative medicine (代替医療) の一種であり, conventional medicine の反対に位置するものか, あるいは補完的なものである.

mainstream [ふつう名詞の前で] (標準的なので)主流の ◇Many sports are not adequately covered in the *mainstream* media. 多くのスポーツは主流メディアで適切に報道されていない ◇She was an important figure in both avant-garde and *mainstream* cinema. 彼女は前衛映画と主流映画のどちらにおいても大立て者だった
classical [ふつう名詞の前で] クラシックの, 古典派の；(様式・考えが)古典様式の, 古典主義の ◇the *classical* economics of Smith and Ricardo スミスとリカードの古典派経済学 ◇the *classical* theory of unemployment 古典派の失業論 ◇*classical* and modern ballet/dance クラシックバレエとモダンバレエ/クラシックダンスとモダンダンス
orthodox 《ややフォーマル》(信念・行動が)正統的な；正統派の ◇At that time the *orthodox* view was that secondary education should be selective. 当時, 正統的な見方は中等教育は選択的であるべきだというものであった ◇More *orthodox* scholars scoff at such theories. より正統派の学者たちはそういった理論をあざける 反意 **unorthodox** (UNUSUAL)

traffic 名

traffic・congestion・traffic jam・bottleneck・gridlock
特定の時間に道路上に乗り物がある状態
【類語訳】交通, 交通渋滞, 交通渋滞区間, 交通麻痺

文型&コロケーション
▶ **severe** congestion/ traffic jams
▶ **urban** traffic/ congestion
▶ to **increase/ reduce** traffic/ congestion
▶ to **cause** congestion/ traffic jams

▶ to **be stuck/ caught** in traffic/ a traffic jam

traffic [U] 交通 ◇I was stuck in *heavy traffic* for over an hour. 交通渋滞で1時間以上立ち往生した ◇The area is closed to *through traffic* (= traffic that will not be stopping). その場所は車の通り抜けができなくなっている ◇There will be an increase in the *volume of traffic*. 交流量は増加するでしょう ◇Flooding caused *traffic chaos*. 洪水で交通が混乱した
congestion [U] 《ややフォーマル》(特定の地域における)渋滞 ◇Better public transport would help ease traffic *congestion*. よりよい公共交通機関により交通渋滞は緩和されるでしょう ☞ **congested** (FULL)
'**traffic jam** [C] (道路上の)交通渋滞 ◇Why sit in a *traffic jam* when it's quicker to walk? 歩いたほうが早いのに, どうして交通渋滞の中でじっとしているの
bottleneck [C] (交通渋滞を引き起こす)狭い道路[区間] ◇I came this way to avoid the *bottleneck* at the traffic lights. 信号での交通渋滞区間を避けるためにこちらに来たのです
gridlock [U] (都市部における)交通渋滞[麻痺] ◇The protest march created *gridlock*. 抗議のデモ行進で交通渋滞になった

train 動

1 ☞ TEACH
train・teach・coach・show・educate・groom・instruct
特定の仕事[活動]のために人, 自分自身, 動物に技術を教える
【類語訳】訓練する, 教育する, 養成する, 調教する, 訓練を受ける, 教育を受ける, 教える, 指導する, コーチを務める

文型&コロケーション
▶ to train/ coach/ educate/ instruct sb **in** sth
▶ to train/ coach/ groom sb **for** sth
▶ to teach/ educate sb **about** sth
▶ to train/ groom sb **as** sth
▶ to train/ teach/ groom sb **to do** sth
▶ to teach/ show sb **how to** do sth
▶ to teach/ show sb **that**...
▶ to train/ teach/ educate/ instruct a **pupil**
▶ to train/ teach/ educate a **teacher/ doctor/ nurse/ student**
▶ to train/ teach/ educate the **workforce**
▶ to train/ coach a **gymnast/ athlete/ footballer/ player/ team**
▶ to teach/ coach **athletics/ basketball/ boxing/ football/ gymnastics/ hockey/ rugby/ soccer**
▶ be **well** trained/ taught/ coached/ instructed

train [他, 自] (人・動物を)訓練[教育, 養成, 調教]する；訓練[教育, 養成, 調教]を受ける ◇They *train* dogs to sniff out drugs. 彼らは薬を嗅ぎ分ける訓練を犬に行っている ◇All members of the team have been *trained* in first aid. チームのメンバー全員が応急手当の訓練を受けている ◇He *trained* as a teacher before becoming an actor. 彼は俳優になる前に教員の養成を受けた ☞ **training** (EDUCATION), **untrained** (IGNORANT)
teach [他] (人に方法を)教える；(人に異なる感じ方・考え方を)学ばせる ◇My father *taught* me how to ride a bike. 父は私に自転車の乗り方を教えてくれた ◇Could you

↳train

training

teach me to do that? そのやり方を教えていただけますか ◇She *taught* me to be less critical of other people. 私は彼女から他人に対してあまり批判的にならないように教わった ◇My parents *taught* me that honesty was always the best policy. 私は両親から正直こそが常に最善の策であることを学んだ ◇Our experience as refugees *taught* us many valuable lessons. 難民としての経験から我々は多くの貴重な教訓を学んだ ☞ **teach** (TEACH)

coach [他] (人にスポーツのやり方[技術の上達法]を)指導する、コーチを務める ◇Her father *coached* her for the Olympics. 彼女の父はオリンピックに向けて彼女を指導した ◇She has *coached* hundreds of young singers. 彼女は何百人もの若い歌手たちを指導してきた ◇He *coaches* basketball and soccer. 彼はバスケットボールとサッカーを指導している ☞ **coaching** (EDUCATION)

> ノート **train**と**coach**の使い分け：これらの語はどちらもスポーツ選手に競技会の準備をさせたり、ミュージシャンなどに公演の準備をさせたりする場合に用いられる。人を仕事のために技術訓練するときには**train**を用いるが、**coach**は不可。×All members of the team have been *coached* in first aid. ×They *coach* dogs to sniff out drugs. **coach**は人・スポーツを目的語に取ることができるが、**train**は人しか目的語に取ることができない。×He *trains* basketball.

show [他] (やって見せて[説明して])教える ◇She *showed* her students the technique. 彼女は学生たちにその技術を教えた ◇Can you *show* me how to do it? そのやり方を教えていただきますか

educate [他] (ややフォーマル)(責任のある行動を促すために人を)教育する ◇Children need to be *educated on* the dangers of drug-taking. 子どもたちは麻薬服用の危険性について教育を受ける必要がある ◇Their task was to inform, *educate* and entertain the viewers. 彼らの仕事はテレビ視聴者に情報と教育と娯楽を提供することだった ☞ **education** (EDUCATION)

groom [他、しばしば受身で] (特に進行形で)(ジャーナリズム)(重要な職(位)に向けて人を)訓練[教育、養成]する ◇She is already being *groomed* for the top job in the firm. 彼女はすでに会社の最高位職への養成を受けているところだ

instruct [他] (フォーマル)(人に実用的な技術を)教える、教育する ◇All our staff have been *instructed* in sign language. 当社の従業員は全員、手話の訓練を受けています ☞ **instruction** (EDUCATION)

2 ☞ PRACTISE
train・exercise・work out・keep fit・warm up
身体活動に備えて体の準備をする[体力や健康を向上させるために体を動かす]
【類語訳】トレーニングをする[させる]、練習をする[させる]、指導する、調教する、運動をする[させる]、鍛える、体を鍛える、健康を保つ

> 文型&コロケーション
> ▸ to train/ exercise/ warm up **properly**
> ▸ to train/ exercise/ work out **regularly**
> ▸ to train/ exercise a **horse/ dog**

train [自、他] (スポーツに備えて)トレーニング[練習]をする；(人・動物に)トレーニング[練習]をさせる、指導[調教]する ◇We watched the athletes *training* for the Olympics. 私たちは運動選手がオリンピックに向けてトレーニングしているのを見た ◇I *train* in the gym for two hours a day. 私は1日に2時間ジムでトレーニングしている ◇She *trains* horses. 彼女は馬の調教をしている ◇He *trains* the Olympic team. 彼はオリンピックチームを指導している

exercise [自、他] (健康維持・体力向上のために)運動をする；(動物に)運動[散歩]をさせる；(体の部位を)鍛える ◇How often do you *exercise*? どのくらいの頻度で運動しますか ◇Horses need to be *exercised* regularly. 馬は規則正しく運動をする必要がある ◇These movements will *exercise* your arms and shoulders. これらの動きは腕と肩を鍛えます ☞ **exercise** (SPORT)

work out [句動] (ジムの器具を用いて)体を鍛える ◇I *work out* regularly to keep fit. 私は健康を保つために定期的に体を鍛えています ☞ **workout** (SPORT)

keep 'fit [行it] (特に英)(定期的に運動をして)健康を保つ ◇She tries to *keep fit* by jogging every day. 彼女は毎日ジョギングをして健康を保つようにしている

warm 'up [句動] (運動・演奏・演技のための軽い)準備運動[ウォーミングアップ]をする ◇We arrived just as the players were *warming up*. 私たちは選手たちがちょうど準備運動をしているときに到着した ❶スポーツ選手と同様にダンサーなどの演者も warm up する必要がある.

▸ **'warm-up** 名 [C, 単数で] ◇He swam ten lengths of the pool as a *warm-up*. 彼はウォーミングアップとしてプールを5往復泳いだ ◇*warm-up* exercises 準備運動

training 名

training・rehearsal・practice・drill
活動や行事に備えての準備の過程を表す
【類語訳】トレーニング、練習、下稽古、リハーサル、予行演習、練習時間、訓練、演習

> 文型&コロケーション
> ▸ training/ rehearsals **for** sth
> ▸ **in** training/ rehearsal
> ▸ **regular** training/ rehearsals/ practice/ drills
> ▸ **football/ hockey, etc.** training/ practice
> ▸ to **do** training/ rehearsals/ practice
> ▸ to **have** rehearsals/ practice
> ▸ a training/ rehearsal/ practice **session/ schedule**

training [U] (スポーツ競技会に参加するための)トレーニング、練習 ◇Phillips is in serious *training* for the Olympics. フィリップスはオリンピックに向けて本格的にトレーニング中です ◇She did six months' hard *training* before the marathon. 彼女はマラソンの前に半年間の厳しいトレーニングを積んだ ❶(米)では、training は大きな行事のための本格的な準備を指す。(英)では、本格的であってもそれほど本格的でなくてもよい。(米)では、それほど本格的ではないトレーニングには practice を用いる。◆I go to football *training* after school. ((英))放課後にサッカーの練習に行っています) ◆I go to soccer *practice* after school. ((米、英))放課後にサッカーの練習に行っています) ☞ **exercise** (SPORT)

rehearsal [U, C] (劇団・楽団などの公演に向けての)下稽古、リハーサル；(将来に備える)予行演習 ◇Our new production of 'Hamlet' is currently in *rehearsal*. 我々が新たに上演する「ハムレット」は現在、リハーサル中です ◇During the *dress rehearsal* (= the final rehearsal in full costume) she suddenly forgot her lines. (衣裳を着ての)本稽古中に彼女は突然台詞を忘れた ◇These training exercises are designed to be a *rehearsal* for the invasion. これらの訓練演習は侵略に備えた予行演習を目指しています ☞ **rehearse** (PRACTISE)

practice [U, C] (技術を向上させるための定期的な)練習；練習時間 ◇The trainees need more *practice in* using the compass. 訓練生には羅針盤を使った練習がもっと必要です ◇His accent should improve *with practice*. 彼のアクセントは練習すれば改善するはずだ ◇If you don't play regularly you soon get *out of practice*. 定期的に演奏しないと、すぐに腕がなまります ◇It *takes a lot of practice* to play the violin well. ヴァイオリンを上手に弾くにはかなりの練習(時間)が必要です ◇There's a basketball *practice* every Friday evening. 毎週金曜の夜にはバスケットボールの練習があります ☞ **practise** (PRACTISE)

drill [C] (緊急事態に備える)訓練, 演習 ◇There'll be a *fire drill* sometime this morning. 今日の午前中のいつか消防訓練があります

travel 名

travel・tourism・sightseeing・travelling
場所に出向く行為[活動]
【類語訳】旅行, 移動, 紀行, 観光産業, 観光

文型&コロケーション
▶travel/ travelling **by** sth
▶a **day's** travel/ sightseeing/ travelling
▶to **go** sightseeing/ travelling
▶travel/ travelling **costs/ expenses/ arrangements**

travel [U] (長距離にわたる仕事・楽しみでの)旅行, 移動, 紀行 ◇Her interests include music and foreign *travel*. 彼女の興味には音楽と外国旅行が含まれます ◇Continued fighting makes *travel* in the area dangerous. 引き続く戦闘で、その地域の旅行は危険になっている ◇air/rail/space *travel* 飛行機/鉄道/宇宙旅行 ◇Expenditure on business *travel* was reduced. 出張旅費は削減された ◇*travel* insurance/documents 旅行保険/旅券 ◇a *travel* guide/writer 旅行案内書/紀行作家 ◇Do you suffer from *travel* sickness? 乗り物酔いしますか ☞ **travel** (GO 2)

tourism [U] (宿泊設備・サービス・娯楽の提供に関連する)観光産業 ◇We hope that this investment will lead to increased *tourism* in the area. この投資でその地域の観光産業が盛んになることを期待しています ☞ **tour** (TRIP), **tourist** (TOURIST)

sightseeing [U] (興味深い場所・建物を訪れる)観光 ◇Did you have a chance to *do any sightseeing*? どこか観光する機会はありましたか ◇They were on a *sightseeing* trip to the Pyramids. 彼らはピラミッドへの観光旅行中だった ☞ **sightseer** (TOURIST)

▶, **see the 'sights** フレーズ In the afternoon there'll be a chance to *see the sights* of Brussels. 午後にはブリュッセルの名所を観光するチャンスがあるでしょう

travelling 《特に英》《米でふつう **traveling**》 [U] (長距離にわたる仕事・楽しみでの)旅行, 移動, 紀行 ◇She enjoys skiing, *travelling* and music. 彼女はスキーと旅行と音楽が好きです ◇She was joined in London by her *travelling* companions (= the people who would make the journey with her). ロンドンで旅行仲間が彼女に合流した

ノート **travel** と **travelling** の使い分け : travel は一般の人々の旅行について用いられることが多く、travelling は特定の人の旅行について用いられることが多い。◆The pass allows unlimited *travel* on all public transport. (そのパスですべての公共交通機関は乗り放題です) ◆My job involves a lot of *travelling*. (私の仕事には多くの移動が伴います)。 travel は特定の種類の旅行を表すために、名詞・形容詞の後で用いられることが多い。◆air/rail/space/business/foreign *travel* (飛行機/鉄道/宇宙/出張/外国旅行) ×air/rail/space/business/foreign *travelling*.

treatment 名

treatment・surgery・medicine・therapy・operation・healing・medical care・cure・nursing
病気[怪我]の後に人々を健康にする営み[研究]
【類語訳】治療, 処置, 手当て, 手術, 外科, 医学, 療法, 治癒, 医療, 快復, 看護

文型&コロケーション
▶treatment/ surgery/ therapy/ an operation **for** sth
▶surgery/ an operation **on** sb/ sth
▶(an) **emergency** treatment/ surgery/ operation
▶(a/ an) **alternative/ orthodox/ conventional** treatment/ medicine/ therapy
▶to **have** treatment/ surgery/ therapy/ an operation/ medical care
▶to **undergo** treatment/ surgery/ therapy/ an operation
▶to **receive** treatment/ surgery/ therapy/ medical care
▶to **need/ require** treatment/ surgery/ therapy/ an operation/ medical care
▶to **give sb** treatment/ therapy/ medical care
▶to **carry out** treatment/ surgery/ an operation
▶to **perform** surgery/ an operation

treatment [U, C] (病気・けがを治す)治療, 処置, 手当て ◇He is receiving *treatment* for shock. 彼はショック(症)の治療を受けているところだ ◇She is *responding well to treatment*. 彼女は治療に対してよい反応を示している ◇Guests at the health spa receive a range of beauty and fitness *treatments*. 健康スパの客はさまざまな美容と健康のための治療を受けます

surgery [U] 手術；外科 ◇The doctor had to perform emergency *surgery* to the patient's head. 医師はその患者の頭部に緊急手術を施さなければならなかった ◇She will require *surgery* on her left knee. 彼女は左膝の手術が必要になるだろう ◇My brother went on to study *surgery*. 私の兄は手術の勉強を続けた ❶plastic surgery (形成外科), あるいは cosmetic surgery (美容整形外科)は、人の皮膚の損傷を治療する[外見を改善する]医療手術を指す。

medicine [U] (病気・けがの研究・治療をする)医学, 医療 ◇She went on to practise *medicine* after completing her studies. 彼女は研究を終えた後、続けて医院を開業した ◇Which *branch of medicine* are you going to train in? どの医学分野の研修を受けるつもりですか ◇He gave up general *medicine* to specialize in geriatric *medicine*. 彼は老齢病医学を専攻するために一般内科をあきらめた ☞ **medicine** (DRUG 2)

therapy [U, C] (病気・身体的障害に対する特定の)治療, 療法 ◇Most patients undergo some sort of drug *ther-*

↳**treatment**

apy for leukaemia. ほとんどの患者は白血病のためのある種の薬物療法を受けている ◇She has trained in alternative *therapies* (= therapies that do not use traditional drugs). 彼女は代替療法の研修を受けている ❶ *therapy* は特定の種類の治療法を意味する複合語で用いられることが多い。 physiotherapy (物理療法), chemotherapy (化学療法), radiotherapy (放射線療法), occupational therapy (作業療法), speech therapy (言語療法), psychotherapy (心理療法) など。また、therapyは薬を投与するのではなく、話し合いを通じて精神障害を治療するpsychotherapy (心理療法) を表す語でもある。

operation [C] 手術 ◇Will I need to have an *operation*? 手術を受けなければなりませんか ◇an *operation* on her lung to remove a tumour 腫瘍の摘出のための肺手術 ◇He underwent a three-hour heart *operation*. 彼は3時間の心臓手術を受けた

▶**operate** 動 [自] ◇The doctors *operated* last night. 医師たちは昨晩手術をした ◇We will have to *operate* on his eyes. 我々は彼の目の手術をしなければならないだろう

ノート **surgery** と **operation** の使い分け: surgery は不可算, operationは可算である。 ◆The doctor recommended *surgery*. (医師は手術を勧めた) ◆She's had three *operations* in the past two years. 彼女はここ2年で三度の手術を受けた

healing [U] (自然な方法による) 治癒, 治療 ◇Homeopathy aims to reinforce the body's natural *healing* powers. 類似療法は体の自然治癒力を強化することを目的としている ◇Rest is an important part of the *healing* process. 安静は治癒過程の重要な一部である ❶ faith healing (信仰療法) は、信仰と祈りの力によって病気を治療する方法を指す。 ☞ **heal** (CURE)

¹medical care [U] (病人・けが人の看護をする) 医療 ◇Many people didn't receive *proper medical care* after the explosion. その爆発後、多くの人々は適切な医療を受けなかった

cure [C] (病気の)治療; 快復 ◇Doctors cannot effect a *cure* if the illness has spread too far. 病気が広く蔓延すると医師たちは治療を施せない ◇The *cure* took six weeks. 回復には6週間かかった ☞ **cure** (CURE), **cure** (DRUG 2)

nursing [U] (仕事・技術としての)看護 ◇He is planning to follow a career in *nursing*. 彼は看護の道に進むつもりである

trend 名

trend・tendency・movement・drift
ゆっくりと起こる状況 [人々の考え方, 振る舞い方] の変化を表す
【類語訳】傾向, 動向, 趨勢, 時代の風潮, 風潮, 動き, 傾斜

文型&コロケーション
▶the trend/ tendency/ movement/ drift **towards** sth
▶the trend/ movement/ drift **away from** sth
▶a trend/ tendency **to do** sth
▶a **general** trend/ tendency/ movement/ drift
▶a **downward/ gradual** trend/ movement/ drift

trend [C] (一般的な)傾向, 動向, 趨勢, 時代の風潮 ◇a survey of social *trends* 社会動向の調査 ◇a downward/upward *trend* in sales 売上高の減少 [増加] 傾向 ◇There is a growing *trend* towards earlier retirement. 早期退職は増加傾向にある ◇The company managed to *buck the trend* (= to be different from most others) and increase profits this year. その会社は大半の会社とは異なり、何とか今年は利益増を果たした ☞ **trend** (FASHION)

tendency [C] (新しい)傾向, 風潮 ◇There is a growing *tendency* among employers to hire casual workers. 雇用者間では臨時労働者を雇う傾向が強くなっている ☞ **tendency** (TENDENCY)

movement [単数で] (段階的な) 動向, 傾向, 動き ◇A *movement* away from this idea can be seen in the second half of the century. この考えから脱却する動きは今世紀後半に見られる ◇The *movement* to greater liberalization was halted. いっそうの自由化への動きは中断させられた

drift [単数で] (悪い方向への段階的な)傾向, 傾斜, 風潮 ◇Action is needed to prevent a *drift* into lawlessness. 無法と化すのを防ぐために行動は必要である ◇The polls show a *drift* back towards Labour. 世論調査は労働党への回帰傾向を示している

trick 名 ☞ TACTIC

trick・trap・hoax・device・bluff・ruse・set-up
人をだますために行う物事
【類語訳】策略, いたずら, 引っ掛け, 罠, でっち上げ, だまし, 嘘, 計略, はったり

文型&コロケーション
▶a **clever** trick/ trap/ device/ ruse
▶a **simple** trick/ device/ ruse
▶to **try** a trick/ device/ ruse
▶to **use/ resort to** a trick/ device
▶a trick/ trap/ device/ bluff/ ruse **works**

trick [C] (人をだますための)策略, いたずら, 引っ掛け ◇They had to think of a *trick* to get past the guards. 彼らは警備員のそばを通り抜けるために策を練らなければならなかった ◇The kids are always *playing tricks on* their teacher. 子どもたちはいつも先生にいたずらばかりしている ◇She won't *fall for* such a stupid trick. 彼女はそんなばかげた手は食わないよ ◇It was a *trick question* (= one to which the answer seems easy but actually is not). それは引っ掛け問題だった ☞ **trick** (CHEAT 動), **prank** (JOKE)

trap [C] 罠 ◇She had *set a trap* for him and he had *walked* straight *into* it. 彼女が彼に罠を仕掛けたら、彼はもろにはまってしまった

hoax [C] 《特にジャーナリズム》でっち上げ, だまし, 嘘, いたずら ◇She described the deception as a cruel *hoax*. 彼女はその手口を悪質なでっち上げだと評した ◇He was accused of using a *bomb hoax* to empty a rival restaurant. 彼は競争相手のレストランをがらがらにするために、爆破予告をして起訴された ◇Detectives are still investigating the *hoax calls*. 刑事たちは依然としてそのいたずら電話の捜査をしている

device [C] (ややフォーマル) (ほしい物を手に入れるための不誠実な)策略, 計略 ◇The report was a *device* used to hide rather than reveal problems. その報告書は問題点を明らかにするというよりは、むしろ隠蔽するために用いられた策略だった ❶ *device* は必ずしも不誠実とは限らない。物事を行う巧妙で有効な方法にすぎないこともある。☞ **device** (TACTIC)

bluff [C, U] はったり ◇He said he would resign if he didn't get more money, but it was only a *bluff*. 彼はもっと金をもらわないと辞めると言ったが、それは単なるはったりにすぎなかった ◇He threatened to resign but it was all *bluff*. 彼は辞めると脅したが、まったくのはったりだった ❶ call sb's *bluff* は相手が実行するほど無慈悲[勇敢]ではないと思い込ませ、脅しを実行に移すことを命じるような場合に用いられる。◆ She was tempted to *call his bluff*, hardly able to believe he'd carry out his threat. (彼女は、彼の脅しがはったりとしか思えなかったので、やれるならやってみなさいと開き直って見せた). ☞ **bluff** (PRETEND)

ruse [C] (ややフォーマル、書き言葉、時にけなして) (ほしい物を手に入れるために人をだます) 策略、計略 ◇She tried to think of a *ruse* to get him out of the house. 彼女は彼を家から追い出す策略を練ろうとした

ノート device と ruse の使い分け: ruse は device よりも悪質なことが多い。それは真実でない事を人に信じさせようと故意に意図しているからである。device は実際に嘘をつくことなく本当の意図[理由]を隠すことが多い。

'set-up [C, ふつう単数で]《インフォーマル、ふつうけなして》罠 ◇He didn't steal the goods. It was a *set-up*. 彼は商品は盗まなかった。それは罠だったのだ

trip 图 ☞ HOLIDAY 2

trip・journey・tour・expedition・excursion・pilgrimage・outing・travels・day out
ある場所へ旅する行為
【類義訳】旅行、周遊旅行、探検、小旅行、遠足、巡礼の旅、行脚、ピクニック、日帰り旅行

【文型&コロケーション】
▶ a **trip**/ a **journey**/ a **tour**/ an **expedition**/ an **excursion**/ a **pilgrimage**/ an **outing**/ a **day out to** sth/ somewhere
▶ **on** a **trip**/ a **journey**/ a **tour**/ an **expedition**/ an **excursion**/ (a) **pilgrimage**/ an **outing**/ your **travels**/ a **day out**
▶ a **long trip**/ **journey**/ **tour**/ **expedition**/ **day out**
▶ a **short trip**/ **journey**/ **tour**/ **expedition**/ **excursion**
▶ a **pleasant trip**/ **journey**/ **tour**/ **outing**/ **day out**
▶ a **successful trip**/ **journey**/ **tour**/ **expedition**/ **outing**
▶ a **foreign**/ **overseas trip**/ **journey**/ **tour**/ **expedition**
▶ a **bus**/ **coach**/ **train**/ **rail trip**/ **journey**/ **tour**
▶ a **shopping trip**/ **expedition**/ **excursion**
▶ to **go on** a **trip**/ a **journey**/ a **tour**/ an **expedition**/ an **excursion**/ a **pilgrimage**/ an **outing**/ your **travels**/ a **day out**
▶ to **set out on**/ **set off on** a **trip**/ a **journey**/ a **tour**/ an expedition/ an excursion/ a pilgrimage/ your travels
▶ to **come back from**/ **return from** a **trip**/ a **journey**/ a **tour**/ an **expedition**/ an **excursion**/ a **pilgrimage**/ an **outing**/ your **travels**/ a **day out**
▶ to **make** a **trip**/ a **journey**/ a **tour**/ an **expedition**/ an **excursion**/ a **pilgrimage**

trip [C] 旅行 ◇a business *trip* 出張旅行 ◇a school *trip* to France フランスへの修学旅行 ◇Tomorrow there will be a *boat trip* to the island. 明日はその島への船旅をします ◇We took a *day trip* to Siena. 私たちはシエナに日帰り旅行をしました ◇They had to make several *trips* to bring all the equipment over. 彼らはすべての設備を引き渡すために数回の旅をしなければならなかった ◇From London to Oxford is a *round trip* of over 100 miles (=

it is over 100 miles there and back again). ロンドンからオックスフォードまでは往復100マイル以上の旅行

journey [C] (長距離の)旅行 ◇It was a long and difficult *journey* across the mountains. それは山脈を越える長く困難な旅だった ◇They continued their *journey* on foot. 彼らは徒歩で旅を続けた ◇We *broke our journey* (= stopped for a short time) in Madrid. 私たちは旅の途中でマドリードに立ち寄った

ノート trip と journey の使い分け: trip はこのグループで最も基本的な語であるが、journey はそうではない。trip は journey より幅広い文脈で用いられる。trip はふつうある場所へ向かい再び戻って来る旅行を指す。journey はふつう片道である。trip は、必ずしもそうである必要はないが、journey より短い距離であることが多い。◆ a *trip* to New York (ニューヨーク旅行) ◆ a round-the-world *trip* (世界一周旅行). trip はたとえ距離が長くても時間的には短いことが多い。journey は移動に長い時間がかかり、困難な場合に用いられることが多い。✕ It was a long and difficult *trip* across the mountains. 《米》では、journey は短い旅行とは限らない。◆ How far is your *journey* to work? 《特に英》通勤はどのくらい違いのですか。trip は特に楽しみ[特定]の目的の旅行に用いられる。◆ a day/school/business *trip* (日帰り/修学/出張旅行). ✕ a day/school/business *journey*.

tour [C] (異なる場所を数箇所訪れる) 周遊旅行 ◇We're going on a *tour of* Bavaria. 私たちはバイエルン地方を周遊旅行中です ◇After a *whirlwind tour* (= a very fast tour) of the temples, it was time to find a hotel. 駆け足でお寺巡りをしたら、ホテルを探す時間となった ◇If there are any problems, contact your *tour operator* (= a company that arranges organized tours). 何か問題があれば添乗員にご連絡ください ☞ **tourism** (TRAVEL), **tourist** (TOURIST)

expedition [C] (調査のための)探検；(ほしい物を手に入れるための)小旅行 ◇He *led* the first *expedition* to the South Pole. 彼は南極を初めて探検した ◇She made two *expeditions* to Brazil to study wild plants. 野生植物を研究するために彼女はブラジルへ二度探検に出かけた ◇Win a fantastic shopping *expedition* to New York! ニューヨークへの素晴らしい買い物旅行を勝ち取ってください

excursion [C] (団体の)小旅行, 遠足 ◇We decided to make an all-day *excursion* to the island. 私たちはその島に1日がかりの小旅行することにした

pilgrimage [C, U] (聖地への)巡礼の旅；(讃美[尊敬]している人との)旅行, 行脚 ◇the annual *pilgrimage* to Mecca 毎年恒例のメッカへの巡礼の旅 ◇His grave has become a *place of pilgrimage* (= a place that people go on pilgrimages to). 彼の墓は巡礼の地となった ☞ **pilgrim** (TOURIST)

outing [C] (ややフォーマル) (団体でする日帰りの)ピクニック, 遠足 ◇a family *outing* to the seaside 海辺への家族ピクニック ◇The children were on a day's *outing* from school. 子どもたちは学校から一日がかりの遠足だった

travels [複数で] (外国への)旅行 ◇The novel is based on his *travels* in Asia. その小説は彼のアジア旅行に基づいている ◇When are you *off on your travels* (= going travelling)? いつ旅に出るのですか

,day 'out (複 **days out**) [C] (特に英) 日帰り旅行 ◇We had a *day out* at the beach. 私たちはビーチに日帰り旅行をした

trouble 名

1 trouble・unrest・disturbance・disorder・anarchy・agitation
暴力的な行動[抗議]を伴う状況を表す
【類語訳】もめごと, いざこざ, トラブル, 不安, 不穏, 騒動, 動乱, 治安紊乱(㊨), 無政府状態, 抗議運動

▸文型&コロケーション
▸ trouble/ unrest/ disturbances/ disorder/ agitation **among** sb
▸ **serious** trouble/ unrest/ disturbances/ disorder
▸ **public/ political** trouble/ unrest/ disturbances/ disorder/ agitation
▸ **violent/ civil/ urban/ social** unrest/ disturbances/ disorder
▸ to **cause** trouble/ unrest/ a disturbance
▸ to **lead to** unrest/ a disturbance/ disorder/ anarchy
▸ to **quell** the unrest/ disturbance/ disorder
▸ trouble/ unrest/ a disturbance/ disorder **occurs**

trouble [U] (暴力的な)もめごと, いざこざ, トラブル ◇As the bars closed the town was full of youths *looking for trouble*. バーが閉まると町は軽はずみな行動に走る若者であふれていた ◇The police were *expecting trouble* after the game. 警察は試合後の混乱を予想していた ◇Troops were stationed nearby in case of crowd *trouble*. 群衆によるトラブルに備えて近くに軍隊が配置された
unrest [U] 《ややフォーマル》(政治上の)不安, 不穏 ◇There was growing *unrest* among the city's ethnic minorities. その都市の少数民族の間に不穏な空気が広がり始めていた
disturbance [C, U] 《ややフォーマル》(公共の場での暴力的な)騒動, 動乱 ◇News of the arrests provoked serious *disturbances* in the streets. 逮捕のニュースで市街に深刻な騒動が巻き起こった ◇The army is trained to deal with riots and civil *disturbance*. 軍隊は暴動と市民の騒動に対処するよう訓練を受けている
disorder [U] 《ややフォーマル》(公共の場での暴力的な)騒動, 治安紊乱 ◇The food crisis led to outbreaks of rioting and public *disorder*. 食糧危機により暴動と治安紊乱が発生した 反意 **order** (PEACE), ☞ **disorderly** (WILD)
anarchy [U] 無政府状態 ◇Our nation is descending into *anarchy*. 我が国は無政府状態に陥りつつある ❶国は anarchy の状態に descend into (傾斜する), slide into (次第に陥る), fall into (陥る)ことがある.
agitation [U, C] 《ややフォーマル》(政治的変革を達成するための民衆の)抗議運動 ◇There has been widespread *agitation for* social reform. 社会改革を求める抗議運動が広がっている ◇His political opponents have threatened to launch a mass *agitation against* the agreement. 彼の政敵たちは, その協定に反対する大規模な運動を始めると脅していた ☞ **agitate** (CAMPAIGN 動)

2 trouble・hardship・misfortune・adversity
人が巻き込まれる困難な[危険な]状況
【類語訳】災難, 困難, トラブル, 厄介な状況, もめごと, 苦労, 辛苦, 不運, 不幸, 逆境, 不運な事故

▸文型&コロケーション
▸ **great/ real** trouble/ hardship/ misfortune/ adversity
▸ **financial** trouble/ hardship
▸ to **cause** trouble/ hardship
▸ to **suffer/ face/ meet with** hardship/ misfortune/ adversity
▸ **in times of** trouble/ hardship/ adversity

trouble [U] 《ふつう in や into の後で》災難, 困難, トラブル; (非難・処罰を受けるかもしれない)厄介な状況, もめごと ◇A yachtsman *got into trouble* off the coast and had to be rescued. ヨットマンが沖でトラブルに陥り, 救助を必要としていた ◇The company *ran into trouble* early on, when a major order was cancelled. その会社は, 大口注文をキャンセルされて早々に困難に陥った ◇He's *in trouble with* the police. 彼は警察沙汰を起こした ◇My brother was always *getting me into trouble* with my parents. 兄はいつも両親とのもめごとに私を巻き込んでばかりいた
hardship [U, C] 《ややフォーマル》(お金・食糧・衣類などのない)苦難, 辛苦 ◇The two men endured great *hardship* during their trek across Antarctica. その二人の男は南極大陸横断中に大変な困難に耐えた ◇People suffered many *hardships* during that long winter. 人々はその長い冬の間, 多くの苦難を味わった ◇It was *no hardship* to walk home on such a lovely evening. あんなすてきな夜に歩いて帰宅してつらくもなんともなかった ☞ **hard** (DIFFICULT 2), **poverty** (POVERTY)
misfortune [U] 《フォーマル》不運, 不幸, 逆境; 不運[不幸]な事故[状況, 出来事], 災難 ◇He has known great *misfortune* in his life. 彼は人生で大きな不運を経験していた ◇We *had the misfortune to* run into a violent storm. 私たちは不運にもひどい嵐に遭った ◇She bore her *misfortunes* bravely. 彼女は立派に不運に耐えた
adversity [U, C] 《フォーマル》逆境, 不運, 不幸 ◇She has shown great courage in the face of *adversity*. 彼女は逆境に直面して並外れた勇気を見せた ◇He overcame many personal *adversities*. 彼は多くの個人的な逆境を乗り越えた

true 形 ☞ RELIABLE 2

true・right・correct
物事が事実として疑いの余地のないことを表す
【類語訳】真実の, 本当の, 事実どおりの, 正しい, 適当な

▸文型&コロケーション
▸ **right/ correct about** sb/ sth
▸ the **true/ right/ correct answer**
▸ the **right/ correct time**
▸ **quite/ absolutely/ more or less** true/ right/ correct

true 真実の, 本当の, 事実どおりの ◇That's not *strictly true* (= completely true). それは厳密に言えば真実ではない ◇Indicate whether the following statements are *true or false*. 次の文が正しいか誤っているか答えなさい ◇Is it *true (that)* she's leaving? 彼女が出て行くというのは本当ですか ◇The novel is based on a *true story*. その小説は実話に基づいている ❶他の事柄より重要だと思っても, 特定の事実[供述]が真実であることを認めるときに true を用いることができる. ◆'We could get it cheaper.' '*True*, but would it be as good?' (「それはもっと安くできますよ」「こもっともだが, 質も同じくらいいいんでしょうか」) ❶true は複写版がその中身・趣旨において原物と同じであると言うときにも用いられる. ◆The movie isn't really *true to* the book.

(その映画はあまり原作(本)に忠実ではない). **反意 untrue, false** (WRONG1), ☞ **the truth** (FACT)

right (疑いの余地がなく)正しい, 適当な ◇I got about half the answers *right*. 半分くらい正解でした ◇What's the *right* time? 正確に何時ですか ◇'David, isn't it?' 'Yes, that's *right*.'「デイヴィッドだよね」「ああ, そうだよ」◇It was Monday you went to see Angie, *right*? (= is that right?) 君がアンジーに会いに行ったのは月曜日, そうだったよね **反意 wrong** (WRONG1)
▷ **right** 副 You guessed *right*. 当たりだ
correct (ややフォーマル)(何の間違いもなく)正しい ◇Only one of the answers is *correct*. その答えのうち一つだけが正しい ◇Check that all the details are *correct*. 詳細すべてに誤りがないことを確認しなさい ◇Are you in charge here?' 'That's *correct*.'「ここはあなたの担当」「そうです」**反意 incorrect** (WRONG1)
▷ **correctly** 副 Have you spelled it *correctly*? それを正しく綴りましたか

ノート right と correct の使い分け: correct は right よりもフォーマルで, 公式[正式]な指示・文書で用いられる傾向が強い.

trust 動

trust・depend on/upon sb/sth・rely on/upon sb/sth・take sb/sth for granted・count on sb/sth・believe in sb・pin your hopes on sb/sth・have confidence in sb

人や物事が自分の望み[期待]どおりになると思う, 人や物事が伝える中身が正しい[真実である]と思う
【類語訳】信用する, 信頼する, 当てにする, 頼りにする, 信じる, 期待する, 当然のことと思う, 期待をかける, 望みを託す

文型&コロケーション
▶ to trust/ depend on/ rely on/ count on sb **to do sth**
▶ to trust/ believe/ have confidence **in** sb/ sth
▶ to trust/ rely on/ believe in/ have confidence in **yourself**
▶ to trust/ rely on/ have confidence in **sb's judgement**
▶ to trust/ rely on **sb's advice**
▶ to depend on/ rely on/ count on **sb's support**
▶ to trust/ rely on **sb's figures/ what sb tells you/ what you read**
▶ to **completely** trust sb/ depend on/ rely on/ take sb for granted/ believe in sb
▶ to **really** trust/ depend on/ rely on/ believe in sb

trust [他] (人を)信用[信頼]する, 当て[頼り]にする;(物事が真実である[正しい]と)信じる ◇It seems you can't *trust* anyone these days. 最近あなたは誰も信用していないようだね ◇You can *trust* me not to tell anyone. 誰にも言わないからぼくを信じてくれて大丈夫だ ◇I'd *trust* him with my life. 命がけで彼を信頼したい ◇I don't really *trust* his judgement. 彼の判断をそれほど信じていません ◆Don't *trust* what you read in the newspapers! 新聞で読んだことを信じるな ◇Such figures are *not to be trusted*. そんな数字は当てにならない ❶ trust は常に目的語を取る. 特に(英)では, trust in sb/sth, trust to sth といった句動詞で用いられることもある. ◆She needs to *trust* more in her own abilities. (彼女は自分の能力にもっと自信を持つ必要がある.) ◆I stumbled along in the dark, *trusting to luck* to find the right door (= hoping that I would be lucky enough to find the right door, as I had nothing to guide me). (私は目当てのドアを見つけようと運を天に任せて暗闇の中をすすきながら進んだ). **反意 distrust** (SUSPECT), ☞ **trust** (FAITH), **trusted** (RELIABLE1), **trusting** (NAIVE)

de'pend on/upon sb/sth 句動詞 ≪しばしば can/cannot/could/could not と共に≫ (人・物事を)信用[信頼]する, 当て[頼り]にする;(人・物事が真実である[正しい]と)信じる;(物事が起こると)確信[期待]する ◇He was the sort of person you could *depend on*. 彼は信頼できるタイプの人間だった ◇He knew he could *depend on* her to deal with the situation. 彼はその状況に対処する際に彼女は当てになると彼にはわかっていた ◇Can you *depend on* her version of what happened? 何が起きたかについての彼女の説明を信じられますか ◇You can *depend on* her to be (= she always is) late. ≪皮肉で≫彼女は遅れて来ると思っていいよ ❶ depend upon sb/sth は depend on sb/sth よりもフォーマルである.

re'ly on/upon sb/sth 句動詞 ≪特に can/cannot/could/could not および should/should not と共に≫ (人・物事を)信用[信頼]する, 当て[頼り]にする;(人・物事が十分正直である[正しい], 善良である]と)信じる ◇Can I *rely on* you to keep this secret? この秘密は守ってくれると信じていいのかい ◇You can't *rely on* any figures you get from them. 彼らから入手するどの数字も信頼しては駄目だ ◇You can *rely on* our support. 私たちの支援を当てにしてくださっていいです ◇The local transport system can't be *relied on*. 地方の交通網は頼りにならない ❶ rely upon sb/sth は rely on sb/sth よりもフォーマルである. ☞ **rely on/upon sb/sth** (NEED 動), **reliable** (RELIABLE1)

ノート trust, depend on/upon sb/sth, rely on/upon sb/sth の使い分け: trust は目的語に人を取るが, 物やシステムを取ることはできない. ×The local transport system can't be *trusted*. また, trust は人の judgement (判断)や advice (忠告)を目的語に取るが, 人の support (支援)を取ることはできない. depend on は support を目的語に取るが, judgement や advice を取ることはできない. rely on/upon sb/sth は特に忠告[約束する]ために, you can/could や you should と共に用いられる. ×I don't really *rely on* his judgement. ◆You can't really *rely on* his judgement. (彼の判断はさほど頼りになりません).

take sb/sth for 'granted, take it for 'granted (that…) フレーズ ≪時にけなして≫(物事を)当然のこととする;(人・物事を)当然のこととしておろそかにする, 軽視する ◇Her husband was always there and she just *took* him *for granted*. 夫がいつもそこにいてくれて, 彼女はそれを当然のことと思っていた ◇We *take* having an endless supply of clean water *for granted*. 私たちは清浄水が無制限に供給されるのを当たり前のことと考えている ◇I just *took it for granted that* he'd always be around. 彼がいつも周りにいるのに慣れっこになってしまっていただけだ

'count on sb/sth 句動詞 ≪しばしば can/cannot/could/could not と共に≫ (人・物事を)確信[期待]する, 当て[頼り]にする ◇I'm *counting on* you to help me. あなたが手伝ってくれるのを期待しています ◇We can't *count on* the good weather lasting. 晴天が続くことは当てにできません ◇Can we *count on* your support in the next election? 次の選挙であなた方の支援を期待していいですか ◇I'm sure he'll help.' '*Don't count on it*.'「彼はきっと手伝ってくれるよ」「当てにするな」❶ count on sb の目的は, 必要とするときに助けてもらうことで, 忠告してもらうことではない. ×You can

↳trust

count on his judgement. count on sb/sth は、助けを要請する[約束する]、自分の考えが正しいことを述べる[際に can/could と共に用いられることが多い]

be'lieve in sb 句動 (人を)信じる、信用[信頼]する ◇They need a leader they can *believe in*. 彼らは信頼できる指導者を必要としている ◇You've got to *believe in* yourself. 自分を信じなくては駄目だ ☞ **belief** (FAITH)

,pin your 'hopes on sb/sth 仔社 (-nn-) (人・物事の成功・支援に)期待をかける、望みを託す ◇The company is *pinning* all *its hopes on* the new project. 会社は新事業にすべての望みを託している

have 'confidence in sb/sth フレーズ (人・物事の能力・資質を)信頼する ◇The players all *have confidence in* their manager. 選手たちは全員、監督を信頼している ◇I *have* absolute *confidence in* her abilities. 彼女の能力に絶対の信頼を置いています ☞ **confidence** (FAITH)

try 動

1 try・attempt・seek・struggle・strive・endeavour・have a go・go for sth
物事を行おう[達成しよう]とする
【類語訳】努力する、試みる、挑む、企てる、努める、奮闘する、一生懸命になる、悪戦苦闘する、挑戦する

文型&コロケーション

▶ to try/ attempt/ seek/ struggle/ strive/ endeavour **to do sth**
▶ to try/ attempt/ seek/ struggle/ strive **for/ against** sth
▶ to try/ attempt/ seek/ struggle/ strive **desperately/ in vain**
▶ to be **constantly** trying/ seeking/ struggling/ striving to do sth
▶ to **consciously** try/ attempt/ seek/ strive to do sth
▶ to **deliberately** try/ attempt/ seek/ endeavour to do sth
▶ to try/ struggle/ strive **hard**

try [自, 他] 努力する、試みる ◇I don't know if I can come but I'll *try*. 来られるかどうかわからないけど努力してみるよ ◇What are you *trying* to do? 何をしようと頑張ってるの ◇I *tried* hard not to laugh. 笑わないようにしようと懸命に努めた ◇She *tried her best* to solve the problem. 彼女は問題を解決するために最善の努力をした ◇Just *try your hardest*. ただ精一杯努力しなさい ❶話し言葉では、try は to 不定詞の代わりに and + 他の動詞の形で用いられる。◆ I'll *try and* get you a new one tomorrow. (明日は新しいのを手に入れてあげられるよう努力します)。◆ *Try and* finish quickly. (早く終わるよう努力しなさい)。この構文では、try は不定詞でしか用いることができず、人にどうすべきか指図するときにも用いることができる。☞ **try** (ATTEMPT)

attempt [他] (ややフォーマル) (困難[危険]な事に[を])挑む、試みる、企てる ◇The prisoner was shot while *attempting* to escape. その囚人は脱走を試みて撃たれた ◇The coastguard had advised them not to *attempt* a rescue. 沿岸警備隊は彼らに救助を試みては駄目だと忠告した ◇More than once, depression drove him to *attempt suicide*. うつ病から彼は一度ならず自殺未遂に追いやられた ☞ **attempt** (ATTEMPT)

▶ **attempted** 形 《名詞の前で》 ◇*attempted* rape/ murder/robbery (= that was attempted but was not successful) 強姦／殺人／強盗未遂

try

ノート **try** と **attempt** の使い分け：try のほうが一般的で、インフォーマルな会話で用いられることが多い。attempt はフォーマルで、達成するための努力ではなく、行為の始まりに重点を置く。名詞を伴う場合、attempt はふつう成功しなかった[成功しそうにない]事柄への努力を指す。◆ The prisoners *attempted* an escape, but failed. (囚人たちは脱走を試みたが失敗した)。

seek [他] 《seek to do sth の形で》《フォーマル》(長い時間かかるかもしれない事を行おうと)努める、試みる ◇The research project will *seek* to find an answer to this question. その研究プロジェクトはこの問題の答えを見つけ出そうとするでしょう ☞ **seek** (ASK 2), **seek** (LOOK 動 2)

struggle [自, 他] (困難な問題で)努力[奮闘]する、一生懸命になる、悪戦苦闘する ◇Shona *struggled* for breath. ショーナは息を吸おうともがいた ◇The family *struggled through* the next few years. その後数年、家族は悪戦苦闘した ◇I'm really *struggling with* this essay. 私はこのエッセーに必死で取り組んでいる ◇They *struggled* just to pay their bills. 彼らは支払いをするためだけに一生懸命だった ☞ **struggle** (EFFORT)

strive [自] 《フォーマル》 (長きにわたって)一生懸命に努力する、奮闘する ◇We constantly *strive* for excellence in design. 私どもは常にデザインの優秀性を追求して懸命にしています ◇They were always *striving towards* perfection. 彼らはいつも完璧を求めて奮闘していた

endeavour 《英》 《米 endeavor》 [他] 《to 不定詞を伴って》《フォーマル》 一生懸命に努力する ◇I will *endeavour* to do my best for my country. 国のために最善を尽くすよう努力します ☞ **endeavour** (EFFORT)

have a 'go 仔社 《インフォーマル, 特に話し言葉》試みる、挑戦する ◇'I can't start the engine.' 'Let me *have a go*.' 「エンジンがかからないよ」「ぼくがやってみるよ」 ◇I've always wanted to *have a go* at windsurfing. ずっとウインドサーフィンに挑戦してみたいと思っていました

'go for sth 句動 《インフォーマル, 話し言葉》 (物事を手に入れよう[達成しよう]と)懸命に努力する[頑張る] ◇*Go for it*, John! You know you can beat him. 頑張れ、ジョン。お前ならあいつを倒せる ◇She'll be *going for gold* in the Olympics. 彼女はオリンピックで金メダルを取りにいくでしょう

2 ☞ TEST 動 1
try・taste・sample
どんなものか確かめるために使う[行う、経験する]
【類語訳】試す、試しに使う、味見する、試食する、試飲する

文型&コロケーション

▶ to try/ sample a **new product**
▶ to try/ taste/ sample **food/ wine**

try [他] 試す、試しに使う[行う、食べる、飲む] ◇Have you *tried* this new coffee? It's very good. この新しいコーヒーは飲んでみたかい。とってもおいしいよ ◇*Try* these shoes *for size* — they should fit you. この靴のサイズが合うかどうか履いてみてですよ ◇She *tried* the door, but it was locked. 彼女はドアを開けようとしたが鍵がかかっていた ◇John isn't here. *Try phoning* his home number. ジョンはここにはいません。自宅の番号に電話してみなさい ☞ **try sb/sth out** (TEST 動 1)

taste [他] 味見[試食, 試飲]する ◇*Taste* it and see if you think there's enough salt in it. 塩加減が十分かどうか味見して確かめなさい

sample [他]《書き言葉》(物を少量だけ)味見[試食]する, (物事を短時間だけ)味わう ◇I *sampled* the delights of Greek cooking for the first time. ギリシャ料理のおいしさを初めて体験しました ◇He put his head out of the window and *sampled* the morning air. 彼は窓から頭を出して朝の空気を味わった

tumour 《英》(《米》tumor) 名

tumour・ulcer・sore・swelling・inflammation・blister・lump・bump・abscess・boil
病気[けが]の結果として, 不健康で通常より大きくなった皮膚上[体内]の箇所
【類語訳】腫瘍, 潰瘍, 腫れ物, 腫れ, 炎症, 水ぶくれ, こぶ, しこり, 打撲傷, 打ち身, 膿瘍, おでき

▸文型&コロケーション

▸ a tumour/ an ulcer/ sores/ a swelling/ a blister/ a lump/ an abscess/ a boil **on** a part of the body
▸ a tumour/ an ulcer/ a swelling/ inflammation/ a lump/ an abscess **in** a part of the body
▸ (a) **painful** ulcers/ sores/ swelling/ inflammation/ blisters/ lump/ abscess/ boil
▸ to **have** a tumour/ an ulcer/ a sore/ a swelling/ inflammation/ a blister/ a lump/ a bump/ an abscess/ a boil
▸ to **develop** a tumour/ an ulcer/ a blister/ an abscess
▸ to **get** an ulcer/ sores/ a blister/ a bump/ a boil
▸ to **treat** a tumour/ an ulcer/ a boil
▸ a tumour/ an ulcer/ a blister/ an abscess **forms/ develops**
▸ an ulcer/ a blister/ an abscess/ a boil **bursts**

tumour 《英》(《米》**tumor**) [C] 腫瘍 ◇He has a *malignant* (= harmful) *brain tumour*. 彼は悪性の脳腫瘍を患っている ◇They were relieved to hear that the *tumour* was *benign* (= not dangerous). 腫瘍が良性だと聞いて彼らは安堵した

ulcer [C] 潰瘍 ◇a stomach *ulcer* 胃潰瘍 ◇a mouth *ulcer*《英》口内炎 ❶《米》で mouth ulcer は, canker sore と呼ばれる

sore [C] 腫れ物, 潰瘍 ◇The illness left them with *open sores* all over their backs. その病気で, 彼らの背中じゅうに口の開いた潰瘍が残った ❶cold sore (ヘルペス)は, ウィルスによって引き起こされる唇上[口内]に痛みを伴う発疹である。canker sore (口内炎)は, mouth ulcer を意味するが,《米》の語句で, ウィルスによって引き起こされるものではない。
☞ **sore** (PAINFUL1)

swelling [U, C] 腫れ；腫れ物 ◇Use ice to reduce the *swelling*. 氷を使って腫れを抑えなさい ◇The fall left her with a painful *swelling* above her eye. 彼女は転んで, 目の上に痛みを伴う腫れができた

inflammation [U, C] 炎症 ◇The doctor's notes recorded *inflammation* of the ear. 医師のメモには耳の炎症と記録されていた ☞ **inflamed** (PAINFUL1)

blister [C] 水ぶくれ ◇He'd got *blisters* on his feet from running. 彼は走って足に水ぶくれができた

lump [C] (重病の兆候でもありうる)こぶ, しこり, 腫れ物 ◇He was unhurt except for a *lump* on his head. 頭のこぶ以外は彼は無傷だった ◇Check your breasts for *lumps* every month. 毎月胸のしこりを検査しなさい

bump [C] (ややインフォーマル)(物に当たってできる)こぶ, 打撲傷, 打ち身 ◇She was covered in *bumps* and bruises. 彼女は打ち身とあざだらけだった

abscess [C] 膿瘍 ◇He had a painful *abscess* on his gum. 彼は歯肉に痛みのある膿瘍ができた

boil [C] おでき ◇The *boil* on his back was painful. 彼の背中のおできが痛んだ

ノート abscess と boil の使い分け：boil は常に体の表面の皮膚下にしかできず, ふつう abscess ほど深刻なものではない。abscess は体内に深く進行することがあり, ふつう医師の治療が必要となる。

turn 動

1 turn・turn (sb/sth) around/round・swing・twist・spin・wheel・whirl・swivel・pivot
他の方向に向くために体(の一部)を動かす
【類語訳】向きを変える, 振り向く, 回転させる, 振り向かせる, ねじる, ひねる, くるりと回す, さっと向ける, 旋回する

▸文型&コロケーション

▸ to turn/ swing/ twist/ spin/ wheel/ whirl/ swivel/ pivot **around/ round**
▸ to turn/ swing/ spin/ wheel/ whirl/ swivel **back/ away**
▸ to turn/ turn around/ swing/ spin/ whirl/ swivel/ pivot **on** sth
▸ to turn/ twist/ swivel your **head**
▸ to turn/ turn around/ swing/ twist/ spin/ wheel/ whirl around/ swivel **to face** sb/ sth
▸ to turn/ turn around/ swing/ spin/ wheel/ whirl **suddenly**
▸ to turn/ turn around/ swing/ spin/ wheel **sharply/ quickly**
▸ to turn/ turn around/ twist **slowly**

turn [自, 他]《ふつう副詞や前置詞と共に》(体(の一部))の向きを変える ◇We *turned* and headed for home. 私たちは向きを変えて自宅に向かった ◇Anne flushed and *turned* back to his work. 彼は職場に引き返した ◇Anne flushed and *turned* her head away. アンは顔を赤らめて横を向いた ◇While his *back was turned* I sneaked a look at his notes. 彼が背中を向けている間に彼のメモを盗み見た

ˌturn aˈround/ˈround, ˌturn sb/sth aˈround/ˈround 句動詞 向きを変える, 振り向く, (人・物)を回転させる, 振り向かせる ◇*Turn around* and let me look at you. 振り向いて顔を見せて ◇*Turn* your chair *round*. 椅子を回転させて ❶ turn around/round などの句動詞において, round は特に《英》で用いられ, around は特に《米》で用いられる。

swing [自, 他]《副詞や前置詞と共に》(突然)くるりと向きを変える, 振り向く；(人・物)を回転させる, 振り向かせる ◇The bus *swung* sharply to the left. バスは左に急旋回した ◇She *swung* around angrily, her eyes blazing. 彼女は目を血走らせて怒って振り返った ◇He *swung* the car round in a dangerous U-turn. 彼は危険な急旋回で車をUターンさせた

twist [自, 他]《ふつう副詞や前置詞と共に》(体の部位を)ねじる, ひねる ◇She *twisted* in her chair to look. 彼女は椅子にすわったまま体をねじって見た ◇Hold your arms out to the sides and *twist* your upper body. 腕を両側に伸ばして腰をひねりなさい

spin [自, 他]《副詞や前置詞と共に》(素早く)くるりと向きを変える, 振り向く；(人・物)を回転させる, 振り向かせる ◇She *spun* on her heel and walked out. 彼女はくるりと向きを変えて歩み出した ◇He *spun* the child roughly around.

彼は手荒く子どもを振り向かせた

wheel [自, 他]《副詞や前置詞と共に》《書き言葉》[素早く[突然]]くるりと向きを変える, 振り向く ; (人・物を)回転させる, 振り向かせる ◇Jim *wheeled* back to face me. ジムはくるりと振り返って私と向かい合った ◇He *wheeled* his horse around. 彼はさっと馬の向きを変えた

whirl [自, 他]《ふつう副詞や前置詞と共に》《書き言葉》[素早く[突然]]くるりと向きを変える, 振り向く ; (人・物を)回転させる, 振り向かせる ◇She *whirled* on him, furious. 彼女は激怒して彼の方をくるりと向いた ◇He grasped her wrist and *whirled* her back to face him. 彼は彼女の手首をつかんで自分のほうにさっと向かせた ❶この意味では, whirl は人についてしか用いられない. ふつう, その人は強い感情, 特に怒りの下に行動している.

swivel (-ll-, 米 -l-) [自, 他]《書き言葉》[素早く]くるりと振り向く, (体・目・頭を)くるりと回す, さっと向ける ◇He *swivelled* around to look at her. 彼はくるりと振り返って彼女を見た ◇I *swivelled* my head to peer at him. 私は首をくるりと回して彼を見つめた

pivot [自]《ふつう副詞や前置詞と共に》(中心点の上で)向きを変える, 回転[旋回]する ◇He *pivoted* on one foot and threw the ball to Gary. 彼は片足を軸に回転し, ゲーリーにボールを投げた ◇The mechanism *pivots* around a central point. その機械は中心点を支点に旋回する

2 turn・transform・convert・change・translate・evolve・mutate・metamorphose
外見[特徴]が異なる, 外見[特徴]を異ならせる
【類語訳】変わる, 変える, 一変させる, 変形させる, 変容させる, 進化する, 突然変異する, 突然変異させる

文型&コロケーション
▶to turn/ transform sth/ convert/ change/ translate/ evolve/ mutate/ metamorphose **into** sth
▶to turn/ transform sth/ convert/ change/ evolve/ mutate/ metamorphose **from** sth **into** sth
▶to turn/ transform sth/ convert/ evolve/ mutate **rapidly** (into sth)
▶to turn/ transform sth/ convert/ change/ evolve **quickly/ slowly/ gradually** (into sth)
▶to turn/ transform sth/ convert/ change **suddenly/ miraculously/ overnight** (into sth)
▶to transform/ convert/ change sth **completely**
▶to **easily/ automatically** turn/ transform sth/ convert/ change/ translate (into sth)

turn [自, 他]《into や from と to と共に》(…に)変わる ; (…に)変える ◇The natural sugars *turn* into alcohol during brewing. 天然糖は醸造中にアルコールに変化する ◇The problem *turned* into an advantage. その問題は利点に転じた ◇The leaves gradually *turn* from green to orange. 葉は緑色から次第にオレンジ色に変わる ◇There are plans to *turn* the old station into a hotel. 古い駅をホテルに変える計画がある ❶童話では, 魔法使いが turn sb into sth (人を物に変える)ことがある. ◆With a wave of her wand, she *turned* him *into* a frog. 魔法の杖を一振りして彼女は彼を蛙に変えてしまった. 日常会話の場合は, 人は犯罪者, ギャンブラー, 暴君, 英雄, 映画スターに turn into sth (変わる)するし, 周りの環境が人をそういったものに turn sb into sth (変える)人. 人は建物をホテルに, 家屋を住居に turn sth into sth することもある. また, 状況が…に変わる, 状況を…に変えると言う場合にも turn sth, turn sth into sth で表

現することができる. ◆What began as a minor disagreement has *turned into* a major crisis. 小さな不一致として始まったことが重大な危機に変わってしまった ◆I managed to *turn* the whole thing *into* a joke. 私はすべてを何とかジョークにした.

transform [他](よりよくするために つくり)変える, 一変させる ; (物事を)変形[変容]させる ◇A new colour scheme will *transform* your bedroom. 新しい色彩設計は寝室を一変させるでしょう ◇It was an event that would *transform* my life. それは私の生活を一変させる出来事だった ◇The photochemical reactions *transform* the light into electrical impulses. 光化学反応は光を電気インパルスに変換する ❶日常会話では, transform はふつう変化が劇的だったことを示唆する. 科学的な文脈では, transform は必ずしも劇的な変化を示すとは限らない.

▶**transformation** [名] [C, U] ◇The country's *transformation* from dictatorship to democracy has been peaceful. 《書き言葉》その国の独裁制から民主制への転換は平和的だった ◇What a *transformation*! You look great. 何て変わりようなの. すごく決まってるじゃない

convert [他, 自](形態・目的・システムが[を])変わる, 変える ; (ある形態・目的・システムに)変わることのできる ◇The hotel is going to be *converted* into a nursing home. そのホテルは養護施設に改装される予定である ◇Hot water is *converted* to electricity by a turbine. 熱湯はタービンによって電気に変えられる ◇We've *converted* from coal to gas central heating. 私たちは石炭暖房から集中ガス暖房に切り替えました ◇We need a sofa that *converts* into a bed. 私たちとしてはソファーベッドがほしい ❶convert は人々が住むのにふさわしいものにするために古い建物を変えることについて用いられることが多い. ◆to *convert* a church/ farm buildings/a barn/a house/stables/a mill (into sth) (教会/農舎/納屋/家/厩舎/工場を(…に)改装する). ◆They now live in a *converted* church/barn/mill. (彼らは教会/納屋/工場を改装した家に住んでいる). convert は目的語を取らずに, ある種のサービスから別のサービスに変わることについて用いられることが多い. ◆All homes must *convert* to digital TV by 2012, when the analogue signal will be switched off. (すべての家庭はアナログ信号が止まる2012年までにデジタルテレビに変えなくてはならない). また, ある通貨から別の通貨に換えること, お金の保有形式を変えることについても用いられる. ◆to *convert* securities into shares (有価証券を株式に換える). ☞**conversion** (CHANGE [名] 2), **convertible** (FLEXIBLE 1)

change [自, 他]《into や from と共に》(状態が[を])変わる, 変える ◇Caterpillars *change* into butterflies. 毛虫は蝶に変わる ◇The lights *changed* from red to green. 信号は赤から青に変わった ◇With a wave of her wand, she *changed* the frog into a handsome prince. 魔法の杖を一振りして彼女は蛙をハンサムな王子に変えた

ノート turn と change の使い分け: change は物事が自然に[自動的に, 魔法で]変化する場合にしか用いられない. これらの場合には turn を用いることが多い. change は人々が努力を払って[技術を使って]ある物[状況]を別の物[状況]に変える場合や環境が状況を変える場合にいつも用いられるとは限らない. ×There are plans to *change* the old station into a hotel. ×I managed to *change* the whole thing into a joke. ×A minor disagreement has *changed* into a major crisis.

translate [他, 自]《ややフォーマル》(形態が[を])変わる, 変える ◇It's time to *translate* words into action. 言

葉を行動に移すときだ ◇I hope all the hard work will *translate* into profits. あらゆる努力が利益に変わることを望んでいる ◇Most attempts to *translate* Shakespeare to the small screen (= television) are not successful. シェイクスピア作品のテレビドラマ化の試みはほとんど日の目を見ていない ❶ translate は人々が好結果を得たいと思っていることについて用いられることが多い. ◆You need to *translate* your ideas into practice/your enthusiasm into success. (自分の考えを実践に/熱意を成功に変えなければなりません). また, 例えば(劇場向きに企画された)テレビドラマの制作など, 異なる媒体を使って同じ物を生み出すことがいかに容易[困難]かについて用いられたり, システムの別の場所への導入について用いられたりすることが多い. ◆I'm not sure how well the American system would *translate* to a European context. (米国のシステムがいかにうまくヨーロッパの事情に合わせて変わるか確信がない).

evolve [自, 他] 《生物》《動植物が》進化する; 進化させる ◇The three species *evolved* from a single ancestor. その3つの種は単一の祖先から進化した ◇The dolphin has *evolved* a highly developed jaw. イルカは非常に発達した顎を進化させた ☞ **evolve** (DEVELOP 1)
▶ **evolution** [名] [U] ◇the *evolution* of the human species 人類の進化

mutate [自, 他] 《生物 or 書き言葉》突然変異する[させる]; (新しい形態に)変わる ◆We are studying the ability of the virus to *mutate* into new forms. 私たちはウィルスが新しい形態に突然変異する能力を研究しています ◆Scientists have been able to replace the *mutated* gene with a normal one. 科学者たちは突然変異した遺伝子を正常な遺伝子に置き換えることができるようになっている ◇Rhythm and blues *mutated* into rock and roll. リズム&ブルースはロックンロールに変化した ❶遺伝子変化(genetic change)は生物の細胞の中にある身体的特徴を制御する遺伝因子に関連するものをいい, 不快な物への段階的変化を表す. ◆to *mutate* into a monster/a writhing, biting snake/rotting vegetation (怪物/のたくる噛みつき蛇/腐敗ゆう種に変化する). また, しばしば奇妙な[不可解な]形で単独で徐々に起こるように思える変化を表すこともある. ◆Memories had *mutated* into bizarre myths. (記憶は奇妙な作り話に変わった).
▶ **mutation** [名] [U, C] ◇These cells have been affected by *mutation*. これらの細胞は突然変異の影響を受けてきた ◇The disease is caused by genetic *mutations*. その病気は遺伝子の突然変異によって引き起こされる

metamorphose [自]《フォーマル》《一定期間をかけて》変わる ◇The caterpillar will eventually *metamorphose* into a butterfly. 毛虫は最終的には蝶に変化するでしょう ◇She had *metamorphosed* from an awkward schoolgirl into a beautiful woman. 彼女は垢抜けしない女生徒から美しい女性へと変身した
▶ **metamorphosis** [名] [C, U] ◇We studied the *metamorphosis* of a caterpillar into a butterfly. 《フォーマル》私たちは毛虫から蝶への変態を学んだ

turn out [句動詞]

turn out・emerge・come out・come to light・get out・transpire・leak out
未知の情報が知れ渡る
【類語訳】わかる, 判明する, 明らかになる, わかってくる, 明るみに出る, 漏れる, 発覚する

【文型&コロケーション】
▶ news/ the truth emerges/ comes out/ gets out/ leaks out
▶ It turns out/ emerges/ transpires that...
▶ it now turns out/ emerges/ transpires...
▶ to turn out/ emerge/ come out/ come to light/ transpire later
▶ to turn out/ emerge/ transpire/ leak out subsequently
▶ to turn out/ emerge/ come out/ come to light finally

,turn 'out [句動詞] 《予期せずに結局…であることが》わかる, 判明する ◇The job *turned out to be* harder than we thought. その仕事は我々が思う以上に大変だとわかった ◇It *turned out* that she was a friend of my sister. 彼女は姉の友人であることが判明した

emerge [自] 《ややフォーマル》《事実・考え・証拠が》明らかになる, わかってくる, 明るみに出る ◇No new evidence *emerged* during the investigation. 捜査中に新たな証拠は何も出て来なかった ◇It *emerged* that the company was going to be sold. その会社は売却される予定であることが明らかになった ◇One thing *emerges* very clearly *from* this study. この研究から一つのことが非常にはっきりとわかってくる

,come 'out [句動詞] 《ニュース・話・真実が》明らかになる, 判明する ◇The full story *came out* at the trial. 裁判でその話の一部始終が判明した ◇It *came out* that he'd been telling lies. 彼がずっと嘘をついてきたことが明らかになった

come to 'light [行idiom] 《証拠・知識が》明るみに出る ◇New evidence has recently *come to light*. 最近, 新たな証拠が明るみに出た

,get 'out [句動詞] 《進行形がまれ》《ややインフォーマル》《秘密情報が》漏れる, 発覚する ◇If this *gets out* there'll be trouble. これが漏れれば問題になるでしょう

transpire [動] [自]《進行形がまれ》《フォーマル》《秘密・未知の情報が》明るみに出る, 発覚する ◇It *transpired* that the gang had had a contact inside the bank. 銀行内部にギャングの密通者がいたことが発覚した ◇This story, it later *transpired*, was untrue. 後でわかったことだが, この話は虚偽であった

,leak 'out [句動詞] 《進行形がまれ》《ややインフォーマル》《秘密情報が》漏れる, 発覚する ◇Details of the plan soon *leaked out*. 計画の詳細がまもなく漏れた ☞ **leak** (REVEAL)

【ノート】get out と leak out の使い分け: leak out は特定の組織, 例えば政府などの内部の人間しか知らない情報について用いられる. get out は情報が偶然[故意]に漏らされる場合. leak out はふつう, 例えば組織に影響・損害を与えるために故意に漏らされる場合に用いられる.

turn sth off [句動詞]

turn sth off・switch (sth) off・shut sth off・disconnect・turn sth out・unplug
スイッチ[ボタンなど]を動かして電気[ガス, 水道など]の流れを止める
【類語訳】電源を切る, 消す, 栓を締める, 止める, スイッチを切る, 電話が切れる, プラグを抜く

【文型&コロケーション】
▶ to turn off/ switch off/ disconnect/ unplug a/ the machine/ phone
▶ to turn off/ switch off/ shut off/ disconnect the power/

turn sth off

electricity supply
- to turn off/ shut off/ disconnect the **gas/ water**
- to turn off/ switch off/ turn out a **light/ lamp**
- to turn off/ switch off/ unplug an/ the **appliance/ TV**
- to turn off/ switch off/ shut off the **engine**
- to turn off/ switch off the **motor/ ignition/ wipers/ alarm/ torch/ computer**

,turn sth 'off 句動詞 《特に話し言葉》（機械・照明の）電源を切る，消す（電気・ガス・水道の）栓を締める，止める ◇Please *turn* the television *off* before you go to bed. 就寝前にテレビを消してください ◇*Turn* that tap *off*! その栓を締めて ◇They've *turned off* the water while they repair a burst pipe. 破裂したパイプを修理している間，彼らは水を止めた ❶ *turn off*は水・ガスが流れ出るのを防ぐために栓を締める場合にも，電気機器・機械の動作を止める場合にも用いられる．反意 **turn sth on** (TURN STH ON), ☞ **turn sth down** (REDUCE)

,switch sth 'off 句動詞 （機械・照明・電気の供給の）スイッチ[電源]を切る ◇How do you *switch* this thing *off*? どうやってこの電源を切るのですか ◇The electricity has been *switched off*. 電気はスイッチが切られていた ❶ *switch off*はスイッチ・ボタンを用いる電気装置にしか用いず，水道・ガス・栓には用いない．《英》では，switch offはテレビ・ラジオについて用いる場合には目的語なしで用いることもできる．◆I *switched off* (= the television/radio) after five minutes — I thought the show was awful. 《英》5分でテレビ[ラジオ]を消したよ—ひどい番組だと思った．反意 **switch sth on** (TURN STH ON), ☞ **switch** (BUTTON 1)

,shut sth 'off 句動詞《特に書き言葉 or 専門語》（エンジン・電気・水道・ガスを）止める ◇He *shut off* the engine and silence enfolded them. 彼がエンジンを止めると彼らは沈黙に包まれた ◇A valve *shuts off* the gas when the lid is closed. ふたが閉じられるとバルブがガスを止めます

dis'connect 他，しばしば受身《特に書き言葉》（ガス・水・電気の供給設備を）外す；（電話回線・水・電気・ガスの供給を）止める；（電話中に）電話が切れる ◇First, *disconnect* the boiler from the water mains. まず，ボイラーを給水本管から外してください ◇You may be *disconnected* if you do not pay the bill. 支払わなければ（電話）止められるかもしれません ◇We were suddenly *disconnected*. 私たちの電話は突然切れた 反意 **connect**

,turn sth 'out 句動詞 （照明の）スイッチ[電源]を切る，消す ◇Remember to *turn out* the lights when you go to bed. 寝寝するときは明かりを消し忘れないように 反意 **turn sth on** (TURN STH ON)

un'plug (-gg-) 他（電気装置の）プラグを抜く ◇If I'm very busy, I *unplug* the phone. とても忙しいときは電話線を抜いておくんだ 反意 **plug sth in** (TURN STH ON)

turn sth on 句動詞

turn sth on • switch sth on • start • plug sth in(to sth) • set sth off • start (sth) up • put sth on

機械[電気装置など]を作動させる
【類語訳】（電気などを）つける，栓を開ける，スイッチを入れる，電源を入れる，始動させる，始動する，爆発させる，再生する

文型&コロケーション
- to turn on/ switch on/ start/ plug in/ start up a **machine**
- to turn on/ switch on/ plug in/ start up a **computer**
- to turn on/ switch on/ plug in an **appliance**
- to turn on/ switch on/ start/ start up the **motor/ engine**
- to turn on/ switch on/ start the **ignition**
- to turn on/ switch on/ plug in/ put on the **lamp/ light/ television/ radio/ fire/ heater**
- to turn on/ switch on/ put on the **gas/ heating/ oven/ headlights/ wipers**
- to switch on/ plug in/ put on the **kettle**

,turn sth 'on 句動詞《特に話し言葉》（電気・ガス・水道などを）つける，栓を開ける ◇He *turned on* the taps and washed his hands. 彼は栓をひねって手を洗った ◇I'll *turn* the television *on*. テレビをつけるよ ❶ *turn sth on*は水・ガスを流れさせるために栓をひねる場合にも，電気装置・機械を作動させる場合にも用いられる．反意 **turn sth out** (TURN STH OFF), ☞ **turn sth up** (INCREASE)

,switch sth 'on 句動詞 （照明・機械などの）スイッチ[電源]を入れる ◇How do you *switch* this thing *on*? これはどうやってスイッチを入れるの ❶ *switch sth on*は電気装置を作動させることにしか用いられない．《英》では switch onはテレビ・ラジオについて用いる場合には目的語なしで用いることもできる．◆We only *switched on* (= the television/radio) halfway through the show. 《英》私たちは番組の途中でテレビ[ラジオ]をつけた．反意 **switch off** (TURN STH OFF), ☞ **switch** (BUTTON 1)

start [他，自]（乗り物・機械を）始動させる；（乗り物・機械が）始動する ◇*Start* the engines! エンジンをかけろ ◇I can't get the car *started*. 車が動かない ◇The car won't *start*. 車はどうしても動かない

,plug sth 'in, ,plug sth 'into sth 句動詞 (-gg-) （電気装置を[に]）プラグで接続する，プラグを差し込む ◇Is the printer *plugged in*? プリンターはコンセントが入っていますか ◇Simply *plug* the lamp *into* a 13-amp socket. 単にランプのプラグを13アンペアのソケットに差し込むだけでいいんだ 反意 **unplug** (TURN STH OFF)

,set sth 'off 句動詞 （爆弾などを）爆発させる；（警報装置を）鳴らす ◇A gang of boys were *setting off* fireworks in the street. 少年のグループが通りで花火を打ち上げていた ◇Opening this door will *set off* the alarm. このドアを開けると警報が鳴ります

,start sth 'up, ,start 'up 句動詞 （乗り物・機械を）始動させる；（乗り物・機械が）始動する ◇The first thing I do is *start up* my computer. まず最初にすることはコンピューターを起動させることです ◇I heard his car *start up*. 彼の車のエンジンがかかるのが聞こえた 反意 **shut down** ❶ shut downはコンピューターなどの機械を起動させることと反対のことを意味する．乗り物を停止(stop)させてから，エンジンを切る(turn off)ので turn off the car/vehicleとは言わない．

> ノート startと start upの使い分け：場合によって両語も使用可能．◆*Start/start up* the engine!（エンジンをかけろ）．startのみ get sth started, sth won't start などで用いられる．×I can't get the car *started up*. ×The car won't *start up*. start sth upはコンピューターについて用いられる一般的な語句である．×The first thing I do is *start* my computer.

,put sth 'on 句動詞《特に話し言葉》（機器の）スイッチ[電源]を入れる；（テープ・CDなどを）再生する，かける ◇She *put on* the brakes suddenly. 彼女は突然ブレーキをかけた ◇I'll *put* the kettle *on* for tea.《英》お茶の用意にやかんをかけよう ◇Do you mind if I *put* some music on? 音楽をかけても構いませんか ❶put sth on は車の部位を作動させることについて用いられることが多い. ◆to put on the brakes/headlights/indicator/turn signal/windscreen wipers/windshield wipers (ブレーキをかける/ヘッドライトをつける/方向指示器をつける/ウィンカーを出す/フロントガラスのワイパーを動かす/フロントガラスのワイパーを動かす). 音楽を聴くことについても用いられることが多い. ◆to put on a CD/some music (CD/音楽をかける). 家庭では, put on the kettle/the air conditioning/(英)the heating/(米)the heat の形で用いられる傾向が最も強い.

typical 形

typical・characteristic・symbolic・representative・classic・archetypal・stereotypical・quintessential
特定のタイプの人[物事, 集団]に性質[特徴]がふつうに備わっていることを表す
【類語訳】典型的な, 代表的な, 特有の, 独特の, 象徴となる, 象徴的な

文型&コロケーション
▶ typical/ characteristic/ symbolic/ representative of sth
▶ a typical/ a characteristic/ a representative/ a classic/ an archetypal **example** of sth
▶ a typical/ a characteristic/ a symbolic/ a representative/ an archetypal **figure**
▶ a typical/ characteristic/ symbolic **gesture**
▶ typical/ characteristic/ stereotypical **behaviour**
▶ very typical/ characteristic/ symbolic/ representative/ stereotypical
▶ highly typical/ characteristic/ symbolic
▶ fairly typical/ characteristic/ representative/ stereotypical

typical (特定のタイプの人・物事・集団に)典型的な, 代表的な, 特有の ◇It's a typical Italian café. それって典型的なイタリアンカフェだね ◇This meal is typical of local cookery. この料理は代表的な郷土料理法によるものだ ◇The weather at the moment is not typical for July. 現在の天気は7月特有のものではない ❶typical はまた, 性格がわかっていて, その行動パターンが読める人について語るときにも用いられる. この用法は不満を示すことが多い. ◆It was typical of her to forget. (彼女が忘れるのはよくあることだった). ◆He spoke with typical enthusiasm. (彼はいつもながら熱心に語った). ◆She's late again — typical! ((インフォーマル, 話し言葉, けなして)彼女はまた遅刻だ — いつものことだ). 反意 **atypical** (UNUSUAL)
▶ **typically** 副 ◇They treated us to some typically American hospitality. 彼らは私たちをアメリカ独特のサービスでもてなしてくれた ◇Typically, she couldn't find her keys. 例によって彼女は鍵を見つけられなかった

characteristic (ややフォーマル)(物事・人の性格[行動]に)特有の, 独特の ◇With characteristic modesty she insisted on sharing the credit with the whole team. 彼女特有の慎み深さから, 彼女はチーム全体で賞賛を分かち合おうと主張した ◇They suffer from many of the environmental problems that are characteristic of inner-city areas. 彼らは都心部にありがちな多くの環境問題

に悩んでいる 反意 **uncharacteristic** ❶uncharacteristic は人・物事に特有[人の通常の振る舞い方]でないことを表す. ◆The remark was quite uncharacteristic of her. (その発言には彼女らしさがまったくなかった).
▶ **characteristically** 副 ◇Characteristically, Helen paid for everyone. いかにもだけヘレンがみんなの分の支払いをしたんだよ

ノート **typical** と **characteristic** の使い分け: 予期するとおりに人が振る舞うことを意味して用いられる両語であるが, typical はふつう(称賛の場合もなくはないが)非難の意味合いを持つのに対して, characteristic は称賛の意味合いで用いられる. ◆It was typical of her to forget. (彼女が忘れるのはよくあることだった). ◆Such generosity was characteristic of Mike. (そういった気前のよさがマイクらしかった).

symbolic 象徴となる; 象徴的な ◇The dove is symbolic of peace. 鳩は平和の象徴である ◇He shook his fist in a symbolic gesture of defiance. 彼は象徴的な反抗のしぐさとして拳を振り回した ◇The new regulations are largely symbolic (= they will not have any real effect). 新たな規則は概して象徴的なだけです
▶ **symbolically** 副 ◇a symbolically significant gesture 象徴的に重要なしぐさ

representative (ややフォーマル) (特定の集団に)代表的な; (大きな集団に)典型的な ◇The paper-thin models in magazines are not representative of most women. 雑誌に載る紙のように細いモデルたちは大多数の女性とはかけ離れている ◇We interviewed a representative sample of teachers. 我々は教師の典型とも言うべき人にインタビューした 反意 **unrepresentative** ❶unrepresentative は, 物事・人々の集団に典型的ではなく, その集団の情報源として有用でない場合に用いられる. ◆an unrepresentative sample (典型的でない見本).

classic (非常に)典型的な ◇It was a classic example of poor communication. それはコミュニケーション不足の典型的な例だった ◇She displayed the classic symptoms of depression. 彼女はうつ病の典型的な症状を示していた ❶この意味でのclassicが最も頻繁に結びつく語はexampleである.

archetypal (ふつう名詞の前で)(ややフォーマル, 書き言葉)(重要な性質・特徴をすべて備えていて)典型的な ◇The Beatles were the archetypal pop group. ビートルズは典型的なポップグループだった ◇It was the archetypal British suburb, built in the 1930s. そこは1930年代に築かれた典型的な英国の郊外だった

stereotypical (しばしばけなして) (固定観念として抱かれていて)典型的な ◇She did not conform to his stereotypical image of feminine behaviour. 彼女は, 彼が考えている女性らしい振る舞いの典型的なイメージに合っていなかった

quintessential [名詞の前で](フォーマル)(完璧に)典型的な ◇He was the quintessential tough guy. 彼はまさにタフガイだった
▶ **quintessentially** 副 ◇a sense of humour that is quintessentially British まさにイギリス的なユーモアのセンス

U u

ugly 形

ugly・hideous・unattractive・grotesque・plain・unsightly

人や物が見るのに愉快でないことを表す
【類語訳】見苦しい, 醜い, ぞっとする, 忌まわしい, 魅力のない, 異様な, 奇怪な, 美しくない, かわいくない, 目障りな

unattractive	ugly	hideous
plain	unsightly	grotesque

文型&コロケーション
- an ugly/ a hideous/ a grotesque/ a plain **face**
- an ugly/ an unattractive/ a plain **girl/ woman**
- an ugly/ unattractive **man**
- to **look** ugly/ hideous/ unattractive/ grotesque/ unsightly
- **very** ugly/ unattractive/ plain/ unsightly
- **pretty** ugly/ hideous/ unattractive
- **quite** ugly/ hideous/ grotesque
- **rather/ extremely** ugly/ unattractive/ plain

ugly 見苦しい, 醜い ◇The room was full of heavy, *ugly* furniture. その部屋は重くて見苦しい家具で一杯だった ◇The screaming child in her arms was an *ugly* little thing. 彼女の腕の中で泣きわめく子どもは小さな醜い存在でしかなかった 反意 beautiful (BEAUTIFUL 1, 2)

hideous 《ややインフォーマル, 特に話し言葉》《非常に醜くて[不快で]》ぞっとする, 忌まわしい ◇The curtains were a *hideous* brown colour. カーテンはぞっとするような茶色だった ◇The whole experience had been like some *hideous* nightmare. その経験すべては忌まわしい悪夢のようだった
▶ **hideously** 副 ◇His face was *hideously* deformed. 彼の顔はぞっとするほど変形していた

unattractive 《特に書き言葉》魅力のない, 醜い ◇His face creased into an *unattractive* smile. 彼は顔にしわを寄せて醜い笑顔を浮かべた ◇The women were young and not *unattractive* (= they were attractive). 女性たちは若く魅力的だった 反意 attractive (BEAUTIFUL 1, 2)

grotesque 《(恐怖・笑いを引き起こすほど)異様な, 奇怪な ◇It was a *grotesque* figure with a snarling beast's head. それは歯をむき出してうなる獣の頭を持つ奇怪な姿だった

plain 《特に書き言葉》《女性・少女が》美しく[かわいく]ない, 不器量な ◇As a child she was rather *plain*. 子どもの頃, 彼女はかなり不器量だった 反意 pretty (BEAUTIFUL 1), ☞ **plain** (PLAIN 1)

unsightly 《ややフォーマル》見苦しい, 醜い, 目障りな ◇There were *unsightly* marks on the walls caused by damp. 壁には湿気でできた見苦しい跡があった ◇It was an area of *unsightly* derelict buildings. そこは目障りな廃屋が立ち並ぶ地域だった ❶ unsightly は人ではなく物に用いられる. 魅力さを損なう marks (跡), patches (継ぎ) などに用いられることが多い.

unacceptable 形

unacceptable・unreasonable・too much・intolerable・unbearable・out of line・out of order・insufferable

とても悪くて受容[忍耐]不可能であることを表す
【類語訳】受け入れられない, 容認できない, 許容できない, 承服できない, 理性を欠いた, 耐えられない, 我慢できない

文型&コロケーション
- unacceptable/ intolerable **to** sb
- too much/ intolerable/ unbearable **for** sb
- unacceptable/ unreasonable/ intolerable/ unbearable **that**…
- unacceptable/ unreasonable/ too much/ intolerable/ unbearable/ out of order **to do sth**
- unacceptable/ unreasonable/ intolerable **behaviour/ demands/ interference/ levels**
- an unacceptable/ unreasonable/ intolerable **burden**
- an unacceptable/ intolerable/ unbearable **situation**
- **quite/ completely/ totally** unacceptable/ unreasonable/ intolerable/ unbearable/ out of order
- **absolutely/ increasingly** unacceptable/ intolerable/ unbearable
- **a bit** unreasonable/ too much/ out of order
- **almost/ nearly** too much/ intolerable/ unbearable

unacceptable 《ややフォーマル》受け入れられない, 容認[許容, 承服]できない ◇Such behaviour is totally *unacceptable* in a civilized society. そのような行動は文明社会ではまったく受け入れられない ◇Such a solution would be quite *unacceptable* to the majority of people. そのような解決策では大多数の人々にまったく受け入れられないだろう ◇Noise from the factory has reached an *unacceptable* level. 工場の騒音は許容できない水準にまで達した 反意 acceptable (FINE), acceptable (RIGHT 形 2)
▶ **unacceptably** 副 ◇*unacceptably* high levels of unemployment 容認できないほど高い失業率の水準

unreasonable 《適当でなく》無理な, 無分別な, 理性を欠いた;《(過度な要求で)法外な, 不当な, 理不尽な ◇It would be *unreasonable* to expect somebody to come at such short notice. そんな急に誰かが来てくれると思っても無理だろう ◇The fees they charge are not *unreasonable*. その請求金額は法外ではない ◇He was being totally *unreasonable* about it. 彼はそのことについてすっかり理性を失っていた 反意 reasonable (REASONABLE)

too much 《ややインフォーマル, 話し言葉》《(持っている以上の技術・体力を必要として)手に負えない, 過酷である;耐えられない, まいらせる ◇What with the exams, and then his illness, things have become *too much* for him. 試験やら病気やらで, 彼にとって事態は過酷なものとなっている ◇This is *too much*! First she complains that I'm never in the office, then she wants to know why I'm not visiting so many clients. いやम, まいったよ. まず, 彼女は私が事務所に全然いないと文句を言うかと思うと, 次にどうして私があまり顧客を訪問しないのかを知りたがりもするんだ

intolerable

intolerable 《ややフォーマル》(状況・感情・行動が)耐えられない, 我慢できない, 目に余る ◇Keeping the secret put an *intolerable* burden on him. その秘密を守ることが彼には我慢ならないほどの負担になった ◇Her behaviour has become *intolerable*. 彼女の行動は目に余るものとなった ◇It seems to me *intolerable* that children do not have the same legal protection as adults. 子どもたちが大人と同じ法的保護を受けないのは, 私には耐えがたいものに映る 反意 tolerable ❶反意語の tolerable はふつう, almost intolerable を表現する文脈の中で用いられる. ◆ At times, the heat was barely *tolerable*. (時折, 暑さはかろうじて耐えられた).

▶**intolerably** 副 ◇It became *intolerably* hot by day. 昼間は我慢できないほど暑くなった

unbearable (状況・感情・人に[が])耐えられない, 我慢できない, 鼻持ちならない ◇Some of the victims were suffering *unbearable* pain. 犠牲者の中には耐えられないほどの痛みに苦しんでいる者もいた ◇The heat was becoming *unbearable*. 暑さは耐えがたいものとなりつつあった ◇He's been *unbearable* since he won that prize. 彼はその賞を取ってから鼻持ちならない奴になった 反意 **bearable** ❶反意語の bearable はふつう, almost unbearable を表現する文脈の中で用いられる. ◆ She was the only thing that made life *bearable*. (彼女が人生を何とか我慢できるものにしてくれる唯一の存在だった).

▶**unbearably** 副 ◇*unbearably* hot/painful/arrogant 耐えがたいほど暑い/痛い/横柄さ

ノート **intolerable** と **unbearable** の使い分け: 多くの場合, 両語とも使用可能. ◆ *intolerable*/*unbearable* heat/pain/suffering/tension/excitement (耐えがたい暑さ/痛み/苦しみ/緊張/興奮). しかしながら, unbearable は単に感情と言うより正義感を害するという事柄に関していつも用いられるわけではない. ✕It is *unbearable* that children do not have the same legal protection as adults. unbearable は精神的苦痛よりも肉体的苦痛について用いられることが多く, 人があまりにも困難なことを行わなければならないような状況では用いられない. ✕Keeping the secret was an *unbearable* burden. unbearable は人を主語に取ることができるが, intolerable は不可. ✕He's been *intolerable* since he won that prize.

,out of 'line 行私 《特に米, インフォーマル, 話し言葉》(人が容認できないほど)やり[言い]過ぎの;(言動が容認できないほど)行き過ぎの, 常軌を逸した, 規則に反した ◇You'd better better calm down — you're way *out of line*. 落ち着け, 落ち着いたほうがいいって—君は言い過ぎなんだよ ◇If you **step out of 'line** one more time, you're fired. もう一度規則に反した行動をとったら, 君は首だ

,out of 'order 行私 《英, インフォーマル, 話し言葉》(人が容認できないほど)やり[言い]過ぎの;(言動が容認できないほど)行き過ぎの, 常軌を逸した, 規則に反した ◇What he did was right *out of order*. 彼がしたことはまったく常軌を逸していた

ノート **out of line** と **out of order** の使い分け:《英》では, out of order は out of line よりも頻繁に用いられるが,《米》では用いられない. 人を主語に, get/step out of line と言えるが, get/step out of order とは言えない.

insufferable 《ややフォーマル》(人・人格が)耐えられない, 我慢できない, しゃくに障る ◇She's totally *insufferable*! 彼女には我慢ならない ◇He bore a look of *insuf-*

ferable smugness. 彼はしゃくに障るうぬぼれた表情をした

unclear 形

unclear • uncertain • unresolved • in doubt • indefinite • in the balance • undecided
物事が明確でない[決定されていない]状態を表す
【類語訳】はっきりしない, 不明確な, わかりづらい, 不明瞭な, 不確かな, 未決定の, 未解決の, 未回答の

文型&コロケーション
▶ It is unclear/ uncertain **what**/ **whether**...
▶ to **remain** unclear/ uncertain/ unresolved/ in doubt/ in the balance/ undecided
▶ to **leave sth** unclear/ uncertain/ unresolved/ in doubt/ undecided
▶ **still** unclear/ uncertain/ unresolved/ in doubt/ in the balance/ undecided

unclear はっきりしない, 不明確[不確定]な;わかりづらい, 不明瞭, 不明な, 不確かな ◇His motives are *unclear*. 彼の動機ははっきりしない ◇Our plans are *unclear* at the moment. 我々の計画はまだ不確定だ ◇It is *unclear* whether there is any damage. 被害があるかどうかは不明である ◇Some of your diagrams are *unclear*. 君が描いた図解の中にはわかりにくいものがある 反意 **clear** (CLEAR 形 1, 2)

uncertain 不明確[不確定]な, 未決定の ◇It is *uncertain* what his role in the company will be. 会社における彼の役割がどんなものになるかは未定である ☞ **uncertain** (UNSURE), **uncertainty** (DOUBT 名 2)

unresolved 《フォーマル》(問題・質問が)未解決[未回答, 未決定]の ◇These *unresolved* issues must be addressed. これらの未解決問題には本気で取り組まなければならない

in 'doubt フレーズ 《しばしば否定的な文で》不明確[不確定]な, 未決定の ◇The success of the system is not *in doubt*. そのシステムの成功は確実だ ❶ in doubt は特に物事の結果・将来・成功・本質について用いられる.

indefinite 無期限の ◇She will be away for the *indefinite* future. 彼女は将来無期限にわたって不在であろう ◇The workers have been on *indefinite* strike since July. 労働者たちは7月以来無期限のストライキを敢行中だ

▶**indefinitely** 副 ◇The trial was postponed *indefinitely*. 裁判は無期限に延期された

in the 'balance 行私 不確定[不安定]な, 未決定な ◇The long-term future of the space programme hangs *in the balance*. 宇宙計画の長期的な未来は不確定の状態にある ◇His life hung *in the balance* for two weeks as he lay in a coma. 彼の命は昏睡状態で横になったまま, 2週間の間不安定な状態が続いた ❶ in the balance は人・物事の将来・結果が当面非常に不確かである状況を表す. 将来の結果が, 成功と失敗[生と死]といった正反対の一方になることが予想される場合に用いられることが多い.

undecided [名詞の前まれ] 未決定の ◇The venue for the World Cup remains *undecided*. ワールドカップの開催地は未決定のままだ

unconscious 形

unconscious • unintended • unplanned • subconscious • unintentional

意識的に自覚していなくても、行動[考え]に影響を与える
【類語訳】無意識下の, 意図的でない, 知らず知らずの, 故意でない, 潜在意識下の

文型&コロケーション

- an unconscious/ unplanned/ unintentional **action**
- an unintended/ unplanned **consequence**
- an unintended/ unintentional **effect**
- at an unconscious/ a subconscious **level**
- an unconscious/ a subconscious **desire/ feeling/ fear/ memory**
- the unconscious/ subconscious **mind**
- largely unconscious/ unintended/ unintentional

unconscious (感情・考え・行動が)無意識(下)の; 意図的でない, 知らず知らずの ◇Human beings are driven by many *unconscious* impulses. 人間は多くの無意識の衝動に突き動かされている ◇The brochure is full of *unconscious* humour. そのパンフレットは巧まざるユーモアにあふれている ◇She researches into the depths of the *unconscious* mind. 彼女は無意識の精神の深遠さを研究している 反意 **conscious** (DELIBERATE)
▶**the unconscious** 名 [単数で] ◆the concept of *the unconscious* as first developed by Freud《心理》フロイトが初めて発展させた無意識の概念
▶**unconsciously** 副 ◆She *unconsciously* began to relax in his company. 彼女は彼と一緒にいることで知らず知らずのうちにくつろぎ始めた 反意 **consciously** (DELIBERATE)

unintended (効果・結果・意味が)意図(的)[故意]でない ◇an *unintended* insult 故意でない侮辱 ◇In law you are considered responsible for the *unintended* consequences of your actions. 法律では, 君は君の行動の意図せぬ結果に対して責任があると考えられる 反意 **intended** (DELIBERATE)

unplanned 予定外の, 無計画の ◇The clinic provides advice on *unplanned* pregnancies. その診療所では予定外妊娠について助言をしている

subconscious [ふつう名詞の前で] 潜在意識(下)の ◇Some patients have a *subconscious* fear that they will die under anaesthetic. 患者の中には麻酔薬で死ぬのではないかという潜在意識下の恐怖を抱く者もいる ◇Early childhood events are stored in the *subconscious* memory. 幼児期早期の出来事は潜在意識下の記憶に蓄積される 反意 **conscious** (DELIBERATE), ☞ **the/your subconscious** (MIND)
▶**subconsciously** 副 ◇*Subconsciously*, she was looking for the father she'd never known. 彼女はまったく知らない父親を潜在意識下で捜していた

ノート **unconscious** と **subconscious** の使い分け:
感情は unconscious, subconscious で形容できるが, 行動は unconscious でしか形容できない。◆He pushed back his hair in an *unconscious* gesture of annoyance. (彼はいら立ったときの無意識の仕草として, 髪をかき上げた)。×He pushed back his hair in a *subconscious* gesture. 両語とも意識していない感情を含む精神の一部を表すことができるが, **the unconscious** (無意識) は心理学におけるより専門的な用語である。

unintentional 意図的[故意]でない ◇Perhaps I misled you, but it was quite *unintentional*. 私は君に誤解させたかもしれないが, まったく故意ではなかったんだ 反意 **intentional** (DELIBERATE)
▶**unintentionally** 副 ◇They had *unintentionally* provided wrong information. 彼らは意図せず誤った情報を与えていた 反意 **intentionally** (DELIBERATE)

uncontrollable 形

uncontrollable・overwhelming・intractable・irresistible・unmanageable
物事が管理[対処]困難[不可能]であることを表す
【類語訳】抑えがたい, 手に負えない, 抗しがたい, 扱いにくい

文型&コロケーション

- an uncontrollable/ overwhelming/ irresistible **urge/ impulse**
- an overwhelming/ irresistible **force/ influence/ pressure/ temptation/ desire**
- apparently uncontrollable/ overwhelming/ intractable/ irresistible/ unmanageable
- completely uncontrollable/ overwhelming/ irresistible/ unmanageable

uncontrollable (感情・物事・人が)抑えがたい, 手に負えない ◇I had an *uncontrollable* urge to laugh. 私には抑え難い笑いたくなる衝動があった ◇That child is *uncontrollable* (= behaves very badly and cannot be controlled). あの子は手に負えない
▶**uncontrollably** 副 ◇She began shaking *uncontrollably*. 彼女は震え出すのを抑えきれなかった

overwhelming (感情・経験が)抗しがたい[抑え]がたい, 圧倒的な ◇She had an almost *overwhelming* desire to tell him the truth. 彼女は彼に真実を話したいというほとんど抗しがたい欲求を覚えた ◇You may find the whole experience somewhat *overwhelming*. その体験全体を何やら圧倒的なものに感じるかもしれない

intractable《フォーマル》(問題・人が)扱いにくい, 対処の難しい ◇Unemployment was proving to be an *intractable* problem. 失業は対処の難しい問題だと判明しつつあった ◇There was no pleasing this *intractable* man. この扱いにくい男を満足させることはできなかった

irresistible (感情・出来事・議論が)抗し[抑え]がたい, 圧倒的な ◇The temptation to take a look proved to be *irresistible*. 一目見たいという衝動はとても抑えられるものではなかった ◇His arguments were *irresistible*. 彼の主張は有無を言わさぬものだった
▶**irresistibly** 副 ◇They were *irresistibly* drawn to each other. 彼らは抗しがたいほど互いに惹かれ合った

unmanageable (問題・人が)扱いにくい, 管理[対処]の難しい, 手に負えない, 収拾のつかない ◇The costs involved had become *unmanageable*. 関連費用は手に負えなくなっていた 反意 **manageable** ❶ 管理・対処が可能であることを表す。◆The debt has been reduced to a more *manageable* level. (負債はより対処可能な水準にまで減っている)。

understand 動

1 understand・see・get・follow・grasp・comprehend・catch on・take sth in
物事がなぜ起こるのか, 物事がどう機能するのか, 物事が何を意味するのかなどを知る
【類語訳】わかる, 理解する, 把握する

understand

文型&コロケーション

▶ to understand/ see/ get/ follow/ grasp/ comprehend/ catch on to/ take in **what/ why/ how**...
▶ to understand/ see/ get/ grasp/ comprehend/ take in **that**...
▶ to understand/ see/ get/ grasp/ take in the **meaning** (of sth)
▶ to understand/ see/ get/ grasp the **point/ idea** (of sth)
▶ to understand/ grasp a **concept/ principle**
▶ to understand/ follow the **instructions**
▶ **can/ can't** understand/ see/ follow/ grasp/ comprehend/ take in sth
▶ to **try to** understand/ see/ follow/ grasp/ comprehend/ take in sth
▶ to **begin to** understand/ see/ grasp/ comprehend/ take in sth
▶ to be **easy/ difficult/ hard** to understand/ see/ follow/ grasp/ comprehend/ take in
▶ to **easily** understand/ see/ grasp/ comprehend
▶ to **(not) quite** understand/ see/ get/ follow/ grasp sth
▶ to **fully** understand/ see/ grasp/ comprehend/ take in sth

understand [他, 自]《進行形なし》わかる；理解する ◇Do you *understand* French? フランス語がわかりますか ◇He couldn't *understand* what she was saying. 彼は彼女が何を言っているのか理解できなかった ◇Doctors still don't *understand* much about the disease. 医師たちはまだこの病気についてあまり理解していない ◇The disease is still not fully *understood*. その病気はまだ十分に理解されていない ◇I could never *understand* why she was fired. なぜ彼女が解雇されるのかまったく理解できなかった ◇I just don't *understand*! どうにも理解できないよ ◇I don't want you doing that again. Do you *understand*? あなたにそれをもう一度やってほしくないんだ。わかるかい 反義 **misunderstand** (MISUNDERSTAND)

see [自, 他]《進行形なし》《特に話し言葉》理解する, わかる ◇It opens like this.' ' Oh, *I see*.' 「こんなふうに開きます」「ああ、なるほど」◇*You see*, she only heard about the plan yesterday. いいかい、彼女はその計画について昨日聞いたばかりなんだよ ◇I don't think she *saw* the point of the story. 彼女は話の要点をわかっていないと思う ◇Oh yes, *I see what you mean*. ええ、おっしゃることはわかります ◇Can't you *see* that he's taking advantage of you? 彼に利用されているのがわからないの

get [他, 受身なし]《進行形なし》《インフォーマル、特に話し言葉》(冗談[人が言おうとしていること, 人が描写しようとしている状況]を)理解する、わかる ◇She didn't *get* the joke. 彼女はその冗談がわからなかった ◇I don't *get* you. あなたの言っていることがわかりません ◇I don't *get it* — why would she do a thing like that? わからないなあ—どうして彼女はそんなことをするんだろう ◇I *get the message* — you don't want me to come. 言ってることはわかるよ—私に来てほしくないんだろう

follow [自, 他]《進行形なし》(説明・話・物事の意味を)理解する, わかる ◇Sorry — I don't quite *follow*. すみません—まったくわかりません ◇I don't *follow* you. おっしゃることがわかりません ◇The plot is almost impossible to *follow*. その筋はほとんど理解不能

grasp [他]《進行形なし》(事実・考え・物事のやり方を)把握する, 理解する, わかる ◇They failed to *grasp* the importance of his words. 彼らは彼の言葉の重要性を把握できなかった ◇She was unable to *grasp* how to do it. 彼女はどうやったらいいのかがわからなかった

ノート understand と grasp の使い分け：物事の意味・重要性を初めて理解する場合に understand, grasp を用いることができる。◆It's a difficult concept for children to *understand*/*grasp*. (それは子どもが理解するには難しい概念である)．物事の意味・重要性を知っている状態に対しては understand, have grasped を用いる。◆By this time, engineers *understood*/*had grasped* the basic principles of aerodynamics. (このときまでには、技師たちは空気力学の基本原理を理解していた)．×By this time, engineers *grasped* the basic principles... understandだけが言語・単語・書かれた物について用いることができる。×I don't *grasp* French/the instructions.

comprehend [他, 自]《進行形では用いない；しばしば否定的な文で》《フォーマル》(事実・考え・理由を)理解する ◇The concept of infinity is almost impossible for the human mind to *comprehend*. 無限の概念を人間の頭で理解するのはほぼ不可能である ◇He stood staring at the body, unable to *comprehend*. 彼は理解できずに、死体を見つめて立っていた

,**catch 'on** 句動詞《進行形なし》《インフォーマル、特に話し言葉》(状況を)把握する、理解する、わかる ◇She still didn't *catch on*, even after all those hints. それらすべてのヒントをもらってもなお、彼女はわかっていなかった ◇He finally *caught on to* what was going on. 彼はようやく何が起きているのかを把握した

,**take sth 'in** 句動詞《しばしば否定的な文で》(聞いて[読んで]物事を)理解する ◇I realized I was reading without *taking* anything *in*. 私は自分が何も理解せずに読んでいたことがわかった

2 understand・relate to sb/sth・identify with sb/sth・empathize

他の人が感じる[経験する]ことを知って[共有して]いる
【類語訳】理解している、わかっている、共感する、感情移入する

文型&コロケーション

▶ to **try to** understand/ relate to/ identify with/ empathize (with) (sb/ sth)
▶ to **be able/ unable to** understand/ relate to/ identify with/ empathize (with) (sb/ sth)
▶ I, you, he, etc. **can/ could** understand/ relate to/ identify with/ empathize with sb/ sth
▶ It's **easy/ difficult/ hard to** understand/ relate to/ identify with/ empathize (with) (sb/ sth)
▶ to **really/ totally** understand/ relate to/ identify with/ empathize (with) (sb/ sth)
▶ to **easily** understand/ relate to/ identify with (sb/ sth)

understand [他, 自] (人のことを[が])理解している、わかっている ◇Nobody *understands* me. 誰も私のことを理解していない ◇He doesn't *understand* women at all. 彼は女性というものがまったくわかっていない ◇They *understand* what I have been through. 彼らは私が何を体験してきたかわかっている ◇If you want to leave early, I'm sure he'll *understand*. もし早退したいのなら、きっと彼はわかってくれると思う ☞ **understanding** (SENSITIVE 1)

re'late to sb/sth 句動詞 (共感して人・物事のことを)理解している、わかっている ◇Many adults can't *relate to* children. 多くの大人は子どものことが理解できない ◇Our product needs an image that people can *relate to*. 我々の製品には人々が共感できるイメージが必要だ

i'dentify with sb/sth 句動詞 （共感して他の人に）自分を重ね合わせる、感情移入する ◇I didn't enjoy the book because I couldn't *identify with* any of the main characters. 主要な登場人物の誰にも感情移入できなかったので、その本は楽しくなかった

ノート **relate to sb/sth**と**identify with sb/sth**の使い分け：relate to sb/sthはふつう個人的な関係について用いられ、例えば、先生と生徒、親と子、社長と従業員などの関係がいかにうまくいっているかを表すことができる。◆He's a successful and popular teacher because he really *relates to* the children. （子どものことを本当に理解しているがために、彼は人気のある名教師なのだ）。一方、identify with sbは、ある人と何かしらよく似ている、あるいはある人と同じ経験を持っていると感じる場合に用いられる。さらに、本や映画の登場人物、作家や俳優といった有名人に対する好意的な感情を表すこともある。◆Which character do you *identify with* most, the father or his son?（どちらの登場人物に一番共感しますか、父親ですか、息子ですか）

empathize [英でまた **-ise**] [自] 他人の身になれる、共感[感情移入]する ◇A glamorous 20-year-old stylist is unlikely to *empathize* with a working mother of three. 20歳の色っぽいスタイリストが3人の子持ちの働く母親の身にはなれそうにない ☞ **sympathize (SORRY FOR SB)**

understanding 名

understanding・sense・insight・conception・comprehension・grasp・appreciation・depth
状況やテーマなどを理解する人の能力
【類語訳】理解、知識、感覚、意識、センス、理解力、鑑賞力、洞察、洞察力、見識、概念、観念、造詣

文型&コロケーション

▶ sb's understanding/ sense/ conception/ comprehension/ grasp/ appreciation/ depth **of** sth
▶ **beyond** (sb's) understanding/ (sb's) conception/ (sb's) comprehension/ sb's grasp
▶ an understanding/ a sense/ an insight/ the conception/ an appreciation **that**...
▶ (a) **good** understanding/ sense/ conception/ grasp/ appreciation
▶ a **proper** understanding/ sense/ grasp/ appreciation
▶ a **thorough** understanding/ comprehension/ grasp/ appreciation
▶ an **adequate** understanding/ conception/ comprehension/ grasp/ appreciation
▶ (a) **historical/ musical** understanding/ sense/ insight/ appreciation
▶ to **have** an understanding/ a sense/ (an) insight/ a conception/ a comprehension/ a grasp/ an appreciation/ depth
▶ to **show** understanding/ a sense/ insight/ a grasp/ an appreciation
▶ to **increase/ enhance** your understanding/ your sense/ insight/ comprehension/ your appreciation
▶ to **improve** your understanding/ your sense/ insight/ comprehension/ grasp
▶ to **develop/ gain** an understanding/ a sense/ an insight/ an appreciation
▶ a **level** of understanding/ insight/ comprehension/ appreciation

▶ a **lack** of understanding/ insight/ comprehension/ appreciation/ depth

understanding [U, 単数で] （特定のテーマ[状況]に対する）理解、知識 ◇The committee has little or no *understanding* of the problem. 委員会は問題をほとんど、あるいはまったく理解していない ◇The vastness of the universe is beyond human *understanding*. 宇宙の広大さは人知を越えている ◇His writings reflect a good *understanding* of the society he lived in. 彼の著書が、彼が暮らしていた社会に対する十分な理解が反映されている 反意 **misunderstanding (ILLUSION)**

sense [単数で]（物事に対する）感覚、意識；（物事に関して賢明な判断をする）感覚、センス、理解力[鑑賞]力 ◇She always had a strong *sense* of personal responsibility (= an understanding that she is responsible for her own actions). 彼女はいつも自ら責任を取る気持ちが強かった ◇Babies seem to have an innate *sense* of rhythm (= an ability to respond to the beat of music). 赤ん坊は生まれながらにしてリズム感を持っているようだ ◇One of the most important things in a partner is a *sense of humour* (= the ability to find things funny or make people laugh). パートナーに最も重要なことの一つはユーモアのセンスである ◇I've got a hopeless *sense of direction* (= ability to know where I am and where I am going in relation to other places). 私には絶望的なほど方向感覚がない ◇Always try to keep a *sense of proportion* (= the ability to know what is important in relation to other things). 常に平衡感覚を保とうと努力しなさい ◇Ed doesn't have any *dress sense* (= the ability to know what clothes look good) at all! エドは服のセンスがまったくない ◇I developed a certain *road sense* (= the ability to travel on roads safely) during my years as a cyclist. 自転車に乗っている数年の間にいくぶん交通安全の感覚を養った ❶この意味では、senseはほとんど常に **a/sb's sense of sth**, **dress/road sense** の句で用いられる。

insight [U, C]《しばしばほめて》（真実を理解する）洞察力；（物事に対する）洞察、看破、見識 ◇She was a writer of great *insight*. 彼女は洞察力の鋭い作家だった ◇I hope you've gained some *insight into* the difficulties we face. あなたは我々の直面している困難をある程度察しておられることと思います ◇The book gives us some fascinating *insights* into life in Mexico. その本はメキシコの暮らしについて見事に看破している

conception [U, C]《ややフォーマル》（物事に関する）概念、観念 ◇He has no *conception* of what it's like to be unemployed. 失業しているとはどういうものか、彼には見当がつかない ◇I had a rather romantic *conception* of life in the country. 私はその国での生活[田舎の暮らし]をかなりロマンチックなものだと思い描いていた

comprehension [U, 単数で]《ややフォーマル、特に書き言葉》理解（力）◇His behaviour was beyond *comprehension*. 彼の行動は理解できなかった ◇The task requires a good *comprehension* of complex instructions. その任務には複雑な指示に対する十分な理解力が求められる

grasp [単数で]（テーマに対する）理解 ◇She has an excellent *grasp* of English grammar. 彼女は英文法を見事に理解している ◇Such complicated instructions are beyond the *grasp* of most of our students. そういった複雑な指示は私たちの学生ほとんどの理解を越えている

appreciation [U, 単数で]《ややフォーマル》（状況・問題・

テーマに対する十分[好意的]な)理解 ◇I had no *appreciation* of the problems they faced. 私は彼らが直面している問題を正しく理解していなかった ◇Candidates should have a broad *appreciation* of contemporary issues. 候補者たちは現代の問題を幅広く理解していなければなりません ☞ **appreciate** (KNOW)

depth [U] 《ほめて》深い知識, 造詣; (深い知識を提供[説明]する)深み, 深遠さ ◇a writer of great wisdom and *depth* 素晴らしい知恵と深い知識を備えた作家 ◇a job that doesn't require any great **depth of knowledge** 深い知識を大して必要としない仕事 ◇His ideas lack *depth*. 彼の考えは深みに欠ける

undo 動

undo・open・untie・unbutton・detach・unfasten・unzip・unwrap

しっかりと固定された[縛られた, 包まれた]物を開ける, 結合された二つの物を分ける
【類語訳】開ける, ほどく, 外す, ボタンを外す, 取り外す, 引き離す, ジッパーを外す, 包装を解く

▸文型&コロケーション

▸to undo/ open/ untie/ unwrap a **parcel/ package**
▸to undo/ untie a **knot/ rope/ string/ ribbon/ lace/ shoelace**
▸to open/ unwrap a **present**
▸to undo/ unbutton/ unfasten/ unzip a **jacket/ coat/ fly**
▸to undo/ unbutton/ detach/ unfasten a **collar**
▸to undo/ unfasten a **belt/ button/ clip/ strap/ zip/ buckle/ catch/ seat belt**
▸to undo/ unbutton a **blouse/ shirt**

undo [他] (固定された[縛られた, 包まれた]物を)開ける, ほどく, 外す, 脱ぐ ◇I can't *undo* this zip — it seems to be stuck. このジッパーを開けられない—ひっかかっているみたいだ ◇He *undid* his jacket and threw it over a chair. 彼はジャケットを脱いで椅子の上に放り投げた ◇I *undid* the package and took out the books. 私は包みを開けて本を取り出した

open [他] (容器などを)開ける ◇Shall I *open* another bottle? もう一瓶開けましょうか ◇He *opened* the letter and read it. 彼は手紙を開けて読んだ

untie [他] (結び目・縛られた物を)ほどく ◇Can you *untie* this knot for me? この結び目をほどいてもらえますか ◇He *untied* the rope and pushed the boat into the water. 彼はロープをほどいてボートを水の中に押し出した ◇She *untied* his hands and let him go. 彼女は彼の手をほどいて, 彼を行かせた 反意 **tie** (ATTACH)

unbutton [他] (衣服の)ボタンを外す ◇He *unbuttoned* his shirt. 彼はシャツのボタンを外した 反意 **button** (TIE), ☞ **button** (BUTTON 2)

detach [他, 自] 《ややフォーマル》(大きな物から物を)取り外す, 引き[切り]離す (物から)分離する, 外れる ◇*Detach* the coupon and return it as soon as possible. できるだけ早く無料引換券を切り離してご返送ください ◇One of the panels had become *detached* from the main structure. 一枚のパネルが主要構造からはがれていた ◇The skis should *detach* from the boot if you fall. 転んだらスキー板がブーツから外れるはずです 反意 **attach** (ATTACH)

unfasten [他] 《ややフォーマル》(固定された物を)開ける, ほどく, 外す ◇Passengers are permitted to *unfasten* their seat belts. 乗客の皆さんはシートベルトを外してかまいません 反意 **fasten**, ☞ **fastener** (BUTTON 2)

unzip (-pp-) [他] (かばん・衣服の)ジッパーを外す; (かばん・衣服が)ジッパーで開く ❶《英》zipや《米》zipperは, 引き合わせて閉め, 引き出して開ける 歯のついたプラスチックの2列の歯からなるファスナーの一種である. ◆She *unzipped* his jacket, as if he were a child. (彼女は彼がまるで子どもであるかのように, 彼のジャケットのジッパーを開けてやった) ◆The bag *unzips* at the side. (そのかばんは横のジッパーが開きます). 反意 **zip**, ☞ **zip, zipper** (BUTTON 2)

unwrap (-pp-) [他] 包み紙を取り去る, 包装を解く, 開ける ◇Don't *unwrap* your present until your birthday. 誕生日までプレゼントを開けちゃ駄目よ 反意 **wrap** ❶ wrap sth (up)は, 例えばプレゼントとしてあげようとする場合などに, 紙などの材料で物を覆うことをいう. ◆He spent the evening *wrapping* up the Christmas presents. (彼はその夜をクリスマスプレゼントの包装に費やした) ◆individually *wrapped* chocolates (個別に包装されたチョコレート).

undoubted 形

undoubted・unchallenged・undisputed・unquestioned・uncontested

誰もが正しい[真実である]と認めることを表す
【類語訳】疑問の余地のない, 紛れもない, 確かな, 揺るぎない, 議論の余地のない, 異論のない, 異議のない

▸文型&コロケーション

▸an undoubted/ undisputed/ uncontested **fact**
▸unchallenged/ undisputed/ unquestioned **authority**
▸the unchallenged/ undisputed **leader**
▸undisputed/ uncontested **supremacy**
▸to go unchallenged/ unquestioned/ uncontested

undoubted [ふつう名詞の前で] (存在[真実]に[が])疑問の余地のない, 紛れもない, 確かな ◇She has an *undoubted* talent as an organizer. 彼女はまとめ役としての紛れもない才能を持っている ◇The event was an *undoubted* success. そのイベントは確かに成功だった ☞ **doubt** (DOUBT 動)

▸**undoubtedly** 副 ◇There is *undoubtedly* a great deal of truth in what he says. 彼が言うことに大いに真実味があるのは確かだ

unchallenged 疑問の余地のない; (疑いなく受け入れられて)問題にされない, まかり通る; (支配者・指導者(の地位)が)確固たる, 揺るぎない ◇She could not allow such a claim to go *unchallenged*. 彼女はそんな主張がまかり通ることが許せなかった ◇He is in a position of *unchallenged* authority. 彼は確固たる権限を持った地位にある ☞ **challenge** (DOUBT 動)

undisputed 疑問[議論]の余地のない, 異論[異議]のない, 明白な ◇She began by laying out the *undisputed* facts of the case. 彼女は事件の明白な事実の説明から始めた ◇The film is an *undisputed* masterpiece of the twentieth century. その映画は議論の余地なく20世紀の傑作である ☞ **dispute** (DOUBT 動)

unquestioned 《フォーマル》(とても明白で)疑問の余地のない; (正しいとして)疑われない ◇His courage remains *unquestioned*. 彼の勇敢さに疑問の余地は依然としてない ◇There was an *unquestioned* assumption that the war would be short and relatively painless. その戦争は短期的で災禍は比較的軽微に終わるものと疑いもなく思い込まれていた ☞ **question** (DOUBT 動)

↪undoubted **unemployed, unemployment, unfortunate**

▶**unquestioningly** 副 ◇They accepted *unquestioningly* the rules he had laid down. 彼らは彼が定めた規則を疑わずに受け入れた
uncontested 対抗者のいない, 論争の余地のない ◇He was officially elected mayor in an *uncontested* election. 彼は対抗馬のいない選挙で公選された市長だった ◇These claims have not gone *uncontested* (= they have been contested). これらの主張は論争の的とならずにすんできたのではない ☞ **contest** (DOUBT 動)

unemployed 形

unemployed・jobless・out of work・redundant・on the dole・on welfare
人が職を持っていないことを表す
【類語訳】失業した, 失業中の, 解雇された, 失業手当を受けて, 生活保護を受けて

〖文型&コロケーション〗
▶ unemployed/ jobless **people**
▶ unemployed/ redundant **workers**
▶ **currently/ still** unemployed/ out of work
▶ **newly** unemployed/ redundant
▶ **the long-term** unemployed/ jobless

unemployed 失業した, 失業中の ◇How long have you been *unemployed*? どのくらいの間, 失業しているのですか ◇He's an *unemployed* builder. 彼は失業中の建設労働者だ ☞ **be employed** (WORK 動 1)
▶**the unemployed** 名 [複数扱い] ◇We're working on a programme to get *the* long-term *unemployed* back to work. 我々は長期失業者たちを職場に戻すプログラムに取り組んでいます
jobless 《ジャーナリズム》失業した, 失業中の ◇The closure left 500 people *jobless*. 閉鎖で500人が失業したままだった ❶*jobless*は特にジャーナリズムで, 集団としての失業者について用いられる。個々の失業者については用いられない。×How long have you been *jobless*?
,**out of 'work** 失業して, 失業中で ◇She had been *out of work* for a year. 彼女は一年間失業していた ☞ **be in work** (WORK 動 1)

[ノート] **unemployed**と**out of work**の使い分け: out of workは日常会話で, 特定の人について言う場合に用いられることが多く, unemployedほどは長く続かない響きがあるため, より丁寧な語である。

redundant 《英》余剰人員となった, (一時)解雇となった ◇I've been expecting to be *made redundant* for a year now. 現在, 私は一年間の一時解雇となりそうな状態です ☞ **make sb redundant** (FIRE)
,**on the 'dole** 《英, インフォーマル》失業手当を受けて ◇He's been *on the dole* for a year. 彼は一年間失業手当を受けている ❶*on the dole*のよりフォーマルな言い方は, claiming social security/unemployment benefitである。
,**on 'welfare** 《特に米》生活保護を受けて ◇They would rather work than live *on welfare*. 生活保護を受けて生活するより働きたいと彼らは思っている ☞ **welfare** (AID)

unemployment 名

unemployment・redundancy・dismissal・sacking・lay-off・discharge
職を持っていない状態, 職を失うという事実, 公式に人を解雇する行為
【類語訳】失業, 失業率, 失業者数, 解雇, 退職, 解散, 免職, 除隊

〖文型&コロケーション〗
▶ **mass** unemployment/ redundancies/ dismissals/ lay-offs
▶ **large-scale** unemployment/ redundancies/ lay-offs
▶ **to face** unemployment/ redundancy/ dismissal
▶ **to lead to/ avoid** unemployment/ redundancies/ dismissal

unemployment [U] 失業(状態); 失業率, 失業者数 ◇Thousands of young people are facing long-term *unemployment*. 多数の若者が長期にわたる失業に直面している ◇It's an area of high *unemployment*. そこは失業率の高い地域である ◇Last month saw a rise in both inflation and *unemployment*. 先月はインフレ率と失業者数の両方が上昇した 反意 **employment** (WORK 名 1)
redundancy [U, C] 《英, ふつう複数で》《英, ややフォーマル》(会社にできる仕事がないことによる)失業(状態), (一時)解雇, 退職 ◇Thousands of factory workers are facing *redundancy* in the New Year. 多数の工場労働者が新年には失業するだろう ◇She decided to take *voluntary redundancy* (= to offer to leave her job). 彼女は希望退職を受け入れる決意をした ◇The threat of *compulsory redundancies* still hangs over the firm. 依然として, 強制退職の脅威が会社の行く手にのしかかっている ◇200 workers have been issued with *redundancy notices*. 200人の労働者に解雇予告が出された ☞ **make sb redundant** (FIRE)
dismissal [U, C] 《ややフォーマル or 法律》(公式の)解雇, 解散 ◇He still hopes to win his claim against *unfair dismissal*. 彼は不当解雇に対する請求金を獲得することを今もなお望んでいる ◇The *dismissals* followed the resignation of the chairman. 議長の辞任に続いて, 何人もが解雇された ☞ **dismiss** (FIRE)
sacking [C] 《英, ややインフォーマル, 特にジャーナリズム》(不正行為による)免職 ◇A council chief faced calls for his *sacking* yesterday over allegations that he had accepted bribes. 地方議会のトップが昨日, 賄賂を受け取ったという申し立てをめぐって免職要求に直面した ☞ **sack** (FIRE)
'lay-off [C] 《ややインフォーマル, 特にジャーナリズム》(会社にできる仕事がないことによる)(一時)解雇, レイオフ ◇We do not want to risk further *lay-offs* in the factory. 我々は工場におけるさらなる一時解雇の危険を冒したくない ❶この文脈では, job cutsも使える。 ☞ **cut** (REDUCTION), **lay sb off** (FIRE)
discharge [C, U] (軍における公式の)除隊 ◇The illness resulted in his *discharge* from the army. 彼は病気で軍からの除隊という結果になった ☞ **discharge** (FIRE)

unfortunate 形

1 unfortunate・unlucky・ill-fated・out of luck
人や物事が不運を招くことを表す
【類語訳】不運な, 不幸な, 縁起の悪い, 不吉な, 不運で, ついていなくて

〖文型&コロケーション〗
▶ to be unfortunate/ unlucky **for** sb
▶ to be unfortunate/ unlucky **in** sth

unfortunate

▶ to be unfortunate/ unlucky that...
▶ to be unfortunate/ unlucky (not) to do sth
▶ very/ extremely/ a bit/ a little unfortunate/ unlucky

unfortunate (《ややフォーマル》) 不運な, 不幸な; 縁起の悪い, 不吉な ◇He was *unfortunate* to lose in the final round. 彼は不運にも決勝戦で敗れた ◇It was an *unfortunate* accident. それは不幸な事故だった ◇The *unfortunate* animal was locked inside the house for a week. その動物は不運にも一週間家の中に閉じ込められた 反意 fortunate

➤ **unfortunately** 副 ◇*Unfortunately* for him, the police had been informed and were waiting outside. 彼にとっては不幸なことだが, 警察に通報を受けて外で待っていた

unlucky 不運な, 不幸な; 縁起の悪い, 不吉な ◇She has been *unlucky* with injuries this year. 彼女は今年はけがをしてついていなかった ◇She was desperately *unlucky* not to win. 彼女はひどく不運にも勝てなかった ◇By some *unlucky* chance, her name was left off the list. 不運にも何かの拍子で, 彼女の名前はリストから除外された ◇Some people think it's *unlucky* to walk under a ladder. はしごの下を歩くのは縁起が悪いと考える人々もいる 反意 lucky (TIMELY)

➤ **unluckily** 副 ◇He was injured in the first game and *unluckily* missed the final. 彼は最初の試合でけがをして, 不運にも決勝戦に出られなかった

ill-'fated 《書き言葉》 (出来事・旅・事業が死・失敗を招き)不運な, 不幸な ◇It is the story of their *ill-fated* 1970 expedition. それは1970年の不運な結末を迎えた探険話である ◇She regretted ever meeting him at that *ill-fated* party. 彼女はそのパーティーで不運にも彼と出会う羽目になったことを悔やんだ

,out of 'luck フレーズ 《ややインフォーマル》 (見つけよう[達成しよう]とする際に)不運で, ついていなくて ◇If you're looking for Rachel, you're *out of luck*. She left 10 minutes ago. レイチェルを捜しているなら, ついてないよ 彼女は10分前に出てったよ 反意 in luck

---

2 unfortunate • pity • shame • pathetic • too bad • sad • sorry • feeble • regrettable
弱い[役に立たない, 成功しない, 失望させる]ことを表す
【類語訳】残念な, あいにくの, 情けない, お粗末な, 嘆かわしい, 悲しむべき, 哀れむべき, 惨めな, 遺憾な, 気の毒な

文型&コロケーション
▶ It's a pity/ a shame/ too bad **about** sb/ sth.
▶ unfortunate/ a pity/ a shame/ pathetic/ too bad/ regrettable **that**...
▶ an unfortunate/ a pathetic/ a sad/ a sorry **sight/ story/ state (of affairs)**
▶ an unfortunate/ a sad/ a sorry **affair/ business/ episode/ saga/ tale/ plight**
▶ **rather** unfortunate/ a pity/ a shame/ pathetic/ feeble/ regrettable
▶ **pretty/ a bit/ a little** unfortunate/ pathetic/ feeble
▶ **very** unfortunate/ feeble/ regrettable
▶ **a great/ real/ terrible** pity/ shame
▶ **What** a pity/ shame.

unfortunate (結果)残念な, あいにくの; 不適当な, 的外れな ◇It was *unfortunate* that he couldn't speak English. あいにく彼は英語が話せなかった ◇It was an *unfortunate* choice of words. それは的外れな言葉の選択だった 反意 fortunate (TIMELY)

➤ **unfortunately** 副 ◇*Unfortunately* I won't be able to attend the meeting. あいにく, 会議には出席できないだろう

pity 名 (ふつう **a** pity) 〔単数で〕《特に話し言葉》残念な[惜しい]こと ◇It's a *pity* that you can't stay longer. あなたがこれ以上いられないのは残念です ◇'I've lost it!' 'Oh, what a *pity*.' 「それをなくしちゃったんだ」「ああ, もったいない」 ◇It seems a *pity* to waste this food. この食べ物を無駄にするのはもったいないように思える ◇Oh, that's a *pity*. ああ, かわいそうに ◇It would be a great *pity* if you gave up now. 今君があきらめることになれば, 非常に残念だな

shame 名 (ふつう **a** shame) 〔単数で〕《ややインフォーマル, 特に話し言葉》〔惜しい〕こと ◇It's such a *shame* that she wasn't here to see it. 彼女がここにいてそれを見なかったのは本当に残念です ◇What a *shame* they couldn't come. 彼らが来られなかったのは残念です ◇It would be *a crying shame* (= a great shame) to let all that talent go to waste. その才能を全部無駄にしてしまうことになれば非常に惜しい

ノート **pity と shame の使い分け** : pity も shame も書き言葉よりも話し言葉で用いられることが多いが, **shame** のほうが pity よりもはるかに頻繁に話し言葉で用いられる.

pathetic (《インフォーマル, けなして》) (人・試みが)情けない, お粗末な ◇That was an absolutely *pathetic* excuse. それはまったくお粗末な言い訳だった ◇I know it sounds *pathetic*, but I can't ride a bike. 情けなく聞こえると思いますが, 私は自転車に乗れないんです ◇You're *pathetic*! 情けない奴だな

➤ **pathetically** 副 ◇His attempt to fool the guard was *pathetically* unconvincing. 護衛をだまそうという彼の試みは, 情けないほど説得力に欠けていた

too bad フレーズ 《インフォーマル, 話し言葉》残念な[惜しい]こと ◇*Too bad* every day can't be as good as this. 毎日がこんなについてたら, と思うけどそうはいかないんだよね ❶ too bad は本当はそう思っていない場合に, 「不運[残念]です」と言うのに皮肉的に用いられることが多い. ◆ If sometimes they're the wrong decisions, *too bad*. 《皮肉で》もしそれらが時に間違った決定であるとすれば, 残念だね.

sad 〔名詞の前で〕《しばしばなして》 (批判に値して[を招いて]) 嘆かわしい, けしからぬ, ひどい ; (同情して)悲しむべき ◇This *sad* state of affairs does not have to continue. この嘆かわしい事態を放置してよいわけがない ◇It's a *sad* fact that many of those killed were children. 殺された人たちの多くが子どもだったということは悲しい事実です

➤ **sadly** 副 ◇If you think I'm going to help you again, you're *sadly* mistaken. 私がもう一度手助けすると考えているなら, ひどい思い違いだね

sorry 〔名詞の前で〕哀れむべき, 嘆かわしい, 情けない, 惨めな ◇The business is in a *sorry* state. 経営は嘆かわしい状態にある ◇They were a *sorry* sight when they eventually got off the boat. ようやく下船した時の彼らは惨めな姿だった

ノート **sad と sorry の使い分け** : 多くの場合, 両語とも使用可能. ◆ a *sad/sorry* affair/business/episode/story/tale/saga/plight/sight (悲しい[哀れな]事態/出来事/エピソード/話/物語/武勇談/窮状/光景). しかし, sorry は哀れを感じる場合に用いられることが多く, sad は不満を感

じる場合に用いられることが多い. sad は社会・制度に存在する truth, reality, fact, comment, example, indictment, reflection, reminder などの語と共に用いられることが多いが, sorry はそうではない.

feeble (人・試みが)情けない, お粗末な ◇He told a few *feeble* jokes. 彼はつまらないジョークをいくつか言った ◇Don't be so *feeble*! Tell her you don't want to go. 情けないな. 行きたくないって彼女に言えよ

ノート **pathetic** と **feeble** の使い分け：pathetic は feeble よりもインフォーマルで, より強い不満・軽蔑を表す.

regrettable 《フォーマル》(結果が)遺憾な, 気の毒な ◇It is *regrettable* that the police were not informed sooner. もっと早く警察に通報されなかったのは遺憾である ◇The loss of jobs is highly *regrettable*. 失職は非常に気の毒です
▷**regrettably** 副 ◇*Regrettably*, crime has been increasing in this area. 遺憾ながら, この地域では犯罪が増加を続けている

ノート **unfortunate** と **regrettable** の使い分け：unfortunate も regrettable も, 物事に用いることができ, incident, occurrence, error, consequence, tendency などと結びつく. しかし, regrettable な物事はふつう, 少なくとも部分的に人の力の及ぶ範囲内にあると考えられる. regrettable を用いることで, 責任を認める[責任を転嫁する]ことを人が望んでいることを示唆する. unfortunate な物事は不運の結果であると考えられることが多い.

unhappy 形

1 ☞ SAD, DEPRESSED
unhappy・sad・miserable・melancholy・mournful・heartbroken
人が幸せでないと感じたり, 示したりすることを表す
【類語訳】不幸せな, 悲しい, 寂しい, 惨めな, 憂鬱な, ふさぎ込んだ, 悲しみに沈んだ, 悲嘆に暮れた

```
unhappy        miserable          heartbroken
sad
melancholy
mournful
```

文型&コロケーション
▶ unhappy/ sad/ miserable/ heartbroken **about** sth
▶ unhappy/ sad/ miserable/ heartbroken **when/ that**...
▶ an unhappy/ a sad/ a miserable/ a melancholy/ a mournful **face**
▶ an unhappy/ a sad/ a melancholy/ a mournful **expression**
▶ sad/ melancholy/ mournful **eyes**
▶ to **feel** unhappy/ sad/ miserable
▶ to **look** unhappy/ sad/ miserable/ mournful
▶ **very** unhappy/ sad/ miserable

unhappy 不幸せな, 悲しい；不幸せそうな, 悲しそうな ◇He grew more *unhappy* as the years went by. 彼は年が経つにつれてより不幸せになった ◇She sounded so *unhappy* when I left her. 私が彼女の元を去るとき, 彼女はとても悲しそうだった ◇He had an *unhappy* childhood. 彼は不幸せな幼少期を送った 反意 **happy** (HAPPY), ☞ **unhappiness** (GRIEF)
▷**unhappily** 副 ◇He sighed *unhappily*. 彼は悲しそうにため息をついた

sad 悲しい, 寂しい；悲しそうな, 寂しそうな ◇She was still feeling very *sad* about her father's death. 彼女はいまだに父親の死をとても悲しんでいた ◇We are *sad to* hear that you are leaving. お発ちになると聞いて, 私たちはとても寂しいです ◇He gave a slight, *sad* smile. 彼は少し悲しげな笑みを見せた 反意 **happy** (HAPPY), ☞ **sadness** (GRIEF)
▷**sadly** 副 ◇She shook her head *sadly*. 彼女は悲しそうに首を振った

ノート **unhappy** と **sad** の使い分け：ふつう unhappy と感じるのは, 自分の身に起こった物事のためである. sad と感じるのはふつう他の人の身に起こった物事についてである. ×He grew *sadder* as the years went by. ×She was very *unhappy* about her father's death. 人生における期間・体験は unhappy となりうる. 見聞きする物事は sad となりうる. ◆an *unhappy* childhood/marriage (不幸な幼少期/不幸せな結婚生活). ×a *sad* childhood/marriage. ◆*sad* news (悲しい知らせ). ◆a *sad* story (悲しい話). ×*unhappy* news. ×an *unhappy* story. ☞ **sad** (SAD)

miserable 惨めな ◇We were cold, wet and thoroughly *miserable*. 私たちは寒く, ずぶ濡れで, 本当に惨めだった ◇She knows how to **make life miserable** for her employees. 彼女はどうすれば従業員の生活が悲惨なものになるか知りぬいている 反意 **cheerful** (CHEERFUL), ☞ **misery** (DISTRESS)
▷**miserably** 副 ◇They wandered around *miserably* in the rain. 彼らは雨の中を惨めにさまよい歩いた

melancholy 《文語》(長期的に明白な理由もなく)憂鬱な, ふさぎ込んだ ◇He was a tall man with a long, *melancholy* face. 彼は面長で陰気な顔つきをした背の高い男だった ☞ **melancholy** (GRIEF)

mournful 《書き言葉》(人の様子が)悲しそうな, 悲しみに沈んだ ◇I couldn't bear the *mournful* look on her face. 私は彼女の悲しみに沈んだ表情に耐えられなかった
▷**mournfully** 副 ◇The dog looked *mournfully* after its owner. 犬は悲しげに飼い主を見送った

heartbroken (起こった事のために)悲嘆に暮れた, 悲しみに打ちひしがれた ◇He was *heartbroken* when she left him. 彼は彼女が去って悲嘆に暮れた ☞ **heartbreak** (GRIEF), **heartbreaking** (SAD)

2 unhappy・dissatisfied・frustrated・disgruntled・aggrieved・displeased・discontented
人が起こった状況[物事]のために不愉快に感じる[満足を覚えない]ことを表す
【類語訳】不満な, 不服な, 欲求不満を抱いた, いらいらした, 不機嫌な, 気に入らない, 不満で, 飽き足りない

文型&コロケーション
▶ unhappy/ dissatisfied/ frustrated/ disgruntled/ displeased/ discontented **with** sth
▶ unhappy/ frustrated/ disgruntled/ aggrieved/ displeased **at** sth
▶ unhappy/ frustrated/ disgruntled/ aggrieved **about** sth
▶ unhappy/ frustrated/ disgruntled/ displeased **that**...
▶ an unhappy/ a dissatisfied **customer**
▶ to **feel** unhappy/ dissatisfied/ frustrated/ disgruntled/ ag-

grieved
▶**deeply** unhappy/ dissatisfied/ frustrated/ aggrieved
▶**increasingly** unhappy/ dissatisfied/ frustrated

unhappy 不満な ◇They were *unhappy* with their accommodation. 彼らは宿泊設備に不満を感じていた ◇He was *unhappy* at being left out of the team. 彼はチームから外されて不満だった 反意 **happy** (HAPPY)

dissatisfied 《ややフォーマル》不満な, 不服な ◇If you are *dissatisfied* with our service, please write to the manager. 私どものサービスにご不満でしたら, どうぞ支配人に書面でお申しつけください ◇The decision left us feeling deeply *dissatisfied*. 私たちはその決定にひどく不満を抱いたままだった ◇He has to deal with complaints from *dissatisfied* guests. 彼は不満を抱いた客の苦情に対処しなければならない 反意 **satisfied** (HAPPY)
▶**dissatisfaction** 名 [U] ◇Many people have expressed their *dissatisfaction* with the arrangement. 多くの人々がその取り決めへの不満を表した 反意 **satisfaction** (SATISFACTION)

ノート **unhappy** と **dissatisfied** の使い分け: dissatisfied は unhappy よりもフォーマルで, 特にビジネスや政治の文脈において, 人々が受けたサービス・購入した商品・公的な決定 [政策, 活動] に満足していない場合に用いられる. unhappy もこのような場合にも用いることはできるが, 特により個人的な失望の場合に用いられる. ♦*unhappy/dissatisfied* customers (満足していない顧客たち) ×He was *dissatisfied* at being left out of the team.

frustrated (望みがかなわないために) 欲求不満を抱いた, いらいらした ◇They felt *frustrated* at the lack of progress. 彼らは進展がないことに欲求不満を感じていた ◇Sometimes he gets really *frustrated* with his own violin playing. 彼は時々, 自分のヴァイオリン演奏に本当にいらいらする ☞ **frustrate** (ANNOY), **frustrating** (ANNOYING), **frustration** (FRUSTRATION)

disgruntled (気分を害する事が起こって) 不機嫌な, 不満な ◇I left feeling *disgruntled* at the way I'd been treated. 私は自分の待遇に不満を覚えながら去った ◇Police believe it was probably sabotage by a *disgruntled* employee. 警察はそれはおそらく不満を抱く従業員による妨害行為であっただろうと考えている

aggrieved 《ややフォーマル, 書き言葉》不当な扱いと感じた, 不機嫌な ◇He had every right to feel *aggrieved* at the decision. 彼はその決定を不当な扱いだと感じるのもしごく当然だった ◇'What am I supposed to do about it?' he said in an *aggrieved* tone. 「僕はそれについてどうすればいいわけ」と彼は不機嫌な口調で言った

displeased [名詞の前では用いない]《フォーマル》気に入らない, 不満な ◇Are you *displeased* with my work? 私の仕事が気に入らないの 反意 **pleased** (GLAD)

discontented (自分の境遇に) 不満な, 飽き足りない ◇He felt *discontented* with the way his life had turned out. 彼は自分の人生の進展ぶりに不満を感じていた 反意 **contented** (HAPPY)

union 名 ☞ GROUP 3, ORGANIZATION

union・club・association・society・alliance・league・coalition・federation・guild
共通の利益や目的を持つ人々 [労働者, 政党] などの集団
【類語訳】労働組合, 連合, 連盟, 組合, 同好会, クラブ, 団体, ギルド

文型&コロケーション
▶a **national** union/ club/ association/ society/ league/ coalition/ federation
▶a **local** union/ club/ association/ society/ coalition/ federation
▶an **international** union/ club/ association/ league/ coalition/ federation
▶a **strong** union/ alliance/ coalition/ guild
▶a **loose** association/ alliance/ coalition/ federation
▶a **trade** union/ association/ federation/ guild
▶a **political** club/ association/ society/ alliance/ coalition
▶a **professional** union/ club/ association/ society
▶to **form** a union/ a club/ an association/ a society/ an alliance/ a league/ a coalition/ a federation
▶to **set up** a union/ a club/ an association/ a society/ a league/ a federation
▶to **join** a union/ a club/ an association/ a society/ an alliance/ a league/ a coalition/ a federation
▶to **belong to** a union/ a club/ an association/ a society/ an alliance/ a federation
▶a union/ a club/ an association/ a society **meets**
▶a **member of** a union/ a club/ an association/ a society/ an alliance/ a league/ a coalition/ a federation/ a guild

union [C]《(同一産業の)》労働組合; (共通の利益を持つ) 連合 [連盟] (組織), 組合, 協会 ◇The *union* represents 40% of all hospital workers. その労働組合は病院の全労働者の4割を代表している ◇He has been appointed head of the Welsh Rugby *Union* (= sports organization). 彼はウェールズ・ラグビー協会の会長に指名された ❶「労働組合」としての union は, 《英》では trade union または trades union, 《米》では labor union とも呼ばれる. trade union は労働者の利益を保護し, 労働条件を改善するために存在する.

club [C+単数・複数動詞]《(特に複合語)》(特定の活動・スポーツの) 同好会, クラブ ◇She plays at the local tennis *club*. 彼女は地元のテニスクラブでプレーしている ◇She gives talks at local schools and **youth clubs**. 彼女は地元の学校やユースクラブで講演を行っている ◇*Fan club* members can get concert tickets at a discount. ファンクラブの会員はコンサートのチケットを割引料金で入手できます ❶《英》では, club は選手・監督・オーナー・団員を含むプロスポーツ団体も指す. ☞ **club** (TEAM 2)

association [C+単数・複数動詞]《(特定の目的のための公式の)》組合, 団体, 協会 ◇The Football *Association* has launched an investigation into the incident. イングランドサッカー協会はその事件の調査を開始した ◇Local councils have begun to work closely with *housing associations*. 地元議会は住宅協会と緊密に協力し始めた ◇Do you belong to any professional or trade *associations*? あなたはどこかの専門職協会か同業組合に所属していますか

society [C]《(特に名前で)》(特定の目的のための) 組合, 団体, 協会 ◇the American *Society* of Newspaper Editors 米国新聞編集者協会 ◇the Royal *Society for the Protection of Birds* 王立鳥類保護協会 ◇He made few friends and joined few clubs or *societies*. 彼は友達をほとんど作らずクラブや団体にもほとんど参加しなかった

ノート **club, association, society** の使い分け: 共通の利益・目的を持つ人々の集団は, しばしば歴史的な理由か

↳union

ら、これらの単語を集団の名称の一部として用いている。**club** はスポーツ・趣味に関わり、かなりインフォーマルである。例えば drama **club** はより伝統的な dramatic **society** よりもインフォーマルなものである。**association** はふつう専門領域や社会問題に関係している公的な団体を指す。◆a trade/professional/residents'/housing **association**（同業組合／専門職協会／自治会／住宅協会）。**society** は学術的な関心を持つことが多い。ほとんどの大学には、歴史・政治・音楽といった特定の関心を持つ学生たちが参加できる無数の **society** がある。**society** はまた慈善団体の名称に用いられることも多い。

alliance [C]（特定の目的のための異なる政党で構成される）連合（組織）◇The Movement for Multiparty Democracy was a loose *alliance* of opposition parties. 複数政党制民主主義運動は、緩やかな野党連合だった

league [C]（しばしば組織の名称で用いて）（特定の目的のための）連盟（組織）◇the *League* of Nations 国際連盟 ◇a meeting of the Women's *League* for Peace 婦人平和連盟の会議

coalition [C]（特定の目的のための異なる政党で構成される）連合（組織）◇The network is a global *coalition* of environmental and consumer groups. そのネットワークは環境団体と消費者団体の世界的な連合組織である

ノート alliance と coalition の使い分け：alliance は、さまざまな人々や集団が一緒になって形成されるもの、coalition は、単に既存の二つ以上の集団が寄り集まったものである。

federation [C]（クラブ・労働組合などの）連合［連盟］（組織）◇He proposed a loose *federation* of small, local groups. 彼は地元の小グループの緩やかな連合を提案した ◇the British Athletics *Federation* 英国陸上競技連盟

guild [C＋単数・複数動詞]（同じ仕事をする［共通の利益・目的を持つ]）組合、団体、協会；（中世における熟練工の組合である）ギルド ◇He is an active member of the Screen Actors' *Guild*. 彼は映画俳優組合の活動的なメンバーである ◇The building originally belonged to the *guild* of clockmakers. その建物は元々、時計師のギルドの所有だった ❶名称の一部に guild が入る職業集団は、過去において職人のギルドとして始まった場合が多い。

unique 形 ☞SPECIAL

─────────────────────────

unique・special・distinctive・peculiar・individual・idiosyncratic
一人の人［一つの集団や事物］にのみ関連することを表す
【類義訳】唯一の、特有の、独特の、独自の、特別の、専用の、個性的な、特異な

📝文型&コロケーション

▸sth unique/ special/ distinctive/ individual **about** sth
▸a species, etc. unique/ peculiar **to** ...
▸sb's **own** unique/ special/ distinctive/ peculiar/ individual...
▸a unique/ a special/ a distinctive/ a peculiar/ an individual/ an idiosyncratic **style/ character**
▸the unique/ special/ distinctive/ peculiar/ individual/ idiosyncratic **nature** of sth
▸unique/ special/ distinctive/ peculiar/ individual/ idiosyncratic **features**
▸a unique/ a special/ a distinctive/ a peculiar/ an individual **flavour**
▸a unique/ a distinctive/ an individual/ an idiosyncratic **personality**
▸a unique/ a special/ a distinctive/ an individual/ an idiosyncratic **approach**
▸sb/ sth's unique/ special/ distinctive/ peculiar **brand** of sth
▸the unique/ special/ peculiar/ individual **circumstances** of sth
▸**quite** unique/ distinctive
▸**highly/ very** distinctive/ individual/ idiosyncratic

unique （同種類のうちで）唯一の、ただ一つしかない；（特定の人・場所・事物にのみ）特有の、固有の、独特の、独自の、特別の ◇Every human being has a *unique* fingerprint that does not change over time. 人間には誰しも、時と共に変化することのない その人固有の指紋がある ◇Each item has a *unique* 6-digit code. どの品目にも6桁の固有のコードがついている ◇Her lawyer said the case was *unique in* French law. その判例はフランスの法律に特有のものだと彼女の弁護士は言った ◇There's nothing *unique* about the case. その事例に特別なものは何もない ◇The pattern of stripes is *unique* to each individual animal. 縞模様は個々の動物に固有のものである ☞ **unique** (REMARKABLE), **uniqueness** (IDENTITY)

▸**uniquely** 副 ◇Some of the regulations apply *uniquely* to the 16-19 age group. いくつかの条件は16－19歳のグループのみに適用される

special （特定の人・集団に）特有の、固有の、独特の、独自の、特別（用）の、専用の ◇She has a *special* way of smiling. 彼女は独特な笑い方をする ◇The President ended with a *special* message for the people of Texas. 大統領はテキサス市民に向けた特別なメッセージで締めくくった ◇The directors have their own *special* pension fund. 重役たちには独自の特別年金基金がある ☞ **special** (SPECIAL)

▸**specially** 副 ◇She has to have her shoes *specially* made. 彼女は特製の靴を注文する必要がある

distinctive （性質・特徴が）他との区別を示す、特有の、独特の ◇The male bird has *distinctive* black and white markings on the head. 雄の鳥には頭に独特の白黒の斑点がある ◇There was nothing *distinctive* about the envelope in which the letter came. 手紙が入っていた封筒には特別変わったことは何もなかった

▸**distinctively** 副 ◇It's a blue cheese with a *distinctively* sharp taste. それはぴりっとした独特の味のするブルーチーズです

peculiar （特定の場所・状況・人・事物に）特有の、固有の、独特の、独自の、特別の ◇The species is *peculiar* to China. その種は中国固有である ◇Each house had its own *peculiar* smell. どの家にもその家特有の匂いがあった

▸**peculiarity** 名 [C] ◇the cultural *peculiarities* of the English 英国人の文化的特性

▸**peculiarly** 副 ◇It is a *peculiarly* English design. それは独特の英国的デザインだ

ノート unique と peculiar の使い分け：多くの場合、両語とも使用可能。◆The problem is not *unique/peculiar* to this country. (この問題はこの国特有のものではない)。peculiar は特に場所について用いられる。unique は個々の人々・動物について用いられることが多い。unique は人・事物が特別[まれ]であることを示唆し、peculiar よりも肯定的である場合が多い（必ずしもそうとは限らないがいくぶん否定的で、人・事物がある意味で変わっていることを示唆することもある。☞ **peculiar** (STRANGE 1)

individual《ふつうほめて》(特定の人・物事が興味深く典型的で)それぞれ異なった，独特な，個性的な ◇A player's style is almost as *individual* as his DNA. 演奏者のスタイルはDNAと同じくらい個々に違う ☞ **individuality** (IDENTITY)

idiosyncratic《ややフォーマル》(人の振る舞い方・考え方が)特異な，独特の ◇She had an odd, *idiosyncratic* way of looking at things. 彼女は奇妙で特異な物の見方をした

unlikely 形

1 unlikely・doubtful・improbable
物事が生じそうにもない[真実でありそうにもない]ことを表す
【類語訳】起こりそうにもない，ありそうにもない，疑わしい，不確かな

文型&コロケーション
▶ to be unlikely/ doubtful/ improbable **that**...
▶ to **seem/ look/ make sth** unlikely/ doubtful/ improbable
▶ **very/ highly/ extremely/ rather/ somewhat** unlikely/ doubtful/ improbable

unlikely 起こりそうにもない，(真実で)ありそうにもない ◇The project seemed *unlikely to* succeed. その事業は成功しそうにないように思えた ◇It's most *unlikely* that she'll arrive before seven. 彼女が7時前に到着するなんてとてもありそうにない ◇*In the unlikely event of* a problem arising, please contact the hotel manager. 万が一問題が起きましたら，どうぞホテル支配人までお知らせください ☞ **likely** (LIKELY)

doubtful [名詞の前はまれ]《ややフォーマル，特に書き言葉》(起こりそう[真実でありそう]にもない)疑わしい，不確かな ◇It is *doubtful if* this painting is a Picasso. この絵がピカソのものであるかどうか疑わしい ◇It is *doubtful whether* the car will last another year. 車があと一年もつかどうか疑わしい ◇Terry is injured and is *doubtful for* the game tomorrow (= unlikely to play). テリーが負傷し，明日の試合の出場が危ぶまれている ❶この意味では，doubtfulはほとんど常に，後に if, whether, for, that...を伴う。☞ **doubt** (DOUBT 名 1), **doubt** (DOUBT 動)

improbable《ややフォーマル，書き言葉》起こりそうにもない，(真実で)ありそうにもない ◇The whole story sounded highly *improbable*. その話全体がほとんどありえないように思えた ◇It seemed *improbable* that the fine weather would continue. 好天が続くことはなさそうに思えた ❶ improbableはunlikelyよりもフォーマルで，後にto不定詞を伴うことはできない。×The project seemed *improbable* to succeed. 反意 **probable** (LIKELY)

2 ☞ INCREDIBLE
unlikely・weak・far-fetched・implausible・unconvincing・improbable
信じるのが難しい[ふつうには予測できない]ことを表す
【類語訳】信じがたい，疑わしい，考えられない，思いもよらない，とっぴな，こじつけの，真実味のない，説得力のない，納得のいかない

文型&コロケーション
▶ an unlikely/ a far-fetched/ an implausible/ an unconvincing **explanation**
▶ an unlikely/ a far-fetched/ an implausible/ an improbable **story**
▶ an unlikely/ improbable **situation**
▶ **rather** unlikely/ weak/ far-fetched/ implausible/ unconvincing/ improbable
▶ **very** unlikely/ weak/ far-fetched/ unconvincing/ improbable
▶ **highly/ inherently** unlikely/ implausible/ improbable
▶ **completely** unlikely/ unconvincing/ improbable

unlikely [名詞の前で]信じがたい，疑わしい；(人・物事・場所について)考えられない，思いもよらない ◇She gave me a rather *unlikely* explanation for her behaviour. 彼女は自分の振る舞いについてとても信じがたい説明をした ◇He seems a most *unlikely* candidate for the job. 彼はその仕事の候補者にはまず考えられないように思える ◇They have built hotels in the most *unlikely* places. まったく思いも寄らない場所にホテルが建てられている ❶ unlikelyは思いもよらず成功する人に用いることもある。◆ an *unlikely* hero/winner/rock star/celebrity (思いもよらないヒーロー/勝者/ロックスター/有名人)。または，普通に考えてふさわしいとは思えない場合に，選んでもらおうとする人に用いることもある。◆ an *unlikely* candidate/applicant/contender (考えにくい候補者/志願者/競争相手)

weak (人々が信じそうもなく[納得しそうもなく])根拠の弱い，説得力[論理性，迫力]に欠ける，感銘[印象]の薄い ◇*weak* arguments/evidence 説得力に欠ける議論/根拠の弱い議論 ◇The case for the prosecution was rather *weak*. 起訴理由はやや根拠が弱かった ◇I enjoyed the movie but I thought the ending was very *weak*. 映画は面白かったが，結末はどうにも納得がいかなかった ❶ weakは特に説得して物事を信じさせる論法について用いられる。反意 **strong** (CONVINCING)

far-'fetched (非常に信じがたく)かけ離れた，無理な，とっぴな，こじつけの ◇The whole story sounds very *far-fetched*. その話全体がとてもとっぴに聞こえる ❶一般的な表現は，sth is a bit far-fetched (…が少しかけ離れている), sth seems/sounds far-fetched (…が信じにくく聞こえる[聞こえる])がある。たとえ信じがたくとも物事が真実であることを主張する場合には，sth may seem/sound far-fetched, but... (…はとっぴに思える[聞こえる]かもしれないが…)の表現も一般的である。

implausible《ややフォーマル》(理にかなっておらず)信じがたい ◇This is a highly *implausible* claim. これはとても信じがたい要求です ◇Her explanation is not *implausible* (= it is plausible). 彼女の説明は考えられなくもない 反意 **plausible** (POSSIBLE 2)

▶ **implausibly** 副 ◇He argued, somewhat *implausibly*, that the accident could not have been prevented. 少々信じがたいのだが，彼は事故は防ぎようがなかったと論じた

unconvincing 真実[現実]味のない；説得力のない，納得のいかない ◇I find the characters in the book very *unconvincing*. その本の登場人物は非常に現実味がないように思う ◇His argument was *unconvincing*. 彼の主張には納得がいかなかった ◇She managed a weak, *unconvincing* smile. 彼女は何とか弱々しい作り笑いをした ❶ unconvincingは argument, attempt, explanation, reason, story など，人が発言する事柄について用いられることが多い。しかし，笑っている人が実際にはうれしいと思う場合には an unconvincing smile, 登場人物を俳優があまり上手に演じていないと思う場合には an unconvincing performance と言うことがある。反意 **convincing** (CONVINCING)

▶ **unconvincingly** 副 ◇He laughed *unconvincingly*. 彼は取ってつけたような笑い方をした

improbable [ふつう名詞の前で]《書き言葉》(思いもよらない)奇抜な，妙な，奇想天外な ◇Her hair was an *improba-*

ble shade of yellow. 彼女の髪は黄色い奇抜な色合いだった ❶ improbableは思いもよらないが、うまくいっているcombination, match, friendshipについて用いられることが多い。

unofficial 形 ☞ IRRATIONAL

unofficial・unauthorized・unlicensed・off the record
権威者に承認されていないことを表す
【類語訳】非公式の、非公認の、無許可の、無認可の、権威のない、無免許の、オフレコで

文型&コロケーション
▶ an unofficial/ unauthorized **biography/ copy**

unofficial 非公式[非公認]の ◊According to *unofficial* estimates about 200 died. 非公式の見積もりでは約200名が死亡した ◊There will be a review of the law on *unofficial* action and strikes in essential services. 必要不可欠なサービスにおける非公認活動やストライキに関する法律は見直されることになる ◊The result for the athlete was an *unofficial* world best of 2 minutes 27 seconds. その陸上選手の結果は2分27秒という非公認の世界最高記録だった ◊It's one of numerous *unofficial* Harry Potter websites/fan clubs. それはハリー・ポッターのおびただしい数の非公式ウェブサイト/ファンクラブの一つである 反意 **official** (OFFICIAL 形)
➤**unofficially** 副 ◊The cost was *unofficially* estimated at £2 million. 経費は非公式には200万ポンドと見積もられた

unauthorized (英でまた **-sed**)《フォーマル》無許可[無認可]の、権限のない ◊There are special precautions to prevent *unauthorized* personnel from gaining access. 権限のない職員のアクセスを防ぐ特別な予防措置がある ◊Failure to complete the form will result in absences being regarded as *unauthorized*. 書類を記入し損なうと、欠席が無許可と見なされることになります 反意 **authorized** (OFFICIAL 形)

ノート **unofficial** と **unauthorized** の使い分け：unofficialな行動・陳述内容は、まだ権威者によって承認されていないが、後で承認されるかもしれない。行動がunauthorizedである場合は、その行動に対する許可は与えられておらず、それどころか却下されているかもしれない。陳述内容はふつうunauthorizedと表すことはできない。

unlicensed 《ややフォーマル》無免許の、許可[認可]証のない ◊Tourists were warned never to use *unlicensed* taxis. 観光客は無免許タクシーを利用しないよう警告された ◊The Act prohibits the *unlicensed* disposal of controlled waste. 法令は規制廃棄物の無免許廃棄を禁じている 反意 **licensed** (OFFICIAL 形)

off the 'record 形副 非公式で、オフレコで(ふつうジャーナリストに向けて用いられて、まだ公式でない[情報の出所が自分であることを知られたくない]場合に用いられる) ◊Stop the tape. This is *off the record*. テープを止めてください。これはオフレコです ◊Can I tell you something strictly *off the record*? 完全に非公式でお話しすることがあるのですが

unsure 形

unsure・undecided・uncertain・hesitant・ambivalent・doubtful・dubious・in doubt

人が疑問[疑念]を抱いていることを表す
【類語訳】確信がない、自信がない、疑いを抱いた、迷った、未決定の、ためらった、あいまいな、どっちつかずの、疑わしい

文型&コロケーション
▶ unsure/ undecided/ uncertain/ hesitant/ ambivalent/ doubtful/ dubious/ in doubt **about** sth
▶ unsure/ undecided/ uncertain/ doubtful/ dubious/ in doubt **as to** sth
▶ unsure/ uncertain/ hesitant/ doubtful/ dubious **of** sth
▶ unsure/ undecided/ uncertain **what**...
▶ unsure/ uncertain **how**...
▶ **a bit/ rather/ somewhat** unsure/ hesitant/ ambivalent/ doubtful/ dubious
▶ **somewhat** unsure/ hesitant/ ambivalent/ doubtful/ dubious
▶ **very** unsure/ undecided/ uncertain/ hesitant/ ambivalent/ doubtful/ dubious

unsure [名詞の前では用いない]（物事について）確信[自信]がない；疑いを抱いた、（判断に）迷った ◊There were a lot of things I was *unsure* about. 私が確信の持てないことがたくさんあった ◊He was *unsure* of what to do next. 彼は次に何をすべきか迷っていた ◊I was *unsure* how to reply to this question. この質問にどう答えるべきか自信がなかった 反意 **sure** (SURE)

undecided [名詞の前はまれ]（人・物事について）未決定の ◊I'm still *undecided* about who to vote for. 誰に投票するかまだ決めていません 反意 **decide** (DECIDE)

uncertain [名詞の前はまれ]（物事について）確信[自信]がない；疑いを抱いた、（判断に）迷った ◊They're both *uncertain* about what to do. 彼らは二人とも何をすべきか迷っている ◊I'm still *uncertain* of my feelings for him. まだ彼に対する自分の思いに確信が持てない 反意 **certain** (SURE), ☞ **uncertainty** (DOUBT 名)

ノート **unsure** と **uncertain** の使い分け：人の感情について用いる場合には、これらの語に実質的な意味の違いはないが、unsureは話し言葉・書き言葉の両方においてほぼ倍の頻度で用いられ、uncertainはいくぶんフォーマルである。uncertainは明確でない[確定していない]事実・状況について用いられることが多いが、unsureはそうではない。☞ **uncertain** (UNCLEAR)

hesitant [名詞の前では用いない]（確信・自信がない[恥ずかしい、気が進まない]）ためらった ◊She's *hesitant* about signing the contract. 彼女は契約書にサインをするのをためらっている ◊Doctors are *hesitant to* comment on the new treatment. 医師たちは新しい治療法についてコメントするのを躊躇している

ambivalent 《ややフォーマル、特に書き言葉》（人・物事が）相反する、あいまいな、どっちつかずの ◊She is deeply *ambivalent* about her feelings for him. 彼女の彼への気持ちにはひどく相反する思いが交錯している ◊He has an *ambivalent* attitude towards her. 彼は彼女に対してあいまいな態度をとっている

doubtful （物事に）確信[自信]がない、迷った；疑いを示した、疑わしそうな ◊He was *doubtful* about accepting extra work. 彼は追加の仕事を受け入れることを迷っていた ◊A *doubtful* look crossed her face. 疑いの表情が彼女の顔をよぎった ☞ **doubt** (DOUBT 名 1)
➤**doubtfully** 副 ◊He shook his head *doubtfully*. 彼は疑わしげに首を振った

untidy, unusual

dubious [名詞の前はまれ]（物事に）確信[自信]がない, 迷っていた；疑いを示した, 疑わしそうな ◇I was rather *dubious* about the whole idea. 私はその考え全体にやや疑念を抱いていた ◇Kate looked *dubious*, but did as she was asked. ケイトは怪しんでいるようだったが, 言われたとおりにした
▶**dubiously** 副 ◇He looked *dubiously* at her. 彼は疑わしげに彼女を見た

ノート **doubtful** と **dubious** の使い分け：これらの語に実質的な意味の違いはない。dubious は話し言葉で用いられることがいくぶん多いが, 名詞の前ではそれほど頻繁には用いられない。

in 'doubt フレーズ （何をすべきかについて）確信[自信]がない, 迷った ◇*If in doubt*, wear black. 迷うのなら, 黒を着なさい

untidy 形

untidy・messy・cluttered・all over the place・disordered・out of place・jumbled
物が適切な場所になくて乱雑な状態であることを表す
【類語訳】きちんとしていない, だらしのない, 取り散らかった, 乱雑な, 汚い, 無秩序な, ごちゃ混ぜになった, 雑然とした

文型&コロケーション
▶ an untidy/ a messy/ a cluttered **house**
▶ an untidy/ a cluttered **room/ desk**
▶ an untidy/ a disordered **state**
▶ untidy/ disordered **hair**
▶ an untidy/ a messy/ a jumbled **heap/ pile** of sth
▶ an untidy/ a jumbled **collection** of sth
▶ cluttered/ jumbled **up**

untidy 《特に英, 時にけなして》きちんとしていない, だらしのない, 取り散らかった, 乱雑な ◇Try not to make the place *untidy*. その場所を散らかさないようにしなさい ◇The books were piled an *untidy* heap. 本が乱雑に山積みされていた ◇Your hair is a little *untidy*. あなたの髪, 少し乱れてるよ
反意 **tidy** (NEAT)
▶**untidily** 副 ◇Her hair fell *untidily* about her shoulders. 彼女の髪は肩の辺りでだらしなく垂れ下がっていた
messy 《ややインフォーマル, 時にけなして》取り散らかした, 乱雑な, 汚い ◇The house always looked *messy*. その家はいつも散らかっているようだった ◇Sorry, it's a bit *messy* in here. ごめんね, ここ, ちょっと散らかってるんだ ◇How did the place *get* so *messy*? どうしてそこはそんなに散らかったの ☞ **mess** (MESS1)

ノート **untidy** と **messy** の使い分け：《米》では, messy がこれらの語の中で最も頻繁に用いられ, untidy はあまり用いられない。《英》では, untidy がこの意味で最も頻繁に用いられ, messy は「汚い」という意味で用いられるほうが多い。
☞ **messy** (DIRTY)

cluttered 《ややインフォーマル, けなして》（表面・場所が多くの物で）ごちゃごちゃに取り散らかった ◇His apartment was small, *cluttered* and dirty. 彼の部屋は小さくてごちゃごちゃしていて汚かった ◇The study was *cluttered with* furniture. その書斎は家具がごちゃごちゃに置かれていた 反意 **uncluttered** (NEAT), ☞ **clutter** (MESS1)
all 'over the place 行動 《インフォーマル》ごちゃごちゃに取り散らかって, すっかり乱雑で ◇She arrived out of breath and with her hair *all over the place*. 彼女は息を切らして, 髪を振り乱して到着した

disordered 《ややフォーマル》(物の配置が)無秩序な ◇It is likely that the universe started out in a chaotic and *disordered* state. 宇宙は混沌とした無秩序な状態で始まったようだ 反意 **ordered** (NEAT), ☞ **disorder** (MESS1)
out of 'place 行動 《ふつう否定的な文で》（あるべき場所になくて）整理整頓されてなくて, きちんとしていなくて ◇He does not like things *out of place*. 彼は物が整理整頓されていないのを嫌った ◇She never has a hair *out of place*. 彼女はいつも身だしなみがきちんとしている
jumbled ごちゃ混ぜになった, 雑然とした ◇There was a *jumbled* collection of objects on the mantelpiece. 炉棚の上には物が雑然と集められていた ◇The drawer was full of letters all *jumbled together*. 引き出しはごちゃごちゃの手紙であふれていた ☞ **jumble** (MESS1)

unusual 形 ☞ STRANGE1

unusual・eccentric・unorthodox・unconventional・atypical・different・offbeat・out of the ordinary
物事が通常とは異なることを表す
【類語訳】普通でない, いつもと異なる, 異例の, 珍しい, 一風変わった, 独特の, 奇妙な, 常軌を逸した, 慣習にとらわれない

文型&コロケーション
▶ unusual/ eccentric/ unorthodox/ unconventional/ atypical **behaviour**
▶ unusual/ eccentric/ unorthodox/ unconventional **ideas/ views/ ways**
▶ an unusual/ an unorthodox/ an unconventional/ an offbeat **approach**
▶ unusual/ unorthodox/ unconventional **methods**
▶ sb's **approach/ ideas/ methods/ views is/ are different**
▶ **very** unusual/ eccentric/ unorthodox/ unconventional
▶ **highly/ rather** unusual/ eccentric/ unorthodox
▶ **pretty** unusual/ eccentric/ unconventional
▶ **somewhat** unusual/ eccentric/ unorthodox/ atypical
▶ **a bit** unusual/ eccentric/ different/ out of the ordinary

unusual 普通でない, いつもと異なる, 異常な, 異例の, まれな；(他とは)異なっていて面白く魅力的な)珍しい, 一風変わった, 独特の ◇She has a very *unusual* name. 彼女は非常に珍しい名前だ ◇It was *unusual* to see anyone out on the streets at this hour. この時間に通りに人が出ているのを見かけるのはまれだった ◇It's *not unusual* for junior doctors to work 60 hours a week. 若手の医師が週に60時間働くことは珍しくない 反意 **usual** (USUAL)
▶**unusually** 副 ◇*Unusually* for him, he was dressed in a suit. 彼としては異例だが, スーツを着ていた ◇She was *unusually* quiet that evening. 彼女はその夜, いつになく静かだった
eccentric （人・振る舞いが危害はないが）奇妙な, 変な, 常軌を逸した, 異常な ◇She was the classic *eccentric* old lady, living with a houseful of cats. 彼女は家一杯に猫を飼っている典型的な変わり者の老婆だった ◇His behaviour grew increasingly *eccentric* as time went on. 彼の行動は時が経つにつれてますます常軌を逸するようになった
▶**eccentric** 名 [C] ◇Most people considered him a harmless *eccentric*. たいていの人が彼を害のない変人だと見なしていた
unorthodox （方法・考え・振る舞いが批判を招く形で）正統でない, 異端の ◇His methods have been criticized as

somewhat *unorthodox*. 彼のやり方はいささか正統でないと批判されてきた ◇Their *unorthodox* beliefs often landed them in trouble with the authorities. 彼らは異端教義のために当局と衝突することがしばしばあった 反意 **orthodox** (TRADITIONAL)

unconventional 《しばしばほめて》(面白い形で)慣習[因習]にとらわれない、型にはまらない ◇She's known for her *unconventional* approach to child-rearing. 彼女は育児に対して慣習にとらわれない取組みで知られる ◇He thought of their lifestyle as daringly *unconventional*. 彼は彼らの生活様式を大胆なほど型破りなものと考えた 反意 **conventional** (CONSERVATIVE)
➤**unconventionally** ◇She dresses *unconventionally*. 彼女は因習にとらわれない服装をする

atypical (特定の種類の人・事物・集団に)典型的でない、異例の ◇The so-called 'norm' of the nuclear family is in fact *atypical* of many families. いわゆる核家族の「標準」は実際には多くの家庭の典型ではない 反意 **typical** (TYPICAL), **typical** (NORMAL)

different [名詞の前はまれ]《特に話し言葉》(他とは異なって)変わった ◇'Did you enjoy the play?' 'Well, it was certainly *different*.'「お芝居、面白かった?」「ああ、確かに変わってたね」❶ *different* は物事を批判するのを避ける語として用いられることが多い。現に物事が奇妙だと思っていて、実際にそれを好きか[好意的に判断するか]どうかはっきりしない場合に、人々はその物事が *different* であると言う。

offbeat [ふつう名詞の前で][インフォーマル]《大半の人が考えるものとは異なり》一風変わった ◇He has a rather *offbeat* sense of humour. 彼にはやや一風変わったユーモアセンスがある

out of the 'ordinary 行政 普通でない、いつもと異なる、異常な、異例の、変わった ◇There seems to be nothing *out of the ordinary* about his application. 彼の願書に変わったところは何もないようだ

unwanted 形

unwanted・unpopular・unwelcome・unsolicited・undesirable・uninvited・unloved
欲せられていないことを表す
【類語訳】望まれていない、求められていない、人気のない、歓迎されていない、招かれていない、愛されていない

文型&コロケーション
▶ an unwanted/ an unpopular/ an unloved **child**
▶ an unwanted/ unloved **baby**
▶ an unwanted/ unwelcome/ unsolicited **call**
▶ an unwanted/ unwelcome/ undesirable **change/ effect**
▶ an unwanted/ unwelcome/ uninvited **guest/ visitor**
▶ an unwanted/ unwelcome **intruder/ intrusion**
▶ unwanted/ unwelcome **attention/ publicity**
▶ unwanted/ unsolicited **advice/ goods/ material**

unwanted 望まれていない、求められていない ◇They aim to reduce *unwanted* pregnancies. 彼らは望まれていない妊娠を減らすことを目標としている ◇It is very sad when children feel *unwanted* (= feel that other people do not care about them). 子どもが自分は望まれていないと感じるならば、非常に悲しいことだ

unpopular 人気のない、不評判の ◇He made several *unpopular* decisions during his leadership. 彼は指導者の在任期間、いくつか評判の悪い決定を下した ◇The proposed increase in income tax proved deeply *unpopular with* the electorate. 提案された所得税増税は、有権者たちにひどく評判が悪いとわかった ◇The party is increasingly *unpopular among* young people. その党は次第に若者たちの人気を失っている 反意 **popular** (POPULAR)
➤**unpopularity** 名 [U] ◇the growing *unpopularity* of the military regime 軍事政権の高まる不評判

unwelcome 歓迎されていない、嫌な、不快な ◇Security cameras around the building keep out *unwelcome* visitors. ビルの周りの防犯カメラが望ましくない訪問者たちの侵入を防止している ◇Jones's book revealed an *unwelcome* truth which no one really wanted to hear. ジョーンズの本は、誰もが本当は聞きたくもない不愉快な真実を暴露した 反意 **welcome** ❶welcomeは会って[招いて]、取って、持って、など]うれしい人・事物を指すのに用いられる ◆Children are always *welcome* at the hotel. (そのホテルはいつも子どもたちを歓迎しています) ◆The fine weather *made a welcome change*. (好天のおかげで、うれしい変化が起きた)

ノート **unwanted** と **unwelcome** の使い分け: guests, visitors, intruders, attention, publicity, changes, effects は unwanted でも unwelcome でも修飾可能. children, babies, pregnancies, goods, advice は unwantedで修飾可能. news, facts, the truth は unwelcome で修飾可能.

unsolicited 《ややフォーマル》求められていない、望まれていない ◇I didn't appreciate his *unsolicited* advice. 頼んでもいないのに彼がする助言は迷惑だった ◇The record company receives dozens of *unsolicited* demo tapes each week. レコード会社は毎週、求めてもいないのに多数のデモテープを受け取る

undesirable 《ややフォーマル》好ましくない;(トラブル・問題を招きそうで)望ましくない、嫌な、不快な ◇What is the best way to deal with *undesirable* behaviour? 好ましくない振る舞いに対処する最善の方法は何ですか ◇It would be highly *undesirable* to increase class sizes further. 1クラスの人数をさらに増やすことは、極めて望ましくないだろう 反意 **desirable** (POPULAR), **desirable** (BEST)

uninvited 《しばしば動詞の後で》招かれていない、求められていない ◇There were one or two *uninvited* guests at the party. そのパーティーには一人二人招かれざる客がいた ◇He turned up *uninvited*. 彼は招かれてもいないのに姿を現した

unloved 《ややフォーマル》愛されていない ◇According to the theory, *unloved* children become bad parents. その説によれば、愛されていない子どもは悪い親となる

upset 形

upset・sorry・distressed・devastated・hurt・distraught・dismayed・anguished
人が不快な事が起きて沈んでいる様子を表す
【類語訳】悲しんで、がっかりして、気の毒に思って、かわいそうに思って、落胆しきった、取り乱した、うろたえた、苦悶の

upset	distressed	devastated
sorry	anguished	distraught
hurt		
dismayed		

文型&コロケーション

▶upset/ distressed/ devastated/ hurt/ dismayed **by** sth
▶upset/ distressed/ devastated/ dismayed **at** sth
▶upset/ sorry/ distressed/ devastated **about** sth
▶upset/ sorry/ distressed/ devastated/ hurt/ distraught/ dismayed **that**...
▶to be sorry/ distressed/ devastated/ dismayed **to see/ hear/ find, etc**....
▶a distressed/ distraught **mother/ relative**
▶to **feel** upset/ sorry/ distressed/ devastated/ hurt/ dismayed
▶to **look** upset/ sorry/ distressed/ devastated/ hurt/ distraught/ dismayed/ anguished
▶**very** upset/ sorry/ distressed/ hurt
▶**deeply** distressed/ distressed/ hurt
▶**extremely** upset/ sorry/ distressed/ distraught
▶**absolutely/ completely** devastated/ distraught
▶**too** upset/ distressed/ distraught **to do sth**

upset ［名詞の前では用いない］（不快な事が起きて）悲しんで，がっかりして ◇There's no point *getting upset* about it. そんなこと，がっかりすることじゃないよ ◇I think she may be a bit *upset with* you. 彼女はちょっと君にがっかりしているかもしれないよ ◇She was *upset* that he had left without saying goodbye. 彼女は彼が別れも告げずに去ってしまったことを悲しんだ ☞ **upset** (HURT 1), **upsetting** (PAINFUL 2)

sorry ［名詞の前では用いない］（不快な事が他人の身に起きて）気の毒［かわいそう］に思って ◇I'm *sorry* that your husband lost his job. ご主人が失業されたとはお気の毒に ◇We're *sorry* to hear that your father's in hospital again. お気の毒に，お父様がまた入院されたとか ◇No one is *sorrier* than I am about what happened. 起こったことを気の毒に思う気持ちは誰にも負けません 反意 **glad, happy** (GLAD), ☞ **sympathetic** (SENSITIVE 1)

distressed （不快な事が起きて非常に）落胆しきった，思い悩んだ ◇He was too *distressed* and confused to answer their questions. 彼はあまりにも落胆しきってうろたえていたので，彼らの質問に答えられなかった ◇She was in a somewhat *distressed state* when she came to see me. 彼女は私に会いに来たとき，いくぶん思い悩んでいる状態だった ☞ **distress** (DISTRESS), **distress** (HURT 1), **distressing** (PAINFUL 2)

devastated （ややインフォーマル）（ひどく悲しんで［ショックを受けて］）がく然とした，打ちひしがれた ◇I felt *devastated* at losing my job. 私は仕事を失ってがく然とした ◇His family is absolutely *devastated*. 彼の家族はすっかり打ちひしがれている

hurt （人の言動に）傷ついた ◇a *hurt* look/expression 傷ついた顔つき／表情 ◇She was deeply *hurt* that she had not been invited. 彼女は招かれなかったことにひどく傷ついていた ◇Martha's *hurt* pride showed in her eyes. マーサの傷ついたプライドは，その目に見てとれた ☞ **hurt** (DISTRESS), **hurt** (HURT 1)

distraught （悲しみ・心配で）取り乱した ◇She's still too *distraught* to talk about the tragedy. 彼女はまだとても取り乱していて，その悲劇について語ることができない ◇The child's *distraught* parents pleaded for witnesses to contact the police. 取り乱したその子どもの両親は目撃者に警察へ連絡してくれるよう懇願した

dismayed （ショックで落胆して）うろたえた ◇He was *dismayed* at the change in his old friend. 彼は旧友の変わり様にうろたえた ◇They were *dismayed* to find that the ferry had already left. フェリーがすでに出てしまったことを知って，彼らはがっくりした ☞ **dismay** (SHOCK 名), **dismay** (SHOCK 動)

anguished （ややフォーマル）苦悶の ◇She read the letter, gave an *anguished cry* and collapsed. 彼女は手紙を読み，苦悶の叫び声を上げてくずおれた ◇He looked across at Kate's *anguished* face. 彼はケイトの苦悶の表情を遠巻きに見た ☞ **anguish** (DISTRESS)

urgent 形

urgent • pressing • burning • compelling
即座に対処する必要があることを表す
【類語訳】急を要する，緊急の，至急の，切迫した，差し迫った，火急の，抑えきれない，…せずにはいられない

文型&コロケーション

▶an urgent/ a pressing/ a burning/ a compelling **desire/ need**
▶an urgent/ a pressing/ a burning **issue/ question**
▶urgent/ pressing **business/ demands**
▶an urgent/ a pressing **problem/ matter/ task**

urgent 急を要する，緊急の，至急の，切迫した ◇'Can I see you for a moment?' 'I'm very busy — is it *urgent*?' 「ちょっとお時間よろしいですか」「とても忙しいんだ一急ぎかい」 ◇The situation calls for *urgent* action. 事態は緊急の行動を要している ◇The law is *in urgent need of* reform. その法律の改正が緊急に必要である ☞ **urgency** (IMPORTANCE), **urge** (DESIRE)
▶**urgently** 副 ◇New equipment is *urgently* needed. 新しい設備が緊急に必要である ◇I need to speak to her *urgently*. 至急，彼女と話す必要がある

pressing ［ふつう名詞の前で］（ややフォーマル，特に書き言葉）急を要する，緊急の，至急の，切迫した ◇There is a *pressing* need for more specialist nurses. より専門的な看護師が至急にいります ◇The government seems to think that international problems are more *pressing* than domestic ones. 政府は国際問題は国内問題より緊急性が高いと考えているようだ

[ノート] **urgent**と**pressing**の使い分け：両語とも必要性・問題・要求・ビジネス問題を表すのに用いることができる。urgentは attention, consideration, action, measure, step, meeting, talks, letter, message, repair など幅広い語と結びつく。pressingはurgentよりもフォーマルで，特に書き言葉で用いられる。

burning ［名詞の前で］（欲求・願望が）激しい，燃えたぎる；（問題・質問が）差し迫った，火急の ◇He had a *burning ambition* to start his own business. 彼には自分で新しい仕事をするという燃えたぎる野心があった ◇Immigration was one of the *burning* issues of the day. 移民問題は当時の火急の問題の一つだった

compelling 《書き言葉》（欲求・願望が）抑えきれない，…せずにはいられない ◇He was a sad man with a *compelling* need to talk about his unhappiness. 彼は自分の不幸についてどうしても語らずにはいられない悲しい男だった ☞ **compulsion** (DESIRE)

use 名

use • application • practice • exercise

↪use

物事を使う[行う]行為
【類語訳】応用, 適用, 活用, 利用, 実践, 実見, 行使, 使用, 行使権

文型&コロケーション

▶ **effective/ proper/ continued/ normal** use/ application/ practice/ exercise
▶ **full/ constant** use/ application/ exercise
▶ **free** use/ practice/ exercise
▶ **common/ current/ correct/ safe/ commercial/ industrial/ clinical** use/ application/ practice
▶ sth **has** a use/ an application
▶ to **limit/ regulate/ justify** the use/ practice/ exercise of sth

use [U, 単数で] 使用[利用]すること；使用[利用]されている状態；(他人の物を)使用[利用]する権利[機会]；(精神・肉体を)使用させる[働かせる]能力 ◇The software is designed for *use* in schools. そのソフトウェアは学校での使用を意図したものだ ◇The chapel was built in the 12th century and is still *in use* today. その礼拝堂は12世紀に建てられ, 今もまだ使用されている ◇The bar is *for the use of* members only. そのバーは会員のみ利用できます ◇I have the *use* of the car this week. 今週, 私にはその車の使用権がある ◇He lost the *use* of his legs (= became unable to walk) in an accident. 彼は事故で両脚が使えなくなった

application [U, C] 《ややフォーマル》(理論・発見・発明の)応用, 適用, 活用, 利用 ◇This essay examines the *application* of new technology to teaching. この小論は新しい科学技術の教育への応用について精査している ◇The new invention would have a wide range of *applications* in industry. その新発明は産業界で幅広く応用されるでしょう ☞ apply (APPLY)

practice [U] 実践, 実行 ◇The book is about the *theory and practice* of teaching. その本は指導法の理論と実践について書かれたものである ◇She's determined to *put* her new ideas *into practice*. 彼女は新しい考えを実行に移そうと心に決めている ☞ **put sth into practice** (APPLY), **practise** (DO)

exercise [U] 《of を伴って》《ややフォーマル》(権力・技術・特質の)行使, 使用, 働かせること, (物事を発動する)行使権 ◇Sovereignty means more than just the *exercise* of power. 主権とは単なる権力の行使以上のことを意味する ◇One of these powers is the *exercise* of discretion by police officers. これらの権力の一つに, 警官による裁量権の行使がある

use 動

1 ☞ APPLY
use・exercise・employ・draw on/upon sth・exert・make use of sb/sth・utilize・resort to sth・fall back on sb/sth

特定の目的のために機械[方法, 物, 技術, 機会]を駆使して事を行う
【類語訳】使う, 用いる, 使用する, 利用する, 働かせる, 行使する, 活用する

文型&コロケーション

▶ to use/ employ/ utilize sth **as** sth
▶ to use/ employ/ draw on/ make use of/ utilize/ resort to/ fall back on sth **to do** sth
▶ to use/ exercise/ employ/ draw on/ make use of/ utilize/ fall back on (a) **skill**
▶ to use/ employ/ make use of/ utilize/ resort to/ fall back on a **method/ technique**
▶ to use/ exercise/ employ/ resort to **violence**
▶ to use/ exercise/ exert your **influence/ power/ authority**
▶ to use/ employ/ draw on/ make use of/ utilize **resources**
▶ to use/ make use of/ utilize the **facilities/ a service/ an opportunity**
▶ to **often/ frequently** use/ exercise/ employ/ draw on/ make use of/ utilize/ resort to sb/ sth
▶ to **usually** use/ exercise/ employ/ resort to sb/ sth
▶ to **commonly/ occasionally** use/ employ/ resort to sb/ sth
▶ to **rarely** use/ exercise/ employ/ draw on/ resort to sb/ sth
▶ to use/ exercise/ employ sb/ sth **widely**
▶ to use/ employ/ draw on/ utilize sb/ sth **extensively**
▶ to use/ draw on/ utilize sb/ sth **heavily**

use [他] (特定の目的のために機械・方法・物・技術・機会を)使う, 用いる, 使用[利用]する, 働かせる ◇Can I *use* your phone? 電話を使わせてもらえる ◇Have you ever *used* this software before? 前にこのソフトを使ったことはありますか ◇How often do you *use* (= travel by) the bus? どのくらいバスを利用しますか ◇The blue files are *used for* storing old invoices. 青いファイルは古い送り状を保存するために使われている ◇Police *used* tear gas to disperse the crowds. 警察は群集を追い払うために催涙ガスを使用した ◇Don't keep asking me what to do — just *use* your common sense! どうすべきか私に聞いてばかりいないで—少しは常識を働かせなさい ❶このグループのすべての同義語の中で, use は物を使って事を行うことについて最も頻繁に用いられる. ◆ to *use* a computer/comb/dictionary/fork/pen/pencil/phone/spoon/weapon, etc. (コンピューター/くし/辞書/フォーク/ペン/鉛筆/電話/スプーン/武器などを使う).

exercise [他] 《フォーマル》(物事を達成するために権力・権利・個性を)行使[使用]する, 働かせる ◇He was a man who *exercised* considerable influence over people. 彼は人々に対してかなりの影響力を行使する人だった ◇When she appeared in court she *exercised* her right to remain silent. 彼女は出廷すると, 黙秘権を行使した

employ [他] 《フォーマル》(特定の目的のために技術・方法などを)使う, 用いる ◇He criticized the repressive methods *employed* by the country's government. 彼はその国の政府が用いている弾圧的手法を批判した ◇The police had to *employ* force to enter the building. 警察はその建物に入るために武力を用いなければならなかった

'draw on/upon sth [句動詞] 《ややフォーマル》(利用可能なものを)使う, 用いる, 頼る, 当てにする ◇I'll have to *draw on* my savings. 貯金を使わなければならないだろう ◇The novelist *draws* heavily *on* her personal experiences. その小説家は自らの個人的な体験に大いに依存している ❶ draw on/upon sth はほとんどの場合, 人が仕事において, 経験・方法・情報・データ・理論・研究結果・知識を使う場合に用いる.

exert [他] 《ややフォーマル》(物事を達成するために権力・影響力を)行使する, 及ぼす；(人・物事に)大きな影響力を及ぼす ◇He *exerted* all his authority to make them accept the plan. 彼は彼らに計画を受け入れさせるために全権力を行使した ◇The moon *exerts* a force on the earth that causes the tides. 月は地球に潮の干満を引き起こす力を及ぼす

> **ノート** exercise と exert の使い分け：exert は人・物事を主語にして、目的語に power, authority, influence, pressure, force を取り、影響を及ぼすことを表す。exercise は人のみを主語にして、目的語には power, authority, influence だけでなく、right, privilege や、care, caution, tact, discretion, diplomacy, judgement, discipline, restraint, self-control などの個人的資質も取ることができる。

make 'use of sb/sth [フレーズ] （優位に立つために人・物事を）使用[利用、活用]する ◇We could *make* better *use of* our resources. 私たちは資源をもっと有効に使えるはずだ ◇You should *make use of* your contacts. 縁故を利用すべきです

utilize (英でまた **-ise**) [他]《フォーマル》（実用的な目的のために物を）利用[活用]する ◇The Romans were the first to *utilize* concrete as a building material. ローマ人はコンクリートを初めて建築資材として利用した ◇The resources at our disposal could have been better *utilized*. 私たちが自由に使える資源をもっと活用することができたはずなのに

resort to sth [句動詞] （解決策がないため好ましくない物事を）使う、用いる、頼る、訴える ◇They felt obliged to *resort to* violence. 彼らは暴力に訴えるざるをえないと感じた ◇We may have to *resort to* using untrained workers. 我々は未熟練労働者の投入に頼らなければならないかもしれない ❶ *resort to* の典型的な連語には bribery, force, terror, violence が挙げられる。

,fall 'back on sb/sth [句動詞] [受身なし]（困難な状況にあるときに人・物事に）頼る、当てにする ◇I have a little money in the bank to *fall back on*. 銀行に頼みの綱とする少しの金がある ◇She *fell back on* her usual excuse of having no time. 彼女は時間がないといういつもの言い訳に頼った

2 use・use sth up・consume・expend・deplete・drain・absorb・exhaust・get through sth
（ほとんど）何も残らないように、特定の目的に向けて
【類語訳】費やす、消費する、使いきる、使い果たす、枯渇させる、消耗させる、疲弊させる、使い尽くす

[文型＆コロケーション]
▶ to use/ use up/ consume/ expend/ deplete/ drain/ absorb/ exhaust **resources**
▶ to use/ use up/ deplete/ exhaust **a supply/ supplies** of sth
▶ to use/ deplete/ drain/ exhaust **reserves** of sth
▶ to use/ use up/ consume/ expend **money**
▶ to use/ deplete/ drain/ exhaust **funds**
▶ to use/ consume/ expend/ absorb **time**
▶ to use/ use up/ consume/ expend/ drain/ absorb/ exhaust **energy**
▶ to use/ use up/ consume/ deplete/ absorb/ exhaust sth **quickly**
▶ to consume/ deplete/ absorb/ exhaust sth **rapidly**
▶ to use up/ consume/ drain/ absorb/ exhaust sth **completely**

use [他] （時間・金・エネルギー・材料を）費やす、使う、使いきる ◇This type of heater *uses* a lot of electricity. このタイプのヒーターは電力をたくさん食う ◇I hope you haven't *used* all the milk. 君は牛乳を全部使いきっていないよね ◇You should learn to *use* your time more efficiently. 時間をもっと効率的に使うことを学ぶべきです

,use sth 'up [句動詞] （物を）使いきる ◇Making soup is a good way of *using up* leftover vegetables. スープ作りは残りの野菜を使いきるよい方法です ◇I'm wondering how to arrange the furniture without *using up* too much space. スペースを使いすぎずに、どうやって家具を配置したらいいか考えているところです

consume [他] 《ややフォーマル、書き言葉》（燃料・エネルギー・時間を）費やす、消費する、使う、使い果たす ◇My new car *consumes* much less fuel. 私の新車は燃費がずっといい ◇The production of new paper from wood pulp *consumes* vast amounts of energy. 木材パルプからの新しい紙の生産には、膨大なエネルギーが消費される ❶ *consume* は目的語に資源を取り、ふつう人ではなく物事・過程を主語に取る。×The government has *consumed* large sums of public money. ◆Bureaucracy *consumes* money that could have been spent on public services. （官僚制により公共サービスに使えたかもしれない金が使い果たされている）。☞ **consume** (EAT)
▶ **consumption** [名] [U] ◇Gas and oil *consumption* always increases in cold weather. ガソリンと石油の消費は寒波が来るといつも増加する

expend [他] 《フォーマル》（時間・金・エネルギー・努力を）費やす、消費する、使う、使い果たす ◇The government has *expended* large sums of public money on a failing project. 政府は多額の公金を破綻しつつある事業に費やしてきた ◇Unlike most animals, mussels do not *expend* energy looking for food. ほとんどの動物と違い、イガイは餌を探すのにエネルギーを使わない
▶ **expenditure** [名] [U] ◇This study represents a major *expenditure* of time and effort. この研究は時間と労力を大いに費やす典型です

deplete [他、ふつう受身で]《ややフォーマル》（物を）激減させる、枯渇させる ◇Food supplies were severely *depleted*. 食糧供給は大幅に減少した ◇Fossil fuel reserves are being *depleted* at an alarming rate. 化石燃料の埋蔵量は、驚くべき速さで枯渇しつつある
▶ **depletion** [名] [U] ◇ozone *depletion* オゾンの激減 ◇the *depletion* of fish stocks 魚種資源の激減

drain [他] （金・体力を使い果たして人・物を）消耗させる、枯渇させる、疲弊させる ◇My mother's hospital expenses were slowly *draining away* my income. 母の入院費用で徐々に私の収入が枯渇しつつあった ◇I felt *drained of* energy. 活力が失せていく気がした ◇The experience left her *emotionally drained*. その経験で彼女は精神的に疲れ切ってしまった
▶ **a drain on sth** [名] [単数で] ◇Military spending is *a* huge *drain on* the country's resources. 軍事費がその国の財源をひどく枯渇させている

absorb [他] （金・時間を大量に）かける、取る ◇The new proposals would *absorb* $80 million of the federal budget. 新しい案には8000万ドルもの連邦予算がかかるだろう

exhaust [他] 《ややフォーマル》（物を）使い尽くす ◇Within three days they had *exhausted* their supply of food. 彼らは3日のうちに、供給された食糧を食べ尽くしてしまった ◇Don't give up until you have *exhausted* all the *possibilities*. すべてあきらめてはいけない

> **ノート** use sth up と exhaust の使い分け：exhaust はややフォーマルで、特に大量の[非常に重要な]物事を使い果た

すことについて用いられる。use sth up は特に比較的少量でそれほど重要でない物事について用いられる。◆They had *exhausted* their food supply.（彼らは供給された食糧を食べ尽くしてしまっていた）×They had *used up* their food supply. ◆Sorry — I've *used up* the milk. （ごめん—牛乳全部使いきっちゃった）×Sorry — I've *exhausted* the milk.

'get through sth 句動詞 （物を大量に）費やす、消費する、使う、使い果たす ◇We *got through* a fortune while we were in New York! ニューヨークにいる間に、私たちは大金を使い果たした ◇We *get through* a lot of paper in the office. 私たちはオフィスで大量の紙を消費している

used to sth 形

used to (doing) sth・familiar with sth・accustomed to (doing) sth・up to date
物事についてよくわかっていることを表す
【類語訳】慣れた、よく知った、詳しい、精通した、熟知した、通じた、なじみのある、習慣の

▷文型&コロケーション
▶ used/ accustomed **to** sth
▶ to be familiar/ up to date **with** sth
▶ to **get**/ **grow** used to/ accustomed to sth
▶ to **keep** (sb) familiar with sth/ up to date
▶ **already** used to sth/ familiar with sth/ accustomed to sth/ up to date
▶ **fully** familiar with sth/ up to date

used to sth, used to doing sth フレーズ （経験して）慣れた ◇I'm not *used to* e*a*ting so much at lunchtime. 昼food時にそんなにたくさん食べることに慣れていない ◇I found the job tiring at first but I soon got *used to* it. 最初は仕事を骨が折れると感じたが、すぐに慣れた 反意 **unused to sth** (NEW 3)
familiar with sth フレーズ （物事を）よく知った、詳しい、精通した、熟知した、通じた、なじみのある ◇I wasn't *familiar with* the area. 私はその地域にはなじみがなかった ◇You will need to be thoroughly *familiar with* the software. そのソフトに熟知する必要があるでしょう 反意 **unfamiliar with sth** (NEW 3)
accustomed to sth, accustomed to doing sth フレーズ （ややフォーマル）（物事［…すること］に）慣れた、習慣の ◇My eyes slowly grew *accustomed to* the dark. 私の目はだんだん闇に慣れてきた ◇She was a person *accustomed to* having eight hours' sleep a night. 彼女は一晩に8時間眠るのが習慣の人だった 反意 **unaccustomed to sth** (NEW 3)
up to 'date [名詞の前では用いない] 最新の情報を持った ◇I need to be kept *up to date* with any developments. あらゆる開発についての最新情報を得ている必要が私にはある ◇She brought him *up to date* with what had happened. 彼女は彼に何が起きたかについての最新情報を伝えた ◇*up-to-date* information/records 最新情報／記録 反意 **out of date** (OLD-FASHIONED)

useful 形

useful・convenient・handy・practical・usable・great for sth・of use・functional
物事が手助けになったり、特定の目的に適っていることを表す
【類語訳】有用な、有効な、有益な、役に立つ、助けになる、便利な、手ごろな、使い勝手のよい、実用的な、機能的な

▷文型&コロケーション
▶ to be useful/ of use **to** sb
▶ to be useful/ convenient/ handy/ great **for doing** sth
▶ useful/ handy/ practical **tips**/ **hints**
▶ to **come in** useful/ handy
▶ **very**/ **quite** useful/ convenient/ handy/ practical/ usable/ functional
▶ **highly** useful/ convenient/ practical/ functional
▶ **extremely** useful/ convenient/ practical

useful （望みをかなえるのに）有用な、有効な、有益な、役に立つ、助けになる ◇a *useful* book/gadget 役に立つ本／装置 ◇It can be *useful* to write a short summary of your argument first. まず自分の主張の簡単な要約を書くことが助けになるかもしれない ◇He might be *useful* to us. 彼は私たちの役に立つかもしれない ◇Don't just sit watching TV — *make yourself useful*! ただ座ってテレビを見てるんじゃない—役に立つことをしなさい ◇Some products can be recycled at the end of their *useful* life. 製品の中には耐用年数の終わりにリサイクルできるものもある 反意 **useless** (USELESS)
▷ **usefully** 副 ◇The money could more *usefully* be spent on new equipment. その金はもっと有効に新しい装置に使うことができるのに
convenient （使う［行う］のに）便利な、都合のよい、手ごろな、使い勝手のよい ◇A bicycle is often more *convenient* than a car in towns. 町では自動車よりも自転車のほうが都合のいいことが多い ◇It is very *convenient* to pay by credit card. クレジットカードで支払うととても便利です ◇Fruit is a *convenient* source of vitamins and energy. 果物はビタミンとエネルギーの手ごろな供給源である ◇He used his wife's birthday as a *convenient* excuse for not going to the meeting. 《けなして》彼は妻の誕生日を会議に出ないための都合のいい言い訳に使った
▷ **conveniently** 副 ◇The report can be *conveniently* divided into three main sections. その報告書は便宜上3つの主な部分に分けることができる
handy （インフォーマル）（使うのに）便利な、役に立つ ◇The introductory booklet contains some *handy* tips for getting started. 入門用の小冊子にはスタートのためのちょっとした秘訣が載っている ◇Take your penknife — you never know when it might come in *handy* (= be handy). ペンナイフを持って行きなさい—いつ役に立つかわからないから
practical （特定の状況で）実用的な、実際に役立つ ◇It's a *practical* little car — ideal for the city. これは実用的な小型車です—都会には理想的です ◇Travel by boat was often faster and more *practical* than travel along the primitive roads. ボートでの移動は昔ながらの道路を走るよりも速く、かつ実際に役立つことが多かった
usable 使用［利用］できる；使用［利用］できる状態の ◇How can we display this data in a *usable* form? どうやったらこのデータを利用できる形で表示できるだろう ◇Take my bike — it's rusty, but it's perfectly *usable*. 僕の自転車を使いなよ—一錆びてるけどばっちり使えるから 反意 **unusable** (USELESS)
great for sth フレーズ （インフォーマル、特に話し言葉）（物事に）最適の、効果てきめんの ◇This gadget's *great for* open-

ing jars. この道具は広口瓶を開けるのに最適です ◇Try this cream — it's *great for* spots. このクリーム試してごらん—にきびに効果てきめんだよ
- **of use** [フレーズ] 《フォーマル》(望みをかなえるのに)有用な, 有効な, 有益な, 役に立つ, 助けになる ◇Can I be *of any use* (= can I help)? どんなご用件でしょうか ◇Your suggestion will be kept on file and may be *of use* should circumstances change. あなたの提言はファイルに収めておきます, 万一状況が変われば役に立つかもしれません
- **functional** (役に立って)機能的な ; (装飾がなくて)機能性を重視した ◇Bathrooms don't have to be *purely functional*. 浴室は機能性のみを求める必要はない ◇The office is a *functional* working area, designed with efficiency in mind. そのオフィスは効率性を考慮して設計されており, 機能性を重視した作業域だ

useless [形]

useless・in vain・pointless・futile・hopeless・fruitless・vain・unusable

その物事では目的もなく望みの達成も不可能であることを表す
【類語訳】役に立たない, 使い物にならない, 無用の, 無益な, 無駄な, 無意味な, 効果のない, 望みのない, 成果のない

[文型&コロケーション]
▶to be useless/ pointless/ futile/ hopeless/ fruitless/ vain **to do sth**
▶to be useless/ pointless **doing sth**
▶a useless/ pointless/ futile/ fruitless **exercise**
▶a futile/ hopeless/ fruitless/ vain **attempt**
▶a futile/ fruitless/ vain **effort**
▶a hopeless/ fruitless/ vain **task**
▶a futile/ hopeless/ fruitless/ vain **search**
▶**largely** useless/ in vain/ pointless/ futile/ hopeless/ fruitless/ vain
▶**seemingly** useless/ in vain/ pointless/ futile/ hopeless
▶**completely** useless/ pointless/ futile/ hopeless/ unusable
▶**utterly** useless/ pointless/ futile/ hopeless

useless 役に立たない, 使い物にならない, 無用の ; (必要なことを行わず[達成せず]に)無益な, 無駄な ◇This pen is *useless*. このペンは使い物にならない ◇He knew it was *useless* to protest. 彼は抗議しても無駄なことを知っていた ◇It's *useless* worrying about it. それについて心配しても無駄だ ◇The letter is *useless as* evidence. その手紙は証拠としては役に立たない ◇The land is *useless for* cattle. その土地は畜牛にとっては無益である ◇The drug is *useless in* the treatment of patients with AIDS. その薬はエイズ患者の治療には役に立たない ◇The information was *useless to* him. その情報は彼にとって無用だった ◇The quality ranged from acceptable to *worse than useless*. 品質は満足のいくものから, まったく使い物にならないものまで多岐にわたった [反意] **useful** (USEFUL), **valuable** (VALUABLE 2)
▶**uselessly** [副] ◇The sail flapped *uselessly*. 帆は無駄にはためいていた

in 'vain [イディオム] 《書き言葉》(必要なことを達成せずに)無益で, 無駄で ; (成功せずに)無駄で, 駄目で ◇All their efforts were *in vain*. 彼らの努力はすべて無駄であった ◇They *tried in vain* to persuade her to go. 彼らは彼女を説得して行かせようとしたが, 駄目だった ◇She *waited in vain*

for her son to return. 彼女は息子の帰りを待っていたが, 無駄だった
pointless (何の目的もなくて)無意味な ; (成功の見込みがないために行う価値がなくて)無益な, 無駄な ◇Trying to foresee the future is a *pointless* exercise. 未来を予知しようとするのは無意味な行いである ◇It would be *pointless for* both of you to work on the same thing. 二人ともが同じことに取り組むのは無駄でしょう ◇I knew it was *pointless* expecting him to change his mind. 彼の気が変わることを期待するのは無駄だとわかっていた [反意] **worthwhile** (VALUABLE 2)
▶**pointlessly** [副] ◇He would argue *pointlessly* with his parents. 彼は両親とかみ合わぬ議論をよくした

futile 《ややフォーマル》(失敗に終わって)無益な, 無駄な ; 効果[意味]のない ◇It was a *futile gesture* as the real damage had already been done. すでに実害を受けていたので, そんなジェスチャーは無駄だった ◇Their efforts to revive him were *futile*. 彼を甦らせる彼らの努力は無駄に終わった
▶**futility** [名] [U] ◇a sense of *futility* 徒労感 ◇the *futility* of war 戦争のむなしさ

hopeless (成功・改善・効果の)望み[見込み]のない ◇*It's hopeless* trying to convince her. 彼女を説得しようとしても見込みはない ◇Most students are making good progress, but Michael is *a hopeless case*. たいていの学生は順調に進歩しつつあるが, マイケルの場合は望みがない [反意] **hopeful** (PROMISING)

fruitless 《ややフォーマル》無益な, 無駄な, 成果[実り]のない ◇He returned home after weeks of *fruitless* negotiations. 数週間にわたる実りのない交渉の末, 彼は帰国した ◇The search proved *fruitless*. その捜索は無駄であることがわかった [反意] **fruitful** (PRODUCTIVE)

vain (ふつう名詞の前で)《書き言葉》無益な, 無駄な, むなしい, はかない ◇I knocked loudly *in the vain hope* that someone might answer. 誰かが答えてくれるかもしれないといういはかない望みを抱いて大きくノックした

unusable [名詞の前はまれ](状態・品質が悪くて)使用[利用]できない ◇The damage rendered the building *unusable*. 損傷でその建物は利用できなくなった ◇The plutonium is *unusable* for anything until it is reprocessed. プルトニウムは再処理されるまではどんな用にも使用できない [反意] **usable** (USEFUL)

usual [形]

usual・traditional・standard・general・routine・regular・habitual

物事が長期間にわたってほとんどの場合に起こる, 人に典型的であることを表す
【類語訳】通常の, 通例の, 普通の, 普段の, いつもの, ありふれた, 標準の, 一般的の, 日常の, ごく普通の, 平凡な

[文型&コロケーション]
▶to be usual/ traditional/ routine **to do sth**
▶usual/ traditional/ routine **for sb/ sth**
▶the usual/ traditional/ standard/ general/ routine/ regular **procedure/ practice**
▶the usual/ traditional/ standard/ general/ routine/ regular/ habitual **way**
▶the usual/ traditional/ standard/ general **approach**
▶the usual/ traditional/ general **sense/ style**
▶sb's usual/ traditional/ habitual **role**

→usual

- usual/ standard/ general/ routine/ regular/ habitual **behaviour**
- in the/ sb's usual/ traditional/ standard/ habitual **manner**
- **very** traditional/ general/ routine
- **fairly** usual/ traditional/ standard/ general/ routine

usual 通常の, 平常の, 通例の, 普通の, 普段の, いつもの, ありふれた, ありきたりの ◇It is *usual* to start a speech by thanking everybody for coming. 来てくれたことを全員に感謝して演説を始めるのが普通です ◇It is *usual* for the employer to pay the costs. 雇い主がその費用を支払うのが通例です ◇He came home later than *usual*. 彼はいつもより遅く帰宅した ◇She arrived at the *usual* time. 彼女は通常の時間に到着した ◇She made all the *usual* excuses. 彼女はことごとくありきたりの言い訳をした ◇He didn't sound like his *usual* happy self. 彼はいつもの幸せそうな声ではなかった ◇Despite the problems staff arrived for work *as usual*. 問題があったにもかかわらず, 職員たちは平常どおりに出勤した 反意 **unusual (UNUSUAL)**

traditional 伝統的な ◇The band plays *traditional* Celtic music. そのバンドは伝統的なケルト音楽を演奏します ◇Most of the buildings are in the *traditional* style. そのほとんどの建物は伝統様式です ◇It's *traditional* in America to eat turkey on Thanksgiving Day. 感謝祭に七面鳥を食べるのはアメリカでは伝統である
  ▸ **traditionally** 副 ◇*Traditionally*, markets are held in the open air. 伝統的に, 市場は野外で開かれます

standard (特別な[珍しい]特徴を持たずに)標準の, 通常の, 普通の ◇Pizza dough is oilier than *standard* bread dough. ピザ生地は普通のパン生地よりも油分を多く含んでいる ◇Calls will be charged at the *standard* rate. 通話は標準料率で課金されます ◇The rifle was *standard issue* for the British army before the First World War. 第一次大戦以前の英国の軍隊では, そのライフルは標準仕様だった ◇All vehicles come with a catalytic converter *as standard*. 自動車にはすべて, 触媒コンバーターが標準装備されている 反意 **non-standard**

general [ふつう名詞の前で] 一般的な ◇The machines all operate on the same *general* principle. それらの機械はすべて同じ一般原理で稼動します ◇*As a general rule*, the paler the roast the milder the coffee. 一般に, 焙煎したものの色が薄ければ薄いほど, コーヒーも口当たりがまろやかです ◇*In general*, Japanese cars are very reliable. 一般的に, 日本車は非常に信頼性が高い ☞ **general (GENERAL)**

routine [ふつう名詞の前で] (仕事・状況・過程の一部として)日常の, ごく普通の; (あらゆる点で)平凡な, ありきたりの ◇The fault was discovered during a *routine* check. その欠陥は日常点検で発見された ◇Don't worry — these are just *routine* enquiries. ご心配なく — これらはごく型どおりの取り調べにすぎませんから ◇He died of heart failure during a *routine* operation. 彼は平凡な手術の最中に心不全で死亡した ☞ **routinely (OFTEN)**

regular [名詞の前で] (行動・物事が)通常の, 平常の, 普通の, 通例の; (人が)常勤の, 正規の ◇On Monday he would have to return to his *regular* duties. 月曜日には彼は通常の職務に戻らなくてはならないだろう ◇The other bag had my *regular* clothes in it. もう一つのカバンには私の普段着が入っていました ◇I couldn't see my *regular* doctor today. 今日はいつもの[常勤の]先生に診てもらえなかった
  ▸ **regularly** ◇He *regularly* got up at four in the morning. 彼は普段は, 朝4時に起きていた

usually

habitual [名詞の前で] 《ややフォーマル》 (人が)いつもの ◇She reverted to her *habitual* frown. 彼女はいつものしかめ面に戻った ◇He sat smoking his *habitual* cigarette. 彼は腰を下ろしていつものタバコを吸っていた ☞ **habit (HABIT), habitually (OFTEN)**

usually 副

usually • often • normally • generally • commonly • mostly • most of the time • in general • as a rule • more often than not/as often as not

物事がほとんどの場合に行われる[起こる]ことを表す
【類義訳】通常は, 平常は, 通例は, 普通は, 普段は, いつもは, たいてい, ほとんどの場合, 多くの場合, いつものように

文型&コロケーション

- usually/ often/ generally/ commonly/ mostly **known as...**
- usually/ often/ normally/ generally/ commonly/ mostly **called/ found...**
- usually/ often/ normally/ generally/ commonly/ mostly **used**
- usually/ normally/ generally/ commonly **accepted**
- **to** usually/ often/ normally/ generally/ commonly **happen**
- **not** usually/ often/ normally/ generally/ commonly/ in general/ as a (general) rule
- **most** usually/ often/ normally/ generally/ commonly
- **quite** often/ generally/ commonly

usually 通常は, 平常は, 通例は, 普通は, 普段は, いつもは; たいてい, ほとんどの場合 ◇The journey *usually* takes an hour. その道のりはふつう一時間かかる ◇*Usually*, there's no extra charge for delivery. たいてい, 配達に追加料金は掛かりません ◇Planning permission is not *usually* needed. 通例, 建築許可は必要ありません ◇Describe what *usually* happens. ふだん起こることを説明しなさい

often たいてい, 多くの場合 ◇Old houses are *often* damp. 古い家はたいていじめじめしている ◇People *often* find it difficult to say goodbye. 人々は別れの一言がなかなか言えないことが多い ◇She's mean. Rich people very *often* are. 彼女はけちだ. 金持ちにはよくあることだが ◇Traffic has increased and the roads are *all too often* inadequate. 交通量は多くなるが道路の整備が追いつかないことがあまりに多い ☞ **often (OFTEN)**

normally 通常は, 平常は, 通例は, 普通は, 普段は, いつもは ◇The journey to work *normally* takes an hour. 通勤にはふつう一時間かかる ◇The Prime Minister would not *normally* be expected to attend the meeting. 首相のその会議への出席は通常はありえないだろう ◇*Normally*, it takes three or four years to complete the training. 訓練を完了するには通例, 3, 4年かかる

ノート usually と normally の使い分け：usually はほとんどの場合に起こるというような文脈で用いられる. normally は通常の場合と特定の場合を比べるような文脈で用いられる. ◆ It's *normally* much warmer than this in July (= but this July is unusually cold). (ふつう7月はこれよりずっと暖かい). ◆ He *normally* stayed in luxury hotels (= but this time he could not afford to do so). (彼はいつもは豪華なホテルに泊まっていた)

generally 一般的に, たいてい; 通常は, 通例は, 普通は, 普段は, いつもは ◇Payments are *generally* made on an annual basis. 支払いは一般的に，一年単位で行われる ◇Repairs are occasionally needed but *generally* the machine is quite reliable. 時折修理は必要ですが，通常，その機械は十分信頼性が高いです ❶ *generally* は *usually* よりもいくぶんフォーマルであることが多い．*generally* は書き言葉において受身の文で用いられることがいくぶん多く，個人的な習慣ではなく一般的な状況について用いられる．

commonly 通例の場合，たいてい，ほとんどの場合；一般的に ◇To receive satellite TV you need an antenna (*commonly* known as a dish). 衛星テレビを受信するには，(通例，ディッシュとして知られる)アンテナが必要です ◇These companies are *commonly* thought of as models of efficiency. これらの会社は一般的に，効率性の模範と考えられている ☞ **common (GENERAL)**

mostly たいてい，ほとんどの場合；通常は，平常は，通例は，普通は，普段は，いつもは ◇People *mostly* grew their own vegetables. 人々はたいてい，自分たちで自家用の野菜を栽培した ◇She *mostly* calls me by my last name. 彼女はふつう，私を苗字で呼ぶ ◇*Mostly* he eats in a restaurant. 彼はたいてい，レストランで食事をする ❶ *mostly* は *usually* よりもいくぶんインフォーマルであることが多く，特に話し言葉やよりインフォーマルな書き言葉において用いられる．*mostly* は人々が一般に行う[特定の人がふだん行う]ことを表すような場合に用いられ，ふだん起こることを表すような場合には用いられない．✕The journey *mostly* takes an hour. ✕Describe what *mostly* happens.

'most of the time 行札 ほとんど常に ◇*Most of the time* I quite liked being on my own. ほとんどいつも，私は自分ひとりでいるのがとても好きだった ◇The weather was cold and it rained *most of the time*. 天候は寒く，ほとんど常に雨が降った

in 'general 行札 《ややフォーマル，特に書き言葉》一般的に，たいてい；通常は，平常は，通例は，普通は，普段は，いつもは ◇*In general* the instruments are extremely reliable. 一般的に，それらの器具は非常に信頼できる ◇The attacks were *in general* not reported in the media. そうした攻撃は通常，マスコミで報じられなかった ❶ *in general* は *generally* のいくぶんフォーマルな表現である．

,as a 'rule 行札 たいてい，ほとんどの場合；通常は，通例は，普通は，普段は，いつもは ◇*As a rule* students have one piano lesson a week. たいてい，学生は週に1回ピアノのレッスンを受けます ◇*As a general rule* the softer cheeses are less fattening. 一般に，柔らかい種類に属するチーズは比較的太りにくい ❶ *as a general rule* は何をすべきかについて助言するために，「指針として」を意味するのに用いられることが多い．◆*As a general rule*, mild mustards should be served with spicy food. (原則的に，スパイスのよく効いた食べ物にはまろやかなマスタードを添えて出すといいです). ☞ **rule (HABIT), rule (PRINCIPLE 1)**

more ,often than 'not, as ,often as 'not フレーズ 通常は，平常は，通例は，普通は，普段は，いつもは；(人・物事が)いつものように ◇*More often than not*, the victims have serious medical problems. 通例，そうした被害者は深刻な健康問題を抱えている ◇As a teenager he was in trouble at school *as often as not*. 十代の若者だったときは，彼は学校でトラブルの渦中にあるのが常だった

V v

vague 形

vague・approximate・rough・indeterminate・indistinct・imprecise・ill-defined・borderline
明確[正確]でないことを表す
【類語訳】あやふやな、漠然とした、ぼんやりとした、あいまいな、はっきりしない、近似的な、おおよその、どっちつかずの

文型&コロケーション
- vague/ imprecise **about** sth
- a vague/ an approximate/ a rough **idea**
- a vague/ an imprecise/ an ill-defined **term**
- a vague/ an ill-defined **concept**
- an approximate/ a rough **calculation/ figure/ estimate/ guide/ translation**
- **very** vague/ approximate/ rough/ indistinct/ imprecise/ ill-defined/ borderline
- **somewhat** vague/ indeterminate/ indistinct/ imprecise/ ill-defined
- **rather** vague/ imprecise/ ill-defined

vague (考えが)あやふやな、漠然とした、ぼんやりとした；(情報・詳細が)明言されていない、はっきりしない ◇I have a *vague* recollection of meeting him when I was a child. 子どもの頃彼に会ったことはぼんやりとしか覚えていない ◇She's a little *vague* about her plans for next year. 彼女の来年の計画については少しあやふやです ◇He was accused of being deliberately *vague*. 彼は故意に明言を避けているとして非難された 反意 **clear** (SURE), **precise** (EXACT)
▷**vaguely** 副 ◇I can *vaguely* remember my first day at school. 初めて学校に行った日のことはぼんやりとしか思い出せない ◇a *vaguely* worded statement あいまいな言葉づかいの陳述

approximate (ややフォーマル、特に書き言葉) (数量が)ほぼ正確な、近似的な；おおよその、概略の ◇The cost given is only *approximate*. 算出された費用は近似値にすぎない ◇Use these figures as an *approximate* guide in your calculations. これらの数字を計算のおおよその指標に使いなさい 反意 **exact** (EXACT)
▷**approximately** 副 ◇The journey took *approximately* seven hours. 旅はほぼ7時間かかった ◇The two buildings were *approximately* equal in size. その二つのビルの大きさはほぼ同じだった

rough おおよその、概略の、あらましの；大ざっぱな、大まかな、下書きの ◇There were about 20 people there, at a *rough* guess. 大まかな推測では、そこには約20人の人たちがいた ◇I made a *rough* sketch of the inside of the church. 教会内部の見取り図の下書きを書いた 反意 **exact** (EXACT)
▷**roughly** 副 ◇We live *roughly* halfway between here and the coast. 私たちはここと海岸のほぼ中間に住んでいます ◇*Roughly speaking*, we receive about fifty letters a week on the subject. 大まかに言うと、その問題について週に約50通の手紙を受け取ります

ノート **approximate** と **rough** の使い分け：approximate は数・量・費用などについての(推測(guess)でなく)見積もり(estimate)・見当(idea)を表すこともできるが、数・量・費用などそのものを表すことが最も多い. rough は数・量・費用を表すこともできるが、見積もり・見当・推測のほうが多い. rough は著述(writing)・素描(drawing)を表すのに用いることができるが、approximate は不可. ×an *approximate* draft/sketch of sth.

indeterminate (ややフォーマル、特に書き言葉) (簡単[正確]に識別できずに)不確かな、あいまいな、はっきりしない ◇Her eyes were an *indeterminate* colour. 彼女の瞳ははっきりしない色合いだった ◇She was a tall woman of *indeterminate* age. 彼女の年齢ははっきりわからないが背の高い女性だった

indistinct (明確に見えず[聞こえず、思い出せず]に)はっきりしない、不明瞭な、ぼやけた、あやふやな、ぼんやりした ◇an *indistinct* figure in the distance 遠方にあるぼんやりした物の姿 ◇His memory of the incident was somewhat *indistinct*. その事件についての彼の記憶は少々あやふやだった 反意 **distinct** (MARKED)

imprecise 不正確な；(詳細を伝えず)あいまいな、漠然とした、はっきりしない ◇The problems arise from an *imprecise* definition of terms. それらの問題は用語の不確な定義から発生している ◇The witness's descriptions were too *imprecise* to be of any real value. 目撃者の説明はあまりにあいまいで、何ら実質的な価値はなかった 反意 **precise** (EXACT), ☞ **ambiguous** (MISLEADING)
▷**imprecisely** 副 ◇These terms are often used *imprecisely*. これらの用語は不正確に用いられることが多い

ill-de'fined (ややフォーマル、けなして) (明確に定義されておらず)不明確な、あいまいな ◇The precise aims of the committee remain *ill-defined*. その委員会の明確な目的はあいまいなままである

borderline どちらとも決めかねる、どっちつかずの；きわどい ◇In doubtful and *borderline* cases teachers will take the final decision. 疑わしくどちらとも決めかねる場合は、教師が最終決定を下します ☞ **borderline** (LIMIT 2)

valuable 形

1 valuable・precious・priceless・irreplaceable
物が人にとって大金に値する[非常に重要である]ことを表す
【類語訳】高価な、貴重な、希少価値の高い、金では買えない、かけがえのない

文型&コロケーション
- valuable/ precious/ priceless/ irreplaceable **to** sb
- valuable/ precious/ priceless/ irreplaceable **possessions**
- valuable/ precious/ priceless **antiques/ jewels/ jewellery/ gems**

valuable 金銭的価値の高い、高価な、貴重な ◇My home is my most *valuable* asset. 自宅は私の最も高価な資産です 反意 **worthless** (PRICE), ☞ **value** (PRICE)

precious 希少価値の高い, 高価な, 貴重な ◇The crown was set with *precious stones* — diamonds, rubies and emeralds. 王冠は宝石のダイヤモンドとルビーとエメラルドで飾られていた ◇*precious metals* (= gold and silver) 貴金属

priceless (非常に[値の付けられないほど])高価[貴重]な; 金では買えない ◇a *priceless* collection of antiques 値の付けられないほど高価な骨董品のコレクション ◇Our family photos are *priceless*. 私たちの家族写真はお金では買えません

irreplaceable (あまりに貴重で)置き[取り]換えられない, かけがえのない ◇These paintings are *irreplaceable*. これらの絵画はかけがえのないものです

2 **valuable**・**helpful**・**good**・**favourable**・**worthwhile**・**beneficial**・**constructive**・**positive**・**advantageous**
人や物事にとって無益ではなく, 重要であることを表す
【類語訳】利用価値の高い, 貴重な, 有用な, 有益な, 役立つ, 順調な, 有利な, やりがいのある, 利益になる, ためになる

▶ valuable/ helpful/ good/ favourable/ beneficial/ advantageous **for** sb/ sth
▶ valuable/ helpful/ favourable/ beneficial/ advantageous **to** sb/ sth
▶ to be valuable/ helpful/ good/ worthwhile/ beneficial/ advantageous **to do sth**
▶ valuable/ helpful/ good/ constructive/ positive **suggestions/ advice**
▶ a valuable/ helpful/ worthwhile/ beneficial/ constructive/ positive **contribution**
▶ a valuable/ good/ worthwhile/ beneficial/ constructive/ positive **experience**
▶ a valuable/ good/ positive **lesson**
▶ a good/ a favourable/ a beneficial/ a constructive/ a positive/ an advantageous **effect**
▶ a good/ favourable/ beneficial/ constructive/ positive **influence**
▶ a good/ favourable/ beneficial/ positive **result**
▶ a good/ a favourable/ an advantageous **position**
▶ **very** valuable/ helpful/ good/ favourable/ worthwhile/ beneficial/ constructive/ positive/ advantageous
▶ **highly** valuable/ favourable/ beneficial/ constructive/ positive/ advantageous
▶ **extremely** valuable/ helpful/ good/ favourable/ worthwhile/ beneficial/ positive/ advantageous
▶ **mutually** helpful/ beneficial/ advantageous

valuable 《ほめて》(非常に有益かつ重要で)利用価値の高い, 貴重な ◇The Internet can be a very *valuable* learning tool. インターネットは非常に利用価値の高い教材になりうる ◇You should gain some *valuable* insights into the world of business. 実業界への貴重な洞察が得られるはずです ◇Spinach is a *valuable* source of iron. ホウレン草は鉄分の貴重な供給源である 反意 **useless** (USELESS), ☞ **fruitful** (PRODUCTIVE), **value** (APPRECIATE)

helpful (特定の状況を改善するのに)有用な, 有益な, 役立つ, 助けになる ◇Here are some *helpful* hints for successful revision. ここに改正がうまくいくのに役立つヒントがいくつかあります ◇Sorry I can't be more *helpful*. ごめ んね, これ以上力になれなくて ◇Role-play is *helpful in* developing communication skills. ロールプレイングはコミュニケーション能力を向上させるのに役立ちます ◇You might find it *helpful* to contact a self-help group. 自助グループと連絡を取ってみたら何か助けになるかもしれませんよ 反意 **unhelpful,** ☞ **help** (HELP 名), **help** (HELP 動)
▶**helpfully** 副 ◇She *helpfully* suggested that I try the local library. 彼女は地元の図書館に行ってみるよう助けとなるような提案をしてくれた

good (人・物事に)有益な, 役立つ, よい, 好適な ◇Too much sun isn't *good* for you. 日光に当たりすぎるのは体によくありません ◇My father once gave me some *good* advice. 以前父は役に立つ助言をしてくれた ◇It's *no good* complaining — they never listen. 文句を言っても無駄だ―彼らは全然聞こうとしない ◇This book is *no good to* me: I need the new edition. この本は私には何の役にも立たない, 新版が欲しい 反意 **bad**

favourable 《英》《米 **favorable**》《ややフォーマル》(物事にとって)良好な, 好適な, 順調な, 有利な ◇The terms of the agreement are *favourable* to both sides. その合意の条件は双方に利益をもたらします ◇An area with a *favourable* climate will inevitably be richer than one without. 気候が良好な地域はそうでない地域より確実に豊かになるでしょう ◇Winning the debate put him in a very *favourable* position. 論争に勝つことで, 彼は非常に有利な立場に立った 反意 **unfavourable** (DIFFICULT 2)

worthwhile 《ほめて》(重要な[楽しい, 興味深い]ので)時間[金, 努力]をかける価値のある, やりがいのある ◇a *worthwhile* cause/discussion/job 努力を傾ける価値のある運動[目標]/時間をかける価値のある議論/やりがいのある仕事 ◇The smile on her face made it all *worthwhile*. 彼女の笑顔で, それはすべてやりがいのあるものになった ◇High prices in the UK make it *worthwhile* for buyers to look abroad. イギリスは物価が高いのでバイヤーたちが海外に目を向けてみる価値はある ◇It didn't seem *worthwhile* writing it all out again. それをまた全部書き改める価値はないように思えた 反意 **pointless** (USELESS)

beneficial 《フォーマル》有益な, 役立つ, 利益となる, ためになる ◇Relaxation classes can be *beneficial* to people of all ages. リラクゼーションのクラスは, すべての年代の人々のためになります ◇Lowering salt intake has a *beneficial* effect on blood pressure. 塩分の摂取量を減らすことは血圧に有益な効果がある 反意 **detrimental** (HARMFUL), ☞ **benefit** (BENEFIT), **benefit** (HELP 動 2)

ノート **good** と **beneficial** の使い分け : **beneficial** は **good** よりもはるかにフォーマルな語である。この意味では, **good** はほとんどの場合, **good for** sb/sth, **no good doing** sth, **no good to** sb の句で用いられる。

constructive 《ほめて》建設的な ◇You should always welcome *constructive criticism* of your work. 自分の仕事に対する建設的な批判は常に喜んで受け入れるべきだ ◇Can't you find something more *constructive* to do? もっと建設的なやるべきことを見つけられないの

positive [ふつう名詞の前で] 《ほめて》(人・物事に対して)好意的な, 肯定的な, 前向きな ◇Local residents made a very *positive* contribution to the debate. 地元住民はその議論に対して非常に積極的に貢献してくれた 反意 **negative** (HARMFUL)

advantageous (特定の人・集団にとって)有利な, 有益な, 好都合な ◇An agreement would be *advantageous* to both sides. 合意ということになれば双方にとって好都合だろう 反意 **disadvantageous** (DIFFICULT 2)

valuation 名

valuation・estimate・quote・quotation・costing
物事にいくら金銭的価値がある[費用がかかる]かについての判断
【類語訳】評価、査定、見積もり、鑑定、評価価格、原価計算

▶文型&コロケーション
▶ an estimate/ a quote/ a quotation **for** a piece of work
▶ a **high/ low** valuation/ estimate/ quote/ quotation
▶ a **detailed** valuation/ estimate/ quote/ quotation/ costing
▶ a **stock/ market/ share** valuation/ quote/ quotation
▶ to **give/ provide/ get/ obtain/ accept** a valuation/ an estimate/ a quote/ a quotation

valuation [C, U] (金銭的価値についての専門的な)評価、査定、見積もり、鑑定；評価[査定、見積もり、鑑定]価格 ◊Surveyors carried out a *valuation* of the property. 鑑定人たちがその資産の査定を行った ◊methods of land *valuation* 土地の評価法 ◊Experts set a high *valuation* on the painting. 専門家たちはその絵画に高い鑑定額を付けた

estimate [C] (仕事の費用についての)見積もり ◊We got *estimates* for the repair work from three firms and accepted the lowest. 私たちは補修工事について3社から見積もりを得て、最低価格を受け入れた ☞ **estimate** (ESTIMATE 動)

quote [C] (《インフォーマル、特に話し言葉》)(仕事の厳密な費用の)見積もり ◊Theirs was the lowest *quote*, so we went with them (= got them to do the work). 彼らのが最も安い見積もりだったので、我々は彼らに落札させた
▶ **quote** 動 [他] ◊They *quoted* us £300 for installing a shower unit. 彼らはシャワーユニットの取り付けについて、300ポンドの見積もり額を我々に提示した

quotation [C] (《ややフォーマル》)(仕事の厳密な費用の)見積もり ◊You should always get a written *quotation* from builders before they start work. 仕事に着手する前に必ず、建設業者から書面による見積もりをもらうべきです

ノート **quote** と **quotation** の使い分け：これらの語は厳密には同じ意味だが、quote のほうがインフォーマルである。《英》では、quote も quotation も「株式市場における商品・会社の時価・相場」を意味する。◆ It was the first football club to have a full stock market *quotation*. (そこが完全な株式市場を導入した最初のサッカークラブだった)。◆ Check stock *quotes* and email messages on your mobile phone. ((《インフォーマル》)携帯電話で株価と電子メールをチェックしなさい)。ビジネス報道では、かなりインフォーマルな言い回しを用いることが多い。ビジネスレターでは比較的フォーマルな語を用いる。

costing [C] (《英》)(新サービス・新製品の)原価計算 ◊Here is a detailed *costing* of our proposals. ここに我々の企画についての詳しい原価計算ができています ◊You'd better do some *costings*. 少しは原価計算を行ったほうがいい

ノート **estimate** と **costing** の使い分け：estimate はふつう単一の仕事に対するもの。costing, costings はサービス・製品に対するもので、それに関連するすべての仕事を含んだものを指す。estimate は最終的な価格に重点を置き、costing はその価格を算出する過程に重点が置かれる。

value 名

value・quality・merit・worth・excellence・distinction・meaning
優秀[有用]な質を表す
【類語訳】価値、真価、質、高品質、美点、功績、長所、優秀さ、卓越、非凡さ、名声、栄誉、重要性

▶文型&コロケーション
▶ sb/ sth **of** value/ quality/ merit/ worth/ excellence/ distinction
▶ value/ merit/ excellence/ distinction **in** sth
▶ **without** value/ merit/ worth/ distinction/ meaning
▶ **great/ real** value/ quality/ merit/ worth/ distinction/ meaning
▶ **true** value/ quality/ worth/ excellence/ meaning
▶ **considerable** value/ quality/ merit/ distinction
▶ **dubious** value/ quality/ merit/ distinction
▶ **artistic** value/ quality/ merit/ worth/ excellence
▶ **academic** merit/ excellence/ distinction
▶ to **have** value/ quality/ merit/ worth/ distinction/ meaning
▶ sb/ sth **proves** their/ its value/ quality/ merit/ worth

value [U] (優秀[有用、重要]な)価値；真価 ◊The *value* of regular exercise should not be underestimated. 定期的な運動の価値は過小評価されてはならない ◊The arrival of canals was of great *value to* many industries. 運河の出現は多くの産業にとって大きな価値があった ◊This ring has great *sentimental value* for me (= it is important because I associate it with people or places that are emotionally important to me). この指輪は私にとって思い入れが大いにある ◊I suppose it has a certain *novelty value* (= it's interesting because it's new) but you'll soon get bored of it. それにはある種の目新しさの価値があると思うが、じきに飽きてしまうようなものです ☞ **value** (APPRECIATE)

quality [U] (良)質、高品質 ◊We aim to provide *quality* at reasonable prices. 手ごろな価格で高品質なものを提供するのが我々の目的です ◊Get it right, even if it takes time; it's *quality* not quantity that matters. 時間をかけても正しく理解しなさい。問題なのは量ではなく質です ☞ **quality** (GOOD 1)

merit [U] (《ややフォーマル》)(賞賛[報酬、感嘆]に値する)価値、美点、功績、長所 ◊It's a work of outstanding artistic *merit*. それは目覚ましい芸術的な価値のある作品である ◊The plan is entirely without *merit*. その計画にはまったくよい点がない ◊I want to get the job **on merit** (= because I deserve it, not as a favour). 私は実力[功績]でその仕事に就きたい

worth [U] (実際的[道徳的])な)価値、真価 ◊The children here quickly gain a sense of their own *worth*. ここの子どもたちはすぐに子どもたち自身の価値に目覚める ◊A good job interview should help candidates prove their *worth*. よい就職面接とは志願者が自分の真価を証明する手助けとなるはずのものです ❶ worth はまた物事の「金銭的な価値」にも用いられる。反意 **worthless**, ☞ **worth** (PRICE)

excellence [U] 優秀さ、卓越(性) ◊The college has a reputation for academic *excellence*. その大学は学問的優秀さで評判を得ている ◊We want this hospital to be a ***centre of excellence***. 我々はこの病院を卓越したセンターにしたい ☞ **excellent** (EXCELLENT)

distinction [U, 単数で] 《ややフォーマル》非凡さ, 傑出, 著名, 名声, 栄誉, 特異性 ◇a writer of great *distinction* 非凡にも傑出した作家 ◇She had the *distinction* of being the first woman to fly the Atlantic. 彼女は大西洋を横断飛行した最初の女性となる栄誉に与った
meaning [U] (感情・経験の実質的な)重要性, 意味 ; (人生の)意義 ◇With Anna he learned the *meaning* of love. アンナと一緒になって, 彼は愛の意味を知った ◇Her life seemed to have lost all *meaning*. 彼女の人生はすべての意義を失ってしまったようだった

values 图 ☞ PRINCIPLE 1, VIEW 1

values・teaching・belief・ideology・doctrine・philosophy・code・ethic・ethos
何が道徳的[政治的]に善であり悪であるかについての(一連の)考え
【類語訳】価値観, 教え, 教義, 教訓, 信条, イデオロギー, 主義, 哲学, 人生観, おきて, 規範, 作法, 倫理, 道徳

▶ 文型&コロケーション
- sb's **religious** values/ teaching/ beliefs/ ideology/ doctrine/ philosophy/ code/ ethic/ ethos
- sb's **moral** values/ teaching/ beliefs/ doctrine/ philosophy/ code
- sb's **political** values/ beliefs/ ideology/ doctrine/ philosophy/ ethic/ ethos
- sb's **social** values/ beliefs/ ideology/ philosophy/ code/ ethic/ ethos
- sb's **cultural** values/ beliefs/ ideology/ code/ ethos
- **traditional** values/ teaching/ beliefs/ ideology/ doctrine/ philosophy/ code/ ethic
- **conservative/ liberal** values/ beliefs/ ideology/ philosophy
- to **have** values/ beliefs/ an ideology/ a doctrine/ a philosophy/ a code/ an ethic/ an ethos
- to **subscribe to** values/ teaching/ an ideology/ a doctrine/ a philosophy/ a code/ an ethic
- to **hold** values/ beliefs
- to **go/ be against** sb's values/ teaching/ beliefs/ doctrine/ philosophy/ code/ ethos

values [複数で] 価値観 ◇All major religions have certain *values* in common. 主な宗教はすべてある種の価値観を共有している ◇Conservatives often talk about a return to ***family values*** without actually explaining what these are. 保守党員が, それが何であるかを実際に説明することなく, 家庭内の価値観への回帰について語ることが多い
teaching [U, C, ふつう複数で] (政治[宗教, 社会]的な)教え, 教義, 教訓 ◇These views go against traditional Christian *teaching*. これらの考え方は伝統的なキリスト教の教義に反する ◇The culture is based in the *teachings* of Confucius. その文化は孔子の教えに基づいている
belief [C, ふつう複数で] (宗教上の)信条 ◇You need to examine your own attitudes and *beliefs*. ご自分の態度と信条とを吟味する必要があります
ideology [U, C] 《時にはなして》(経済的[政治的]な)イデオロギー ; (特定集団に影響を与える)ideology. 個人主義は資本主義イデオロギーの中核である ◇It's difficult to stand outside the dominant *ideology* of your own society.

自分の社会における支配的なイデオロギーの及ばないところに身を置くのは難しい
doctrine [C, U] (宗教・政党の)教義, 主義, 信条 ◇She was deeply committed to political *doctrines* of social equality. 彼女は社会的平等という政治信条に専心的に取り組んでいた ◇He has written books on Catholic *doctrine*. 彼はカトリック教義に関する著書が(何冊か)ある
philosophy [C] 哲学 ; 人生観 ◇He holds firmly to a Buddhist *philosophy* of life. 彼は仏教的な人生哲学をしっかり固守している ◇My own *philosophy* is to take all the opportunities you can in life. 私独自の人生観とは, 人生における可能な機会はすべて利用することである
code [C] (集団・社会の)決まり, おきて, 規則, 規定, 規範, 作法 ◇The school enforces a strict ***code of conduct***. その学校は行動に厳しい規則を課している ◇There was a rigid ***code of honour*** associated with the cult. その教団には厳格な信義のおきてがあった ◇Young people unconsciously conform to a ***dress code*** but reject any kind of uniform. 若者たちは無意識にある服装規定に従っているのに, どんな種類の制服も受け入れない
ethic [単数で] (行動の規範となる)倫理, 道徳 ◇They have a very strong ***work ethic*** (= the principle that people should work hard). 彼らには非常に強い労働倫理がある ❶ *ethic* は, 勤勉の価値と個人的な道徳心の向上を教授するプロテスタント教会と強く結びついており, 最も強く結びつく語に Protestant, work が挙げられる. ☞ **ethics** (PRINCIPLE 1), **ethical** (MORAL)
ethos [単数で] 《フォーマル》(特定集団・社会の道徳的な)精神, 理念 ◇They tried to develop an *ethos* of public service. 彼らは公益事業の精神を発展させようとした

variable 图

variable・dynamic・irregular・inconsistent・fluid・uneven
物事がしばしば変化する[変化しがちである]ことを表す
【類語訳】変わりやすい, 不定の, 動的な, 活発な, ふぞろいの, 不定期の, 不規則な, 首尾一貫しない, 流動的な

▶ 文型&コロケーション
- variable/ inconsistent/ uneven **quality**
- a variable/ dynamic/ fluid **environment**
- a variable/ fluid **situation**
- irregular/ uneven **breathing/ rhythms**
- **very** variable/ irregular/ inconsistent/ fluid/ uneven
- **highly** variable/ dynamic/ irregular/ inconsistent/ fluid
- **somewhat** variable/ irregular/ inconsistent/ uneven

variable 変わりやすい ; 不定の ◇The forecast is based on assumptions of *variable* temperature. その天気予報は気温が変わりやすいという前提に基づいている ◇The acting is of *variable* quality (= some of it is good and some of it is bad). その演技の質は定まっていない ☞ **variability** (CHANGE 图 1), **vary** (DIFFER)
dynamic 《ふつうほめて, 特にビジネス》(過程・状況が)(流)動的な, 活発な, 活動的な, 精力的な ◇They want to promote a *dynamic* economy with a high level of employment. 彼らは雇用水準の高い活発な経済を進展させたがっている ◇The business has managed to change and remain *dynamic*. その企業は何とか変化し活動的であり続けてきた 反意 **static** (STEADY)
irregular 《ふつうけなして》不整の, ふぞろいの ; 不定期の,

不規則な ◇an *irregular* heartbeat 不整脈 ◇*irregular* attendance at school 不定期登校 ◇He visited his parents *at irregular intervals*. 彼は不定期に両親を訪ねた 反意 **regular** (STEADY), **regular** (FREQUENT)

inconsistent (けなして) 首尾一貫しない, 矛盾した; 無節操な, 気まぐれな ◇The tests gave *inconsistent* results. 検査の結果は首尾一貫しなかった ◇Children find it difficult if a parent is *inconsistent*. 親が気まぐれだと, 子供たちはつらい思いをする 反意 **consistent** (STEADY)

fluid 《フォーマル》(状況が)変わりやすい, 流動的な; 固定していない ◇The *fluid* political situation made investment impossible. 流動的な政治状況で投資が不可能になった ◇There is a *fluid* relationship between managers and workers. 労使関係は固まっていない ❶ **fluid** はほとんどの場合, **state**, **situation**, **relationship** と共に用いられる

uneven 不ぞろいの, 不規則な, むらのある, 一様でない ◇Her breathing was quick and *uneven*. 彼女の呼吸は速く不規則だった ❶ **uneven** の典型的な連語は人々の動作に関連している. ◆an *uneven* voice/laugh/pace/tread (むらのある声/一様でない笑い声/一定しない歩調/不規則な足どり). 反意 **even** (STEADY)

very 形

very・actual・exact・precise
特定の物事[時]について話していることを強調するのに用いる 【類語訳】他ならぬ, まさにその, 当の, 実際の, 正確な, ちょうどの, まったくの

▶文型&コロケーション
▶the very/ actual/ exact/ precise **moment**
▶sb's very/ actual/ exact **words**
▶the actual/ exact/ precise **nature** of sth
▶the very/ exact **same** sth

very [名詞の前で] (特定の物事・人について話していることを強調して) 他ならぬ, まさにその, 当の ◇Those were her *very* words. それは他ならぬ彼女の言葉だった ◇That's *the very thing* I need. それはまさに私が必要としているものだ

actual [名詞の前で] (物事の最も重要な部分を強調して) 実際の, 本番の ◇The wedding preparations take weeks but the *actual* ceremony takes less than an hour. 結婚の準備には数週間かかるが, 実際の結婚式は一時間足らずしかかからない

exact [名詞の前で] (物事が特定の時に[方法で]起こることを強調して) 正確な, まさにその, きっちりの, ちょうどの, まったくの ◇We need to know the *exact* time the incident occurred. 我々はその事件が起こった正確な時間を知る必要がある ◇I had the *exact* same problem as you when I first started. 《ややインフォーマル, 特に話し言葉》私が最初に始めたときは, 君とまったく同じ問題をかかえていた ☞ **exact** (EXACT)

▶**exactly** 副 ◇It happened almost *exactly* a year ago. それはちょうど一年前に起こった

precise [名詞の前で] 《ややフォーマル》(物事が特定の時に[方法で]起こることを強調して) 正確な, まさにその, きっちりの, ちょうどの, まったくの ◇Doctors found it hard to establish the *precise* nature of her illness. 医師たちは彼女の病気の正確な種類を明らかにするのは気づいていた ☞ **precise** (EXACT)

▶**precisely** 副 ◇The meeting starts at 2 o'clock *precisely*. 会議は2時きっかりに始まります

ノート **exact** と **precise** の使い分け：多くの場合, 両語とも使用可能. ◆at that *exact*/*precise* moment (まさにその瞬間). ◆the *exact*/*precise* nature of sth (…の正確な性質[種類]). しかしながら, **precise** は **exact** よりもフォーマルであることが多く, インフォーマルな表現では用いられない. ✗I had the *precise* same problem.

very 副

very・well・so・really・quite・extremely・highly・most・desperately・truly・bloody
形容詞や副詞, 動詞の前で用いられ, 「高度に」を意味する 【類語訳】非常に, 大いに, とても, 実に, かなり, 相当に, ずいぶん, たいへん, すごく, 本当に, きわめて, すっかり, まったく

▶文型&コロケーション
▶very/ so/ really/ quite/ extremely/ highly **successful**/ **intelligent**/ **competitive**/ **critical**/ **sensitive**
▶very/ so/ really/ quite/ extremely/ most/ desperately **anxious**/ **concerned**/ **disappointed**/ **unhappy**/ **important**
▶very/ so/ really/ quite/ extremely/ desperately/ truly **sorry**
▶very/ so/ really/ extremely/ most/ desperately **worried**
▶very/ so/ really/ quite/ extremely/ desperately **ill**/ **sick**/ **tired**/ **poor**/ **lonely**/ **hard**/ **close**
▶very/ so/ really/ quite/ extremely/ bloody **good**/ **hot**
▶so/ really/ truly/ bloody **awful**
▶very/ so/ really/ quite/ extremely/ bloody **well**
▶very/ so/ really/ extremely **few**
▶**not** very/ so/ really **happy**/ **expensive**
▶to really/ desperately/ truly **want**/ **need**/ **love** sb/ sth

very 非常に, 大いに, とても, 実に, ごく ◇This room is *very* small/hot/useful. この部屋は非常に狭い/暑い/実用的である ◇They left *very* quickly/soon. 彼らはとても早く立ち去った ◇*Very* few people know that. それを知っている人はほとんどいない ◇'Do you like it?' 'Yes, I do. *Very much*.' 「それ, 好き」「ええ, 好きです. とってもね」 ◇'Is it what you expected?' 'Oh yes, *very much so*.'「それは期待していたことですか」「ああ, そうだよ, 大いにね」 ◇'Are you busy?' 'Not *very*.' 「忙しい」「それほどでも」 ◇The new building has been *very* much admired. その新しいビルは非常に高い評価を受けている ◇I'm *not very* (= not at all) impressed. ちっとも感動しない

well 大いに, とても, かなり, 相当に, ずいぶん, よほど ◇He was driving at *well* over the speed limit. 彼は制限速度をかなりオーバーして運転していた ◇It's a *well*-loved tale of love and romance. それはとても愛されている愛とロマンスの物語である ◇The castle is *well* worth a visit. その城は訪れてみる価値が大いにある ◇He liked her *well enough* (= to a reasonable degree) but he wasn't going to make a close friend of her. 彼は彼女のことをそこそこ好きだったが, 親友になろうとはしていなかった ❶《インフォーマルな《英》の話し言葉では, **well** は **very** の代わりに用いられる. ◆I was *well* annoyed, I can tell you. 《《英》, 話し言葉》正直なところ, 私はずいぶん困っていた)

so 《インフォーマル, 特に話し言葉》非常に, たいへん, とても, 実に, すごく ◇The girls looked *so* pretty in their summer dresses. 少女たちはサマードレスに身を包み, とてもかわいく見えた ◇I'm *so* glad to see you. お会いできてとてもうれしいです ◇We have *so* much to do. 私たちにはやること

がすごくたくさんある ◇Their attitude is *so very* English. 彼らの態度はいかにも英国人らしい ◇He sat there *ever so* quietly. 《英》彼は実に静かにそこに座っていた

really 《ややインフォーマル, 特に話し言葉》本当に, とても, かなり, ずいぶん, 実に ◇This is a *really* nice place. ここはとても素晴らしい場所です ◇I'm *really* sorry. 本当にごめんなさい ◇She was driving *really* fast. 彼女はずいぶん車を飛ばしていた ◇I *really* hope we can meet up again soon. またすぐにお会いできることを心から願っています
☞ **real** (COMPLETE)

ノート **very, so, really の使い分け**: very はこれらの語の中で最も頻繁に用いられ, 最も当たり障りのない語である。really はよりインフォーマルで, 程度がより強い場合もある。so もまた, 程度がより強く, コメント・意見を強調するのに用いられることが多い。so はこれらの語の中では最もインフォーマルで, 書き言葉では誤用であると考える人々もいる。so と really は意味の弱い・強い形容詞のどちらとも用いることができる。◆ *so/really* good (= weak) (とてもよい). ◆ *so/really* wonderful (= strong) (とても素晴らしい). very は意味の強い形容詞とは用いられない。◆ *very* good (とてもよい). × *very* wonderful. very は形容詞を伴って, 連結動詞の後でも, 名詞句の前でも用いることができる。◆ This place is *very/really* nice. (この場所はとても素晴らしい). ◆ This is a *very/really* nice place. (ここはとても素晴らしい場所だ). so は連結動詞の後でしか用いることができず, 名詞句の前では, such a... を用いる。◆ This place is *so* nice. (この場所はとても素晴らしい). ◆ This is *such a* nice place. (ここはとても素晴らしい場所だ). really はまた動詞と共に用いることができる。◆ I *really* love it here. (私はここが大好きだ). very はこの形で用いることはできないが, 場合によっては very much を用いることができる。◆ I *very* much like the way they've arranged everything. (私は彼らのすべての段取りの仕方がとても気に入っている)。

quite 《ふつう形容詞や副詞と共に》非常に, たいへん, とても, 実に, すごく, かなり ◇You'll be *quite* comfortable here. ここならとても落ち着けるでしょう ◇I can see it *quite* clearly. とてもはっきりそれを見ることができます ❶ この意味は《米》では最も頻繁に用いられる意味である。《英》では rather (やや), completely (すっかり) の意味で用いられることが多い。☞ **quite** (QUITE 1, 2)

extremely 《ふつう形容詞や副詞と共に》きわめて, たいへん ◇This issue is *extremely* complicated. この問題はきわめて複雑です ◇I would be *extremely* grateful if you could have a word with her. あなたが彼女と言葉を交わしていただけるならたいへんありがたく思います ◇Mark knew he had behaved *extremely* badly. マークは自分の振る舞いがきわめてよくなかったことを承知していた ❶ extremely は very, so, really よりも程度が強い。また, いくぶんフォーマルでもある。

highly 非常に, たいへん, とても, 実に, すごく, かなり ◇a *highly* skilled workforce 高度な技能を持つ労働力 ◇It is *highly* unlikely that she'll be late. 彼女が遅刻するなどまずありえない ❶ highly は, このグループの他の類語に比べて限られた形容詞としか結びつかない。特に評価・位置づけを表す形容詞, または人の個人的な性質を表す形容詞と共に用いられる。◆ *highly* successful/intelligent/skilled/motivated/competitive (とても成功した/知的な/熟練した/意欲のある/競争心旺盛な). ◆ *highly* critical/sensitive (非常に批判的な/敏感な).

most 《フォーマル》非常に, とても, 実に, すごく; きわめ

て, たいへん; すっかり, まったく ◇It was *most* kind of you to meet me. 会っていただいて誠にありがとうございました ◇We shall *most* probably never meet again. 私たちはまずおそらく再会することはないでしょう ◇This technique looks easy, but it *most* certainly is not. この技術は簡単そうに見えるが, 実際はまったくそうではない

desperately 《困難[不幸]な状況において》ひどく, すごく, 必死に, 是が非でも ◇*desperately* ill/unhappy/lonely 重態の/ひどく不幸な/ひどく心細い ◇He took a deep breath, *desperately* trying to keep calm. 彼は必死に落ち着こうとして深呼吸をした ◇They *desperately* wanted a child. 彼らは是が非でも子どもがほしかった

truly 《ややフォーマル》《良質[印象的]であることを強調して》実に, 本当に ◇It was a *truly* memorable occasion. それは実に記念すべき出来事だった ◇They gave a *truly* magnificent performance. 彼らは本当に素晴らしい演技をした

bloody 《英, 卑語, 話し言葉》《コメント・怒りに満ちた発言を強調して》とんでもなく, ひどく, すごく, どえらく, まったく (多くの人々が攻撃的だと感じる汚い言葉) ◇What *bloody* awful weather! まったくとんでもねぇひでぇ天気だ ◇She did *bloody* well to win that race. 彼女がそのレースに勝つなんてすげぇよ ◇'I'm not coming.' 'Yes, you *bloody well* are.' 「僕は行かないよ」「いや, 絶対に来るね」 ◇'Will you apologize to him?' '*Not bloody likely* (= Certainly not)!' 「彼に謝るの?」「謝るわけないじゃない」 ◇He doesn't *bloody* care about anybody. 彼は誰のことも気になんかしちゃいない ◇I can't get this *bloody* thing to work. こん畜生, これ動かないよ

victory 名

victory・win・landslide・defeat・upset・result
試合[競技, 選挙, 戦争]における成功
【類語訳】勝利, 圧倒的勝利, 地滑り的勝利, 番狂わせ, 結果

文型&コロケーション
▶ a victory/ a win/ a landslide/ an upset/ a result **for** sb
▶ a victory/ a win/ an upset/ a result **against** sb
▶ a victory/ win **over** sb
▶ a victory/ a win/ a landslide/ an upset **in** sth
▶ a **stunning/ surprise** victory/ win/ defeat/ upset/ result
▶ a **comprehensive/ decisive/ crushing/ narrow** victory/ win/ defeat
▶ a **great** victory/ win/ upset/ result
▶ a **Democrat/ Labour, etc.** victory/ win/ landslide
▶ to **pull off/ get** a victory/ win/ result
▶ to **clinch/ secure/ snatch/ score/ notch up/ chalk up/ gain/ earn** a victory/ win
▶ to **cruise to/ sweep to/ romp to/ claim/ deserve/ celebrate** victory/ a win
▶ to **win** a victory/ by a landslide

victory [C, U] 《試合・競技・選挙・議論・戦争における》勝利 ◇The team are celebrating a 3-2 *victory* over Poland. チームはポーランドに対する3-2の勝利を祝っている ◇Labour swept to *victory* in the 1997 election. 労働党は1997年の選挙で圧勝した ❶ moral *victory* は, 実際の結果に関して成功せずとも, 自分の考え・信条が正しいことが証明されたことを指す。◆ In spite of the result, we felt we had won a *moral victory*. (結果に関わらず, 我々は精神的な勝利を勝ち取ったのだと感じた) 反意 **defeat** (DEFEAT)

win [C] 《ややインフォーマル》《試合・競技・選挙における》勝

↪victory

利 ◇People still talk about the famous *win* against Brazil. 人々はいまだにかの有名な対ブラジル戦の勝利を話題にしている ◇Torino notched up a 2-1 *win* at Lazio. トリノはラツィオに2-1で勝利した ◇They have now gone 10 games *without a win*. 彼らは現在、10戦して勝利がない ◇After this year's election *win*, they have time on their side. 今年の選挙戦での勝利の後、彼らは時を味方につけている ❶*win*はいくぶんインフォーマルな語で、特にスポーツ報道で用いられる。議論・戦争における勝利については用いられない。 反意 **loss** ❶*loss*は試合・競技・選挙に勝利できないことを指す。◆Argentina's 2-1 *loss* to Brazil(アルゼンチンの対ブラジル戦2-1での敗北). ☞ **win (WIN)**

landslide [C, ふつう単数で]《選挙における人・党の》圧倒[地滑り]的勝利 ◇The National Party won by a *landslide*. 国民党は圧倒的な勝利を収めた ◇No one expected a repeat of Labour's 1997 *landslide victory*. 誰も労働党の1997年の地滑り的勝利の再現を期待していなかった

defeat [C, ふつう単数で]《試合・競技・選挙・戦争において達成する》勝利 ◇They played a key role in Wellington's *defeat of* Napoleon at Waterloo. 彼らはワーテルローでのウェリントンのナポレオンに対する勝利において重要な役割を果たした ◇He almost pulled off a *shock defeat* of the reigning champion. 彼はもう少しのところで現チャンピオンから大金星を挙げるところだった ☞ **defeat (DEFEAT)**

upset [C]《ややインフォーマル、特にジャーナリズム》(競技における)番狂わせ ◇The war veteran came close to pulling a stunning political *upset* in Ohio this summer (= by nearly winning an election). この夏オハイオでの退役軍人は、もう少しで驚くべき政治的番狂わせを演じるところだった

result [C, ふつう単数で]《英、インフォーマル》(サッカー試合における勝利としての)結果 ◇We badly need to get a *result* from this match. 我々はこの試合で、どうしても結果を出す必要がある ◇This was a great *result* for us. これは私たちにとって素晴らしい結果だった

view 名

1 ☞ ATTITUDE, VALUES

view • opinion • point • belief • idea • point of view • feeling • judgement • conviction • sentiment
特定の問題について思いをめぐらして抱くことを表す
【類語訳】考え、意見、見解、認識、見方、…観、所見、評価、主張、言い分、信念、観点、視点、感想、所感、判断、意向

文型&コロケーション

▶ sb's view/ opinion/ point/ beliefs/ ideas/ feelings/ judgement/ conviction/ sentiments **about** sb/ sth
▶ sb's view/ opinion/ ideas/ point of view/ feelings **on** sb/ sth
▶ sb's view/ opinion **of** sb/ sth
▶ **in** sb's view/ opinion/ judgement
▶ the view/ opinion/ point/ belief/ idea/ point of view/ feeling/ judgement/ conviction **that**...
▶ **different** views/ opinions/ beliefs/ ideas/ points of view/ convictions/ sentiments
▶ a **general** view/ opinion/ belief/ point of view/ feeling/ conviction/ sentiment
▶ a **popular** view/ opinion/ belief/ feeling/ sentiment
▶ a **strong** view/ opinion/ belief/ feelings/ conviction/ sentiment
▶ a **firm** view/ opinion/ belief/ conviction

view

▶ a **personal/ private** view/ opinion/ belief/ point of view/ feeling/ judgement/ conviction/ sentiment
▶ a **political/ religious** view/ opinion/ belief/ idea/ feelings/ conviction/ sentiment
▶ to **have/ hold** a view/ an opinion/ a belief/ a point of view/ a conviction
▶ to **be of** the view/ opinion/ belief (that...)
▶ to **express** your view/ opinion/ beliefs/ ideas/ point of view/ feelings/ conviction/ sentiments
▶ to **hear** sb's views/ opinion/ ideas/ point of view
▶ to **change** your view/ opinion/ beliefs/ ideas/ point of view/ judgement
▶ to **support** a view/ opinion/ belief/ an idea/ a point of view/ a conviction

view [C]《人・物事に関する》考え、意見、見解；《人・物事に対する》認識、見方、…観 ◇We have widely differing *views* on how to raise children. 育児法については非常に多様な意見がある ◇We take the *view* that it would be wrong to interfere. 私たちは干渉するのは間違いだろうという見方です ◇In my *view* it would be a complete waste of time. 私の意見では、それはまったくの時間の浪費だと思う

opinion [C, U]《人・物事に関する》意見；《物事に関する専門家の》見解、所見；《人・物事に関する集団の》考え、意見、評価 ◇I've recently changed my *opinion* of her. 最近、彼女に対する私の意見は変わった ◇You can always ask for a *second opinion* (= the opinion of another professional person) if you're not sure. 確信がなければ、常にセカンドオピニオンを要求できます ◇You need to be able to distinguish between fact and *opinion*. 事実と意見を区別することができるようになる必要がある ◇*Public opinion* (= what most people think) is shifting in favour of change. 世論は変化を支持する方向に移り変わりつつある ◇*Opinion is divided* about whether to join the new currency. 新通貨に参加するかどうかについては意見が分かれている ◇'I think she's great.' 'Well, that's *a matter of opinion* (= other people may disagree)'. 「彼女は素晴らしいと思う」「まあ、それは意見の分かれる問題だね」

point [C]《言ったり書いたりして伝えようとする》意見、主張、言い分、言いたいこと ◇I *take your point* (= I understand and accept what you are saying). おっしゃっていることはわかります ◇He's just saying that to *prove a point* (= to show his idea is right). 彼は自分の言い分の正当性を証明するためにそう言っているだけのことです ◇OK, you've *made your point*! わかりました、ご自分の主張はなされましたね ❶*point*は意見・主張と同様に事実をも指すことがある。☞ **point (FACTOR)**

belief [C, U]《人・物事に関して真実であると》信じていること、信念 ◇She acted in the *belief* that she was doing the right thing. 彼女は正しいことをしていると信じて行動した ◇*Contrary to popular belief* (= despite what most people think) he was not involved in the affair. 世間一般に信じられているのとは反対に、彼はその一件に関わっていなかった ☞ **believe (THINK)**

idea [C, ふつう複数で]考え、意見 ◇He has some very strange *ideas* about education. 彼は教育について非常に変わった考えを持っている ◇The *idea* that I was only interested in making money is ludicrous. 私が金儲けにしか興味がなかったという意見はばかげている

,point of 'view (複 **points of view**) [C]《物事への特定の》考え、意見、見解、見方、観点、視点 ◇You have to try to see your opponent's *point of view*. 相手の見解に目を向けるようにしなければなりません ◇He has always taken the opposite *point of view*. 彼はいつも逆の観点に立ってきた

feeling [C, U]《ややインフォーマル》(人・物事に関する)考え, 意見, 感想, 所感, 気持ち ◇I don't have any strong *feelings* about it one way or another. どちらにしても, 私はそれについて断固たる意見は何も持っていません ◇My own *feeling* is that we should go for the cheaper option. 私自身の考えでは, 我々はより安価なほうを選ぶべきです ◇She **had mixed feelings** about giving up her job. 彼女は仕事を辞めることについて複雑な思いだった ◇The general *feeling* of the meeting was against the decision. 会議の全体的な印象はその決定に反対というものだった ☞ **feel** (THINK)

▶ノート **idea** と **feeling** の使い分け: idea はより主義・信条に基づいたものであり, feeling はいくぶんより感情に基づいたものである.

judgement (または特に米で **judgment**) [C, U] (物事に関する慎重に考えた末の)考え, 意見, 見解；評価, 判断 ◇It's not for me to make any *judgements* about the situation. 私はその状況について何らかの判断を下す立場にない ◇He's always very ready to **pass** *judgement* on others. 彼は他人に対して評価を下したくていつもうずうずしている ◇I'd like to **reserve** *judgement* until I see the report (= not form an opinion until I have seen it). 報告書を見るまでは判断を差し控えたいと思います ◇I gave him the money **against my better** *judgement* (= even though I knew it was probably the wrong thing to do). よくないと思いながらも, 私は彼に金を与えた ☞ **judge** (JUDGE 動)

conviction [C, U]《ややフォーマル》(強い)信念 ◇We were sustained by the *conviction* that all would be well in the end. 我々は最後にはすべてがうまくいくという強い信念に支えられていた ◇She was motivated by deep religious *conviction*. 彼女は深い宗教的信念に動機づけられていた

sentiment [C, U]《フォーマル》(感情に基づいた)考え, 意見, 意向, 感想, 所感 ◇This is a *sentiment* that I totally agree with. これは私が全面的に同意する考えです ◇Nationalist *sentiment* spread quickly, especially in the cities. 特に都市において, 国粋主義的な考えが急速に広まった

2 view・sight・scene・panorama
特定の場所から見ることのできる物
【類語訳】景色, 風景, 眺め, 光景, 全景, パノラマ

▶文型&コロケーション
▶ a view/ panorama **of** sth
▶ a **beautiful/ breathtaking** view/ sight/ scene/ panorama
▶ a **magnificent/ spectacular** view/ sight/ panorama
▶ a **picturesque** view/ scene/ panorama
▶ to **enjoy** the view/ sight/ scene/ panorama
▶ to **take in** the view/ sight/ scene
▶ to **admire** the view/ sight

view [C] (美しい自然の)景色, 風景, 眺め ◇The *view* **from** the top of the tower was spectacular. 塔のてっぺんから見る風景は壮観だった ◇The cottage had a delightful sea *view*. コテージからきれいな海の景色が見えた ◇I'd like a room with a *view*, please. 眺めのいい部屋をお願いします ☞ **view** (SIGHT)

sight [C] (印象的な[珍しい])光景, 姿, 見えるもの ◇He became a familiar *sight* on the streets of Oxford. 彼の姿をオックスフォードの街並みでよく見かけるようになった ◇He was a sorry *sight*, soaked to the skin and shivering. 彼はずぶ濡れで震えていて気の毒な姿だった ◇The museum attempts to recreate **the sights and sounds** of wartime Britain. 博物館は戦時中の英国を視覚と聴覚の両面で再現しようと試みている ☞ **sight** (SIGHT)

scene [C] (人々・動物のいる)光景, 景色, 風景, 眺め ◇It was a delightful rural *scene*. それはきれいな田園風景だった ◇They went abroad for **a change of scene** (= to see and experience new surroundings). 彼らは環境の変化を求めて海外へ出かけた ❶《米》a change of sceneryと言うほうが一般的である. ☞ **scenery** (COUNTRY 2)

panorama [C] (広大な土地の)全景, パノラマ ◇There is a wonderful *panorama* of the mountains from the hotel. ホテルからは山並みの素晴らしい全景が見える

violent 形

violent・bloody・rough・murderous・homicidal・bloodthirsty
人が人を力ずくで傷つける[殺害する]ことを意図したことを表す
【類語訳】暴力的な, 暴力による, 流血の, 血みどろの, 血生臭い, 乱暴な, 荒っぽい, 凶悪な, 残忍な, 残虐な, 殺意のある

rough	violent	murderous
	bloody	homicidal
		bloodthirsty

▶文型&コロケーション
▶ violent/ murderous/ homicidal **towards** sb
▶ a violent/ murderous/ homicidal **attack**
▶ violent/ murderous/ homicidal **tendencies**

violent (人を傷つける[殺害する]ことを意図して)暴力的な, 暴力による ◇*Violent* crime has increased by 15 per cent. 凶悪犯罪は15%増加した ◇Her husband was a *violent* man. 彼女の夫は凶暴な男だった ◇He later met a *violent* death on the battlefield. 彼はのちに, 戦場で非業の死を遂げた ◇Children should not be allowed to watch *violent* movies (= that show a lot of violence). 子どもたちが暴力的な映画を見るのを許してはならない ◇The crowd suddenly turned *violent*. 群衆は突然暴徒化した
▶ **violence** 名 [U] ◇crimes/acts/threats of *violence* 暴力的な犯罪/行為/脅迫 ◇He condemned the protesters' use of *violence* against the police. 彼は抗議団体の警察への暴力の行使を糾弾した ◇**domestic** *violence* (= between family members) 家庭内暴力
▶ **violently** 副 ◇The crowd reacted *violently*. 群衆は暴力的な反応を示した

bloody [ふつう名詞の前で]《特にジャーナリズム》(大量の暴力と殺害を伴って)流血の, 血みどろの, 血生臭い ◇A *bloody* battle has been fought in the region. その地域では血みどろの戦闘が行われてきた ◇The terrorists have halted their *bloody* campaign of violence. テロリストたちは激しい流血闘争をやめた ❶ bloodyは戦争・戦闘に用いられる

→violent

が, それに関わる人には用いられない. ✗Her husband was a *bloody* man.

rough〈ややインフォーマル〉乱暴な, 荒っぽい, 手荒な; 暴力的な, 暴力による ◇They complained of *rough* handling by the guards. 彼らは警備員たちの手荒な扱いに苦情を申し立てた ◇She doesn't like playing with the *rough* kids. 彼女はその乱暴な子どもたちと遊ぶのが嫌いだ ◇Don't try any *rough stuff* with me.〈話し言葉〉私には乱暴なまねはしないでね ☞ **gentle** (SENSITIVE 1)
▶**roughly** ◇He pushed her *roughly* out of the way. 彼は彼女を乱暴に押しのけた

murderous〈書き言葉〉(他人を殺そうと意図して)凶悪な, 残忍な, 残虐な, 殺意のある, 殺人を犯す傾向のある;(人に)殺人をさせかねない ◇The film turns a *murderous* villain into a hero. その映画では残忍な悪党を英雄に仕立てている ◇Some of the patients had suicidal or *murderous* tendencies. 中には自殺性向や殺人性向のある患者もいた ❶ *murderous*は怒り・憎悪を覚える人々を表すのに用いられることが多い. ◆a *murderous* look/glance/mood (殺意のある顔つき/一瞥/雰囲気), a *murderous* intent/rage/jealousy (殺意/殺意に満ちた激しい怒り/殺人を犯しかねない嫉妬). ☞ **murder** (MURDER), **murder** (KILL)

homicidal〈ややフォーマル〉(他人を殺そうと意図して)凶悪な, 残忍な, 残虐な, 殺意のある, 殺人を犯す傾向のある;(人に)殺人をさせかねない ◇He's a *homicidal* maniac. 彼は殺人狂だ ◇She had clear *homicidal* tendencies. 彼女には明らかに殺人性向があった ☞ **homicide** (MURDER)

┏━━━━━━━━━━━━━━━━━━━━━━━━━━━━━━━━┓
ノート **murderous** と **homicidal** の使い分け：*murderous* は *homicidal* よりも強い恐怖感・嫌悪感を表す. 怒り・憎悪などの強い感情によって引き起こされる行動を表すのに用いられることが多い. *homicidal* はより専門的で, それほど情緒的でない用語である. 精神病によって引き起こされる行動を表すのに用いられることが多い.
┗━━━━━━━━━━━━━━━━━━━━━━━━━━━━━━━━┛

bloodthirsty(人を殺し[傷つけ]たがって)凶悪な, 残忍な, (殺人・暴力を見聞きするのを楽しんで)血に飢えた, 残虐な; 殺人・暴力の場面の多い ◇We are not a *bloodthirsty* people. 我々は残忍な人間ではない ◇It's a *bloodthirsty* tale of murder and revenge. それは暴力シーンの多い殺人と復讐の物語である

visible 形 ☞ MARKED

visible・on display・noticeable・in evidence・discernible・in view
人や物事を目にする[気づく]ことができることを表す
【類語訳】目に見える, 展示されて, 陳列されて, 目立つ, はっきり見える, 明らかな, 認識できる, 見分けのつく

文型&コロケーション
▶ visible/ noticeable/ discernible **to/ in/ from** sb/ sth
▶ a visible/ a noticeable/ a discernible **effect/ feature/ difference/ change**
▶ **clearly** visible/ in evidence/ discernible/ in view
▶ **still** visible/ on display/ noticeable/ in evidence
▶ **particularly** visible/ noticeable/ in evidence
▶ **just/ barely** visible/ noticeable/ discernible

visible 目に見える; 目に見えて明らかな ◇The house is clearly *visible* from the beach. 家は浜辺からはっきり見える ◇Most stars are not *visible to the naked eye*. ほとんどの星は肉眼では見えない ◇He showed no *visible* sign of emotion. 彼は感情を目に見える形で表さなかった 反 **invisible**
▶**visibly** ◇He was *visibly* shocked. 彼は目に見えてショックを受けていた

on di'splay フレーズ 展示[陳列]されて ◇Designs for the new sports hall are *on display* in the library. 新しいスポーツ会館の設計図が図書館に展示されている ◇The old carriages were put *on* permanent *display* in the Museum of Transport. 古い四輪馬車が交通博物館で常設展示されていた

noticeable 目立つ, はっきり見える, 顕著な; 明白な, 明らかな ◇Her scars are hardly *noticeable* now. 彼女の傷跡は今ではほとんど目立たない ◇It was *noticeable that* none of the family were present. その家族の誰も出席していないのは目を引いた ◇The new filing system is a *noticeable* improvement on the old one. 新しいファイリングシステムは古いものに顕著な改善を施したものだ ☞ **notice** (NOTICE)
▶**noticeably** ◇Her hand was shaking *noticeably*. 彼女の手が震えているのがはっきり見えた ◇Marks were *noticeably* higher for girls than for boys. 得点は男子より女子のほうが明らかに高かった

in 'evidence フレーズ 目立って, はっきり見えて ◇The police were much *in evidence* at today's demonstration. 今日のデモでは警察の姿がすごく目立っていた

discernible《フォーマル》認識[識別]できる, 見分けのつく ◇There is often no *discernible* difference between rival brands. 競合会社のブランド商品の間には見分けのつく違いがないことが多い ◇His face was barely *discernible* in the gloom. 彼の顔は薄暗がりの中でほとんど識別できなかった ☞ **discern** (IDENTIFY)

in 'view フレーズ (人・物が)見える所に, 視界内に ◇There was nobody *in view*. 視界には誰もいなかった ◇They cleared the fence and lay down *in view of* (= where they could see) the camp. 彼らは柵を取り除いて野営地の見える所に横たわった ◇He was shot *in full view* of (= where he could be clearly seen by) a large crowd. 彼は大群衆に丸見えの場所で撃たれた 反 **out of sight**

visit 名

visit・tour・stay・call・stopover
人が人に会いに[場所を見に]行ってそこで時間を過ごす機会[期間]を表す
【類語訳】訪問, 来訪, 見物, 観光, 見学, 視察, 滞在, 立ち寄り, 往診, 短期滞在

文型&コロケーション
▶ **on** a visit/ tour/ call
▶ **during** sb's visit/ tour/ stay
▶ **an overnight** stay/ stopover
▶ to **go on** a visit/ tour
▶ to **make** a visit/ stay/ call
▶ to **pay sb** a visit/ call
▶ to **cut short** a visit/ tour/ stay
▶ to **cancel** a visit/ tour

visit [C] (人・場所への)訪問, 来訪, 見物, 観光 ◇Is this your first *visit to* New York? ニューヨーク訪問は今回が初めてですか ◇We had a *visit from* the police last night. 昨晩, 警察が私たちのところにやってきた ◇Enjoy your *visit*! 滞在を楽しんでください ◇If you have time,

visit, voluntary

pay a *visit* to the local museum. 時間があれば、地元の美術館を訪ねてみてください ◇The prime minister is on an official *visit* to Jamaica. 首相はジャマイカを公式訪問中です ☞ **visit** (STAY 2), **visitor** (TOURIST)

tour [C] (訪問者・観光客としての)見学, 視察, 観光 ◇In the afternoon we went on a *tour* of the ruins. 私たちは午後, 遺跡を巡るツアーに出かけた ◇We were given a *guided tour* of the palace. 私たちは宮殿をガイド付きで案内してもらった ◇The minister continued with his *tour of inspection* (= an official visit to examine a place) of the prison. 大臣は刑務所の視察を続けた

stay [C] (訪問[観光旅行]中の)滞在(期間) ◇I enjoyed my *stay* in Prague. 私はプラハ滞在を楽しんだ ☞ **stay** (STAY 2)

call [C] (人の家への短時間の)訪問, 立ち寄り, (医者による)往診 ◇I'm afraid this isn't a social *call*. 残念ながら, 今回はお付き合いで伺ったのではありません ◇The doctor's out on a *call* at the moment. 先生はただ今往診に出かけています ❶ *call* は専門家, 特に医者・看護師による人の家への短い訪問について用いられる。また, 互いに訪問し合う友人についても用いられるが, 今ではかなり古風に聞こえる。 ◆ He decided to pay a *call* on his old friend. (彼は旧友を訪ねることにした)

stopover [C] (旅行の前半と後半の間の短期間の)立ち寄り, 短期滞在 ◇We had a two-day *stopover* in Fiji on the way to Australia. オーストラリアに向かう途中で, 2日間フィジーに立ち寄った ☞ **stop over** (STAY 2)

visit 動

visit • go to sth • see • attend • call • drop in/round/by, drop into sth • pop in/round/over • stop by (sth) • look in on sb • look sb up
ある期間, 人に会いに[場所を見に]行く
【類語訳】訪れる, 訪問する, 見物する, 出かける, 会いに行く, 通う, 訪ねる, 立ち寄る, 見舞いに行く

▸文型&コロケーション
▸ to **call**/ drop in/ pop in/ **look in on** sb
▸ to visit/ see a/ the **doctor/ dentist**
▸ to go to the **doctor's/ dentist's**
▸ to **come/ go to** visit/ see sb
▸ to **come/ go and** visit/ see sb
▸ to call/ drop in/ pop in/ stop by **to see** sb
▸ to **often** visit/ go to sth/ see/ drop in/ pop in/ stop by/ look in
▸ to **regularly** visit/ go to sth/ see/ attend/ call/ pop in
▸ to **occasionally** visit/ go to sth/ see/ attend/ call/ drop in/ look in

visit [他] (ややフォーマル) (人・場所を)訪れる, 訪問する, 見物する ◇The President will be *visiting* six European capitals. 大統領はヨーロッパの6つの首都を訪れる予定です ◇I *visited* her in hospital. 私は彼女を病院に見舞った

'go to sth 句動詞 (受身なし) (特定の目的のために場所に)行く, 出かける ◇I have to *go to* the doctor's for a check-up. 健康診断のために病院に行かなければならない ◇Do you *go to* church (= regularly attend church services)? 礼拝に行っていますか ◇I'm not prepared to *go to* prison for a crime I didn't commit. 犯してもいない罪のために, 刑務所に入る覚悟はない ◇They sometimes *go to* the pub after work. 彼らは仕事の後, 時々パブに出かける

see [他] (人に)会いに行く ◇When was the last time you *saw* a dentist? 最後に歯医者に行ったのはいつでしたか ◇Come and *see* us again soon! またすぐに私たちに会いに来てください ◇He said he'd been to *see* his sister. 彼は姉に会いに行っていたと言った ❶ この意味では, see は特に come/go and see sb, come/go to see sb の表現で用いられる

attend [他] (フォーマル) (教会・学校・病院などに定期的に)通う ◇The children *attended* the local school. 子どもたちは地元の学校に通った ◇The patients all *attend* the clinic monthly. 患者たちは皆, 毎月診療所に通っている

call [自] (特に英, ややフォーマル) (人の家を短時間)訪ねる, 立ち寄る ◇We *called* but they were out. 私たちが訪ねて行ったが, 彼らは出かけていた ◇I *called* round at the house to check how things were. 私は彼の家に立ち寄って, 事態がどうなっているか確かめた

,drop 'in/'round/'by, ,drop 'into sth 句動詞 (-pp-) [受身なし] (ややインフォーマル) (予告なしに人・場所を短時間)訪ねる, 立ち寄る ◇Don't forget to *drop in* on Harry. ハリーのところに立ち寄るのを忘れないでね ◇They *dropped round* for a drink. 彼らは一杯飲みに立ち寄った ◇I'll *drop by* some time next week. 来週のいつか顔を出すよ ◇I sometimes *drop into* the National Gallery for an hour or so. 私は時々, 一時間かそこらナショナルギャラリーに立ち寄ります

▸ **'drop-in** 形 a *drop-in* advice centre 気軽に寄れる相談センター

,pop 'in/'round/'over 句動詞 (-pp-) (英, インフォーマル) (予告なしに人・場所を短時間)訪ねる, 立ち寄る ◇I was just passing and thought I'd *pop in*. ちょうど通りがかったから, ちょっと立ち寄ろうと思ったんだよ

,stop 'by, ,stop 'by sth 句動詞 (-pp-) (受身なし) (ややインフォーマル) (場所に短時間)立ち寄る ◇He used to *stop by* every day. 彼は毎日立ち寄ったものだった ◇She *stopped by* the store at about five o'clock. 彼女は5時くらいに店に立ち寄った ☞ **stop** (STAY 1), **stop over** (STAY 2)

,look 'in on sb 句動詞 (ややインフォーマル) (老人・病人を短時間)訪ねる, 見舞いに(家を)訪れる ◇Could you *look in on* Dad some time? いつか父の見舞いに来てもらえますか

,look sb 'up 句動詞 [受身なし] (インフォーマル) (遠くに住んでいる[長いこと会っていない]人を)訪ねる, 連絡をとる ◇I promised to *look* her *up* next time I was in England. 次にイングランドに行ったときに彼女を訪ねると約束した

voluntary 形

1 voluntary • optional • discretionary
人が義務ではなく, 自ら好んで行う[決める, 持つ]ことを表す
【類語訳】自発的な, 自由意志の, 任意の, 随意の, 志願の, 選択の, オプションの, 自由裁量の

▸文型&コロケーション
▸ a **voluntary**/ an optional **course/ procedure/ scheme**
▸ **entirely** voluntary/ optional/ discretionary
▸ **purely/ largely** voluntary/ optional

voluntary 自発的な, 自由意志の, 任意の, 随意の, 志願の, 希望の ◇Many people pay *voluntary* contributions into a pension fund. 多くの人々が年金基金に自発的に拠出金を支払っています ◇Attendance at classes is purely *voluntary*. クラスへの出席はまったく任意です ◇He took

voluntary redundancy.《英》彼は希望退職に応じた 反意 **involuntary, compulsory** (NECESSARY)
▶**voluntarily** 副 ◇He was not asked to leave ― he went *voluntarily*. 彼は求められて出て行ったのではない―自発的に行ったんだ

optional 選択の, 任意の, 随意の, オプションの ◇Certain classes are compulsory, others are *optional*. あるクラスは必修で, 他のクラスは選択制である ◇This model comes with a number of *optional extras* (= things you can choose to have but which you pay extra for).《英》このモデルには, 追加料金による数々のオプションが付いています 反意 **compulsory, obligatory** (NECESSARY), ☞ **option** (OPTION)

ノート **voluntary** と **optional** の使い分け：voluntary は規則・法律によって強制されることなく自らの意志で物事を行う[持つ]ことを強調する. optional は物事が必須部分でなく追加部分である場合に, 望めば選択して利用できることを強調する.

discretionary [ふつう名詞の前で]《フォーマル》《権威者の》自由裁量の；(規則によって決められずに)任意に決定できる, 任意の ◇Such awards are allocated on a *discretionary* basis. そういった賞は自由裁量で割り当てられる
▶**discretion** 名 [U] ◇Bail is granted *at the discretion of* the court. 保釈は裁判所の自由裁量で認められる

2 voluntary・unpaid・honorary
報酬を受けずに仕事を行うことを表す
【類語訳】ボランティアの, 無償の, ボランティアで働く, 無給の, 無給で働く, 名誉職の

文型&コロケーション
▶**on** a voluntary/ an unpaid/ an honorary **basis**
▶voluntary/ unpaid **work/ service/ overtime**
▶a voluntary/ an unpaid **worker/ carer/ helper**

voluntary [ふつう名詞の前で] (仕事が)ボランティアの, 無償の；(人が)ボランティア[無償]で働く ◇I do some *voluntary* work at the local hospital. 私は地元の病院でボランティア活動をしています ◇The day centre is operated by a *voluntary organization*. そのデイ・センターはボランティア団体によって運営されている

unpaid (仕事・休暇が)無給の；(人が)無給で働く ◇Many of the children are used as *unpaid* labour. 多くの子どもたちが無給労働者として使われている ◇He chose to take 6 weeks of *unpaid leave*. 彼は6週間の無給休暇をとることにした ◇The canteen is run by *unpaid* volunteers. 酒保は無給の志願兵によって運営されています

honorary 名誉職の ◇The post of treasurer is a purely *honorary* position. 財務部長の地位はまったくの名誉職です ◇He became *honorary* president of the club. 彼はそのクラブの名誉会長になった

vulnerable 形

vulnerable・at risk・helpless・endangered・open to sth・exposed・defenceless
人や物事が十分に保護されていないことを表す
【類語訳】弱い, 無力の, 脆弱な, 傷つきやすい, 危険にさらされた, 絶滅の危機に瀕した, 無防備な

文型&コロケーション
▶vulnerable/ open/ exposed **to** criticism, attack, etc.
▶helpless/ defenceless **against** sth
▶vulnerable/ helpless/ defenceless **people/ children**
▶helpless/ defenceless **civilians/ victims**
▶a vulnerable/ an endangered **species**
▶a vulnerable/ a helpless/ an exposed **position**
▶to **feel** vulnerable/ at risk/ helpless/ exposed/ defenceless
▶to **leave sb/ sth** vulnerable/ at risk/ helpless/ open to sth/ exposed/ defenceless
▶**totally/ completely** vulnerable/ helpless/ defenceless
▶**highly** vulnerable/ endangered/ exposed
▶**increasingly** vulnerable/ at risk/ exposed

vulnerable (身体的[精神的]に)弱い, 無力な, 脆弱な, 傷つきやすい, 攻撃を受けやすい ◇Exhaustion from their long and fruitless war had left them *vulnerable* to attack. 長く無益な戦争による疲弊で, 彼らは攻撃に脆弱になっていた ◇We should protect the most *vulnerable* members of our society. 私たちは社会で最も弱い人たちを守らねばならない

,at 'risk フレーズ 危険にさらされて ◇Butterflies are *at risk from* attack by birds. 蝶は鳥の攻撃を受ける危険にさらされている ◇Lone parent families with young children are particularly *at risk of* becoming homeless. 幼児を抱える片親の家族は特にホームレスになる危険にさらされている ◇If we go to war, innocent lives will be *put at risk*. 我々が戦争に行けば, 罪のない人々の命が危険にさらされるだろう ☞ **risk** (RISK 1)

helpless 自分ではどうすることもできない, 無力な ◇Paul threw up his hands in a *helpless* gesture of surrender. ポールはどうすることもできない降伏の仕草で両手を挙げた ◇He lay *helpless* on the floor. 彼は力なく床に横たわった ◇It's natural to feel *helpless* against such abuse. そのような虐待に対して無力感を覚えるのは当然である
▶**helplessly** 副 ◇They watched *helplessly* as their home went up in flames. 彼らは自分の家が焼け落ちるのをなすすべなく見つめていた

endangered 絶滅の危機に瀕した, 存続が危ぶまれる ◇The sea turtle is an *endangered species* (= it may soon no longer exist). ウミガメは絶滅危惧種である ◇The group has campaigned to save several *endangered* buildings in the area. そのグループはその地域にあるいくつかの存続の危ぶまれる建物を残しておくために運動を行ってきた ☞ **endanger** (THREATEN)

open to sth (攻撃・損傷・批判などを[に])受けやすい, さらされた ◇The system is *open to* abuse. その制度は悪用される危険がある

exposed (人が危険・攻撃・批判を[に])受けやすい, さらされた ◇She was left feeling *exposed* and vulnerable. 彼女は一人ぼっちで大きな不安を感じていた ◇From the moment of birth, a baby is *exposed* to all the hazards in the external environment. 生まれた瞬間から赤ん坊は外的環境のあらゆる危険にさらされている

defenceless《英》《米 **defenseless**》自分で自分の身を守れない, 弱い, 無力な；無防備な ◇I can't believe that we persist in such cruelty to *defenceless* animals. 我々が無力な動物たちに対してそういった残虐行為を続けていることが私には信じられない ◇The village is *defenceless against* attack. その村は攻撃に対して無防備である

W w

walk [動]

1 walk・step・stride・stroll・pace・march・tread・prowl
地面上で一歩前に踏み出すことでどこかへ移動する
【類語訳】歩く, 歩を進める, 進む, ぶらつく, 行ったり来たりする, 行進する, うろつく, 徘徊することもある

文型&コロケーション
- to walk/ step/ stride/ stroll/ march **to/ towards** sb/ sth
- to walk/ step/ stroll/ pace/ march/ prowl **around/ round** (sth)
- to walk/ stroll/ pace/ march/ prowl **up and down**
- to walk/ pace/ prowl **to and fro/ back and forth**
- to step/ tread **in/ on** sth
- to walk/ step/ stride/ march **briskly**
- to walk/ step/ stride **quickly**
- to walk/ step/ tread **carefully/ gingerly/ lightly**
- to pace/ prowl **nervously/ restlessly**
- to walk/ pace/ prowl **the streets/ corridors**

walk [自, 他]《ふつう副詞や前置詞と共に》(走らずに)歩いて行く[来る] ◇How did you get here?' 'I *walked*'. 「どうやってここに来たの」「歩いて来たよ」 ◇The baby is just learning to *walk*. 赤ん坊はやっと歩けるようになりかけたところです ◇The door opened and Jo *walked* in. ドアが開いてジョーが中に入ってきた ◇I had to *walk* all the way home. ずっと家まで歩かなければならなかった ◇Women have to *walk* several miles each day to get water. 女性たちは水を手に入れるために毎日数マイル歩かなければならない

step (-pp-) [自]《副詞や前置詞と共に》(特定の方向[場所]に)歩を進める, 進む; (短い距離を)歩いて行く[来る] ◇*Step* forward when your name is called out. 名前を呼ばれたら前に出てください ◇I accidentally *stepped* on her toe. 誤って彼女のつま先を踏んだ ◇We had to *step* carefully to avoid the broken glass. 私たちは割れたガラスを避けて注意深く歩かなければならなかった ◇She *stepped aside* to let them pass. 彼女は彼らを通すために脇に寄った ◇Could you *step* inside for a moment? ちょっと中に入ってもらえますか ☞ **step** (STEP)

stride [自]《完了形では用いない;特定の方向に》大股で歩く ◇He *strode* off in search of a taxi. 彼はタクシーを捜し求めて大股で立ち去った ◇She *strode* angrily into his office. 彼女は腹立たしげに大股で彼のオフィスに入って行った ☞ **stride** (STEP)

stroll [自]《ふつう副詞や前置詞と共に》(楽しげにゆっくりくつろいで)ぶらぶら歩く, ぶらつく ◇People were *strolling* around in the grounds. 人々が構内をぶらぶら歩き回っていた

pace [自, 他]《副詞や前置詞と共に》(緊張して[怒って])行ったり来たりする ◇She *paced* up and down outside the interview room. 彼女は面接室の外で行ったり来たりしていた ◇He was *pacing* the room like a caged animal. 彼は檻に入れられた動物のように部屋の中を行ったり来たりしていた

いた ☞ **pace** (STEP)

march [自]《ふつう副詞や前置詞と共に》(人の集団・兵隊が)行進[行軍]する ◇Guards were *marching* up and down outside the building. 護衛隊が建物の外を行ったり来たりして行進していた ◇They *marched* 20 miles to reach the capital. 彼らは20マイルを行進して首都にたどり着いた ◇Troops *marched on* the town. 兵士が町へ進軍した ❶ march はまた「どこかへ決然と素早く歩いて行く」の意味で, 個人について用いられることもある.

tread [自]《副詞や前置詞と共に》《英》(歩いているときに)足を踏み下ろす ◇Ouch! You *trod* on my toe! 痛いっ. ぼくの足を踏んだよ ◇Careful you don't *tread* in that puddle. その水たまりに足を踏み込まないように気をつけなさい

📝 **step, stride, pace, tread** の使い分け: これらの語はそれぞれ, 一緒に用いる傾向のある副詞が異なる. **step** は briskly, quickly, carefully, lightly, gingerly を, **stride** は briskly, quickly, angrily, confidently, purposefully を, **pace** は nervously, restlessly, slowly を, **tread** は carefully, gingerly, softly, lightly, heavily, warily をそれぞれ伴うことができる. しかし《米》では, 意味が比喩的でなければ, tread の代わりに step が用いられる. ●We must *tread* carefully (= be careful about how we do this) — we don't want to offend anyone. (比喩的)私たちは注意深く事を運ばなければならない—誰の気分も害したくないんだ).

prowl [他, 自]《書き言葉》《ふつう副詞や前置詞と共に》(退屈・心配で)うろつく, 徘徊する ◇He *prowled* the empty rooms of the house at night. 彼は夜, その家の空き部屋をうろついた ◇Her husband was *prowling* restlessly around the room. 彼女の夫はそわそわと部屋の周りをうろついていた

2 walk・hike・trek
楽しみのために歩行で時間を過ごす
【類語訳】歩く, 散歩する, ハイキングをする, トレッキングをする

文型&コロケーション
- to go **walking/ hiking/ trekking**

walk (または **go walking**) [自]《特に英》(楽しみのために) 歩く, 散歩する ◇We're *going walking* in the mountains this summer. この夏, 私たちは山歩きに出かける予定だ ◇I *walked* across Scotland with a friend. 私は友だちと一緒にスコットランドを歩いて横断した ◇Have you ever *walked* the Pennine Way? ペナイン・ウェイを歩いたことはありますか

▶ **walk** [名] [C] ◇Let's *go for a walk*. 散歩に出かけよう ◇She's taken the dog for a *walk*. 彼女は犬を散歩に連れて行った ◇It's only a short *walk* to the beach. 浜辺までは少し歩くだけです ◇There are some interesting *walks* (= routes for walking) around here. このあたりには面白い散歩道があります ◇He set out on the long *walk* home. 彼は長い道のりを歩いて家路についた

▶ **walking** [名] [U] ◇Activities on offer include *walking* and bird watching. 散策やバードウォッチングも楽しむ

↪**walk**

ことができます ◇This is superb *walking* country. ここは散歩に適した素晴らしい田園地方である
hike [自] (または **go hiking**) (田園地方で)長距離歩行する;(楽しみのために田園地方で)ハイキングをする ◇If the weather's fine, we'll *go hiking* this weekend. もし天気がよければ、私たちは今週末ハイキングに出かけます ◇You'll need some strong boots for *hiking* over rough country. 起伏のある田園地方をハイキングするには、頑丈なブーツが必要でしょう ❶(米)では、hikeは目的語と共に用いられることもある。◆I always wanted to *hike* the Rockies. (《米》私はずっとロッキー山脈をハイキングしたいと思っていた).
▶**hike** [名] [C] ◇They *went on a* ten-mile *hike* through the forest. 彼らは森を抜ける10マイルのハイキングに出かけた
trek (または **go trekking**) (-kk-) [自, 他] (山中を長い距離にわたって楽しみのために)トレッキングをする ◇Last autumn we *went trekking* in Nepal. 昨年の秋、私たちはネパールにトレッキングに出かけた ◇They *trekked* the 45 miles across the glacier. 彼らはトレッキングで氷河を45マイル横断した
▶**trek** [名] [C] ◇They reached the camp after an arduous two-day *trek* across the mountains. 彼らは2日間にわたり険しい山並みをトレッキングした後、キャンプにたどり着いた

want [動]

want・would like sth・wish・like・feel like sth・desire・fancy
物事に対し欲求を抱く
【類語訳】欲する、ほしがる、望む、…したい、…してほしい、願う、好む、気が向く

文型&コロケーション
▶sb wants/ would like/ wishes/ likes/ desires **to do** sth
▶to feel like/ fancy **doing** sth
▶**if you** want/ wish/ like
▶**if you** feel like it
▶sb **really** wants/ would like/ wishes/ feels like/ desires/ fancies sth
▶to **truly** want/ wish/ desire sth
▶sb **just** wants/ would like/ feels like/ fancies sth
▶to **only** want/ wish/ desire sth
▶to **always** want/ wish/ feel like/ desire/ fancy sth
▶sb wants/ would like/ desires sth **very much**
▶to want/ wish **desperately** to do sth

want [他] 《進行形はまれ》《ややフォーマル、特に話し言葉》欲する、ほしがる、望む、…したい、…してほしい ◇Do you *want* some more tea? お茶をもう少しいかがですか ◇*All I want* is the truth. 私が望むのは真実だけです ◇I can do whatever I *want*. したいことは何でもできます ◇What do you *want* to do tomorrow? 明日何をしたいですか ◇'It's time you did your homework.' 'I don't *want* to!'「宿題をする時間よ」「やりたくない」◇Do you *want* me to help? 手伝ってほしいかい ❶want that...とは言えないことに注意。×I *want that* you do it quickly. ◆I *want* it done quickly.(すぐにそれをやってもらいたい). wantの後に不定詞を用いる場合は、to不定詞でなければならない。×I *want study* in America. ◆I *want to study* in America. (アメリカで勉強したい). ☞ **want** (DESIRE)

want, war

would like sth フレーズ 《ややフォーマル、特に話し言葉》(丁寧に)欲する、望む、…したい、…してほしい ◇*Would* you *like* a drink? 飲み物はいかがですか ◇I'd *like* to think it over. よく考えてみたい ◇We'd *like* you to come and visit us. 私たちに会いに来ていただきたい ◇We *would like* to apologize for the delay. 《フォーマル》遅れて誠に申し訳ありません ❶話し言葉では、I would likeはほぼ常にI'd likeと短縮される。
wish [他] 《進行形はまれ》(物事が起こって[本当であって]ほしいと)欲する、望む、願う ◇I *wish* I were taller. もっと背が高ければなあ ◇I *wish* I hadn't eaten so much. あんなにたくさん食べなければよかった ◇I *wish* you wouldn't leave your clothes all over the floor. 床じゅう至るところに服を散らかっぱなしにしないでほしいんだけど ◇She *wished* herself a million miles away. 彼女はずっと遠くに行ってしまいたい思いであった ❶フォーマルな言い回しでは特に《英》で、wishはまた「…したい」の意味もある。◆I *wish* to speak to the manager. (「(『支配人と話したいのですが』). ☞ **wish** (DESIRE), **wish** (HOPE [動])
like [他, 受身なし]《進行形なし》《特に英、ややインフォーマル、特に話し言葉》(…する[…を持つ])ことを欲する、好む、望む ◇Do what you *like* — I don't care. 好きなようにしなさい — 私はかまわないから ◇You can dye your hair whatever colour you *like*. お好きなどんな色にでも髪を染められます ◇You can come too if you *like*. よければ、あなたもお越しください ❶この意味では、like は what [whatever, if]節でしか用いられない。たとえある物事をしようと自分で決めなくとも、提案に同意するためにif you *like*が用いられることがある。◆'Let's go and see "The Last Samurai."' 'OK, if you *like*.'(『『ラストサムライ』を見に行こう』「いいとも、お望みなら」). likeのこの意味は、《英》で用いられるのがほとんどである。《米》では、ふつうwantを用いる。◆Do what you *want* — I don't care. (したいようにしなさい — 私はかまわないから).
feel like sth フレーズ 《進行形なし》《インフォーマル、話し言葉》(…を持ちたい[…したい])気分である、(…への)気が向く ◇I *feel like* a drink. 一杯やりたい気分だ ◇He *felt like* bursting into tears. 彼はわっと泣き出したい気分だった ◇We'll go for a walk if you *feel like* it. 気が向いたら散歩に出かけよう
desire [他] 《進行形なし》《フォーマル》(…を持つこと[…すること]を)欲する、望む、好む ◇The house had everything you could *desire*. その家には望みうるものは何でもあった ◇The dessert can be topped with cream, *if desired* (= if you like). お好みでデザートにはクリームをトッピングできます ◇The medicine did not achieve *the desired effect*. その薬は期待された効果がなかった ☞ **desire** (DESIRE)
fancy [他] 《進行形なし》《英、インフォーマル、特に話し言葉》(…を持つこと[…すること]を)欲する、望む、好む ◇*Fancy* a drink? 一杯飲みたい ◇I *fancied* a change of scene. 私は転地したいと望んだ

war [名]

war・battle・action・conflict・fighting・combat・warfare・campaign・hostilities・skirmish
二つ以上の国[人々の集団]が互いに交じり合って争う状況
【類語訳】戦争、交戦、戦い、戦闘、実戦、争い、紛争、闘争、小競り合い

文型&コロケーション
▶a war/ a battle/ action/ a conflict/ fighting/ combat/ war-

fare/ a campaign/ hostilities/ a skirmish **with/ against/ between** sb/ sth
▸ **in** war/ battle/ action/ conflict/ fighting/ combat/ warfare/ hostilities
▸ **in a** war/ battle/ conflict/ campaign/ skirmish
▸ **(a) civil/ nuclear** war/ conflict/ warfare
▸ **(a) fierce/ bloody** action/ conflict/ fighting/ combat/ warfare
▸ **(a) decisive** war/ battle/ action/ conflict/ campaign
▸ **(a) military** battle/ action/ conflict/ combat/ campaign
▸ **to win/ lose** a war/ battle/ conflict/ campaign/ skirmish
▸ **to fight** a war/ battle/ campaign
▸ a war/ a battle/ action/ a conflict/ fighting/ combat/ a campaign/ a skirmish **takes place**
▸ war/ conflict/ fighting/ hostilities **breaks out/ break out**
▸ a war/ a battle/ action/ a conflict/ fighting/ combat/ a campaign/ hostilities **begins/ begin**
▸ a war/ a battle/ a conflict/ fighting/ combat/ a campaign/ hostilities **ends/ end**
▸ a war/ a battle/ a conflict/ fighting/ combat/ warfare/ a campaign **continues**
▸ a war/ a battle/ a conflict/ fighting/ combat/ warfare/ a campaign **goes on**
▸ **the outbreak of** war/ conflict/ fighting/ combat/ hostilities

war [U, C] (国・人々による)戦争(状態), 交戦 ◇The two countries were *at war* for eight years. その2か国は8年間交戦中だった ◇The USA *declared war* on Germany in 1917. アメリカ合衆国は1917年にドイツに宣戦布告した ◇The terrorists were charged with *waging war* against the state. テロリストたちは国家に対して戦争を仕掛けたかどで告発された ◇My grandfather fought in two *world wars*. 祖父は二つの世界大戦で戦った ◇The country *went to* war in 1914. その国は1914年に戦争を始めた
反戦 **peace** (PEACE)

battle [C, U] (軍隊による)戦い, 戦闘; (人々による)交戦 ◇Napoleon was defeated at the *Battle* of Waterloo. ナポレオンはワーテルローの戦いで敗れた ◇His father had been killed in *battle*. 彼の父は戦死してしまっていた ◇Many young men were *sent into battle* without proper training. 多くの若者がまともな訓練を受けることなく戦地に送られた ◇Scores of people have been hurt in running *battles* with police. 警察との交戦が長引いて多くの人々が負傷した

action [U] 《特にジャーナリズム》(戦闘・戦争における)軍事行動, 交戦, 実戦 ◇He was killed during enemy *action*. 彼は敵との交戦中に死亡した ◇He was reported missing in *action*. 彼は交戦中に行方不明になったと伝えられた ◇I never *saw action* during the war. 私は戦時中に一度も実戦を経験しなかった

conflict [C, U] (2か国間の)争い, 紛争, 闘争 ◇Peace talks have failed to end the 6-year-old *conflict*. 和平交渉が6年にわたる紛争を終結させられなかった ◇*Conflict* between the two groups has left more than 8,000 dead. その二つの集団間の争いは, 8千人以上の死者を出した

fighting [U] (人々による)戦い, 戦闘, 交戦 ◇Heavy *fighting* broke out in the east of the country. 国の東部で激しい戦闘が勃発した ◇There were outbreaks of street *fighting* in three districts of the city last night. 昨晩, その都市の3つの地区で市街戦が勃発した

combat [U] 戦い, 戦闘, 交戦 ◇The soldiers are in *combat* with rebel forces. 兵士たちは反乱軍との戦闘中

である ◇The troops were locked in hand-to-hand *combat*. 両軍とも白兵戦で互角の戦いをした

warfare [U] (特定の武器・方法の使用による)戦争(行為), 交戦 ◇He denied his country has developed the capability for chemical *warfare*. 彼は母国が化学兵器戦争のための能力を開発してきていることを否定した ◇The fighting quickly turned into full-scale guerrilla *warfare*. その戦闘はすぐに全面的なゲリラ戦に転じた

campaign [C] (特定の軍事目的を達成するための)軍事[作戦]行動, …方面作戦 ◇The Russian *campaign* ended with the German defeat at Stalingrad. ロシア方面作戦はスターリングラードにおけるドイツの敗北で終結した ◇The terrorists responded with a bombing *campaign* directed at business and commerce. テロリストたちは商業と通商に対する爆撃作戦で応酬した

hostilities [複数形で]《ややフォーマル, 特にジャーナリズム》戦闘(行為), 交戦 ◇*Hostilities* between the two countries ended in a ceasefire. その2か国間の戦闘は停戦という形で終結した ❶ hostilities は特に戦闘が始まる[終わる], 中止する, 再開する]ときに用いられる. 動詞の連語には, begin, break out, cease, end, suspend, resume などが挙げられる. 句としては, the outbreak/cessation/suspension/resumption of hostilities などがある.

skirmish [C] (小隊同士の偶発的な)小競り合い ◇Minor *skirmishes* broke out all along the border. ちょっとした小競り合いが国境の至るところで起こった

wash 動

wash • bath/bathe • shower • freshen (yourself) up • wash up • clean yourself up/get (yourself) cleaned up
水と石けんを使って自分や他人を清潔にする
【類義訳】洗う, 入浴させる, 風呂に入れる, シャワーを浴びる, さっぱりする

文型&コロケーション
▸ to wash/ shower **quickly**
▸ to wash/ bath/ bathe/ shower **and change/ dress**

wash [自, 他]《特に英》洗う, 体を洗う ◇I *washed* and changed before going out. 出かける前に体を洗って着替えた ◇She was no longer able to *wash* herself. 彼女はもはや自分の体を洗うことができなかった ❶《英》では, have a wash と言うこともできる. 《米》では, より具体的で, 体をどのように洗うかを言うほうが普通である. ◆He *washed* his face. (彼は顔を洗った). ◆I took a shower. (シャワーを浴びた).
☞ **wash** (CLEAN) 動

bath 《英》《米 **bathe**》[他] (人を)入浴させる, 風呂に入れる ◇He never *bathed* the kids when they were little. 彼は子どもたちが小さい頃, 風呂に入れてやることはまったくなかった ❶「入浴する」という意味では, bath, bathe を用いることも可能であるが, この用法は古風なので, have a bath《英》, take a bath《米》と言うほうがずっと普通である.

shower [自] シャワーを浴びる ◇She *showered* and dressed and went downstairs. 彼女はシャワーを浴び, 身仕度をしてから階下へ下りていった ❶ have a shower《英》, take a shower《米》と言うほうが普通である.

freshen 'up, freshen yourself 'up 句動 (入浴・シャワー以外で体を)さっぱりする ◇I'll just go and *freshen up* before supper. 夕食前にちょっとさっぱりして行ってくるよ ◇She kicked off her shoes and *freshened herself up* in the bathroom. 彼女は靴を脱ぎ捨て, 風呂

↪wash

場でさっぱりした

,wash 'up 句動詞 《米》(顔・手を)洗う ◇Go get *washed up* ― it's time to eat. 手を洗ってきなさい―一食事の時間よ ❶《英》では, wash up は「食後に皿・鍋などを洗うこと」を意味する. ◆Since you made lunch, I'll *wash up*. (君が昼食を作ってくれたから, 僕が洗い物をするよ). ☞ **wash** (CLEAN 動)

,clean yourself 'up, get (yourself) ,cleaned 'up 句動詞 《米》(シャワーを浴びたりして)体を洗う ◇You need to *clean yourself up* ― you've been outside all day. あなた, 体を洗わなきゃ――一日中外にいたんだから

waste 名

waste・garbage・rubbish・trash・litter・debris・scrap・refuse
もはや不必要になってどこかに捨てられる[置き去られる]物
【類語訳】廃棄物, 廃水, 生ごみ, ごみ, くず, 廃品, スクラップ

文型&コロケーション
▶ **organic** waste/ garbage/ rubbish/ debris
▶ **household/ domestic** waste/ garbage/ rubbish/ trash/ refuse
▶ to **dump** waste/ garbage/ rubbish/ trash/ debris/ refuse
▶ to **produce** waste/ garbage/ rubbish/ trash/ debris
▶ to **take out** the garbage/ rubbish/ trash
▶ waste/ garbage/ rubbish/ trash/ refuse **disposal/ collection**
▶ a waste/ garbage/ rubbish/ trash **dump**
▶ a garbage/ rubbish/ trash/ scrap **heap**
▶ a waste/ rubbish/ trash/ litter **bin**
▶ a garbage/ trash **can**

waste [U] (または《専門語》**wastes** [複数で]) 廃棄物, 廃水 [液] ◇Around four million tons of industrial *waste* are disposed of each year. 毎年, 約400万トンの産業廃棄物が処分されている ◇the disposal of toxic/radioactive *wastes* 有毒/放射性廃棄物の廃棄 ◇*Waste* water is pumped from the factory into a nearby river. 廃水が工場から近くの川にポンプで垂れ流されている

garbage [U] 《特に米》(水分を含んだ)生ごみ ◇The *garbage* cans had just been emptied. 生ごみ入れは空にしたばかりだった ◇The canal is full of *garbage* and bits of wood. 用水路は生ごみと木片であふれている

rubbish [U] 《特に英》(乾燥した)ごみ ◇The streets were littered with *rubbish*. 通りにはごみが散乱していた ◇Over a third of British household *rubbish* is packaging. 英国の家庭ごみの3分の1以上が梱包材である ☞ **junk** (THING 2)

trash [U] 《米》(乾燥した)ごみ ◇The subway entrance was blocked with *trash*. 地下鉄の入口はごみでふさがっていた ◇What are these letters doing in the *trash*? どうしてこれらの手紙がごみの中にあるんだい ◇Don't forget to take out the *trash*. 忘れずにごみを出してね

litter [U] (公共の場に放置された紙・缶・瓶などの小さな)ごみ ◇There will be fines for people who *drop litter*. ごみを捨てる人には罰金が科せられる

debris [U] 《フォーマル》(放置された不用な)くず ◇Clear away leaves and other garden *debris* from the pond. 池から葉っぱなどの庭くずを片づけてください

scrap [U] (元の目的に使用できない)くず, 廃品, スクラップ ◇We sold the car *for scrap* (= so that any good

parts could be used again). 我々はその車をスクラップとして売った ◇*scrap* metal/iron くず金属/鉄 ☞ **scrap** (REMOVE)

refuse [U] 《フォーマル》(投棄された)廃棄物, ごみ ◇Domestic *refuse* can be burnt to produce electricity. 家庭ごみは燃やして発電に使うことができます

ノート **waste, garbage, rubbish, trash, refuse** の使い分け: rubbish は《英》で, もはや必要とされないために捨てられる「ごみ」を指す一般的な語. garbage と trash は両語とも《米》で用いられる. 家庭では, garbage は残飯など水分を含んだ「生ごみ」を指す傾向がある. trash は紙・ボール紙など乾燥した「ごみ」を指す傾向が多いが, 実際にはどちらの不用物に対しても, 両語とも用いることができる. waste は特に非常に大量な「廃棄物」を指し, 家庭の文脈ではあまり用いられない. waste は人間の体がもはや必要としない固体や液体を指すこともできる一般的な語である. ◆There were no toilet facilities and no way to dispose of human *waste* in a sanitary manner. (トイレ設備も人間の排泄物を衛生的に処理する方法もなかった). 《英》では, dustman (清掃作業員)が集めるために, 通りにある dustbin (ごみ入れ)に rubbish を入れる. 《米》では, garbage と trash が通りにある garbage/trash can (ごみ入れ)に入れられ, garbage man/collector (清掃作業員)によって集められる. refuse はフォーマルな語で,《英》《米》の両方で用いられる. refuse collector (清掃作業員)は dustman や garbage collector を表すフォーマルな語である. ☞ **junk** (THING 2)

way 名

1 way・approach・style・manner
誰かが何かをするときの特別な手段
【類語訳】やり方, 仕方, 方法, 取り組み方, 流儀

文型&コロケーション
▶ a **way/ style/ manner of** (doing) sth
▶ **in** a (...) way/ style/ manner
▶ a **traditional/ conventional/ different** way/ approach/ style/ manner
▶ a/ an **casual/ informal/ formal** way/ approach/ style/ manner
▶ the **usual** way/ approach/ style/ manner
▶ a **new** way/ approach/ style
▶ an **effective** way/ approach/ manner
▶ the **right/ wrong** way/ approach/ manner
▶ to **have/ adopt** a way/ an approach/ a style/ a manner
▶ to **change** a way/ your approach/ a style
▶ to **develop** a way/ an approach/ a style
▶ to **try** a way/ an approach

way [C] やり方, 仕方, 方法 ◇Try to approach this in a sensible *way*. 賢明なやり方でこれに取り組んでみなさい ◇He has a *way* of staring at you that is very unnerving. 彼にじっと見られると君は落ち着かなくなるよね ◇You won't impress the judges that *way*. 裁判官にそんな心証を与えないように ◇I like *the way (that)* you did that. 君のそのやり方が気に入っている ◇Infectious diseases can be passed on in several different *ways*. 感染症にはいくつかの異なる感染経路がある

approach [C] 取り組み方 ◇The school has adopted a firmer *approach to* discipline. その学校は規律への取り組みをより厳しくした ◇She favoured the direct *ap-*

proach. 彼女は直接的なやり方を好んだ
style [C] (特定の)やり方, 仕方, 方法, 流儀 ◇His aggressive *style* of play sometimes got him into trouble. 自らの攻撃的プレースタイルによって彼は時々トラブルに陥った ◇What's her teaching *style* like? 彼女の教え方ってどんなふうなの ◇I like your *style*! あなたのやり方が気に入っています ◇Caution was not her *style* (= not the way she usually behaved). 用心するのはいつもの彼女らしくなかった

ノート **way**と**style**の使い分け：wayは, ある特定の場合に人が物事をどのように行うかを表す. styleは, 人が物事をふだんどのようにするかを表し, 個性の一部である.

manner [単数形]《フォーマル》(人に対する)方法, やり方 ◇She answered in a business-like *manner*. 彼女は事務的に答えた ◇The *manner* in which the decision was taken is extremely regrettable. その決定の下され方はきわめて遺憾である

2 way・method・technique・means・process・mechanism・system・methodology
何かをしたり, 成し遂げたりするために行う特別なことを表す
【類語訳】方法, 手段, 方式, 技術, 技法, 技巧, 製法, 工程, 手順

文型&コロケーション
▶a method/ technique/ means/ process/ mechanism/ system/ methodology **for** (doing) sth
▶a way/ method/ technique/ means/ system/ methodology **of** (doing) sth
▶an **effective** way/ method/ technique/ means/ mechanism/ system
▶a **good/ practical** way/ method/ technique/ means/ system
▶a **simple** way/ method/ technique/ means/ process/ system
▶a/ the **traditional** way/ method/ technique/ means/ system/ methodology
▶a **new** way/ method/ technique/ means/ system/ methodology
▶an **alternative** way/ method/ technique/ means/ methodology
▶to **use** a method/ technique/ means/ process/ system/ methodology
▶to **adopt** a method/ technique/ system/ methodology
▶to **devise/ develop** a way/ method/ technique/ means/ process/ system/ methodology
▶to **find** a way/ method/ means/ system
▶to **change** a way/ method/ system/ methodology
▶a method/ technique/ mechanism/ system **works**

way [C] (目的達成の)方法, 手段 ◇There are several possible *ways* of dealing with this problem. この問題に対処する方法がいくつかあります ◇That's not the *way* to hold a pair of scissors! はさみの持ち方はそうじゃないよ ◇I prefer to do things the easy *way*. 私は物事を簡単な方法でやるのが好きだ ◇We should have done it *my way*! 我々はそれをぼくのやり方でやるべきだったのに ◇I generally get what I want *one way or another*. 私は通常何とかして自分がほしいものは手に入れている

method [C] (何段階かに分かれる)方法, 方式 ◇He's quite critical of modern teaching *methods*. 彼は現代の教授法に対してきわめて批判的である ◇This is a sim-pler *method* for making bread. こちらのほうがパン作りの簡単な方法だ ◇There are various *methods* of dealing with this problem. この問題に対処する方法はいろいろある

technique [C] 技術, 技法, 技巧 ◇The artist combines different *techniques* in the same painting. その芸術家は1枚の絵の中で異なる技法を組み合わせている ◇You will learn various *techniques* for dealing with difficult customers. 気難しい顧客の扱い方をいろいろ身に付けることになるでしょう ◇He needs to improve his throwing *technique*. 彼は投げ方を改善する必要がある

means [C] (使用する)手段, 方法 ◇TV is a highly effective *means* of communication. テレビはきわめて有効な通信手段である ◇What **means of transport** did they use? 彼らはどんな交通手段を使ったのですか ◇We will use whatever *means* are necessary. 我々は必要なあらゆる手段を使うことになります ◇The load was lifted *by means of* (= using) a crane. その積み荷はクレーンで持ち上げられた

process [C] (産業における)製法, 工程 ◇They are made using the most advanced manufacturing *processes*. それらは最先端の製造工程を経て作られる

mechanism [C] 《ややフォーマル》(目的達成の)方法 ◇Various *mechanisms* are in place for dealing with emergencies. 緊急事態に対処するいろいろな方法がとられている ◇Simple repetition was regarded as an effective learning *mechanism*. 単純な繰り返しが効果的な学習方法と見なされていた

system [C] (体系的な)方式, 手順 ◇This is a highly effective *system* for storing data. これはデータ蓄積にきわめて有効な方式だ ◇Once your *systems* are in place you can concentrate on the main focus of your business. いったん手順が整えば業務の一番の中心に全力を注ぐことができます ☞ **systematic** (EFFICIENT)

methodology [U, C] 《フォーマル》方法[原理]体系 ◇Please give a brief outline of your research *methodology*. ご自分の研究の方法体系の短い概略をお示しください ◇Different people adopt different *methodologies*. 人によって取るやり方はまちまちだ

3 way・route・direction・line・path・orbit・course・bearing
どこかへ行くための陸路や水路や空路を表す
【類語訳】道, 道筋, 進路, 通り道, 行く手, 方向, 進行方向, 経路, 道順, ルート, 路線, 方面, 軌道, 針路, 航路, 方位, 方角

文型&コロケーション
▶a way/ route/ path/ course **to** sth
▶a/ the way/ route/ line/ path/ course **from...to...**
▶a/ the way/ route/ line/ path/ course **through/ along/ across** sth
▶**on** the way/ route/ path
▶**in** sb/ sth's way/ line/ path
▶**in** the direction/ line/ path **of** sth
▶the **right/ wrong** way/ route/ direction/ path/ course
▶the **shortest** way/ route/ line/ path/ course
▶the **quickest** way/ route
▶a **straight** line/ path/ course
▶the **opposite/ other** way/ direction
▶a **direct** way/ route/ line/ path/ course
▶to **follow** a way/ a route/ a line/ a path/ an orbit/ a course
▶to **take** a way/ route/ direction/ path/ course
▶to **block** the/ sb/ sth's way/ route/ line/ path

↪**way**

▸ to **know** the way/ route
▸ to **change** direction/ course

way [C, ふつう単数で] (場所への)道, 道筋；(人・物への)進路, 通り道, 行く手；(人・物が向かう移動する)方向, 進行方向 ◇I stopped to **ask the way**. 立ち止まって道を尋ねた ◇They had to **fight their way** through the crowd. 彼らは人込みの中を苦労して通り抜けねばならなかった ◇**Get out of my way!** I'm in a hurry! どけ、急いでるんだ ◇She was **going my way**, so we talked as we walked. 彼女の向かっている先が私と同じでしたので, 私たちは歩きながら話した ◇They bought some supplies on the **way**. 彼らは途中で必需品をいくらか買った ◇Which **way** did they go? 彼らはどっちの方へ行ったの ◇He narrowly avoided a car coming the other **way** (= towards him). 彼は自分に向かってくる車をかろうじてよけた

route [C] (計画的な)経路, 道順, ルート；(バス・列車などの)路線, (商品の)配達／輸送)路 ◇It's the best **route** into the city from the south. それが南部からその都市へ入る最善のルートである ◇Motorists are being advised to take an alternative **route**. 車のドライバーには代替ルートを取るよう勧めている ◇We'll have to plan our **route** carefully. 私たちは慎重に順路を計画しなければならないだろう ◇We took the **scenic route** through the hills. 私たちは丘を通る景色のよいルートをとった ◇Is the hotel on a **bus route**? そのホテルはバス路線沿いにありますか ◇These were the ancient trade **routes** between Europe and Asia. これらはヨーロッパとアジアの間における古代の通商路だった

▸**route** [動] [他] 《ふつう副詞や前置詞と共に》◇Satellites **route** data all over the globe. 衛星が世界中にデータを送っている

direction [C, U] (人・物が向かう)方向, 方面, 進行方向；(人・物事がやって来る)方向, 方面, 方向 ◇He ran off in the **direction** of the river. 彼は川の方向に走り去った ◇The plane was flying in a northerly **direction**. 飛行機は北に向かって飛んでいた ◇The road was blocked in both **directions**. 道路はどちらの方向もふさがれていた ◇When the police arrived, the crowd scattered **in all directions**. 警察が到着すると, 群衆は四散した ◇I had lost all **sense of direction** = I did not know which way to go). 私はすっかり方向感覚を失ってしまっていた ◇Support came from an unexpected **direction**. 思ってもみなかった方面から支援を受けた ☞ **direct** (TAKE 2)

line [C, ふつう単数で] (人・物が移動(位置)する)方向, 進行方向；(特定的に使用される)進路, 経路 ◇They followed the **line** of the river for three miles. 彼らは川に沿って3マイル進んだ ◇Try to keep the boat sailing **in a straight line**. 船を一直線に航行させ続けるよう努めなさい ◇They were directly **in the line of fire** (= the direction that sb is shooting in). 彼らは銃弾が飛び交う真っ只中にいた ◇Their aim was to block the enemy's **supply lines** (= the route that supplies come along). 彼らの目的は敵の補給路を断つことだった

path [C] (人・物が移動する)進路, 通り道；(移動の際の) 行く手 ◇The diagram shows the **path** of the satellite between 10.20 and 10.34. その図では10時20分から34分までの衛星の軌道が示されている ◇The avalanche destroyed everything in its **path**. 雪崩は通り道にあるあらゆるものを破壊した

orbit [C, U] (惑星・物体の)軌道 ◇There are slight changes in the Earth's **orbit around** the Sun. 太陽を

---

wear

回る地球の軌道にわずかな変化がある ◇The satellite **went into orbit** last month. 衛星は先月, 軌道に乗った ◇He spent eleven months **in orbit** (= in space). 彼は軌道上で11か月間過ごした ☞ **orbit** (SPIN)

course [U, C, ふつう単数で] (船・飛行機の)針路, 航路 ◇The plane was **off course** (= was not following the correct route). その機は針路を外れていた ◇The ship **set a course for** (= started to sail towards) the Christmas Islands. 船はクリスマス諸島へ針路を定めた

bearing [C, ふつう複数で] 《専門語》(コンパスで測定した)相対的位置, 方位, 方角, 方向 ◇The log records the ship's **bearings**, wind direction and speed. 測程儀は船の相対的位置・風向・風速を記録する ◇You'll learn how to **take your bearings** with a compass. コンパスで自分の位置を確かめる方法を学習してもらいます ◇They took **compass bearings** on the tower. 彼らは塔の上でコンパスを使って方向を定めた

wear [動]

wear・put sth on・dress・get dressed・have (got) sth on・change
衣服を自分の身にまとう
【類意訳】身に着ける, 着る, 服を着る, 正装する, 着替える

[文型&コロケーション]
▸ to wear/ put on/ have on a **coat/ jacket/ suit/ hat**
▸ to wear/ put on/ have on a **ring/ badge/ watch**
▸ to wear/ put on/ have on your **glasses**
▸ to wear/ put on/ have on **make-up/ lipstick**

wear [他] (衣類・装飾品などを)身に着けている, 着ている ◇Do I have to **wear** a tie? ネクタイをしないといけないかな ◇Was he **wearing** a seat belt? 彼はシートベルトをしていましたか ◇She always **wears** black (= black clothes). 彼女はいつも黒い服を着ている

put sth 'on [句動] (衣類・装飾品などを)身に着ける, 着る ◇Hurry up! **Put** your coat **on**. 急いで, コートを着て ◇She's just **putting on** her make-up. 彼女はちょうど化粧をしているところだ [反意] **take sth off** (TAKE STH OFF)

dress [自, 他] (自分・人に)服を着せる, 服を着る；(特定の種類・型の)服を着ている, 服装にする；正装する ◇I **dressed** quickly. 私は素早く服を着た ◇She **dressed** herself and the children in their best clothes. 彼女は一張羅を着て, 子どもたちにも一張羅を着させた ◇to **dress** well/badly/ fashionably/comfortably きちんとした／ひどい／おしゃれな／快適な服装をする ◇You should **dress** for cold weather today. 今日は寒い天候に備えた服装をしなさい ◇She always **dressed** entirely **in** black. 彼女はいつも黒ずくめの服装をしていた ❶ **dress up** は特にいつもと違ったような人・物に見せかけるために, ふだん着ているものよりもフォーマルな服を着ること, 特別な服装にすることを指す。◆There's no need to **dress up** — come as you are. (めかし込む必要はない — いつもどおりの服装で来て). ◆The kids love **dressing up**. (子どもたちはおしゃれが大好きだ). ◆The boys were all **dressed up** as pirates. (少年たちは皆, 海賊に扮していた). **dress down** は, 例えば職場などで, ふだん着ているものよりインフォーマルな服を着ることを指す。◆Everyone **dresses down** on Fridays. (金曜日は皆, カジュアルな服装をする). [反意] **undress** (TAKE STH OFF)

,get 'dressed [フレーズ] (何も身に着けていないときに)服を着る ◇Get up and **get dressed!** 起きて服を着なさい ❶朝

well

起きたときや、シャワーを浴びたばかりのときなど、何も服を身に着けていない場合に、get dressed は用いられる。ある衣服一式を脱いで別の衣服を身に着ける場合は、change または get changed を用いる。 反意 **get undressed** (TAKE STH OFF)

,have sth 'on (または ,have got sth 'on) 句動詞 [進行形なし] (衣類を)身に着けている、着ている ◇She *had* a red jacket *on*. 彼女は赤い上着を着ていた ◇He *had* nothing (= no clothes) *on*. 彼は何も着ていなかった

change [自, 他] (異なる[清潔な]服に)着替える、(服を)着替える ◇I went into the bedroom to *change*. 寝室に着替えに行った ◇She *changed into* her swimsuit. 彼女は水着に着替えた ◇You need to *change out of* those wet things. その濡れた服を着替えなくちゃ ◇I didn't have time to *get changed* before the party. 《特に英》パーティーの前に服を着替える時間がなかった ◇I didn't have time to *change clothes* before the party. 《特に米》パーティーの前に服を着替える時間がなかった

well 形

well・all right・OK・fine・healthy・strong・fit・good・great
人が病気でないことを表す
【類語訳】健康な、元気な、丈夫な、気分のよい、大丈夫で、体調のよい

all right	well	fine
OK	healthy	great
	strong	
	fit	
	good	

文型&コロケーション
▸ all right/ OK/ fit **for** sth
▸ all right/ OK/ fit **to do** sth
▸ **to feel/ look** well/ all right/ OK/ fine/ healthy/ strong/ fit/ good/ great
▸ **to keep (sb)** well/ healthy/ fit
▸ **to get** well/ strong/ fit
▸ **perfectly** well/ all right/ OK/ fine/ healthy/ fit
▸ **very/ extremely/ apparently** well/ healthy/ fit
▸ **physically** well/ healthy/ strong/ fit
▸ **fit and** well/ healthy/ strong

well [名詞の前まれ]《特に話し言葉》健康な、元気な、丈夫な、気分のよい ◇I'm not feeling very *well*. あまり気分がよくない ◇You're looking *well*. 元気そうだね ◇Is he *well* enough to travel? 旅に出られるほど彼は元気なの ◇Wait till you're *better* before you go back to work. 仕事に戻るのは、もっと元気になってからにしなさい ◇I hope you're keeping *well*. あなたが元気にしているのを願っています ◇'How are you?' 'Very *well*, thanks.' 「元気だ」「とても元気だよ、ありがとう」 ◇*Get well soon* (= a message on a greetings card to sb who is ill). 早く元気になってね ◇He's not a *well* man. 《インフォーマル》彼は丈夫な男ではない ❶ *well* は特に自分の健康について話すため、人に体調を尋ねたり、それに対してあれこれ言うために用いられる。また、例えば病気が快復したときなど、特定の時に人の健康について話すのにも用いられる。 反意 **sick, ill, unwell** (SICK 1)

all 'right [名詞の前では用いない]《ややインフォーマル、話し言葉》気分が悪くない、けがしていない、大丈夫で ◇Are you feeling *all right*? 気分は悪くないかい ◇I'm *all right* now. もう大丈夫だ

OK (または **okay**) [名詞の前では用いない]《インフォーマル、話し言葉》気分が悪くない、けがしていない、大丈夫で ◇Are you *OK*? 大丈夫かい ◇He should be *OK* for the game on Saturday. 彼は土曜の試合には大丈夫だろう

ノート **all right と OK の使い分け**：これらの語はこのグループの他の類語ほどは肯定的ではない。まったく健康であるというよりは実際には病気でない[けがしていない]と言う場合に、話し言葉で用いられる。どちらもかなりインフォーマルだが、OKのほうがいくぶん all right よりもさらにインフォーマルである。どちらの語にも「安全な」の意味もある。 ☞ **SAFE**

fine [名詞の前では用いない]《否定文では用いない；比較・最上級では用いない》《特に話し言葉》すっかり健康[元気]な ◇'How are you?' '*Fine*, thanks.' 「元気」「元気だよ、ありがとう」 ◇She was absolutely *fine* throughout the pregnancy. 彼女は妊娠中ずっとまったく健康だった ❶ *fine* は特に人に体調を尋ねられた際に、自分の健康について言うのに用いられる。また、人に話しかける際に、相手の健康について話すのにも用いられる。well と違い、人に体調を尋ねる[人の体調についてあれこれ言う]場合に用いられることは少ない。 ✕ Are you keeping *fine*? ✓ You're looking *fine*!

healthy (病気になりそうにない)健康な、元気な ◇Keep *healthy* by eating well and exercising regularly. よく食べて、定期的に運動して、健康を保ってください ◇She gave birth to a *healthy* boy. 彼女は元気な男の子を出産した ◇Here are ten tips for a *healthy* heart. ここに健康な心臓のための10の秘訣があります 反意 **sickly, unhealthy** (SICK 1), ☞ **health** (HEALTH)

strong (病気を患っておらず)健康な、元気な ◇After a few weeks she was feeling *stronger*. 数週間後、彼女はさらに元気になっていた ❶ *strong* は病後に健康を回復することに用いられる。 反意 **weak**, ☞ **strength** (FORCE 名)

fit 《特に英》(定期的な運動のおかげで)健康な、元気な、体調[調子]のよい ◇I used to go swimming every day in order to keep *fit*. 健康を保つために、毎日泳ぎに行ったものだ ◇A reasonably *fit* adult should have no difficulty with the climb. そこそこ健康な成人なら、登るのに困難はないはずです ❶ *fit* は「物事を行うのに十分健康な」を意味して、fit for sth, fit to do sth の句で用いられることがある。スポーツ選手がけがから回復してプレー[競技]できることを言うために、スポーツの文脈で用いられることが多い。 ◆ He's been ill and isn't *fit enough for* work yet. (彼はしばらく病気で、まだ働くのに万全の健康状態ではない)。 ◆ He should be *fit to* play in the match tomorrow. (彼は明日には、試合でプレーできるほど体調がよくなっているはずです)。 ◆ She won't compete unless she's *fully fit*. (彼女は十分に体調がよくなければ、競技に出ないでしょう)。 反意 **unfit** (SICK 1), ☞ **fitness** (HEALTH)

good (人・体の部位が)健康な、元気な、体調[調子]のよい ❶ *good* がこの意味で、人について用いられる場合は、ふつう否定的な文で用いられる。 ◆ I don't feel too *good* today. (今日はあまり体調がすぐれない)。しかし、インフォーマルな《米》の言い回しでは、形容詞・副詞のどちらの形でも、肯定的な文で用いられることもある。 ◆ 'How are you?' 'I'm *good*, thanks!' (《米, インフォーマル》「調子はどう」「いいよ、ありがとう」)。 ◆ I'm doing *good*. (元気にやってるよ)。 ❷ *good* はまた、特に目・耳について、片方が不全な[うまく機能しない]場合に用いられることもある。 ◆ Can you speak into my *good* ear? (よ

〈聞こえるほうの耳に向かって話してもらえますか〉. 反意 **bad** (SICK 1)
great (ややインフォーマル, 特に話し言葉)(身体的[精神的]に)非常に元気な[気分のよい] ◇I feel *great* today. 今日はとても気分がいい ◇Everyone's in *great* form. 皆, 元気一杯だ ◇She seemed in *great* spirits (= very cheerful). 彼女はとてもはつらつとしているようだった

wet 形 ☞ SOFT

wet・moist・damp・soaked・sodden・drenched・saturated
物が液体や水で覆われていることを表す
【類語訳】濡れた, 湿った, しっとりした, じめじめした, びしょ濡れの

moist	wet	soaked
damp		sodden
		drenched
		saturated

文型&コロケーション

▶ wet/ moist/ damp/ soaked/ drenched/ saturated **with** sth
▶ soaked/ drenched **in** sth
▶ sb's **clothes/ hair** is/ are wet/ damp/ soaked/ sodden/ drenched
▶ sb's **coat/ shirt** is wet/ damp/ soaked/ drenched
▶ sb's **shoes** are wet/ damp/ soaked/ drenched
▶ wet/ moist/ damp/ sodden/ saturated **ground/ earth**
▶ wet/ moist/ damp/ saturated **soil**
▶ to **become** wet/ moist/ damp/ soaked/ sodden/ saturated
▶ to **get** wet/ moist/ damp/ soaked/ sodden/ drenched
▶ **very/ slightly** wet/ moist/ damp
▶ **absolutely/ thoroughly/ completely** soaked/ drenched/ saturated

wet (液体・水で)濡れた ◇The car had skidded in the *wet* road. 車は濡れた道路でスリップしてしまった ◇You'll get *wet* (= in the rain) if you go out now. 今出かけたら濡れるよ ◇Try not to get your shoes *wet*. 靴を濡らさないようにね ◇We were all *soaking wet* (= extremely wet). 私たちは皆, ずぶ濡れだった ◇My shirt was *wet through* (= completely wet). (英) シャツはびしょ濡れだった 反意 **dry** ❶この意味での反対語の dry には類義語がない。◆Is my shirt *dry* yet? (私のシャツはもう乾いた?) ◆Store onions in a cool *dry* place. (タマネギは乾燥した涼しい場所で保存しなさい). ☞ **wet** (SOAK)

moist (しばしばほめて)(心地よく[役に立つ程度に])湿った, 濡れた, しっとりした ◇The warm *moist* air is perfect for growing fruit trees. 暖かく湿った空気は, 果樹が生長するのにうってつけである ◇a lovely rich *moist* cake 素晴らしくコクのあるしっとりしたケーキ ◇Water the plants regularly to keep the soil *moist*. 土の湿り気を保つために, 定期的に植物に水をやりなさい ☞ **moisture** (MOISTURE), **moisten** (SOAK)

damp (時にけなして)(不快に)湿った, 濡れた, じめじめした ◇The cottage was cold and *damp*. そのコテージは寒くじめじめしていた ◇Wipe the surface with a *damp* cloth. 濡れた布で表面を拭いてください ☞ **damp** (MOISTURE), **dampen** (SOAK)

soaked (ややインフォーマル)びしょ(ずぶ)濡れの ◇He woke up *soaked* with sweat. 彼は汗びっしょりで目覚めた ◇His *soaked* shirt stuck to his chest. ずぶ濡れのシャツが彼の胸に張りついていた ◇You're *soaked to the skin* (= completely wet)! (特に英) びしょ濡れじゃない ☞ **soak** (SOAK)

sodden びしょ[ずぶ]濡れの ◇I had to get out of my *sodden* clothes. ずぶ濡れの服を脱がなければならなかった ◇I preferred not to sit on the *sodden* grass. びしょ濡れの芝の上に座りたくなかった

drenched [名詞の前のみ] びしょ[ずぶ]濡れの ◇His face was *drenched* with sweat. 彼の顔は汗びっしょりだった ◇Her clothes were *drenched* in blood. 彼女の服は血まみれだった ☞ **drench** (SOAK)

ノート **soaked, sodden, drenched** の使い分け:
soaked と drenched は, with または in と共に用いられるが, sodden は不可. ◆*soaked/drenched* with/in sweat/blood/tears/perspiration (汗びっしょりの/血まみれの/涙でぐしょぐしょの/汗びっしょりの). ×*sodden* with/in sweat/blood/tears/perspiration. また, soaked と sodden は名詞の前で用いることもできるが, drenched はふつう不可. ◆their *soaked/sodden* clothes/sheets (彼らのびしょ濡れの服/シーツ). ×their *drenched* clothes/sheets. sodden はふつう水や雨で濡れた物・地面に用いられることが多い. ◆the *sodden* earth/ground/grass/turf/fields (びしょ濡れの土/地面/草地/芝/野原). soaked と drenched は水・汗・血で濡れた物に用いるが, 地面には用いられない. ×the *soaked/drenched* earth/ground/grass/turf/fields.

saturated (ややフォーマル, 書き言葉) びしょびしょに濡れた, 飽和状態になった ◇*Saturated* soil lacks air, without which plant roots die. 飽和土は空気が乏しく, 空気なしでは植物の根は死んでしまう

whisper 動

whisper・murmur・mutter・sigh・mumble・groan・mouth・moan
静かな声で何かを言う
【類語訳】ささやく, 小声で話す, ひそひそ話す, つぶやく, ほそぼそ言う, ぶつぶつ言う, ため息をつく, うめく, うなる

文型&コロケーション

▶ to whisper/ murmur/ mutter/ mumble/ groan/ mouth/ moan (sth) **to** sb
▶ to whisper/ murmur/ mutter/ mumble **about** sth
▶ to groan/ moan **with** pain/ pleasure etc.
▶ to whisper/ murmur/ mutter/ mumble **that**...
▶ to whisper/ murmur/ mutter/ mumble/ mouth **something/ an apology**
▶ to whisper/ murmur/ mutter/ sigh/ groan/ moan **softly**
▶ to whisper/ mutter/ sigh/ groan/ moan **loudly**
▶ to whisper/ murmur/ mutter **thickly/ incoherently**

whisper [自, 他] (声を出さないで)ささやく, 小声で[ひそひそ]話す ◇Don't you know it's rude to *whisper*? ひそひそ話は失礼だって知らないの ◇What are you two *whispering* about? あなたたち二人, 何をひそひそ話してるの ◇'Can you meet me tonight?' he *whispered*. 「今夜会える」と彼は小声で言った ◇She leaned over and *whispered* something in his ear. 彼女は身を乗り出して, 彼の耳元で何かをささやいた 反意 **shout** (SHOUT)

▶**whisper** 图 [C] ◇They spoke in barely audible whispers. 彼らはかろうじて聞き取れるような小声で話した ◇Her voice dropped to a whisper. 彼女の声は小さくなってささやき声になった
murmur [自, 他] (聞き取りづらいほど静かな声で)つぶやく, 小声で[ひそひそ]話す ◇She was murmuring in his ear. 彼女は彼の耳元でひそひそ話していた ◇She murmured her agreement. 彼女は消え入るような声で承諾した
▶**murmur** 图 ◇He took the mug of coffee with a murmur of thanks. 彼はありがとうとつぶやいて, マグカップのコーヒーを手にとった
mutter [自, 他] (何かに困って聞き取りづらいほど静かな声で)ほそほそ[ぶつぶつ]言う, つぶやく ◇She just sat there muttering to herself. 彼女はただそこに座ってぶつぶつ独り言を言っていた ◇I muttered something about needing to get back to work. 私は仕事に戻らなくちゃ, というようなことをつぶやいた
▶**mutter** 图 [C] ◇She gave a low mutter of apology. 彼女は小声でほそぼそ詫びた
sigh [他] (失望・悲嘆・疲労のために)ため息まじりに言う, ため息をつく ◇'Oh well, better luck next time,' she sighed. 「まあともかく, 次回はつきが回ってくるわ」と彼女はため息まじりに言った
▶**sigh** 图 [C] ◇We all breathed/heaved a great sigh of relief when it was over. それが終わると, 私たちは皆, 深く安堵のため息をついた ◇'I'll wait,' he said with a sigh. 「待つよ」と彼はため息まじりに言った
mumble [自, 他] (恥ずかしい[ばつが悪い, 腹を立てている]ために)ほそほそ[ぶつぶつ]言う, つぶやく ◇I could hear him mumbling to himself. 彼がぶつぶつ独り言を言っているのが聞こえた ◇'Sorry,' she mumbled. 「ごめんなさい」と彼女はつぶやくように言った ◇She mumbled an apology and left. 彼女は詫びの言葉をぼそっと言って立ち去った
▶**mumble** 图 [C, ふつう単数で] ◇He spoke in a low mumble, as if to himself. 彼はまるで独り言のように, 小声でほそほそと話した
groan [自] (失望・動揺・苦痛・快感で)うめく; 不満の声を上げる ◇He lay on the floor groaning. 彼は床に横たわってうめき声を上げた ◇We all groaned at his terrible jokes. 私たちは皆, 彼のつまらないジョークに不満の声を上げた
▶**groan** 图 ◇She let out a groan of dismay. 彼女は落胆のうめき声を上げた
mouth [他] (声は出さずに)口だけを動かして言う[伝える] ◇He mouthed a few obscenities at us and then moved off. 彼は我々に卑猥な言葉をいくつか, 口だけを動かして伝え, その後立ち去った
moan [自] (悲哀・苦痛・快感で)うめく, うなる ◇He moaned with sheer pleasure. 彼はこの上ない喜びを感じてうめき声を上げた ◇Most of the patients were moaning in pain. 患者のほとんどが痛みでうめき声を上げていた ☞ **moan** (COMPLAIN)
▶**moan** 图 ◇A low moan of despair escaped her. 彼女の口から低い絶望のうめき声が漏れた

┌─────────────────────────────────────┐
│ ノート groanとmoanの使い分け: moanのほうがgroan
│ よりも強い感情, つまり強い苦痛・快感だけでなく, 単なる失望
│ ではない深い悲哀・絶望を表すことがある.
└─────────────────────────────────────┘

whole 形

whole・full・total・entire・complete
最大の大きさや合体した状態を表す

【類語訳】全体の, 全部の, 全員の, すべての, まるごとの, まる…, まったくの, 完全な, 総計の, 合計の

[文型&コロケーション]
▶a whole/ a full/ an entire/ a complete **day/ set**
▶the whole/ full/ complete **truth/ story**
▶full/ complete **details**
▶full/ a total **membership**
▶your whole/ a full/ your entire **life**
▶the whole/ total/ entire **population**
▶**unusually/ nearly/ fairly/ reasonably** full/ complete
▶**almost** full/ total/ complete

whole [名詞の前で] (物事について)全体の, 全部の, 全員の, すべての, まるごとの, まる…, …の間中ずっと; (物事について)大きな, 非常な, まったくの, まさにその ◇We drank a whole bottle each. 私たちはそれぞれ, 一瓶まるまる飲み干した ◇The whole country (= all the people in it) mourned her death. 国中の人々が彼女の死を悼んだ ◇She wasn't telling the whole truth. 彼女はまったくありのままを話していたのではなかった ◇Let's forget the whole thing. すべてを忘れよう ◇We offer a whole variety of weekend breaks. 私どもは非常にバラエティーに富んだ週末の休暇をご提案いたします ◇I can't afford it — that's the whole point (= that's exactly what I've been trying to explain). そんなことに使う金の余裕はない—そこがまさに肝心なところなんだ

full [ふつう名詞の前で] (人・物事について)全部の, すべての, 全部[すべて]そろった; (水準・程度・量について)最大限の, 最高の, 完全な ◇A full refund will be given if the item is faulty. 品物に欠陥があれば, 全額払い戻しいたします ◇The address must be printed in full. 住所は(省略せずに)すべて活字体で書くこと ◇Many people don't use their computers to their full potential. 多くの人々はコンピューターの潜在能力を最大限に活用していない ◇Students should take full advantage of the college's facilities. 学生は大学の施設を最大限に利用すべきです ◇measures to achieve full employment 完全雇用を達成する方策 ◇I've always believed in living life to the full. 私は人生を精一杯生きることがよいと常に信じてきた ☞ fully (QUITE 2)

total [ふつう名詞の前で] (量・数について)全部の, 総計の, 合計の ◇The total profit was more than £500. 利益総額は500ポンド以上だった ◇The club has a total membership of about 300. クラブの全会員数はおよそ300名です ☞ **total** (COMPLETE), **total** (COUNT), **totally** (QUITE 2)
▶**total** 图 ◇You got 47 points in the last game and 18 in this one, making a total of 65. 前回の試合で47点, 今回の試合で18点獲得で, あなたの合計点は65点です ◇Out of a total of 15 games, they only won 2. 全15試合で, 彼らの勝利はたったの2試合だった ◇The repairs come to over £500 in total (= including everything). 修繕費はしめて500ポンド以上になる

entire [名詞の前で] (物事について)全体の, 全部の, 全員の, すべての, まるごとの, まる…, …の間中ずっと ◇I have never in my entire life heard such nonsense! 生まれてこの方, 私はこんなばかげた話を聞いたことがない ◇The disease threatens to wipe out the entire population. その病気は全人口を絶滅させる恐れがある ☞ **entirely** (QUITE 2)

┌─────────────────────────────────────┐
│ ノート wholeとentireの使い分け: entireはwholeより
│ も物事を強調し, 特に物事がいかに望ましくないかを強調するの
│ に用いられる. ◆I wasted a whole/an entire day on

it. (私はそれにまるまる一日を費やした). ◆We spent the *whole* day on the beach. (私たちはビーチで一日中過ごした). ×We spent the *entire* day on the beach.

complete (必要な部分をすべて含んで)全部[すべて]そろった, 完全な ◇A *complete* guide to events in Oxford is available from the office. オックスフォードでのイベントの完全ガイドが営業所で入手いただけます ◇the *complete works* of Tolstoy トルストイ全集 反意 **incomplete**

wide 形

1 ☞ DIVERSE, GENERAL
wide・broad・extensive・large-scale・mass・sweeping・wide-ranging・far-reaching・wholesale
物事が多くの人々[物事]に影響を与える[を関わらせる]こと, 物事が多くの異なるテーマを網羅することを表す
【語義訳】さまざまな, 幅広い, 広範な, 広い, 大規模な, 大量の, 大衆向けの, 集団の, 大々的な, 全面的な

文型&コロケーション
▶a wide/ a broad/ an extensive **range**
▶a broad/ an extensive/ a large-scale/ a mass/ a sweeping/ a wide-ranging/ a far-reaching **programme**
▶broad/ extensive/ large-scale/ sweeping/ wide-ranging/ far-reaching/ wholesale **changes**
▶a broad/ an extensive/ a sweeping/ a wide-ranging/ a wholesale **review**
▶a wide/ a broad/ an extensive/ a wide-ranging **debate**
▶wide/ broad/ extensive/ large-scale/ mass **support**
▶a broad/ extensive/ sweeping/ wide-ranging **powers**
▶a wide/ a broad/ an extensive/ a far-reaching **influence**
▶a wide/ broad/ mass **appeal**
▶wide/ broad/ extensive/ wide-ranging **interests**
▶wide/ broad/ extensive **knowledge**
▶extensive/ large-scale/ mass/ wholesale **destruction**

wide (人・物事の数・種類が)さまざまな, 幅広い, 広範な; (地理的範囲が)広い, 広範囲にわたる ◇We stock a *wide* range of goods. 私たちはさまざまな商品を取り揃えています ◇Jenny has a *wide* circle of friends. ジェニーは幅広い交友関係を持っている ◇The museum is trying to attract a *wider* audience. その美術館はより幅広い客層を引きつけようとしている ◇The festival attracts people from a *wide* area. その祭りは広範にわたる地域の人々を魅了している 反意 **narrow** (LIMITED 1)
▷**widely** 副 ◇The idea is now *widely* accepted. その考えは現在では広く受け入れられている ◇He has travelled *widely* in Asia. 彼はアジアを広範囲に旅してきた

broad (人・物事の数・種類が)さまざまな, 幅広い, 広範な, 広範囲にわたる ◇The course caters for a *broad* spectrum of interests. その講座は人々のさまざまな好奇心にこたえます ◇We have devised a *broad* and balanced curriculum. 私たちは幅広くバランスのとれたカリキュラムとなるよう工夫しました ◇Having children gave her a *broader* outlook on life. 子どもを持つことで, 彼女はより幅広い人生観を得た ◇The novel is about education in its *broadest* sense. その小説は最も広い意味での教育を扱っています 反意 **narrow** (LIMITED 1), ☞ **breadth** (RANGE 2)

ノート **wide** と **broad** の使い分け: 多くの場合, 両語とも使用可能. しかし, **wide** は物事や人々の精選・選択・種類を表すについて用いられることが多い. ×a *broad* audience. ×a *broad* circle of friends. **wide** は広大な地理的範囲に影響を与える物事について用いられるが, **broad** は不可. ×The festival attracts people from a *broad* area. **broad** は数多くの人々に対する物事の影響について用いられることが多い. ◆to have a *broad* appeal (幅広い層の支持を得ている). ◆to attract *broad* support (幅広い支持を集める). **broad** はまた知識・教育に用いられることも多い. ◆a *broad* curriculum (広範なカリキュラム). ◆*broad* experience/knowledge (幅広い経験/知識). また, ビジネスに関連する文脈でも用いられる. ◆There is *broad* support amongst clients for the new initiative. (新しい構想を求める依頼人たちの幅広い支持を受けている).

extensive (ややフォーマル) (情報が)幅広い, 広範な, 広範囲にわたる ◇*Extensive* research has been done into this disease. この病気について広範にわたる研究が行われてきた ◇His knowledge of music is *extensive*. 彼の音楽に対する知識は広範だ ◇She has *extensive* experience in computers. 彼女はコンピューターについて幅広い経験がある

large-scale [ふつう名詞の前で] (人・物事に関して)大規模な, 広範囲にわたる ◇The proposals include *large-scale* investment in agriculture and industry. その提案には農産業に対する大規模な投資が含まれている ◇Large areas of the forest will be cleared for ranching as part of a *large-scale* development plan. 広範囲にわたる開発計画の一部としての牧場経営のために, その森林の広い部分が裸地にされることになる

mass [名詞の前で] (人・物事に影響を与えて[関して])大量の, 大衆[一般]向けの, 集団の ◇Their latest product is aimed at the *mass market*. 彼らの最新製品は大衆向けの市場に狙いを定めている ◇The play was so awful that there was a *mass exodus* from the theatre at the interval. その劇の出来はとてもひどく, 幕間で数多くの観衆が劇場を後にした

ノート **large-scale** と **mass** の使い分け: 両語ともビジネスや産業について用いられる. ◆*large-scale/mass* production/unemployment (大規模[大量]生産/の[な]失業). **large-scale** は特に大量の資源を必要とし広範囲の地域に影響を与えるビジネス活動について用いられる. ◆a *large-scale* enterprise/project/operation (大企業/大規模事業/大規模操業). **mass** は特に一か所で一斉に, 多くの人々が影響を受ける[関係する]場合に用いられることが多い. ◆the *mass* media/market (マスメディア/大衆向けの市場). ◆a *mass* movement/audience/protest/demonstration (大衆運動/一般聴衆/集団抗議運動/集団デモ). また, 多くの人々を殺害することを表す語とも結びつく. ◆a *mass* murderer/grave (大量殺人/死). ◆weapons of *mass* destruction (大量破壊兵器).

sweeping [ふつう名詞の前で] (人・物事に重大な影響を与えて)大々的な, 全面的な, 広範な ◇Shareholders have agreed to a series of *sweeping* changes in the organization of the company. 株主たちは会社の組織内の一連の全面改革に同意している ◇Security forces have given *sweeping* powers to search homes. 治安部隊は家宅捜索をする広範な権限を与えられていた ❶この意味での *sweeping* の典型的な連語に: changes, reforms, powers が挙げられる.

wide-'ranging (書き言葉) (テーマ・範囲が)多方面にわたる, 幅広い ◇The commission has been given *wide-ranging* powers. 委員会は多方面にわたる権限を与えられいた ◇The activities stimulated a *wide-ranging* discussion. 活動は幅広い議論を促した ❶ *wide-ranging* は一般的に議論や変化に関連する語と結びつく。◆a *wide-ranging* debate/discussion/review (幅広い討論／議論／見直し). ◆*wide-ranging* talks (多方面にわたる交渉). ◆*wide-ranging* reforms/changes/recommendations (広範にわたる改革／変化／推奨)

,far-'reaching [ふつう名詞の前で]《ややフォーマル》(影響・効果)が幅広い, 広範な, 広範囲にわたる ◇The decision by the European Court will have *far-reaching consequences*. 欧州裁判所による決定は広範囲にわたる影響を及ぼすだろう

wholesale [名詞の前で]《望ましくない物事が》大量の, 大規模な ◇Localized tensions had developed into *wholesale* slaughter. 局地的な緊張関係が大量殺人に発展してしまっていた

2 wide・thick・broad
一方の側から他方の側までの間隔が大きい, 向かい合う側[面]の間隔が大きい
【類語訳】幅の広い, 幅が…の, 厚い, 厚さが…の

▶a wide/ broad **road/ street/ river/ stream/ staircase/ mouth/ smile/ grin**
▶very/ extremely/ quite/ fairly/ rather/ relatively wide/ thick/ broad

wide 幅の広い[大きい]；幅が…の ◇Her face broke into a *wide* grin. 彼女は突然, 大きくにっこり笑った ◇He wore a jacket with *wide* lapels. 彼は幅の広い上着を着ていた ◇How *wide* is that stream? その小川はどのくらいの幅がありますか ◇It's about 2 metres *wide*. 幅は約2mです ◇The road was just *wide* enough for two vehicles to pass. その道路はやっと2台の車が通れるくらいの幅だった 反意 **narrow** (NARROW)

thick 厚い；厚さが…の ◇He cut two *thick* slices of bread. 彼はパンを2枚厚切りにした ◇That's a very *thick* book (= one that has a lot of pages). それは非常に厚い本である ◇She padded noiselessly across the *thick* carpet. 彼女は音を立てずに分厚いカーペットを歩いて横切った ◇Everything was covered in a *thick* layer of dust. すべての物が分厚いほこりの層で覆われていた ◇How *thick* are the walls? 壁はどれくらいの厚いですか ◇They're two feet *thick*. それらは厚さが2フィートある ❶ *thick* は本・壁・ドア・一切れの食べ物などの固形物, 物質・材料の層について用いられる。反意 **thin** (NARROW)

ノート wideとthickの使い分け：wideは時に, ドアなどについて用いられることもある。wide doorは, 正面から見て一方の側から他方の側までの「幅の広い」ドアを指す。thick doorは, 表面と裏面の間が普通よりも「厚い」ドアを指す。thick doorは重くて, thick wallsと同様に, 音を通しにくい。

broad 《しばしばほめて, 特に書き言葉》幅の広い[大きい]；幅が…の ◇We drove down a *broad* avenue lined with trees. 私たちは並木の植わった道幅の広い大通りを車で通った ◇He's got *broad* shoulders. 彼は肩幅が広い 反意 **narrow** (NARROW)

ノート wideとbroadの使い分け：broadはwideほど頻繁には用いられず, 話し言葉よりも書き言葉で用いられることが多い。物が魅力的な形で幅が広いことを示唆するのに用いられることが多い。◆a *broad* avenue lined with trees (並木の植わった道幅の広い大通り). ◆He was gorgeous — *broad* shoulders and twinkling eyes. (彼はかっこよかった―肩幅が広く目が輝いていた). しかし体の部位について*wide*よりも頻繁に用いられる。◆a *broad* back/ chest/face/forehead (広い背中/胸/顔/額). しかし両語とも, grin, smileとは用いることができる。

wild 形

wild・disruptive・unruly・disorderly・rowdy
人や行動, 感情が抑制が利かない[制御が難しい]ことを表す
【類語訳】乱暴な, 凶暴な, 荒っぽい, 無法な, 自由奔放な, 自堕落な, 破壊的な, 手に負えない, 抑えがたい, 騒々しい

▶wild/ disruptive/ unruly/ disorderly/ rowdy **behaviour**
▶an unruly/ a disorderly/ a rowdy **crowd**

wild 乱暴な, 凶暴な, 荒っぽい, 無法な, 自由奔放な, 自堕落な ◇There is a *wild* side to him. 彼には荒っぽい側面がある ◇He had a *wild* look in his eyes. 彼は凶暴な目つきをしていた ◇Those girls have been allowed to **run *wild*** (= behave as they like because nobody is controlling them). その少女たちは自由奔放に振る舞うことを許されてきた

disruptive 《通常の形で持続[機能]できなくなるほど》崩壊[分裂]させる, 破壊的な ◇She was a *disruptive influence* on the rest of the class. 彼女はクラス全体を分裂させる影響力を持っていた ◇Working such long hours can be extremely *disruptive* to home life. そんなに長い時間働くと, 家庭生活をひどく崩壊させることになるかもしれない

unruly 《ややフォーマル》乱暴な, 無法な, 手に負えない, 抑えがたい ◇The police were attacked by an *unruly* mob. 警察は無法な暴徒たちに攻撃された ◇He struggled hard to control his *unruly* emotions. 彼は抑えがたい感情を必死に抑えようとした

disorderly [ふつう名詞の前で]《フォーマル》(公共の場で)乱暴な, 無法な, 騒々しい, 治安びん乱の, 風紀を乱す ◇He has been charged with *disorderly conduct*. 彼は治安びん乱行為の容疑で告発された ◇They were arrested for being *drunk and disorderly*. 彼らは酔って風紀を乱したとして逮捕された 反意 **orderly** (EFFICIENT), ☞ **disorder** (TROUBLE 1)

rowdy 《集団で》乱暴な, 無法な, 騒々しい ◇Some lads were getting a bit *rowdy*. 何人かの若者たちが少し暴れていた ◇The meeting had been quite *rowdy*. 会議は実に騒然としていた

win 動 ☞ DEFEAT

win・prevail・win out・triumph・win the day・come out on top
人より[困難にもかかわらず]優れている
【類語訳】勝つ, 勝利する, 優勝する, 勝ち取る, 優勢である, 勝つ, うまくいく, 奏功する, 打ち勝つ, 成功する

▶to win/ prevail/ win the day **against** sb
▶to prevail/ win out/ triumph **over** sb/ sth

▶to win/ prevail/ win out/ triumph **in the end**
▶to **eventually/ ultimately** win/ prevail/ triumph/ win the day/ come out on top
▶to **finally** win/ prevail/ win out/ triumph/ win the day

win [自, 他]（競技・競走・選挙・議論・戦闘・戦争で）勝利する, 優勢する, 勝ち取る ◇Which team *won*? どちらのチームが勝ったの ◇France *won* by six goals to two against Denmark. フランスが6対2でデンマークに勝利した ◇He always *won at* cards. 彼はトランプではいつも勝った ◇He *narrowly won* (= by a small margin) the seat for Labour. 彼は労働党の議席をかろうじて勝ち取った ◇I think I *won* the argument. 議論に勝ったと思う ◇Historians still argue about who really *won* the war of 1812. 歴史家たちはいまだに1812年戦争で実際には（米英）どちらの国が勝利したのかについて議論している [反意] **lose**, ☞ **win** (VICTORY)

prevail [自]《フォーマル》(考え・意見が奮闘[議論])広まっている, 普及している, 優勢である, 勝つ ◇Justice will *prevail* over tyranny. 正義は専制政治に打ち勝つだろう ◇Fortunately, *common sense prevailed*. 幸いにも, 常識が勝った ❶ *prevail* にはスポーツで相手を「打ち破る」の意味もある. ☞ **prevail** (DEFEAT)

,win 'out [句動]《ややインフォーマル》(困難にもかかわらず) 勝利する, うまくいく, 奏功する ◇It remains to be seen whether the archaeologists will *win out* over the planners in this dispute. この論争で考古学者たちが施工計画者たちに勝つかどうかはまだわからない ◇Economic efficiency will always *win out* in the end. 最終的には, 経済効率が常に優先されるだろう

triumph [自]《書き言葉》(人・物事に)勝利する, 打ち勝つ ; (困難にもかかわらず)成功する, うまくいく ◇Italy *triumphed* 3-0 in the quarter-finals. イタリアは準々決勝で3-0で勝利した ◇As usual in this kind of movie, good *triumphs* over evil in the end. この種の映画によくあるように, 最終的には善が悪に打つのだ

win the 'day [句動]《書き言葉, 特にジャーナリズム》(議論[困難な状況])の末に人・物事に)勝利する ◇Consumer pressure has finally *won the day* and forced a change in the law. 消費者の圧力がついには勝利を収め, 法改正を余儀なくさせた

come out on 'top [句動]《ややインフォーマル》(競技・議論で人に)勝つ, 勝利する ◇The older child, stronger and more experienced, is bound to *come out on top*. 力が強く経験豊富な年上の子がきっと勝つ

wise [形]

wise・sensible・prudent
人が経験と知識のおかげで, 的確な判断を下す[よい助言を与える]ことができることを表す
【類語訳】賢い, 賢明な, 知恵のある, 分別のある, 思慮深い, 慎重な

[文型&コロケーション]
▶a wise/ sensible/ prudent **person/ man/ woman**

wise 賢い, 賢明な, 知恵のある ◇He was too *wise* and experienced to try to escape. 彼はあまりに賢くて経験豊富なため, 逃げ出そうとしなかった ◇I'm *older and wiser* after ten years in the business. 私はその仕事に10年携わった結果, 相応の年齢と知恵を身につけている [反意] **fool-**

ish (CRAZY), ☞ **wisdom** (KNOWLEDGE)
▶**wisely** [副] ◇She *wisely* turned down the offer. 彼女は賢明にもその申し出を断った

sensible 分別[良識]のある, 賢明な ◇I wish you'd be *sensible* for once! 今回に限ってはあなたに分別があればなあと思う ◇She was a pleasant, *sensible* woman. 彼女は愛想よく良識のある女性だった [反意] **stupid** (CRAZY), ☞ **mature** (ADULT)
▶**sensibly** [副] ◇*Sensibly* they decided not to oppose the case. 彼らは賢明にもその主張に反対しないことにした

> [ノート] **wise** と **sensible** の使い分け : **wise** は経験を通じて獲得され, よいことに使われる知識によって尊敬される年上の人々を指すのにも用いられることが多い. **sensible** は日常の実際問題において適切な判断を下すあらゆる年齢の人々を指すのに用いられる. **sensible** であることはよい性質であるのだが, 時としてかなり退屈だとみなされることもある.

prudent 思慮[用心]深い, 慎重な ◇She has always been a *prudent* businesswoman. 彼女は常に思慮深い実業家としてやってきた ❶ *prudent* の反意語である *imprudent* は, 人についてよりもはるかに頻繁に行動・決定について用いられる.

wish [名]

wish・request・will
人が持ちたい[起こってほしい]と思う気持ちを表す
【類語訳】願い, 望み, 願望, 意向, 頼み, 依頼, 要望, 要求, 要請, リクエスト, 意思

[文型&コロケーション]
▶a wish/ request **for** sth
▶**against** sb's wish/ will
▶sb's **particular/ personal/ dying** wish/ request
▶sb's **conscious** wish/ will
▶to **have/ express/ consider/ comply with/ ignore** a wish/ request
▶to **obey/ go against** sb's wishes/ will

wish [C]《ややフォーマル》願い(事), 望み(事), 願望, 意向 ◇He refused to carry out her *wishes*. 彼は彼女の願いを叶えようとはしなかった ◇I'm sure that you will *get your wish*. あなたの望みはきっと叶うと思います ◇She married against her parents' *wishes*. 彼女は両親の意に反した結婚をした ☞ **wish** (DESIRE), **wish** (HOPE) [動]

request [C]《ややフォーマル》(正式な)頼み(事), 依頼, 要望, 要求, 要請, リクエスト ◇My *request* was granted. 私の頼み事は聞き入れられた ◇a radio *request* programme (= a programme of music that listeners have asked for) ラジオのリクエスト番組 ☞ **request** (REQUEST), **request** (ASK 2)

will [単数で]《フォーマル》(特定の状況での)意思, 意向, 願望 ◇I don't want to go against your *will*. 私はあなたの意向に反したくはない ◇They governed according to the *will* of the people. 国民の意思に従って統治が行われた ❶ *will* は人民の生活に関連する文脈で用いられることが多い.
◆ the collective/general/majority/national/popular/public *will*（総体的な/一般の/多数の/国家としての/大衆の/人民の意思）

witness, woman, wonderful

witness 名 ☞AUDIENCE

witness・observer・onlooker・passer-by・bystander・eyewitness
物事が起こるのを見る人
【類語訳】目撃者, 証人, 観察者, 見物人, 通行人

文型&コロケーション
▶ a witness/ an observer/ an onlooker/ a passer-by/ a bystander/ an eyewitness **sees** sb/ sth
▶ an observer/ an onlooker/ a passer-by/ a bystander **witnesses** sth

witness [C] 目撃者；(法廷での)証人 ◇Police have appealed for *witnesses to* the accident. 警察はその事故の目撃者が名乗りでてくれるよう呼びかけをしている ◇a prosecution/defence *witness* 検察/弁護側の証人 ◇She appeared as a *witness for* the prosecution. 彼女は検察側の証人として登場した ◇Several *witnesses* testified that there had been two gunmen. 銃を持った人間が二人いたと, 数人の目撃者が証言した ☞ **witness** (NOTICE)
observer [C] 観察者, 見物人 ◇*To the casual observer*, it would have looked like any other domestic argument. 事情を知らない人が見たら, それはよくある家庭内の口論のように見えただろう ◇According to *observers*, the plane exploded shortly after take-off. 見ていた人たちによれば, その飛行機は離陸後間もなく爆発したとのことだ ☞ **observe** (NOTICE)
onlooker [C] (巻き込まれなかった)見物人 ◇A crowd of *onlookers* gathered at the scene of the crash. 大勢の見物人が墜落現場に集まった
‚passer-'by (複 passers-by) [C] (偶然その場を通りがかった)通行人 ◇Police asked *passers-by* if they had witnessed the accident. 警察はその事故を目撃したかどうか通行人に尋ねた
bystander [C] (事故・けんかなどの)近くにいた人 ◇Three innocent *bystanders* were killed in the crossfire. 近くにいた罪のない3人の人が十字砲火で殺された
eyewitness [C] (犯罪・事故などの)目撃者 ◇One *eyewitness* saw the gunmen leave the building. 一人の目撃者が銃を持った男たちがビルから出て来るのを見た ◇He gave an *eyewitness account* of the suffering of the refugees. 彼は難民の苦難について目撃証言を行った

woman 名

woman・lady・female
成人で男性ではない人
【類語訳】女, 女性, 婦人, 淑女, 女子

文型&コロケーション
▶ a/ an **young/ older** woman/ lady/ female
▶ a/ an **middle-aged/ old/ elderly** woman/ lady/ female
▶ a **black/ white** woman/ lady/ female
▶ a **married/ single/ unmarried** woman/ lady
▶ a **beautiful/ attractive** woman/ lady/ female
▶ a **nice/ fine/ charming** woman/ lady

woman [C] (成人の)女, 女性 ◇a 24-year-old *woman* 24歳の女性 ◇Alcohol affects men and *women* differently. アルコールは男女に対して異なる影響を与える ◇I prefer to see a *woman* doctor. 女医さんに診てもらいたい 反意 **man** (MAN 1)
lady [C] 女性, 婦人, 淑女(見知らぬ女性に対する丁寧な表現) ◇There's a *lady* waiting to see you. あなたにお会いしたいという女性がお待ちです ❶複数形の ladies は, 二人以上の女性に対する丁寧かフォーマルな呼びかけに用いられる. ◆Can I take your coats, *ladies*? (ご婦人方, コートをお預りしましょうか) ◆*Ladies and gentlemen*! Can I have your attention, please? (紳士淑女の皆さん, ご注目ください) 一人の女性に呼びかける場合は, madam または ma'am を用いることができる. ◆Can I take your coat, *madam/ma'am*? (奥様, コートをお預りしましょうか). しかし, 中には lady や madam と呼ばれたくない女性もいるため, 使わないという人もいる. ◆There's someone waiting to see you. (あなたにお会いしたいという方がお待ちです) ◆Can I take your coats? (コートをお預りしましょうか) 反意 **gentleman** (MAN 1)
female [C] 《フォーマル or 専門語》(少女を含む)女, 女性, 女子 ◇The body is that of a white *female* aged about 30. 遺体は30歳くらいの白人女性のものだ ◇More *females* than males are employed in the factory. その工場では男性よりも女性のほうがたくさん雇われている ❶名詞の female はほとんどの場合, フォーマル[公式, 科学的, 医学的]な文脈で用いられる. 反意 **male** (MAN 1)

wonderful 形 ☞EXCELLENT, GOOD 1, MAGNIFICENT, NICE 1, SATISFYING

wonderful・lovely・marvellous・delightful・delicious
大きな喜び[楽しみ]を与えてくれる経験[感情, 光景]を表す
【類語訳】すてきな, 最高の, うれしい, 素晴らしい, 見事な, 美しい, 驚くべき, 絶好の, 楽しい, 心地よい

文型&コロケーション
▶ a wonderful/ lovely/ marvellous/ delightful/ delicious **feeling/ sensation**
▶ (a) wonderful/ lovely/ marvellous/ delightful **experience/ evening/ time/ party/ place/ views/ scenery/ weather**
▶ What a wonderful/ lovely/ marvellous/ delightful/ delicious **surprise**!
▶ It would be wonderful/ lovely/ delightful **if**...
▶ It's wonderful/ lovely/ marvellous **that**...
▶ It's wonderful/ lovely/ marvellous **to be/ feel/ find/ have/ know/ see**...
▶ That **sounds** wonderful/ lovely/ marvellous/ delightful.
▶ **really/ quite/ absolutely** wonderful/ lovely/ marvellous/ delightful

wonderful (大いに楽しんで)すてきな, 最高の；(大きな喜び[楽しみ]を与えてくれて)うれしい；(極めてよくて)素晴らしい, 見事な ◇We had a *wonderful* time last night. 私たちは昨晩, すてきな時間を過ごした ◇It's *wonderful* to see you! お会いできてうれしいです ◇The weather was absolutely *wonderful*. 実に素晴らしいお天気だった ◇Note the *wonderful* skill in these sculpted hands and faces. これらの手と顔の彫刻の見事な技にご注目ください ☞ **wonder** (MIRACLE)
▷**wonderfully** 副 ◇The hotel is *wonderfully* comfortable. そのホテルは素晴らしく快適です ◇Things have worked out *wonderfully* (well). 物事が最高にうまくいった

lovely《特に英、ややインフォーマル、特に話し言葉》(大いに楽しんで)素晴らしい、すてきな；(大きな喜び[楽しみ]を与えてくれて)；(非常に魅力的で)美しい ◇We had a *lovely* day (= we really enjoyed ourselves). すてきな一日だった ◇What a *lovely* day (= the weather is very good)! 何て素晴らしい日和なの ◇'Can I get you anything?' 'A cup of tea would be *lovely*.' 「何かほしいものは」「お茶を一杯いただけますか」 ◇It's been *lovely* having you here. あなたがここにいてくれてうれしい ◇It's a *lovely* old farmhouse. それは美しい古い農家です ❶《英》の話し言葉では、lovely は物事がいかに心地よいかを強調するために、形容詞の前で用いることがある。◆a *lovely* cool drink (素晴らしい冷たい飲み物)。◇It's *lovely* and warm in here.(ここは暖かくていいところね)。「lovely＋形容詞」は名詞の前で用いることはできない。×a *lovely* and warm place.

marvellous《英》(《米》**marvelous**)《ややインフォーマル、特に話し言葉》(大きな喜び[楽しみ]を与えてくれて)素晴らしい、驚くべき；(極めてよくて)絶好の ◇The food smells absolutely *marvellous*. その食べ物の匂いはこの上なく素晴らしい匂いがする ◇This will be a *marvellous* opportunity for her. これは彼女にとって絶好の機会となるでしょう ◇It's *marvellous* what modern technology can do. 現代技術が可能にしてくれることは素晴らしいわ ☞ **marvel** (MIRACLE)

▷ **marvellously** 副 《英》(《米》**marvelously**) ◇This recipe is *marvellously* simple and quick. このレシピは驚くほど簡単で素早くできます

【ノート】**wonderful と marvellous の使い分け**：marvellousのほうがいくぶん wonderful よりもインフォーマルで、特に話し言葉で用いられる。

delightful(大きな喜び[楽しみ]を与えてくれて)うれしい、楽しい；(非常に魅力的で)美しい ◇It has been a most *delightful* evening. すごく楽しい夜だったね ◇It was a *delightful* little fishing village. そこは美しい小さな漁村だった

▷ **delightfully** 副 ◇The hotel is *delightfully* situated on the edge of the lake. うれしいことに、そのホテルは湖畔にあるの

【ノート】**wonderful, lovely, delightful の使い分け**：これらの語はすべて、時間・出来事・場所、光景・感情・天気に用いることができる。wonderful はまた機会・能力にも用いることもできる。×a *lovely/delightful* opportunity/skill. lovely は《英》の話し言葉で最も頻繁に用いられるが、《米》では、話し言葉でも書き言葉でも wonderful が最も使用頻度が高い。delightful は特に、時間・出来事・場所について用いられる

delicious《文語》(肉体的に大きな喜び[楽しみ]を与えてくれて)心地よい ◇the *delicious* coolness of the breeze そよ風の心地よい涼しさ ◇A *delicious* shiver of excitement ran through his body. 彼の体に心地よい武者震いが走った

▷ **deliciously** 副 ◇The water was *deliciously* cool. 水は心地よく冷たかった

work 名

1 ☞ **JOB**

work・employment・career・profession・occupation・practice・trade

長期間にわたって人が報酬の見返りに行う働き

【類語訳】仕事、職業、雇用、就業、経歴、専門職、開業

【文型&コロケーション】

- sb's **chosen** work/ employment/ career/ profession/ occupation/ trade
- (a) **skilled/ manual** work/ employment/ occupation/ trade
- (a) **professional** work/ employment/ career/ occupation/ practice
- (a) **full-time/ part-time/ permanent** work/ employment/ career/ occupation
- (a) **regular** work/ employment/ occupation/ trade
- (a) **casual/ seasonal** work/ employment/ occupation
- (a) **well-paid** work/ employment/ profession/ occupation
- (a) **low-paid** work/ employment/ occupation
- to **have/ pursue** work/ employment/ a career/ a profession/ an occupation/ a trade
- to **take up** work/ employment/ a career/ a profession/ an occupation/ ...practice/ a trade
- to **go back/ return** to work/ employment/ a career/ a profession/ ...practice
- to **look for/ seek/ find** work/ employment/ a career/ an occupation

work [U] 仕事、職業 ◇He's been *out of work* for over a year. 彼は一年以上失業している ◇It is a country where most women with young children are *in paid work*.《英》その国では幼い子どものいる女性のほとんどが有給の仕事に就いている ◇She's planning to return to *work* in September. 彼女は9月に職場復帰する予定だ ◇Would you give up *work* if you won the lottery? もし宝くじが当たったら、仕事を辞めるかい ◇Any kind of *work with* kids would suit him fine. 子どもに関わる仕事ならどんなものでも彼には向いているだろうな ◇'Where's John?' 'He's still *at work*.' 「ジョンはどこ」「彼はまだ職場だよ」 ◇She's been *off work* (= not at work) for three weeks. 彼女は3週間仕事から離れている ◇He *started work* as a security guard. 彼は警備員の仕事を始めた

employment [U]《ややフォーマル》仕事、職業；雇用[就業](状態) ◇It's getting more and more difficult for young people to find regular *employment*. 若者が定職に就くのがますます難しくなってきている ◇The government aims to have *full employment* (= a situation in which everyone who wants a job has one) within five years. 政府は5年以内に完全雇用を実現することを目指している 反意 **unemployment** (UNEMPLOYMENT), ☞ **employ** (EMPLOY)

career [C] (時が経つにつれ大きな責任を伴う特定分野の)仕事、職業、経歴 ◇I never wanted a military *career*. 兵役には就きたいと思ったことはない ◇Kelly's *career* took off (= started to be successful) when she was spotted at a talent contest. タレント・コンテストで注目されたときにケリーの成功への経歴は始まった ◇His *career* spanned (= continued over) four decades. 彼の経歴は40年に及んだ ◇By 2001, she was at *the peak of her career* (= at the most successful point in her career). 2001年には、彼女はキャリアの頂点に達していた ◇I didn't think it was a very good *career move*. あまりいい転職だったとは思わなかった ◇It's time for a *career change*. 転職する時だ

profession [C]《特別な訓練・技術・教育を必要とする》職業、知的職業、専門職 ◇Alan's a teacher *by profes-*

sion. アランの職業は教師です ◇He hopes to **enter** the medical *profession*. 彼は医療の世界に入りたいと思っている ◇I **joined** the *profession* when I was in my early twenties. 私は20代の初めにその職業に就いた ◇She's at the **top of** her *profession*. 彼女は自分の職業の上で今盛期を迎えている ❶特に《英》では、複数形の professions は、医師・弁護士など、高水準の教育・訓練を必要とする伝統的な職業を指す。◆ employment in industry and the *professions*（産業および知的職業における雇用）. the profession[単数形＋単数・複数動詞]は特定の業界で働くすべての人々を指す

▶**professional** [形] ◇Most of the people on the course were *professional* women. その講座に出ていた人のほとんどが専門職に就いている女性だった ◆ *professional* qualifications/skills 専門職の資格/技術

occupation [C]《ややフォーマル》仕事、職業 ◇Please state your name, age, and *occupation*. お名前、年齢、ご職業をおっしゃってください ◇Why is nursing still seen as a female *occupation*? なぜいまだに看護は女性の仕事だと見なされているのか

practice [U]（医師・弁護士などの）仕事、開業 ◇Students should have prior experience of veterinary *practice*. 学生たちは獣医の仕事を事前に体験しておくとよい ◇My analyst is no longer in *practice*. 私の精神分析医はもう開業していない ☞ **practice** (COMPANY).

trade [C]（手仕事を伴う特別な訓練・技術を必要とする）仕事、職業 ◇She's now a carpenter **by** *trade*. 彼女は今大工（職人）です ◇My parents always wanted me to leave school early and **learn a** *trade*. 両親はいつも私に早く学校を辞めて、仕事を覚えてほしがっていた ☞ **trade** (INDUSTRY).

2 work・writings・piece・masterpiece・composition・work of art・oeuvre

画家[作家、音楽家]によって創り出される物
【類語訳】作品、楽曲、著書、著作集、詩、傑作、芸術作品

〖文型&コロケーション〗
▶a work/ piece/ masterpiece/ composition/ work of art **by** sb
▶a/ an **great/ original** work/ piece/ masterpiece/ composition/ work of art
▶a/ an **orchestral/ choral** work/ piece/ masterpiece/ composition
▶a/ an **classical/ abstract** work/ piece/ composition
▶sb's **collected/ complete** works/ writings
▶to **perform** a work/ piece/ composition

work [C]（本・絵画の）作品、（音楽の）楽曲 ◇The film is based on an early *work* by Alan Moore. その映画はアラン・ムーアの初期の作品に基づいている ◆ *works* of fiction/literature 小説／文学作品 ◆ Chopin's piano *works* ショパンのピアノ曲

writings [複数形]（特定の人による）（特定のテーマに関する）著書、著作集 ◇His experiences in Morocco influenced his later *writings*. モロッコにおける体験が彼の後期の著作に影響を与えた ◆ the *writings* of Sun Tzu 孫子の著作集

piece [C]（音楽の）楽曲、（一編の）詩、（著作・美術の）作品 ◇The orchestra performed *pieces* by Ravel and Prokofiev. オーケストラはラヴェルとプロコフィエフの楽曲を演奏した ❶ piece of music/writing/poetry/art（楽曲／著

一編の詩／美術品）と言えるが、piece 自体はふつう、フォーマルな言い回しや文脈が明らかな場合を除いて、「楽曲」を意味する。◆ Auditioning students are required to play a solo *piece* of their choice.（オーディションを受ける学生は、自分で選んだソロの楽曲を演奏することが求められる）. ◆ They have some beautiful *pieces* (= paintings, drawings, etc.) in their home.《フォーマル》彼らは自宅に美術品を所有しています ☞ **piece** (ARTICLE).

masterpiece [C]（美術・文学などの）（最高）傑作、代表作 ◇The work has been described as a literary *masterpiece*. その作品は文学の最高傑作と評されてきた ◇This is an excellent production of Verdi's *masterpiece*. これはヴェルディの代表作の傑出した上演である ◇Her work is a *masterpiece* of simplicity (= an excellent example of sth simple). 彼女の作品は見事なまでにシンプルである

composition [C]《フォーマル》（音楽の）楽曲、（一編の）詩、（美術の）作品 ◇one of Stravinsky's finest *compositions* ストラヴィンスキーの最高の楽曲の一つ

〖ノート〗**work, piece, composition** の使い分け：work は人が努力して創り出した物を強調し、あらゆる種類の芸術・文学・音楽の作品について用いることができる。piece は短い楽曲について用いられることが多い。composition もまた音楽について用いられることがほとんどだが、詩・美術について用いられることもある。

,work of 'art (複 **works of art**) [C]（絵画・線画・彫像の）芸術作品 ◇A number of priceless *works of art* were stolen from the gallery. いくつもの値の付けられないほど貴重な芸術作品が美術館から盗まれた

oeuvre [単数形で]《フランス語から、フォーマル》（作家・画家・作曲家の）（全）作品 ◇She created an *oeuvre* that is both refreshing and overwhelming. 彼女は清々しくかつ人を圧倒するような作品を創作した

work [動]

1 work・be employed・have a job・earn a/your living・be in work・practise

仕事を通じて金を稼ぐ
【類語訳】働いている、携わっている、生計を立てる、開業している

〖文型&コロケーション〗
▶to work/ be employed/ have a job/ earn a living/ practise **as** sth
▶to work/ be employed/ have a job **at** a place

work [自] 仕事をしている、働いている ◇Both my parents *work*. 私の両親は二人とも働いている ◇She *works* **for** an engineering company. 彼女は工学系の会社で働いている ◇I've always *worked* in education. 私はずっと教育界で働いてきた ◇Do you enjoy *working* **with** children? 子どもたちと関わる仕事は楽しいですか

be em'ployed [他, 受身で]《ややフォーマル》仕事をしている、働いている、携わっている ◇For the past three years he has *been employed* as a firefighter. 彼はこの3年間、消防士として働いてきた ◇A number of people are *employed* **to** deal with the backlog of work. 相当数の人々が残務処理にあたるために雇われている ☞ **employ** (EMPLOY), **unemployed** (UNEMPLOYED).

,have a 'job [フレ] 仕事をしている、働いている、職に就いている ◇She *had a job* as a waitress. 彼女はウェイトレス

仕事をしていた ◇I've got a temporary job at the moment. 私は現在, 臨時の仕事に就いています ◇She's never had a steady job (= a job that is not going to end suddenly). 彼女は定職に就いたことがない

ノート work, be employed, have a jobの使い分け：
workはこれらの語の中で最も一般的な語で, 人が特定の仕事に就く特定の仕事, 一般的な種類の仕事, 単に働いているという事実について用いられる。be employedはしばしばasやtoを伴って, ほとんどの場合, 特定の仕事や一般的な種類の仕事について用いられる。◆ be employed as a teacher (教師として働いていて), ◆ be employed to train users in the new system (新システムの利用者の訓練に携わっている). have a jobは失業していないという事実について用いられることが多い。◆ Do you have a job? (仕事はしてるの). また, workと同じようにasと共に用いられることもある。◆ She worked/had a job as a waitress in a cocktail bar. (彼女はカクテルバーでウェイトレスとして働いていた). have a jobはほとんどの場合, 過去形で用いられ, 雇用期間がより一時的であることも示唆する。have a jobはworkよりもいくぶんインフォーマルなことがある。

,earn a/your 'living フレーズ 生計を立てる ◇She earns her living as a freelance journalist. 彼女はフリージャーナリストとして生計を立てている
be in work フレーズ (英) (失業状態との対比で)職に就いている ◇Most of those who were in work had temporary jobs. 仕事に就いている人のほとんどが臨時職だった
☞ **out of work** (UNEMPLOYED)
practise (英) (米**practice**) [自, 他] (医師・弁護士などとして)開業している ◇There are over 50,000 solicitors practising in England and Wales. イングランドおよびウェールズで開業している事務弁護士は5万人以上います ◇He practised as a lawyer for many years. 彼は長年, 弁護士を開業していた ◇She was banned from practising medicine. 彼女は医師としての業務に携わることを禁じられた

2 ☞ OPERATE
work・function・run・operate・go
機械[システム, 装置]を正しく形で運用することができる
【類語訳】作動する, 稼動する, 機能する, 動く, 作用する, 営業している

▸to **actually/ still** work/ function/ go
▸to work/ function/ run/ operate **efficiently/ satisfactorily/ smoothly/ independently/ successfully/ normally/ reliably**
▸to work/ function/ run **perfectly**
▸to work/ function/ operate **effectively/ properly/ correctly**
▸to work/ function **well**
▸to run/ operate **continuously**
▸**fully** functioning/ operating

work [自] (機械・装置が)作動[稼動, 機能]する, 動く, 働く ◇The phone isn't working. その電話は通じていない ◇It works by electricity. それは電気で動きます ◇Are they any closer to understanding how the brain works? 彼らは脳の仕組みについての理解が少しは進んでいるのでしょうか ☞ work (OPERATE)
function [自] (ふつう副詞や前置詞と共に) (ややフォーマル) 機

能[作用, 作動]する, 働く ◇Despite the power cuts, the hospital continued to function normally. 停電にもかかわらず, 病院は正常に機能し続けた ◇Many children can't function effectively in large classes. 大学級では, 多くの子どもたちの学習効果が上がっていない ◇We now have a functioning shower. 私たちは今, シャワーが使えるようになっています
run [自] 作動[稼動]する, 動く ◇Stan had the chainsaw running. スタンはチェーンソーを作動させていた ◇Our van runs on (= uses) diesel. うちのバンはディーゼルエンジンです ◇Which operating system have you got running? どのオペレーティングシステムを作動させているのですか ❶ runはふつうエンジン, モーター, エンジン[モーター]で動く機械, コンピュータープログラムについて用いられる。☞ **run** (OPERATE), **up and running** (ACTIVE)
operate [自] (ふつう副詞や前置詞と共に) (ややフォーマル) (機械が特定の形で)作動[稼動, 機能]する, 動く, 働く ;(サービス・システムが)営業[作動]している ◇Solar panels can only operate in sunlight. 太陽パネルは日光が当たらないと機能しない ◇Some people can only operate well under pressure. 圧力がかからないとよく動かない人もいる ◇A new late-night service is now operating. 現在, 新たな深夜営業を実施しております ☞ **operate** (OPERATE)
▸ **operation** [名] [U] ◇Regular servicing guarantees the smooth operation of the engine. 定期点検をさせていただくことで, エンジンのスムーズな作動が保証されます ☞ **in operation, operational** (ACTIVE)

ノート functionとoperateの使い分け：functionは物事が機能するかどうか[いかにうまく[まずく]機能するか]について用いられることが多い。operateは物事が機能するのに必要な条件について用いられる。

go [自] (インフォーマル, 特に話し言葉) (機械が)作動する, 動く ◇What makes it go? それは何で動くの

worker [名]

1 ☞ STAFF
worker・employee・staff member・member of staff
会社などの組織で働く人
【類語訳】労働者, 従業員, 職員, 作業員, 工員, 社員

▸a/ an **full-time/ part-time/ female/ male/ experienced/ key** worker/ employee/ staff member/ member of staff
▸a **permanent/ junior/ senior** employee/ staff member/ member of staff
▸to **have/ employ/ dismiss** a worker/ an employee/ a staff member/ a member of staff
▸to **fire** a worker/ an employee/ a staff member
▸to **sack** a worker/ an employee/ a staff member
▸a worker/ an employee/ a staff member/ a member of staff **works**

worker [C] (しばしば複合語で) 仕事をする[働く]人, (特定の種類の仕事をする)労働者, 従業員, 職員, 作業員, 工員 ◇Aid workers quickly arrived at the scene of the disaster. 救援隊員たちが災害現場にすぐに到着した ◇There are few jobs available for manual workers. 肉体労働者向けの仕事はほとんどない ◇We will take on several casual workers over the summer months. 私たちは夏の数か月, 数人の臨時工を雇い入れる予定です ❶ こ

の意味の worker は人が働く場所，仕事の種類，結ぶ雇用契約の種類を表す複合語で用いられることが多い．◆ office/ farm/factory workers（内勤者／農業労働者／工場労働者）．◆ rescue/aid/research workers（救助隊員／救援隊員／研究員）．◆ skilled/unskilled/manual/blue-collar/white-collar workers（熟練工／未熟練工／肉体労働者／ブルーカラー／ホワイトカラー）．◆ temporary/part-time/casual/seasonal/migrant workers（臨時工／パート従業員／臨時雇い／季節労働者／移民労働者）．

employee [C]（人のために働いて報酬を受ける）従業員，社員 ◇The firm has over 500 *employees*. その企業には500人以上の従業員がいる

staff member [C]《特に米》(組織に雇われている) 職員 ◇Three hospital *staff members* were suspended after the incident. その事件の後で，3人の病院職員が停職になった

,member of 'staff [C]《英》(組織に雇われている) 職員 ◇All *members of staff* work as a team to achieve customer satisfaction. すべての職員が顧客の満足を達成するためにチームとして働いている

ノート **employee, staff member, member of staff の使い分け**：employee は多数の従業員がいる会社の従業員である場合も，他に従業員がいない個人の元での従業員である場合もある．staff member, member of staff は少なくとも数人の人を雇っている会社・組織のために働く従業員に用いられる．しかし，employee はほとんどの場合，従業員全体，特に雇用条件 [条項] を問題にする場合に用いられる．個人 (が行う仕事) に言及する場合は，ふつう staff member, member of staff を用いる．☞ **staff** (STAFF)

2 worker・labourer・staff・workman
組織において経営者よりも下位にいて，物事を組織したり人々を管理するのではなく，体を使って働く人のことを表す
【類語訳】労働者，職員，肉体労働者

文型&コロケーション
▶ (a) **skilled** worker/ labourer/ workman
▶ (an) **unskilled** worker/ labourer
▶ (a) **female/ male** worker/ staff
▶ an **unemployed** worker/ labourer/ workman
▶ to **employ** a worker/ a labourer/ staff/ a workman
▶ workers/ labourers/ staff/ workmen **work**

worker [C]（経営者に対する）労働者 ◇Conflict between employers and *workers* intensified. 労使紛争は激化した ◇Talks between *workers* and management have ended today. 労使交渉は今日終わった

labourer《英》《米 **laborer**》[C]（屋外労働に携わる未熟練の）(肉体) 労働者 ◇He managed to get a job as an agricultural *labourer*. 彼はやっとのことで農業労働者の仕事を得た

staff［単数で］《米》(学校・大学の教員以外の) 職員 ◇Students, faculty and *staff* were all men in those days. 学生・教員・職員は当時，全員男性だった ☞ **staff** (STAFF)

workman [C] 肉体労働者 ◇A gang of *workmen* were shovelling rubble into a truck. 肉体労働者の一団が瓦礫をシャベルですくってトラックに投げ込んでいた

ノート **labourer と workman の使い分け**：labourer はしばしば農場・地方で，きつい肉体労働を行う．workman はふつう建設 [補修] 工事を行う．labourer, workman は両語とも熟練している場合にも熟練していない場合にも用いることができるが，一般的には workman は labourer よりも熟練していて，機械や技術を使える傾向にある．例えば，builder（建設労働者）は workman と呼べるだろう．builder's labourer は，それほど熟練を必要としない仕事をして builder の補佐をする人を指す．

worried 形 ☞ AFRAID, RESTLESS

worried・concerned・nervous・anxious・uneasy・bothered・troubled・disturbed・apprehensive
不快な物事が起こる [起きた] かもしれないと考えて，冷静さをなくすことを表す
【類語訳】不安な，緊張した，びくびくした，怖がった，落ち着かない，そわそわした，動揺した，気がかりな

文型&コロケーション
▶ to be worried/ concerned/ nervous/ anxious/ uneasy/ bothered/ troubled/ disturbed/ apprehensive **about** sth
▶ to be worried/ concerned/ anxious **for** sb/ sth
▶ to be worried/ concerned/ nervous/ anxious/ bothered/ disturbed/ apprehensive **that** ...
▶ a worried/ a concerned/ a nervous/ an anxious/ an uneasy/ a troubled/ an apprehensive **expression/ look/ smile**
▶ a worried/ a concerned/ a nervous/ an anxious/ a troubled **voice**
▶ to **get** worried/ nervous/ anxious/ apprehensive

worried 心配した，不安な ◇Don't look so *worried*! そんなに心配そうな顔しないで ◇I'm not *worried* about her — she can take care of herself. 私は彼女のことは心配していない—彼女は自分のことは自分でできるからさ ◇I was *worried* (that) I would fail the exam. 試験に落ちるんじゃないかと不安だった ◇Where have you been? I've been *worried sick* (= extremely worried). どこにいたの．とっても心配してたんだよ ☞ **worry** (CONCERN)
▶**worriedly** 副 ◇He glanced *worriedly* at his father. 彼は心配そうに父親をちらっと見た

concerned 心配 [懸念] した ◇The President is deeply *concerned* about this issue. 大統領はこの問題について深く懸念している ◇I was rather *concerned* at the severity of the punishment. 私はその刑罰の厳しさをかなり心配していた ◇*Concerned* parents held a meeting. 心配した親たちは集会を開いた ☞ **concern** (CONCERN)

ノート **worried と concerned の使い分け**：concerned はふつう他人 [社会，世界など] に影響を与える問題について用いられる．worried もそれについて用いることもあるが，より個人的な問題について用いることもできる．

nervous 心配した，緊張した，びくびくした，怖がった ◇Consumers are very *nervous* about the future. 消費者たちは将来についてかなり心配している ◇The horse may be *nervous* of cars. その馬は車を怖がるかもしれない ◇By the time the police arrived, I was a *nervous wreck*. 警察が到着するまで，私はびくびくしていた 反意 **relaxed** (CALM), **confident** (CONFIDENT), ☞ **nerve-racking** (STRESSFUL)
▶**nervously** 副 ◇She smiled *nervously*. 彼女は緊張した面持ちではほほ笑んだ

anxious 心配した，不安な，気をもんだ ◇He grew in-

↳worried

creasingly *anxious* as time went on. 彼は時が経つにつれだんだん不安になってきた ☞**anxious** (STRESSFUL), **anxiety** (CONCERN)
▶**anxiously** 副 ◇to ask/look/wait *anxiously* 心配そうに尋ねる／見る／待つ ◇Residents are *anxiously* awaiting a decision. 住民たちは心配そうに決定を待ち構えている

【ノート】**worried, nervous, anxious の使い分け**：**worried** は起こるかもしれない問題［悪い物事］について考えるときにどう感じるかを表すために、最も頻繁に用いられる語である。**anxious** はより強い感情を表すことができ、よりフォーマルである。**nervous** は試験・面接・不快［困難］な物事などを前にどう感じるかを表すのに用いられることが多い。**nervous** は人の性格を表すことができる。a very nervous girl は、しばしば［いつも］**nervous** である。a worried girl は、特定の場で［特定の物事について］**worried** である。**nervous** は人の性格を表すことができるが、特定の感情を表す。**anxious** は感情や性格を表すことができる。

uneasy （望ましくない物事が起こるかもしれないと思って［行っていることが正しいかどうか確信がなくて］）心配した、不安、落ち着かない、そわそわした ◇He had an *uneasy* feeling that something terrible was going to happen. 彼は何か恐ろしいことが起こりそうだという不安を覚えた ◇She felt *uneasy* about leaving the children with him. 彼女は子どもたちを彼に預けたことで落ち着かなかった
反意 **easy** (EASY 2), ☞ **unease** (CONCERN)
▶**uneasily** 副 ◇I wondered *uneasily* what he was thinking. 彼が何を考えているのだろうか不安に思った

bothered （しばしば否定文で）《ややインフォーマル》 気をもんだ、思い悩んだ、苦にした ◇You don't sound too *bothered* about it. Don't you mind? あまりそのことを苦にしていないようね。気にならないの

troubled 《書き言葉》 心配した、不安な、気をもんだ ◇She looked into his *troubled* face. 彼女は彼の不安そうな顔を覗き込んだ ❶ **troubled** は特に人々の表情・顔・目と共に用いられる。

disturbed 《ややフォーマル、特に書き言葉》 心配した、動揺した、気がかりな ◇I was deeply *disturbed* and depressed by the news. 私はその知らせに深く動揺して落ち込んだ

apprehensive 《フォーマル》（望ましくない物事が起こるかもしれないと思って少し）心配［懸念］した、不安な、気がかりな ◇I was a little *apprehensive* about the effects of what I had said. 自分が言ったことの影響がちょっと気がかりだった ☞ **apprehension** (CONCERN)
▶**apprehensively** 副 ◇He was looking at me *apprehensively*. 彼は私を不安げに見つめていた

worry 動

worry・bother・concern・trouble・disturb・unsettle
人を落ち着かなくさせる［不安にさせる］
【類語訳】心配させる、悩ませる、困らせる、いらいらさせる、動揺させる

bother	concern	worry
	disturb	trouble
	unsettle	

文型&コロケーション
▶It worries/ bothers/ concerns/ troubles/ disturbs **sb that** ...

worry, worrying

▶Is there something worrying/ bothering/ troubling **you**?
▶to worry/ bother/ concern/ trouble sb **with sth**
▶to worry/ bother/ concern/ trouble **yourself about** sth
▶sth doesn't worry/ bother/ concern sb **in the slightest/ least**
▶What worries/ bothers/ concerns/ troubles/ disturbs **me is...**

worry ［他］ 心配させる、不安にさせる、悩ませる；困らせる、いらいらさせる ◇What *worries* me is how I'm going to get another job. 私の悩みは、どうやって他の職に就くかということだ ◇He's *worried himself sick* about his daughter. 彼は自分自身が病気になるほど娘のことを心配している ◇The noise never seems to *worry* her. 彼女はその音にいらいらすることはまったくないようだ

bother ［他］《ややインフォーマル》 気をもませる、悩ませる ◇Does it *bother* you that she earns more than you? 彼女があなたよりたくさん稼いでいることが気になるのですか ◇It *bothers* me to think of her alone in that big house. あんな大きな家に彼女が一人だと思うと気になる ◇'I'm sorry he was so rude to you.' 'It doesn't *bother* me.'「彼があなたに対してとても無作法だったことをお詫びします」「気にならないよ」

concern ［他］《進行形はまれ》 心配させる、不安にさせる、気にかけさせる ◇What *concerns* me is our lack of preparation for the change. 私が気がかりなのは、その変化に対して我々が準備不足なことです ☞ **concern** (CONCERN)

trouble ［他］ 心配させる、不安にさせる、気をもませる、悩ませる ◇What is it that's *troubling* you? 何を悩んでいるのですか

disturb ［他］ 心配させる、動揺させる、心をかき乱す ◇The letter shocked and *disturbed* me. その手紙にショックを受け私は動揺した ◇It *disturbed* her to realize that she was missing him already. 彼がいないことをもう寂しがっていると自覚して、彼女は当惑した

【ノート】**worry, bother, concern, trouble, disturb の使い分け**：これらの語はすべて、非常に似た意味を持つが、意味の強さ・頻度・言語使用域に少し違いがある。**bother** が最もインフォーマルで、特に It doesn't bother me., I'm not bothered. といった話し言葉の文句で用いられる。**concern** が最もフォーマルで、ふつう進行形では用いられない。×What is it that's *concerning* you?

unsettle ［他］（状況の変化によって）動揺させる、不安にさせる ◇Changing schools might *unsettle* the kids. 転校で子どもたちは不安になるかもしれない

worrying 形 ☞ FRIGHTENING, PAINFUL 2

worrying・disturbing・unsettling・disconcerting・unnerving
行為［出来事、状況など］が自分を心配［緊張、不安］にさせること
【類語訳】心配な、厄介な、悩ませる、いらいらさせる、動揺させる、気がかりな、落ち着かない、まごつかせる、びくびくさせる

文型&コロケーション
▶worrying/ disturbing/ unsettling/ disconcerting/ unnerving **for** sb
▶a worrying/ disturbing **thought**
▶a disturbing/ an unsettling/ an unnerving **effect/ experience**
▶to find sth worrying/ disturbing/ disconcert-

ing/ unnerving
▶**very** worrying/ disturbing/ unsettling/ disconcerting/ unnerving

worrying 心配な、厄介な、悩ませる、いらいらさせる ◇a *worrying* development/sign/trend 厄介な展開/兆し/動向 ◇It must be *worrying* not to know where he is. 彼の所在がわからなくていらいらするに違いない

disturbing 心配な、動揺させる、気がかりな ◇This is an extremely *disturbing* piece of news. これはきわめて気がかりなニュースだ

unsettling 動揺させる、不安にさせる、落ち着かない ◇She found his questions deeply *unsettling*. 彼女は彼の質問がひどく心を動揺させるものだとわかった ☞**unsettled** (RESTLESS)

disconcerting 悩ませる、心をかき乱す、まごつかせる ◇She had the *disconcerting* habit of saying exactly what she thought. 彼女には、思ったことをそのまま口にして人をまごつかせる癖があった

unnerving びくびくさせる、自信をなくさせる ◇The whole experience was a little *unnerving*. その経験すべては少々自信をなくさせるものだった

┃ノート┃ **unsettling, disconcerting, unnerving** の使い分け：これらの語はすべて、不快にさせる[自信と平静さを失わせる]物事・出来事などに用いられる. disconcerting は特に人の行為・外見・性格について用いられ、unsettling と unnerving は状況・出来事・雰囲気に用いられることが多い.

worsen 動

worsen・get worse・weaken・deteriorate・decline・slip・degenerate・fail・relapse
何らかの形で今より小さく[弱く、悪く]なることを表す
【類語訳】悪化する、弱まる、劣化する、衰える、低下する、減少する、衰退する、落ちる

┃文型&コロケーション┃
▶to deteriorate/ degenerate/ relapse **into** sth
▶sb's **health** worsens/ gets worse/ deteriorates/ declines/ fails
▶a **situation** worsens/ gets worse/ deteriorates/ degenerates
▶**conditions** worsen/ get worse/ deteriorate
▶the **weather** worsens/ gets worse/ deteriorates
▶**sales** weaken/ deteriorate/ decline/ slip
▶sb/ sth's **popularity** weakens/ declines/ slips
▶**quality** deteriorates/ declines/ slips
▶to worsen/ weaken/ deteriorate/ decline/ degenerate **rapidly**
▶to worsen/ weaken/ deteriorate/ decline **significantly/ steadily**
▶to worsen/ weaken/ decline/ slip **considerably**
▶to worsen/ weaken/ decline **slightly**
▶to worsen/ deteriorate/ decline **dramatically**
▶to get **steadily/ considerably/ slightly** worse

worsen [自]《ややフォーマル》悪化する ◇The political situation is steadily *worsening*. 政情はじわじわと悪化している ◇Her symptoms have *worsened* considerably since we last saw her. 最後に会って以来、彼女の症状はかなり悪化している ┃反意┃ **improve** (IMPROVE 2)

get 'worse ┃フレーズ┃《ややインフォーマル、特に話し言葉》悪化する；体調が悪くなる ◇Things are just *getting worse and worse*. 事態はますます悪化するばかりである ◇If he *gets* any *worse* we'll call the doctor. これ以上彼の体調が悪くなるなら、医者を呼びましょう ┃反意┃ **get better** (IMPROVE 2)

weaken [自]弱くなる、弱まる ◇His authority is steadily *weakening*. 彼の権限は次第に弱まりつつある ┃反意┃ **strengthen**

deteriorate [自]《ややフォーマル》悪化[劣化]する ◇The overall quality of rivers and canals has *deteriorated*. 川と運河の質が全般的に悪化している ◇The discussion quickly *deteriorated* into an angry argument. 議論はすぐにとげとげしい言い争いに陥った ┃反意┃ **improve** (IMPROVE 2)

┃ノート┃ **worsen** と **deteriorate** の使い分け：多くの場合、両語とも使用可能. ●sb's health/a situation/conditions/the weather/a relationship worsens/deteriorates（人の健康/状況/状態/天気/関係が悪化する）. worsen は problem, crisis, position, symptom などの可算名詞で表される特定の問題について用いられることが多い. ×Her symptoms have *deteriorated* considerably. deteriorate は life, work, behaviour, morale, quality などの不可算名詞によって表される、より一般的な事柄に用いられることが多い. また、sth deteriorates into sth の句でも用いられる. ×The overall quality of rivers and canals has *worsened*. ×The discussion *worsened* into an angry argument.

decline [自]《ややフォーマル》衰える、低下[減少]する ◇Support for the party continues to *decline*. その党への支持は低下し続けている ◇Her health was *declining* rapidly. 彼女の健康は急速に衰えつつあった ❶この意味の decline は、人の健康・国家[地域, 会社]の経済力・人[物事]への支持について用いられる. health, economy, industry, fortunes, prosperity, support, popularity などと結びつく. decline には「水準[数]において低下[減少]する」という関連する意味がある. ☞**decline** (REDUCTION)

slip (-pp-) [自]《ややフォーマル、特にビジネス》（水準がいくぶん）低下[減少]する；(徐々に)悪化する、弱まる ◇His popularity has *slipped* recently. 最近、彼の人気が下がっている ◇That's three times she's beaten me — I must be *slipping*! 彼女に3度負けたよ—私の腕が落ちているに違いない ◇Pre-tax profits *slipped* to $3.7 million, from $3.9 million the previous year. 税込利益は前年の390万ドルから370万ドルに減少した

degenerate [自]《ややフォーマル》悪化[衰退]する ◇The march rapidly *degenerated* into a riot. デモ行進は急速に暴動に堕ちた ❶degenerate はほとんどの場合、degenerate into sth の句で用いられる. よく、degenerate into a conflict/a riot/a battle/chaos/violence/a farce/a brawl などの結びつきで用いられる.

fail [自]《特に進行形で》（健康・視力が）衰える、落ちる ◇Her eyesight is *failing*. 彼女の視力が落ちてきている ◇His last months in office were marred by *failing* health. 健康の衰えで、彼の先月の仕事は台無しになった

relapse [自]《ややフォーマル》（快復後に）病気がぶり返す[再発する] ◇Two days after leaving the hospital she *relapsed* into a coma. 退院後2日で、彼女は再び昏睡状態に陥った ┃反意┃ **recover** (RECOVER)

▶**relapse** 名 [C, U] to have/suffer a *relapse* 病気がぶり返す

worthy 〖形〗

worthy・fine・noble・admirable・deserving・honourable・creditable
賞賛と尊敬を払える人や物事を表す
【類語訳】値する, 価値がある, ふさわしい, 立派な, 優れた, 素晴らしい, 見事な, 気高い, 高潔な, 賞賛すべき, 尊敬に値する

文型&コロケーション

▶ to be worthy/ deserving **of** sth
▶ a worthy/ a fine/ a noble/ an admirable **man/ woman**
▶ a worthy/ a fine/ a noble/ an admirable/ a creditable **effort**
▶ a worthy/ a fine/ a noble/ a deserving/ an honourable **cause**
▶ worthy/ fine/ noble **ideals/ principles**
▶ fine/ noble/ admirable **work**
▶ a fine/ an admirable/ a creditable **performance**

worthy 《フォーマル, しばしばほめて》(尊敬・注目・賞賛などに)値する, 価値がある, ふさわしい, 立派な ◇A number of the report's findings are *worthy of note*. 報告書の調査結果のいくつかは注目に値する ◇Several of our members are *worthy of* particular *mention*. 我々のメンバーのうち数人は特筆に値します ◇He felt he was not *worthy* of her (= that he did not deserve her love). 彼は自分は彼女にふさわしくないと思った ◇In Mason we have a *worthy* new champion (= one who deserves to win). メーソンには, 我々の新しいチャンピオンにふさわしい資質がある ◇The money we raise will be going to a very *worthy* cause. 調達される資金は非常に価値ある目的に使われることになります ◇He's a very *worthy* man, I suppose, but he's very dull. 彼はとても立派な人だとは思うのだが, でもとても退屈だ 反意 **unworthy** ❶ unworthy な人・物事は, それにふさわしい[尊敬に値する]性質を備えていない. ◆He considered himself *unworthy of* the honour they had bestowed on him. 彼は自分のことを, 与えられた栄誉に値しないと考えた.

fine 〔名詞の前で〕《ややフォーマル, ほめて》(誠実さ・プロ意識などが尊敬[賞賛]に値して)優れた, 素晴らしい, 見事な ◇He was a *fine* man and a *fine* soldier (= respected both as a man and as a soldier). 彼は優れた人間であり, 優れた兵士でもあった ◇It was a *fine* example of leadership. それは指導力の素晴らしい一例だった

noble 《ややフォーマル, ほめて》(勇敢[誠実]さ・他人への配慮などが賞賛に値して)気高い, 高潔な, 崇高な ◇She died in a *noble* cause. 彼女は崇高な目的のために亡くなった ◇It was very *noble* of you to go so far to take him home. 彼を連れ帰るためにそんなに遠くまで出かけるなんて, あなたはとても高潔だった

▶ **nobly** 〖副〗 ◇They acted generously and *nobly*. 彼らは寛大にかつ気高く振る舞った

admirable 《フォーマル, ほめて》賞賛[尊敬]すべき, 感心な, 立派な, 見事な ◇Her dedication to her work is *admirable*. 彼女の仕事への専心には感心する ◇He made his point with *admirable* clarity. 彼は見事にはっきりと自分の主張を述べた

▶ **admirably** 〖副〗 ◇They cope *admirably* with the many demands put upon them. 彼らは自分たちに課せられる多くの要求に立派に対処する

deserving 《フォーマル》援助[支持, 注目]に値する, ふさわしい ◇Only the most *deserving cases* ever get any state help. そもそも国の支援が受けられるのは, 誰よりもそれを必要としている人に限られる ◇A distinction was made between the *deserving* and the undeserving poor. 支援に値する貧民と値しない貧民の区別がなされた 反意 **undeserving** ❶ undeserving は物事を持つ[受ける]に値しないことを表す. ◆He was *undeserving of* her affections. 彼は彼女の愛情を受けるにふさわしくなかった.

honourable 《英》(米 **honorable**) 尊敬すべき; 面目の保てる ◇She had a long and *honourable* career in government. 彼女は政府機関で長きにわたる尊敬に値する経歴を築いた ◇The team managed an *honourable* 2-2 draw. チームは2-2の引き分けで何とか面目を保った 反意 **dishonourable**, ☞ **honour** (REPUTATION)

〖ノート〗 **fine, noble, admirable, honourable** の使い分け: noble はこれらの語の中で最も意味の強い語で, 何かのために死のような行動について用いられる. fine は人が誠実に申し分なく義務を果たすことを示唆する. admirable はバランス・明快さといったそれほど個人的でない性質を表すことが多い. この意味の honourable は, いくぶん否定的な語である. 特に困難な環境でなかがい物事を行う場合に, 恥じることは何もないということを言うのに用いられることが多い. ×a *fine/noble/admirable* 2-2 draw. スポーツの結果は, a fine win とは言えるかもしれないが, ×a *fine/noble/admirable* draw とは言えない. この意味では, a fine/noble/admirable man/woman と言うことはできる. しかし, an honourable man/woman と言うと, 高い道徳水準を持った人を意味することになる. ☞ **honourable** (RESPECTABLE)

creditable 《フォーマル》(かなりよい水準なので)尊敬[賞賛]に値する, 立派な, 見事な ◇The chairman welcomed the company's *creditable* performance in the previous year. 会長は前年度における会社の見事な実績を歓迎した ◇Although they struggled, they ended up coming a *creditable* second (= second in a race or competition). 彼らはもがき苦しんだが, 結局見事に2着に入った ❶ creditable は努力よりも功績について用いられる. 一般的には, performance, result, achievement, showing と結びつく. かなり高いが抜群ではない水準の功績に用いられる.

▶ **creditably** 〖副〗 ◇All three players performed *creditably*. 3人の選手は皆, 立派な成績を残した

write 〖動〗

write・sign・write sth down・put sth down・scribble・copy・scrawl・transcribe
ペン[鉛筆]を使って, 表面に文字[数字]を形作る
【類語訳】書く, 署名する, サインする, 書き留める, 走り書きする, 落書きする, 書き写す, 書き起こす

文型&コロケーション

▶ to write/ sign/ write sth down/ put sth down/ scribble/ scrawl **on** sth
▶ to write/ write sth down/ put sth down/ scribble/ scrawl **in** sth
▶ to copy/ transcribe sth **into** sth
▶ to write/ sign/ write sth down/ put sth down/ scribble/ scrawl **with** sth
▶ to write/ put/ scribble/ copy/ scrawl sth **down**
▶ to write/ copy sth **out**
▶ to write/ write down/ put down/ scribble/ copy/ transcribe some **notes**

▶to write/ sign/ write down/ put down/ scribble/ scrawl your **name**
▶to write/ scribble/ scrawl your **signature**

write [自, 他]（ペン・鉛筆を使って紙などに文字・数字を）書く ◇I haven't got anything to *write* with. 書く物を何も持っていません ◇Please *write* clearly in black ink. 黒いインクではっきり書いてください ◇In some countries children don't start learning to *read and write* until they are six. 国によっては、子供が6歳になるまで読み書きを学習し始めない ◇*Write* your answer out again on a new sheet of paper. もう一度新しい紙に答えを書きなさい ◇Ancient historians *wrote of* a lost continent beneath the ocean. 古代の歴史学者たちは、海底の失われた大陸について書き記した ◇In his latest book he *writes that* the theory has since been disproved. 彼はその最新の著書で、その説はその後反証されてきたと書いている ◇I'll *write* you a receipt. 領収書をお書きしますね

▶**writing** [名] [U] ◇Our son's having problems with his *reading and writing*. うちの息子は読み書きに問題があるんです ◇There was *writing* all over the desk. 机の上一面に書き込みがあった ◇Who's this from? I don't recognize the *writing*. これは誰から。筆跡ではわからない

sign [自, 他]（文書・書類に）署名する, 記名調印する, サインする ◇*Sign* here, please. ここに署名をお願いします ◇*Sign* your name here, please. ここに署名をお願いします ◇You haven't *signed* the letter. 手紙に署名がありませんよ ◇The treaty was *signed* on 24 March. その条約は3月24日に調印された ◇The player was *signing* autographs for a group of fans. その選手はファンの一団にサインを書いていた ◇He *signed* himself 'Jimmy'. 彼は自分のことを「ジミー」と署名した

▶**signature** [名] [C, U] ◇Someone had forged her *signature* on the cheque. 誰かが小切手に彼女の筆跡をまねて署名していた ◇Two copies of the contract will be sent to you for *signature*.《フォーマル》ご署名をいただくために、契約書の写しが2枚お手元に届きます

,**write sth 'down** [句動詞]（覚えて［記録して］おくために物事を）書き留める ◇*Write down* the address before you forget it. 忘れないうちに住所を書き留めてください ◇Everything he said was *written down*. 彼が言ったことは全部書き留められた

,**put sth 'down** [句動詞]（覚えて［記録して］おくために物事を）書き留める ◇The meeting's on the 23rd. *Put it down* in your diary. 会議は23日だよ。手帳に書き留めておいてね ◇One day I'm going to *put it all down on paper*. いつか全部それを紙に書き留めるつもりだ

[ノート] write sth down と put sth down の使い分け：この二つの句動詞の間に実質的な意味の違いはない。put sth down はふつう物事がどこに［どのように］書かれるかを示す前置詞句と共に用いられる。◆*Put* it *down* in your diary/ on paper/in writing.（それを手帳に書き留めて／紙に書き留めて／書面にしておいてください）

scribble [他, 自]（時間がないので）走り［殴り］書きする；落書きする ◇He *scribbled* a note to his sister before leaving. 彼は発つ前に姉に走り書きのメモを書いた ◇Throughout the interview, the journalists *scribbled away* furiously. インタビューの間ずっと、報道陣は猛烈な勢いで殴り書きを続けた ◇Someone had *scribbled* all over the table in crayon. 誰かがテーブルの上一面にクレヨンで落書きをしていた

▶**scribble** [名] [U, 複数で] ◇How do you expect me to read this *scribble*? 私にどうやってこの走り書きを読めって言うの ◇The page was covered with a mass of *scribbles*. そのページは一面落書きだらけだった

copy [他]（書かれている通りに）書き写す ◇She *copied* the phone number into her address book. 彼女はアドレス帳にその電話番号を写した ◇I *copied* out several poems. いくつかの詩をすっかり書き写した

scrawl [他, 自]（読みづらいほどに）走り［殴り］書きする ◇She had *scrawled* the directions on a piece of paper. 彼女は紙に指示を走り書きしておいた ◇Someone had *scrawled* all over my notes. 誰かが私のノートの至る所に走り書きをした

▶**scrawl** [名] [C, U] ◇Her signature was an illegible *scrawl*. 彼女のサインは判読のできない走り書きだった ◇I can't be expected to read this *scrawl*! この走り書きは読めるわけがない

[ノート] **scribble** と **scrawl** の使い分け：scrawl はぞんざいに書くことを表すが、それは特にあまり時間がないからというわけではない。×The journalists *scrawled* away furiously.

transcribe [他]（考え・演説・データを文書として［元の形と異なる形式で］）書き起こす, 文字化する ◇Clerks *transcribe* everything that is said in court. 書記は法廷での発言をすべて書き起こします ◇The interview was recorded and then *transcribed*. 会見は録音されてから文字に起こされた ☞ **transcript** (COPY [名] 1)

writer [名] ☞ REPORTER

writer・author・poet・novelist・playwright・biographer・scribe・scriptwriter・dramatist・screenwriter
書くことを仕事とする人
【類語訳】作家, 文筆家, 書き手, 筆者, 著者, 作者, 詩人, 小説家, 劇作家, 脚本家, 伝記作家, シナリオライター

[文型&コロケーション]

▶an **award-winning** writer/ author/ poet/ novelist/ playwright/ screenwriter
▶a/ an **famous/ aspiring** writer/ author/ poet/ novelist/ playwright/ screenwriter
▶a **best-selling/ romantic** writer/ author/ poet/ novelist
▶a **historical/ science fiction** writer/ author/ novelist
▶a writer/ an author/ a poet/ a novelist/ a playwright/ a biographer/ a scribe/ a scriptwriter/ a dramatist/ a screenwriter **writes** sth

writer [C] 作家, 文筆家；書き手, 筆者, 著者, 作成者 ◇a travel/science/cookery *writer* 紀行／科学書／料理本作家 ◇the *writer* of this letter/article/computer program この手紙の書き手／記事の筆者／コンピュータープログラムの作成者

author [C]（本・物語・記事などの）作家, 作者, 筆者, 著者 ◇She is a published *author*. 彼女は出版作品のある作家である ◇Who's the *author*? 著者は誰ですか

poet [C] 詩人 ◇the Romantic *poets* ロマン派の詩人

novelist [C] 小説家 ◇She is now a best-selling *novelist*. 彼女は今やベストセラー作家だ ☞ **novel** (BOOK)

playwright [C]（演劇・テレビ・ラジオの）劇作家, 脚本家

◇The famous *playwright* died in 1616 at the age of 52. その有名な劇作家は1616年に52歳で亡くなった ☞ **play** (PLAY 名)

biographer [C] 伝記作家 ◇As Dr Johnson's *biographer*, Boswell became quite famous in his own right. ボズウェルはジョンソン博士の伝記作家として、彼自身もまたとても有名になった

scribe [C] （印刷術発明以前に文書の写しを作成した）筆写者 ◇Before paper was common, medieval *scribes* used parchment or vellum. 紙が広く行きわたる以前、中世の筆写者は羊皮紙か子牛皮を使った

scriptwriter [C] （劇・映画・放送番組の）脚本家 ◇Not even Hollywood *scriptwriters* had dreamt up such a horrific chain of events. ハリウッドの脚本家でさえ、そんな恐ろしい一連の出来事を思いついたことはなかった

dramatist [C] 《ややフォーマル》（演劇・テレビ・ラジオの）劇作家, 脚本家 ◇It is a powerful story written by a great *dramatist*. それは著名な劇作家の書いた力強い物語だ ☞ **drama** (PLAY 名)

▸**dramatize** 《英でまた **-ise**》動 [他] ◇The book has been *dramatized* on television. その本はテレビでドラマ化された

▸**dramatization** 《英でまた **-isation**》名 [C, U] ◇a television *dramatization* of the trial その裁判のテレビドラマ化

ノート **playwright と dramatist の使い分け**：これらの語に意味や用法の違いはほとんどない。どちらも特に演劇のために劇を書く人について用いられるが、テレビ[ラジオ]用の作家も指すことができる。playwright は、現代の作家や過去の作家について同じような用いられ方をする。dramatist は、いくぶん過去の作家について用いられることのほうが多いが、現代の dramatist についても用いることができる。

screenwriter [C] （映画・テレビの）シナリオライター, 脚本家 ◇an Oscar-winning *screenwriter* アカデミー賞受賞の映画脚本家

wrong 形

1 wrong・false・mistaken・incorrect・inaccurate・misguided・untrue
正しくないことを表す
【類語訳】間違った, 誤った, 反対の, 逆の, 虚偽の, ごまかしの, 見せかけの, 不正確な, 見当違いの

文型&コロケーション
▸to be wrong/ mistaken **about** sth
▸a **prediction** is wrong/ false/ incorrect/ inaccurate
▸a **guess** is wrong/ incorrect
▸wrong/ false/ mistaken/ incorrect/ inaccurate/ untrue **information**
▸a wrong/ a false/ a mistaken/ an incorrect/ an inaccurate/ a misguided **assumption**
▸a false/ a mistaken/ an inaccurate/ a misguided **belief**
▸to **give**/ **get** the wrong/ a false/ a mistaken/ an inaccurate **impression**
▸a wrong/ an incorrect **answer**
▸**totally** wrong/ false/ mistaken/ incorrect/ inaccurate/ misguided/ untrue
▸**completely** wrong/ false/ mistaken/ incorrect/ misguided/ untrue
▸**quite** wrong/ false/ mistaken/ incorrect/ inaccurate/ misguided/ untrue
▸**clearly** wrong/ false/ incorrect/ untrue
▸**seriously** wrong/ mistaken/ incorrect/ inaccurate
▸**hopelessly** wrong/ inaccurate/ misguided
▸**grossly** wrong/ mistaken/ incorrect/ inaccurate/ misguided
▸**simply** wrong/ incorrect/ misguided/ untrue
▸**sadly** wrong/ mistaken/ misguided
▸**It is**/ **would be** wrong/ false/ incorrect/ inaccurate/ untrue **to say**...

wrong 間違った, 誤った；反対の, 逆の ◇I got all the answers *wrong*. 私の答えはすべて間違っていた ◇He was driving on the *wrong* side of the road. 彼は道路の対向車線を走行していた ◇Sorry, I must have dialled the *wrong* number. すみません、どうも番号を間違えたようです ◇You're holding the camera the ***wrong way up***. そのカメラ、上下反対ですよ ◇That picture is the ***wrong way round***. 《英》その絵は逆さまです ◇***the wrong way around*** 《米》逆さまで ◇I think she lives at number 40, but I could be *wrong*. 彼女は40番地に住んでいると思うけど、間違ってるかも ◇She would prove him *wrong* whatever happened. 彼女は何が何でも彼の間違いを証明するつもりだった 反意 **right** (RIGHT 形 1), **right** (TRUE), ☞ **the wrong idea** (ILLUSION)

▸**wrongly** 副 ◇The sentence had been *wrongly* translated. その文は間違って翻訳されてしまっていた ◇He assumed, *wrongly*, that she did not care. 彼女は気にかけていないのだと彼は誤って決めてかかった

false 間違った, 誤った；虚偽の, ごまかしの, 見せかけの ◇A whale is a fish. ***True or false?*** クジラは魚類である。○か×か ◇He used a *false* name to get the job. 彼はその仕事を得るために偽名を使った ◇I don't want to raise any *false* hopes, but I think he's still alive. ぬか喜びさせたくないけど、彼はまだ生きていると思う ◇We had been lulled into a ***false sense of security*** (= wrongly made to feel safe). 我々は（だまされて）安心だと思い込まれた ◇Buying a cheap computer is a ***false economy*** (= it will not save you money). 安いコンピュータを買うのは安物買いの銭失いだ 反意 **true** (TRUE), ☞ **false impression** (ILLUSION)

▸**falsely** 副 ◇He had been *falsely* accused of murder. 彼は殺人の濡れ衣を着せられていた

mistaken （意見・判断が）間違った, 誤った；誤解[思い違い]による ◇I thought I knew him, but I must have been *mistaken*. 彼のことを知っているつもりだったが、考え違いだったようだ ◇I told her my secret ***in the mistaken belief*** that I could trust her. 信頼できると思い違いをして彼女に秘密を話した ◇It was a case of ***mistaken identity*** (= when you think sb is a particular person but they are not). それは人違いのケースだった ☞ **mistake** (MISTAKE 1), **mistake** (MISUNDERSTAND)

▸**mistakenly** 副 ◇He *mistakenly* believed that his family would stand by him. 彼は家族が力になってくれるものと誤解していた

incorrect 《ややフォーマル》事実に反した, 正しくない, 不正確な；間違った, 誤った ◇Many of the figures were *incorrect*. 多くの数字が正しくなかった ◇Marks will be taken off for *incorrect* spellings. 綴りの間違いは減点されます ◇His version of what happened is *incorrect*. 何が起きたかについての彼の説明は事実に反している ◇It's technically *incorrect* to talk about bats 'hearing'

wrong

things. 物音を「聞く」コウモリについて話すのは、専門的には正しいことではない 反意 **correct** (TRUE).
▶**incorrectly** 副 ◇A lot of people spell this *incorrectly*. 多くの人々がこの綴りを間違える
inaccurate 事実に反した、正しくない、不正確な；間違った、誤った ◇The movie is historically *inaccurate*, but well worth seeing. その映画は歴史的事実に反しているが、観る価値は十分にある ◇All the maps we had were *wildly inaccurate*. 私たちが持っている地図は全部、ひどく不正確だった 反意 **accurate** (EXACT), ☞ **inaccuracy** (MISTAKE 2)
▶**inaccurately** 副 ◇She has been *inaccurately* described as a soul singer. 彼女はソウル歌手という間違ったレッテルを貼られてきた

ノート **incorrect** と **inaccurate** の使い分け：間違った事実・数字・綴りは incorrect と表現し、不正確な事実に基づいた確信・説明は incorrect, inaccurate と表現できる。不正確な事実を含んだ、映画・報告書・地図などの制作物については inaccurate を用いる。

misguided （状況を正しく理解[判断]しなかったために）見当違いの、間違った ◇The new proposals are totally *misguided*. 新しい提案はまったく見当違いである ◇In her *misguided* attempts to help, she only made the situation worse. 彼女は助けようとあれこれ試みたが、どれも見当違いだったので、事態を悪化させただけだった
untrue [名詞の前はまれ] 虚偽の、見当違いの ◇These accusations are totally *untrue*. これらの告発はまったくの虚偽である ◇It would be *untrue* to say that something like this could never happen again. こういったことは二度と起きえないと言うのは見当違いだろう 反意 **true** (TRUE)

2 wrong・inappropriate・unsuitable・bad・inconvenient・unfit・awkward
人や物事が特定の状況に適切でないことを表す
【類語訳】不適切な、そぐわない、不適当な、不都合な、まずい、不適格な

文型&コロケーション
▶wrong/ inappropriate/ unsuitable/ inconvenient/ unfit/ awkward **for** sb/ sth
▶wrong/ inappropriate/ unsuitable/ inconvenient/ unfit **to do sth**
▶the wrong/ an inappropriate/ a bad/ an inconvenient/ an awkward **time**
▶**most/ rather** inappropriate/ unsuitable/ inconvenient/ awkward
▶**highly/ somewhat** inappropriate/ unsuitable/ inconvenient
▶**quite/ completely/ totally** inappropriate/ unsuitable/ unfit
▶**very/ extremely** unsuitable/ inconvenient/ awkward

wrong [ふつう名詞の前で]（特定の状況・目的に）不適切な、そぐわない ◇He's the *wrong* person for the job. 彼はその仕事にふさわしくない人物だ ◇I realized that it was the *wrong* thing to say. 私はそれが不適切な発言だったと悟った ◇We don't want this document *falling into the wrong hands*. 我々はこの文書が不適切な人物の手に渡ってほしくないのだ ❶この意味のwrongはふつうthe の後で用いられる。 反意 **right** (GOOD 2)
inappropriate 《ややフォーマル》（特定の状況に）不適切な、ふさわしくない、そぐわない ◇What's the best way for a teacher to deal with *inappropriate* behaviour? 教師が不適切な行動に対処する際の最善の方法は何ですか ◇It would be *inappropriate* for me to comment on what your tutor said. あなたの個人指導教師が言ったことに私がコメントするのは不適切でしょう 反意 **appropriate** (GOOD 2)
▶**inappropriately** 副 ◇She was *inappropriately* dressed for a funeral. 彼女は葬儀にそぐわない服装をしていた
unsuitable （特定の目的・場・人に）不適切な、ふさわしくない、不似合いの ◇He was wearing shoes that were totally *unsuitable* for climbing. 彼は登山にまったくふさわしくない靴を履いていた ◇They considered him quite *unsuitable* for their daughter. 彼らは彼のことを娘にまったく不似合いだと思った 反意 **suitable** (GOOD 2)
▶**unsuitably** 副 ◇They were *unsuitably* dressed for the occasion. 彼らはその場にふさわしくない服装をしていた

ノート **inappropriate** と **unsuitable** の使い分け：unsuitable な服装・設備・施設はふつう、特定の目的に不適切である。inappropriate な行動・服装はふつう、社交上の理由から不適切である。

bad [名詞の前で]（問題を引き起こして）不適当な、不都合な；（適切な判断に基づかずに）まずい ◇I know that this is a *bad* time to ask for help. 今は援助を求めるには不適当なタイミングだと承知している ◇He now realized that it had been a *bad* decision on his part. それが自分にとって不都合な決定だったと、彼は今になって悟った ❶この意味のbadはふつう time, timing, decision, reason と結びつく。 反意 **good** (GOOD 2), **good** (GOOD 3)
inconvenient （ややフォーマル）（欲求・意向に関した面倒・問題を引き起こして）不適当な、不都合な ◇That's most *inconvenient* for me. I'm working that weekend. それは私にはすごく都合が悪い。その週末は仕事なんだ 反意 **convenient** (GOOD 2)
unfit 資格のない、不適格な；不適切な、ふさわしくない ◇They described him as *unfit* to govern. 彼らは彼を統治する資格はないと評した ◇The meat was *unfit for* human consumption. その肉は人間が食べるのには適さなかった ◇The court claims she is an *unfit* mother. 裁判所は彼女が母親として不適格だと断じている ❶unfitはふつう to do sth, unfit for sth の句で用いられる。 ◆*unfit to* govern/rule/stand trial/drive（統治する／支配する／裁判を受ける／運転する資格がない）。 ◆*unfit for* human consumption/habitation （人間が食べる／住むのに適さない）。unfit が名詞の前にくるときはほぼ unfit mother の句で用いられる。 反意 **fit** (GOOD 2)
awkward 不都合な ◇Have I come at an *awkward* time? 都合の悪いときに来ちゃったかな ◇That's a bit *awkward* for me — could we make it earlier? それはちょっと都合が悪いですね—もうちょっと早くなりますか

ノート **inconvenient** と **awkward** の使い分け：inconvenient のほうが awkward よりもフォーマルで、不都合の度合いがより大きいことを示唆する。

3 ☞ ILLEGAL
wrong・unfair・unjust・unequal・immoral・unethical・inequitable
人や物事が公正で[道徳的に正しく]ないことを表す

wrong

【類語訳】悪い、邪悪な、不正な、不公平な、不当な、不条理な、不平等な、不釣合いな、不道徳な、不品行な

文型&コロケーション
▶ wrong/ unfair/ unjust **of** sb
▶ wrong/ unfair/ unjust/ immoral/ unethical **to do sth**
▶ to be wrong/ unfair/ unjust **that**...
▶ an unfair/ unequal/ inequitable **share/ distribution** of sth
▶ immoral/ unethical **behaviour/ conduct**
▶ **very** wrong/ unfair/ unjust/ unequal
▶ **highly** unfair/ unjust/ unequal/ immoral/ unethical
▶ **quite/ totally** wrong/ unfair/ unjust/ immoral
▶ **patently** wrong/ unfair/ unjust

wrong [名詞の前はまれ] (道徳的に)正しくない、よくない、悪い、邪悪な ◇Paying people such low wages is simply *wrong*. 人々にそんな低賃金しか支払わないのは断じてよくない ◇It's *wrong* to tell lies. 嘘をつくのはよくない ◇It was *wrong* of me to lose my temper. 短気を起こしたのは私が悪かった ◇This man has done nothing *wrong*. この男は何も悪いことはしていない ◇He knows that he's *done wrong*. 彼は自分が悪いことをしたとわかっている ◇There's *nothing wrong with* eating meat. 肉を食べることは何も悪いことではない ◇What's *wrong with* leading a comfortable life? 快適な生活を送ることのどこが悪いんだ 反意 **right** (RIGHT 形 2), ☞ **wrong** (EVIL 名)
▶ **wrongly** 副 ◇She was *wrongly* accused of stealing. 彼女は窃盗の濡れ衣を着せられた

unfair [規則・道徳規範に照らして]不正な; (平等に扱わず[ふさわしい扱いをせず]に)不公平な、不当な ◇Most of his criticisms were grossly *unfair*. 彼の批判のほとんどははなはだ公正を欠いていた ◇It would be *unfair* not to let you have a choice. あなたに選択肢を与えないのはフェアじゃないだろう ◇Life seems so *unfair* sometimes. 人生は時として、とても不公平に思える ◇The other team had definitely been given an *unfair* advantage. 相手チームが不当に有利な扱いを受けたのは明らかだった ◇I don't want to be *unfair to* anyone, so you'll all get an equal chance. 誰に対しても不公平にしたくないので、あなたたちみんなにも平等にチャンスが与えられるでしょう ◇I don't want to be *unfair on* anyone ...《英でまた》誰に対しても不公平でありたくない… 反意 **fair** (REASONABLE), ☞ **unfairness** (INEQUALITY)
▶ **unfairly** 副 ◇He was beginning to wonder if he had treated her *unfairly*. 彼は自分が彼女を不当に扱ったのではないかと思い始めていた

unjust 《ややフォーマル》不公平な、不当な、不条理な ◇Such *unjust* laws should be abolished. そんな不当な法律は廃止されるべきだ ◇It's an *unjust* world that we live in. 私たちが生きているのは不条理な世界である ◇The system is corrupt and *unjust*. その制度は腐敗していて不公平である ❶ unjustは特に社会・法制度に用いられる. accusation, law, punishment, regime, society, system, worldと結びつく. 反意 **just** (REASONABLE), ☞ **injustice** (INEQUALITY)
▶ **unjustly** 副 ◇She felt that she had been *unjustly* punished. 彼女は自分は不当な処罰を受けたのだと思った

unequal [ふつう名詞の前で]不平等な、不釣合いな ◇an *unequal* distribution of wealth 富の不平等な分配 ◇They saw the war as an *unequal* contest between a massive superpower and a small and defenceless country. 彼らはその戦争を、圧倒的な超大国と無防備な小国との不釣合いな争いとみなした 反意 **equal** (REASONABLE), ☞ **inequality** (INEQUALITY)

immoral (人・行動が)不道徳な、不品行な ◇There's nothing *immoral* about wanting to earn more money. もっと金を稼ぎたいと思うことに、何の不道徳なところもない ◇I think this is an unjust and *immoral* war. これは不当で道義に反する戦争だと思う 反意 **moral** (GOOD 5), ☞ **immoral** (EVIL 形)

unethical (特定の職業・制度の基準から見て)非倫理的な ◇Although it's not illegal, many people would consider it *unethical*. それは違法ではないが、多くの人々は倫理に反すると考えるだろう 反意 **ethical** (GOOD 5)

inequitable 《フォーマル》不公平な; 不平等な ◇Distribution of wealth in the country is highly *inequitable*. その国の富の分配はきわめて不公平である 反意 **equitable** (REASONABLE)

Y y

young 形

young・teenage・juvenile・junior・adolescent・teen
人や物事が短い期間の生存[存在]ゆえに十分には発達していないことを表す
【類語訳】若い, 幼い, 歴史の浅い, 新興の, ティーンエイジャーの, 少年少女の, 児童の, ジュニアの, 思春期の, 青年期の

文型&コロケーション
- a young/ a teenage/ an adolescent **boy/ girl**
- a young/ juvenile **offender**
- a young/ teenage **fan**
- a teenage/ teen **idol**

young 若い, 幼い；歴史の浅い, 建国[創業]間もない, 新興の；古くない, 新鮮な；若者[幼児]から成る ◇*young* babies/children/animals 幼い赤ん坊/幼児/幼獣 ◇Caterpillars eat the *young* leaves of this plant. 毛虫はこの植物の若い葉っぱを食べる ◇Fruit Fresh is a *young* company that is growing fast. フルート・フレッシュ社は急成長を遂げている創業間もない会社である ◇The team is full of talented *young* players. そのチームは才能ある若い選手をたくさん抱えている ◇I am the *youngest* of four sisters. 私は四人姉妹の末っ子です ◇They **married** *young* (= at an early age). 彼らは若くして結婚した ◇This cottage would be perfect for a couple with a *young* family (= a couple with young children). このコテージは幼い子のいる夫婦にはうってつけでしょう 反意 **old, elderly, aged** (OLD 2)

teenage [ふつう名詞の前で] 13〜19歳の[に特有の], ティーンエイジャーの[向けの] ◇The place was full of giggling *teenage* girls. そこはくすくす笑うティーンエイジャーの少女たちであふれていた ◇He went through a brief period of *teenage* rebellion when he was 16. 彼は16歳のときに, ティーンエイジャーとしての短い反抗期を経験した ☞ **teenager** (GIRL)

juvenile [名詞の前で]《フォーマル or 法律》少年少女の[に特有の], 児童の[向けの] ◇What can be done to help these *juvenile delinquents* turn away from crime? この非行少年たちが犯罪に手を染めないように支援するために何ができますか ◇The government has failed to deal with the problem of *juvenile* crime. 政府は少年犯罪の問題に対処することができなかった 反意 **adult** (ADULT), ☞ **juvenile** (GIRL)

junior [名詞の前で]（スポーツで）ジュニアの ◇The world *junior* tennis championships will be held in Paris next month. 世界ジュニアテニス選手権は来月パリで開催されます ❶《英》では, junior はまた7〜11[13]歳の間の子どもたちのための学校(の一部)も指す. ◆My daughter goes into the *junior* school next year. (来年, 私の娘はその小学校へ上がります) ◆the *junior* department (児童部).

adolescent (12〜18歳の)思春期の, 青年期の ◇the attitudes of *adolescent* girls 思春期の少女たちの態度 ☞ **adolescent** (GIRL)

teen [ふつう名詞の前で]《特に米, インフォーマル》13〜19歳の[に特有の], ティーンエイジャーの[向けの] ◇It was a *teen* magazine, full of glossy pictures of the latest pop idols. それは最新のアイドル歌手の光沢紙を使った写真がいっぱい載った, ティーンエイジャー向けの雑誌だった ☞ **teenager** (GIRL)

INDEX

このインデックスは，親見出しとすべての類語をアルファベット順に配列したものです。スモールキャピタルで示された英語は親見出しを表し，親見出しの収録ページと，個々の類語が収録されている親見出しがわかります。例えば，以下のようになります。

ABILITY 名 *p.1* → 親見出し ability が1ページに収録されています。
abandon 動 ▶LEAVE 4, STOP → abandon という類語が親見出し leave 4 と stop の2か所に収録されています。

A

absurd 形
  ▶RIDICULOUS
abandon 動
  ▶LEAVE 4, STOP
abandoned 形
  ▶DESERTED
abbey 名
  ▶CHURCH
abbreviated 形
  ▶SHORT 3
abduct 動
  ▶KIDNAP
abhor 動
  ▶HATE
abide by sth
  ▶FOLLOW 3
ABILITY 名 *p.1*
ability 名
  ▶ABILITY, SKILL 1
able 形
  ▶GOOD 4
abode 名
  ▶HOME
ABOLISH 動 *p.1*
abolish 動
  ▶ABOLISH
abominable 形
  ▶DISGUSTING 2
about 副
  ▶ALMOST
abscess 名
  ▶TUMOUR
absence 名
  ▶LACK
absent-minded 形
  ▶CARELESS
absolute 形
  ▶COMPLETE, FINAL
absolutely 副
  ▶QUITE 2
absorb 動
  ▶INTEREST 動, USE 動 2
absorbed 形
  ▶INTERESTED
absorbing 形
  ▶INTERESTING
abstract 形
  ▶INTELLECTUAL 1
abstract 名
  ▶SUMMARY
abstraction 名
  ▶IDEA 1

abuse 動
  ▶OFFEND
abusive 形
  ▶OFFENSIVE
academic 形
  ▶EDUCATIONAL, INTELLECTUAL 1
ACCELERATE 動 *p.2*
accelerate 動
  ▶ACCELERATE
accept 動
  ▶AGREE, GET 2, GREET, LET SB IN, TAKE 4
acceptable 形
  ▶ADEQUATE, FINE, RIGHT 形 2
acceptance 名
  ▶APPROVAL
ACCESS 名 *p.2*
access 名
  ▶ACCESS
accessible 形
  ▶CLEAR 形 2
accessory 名
  ▶DECORATION
ACCIDENT 名 *p.3*
accident 名
  ▶ACCIDENT, LUCK
acclaim 名
  ▶PRAISE 名
acclaim 動
  ▶PRAISE 動
accommodating 形
  ▶HELPFUL
accomplish 動
  ▶ACHIEVE
accomplished 形
  ▶GOOD 4
accord 名
  ▶CONTRACT
accord 動
  ▶GIVE 1
account 名
  ▶BILL, FUND 名, REPORT 2
accountability 名
  ▶RESPONSIBILITY
account for sth
  ▶EXPLAIN 2

accredited 形
  ▶OFFICIAL 形
accrue 動
  ▶COLLECT
accumulate 動
  ▶COLLECT
accurate 形
  ▶EXACT
accusation 名
  ▶CHARGE 名
ACCUSE 動 *p.3*
accuse 動
  ▶ACCUSE
accustomed to sth
  ▶USED TO STH
ache 名
  ▶PAIN
ache 動
  ▶HURT 2
achievable 形
  ▶POSSIBLE 1
ACHIEVE 動 *p.4*
achieve 動
  ▶ACHIEVE, SUCCEED
acid 形
  ▶BITTER
acknowledge 動
  ▶ADMIT, ANSWER 動
acknowledgement 名
  ▶ANSWER 名
acquaintance 名
  ▶FRIEND, FRIENDSHIP
acquiesce 動
  ▶AGREE
acquiescence 名
  ▶APPROVAL
acquire 動
  ▶BUY, GET 1, LEARN
acrid 形
  ▶BITTER
act 名
  ▶ACTION, PERFORMANCE, RULE 名
act 動
  ▶AFFECT, PLAY 動 2, PRETEND
acting 名
  ▶DRAMA
ACTION 名 *p.5*

action 名
  ▶ACTION, CASE, EFFECT, WAR
ACTIVE 形 *p.6*
active 形
  ▶ACTIVE, BUSY 1, ENERGETIC
activity 名
  ▶PROJECT
act on/upon sth
  ▶FOLLOW 3
ACTOR 名 *p.6*
actor 名
  ▶ACTOR
actress 名
  ▶ACTOR
actual 形
  ▶REAL, VERY 形
acute 形
  ▶SERIOUS 1
ad 名
  ▶ADVERTISEMENT
adapt 動
  ▶CHANGE 動 1
adaptable 形
  ▶FLEXIBLE 1
adaptation 名
  ▶CHANGE 名 2
add 動
  ▶COUNT
addict 名
  ▶FAN
ADDICTIVE 形 *p.6*
addictive 形
  ▶ADDICTIVE
address 名
  ▶HOME, SPEECH
address 動
  ▶CALL 1, FOCUS, SEND
add up to sth
  ▶REPRESENT 1
ADEQUATE 形 *p.7*
adequate 形
  ▶ADEQUATE
adhere to sth
  ▶FOLLOW 3
adjourn 動
  ▶DELAY
ADJUST 動 *p.7*
adjust 動
  ▶ADJUST

adjustable → also-ran

adjustable 形
▶ FLEXIBLE 1
adjustment 名
▶ CHANGE 名 2
administer 動
▶ REGULATE, RUN 2
administration 名
▶ GOVERNMENT 1, 2, MANAGEMENT
administrator 名
▶ ORGANIZER
admirable 形
▶ WORTHY
ADMIRATION 名 p.8
admiration 名
▶ ADMIRATION
admire 動
▶ APPRECIATE, RESPECT
admirer 名
▶ FAN, PARTNER 2
admiring 形
▶ GOOD 6
admission 名
▶ ACCESS
ADMIT 動 p.8
admit 動
▶ ADMIT, LET SB IN
adolescence 名
▶ CHILDHOOD
adolescent 形
▶ YOUNG
adolescent 名
▶ GIRL
adopt 動
▶ BRING SB UP, CHOOSE, PRETEND
adorable 形
▶ SWEET
adore 動
▶ LIKE 動, LOVE 動
adoring 形
▶ LOVING
adorn 動
▶ DECORATE
adulation 名
▶ PRAISE 名
ADULT 名 p.9
adult 形
▶ ADULT
advance 名
▶ LOAN, PROGRESS
advance 動
▶ DEVELOP 1, GO 1, PROPOSE
advanced 形
▶ MODERN
advancement 名
▶ PROGRESS
advances 名
▶ OFFER 1
advantage 名
▶ BENEFIT
advantageous 形
▶ VALUABLE 2

advent 名
▶ ARRIVAL
adventurous 形
▶ BOLD
adversary 名
▶ ENEMY
adverse 形
▶ DIFFICULT 2
adversity 名
▶ TROUBLE 2
advert 名
▶ ADVERTISEMENT
ADVERTISE 動 p.10
advertise 動
▶ ADVERTISE, PUBLISH 1
ADVERTISEMENT 名 p.10
advertisement 名
▶ ADVERTISEMENT
ADVICE 名 p.11
advice 名
▶ ADVICE
advisable 形
▶ BEST
advise 動
▶ RECOMMEND 1
ADVISER 名 p.11
adviser 名
▶ ADVISER
advocate 名
▶ LAWYER
advocate 動
▶ RECOMMEND 1
aerobics 名
▶ SPORT
affair 名
▶ BUSINESS, EVENT 1, RELATIONSHIP 2
AFFECT 動 p.11
affect 動
▶ AFFECT, IMPRESS
affection 名
▶ LOVE 名 2
affectionate 形
▶ LOVING
affiliation 名
▶ RELATIONSHIP 1
affinity 名
▶ SIMILARITY
affirm 動
▶ CLAIM
affirmative action 名
▶ DISCRIMINATION
affluence 名
▶ MONEY 3
affluent 形
▶ RICH
affordable 形
▶ CHEAP
aficionado 名
▶ EXPERT
AFRAID 形 p.12
afraid 形
▶ AFRAID
AGAINST SB/STH p.13

age 名
▶ PERIOD
aged 形
▶ OLD 2
ageism 名
▶ RACISM
agency 名
▶ SERVICE
agenda 名
▶ SCHEDULE
aggression 名
▶ ATTACK 名 1, TENSION
AGGRESSIVE 形 p.13
aggressive 形
▶ AGGRESSIVE 1, 2
aggrieved 形
▶ UNHAPPY 2
agitate 動
▶ CAMPAIGN 動
agitated 形
▶ RESTLESS
agitation 名
▶ CONCERN, TROUBLE 1
agonizing 形
▶ PAINFUL 2
agony 名
▶ DISTRESS, PAIN
AGREE 動 p.14
agree 動
▶ AGREE, MATCH 1
AGREEMENT 名 p.15
agreement 名
▶ AGREEMENT, APPROVAL
AID 名 p.16
aid 名
▶ AID, HELP 名, TOOL
aid 動
▶ HELP 動 1, 2
aid and abet
▶ HELP 動 1
ailing 形
▶ SICK 1
ailment 名
▶ DISEASE
aim 名
▶ PURPOSE
aim 動
▶ INTEND
air 名
▶ APPEARANCE
air 動
▶ SAY 2
airless 形
▶ HUMID
aisle 名
▶ CORRIDOR
alarm 名
▶ FEAR
alarm 動
▶ FRIGHTEN
alarmed 形
▶ AFRAID
alarming 形
▶ FRIGHTENING

alcohol 名
▶ DRINK 名
alert to sth 形
▶ AWARE
alert sb to sth
▶ TELL 1
alien 形
▶ FOREIGN, STRANGE 2
alienate 動
▶ DIVIDE 2
alienation 名
▶ DIVISION 2
align 動
▶ ARRANGE
alike 形
▶ LIKE 前 形
ALIVE 形 p.16
alive 形
▶ ALIVE
alive and well
▶ SAFE
allay 動
▶ EASE
allege 動
▶ CLAIM
alleged 形
▶ SUPPOSED
alleviate 動
▶ EASE
alley 名
▶ ROAD
alliance 名
▶ UNION
allocation 名
▶ SHARE 名
all over the place
▶ UNTIDY
ALLOW 動 p.17
allow 動
▶ ALLOW
allowance 名
▶ SHARE 名
all-purpose 形
▶ FLEXIBLE 1
all right 形
▶ ADEQUATE, FINE, SAFE, WELL
allude to sb/sth
▶ MENTION
allusion 名
▶ REFERENCE
ally 名
▶ PARTNER 1
ALMOST 副 p.18
almost 副
▶ ALMOST
alone 形
▶ LONELY
aloof 形
▶ COLD 2
a lot 副
▶ OFTEN
also-ran 名
▶ LOSER 1

867

alter 動
▶ CHANGE 動 1, 2
alteration 名
▶ CHANGE 名 2
alternate 動
▶ CHANGE 動 2
alternation 名
▶ CHANGE 名 1
alternative 名
▶ OPTION
amass 動
▶ COLLECT
amaze 動
▶ SURPRISE
AMAZING 形 p.18
amazing 形
▶ AMAZING
ambiguous 形
▶ MISLEADING
ambition 名
▶ HOPE 名 2
ambitious 形
▶ AGGRESSIVE 2
ambivalent 形
▶ UNSURE
amend 動
▶ ADJUST
amendment 名
▶ CHANGE 名 2
amenity 名
▶ FACILITIES
amiable 形
▶ FRIENDLY 1
amicable 形
▶ FRIENDLY 2
amoral 形
▶ CORRUPT
amount 名
▶ NUMBER
amount to sth
▶ REPRESENT 1
amphitheatre 名
▶ HALL 1
amusement 名
▶ ENTERTAINMENT, INTEREST 名 2
amusing 形
▶ FUNNY
analogous 形
▶ EQUIVALENT
analyse 動
▶ EXAMINE
analysis 名
▶ RESEARCH
ANALYST 形 p.19
analyst 名
▶ ANALYST
anarchy 名
▶ TROUBLE 1
ancestry 名
▶ FAMILY 3
anchor 名
▶ PRESENTER
ancient 形
▶ OLD 1

anecdote 名
▶ STORY
ANGER 名 p.20
ANGER 動 p.20
anger 名
▶ ANGER 名
anger 動
▶ ANGER 動
angle 名
▶ ATTITUDE
angle 動
▶ LEAN
ANGRY 形 p.21
angry 形
▶ ANGRY
angst 名
▶ CONCERN
anguish 名
▶ DISTRESS
anguished 形
▶ UPSET
animate 動
▶ ALIVE
animated 形
▶ LIVELY
animosity 名
▶ TENSION
annex 動
▶ INVADE
annihilate 動
▶ DESTROY
anniversary 名
▶ BIRTHDAY
announce 動
▶ DECLARE
announcement 名
▶ STATEMENT
announcer 名
▶ PRESENTER
ANNOY 動 p.21
annoy 動
▶ ANNOY
annoyance 名
▶ FRUSTRATION
ANNOYED 形 p.22
annoyed 形
▶ ANNOYED
ANNOYING 形 p.22
annoying 形
▶ ANNOYING
annul 動
▶ CANCEL
ANSWER 名 p.23
ANSWER 動 p.23
answer 名
▶ ANSWER 名, SOLUTION
answer 動
▶ ANSWER 動
antagonism 名
▶ TENSION
antagonistic 形
▶ AGAINST SB/STH
antagonize 動
▶ ANGER 動

anticipate 動
▶ EXPECT
anticipation 名
▶ EXPECTATION
antidote 名
▶ DRUG 2
antipathy 名
▶ TENSION
antiquated 形
▶ OLD-FASHIONED
antique 形
▶ OLD 1
antisocial 形
▶ SOLITARY
antonym 名
▶ OPPOSITE 2
anxiety 名
▶ CONCERN
anxious 形
▶ EAGER, STRESSFUL, WORRIED
apartheid 名
▶ DISCRIMINATION
apathetic 形
▶ INDIFFERENT
aperture 名
▶ HOLE 1
aplomb 名
▶ CONFIDENCE
apologetic 形
▶ SORRY
appal 動
▶ SHOCK 動
appalling 形
▶ TERRIBLE 3
apparatus 名
▶ EQUIPMENT, SYSTEM
apparel 名
▶ CLOTHES
APPARENT 形 p.24
apparent 形
▶ APPARENT, CLEAR 形 1
appeal 名
▶ CASE, INTEREST 名 1, REQUEST
appeal 動
▶ ASK 2, INTEREST 動
appealing 形
▶ POPULAR
APPEAR 動 p.25
appear 動
▶ APPEAR, ARRIVE, FEATURE 動
appear 連結動詞
▶ SEEM
APPEARANCE 名 p.25
appearance 名
▶ APPEARANCE, ARRIVAL
appetizing 形
▶ DELICIOUS
applaud 動
▶ PRAISE 動
applicable 形
▶ RELEVANT

applicant 名
▶ CANDIDATE
application 名
▶ REQUEST, USE 名
APPLY 動 p.26
apply 動
▶ APPLY, ASK 2
APPOINT 動 p.26
appoint 動
▶ APPOINT
appointment 名
▶ JOB, MEETING 2
appraisal 名
▶ ASSESSMENT
APPRECIATE 動 p.27
appreciate 動
▶ APPRECIATE, KNOW
appreciation 名
▶ ADMIRATION, THANKS, UNDERSTANDING
appreciative 形
▶ GOOD 6, GRATEFUL
apprehension 名
▶ CONCERN
apprehensive 形
▶ WORRIED
apprentice 名
▶ RECRUIT
approach 名
▶ ARRIVAL, OFFER 1, WAY 1
approach 動
▶ COME 1, 2
approachable 形
▶ FRIENDLY 1
appropriate 形
▶ GOOD 2
APPROVAL 名 p.27
approval 名
▶ APPROVAL, PRAISE 名
APPROVE 動 p.28
approve 動
▶ AGREE, APPROVE, IN FAVOUR (OF SB/STH)
approving 形
▶ GOOD 6
approximate 形
▶ VAGUE
apt 形
▶ GOOD 2
aptitude 名
▶ SKILL 1
arbiter 名
▶ JUDGE 名
arbitrate 動
▶ INTERVENE
arbitrator 名
▶ NEGOTIATOR
arc 動
▶ CURVE
archetypal 形
▶ TYPICAL
archetype 名
▶ EXAMPLE 2

archive 名
▶ DOCUMENT
ardent 形
▶ INTENSE
arduous 形
▶ HARD
AREA 形 p.28
area 名
▶ AREA 1, 2, PLACE
ARGUE 動 p.30
argue 動
▶ ARGUE, CLAIM
ARGUMENT 名 p.30
argument 名
▶ ARGUMENT 1, 2
arise 動
▶ FOLLOW 2, HAPPEN
the aristocracy 名
▶ ELITE
arm 名
▶ DEPARTMENT
arm 動
▶ EQUIP
arms 名
▶ LOGO
ARMY 名 p.31
army 名
▶ ARMY
aroma 名
▶ SMELL
arouse 動
▶ STIMULATE
ARRANGE 動 p.32
arrange 動
▶ ARRANGE, ORGANIZE
arrangement 名
▶ AGREEMENT, DESIGN 名, PLANNING
array 名
▶ RANGE 1
arrears 名
▶ DEBT
ARRIVAL 名 p.32
arrival 名
▶ ARRIVAL
ARRIVE 動 p.33
arrive 動
▶ ARRIVE, COME 2, SUCCEED
arrive at sth
▶ ACHIEVE
arrogance 名
▶ PRIDE
arrogant 形
▶ PROUD 2
arsenal 名
▶ SUPPLY
art 名
▶ SKILL 1
artefact 名
▶ THING 1
ARTICLE 名 p.34
article 名
▶ ARTICLE
ARTIFICIAL 形 p.34

artificial 形
▶ ARTIFICIAL
artist 名
▶ ACTOR
artiste 名
▶ ACTOR
artistic 形
▶ CREATIVE
artistry 名
▶ SKILL 2
artwork 名
▶ PICTURE
as a rule
▶ USUALLY
ascend 動
▶ CLIMB
ascertain 動
▶ FIND 3
ashamed 形
▶ SORRY
ASK 動 p.34
ask 動
▶ ASK 1, 2, CHARGE 動, DEMAND 動
aspiration 名
▶ HOPE 名 2
aspire 動
▶ HOPE 動
assassinate 動
▶ KILL
assassination 名
▶ MURDER
assault 名
▶ ATTACK 名 1, 2, CRITICISM
assault 動
▶ ATTACK 動 1
assemble 動
▶ BUILD, MEET 1
assembly 名
▶ MEETING 1, PRODUCTION
assent 名
▶ APPROVAL
assert 動
▶ CLAIM
assertive 形
▶ AGGRESSIVE 2
assertiveness 名
▶ CONFIDENCE
assess 動
▶ JUDGE 動, TEST 動 2
ASSESSMENT 名 p.36
assessment 名
▶ ASSESSMENT
asset 名
▶ BENEFIT, THING 2
ASSIGNMENT 名 p.36
assignment 名
▶ ASSIGNMENT
assist 動
▶ HELP 動 1, 2
assistance 名
▶ HELP 名

assistant 名
▶ SALESMAN
associate 名
▶ PARTNER 1
associate 動
▶ RELATE
associated 形
▶ RELATED
association 名
▶ RELATION, RELATIONSHIP 1, UNION
assorted 形
▶ DIVERSE
assortment 名
▶ RANGE 1
assume 動
▶ PRETEND, SUPPOSE
assumed 形
▶ SUPPOSED
assumption 名
▶ SPECULATION
assurance 名
▶ CONFIDENCE, PROMISE 名
assure 動
▶ ENSURE, PROMISE 動
assured 形
▶ CERTAIN
assure yourself 動
▶ CHECK 2
astonish 動
▶ SURPRISE
astonishing 形
▶ AMAZING
astound 動
▶ SURPRISE
astronomical 形
▶ HIGH 1
astute 形
▶ SHREWD
asylum 名
▶ SHELTER
asylum seeker 名
▶ REFUGEE
at a loss
▶ CONFUSED
at a standstill
▶ STILL
at fault
▶ GUILTY
at large
▶ FREE 形 1
atlas 名
▶ MAP
at leisure 形
▶ EASY 2
ATMOSPHERE 名 p.37
atmosphere 名
▶ ATMOSPHERE
at odds
▶ INCONSISTENT
at peace
▶ DEAD

at risk
▶ VULNERABLE
atrocity 名
▶ CRIME 2
ATTACH 動 p.38
attach 動
▶ ATTACH
attachment 名
▶ LOVE 名 2
ATTACK 名 p.38
ATTACK 動 p.39
attack 名
▶ ATTACK 名 1, 2, CRITICISM
attack 動
▶ ATTACK 動 1, 2, BLAME
attain 動
▶ ACHIEVE
ATTEMPT 名 p.40
attempt 名
▶ ATTACK 名 2, ATTEMPT
attempt 動
▶ TRY 1
attend 動
▶ VISIT 動
attendant 形
▶ RELATED
attend to sb/sth
▶ LOOK AFTER SB
ATTENTION 名 p.40
attention 名
▶ ATTENTION
attentive 形
▶ INTERESTED
at times
▶ SOMETIMES
ATTITUDE 名 p.41
attitude 名
▶ ATTITUDE
attorney 名
▶ LAWYER
attract 動
▶ INTEREST 動
attraction 名
▶ INTEREST 名 1, LOVE 名 1
attractive 形
▶ BEAUTIFUL 1, 2, POPULAR
attribute 名
▶ FEATURE 名
at work 形
▶ BUSY 1
atypical 形
▶ UNUSUAL
auction 動
▶ SELL 1
auctioneer 名
▶ SALESMAN
auction sth off
▶ SELL 1
audacity 名
▶ COURAGE
AUDIENCE 名 p.42

audience 名
▶ AUDIENCE, INTERVIEW 1, MARKET 1
audit 名
▶ INSPECTION
audit 動
▶ CHECK 1
audition 名
▶ INTERVIEW 2
auditorium 名
▶ HALL 1
aura 名
▶ ATMOSPHERE
auspicious 形
▶ PROMISING
austere 形
▶ PLAIN 1
authentic 形
▶ REAL, RELIABLE 2
authenticate 動
▶ CONFIRM 1
author 名
▶ WRITER
authoritative 形
▶ RELIABLE 2
THE AUTHORITIES 名 p.42
the authorities 名
▶ AUTHORITIES
authority 名
▶ CONTROL, EXPERT, PERMISSION, RIGHT
authorization 名
▶ LICENCE, PERMISSION
authorize 動
▶ ALLOW
authorized 形
▶ OFFICIAL 1
autocrat 名
▶ DICTATOR
autocratic 形
▶ REPRESSIVE
autonomy 名
▶ FREEDOM, INDEPENDENCE
AVAILABLE 形 p.43
available 形
▶ AVAILABLE, FREE 3
avant-garde 形
▶ EXPERIMENTAL
avenue 名
▶ ROAD
AVERAGE 形 p.43
average 形
▶ AVERAGE, NORMAL
aversion 名
▶ HATRED
avert 動
▶ PREVENT
avid 形
▶ EAGER
avoid 動
▶ PREVENT
await 動
▶ EXPECT

AWARD 名 p.43
award 名
▶ AWARD, COMPENSATION
award 動
▶ GIVE 1
AWARE 形 p.44
aware 形
▶ AWARE
AWARENESS 名 p.44
awareness 名
▶ AWARENESS
awe 名
▶ ADMIRATION
awesome 形
▶ AMAZING, GREAT 1
awful 形
▶ TERRIBLE 1, 2, 3
awkward 形
▶ EMBARRASSED, SENSITIVE 2, WRONG 2
axe 動
▶ ABOLISH, FIRE

B

babe 名
▶ DARLING
baby 名
▶ CHILD, DARLING
back 名
▶ SUPPORT
back down
▶ GIVE WAY
backdrop 名
▶ CONTEXT, ENVIRONMENT
backer 名
▶ SPONSOR
backfire 動
▶ FAIL 2
background 名
▶ CONTEXT, ENVIRONMENT
backing 名
▶ INVESTMENT
backpacker 名
▶ TOURIST
backtrack 動
▶ BREAK 4
backup 名
▶ HELP 名
back sb/sth up
▶ CONFIRM 2
BAD 形 p.46
bad 形
▶ BAD, DIFFICULT 2, EVIL 形, HARMFUL, INCOMPETENT, OFFENSIVE, POOR 2, ROTTEN, SERIOUS 1, SICK 1, SORRY, WRONG 2
bad-tempered 形
▶ IRRITABLE

baffling 形
▶ CONFUSING
bail sb out
▶ SAVE 1
bait 名
▶ BRIBE
balance sth against sth
▶ COMPARE 1
bald 形
▶ PLAIN 2
ballot 名
▶ ELECTION
ballot 名
▶ SURVEY
ballroom 名
▶ HALL 1
BAN 名 p.46
BAN 動 p.47
ban 名
▶ BAN 名
ban 動
▶ BAN 動
band 名
▶ PARTY 2
bandit 名
▶ THIEF
BANG 動 p.47
bang 動
▶ BANG 1, 2, HIT 1
bang into sth
▶ CRASH
banish 動
▶ EXPEL
bank 名
▶ SUPPLY
bank 動
▶ LEAN, SAVE 3
banking 名
▶ FINANCE
bankroll 動
▶ FUND 動
BANKRUPT 形 p.48
bankrupt 形
▶ BANKRUPT
banned 形
▶ FORBIDDEN
banter 名
▶ HUMOUR
bar 名
▶ LAWYER, PIECE
bar 動
▶ BAN 動, BLOCK 2
barbaric 形
▶ CRUEL
bare 形
▶ EMPTY, NAKED, PLAIN 1, 2
bargain 名
▶ AGREEMENT
bargain 動
▶ NEGOTIATE
bargain for/on sth
▶ EXPECT
barge 動
▶ PUSH 2

barge in
▶ INTERRUPT
barrage 名
▶ FLOOD 名 2
barricade 名
▶ BARRIER
barricade 動
▶ BLOCK 2
BARRIER 名 p.48
barrier 名
▶ BARRIER, OBSTACLE
barrister 名
▶ LAWYER
barter 名
▶ EXCHANGE
barter 動
▶ REPLACE 2
BASE 動 p.49
base 名
▶ BOTTOM
base 動
▶ BASE
base 形
▶ EVIL 形
bash 動
▶ HIT 1
basic 形
▶ FUNDAMENTAL
BASICS 名 p.49
basics 名
▶ BASICS
basis 名
▶ REASON
bass 形
▶ DEEP 2
bath 動
▶ WASH
bathe 動
▶ CLEAN 動
bathroom 名
▶ TOILET
batter 動
▶ BEAT
battery 名
▶ FLOOD 名 2
battle 名
▶ CAMPAIGN 名, WAR
battle 動
▶ COMPETE
batty 形
▶ MAD
baulk 動
▶ HESITATE
bawl 動
▶ SHOUT
beach 名
▶ COAST
bead 名
▶ DROP
be against sb/sth
▶ AGAINST SB/STH
be aimed at sb
▶ FOCUS
be aimed at sth
▶ DESIGN 動 2

be all for sth/for doing sth
▶ IN FAVOUR (OF SB/STH)
beam 動
▶ SMILE
bear 動
▶ HATE, STAND 2
bearing 名
▶ WAY 3
bear sb/sth in mind
▶ REMEMBER
bear sb/sth out
▶ CONFIRM 2
bear witness
▶ CONFIRM 1
BEAT 動 p.50
beat 動
▶ BEAT, DEFEAT, SHAKE 1, STIR
be at odds
▶ CONFLICT 動, DISAGREE
beat sb up
▶ ATTACK 動 1
BEAUTIFUL 形 p.50
beautiful 形
▶ BEAUTIFUL 1, 2
be blessed with sb/sth
▶ HAVE 2
be/get bogged down
▶ HOLD SB/STH UP
be born and bred
▶ BRING SB UP
be bothered
▶ CARE
BECOME 連結動 p.52
become 連結動
▶ BECOME
be devoted to sb
▶ LOVE 動
be done
▶ FINISH
be employed
▶ WORK 動 1
be endowed with sth
▶ HAVE 2
be/become estranged
▶ DIVIDE 2
be fond of sb
▶ LOVE 動
be fond of sth
▶ LIKE 動
BEGIN 動 p.53
begin 動
▶ BEGIN, START 動
BEGINNER 名 p.53
beginner 名
▶ BEGINNER
beginning 名
▶ START 名
beginnings
▶ SOURCE
be going places
▶ DO WELL

be/stand in awe of sb/sth
▶ RESPECT 動
be in charge
▶ RUN 2
be in power
▶ RULE 動 1
be/have sb in stitches
▶ LAUGH
be in tears
▶ CRY
be intended for/as/to be sth
▶ DESIGN 動 2
be/get involved
▶ JOIN
be/get in sb's/the way
▶ BLOCK 2
be in work
▶ WORK 動 1
be keen on sth
▶ LIKE 動
belated 形
▶ LATE
be left 動
▶ REMAIN
belief 名
▶ FAITH, VALUES, VIEW 1
believable 形
▶ POSSIBLE 2
believe 動
▶ THINK
believe in sb
▶ TRUST
believe in sth/in doing sth
▶ IN FAVOUR (OF SB/STH)
bellow 動
▶ SHOUT
belongings 名
▶ THING 2
beloved 形
▶ DEAR
beloved 名
▶ DARLING
belt 名
▶ AREA 1
bemused 形
▶ CONFUSED
benchmark 名
▶ CRITERION
bend 動
▶ CORNER
bend 動
▶ CURVE
benefactor 名
▶ SPONSOR
beneficial 形
▶ VALUABLE 2
BENEFIT 名 p.54
benefit 名
▶ BENEFIT
benefit 動
▶ HELP 動 2

benevolent 形
▶ KIND 形
benign 形
▶ KIND 形
bent 名
▶ TENDENCY
be off
▶ LEAVE 1
be of service
▶ HELP 動 1
be on a par with sb/sth
▶ COMPARE 2
be on your feet
▶ STAND 1
be/go on your way
▶ GO AWAY
berate 動
▶ SCOLD
bereft 形
▶ LONELY
be responsible for sb/sth
▶ RUN 2
be seated 動
▶ SIT
beside the point
▶ IRRELEVANT
beside yourself
▶ HYSTERICAL
be situated 動
▶ BASE
be/feel sorry for sb
▶ SORRY FOR SB
besotted 形
▶ IN LOVE
BEST 形 p.54
best 形
▶ BEST
best 動
▶ DEFEAT
the/your best bet
▶ OPTION
best-loved 形
▶ FAVOURITE
bestow 動
▶ GIVE 1
be together
▶ GO OUT
betray 動
▶ CHEAT 動, REVEAL, TELL 2
BETTER 形 p.55
better 形
▶ BETTER
be under the impression that…
▶ THINK
bewildered 形
▶ CONFUSED
bewildering 形
▶ CONFUSING
bewitch 動
▶ DELIGHT
beyond belief
▶ INCREDIBLE

bias 名
▶ DISCRIMINATION, TENDENCY
bias 動
▶ INFLUENCE 動
BIASED 形 p.55
biased 形
▶ BIASED
bicker 動
▶ ARGUE
bid 名
▶ OFFER 2
big 形
▶ IMPORTANT, LARGE
bigotry 名
▶ RACISM
bilk 動
▶ DEFRAUD
BILL 名 p.56
bill 名
▶ BILL
bill 動
▶ CHARGE 動
bimbo 名
▶ FOOL
biographer 名
▶ WRITER
birth 名
▶ FAMILY 3, START 名
BIRTHDAY 名 p.56
birthday 名
▶ BIRTHDAY
BIT 名 p.57
bit 名
▶ BIT, MINUTE
BITE 動 p.57
bite 動
▶ BITE
a bit much 形
▶ EXCESSIVE
BITTER 形 p.58
bitter 形
▶ BITTER, FREEZING
bizarre 形
▶ STRANGE 1
blab 動
▶ TELL 2
black 形
▶ DARK 1, NEGATIVE
blacklist 動
▶ EXCLUDE 2
blackmail 名
▶ CORRUPTION
BLAME 動 p.58
blame 名
▶ FAULT
blame 動
▶ BLAME
blameless 形
▶ INNOCENT
blast 名
▶ FUN
bleak 形
▶ NEGATIVE

blemish 名
▶ MARK
blend 動
▶ MATCH 2
blessing 名
▶ APPROVAL
bliss 名
▶ JOY
blissful 形
▶ HAPPY
blister 名
▶ TUMOUR
blob 名
▶ DROP
BLOCK 動 p.59
block 名
▶ PIECE
block 動
▶ BLOCK 1, 2
block sth off
▶ BLOCK 2
bloke 名
▶ MAN 1
blood 名
▶ FAMILY 3
bloodthirsty 形
▶ VIOLENT
bloody 形
▶ VIOLENT
bloody 副
▶ VERY
bloom 動
▶ DO WELL
blossom 動
▶ DO WELL
blot 名
▶ MARK
blow the whistle on sb/sth
▶ TELL 2
blueprint 名
▶ PLAN 2
the blues 名
▶ GLOOM
bluff 名
▶ TRICK
bluff 動
▶ PRETEND
blunder 名
▶ MISTAKE 1
blunt 形
▶ HONEST
blurb 名
▶ ADVERTISEMENT
blush 動
▶ FLUSH
board 名
▶ COMMITTEE, SIGN 2
BOAST 動 p.60
boast 動
▶ BOAST, HAVE 2
boastful 形
▶ PROUD 2
body 名
▶ COMMITTEE, POINT

bodyguard 名
▶ GUARD
boil 動
▶ TUMOUR
boiling 形
▶ HOT
BOLD 形 p.60
bold 形
▶ BOLD, BRIGHT
bolt 動
▶ CLOSE, FLEE
bomber 名
▶ GUERRILLA
BOOK 名 p.61
book 名
▶ BOOK
book 動
▶ ORDER 2
bookish 形
▶ INTELLECTUAL 2
booklet 名
▶ LEAFLET
boom 動
▶ DO WELL
boost 動
▶ INCREASE
booth 名
▶ STALL
booze 名
▶ DRINK 名
booze 動
▶ DRINK 動
borderline 形
▶ VAGUE
borderline 名
▶ LIMIT 2
BORING 形 p.61
boring 形
▶ BORING
borough 名
▶ CITY
boss 名
▶ LEADER 1, MANAGER
bother 動
▶ INTERRUPT, WORRY
bothered 形
▶ WORRIED
bottleneck 名
▶ TRAFFIC
BOTTOM 名 p.62
bottom 名
▶ BOTTOM
boulevard 名
▶ ROAD
bounce 動
▶ JUMP
bouncer 名
▶ GUARD
bound 形
▶ CERTAIN
bound 動
▶ RUN 1
boundary 名
▶ LIMIT 2

bounds 名
▶ LIMIT 2
bout 名
▶ GAME
bowl 動
▶ THROW
bowl sb over
▶ SURPRISE
bow to sth
▶ GIVE WAY
box 動
▶ FIGHT 動
boy 名
▶ CHILD
boycott 動
▶ BAN 動
boyfriend 名
▶ PARTNER 2
boyish 形
▶ CHILDISH
the boys 名
▶ FRIEND
bracket 名
▶ CATEGORY
bracket 動
▶ CLASSIFY
brag 動
▶ BOAST
brain 名
▶ GENIUS, INTELLIGENCE, MIND
branch 名
▶ AREA 2, DEPARTMENT
brand 名
▶ KIND
brand 動
▶ CALL 1
brand new 形
▶ NEW 2
brash 形
▶ CONFIDENT
brat 名
▶ CHILD
BRAVE 形 p.62
brave 形
▶ BRAVE
bravery 名
▶ COURAGE
brawl 名
▶ FIGHT 名
brawl 動
▶ FIGHT 動
breach 動
▶ BREAK 3
breadth 名
▶ RANGE 2
BREAK 動 p.63
break 名
▶ HOLIDAY 1, 2, OPPORTUNITY, PAUSE
break 動
▶ BREAK 1, 2, 3, 4, CONVEY
breakdown 名
▶ FAILURE

break down
▶ BREAK 2, FAIL 2
break sb's heart
▶ HURT 1
break-in 名
▶ THEFT
break into sth
▶ ROB
break up
▶ DIVIDE 1
breathtaking 形
▶ AMAZING
breed 動
▶ KEEP 4
BRIBE 名 p.65
bribe 名
▶ BRIBE
bribery 名
▶ CORRUPTION
brief 形
▶ SHORT 1, 3
brief 動
▶ TELL 1
BRIGHT 形 p.65
bright 形
▶ BRIGHT, CHEERFUL, INTELLIGENT, PROMISING
brilliant 形
▶ BRIGHT, GREAT 1, INTELLIGENT
bring 動
▶ TAKE 1
bring sth about
▶ CAUSE
bring sth down
▶ REDUCE
bring sth in
▶ INTRODUCE
bring sb in sth
▶ MAKE 2
bring sth to light
▶ REVEAL
BRING SB UP p.65
bring sb up
▶ BRING SB UP
brisk 形
▶ FAST
brittle 形
▶ FRAGILE
broad 形
▶ WIDE 1, 2
broadcaster 名
▶ PRESENTER
broaden 動
▶ EXPAND
brochure 名
▶ LEAFLET
broke 形
▶ BANKRUPT
bruise 名
▶ INJURY
bruise 動
▶ INJURE
BRUSH 動 p.66

brush → cast about/around for sth

brush 動
▶ BRUSH, TOUCH
brutal 形
▶ CRUEL, RUTHLESS
B.S. 略
▶ NONSENSE
bubbly 形
▶ LIVELY
buckle 動
▶ BUTTON 2
buddy 名
▶ FRIEND
budget 形
▶ CHEAP
budget 名
▶ FUND
budget 動
▶ SAVE 2
budgetary 形
▶ ECONOMIC
buff 名
▶ EXPERT
buffer 名
▶ PRECAUTION
bug 名
▶ DEFECT, DISEASE
bug 動
▶ ANNOY
BUILD 動 p.66
build 動
▶ BUILD, MAKE 1
builder 名
▶ MAKER
build sth in
▶ INCLUDE
building 名
▶ PRODUCTION
bull 名
▶ NONSENSE
bulldoze 動
▶ DEMOLISH
bulletin board 名
▶ SIGN 2
bullish 形
▶ OPTIMISTIC
bullshit 名
▶ NONSENSE
bullying 名
▶ REPRESSION
bump 名
▶ TUMOUR
bump 動
▶ BANG 2, HIT 1, SHAKE 2
bumper 形
▶ LARGE
bump into sb
▶ MEET 2
bump sb off
▶ KILL
bunch 名
▶ GROUP 1, 2
buoyant 形
▶ SUCCESSFUL 2

burden 名
▶ CARGO, RESPONSIBILITY
bureau 名
▶ SERVICE
BUREAUCRACY 名 p.67
bureaucracy 名
▶ AUTHORITIES, BUREAUCRACY
bureaucrat 名
▶ OFFICIAL
burglar 名
▶ THIEF
burglarize 動
▶ ROB
burglary 名
▶ THEFT
burgle 動
▶ ROB
burn 動
▶ FLUSH, HURT 2
burning 形
▶ HOT, PAINFUL 1, URGENT
burst its banks
▶ FLOOD
bury 動
▶ HIDE
BUSINESS 名 p.67
business 名
▶ BUSINESS, COMPANY, EVENT 1, INDUSTRY, TASK, TRADE
businesslike 形
▶ EFFICIENT
businessman 名
▶ EXECUTIVE
bust 形
▶ BANKRUPT
bustling 形
▶ CROWDED
BUSY 形 p.68
busy 形
▶ BUSY 1, 2, CROWDED
BUTTON 名 p.69
button 名
▶ BUTTON 1, 2
BUY 動 p.70
buy 動
▶ BUY
buyer 名
▶ CUSTOMER
buzz 名
▶ EXCITEMENT
bygone 形
▶ PREVIOUS
bystander 名
▶ WITNESS

C

cabinet 名
▶ GOVERNMENT 1
cadet 名
▶ RECRUIT

cajole 動
▶ PERSUADE
calamity 名
▶ CRISIS
CALCULATE 動 p.72
calculate 動
▶ CALCULATE, ESTIMATE
calculated 形
▶ DELIBERATE
calculation 名
▶ ESTIMATE
calendar 名
▶ SCHEDULE
calibre 名
▶ QUALITY
CALL 動 p.72
call 名
▶ REQUEST, VISIT
call 動
▶ CALL 1, 2, HAVE 4, REGARD, VISIT
call for sth
▶ ASK 2, NEED
(no) call for sth
▶ DEMAND
call sth off
▶ ABOLISH
callous 形
▶ RUTHLESS
call sb up
▶ CALL 2
CALM 形 p.74
calm 形
▶ CALM, QUIET 1
calm 名
▶ PEACE, SILENCE
camaraderie 名
▶ FRIENDSHIP
camouflage 動
▶ HIDE
camp 名
▶ PARTY 1
CAMPAIGN 名 p.74
CAMPAIGN 動 p.75
campaign 名
▶ CAMPAIGN, WAR
campaign 動
▶ CAMPAIGN
CANCEL 動 p.76
cancel 動
▶ ABOLISH, CANCEL
candid 形
▶ HONEST
CANDIDATE 名 p.76
candidate 名
▶ CANDIDATE
canny 形
▶ SHREWD
canvass 動
▶ SURVEY
capability 名
▶ ABILITY
capable 形
▶ GOOD 4

capacity 名
▶ ABILITY
capital 名
▶ MONEY 1
captain 動
▶ LEAD
captaincy 名
▶ MANAGEMENT
captivate 動
▶ DELIGHT
capture 動
▶ INVADE
CARE 動 p.77
care 動
▶ CARE
career 名
▶ LIFE 2, WORK 名 1
care for sb
▶ LOOK AFTER SB, LOVE 動
careful 形
▶ DETAILED
CARELESS 形 p.77
careless 形
▶ CARELESS
CARGO 名 p.77
cargo 名
▶ CARGO
caricature 名
▶ PARODY
caring 形
▶ LOVING
carp 動
▶ COMPLAIN
carry 動
▶ SELL 2, TAKE 1
carry on
▶ CONTINUE 1, 2
carry sth out
▶ DO, FOLLOW 3
cartoon 名
▶ PICTURE
carve 動
▶ CUT 2
carve sth up
▶ SHARE 動
cascade 動
▶ FLOW
CASE 名 p.78
case 名
▶ ARGUMENT 2, CASE, EXAMPLE 1, INVESTIGATION, PATIENT, SITUATION
CASH 動 p.78
cash 名
▶ MONEY 1, 2
cash 動
▶ CASH
cash sth in
▶ CASH
cast about/around for sth
▶ LOOK 動 2

castigate 動
▶ SCOLD
casual 形
▶ INFORMAL
catalogue 名
▶ LIST 名, SERIES
catastrophe 名
▶ CRISIS, DISASTER
catch 名
▶ BUTTON 2, DISADVANTAGE
catch 動
▶ FIND 2, HEAR, LOOK 動 1, SEE, SUFFER FROM STH, TAKE 3
catch on
▶ UNDERSTAND 1
catchphrase 名
▶ SLOGAN
catch up 動
▶ GET 3
categorical 形
▶ FINAL
categorize 動
▶ CLASSIFY
CATEGORY 名 *p.79*
category 名
▶ CATEGORY
cathedral 名
▶ CHURCH
catwalk 名
▶ CORRIDOR
caucus 名
▶ MEETING 1
CAUSE 動 *p.79*
cause 名
▶ CHARITY, REASON, SOURCE
cause 動
▶ CAUSE
cavity 名
▶ HOLE 2
cease 動
▶ STOP
ceiling 名
▶ LIMIT 1
celebrate 動
▶ PLAY 動 1, PRAISE 動
celebrated 形
▶ FAMOUS
celebration 名
▶ EVENT 2
celebrity 名
▶ FAME, STAR
censure 名
▶ CRITICISM
censure 動
▶ BLAME
central 形
▶ MAIN
centre 名
▶ ORGANIZATION
century 名
▶ PERIOD

CERTAIN 形 *p.80*
certain 形
▶ CERTAIN, PARTICULAR, SURE
certainty 名
▶ FAITH
CERTIFICATE 名 *p.81*
certificate 名
▶ CERTIFICATE
certify 動
▶ APPROVE, CONFIRM 2
cessation 名
▶ END 名
chagrin 名
▶ FRUSTRATION
chain 名
▶ SERIES
chair 名
▶ LEADER 1
chair 動
▶ LEAD
chairman 名
▶ LEADER 1
challenge 名
▶ PROBLEM
challenge 動
▶ DOUBT 動
challenger 名
▶ PARTICIPANT
challenging 形
▶ DIFFICULT 1
chamber 名
▶ HALL 1
champion 動
▶ SUPPORT
championship 名
▶ AWARD
chance 名
▶ LUCK, OPPORTUNITY, POSSIBILITY, RISK 2
chance 動
▶ DARE
(the) chances are...
▶ PROBABLY
CHANGE 名 *p.81*
CHANGE 動 *p.83*
change 名
▶ CHANGE 名 1, 2, MONEY 2
change 動
▶ CASH, CHANGE 動 1, 2, REPLACE 2, TURN 2, WEAR
change over
▶ SWITCH
chapel 名
▶ CHURCH
character 名
▶ CHARM, NATURE 1, PERSON, PERSONALITY, REPUTATION
characteristic 形
▶ TYPICAL

characteristic 名
▶ FEATURE 名
CHARGE 名 *p.84*
CHARGE 動 *p.85*
charge 名
▶ CHARGE 名, EXCITEMENT, RATE, RESPONSIBILITY
charge 動
▶ ACCUSE, ATTACK 動 2, CHARGE 動, RUN 1
charisma 名
▶ CHARM
charismatic 形
▶ NICE 2
CHARITY 名 *p.85*
charity 名
▶ AID, CHARITY
CHARM 名 *p.86*
charm 名
▶ CHARM, INTEREST 名 1
charm 動
▶ DELIGHT
charming 形
▶ BEAUTIFUL 2, NICE 2
chart 名
▶ MAP
chart 動
▶ RECORD
charter 名
▶ LAW, LICENCE
charter 動
▶ ORDER 2
chase 動
▶ FOLLOW 1
chat 名
▶ DISCUSSION
chatter 名
▶ DISCUSSION
chat sb up
▶ FLIRT
chauvinism 名
▶ RACISM
CHEAP 形 *p.86*
cheap 形
▶ CHEAP, POOR 2
CHEAT 名 *p.87*
CHEAT 動 *p.87*
cheat 名
▶ CHEAT 名
cheat 動
▶ CHEAT 動
cheater 名
▶ CHEAT 名
CHECK 動 *p.88*
check 名
▶ BILL, INSPECTION, INVESTIGATION, LIMIT 1
check 動
▶ CHECK 1, 2, SUPPRESS 2
checklist 名
▶ LIST 名

check sth out
▶ LOOK 動 1
check over sb/sth
▶ CHECK 1
check through sth
▶ CHECK 1
check-up 名
▶ INSPECTION
cheeky 形
▶ RUDE
cheer 動
▶ ENCOURAGE, SHOUT
CHEERFUL 形 *p.89*
cheerful 形
▶ CHEERFUL
cheer sb up
▶ ENCOURAGE
cheery 形
▶ CHEERFUL
chemical 名
▶ MATERIAL
cherish 動
▶ APPRECIATE
cherished 形
▶ DEAR
chew 動
▶ BITE
chicken 名
▶ COWARD
chicken out 動
▶ PANIC
chide 動
▶ SCOLD
chief 形
▶ MAIN, TOP
chief 名
▶ LEADER 1
chief executive 名
▶ LEADER 1
CHILD 名 *p.89*
child 名
▶ CHILD
CHILDHOOD 名 *p.90*
childhood 名
▶ CHILDHOOD
CHILDISH 形 *p.90*
childish 形
▶ CHILDISH
childlike 形
▶ CHILDISH
chill 名
▶ COLD 1
chill 動
▶ COOL
chilling 形
▶ FRIGHTENING
chill out
▶ REST
chilly 形
▶ COLD 1
chip 名
▶ FRAGMENT
chip in
▶ GIVE 3, INTERRUPT
CHOICE 名 *p.91*

choice → collective

choice 名
▶ CHOICE 1, 2, OPTION, RANGE 1
choke 動
▶ COUGH
CHOOSE 動 p.91
choose 動
▶ CHOOSE, DECIDE
chop 動
▶ CUT 2
choppy 形
▶ ROUGH
chore 名
▶ TASK
christen 動
▶ CALL 1
chronicle 動
▶ DESCRIBE
chronology 名
▶ SERIES
chubby 形
▶ FAT
chuck 動
▶ THROW
chuckle 動
▶ LAUGH
chunk 名
▶ PIECE
CHURCH 名 p.92
church 名
▶ CHURCH
churlish 形
▶ RUDE
churn sth out
▶ MANUFACTURE
circle 名
▶ GROUP 2
circle 動
▶ SPIN
circular 形
▶ LEAFLET
circulate 動
▶ FLOW, PUBLISH 1
circumstance 名
▶ SITUATION
citation 名
▶ REFERENCE
cite 動
▶ ACCUSE, MENTION, QUOTE
CITIZEN 名 p.93
citizen 名
▶ CITIZEN, RESIDENT
CITY 名 p.93
city 名
▶ CITY
civic 形
▶ SOCIAL
civil 形
▶ NATIONAL, POLITE
civility 名
▶ RESPECT
civil servant 名
▶ OFFICIAL
CLAIM 動 p.94

claim 名
▶ REQUEST, RIGHT
claim 動
▶ ASK 2, CLAIM
clamber 動
▶ CLIMB
clamour 動
▶ DEMAND
clan 名
▶ PEOPLE
clarify 動
▶ EXPLAIN 1
clash 名
▶ CONFLICT 名, FIGHT 名
clash 動
▶ ARGUE, BANG 1, CONFLICT 動, FIGHT 動
clasp 名
▶ BUTTON 2
clasp 動
▶ HOLD
CLASS 名 p.94
class 名
▶ CATEGORY, CLASS 1, 2, 3, STYLE
class 動
▶ CLASSIFY
classic 形
▶ ELEGANT, EXCELLENT, TYPICAL
classical 形
▶ TRADITIONAL
classification 名
▶ CATEGORY
classified 形
▶ SECRET
CLASSIFY 動 p.97
classify 動
▶ CLASSIFY
classmate 名
▶ PARTNER 1
classy 形
▶ FASHIONABLE
clatter 動
▶ SHAKE 2
clay 名
▶ SOIL
CLEAN 動 p.97
CLEAN 形 p.98
clean 動
▶ CLEAN
clean 形
▶ CLEAN
cleanse 動
▶ CLEAN
clean up
▶ TIDY
clean yourself up
▶ WASH
CLEAR 動 p.98
CLEAR 形 p.99
clear 動
▶ ALLOW, CASH, CLEAR 動, DISAPPEAR

clear 形
▶ CLEAR 形 1, 2, 3, SUNNY, SURE
clearance 名
▶ PERMISSION
clear out
▶ GO AWAY
clear the way
▶ HELP 動 2
clear up
▶ TIDY
clear your throat
▶ COUGH
clench 動
▶ TIGHTEN
clerk 名
▶ SALESMAN
clever 形
▶ INTELLIGENT
client 名
▶ CUSTOMER
clientele 名
▶ MARKET 1
climate 名
▶ AREA 1, ATMOSPHERE
climax 名
▶ PEAK
CLIMB 動 p.101
climb 動
▶ CLIMB, RISE
clinch 動
▶ CONFIRM 3
cling 動
▶ HOLD
clique 名
▶ GROUP 2
CLOSE 動 p.101
CLOSE 形 p.102
close 名
▶ END 名
close 動
▶ CLOSE 動, END 動
close 形
▶ CLOSE 形, DETAILED, LIKE 前 形
close in
▶ COME 1
closeness 名
▶ FRIENDSHIP
closing 形
▶ LAST 1
CLOTHES 名 p.103
clothes 名
▶ CLOTHES
clothing 名
▶ CLOTHES
CLOUDY 形 p.103
cloudy 形
▶ CLOUDY
club 名
▶ TEAM 2, UNION
clue 名
▶ SUGGESTION
clueless 形
▶ IGNORANT

clump 名
▶ GROUP 1
cluster 名
▶ GROUP 1
clutch 動
▶ HOLD
clutter 名
▶ MESS 1
cluttered 形
▶ UNTIDY
coach 動
▶ TRAIN 1
coaching 名
▶ EDUCATION
coal 名
▶ OIL
coalition 名
▶ UNION
coarse 形
▶ OFFENSIVE
COAST 名 p.104
coast 名
▶ COAST
coastline 名
▶ COAST
coax 動
▶ PERSUADE
cocky 形
▶ PROUD 2
code 名
▶ LAW, VALUES
coerce 動
▶ PRESS 2
coercion 名
▶ PRESSURE 2
cogent 形
▶ CONVINCING
coherence 名
▶ EFFICIENCY
coherent 形
▶ RATIONAL
coincide 動
▶ MATCH 1
coincidence 名
▶ LUCK
COLD 形 p.104
cold 形
▶ COLD 1, 2
cold-blooded 形
▶ RUTHLESS
collaborator 名
▶ PARTNER 1
collapse 名
▶ FAILURE
collapse 動
▶ FAIL 2
colleague 名
▶ PARTNER 1
COLLECT 動 p.106
collect 動
▶ COLLECT, GET 2
collection 名
▶ GROUP 1
collective 形
▶ COMMON

collide 動
  ▶ CRASH
collision 名
  ▶ ACCIDENT, CONFLICT 名
collude 動
  ▶ PLOT
collusion 名
  ▶ CONSPIRACY
colony 名
  ▶ TERRITORY
colossal 形
  ▶ HUGE
colour 動
  ▶ AFFECT, DRAW, FLUSH, PAINT
colourless 形
  ▶ CLEAR 形 3
colours 名
  ▶ LOGO
column 名
  ▶ ARTICLE
columnist 名
  ▶ REPORTER
comb 動
  ▶ BRUSH
combat 名
  ▶ WAR
combat 動
  ▶ OPPOSE
COMBINE 動 p.106
combine 動
  ▶ COMBINE
COME 動 p.107
come 動
  ▶ ARRIVE, COME 1, 2, GO 2
come 連結動詞
  ▶ BECOME
come about
  ▶ HAPPEN
come across
  ▶ SEEM
come across sb/sth
  ▶ FIND 2
come along
  ▶ COME 1
come back
  ▶ RETURN 1
come between sb and sb
  ▶ DIVIDE 2
comedian 名
  ▶ ACTOR
come down
  ▶ FALL 1
come down sth
  ▶ FALL 2, RAIN
come down to sth
  ▶ REPRESENT 1
come down with sth
  ▶ SUFFER FROM STH
comedy 名
  ▶ HUMOUR, PLAY 名

come in
  ▶ ARRIVE, ENTER
come on/along
  ▶ DEVELOP 1
come on to sb
  ▶ FLIRT
come out
  ▶ APPEAR, TURN OUT
come out on top
  ▶ WIN
come over
  ▶ SEEM
come through sth
  ▶ SURVIVE
come to light
  ▶ TURN OUT
come to nothing
  ▶ FAIL 2
come up
  ▶ HAPPEN
come upon sb/sth
  ▶ FIND 2
comfort 名
  ▶ RELIEF
COMFORTABLE 形 p.108
comfortable 形
  ▶ COMFORTABLE, RICH
comfy 形
  ▶ COMFORTABLE
comic 形
  ▶ FUNNY
coming 形
  ▶ NEXT
coming 名
  ▶ ARRIVAL
command 名
  ▶ CONTROL
command 動
  ▶ ORDER 1, RUN 2
commandment 名
  ▶ RULE 名
commemoration 名
  ▶ BIRTHDAY
commence 動
  ▶ BEGIN, START 動
commend 動
  ▶ PRAISE 動
COMMENT 動 p.109
comment 名
  ▶ STATEMENT
comment 動
  ▶ COMMENT
commentary 名
  ▶ ASSESSMENT, REPORT 2
commentator 名
  ▶ ANALYST, PRESENTER
commerce 名
  ▶ TRADE
commercial 形
  ▶ ECONOMIC, SUCCESSFUL 2
commercial 名
  ▶ ADVERTISEMENT

commiserate 動
  ▶ SORRY FOR SB
commission 名
  ▶ COMMITTEE, SHARE 名, TASK
commission 動
  ▶ APPOINT
commissioner 名
  ▶ OFFICIAL 名
commit 動
  ▶ DEVOTE, DO, PROMISE 動
commitment 名
  ▶ PROMISE 名, RESPONSIBILITY
committed 形
  ▶ RELIABLE 1
COMMITTEE 名 p.109
committee 名
  ▶ COMMITTEE
commodity 名
  ▶ PRODUCT, THING 1
COMMON 形 p.110
common 形
  ▶ COMMON, GENERAL, NORMAL
commonly 副
  ▶ USUALLY
commonplace 形
  ▶ GENERAL
communal 形
  ▶ COMMON
communicate 動
  ▶ CONVEY, TALK
COMMUNICATION 名 p.111
communication 名
  ▶ COMMUNICATION, LETTER
compact 形
  ▶ SMALL
companion 名
  ▶ FRIEND
companionship 名
  ▶ FRIENDSHIP
COMPANY 名 p.112
company 名
  ▶ COMPANY, PARTY 2
comparable 形
  ▶ EQUIVALENT
COMPARE 動 p.112
compare 動
  ▶ COMPARE 1, 2
compassion 名
  ▶ SYMPATHY
compassionate 形
  ▶ SENSITIVE 1
compel 動
  ▶ FORCE 動
compelling 形
  ▶ CONVINCING, INTERESTING, URGENT
COMPENSATION 名 p.113
compensation 名
  ▶ COMPENSATION
COMPETE 動 p.114

compete 動
  ▶ COMPETE
competence 名
  ▶ SKILL 2
competent 形
  ▶ GOOD 4
COMPETITION 名 p.114
competition 名
  ▶ COMPETITION 1, 2, ENEMY
competitive 形
  ▶ AGGRESSIVE 2, CHEAP
competitiveness 名
  ▶ COMPETITION 2
competitor 名
  ▶ ENEMY, PARTICIPANT
COMPLAIN 動 p.116
complain 動
  ▶ COMPLAIN
complaint 名
  ▶ DISEASE
COMPLETE 形 p.116
complete 形
  ▶ COMPLETE, WHOLE
complete 動
  ▶ FINISH
completely 副
  ▶ QUITE 2
COMPLEX 形 p.117
complex 形
  ▶ COMPLEX
complex 名
  ▶ OBSESSION
complicated 形
  ▶ COMPLEX
complication 名
  ▶ PROBLEM
compliment 動
  ▶ PRAISE 動
complimentary 形
  ▶ FREE 形 2, GOOD 6
comply 動
  ▶ FOLLOW 3
component 名
  ▶ ELEMENT
composed 形
  ▶ CALM
composition 名
  ▶ STRUCTURE, WORK 名 2
comprehend 動
  ▶ UNDERSTAND 1
comprehensible 形
  ▶ CLEAR 形 2
comprehension 名
  ▶ UNDERSTANDING
comprehensive 形
  ▶ DETAILED
COMPROMISE 名 p.118
compromise 名
  ▶ COMPROMISE
compromise 動
  ▶ DAMAGE 動
compulsion 名
  ▶ DESIRE, PRESSURE 2

compulsive 形
▶ ADDICTIVE
compulsory 形
▶ NECESSARY
compunction 名
▶ DOUBT 名 2
compute 動
▶ CALCULATE
comradeship 名
▶ FRIENDSHIP
con 名
▶ FRAUD 2
con 動
▶ CHEAT 動
conceal 動
▶ HIDE
concede 動
▶ ADMIT
conceit 名
▶ PRIDE
conceited 形
▶ PROUD 2
conceivable 形
▶ POSSIBLE 2
concentration 名
▶ ATTENTION
concept 名
▶ IDEA 1
conception 名
▶ UNDERSTANDING
conceptual 形
▶ INTELLECTUAL 1
conceptualize 動
▶ IMAGINE
CONCERN 名 p.118
concern 名
▶ BUSINESS, CONCERN,
ISSUE, SYMPATHY
concern 動
▶ AFFECT, WORRY
concerned 形
▶ WORRIED
concession 名
▶ COMPROMISE
concise 形
▶ SHORT 3
CONCLUDE 動 p.119
conclude 動
▶ CONCLUDE, END
CONCLUSION 名 p.119
conclusion 名
▶ CONCLUSION, END 名
concrete 形
▶ FINAL
concurrent 形
▶ PARALLEL
condemn 動
▶ BLAME
condemnation 名
▶ CRITICISM
condensation 名
▶ MOISTURE
CONDITION 名 p.120

condition 名
▶ CONDITION, DISEASE,
HEALTH, STATE
conditions 名
▶ SITUATION
condolence 名
▶ SYMPATHY
condone 動
▶ FORGIVE
conduct 動
▶ DO
confer 動
▶ GIVE 1, TALK
conference 名
▶ MEETING 1
confess 動
▶ ADMIT
confidant 名
▶ FRIEND
CONFIDENCE 名 p.121
confidence 名
▶ CONFIDENCE, FAITH
CONFIDENT 形 p.122
confident 形
▶ CONFIDENT, SURE
confidential 形
▶ SECRET
configuration 名
▶ DESIGN 名
confines 名
▶ LIMIT 2
CONFIRM 動 p.122
confirm 動
▶ APPROVE,
CONFIRM 1, 2, 3
CONFLICT 名 p.123
CONFLICT 動 p.124
conflict 名
▶ CONFLICT 名, DEBATE,
WAR
conflict 動
▶ CONFLICT 動
conformist 形
▶ CONSERVATIVE
confound 動
▶ DISPROVE
CONFUSED 形 p.124
confused 形
▶ CONFUSED
CONFUSING 形 p.125
confusing 形
▶ CONFUSING
confusion 名
▶ DOUBT 名 1
congenital 形
▶ NATURAL
congested 形
▶ FULL
congestion 名
▶ TRAFFIC
conglomerate 名
▶ GROUP 3
congratulate 動
▶ PRAISE 動

congratulate yourself
▶ BOAST
Congressman 名
▶ POLITICIAN
conjecture 名
▶ SPECULATION
con man 名
▶ CHEAT 名
connect 動
▶ RELATE
connected 形
▶ RELATED
connection 名
▶ RELATION
connections 名
▶ FAMILY 2
connive 動
▶ PLOT
connoisseur 名
▶ EXPERT
conquer 動
▶ INVADE, SUCCEED
conscious 形
▶ AWARE, DELIBERATE
consciousness 名
▶ AWARENESS
consent 名
▶ PERMISSION
consent 動
▶ AGREE
consequence 名
▶ IMPORTANCE, RESULT
consequent 形
▶ RELATED
CONSERVATIVE 形 p.125
conservative 形
▶ CONSERVATIVE
CONSIDER 動 p.126
consider 動
▶ CONSIDER, REGARD
considerable 形
▶ LARGE
considerate 形
▶ KIND 形
CONSIDERATION 名 p.127
consideration 名
▶ CONSIDERATION,
FACTOR
consistent 形
▶ STEADY
consolation 名
▶ RELIEF
consolidate 動
▶ COMBINE
consortium 名
▶ GROUP 3
conspicuous 形
▶ MARKED
CONSPIRACY 名 p.127
conspiracy 名
▶ CONSPIRACY
conspire 動
▶ PLOT
constable 名
▶ POLICEMAN

constant 形
▶ FREQUENT, STEADY
constitute 連結動詞
▶ REPRESENT 1
constitution 名
▶ HEALTH, LAW
constitutional 形
▶ LEGAL
constraint 名
▶ LIMIT 1
construct 動
▶ BUILD
construction 名
▶ PRODUCTION,
STRUCTURE
constructive 形
▶ VALUABLE 2
consult 動
▶ ASK 1, TALK
consultant 名
▶ ADVISER
consultation 名
▶ DISCUSSION,
INTERVIEW 1
consume 動
▶ EAT, USE 動 2
consumer 名
▶ CUSTOMER
consumer group 名
▶ INSPECTOR
consuming 形
▶ ADDICTIVE
consummate 形
▶ IMPRESSIVE
contact 名
▶ COMMUNICATION,
PARTNER 1,
RELATIONSHIP 1
contain 動
▶ INCLUDE, SUPPRESS 2
contemplate 動
▶ CONSIDER, LOOK 動 1
contemplation 名
▶ CONSIDERATION
contemporary 形
▶ RECENT
CONTEMPT 名 p.128
contempt 名
▶ CONTEMPT
contend 動
▶ CLAIM
contender 名
▶ PARTICIPANT
contend with sb/sth
▶ DEAL WITH SB/STH
content 形
▶ HAPPY
content 名
▶ MESSAGE
contented 形
▶ HAPPY
contention 名
▶ DEBATE
contentment 名
▶ SATISFACTION

contest 名
▶ COMPETITION 1, 2
contest 動
▶ COMPETE, DOUBT 動
contestant 名
▶ PARTICIPANT
CONTEXT 名 p.128
context 名
▶ CONTEXT
contingent 形
▶ ARMY, PARTY 2
continual 形
▶ CONTINUOUS, FREQUENT
CONTINUE 動 p.129
continue 動
▶ CONTINUE 1, 2, 3, REMAIN
CONTINUOUS 形 p.131
continuous 形
▶ CONTINUOUS, FREQUENT
contour 名
▶ SHAPE
CONTRACT 名 p.132
contract 名
▶ CONTRACT
contract 動
▶ EMPLOY, SHRINK, SUFFER FROM STH
contradict 動
▶ CONFLICT 動, DENY
contradiction 名
▶ CONFLICT 名
contradictory 形
▶ INCONSISTENT
contrary 形
▶ OPPOSITE 形
the contrary 名
▶ OPPOSITE 名
contrast 名
▶ DIFFERENCE, OPPOSITE 名
contrast 動
▶ COMPARE 1, CONFLICT 動
contrasting 形
▶ DIFFERENT
contribute 動
▶ GIVE 3
contribution 名
▶ GIFT, INVOLVEMENT, PAYMENT
contributor 名
▶ REPORTER, SPONSOR
CONTROL 名 p.132
control 名
▶ BUTTON 1, CONTROL, LIMIT 1
control 動
▶ OPERATE, RUN 2, SUPPRESS 2
controlled 形
▶ CALM, LIMITED 2

controversy 名
▶ DEBATE
conurbation 名
▶ CITY
convalesce 動
▶ RECOVER
convene 動
▶ HAVE 4, MEET 1
convenient 形
▶ GOOD 2, USEFUL
convention 名
▶ CONTRACT, MEETING 1, TRADITION
conventional 形
▶ CONSERVATIVE, TRADITIONAL
converge 動
▶ COME 1
conversation 名
▶ DISCUSSION
conversion 名
▶ CHANGE 名 2
convert 動
▶ PERSUADE, SWITCH, TURN 2
convertible 形
▶ FLEXIBLE 1
CONVEY 動 p.133
convey 動
▶ CONVEY
conviction 名
▶ FAITH, VIEW 1
CONVINCE 動 p.134
convince 動
▶ CONVINCE
convinced 形
▶ SURE
convince sb to do sth
▶ PERSUADE
CONVINCING 形 p.134
convincing 形
▶ CONVINCING
convoluted 形
▶ COMPLEX
convulse 動
▶ SHAKE 3
convulsion 名
▶ SHIVER
COOL 動 p.135
cool 動
▶ COOL
cool 形
▶ CALM, COLD 1, 2, GREAT 1, PALE
cool down
▶ COOL
cooperate 動
▶ HELP 動 1
cooperation 名
▶ HELP 名
cooperative 形
▶ COMMON, HELPFUL
cooperative 名
▶ GROUP 3

co-opt 動
▶ APPOINT
coordinate 動
▶ MATCH 2
coordination 名
▶ PLANNING
cop 名
▶ POLICEMAN
COPY 名 p.135
COPY 動 p.136
copy 名
▶ COPY 名 1, 2
copy 動
▶ COPY 動, FOLLOW 4, WRITE
cordial 形
▶ FRIENDLY 2
core 名
▶ POINT
CORNER 名 p.137
corner 名
▶ CORNER, MESS 2
corporation 名
▶ COMPANY
corps 名
▶ TEAM 1
CORRECT 動 p.137
correct 動
▶ CORRECT
correct 形
▶ RIGHT 形 1, TRUE
correlate 動
▶ MATCH 1
correlation 名
▶ RELATION
correspond 動
▶ MATCH 1
correspondence 名
▶ COMMUNICATION, LETTER, SIMILARITY
correspondent 名
▶ REPORTER
corresponding 形
▶ EQUIVALENT
CORRIDOR 名 p.138
corridor 名
▶ CORRIDOR
corroborate 動
▶ CONFIRM 1
CORRUPT 形 p.138
corrupt 形
▶ CORRUPT
CORRUPTION 名 p.139
corruption 名
▶ CORRUPTION
cosmopolitan 形
▶ INTERNATIONAL
cost 名
▶ PRICE
costing 名
▶ VALUATION
costly 形
▶ EXPENSIVE
COSTS 名 p.139

costs 名
▶ COSTS
costume 名
▶ CLOTHES
cosy 形
▶ COMFORTABLE
COUGH 動 p.140
cough 動
▶ COUGH
council 名
▶ COMMITTEE
councillor 名
▶ OFFICIAL 名
councilman 名
▶ OFFICIAL 名
counsel 名
▶ LAWYER
counselling 名
▶ ADVICE
counsellor 名
▶ ADVISER
COUNT 動 p.140
count 動
▶ ESTIMATE 動
count 動
▶ COUNT, REGARD
counterproductive 形
▶ INEFFECTIVE
count on sb/sth
▶ TRUST
COUNTRY 名 p.141
country 名
▶ COUNTRY 1, 2
countryside 名
▶ COUNTRY 2
COUNTY 名 p.142
county 名
▶ COUNTY
coup 名
▶ REVOLUTION
COURAGE 名 p.142
courage 名
▶ COURAGE
courageous 形
▶ BRAVE
course 名
▶ CLASS 1, WAY 3
COURT 名 p.143
court 名
▶ COURT
court 動
▶ GO OUT
courteous 形
▶ POLITE
courtesy 名
▶ RESPECT 名
courthouse 名
▶ COURT
court martial 名
▶ CASE
court of appeal 名
▶ COURT
court of law 名
▶ COURT

courtroom 名
▶ COURT
courtship 名
▶ RELATIONSHIP 2
cover 名
▶ REPLACEMENT,
SECURITY, SHELTER
cover 動
▶ DESCRIBE, GO 2, HIDE,
INCLUDE
cover for sb
▶ REPLACE 1
COWARD 名 p.144
coward 名
▶ COWARD
co-worker 名
▶ PARTNER 1
coy 形
▶ SHY
crack 動
▶ BANG 1, 2, BREAK 1
crack up
▶ LAUGH
cradle 動
▶ HUG
craftsman 名
▶ MAKER
cram 動
▶ PACK
crammed 形
▶ FULL
crap 形
▶ POOR 2
crap 名
▶ NONSENSE
CRASH 動 p.144
crash 名
▶ ACCIDENT
crash 動
▶ BANG 1, BREAK 2,
CRASH, FALL 2
crater 名
▶ HOLE 2
craze 名
▶ FASHION
CRAZY 形 p.145
crazy 形
▶ CRAZY, MAD
crazy about sb
▶ IN LOVE
create 動
▶ CAUSE, MAKE 1
creation 名
▶ DEVELOPMENT
CREATIVE 形 p.145
creative 形
▶ CREATIVE
creativity 名
▶ INSPIRATION
credentials 名
▶ CERTIFICATE
credible 形
▶ POSSIBLE 2
credit 名
▶ LOAN, PRAISE 名

creditable 形
▶ WORTHY
creepy 形
▶ FRIGHTENING
crest 名
▶ LOGO
crew 名
▶ TEAM 1
CRIME 名 p.146
crime 名
▶ CRIME 1, 2
CRIMINAL 名 p.147
criminal 名
▶ CRIMINAL
criminal 形
▶ ILLEGAL,
OUTRAGEOUS
CRISIS 名 p.148
crisis 名
▶ CRISIS
crisp 形
▶ COLD 1
CRITERION 名 p.149
criterion 名
▶ CRITERION
critic 名
▶ ANALYST
CRITICAL 形 p.149
critical 形
▶ CRITICAL, ESSENTIAL,
SERIOUS 1
CRITICISM 名 p.150
criticism 名
▶ ASSESSMENT,
CRITICISM
criticize 動
▶ BLAME
critique 名
▶ ASSESSMENT
crony 名
▶ FRIEND
crook 名
▶ CRIMINAL
crooked 形
▶ CORRUPT
crop up
▶ HAPPEN
cross 形
▶ ANGRY
cross-examine 動
▶ QUESTION 動
cross sb/sth off
▶ DELETE
cross sth out
▶ DELETE
CROWD 名 p.151
crowd 名
▶ CROWD, GROUP 2
CROWDED 形 p.151
crowded 形
▶ CROWDED
crucial 形
▶ ESSENTIAL
CRUEL 形 p.151

cruel 形
▶ CRUEL
crumb 名
▶ FRAGMENT
crunch 動
▶ BITE
crusade 名
▶ CAMPAIGN 名
crush 名
▶ CROWD, LOVE 名 1
crush 動
▶ DISCOURAGE 2,
SUPPRESS 1
crux 名
▶ POINT
CRY 動 p.152
cry 動
▶ CRY, SHOUT
cry out
▶ SCREAM
cube 名
▶ PIECE
cuddle 動
▶ HUG
cuddly 形
▶ SWEET
cue 名
▶ SIGNAL
culmination 名
▶ PEAK
culprit 名
▶ CRIMINAL
CULTURAL 形 p.153
cultural 形
▶ CULTURAL
cultured 形
▶ INTELLECTUAL 2
cup 名
▶ AWARD
curb 名
▶ LIMIT 1
curb 動
▶ SUPPRESS 2
CURE 動 p.154
cure 名
▶ DRUG 2, TREATMENT
cure 動
▶ CORRECT, CURE
curious 形
▶ STRANGE 1
current 形
▶ RECENT
curriculum 名
▶ CLASS 1
CURVE 動 p.154
curve 動
▶ CURVE
cushion 動
▶ EASE
cushy 形
▶ EASY 1
custom 名
▶ TRADITION
CUSTOMER 名 p.154

customer 名
▶ CUSTOMER
customs 名
▶ TAX
CUT 動 p.155
cut 名
▶ INJURY, REDUCTION,
SHARE
cut 動
▶ CUT 1, 2, DELETE,
FREE 動
cutback 名
▶ REDUCTION
cut sth back
▶ CUT 1
cut sth down
▶ CUT 1, DEMOLISH
cute 形
▶ BEAUTIFUL 1, SWEET
cut in
▶ INTERRUPT
cut sb/sth off
▶ ISOLATE
cut sth off
▶ BLOCK 2
cut out for sth
▶ GOOD 2
cut sth up
▶ DIVIDE 1
cynical 形
▶ SUSPICIOUS 1
cynicism 名
▶ SCEPTICISM

D

DAMAGE 名 p.157
DAMAGE 動 p.157
damage 名
▶ DAMAGE 名
damage 動
▶ DAMAGE 動
damaging 形
▶ HARMFUL
damning 形
▶ CRITICAL
damp 形
▶ WET
damp 名
▶ MOISTURE
dampen 動
▶ SOAK
danger 名
▶ RISK 1, THREAT
DANGEROUS 形 p.158
dangerous 形
▶ DANGEROUS
DARE 動 p.158
dare 動
▶ DARE
daring 形
▶ BOLD
daring 名
▶ COURAGE
DARK 形 p.159

dark → demand

- dark 形
  - ▶ DARK 1, 2, EVIL 形, NEGATIVE
- DARLING 名 p.160
- darling 名
  - ▶ DARLING
- darling 形
  - ▶ DEAR
- darn 動
  - ▶ REPAIR
- dash 動
  - ▶ BEAT, HURRY
- data 名
  - ▶ INFORMATION
- date 名
  - ▶ MEETING 2, PARTNER 2, TIME
- date 動
  - ▶ GO OUT
- dated 形
  - ▶ OLD-FASHIONED
- daunt 動
  - ▶ DISCOURAGE 2
- daunting 形
  - ▶ FRIGHTENING
- dawn 名
  - ▶ START 名
- day 名
  - ▶ PERIOD
- day off 名
  - ▶ HOLIDAY 1
- day out 名
  - ▶ TRIP
- dazed 形
  - ▶ CONFUSED
- dazzle 動
  - ▶ IMPRESS
- DEAD 形 p.160
- dead 形
  - ▶ DEAD
- deadly 形
  - ▶ FATAL
- deafening 形
  - ▶ LOUD
- deal 名
  - ▶ AGREEMENT
- deal 動
  - ▶ DISTRIBUTE, SELL 2
- DEALER 名 p.160
- dealer 名
  - ▶ DEALER
- deal in sth
  - ▶ SELL 2
- dealing 名
  - ▶ TRADE
- dealings 名
  - ▶ COMMUNICATION
- DEAL WITH SB/STH p.161
- deal with sb/sth
  - ▶ DEAL WITH SB/STH, NEGOTIATE
- DEAR 形 p.162
- dear 形
  - ▶ DEAR

- dear 名
  - ▶ DARLING
- dear old/little... 形
  - ▶ SWEET
- debacle 名
  - ▶ DISASTER
- DEBATE 名 p.162
- debate 名
  - ▶ DEBATE, DISCUSSION
- debate 動
  - ▶ TALK
- debit 名
  - ▶ DEBT
- debit 動
  - ▶ DISCOUNT
- debrief 動
  - ▶ QUESTION 動
- debris 名
  - ▶ REMAINS, WASTE
- DEBT 名 p.163
- debt 名
  - ▶ DEBT
- debunk 動
  - ▶ DISPROVE
- decade 名
  - ▶ PERIOD
- decamp 動
  - ▶ GO AWAY
- deceased 形
  - ▶ DEAD
- deceit 名
  - ▶ FRAUD 1
- deceitful 形
  - ▶ DISHONEST
- deceive 動
  - ▶ CHEAT 動
- decent 形
  - ▶ RESPECTABLE, RIGHT 形 2
- deception 名
  - ▶ FRAUD 1
- deceptive 形
  - ▶ MISLEADING
- DECIDE 動 p.164
- decide 動
  - ▶ CHOOSE, CONFIRM 3, DECIDE, DETERMINE
- decided 形
  - ▶ MARKED
- decimate 動
  - ▶ DESTROY
- decisive 形
  - ▶ ESSENTIAL
- deck 名
  - ▶ FLOOR
- deck 動
  - ▶ DECORATE
- declaration 名
  - ▶ STATEMENT
- DECLARE 動 p.164
- declare 動
  - ▶ DECLARE
- decline 名
  - ▶ REDUCTION

- decline 動
  - ▶ FALL 1, REFUSE, WORSEN
- DECORATE 動 p.165
- decorate 動
  - ▶ DECORATE
- DECORATION 名 p.166
- decoration 名
  - ▶ DECORATION
- decrease 名
  - ▶ REDUCTION
- decrease 動
  - ▶ FALL 1, REDUCE
- decree 動
  - ▶ RULE 動 2
- dedicate 動
  - ▶ DEVOTE
- dedicated 形
  - ▶ RELIABLE 1
- deduce 動
  - ▶ CONCLUDE
- deduct 動
  - ▶ DISCOUNT
- deduction 名
  - ▶ CONCLUSION
- deed 名
  - ▶ ACTION, DOCUMENT
- DEEP 形 p.166
- deep 形
  - ▶ DARK 2, DEEP 1, 2
- DEFEAT 動 p.167
- defeat 名
  - ▶ VICTORY
- defeat 動
  - ▶ DEFEAT
- DEFECT 名 p.168
- defect 名
  - ▶ DEFECT
- defence 名
  - ▶ ARGUMENT 2, PRECAUTION, SECURITY
- defenceless 形
  - ▶ VULNERABLE
- defend 動
  - ▶ EXPLAIN 2, PROTECT
- defer 動
  - ▶ DELAY
- deferential 形
  - ▶ POLITE
- deficiency 名
  - ▶ LACK
- deficient 形
  - ▶ INADEQUATE
- deficit 名
  - ▶ LACK
- define 動
  - ▶ EXPLAIN 1, LIST 動
- definite 形
  - ▶ CERTAIN, MARKED
- DEFINITION 名 p.168
- definition 名
  - ▶ DEFINITION
- definitive 形
  - ▶ FINAL

- DEFRAUD 動 p.169
- defraud 動
  - ▶ DEFRAUD
- defy 動
  - ▶ OPPOSE
- degenerate 動
  - ▶ WORSEN
- dejected 形
  - ▶ DEPRESSED
- DELAY 動 p.169
- delay 動
  - ▶ DELAY, HOLD SB/STH UP
- delegation 名
  - ▶ COMMITTEE
- DELETE 動 p.170
- delete 動
  - ▶ DELETE
- DELIBERATE 形 p.171
- deliberate 形
  - ▶ DELIBERATE
- deliberate 動
  - ▶ CONSIDER
- deliberation 名
  - ▶ CONSIDERATION
- delicate 形
  - ▶ FRAGILE, SENSITIVE 2
- DELICIOUS 形 p.171
- delicious 形
  - ▶ DELICIOUS, WONDERFUL
- DELIGHT 動 p.172
- delight 名
  - ▶ JOY, PLEASURE
- delight 動
  - ▶ DELIGHT
- delighted 形
  - ▶ GLAD
- delightful 形
  - ▶ WONDERFUL
- delinquency 名
  - ▶ CRIME 1
- delinquent 形
  - ▶ ILLEGAL
- delinquent 名
  - ▶ CRIMINAL
- delirious 形
  - ▶ HYSTERICAL
- deliver 動
  - ▶ TAKE 1
- DELIVERY 名 p.172
- delivery 名
  - ▶ DELIVERY
- deluge 名
  - ▶ FLOOD 名 1
- delusion 名
  - ▶ ILLUSION
- delve into sth
  - ▶ INVESTIGATE
- DEMAND 動 p.173
- DEMAND 動 p.174
- demand 動
  - ▶ DEMAND 名, REQUEST

demand 動
▶ ASK 1, DEMAND 動, NEED
demanding 形
▶ DIFFICULT 1
demands 名
▶ PRESSURE 1
demo
▶ PRESENTATION
DEMOLISH 動 p.174
demolish 動
▶ DEMOLISH, DISPROVE
demonic 形
▶ EVIL 1
demonstrate 動
▶ SHOW 1
demonstration 名
▶ EVIDENCE, EXPRESSION, PRESENTATION
demonstrative 形
▶ SOCIABLE
demonstrator 名
▶ PROTESTER
demoralize 動
▶ DISCOURAGE 2
demoralized 形
▶ DEPRESSED
denial 名
▶ REFUSAL
denote 動
▶ MEAN 動 1
denounce 動
▶ BLAME
denunciation 名
▶ CRITICISM
DENY 動 p.175
deny 動
▶ DENY, REFUSE
depart 動
▶ LEAVE 1, 3
DEPARTMENT 名 p.175
department 名
▶ DEPARTMENT
DEPEND ON/UPON STH p.176
depend on/upon sb/sth
▶ TRUST
depend on/upon sth
▶ DEPEND ON/UPON STH
depict 動
▶ PRESENT 2
depiction 名
▶ DESCRIPTION
deplete 動
▶ USE 動 2
deplorable 形
▶ OUTRAGEOUS
deplore 動
▶ DISAPPROVE
deport 動
▶ EXPEL
deposit 名
▶ PAYMENT

deposit 動
▶ SAVE 3
depress 動
▶ DISCOURAGE 2
DEPRESSED 形 p.176
depressed 形
▶ DEPRESSED
depressing 形
▶ NEGATIVE
depression 名
▶ GLOOM, RECESSION
deprivation 名
▶ POVERTY
deprived 形
▶ POOR 1
depth 名
▶ UNDERSTANDING
deputize 動
▶ REPLACE 1
derision 名
▶ CONTEMPT
derive sth from sth
▶ GET 2
derogatory 形
▶ INSULTING
descend 動
▶ FALL 2
descent 名
▶ FAMILY 3
DESCRIBE 動 p.177
describe 動
▶ DESCRIBE, REGARD
DESCRIPTION 名 p.178
description 名
▶ DESCRIPTION
DESCRIPTIVE 形 p.178
descriptive 形
▶ DESCRIPTIVE
desert 動
▶ LEAVE 4
DESERTED 形 p.179
deserted 形
▶ DESERTED
deserving 形
▶ WORTHY
DESIGN 名 p.179
DESIGN 動 p.180
design 名
▶ DESIGN 名, DEVELOPMENT, PLAN 2
design 動
▶ DESIGN 動 1, 2
designate 動
▶ APPOINT, CALL 1
desirable 形
▶ BEST, POPULAR
DESIRE 名 p.180
desire 名
▶ DESIRE, LOVE 名 1
desire 動
▶ WANT
desolate 形
▶ LONELY
desperate 形
▶ SERIOUS 1

desperately 副
▶ VERY 副
despise 動
▶ HATE
despondency 名
▶ GLOOM
despondent 形
▶ DEPRESSED
despot 名
▶ DICTATOR
destined 形
▶ CERTAIN
destiny 名
▶ LUCK
destitute 形
▶ POOR 1
destitution 名
▶ POVERTY
DESTROY 動 p.181
destroy 動
▶ DESTROY
destructive 形
▶ HARMFUL
detach 動
▶ UNDO
detached 形
▶ INDIFFERENT
detachment 名
▶ TEAM 1
detail 名
▶ INFORMATION
detail 動
▶ LIST 動
DETAILED 形 p.182
detailed 形
▶ DETAILED
detain 動
▶ HOLD SB/STH UP, JAIL
detect 動
▶ NOTICE
detective 名
▶ POLICEMAN
deteriorate 動
▶ WORSEN
DETERMINATION 名 p.183
determination 名
▶ DETERMINATION
DETERMINE 動 p.184
determine 動
▶ DECIDE, DETERMINE, FIND 3
detest 動
▶ HATE
detriment 名
▶ DAMAGE
detrimental 形
▶ HARMFUL
devastate 動
▶ DESTROY
devastated 形
▶ UPSET
DEVELOP 動 p.184
develop 動
▶ DEVELOP 1, 2, SUFFER FROM STH

DEVELOPMENT 名 p.185
development 名
▶ DEVELOPMENT, EVENT 1, PROGRESS
device 名
▶ TACTIC, TOOL, TRICK
devious 形
▶ DISHONEST
DEVOTE 動 p.186
devote 動
▶ DEVOTE
devoted 形
▶ LOVING
devotee 名
▶ FAN
devotion 名
▶ LOVE 名 2
devour 動
▶ EAT
dew 名
▶ MOISTURE
dexterity 名
▶ SKILL 2
dial 名
▶ BUTTON 1
dial 動
▶ CALL 2
dialogue 名
▶ DISCUSSION
diary 名
▶ SCHEDULE
dice 動
▶ CUT 2
dictate 動
▶ DETERMINE, QUOTE, RULE 動 2
DICTATOR 名 p.186
dictator 名
▶ DICTATOR
dictatorial 形
▶ REPRESSIVE
dictatorship 名
▶ REPRESSION
didactic 形
▶ EDUCATIONAL
DIE 動 p.187
die 動
▶ DIE
die out
▶ DISAPPEAR
diesel 名
▶ OIL
diet 名
▶ FOOD
DIFFER 動 p.187
differ 動
▶ DIFFER, DISAGREE
DIFFERENCE 名 p.187
difference 名
▶ DEBATE, DIFFERENCE
DIFFERENT 形 p.188
different 形
▶ DIFFERENT, UNUSUAL
DIFFICULT 形 p.189

difficult 形
 ▶ DIFFICULT 1, 2
difficulty 名
 ▶ PROBLEM
diffident 形
 ▶ SHY
dignified 形
 ▶ PROUD 1
DIGNITY 名 p.190
dignity 名
 ▶ DIGNITY
dilemma 名
 ▶ MESS 2
DIM p.191
dim 形
 ▶ DIM
diminish 動
 ▶ FALL 1
diminutive 形
 ▶ SHORT 2
dip 動
 ▶ SOAK
dip into sth
 ▶ READ
diplomacy 名
 ▶ TACT
dire 形
 ▶ SERIOUS 1
direct 形
 ▶ HONEST
direct 動
 ▶ FOCUS, ORDER 1, RUN 2, TAKE 2
direction 名
 ▶ GOVERNMENT 2, WAY 3
director 名
 ▶ MANAGER
directorate 名
 ▶ MANAGEMENT
directorship 名
 ▶ MANAGEMENT
directory 名
 ▶ LIST
dirt 名
 ▶ SOIL
DIRTY 形 p.191
dirty 形
 ▶ CORRUPT, DIRTY
DISABLED 形 p.192
disabled 形
 ▶ DISABLED
DISADVANTAGE 名 p.192
disadvantage 名
 ▶ DISADVANTAGE
disadvantaged 形
 ▶ POOR 1
disadvantageous 形
 ▶ DIFFICULT 2
DISAGREE 動 p.193
disagree 動
 ▶ DISAGREE
disagreement 名
 ▶ DEBATE
disallow 動
 ▶ REFUSE

DISAPPEAR 動 p.193
disappear 動
 ▶ DISAPPEAR
DISAPPOINT 動 p.194
disappoint 動
 ▶ DISAPPOINT
DISAPPOINTING 形 p.194
disappointing 形
 ▶ DISAPPOINTING
disappointment 名
 ▶ LOSER 2
disapproval 名
 ▶ CRITICISM
DISAPPROVE 動 p.195
disapprove 動
 ▶ DISAPPROVE
disapproving 形
 ▶ CRITICAL
DISASTER 名 p.195
disaster 名
 ▶ CRISIS, DISASTER, LOSER 2
disbelief 名
 ▶ SCEPTICISM
disbelieve 動
 ▶ SUSPECT
disbelieving 形
 ▶ SUSPICIOUS 1
discard 動
 ▶ REMOVE
discernible 形
 ▶ VISIBLE
discerning 形
 ▶ SHREWD
discharge 名
 ▶ UNEMPLOYMENT
discharge 動
 ▶ FIRE
discipline 名
 ▶ AREA 2, CONTROL
disclaim 動
 ▶ DENY
disclose 動
 ▶ REVEAL
discomfort 名
 ▶ PAIN
disconcerting 形
 ▶ WORRYING
disconnect 動
 ▶ TURN STH OFF
discontented 形
 ▶ UNHAPPY 2
discontinue 動
 ▶ STOP
DISCOUNT 動 p.195
discount 名
 ▶ DISCOUNT
DISCOURAGE 動 p.196
discourage 動
 ▶ DISCOURAGE 1, 2
discouraging 形
 ▶ DISAPPOINTING
discourteous 形
 ▶ RUDE

discover 動
 ▶ FIND 1, 2, 3
discredit 名
 ▶ DISGRACE
discredit 動
 ▶ DISPROVE
discretion 名
 ▶ TACT
discretionary 形
 ▶ VOLUNTARY 1
discriminating 形
 ▶ SHREWD
DISCRIMINATION 名 p.197
discrimination 名
 ▶ DISCRIMINATION
discriminatory 形
 ▶ BIASED
discuss 動
 ▶ EXAMINE, TALK
DISCUSSION 名 p.198
discussion 名
 ▶ DISCUSSION, RESEARCH
disdain 名
 ▶ CONTEMPT
DISEASE 名 p.199
disease 名
 ▶ DISEASE
disenfranchise 動
 ▶ SUPPRESS 1
disengage 動
 ▶ FREE
disentangle 動
 ▶ FREE
DISGRACE 名 p.200
disgrace 名
 ▶ DISGRACE
disgraceful 形
 ▶ OUTRAGEOUS
disgruntled 形
 ▶ UNHAPPY 2
disguise 動
 ▶ HIDE
disgust 名
 ▶ SHOCK
DISGUSTING 形 p.200
disgusting 形
 ▶ DISGUSTING 1, 2
DISHONEST 形 p.201
dishonest 形
 ▶ DISHONEST
dishonesty 名
 ▶ FRAUD 1
dishonour 動
 ▶ DISGRACE
dish sth out
 ▶ DISTRIBUTE
disinherit 動
 ▶ REJECT
disinterested 形
 ▶ OBJECTIVE
dislike 名
 ▶ HATRED
dislike 動
 ▶ HATE

dismal 形
 ▶ POOR 2
dismay 名
 ▶ SHOCK
dismay 動
 ▶ SHOCK
dismayed 形
 ▶ UPSET
dismiss 動
 ▶ ABOLISH, FIRE
dismissal 名
 ▶ UNEMPLOYMENT
disobey 動
 ▶ OPPOSE
disorder 名
 ▶ DISEASE, MESS 1, TROUBLE 1
disordered 形
 ▶ UNTIDY
disorderly 形
 ▶ WILD
disorganized 形
 ▶ RANDOM
disorientated 形
 ▶ CONFUSED
disoriented 形
 ▶ CONFUSED
disown 動
 ▶ REJECT
disparaging 形
 ▶ INSULTING
disparate 形
 ▶ DIFFERENT
disparity 名
 ▶ DIFFERENCE
dispatch 動
 ▶ SEND
dispense 動
 ▶ DISTRIBUTE
dispense with sb/sth
 ▶ REMOVE
displace 動
 ▶ EXPEL
display 名
 ▶ EXHIBITION, EXPRESSION, PERFORMANCE
display 動
 ▶ PRESENT 1
displease 動
 ▶ ANNOY
displeased 形
 ▶ UNHAPPY 2
displeasure 名
 ▶ FRUSTRATION
dispose of sb/sth
 ▶ REMOVE
disposition 名
 ▶ PERSONALITY
disproportionate 形
 ▶ EXCESSIVE
DISPROVE 動 p.202
disprove 動
 ▶ DISPROVE

dispute 名
▶ DEBATE
dispute 動
▶ DISAGREE, DOUBT
disregard 動
▶ IGNORE
disrepute 名
▶ DISGRACE
disrespect 名
▶ CONTEMPT
disrespectful 形
▶ RUDE
disruptive 形
▶ WILD
dissatisfied 形
▶ UNHAPPY 2
dissent 名
▶ DEBATE
dissertation 名
▶ PAPER
dissident 名
▶ PROTESTER
dissimilar 形
▶ DIFFERENT
dissolution 名
▶ DIVISION 1
dissolve 動
▶ DISAPPEAR
dissuade 動
▶ DISCOURAGE 1
distance 名
▶ DIVISION 2
distant 形
▶ COLD 2, PREVIOUS
distasteful 形
▶ DISGUSTING 2
distinct 形
▶ MARKED, PARTICULAR
distinction 名
▶ DIFFERENCE, VALUE
distinctive 形
▶ UNIQUE
distinguished 形
▶ GREAT 2
distraught 形
▶ UPSET
DISTRESS 名 p.203
distress 名
▶ DISTRESS
distress 動
▶ HURT 1
distressed 形
▶ UPSET
distressing 形
▶ PAINFUL 2
DISTRIBUTE 動 p.204
distribute 動
▶ DISTRIBUTE
distribution 名
▶ DELIVERY
distributor 名
▶ DEALER
district 名
▶ AREA 1, COUNTY

distrust 名
▶ SCEPTICISM
distrust 動
▶ SUSPECT
disturb 動
▶ INTERRUPT, WORRY
disturbance 名
▶ TROUBLE 1
disturbed 形
▶ WORRIED
disturbing 形
▶ WORRYING
disunity 名
▶ DIVISION 2
disused 形
▶ DESERTED
diverge 動
▶ DIFFER
divergence 名
▶ DIFFERENCE
DIVERSE 形 p.204
diverse 形
▶ DIVERSE
diversity 名
▶ RANGE 1
DIVIDE 動 p.205
divide 動
▶ DIVIDE 1, 2, ISOLATE, SHARE 1
dividend 名
▶ PROFIT
DIVISION 名 p.206
division 名
▶ DEPARTMENT, DIVISION 1, 2
divorced 形
▶ SINGLE
divulge 動
▶ REVEAL
DO 動 p.207
do 動
▶ DO, GO 2, LEARN, MAKE 1, PLAY 動 2, STAY 2
do a deal
▶ NEGOTIATE
do a U-turn 動
▶ BREAK 4
do away with sth
▶ ABOLISH
do business
▶ SELL 2
dock 動
▶ DISCOUNT
doctrine 名
▶ VALUES
DOCUMENT 名 p.208
document 名
▶ DOCUMENT
document 動
▶ RECORD
documentation 名
▶ CERTIFICATE
dodgy 形
▶ SUSPICIOUS 2

doing 名
▶ ACTION
dole sth out
▶ DISTRIBUTE
domain 名
▶ AREA 2
domestic 形
▶ NATIONAL
dominant 形
▶ POWERFUL
dominion 名
▶ TERRITORY
don 名
▶ LECTURER
donate 動
▶ GIVE 3
donation 名
▶ GIFT
donor 名
▶ SPONSOR
dope 名
▶ DRUG 1
dork 名
▶ FOOL
dossier 名
▶ DOCUMENT
dote on/upon sb
▶ LOVE 動
DOUBT 名 p.209
DOUBT 動 p.210
doubt 名
▶ DOUBT 名 1, 2
doubt 動
▶ DOUBT 動, SUSPECT
doubtful 形
▶ UNLIKELY 1, UNSURE
doubtless 副
▶ PROBABLY
dour 形
▶ STERN
douse 動
▶ SOAK
DO WELL 動 p.211
do well 動
▶ DO WELL
down 動
▶ DEPRESSED
downbeat 形
▶ NEGATIVE
downright 形
▶ COMPLETE
downside 名
▶ DISADVANTAGE
downsize 動
▶ CUT 1
down-to-earth 形
▶ REALISTIC
downturn 名
▶ REDUCTION
doze 動
▶ SLEEP
draft 名
▶ PLAN 2
draft 動
▶ PREPARE 1

drag 動
▶ PULL 1
drag on
▶ CONTINUE 1
drain 動
▶ CLEAR 動, DRINK 動, PUMP, USE 動 2
drained 形
▶ TIRED
DRAMA 名 p.211
drama 名
▶ DRAMA, PLAY 名
dramatic 形
▶ EXCITING
dramatist 名
▶ WRITER
dramatize 動
▶ EXAGGERATE
drastic 形
▶ SERIOUS 1
DRAW 動 p.212
draw 動
▶ CLOSE 動, COME 1, DRAW, PULL 1, PUMP
draw attention to sb/sth
▶ POINT STH OUT
drawback 名
▶ DISADVANTAGE
drawing 名
▶ PICTURE
draw near 動
▶ COME 2
draw on/upon sth
▶ USE 動 1
drawstring 名
▶ BUTTON 2
draw sth up
▶ PREPARE 1
dread 名
▶ FEAR
dreadful 形
▶ TERRIBLE 1, 3
dream 名
▶ HOPE 名 2
drench 動
▶ SOAK
drenched 形
▶ WET
dress 名
▶ CLOTHES
dress 動
▶ WEAR
drift 動
▶ TREND
drill 動
▶ TRAINING
DRINK 名 p.212
DRINK 動 p.212
drink 名
▶ DRINK 名
drink 動
▶ DRINK 動
drip 名
▶ DROP

drive 名
▶ CAMPAIGN 名
drive 動
▶ FORCE 動, GO 2, PUSH 1, TAKE 2
drive sb mad/crazy
▶ ANGER 動
drizzle 動
▶ RAIN
DROP 名 p.213
drop 名
▶ DROP, REDUCTION
drop 動
▶ EXCLUDE 2, FALL 1, 2, STOP
drop in/round/by
▶ VISIT 動
drove 名
▶ CROWD
drowsy 形
▶ TIRED
DRUG 名 p.213
drug 名
▶ DRUG 1, 2
drum 動
▶ KNOCK
dry 形
▶ BORING, IRONIC, SUNNY
dry-clean 動
▶ CLEAN 動
dub 動
▶ CALL 1
dubious 形
▶ SUSPICIOUS 2, UNSURE
dude 名
▶ MAN 1
due 形
▶ RIGHT 形 2
due 名
▶ RIGHT 名
dues 名
▶ RATE
dull 形
▶ BORING, CLOUDY, PALE, QUIET 2
dumb 形
▶ CRAZY, SILENT, STUPID
dummy 形
▶ FAKE
dump 動
▶ LEAVE 4, PUT, REMOVE
dumpy 形
▶ SHORT 2
dupe 動
▶ CHEAT 動
duplicate 名
▶ COPY 名 2
duplicate 動
▶ COPY 動
dusk 名
▶ NIGHT 2
dusky 形
▶ PALE

dust 名
▶ SOIL
dust 動
▶ BRUSH
dusty 形
▶ DIRTY
dutiful 形
▶ GOOD 7
duty 名
▶ RESPONSIBILITY, TASK, TAX
dweller 名
▶ RESIDENT
dwelling 名
▶ HOME
dye 動
▶ PAINT
the dying 名
▶ PATIENT
dynamic 形
▶ ENERGETIC, VARIABLE
dynasty 名
▶ FAMILY 3

E

EAGER 形 p.215
eager 形
▶ EAGER
earliest 形
▶ FIRST
the early hours
▶ NIGHT 1
earn 動
▶ GAIN, MAKE 2
earn a/your living
▶ WORK 動 1
earnest 形
▶ SERIOUS 2
earnings 名
▶ INCOME, PROFIT
ear-splitting 形
▶ LOUD
earth 名
▶ SOIL
EASE 動 p.216
ease 動
▶ EASE, HELP 動 2
EASY 形 p.216
easy 形
▶ EASY 1, 2, FRIENDLY 2
easy-going 形
▶ CALM
EAT 動 p.218
eat 動
▶ EAT
ebullient 形
▶ LIVELY
eccentric 形
▶ UNUSUAL
echo 動
▶ REPEAT
eclectic 形
▶ DIVERSE
ECONOMIC 形 p.219

economic 形
▶ ECONOMIC, SUCCESSFUL 2
economical 形
▶ CHEAP, SHORT 3
economics 名
▶ FINANCE
economize 動
▶ SAVE 2
ecosystem 名
▶ NATURE 2
ecstasy 名
▶ JOY
ecstatic 形
▶ EXCITED
EDGE 名 p.219
edge 名
▶ EDGE
edge 動
▶ DECORATE
editor 名
▶ REPORTER
editorial 名
▶ ARTICLE
educate 動
▶ TEACH, TRAIN 1
educated 形
▶ INFORMED
EDUCATION 名 p.220
education 名
▶ EDUCATION
EDUCATIONAL 形 p.221
educational 形
▶ EDUCATIONAL
educationalist 名
▶ TEACHER
educator 名
▶ TEACHER
eerie 形
▶ FRIGHTENING
EFFECT 名 p.221
effect 名
▶ EFFECT
effect 動
▶ ACHIEVE
effective 形
▶ SUCCESSFUL 1
EFFICIENCY 名 p.222
efficiency 名
▶ EFFICIENCY
EFFICIENT 形 p.222
efficient 形
▶ EFFICIENT
EFFORT 名 p.223
effort 名
▶ ATTEMPT, EFFORT
effortless 形
▶ EASY 1
ego 名
▶ DIGNITY, MIND
egocentric 形
▶ SELFISH
egoism 名
▶ PRIDE

egotistical 形
▶ SELFISH
elaborate 形
▶ COMPLEX
elastic 形
▶ FLEXIBLE 2
elated 形
▶ EXCITED
elbow 動
▶ PUSH 2
elderly 形
▶ OLD 2
elect 動
▶ APPOINT, DECIDE
ELECTION 名 p.224
election 名
▶ CHOICE 1, ELECTION
elegance 名
▶ STYLE
ELEGANT 形 p.224
elegant 形
▶ ELEGANT
ELEMENT 名 p.225
element 名
▶ ELEMENT, MATERIAL
elementary 形
▶ FUNDAMENTAL
eliminate 動
▶ EXCLUDE 1, KILL, REMOVE
ELITE 名 p.225
elite 名
▶ ELITE
elite 形
▶ TOP
elude 動
▶ ESCAPE
email 名
▶ LETTER
emancipate 動
▶ RELEASE
embargo 名
▶ BAN 名
embark on/upon sth
▶ BEGIN
EMBARRASS 動 p.226
embarrass 動
▶ EMBARRASS
EMBARRASSED 形 p.226
embarrassed 形
▶ EMBARRASSED
embellish 動
▶ EXAGGERATE
embezzle 動
▶ STEAL
embezzlement 名
▶ THEFT
emblem 名
▶ LOGO
embodiment 名
▶ EXAMPLE 2
embody 動
▶ REPRESENT 2
embrace 動
▶ HUG, INCLUDE

emerge 動
▶ APPEAR, TURN OUT
emergency 名
▶ CRISIS
emigrant 名
▶ REFUGEE
emigrate 動
▶ LEAVE 2
eminent 形
▶ GREAT 2
EMOTION 名 p.227
emotion 名
▶ EMOTION
emotional 形
▶ INTENSE
emotive 形
▶ SENSITIVE 2
empathize 動
▶ UNDERSTAND 2
emphasis 名
▶ PRIORITY
emphasize 動
▶ STRESS
EMPLOY 動 p.228
employ 動
▶ EMPLOY, USE 動 1
employee 名
▶ WORKER 1
employer 名
▶ MANAGER
employment 名
▶ WORK 名 1
empower 動
▶ ALLOW
EMPTY 形 p.228
empty 形
▶ EMPTY
empty 動
▶ CLEAR 動
emulate 動
▶ FOLLOW 4
enchant 動
▶ DELIGHT
enclave 名
▶ TERRITORY
encompass 動
▶ INCLUDE
encounter 名
▶ MEETING 2
encounter 動
▶ HAVE 3, MEET 2
ENCOURAGE 動 p.229
encourage 動
▶ ENCOURAGE
encouraging 形
▶ PROMISING
END 名 p.229
END 動 p.230
end 名
▶ EDGE, END 名, TARGET
end 動
▶ END 動
endanger 動
▶ THREATEN

endangered 形
▶ VULNERABLE
endearing 形
▶ SWEET
endeavour 名
▶ EFFORT
endeavour 動
▶ TRY 1
ending 名
▶ END 名
endorse 動
▶ RECOMMEND 2
ENDORSEMENT 名 p.230
endorsement 名
▶ ENDORSEMENT
endow 動
▶ FUND 動
endowment 名
▶ INVESTMENT
endure 動
▶ STAND 2
enduring 形
▶ PERMANENT
end-user 名
▶ CUSTOMER
ENEMY 名 p.231
enemy 名
▶ ENEMY
ENERGETIC 形 p.231
energetic 形
▶ ENERGETIC
energy 名
▶ EFFORT
enforce 動
▶ APPLY
engage 動
▶ EMPLOY
engaged 形
▶ BUSY 1
engage in sth
▶ JOIN
engagement 名
▶ INVOLVEMENT, MEETING 2
engaging 形
▶ NICE 2
engineer 動
▶ DESIGN 動 1
engrossed 形
▶ INTERESTED
enhance 動
▶ IMPROVE 1
enjoy 動
▶ HAVE 2
enjoyable 形
▶ NICE 1
enjoyment 名
▶ FUN
enjoy yourself
▶ PLAY 動 1
enlarge 動
▶ EXPAND
enlighten 動
▶ TELL 1

enlightened 形
▶ TOLERANT
enlightening 形
▶ INFORMATIVE
enlightenment 名
▶ KNOWLEDGE
enmity 名
▶ TENSION
enormous 形
▶ HUGE
enquire 動
▶ ASK 1
enquire into sth
▶ INVESTIGATE
enquiry 名
▶ INVESTIGATION, QUESTION 名, RESEARCH
enrage 動
▶ ANGER 動
enraged 形
▶ FURIOUS
enrich 動
▶ IMPROVE 1
enrol 動
▶ LET SB IN
ensue 動
▶ FOLLOW 2
ensuing 形
▶ RELATED
ENSURE 動 p.232
ensure 動
▶ ENSURE
ENTER 動 p.232
enter 動
▶ ENTER, JOIN, RECORD
enter into sth
▶ JOIN
enterprise 名
▶ COMPANY, PROJECT, TRADE
entertain 動
▶ GREET
entertainer 名
▶ ACTOR
entertaining 形
▶ FUNNY
ENTERTAINMENT 名 p.233
entertainment 名
▶ ENTERTAINMENT, INTEREST 名 2
enthral 動
▶ DELIGHT
enthusiast 名
▶ FAN
enthusiastic 形
▶ EAGER
entire 形
▶ WHOLE
entirely 副
▶ QUITE 2
entitle 動
▶ ALLOW, CALL 1
entitlement 名
▶ RIGHT 名

entity 名
▶ THING 1
entrance 名
▶ ACCESS, ARRIVAL
entrance 動
▶ DELIGHT
entrant 名
▶ CANDIDATE
entrepreneur 名
▶ EXECUTIVE
entry 名
▶ ACCESS, HALL 2
entryway 名
▶ HALL 2
enviable 形
▶ POPULAR
ENVIRONMENT 名 p.233
environment 名
▶ ENVIRONMENT, NATURE 2
envisage 動
▶ IMAGINE
envision 動
▶ IMAGINE
envy 名
▶ JEALOUSY
episode 名
▶ EVENT 1
epitome 名
▶ EXAMPLE 2
epitomize 動
▶ REPRESENT 2
epoch 名
▶ PERIOD
EQUAL 形 p.234
equal 形
▶ EQUAL, REASONABLE
equal 動
▶ COMPARE 2
equality 名
▶ JUSTICE
EQUIP 動 p.235
equip 動
▶ EQUIP
EQUIPMENT 名 p.235
equipment 名
▶ EQUIPMENT
equitable 形
▶ REASONABLE
equity 名
▶ JUSTICE
equivalence 名
▶ SIMILARITY
EQUIVALENT 形 p.236
equivalent 形
▶ EQUIVALENT
era 名
▶ PERIOD
erase 動
▶ DELETE
erect 動
▶ BUILD
errand 名
▶ TASK

INDEX

error 名
▶ MISTAKE 1, 2
escalate 動
▶ RISE
ESCAPE 動 p.236
escape 動
▶ ESCAPE
escort 動
▶ TAKE 2
essay 名
▶ PAPER
essence 名
▶ NATURE 1
ESSENTIAL 形 p.237
essential 形
▶ ESSENTIAL, FUNDAMENTAL
essential 名
▶ NEED
essentials 名
▶ BASICS
ESTABLISH 動 p.238
establish 動
▶ ESTABLISH, FIND 3
the establishment 名
▶ AUTHORITIES
estate 名
▶ LAND 1
esteem 名
▶ ADMIRATION
esteem 動
▶ RESPECT
ESTIMATE 名 p.238
ESTIMATE 動 p.239
estimate 名
▶ ESTIMATE, VALUATION
estimate 動
▶ ESTIMATE
estimation 名
▶ ASSESSMENT
estranged 形
▶ SINGLE
estrangement 名
▶ DIVISION 2
eternal 形
▶ PERMANENT
ethic 名
▶ VALUES
ethical 形
▶ GOOD 5, MORAL
ethics 名
▶ PRINCIPLE 1
ethnic 形
▶ CULTURAL
ethnic group 名
▶ PEOPLE
ethos 名
▶ VALUES
etiquette 名
▶ RESPECT 名
euphoria 名
▶ JOY
euphoric 形
▶ EXCITED

euthanasia 名
▶ MURDER
evacuee 名
▶ REFUGEE
evade 動
▶ ESCAPE
evaluate 動
▶ JUDGE 動
evaluation 名
▶ ASSESSMENT
even 形
▶ CLOSE 形, STEADY
even-handed 形
▶ REASONABLE
evening 名
▶ NIGHT 2
EVENT 名 p.240
event 名
▶ EVENT 1, 2
eventful 形
▶ BUSY 2
eventual 形
▶ LAST 1
eventuality 名
▶ EVENT 1
every so often
▶ SOMETIMES
EVIDENCE 名 p.241
evidence 名
▶ EVIDENCE
evidence 動
▶ CONFIRM 1
evident 形
▶ CLEAR 形 1
EVIL 名 p.242
EVIL 形 p.242
evil 名
▶ EVIL 名
evil 形
▶ EVIL 形
evocation 名
▶ DESCRIPTION
evolve 動
▶ DEVELOP 1, 2, TURN 2
ex- 連結形
▶ FORMER
EXACT 形 p.242
exact 形
▶ EXACT, VERY 形
exact 動
▶ DEMAND 動
EXAGGERATE 動 p.243
exaggerate 動
▶ EXAGGERATE
exalted 形
▶ GREAT 2
exam 名
▶ TEST 名 2
examination 名
▶ INSPECTION, RESEARCH, TEST 名 2
EXAMINE 動 p.244
examine 動
▶ CHECK 1, EXAMINE, TEST 動 2

examiner 名
▶ INSPECTOR, JUDGE 名
EXAMPLE 名 p.244
example 名
▶ EXAMPLE 1, 2, INFLUENCE 名
exasperate 動
▶ ANNOY
exasperated 形
▶ ANNOYED
exasperation 名
▶ FRUSTRATION
excellence 名
▶ VALUE
EXCELLENT 形 p.245
excellent 形
▶ EXCELLENT
exceptional 形
▶ REMARKABLE, SPECIAL
EXCESS 形 p.246
excess 形
▶ EXCESS
EXCESSIVE 形 p.246
excessive 形
▶ EXCESSIVE
EXCHANGE 名 p.247
exchange 名
▶ DISCUSSION, EXCHANGE
exchange 動
▶ CASH, REPLACE 2
excite 動
▶ STIMULATE
EXCITED 形 p.247
excited 形
▶ EXCITED
EXCITEMENT 名 p.248
excitement 名
▶ EXCITEMENT
EXCITING 形 p.248
exciting 形
▶ EXCITING
EXCLUDE 動 p.249
exclude 動
▶ EXCLUDE 1, 2
exclusive 形
▶ OWN
excommunicate 動
▶ EXCLUDE 2
excruciating 形
▶ PAINFUL 1
excursion 名
▶ TRIP
excuse 名
▶ REASON
excuse 動
▶ FORGIVE
execute 動
▶ KILL
EXECUTIVE 名 p.250
executive 名
▶ EXECUTIVE, GOVERNMENT 1, MANAGEMENT

exemplary 形
▶ PERFECT
exemplify 動
▶ REPRESENT 2
exercise 名
▶ ASSIGNMENT, PROJECT, SPORT, USE 名
exercise 動
▶ TRAIN 2, USE 動 1
exert 動
▶ USE 動 1
exertion 名
▶ EFFORT
exhaust 動
▶ USE 動 2
exhausted 形
▶ TIRED
exhaustive 形
▶ DETAILED
exhibit 名
▶ EXHIBITION
EXHIBITION 名 p.250
exhibition 名
▶ EXHIBITION, EXPRESSION
exhilarated 形
▶ EXCITED
exhilarating 形
▶ EXCITING
exhilaration 名
▶ EXCITEMENT
exile 名
▶ REFUGEE
exile 動
▶ EXPEL
existence 名
▶ LIFE 1, 3
exit 動
▶ LEAVE 1
exit poll 名
▶ ELECTION
exorbitant 形
▶ HIGH 1
EXPAND 動 p.251
expand 動
▶ EXPAND
expatriate 名
▶ REFUGEE
EXPECT 動 p.252
expect 動
▶ DEMAND 動, EXPECT, SUPPOSE
expectancy 名
▶ HOPE 名 1
expectant 形
▶ OPTIMISTIC
EXPECTATION 名 p.253
expectation 名
▶ EXPECTATION, HOPE 名 2
expedition 名
▶ TRIP
EXPEL 動 p.253

expel → fate

expel 動
▶ EXCLUDE 2, EXPEL
expend 動
▶ USE 動 2
expenditure 名
▶ COSTS
expense 名
▶ PRICE
expenses 名
▶ COSTS
EXPENSIVE 形 p.254
expensive 形
▶ EXPENSIVE
experience 名
▶ EVENT 1, KNOWLEDGE, LIFE 3
experience 動
▶ FEEL, HAVE 3
EXPERIENCED 形 p.254
experienced 形
▶ EXPERIENCED, SOPHISTICATED
experiment 名
▶ TEST 名 1
experiment 動
▶ TEST 動 1
EXPERIMENTAL 形 p.255
experimental 形
▶ EXPERIMENTAL
EXPERT 名 p.255
expert 名
▶ EXPERT
expert 形
▶ IMPRESSIVE
expertise 名
▶ SKILL 2
EXPLAIN 動 p.256
explain 動
▶ EXPLAIN 1, 2
explanation 名
▶ REASON
explanatory 形
▶ DESCRIPTIVE
explicit 形
▶ CLEAR 形 2
explode 動
▶ BANG 1, DISPROVE
exploration 名
▶ RESEARCH
explore 動
▶ INVESTIGATE
export 動
▶ SELL 2
expose 動
▶ REVEAL, SHOW 2
exposed 形
▶ VULNERABLE
expound 動
▶ EXPLAIN 1
express 動
▶ CLEAR 形 2, FAST
express 動
▶ SAY 2
EXPRESSION 名 p.257

expression 名
▶ EXPRESSION
exquisite 形
▶ BEAUTIFUL 2
extend 動
▶ EXPAND, MAINTAIN
extended 形
▶ LONG
extensive 形
▶ LARGE, WIDE 1
exterminate 動
▶ DESTROY
external 形
▶ FOREIGN
extortion 名
▶ CORRUPTION
extortionate 形
▶ HIGH 1
extract 動
▶ PUMP
extradite 動
▶ EXPEL
extraneous 形
▶ IRRELEVANT
extraordinary 形
▶ REMARKABLE, SPECIAL, SURPRISING
extrapolate 動
▶ ESTIMATE 1
extreme 形
▶ RADICAL, SERIOUS 1
extremely 副
▶ VERY 副
extrovert 形
▶ SOCIABLE
exuberant 形
▶ LIVELY
eyewitness 名
▶ WITNESS

F

fabric 名
▶ STRUCTURE
fabrication 名
▶ LIE
fabulous 形
▶ GREAT 1
facilitate 動
▶ HELP 動 2
FACILITIES 名 p.258
facilities 名
▶ FACILITIES
facsimile 名
▶ COPY 名 2
FACT 名 p.258
fact 名
▶ FACT, INFORMATION
faction 名
▶ PARTY 1
FACTOR 名 p.259
factor 名
▶ FACTOR
FACTORY 名 p.259

factory 名
▶ FACTORY
factual 形
▶ RELIABLE 2
fad 名
▶ FASHION
fade 動
▶ DISAPPEAR
FAIL 動 p.259
fail 動
▶ BREAK 2, DISAPPOINT, FAIL 1, 2, 3, WORSEN
FAILURE 名 p.261
failure 名
▶ DISASTER, FAILURE, LOSER 2
faint 形
▶ DIM, QUIET 2
fair 形
▶ FINE, REASONABLE
fair 名
▶ EXHIBITION
fairly 副
▶ QUITE 1
fairness 名
▶ JUSTICE
fair play 名
▶ JUSTICE
FAITH 名 p.261
faith 名
▶ FAITH
faithful 形
▶ RELIABLE 1
FAKE 名 p.262
fake 名
▶ FAKE
fake 動
▶ PRETEND
fake 形
▶ ARTIFICIAL
FALL 動 p.262
fall 名
▶ REDUCTION
fall 動
▶ FALL 1, 2, 3, RAIN
fallacy 名
▶ ILLUSION
fall back on sb/sth
▶ USE 動 1
fall down
▶ FALL 3
fall out
▶ ARGUE
fall over
▶ FALL 3
fall through
▶ FAIL 2
false 形
▶ ARTIFICIAL, WRONG 1
falsehood 名
▶ LIE
false impression 名
▶ ILLUSION
FAME 名 p.264

fame 名
▶ FAME
famed 形
▶ FAMOUS
familiar with sth
▶ USED TO STH
FAMILY 名 p.264
family 名
▶ FAMILY 1, 2, 3
FAMOUS 形 p.266
famous 形
▶ FAMOUS
FAN 名 p.267
fan 名
▶ FAN
fanatic 名
▶ FAN
fancy 動
▶ WANT
fantastic 形
▶ GREAT 1
fantasy 名
▶ HOPE 名 2, IMAGINATION
farce 名
▶ PLAY 名
fare 名
▶ FOOD, RATE
far-fetched 形
▶ UNLIKELY 2
farmers' market 名
▶ MARKET 2
farmland 名
▶ LAND 1
far-reaching 形
▶ WIDE 1
fascinate 動
▶ INTEREST 動
fascinated 形
▶ INTERESTED
fascinating 形
▶ INTERESTING
fascination 名
▶ INTEREST 名 1
FASHION 名 p.268
fashion 名
▶ FASHION
FASHIONABLE 形 p.268
fashionable 形
▶ FASHIONABLE
FAST 形 p.269
fast 形
▶ FAST, QUICK
fasten 動
▶ ATTACH
fastener 名
▶ BUTTON 2
FAT 形 p.269
fat 形
▶ FAT
FATAL 形 p.270
fatal 形
▶ FATAL
fate 名
▶ LUCK

fatigued 形
▶ TIRED
FAULT 名 p.270
fault 名
▶ DEFECT, FAULT
faultless 形
▶ PERFECT
favour 名
▶ APPROVAL
favour 動
▶ PREFER
favourable 形
▶ GOOD 6, VALUABLE 2
favoured 形
▶ FAVOURITE
FAVOURITE 形 p.271
favourite 形
▶ FAVOURITE
favourite 名
▶ CHOICE 2
favouritism 名
▶ DISCRIMINATION
fax 名
▶ LETTER
FEAR 名 p.272
fear 名
▶ FEAR, RISK 1
fearful 形
▶ AFRAID
fearless 形
▶ BRAVE
feasible 形
▶ POSSIBLE 1
FEATURE 名 p.273
FEATURE 動 p.273
feature 名
▶ ARTICLE, FEATURE 名
feature 動
▶ FEATURE
federal 形
▶ PUBLIC
federation 名
▶ UNION
fee 名
▶ RATE
feeble 形
▶ UNFORTUNATE 2
FEEL 動 p.274
feel 名
▶ ATMOSPHERE
feel 動
▶ FEEL, HAVE 3, THINK, TOUCH
feel 連結動詞
▶ SEEM
feel for sb
▶ SORRY FOR SB
feeling 名
▶ ATMOSPHERE, EMOTION, IDEA 2, SENSE, VIEW 1
feelings 名
▶ DIGNITY
feel like sth
▶ WANT

feign 動
▶ PRETEND
fell 名
▶ HILL
fell 動
▶ DEMOLISH
fellow 名
▶ LECTURER
fellowship 名
▶ FRIENDSHIP
felon 名
▶ CRIMINAL
felony 名
▶ CRIME 2
female 名
▶ WOMAN
fend for yourself
▶ TAKE CARE OF YOURSELF
ferry 動
▶ TAKE 1
fertile 形
▶ PRODUCTIVE
fervent 形
▶ INTENSE
fervour 名
▶ EMOTION
festivities 名
▶ EVENT 2
festoon 動
▶ DECORATE
feverish 形
▶ HOT
few and far between
▶ SCARCE
fiancé 名
▶ PARTNER 2
fiancée 名
▶ PARTNER 2
fiasco 名
▶ DISASTER
fib 名
▶ LIE
fiction 名
▶ LIE
FICTIONAL 形 p.274
fictional 形
▶ FICTIONAL
fictitious 形
▶ FICTIONAL
field 名
▶ AREA 2
fierce 形
▶ INTENSE
fiery 形
▶ INTENSE
FIGHT 名 p.275
FIGHT 動 p.275
fight 名
▶ ARGUMENT 1, CAMPAIGN 名, FIGHT 名, GAME

fight 動
▶ ARGUE, CAMPAIGN 動, COMPETE, FIGHT 動, OPPOSE
fighting 名
▶ WAR
FIGURE 名 p.276
figure 名
▶ FIGURE, PERSON, SHAPE
figure 動
▶ CALCULATE, CONCLUDE, ESTIMATE 動, FEATURE
figure sth out
▶ CALCULATE
file 名
▶ DOCUMENT
file 動
▶ CLASSIFY, PRESENT 3
filings 名
▶ FRAGMENT
FILL 動 p.276
fill 動
▶ FILL
fill sb in
▶ TELL 1
fill in for sb/sth
▶ REPLACE 1
fill up
▶ FILL
filthy 形
▶ DIRTY, OFFENSIVE
FINAL 形 p.277
final 形
▶ FINAL, LAST 1
final 名
▶ GAME
finale 名
▶ END 名
finalize 動
▶ FINISH
FINANCE 名 p.277
finance 名
▶ FINANCE, MONEY 1
finance 動
▶ FUND
financial 形
▶ ECONOMIC
FIND 動 p.278
find 動
▶ FIND 1, 2, 3, 4, REGARD
finding 名
▶ CONCLUSION
find out
▶ FIND 1
FINE 形 p.280
fine 形
▶ FINE, GOOD 1, NARROW, SUNNY, WELL, WORTHY
fine 名
▶ RATE

fine 動
▶ CHARGE 動
finery 名
▶ DECORATION
finger 動
▶ TELL 2
fingerprint 名
▶ MARK
FINISH 動 p.281
finish 名
▶ END 名
finish 動
▶ EAT, END 動, FINISH
finish sb/sth off
▶ KILL
FIRE 動 p.282
fire 動
▶ FIRE
fire sb up
▶ INSPIRE
FIRM 形 p.283
firm 形
▶ FINAL, FIRM, SOLID, STRICT, TIGHT
firm 名
▶ COMPANY
FIRST 限定詞 p.283
first 限定詞
▶ FIRST, TOP
first-rate 形
▶ EXCELLENT
fishy 形
▶ SUSPICIOUS 2
fit 形
▶ GOOD 2, WELL
fit 動
▶ MATCH 1
fitness 名
▶ HEALTH
fit sb/sth out
▶ EQUIP
fitting 形
▶ GOOD 2
fix 名
▶ SOLUTION
fix 動
▶ ATTACH, CORRECT, REPAIR
fixation 名
▶ OBSESSION
fixture 名
▶ GAME
flair 名
▶ SKILL 1, STYLE
flak 名
▶ CRITICISM
flake 名
▶ FRAGMENT
flap 動
▶ SHAKE 1
flash flood 名
▶ FLOOD 名 1
FLAT 形 p.284
flat 形
▶ FLAT

flatten → free of charge

flatten 動
  ▶ DEMOLISH
flattering 形
  ▶ GOOD 6
flattery 名
  ▶ PRAISE 名
flavour 名
  ▶ ATMOSPHERE
flaw 名
  ▶ DEFECT
flawless 形
  ▶ PERFECT
FLEE 動 p.284
flee 動
  ▶ FLEE
fleece 動
  ▶ DEFRAUD
fleeting 形
  ▶ SHORT 1
FLEXIBLE 形 p.285
flexible 形
  ▶ FLEXIBLE 1, 2
flick through sth
  ▶ READ
fling 動
  ▶ THROW
FLIRT 動 p.286
flirt 動
  ▶ FLIRT
FLOOD 名 p.286
FLOOD 動 p.287
flood 名
  ▶ FLOOD 名 1, 2
flood 動
  ▶ FLOOD 動, SOAK
FLOOR 名 p.287
floor 名
  ▶ FLOOR
flop 動
  ▶ DISASTER
flourish 動
  ▶ DO WELL
flout 動
  ▶ OPPOSE
FLOW 動 p.288
flow 動
  ▶ FLOW
fluctuate 動
  ▶ CHANGE 動 2
fluctuation 名
  ▶ CHANGE 名 1
fluid 形
  ▶ VARIABLE
fluid 名
  ▶ MATERIAL
fluke 名
  ▶ MIRACLE
flunk 動
  ▶ FAIL 3
FLUSH 動 p.289
flush 動
  ▶ FLUSH
flustered 形
  ▶ RESTLESS

fly 動
  ▶ GO 2, HURRY, TAKE 1
flyer 名
  ▶ LEAFLET
FOCUS 動 p.289
focus 動
  ▶ FOCUS
foe 名
  ▶ ENEMY
foggy 形
  ▶ CLOUDY
folk 形
  ▶ CULTURAL
FOLLOW 動 p.290
follow 動
  ▶ FOLLOW 1, 2, 3, 4,
    UNDERSTAND 1
follower 名
  ▶ FAN
follow in sb's footsteps
  ▶ FOLLOW 4
the following 形
  ▶ NEXT
follow suit
  ▶ FOLLOW 4
follow through
  ▶ FINISH
fond 形
  ▶ LOVING
FOOD 名 p.292
food 名
  ▶ FOOD
foodstuff 名
  ▶ FOOD
FOOL 名 p.293
fool 名
  ▶ FOOL
fool 動
  ▶ CHEAT 動
foolish 形
  ▶ CRAZY, RIDICULOUS
foot 名
  ▶ BOTTOM
foothills 名
  ▶ HILL
footpath 名
  ▶ PATH
footstep 名
  ▶ STEP
forage 動
  ▶ LOOK 動 2
forbid 動
  ▶ BAN
FORBIDDEN 形 p.293
forbidden 形
  ▶ FORBIDDEN
FORCE 名 p.294
FORCE 動 p.294
force 名
  ▶ ARMY, CONTROL,
    EFFECT, FORCE 名,
    INFLUENCE 名,
    PRESSURE 2
force 動
  ▶ FORCE 動, PUSH 1

forced 形
  ▶ NECESSARY
forceful 形
  ▶ AGGRESSIVE 2,
    CONVINCING
foreboding 名
  ▶ IDEA 2
forecast 名
  ▶ EXPECTATION
forecast 動
  ▶ PREDICT
FOREIGN 形 p.294
foreign 形
  ▶ FOREIGN
foreman 名
  ▶ MANAGER
foremost 形
  ▶ TOP
foresee 動
  ▶ PREDICT
foreseeable 形
  ▶ PREDICTABLE
foresight 名
  ▶ EXPECTATION
foreword 名
  ▶ INTRODUCTION
forgery 名
  ▶ FAKE
forget 動
  ▶ FAIL 1
forgetful 形
  ▶ CARELESS
FORGIVE 動 p.295
forgive 動
  ▶ FORGIVE
forlorn 形
  ▶ LONELY
form 名
  ▶ KIND 名, SHAPE,
    STRUCTURE
form 動
  ▶ APPEAR, DETERMINE,
    ESTABLISH, MAKE 1
FORMAL 形 p.295
formal 形
  ▶ FORMAL, OFFICIAL 形
formality 名
  ▶ RESPECT 名
format 名
  ▶ DESIGN
FORMER 形 p.296
former 形
  ▶ FORMER, PREVIOUS
formula 名
  ▶ SLOGAN
for nothing
  ▶ FREE 形 2
for sale
  ▶ AVAILABLE
forthcoming 形
  ▶ NEXT
forthright 形
  ▶ HONEST
fortunate 形
  ▶ TIMELY

fortune 名
  ▶ LUCK, MONEY 3
forward 動
  ▶ SEND
fossil fuel 名
  ▶ OIL
foster 動
  ▶ BRING SB UP
foul 形
  ▶ DISGUSTING 1,
    OFFENSIVE
found 動
  ▶ ESTABLISH
foundation 名
  ▶ BOTTOM, CHARITY
founder 名
  ▶ FAIL 2
foundry 名
  ▶ FACTORY
foyer 名
  ▶ HALL 2
fraction 名
  ▶ FIGURE
fracture 動
  ▶ BREAK 1
FRAGILE 形 p.296
fragile 形
  ▶ FRAGILE
FRAGMENT 名 p.296
fragment 名
  ▶ FRAGMENT
fragrance 名
  ▶ SMELL
frame of mind 名
  ▶ MOOD
framework 名
  ▶ STRUCTURE
franchise 名
  ▶ LICENCE
frank 形
  ▶ HONEST
frantic 形
  ▶ HYSTERICAL
FRAUD 名 p.297
fraud 名
  ▶ FRAUD 1, 2
fraudulent 形
  ▶ CORRUPT
fraught 形
  ▶ STRESSFUL
freak 名
  ▶ FAN
freak out
  ▶ PANIC
FREE 形 p.298
FREE 形 p.298
free 動
  ▶ FREE 動, RELEASE
free 形
  ▶ EMPTY, FREE 形 1, 2, 3
FREEDOM 名 p.299
freedom 名
  ▶ FREEDOM
free of charge
  ▶ FREE 形 2

889

INDEX

free time 名
▶ LEISURE
freeze 動
▶ COOL
FREEZING 形 p.300
freezing 形
▶ FREEZING
freight 名
▶ CARGO, DELIVERY
FREQUENT 形 p.300
frequent 形
▶ FREQUENT
frequently 副
▶ OFTEN
fresh 形
▶ NEW 1
freshen up
▶ WASH
FRIEND 名 p.301
friend 名
▶ FRIEND
FRIENDLY 形 p.302
friendly 形
▶ FRIENDLY 1, 2
FRIENDSHIP 名 p.303
friendship 名
▶ FRIENDSHIP
fright 名
▶ FEAR
FRIGHTEN 動 p.304
frighten 動
▶ FRIGHTEN
frightened 形
▶ AFRAID
FRIGHTENING 形 p.304
frightening 形
▶ FRIGHTENING
frills 名
▶ DECORATION
fringe 名
▶ EDGE
from the (bottom of your) heart
▶ DEEP 1
from time to time
▶ SOMETIMES
frontier 名
▶ LIMIT 2
front runner 名
▶ LEADER 2
frosty 形
▶ COLD 2, FREEZING
frown on/upon sth
▶ DISAPPROVE
frozen 形
▶ FREEZING
the fruit/fruits of sth
▶ RESULT
fruitful 形
▶ PRODUCTIVE
fruitless 形
▶ USELESS
frustrate 動
▶ ANNOY

frustrated 形
▶ UNHAPPY 2
frustrating 形
▶ ANNOYING
FRUSTRATION 名 p.305
frustration 名
▶ FRUSTRATION
fuel 名
▶ OIL
fulfil 動
▶ ACHIEVE, MEET 4
fulfilling 形
▶ SATISFYING
fulfilment 名
▶ SATISFACTION
FULL 形 p.306
full 形
▶ BUSY 2, DEEP 2, FULL, WHOLE
full-scale 形
▶ DETAILED
fully 副
▶ QUITE 2
fuming 形
▶ FURIOUS
FUN 名 p.306
fun 名
▶ ENTERTAINMENT, FUN
function 名
▶ EVENT 2
function 動
▶ WORK 動 2
functional 形
▶ USEFUL
FUND 名 p.307
FUND 動 p.307
fund 名
▶ FUND
fund 動
▶ FUND
FUNDAMENTAL 形 p.308
fundamental 形
▶ FUNDAMENTAL
fundamentals 名
▶ BASICS
funding 名
▶ INVESTMENT
funds 名
▶ MONEY 1
FUNNY 形 p.309
funny 形
▶ FUNNY, STRANGE 1
funny side 名
▶ HUMOUR
FURIOUS 形 p.310
furious 形
▶ FURIOUS
fury 名
▶ ANGER
fuse 動
▶ COMBINE
futile 形
▶ USELESS
future 形
▶ NEXT

frustrated 形
▶ UNHAPPY 2
futuristic 形
▶ EXPERIMENTAL

G

gadget 名
▶ TOOL
gaffe 名
▶ MISTAKE 1
gag 名
▶ JOKE
GAIN 動 p.311
gain 名
▶ INCREASE 名, PROFIT
gain 動
▶ GAIN
gain ground
▶ DEVELOP 1
gallant 形
▶ BRAVE
galling 形
▶ ANNOYING
gallop 動
▶ RUN 1
gamble 動
▶ RISK 2
GAME 名 p.311
game 名
▶ FRAUD 2, GAME, INTEREST 名 2
gang 名
▶ GROUP 2, PARTY 2, TEAM 1
GAP 名 p.312
gap 名
▶ GAP, HOLE 1, PAUSE
garbage 名
▶ NONSENSE, WASTE
garment 名
▶ CLOTHES
garnish 名
▶ DECORATION
garnish 動
▶ DECORATE
garrison 名
▶ GUARD
gas 名
▶ MATERIAL, OIL
gash 名
▶ INJURY
gasoline 名
▶ OIL
gather 動
▶ COLLECT, CONCLUDE, MEET 1
gathering 名
▶ MEETING 1
gauge 名
▶ CRITERION
gauge 動
▶ ESTIMATE 動, JUDGE 動
gawk 動
▶ STARE

gaze 名
▶ LOOK 名
gaze 動
▶ STARE
gear 名
▶ CLOTHES, EQUIPMENT
gear up
▶ PREPARE 2
GENERAL 形 p.312
general 形
▶ GENERAL, USUAL
generally 副
▶ USUALLY
generate 動
▶ MAKE 1
generation 名
▶ PERIOD
generous 形
▶ KIND 形
genetic 形
▶ NATURAL
genial 形
▶ FRIENDLY 1
GENIUS 名 p.313
genius 名
▶ GENIUS, INTELLIGENCE
genre 名
▶ KIND 名
GENTLE 形 p.313
gentle 形
▶ GENTLE, SENSITIVE 1
gentleman 名
▶ MAN 1
gentlemanly 形
▶ POLITE
the gentry 名
▶ ELITE
genuine 形
▶ DEEP 1, REAL
geography 名
▶ DESIGN 名
gesture 名
▶ ACTION, MOVEMENT
GET 動 p.314
get 動
▶ BUY, GET 1, 2, 3, GO 1, PERSUADE, SUFFER FROM STH, UNDERSTAND 1
get 連結動詞
▶ BECOME
get sth across
▶ CONVEY
get a move on
▶ HURRY
get angry
▶ LOSE YOUR TEMPER
getaway 名
▶ HOLIDAY 2
get away
▶ ESCAPE, GO AWAY
get back
▶ RETURN 1
get back to sb
▶ ANSWER 動

get better
▶ IMPROVE 2, RECOVER
get sb down
▶ DISCOURAGE 2
get dressed
▶ WEAR
get here/there
▶ ARRIVE
get hold of sth
▶ GET 1
get in
▶ ARRIVE
get mad
▶ LOSE YOUR TEMPER
get/go nowhere
▶ FAIL 2
get on
▶ SUCCEED
get on sb's nerves
▶ ANNOY
get out
▶ TURN OUT
get out of here
▶ GO AWAY
get ready
▶ PREPARE 2
get sb/sth ready
▶ PREPARE 1
get rid of sb/sth
▶ REMOVE
get round sb
▶ PERSUADE
get the better of sb
▶ DEFEAT
get the hang of sth
▶ LEARN
get there
▶ ACHIEVE
get through sth
▶ GRADUATE, USE 動 2
get-together 名
▶ EVENT 2
get together
▶ MEET 1
get to know sb
▶ MEET 3
get to your feet
▶ STAND 1
get undressed
▶ TAKE STH OFF
get up
▶ STAND 1
get well
▶ RECOVER
get worse
▶ WORSEN
get sb wrong
▶ MISUNDERSTAND
get sth wrong
▶ MISUNDERSTAND
ghastly 形
▶ BAD
giant 形
▶ HUGE

gibberish 名
▶ NONSENSE
GIFT 名 p.315
gift 名
▶ GIFT, SKILL 1
gifted 形
▶ GOOD 4
gigantic 形
▶ HUGE
giggle 動
▶ LAUGH
GIRL 名 p.316
girl 名
▶ CHILD, GIRL
girlfriend 名
▶ PARTNER 2
girlish 形
▶ CHILDISH
the girls 名
▶ FRIEND
gist 名
▶ MESSAGE
GIVE 動 p.317
give 動
▶ GIVE 1, 2, 3, HAVE 4, PROVIDE
give and take
▶ COMPROMISE
give sb/sth away
▶ REVEAL
give sth back
▶ RETURN 2
give in
▶ GIVE WAY
give in/hand in your notice
▶ LEAVE 3
give sth out
▶ DISTRIBUTE
give sth over to sth
▶ DEVOTE
give rise to sth
▶ CAUSE
give sb the sack
▶ FIRE
give sth up
▶ STOP
GIVE WAY 動 p.318
give way
▶ GIVE WAY
GLAD 形 p.319
glad 形
▶ GLAD, GRATEFUL
glamorous 形
▶ FASHIONABLE
glamour 名
▶ INTEREST 名 1, STYLE
glance 名
▶ LOOK 名
glare 名
▶ LOOK 名
glare 動
▶ STARE
gleam 動
▶ SHINE

glimpse 名
▶ LOOK 名
glimpse 動
▶ SEE
glint 動
▶ SHINE
glisten 動
▶ SHINE
glitch 名
▶ DEFECT
glitter 動
▶ SHINE
gloat 動
▶ BOAST
global 形
▶ INTERNATIONAL
globe 名
▶ MAP
globule 名
▶ DROP
GLOOM 名 p.319
gloom 名
▶ GLOOM
gloomy 形
▶ DEPRESSED, NEGATIVE
glorify 動
▶ PRAISE 動
glorious 形
▶ FAMOUS, MAGNIFICENT, SUNNY
glory 名
▶ STATUS
gloss over sth
▶ IGNORE
glow 動
▶ FLUSH, SHINE
glowing 形
▶ GOOD 6
glue 動
▶ ATTACH
glum 形
▶ DEPRESSED
gnaw 動
▶ BITE
GO 動 p.320
go 名
▶ ATTEMPT, OPPORTUNITY
go 動
▶ GO 1, LEAVE 1, MATCH 2, WORK 動 2
go 連結動詞
▶ BECOME
go about sth
▶ BEGIN
go against sb/sth
▶ OPPOSE
go against sth
▶ CONFLICT 動
the go-ahead 名
▶ PERMISSION
goal 名
▶ TARGET
go along with sb/sth
▶ AGREE

go around/round
▶ SPIN
GO AWAY p.321
go away
▶ GO AWAY
go back
▶ RETURN 1
go back on sth
▶ BREAK 4
go berserk
▶ LOSE YOUR TEMPER
go-between 名
▶ NEGOTIATOR
go down
▶ BREAK 2
go down sth
▶ FALL 2
go for sb/sth
▶ LIKE 動, TRY 1
go for sth
▶ CHOOSE
go in
▶ ENTER
go into sth
▶ EXAMINE
go mad
▶ LOSE YOUR TEMPER
GOOD 形 p.322
good 形
▶ GOOD 1, 2, 3, 4, 5, 6, 7, HEALTHY, KIND 形, NICE 1, SUNNY, VALUABLE 2, WELL
good 名
▶ BENEFIT, MORALITY
good-looking 形
▶ BEAUTIFUL 1
good-natured 形
▶ FRIENDLY 1
goodness 名
▶ MORALITY
good point 名
▶ BENEFIT
goods 名
▶ CARGO, PRODUCT, THING 2
good time 名
▶ FUN
gooey 形
▶ SOFT
go off
▶ GO AWAY
go on
▶ CONTINUE 1, 3
go on with sth
▶ CONTINUE 2
GO OUT p.327
go out
▶ GO OUT
go over sth
▶ CHECK 1, PRACTISE
gorgeous 形
▶ BEAUTIFUL 1
go so/as far as to...
▶ DARE

INDEX

gossip 名
▶ DISCUSSION
go through sth
▶ DO, HAVE 3
go to sth
▶ VISIT 動
go up
▶ RISE
go up sth
▶ CLIMB
govern 動
▶ DETERMINE, RULE 動 1
governess 名
▶ TEACHER
GOVERNMENT 名 p.327
government 名
▶ GOVERNMENT 1, 2
governor 名
▶ LEADER 1, MANAGER
go wrong
▶ FAIL 2
go wrong
▶ BREAK 2
grab 動
▶ TAKE 3
grace 名
▶ RESPECT 名, STYLE
graceful 形
▶ ELEGANT
gracious 形
▶ POLITE
grade 名
▶ CLASS 3, QUALITY
grade 動
▶ RANK
gradual 形
▶ SLOW
GRADUATE 動 p.329
graduate 動
▶ GRADUATE
grain 名
▶ BIT
grand 形
▶ MAGNIFICENT
grant 名
▶ INVESTMENT
grant 動
▶ ADMIT, ALLOW
graphics 名
▶ PICTURE
grapple 動
▶ FIGHT 動
grasp 名
▶ CONTROL, UNDERSTANDING
grasp 動
▶ HOLD, UNDERSTAND 1
grass 動
▶ TELL 2
GRATEFUL 形 p.329
grateful 形
▶ GRATEFUL
gratify 動
▶ PLEASE

gratifying 形
▶ SATISFYING
gratitude 名
▶ THANKS
gratuity 名
▶ GIFT
grave 形
▶ SERIOUS 1, 2
gravity 名
▶ IMPORTANCE
graze 名
▶ INJURY
graze 動
▶ SCRATCH, TOUCH
GREAT 形 p.329
great 形
▶ GOOD 4, GREAT 1, 2, IMPORTANT, LARGE, POWERFUL, WELL
great 名
▶ STAR
great for sth
▶ USEFUL
great time 名
▶ FUN
GREET 動 p.331
greet 動
▶ GREET
gregarious 形
▶ SOCIABLE
grey 形
▶ CLOUDY
gridlock 名
▶ TRAFFIC
GRIEF 名 p.331
grief 名
▶ GRIEF
grill 動
▶ QUESTION 動
grim 形
▶ BAD, STERN
grimy 形
▶ DIRTY
grin 動
▶ SMILE
grip 動
▶ HOLD, INTEREST 動
gripping 形
▶ INTERESTING
grit your teeth
▶ TIGHTEN
groan 動
▶ WHISPER
groom 動
▶ BRUSH, TRAIN 1
gross 形
▶ DISGUSTING 1
gross 動
▶ MAKE 2
grotesque 形
▶ UGLY
ground 名
▶ LAND 2, SOIL
groundless 形
▶ IRRATIONAL

grounds 名
▶ REASON
GROUP 名 p.332
group 名
▶ GROUP 1, 2, 3
group 動
▶ CLASSIFY
groupie 名
▶ FAN
grow 動
▶ RISE
grow 連結動
▶ BECOME
grown 形
▶ ADULT
grown-up 形
▶ ADULT
growth 名
▶ INCREASE 名
grubby 形
▶ DIRTY
grudging 形
▶ RELUCTANT
gruelling 形
▶ HARD
gruesome 形
▶ TERRIBLE 3
grumble 動
▶ COMPLAIN
grumpy 形
▶ IRRITABLE
guarantee 名
▶ PROMISE 名
guarantee 動
▶ ENSURE, FUND 動, PROMISE 動
guaranteed 形
▶ CERTAIN
GUARD 名 p.334
guard 名
▶ GUARD
guard 動
▶ PROTECT
GUERRILLA 名 p.334
guerrilla 名
▶ GUERRILLA
guess 名
▶ SPECULATION
guess 動
▶ ESTIMATE 動, SUPPOSE
guesswork 名
▶ SPECULATION
guest 名
▶ TENANT
guidance 名
▶ ADVICE
guide 名
▶ ADVISER, BOOK, CRITERION
guide 動
▶ TAKE 2
guideline 名
▶ CRITERION
guild 名
▶ UNION

GUILT 名 p.335
guilt 名
▶ FAULT, GUILT
GUILTY 形 p.335
guilty 形
▶ GUILTY, SORRY
gulf 名
▶ GAP
gullible 形
▶ NAIVE
guru 名
▶ EXPERT
gush 動
▶ FLOW
guts 名
▶ COURAGE
gutsy 形
▶ BRAVE
guy 名
▶ MAN 1

H

HABIT 名 p.337
habit 名
▶ HABIT
habitual 形
▶ FREQUENT, USUAL
habitually 副
▶ OFTEN
hack 名
▶ REPORTER
haggle 動
▶ NEGOTIATE
hail 名
▶ FLOOD 名 2
hail 動
▶ PRAISE 動
hairpin bend 名
▶ CORNER
hair-raising 形
▶ FRIGHTENING
half 副
▶ PARTLY
half-hearted 形
▶ INDIFFERENT
half-price 形
▶ CHEAP
HALL 名 p.337
hall 名
▶ CORRIDOR, HALL 1, 2
hallmark 名
▶ SIGN 1
hallway 名
▶ CORRIDOR, HALL 2
hammer 動
▶ BEAT
hamper 動
▶ BLOCK 1
hand 名
▶ INVOLVEMENT
hand 動
▶ GIVE 2
hand sth back
▶ RETURN 2

handicap 名
▶ OBSTACLE
handicap 動
▶ BLOCK 1
handicapped 形
▶ DISABLED
hand sth in
▶ PRESENT 3
handle 名
▶ BUTTON 1
handle 動
▶ DEAL WITH SB/STH, HOLD, SELL 2
handling 名
▶ DELIVERY
handout 名
▶ AID, GIFT, LEAFLET
hand sth out
▶ DISTRIBUTE
hand sb/sth over
▶ GIVE 2
handsome 形
▶ BEAUTIFUL 1, LARGE
handy 形
▶ USEFUL
hang 動
▶ DECORATE
hang around
▶ STAY 1
hang on
▶ HOLD, PERSIST
hang on sth
▶ DEPEND ON/UPON STH
hang out
▶ REST
hang-up 名
▶ OBSESSION
haphazard 形
▶ RANDOM
HAPPEN 動 *p.338*
happen 動
▶ HAPPEN
happiness 名
▶ SATISFACTION
HAPPY 形 *p.339*
happy 形
▶ GLAD, HAPPY, TIMELY
HARD 形 *p.339*
hard 形
▶ DIFFICULT 1, 2, FINAL, HARD, RUTHLESS, SOLID
hard copy 名
▶ COPY 1
hard-fought 形
▶ CLOSE 1
hardly ever 副
▶ RARELY
hard-pressed 形
▶ BUSY 1
hardship 名
▶ TROUBLE 2
hard up 形
▶ POOR 1

hardware 名
▶ EQUIPMENT
hard work 名
▶ EFFORT
harm 名
▶ DAMAGE 名
harm 動
▶ DAMAGE 動
HARMFUL 形 *p.340*
harmful 形
▶ HARMFUL
harrowing 形
▶ PAINFUL 2
harsh 形
▶ STRICT
has-been 名
▶ LOSER 2
haste 名
▶ SPEED
hasten 動
▶ ACCELERATE, HURRY
hasty 形
▶ QUICK, RECKLESS
HATE 動 *p.341*
hate 名
▶ HATRED
hate 動
▶ HATE
hateful 形
▶ DISGUSTING 2
HATRED 名 *p.342*
hatred 名
▶ HATRED
haughty 形
▶ PROUD 2
haul 動
▶ PULL 1
haulage 名
▶ DELIVERY
HAVE 動 *p.342*
have 動
▶ EAT, HAVE 1, 2, 3, 4, SUFFER FROM STH
have a go
▶ TRY 1
have a good time
▶ PLAY 動 1
have a job
▶ WORK 動 1
have/play a part
▶ JOIN
have confidence in sb/sth
▶ TRUST
have fun
▶ PLAY 動 1
have got 動
▶ HAVE 1, 2
have sb/sth in mind
▶ INTEND
haven 名
▶ REFUGE
have sth on
▶ WEAR

hazard 名
▶ THREAT
hazard 動
▶ DARE
hazardous 形
▶ DANGEROUS
hazy 形
▶ CLOUDY
head 名
▶ LEADER 1, MIND
head 動
▶ GO 1, LEAD
heading 名
▶ CATEGORY
headship 名
▶ MANAGEMENT
headstrong 形
▶ STUBBORN
heady 形
▶ EXCITING
heal 動
▶ CURE, RECOVER
healing 名
▶ TREATMENT
HEALTH 名 *p.345*
health 名
▶ HEALTH
HEALTHY 形 *p.345*
healthy 形
▶ HEALTHY, WELL
HEAR 動 *p.345*
hear 動
▶ FIND 1, HEAR
hearing 名
▶ CASE
heart 名
▶ POINT
heartache 名
▶ GRIEF
heartbreak 名
▶ GRIEF
heartbreaking 形
▶ SAD
heartbroken 形
▶ UNHAPPY 1
heartening 形
▶ PROMISING
heartfelt 形
▶ DEEP 1
heartless 形
▶ RUTHLESS
hearty 形
▶ LIVELY
HEAT 動 *p.346*
heat 名
▶ EMOTION, PRESSURE 1
heat 動
▶ HEAT
heated 形
▶ HOT, INTENSE
heat sth up
▶ HEAT
hectic 形
▶ BUSY 2

heed 動
▶ HEAR
hefty 形
▶ LARGE
height 名
▶ PEAK
heighten 動
▶ INCREASE 動
heist 名
▶ THEFT
HELP 名 *p.347*
HELP 動 *p.347*
help 名
▶ AID, HELP 名
help 動
▶ HELP 動 1, 2
HELPFUL 形 *p.349*
helpful 形
▶ HELPFUL, VALUABLE 2
helpless 形
▶ VULNERABLE
help out
▶ HELP 動 1
hereditary 形
▶ NATURAL
heroic 形
▶ BRAVE
heroism 名
▶ COURAGE
hesitant 形
▶ UNSURE
HESITATE 動 *p.349*
hesitate 動
▶ HESITATE
heterogeneous 形
▶ DIVERSE
heyday 名
▶ PEAK
HIDE 動 *p.350*
hide 動
▶ HIDE
hideous 形
▶ UGLY
hideout 名
▶ REFUGE
hiding place 名
▶ REFUGE
HIGH 形 *p.350*
high 形
▶ HIGH 1, 2, 3, TOP
high 名
▶ EXCITEMENT, PEAK
highbrow 形
▶ INTELLECTUAL 2
high-handed 形
▶ PROUD 2
highlands 名
▶ HILL
highlight 名
▶ PEAK
highlight 動
▶ POINT STH OUT
highly 副
▶ VERY 副

high-pitched → HURRY

high-pitched 形
  ▶ HIGH 3
high point 名
  ▶ PEAK
high-powered 形
  ▶ POWERFUL
high quality 名
  ▶ GOOD 1
high-ranking 形
  ▶ TOP
high-rise 形
  ▶ HIGH 2
high-risk 形
  ▶ DANGEROUS
high-speed 形
  ▶ FAST
highwayman 名
  ▶ THIEF
hike 名
  ▶ INCREASE 名
hike 動
  ▶ WALK 2
hilarious 形
  ▶ FUNNY
HILL 名 *p.352*
hill 名
  ▶ HILL
hinder 動
  ▶ BLOCK 1
hindrance 名
  ▶ OBSTACLE
hinge on/upon sth
  ▶ DEPEND ON/UPON STH
hint 名
  ▶ SUGGESTION
hint 動
  ▶ MEAN 動 2
hip 形
  ▶ FASHIONABLE
hire 動
  ▶ EMPLOY, ORDER 2
historic 形
  ▶ FAMOUS
HIT 動 *p.353*
hit 動
  ▶ BANG 2, GET 3, HIT 1, 2
hoard 名
  ▶ SUPPLY
hoard 動
  ▶ KEEP 1
hoax 名
  ▶ TRICK
hobby 名
  ▶ INTEREST 名 2
HOLD 動 *p.354*
hold 名
  ▶ CONTROL
hold 動
  ▶ HAVE 1, 4, HOLD, JAIL, KEEP 3, THINK
hold/keep sb/sth at bay
  ▶ RESIST

hold back
  ▶ HESITATE
hold sb/sth back
  ▶ BLOCK 1
hold sth back
  ▶ SUPPRESS 2
holding 名
  ▶ THING 2
hold on
  ▶ HOLD
hold on to sth
  ▶ KEEP 2
hold out against sb/sth
  ▶ RESIST
hold out for sth
  ▶ DEMAND 動
hold talks
  ▶ NEGOTIATE
HOLD SB/STH UP *p.355*
hold sb/sth up
  ▶ HOLD SB/STH UP
hold up sb/sth
  ▶ ROB
hold/stand your ground
  ▶ RESIST
HOLE 名 *p.355*
hole 名
  ▶ HOLE 1, 2
HOLIDAY 名 *p.356*
holiday 名
  ▶ HOLIDAY 1, 2
holidaymaker 名
  ▶ TOURIST
holler 動
  ▶ SHOUT
hollow 形
  ▶ HOLE 2
HOME 名 *p.357*
home 名
  ▶ FAMILY 1, HOME
home 形
  ▶ NATIONAL
homely 形
  ▶ COMFORTABLE
homesick 形
  ▶ LONELY
homework 名
  ▶ ASSIGNMENT
homey 形
  ▶ COMFORTABLE
homicidal 形
  ▶ VIOLENT
homicide 名
  ▶ MURDER
homogeneous 形
  ▶ EQUAL
HONEST 形 *p.358*
honest 形
  ▶ HONEST
honesty 名
  ▶ INTEGRITY
honey 名
  ▶ DARLING

honorary 形
  ▶ VOLUNTARY 2
honour 動
  ▶ AWARD, INTEGRITY, PLEASURE, REPUTATION, STATUS
honourable 形
  ▶ RESPECTABLE, WORTHY
hop 動
  ▶ JUMP
HOPE 名 *p.359*
HOPE 動 *p.360*
hope 名
  ▶ HOPE 名 1, 2
hope 動
  ▶ HOPE 動
hopeful 形
  ▶ OPTIMISTIC, PROMISING
hopeless 形
  ▶ POOR 2, USELESS
horde 名
  ▶ CROWD
horizontal 形
  ▶ FLAT
horrendous 形
  ▶ TERRIBLE 1
horrible 形
  ▶ TERRIBLE 1, 3
horrific 形
  ▶ TERRIBLE 3
horrify 動
  ▶ SHOCK 動
horrifying 形
  ▶ TERRIBLE 3
horror 名
  ▶ SHOCK 名
hose 動
  ▶ CLEAN 動
hospitable 形
  ▶ FRIENDLY 1
host 名
  ▶ PRESENTER
host 動
  ▶ HAVE 4, PRESENT 4
hostile 形
  ▶ AGAINST SB/STH, AGGRESSIVE 1
hostilities 名
  ▶ WAR
hostility 名
  ▶ OPPOSITION, TENSION
HOT 形 *p.361*
hot 形
  ▶ HOT, POPULAR, STRONG 2
hour 名
  ▶ TIME
house 名
  ▶ COMPANY, FAMILY 1
household 名
  ▶ FAMILY 1
householder 名
  ▶ RESIDENT

housework 名
  ▶ TASK
howl 動
  ▶ SCREAM
howler 名
  ▶ MISTAKE 2
hubris 名
  ▶ PRIDE
huff 名
  ▶ TEMPER
HUG 動 *p.361*
hug 動
  ▶ HUG
HUGE 形 *p.362*
huge 形
  ▶ HUGE
human 形
  ▶ PERSON
human being 名
  ▶ PERSON
humane 形
  ▶ SENSITIVE 1
humanity 名
  ▶ MAN 2, SYMPATHY
humankind 名
  ▶ MAN 2
the human race 名
  ▶ MAN 2
human resources 名
  ▶ STAFF
HUMID 形 *p.363*
humid 形
  ▶ HUMID
humidity 名
  ▶ MOISTURE
humiliate 動
  ▶ EMBARRASS
humorous 形
  ▶ FUNNY
HUMOUR 名 *p.363*
humour 名
  ▶ HUMOUR
humourless 形
  ▶ SERIOUS 2
hunch 名
  ▶ IDEA 2
HUNGRY 形 *p.363*
hungry 形
  ▶ EAGER, HUNGRY
hunk 名
  ▶ PIECE
hunt 名
  ▶ SEARCH
hunt 動
  ▶ FOLLOW 1, LOOK 動 2
hurdle 名
  ▶ BARRIER, OBSTACLE
hurdle 動
  ▶ JUMP
hurl 動
  ▶ THROW
hurried 形
  ▶ QUICK
HURRY 動 *p.364*

hurry → in action

hurry 動
▶ HURRY
HURT 動 p.364
hurt 名
▶ DISTRESS
hurt 動
▶ DAMAGE 動, HURT 1, 2, INJURE
hurt 動
▶ UPSET
hurtful 形
▶ MEAN 形
hush 名
▶ SILENCE
hushed 形
▶ QUIET 2
hustler 名
▶ CHEAT 名
hygienic 形
▶ CLEAN 形
hype 動
▶ ADVERTISE
hypocritical 形
▶ DISHONEST
hypothesis 名
▶ THEORY 2
hypothetical 形
▶ SUPPOSED
hysteria 名
▶ FEAR
HYSTERICAL 形 p.366
hysterical 形
▶ HYSTERICAL

I

icy 形
▶ FREEZING
ID 名
▶ CERTIFICATE
I dare say
▶ SUPPOSE
IDEA 名 p.367
idea 名
▶ IDEA 1, 2, PURPOSE, SENSE, VIEW 1
IDEAL 形 p.368
ideal 形
▶ IDEAL
ideal 名
▶ EXAMPLE 2, PRINCIPLE 1
identical 形
▶ EQUAL
identify 動
▶ FIND 3
identify with sb/sth
▶ UNDERSTAND 2
IDENTITY 名 p.369
identity 名
▶ IDENTITY
ideology 名
▶ VALUES
idiosyncratic 形
▶ UNIQUE

idiot 名
▶ FOOL
idiotic 形
▶ CRAZY
idolize 動
▶ LOVE 動
IGNORANCE 名 p.369
ignorance 名
▶ IGNORANCE
IGNORANT 形 p.369
ignorant 形
▶ IGNORANT
IGNORE 動 p.370
ignore 動
▶ IGNORE
ill 形
▶ HARMFUL, SICK 1
ill-defined 形
▶ VAGUE
ILLEGAL 形 p.370
illegal 形
▶ ILLEGAL
illegitimate 形
▶ ILLEGAL
ill-fated 形
▶ UNFORTUNATE 1
ill health
▶ ILLNESS
illicit 形
▶ ILLEGAL
illiterate 形
▶ IGNORANT
ILLNESS 名 p.371
illness 名
▶ DISEASE, ILLNESS
illogical 形
▶ IRRATIONAL
illuminating 形
▶ INFORMATIVE
ILLUSION 名 p.371
illusion 名
▶ ILLUSION
illustrate 動
▶ DECORATE, EXPLAIN 1, SHOW 1
illustration 名
▶ EXAMPLE 1
illustrative 形
▶ DESCRIPTIVE
I'm afraid
▶ SORRY
image 名
▶ IDEA 1, PICTURE, REPUTATION
imaginable 形
▶ POSSIBLE 2
imaginary 形
▶ FICTIONAL
IMAGINATION 名 p.372
imagination 名
▶ IMAGINATION, INSPIRATION
imaginative 形
▶ CREATIVE
IMAGINE 動 p.372

imagine 動
▶ IMAGINE, SUPPOSE
imbalance 名
▶ DIFFERENCE
imitate 動
▶ FOLLOW 4
imitation 名
▶ ARTIFICIAL
imitation 名
▶ FAKE, PARODY
immaculate 形
▶ PERFECT
immaterial 形
▶ IRRELEVANT
immature 形
▶ CHILDISH
IMMEDIATE 形 p.373
immediate 形
▶ IMMEDIATE
immense 形
▶ HUGE
immerse 動
▶ SOAK
immigrant 名
▶ REFUGEE
immobile 形
▶ STILL
immoral 形
▶ WRONG 3
immorality 名
▶ EVIL 名
immortal 形
▶ PERMANENT
impact 名
▶ EFFECT
impact 動
▶ AFFECT
impair 動
▶ DAMAGE 動
impart 動
▶ CONVEY
impartial 形
▶ OBJECTIVE
impatient 形
▶ EAGER, RESTLESS
impeach 動
▶ ACCUSE
impeachment 名
▶ CHARGE 名
impeccable 形
▶ PERFECT
impediment 名
▶ OBSTACLE
impel 動
▶ FORCE 動
imperative 形
▶ ESSENTIAL
imperfection 名
▶ DEFECT
impersonal 形
▶ COLD 2
impersonation 名
▶ PARODY
impertinent 形
▶ RUDE

impetus 名
▶ INCENTIVE
implausible 形
▶ UNLIKELY 2
implement 名
▶ TOOL
implement 動
▶ DO
implication 名
▶ RESULT
imply 動
▶ MEAN 動 2, SUGGEST
impolite 形
▶ RUDE
import 動
▶ SELL 2
IMPORTANCE 名 p.374
importance 名
▶ IMPORTANCE
IMPORTANT 形 p.374
important 形
▶ IMPORTANT, POWERFUL
impose 動
▶ APPLY
imposing 形
▶ MAGNIFICENT
IMPOSSIBLE 形 p.375
impossible 形
▶ IMPOSSIBLE
impoverished 形
▶ POOR 1
imprecise 形
▶ VAGUE
IMPRESS 動 p.376
impress 動
▶ IMPRESS
impression 名
▶ EFFECT, PARODY, SENSE
impressionable 形
▶ NAIVE
IMPRESSIVE 形 p.376
impressive 形
▶ IMPRESSIVE, MAGNIFICENT
imprison 動
▶ JAIL
improbable 形
▶ UNLIKELY 1, 2
impromptu 形
▶ SPONTANEOUS
IMPROVE 動 p.377
improve 動
▶ IMPROVE 1, 2
impulse 名
▶ DESIRE
impulsive 形
▶ SPONTANEOUS
inaccuracy 名
▶ MISTAKE 2
inaccurate 形
▶ WRONG 1
in action
▶ ACTIVE

INADEQUATE 形 *p.378*
inadequate 形
  ▶ INADEQUATE, INCOMPETENT
in a good mood
  ▶ CHEERFUL
in all probability...
  ▶ PROBABLY
inapplicable 形
  ▶ IRRELEVANT
inappropriate 形
  ▶ WRONG 2
inarticulate 形
  ▶ SILENT
inaudible 形
  ▶ QUIET 2
incarcerate 動
  ▶ JAIL
incense 動
  ▶ ANGER 動
incensed 形
  ▶ FURIOUS
INCENTIVE 名 *p.378*
incentive 名
  ▶ INCENTIVE
incessant 形
  ▶ CONTINUOUS
incident 名
  ▶ EVENT 1
incisive 形
  ▶ SHREWD
inclination 名
  ▶ DESIRE
INCLUDE 動 *p.379*
include 動
  ▶ INCLUDE
incoherent 形
  ▶ HYSTERICAL
INCOME 名 *p.380*
income 名
  ▶ INCOME, REVENUE
incompatible 形
  ▶ INCONSISTENT
INCOMPETENT 形 *p.381*
incompetent 形
  ▶ INCOMPETENT
incompetent 形
  ▶ LOSER 2
incomprehensible 形
  ▶ CONFUSING
incomprehension 名
  ▶ IGNORANCE
inconceivable 形
  ▶ IMPOSSIBLE
inconsiderate 形
  ▶ INSENSITIVE
INCONSISTENT 形 *p.381*
inconsistent 形
  ▶ INCONSISTENT, VARIABLE
inconvenient 形
  ▶ WRONG 2
incorporate 動
  ▶ INCLUDE

incorrect 形
  ▶ WRONG 1
INCREASE 名 *p.382*
INCREASE 動 *p.383*
increase 名
  ▶ INCREASE
increase 動
  ▶ INCREASE 動, RISE
INCREDIBLE 形 *p.384*
incredible 形
  ▶ INCREDIBLE, REMARKABLE
incredulous 形
  ▶ SUSPICIOUS 1
incurable 形
  ▶ FATAL
incursion 名
  ▶ ATTACK 名 1
in sb's day
  ▶ LIFE 2
indebted 形
  ▶ GRATEFUL
indecision 名
  ▶ DOUBT 名 1
indefinite 形
  ▶ UNCLEAR
in demand
  ▶ POPULAR
INDEPENDENCE 名 *p.384*
independence 名
  ▶ FREEDOM, INDEPENDENCE
independent 形
  ▶ CONFIDENT
in-depth 形
  ▶ DETAILED
indeterminate 形
  ▶ VAGUE
index 名
  ▶ LIST 名
indicate 動
  ▶ DECLARE, SHOW 1, SUGGEST
indication 名
  ▶ SIGN 1
indicator 名
  ▶ SIGN 1
indict 動
  ▶ ACCUSE
indictment 名
  ▶ CHARGE 名
INDIFFERENT 形 *p.385*
indifferent 形
  ▶ INDIFFERENT
indigenous 形
  ▶ CULTURAL
indignant 形
  ▶ ANGRY
indignation 名
  ▶ ANGER 名
indiscriminate 形
  ▶ RANDOM
indispensable 形
  ▶ ESSENTIAL

indistinct 形
  ▶ VAGUE
indistinguishable 形
  ▶ EQUAL
individual 形
  ▶ OWN, PARTICULAR, UNIQUE
individual 名
  ▶ PERSON
individuality 名
  ▶ IDENTITY
in doubt
  ▶ UNCLEAR, UNSURE
induce 動
  ▶ CAUSE
inducement 名
  ▶ INCENTIVE
indulgent 形
  ▶ TOLERANT
industrialist 名
  ▶ EXECUTIVE
INDUSTRY 名 *p.385*
industry 名
  ▶ INDUSTRY, PRODUCTION
INEFFECTIVE 形 *p.386*
ineffective 形
  ▶ INEFFECTIVE
ineffectual 形
  ▶ INEFFECTIVE
inefficient 形
  ▶ INEFFECTIVE
inept 形
  ▶ INCOMPETENT
INEQUALITY 名 *p.386*
inequality 名
  ▶ INEQUALITY
inequitable 形
  ▶ WRONG 3
inequity 名
  ▶ INEQUALITY
inert 形
  ▶ STILL
inescapable 形
  ▶ INEVITABLE
in evidence
  ▶ VISIBLE
INEVITABLE 形 *p.387*
inevitable 形
  ▶ INEVITABLE
inexorable 形
  ▶ INEVITABLE
inexpensive 形
  ▶ CHEAP
inexperience 名
  ▶ IGNORANCE
inexperienced 形
  ▶ NAIVE
inexplicable 形
  ▶ CONFUSING
infancy 名
  ▶ CHILDHOOD
infant 名
  ▶ CHILD

infatuated 形
  ▶ IN LOVE
infatuation 名
  ▶ LOVE 名 1
IN FAVOUR (OF SB/STH) *p.387*
(be) in favour (of sb/sth)
  ▶ IN FAVOUR (OF SB/STH)
infection 名
  ▶ DISEASE
infer 動
  ▶ CONCLUDE
inference 名
  ▶ CONCLUSION
inferior 形
  ▶ POOR 2
inflamed 形
  ▶ PAINFUL 1
inflammation 名
  ▶ TUMOUR
inflate 動
  ▶ EXAGGERATE, INCREASE 動
inflated 形
  ▶ HIGH 1
inflation 名
  ▶ INCREASE 名
INFLUENCE 名 *p.388*
INFLUENCE 動 *p.389*
influence 名
  ▶ EFFECT, INFLUENCE 名
influence 動
  ▶ AFFECT, INFLUENCE 動
influential 形
  ▶ POWERFUL
info 名
  ▶ INFORMATION
in force
  ▶ ACTIVE
inform 動
  ▶ TELL 1
INFORMAL 形 *p.389*
informal 形
  ▶ INFORMAL
INFORMATION 名 *p.389*
information 名
  ▶ INFORMATION
informational 形
  ▶ EDUCATIONAL
INFORMATIVE 形 *p.390*
informative 形
  ▶ INFORMATIVE
INFORMED 形 *p.391*
informed 形
  ▶ INFORMED
inform on sb
  ▶ TELL 2
infrequent 形
  ▶ RARE
infrequently 副
  ▶ RARELY
infringe 動
  ▶ BREAK 3

infuriate → interview

897

INDEX

infuriate 動
▶ ANGER 動
infuriating 形
▶ ANNOYING
in general
▶ USUALLY
ingenious 形
▶ CREATIVE
ingenuity 名
▶ INSPIRATION
ingest 動
▶ EAT
ingredient 名
▶ ELEMENT
inhabit 動
▶ LIVE
inhabitant 名
▶ RESIDENT
inhibit 動
▶ BLOCK 1
inhibited 形
▶ SHY
inhuman 形
▶ CRUEL
inhumane 形
▶ CRUEL
initial 形
▶ FIRST
initiate 動
▶ INTRODUCE
initiative 名
▶ PLAN 1
INJURE 動 p.391
injure 動
▶ INJURE
INJURY 名 p.392
injury 名
▶ INJURY
injustice 名
▶ INEQUALITY
inkling 名
▶ IDEA 2
IN LOVE 形 p.393
in love
▶ IN LOVE
innate 形
▶ NATURAL
innocence 名
▶ IGNORANCE
INNOCENT 形 p.393
innocent 形
▶ INNOCENT, NAIVE
innovation 名
▶ DEVELOPMENT
innovative 形
▶ CREATIVE
innovator 名
▶ LEADER 2
in one piece
▶ SAFE
inoperable 形
▶ FATAL
in operation
▶ ACTIVE

in order
▶ FINE
inordinate 形
▶ EXCESSIVE
in part
▶ PARTLY
input 名
▶ INVOLVEMENT
inquest 名
▶ INVESTIGATION
insane 形
▶ CRAZY
insecure 形
▶ SHY
INSENSITIVE 形 p.393
insensitive 形
▶ INSENSITIVE
in short supply
▶ SCARCE
insight 名
▶ UNDERSTANDING
insignia 名
▶ LOGO
insignificant 形
▶ MINOR
insinuate 動
▶ MEAN 動 2
insist 動
▶ CLAIM, DEMAND 動
insolent 形
▶ RUDE
insolvent 形
▶ BANKRUPT
inspect 動
▶ CHECK 1
INSPECTION 名 p.394
inspection 名
▶ INSPECTION
INSPECTOR 名 p.395
inspector 名
▶ INSPECTOR
INSPIRATION 名 p.395
inspiration 名
▶ EXAMPLE 2, INCENTIVE, INSPIRATION
INSPIRE 動 p.396
inspire 動
▶ INSPIRE, STIMULATE
instalment 名
▶ PAYMENT
instance 名
▶ EXAMPLE 1
instant 形
▶ IMMEDIATE
instant 名
▶ MINUTE, TIME
instantaneous 形
▶ IMMEDIATE
instigate 動
▶ INTRODUCE
INSTINCT 名 p.396
instinct 名
▶ IDEA 2, INSTINCT

instinctive 形
▶ NATURAL
institute 名
▶ ORGANIZATION
institute 動
▶ INTRODUCE
institution 名
▶ ORGANIZATION
instruct 動
▶ ORDER 1, TRAIN 1
instruction 名
▶ EDUCATION
instructional 形
▶ EDUCATIONAL
instructive 形
▶ INFORMATIVE
instrument 名
▶ TOOL
instrumental 形
▶ POWERFUL
insufferable 形
▶ UNACCEPTABLE
insufficient 形
▶ INADEQUATE
insult 動
▶ OFFEND
INSULTING 形 p.396
insulting 形
▶ INSULTING
insurgency 名
▶ REVOLUTION
insurgent 名
▶ GUERRILLA
integrate 動
▶ COMBINE
INTEGRITY 名 p.397
integrity 名
▶ INTEGRITY
intellect 名
▶ INTELLIGENCE
INTELLECTUAL 形 p.397
intellectual 形
▶ INTELLECTUAL 1, 2
INTELLIGENCE 名 p.399
intelligence 名
▶ INFORMATION, INTELLIGENCE
INTELLIGENT 形 p.399
intelligent 形
▶ INTELLIGENT
intelligible 形
▶ CLEAR 形 2
INTEND 動 p.400
intend 動
▶ INTEND, MEAN 動 2
intended 形
▶ DELIBERATE
INTENSE 形 p.400
intense 形
▶ INTENSE
intensify 動
▶ INCREASE
intent 名
▶ PURPOSE

intention 名
▶ PURPOSE
intentional 形
▶ DELIBERATE
intercede 動
▶ INTERVENE
interchangeable 形
▶ EQUAL
intercontinental 形
▶ INTERNATIONAL
interdependence 名
▶ RELATION
INTEREST 名 p.401
INTEREST 動 p.402
interest 名
▶ ATTENTION, INTEREST 名 1, 2, INVOLVEMENT, PROFIT
interest 動
▶ INTEREST 動
INTERESTED 形 p.403
interested 形
▶ INTERESTED
INTERESTING 形 p.403
interesting 形
▶ INTERESTING
interfere with sth
▶ BLOCK 1
intermediary 名
▶ NEGOTIATOR
intermittent 形
▶ OCCASIONAL
intern 名
▶ RECRUIT
intern 動
▶ JAIL
internal 形
▶ NATIONAL
INTERNATIONAL 形 p.404
international 形
▶ INTERNATIONAL
interpret 動
▶ EXPLAIN 1
interpretation 名
▶ DEFINITION
interpretative 形
▶ DESCRIPTIVE
interrogate 動
▶ QUESTION 動
interrogation 名
▶ INTERVIEW 1
INTERRUPT 動 p.405
interrupt 動
▶ INTERRUPT
interruption 名
▶ PAUSE
INTERVENE 動 p.405
intervene 動
▶ INTERVENE
INTERVIEW 名 p.406
interview 名
▶ INTERVIEW 1, 2
interview 動
▶ QUESTION 動

in the balance
▶ UNCLEAR
in the clear
▶ INNOCENT
in the nude
▶ NAKED
in the wrong
▶ GUILTY
intimacy 名
▶ FRIENDSHIP
intimate 形
▶ SECRET
intimidated 形
▶ AFRAID
intimidating 形
▶ FRIGHTENING
intolerable 形
▶ UNACCEPTABLE
intolerance 名
▶ DISCRIMINATION
intolerant 形
▶ BIASED
intractable 形
▶ UNCONTROLLABLE
intricate 形
▶ COMPLEX
intrigue 名
▶ CONSPIRACY
intrigue 動
▶ INTEREST
INTRODUCE 動 p.407
introduce 動
▶ INTRODUCE, PRESENT 4
INTRODUCTION 名 p.408
introduction 名
▶ BASICS, INTRODUCTION, MEETING 2
introductory 形
▶ FIRST
introverted 形
▶ SOLITARY
intrude 動
▶ INTERRUPT
intuition 名
▶ IDEA 2, INSTINCT
intuitive 形
▶ NATURAL
INVADE 動 p.408
invade 動
▶ INVADE
in vain
▶ USELESS
invalid 形
▶ PATIENT
invalidate 動
▶ CANCEL, DISPROVE
invasion 名
▶ ATTACK 1
invent 動
▶ DESIGN 動 1
invention 名
▶ DEVELOPMENT

inventive 形
▶ CREATIVE
inventiveness 名
▶ INSPIRATION
inventory 名
▶ LIST 名
inverse 形
▶ OPPOSITE 形
INVESTIGATE 動 p.408
investigate 動
▶ INVESTIGATE
INVESTIGATION 名 p.409
investigation 名
▶ INVESTIGATION, REPORT 1
INVESTMENT 名 p.410
investment 名
▶ INVESTMENT
in view
▶ VISIBLE
invite 動
▶ ASK 2
invoice 名
▶ BILL
invoice 動
▶ CHARGE 動
involuntary 形
▶ NECESSARY
involve 動
▶ AFFECT, INCLUDE
involved 形
▶ BUSY 1, COMPLEX
INVOLVEMENT 名 p.411
involvement 名
▶ INVOLVEMENT
(not) in your right mind
▶ MAD
irate 形
▶ ANGRY
IRONIC 形 p.412
ironic 形
▶ IRONIC
IRRATIONAL 形 p.412
irrational 形
▶ IRRATIONAL
irreconcilable 形
▶ INCONSISTENT
irregular 形
▶ VARIABLE
IRRELEVANT 形 p.413
irrelevant 形
▶ IRRELEVANT
irreplaceable 形
▶ VALUABLE 1
irresistible 形
▶ UNCONTROLLABLE
irresponsible 形
▶ RECKLESS
irreverent 形
▶ RUDE
IRRITABLE 形 p.413
irritable 形
▶ IRRITABLE
irritate 動
▶ ANNOY

irritated 形
▶ ANNOYED
irritating 形
▶ ANNOYING
irritation 名
▶ FRUSTRATION
ISOLATE 動 p.414
isolate 動
▶ ISOLATE
isolated 形
▶ LONELY
isolation 名
▶ DIVISION 1
ISSUE 名 p.414
issue 名
▶ ISSUE, PROBLEM
issue 動
▶ PROVIDE, PUBLISH 1, 2
itch 動
▶ HURT 2
itchy 形
▶ PAINFUL 1
item 名
▶ ISSUE, REPORT 2, THING 1
itemize 動
▶ LIST 動
itinerary 名
▶ SCHEDULE

J

JAIL 動 p.416
jail 動
▶ JAIL
jam 動
▶ PACK
jar 動
▶ SHAKE 2
JEALOUSY 名 p.416
jealousy 名
▶ JEALOUSY
jeopardize 動
▶ THREATEN
jerk 名
▶ FOOL
jerk 動
▶ PULL 2
jiggle 動
▶ SHAKE 2
JOB 名 p.417
job 名
▶ JOB, RESPONSIBILITY, TASK
jobless 形
▶ UNEMPLOYED
jog 動
▶ RUN 1
JOIN 動 p.417
join 動
▶ JOIN
join in
▶ JOIN
joint 形
▶ COMMON

JOKE 名 p.418
joke 名
▶ JOKE
jolly 形
▶ CHEERFUL
jolt 動
▶ SHAKE 2
jostle 動
▶ PUSH 2
journalist 名
▶ REPORTER
journey 名
▶ TRIP
JOY 名 p.419
joy 名
▶ JOY, PLEASURE
joyful 形
▶ HAPPY
jubilee 名
▶ BIRTHDAY
JUDGE 名 p.419
JUDGE 動 p.419
judge 名
▶ JUDGE 名
judge 動
▶ ESTIMATE 動, JUDGE 動
judgement 名
▶ VIEW 1
judgemental 形
▶ CRITICAL
judgment 名
▶ CONCLUSION
jumble 名
▶ MESS 1
jumbled 形
▶ UNTIDY
JUMP 動 p.420
jump 動
▶ JUMP, SOAR
junior 形
▶ YOUNG
junior 名
▶ CHILD
junk 名
▶ THING 2
jurisdiction 名
▶ CONTROL
jury 名
▶ COMMITTEE
just 形
▶ REASONABLE
JUSTICE 名 p.421
justice 名
▶ JUSTICE
justifiable 形
▶ RIGHT 形 2
justification 名
▶ REASON
justified 形
▶ RIGHT 形 2
justify 動
▶ EXPLAIN 2
just right
▶ IDEAL

juvenile → learn/know sth by heart

K

juvenile 形
▶ YOUNG
juvenile 名
▶ GIRL
juxtapose 動
▶ COMPARE 1

keen 形
▶ EAGER
KEEP 動 p.422
keep 動
▶ CONTINUE 2, HOLD SB/STH UP, KEEP 1, 2, 3, 4, REMAIN
keep at sth
▶ PERSIST
keep fit
▶ TRAIN 2
keep from sth
▶ SUPPRESS 2
keep sb from sth
▶ PREVENT
keep going
▶ PERSIST
keep sth going
▶ MAINTAIN
keep on
▶ CONTINUE 1
keep sb/sth out
▶ EXCLUDE 2
keep sth up
▶ CONTINUE 2, MAINTAIN
key 形
▶ MAIN
key 名
▶ BUTTON 1, SOLUTION
keynote 名
▶ SUBJECT
kick 名
▶ EXCITEMENT
kickback 名
▶ BRIBE
kick-off 名
▶ START 1
kick off 動
▶ START 動
kid 名
▶ CHILD
KIDNAP 動 p.423
kidnap 動
▶ KIDNAP
KILL 動 p.423
kill 動
▶ KILL
killing 名
▶ MURDER
kin 名
▶ FAMILY 2
KIND 名 p.424
KIND 形 p.425
kind 名
▶ KIND 形

kind 形
▶ KIND 形
kiosk 名
▶ STALL
kit 名
▶ EQUIPMENT
kit sb/sth out
▶ EQUIP
knack 名
▶ SKILL 1
knob 名
▶ BUTTON 1
KNOCK 動 p.425
knock 動
▶ BANG 2, HIT 1, KNOCK
knock sth down
▶ DEMOLISH
knock off
▶ STOP
knock sth off
▶ DISCOUNT
KNOW 動 p.426
know 動
▶ FEEL, KNOW, LEARN
know-how 名
▶ SKILL 2
KNOWLEDGE 名 p.426
knowledge 名
▶ AWARENESS, KNOWLEDGE
knowledgeable 形
▶ INFORMED

L

label 動
▶ CALL 1
labourer 名
▶ WORKER 2
lace 名
▶ BUTTON 2
LACK 名 p.428
lack 動
▶ LACK
lacking 形
▶ INADEQUATE
lad 名
▶ GIRL
ladies' room 名
▶ TOILET
lady 名
▶ WOMAN
laid-back 形
▶ CALM
lakeside 名
▶ COAST
lame 形
▶ DISABLED
LAND 名 p.428
land 名
▶ COUNTRY 1, 2, LAND 1, 2, SOIL
land 動
▶ ARRIVE, GAIN

landscape 名
▶ COUNTRY 2
landslide 名
▶ VICTORY
lane 名
▶ ROAD
LANGUAGE 名 p.429
language 名
▶ LANGUAGE
languid 形
▶ EASY 2
larceny 名
▶ THEFT
LARGE 形 p.429
large 形
▶ LARGE
large-scale 形
▶ WIDE 1
lash 動
▶ BEAT
LAST 限定詞 p.431
last 限定詞
▶ LAST 2
last 限定詞 形
▶ LAST 1
last 動
▶ CONTINUE 1, REMAIN
lasting 形
▶ PERMANENT
LATE 形 p.432
late 形
▶ DEAD, LATE
later 形
▶ LAST 1, NEXT
latest 形
▶ RECENT
latrine 名
▶ TOILET
latter 形
▶ LAST 1
LAUGH 動 p.432
laugh 動
▶ LAUGH
laughable 形
▶ RIDICULOUS
LAUGH AT SB/STH p.433
laugh at sb/sth
▶ LAUGH AT SB/STH
launch 動
▶ INTRODUCE, PRESENT 1
lavatory 名
▶ TOILET
lavish sth on/upon sb/sth
▶ GIVE 1
LAW 名 p.433
law 名
▶ LAW, PRINCIPLE 2, RULE 2, THEORY 1
law-abiding 形
▶ RESPECTABLE
law and order
▶ PEACE

law court 名
▶ COURT
lawful 形
▶ LEGAL
lawmaker 名
▶ POLITICIAN
lawsuit 名
▶ CASE
LAWYER 名 p.434
lawyer 名
▶ LAWYER
lay 動
▶ PUT, SPREAD
lay sth down
▶ RULE 動 2
lay-off 名
▶ UNEMPLOYMENT
lay sb off
▶ FIRE
layout 名
▶ DESIGN 名
lay sth out
▶ ARRANGE, SPREAD
lazy 形
▶ EASY 2
LEAD 動 p.435
lead 名
▶ INFLUENCE 名
lead 動
▶ LEAD, TAKE 2
LEADER 名 p.435
leader 名
▶ LEADER 1, 2
leadership 名
▶ GOVERNMENT 2, MANAGEMENT
leading 形
▶ TOP
lead to sth
▶ CAUSE
LEAFLET 名 p.437
leaflet 名
▶ LEAFLET
leaf through sth
▶ READ
league 名
▶ CATEGORY, UNION
leak 動
▶ REVEAL
leak out
▶ TURN OUT
LEAN 動 p.437
lean 動
▶ LEAN
lean 形
▶ THIN
leap 動
▶ JUMP, SOAR
LEARN 動 p.438
learn 動
▶ FIND 1, LEARN
learn/know sth by heart
▶ LEARN

learned 形
▶ INTELLECTUAL 2
learning 名
▶ EDUCATION, KNOWLEDGE
LEAVE 動 *p.439*
leave
▶ HOLIDAY 1, PERMISSION
leave 動
▶ LEAVE 1, 2, 3, 4, TAKE 1
leave sb in the lurch
▶ DISAPPOINT
leave off
▶ STOP
leave your/its/a mark
▶ AFFECT
lecture 名
▶ SPEECH
lecture 動
▶ SCOLD, TEACH
LECTURER 名 *p.441*
lecturer 名
▶ LECTURER
leeway 名
▶ FREEDOM
leftover 形
▶ EXCESS
leg 名
▶ STAGE
LEGAL 形 *p.442*
legal 形
▶ LEGAL
legend 名
▶ STAR
legendary 形
▶ FAMOUS
legion 名
▶ ARMY
legislate 動
▶ RULE 動 2
legislation 名
▶ LAW
legislator 名
▶ POLITICIAN
legitimate 形
▶ GOOD 3, LEGAL
LEISURE 名 *p.442*
leisure 名
▶ LEISURE
leisurely 形
▶ EASY 2
lend 動
▶ PROVIDE
lend (sb) a hand
▶ HELP 動 1
length 名
▶ PIECE
lengthen 動
▶ EXPAND
lengthy 形
▶ LONG
lesson 名
▶ CLASS 2

let 動
▶ ALLOW
let sb down
▶ DISAPPOINT
let sb go
▶ FIRE
let go
▶ FREE 動
let sb go
▶ RELEASE
lethal 形
▶ FATAL
LET SB IN *p.443*
let sb in
▶ LET SB IN
let sb/sth loose
▶ RELEASE
LETTER 名 *p.443*
letter 名
▶ LETTER
level 形
▶ CLOSE 形, FLAT
level 名
▶ ATTITUDE, CLASS 3, FLOOR, QUALITY
level 動
▶ DEMOLISH
level-headed 形
▶ REALISTIC
lever 名
▶ BUTTON 1
levy 動
▶ CHARGE 動
liability 名
▶ DEBT, RESPONSIBILITY
liaison 名
▶ RELATIONSHIP 2
liaison officer
▶ NEGOTIATOR
liberal 形
▶ TOLERANT
liberate 動
▶ RELEASE
liberty 名
▶ FREEDOM, RIGHT 名
LICENCE 名 *p.444*
licence 名
▶ LICENCE
license 動
▶ ALLOW
licensed 形
▶ OFFICIAL 形
LIE 名 *p.445*
lie 名
▶ LIE
LIFE 名 *p.445*
life 名
▶ LIFE 1, 2, 3, NATURE 2
lifeless 形
▶ DEAD
lifestyle 名
▶ LIFE 3
life-threatening 形
▶ SERIOUS 1

lifetime 名
▶ LIFE 2
lift 動
▶ CANCEL
lift/raise sb's spirits
▶ ENCOURAGE
light 形
▶ GENTLE, MINOR, PALE
lighten 動
▶ EASE
light-hearted 形
▶ FUNNY
LIKE 動 *p.447*
LIKE 前 形 *p.448*
like 動
▶ LIKE 動, LOVE 動, WANT
like 前 形
▶ LIKE 前 形
likeable 形
▶ NICE 2
likelihood 名
▶ POSSIBILITY
LIKELY 形 *p.448*
likely 形
▶ LIKELY
likeness 名
▶ SIMILARITY
liking 名
▶ LOVE 名 2, TASTE
LIMIT 名 *p.449*
limit 名
▶ EDGE, LIMIT 1, 2
limitation 名
▶ LIMIT 1
LIMITED 形 *p.451*
limited 形
▶ LIMITED 1, 2
line 名
▶ ATTITUDE, LIMIT 2, SERIES, SHAPE, WAY 3
lineage 名
▶ FAMILY 3
line-up 名
▶ TEAM 2
line sb/sth up
▶ ARRANGE
linger 動
▶ REMAIN, STAY 1
link 名
▶ RELATION, RELATIONSHIP 1
link 動
▶ RELATE
liquid 名
▶ MATERIAL
liquidate 動
▶ SELL 1
liquor 名
▶ DRINK 名
LIST 名 *p.451*
LIST 動 *p.452*
list 名
▶ LIST

list 動
▶ LIST 動
listen 動
▶ HEAR
listener 名
▶ AUDIENCE
listing 名
▶ LIST 動
literacy 名
▶ KNOWLEDGE
literary 形
▶ INTELLECTUAL 2
litigation 名
▶ CASE
litter 名
▶ WASTE
little 形
▶ SLIGHT, SMALL
LIVE 動 *p.453*
live 動
▶ LIVE, REMAIN, SURVIVE
live 形
▶ ALIVE
live it up
▶ PLAY 動 1
LIVELY 形 *p.453*
lively 形
▶ BUSY 2, CROWDED, LIVELY
live on sth
▶ SURVIVE
live through sth
▶ SURVIVE
living 形
▶ ALIVE
living 名
▶ LIFE 3
load 名
▶ CARGO
load 動
▶ FILL
loaded 形
▶ RICH
loaf 名
▶ PIECE
LOAN 名 *p.454*
loan 名
▶ LOAN
loathe 動
▶ HATE
loathing 名
▶ HATRED
lob 動
▶ THROW
lobby 名
▶ HALL 2, PARTY 1
lobby 動
▶ CAMPAIGN 動
local 名
▶ RESIDENT
locate 動
▶ BASE, FIND 4
location 名
▶ PLACE

lock → making

lock 動
  ▶ CLOSE
lock sb up/away
  ▶ JAIL
lodge 動
  ▶ PRESENT 3
lodger 名
  ▶ TENANT
lofty 形
  ▶ HIGH 2
log 動
  ▶ RECORD
LOGIC 名 *p.454*
logic 名
  ▶ LOGIC
logical 形
  ▶ OBVIOUS, RATIONAL
logistics 名
  ▶ PLANNING
LOGO 名 *p.455*
logo 名
  ▶ LOGO
loiter 動
  ▶ STAY 1
lone 形
  ▶ SINGLE
LONELY 形 *p.455*
lonely 形
  ▶ LONELY
LONG 形 *p.456*
long 形
  ▶ LONG
long-lasting 形
  ▶ LONG
long-lived 形
  ▶ OLD 2
long-serving 形
  ▶ EXPERIENCED
long-standing 形
  ▶ OLD 1
loo 名
  ▶ TOILET
LOOK 名 *p.456*
LOOK 動 *p.457*
look 名
  ▶ APPEARANCE, CONSIDERATION, FASHION, LOOK 名, SEARCH
look 動
  ▶ LOOK 動 1, 2
look 連結動詞
  ▶ SEEM
LOOK AFTER SB *p.458*
look after sb
  ▶ LOOK AFTER SB
look after sth
  ▶ DEAL WITH SB/STH
look after yourself
  ▶ TAKE CARE OF YOURSELF
look ahead
  ▶ EXPECT

look at sth
  ▶ CHECK 1, CONSIDER, REGARD
look back
  ▶ REMEMBER
look for sth
  ▶ EXPECT
look forward to sth
  ▶ EXPECT
look in on sb
  ▶ VISIT 動
look into sth
  ▶ INVESTIGATE
lookout 名
  ▶ GUARD
look sb/sth over
  ▶ CHECK 1
looks 名
  ▶ APPEARANCE
look through sth
  ▶ READ
look up
  ▶ IMPROVE 2
look sb up
  ▶ VISIT 動
look up to sb
  ▶ RESPECT 動
loom 動
  ▶ APPEAR
loose 形
  ▶ FREE 形 1
loot 動
  ▶ ROB
looter 名
  ▶ THIEF
lore 名
  ▶ KNOWLEDGE
lose 動
  ▶ ESCAPE
lose patience
  ▶ LOSE YOUR TEMPER
LOSER 名 *p.459*
loser 名
  ▶ LOSER 1, 2
lose your nerve
  ▶ PANIC
LOSE YOUR TEMPER *p.460*
lose your temper
  ▶ LOSE YOUR TEMPER
loss 名
  ▶ DEBT
LOSS-MAKING 形 *p.460*
loss-making 形
  ▶ LOSS-MAKING
lot 名
  ▶ LAND 2
lottery 名
  ▶ RISK 2
LOUD 形 *p.460*
loud 形
  ▶ LOUD
lousy 形
  ▶ BAD
lovable 形
  ▶ SWEET

LOVE 名 *p.461*
LOVE 動 *p.462*
love 名
  ▶ DARLING, LOVE 名 1, 2, TASTE
love 動
  ▶ LIKE 動, LOVE 動
love affair 名
  ▶ RELATIONSHIP 2
loved one 名
  ▶ DARLING
lovely 形
  ▶ BEAUTIFUL 1, 2, NICE 2, WONDERFUL
lover 名
  ▶ FAN
LOVING 形 *p.463*
loving 形
  ▶ LOVING
low 形
  ▶ DEEP 2, POOR 2, SCARCE
lower 動
  ▶ REDUCE
loyal 形
  ▶ RELIABLE 1
lucid 形
  ▶ CLEAR 形 2
LUCK 名 *p.463*
luck 名
  ▶ LUCK
lucky 形
  ▶ TIMELY
lucrative 形
  ▶ SUCCESSFUL 2
ludicrous 形
  ▶ RIDICULOUS
lukewarm 形
  ▶ COLD 1, INDIFFERENT
lull 名
  ▶ PAUSE
lump 名
  ▶ PIECE, TUMOUR
lust 名
  ▶ LOVE 名 1
lying 形
  ▶ DISHONEST

M

MAD 形 *p.465*
mad 形
  ▶ ANGRY, CRAZY, EAGER, MAD
maddening 形
  ▶ ANNOYING
magic 名
  ▶ INTEREST 名 1
magnate 名
  ▶ EXECUTIVE
MAGNIFICENT 形 *p.465*
magnificent 形
  ▶ MAGNIFICENT
mail 名
  ▶ LETTER

mail 動
  ▶ SEND
maim 動
  ▶ INJURE
MAIN 形 *p.466*
main 形
  ▶ MAIN
mainstream 形
  ▶ TRADITIONAL
MAINTAIN 動 *p.467*
maintain 動
  ▶ CLAIM, MAINTAIN
majestic 形
  ▶ MAGNIFICENT
major 形
  ▶ MAIN
MAKE 動 *p.468*
make 動
  ▶ CAUSE, FORCE 動, GET 3, MAKE 1, 2
make sb's acquaintance
  ▶ MEET 3
make a name for yourself
  ▶ SUCCEED
make a pass at sb
  ▶ FLIRT
make-believe 名
  ▶ IMAGINATION
make sb better
  ▶ CURE
make sb's day
  ▶ PLEASE
make for sth
  ▶ GO 1
make fun of sb/sth
  ▶ LAUGH AT SB/STH
make it
  ▶ GET 3, SUCCEED, SURVIVE
make sth of sb/sth
  ▶ THINK
make off
  ▶ FLEE
MAKER 名 *p.469*
maker 名
  ▶ MAKER
make sb redundant
  ▶ FIRE
make sure
  ▶ CHECK 2, ENSURE
make-up 名
  ▶ PERSONALITY, STRUCTURE
make up your mind 動
  ▶ DECIDE
make use of sb/sth
  ▶ USE 動 1
make your/a mark
  ▶ SUCCEED
make your way
  ▶ GO 1
making 名
  ▶ PRODUCTION

male 名
▶ MAN 1
malignant 形
▶ FATAL
mall 名
▶ MARKET 2
MAN 名 p.470
man 名
▶ MAN 1, 2, PARTNER 2
manage 動
▶ ACHIEVE, ARRANGE, RUN 2
MANAGEMENT 名 p.471
management 名
▶ GOVERNMENT 2, MANAGEMENT
MANAGER 名 p.472
manager 名
▶ MANAGER
managing director 名
▶ LEADER 1
mandatory 形
▶ NECESSARY
mania 名
▶ OBSESSION
manifest itself 動
▶ APPEAR
manifesto 名
▶ PLAN 1
manipulate 動
▶ OPERATE
mankind 名
▶ MAN 2
man-made 形
▶ ARTIFICIAL
manner 名
▶ APPEARANCE, WAY 1
manners 名
▶ RESPECT 名
manoeuvre 名
▶ TACTIC
manpower 名
▶ STAFF
manslaughter 名
▶ MURDER
mantra 名
▶ SLOGAN
manual 名
▶ BOOK
MANUFACTURE 動 p.472
manufacture 名
▶ PRODUCTION
manufacture 動
▶ MANUFACTURE
manufacturer 名
▶ MAKER
manufacturing 名
▶ PRODUCTION
MAP 名 p.473
map 名
▶ MAP
mar 動
▶ RUIN
march 動
▶ WALK 1

margin 名
▶ EDGE, GAP
marginal 形
▶ CLOSE 形, SLIGHT
MARK 名 p.473
mark 名
▶ MARK, SIGN 1
mark 動
▶ MEAN 動 1
MARKED 形 p.474
marked 形
▶ MARKED
MARKET 名 p.474
market 名
▶ DEMAND 名, MARKET 1, 2, TRADE
market 動
▶ ADVERTISE
market leader 名
▶ LEADER 2
marketplace 名
▶ TRADE
marvel 名
▶ MIRACLE
marvellous 形
▶ WONDERFUL
mask 動
▶ HIDE
mass 形
▶ WIDE 1
mass 動
▶ MEET 1
massive 形
▶ HUGE
mass-produce 動
▶ MANUFACTURE
master 動
▶ LEARN
masterly 形
▶ IMPRESSIVE
mastermind 名
▶ GENIUS
masterpiece 名
▶ WORK 名 2
MATCH 動 p.475
match 名
▶ GAME
match 動
▶ COMPARE 2, MATCH 1, 2, RELATE
match sth against sth
▶ COMPARE 1
matching 形
▶ EQUIVALENT
mate 名
▶ FRIEND
MATERIAL 名 p.476
material 名
▶ EQUIPMENT, INFORMATION, MATERIAL
material 形
▶ RELEVANT
materialize 動
▶ HAPPEN

matter 名
▶ ISSUE, MATERIAL, PROBLEM
matter-of-fact 形
▶ REALISTIC
mature 形
▶ ADULT, OLD 2
mature 動
▶ DEVELOP 1
maximize 動
▶ INCREASE 動
mayor 名
▶ OFFICIAL 名
meagre 形
▶ INADEQUATE
meal 名
▶ FOOD
MEAN 動 p.477
MEAN 形 p.478
mean 動
▶ DESIGN 動 2, INTEND, MEAN 動 1, 2
mean 形
▶ MEAN 形
MEANING 名 p.478
meaning 名
▶ MEANING, VALUE
means 名
▶ MONEY 1, WAY 2
measure 名
▶ ACTION, CRITERION
measured 形
▶ SLOW
mechanism 名
▶ WAY 2
medal 名
▶ AWARD
mediate 動
▶ INTERVENE
mediator 名
▶ NEGOTIATOR
medical care 名
▶ TREATMENT
medication 名
▶ DRUG 2
medicine 名
▶ DRUG 2, TREATMENT
meditate 動
▶ CONSIDER
meditation 名
▶ CONSIDERATION
MEET 動 p.479
meet 動
▶ GREET, HAVE 3, MEET 1, 2, 3, 4
MEETING 名 p.480
meeting 名
▶ MEETING 1, 2
meet up
▶ MEET 1
meet with sb
▶ MEET 1
melancholy 形
▶ UNHAPPY 1

melancholy 名
▶ GRIEF
mellow 形
▶ DARK 2
melt 動
▶ DISAPPEAR
Member of Parliament 名
▶ POLITICIAN
member of staff 名
▶ WORKER 1
memo 名
▶ LETTER
memorize 動
▶ LEARN
MEMORY 名 p.482
memory 名
▶ MEMORY
menace 名
▶ THREAT
mend 動
▶ REPAIR, RESOLVE
men's room 名
▶ TOILET
mental 形
▶ INTELLECTUAL 1
MENTION 動 p.482
mention 名
▶ REFERENCE
mention 動
▶ MENTION
mentor 名
▶ ADVISER
mentoring 名
▶ EDUCATION
merchandise 名
▶ PRODUCT
merchandise 動
▶ ADVERTISE
merchant 名
▶ DEALER
merciless 形
▶ RUTHLESS
merge 動
▶ COMBINE
merit 名
▶ BENEFIT, VALUE
MESS 名 p.483
mess 名
▶ MESS 1, 2
MESSAGE 名 p.484
message 名
▶ LETTER, MESSAGE
messy 形
▶ DIRTY, UNTIDY
metamorphose 動
▶ TURN 2
method 名
▶ EFFICIENCY, WAY 2
methodical 形
▶ EFFICIENT
methodology 名
▶ WAY 2
metropolis 名
▶ CITY

microscopic → move

microscopic 形
▶ SMALL
middle ground 名
▶ COMPROMISE
the middle of the night
▶ NIGHT 1
midnight 名
▶ NIGHT 1
might 名
▶ FORCE 名
migrant 名
▶ REFUGEE
migrate 動
▶ LEAVE 2
mild 形
▶ GENTLE, SUNNY
milieu 名
▶ CONTEXT
militant 形
▶ AGGRESSIVE 1
mill 名
▶ FACTORY
mimic 動
▶ FOLLOW 4
MIND 名 p.484
mind 名
▶ INTELLIGENCE, MEMORY, MIND
mind 動
▶ CARE
minder 名
▶ GUARD
mindful 形
▶ AWARE
miniature 形
▶ SMALL
minimal 形
▶ SLIGHT
minimize 動
▶ REDUCE
ministry 名
▶ SERVICE
MINOR 形 p.485
minor 形
▶ MINOR
minor 名
▶ CHILD
MINUTE 名 p.486
minute 名
▶ MINUTE
minute 名
▶ RECORD
minute 形
▶ DETAILED, SMALL
MIRACLE 名 p.486
miracle 名
▶ MIRACLE
miraculous 形
▶ AMAZING
miscellaneous 形
▶ DIVERSE
misconception 名
▶ ILLUSION
misconduct 名
▶ CRIME 1

misdemeanour 名
▶ CRIME 2
miserable 形
▶ NEGATIVE, UNHAPPY 1
misery 名
▶ DISTRESS
misfortune 名
▶ TROUBLE 2
misgiving 名
▶ DOUBT 2
misguided 形
▶ WRONG 1
mishap 名
▶ ACCIDENT
misinterpret 動
▶ MISUNDERSTAND
misinterpretation 名
▶ ILLUSION
misjudge 動
▶ MISUNDERSTAND
MISLEADING 形 p.487
misleading 形
▶ MISLEADING
misprint 名
▶ MISTAKE 2
misread 動
▶ MISUNDERSTAND
mission 名
▶ COMMITTEE, TASK
MISTAKE 名 p.487
mistake 名
▶ MISTAKE 1, 2
mistake 動
▶ MISUNDERSTAND
mistaken 形
▶ WRONG 1
misty 形
▶ CLOUDY
MISUNDERSTAND 動 p.488
misunderstand 動
▶ MISUNDERSTAND
misunderstanding 名
▶ ILLUSION
mix 動
▶ MATCH 2
mixed 形
▶ DIVERSE
moan 動
▶ COMPLAIN, WHISPER
mob 名
▶ CROWD
mobile 形
▶ ENERGETIC
mock 動
▶ LAUGH AT SB/STH
mockery 名
▶ CONTEMPT
mock-up 名
▶ COPY 名 2
model 名
▶ COPY 名 2, EXAMPLE 2
model yourself/sth on sb/sth
▶ FOLLOW 4

moderately 副
▶ PARTLY
moderator 名
▶ JUDGE 名
MODERN 形 p.489
modern 形
▶ EXPERIMENTAL, MODERN, RECENT
modern-day 形
▶ RECENT
modernist 形
▶ EXPERIMENTAL
modest 形
▶ SLIGHT
modification 名
▶ CHANGE 名 2
modify 動
▶ ADJUST
module 名
▶ ELEMENT
moist 形
▶ WET
moisten 動
▶ SOAK
MOISTURE 名 p.489
moisture 名
▶ MOISTURE
moment 名
▶ MINUTE, OPPORTUNITY, TIME
momentary 形
▶ SHORT 1
momentous 形
▶ IMPORTANT
monetary 形
▶ ECONOMIC
MONEY 名 p.489
money 名
▶ MONEY 1, 2, 3
monitor 名
▶ INSPECTOR
monograph 名
▶ PAPER
monotonous 形
▶ BORING
monumental 形
▶ HUGE
MOOD 名 p.491
mood 名
▶ ATMOSPHERE, MOOD, TEMPER
moor 動
▶ HILL
moorland 名
▶ HILL
moot 動
▶ PROPOSE
MORAL 形 p.491
moral 形
▶ GOOD 5, MORAL
morale 名
▶ MOOD
MORALITY 名 p.492

morality 名
▶ MORALITY, PRINCIPLE 1
morals 名
▶ PRINCIPLE 1
moratorium 名
▶ BAN 名
more often than not
▶ USUALLY
more or less
▶ ALMOST
moron 名
▶ FOOL
morose 形
▶ IRRITABLE
morsel 名
▶ BIT
mortal 名
▶ PERSON
mortgage 名
▶ LOAN
mortify 動
▶ EMBARRASS
mosque 名
▶ CHURCH
most 副
▶ VERY 副
most likely 副
▶ PROBABLY
mostly 副
▶ USUALLY
most of the time
▶ USUALLY
motif 名
▶ SUBJECT
motion 名
▶ MOVEMENT, PROPOSAL
motionless 形
▶ STILL
motivate 動
▶ INSPIRE
motivation 名
▶ INCENTIVE
motive 名
▶ REASON
motley 形
▶ DIVERSE
motto 名
▶ SLOGAN
mouldy 形
▶ ROTTEN
mound 名
▶ HILL
mount 動
▶ CLIMB, ORGANIZE
mountain 名
▶ HILL
mournful 形
▶ UNHAPPY 1
mouth 動
▶ WHISPER
mouth-watering 形
▶ DELICIOUS
move 動
▶ ACTION, MOVEMENT

move → normal

move 動
▶ DEVELOP 1, GO 1, IMPRESS, LEAVE 2, PROPOSE
MOVEMENT 名 p.492
movement 名
▶ MOVEMENT, TREND
move out
▶ LEAVE 2
movie star 名
▶ ACTOR
MP 名
▶ POLITICIAN
much loved 形
▶ DEAR
mud 名
▶ SOIL
muddle 名
▶ MESS 1
muddled 形
▶ CONFUSED
muddy 形
▶ DIRTY
muffled 形
▶ QUIET 2
mug 動
▶ ATTACK 動 1
mull sth over
▶ CONSIDER
multinational 形
▶ INTERNATIONAL
multi-purpose 形
▶ FLEXIBLE 1
multiracial 形
▶ INTERNATIONAL
mumble 動
▶ WHISPER
munch 動
▶ BITE
municipality 名
▶ CITY
MURDER 名 p.492
murder 名
▶ MURDER
murder 動
▶ KILL
murderous 形
▶ VIOLENT
murky 形
▶ CLOUDY
murmur 動
▶ WHISPER
muscular 形
▶ STRONG 1
mushy 形
▶ SOFT
mutate 動
▶ TURN 2
mute 形
▶ SILENT
mutiny 名
▶ REVOLUTION
mutter 動
▶ WHISPER

mutually exclusive
▶ INCONSISTENT
mysterious 形
▶ STRANGE 1
myth 名
▶ ILLUSION

N

NAIVE 形 p.494
naive 形
▶ NAIVE
naivety 名
▶ IGNORANCE
NAKED 形 p.494
naked 形
▶ NAKED
name 名
▶ REPUTATION, STAR
name 動
▶ APPOINT, CALL 1, LIST 動
nap 動
▶ SLEEP
narcotic 名
▶ DRUG 1
narrate 動
▶ DESCRIBE, QUOTE
narrative 形
▶ STORY
NARROW 形 p.495
narrow 形
▶ CLOSE 形, LIMITED 1, NARROW
narrow 動
▶ SHRINK
nasty 形
▶ BAD, MEAN 形
nation 名
▶ COUNTRY 1
NATIONAL 形 p.495
national 形
▶ CULTURAL, NATIONAL, PUBLIC
national 名
▶ CITIZEN
nationalism 名
▶ RACISM
nationality 名
▶ PEOPLE
nationwide 形
▶ NATIONAL
native 形
▶ CULTURAL
native 名
▶ CITIZEN, RESIDENT
NATURAL 形 p.496
natural 形
▶ NATURAL, OBVIOUS
the natural world 名
▶ NATURE 2
NATURE 名 p.497
nature 名
▶ KIND 名, NATURE 1, 2, PERSONALITY

nauseating 形
▶ DISGUSTING 1
nauseous 形
▶ SICK 2
near 形
▶ CLOSE 形
near 動
▶ COME 1, 2
nearly 副
▶ ALMOST
NEAT 形 p.498
neat 形
▶ EFFICIENT, NEAT
NECESSARY 形 p.498
necessary 形
▶ INEVITABLE, NECESSARY
necessity 名
▶ NEED 名
neck and neck
▶ CLOSE 形
NEED 名 p.499
NEED 動 p.499
need 名
▶ DESIRE, NEED 名, POVERTY, REASON
need 動
▶ NEED 動
needy 形
▶ POOR 1
NEGATIVE 形 p.500
negative 形
▶ HARMFUL, NEGATIVE
neglect 動
▶ FAIL 1, IGNORE, LEAVE 4
negligent 形
▶ CARELESS
negligible 形
▶ SLIGHT
NEGOTIATE 動 p.501
negotiate 動
▶ NEGOTIATE
NEGOTIATOR 名 p.501
negotiator 名
▶ NEGOTIATOR
neighbourhood 名
▶ AREA 1
neighbourly 形
▶ HELPFUL
nerve 名
▶ COURAGE
nerve-racking 形
▶ STRESSFUL
nervous 形
▶ WORRIED
nervous wreck 名
▶ COWARD
net 動
▶ GAIN, MAKE 2
network 名
▶ SYSTEM
neurosis 名
▶ OBSESSION

neutral 形
▶ OBJECTIVE, PALE
NEW 形 p.502
new 形
▶ NEW 1, 2, 3, RECENT
newscaster 名
▶ PRESENTER
newsreader 名
▶ PRESENTER
NEXT 形 p.503
next 形
▶ NEXT
nibble 動
▶ BITE
NICE 形 p.504
nice 形
▶ NICE 1, 2
nick 動
▶ STEAL
nickname 動
▶ CALL 1
NIGHT 名 p.505
night 名
▶ NIGHT 1, 2
nightfall 名
▶ NIGHT 2
night-time 名
▶ NIGHT 1
no 名
▶ REFUSAL
the nobility 名
▶ ELITE
noble 形
▶ WORTHY
no doubt 副
▶ PROBABLY
no-hoper 名
▶ LOSER 2
noisy 形
▶ LOUD
nominate 動
▶ APPOINT, RECOMMEND 2
nomination 名
▶ CHOICE 1
nominee 名
▶ CANDIDATE
non-existent 形
▶ FICTIONAL
no-nonsense 形
▶ REALISTIC
non-partisan 形
▶ OBJECTIVE
non-profit 形
▶ LOSS-MAKING
NONSENSE 名 p.506
nonsense 名
▶ NONSENSE
non-stop 形
▶ CONTINUOUS
norm 名
▶ CRITERION
NORMAL 形 p.507
normal 形
▶ NORMAL

normally → on welfare

normally 副
▶ USUALLY
norms 名
▶ TRADITION
not (very) well 形
▶ SICK 1
notable 形
▶ IMPORTANT
not bad 形
▶ ADEQUATE
note 名
▶ LETTER
note 動
▶ COMMENT, NOTICE
not guilty
▶ INNOCENT
NOTICE 動 p.508
notice 名
▶ ATTENTION, SIGN 2
notice 動
▶ NOTICE
noticeable 形
▶ VISIBLE
noticeboard 名
▶ SIGN 2
notify 動
▶ TELL 1
notion 名
▶ IDEA 1
notional 形
▶ SUPPOSED
not quite 副
▶ ALMOST
not see eye to eye with sb
▶ DISAGREE
nourishing 形
▶ HEALTHY
nourishment 名
▶ FOOD
novel 形
▶ NEW 1
novel 名
▶ BOOK
novelist 名
▶ WRITER
novice 名
▶ BEGINNER
now and again/then
▶ SOMETIMES
nucleus 名
▶ POINT
nude 形
▶ NAKED
NUMBER 名 p.508
number 名
▶ FIGURE, NUMBER
number one 形
▶ MAIN
nursing 名
▶ TREATMENT
nutritional 形
▶ HEALTHY
nutritious 形
▶ HEALTHY

nuts 名
▶ MAD

O

oath 名
▶ PROMISE 2
obedient 形
▶ GOOD 7
obese 形
▶ FAT
obey 動
▶ FOLLOW 3
object 名
▶ TARGET, THING 1
object 動
▶ COMPLAIN
objection 名
▶ OPPOSITION
objectionable 形
▶ MEAN 形
OBJECTIVE 形 p.510
objective 形
▶ OBJECTIVE
objective 名
▶ TARGET
obligation 名
▶ RESPONSIBILITY
obligatory 形
▶ NECESSARY
oblige 動
▶ FORCE 動
obliging 形
▶ HELPFUL
obnoxious 形
▶ MEAN 形
observation 名
▶ INSPECTION, STATEMENT
observe 動
▶ COMMENT, FOLLOW 3, LOOK 動 1, NOTICE
observer 名
▶ ANALYST, INSPECTOR, WITNESS
OBSESSION 名 p.510
obsession 名
▶ OBSESSION
obsessional 形
▶ ADDICTIVE
obsessive 形
▶ ADDICTIVE
obsolete 形
▶ OLD-FASHIONED
OBSTACLE 名 p.511
obstacle 名
▶ BARRIER, OBSTACLE
obstinate 形
▶ STUBBORN
obstruct 動
▶ BLOCK 1, 2
obstruction 名
▶ BARRIER
obtain 動
▶ GET 1

obtuse 形
▶ STUPID
OBVIOUS 形 p.511
obvious 形
▶ CLEAR 形 1, OBVIOUS
occasion 名
▶ EVENT 2, OPPORTUNITY, TIME
OCCASIONAL 形 p.512
occasional 形
▶ OCCASIONAL
occasionally 副
▶ SOMETIMES
occupant 名
▶ TENANT
occupation 名
▶ PROJECT, WORK 名 1
occupied 形
▶ BUSY 1
occupy 動
▶ INVADE, LIVE
occur 動
▶ HAPPEN
occurrence 名
▶ EVENT 1
ocean 名
▶ SEA
the odd... 形
▶ OCCASIONAL
odd 形
▶ STRANGE 1
odds 名
▶ POSSIBILITY
ODOUR 名 p.512
odour 名
▶ ODOUR
oeuvre 名
▶ WORK 名 2
of choice
▶ FAVOURITE
off 形
▶ ROTTEN
off and on
▶ SOMETIMES
offbeat 形
▶ UNUSUAL
offence 名
▶ CRIME 2
OFFEND 動 p.513
offend 動
▶ OFFEND
offender 名
▶ CRIMINAL
OFFENSIVE 形 p.513
offensive 形
▶ DISGUSTING 1, OFFENSIVE
offensive 名
▶ ATTACK 名 1
OFFER 名 p.514
offer 名
▶ OFFER 1, 2
office 名
▶ SERVICE

officer 名
▶ OFFICIAL 名, POLICEMAN
OFFICIAL 名 p.515
OFFICIAL 形 p.515
official 名
▶ OFFICIAL
official 形
▶ OFFICIAL
officialdom
▶ AUTHORITIES
off-the-cuff 形
▶ SPONTANEOUS
off the record
▶ UNOFFICIAL
OFTEN 副 p.516
often 副
▶ OFTEN, USUALLY
of the essence
▶ ESSENTIAL
of use
▶ USEFUL
OIL 名 p.516
oil 名
▶ OIL
OK 形
▶ FINE, SAFE, WELL
OK 動
▶ ALLOW
OLD 形 p.517
old 形
▶ FORMER, OLD 1, 2, PREVIOUS
OLD-FASHIONED 形 p.518
old-fashioned 形
▶ OLD-FASHIONED
omission 名
▶ MISTAKE 1
omit 動
▶ FAIL 1
once in a while
▶ SOMETIMES
on display
▶ VISIBLE
one-liner 名
▶ JOKE
one-sided 形
▶ BIASED
onlooker 名
▶ WITNESS
on occasion(s)
▶ SOMETIMES
on sale
▶ AVAILABLE
onset 名
▶ START 名
on the dole
▶ UNEMPLOYED
on the house
▶ FREE 形 2
on the market
▶ AVAILABLE
on welfare 形
▶ UNEMPLOYED

open 形
▶ HONEST
open 動
▶ BEGIN, SPREAD, START 動, UNDO
opening 形
▶ FIRST
opening 名
▶ HOLE 1, JOB, START 名
open-minded 形
▶ TOLERANT
open the way
▶ HELP 動 2
open to sth
▶ VULNERABLE
OPERATE 動 p.518
operate 動
▶ OPERATE, ORGANIZE, WORK 動 2
operation 名
▶ COMPANY, PROJECT, TRADE, TREATMENT
operational 形
▶ ACTIVE
opinion 名
▶ VIEW 1
opponent 名
▶ ENEMY, PROTESTER
OPPORTUNITY 名 p.519
opportunity 名
▶ OPPORTUNITY
OPPOSE 動 p.520
oppose 動
▶ OPPOSE
opposed 形
▶ AGAINST SB/STH, OPPOSITE 形
OPPOSITE 名 p.520
OPPOSITE 形 p.521
opposite 名
▶ OPPOSITE 名
opposite 形
▶ OPPOSITE 形
OPPOSITION 名 p.522
opposition 名
▶ CONFLICT 名, ENEMY, OPPOSITION
oppress 動
▶ DISCOURAGE 2, SUPPRESS 1
oppression 名
▶ REPRESSION
oppressive 形
▶ REPRESSIVE
opt 動
▶ CHOOSE
optimism 名
▶ HOPE 名 1
OPTIMISTIC 形 p.522
optimistic 形
▶ OPTIMISTIC
optimum 形
▶ IDEAL
OPTION 名 p.523

option 名
▶ OPTION
optional 形
▶ VOLUNTARY 1
oral 名
▶ TEST 名 2
orbit 名
▶ WAY 3
orbit 動
▶ SPIN
orchestrate 動
▶ ORGANIZE
ORDER 動 p.523
order 名
▶ EFFICIENCY, PEACE, REQUEST, SERIES
order 動
▶ ORDER 1, 2, RANK, RULE 動 2
ordered 形
▶ NEAT
orderly 形
▶ EFFICIENT, NEAT
ordinary 形
▶ AVERAGE, NORMAL
ORGANIZATION 名 p.524
organization 名
▶ EFFICIENCY, ORGANIZATION, PLANNING, SYSTEM
ORGANIZE 動 p.525
organize 動
▶ ARRANGE, ORGANIZE
organized 形
▶ EFFICIENT
ORGANIZER 名 p.526
organizer 名
▶ ORGANIZER
orient 動
▶ FOCUS
orientation 名
▶ TENDENCY
origin 名
▶ FAMILY 3, SOURCE
original 形
▶ CREATIVE, FIRST
originality 名
▶ INSPIRATION
ornament 名
▶ DECORATION
ornament 動
▶ DECORATE
orthodox 形
▶ TRADITIONAL
ostensible 形
▶ APPARENT
ostracize 動
▶ EXCLUDE 2
outcome 名
▶ RESULT
outdated 形
▶ OLD-FASHIONED
outfit 名
▶ GROUP 3

outfit 動
▶ EQUIP
outgoing 形
▶ SOCIABLE
outing 名
▶ TRIP
outlaw 動
▶ BAN 動
outlay 名
▶ COSTS
outline 名
▶ SHAPE, SUMMARY
outlook 名
▶ ATTITUDE
out of date 形
▶ OLD-FASHIONED
out of harm's way
▶ SAFE
out of line
▶ UNACCEPTABLE
out of luck
▶ UNFORTUNATE 1
out of order
▶ UNACCEPTABLE
out of place
▶ UNTIDY
out of the ordinary
▶ UNUSUAL
out of the question
▶ IMPOSSIBLE
out of work 形
▶ UNEMPLOYED
out of your mind
▶ MAD
outpouring 名
▶ FLOOD 名 2
OUTPUT 名 p.526
output 動
▶ OUTPUT
outrage 名
▶ ANGER 名, CRIME 2
outrage 動
▶ ANGER 動
outraged 形
▶ FURIOUS
OUTRAGEOUS 形 p.526
outrageous 形
▶ OUTRAGEOUS
outright 形
▶ COMPLETE
outset 名
▶ START 名
outspoken 形
▶ HONEST
outstanding 形
▶ EXCELLENT
outward 形
▶ APPARENT
overcast 形
▶ CLOUDY
overcome 動
▶ DEFEAT
overcrowded 形
▶ FULL

overdraft 名
▶ LOAN
overdue 形
▶ LATE
overflow 動
▶ FLOOD 動
overhaul 動
▶ REPAIR
overheads 名
▶ COSTS
overjoyed 形
▶ GLAD
overlook 動
▶ IGNORE
overpriced 形
▶ EXPENSIVE
overseas 形
▶ FOREIGN
oversee 動
▶ REGULATE
oversight 名
▶ MISTAKE 1
overstate 動
▶ EXAGGERATE
over the top
▶ EXCESSIVE
overture 名
▶ OFFER 1
overview 名
▶ SUMMARY
overweight 形
▶ FAT
overwhelming 形
▶ UNCONTROLLABLE
overwrought 形
▶ HYSTERICAL
OWN 形 p.527
own 形
▶ OWN
own 動
▶ HAVE 1

P

pace 名
▶ STEP
pace 動
▶ WALK 1
PACK 動 p.529
pack 名
▶ PARTY 2
pack 動
▶ FILL, PACK
packed 形
▶ FULL
pack sth in
▶ STOP
pact 名
▶ AGREEMENT
PAIN 名 p.529
pain 名
▶ DISTRESS, PAIN
pain 動
▶ HURT 1
PAINFUL 形 p.530

painful → perpetual

painful 形
▶ PAINFUL 1, 2
painless 形
▶ EASY 1
PAINT 動 p.531
paint 動
▶ DRAW, PAINT
painting 名
▶ PICTURE
pal 名
▶ FRIEND
PALE 形 p.531
pale 形
▶ PALE
paltry 形
▶ INADEQUATE
pamphlet 名
▶ LEAFLET
panel 名
▶ COMMITTEE
PANIC 動 p.532
panic 名
▶ FEAR
panic 動
▶ PANIC
panicky 形
▶ HYSTERICAL
panic-stricken 形
▶ HYSTERICAL
panorama 名
▶ VIEW 2
PAPER 名 p.532
paper 名
▶ PAPER, TEST 名 2
papers 名
▶ CERTIFICATE, DOCUMENT
paperwork 名
▶ BUREAUCRACY, DOCUMENT
PARALLEL 形 p.533
parallel 形
▶ PARALLEL
parallel 名
▶ SIMILARITY
parameter 名
▶ LIMIT 2
paramilitary 名
▶ GUERRILLA
paranoia 名
▶ FEAR
paranoid 形
▶ AFRAID
pardon 動
▶ FORGIVE
parentage 名
▶ FAMILY 3
parliament 名
▶ GOVERNMENT 1
PARODY 名 p.533
parody 名
▶ PARODY
part 名
▶ AREA 1, ELEMENT, INVOLVEMENT

part 動
▶ ISOLATE, LEAVE 1
partially 副
▶ PARTLY
PARTICIPANT 名 p.534
participant 名
▶ PARTICIPANT
participate 動
▶ JOIN
participation 名
▶ INVOLVEMENT
particle 名
▶ BIT
PARTICULAR 形 p.534
particular 形
▶ PARTICULAR, SPECIAL
particular 名
▶ INFORMATION
partisan 名
▶ BIASED
partisan 名
▶ GUERRILLA
partition 名
▶ DIVISION 1
PARTLY 副 p.535
partly 副
▶ PARTLY
PARTNER 名 p.536
partner 名
▶ PARTNER 1, 2
partnership 名
▶ GROUP 3, RELATIONSHIP 1
PARTY 名 p.537
party 名
▶ PARTY 1, 2
party 動
▶ PLAY 動 1
pass 名
▶ LICENCE
pass 動
▶ GIVE 2, GO 1, GRADUATE
passage 名
▶ CORRIDOR
passageway 名
▶ CORRIDOR
pass away
▶ DIE
passer-by 名
▶ WITNESS
passing 形
▶ SHORT 1
passion 名
▶ EMOTION, LOVE 名 1, TASTE
passionate 形
▶ INTENSE
pass sth on
▶ CONVEY
pass sth out
▶ DISTRIBUTE
past 形
▶ LAST 2, PREVIOUS

pastel 形
▶ PALE
pastime 名
▶ INTEREST 名 2
patch 動
▶ REPAIR
patch sth up
▶ RESOLVE
PATH 名 p.538
path 名
▶ PATH, WAY 3
pathetic 形
▶ SAD, UNFORTUNATE 2
PATIENCE 名 p.538
patience 名
▶ PATIENCE
patient 形
▶ CALM
PATIENT 名 p.539
patient 名
▶ PATIENT
a pat on the back
▶ PRAISE 名
patriotism 名
▶ RACISM
patron 名
▶ CUSTOMER, SPONSOR
PAUSE 名 p.539
pause 名
▶ PAUSE
pavement 名
▶ PATH
pay 名
▶ INCOME
pay attention
▶ HEAR
PAYMENT 名 p.540
payment 名
▶ PAYMENT
pay-off 名
▶ BRIBE
PC 名
▶ POLICEMAN
PE 名
▶ SPORT
PEACE 名 p.540
peace 名
▶ PEACE, SILENCE
peaceful 形
▶ QUIET 1
peacemaker 名
▶ NEGOTIATOR
PEAK 名 p.541
peak 名
▶ HILL, PEAK
peat 名
▶ SOIL
peculiar 形
▶ STRANGE 1, UNIQUE
pedagogic 形
▶ EDUCATIONAL
pedigree 名
▶ FAMILY 3
peer 動
▶ STARE

pejorative 形
▶ INSULTING
penniless 形
▶ POOR 1
PEOPLE 名 p.542
people 名
▶ PEOPLE
people 動
▶ LIVE
perceive 動
▶ NOTICE
percentage 名
▶ SHARE 名
perception 名
▶ AWARENESS
perceptive 形
▶ SHREWD
perch 動
▶ SIT
PERFECT 形 p.542
perfect 形
▶ COMPLETE, EXCELLENT, IDEAL, PERFECT
perfectly 副
▶ QUITE 2
perform 動
▶ DO, PLAY 動 2
PERFORMANCE 名 p.543
performance 名
▶ PERFORMANCE
performer 名
▶ ACTOR
the performing arts 名
▶ DRAMA
perimeter 名
▶ EDGE
PERIOD 名 p.544
period 名
▶ CLASS 2, PERIOD
peripheral 形
▶ MINOR
periphery 名
▶ EDGE
perish 動
▶ DIE
perjury 名
▶ LIE
PERMANENT 形 p.545
permanent 形
▶ PERMANENT
PERMISSION 名 p.545
permission 名
▶ PERMISSION
permissive 形
▶ TOLERANT
permit 名
▶ LICENCE
permit 動
▶ ALLOW
pernicious 形
▶ HARMFUL
perpetual 形
▶ FREQUENT

perpetuate 動
▶ MAINTAIN
perplexed 形
▶ CONFUSED
persecute 動
▶ SUPPRESS 1
persecution 名
▶ REPRESSION
perseverance 名
▶ DETERMINATION
persevere 動
▶ PERSIST
PERSIST 動 p.546
persist 動
▶ PERSIST
persistence 名
▶ DETERMINATION
persistent 形
▶ CONTINUOUS, FREQUENT
PERSON 名 p.546
person 名
▶ PERSON
persona 名
▶ PERSONALITY
personable 形
▶ NICE 2
personal 形
▶ OWN, SECRET
PERSONALITY 名 p.547
personality 名
▶ CHARM, PERSONALITY, STAR
personnel 名
▶ STAFF
perspective 名
▶ ATTITUDE
PERSUADE 動 p.548
persuade 動
▶ CONVINCE, PERSUADE
persuasive 形
▶ CONVINCING
pertinent 形
▶ RELEVANT
pesky 形
▶ ANNOYING
pessimistic 形
▶ NEGATIVE
pet 名
▶ FAVOURITE
petite 形
▶ SHORT 2
petition 名
▶ REQUEST
petition 動
▶ ASK 2
petrified 形
▶ AFRAID
petrol 名
▶ OIL
petroleum 名
▶ OIL
petty 形
▶ MINOR

petulant 形
▶ IRRITABLE
phase 名
▶ STAGE
phase sth in
▶ INTRODUCE
phenomenal 形
▶ REMARKABLE
phenomenon 名
▶ EVENT 1, MIRACLE
philanthropist 名
▶ SPONSOR
philosophical 形
▶ INTELLECTUAL 1
philosophy 名
▶ VALUES
phobia 名
▶ FEAR
phone 動
▶ CALL 2
photocopy 名
▶ COPY 名 1
photocopy 動
▶ COPY 動
phrase 動
▶ SAY 2
pick 名
▶ CHOICE 1, 2
pick 動
▶ CHOOSE
pickpocket 名
▶ THIEF
pick up
▶ IMPROVE 2, LEARN
pick sth up
▶ BUY, GET 1
pick yourself up
▶ STAND 1
PICTURE 名 p.549
picture 名
▶ DESCRIPTION, IDEA 1, PICTURE
picture 動
▶ IMAGINE
picturesque 形
▶ BEAUTIFUL 2
PIECE 名 p.550
piece 名
▶ ARTICLE, BIT, ELEMENT, PIECE, WORK 名 2
piercing 形
▶ HIGH 3
pile-up 名
▶ ACCIDENT
pilgrim 名
▶ TOURIST
pilgrimage 名
▶ TRIP
pilot 動
▶ TEST 動 1
pilot study 名
▶ TEST 名 1
pin 名
▶ BUTTON 2

pin your hopes on sb/sth
▶ TRUST
pioneer 名
▶ LEADER 2
pioneer 動
▶ DEVELOP 2
pique 名
▶ FRUSTRATION
pirate 名
▶ ILLEGAL
pirate 動
▶ THIEF
pissed off 形
▶ ANGRY
piss sb off
▶ ANGER 動
pit 名
▶ HOLE 2
pit sb/sth against sb/sth
▶ COMPETE
pitch 動
▶ FOCUS, THROW
pitfall 名
▶ DISADVANTAGE
pithy 形
▶ SHORT 3
pity 名
▶ SYMPATHY, UNFORTUNATE 2
pity 動
▶ SORRY FOR SB
pivot 動
▶ TURN 1
pivotal 形
▶ ESSENTIAL
PLACE 名 p.551
place 名
▶ HOME, PLACE
place 動
▶ PUT, RANK
placebo 名
▶ DRUG 2
place of worship 名
▶ CHURCH
placid 形
▶ CALM
PLAIN 形 p.552
plain 形
▶ AVERAGE, CLEAR 形 1, 2, PLAIN 1, 2, UGLY
plain sailing
▶ EASY 1
PLAN 名 p.553
plan 名
▶ MAP, PLAN 1, 2, PURPOSE
plan 動
▶ INTEND, ORGANIZE
planner 名
▶ ORGANIZER
PLANNING 名 p.554

planning 名
▶ PLANNING
plant 名
▶ FACTORY
plant 動
▶ PUT
plaque 名
▶ SIGN 2
plate 名
▶ SIGN 2
platform 名
▶ PLAN 1
plausible 形
▶ POSSIBLE 2
PLAY 名 p.555
PLAY 動 p.555
play 名
▶ ENTERTAINMENT, PLAY 名
play 動
▶ PLAY 動 1, 2
play-off 名
▶ GAME
playwright 名
▶ WRITER
plea 名
▶ ARGUMENT 2, REQUEST
pleasant 形
▶ FRIENDLY 1, NICE 1
PLEASE 動 p.556
please 動
▶ PLEASE
pleased 形
▶ GLAD
pleasing 形
▶ SATISFYING
pleasurable 形
▶ NICE 1
PLEASURE 名 p.557
pleasure 名
▶ ENTERTAINMENT, FUN, PLEASURE
pledge 名
▶ PROMISE 名
pledge 動
▶ PROMISE 動
plight 名
▶ MESS 2
PLOT 動 p.557
plot 名
▶ CONSPIRACY, LAND 2, STORY
plot 動
▶ PLOT
plough into sth
▶ CRASH
plough through sth
▶ READ
ploy 名
▶ TACTIC
pluck up (the) courage
▶ DARE
plug 名
▶ ADVERTISEMENT

plug → premonition

plug 動
▶ ADVERTISE
plug sth in
▶ TURN STH ON
plummet 動
▶ SLUMP
plump 形
▶ FAT
plunder 動
▶ ROB
plunge 動
▶ FALL 2, SLUMP
plus 名
▶ BENEFIT
poach 動
▶ STEAL
poacher 名
▶ THIEF
pocket 名
▶ FUND 名
pocket 動
▶ MAKE 2
poet 名
▶ WRITER
POINT 名 p.558
point 名
▶ FACTOR, FEATURE 名, INFORMATION, PLACE, POINT, PURPOSE, TIME, VIEW 1
point 動
▶ SUGGEST
pointer 名
▶ SUGGESTION
pointless 形
▶ USELESS
point of view 名
▶ ATTITUDE, VIEW 1
POINT STH OUT p.558
point sth out
▶ POINT STH OUT
point to sth
▶ POINT STH OUT
point sth up
▶ POINT STH OUT
poison 動
▶ INFLUENCE 動
poke 動
▶ PUSH 1
poke fun at sb/sth
▶ LAUGH AT SB/STH
police 動
▶ REGULATE
POLICEMAN 名 p.559
policeman 名
▶ POLICEMAN
police officer 名
▶ POLICEMAN
policewoman 名
▶ POLICEMAN
policy 名
▶ HABIT, PLAN 1
POLITE 形 p.560
polite 形
▶ POLITE

politeness 名
▶ RESPECT 名
POLITICIAN 名 p.560
politician 名
▶ POLITICIAN
poll 名
▶ ELECTION, INVESTIGATION
poll 動
▶ SURVEY
pompous 形
▶ PROUD 2
ponder 動
▶ CONSIDER
pool 名
▶ SUPPLY
pool 動
▶ SHARE 動
pooped 形
▶ TIRED
POOR 形 p.561
poor 形
▶ INCOMPETENT, POOR 1, 2
pop 動
▶ APPEAR, BANG 1, PUT
pop in/round/over
▶ VISIT
POPULAR 形 p.563
popular 形
▶ COMMON, POPULAR, SOCIAL
portrait 名
▶ DESCRIPTION, PICTURE
portray 動
▶ PRESENT 2
portrayal 名
▶ DESCRIPTION
pose 名
▶ POSITION
pose 動
▶ ASK 1, REPRESENT 1
POSITION 名 p.563
position 名
▶ ATTITUDE, CLASS 3, JOB, PLACE, POSITION, SITUATION
position 動
▶ PUT
positive 形
▶ COMPLETE, FINAL, GOOD 6, OPTIMISTIC, SURE, VALUABLE 2
possess 動
▶ HAVE 1, 2
possession 名
▶ TERRITORY, THING 2
possibilities 名
▶ POTENTIAL
POSSIBILITY 名 p.564
possibility 名
▶ OPPORTUNITY, OPTION, POSSIBILITY
POSSIBLE 形 p.565

possible 形
▶ LIKELY, POSSIBLE 1, 2
post 名
▶ JOB, LETTER
post 動
▶ SEND
posting 名
▶ JOB
postmodernist 形
▶ EXPERIMENTAL
postpone 動
▶ DELAY
postulate 動
▶ SAY 3
posture 名
▶ POSITION
POTENTIAL 名 p.566
potential 名
▶ POTENTIAL
potential 形
▶ LIKELY
potter 動
▶ REST
potty 名
▶ TOILET
pound 動
▶ BEAT, RUN 1
pour 動
▶ FLOW, RAIN
POVERTY 名 p.566
poverty 名
▶ POVERTY
power 名
▶ ABILITY, CONTROL, COUNTRY 1, EFFECT, FORCE 名, RIGHT 名
POWERFUL 形 p.567
powerful 形
▶ POWERFUL, STRONG 1
practical 形
▶ POSSIBLE 1, REALISTIC, USEFUL
practical 名
▶ TEST 名 2
practicalities 名
▶ BASICS
practically 動
▶ ALMOST
practice 名
▶ COMPANY, HABIT, TRADITION, TRAINING, USE 名, WORK 名 1
PRACTISE 動 p.568
practise 動
▶ DO, PRACTISE, WORK 動 1
practised 形
▶ EXPERIENCED
pragmatic 形
▶ REALISTIC
PRAISE 名 p.568
PRAISE 動 p.569
praise 名
▶ PRAISE

praise 動
▶ PRAISE
prank 名
▶ JOKE
prat 名
▶ FOOL
preamble 名
▶ INTRODUCTION
PRECAUTION 名 p.570
precaution 名
▶ PRECAUTION
precedence 名
▶ PRIORITY
preceding 形
▶ LAST 2
precious 形
▶ DEAR, VALUABLE 1
precise 形
▶ EXACT, VERY 形
preclude 動
▶ PREVENT
predicament 名
▶ MESS 2
PREDICT 動 p.570
predict 動
▶ PREDICT
PREDICTABLE 形 p.571
predictable 形
▶ PREDICTABLE
prediction 名
▶ EXPECTATION
predominant 形
▶ MAIN
preface 名
▶ INTRODUCTION
PREFER 動 p.571
prefer 動
▶ PREFER
preferable 形
▶ BETTER
preference 名
▶ CHOICE 2, TASTE
preferred 形
▶ FAVOURITE
prejudice 名
▶ DISCRIMINATION
prejudice 動
▶ INFLUENCE 動
prejudiced 形
▶ BIASED
preliminary 形
▶ FIRST
premature 形
▶ RECKLESS
premeditated 形
▶ DELIBERATE
premier 形
▶ TOP
premise 名
▶ THEORY 2
premium 名
▶ PAYMENT
premonition 名
▶ IDEA 2

preoccupation 名
▶ OBSESSION
preparation 名
▶ PLANNING
preparatory 形
▶ FIRST
PREPARE 動 p.571
prepare 動
▶ PREPARE 1, 2, TEACH
prerequisite 名
▶ CONDITION
prescribe 動
▶ RULE 動 2
prescription 名
▶ DRUG 2
presence 名
▶ CHARM
PRESENT 動 p.572
present 名
▶ GIFT
present 動
▶ GIVE 1, PLAY 動 2, PRESENT 1, 2, 3, 4
present 形
▶ RECENT
PRESENTATION 名 p.574
presentation 名
▶ PRESENTATION
present-day 形
▶ RECENT
PRESENTER 名 p.574
presenter 名
▶ PRESENTER
preserve 名
▶ BUSINESS
preserve 動
▶ MAINTAIN, PROTECT
preside 動
▶ LEAD
president 名
▶ LEADER 1
PRESS 動 p.574
press 動
▶ PRESS 1, 2, PUSH 1
press ahead/on
▶ CONTINUE 2
press for sth
▶ DEMAND 動
pressing 形
▶ URGENT
PRESSURE 名 p.575
pressure 名
▶ PRESSURE 1, 2
pressure 動
▶ PRESS 2
pressurize 動
▶ PRESS 2
prestige 名
▶ STATUS
prestigious 形
▶ GREAT 2
presumably 副
▶ PROBABLY

presume 動
▶ DARE, SAY 3, SUPPOSE
presumption 名
▶ SPECULATION
presuppose 動
▶ SAY 3
presupposition 名
▶ SPECULATION
PRETEND 動 p.576
pretend 動
▶ IMAGINE, PRETEND
pretend 形
▶ FICTIONAL
pretext 名
▶ REASON
pretty 形
▶ BEAUTIFUL 1, 2
pretty 副
▶ QUITE 1
pretty much/well 副
▶ ALMOST
prevail 動
▶ DEFEAT, WIN
prevalent 形
▶ GENERAL
PREVENT 動 p.577
prevent 動
▶ PREVENT
PREVIOUS 形 p.577
previous 形
▶ LAST 2, PREVIOUS
PRICE 名 p.578
price 名
▶ PRICE
priceless 形
▶ VALUABLE 1
pricey 形
▶ EXPENSIVE
prickly 形
▶ SENSITIVE 3
PRIDE 名 p.579
pride 名
▶ DIGNITY, PLEASURE, PRIDE, SATISFACTION
pride yourself on sth
▶ BOAST
primary 形
▶ FIRST, MAIN
prime 形
▶ GOOD 1, MAIN
prime 名
▶ PEAK
principal 形
▶ MAIN
PRINCIPLE 名 p.579
principle 名
▶ PRINCIPLE 1, 2, THEORY 1
principled 形
▶ GOOD 5
print 動
▶ PICTURE
print 動
▶ PUBLISH 1, 2

printout 名
▶ COPY 名 1
prior 形
▶ PREVIOUS
prioritize 動
▶ STRESS
PRIORITY 名 p.580
priority 名
▶ PRIORITY
pristine 形
▶ PERFECT
private 形
▶ OWN, SECRET
privation 名
▶ POVERTY
privilege 名
▶ PLEASURE, RIGHT 名
privileged 形
▶ RICH
prize 名
▶ AWARD
prize 動
▶ APPRECIATE
prized 形
▶ DEAR
probability 名
▶ POSSIBILITY
probable 形
▶ LIKELY
PROBABLY 副 p.581
probably 副
▶ PROBABLY
probe 名
▶ INVESTIGATION
probe 動
▶ INVESTIGATE
probity 名
▶ INTEGRITY
PROBLEM 名 p.581
problem 名
▶ PROBLEM
problematic 形
▶ SENSITIVE 2
proceed 動
▶ CONTINUE 2, GO 1
proceeding 名
▶ CASE
proceedings 名
▶ EVENT 1
proceeds 名
▶ REVENUE
process 名
▶ WAY 2
proclaim 動
▶ DECLARE
procure 動
▶ GAIN
prodigy 名
▶ GENIUS
produce 名
▶ PRODUCT
produce 動
▶ CAUSE, MAKE 1, MANUFACTURE, PLAY 動 2, PRESENT 1

producer 名
▶ MAKER
PRODUCT 名 p.582
product 名
▶ PRODUCT, RESULT
PRODUCTION 名 p.583
production 名
▶ OUTPUT, PERFORMANCE, PRODUCTION
PRODUCTIVE 形 p.583
productive 形
▶ PRODUCTIVE
productivity 名
▶ OUTPUT
profession 名
▶ WORK 名 1
professional 形
▶ GOOD 4
professor 名
▶ LECTURER
proficiency 名
▶ SKILL 2
proficient 形
▶ GOOD 4
profile 名
▶ DESCRIPTION, REPUTATION, SHAPE
PROFIT 名 p.584
profit 名
▶ PROFIT
profit 動
▶ MAKE 2
profitable 形
▶ SUCCESSFUL 2
profit-making 形
▶ SUCCESSFUL 2
programme 名
▶ CLASS 1, PLAN 1, SCHEDULE
PROGRESS 名 p.584
progress 名
▶ PROGRESS
progress 動
▶ DEVELOP 1
progression 名
▶ PROGRESS
progressive 形
▶ RADICAL
prohibit 動
▶ BAN 動
prohibited 形
▶ FORBIDDEN
prohibition 名
▶ BAN 名
prohibitive 形
▶ HIGH 1
PROJECT 名 p.585
project 名
▶ ASSIGNMENT, PROJECT
project 動
▶ PREDICT
projection 名
▶ EXPECTATION

prolific → QUALITY

prolific 形
▶ PRODUCTIVE
prologue 名
▶ INTRODUCTION
prolong 動
▶ MAINTAIN
prolonged 形
▶ LONG
prominence 名
▶ FAME
prominent 形
▶ FAMOUS
PROMISE 名 p.586
PROMISE 動 p.587
promise 名
▶ POTENTIAL, PROMISE
promise 動
▶ PROMISE
PROMISING 形 p.588
promising 形
▶ PROMISING
promote 動
▶ ADVERTISE
promoter 名
▶ SPONSOR
promotion 名
▶ ADVERTISEMENT, PROGRESS
prompt 形
▶ IMMEDIATE
pronounce 動
▶ DECLARE
pronounced 形
▶ MARKED
proof 名
▶ EVIDENCE
propensity 名
▶ TENDENCY
proper 形
▶ REAL, RIGHT 形 1, 2
property 名
▶ FEATURE 名, THING 2
prophecy 名
▶ EXPECTATION
prophesy 動
▶ PREDICT
proportion 名
▶ RATIO
proportional 形
▶ RELATIVE
proportionate 形
▶ RELATIVE
PROPOSAL 名 p.589
proposal 名
▶ OFFER 1, PROPOSAL
PROPOSE 動 p.589
propose 動
▶ INTEND, PROPOSE
proposition 名
▶ PROPOSAL, THEORY 2
prop sth up
▶ MAINTAIN
prosecute 動
▶ ACCUSE

prosecution 名
▶ CASE
prospect 名
▶ IDEA 1, POSSIBILITY
prospective 形
▶ LIKELY, NEXT
prospects 名
▶ POTENTIAL
prosper 動
▶ DO WELL
prosperity 名
▶ MONEY 3
prosperous 形
▶ RICH
PROTECT 動 p.590
protect 動
▶ PROTECT
protection 名
▶ SECURITY
protest 名
▶ OPPOSITION
protest 動
▶ CLAIM, COMPLAIN
PROTESTER 名 p.591
protester 名
▶ PROTESTER
protracted 形
▶ LONG
PROUD 形 p.591
proud 形
▶ GLAD, PROUD 1, 2
prove 動
▶ SHOW 1
proven 形
▶ FINAL
PROVIDE 動 p.592
provide 動
▶ PROVIDE
provide for sth
▶ PREPARE 2
providence 名
▶ LUCK
province 名
▶ COUNTY
provision 名
▶ CONDITION, PLANNING
provision 動
▶ EQUIP
proviso 名
▶ CONDITION
prowess 名
▶ SKILL 2
prowl 動
▶ WALK 1
proxy 名
▶ REPLACEMENT
prudent 形
▶ WISE
psychological 形
▶ INTELLECTUAL 1
puberty 名
▶ CHILDHOOD
PUBLIC 形 p.592

public 形
▶ COMMON, FAMOUS, PUBLIC, SOCIAL
public 名
▶ MARKET 1
publication 名
▶ BOOK
public figure 名
▶ STAR
publicity 名
▶ ADVERTISEMENT, FAME
publicize 動
▶ PUBLISH 1
PUBLISH 動 p.593
publish 動
▶ PUBLISH 1, 2
PULL 動 p.594
pull 動
▶ INJURE, PULL 1, 2
pull sth apart
▶ TEAR
pull sth in
▶ MAKE 2
pull sth off
▶ ACHIEVE
pull through
▶ RECOVER
pummel 動
▶ BEAT
PUMP 動 p.595
pump 動
▶ FLOW, PUMP
pun 名
▶ JOKE
punch 動
▶ HIT 2
pundit 名
▶ EXPERT
pungent 形
▶ BITTER
punishable 形
▶ ILLEGAL
punishing 形
▶ HARD
punitive 形
▶ STRICT
punter 名
▶ CUSTOMER
purchase 動
▶ BUY
purchaser 名
▶ CUSTOMER
pure 形
▶ CLEAN 形
purity 名
▶ MORALITY
purported 形
▶ APPARENT
PURPOSE 名 p.596
purpose 名
▶ DETERMINATION, PURPOSE
purposeful 形
▶ DELIBERATE

purse 名
▶ FUND 名
pursue 動
▶ CONTINUE 2, FOLLOW 1
pursuit 名
▶ PROJECT, SEARCH
PUSH 動 p.596
push 動
▶ ADVERTISE, PRESS 1, 2, PUSH 1, 2
pushy 形
▶ AGGRESSIVE 2
PUT 動 p.597
put 動
▶ ATTACH, PUT, RANK, SAY 2
put a figure on sth
▶ CALCULATE
put/set sth aside
▶ SAVE 3
put sth back
▶ RETURN 2
put sth down
▶ SUPPRESS 1, WRITE
put sth forward
▶ PROPOSE
put sth in
▶ PRESENT 3
put sth into effect
▶ APPLY
put sth into practice
▶ APPLY
put sth off
▶ DELAY
put sth on
▶ PLAY 動 2, PRETEND, TURN STH ON, WEAR
put out 動
▶ ANNOYED
put sth right
▶ CORRECT
put sth together
▶ PREPARE 1
put sb/sth to the test
▶ TEST 動 1
put sth up
▶ BUILD, PROVIDE
put up with sb/sth
▶ STAND 2
put your feet up
▶ REST
puzzled 形
▶ CONFUSED
puzzling 形
▶ CONFUSING

Q

qualification 名
▶ CONDITION
qualify 動
▶ ADJUST, ALLOW, GRADUATE
QUALITY 名 p.599

quality

- **quality** 名
  - ▶ FEATURE 名, QUALITY, VALUE
- **quality** 形
  - ▶ GOOD 1
- **qualm** 名
  - ▶ DOUBT 名 2
- **quantify** 動
  - ▶ CALCULATE
- **quantity** 名
  - ▶ NUMBER
- **quarantine** 名
  - ▶ DIVISION 1
- **quarantine** 動
  - ▶ ISOLATE
- **quarrel** 名
  - ▶ ARGUMENT 1
- **quarrel** 動
  - ▶ ARGUE
- **quarter** 名
  - ▶ AREA 1
- **queasy** 形
  - ▶ SICK 2
- **quell** 動
  - ▶ SUPPRESS 1
- **query** 名
  - ▶ QUESTION 名
- **query** 動
  - ▶ DOUBT 動
- **quest** 名
  - ▶ SEARCH
- **QUESTION** 名 *p.599*
- **QUESTION** 動 *p.599*
- **question** 名
  - ▶ DOUBT 名 1, ISSUE, QUESTION 名
- **question** 動
  - ▶ DOUBT 動, QUESTION 動
- **questionable** 形
  - ▶ SUSPICIOUS 2
- **a question mark over sth**
  - ▶ DOUBT 名 1
- **quibble** 名
  - ▶ CRITICISM
- **QUICK** 形 *p.600*
- **quick** 形
  - ▶ FAST, QUICK
- **quicken** 動
  - ▶ ACCELERATE
- **QUIET** 形 *p.601*
- **quiet** 形
  - ▶ QUIET 1, 2, 3
- **quiet** 名
  - ▶ SILENCE
- **quintessential** 形
  - ▶ TYPICAL
- **quip** 名
  - ▶ JOKE
- **quit** 動
  - ▶ LEAVE 2, 3, STOP
- **QUITE** 副 *p.602*
- **quite** 副
  - ▶ QUITE 1, 2, VERY 副
- **quiver** 動
  - ▶ SHIVER
- **quiz** 名
  - ▶ COMPETITION 1, TEST 名 2
- **quiz** 動
  - ▶ QUESTION 動, TEST 動 2
- **quota** 名
  - ▶ SHARE 名
- **quotation** 名
  - ▶ REFERENCE, VALUATION
- **QUOTE** 動 *p.604*
- **quote** 名
  - ▶ REFERENCE, VALUATION
- **quote** 動
  - ▶ MENTION, QUOTE

R

- **rabble** 名
  - ▶ CROWD
- **race** 名
  - ▶ COMPETITION 2, PEOPLE
- **race** 動
  - ▶ RUN 1
- **racial** 形
  - ▶ CULTURAL
- **RACISM** 名 *p.605*
- **racism** 名
  - ▶ RACISM
- **racket** 名
  - ▶ FRAUD 2
- **rack up sth**
  - ▶ COLLECT
- **RADICAL** 形 *p.605*
- **radical** 形
  - ▶ FUNDAMENTAL, RADICAL
- **rage** 名
  - ▶ ANGER 名, TEMPER
- **raging** 形
  - ▶ ROUGH
- **raid** 名
  - ▶ ATTACK 名 1, THEFT
- **raid** 動
  - ▶ ATTACK 動 2, ROB
- **raider** 名
  - ▶ THIEF
- **RAIN** 動 *p.606*
- **rain** 動
  - ▶ RAIN
- **raise** 名
  - ▶ INCREASE 名
- **raise** 動
  - ▶ BRING SB UP, INCREASE 動, KEEP 4
- **raise your voice**
  - ▶ SHOUT
- **rake sth in**
  - ▶ MAKE 2
- **rally** 動
  - ▶ MEET 1
- **ram** 動
  - ▶ PUSH 1
- **RANDOM** 形 *p.606*
- **random** 形
  - ▶ RANDOM
- **RANGE** 名 *p.607*
- **range** 名
  - ▶ RANGE 1, 2
- **range** 動
  - ▶ DIFFER
- **RANK** 動 *p.608*
- **rank** 名
  - ▶ CLASS 3
- **rank** 動
  - ▶ RANK
- **ranking** 名
  - ▶ CLASS 3
- **rankle** 動
  - ▶ ANGER 動
- **ransack** 動
  - ▶ ROB
- **ransom** 動
  - ▶ RELEASE
- **rap** 名
  - ▶ CRITICISM
- **rap** 動
  - ▶ KNOCK
- **rape** 名
  - ▶ ATTACK 名 2
- **rapid** 形
  - ▶ QUICK
- **rapidity** 名
  - ▶ SPEED
- **rapt** 形
  - ▶ INTERESTED
- **rapturous** 形
  - ▶ EXCITED
- **RARE** 形 *p.608*
- **rare** 形
  - ▶ RARE
- **RARELY** 副 *p.609*
- **rarely** 副
  - ▶ RARELY
- **rash** 形
  - ▶ RECKLESS
- **rasher** 名
  - ▶ PIECE
- **RATE** 名 *p.609*
- **rate** 名
  - ▶ RATE
- **rate** 動
  - ▶ JUDGE 動, RANK
- **rates** 名
  - ▶ TAX
- **rather** 副
  - ▶ QUITE 1
- **ratify** 動
  - ▶ APPROVE
- **rating** 名
  - ▶ CLASS 3
- **RATIO** 名 *p.610*
- **ratio** 名
  - ▶ RATIO
- **ration** 名
  - ▶ SHARE 名
- **RATIONAL** 形 *p.610*
- **rational** 形
  - ▶ RATIONAL
- **rationality** 名
  - ▶ LOGIC
- **rationalize** 動
  - ▶ CUT 1
- **rattle** 動
  - ▶ SHAKE 2
- **ravage** 動
  - ▶ DESTROY
- **rave** 動
  - ▶ PRAISE 動
- **ravenous** 形
  - ▶ HUNGRY
- **raw** 形
  - ▶ PAINFUL 1
- **raze** 動
  - ▶ DEMOLISH
- **reach** 名
  - ▶ RANGE 2
- **reach** 動
  - ▶ ACHIEVE, CALL 2, GET 3
- **READ** 動 *p.611*
- **read** 動
  - ▶ READ
- **reading** 名
  - ▶ DEFINITION
- **read sth into sth**
  - ▶ CONCLUDE
- **REAL** 形 *p.612*
- **real** 形
  - ▶ COMPLETE, DEEP 1, REAL
- **real estate** 名
  - ▶ LAND 1
- **REALISTIC** 形 *p.612*
- **realistic** 形
  - ▶ POSSIBLE 1, REALISTIC
- **reality** 名
  - ▶ FACT
- **realization** 名
  - ▶ AWARENESS
- **realize** 動
  - ▶ KNOW
- **real-life** 形
  - ▶ RELIABLE 2
- **real life**
  - ▶ FACT
- **really** 副
  - ▶ VERY 副
- **realm** 名
  - ▶ AREA 2
- **the real world**
  - ▶ FACT
- **reap** 動
  - ▶ GET 2
- **rear** 動
  - ▶ BRING SB UP, KEEP 4
- **REASON** 名 *p.613*
- **reason** 名
  - ▶ LOGIC, REASON

reason 動
▶ CONCLUDE
REASONABLE 形 p.614
reasonable 形
▶ ADEQUATE, CHEAP, FINE, REASONABLE
reasonably 副
▶ QUITE 1
reasoned 形
▶ RATIONAL
reassurance 名
▶ RELIEF
rebate 名
▶ COMPENSATION
rebel 名
▶ GUERRILLA, PROTESTER
rebel 動
▶ OPPOSE
rebellion 名
▶ REVOLUTION
rebuff 名
▶ REFUSAL
rebuff 動
▶ REFUSE
rebuke 動
▶ SCOLD
rebut 動
▶ DISPROVE
recall 名
▶ MEMORY
recall 動
▶ REMEMBER
recant 動
▶ BREAK 4
receipts 名
▶ REVENUE
receive 動
▶ GET 2, GREET, HAVE 3, LET SB IN
RECENT 形 p.615
recent 形
▶ RECENT
reception 名
▶ EVENT 2, HALL 2
recess 名
▶ HOLIDAY 1
RECESSION 名 p.616
recession 名
▶ RECESSION
recite 動
▶ QUOTE
RECKLESS 形 p.616
reckless 形
▶ RECKLESS
reckon 動
▶ ESTIMATE 動, REGARD, THINK
reckoning 名
▶ ESTIMATE
reclusive 形
▶ SOLITARY
recognition 名
▶ ADMIRATION

recognize 動
▶ ADMIT, APPROVE
recoil 動
▶ HESITATE
recollect 動
▶ REMEMBER
recollection 名
▶ MEMORY
RECOMMEND 動 p.617
recommend 動
▶ RECOMMEND 1, 2
recommendation 名
▶ ENDORSEMENT, PROPOSAL
reconstruction 名
▶ COPY 名 2
RECORD 動 p.618
record 動
▶ RECORD
recount 動
▶ DESCRIBE
RECOVER 動 p.619
recover 動
▶ RECOVER
recreation 名
▶ ENTERTAINMENT
recrimination 名
▶ CHARGE 名
RECRUIT 名 p.619
recruit 名
▶ RECRUIT
recruit 動
▶ EMPLOY
rectify 動
▶ CORRECT
recuperate 動
▶ RECOVER
redeem 動
▶ SAVE 1
red-hot 形
▶ HOT
redress 動
▶ CORRECT
red tape 名
▶ BUREAUCRACY
REDUCE 動 p.620
reduce 動
▶ REDUCE
REDUCTION 名 p.620
reduction 名
▶ REDUCTION
redundancy 名
▶ UNEMPLOYMENT
redundant 形
▶ UNEMPLOYED
reek 名
▶ ODOUR
ref 名
▶ JUDGE 名
referee 名
▶ JUDGE 名
REFERENCE 名 p.621
reference 名
▶ ENDORSEMENT, REFERENCE

referendum 名
▶ ELECTION
refer to sb/sth
▶ MENTION
refill 動
▶ FILL
refine 動
▶ IMPROVE 1
reflect 動
▶ CONSIDER
reflection 名
▶ CONSIDERATION
reform 動
▶ IMPROVE 1
refreshment 名
▶ FOOD
refrigerate 動
▶ COOL
REFUGE 名 p.622
refuge 名
▶ REFUGE, SHELTER
REFUGEE 名 p.622
refugee 名
▶ REFUGEE
refund 名
▶ COMPENSATION
REFUSAL 名 p.623
refusal 名
▶ REFUSAL
REFUSE 動 p.623
refuse 名
▶ WASTE
refuse 動
▶ REFUSE
refute 動
▶ DENY, DISPROVE
REGARD 動 p.624
regard 名
▶ ATTENTION
regard 動
▶ LOOK 動 1, REGARD
regime 名
▶ GOVERNMENT 1
region 名
▶ AREA 1, COUNTY
register 名
▶ LIST 名
register 動
▶ PRESENT 3, RECORD
regret 名
▶ GRIEF, GUILT
regrettable 形
▶ UNFORTUNATE 2
regular 形
▶ FREQUENT, STEADY, USUAL
regular 名
▶ CUSTOMER
REGULATE 動 p.625
regulate 動
▶ REGULATE
regulation 名
▶ GOVERNMENT 2, RULE 名

regulator 名
▶ INSPECTOR
rehabilitate 動
▶ CURE
rehearsal 名
▶ TRAINING
rehearse 動
▶ PRACTISE
reheat 動
▶ HEAT
reign 名
▶ GOVERNMENT 1
reign 動
▶ RULE 動 1
reimbursement 名
▶ COMPENSATION
reiterate 動
▶ REPEAT
REJECT 動 p.626
reject 動
▶ REFUSE, REJECT
rejection 名
▶ REFUSAL
relapse 動
▶ WORSEN
RELATE 動 p.626
relate 動
▶ DESCRIBE, RELATE
RELATED 形 p.627
related 形
▶ RELATED
relate to sb/sth
▶ UNDERSTAND 2
RELATION 名 p.628
relation 名
▶ FAMILY 2, RELATION
relations 名
▶ RELATIONSHIP 1
RELATIONSHIP 名 p.628
relationship 名
▶ RELATION, RELATIONSHIP 1, 2
RELATIVE 形 p.630
relative 形
▶ RELATIVE
relative 名
▶ FAMILY 2
relax 動
▶ REST
relaxation 名
▶ ENTERTAINMENT
relaxed 形
▶ CALM, INFORMAL
relay 動
▶ CONVEY
RELEASE 動 p.630
release 動
▶ FREE 動, PUBLISH 1, 2, RELEASE
relent 動
▶ GIVE WAY
relentless 形
▶ CONTINUOUS
RELEVANT 形 p.631

relevant → restless

relevant 形
  ▶ RELEVANT
RELIABLE 形 p.632
reliable 形
  ▶ RELIABLE 1, 2
RELIEF 名 p.633
relief 名
  ▶ AID, RELIEF, REPLACEMENT
relieve 動
  ▶ EASE, REPLACE 1
relieved 形
  ▶ GLAD
relocate 動
  ▶ LEAVE 2
RELUCTANT 形 p.634
reluctant 形
  ▶ RELUCTANT
rely on/upon sb/sth
  ▶ NEED 動, TRUST
REMAIN 動 p.634
remain 動
  ▶ REMAIN, STAY 1
REMAINS 名 p.635
remains 名
  ▶ REMAINS
remark 名
  ▶ STATEMENT
remark 動
  ▶ COMMENT
REMARKABLE 形 p.635
remarkable 形
  ▶ REMARKABLE
remedy 名
  ▶ DRUG 2, SOLUTION
remedy 動
  ▶ CORRECT
REMEMBER 動 p.636
remember 動
  ▶ REMEMBER
remembrance 名
  ▶ MEMORY
reminisce 動
  ▶ REMEMBER
reminiscence 名
  ▶ MEMORY
remorse 名
  ▶ GUILT
remote 形
  ▶ COLD 2, PREVIOUS
REMOVE 動 p.637
remove 動
  ▶ REMOVE, TAKE STH OFF
renew 動
  ▶ CONTINUE 3
renowned 形
  ▶ FAMOUS
rent 名
  ▶ RATE
rent 動
  ▶ ORDER 2
rental 名
  ▶ RATE

reopen 動
  ▶ CONTINUE 3
rep 名
  ▶ SALESMAN
REPAIR 動 p.638
repair 名
  ▶ STATE
repair 動
  ▶ REPAIR, RESOLVE
repatriate 動
  ▶ EXPEL
repayment 名
  ▶ PAYMENT
repeal 動
  ▶ CANCEL
REPEAT 動 p.639
repeat 動
  ▶ CONVEY, QUOTE, REPEAT
repel 動
  ▶ SHOCK
repentance 名
  ▶ GUILT
repercussion 名
  ▶ RESULT
repetitive 形
  ▶ BORING
REPLACE 動 p.639
replace 動
  ▶ REPLACE 1, 2, RETURN 2
REPLACEMENT 名 p.641
replacement 名
  ▶ EXCHANGE, REPLACEMENT
replay 名
  ▶ GAME
replenish 動
  ▶ FILL
replica 名
  ▶ COPY 名 2
reply 名
  ▶ ANSWER 名
reply 動
  ▶ ANSWER 動
REPORT 名 p.641
report 名
  ▶ REPORT 1, 2
report 動
  ▶ DESCRIBE, TELL 1
REPORTER 名 p.643
reporter 名
  ▶ REPORTER
REPRESENT 動 p.643
represent 動
  ▶ PRESENT 2, REPRESENT 2
represent 連結動
  ▶ REPRESENT 1
representation 名
  ▶ DESCRIPTION
representative 形
  ▶ TYPICAL
representative 名
  ▶ POLITICIAN, SALESMAN

repress 動
  ▶ SUPPRESS 1, 2
REPRESSION 名 p.644
repression 名
  ▶ REPRESSION
REPRESSIVE 形 p.645
repressive 形
  ▶ REPRESSIVE
reprimand 動
  ▶ SCOLD
reprisal 名
  ▶ REVENGE
reproach 動
  ▶ SCOLD
reproduce 動
  ▶ COPY 動
reproduction 名
  ▶ COPY 名 2
repudiate 動
  ▶ DENY
repugnant 形
  ▶ DISGUSTING 2
repulsive 形
  ▶ DISGUSTING 1
reputable 形
  ▶ RESPECTABLE
REPUTATION 名 p.645
reputation 名
  ▶ REPUTATION
REQUEST 名 p.646
request 名
  ▶ REQUEST, WISH
request 動
  ▶ ASK 2
require 動
  ▶ DEMAND 動, NEED 動
requirement 名
  ▶ CONDITION, NEED 名
requisite 形
  ▶ NECESSARY
reschedule 動
  ▶ DELAY
rescue 動
  ▶ SAVE 1
RESEARCH 名 p.647
research 名
  ▶ RESEARCH
research 動
  ▶ INVESTIGATE
resemblance 名
  ▶ SIMILARITY
reservation 名
  ▶ REQUEST
reserve 名
  ▶ FUND 名, REPLACEMENT, SUPPLY
reserve 動
  ▶ ORDER 2
reserved 形
  ▶ QUIET 3
reside 動
  ▶ LIVE
residence 名
  ▶ HOME

RESIDENT 名 p.648
resident 名
  ▶ RESIDENT, TENANT
resign 動
  ▶ LEAVE 3
resignation 名
  ▶ PATIENCE
RESIST 動 p.648
resist 動
  ▶ OPPOSE, RESIST
resistance 名
  ▶ OPPOSITION
resistant 形
  ▶ AGAINST SB/STH
resolution 名
  ▶ SOLUTION
RESOLVE 動 p.649
resolve 名
  ▶ DETERMINATION
resolve 動
  ▶ DECIDE, RESOLVE
resort to sth
  ▶ USE 動 1
resounding 形
  ▶ DEEP 2
resource 名
  ▶ FACILITIES, SUPPLY
RESPECT 名 p.649
RESPECT 動 p.650
respect 名
  ▶ ADMIRATION, RESPECT
respect 動
  ▶ FOLLOW 3, RESPECT
RESPECTABLE 形 p.650
respectable 形
  ▶ RESPECTABLE
respectful 形
  ▶ POLITE
respective 形
  ▶ PARTICULAR
respond 動
  ▶ ANSWER 動
response 名
  ▶ ANSWER 名
RESPONSIBILITY 名 p.651
responsibility 名
  ▶ FAULT, RESPONSIBILITY
responsible 形
  ▶ GUILTY, RELIABLE 1
REST p.652
rest 動
  ▶ REST
restart 動
  ▶ CONTINUE 3
restate 動
  ▶ REPEAT
restitution 名
  ▶ COMPENSATION
RESTLESS 形 p.653
restless 形
  ▶ RESTLESS

restock 動
  ▶ FILL
rest on sth
  ▶ DEPEND ON/UPON STH
restore 動
  ▶ RETURN 2
restrain 動
  ▶ PREVENT, SUPPRESS 2
restraint 名
  ▶ LIMIT 1
restricted 形
  ▶ LIMITED 1, 2
restriction 名
  ▶ LIMIT 1
restroom 名
  ▶ TOILET
RESULT 名 p.653
result 名
  ▶ RESULT, VICTORY
result 動
  ▶ FOLLOW 2
resultant 形
  ▶ RELATED
result in sth
  ▶ CAUSE
resulting 形
  ▶ RELATED
resume 動
  ▶ CONTINUE 3
resuscitate 動
  ▶ CURE
retail 動
  ▶ SELL 2
retailer 名
  ▶ DEALER
retain 動
  ▶ EMPLOY, KEEP 2, 3
retaliation 名
  ▶ REVENGE
retard 動
  ▶ HOLD SB/STH UP
reticent 形
  ▶ QUIET 3
retire 動
  ▶ LEAVE 3
retort 名
  ▶ ANSWER 名
retort 動
  ▶ ANSWER 動
retract 動
  ▶ BREAK 4
retreat 名
  ▶ REFUGE
RETURN 動 p.654
return 名
  ▶ PROFIT
return 動
  ▶ RETURN 1, 2
return to sth
  ▶ CONTINUE 3
reunion 名
  ▶ EVENT 2
REVEAL 動 p.655
reveal 動
  ▶ REVEAL, SHOW 2

revealing 形
  ▶ INFORMATIVE
REVENGE 名 p.656
revenge 動
  ▶ REVENGE
REVENUE 名 p.656
revenue 名
  ▶ REVENUE
reversal 名
  ▶ EXCHANGE
reverse 形
  ▶ OPPOSITE 形
reverse 動
  ▶ REPLACE 2
the reverse 名
  ▶ OPPOSITE 名
review 名
  ▶ ASSESSMENT,
    REPORT 1
review 動
  ▶ EXAMINE, LEARN
reviewer 名
  ▶ REPORTER
revise 動
  ▶ ADJUST, LEARN
revision 名
  ▶ CHANGE 名 2
revoke 動
  ▶ CANCEL
revolt 名
  ▶ REVOLUTION
revolting 形
  ▶ DISGUSTING 1
REVOLUTION 名 p.657
revolution 名
  ▶ REVOLUTION
revolutionary 形
  ▶ RADICAL
revolutionary 名
  ▶ GUERRILLA
revolve 動
  ▶ SPIN
reward 名
  ▶ AWARD
rewarding 形
  ▶ SATISFYING
RICH 形 p.657
rich 形
  ▶ DARK 2, DEEP 2,
    PRODUCTIVE, RICH
riches 名
  ▶ MONEY 3
ride 動
  ▶ GO 2
ridge 名
  ▶ HILL
ridicule 名
  ▶ CONTEMPT
ridicule 動
  ▶ LAUGH AT SB/STH
RIDICULOUS 形 p.658
ridiculous 形
  ▶ RIDICULOUS
rife 形
  ▶ GENERAL

rift 名
  ▶ DIVISION 2
RIGHT 名 p.659
RIGHT 形 p.660
right 名
  ▶ MORALITY, RIGHT 名
right 形
  ▶ FINE, GOOD 2,
    RIGHT 形 1, 2, TRUE
righteousness 名
  ▶ MORALITY
rigid 形
  ▶ SOLID, STRICT
rigorous 形
  ▶ DETAILED
rile 動
  ▶ ANGER 動
ring 名
  ▶ TEAM 1
ring 動
  ▶ CALL 2
rinse 動
  ▶ CLEAN 動
riot 名
  ▶ REVOLUTION
rioting 名
  ▶ REVOLUTION
rip 動
  ▶ TEAR
rip sb off
  ▶ DEFRAUD
RISE 動 p.661
rise 名
  ▶ INCREASE 名,
    PROGRESS
rise 動
  ▶ RISE, STAND 1
RISK 名 p.662
risk 名
  ▶ RISK 1, 2, THREAT
risk 動
  ▶ DARE, THREATEN
risky 形
  ▶ DANGEROUS
ritual 名
  ▶ HABIT
rival 名
  ▶ ENEMY
rival 動
  ▶ COMPARE 2
rivalry 名
  ▶ COMPETITION 2
rivet 動
  ▶ INTEREST 動
riveting 形
  ▶ INTERESTING
ROAD 名 p.663
road 名
  ▶ ROAD
roadblock 名
  ▶ BARRIER, OBSTACLE
roar 動
  ▶ LAUGH, SHOUT
roaring 形
  ▶ LOUD

ROB 動 p.664
rob 動
  ▶ ROB
robber 名
  ▶ THIEF
robbery 名
  ▶ THEFT
rock 動
  ▶ SHAKE 2, SHOCK 動
rocket 動
  ▶ SOAR
role 名
  ▶ INVOLVEMENT
role model 名
  ▶ EXAMPLE 2
roll 名
  ▶ LIST 名
roll 動
  ▶ SPIN
roll in
  ▶ ARRIVE
romance 名
  ▶ LOVE 名 1,
    RELATIONSHIP 2
romantic 形
  ▶ LOVING
rookie 名
  ▶ BEGINNER
root 名
  ▶ SOURCE
roots 名
  ▶ FAMILY 3
rosy 形
  ▶ PROMISING
rotate 動
  ▶ SPIN
ROTTEN 形 p.664
rotten 形
  ▶ CORRUPT,
    INCOMPETENT, ROTTEN
ROUGH 形 p.665
rough 形
  ▶ DIFFICULT 2, ROUGH,
    VAGUE, VIOLENT
round 名
  ▶ GAME, STAGE
round sth off
  ▶ FINISH
round sth out
  ▶ FINISH
round-the-clock 形
  ▶ CONTINUOUS
rout 動
  ▶ DEFEAT
route 名
  ▶ WAY 3
routine 形
  ▶ USUAL
routinely 副
  ▶ OFTEN
row 名
  ▶ ARGUMENT 1, ROAD
row 動
  ▶ ARGUE

rowdy 形
▶ WILD
rub 動
▶ SCRATCH
rubbish 名
▶ NONSENSE, WASTE
rubble 名
▶ REMAINS
rub sth out
▶ DELETE
RUDE 形 p.665
rude 形
▶ OFFENSIVE, RUDE
rudimentary 形
▶ FUNDAMENTAL
RUIN 動 p.666
ruin 名
▶ REMAINS
ruin 動
▶ RUIN
RULE 名 p.666
RULE 動 p.667
rule 名
▶ CONTROL, HABIT, PRINCIPLE 2, RULE 名, THEORY 1
rule 動
▶ DETERMINE, RULE 動 1, 2
the rule of law
▶ PEACE
rule sb/sth out
▶ EXCLUDE 1, PREVENT
rules and regulations
▶ BUREAUCRACY
ruling 名
▶ CONCLUSION
RUN 動 p.668
run 動
▶ FLOW, GO 1, 2, HURRY, OPERATE, ORGANIZE, RUN 1, 2, WORK 動 2
run away
▶ FLEE
rundown 名
▶ SUMMARY
run for it
▶ FLEE
run into sb
▶ MEET 2
run into sth
▶ HAVE 3
runner-up 名
▶ LOSER 1
run off
▶ FLEE
a run on sth
▶ DEMAND 名
run through sth
▶ PRACTISE
run sth up
▶ COLLECT
ruse 名
▶ TRICK

rush 動
▶ HURRY
RUTHLESS 形 p.669
ruthless 形
▶ RUTHLESS

S

sabbatical 名
▶ HOLIDAY 1
sack 動
▶ FIRE
sacking 名
▶ UNEMPLOYMENT
SAD 形 p.671
sad 形
▶ SAD, UNFORTUNATE 2, UNHAPPY 1
sadden 動
▶ HURT 1
sadistic 形
▶ CRUEL
sadness 名
▶ GRIEF
SAFE 形 p.671
safe 形
▶ SAFE
safeguard 名
▶ PRECAUTION
safeguard 動
▶ PROTECT
safe house 名
▶ REFUGE
safety 名
▶ SHELTER
saga 名
▶ STORY
sail through sth
▶ GRADUATE
salary 名
▶ INCOME
sales force 名
▶ STAFF
SALESMAN 名 p.672
salesman 名
▶ SALESMAN
the same 形
▶ EQUAL
sample 動
▶ SURVEY, TRY 2
sanction 名
▶ BAN 名
sanction 動
▶ ALLOW
sanctuary 名
▶ CHURCH, REFUGE, SHELTER
sand 名
▶ COAST
sarcastic 形
▶ IRONIC
sardonic 形
▶ IRONIC
satanic 形
▶ EVIL 形

satellite 名
▶ TERRITORY
satirical 形
▶ IRONIC
SATISFACTION 名 p.672
satisfaction 名
▶ SATISFACTION
satisfactory 形
▶ FINE
satisfied 形
▶ HAPPY, SURE
satisfy 動
▶ CONVINCE, MEET 4, PLEASE
SATISFYING 形 p.673
satisfying 形
▶ SATISFYING
saturated 形
▶ WET
savage 形
▶ CRUEL
SAVE 動 p.673
save 動
▶ KEEP 2, SAVE 1, 2, 3
savings 名
▶ FUND
savoury 形
▶ STRONG 2
SAY 動 p.674
say 動
▶ PREDICT, QUOTE, SAY 1, 2, 3
scale 名
▶ RATIO
scale 動
▶ CLIMB
scale sth back
▶ CUT 1
scale sth down
▶ CUT 1
scam 名
▶ FRAUD 2
scan 名
▶ INSPECTION
scan 動
▶ READ
scandalize 動
▶ SHOCK 動
scandalous 形
▶ OUTRAGEOUS
scant 形
▶ INADEQUATE
SCARCE 形 p.676
scarce 形
▶ SCARCE
scarcity 名
▶ LACK
scare 動
▶ FRIGHTEN
scared 形
▶ AFRAID
scary 形
▶ FRIGHTENING
scene 名
▶ PLACE, VIEW 2

scenery 名
▶ COUNTRY 2
scenic 形
▶ BEAUTIFUL 2
scent 名
▶ SMELL
sceptical 形
▶ SUSPICIOUS 1
SCEPTICISM 名 p.676
scepticism 名
▶ SCEPTICISM
SCHEDULE 名 p.677
schedule 名
▶ SCHEDULE
scheme 名
▶ CONSPIRACY, PLAN 1
scheme 動
▶ PLOT
schism 名
▶ DIVISION 2
scholarly 形
▶ EDUCATIONAL, INTELLECTUAL 2
scholarship 名
▶ KNOWLEDGE
schooling 名
▶ EDUCATION
schoolteacher 名
▶ TEACHER
scientific 形
▶ RATIONAL
SCOLD 動 p.678
scold 動
▶ SCOLD
scope 名
▶ RANGE 2
scorn 名
▶ CONTEMPT
scout 動
▶ LOOK 2
scramble 動
▶ CLIMB
scrap 名
▶ BIT, WASTE
scrap 動
▶ ABOLISH, REMOVE
scrape 動
▶ SCRATCH
SCRATCH 動 p.679
scratch 名
▶ INJURY
scratch 動
▶ SCRATCH
scrawl 動
▶ WRITE
SCREAM 動 p.679
scream 動
▶ SCREAM, SHOUT
screech 動
▶ SCREAM
screen 名
▶ PRECAUTION
screen 動
▶ TEST 動 1

screen test → set-up

screen test 名
▶ INTERVIEW 2
screenwriter 名
▶ WRITER
screw 動
▶ DEFRAUD
screw your eyes/face up
▶ TIGHTEN
scribble 動
▶ WRITE
scribe 名
▶ WRITER
scriptwriter 名
▶ WRITER
scrub 動
▶ BRUSH
scruple 名
▶ DOUBT 名 2
scrupulous 形
▶ GOOD 5
scrutiny 名
▶ RESEARCH
scuff 動
▶ SCRATCH
scuffle 名
▶ FIGHT 名
scuffle 動
▶ FIGHT 動
SEA 名 p.680
sea 名
▶ SEA
seaboard 名
▶ COAST
seal 名
▶ LOGO
seal 動
▶ BLOCK 2
SEARCH 名 p.680
search 名
▶ SEARCH
search 動
▶ LOOK 動 2
search sb/sth out
▶ FIND 4
seashore 名
▶ COAST
seaside 名
▶ COAST
seasoned 形
▶ EXPERIENCED
sec 名
▶ MINUTE
second 名
▶ MINUTE
second 動
▶ SUPPORT
second-rate 形
▶ POOR 2
second thoughts
▶ DOUBT 名 2
SECRET 形 p.681
secret 形
▶ SECRET

secretary 名
▶ OFFICIAL 名
sectarianism 名
▶ RACISM
section 名
▶ ELEMENT
sector 名
▶ AREA 2
secure 形
▶ FIRM, SAFE
secure 動
▶ ATTACH, GAIN, PROTECT
SECURITY 名 p.682
security 名
▶ SECURITY
SEE 動 p.682
see 動
▶ GO OUT, IMAGINE, LOOK 動 1, REGARD, SEE, UNDERSTAND 1, VISIT 動
seek 動
▶ ASK 2, LOOK 動 2, TRY 1
SEEM 連結動詞 p.683
seem 連結動詞
▶ SEEM
seeming 形
▶ APPARENT
seething 形
▶ FURIOUS
see-through 形
▶ CLEAR 形 3
see to sth
▶ DEAL WITH SB/STH
see to it that...
▶ ENSURE
segregate 動
▶ ISOLATE
segregation 名
▶ DIVISION 1
seize 動
▶ INVADE, KIDNAP, TAKE 3
seldom 副
▶ RARELY
select 動
▶ CHOOSE
selection 名
▶ CHOICE 1, 2, RANGE 1
self
▶ IDENTITY, PERSONALITY
self-centred 形
▶ SELFISH
self-confidence 名
▶ CONFIDENCE
self-confident 形
▶ CONFIDENT
self-conscious 形
▶ EMBARRASSED
self-defeating 形
▶ INEFFECTIVE

self-determination 名
▶ INDEPENDENCE
self-esteem 名
▶ DIGNITY
self-evident 形
▶ CLEAR 形 1
self-government 名
▶ INDEPENDENCE
self-image 名
▶ DIGNITY
self-important 形
▶ PROUD 2
SELFISH 形 p.684
selfish 形
▶ SELFISH
self-respect 名
▶ DIGNITY
self-respecting 形
▶ PROUD 1
self-serving 形
▶ SELFISH
SELL 動 p.684
sell 動
▶ SELL 1, 2
seller 名
▶ DEALER
sell sth off
▶ SELL 1
sell up
▶ SELL 1
seminar 名
▶ CLASS 2
senator 名
▶ POLITICIAN
SEND 動 p.685
send 動
▶ CONVEY, SEND
send sth in
▶ PRESENT 3
send sth on
▶ SEND
send sb to prison
▶ JAIL
senior 形
▶ TOP
sensation 名
▶ SENSE
sensational 形
▶ AMAZING
SENSE 名 p.686
sense 名
▶ MEANING, SENSE, UNDERSTANDING
sense 動
▶ FEEL
sensibilities 名
▶ DIGNITY
sensible 形
▶ BEST, WISE
SENSITIVE 形 p.687
sensitive 形
▶ SENSITIVE 1, 2, 3
sensitivity 名
▶ TACT

sentiment 名
▶ EMOTION, VIEW 1
sentry 名
▶ GUARD
separate 形
▶ PARTICULAR
separate 動
▶ DIVIDE 2
separated 形
▶ SINGLE
separate out
▶ DIVIDE 1
separation 名
▶ DIVISION 1
sequence 名
▶ SERIES
SERIES 名 p.688
series 名
▶ SERIES
SERIOUS 形 p.689
serious 形
▶ SERIOUS 1, 2
seriousness 名
▶ IMPORTANCE
sermon 名
▶ SPEECH
serve 動
▶ MEET 4
SERVICE 名 p.691
service 名
▶ FACILITIES, HELP 名, INDUSTRY, SERVICE
session 名
▶ CLASS 2, MEETING 1
set 名
▶ GROUP 1, 2
set 動
▶ PUT
set about sth
▶ BEGIN
set sb/sth back
▶ HOLD SB/STH UP
set foot in/on sth
▶ ENTER
set sb/sth free
▶ RELEASE
set/put sth in motion
▶ INTRODUCE
set sth off
▶ TURN STH ON
set sth out
▶ ARRANGE
set sb/sth straight
▶ CORRECT
setting 名
▶ CONTEXT, ENVIRONMENT
settle 動
▶ CONFIRM 3, PUT, RESOLVE
settlement 名
▶ AGREEMENT, PAYMENT
set-up 名
▶ TRICK

INDEX

917

set sth up → **silence**

set sth up
▶ BUILD, ESTABLISH
set your heart on sth
▶ HOPE
set your sights on sth
▶ HOPE
severe 形
▶ PLAIN 1, SERIOUS 1, STERN, STRICT
sexism 名
▶ RACISM
shadow 名
▶ SHAPE
shadowy 形
▶ DARK 1
shady 形
▶ DARK 1, SUSPICIOUS 2
SHAKE 動 p.691
shake 動
▶ SHAKE 1, 2, 3
shake sth off
▶ RECOVER
shaking 名
▶ SHIVER
shame 名
▶ DISGRACE, GUILT, UNFORTUNATE 2
shame 動
▶ EMBARRASS
shameful 形
▶ OUTRAGEOUS
shampoo 動
▶ CLEAN
SHAPE 名 p.693
shape 名
▶ HEALTH, SHAPE, STATE
shape 動
▶ DETERMINE
shape up
▶ DEVELOP 1
shard 名
▶ FRAGMENT
SHARE 名 p.694
SHARE 動 p.695
share 名
▶ SHARE
share 動
▶ JOIN, SHARE
sharp 形
▶ BITTER, HIGH 3, MARKED
shattered 形
▶ TIRED
shavings 名
▶ FRAGMENT
shed 動
▶ REMOVE
shed/cast/throw light on sth
▶ EXPLAIN 1
sheepish 形
▶ EMBARRASSED
SHELTER 名 p.695

shelter 名
▶ REFUGE, SHELTER
shelter 動
▶ PROTECT
shelve 動
▶ DELAY
shield 名
▶ PRECAUTION
shield 動
▶ PROTECT
shift 名
▶ CHANGE 名 1, TEAM 1
shift 動
▶ CHANGE 動 1, 2
shifty 形
▶ SUSPICIOUS 2
shimmer 動
▶ SHINE
SHINE 動 p.696
shine 動
▶ SHINE
ship 動
▶ TAKE 1
shipment 名
▶ DELIVERY
shipping 名
▶ DELIVERY
shit 形
▶ POOR 2
SHIVER 名 p.696
shiver 名
▶ SHIVER
shiver 動
▶ SHAKE 3
SHOCK 名 p.697
SHOCK 動 p.697
shock 名
▶ SHOCK
shock 動
▶ OFFEND, SHOCK
shocking 形
▶ OUTRAGEOUS
shoot up
▶ SOAR
shop 動
▶ BUY
shopkeeper 名
▶ DEALER
shoplift 動
▶ STEAL
shoplifter 名
▶ THIEF
shoplifting 名
▶ THEFT
shopper 名
▶ CUSTOMER
shopping centre 名
▶ MARKET 2
shoreline 名
▶ COAST
SHORT 形 p.698
short 形
▶ SCARCE, SHORT 1, 2, 3
shortage 名
▶ LACK

short-change 動
▶ DEFRAUD
shorten 動
▶ SHRINK
shortfall 名
▶ LACK
short-lived 形
▶ SHORT 1
shot 名
▶ ATTEMPT
shoulder 動
▶ PUSH 2
SHOUT 動 p.700
shout 動
▶ SHOUT
shouting match 名
▶ ARGUMENT 1
shove 動
▶ PUSH 1, 2
SHOW 動 p.701
show 名
▶ EXHIBITION, EXPRESSION, PERFORMANCE
show 動
▶ APPEAR, ARRIVE, PRESENT 1, 2, SHOW 1, 2, TAKE 2, TRAIN 1
showbiz 名
▶ DRAMA
show business 名
▶ DRAMA
shower 名
▶ FLOOD 名 2
shower 動
▶ WASH
show off
▶ BOAST
show of hands
▶ ELECTION
show up
▶ ARRIVE
shred 名
▶ FRAGMENT
shred 動
▶ TEAR
SHREWD 形 p.702
shrewd 形
▶ SHREWD
shriek 名
▶ SCREAM
shrill 形
▶ HIGH 3
shrine 名
▶ CHURCH
SHRINK 動 p.702
shrink 動
▶ SHRINK
shrink from sth
▶ HESITATE
shudder 名
▶ SHIVER
shudder 動
▶ SHAKE 2, 3

shut 動
▶ CLOSE
shut sth off
▶ TURN STH OFF
shut sb/sth out
▶ EXCLUDE 2
SHY 形 p.703
shy 形
▶ SHY
shy away from sth
▶ HESITATE
SICK 形 p.703
sick 形
▶ SICK 1, 2
the sick 名
▶ PATIENT
sicken 動
▶ SHOCK 動
sickening 形
▶ DISGUSTING 2
sickly 形
▶ SICK 1
sickness 名
▶ DISEASE, ILLNESS
side 名
▶ ATTITUDE, EDGE, TEAM 2
side by side
▶ PARALLEL
sidewalk 名
▶ PATH
side with sb
▶ SUPPORT
sigh 動
▶ WHISPER
SIGHT 名 p.704
sight 名
▶ LOOK 名, SIGHT, VIEW 2
sight 動
▶ SEE
sightseeing 名
▶ TRAVEL
sightseer 名
▶ TOURIST
SIGN 名 p.705
sign 名
▶ SIGN 1, 2, SIGNAL
sign 動
▶ EMPLOY, WRITE
SIGNAL 名 p.706
signal 名
▶ SIGN 1, SIGNAL
signal 動
▶ MEAN 動 1
significance 名
▶ IMPORTANCE, MEANING
significant 形
▶ IMPORTANT
signify 動
▶ MEAN 動 1
SILENCE 名 p.706
silence 名
▶ SILENCE

SILENT 形 *p.707*
silent 形
▶ QUIET 1, 2, 3, SILENT
silhouette 名
▶ SHAPE
silly 形
▶ CRAZY, RIDICULOUS
similar 形
▶ LIKE 前 形
SIMILARITY 名 *p.707*
similarity 名
▶ SIMILARITY
simper 動
▶ SMILE
simple 形
▶ AVERAGE, EASY 1, PLAIN 1, 2
simultaneous 形
▶ PARALLEL
sin 名
▶ CRIME 2, EVIL 名
sincere 形
▶ DEEP 1, HONEST
sinful 形
▶ EVIL 形
SINGLE 形 *p.708*
single 形
▶ PARTICULAR, SINGLE
single sb/sth out
▶ CHOOSE
sink 動
▶ FALL 1, 2
sinner 名
▶ CRIMINAL
sip 動
▶ DRINK 動
siphon 動
▶ PUMP
sissy 名
▶ COWARD
SIT 動 *p.709*
sit 動
▶ SIT
sit back
▶ REST
sit down
▶ SIT
site 名
▶ PLACE
site 動
▶ BASE
SITUATION 名 *p.709*
situation 名
▶ SITUATION
sixth sense 名
▶ INSTINCT
sizeable 形
▶ LARGE
size sb/sth up
▶ JUDGE 動
sketch 名
▶ PICTURE, PLAY 名, SUMMARY
sketch 動
▶ DRAW

skilful 形
▶ GOOD 4
SKILL 名 *p.710*
skill 名
▶ SKILL 1, 2
skilled 形
▶ GOOD 4
skim 動
▶ READ
skimp 動
▶ SAVE 2
skinny 形
▶ THIN
skirmish 名
▶ WAR
slab 名
▶ PIECE
slam 動
▶ CLOSE 動, CRASH
slant 動
▶ LEAN
slap 動
▶ HIT 2
slash 動
▶ CUT 1
slay 動
▶ KILL
slaying 名
▶ MURDER
SLEEP 動 *p.712*
sleep 動
▶ SLEEP
sleepy 形
▶ QUIET 1, TIRED
slender 形
▶ THIN
slice 名
▶ PIECE
slice 動
▶ CUT 2
SLIGHT 形 *p.712*
slight 形
▶ SLIGHT, THIN
slim 形
▶ THIN
slimy 形
▶ SOFT
slip 名
▶ MISTAKE 2
slip 動
▶ WORSEN
sliver 名
▶ FRAGMENT
SLOGAN 名 *p.713*
slogan 名
▶ SLOGAN
slope 動
▶ LEAN
slot 名
▶ HOLE 1
SLOW 形 *p.713*
slow 形
▶ LATE, SLOW
slowdown 名
▶ RECESSION

sluggish 形
▶ SLOW
SLUMP 動 *p.714*
slump 名
▶ RECESSION, REDUCTION
slump 動
▶ SLUMP
smack 動
▶ HIT 2
SMALL 形 *p.714*
small 形
▶ SLIGHT, SMALL
the small hours
▶ NIGHT 1
the small print 名
▶ CONDITION
smart 形
▶ ELEGANT, FASHIONABLE, INTELLIGENT
smarts 名
▶ INTELLIGENCE
smash 動
▶ CRASH
smear 名
▶ MARK
SMELL 名 *p.715*
smell 名
▶ ODOUR, SMELL
SMILE 名 *p.715*
smile 動
▶ SMILE
smirk 動
▶ SMILE
smitten 形
▶ IN LOVE
smooth 形
▶ FLAT
smudge 名
▶ MARK
snag 名
▶ DISADVANTAGE
snake 動
▶ CURVE
snap 動
▶ BREAK 1
snap sth up
▶ BUY
snatch 動
▶ TAKE 3
sneer 動
▶ LAUGH AT SB/STH
sneeze 動
▶ COUGH
snicker 動
▶ LAUGH
sniff sb/sth out
▶ FIND 4
snigger 動
▶ LAUGH
snivel 動
▶ CRY
snooze 動
▶ SLEEP

snowy 形
▶ FREEZING
snug 形
▶ COMFORTABLE
snuggle 動
▶ HUG
so 副
▶ FACT, VERY 副
SOAK 動 *p.716*
soak 動
▶ SOAK
soaked 形
▶ WET
SOAR 動 *p.717*
soar 動
▶ SOAR
sob 動
▶ CRY
sober 形
▶ SERIOUS 2
SOCIABLE 形 *p.717*
sociable 形
▶ SOCIABLE
SOCIAL 形 *p.718*
social 形
▶ SOCIABLE, SOCIAL
social security 名
▶ AID
society 名
▶ ELITE, UNION
sock 名
▶ HIT 2
sodden 形
▶ WET
SOFT 形 *p.718*
soft 形
▶ DIM, PALE, QUIET 2, SENSITIVE 1, SOFT
soften 動
▶ EASE
soggy 形
▶ SOFT
SOIL 名 *p.718*
soil 名
▶ SOIL
soiled 形
▶ DIRTY
solemn 形
▶ SERIOUS 2
solicitor 名
▶ LAWYER
SOLID 形 *p.719*
solid 形
▶ GOOD 3, SOLID
solid 名
▶ MATERIAL
SOLITARY 形 *p.720*
solitary 形
▶ SOLITARY
SOLUTION 名 *p.720*
solution 名
▶ SOLUTION
sombre 形
▶ SERIOUS 2
SOMETIMES 副 *p.721*

sometimes 副
▶ SOMETIMES
somewhat 副
▶ PARTLY
sonorous 形
▶ DEEP 2
soothe 動
▶ EASE
sop 名
▶ COMPROMISE
SOPHISTICATED 形 *p.721*
sophisticated 形
▶ SOPHISTICATED
sore 形
▶ PAINFUL 1
sore 名
▶ TUMOUR
sorrow 名
▶ GRIEF
SORRY 形 *p.722*
sorry 形
▶ SORRY, UNFORTUNATE 2, UPSET
SORRY FOR SB 動 *p.722*
sort 名
▶ KIND 名
sort 動
▶ CLASSIFY
sort sth out
▶ ARRANGE, ORGANIZE, TIDY
soul 名
▶ MIND, PERSON
sound 連結動
▶ SEEM
sound 形
▶ GOOD 3
sour 形
▶ BITTER, ROTTEN
sour 動
▶ INFLUENCE 1
SOURCE 名 *p.723*
source 名
▶ SOURCE
sovereignty 名
▶ INDEPENDENCE
space 名
▶ HOLE 1, LAND 2
spank 動
▶ HIT 2
spare 形
▶ EXCESS, FREE 形 3
spare time 名
▶ LEISURE
sparkle 動
▶ SHINE
sparse 形
▶ INADEQUATE
spasm 名
▶ SHIVER
speak 動
▶ MENTION, SAY 1, TALK
spearhead 動
▶ LEAD

SPECIAL 形 *p.724*
special 形
▶ SPECIAL, UNIQUE
specialism 名
▶ AREA 2
specialist 名
▶ EXPERT
specialty 名
▶ AREA 2
specific 形
▶ EXACT, PARTICULAR
specify 動
▶ LIST 動
specimen 名
▶ EXAMPLE 1
speck 名
▶ BIT, MARK
spectacle 名
▶ PERFORMANCE
spectacular 形
▶ IMPRESSIVE, MAGNIFICENT
spectator 名
▶ AUDIENCE
spectrum 名
▶ RANGE 2
speculate 動
▶ SAY 3
SPECULATION 名 *p.724*
speculation 名
▶ SPECULATION
speculative 形
▶ SUPPOSED
SPEECH 名 *p.725*
speech 名
▶ SPEECH
speechless 形
▶ SILENT
SPEED 名 *p.725*
speed 名
▶ SPEED
speed 動
▶ ACCELERATE
speed up
▶ ACCELERATE
speedy 形
▶ QUICK
spell 名
▶ INTEREST 1
spell sth out
▶ EXPLAIN 1
spending 名
▶ COSTS
spew 動
▶ FLOW
sphere 名
▶ AREA 2
spicy 形
▶ STRONG 2
spill over
▶ FLOOD
SPIN 動 *p.725*
spin 動
▶ SPIN, TURN 1

spiral 名
▶ INCREASE 名
spiral 動
▶ SOAR
spirit 名
▶ ATMOSPHERE, DETERMINATION, DRINK 名, MIND, NATURE 1
spirited 形
▶ LIVELY
spirits 名
▶ MOOD
splash 名
▶ DROP
splinter 名
▶ FRAGMENT
split 名
▶ DIVISION 1, 2
split 動
▶ DIVIDE 1, 2, SHARE 動, TEAR
split second 名
▶ MINUTE
split up
▶ DIVIDE 1
spoil 動
▶ RUIN
spongy 形
▶ SOFT
SPONSOR 名 *p.726*
sponsor 名
▶ SPONSOR
sponsor 動
▶ FUND
sponsorship 名
▶ INVESTMENT
SPONTANEOUS 形 *p.727*
spontaneous 形
▶ SPONTANEOUS
spoof 名
▶ PARODY
spook 動
▶ FRIGHTEN
spooky 形
▶ FRIGHTENING
sporadic 形
▶ OCCASIONAL
SPORT 名 *p.727*
sport 名
▶ SPORT
spot 名
▶ MARK, PLACE
spot 動
▶ SEE
spotless 形
▶ CLEAN 形
sprain 動
▶ INJURE
spray 動
▶ MOISTURE
SPREAD 動 *p.728*
spread 動
▶ SPREAD

springy 形
▶ FLEXIBLE 2
sprint 動
▶ RUN 1
spurious 形
▶ MISLEADING
spurt 動
▶ FLOW
squabble 名
▶ ARGUMENT 1
squabble 動
▶ ARGUE
squad 名
▶ TEAM 1, 2
squeal 動
▶ SCREAM
squeeze 動
▶ PACK, PRESS 1, PUMP
squint 動
▶ STARE
squishy 形
▶ SOFT
stab 名
▶ ATTEMPT
stab sb in the back
▶ TELL 2
stable 形
▶ FIRM, STEADY
STAFF 名 *p.728*
staff 名
▶ STAFF, WORKER 2
staff member 名
▶ WORKER 1
STAGE 名 *p.729*
stage 名
▶ DRAMA, STAGE
stage 動
▶ PLAY 動 2
stagger 動
▶ SURPRISE
staggering 形
▶ AMAZING
staid 形
▶ FORMAL
stain 名
▶ MARK
stain 動
▶ PAINT
stained 形
▶ DIRTY
stake 名
▶ INVOLVEMENT
stale 形
▶ ROTTEN
stalk 動
▶ FOLLOW 1
STALL 名 *p.729*
stall 名
▶ STALL
stall 動
▶ HOLD SB/STH UP
stamp 名
▶ LOGO
stampede 動
▶ RUN 1

stance 名
▶ ATTITUDE, POSITION
STAND 動 p.729
stand 名
▶ ATTITUDE, STALL
stand 動
▶ HATE, REMAIN, STAND 1, 2
standard 形
▶ USUAL
standard 名
▶ CRITERION, QUALITY
standards 名
▶ PRINCIPLE 1
stand down
▶ LEAVE 3
stand for sth
▶ SUPPORT
stand-in 名
▶ REPLACEMENT
stand in for sb/sth
▶ REPLACE 1
standing 名
▶ CLASS 3
stand on your own (two) feet
▶ TAKE CARE OF YOURSELF
stand up
▶ STAND 1
stand up for sb/sth
▶ EXPLAIN 2
stand up to sb
▶ OPPOSE
STAR 名 p.730
star 名
▶ STAR
star 動
▶ FEATURE 動
stardom 名
▶ FAME
STARE 動 p.731
stare 名
▶ LOOK 名
stare 動
▶ STARE
stark 形
▶ PLAIN 1, 2
START 名 p.731
START 動 p.732
start 名
▶ OPPORTUNITY, START 名
start 動
▶ BEGIN, START 動, TURN STH ON
starting point
▶ SOURCE
startle 動
▶ SURPRISE
startled 形
▶ AFRAID
start off
▶ START 動

start sth up
▶ TURN STH ON
starving 形
▶ HUNGRY
stash 名
▶ FUND 名
stash 動
▶ KEEP 1
STATE 名 p.733
state 名
▶ COUNTRY 1, COUNTY, STATE
state 形
▶ DECLARE, LIST 動
state 形
▶ PUBLIC
STATEMENT 名 p.733
statement 名
▶ STATEMENT
state of affairs 名
▶ SITUATION
state of the art 形
▶ MODERN
statesman 名
▶ POLITICIAN
static 形
▶ STEADY
stationary 形
▶ STILL
statistics 名
▶ FIGURE
stats 名
▶ FIGURE
stature 名
▶ REPUTATION
STATUS 名 p.734
status 名
▶ CLASS 3, STATUS
statute 名
▶ RULE 名
statutory 形
▶ LEGAL
staunch 形
▶ RELIABLE 1
STAY 動 p.734
stay 名
▶ VISIT 名
stay 動
▶ REMAIN, STAY 1, 2
stay put
▶ STAY 1
STEADY 形 p.735
steady 形
▶ FIRM, STEADY
STEAL 動 p.736
steal 動
▶ STEAL
steamy 形
▶ HUMID
steely 形
▶ STERN
steep 形
▶ HIGH 1
stem from sth
▶ FOLLOW 2

stench 名
▶ ODOUR
STEP 名 p.737
step 名
▶ ACTION, STAGE, STEP
step 動
▶ WALK 1
step down
▶ LEAVE 3
step sth up
▶ INCREASE 動
stereotypical 形
▶ TYPICAL
sterile 形
▶ CLEAN 形
sterling 形
▶ GOOD 1
STERN 形 p.737
stern 形
▶ STERN
stick 動
▶ ATTACH, PUSH 1, PUT
stick around
▶ STAY 1
stick up for sb/sth
▶ EXPLAIN 2
stick with sb/sth
▶ CONTINUE 2
stick your neck out
▶ DARE
stiff 形
▶ FORMAL, SOLID, TIGHT
stifle 動
▶ SUPPRESS 2
stifling 形
▶ HUMID
STILL 形 p.737
still 形
▶ STILL
stimulant 名
▶ DRUG 1
STIMULATE 動 p.738
stimulate 動
▶ INSPIRE, STIMULATE
stimulating 形
▶ INTERESTING
stimulus 名
▶ INCENTIVE
sting 名
▶ CONSPIRACY
sting 動
▶ HURT 1, 2
stink 動
▶ ODOUR
stipulate 動
▶ DEMAND 動
STIR 動 p.738
stir 動
▶ STIMULATE, STIR
stirring 形
▶ EXCITING
stock 名
▶ SUPPLY
stock 動
▶ EQUIP, SELL 2

stockpile 名
▶ SUPPLY
stockpile 動
▶ KEEP 1
stock up
▶ KEEP 1
STOP 動 p.738
stop 動
▶ END 動, PREVENT, STAY 1, STOP
stop by
▶ VISIT 動
stopover 名
▶ VISIT 名
stop over
▶ STAY 2
store 名
▶ SUPPLY
store 動
▶ KEEP 1, 3
storey 名
▶ FLOOR
storm 動
▶ ATTACK 動 2
stormy 形
▶ ROUGH
STORY 名 p.739
story 名
▶ LIE, REPORT 2, STORY
storyline 名
▶ STORY
stout 形
▶ FAT
straight 形
▶ HONEST
straightforward 形
▶ EASY 1, HONEST
strain 名
▶ PRESSURE 1
strain 動
▶ INJURE
strained 形
▶ STRESSFUL, TENSE
straits 名
▶ MESS 2
strand 動
▶ LEAVE 4
STRANGE 形 p.740
strange 形
▶ STRANGE 1, 2
strap 動
▶ ATTACH
strategy 名
▶ PLAN 1
straw poll 名
▶ ELECTION
streak 名
▶ MARK
stream 名
▶ FLOOD 名 2
stream 動
▶ FLOW
street 名
▶ ROAD

strength 名
▶ BENEFIT, FORCE
strenuous 形
▶ HARD
STRESS 動 p.741
stress 名
▶ PRESSURE 1, PRIORITY
stress 動
▶ STRESS
stressed 形
▶ TENSE
STRESSFUL 形 p.742
stressful 形
▶ STRESSFUL
stretch 動
▶ EXPAND
STRICT p.743
strict 形
▶ STRICT
stride 名
▶ STEP
stride 動
▶ WALK 1
strike 名
▶ ATTACK 名 1
strike 動
▶ ATTACK 動 1, 2, HIT 1, 2
strike 連結動詞
▶ SEEM
strike sth out
▶ DELETE
striking 形
▶ BEAUTIFUL 1, MARKED
string 名
▶ SERIES
stringent 形
▶ STRICT
strip 動
▶ TAKE STH OFF
strip mall 名
▶ MARKET 2
strive 動
▶ TRY 1
stroll 動
▶ WALK 1
STRONG 形 p.744
strong 形
▶ CONVINCING, POWERFUL, STRONG 1, 2, WELL
strong-willed 形
▶ STUBBORN
STRUCTURE 名 p.744
structure 名
▶ EFFICIENCY, STRUCTURE
struggle 名
▶ CAMPAIGN 名, EFFORT, FIGHT
struggle 動
▶ COMPETE, FIGHT 動, RESIST, TRY 1
struggle along/on
▶ PERSIST

STUBBORN 形 p.745
stubborn 形
▶ STUBBORN
stubby 形
▶ SHORT 2
studious 形
▶ INTELLECTUAL 2
study 名
▶ EDUCATION, REPORT 1, RESEARCH
study 動
▶ EXAMINE, LEARN
stuff 名
▶ MATERIAL, NATURE 1, THING 2
stuff 動
▶ EAT, PACK, PUT
stuffed 形
▶ FULL
stuffy 形
▶ FORMAL, HUMID
stumble 動
▶ FALL 3
stumble on/upon/across sb/sth
▶ FIND 2
stumbling block 名
▶ OBSTACLE
stun 動
▶ SURPRISE
stunning 形
▶ AMAZING, BEAUTIFUL 1
stunt 名
▶ ACTION
stunt 動
▶ HOLD SB/STH UP
stunted 形
▶ SHORT 2
STUPID 形 p.745
stupid 形
▶ CRAZY, STUPID
STYLE 名 p.745
style 名
▶ FASHION, KIND 名, STYLE, WAY 1
stylish 形
▶ ELEGANT
suave 形
▶ SOPHISTICATED
subconscious 形
▶ UNCONSCIOUS
the/your subconscious 名
▶ MIND
subdivide 動
▶ DIVIDE 1
subdue 動
▶ SUPPRESS 1
SUBJECT 名 p.746
subject 名
▶ AREA 2, CITIZEN, SUBJECT
subjective 形
▶ OWN

subject matter 名
▶ MESSAGE
submit 動
▶ GIVE WAY, PRESENT 3
subscribe to sth
▶ IN FAVOUR (OF SB/STH)
subscription 名
▶ PAYMENT
subsequent 形
▶ NEXT
subsidize 動
▶ FUND
subsidy 名
▶ INVESTMENT
substance 名
▶ IMPORTANCE, MATERIAL, MESSAGE
substantial 形
▶ LARGE
substantiate 動
▶ CONFIRM 1
substitute 名
▶ REPLACEMENT
substitute 動
▶ REPLACE 2
substitute for sb/sth
▶ REPLACE 1
substitution 名
▶ EXCHANGE
subtle 形
▶ PALE
subtract 動
▶ DISCOUNT
SUCCEED 動 p.746
succeed 動
▶ ACHIEVE, SUCCEED
SUCCESSFUL 形 p.747
successful 形
▶ SUCCESSFUL 1, 2
succession 名
▶ SERIES
succinct 形
▶ SHORT 3
suck 動
▶ DRINK 動
suffer 動
▶ HAVE 3
sufferer 名
▶ PATIENT
SUFFER FROM STH 動 p.748
suffer from sth
▶ SUFFER FROM STH
suffering 名
▶ DISTRESS, PAIN
SUGGEST 動 p.748
suggest 動
▶ MEAN 動 2, PROPOSE, RECOMMEND 2, SUGGEST
SUGGESTION 名 p.749
suggestion 名
▶ PROPOSAL, SUGGESTION
suicide 名
▶ MURDER

suit 名
▶ CASE
suit 動
▶ MEET 4
suitable 形
▶ GOOD 2
suitor 名
▶ PARTNER 2
sulk 動
▶ TEMPER
sulky 形
▶ IRRITABLE
sullen 形
▶ IRRITABLE
sultry 形
▶ HUMID
sum 名
▶ NUMBER
SUMMARY 名 p.749
summary 名
▶ SUMMARY
summit 名
▶ HILL, MEETING 1
sundown 名
▶ NIGHT 2
SUNNY 形 p.750
sunny 形
▶ SUNNY
sunset 名
▶ NIGHT 2
superb 形
▶ EXCELLENT
superficial 形
▶ APPARENT
superfluous 形
▶ EXCESS
superintend 動
▶ REGULATE
superintendent 名
▶ MANAGER
superior 形
▶ BETTER, GOOD 1, TOP
superpower 名
▶ COUNTRY 1
supersonic 形
▶ FAST
superstar 名
▶ STAR
supervise 動
▶ REGULATE
supervision 名
▶ GOVERNMENT 2
supervisor 名
▶ MANAGER
supple 形
▶ FLEXIBLE 2
supplier 名
▶ DEALER
SUPPLY 名 p.750
supply 名
▶ SUPPLY
supply 動
▶ PROVIDE
SUPPORT 動 p.751

support 名
 ▶ EVIDENCE, HELP 名
support 動
 ▶ CONFIRM 1, FUND 動,
   HELP 動 1, SUPPORT
supporter 名
 ▶ FAN
SUPPOSE 動 p.752
suppose 動
 ▶ SAY 3, SUPPOSE
SUPPOSED 形 p.752
supposed 形
 ▶ SUPPOSED
SUPPRESS 動 p.753
suppress 動
 ▶ SUPPRESS 1, 2
SURE 形 p.755
sure 形
 ▶ CERTAIN, SURE
surge 名
 ▶ INCREASE 名
surge 動
 ▶ SOAR
surgery 名
 ▶ TREATMENT
surplus 形
 ▶ EXCESS
surplus 名
 ▶ PROFIT
SURPRISE 動 p.755
surprise 動
 ▶ SURPRISE
SURPRISING 形 p.756
surprising 形
 ▶ SURPRISING
surrogate 名
 ▶ REPLACEMENT
surroundings 名
 ▶ ENVIRONMENT
surveillance 名
 ▶ INSPECTION
SURVEY 動 p.757
survey 動
 ▶ INSPECTION,
   INVESTIGATION,
   REPORT 1
survey 動
 ▶ EXAMINE, SURVEY
survival 名
 ▶ LIFE 1
SURVIVE 動 p.757
survive 動
 ▶ SURVIVE
SUSPECT 動 p.758
suspect 動
 ▶ SUPPOSE, SUSPECT
suspect 形
 ▶ SUSPICIOUS 2
suspend 動
 ▶ DELAY
suspicion 名
 ▶ DOUBT 名 2, IDEA 2,
   SCEPTICISM
SUSPICIOUS 形 p.758

suspicious 形
 ▶ SUSPICIOUS 1, 2
sustain 動
 ▶ APPROVE, MAINTAIN
swallow 動
 ▶ EAT
swap 名
 ▶ EXCHANGE
swap 動
 ▶ REPLACE 2, SWITCH
swat 動
 ▶ HIT 2
sway 動
 ▶ INFLUENCE 動
swear 動
 ▶ PROMISE 動
sweep 動
 ▶ BRUSH
sweeping 形
 ▶ WIDE 1
SWEET 形 p.759
sweet 形
 ▶ KIND 形, SWEET
sweetheart 名
 ▶ DARLING, PARTNER 2
sweetie 名
 ▶ DARLING
swelling 名
 ▶ TUMOUR
swift 形
 ▶ QUICK
swig 動
 ▶ DRINK 動
swindle 動
 ▶ DEFRAUD
swindler 名
 ▶ CHEAT 名
swing 名
 ▶ CHANGE 名 1
swing 動
 ▶ CHANGE 動 2, TURN 1
swish 動
 ▶ SHAKE 1
SWITCH 動 p.760
switch 名
 ▶ BUTTON 1,
   CHANGE 名 2
switch 動
 ▶ REPLACE 2, SWITCH
switch sth off
 ▶ TURN STH OFF
switch sth on
 ▶ TURN STH ON
swivel 動
 ▶ SPIN, TURN 1
syllabus 名
 ▶ CLASS 1
symbol 名
 ▶ SIGN 1
symbolic 形
 ▶ TYPICAL
symbolize 動
 ▶ REPRESENT 2
sympathetic 形
 ▶ SENSITIVE 1

sympathize 動
 ▶ SORRY FOR SB
SYMPATHY 名 p.760
sympathy 名
 ▶ SYMPATHY
symptom 名
 ▶ SIGN 1
synagogue 名
 ▶ CHURCH
syndicate 名
 ▶ GROUP 3
synonymous 形
 ▶ EQUAL
synopsis 名
 ▶ SUMMARY
synthetic 形
 ▶ ARTIFICIAL
SYSTEM 名 p.761
system 名
 ▶ AUTHORITIES, SYSTEM,
   WAY 2
systematic 形
 ▶ EFFICIENT

T

tab 名
 ▶ BILL
table 名
 ▶ LIST 2
table 動
 ▶ PRESENT 3
taboo 形
 ▶ FORBIDDEN
taboo 名
 ▶ BAN 名
taciturn 形
 ▶ QUIET 3
tackle 動
 ▶ EQUIPMENT
TACT 名 p.762
tact 名
 ▶ TACT
TACTIC 名 p.762
tactic 名
 ▶ TACTIC
tactless 形
 ▶ INSENSITIVE
tail 動
 ▶ FOLLOW 1
tailor 動
 ▶ CHANGE 動 1
tailor-made 形
 ▶ IDEAL
TAKE 動 p.762
take 名
 ▶ REVENUE
take 動
 ▶ BUY, CONSIDER,
   CONTINUE 1,
   DISCOUNT, GET 1,
   HAVE 3, INVADE,
   STAND 2, STEAL,
   TAKE 1, 2, 3, 4

take (a) hold
 ▶ AFFECT
take sb aback
 ▶ SURPRISE
take a seat
 ▶ SIT
take sth back
 ▶ BREAK 4, RETURN 2
take sb's breath away
 ▶ IMPRESS
take care of sb
 ▶ LOOK AFTER SB
take care of sth
 ▶ DEAL WITH SB/STH
TAKE CARE OF YOURSELF
 動 p.765
take care of yourself
 ▶ TAKE CARE OF YOUR-
   SELF
take sb/sth for granted
 ▶ TRUST
take fright
 ▶ PANIC
take sb in
 ▶ CHEAT 動
take sth in
 ▶ INCLUDE, NOTICE,
   UNDERSTAND 1
take issue with sb
 ▶ DISAGREE
take it
 ▶ SUPPOSE
take it/things easy
 ▶ REST
take no notice
 ▶ IGNORE
take off
 ▶ FLEE
TAKE STH OFF p.765
take sth off
 ▶ TAKE STH OFF
take sth off sth
 ▶ DISCOUNT
take sb on
 ▶ COMPETE, EMPLOY
take sb/sth on
 ▶ TAKE 4
take sth on board
 ▶ AGREE
take sb/sth out
 ▶ KILL
take sth out
 ▶ GET 1
take sth out of sth
 ▶ DISCOUNT
take part
 ▶ JOIN
take place
 ▶ HAPPEN
take stock
 ▶ EXAMINE
take sth up
 ▶ BEGIN, CONTINUE 3,
   TAKE 4

INDEX

takings 名
▶ REVENUE
tale 名
▶ STORY
talent 名
▶ SKILL 1
talented 形
▶ GOOD 4
TALK 動 p.766
talk 名
▶ DISCUSSION, SPEECH
talk 動
▶ SAY 1, 2, TALK
talk sb into sth
▶ PERSUADE
talk sb out of sth
▶ DISCOURAGE 1
tall 形
▶ HIGH 2
tally 名
▶ ESTIMATE 名
tally 動
▶ COUNT
tangled 形
▶ COMPLEX
tantamount to sth
▶ EQUAL
tantrum 名
▶ TEMPER
tap 動
▶ KNOCK
tape 動
▶ ATTACH
TARGET 名 p.766
target 名
▶ TARGET
target 動
▶ FOCUS
tariff 名
▶ TAX
TASK 名 p.767
task 名
▶ TASK
task force 名
▶ COMMITTEE
TASTE 名 p.768
taste 名
▶ TASTE
taste 動
▶ EAT, FEEL, TRY 2
tasty 形
▶ DELICIOUS
taut 形
▶ TIGHT
TAX 名 p.769
tax 動
▶ TAX
taxing 形
▶ DIFFICULT 1
taxpayer 名
▶ CITIZEN
TEACH 動 p.769
teach 動
▶ TEACH, TRAIN 1
TEACHER 名 p.769

teacher 名
▶ TEACHER
teaching 名
▶ EDUCATION, VALUES
TEAM 名 p.770
team 名
▶ TEAM 1, 2
teammate 名
▶ PARTNER 1
TEAR 動 p.771
tear 動
▶ INJURE, RUN 1, TEAR
tear sth down
▶ DEMOLISH
tease 動
▶ FLIRT, LAUGH AT SB/STH
technique 名
▶ SKILL 2, WAY 2
tedious 形
▶ BORING
teen 形
▶ YOUNG
teen 名
▶ GIRL
teenage 形
▶ YOUNG
teenager 名
▶ GIRL
teens 名
▶ CHILDHOOD
telephone 動
▶ CALL 2
TELL 動 p.772
tell 動
▶ DESCRIBE, ORDER 1, TELL 1, 2
telling 形
▶ INFORMATIVE
tell sb off
▶ SCOLD
TEMPER 名 p.773
temper 動
▶ TEMPER
temperament 名
▶ PERSONALITY
temperate 形
▶ SUNNY
temple 名
▶ CHURCH
temporary 形
▶ SHORT 1
temptation 名
▶ DESIRE
tenacity 名
▶ DETERMINATION
TENANT 名 p.773
tenant 名
▶ TENANT
tend 動
▶ LOOK AFTER SB
TENDENCY 名 p.774
tendency 名
▶ TENDENCY, TREND

tender 形
▶ LOVING
tender 名
▶ OFFER 2
tenderness 名
▶ LOVE 名 2
tenet 名
▶ PRINCIPLE 2
TENSE 形 p.774
tense 形
▶ STRESSFUL, TENSE
tense 動
▶ TIGHTEN
TENSION 名 p.774
tension 名
▶ PRESSURE 1, TENSION
tepid 形
▶ COLD 1, INDIFFERENT
term 動
▶ CALL 1
terminal 形
▶ FATAL
terminate 動
▶ END 動
termination 名
▶ END 名
terminology 名
▶ LANGUAGE
terms 名
▶ CONDITION, LANGUAGE, RATE
terrace 名
▶ ROAD
terrain 名
▶ COUNTRY 2
TERRIBLE 形 p.775
terrible 形
▶ TERRIBLE 1, 2, 3
terrific 形
▶ GREAT 1
terrified 形
▶ AFRAID
terrify 動
▶ FRIGHTEN
terrifying 形
▶ FRIGHTENING
TERRITORY 名 p.777
territory 名
▶ TERRITORY
terror 名
▶ FEAR
terrorist 名
▶ GUERRILLA
TEST 名 p.777
TEST 動 p.778
test 名
▶ CRITERION, GAME, TEST 名 1, 2
test 動
▶ TEST 動 1, 2
testify 動
▶ CONFIRM 2
testify to sth
▶ CONFIRM 1

testimonial 名
▶ ENDORSEMENT
testimony 名
▶ EVIDENCE
testing 形
▶ DIFFICULT 1
testing 名
▶ TEST 名 1
text 名
▶ BOOK, LETTER
textbook 名
▶ BOOK
thankful 形
▶ GRATEFUL
THANKS 名 p.779
thanks 名
▶ THANKS
theatre 名
▶ DRAMA, HALL 1
THEFT 名 p.780
theft 名
▶ THEFT
theme 名
▶ SUBJECT
then 形
▶ FORMER
theorem 名
▶ THEORY 1
theoretical 形
▶ INTELLECTUAL 1, SUPPOSED
THEORY 名 p.780
theory 名
▶ THEORY 1, 2
therapy 名
▶ TREATMENT
there's no comparison
▶ SIMILARITY
thesis 名
▶ PAPER, THEORY 2
thick 形
▶ STUPID, WIDE 2
THIEF 名 p.781
thief 名
▶ THIEF
THIN 形 p.782
thin 形
▶ DIM, NARROW, THIN
THING 名 p.782
thing 名
▶ PERSON, THING 1
things 名
▶ SITUATION, THING 2
thingy 名
▶ THING 1
THINK 動 p.784
think 動
▶ CONSIDER, EXPECT, IMAGINE, THINK
think back
▶ REMEMBER
thinking 形
▶ INFORMED
think twice
▶ HESITATE

thorough 形
▶ DETAILED
thought 名
▶ CONSIDERATION, IDEA 1
thoughtful 形
▶ KIND 形
thoughtless 形
▶ INSENSITIVE
thrash 動
▶ DEFEAT
thread 名
▶ MESSAGE
THREAT 名 p.785
threat 名
▶ RISK 1, THREAT
THREATEN 動 p.785
threaten 動
▶ THREATEN
thrill 名
▶ EXCITEMENT
thrilled 形
▶ GLAD
thrilling 形
▶ EXCITING
thrive 動
▶ DO WELL
thriving 形
▶ SUCCESSFUL 2
throb 動
▶ HURT 2
throng 名
▶ CROWD
THROW 動 p.786
throw 動
▶ HAVE 4, THROW
throw sth away/out
▶ REMOVE
throw sth out
▶ REFUSE
thrust 動
▶ PUSH 1
the thrust 名
▶ MESSAGE
thumbs up
▶ APPROVAL
thump 動
▶ HIT 2
tic 名
▶ SHIVER
tickle 動
▶ HURT 2
tidal wave 名
▶ FLOOD 名 1
TIDY 動 p.786
tidy 動
▶ TIDY
tidy 形
▶ EFFICIENT, NEAT
tie 名
▶ GAME, RELATIONSHIP 1
tie 動
▶ ATTACH

tie in
▶ MATCH 1
tier 名
▶ FLOOR
tiff 名
▶ ARGUMENT 1
TIGHT 形 p.786
tight 形
▶ TIGHT
TIGHTEN 動 p.787
tighten 動
▶ TIGHTEN
tighten your belt
▶ SAVE 2
tilt 動
▶ LEAN
TIME 名 p.787
time 名
▶ PERIOD, TIME
TIMELY 形 p.788
timely 形
▶ TIMELY
time off 名
▶ HOLIDAY 1
timetable 名
▶ SCHEDULE
timid 形
▶ SHY
tingle 動
▶ HURT 2
tint 動
▶ PAINT
tiny 形
▶ SMALL
tip 名
▶ ADVICE, GIFT
tip 動
▶ LEAN
TIRED 形 p.789
tired 形
▶ TIRED
tiresome 形
▶ ANNOYING
title 名
▶ AWARD, BOOK, RIGHT 名
titter 動
▶ LAUGH
to be expected
▶ PREDICTABLE
to blame
▶ GUILTY
toddler 名
▶ CHILD
togetherness 名
▶ FRIENDSHIP
TOILET 名 p.789
toilet 名
▶ TOILET
tolerance 名
▶ PATIENCE
TOLERANT 形 p.790
tolerant 形
▶ TOLERANT

tolerate 動
▶ STAND 2
toll 名
▶ RATE
tone 名
▶ ATMOSPHERE
too bad
▶ UNFORTUNATE 2
TOOL 名 p.790
tool 名
▶ TOOL
too much 形
▶ UNACCEPTABLE
TOP 形 p.791
top 形
▶ TOP
top 名
▶ PEAK
the top brass 名
▶ AUTHORITIES
topic 名
▶ SUBJECT
topography 名
▶ COUNTRY 2
topple 動
▶ FALL 2
top sb/sth up
▶ FILL
torrent 名
▶ FLOOD 名 1, 2
tortuous 形
▶ COMPLEX
torture 名
▶ DISTRESS
to some extent
▶ PARTLY
toss 動
▶ THROW
total 形
▶ COMPLETE, WHOLE
total 名
▶ COUNT, CRASH
totalitarian 形
▶ REPRESSIVE
totally 副
▶ QUITE 2
to the point
▶ RELEVANT
tot sth up
▶ COUNT
TOUCH 動 p.792
touch 動
▶ IMPRESS, TOUCH
touchy 形
▶ SENSITIVE 3
tough 形
▶ DIFFICULT 2, STRICT
tour 名
▶ TRIP, VISIT 名
tourism 名
▶ TRAVEL
TOURIST 名 p.792
tourist 名
▶ TOURIST

tow 動
▶ PULL 1
towering 形
▶ HIGH 2
town 名
▶ CITY
trace 名
▶ SIGN 1
trace 動
▶ FIND 4
track 名
▶ PATH
track 動
▶ FOLLOW 1
track sb/sth down
▶ FIND 4
tract 名
▶ PAPER
TRADE 名 p.793
trade 名
▶ INDUSTRY, TRADE, WORK 名 1
trade 動
▶ REPLACE 2, SELL 2
trademark 名
▶ LOGO
trade-off 名
▶ COMPROMISE
trader 名
▶ DEALER
trade show 名
▶ EXHIBITION
trading 名
▶ TRADE
TRADITION 名 p.794
tradition 名
▶ TRADITION
TRADITIONAL 形 p.794
traditional 形
▶ TRADITIONAL, USUAL
traditionalist 形
▶ CONSERVATIVE
TRAFFIC 名 p.795
traffic 名
▶ TRAFFIC
traffic jam 名
▶ TRAFFIC
trafficking 名
▶ TRADE
tragedy 名
▶ CRISIS, PLAY 名
tragic 形
▶ SAD
trail 名
▶ PATH
trail 動
▶ FOLLOW 1, PULL 1
trailer 名
▶ ADVERTISEMENT
TRAIN 名 p.795
train 動
▶ TRAIN 1, 2
trainee 名
▶ RECRUIT
TRAINING 名 p.796

training 名
▶ EDUCATION, TRAINING
trait 名
▶ FEATURE 名
tranquil 形
▶ QUIET 1
tranquillity 名
▶ SILENCE
transcribe 動
▶ WRITE
transcript 名
▶ COPY 名 1
transfer 動
▶ GIVE 1
transform 動
▶ TURN 2
transit 名
▶ DELIVERY
transition 名
▶ CHANGE 名 2
translate 動
▶ TURN 2
translucent 形
▶ CLEAR 形 3
transparent 形
▶ CLEAR 形 3
transpire 動
▶ TURN OUT
transport 名
▶ DELIVERY
transport 動
▶ TAKE 1
trap 名
▶ TRICK
trash 名
▶ WASTE
traumatic 形
▶ PAINFUL 2
traumatize 動
▶ FRIGHTEN
TRAVEL 名 p.797
travel 名
▶ TRAVEL
travel 動
▶ GO 1, 2
travelling 名
▶ TRAVEL
travels 名
▶ TRIP
treacherous 形
▶ DANGEROUS
tread 動
▶ WALK 1
treasure 動
▶ APPRECIATE
treasured 形
▶ DEAR
treat 名
▶ PLEASURE
treatise 名
▶ PAPER
TREATMENT 名 p.797
treatment 名
▶ TREATMENT

treaty 名
▶ CONTRACT
treble 形
▶ HIGH 3
trek 動
▶ WALK 2
tremble 名
▶ SHIVER
tremble 動
▶ SHAKE 3
tremendous 形
▶ GREAT 1, HUGE
tremor 名
▶ SHIVER
TREND 名 p.798
trend 名
▶ FASHION, TREND
trendy 形
▶ FASHIONABLE
trial 名
▶ CASE, INTERVIEW 2, TEST 名 1
tribal 形
▶ CULTURAL
tribe 名
▶ PEOPLE
tribunal 名
▶ COURT
TRICK 名 p.798
trick 名
▶ TRICK
trick 動
▶ CHEAT 動
tricky 形
▶ SENSITIVE 2
trim 動
▶ DECORATE
TRIP 名 p.799
trip 名
▶ TRIP
trip 動
▶ FALL 3
triumph 動
▶ WIN
triumphant 形
▶ SUCCESSFUL 1
trivial 形
▶ MINOR
trooper 名
▶ POLICEMAN
trophy 名
▶ AWARD
trot 動
▶ RUN 1
TROUBLE 名 p.800
trouble 名
▶ ILLNESS, PROBLEM, TROUBLE 1, 2
trouble 動
▶ INTERRUPT, WORRY
troubled 形
▶ WORRIED
trough 名
▶ RECESSION

trounce 動
▶ DEFEAT
TRUE 形 p.800
true 形
▶ REAL, RELIABLE 1, TRUE
truly 副
▶ VERY 副
TRUST 動 p.801
trust 名
▶ CHARITY, FAITH
trust 動
▶ TRUST
trusted 形
▶ RELIABLE 1
trusting 形
▶ NAIVE
trustworthy 形
▶ RELIABLE 1
the truth 名
▶ FACT
truthful 形
▶ HONEST
TRY 動 p.802
try 名
▶ ATTEMPT
try 動
▶ TRY 1, 2
trying 形
▶ ANNOYING
tryout 名
▶ INTERVIEW 2
try sb/sth out
▶ TEST 動 1
tsunami 名
▶ FLOOD 名 1
tuck in
▶ EAT
tug 動
▶ PULL 1, 2
tuition 名
▶ EDUCATION
tumble 動
▶ FALL 2, SLUMP
TUMOUR 名 p.803
tumour 名
▶ TUMOUR
tune in
▶ HEAR
turbulent 形
▶ ROUGH
TURN 動 p.803
turn 名
▶ CORNER, OPPORTUNITY
turn 動
▶ CURVE, FOCUS, SPIN, TURN 1, 2
turn 連結動詞
▶ BECOME
turn a blind eye
▶ IGNORE
turn around/round
▶ TURN 1

turn back
▶ RETURN 1
turn sb/sth down
▶ REFUSE
turn sth down
▶ REDUCE
turn King's/Queen's evidence
▶ TELL 2
TURN STH OFF p.805
turn sth off
▶ TURN STH OFF
TURN STH ON p.806
turn sth on
▶ TURN STH ON
TURN OUT p.805
turn out
▶ HAPPEN
turn sb/sth out
▶ MANUFACTURE, TURN OUT
turn sth out
▶ TURN STH OFF
turnover 名
▶ REVENUE
turn up
▶ ARRIVE
turn sth up
▶ FIND 2, INCREASE 動
turn your back on sb/sth
▶ LEAVE 4
tussle 名
▶ FIGHT 名
tutor 名
▶ TEACHER
tutor 動
▶ TEACH
tutorial 名
▶ CLASS 2
tutoring 名
▶ EDUCATION
twilight 名
▶ NIGHT 2
twinkle 動
▶ SHINE
twirl 動
▶ SPIN
twist 名
▶ CORNER
twist 動
▶ CURVE, INJURE, SPIN, TURN 1
twist sb's arm
▶ PRESS 2
twitch 名
▶ SHIVER
twitch 動
▶ SHAKE 3
two-faced 形
▶ DISHONEST
tycoon 名
▶ EXECUTIVE
type 名
▶ KIND 名, PERSON

TYPICAL 形 p.807
typical 形
▶ NORMAL, TYPICAL
typify 動
▶ REPRESENT 2
tyrannical 形
▶ REPRESSIVE
tyranny 名
▶ REPRESSION
tyrant 名
▶ DICTATOR

U

ubiquitous 形
▶ GENERAL
UGLY 形 p.808
ugly 形
▶ UGLY
ulcer 名
▶ TUMOUR
ultimate 形
▶ FUNDAMENTAL, LAST 1
umpire 名
▶ JUDGE 名
UNACCEPTABLE 形 p.808
unacceptable 形
▶ UNACCEPTABLE
unaccustomed to sth 形
▶ NEW 3
unambiguous 形
▶ CLEAR 形 2
unattainable 形
▶ IMPOSSIBLE
unattractive 形
▶ UGLY
unauthorized 形
▶ UNOFFICIAL
unavoidable 形
▶ INEVITABLE
unbalanced 形
▶ BIASED
unbearable 形
▶ UNACCEPTABLE
unbelievable 形
▶ INCREDIBLE, REMARKABLE
unbiased 形
▶ OBJECTIVE
unbroken 形
▶ CONTINUOUS
unbutton 動
▶ UNDO
uncanny 形
▶ STRANGE 1
uncaring 形
▶ INSENSITIVE
uncertain 形
▶ UNCLEAR, UNSURE
uncertainty 名
▶ DOUBT 名 1, 2
unchallenged 形
▶ UNDOUBTED

unchanging 形
▶ STEADY
UNCLEAR 形 p.809
unclear 形
▶ UNCLEAR
uncluttered 形
▶ NEAT
uncomfortable 形
▶ EMBARRASSED
uncommon 形
▶ RARE
uncomplicated 形
▶ EASY 1
unconfirmed 形
▶ IRRATIONAL
UNCONSCIOUS 形 p.809
unconscious 形
▶ UNCONSCIOUS
unconstitutional 形
▶ ILLEGAL
uncontested 形
▶ UNDOUBTED
UNCONTROLLABLE 形 p.810
uncontrollable 形
▶ UNCONTROLLABLE
unconventional 形
▶ UNUSUAL
unconvincing 形
▶ UNLIKELY 2
uncover 動
▶ REVEAL
undecided 形
▶ UNCLEAR, UNSURE
undemanding 形
▶ EASY 1
undemocratic 形
▶ REPRESSIVE
underachiever 名
▶ LOSER 2
undergo 動
▶ HAVE 3
underhand 形
▶ DISHONEST
underline 動
▶ STRESS
underlying 形
▶ FUNDAMENTAL
under pressure
▶ TENSE
underscore 動
▶ STRESS
UNDERSTAND 動 p.810
understand 動
▶ CONCLUDE, UNDERSTAND 1, 2
understandable 形
▶ OBVIOUS
understanding 形
▶ SENSITIVE 1
UNDERSTANDING 名 p.812
understanding 名
▶ AGREEMENT, DEFINITION, SYMPATHY, UNDERSTANDING

understudy 名
▶ REPLACEMENT
undertake 動
▶ DO, PROMISE 動
undertaking 名
▶ PROJECT
underweight 形
▶ THIN
underwrite 動
▶ FUND 動
undesirable 形
▶ UNWANTED
undisclosed 形
▶ SECRET
undisputed 形
▶ UNDOUBTED
UNDO 動 p.813
undo 動
▶ UNDO
UNDOUBTED 形 p.813
undoubted 形
▶ UNDOUBTED
undress 動
▶ TAKE STH OFF
undressed 形
▶ NAKED
undue 形
▶ EXCESSIVE
unearth 動
▶ FIND 2
unease 名
▶ CONCERN
uneasy 形
▶ WORRIED
uneconomic 形
▶ LOSS-MAKING
uneducated 形
▶ IGNORANT
UNEMPLOYED 形 p.814
unemployed 形
▶ UNEMPLOYED
UNEMPLOYMENT 名 p.814
unemployment 名
▶ UNEMPLOYMENT
unequal 形
▶ DIFFERENT, WRONG 3
unequivocal 形
▶ PLAIN 2
unethical 形
▶ WRONG 3
uneven 形
▶ VARIABLE
unexpected 形
▶ SURPRISING
unfair 形
▶ WRONG 3
unfairness 名
▶ INEQUALITY
unfamiliar 形
▶ STRANGE 2
unfamiliar with sth 形
▶ NEW 3
unfasten 動
▶ UNDO

unfavourable 形
▶ DIFFICULT 2
unfazed 形
▶ CALM
unfit 形
▶ SICK 1, WRONG 2
unfold 動
▶ DESCRIBE, SPREAD
unforeseeable 形
▶ SURPRISING
unforeseen 形
▶ SURPRISING
unforgivable 形
▶ OUTRAGEOUS
unforgiving 形
▶ STERN
UNFORTUNATE 形 p.814
unfortunate 形
▶ UNFORTUNATE 1, 2
unfounded 形
▶ IRRATIONAL
unfriendly 形
▶ COLD 2
unhappiness 名
▶ GRIEF
UNHAPPY 形 p.816
unhappy 形
▶ UNHAPPY 1, 2
unharmed 形
▶ SAFE
unhealthy 形
▶ SICK 1
unhurried 形
▶ EASY 2
unhurt 形
▶ SAFE
uniform 形
▶ EQUAL
uniformity 名
▶ SIMILARITY
unify 動
▶ COMBINE
unimportant 形
▶ MINOR
unimpressed 形
▶ INDIFFERENT
uninformed 形
▶ IGNORANT
uninhabited 形
▶ DESERTED
uninhibited 形
▶ SOCIABLE
uninjured 形
▶ SAFE
unintelligible 形
▶ CONFUSING
unintended 形
▶ UNCONSCIOUS
unintentional 形
▶ UNCONSCIOUS
uninterested 形
▶ INDIFFERENT
uninteresting 形
▶ BORING

uninterrupted 形
  ▶ CONTINUOUS
uninvited 形
  ▶ UNWANTED
UNION 名 p.817
union 名
  ▶ UNION
UNIQUE 形 p.818
unique 形
  ▶ REMARKABLE, UNIQUE
uniqueness 名
  ▶ IDENTITY
unit 名
  ▶ ARMY, DEPARTMENT, ELEMENT
unite 動
  ▶ COMBINE
universal 形
  ▶ GENERAL
unjust 形
  ▶ WRONG 3
unkind 形
  ▶ MEAN 形
unknown 形
  ▶ STRANGE 2
unlawful 形
  ▶ ILLEGAL
unlicensed 形
  ▶ UNOFFICIAL
unlike 形
  ▶ DIFFERENT
UNLIKELY 形 p.819
unlikely 形
  ▶ UNLIKELY 1, 2
unlit 形
  ▶ DARK 1
unload 動
  ▶ CLEAR 動
unloved 形
  ▶ UNWANTED
unlucky 形
  ▶ UNFORTUNATE 1
unmanageable 形
  ▶ UNCONTROLLABLE
unmarried 形
  ▶ SINGLE
unmistakable 形
  ▶ MARKED
unmoved 形
  ▶ RUTHLESS
unnerving 形
  ▶ WORRYING
unoccupied 形
  ▶ DESERTED
UNOFFICIAL 形 p.820
unofficial 形
  ▶ UNOFFICIAL
unorthodox 形
  ▶ UNUSUAL
unpack 動
  ▶ CLEAR 動
unpaid 形
  ▶ VOLUNTARY 2
unperturbed 形
  ▶ CALM

unplanned 形
  ▶ UNCONSCIOUS
unpleasant 形
  ▶ BAD, MEAN 形
unplug 動
  ▶ TURN STH OFF
unpopular 形
  ▶ UNWANTED
unpredictable 形
  ▶ SURPRISING
unprincipled 形
  ▶ CORRUPT
unproductive 形
  ▶ INEFFECTIVE
unprofitable 形
  ▶ LOSS-MAKING
unquestioned 形
  ▶ UNDOUBTED
unreasonable 形
  ▶ HIGH 1, UNACCEPTABLE
unremarkable 形
  ▶ AVERAGE
unresolved 形
  ▶ UNCLEAR
unrest 名
  ▶ TROUBLE 1
unroll 動
  ▶ SPREAD
unruly 形
  ▶ WILD
unsafe 形
  ▶ DANGEROUS
unsatisfactory 形
  ▶ DISAPPOINTING
unscathed 形
  ▶ SAFE
unscientific 形
  ▶ IRRATIONAL
unscrupulous 形
  ▶ CORRUPT
unsettle 動
  ▶ WORRY
unsettled 形
  ▶ RESTLESS
unsettling 形
  ▶ WORRYING
unsightly 形
  ▶ UGLY
unsociable 形
  ▶ SOLITARY
unsolicited 形
  ▶ UNWANTED
unspoiled 形
  ▶ PERFECT
unsubstantiated 形
  ▶ IRRATIONAL
unsuitable 形
  ▶ WRONG 2
unsupported 形
  ▶ IRRATIONAL
UNSURE 形 p.820
unsure 形
  ▶ UNSURE

unsurprising 形
  ▶ PREDICTABLE
unsympathetic 形
  ▶ INSENSITIVE
unsystematic 形
  ▶ RANDOM
unthinkable 形
  ▶ IMPOSSIBLE
unthinking 形
  ▶ INSENSITIVE
UNTIDY 形 p.821
untidy 形
  ▶ RANDOM, UNTIDY
untie 動
  ▶ UNDO
untrained 形
  ▶ IGNORANT
untried 形
  ▶ NEW 2
untrue 形
  ▶ WRONG 1
unusable 形
  ▶ USELESS
unused to sth 形
  ▶ NEW 3
UNUSUAL 形 p.821
unusual 形
  ▶ REMARKABLE, UNUSUAL
unveil 動
  ▶ PRESENT 1
UNWANTED 形 p.822
unwanted 形
  ▶ UNWANTED
unwashed 形
  ▶ DIRTY
unwelcome 形
  ▶ UNWANTED
unwell 形
  ▶ SICK 1
unwilling 形
  ▶ RELUCTANT
unwind 動
  ▶ REST
unwise 形
  ▶ RECKLESS
unwrap 動
  ▶ UNDO
unzip 動
  ▶ UNDO
up and running
  ▶ ACTIVE
upbeat 形
  ▶ OPTIMISTIC
upcoming 形
  ▶ NEXT
uphold 動
  ▶ APPROVE
uplift 動
  ▶ ENCOURAGE
the upper class 名
  ▶ ELITE
uprising 名
  ▶ REVOLUTION
UPSET 形 p.822

upset 形
  ▶ UPSET
upset 名
  ▶ VICTORY
upset 動
  ▶ HURT 1
upsetting 形
  ▶ PAINFUL 2
upshot 名
  ▶ RESULT
uptight 形
  ▶ TENSE
up to a point
  ▶ PARTLY
up to date 形
  ▶ MODERN, USED TO STH
upturn 名
  ▶ INCREASE 名
urbane 形
  ▶ SOPHISTICATED
urge 名
  ▶ DESIRE
urge 動
  ▶ RECOMMEND 1
urgency 名
  ▶ IMPORTANCE
URGENT 形 p.823
urgent 形
  ▶ URGENT
urinal 名
  ▶ TOILET
usable 形
  ▶ USEFUL
usage 名
  ▶ LANGUAGE
USE 名 p.823
USE 動 p.824
use 名
  ▶ USE 名
use 動
  ▶ USE 動 1, 2
USED TO STH 形 p.826
used to sth
  ▶ USED TO STH
USEFUL 形 p.826
useful 形
  ▶ USEFUL
USELESS 形 p.827
useless 形
  ▶ INCOMPETENT, USELESS
use sth up
  ▶ USE 動 2
usher 動
  ▶ TAKE 2
USUAL 形 p.827
usual 形
  ▶ USUAL
USUALLY 副 p.828
usually 副
  ▶ USUALLY
utensil 名
  ▶ TOOL
utility 名
  ▶ FACILITIES

V

utilize 動
▶ USE 動 1
utter
▶ COMPLETE
utterly 副
▶ QUITE 2

vacancy 名
▶ JOB
vacant 形
▶ EMPTY
vacation 名
▶ HOLIDAY 1, 2
vacationer 名
▶ TOURIST
VAGUE 形 p.830
vague 形
▶ VAGUE
vain 形
▶ PROUD 2, USELESS
valid 形
▶ GOOD 3, LEGAL
validate 動
▶ APPROVE, CONFIRM 1
valour 名
▶ COURAGE
VALUABLE 形 p.830
valuable 形
▶ VALUABLE 1, 2
valuables 名
▶ THING 2
VALUATION 名 p.832
valuation 名
▶ VALUATION
VALUE 名 p.832
value 名
▶ PRICE, VALUE
value 動
▶ APPRECIATE
VALUES 名 p.833
values 名
▶ VALUES
vanish 動
▶ DISAPPEAR
vanity 名
▶ PRIDE
vanquish 動
▶ DEFEAT
variability 名
▶ CHANGE 名 1
VARIABLE 形 p.833
variable 形
▶ VARIABLE
variance 名
▶ DIFFERENCE
variation 名
▶ CHANGE 名 1, DIFFERENCE
varied 形
▶ DIVERSE
variety 名
▶ KIND 名, RANGE 1

vary 動
▶ CHANGE 動 1, 2, DIFFER
vast 形
▶ HUGE
vault 動
▶ JUMP
Velcro™ 名
▶ BUTTON 2
velocity 名
▶ SPEED
vendor 名
▶ DEALER
vengeance 名
▶ REVENGE
venture 名
▶ PROJECT
venture 動
▶ DARE
venue 名
▶ PLACE
verdict 名
▶ CONCLUSION
verifiable 形
▶ RELIABLE 2
verify 動
▶ CHECK 2, CONFIRM 2
versatile 形
▶ FLEXIBLE 1
version 名
▶ KIND 名, REPORT 2
VERY 形 p.834
VERY 副 p.834
very 形
▶ VERY
very 副
▶ VERY
veteran 形
▶ EXPERIENCED
veto 名
▶ BAN 名, REFUSAL
veto 動
▶ REFUSE
viable 形
▶ POSSIBLE 1
vibrant 形
▶ BRIGHT, CROWDED
vibrate 動
▶ SHAKE 2
vice 名
▶ CRIME 1, EVIL 名
vicious 形
▶ CRUEL
vicious circle 名
▶ MESS 2
victim 名
▶ PATIENT
victorious 形
▶ SUCCESSFUL 1
VICTORY 名 p.835
victory 名
▶ VICTORY
vie 動
▶ COMPETE
VIEW 名 p.836

view 名
▶ ATTITUDE, SIGHT, VIEW 1, 2
view 動
▶ CHECK 1, LOOK 1, REGARD
viewer 名
▶ AUDIENCE
vigorous 形
▶ ENERGETIC
vile 形
▶ TERRIBLE 1
village 名
▶ CITY
violate 動
▶ BREAK 3
VIOLENT 形 p.837
violent 形
▶ INTENSE, ROUGH, VIOLENT
virtual 形
▶ FICTIONAL
virtually 副
▶ ALMOST
virtue 名
▶ BENEFIT, MORALITY
virtuoso 形
▶ IMPRESSIVE
virtuous 形
▶ GOOD 5
virus 名
▶ DEFECT, DISEASE
VISIBLE 形 p.838
visible 形
▶ VISIBLE
vision 名
▶ IMAGINATION, INSPIRATION, SIGHT
VISIT 名 p.838
VISIT 動 p.839
visit 名
▶ VISIT
visit 動
▶ CHECK 1, STAY 2, VISIT
visitor 名
▶ TOURIST
visualize 動
▶ IMAGINE
vital 形
▶ ESSENTIAL
vivacious 形
▶ LIVELY
vivid 形
▶ BRIGHT
vocabulary 名
▶ LANGUAGE
vogue 名
▶ FASHION
voice 動
▶ SAY 2
volley 名
▶ FLOOD 名 2
volume 名
▶ BOOK, NUMBER

VOLUNTARY 形 p.839
voluntary 形
▶ VOLUNTARY 1, 2
vote 名
▶ ELECTION
vote 動
▶ SUPPORT
vote sb in
▶ APPOINT
voter 名
▶ CITIZEN
vouch for sb/sth
▶ CONFIRM 2
vow 名
▶ PROMISE 名
vow 動
▶ PROMISE 動
VULNERABLE 形 p.840
vulnerable 形
▶ VULNERABLE

W

wag 動
▶ SHAKE 1
wage 名
▶ INCOME
wail 動
▶ SCREAM
wait 動
▶ DELAY, HOPE 動
WALK 動 p.841
walk 動
▶ TAKE 2, WALK 1, 2
walk out
▶ LEAVE 4
walkway 名
▶ CORRIDOR
WANT 動 p.842
want 名
▶ DESIRE, NEED 名
want 動
▶ NEED 動, WANT
wanting 形
▶ DISAPPOINTING
WAR 名 p.842
war 名
▶ CAMPAIGN 名, DEBATE, WAR
wardrobe 名
▶ CLOTHES
warfare 名
▶ WAR
warlike 形
▶ AGGRESSIVE 1
warm 形
▶ DARK 2, FRIENDLY 1, HOT
warm 動
▶ HEAT
warm up
▶ TRAIN 2
warm sth up
▶ HEAT

warn sb off
- ▶ DISCOURAGE 1

warrant
- ▶ LICENCE

WASH 動 *p.843*

wash 動
- ▶ CLEAN 動, WASH

washout 名
- ▶ DISASTER

wash up
- ▶ WASH

wash your hands of sb/sth
- ▶ REJECT

WASTE 名 *p.844*

waste 名
- ▶ WASTE

watch 動
- ▶ LOOK 動 1

watchdog 名
- ▶ INSPECTOR

watcher 名
- ▶ ANALYST

watch for sb/sth
- ▶ EXPECT

waterfront 名
- ▶ COAST

waters 名
- ▶ SEA

wave 名
- ▶ MOVEMENT

wave 動
- ▶ SHAKE 1

WAY 名 *p.844*

way 名
- ▶ WAY 1, 2, 3

a/the/sb's way of life
- ▶ LIFE 3

way out 名
- ▶ SOLUTION

ways 名
- ▶ HABIT

weak 形
- ▶ DIM, UNLIKELY 2

weaken 動
- ▶ WORSEN

weakness 名
- ▶ TASTE

wealth 名
- ▶ MONEY 3

wealthy 形
- ▶ RICH

WEAR 動 *p.846*

wear 名
- ▶ CLOTHES

wear 動
- ▶ WEAR

weary 形
- ▶ TIRED

weather 動
- ▶ SURVIVE

weave 動
- ▶ DESCRIBE

web 名
- ▶ SYSTEM

wedge 名
- ▶ PIECE

wedge 動
- ▶ PACK

weep 動
- ▶ CRY

weight 名
- ▶ STRESS

weird 形
- ▶ STRANGE 1

welcome 動
- ▶ GREET, LET SB IN

welcoming 形
- ▶ FRIENDLY 1

welfare 名
- ▶ AID

WELL 形 *p.847*

well 形
- ▶ WELL

well 副
- ▶ VERY

well behaved 形
- ▶ GOOD 7

well-being 名
- ▶ HEALTH

well dressed 形
- ▶ ELEGANT

well founded 形
- ▶ GOOD 3

well known 形
- ▶ FAMOUS

well off 形
- ▶ RICH

well read 形
- ▶ INFORMED

WET 形 *p.848*

wet 形
- ▶ WET

wet 動
- ▶ SOAK

whack 動
- ▶ HIT 2

what sb is getting/driving at
- ▶ MEAN 動 2

wheel 名
- ▶ BUTTON 1

wheel 動
- ▶ TURN 1

whereabouts 名
- ▶ PLACE

whiff 名
- ▶ SMELL

whim 名
- ▶ DESIRE

whimper 動
- ▶ CRY

whine 動
- ▶ COMPLAIN, CRY

whip 動
- ▶ STIR

whirl 動
- ▶ SPIN, TURN 1

whisk 動
- ▶ STIR

WHISPER 動 *p.848*

whisper 名
- ▶ WHISPER

WHOLE 形 *p.849*

whole 形
- ▶ WHOLE

whole 名
- ▶ THING 1

wholehearted 形
- ▶ DEEP 1

wholesale 形
- ▶ WIDE 1

wholesaler 名
- ▶ DEALER

wicked 形
- ▶ EVIL 形, GREAT 1

wickedness 名
- ▶ EVIL

WIDE 形 *p.850*

wide 形
- ▶ WIDE 1, 2

widen 動
- ▶ EXPAND

wide-ranging 形
- ▶ WIDE 1

widespread 形
- ▶ GENERAL

widowed 形
- ▶ SINGLE

WILD 形 *p.851*

wild 形
- ▶ WILD

the wild 名
- ▶ NATURE 2

wildlife 名
- ▶ NATURE 2

wilful 形
- ▶ DELIBERATE, STUBBORN

will 名
- ▶ WISH

willing 形
- ▶ HELPFUL

wimp 名
- ▶ COWARD

WIN 名 *p.851*

win 名
- ▶ VICTORY

win 動
- ▶ GAIN, WIN

wind 動
- ▶ CURVE

window 名
- ▶ OPPORTUNITY

wind up
- ▶ END

wind sb up
- ▶ ANNOY

wing 名
- ▶ DEPARTMENT

winning 形
- ▶ SUCCESSFUL 1

win out
- ▶ WIN

win sb over
- ▶ PERSUADE

win the day
- ▶ WIN

wintry 形
- ▶ FREEZING

wipe 動
- ▶ DELETE

wipe sb/sth out
- ▶ DESTROY

wisdom 名
- ▶ KNOWLEDGE

WISE 形 *p.852*

wise 形
- ▶ BEST, WISE

wisecrack 名
- ▶ JOKE

WISH 名 *p.852*

wish 名
- ▶ DESIRE, WISH

wish 動
- ▶ HOPE 動, WANT

wishful thinking 名
- ▶ HOPE 名 1

wit 名
- ▶ HUMOUR

withdraw 動
- ▶ BREAK 4

withdrawn 形
- ▶ SOLITARY

WITNESS 名 *p.853*

witness 名
- ▶ WITNESS

witness 動
- ▶ NOTICE

wits 名
- ▶ INTELLIGENCE

witty 形
- ▶ FUNNY

wobble 動
- ▶ SHAKE 2

wolf 動
- ▶ EAT

WOMAN 名 *p.853*

woman 名
- ▶ WOMAN

wonder 名
- ▶ MIRACLE

wonder 動
- ▶ CONSIDER

WONDERFUL 形 *p.853*

wonderful 形
- ▶ NICE 2, WONDERFUL

woo 動
- ▶ GO OUT

word 名
- ▶ PROMISE 名

wording 名
- ▶ LANGUAGE

WORK 名 *p.854*

WORK 動 *p.855*

work 名
- ▶ TASK, WORK 名 1, 2

work 動
- ▶ AFFECT, CAMPAIGN 動, OPERATE, WORK 動 1, 2

workable 形
- ▶ POSSIBLE 1

worked up 形
- ▶ HYSTERICAL

WORKER 名 p.856

worker 名
- ▶ WORKER 1, 2

workforce 名
- ▶ STAFF

workings 名
- ▶ SYSTEM

workman 名
- ▶ WORKER 2

workmate 名
- ▶ PARTNER 1

work of art 名
- ▶ WORK 名 2

workout 名
- ▶ SPORT

work out
- ▶ TRAIN 2

work sth out
- ▶ CALCULATE

works 名
- ▶ FACTORY

workshop 名
- ▶ CLASS 2, FACTORY

worldwide 形
- ▶ INTERNATIONAL

worn out 形
- ▶ TIRED

WORRIED 形 p.857

worried 形
- ▶ WORRIED

WORRY 動 p.858

worry 名
- ▶ CONCERN

worry 動
- ▶ WORRY

WORRYING 形 p.858

worrying 形
- ▶ WORRYING

WORSEN 動 p.859

worsen 動
- ▶ WORSEN

worth 動
- ▶ PRICE, VALUE

worthwhile 形
- ▶ VALUABLE 2

WORTHY 形 p.860

worthy 形
- ▶ WORTHY

would like sth
- ▶ WANT

would rather...
- ▶ PREFER

wound 名
- ▶ INJURY

wound 動
- ▶ HURT 1, INJURE

wrap sth up
- ▶ FINISH

wreck 名
- ▶ ACCIDENT, REMAINS

wreck 動
- ▶ CRASH, RUIN

wreckage 名
- ▶ REMAINS

wrestle 動
- ▶ FIGHT 動

wretched 形
- ▶ BAD

WRITE 動 p.860

write 動
- ▶ WRITE

write back
- ▶ ANSWER 動

write sth down
- ▶ WRITE

write sth off
- ▶ CRASH

WRITER 名 p.861

writer 名
- ▶ WRITER

writings 名
- ▶ WORK 名 2

WRONG 形 p.862

wrong 形
- ▶ WRONG 1, 2, 3

wrong 名
- ▶ CRIME 2, EVIL 名

wrongdoing 名
- ▶ CRIME 1

the wrong idea
- ▶ ILLUSION

wry 形
- ▶ IRONIC

wuss 名
- ▶ COWARD

X

xenophobia 名
- ▶ RACISM

Y

yank 動
- ▶ PULL 2

yard 名
- ▶ FACTORY

yardstick 名
- ▶ CRITERION

yell 動
- ▶ SHOUT

yelp 動
- ▶ SCREAM

yield 名
- ▶ OUTPUT

yield 動
- ▶ GIVE WAY, PROVIDE

YOUNG 形 p.865

young 形
- ▶ YOUNG

youngster 名
- ▶ CHILD

youth 名
- ▶ CHILDHOOD, GIRL

youthful 形
- ▶ CHILDISH

yummy 形
- ▶ DELICIOUS

Z

zap 動
- ▶ DESTROY

zealous 形
- ▶ EAGER

zigzag 名
- ▶ CORNER

zigzag 動
- ▶ CURVE

zip 名
- ▶ BUTTON 2

zipper 名
- ▶ BUTTON 2

zone 名
- ▶ AREA 1, COUNTY

小学館 オックスフォード英語類語辞典

2011年6月20日　　初版　第1刷発行

監修者　田中　実
発行者　大澤　昇
発行所　株式会社　小学館
　　　　〒101-8001 東京都千代田区一ツ橋2-3-1
　　　　電話　編集　03-3230-5169
　　　　　　　販売　03-5281-3555
印刷所　萩原印刷株式会社
製本所　株式会社若林製本工場

© Shogakukan 2011

造本には十分注意しておりますが、印刷・製本など製造上の不備がございましたら、「制作局コールセンター」(フリーダイヤル 0120-336-340) にご連絡ください。(電話受付は、土・日・祝日を除く9:30～17:30です)

Ⓡ〈日本複写権センター委託出版物〉
本書を無断で複写(コピー)することは、著作権法上の例外を除き、禁じられています。本書をコピーされる場合は、事前に日本複写権センター(JRRC)の許諾を受けてください。
JRRC　　URL: http://www.jrrc.or.jp
　　　　email: info@jrrc.or.jp
　　　　電話 03-3401-2382

本書の電子データ化等の無断複製は著作権法上の例外を除き禁じられています。代行業者等の第三者による本書の電子的複製も認められておりません。

★小学館外国語編集部のウェブサイト『小学館ランゲージワールド』
　http://www.l-world.shogakukan.co.jp/
Printed in Japan　　　　　　　　ISBN 978-4-09-506731-5